Oxford
Desk
Dictionary
of
People
and
Places

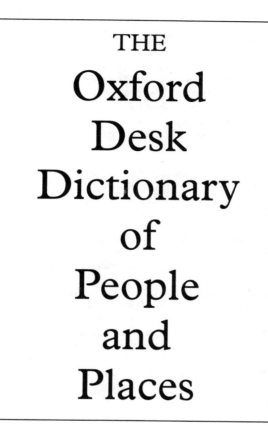

THE

Oxford Desk Dictionary of People and Places

Edited by

Frank Abate

New York   Oxford
Oxford University Press
1999

Oxford University Press

New York   Oxford
Athens   Auckland   Bangkok   Bogotà
Buenos Aires   Calcutta   Cape Town   Chennai   Dar es Salaam
Delhi   Florence   Hong Kong   Istanbul   Karachi
Kuala Lumpur   Madrid   Melbourne
Mexico City   Mumbai   Nairobi   Paris   São Paulo   Singapore
Taipei   Tokyo   Toronto   Warsaw

and associated companies in
Berlin   Ibadan

This is a compilation of *The Oxford Essential Biographical Dictionary* and
The Oxford Essential Geographical Dictionary, prepared by Oxford University Press
for publication in 1999 by The Berkley Publishing Group.

Published by Oxford University Press, Inc.,
198 Madison Avenue, New York, New York 10016
Oxford is a registered trademark of Oxford University Press.

ISBN 0-19-513872-4

1 3 5 7 9 8 6 4 2
Printed in the United States of America
on acid free paper

Contents

Staff

Introduction

The Oxford Desk Dictionary of People and Places offers, for the first time, comprehensive coverage of the sort of encyclopedic information that people need answers to the most—notable people and significant places—from today's world and throughout history.

The biographical section includes more than 7,500 prominent individuals, living and dead, selected from the annals of history, statecraft, science, business, entertainment, sports—indeed, any fields of human activity that are of interest to people generally.

For each entry the user will find the following information: the name of the individual, an indication of correct word division of the surname (if applicable), the pronunciation (unless an accurate pronunciation could not be determined); alternate names, nicknames, names at birth, and other names by which an individual may be known; and a concise definition identifying the individual's nationality/country of origin and principal occupation(s), as well as (in most cases) an indication of the particular significance of that individual in human affairs or in a certain field of activity.

The geographical section covers some 10,000 places of all kinds, including all continents and countries of the world (with helpful locator maps), capitals, major or historic cities and towns, plus important regions of the world, notable geographic features, and places that have played a part in world history and culture. For each entry, the user will find the name of the place, an indication of correct word division, pronunciation (unless an accurate pronunciation could not be determined), alternate spellings of the name or alternate names of the place, and a concise definition that gives the location of the place and some indication of its significance. Where appropriate, figures are given for area or population.

About one-third of the places covered in *The Oxford Desk Dictionary of People and Places* are in North America. This focus on material of particular interest to American readers is also reflected in the handling of all 50 U.S. states in special feature boxes, which give an expanded range of information, including such items as state flowers and nicknames, and in the inclusion of more information on Canadian provinces and territories and on Mexican states than on analogous political entities elsewhere in the world.

No other single-volume dictionary has anything like this scope. Even the largest "unabridged" general dictionaries do not come close to *The Oxford Desk Dictionary of People and Places* for biographical and geographical coverage.

How to Use This Book

The "entry map" below shows the different parts of a typical entry for a **person** in this dictionary: surname and given name(s), pronunciation, life date(s), any alternate names, the identifying information on that individual, and any information indicating significance.

> **Buck** |bək|, Pearl S. (1892–1973) U.S. writer; full name *Pearl Sydenstricker Buck*. Her upbringing and work in China inspired her earliest novels, including *The Good Earth* (Pulitzer Prize, 1931). Nobel Prize for Literature (1938).

The "entry map" below shows the different parts of a typical entry for a **place** in this dictionary: place name, pronunciation, population figure (for populated places), location, and capital city (where appropriate):

> **Ka•li•nin•grad** |kə'lēnen,grəd| **1** port on the Baltic Sea, capital of the Russian region of Kaliningrad. Pop. 406,000. It was known by its German name of Königsberg until 1946, when it was ceded to the Soviet Union and renamed in honor of Soviet President Mikhail Kalinin. Its port is ice-free all year round and is a major naval base. **2** region of Russia, an exclave on the Baltic coast of E Europe. Capital: Kaliningrad. It is separated from Russia by the territory of Lithuania, Latvia, and Belarus.

1. **Boldface:** Main entries, alternate names, and derivative forms appear in boldface.

1a. **Word division:** Dots within the main entries mark places where a name can be divided correctly, as at the end of a line of text. Many names will not have dots at each syllable, because the dots are intended to show optimum word division points. Thus, one-letter syllables at the beginning or end of a name are not separated by dots (**Aus•tria**, not **Aus•tri•a; Avon**, not **A•von**). No divisions are marked in hyphenated names, because they are best divided at the hyphen. Standard generic terms that are used in many place names, such as *River* and *Mountain*, are not marked for word division.

2. **Cross references** appear in small capital letters.

> **Llo•sa** |'yōsə|, Mario Vargas see VARGAS
> LLOSA.

3. **Sense numbers** are used to group closely related places under a single main entry where the places occur within a single country.

> **Oa•xa•ca** |wä'häkə| **1** state of S Mexico.
> Area: 36,289 sq. mi./93,952 sq. km. Pop.
> 3,022,000. **2** its capital city, an historic cultural and commercial center. Pop. 213,000.
> Full name **Oaxaca de Juárez**.

But where a single place name occurs in more than one country—as in the case of **Perth**, Scotland, and **Perth**, Australia—each place is treated as a separate entry and appears in alphabetical order by the country name, or by the name of the most commonly known next higher political division. In the case of such "homographs" (two or more names spelled exactly the same, although the two are separate places, and the names may have no relation to each other), entry order is indicated by a superscript number.

> **Perth**[1] |pərTH| the capital of the state of Western Australia, on the Indian Ocean. Pop.
> 1,019,000 (including the port of Fremantle). Founded by the British in 1829, it developed rapidly after the discovery in 1890 of nearby gold.
> **Perth**[2] |pərTH| town in E Scotland, at the head of the Tay estuary. Pop. 41,000. The administrative center of Perth and Kinross region, it was the capital of Scotland from 1210 until 1452.

4. **Family names:** Individuals who are members of the same family are covered under one main entry. Individuals in the single family entry are given in order chronologically by birth date, for example:

> **Ad•ams** |'ædəmz| U.S. political family,
> including: **John Adams** see box. **Abigail
> Smith Adams** (1744–1818), wife of
> John Adams and U.S. first lady (1797–
> 1801). **John Quincy Adams** see box.
> **Louisa Catherine Johnson Adams**
> (1775–1852), wife of John Quincy
> Adams and U.S. first lady (1825–29).
> **Charles Francis Adams** (1807–86),
> U.S. diplomat and author. The son of
> John Quincy Adams, he was a member of
> the Massachusetts House of Representatives (1859–61) and U.S. ambassador to
> Great Britain (1861–68). **Charles Francis Adams** (1835–1915), U.S. historian.
> The son of Charles Francis (1807–86),
> he was an expert on railroads.

But where a single surname and given name combination is spelled exactly the same for two *unrelated* individuals, two separate main entries are given, distinguished by a superscript number given after each surname. In the case of such "homographs" (names spelled exactly the same, although the two individuals have no familial relation to one another), entry order is chronological by birth date.

> **Ba•con**[1] |'bākən|, Francis, Baron Verulam and Viscount St. Albans (1561–1626) English statesman and philosopher. As a scientist he advocated the inductive method; his views were instrumental in the founding of the Royal Society in 1660. Notable works: *The Advancement of Learning* (1605) and *Novum Organum* (1620).
>
> **Ba•con**[2] |'bākən|, Francis (1909–92) Irish painter. His work chiefly depicts human figures in grotesquely distorted postures, their features blurred or erased.

5. The name under which a person or place is listed is, in some cases (for example, *Venice, Rome,* and *Italy*) not the official "native" form or spelling, but is the form in which Americans are likely to use the name. In some other cases, the form under which a name is entered is better known than the official form or spelling; for example, San Buenaventura, California, is not as well known by that (official) name as by the entry form given, **Ventura**.

6. The characterization of the **status** of a place, it should be noted, is also subject to language and national differences. For entries in the United States and Canada, terms like *city, town,* and *village* used in this dictionary reflect official usage, which is a matter of municipal organization, not population or land area; for example, the town of Hempstead, New York; the village of Skokie, Illinois; and the city of Sitka, Alaska. In other parts of the world, governmental form and municipal designation take many forms (and are sometimes difficult to determine with certainty). For places outside the United States and Canada, this book adopts general usage, and the term *city,* for example, usually denotes an urban place larger than a town or village. There are, of course, many different designations for populated places, some more familiar than others, such as *commune, borough,* and *parish*; some of these are used here, following the most reliable source information that could be obtained.

7. **Population figures:** For populated places in the United States and Canada, the latest official census figures are used. For populated places in the rest of the world, sources vary, but recently released figures are used (rounded off, in almost all cases, to the nearest thousand).

8. **Measurements** are given in standard units first, followed by a conversion into metric measurement. This conforms to prevalent usage in the United States. Thus miles (mi.) are also given in kilometers (km.), feet (ft.) in meters (m.), and square miles (sq. mi.) in square kilometers (sq. km.).

Abbreviations

Abbreviations (besides those that are quite standard and familiar) used in the text of the entries include the following:

AFL	American Football League
c.	circa
CIA	Central Intelligence Agency
Co.	Company
Corp.	Corporation
FBI	Federal Bureau of Investigation
fl.	floruit (date of prominence)
Inc.	Incorporated
LPGA	Ladies Professional Golfers Association
NAACP	National Association for the Advancement of Colored People
NASA	National Aeronautics and Space Administration
NATO	North Atlantic Treaty Organization
NBA	National Basketball Association
NCAA	National Collegiate Athletic Association
NFL	National Football League
NHL	National Hockey League
PGA	Professional Golfers Association
U.S.	United States (of America)
UK	United Kingdom (Great Britain)
UN	United Nations
USSR	Union of Soviet Socialist Republics (Soviet Union)

Pronunciation Key

Main entries are normally followed by a pronunciation, which appears within upright vertical lines immediately after the main entry, for example:

Ker•ou•ac |'kerəwæk|

The pronunciations use a simple respelling system to represent English and some non-English sounds, as shown below. Pronunciations generally are an "Americanized" rendering that is acceptable in almost all contexts. In certain cases, especially with unusual names (sometimes of non-English origin) whose pronunciations are less familiar, the pronunciations are approximations of the way the name is pronounced in the particular foreign language of origin. Where information on the pronunciations preferred by a certain individual or family could be determined, that preferred pronunciation is given. In a small percentage of entries, when reliable data could not be obtained, no pronunciation is given.

VOWELS:

Symbol:	as in:	Example:
æ	cat	**Nash** |næsʜ|
ā	mate	**Ma•con** |'mākən|
ä	father	**Scott** |skät|
e	let	**Penn** |pen|
ē	feet	**Eden** |'ēdn|
i	it	**Mil•ler** |'milər|
ī	tide	**Eif•fel Tower** |'īfəl|
aw	fall	**Al•bright** |'awlbrīt|
ō	cove	**Ohio** |ō'hīō|
o͝o	hook	**Bush** |bo͝osʜ|
o͞o	loose	**Shu•la** |'sʜo͞olə|
ə	but; banana	**Aca•dia** |ə'kādēə|

DIPHTHONGS:

oi	foil	**Con•roy** |'kän,roi|
ow	couch	**Ei•sen•how•er** |'īzən,howər|

CONSONANTS:

b	boot	**Bom·beck** |'bäm,bek|
CH	church	**Chad** |CHæd|
d	dog	**Da·vis** |'dāvəs|
f	fate	**Flag·staff** |'flæg,stæf|
g	go; bigger	**Get·tys·burg** |'getēz,bərg|
h	hot; behave	**Har·ri·son** |'herəsən|
j	jack; magic	**Ja·pan** |jə'pæn|
k	kettle; cut	**Can·a·da** |'kænədə|
l	lap; cellar; cradle	**La·Belle** |lə'bel|
m	main	**Mc·Mil·lan** |mək'milən|
n	honor; maiden	**No·lan** |'nōlən|
NG	singer	**Fin·ger Lakes** |'fiNGgər|
p	put	**Pam·plo·na** |pæm'plōnə|
r	root; carry	**Rich·ards** |'riCHərdz|
s	sit	**Scripps** |skrips|
SH	shape; wish	**Marsh** |märSH|
t	top; butter	**Trot·sky** |'trätskē|
TH	thing; path	**Lu·ther** |'lⁿⁿTHər|
TH	this; mother	**Neth·er·lands** |'neTHərlən(d)z|
v	never	**Ven·ice** |'venəs|
w	wait; quick	**Wales** |wālz|
y	yes; beyond	**Young** |yəNG|
z	lazy; fuse	**Za·pa·ta** |zə'pätə|
ZH	beige; leisure	**Bei·jing** |'bā'zHiNG|

FOREIGN SOUNDS:

KH	Bach	**Feu·er·bach** |'foiər,bäKH|
N	vin	**Gau·guin** |gō'gæN|
Œ	Goethe	**Köln** |kŒln|
Y	über	**Lul·ly** |lY'lē|

STRESS

Each stressed syllable is preceded by a small upright stroke, showing that the following syllable has a stressed vowel sound. Primary stress is shown by an upright stroke above the line, while secondary stress is shown by an upright stroke below the line:

Col·os·se·um \|,kälə'sēəm\|

Dictionary of People

Aa

Aal·to |'ältaw|, Alvar (1898–1976) Finnish architect and designer. Full name *Hugo Alvar Henrik Aalto.* As a designer he is known as the inventor of bent plywood furniture.

Aar·on |'erən|, Hank (1934–) U.S. baseball player. Full name *Henry Louis Aaron.* He set the all-time career record for home runs (755) and runs batted in (2,297). Elected to the Baseball Hall of Fame (1982).

Ab·bas |'æbəs|, Ferhat (1899–1985) Algerian nationalist leader. He was president of the Algerian provisional government from 1958, and president of the constituent assembly of independent Algeria (1962–63).

Ab·be |'äbə|, Ernst (1840–1905) German physicist. He invented the apochromatic lens.

Ab·bey |'æbē|, Edwin Austin (1852–1911) U.S. painter and illustrator. He was a *Harper's Weekly* staff illustrator.

Ab·bot |'æbət|, Charles Greeley (1872–1973) U.S. astrophysicist. He was director of the astrophysical observatory of the Smithsonian Institution (1907–44).

Ab·bott |'æbət|, Berenice (1898–1991) U.S. photographer and author. She is known for her photographs of New York City and for preserving the photographs of Eugène Atget.

Ab·bott |'æbət|, Robert Sengstacke (1868–1940) U.S. publisher and editor. He founded and edited the *Chicago Defender* (1905–40).

Ab·duh |'äbdoo|, Muhammad (1849–1905) Egyptian Islamic scholar, jurist, and liberal reformer.

Ab·dul Ha·mid II |əb‚dool hä'mēd| (1842–1918) The last sultan of Turkey (1876–1909). An autocratic ruler, he was deposed after the revolt of the Young Turks (1908). He is remembered for the massacres of Christian Armenians (1894–96).

Abdul-Jabbar |æb‚doolja'bär|, Kareem (1947–) U.S. basketball player. Born *Ferdinand Lewis Alcindor;* known (until 1968) as **Lew Alcindor.** He set

more than 20 all-time records, including most games played (1,560) and most career points (38,387). Elected to the Basketball Hall of Fame (1995).

Ab·dul·lah ibn Hus·sein |äb'doolə ib(ə)n hoo'sān| (1882–1951) king of Jordan (1946–51). He served as emir of Transjordan from 1921, becoming king of Jordan on its independence. He was assassinated in 1951.

Ab·dul Rah·man |əb'dool rä'män|, Tunku (1903–90) Malayan statesman. He was the first prime minister of independent Malaya (1957–63) and of Malaysia (1963–70).

Abe |'äbä|, Kōbō (1924–93) Japanese author. Real name *Abe Kimifusa.*

Abel |'äbəl|, Niels Henrik (1802–29) Norwegian mathematician. He proved that equations of the fifth degree cannot be solved by conventional algebraic methods, and made advances in the fields of power series and elliptic functions.

Ab·e·lard |'æbə‚lärd|, Peter (1079–1144) French scholar, theologian, and philosopher. He is famous for his tragic love affair with his pupil Héloïse (see HÉLOÏSE).

Ab·er·crom·bie |'æbər'krämbē|, Sir (Leslie) Patrick (1879–1957) English town planner and architect. He is known for his postwar "Greater London Plan," for which he was knighted in 1945.

Ab·er·deen |'æbər‚dēn|, George Hamilton-Gordon, 4th Earl of (1784–1860) British Conservative statesman. He was prime minister (1852–55).

Ab·er·nathy |'æbər‚næTHē|, Ralph David (1926–90) U.S. clergyman and civil rights activist. With Martin Luther King, Jr., he led the U.S. civil rights movement in the 1950s and 1960s and founded (1957) the Southern Christian Leadership Conference. He published his autobiography, *And the Walls Came Tumbling Down,* in 1989.

Abra·hams |'äbrə‚hæmz|, Harold (Maurice) (1899–1978) English athlete. In 1924 he became the first Englishman to win the 100 meters in the

Olympic Games. His story was the subject of the movie *Chariots of Fire* (1981).

Abram·o·vitz |ə'brämə‚vits|, Max (1908–) U.S. architect.

Abrams |'ābrəmz|, Creighton William (1914–74) U.S. army officer. He became major general (1965) and vice-chief of the U.S. Army (1964–67) before commanding U.S. troops in Vietnam (1968–72) and overseeing U.S. withdrawal; he then served as army chief of staff (1972–74).

Ab·zug |'æbzo͞og|, Bella Savitsky (1920–98) U.S. antiwar, feminist and gay rights activist. She was a New York attorney and U.S. congresswoman (1971–77) and a founding member of the National Organization for Women.

Ache·be |ə'CHäbā|, Chinua (1930–) Nigerian novelist, poet, short-story writer, and essayist. Born *Albert Chinualumgu*. Notable works: *Things Fall Apart* (1958) and *Anthills of the Savanna* (1987). Nobel Prize for Literature (1989).

Ach·e·son |'æCHəsən|, Dean (Gooderham) (1893–1971) U.S. statesman and secretary of state (1949-53). He urged international control of nuclear power, was instrumental in the formation of NATO, and implemented the Marshall Plan and the Truman Doctrine.

Acuff |'ā‚kəf|, Roy (1903–92) U.S. country musician. Known as the "King of Country Music," he was a star of the Grand Ole Opry, and with Fred Rose he formed the Acuff-Rose Music Publishing Co. (1942).

Ad·am |'ædəm|, Robert (1728–92) Scottish architect. He was influenced by neoclassical theory and, assisted by his brother **James** (1730–94), he initiated a lighter, more decorative style than the Palladianism favored by the British architecture of the previous half-century.

Ad·ams |'ædəmz| U.S. political family, including: **John Adams** see box. **Abigail Smith Adams** (1744–1818), wife of John Adams and U.S. first lady (1797–1801). **John Quincy Adams** see box. **Louisa Catherine Johnson Adams** (1775–1852), wife of John Quincy Adams and U.S. first lady (1825–29). **Charles Francis Adams**

Adams, John
2nd U.S. president

Life dates: 1735–1826
Place of birth: Braintree (now Quincy), Massachusetts
Mother: Susanna Boylston Adams
Father: John Adams
Wife: Abigail Smith Adams
Children: Abigail, John Quincy (6th U.S. president), Susanna, Charles, Thomas
College/University: Harvard
Career: Lawyer; schoolmaster; writer
Political career: Massachusetts legislature; First Continental Congress; Second Continental Congress; minister to Great Britain and the Netherlands; vice president (under Washington); president
Party: Federalist
Home state: Massachusetts
Opponent in presidential race: Thomas Jefferson
Term of office: March 4, 1797–March 3, 1801
Vice president: Thomas Jefferson
Notable events of presidency: XYZ Affair; Judiciary Act; Alien and Sedition Acts
Other achievements: Admitted to the Massachusetts bar; president of the Massachusetts Society for Promoting Agriculture; wrote articles for the Boston *Patriot*
Place of burial: Quincy, Massachusetts

(1807–86), U.S. diplomat and author. The son of John Quincy Adams, he was a member of the Massachusetts House of Representatives (1859–61) and U.S. ambassador to Great Britain (1861–68). **Charles Francis Adams** (1835–1915), U.S. historian. The son of Charles Francis Adams (1807–86), he was an expert on railroads.

Ad·ams |'ædəmz|, Alice (1926–) U.S. author and editor.

Ad·ams |'ædəmz|, Ansel (Easton) (1902–84) U.S. photographer. He was noted for his black-and-white photographs of American landscapes. Many of Adams's collections, such as *My Camera in the National Parks* (1950) and *This is the American Earth* (1960), reflect his interest in conservation.

Ad·ams |'ædəmz|, Harriet Stratemeyer (c. 1893–1982) U.S. author. After the

Adams, John Quincy
6th U.S. president

Life dates: 1767–1848
Place of birth: Braintree (now Quincy), Massachusetts
Mother: Abigail Smith Adams
Father: John Adams (2nd U.S. president)
Wife: Louisa Catherine Johnson Adams
Children: George, John, Charles, Louisa
College/University: Harvard; also attended University of Leiden
Career: Lawyer
Political career: Massachusetts Senate; U.S. Senate; minister to Great Britain, Netherlands, Portugal, Prussia, and Russia; U.S. secretary of state; president; U.S. House of Representatives
Party: Whig; Federalist; Democratic-Republican
Home state: Massachusetts
Opponents in presidential race: Henry Clay; Andrew Jackson; William H. Crawford
Term of office: March 4, 1825–March 3, 1829
Vice president: John C. Calhoun
Notable events of presidency: Erie Canal opened; Pan-American Congress; Tariff of Abominations; construction of Baltimore and Ohio Railroad began; Treaty of Paris; Treaty of Ghent; South Carolina Exposition on nullification of federal tariffs
Other achievements: Admitted to the Massachusetts bar; only U.S. president elected to the House after presidency; secretary to his father, John Adams; wrote pamphlets and articles under the pseudonyms of "Publicola," "Marcellus," "Columbus," etc.; professor of rhetoric and belles lettres, Harvard College; nominated to U.S. Supreme Court, but declined
Place of burial: Quincy, Massachusetts

death of her father, Edward Stratemeyer (1862–1930), she continued to write the series of books he created, especially the Nancy Drew and Hardy Boys series.

Ad•ams |'ædəmz|, Henry Brooks (1838–1918) U.S. historian and scholar. Notable works: *Democracy* (1880) and *The Education of Henry Adams* (1907, Pulitzer Prize).

Ad•ams |'ædəmz|, Herbert Samuel (1858–1945) U.S. sculptor. He executed busts of John Marshall, William Ellery Channing, William Cullen Bryant, Will Rogers, and Joseph Story; he also created the bronze doors of St. Bartholomew's Church in New York City, and those of the Library of Congress.

Ad•ams |'ædəmz|, James Truslow (1878–1949) U.S. historian. He wrote *The Founding of New England* (1921, Pulitzer Prize) and edited the *Dictionary of American History* (1940) and *Atlas of American History* (1943).

Ad•ams |'ædəmz|, John Couch (1819–92) English astronomer. In 1843 he calculated the position of a supposed planet beyond Uranus; similar calculations performed by Le Verrier resulted in the discovery of Neptune three years later.

Ad•ams |'ædəmz|, Richard George (1920–) British novelist. Notable works: *Watership Down* (1972).

Ad•ams |'ædəmz|, Samuel (1722–1803) American Revolutionary politician. He was a leader of the Boston Tea Party (1773), a delegate to the First and Second Continental Congresses, and a signer of the Declaration of Independence.

Ad•ams |'ædəmz|, Scott (1957–) U.S. cartoonist. He created the comic strip "Dilbert."

Ad•ams |'ædəmz|, Thomas. U.S. inventor. He was the first person to make sticks of chewing gum from the plant sap chicle (1870).

Ad•dams |'ædəmz|, Charles (1912–88) U.S. cartoonist. He created macabre cartoons, many of which were published in *The New Yorker*.

Ad•dams |'ædəmz|, Jane (1860–1935) U.S. social reformer, feminist, and pacifist. In 1889 she founded Hull House, a center for the care and education of the poor of Chicago, and a national model for the combat of urban poverty and the treatment of young offenders. She was a leader of the women's suffrage movement and an active pacifist. Nobel Peace Prize (1931).

Ad•der•ly |'ædərlē|, Cannonball (1928–75) U.S. jazz alto saxophonist. Born *Julian Edwin Adderly*. He played in the Miles Davis Quintet (1957–59) and later formed a second quintet with his brother, Nat Adderly.

Ad•ding•ton |'ædiNGtən|, Henry, 1st Viscount Sidmouth (1757–1844) British Tory statesman, prime minister (1801–04), and home secretary (1812–21).

Ad•di•son |'ædəsən|, Joseph (1672–1719) English essayist, poet, dramatist, and Whig politician. In 1711 he founded the *Spectator* with Sir Richard Steele.

Ad•di•son |'ædəsən|, Thomas (1793–1860) English physician. A renowned clinical teacher, he described the disease now named for him, ascribing it correctly to defective functioning of the adrenal glands.

Ade•nau•er |'ædə,nowər|, Konrad (1876–1967) German statesman. He was first chancellor of the Federal Republic of Germany (1949–63).

Ad•ler |'ædlər|, Alfred (1870–1937) Austrian psychologist and psychiatrist. Adler disagreed with Freud's idea that mental illness was caused by sexual conflicts in infancy, arguing that society and culture were significant factors. He introduced the concept of the inferiority complex.

Ador•no |ä'dôrnō|, Theodor Wiesengrund (1903–69) German philosopher, sociologist, and musicologist. Born *Theodor Wiesengrund*. A member of the Frankfurt School, Adorno argued that philosophical authoritarianism is inevitably oppressive.

Adri•an IV |'ädri,än| (c. 1100–59) Pope (1154–59). Born *Nicholas Breakspear*. He is the only Englishman to have held this office.

Ael•fric |'ælfrik| (c. 955–c. 1020) Anglo-Saxon monk, writer, and grammarian. Called **Grammaticus**. Notable works: *Lives of the Saints* (993–996).

Aes•chi•nes |'eskənēz| (c. 389–c. 314 BC) Athenian orator and statesman. He opposed Demosthenes' efforts to unite the Greek city states against Macedon, with which he attempted to make peace.

Aes•chy•lus |'eskələs| (c. 525–c. 456 BC) Greek dramatist. Aeschylus is best known for his trilogy the *Oresteia* (458 BC, consisting of the tragedies *Agamemnon*, *Choephoroe*, and *Eumenides*), which tells the story of Agamemnon's murder at the hands of his wife Clytemnestra and the vengeance of their son Orestes.

Ae•sop |'ē,säp| (c. 550 BC) Greek storyteller. The moral animal fables associated with him were probably collected from many sources and initially communicated orally.

Af•fleck |'æf,lek|, Ben (1972–) U.S. actor and screenwriter. Full name *Benjamin Geza Affleck*. His screenplay for the movie *Good Will Hunting* (1997) won an Academy Award.

Agas•si |'ægəsē|, André (1970–) U.S. tennis player. He won at Wimbledon (1992), the U.S. Open (1994), and the Australian Open (1995).

Ag•as•siz |'ægəsē|, Jean Louis Rodolphe (1807–73) Swiss-born U.S. zoologist, geologist, and paleontologist. In 1837 Agassiz was the first to propose that much of Europe had once been in the grip of an ice age.

Agee |'ā,jē|, James Rufus (1909–55) U.S. author. He was widely recognized for *Let Us Now Praise Famous Men* (1941), his study of Alabama tenant farmers, co-authored with photographer Walker Evans. He also wrote poetry; movie scripts, including *The African Queen* (1952); and novels, including *A Death in the Family* (1957, Pulitzer Prize).

Ag•nes[1] |'ægnəs|, St. (died c. 304) Roman martyr. She is the patron saint of virgins and her emblem is a lamb (Latin *agnus*). Feast day, January 21.

Ag•nes[2] |'ægnəs|, St. (c. 1211–82) patron saint of Bohemia. She was canonized in 1989. Feast day, March 2.

Agne•si |än'yäzē|, Maria Gaetana (1718–99) Italian mathematician and philosopher. She is regarded as the first female mathematician of the Western world.

Ag•new |'ægnōō|, Spiro T. (1918–96) vice president of the U.S. (1969–73). He pleaded nolo contendere to charges of tax evasion on contractors' payments to him as governor of Maryland; as a result of this scandal, he resigned the vice presidency in 1973.

Agri•co•la |ə'grikələ|, Gnaeus Julius (AD 40–93) Roman general and governor of Britain (78–84). As governor he completed the subjugation of Wales and defeated the Scottish Highland tribes.

Agrip·pa |əˈgripə|, Marcus Vipsanius (63?–12 BC) Roman general. Augustus's adviser and son-in-law, he played an important part in the naval victories over Mark Antony.

Ai·dan |ˈadən|, St. (died AD 651) Irish missionary and evangelist of northern England.

Ai·ken |ˈākən|, Conrad Potter (1889–1973) U.S. poet, critic, and writer. Notable works: *Selected Poems*, which won the 1929 Pulitzer Prize.

Ai·ken |ˈākən|, Howard Hathaway (1900–73) U.S. mathematician and computer scientist.

Ai·ley |ˈālē|, Alvin (1931–89) U.S. dancer and choreographer. He founded the American Dance Theatre (1958), which helped to establish modern dance as an American art form; he incorporated ballet, jazz, and Afro-Carribbean idioms in his choreography.

Ait·ken |ˈātkən|, William Maxwell see BEAVERBROOK.

Ak·bar |ˈæk,bär|, Jala-lu-Din Muhammad (1542–1605) Mogul emperor of India (1556–1605). Called **Akbar the Great**. Akbar expanded the Mogul empire to incorporate northern India.

Akhe·na·ton |äkˈnätən| (14th century BC) Egyptian pharaoh. Also **Amenhotep** or **Ikhnaton**. A pharaoh of the 18th dynasty, he came to the throne as *Amenhotep IV* and reigned 1379–1362 BC. The husband of Nefertiti, he introduced the monotheistic solar cult of Aten and moved the capital from Thebes to the newly built city of Akhetaten.

Akh·ma·to·va |ækˈmätəvə|, Anna (1889–1966) Russian poet. Pseudonym of *Anna Andreevna Gorenko*. Akhmatova was a member of the Acmeist group of poets.

Aki·hi·to |äkēˈhētō| (1933–) emperor of Japan (1989–). Full name *Tsugu Akihito*. The son of Emperor Hirohito.

Alain-Fournier |äˈlan fŏorˈnyä| (1886–1914) French novelist. Pseudonym of *Henri-Alban Fournier*.

al-Amin, Jamil Abdullah (1943–) U.S. political activist and author. Formerly known as **H. Rap Brown**, he was chairman of the Student Nonviolent Coordinating Committee and, with Stokely Carmichael, an outspoken advocate of black power in the 1960s.

Alar·cón |älärˈkawn|, Pedro Antonio de (1833–91) Spanish novelist and short-story writer. Notable works: *The Three-Cornered Hat* (1874).

Alarcón y Mendoza |ˌälärˈkawn ē ˌmen ˈdōsə| see RUIZ DE ALARCÓN Y MENDOZA.

Al·a·ric |ˈælərik| (c. 370–410) king of the Visigoths (395–410). He captured Rome in 410.

Al·ban |ˈälbən|, St. (3rd century) the first British Christian martyr. He was a native of Verulamium (now St. Albans).

Al·bee |ˈälbē|, Edward Franklin (1928–) U.S. dramatist. He was initially associated with the Theater of the Absurd, but *Who's Afraid of Virginia Woolf* (1962) marked a more naturalistic departure. Another notable play is *A Delicate Balance* (1966).

Al·bers |ˈälbərz|, Josef (1888–1976) U.S. artist, designer, and teacher, born in Germany. His work is associated with the Bauhaus and constructivism.

Al·bert |ˈælbərt|, Prince (1819–61) consort to Queen Victoria of Great Britain and prince of Saxe-Coburg-Gotha. Full name *Albert Francis Charles Augustus Emmanuel*.

Al·ber·ti |älˈbərtē|, Leon Battista (1404–72) Italian architect, humanist, painter, and art critic. His book *On Painting* (1435) was the first account of the theory of perspective in the Renaissance.

Al·bert·son |ˈælbərt,sən|, Jack (1907–81) U.S. actor. He was a character player in vaudeville, burlesque, Broadway, television, and movies. Notable movies: *The Subject Was Roses* (1968, Academy Award).

Al·ber·tus Mag·nus |ælˈbərtəs ˈmæg nəs|, St. (c. 1200–80) Dominican theologian, philosopher, and scientist. Known as **Doctor Universalis**. A teacher of St. Thomas Aquinas, he was a pioneer in the study of Aristotle and contributed significantly to the comparison of Christian theology and pagan philosophy. Feast day, November 15.

Al·bi·no·ni |ˌælbəˈnōnē|, Tomaso

Giovanni (1671–1751) Italian composer of opera and instrumental works.

Al•bi•nus |æl'bēnəs| Another name for ALCUIN.

Al•bright |'awlbrīt|, Madeleine Korbel (1937–) U.S. secretary of state (1997–), born in Czechoslovakia. She was the first woman to head the U.S. State Department.

Al•bu•quer•que |'ælbə‚kerkē|, Alfonso de (1453–1515) Portuguese colonial statesman. He conquered Goa (1510) and made it the capital of the Portuguese empire in the east.

Al•cae•us |'æl‚sēəs| (c. 620–c. 580 BC) Greek lyric poet. He invented a new form of lyric meter, called the alcaic. His works were a model for the Roman poet Horace and the verse of the Renaissance.

Al•ci•bi•a•des |‚ælsə'bīədēz| (c. 450–404 BC) Athenian general and statesman. He led the unsuccessful Athenian expeditions against Sparta and Sicily during the Peloponnesian War but fled to Sparta after being charged with sacrilege.

Al•cock |'awl‚käk|, Sir John William (1892–1919) English aviator. Together with Sir Arthur Whitten Brown, he made the first nonstop transatlantic flight in June 1919.

Al•cott |'awl‚kət| U.S. family name of: **Bronson Alcott** (1799–1888), an educator. Full name Amos Bronson Alcott. He advocated radical reforms in education, including racial integration in the classroom. Appointed superintendent of schools in Concord, Massachusetts, in 1859, he created the first parent-teacher association. His daughter, **Louisa May Alcott** (1832–88), was a novelist whose best known work was Little Women (1868–69).

Al•cuin |'ælkwən| (c. 735–804) English scholar, theologian, and adviser to Charlemagne. Also known as **Albinus**. He is credited with the transformation of Charlemagne's court into a cultural center in the period known as the Carolingian Renaissance.

Al•da |'awldə|, Alan (1936–) U.S. actor, director, and writer. He won five Emmys for his role as Hawkeye Pierce on the television series "M*A*S*H" (1972–83).

Al•diss |'awldəs|, Brian (Wilson) (1925–) English novelist and critic. He is best known for his science fiction. Notable works: Frankenstein Unbound (1973).

Al•drin |'awldrin|, Buzz (1930–) U.S. astronaut. Full name Edwin Eugene Aldrin, Jr.. In 1969 he took part in the first moon landing, the Apollo 11 mission, becoming the second person to set foot on the moon, after Neil Armstrong.

Al•dus Ma•nu•ti•us |'awldəs mə-'nōōsh(ē)əs| (1450–1515) Italian scholar, printer, and publisher. Latinized name of Teobaldo Manucci; also known as **Aldo Manuzio**. He printed fine first editions of many Greek and Latin classics.

Ale•khine |‚əl'yōκHyin|, Alexander (1892–1946) Russian-born French chess player. He was world champion from 1927 to 1935 and from 1937 until his death.

Al•ex•an•der[1] |‚æləg'zændər| (356–323 BC) king of Macedon (336–323). Known as **Alexander the Great**. The son of Philip II, he conquered Persia, Egypt, Syria, Mesopotamia, Bactria, and the Punjab; in Egypt he founded the city of Alexandria.

Al•ex•an•der[2] |‚æləg'zændər| (1777–1825) The name of three czars of Russia: **Alexander I** (1777–1825; reigned 1801–25); **Alexander II** (1818–81; reigned 1855–81), the son of Nicholas I. He was known as **Alexander the Liberator** after the emancipation of the serfs (1861). **Alexander III** (1845–94; reigned 1881–94), the son of Alexander II.

Al•ex•an•der[3] |‚æləg'zændər| (c. 1080–1124) The name of three kings of Scotland: **Alexander I** (c. 1077–1124; reigned 1107–24), the son of Malcolm III; **Alexander II** (1198–1249; reigned 1214–49), the son of William I of Scotland; and **Alexander III** (1241–86; reigned 1249–86), the son of Alexander II.

Al•ex•an•der |‚æləg'zændər|, Grover Cleveland (1887–1950) U.S. baseball player. Known as **Pete**. A 20-season pitcher (1911–30), he retired with 373 career wins and 90 shutouts. Elected to the Baseball Hall of Fame (1938).

Al·ex·an·der |ˌæləgˈzændər|, Harold (Rupert Leofric George), 1st Earl Alexander of Tunis (1891–1969) British field marshal and Conservative statesman.

Al·ex·an·der |ˌæləgˈzændər|, (Andrew) Lamar (1940–   ) U.S. politician and administrator. He was the governor of Tennessee (1979–87) and President Bush's secretary of education (1991–93).

Al·ex·an·der Nev·sky |ˌæləgˈzændər ˈnyefskē| (c. 1220–63) prince of Novgorod (1236–63). Also **Nevski**. He defeated the Swedes on the banks of the River Neva in 1240. Feast day, August 30 or November 23.

Al·ex·and·er·son |ˌæləgˈzændərsən|, Ernst Frederik Werner (1878–1975) U.S. electrical engineer and inventor, born in Sweden. Having invented and perfected radio receiving and transmitting systems, he produced a complete television system (1927) and a color television receiver (1955).

Al·fon·so XIII |ælˈfänsō| (1886–1941) king of Spain (1886–1931). He was forced into exile after elections indicating a preference for a republic.

Al·ford |ˈawlfərd|, Andrew (1904–92) U.S. inventor, born in Russia. He invented and developed antennas for radio-navigation and instrument-landing systems.

Al·fred |ˈælfrəd| (849–99) king of Wessex (871–99). Known as **Alfred the Great**. Alfred's military resistance saved SW England from Viking occupation. A great reformer, he is credited with the foundation of the English navy and with a revival of learning.

Alf·vén |älˈvän|, Hannes Olof Gösta (1908–95) Swedish theoretical physicist. His work was important for controlled thermonuclear fusion. Nobel Prize for Physics (1970).

Al·ger |ˈæljər|, Horatio, Jr. (1832–99) U.S. author. His novels, most notably *Ragged Dick* (1867), were infused with the message that honest hard work can overcome poverty.

Al·gren |ˈawlgrən|, Nelson (Abraham) (1909–81) U.S. novelist. He drew on his childhood experiences in the slums of Chicago for his novels of social realism,

for example *The Man with the Golden Arm* (1949) and *Walk on the Wild Side* (1956).

Ali[1] |äˈlē|, Muhammad see MUHAMMAD ALI[1].

Ali[2] |äˈlē|, Muhammad see MUHAMMAD ALI[2].

Ali·ghie·ri |äˌligˈyerē|, Dante see DANTE.

Al·len |ˈælən|, Ethan (1738–89) American Revolutionary soldier. He fought the British in the Revolutionary War and led an irregular force, the Green Mountain Boys, in their campaign to gain independence for Vermont, which became a state after his death.

Al·len |ˈælən|, Frederick Lewis (1890–1954) U.S. historian and editor. He worked for *Harper's Magazine* on staff (1923–41) and as editor (1941–53). Notable books: *Only Yesterday* (1931) and *The Big Change* (1952).

Al·len |ˈælən|, Gracie (c. 1905–64) U.S. comedian and television actress. She was the wife and comedy partner of George Burns.

Al·len |ˈælən|, Sam Leeds U.S. businessman. He founded the Flexible Flyer sled company.

Al·len |ˈælən|, Steve (1921–   ) U.S. television humorist and songwriter. Full name *Stephen Valentine Patrick William Allen*. He was host and creator of "The Tonight Show" (1953–57) and host of "The Steve Allen Show" (1956–60).

Al·len |ˈælən|, Tim (1953–   ) U.S. actor. Born *Tim Allen Dick*. A comedian and writer, he starred in the television sitcom "Home Improvement" (1991–99).

Al·len |ˈælən|, Woody (1935–   ) U.S. movie director, writer, and actor. Born *Allen Stewart Konigsberg*. Notable movies: *Play it Again, Sam* (1972), *Annie Hall* (1977, Academy Award), and *Hannah and Her Sisters* (1986, Academy Award).

Al·len·by |ˈælənbē|, Edmund Henry Hynman, 1st Viscount (1861–1936) British soldier. Commander of the Egyptian Expeditionary Force against the Turks, he captured Jerusalem in 1917 and defeated the Turkish forces at Megiddo in 1918.

Al·len·de |äˈyenˌdā| Family name of:
Salvador Allende (1908–73), Chilean

president (1970–73). The first avowed Marxist to win a presidency in a free election, Allende was overthrown and killed in a military coup led by General Pinochet. **Isabel Allende** (1942–), Chilean author, born in Peru. Notable novels: *The House of the Spirits* (1985, Lillian Gish Prize) and *The Infinite Plan* (1993). She is the niece of Salvador Allende.

Al·li·son |'æləsən|, Dorothy (1949–) U.S. author. She was a National Book Award finalist (1992) for her novel *Bastard Out of Carolina*.

All·man |'awlmən| U.S. musicians. **Duane Allman** (1946–71) was a guitarist for The Allman Brothers Band. His brother **Gregg** (1947–) was keyboardist and guitarist for The Allman Brothers Band.

All·ston |'awlstən|, Washington (1779–1843) U.S. landscape painter. He was the first major artist of the American romantic movement.

Alma-Tadema |'ælmə 'tædəmə|, Sir Lawrence (1836–1912) British painter, born in the Netherlands. He is known for his lush genre scenes set in the ancient world.

Al·pert |'ælpərt|, Herb (1935–) U.S. musician and producer. A jazz trumpeter, he cofounded A & M Records (1962) with Jerry Moss.

Alt·dor·fer |'ält,dawrfər|, Albrecht (*c.* 1480–1538) German painter and engraver. He was one of the first modern European landscape painters and was principal artist of the Danube School.

Alt·hus·ser |'ält,hoosər|, Louis (1918–90) French philosopher. In giving a reinterpretation of traditional Marxism in the light of structuralist theories, his work had a significant influence on literary and cultural theory.

Alt·man |'awltmən|, Robert (1925–) U.S. movie director. Notable movies: *M*A*S*H* (1970) and *The Player* (1992).

Al·va·rez |'ælvə,rez|, Luis Walter (1911–88) U.S. physicist. In 1980 Alvarez and his son identified iridium in sediment from the Cretaceous–Tertiary boundary and proposed that this resulted from a catastrophic meteorite impact.

Ama·do |ä'mäṮHō|, Jorge (1912–) Brazilian author. Notable novels: *The Violent Land* (1944) and *Pen, Sword and Camisole: A Fable to Kindle Hope* (1985).

Ama·ti |ä'mätē| a family of Italian violin-makers from Cremona. In the 16th and 17th centuries, three generations of the Amatis developed the basic proportions of the violin, viola, and cello.

Ama·to |ə'mätō|, Pasquale (1878–1942) Italian operatic baritone. He sang 446 performances with the Metropolitan Opera, beginning in 1908.

Am·brose |'æm,brōz|, St. (*c.* 339–97) Doctor of the Church, a champion of orthodoxy, who introduced much Eastern theology and liturgical practice into the West. Feast day, December 7.

Ame·che |ə'mēcHē|, Don (1908–93) U.S. actor. Born *Dominic Felix Amici*. Notable movies: *Cocoon* (1985, Academy Award).

Amen·ho·tep |,æmən'hōtəp| see AKHENATON.

Am·herst |'æm(h)ərst|, Lord Jeffrey (1717–97) English soldier and military commander in North America. He was appointed Governor General of British North America (1760–63) and served as commander in chief of the British army (1772–95).

Am·i·don, Tom U.S. entrepreneur. He created Cream of Wheat cereal.

Amin |ä'mēn|, Idi (1925–) Ugandan soldier and head of state (1971–79); full name *Idi Amin Dada*. He was deposed after a period of rule characterized by the murder of political opponents.

Amis |'ämis| English novelists. **Sir Kingsley Amis** (1922–95) achieved popular success with his first novel *Lucky Jim* (1954); his later novels include *The Old Devils* (1986, Booker Prize) and *The Folks that Live on the Hill* (1990). His son, **Martin (Louis) Amis** (1949–), wrote *The Rachel Papers* (1973), *Money* (1984), and *Time's Arrow* (1991).

Am·mons, A. R. (1926–) U.S. poet. Full name *Archie Randolph Ammons*. He is considered one of the leading transcendentalist American poets. He received the National Book Award for *Garbage* (1993).

Amos |'äməs|, Tori (1963–) U.S. pop

singer. She was the youngest student ever to attend Peabody Conservatory in Baltimore.

Am·père |'æm,piər|, André-Marie (1775–1836) French physicist, mathematician, and philosopher, who analyzed the relationship between magnetic force and electric current.

Amund·sen |'æmənsən|, Roald (1872–1928) Norwegian explorer. Amundsen was the first to navigate the Northwest Passage (1903–6), during which expedition he located the site of the magnetic north pole. In 1911 he became the first to reach the South Pole.

Anac·re·on |ə'nækrēən| (c. 570–c. 478 BC) Greek lyric poet. He is best known for his celebrations of love and wine.

An·ax·ag·o·ras |ˌænək'sægərəs| (c. 500–c. 428 BC) Greek philosopher. He taught in Athens and believed that all matter was infinitely divisible and motionless until animated by mind (nous).

An·ax·i·man·der |ə,næksə'mændər| (c. 610–c. 547 BC) Greek scientist who lived at Miletus. He believed the earth to be cylindrical and poised in space, and is reputed to have taught that life began in water and that humans originated from fish.

An·ax·im·e·nes |ˌænək'simənēz| (c. 546 BC) Greek philosopher and scientist, who lived at Miletus. Anaximenes believed the earth to be flat and shallow, a view of astronomy that was a retrograde step from that of Anaximander.

An·der·sen |'ændərsən|, Hans Christian (1805–75) Danish author. He is famous for his fairy tales, published from 1835, such as "The Snow Queen," "The Ugly Duckling," and "The Little Match Girl."

An·der·son |'ændərsən|, Bradley Jay (1924–) U.S. cartoonist. He created the syndicated cartoons "Marmaduke" (1954) and "Grandpa's Boy" (1954).

An·der·son |'ændərsən|, Carl David (1905–91) U.S. physicist. In 1932 he discovered the positron—the first antiparticle known. Nobel Prize for Physics (1936, shared).

An·der·son |'ændərsən|, Elizabeth Garrett (1836–1917) English physician. She established a clinic for women and children in London and was the first woman elected to the British Medical Association (1873).

An·der·son |'ændərsən|, Gillian (1968–) U.S. actress. She has won Emmy Awards for her role as FBI agent Dana Scully on the television show "The X-Files."

An·der·son |'ændərsən|, Ian (1947–) British flutist, born in Scotland. He performed with the rock group Jethro Tull.

An·der·son |'ændərsən|, John Bayard (1922–) U.S. lawyer and politician. He was an Independent Party presidential candidate in 1980.

An·der·son |'ændərsən|, Marian (c. 1902–93) U.S. operatic contralto. In 1955 she became the first black singer to perform at the New York Metropolitan Opera.

An·der·son |'ændərsən|, Maxwell (1888–1959) U.S. playwright. His plays, many of which are written in verse, deal with social and moral problems. He also wrote many historical dramas. Notable works: *Elizabeth the Queen* (1930), *Key Largo* (1939), *Anne of the Thousand Days* (1948), and *The Bad Seed* (1954).

An·der·son |'ændərsən|, Philip Warren (1923–) U.S. physicist. He made contributions to the study of solid-state physics, investigating magnetism and superconductivity. Research on molecular interactions has also been facilitated by his work on the spectroscopy of gases. Nobel Prize for Physics (1977).

An·der·son |'ændərsən|, Robert Woodruff (1917–) U.S. playwright and educator. Notable plays: *Tea and Sympathy* (1953), *You Know I Can't Hear You When the Water's Running* (1967), and *I Never Sang for My Father* (1968).

An·der·son |'ændərsən|, Sherwood (1876–1941) U.S. author. He is best known for *Winesburg, Ohio* (1919), a collection of interrelated short stories that explore the loneliness and frustration of small town life.

An·dré |'än,drā|, Carl (1935–) U.S. minimalist sculptor. His most famous works consist of ready-made units such as bricks, stacked according to a mathematical system and without adhesives or joints.

An·dré |'än,drā|, John (1750–80)

British soldier. He successfully negotiated with Benedict Arnold for the betrayal of West Point to the British (1779–80). Captured while on his return to New York, he was tried and hanged as a spy.

An·dret·ti |æn'dretē|, Mario (Gabriele) (1940–) Italian-born U.S. race-car driver.

An·drew |'æn,drōō|, Prince, Duke of York (1960–) British prince. Full name *Andrew Albert Christian Edward.* He is the second son of Elizabeth II. He married Sarah Ferguson in 1986 but the couple divorced in 1993; they have two children, Princess Beatrice (1988–) and Princess Eugenie (1990–).

An·drew |'æn,drōō|, St. died (c. 60 AD) an Apostle. He was the brother of St. Peter. The X-shaped cross is associated with him because he is said to have been crucified on such a cross. St. Andrew is the patron saint of Scotland and Russia. Feast day, November 30.

An·drews |'æn,drōōz|, Julie (1935–) English actress and singer. Born *Julia Elizabeth Wells.* She is best known for the movies *Mary Poppins* (1964) and *The Sound of Music* (1965).

An·drews |'æn,drōōz|, Roy Chapman (1884–1960) U.S. naturalist, explorer, and author. He discovered the first known clutch of fossil dinosaur eggs in Mongolia (1925).

An·drews |'æn,drōōz|, Thomas (1813–85) Irish physical chemist. He discovered the critical temperature of carbon dioxide and showed that ozone is an allotrope of oxygen.

An·drić |'ändrēt|, Ivo (1892–1975) Yugoslav novelist, essayist, and short-story writer. Nobel Prize for Literature (1961).

An·dro·pov |æn'drō,pawf|, Yuri (Vladimirovich) (1914–84) Soviet statesman, general secretary of the Communist Party of the USSR (1982–84) and president (1983–84). As president he initiated the reform process carried through by Mikhail Gorbachev, his chosen successor.

An·gel·ic Doctor the nickname of St. Thomas AQUINAS.

An·ge·li·co |'ænje,likō|, Fra (c. 1400–55) Italian painter and Dominican friar.

Born *Guido di Pietro*; monastic name *Fra Giovanni da Fiesole.* Notable works: the frescoes in the convent of San Marco, Florence (c. 1438–47).

An·ge·lou |'ænjəlō|, Maya (1928–) U.S. novelist and poet. acclaimed for the first volume of her autobiography, *I Know Why the Caged Bird Sings* (1970).

Ång·ström |'ænGstrəm|, Anders Jonas (1814–1874) Swedish physicist. He proposed a relationship between the emission and absorption spectra of chemical elements, and measured optical wavelengths in the unit later named in his honor.

An·ka |'ænGkə|, Paul (1941–) Canadian musician. Among the hits that he composed and sang are "Lonely Boy" (1959) and "Put Your Head on My Shoulder" (1959).

An·nan |'ænən|, Kofi (Atta) (1938–) Ghanaian diplomat; secretary general of the United Nations (1997–).

Anne |æn| (1665–1714) queen of England and Scotland (known as Great Britain from 1707) and Ireland (1702–14). The last of the Stuart monarchs, daughter of the Catholic James II (but herself a Protestant), she succeeded her brother-in-law William III to the throne.

Anne |æn|, Princess (1950–) British princess. Full name *Anne Elizabeth Alice Louise*, the Princess Royal. Daughter of Elizabeth II.

Anne, St. traditionally the mother of the Virgin Mary. First mentioned by name in the apocryphal gospel of James (2nd century). Feast day, July 26.

Anne Boleyn |æn bŏŏ'lin| see BOLEYN.

An·nen·berg |'ænən,bərg|, Walter (Hubert) (1908–) U.S. publisher and philanthropist. He founded the magazines *Seventeen* (1944) and *TV Guide* (1953) and was US ambassador to Britain (1969–74).

Anne of Cleves |'æn| (1515–57) fourth wife of Henry VIII. Arranged for political purposes, the marriage was dissolved after only six months; Henry, initially deceived by a flattering portrait of Anne by Holbein, took an instant dislike to her.

An·ni·go·ni |,ænə'gawnē|, Pietro (1910–88) Italian painter. He is famous for his portraits of Queen Elizabeth II (1955, 1970) and President Kennedy (1961).

An•no |'änō|, Mitsumasu (1926–) Japanese author and illustrator of children's books.

Anouilh |ä'n⊽⊽ē|, Jean (1910–87) French dramatist. He wrote many plays but is best known for his reworking of the Greek myth of Antigone in *Antigone* (1944).

An•selm |'ænsəlm|, St. (*c.* 1033–1109) Italian-born philosopher and theologian, Archbishop of Canterbury (1093–1109).

Antall |'æntæ|, Jozsef (1933–93) Hungarian statesman. He was prime minister (1990–93), elected premier in the country's first free elections for over forty years.

An•the•mi•us |æn'THēmē₁əs| (6th century AD) Greek mathematician, engineer, and artist; known as **Anthemius of Tralles**.

An•tho•ny |'ænTHənē|, St. (*c.* 250–356) Also **Antony**. Egyptian hermit, the founder of monasticism. Feast day, January 17.

An•tho•ny |'ænTHənē|, Susan Brownell (1820–1906) U.S. social reformer and leader of the woman suffrage movement. She traveled, lectured, and campaigned throughout her life for women's rights. With Elizabeth Cady Stanton, she organized (1869) the National Woman Suffrage Association. With Stanton and Matilda Joslyn Gage, she compiled Volumes I to III of the *History of Woman Suffrage* (1881–86).

An•tho•ny of Pad•ua |'ænTHənē|, St. (1195–1231) Portuguese Franciscan friar. His devotion to the poor is commemorated by alms known as St. Anthony's bread; he is invoked to find lost articles. Feast day, June 13.

An•ti•o•chus |æn'tīəkəs| (*c.* 242–187) BC) the name of eight Seleucid kings, notably: **Antiochus III** (*c.* 242–187 BC; reigned 223–187 BC); known as **Antiochus the Great**. He restored and expanded the Seleucid empire. **Antiochus IV** (*c.* 215–163 BC; reigned 175–163 BC). Known as **Antiochus Epiphanes**. His firm control of Judaea and his attempt to Hellenize the Jews re-

sulted in the revival of Jewish nationalism and the Maccabean revolt.

An•to•ni•nus Pi•us |æntə'nīnəs 'pīəs| (86–161) Roman emperor 138–61. The adopted son and successor of Hadrian, he had a generally peaceful and harmonious reign.

An•to•nio•ni |æn'tōnē₁ōnē|, Michelangelo (1912–) Italian movie director. Notable movies: *L'avventura* (1960), *Blow-Up* (1966), and *Zabriskie Point* (1970).

An•to•ny |'æntənē|, Mark (*c.* 82 or 81–30 BC) Roman general and triumvir; Latin name *Marcus Antonius*. A supporter of Julius Caesar, following Caesar's assassination in 44 he took charge of the Eastern Empire, where he established his association with Cleopatra. Quarrels with Octavian led finally to his defeat at the battle of Actium and to his suicide.

An•to•ny |'æntənē|, St. see ANTHONY, ST.

An•to•ny of Padua |'æntənē|, St. see ANTHONY OF PADUA, ST.

Apel•les |ə'pelēz| (4th century BC) Greek painter. He is now known only from written sources, but was highly acclaimed throughout the ancient world.

Apol•li•naire |ə₁pälə'ner|, Guillaume (1880–1918) French poet. Pseudonym of *Wilhelm Apollinaris de Kostrowitzki*. He coined the term *surrealist* and was acknowledged by the surrealist poets as their precursor. Notable works: *Les Alcools* (1913) and *Calligrammes* (1918).

Ap•ol•lo•ni•us[1] |₁æpə'lōnēəs| 3rd cent. BC. Greek poet called **Appollonius of Rhodes**. Notable work: *Argonautica*.

Ap•ol•lo•ni•us[2] |₁æpə'lōnēəs| (*c.* 262–190 BC) Greek mathematician; **Apollonius of Perga**. He was the first to use the terms *ellipse, parabola*, and *hyperbola*.

Ap•pel |'æpəl|, Karel (1921–) Dutch painter, sculptor, and graphic artist.

Ap•ple |'æpəl|, Fiona (1977–) U.S. rock singer and songwriter. Born *Fiona Apple Maggart*. She won a 1998 Grammy Award for "Criminal."

Ap•ple•seed |'æpəl₁sēd|, Johnny (1774–1845) U.S. folk hero. Born *John Chapman*. A missionary, he traveled throughout Ohio and Indiana planting and caring for apple orchards.

Ap·ple·ton |'æpəltən|, Sir Edward Victor (1892–1965) English physicist. He discovered a region of ionized gases (the Appleton layer) in the atmosphere above the Heaviside or E layer, and won the Nobel Prize for Physics in 1947.

Ap·u·le·ius |,apyə'lēəs| (c. 124–c. 170) Roman writer, born in Africa. Notable works: *Metamorphoses (The Golden Ass)*.

Aqui·nas |ə'kwīnəs|, St. Thomas (1225–74) Italian philosopher, theologian, and Dominican friar. Known as *the Angelic Doctor*. He is regarded as the greatest figure of scholasticism; one of his most important achievements was the introduction of the work of Aristotle to Christian western Europe. Feast day, January 28.

Aqui·no |ə'kēnō|, (Maria) Corazon (1933–) Filipino stateswoman and president (1986–92).

Aq·ui·taine |'ækwi,tān|, Eleanor of see ELEANOR OF AQUITAINE.

Á·vila |'ävēlə|, Teresa of see TERESA OF ÁVILA, ST.

Ar·a·fat |'erə,fæt|, Yasser (1929–) Palestinian statesman, chairman of the Palestine Liberation Organization from 1968 and Palestinian president since 1996.

Ar·a·gon |'erə,gän|, Catherine of see CATHERINE OF ARAGON.

Ar·bus |'ärbəs|, Diane (1923–71) U.S. photographer. She is best known for her disturbing images of people on the streets of U.S. cities.

Ar·buth·not |är'bəTHnət|, John (1667–1735) Scottish physician and writer. His satirical *History of John Bull* (1712) was the origin of John Bull as the personification of the typical Englishman.

Ar·ca·ro |är'kærō; är'kerō|, Eddie (1916–) U.S. jockey. Full name *George Edward Arcaro*. He was the first two-time Triple Crown winner, riding Whirlaway (1941) and Citation (1948).

Ar·chil·o·chus |är'kiləkəs| (7th century BC) Greek poet. He is credited with the invention of iambic meter.

Ar·chi·me·des |,ärkə'mēdēz| (c. 287–212 BC) Greek mathematician and inventor, of Syracuse. He is famous for his discovery of Archimedes' principle (legend has it that he made this discovery while taking a bath, and ran through the

streets shouting "Eureka!"); among his mathematical discoveries are the ratio of the radius of a circle to its circumference, and formulas for the surface area and volume of a sphere and of a cylinder.

Ar·chi·pen·ko |,ärki'peNGkō|, Alexander (Porfirevich) (1887–1964) Russianborn U.S. sculptor. He adapted cubist techniques to sculpture.

Ar·den |'ärdən|, Elizabeth (c. 1884–1966) Canadian-born U.S. executive in the cosmetics industry; born *Florence Nightingale Graham*.

Arendt |ə'rent|, Hannah (1906–75) German-born U.S. philosopher and political theorist.

Ari·as San·chez |'ärēäs 'sänCHez|, Oscar (1941–) Costa Rican president (1986–94). Nobel Peace Prize (1987).

Ari·os·to |,ärē'ästō|, Ludovico (1474–1533) Italian poet. He was noted for his romantic epic *Orlando Furioso* (final version 1532).

Ar·is·tar·chus[1] |,erə'stärkəs| (3rd century BC) Greek astronomer. Known as **Aristarchus of Samos**. Founder of an important school of Hellenic astronomy, he was aware of the rotation of the earth around the sun and so was able to account for the seasons.

Ar·is·tar·chus[2] |,erə'stärkəs| (c. 215–145 BC) Greek scholar. Known as **Aristarchus of Samothrace**. He was noted for his editions of the writings of Homer and other Greek authors.

Ari·stide |,ærə'stēd|, Jean-Bertrand (1953–) Haitian president (1990–96). He led a movement against the dictatorship of Duvalier in the 1980s and was elected president of Haiti in 1990, but was forced into exile (1991–94) by a military coup. In 1994, the presence of U.S. troops facilitated his return.

Ar·is·ti·des |,erə'stīdēz| (c. 530–468 BC) Athenian statesman and general. Known as **Aristides the Just**.

Ar·is·tip·pus |,erə'stipəs| (c. 435–366 BC) Greek philosopher. Known as **Aristippus the Elder**. He is considered the founder of the Cyrenaic school.

Ar·is·toph·a·nes |,erə'stäfənēz| (c. 450–c. 388 BC) Greek comic dramatist. Notable works: *Lysistrata*, the *Birds*, and the *Frogs*.

Ar·is·tot·le |'erəs'tädəl| (384–322 BC)

Greek philosopher and scientist. A pupil of Plato and tutor to Alexander the Great, he founded a school (the Lyceum) outside Athens. He is one of the most influential thinkers in the history of Western thought. His surviving works cover a vast range of subjects, including logic, ethics, metaphysics, politics, natural science, and physics.

Ark·wright |'ärk,rīt|, Sir Richard (1732–92) English inventor and industrialist. In 1767 he patented a water-powered spinning machine.

Ar·ledge |'ärlij|, Roone (1931–   ) U.S. television executive. He has won 36 Emmys for technical and editorial innovation in sports coverage, including 10 Olympic Games and "Monday Night Football."

Ar·ma·ni |är'mänē|, Giorgio (1935–   ) Italian fashion designer.

Ar·ma·tra·ding |'ärmə,trādiNG|, Joan (1950–   ) British musician, born in St. Kitts. Her music is a blend of folk, reggae, soul, and rock.

Ar·mour |'ärmər|, Philip Danforth (1832–1901) U.S. industrialist. He reorganized his brother Herman's grain commission house into the Armour & Co. meat-packing plant (1870).

Arm·strong |'ärm,strawNG|, Edwin Howard (1890–1954) U.S. electrical engineer, inventor of the superheterodyne radio receiver and the frequency modulation (FM) system.

Arm·strong |'ärm,strawNG|, Louis (Daniel) (1901–71) U.S. jazz musician. Known as **Satchmo**. A major influence on Dixieland jazz, he was a trumpet and cornet player as well as a bandleader and a distinctive singer.

Arm·strong |'ärm,strawNG|, Neil (Alden) (1930–   ) U.S. astronaut. He commanded the Apollo 11 mission, during which he became the first man to set foot on the moon (July 20, 1969).

Arne |ärn|, Thomas (1710–78) English composer of the tune for "Rule, Britannia," and of Shakespearean songs.

Ar·no |'är,nō|, Peter (1904–68) U.S. cartoonist. Born *Curtis Arnoux Peters*. He published satirical cartoons of New York society in *The New Yorker* and wrote musical revues.

Ar·nold |'ärnəld|, Benedict (1741–

1801) Revolutionary War general and traitor to the American side. With Ethan Allan, he captured Fort Ticonderoga but later planned to betray West Point to the British. He was captured and hanged by the Americans, and his name became a synonym for "traitor."

Ar·nold |'ärnəld|, Hap (1886–1950) U.S. airman and author. Full name *Henry Harley Arnold*. He helped develop the U.S. Army Air Corps during the 1930s; later he served as general of the army (1944) and general of the air force (1949).

Ar·nold |'ärnəld|, Sir Malcolm (Henry) (1921–   ) English composer and trumpeter, noted especially for his orchestral works and movie scores.

Ar·nold |'ärnəld|, Matthew (1822–88) English poet, essayist, and social critic. In works such as *Culture and Anarchy* (1869) he criticized the Victorian age in terms of its materialism, philistinism, and complacency. Notable poems: "The Scholar Gipsy" (1853) and "Dover Beach" (1867.

Arp |ärp|, Jean (1887–1966) French painter, sculptor, and poet. Also known as **Hans Arp**. He was a co-founder of the Dada movement.

Ar·rhe·ni·us |ə'rānēəs|, Svante August (1859–1927) Swedish chemist, noted for his work on electrolytes. Nobel Prize for Chemistry (1903).

Ar·row |'erō|, Kenneth Joseph (1921–   ) U.S. economist. He is noted chiefly for his work on general economic equilibrium and social choice. Nobel Prize for Economics (1972).

Ar·taud |'är'tō|, Antonin (1896–1948) French actor, director, and poet. He developed the concept of the nonverbal Theater of Cruelty, which concentrated on the use of sound, mime, and lighting.

Ar·ta·xer·xes |,ärtə'zərksēz| the name of three kings of ancient Persia: **Artaxerxes I** son of Xerxes I, reigned 464–424 BC. **Artaxerxes II** son of Darius II, reigned 404–358 BC. **Artaxerxes III** son of Artaxerxes II, reigned 358–338 BC.

Ar·thur |'ärTHər| (5th or 6th century) A legendary king of Britain, historically perhaps a 5th- or 6th-century Romano-British chieftain or general. Stories of his life, the exploits of his knights, and the

Round Table of the court at Camelot were developed by Malory, Chrétien de Troyes, and other medieval writers and became the subject of many legends.

Ar•thur |'ärтнәr|, Chester Alan see box.

Ellen Lewis Herndon Arthur (1837–80), wife of Chester Alan Arthur; she died before her husband became president.

Ar•ya•bha•ta I |'æryә'bәtә| (476–c. 550) Indian astronomer and mathematician. His surviving work, the *Aryabhatiya* (499, has sections dealing with mathematics, the measurement of time, planetary models, the sphere, and eclipses.

Asch |äsн; æsн|, Sholem (1880–1957) U.S. author and playwright, born in Poland. Notable plays: *The God of Vengeance* (1910). Notable novels: *Mottke the Thief* (1935) and *The Prophet* (1955).

As•cham |'æskәm|, Roger (1515–68) English humanist scholar and writer. He was noted for his treatise on archery, *Toxophilus* (1545), and *The Scholemaster* (1570), a practical and influential tract on education.

Ash•bery |'æsнberē|, John Lawrence (1927–) U.S. poet. He is noted for his visionary poetry, as in *Self-Portrait in a Convex Mirror* (1975, National Book Award).

Ash•croft |'æsн,krawft|, Dame Peggy (1907–91) English actress; born *Edith Margaret Emily Ashcroft*. She made her name on the stage with a number of Shakespearean roles.

Ashe |æsн|, Arthur (Robert) (1943–93) U.S. tennis player. He won the U.S. Open championship in 1968 and Wimbledon in 1975, and was the first black male player to achieve world rankings.

Ash•ke•na•zy |,äsнkә'näzē|, Vladimir (Davidovich) (1937–) Russian-born pianist. A child prodigy, he left the Soviet Union in 1963, finally settling in Iceland in 1973.

Ash•ley |'æsнlē|, Laura (1925–85) Welsh fashion and textile designer, known for her use of floral patterns and romantic Victorian and Edwardian styles.

Ash•man |'æsн,mәn|, Howard (1950–91) U.S. lyricist. His songs are featured

---

Arthur, Chester Alan
21st U.S. president

Life dates: 1829–1886
Place of birth: Fairfield, Vermont
Mother: Malvina Stone Arthur
Father: William Arthur
Wife: Ellen Lewis Herndon Arthur
Children: William, Chester, Ellen
College/University: Union College
Military service: during Civil War, brigadier-general, quartermaster-general in New York State Militia
Career: Lawyer; teacher
Political career: Collector, New York Custom House; vice president (under Garfield); president
Party: Republican
Home state: New York
Opponents in presidential race: none; succeeded to the presidency on the assassination of James Garfield
Term of office: Sept. 20, 1881 (following the death of Garfield)–March 3, 1885
Vice president: none
Notable events of presidency: Panic of 1883; Pendleton Act; Chinese Exclusion Act; Edmunds Anti-Polygamy Act; adoption of standard time; Korean Treaty of Peace, Amity, Commerce and Navigation; dedication of the Washington Monument; Civil Service Commission organized; establishment of territorial government in Alaska; Nicaragua Canal Treaty (later Panama Canal Treaty)
Other achievements: Admitted to the New York bar; delegate from New York to Republican National Convention, Chicago
Place of burial: Albany, New York

---

in *Little Shop of Horrors* and *The Little Mermaid*.

Ash•mole |'æsн,mōl|, Elias (1617–92) English antiquary. His collection of rarities, presented to Oxford University in 1677, formed the nucleus of the Ashmolean Museum.

Ash•ton |'æsнtәn|, Sir Frederick (William Mallandaine) (1904–88) British ballet dancer, choreographer, and director. As a choreographer he created successful new works as well as popular adaptations of classical ballets.

Ashur•ba•ni•pal |ä,sнōor'bänipäl| (c. 668–627 BC) grandson of Sennacherib.

A patron of the arts, he established a library of more than 20,000 clay tablets at Nineveh.

As·i·mov |ˈæzəˌmawv|, Isaac (1920–92) Russian-born U.S. writer and scientist, particularly known for his works of science fiction and books on science for nonscientists. Notable science-fiction works: *I, Robot* (1950) and *Foundation* (trilogy, 1951–53).

As·ner |ˈæzner|, Edward (1929–) U.S. actor. He starred in *The Mary Tyler Moore Show* (1970–77) and *The Lou Grant Show* (1977–82), and has won 7 Emmys.

Aso·ka |əˈsōkə| (died *c*. 232 BC) emperor of India *c*. 269–232 BC. Also **Ashoka**. He converted to Buddhism and established it as the state religion.

As·quith |ˈæskwəTH|, Herbert Henry, 1st Earl of Oxford and Asquith (1852–1928) British Liberal statesman, prime minister (1908–16).

As·sad |äˈsäd|, Hafiz al- (1928–) Syrian Baath statesman, president since 1971.

As·san·te |äˈsän‚te|, Armand (1949–) U.S. actor. His films include *Fatal Instinct* (1993); he has also won Emmy Awards for the television special "The Odyssey."

As·si·si[1] |əˈsēsē| see CLARE OF ASSISI, ST.

As·si·si[2] |əˈsēsē| see FRANCIS OF ASSISI, ST.

Astaire |əˈstær|, Fred (1899–1987) U.S. dancer, singer, and actor; born *Frederick Austerlitz*. He is famous for starring in a number of movie musicals, including *Top Hat* (1935), in a successful partnership with Ginger Rogers.

As·ton |ˈæstən|, Francis William (1877–1945) English physicist. He invented the mass spectrograph (with J. J. Thomson) and eventually discovered many of the 287 naturally occurring isotopes of nonradioactive elements. Nobel Prize for Chemistry (1922).

As·tor |ˈæstər|, John Jacob (1763–1848) U.S. merchant, born in Germany. He emigrated to the U.S. in 1784 and made a fortune in the fur trade.

As·tor |ˈæstər|, Nancy Witcher Langhorne, Viscountess (1879–1964) U.S.-born British Conservative politician.

She became the first woman to sit in the House of Commons when she succeeded her husband as a member of Parliament.

As·tu·ri·as |äˈsto͞or‚yäs|, Miguel Angel (1899–1974) Guatemalan novelist and poet, best known for his experimental novel *The President* (1946). Nobel Prize for Literature (1967).

Ata·türk |ˈætətərk|, Kemal (1881–1938) Turkish general and statesman, president (1923–38); also called **Kemal Pasha**. He was elected the first president of the Turkish republic. He abolished the caliphate and introduced other policies designed to make Turkey a modern secular state.

At·get |ätzHe|, Eugène (1856–1927) French photographer. Full name *Jean-Eugène-Auguste Atget*. His is noted for his photographs of Paris, especially historic buildings, architectural decoration, and tradespeople.

Ath·a·na·sius |‚æTHəˈnāsHəs|, St. (*c*. 293–373) Greek theologian and upholder of Christian orthodoxy against the Arian heresy. Feast day, May 2.

Ath·el·stan |ˈæTHəl‚stæn| (895–939) king of England (925–39). Athelstan came to the thrones of Wessex and Mercia in 924 before effectively becoming the first king of all England.

At·kins |ˈætkinz|, Chet (1924–) U.S. musician. A guitarist and country music producer, he established the "Nashville Sound" at RCA Records.

At·kin·son |ˈætkinsən|, Sir Harry (Albert) (1831–92) British-born New Zealand statesman, prime minister (1876–77, 1883–84, and 1887–91).

At·ten·bor·ough |ˈætn‚bərə| Family name of: **Richard (Samuel) Attenborough, Baron Attenborough of Richmond-upon-Thames** (1923–), English movie actor, producer, and director. His brother, **Sir David (Frederick) Attenborough** (1926–), English naturalist and broadcaster. He is known for movies of animals in their natural habitats, including *Life on Earth* (1979), *The Living Planet* (1983), and *The Trials of Life* (1990).

At·ti·la |əˈtilə| (*c*. 406–53) king of the Huns (434–53). Known as **Attila the Hun**. He ravaged vast areas between the

Rhine and the Caspian Sea, before being defeated by the joint forces of the Roman army and the Visigoths at Chèlons in 451.

Att•lee |'æt,lē|, Clement Richard, 1st Earl Attlee (1883–1967) British Labour statesman, prime minister (1945–51). His term saw the creation of the modern welfare state and nationalization of major industries.

At•tucks |'ætəks|, Crispus (1723?–1770) American revolutionary. Believed to be either an escaped or freed slave, he was one of five colonists killed by British soldiers in the Boston Massacre (March 5, 1770).

At•wood |'æt,wŏod|, Margaret (Eleanor) (1939–) Canadian novelist, poet, critic, and short-story writer. Notable novels: *The Edible Woman* (1969), *Cat's Eye* (1989).

Au•brey |'awbrē|, John (1626–97) English antiquarian and author. He is chiefly remembered for *Brief Lives*, a collection of biographies of eminent people.

Au•chin•closs |'awkən,kläs|, Louis Stanton (1917–) U.S. lawyer and author. Pseudonym (early novels) **Andrew Lee**.

Au•den |'awdən|, W. H. (1907–73) British-born poet, resident in America from 1939. Full name *Wystan Hugh Auden*. *Look, Stranger!* (1936) and *Spain* (1937, on the Civil War) secured his position as a leading left-wing poet. He was awarded the Pulitzer Prize for *The Age of Anxiety* (1947).

Au•du•bon |'awdə,bän|, John James (1785–1851) U.S. naturalist and artist. Notable works: *The Birds of America* (1827–38), in which he portrayed even the largest birds life-size, and painted them in action.

Au•er |'ow(ə)r|, Carl, Baron von Welsbach (1858–1929) Austrian chemist, who separated the supposed rare earth element didymium into neodymium and praseodymium.

Au•er•bach |'ow(ə)r,bäk|, Frank (1931–) German-born British painter.

Au•er•bach |'ow(ə)r,bäk|, Red (1917–) U.S. basketball coach. Full name *Arnold Jacob Auerach*. As coach of the Boston Celtics (1950 –66), he led the team to nine NBA championships, eight of them consecutively (1959–66).

Au•gus•tine[1] |'awgə,stēn; ə'gəstin|, St. (354–430) Doctor of the Church; known as **St. Augustine of Hippo**. He became bishop of Hippo in North Africa in 396. His writings, such as the *City of God*, dominated subsequent Western theology. Feast day, August 28.

Au•gus•tine[2] |'awgə,stēn|, St. (died *c.* 604) Italian churchman. Known as **St. Augustine of Canterbury**. Sent from Rome by Pope Gregory the Great to refound the Church of England in 597, he founded a monastery at Canterbury and became its first archbishop. Feast day, May 26.

Au•gus•tus |ə'gəstəs| (63 BC–AD14) the first Roman emperor; born *Gaius Octavianus*; also called **Octavian**. He was adopted in the will of his great-uncle Julius Caesar and gained supreme power by his defeat of Antony in 31 BC. In 27 BC he was given the title Augustus ('venerable') and became in effect emperor.

Aung San |'owNG 'sän| (*c.* 1914–47) Burmese nationalist leader. As leader of the Council of Ministers he negotiated a promise of self-government from the British shortly before his assassination.

Aung San Suu Kyi |'owNG 'sän 'sŏo 'CHē|, Daw (1945–) Burmese political leader, daughter of Aung San and leader of the National League for Democracy (NLD) since 1988. She was kept under house arrest from 1989 to 1995, and the military government refused to recognize her party's victory in the 1990 elections. Nobel Peace Prize (1991).

Au•rang•zeb |aw,ræNG'zeb| (1618–1707) Mogul emperor of Hindustan (1658–1707), who increased the Mogul empire to its greatest extent.

Au•re•li•an |aw'rēlēən| (*c.* 215–75) Roman emperor (270–75); Latin name *Lucius Domitius Aurelianus*. Originally a common soldier, he rose through the ranks and was elected emperor by the army.

Au•re•li•us |aw'rēlēəs|, Marcus (121–80) Roman emperor (161–80); full name *Caesar Marcus Aurelius Antoninus Augustus*. He was occupied for much of his reign with wars against invading Germanic tribes. His *Meditations*, a collection of aphorisms and reflections, are evidence of his philosophical interests.

Au·ric |'awrik|, Georges (1899–1983) French composer. Auric was one of the anti-romantic group Les Six. He is probably best known for his scores for movies such as *The Lavender Hill Mob* (1951) and *Moulin Rouge* (1952).

Aus·ten |'awstən|, Jane (1775–1817) English novelist. Her major novels are *Sense and Sensibility* (1811), *Pride and Prejudice* (1813), *Mansfield Park* (1814), *Emma* (1815), *Northanger Abbey* (1818), and *Persuasion* (1818). They are notable for skillful characterization, dry wit, and penetrating social observation.

Aus·tin |'awstən|, Herbert, 1st Baron Austin of Longbridge (1866–1941) British automobile manufacturer. Among the cars produced by his factory the Austin Seven ("Baby Austin") was particularly popular. His company merged with Morris Motors in 1952 to form the British Motor Corp.

Aus·tin |'awstən|, J. L. (1911–60) English philosopher. Full name *John Langshaw Austin*. A careful exponent of linguistic philosophy, he pioneered the theory of speech acts, pointing out that utterances can be used to perform actions as well as to convey information. Notable works: *Sense and Sensibilia* and *How to Do Things with Words* (both 1962).

Aus·tin |'awstən|, John (1790–1859) English jurist. His work is significant for its strict delimitation of the sphere of law and its distinction from that of morality.

Aus·tin |'awstən|, Stephen Fuller (1793–1836) colonizer of Texas. He founded the first recognized Anglo-American settlement in Texas (1822) and served briefly as secretary of state of the Republic of Texas (1836).

Au·try |'awtrē|, (Orvon) Gene (1907–98) U.S. singer and actor. Known as **the Singing Cowboy**. His credits include the first cowboy song recording (1929) and 88 musical Westerns.

Av·a·lon |'ævə,län|, Frankie (1939–) U.S. musician. Full name *Francis Avalon*. He was a singer who made regular appearances on television's "American Bandstand" and costarred with Annette Funicello in several beach party movies.

Av·e·don |'ævədän|, Richard (1923–) U.S. photographer and photojournalist. Among his noted works is *Observations* (1959), a book of celebrity portraits. His series of photos chronicling the civil rights and antiwar movements of the 1960s gained critical acclaim.

Aver·ro·ës |ə'verə,wēz; ˌævə'rōēz| (1126–98) Spanish-born Islamic philosopher, judge, and physician; Arabic name *ibn-Rushd*. His highly influential commentaries on Aristotle sought to reconcile Aristotle with Plato and the Greek philosophical tradition with the Arabic.

Avery |'ævərē|, Tex (1907–80) U.S. animator. Born *Frederick Bean Avery*. He created the cartoon characters Bugs Bunny and Porky Pig.

Av·i·cen·na |ˌævə'senə| (980–1037) Persian-born Islamic philosopher and physician; Arabic name *ibn-Sina*. His philosophical system, drawing on Aristotle but in many ways closer to Neoplatonism, was the major influence on the development of scholasticism. His *Canon of Medicine* was a standard medieval medical text.

Avo·ga·dro |ˌävə'gädrō|, Amedeo (1776–1856) Italian chemist and physicist. His law, formulated in 1811, was used to derive both molecular weights and a system of atomic weights.

Ax |æks|, Emanuel (1949–) U.S. pianist, born in Poland. A soloist with major international orchestras, he has won four Grammys and the Arthur Rubinstein International Competition (1974).

Ayatollah Kho·mei·ni |kō'mānē| see KHOMEINI.

Ayck·bourn |'īk,baw(ə)rn|, Sir Alan (1939–) English dramatist, known chiefly for comedies dealing with suburban and middle-class life. Notable plays: *Relatively Speaking* (1967), *Absurd Person Singular* (1973).

Ay·er |ær|, Sir A. J. (1910–89) English philosopher. Full name *Alfred Jules Ayer*. Involved with the Vienna Circle in 1932, he was an important proponent of logical positivism. Notable works: *Language, Truth, and Logic* (1936).

Ayl•ward |ˈālwawrd|, Gladys (May) (1902–70) English missionary. In 1932 she helped found an inn in Yangsheng (later portrayed in the 1959 movie *The Inn of the Sixth Happiness*). During the Sino-Japanese war she made a perilous journey to lead a hundred children to safety. She later settled in Taiwan as head of an orphanage.

Ayub Khan |äˈo͞obˈkän|, Muhammad (1907–74) Pakistani soldier and statesman; he was president (1958–69).

Azi•ki•we, (Benjamin) Nnamdi (1904–96) Nigerian statesman, the first governor general of an independent Nigeria (1960–63) and its first president (1963–66).

Bb

Baa·de |'bädə|, (Wilhelm Heinrich) Walter (1893–1960) German-born U.S. astronomer. He proved that the Andromeda galaxy was much farther away than had been thought, which implied that the universe was much older and more extensive than had been supposed.

Bab·bage |'bæbij|, Charles (1792–1871) English mathematician, inventor, and pioneer of machine computing. He designed a mechanical computer with Ada Lovelace but was unable to complete it in his lifetime.

Bab·bitt |'bæbət|, Arthur (1907–92) U.S. cartoonist. He worked on several Disney projects, including "Snow White."

Bab·bitt |'bæbət|, Bruce Edward (1938–) U.S. politician. He has served as the governor of Arizona (1978–87) and the U.S. Secretary of the Interior (1993–).

Bab·bitt |'bæbət|, Milton (Byron) (1916–) U.S. composer and mathematician. His compositions developed from the twelve-note system of Schoenberg and Webern.

Ba·bel |'bæbəl|, Isaac Emmanuilovich (1894–1941) Russian author. He was exiled to Siberia *c.* 1937. Notable works: *Odessa Tales* (1916), *Konarmiya* (1926), and the plays *Zakat* (1928) and *Mariya* (1935).

Ba·bur |'bä,bŏŏr| (1483–1530) first Mogul emperor of India *c.* 1525–30, descendant of Tamerlane; born *Zahir ad-Din Muhammad*. He invaded India *c.* 1525 and conquered the territory from the Oxus to Patna.

Ba·call |bə'kawl|, Lauren (1924–) U.S. actress; born *Betty Jean Perske*. She co-starred with her husband, Humphrey Bogart, in a number of successful movies.

Bach |bäKH|, Johann Sebastian (1685–1750) German composer. An exceptional and prolific baroque composer, he produced works ranging from violin concertos, suites, and the six *Brandenburg Concertos* (1720–21) to clavier works and sacred cantatas. Large-scale choral works include *The Passion according to St. John* (1723), *The Passion according to St. Matthew* (1729), and the *Mass in B minor* (1733–38). He had twenty children: **Carl Philipp Emanuel Bach** (1714–88) wrote church music, keyboard sonatas, and a celebrated treatise on clavier playing, and **Johann Christian Bach** (1735–82) became music master to the British royal family and composed thirteen operas.

Bach·a·rach |'bækə,ræk|, Burt (1929–) U.S. writer of popular songs, many of which were written with lyricist Hal David (1921–).

Ba·con[1] |'bākən|, Francis, Baron Verulam and Viscount St. Albans (1561–1626) English statesman and philosopher. As a scientist he advocated the inductive method; his views were instrumental in the founding of the Royal Society in 1660. Notable works: *The Advancement of Learning* (1605) and *Novum Organum* (1620).

Ba·con[2] |'bākən|, Francis (1909–92) Irish painter. His work chiefly depicts human figures in grotesquely distorted postures, their features blurred or erased.

Ba·con |'bākən|, Henry (1866–1924) U.S. architect. He collaborated with sculptor Daniel Chester French in the creation of several American memorials, most notably the Lincoln Memorial (1911) in Washington, D.C., the design of which was Bacon's last major work.

Ba·con |'bākən|, Kevin (1958–) U.S. actor. In 1996 he made his directorial debut in the film *Losing Chase*.

Ba·con |'bākən|, Roger (1220–92) English philosopher, scientist, and Franciscan monk. Most notable for his work in the field of optics, he emphasized the need for an empirical approach to scientific study.

Baden-Powell |'bādn 'pōəl|, Robert (Stephenson Smyth), 1st Baron Baden-Powell of Gilwell (1857–1941) English soldier and founder of the Boy Scout movement.

Ba·der |'bādər|, Sir Douglas (Robert

Stuart) (1910–82) British airman. Despite having lost both legs in a flying accident in 1931, he saw action as a fighter pilot during the Battle of Britain (1940–41). After the war he was noted for his work on behalf of disabled people.

Ba•du |ˌbäˈdo͞o|, Erykah (1971–) U.S. rhythm and blues musician. Born *Erica Wright*. Grammy Award, 1998.

Baeck, Leo (1873–1956) German rabbi and theologian. As leader of the National Agency of Jews in Germany (1933–42), he was eventually sent (1942–45) to a German concentration camp. After the war, he became president of the World Union for Progressive Judaism in London and taught at the Hebrew Union College in Cincinnati, Ohio.

Bae•de•ker |ˈbäˌdekər|, Karl (1801–59) German publisher. He is remembered chiefly for the series of travel guidebooks to which he gave his name and which are still published today.

Baeke•land |ˈbäkˌlənd|, Leo Hendrik (1863–1944) U.S. chemist and inventor, born in Belgium. He invented and developed the synthetic resin Bakelite (1907).

Baer |bär|, Karl Ernst von (1792–1876) German biologist. He discovered that ova were particles within the ovarian follicles, and he formulated the principle that in the developing embryo general characteristics appear before special ones. His studies were used by Darwin in the theory of evolution.

Baer |bär|, Ralph U.S. engineer and inventor. He devised the first video game.

Baey•er |ˈbeyər|, (Johann Friedrich Wilhelm) Adolf von (1835–1917) German organic chemist. He prepared the first barbiturates and investigated dyes, synthesizing indigo and determining its structural formula. Nobel Prize for Chemistry (1905).

Ba•ez |bīˈez|, Joan (1941–) U.S. folk singer and civil rights activist

Baf•fin |ˈbæfən|, William (*c.* 1584–1622) English navigator and explorer, the pilot of several expeditions in search of the Northwest Passage (1612–16).

Bage•hot |ˈbæjət|, Walter (1826–77) English economist and journalist; editor of the *Economist* (1860–77).

Bai•ley |ˈbālē|, Donovan (1967–) Canadian sprinter, born in Jamaica. He set the world record for the 100 meters (9.84 seconds) at the 1996 Olympic Games.

Bai•ley |ˈbālē|, Mildred (1907–51) U.S. jazz and blues singer and pianist. She was the first white singer to successfully emulate jazz as performed by black contemporaries.

Baird |bærd|, John Logie (1888–1946) Scottish pioneer of television. He made the first transatlantic transmission and demonstration of color television in 1928 using a mechanical system which was soon superseded by an electronic system.

Bai•ul |bīˈo͞ol|, Oksana (1977–) Ukranian figure skater. She was the 1993 world champion at age 15 and a 1994 Olympic gold medalist.

Ba•ker |ˈbākər|, Chet (1929–87) U.S. jazz trumpeter. Full name *Chesney Henry Baker*. He played with Gerry Mulligan in his "pianoless" quartet, as well as with others and on his own.

Ba•ker |ˈbākər|, George (1915–75) U.S. cartoonist. He created the syndicated comic strip "Sad Sack," depicting the beleaguered enlisted military man.

Ba•ker |ˈbākər|, Dame Janet (Abbott) (1933–) English operatic mezzo-soprano.

Ba•ker |ˈbākər|, Josephine (1906–75) U.S. dancer. She was a star of the Folies-Bergère in the 1930s, famed for her exotic dancing and risqué clothing.

Ba•ker |ˈbākər|, Russell (1925–) U.S. journalist. He won a Pulitzer Prize in 1983 for *Growing Up* and in 1979 for *Commentary.*

Bake•well |ˈbākˌwel|, Robert (1725–95) English pioneer in scientific methods of livestock breeding and husbandry. He produced pedigree herds of sheep and cattle and increased the meat production from his animals through selective breeding.

Bak•er |ˈbākər|, Robert T. (1945–) U.S. paleontologist. He proposed the controversial idea that dinosaurs were both active and warm-blooded.

Bakst |bækst|, Léon (1866–1924) Russian painter and designer; born *Lev Samuilovich Rozenberg.* He was a member of the Diaghilev circle and the Ballets Russes, for which he designed exotic, richly colored sets and costumes.

Ba•ku•nin |bə'kॿ̄,nyēn|, Mikhail (Aleksandrovich) (1814–76) Russian anarchist. He took part in the revolutions of 1848, and participated in the First International until his expulsion in 1872.

Bal•an•chine |bælən,SHēn|, George (1904–83) Russian-born U.S. ballet dancer and choreographer; born *Georgi Melitonovich Balanchivadze.* He was chief choreographer of Diaghilev's Ballets Russes during the 1920s, and in 1934 he co-founded the company which later became the New York City Ballet.

Bal•boa |bæl'bōə|, Vasco Núñez de (1475–1519) Spanish explorer. In 1513 he reached the western coast of the isthmus of Darien (Panama), thereby becoming the first European to see the eastern shores of Pacific Ocean.

Bald•win |'bawldwən|, Henry (1780–1844) U.S. Supreme Court Justice (1830–44). He was a member of the U.S. House of Representatives from Pennsylvania (1817–22).

Bald•win |'bawldwən|, James (Arthur) (1924–87) U.S. novelist and black civil rights activist. Notable works: *Go Tell It on the Mountain* (1953) and *Giovanni's Room* (1956).

Bald•win |'bawldwən|, Stanley, 1st Earl Baldwin of Bewdley (1867–1947) British Conservative statesman and prime minister (1923–24, 1924–29, and 1935–37). Despite the German occupation of the Rhineland and the outbreak of the Spanish Civil War (both 1936), Baldwin opposed demands for rearmament, believing that the public would not support it.

Ba•len•cia•ga |bə,lensē'ägə|, Cristóbal (1895–1972) Spanish couturier. In the 1950s he contributed to the move away from the tight-waisted New Look originated by Christian Dior to a looser, semifitted style.

Bal•four |'bæl,fər|, Arthur James, 1st Earl of Balfour (1848–1930) British Conservative statesman, prime minister (1902–05). In 1917, in his capacity as

foreign secretary, Balfour issued the declaration in favor of a Jewish national home in Palestine that came to be known as the Balfour Declaration.

Ball |bawl|, John (died 1381) English rebel, a priest who preached an egalitarian social message. Following the Peasants' Revolt, he was hanged as a traitor.

Ball |bawl|, Lucille (1911–89) U.S. comedienne, known in particular for the popular television series "I Love Lucy" (1951–55).

Bal•la |'bälä|, Giacomo (1871–1958) Italian futurist painter. He created some of the earliest nonobjective paintings.

Bal•lan•tine |'bælən,tīn|, Ian (1916–95) U.S. publisher. He founded Penguin USA, Bantam Books, and Ballantine Books.

Bal•lan•tyne |'bælən,tīn|, R. M. (Robert Michael) (1825–94) Scottish author. He wrote acclaimed stories for boys, such as *The Coral Island* (1857).

Bal•lard |'bælərd|, J. G. (James Graham) (1930–) British novelist and short-story writer. He is known for dystopian science fiction such as his first novel, *The Drowned World* (1962), and *Crash* (1973).

Bal•lard |'bælərd|, Robert Duane (1942–) U.S. marine biologist and explorer. He found the wrecks of the *Bismarck* and the *Titanic* (1985).

Bal•le•ste•ros |bælə'ste,rōs|, Severiano (1957–) Spanish professional golfer. Known as **Sevvy**.

Bal•sam |'bawlsəm|, Martin (1919–96) U.S. actor. He won an Academy Award for *A Thousand Clowns* (1965).

Bal•zac |bawl'zäk|, Honoré de (1799–1850) French novelist. He is chiefly remembered for his series of ninety-one interconnected novels and stories known collectively as *La Comédie humaine*, which includes *Eugénie Grandet* (1833) and *Le Père Goriot* (1835).

Ban•croft |'bæn,krawft|, Anne (1931–) U.S. actress. Born *Anna Maria Luisa Italiano.* She won a 1959 Tony Award for her performance in the play *The Miracle Worker,* and an Academy Award for her performance in the movie version (1962) of the same work.

Ban•croft |'bæn,krawft|, George

(1800–91) U.S. historian and statesman. As U.S. secretary of the navy (1845–46), he established the U.S. Naval Academy at Annapolis (1845). He was ambassador to Great Britain (1846–49) and to Prussia and Germany (1867–74). Notable works: *History of the United States* (ten volumes, 1834–74).

Ban•da |'bændə|, Hastings Kamuzu (*c.* 1906–) Malawian statesman, prime minister (1964–94) and the first president of the Republic of Malawi (1966–94).

Ban•da•ra•nai•ke |ˌbændərə'nīkə|, Sirimavo Ratwatte Dias (1916–) Sinhalese stateswoman and prime minister of Sri Lanka (1960–65, 1970–77, and from 1994). The world's first woman prime minister, she succeeded her husband, S. W. R. D. Bandaranaike, after his assassination.

Ban•de•ras |ˌbæn'därəs|, Antonio (1960–) U.S. actor and director, born in Spain.

Bank•head |'bæŋk,hed|, Tallulah (1903–68) U.S. actress.

Banks |bæŋks|, Ernie (1931–) U.S. baseball player. Full name *Ernest Banks*; known as **Mr. Cub**. Elected to the Baseball Hall of Fame (1977).

Banks |bæŋks|, Sir Joseph (1743–1820) English botanist. He accompanied Captain James Cook on his first voyage to the Pacific, and helped to establish the Royal Botanic Gardens at Kew.

Ban•ne•ker |'bænəkər|, Benjamin (1731–1806) U.S. inventor, astronomer, and mathematician. Born to a slave father and freed slave mother, he published an almanac (1792–1802) that featured his astronomical and tide calculations. On the recommendation of Thomas Jefferson, he was hired to assist in the surveying of the District of Columbia (1791).

Ban•nis•ter |'bænəstər|, Sir Roger (Gilbert) (1929–) British middle-distance runner and neurologist. In May 1954 he became the first man to run a mile in under four minutes.

Ban•ting |'bæntiNG|, Sir Frederick Grant (1891–1941) Canadian physiologist and surgeon. With the assistance of C. H. Best, Banting discovered insulin

(1921–22), using it to treat the previously incurable and fatal disease diabetes. Nobel Prize for Physiology or Medicine (1923, shared with J. J. R. Macleod).

Ba•ra•ka |bə'räkə; 'bä'räkə |, Imamu Amiri (1934–) U.S. author. Born *LeRoi Jones*. An African-American Muslim, he has written plays, short stories, and nonfiction that reflect his black nationalism.

Bar•ba•ros•sa¹ |ˌbärbə'rawsə| (died 1546) Barbary pirate; born *Khair ad-Din*. He was notorious for his successes against Christian vessels in the eastern Mediterranean.

Bar•ba•ros•sa² |ˌbärbə'rawsə| see FREDERICK I.

Bar•ber |'bärbər|, Samuel (1910–81) U.S. composer. He developed a style based on romanticism allied to classical forms; his music includes operas and orchestral and chamber music.

Bar•be•ra |ˌbär'bärə|, Joseph (1911–) U.S. animator. He was co-chairman and cofounder of Hanna-Barbera Cartoons, Inc., with partner William Hanna; together they created characters such as the Flintstones, Tom and Jerry, The Jetsons, Yogi Bear, and Scooby Doo. He won seven Academy Awards between 1943 and 1953 for MGM's animated shorts.

Bar•bi•rol•li |ˌbärbə'rōlē|, Sir John (Giovanni Battista) (1899–1970) English conductor, of Franco-Italian descent.

Bar•bour |'bärbər|, John (*c.* 1325–95) Scottish poet and prelate. The only poem ascribed to him with certainty is *The Bruce*, a verse chronicle relating the deeds of Robert the Bruce.

Bar•bour |'bärbər|, Philip P. (1783–1841) U.S. Supreme Court Justice (1836–41).

Bar-Cochba |'bär 'kawKHbä| Jewish rebel leader; known as **Simeon** in Jewish sources. He led the rebellion in AD 132 against the Romans, and was accepted by some of his Jewish contemporaries as the Messiah.

Bar•deen |ˌbär'dēn|, John (1908–91) U.S. physicist. He won the Nobel Prize in 1956 with William Shockley and Walter Brattain for developing a point-contact transistor and again in 1972 with Leon N. Cooper and John R. Schreiffer for the theory of superconductivity.

Bar·dot |bär'dō|, Brigitte (1934–) French actress; born *Camille Javal*. The movie *And God Created Woman* (1956) established her reputation as an international sex symbol.

Bar·en·boim |'bærən,boim|, Daniel (1942–) Israeli pianist and conductor, musical director of the Orchestre de Paris 1975–88 and of the Chicago Symphony Orchestra from 1991.

Ba·rents |'berənts|, Willem (c. 1550–1597) Dutch explorer. The leader of several expeditions in search of the Northeast Passage to Asia, Barents discovered Spitsbergen and reached Novaya Zemlya, off the coast of which he died.

Bar·ker |'bärkər|, George (Granville) (1913–91) English poet, noted for his penchant for puns, distortion, and abrupt changes of tone.

Bark·ley |'bärklē|, Alben William (1877–1956) vice president of the U.S. (1949–53).

Bark·ley |'bärklē|, Charles (1963–) U.S. basketball player. He was a five-time All-NBA player, first with Philadelphia and then with Phoenix; he was also a member of the U.S. Olympic Dream Team (1992).

Bar·na·bas |'bärnəbəs|, St. (1st century AD) Cypriot Levite and Apostle. He accompanied St. Paul on the first missionary journey to Cyprus and Asia Minor. The traditional founder of the Cypriot Church, he is said to have been martyred in Cyprus. Feast day, June 11.

Bar·nard |'bär,närd|, Christiaan Neethling (1922–) South African surgeon. He pioneered human heart transplantation, performing the first operation of this kind in December 1967.

Bar·nard |'bär,närd|, Henry (1811–1900) U.S. educator. He was a public school system reformer and the first U.S. commissioner of education (1867–70).

Barnes |bärnz|, Djuna (1892–1982) U.S. poet, author, and artist. Also known by pseudonym **Linda Steptoe**. Notable works of verse: *Creatures in an Alphabet* (1982). Notable novels: *Ryder* (1928) and *Nightwood* (1936).

Bar·num |'bärnəm|, P. T. (Phineas Taylor) (1810–91) U.S. showman. He billed his circus, opened in 1871, as "The Greatest Show on Earth"; ten years later he founded the Barnum and Bailey Circus with his former rival Anthony Bailey (1847–1906).

Ba·ro·ja (y Nes·si) |,bä'rōKHə ē 'nesē|, Pío (1872–1956) Spanish novelist. He was a physician in Basque country who wrote nearly 100 novels, including the 22-volume *Memorias de un hombre de acción*.

Bar·rault |bä'rō|, Jean-Louis (1910–94) French actor and director. He directed a number of movies, including *Les Enfants du Paradis* (1945).

Bar·rett |'berət|, Elizabeth see BROWNING, ELIZABETH BARRETT.

Bar·rie |'berē|, Sir J. M. (James Matthew) (1860–1937) Scottish dramatist and novelist. Barrie's most famous play is *Peter Pan* (1904), a fantasy for children about a boy who would not grow up.

Bar·row |'berō|, Clyde (1909–34) U.S. bank robber and murderer. He and his partner, Bonnie Parker, shot and killed at least 13 persons during a notorious two-year crime spree across the Southwest. They were finally stopped and shot to death at a Louisiana roadblock.

Bar·ry |'berē|, Sir Charles (1795–1860) English architect, designer of the Houses of Parliament.

Bar·ry |'berē|, Dave (1947–) U.S. newspaper columnist and author. He writes a column for the *Miami Herald* (1983–), won the 1988 Pulitzer Prize for *Criticism or Commentary*, and has written humorous books.

Bar·ry[1] |'berē|, John (1745–1803) American naval officer, born in Ireland. After John Paul Jones, Barry ranks as the foremost naval hero of the American Revolution.

Bar·ry[2] |'berē|, John (1933–) English composer. A three-time Academy Award winner, he gained fame for the music of several James Bond movies.

Bar·ry |'berē|, Marion Shepilov, Jr. (1936–) U.S. politician. He was the mayor of Washington, D.C. (1979–91; 1995–98).

Bar·ry |'berē|, Philip James Quinn (1896–1949) U.S. playwright. Notable plays: *Holiday* (1928) and *The Philadelphia Story* (1939).

Bar·ry |'berē|, Rick (1944–) U.S. basketball player. Elected to the Basketball Hall of Fame (1986).

Bar·ry·more |'berē,mŏŏr| U.S. family of movie and stage actors, notably **Lionel** (1878–1954), his sister **Ethel** (1879–1959), their brother **John** (1882–1942), and John's granddaughter **Drew** (1975–).

Bart |bärt|, Lionel (1930–1999) English composer and lyricist. His musicals include *Oliver!* (1960).

Barth |bärt.|, John (Simmons) (1930–) U.S. novelist and short-story writer noted for complex experimental novels such as *The Sot-Weed Factor* (1960).

Barth |bärTH|, Karl (1886–1968) Swiss Protestant theologian. His seminal work *Epistle to the Romans* (1919) established a neo-orthodox or theocentric approach to contemporary religious thought that remains influential on Protestant theology.

Bar·thelme, Donald (1931–1989) U.S. author. Notable works: *Come Back, Dr. Caligari* (1964) and *Paradise* (1986).

Barthes |bärt|, Roland (1915–80) French writer and critic. Barthes was a leading exponent of structuralism and semiology in literary criticism, while later works were influential in the development of deconstruction and post-structuralism.

Bar·thol·di |bär'tōldē|, Frédéric-Auguste (1834–1904) French sculptor, known especially as the designer of the Statue of Liberty, which was presented to the U.S. in 1886.

Bar·thol·o·mew |bär'THälə,myōō|, St. an Apostle, regarded as the patron saint of tanners. Feast day, August 24.

Bart·lett |'bärtlət|, John (1820–1905) U.S. publisher and lexicographer. His most famous work, Bartlett's *Familiar Quotations*, was first published in 1855.

Bart·lett |'bärtlət|, John Russell (1805–86) U.S. bibliographer and librarian. He served as Rhode Island's secretary of state (1855–72); his works include *Dictionary of Americanisms* (1848) and *Records of the Colony of Rhode Island, 1636–1792*.

Bart·lett |'bärtlət|, Josiah (1729–95) American Revolutionary leader and physician. He was a signer of the Declaration of Independence and the first governor of New Hampshire (1793–94).

Bart·lett |'bärtlət|, Paul Wayland (1865–1925) U.S. sculptor. He created the pediment on the House wing of the U.S. Capitol (1916).

Bart·lett |'bärtlət|, Robert Abram (1875–1946) U.S. explorer and author. Known as **Captain Bob Bartlett**. He commanded the ship *Roosevelt* on Robert Peary's Arctic voyages (1905–09) and made numerous other northern expeditions.

Bar·tók |'bär,tawk|, Béla (1881–1945) Hungarian composer. His work owes much to Hungarian folk music and includes six string quartets, three piano concertos, and the *Concerto for Orchestra* (1943).

Bar·to·lom·meo |,bärtōlō'meō|, Fra (*c.* 1472–1517) Italian painter; born *Baccio della Porta*. He was a Dominican friar and worked chiefly in Florence.

Bar·ton |'bärtən|, Clara (1821–1912) U.S. founder of the American Red Cross and its first president (1882–1904).

Bar·ton |'bärtən|, Sir Derek Harold Richard (1918–98) English chemist and educator. He added a third dimension to chemical analysis, which became central to research on new drugs. Nobel Prize, 1969.

Bar·ton |'bärtən|, Sir Edmund (1849–1920) Australian statesman and jurist, first prime minister of Australia (1901–03).

Ba·ruch |bə'rŏŏk|, Bernard Mannes (1870–1965) U.S. financier and economic adviser. As a sought-after presidential adviser, his many appointments included chairman of the War Industries Board (1918–19) and U.S. representative on the United Nations Atomic Energy Commision (1946).

Ba·rysh·ni·kov |bə'risHnə,kawv|, Mikhail (Nikolaevich) (1948–) U.S. ballet dancer, born in Latvia of Russian parents. In 1974 he defected to the West while touring with the Kirov Ballet.

Bar•zun |ˌbärˈzən|, Jacques Martin (1907–) U.S. educator, author, and literary critic, born in France. He is known as a staunch and outspoken supporter of traditional standards of language and education. Notable books: *Teacher in America* (1945), *Music in American Life* (1956), and *Clio and the Doctors* (1974).

Ba•sie |ˈbāsē|, Count (William) (1904–84) U.S. jazz pianist, organist, and bandleader. In 1935 he formed the Count Basie Orchestra, which became one of the most successful bands of the swing era.

Bas•il |ˈbæzəl|, St. (*c.* 329–79) Doctor of the Church, bishop of Caesarea; known as **St. Basil the Great**. Brother of St. Gregory of Nyssa, he staunchly opposed the Arian heresy and put forward a monastic rule that is still the basis of monasticism in the Eastern Church. Feast day, June 14.

Ba•sing•er |ˈbāˌsiNGgər|, Kim (1953–) U.S. actress. Academy Award, 1997.

Bas•ker•ville |ˈbæskərˌvil|, John (1706–75) British printer and typographer. His experiments in typefounding (1750s) led him to design the Baskerville type styles. He served as printer to Cambridge University (1758–68).

Bas•kin |ˈbæskən|, Burton (1913–67) U.S. businessman. He formed the Baskin-Robbins ice cream business in 1947 with brother-in-law Irvine Robbins (1917–).

Bas•qui•at, Jean-Michel (1960–1988) U.S. painter, sculptor, and draughtsman. He was a graffiti artist in New York City who eventually had exhibitions of his artwork.

Bate•man |ˈbātmən|, H. M. (Henry Mayo) (1887–1970) Australian-born British cartoonist.

Bates |bāts|, Daisy. U.S. civil rights activist. She was one of the students who integrated Central High School in Little Rock, Arkansas (1957); she recounted her experiences in *The Long Shadow of Little Rock*. She served as president of the Arkansas chapter of the NAACP. Spingarn Medal, 1958.

Bates |bāts|, H. E (1905–74) English novelist and short-story writer; full name *Herbert Ernest Bates*.

Bates |bāts|, Kathy (1948–) U.S. actress. Notable movies: *Misery* (1990, Academy Award), *Fried Green Tomatoes* (1991), and *Titanic* (1997).

Bate•son |ˈbātsən|, William (1861–1926) English geneticist. He coined the term *genetics* in its current sense and publicized the work of Mendel.

Ba•tis•ta |bəˈtēstə|, Fulgencio (1901–73) Cuban soldier and statesman, president (1940–44 and 1952–59); full name *Fulgencio Batista y Zaldívar*. Despite support from the U.S. his second government was overthrown by Fidel Castro.

Bat•ten |ˈbætn|, Jean (1909–82) New Zealand aviator. She was the first woman to fly from England to Australia and back (1934–5), and in 1936 she made the first direct solo flight from England to New Zealand.

Bau•de•laire |ˌbōdəˈler|, Charles-Pierre (1821–67) French poet and critic. He is largely known for *Les Fleurs du mal* (1857), a series of 101 lyrics that explore his isolation and melancholy and the attraction of evil and the macabre.

Bau•dril•lard, Jean (1929–) French sociologist and cultural critic, associated with postmodernism.

Baugh |baw|, Sammy (1914–) U.S.football player. Full name *Samuel A. Baugh*; known as **Slingin' Sammy**. His trademark pinpoint passing revolutionized professional football by making the forward pass a routine play from scrimmage. He became the only player to lead the NFL in passing, punting, and interceptions in the same season (1943).

Baum |bawm|, L. Frank (1856–1919) U.S. journalist and author. Full name *Lyman Frank Baum*. Notable children's books: *Father Goose: His Book* (1899) and *The Wonderful Wizard of Oz* (1900). He also wrote under numerous pseudonyms, including Edith Van Dyne, Laura Bancroft, and Captain Hugh Fitzgerald.

Bausch |bowSH|, John Jacob (1830–1926) U.S. businessman. He was a co-founder of the Bausch & Lomb Optical Co. (1853).

Bax |bæks|, Sir Arnold (Edward Trevor)

(1883–1953) English composer, noted for tone poems such as *Tintagel* (1917).

Bax·ter |'bækstər|, Anne (1923–85) U.S. actress. She won an Academy Award in 1946 for *The Razor's Edge*.

Bax·ter |'bækstər|, James Keir (1926–72) New Zealand poet, dramatist, and critic.

Ba·yard |bī'är; 'bāərd|, Pierre du Terrail, Chevalier de (*c.* 1473–1524) French soldier. He became known as the knight "sans peur et sans reproche" (fearless and above reproach).

Bay·lor |'bālər|, Elgin Gay (1934–) U.S. basketball player. Elected to the Basketball of Fame (1976).

Bea·dle |'bēdl|, Erastus Flavel (1821–94) U.S. publisher. He introduced the Dime Novel series (631 titles), Dime Library (1103 titles), and Half Dime Library (1168 titles).

Beale |bēl|, Dorothea (1831–1906) English educationist. She was principal of Cheltenham Ladies' College 1858–1906 and a campaigner for women's suffrage and higher education.

Bea·mon |'bēmən|, Bob (1946–) U.S. long jumper; full name *Robert Beamon*. At the 1968 Olympic Games he set a world record that stood until 1991.

Bean |bēn|, Leon Lenwood (1872–1967) U.S. outdoorsman and entrepreneur. He created the Maine Hunting Shoe and started the L.L. Bean Co.

Bean |bēn|, Roy (1825?–1903) U.S. frontiersman. Known as **Judge**. In 1882 he named himself justice of the peace in the Texas camp "Vinegaroon," which he renamed Langtry after his idol Lillie Langtry. He held court in his saloon, the Jersey Lily.

Beard |bird|, Charles Austin (1874–1948) U.S. historian and educator. He cowrote *The Development of Modern Europe* (1907), a pioneer text of economic, political and cultural history.

Beard |bird|, Daniel Carter (1850–1941) U.S. illustrator, author, and outsdoorsman. He founded the Sons of Daniel Boone (1905), a forerunner of the Boy Scouts of America, and authored the *American Boy's Handy Book* (1882).

Beard |bird|, James (1903–85) U.S. gastronome and author. He wrote many cookbooks, including *James Beard's American Cookery* (1980).

Beards·ley |'birdzlē|, Aubrey (Vincent) (1872–98) English artist and illustrator, associated with art nouveau and the Aesthetic movement. He is known for original and controversial illustrations, such as those for Oscar Wilde's *Salome* (1894).

Beas·ley |'bēzlē|, Delilah Leontium (1871–1934) U.S. journalist and historian. She wrote *The Negro Trail Blazers of California* (1919), which documented the role of blacks in the American westward expansion.

Bea·ton |'bētn|, Sir Cecil (Walter Hardy) (1904–80) English photographer, famous for his fashion features and portraits of celebrities, particularly the British royal family. He later diversified into costume and set design, winning two Oscars for the movie *My Fair Lady* (1964).

Be·a·trix |'bēətrics| (1938–) queen of the Netherlands (1980–).

Beat·tie |'be‚tē|, Ann (1947–) U.S. author. Notable works of fiction: *Another You* (1995) and *Park City: New and Selected Stories* (1998).

Beat·ty |'bētē|, David, 1st Earl Beatty of the North Sea and of Brooksby (1871–1936) British admiral during World War I.

Beat·ty |'bātē|, Warren (1937–) U.S. movie actor, director, and screenwriter; born *Henry Warren Beaty*.

Beau·mar·chais |bō‚mär'sHā|, Pierre-Augustin Caron de (1732–99) French dramatist. He is chiefly remembered for his comedies *The Barber of Seville* (1775) and *The Marriage of Figaro* (1784), which inspired operas by Rossini and Mozart.

Beau·mont |'bō‚mänt|, Francis (1584–1616) English dramatist. He collaborated with John Fletcher on *Philaster* (1609), *The Maid's Tragedy* (1610–11), and many other plays.

Beau Nash |bō 'næsH| see NASH, RICHARD.

Beau·re·gard |'bōrə‚gärd|, Pierre Gustave Toutant (1818–93) U.S. army officer. He served as superintendent of the U.S. Military Academy at West Point; on the eve of the Civil War, he resigned to join the Confederate army as a brigadier general.

Beck |bek|, C. C. (1910–89) U.S. cartoonist and artist. Full name *Charles Clarence Beck.* He was co-creator of the original "Captain Marvel."

Beck |bek|, Jeff (1944–   ) British musician. He played lead guitar in rock, blues rock, psychedelia and heavy metal bands.

Beck·en·bau·er |'bekən,bowər|, Franz (1945–   ) German professional soccer player and team manager.

Beck·er |'bekər|, Boris (1967–   ) German professional tennis player.

Beck·et |'bekət|, St. Thomas à (c. 1118–70) English prelate and statesman, Archbishop of Canterbury (1162–70). He came into open opposition with King Henry II, who uttered words in anger which led four knights to assissinate Becket in his cathedral. Becket's tomb became a major center of pilgrimage until its destruction under Henry VIII (1538). Feast Day, December 29.

Beck·ett |'bekət|, Samuel (Barclay) (1906–89)) Irish dramatist, novelist, and poet. He is best known for his plays, especially *Waiting for Godot* (1952), a seminal work in the Theater of the Absurd. Nobel Prize for Literature (1969).

Beck·ford |'bekfərd|, William (1760–1844) English writer and collector. As an author he is remembered for the oriental romance *Vathek* (1786, originally written in French).

Beck·man |'bekmən|, Arnold Orville (1900–   ) U.S. electrical engineer and inventor. He invented a quartz spectrophotometer, which made automatic chemical analysis possible.

Beck·mann |'bekmən|, Ernst Otto (1853–1923) German chemist. He devised a method of determining a compound's molecular weight by measuring the rise in boiling point of a solvent containing the compound.

Beck·mann |'bekmən|, Max (1884–1950) German painter and graphic artist. Beckmann's paintings reflect his first-hand experience of human evil during World War I.

Beck·wourth |'bek,wərTH|, James P. (1798–1867) U.S. western pioneer and fur trader. Born into slavery, but raised free in Missouri, he traveled west on fur-trading expeditions (1823–26) and lived among the Crow Indians (1826–37). The pass he discovered (1850) in the Sierra Nevada Mountains opened a route to California's Sacramento Valley. His *Life and Adventures of James P. Beckwourth* (1856) documents the life of the mountain men of the American West.

Bec·que·rel |bek'rel|, Antonie-Henri (1852–1908) French physicist. With Marie and Pierre Curie he discovered the natural radioactivity in uranium salts. Nobel Prize for Physics (1903, shared with the Curies).

Bede |bēd|, St. (c. 673–735) English monk, theologian, and historian; known as the **Venerable Bede**. Bede wrote *The Ecclesiastical History of the English People* (written in Latin, completed in 731), a primary source for early English history. Feast day, May 27.

Bee·cham |'bēCHəm|, Sir Thomas (1879–1961) English conductor and impresario, founder of the London Philharmonic (1932) and the Royal Philharmonic (1947). He did much to stimulate interest in new or neglected composers such as Sibelius, Delius, and Richard Strauss.

Bee·cher |'bēCHər|, Henry Ward (1813–87) U.S. Congregationalist clergyman, orator, and writer. He became famous as an orator attacking political corruption and slavery.

Beene |bēn|, Geoffrey (1927–   ) U.S. fashion designer. He won eight Coty Awards.

Beer·bohm |'bir,bōm|, Max (1872–1956) English caricaturist, essayist, and critic; full name *Sir Henry Maximilian Beerbohm.* A central figure of the Aesthetic Movement, he is remembered chiefly for his novel, *Zuleika Dobson* (1911).

Beers |bērz|, Clifford Whittingham (1876–1943) U.S. mental health reformer. After careful notations of his own mental breakdown and recovery, he founded the Connecticut Society for Mental Hygiene (1908) and the National Commission for Mental Hygiene (1909).

Bee·tho·ven |'bā,tōvən|, Ludwig van

(1770–1827) German composer. Despite increasing deafness Beethoven was responsible for a prodigious output; nine symphonies, thirty-two piano sonatas, sixteen string quartets, the opera *Fidelio* (1814), and the Mass in D (the *Missa Solemnis*, 1823). He is often seen as bridging the classical and romantic movements.

Bee·ton |'bētn|, Mrs. Isabella Mary (1836–65) English author on cookery, famous for her best-selling *Book of Cookery and Household Management* (1861).

Be·gin |bā'gin|, Menachem (1913–92) Israeli statesman and prime minister (1977–84). His hard line on Arab–Israeli relations softened in a series of meetings with President Sadat of Egypt, which led to a peace treaty between the countries. Nobel Peace Prize (1978, shared with Sadat).

Be·han |'bēən|, Brendan (Francis) (1923–64) Irish dramatist and poet who supported Irish nationalism and was convicted for terrorism. Notable works: *Borstal Boy* (novel, 1958) and *The Quare Fellow* (play, 1956).

Behn |bān|, Aphra (1640–89) English novelist and dramatist, regarded as the first professional woman writer in England. Notable works: *The Rover* (comic play, 1678) and *Oroonoko, or the History of the Royal Slave* (novel, 1688).

Beh·rens |'bārəns|, Peter (1868–1940) German architect and designer. He trained Walter Gropius and Le Corbusier.

Beh·ring |'beriNG|, Emil Adolf von (1854–1917) German bacteriologist and one of the founders of immunology. Nobel Prize for Physiology or Medicine (1901).

Bei·der·becke |'bīdər‚bek|, Bix (1903–31) U.S. jazz musician and composer; born *Leon Bismarck Beiderbecke*. A self-taught cornettist and pianist, he was one of a handful of white musicians who profoundly influenced the development of jazz.

Bé·jart |bā'zHär|, Maurice (1927–) French ballet choreographer; born *Maurice Jean Berger*.

Bel·i·veau, Jean (1931–) Canadian hockey player. Known as **Le Gros Bill**.

Bell |bel|, Alexander Graham (1847–

1922) Scottish-born U.S. scientist, the inventor of the telephone; he also made improvements to the telegraph and the phonograph.

Bell |bel|, Gertrude (Margaret Lowthian) (1868–1926) English archaeologist, traveler, and supporter of Arab independence.

Bell |bel|, Jocelyn (1943–) British radio astronomer. Full name *Susan Jocelyn Bell Burnell*. As a research student at Cambridge, working with Professor Antony Hewish, she discovered pulsars (1967).

Bell |bel|, Lawrence Dale (1894–1956) U.S. aircraft designer. The president of Bell Aircraft (1935–56), he designed and produced the first rocket-propelled airplane. Named the X-1, it was the first aircraft to break the sound barrier (1947).

Bell |bel|, Vanessa (1879–1961) English painter and designer; born *Vanessa Stephen*. Together with her sister Virginia Woolf she was a prominent member of the Bloomsbury Group.

Bel·la·my |'beləmē|, Edward (1850–1898) U.S. journalist and novelist. His utopian romance *Looking Backward: 2000–1887* (1888) led to the founding of the Nationalist party, which advocated socialist economic principles.

Bel·li·ni |bə'lēnē| Family of Italian painters in Venice: **Jacopo** (*c.*1400–70), **Gentile** (*c.*1429–1507), and **Giovanni** (*c.*1430–1516).

Bel·li·ni |bə'lēnē|, Vincenzo (1801–35) Italian opera composer. Notable operas: *La Sonnambula* (1831), *Norma* (1831), and *I Puritani* (1835).

Bel·loc |'belawk|, (Joseph) Hilaire (Pierre René) (1870–1953) French-born British writer, historian, and poet remembered chiefly for *Cautionary Tales* (1907).

Bel·low |'belō|, Saul (1915–) Canadian-born U.S. novelist, of Russian-Jewish descent. Notable works: *The Adventures of Augie March* (1953) and *Herzog* (1964). Nobel Prize for Literature (1976).

Bel·lows |'bel‚ōz|, George Wesley (1882–1925) U.S. artist and lithographer. Known for his sporting scenes, portraits, and landscapes, he was also noted for a compelling series of antiwar paintings during World War I.

Bel·lus·chi, Pietro (1899–1994) U.S. architect, born in Italy. Noted for his use of "curtain wall" construction, he designed more than 1,000 buildings, including the Equitable Building (1945–48) in Portland, Oregon.

Bel·shaz·zar |bel'sHæ,zər| (died *c.* 539 BC) viceroy and son of the last king of Babylon. The Bible (Daniel 5) tells how his death in the sack of the city was foretold by a mysterious hand that wrote on the palace wall at a banquet.

Be·lu·shi |bə'lo͞o,sHē|, John (1949–82) U.S. comedian and actor. He is best known for his comic characterizations on television's "Saturday Night Live" (1975–79) and as one of the title characters in the movie *The Blues Brothers* (1980).

Be·mel·mans |'bēməlmənz|, Ludwig (1898–1962) U.S. restaurant proprietor and author, born in the Austrian Tyrol. He wrote the *Madeleine* series of books for children, as well as nonfiction travel literature for adults.

Ben Bel·la |'ben 'belə|, (Mohammed) Ahmed (1918–) Algerian statesman, prime minister (1962–63) and president (1963–65). The first president of an independent Algeria, he was overthrown in a military coup.

Bench |benCH|, Johnny Lee (1947–) U.S. baseball player. Elected to the Baseball Hall of Fame (1989).

Bench·ley |'benCH,lē| Family of U.S. authors, including: **Robert Charles** (1889–1945), drama critic, actor, and humorist. He was a theater critic for *Life* magazine (1920–29) and *The New Yorker* (1929–40). His son, **Nathaniel Benchley** (1915–81), was the author of humorous novels, including *Lassiter's Folly* (1971). **Peter Benchley** (1940–), the son of Nathaniel, wrote *Jaws* (1974) and *The Deep* (1976).

Ben·e·dict |'benədikt|, St. (*c.* 480–*c.* 547) Italian hermit. He established a monastery at Monte Cassino and his *Regula Monachorum* (known as the Rule of St. Benedict) formed the basis of the Western monasticism. Feast day, July 11 (formerly March 21).

Be·neš |'ben,esH|, Edvard (1884–

1948) Czechoslovak statesman, prime minister (1921–22), and president (1935–38 and 1945–48). During World War II he served in London as head of the Czechoslovakian government in exile. In 1945 he regained the presidency but resigned after the 1948 communist coup.

Be·nét |bə'nā| . Family of U.S. authors, including: **William Rose Benét** (1886–1950), poet, novelist, and editor. Husband of Elinor Wylie, he won the Pulitzer Prize in 1941 for *The Dust Which Is God*. His brother, **Stephen Vincent Benét** (1898–1943), was the author of *John Brown's Body* (1928, Pulitzer Prize) and *Western Star* (1943, Pulitzer Prize).

Be·net·ton |'benə,tän| Italian entrepreneurs: **Luciano Benetton** (1938–) and his sister **Giuliana Benetton** (1938–) founded the multinational Benetton clothing company.

Ben-Gurion |ben'gəryən|, David (1886–1973) Israeli statesman, prime minister (1948–53 and 1955–63), Israel's first prime minister and minister of defense.

Ben·nett |'benət| U.S. journalists, including: Scottish-born **James Gordon Bennett** (1795–1872), who founded *The New York Herald*. His son **James Gordon Bennett** (1841–1918) sponsored Henry Stanley's expedition into Africa (1870–71) to find David Livingstone.

Ben·nett |'benət|, (Enoch) Arnold (1867–1931) English novelist, dramatist, and critic. His fame rests on the novels and stories set in the Potteries ("the Five Towns") of his youth, notably *Anna of the Five Towns* (1902), *The Old Wives' Tale* (1908), and the *Clayhanger* series (1902–08).

Ben·nett |'benət|, Michael (1943–87) U.S. choreographer and stage director. Notable productions *Promises, Promises* (1968) and *A Chorus Line* (1975).

Ben·nett |'benət|, Sir Richard Rodney (1936–) English composer, whose works include movie scores, operas, concertos, and chamber pieces.

Ben·nett |'benət|, Tony (1926–) U.S. musician. Born *Anthony Dominick Benedetto*. He was a popular jazz-inflected singer in the early 1950s. Grammy Award, 1998.

Ben·nett |'benət|, William John (1943–) U.S. statesman. He was chairman of the National Endowment for the Humanities (1981–85) and secretary of the U.S. Department of Education (1985–88).

Ben·nett |'benət|, Willard Harrison (1903–87) U.S. physicist. He invented the radio frequency mass spectrometer, which was first used in space by the Soviets aboard their satellite Sputnik (1957).

Ben·ny |'benē|, Jack (1894–1974) U.S. comedian and actor; born *Benjamin Kubelsky*. Working notably on radio and then television, he was renowned for his timing, delivery, and mordant, self-effacing humour.

Ben·tham |'benTHəm|, Jeremy (1748–1832) English philosopher and jurist, the first major proponent of utilitarianism. Bentham wanted to reform the law, arguing that the proper object of all legislation and conduct was to secure "the greatest happiness of the greatest number." Notable works: *Introduction to the Principles of Morals and Legislation* (1789).

Bent·ley |'bentlē|, Edmund Clerihew (1875–1956) English journalist and novelist, inventor of the comic verse form, the clerihew. Notable works: *Trent's Last Case* (detective novel, 1913) and *Clerihews Complete* (1951).

Ben·ton[1] |'bentən|, Thomas Hart (1782–1858) U.S. politician. He was a Democratic member of the U.S. Senate from Missouri (1820–50) and a supporter of frontier explorations.

Ben·ton[2] |'bentən|, Thomas Hart (1889–1975) U.S. painter. He was a leader of the American naturalist school and a great-nephew of Thomas Hart Benton.

Bent·sen |'bentsen|, Lloyd (1921–) U.S. politician. He was a member of the U.S. Senate from Texas (1971–93), a Democratic vice presidential candidate (1988), and secretary of the treasury (1993–94).

Benz |benz|, Carl Friedrich (1844–1929) German engineer and automotive manufacturer. In 1885 he built the first vehicle to be powered by an internal combustion engine.

Ber·e·nice |ˌberə'nēs| (3rd century BC) Egyptian queen, wife of Ptolemy III. She dedicated her hair as an offering for the safe return of her husband from an expedition; the hair was stolen and (according to legend) placed in the heavens. She is commemorated in the name of the constellation Coma Berenices (*Berenice's hair*).

Ber·en·son |'berənsən|, Bernard (1865–1959) U.S. art critic, born in Lithuania. He was an authority on Italian Renaissance art.

Berg |bərg|, Alban (Maria Johannes) (1885–1935) Austrian composer, a leading exponent of twelve-note composition. Notable works: the operas *Wozzeck* (1914–21) and *Lulu* (1928–35) and his violin concerto (1935).

Berg |bərg|, Patty (1918–) U.S. golfer. Full name *Patricia Jane Berg*.

Ber·gen |'bərgən|, Candice (1946–) U.S. actress and photojournalist. She won five Emmy Awards for her title role in television's "Murphy Brown" (1988–98). Notable movies: *Carnal Knowledge* (1971) and *Rich and Famous* (1981). She was the wife of director Louis Malle.

Ber·ger |'bərgər|, Hans (1873–1941) German psychiatrist who detected electric currents in the cerebral cortex and developed encephalography.

Ber·ger |'bərgər|, Thomas (1924–) U.S. author. Notable works: *Crazy in Berlin* (1958), *Little Big Man* (1964), and *The Feud* (1983).

Ber·ge·rac |'bərzHəˌræk| see CYRANO DE BERGERAC.

Ber·gi·us |'bərˌgēyəs|, Friedrich Karl Rudolf (1884–1949) German industrial chemist. Nobel Prize for Chemistry (1931).

Berg·man |'bərgmən|, (Ernst) Ingmar (1918–) Swedish movie and theater director. He used haunting imagery and symbolism often derived from Jungian dream analysis. Notable movies: *Smiles of a Summer Night* (1955), *The Seventh Seal* (1956), and *Hour of the Wolf* (1968).

Berg·man |'bərgmən|, Ingrid (1915–82) Swedish actress. Notable roles: *Casablanca* (1942), *Anastasia* (1956), and *Murder on the Orient Express* (1974).

Berg·son |'bərgsən|, Henri (Louis) (1859–1941) French philosopher. Dividing the world into life (or consciousness) and matter, he rejected Darwinian evolution and argued that life possesses an inherent creative impulse (*elan vital*) that creates new forms as life seeks to impose itself on matter. Nobel Prize for Literature (1927).

Be·ria |'byer,yä|, Lavrenti (Pavlovich) (1899–1953) Soviet politician and head of the secret police 1938–53. He was involved in the elimination or deportation of Stalin's opponents, but after Stalin's death he was arrested and executed.

Ber·i·gan |'berə,gən|, Bunny (1908–42) U.S. jazz trumpeter and orchestra leader. Full name *Rowland Bernart Berigan*. He played with various bands, including Tommy Dorsey and Benny Goodman, until he started his own (1937).

Be·ring |'beriNG|, Vitus (Jonassen) (1681–1741) Danish navigator and explorer. He led several Russian expeditions aimed at discovering whether Asia and North America were connected by land. He sailed along the coast of Siberia and in 1741 reached Alaska from the east but died on the return journey; the Bering Sea and Bering Strait are named after him.

Ber·io |'berēō|, Luciano (1925–) Italian composer, an experimentalist who has adopted serial, aleatory, and electronic techniques. Notable works: *Circles* (1960), *Sequenza* series (1958–75), and *Un Re in Ascolto* (opera, 1984).

Berke·ley |'bərklē|, Busby (1895–1976) U.S. choreographer and movie director; born *William Berkeley Enos*. He is remembered for spectacular sequences in which dancers formed kaleidoscopic patterns on the screen. Notable movies: the *Gold Diggers* series (1922–37) and *Babes in Arms* (1939).

Berke·ley |'bərklē|, George (1685–1753) Irish philosopher and bishop. He argued that material objects exist solely by being perceived, so there are only minds and mental events. Since God perceives everything all the time, objects have a continuous existence in the mind of God. Notable works: *A Treatise Concerning the Principles of Human Knowledge* (1710).

Berke·ley |'bərklē|, Sir Lennox (Randall Francis) (1903–89) English composer of four operas, four symphonies, music for ballet and movie, and sacred choral music.

Ber·ko·witz |'bərkō,wits|, David (1953–) U.S. murderer. Known as **Son of Sam**.

Berle |bərl|, Milton (1908–) U.S. actor. Born *Milton Berlinger*. He began as a vaudeville entertainer and went on to star in radio, stage, movies, and television.

Ber·lin |bər'lin|, Irving (1888–1989) Russian-born U.S. composer of popular music; born *Israel Baline*. He wrote more than 800 songs many of which are regarded as popular "standards" or classics. Notable works: the songs "God Bless America" (1939) and "White Christmas" (1942) and the score for *Annie get Your Gun* (1946).

Ber·lin |bər'lin|, Sir Isaiah (1909–) Latvian-born British philosopher who concerned himself with the history of ideas. Notable works: *Karl Marx* (1939), *Four Essays on Liberty* (1959), and *Vico and Herder* (1976).

Ber·li·ner |'bərlənər|, Emile (1851–1929) U.S. inventor, born in Germany. He invented the Berliner loose-contact telephone transmitter (1877), devised a method of duplicating flat disk recordings (1888), and developed the first acoustic tiles (1915).

Ber·lioz |'berlē,ōz|, Hector (1803–69) French composer; full name *Louis-Hector Berlioz*. Notable works: *Les Troyens* (opera, 1856–9), *Symphonie fantastique* (1830), and *La Damnation de Faust* (cantata, 1846).

Ber·na·dette |'bərnədet|, St. (1844–79) French peasant girl; born *Marie Bernarde Soubirous*. Her visions of the Virgin Mary in Lourdes in 1858 led to the town's establishment as a center of pilgrimage. Feast day, February 18.

Ber·na·dotte |'bernədät|, Jean Baptiste Jules (1763–1844) French soldier, king of Sweden (as Charles XIV) (1818–44). One of Napoleon's marshals, he was adopted by Charles XIII of Sweden in

1810 and later became king, thus founding Sweden's present royal house.

Ber·na·dotte |'bernədät|, Folke, Count Bernadotte of Wisborg (1895–1948) Swedish statesman. As vice-president of the Swedish Red Cross he arranged the exchange of prisoners of war and in 1945 conveyed a German offer of capitulation to the Allies.

Ber·nard |bər'närd|, Claude (1813–78) French physiologist. Bernard showed the role of the pancreas in digestion, the method of regulation of body temperature, and the function of nerves supplying the internal organs.

Ber·nard |bər'närd|, St (died c. 1081) French monk who founded two hospices for travelers in the Alps. The St. Bernard passes, where the hospices were situated, and St. Bernard dogs, once kept by the monks and trained to aid travelers, are named after him. Feast day, May 28.

Ber·nard of Clair·vaux |ˌbər'närd əv kler'vō|, St. (1090–1153) French theologian and abbot. He was the first abbot of Clairvaux, and his monastery became one of the chief centers of the Cistercian order. Feast day, August 20.

Berners-Lee |'bərnərz 'lē|, Tim. U.S. computer scientist. He developed the World Wide Web (1989) and directs the W3 Consortium at MIT's Laboratory for Computer Science.

Bern·hard |'bərn,härt|, Sandra (1955–) U.S. actress and singer. Her movie and television credits include *The Apocalypse* (1997) and appearances on "Late Night with David Letterman" and "Roseanne."

Bern·hardt |'bərn,härt|, Sarah (1844–1923) French actress; born *Henriette Rosine Bernard*. She was best known for her portrayal of Marguerite in *La Dame aux Camélias* and Cordelia in *King Lear.*

Ber·ni·ni |bər'nēnē|, Gian Lorenzo (1598–1680) Italian baroque sculptor, painter, and architect. His work includes the great canopy over the altar and the colonnade round the piazza at St. Peter's in Rome.

Ber·noul·li |ˌbər'no͞olē| Family of Swiss mathematicians, including **Jakob Bernoulli** (1655–1705); also known as *Jacques* or *James*. He made discoveries

in calculus and contributed to geometry and the theory of probabilities. His brother, **Johann Bernoulli** (1667–1748), was also known as *Jean* or *John*. He contributed to differential and integral calculus. Johann's son, **Daniel Bernoulli** (1700–82), contributed to hydrodynamics and mathematical physics.

Bern·stein |'bərnstēn|, Carl (1944–) U.S. journalist and author. He was the *Washington Post* reporter who, with Bob Woodward, broke the story of the Watergate burglary and traced the financial payoffs to President Nixon.

Bern·stein |'bərnstīn|, Leonard (1918–90) U.S. composer, conductor, and pianist. He worked as a conductor with the New York Philharmonic Orchestra (1945–48 and 1957–69). As a composer he encompassed a wide range of forms and styles in his music. Notable works: *Candide* (operetta, 1954–6), *West Side Story* (musical, 1957), *Chichester Psalms* (1965), and movie music for *On the Waterfront* (1954).

Ber·ra |'berə|, Yogi (1925–) U.S. baseball player; born *Lawrence Peter Berra.* He was especially famous as a catcher with the New York Yankees, setting the record for the most home runs (313) by a catcher in the American League. He became known for his pithy saying such as (on baseball) "You can't think and hit at the same time".

Ber·ri·gan |'berə,gən| U.S. family that includes two brothers, priests and political activists: **Daniel** (1921–), a Jesuit priest, devoted his time to civil rights, antipoverty, and antiwar causes. He was convicted and sentenced to three years in prison for destroying selective service files in 1968. He later wrote his prison memoirs, *Lights On in the House of the Dead* (1974). His brother, **Philip** (1923–), a Roman Catholic priest, founded the Catholic Peace Fellowship. He, too, was convicted and sent to prison for destroying selective service files in 1967 and 1968. Notable works: *Prison Journals of a Revolutionary Priest* (1970) and *Widen the Prison Gates* (1973).

Ber·ry |'berē|, Chuck (1926–) U.S. rock-and-roll singer, guitarist, and songwriter; born *Charles Edward Berry*. Notable songs: "Johnny B Goode" (1958).

Ber•ry |'berē|, Jim (1932–   ) U.S. cartoonist and author. Full name *James Berry*. He created the comic "Berry's World."

Ber•ry |'berē|, Wendell (1934–   ) U.S. author and professor. His poems, novels, and essays reflect his native state of Kentucky.

Ber•ry•man |'berē,mən|, John (1914–1972) U.S. poet and educator. Notable works: *77 Dream Songs* (1964), which won the Pulitzer Prize.

Ber•til•lon |bertē'yōn|, Alphonse (1853–1914) French criminologist. He devised a system of body measurements for the identification of criminals, which was widely used until superseded by fingerprinting at the beginning of the 20th century.

Ber•to•luc•ci |,bərtə'lōōCHē|, Bernardo (1940–   ) Italian movie director. Notable works: *The Spider's Stratagem* (1970), *Last Tango in Paris* (1972), and *The Last Emperor* (1988).

Ber•ze•li•us |bər'zēlēəs|, Jöns Jakob (1779–1848) Swedish analytical chemist. He determined the atomic weights of many elements and discovered cerium, selenium, and thorium.

Bes•ant |'bezənt|, Annie (1847–1933) English theosophist, writer, and politician, president of the Theosophical Society. She settled in Madras, where she worked for Indian self-government.

Bes•sel |'besəl|, Friedrich Wilhelm (1784–1846) German astronomer and mathematician. He determined the positions of some 75,000 stars, obtained accurate measurements of stellar distances, and following a study of the orbit of Uranus, predicted the existence of an eighth planet.

Bes•se•mer |'besəmər|, Sir Henry (1813–98) English engineer and inventor. By 1860 he had developed the Bessemer process, the first successful method of making steel in quantity at low cost.

Best |best|, Charles Herbert (1899–1978) American-born Canadian physiologist who assisted F. G. Banting in research leading to the discovery of insulin in 1922.

Be•thune |bə'THyōōn|, Henry Norman (1899–1939) Canadian surgeon. He joined the Communist Party in 1935 and served in the Spanish Civil War against the Fascists, organizing the first mobile blood-transfusion service. Bethune then joined the Chinese army in their war against Japan as a surgeon, becoming a hero in the People's Republic; he died while in China.

Be•thune |bə'THyōōn|, Mary McLeod (1875–1955) U.S. educator. She was founder and first president (1935–49) of the National Council of Negro Women.

Bet•je•man |'beCHəmən|, Sir John (1906–84) British poet and author. He received the Queen's Medal for Poetry in 1960, was knighted in 1969, and became Poet Laureate in 1972.

Bet•tel•heim |'betl,hīm|, Bruno (1903–90) U.S. psychologist and author, born in Austria. His experiences in Nazi Germany helped him develop revolutionary theories and therapies for emotionally disturbed children

Bet•ter•ton |'betərtən|, Thomas (1635–1710) English actor. A leading actor of the Restoration period, he also adapted the plays of John Webster, Molière, and Beaumont and Fletcher for his own productions.

Bet•ti |'betē|, Ugo (1892–1953) Italian dramatist, poet, and short-story writer. Notable plays: *Corruption in the Palace of Justice* (1949), *Crime on Goat Island* (1950).

Bett•man |'betmən|, Otto Ludwig (1903–98) U.S. picture archivist and graphic historian, born in Germany. He founded the archive of photographs (1941) and was the author of many books of photographs, including *A Pictorial History of American Sports* (1952) and *A Pictorial History of Medicine* (1956).

Beuys |bois|, Joseph (1921–86) German artist. One of the most influential figures of the avant-garde movement in Europe in the 1970s and 1980s, his work consisted of "assemblages" of various articles of rubbish. In 1979 he co-founded the German Green Party.

Bew•ick |'byōōik|, Thomas (1753–1828) English artist and wood engraver, noted especially for the animal studies in such books as *A History of British Birds* (1797, 1804).

Be·zos, Jeff. U.S. businessman. He founded Amazon.com, the Internet bookstore (1995).

Bhut·to |'bŏŏtō| Family of Pakistani politicians, including: **Zulfikar Ali Bhutto** (1928–79), president (1971–73) and prime minister (1973–77). He was ousted by a military coup and executed for conspiring to murder a political rival. His daughter, **Benazir Bhutto** (1953–), was prime minister (1988–90 and 1993–96). She was the first woman prime minister of a Muslim country and took Pakistan back into the British Commonwealth.

Bich, Marcel (1914–) French manufacturer and inventor. He invented the Bic disposable ballpoint pen and cigarette lighter.

Bi·den |'bīdən|, Joseph Robinette, Jr. (1942–) U.S. politician. He is a member of the U.S. Senate from Delaware (1972–)

Bierce |birs|, Ambrose (Gwinnett) (1842–*c.* 1914) U.S. writer, best known for his sardonic short stories and *The Devil's Dictionary* (1911). In 1913 he traveled to Mexico and mysteriously disappeared.

Bier·stadt |'bir‚stät|, Albert (1830–1902) U.S. painter, born in Germany. He was a member of the Hudson River school of landscape painters.

Bi·ko |'bēkō|, Steve (1946–77) South African radical leader; full name *Stephen Biko*. He was banned from political activity in 1973; after his death in police custody he became a symbol of heroic resistance to apartheid.

Bi·net |bə'nā|, Alfred (1857–1911) French psychologist. He devised a mental age scale that described performance in relation to the average performance of students of the same physical age, and with the psychiatrist **Théodore Simon**, (1873–1961) was responsible for a pioneering system of intelligence tests.

Bing |biNG|, Rudolf (1902–97) U.S. opera conductor and manager, born in Vienna. He was conductor and director of the Metropolitan Opera in New York

(1950–72); in 1955, he hired Marian Anderson, ending the Met's unwritten ban against African Americans.

Bing·ham |'biNGəm|, George Caleb (1811–79) U.S. artist. His paintings of the American frontier include *The Fur Traders Descending the Missouri* (1845) and *The Trappers Return* (1851). Several of his works, notably *The County Election* (1851–52), reflect a political theme.

Bing·ham |'biNGəm|, Hiram (1875–1956) U.S. explorer and politican. A Yale professor (1907–24), he discovered the Inca ruins of Machu Picchu (1911). He served as governor of Connecticut (1924–25) and in the U.S. Senate (1925–33).

Bin·ney |'bi‚nē|, Edwin (1866–1934) U.S. entrepreneur. He was a cofounder of Crayola crayons.

Bin·nig |'bi‚niKH|, Gerd Karl (1947–) German physicist and inventor. With Heinrich Rohrer, he developed the scanning tunneling microscope. Nobel Prize in Physics (1986).

Bi·on·di |bē'awndē|, Matt (1965–) U.S. swimmer. Full name *Matthew Biondi*. At the 1986 world championships, he won a record seven medals (three gold). He won eight Olympic gold medals (1984, 1988, 1992).

Bird |bərd|, Larry (1956–) U.S. basketball player and coach. Elected to the Basketball Hall of Fame (1998).

Birds·eye |'bərdz‚ī|, Clarence (1886–1956) U.S. businessman and inventor. A former fur trader, he had observed food preservation techniques practiced by local people in Labrador. He developed a process of rapid freezing of foods in small packages suitable for retail, creating a revolution in eating habits.

Birk·hoff |'bər‚kawf|, George David (1884–1944) U.S. mathematician. He proved Poincaré's last theorem, now known as the Poincaré-Birkhoff fixed-point theorem (1912).

Bish·op |'biSHəp|, Elizabeth (1911–79) U.S. poet awarded the Pulitzer Prize for her first two collections, *North and South* (1946) and *A Cold Spring* (1955).

Bis·marck |'bizmärk|, Otto Eduard Leopold von, Prince of Bismarck, Duke of Lauenburg (1815–98) Prussian minister and German statesman, chancellor of the German Empire (1871–90); known as the **Iron Chancellor**. He was the driving force behind the unification of Germany, orchestrating wars with Denmark (1864), Austria (1866), and France (1870–71) in order to achieve this end.

Bi•zet |bi'zā|, Georges (1838–75) French composer; born *Alexandre César Léopold Bizet*. He is best known for the opera *Carmen* (1875).

Bjerk•nes |'byərk,näs|, Vilhelm Friman Koren (1862–1951) Norwegian geophysicist and meteorologist. He developed a theory of physical hydrodynamics for atmospheric and oceanic circulation, and mathematical models for weather prediction.

Björ•ling |'byœrling|, Jussi (1911–60) Swedish operatic tenor. He made his debut with the Metropolitan Opera in 1938 as Rudolfo in *La Bohème*, and he excelled in roles from Verdi and Puccini.

Black |blæk|, Harold Stephen (1898–1983) U.S. electrical engineer and inventor. In the late 1920s, he invented and developed a negative feedback amplifier, which countered the problem of distortion in telephone communications. He later applied this technology to systems useful to the blind and deaf.

Black |blæk|, Hugo Lafayette (1886–1971) U.S. Supreme Court Justice (1937–71). He was also a U.S. senator from Alabama (1927–37).

Black |blæk|, Joseph (1728–99) Scottish chemist. He was important in developing accurate techniques for following chemical reactions by weighing reactants and products, and formulated the concepts of latent heat and thermal capacity.

Black•beard |'blækbērd| (died 1718) pirate in the West Indies and Virginia–North Carolina coast. Born *Edward Teach* (also *Thatch* or *Thack*). He was originally a privateer during the War of the Spanish Succession (1701–14).

Black•ett |'blækət|, Patrick Maynard Stuart (Baron) (1897–1974) English physicist. Blackett was a member of the Maud Committee that dealt with the development of the atom bomb. He also

modified the cloud chamber for the study of cosmic rays. Nobel Prize for Physics (1948).

Black Hawk |'blæk ,hawk| (1767–1838) chief of the Sauk and Fox Indians. He was a leader in the Black Hawk War (1832); in 1833 he published his *Autobiography*.

Black•more |'blæk,mōr|, R. D. (Richard Doddridge) (1825–1900) English novelist and poet. He is known for his romantic novel *Lorna Doone* (1869).

Black•mun |'blækmən|, Harry Andrew (1908–1999) U.S. Supreme Court Justice (1970–94).

Black•mur |'blækmər|, R. P. (1904–65) U.S. poet and literary critic. Full name *Richard Palmer Blackmur*. With no formal education after high school, he served as a resident fellow (1940–48) and professor (1948–65) at Princeton. He was a prominent advocate of the New Criticism.

Black Prince |'blæk 'prins| (1330–76) eldest son of Edward III of England; name given to Edward, Prince of Wales and Duke of Cornwall. He was responsible for the English victory at Poitiers in 1356. He predeceased his father, but his son became king as King Richard II; the name Black Prince apparently derives from the black armor he wore when fighting.

Black•stone |'blæk,stōn|, Sir William (1723–80) English jurist. His major work was the *Commentaries on the Laws of England* (1765–9), an exposition of English law.

Blair |bler| U.S. political family, including: **Francis Preston Blair** (1791–1876), a journalist and politician. He was a member of President Andrew Jackson's "kitchen cabinet" and helped organize the Republican Party (1856), later becoming one of Abraham Lincoln's advisers. His son **Montgomery Blair** (1813–83), a jurist and politician, represented Dred Scott before the Supreme Court (1857). **Francis Preston Blair, Jr.**, (1821–75), the son of Francis Preston Blair and brother of Montgomery Blair, was a politician who helped establish the Free Soil Party (1848) and was an unsuccessful

Democratic vice presidential candidate (1868).

Blair |bler|, Bonnie (1964–) U.S. speed skater. She is the only U.S. woman to win five Olympic gold medals (500m, 1988; 500m and 1000m, 1992 and 1994).

Blair |bler|, Henry. U.S. inventor. He obtained patents for a corn planter (1834) and a cotton planter (1836).

Blair |bler|, John (1732–1800) U.S. Supreme Court Justice (1789–96). He was a member of the Consitutional Convention (1787).

Blair |bler|, Tony (1953–) British Labour statesman, prime minister from 1997; full name *Anthony Charles Lynton Blair*. His landslide victory in the election of 1997 gave his party its biggest-ever majority and made him the youngest prime minister since Lord Liverpool in 1812.

Blake |blāk|, Eubie (1883–1983) U.S. jazz pianist and composer. One of the foremost ragtime pianists, he wrote over 300 songs, many in collaboration with Noble Sissle.

Blake |blāk|, Peter (1932–) English painter, prominent in the pop art movement in the late 1950s and early 1960s. He is best known for the cover design for the Beatles album *Sergeant Pepper's Lonely Hearts Club Band* (1967).

Blake |blāk|, William (1757–1827) English artist and poet. Blake's poems mark the beginning of romanticism and a rejection of the Age of Enlightenment. His watercolors and engravings, like his writings, were only fully appreciated after his death. Notable collections of poems: *Songs of Innocence* (1789) and *Songs of Experience* (1794).

Bla·key |'blākē|, Art (1919–90) U.S. jazz drummer, a pioneer of the bebop movement, known for his group the Jazz Messengers; full name *Arthur Blakey*.

Blan·chard |'blænCHərd|, Jean-Pierre-François (1753–1809) French balloonist. He made the first crossing of the English Channel by air, flying by balloon, on January 7, 1785.

Blan·da |'blændə|, George Frederick (1927–) U.S. football player. He is the all-time leading scorer (2,002 points) in professional football.

Blan·ding |'blæn,diNG|, Sarah G. (1899–1985) U.S. educator. She was president of Vassar College (1946–64).

Blan·ton |'blæntən|, Jimmy (1918–42) U.S. jazz bassist. He was hired by Duke Ellington in 1939.

Blass |'blæs|, Bill (1922–) U.S. fashion designer. Full name *William Ralph Blass*.

Blatch·ford |'blæcHfərd|, Samuel (1820–1893) U.S. Supreme Court Justice (1882–93).

Bla·vat·sky |blə'vætskē|, Helena (Petrovna) (1831–91) Russian spiritualist, born in Ukraine; born *Helena Petrovna Hahn*; known as **Madame Blavatsky**. In 1875 she co-founded the Theosophical Society in New York together with the American Henry Steel Olcott.

Blé·riot |'blārȳō; 'blerē,ō|, Louis (1872–1936) French aviation pioneer. On July 25, 1909 he became the first to fly the English Channel (Calais to Dover), in a monoplane of his own design.

Blessed Virgin Mary Also **Blessed Virgin**. (abbrev.: **BVM**) a title given to Mary, the mother of Jesus. (see MARY 1).

Bligh |blī|, William (1754–1817) British naval officer, captain of HMS *Bounty*. In 1789 part of his crew, led by the first mate Fletcher Christian, mutinied and set Bligh adrift in an open boat, arriving safely at Timor, nearly 4,000 miles (6,400 km) away, a few weeks later.

Bliss |blis|, Sir Arthur (Edward Drummond) (1891–1975) English composer. He moved from the influence of Stravinsky, in works such as *A Colour Symphony* (1922), to a rich style closer to Elgar, as in his choral symphony *Morning Heroes* (1930).

Blixen, Karen (Christence), Baroness Blixen-Finecke (1885–1962) Danish novelist and short-story writer; born *Karen Dinesen*; also known by the pseudonym of **Isak Dinesen**. She is best known for *Seven Gothic Tales* (1934) and her autobiography *Out of Africa* (1937).

Bloch |blāk|, Ernest (1880–1959) Swiss-born U.S. composer, of Jewish descent. His work reflects the influence of the late 19th-century romanticism of Liszt and Richard Strauss and Jewish musical forms. Notable works: the *Israel Symphony* (1912–16) and *Solomon* (1916).

Bloch |bläk|, Felix (1905–83) U.S. physicist, born in Switzerland. With Edward Mills Purcell, he won the 1952 Nobel Prize for Physics for the discovery of nuclear magnetic resonance.

Bloch |bläk|, Henry Wollman (1922–) U.S. businessman. He founded the tax-preparation company H & R Block (1955).

Block |bläk|, Herbert L. (1909–) U.S. editorial cartoonist, author, and artist. Known as **Herblock**. He is a two-time winner of the Pulitzer Prize for cartooning (1942, 1954) and the recipient of several journalism awards.

Blon•din |'bländēn|, Charles (1824–97) French acrobat; born *Jean-François Gravelet*. He is famous for on several occasions walking across a tightrope suspended over Niagara Falls.

Bloody Mary the nickname of Mary I of England (see MARY 2).

Bloom |bloōm|, Allan David (1936–92) U.S. political scientist and author. In his best-selling *The Closing of the American Mind: How Higher Education Has Failed Democracy and Impoverished the Souls of Today's Students* (1987), he denounced the decline of liberal education in the U.S.

Bloom |bloōm|, Harold (1930–) U.S. literary critic, educator, and author. Notable works: *The Anxiety of Influence* (1973) and *Omens of Millennium* (1996).

Bloom•berg |'bloōmbərg|, Michael Rubens (1942–) U.S. businessman. He is founder, chairman, and CEO of the business news service, Bloomberg Financial Markets (begun 1981).

Bloom•er |'bloōmər|, Amelia Jenks (1818–94) U.S. suffragette and social reformer. She founded and edited the feminist paper *Lily* (1849–55), and she wore full pants that came to be known as "bloomers."

Bloom•field |'bloōm,fēld|, Leonard (1887–1949) U.S. linguist, one of the founders of American structural linguistics. His primary aim was to establish linguistics as an autonomous and

scientific discipline. Notable works: *Language* (1933).

Blü•cher |'bloōkər|, Gebhard Leberecht von, Prince of Wahlstatt (1742–1819) Prussian field marshal. Nickname **Marschall Vorwäts.** He served in the war against Napoléon (1813).

Blum |bloōm|, Léon (1872–1950) French statesman, prime minister (1936–37, 1938, 1946–47). As France's first socialist and Jewish prime minister, Blum introduced significant labor reforms.

Blum•berg |'bloōmbərg; 'bləmbərg|, Baruch Samuel (1925–) U.S. research physician. He discovered a causative agent for hepatitis B (1963) and developed a hepatitis B vaccine (1982).

Blume |bloōm|, Judy Sussman (1938–) U.S. author. She wrote bestselling children's fiction, including *Are You There, God? It's Me, Margaret* (1970), and adult fiction, including *Summer Sisters* (1998).

Blu•men•bach |'bloōmən,bäk|, Johann Friedrich (1752–1840) German physiologist and anatomist. He is regarded as the founder of physical anthropology, though his approach has since been much modified. He classified modern humans into five broad categories (Caucasian, Mongoloid, Malayan, Ethiopian, and American) based mainly on cranial measurements.

Blun•den |'bləndən|, Edmund (Charles) (1896–1974) English poet and critic. His poetry reveals his love of the English countryside, while his prose work *Undertones of War* (1928) deals with his experiences in the First World War.

Blunt |blənt|, Anthony (Frederick) (1907–83) British art historian, Foreign Office official, and Soviet spy. He confessed in 1965 that he had been a Soviet agent since the 1930s and had facilitated the escape of Guy Burgess and Donald Maclean. When these facts were made public in 1979 he was stripped of his knighthood.

Bly |blī|, Robert Elwood (1926–) U.S. poet and author. Notable works: *The Light Around the Body* (1967, National Book Award) and *Iron John: A Book about Men* (1990).

Bly·ton |'blītn|, Enid (1897–1968) English writer of children's fiction. Her best-known creation for young children is the character Noddy, who first appeared in 1949; her books for older children include the series of *Famous Five* and *Secret Seven* adventure stories.

Bo·as |'bōæz|, Franz (1858–1942) German-born U.S. anthropologist. A pioneer of modern anthropology, he developed the linguistic and cultural components of ethnology. He did much to overturn the theory that Nordic peoples constitute an essentially superior race; his writings were burnt by the Nazis.

Boc·cac·cio |bō'käCHēō|, Giovanni (1313–75) Italian writer, poet, and humanist. He is most famous for the *Decameron* (1348–58), a collection of a hundred tales told by ten young people who have moved to the country to escape the Black Death.

Boc·che·ri·ni |,bōkə'rēnē|, Luigi (1743–1805) Italian composer and cellist, known chiefly for his cello concertos and sonatas.

Boch·co |'bäCH,kō|, Steven (1943–) U.S. television producer and screenwriter. He cocreated the Emmy Award-winning television series "Hill Street Blues" and was executive producer of the series "LA Law" and "NYPD Blue."

Bod·ley |'bädlē|, Sir Thomas (1545–1613) English scholar and diplomat. He refounded and greatly enlarged the Oxford University library, which was renamed the Bodleian in 1604.

Bo·do·ni |bō'dōnē|, Giambattista (1740–1813) Italian printer. He designed a typeface that is characterized by extreme contrast between uprights and diagonals.

Boe·ing |'bōiNG|, William Edward (1881–1956) U.S. industrialist. He founded the Boeing Aircraft Co.

Boe·sky |'bō,skē|, F. Ivan (1936–) U.S. stockbroker. Accused of insider trading on Wall Street, he pleaded guilty to an unspecified criminal count and paid a $100 million fine.

Bo·e·thi·us |bō'ēTHēəs|, Anicius Manlius Severinus (c. 480–524) Roman statesman and philosopher, best known for *The Consolation of Philosophy*, which he wrote while in prison on a charge of treason.

Bo·gan |,bō'gæn|, Louise (1897–1970) U.S. poet and critic. She was poetry editor of the *New Yorker* magazine for many years. Notable works: *Body of This Death* (1923), *The Blue Estuaries: Poems 1923–1968* (1968), and the literary history *Achievement in American Poetry, 1900–1950* (1951).

Bo·garde |'bō,gärd|, Sir Dirk (1921–) British actor and writer, of Dutch descent. Born *Derek Niven van den Bogaerde*. Notable movies: *The Servant* (1963) and *Death in Venice* (1971).

Bo·gart |'bōgärt|, Humphrey (DeForest) (1899–1957) U.S. actor. His many movies include *Casablanca* (1942), *The Big Sleep* (1946, in which he played opposite his fourth wife, Lauren Bacall), and *The African Queen* (1951, for which he won an Oscar).

Bohr |bōr|, Niels Henrik David (1885–1962) Danish physicist and pioneer in quantum physics. Bohr's theory of the structure of the atom incorporated quantum theory for the first time, and is the basis for present-day quantum-mechanical models. Bohr helped to develop the atom bomb in Britain and then in the US. Nobel Prize for Physics (1922).

Boi·leau |,bwä'lō|, Nicolas (1636–1711) French critic and poet; full name *Nicholas Boileau-Despréaux*. Boileau is considered particularly important as one of the founders of French literary criticism. His didactic poem *Art poétique* (1674) defined principles of composition and criticism.

Bo·kas·sa |bō'käsə|, Jean Bédel (1921–96) African statesman and military leader, president (1972–76) of the Central African Republic, and self-styled emperor (1976–79).

Bol·den |'bōl,dən|, Buddy (1877–1931) U.S. jazz musician. Born *Charles Joseph Bolden*. He was a cornetist and leader of several New Orleans bands in the 1890s.

Bol·dre·wood |'bōldər,wo͝od|, Rolf (1826–1915) Australian novelist; pseudonym of *Thomas Alexander Browne*. His most enduring work was *Robbery Under Arms* (first published as a serial in 1882–

83), a narration of the life and crimes of a bushranger under sentence of death.

Bol•eyn |boo'lin|, Anne (1507?–36) second wife of Henry VIII and mother of Elizabeth I. Henry divorced Catherine of Aragon in order to marry Anne (1533), but she fell from favor when she failed to provide him with a male heir, and she was eventually executed because of alleged infidelities.

Bol•ger |'bōljər|, James (Brendan) (1935–) New Zealand National Party statesman and prime minister (1990–97).

Bo•ling•broke |'bawliNG,brŏŏk; 'bōliNG ,brōk|, Henry the surname of Henry IV of England (see HENRY1).

Bo•lí•var |'bələ,vär|, Simón (1783–1830) Venezuelan patriot and statesman; known as **the Liberator**. He succeeded in driving the Spanish from Venezuela, Colombia, Peru, and Ecuador although his dream of South American federation was never realized. Upper Peru was named Bolivia in his honor.

Böll |bäl|, Heinrich (Theodor) (1917–85) German novelist and short-story writer. His later work, such as *The Lost Honour of Katharina Blum* (1974), is frequently critical of post-war German society. Nobel Prize for Literature (1972).

Bolt |bōlt|, Robert (Oxton) (1924–95) English writer best known for the play *A Man for All Seasons* (1960) and the screenplays for *Lawrence of Arabia* (1962) and *Dr Zhivago* (1965).

Boltz•mann |'bawltsmən|, Ludwig Eduard (1844–1906) Austrian physicist, who made contributions to the kinetic theory of gases, statistical mechanics, and thermodynamics.

Bom•beck |'bäm,bek|, Erma Louise (1927–96) U.S. journalist and author. Her syndicated column appeared in newspapers throughout the U.S. from 1965 until her death. Notable works: *Motherhood: The Second Oldest Profession* (1983); *Family: The Ties That Bind...and Gag!* (1987).

Bo•na•parte |'bōnə,pärt|, Napoleon a Corsican family including the three French rulers named Napoleon.

Bon•a•ven•tu•re |,bänəvən'cHŏŏr|, St. (c. 1217–74) Franciscan theologian;

born *Giovanni di Fidanza*; known as **the Seraphic Doctor**. He wrote the official biography of St. Francis and had a lasting influence as a spiritual writer. Feast day, July 15 (formerly 14).

Bond |bänd|, Edward (1934–) English dramatist. Many of his plays are marked by scenes of violence and cruelty. Notable works: *Saved* (1965) and *Lear* (1971).

Bon•hoef•fer |'bän,hawfər|, Dietrich (1906–45) German Lutheran theologian and pastor. He was an active opponent of Nazism and was involved in the German resistance movement. Arrested in 1943, he was sent to Buchenwald concentration camp and later executed.

Bon•i•face |'bänəfəs|, St. (c. 675–754) Anglo-Saxon missionary; born *Wynfrith*; known as **the Apostle of Germany**. He was sent to Frisia and Germany to spread the Christian faith and was appointed Primate of Germany in 732; he was martyred in Frisia. Feast day, June 5.

Bon•nard |baw'när|, Pierre (1867–1947) French painter and graphic artist, member of the Nabi Group.

Bon•ney |'bänē|, William H. (1859–81) U.S. outlaw; born *Henry McCarty*; known as **Billy the Kid**. A notorious robber and murderer, he was captured by Sheriff Pat Garrett in 1880, and was shot by Garrett after he escaped.

Bonnie Prince Charlie see STUART 1.

Bon•nin |'bawnin|, Gertrude Simmons (1876–1938) Sioux-American author and Indian activist. Also known as **Zitkala-Sa** ("Red Bird."). One of the first Native Americans to translate and publish traditional Indian stories, she published her first book, *Old Indian Legends*, in 1901. She founded the National Council of American Indians (1926).

Bo•no |'bō,nō|, Sonny (1935–98) U.S. entertainer and politician. Born *Salvatore Bono*. Famed as half of the singing duo Sonny and Cher (1964–74), he became a Republican politician. He served as mayor of Palm Springs, California (1988–92) and in the U.S. House of Representatives (1994–98).

Bon•temps |,bän'täm|, Arna Wendell (1902–73) U.S. author and librarian. He was librarian of Fisk University and the author of novels about African American life; his nonfiction includes correspondence with Langston Hughes, published in 1979.

Boole |bōōl|, George (1815–64) English mathematician responsible for Boolean algebra. The study of mathematical or symbolic logic developed mainly from his ideas.

Boone |bōōn|, Daniel (c. 1734–1820) American pioneer. Boone made trips west from Pennsylvania into the unexplored area of Kentucky, organizing settlements and successfully defending them against hostile American Indians.

Boor•stin |'bawrstən; 'bərstən|, Daniel J. (1914–) U.S. educator and author. He was Librarian of Congress (1975–87). Notable works: *The Democratic Experience* (1973, Pulitzer Prize).

Booth |bōōTH|, George (1926–) U.S. cartoonist, artist, and author. He was on staff at *The New Yorker* magazine

Booth |bōōTH|, John Wilkes (1838–65) U.S. actor and assassin of Abraham Lincoln.

Booth |bōōTH|, Shirley (1898–1992) U.S. actress. She won an Academy Award in 1952 for *Come Back, Little Sheba.*

Booth |bōōTH|, William (1829–1912) English religious leader, founder and first general of the Salvation Army. A Methodist revivalist preacher, in 1865 he established a mission in the East End of London that later became the Salvation Army.

Bor•den |'bawrdən|, Gail (1801–74) U.S. businessman and inventor. He invented the process for making condensed milk and founded Borden's Milk & Ice Cream Co.

Bor•den |'bawrdən|, Lizzie Andrew (1860–1927) U.S. accused murderess. Accused of the murder of her father and stepmother in Fall River, Massachusetts, in 1892, she was acquitted in a trial that became a national sensation.

Bor•det |bawr'dā|, Jules-Jean-Baptiste-Vincent (1870–1961) Belgian bacteriologist and immunologist. He discovered the complement system of blood serum, and developed a vaccine for whooping cough. Nobel Prize for Physiology or Medicine (1919).

Borg |bawrg|, Björn (Rune) (1956–) Swedish tennis player. He won five consecutive men's singles titles at Wimbledon (1976–80), beating the record of three consecutive wins held by Fred Perry.

Bor•ges |'bawr,hās|, Jorge Luis (1899–1986) Argentinian poet, short-story writer, and essayist. The volume of short stories *A Universal History of Infamy* (1935, revised 1954) is regarded as founding work of magic realism.

Bor•gia |'bawrzHə| Italian family, including: **Cesare Borgia** (c. 1476–1507), a statesman, cardinal, and general. The illegitimate son of Cardinal Rodrigo Borgia (later Pope Alexander VI) and brother of Lucrezia Borgia, he was captain general of the papal army from 1499, and became master of a large portion of central Italy. His sister, **Lucrezia Borgia** (1480–1519), married three times, according to the political alliances useful to her family; after her third marriage in 1501 she established herself as a patron of the arts.

Bor•glum |'bawrgləm|, Gutzon (1867–1941) U.S. sculptor. Full name *John Gutzon de la Mothe Borglum.* His most famous work is the Mount Rushmore National Memorial in South Dakota, which features the monumental heads of Presidents Washington, Jefferson, Lincoln, and T. Roosevelt. The work, begun in 1927, was completed in 1941 with the help of his son Lincoln Borglum (1912–86).

Borg•nine |'bawrg,nīn|, Ernest (1917–) U.S. actor. He won an Academy Award in 1955 for *Marty.*

Bo•ri |'bawrē|, Lucrezia (1887–1960) Italian operatic soprano, born in Spain. She made her debut with the Metropolitan Opera in 1912 as Manon in *Manon Lescaut* and sang there for 19 seasons; in 1935, she was first woman and first active artist to be elected a director of the Metropolitan Opera Association.

Boris Godunov |'bawris 'gōd(ə),nawf; 'gawd(ə),nawf| see GODUNOV.

Bork |bawrk|, Robert Heron (1927–) U.S. jurist and legal scholar. He was nominated to the Supreme Court by Ronald Reagan but rejected by the Senate in a controversial vote.

Bor·laug |'bawr,lawg|, Norman Ernest (1914–) U.S. agronomist. He developed high-yielding cereals for cultivation in the Third World. Nobel Peace Prize (1970).

Bor·mann |'bawrmən|, Martin Ludwig (1900–c. 1945) German Nazi politician. Considered to be Hitler's closest collaborator, he disappeared at the end of World War II; his skeleton, exhumed in Berlin, was identified in 1973.

Born |bawrn|, Max (1882–1970) German theoretical physicist, a founder of quantum mechanics. Nobel Prize for Physics (1954).

Bo·ro·din |bawrə'dēn|, Aleksandr (Porfiryevich) (1833–87) Russian composer. He is best known for the epic opera *Prince Igor* (completed after his death by Rimsky-Korsakov and Glazunov).

Bor·ro·mi·ni |,bawrə'mēnē|, Francesco (1599–1667) Italian architect, a leading figure of the Italian baroque.

Bor·row |'bärō|, George (Henry) (1803–81) English writer. His travels with gypsies provided material for the picaresque narrative *Lavengro* (1851) and its sequel *The Romany Rye* (1857).

Bosch |bawsн|, Carl (1874–1940) German industrial chemist. He was recognized for his invention and development of chemical high-pressure methods, specifically the Haber-Bosch process, by which hydrogen is obtained from water gas and superheated steam. Nobel Prize for Chemistry (1931).

Bosch |bawsн|, Hieronymus (1450–1516) Dutch painter. Bosch's highly detailed works are typically crowded with half-human, half-animal creatures and grotesque demons in settings symbolic of sin and folly. His individual style prefigures that of the surrealists.

Bose |bōz|, Sir Jagadis Chandra (1858–1937) Indian physicist and plant physiologist. He investigated the properties of very short radio waves, wireless telegraphy, and radiation-induced fatigue in inorganic materials. His physiological work involved comparative measurements of the responses of plants exposed to stress.

Bose |bōz|, Satyendra Nath (1894–1974) Indian physicist. With Einstein he described fundamental particles which later came to be known as *bosons*.

Boswell |'bäzwel|, James (1740–95) Scottish author, companion and biographer of Samuel Johnson. He is known for *Journal of a Tour to the Hebrides* (1785) and *The Life of Samuel Johnson* (1791).

Bo·tha |'bōtə|, Louis (1862–1919) South African soldier and statesman, first prime minister of the Union of South Africa (1910–19).

Bo·tha, P. W (1916–) South African statesman, prime minister (1978–84), state president (1984–89); full name *Pieter Willem Botha*. An authoritarian leader, he continued to enforce apartheid but in response to pressure introduced limited reforms; his resistance to more radical changes ultimately led to his fall from power.

Both·well |'bäтнwəl|, James Hepburn, 4th Earl of (c. 1535–78) Scottish nobleman and third husband of Mary, Queen of Scots. He was implicated in the murder of Mary's previous husband, Lord Darnley (1567), a crime for which he was tried but acquitted; he married Mary later the same year.

Bot·ti·cel·li |,bätə'cнelē|, Sandro (1445–1510) Italian painter; born *Alessandro di Mariano Filipepi*. He worked in Renaissance Florence under the patronage of the Medicis. Botticelli is best known for his mythological works such as *Primavera* (c.1478) and *The Birth of Venus* (c.1480).

Bou·cher |bōō'sнā|, François (1703–70) French painter and decorative artist, one of the foremost artists of the rococo style in France. Notable paintings: *The Rising of the Sun* (1753) and *Summer Pastoral* (1749).

Bou·cher de Crèvecoeur de Perthes |bōō'sнā də pert|, Jacques (1788–1868) French archaeologist. In 1837 he discovered some of the first evidence of man-made stone tools near the bones of extinct (Pleistocene) animals in the valley of the River Somme. He argued that these tools (and their makers) belonged to a pre-Celtic "antediluvian" age, but his findings were not accepted until the 1850s.

Bou·chet |boo͞'shā|, Edward Alexander (1852–1918) U.S. physicist. He became the first African American to earn a Ph.D. from an American university (Yale, 1876).

Bou·dic·ca |boo͞'dikə| (died AD 60) a queen of the Britons, ruler of the Iceni tribe in eastern England; also known as **Boadicea**. Boudicca led her forces in revolt against the Romans and sacked Colchester, St. Albans, and London before being defeated by the Roman governor Suetonius Paulinus.

Bou·gain·ville |boo͞gən'vēl|, Louis-Antoine de (1729–1811) French explorer. Bougainville led the first French circumnavigation of the globe 1766–69, visiting many of the islands of the South Pacific and compiling an invaluable scientific record of his findings.

Bou·lan·ger |boo͞län'zhā|, Nadia-Juliette (1887–1979) French music teacher, conductor, and composer. Her students included Aaron Copland, Roger Sessions, Virgil Thomson, and Leonard Bernstein.

Bou·lez |boo͞'lez|, Pierre (1925–) French composer and conductor. His works explore and develop serialism and aleatory music, making use of both traditional and electronic instruments.

Boult |bōlt|, Sir Adrian (Cedric) (1899–1983) English conductor. Music director of the BBC 1930–49 and principal conductor of the London Philharmonic Orchestra 1950–57.

Boul·ton |'bōltən|, Matthew (1728–1809) English engineer and manufacturer. With his partner James Watt he pioneered the manufacture of steam engines, which they began to produce in 1774.

Bour·gui·ba |boo͞r'gēbə|, Habib ibn Ali (1903–) Tunisian nationalist and statesman and the first president of independent Tunisia (1957–87).

Bourke-White |'boo͞rk '(h)wīt|, Margaret (1906–71) U.S. photojournalist. During World War II she was the first female photographer with the U.S. armed forces, at the end of the war accompanying the Allied forces when they entered the Nazi concentration camps.

Boutros Ghali |ˌboo͞trōs'gälē|, Boutros (1922–) Egyptian diplomat and politician and Secretary General of the United Nations (1992–97).

Bow |bō|, Clara (1905–65) U.S. actress. One of the most popular stars and sex symbols of the 1920s, she was known as the "It Girl."

Bow·ditch |'baw,dich|, Nathaniel (1773–1838) U.S. mathematician and astronomer. He expanded *The Practical Navigator* into *The New American Practical Navigator* (1802).

Bow·en |'bōən|, Elizabeth (Dorothea Cole) (1899–1973) British novelist and short-story writer, born in Ireland. Notable novels: *The Death of the Heart* (1938) and *The Heat of the Day* (1949).

Bow·er·man |'bowər,mən|, William J (1909–) U.S. businessman. While coaching track at the University of Oregon (1960–75), he founded the Nike company (1973–).

Bow·ie |'bōē|, David (1947–) English rock singer, songwriter, and actor; born *David Robert Jones*. He is known for his theatrical performances and unconventional stage personae.

Bow·ie |'bōē; 'boo͞ē|, Jim (1796–1836) American frontiersman Full name *James Bowie*. The Bowie knife was designed either by him or by his brother Rezin. He became a leader among the American settlers who opposed Mexican rule in Texas. He shared command of the garrison that resisted the Mexican attack on the Alamo, where he died.

Bow·ker |'bowkər|, Richard Rogers (1848–1933) U.S. editor and author. He was founder (with F. Leypoldt and Melvil Dewey) and editor of *The Library Journal*, publisher and editor of *Publishers' Weekly*, and founder of the American Library Association (1876).

Bow·les |bōlz|, Paul (Frederick) (1910–) U.S. writer and composer. His novels, which include *The Sheltering Sky* (1949) and *The Spider's House* (1966), typically concern westerners in the Arab world.

Boyce |bois|, William (1711–79) English composer and organist. His compositions include songs, overtures, and eight symphonies; one of his most famous songs is "Hearts of Oak". He is also noted for his *Cathedral Music* (1760–73).

Boyd |boid|, Arthur (Merric Bloomfield) (1920–) Australian painter, potter, etcher, and ceramic artist. He is famous for his large ceramic sculptures and for his pictures inspired by his travels among the native people of Australia.

Boyd |boid|, John R (1927–97) U.S. military strategist. He was an expert on air-to-air combat and the architect of military reform in the U.S. Deptartment of Defense in the 1970s and 1980s.

Boyer |'boiər|, Charles (1899–1978) French-born U.S. actor. Before going to Hollywood in the 1930s he enjoyed a successful stage career in France. Notable movies: *Mayerling* (1936), *Gaslight* (1944), and *Barefoot in the Park* (1968).

Boyle |boil|, Robert (1627–91) Irishborn scientist. Boyle put forward a view of matter based on particles that was a precursor of the modern theory of chemical elements. He is best known for his experiments with the air pump, which led to the law named after him.

Boyle |boil|, T. Coraghessan (1948–) U.S. author. Notable works: *The Road to Wellville* (1993).

Boz |bäz| the pseudonym used by Charles Dickens in his *Pickwick Papers* and contributions to the *Morning Chronicle*.

Brad·bury |'bræd,berē|, Ray (1920–) U.S. writer of science fiction; full name *Raymond Douglas Bradbury*. Notable works: *The Martian Chronicles* (short story collection, 1950) and *Fahrenheit 451* (novel, 1951).

Brad·dock |'brædək|, Edward (1695–1755) British soldier. He was major general and commander in chief of the British forces in America in 1754.

Brad·ford |'brædfərd|, Barbara Taylor (1933–) U.S. author, born in England. Notable novels: *A Woman of Substance* (1974) and *A Sudden Change of Heart* (1999).

Brad·ford |'brædfərd|, William (1590–1657) U.S. religious and colonial leader. He was a signer of the Mayflower Compact (1620) and Governor of Plymouth Colony (1621–32; 1635; 1637; 1639–43; 1645–56).

Brad·ham |'brædəm|, Caleb D. U.S. inventor. He created the formula used in Pepsi-Cola.

Brad·lee |'brædlē|, Benjamin Crowninshield (1921–) U.S. journalist. He is the executive editor of the *Washington Post* (1968–).

Brad·ley |'brædlē|, Bill (1943–) U.S. basketball player and politician. He played for the New York Knicks in the NBA (1967–77) before entering politics. A New Jersey Democrat, he was elected to the U.S. Senate (1979–). Elected to the Basketball Hall of Fame (1983).

Brad·ley |'brædlē|, Edward R. (1941–) U.S. journalist. He is a news correspondent for the CBS television news show "60 Minutes" (1981–).

Brad·ley |'brædlē|, James (1693–1762) English astronomer. Bradley was appointed Astronomer Royal in 1742. He discovered the aberration of light and also observed the oscillation of the earth's axis, which he termed *nutation*. His star catalogue was published posthumously.

Brad·ley |'brædlē|, Joseph P. (1813–92) U.S. Supreme Court justice (1870–92).

Brad·ley |'brædlē|, Milton (1836–1911) U.S. publisher and manufacturer. His board game *The Checkered Game of Life* (1860) led to the formation of the Milton Bradley Co. (1864).

Brad·ley |'brædlē|, Omar Nelson (1893–1981) U.S. general. He was in charge of the land contingent during the Normandy campaign (1944–45) and served as chief of staff of the U.S. Army (1948–49), chairman of the U.S. Joint Chiefs of Staff (1949–53), and General of the Army (1950).

Brad·ley |'brædlē|, Thomas (1917–98) U.S. politician and lawyer. Elected mayor of Los Angeles (1973–93), he became the first African-American mayor of a largely white city. Awarded Spingarn Medal (1984).

Brad·shaw |'bræd,sHaw|, Terry Paxton (1948–) U.S. football player.

Brad·street |'bræd,strēt|, Anne Dudley (1612–72) U.S. poet. She came from England with her husband Simon Bradstreet to the Massachusetts Bay Colony in 1630. She was the first American poetess. Notable works: *The Tenth Muse Lately Sprung Up in America* (1650).

Bra·dy |'brādē|, James Buchanan (1856–1917) U.S. financier. He was a salesman for a railroad supply house and was known for his ostentatious display of jewelry, which gave him the nickname "Diamond Jim."

Bra·dy |'brādē|, Mathew B. (1823?–96) U.S. photographer. His photographs of Union armies taken during the Civil War became the basis for his National Photographic Collection, and the publication of his *Gallery of Illustrious Americans* (1850) established him as a leading American photographer.

Bragg |brag|, Sir William Henry (1862–1942) English physicist, a founder of solid-state physics. He collaborated with his son, **Sir (William) Lawrence Bragg**, (1890–1971, in developing the technique of X-ray diffraction for determining the atomic structure of crystals; for this they shared the 1915 Nobel Prize for Physics.

Bra·he |'brä,hē|, Tycho (1546–1601) Danish astronomer. He built an observatory equipped with precision instruments, but despite demonstrating that comets follow sun-centered paths, he adhered to a geocentric view of the planets.

Brahms |brämz|, Johannes (1833–97) German composer and pianist. He eschewed program music and opera and concentrated on traditional forms. He wrote four symphonies, four concertos, chamber and piano music, choral works including the *German Requiem* (1857–68), and nearly 200 songs including *Wiegenlied*, (op. 49), for the melody for "Brahms Lullaby."

Braille |brāl|, Louis (1809–52) French educationist. Blind from the age of 3, by the age of 15 he had developed his own system of raised-point reading and writing, which was officially adopted two years after his death.

Braine |brān|, John (Gerard) (1922–86) English novelist, famous for his first novel, *Room at the Top* (1957), whose opportunistic hero was hailed as a representative example of an "angry young man."

Brai·thwaite |'brāTH,wāt|, William

Stanley Beaumont (1878–1962) U.S. poet and anthologist. He is noted for his poetry collection *The House of Falling Leaves* (1904) and for editing annual anthologies of magazine verse (1913–39). Spingarn Medal, 1918.

Bra·mah |'brämə|, Joseph (1748–1814) English inventor. One of the most influential engineers of the Industrial Revolution, Bramah is best known for his hydraulic press, used for heavy forging.

Bra·man·te |brä'mäntä|, Donato (d' Angelo) (1444–1514) Italian architect. As architect to Pope Julius II he drew up the first plan for the new St. Peter's (begun in 1506), instigating the concept of a huge central dome.

Bran·agh |'branə|, Kenneth (Charles) (1960–) English actor, producer, and director. With the Royal Shakespeare Company he attracted critical acclaim for roles such as Henry V. He has also directed and starred in movies such as *Hamlet* (1996).

Bran·cu·şi |'bränkoosh|, Constantin (1876–1957) Romanian sculptor, who spent much of his working life in France. His sculpture represents an attempt to move away from a representational art and to capture the essence of forms by reducing them to their ultimate, almost abstract, simplicity.

Bran·deis |'bran,dīs|, Louis Dembitz (1856–1941) U.S. Supreme Court justice (1916–39). He gained an early reputation as the "people's attorney" by defending without a fee Boston residents seeking regulation of local public utilities. His "Brandeis brief" made use of social facts, rather than relying solely on precedent and general argument.

Bran·do |'brandō|, Marlon (1924–) U.S. actor. An exponent of method acting, he first attracted critical acclaim in the stage production of *A Streetcar Named Desire* (1947); he starred in the movie version four years later. Other notable movies: *On the Waterfront* (1954, for which he won an Oscar) and *The Godfather* (1972).

Brandt |brant|, Bill (1904?–83) German-born British photographer; full name *Hermann Wilhelm Brandt*. He is best known for his almost abstract treatment of the nude, as in *Perspectives of Nudes* (1961).

Brandt |brænt|, Willy (1913–92) German statesman, chancellor of West Germany 1969–74; born *Karl Herbert Frahm*. He achieved international recognition for his policy of détente and the opening of relations with the countries of the Eastern bloc (Ostpolitik). Nobel Peace Prize (1971).

Bran·son |'brænsən|, Richard (1950–) English businessman and adventurer. He made his name with the company Virgin Records, which he set up in 1969. He later influenced the opening up of air routes with Virgin Atlantic Airways, established in 1984.

Braque |bräk|, Georges (1882–1963) French painter. His collages, which introduced commercial lettering and fragmented objects into pictures to contrast the real with the "illusory" painted image, were the first stage in the development of synthetic cubism.

Bras·sey |'bræsē|, Thomas (1805–70) English engineer and railway contractor. He built more than 10,000 km (6,500 miles) of railways in Europe, India, South America, and Australia.

Brat·tain |'brætn|, Walter Houser (1902–87) U.S. inventor. He co-invented the point-contact transistor (1947) with John Bardeen and William Shockley, with whom he share a Nobel Prize for Physics (1956).

Braun |brown|, Eva (1912–45) German mistress of Adolf Hitler. Braun and Hitler are thought to have married during the fall of Berlin, shortly before committing suicide together in the air-raid shelter of his Berlin headquarters.

Braun |brown|, Karl Ferdinand (1850–1918) German physicist. Braun invented the coupled system of radio transmission and the Braun tube (forerunner of the cathode ray tube), in which a beam of electrons could be deflected. Nobel Prize for Physics (1909).

Braun |brown|, Wernher Magnus Maximilian von (1912–77) German-born U.S. rocket engineer. Braun led development on the V-2 rockets used by Germany in World War II. After the war he moved to the U.S., where he pioneered

the work that resulted in the U.S. space program.

Brau·ti·gan |'brawtə,gən|, Richard (1935–84) U.S. author. His novels, particularly *Trout Fishing in America* (1967), reflect the ethos of the Beat generation.

Brax·ton |'brækstən|, Toni (1968–) U.S. pop singer. Grammy Award, 1997.

Braz·le·ton |'bræzl,tən; 'brāzl,tən|, T. Berry (1918–) U.S. pediatrician and educator. He was director of the child development unit at Children's Hospital Medical Center in Boston (1972–) and the author of *Infants and Mothers: Individual Differences in Development* (1970).

Bream |brēm|, Julian (Alexander) (1933–) English guitarist and lute player. He formed the Julian Bream Consort for the performance of early consort music and revived and edited much early music. Britten, Walton, and others composed works for him.

Breath·ed |'breTH,əd|, Berke (1957–) U.S. cartoonist. Full name *Guy Berkeley Breathed*. He created the Pulitzer Prize-winning comic strip "Bloom County."

Brecht |brekt|, (Eugen) Bertolt (Friedrich) (1898–1956) German dramatist, producer, and poet. His interest in combining music and drama led to collaboration with Kurt Weill, for example in *The Threepenny Opera* (1928), an adaptation of John Gay's *The Beggar's Opera*. Brecht's later drama, written in exile after Hitler's rise to power, uses techniques of theatrical alienation and includes *Mother Courage* (1941) and *The Caucasian Chalk Circle* (1948).

Breck·in·ridge |'brekən,rij|, John Cabell (1821–75) U.S. politician and vice president of the U.S. (1857–61).

Brel |brel|, Jacques (1929–78) Belgian singer and composer. He gained a reputation in Paris as an original songwriter whose satirical wit was balanced by his idealism and hope.

Bren·dan |'brendən|, St (*c*. 486–*c*. 578) Irish abbot. The legend of the "Navigation of St. Brendan" (*c*.1050), describing his voyage with a band of monks to a promised land (possibly Orkney or the Hebrides), was widely popular in the Middle Ages. Feast day, May 16.

Bren·del |'brendəl|, Alfred (1931–)
Austrian pianist.

Bren·nan |'brenən|, Walter (1894–
1974) U.S. actor. He was the first actor
to win three Academy Awards (1936,
Come and Get It; 1938, *Kentucky*; 1940,
The Westerner).

Bren·nan |'brenən|, William J., Jr
(1906–97) U.S. Supreme Court Justice
(1956–90).

Bres·lin |'brez,lin|, Jimmy (1930–)
U.S. journalist and author. A syndicat-
ed columnist, he won a 1986 Pulitzer
Prize in 1986. He wrote *The Gang That
Couldn't Shoot Straight* (1969) and *He
Got Hungry and Forgot His Manners*
(1988).

Bre·ton |'bretn|, André (1896–1966)
French poet, essayist, and critic. First involved with Dadaism, Breton later
launched the surrealist movement, out-
lining the movement's philosophy in his
manifesto of 1924. His creative writing
is characterized by surrealist techniques
such as "automatic" writing.

Brett |bret|, George (1953–) U.S.
baseball player. He was the American
League batting champion in three different decades (1976, 1980, 1990).
Elected to the Baseball Hall of Fame
(1999).

Brett |bret|, Jan (1949–) U.S. author
and illustrator. Her lavishly illustrated
children's books include *Trouble with
Trolls* (1992).

Breu·er |'broiər|, Marcel Lajos (1902–
81) U.S. architect, born in Hungary.
Notable designs: UNESCO headquar-
ters (1953–58) in Paris and the Whitney
Museum of American Art (1965–66) in
New York City.

Breuil |'broEy|, Henri-Édouard Prosper
(1877–1961) French archaeologist. He
is noted for his work on Paleolithic cave
paintings, in particular those at Altami-
ra in Spain, which he was able to au-
thenticate.

Brew·er |'broŏər|, David J. (1837–
1910) U.S. Supreme Court Justice
(1889–1910).

Brew·ster |'broŏstər|, Sir David (1781–
1868) Scottish physicist. He is best
known for his work on the laws govern-
ing the polarization of light, and for his
invention of the kaleidoscope.

Brey·er |'brīər|, Stephen Gerald
(1938–) U.S. Supeme Court justice
(1994–)

Brezh·nev |'brezH,nev|, Leonid
(Ilyich) (1906–82) Soviet statesman,
general secretary of the Communist
Party of the USSR (1966–82) and president (1977–82). His period in power
was marked by intensified persecution
of dissidents at home and by attempted
détente followed by renewed Cold War
in 1968; he was largely responsible for
the invasion of Czechoslovakia (1968).

Brick·er |'brikər|, John W. (1893–1986)
U.S. politician. He was a Republican
vice presidential candidate (1944).

Bride, St. see BRIDGET, ST.

Bridge |brij|, Frank (1879–1941) Eng-
lish composer, conductor, and violist.
His compositions include chamber
music, songs, and orchestral works,
among them *The Sea* (1910–11) and
Oration (for cello and orchestra, 1930).

Bridg·es |'brijəz|, Lloyd Vernet, Jr.
(1913–98) U.S. actor. Father of Jeff
Bridges and Beau Bridges. His many
movie credits include *High Noon* (1952)
and *Airplane* (1980).

Bridg·es |'brijəz|, Robert (Seymour)
(1844–1930) English poet and literary
critic. His long philosophical poem *The
Testament of Beauty* (1929), written in
the Victorian tradition, was instantly
popular. He was Poet Laureate 1913–
30.

Bridg·et[1] |'brijət|, St. (*c.* 453–524) Irish
abbess. Also **Bride** or **Brigid**; also
known as **St. Bridget of Ireland**. She
was venerated in Ireland as a virgin saint
and noted in miracle stories for her com-
passion; her cult soon spread over most
of western Europe. Feast day, July 23.

Bridg·et[2] |'brijət|, St. (*c.* 1303–73)
Swedish nun and visionary. Also **Birgit-
ta**; also known as **St. Bridget of Sweden**. She experienced her first vision of
the Virgin Mary at the age of seven. Feast
day, July 23.

Bridg·man |'brijmən|, Percy Williams
(1882–1961) U.S. physicist. He worked
with liquids and solids under very high
pressures, and his techniques were later
used in making artificial minerals (including diamonds). Nobel Prize for
Physics (1946).

Briggs |brigz|, Clare A. (1875–1930) U.S. cartoonist. He created the comic strip "Mr. & Mrs."

Briggs |brigz|, Henry (1561–1630) English mathematician. He was renowned for his work on logarithms, in which he introduced the decimal base, made the thousands of calculations necessary for the tables, and popularized their use. Briggs also devised a standard method used for long division.

Bright |brīt|, John (1811–89) English Liberal politician and reformer. A noted orator, Bright was the leader, along with Richard Cobden, of the campaign to repeal the Corn Laws. He was also a vociferous opponent of the Crimean War (1854) and was closely identified with the 1867 Reform Act.

Brigid, St. see BRIDGET, ST.

Brind·ley |'brindlē|, James (1716–72) pioneering English canal-builder. He designed some 600 km (375 miles) of waterway with a minimum of locks, cuttings, or tunnels, connecting most of the major rivers of England.

Brink |briNGk|, André (1935–) South African novelist, short-story writer, and dramatist. He gained international recognition with his novel *Looking on Darkness* (1973), which became the first novel in Afrikaans to be banned by the South African government. Other notable novels: *A Dry White Season* (1979) and *A Chain of Voices* (1982).

Brink·ley |'briNGk,lē|, David (1920–) U.S. news commentator. He reported news for NBC (1951–81) and anchored ABC's *This Week* (1981–97).

Bris·bane |'brizbən|, Sir Thomas Makdougall (1773–1860) Scottish soldier and astronomer. In 1790 he joined the army, becoming major general in 1813. He was governor of New South Wales (1821–25) and became an acclaimed astronomer.

Brit·ten |'britn|, (Edward) Benjamin, Lord Britten of Aldeburgh (1913–76) English composer, pianist, and conductor. Notable operas: *Peter Grimes* (1945), *A Midsummer Night's Dream* (1960), and *Death in Venice* (1973) .

Brock |bräk|, Lou (1939–) U.S. baseball player. He was the National League stolen base leader eight times, and (until 1991) held the record for career stolen bases (938).

Bro·der |'brōdər|, David Salzer (1929–) U.S. journalist and author. A syndicated columnist, he won a Pulitzer Prize in 1973 and became an associate editor of *The Washington Post* (1975–).

Brod·key |'brawd,kē|, Harold (1930–1996) U.S. author. He wrote about Jewish family life in small-town midwestern America. Notable works: *First Love and Other Sorrows* (1958) and *Stories in an Almost Classical Mode* (1988).

Brod·sky |'brädskē|, Joseph (1940–96) Russian-born U.S. poet; born *Iosif Aleksandrovich Brodsky*. Writing both in Russian and in English, he was most famous for his collection *The End of a Beautiful Era* (1977). Nobel Prize for Literature (1987); U.S. Poet Laureate (1991).

Bro·dy |'brō,dē|, Jane (1941–) U.S. journalist and author. A science writer and personal health columnist for the *New York Times* (1965–), she also wrote *Jane Brody's Good Food Book* (1985).

Broglie, de see DE BROGLIE.

Bro·now·ski |,brə'nowskē|, Jacob (1908–74) Polish-born British scientist, writer, and broadcaster. He popularized science with such books as *The Common Sense of Science* (1951) and the 1970s television documentary series "The Ascent of Man."

Bron·të |'bräntē| Family of English novelists, including: **Charlotte Brontë** (1816–55). Under the pseudonym *Currer Bell*, she published *Jane Eyre* (1847). Her sister **Emily Brontë** (1818–48), under the pseudonym *Ellis Bell*, published *Wuthering Heights* (1847). **Anne Brontë** (1820–49) was the sister of Charlotte and Emily. Under the pseudonym *Acton Bell*, she published *The Tenant of Wildfell Hall* (1847).

Bron·zi·no |,brawn'zēnō|, Agnolo (1503–72) Italian mannerist painter; born *Agnolo di Cosimo*. He spent most of his career in Florence as court painter to Cosimo de' Medici. Notable works: *Venus, Cupid, Folly, and Time* (c.1546).

Brooke |broŏk|, Edward William (1919–) U.S. attorney and politician. He was a Republican member of the U.S. Senate from Massachusetts (1966–

79) and the first African American senator elected in 85 years. Spingarn Medal, 1967.

Brooke |brook|, Rupert (Chawner) (1887–1915) English poet. He is most famous for his wartime poetry *1914 and Other Poems* (1915). He died while on naval service in the Mediterranean.

Brook•ner |'brooknər|, Anita (1928–) English novelist and art historian.

Brooks |brooks|, Cleanth (1906–94) U.S. teacher and critic. A leading proponent of the New Criticism movement, he edited *The Southern Review* from 1935 to 1942 and taught at Yale University (1947–75). Notable works: *Modern Poetry and Tradition* (1939).

Brooks |brooks|, Garth (1962–) U.S. country music singer and songwriter. Full name *Troyal Garth Brooks*. Notable albums: *No Fences* (1990) and *Ropin' the Wind* (1991).

Brooks |brooks|, Gwendolyn (1917–) U.S. poet and author. She was the first African-American woman named as Poetry Consultant to the Library of Congress (1985–86). Notable works: *Annie Allen* (1949), which won the Pulitzer Prize.

Brooks |brooks|, Henry Sands (1770?– 1833) U.S. entrepreneur. A pioneer in men's ready-to-wear clothing, he was the founder of Brooks Brothers clothing stores.

Brooks |brooks|, James L. (1940–) U.S. director. Notable movies: *Terms of Endearment* (1983, Academy Award).

Brooks |brooks|, Mel (1926–) U.S. comedian, movie director and comic actor; born *Melvin Kaminsky*. He is known especially for his parodies and farces. His movie debut *The Producers* (1967) was followed by the spoof western *Blazing Saddles* (1974).

Brooks |brooks|, Van Wyck (1886–1963) U.S. literary critic. Notable works: *The Wine of the Puritans* (1909), *America's Coming-of-Age* (1915), and *The Flowering of New England* (1936), which won the Pulitzer Prize.

Broon•zy |'broon,zē|, Big Bill (1893–1958) U.S. guitarist and blues singer. Full name *William Lee Conley Broonzy*.

Brou•wer |'brow,ər|, Adriaen (*c.* 1605–?8) Flemish painter. Providing an im-

porant link between Dutch and Flemish genre painting, his most typical works represent peasant scenes in taverns.

Brown |brown|, Sir Arthur Whitten (1886–1948) Scottish aviator. He made the first transatlantic flight in 1919 with Sir John William Alcock.

Brown |brown|, Ford Madox (1821–93) English painter. His early work was inspired by the Pre-Raphaelites, and in 1861 he became a founding member of William Morris's company, designing stained glass and furniture.

Brown |brown|, Helen Gurley (1922–) U.S. editor and author. She was editor in chief of *Cosmopolitan* magazine (1972–) and author of *Sex and the Single Girl* (1962).

Brown |brown|, Henry Billings (1836–1913) U.S. Supreme Court Justice (1890–1906).

Brown |brown|, H. Rap (1943–) see AL-AMIN, Jamil Abdullah.

Brown[1] |brown|, James (1800–55) U.S. publisher. In partnership with Charles C. Little, he founded Little, Brown & Co. (1847).

Brown[2] |brown|, James (1928–) U.S. soul and funk singer and songwriter. In the 1960s he played a leading role in the development of funk with songs such as "Papa's Got a Brand New Bag" (1965).

Brown |brown|, Jerry, Jr. (1938–) U.S. politician. Full name *Edmund Gerald Brown*. He was governor of California (1975–83) and a Democratic presidential candidate (1990).

Brown |brown|, Jim (1936–) U.S. football player and actor. He was the NFL's premier running back, leading the league in rushing in eight of his nine seasons (1957–66). He was later featured in several action-adventure movies, including *Ice Station Zebra* (1968).

Brown |brown|, John (1800–59) U.S. radical abolitionist. In 1859 he was executed after raiding a government arsenal at Harpers Ferry, Virginia, intending to arm black slaves and start a revolt. He became a hero of the abolitionists in the Civil War; he is commemorated in the song "John Brown's Body."

Brown |brown|, John Carter (1797–

1874) U.S. bibliophile. He assembled over 7,500 volumes of early Americana, which became the John Carter Brown Library at Brown University.

Brown |brown|, Lancelot (1715–83) English landscape gardener; known as **Capability Brown**. He evolved an English style of natural-looking landscape parks. Notable examples of his work are at Blenheim Palace, Chatsworth House in Derbyshire, and Kew Gardens.

Brown |brown|, Marc Tolon (1946–) U.S. author and artist. He wrote the "Arthur" series of books for children.

Brown |brown|, Margaret Wise (1910–52) U.S. author. She was a prolific writer of books for young children, including "Good Night, Moon" (1947).

Brown |brown|, Paul (1908–91) U.S. football coach. He led the Cleveland Browns to three NFL titles (1950, 1954, 1955). He founded the Cincinnati Bengals (1968).

Brown |brown|, Rachel Fuller (1898–1980) U.S. inventor. With Elizabeth Lee Hazen, she developed Nystatin, the first nontoxic antifungal antibiotic.

Brown |brown|, Sterling Allen (1901–89) U.S. poet, literary critic, and educator. Considered a founder of black literary criticism, he wrote *Negro Poetry and Drama* (1937).

Brown |brown|, Tina (1953–) U.S. editor, born in England. She edited *Vanity Fair* (1984–92) and *The New Yorker* (1992–98).

Brown |brown|, William Wells (1816?–84) U.S. author. After securing freedom from slavery, Brown aided other fugitive slaves. Notable works: *Clotelle: or, The President's Daughter* (1852), said to be the first novel published by an African American.

Browne |brown|, Dik (1917–89) U.S. cartoonist, advertising artist, and author. Full name *Richard Arthur Allen*. He was creator of the comic strip "Hagar the Horrible" and co-creator of the comic strip "Hi and Lois."

Browne |brown|, Jackson (1948–) U.S. rock singer and songwriter.

Browne |brown|, Sir Thomas (1605–82) English author and physician. He achieved prominence with *Religio Medici* (1642), a collection of opinions

on a vast number of subjects connected with religion.

Brow•ning |'browniNG| English poets: **Elizabeth Barrett Browning** (1806–61); born *Elizabeth Barrett*. She established her reputation with *Poems* (1844). In 1846 she eloped to Italy with **Robert Browning** (1812–89). In 1842 he established his name with *Dramatic Lyrics*, containing "The Pied Piper of Hamelin" and "My Last Duchess."

Bru•beck |'broobek|, Dave (1920–) U.S. jazz pianist, composer, and bandleader; full name *David Warren Brubeck*. He formed the Dave Brubeck Quartet in 1951 and won international recognition with the album *Time Out*, which included "Take Five" (1959).

Bruce |broos|, Lenny (1925–66) U.S. comedian; born *Leonard Alfred Schneider*. He gained notoriety for flouting the bounds of respectability with his humor, and was imprisoned for obscenity in 1961. He died following an accidental drug overdose.

Bruce |broos|, James (1730–94) Scottish explorer. In 1770 he was the first European to discover the source of the Blue Nile, although his *Travels to Discover the Sources of the Nile* (1790), recounting his expedition, was dismissed by his contemporaries as fabrication.

Bruce |broos|, Robert the see ROBERT I.

Bruck•ner |'brooknər|, Anton (1824–1896) Austrian composer and organist. He wrote ten symphonies, four masses, and a *Te Deum* (1884).

Brue•gel |'broigəl|, Pieter (c. 1525–69) Flemish artist Family of Flemish artists, including: **Pieter Bruegel** (c. 1525–69); known as **Pieter Bruegel the Elder**. He produced landscapes, religious allegories, and satires of peasant life. Notable works: *The Procession to Calvary* (1564), *The Blind Leading the Blind* (1568), and *The Peasant Dance* (1568). His son, **Pieter Bruegel** (1564–1638), known as **Pieter Bruegel the Younger** or as **Hell Bruegel**, was a very able copyist of his father's work; he is also noted for his paintings of devils. **Jan Bruegel** (1568–1625), son of Pieter Bruegel the Elder, was known as **Velvet**. He was a celebrated painter of flower, landscape, and mythological pictures.

Brum·mell |'brəməl|, George Bryan (1778–1840) English dandy; known as **Beau Brummell**. He was the arbiter of British fashion for the first decade and a half of the 19th century, owing his social position to his friendship with the Prince Regent.

Brundt·land |'brənt,lənd|, Gro Harlem (1939–) Norwegian Labor stateswoman and prime minister (1981, 1986–89, and 1990–96). As Norway's first woman prime minister, she chaired the World Commission on Environment and Development (known as the Brundtland Commission), which produced the report *Our Common Future* in 1987.

Bru·nel |brə'nel| Family of English engineers, including French-born **Sir Marc Isambard Brunel** (1769–1849). He introduced mass-production machinery to the Portsmouth dockyard and designed other machines for woodworking, bootmaking, knitting, and printing. He also worked to construct the first tunnel under the Thames (1825–43). His son, **Isambard Kingdom Brunel** (1806–59), was chief engineer of the Great Western Railway. His achievements include designing the Clifton suspension bridge (1829–30) and the first transatlantic steamship, the *Great Western* (1838).

Bru·nel·les·chi |,brōōnl-'eskē|, Filippo (1377–1446) Italian architect; born *Filippo di Ser Brunellesco*. He is especially noted for the dome of Florence cathedral (1420–61), which he raised without the use of temporary supports. He is often credited with the Renaissance "discovery" of perspective.

Bru·no |'brōōnō|, Frank (1961–) English heavyweight boxing champion. Full name *Franklin Ray Bruno*.

Bru·no |'brōōnō|, Giordano (1548–1600) Italian philosopher. He was a follower of Hermes Trismegistus and a supporter of the heliocentric Copernican view of the solar system. Bruno was tried by the Inquisition for heresy and burned at the stake.

Bru·no |'brōōnō|, St. (c. 1030–1101) German-born French churchman. In 1084 he withdrew to the mountains of Chartreuse and founded the Carthusian

order at La Grande Chartreuse. Feast day, October 6.

Bru·ton |'brōōtən|, John (Gerard) (1947–) Irish Fine Gael statesman and Taoiseach (prime minister) (1994–97).

Bru·tus |'brōōtəs|, Lucius Junius (6th century BC) legendary founder of the Roman Republic. Traditionally he led a popular uprising, after the rape of Lucretia, against the king (his uncle) and drove him from Rome. He and the father of Lucretia were elected as the first consols of the Republic (509 BC).

Bru·tus |'bōōtəs|, Marcus Junius (85–42 BC) Roman senator. With Cassius he led the conspirators who assassinated Julius Caesar in 44 BC. They were defeated by Caesar's supporters, Antony and Octavian, at the battle of Philippi in 42 BC, after which Brutus committed suicide.

Bry·an |'brīən| U.S. political family, including **William Jennings Bryan** (1860–1925); known as **The Great Commoner**. His "Cross of Gold" speech (1896) won him the Democratic nomination for the U.S. presidency, and he was nominated and defeated two other times (1900 and 1908). He was the prosecutor of evolutionist John T. Scopes and had notable debates with Clarence Darrow (1925). His brother, **Charles Wayland Bryan** (1867–1945), served as governor of Nebraska (1923–25) and was a Democratic vice presidential candidate in 1924.

Bry·ant |'brīənt|, Lane (1879–1951) U.S. businesswoman, born in Lithuania. Born *Lena Himmelstein Bryant*. She founded Lane Bryant Apparel, which specializes in women's garments in larger sizes.

Bry·ant |'brīənt|, Paul William (1913–83) U.S. college football coach. Known as **Bear**. He set a record for most career wins (323) for a collegiate football coach.

Bry·ant |'brīənt|, William Cullen (1794–1878) U.S. poet and editor. He was co-owner and editor of the *New York Evening Post* (1829–78); his poems "Thanatopsis" and "An Indian at the Burial Place of His Fathers" established him as the leading poet of his time.

Bryn·ner |'brinər|, Yul (1920–85) U.S. actor, born in Russia. Born *Taidje Khan.* He is best known as the king of Siam in the musical *The King and I,* a role he performed on stage more than 4,500 times (1951–85). Notable movies: *The King and I* (1956, Academy Award) and *The Magnificent Seven* (1960).

Buat·ta, Mario (1935–) U.S. interior designer. Known as the "prince of chintz," with Mark Hampton, he redecorated Blair House in Washington, D.C. (1985).

Buber, Martin (1878–1965) Israeli religious philosopher, born in Austria. In his existentialist work *I and Thou* (1923), he argues that religious experience involves reciprocal relationships with a personal subject, rather than knowledge of some "thing."

Bub·ka |'bəbkə|, Sergei (1963–) Ukrainian pole vaulter. A six-time world champion and Olympic gold medalist (1991), he became the first man to clear 20 feet both indoors and out (1991).

Buch·an |'bəkən|, Alexander (1829–1907) Scottish meteorologist. He wrote a textbook on meteorology and produced maps and tables of atmospheric circulation, and of ocean currents and temperatures, based largely on information gathered on the voyage of HMS *Challenger* in 1872–6.

Buch·an |'bəkən|, John, 1st Baron Tweedsmuir (1875–1940) Scottish novelist. His adventure stories feature recurring heroes such as Richard Hannay. Notable works: *The Thirty-Nine Steps* (1915).

Bu·chan·an |byoō'kænən|, James see box.

Bu·chan·an |byoō'kænən|, Pat (1938–) U.S. journalist. Full name *Patrick Joseph Buchanan.* Noted for his political conservatism, he has been a syndicated newspaper columnist, radio commentator, and cohost of a television forum of political discussion.

Buch·ner |'boōkнnər|, Eduard (1860–1917) German organic chemist. He studied the chemistry of alcoholic fermentation and identified several enzymes, notably zymase. Nobel Prize for Chemistry (1907).

Buch·wald |'bək,wawld|, Art (1925–)

Buchanan, James
15th U.S. president

Life dates: 1791–1868
Place of birth: Stony Batter, Pennsylvania
Mother: Elizabeth Speer Buchanan
Father: James Buchanan
Wife: none
Children: none
College/University: Dickinson College
Military service: Company of Dragoons, War of 1812
Career: Lawyer; writer
Political career: Pennsylvania legislature; U.S. House of Representatives; minister to Russia; U.S. Senate; minister to Great Britain; U.S. secretary of state; president
Party: Federalist (till 1824); Democratic
Home state: Pennsylvania
Opponents in presidential race: John Charles Frémont; Millard Fillmore
Term of office: March 4, 1857–March 3, 1861
Vice president: John C. Breckinridge
Notable events of presidency: Panic of 1857; Pony Express; raid by John Brown on Harper's Ferry; Dred Scott decision; Minnesota admitted as the 32nd state, Oregon admitted as the 33rd state; Kansas admitted as the 34th state; secession of South Carolina, Mississippi, Florida, Alabama, Georgia, Louisiana, and Texas from the Union; Confederate States of America organized
Other achievements: Admitted to the Pennsylvania bar; co-author of pro-slavery Ostend Manifesto calling for immediate acquisition of Cuba
Place of burial: Lancaster, Pennsylvania

U.S. journalist and author. A syndicated columnist and 1982 Pulitzer Prize winner, he wrote *I Am Not A Crook* (1974) and *I Think I Don't Remember* (1987).

Buck |bək|, Pearl S. (1892–1973) U.S. writer; full name *Pearl Sydenstricker Buck.* Her upbringing and work in China inspired her earliest novels, including *The Good Earth* (Pulitzer Prize, 1931). Nobel Prize for Literature (1938).

Buck·land |'bəklənd|, William (1784–1856) English geologist. He helped to redefine geology, correlating deposits and associated fossils with former conditions, and developed the idea of an ice age. He was the first to describe and name a dinosaur (*Megalosaurus*), in 1824.

Buck•ley |'bəklē|, William F., Jr. (1925–) U.S. journalist and author. Full name *William Frank Buckley, Jr.*. Founder of the politically conservative *National Review* magazine (1955), he has hosted the television discussion program "Firing Line" since 1966.

Bud•dha |'boŏdə| Often **the Buddha**, a title given to the founder of Buddhism, Siddartha Gautama (*c.* 563–*c.* 460 BC). Born an Indian prince, he renounced wealth and family to become an ascetic, and after achieving enlightenment while meditating, taught all who came to learn from him.

Budge |bəj|, Don (1915–) U.S. tennis champion; born *John Donald Budge.* He was the first to win the four major singles championships, the "Grand Slam"—Australia, France, Wimbledon, and the U.S.—in one year (1938).

Bu•ell |'byoŏl|, Marjorie (1904–93) U.S. cartoonist. She created "Little Lulu," originally a panel in the *Saturday Evening Post.*

Buf•fa•lo Bill |'bəfə,lō'bil| (1846–1917) U.S. showman; born *William Frederick Cody.* He gained his nickname for killing 4,280 buffalo in eight months to feed the Union Pacific Railroad workers, and subsequently devoted his career to his traveling Wild West Show.

Buf•fett |'bəfət|, Jimmy (1946–) U.S. musician and author. He is known for the hit song "Margaritaville."

Buf•fett |'bəfət|, Warren Edward (1930–) U.S. businessman. He is the CEO of Berkshire Hathaway and an influential board member of Salomon Brothers.

Buf•fon |,byoŏ'fōn|, Georges-Louis Leclerc, Comte de (1707–88) French naturalist. A founder of paleontology, he emphasized the unity of all living species, minimizing the apparent differences between animals and plants. He produced a compilation of the animal kingdom, the *Histoire Naturelle*, which had reached thirty-six volumes by the time of his death.

Bu•ick |'byoŏik|, David Dunbar (1854–1929) U.S. inventor and manufacturer. He formed the Buick Manufacturing Co. (1902) to build automobiles.

Bu•kha•rin |boŏ'kär,yēn|, Nikolay (Ivanovich) (1888–1938) Russian revolutionary activist and theorist. Editor of *Pravda* (1918–29) and *Izvestia* (1934–37), a member of the Politburo (1924–29), and chairman of Comintern from 1926, he was executed in one of Stalin's purges.

Bul•finch |'boŏl,finCH| U.S. family, including: **Charles Bullfinch** (1763–1844), an architect. He was the first professional architect in the U.S. and designed many buildings in his native Boston, including the Boston State House (1795–98). He succeeded Benjamin Henry Latrobe as architect of the National Capitol (1817–30). His son, **Thomas Bullfinch** (1796–1867), was an author. Notable works: *The Age of Fable* (1855) and *The Age of Chivalry* (1958).

Bul•ga•kov |,boŏl'gäkəf|, Mikhail Afanasyevich (1891–1940) Russian author. Notable novels: *The White Guard* (1925) and *The Master and Margarita* (1938). Such satirical works were banned and did not reemerge until the 1960s.

Bul•ga•nin |,boŏl'gänyēn|, Nikolay (Aleksandrovich) (1895–1975) Soviet statesman and chairman of the Council of Ministers (premier) (1955–58). He was vice-premier in the government of Georgi Malenkov in 1953, and in 1955 shared the premiership with Khrushchev.

Bult•mann |'boŏlt,män|, Rudolf (Karl) (1884–1976) German Lutheran theologian. He emphasized the "existential" rather than the historical significance of the Gospel story. Notable works: *The History of the Synoptic Tradition* (1921).

Bulwer-Lytton |,boŏlwər 'lit(ə)n| see LYTTON.

Bunche |'bənCH|, Ralph Johnson (1904–71) U.S. diplomat. Nobel Peace Prize, 1950.

Bu•nin |'boŏn,yin|, Ivan (Alekseyevich) (1870–1953) Russian poet and prose writer. An opponent of modernism, he concentrated on the themes of peasant life and love. Nobel Prize for Literature (1933, the first Russian prizewinner).

Bun·sen |'bənsən|, Robert Wilhelm Eberhard (1811–99) German chemist. With Gustav Kirchhoff he pioneered spectroscopy, detecting new elements (caesium and rubidium) and determining the composition of many substances and of the sun and stars. He designed numerous items of chemical apparatus, notably the Bunsen burner (1855).

Bun·shaft |'bən,sHæft|, Gordon (1909–90) U.S. architect. He is best known for his use of the International style in corporate architecture. Notable designs: Pepsi-Cola Building (1960) in New York City, and the Hirshhorn Museum and Sculpture Garden (1974) in Washington, D.C.

Bu·ñu·el |,bōōnyə'wel|, Luis (1900–83) Spanish movie director. Influenced by surrealism, he wrote and directed his first movie, *Un Chien andalou* (1928), jointly with Salvador Dali. Other notable movies: *Belle de jour* (1967) and *The Discreet Charm of the Bourgeoisie* (1972).

Bun·yan |'bənyən|, John (1628–88) English writer. A Nonconformist, he was imprisoned twice for unlicensed preaching, during which time he wrote his spiritual autobiography, *Grace Abounding* (1666), and began his major work, *The Pilgrim's Progress* (1678–84).

Buon·a·parte |,bwōnä'pärte| see BONAPARTE.

Buo·nar·ro·ti |,bwōnä'rōtē|, Michelangelo see MICHELANGELO.

Bur·bage |'bərbij|, Richard (*c.* 1567–1619) English actor. He was the creator of most of Shakespeare's great tragic roles: Hamlet, Othello, Lear, and Richard III, and was also associated with the building of the Globe Theatre.

Bur·bank |'bər,bæNGk|, Luther (1849–1926) U.S. horticulturist. His experiments in cross-breeding led to new types and improved varieties of plants, especially the Shasta daisy and the potato.

Burck·hal·ter |'bərk,hawltər|, Joseph H. (1912–) U.S. inventor. With Robert J. Seiwald, he developed dyes that could be utilized in the diagnosis of infectious diseases.

Bur·don |'bərdən|, Eric (1941–) British rock singer and guitarist.

Bur·ger |'bərgər|, Warren Earl (1907–95) U.S. Supreme Court justice (1969–86). Appointed as chief justice to the Supreme Court by President Richard Nixon, he was a conservative and an advocate of judicial restraint.

Bur·gess |'bərjəs|, Anthony (1917–93) English novelist and critic; pseudonym of *John Anthony Burgess Wilson*. One of his best-known novels is *A Clockwork Orange* (1962), a disturbing, futuristic vision of juvenile delinquency, violence, and high technology. Other notable works: *The Malayan Trilogy* (1956–59) and *Earthly Powers* (1980).

Bur·gess |'bərjəs|, Edward (1848–91) U.S. naval architect. He designed the America's Cup winners *Puritan* (1850), *Mayflower* (1886), and *Volunteer* (1887).

Bur·gess |'bərjəs|, Thornton Waldo (1874–1965) U.S. author of children's books. He wrote the *Old Mother West Wind* series (1910–18), as well as hundreds of stories about Peter Rabbit.

Burgh·ley |'bərlē|, William Cecil, 1st Baron (1520–98) English statesman. Secretary of State to Queen Elizabeth I 1558–72 and Lord High Treasurer 1572–98, he was the queen's most trusted councilor and minister.

Bur·goyne |'bər,goin|, John (1722–92) English general and dramatist; known as **Gentleman Johnny**. He surrendered to the Americans at Saratoga (1777) in the Revolutionary War.

Burke |bərk|, Edmund (1729–97) British man of letters and Whig politician. Burke wrote on the issues of political emancipation and moderation, notably with respect to Roman Catholics and the American colonies.

Burke |bərk|, John (1787–1848) Irish genealogical and heraldic writer. He compiled the first edition of *Burke's Peerage* (1826), still regarded as the authoritative guide to the British aristocracy.

Burke |bərk|, Robert O'Hara (1820–61) Irish explorer. He led a successful expedition from south to north across Australia in the company of William Wills and two others—the first white men to make this journey. On the return journey, however, Burke, Wills, and a third companion died of starvation.

Burke |bərk|, William (1792–1829)

Irish murderer. He was a bodysnatcher operating in Edinburgh with his accomplice **William Hare**. Burke was hanged for his crimes.

Bur•leigh |'bərlē|, Harry Thacker (1866–1949) U.S. singer and composer. He is known especially for his arrangements of negro spirituals.

Burne-Jones |'bərn'jōnz|, Sir Edward (Coley) (1833–98) English painter and designer. His work, which included tapestry and stained-glass window designs, reflected his interest in medieval and literary themes and is typical of the later Pre-Raphaelite style. Notable paintings: *The Golden Stairs* (1880) and *The Mirror of Venus* (1867–77).

Bur•nett |bər'net|, Carol (1936–) U.S. actress. A five-time Emmy Award winner, she is best known for the television program "The Carol Burnett Show" (1966–77).

Bur•nett |bər'net|, Frances (Eliza) Hodgson (1849–1924) British-born U.S. novelist. She is remembered chiefly for her novels for children, including *Little Lord Fauntleroy* (1886), *A Little Princess* (1905), and *The Secret Garden* (1911).

Bur•ney |'bərnē|, Fanny (1752–1840) English novelist; born *Frances Burney*. Notable works: *Evelina* (1778), *Cecilia* (1782), and *Letters and Diaries* (1846).

Burn•ham |'bərnəm|, Daniel H. (1846–1912) U.S. architect. Notable designs: Flatiron Building (1901) in New York City, and Union Railroad Station (1909) in Washington, D.C.

Burns |bərnz|, George (1896–1996) U.S. comedian. Born *Nathan Birnbaum*. Known for his comedy partnership with his wife Gracie Allen (*c.* 1905–64), he won an Academy Award for the movie *The Sunshine Boys* (1975).

Burns |bərnz|, Ken (1953–) U.S. filmmaker. He has created American historical documentary epics, including *The Civil War* (1990) and *Baseball* (1994).

Burns |bərnz|, Robert (1759–96) Scottish poet, best known for poems such as "The Jolly Beggars" (1786) and "Tam o' Shanter" (1791), and for old Scottish songs that he collected, including "Auld Lang Syne". Burns Night celebrations are held in Scotland and elsewhere on his birthday, January 25.

Burn•side |'bərn,sīd|, Ambrose Everett (1824–81) U.S. army officer. He was appointed General of the Army of the Potomac (1862), but his incompetence at the Battle of Fredericksburg (1862) led to his transfer to Ohio.

Bur•pee |'bər,pē|, Washington Atlee (1858–1915) U.S. businessman. He began a mail-order poultry business at age 17, and incorporated the W. Atlee Burpee & Co. (1878), which sold livestock and farm seed.

Burr |bər|, Aaron (1756–1836) U.S. statesman. In 1804, while vice-president, he killed his rival Alexander Hamilton in a duel. He then plotted to form an independent administration in Mexico and was tried for treason but acquitted.

Bur•ra |'bərə|, Edward (1905–76) English painter, noted for his low-life subjects, as in *Harlem* (1934), and the bizarre and fantastic, as in *Dancing Skeletons* (1934).

Bur•roughs |'bərōz|, Edgar Rice (1875–1950) U.S. novelist and writer of science fiction. He is chiefly remembered for his adventure stories about Tarzan, who first appeared in *Tarzan of the Apes* (1914).

Bur•roughs |'bərōz|, William (Seward) (1914–97) U.S. novelist. In the 1940s he became addicted to heroin, and his best-known writing, for example *Junkie* (1953) and *The Naked Lunch* (1959), deals with life as a drug addict in a unique, surreal style.

Burt |bərt|, Cyril (Lodowic) (1883–1971) English psychologist. Using studies of identical twins, he claimed that intelligence is inherited, but he was later accused of fabricating data.

Bur•ton |'bərtən|, Harold Hitz (1888–1964) U.S. Supreme Court Justice (1945–58).

Bur•ton |'bərtən|, Richard (1925–84) Welsh actor; born *Richard Jenkins*. He often co-starred with Elizabeth Taylor (to whom he was twice married). Notable movies: *The Spy Who Came in from the Cold* (1966) and *Who's Afraid of Virginia Woolf* (1966).

Bur•ton |'bərtən|, Sir Richard (Francis)

(1821–90) English explorer, anthropologist, and translator. He and John Hanning Speke were the first Europeans to see Lake Tanganyika (1858). Notable translations: the *Arabian Nights* (1885–8), the *Kama Sutra* (1883), and *The Perfumed Garden* (1886).

Bur•ton |'bərtən|, William Meriam (1865–1954) U.S. chemist. He developed a thermal process of manufacturing gasoline (1912). He was president of the Standard Oil Co. (1918–27).

Bu•sca•glia |,bəs'kælia|, Leo (1924–98) U.S. educator and author. Full name *Felice Leonardo Buscaglia*. His works include *The Fall of Freddie the Leaf* (1982) and *Loving Each Other: The Challenge of Human Relationships* (1984).

Busch |bŏŏSH|, Adolphus (1839–1913) U.S. businessman, born in Germany. As president of the Anheuser-Busch Brewing Association (1879–1913), he was a pioneer in the pasteurization of beer and introduced the Budweiser brand.

Bush |bŏŏSH|, George (Herbert Walker) see box. **Barbara Pierce Bush** (1925–   ), wife of George Bush and U.S. first lady (1989–93).

Bush•mil•ler |'bŏŏSH,milər|, Ernie (1905–82) U.S. cartoonist, comedy writer, and author. Full name *Ernest Paul Bushmiller*. He created the comic strips "Fritzi Ritz" and the internationally syndicated "Nancy."

Bush•nell |'bŏŏSH,nel|, David (1742?–1824) U.S. inventor. He invented a submarine that was first used in warfare (1775) called "Bushnell's Turtle."

Bu•so•ni |,bŏŏ'zōnē|, Ferruccio (Benvenuto) (1866–1924) Italian composer, conductor, and pianist. As a composer he is best known for his piano works and his unfinished opera *Doktor Faust* (1925).

Buss |bəs|, Frances Mary (1827–94) English educationist. She was in charge of the North London Collegiate School for Ladies (1850–94) and campaigned for higher education for women with her friend Dorothea Beale.

Bute |byŏŏt|, John Stuart, 3rd Earl of (1713–92) Scottish courtier and Tory statesman, prime minister (1762–63).

Bu•the•le•zi |'bŏŏdə,lāzē|, Chief Mangosuthu (Gatsha) (1928–   ) South

---

Bush, George Herbert Walker
41st U.S. president

Life dates: 1924–
Place of birth: Milton, Massachusetts
Mother: Dorothy Walker Bush
Father: Prescott Sheldon Bush
Wife: Barbara Pierce Bush
Children: George, Robin, John, Neil, Marvin, Dorothy
College/University: Yale
Military service: U.S. Navy pilot
Career: Businessman
Political career: U.S. House of Representatives; ambassador to the United Nations; director of the Central Intelligence Agency; vice president (under Reagan); president
Party: Republican
Home state: Texas
Opponent in presidential races: Michael Dukakis; Bill Clinton
Term of office: Jan. 20, 1989–Jan. 20, 1993
Vice president: Dan (James Danforth) Quayle
Notable events of presidency: Americans with Disabilities Act; Iraq's invasion of Kuwait and Persian Gulf War; Iran-Contra Affair
Other achievements: Distinguished Flying Cross and three air medals for combat in the Pacific in World War II

African politician. He became leader of the Inkatha movement in 1975 and minister of home affairs in 1994.

But•kus |'bətkəs|, Dick (1942–   ) U.S. football player. Elected to the Football Hall of Fame (1979).

But•ler |'bətlər|, Nicholas Murray (1862–1947) U.S. educator. He was organizer and first president of the New York College for Training of Teachers, now Teachers College, Columbia University. Nobel Peace Prize, 1931.

But•ler |'bətlər|, Pierce (1866–1939) U.S. Supreme Court Justice (1922–39).

But•ler[1] |'bətlər|, Samuel (1612–80) English poet, most notable for his three-part satirical poem *Hudibras* (1663–78).

But•ler[2] |'bətlər|, Samuel (1835–1902) English novelist. Notable works: *Erewhon* (1872), *Erewhon Revisited* (1901), and *The Way of All Flesh* (1903).

But•ter•field |'bətər,fēld|, William (1814–1900) English architect, an exponent of the Gothic revival. Notable designs: All Saints', Margaret Street, London (1850–59) and Keble College, Oxford (1867–83).

But·ter·ick |'bətər,ik|, Ebenezer (1826–1903) U.S. tailor and inventor. He invented the dress pattern made of tissue paper (1859).

But·ton |'bətn|, Dick (1929–) U.S. figure skater. Full name *Richard Button.* He was five-time world champion (1948–52) and won two Olympic gold medals (1948, 1952).

But·tons |'bətnz|, Red (1919–) U.S. actor. Born *Aaron Chwatt.* Notable movies: *Sayonara* (1957, Academy Award).

Bux·te·hu·de |bəkstə'hoödə|, Dietrich (1637–1707) Danish organist and composer. Working in Lübeck, Germany, he wrote mainly for the organ.

By·as |'bīəs|, Don (1912–72) U.S. jazz tenor saxophonist. Born *Carlos Wesley.* He played with various bands, including those led by Lionel Hampton, Coleman Hawkins, Dizzy Gillespie, Cout Basie, and Duke Ellington, as well as his own.

By·att |'bīət|, A. S. (1936–) English novelist and literary critic; born *Antonia Susan Byatt.* She is the elder sister of Margaret Drabble. Notable novels: *The Virgin in the Garden* (1978) and *Possession* (1990).

Byrd |bərd|, Richard (Evelyn) (1888–1957) American explorer, naval officer, and aviator. He claimed to have made the first aircraft flight over the North Pole (1926, although his actual course has been disputed). He was the first to fly over the South Pole (1929).

Byrd |bərd|, Robert (1917–) U.S. senator from West Virginia (1950–52; 1959–).

Byrd |bərd|, William (1543–1623) English composer. He was joint organist of the Chapel Royal with Tallis and is famous for his Latin masses and his Anglican Great Service.

Byrnes |bərnz|, James F. (1879–1972) U.S. Supreme Court Justice (1941–42), politician, and author. He served as director of the Office of Economic Stabilization (1942–43), as director of war mobilization (1943–45); and as secretary of state (1945–47).

By·ron |'bīrən|, George Gordon, 6th Baron (1788–1824) English poet. Byron's poetry exerted considerable influence on the romantic movement, particularly on the Continent. Having joined the fight for Greek independence, he died of malaria before seeing serious action. Notable works: *Childe Harold's Pilgrimage* (1812–18) and *Don Juan* (1819–24)

Cc

Ca·bal·lé |kə'bälyä; kəbäl'yā|, Montserrat (1933–) Spanish operatic soprano.

Cab·ell |'kæbəl|, James Branch (1879–1958) U.S. author. He wrote novels, poetry, criticism, and nonfiction, including the 18-volume *Biography of Manuel* (1917–29).

Ca·be·za de Va·ca |kä,besə de 'väkə|, Á Núñez (c. 1490–c. 1560) Spanish explorer. He began an expedition to Florida in 1528 that eventually led him across the Southwest to the Gulf of California.

Cab·ot |'kæbət|, George (1752–1823) U.S. businessman and senator from Massachusetts (1791–96).

Cab·ot |'kæbət|, Italian explorers, including: **John Cabot** (c. 1450–c. 1499). While in the service of England, he sailed from Bristol in 1497 in search of Asia, but in fact discovered the mainland of North America. His son, **Sebastian Cabot** (c. 1476–1557), accompanied his father on his voyage in 1497 and made further voyages after the latter's death, most notably to Brazil and the River Plate (1526).

Ca·bri·ni |kə'brēnē|, St. Frances Xavier (1850–1917) U.S. religious leader, born in Italy. Born *Maria Francesca Cabrini*; known as **Mother Cabrini**. She became the first American saint in 1946.

Cad·bury |'kædbərē| **George** (1839–1922) and **Richard** (1835–99) English cocoa and chocolate manufacturers and social reformers.

Cade |kād|, Jack (died 1450) Irish rebel. Full name *John Cade*. In 1450 he assumed the name of Mortimer and led the Kentish rebels against Henry VI. They occupied London for three days and executed the treasurer of England and the sheriff of Kent.

Ca·dil·lac |'kædə,læk|, Antoine Laumet de La Mothe (1658–1730) French soldier and colonialist. He founded military posts at Mackinac (1694) and Detroit; from 1713 to 1716 he was governor of Louisiana.

Caed·mon |'kædmən| (7th century) Anglo-Saxon monk and poet, said to have been an illiterate herdsman inspired in a vision to compose poetry on biblical themes. The only authentic fragment of his work is a song in praise of the Creation, quoted by Bede.

Caen |kän|, Herb (1916–97) U.S. journalist and author. He wrote for San Francisco newspapers (1936–58) and authored numerous books. He received a special Pulitzer citation for journalism in 1996.

Caesar, Gaius Julius (100–44 BC) Roman general and statesman. He established the First Triumvirate with Pompey and Crassus (60), and became consul in 59. Between 58 and 51 he fought the Gallic Wars, invaded Britain (55–54), and acquired immense power. After civil war with Pompey, which ended in Pompey's defeat at Pharsalus (48), Caesar became dictator of the Roman Empire; he was murdered on the Ides (15th) of March in a conspiracy led by Brutus and Cassius.

Cae·sar |'sēzər|, Sid (1922–) U.S. actor. He was one of the comedy stars featured on television's "Your Show of Shows" (1950–54).

Cage |kāj|, John (Milton) (1912–92) U.S. composer, pianist, and writer. He was notable for his experimental approach, which included the use of aleatory music and periods of silence.

Cag·ney |'kægnē|, James (1899–1986) U.S. actor. He is chiefly remembered for playing gangster roles in movies such as *The Public Enemy* (1931).

Cahn |kän|, Sammy (1913–93) U.S. lyricist. Notable songs: "High Hopes," "Love and Marriage," and "The Second Time Around."

Cain |kān|, James Mallahan (1892–1977) U.S. novelist and journalist. Notable works: *The Postman Always Rings Twice* (1934) and *Double Indemnity* (1936).

Caine |kān|, Sir Michael (1933–) English actor. Born *Maurice Micklewhite*. Notable movies: *The Ipcress File* (1965) and *Hannah and Her Sisters* (1986, Academy Award).

Ca·lam·i·ty Jane |ˌkə'læmitē 'jān| (c. 1852–1903) U.S. frontierswoman. Born *Martha Jane Cannary*. She was noted for her skill at shooting and riding.

Cal·de·cott |'käldəˌkät|, Randolph (1846–86) English graphic artist and watercolor painter. He is best known for his illustrations for children's books.

Cal·der |'käldər|, Alexander (1898–1976) U.S. sculptor and painter. He introduced movement into sculpture, making the first pieces to be called "mobiles." His static sculptures are known by contrast as "stabiles."

Cal·de·rón de la Bar·ca |ˌkäldə'rōn de lä 'bärkə|, Pedro (1600–81) Spanish dramatist and poet. He wrote some 120 plays and more than 70 of them religious dramas.

Cal·de·rone |ˌkäldə'rōn|, Mary Steichen (1904–98) U.S. physician. The daughter of Edward Steichen, she was an advocate of family planning and sexual education in schools and communities. She cofounded the Sex Information and Education Council of the U.S. (SIECUS, 1964) and wrote *Talking With Your Child About Sex* (1982).

Cald·well |'kawldwel|, Erskine Preston (1903–87) U.S. novelist and short-story writer. He reproduced the dialect of poor whites in his realistic, earthy, and popular novels, such as *Tobacco Road* (1932).

Cal·houn |kæl'hōōn|, John Caldwell (1782–1850) U.S. politician. A South Carolina Democrat, he served as U.S. vice president (1825–32) and in the U.S. Senate (1832–1844).

Ca·lig·u·la |kə'ligyələ| (AD 12–41) Roman emperor (37–41). Born *Gaius Julius Caesar Germanicus*. His reign was notorious for its tyrannical excesses.

Cal·i·sher |'kælisHər|, Hortense (1911–) U.S. author.

Cal·la·ghan |'kæləˌhæn|, (Leonard) James, Baron Callaghan of Cardiff (1912–) British Labour statesman; prime minister (1976–79).

Cal·las |'kæləs|, Maria (1923–77) U.S.-born operatic soprano, of Greek parentage. Born *Maria Cecilia Anna Kalageropoulos*. She was a coloratura soprano whose bel canto style of singing was especially suited to early Italian opera.

Ca·lles |'kīyäs|, Plutarco Elías (1877–1945) Mexican president (1924–28). Opposed to the the the policies of President Cardenas, he was forced into exile in the U.S. (1936–41).

Cal·ley |'kælē|, William Laws, Jr. (1943–) U.S. army officer. He was convicted in 1971 of the premeditated murder of 22 South Vietnamese at My Lai (1968).

Cal·lic·ra·tes |ˌkə'likrətēz| (5th century BC) Greek architect. He was the leading architect in Periclean Athens, and with Ictinus designed the Parthenon (447–438 BC).

Cal·lil |kə'lil|, Carmen (Thérèse) (1938–) Australian publisher. She founded the feminist publishing house Virago in 1972.

Cal·lim·a·chus |kə'liməkəs| (c. 305–c. 240 BC) Greek poet and scholar. He is famed for his hymns and epigrams, and was head of the library at Alexandria.

Cal·lo·way |'kæləwā|, Cab (1907–94) U.S. jazz singer and bandleader. Full name *Cabell Calloway*. He was famous for his style of scat singing and for songs such as "Minnie the Moocher" (1931).

Cal·vert |'kælvərt| British and colonial American family, including **George Calvert, 1st Baron Baltimore** (c. 1580–1632), who was granted the territory of what is now Maryland but died before the charter was issued. The charter was instead issued to his son, **Cecilius Calvert, 2nd Baron Baltimore** (1605–75), who established the colony of Maryland. His brother **Leonard Calvert** (1606–47) was the first governor (1634–47) of the province of Maryland. **Charles Calvert, 3rd Baron Baltimore** (1637–1715) was the son of Cecilius Calvert. He served as governor of Maryland (1661–75) and as proprietor (1675–89).

Cal·vin |'kælvən|, John (1509–64) French Protestant theologian and reformer. He established the first Presbyterian government in Geneva (1536–38). His *Institutes of the Christian Religion* (1536) was the first systematic account of reformed Christian doctrine.

Cal·vin |'kælvən|, Melvin (1911–97)

U.S. biochemist. He investigated photosynthesis and discovered the cycle of reactions (the *Calvin cycle*) that constitute the dark reaction. Nobel Prize for Chemistry (1961).

Cal•vi•no |käl'vēnō|, Italo (1923–85) Italian novelist and short-story writer, born in Cuba. His later works, such as *If on a Winter's Night a Traveler* (1979), are associated with magic realism.

Cam•by•ses II |kæm'bīsēz| (died 522 BC) King of Persia (529–522 BC), son of Cyrus. He is chiefly remembered for his conquest of Egypt in 525 BC.

Cam•er•on |'kæmrən| U.S. political family, including: **Simon Cameron** (1799–1889), a financier and U.S. senator (1845–49, 1857–61, 1867–77). He established and maintained control of the Republican party machine in Pennsylvania. **James Donald Cameron** (1833–1918), the son of Simon Cameron, was U.S. secretary of war (1876–77) and a U.S. senator from Pennsylvania (1877–97).

Cam•er•on |'kæmrən|, James (1954–) U.S. director, born in Canada. Notable movies: *The Terminator* (1984) and *Titanic* (1997, Academy Award).

Cam•er•on |'kæmrən|, Julia Margaret (1815–79) English photographer, credited with being the first to use soft-focus techniques. Her work often reflects the influence of contemporary painting, especially that of the Pre-Raphaelites.

Ca•mõ•es |kə'moiSH|, Luis (Vaz) de (*c.* 1524–80) Portuguese poet. Also **Camoëns**. His most famous work, *The Lusiads* (1572), describes Vasco da Gama's discovery of the sea route to India.

Camp |kæmp|, Walter Chauncey (1859–1925) U.S. football coach. One of the first to play American football, he coached at Yale and was influential in shaping the rules of the sport.

Cam•pa•nel•la |ˌkæmpə'nelə|, Roy (1921–93) U.S. baseball player. Known as **Campy**. Elected to Baseball Hall of Fame (1969).

Camp•bell |'kæmbəl|, Earl (1955–) U.S. football player. Awarded the Heisman Trophy (1977).

Camp•bell |'kæmbəl|, John A. (1811–

89) U.S. Supreme Court justice (1853–61). He served as assistant secretary of war in the Confederate cabinet (1862–65).

Camp•bell |'kæmbəl|, Joseph (1817–1900) U.S. businessman. He entered the canning business in 1869 and introduced the Campbell Soup Co. in 1898.

Camp•bell |'kæmbəl|, Mrs. Patrick (1865–1940) English actress. Born *Beatrice Stella Tanner*. George Bernard Shaw wrote the part of Eliza Doolittle in *Pygmalion* (1914) for her.

Camp•bell |'kæmbəl|, Roy (1901–57) South African poet. Full name *Ignatius Royston Dunnachie Campbell*. His long poem *Flowering Rifle* (1939) shows strong right-wing sympathies. He fought for Franco's side in the Spanish Civil War.

Camp•bell |'kæmbəl|, Thomas (1777–1844) Scottish poet. He published *Gertrude of Wyoming* (1809) among other volumes of verse, and is known for his patriotic lyrics such as "The Battle of Hohenlinden" and "Ye Mariners of England."

Campbell-Bannerman |'kæmbəl 'bænərmən|, Sir Henry (1836–1908) British Liberal statesman and prime minister (1905–08).

Cam•pi•on |'kæmpēən|, St. Edmund (1540–81) English Jesuit priest and martyr. Feast day, December 1.

Cam•pi•on |'kæmpēən|, Jane (1954–) New Zealand movie director and screenwriter. Notable works: *An Angel at My Table* (1990) and *The Piano* (1993).

Cam•ras |'kæmrəs|, Marvin (1916–95) U.S. inventor. In the 1930s, he developed a wire recorder. His inventions revolutionized the field of electronic communications.

Ca•mus |kä'moo|, Albert (1913–60) French novelist, dramatist, and essayist, closely aligned with existentialism. Notable works: *The Outsider* (novel, 1942), *The Plague* (novel, 1947), and *The Rebel* (essay, 1951). Nobel Prize for Literature (1957).

Ca•na•let•to |ˌkänə'letō| (1697–1768) Italian painter. Born *Giovanni Antonio Canale*. He is well known for his paintings of Venetian festivals and scenery.

Can·dler |'kæn(də)lər|, Asa Griggs (1851–1929) U.S. manufacturer and politician. He bought the formula for Coca-Cola (1887) and was president and organizer of the Coca-Cola Co. (until 1916); after selling the company he became mayor of Atlanta (1917–18).

Can·dolle |kæn'dawl|, Augustin-Pyrame de (1778–1841) Swiss botanist. He introduced a new scheme of plant classification based on morphological characteristics, which prevailed for many years.

Can·dy |'kændē|, John (1950–94) U.S. comedian, born in Canada. He acted in television and movies, including *The Blues Brothers* (1980) and *Planes, Trains, and Automobiles* (1987).

Ca·net·ti |kə'netē|, Elias (1905–94) Bulgarian-born British writer. Notable works: *Auto-da-Fé* (1936) and *Crowds and Power* (1960). Nobel Prize for Literature (1981).

Ca·niff |kə'nif|, Milton Arthur (1907–88) U.S. cartoonist. He created two of the longest-running comic strips in daily newspaper syndication history, "Terry and the Pirates" and "Steve Canyon."

Can·ion |'kænyən|, Joseph Rod (1945–) U.S. businessman. He founded Compaq Computers (1982).

Can·more |'kaenmawr| the nickname of Malcolm III of Scotland (see MALCOLM).

Can·ning |'kæniNG|, George (1770–1827) British Tory statesman; prime minister (1827).

Can·niz·za·ro |ˌkænəd'zärō|, Stanislao (1826–1910) Italian chemist. He revived Avogadro's hypothesis and used it to distinguish clearly between atoms and molecules, and to introduce the unified system of atomic and molecular weights.

Can·non |'kænən|, James W. (1852–1921) U.S. manufacturer. He began producing towels in 1894.

Ca·no·va |kə'nōvə|, Antonio (1757–1822) Italian sculptor, a leading exponent of neoclassicism. Notable works: *Cupid and Psyche* (1792) and *The Three Graces* (1813–16).

Can·tor |'kæntər|, Georg (1845–1918) Russian-born German mathematician. His work on numbers laid the foundations for the theory of sets and stimu-

lated 20th-century exploration of number theory.

Ca·nute |kə'nyo͞ot| (died 1035) Danish king of England (1017–35), Denmark (1018–35), and Norway (1028–35), son of Sweyn I. Also **Cnut** or **Knut**.

Çapability Brown see BROWN.

Ča·pek, Karel (1890–1938) Czech novelist and dramatist He is known for *R. U. R. (Rossum's Universal Robots)* (1920), which introduced the word *robot* to the English language, and *The Insect Play* (1921), written with his brother **Josef** (1887–1945).

Ca·pet |'kāpət; kä'pā|, Hugh (938–96) king of France 987–96, founder of the Capetian dynasty.

Ca·pone |kə'pōn|, Al (1899–1947) U.S. gangster. Full name *Alphonse Capone*; known as **Scarface**. He dominated organized crime in Chicago in the 1920s and was believed responsible for many murders, including the St. Valentine's Day Massacre. However, it was for federal income tax evasion that he was eventually imprisoned in 1931.

Ca·po·te |kə'pō͵tē |, Truman (1924–84) U.S. writer. Born *Truman Streckfus Persons*. Notable works: *Breakfast at Tiffany's* (1958) and *In Cold Blood* (1966), a meticulous re-creation of a brutal multiple murder.

Capp |kæp|, Al (1909–79) U.S. cartoonist. Born *Alfred Gerald Caplin*. He is best known for his comic strip "Li'l Abner" (1934–1977).

Cap·ra |'kæprə|, Frank (1897–1991) Italian-born U.S. movie director. Notable movies: *It Happened One Night* (1934), *Arsenic and Old Lace* (1944), and *It's a Wonderful Life* (1946). He won six Academy Awards.

Ca·ra·cal·la |ˌkerə'kälə| (188–217) Roman emperor 211–17. Born *Septimius Bassianus*; later called *Marcus Aurelius Severus Antoninus Augustus*. In 212 he granted Roman citizenship to all free inhabitants of the Roman Empire.

Ca·rac·ta·cus |kə'ræktəkəs| variant spelling of CARATACUS.

Ca·rat·a·cus |kə'rätəkəs| (1st century AD) British chieftain, son of Cymbeline. Also **Caractacus**. He took part in the resistance to the Roman invasion of AD 43.

Ca·ra·vag·gio |ˌkerəˈväjēō|, Michelangelo Merisi da (*c.* 1573–1610) Italian painter. An influential figure in the transition from late mannerism to baroque, he made use of naturalistic realism and dramatic light and shade.

Cár·de·nas |ˈkärdənəs|, Lázaro (1895–1970) Mexican revolutionary leader and president (1934–40).

Car·din |kärˈdæn|, Pierre (1922–) French couturier, the first designer in the field of haute couture to show a collection of clothes for men as well as women.

Car·do·zo |kärˈdōzō|, Benjamin Nathan (1870–1938) U.S. Supreme Court justice (1932–38).

Ca·rew |kəˈrōō|, Rod (1945–) U.S. baseball player. Born *Rodney Cline Carew.* He was a seven-time American League batting champion.

Car·ey |ˈkerē|, George (Leonard) (1935–) English Anglican churchman, Archbishop of Canterbury from 1991. The controversial introduction of women priests into the Church of England was approved under his leadership.

Car·ey |ˈkerē|, Mariah (1970–) U.S. singer and songwriter. Grammy Awards (1991).

Carle |kärl|, Eric (1929–) U.S. author and illustrator of children's books. Notable works: The Very Busy Spider (1984).

Carl·son |ˈkärlsən|, Chester Floyd (1906–68) U.S. inventor. He invented the electrostatic "xerography" process (1938), the development of which gave rise to the Xerox Corp.

Carl·ton |ˈkärltn|, Effie (1857–1940) U.S. actress. Under the pen name **Effie Canning** she wrote the lullaby *Rock-a-Bye-Baby* (1887).

Carl·ton |ˈkärltn|, Steve (1944–) U.S. baseball player. Born *Steven Norman Carlton.* He was the first pitcher to win four Cy Young Awards (1972, 1977, 1980, 1982). Elected to Baseball Hall of Fame (1994).

Car·lyle |ˈkärˌlīl|, Thomas (1795–1881) Scottish historian and political philosopher. He established his reputation as a historian with his *History of the French Revolution* (1837). Influenced by German Romanticism, many of his works,

including *Sartor Resartus* (1833–34), celebrate the force of the "strong, just man" as against the degraded masses.

Car·mi·chael |ˈkärˌmīkl|, Hoagy (1899–1981) U.S. jazz pianist, composer, and singer. Born *Howard Hoagland Carmichael.* His best-known songs include "Stardust" (1929), "Georgia on My Mind" (1930), and "In the Cool, Cool, Cool of the Evening" (1951).

Car·nap |ˈkärnəp|, Rudolf (1891–1970) German-born U.S. philosopher, a founding member of the logical positivist Vienna Circle. Notable works: *The Logical Structure of the World* (1928) and *The Logical Foundations of Probability* (1950).

Car·né |kärˈnä|, Marcel (1906?–96) French movie director. He gained his reputation for the movies he made with the poet and scriptwriter **Jacques Prévert** (1900–77), notably *Le Jour se lève* (1939) and *Les Enfants du paradis* (1945).

Car·ne·gie |ˈkärnəgē; kärˈnegē|, Andrew (1835–1919) Scottish-born U.S. industrialist and philanthropist. He built up a fortune in the steel industry in the U.S., then retired from business in 1901 and devoted his wealth to charitable purposes, in particular libraries, education, and the arts.

Car·ne·gie |ˈkärnəgē; kärˈnegē|, Dale (1888–1955) U.S. lecturer and author. Born *Dale Carnagey.* He wrote *How to Win Friends and Influence People* (1936).

Car·ne·gie |ˈkärnəgē; kärˈnegē|, Hattie (1889–1956) U.S. fashion designer, born in Austria. Born *Henriette Kanengesier.* She popularized the "little Carnegie suit" and the simple black cocktail dress

Car·ney |ˈkärnē|, Art (1918–) U.S. actor. He played Ed Norton, upstairs neighbor to Ralph Cramden, on television's "The Honeymooners." Notable movies: *Harry and Tonto* (1974, Academy Award).

Car·ney |ˈkärnē|, Harry (Howell) (1910–74) U.S. jazz baritone saxonphonist. He was the first and for many years the only soloist on his instrument.

Car·not |kärˈnō|, Nicolas-Léonard-Sadi (1796–1832) French scientist. His work in analyzing the efficiency of steam engines was posthumously recognized as being of crucial importance to the theory of thermodynamics.

Ca·roth·ers |kə'rəṮHərz|, Wallace Hume (1896–1937) U.S. industrial chemist. He developed the first successful synthetic rubber, neoprene, and the synthetic fiber nylon 6.6.

Car·pac·cio |kär'pätСНŌ|, Vittore (c. 1460–c. 1525) Italian painter noted especially for his paintings of Venice.

Car·pen·ter |'kärpəntər|, John Alden (1876–1951) U.S. composer. Works include the ballets *Krazy Kat* (1921) and *Skyscraper* (1923–24) and the suite *Jazz Orchestra Pieces* (1925–26).

Carr |kär|, Emily (1871–1945) Canadian painter and writer. Her paintings, inspired by the wilderness of British Columbia, often drew on motifs of American Indian folk art. From 1927 she came into contact with the Group of Seven and produced such expressionist works as *Forest Landscape II* and *Sky* (both 1934–35).

Car·rac·ci |kä'rätСНē| Italian painters. **Lidovico Carracci** (1555–1619) is remembered chiefly as a distinguished teacher. With his cousins **Annibale Carracci** (1560–1609) and **Agostino Carracci** (1557–1602) he established an academy at Bologna which was responsible for training many important painters. Annibale is is famed for the ceiling of the Farnese Gallery (1597–1600) in Rome; he developed a style that was the foundation of the Italian baroque and is also remembered for his invention of the caricature. Agostino was chiefly an engraver but he also worked with his brother in the Farnese Gallery.

Car·rel |'kerəl|, Alexis (1873–1944) French surgeon and biologist. He developed improved techniques for suturing arteries and veins, and carried out some of the first organ transplants. Nobel Prize for Physiology or Medicine (1912).

Car·re·ras |kə'rerəs|, José (1946–) Spanish operatic tenor.

Car·rère |kə'rer|, John Merven (1858–1911) U.S. architect, born in Brazil. He designed the Hotel Ponce de Leon (St. Augustine, Florida, 1887), the Carnegie

Institution (Washington, D.C., 1906) and the New York Public Library (completed 1911).

Car·rey |'kerē|, Jim (1962–) U.S. actor, born in Canada. Notable movies: *Liar, Liar* (1996), *The Cable Guy* (1996), and *The Truman Show* (1997).

Car·ri·er |'kerēər|, Willis Haviland (1876–1950) U.S. engineer and inventor. He invented and developed air-conditioning technology and was the first to create an air-conditioning system for skyscrapers (1939).

Car·ring·ton |'keriNGtən|, Dora (1893–1932) English painter. She was a member of the Bloomsbury Group.

Car·roll |'kerəl|, Earl (1893–1948) U.S. theatrical producer and composer. He produced Broadway shows and lavish revues, including *The Earl Carroll Vanities* (1923–35).

Car·roll |'kerəl|, Lewis (1832–98) English writer; pseudonym of *Charles Lutwidge Dodgson*. He wrote the children's classics *Alice's Adventures in Wonderland* (1865) and *Through the Looking Glass* (1871), which were inspired by Alice Liddell, the young daughter of the dean at the Oxford college where Carroll was a mathematics lecturer.

Car·ruth |kə'rо͞оTH|, Hayden (1921–) U.S. poet. National Book Award (1996).

Car·sey |'kärsē|, Marcia Lee Peterson (1944–) U.S. television producer. Co-owner of the Carsey-Werner Co. (1982–), she was executive producer of "The Cosby Show" and "A Different World."

Car·son |'kärsən|, Kit (1809–68) U.S. frontiersman and scout. Full name *Christopher Carson*. He was a U.S. Indian agent in the Southwest (1853–60, 1865–68) and organized Union scouts in the West during the Civil War.

Car·son |'kärsən|, Johnny (1925–) U.S. television personality. Full name *John William Carson*, host of "The Tonight Show" (1962–92).

Car·son |'kärsən|, Rachel Louise (1907–64) U.S. biologist and author. Works include *The Sea Around Us* (1941) and *Silent Spring* (1962).

Car·ter |'kärtər|, Angela (1940–92) English novelist and short-story writer, whose fiction is characterized by fantasy, black humor, and eroticism. Notable works: *The Magic Toyshop* (1967) and *Nights at the Circus* (1984).

Car•ter |'kärtər|, U.S. musicians, including: **A. P. Carter** (1891–1960). Full name *Alvin Pleasant Carter*. He was the founder of the Carter Family Singers (1927–43), who popularized Appalachian folk music. His sister-in-law, **Maybelle Addington Carter** (1909–78), was the featured singer of the Carter Family.

Car•ter |'kärtər|, Elliott (Cook) (1908–) U.S. composer. He is noted for his innovative approach to meter and his choice of sources as diverse as modern jazz and Renaissance madrigals.

Car•ter |'kärtər|, Howard (1873–1939) English archeologist. In 1922, while excavating in the Valley of the Kings at Thebes, he discovered the tomb of Tutankhamen.

Car•ter |'kärtər|, Jimmy see box.

(Eleanor) Rosalynn Smith Carter (1927–), wife of Jimmy Carter and U.S. first lady (1977–81).

Car•tier |kärtē'ā|, Jacques (1491–1557) French explorer. The first to establish France's claim to North America, he made three voyages to Canada between 1534 and 1541.

Cartier-Bresson |ˌkärtē'ā bres'ōN|, Henri (1908–) French photographer and film director. He is famed for his collection of photographs *The Decisive Moment* (1952) and his documentary film about the Spanish Civil War, *Return to Life* (1937).

Cart•land |'kärtlənd|, Dame Barbara (1901–) English author. Full name *Mary Barbara Hamilton Cartland*. She is best known for her light romantic fiction.

Cart•wright |'kärt,rīt|, Alexander Joy (1820–92) U.S. sportsman. He founded the Knickerbocker Baseball Club and was influential in developing the rules of baseball. Elected to Baseball Hall of Fame (1938).

Cart•wright |'kärt,rīt|, Edmund (1743–1823) English engineer, inventor of the power loom.

Ca•ru•so |kə'ro͞osō|, Enrico (1873–1921) Italian operatic tenor. He was the

---

Carter, Jimmy (James Earl, Jr.)
39th U.S. president

Life dates: 1924–
Place of birth: Plains, Georgia
Mother: Lillian Gordy Carter
Father: James Earl Carter, Sr.
Wife: Rosalynn Smith Carter
Children: John (Jack), James (Chip), Donnel Jeffrey (Jeff), Amy
College/University: Georgia Southwestern College; Georgia Institute of Technology; U.S. Naval Academy
Military service: Lieutenant senior grade, U.S. Navy
Career: Peanut farmer; lecturer; writer
Political career: Georgia Senate; governor of Georgia; president
Party: Democratic
Home state: Georgia
Opponents in presidential races: Gerald R. Ford, Eugene McCarthy; Ronald Reagan
Term of office: Jan. 20, 1977–Jan. 20, 1981
Vice president: Walter Mondale
Notable events of presidency: SALT II Treaty; fall of the shah of Iran and seizure of U.S. embassy and American hostages in Teheran; Camp David accords; Panama Canal treaty; Department of Education created; U.S. boycott of Moscow Olympics
Other achievements: Led several international election observer teams

---

first major tenor to be recorded on phonograph records.

Car•ver |'kärvər|, George Washington (1864?–1943) U.S. botanist. He was born into slavery; later, he became the director of agricultural research at Tuskegee Institute (1896) and developed many products from soybeans, sweet potatoes, and peanuts.

Car•ville |'kärvil|, James (1944–) U.S. political strategist and author. He managed Bill Clinton's presidential campaign in 1992 and wrote *We're Right, They're Wrong* (1996).

Cary |'kerē|, Joyce (1888–1957) English novelist. Full name *Arthur Joyce Lunel Cary*. Notable works: *The Horse's Mouth* (1944) and *Not Honour More* (1955).

Ca•sals |kə'säls|, Pablo (1876–1973) Spanish cellist, conductor, and composer.

Cas·a·no·va |ˌkæsə'nōvə|, Giovanni (1725–98) Full name *Giovanni Jacopo Casanova de Seingalt*. Italian adventurer.

Case·ment |'kāsmənt|, Sir Roger (David) (1864–1916) Irish diplomat and nationalist. In 1914 he sought German support for an Irish uprising, and was subsequently hanged by the British for treason.

Ca·sey |'kāsē|, William Joseph (1913–87) U.S. intelligence official. He was the director of the CIA (1981–87). Under his leadership, the CIA assisted Nicaraguan contras and was alleged to have been involved in the arms-for-hostages deal known as the "Iran-contra affair."

Cash |kæsH|, Johnny (1932–) U.S. country music singer and songwriter. Notable songs: "I Walk the Line" (1956) and "A Boy Named Sue" (1969).

Cas·per |'kæspər|, Billy (1931–) U.S. golfer.

Cas·satt |kə'sæt|, Mary Stevenson (1844–1926) U.S. painter, who worked mostly in Paris. Her paintings display a close interest in everyday subject matter.

Cas·si·ni |kə'sēnē|, Giovanni Domenico (1625–1712) Italian-born French astronomer. He discovered the gap in the rings of Saturn known as Cassini's division.

Cas·sius |'kæsHəs|, Gaius (died 42 BC) Roman general; full name *Gaius Cassius Longinus*. He was one of the leaders of the conspiracy in 44 BC to assassinate Julius Caesar.

Cas·ta·ne·da |ˌkästə'nädə|, Carlos (1931–98) Brazilian author. His works include *The Teachings of Don Juan* (1968).

Cas·te·lla·nos |ˌkästə'yänōs|, Rosario (1925–74) Mexican author and literary critic.

Cas·tle |'kæsəl|, Vernon Blythe (1887–1918) British dancer and aviator. Born *Vernon Blythe*. With his wife Irene (1893–1969), he originated the one-step, the turkey trot, the Castle walk, and the hesitation waltz.

Cas·tle·reagh |'kæsəlrā|, Robert Stewart, Viscount (1769–1822) British Tory statesman. He became foreign secretary

in 1812 and represented Britain at the Congress of Vienna (1814–15).

Cas·tro |'kæstrō|, Fidel (1927–) Cuban statesman, prime minister (1959–76), and president from 1976. After overthrowing President Batista, he set up a communist regime that survived the abortive Bay of Pigs invasion, the Cuban Missile Crisis, and the collapse of the Soviet bloc.

Cas·tro |'kæstrō|, José María (1818–93) Costa Rican politician. He was president (1847–49) at the time of the Costa Rican Declaration of Independence (1848), and again for a later term (1866–68).

Cath·er |'kæTHər|, Willa (Sibert) (1873–1947) U.S. novelist and short-story writer. Her home state of Nebraska provides the setting for some of her best writing. Notable novels: *O Pioneers!* (1913) and *Death Comes for the Archbishop* (1927).

Cath·e·rine |'kæTHrən|, St. (died *c.* 307) early Christian martyr; known as **St. Catherine of Alexandria**. According to tradition she opposed the persecution of Christians under the emperor Maxentius and refused to recant or to marry the emperor. She is said to have been tortured on a spiked wheel and then beheaded. Feast day, November 25.

Ca·the·rine de' Me·di·ci |kəˌträn də me 'dēcHē| (1519–89) queen of France, wife of Henry II. She ruled as regent (1560–74) during the minority reigns of her three sons, Francis II, Charles IX, and Henry III, and it was at her instigation that Huguenots were killed in the Massacre of St. Bartholomew (1572).

Cath·e·rine II |'kæTHrən| (1729–96) empress of Russia, reigned 1762–96; known as **Catherine the Great**. She became empress after her husband, Peter III, was deposed; her attempted social and political reforms were impeded by the aristocracy. She formed alliances with Prussia and Austria, and made territorial advances at the expense of the Turks and Tartars.

Cath·e·rine of Ar·a·gon |ˌkæTHrən əv 'erə,gän| (1485–1536) first wife of Henry VIII, youngest daughter of Ferdinand and Isabella of Castile, mother of Mary I. Henry's wish to annul his marriage to Catherine (due to her failure to produce a male heir) led eventually to England's break with the Roman Catholic Church.

Cat·i·line |'kætə,līn| (c. 108–162 BC) Roman nobleman and conspirator; Latin name *Lucius Sergius Catilina*. In 63 BC he planned an uprising which was suppressed; his fellow conspirators were executed and he died in battle in Etruria.

Cat·lin |'kætlən|, George (1796–1872) U.S. artist and author. He contributed 300 engravings to *The Manners, Customs and Condition of North American Indians* (1841), *Last Rambles Amongst the Indians of the Rocky Mountains and the Andes* (1867), and *Life Among the Indians* (1867).

Ca·to |'kātō|, Marcus Porcius (234–149 BC) Roman statesman, orator, and writer; known as **Cato the Elder** or **Cato the Censor**. As censor he initiated a vigorous program of reform, and attempted to stem the growing influence of Greek culture.

Ca·tron |'kātrən|, John (1786?–1865) U.S. Supreme Court justice (1837–65).

Catt |kæt|, Carrie Clinton Chapman Lane (1859–1947) U.S. suffragist. As president of the National American Woman Suffrage Association (1900–04; 1915–47) and of the International Woman Suffrage Alliance (1904–23), she was instrumental in the adoption of the 19th amendment to U.S. Constitution (1920).

Cat·tell |kə'tel|, James McKeen (1860–1944) U.S. psychologist. He was a pioneer in developing psychological tests and experimental methods.

Ca·tul·lus |kə'tələs|, Gaius Valerius (c. 84–c. 54 BC) Roman poet. He is best known for his love poems.

Cau·chy |kō'SHē|, Augustin-Louis, Baron (1789–1857) French mathematician. He transformed the theory of complex functions by developing his integral theorems. He founded the modern theory of elasticity, and contributed substantially to the founding of group theory and analysis.

Ca·va·fy |kä'väfē|, Constantine (Peter) (1863–1933) Greek poet; born *Konstantinos Petrou Kavafis*. His poems refer mainly to the Hellenistic and Graeco-Roman period of his native Alexandria.

Cav·ell |'kævəl|, Edith (Louisa) (1865–1915) English nurse. During World War I, she helped Allied soldiers to escape from occupied Belgium. She was subsequently executed by the Germans and became a heroine of the Allied cause.

Cav·en·dish |'kævəndisH|, Henry (1731–1810) English chemist and physicist. He identified hydrogen, studied carbon dioxide, and determined their densities relative to atmospheric air. He also established that water is a compound, and determined the density of the earth.

Ca·vour |kə'vōor|, Camillo Benso, Conte di (1810–61) Italian statesman. A supporter of Italian unification under Victor Emmanuel II, he was premier of Piedmont (1852–59; 1860–61), and in 1861 became the first premier of a unified Italy.

Caw·ley |'kawlē|, Yvonne (Fay) (1951–) Australian professional tennis player; born *Evonne Fay Goolagong*.

Cax·ton |'kækstən|, William (c. 1422–91) English printer. He printed the first book in English in 1474 and went on to produce about eighty other texts, including editions of *Le Morte d'Arthur* and *Canterbury Tales*.

Cay·ley |'kālē|, Arthur (1821–95) English mathematician and barrister. He wrote almost a thousand mathematical papers, including articles on determinants, group theory, and the algebra of matrices. The *Cayley numbers*, a generalization of complex numbers, are named after him.

Cay·ley |'kālē|, Sir George (1773–1857) British engineer, the father of British aeronautics. He is best known for his understanding of the principles of flight and for building the first manned glider, which was flown in 1853. He was also a founder of the original Polytechnic Institution.

Ceau·şescu |CHOW'CHeskōō|, Nicolae (1918–89) Romanian Communist statesman, first president of the Socialist Republic of Romania (1974–89). His regime became increasingly totalitarian and corrupt; a popular uprising in December 1989 resulted in its downfall and in his execution.

Ce•cil |'sesəl|, William see BURGHLEY.

Ce•cil•ia |sə'sēlyə|, St. (2nd or 3rd century) Roman martyr. According to legend, she took a vow of celibacy but when forced to marry converted her husband to Christianity and both were martyred. She is the patron saint of church music. Feast day, November 22.

Cé•line |sā'lēn|, Louis-Ferdinand (1894–1961) French novelist; pseudonym of *Louis-Ferdinand Destouches*. He is best known for his autobiographical novel, the satirical *Voyage au bout de la nuit* (1932).

Cel•li•ni |CHə'lēnē|, Benvenuto (1500–71) Italian goldsmith and sculptor, the most renowned goldsmith of his day.

Cel•si•us |'selsēəs|, Anders (1701–44) Swedish astronomer, best known for his temperature scale.

Cerf |sərf|, Bennett Alfred (1898–1971) U.S. publisher, editor, and author. He was a cofounder of Random House publishers (1927).

Cer•van•tes |sər'väntās|, Miguel de (1547–1616) Spanish novelist and dramatist; full name *Miguel de Cervantes Saavedra*. His most famous work is *Don Quixote* (1605–15), a satire on chivalric romances that greatly influenced the development of the novel.

Cet•shwayo |keCH'wīō| (c. 1826–84) Zulu king. Also **Cetewayo**. He became ruler of Zululand in 1873 and was involved in a series of battles with the Afrikaners and British; he was deposed as leader after the capture of his capital by the British in 1879.

Cé•zanne |sā'zän|, Paul (1839–1906) French painter. He is closely identified with post-Impressionism and his later work had an important influence on cubism. Notable works: *Bathers* (sequence of paintings 1890–1905).

Cha•brol |sHä'brōl|, Claude (1930–) French movie director, a member of the *nouvelle vague*. His movies typically combine suspense with studies of personal relationships, and include *Les Biches* (1968).

Chad•wick |'CHæd,wik|, George Whitefield (1854–1931) U.S. conductor and composer. He was director of the New England Conservatory of Music (from 1897).

Chad•wick |'CHæd,wik|, Henry (1824–1908) U.S. sportswriter. Compiled a baseball handbook that later became *Spalding's Official Baseball Guide*. Elected to Baseball Hall of Fame (1938).

Chad•wick |'CHæd,wik|, Sir James (1891–1974) English physicist. He discovered the neutron, for which he received the 1935 Nobel Prize for Physics.

Chaf•fee |'CHæfē|, Roger Bruce (1935–67) U.S. astronaut. He died in a flash fire in the Apollo 1 space capsule.

Cha•gall |sHə'gäl|, Marc (1887–1985) Russian-born French painter and graphic artist. His work was characterized by the use of rich emotive color and dream imagery, and had a significant influence on surrealism.

Chain |CHān|, Sir Ernst Boris (1906–79) German-born British biochemist. With Howard Florey he isolated and purified penicillin and in 1945 they shared a Nobel Prize with Alexander Fleming.

Cha•lia•pin |sHäl'yä,pyin|, Fyodor (Ivanovich) (1873–1938) Russian operatic bass.

Cham•ber•lain |'CHāmbərlən|, Neville (1869–1940) British Conservative statesman, prime minister (1937–40). Full name *Arthur Neville Chamberlain*. He pursued a policy of appeasement with Nazi Germany, signing the Munich Agreement (1938), but was forced to abandon this policy following Hitler's invasion of Czechoslovakia in 1939.

Cham•ber•lain |'CHāmbərlən|, Owen (1920–) American physicist. He investigated subatomic particles and in 1955 discovered the antiproton with **E. G. Segrè**, 1905–89, for which they shared the 1959 Nobel Prize for Physics.

Cham•ber•lain |'CHāmbərlən|, Wilt (1936–) U.S. basketball player. Full name *Wilton Norman Chamberlain*; known as **Wilt the Stilt**. Elected to the Basketball Hall of Fame (1978).

Cham•ber•lin |'CHāmbərlən|, Thomas Chrowder (1843–1928) U.S. geologist. He founded the *Journal of Geology*.

Cham•bers |'CHāmbərz|, Whittaker (1901–61) U.S. journalist. Full name *Jay David Whittaker Chamberlain*. He accused Alger Hiss of Communist party membership and of passing State Department documents to Soviet agents.

Cham·pion |'CHæmpēən|, Gower (1921–80) U.S. choreographer, dancer, and director.

Cham·plain |ˌSHæm'plān|, Samuel de (1567–1635) French explorer and colonial statesman. He established a settlement at Quebec (Canada) in 1608, developing alliances with the native peoples, and was appointed lieutenant governor in 1612.

Cham·pol·lion |ˌSHämpawl'yawn|, Jean-François (1790–1832) French Egyptologist. A pioneer in the study of ancient Egypt, he is best known for his success in deciphering some of the hieroglyphic inscriptions on the Rosetta Stone in 1822.

Chan |CHæn|, Jackie (1954–) U.S. actor, director, and screenwriter, born in China. He is known for his stunts, which he choreographs and performs himself.

Chan·cel·lor |'CHænsələr|, John William (1927–) U.S. journalist. He has provided news coverage for NBC since 1967 as a correspondent, television anchorman, and commentator.

Chan·dler |'CHændlər|, Raymond (Thornton) (1888–1959) U.S. novelist. He is remembered as the creator of the private detective Philip Marlowe. Notable novels: *The Big Sleep* (1939).

Chan·dra·gup·ta Maurya |ˌCHəndrə 'gŏŏptə| (c. 325–297 BC) Indian emperor. He founded the Mauryan empire and annexed provinces deep into Afghanistan from Alexander's Greek successors.

Chan·dra·se·khar |ˌCHändrə'sākər|, Subrahmanyan (1910–95) Indian-born American astronomer. He suggested how some stars could eventually collapse to form a dense white dwarf, provided that their mass does not exceed an upper limit (the *Chandrasekhar limit*).

Cha·nel |SHə'nel|, Coco (1883–1971) French couturière; born *Gabrielle Bonheur Chanel*. Her simple but sophisticated garments were a radical departure from the stiff corseted styles of the day. She also diversified into perfumes, costume jewelry, and textiles.

Cha·ney |'CHānē|, Lon (1883–1930) U.S. movie actor; born *Alonso Chaney*. He played a wide variety of deformed villains and macabre characters in more than 150 movies, including *The Hunchback of Notre Dame* (1923).

Chan·ning |'CHæniNG|, Carol (1923–) U.S. actress. She starred on Broadway in *Hello, Dolly!* (1964–67; Tony Award 1964) and has received a Tony Lifetime Achievement Award (1995).

Chan·ning |'CHæniNG|, Walter (1786–1876) U.S. obstetrician. Professor and dean at Harvard Medical School (1819–47), he introduced the use of ether in childbirth delivery (1847).

Chan·ning |'CHæniNG|, William Ellery (1818–1901) U.S. poet. He was a transcendentalist colleague of Thoreau and Emerson.

Cha·nute |SHə'nŏŏt|, Octave (1832–1910) French-born American aviation pioneer. From 1898 he produced a number of gliders, including a biplane that made over 700 flights. He assisted the Wright brothers in making the world's first controlled powered flight.

Cha·pin |'CHāpən|, Roy Dikeman (1880–1936) U.S. industrialist. He was the organizer of the Hudson Motor Car Co. (with Howard E. Coffin, 1909) and the U.S. secretary of commerce (1932–33).

Chap·lin |'CHæplən|, Charlie (1889–1977) British movie actor and director. Full name *Sir Charles Spencer Chaplin*. He directed and starred in many short silent comedies, mostly playing a bowler-hatted tramp, a character that was his trademark for more than 25 years. A master who combined pathos with slapstick clowning, he was best suited to the silent medium. Notable movies: *The Kid* (1921).

Chap·man |'CHæpmən|, Frank Michler (1864–1945) U.S. ornithologist and author. Author of *Handbook of Birds of Eastern North America* (1895), he became curator of the American Museum of Natural History (1908–42).

Chap·man |'CHæpmən|, George (c. 1559–1634) English poet and dramatist. He is chiefly known for his translations of Homer; the complete *Iliad* and *Odyssey* were published in 1616. They are commemorated in Keats's sonnet *"On First Looking into Chapman's Homer"* (1817).

Chap·man, John see APPLESEED, JOHNNY.

Chap·man |'CHæpmən|, Mark David (1955–) U.S. convicted murderer of John Lennon.

Chap·man |'CHæpmən|, Tracy (1964–) U.S. folk-rock singer and songwriter. Grammy Awards, 1988 and 1997.

Char·cot |SHär'kō|, Jean-Martin (1825–93) French neurologist, regarded as one of the founders of modern neurology. He established links between neurological conditions and particular lesions in the central nervous system. His work on hysteria was taken up by his pupil Sigmund Freud.

Char·don·net |SHärdə'nā|, Louis-Marie-Hilaire, Comte de Bernigaud (1839–1924) French chemist. He patented rayon (1884) and established factories for its manufacture.

Char·le·magne |'SHärlə,mān| (742–814) king of the Franks (768–814) and Holy Roman emperor (as Charles I) (800–814). Latin name *Carolus Magnus*; known as **Charles the Great**. As the first Holy Roman emperor, Charlemagne promoted the arts and education, and his court became the cultural center of the Carolingian Renaissance, the influence of which outlasted his empire.

Charles[1] |CHärlz| the name of two kings of England, Scotland, and Ireland: **Charles I** (1600–49; reigned 1625–49), the son of James I. His reign was dominated by the deepening religious and constitutional crisis that resulted in the English Civil War (1642–49). After the battle of Naseby, Charles tried to regain power in alliance with the Scots, but his forces were defeated in 1648 and he was tried by a special Parliamentary court and beheaded. **Charles II** (1630–85; reigned 1660–85), the son of Charles I. Charles was restored to the throne after the collapse of Cromwell's regime and displayed considerable adroitness in handling the difficult constitutional situation, although continuing religious and political strife dogged his reign.

Charles[2] |CHärlz| the name of four kings of Spain: **Charles I** (1500–58; reigned 1516–56), the son of Philip I. He was Holy Roman emperor (as Charles V) (1519–56). His reign was characterized by the struggle against Protestantism in Germany, rebellion in Castile, and war with France (1521–44). Exhausted by these struggles, Charles handed Naples, the Netherlands, and Spain over to his son Philip II and the imperial crown to his brother Ferdinand, and retired to a monastery. **Charles II** (1661–1700; reigned 1665–1700). He inherited a kingdom already in a decline which he was unable to halt. His choice of Philip of Anjou, grandson of Louis XIV of France, as his successor gave rise to the War of the Spanish Succession. **Charles III** (1716–88; reigned 1759–88). He improved Spain's position as an international power through an increase in foreign trade, and brought Spain a brief cultural and economic revival. **Charles IV** (1748–1819; reigned 1788–1808). During the Napoleonic Wars he suffered the loss of the Spanish fleet, destroyed along with that of France at Trafalgar in 1805. Following the French invasion of Spain in 1807, Charles was forced to abdicate.

Charles[3] |CHärlz| the name of seven Holy Roman Emperors. **Charles I** see CHARLEMAGNE. **Charles II** (823–877; reigned 875–877). **Charles III** (839–888; reigned 881–887). **Charles IV** (1316–1378; reigned 1355–1378). **Charles V** Charles I of Spain (see CHARLES[2]). **Charles VI** (1685–1740; reigned 1711–40). His claim to the Spanish throne instigated the War of the Spanish Succession, but he was ultimately unsuccessful. He drafted the Pragmatic Sanction in an attempt to ensure that his daughter succeeded to the Habsburg dominions; this triggered the War of the Austrian Succession after his death. **Charles VII** (1697–1745; reigned 1742–45).

Charles VII |CHärlz| (1403–61) king of France; reigned 1422–61. At the time of his accession, much of northern France was under English occupation. After the intervention of Joan of Arc, however, the French experienced a dramatic military revival, and the defeat of the English ended the Hundred Years War.

Charles XII |CHärlz| (1682–1718) king of Sweden. Also **Karl XII**. In 1700 he embarked on the Great Northern War against Denmark, Poland-Saxony, and Russia. Initially successful, in 1709 he embarked on an expedition into Russia that ended in the destruction of his army and his internment.

Charles |CHärlz|, Prince (1948–   ) British prince. Full name **Charles Philip Arthur George**, Prince of Wales (1948–   ), heir apparent to Elizabeth II. He married Lady Diana Spencer in 1981; the couple had two children, Prince William Arthur Philip Louis (1982–   ) and Prince Henry Charles Albert David (known as Prince Harry; 1984–   ), and were divorced in 1996.

Charles |CHärlz|, Ray (1930–   ) U.S. pianist and singer; born *Ray Charles Robinson*. Totally blind from the age of 6, he drew on blues, jazz, and country music for songs such as "What'd I Say" (1959), "Georgia On My Mind" (1960), and "Busted" (1963).

Charles Mar•tel |,CHärlz mär'tel| (*c.* 688–741) Frankish ruler. He ruled the eastern part of the Frankish kingdom from 715 and the whole kingdom from 719 and was the grandfather of Charlemagne. His rule marked the beginning of Carolingian power.

Chase |CHās|, Salmon Portland (1808– 73) Chief Justice of the U.S. (1864–73). He defended fugitive slaves; as U.S. secretary of the treasury (1861–64), he issued the first "greenbacks" (1863).

Chase |CHās|, Samuel (1741–1811) U.S. Supreme Court justice (1796– 1811). He was a delegate to the Continental Congress (1774–78, 1784, 1785) and a signer of the Declaration of Independence. In 1804 he was impeached but was reinstated to the bench in 1805.

Chast |CHæst|, Roz (1954–   ) U.S. cartoonist and illustrator. She was on staff with the *New Yorker* magazine and has illustrated several children's books.

Chat•eau•bri•and |SHæ,tōbrē'awn|, François-Auguste-René, Vicomte de (1768–1848) French writer and diplomat. He was an important figure in early French romanticism. Notable works: *Le Génie du Christianisme* (1802) and *Mémoires d'outre-tombe* (autobiography, 1849–50).

Chat•ham |'CHætəm|, 1st Earl of see PITT.

Chat•ter•ton |'CHætərtən|, Thomas (1752–70) English poet. He is chiefly remembered for his fabricated poems professing to be those of a 15th-century monk. He committed suicide at the age of 17.

Chau•cer |'CHawsər|, Geoffrey (*c.* 1342–1400) English poet. His most famous work, *The Canterbury Tales* (*c.*1387–1400), is a cycle of linked tales told by a group of pilgrims. His skills of characterization, humor, and versatility established him as the first great English poet. Other notable works: *Troilus and Criseyde* (1385).

Chau•liac |SHōl'yäk|, Guy de (*c.* 1300– 68) French physician. His *Chirurgia Magna* (1363) was the first work to describe many surgical techniques.

Cha•vez |'SHävez|, Cesar Estrada (1927–93) U.S. labor leader. He founded the organization that became the United Farm Workers (1962), and used nonviolent tactics to gain union contracts with California vineyard owners.

Cha•vis |'CHävəs; 'CHævəs| , Benjamin U.S. minister and black activist. He was executive director of the NAACP (1993–94) until fired for misuse of funds.

Cha•yef•sky |,CHī'efskē; ,CHī'evskē|, Paddy (Sidney) (1923–81) U.S. writer. He wrote television dramas, films, plays, and a science fiction novel, *Altered States* (1978).

Chea•tam |'CHētəm|, Adolphus (1905– 97) U.S. jazz trumpeter.

Cheat•ham |'CHētəm|, Doc (1906–97) U.S. musician. He was a jazz and big band trumpeter whose career spanned eight decades.

Check•er |'CHekər|, Chubby (1941–   ) U.S. singer. Born *Ernest Evans*. He popularized dance crazes such as "The Twist" (1960).

Chee•ver |'CHēvər|, John (1912–82) U.S. short-story writer and novelist. His stories frequently satirize affluent suburban New Englanders. Notable novels: *The Wapshot Chronicle* (1957).

Che·khov |'CHekawv|, Anton (Pavlovich) (1860–1904) Russian dramatist and short-story writer. Chekhov's work, portraying upper-class life in prerevolutionary Russia with a blend of naturalism and symbolism, had a considerable influence on 20th-century drama. Notable plays: *The Seagull* (1895), *Uncle Vanya* (1900), *The Three Sisters* (1901), and *The Cherry Orchard* (1904).

Cheng Ho |'jeNG 'hō| (*c.* 1371–*c.* 1433) Chinese admiral and explorer.

Chen·nault |SHə'nält|, Claire Lee (1890–1958) U.S. aviator. In 1941 she formed the American volunteer group the "Flying Tigers" to aid China.

Che·ops |'kē,äps| (26th century BC) Egyptian pharaoh of the 4th dynasty. Egyptian name **Khufu**. He commissioned the building of the Great Pyramid at Giza.

Cher |SHer| (1946–) U.S. actress and singer. Born *Cherilyn LaPiere Sarkisian*. She was married to Sonny Bono, with whom she cohosted a television show, and to musician Gregg Allman. Notable movies: *Moonstruck* (1987, Academy Award) and *Tea With Mussolini* (1999).

Che·ren·kov |CHə'reNG,kawv|, Pavel (Alekseyevich) (1904–90) Soviet physicist. Also **Cerenkov**. He investigated the effects of high-energy particles and shared the 1958 Nobel Prize for Physics for discovering the cause of blue light (now called *Cerenkov Radiation*) emitted by radioactive substances underwater.

Cher·nen·ko |CHer'nyeNGkō|, Konstantin (Ustinovich) (1911–85) Soviet statesman. He was General Secretary of the Communist Party of the USSR and president (1984–85). He died after only thirteen months in office and was succeeded by Mikhail Gorbachev.

Cher·ry |'CHere|, Don (1936–95) U.S. jazz trumpeter. Full name *Donald Eugene Cherry*. He was a leading figure in free jazz.

Che·ru·bi·ni |,kərə'bēnē|, (Maria) Luigi (Carlo Zenobio Salvadore) (1760–1842) Italian composer. He spent most of his composing career in Paris and is principally known for his church music and operas.

Cher·well |'CHer,wel|, Frederick Alexander Lindemann, 1st Viscount (1886–1957) German-born British physicist. He was Winston Churchill's scientific adviser during World War II.

Chese·brough |'CHēzbrə|, Robert (1837–1933) U.S. inventor. He discovered and patented Vaseline (1870).

Ches·ter·ton |'CHestərtən|, G. K. (1874–1936) English essayist, novelist, and critic. Full name *Gilbert Keith Chesterton*. His novels include *The Napoleon of Notting Hill* (1904) and a series of detective stories featuring Father Brown, a priest with a talent for crime detection.

Chest·nutt |'CHestnət|, Charles Waddell (1858–1932) U.S. author. He wrote *Life of Frederick Douglass* (1899), as well as novels and short stories with a subtle treatment of racial themes.

Che·va·lier |SHevä'lyä|, Maurice-Auguste (1888–1972) French singer and actor. Notable movies: *Innocents of Paris* (1929), *Love Me Tonight* (1932), and *Gigi* (1958).

Chev·ro·let |,SHevrə'lā|, Louis (1879–1941) U.S. automobile racer, designer, and manufacturer. He founded the Chevrolet Motor Co. (1911) and designed its first car.

Chiang Kai-shek |'CHæNG 'kī 'SHek| (1887–1975) Chinese statesman and general. Also **Jiang Jie Shi**. He was president of China (1928–31, 1943–49) and of Taiwan (1950–75). He tried to unite China by military means in the 1930s but was defeated by the Communists. Forced to abandon mainland China in 1949, he set up a separate Nationalist Chinese State in Taiwan.

Chi·ches·ter |'CHiCHəstər|, Sir Francis (Charles) (1901–72) English yachtsman. In his yacht *Gipsy Moth IV* he was the first person to sail alone around the world with only one stop (1966–67).

Chif·ley |'CHiflē|, Joseph Benedict (1885–1951) Australian Labour statesman. He was prime minister (1945–49).

Child |CHīld|, Julia (McWilliams) (1912–) U.S. chef and author. Known as **the French Chef**. She has hosted several televsion cooking programs since

1963. She co-authored the two-volume *Mastering the Art of French Cooking* (1961–70).

Child |CHīld|, Lydia Marie (1802–80) U.S. abolitionist and author. She was editor of the *National Anti-Slavery Standard* (1841–43) and the author of novels, children's books, and the poem "Thanksgiving Day," which begins, "Over the river and through the woods."

Chil•ders |'CHildərz|, (Robert) Erskine (1870–1922) English-born Irish writer and political activist. He was court-martialed and shot for his involvement in the Irish civil war. Notable works: *The Riddle of the Sands* (novel, 1903). His son **Erskine Hamilton Childers** (1905–74) was president of Ireland (1973–74).

Chip•pen•dale |'CHipən‚dāl|, Thomas (1718–79) English furniture-maker and designer. He produced furniture in a neoclassical vein, with elements of the French rococo, chinoiserie, and Gothic revival styles, and his book of furniture designs *The Gentleman and Cabinetmaker's Director* (1754) was immensely influential.

Chi•rac |SHi'räk|, Jacques (René) (1932–) French statesman. He was prime minister (1974–76 and 1986–88) and president from 1995.

Chi•ri•co |'kēri‚kō|, Giorgio de (1888–1978) Greek-born Italian painter. His disconnected and unsettling dream images exerted a significant influence on surrealism.

Chis•holm |'CHizəm|, Shirley Anita St. Hill (1924–) U.S. politician and educator. The first African-American woman elected to Congress, she was a member of the U.S. House of Representatives from New York (1968–83).

Chis•um |'CHizəm|, John Simpson (1824–84) U.S. rancher frontiersman. He developed the largest cattle herd in the U.S. during the 1870s.

Choate |CHōt|, Joseph Hodges (1832–1917) U.S. lawyer and diplomat. He was U.S. ambassador to Britain (1899–1905) and head of the U.S. delegation to the second International Peace Conference at The Hague (1907).

Choate |CHōt|, Rufus (1799–1859) U.S. lawyer. He was a Massachusetts member of the U.S. House of Repre-

sentatives (1831–34) and the U.S. Senate (1841–45).

Chom•sky |'CHämskē|, (Avram) Noam (1928–) U.S. theoretical linguist. He is noted for expounding the theory of generative grammar. He also theorized that linguistic behavior is innate, not learned, and that all languages share the same underlying grammatical base. Chomsky is known also for his opposition to U.S. involvement in the Vietnam War and the Gulf War. Notable works: *Syntactic Structures* (1957) and *Aspects of the Theory of Syntax* (1965).

Cho•pin |SHō'pæn|, Frédéric (François) (1810–49) Polish-born French composer and pianist. Polish name *Fryderyk Franciszek Szopen*. Writing almost exclusively for the piano, he composed numerous mazurkas and polonaises inspired by Polish folk music, as well as nocturnes, preludes, and two piano concertos (1829; 1830).

Cho•pin |'SHō'pən|, Kate (O'Flaherty) (1851–1904) U.S. novelist and short-story writer. Notable works: *Bayou Folk* (1894), *A Night in Acadie* (1897), and *The Awakening* (1899).

Chré•tien |krā'tyen|, Jean (1934–) Canadian Liberal statesman. Full name *Joseph-Jacques Jean* He became prime minister in 1993.

Chré•tien de Troyes |krā‚tyen də 'trwä| (1130–1183) French poet. His courtly romances on Arthurian themes include *Lancelot* (*c.*1177–88) and *Perceval* (1181–90, unfinished).

Chris•tian |'krisCHən|, Charles (1919–42) U.S. jazz guitarist. He was a pioneer of electrically amplified guitar and played with Benny Goodman's band (1939–42).

Chris•tian |'krisCHən|, Fletcher (*c.* 1764–*c.* 1793) English seaman and mutineer. As first mate under Captain Bligh on the HMS *Bounty*, in April 1789 Christian seized the ship and cast Bligh and others adrift. In 1790 the mutineers settled on Pitcairn Island, where Christian was probably killed by Tahitians.

Chris•tie |'kristē|, Dame Agatha (1890–1976) English writer of detective fiction. Notable works: *Murder on the Orient Express* (1934), *Death on the Nile* (1937), and *The Mousetrap* (play, 1952). She created the detectives Miss Marple and Hercule Poirot.

Chris·tie |'kristē|, Julie (1940–) British actress, born in India. Notable movies: *Darling* (1965, Academy Award), *Dr. Zhivago* (1965), and *Shampoo* (1975).

Chris·to·pher |'kristəfər|, Warren (1925–) U.S. statesman and lawyer. He served as Bill Clinton's secretary of state (1993–97).

Chris·ty |'kristē|, Edwin Pearce (1815–62) U.S. actor and singer. He founded the Christy Minstrels singing group.

Chris·ty |'kristē|, Howard Chandler (1873–1952) U.S. illustrator and painter. An illustrator for periodicals, he popularized the image of the "Christy girl."

Chrys·ler |'krīslər|, Walter Percy (1875–1940) U.S. automobile manufacturer. He was president and general manager of Buick Motor Co. (1916–19). He introduced the Chrysler automobile (1924) and became chairman of Chrysler Corp. (1935–40).

Chrys·os·tom |'krisəstəm|, St. John (*c.* 347–407) Doctor of the Church, bishop of Constantinople. He attempted to reform the corrupt state of the court, clergy, and people; this offended many, including the Empress Eudoxia, who banished him in 403. His name means "golden-mouthed" in Greek, referring to his preaching ability. Feast day, January 27.

Chung |CHəNG|, Connie (1946–) U.S. broadcast journalist. Full name *Constance Yu-Hwa Chung.*Since 1987 she has been a news correspondent and anchor for NBC.

Church |CHərCH|, Frank Forrester (1924–84) U.S. politician. A U.S. senator from Idaho, he was a leading liberal voice and civil rights champion who opposed the Vietnam War.

Church |CHərCH|, Frederick Edwin (1826–1900) U.S. painter. He was a student of Thomas Cole and was known for his landscapes.

Chur·chill |'CHərCHəl|, Sir Winston (Leonard Spencer) (1874–1965) British Conservative statesman. He served as prime minister (1940–45, 1951–55). A consistent opponent of appeasement during the 1930s, he replaced Neville Chamberlain as British prime minister in 1940 and led Britain throughout World War II, forging and maintaining the alliance that defeated the Axis Powers. His writings include *The Second World War* (1948–53) and *A History of the English-Speaking Peoples* (1956–58); he won the Nobel Prize for Literature in 1953.

Church·ward |'CHərCHwərd|, George Jackson (1857–1933) English railway engineer. The standard 4-6-0 locomotives that he built at the Swindon works of the Great Western Railway were the basis of many later designs.

Cic·e·ro |'sisərō|, Marcus Tullius (106–43 BC) Roman statesman, orator, and writer. As an orator and writer Cicero established a model for Latin prose; his surviving works include speeches, treatises on rhetoric, philosophical works, and letters. A supporter of Pompey against Julius Caesar, in the *Philippics* (43 BC) he attacked Mark Antony, who had him put to death.

Cid, El |sid|, Count of Bivar (*c.* 1043–99) Spanish soldier. Born *Rodrigo Díaz de Vivar.* He was a champion of Christianity against the Moors. In 1094 he captured Valencia, which he went on to rule. He is immortalized in the Spanish *Poema de Cid* (12th century) and in Corneille's play *Le Cid* (1637).

Ciof·fi |'CHōfē|, Lou (1926–98) U.S. journalist. He covered the Korean and Vietnam wars.

Cis·ne·ros |ˌsis'nerəs|, Sandra (1954–) U.S. poet and author. Works include *The House on Mango Street* (1983), which received an American Book Award.

Clai·borne |'klā،bawrn|, Craig (1920–) U.S. editor and cookbook author. He is the food editor for the New York Times and author of *Classic French Cuisine* (1970).

Clai·borne |'klā،bawrn|, Liz (1929–) U.S. fashion designer and manufacturer. Full name *Elisabeth Claiborne Ortenberg.*

Clan·cy |'klænsē|, Tom (1947–) U.S. author. Notable novels: *Hunt for Red October* (1985), *Patriot Games* (1987), and *Rainbow Six* (1998).

Clap·ton |'klæptən|, Eric (1945–)
English blues and rock guitarist, singer,
and composer. He is noted as a virtuoso
guitarist and interpreter of the blues.

Clare |kler|, John (1793–1864) English
poet. He wrote in celebration of the natural world. In 1837 he was certified in-
sane and spent the rest of his life in an
asylum. Notable works: *Poems Descrip-
tive of Rural Life and Scenery* (1820) and
The Rural Muse (1835).

Clar·en·don |'klerəndən|, Edward
Hyde, Earl of (1609–74) English statesman and historian. He was chief advis-
er to Charles II and chancellor of Oxford University (1660–67). Notable
works: *History of the Rebellion and Civil
Wars in England* (published posthumously 1702–04).

Clare of As·si·si |ˌkler əv ə'sēsē|, St.
(1194–1253) Italian saint and abbess.
With St. Francis she founded the order
of Poor Ladies of San Damiano ("Poor
Clares"), of which she was abbess. Feast
day, August 11 (formerly 12).

Clark |klärk|, Dick (1929–) U.S. per-
former and producer. He hosted television's "American Bandstand" (1952–
87) and formed Dick Clark Productions
in 1956.

Clark |klärk|, George Rogers (1752–
1818) American Revolutionary War
leader and frontiersman. He defended
the Illinois frontier against the British.

Clark |klärk|, Joe (1939–) Canadian
statesman. Full name *Charles Joseph
Clark*. A leader of the Progressive Conservative Party (1976–83), he became
Canada's youngest prime minister
(1979–80).

Clark |klärk|, Kenneth Bancroft
(1914–) U.S. educator, author, and
psychologist. Notable works: *Desegrega-
tion: An Appraisal of the Evidence* (1953)
and *The War Against Poverty* (1968). Spingarn Medal, 1961.

Clark |klärk|, Mark Wayne (1896–1984)
U.S. army officer. He served as chief of
staff of the U.S. Army ground forces
(1942), as UN commander and commander in chief of the U.S. Far East
command (1952–53). He signed the
Korean armistice.

Clark |klärk|, Mary Higgins (1931–)
U.S. author. Notable novels: *A Stranger
is Watching* (1978) and *All Through the
Night* (1998).

Clark |klärk|, Tom Campbell (1899–
1977) U.S. Supreme Court justice
(1949–67).

Clark |klärk|, William (1770–1838) U.S.
explorer. With Meriwether Lewis, he
commanded the Lewis and Clark expedition (1804–06) across the North
American continent.

Clarke |klärk|, Sir Arthur Charles
(1917–) English writer of science fiction. He wrote the book *2001: A Space
Odyssey* in 1968 and cowrote (with Stanley Kubrick) the screenplay for the
movie in the same year.

Clarke |klärk|, Bobby (1949–) U.S.
hockey player.

Clarke |klärk|, John H. (1857–1945)
U.S. Supreme Court justice (1916–22).
He was president of the League of Nations Non-Partisan Committee (1922–
28).

Clarke |klärk|, Kenny (1914–85) U.S.
jazz drummer and bandleader. Full
name *Kenneth Spearman Clarke*. A pioneer of modern drums, he composed
"Salt Peanuts" with Dizzy Gillespie and
"Epistrophy" with Thelonius Monk.

Claude Lor·rain |ˌklawd law'rān|
(1600–82) Also **Lorrain**. French
painter; born *Claude Gellée*. He is noted
for the use of light in his landscapes. Notable works: *Ascanius and the Stag*
(1682).

Claudius (10 BC–AD 54) Roman emperor (41–54); full name *Tiberius
Claudius Drusus Nero Germanicus*. His
reign was noted for its restoration of
order after Caligula's decadence and for
its expansion of the Empire, in particular the invasion of Britain in AD 43. His
fourth wife, Agrippina, is said to have
poisoned him.

Clau·se·witz |'klowzə,vits|, Carl von
(1780–1831) Prussian general and military theorist. His study *On War* (1833)
had a marked influence on strategic
studies in the 19th and 20th centuries.

Clau·si·us |'kläzēəs|, Rudolf (1822–88)
German physicist, one of the founders
of modern thermodynamics. He was the
first, in 1850, to formulate the second
law of thermodynamics, developing the
concept of a system's available thermal

energy and coining the term *entropy* for it.

Cla·vell |klə'vel|, James (1924–94) Australian author and filmmaker. Born *Charles Edmund DuMaresq de Clavell*. Notable novels: *King Rat* (1962) and *Shogun* (1975). Notable movies (as writer and producer): *The Great Escape* (1963) and *To Sir with Love* (also directed; 1967).

Clay, Cassius see MUHAMMAD ALI.

Clay |klā|, Henry (1777–1852) U.S. politician and statesman. He was a leader of the "War Hawks" (1811); for his role as a champion of the Missouri Compromise (1820), he was nicknamed "the Great Pacificator." He served as U.S. secretary of state (1825–29) and as a U.S. senator from Kentucky (1831–42); his oratory favoring the Compromise of 1850 earned him a second nickname, "the Great Compromiser."

Clay |klā|, Lucius DuBignon (1897–1978) U.S. army officer. He served as commander in chief of U.S. forces in Europe (1947–49) and was in charge of the Berlin airlift (1948).

Clay·ton |'klātn|, Buck (1911–91) U.S. jazz trumpeter and arranger. Full name *Wilbur Dorsey Clayton*. He was a leading soloist with Count Basie's band and a central figure of mainstream jazz.

Cleary |'klirē|, Beverly (Bunn) (1916–) U.S. author. Notable children's books: *Henry Huggins* (1950) and *Ramona the Pest* (1968).

Clea·ver |'klēvər|, Eldridge (1935–98) U.S. civil rights activist.

Cleese |klēz|, John (Marwood) (1939–) English comic actor and writer. He became famous for television's "Monty Python's Flying Circus" (1969–74) and the situation comedy "Fawlty Towers" (1975–79).

Cleis·the·nes |'klīsTHə,nēz| (c. 570 BC–c. 508 BC) Athenian statesman. His reforms consolidated the Athenian democratic process begun by Solon and influenced the policies of Pericles.

Cle·men·ceau |,klemən'sō|, Georges (Eugène Benjamin) (1841–1929) French statesman, prime minister (1906–09, 1917–20). At the Versailles peace talks he pushed hard for a punitive settlement with Germany, but failed to obtain all that he demanded (notably the Rhine River as a frontier).

Clem·ens |'klemɘns|, Roger (1962–) U.S. baseball player. Full name *William Roger Clemens*, known as **the Rocket**. He set a major league record by twice striking out 20 batters during a nine-inning game. Received four Cy Young Awards (1986, 1987, 1991, 1997).

Clemens, Samuel Langhorne see TWAIN, MARK.

Clem·ent |'klemɘnt|, St. (1st century AD) Pope (bishop of Rome) c. 88–c. 97. He was probably the third pope after St. Peter; known as **St. Clement of Rome**. Feast day, November 23.

Cle·men·te |klə'mentē|, Roberto Walker (1934–72) U.S. baseball player, born in Puerto Rico. He was a four-time National League batting champion. Elected to the Baseball Hall of Fame (1973).

Clem·ent of Al·ex·an·dria |'klemɘnt ɘv ,æleg'zændrēɘ|, St. (c. 150–c. 215) Greek theologian. Latin name *Titus Flavius Clemens*. His main contribution to theological scholarship was to relate the ideas of Greek philosophy to the Christian faith. Feast day, December 5.

Cle·o·pat·ra |,klēɘ'pætrɘ| (69–30 BC) queen of Egypt (47–30). Also called **Cleopatra VII**. She was the last Ptolemaic (Macedonian dynasty) ruler. After a brief liaison with Julius Caesar she formed a political and romantic alliance with Mark Antony. Their ambitions ultimately brought them into conflict with Rome, and she and Antony were defeated at the battle of Actium in 31. She is reputed to have committed suicide by allowing herself to be bitten by an asp.

Cleve·land |'klēvlɘnd|, (Stephen) Grover (1837–1908) see box. **Frances Folsom Cleveland** (1864–1947), wife of Grover Cleveland and U.S. first lady (1886–89, 1893–97).

Cleve·land |'klēvlɘnd|, James (1931–91) U.S. gospel singer and composer.

Clif·ford |'klifɘrd|, Clark M. (1906–98) U.S. attorney and public official. A key adviser to four Democratic presidents, he helped draft legislation establishing the CIA.

Clif·ford |'klifɘrd|, Nathan (1803–81) U.S. Supreme Court justice (1858–81).

Cleveland, Grover
*22nd and 24th U.S. president
(two separate terms)*

Life dates: 1837–1908
Place of birth: Caldwell, New Jersey
Mother: Anne Neal Cleveland
Father: Richard Falley Cleveland
Wife: Frances Folsom Cleveland
Children: Ruth, Esther, Marion, Richard, Francis
College/University: none
Career: Lawyer; sheriff
Political career: Mayor of Buffalo, New York; governor of New York; president
Party: Democratic
Home state: New York
Opponents in presidential races: James G. Blaine (in 1884); Benjamin Harrison, James B. Weaver (in 1888 and 1892)
Terms of office: March 4, 1885–March 3, 1889 (first term); March 4, 1893–March 3, 1897 (second term)
Vice presidents: Thomas A. Hendricks (first term); Adlai E. Stevenson (second term)
Notable events of presidency: (first term) Interstate Commerce Act; Presidential Succession Act; (second term) financial panic of 1893; labor unrest, including Pullman strike of 1894; gold crisis of 1895; Statue of Liberty dedication; Department of Agriculture established; Utah admitted as 45th state
Place of burial: Princeton, New Jersey

He helped negotiate the Treaty of Guadeloupe Hidalgo with Mexico (1848).

Clift |klift|, Montgomery (1920–66) U.S. actor. Full name *Edward Montgomery Clift*. He received four Oscar nominations for movies that included *From Here to Eternity* (1953) and *Judgment at Nuremberg* (1961).

Cline |klīn|, Patsy (1932–63) U.S. country singer. Born *Virginia Petterson Hensley*. She was discovered in 1957 when she sang "Walkin' After Midnight" on a television show. She had hits with "Crazy" (1961) and "Sweet Dreams of You" (1963).

Clin•ton |'klintən|, DeWitt (1769–1828) U.S. politician. Among his political positions, he was a member of the New York legislature (1798–1802), a

U.S. senator (1802–03), and mayor of New York City (1803–07, 1808–10, 1811–15). As governor of New York (1817–23, 1825–28), he was a champion of the Erie Canal.

Clin•ton |'klintən|, George (1739–1812) U.S. politician. He was governor of New York (1777–95) and vice president of the U.S. (1805–12).

Clin•ton |'klintən|, Sir Henry (1738–95) English soldier. He fought at the battles of Bunker Hill (1775) and Long Island (1776) and became commander in chief of British troops in America (1778).

Clin•ton |'klintən|, William Jefferson (1946–   ) see box. **Hillary Rodham**

Clinton, Bill (William Jefferson)
42nd U.S. president

Life dates: 1946–
Place of birth: Hope, Arkansas
Name at birth: William Jefferson Blythe IV
Mother: Virginia Cassidy Blythe (later married Roger Clinton, Sr.)
Father: William Jefferson Blythe II (died before son's birth)
Stepfather: (from the age of 4) Roger Clinton, Sr.
Wife: Hillary Rodham Clinton (married 1975; adopted her husband's last name in 1982)
Child: Chelsea
College/University: Georgetown; Oxford (as Rhodes scholar); Yale Law School
Career: Lawyer
Political career: Governor of Arkansas (two separate terms); president
Party: Democratic
Home state: Arkansas
Opponents in presidential races: George Bush; Robert Dole
Term of office: Jan. 20, 1993–
Vice president: Albert Gore, Jr.
Notable events of presidency: North American Free Trade Agreement (NAFTA); Anti-Crime Bill; Israeli-PLO Peace Accord; Bosnian Civil War treaty (Dayton accords); Good Friday Peace Agreement in Northern Ireland; Paula Jones sexual-harassment lawsuit; Monica Lewinsky scandal; impeachment in the U.S. House of Representatives and acquittal in U.S. Senate trial

Clinton (1947–), wife of Bill Clinton and U.S. first lady (1993–).

Clive |klīv|, Robert (1725–74) (1st Baron Clive of Plassey) British general and colonial administrator; known as **Clive of India**. In 1757 he recaptured Calcutta, following the Black Hole incident, and gained control of Bengal. He served as governor of Bengal 1765–67, but was implicated in the East India company's corruption scandals and committed suicide.

Close |klōz|, Glenn (1947–) U.S. actress. Her movies include *Fatal Attraction* (1987), and her stage appearances include *The Real Thing* (1984–85) and *Sunset Boulevard* (1995).

Clou·et |klōō'ā| French court portrait painters. **Jean Clouet** (*c.* 1485–1541) worked as court painter to Francis I; the monarch's portrait in the Louvre is attributed to him. His son **François Clouet** (*c.* 1516–72) succeeded his father as court painter, and is chiefly known for his undated portraits of Elizabeth of Austria (now in the Louvre) and Mary, Queen of Scots (now in the Wallace Collection in London).

Clough |klŭf|, Arthur Hugh (1819–61) English poet. Notable poems: "Amours de Voyage" (1858).

Clo·vis |'klōvəs| (*c.* 466–511) king of the Franks (481–511). He extended Merovingian rule to Gaul and Germany, making Paris his capital. After his conversion to Christianity he championed orthodoxy against the Arian Visigoths, finally defeating them in the battle of Poitiers (507).

Clu·ett |'klōō͝ət|, Sanford Lockwood (1874–1968) U.S. engineer. He invented the Sanforizing process of mechanically preshrinking fabrics.

Co·bain |'kō'bān|, Kurt (Donald) (1967–94) U.S. rock singer, guitarist, and songwriter. As leader of the Seattle band Nirvana, his style helped characterize the alternative music scene. His notoriety reached cult proportions, undiminished by his suicide in April 1994.

Cobb |käb|, Ty (1886–1961) U.S. baseball player. Full name *Tyrus Raymond Cobb*; also known as **Georgia Peach**. He holds the highest lifetime batting average (.367) in baseball history.

Cob·bett |'käbət|, William (1763–1835) English writer and political reformer. He started his political life as a Tory, but later became a radical and in 1802 founded the periodical *Cobbett's Political Register*. Notable works: *Rural Rides* (1830).

Cob·den |'käbdn|, Richard (1804–65) English political reformer. He was one of the leading spokesmen of the free-trade movement in Britain. From 1838, together with John Bright, he led the Anti-Corn Law League in its successful campaign for the repeal of the Corn Laws (1846).

Co·burn |'kōbərn|, Charles (1877–1961) U.S. actor. Notable movies: *The Devil and Miss Jones* (1941) and *The More the Merrier* (1943, Academy Award).

Co·chise |kō'CHēs| (1812?–74) Apache Indian chief.

Coch·ran |'käkrən|, Sir Charles Blake (1872–1951) English theatrical producer. He was noted for musical revues including Noël Coward's *Bitter Sweet* (1929) and *Cavalcade* (1931). He was also agent for Houdini.

Coch·ran |'käkrən|, Eddie (1938–60) U.S. rock-and-roll singer and songwriter. Full name *Edward Cochrane*. He was killed in a car crash during a British tour. Notable songs: "Summertime Blues" (1958) and "Three Steps to Heaven" (1960).

Coch·ran |'käkrən|, Jacqueline (1910?–80) U.S. aviator. The first woman to break the sound barrier, she set many speed and altitude records

Coch·ran |'käkrən|, Johnnie L., Jr. (1937–) U.S. attorney. He was the lead defense attorney for O. J. Simpson in his murder trial (1995)

Cock·croft |'kä͵krawft|, Sir John Douglas (1897–1967) English physicist. In 1932 he succeeded (with E. T. S. Walton) in splitting the atom, ushering in the whole field of nuclear and particle physics. Nobel Prize for Physics (1951, shared with Walton).

Cock·er |'käkər|, Joe (1944–) British musician. Full name *Robert John Cocker*. Known for his gritty, powerful white-soul and rock voice, his performance at Woodstock of "A Little Help from My

Friends" became an archetypal rock performance.

Cock·er·ell |'käkrəl|, Sir Christopher Sydney (1910–) English engineer, the inventor of the hovercraft.

Coc·teau |käk'tō|, Jean (1889–1963) French dramatist, novelist, and movie director. His plays are noted for their striking blend of poetry, irony, and fantasy. Notable works: *La Machine infernale* (play, 1934), *La Belle et la bête* (movie, 1946), and *Les Enfants terribles* (novel, 1929).

Co·dy |'kōdē|, William Frederick see BUFFALO BILL.

Coe |kō|, Sebastian (1956–) British middle-distance runner and Conservative politician. He was an Olympic gold medal winner in the 1,500 meters in 1980 and 1984.

Coen |kōn| U.S. filmmakers. **Joel Coen** (1954–), a director, and his brother **Ethan Coen** (1957–), a producer, together created such movies as *Barton Fink* (1991) and *Fargo* (1996, Academy Award).

Coet·zee |'kōōtsir|, J. M. (1940–) South African novelist; full name *John Maxwell Coetzee*. Notable novels: *In the Heart of the Country* (1977) and *Life and Times of Michael K* (1983).

Cof·fin |'kawfən|, Howard Earle (1873–1937) U.S. engineer. He designed the Hudson automobile and helped found National Air Transport (1925), which was the forerunner of United Airlines.

Cof·fin |'kawfən|, Levi (1798–1877) U.S. abolitionist. He was active in the Underground Railroad and opened a Quaker school for slaves.

Cof·fin |'kawfən|, William Sloan (1924–) U. S. minister. As a Presbyterian clergyman and Yale University chaplain during the 1960s, he was a leader of antiwar protests.

Co·han |'kō,hæn|, George Michael (1878–1942) U.S. actor, playwright, composer, and producer. Among his most famous tunes are "Yankee Doodle Dandy" and "Give My Regards to Broadway."

Cohn |kōn|, Al (1925–88) U.S. jazz tenor saxophonist and composer. Full name *Alvin Gilbert Cohn*. He was the principal arranger for the musicals *Raisin* (1973), *Music, Music, Music* (1974), and *Sophisticated Ladies* (1981).

Cohn |kōn|, Ferdinand Julius (1828–98) German botanist, a founder of bacteriology and the first to devise a systematic classification of bacteria into genera and species.

Cohn |kōn|, Harry (1891–1958) U.S. founder of Columbia Pictures.

Col·bert |kōl'bert|, Jean Baptiste (1619–83) French statesman, chief minister to Louis XIV 1665–83. He was responsible for reforming the country's finances and the navy, and for boosting industry and commerce.

Cole |kōl| U.S. musicians: **Nat King Cole** (1919–65), a singer and pianist, was born *Nathaniel Adams Coles*. His mellow vocal tones won him international recognition as a singer. He became the first black man to have his own radio (1948–49) and television (1956–57) series. Notable songs: "Mona Lisa" (1950) and "Ramblin' Rose" (1962). His daughter **Natalie Cole** (1950–), a singer, won three Grammy Awards for her album *Unforgettable* (1991).

Cole |kōl|, Cozy (1909–81) U.S. jazz drummer. Born *William Randolph Cole*. He performed with Cab Calloway's orchestra (1938–42) and with Louis Armstrong's All Stars (1949–53). He opened a drum school in New York with Gene Krupa.

Cole |kōl|, Thomas (1801–48) U.S. artist. He was founder of the Hudson River School.

Cole·man |'kōlmən|, Ornette (1930–) U.S. jazz saxophonist, trumpeter, violinist, and composer, whose music is noted for its lack of harmony and chordal structure.

Cole·man |'kōlmən|, William (1870–1957) U.S. businessman. He founded Coleman Camping Equipment and marketed the "Coleman Arc Lamp" gas lamp to homes without electricity in 1903.

Cole·ridge |'kōl(ə)rij|, Samuel Taylor (1772–1834) English poet, critic, and philosopher. His *Lyrical Ballads* (1798), written with William Wordsworth, marked the start of English romanticism and included "The Rime of the Ancient Mariner." Other notable poems:

"Christabel" and "Kubla Khan" (both 1816).

Coles |kōl|, Joanna (1944–) U.S. author. Her nonfiction books for children include the *Magic School Bus* series.

Coles |kōlz|, Robert Martin (1929–) U.S. psychiatrist, educator, and author. A specialist in child psychology, he wrote the Pulitzer Prize–winning series *Children of Crisis* (1967–78).

Co•lette |kō'let| (1873–1954) French novelist. Born *Sidonie Gabrielle Claudine*. Notable novels: *Chéri* (1920) and *La Fin de Chéri* (1926). Her novel *Gigi* (1945) was filmed in 1948 and again as a musical in 1958.

Col•fax |'kawlfæks|, Schuyler (1823–85) U.S. vice president (1869–73).

Col•gate |'kōl‚gāt|, William (1783–1857) U.S. manufacturer and philanthropist, born in England. He started out making candles and then (1806) set up a tallow factory in New York to make soap. His firm later became the Colgate-Palmolive-Peet Co. Colgate University was named in his honor.

Col•lier |'kälyər|, Peter Fenelon (1849–1909) U.S. publisher. He founded *Collier's Weekly* (1896).

Col•lins |'kälənz|, Edward Knight (1802–78) U.S. shipowner. He founded the Collins Line (1847), with steamships that were then the fastest in transatlantic service.

Col•lins |'kälənz|, Joan (Henrietta) (1933–) English actress. She was a sex symbol in movies such as *Our Girl Friday* (1953) and was later known for the television series "Dynasty" (1981–89). She is the sister of the novelist Jackie Collins.

Col•lins |'kälənz|, Judy (1939–) U.S. singer, songwriter, author, and actress Her lyrical voice helped to define folk rock in the 1960s.

Col•lins |'kälənz|, Michael (1890–1922) Irish nationalist leader and politician. A member of Parliament for Sinn Fein, he was one of the negotiators of the Anglo-Irish Treaty of 1921. He commanded the Irish Free State forces in the civil war and became head of state but was assassinated ten days later.

Col•lins |'kälənz|, Phil (1951–) U.S. rock musician. Full name *Phillip David*

Charles Collins. He was a singer with many top hits and a drummer for Genesis, Eric Clapton, and Led Zeppelin.

Col•lins |'kälənz|, (William) Wilkie (1824–89) English novelist. He is noted for his detective stories *The Woman in White* (1860) and *The Moonstone* (1868).

Col•man |'kōlmən|, Ronald (1891–1958) English actor. Notable movies: *A Tale of Two Cities* (1935), *The Prisoner of Zenda* (1937), and *Random Harvest* (1942).

Col•son |'kōlsən|, Charles Wendell (1931–) U.S. lay minister. As special counsel to President Nixon (1969–72), he became a principal in the Watergate scandal.

Colt |kōlt|, Samuel (1814–62) U.S. inventor. He is remembered chiefly for the revolver named after him, which was patented originally in 1836; it was adopted by the U.S. Army in 1846. His armory at Hartford, Connecticut, advanced the manufacturing techniques of interchangeable parts and the production line.

Col•ton |'kawltn|, Frank Benjamin (1923–) U.S. chemist, born in Poland. He developed Enovid, the first oral contraceptive (1960).

Col•trane |'kōl‚trān|, John William (1926–67) U.S. jazz saxophonist. He was a leading figure in avant-garde jazz, bridging the gap between the harmonically dense jazz of the 1950s and the free jazz that evolved in the 1960s. Notable recordings: *My Favorite Things* (1960).

Co•lum•ba |kə'ləmbə|, St. (*c.* 521–97) Irish abbot and missionary. He established the monastery at Iona *c.*563 and converted the Picts to Christianity. Feast day, June 9.

Co•lum•bus |kə'ləmbəs|, Christopher (1451–1506) Italian-born Spanish explorer. Spanish name *Cristóbal Colón*. His four pioneering voyages to the Americas (1492–1504) led to Spanish colonization of the New World.

Co•ma•ne•ci |kōmə'nēCH|, Nadia (1961–) Romanian gymnast; emigrated to the U.S. in 1989. In 1976 she became the first Olympic gymnast to earn seven perfect scores and won three gold medals at the 1976 Olympics.

Co·mis·key |kə'miskē|, Charles Albert (1859–1931) U.S. baseball executive. A professional baseball player and the founder, owner, and president of the Chicago White Sox (1900), he built Comiskey Park and was inducted into the Baseball Hall of Fame (1939).

Com·ma·ger |'kəmə,jər|, Henry Steele (1902–98) U.S. educator and author. Notable works: *The American Mind* (1951) and *Freedom, Loyalty, Dissent* (1954).

Co·mo |'kō,mō|, Perry (1912–) U.S. singer. A nightclub entertainer with movie and television credits, he starred in the television program "The Perry Como Show."

Comp·ton |'kämptn|, Arthur Holly (1892–1962) American physicist. He observed the Compton effect and thus demonstrated the dual particle and wave properties of electromagnetic radiation and matter, as predicted by quantum theory. Nobel Prize for Physics (1927).

Compton-Burnett |'kämptn bər'net|, Dame Ivy (1884–1969) English novelist. Notable novels: *Brothers and Sisters* (1929), *A Family and a Fortune* (1939), and *Manservant and Maidservant* (1947).

Com·stock |'käm,stäk|, John Henry (1849–1931) U.S. entomologist and author. He wrote pioneering work in the classification of scale insects, moths, and butterflies.

Com·stock |'käm,stäk|, Anthony (1844–1915) U.S. reformer. He campaigned against pornographic literature and helped pass the federal Comstock Law (1873) banning such literature from the mails. As founder and secretary for the Society for the Suppression of Vice in New York, he carried out raids on publishers and vendors of "obscene" materials.

Comte |kawnt|, Auguste (1798–1857) French philosopher, one of the founders of sociology. Comte's positivist philosophy attempted to define the laws of social evolution and to found a genuine social science that could be used for social reconstruction.

Co·nan Doyle |'kōnən 'doil| see DOYLE.

Co·ne·glia·no |kawnel'yänō|, Emmanuele see DA PONTE.

Con·fu·cius |kən'fyōoSHəs| (551–479 BC) Chinese philosopher. Latinized name of *Kongfuze* (*K'ung Fu-tzu*). Known as **Kong the master**. His ideas about the importance of practical moral values, collected by his disciples in the *Analects*, formed the basis of the philosophy known as Confucianism.

Con·greve |'käNG,grēv|, William (1670–1729) English dramatist. A close associate of Swift, Pope, and Steele, he wrote plays such as *Love for Love* (1695) and *The Way of the World* (1700), which epitomize the wit and satire of Restoration comedy.

Con·nell |'känəl|, Evan Shelby, Jr. (1924–) U.S. author. His works of nonfiction include the historical *Son of the Morning Star* (1984). Notable novels: *Mrs. Bridge* (1959) and *Mr. Bridge* (1969).

Con·nery |'känərē|, Sean (1930–) Scottish actor. Born *Thomas Connery*. He is best known for his portrayal of British secret agent James Bond in a number of movies. Other notable work: *The Untouchables* (1987, Academy Award).

Con·nol·ly |'känəlē|, Cyril (Vernon) (1903–74) English writer and journalist. His works include one novel, *The Rock Pool* (1936), and collections of essays, aphorisms, and reflections, among which are *Enemies of Promise* (1938) and *The Unquiet Grave* (1944). He worked for the *Sunday Times* from 1951 until 1974.

Con·nol·ly |'känəlē|, Maureen Catherine (1934–69) U.S. tennis player. Known as **Little Mo**. She was 16 when she first won the U.S. singles title and 17 when she took the Wimbledon title. In 1953 she became the first woman to win the tennis Grand Slam. She retired in 1954 after a riding accident.

Con·nor |'känər|, Dennis (1942–) U.S. yachtsman. Three-time winner of the America's Cup (1980, 1987, 1988), he is also the first American skipper to lose the Cup (1983).

Con·nors |'känərz|, Jimmy (1952–) U.S. professional tennis player. Full name *James Scott Connors*. He won Wimbledon in 1974 and 1982, and the U.S. Open championship five times.

Con•over |'känəvər|, Lloyd H. (1923–) U.S. inventor. He created the broad-spectrum antibiotic tetracycline (patented 1955).

Con•rad |'kän,ræd|, Paul Francis (1924–) U.S. political cartoonist. Pulitzer Prizes, 1964 and 1971.

Con•rad |'kän,ræd|, Joseph (1857–1924) Polish-born British novelist. Born *Józef Teodor Konrad Korzeniowski*. Although French was his first foreign language, Conrad wrote in English and became a British citizen in 1886. Much of his work, including his story *Heart of Darkness* (1902) and the novel *Nostromo* (1904), explores the darkness within human nature.

Con•roy |'kän,roi|, Pat (1945–) U.S. author. Full name *Donald Patrick Conroy*. Notable novels: *The Great Santini* (1976) and *The Prince of Tides* (1986).

Con•sta•ble |'känstəbəl|, John (1776–1837) English painter. Among his best-known works are early paintings like *Flatford Mill* (1817) and *The Hay Wain* (1821), inspired by the landscape of his native Suffolk.

Con•stan•tine |'känstən,tēn| (*c.* 274–337) Roman emperor. Known as **Constantine the Great**. He was the first Roman emperor to be converted to Christianity and in 324 made Christianity the Empire's state religion. In 330 he moved his capital from Rome to Byzantium, renaming it Constantinopolis (Constantinople). In the Orthodox Church he is venerated as a saint.

Cook |kook|, George Cram (1873–1924) U.S. playwright, novelist, and poet.

Cook |kook|, Captain James (1728–79) English explorer. On his first expedition to the Pacific (1768–71), he charted the coasts of New Zealand and New Guinea as well as exploring the east coast of Australia and claiming it for Britain. He made two more voyages to the Pacific before being killed in a skirmish with native people in Hawaii.

Cook |kook|, Peter (Edward) (1937–95) English comedian and actor.

Cook |kook|, Robin (1940–) U.S. author. He is known as the master of the medical thriller. Notable novels: *Fatal Cure* (1994) and *Chromosome 6* (1997).

Cook |kook|, Thomas (1808–92) English founder of the travel firm Thomas Cook. In 1841 he organized the first publicly advertised excursion train in England; the success of this venture led him to organize further excursions both in Britain and abroad, laying the foundations for the British tourist and travel-agent industry.

Cooke |kook|, Jay (1821–1905) U.S. financier. He was the founder of Jay Cooke and Co., a leading Philadelphia bank (1861); his financing of western railroads precipitated the Panic of 1873.

Cooke |kook|, Sam (1935–64) U.S. musician. He was a singer, songwriter, and producer who mixed gospel and rock to provide the foundation of soul music.

Cooke |kook|, Sir William Fothergill (1806–79) English inventor. With Sir Charles Wheatstone he invented the electric telegraph alarm.

Cook•son |'kooksən|, Dame Catherine (Ann) (1906–1998) English writer. She is a prolific author of romantic fiction.

Coo•lidge |'koolij|, (John) Calvin (1872–1933) see box. **Grace Anna Goodhue Coolidge** (1879–1957), wife of Calvin Coolidge and U.S. first lady (1923–29).

Coo•lidge |'koolij|, William David (1873–1975) U.S. physical chemist and inventor. His invention of ductile tungsten (1908) revolutionized the production of light bulbs and enabled him to make significant strides in x-ray technology.

Coo•ney |'koonē|, Joan Ganz (1929–) U.S. broadcasting executive. A pioneer of educational children's television, she founded the Children's Television Workshop (1968) and created "Sesame Street" (1968–) for the Public Broadcasting System.

Coo•per |'koopər|, Alice (Vincent Damon Furnier) (1948–) U.S. rock singer and songwriter.

Coo•per |'koopər|, Gary (1901–61) U.S. movie actor. Born *Frank James Cooper*. He is noted for his performances in such westerns as *The Virginian* (1929) and *High Noon* (1952).

Coo•per |'koopər|, James Fenimore

Coolidge, Calvin (born John Calvin)
30th U.S. president

Life dates: 1872–1933
Place of birth: Plymouth Notch, Vermont
Mother: Victoria Josephine Moor Coolidge
Stepmother: Caroline Athelia Brown Coolidge
Father: John Calvin Coolidge
Wife: Grace Anna Goodhue Coolidge
Children: John; Calvin, Jr.
Nickname: "Silent Cal"
College/University: Amherst College
Career: Lawyer; bank vice president; newspaper columnist
Political career: Massachusetts House of Representatives; mayor, Northampton, Mass.; Massachusetts Senate; lieutenant governor and governor of Massachusetts; vice president (under Harding); president
Party: Republican
Home state: Massachusetts
Opponents in presidential race: John W. Davis, Robert M. La Follette
Term of office: Aug. 3, 1923–March 3, 1929 (succeeded to the presidency on the death of Warren G. Harding; won 1924 election)
Vice president: none (1st term); Charles G. Dawes (2nd term)
Notable events of presidency: Teapot Dome scandal; Immigration Act of 1924; Scopes monkey trials; Japanese Exclusion Act; Charles Lindbergh's transatlantic solo flight; Kellogg-Briand Peace Pact; U.S. Foreign Service created
Other achievements: Admitted to the Pennsylvania bar; settled Boston police strike; chairman, Nonpartisan Railroad Commission; president, American Antiquarian Society; wrote syndicated newspaper column
Place of burial: Plymouth Notch, Vermont

(1789–1851) U.S. novelist. He is renowned for his tales of American Indians and frontier life, in particular *The Last of the Mohicans* (1826).

Coo·per |'kōōpər|, Peter (1791–1883) U.S. manufacturer and philanthropist. He designed and built the first steam locomotive, *Tom Thumb* (1830), and founded Cooper Union in New York City (1859).

Coo·per |'kōōpər|, Susie (1902–95) English ceramic designer and manufacturer. Full name *Susan Vera Cooper*. Her work was noted for its functional shapes and simple, vivid designs.

Coors |kōōrz|, Adolph (1847–1929) U.S. businessman, born in Germany. He founded the Coors brewery.

Co·per·ni·cus |kə'pərnəkəs|, Nicolaus (1473–1543) Polish astronomer. Latinized name of *Mikołaj Kopernik*. He proposed a model of the solar system in which the planets orbited in perfect circles around the sun, and his work ultimately led to the overthrow of the established geocentric cosmology. He published his astronomical theories in *De Revolutionibus Orbium Coelestium* (1543).

Cop·land |'kōplənd|, Aaron (1900–90) U.S. composer, pianist, and conductor, of Lithuanian descent. He established a distinctive American style in his compositions, borrowing from jazz, folk, and other traditional music. Notable works: *Appalachian Spring* (1944), *Fanfare for the Common Man* (1942), and *Music for the Theater* (1925).

Cop·ley |'käplē|, John Singleton (1738–1815) U.S. painter. He is noted for his portraits and for paintings such as *The Death of Chatham* (1779–80), one of the first large-scale paintings of contemporary events.

Cop·per·field |'käpər,fēld|, David (1956–) U.S. magician. Born *David Seth Kotkin*. He has appeared extensively on television and Broadway, performing illusions such as walking through the Great Wall of China.

Cop·po·la |'käpələ|, Francis Ford (1939–) U.S. movie director, writer, and producer. Notable movies: *The Godfather* (1972) and *Apocalypse Now* (1979).

Cor·bett |'kawrbət|, James John (1866–1933) U.S. boxer. Known as **Gentleman Jim**. He won two world heavyweight championships (1892, 1897).

Cor·bin |'kawrbin|, Margaret (1751–1800) American Revolutionary heroine. After her husband's death in the attack on Fort Washington (1776), she took his place at his cannon until becoming severly wounded. She was the first woman to be pensioned by the American government.

Cor·day |kawr'dā|, Charlotte (1768–93) French political assassin. Full name *Marie Anne Charlotte Corday d'Armont*. She became involved with the Girondists and in 1793 assassinated the revolutionary leader Jean Paul Marat in his bath; she was found guilty of treason and guillotined.

Cor·dero |kawrderō|, Angel (1942–) U.S. jockey, born in Puerto Rico.

Co·rel·li |kə'relē|, Arcangelo (1653–1713) Italian violinist and composer. His best-known works are his trio and solo sonatas for the violin and his concerti grossi (published posthumously in 1714), especially the "Christmas" concerto.

Co·rel·li |kə'relē|, Marie (1855–1924) English writer of romantic fiction; pseudonym of *Mary Mackay*. The sales of her novels *Thelma* (1887), *Barabbas* (1893), and *The Sorrows of Satan* (1895) broke records for book sales in the UK, although her popularity was not matched by critical acclaim.

Cor·i·o·la·nus |ˌkawrēə'lānəs|, Gnaeus Marcius (6th–5th century BC) Roman general, who got his name from the capture of the Volscian town of Corioli. According to legend, after his banishment from Rome he led a Volscian army against the city and was turned back only by the pleas of his mother and wife.

Cor·mack |'kawrmək|, Allan MacLeod (1924–98) U.S. physicist and educator, born in South Africa. He helped to invent the CAT scan. Nobel Prize, 1979.

Cor·neille |kawr'nā|, Pierre (1606–84) French dramatist, generally regarded as the founder of classical French tragedy. Notable plays: *Le Cid* (1637), *Cinna* (1641), and *Polyeucte* (1643).

Cor·nell |kawr'nel|, Ezra (1807–74) U.S. financier and philanthropist. He was an organizer of the Magnetic Telegraph Co., which connected New York and Washington. He later helped found the Western Union Telegraph Co.

Cor·nish |'kawrniSH|, Samuel E (1793–1858) U.S. journalist. He cofounded the first newspaper for African Americans, *Freedom's Journal* (1827).

Corn·wal·lis |ˌkawrn'wäləs|, Charles, 1st Marquis (1738–1805) English soldier. He surrendered the British forces at Yorktown (1781), ending the fighting in the American Revolution.

Co·ro·na·do |ˌkawrə'nädō|, Francisco Vásquez de (1510?–54) Spanish explorer. His explorations into Arizona and New Mexico from Mexico opened the Southwest to Spanish colonization.

Co·rot |kə'rō|, Jean-Baptiste-Camille (1796–1875) French landscape painter, who worked in an essentially classical style despite his contact with the Barbizon School. Corot had a significant influence on the Impressionists.

Cor·reg·gio |kə'rejēō|, Antonio Allegri da (1494–1534) Italian painter. The soft, sensual style of his devotional and mythological paintings influenced the rococo of the 18th century. He is best known for his frescoes in Parma Cathedral.

Cort |kawrt|, Henry (1740–1800) English ironmaster. He patented a process for producing iron bars by passing iron through grooved rollers, thus avoiding a hammering stage.

Côrte-Real |'kawrˌtə rē'äl|, Gaspar (1450?–?1501) Portuguese navigator and explorer. He explored the coasts of Labrador and Newfoundland (1500).

Cor·tés |kawr'tez|, Hernando (1485–1547) First of the Spanish conquistadors. Also **Cortez**. Cortés overthrew the Aztec empire, conquering its capital, Tenochtitlán, in 1519 and deposing its emperor, Montezuma. In 1521 he destroyed Tenochtitlán completely and established Mexico City as the new capital of Mexico (then called New Spain).

Cos·by |'käzbē|, Bill (1937–) U.S. comedian, actor, and author. Full name *William Henry Cosby, Jr.* He was the first African American to star in a weekly television drama ("I Spy"; 1965–68). His comedy series "The Cosby Show" (1984–92) was one of the most successful programs in television history. Notable books: *Fatherhood* (1987) and *Congratulations! Now What?: A Book for Graduates* (1999).

Co·sell |kō'sel|, Howard (1918–95)

U.S. sports journalist. He was a television and radio commentator whose abrasive "tell it like it is" style found many followers.

Cos·i·mo de' Me·di·ci |'käzə͵mō de me 'dēCHē| (1389–1464) Italian statesman and banker. Known as **Cosimo the Elder**. He laid the foundations for the Medici family's power in Florence, becoming the city's ruler in 1434 and using his considerable wealth to promote the arts and learning.

Cos·ta |'kawstə|, Lúcio (1902–63) French-born Brazilian architect, town planner, and architectural historian. He achieved a worldwide reputation with his design for Brazil's new capital, Brasilia, which was chosen by an international jury in 1956.

Cost·ner |'kawstnər|, Kevin (1955–) U.S. actor, director, and producer. Notable movies: *Dances with Wolves* (1990, Academy Award).

Cot·man |'kätmən|, John Sell (1782–1842) English watercolorist and landscape painter. He is regarded as one of the leading figures of the Norwich School.

Cot·sa·kos |kət'säkōs|, Christos Michael (1948–) U.S. businessman. He is the president and CEO of E*Trade Group, Inc. (1996–).

Cot·ten |'kätn|, Joseph (1905–94) U.S. actor. A star of Broadway (*The Philadelphia Story*, 1939), Hollywood (*Citizen Kane*, 1941), and television, his credits include over 60 movies.

Cot·ton |'kätn|, John (1585–1652) English Puritan clergyman. He was a 1633 emigrant to the Massachusetts Bay Colony and a leading exponent of Congregationalism.

Cot·trell |'kätrəl|, Frederick Gardner (1877–1948) U.S. physical chemist and inventor. He invented electrostatic precipitators (1911) and developed practical methods for producing synthetic ammonia.

Cou·ber·tin |kōō'bərtän|, Pierre de, Baron (1863–1937) French educator and sportsman. As president of the International Olympic Committee (1894–1925), he revived the Olympic Games.

Cou·lomb |'kōō͵läm|, Charles-Augustin de (1736–1806) French military

engineer. He is best known for Coulomb's Law (1785), which describes the inverse square law of electrostatic force. From this a quantity of electric charge may be defined.

Coul·ter |'kōltər|, Ernest Kent (1871?–1952) U.S. lawyer and humanitarian. A children's rights advocate in the legal system, he founded the Big Brother movement (1904) and was president of the Society for the Prevention of Cruelty to Children (1914–36).

Cou·pe·rin |͵kōōp'rän|, François (1668–1733) French composer, organist, and harpsichordist. A composer at the court of Louis XIV, he is principally known for his harpsichord works.

Cour·bet |kōōr'bā|, Gustave (1819–77) French painter. A leader of the 19th-century realist school of painting, he favored an unidealized choice of subject matter that did not exclude the ugly or vulgar. Notable works: *Burial at Ornans* (1850) and *Painter in his Studio* (1855).

Cour·ic |'kōōrik|, Katie (1957–) U.S. TV journalist. She coanchors NBC's *The Today Show* (1991–).

Cour·règes |kaw'reZH|, André (1923–) French fashion designer. He is famous for his futuristic and youth-oriented styles, in particular the use of plastic and metal and unisex fashion such as trouser suits for women.

Court |kawrt|, Margaret Smith (1942–) Australian tennis player. She won more Grand Slam events (66) than any other player.

Cour·tauld |kawr'tōld|, Samuel (1876–1947) English industrialist. He was a director of his family's silk firm and a collector of French Impressionist and post-Impressionist paintings. He presented his collection to the University of London, endowed the Courtauld Institute of Art, and bequeathed to it his house in Portman Square, London.

Cous·teau |kōō'stō|, Jacques-Yves (1910–97) French oceanographer and movie director. He devised the scuba apparatus, but is known primarily for several feature films and a popular television series on marine life.

Cou·sy |'kōōzē|, Bob (1928–) U.S. basketball player. Full name *Robert*

Joseph Cousy. Elected to the Basketball Hall of Fame (1970).

Cov·er·dale |'kəvər,dāl|, Miles (1488?–1569) English biblical scholar. He translated the first complete printed English Bible (1535), published in Zurich while he was in exile for preaching against confession and images. He also edited the Great Bible of 1539.

Cow·ard |'kowərd|, Sir Noël (Pierce) (1899–1973) English dramatist, actor, and composer. He is remembered for witty, satirical plays, such as *Hay Fever* (1925) and *Private Lives* (1930), as well as revues and musicals featuring songs such as "Mad Dogs and Englishmen" (1932).

Cow·en |'kowən|, Joshua Lionel (1877–1965) U.S. inventor. He invented batteries, electric fuses, and Lionel trains.

Cow·per |'ko͞opər|, William (1731–1800) English poet. He is best known for his long poem *The Task* (1785) and the comic ballad *John Gilpin* (1782).

Cox |käks|, James Middleton (1870–1957) U.S. newspaper publisher and politician. He was owner of the Dayton (Ohio) *Daily News*, the Springfield (Ohio) *Press-Republican*, and the Springfield *Sun*, and was a Democratic nominee for president of the U.S. in 1920.

Coxe |käks|, Tench (1755–1824) U.S. political economist. He was assistant U.S. secretary of the treasury (1790–92), commissioner of the revenue (1792–98), and purveyor of public supplies (1803–12).

Coz·zens |'kəzənz|, James Gould (1903–78) U.S. author. Notable works: *Guard of Honor* (1948, Pulitzer Prize) and *By Love Possessed* (1957).

Crabbe |kræb|, George (1754–1832) English poet. He is best known for grimly realistic narrative poems, such as "The Village" (1783) and "The Borough" (1810); the latter included tales of Peter Grimes and Ellen Orford and later provided the subject matter for Benjamin Britten's opera *Peter Grimes* (1945).

Cram |kræm|, Ralph Adams (1863–1942) U.S. architect. Notable designs: Cathedral of St. John the Divine (1912) in New York City, and Princeton University (1909–31).

Cra·nach |'krænək| German painters. **Lucas Cranach** (1472–1553); known as **Cranach the Elder**. He was a member of the Danube School who was noted for his early religious pictures, such as *The Rest of the Flight into Egypt* (1504). He also painted portraits, including several of Martin Luther. His son, **Lucas Cranach** (1515–86), was known as **Cranach the Younger**. He continued to work in the same tradition as his father.

Crane |krān|, Hart (1899–1932) U.S. poet. Full name *Harold Hart Crane*. He published only two books before committing suicide: the collection *White Buildings* (1926) and *The Bridge* (1930), a mystical epic poem concerned with American life and consciousness.

Crane |krān|, Roy (1901–77) U.S. cartoonist. Full name *Royston C. Crane*. One of the earliest cartoonists to produce an adventure strip, he was the creator of the characters Wash Tubbs, Captain Easy, and Buz Sawyer.

Crane |krān|, Stephen (1871–1900) U.S. writer. His reputation rests on his novel *The Red Badge of Courage* (1895), a study of an inexperienced soldier in the Civil War. It was hailed as a masterpiece of psychological realism, even though Crane himself had no personal experience of war.

Cran·mer |'krænmər|, Thomas (1489–1556) English Protestant cleric and martyr. After helping to negotiate Henry VIII's divorce from Catherine of Aragon, he was appointed the first Protestant Archbishop of Canterbury in 1532. He was responsible for liturgical reform and the compilation of the Book of Common Prayer (1549). In the reign of Mary Tudor, Cranmer was tried for treason and heresy and burned at the stake.

Cras·sus |'kræsəs|, Marcus Licinius (*c.* 115–53 BC) Roman politician. After defeating the slave rebellion led by Spartacus in 71 BC, Crassus joined Caesar and Pompey in the First Triumvirate in 60. In 55 he was made consul and given a special command in Syria, where, after some successes, he was defeated and killed.

Cra•ter |'krātər|, Joseph Force (1889–?1937) U.S. jurist. He disappeared on August 6, 1930, while hearing a case on the New York Supreme Court; his disappearance was linked to possible political corruption. He was never found but was declared dead in July 1937.

Craw•ford |'krawfərd| Family name of **Thomas Crawford** (1814–57), a U.S. sculptor. His "Armed Freedom" crowns the dome of the National Capitol; he also sculpted the pediments in the Senate wing of the Capitol. His son, **Francis Marion Crawford** (1854–1909), was a U.S. novelist, born in Italy.

Craw•ford |'krawfərd|, Cindy (1966–) U.S. model.

Craw•ford |'krawfərd|, Joan (1908–73) U.S. movie actress. Born *Lucille LeSueur*. Her movie career lasted for over forty years, during which she played the female lead in movies such as *Rain* (1932), *The Women* (1939), and *Mildred Pierce* (1945). She later appeared in mature roles, such as in the horror movie *Whatever Happened to Baby Jane?* (1962).

Craw•ford |'krawfərd|, Osbert Guy Stanhope (1886–1957) British archaeologist. He pioneered the use of aerial photography in the detection of previously unlocated or buried archeological sites and monuments.

Cray |krā|, Seymour Robert (1925–96) U.S. computer designer. He designed the first computer made with transistors, the Cray-1 and Cray-2.

Cra•zy Horse |'krāzē ,hawrs| (*c.* 1842–77) Sioux chief. Sioux name *Ta-Sunko-Witko*. In 1876 he led a successful rearguard action of Sioux and Cheyenne warriors against U.S. army forces in Montana. A leading figure in the resistance to white settlement on American Indian land, he was at the center of the confederation that defeated General Custer at Little Bighorn (1876). He surrendered in 1877 and was killed in custody.

Creel |krēl|, George Edward (1876–1953) U.S. journalist and author. He founded and edited the *Kansas City Independent* (1899–1909).

Cree•ley |'krēlē|, Robert White (1926–) U.S. poet. He was editor of *Black Mountain Review* (1954–57).

Cret |krā|, Paul Philippe (1876–1945) U.S. architect, born in France. He designed the Folger Shakespeare Library and the Federal Reserve Board building in Washington, D.C.

Crews |krōoz|, Harry (1935–) U.S. author and educator.

Crich•ton |'krītn|, James (1560–1582) Scottish adventurer. Known as **the Admirable Crichton**. Crichton was an accomplished swordsman, poet, and scholar. He served in the French army and made a considerable impression on French and Italian universities with his skills as a polyglot orator.

Crich•ton |'krītn|, Michael (1942–) U.S. author. Notable novels: *Jurassic Park* (1990) and *The Lost World* (1995).

Crick |krik|, Francis Harry Compton (1916–) English biophysicist. Together with J. D. Watson he proposed the double helix structure of the DNA molecule, thus broadly explaining how genetic information is carried in living organisms and how genes replicate. Shared the Nobel Prize for Physiology or Medicine (1962).

Crip•pen |'kripən|, Hawley Harvey (1862–1910) U.S.-born British murderer. Known as **Doctor Crippen**. Crippen poisoned his wife at their London home and sailed to Canada with his former secretary. His arrest in Canada was achieved through the intervention of radiotelegraphy, the first case of its use in apprehending a criminal; Crippen was later hanged.

Cro•ce |'krōcHā|, Benedetto (1866–1952) Italian philosopher and politician. In his *Philosophy of Spirit*, he denied the physical reality of a work of art and identified philosophical endeavor with a methodological approach to history. A former minister of education, he helped to rebuild democracy in Italy after the fall of Mussolini.

Crock•er |'kräkər|, Charles (1822–88) U.S. financier. He merged the Southern Pacific and Central Pacific railroads (1884).

Crock•er |'kräkər|, Francis Bacon (1861–1921) U.S. electrical engineer. Along with others, he developed the standard electrical motor (1886).

Crock•ett |'kräkət|, Davy (1786–1836)

U.S. frontiersman, soldier, and politician. Full name *David Crockett*. He was a member of the U.S. House of Representatives (1827–35) and cultivated the image of a rough backwoods legislator. On leaving politics he returned to the frontier, where he took up the cause of independence for Texas and was killed at the siege of the Alamo.

Croe·sus |'krēsəs| (died *c*. 546 BC) The last king of Lydia (*c*. 560–546 BC). Renowned for his great wealth, he subjugated the Greek cities on the coast of Asia Minor before being overthrown by Cyrus the Great of Persia.

Cro·ker |'krōkər|, Richard (1841–1922) U.S. politician, born in Ireland. Known as **Boss Croker**. He was recognized as the leader of Tammany Hall (1884–1901).

Cro·ly |'krōlē| U.S. family of editors. Irish-born **David Goodman Croly** (1829–89), a journalist, was the managing editor of *New York World* (1862–72) and editor of the *Daily Graphic* (1873–78). His wife, **Jane Cunningham Croly** (1829–1901), born in England, was an editor. Pseudonym **Jennie June**. She founded the women's club Sorosis and the Woman's Press Club in New York. Their son, **Herbert David Croly** (1869–1930), an editor and author, founded *The New Republic*.

Crome |krōm|, John (1768–1821) English painter. Founder and leading member of the Norwich School, he later developed a distinctive romantic style of his own, exemplified in such landscapes as *Slate Quarries*.

Cromp·ton |'krämtn|, Richmal (1890–1969) English writer. Pseudonym of *Richmal Crompton Lamburn*. She made her name with *Just William* (1922), a collection of stories for children about a mischievous schoolboy, William Brown. She published a further thirty-seven collections based on the same character, as well as some fifty books for adults.

Cromp·ton |'krämtn|, Samuel (1753–1827) English inventor. Famed for his invention of the spinning mule, he lacked the means to obtain a patent and sold his rights to an industrialist for £67. The House of Commons subse-quently gave him £5,000 in compensation.

Crom·well |'krämwel|, Oliver (1599–1658) English general and statesman. He was Lord Protector of the Commonwealth (1653–58). Cromwell was the leader of the victorious Parliamentary forces (or Roundheads) in the English Civil War. As head of state he styled himself Lord Protector, and refused Parliament's offer of the Crown in 1657. His rule was notable for its Puritan reforms in the Church of England. He was briefly succeeded by his son **Richard** (1626–1712), who was forced into exile in 1659.

Crom·well |'krämwel|, Thomas (1485?–1540) English statesman. He was chief minister to Henry VIII (1531–40). He presided over the king's divorce from Catherine of Aragon (1533) and his break with the Roman Catholic Church as well as the dissolution of the monasteries and the 1534 Act of Supremacy. He fell from favor over Henry's marriage to Anne of Cleves and was executed on a charge of treason.

Cro·nin |'krōnən|, A. J. (1896–1981) Scottish novelist. Full name *Archibald Joseph Cronin*. His novels, including *The Citadel* (1937), often reflect his early experiences as a doctor.

Cron·kite |'kräNGkīt|, Walter Leland, Jr. (1916–) U.S. television journalist. He anchored the "CBS Evening News" from its debut (1962) until his retirement (1981).

Crook |krŏŏk|, George (1829–90) U.S. army officer. He fought against American Indians and was defeated by Crazy Horse (1876); he also fought against the Apaches and Geronimo (1882–85).

Crookes |krŏŏks|, Sir William (1832–1919) English physicist and chemist. In 1861 he discovered the element thallium. This led him indirectly to the invention of the radiometer in 1875. He later developed a vacuum tube (the precursor of the X-ray tube) and in 1903 invented the spinthariscope.

Cros·by |'krawzbē|, Bing (1904–77) U.S. singer and actor; born *Harry Lillis Crosby*. His songs include "White Christmas" (from the movie *Holiday*

Inn, 1942) one of the best selling songs of all time. He also starred in the series of *Road* movies (1940–62) with Bob Hope and Dorothy Lamour.

Cros·by |'krawzbē|, David (1941–) U.S. rock guitarist and singer. Born *David Van Cartland*. He was a member of the Byrds and of Crosby, Stills, Nash (and Young).

Cross |kraws|, (Charles) Whitman (1854–1949) U.S. geologist. With Iddings, Pirsson, and Washington, he wrote *Quantitative Classification of Igneous Rocks* (1903).

Crow |krō|, Sheryl (1963–) U.S. rock singer, songwriter, and guitarist. Grammy Awards, 1997.

Crown·in·shield |'krownən,SHēld|, Francis Welch (1872–1947) U.S. editor, born in France. He was the publisher of *The Bookman* (1895–1900) and editor of *Vanity Fair* (1914–36).

Cruik·shank |'krŏŏk,SHæNGk|, George (1792–1878) English painter, illustrator, and caricaturist, the most eminent political cartoonist of his day. His later work includes illustrations for Charles Dickens's *Sketches by Boz* (1836), and a series of etchings supporting the temperance movement.

Cruise |krŏŏz|, Tom (1962–) U.S. actor. Born *Thomas Cruise Mapother, IV*.

Crumb |krəm|, Robert (1943–) U.S. cartoonist and author. He was the leading member of a group of "underground" cartoonists producing controversial work satirizing American society.

Crys·tal |'kristl|, Billy (1947–) U.S. actor, comedian, writer, and director.

Cu·kor |'kŏŏkər|, George Dewey (1899–1983) U.S. movie director. Notable movies: *My Fair Lady* (1964, Academy Award).

Cul·bert·son |'kəlbərtsən|, Ely (1891–1955) U.S. bridge player. An authority on contract bridge, he revolutionized the game by formalizing a system of bidding. This helped to establish this form of the game in preference to auction bridge.

Cul·ha·ne |kəl'hānē|, Shamus (1908–96) U.S. producer and animator. He was an animator with Walt Disney Studios and others before opening his own studio (1946). Notable movies: *Snow White* (1937, Academy Award).

Cul·len |'kələn|, Countee (1903–46) U.S. poet and leader of the Harlem Renaissance.

Cul·pep·er |'kəl,pepər|, Nicholas (1616–54) English herbalist. His *Complete Herbal* (1653) popularized herbalism and, despite embracing ideas of astrology and the doctrine of signatures, was important in the development of botany and pharmacology.

Cum·ber·land |'kəmbərlənd|, William Augustus, Duke of (1721–65) English military commander, third son of King George II. He gained great notoriety (and his nickname "the Butcher") for the severity of his suppression of the Jacobite clans in the aftermath of his victory at the Battle of Culloden in Scotland (1746).

cum·mings |'kəmiNGz|, e. e. (1894–1962) U.S. poet and novelist; full name *Edward Estlin Cummings*. His poems are characterized by their experimental typography (most notably in the avoidance of capital letters), technical skill, frank vocabulary, and the sharpness of his satire.

Cum·mings |'kəmiNGz|, Homer Stillé (1870–1956) U.S. lawyer and politician. As U.S. attorney general (1933–39), he drafted Pres. Franklin D. Roosevelt's plan to "pack" the U.S. Supreme Court (1937).

Cu·nard |kyŏŏ'närd|, Sir Samuel (1787–1865) Canadian-born British shipowner. One of the pioneers of the regular transatlantic passenger service, he founded the steamship company that still bears his name with the aid of a contract to carry the mail between Britain and Canada. The first such voyage for the company was made in 1840.

Cun·ning·ham |'kəniNG,hæm|, Imogen (1883–1976) U.S. photographer. She is best known for her black-and-white portraits and nature studies.

Cun·ning·ham |'kəniNG,hæm|, Merce (1919–) U.S. dancer and choreographer. A dancer with the Martha Graham Dance Company (1939–45), he began to experiment with choreography, collaborating with the composer John Cage in solo performances in 1944. He formed his own company in 1953 and explored new abstract directions for modern dance.

Cu·rie |'kyŏŏrē| French physicists. **Pierre Curie** (1859–1906) and his wife, Polish-born **Marie Curie** 1867–1934), were pioneers in studying radioactivity. Working together on the mineral pitchblende, they discovered the elements polonium and radium, for which they shared the 1903 Nobel Prize for Physics with A. H. Becquerel. After her husband's accidental death Marie received another Nobel Prize (for chemistry) in 1911 for her isolation of radium. She died of leukemia, caused by prolonged exposure to radioactive materials.

Cur·ley |'kərlē|, James Michael (1874–1958) U.S. politician. An urban political boss, he was a member of the U.S. House of Representatives (1911–14, 1943–47), mayor of Boston (four terms between 1914 and 1950), and governor of Massachusetts (1935–37).

Cur·ri·er |'kərēər|, Nathaniel (1813–88) U.S. lithographer. He partnered with James Ives in 1857 to establish the company of Currier & Ives, which produced hand-colored prints of American scenes.

Cur·ry |'kərē|, John (Anthony) (1949–94) English figure skater.

Cur·ry |'kərē|, John Steuart (1897–1946) U.S. artist. Much of his work portrayed legendary American folk heroes, such as his depiction of abolitionist John Brown in *Tragic Prelude*, part of a mural series (1938–40) in the Kansas State Capitol.

Cur·tin |'kərtn|, Jane (1947–) U.S. actress. She was an original cast member of television's "Saturday Night Live" (1975–80) and later starred in the television sitcom "Third Rock from the Sun."

Cur·tin |'kərtn|, John (Joseph Ambrose) (1885–1945) Australian Labour statesman, prime minister (1941–45).

Cur·tis |'kərtəs| U.S. family, including: **Benjamin Robbins Curtis** (1809–74), a U.S. Supreme Court justice (1851–57). He resigned in protest over the Supreme Court's handling of the Dred Scott case. He served as chief counsel to Andrew Johnson during Johnson's impeachment. His brother, **George Tick-**nor Curtis** (1812–94), a lawyer and author, argued for the plaintiff before the U.S. Supreme Court in the Dred Scott case.

Cur·tis |'kərtəs|, Charles (1860–1936) U.S. politician. A member from Kansas of the U.S. House of Representatives (1893–1907) and the U.S. Senate (1907–13, 1915–29), he was vice president of the U.S. (1929–33) under Herbert Hoover.

Cur·tis |'kərtəs|, Cyrus Hermann Kotzschmar (1850–1933) U.S. publisher. He was head of the Curtis Publishing Co. (1890–1933), which published the *Ladies' Home Journal*, the *Saturday Evening Post*, and the *Philadelphia Inquirer*.

Cur·tis |'kərtəs|, Edward Sheriff (1868–1952) U.S. photographer. He photographed the Harriman Alaskan expedition (1899) and was known for his photographs of American Indians.

Cur·tis |'kərtəs|, George William (1824–92) U.S. author. He was a member of the Brook Farm community, a leader in civil service reform, and the editor of *Harper's Weekly* from 1863.

Cur·tiss |'kərtəs|, Glenn (Hammond) (1878–1930) U.S. air pioneer and aircraft designer. In 1908 Curtiss made the first public U.S. flight of more than a kilometer. He built his first airplane in 1909, invented the aileron, and demonstrated the first practical seaplane two years later.

Cur·tiz |'kərtəs|, Michael (1888–1962) U.S. director, born in Hungary. Notable movies: *Casablanca* (1943, Academy Award)

Cush·ing |'kŏŏSHiNG|, Harvey Williams (1869–1939) American surgeon. He introduced techniques that greatly increased the likelihood of success in neurosurgical operations, and described the hormonal disorder that was later named after him.

Cush·ing |'kŏŏSHiNG|, Peter (1913–94) English actor, known particularly for his roles in horror movies.

Cush·ing |'kŏŏSHiNG|, William (1732–1810) U.S. Supreme Court justice (1789–1810). He also served as Chief Justice of the Massachusetts Supreme Court (1777–89).

Cus·ter |'kəstər|, George Armstrong (1839–76) U.S. cavalry officer He served with distinction in the Civil War, but led his 266 men to their deaths in a clash (popularly known as Custer's Last Stand) with the Sioux at Little Bighorn in Montana (1876). Controversy over his conduct in the final battle still continues.

Cuth·bert |'kəTHbərt|, St. (635–687) English monk, bishop, and missionary to Northumbria. Feast day, March 20.

Cut·ter |'kətər|, Charles Ammi (1837–1903) U.S. librarian. He developed a system of labeling books using initial letters and numbers for the authors' names.

Cu·vier |koōvē'ā|, Georges Léopold Chrétien Frédéric Dagobert, Baron (1769–1832) French naturalist. Cuvier founded the science of paleontology and made pioneering studies in comparative anatomy and classification.

Cym·be·line |'simbəlēn| (died c. 42 AD) British chieftain. Also **Cunobelinus**. A powerful ruler, he made Camulodunum (Colchester) his capital, and established a mint there. He was the subject of a medieval fable used by Shakespeare for his play *Cymbeline.*

Cyn·e·wulf |'kinə,woolf| (9th century) Anglo-Saxon poet. Modern scholarship attributes four poems to him: *Juliana, Elene, The Fates of the Apostles,* and *Christ II.*

Cyp·ri·an |'siprēən|, St. (died 258) Carthaginian bishop and martyr. The author of a work on the nature of true unity in the Church in its relation to the episcopate, he was martyred in the reign of the Roman emperor Valerian. Feast day, September 16 or 26.

Cyr·a·no de Ber·ge·rac |,sirənō də 'bərzHəræk|, Savinien (1619–55) French soldier, duelist, and writer. He is chiefly remembered for the large number of duels that he fought (many on ac-

count of his proverbially large nose), as immortalized in a play by Edmond Rostand (*Cyrano de Bergerac,* 1897).

Cyr·il |'sirəl|, St. (c. 827–69) Greek missionary. The invention of the Cyrillic alphabet is ascribed to him. He and his brother, St. Methodius, were sent to Moravia where they taught in the vernacular, which they adopted also for the liturgy, and circulated a Slavic version of the scriptures. Feast day (in the Eastern Church) May 11; (in the Western Church) February 14.

Cyr·il of Al·ex·an·dria |,sirəl əv æleg-'zændrēə|, St. (c. 375–444) Doctor of the Church and patriarch of Alexandria. A champion of orthodoxy, he is best known for his vehement opposition to the views of the patriarch of Constantinople, Nestorius, whose condemnation he secured at the Council of Ephesus in 431. Feast day, February 9.

Cy·rus[1] |'sīrəs| (died c. 530 BC) king of Persia 559–530 BC and founder of the Achaemenid dynasty, father of Cambyses; known as **Cyrus the Great**. He defeated the Median empire in 550 BC and went on to conquer Asia Minor, Babylonia, Syria, Palestine, and most of the Iranian plateau. He is said to have ruled with wisdom and moderation, maintaining good relations with the Jews (whom he freed from the Babylonian Captivity) and the Phoenicians.

Cy·rus[2] |'sīrəs| (424–401 BC) Persian prince; known as **Cyrus the Younger**. On the death of his father, Darius II, in 405 BC, Cyrus led an army of mercenaries against his elder brother, who had succeeded to the throne as Artaxerxes II. His campaign is recounted by the historian Xenophon.

Czer·ny |'cHərnē|, Karl (1791–1857) Austrian pianist, teacher, and composer. The bulk of his output is made up of more than 1,000 exercises and studies for the piano.

Dd

Dadd |dæd|, Richard (1819–87) English painter. After killing his father while suffering a mental breakdown, he was confined in asylums, where he produced a series of visionary paintings.

da Ga•ma |dəˈgämə|, Vasco (*c.*1469–1524) Portuguese explorer. He led the first European expedition around the Cape of Good Hope in 1497, sighting and naming Natal on Christmas Day before crossing the Indian Ocean and arriving in Calicut (Kozhikode, in India) in 1498. He also established colonies in Mozambique.

Da•guerre |dəˈger|, Louis-Jacques-Mandé (1789–1851) French physicist, painter, and inventor of the first practical photographic process. He went into partnership with **Joseph-Nicéphore Niépce**, (1765–1833) to improve the latter's heliography process, and in 1839 he presented his daguerreotype process to the French Academy of Sciences.

Dahl |däl|, Roald (1916–90) British writer, of Norwegian descent. His fiction and drama, such as the short-story collection *Tales of the Unexpected* (1979), typically include macabre plots and unexpected outcomes. Notable works for children: *Charlie and the Chocolate Factory* (1964), and *The BFG* (1982).

Dahl•berg |ˈdälber|, Edward (1900–77) U.S. author. He wrote novels, including *Kentucky Blue Grass* (1932); essays, including *Can These Bones Live?* (1941); and an autobiography, *Because I Was Flesh* (1964).

Dai•ley |ˈdälē|, Janet (1944–) U.S. author. She wrote many historical and romantic novels.

Daim•ler |ˈdämlər|, Gottlieb Wilhelm (1834–1900) German engineer and automobile manufacturer. An employee of Nikolaus Otto, he produced a small engine using the Otto cycle in 1884 and made it propel a bicycle using gasoline. He founded the Daimler automobile company in 1890.

Da•la•dier |dälä'dyā|, Édouard (1884–1970) French prime minister (1933, 1934, 1938–40).

Da•lai La•ma |ˈdälē ˈlämə| (1935–) Tibetan Buddhist leader. Born *Tenzin Gyatso*. He won a Nobel Peace Prize (1989) for his nonviolent movement to end Chinese domination of Tibet.

Dale |dāl|, Sir Henry Hallett (1875–1968) English physiologist and pharmacologist. He investigated the role of histamine in anaphylactic shock and allergy, and the role of acetylcholine as a natural neurotransmitter. Nobel Prize for Physiology or Medicine (1936).

Dale |dāl|, Sir Thomas (died 1619) English naval commander and colonial administrator. As colonial governor of Virginia, he enforced "Dale's Code," a legislative code that caused 1611–16 to be known as "5 years of slavery."

d'Alem•bert |dälän'ber|, Jean Le Rond (1717–83) French mathematician, physicist, and philosopher. His most famous work was the *Traité de dynamique* (1743), in which he developed his own laws of motion. From 1746 to 1758 he was Diderot's chief collaborator on the *Encyclopédie*.

Da•ley |ˈdālē|, Richard Joseph (1902–76) U.S. politician. As mayor of Chicago (1955–76) he was known as a big-city boss; he also led the National Democratic Party.

Dal•hou•sie |dælˈhoōzē|, James Andrew Broun Ramsay, 1st Marquess of (1812–60) A British colonial administrator, he was a progressive governor general of India (1847–56).

Da•li |ˈdälē; däˈlē|, Salvador Felipe Jacinto (1904–89) Spanish painter. A surrealist, he portrayed dream images with almost photographic realism against backgrounds of arid Catalan landscapes. Dali also collaborated with Buñuel in the production of the movie *Un Chien andalou* (1928). Notable works: *The Persistence of Memory* (1931).

Dal•la•pic•co•la |ˌdäläpi'kōlə|, Luigi (1904–75) Italian composer. He combined serialism with lyrical polyphonic writing. Notable works: *Songs of Prison* (1938–41).

Dal•las |ˈdæləs|, U.S. political family.

Jamaican-born **Alexander James Dallas** (1759–1817) was a lawyer and secretary of the treasury (1814–16). He restored public faith in U.S. credit after the War of 1812; he also established the second bank of the U.S. His son **George Mifflin Dallas** (1792–1864) was U.S. vice president (1845–49). The city of Dallas, Texas, is named for him.

Dal·ton |'dawltən|, John (1766–1844) English chemist, father of modern atomic theory. He defined an atom as the smallest part of a substance that could participate in a chemical reaction and argued that elements are composed of atoms. He stated that elements combine in definite proportion and produced the first table of comparative atomic weights.

Dal·trey |'dältrē; 'dawltrē|, Roger Harry (1944–   ) British rock singer. He was a member of the rock band The Who.

Da·ly |'dālē|, (John) Augustin (1838–99) U.S. playwright and theatrical manager. He managed theaters in New York and London while also writing drama criticism for New York daily newspapers.

Da·ly |'dālē|, Marcus (1841–1900) U.S. businessman. In partnership with others, he organized the Anaconda Mining Company (1891) and the Amalgamated Copper Company (1891).

Da·ly |'dālē|, Tyne (1947–   ) U.S. actress. She won four Emmys as costar of the television series "Cagney and Lacey."

Dam |dæm|, (Carl Peter) Henrik (1895–1976) Danish biochemist. He discovered vitamin K and shared the 1943 Nobel Prize for Medicine or Physiology with E. A. Doisy.

Da·ma·di·an, Raymond Vahan (1936–   ) U.S. biophysicist. He invented the magnetic resonance imaging (MRI) scanner (1989).

Da·mien |'dāmēən|, Father Joseph (1840–89) Belgian priest. Born *Joseph Damien de Veuster*. He ministered to a Hawaiian leper colony from 1873 until his death from leprosy.

Da·mon |'dāmən|, Matt (1970–   ) U.S. actor. Notable movies: *Good Will Hunting* (1997, Academy Award).

Dam·pi·er |'dæmpēər|, William (1652–1715) English explorer, buccaneer, and adventurer. He is notable for having sailed around the world twice. In 1683 he set out from Panama, crossing the Pacific and reaching England again in 1691; in 1699 the government commissioned him to explore the northwest coast of Australia.

Dam·rosch |'däm,rawsH|, Leopold (1832–85) U.S. symphony conductor, born in Prussia. As founder and conductor of the New York Symphony, he introduced U.S. audiences to operas by Wagner and symphonic music by Brahms and other Europeans. When he died, his son Walter (1862–1950) assumed his post at the New York Symphony and also conducted at the Metropolitan Opera.

Da·na |'dānə|, Charles Anderson (1819–97) U.S. newspaper editor. He was a resident of the Brook Farm commune (1841–46) and the owner and editor of the *New York Sun* (1868–97).

Da·na |'dānə|, James Dwight (1813–95) U.S. naturalist, geologist, and mineralogist. He founded an important classification of minerals based on chemistry and physics. His view of the earth as a unit was an evolutionary one, but he was slow to accept Darwin's theory of evolution.

Da·na |'dānə|, Richard Henry (1815–82) U.S. adventurer, lawyer, and writer, known for his classic account of his voyage on a brig from Boston around Cape Horn to California, *Two Years Before the Mast* (1840).

Dan·dridge |'dændrij|, Dorothy (1923–65) U.S. actress. She was the first African-American woman nominated for an Oscar in the Best Actress category (*Carmen Jones*, 1954).

Dane |dān|, Nathan (1752–1835) U.S. jurist. He was a delegate to the Continental Congress (1785–87), and as a Massachusetts state senator (1790–98) revised many Massachusetts laws.

Dan·iel |'dænyəl|, Jack Newton (1846–1911) U.S. entrepreneur. He founded the Jack Daniels distillery.

Dan·iel |'dænyəl|, Peter Vivian (1784–1860) U.S. Supreme Court justice (1841–60).

Da·ni·lo·va |də'nēləvə|, Alexandra (1904–97) U.S. ballet dancer and teacher, born in Russia. She taught at the School of American Ballet (1964–89).

Dan·nay |də'nā|, Frederic (1905–82) U.S. author. With Manfred Bennington Lee (1905–71), he wrote over 40 detective novels under the pseudonym **Ellery Queen** and a series of novels under the pseudonym **Barnaby Ross.**

d'An·nun·zio |dän'nŏŏntsyō|, Gabriele (1863–1938) Italian novelist, dramatist, and poet. He is best known for his "Romances of the Rose" trilogy, including *The Triumph of Death* (1894), which shows the influence of Nietzsche.

Dan·te |'däntā| (1265–1321) Italian poet; full name *Dante Alighieri*. His reputation rests chiefly on *The Divine Comedy* (c.1309–20), an epic poem describing his spiritual journey through Hell and Purgatory and finally to Paradise. His love for Beatrice Portinari is described in *Vita nuova* (c.1290).

Dan·ton |'dæntən|, Georges-Jacques (1759–94) French revolutionary. A noted orator, he won great popularity in the early days of the French Revolution. He was initially an ally of Robespierre but later revolted against the severity of the Revolutionary Tribunal and was executed on Robespierre's orders.

Da Pon·te |dä'pōntā|, Lorenzo (1749–1838) Italian poet and librettist; born *Emmanuele Conegliano*. He became poet to the Court Opera in Vienna in 1784 and wrote the libretti for Mozart's *Marriage of Figaro* (1786), *Don Giovanni* (1787), and *Così fan tutte* (1790).

Dare |der|, Virginia (1587–?) First English child born in North America. Born on Roanoke Island, Virginia, to Ananias Dare and Elinor White, she disappeared with the other 117 Roanoke colonists, as was discovered in 1591.

Dar·in |'derən|, Bobby (1936–73) U.S. pop singer and songwriter. Born *Walden Robert Cassotto*. He was a film star and teen idol of the 1950s. Notable songs: "Splish Splash" and "Mack the Knife."

Da·ri·us I |də'rīəs; 'derdə'rīəs; 'derēəs| (550–486 BC) king of Persia 521–486 BC. Known as **Darius the Great**. He divided the empire into provinces, governed by satraps, developed commerce, built a network of roads, and connected the Nile with the Red Sea by canal. After a revolt by the Greek cities in Ionia (499–494 BC) he invaded Greece but was defeated at Marathon (490 BC).

Dar·ley |'därlē|, Felix Octavius Carr (1822–88) U.S. illustrator and author. He illustrated the works of Irving, Cooper, Longfellow, Dickens, and others.

Dar·ling |'därliNG|, Jay Norwood (1876–1962) U.S. political cartoonist. Pseudonym **Ding**. He worked for the *Des Moines Register* (1906–11; 1913–49) and was nationally syndicated from 1917. Pulitzer Prizes, 1923 and 1943.

Darn·ley |'därnlē|, Henry Stewart, Lord (1545–65) Scottish nobleman, second husband of Mary, Queen of Scots, and father of James I of England. Also **Henry Stuart**. He was implicated in the murder of his wife's secretary Rizzio in 1566, and was later killed in a mysterious gunpowder explosion in Edinburgh.

Dar·row |'derō|, Clarence Seward (1857–1938) U.S. lawyer. He served as defense counsel in several well-publicized trials, including that of John T. Scopes of Dayton, Tennessee, who was charged with violating state law for teaching evolution in a public school (1925).

Dart |därt|, Raymond Arthur (1893–1988) Australian-born South African anthropologist and anatomist. In 1925 he found the first specimen of a hominid for which he coined the genus name *Australopithecus*.

Dar·win |'därwən| English scientists. **Erasmus Darwin** (1731–1802) was a physician, scientist, inventor, and poet. He is chiefly remembered for his scientific and technical writing, much of which appeared in the form of long poems. These include *Zoonomia* (1794–96), which proposed a Lamarckian view of evolution. He was the grandfather of Francis Galton (see GALTON, FRANCIS) and **Charles (Robert) Darwin** (1809–82), a natural historian and geologist, proponent of the theory of evolution by natural selection. Darwin was the naturalist on HMS *Beagle* for its voyage around the southern hemisphere (1831–36), during which he collected the material that became the basis for his ideas on natural selection. His works *On the Origin of Species* (1859) and *The Descent of Man* (1871) had a fundamental effect on the concepts of nature and humanity's place within it.

Dau•bi•gny |ˌdōbē'nyā|, Charles-François (1817–78) French landscape painter. He was a member of the Barbizon School and is often regarded as a linking figure between this group and the Impressionists.

Dau•det |dō'dā|, Alphonse (1840–97) French novelist and dramatist. He is best known for his sketches of life in his native Provence, particularly the *Lettres de mon moulin* (1869).

Daugh•er•ty |'dōərtē|, Harry Micajah (1860–1941) U.S. politician. A U.S. attorney general (1921–24), he managed the political career of Warren Harding. In 1927, he was tried and acquitted of charges of conspiracy to defraud the U.S. government.

Daum•ier |dōm'yā|, Honoré (1840–97) French painter and lithographer. From the 1830s he worked as a cartoonist for periodicals such as *Charivari*, where he produced lithographs satirizing French society and politics.

Dav•en•port |'dævən‚pawrt|, Charles Benedict (1866–1944) U.S. zoologist, eugenicist, and author.

Dav•en•port |'dævən‚pawrt|, John (1597–1670) U.S. clergyman, born in England. He was the Puritan founder of the New Haven Colony and of the Third (Old South) Church, Boston.

Da•vid |'dāvəd| (died *c.* 962 BC) king of Judah and Israel *c.*1000–*c.*962 BC. In the biblical account, he was the youngest son of Jesse. He killed the Philistine Goliath and, on Saul's death, became king, making Jerusalem his capital. He is traditionally regarded as the author of the Psalms, although this has been disputed.

Da•vid |'dāvəd| the name of two kings of Scotland: **David I** (*c.* 1084–1153; reigned 1124–53). He was the sixth son of Malcolm III. In 1136 he invaded England in support of his niece Matilda's claim to the throne, but was defeated at the Battle of the Standard in 1138. **David II** (1324–71; reigned 1329–71)

was the son of Robert the Bruce. His reign witnessed a renewal of fighting with England, with Edward III supporting the pretender Edward de Baliol. His death without issue left the throne to the Stuarts.

Da•vid |'dāvəd|, Jacques-Louis (1748–1825) French painter, famous for neoclassical paintings such as *The Oath of the Horatii* (1784). He became actively involved in the French Revolution, voting for the death of Louis XVI and supporting Robespierre.

Da•vid |'dāvəd|, St. (*c.* 520–600) Welsh monk; Welsh name **Dewi**. Since the 12th century he has been regarded as the patron saint of Wales. Little is known of his life, but it is generally accepted that he transferred the center of Welsh ecclesiastical administration from Caerleon to Mynyw (now St. David's). Feast day, March 1.

Da•vies |'dāvēz|, W. H. (1871–1940) English poet; full name *William Henry Davies*. He emigrated to the U.S. and lived as a vagrant and laborer, writing *The Autobiography of a Super-Tramp* (1908) about his experiences.

Da•vies |'dāvēz|, Arthur Bowen (1862–1928) U.S. artist. He painted romantic landscapes and experimented with Cubism.

Da•vies |'dāvēz|, Ray (1944–) British musician. He was a rock guitarist and vocalist with The Kinks.

Da•vies |'dāvēz|, (William) Robertson (1913–95) Canadian novelist, dramatist, and journalist. He won international recognition with his Deptford trilogy of novels, comprising *Fifth Business* (1970), *The Manticore* (1972), and *World of Wonders* (1975).

da Vin•ci |də'vinCHē|, Leonardo (1452–1519) see LEONARDO DA VINCI.

Da•vis |'dāvəs|, Alexander Jackson (1803–92) U.S. architect. He is known for his Gothic and Italianate country houses.

Da•vis |'dāvəs|, Angela Yvonne (1944–) U.S. civil rights leader and author.

Da•vis |'dāvəs|, Benjamin Oliver (1877–1970) U.S. military leader. He was the first African-American general in the U.S. Army (1940).

Da•vis |'dāvəs|, Bette (1908–89) U.S. actress; born *Ruth Elizabeth Davis*. She established her Hollywood career playing a number of strong, independent female characters in such movies as *Dangerous* (1935). Her flair for suggesting the macabre and menacing emerged in later movies, such as *Whatever Happened to Baby Jane?* (1962).

Da•vis |'dāvəs|, Charles Henry (1807–77) U.S. naval officer. He commanded a Union gunboat flotilla on the Mississippi (1862).

Da•vis |'dāvəs|, David (1815–86) U.S. Supreme Court justice (1862–77).

Da•vis |'dāvəs|, Dwight Filley (1879–1945) U.S. public official. An independently wealthy amateur tennis player, he donated the Davis Cup (1900); he later became U.S. secretary of war (1925–29) and governor general of the Philippines (1929–32). A founding trustee of the Brookings Institution, he was also its chairman (1937–45).

Da•vis |'dāvəs|, Geena (1957–   ) U.S. actress. Notable movies: *The Accidental Tourist* (1988, Academy Award)

Da•vis |'dāvəs|, Henry Winter (1817–65) U.S. politician. As a member of the U.S. House of Representatives from Maryland (1855–61, 1863–65), he was a leader of the Radical Republicans.

Da•vis |'dāvəs|, Jefferson (1808–89) U.S. politician and president of the Confederate States of America. As a U.S. senator from Mississippi (1847–51) and a defender of slavery, he withdrew from the Senate when Mississippi seceded from the union and was later elected president of the Confederate States of America (1862). He wrote *The Rise and Fall of the Confederate Government* (1881).

Da•vis |'dāvəs|, Jim (1945–   ) U.S. cartoonist. Full name *James Robert Davis*. He created the "Garfield" comic strip (1978), as well as books and television scripts based on the Garfield character.

Da•vis |'dāvəs|, John (*c.* 1550–1605) English navigator. On searches for the Northwest Passage to Asia, he discovered Cumberland Sound off Baffin Island (1585) and sailed through Davis Strait (1587) into Baffin Bay.

Da•vis |'dāvəs|, John William (1873–

1955) U.S. politician. He was a Democratic presidential candidate in 1924.

Da•vis |'dāvəs|, Miles (Dewey) (1926–91) U.S. jazz trumpeter, composer, and bandleader. In the 1950s he played and recorded arrangements in a new style that became known as "cool" jazz, heard on albums such as *Kind of Blue* (1959). In the 1960s he pioneered the fusion of jazz and rock.

Da•vis |'dāvəs|, Sammy, Jr (1925–90) U.S. actor, singer and dancer. Spingarn Medal, 1968.

Da•vis |'dāvəs|, Stuart (1894–1964) U.S. artist. He experimented with Cubism and abstract paintings.

Da•vis |'dāvəs|, William Augustine (1809–75) U.S. postal authority. He devised a system of sorting mail on trains, originating railroad post-office service.

Da•vi•son |'dāvəsən|, Wild Bill (1906–89) U.S. Chicago jazz cornetist. Full name *William Edward Davison*.

Da•vis•son |'dāvəsən|, Clinton Joseph (1881–1958) U.S. physicist. With **L. H. Germer** (1896–1971), he discovered electron diffraction, thus confirming de Broglie's theory of the wave nature of electrons. Nobel Prize for Physics (1937).

Da•vy |'dāvē|, Sir Humphry (1778–1829) English chemist, a pioneer of electrochemistry. He discovered nitrous oxide (laughing gas) and the elements sodium, potassium, magnesium, calcium, strontium, and barium. He also identified and named the element chlorine, determined the properties of iodine, and demonstrated that diamond was a form of carbon. In 1815 he invented the miner's safety lamp.

Dawes |dawz|, Charles Gates (1865–1951) U.S. politican, lawyer, and financier. He was vice president of the U.S. (1925–29). Nobel peace prize, 1925, with Sir Austen Chamberlain.

Dawes |dawz|, Henry Laurens (1816–1903) U.S. politician. As a U.S. senator from Massachusetts (1875–93), he was chairman of the Senate Committee on Indian Affairs. The Dawes Act (1887) ended the status of Indian tribal lands as "domestic nations."

Dawes |dawz|, William (1745–99) U.S. patriot. With Paul Revere, he rode from

Lexington to Concord, Massachusetts, to warn of approaching British soldiers (April 18, 1775).

Daw•kins |'dawkənz|, Richard (1941–) English biologist. Dawkins's book *The Selfish Gene* (1976) did much to popularize the theory of sociobiology. In *The Blind Watchmaker* (1986) Dawkins discussed evolution by natural selection and suggested that the theory could answer the fundamental question of why life exists.

Daw•son |'dawsən|, William Levi (1886–1970) U.S. politician. A member of the U.S. House of Representatives from Illinois (1943–70), he was the first African-American chairman of a major House committee.

Day |dā| U.S. family, including: **Benjamin Henry Day** (1810–89), a newspaperman. He founded the first one-cent daily paper, the *New York Sun* (1833). His son, **Benjamin Day** (1838–1916), a printer, invented the Ben Day process for shading and color in printing illustrations. Benjamin Henry Day's grandson, **Clarence Shepard Day, Jr.** (1874–1935), was a writer. Notable works: *Life with Father* (1935).

Day |dā|, Doris (1924–) U.S. actress and singer. Born *Doris Kappelhoff*. She became a movie star in the 1950s with roles in light-hearted musicals, comedies, and romances such as *Calamity Jane* (1953) and *Pillow Talk* (1959).

Day |dā|, Dorothy (1897–1980) U.S. journalist and reformer. She founded the Catholic Worker newspaper with Peter Maurin (1933).

Day |dā|, William Rufus (1849–1923) U.S. Supreme Court justice (1903–22).

Da•yan |dī'yän|, Moshe (1915–81) Israeli statesman and general. As Minister of Defense he oversaw Israel's victory in the Six Day War and as Foreign Minister he played a prominent role in negotiations towards the Camp David agreements of 1979.

Day-Lewis |'dā 'lōōwəs|, C(ecil) (1904–72) English poet and critic. His early verse, such as *Transitional Poems* (1929), reflects the influence of revolutionary thinking. After 1940, he increasingly became an Establishment figure and was Poet Laureate 1968–72.

Dea•kin |'dēkən|, Alfred (1856–1919) Australian Liberal statesman, prime minister (1903–04, 1905–08, and 1909–10).

Dean |dēn|, Dizzy (1911–74) U.S. baseball player. Born *Jay Hanna Dean*. He led National League pitchers in strikeouts (1932–36).

Dean |dēn|, James (1931–55) U.S. actor. Although he starred in only three movies before dying in a car accident, he became a cult figure closely identified with the title role of *Rebel Without a Cause* (1955), symbolizing for many the disaffected youth of the postwar era.

Dean |dēn|, John, III (1938–) U.S. political adviser. After serving as presidential counsel to Richard Nixon, he became the chief witness in the Watergate hearings. He was convicted of conspiracy and served four months in prison.

de Beau•voir |dəbōv'wär|, Simone (1908–86) French existentialist philosopher, novelist, and feminist. Her best-known work is *The Second Sex* (1949), a central book of the "second wave" of feminism. She is strongly associated with Jean-Paul Sartre, with whom she had a lifelong association.

De•Beck, Billy (1890–1942) U.S. cartoonist. Full name *William Morgan De-Beck*. He created Barney Google, Spark Plug, and other popular cartoon characters.

De•brett |də'bret|, John (c. 1750–1822) English publisher. He compiled *The Peerage of England, Scotland, and Ireland* (first issued in 1803), which, with its periodic updatings, is regarded as the authority on the British nobility.

de Bro•glie |də 'brawglē|, Louis-Victor-Pierre-Raymond (1892–1987) French physicist. His experiments initiated the study of wave mechanics. Nobel Prize for Physics (1929).

Debs |debz|, Eugene Victor (1855–1926) U.S. labor leader. The chief organizer of the Social Democratic Party (1897), he ran as a Socialist candidate for U.S. president five times from 1900 to 1920. He was a founder of the Industrial Workers of the World (1905).

De•Buss•chere |də'bōōsHər|, Dave (1940–) U.S. professional athlete. After playing at the major league level in both baseball and basketball, he became the youngest coach in NBA history.

De·bus·sy |ˌdebyoo'sē|, (Achille) Claude (1862–1918) French composer and critic. Debussy carried the ideas of Impressionist art and symbolist poetry into music, using melodies based on the whole-tone scale and delicate harmonies exploiting overtones. Notable works: *Prélude à l'après-midi d'un faune* (1894).

De·bye |də'bī|, Peter Joseph William (1884–1966) Dutch-born U.S. chemical physicist. Debye is best known for establishing the existence of permanent electric dipole moments in many molecules, demonstrating the use of these to determine molecular size and shape, and modifying Einstein's theory of specific heats as applied to solids. Nobel Prize for Chemistry (1936).

De·ca·tur |də'kātər|, Stephen (1779–1820) U.S. naval officer. He was a daring commander in the Tripolitan War and gave the famous toast, "Our Country! In her intercourse with foreign nations may she always be in the right; but our country, right or wrong!"

De·cius |'dēsHēəs|, Gaius Messius Quintus Trajanus (*c.*201–251) Roman emperor (249–51). He was the first Roman emperor to promote systematic persecution of the Christians in the empire.

De·de·kind |'dādəkint|, (Julius Wilhem) Richard (1831–1916) Full name *Julius Wilhelm Richard Didekind.* German mathematician, one the founders of abstract algebra and modern mathematics.

de Du·ve |ˌdə'doovə|, Christian René (1917–) British-born Belgian biochemist. A pioneer in the study of cell biology, he won the Nobel Prize for Physiology or Medicine in 1974.

Dee |dē|, John (1527–1608) English alchemist, mathematician, and geographer. He was Elizabeth I's astrologer, and in later life he absorbed himself in alchemy and acquired notoriety as a sorcerer.

Deere |dir|, John (1804—86) U.S. manufacturer. He founded John Deere & Co. (1868), originally manufacturing plows.

Deer·ing |'dēriNG|, William (1826–

1913) U.S. industrialist. He established a harvester manufacturing business and merged with International Harvester Co. (1902).

de Falla |də 'fäyə|, Manuel see FALLA.

De·foe |də'fō|, Daniel (1660–1731) English novelist and journalist. His best-known novel, *Robinson Crusoe* (1719), is loosely based on the true story of the shipwrecked sailor Alexander Selkirk; it has a claim to being the first English novel. Other notable works: *Moll Flanders* (novel, 1722) and *A Journal of the Plague Year* (historical fiction, 1722).

De For·est |dē'fawrəst|, John William (1826–1906) U.S. author. He wrote the first American realistic novel, *Miss Ravenel's Conversion* (1867).

De For·est |dē'fawrəst|, Lee (1873–1961) U.S. physicist and electrical engineer. He designed a triode valve that was crucial to the development of radio communication, television, and computers.

De For·est |dē'fawrəst|, Robert Weeks (1848–1931) U.S. lawyer. He helped found the New York Charity Organization Society (1882), where he served as president (1888–1931).

De·Frantz, Anita Lucette (1952–) U.S. sports executive and attorney. After winning an Olympic bronze medal in rowing (1976), she became one of two U.S. delegates to the International Olympic Committee and a member of the USOC Executive Committee.

De·gas |dā'gä|, (Hilaire-Germain) Edgar (1834–1917) French painter and sculptor. An Impressionist painter, Degas is best known for his paintings of ballet dancers.

de Gaulle |də 'gawl|, Charles (André Joseph Marie) (1890–1970) French general and statesman, head of government (1944–46), president (1959–69). A wartime organizer of the Free French movement, de Gaulle became President after having been asked to form a government, going on to establish the French presidency as a democratically elected office (1962). He is remembered particularly for his assertive foreign policy and for quelling the student uprisings and strikes of May 1968.

De·gen·er·es |də'generəs|, Ellen

(1958–) U.S. actress and comedian. She was star of the sitcom "Ellen," a television show whose main character is revealed to be a homosexual.

de Hav·il·land |dəˈhævələnd|, Sir Geoffrey (1882–1965) English aircraft designer and manufacturer. He designed and built many aircraft, including the Mosquito of World War II.

de Hav·il·land |dəˈhævələnd|, Olivia (1916–) U.S. actress, born in Japan. Notable movies: *To Each His Own* (1946, Academy Award) and *The Heiress* (1949, Academy Award).

de Hooch |dəˈhōk|, Pieter (c.1629–c.1684) Also **de Hoogh**. Dutch genre painter. He is noted for his depictions of domestic interior and courtyard scenes.

Deigh·ton |ˈdātn|, Len (1929–) English writer; full name *Leonard Cyril Deighton*. His reputation is based on his spy thrillers, several of which have been adapted as movies and for television.

Dek·ker |ˈdekər|, Thomas (c.1572–c.1632) English dramatist, author of the revenge tragedy *The Witch of Edmonton* (1623), in which he collaborated with John Ford and William Rowley, and *The Honest Whore* (1604) with Thomas Middleton.

de Klerk |dəˈklerk|, F. W. (1936–) South African statesman, president (1989–94); full name *Frederik Willem de Klerk*. As state president, he freed Nelson Mandela in 1990, lifted the ban on membership in the African National Congress (ANC), and opened the negotiations that led to the first democratic elections in 1994. Nobel Peace Prize with Nelson Mandela (1993).

de Koon·ing |dəˈkooniNG|, Willem (1904–97) Dutch-born U.S. painter, a leading exponent of abstract expressionism. The female form became a central theme in his later work, notably in the *Women* series (1950–53).

De Ko·ven |dəˈkōvən|, (Henry Louis) Reginald (1859–1920) U.S. composer. He composed operas and songs.

de la Beche |ˈdelə,beSH|, Sir Henry Thomas (1796–1855) English geologist. He traveled extensively and produced the first geological description and map of Jamaica. He was involved in the establishment of the Geological Sur-

vey of Great Britain in 1835, directing it from then until his death.

De·la·croix |ˌdeləˈkrwä|, (Ferdinand Victor) Eugène (1798–1863) French painter, the chief painter of the French romantic school. He is known for his use of vivid color, free drawing, and exotic, violent, or macabre subject matter. Notable works: *The Massacre at Chios* (1824).

de la Hoya |ˌdələˈhoiyə|, Oscar (1973–) U.S. boxer. A 1992 Olympic gold medalist, he has been the world lightweight (1995), super lightweight (1996), and welterweight (1997) champion.

de la Mare |ˌdeləˈmær|, Walter (John) (1873–1956) English poet. He is known particularly for his verse for children. Notable work: *The Listeners* (1912).

De·la·ney |dəˈlānē|, Kim (1961–) U.S. television actress. She won Emmy Awards (1996, 1997) for her role in "NYPD Blue."

de la Ren·ta |dāləˈrentə|, Oscar (1932–) U.S. fashion designer, born in the Dominican Republic. He is known especially for lavish evening gowns.

de la Roche |dələˈrawSH|, Mazo (1885–1961) Canadian novelist. She won acclaim for *Jalna* (1927), the first of a series of novels about the Whiteoak family. The "Jalna" cycle was noted for its characterization and its evocation of rural Ontario.

De·lau·nay |dəlawˈnā|, Robert (1885–1941) French painter. For most of his career he experimented with the abstract qualities of color, and he painted some of the first purely abstract pictures. He was one of the founding members of Orphism together with Sonia Delaunay-Terk.

Delaunay-Terk |dəlawˈnā ˈtərk|, Sonia (Terk) (1885–1979) Russian-born French painter and textile designer, wife of Robert Delaunay. She created abstract paintings based on harmonies of form and color.

Del·brück |ˈdel,brook|, Max (1906–81) U.S. biologist, born in Germany. With Salvador Luria and Alfred Hershey, he discovered the recombination of viral DNA (1946) and won a Nobel Prize in Physiology or Medicine (1969).

de Len•clos, Ninon see LENCLOS.

Del•font |del'fänt|, Bernard, Baron Delfont of Stepney (1909–94) Russianborn British impresario; born *Boris Winogradsky*. From the early 1940s onward he presented more than 200 shows in London's West End theatrical district.

De•libes |də'lēb|, (Clément Philibert) Léo (1836–91) French composer and organist. His best-known works are the ballets *Coppélia* (1870) and *Sylvia* (1876).

De Lil•lo, Don (1936–) U.S. author. Notable works: *White Noise* (1985).

De•li•us |'dēlēəs|, Frederick Theodore Albert (1862–1934) English composer, of German and Scandinavian descent. He is best known for pastoral works such as *Brigg Fair* (1907), but he also wrote songs, concertos, and choral and theater music.

Dell |del|, Michael (1965–) U.S. manufacturing executive. He founded the Dell Computer Corp. (1984).

del•la Fran•ces•ca |,delə ,frän-'cheskə| see PIERO DELLA FRANCESCA.

della Quer•cia |,dälä 'kwerchä|, Jacopo (*c.*1374–1438) Italian sculptor. He is noted for his tomb of Ilaria del Carretto in Lucca cathedral (*c.*1406) and for the biblical reliefs on the portal of San Petronio in Bologna (1425–35).

Della Rob•bia |,dälä'rawbyä|, Luca (*c.*1400–82) Italian sculptor and ceramicist. He is best known for his relief panels in Florence cathedral and his color-glazed terracotta figures.

De•Lor•e•an |də 'lawrēən|, John Z. (1925–) U.S. automobile designer and manufacturer.

De•lors |də'lawr|, Jacques (Lucien Jean) (1925–) French socialist politician, president of the European Commission (1985–94). During his presidency he pressed for closer European union and oversaw the introduction of a single market within the European Community, which came into effect on January 1, 1993.

del Sar•to |del 'särtō|, Andrea see SARTO

de Main•te•non |də ,mænt(ə)nawN| see MAINTENON.

de Mau•pas•sant |də ,mōpə'sän|, Guy see MAUPASSANT.

de' Medici, Catherine see CATHERINE DE' MEDICI.

de' Medici, Cosimo see COSIMO DE' MEDICI.

de Medici, Giovanni the name of Pope Leo X (see LEO).

de' Medici, Lorenzo see LORENZO DE' MEDICI.

de' Medici see MEDICI.

de Mé•di•cis |də ,medə'sēs|, Marie see MARIE DE MÉDICIS.

De•Mille |də'mil|, Cecil B. (1881–1959) U.S. movie producer and director, famous for his spectacular epics; full name *Cecil Blount DeMille*. Notable movies: *The Ten Commandments* (1923; remade 1956) and *Samson and Delilah* (1949).

de Mille |də'mil|, Agnes (George) (*c.* 1905–93) U.S. dancer and choreographer. She is known for her choreography of the ballet *Rodeo* (1942) and the Broadway musical *Oklahoma* (1943). She is a niece of Cecil B. DeMille.

De•moc•ri•tus |də'mäkrətəs| (*c.* 460–*c.* 370 BC) Greek philosopher. He developed the atomic theory originated by his teacher, Leucippus, which explained natural phenomena in terms of the arrangement and rearrangement of atoms moving in a void.

de Mon•tes•pan |də ,mawntəs'pän|, Marquise de see MONTESPAN.

de Mont•fort |də 'män(t)fərt|, Simon see MONTFORT.

De•mos•the•nes |də'mästHənēz| (384–322 BC) Athenian orator and statesman. He is best known for his political speeches on the need to resist aggressive tendencies of Philip II of Macedon (the *Philippics*).

Demp•sey |'dempsē|, Jack (1895–1983) U.S. profesional boxer; full name *William Harrison Dempsey*. He was world heavyweight champion 1919–26.

Den•by |'denbē|, Edwin (1870–1929) U.S. politician. He resigned as U.S. secretary of the navy (1921–24) after being implicated in the Teapot Dome Scandal.

Dench |'dench|, Dame Judi (1934–) English actress; full name *Judith Olivia Dench*. She has performed in numerous theatrical, movie, and television productions. She won an Oscar as best supporting actress for *Shakespeare in Love* (1998).

De·neuve |də'nŏŏv|, Catherine (1943–) French actress; born *Catherine Dorléac*. Notable movies: *Repulsion* (1965) and *Belle de jour* (1967).

Deng Xiao·ping |'dəNG'sHOW'piNG| (1904–97) Also **Teng Hsiao-p'ing**. Chinese communist statesman, vice premier (1973–76, 1977–80); vice chairman of the Central Committee of the Chinese Communist Party (1977–80). Discredited during the Cultural Revolution, he was reinstated in 1977, becoming the de facto leader of China. He worked to modernize the economy and improve relations with the West, although in 1989 his orders led to the massacre of some 2,000 prodemocracy demonstrators in Beijing's Tiananmen Square.

De·ni·kin |dyin'yēkyin|, Anton Ivanovich (1872–1947) Russian soldier. He established the South Russian government but was defeated by the Bolsheviks (1919).

De·Niro |də'nērō|, Robert (1943–) U.S. actor and director. He has starred in many movies, often playing tough characters, and has worked frequently with director Martin Scorsese. He won Oscars for *The Godfather, Part II* (1974) and *Raging Bull* (1980). Other movies include *Taxi Driver* (1976), *The Deer Hunter* (1978), *the Untouchables* (1987), *Goodfellas* (1990), and *Casino* (1995).

Den·is |'denəs|, St. (died *c.*250) Also **Denys**. Italian-born French bishop, patron saint of France; Roman name *Dionysius*. According to tradition he was one of a group of seven missionaries sent from Rome to convert Gaul; he became bishop of Paris and was martyred in the reign of the emperor Valerian. Feast day, October 9.

Den·is |'denəs|, Maurice (1870–1943) French painter, designer, and art theorist. A member of the Nabi Group, he wrote many works on art, including *Théories* (1913) and *Nouvelles Théories* (1921).

Den·ver |'denvər|, John (1943–97) U.S. country and pop singer and songwriter. Born *John Henry Deutschendorf*. He celebrated the state of Colorado in his music.

Denys, St. see DENIS, ST.

de Pao·la, Tomie (1934–) U.S. author and illustrator. Full name *Thomas Anthony de Paola*. His children's books, including the "Strega Nona" stories, have received several awards for typography and illustration.

Dé·par·dieu |dāpär'dyŏŏ|, Gérard (1948–) French actor.

de Pi·san, Christine (*c.*1364–*c.*1430) Also **de Pizan**. Italian writer, resident in France from 1369. The first professional woman writer in France, she is best known for her works in defense of women's virtues and achievements, such as *Le Livre des trois vertus* (1406).

De Quin·cey |di'kwinsē|, Thomas (1785–1859) English essayist and critic. He achieved fame with his *Confessions of an English Opium Eater* (1822), a study of his addiction to opium and its psychological effects.

De·rain |də'ræn|, André (1880–1954) French painter, one of the exponents of fauvism. He also designed theater sets and costumes, notably for the Ballets Russes.

Der·by |'dərbē|, Edward George Geoffrey Smith Stanley, 14th Earl of (1799–1869) British Conservative statesman, prime minister (1852, 1858–59, 1866–68).

Der·in·ger |'derənjər|, Henry (1786–1869) U.S. gun manufacturer. He invented the pistol that became known as the Derringer.

Dern |dern|, George Henry (1872–1936) U.S. mining executive and politician. He was governor of Utah (1925–32) and author of the workmen's compensation law.

Der·r·da |dəri'dä|, Jacques (1930–) French philosopher and literary critic, the most important figure in the theory of deconstructionism. Notable works: *Of Grammatology* (1967) and *Writing and Difference* (1967).

de Sade |də'säd|, Marquis see SADE.

De·sai |də'sī|, (Shri) Morarji (Ranchhodji) (1896–1995) Indian prime minister (1977–79).

Des·cartes |dā'kärt|, René (1596–1650) French philosopher, mathematician, and man of science. Aiming to reach totally secure foundations for knowledge, he concluded that everything was open to doubt except his own conscious experience, and his existence as a necessary condition of this: "*Cogito, ergo sum*" (I think, therefore I am). From this certainty he developed a dualistic theory regarding mind and matter as separate though interacting. In mathematics, Descartes developed the use of coordinates to locate a point in two or three dimensions.

De Si·ca |də'sēkə|, Vittorio (1901–74) Italian movie director and actor, a key figure in Italian neorealist cinema. Notable movies: *The Bicycle Thief* (1948) and *Two Women* (1960), both of which won Oscars.

de So·to |də'sōtō|, Hernando (*c.* 1496–1542) Spanish soldier and explorer. Landing in Florida in 1539, he explored much of what is now the southeastern U.S., as far west as Oklahoma. He died of a fever on the banks of the Mississippi River.

de Spinoza, Baruch see SPINOZA.

des Prez |dā'prā|, Josquin (*c.*1440–1521) Also **des Prés** or **Desprez**. Flemish musician, he was a leading Renaissance composer.

de Staël |də 'stäl|, Madame (1766–1817) French novelist and critic, a precursor of the French romantics, born *Anne Louise Germaine Necker*. Her best-known critical work, *De l'Allemagne* (1810), introduced late 18th-century German writers and thinkers to France.

de Troyes, Chrétien see CHRÉTIEN DE TROYES.

Dett |det|, Robert Nathaniel (1882–1943) U.S. conductor and composer. He authored *The Dett Collection of Negro Spirituals* (1937).

de Va·le·ra |ˌdəvə'lerə|, Eamon (1882–1975) U.S.-born Irish statesman, prime minister (1937–48, 1951–54, and 1957–59), and president of the Republic of Ireland (1959–73). He was the leader of Sinn Fein (1917–26) and the founder of the Fianna Fáil Party in 1926. As president of the Irish Free State from 1932, de Valera was largely responsible for the new constitution of 1937 that created the state of Eire.

de Val·ois |də väl'wä|, Dame Ninette (1898–) Irish choreographer, ballet dancer, and teacher; born *Edris Stannus*.

A former soloist with Diaghilev's Ballets Russes, she formed the Vic-Wells Ballet (which eventually became the Royal Ballet) and the Sadler's Wells ballet school.

de Va·ro·na |ˌdəvə'rōnə|, Donna (1947–) U.S. swimmer. Winner of 2 gold medals in the 1964 Olympic Games, she set 18 world records during her career; she was a cofounder of the Women's Sports Foundation (1974).

De·vers |'dēvərz|, Gail (1966–) U.S. track and field athlete. She won Olympic gold medals in the 100 meters (1992, 1996) and was a 3-time world champion in the 100 meters and 100-meter hurdles.

De Vinne |də'vinē|, Theodore Low (1828–1914) U.S. printer and author. He founded and served as the first president of the Grolier Club (1884).

De Vo·to |di'vōtō|, Bernard Augustine (1897–1955) U.S. author, editor, and educator. He edited "The Easy Chair" in *Harper's Magazine* (1935–55). Notable works: *Across the Wide Missouri* (1947, Pulitzer Prize).

de Vries |dəv'rēs|, Hugo Marie (1848–1935) Dutch plant physiologist and geneticist. De Vries did much work on osmosis and water relations in plants, coining the term *plasmolysis*. His subsequent work on heredity and variation contributed substantially to the chromosome theory of heredity.

De Vries |di'vrēs|, Peter (1910–93) U.S. author. Although known for his comic touch, he also wrote a harrowing autobiographical novel, *The Blood of the Lamb* (1961), after his young daughter died of leukemia. Notable works: *No, But I Saw the Movie(s)* (1952), *Reuben, Reuben* (1964), and *Slouching Towards Kalamazoo* (1983).

Dew·ar |'dōōwər|, Sir James (1842–1923) Scottish chemist and physicist. He is chiefly remembered for his work in cryogenics, in which he devised the vacuum flask, achieved temperatures close to absolute zero, and was the first to produce liquid oxygen and hydrogen in quantity.

Dew·ey |'dōōē|, George (1837–1917) U.S. naval officer. Appointed commodore of the navy in 1896, he was the hero of the battle of Manila (May 1, 1898) during the Spanish-American War.

Dew·ey |'do͞oē|, John (1859–1952) U.S. philosopher and educational theorist. Working in the pragmatic tradition of William James and C. S. Pierce, he defined knowledge as successful practice, and evolved the educational theory that children would learn best by doing. Notable work: *The School and Society* (1899).

Dew·ey |'do͞oē|, Melvil (1851–1931) U.S. librarian. He devised a decimal system of classifying books, using ten main subject categories.

Dew·ey |'do͞oē|, Thomas Edmund (1902–71) U.S. attorney. He served as governor of New York (1943–55) and was a Republican presidential candidate (1944,1948).

Dew·hurst |'do͞o,hərst|, Colleen (1926–1991) U.S. actress. A star of film and stage, she has won two Tony Awards (1960, 1973).

Dia·ghi·lev |'dyägyəlyəf|, Sergey (Pavlovich) (1872–1929) Russian ballet impresario. In 1909 he formed the Ballets Russes, which he directed until his death. With Nijinsky, and later Massine, as his star performer, he transformed the European ballet scene, pooling the talents of leading choreographers, painters, and composers of his day.

Dia·mond |'dīmənd|, Neil (1941–) U.S. pop singer and songwriter.

Di·ana, Prin·cess of Wales |dī'ænə| (1961–1997) Former wife of Prince Charles; her title before marriage was *Lady Diana Frances Spencer*. The daughter of the 8th Earl Spencer, she married Prince Charles in 1981; the couple were divorced in 1996. They had two children, *Prince William Arthur* (1982–) and *Prince Henry Charles Albert David* (known as Prince Harry, 1984–). She became a popular figure through her charity work and media appearances, and her death in a car crash in Paris gave rise to intense international mourning.

Di·as |'dēäSH|, Bartolomeu (c.1450–1500) Also **Diaz**. Portuguese navigator and explorer. He was the first European to round the Cape of Good Hope (1488), thereby establishing a sea route from the Atlantic to Asia.

Dí·az |'dēæz|, Porfirio (1830–1915) Mexican general and statesman, president (1877–80, 1884–1911).

Diaz variant spelling of DIAS.

Dick·ens |'dikənz|, Charles (John Huffam) (1812–70) English novelist. His novels and stories are notable for their satirical humor and treatment of contemporary social problems, including the plight of the urban poor and the corruption and inefficiency of the legal system. Memorable characters such as Scrooge and Mr. Micawber contributed to his work's popular appeal. Some of his most famous works are *Oliver Twist* (1837–38), *Nicholas Nickleby* (1838–39), *A Christmas Carol* (1843), *David Copperfield* (1850), *Bleak House* (1852–53), and *Great Expectations* (1860–61).

Dick·en·son |'dikənsən|, Vic (1906–84) U.S. jazz trombonist and composer. He played with many groups and was known as one of the most consistent mainstream jazz musicians.

Dick·er·son |'dikərsən|, Eric (1960–) U.S. football player. He set the NFL's single-season rushing record of 2,105 yards in 1984.

Dick·ey |'dikē|, James (Lafayette) (1923–97) U.S. poet and author. Notable works: *Buckdancer's Choice* (1965, National Book Award) and *Deliverance* (1970).

Dick·in·son |'dikənsən|, Emily (Elizabeth) (1830–86) U.S. poet. From the age of 24, she led the life of a recluse; her poems use an elliptical language, emphasizing assonance and alliteration rather than rhyme, reflecting the struggles of her reclusive life. Although she wrote nearly 2,000 poems, only seven were published in her lifetime; the first notable collection appeared in 1890.

Did·ley |'didlē|, Bo (1928–) U.S. rock singer and songwriter. Born *Ellas Bates*.

Di·de·rot |'dēdə,rō|, Denis (1713–84) French philosopher, writer, and critic. A leading figure of the Enlightenment in France, he was principal editor of the *Encyclopédie* (1751–76), through which he disseminated and popularized philosophy and scientific knowledge. Other notable works: *Le Rêve de D'Alembert* (1782) and *Le Neveu de Rameau* (1805).

Did·i·on |'didiən|, Joan (1934–) U.S. author. Winner of the National Book Award for *Play It As It Lays* (1970), she is best known for writing about the extremes of life in her native California. Notable works: *Run, River* (1963), *Slouching Towards Bethlehem* (1968), and *After Henry* (1992).

Die·fen·ba·ker |'dēfən,bäkər|, John George (1895–1979) Canadian politician. He was prime minister (1957-63) and a member of the House of Commons (1940-79).

Die·sel |'dēzəl|, Rudolf (Christian Karl) (1858–1913) French-born German engineer, inventor of the diesel engine. In 1892 he patented a design for his new type of internal combustion engine, and developed it, exhibiting the prototype in 1897.

Die·trich |'dē,trik|, Marlene (c.1901–92) German-born U.S. actress and singer; born *Maria Magdelene von Losch*. She became famous for her part as Lola in *The Blue Angel* (1930), one of many movies she made with Josef von Sternberg. From the 1950s she was also successful as an international cabaret star.

Dietz |dēts|, Howard (1896–1983) U.S. lyricist. In collaboration with George Gershwin, Jerome Kern, and Arthur Schwartz, he wrote over 500 songs, including *You and the Night and the Music, Dancing in the Dark,* and *That's Entertainment.*

Di·fran·co |də'fræNkō|, Ani (1970–) U.S. musician and punk-folk feminist.

Dil·lard |'dilərd|, Annie (1945–) U.S. author. She is the writer of essays on ecological subjects, including *Pilgrim at Tinker Creek* (1974, Pulitzer Prize).

Dil·ler |'dilər|, Barry (1942–) U.S. corporate executive. He has been chairman of the board of Paramount Pictures Corp. (1974–84) and CEO of 20th Century Fox (1984–) and Fox Television (1985–).

Dil·lin·ger |'dilənjər|, John (1903–34) U.S. outlaw. He was a bank robber who made daring escapes from jail and was named "Public Enemy Number 1" by the FBI; he was eventually betrayed by the "Lady in Red."

Di·Mag·gio |di'mæjēō|, Joe (1914–99) U.S. baseball player; Full name *Joseph Paul DiMaggio*; called *Joltin' Joe* and *the Yankee Clipper*. Star of the New York Yankees teams of 1936–51, he was renowned for his outstanding batting ability and for his outfield play. In 1941 he hit safely in 56 consecutive games, a record that has not been challenged. He was briefly married to Marilyn Monroe in 1954.

Ding·ley |'diNGlē|, Nelson (1832–99) U.S. politician. As a member of the U.S. House of Representatives from Maine (1881–99), he authored the Dingley Tariff Act (1897).

Di·o·cle·tian |,dīə'klēsHən| (c.245–c.313) Roman emperor (284–305); full name *Gaius Aurelius Valerius Diocletianus*. Faced with mounting military problems, in 286 he divided the empire between himself in the east and Maximian in the west. Diocletian launched the final persecution of the Christians (303).

Di·og·e·nes |dī'äjənēz| (c.412–c.323 BC) Greek philosopher. The most famous of the Cynics, he lived ascetically in Athens (according to legend, he lived in a tub) and was accordingly nicknamed *Kuōn* ("the dog"), from which the Cynics derived their name. He emphasized self-sufficiency and the need for natural, uninhibited behaviour, regardless of social conventions.

Di·on |'dē,än|, Celine (1968–) Canadian rock singer. She won a Grammy Award for the song "My Heart Will Go On," from the movie *Titanic* (1997).

Di·o·ny·sius |,dīə'nisēəs; ,dīə'nisHəs| name of two rulers of Syracuse: **Dionysius I** (c.430–367 BC; reigned 405–367); known as **Dionysius the Elder**. A tyrannical ruler, he waged three wars against the Carthaginians for control of Sicily, later becoming the principal power of Greek Italy after the capture of Rhegium (386) and other Greek cities in southern Italy. His son, **Dionysius II** (c. 397–344 BC; reigned 367-357 and 346-344), was known as **Dionysius the Younger**. He lacked his father's military ambitions and signed a peace treaty with Carthage in 367. Despite his patronage of philosophers, he resisted the attempt by Plato to turn him into a philosopher king.

Di·o·ny·sius Ex·i·gu·us |eg'zigyŏŏəs| (*c.*500–*c.*560) Scythian-born monk and scholar. He is notable for having developed in 525, at the behest of Pope John I, the system of dates BC and AD that is still in use today, calculating 753 years from the founding of Rome as the year of Jesus Christ's Incarnation; this has since been shown to be mistaken by several years. He is said to have taken the nickname *Exiguus* ('little') as a sign of humility.

Di·o·ny·sius of Hal·i·car·nas·sus |,hælicär'næsəs| (1st century BC) Greek historian, literary critic, and rhetorician. He lived in Rome from 30 BC and is best known for his detailed history of the city, written in Greek; this covers the period from the earliest times until the outbreak of the first Punic War (264 BC).

Di·o·ny·sius the Are·op·a·gite |,ærē-'äpə,gīt| (1st century AD) Greek churchman. His conversion by St. Paul is recorded in Acts 17:34, and according to tradition he went on to become the first bishop of Athens. He was later confused with St. Denis and with a mystical theologian, Pseudo-Dionysius the Areopagite, who exercised a profound influence on medieval theology.

Di·o·phan·tus |,dīə'fæntəs| (*fl. c.*250) Greek mathematician. Diophantus was the first to attempt an algebraical notation, showing in *Arithmetica* how to solve simple and quadratic equations. His work led to Pierre de Fermat's discoveries in the theory of numbers.

Di·or |dē'awr|, Christian (1905–57) French fashion designer. His first collection (1947) featured narrow-waisted tightly fitted bodices and full pleated skirts; this became known as the New Look. He later created the first A-line garments and built up a range of quality accessories.

Di·rac |də'räk|, Paul Adrien Maurice (1902–84) English theoretical physicist. He described the properties of the electron, including its spin, and postulated the existence of the positron by applying Einstein's theory of relativity to quantum mechanics. Nobel Prize for Physics (1933).

Dirks |dərks|, Rudolph (1877–1968) U.S. cartoonist, born in Germany. He was creator of "The Katzenjammer Kids."

Dirk·sen |'dərksən|, Everett McKinley (1896–1969) U.S. politician. An Illinois Republican, he was a member of the U.S. House of Representatives (1933–48), a U.S. Senator (1950–69), and a Senate Republican leader (1959–69).

Dis·ney |'diznē|, Walt (1901–1966) U.S. animator and movie and television producer. Founder of Disney entertainment company; full name *Walter Elias Disney*. He made his name with the creation of cartoon characters such as Mickey Mouse (who first appeared in 1928), Donald Duck, Goofy, and Pluto. *Snow White and the Seven Dwarfs* (1937) was the first full-length cartoon feature film with sound and color. Other notable films: *Pinocchio* (1940), *Dumbo* (1941), and *Bambi* (1942). He also founded the Disneyland amusement park in California.

Dis·rae·li |diz'rālē|, Benjamin, 1st Earl of Beaconsfield (1804–81) British Tory statesman, of Italian-Jewish descent; prime minister (1868, 1874–80). He was largely responsible for the introduction of the second Reform Act (1867), which doubled the electorate, and introduced measures to improve public health and working conditions in factories. He also ensured that Britain bought a controlling interest in the Suez Canal (1875) and made Queen Victoria Empress of India.

Dit·ko |'ditkō|, Steven (1927–   ) U.S. cartoonist. He created the character Spider-Man.

Dix |diks|, Dorothea Lynde (1802–87) U.S. reformer. She was a pioneer of American prison reform, a creator of almshouses and insane asylums, and superintendent of women nurses in the Civil War.

Dix·on |'diksən|, George (*c.* 1755–*c.* 1800) English navigator. He sailed with Cook on his third expedition (1776–69), and in 1787 discovered Queen Charlotte Islands, Norfolk Sound, Port Mulgrave, Dixon Entrance, and Alexander Archipelago.

Dix·on |'diksən|, George (1870–1909)

U.S. boxer, born in Canada. He was the first African-American boxer to win a world bantamweight title (1980), and he later became the world featherweight champion (1891–97 and 1898–1900).

Dix·on |'diksən|, Jeremiah (died 1777) English surveyor. With Charles Mason, he determined the boundary between Maryland and Pennsylvania that became known as the Mason-Dixon line.

Dix·on |'diksən|, Thomas (1864–1946) U.S. clergyman and writer. He was an extremist Southerner, strongly supportive of the Ku Klux Klan; his 20 novels include the trilogy *The Leopard's Spots* (1902), *The Clansman* (1905), and *The Traitor* (1907).

Dix·on |'diksən|, Willie (1915–92) U.S. songwriter. His classics, such as "You Shook Me," "Little Red Rooster," and "Bring It On Home, " linked rock and roll with the blues.

Dje·ras·si, Carl (1923–) U.S. physician, born in Bulgaria. He invented a machine for white blood cell transfusions (1970); his contributions to cancer therapy include chemotherapy and platelet transfusions.

Do·bell |dō'bel|, Sir William (1899–1970) Australian painter.

Dö·be·rei·ner |'doEbə,rīnər|, Johann Wolfgang (1780–1849) German chemist. His work contributed to the formation of the periodic table of elements.

Do·by |'dōbē|, Larry (1924–) U.S. baseball player and manager.

Dob·zhan·sky |dəb'zHänskē |, Theodosius Grigorievich (1900–75) U.S. geneticist, author, and educator, born in Ukraine. He studied genetic variation and the philosophical implications of evolution.

Doc·tor·ow |'däktə,rō |, E. L. (1931–) U.S. author. Born *Edgar Lawrence Doctorow*. He won a National Book Critics Circle Award for *Ragtime* (1975).

Dodge |däj| U.S. family, including **David Low Dodge** (1774–1852), a businessman and pacifist. He founded the New York Peace Society (1815), the first group of its kind. His son, **William Earl Dodge** (1805–83), a businessman and philanthropist, founded Phelps, Dodge & Co. (1883), and was an orga-

nizer of the YMCA in the U.S. David Low Dodge's great-granddaughter, **Grace Hoadley Dodge** (1856–1914), was a social worker. She organized a club for young working women (1885).

Dodge |däj|, Grenville Mellen (1831–1916) U.S. Army officer and civil engineer. He supervised the building of the Union Pacific Railroad (1866–70).

Dodge |däj|, Mary Elizabeth Mapes (1831–1905) U.S. author. Notable works: *Hans Brinker, or The Silver Skates* (1865).

Dodgson, Charles Lutwidge see CARROLL.

Doe·nitz |'dənits|, Karl (1891–1980) German admiral. He was commander in chief of the German navy (1943) and delivered the German surrender (1945).

Doi, Takako (1935–) Japanese author. Works include *Chinese Painting* (1983).

Dois·neau, Robert (1912–94) French photographer, best known for his photos of the city and inhabitants of Paris. Notable works: "The Kiss at the Hôtel de Ville" (1950).

Doi·sy |'doizē|, Edward Adelbert (1893–1986) U.S. biochemist. He isolated sex homones and discovered Vitamin K, and with Henrik Dam won the Nobel Prize (1943) for Physiology or Medicine.

Dole |dōl| U.S. political family, including: **Bob Dole** (1923–); full name *Robert Joseph Dole*. A senator from 1968, he became leader of the Republican Party in 1992, and was defeated by Bill Clinton in the presidential election of 1996. His wife, **Elizabeth Hanford Dole** (1936–), was U.S. secretary of transportation (1983–89) and U.S. secretary of labor (1989–91) before becoming president of the American Red Cross (1991–99).

Do·lin |'dōlən|, Sir Anton (1904–83) English ballet dancer and choreographer; born *Sydney Francis Patrick Chippendall Healey-Kay*. He was the first artistic director of the London Festival Ballet (1950–61), as well as first soloist.

Doll |däl|, Sir Richard (1912–) English physician. Full name *William Richard Shaboe Doll*. With **Sir A. Bradford Hill** (1897–1991), he was the first to show a statistical link between smoking and lung cancer.

Dol·lar |'dälər|, Robert (1844–1932) U.S. businessman, born in Scotland. He founded Dollar Steamship Co. (1901) for trade with Asia and expanded to around-the-world passenger service (1924).

Doll·fuss |'dälfəs|, Engelbert (1892–1934) Austrian statesman, chancellor of Austria 1932–34. From 1933 Dollfuss attempted to block Austrian Nazi plans to force the *Anschluss* (German annexation of Austria) by governing without Parliament. He was assassinated by Austrian Nazis.

Do·magk |'dō,mäk|, Gerhard (1895–1964) German bacteriologist and pathologist. Nobel Prize for Physiology or Medicine, 1939.

Do·men·i·ci |də'menəCHē|, Pete (1932–) U.S. politician and lawyer. He was a member of the U.S. Senate from New Mexico (1972–).

Do·min·go |də'miNGgō|, Placido (1941–) Spanish-born operatic tenor; emigrated to Mexico in 1950.

Dom·i·nic |'dämənik|, St. (*c.*1170–1221) Spanish priest and friar; Spanish name *Domingo de Guzmán.* In 1216 he founded the Order of Friars Preachers at Toulouse in France; its members became known as Dominicans or Black Friars. Feast day, August 8.

Do·mi·nio |'dämə,nō|, Fats (1928–) U.S. pianist, singer, and songwriter; born *Antoine Domino.* His music represents part of the transition from rhythm and blues to rock and roll, and shows the influence of jazz, boogie-woogie, and gospel music. Notable songs: "Ain't That a Shame" (1955) and "Blueberry Hill" (1956).

Do·mi·tian |də'misHən| (AD 51–96) Son of Vespasian, Roman emperor (81–96); full name *Titus Flavius Domitianus.* An energetic but autocratic ruler, he embarked on a major building program, but was assassinated following a lengthy period of terror.

Don·a·hue |'dänə,hyōō|, Phil (1935–) U.S. talk show host. He began the award-winning *Phil Donahue Show* in 1967 and retired in 1996.

Don·ald |'dawnəld|, David Herbert (1920–) U.S. historian and biographer. Notable works: *Charles Sumner and the Coming of the Civil War* (1960, Pulitzer prize) and *Look Homeward: A Life of Thomas Wolfe* (1987, Pulitzer prize).

Don·a·tel·lo |,dänə'telō| (*c.*1386–1466) Italian sculptor; born *Donato di Betto Bardi.* He was one of the pioneers of scientific perspective, and is especially famous for his lifelike sculptures, including the bronze *David* (*c.*1430–60).

Do·na·tus |,dō'nätəs|, Aelius (4th century) Roman grammarian. The *Ars Grammatica,* containing his treatises on Latin grammar, was the sole textbook used in schools in the Middle Ages.

Don·i·zet·ti |,dänə'zetē|, Gaetano (1797–1848) Italian composer. His operas include tragedies such as *Lucia di Lammermoor* (1835) and comedies such as *Don Pasquale* (1843).

Don·kin |'däNkən|, Bryan (1768–1855) English engineer. He developed a method of food preservation by heat sterilization, sealing the food inside a container made of sheet steel and so producing the first tin can.

Donne |'dən|, John (1572–1631) English poet and preacher. A metaphysical poet, he is most famous for his *Satires* (*c.*1590–99), *Elegies* (*c.*1590–99), and love poems, which appeared in the collection *Songs and Sonnets.* He also wrote religious poems and, as dean of St. Paul's in London from 1621, was one of the most celebrated preachers of his age.

Don·o·van |'dänəvən| (1946–) British folk-rock singer. Born *Donovan Leitch.* Notable songs: "Mellow Yellow" (1966).

Doo·ley |'dōōlē|, Thomas Anthony (1927–61) U.S. physician and author. He established a medical mission in Northern Laos (1956) and hospitals in Cambodia, Laos, and Vietnam; in 1957 he established Medico, an international medical aid mission.

Doo·lit·tle |'dōō,litəl|, Hilda (1886–1961) U.S. poet; Pseudonym **H. D.** Her work shows the influence of Ezra Pound and other imagist poets. Notable works: *Sea Garden* (1916).

Dop·pler |'däplər|, Christian Johann (1803–53) Austrian physicist, famous for his discovery, in 1842, of what is now known as the Doppler effect.

Do•ran |'dōrən|, George Henry (1869–1956) U.S. publisher, born in Canada. He joined with F. N. Doubleday to form Doubleday, Doran & Co. (1927).

Do•ra•ti |də'rätē|, Antal (1906–88) U.S. composer and conductor, born in Budapest. As musical director of symphonies in Dallas; Minneapolis; Stockholm; Washington, D.C.; and Detroit, he made over 500 recordings.

Do•ré |daw'rā|, Gustave (1832–83) French book illustrator, known for his woodcut illustrations of books such as Dante's *Inferno* (1861), Cervantes' *Don Quixote* (1863), and the Bible (1865–66).

Dorr |'dawr|, Thomas Wilson (1805–54) U.S. lawyer and political reformer. He formed the "People's Party" in Rhode Island and was elected governor (1842). As a result of his attempts to reform established government, civil war broke out in the state (Dorr's Rebellion). He was sentenced to prison in 1844.

Dor•sey |'dawrsē| U.S. musicians. **Jimmy Dorsey** (1904–57), a jazz clarinetist and alto saxophonist, and his brother **Tommy Dorsey** (1905–56), a jazz trombonist, led popular dance and jazz bands both individually and jointly.

Dos Pas•sos |də'spæsəs|, John (Roderigo) (1896–1970) U.S. novelist, chiefly remembered for his portrayal of American life in such novels as *Manhattan Transfer* (1925) and *USA* (1938).

Do•sto•ev•sky |,dästə'yefskē|, Fyodor (Mikhailovich) (1821–81) Russian novelist. Also **Dostoyevsky**. Dostoevsky's novels reveal his psychological insight, savage humor, and concern with the religious, political, and moral problems posed by human suffering. Notable novels: *Crime and Punishment* (1866), *The Idiot* (1868), and *The Brothers Karamazov* (1880).

Dou•ble•day |'dəbl,dā|, Abner (1819–93) U.S. army officer. A Union general in the Civil War, he is credited with creating the modern game of baseball, although this claim has been largely disputed.

Dou•ble•day |'dəbl,dā|, Frank Nelson (1862–1934) U.S. publisher. With S. S.

McClure he founded Doubleday & McClure (1897–1900) and with Walter Hines Page he formed Doubleday, Page & Co. (1900–27); he served as chairman of Doubleday, Doran & Co. (1927–34).

Doug•las |'dəgləs| U.S. actors. **Kirk Douglas** (1916–); born *Issur Danielovitch Demsky*. Notable movies: *Lust for Life* (1956) and *Spartacus* (1960). His son, **Michael Douglas** (1944–), is also a director, and producer. Notable movies: *Romancing the Stone* (1984), *Wall Street* (1987, Academy Award), and *The American President* (1995).

Doug•las |'dəgləs|, Aaron (1899–1979) U.S. painter.

Doug•las |'dəgləs|, Lord Alfred (Bruce) (1870–1945) English poet. Enraged by his long intimacy with Oscar Wilde, Douglas's father, the 8th Marquess of Queensberry, cut off Douglas's allowance and had Wilde imprisoned.

Doug•las |'dəgləs|, Donald Wills (1892–1981) U.S. businessman and aircraft engineer. He was an early engineer of passenger and military airplanes and president of the Douglas Aircraft Co. (1928–57), which merged to become the McDonnell Douglas Corp. (1967).

Doug•las |'dəgləs|, Melvyn (1901–81) U.S. actor. Born *Melvyn Hesselberg*. Notable movies: *Being There* (1979, Academy Award).

Doug•las |'dəgləs|, Stephen Arnold (1813–61) U.S. attorney and politician. Known as **the Little Giant**. An Illinois Democrat who served as a U.S. congressman (1843–47) and senator (1847–61), he is best remembered for a series of seven senatorial-campaign debates (1858) with Republican candidate Abraham Lincoln, in which Douglas advocated states' rights. He won the Senate seat in 1858, but lost his 1860 bid for the presidency to Lincoln, after which he was an outspoken supporter of the Lincoln administration.

Doug•las |'dəgləs|, William Orville (1898–1980) U.S. Supreme Court justice (1939–75). He was noted as a consistent liberal, especially concerning freedom of speech.

Douglas-Home |'dəgləs hōm|, Sir Alex, Baron Home of the Hirsel of Coldstream (1903–95) British Conservative statesman, prime minister (1963–64). Full name *Alexander Frederick Douglas-Home.*

Doug•lass |'dəgləs|, Frederick (1817–95) U.S. abolitionist and author. Born *Frederick Augustus Washington Bailey*. He escaped from slavery in 1838 and became an antislavery lecturer. He established an antislavery newspaper, *North Star* (1847–64), and published his autobiography, *Narrative of the Life of Frederick Douglass* (1845, revised 1892).

Dove |dōv|, Rita (1952–) U.S. author. She was the youngest poet and the first African-American woman to hold the post of Poet Laureate of the U.S. (1993–94). Notable works: *Thomas and Beulah* (1986, Pulitzer prize).

Dow |dow|, Charles Henry (1851–1902) U.S. journalist. With Edward D. Jones (1856–1920), he founded Dow Jones & Co.(1882) and *The Wall Street Journal* (1889).

Dow |dow|, Herbert Henry (1866–1930) U.S. chemist and businessman, born in Canada. He founded Dow Chemical Co. (1897) and developed and patented over 100 chemical processes.

Dowd |dowd|, Maureen (1952–) U.S. journalist. She writes an opinion/editorial column for the *New York Times* (1995–).

Dow•ding |'dowdiNG|, Hugh (Caswall Tremenheere), Baron (1882–1970) British Marshal of the Royal Air Force. He was commander in chief of the British air defense forces that defeated the Luftwaffe during the Battle of Britain in 1940.

Dow•son |'dowsən|, Ernest (Christopher) (1867–1900) English poet, associated with the "decadent" school of Oscar Wilde and Aubrey Beardsley. His two books of poems, *Verses* (1896) and *Decorations* (1899), deal with themes of ennui and world-weariness.

Doyle |doil|, Sir Arthur Conan (1859–1930) Scottish novelist and short-story writer, chiefly remembered for his creation of the private detective Sherlock Holmes. Holmes first appeared in *A Study in Scarlet* (1887), and was featured in more than fifty stories and in novels such as *The Hound of the Baskervilles* (1902).

D'Oy•ly Carte |'doilē 'kärt|, Richard (1844–1901) English impresario and producer. He brought together the librettist Sir W. S. Gilbert and the composer Sir Arthur Sullivan, producing many of their operettas in London's Savoy Theatre, which he had established in 1881.

Drab•ble |'dræbəl|, Margaret (1939–) English novelist, the younger sister of A. S. Byatt. Notable works: *The Millstone* (1966), *The Ice Age* (1977), and *The Radiant Way* (1987).

Dra•co |'drākō| (7th century BC) Athenian legislator. His codification of Athenian law was notorious for its severity in that the death penalty was imposed even for trivial crimes; this gave rise to the adjective draconian in English.

Drake |drāk|, Sir Francis (*c.*1540–96) English sailor and explorer. He was the first Englishman to circumnavigate the globe (1577–80), in his ship the *Golden Hind*. He played an important part in the defeat of the Spanish Armada.

Dra•per |'drāpər| U.S. scientists. English-born **John William Draper** (1811–82) was an organizer and president (1850–73) of New York University Medical School and the author of *Human Physiology, Statical and Dynamical* (1856), for many years the field's standard text. His son, **Henry Draper** (1837–82), was an astronomer. In his self-built observatory, he obtained the first photograph of a stellar spectrum (Vega, 1872) and the first photograph of a nebula (Orion, 1880).

Dra•per |'drāpər|, Charles Stark (1901–87) U.S. aeronautical engineer. He invented the gyroscope-stabilized gunsight used by the U.S. armed forces and directed the development of guidance technology for fighter planes, submarines, missiles, and Apollo spacecraft.

Drei•ser |'drīzər|, Theodore (Herman Albert) (1871–1945) U.S. novelist. His first novel, *Sister Carrie* (1900), caused controversy for its frank treatment of the heroine's sexuality and ambition. Other notable works: *America Is Worth Saving* (1941).

Drew |drōō|, Charles Richard (1904–50) U.S. physician. He was a pioneer in the development of blood banks (1940). Spingarn medal, 1944.

Drew |drōō|, Daniel (1797–1879) U.S. financier. In 1844 he joined the Wall Street banking firm, Drew, Robinson and Co.; later, he manipulated the stock of the Erie Railroad to prevent Cornelius Vanderbilt from gaining a majority interest. Drew Theological Seminary (now Drew University) benefitted from his contributions.

Drew |drōō|, Elizabeth (1935–) U.S. journalist. She wrote for *New Yorker* magazine as a Washington correspondent (1973–92) is a commentator on Monitor Radio.

Drex·el |'dreksəl|, Anthony Joseph (1826–93) U.S. banker and philanthropist. He joined his father's brokerage firm (1847) and merged with J. P. Morgan (1871), making Drexel, Morgan and Co. the most powerful investment banking house in the U.S. He was the founder and benefactor (1892) of Drexel Institute of Technology.

Drey·fus |'drāfəs|, Alfred (1859–1935) French army officer, of Jewish descent. In 1894 he was falsely accused of providing military secrets to the Germans; his trial and imprisonment caused a major political crisis in France. He was eventually fully exonerated in 1906.

Drey·fuss |'drīfəs|, Richard (1947–) U.S. actor. Notable movies: *Close Encounters of the Third Kind* (1977) and *The Goodbye Girl* (1977, Academy Award).

Druck·er |'drəkər|, Mort (1929–) U.S. cartoonist and artist. He was on staff at *Mad* magazine.

Dry·den |'drīdən|, John (1631–1700) English poet, critic, and dramatist of the English Augustan Age. He is best known for *Marriage à La mode* (comedy, 1673), *All for Love* (tragedy based on Shakespeare's *Antony and Cleopatra*, 1678), and *Absalom and Achitophel* (verse satire in heroic couplets, 1681).

Drys·dale |'drīz,dāl|, Sir Russell (1912–81) British-born Australian painter. He dealt with life in the Australian bush, for example in *The Rabbiter and Family* (1938), and with the plight of Aboriginals in contact with white settlement, as in *Mullaloonah Tank* (1953).

Duane |dwān| U.S. family, including:

William Duane (1760–1835), a journalist. He was co-editor of the *Philadelphia Aurora*, which strongly supported Jeffersonian policies. His great-grandson, **William Duane** (1872–1935), was a physicist. He developed methods and equipment for using radium and X rays in medicine.

Duar·te |'dwärtē; 'dwärtä|, José Napoleón (1925–90) Salvadoran politician. After a corrupt military deprived him of his elected presidency (1972), he hid in exile in Venezuela for 7 years and returned in 1980 as a figurehead for the ruling junta; he was elected president (1984–89).

Du Bar·ry |dōō 'berē|, Marie Jeanne Bécu, Comtesse (1743–93) French courtier and mistress of Louis XV. During the French Revolution she was arrested by the Revolutionary Tribunal and guillotined.

Dub·ček |'dōōb,CHek|, Alexander (1921–92) Czechoslovak statesman, first secretary of the Czechoslovak Communist Party (1968–69). Dubček was the driving force behind the Czechoslovakian political reforms of 1968 (the Prague Spring), which prompted the Soviet invasion of Czechoslovakia in 1968 and his removal from office. After the collapse of communism in 1989, he was elected speaker of the Federal Assembly in the new Czechoslovak parliament.

Du·bin·sky |də'binskē|, David (1892–1982) U.S. labor leader and social reformer, born in Russia. He served as president of the International Ladies' Garment Workers Union (1932–66).

Du Bois |dōō'bois|, W. E. B. (1868–1963) U.S. writer, sociologist, and political activist; full name *William Edward Burghardt Du Bois*. He was an important figure in campaigning for equality for black Americans arguing in *The Souls of Black Folk* (1903) that racial equality could be achieved only by political organization and struggle. He co-founded the National Association for the Advancement of Colored People (NAACP) in 1909.

Du·buf·fet |dOEbOE'fä|, Jean (1901–85) French painter. He rejected traditional techniques, incorporating materials such as sand and plaster in his paintings and producing sculptures made from rubbish.

Duc·cio |'do͞otCHō|, di Buoninsegna (c.1255–1318) Italian painter, founder of the Sienese school of painting; full name *Duccio di Buoninsegna.* The only fully documented surviving work by him is the *Maestà* for the high altar of Siena Cathedral (completed 1311).

Du·ce |'do͞oCHā|, Il the title assumed by Benito Mussolini in 1922.

Du·champ |do͞o'SHäm|, Marcel (1887–1968) French-born artist, a U.S. citizen from 1955. A leading figure of the Dada movement and originator of conceptual art, he invented "ready-mades," mass-produced articles selected at random and displayed as works of art—most famously a bicycle wheel and a urinal.

Du·chov·ny |do͞o'kəvnē|, David (1960–) U.S. actor. He won awards for his role as FBI agent Fox Mulder on "The X-Files."

Dud·ley |'dədlē|, Robert, Earl of Leicester (c.1532–88) English nobleman, military commander, and court favorite of Elizabeth I.

Due·sen·berg |'do͞ozən,bərg|, Frederick Samuel (1877–1932) U.S. manufacturer, born in Germany. He founded the Duesenberg Motor Co. (1917) and designed racing and luxury cars.

Du·fay |do͞o'fā|, Guillaume (c.1400–74) French composer. He made a significant contribution to the development of Renaissance polyphony.

Dufy, Raoul (1877–1953) French painter and textile designer His characteristic style involved calligraphic outlines sketched on brilliant background washes.

Du·ka·kis |də'käkəs|, Michael Stanley (1933–) U.S. politician. He was governor of Massachusetts (1975–79, 1983–91) and a Democratic presidential candidate (1988). Olympia Dukakis is his cousin.

Du·ka·kis |də'käkəs|, Olympia (1931–) U.S. actress. Notable movies: *Steel Magnolias* (1989) and *Moonstruck* (1987, Academy Award). Michael Dukakis is her cousin.

Duke |do͞ok|, U.S. industrialists. **Benjamin Newton Duke** (1855–1929) and his brother **James Buchanan Duke** (1856–1925) established a tobacco factory (1874) and joined with rival companies in the American Tobacco Co. Benjamin served as the company's president. James founded Duke University. James's daughter, **Doris Duke** (1912–93), was a philanthopist and heiress to the Duke tobacco fortune.

Dul·les |'dələs|, John Foster (1888–1959) U.S. statesman and international lawyer. He was the U.S. adviser at the founding of the United Nations in 1945 and negotiated the peace treaty with Japan in 1951. As U.S. secretary of state at the height of the Cold War (1953–59) he urged the stockpiling of nuclear arms to deter Soviet aggression.

Du·luth |də'lo͞oTH|, Daniel Greysolon (1636–1710) French explorer. He was sent by Comte de Frontenac to establish forts and trading posts in the western part of the Great Lakes region (1678). Duluth, Minnesota, is named after him.

Du·mas |do͞o'mä| French authors, including **Alexandre Dumas** (1802–70); known as **Dumas** *pére* (father). Although he was a pioneer of the romantic theater in France, his reputation now rests on his historical adventure novels *The Three Musketeers* (1844–45) and *The Count of Monte Cristo* (1844–45). His son, **Alexandre Dumas** (1824–95), was known as **Dumas** *fils* (son). He wrote the novel (and play) *La Dame aux camélias* (1848 and 1852), which formed the basis of Verdi's opera *La Traviata* (1853).

Du Mau·ri·er |də'mawrē,ā| English authors, including French-born **George (Louis Palmella Busson) du Maurier** (1834–96), a novelist, cartoonist, and illustrator. He is chiefly remembered for his novel *Trilby* (1894), which included the character Svengali and gave rise to the word *Svengali,* for a person who has a hypnotic influence over someone else. His granddaughter **Dame Daphne du Maurier** (1907–89) was a novelist. Many of her popular novels and period romances are set in the West Country of England, where she spent most of her life. Notable works: *Jamaica Inn* (1936) and *Rebecca* (1938).

Du Mont |'dōō,mänt; ,dōō'mänt|, Allen Balcom (1901–65) U.S. engineer, inventor, and manufacturer. He established Du Mont Laboratories (1931) and developed and manufactured commercial television receivers.

Du•mont d'Ur•ville |dōō'mōndōōr-'vēl|, Jules-Sébastien-César (1790–1842) French naval commander and explorer. He explored Polynesia and the South Seas (1826–29).

Dun |dən|, Robert Graham (1826–1900) U.S. businessman. He established R. G. Dun & Co., which merged into Dun & Bradstreet, Inc. (1933), and published *Dun's Review* business report (from 1893).

Dun•bar |'dən,bär|, Paul Laurence (1872–1906) U.S. poet. The son of escaped slaves, he published a volume of poetry (1893) whose reputation was established by favorable notice from William Dean Howells.

Dun•bar |'dən,bär|, William (*c.*1460–*c.*1520) Scottish poet. He was the author of satires such as the political allegory "The Thrissill and the Rois" ("The Thistle and the Rose", 1503) and of elegies such as "Lament for the Makaris."

Dun•bar |'dən,bär|, William (1749–1810) U.S. scientist. He explored the old Southwest for President Thomas Jefferson, noting the existence of Hot Springs in Arkansas and exploring the Mississippi Delta.

Dun•can |'dəNGkən|, Isadora (1877–1927) U.S. dancer and teacher. She was a pioneer of modern dance, famous for her "free" barefoot dancing. She died in a freak accident, strangled when her long scarf became entangled in the wheels of a car.

Dun•can I |'dəNGkən| (*c.*1010–40) king of Scotland (1034–40). He was killed in battle by Macbeth.

Dun•lap |'dənlawp|, William (1766–1839) U.S. playwright, painter, and historian. He was the first American to make a serious business of writing for the stage and is honored as the father of the American theater.

Dun•lop |'dənläp|, John Boyd (1840–1921) Scottish inventor. He developed the first successful pneumatic bicycle

tire (1888), manufactured by the company he founded.

Dunne |dən|, Finley Peter (1867–1936) U.S. columnist and editor of the *Chicago Journal*. He is best known for creating the character of Mr. Dooley, Irish saloonkeeper and humorous commentator on current events.

Dunne |dən|, John Gregory (1932–   ) U.S. writer. He is the author of fiction such as *True Confessions* (1977) and nonfiction such as *Vegas* (1974).

Dunne |dən|, John William (1875–1949) English philosopher. His work is especially concerned with time and includes *An Experiment with Time* (1927) and *The Serial Universe* (1934), both of which influenced the plays of J. B. Priestley.

Duns Sco•tus |dən'skōtəs|, John (*c.*1266–1308) Scottish theologian and scholar. A profoundly influential figure in the Middle Ages, he was the first major theologian to defend the theory of the Immaculate Conception, and opposed St. Thomas Aquinas in arguing that faith was a matter of will rather than something dependent on logical proofs.

Dun•sta•ble |'dənstəbəl|, John (*c.*1390–1453) English composer. He was a significant early exponent of counterpoint.

Dun•stan |'dənstən|, St. (*c.*924–88) Anglo-Saxon prelate. As Archbishop of Canterbury he introduced the strict Benedictine rule into England and succeeded in restoring monastic life. Feast day, May 19.

du Pont |dōō'pän|, E. I. (1771–1834) U.S. industrialist, born in France. Full name *Eleuthère Irenee du Pont*. The gunpowder manufacturing plant that he established near Wilmington, Delaware, in 1802 became an American corporate giant, due largely to the government contracts that ensured its early success, especially during the War of 1812.

Du Pré |dōō'prā|, Jacqueline (1945–87) English cellist. She made her solo debut at the age of 16 and became famous for her interpretations of cello concertos. Her performing career was halted in 1972 by multiple sclerosis.

Du•rand |də'rænd|, Asher Brown (1796–1886) U.S. artist. He was one of the earliest landscape painters of the Hudson River School.

Du·rand |də'rænd|, William Frederick (1859–1958) U.S. mechanical engineer and educator. He was a consultant for the Hoover, Grand Coulee, and other dams.

Du·rant |də'rænd| U.S. historians. **Will** (1885–1981; full name *William James Durant*) and his wife **Ariel** (1898–1981; born *Chaya "Ida" Kaufman* in Ukraine) wrote the 11-volume "Story of Civilization" series, works that were published over a 40-year period (1935–75). Volume 10, *Rousseau and Revolution* (1967) won a Pulitzer Prize. The Durants were awarded the Presidential Medal of Freedom (1977).

Du·rant |də'rænd|, Graham J. (1934–) English inventor. With John Colin Emmett (1939-) and C. Robin Ganellin (1934-) he discovered antiulcer compounds (trade name Tagamet).

Du·rant |də'rænd|, Thomas Clark (1820–85) U.S. businessman. He was an organizer (1863–69) and president (1863–67) of the Union Pacific Railroad Co.

Du·rant |də'rænd|, William Crapo (1861–1947) U.S. industrialist. He created or took over several automobile companies, including Buick (1904), General Motors (1908), and Chevrolet (1911). He invested poorly and ended his life bankrupt.

Du·ran·te |də'ræntē|, Jimmy (1893–1980) U.S. entertainer. Born *James Francis Durante*. The gravelly-voiced star of Broadway, movies, radio, and television, his career began in vaudeville.

Du·ras |doo'räs|, Marguerite (1914–96) French novelist, movie director, and dramatist; pseudonym of *Marguerite Donnadieu*. She is best known for the screenplay to Alain Resnais' movie *Hiroshima mon amour* (1959) and for her semiautobiographical novel *L'Amant* (1984).

Dü·rer |'dərər|, Albrecht (1471–1528) German engraver and painter. He was the leading German artist of the Renaissance, important for his technically advanced woodcuts and copper engravings and also noted for his watercolors and drawings.

Du·rey |doo'rā|, Louis-Edmond (1888–1979) French composer. A member until 1921 of the group Les Six, he later wrote music of a deliberate mass appeal, in accordance with communist doctrines on art. Notable works: *La Longue marche* (cantata, 1949).

Durk·heim |'dərk,hīm|, Émile (1858–1917) French sociologist, one of the founders of modern sociology. He became the first professor of sociology at the Sorbonne (1913). Notable works: *The Division of Labor in Society* (1893) and *Suicide* (1897).

Du·ro·cher |də'rōsHər|, Leo Ernest (1905–91) U.S. baseball player and manager. He is noted for coining the remark, "nice guys finish last."

Dur·rell |doo'rel| English family, including: **Lawrence (George) Durrell** (1912–90), a novelist, poet, and travel writer. He spent much of his life abroad, particularly in the Mediterranean. Notable works: *Alexandria Quartet* (four novels, 1957–60) and *Prospero's Cell* (travel, 1945). His brother, **Gerald (Malcolm) Durrell** (1925–95), was a zoologist and writer. In 1958 he founded a zoo (later the Jersey Wildlife Preservation Trust) devoted to the conservation and captive breeding of endangered species. Notable works: *My Family and Other Animals* (1956).

Dürrenmatt, Friedrich (1921–90) Swiss playwright, novelist, and critic. Notable works: *The Visit* (1958).

Dur·yea |'door,yä| U.S. inventors and manufacturers. **Charles Edgar Duryea** (1861–1938) and his brother **James Frank Duryea** (1869–1967) built a gasoline automobile (1893) and organized Duryea Motor Wagon Co. (1895).

Du·se |'doozä|, Eleonora (1858–1924) Italian actress, best known for her tragic roles, particularly in plays by Ibsen and Gabriele d'Annunzio.

Dus·ton |'dəstən|, Hannah (1657– c. 1736) American heroine. After being captured by Indians (1697), she escaped and returned home after killing and scalping her captors.

Du Toit |də'toi|, Stephanus Jacobus (1847–1911) South African clergyman and politician. He founded the Society of True South Africans (1875) and helped establish the language (Afrikaans) and political identity of Boers.

Dut•ton |'dətn|, Clarence Edward (1841–1912) U.S. geologist. He worked for the U.S. Geological Survey (1875–90), studying the plateau regions of Utah, Arizona, and New Mexico, and developing the concept of isotasy.

Dut•ton |'dətn|, Edward Payson (1831–1923) U.S. publisher. He founded E. P. Dutton & Co.(1858).

Du•val |dōō'väl|, Gabriel (1752–1844) U.S. Supreme Court justice (1811–35). He served as comptroller of the U.S. Treasury (1802–11).

Du•val•ier |dōō,väl'yā|, François (1907–71) Haitian statesman, president (1957–71); known as **Papa Doc**. His regime was noted for its oppressive nature, opponents being assassinated or forced into exile by his security force, the Tontons Macoutes. He was succeeded by his son **Jean-Claude Duvalier** (1951–) known as **Baby Doc**, who was overthrown by a mass uprising in 1986.

Du•vall |dōō'väl; də'väl|, Robert (1931–) U.S. actor, director, producer, and screenwriter. Notable movies: *Tender Mercies* (1983, Academy Award).

Du•Vig•neaud |dōō'vinyō|, Vincent (1901–78) U.S. biochemist. He studied vitamins and hormones, especially insulin, methionine, and biotin, and isolated and synthesized oxytocin and vasopressin, for which he received the Nobel Prize for Chemistry (1955).

Duy•ckinck |'dī,kiNGk|, Evert Augustus (1816–78) U.S. editor. With his brother George Long (1823–63), he edited the influential *New York Literary World* (1848–53) and compiled the two-volume *Cyclopaedia of American Literature* (1855).

Dvoř•ák |də'vawr,ZHäk|, Antonín (1841–1904) Czech composer Czech composer. Combining ethnic folk elements with the Viennese musical tradition, he wrote chamber music, operas, and songs, but is probably best known for his ninth symphony (*From the New World*, 1892–95).

Dwig•gins |'dwigənz|, William Addison (1880–1956) U.S. book designer. He designed the typefaces Metro (1929), Electra (1935), Caledonia (1939), and Eldorado (1953).

Dwight |dwīt|, John Sullivan (1813–93) U.S. music critic. He founded and edited *Dwight's Journal of Music* (1852–81) and was an organizer of the Boston Philharmonic society (1865).

Dwight |dwīt|, Timothy (1752–1817) U.S. clergyman and educator. He was grandson of Jonathan Edwards and a leading Calvinist and Federalist. From 1795 to 1817, he served as president of Yale University.

Dy•lan |'dilən|, Bob (1941–) U.S. singer and songwriter; born *Robert Allen Zimmerman*. The leader of an urban folk-music revival in the 1960s, he became known for political and protest songs such as "The Times They Are A-Changin" (1964). When on tour in 1966 he caused controversy for using an amplified backing group. His lyrics are noted for their poetic imagery. Notable albums: *Highway 61 Revisited* (1965) and *Blood on the Tracks* (1975).

Dzer•zhin•sky |jər'ZHinskē|, Feliks (Edmundovich) (1877–1926) Russian Bolshevik leader, of Polish descent. He was the organizer and first head of the postrevolutionary Soviet security police (the Cheka, later the OGPU).

Ee

Eads |ēdz|, James Buchanan (1820–87) U.S. engineer and inventor. He invented the diving bell and built the first bridge across the Mississippi at St. Louis (Eads Bridge, 1867–74).

Ead·wig variant spelling of EDWY.

Ea·ker |'ākər|, Ira Clarence (1896–1987) U.S. general. An air force commander during World War II, he was a leader in creating a separate branch of the armed services for the U.S. Air Force (1947).

Ea·kins |'ākinz|, Thomas (1844–1916) U.S. painter and photographer noted for his portraits and genre pictures of life in Philadelphia. His picture *The Gross Clinic* (1875) aroused controversy because of its explicit depiction of surgery.

Eames |ēmz|, Wilberforce (1855–1937) U.S. bibliographer. He was bibliographer of the New York Public Library and the editor of *Sabin's Dictionary*.

Ear·hart |'er,härt|, Amelia (1898–1937) U.S. aviator. In 1932 she became the first woman to fly across the Atlantic solo. Her aircraft disappeared over the Pacific Ocean during a subsequent round-the-world flight.

Ear·ly |'ərlē|, Jubal Anderson (1816–94) U.S. Confederate army officer. He nearly reached the capital in his 1864 raid on Washington, but was defeated several months later by Sheridan in the Shenandoah Valley and was relieved of his command.

Earn·hardt |'ərnhhärt|, Dale (1952–) U.S. racecar driver. He was a seven-time NASCAR national champion.

Earp |ərp|, Wyatt (Berry Stapp) (1848–1929) U.S. marshal and frontiersman. He is famous for the gunfight at the OK Corral (1881), in which Wyatt with his brothers and his friend Doc Holliday fought the Clanton brothers at Tombstone, Arizona.

East·man |'ēs(t)mən|, George (1854–1932) U.S. inventor and manufacturer of photographic equipment. He invented flexible roll film coated with light-sensitive emulsion and, in 1888, the Kodak camera for use with it.

East·wood |'ēs(t),wʊd|, Clint (1930–) U.S. movie actor and director. He became famous with his role in *A Fistful of Dollars* (1964), the first cult "spaghetti western" (movie about the Old West filmed in Italy); other successful movies include *Dirty Harry* (1971). Movies directed include *Bird* (1988) and the western *Unforgiven* (1992).

E·ber·hart, Richard (Ghormley) (1904–) U.S. poet. He won the 1962 Bollingen Prize, the 1966 Pulitzer Prize for his *Selected Poems*, and the National Book Award.

E·bert |'ēbərt|, Roger (1942–) U.S. movie critic. With critic Gene Siskel, he was co-host of a syndicated television program in which they reviewed current films.

Ec·cles |'ekəlz|, Sir John Carew (1903–97) Australian physiologist, who demonstrated the way in which nerve impulses are conducted by means of chemical neurotransmitters. Nobel Prize for Physiology or Medicine (1963).

Eck·ardt |'ekərt|, (Arthur) Roy (1918–98) U.S. clergyman and educator. He was a pioneer in Christian-Jewish relations.

Eck·ert |'ekərt|, John Presper, Jr. (1919–) U.S. electrical engineer. A pioneer in the development of the modern computer working for the Sperry Rand Corp., he designed BINAC, a step towards the UNIVAC 1.

Eco |'e,kō|, Umberto (1932–) Italian novelist and semiotician. Notable works: *The Name of the Rose* (novel, 1981), *Travels in Hyperreality* (writings on semiotics, 1986).

Ed·berg |'edbərg|, Stefan (1966–) Swedish tennis player.

Ed·ding·ton |'ediNGtən|, Sir Arthur Stanley (1882–1944) English astronomer, considered the founder of astrophysics. He used Einstein's theory of relativity to explain the bending of light by gravity that he observed in the 1919 solar eclipse.

Ed·dy |'edē|, Mary Baker (1821–1910) U.S. religious leader and founder of the

Christian Science movement. Long a victim of various ailments, she believed herself cured by a faith healer, Phineas Quimby, and later evolved her own system of spiritual healing.

Edel, (Joseph) Leon (1907–97) U.S. literary critic. His five-volume *Life of Henry James* (1953–72) won a Pulitzer Prize and a National Book Award for two of its volumes.

Edel·man, Marian Wright (1939–) U.S. human rights activist. She was founder and president of the Children's Defense Fund.

Eden |'ēdən|, (Robert) Anthony, 1st Earl of Avon (1897–1977) British Conservative statesman, prime minister (1955–57). His premiership was dominated by the Suez crisis of 1956; widespread opposition to Britain's role in this led to his resignation.

Eder·le, Gertrude Caroline (1906–) U.S. swimmer. The winner of three Olympic medals (1924), she became the first woman to swim the English Channel (1926), breaking the existing men's record by two hours.

Ed·gar |'edgər| king of England (959–75), younger brother of Edwy. He became king of Northumbria and Mercia in 957 when these regions renounced their allegiance to Edwy, succeeding to the throne of England on Edwy's death.

Ed·ger·ton |'ejərtən|, Harold Eugene (1903–90) U.S. electrical engineer. He invented stroboscopic photography.

Edge·worth |'ej,wərTH|, Maria (1767–1849) Irish novelist, born in England. Notable works: *Castle Rackrent* (1800) and *Belinda* (1801).

Ed·in·burgh, Duke of |'ed(ə)n,bərə; 'ed(ə)n,bərō| see PHILIP, PRINCE.

Ed·i·son |'edəsən|, Thomas (Alva) (1847–1931) U.S. inventor. He took out the first of more than a thousand patents at the age of 21. His inventions include automatic telegraph systems, the carbon microphone for telephones, the phonograph, and the carbon filament lamp.

Ed·mund I |'edmənd| (921–46) king of England, reigned 939–46. After succeeding Athelstan, Edmund spent much of his reign trying to win his northern lands back from the Norse control.

Ed·mund II |'edmənd| (*c.*980–1016)

king of England, son of Ethelred the Unready, reigned 1016; known as **Edmund Ironside**. Edmund led the resistance to Canute's forces in 1015, but was eventually defeated and forced to divide the kingdom with Canute. On Edmund's death Canute became king of all England.

Ed·mund |'edmənd|, St. (*c.*1175–1240) English churchman and teacher, archbishop of Canterbury (1234–40); born *Edmund Rich*. He was the last primate of all England. Feast day, November 16.

Ed·mund Cam·pi·on, St. |'edmənd 'kæmpēən| see CAMPION.

Ed·mund Iron·side |'edməd 'iərn,sīd| Edmund II of England (see EDMUND).

Ed·munds |'edmən(d)z|, George Franklin (1828–1919) U.S. lawyer and politician. As a member of the U.S. Senate from Vermont (1866–91), he helped draft the Sherman Antitrust Act (1890) and the Edmunds Act (1882), which outlawed polygamy in the territories.

Ed·mund the Martyr |'edmənd|, St. (*c.*841–70) king of East Anglia (855–70). After the defeat of his army by the invading Danes in 870, tradition holds that he was captured and shot with arrows for refusing to reject the Christian faith or to share power with his pagan conqueror. Feast day, November 20.

Ed·ward |'edwərd| the name of six kings of England and also one of Great Britain and Ireland and one of the United Kingdom: **Edward I** (1239–1307; reigned 1272–1307), the son of Henry III. He was known as **the Hammer of the Scots**. His campaign against Prince Llewelyn ended with the annexation of Wales in 1284, but he failed to conquer Scotland, where resistance was led by Sir William Wallace and later Robert the Bruce. **Edward II** (1284–1327; reigned 1307–27), the son of Edward I. In 1314 he was defeated by Robert the Bruce at Bannockburn. In 1326 Edward's wife, Isabella of France, and her lover, Roger de Mortimer, invaded England; Edward was deposed in favor of his son and murdered. **Edward III** (1312–77; reigned 1327–77), the son of Edward II. In 1330 he took control of his kingdom, banishing Isabella and executing Mortimer.

He supported Edward de Baliol, the pretender to the Scottish throne, and started the Hundred Years War. **Edward IV** (1442–83; reigned 1461–83), the son of Richard, Duke of York. He became king after defeating the Lancastrian Henry VI. Edward was briefly forced into exile (1470–71) by the Earl of Warwick but regained his position with victory at Tewkesbury in 1471. **Edward V** (1470–c. 1483; reigned 1483 but not crowned), the son of Edward IV. Edward and his brother Richard (known as the Princes of the Tower) were probably murdered and the throne was taken by their uncle, Richard III. **Edward VI** (1537–53; reigned 1547–53), the son of Henry VIII. His reign saw the establishment of Protestantism as the state religion. **Edward VII** (1841–1910; reigned 1901–10), the son of Queen Victoria. Although he played little part in government on coming to the throne, his popularity helped revitalize the monarchy. **Edward VIII** (1894–1972; reigned 1936 but not crowned), the son of George V. Edward abdicated eleven months after coming to the throne in order to marry the American divorcee Mrs. Wallis Simpson. Upon the accession by his brother George VI, Edward became Duke of Windsor.

Ed·ward |'edwərd|, Prince (1964–   ) British prince. Full name *Edward Antony Richard Louis*; he is the third son of Elizabeth II.

Edward, Prince of Wales see BLACK PRINCE.

Ed·wards |'edwərdz|, Jonathan (1703–58) American clergyman and theologian. Widely known as a powerful preacher, he served as a missionary to the Indians at Stockbridge, Massachusetts, and is considered the greatest theologian of American Puritanism.

Ed·ward the Confessor |'edwərd|, St. (c. 1003–66) son of Ethelred the Unready, king of England (1042–66). Famed for his piety, Edward founded Westminster Abbey, where he was eventually buried. Feast day, October 13.

Ed·ward the Elder |'edwərd| (c. 870–924) son of Alfred the Great, king of Wessex (899–924). His military successes against the Danes made it possi-

ble for his son Athelstan to become the first king of all England in 925.

Ed·ward the Martyr |'edwərd|, St. (c. 963–78) son of Edgar, king of England (975–78). Edward was faced by a challenge for the throne from supporters of his half-brother, Ethelred, who eventually had him murdered at Corfe Castle in Dorset. Feast day, March 18.

Edwy |'edwē| (died 959) king of England (955–57). Also **Eadwig**. He was probably only 15 years old when he became king; after Mercia and Northumbria renounced him in favor of his brother Edgar, he ruled over only the lands south of the Thames.

Egas Moniz, Antonio Caetano de Abreu Freire (1874–1955) Portuguese neurologist. He developed cerebral angiography as a diagnostic technique, and pioneered the treatment of certain psychotic disorders by the use of prefrontal lobotomy. Nobel Prize for Physiology or Medicine (1949).

Eg·bert |'egbərt| (died 839) king of Wessex (802–39). In 825 he won a decisive victory that temporarily brought Mercian supremacy to an end and foreshadowed the supremacy that Wessex later secured over all England.

Eh·ren·burg |'ārinbərg|, Ilya (Grigorevich) (1891–1967) Russian novelist and journalist. He became famous during World War II for his anti-German propaganda in *Pravda* and *Red Star*. His novels include *The Thaw* (1954), a work criticizing Stalinism.

Eh·ricke |'ārik|, Krafft A. (1917–84) U.S. aeronautical engineer and physicist. The chief scientific adviser to Rockwell International Corp.'s space division, he designed and developed the Atlas and Centaur rockets.

Ehr·lich |'erlik|, Paul (1854–1915) German medical scientist. One of the founders of modern immunology and chemotherapy, he developed techniques for staining specific tissues, believing that a disease organism could be destroyed by an appropriate "magic bullet." The effective treatment of syphilis in 1911 proved his theories.

Ehr·lich·man |'erlikmän|, John Daniel (1925–   ) U.S. government official. A domestic policy adviser to President Nixon, he resigned (1973) and was convicted (1975) of perjury, conspiracy, and obstruction of justice in the Watergate scandal.

Eich·mann |'ĭkmən|, (Karl) Adolf (1906–62) German Nazi administrator who was responsible for administering the concentration camps. In 1960 he was traced by Israeli agents and executed after trial in Israel.

Eif·fel |'ĭfəl|, Alexandre Gustave (1832–1923) French engineer, best known as the designer and builder of the Eiffel Tower and architect of the inner structure of the Statue of Liberty.

Eijk·man |'ĭkmän|, Christiaan (1858–1930) Dutch physician. Eijkman's work resulted in a simple cure for the disease beriberi and led to the discovery of the vitamin thiamine. Nobel Prize for Physiology or Medicine (1929).

Ein·stein |'īn,stīn|, Albert (1879–1955) German-born U.S. theoretical physicist, founder of the theory of relativity. Einstein is often regarded as the greatest scientist of the 20th century. In 1905 he published his special theory of relativity and in 1915 he succeeded in incorporating gravitation in his general theory of relativity, which was vindicated when one of its predictions was observed during the solar eclipse of 1919. However, Einstein searched without success for a unified field theory embracing electromagnetism, gravitation, relativity, and quantum mechanics. He influenced the decision to build an atom bomb, but after World War II he spoke out passionately against nuclear weapons.

Eint·ho·ven |'īnt,hōvən|, Willem (1860–1927) Dutch physiologist. He devised the first electrocardiograph, through which he was able to identify specific muscular contractions in the heart.

Eise·ley |'āzlē|, Loren Corey (1907–77) U.S. anthropologist, educator, and author. Notable works: *The Immense Journey* (1957) and *The Man Who Saw Through Mirrors* (1973).

Ei·sen·how·er |'īzən,howər|, Dwight David (1890–1969) see box. **Mamie Geneva Doud Eisenhower** (1896–

Eisenhower, Dwight David
34th U.S. president

Life dates: 1890–1969
Place of birth: Denison, Texas
Mother: Ida Elizabeth Stover Eisenhower
Father: David Jacob Eisenhower
Wife: Mamie (Marie) Geneva Doud Eisenhower
Children: Dwight, John
Nickname: Ike
College/University: U.S. Military Academy, West Point
Military service: directed tank training during World War I; general staff positions between the wars; commanding general of U.S. forces in the European theater during World War II; directed amphibious invasions of North Africa, Sicily, and Italy; as supreme commander of the Allied Expeditionary Force in Europe, directed Normandy invasion; U.S. Army chief of staff; supreme commander of NATO
Political career: none prior to presidency
Party: Republican
Home state: Kansas (family moved to Abilene in his infancy)
Opponent in presidential races: Adlai E. Stevenson
Term of office: Jan. 20, 1953–Jan. 20, 1961
Vice president: Richard M. Nixon
Notable events of presidency: McCarthy hearings; Supreme Court rules racial segregation of schools unconstitutional; Salk polio vaccine introduced; Suez Canal crisis; National Guard ordered to integrate schools in Little Rock, Ark.; interstate highway system begun; St. Lawrence Seaway completed; Soviet Sputnik launched; first U.S. satellite, Explorer I, launched; Alaska admitted as 49th state; Hawaii admitted as 50th state
Other achievements: Graduated first in his class at Command and General Staff School, Fort Leavenworth, Kansas; president, Columbia University
Place of burial: Abilene, Kansas

1979), wife of Dwight D. Eisenhower and U.S. first lady (1953–61).

Ei·sen·staedt |'īzən,stæt|, Alfred (1898–1995) U.S. photojournalist, born in Dirschau, Germany (now

Tczew, Poland). He was one of the original photographers for *Life* magazine (1932–72).

Ei·sen·stein |'īzən,SHtīn|, Sergei (Mikhailovich) (1898–1948) Soviet movie director, born in Latvia. He is chiefly known for *The Battleship Potemkin* (1925), a commemoration of the Russian Revolution of 1905 celebrated for its pioneering use of montage.

Eis·ner |'īznər|, Michael Dammann (1942–   ) U.S. corporate executive. He is the CEO of Walt Disney Corp. (1984–   ).

Eis·ner |'äznər|, Will (1917–   ) U.S. cartoonist, publisher, and educator. Full name *William E. Eisner*. He created "The Spirit," a weekly adventure series that appeared as an insert in Sunday newspapers (1940–51).

Ek·man |äkmin|, Vagn Walfrid (1874–1954) Swedish oceanographer. He recognized the importance of the Coriolis effect on ocean currents, showing that it can be responsible for surface water moving at an angle to the prevailing wind direction.

El·ton |'eltən|, Charles Sutherland (1900–91) English zoologist. Elton pioneered the study of animal ecology, and his research into rodent populations found practical application in vermin control.

Ed Cid |el 'sid| see CID, EL.

El·dridge |'eldrij|, (David) Roy (1911–89) U.S. jazz trumpeter. He was one of the first African Americans to play in formerly all-white swing bands, including those of Gene Krupa (1941) and Artie Shaw (1944).

El·ea·nor of Aquitaine |'elənər əv 'ækwi,tän; 'elənawr| (*c.* 1122–1204) daughter of the Duke of Aquitaine, queen of France (1137–52) and of England (1154–89). She was married to Louis VII of France in 1137; in 1152, with the annulment of their marriage, she married the future Henry II of England.

El·gar |'elgär|, Sir Edward (William) (1857–1934) British composer He is known particularly for the *Enigma Variations* (1899), the oratorio *The Dream of Gerontius* (1900), and for patriotic

pieces such as the five *Pomp and Circumstance* marches.

El·gin |'el,gən|, James Bruce, 8th Earl of (1811–63) British colonial statesman. As Governor General of Canada (1847–54) he commissioned Louis Hippolyte Lafontaine to form Canada's first cabinet government in 1848. He maintained good relationships with subsequent administrations and successfully negotiated a reciprocity treaty between Canada and the U.S. in 1854.

El·gin |'el,gən|, Thomas Bruce, 7th Earl of (1766–1841) British diplomat and art connoisseur. Between 1803 and 1812 he controversially transported a number of classical sculptures (the "Elgin Marbles") to England from the Parthenon and elsewhere in Greece, which was then under Turkish control.

El Gre·co |el 'grekō| (1541–1614) Cretan-born Spanish painter; born *Domenikos Theotokopoulos*, he is better known by the Spanish name meaning 'the Greek'. El Greco's portraits and religious works are characterized by distorted perspective, elongated figures, and strident use of color.

Elia |'ēlyə| the pseudonym adopted by Charles Lamb in his *Essays of Elia* (1823) and *Last Essays of Elia* (1833).

Eli·jah |ə'lī(d)ZHə| (9th century BC) a Hebrew prophet in the time of Jezebel who maintained the worship of Jehovah against that of Baal and other pagan gods.

El·iot |'elēət|, Charles William (1834–1926) U.S. educator. He was president of Harvard University (1869–1909) and editor of the *Harvard Classics* (1910).

El·iot |'elēət|, George (1819–80) English novelist. Pseudonym of *Mary Ann Evans*. Her novels of provincial life are characterized by their exploration of moral problems and their development of the psychological analysis that marks the modern novel. Notable works: *Adam Bede* (1859), *The Mill on the Floss* (1860), and *Middlemarch* (1871–72).

El·iot |'elēət|, T. S. (1888–1965) U.S.-born British poet, critic, and dramatist; full name *Thomas Stearns Eliot*. Associated with the rise of literary modernism, he was established as the voice of a disillusioned generation by *The Waste Land*

(1922). *Four Quartets* (1943) revealed his increasing involvement with Christianity. Nobel Prize for Literature (1948).

Eli·sha |ə'līsHə| (9th century) Hebrew prophet, disciple and successor of Elijah.

Eliz·a·beth |ə'lizəbəTH| the name of two English monarchs, including: **Elizabeth I** (1533–1603; reigned 1558–1603), the daughter of Henry VIII; queen of England and Ireland. Succeeding her Catholic sister Mary I, Elizabeth re-established a moderate form of Protestantism as the state religion. Her reign was dominated by the threat of a Catholic restoration and by war with Spain, culminating in the defeat of the Armada in 1588. Shakespeare, Marlowe, and Spenser were all active during her reign, which saw a flowering of national culture. Although frequently courted, she never married. **Elizabeth II** (1926–; reigned 1952–), the daughter of George VI. Born *Princess Elizabeth Alexandra Mary*. She married Prince Philip in 1947. They have four children: Prince Charles, Princess Anne, Prince Andrew, and Prince Edward.

Eliz·a·beth |i'lizəbəTH|, the Queen Mother (1903–) wife of George VI; born *Lady Elizabeth Angela Marguerite Bowes-Lyon*. She married George VI in 1923, when he was Duke of York; they had two daughters, Elizabeth (later Queen Elizabeth II) and Margaret.

Eli·zon·do, Hector (1936–) U.S. actor. He won Emmy Awards in 1996 and 1997 for the television series "Chicago Hope".

El·lery |'elərē|, William (1727–1820) U.S. politician. He was a member of the Continental Congress (1776–81 and 1783–85) and a signer of the Declaration of Independence.

El·let |'elət|, Charles (1810–62) U.S. engineer. He built the first wire suspension bridge in America, over the Schuylkill River in Philadelphia (1841–42).

El·li·cott |'eləcət|, Andrew (1754–1820) U.S. surveyor. He surveyed many state boundaries, including those of New York, Pennsylvania, the District of Columbia, Georgia, South Carolina, and Florida.

El·ling·ton |'eliNGtən|, Duke (1899–1974) U.S. jazz pianist, composer, and bandleader; born *Edward Kennedy Ellington*. Coming to fame in the early 1930s, Ellington wrote over 900 compositions and was one of the first popular musicians to write extended pieces. Notable works: *Mood Indigo* (1930).

El·lis |'eləs|, (Henry) Havelock (1859–1939) English psychologist and writer, remembered as the pioneer of the scientific study of sex. His major work was the six-volume *Studies in the Psychology of Sex* (1897–1910, with a seventh volume added in 1928).

El·lis |'eləs|, Perry (1940–86) U.S. fashion designer.

El·li·son |'eləsən|, Ralph (Waldo) (1914–94) U.S. author. Notable works: *Invisible Man* (1952, National Book Award).

Ell·mann |'elmən|, Richard David (1918–87) U.S. literary critic and professor. He won a Pulitzer Prize for the biography *Oscar Wilde* (1988).

Ells·berg |'elzbərg|, Daniel (1931–) U.S. political analyst and activist. A former adviser to President Nixon on policy in Southeast Asia, he became an avid opponent of the Vietnam War. Indicted for leaking classified Vietnam-related papers (the "Pentagon Papers") to the press in 1971, he was freed of charges when it was disclosed that Nixon had authorized the theft of Ellsberg's psychiatric records as a means of discrediting him.

Ells·worth |'elz,wərTH|, Lincoln (1880–1951) U.S. explorer. He participated in a number of polar expeditions and was the first person to fly over both the North (1926) and South (1935) Poles.

Ells·worth |'elz,wərTH|, Oliver (1745–1807) U.S. Supreme Court justice (1796–1800). He was a member of the Continental Congress (1777–84), author of the "Connecticut Compromise," and drafter of the Judiciary Act of 1789.

Éluard |'elwär|, Paul (1895–1952) French poet; pseudonym of *Eugène Grindel*. He was a leading figure in the surrealist movement.

El·ze·vir |'elzə,vir| a family of Dutch printers. Fifteen members were active

Em·er·son |'emərsən|, Ralph Waldo (1803–82) U.S. philosopher and poet. While visiting England in 1832, he met Coleridge, Wordsworth, and Carlyle, through whom he became associated with German idealism. On his return to the U.S. he evolved the concept of Transcendentalism, which found expression in his essay *Nature* (1836).

between 1581 and 1712, including **Louis** (*c.* 1542–1617), who founded the business *c.* 1580. **Bonaventure** (1583–1652) and **Abraham** (1592–1652) managed the firm in its prime.

Em·mett |'emət|, Daniel Decatur (1815–1904) U.S. songwriter and minstrel-show performer. A member of early blackface minstrel troupes, he composed the song "Dixie."

Em·ped·o·cles |em'pedə,klēz| (*c.* 490–430 BC) Greek philosopher, born in Sicily. He taught that the universe is composed of fire, air, water, and earth, which mingle and separate under the influence of the opposing principles of Love and Strife. According to legend he lept into the crater of Mount Etna in order that he might be thought a god.

Emp·son |'em(p)sən|, Sir William (1906–84) English poet and literary critic. His influential literary criticism includes *Seven Types of Ambiguity* (1930).

En·ders |'endərz|, John Franklin (1897–1985) U.S. virologist. With **Frederick C. Robbins** (1916–92) and **Thomas H. Weller** (1915–92), he devised a method of growing viruses in tissue cultures which led to the development of vaccines against mumps, polio, and measles. The three scientists shared a Nobel Prize for Physiology or Medicine in 1954.

Ene·scu |e'neskoō|, George (1881–1955) Romanian violinist, composer, conductor, and teacher. He taught the concert violinist Yehudi Menuhin.

Eng·els |'eNGgəlz|, Friedrich (1820–95) German socialist and political philosopher. He collaborated with Marx in the writing of the *Communist Manifesto* (1848) and translated and edited Marx's later work. Engels's own writings include *The Condition of the Working Classes in England in 1844* (1845).

En·ni·us |'enēəs|, Quintus (239–169 BC) Roman epic poet and dramatist. He was largely responsible for the creation of a native Roman literature based on Greek models, but only fragments of his many works survive.

En·right |'enrīt|, Elizabeth (1909–68) U.S. author. Notable children's books: *Thimble Summer* (1938, Newbery Medal) and *Then There Were Five* (1944).

En·sor |'ensawr|, James (Sydney), Baron (1860–1949) Belgian painter and engraver, noted for his macabre subjects. His work is significant both for symbolism and for the development of 20th-century expressionism.

En·ver Pa·sha |en'vər pä'sHä| (1881–1922) Turkish political and military leader. A leader of the Young Turks in 1908, he came to power as part of a ruling triumvirate following a coup d'état in 1913.

En·ya |'enyə| (1961–) Irish singer and musician. Born *Eithne Ni Bhronain*. Notable songs: "The Memory of Trees" (1997, Grammy Award).

Eph·ron |'efrən|, Nora (1941–) U.S. journalist. A contributing editor for *New York Magazine* and *Esquire*, she also wrote the novel *Heartburn* (1983).

Ep·ic·te·tus |ˌepək'tētəs| (*c.* 55–135) Greek philosopher who preached the common brotherhood of man and advocated a Stoic philosophy.

Ep·i·cu·rus |'epə,kyoōrəs| (341–270 BC) Greek philosopher, founder of Epicureanism. His physics is based on Democritus' theory of a materialist universe composed of indestructible atoms moving in a void, unregulated by divine providence.

Ep·stein |'ep,stīn|, Brian (1935–67) English manager of the Beatles.

Ep·stein |'ep,stīn|, Sir Jacob (1880–1959) U.S.-born British sculptor. A founding member of the vorticist group, he later had great success in his modeled portraits of the famous, in particular his *Einstein* (1933).

Equi·a·no |ˌekwē'änō|, Olaudah (*c.*1750–97) African slave and writer. Known as **Gustavus Vassa**. He became an active abolitionist in England and published his autobiographical narrative in 1789.

Eras·mus |ə'ræzməs|, Desiderius (c.1466–1536) Dutch humanist and scholar. Dutch name *Gerhard Gerhards*. He was the foremost Renaissance scholar of northern Europe, paving the way for the Reformation with his satires on the Church, including the *Colloquia Familiaria* (1518). However, he opposed the violence of the Reformation and condemned Luther in *De Libero Arbitrio* (1523).

Eras·tus |ə'ræstəs| (1524–83) Swiss theologian and physician. Swiss name *Thomas Lieber*; also *Liebler* or *Lüber*. Professor of medicine at Heidleberg from 1558, he opposed the imposition of a Calvinistic system of Church government in the city. The doctrine of Erastianism was later wrongly attributed to him.

Er·a·tos·the·nes |ˌerə'täsTHəˌnēz| (c.276–194 BC) Greek scholar, geographer, and astronomer. The first systematic geographer of antiquity, he accurately calculated the circumference of the earth and attempted (less successfully) to determine the size and distance of the sun and of the moon.

Er·drich |'ərdrik|, Louise (1954–) U.S. author. Notable works: *Love Medicine* (1984, National Book Critics Circle Award).

Er·ics·son |'eriksən|, John (1803–89) Swedish engineer whose inventions included a steam railway locomotive to rival Stephenson's *Rocket*, and the marine screw propeller (1836).

Er·ics·son |'eriksən|, Leif (970–1020) Norse explorer, son of Erik the Red. Also **Ericson** or **Eriksson**. He sailed westward from Greenland (c. 1000) and reputedly discovered land (variously identified as Labrador, Newfoundland, or New England), which he named Vinland because of the vines he claimed to have found growing there.

Er·ik·son |'eriksən|, Erik Homburger (1902–94) U.S. psychoanalyst, born in Germany. His writings include *Childhood and Society* (1950), *Ghandhi's Truth* (1969, Pulitzer Prize), and *Identity and the Life Cycle* (1980).

Er·ik the Red |'erik| (c.940–c.1010) Norse explorer. He left Iceland in 982 in search of land to the west, exploring Greenland and establishing a Norse settlement there in 986.

Er·lang·er |'ərˌlæNGgər|, Abraham Lincoln (1860–1930) U.S. theatrical manager and producer. With others, he formed the Theatrical Syndicate (1896), which virtually monopolized American theatrical business.

Er·lang·er |'ərˌlæNGgər|, Joseph (1874–1965) U.S. physiologist. Collaborating with Herbert Gasser, he showed that the velocity of a nerve impulse is proportional to the diameter of the fiber. Nobel Prize for Physiology or Medicine (1944, shared with Gasser).

Ernst |ərnst|, Max (1891–1976) German artist. He was a leader of the Dada movement and developed the techniques of collage, photomontage, and frottage. He is probably best known for his surrealist paintings, such as *L'Eléphant de Célèbes* (1921).

Erté |'ertä| (1892–1990) Russian fashion illustrator and set designer. Born *Romain de Tirtoff*.

Ertegun, Ahmet Munir (1923–) U.S. record company executive, born in Turkey. He was cofounder of Atlantic Records (1947) and has been elected to the Rock and Roll Hall of Fame.

Er·ving |'ərviNG|, Julius Winfield (1950–) U.S. basketball player. Known as **Dr. J**. He was elected to the Basketball Hall of Fame (1993).

Esaki |i'säkē|, Leo (1925–) Japanese physicist. He investigated and pioneered the development of quantum-mechanical tunneling of electrons in semiconductor devices, and designed the tunnel diode (also called the Esaki diode). Nobel Prize for Physics (1973).

Esch·er |'esHər|, M.C. (1898–1972) Dutch graphic artist. Full name *Maurits Corneille Escher*. His prints are characterized by their sophisticated use of visual illusion.

Es·cof·fier |ˌeskawf'yä|, Georges-Auguste (1846–1935) French chef. He gained an international reputation while working in London at the Savoy Hotel (1890–9) and later at the Carlton (1899–1919).

Es·po·si·to |espə'zētō|, Phil (1942–) U.S. hockey player. He was elected to Hockey Hall of Fame (1984).

Es•py |es'pī|, James Pollard (1785–1860) U.S. meteorologist. As an adviser to the War Department (from 1842) and the Navy Department (from 1848), he pioneered scientific weather forecasting.

Es•qui•vel, Laura (1950–) Mexican author. Notable works: *Like Water for Chocolate* (1992) and *The Law of Love* (1996).

Es•te•fan |'estə,fän|, Gloria (1957–) U.S. musician, born in Cuba. Born *Gloria Fajardo*. A singer and songwriter of the disco-pop and salsa band Miami Sound Machine, she released her first solo album in 1989.

Es•tes |'estēz|, Eleanor (1906–) U.S. author and librarian. Notable children's books: *Rufus M.* (1941) and *Ginger Pye* (1951, Newbery Medal).

Eth•el•red I |'eTHəl,red| (died 871) king of Wessex and Kent (865–71), elder brother of Alfred. His reign was marked by the continuing struggle against the invading Danes. Alfred joined Ethelred's campaigns and succeeded him on his death.

Eth•el•red II |'eTHəl,red| (c.968–1016) king of England (978–1016); known as **Ethelred the Unready**. Ethelred's inability to confront the Danes after he succeeded his murdered half-brother St. Edward the Martyr led to his payment of tribute to prevent their attacks. In 1013 he briefly lost his throne to the Danish king Sweyn I.

Eth•er•idge |,eTH(ə)rəj|, Melissa (1961–) U.S. singer, songwriter and guitarist. She won Grammy Awards in 1992 and 1994.

Eu•clid |'yoo,klid| (c.300 BC) Greek mathematician. His great work, *Elements of Geometry*, which covered plane geometry, the theory of numbers, irrationals, and solid geometry, was the standard text until other kinds of geometry were discovered in the 19th century.

Eugénie |ō'zHänə| (1826–1920) Spanish-born empress of France (1853–70) and wife of Napoleon III; born *Eugénia María de Montijo de Guzmán*. She contributed much to her husband's court and was an important influence on his foreign policy.

Eu•ler |'oilər|, Leonhard (1707–83) Swiss mathematician. He attempted to elucidate the nature of functions, and his study of infinite series led his successors, notably Abel and Cauchy, to introduce ideas of convergence and rigorous argument into mathematics.

Euler-Chelpin |'oilər 'kelpən| Swedish scientists, including: German-born **Hans Karl August Simon von Euler-Chelpin** (1873–1964), a biochemist. He worked mainly on enzymes and vitamins, and explained the role of enzymes in the alcoholic fermentation of sugar. Nobel Prize for Chemistry (1929). His son **Ulf Svante von Euler-Chelpin** (1905–83), a physiologist, was the first to discover a prostaglandin, which he isolated from semen. Euler also identified noradrenaline as the principal chemical neurotransmitter of the sympathetic nervous system. Nobel Prize for Physiology or Medicine (1970).

Eu•rip•i•des |yə'ripə,dēz| (c.484–406 BC) Greek dramatist. His nineteen surviving plays show important innovations in the handling of traditional myths, such as the introduction of realism, an interest in feminine psychology, and the portrayal of abnormal and irrational states of mind. Notable works: *Medea, Hippolytus, Electra, Trojan Women,* and *Bacchae.*

Eusebius (c.264–340 AD) bishop and Church historian; known as **Eusebius of Caesaria**. His *Ecclesiastical History* is the principal source for the history of Christianity (especially in the Eastern Church) from the age of the Apostles until 324.

Ev•ans |'evənz|, Sir Arthur (John) (1851–1941) English archaeologist. His excavations at Knossos (1899–1935) resulted in the discovery of the Bronze Age civilization of Crete, which he named Minoan after the legendary Cretan king Minos.

Ev•ans |'evənz|, Bill (1929–80) U.S. jazz pianist. Full name *William John Evans*. He developed a bop language based on the style of Bud Powell.

Ev•ans |'evənz|, Dame Edith (Mary) (1888–1976) English actress. She appeared in a wide range of Shakespearean and contemporary roles but is particularly remembered as Lady Bracknell in Oscar Wilde's *The Importance of Being Earnest.*

Ev•ans |'evənz|, Gil (1912–87) Canadian jazz pianist, composer, and arranger; born *Ian Ernest Gilmore Green.* In 1947 he began a long association with Miles Davis, producing albums such as *Porgy and Bess* (1958) and *Sketches of Spain* (1959).

Ev•ans |'evənz|, Herbert McLean (1882–1971) U.S. anatomist and educator. He discovered the 48 human chromosomes (1918) and vitamin E (1922).

Ev•ans |'evənz|, Janet (1971–) U.S. swimmer. She won four Olympic gold medals (three in 1988, one in 1992).

Evans-Pritchard |'evənz 'priCHərd|, Sir Edward (Evan) (1902–73) English anthropologist. He is noted for his studies of the Azande and Nuer peoples of the Sudan, with whom he lived in the 1920s and 1930s.

Ev•arts |'evərtz|, William Maxwell (1818–1901) U.S. lawyer and statesman. He was the U.S. secretary of state (1877–81) and a member of the U.S. Senate from New York (1885–91).

Eve•lyn |'ev(ə)lən|, John (1620–1706) English diarist and writer. He is remembered chiefly for his *Diary* (published posthumously in 1818), which describes such important historical events as the Great Plague and the Great Fire of London.

Ev•er•ly |'evərlē| U.S. singers and songwriters. **Don Everly** (1937–) and his brother **Phil Everly** (1939–) formed the rock-folk-country duo known as the Everly Brothers.

Ev•ers |'evərz|, Medgar Wiley (1925–63) U.S. civil rights leader. He was Mississippi field secretary of the NAACP (1952); his assassination was a factor in President Kennedy's call for new, comprehensive civil rights legislation.

Ev•ert |'evərt|, Chris (1954–) U.S. professional tennis player; full name *Christine Marie Evert.*

Ew•ell |'yo͞oəl|, Richard Stoddert (1817–72) U.S. soldier. He resigned from the U.S. Army to join Confederate forces in charge of Richmond defenses (1861).

Ew•ing |'yo͞oiNG|, Patrick (1962–) U.S. basketball player. A center for the New York Knicks, he led the U.S. Olympic team to gold medals in 1984 and 1992.

Ew•ry |'yo͞o(ə)rē|, Ray C. (1873–1937) U.S. track and field athlete. He won eight Olympic gold medals (two in each year:1900, 1904, 1906, 1908).

Eyre |e(ə)r|, Edward John (1815–1901) British-born Australian explorer and colonial statesman. He undertook explorations in the interior deserts of Australia (1840–1) and later served as lieutenant governor of New Zealand and governor of Jamaica.

Ey•senck |'īzəNGk|, Hans (Jürgen) (1916–97) German-born British psychologist. He is best known for his development of behavior therapy.

Ff

Fa·ber |'fābər|, John Eberhard (1822–79) U.S. businessman, born in Germany. He established the Eberhard Faber Pencil Co. in the U.S. (1861) from his family's German pencil-making business.

Fa·ber |'fābər|, Sir Geoffrey Cust (1889–1961) English publisher and author. He was the founding president (1924–61) of Faber and Faber, Ltd.

Fa·ber·gé |'fæbər‚ZHā|, Peter Carl (1846–1920) Russian goldsmith and jeweler, of French descent. He is famous for the intricate Easter eggs that he made for Czar Alexander III and other royal households.

Fa·bi·us |'fābēəs| (died 203 BC) Roman general and statesman; full name *Quintus Fabius Maximus Verrucosus*; known as **Fabius Cunctator** ("Fabius the Delayer"). After Hannibal's defeat of the Roman army at Cannae in 216 BC, Fabius successfully pursued a strategy of caution and delay in order to wear down the Carthaginian invaders.

Fa·bre |fäb(ə)r|, Jean-Henri (1823–1915) French entomologist. Fabre became well known for his meticulous observations of insect behavior, notably the life cycles of dung beetles, oil beetles, and solitary bees and wasps.

Fa·bri·a·no, Gentile da see GENTILE DA FABRIANO.

Fa·bri·ci·us |fä'brētsēo͞os|, Johann Christian (1745–1808) Danish entomologist. Fabricius studied for two years under Linnaeus, and named and described some 10,000 new species of insect.

Fac·tor |'fæktər|, Max (1877–1938) U.S. businessman, born in Russia. A Russian immigrant who founded the Max Factor makeup company, he developed the first greasepaint cream makeup for use on Hollywood movie actors.

Fag·gin, Federico (1941–) U.S. electronics executive and inventor, born in Italy. In the 1960s, he invented the silicon gate technology that enabled him to codesign and build the first microprocessor (1971).

Fahd |fäd| (1923–) king of Saudi Arabia (1982–). Full name *Fahd ibn Abd al-Aziz al Saud.*

Fah·ren·heit |'ferən‚hīt|, Daniel Gabriel (1686–1736) German physicist. Fahrenheit is best known for his thermometer scale, but also set up his own business to manufacture scientific instruments. He also improved the performance of thermometers, developed an instrument to determine atmospheric pressure from the boiling point of water, and designed a hydrometer.

Fair·banks |'ferbæNGks| U.S. actors. **Douglas (Elton) Fairbanks** (1883–1939), was born *Julius Ullman*. He cofounded United Artists in 1919 and became famous for his swashbuckling movie roles. His son, **Douglas Fairbanks, Jr.,** (1909–), played similar roles.

Fair·banks |'ferbæNGks|, Charles Warren (1852–1918) Vice president of the U.S. (1905–09) and member of the U.S. Senate from Indiana (1897–1905).

Fair·fax |'ferfæks|, Thomas, 3rd Baron Fairfax of Cameron (1612–71). English Parliamentary general. Fairfax helped to secure the restoration of Charles II.

Fai·sal |'fīsəl| name of two kings of Iraq: **Faisal I** (1885–1933; reigned 1921–33). A British-sponsored ruler, he was also supported by fervent Arab nationalists. Under his rule Iraq achieved full independence in 1932. His grandson, **Faisal II** (1935–58; reigned 1939–58), was assassinated in a military coup, after which a republic was established.

Fal·do |'fawldō|, Nick (1959–) English professional golfer; full name *Nicholas Alexander Faldo.*

Falk |fawk|, Peter (1927–) U.S. actor. A stage, movie, and television actor, he was the star of the television series "Columbo."

Fal·la |'fälyə; 'fī͡ə|, Manuel de (1876–1946) Spanish composer and pianist. He composed the ballets *Love, the Magician* (1915) and *The Three-Cornered Hat* (1919); the latter was produced by Diaghilev, with designs by Picasso.

Fal·lop·pio |fäl'lōpyō|, Gabriele (1523–62) Italian anatomist. He discovered the function of oviducts (Fallopian tubes).

Fal·well |'fawl,wel|, Jerry L. (1933–   ) U.S. Baptist clergyman. He was the founder and president of the Moral Majority conservative political action group (1979), which later became the Liberty Foundation.

Fan·euil |'fænyəl|, Peter (1700–43) U.S. merchant. He offered the building known as Faneuil Hall to the city of Boston (1742).

Fan·gio |'fänj(ē)ō|, Juan Manuel (1911–95) Argentinian racecar driver. He first won the world championship in 1951 and then held the title from 1954 until 1957.

Far·a·day |'ferə,dā|, Michael (1791–1867) English physicist and chemist. He contributed significantly to the field of electromagnetism, discovering electromagnetic induction and demonstrating electromagnetic rotation (the key to the electric dynamo and motor). Faraday also discovered the laws of electrolysis and set the foundations for the classical field theory of electromagnetic behavior.

Fard |färd|, Wallace D. (1877– *c.*1934) U.S. religious leader. He founded the Black Muslim movement (1930).

Far·go |'färgō|, William George (1818–81) U.S. businessman. He was an organizer of Wells, Fargo & Co. (1852).

Far·ley |'färlē|, Harriet (1817–1907) U.S. factory worker and writer. She edited *Lowell Offering* (1842–45), which became *New England Offering* (1847–50), a periodical collecting the writings of women mill hands.

Far·mer |'färmər|, Fannie Merritt (1857–1915) U.S. educator and author. She opened Miss Farmer's School of Cookery in 1902; her *Boston Cooking School Cook Book* (1896) was known as "the mother of level measurements."

Far·mer |'färmər|, Moses Gerrish (1820–93) U.S. inventor. He was a co-inventor of the electric fire alarm system and helped develop torpedo warfare.

Far·ne·se |fär'neze|, Alessandro, Duke of Parma (1545–92) Italian general and statesman. While in the service of Philip II of Spain he acted as Governor Gen-eral of the Netherlands (1578–92). He captured Antwerp in 1585, securing the southern Netherlands for Spain.

Farn·ham |'färnəm|, Eliza Wood (1815–64) U.S. reformer and author. As matron of the Ossining, New York, prison women's department (1844–48) she instituted many reforms.

Farns·worth |'färns,wərTH|, Philo Taylor (1906–71) U.S. engineer and inventor. A pioneer in television technology, he created the first all-electronic television image (1926). His other inventions include cold cathode ray tubes and an electron microscope.

Fa·rouk |fə'rōōk| (1920–65) king of Egypt, reigned 1936–52. Farouk's defeat in the Arab–Israeli conflict of 1948, together with the general corruption of his reign, led to a military coup in 1952, masterminded by Nasser. Farouk was forced to abdicate in favor of his infant son, Fuad.

Far·quhar |'färkwär|, George (1678–1707) Irish dramatist. He was a principal figure in Restoration comedy. Notable works: *The Recruiting Officer* (1706) and *The Beaux' Stratagem* (1707).

Far·ra·gut |'ferəgət|, David Glasgow (1801–70) U.S. admiral. Tthe outstanding naval commander of the Civil War, he captured the city of New Orleans (April 1862) and extended Union control of the Mississippi north to Vicksburg.

Far·ra·khan |'ferə,kæn|, Louis (1933–   ) U.S. Muslim minister and African-American nationalist.

Far·rand |'färənd|, Livingston (1867–1939) U.S. psychologist, anthropologist, and educator. A scholar specializing in American Indian studies, he served as president of Columbia University (1901–14), the University of Colorado (1914–19), and Cornell University (1921–37).

Far·rar |'färər|, John Chipman (1896–1974) U.S. publisher and author. He was chairman of Farrar, Straus & Giroux (1929–44).

Far·rell |'ferəl|, J. G. (1935–79) English novelist; full name *James Gordon Farrell.* Notable works: *The Siege of Krishnapur* (1973) and *The Singapore Grip* (1978).

Far•rell |'ferəl|, J. T. (1904–79) U.S. novelist. Full name *James Thomas Farrell*. He achieved fame with his trilogy about Studs Lonigan, a young Chicago Catholic of Irish descent, which began with *Young Lonigan* (1932).

Far•rell |'ferəl|, Suzanne (1945–) U.S. dancer. Born *Roberta Sue Ficker*. She performed with the New York City Ballet (1961–69), where she was principal dancer (1965–69). She is noted for her performance in the movie version of *A Midsummer Night's Dream* (1966).

Far•well |'färwel|, Arthur (1877–1952) U.S. composer and critic. He is known for his American Indian songs.

Far•well |'färwel|, John Villiers (1825–1908) U.S. businessman. He donated the land for the first YMCA building in the U.S. (Chicago).

Fass•bin•der |'fæs,bindər|, Rainer Werner (1946–82) German movie director. His movies dealt largely with Germany during World War II and postwar West German society. Notable movies: *The Bitter Tears of Petra von Kant* (1972).

Fast |fæst|, Howard Melvin (1914–) U.S. author. He is best known as a writer of historical novels and as a member of the Communist party (1943–56) who was imprisoned (1950) for refusing to cooperate with the House Committee on Un-American Activities. He was awarded the Stalin Peace Prize in 1953. Notable works: *Spartacus* (1951), *The Naked God* (1957), and *The Immigrant's Daughter* (1985).

Fa•ti•ma |fə'tēmə; 'fætimə| (*c.*616–633 AD) youngest daughter of the prophet Muhammad and wife of the fourth caliph, Ali. The descendants of Muhammad trace their lineage through her; she is revered especially by Shiite Muslims as the mother of the imams Hasan and Husayn.

Faulk•ner |'fawknər|, William (1897–1962) U.S. novelist. His works deal with the history and legends of the American South and have a strong sense of a society in decline. Notable works: *The Sound and the Fury* (1929), *As I Lay Dying* (1930), and *Absalom! Absalom!* (1936). Nobel Prize for Literature (1949).

Fau•ré |faw'rā; fō'rā|, Gabriel-Urbain (1845–1924) French composer and organist. His best-known work is the *Requiem* (1887) for solo voices, choir, and orchestra; he also wrote songs, piano pieces, chamber music, and incidental music for the theater.

Fau•set, Jessie Redmon (1882–1961) U.S. author and editor. She edited DuBois's *The Crisis*; her four novels feature African-American heroines.

Faust |fowst|, Frederick Schiller (1892–1944) U.S. writer. Pseudonym **Max Brand**. He wrote over 100 western novels, including *Destry Rides Again* (1930); he also wrote scripts for the *Dr. Kildare* movie series.

Faust |fowst|, Johann (*c.*1480–1540) German astronomer and necromancer. Also **Faustus**. Reputed to have sold his soul to the Devil, he became the subject of dramas by Marlowe and Goethe, an opera by Gounod, and a novel by Thomas Mann.

Favre |färv|, Brett (1969–) U.S. football player.

Faw•cett |'fawsət|, Farrah (1947–) U.S. actress. She was a star in the "Charlie's Angels" television program, as well as a number of television movies, including *The Burning Bed* (1984).

Fawkes |fawks|, Guy (1570–1606) English conspirator. He was hanged for his part in the Gunpowder Plot of November 5, 1605. The occasion is commemorated annually in England on Bonfire Night with fireworks, bonfires, and the burning of an effigy called *guy*.

FDR the nickname of President Franklin Delano Roosevelt (see ROOSEVELT, FRANKLIN DELANO).

Fech•ner |'feknər|, Gustav Theodor (1801–87) German physicist and psychologist. Fechner hoped to make psychology a truly objective science and coined the termed *psychophysics* to define his study of the quantitative relationship between degrees of physical stimulation and the resulting sensations.

Feif•fer |'fīfər|, Jules (1929–) U.S. cartoonist and author. He is best known for his satirical cartoons, which first appeared in *The Village Voice* and later were internationally syndicated.

Fein•stein |'fīnstīn|, Dianne (1933–) U.S. politician. She was mayor of San

Francisco, California (1978–88), and U.S. senator (1992–).

Fel·ler |'felər|, Bob (1918–) U.S. baseball player. Full name *Robert William Andrew Feller*; known as **Rapid Robert**. He led American League pitchers in strikeouts seven times. Elected to Baseball Hall of Fame (1962).

Fel·li·ni |fə'lēnē|, Federico (1920–93) Italian movie director. He rose to international fame with *La Strada* (1954), which won an Oscar for best foreign movie. Other major movies include *La dolce vita* (1960), a satire on Rome's high society and winner of the Grand Prix at Cannes.

Fen·der |'fendər|, Leo (1907–91) U.S. guitar maker. He pioneered the production of electric guitars, designing the first solid-body electric guitar to be widely available and founding the Fender company.

Fe·nol·lo·sa |ˌfenəl'ōsə|, Ernest Francisco (1853–1908) U.S. educator and author. He led a revival of the Japanese school of painting and a movement to preserve Japanese temples and works of art.

Fer·ber |'fərbər|, Edna (1887–1968) U.S. author. Notable novels: *So Big* (1924, Pulitzer Prize) and *Giant* (1952).

Fer·di·nand II |'fərd(ə)ˌnænd|, of Aragon (1452–1516) king of Castile (1474–1516) and of Aragon (1479–1516); known as **Ferdinand the Catholic**. His marriage to Isabella of Castile in 1469 ensured his accession (as Ferdinand V) to the throne of Castile with her. Ferdinand subsequently succeeded to the throne of Aragon (as Ferdinand II) and was joined as monarch by Isabella. They instituted the Spanish Inquisition in 1478 and supported Columbus's expedition in 1492. Their capture of Granada from the Moors in the same year effectively united Spain as one country.

Fer·en·czi |fə'ren(t)sē|, Sándor (1873–1933) Hungarian psychoanalyst. He was a friend and collaborator of Freud.

Fer·gu·son |'fərgəsən| U.S. politicians. **James Edward Ferguson** (1871–1944) was the governor of Texas until impeached (1915–17). His wife **Miriam Amanda Ferguson** (1875–1961);

known as **Ma** Ferguson. She became governor of Texas (1925–27 and 1933–35) after her husband James was impeached.

Fer·lin·ghet·ti |ˌfərlin'getē|, Lawrence (Monsanto) (1919–) U.S. poet and publisher; born *Lawrence Ferling*. Identified with San Francisco's Beat movement, he founded the publishing house City Lights, which produced works such as Allen Ginsberg's *Howl* (1957). Notable works: *A Coney Island of the Mind* (1958).

Fer·mat |fər'mä(t)|, Pierre de (1601–65) French mathematician. His work on curves led directly to the general methods of calculus introduced by Newton and Leibniz. He is also recognized as the founder of the theory of numbers.

Fer·mi |'ferˌmē|, Enrico (1901–54) Italian-born U.S. atomic physicist, who directed the first controlled nuclear chain reaction in 1942. Nobel Prize for Physics (1938).

Fer·ra·ga·mo |ˌferə'gämō|, Salvatore (1898–1960) Italian shoe designer and manufacturer.

Fer·ran·ti |fə'räntē|, Sebastian Ziani de (1864–1930) English electrical engineer. He was one of the pioneers of electricity generation and distribution in Britain, his chief contribution being the use of high voltages for economical transmission over a distance.

Fer·ra·ri |fə'rärē|, Enzo (1898–1988) Italian car designer and manufacturer. In 1929 he founded the company named after him, producing a range of high-quality sports and racing cars. Since the early 1950s Ferraris have won the greatest number of world championship Grands Prix of any car.

Fer·ra·ro |fə'rärō|, Geraldine Anne (1935–) U.S. politician. She ran unsuccessfully for vice president of the U.S., with Walter Mondale (1984).

Fer·rel |'ferəl|, William (1817–91) U.S. meteorologist and author. His research led to Ferrel's Law (1856) on the deflection of air currents on the rotating earth.

Fer·rer |fə'rär; fə'rer|, José (1912–92) U.S. actor and director, born in Puerto

Rico. Notable movies: *Cyrano de Bergerac* (1950, Academy Award).

Fer·ri·er |'ferēər|, Kathleen (1912–53) English contralto. She is particularly famous for her performance in 1947 of Mahler's song cycle *Das Lied von der Erde.*

Fer·ris |'ferəs|, George Washington Gale, Jr. (1859–96) U.S. engineer and inventor. He invented the Ferris wheel (1893).

Fes·sen·den |'fesəndən|, Reginald Aubrey (1866–1932) Canadian-born U.S. pioneer of radio-telephony, who invented the heterodyne receiver.

Fet·ter·man |'fetərmən|, William Judd (*c.* 1833–66) U.S. army officer. A Civil War Union officer, he was killed by the Sioux and Cheyenne in the "Fetterman massacre" (Dec. 21, 1866).

Feu·er·bach |'fōiər,bäKH|, Ludwig (Andreas) (1804–72) German materialist philosopher. In his best-known work, *The Essence of Christianity* (1841), he argued that the dogmas and beliefs of Christianity are figments of human imagination, fulfilling a need inherent in human nature.

Fey·deau |fā'dō|, Georges (1862–1921) French dramatist. His name has become a byword for French bedroom farce. He wrote some forty plays, including *Hotel Paradiso* (1894) and *Le Dindon* (1896).

Feyn·man |'finmən|, Richard Phillips (1918–88) U.S. theoretical physicist, noted for his work on quantum electrodynamics. Nobel Prize for Physics (1965).

Fi·bo·nac·ci |,fibə'näCHē|, Leonardo (*c.*1170–*c.*1250) Italian mathematician; known as **Fibonacci of Pisa**. Fibonacci popularized the use of the "new" Arabic numerals in Europe. He made many original contributions in complex calculations, algebra, and geometry, and pioneered number theory and indeterminate analysis, discovering the Fibonacci series.

Fich·te |'fiKHtə|, Johann Gottlieb (1762–1814) German philosopher. A pupil of Kant, he postulated that the ego is the basic reality; the world is posited by the ego in defining and delimiting itself. His political addresses had some influence on the development of German nationalism and the overthrow of Napoleon.

Fied·ler |'fēdlər|, Arthur (1894–1979) U.S. conductor. An accomplished violist, he became renowned as conductor of the Boston Pops Orchestra (1930–74).

Fied·ler |'fēdlər|, Leslie A. (1917–) U.S. educator and author. His writings include literary criticism, such as *Love and Death in the American Novel* (1960), and works of fiction.

Field |fēld| U.S. family, including: **David Dudley Field** (1805–94), a lawyer. He wrote the code of civil procedure that was adopted by many U.S. states, Great Britain, and several British colonies. His brother **Stephen Johnson Field** (1816–99) was a U.S. Supreme Court justice (1863–97). David and Stephen's brother, **Cyrus West Field** (1819–92), was an engineer and financier. He promoted the laying of the transatlantic cable (1857–66).

Field |fēld|, Eugene (1850–95) U.S. poet and journalist. He wrote children's verses, including "Little Boy Blue."

Field |fēld|, John (1782–1837) Irish composer and pianist. He is noted for the invention of the nocturne and for his twenty compositions in this form.

Field |fēld|, Marshall (1834–1906) U.S. merchant. He organized the Marshall Field & Co. (1881) and expanded it into the largest wholesale and retail drygoods establishment in the world. He made major donations to the University of Chicago, the Art Institute of Chicago, and the Field Museum of Natural History.

Field |fēld|, Sally (1946–) U.S. actress. Born *Sally Mahoney*. Notable movies: *Norma Rae* (1979, Academy Award).

Field·ing |'fēldiNG|, Henry (1707–54) English novelist. He provoked the introduction of censorship in theaters with his political satire *The Historical Register for 1736*. He then turned to writing picaresque novels, notably *Joseph Andrews* (1742) and *Tom Jones* (1749).

Fields |fēldz|, James Thomas (1817–81) U.S. editor, author, and publisher. He was a partner in the firm Ticknor &

Fields (1854) and editor of *Atlantic Monthly* (1861–70).

Fields |fēldz|, Dorothy (1905–74) U.S. songwriter. She wrote lyrics for Broadway musicals such as *Annie Get Your Gun* (1946) and *Sweet Charity* (1965).

Fields |fēldz|, Dame Gracie (1898–1979) English singer and comedienne; born *Grace Stansfield*.

Fields |fēldz|, W. C. (1880–1946) U.S. comedian; born *William Claude Dukenfield*. Having made his name as a comedy juggler he became a vaudeville star, appearing in the *Ziegfeld Follies* revues between 1915 and 1921. Notable movies: *The Bank Dick* (1940).

Fier·stein, Harvey (1954–   ) U.S. playwright, actor, and AIDS activist. Born *Harvey Forbes*. Notable works: *Torch Song Trilogy* (1981).

Fi·lene |fi'lēn|, Edward Albert (1860–1937) U.S. merchant. The president of Wm. Filene & Sons, he helped establish the Credit Union National Extension Bureau and the International Chamber of Commerce.

Fill·more |'fil,mawr|, Millard see box.

Abigail Powers Fillmore (1798–1853), wife of Millard Fillmore and U.S. first lady (1850–53).

Fil·son |'filsən|, John (c. 1747–88) American frontiersman. He published the earliest account of Daniel Boone's adventures and helped found Cincinnati, Ohio (1788).

Fink |fiNGk|, Albert (1827–97) U.S. engineer. He invented the Fink truss used in railroad bridges, and founded the science of railroad economics.

Fink |fiNGk|, Mike (c. 1770–1823) U.S. frontiersman. He was a famed marksman and Indian scout.

Fin·ley |'finlē|, Martha Farquharson (1828–1909) U.S. author. As Martha Farquharson, she wrote over 100 novels for children, including 28 *Elsie* books.

Fin·sen |'finsən|, Niels Ryberg (1860–1904) Danish physician. He developed the light treatment method for skin diseases. Nobel Prize for Physiology or Medicine (1903).

Fio·ruc·ci |ˌfēə'rōōCHē|, Elio (1935–   ) Italian designer and retailer.

Fire·stone |'firstōn|, Harvey Samuel (1868–1938) U.S. industrialist. He or-

---

Fillmore, Millard
13th U.S. president

Life dates: 1800–1874
Place of birth: Locke, New York
Mother: Phoebe Millard Fillmore
Father: Nathaniel Fillmore
Wives: Abigail Powers Fillmore (died 1853); Caroline Carmichael McIntosh (married 1858)
Children: Millard, Mary (by first wife)
College/University: none
Military service: Commander, Home Guard corps, Mexican War
Career: Lawyer (New York Supreme Court); teacher; wool carder; clothdresser
Political career: New York State Assembly; U.S. House of Representatives; vice president (under Taylor); president
Party: Whig
Home state: New York
Term of office: Jul. 10, 1850–March 3, 1853 (succeeded to the presidency on the death of Zachary Taylor)
Vice president: none
Notable events of presidency: Compromise of 1850; California admitted as 31st state; territorial governments established in Utah and New Mexico; Fugitive Slave Law; Capitol partially destroyed by fire; Washington Territory created
Other achievements: admitted to the New York bar; first chancellor, University of Buffalo; president, Buffalo Historical Society
Place of burial: Buffalo, New York

---

ganized the Firestone Tire & Rubber Co. (1900), which he served as president (1903–32) and chairman (1932–38).

Firth |fərTH|, J. R. (1890–1960) English linguist. Full name *John Rupert Firth*. Noted for his contributions to linguistic semantics and prosodic phonology and for his insistence on studying both speech sounds and words in context. He was a major influence on the development of systemic grammar.

Fisch·er |'fiSHər|, Bobby (1943–   ) U.S. chess player; full name *Robert James Fischer*. He defeated Boris Spassky in 1972 to take the world championship, which he held until 1975. He emerged from seclusion to defeat Gary Kasparov in 1992, although the match was not held under the auspices of the international chess federation.

Fisch·er |'fisHər|, Emil Hermann (1852–1919) German organic chemist. He studied the structure of sugars, other carbohydrates, and purines, and synthesized many of them. He also confirmed that peptides and proteins consist of chains of amino acids. Nobel Prize for Chemistry (1902).

Fisch·er |'fisHər|, Hans (1881–1945) German organic chemist. He determined the structure of the porphyrin group of many natural pigments, including the red oxygen-carrying part of hemoglobin, the green chlorophyll pigments found in plants, and the orange bile pigment bilirubin. Nobel Prize for Chemistry (1930).

Fischer-Dieskau |ˌfisHər'deˌskow|, Dietrich (1925–) German baritone. He is noted for his interpretations of German lieder, in particular Schubert's song cycles.

Fish |fisH|, Hamilton (1808–1893) U.S. politician. He held many political offices, including U.S. secretary of state (1869–77).

Fish·er |'fisHər|, Bud (1884–1954) U.S. cartoonist. Full name *Harry Conway Fisher.* He created in 1907 the world-famous comic strip "Mutt & Jeff," which he drew until his death.

Fish·er |'fisHər|, Ham (1900–55) U.S. cartoonist. Full name *Hammond Edward Fisher.* He was creator of the comic strip "Joe Palooka"

Fish·er |'fisHər|, M. F. K. (1908–92) U.S. author. Full name *Mary Frances Kennedy Fisher.* Her writings, including *How to Cook a Wolf* (1942) and *Long Ago in France* (1991), describe fictional and nonfictional culinary experiences.

Fish·er |'fisHər|, Sir Ronald Aylmer (1890–1962) English statistician and geneticist. Fisher made major contributions to the development of statistics, publishing influential books on statistical theory, the design of experiments, statistical methods for research workers, and the relationship between Mendelian genetics and evolutionary theory.

Fish·er |'fisHər|, St. John (1469–1535) English churchman. In 1504 he became bishop of Rochester and earned the dis-

favor of Henry VIII by opposing his divorce from Catherine of Aragon. When he refused to accept the king as supreme head of the Church, he was condemned to death. Feast day, June 22.

Fisk |fisk|, James (1834–72) U.S. financier. He made his fortune in the stock manipulation that ruined the Erie Railroad, and with Jay Gould he engineered events that involved the U.S. Treasury in the Black Friday scandal (1869).

Fiske |fisk|, Bradley Allen (1854–1942) U.S. naval officer and inventor. He invented electrical military devices, including the electric range finder.

Fiske |fisk|, John (1842–1901) U.S. philosopher, writer, professor, and historian. Born *Edmund Fisk Green.* He was a leading exponent and popularizer of Darwinism.

Fitch |fiCH|, John (1743–98) U.S. inventor. Although he received the U.S. patent and built the first steamboat (1787), he was never commercially successful.

Fit·ti·pal·di |ˌfiti'pawldē|, Emerson (1946–) Brazilian racecar driver. He was the Formula One world champion in 1972 and 1974, and won the Indianapolis 500 in 1989.

Fitts |fits|, Dudley (1903–68) U.S. teacher and translator. He wrote a colloquial metrical translation of Aristophanes' play *Lysistrata* (1954) and edited the Yale Series of Younger Poets (1960–68).

Fitz·ger·ald |ˌfits'jerəld| U.S. authors: **F. Scott Fitzgerald** (1896–1940); full name *Francis Scott Key Fitzgerald.* His novels, in particular *The Great Gatsby* (1925), provide a vivid portrait of the U.S. during the jazz era of the 1920s. His wife, **Zelda Sayre Fitzgerald** (1899–1948), wrote *Save Me the Waltz* (1932), an account of her life with her husband.

Fitz·ger·ald |ˌfits'jerəld|, Barry (1888–1961) U.S. actor, born in Ireland. Born *William Shields.* Notable movies: *Going My Way* (1944, Academy Award).

Fitz·ger·ald |ˌfits'jerəld|, Edward (1809–83) English scholar and poet. Notable works: *The Rubáiyát of Omar Khayyám* (translation, 1859).

Fitz·ger·ald |ˌfitsˈjerəld|, Ella (1918–96) U.S. jazz singer, known for her distinctive style of scat singing.

Fitz·ger·ald |ˌfitsˈjerəld|, Frances (1940–) U.S. author and foreign correspondent. Notable works: *Fire in the Lake: The Vietnamese and the Americans in Vietnam* (1972, Pulitzer Prize and National Book Award).

Fitz·Ger·ald |ˌfitsˈjerəld|, George Francis (1851–1901) Irish physicist. He suggested that length, time, and mass depend on the relative motion of the observer, while the speed of light is constant. This hypothesis, postulated independently by Lorentz, prepared the way for Einstein's special theory of relativity.

Fitz·ger·ald |ˌfitsˈjerəld|, Robert Stuart (1910–85) U.S. educator and writer. He has written poetry and a well-known translation of Homer's *Odyssey* (1961). Bollingen Prize, 1961.

Fitz·patrick |fitsˈpætrək|, Thomas (*c.* 1799–1854) U.S. frontiersman, born in Ireland. A fur trapper, trader, and scout, he was the guide for Frémont's second expedition (1843–44) in the American West and Kearny's expeditions (1845 and 1846).

Fixx |fiks|, Jim (1932–84) U.S. runner. He popularized the sport of running with his bestseller *The Complete Book of Running* (1977).

Flack |flæk|, Roberta (1939–) U.S. pop vocalist.

Flagg |flæg|, James Montgomery (1877–1960) U.S. artist. He created the World War I recruiting poster featuring Uncle Sam's pointing finger and the caption "I Want You."

Flag·ler |ˈflæglər|, Henry Morrison (1830–1913) U.S. financier. With John D. Rockefeller, he developed the Standard Oil Co.

Flah·er·ty |ˈflertē|, Robert Joseph (1884–1951) U.S. movie director, author, and explorer. He is known as the father of documentary film. Notable movies: *Nanook of the North* (1922).

Flam·steed |ˈflæmˌstēd|, John (1646–1719) English astronomer. He was the first Astronomer Royal at the Royal Greenwich Observatory and produced the first star catalog (for use in navigation).

Flan·na·gan |ˈflænəgən|, John Bernard (1895–1942) U.S. sculptor. He is known for his small, primitive sculptures of animals, birds, and fish.

Flat·ley |ˈflætlē|, Michael (1958–) U.S. dancer. He performed Irish step dancing with "Riverdance" before forming his own show, "Lord of the Dance."

Flatt |flæt|, Lester (1914–79) U.S. country singer and guitarist. Notable songs: "Foggy Mountain Breakdown."

Flau·bert |flōˈber|, Gustave (1821–80) French novelist and short-story writer. A dominant figure in the French realist school, he achieved fame with his first published novel, *Madame Bovary* (1857). Its portrayal of the adulteries and suicide of a provincial doctor's wife caused Flaubert to be tried for immorality (and acquitted).

Flax·man |ˈflæksmən|, John (1755–1826) English sculptor and draftsman, noted for his church monuments and his engraved illustrations to Homer (1793).

Fleck·er |ˈflekər|, James (Herman) Elroy (1884–1915) English poet. Notable works: *The Golden Journey to Samarkand* (collection, 1913) and *Hassan* (play, 1922).

Fle·gen·hei·mer |ˈflāgənˌhīmər|, Arthur (1902–35) U.S. gangster. Known as **Dutch Schultz**. As head of the New York crime syndicate, he was notorious for bootlegging, extortion, and the numbers racket.

Fleisch·er |ˈflīsHər|, Max (1883–1972) U.S. cartoonist and animator, born in Austria. He created the character Betty Boop and animated the comic strip character Popeye.

Flem·ing |ˈfleming|, Sir Alexander 1881–1955. Scottish bacteriologist. In 1928, Fleming discovered the effect of penicillin on bacteria.

Flem·ing |ˈfleming|, Ian (Lancaster) (1908–64) English novelist. He is known for his spy novels that feature the secret agent James Bond.

Flem·ing |ˈfleming|, Sir John Ambrose (1849–1945) English electrical engineer, chiefly remembered for his invention of the thermionic valve (1900).

Flem·ing |ˈfleming|, Victor (1883–1949) U.S. movie director. Notable movies: *Gone With the Wind* (1939, Academy Award).

Fletch•er |'fleCHər|, John (1579–1625) English dramatist. A writer of Jacobean tragicomedies, he wrote some fifteen plays with Francis Beaumont, including *The Maid's Tragedy* (1610–11). He is also believed to have collaborated with Shakespeare on such plays as *The Two Noble Kinsmen* and *Henry VIII* (both *c.*1613).

Fletch•er |'fleCHər|, Horace (1849–1919) U.S. nutritionist. He wrote and lectured on the value of thoroughly masticating food.

Flick•in•ger |'flikən,gər|, Donald D. (1907–97) U.S. physician. He helped develop life support systems for high-altitude flight and space travel.

Flin•ders |'flindərz|, Matthew (1774–1814) English explorer. He explored the coast of New South Wales (1795–1800) and circumnavigated Australia (1801–03) for the Royal Navy, charting much of the west coast of the continent for the first time.

Flint |flint|, Austin (1812–86) U.S. physician and educator. He founded Bellevue Hospital Medical College (New York, 1861) and wrote *Treatise on the Principles and Practice of Medicine* (1866).

Flip•per |'flipər|, Henry Ossian (1856–1940) U.S. soldier and engineer. The first black graduate of West Point (1877), he was court-martialed on false charges (1882), to which the army formally admitted in 1976.

Flood |fləd|, Curt (1938–97) U.S. baseball player. He challenged baseball's reserve clause in 1972, which led to new rules for free agency.

Flo•rey |'flawrē|, Howard Walter, Baron (1898–1968) Australian pathologist. With Ernst Chain he isolated and purified penicillin; in 1945 they shared a Nobel Prize for Physiology or Medicine with Alexander Fleming.

Flo•rio |'flawrēō|, John (*c.*1553–1625) English lexicographer, of Italian descent. He produced an Italian–English dictionary entitled *A Worlde of Wordes* (1598) and translated Montaigne's essays into English (1603).

Flynn |flin|, Errol (1909–59) Aus-

tralian-born U.S. actor; born *Leslie Thomas Flynn*. His usual role was the swashbuckling hero of romantic costume dramas in movies such as *Captain Blood* (1935) and *The Adventures of Robin Hood* (1938).

Fo |fō|, Dario (1926–) Italian dramatist. Notable works: *Accidental Death of an Anarchist* (political satire, 1970) and *Open Couple* (farce, 1983). Nobel Prize for Literature (1997).

Foch |'fawSH|, Ferdinand (1851–1929) French general. He supported the use of offensive warfare, which resulted in many of his 20th Corps being killed in August 1914. He was later the senior French representative at the Armistice negotiations.

Fo•gar•ty |'fōgərtē|, Anne (1919–1981) U.S. fashion designer.

Fo•ger•ty |'fōgərtē|, John (1945–) U.S. musician. He performed with Creedence Clearwater Revival. Grammy Award, 1998.

Fo•kine |'fawkyin; faw'kēn|, Michel (1880–1942) Russian-born U.S. dancer and choreographer; born *Mikhail Mikhailovich Fokin*. He was a reformer of modern ballet; as Diaghilev's chief choreographer he staged the premières of Stravinsky's *The Firebird* (1910) and Ravel's *Daphnis and Chloë* (1912).

Fok•ker |'fäkər|, Anthony Herman Gerard (1890–1939) Dutch-born U.S. aircraft designer and pilot. Having built his first aircraft in 1908, he designed fighters used by the Germans in World War I and founded the Fokker Co.

Fo•ley |'fōlē|, Red (1910–68) U.S. country singer. Notable songs: "Blues in My Heart."

Fol•ger |'fōljər|, Henry Clay (1857–1930) U.S. businessman. An executive with Standard Oil (1879–1928), he amassed a large library collection and endowed the Folger Shakespeare Library, Washington, D.C. (1928).

Fol•mer |'fōlmər|, William Frederic (1861–1936) U.S. inventor. He patented over 300 inventions, including gas burners, lamps, and photographic equipment; his photographic manufacturing firm, Folmer & Schwing, was acquired by Eastman Kodak (1905).

Fon•da |'fändə| U.S. actors, including:

Henry Fonda (1905–82). He was noted for his roles in such films as *The Grapes of Wrath* (1939) and *Twelve Angry Men* (1957). He won his only Oscar for his role in his final film, *On Golden Pond* (1981). His daughter, **Jane Fonda** (1937–), is known for films including *Klute* (1971), for which she won an Oscar, and *The China Syndrome* (1979); she also acted alongside her father in *On Golden Pond*. Jane's brother **Peter Fonda** (1939–) and his daughter Bridget Fonda (1964–) are also actors.

Fon·taine |fän'tān|, Joan (1917–) U.S. actress, born in Tokyo. Born *Joan de Havilland*. Notable movies: *Suspicion* (1941, Academy Award).

Fon·tanne |fän'tæn|, Lynn (1887–1983) British actress. She worked with her husband, U.S. actor Alfred Lunt.

Fon·teyn |ˌfän'tān|, Dame Margot (1919–91) English ballet dancer; born *Margaret Hookham*. In 1962 she began a celebrated partnership with Rudolf Nureyev, dancing with him in *Giselle* and *Romeo and Juliet*. In 1979 she was named *prima ballerina assoluta*, a title given only three times in the history of ballet.

Foote |foŏt|, Andrew Hull (1806–63) U.S. naval officer. As a commander off the African coast, he worked at breaking up slave trade (1849–51); he also served as the Union commander of naval operations on the upper Mississippi (1861–62).

Foote |foŏt|, Horton (1916–) U.S. author. He wrote numerous screenplays, including *To Kill a Mockingbird* (1962) and *Tender Mercies* (1983, Academy Award).

Forbes |fawrbz| family of U.S. magazine publishers, including: **Bertie Charles** (1880–1954). Born in Scotland, his full name was *Robert Charles Forbes*. He was the founder, editor, and publisher of *Forbes* magazine (1916). His son **Malcolm Stevenson** (1919–90) published *Forbes* magazine after the death of his father and was a member of the U.S. Senate from New Jersey (1952–58). He was the first person to fly coast-to-coast across the U.S. in a hot air balloon. His son, **Malcolm Stevenson, Jr.** (1947–) worked for *Forbes* from 1970

and served as editor in chief from 1982. He was a U.S. presidential candidate in the Republican primary in 1996.

Forbes |fawrbz|, Esther (1891–1967) U.S. writer. Notable works: *Johnny Tremaine* (1943), *The Running of the Tide* (1948), and *Paul Revere and the World He Lived In* (1942, Pulitzer Prize).

Ford |fawrd|, Gerald (Rudolph) see box.

Betty Ford (1918–); born *Elizabeth Bloomer Warren*; the wife of Gerald Ford and U.S. first lady (1974–77).

Ford |fawrd|, Ford Madox (1873–1939) English novelist and editor; born *Ford Hermann Hueffer*. He is chiefly remembered as the author of the novel *The Good Soldier* (1915). As founder of both the *English Review* (1908) and the *Transatlantic Review* (1924), he published works by such writers as Ernest

---

Ford, Gerald Rudolph
38th U.S. president

Life dates: 1913–
Place of birth: Omaha, Nebraska
Name at birth: Leslie Lynch King, Jr.
Mother: Dorothy Ayer Gardner King
Father: Leslie Lynch King (natural); Gerald R. Ford (adoptive)
Wife: Elizabeth (Betty) Bloomer Ford
Children: Michael, John (Jack), Steven, Susan
College/University: University of Michigan; Yale Law School
Military service: officer in U.S. Navy during World War II
Career: Lawyer
Political career: U.S. House of Representatives; House minority leader; vice president (under Nixon; appointed to replace Spiro Agnew, 1973); president
Party: Republican
Home state: Michigan
Opponent in presidential race: Jimmy Carter
Term of office: Aug. 9, 1974 (succeeded to the presidency on the resignation of Richard M. Nixon)–Jan. 20, 1977
Vice president: Nelson A. Rockefeller
Notable events of presidency: granted unconditional pardon to former President Nixon; clemency for Vietnam draft evaders; end of Vietnam War and evacuation of Americans in Saigon
Other achievements: Eagle Scout; admitted to the Michigan bar

Hemingway, James Joyce, and Ezra Pound. He was the grandson of the Pre-Raphaelite painter Ford Madox Brown.

Ford |ˈfawrd|, Harrison (1942–) U.S. actor. He became internationally famous with the science-fiction movie *Star Wars* (1977) and its two sequels. Other notable movies include *American Graffiti* (1973), *Raiders of the Lost Ark* (1981), *Witness* (1985), and *Air Force One* (1997).

Ford |ˈfawrd|, Henry (1863–1947) U.S. automobile manufacturer. A pioneer of large-scale mass production, he founded the Ford Motor Co., which in 1909 produced his famous Model T. Control of the company passed to his grandson, **Henry Ford II** (1917–1987) in 1945.

Ford[1] |ˈfawrd|, John (1586–*c*.1639) English dramatist. His plays, which include *'Tis Pity She's a Whore* (1633) and *The Broken Heart* (1633), explore human delusion, melancholy, and horror.

Ford[2] |ˈfawrd|, John (1895–1973) U.S. movie director; born *Sean Aloysius O'Feeney*. He is chiefly known for his westerns, including *Stagecoach* (1939) and *She Wore a Yellow Ribbon* (1949).

Ford |ˈfawrd|, Richard (1944–) U.S. writer. Notable works: *The Sportswriter* (1986).

Ford |ˈfawrd|, Tennessee Ernie (1919– 91) U.S. country singer and songwriter. Notable song: "Sixteen Tons."

Ford |ˈfawrd|, Whitey (1928–) U.S. baseball player. Born *Edward Charles Ford*. His career win percentage (.690) is the highest among 20th-century pitchers. Elected to Baseball Hall of Fame (1974).

Fore·man |ˈfawrmən|, Carl (1914–84) U.S. screenwriter. He was blacklisted for being an "uncooperative witness" before the House Committee on Un-American Activities. His movie credits include *High Noon* (1952), *The Bridge on the River Kwai (1957)*, and *The Guns of Navarone* (1961).

Fore·man |ˈfawrmən|, George (1949–) U.S. boxer. Having held the world heavyweight championship (1973–74), he regained the title in 1994, becoming the oldest man to do so.

For·es·ter |ˈfawrəstər|, C. S. (1899– 1966) English novelist. Full name *Cecil Scott Forester*; pseudonym of *Cecil Lewis Troughton Smith*. He is remembered for his seafaring novels set during the Napoleonic Wars, featuring Captain Horatio Hornblower. His other works include *The African Queen* (1935), later made into a celebrated film by John Huston.

Fork·beard |ˈfawrkˌbērd|, Sweyn see SWEYN I.

For·man |ˈfawrmən|, Milos (1932–) Czech-born U.S. movie director. He made *One Flew Over the Cuckoo's Nest* (1975), which won five Oscars, and *Amadeus* (1983), which won eight Oscars, including that for best director.

Form·by |ˈfawrmbē|, George (1904– 61) English comedian; born *George Booth*. He became famous for his numerous musical movies in the 1930s in which he projected the image of a Lancashire working lad and accompanied his songs on the ukulele.

For·rest |ˈfawrəst|, John, 1st Baron (1847–1918) Australian explorer and statesman, first premier of Western Australia (1890–1901).

For·rest |ˈfawrəst|, Nathan Bedford (1821–77) Confederate cavalry officer. He led a massacre of 300 black Union soldiers at the surrender of Fort Pillow, Tennessee (April 12, 1864). He became Grand Wizard of the Ku Klux Klan (1867–69).

For·res·ter |ˈfawrəstər|, Jay Wright (1918–) U.S. computer engineer. He invented the first random-access magnetic core memory storage for electronic digital computers (1949).

Forss·mann |ˈfawrsˌmän|, Werner Theodor Otto (1904–79) German physician. A pioneer in heart research, he shared the 1956 Nobel Prize for Physiology or Medicine with A. Cournand and D. Richards.

For·ster |ˈfawrstər|, E. M. (1879–1970) English novelist and literary critic. Full name *Edward Morgan Forster*. His novels, several of which have been made into successful movies, include *A Room with a View* (1908) and *A Passage to India* (1924).

For·syth |ˈfawrˌsĪTH|, Frederick (1938–) English novelist, known for political thrillers such as *The Day of the*

Jackal (1971), *The Odessa File* (1972), and *The Fourth Protocol* (1984).

For·tas |'fawrtəs|, Abe (1910–82) U.S. Supreme Court justice (1965–69). Criticized for his financial dealings, he was the first justice ever forced to resign due to public scorn.

For·ten |'fawrt(ə)n|, James (1766–1842) U.S. businessman and reformer. An abolitionist born to free black parents, he made his fortune in the sailmaking business.

Fos·bury |'fäs,berē|, Richard (1947–) U.S. high jumper. He originated the now standard style of jumping known as the "Fosbury flop," in which the jumper clears the bar headfirst and with back to the bar. In 1968 he won the Olympic gold medal using this technique.

Fos·se |'fawsē|, Bob (1927–87) U.S. jazz dancer, choreographer, and director. Full name *Robert Louis Fosse*. He directed and choreographed Broadway musicals such as *The Pajama Game* (1954) and movies such as *Cabaret* (1972, Academy Award)

Fos·ter |'fästər|, Hal (1892–1982) U.S. cartoonist, born in Canada. Full name *Harold Rudolf Foster*. He drew the comicstrip versions of adventure heroes Tarzan and Prince Valiant.

Fos·ter |'fästər|, Jodie (1962–) U.S. movie actress and director; born *Alicia Christian Foster*. She won Oscars for her performances in *The Accused* (1988) and *Silence of the Lambs* (1991). She directed *Little Man Tate* (1991).

Fos·ter |'fästər|, Sir Norman (Robert) (1935–) English architect. His work is notable for its sophisticated engineering approach and technological style.

Fos·ter |'fästər|, Stephen (Collins) (1826–64) U.S. composer. He wrote more than 200 songs and, though a Northerner, was best known for songs that captured the Southern plantation spirit, such as "Oh! Susannah" (1848) and "Camptown Races" (1850).

Fos·ter |'fästər|, Vincent, Jr. (1945–93) U.S. attorney. He was deputy White House counsel to President Clinton (1993).

Fos·ter |'fästər|, William Zebulon (1881–1961) U.S. labor leader and politician. He was the Communist Party candidate for president of the U.S.(1924, 1928, and 1932).

Fou·cault |foo'kō|, Jean-Bernard-Léon (1819–68) French physicist. He is chiefly remembered for the huge pendulum which he hung from the roof of the Panthéon in Paris in 1851 to demonstrate the rotation of the earth. He also invented the gyroscope and was the first to determine the velocity of light reasonably accurately.

Fou·cault |foo'kō|, Michel (Paul) (1926–84) French philosopher. A student of Louis Althusser, he was mainly concerned with exploring how society defines categories of abnormality such as insanity, sexuality, and criminality, and the manipulation of social attitudes towards such things by those in power.

Fou·rier |,foorē'ā|, Jean-Baptiste-Joseph, Baron (1768–1830) French mathematician. His studies involved him in the solution of partial differential equations by the method of separation of variables and superposition; this led him to analyze the series and integrals that are now known by his name.

Four·nier |,foorn'yā|, Pierre-Simon (1712–68) French type designer and engraver. He designed many new characters, and was noted for his decorative ornaments in the Rococo style.

Fow·ler |'fowlər|, H. W. (1858–1933) English lexicographer and grammarian. Full name *Henry Watson Fowler*. He compiled the first edition of the *Concise Oxford Dictionary* (1911) with his brother F. G. Fowler, and wrote the moderately prescriptive guide to style and idiom, *Modern English Usage*, first published in 1926.

Fowles |fowls|, John (Robert) (1926–) English novelist. His works include the psychological thriller *The Collector* (1963), the magic realist novel *The Magus* (1966), and the semihistorical novel *The French Lieutenant's Woman* (1969).

Fox |fäks|, Charles James (1749–1806) British statesman. He became a Whig member of Parliament in 1768, supporting American independence and the French Revolution, and collaborated with Lord North to form a coalition government (1783–84).

Fox |fäks|, Fontaine (1884–1964) U.S. cartoonist. He created the suburban-rural town of Toonerville and the panel "Toonerville Folks."

Fox |fäks|, George (1624–91) English preacher and founder of the Society of Friends (Quakers). He taught that truth in the inner voice of God speaking to the soul and rejected priesthood and ritual. Despite repeated imprisonment, he established a society called the "Friends of the Truth" (*c.*1650), which later became the Society of Friends.

Fox |fäks|, Paula (1923–   ) U.S. author of children's fiction. Notable works: *One-Eyed Cat* (1984, Newbery Honor Book).

Fox |fäks|, William (1879–1952) U.S. corporate executive. He founded the Fox Film Corp. (1915), which later became Twentieth Century Fox.

Foxe |fäks|, John (1516–87) English religious writer. He is famous for his *Actes and Monuments* popularly known as *The Book of Martyrs*, which appeared in England in 1563. This passionate account of the persecution of English Protestants fueled hostility to Catholicism for generations.

Fox Tal·bot |'fäks 'tawlbət|, William Henry see TALBOT.

Foxx |fäks|, Jimmie (1907–67) U.S. baseball player. Full name *James Emory Foxx*; known as **Double X** and **the Beast**. Elected to Baseball Hall of Fame (1951).

Foyt |foit|, A. J. (1935–   ) U.S. racecar driver. Full name *Anthony Joseph Foyt*. He was a four-time winner of the Indianapolis 500 (1961, 1964, 1967, 1977).

Fra·go·nard |ˌfrægə'när|, Jean-Honoré (1732–1806) French painter in the rococo style. He is famous for landscapes and for erotic canvases such as *The Progress of Love* (1771).

Frame |frām|, Janet (Paterson) (1924–   ) New Zealand novelist. Her novels draw on her experiences of psychiatric hospitals after she suffered a severe mental breakdown. Her three-volume autobiography (1982–85) was made into the movie *An Angel at My Table* (1990).

France |fräns|, Anatole (1844–1924) French writer; pseudonym of *Jacques-Anatole-François Thibault*. Works include the novel *Le Crime de Sylvestre Bonnard* (1881) and his ironic version of the Dreyfus case, *L'Ile des pingouins* (1908). Nobel Prize for Literature (1921).

Fran·cis I |'frænsəs| (1494–1547) king of France (1515–47). Much of his reign (1521–44) was spent at war with Charles V of Spain. He supported the arts and commissioned new buildings, including the Louvre.

Fran·cis of Assisi |'frænsəs|, St. (1181–1226) Italian monk, founder of the Franciscan order; born *Giovanni di Bernardone*. He founded the Franciscan order in 1209 and drew up its original rule (based on complete poverty). He is revered for his generosity, simple faith, humility, and love of nature. Feast day, October 4.

Fran·cis of Sales |'frænsəs|, St. (1567–1622) French bishop. One of the leaders of the Counter Reformation, he was bishop of Geneva (1602–22). The Salesian order (founded in 1859) is named after him. Feast day, January 24.

Fran·cis Xa·vier |'frænsis 'zāvyər|, St. see XAVIER, ST. FRANCIS.

Franck |fräNGk|, César (Auguste) (1822–90) Belgian-born French composer and organist. His reputation as a composer rests on the *Symphonic Variations* for piano and orchestra (1885), the D minor Symphony (1886–8), and the *String Quartet* (1889).

Franck |fräNGk|, James (1882–1964) German-born U.S. physicist. He worked on the bombardment of atoms by electrons and became involved in the U.S. atom bomb project; he advocated the explosion of the bomb in an uninhabited area to demonstrate its power to Japan.

Fran·co |'frænGkō|, Francisco (1892–1975) Spanish general and statesman, head of state (1939–75). Leader of the Nationalists in the Civil War, in 1937 Franco became head of the Falange Party and proclaimed himself *Caudillo* ("leader") of Spain. With the defeat of the republic in 1939, he took control of the government and established a dictatorship that ruled Spain until his death.

Frank |fræNGk|, Anne (1929–1945) German Jewish girl known for her diary, which records the experiences of her family living for two years in hiding from the Nazis in occupied Amsterdam. They were eventually betrayed and sent to concentration camps; Anne died in Belsen.

Frank•fur•ter |'fræNGk,fərtər|, Felix (1882–1965) U.S. Supreme Court justice (1939–62), born in Austria. He helped found the American Civil Liberties Union (1920) and was awarded the Presidential Medal of Freedom (1963).

Frank•lin |'fræNGklən|, Aretha (1942–) U.S. soul and gospel singer. Her best-known songs include Respect and I Never Loved a Man the Way I Love You (1967).

Frank•lin |'fræNGklən|, Benjamin (1706–90) American statesman, inventor, and scientist. He was one of the signatories to the peace treaty between the U.S. and Great Britain after the American Revolution. His main scientific achievements were the formulation of a theory of electricity, which introduced positive and negative electricity, and a demonstration of the electrical nature of lightning, which led to the invention of the lightning conductor.

Frank•lin |'fræNGklən|, Sir John (1786–1847) British explorer. He and all his crew died during his Arctic expedition (1845–47), but their found remains and records proved the existence of the Northwest Passage.

Frank•lin |'fræNGklən|, John Hope (1915–) U.S. educator, historian, and author. He was the first African American to become president of the American Historical Association (1978–79). Notable works: *From Slavery to Freedom: A History of American Negroes* (1947) and *Racial Equality in America* (1976). Awarded Spingarn Medal (1995).

Frank•lin |'fræNGklən|, (Stella Maria Sarah) Miles (1879–1954) Australian novelist. She wrote the first true Australian novel, *My Brilliant Career* (1901). She also produced a series of chronicle novels under her pseudonym "Brent of Bin Bin" (1928–56).

Frank•lin |'fræNGklən|, Rosalind Elsie (1920–58) English physical chemist and molecular biologist. Together with Maurice Wilkins she investigated the structure of DNA by means of X-ray crystallography, and contributed to the discovery of its helical structure.

Franz |frænz; fränz|, Dennis (1944–) U.S. actor and playwright. He won an Emmy Award (1996–97) for his role in the television show "NYPD Blue."

Franz Josef |'frænz 'yōsef; fränz| (1830–1916) emperor of Austria (1848–1916) and king of Hungary (1867–1916). He gave Hungary equal status with Austria in 1867. His annexation of Bosnia–Herzegovina (1908) contributed to European political tensions, and the assassination in Sarajevo of his heir apparent, Archduke Franz Ferdinand, precipitated World War I.

Fra•ser |'frāzər|, Dawn (1937–) Australian swimmer. She won the Olympic gold medal for the 100-meters freestyle in 1956, 1960, and 1964, the first competitor to win the same title at three successive Olympics.

Fra•ser |'frāzər|, (John) Malcolm (1930–) Australian Liberal statesman, prime minister (1975–83). He was the youngest-ever Australian member of Parliament when elected in 1955.

Fra•ser |'frāzər|, Peter (1884–1950) New Zealand politician, born in Scotland. He was a founder of the Labour Party (1916) and prime minister of New Zealand (1940–49), as well as one of the architects of the United Nations (1945).

Fraun•ho•fer |'frown,hōfər|, Joseph von (1787–1826) German optician and pioneer in spectroscopy. He observed and mapped the dark lines in the solar spectrum (Fraunhofer lines) that result from the absorption of particular frequencies of light by elements present in the outer layers; these are now used to determine the chemical composition of the sun and stars.

Fra•zer |'frāzər|, Sir James George (1854–1941) Scottish anthropologist. In *The Golden Bough* (1809–1915) he proposed an evolutionary theory of the development of human thought, from the magical and religious to the scientific.

Fra•zier |'frāzHər; 'frāzər|, Joe

(1944–) U.S. heavyweight boxing champion; full name *Joseph Frazier*.

Fred·er·ick I |'fred(ə)rik| (*c.*1123–90) king of Germany and Holy Roman emperor (1152–90); known as **Frederick Barbarossa** ("Redbeard"). He made a sustained attempt to subdue Italy and the papacy, but was eventually defeated at the battle of Legnano in 1176.

Fred·er·ick II |'fred(ə)rik| (1712–86) king of Prussia (1740–86); known as **Frederick the Great**. His campaigns in the War of the Austrian Succession (1740–48) and the Seven Years War (1756–63) succeeded in considerably strengthening Prussia's position; by the end of his reign he had doubled the area of his country.

Fred·er·ick Wil·liam |'fred(ə)rik 'wilyəm| (1620–88) elector of Brandenburg (1640–88); known as **the Great Elector**. His program of reconstruction and reorganization following the Thirty Years War brought stability to his country and laid the basis for the expansion of Prussian power in the 18th century.

Freed |frēd|, Alan (1922–65) U.S. radio disc jockey. He helped break barriers in the music industry of the 1950s by broadcasting the rhythm and blues music of black performers to white audiences and by promoting integrated concerts. He is credited with coining the term "rock and roll."

Free·man |'frēmən|, Douglas Southall (1886–1953) U.S. editor, educator, and author. He was editor of the *Richmond News Leader* (1915–33). Notable works: *R. E. Lee* (4 vols., 1934–35, Pulitzer Prize); and *George Washington* (6 vols., 1948–54, Pulitzer Prize).

Fre·ge |'frāgə|, Gottlob (1848–1925) German philosopher and mathematician, founder of modern logic. He developed a logical system for the expression of mathematics. He also worked on general questions of philosophical logic and semantics and devised his influential theory of meaning, based on his use of a distinction between what a linguistic term refers to and what it expresses.

Fre·leng, Friz (1906–95) U.S. animator. Born *Isadore Freleng*. His animation of the cartoon characters Yosemite Sam,

Porky Pig, Sylvester, and Tweety Bird won him three Oscars.

Fré·mont |'frē,mänt|, John Charles (1813–90) U.S. explorer and politician. He was responsible for exploring several viable routes to the Pacific across the Rockies in the 1840s. He made an unsuccessful bid for the presidency in 1856, losing to James Buchanan.

French |frenCH|, Daniel Chester (1850–1931) U.S. sculptor. Among his works is the seated figure of Abraham Lincoln in the Lincoln Memorial, Washington, D.C. (1922).

French |frenCH|, Marilyn (1929–) U.S. author. Notable works: *The Women's Room* (1977).

Fre·neau |fri'nō|, Philip Morin (1752–1832) U.S. poet. He was known as "the poet of the American Revolution" and was publisher of the Jeffersonian newspaper, *The National Gazette*.

Fres·nel |frā'nel|, Augustin Jean (1788–1827) French physicist and civil engineer. He correctly postulated that light has a wavelike motion transverse to the direction of propagation, contrary to the longitudinal direction suggested by Christiaan Huygens and Thomas Young.

Freud |froid| Family name of: **Sigmund Freud** (1856–1939), an Austrian neurologist and psychotherapist. He was the first to emphasize the significance of unconscious processes in normal and neurotic behavior, and was the founder of psychoanalysis as both a theory of personality and a therapeutic practice. He proposed the existence of an unconscious element in the mind that influences consciousness, and of conflicts in it between various sets of forces. Freud also stated the importance of a child's semi-consciousness of sex as a factor in mental development; his theory of the sexual origin of neuroses aroused great controversy. His youngest child, **Anna Freud** (1895–1982), was an Austrian-born British psychoanalyst. She introduced important innovations in method and theory to her father's work, notably with regard to disturbed children, and set up a child therapy course and clinic in London.

Freud |froid|, Lucian (1922–)

German-born British painter, grandson of Sigmund Freud. His subjects, typically portraits and nudes, are painted in a powerful naturalistic style.

Frick |frik|, Henry Clay (1849–1919) U.S. industrialist. He was chairman of the Carnegie Steel Co. (1889–1900); the Frick collection of art is housed in his former house in New York City.

Frie·dan |frē'dæn|, Betty (1921–) U.S. feminist and writer, known for *The Feminine Mystique* (1963), which presented femininity as an artificial construct and traced the ways in which American women are socialized to become mothers and housewives. In 1966 she founded the National Organization for Women, serving as its president until 1970.

Fried·man |'frēdmən|, Bruce Jay (1930–) U.S. author. Notable works: *A Mother's Kisses* (1964), *The Dick* (1970), and *The Lonely Guy's Book of Life* (1978).

Fried·man |'frēdmən|, Milton (1912–) U.S. economist. A principal exponent of monetarism, he acted as a policy adviser to President Reagan from 1981 to 1989. Nobel Prize for Economics (1976).

Frie·drich |'frēdriKH|, Caspar David (1774–1840) German painter, noted for his romantic landscapes. He caused controversy with his altarpiece *The Cross in the Mountains* (1808), which lacked a specifically religious subject.

Friend·ly |'fren(d)lē|, Fred (1915–1998) U.S. journalist. He collaborated with Edward R. Murrow and Walter Cronkite in radio and television to produce various historical series, such as *Hear It Now* and *See It Now*.

Frisch |frisH|, Karl von (1886–1982) Austrian zoologist. He worked mainly on honeybees, studying particularly their vision, navigation, and communication. He showed that they perform an elaborate dance in the hive to indicate the direction and distance of food.

Frisch |frisH|, Otto Robert (1904–79) Austrian-born British physicist. With his aunt, Lise Meitner, he recognized that Otto Hahn's experiments with uranium had produced a new type of nuclear reaction. Frisch named it nuclear fission,

and indicated the explosive potential of its chain reaction.

Frisch |frisH|, Ragnar (Anton Kittil) (1895–1973) Norwegian economist. A pioneer of econometrics, he shared the first Nobel Prize for Economics with Jan Tinbergen (1969).

Frith |friTH|, William Powell (1819–1909) English painter. He is remembered for his panoramic paintings of Victorian life, including *Derby Day* (1858) and *The Railway Station* (1862).

Friz·zell |fri'zel|, Lefty (1928–75) U.S. country singer and guitarist. Full name *William Orville Frizzell*. His honky-tonk, literate country music hits included "If You've Got the Money, I've Got the Time," "Always Late with Your Kisses," and "Long Black Veil."

Fro·bi·sher |'frōbisHər|, Sir Martin (*c.*1535–94) English explorer. In 1576 he led an unsuccessful expedition in search of the Northwest Passage. Frobisher served in Sir Francis Drake's Caribbean expedition of 1585–86 and played a prominent part in the defeat of the Spanish Armada.

Froe·bel |'froEbəl|, Friedrich (Wilhelm August) (1782–1852) German educationist and founder of the kindergarten system. Believing that play materials, practical occupations, and songs are needed to develop a child's real nature, he opened a school for young children in 1837, later naming it the Kindergarten ("children's garden"). He also established a teacher-training school.

Fromm |frōm; främ|, Erich (1900–80) German-born U.S. psychoanalyst and social philosopher. His works, which include *Escape from Freedom* (1941), *Man for Himself* (1947), and *The Sane Society* (1955), emphasize the role of culture in neurosis and strongly criticize materialist values.

Fromm-Reichmann |,främ'rīkmän|, Frieda (1889–1957) U.S. psychiatrist and psychoanalyst, born in Germany.

Fron·te·nac |frawtənäk|, Louis de Buade, Comte de (1622–98) French politician. He served as governor of New France (1672–82, 1689–98).

Frost |frawst|, A. B. (1851–1928) U.S. illustrator and cartoonist. Full name

Arthur Burdett Frost. He illustrated works by Lewis Carroll, Charles Dickens, Mark Twain, and others.

Frost |frawst|, Robert (Lee) (1874–1963) U.S. poet, noted for his ironic tone and simple language. Much of his poetry reflects his affinity with New England, including the collections *North of Boston* (1914) and *New Hampshire* (1923). He won the Pulitzer Prize on three occasions (1924; 1931; 1937).

Frueh |frōō|, Al (1880–1968) U.S. caricaturist and cartoonist. Full name *Alfred Frueh*. He was on staff at the *New Yorker* magazine.

Fry |frī|, Christopher (Harris) (1907–) English dramatist. He is known chiefly for his comic verse dramas, especially *The Lady's not for Burning* (1948) and *Venus Observed* (1950).

Fry |frī|, Elizabeth (1780–1845) English Quaker. She was a leading figure in the early 19th-century campaign for penal reform.

Fry |frī|, Roger (Eliot) (1866–1934) English art critic and painter. He argued for an esthetics of pure form, regarding content as incidental.

Frye |frī|, (Herman) Northrop (1912–91) Canadian literary critic. His work explores the use of myth and symbolism. Notable works: *Fearful Symmetry* (1947) and *The Great Code:The Bible and Literature* (1982).

Fu•ad |fōō'äd| the name of two kings of Egypt: **Fuad I** (1868–1936; reigned 1922–36). Formerly sultan of Egypt (1917–1922), he became Egypt's first king after independence. **Fuad II** (1952–; reigned 1952–53), the grandson of Fuad I. Named king as an infant on the forced abdication of his father, Farouk, he was deposed when Egypt became a republic.

Fuchs |f(y)ōōks|, Klaus (Emil Julius) (1911–88) German-born British physicist. He was a communist who fled Nazi persecution. During the 1940s he passed to the USSR secret information acquired while working on the development of the atom bomb in the U.S., and while engaged in research in Britain.

Fuchs |f(y)ōōks|, Sir Vivian (Ernest) (1908–) English geologist and explorer. He led the Commonwealth

Trans-Antarctic Expedition (1955–58), making the first overland crossing of the Antarctic.

Fuen•tes |'fwentās|, Carlos (1928–) Mexican novelist and writer. Notable works: *Where the Air is Clear* (1958), *Terra nostra* (1975), and *The Old Gringo* (1984).

Fu•gard |'f(y)ōō,gärd|,Athol (1932–) South African dramatist. His plays, including *Blood Knot* (1963) and *The Road to Mecca* (1985), are mostly set in contemporary South Africa and deal with social deprivation and other aspects of life under apartheid.

Ful•bright |'fool,brīt|, (James) William (1905–95) U.S. senator. He sponsored the Fulbright Act of 1946, which authorized funds from the sale of surplus war materials overseas to be used to finance exchange programs of students and teachers between the U.S. and other countries. The program has continued, supported by federal grants.

Ful•ler |'foolər|, Albert Carl (1885–1973) U.S. businessman, born in Canada. He created the Capital Brush Co. (1906), which was later known as the Fuller Brush Co. (1910).

Ful•ler |'foolər|, Charles (1939–) U.S. author. Notable works: *A Soldier's Play* (1981, Pulitzer Prize).

Ful•ler |'foolər|, (Sarah) Margaret (1810–50) U.S. literary critic and social reformer. An advocate of cultural education for women, she conducted "Conversations," a popular series of discussion groups in the Boston area before becoming literary critic of the *New York Tribune* (1844–46). Among her books is the feminist classic *Woman in the Nineteenth Century* (1845).

Ful•ler |'foolər|,MelvilleWeston (1833–1910) U.S. Supreme Court justice (1888–1910). He was also a member of the Court of International Arbitration, The Hague (1900–10).

Ful•ler |'foolər|, R. Buckminster (1895–1983) U.S. designer and architect; full name *Richard Buckminster Fuller*. He is best known for his invention of the geodesic dome and for his ideals of using the world's resources with maximum purpose and least waste.

Ful•ler |'foolər|, Thomas (1608–61)

English cleric and historian. He is chiefly remembered for *The History of the Worthies of England* (1662), a description of counties with short biographies of local personages.

Ful•ton |'foŏltən|, Robert (1765–1815) U.S. pioneer of the steamship. He constructed a steam-propelled "diving-boat" in 1800, which submerged to a depth of 25 ft., and in 1806 he built the first successful paddle steamer, the *Clermont*.

Funk |fəNGk|, Casimir (1884–1967) Polish-born U.S. biochemist. He showed that a number of diseases, including scurvy, rickets, beriberi, and pellagra, were each caused by the deficiency of a particular dietary component, and coined the term *vitamins* for the chemicals concerned.

Furt•wäng•ler |'foŏrt,veNG(g)lər|, Wilhelm ((1886–1954)) German conductor, chief conductor of the Berlin Philharmonic Orchestra from 1922. He is noted particularly for his interpretations of Beethoven and Wagner.

Fu•seli |fyoŏ'zelē|, Henry (1741–1825) Swiss-born British painter and art critic; born *Johann Heinrich Füssli*. A prominent figure of the romantic movement, he tended toward the horrifying and the fantastic, as in *The Nightmare* (1781).

Fus•sell |'fəsəl|, Paul (1924–) U.S. educator and author. Notable works: *The Great War and Modern Memory* (1975, National Book Award).

Gg

Gable |'gābəl|, (William) Clark (1901–60) U.S. actor, famous for leading man roles in movies such as *It Happened One Night* (1934), for which he won an Oscar, *Mutiny on the Bounty* (1935), *Gone with the Wind* (1939), and *The Misfits* (1961).

Ga·bo |'gäbō|, Naum (1890–1977) Russian-born U.S. sculptor, brother of Antoine Pevsner; born *Naum Neemia Pevsner*. A founder of Russian constructivism, Gabo experimented with kinetic art and transparent materials.

Ga·bor |gə'bawr| Hungarian-born U.S. actresses. **Zsa Zsa Gabor** (*c.* 1919–) and her sister **Eva Gabor** (*c.* 1921–95). Eva played the comedic leading role in television's "Green Acres" (1965–71).

Ga·bor |gə'bawr|, Dennis (1900–79) Hungarian-born British electrical engineer, who conceived the idea of holography. Nobel Prize for Physics (1971).

Ga·bri·eli |ˌgäbrē'elē|, Giovanni (*c.* 1556–1612) Italian composer and organist. He was a leading Venetian musician who wrote a large number of motets with instrumental accompaniments for St. Mark's Cathedral.

Gad·dafi |gə'däfē|, Mu'ammar Muhammad al (1942–) Libyan colonel, head of state since 1970. Also **Qaddafi**. After leading the coup that overthrew King Idris in 1969, he established the Libyan Arab Republic and has since pursued an anti-colonial policy at home; he has also been accused of supporting international terrorism.

Gad·dis |'gædis|, William (1922–) U.S. author. Notable works: *J R* (National Book Award, 1975) and *A Frolic of His Own* (National Book Award, 1994).

Ga·ga·rin |gə'gärən|, Yury Alekseyevich (1934–68) Russian cosmonaut. In 1961 he made the first manned space flight, completing a single orbit of the earth in 108 minutes.

Gage |gāj|, Thomas (1596–1656) English priest. He was a Christian missionary to Central America and the West Indies.

Gains·bor·ough |'gānz,bərō|, Thomas (1727–88) English painter. He was famous for his society portraits, including *Mr. And Mrs. Andrews* (1748) and *The Blue Boy* (*c.*1770), and for landscapes such as *The Watering Place* (1777).

Gait·skell |'gātskəl|, Hugh (Todd Naylor) (1906–63) British Labour statesman, chancellor of the exchequer (1950–51) and leader of the Labour Party (1955–63).

Gal·a·had |'gælə,hæd|, Sir the noblest of King Arthur's legendary knights, renowned for immaculate purity and destined to find the Holy Grail.

Gal·ba |'gawlbə|, Servius Sulpicius (*c.* 3BC–69 AD) Roman emperor (AD 68–69). The successor to Nero, he aroused hostility by his severity and parsimony and was murdered in a conspiracy organized by his successor, Otho.

Gal·braith |'gawl,brᴀTH|, John Kenneth (1908–) Canadian-born U.S. economist. He is well known for his criticism of consumerism and of the power of large multinational corporations. Notable works: *The Affluent Society* (1958) and *The New Industrial State* (1967).

Ga·len |'gālən| (129–*c.* 199) Greek physician; full name *Claudios Galenos*; Latin name *Claudius Galenus*. He attempted to systematize the whole of medicine, making important discoveries in anatomy and physiology. His works became influential in Europe when retranslated from Arabic in the 12th century.

Ga·li·leo Ga·li·lei |ˌgælə'lāō ˌgæli'lā(ē)| (1564–1642) Italian astronomer and physicist. He discovered the constancy of a pendulum's swing, formulated the law of uniform acceleration of falling bodies, and described the parabolic trajectory of projectiles. He applied the telescope to astronomy and observed craters on the moon, sunspots, Jupiter's moons, and the phases of Venus.

Gal·la·tin |'gælətən|, (Abraham Alfonse) Albert (1761–1849) U.S. politician, born in Switzerland. As a member of the U.S. House of Representatives from Virginia (1795–1801), he helped establish the House Committee on Finance, now the Ways and Means Committee; he served as U.S. secretary of the treasury (1801–14).

Gal•lau•det |ˌgælə'det|, Thomas Hopkins (1787–1851) U.S. educator. In 1817 he founded the first free American school for the deaf, the Connecticut (later, American) Asylum, in Hartford, Connecticut.

Gal•lo |'gælō| U.S. winemakers. **Ernest Gallo** (1910–) and his brother **Julio Gallo** (1911–93) started a winery to manufacture California wines.

Gal•lo•way |'gælə,wā|, Joseph (1731–1803) U.S. lawyer and politician. He was a loyalist writer and statesman and an adviser to the British crown.

Gal•lup |'gæləp|, George Horace (1901–84) U.S. statistician. He pioneered public opinion polls.

Ga•lois |gäl'wä|, Évariste (1811–32) French mathematician. His memoir on the conditions for solubility of polynomial equations was highly innovative but was not published until 1846, after his death.

Gals•wor•thy |'gawlz,wərTHē|, John (1867–1933) English novelist and dramatist. He is remembered chiefly for *The Forsyte Saga* (1906–28), a series of novels that was adapted for television in 1967. Nobel Prize for Literature (1932).

Gal•ti•eri |ˌgältē'erē|, Leopoldo Fortunato (1926–) Argentinian general and statesman, president (1981–82). Galtieri's military junta ordered the invasion of the Falkland Islands in 1982, precipitating the Falklands War.

Gal•ton |'gawltən|, Sir Francis (1822–1911) English scientist. He founded eugenics and introduced methods of measuring human mental and physical abilities. He also pioneered the use of fingerprints as a means of identification.

Gal•va•ni |gäl'vänē|, Luigi (1737–98) Italian anatomist. He studied the structure of organs and the physiology of tissues, but he is best known for his discovery of the twitching of frogs' legs in an electric field.

Gal•way |'gawl,wā|, James (1939–) British flutist.

Ga•ma |'gämə|, Vasco da see DA GAMA.

Gam•ow |'gæmawf|, George (1904–68) Russian-born U.S. physicist. He was a proponent of the "big bang" theory and also suggested the triplet code of bases in DNA, which governs the synthesis of amino acids.

Gance |gäns|, Abel (1889–1981) French movie director. He was an early pioneer of technical experimentation in movies. Notable movies: *La Roue* (1921) and *Napoléon* (1926).

Gan•dhi |'gändē| Indian political family. **Indira Gandi** (1917–84) was prime minister (1966–77 and 1980–84). The daughter of Jawaharlal Nehru, she sought to establish a secular state and to lead India out of poverty. She was assassinated by her own Sikh bodyguards following prolonged religious disturbances. Her son, **Rajiv Gandi** (1944–91), was prime minister (1984–89) after her assassination. His premiership was marked by continuing unrest, and he was assassinated during an election campaign.

Gan•dhi |'gändē|, Mahatma (1869–1948) Indian nationalist and spiritual leader; full name *Mohandas Karamchand Gandhi*. He became prominent in the opposition to British rule in India, pursuing a policy of non-violent civil disobedience. He never held government office, but was regarded as the country's supreme political and spiritual leader; he was assassinated by a Hindu following his agreement to the creation of the state of Pakistan.

Gar•bo |'gärbō|, Greta (1905–90) Swedish-born U.S. actress. Born *Greta Gustafsson*. She traveled to Hollywood and gained international recognition. Notable movies: *Anna Christie* (1930), *Mata Hari* (1931), and *Anna Karenina* (1935). After her retirement in 1941, she lived as a recluse.

Gar•cia |gär'sēə|, Jerry (1942–95) U.S. rock singer and guitarist; full name *Jerome John Garcia*. Garcia was the central figure of the Grateful Dead, a group formed *c.* 1966. Mixing psychedelic rock with country and blues influences in lengthy improvisations, the band toured extensively until Garcia's death.

Gar•cía Lor•ca |gär'sēə 'lawrkə|, Federico (1899–1936) Spanish poet and dramatist. Notable works: *Romancero gitano* (1953).

Gar·cí·a Már·quez |gär'sēə 'mär,kes|, Gabriel (1928–   ) Colombian novelist. His works include *One Hundred Years of Solitude* (1967), a classic example of magic realism, and *Chronicle of a Death Foretold* (1981). Nobel Prize for Literature (1982).

Gard·ner |'gärdnər|, Alexander (1821–82) U.S. photographer, born in Scotland. His early Civil War photos were credited to Mathew Brady, his employer (1856–63). He published *Gardner's Photographic Sketch Book of the Civil War* (1866) and was hired as the official photographer of the Union Pacific Railroad (1867).

Gard·ner |'gärdnər|, Ava (Lavinnia) (1922–90) U.S. actress. Notable movies: *The Killers* (1946), *Bhowani Junction* (1956), and *The Night of the Iguana* (1964).

Gard·ner |'gärdnər|, Erle Stanley (1889–1970) U.S. novelist and short-story writer. He practiced as a defense lawyer before writing his novels featuring the lawyer-detective Perry Mason.

Gard·ner |'gärdnər|, Isabella Stewart (1840–1924) U.S. socialite and art collector. Her house in Boston was a gathering-place for artists, writers, musicians, and other celebrities. With the help of art connoisseur Bernard Berenson, she assembled an outstanding collection of classical and contemporary art. The palazzo she built in Boston (1903) to house her collection was bequeathed to the city as the Isabella Stewart Gardner Museum.

Gard·ner |'gärdnər|, John Champlin, Jr. (1933–82) U.S. educator and author. Notable works: *October Light* (National Book Critics Circle Award, 1976) and *Mickelsson's Ghosts* (1982).

Gar·field |'gär,fēld|, James Abram see box. **Lucretia Randolph Garfield** (1832–1918), wife of James Garfield and U.S. first lady (1881).

Gar·fun·kel |'gär,fəNGkəl|, Art (1942–   ) U.S. singer and songwriter. He was part of the pop-folk duo Simon and Garfunkel (1958–70), which won four Grammy Awards (1968 and 1970).

Gar·i·bal·di |,geri'bawldē|, Giuseppe

Garfield, James Abram
20th U.S. president

Life dates: 1831–1881
Place of birth: Orange, Ohio
Mother: Eliza Ballou Garfield
Father: Abram Garfield
Wife: Lucretia Rudolph Garfield
Children: Eliza, Harry, James, Mary (Molly), Irvin, Abram, Edward
College/University: Western Reserve Eclectic Institute; Williams College
Military service: during Civil War, rose to rank of major general in the Ohio volunteers
Career: Lawyer; college professor and college president; lay preacher
Political career: Ohio Senate; U.S. House of Representatives; president
Party: Republican
Home state: Ohio
Opponents in presidential race: Neal Dow; James Baird Weaver, John Wolcott Phelps; Winfield Scott Hancock
Term of office: March 4, 1881–Sept. 19, 1881 (died in office after being shot by Charles J. Guiteau on July 2, 1881)
Vice president: Chester Alan Arthur
Other achievements: President, Western Reserve Eclectic Institute; member, Electoral Commission that settled the disputed Tilden-Hayes election of 1876
Place of burial: Cleveland, Ohio

(1807–82) Italian patriot and military leader of the Risorgimento (unification of Italy). With his volunteer force of "Red Shirts" he captured Sicily and southern Italy from the Austrians in 1860–61, thereby playing a key role in the establishment of a united kingdom of Italy.

Gar·land |'gärlənd|, Judy (1922–69) U.S. singer and actress; born *Frances Gumm*. Her most famous early movie role was in *The Wizard of Oz* (1939), in which she played Dorothy and sang "Over the Rainbow". Other notable movies: *Meet Me in St. Louis* (1944) and *A Star is Born* (1954).

Gar·ner |'gärnər|, Errol (Louis) (1923–77) U.S. jazz pianist and composer. He formed his own trio and also recorded with Charlie Parker. Notable songs: "Misty."

Gar·ner |'gärnər|, James (1928–) U.S. actor. Born *James Scott Bumgarner.* He starred in the television series "The Rockford Files" (1974–80). Notable movies: *Victor/Victoria* (1982) and *Murphy's Romance* (1985)

Gar·ner |'gärnər|, John Nance (1868–1967) Vice president of the U.S. (1933–41). Known as **Cactus Jack**. He was a member of the U.S. House of Representatives from Texas (1903–33) and speaker of the House (1931–33).

Gar·ret·son |'gerətsən|, James Edmund (1828–95) U.S. physician. He was a pioneer in oral surgery and published the first textbook on dental surgery.

Gar·rick |'gerik|, David (1717–79) English actor and dramatist. He was a notably versatile actor and the manager of the Drury Lane Theatre.

Gar·ri·son |'gerəsən|, William Lloyd (1805–79) U.S. social liberal and spearhead for New England abolitionism.

Gar·son |'gärsən|, Greer (1908–96) U.S. actress. Notable movies: *Mrs. Miniver* (1942, Academy Award).

Gar·vey |'gärvē|, Marcus (Moziah) (1887–1940) Jamaican political activist and black nationalist leader. He was the leader of the "Back to Africa" movement, which advocated the establishment of an African homeland for black Americans. He attracted a large following in the U.S., and his thinking was later an important influence on Rastafarianism.

Gary |'gerē|, Elbert Henry (1846–1927) U.S. lawyer and businessman. He organized the United States Steel Corp. (1901); Gary, Indiana, is named for him.

Gas·kell |'gæskəl|, Mrs. Elizabeth (Cleghorn) (1810–65) English novelist. Notable works: *Mary Barton* (1848), *Cranford* (1853), and *North and South* (1855). She also wrote a biography (1857) of her friend Charlotte Brontë.

Gass |gæs|, William H(oward) (1924–) U.S. educator and author. Notable works: *Omensetter's Luck* (1966) and *On Being Blue* (1976).

Gas·sen·di |gə'sendē; gä'säNdē|, Pierre (1592–1655) French astronomer and philosopher. He is best known for his atomic theory of matter, which was based on his interpretation of the works of Epicurus.

Gas·ser |'gæsər|, Herbert Spencer (1888–1963) U.S. physiologist. Collaborating with Joseph Erlanger, he used an oscilloscope to show that the velocity of a nerve impulse is proportional to the diameter of the fibre. Nobel Prize for Physiology or Medicine (1944, shared with Erlanger).

Gates |gāts|, Bill (1955–) U.S. computer entrepreneur; full name *William Henry Gates*. He co-founded the computer software company Microsoft. Overseas expansion and the successful marketing of the MS-DOS and Windows operating systems for personal computers made the firm a leading multinational computer company by 1990. He became the youngest multi-billionaire in U.S. history.

Gates |gāts|, Henry Louis, Jr. (1950–) U.S. educator and author. He wrote *The Future of the Race* (1996) and edited *Bearing Witness* (1991).

Gates |gāts|, Horatio (1728–1806) American Revolutionary War army officer, born in England. He was commanding general in the Saratoga Campaign (1777); his friends formed the Conway Cabal in an attempt to replace George Washington with Gates as commander in chief.

Gat·ling |'gætliNG|, Richard Jordan (1818–1903) U.S. inventor. He is best known for the Gatling gun, invented in 1862.

Gau·dí |gow'dē|, Antonio (1852–1926) Spanish architect; full name *Antonio Gaudí y Cornet*. He was a leading but idiosyncratic exponent of art nouveau, known mainly for his ornate and extravagant church of the Sagrada Familia in Barcelona (begun 1884).

Gaudier-Brzeska |ˌgōdyä'bzHeskä|, Henri (1891–1915) French sculptor, a leading member of the vorticist movement. Notable works: the faceted bust of Horace Brodzky (1912) and *Bird Swallowing a Fish* (1913).

Gau·guin |gō'gæN|, (Eugène Henri) Paul (1848–1903) French painter. From 1891 on he lived mainly in Tahiti, painting in a post-Impressionist style that was influenced by primitive art. Notable works: *The Vision after the Sermon* (1888) and *Faa Iheihe* (1898).

Gaulle, Charles de see DE GAULLE.

Gaul·tier |'gōtyā|, Jean Paul (1952–) French fashion designer.

Gaunt, John of see JOHN OF GAUNT.

Gauss |gows|, Carl Friedrich (1777–1855) German mathematician, astronomer, and physicist. Gauss laid the foundations of number theory, and applied rigorous mathematical analysis to geometry, geodesy, electrostatics, and electromagnetism.

Gau·ta·ma |'gowtəmə|, Siddhartha see BUDDHA.

Gau·tier |'gōtyā|, Théophile (1811–72) French author. His works, written in the Romantic tradition, include the novel *Mademoiselle de Maupin* (1835).

Gay |gā|, John (1685–1732) English poet and dramatist. He is chiefly known for *The Beggar's Opera* (1728), a low-life ballad opera combining burlesque and political satire.

Gaye |gā|, Marvin (1939–84) U.S. singer, composer, and musician. Known for hits including "I Heard It Through the Grapevine" (1968), he later recorded the albums *What's Goin' On* (1971), *Let's Get It On* (1973), and *Midnight Love* (1982). He was shot dead by his father in a quarrel.

Gay-Lussac |ˌgālə'sæk|, Joseph-Louis (1778–1850) French chemist and physicist. He is best known for his work on gases, and in 1808 he formulated the law usually known by his name. He also developed techniques of quantitative chemical analysis, confirmed that iodine was an element, discovered cyanogen, and made two balloon ascents to study the atmosphere and terrestrial magnetism.

Ge·ber |'jēbər| (c. 721–c. 815) Arab chemist; Latinized name of *Jabir ibn Hayyan*. Many works are attributed to him, but his name was used by later writers. He was familiar with many chemicals and laboratory techniques, including distillation and sublimation.

Gef·fen |'gefən|, David (1943–) U.S. recording company executive. He founded Asylum Records (1970), Geffen Records (1980), and the Geffen Film Co.

Geh·rig |'gerig|, Lou (Henry Louis) (1903–41) U.S. baseball player. Known as **the Iron Horse**. He played a then-record 2,130 consecutive major league games for the New York Yankees from 1925 to 1939. His consecutive-game streak was ended by the disease that he ultimately died from, amyotrophic lateral sclerosis, often called Lou Gehrig's disease.

Gei·ger |'gīgər|, Johannes Hans Wilhelm (1882–1945) German nuclear physicist. In 1908 he developed his prototype radiation counter for detecting alpha particles, later improved in collaboration with Walther Müller.

Gei·kie |'gīkē|, Sir Archibald (1835–1924) Scottish geologist. He specialized in Pleistocene geology, especially the geomorphological effects of glaciations and the resulting deposits.

Gei·sel |'gīzəl|, Theodor Seuss (1904–91) U.S. author and illustrator. His numerous children's books include *And to Think That I Saw It on Mulberry Street* (1937), *The Cat in the Hat* (1957), and *Green Eggs and Ham* (1960).

Gel·bart |'gelbärt|, Larry (1925–) U.S. movie and television writer. He won an Emmy Award (1972) for his episodes of "M★A★S★H," as well as Tony Awards (1962 and 1989).

Gell·horn |'gelhōrn|, Martha (1908–) U.S. journalist and author. She was a foreign correspondent for *Collier's* Magazine (1937–45) and was married to Ernest Hemingway (1940–43).

Gell-Mann |'gel 'mæn|, Murray (1929–) U.S. theoretical physicist. He coined the word *quark* and proposed the concept of strangeness in quarks. Nobel Prize for Physics (1969).

Ge·may·el |jə'mīəl|, Pierre (1905–84) Lebanese political leader. A Maronite Christian, he founded the right-wing Phalange Party in 1936 and served as a member of Parliament (1960–84). His youngest son, **Bashir** (1947–82), was assassinated while president-elect; his eldest son, **Amin** (1942–), served as president (1982–88).

Ge·net |zHə'nā|, Jean (1910–86) French novelist, poet, and dramatist. Much of his work portrayed life in the criminal and homosexual underworlds, of which he was a part. Notable works: *Our Lady of the Flowers* (novel, 1944), *The Thief's Journal* (autobiography, 1949), and *The Maids* (play, 1947).

Gen•ghis Khan |'geNGgəs 'kän| (1162–1227) founder of the Mongol empire; born *Temujin.* He took the name Genghis Khan ('ruler of all') in 1206 after uniting the nomadic Mongol tribes, and by the time of his death his empire extended from China to the Black Sea. His grandson Kublai Khan completed the conquest of China.

Gen•ti•le |jen'tēlā|, Giovanni (1875–1944) Italian philosopher and educator. He was a proponent of the fascist philosophy of "actualism" and a Mussolini supporter.

Gen•ti•le da Fa•bri•a•no |jen'tēlā dä ˌfäbrē'änō| (*c.* 1370–1427) Italian painter. His major surviving work is the altarpiece *The Adoration of the Magi* (1423), most others having been destroyed.

Geof•frey of Mon•mouth |'jefrē| (*c.* 1110–*c.* 1154) Welsh chronicler. His *Histroia Regum Britanniae* (*c.*1139; first printed in 1508), an account of the kings of Britain, was a major source for English literature but is now thought to contain little historical fact.

George |jawrj| the name of four kings of Great Britain and Ireland, one of Great Britain and Ireland (from 1920 of the United Kingdom), and one of the United Kingdom: **George I** (1660–1727; reigned 1714–27), king of Great Britain and Ireland, great-grandson of James I, Elector of Hanover (1698–1727). He succeeded to the British throne as a result of an Act of Settlement (1701). Unpopular in England as a foreigner who never learned English, he left administration to his ministers. **George II** (1683–1760; reigned 1727–60), son of George I. King of Great Britain and Ireland as well as Elector of Hanover (1727–60). He depended heavily on his ministers, although he took an active part in the War of the Austrian Succession (1740–48). His later withdrawal from active politics allowed the development of constitutional monarchy. **George III** (1738–1820; reigned 1760–1820), grandson of George II. He was

king of Great Britain and Ireland, as well as Elector of Hanover (1760–1815) and King of Hanover (1815–20). He reigned during the time of the Revolutionary War and the War of 1812. He exercised considerable political influence, but it declined from 1788 after bouts of mental illness, as a result of which his son was made regent in 1811. **George IV** (1762–1830; reigned 1820–30), son of George III. King of Great Britain and Ireland. Known as a patron of the arts and *bon vivant,* he gained a bad reputation, which further damaged his attempt to divorce his estranged wife Caroline of Brunswick. **George V** (1865–1936; reigned 1910–36), son of Edward VII. King of Great Britain and Ireland (of the United Kingdom from 1920). He exercised restrained but important influence over British politics, playing an especially significant role in the formation of the government in 1931. **George VI** (1895–1952; reigned 1936–52), son of George V. King of the United Kingdom. He came to the throne on the abdication of his elder brother Edward VIII. Despite a retiring disposition, he became a popular monarch, gaining respect for the staunch example he and his family set during the London Blitz.

George |jawrj|, Henry (1839–97) U.S. economist. He theorized the formula of the single tax, generating taxes from land ownership.

George |jawrj|, St. (*c.* 3rd century) patron saint of England. He is reputed in legend to have slain a dragon, and may have been martyred near Lydda in Palestine some time before the reign of Constantine. His cult did not become popular until the 6th century, and he probably became patron saint of England in the 14th century. Feast day, April 23.

Gep•hardt |'gep,härt|, Richard Andrew (1941–   ) U.S. politician. He is a member of the U.S. House of Representatives from Missouri (1979–   ) and was a 1988 U.S. presidential nominee.

Ge•rard |jə'rärd|, John (1545–1612) English herbalist. He was curator of the physic garden of the College of Surgeons and published his *Herball,* containing over 1,800 woodcuts, in 1597.

Ger·ber |'gərbər|, Daniel Frank (1873–1952) U.S. businessman. He owned a small cannery with his father, and in 1928 he and his wife Dorothy began making and marketing strained baby food.

Gé·ri·cault |ˌZHārē'kō|, (Jean Louis André) Théodore (1791–1824) French painter, criticized for his rejection of classicism in favor of a more realistic style. His most famous work, *The Raft of the Medusa* (1819), depicts the survivors of a famous shipwreck of 1816.

Ger·mer |'germər|, Edmund (1901–87) U.S. scientist, born in Germany. He developed the flourescent lamp and high-pressure mercury-vapor lamp.

Gern·reich, Rudi (1922–85) U.S. fashion designer, born in Austria.

Gerns·back |'gernz,bäk|, Hugo (1884–1967) U.S. inventor and publisher, born in Luxembourg. He patented over 80 electronic inventions and founded *Amazing Stories* magazine (1926), establishing science fiction as literary form. The Hugo Award is named for him.

Ge·ro·ni·mo |jə'ränə,mō| (*c.* 1829–1909) Apache chief. He led his people in resisting white encroachment on tribal reservations in Arizona before surrendering in 1886.

Ger·ry |'jerē|, Elbridge (1744–1814) vice president of the U.S. (1813–14). His political maneuvering in Massachusetts gave rise to the term "gerrymander."

Gersh·win |'gərSHwin| U.S. musicians of Russian-Jewish descent. **Ira Gershwin** (1896–1983), a lyricist, collaborated with his brother **George Gershwin** (1898–1937). Ira won the first Pulitzer Prize awarded to a lyricist for *Of Thee I Sing* (1931). George, who was born *Jacob Gershovitz*, was a composer and pianist. He made his name in 1919 with the song "Swanee." He went on to compose many successful songs and musicals, the orchestral work *Rhapsody in Blue* (1924), and the opera *Porgy and Bess* (1935).

Ger·vin, George (1952–) U.S. basketball player. Known as **the Iceman**.

Get·ty |'getē|, Jean Paul (1892–1976) U.S. industrialist. He made a large for-

tune in the oil industry and was also a noted art collector. He founded the J. Paul Getty Museum in Los Angeles.

Getz |gets|, Stan (1927–91) U.S. jazz saxophonist; born *Stanley Gayetsky*. He was a leader of the "cool" school of jazz; his recordings include "Early Autumn" (1948) and "The Girl from Ipanema" (1963).

Ghi·ber·ti |gē'bertē|, Lorenzo (1378–1455) Italian sculptor and goldsmith. His career was dominated by his work on two successive pairs of bronze doors for the baptistery in Florence.

Ghir·lan·daio |ˌgirlən'däyō| (*c.* 1449–94) Italian painter; born *Domenico di Tommaso Bigordi*. He is noted for his religious frescoes, particularly *Christ Calling Peter and Andrew* (1482–4) in the Sistine Chapel, Rome.

Gia·co·met·ti |ˌjäkə'metē|, Alberto (1901–66) Swiss sculptor and painter. His most typical works feature emaciated and extremely elongated human forms, such as *Pointing Man* (1947).

Gia·mat·ti |j(ē)ə'mäti|, A. Bartlett (1938–89) U.S. educator and sports administrator. He was president of Yale University (1978–86), president of the National Baseball League (1986–89), and the 7th commissioner of baseball (1989).

Giap, Vo Nguyen (1912–) Vietnamese military and political leader. As North Vietnamese vice-premier and defense minister, he was responsible for the strategy leading to the withdrawal of U.S. forces from South Vietnam in 1973 and the subsequent reunification of the country in 1976. His book *People's War, People's Army* (1961) was an influential text for revolutionaries.

Gib·bon |'gibən|, Edward (1737–94) English historian. He is best known for his multi-volume work *The History of the Decline and Fall of the Roman Empire* (1776–88), chapters of which aroused controversy for their critical account of the spread of Christianity.

Gib·bon |'gibən|, Lewis Grassic (1901–35) Scottish writer; pseudonym of *James Leslie Mitchell*.

Gib·bons |'gibənz|, Grinling (1648–1721) Dutch-born English sculptor. He is famous for his decorative carvings, chiefly in wood, as in the choir stalls of St. Paul's Cathedral, London.

Gib•bons |'gibənz|, Orlando (1583–1625) English composer and musician. He was the organist of Westminster Abbey from 1623 and composed mainly sacred music, although he is also known for madrigals such as *The Silver Swan* (1612).

Gibbs |gibz|, Sir Philip Hamilton (1877–1962) British journalist and author. He was knighted for his behind-the-lines work as a correspondent during World War I.

Gibbs |gibz|, James (1682–1754) Scottish architect. He developed Christopher Wren's ideas for London's city churches, especially in his masterpiece, *St. Martin's-in-the-Fields* (1722–26).

Gibbs |gibz|, Josiah Willard (1839–1903) U.S. physical chemist. He pioneered chemical thermodynamics and statistical mechanics, although his theoretical work was not generally appreciated until after his death.

Gibran |jə'brän|, Khalil (1883–1931) Lebanese-born U.S. writer and artist. Also **Jubran**. His writings in both Arabic and English are deeply romantic, displaying his religious and mystical nature.

Gib•son |'gibsən|, Althea (1927–) U.S. tennis player. She was the first black player to succeed at the highest level of tennis, winning all the major world women's singles titles in the late 1950s.

Gib•son |'gibsən|, Bob (1935–) U.S. baseball player. Full name *Robert Gibson*. Elected to Baseball Hall of Fame (1981).

Gib•son |'gibsən|, Charles Dana (1867–1944) U.S. artist. He was a magazine illustrator and creator of the "Gibson Girl."

Gib•son |'gibsən|, Mel (Columcille Gerard) (1956–) U.S.-born Australian actor and director. Notable movies: *Mad Max* (1979), the *Lethal Weapon* series (1987, 1989, 1992, and 1998) and *Braveheart* (1995), which he also directed and which won five Oscars.

Gib•son |'gibsən|, William (1914–) U.S. playwright. Notable works: *The MiracleWorker* (1960) and *Golda* (1977).

Gid•dings |'gidiNGz|, Joshua Reed (1795–1864) U.S. politician and abolitionist. He was a member of the U.S. House of Representatives from the Western Reserve district of Ohio (1838–59) and was censured for his militant abolitionist tactics (1842).

Gide |ZHēd|, André-Paul-Guillaume (1869–1951) French novelist, essayist, and critic, regarded as the father of modern French literature. Notable works: *The Immoralist* (1902), *La Porte Étroite* (1909, *Strait is the Gate*), *The Counterfeiters* (1927), and his *Journal* (1939–50). Nobel Prize for Literature (1947).

Giel•gud |'gēl,go͞od|, Sir (Arthur) John (1904–) English actor and director. A notable Shakespearean actor, particularly remembered for his interpretation of the role of Hamlet, he has also appeared in contemporary plays and films and won an Oscar for his role as a butler in *Arthur* (1980).

Gi•gli |'jēlyē|, Beniamino (1890–1597) Italian operatic tenor. He made his Milan debut with the conductor Toscanini in 1918, and retained his singing talents to a considerable age.

Gil•bert |'gilbərt|, Cass (1859–1934) U.S. architect. He designed the Woolworth building in New York City (1913) and the U.S. Supreme Court building (1935).

Gil•bert |'gilbərt|, Sir Humphrey (*c.* 1539–83) English explorer. He claimed Newfoundland for Elizabeth I in 1583, but was lost when his ship foundered in a storm on the way home.

Gil•bert |'gilbərt|, William (1544–1603) English physician and physicist. He discovered how to make magnets, and coined the term *magnetic pole*. His book *De Magnete* (1600) is an important early work on physics.

Gil•bert |'gilbərt|, Sir W. S. (1836–1911) English dramatist; full name *William Schwenck Gilbert*. He is best known as a librettist who collaborated on light operas with the composer Sir Arthur Sullivan. Notable works: *HMS Pinafore* (1878), *The Pirates of Penzance* (1879), and *The Mikado* (1885).

Gill |gil|, (Arthur) Eric (Rowton) (1882–1940) English sculptor, engraver, and typographer. He designed the first sans serif typeface, Gill Sans.

Gil•les•pie |gi'lespē|, Dizzy (1917–93) U.S. jazz trumpet player and band-leader; born *John Birks Gillespie*. He was a virtuoso trumpet player and a leading exponent of the bebop style.

Gil•lette |jə'let|, King Camp (1855–1932) U.S. inventor and manufacturer. He invented the disposable safety razor.

Gil•man |'gilmən|, Charlotte Anna (Perkins) (1860–1935) U.S. author and feminist lecturer. Notable works: *The Yellow Wallpaper* (1892).

Gil•man |'gilmən|, Daniel Coit (1831–1908) U.S. educator and professor. He founded the Sheffield Scientific School at Yale (1856) and served as the first president of Johns Hopkins University (1875–1901).

Gil•pin |'gilpən|, Charles Sidney (1878–1930) U.S. actor. He was one of the first black actors to gain success on the American stage.

Gil•roy |'gilroi|, Frank D. (1925–) U.S. author. Notable works: *The Subject Was Roses* (1964, Pulitzer Prize).

Gim•bel |'gimbəl|, Isaac (1856–1931) U.S. businessman, born in Germany. With his brothers Charles (1861–1932) and Ellis A. (1865–1950) Gimbel, he founded the department store chain Gimbel Brothers, Inc. (1922).

Ging•rich |'giNG(g)riCH|, Newt (1943–) U.S. politician and speaker of the U.S. House of Representatives. Full name *Newton Leroy Gingrich*. He served as a representative from Georgia (1979-98).

Gins•berg |'ginzbərg|, Allen (1926–97) U.S. poet. A leading poet of the beat generation, and later influential in the hippy movement of the 1960s, he is notable for *Howl and Other Poems* (1956), in which he attacked American society for its materialism and complacency. He later campaigned for civil rights, gay liberation, and the peace movement.

Gins•burg |'ginzbərg|, Charles P. (1920–92) U.S. scientist. He invented a videotape recorder, which was first used by a television network in 1956.

Gins•burg |'ginzbərg|, Ruth Bader (1933–) U.S. Supreme Court justice (1993–).

Gio•lit•ti |jō'lētē|, Giovanni (1842–1928) Italian statesman, prime minister five times between 1892 and 1921. He was responsible for the introduction of a wide range of social reforms, including national insurance (1911) and universal male suffrage (1912).

Gior•gio•ne |jawr'j(ē)awnā| (c. 1477–1511) Italian painter; also called **Giorgio Barbarelli** or **Giorgio da Castelfranco**. An influential figure in Renaissance art, he introduced the small easel picture in oils intended for private collectors. Notable works: *The Tempest* (c.1505) and *Sleeping Venus* (c.1510).

Giot•to |'jawtō| (c. 1266–1337) Italian painter; full name *Giotto di Bondone*. He introduced a naturalistic style showing human expression. His name is associated with the legend of "Giotto's O", in which he is said to have proven his mastery to the pope by drawing a perfect circle freehand. Notable works include the frescoes in the Arena Chapel, Padua (1305–08) and the church of Santa Croce in Florence (c.1320).

Gio•van•ni de' Me•di•ci the name of the Pope Leo X (see LEO).

Gis•card d'Es•taing |zHis'kär des 'tæN|, Valéry (1926–) French statesman, president (1974–81).

Gish |'giSH| U.S. actresses. **Lillian Gish** (1893–1993) and her sister **Dorothy Gish** (1898–1968) appeared in a number of D. W. Griffith's silent movies, including *Hearts of the World* (1918) and *Orphans of the Storm* (1922).

Gis•sing |'gisiNG|, George (Robert) (1857–1903) English novelist. Notable works: *New Grub Street* (1891), *Born in Exile* (1892), and *The Private Papers of Henry Ryecroft* (1903).

Gi•ven•chy |,zHēväN'sHē|, Hubert (1927–) French fashion designer.

Glad•stone |'glæd,stōn|, William Ewart (1809–98) British Liberal statesman, prime minister (1868–74, 1880–85, 1886, and 1892–94).

Glas•gow |'glæz,gō|, Ellen (Anderson Gholson) (1873–1945) U.S. author. Notable works: *In This Our Life* (1941, Pulitzer Prize).

Glash•ow |'glæsHō|, Sheldon Lee (1932–) U.S. theoretical physicist. He independently developed a unified theory to explain electromagnetic interactions and the weak nuclear force, and extended the quark theory of Murray Gell-Mann. Nobel Prize for Physics (1979).

Glas·pell |'glæs,pel|, Susan (1882–1948) U.S. novelist and playwright. She won a Pulitzer Prize for her play *Alison's House* (1930), based on the life of Emily Dickinson.

Glass |glæs|, Philip (1937–   ) U.S. composer, a leading minimalist. Notable works: *Einstein on the Beach* (opera 1976), *Glass Pieces* (ballet 1982), and *Low Symphony* (1993).

Gla·zu·nov |'gläzə,nawf|, Aleksandr (Konstantinovich) (1865–1936) Russian composer, a pupil of Rimsky-Korsakov. Notable work: *The Seasons* (ballet, 1901).

Glea·son |'glēsən|, Jackie (1916–87) U.S. entertainer. Born *Herbert John Gleason*; known as **the Great One**. He is best known for his comedic work in television, especially his role as bus driver Ralph Kramden in "The Honeymooners" (1955–56), one of the most frequently rebroadcast programs in television history.

Glen·dow·er |'glendowər|, Owen (*c.* 1359–*c.* 1416) Also **Glyndwr**. Welsh chief. He proclaimed himself Prince of Wales and led a national uprising against Henry IV.

Glenn |glen|, John Herschel, Jr. (1921–   ) U.S. astronaut and senator. In 1962, he became the first American to orbit the earth. An Ohio Democrat, he served several terms in the U.S. Senate (1975–99). In 1998, he joined the crew of the Space Shuttle in order to help study the effects of space travel on older people.

Glid·den |'glidən|, Joseph Farwell (1813–1906) U.S. farmer and inventor. He invented the first commercially successful barbed wire (1874).

Glin·ka |'gliNGkə|, Mikhail (Ivanovich) (1804–57) Russian composer. Regarded as the father of the Russian national school of music, he is best known for his operas *A Life for the Tsar* (1836) and *Russlan and Ludmilla* (1842).

Glo·ri·a·na |,glawrē'änə| the nickname of Queen Elizabeth I.

Gluck |glŏŏk|, Christoph Willibald (1714–87) German composer, notable for operas in which he sought a balance of music and drama and reduced the emphasis on the star singer. Notable operas: *Orfeo ed Euridice* (1762) and *Iphigénie en Aulide* (1774).

Gob·bi |'gäbē|, Tito (1915–84) Italian operatic baritone, famous for his interpretations of Verdi's baritone roles.

Go·bin·eau |'gäbə,nō|, Joseph-Arthur, Comte de (1816–82) French writer and anthropologist. His stated view that the races are innately unequal and that the white Aryan race is superior to all others later influenced the ideology and policies of the Nazis.

Go·dard |,gō'därd|, Jean-Luc (1930–   ) French movie director. He was one of the leading figures of the *nouvelle vague*. His movies include *Breathless* (1960), *Alphaville* (1965), and the more overtly political *Wind from the East* (1969).

God·dard |'gädərd|, Robert Hutchings (1882–1945) U.S. physicist. He carried out pioneering work in rocketry, and designed and built the first successful liquid-fueled rocket. NASA's Goddard Space Flight Center is named after him.

Gö·del |'gœdəl; 'gōd(ə)l|, Kurt (1906–78) Austrian-born U.S. mathematician. He made several important contributions to mathematical logic, especially the incompleteness theorem.

God·frey |'gädfrē|, Arthur (1903–83) U.S. actor. He starred in radio and television variety shows.

Go·di·va |gə'dīvə|, Lady (*c.* 1140–1180) English noblewoman, wife of Leofric, Earl of Mercia. According to 13th century legend, she agreed to her husband's proposition that he would reduce unpopular taxes only if she rode naked on horseback through the marketplace of Coventry. According to later versions of the story, all the townspeople refrained from watching, except for peeping Tom, who was struck blind in punishment.

Go·du·nov |'gōd(ə),nawf; 'gawd(ə),nawf|, Boris Fyodorovich (1551–1605) czar of Russia (1598–1605). A counselor of Ivan the Terrible, he succeeded Ivan's son as czar. His reign was marked by famine, doubts over his involvement in the earlier death of Ivan's eldest son, and the appearance of a pretender, the so-called False Dmitri.

God·win |'gädwən|, Gail (1937–) U.S. author. Notable works: *A Mother and Two Daughters* (1982).

God·win |'gädwən|, William (1756–1836) English social philosopher and novelist. He advocated a system of anarchism based on a belief in the goodness of human reason and on his doctrine of extreme individualism. His wife was Mary Wollstonecraft, and their daughter, Mary, was the wife of Shelley.

Goeb·bels |'gOEbəlz; 'gəbəlz|, (Paul) Joseph (1897–1945) Also **Göbbels**. German Nazi leader and politician. From 1933 Goebbels was Hitler's Minister of Propaganda, with control of the press, radio, and all aspects of culture, which he manipulated in order to further Nazi aims. He committed suicide rather than surrender to the Allies.

Goe·ring |'gOEriNG; 'gəriNG|, Hermann Wilhelm (1893–1946) German Nazi leader and politician. Goering was responsible for the German rearmament program, founded the Gestapo, and from 1936 until 1943 directed the German economy. He was also the de facto head of the Luftwaffe, the German air force, until he lost face when it failed to win the Battle of Britain or prevent Allied bombing of Germany. Sentenced to death at the Nuremberg war trials, he committed suicide in his cell.

Goes |gOOs|, Hugo van der (c. 1440–82) Flemish painter, born in Ghent. His best-known work is the large-scale *Portinari Altarpiece* (1475), commissioned for a church in Florence.

Goe·thals |'gOTHəlz|, George Washington (1858–1928) U.S. army officer and engineer. As chief engineer and chairman of the Panama Canal Commission (1907), he oversaw construction of the Panama Canal.

Goe·the |'gOEtə|, Johann Wolfgang von (1749–1832) German Romanticist poet, dramatist, and scholar. Involved at first with the *Sturm und Drang* movement, Goethe changed to a more measured and classical style, as in the "Wilhelm Meister" novels (1796–1829). Notable dramas: *Götz von Berlichingen*

(1773), *Tasso* (1790), and *Faust* (1808–32).

Goetz |gets|, Bernhard Hugo (1948–) U.S. murderer. When four teenagers on the New York subway asked him for money, he shot them and killed one, claiming that he was acting in self defense.

Gof·fin |'gawfən|, Gerry (1939–) U.S. lyricist. Notable songs: "Will You Still Love Me Tomorrow" and "Up on the Roof."

Go·gol |'gOgawl|, Nikolay Vasilyevich (1809–52) Russian novelist, dramatist, and short-story writer, born in Ukraine. His writings are satirical, often exploring themes of fantasy and the supernatural. Notable works: *The Government Inspector* (play, 1836), *Notes of a Madman* (short fiction, 1835), and *Dead Souls* (novel, 1842).

Goi·zue·ta, Roberto Crispulo (1931–) U.S. businessman, born in Cuba. With the Coca-Cola Co. since 1954, he became chairman of the board and CEO (1980–).

Go·kha·le |'gOkə,lä|, Gopal Krishna (1866–1915) Indian political leader and social reformer, president of the Indian National Congress from 1905. He was a leading advocate of Indian self-government through constitutional or moderate means.

Gold·berg |'gOl(d),bərg|, Arthur Joseph (1908–90) U.S. Supreme Court justice (1962–65). He served as U.S. ambassador to the U. N. (1965–68) but resigned, protesting the escalation of the Vietnam War.

Gold·berg |'gOl(d),bərg|, Rube (1883–1970) U.S. cartoonist. Full name *Reuben Lucius Goldberg*. As creator of the comic strip characters Professor Lucifer Gorgonzola Butts, Boob McNutt, and Lala Palooza, he satirized American folkways and modern technology. Pulitzer Prize, 1948.

Gold·berg |'gOl(d),bərg|, Whoopi (1955–) U.S. actress. Born *Caryn Johnson*. She has appeared in the movies *The Color Purple* (1985) and *Sister Act* (1992) and in the television series "Star Trek: The Next Generation."

Gold·ber·ger |'gOl(d),bərgər|, Joseph (1874–1929) U.S. physician, born in

Austria. He discovered and developed a cure for pellagra (1913–25).

Gold·ing |ˈgōldiNG|, Sir William (Gerald) (1911–93) English novelist. He achieved literary success with his first novel *Lord of the Flies* (1954), about boys stranded on a desert island who revert to savagery. Nobel Prize for Literature (1983).

Gold·man |ˈgōl(d)mən|, Emma (1869–1940) Lithuanian-born U.S. political activist. Involved in New York's anarchist movement, she was imprisoned in 1917 with lifelong associate Alexander Berkman; in 1919 they were released and deported to Russia. Notable works: *Anarchism and Other Essays* (1910) and *My Disillusionment in Russia* (1923).

Gold·man |ˈgōl(d)mən|, William (1931–) U.S. author of adult and children's fiction. Pseudonym **Harry Longbaugh**. Notable works: *Boys and Girls Together* (1964).

Gold·mark |ˈgōl(d),märk|, Peter Carl (1906–77) Hungarian-born U.S. inventor and engineer. He made the first color television broadcast in 1940, invented the long-playing record in 1948, and pioneered video cassette recording.

Gold·schmidt |ˈgōl(d),SHmit|, Victor Moritz (1888–1947) Swiss-born Norwegian chemist. Considered the founder of modern geochemistry, he carried out fundamental work on crystal structure, suggesting a law relating it to chemical composition.

Gold·smith |ˈgōl(d),smiTH|, Oliver (1730–74) Irish novelist, poet, essayist, and dramatist. Notable works: *The Vicar of Wakefield* (novel, 1766), *The Deserted Village* (poem, 1770), and *She Stoops to Conquer* (play, 1773).

Gold·wa·ter |ˈgōl(d),wawtər|, Barry Morris (1909–98) U.S. politician. He was a member of the U.S. Senate from Arizona (1953–65, 1969–87) and a Republican presidential candidate (1964).

Gold·wyn |ˈgōldwən|, Samuel (1882–1974) Polish-born U.S. movie producer; born *Schmuel Gelbfisz*; changed to *Samuel Goldfish* then *Goldwyn*. He produced his first film in 1913; with Louis B. Mayer, he founded the movie company Metro-Goldwyn-Mayer (MGM) in 1924.

Gol·gi |ˈgawljē|, Camillo (1843–1926) Italian histologist and anatomist. He devised a staining technique to study nerve tissue, classified types of nerve cells, and described the structure of dendritic nerve cells, now called "Golgi cells." Received the Nobel Prize for Physiology or Medicine (1906).

Gol·lancz |gəˈlänts|, Sir Victor (1893–1967) British publisher and philanthropist. A committed socialist, Gollancz compaigned against the rise of Fascism in the 1930s and founded the Left Book Club (1936). He also organized aid for World War I refugees.

Gom·pers |ˈgämpərz|, Samuel (1850–1924) U.S. labor leader, born in England. He helped to found (1881) the Federation of Organized Trades and Labor Unions, which was later reorganized as The American Federation of Labor (1886). He served as president of the A.F. of L. until his death and did much to win respect for organized labor.

Gon·cha·rov |ˈgänCHə,rawf|, Ivan (Aleksandrovich) (1812–91) Russian novelist. His novel *Oblomov* (1857) is regarded as one of the greatest works of Russian realism.

Gon·court |gawnˈko͞or| French novelists and critics. **Edmond de Goncourt** (1822–96) and his brother **Jules de Goncourt** (1830–70) wrote art criticism, realist novels, and social history. In his will Edmond provided for the establishment of the Académie Goncourt, which awards the annual Prix Goncourt to a work of French literature.

Good·all |ˈgo͞odawl|, Jane (1934–) English zoologist. After working with Louis Leakey in Tanzania from 1957, she made prolonged and intimate studies of chimpanzees at the Gombe Stream Reserve by Lake Tanganyika from 1970.

Good·hue |ˈgo͞od(h)yo͞o|, Bertram Grosvenor (1869–1924) U.S. architect. Notable designs: additions to West Point (1903–10) and the Nebraska State Capitol (1920–32).

Good·ing |ˈgo͞odiNG|, Cuba, Jr. (1968–) U.S. actor. Notable movies: *Jerry Maguire* (Academy Award, Best Supporting Actor, 1997); *As Good As It Gets* (1997); and *What Dreams May Come* (1998).

Good·man |'go͝odmən|, Benny (1909–86) U.S. jazz and classical clarinetist and bandleader. Full name *Benjamin David Goodman*; known as **the King of Swing**. He was the first major white bandleader to integrate black and white musicians and the first musician to give a jazz concert at Carnegie Hall (1938).

Good·man |'go͝odmən|, Ellen Holtz (1941–) U.S. journalist and author. An associate editor of the *Boston Globe* (1986–), she writes a syndicated colum of the Washington Post Writers Group (1976–); she won a 1980 Pulitzer Prize in commentary.

Good·man |'go͝odmən|, John (1952–) U.S. actor. He had a leading role in the television series "Roseanne" (1988–96). Notable movies: *Sea of Love* (1989) and *King Ralph* (1991).

Good·man |'go͝odmən|, Paul (1911–72) U.S. psychoanalyst and author. He wrote *Growing Up Absurd* (1960) and *Compulsory Mis-Education* (1964), as well as fiction and poetry.

Good·rich |'go͝odriCH|, Samuel Griswold (1793–1860) U.S. publisher and writer. He published an annual gift book, *The Token* (1827–42); under the pseudonym **Peter Parley,** he wrote 116 children's tales.

Good·son |'go͝odsən|, Mark (1915–) U.S. television producer. He formed Goodson-Todman Productions (1946), which created the television game shows "What's My Line," " Password," "I've Got a Secret," "The Price is Right," and "To Tell the Truth."

Good·win |'go͝odwin|, Doris Kearns (1943–) U.S. journalist, historian, and author. She received the 1995 Pulitzer Prize for *No Ordinary Time.*

Good·year |'go͝od,yir|, Charles (1800–60) U.S. inventor. He developed the vulcanization process for rubber, after accidentally dropping some rubber mixed with sulfur and white lead on a hot stove.

Goos·sens |'go͝osənz|, Sir (Aynsley) Eugene (1893–1962) English conductor, violinist, and composer, of Belgian descent. After conducting in the U.S. (1923–45), he was appointed the director (1947) of the New South Wales Conservatorium and conductor of the Syd-

ney Symphony Orchestra. His compositions include opera, ballet, and symphonies.

Gor·ba·chev |'gawrbə,CHawf|, Mikhail (Sergeyevich) (1931–) Soviet statesman, general secretary of the Communist Party of the USSR (1985–91), and president (1988–91). His foreign policy helped bring about an end to the Cold War, while within the USSR he introduced major reforms, both in the economy and in freedom of information. He resigned following an attempted coup. Nobel Peace Prize (1990).

Gor·di·mer |'gawrdəmər|, Nadine (1923–) South African novelist and short-story writer. Her experience of the effects of apartheid underlies much of her work. Notable novels: *The Conservationist* (1974). Nobel Prize for Literature (1991).

Gor·don |'gawrdən|, Charles George (1833–85) British general and colonial administrator. He made his name by crushing the Taiping Rebellion (1863–64) in China. In 1884 he fought Mahdist forces in Sudan led by Muhammad Ahmad (see MAHDI) but was trapped at Khartoum and killed.

Gor·don |'gawrdən|, Dexter Keith (1923–90) U.S. jazz tenor saxophonist. He defined the bebop style.

Gor·don |'gawrdən|, Jeff (1971–) U.S. racecar driver. He became the youngest winner of the Daytona 500 (1997).

Gor·don |'gawrdən|, Mary Catherine (1949–) U.S. author. Notable works: *The Company of Women* (1981).

Gor·don |'gawrdən|, Ruth (1896–1985) U.S. actress and writer. Born *Ruth Gordon Jones*. Notable movies: *Pat and Mike* (1952), *Rosemary's Baby* (1968, Academy Award), and *Harold and Maude* (1971).

Gor·dy |'gawrdē|, Berry, Jr. (1929–) U.S. recording-company executive and popular music producer. He founded the Motown record company in 1959, which had huge success in the 1960s and 1970s, popularizing black rhythm-and-blues and soul music.

Gore |gawr|, Al (1948–) U.S. vice president (1993–). Full name *Albert Arnold Gore, Jr.* A Tennessee Democrat, he served in the U.S. House of Representatives (1977–85) and U.S. Senate (1985–93). Noted for his commitment to environmental issues, he wrote *Earth in the Balance: Healing the Global Environment* (1992).

Górecki, Henryk Mikolaj (1933–) Polish composer. His works, influenced by religious music, include the *Third Symphony* (1976), known as the *Symphony of Sorrowful Songs*.

Gor·ey |'gawrē|, Edward (St. John) (1925–) U.S. author and illustrator. He published numerous hand-lettered books with brief, cryptic narratives and morbidly comic pen and ink illustrations.

Gor·ges |'gōrjəz|, Sir Ferdinando (*c.* 1566–1647) English soldier and colonizer. He was an organizer of the Plymouth Company (1606) and the Council for New England (1620), which gave rise to the Plymouth Colony and the Massachusetts Bay Company.

Gor·ky |'gawrkē|, Arshile (1905–48) Turkish-born U.S. painter. An exponent of abstract expressionism, he is best known for his work of the early 1940s, for example *Waterfall* (1943).

Gor·ky |'gawrkē|, Maksim (1868–1936) Russian writer and revolutionary; pseudonym of **Aleksei Maksimovich Peshkov**. After the Revolution he was honored as the founder of the new, officially sanctioned socialist realism. His best-known works include the play *The Lower Depths* (1901) and his autobiographical trilogy (1915–23).

Gor·ton |'gawrtən|, Samuel (1592–1677) U.S. religious leader, born in England. He was an Antinomian who was banished to England for heresy (1637–38) but returned and founded a settlement at Warwick, Rhode Island.

Gos·nold |'gäs,nōld|, Bartholomew (*c.* 1572–1607) English navigator. He explored the Maine coast and Narragansett Bay (1602); he was second in command on the Jamestown expedition (1606–07).

Gos·sett |'gäsət|, Louis, Jr. (1936–) U.S. actor. Notable movies: *An Officer and a Gentleman* (1982, Academy Award).

Got·ti |'gätē|, John, Jr. (1940–) U.S.

mobster. He was head of the Gambino underworld crime organization.

Gott·schalk |'gät,SHawk|, Louis Moreau (1829–69) U.S. pianist and composer. He was the first U.S. pianist to tour Europe with critical success.

Gou·dy |'gowdē|, Frederic William (1865–1947) U.S. printer and type designer.

Gould |gōōld|, Chester (1900–85) U.S. cartoonist and author. He was the creator of "Dick Tracy" (1931), the first dramatic comic strip with crime and violence.

Gould |gōōld|, Glenn (Herbert) (1932–82) Canadian pianist and composer. Best known for his performances of works by Bach, he retired from the concert stage in 1964 to concentrate on recording and broadcasting.

Gould |gōōld|, Gordon (1920–) U.S. physicist. A member of the Manhattan Project (1943–45), he worked on the development of the atomic bomb. He devised several laser devices, including a laser amplifier (patented 1978).

Gould |gōōld|, Jay (1836–92) U.S. financier. With James Fisk and Daniel Drew, he gained control of the Erie Railroad (1868) through stock manipulation; with Fisk, he attempted to corner the gold market, which created the Black Friday panic on September 24, 1869.

Gould |gōōld|, John (1804–81) English bird artist. He produced many large illustrated volumes, though it is believed that many of the finest plates were actually drawn by Gould's wife and other employed artists.

Gould |gōōld|, Stephen Jay (1941–) U.S. paleontologist. A noted popularizer of science, he has studied modifications of Darwinian evolutionary theory, proposed the concept of punctuated equilibrium, and written on the social context of scientific theory.

Gou·nod |gōō'nō|, Charles-François (1818–93) French composer, conductor, and organist. He is best known for his opera *Faust* (1859).

Go·won, Yakubu Francisco José de (1934–) Nigerian general and statesman, head of state (1966–75).

Go·ya y Lucientes |'goiə| (1746–1828) Spanish painter and etcher; full name *Francisco José de Goya y Lucientes.* He is famous for his works treating the French occupation of Spain (1808–14), including *The Shootings of May 3rd 1808* (painting, 1814) and *The Disasters of War* (etchings, 1810–14), depicting the cruelty and horror of war.

Gra•ble |'grāb(ə)l|, Betty (1916–73) U.S. actress. Born **Ruth Elizabeth Grable**. A leading movie star, she was most famous for her 1942 pinup poster. Notable movies: *Moon Over Miami* (1941) and *How to Marry a Millionaire* (1953).

Grac•chus |'grækəs| Roman tribunes. **Tiberius Sempronius Gracchus** (*c.* 163–133 BC) and his brother **Gaius Sempronius Gracchus** (*c.*153–121 BC) were also known as **the Gracchi**. They were responsible for radical social and economic legislation, especially concerning the redistribution of land to the poor.

Graf |gräf|, Steffi (1969–   ) German professional tennis player; full name *Stephanie Graf.*

Graf•ton |'græftən|, Augustus Henry Fitzroy, 3rd Duke of (1735–1811) British Whig statesman, prime minister (1768–70).

Graf•ton |'græftən|, Sue (1940–   ) U.S. author. Her alphabet series of mysteries includes *I is for Innocent* (1992), *J is for Judgment* (1994), and *K is for Killer* (1994).

Graham |græm|, Billy (1918–   ) U.S. evangelical preacher and author; full name *William Franklin Graham.* A minister of the Southern Baptist Church. He is world-famous for preaching to mass religious meetings.

Graham |græm|, Katherine Meyer (1917–   ) U.S. publisher. Wife of Philip Graham, head of the communications empire that included *Newsweek* magazine and the *Washington Post,* she became the company's president upon her husband's death (1963), and most notably publisher of the *Post* (1969–79).

Graham |græm|, Martha (1894–1991) U.S. dancer, teacher, and choreographer. She evolved a new dance language using more flexible movements intended to express psychological complexities and emotional power. Notable works:

Appalachian Spring (1931) and *Care of the Heart* (1946).

Graham |græm|, Otto (1921–   ) U.S. football player.

Graham |græm|, Sylvester (1794–1851) U.S. reformer. A promotor of temperance and vegetarianism, he invented the graham cracker and established the breakfast cereal industry.

Graham |græm|, Thomas (1805–69) Scottish physical chemist. He studied diffusion and osmosis, coining the word *osmose* (now *osmosis*) and *colloid* in its modern chemical sense.

Grahame |'graəm|, Kenneth (1859–1932) Scottish-born writer of children's stories, resident in England from 1864. He is remembered for the children's classic *The Wind in the Willows* (1908).

Grain•ger |'gränjər|, (George) Percy (Aldridge) (1882–1961) Australian-born U.S. composer and pianist. From 1901 he lived in London, where he collected, edited, and arranged English folk songs. Notable works: *Shepherd's Hey* (1911).

Gramm |græm|, Phil (1942–   ) U.S. politician. Full name *William Philip Gramm.* He is a member of the U.S. Senate from Texas (1985–   ).

Gram•sci |'græmsHē|, Antonio (1891–1937) Italian political theorist and activist, co-founder and leader of the Italian Communist Party. Imprisoned in 1926 when the Fascists banned the Communist Party, he died shortly after his release. *Letters from Prison* (1947) remains an important work.

Grange |gränj|, Red (1903–91) U.S. football player. Born *Harold Edward Grange*; also called **the Galloping Ghost.** Elected to the NFL Hall of Fame (1963).

Grant |grænt|, Cary (1904–86) British-born U.S. actor; born *Alexander Archibald Leach.* He made his Hollywood screen debut in *This is the Night* (1932) after appearing in Broadway musicals. He acted in more than seventy movies, usually as the debonair male lead, including *Holiday* (1938), *The Philadelphia Story* (1940), *To Catch a Thief* (1955), and *North by Northwest* (1959).

Grant |grænt|, Duncan (James Corrow)

(1885–1978) Scottish painter and designer, a pioneer of abstract art in Britain. He was a cousin of English writer Lytton Strachey and a member of the Bloomsbury Group.

Grant |grænt|, Ulysses S. see box. **Julia Boggs Dent Grant** (1826–1902), wife of Ulysses S. Grant and U.S. first lady (1869–77).

Granville-Barker |'grænvil 'bärkər|, Harley (1877–1946) English dramatist, critic, theater director, and actor. His *Prefaces to Shakespeare* (1927–46) influenced subsequent interpretation of Shakespeare's work. Notable plays: *The Voysey Inheritance* (1905).

Grap·pel·li |grə'pelē|, Stephane (1908–97) French jazz violinist. With Django Reinhardt, he founded the group known as the Quintette du Hot Club de France in 1934.

Grass |græs|, Günter (Wilhelm)

Grant, Ulysses Simpson
18th U.S. president

Life dates: 1822–1885
Place of birth: Point Pleasant, Ohio
Name at birth: Hiram Ulysses Grant
Mother: Hannah Simpson Grant
Father: Jesse Root Grant
Wife: Julia Boggs Dent Grant
Children: Frederick, Ulysses, Ellen ("Nellie"), Jesse
College/University: U.S. Military Academy, West Point
Military service: U.S. Army, Mexican War; during Civil War, officer in and ultimately commander of all Union armies
Career: Farming; real estate
Political career: Secretary of war (interim appointment)
Party: Republican
Home state: Ohio
Opponents in presidential races: Horatio Seymour; Horace Greeley
Term of office: March 4, 1869–March 3, 1877
Vice presidents: Henry Wilson (died in office in 1875); Schuyler Colfax
Notable events of presidency: Black Friday gold panic of 1869; Financial Panic of 1873; Credit Mobilier stock scandal; Whiskey Ring Conspiracy; Colorado admitted as the 38th state
Place of burial: New York, New York

(1927–) German novelist, poet, and dramatist. Notable novels: *The Tin Drum* (1959) and *The Flounder* (1977).

Grau |grow|, Shirley Ann (1929–) U.S. author. Notable works: *The Keepers of the House* (Pulitzer Prize, 1964).

Graup·ner |'growpnər|, (Johann Christian) Gottlieb (1767–1836) U.S. musician, born in Prussia. He organized the Philharmonic Society in Boston (1810–24), the first symphony orchestra in the U.S.

Graves |grāvz|, Robert (Ranke) (1895–1985) English poet, novelist, and critic, known for his interest in classics and mythology. Notable prose works: *Goodbye to All That* (autobiography, 1929), *I, Claudius* (historical fiction, 1934), and *The White Goddess* (non-fiction, 1948).

Gray |grā|, Asa (1810–88) U.S. botanist and author. He wrote many textbooks that greatly popularized botany. He also supported Darwin's theories at a time when they were anathema to many.

Gray |grā|, Elisha (1835–1901) U.S. inventor. He was a rival of Alexander Graham Bell for the telephone patent; his Gray and Barton Co. became Western Electric.

Gray |grā|, Hanna Holborn (1930–) U.S. historian and educator, born in Germany. A history professor, she was president of the University of Chicago (1978–93).

Gray |grā|, Harold Lincoln (1894–1968) U.S. cartoonist. He created the comic strip "Little Orphan Annie" and was the first strip cartoonist to use the medium as a vehicle for expressing political opinions.

Gray |grā|, Horace (1828–1902) U.S. Supreme Court justice (1881–1902).

Gray |grā|, Thomas (1716–71) English poet, best known for "Elegy Written in a Country Church-Yard" (1751).

Gre·co |'grekō|, El see EL GRECO.

Gree·ley |'grēlē|, Horace (1811–72) U.S. journalist and political leader of abolitionism.

Gree·ly |'grēlē|, Adolphus Washington (1844–1935) U.S. army officer and explorer. He conducted an expedition to map unknown segments of Greenland

and Ellesmere Island (1881), and he established telegraph communication in outlying U.S. possessions.

Green |grēn|, Hetty (1834–1916) U.S. financier. Full name *Henrietta Howland Green*; known as the **Witch of Wall Street**. Through shrewd investing, she turned her inherited wealth into the largest fortune held by a woman, but she obscured her identity by living in tenement houses.

Green·a·way |'grēn(ə),wā|, Kate (1846–1901) English artist; full name *Catherine Greenaway*. She is known especially for her illustrations of children's books such as *Mother Goose* (1881).

Green·a·way |'grēn(ə),wā|, Peter (1942–) English movie director. Notable movies: *The Cook, the Thief, His Wife, and Her Lover* (1989) and *The Pillow Book* (1996).

Greene |grēn|, (Henry) Graham (1904–91) English novelist. The moral paradoxes he saw in his Roman Catholic faith underlie much of his work. Notable works: *Brighton Rock* (1938), *The Power and the Glory* (1940), and *The Third Man* (written as a screenplay, and filmed in 1949; novel 1950).

Greene |grēn|, Joe (1946–) U.S. football player. He was chosen All-Pro five times and led Pittsburgh to four Super Bowl titles in the 1970s.

Greene |grēn|, Leonard Michael (1918–) U.S. aerospace inventor and manufacturer. He invented numerous flight safety instruments, most notably the airplane stall warning device, developed during World War II.

Greene |grēn|, Nathanael (1742–86) American revolutionary general. He forced the British out of Georgia and the Carolinas in a series of battles (1781) during the American Revolution and was much admired as a military strategist.

Green·field |'grēn,fēld|, Meg (1930–99) U.S. journalist. An editorial page writer for the *Washington Post* (1979–) and *Newsweek* columnist (1974–), she won a 1978 Pulitzer Prize in editorial writing.

Green·ough |'grēnō|, Horatio (1805–52) U.S. sculptor. His seated *Washington* was intended for the national Capitol rotunda but now resides in the Smithsonian.

Green·span |'grēnspæn|, Alan (1926–) U.S. economist. As chairman of the National Commission on Social Security Reform (1981–83), he helped prevent the bankruptcy of the Social Security system. Appointed chairman of the Federal Reserve Board (1987).

Greer |grir|, Germaine (1939–) Australian feminist and writer. She first achieved recognition with her influential book *The Female Eunuch* (1970), an analysis of women's subordination in a male-dominated society.

Greg·o·ry XIII |'greg(ə)rē| (1502–85) pope (1572–85), born in Italy. He was a major sponsor of numerous educational programs and institutes. The Gregorian calendar, still in use, was introduced in 1582 as a result of his efforts to correct the errors in the Julian calendar.

Greg·o·ry |'greg(ə)rē|, St. (*c.* 540–604) pope (as Gregory I) (590–604) and Doctor of the Church; known as **St. Gregory the Great**. An important reformer, he did much to establish the temporal power of the papacy. He sent St. Augustine to England to lead the country's conversion to Christianity, and is also credited with the introduction of Gregorian chant. Feast day, March 12.

Greg·o·ry of Na·zi·an·zus |'greg(ə)rē əv ,näzē'änzəs|, St. (329–89) Doctor of the Church, bishop of Constantinople. With St. Basil and St. Gregory of Nyssa he upheld orthodoxy against the Arian and Apollinarian heresies, and was influential in restoring adherence to the Nicene Creed. Feast day, (in the Eastern Church) January 25 and 30; (in the Western Church) January 2 (formerly May 9).

Greg·o·ry of Nys·sa |'greg(ə)rē əv 'nisə|, St. (*c.* 330–*c.* 395) Doctor of the Eastern Church, bishop of Nyssa in Cappadocia. The brother of St. Basil, he was an orthodox follower of Origen and joined with St. Basil and St. Gregory of Nazianzus in opposing Arianism. Feast day, March 9.

Greg·o·ry of Tours |'greg(ə)rē əv 'toŏrz|, St. (*c.* 540–94) Frankish bishop and historian. He was elected bishop of Tours in 573; his writings provide the chief authority for the early Merovingian period of French history. Feast day, November 17.

Greg·o·ry the Great |'greg(ə)rē| see GREGORY, ST.

Gren·fell |'gren,fel|, Joyce (Irene Phipps) (1910–79) English entertainer and writer.

Gren·ville |'grenvəl|, George (1712–70) British Whig statesman, prime minister (1763–65). The American Stamp Act (1765), which aroused great opposition in the North American colonies, was passed during his term of office.

Gre·sham |'gresHəm|, Sir Thomas (c. 1519–79) English financier. He founded the Royal Exchange in 1566 and served as the chief financial adviser to the Elizabethan government.

Gres·ley |'grezlē|, Sir (Herbert) Nigel (1876–1941) British railway engineer. He is most famous for designing express steam locomotives, such as the A4 class exemplified by the *Mallard*.

Gretz·ky |'gretskē|, Wayne (1961–) Canadian hockey player. He is the all-time leading point-scorer in the National Hockey League, and was voted Most Valuable Player nine times.

Greuze |grœz|, Jean-Baptiste (1725–1805) French painter, noted for his genre paintings and portraits.

Grey |grā|, Charles, 2nd Earl (1764–1845) British statesman, prime minister (1830–34). His government passed the first Reform Act (1832) as well as important factory legislation and the Act abolishing slavery throughout the British Empire.

Grey |grā|, Sir George (1812–98) British statesman, colonial administrator, and a scholar of Maori culture.

Grey |grā|, Lady Jane (1537–54) queen of England (July 9–19, 1553) and niece of Henry VIII. In 1553, to ensure a Protestant succession, John Dudley, the Duke of Northumberland, forced Jane to marry his son and persuaded the dying Edward VI to name Jane as his successor. She was quickly deposed by forces loyal to Edward's (Catholic) sister Mary, who had popular support, and was executed the following year.

Grey |grā|, Joel (1932–) U.S. actor. Born *Joe Katz*. Notable movies: *Cabaret* (1972, Academy Award).

Grey |grā|, Zane (1872–1939) U.S. writer; born *Pearl Grey*. He wrote 54 westerns in a somewhat romanticized and formulaic style, which sold over 13 million copies during his lifetime.

Grieg |grēg|, Edvard (1843–1907) Norwegian composer, conductor, and violinist. Famous works include the Piano Concerto in A minor (1869) and the incidental music to Ibsen's play *Peer Gynt* (1876).

Grier |grir|, Robert Cooper (1794–1870) U.S. Supreme Court justice (1846–70).

Grif·fey |'grifē|, Ken, Jr. (1969–) U.S. baseball player. Full name *George Kenneth Griffey, Jr.*; known as **Junior**.

Grif·fith |'grifiTH|, Arthur (1872–1922) Irish nationalist leader and statesman, president of the Irish Free State (1922). In 1905 he founded and became president of Sinn Fein. He became vice-president of the newly declared Irish Republic in 1919 and negotiated the Anglo-Irish Treaty (1921).

Grif·fith |'grifiTH|, D. W. (1875–1948) U.S. movie director; full name *David Lewelyn Wark Griffith*. A pioneer in movies, he is responsible for introducing many cinematic techniques, including flashback and fade-out. Notable movies: *The Birth of a Nation* (1915), *Intolerance* (1916), and *Broken Blossoms* (1919).

Gri·mal·di |gri'mäldē|, Francesco Maria (1618–63) Italian physicist and astronomer who discovered the diffraction of light and verified Galileo's law of the uniform acceleration of falling bodies.

Gri·mal·di |gri'mäldē|, Joseph (1779–1837) English circus entertainer who created the role of the circus clown and performed at Covent Garden, where he became famous for his acrobatic skills.

Grim·ké |'grimkē|, Archibald Henry (1849–1930) U.S. lawyer, editor, author, and civil rights leader. He was a member of the original Committee of Forty (1909) who helped found the National Association for the Advancement of Colored People (NAACP). Spingarn Medal, 1919.

Grim·ké |'grimkē| U.S. reformers, abolitionists, and feminists. **Sarah Moore Grimké** (1792–1872) and her sister, **Angelina Emily Grimké** (1805–79), wrote for the American Anti-Slavery Society. Sarah later wrote pamphlets for women's rights, and, with her husband, Theodore Dwight Weld, *American Slavery as It Is: Testimony of a Thousand Witnesses* (1839).

Grimm |grim| German philologists and folklorists. **Jacob (Ludwig Carl) Grimm** (1785–1863) and his brother **Wilhelm (Carl) Grimm** (1786–1859) jointly inaugurated a dictionary of German on historical principles (1852), which was eventually completed by other scholars in 1860. They also compiled an anthology of German fairy tales, which appeared in three volumes between 1812 and 1822.

Gri·mond |'grimənd|, Jo, Baron (1913–93) British Liberal politician, leader of the Liberal Party (1956–67); full name *Joseph Grimond.*

Gris |grēs|, Juan (1887–1927) Spanish painter; born *José Victoriano Gonzales.* His main contribution was to the development of the later phase of synthetic cubism. His work features the use of collage and paint in simple fragmented shapes.

Grish·am |'grishəm|, John (1955–) U.S. author and lawyer. Notable novels: *The Firm* (1991).

Gris·som |'grisəm|, Gus (1926–67) U.S. astronaut. Full name *Virgil Ivan Grissom.* Part of the original Project Mercury astronaut team (1959), he was killed in a flash fire in the Apollo 1 capsule along with Edward H. White and Roger B. Chaffee.

Gri·vas |'grēväs|, George (Theodorou) (1898–1974) Greek Cypriot patriot and soldier. A supporter of the union of Cyprus with Greece, he led the guerrilla campaign against British rule, which culminated in the country's independence in 1959.

Groen·ing |'grāniNG|, Matt (1954–) U.S. cartoonist and author. He created "The Simpsons" television comedy and the weekly comic strip "Life in Hell."

Gro·my·ko |grə'mēkō|, Andrei (Andreevich) (1909–89) Soviet statesman, foreign minister (1957–85), president of the USSR (1985–88). He represented the Soviet Union abroad throughout most of the Cold War.

Gro·pi·us |'grōpēəs|, Walter (1883–1969) German-born U.S. architect. He was the first director of the Bauhaus School of Design (1919–28) and a pioneer of the international style. He settled in the U.S. in 1938, where he was professor of architecture at Harvard University until 1952.

Gross |grōs|, Samuel David (1805–84) U.S. surgeon, educator, and author. He was a founder of the American Surgical Association (1880) and author of *A System of Surgery* (1859), which he constantly revised as a result of his teaching

Grosse·teste |'grōs,test|, Robert (*c.* 1175–1253) English churchman, philosopher, and scholar. His experimental approach to science, especially in optics and mathematics, inspired his pupil, Roger Bacon.

Grosz |grōs|, George (1893–1959) German painter and draughtsman. His satirical drawings and paintings characteristically depict a decadent society in which gluttony and depraved sensuality are juxtaposed with poverty and disease.

Gro·tius |'grōsH(ē)əs|, Hugo (1583–1645) Dutch jurist and diplomat; Latinized name of *Huig de Groot.* His legal treatise *De Jure Belli et Pacis* (1625) established the basis of modern international law.

Grove |grōv|, Sir George (1820–1900) English musicologist. He was the founder and first editor of the multi-volume *Dictionary of Music and Musicians* (1879–89), now named for him in its later editions, and served as the first director of the Royal College of Music (1883–94).

Grove |grōv|, Lefty (1900–75) U.S. baseball player. Full name *Robert Moses Grove.* A pitcher, he led the American League in strikeouts seven times. Elected to Baseball Hall of Fame (1947).

Grü·ne·wald |'grōōnə,vält; grᵢnə,vält|, Mathias (*c.* 1460–1528) German painter; born *Mathis Nithardt*; also called **Mathis Gothardt**. His most famous work is the nine-panel *Isenheim Altar* (completed 1516).

Guar·di |'gärdē|, Francesco (1712–93) Italian painter. A pupil of Canaletto, he produced paintings of Venice notable for their free handling of light and atmosphere.

Guare, John (1938–) U.S. playwright. Notable works: *The House of Blue Leaves* (1971) and *Six Degrees of Separation* (1990).

Guar·ne·ri |gwär'nerē|, Giuseppe (1687–1744) Italian violin-maker; known as **del Gesù**. He is the most famous of a family of three generations of violin-makers based in Cremona.

Gue·ricke |'gārikə|, Otto von (1602–86) German engineer and physicist. He was the first to investigate the properties of a vacuum, and he devised the Magdeburg hemispheres to demonstrate atmospheric pressure.

Guest |gest|, Edgar A. (1881–1959) U.S. journalist and poet, born in England. Full name *Edgar Albert Guest*. He was on the staff of the Detroit *Free Press*. Notable works: *A Heap o' Livin'* (1916), *Just Folks* (1917), and *Life's Highway* (1933).

Gue·va·ra |gwə'värə|, Che (1928–67) Argentinian revolutionary and guerrilla leader; full name *Ernesto Guevara de la Serna*. He played a significant part in the Cuban revolution (1956–59) and became a government minister under Castro. He was captured and executed by the Bolivian army while training guerrillas for a planned uprising in Bolivia.

Gug·gen·heim |'gŏŏgən,hīm|, U.S. family, including: Swiss-born industrialist **Meyer Guggenheim** (1828–1905). With his seven sons he established large mining and metal-processing companies. His son **Solomon Guggenheim** (1861–1949) a philanthropist, set up several foundations providing support for the arts, including the Guggenheim Museum in New York. Meyer's son **Daniel Guggenheim** (1856–1930), an industrialist and philanthropist, expanded the family copper industry to include gold, rubber, and tin; with his wealth he established the Daniel and Florence Guggenheim Foundation (1924) and the Guggenheim Foundation for the Promotion of Aeronautics (1926). Meyer's son

Simon Guggenheim (1867–1941), a politician and philanthropist, was a member of the U.S. Senate from Colorado (1907–13). He established the John Simon Guggenheim Memorial Foundation (1925). Meyer's granddaughter **Peggy Guggenheim** (1898–1979) was a patron of the arts and an author. Full name *Marguerite Guggenheim*. She was a collector of modern art (especially Pollock and Motherwell) and financed galleries in London, New York, and Venice.

Gui·do of Arezzo |'gwēdō əv ə'retsō| (*c.* 991–1050) Italian monk and music theorist. A member of the Benedictine Order, he is credited with devising the four-line musical staff and naming the notes of the scale with syllables.

Giu·li·a·ni |'jŏŏlē'änē|, Rudolph (1944–) U.S. politician. He is the mayor of New York City (1993–).

Guinier, Ewart (1911–90) U.S. educator and union official.

Guin·ness |'ginis|, Sir Alec (1914–) English actor. He gave memorable performances in the movies *Bridge on the River Kwai* (1957) and *Star Wars* (1977) and as espionage chief George Smiley in television versions of John Le Carré's books.

Güi·ral·des |gē'räldäs|, Ricardo (1886–1927) Argentinian author. His novels include *Don Segundo Sombra* (1926).

Guise·wite |'gīz,wīt|, Cathy (1950–) U.S. cartoonist and author. She created the syndicated comic strip "Cathy."

Gu·lick |'g(y)ŏŏlik|, Luther Halsey (1865–1918) U.S. educator. She was a cofounder of the Campfire Girls (1910).

Gunn |'gən|, Thom (1929–) English poet, resident in California from 1954; full name *Thomson William Gunn*. His works, written in a predominantly low-key, laconic, and colloquial style, include *Fighting Terms* (1954), *My Sad Captains* (1961), and *The Passages of Joy* (1982).

Gur·djieff |'gərdyef|, George (Ivanovich) (1877–1949) Russian spiritual leader and occultist. He founded the Institute for the Harmonious Development of Man in Paris (1922).

Gur·ney |'gərnē|, A. R., Jr. (1930–) U.S. educator and playwright. Full name *Albert Ramsdell Gurney.* Notable works: *The Dining Room* (1981) and *The Cocktail Hour* (1987).

Gur•ney |ˈgərnē|, Ivor (Bertie) (1890–1937) English poet and composer He fought on the Western Front during World War I, and wrote the verse collections *Severn and Somme* (1917) and *War's Embers* (1919).

Gus•ta•vus Adol•phus |gəˈstävəs əˈdawlfəs| (1594–1632) king of Sweden (1611–32). His repeated victories in battle made Sweden a European power, and in 1630 he intervened on the Protestant side in the Thirty Years War. His domestic reforms laid the foundation of the modern Swedish state.

Gu•ten•berg |ˈgo͞otn,bərg|, Johannes (*c.* 1400–68) German printer. He was the first in the West to print using movable type; he introduced typecasting using a matrix, an alloy for type metal, and an oil-based ink for printing, and was the first to use a press. By *c.* 1455 he had produced what later became known as the Gutenberg Bible.

Guth•rie |ˈgəTHrē| U.S. folksingers and songwriters. **Woody Guthrie** (1912–67); full name *Woodrow Wilson Guthrie.* His radical politics and the rural hardships of the Depression inspired many of his songs. His son **Arlo Guthrie** (1947–) was the founder of Rising Son Records. Notable songs: "Alice's Restaurant" (1967) and "City of New Orleans."

Gu•tiér•rez |go͞oˈtyerez|, Gustavo (1928–) Peruvian theologian. He was an important figure in the emergence of liberation theology in Latin America, outlining its principles in *A Theology of Liberation* (1971).

Gwynn |gwin|, Nell (1650–87) English actress; full name *Eleanor Gwynn.* She became famous as a comedienne at the Theatre Royal, Drury Lane, London. She was a mistress of Charles II.

Gwynn |gwin|, Tony (1960–) U.S. baseball player. Full name *Anthony Keith Gwynn.*

Hh

Ha·ber·mas, Jürgen (1929–) German philosopher. Notable books: *Theory of Communicative Action* (1982).

Ha·bi·bie |hə'bēbē|, B. J. (1936–) president of Indonesia (1998–). Full name *Bacharuddin Jusuf Habibie.*

Ha·chette |ä'sHet|, Louis-Christophe-François (1800–64) French editor and publisher. He founded the publishing house Hachette et Cie (1826).

Hack·ett |'hækət|, Bobby (1915–76) U.S. jazz cornetist and bandleader. Full name *Robert Leo Hackett.* A melodic improviser, he played in clubs with many different small bands.

Hack·man |'hækmən|, Gene (1930–) U.S. actor. Notable movies: *The French Connection* (1971, Academy Award).

Ha·dri·an |'hādrēən| (AD 76–138) Roman emperor 117–138; full name *Publius Aelius Hadrianus.* The adopted successor of Trajan, he toured the provinces of the Empire and secured the frontiers.

Haeck·el |'hekəl|, Ernst Heinrich (1834–1919) German biologist and philosopher. He popularized Darwin's theories and saw evolution as providing a framework for describing the world, with the German Empire representing the highest evolved form of a civilized nation.

Ha·gen |'hāgən|, Walter Charles (1892–1969) U.S. golfer.

Hag·gard |'hægərd|, Sir (Henry) Rider (1856–1925) English novelist. He is famous for adventure novels such as *King Solomon's Mines* (1885) and *She* (1889).

Hahn |hän|, Otto (1879–1968) German chemist, codiscoverer of nuclear fission. Together with Lise Meitner he discovered the new element protactinium in 1917. The pair discovered nuclear fission in 1938 with **Fritz Strassmann**, (1902–80). Nobel Prize for Chemistry (1944).

Haig |hāg|, Douglas, 1st Earl Haig of Bemersyde (1861–1928) British field marshal during World War I.

Hai·le Se·las·sie |'hīlē sə'læsē| (1892–1975) emperor of Ethiopia 1930–74;

born *Tafari Makonnen.* In exile in Britain during the Italian occupation of Ethiopia (1936–41), he was restored to the throne by the Allies and ruled until deposed by a military coup. He is revered by the Rastafarian religious sect.

Hai·ley |'hālē|, Arthur (1920–) Canadian author. Notable works: *Hotel* (1965) and *Airport* (1968).

Hai·tink |'hītiNGk|, Bernard (Johann Herman) (1929–) Dutch musical director and conductor.

Hak·luyt |'hæklət|, Richard (c. 1552–1616) English geographer and historian. He compiled *Principal Navigations, Voyages, and Discoveries of the English Nation* (1598), a collection of accounts of great voyages of discovery.

Hal·as |'hæləs|, George (1895–1983) U.S. football player, coach, and owner. Full name *George Stanley Halas;* known as **Papa Bear**. He founded the Chicago Bears (originally the Decatur Staleys) in 1920. As a coach, he set an NFL record with 325 wins. Elected to NFL Hall of Fame (1963).

Hal·ber·stam |'hælbər,stæm|, David (1934–) U.S. journalist and author. Notable books: *The Making of a Quagmire* (1965, Pulitzer Prize) and *The Children* (1998).

Hal·dane |'hawl,dān|, J. B. S. (John Burdon Sanderson) (1892–1964) Scottish mathematical biologist. As well as contributing to the development of population genetics, Haldane became well known as a popularizer of science and as an outspoken Marxist.

Hal·de·man |'hawldəmən|, H. R. (1926–93) U.S. government official. Full name *Harry Robbins Haldeman.* White House chief of staff under President Nixon (1969–73), he resigned and was convicted of perjury, conspiracy, and obstruction of justice in the Watergate scandal.

Hale |hāl|, Edward Everett (1822–1909) U.S. clergyman, author, and philanthropist. A Unitarian minister, he wrote *The Man Without a Country* (1863).

Hale |hāl|, George Ellery (1868–1938)

U.S. astronomer. He discovered that sunspots are associated with strong magnetic fields and invented the spectroheliograph. He also initiated the construction of several large telescopes.

Hale |hāl|, Nathan (1755–76) American revolutionary hero. He volunteered (1776) to spy behind British lines on Long Island, disguised as a schoolmaster, but he was captured by the British and hanged without trial. His last words are said to have been, "I only regret that I have but one life to lose for my country."

Hale |hāl|, Sarah Josepha (Buell) (1788–1879) U.S. author. She is best known for the nursery rhyme "Mary Had a Little Lamb," from her *Poems for Our Children* (1830).

Ha·ley |'hālē|, Alex (1921–92) U.S. author. Full name *Alexander Murray Palmer Haley*. His best-selling work *Roots: The Saga of an American Family* chronicled the ancestors of his African-American family from its entry into America as slaves. The book and subsequent television miniseries (1977) each won a Pulitzer Prize.

Ha·ley |'hālē|, Bill (William John Clifton) (1925–81) U.S. rock-and-roll singer; full name *William John Clifton Haley*. His song "Rock Around the Clock" (1954) helped pioneer the popularity of rock and roll.

Hall |hawl|, Arsenio (1955–) U.S. actor and comedian. He was the first African American to host a late night television program (1989–94).

Hall |hawl|, Charles Francis (1821–71) U.S. explorer. He made three expeditions to explore the Arctic (1860–62, 1864–69, and 1871); on his first, he discovered the remains of Martin Frobisher's expedition of 1578.

Hall |hawl|, Charles Martin (1863–1914) U.S. chemist and manufacturer. He devised the commercial method for producing aluminium from bauxite, which involves the electrolysis of alumina dissolved in molten cryolite.

Hall |hawl|, Donald Andrew (1928–) U.S. poet, author, and educator. Notable works: *The Happy Man* (1986), *Seasons at Eagle Pond* (1987), and *Lucy's Summer* (1995).

Hall |hawl|, Granville Stanley (1844–1924) U.S. psychologist and educator. The founder of child psychology in the U.S., he was a leader in the development of educational psychology. He founded the *American Journal of Psychology* (1887) and the American Psychological Association (1891).

Hall |hawl|, James (1793–1868) U.S. lawyer and historian. His books on the early American frontier include *The Romance of Western History* (1857).

Hall |hawl|, J. C. (1891–1982) U.S. businessman. Full name *Joyce Clyde Hall*. He founded Hallmark Greeting Cards.

Hall |hawl|, James, Jr. (1811–98) U.S. geologist and paleontologist. The leading stratigraphic geologist and invertebrate paleontologist of his day, he wrote the 13-volume *Paleontology of New York* (1847–94).

Hall |hawl|, Lyman (1724–90) American revolutionary leader. He was a member of the Continental Congress (1775–78, 1780) and a signer of the Declaration of Independence.

Hall |hawl|, (Marguerite) Radclyffe (1886–1943) English novelist and poet. She is chiefly remembered for her novel *The Well of Loneliness* (1928), an exploration of a lesbian relationship, which caused outrage and was banned in Britain for many years.

Hal·lé |'hälə|, Sir Charles (1819–95) German-born pianist and conductor; born *Karl Halle*. He left Paris in 1848 and settled in Manchester, where he founded the Hallé Orchestra (1858).

Hal·ler |'hälər|, Albrecht von (1708–77) Swiss anatomist and physiologist. He pioneered the study of neurology and experimental physiology and wrote the first textbook of physiology.

Hal·ley |'hælē; 'hālē|, Edmond (1656–1742) English astronomer and mathematician. He is best known for identifying a bright comet (later named after him), and for successfully predicting its return.

Hal·li·day |'hælə₁dā|, Michael (Alexander Kirkwood) (1925–) English linguist. He built on the work of J. R. Firth in pursuit of a psychologically and sociologically realistic overall theory of language and its functions.

Hal·lowes |'hælōz|, Odette (1912–95) French heroine of World War II; born *Marie Céline*. She worked as a British secret agent in occupied France.

Hal·prin |'hælprin|, Lawrence (1916–) U.S. architect. Notable designs: Freeway Park (1972–76) in Seattle, Washington, and Lovejoy Fountain Plaza (1966) in Portland, Oregon.

Hals |häls|, Frans (c. 1581–1666) Dutch portrait and genre painter. He endowed his portraits with vitality and humor, departing from conventional portraiture with works such as *The Banquet of the Officers of the St. George Militia Company* (1616) and *The Laughing Cavalier* (1624).

Hal·sey |'hawlzē|, William Frederick (1882–1959) U.S. naval officer. Known as **Bull**. He was commander of Allied naval forces in the South Pacific (1942–44) and of the U.S. Third Fleet (1944–45), and became a fleet admiral in 1945.

Hal·ston |'hawlstən| (1932–90) U.S. fashion designer. Born *Roy Halston Frowick*.

Ha·ma·da |hə'mädə|, Shoji (1894–1978) Japanese potter. He collaborated with Bernard Leach, working mainly in stoneware to produce utilitarian items of unpretentious simplicity.

Ha·mil·car Bar·ca |hə'mil,kär 'bärkə| (c. 270–229 BC) Carthaginian general, father of Hannibal. He fought Rome in the first Punic War and negotiated the terms of peace after Carthaginian defeat.

Ham·il·ton |'hæməltən|, Sir William Rowan (1806–65) Irish mathematician and theoretical physicist. Hamilton made influential contributions to optics and to the foundations of algebra and quantum mechanics.

Ham·il·ton |'hæməltən|, Alexander (1757–1804) U.S. politician. He established the U.S. central banking system as the first secretary of the treasury under Washington (1789–95), and advocated strong central government. He was killed in a duel with Aaron Burr.

Ham·il·ton |'hæməltən|, Sir Charles (1900–78) New Zealand inventor and automobile-racing driver, best known for his development of the jet boat.

Ham·il·ton |'hæməltən|, Lady Emma (c. 1765–1815) English beauty and mistress of Lord Nelson; born *Amy Lyon* or **Emily Lyon**.

Ham·il·ton |'hæməltən|, Scott (1958–) U.S. figure skater. He won four world championships (1981–84) and an Olympic gold medal (1984).

Ham·il·ton |'hæməltən|, Virginia Esther (1936–) U.S. author. A biographical and children's fiction author, her works include *M. C. Higgins, the Great* (1974), the first book in history to receive the National Book Award and the Newbery Medal.

Ham·lin |'hæmlən|, Hannibal (1809–91) U.S. politician. He was vice president of the U.S. (1861–65), a member of the U.S. Senate (1869–81), and minister to Spain (1881–82).

Ham·lisch |'hæmlisH|, Marvin (1944–) U.S. composer. His compositions include *A Chorus Line* (1975) and *They're Playing Our Song* (1979).

Ham·mar·skjöld |'hämərsHəld|, Dag (Hjalmar Agne Carl) (1905–61) Swedish diplomat and politician. As secretary general of the United Nations (1953–61) he was influential in the establishment of the UN emergency force in Sinai and Gaza (1956), and also initiated peace moves in the Middle East (1957–58). Killed in a plane crash while on a peace mission in Congo, he was posthumously awarded the 1961 Nobel Peace Prize.

Ham·mer |'hæmər|, Armand (1898–1990) U.S. industrialist and philanthropist. He had many business interests in the U.S. and the U.S.S.R. and served as chairman and chief executive officer of Occidental Petroleum Corp. (1957–90).

Ham·mer·stein |'hæmər,stīn|, Oscar II (1895–1960) U.S. lyricist. He collaborated with various composers, most notably Richard Rodgers, with whom he wrote *Oklahoma!* (1943), *South Pacific* (1949), and *The Sound of Music* (1959).

Ham·mett |'hæmət|, (Samuel) Dashiell (1894–1961) U.S. novelist. He developed the hard-boiled style of detective fiction in works such as *The Maltese Falcon* (1930) and *The Thin Man* (1932) (both made into successful movies). He lived for many years with Lillian Hellman; they were both persecuted for their left-wing views during the McCarthy era.

Ham·mon |'hæmən|, Jupiter (c. 1720– c. 1800) U.S. poet. His "An Evening Thought" (1761) was the first published poem by an African American.

Ham·mond |'hæmənd| U.S. engineers. **John Hays Hammond** (1855–1936) was a mining engineer, an associate of Cecil Rhodes in the development of South African mining resources, and a leader in the Transvaal reform movement (1895–96). His son, **John Hays Hammond, Jr.** (1888–1965), was an electrical and radio engineer and inventor. He established the Hammond Radio Research Laboratory (1911).

Ham·mond |'hæmənd|, Dame Joan (1912–96) Australian operatic soprano, born in New Zealand.

Ham·mond |'hæmənd|, Laurens (1895–1973) U.S. inventor. He developed the Hammond electric organ (1933).

Ham·mu·ra·bi |,hæmə'räbē| (died 1750 BC) the sixth king of the first dynasty of Babylonia, reigned 1792–1750 BC. He extended the Babylonian empire and instituted one of the earliest known collections of laws.

Hamp·ton |'hæm(p)tən|, Lionel (1909–) U.S. jazz vibraphonist, drummer, pianist, singer, and bandleader. He played with Benny Goodman in small ensembles before forming his own big band (1940).

Ham·sun |'hämsən|, Knut (1859–1952) Norwegian novelist; pseudonym of Knut Pedersen. Notable works: Hunger (1890) and Growth of the Soil (1917). Nobel Prize for Literature (1920).

Han·cock |'hæn,käk|, John (1737–93) American revolutionary and politician. Noted as the first signer of the Declaration of Independence (1776), he was a member of the Continental Congress (1775–80; 1785; 1786) and its first president (1775–77). He was later governor of Massachusetts (1780–85; 1787–93).

Han·cock |'hæn,käk|, Winfield Scott (1824–86) U.S. army officer. A Union general, he was famed for his defense of Cemetery Ridge in the Battle of Gettysburg (1863). He was the 1880 De-

mocratic presidential candidate, narrowly losing to Garfield.

Hand |hænd|, (Billings) Learned (1872–1961) U.S. jurist and author. He wrote over 2000 opinions as judge of the U.S. Court of Appeals, 2nd Circuit (1924–51). Notable works: The Spirit of Liberty (1952).

Han·del |'hændəl|, George Frideric (1685–1759) German-born composer and organist, resident in England from 1712; born Georg Friedrich Händel. A prolific composer, he is chiefly remembered for his choral works, especially the oratorio Messiah (1742), and for orchestra, his Water Music suite (c.1717) and Music for the Royal Fireworks (1749).

Handley Page, Frederick see PAGE.

Han·dy |'hændē|, W. C. (William Christopher) (1873–1958) U.S. blues musician. He set up a music-publishing house in 1914, and his transcriptions of traditional blues helped establish the pattern of the modern twelve-bar blues.

Hanks |hæNGks|, Tom (1956–) U.S. actor, director and producer; full name Thomas J. Hanks. Light-hearted films such as Splash! (1984) and Big (1988) brought him international success. He won Oscars for his performances in Philadelphia (1993) and Forrest Gump (1994).

Han·na |'hænə|, Bill (1910–) U.S. cartoonist and motion picture and televison producer. Full name William Denby Hanna. With longtime partner Joseph Barbera, he created cartoon characters such as the Flintstones, Top Cat, Huckleberry Hound, Yogi Bear, and Tom and Jerry.

Han·ni·bal |'hænəbəl| (247–183 BC) Carthaginian general. In the second Punic War he attacked Italy via the Alps, repeatedly defeating the Romans, although he failed to take Rome itself.

Hans·ber·ry |'hænz,berē|, Lorraine (1930–65) U.S. playwright. Her A Raisin in the Sun (1959) was the first play by an African-American woman to be produced on Broadway.

Han·sen |'hænsən|, Austin (1910–96) U.S. photographer.

Hap·good |'hæpgood|, Norman (1868–1937) U.S. editor and author. He was editor of the magazines Collier's (1903–

12), *Harper's Weekly* (1913–16), and *Hearst's International* (1923–25).

Har·court |'härkawrt|, Alfred (1881–1954) U.S. publisher. He cofounded the firm that eventually became Harcourt Brace Jovanovich (1919).

Har·die |'härdē|, (James) Keir (1856–1915) Scottish Labour politician. A miner before becoming a member of Parliament in 1892, he became the first leader of both the Independent Labour Party (1893) and the Labour Party (1906).

Har·ding |'härdiNG|, Tonya (1970–) U.S. figure skater. She was a world champion figure skater (1991) involved in a plot to injure competitor Nancy Kerrigan and prevent her from competing on the Olympic team.

Har·ding |'härdiNG|, Warren (Gamaliel) see box. **Florence Kling De Wolfe Harding** (1860–1924), wife of Warren Harding and U.S. first lady (1921–23).

Hard·wick |'härdwik|, Elizabeth (1916–) U.S. author and editor.

Harding, Warren Gamaliel
29th U.S. president

Life dates: 1865–1923
Place of birth: Corsica, Ohio (now Blooming Grove)
Mother: Phoebe Elizabeth Dickerson Harding
Father: George Tryon Harding
Wife: Florence Kling De Wolfe Harding
College/University: Ohio Central College
Career: Publisher; schoolteacher; newspaper editor; insurance salesman
Political career: Ohio Senate; lieutenant governor of Ohio; U.S. Senate; president
Party: Republican
Home state: Ohio
Opponents in presidential race: James M. Cox, Eugene Debs
Term of office: March 4, 1921–Aug. 2, 1923 (died while in office)
Vice president: Calvin Coolidge
Notable events of presidency: peace treaties with Austria, Germany, and Hungary; Teapot Dome Oil Scandal (revealed during Coolidge administration); dedication of the Tomb of the Unknown Soldier at Arlington, Va.
Place of burial: Marion, Ohio

Har·dy |'härdē|, Oliver (1892–1957) see LAUREL, STAN.

Har·dy |'härdē|, Thomas (1840–1928) English novelist and poet. Much of his work deals with the struggle against the indifferent force that inflicts the sufferings and ironies of life. Notable novels: *The Mayor of Casterbridge* (1886), *Tess of the D'Urbervilles* (1891), and *Jude the Obscure* (1896).

Hare, William see BURKE.

Harefoot, Harold see HAROLD.

Har·greaves |'här,grēvz|, James (*c.* 1720–78) English inventor; invented the spinning jenny (*c.* 1764).

Har·i·ot |'hereət|, Thomas (1560–1621) English mathematician and geographer. Also **Thomas Harriot** or **Thomas Harriott**. His *Briefe and True Report of the New-Found Land of Virginia* (1588) was the first English book written about the first English colony in America.

Hark·ness |'härknəs|, Anna M. (1837–1926) U.S. philanthropist. She endowed the Harkness Quadrangle at Yale University (1921) and established the Commonwealth Fund (1920).

Har·lan |'härlən| U.S. jurists. **John Marshall Harlan** (1833–1911) was a U.S. Supreme Court justice (1877–1911). In *Plessy v. Ferguson* (1896), he declared in a dissenting opinion that the Constitution is "color-blind." His grandson, **John Marshall Harlan** (1899–1971), was also a U.S. Supreme Court justice (1955–71).

Har·low |'härlō|, Harry Frederick (1905–81) U.S. ethologist and primate researcher.

Har·low |'härlō|, Jean (1911–37) U.S. movie actress; born *Harlean Carpenter*. Howard Hughes's *Hell's Angels* (1930) launched her career, her platinum blonde hair and sex appeal bringing immediate success. Her movies include *Platinum Blonde* (1931) and six movies with Clark Gable, including *Red Dust* (1932) and *Saratoga* (1937).

Harms·worth |'härmzwərTH|, Alfred Charles William see NORTHCLIFFE.

Har·old I |'herəld| (died 1040) king of England, reigned 1035–40; known as **Harold Harefoot**. An illegitimate son of Canute, he came to the throne when his half-brother Hardecanute (Canute's legitimate heir) was king of Denmark and thus absent when Canute died.

Har•old II |'herəld| (*c.* 1022–66) king of England, reigned 1066, the last Anglo-Saxon king of England. Succeeding Edward the Confessor, he was faced with two invasions within months of his accession. He resisted his half-brother Tostig and the Norse king Harald Hardrada at Stamford Bridge, but was killed and his army defeated by William of Normandy at the Battle of Hastings.

Har•per |'härpər|, Frances Ellen Watkins (1825–1911) U.S. author and social reformer. She was a founding member of the National Association for the Advancement of Colored Women (1896). Notable works: *Poems on Miscellaneous Subjects* (1854) and "The Two Offers" (1859).

Har•per |'härpər|, James (1795–1869) U.S. publisher. With his brothers John (1797–1875), Joseph Wesley (1801–70), and Fletcher (1806–77), he founded Harper & Brothers (1833), which published books and the magazines *Harper's New Monthly* (1850), *Harper's Weekly* (1957), and *Harper's Bazaar* (1867).

Har•per |'härpər|, Valerie (1940–) U.S. actress. Her television credits include the programs "The Mary Tyler Moore Show" (1970–74), "Rhoda" (1974–78), and "Valerie" (1986–87).

Har•ri•man |'herəmən| U.S. family, including: **Edward Henry Harriman** (1848–1909), a financier and railroad executive. His son, **(William) Averell Harriman** (1891–1986), was a U.S. diplomat. He served as U.S. representative to the Paris talks about peace in Vietnam.

Har•ring•ton |'heriNGtən|, Michael (1928–89) U.S. author and educator. He was a democratic socialist whose book *The Other America: Poverty in the United States* (1962) led to President Johnson's War on Poverty programs.

Har•ris |'herəs|, Sir Arthur Travers (1892–1984) British Marshal of the Royal Air Force; known as **Bomber Harris**. As commander in chief of Bomber Command (1942–45) in World War II, he organized mass bombing raids against German towns that resulted in large-scale civilian casualties.

Har•ris |'herəs|, Chapin Aaron (1806–60) U.S. dentist. He founded the first dental periodical, the *American Journal of Dental Science* (1939) and cofounded the first dental college, Baltimore College of Dental Surgery (1840).

Har•ris |'herəs|, Emmylou (1947–) U.S. country musician. Her hits include "If I Could Only Win Your Love" (1975) and "We Believe in Happy Endings" (1988).

Har•ris |'herəs|, Frank (1856–1931) Irish writer; born *James Thomas Harris*.

Har•ris |'herəs|, Joel Chandler (1848–1908) U.S. author. He is best known for his Brer Rabbit and Brer Fox stories as told by the fictional Uncle Remus.

Har•ris |'herəs|, William Torrey (1835–1909) U.S. educator and philosopher. He served as U.S. commissioner of education (1889–1906) and was the leading American interpreter of German philosophical thought.

Har•ri•son |'herəsən|, Benjamin see box. **Caroline Lavinia Scott Harrison** (1832–92), wife of Benjamin Harrison and U.S. first lady (1889–92).

Har•ri•son |'herəsən|, George (1943–) English rock and pop guitarist and songwriter, the lead guitarist of the Beatles.

Har•ri•son |'herəsən|, John (1693–1776) English horologist and inventor. He developed a marine chronometer for determining longitude at sea (1730–63).

Har•ri•son |'herəsən|, Peter (1716–75) U.S. architect.

Har•ri•son |'herəsən|, Sir Rex (1908–90) English actor; full name *Reginald Carey Harrison*. Notable movies: *Blithe Spirit* (1944), *My Fair Lady* (1964), and *Dr. Dolittle* (1967).

Har•ri•son |'herəsən|, Richard Berry (1864–1935) U.S. actor, born in Canada. He won national reputation in the African-American community as a Shakespearean actor and starred in *Green Pastures* (1930, Pulitzer Prize). Spingarn Medal, 1931.

Har•ri•son |'herəsən|, Wallace Kirkman (1895–1981) U.S. architect. His designs in New York City include the Metropolitan Opera House, Lincoln Center, and the United Nations complex.

Harrison, Benjamin
23rd U.S. president

Life dates: 1833–1901
Place of birth: North Bend, Ohio
Mother: Elizabeth Ramsey Irwin Harrison
Father: John Scott Harrison
Wives: Caroline Lavinia Scott Harrison (died 1892); Mary Scott Lord Dimmick Harrison (married 1896)
Children: (by first wife) Russell, Mary; (by second wife) Elizabeth
College/University: Miami University of Ohio
Military service: during Civil War, rose to the rank of brigadier general with Indiana volunteers
Career: Lawyer; law professor
Political career: Indianapolis city attorney; U.S. Senate; president
Party: Republican
Home state: Indiana
Opponents in presidential races: Grover Cleveland
Term of office: March 4, 1889–March 3, 1893
Vice president: Levi P. Morton
Notable events of presidency: Sherman Anti-Trust Act; Sherman Silver Purchase Act; McKinley Tariff Act; Dependent Pension Act; Pan American Union created; Oklahoma opened to settlers; North and South Dakota admitted as the 39th and 40th states; Montana admitted as the 41st state; Wyoming admitted as the 42nd state
Place of burial: Indianapolis, Indiana

Harrison, William Henry
9th U.S. president

Life dates: 1773–1841
Place of birth: Berkeley plantation, Charles City County, Virginia
Mother: Elizabeth Bassett Harrison
Father: Benjamin Harrison
Wife: Anna Tuthill Symmes Harrison
Children: Elizabeth, John (died in infancy), Lucy, William, John, Benjamin, Mary, Carter, Anna, James
College/University: Hampden-Sydney College
Military service: Battle of Tippecanoe (1811); U.S. Army major general in War of 1812
Career: Farmer; soldier
Political career: governor of the Indiana Territory; U.S. House of Representatives; Ohio Senate; U.S. Senate; minister to Colombia; president
Party: Whig
Home state: Ohio
Opponent in presidential races: Martin Van Buren
Term of office: March 4, 1841–Apr. 4, 1841 (died after 31 days in office)
Vice president: John Tyler
Place of burial: North Bend, Ohio

Har·ri·son |'herəsən|, William Henry see box. **Anna Tuthill Symmes Harrison** (1775–1864), wife of William Henry Harrison and U.S. first lady (1841). She had not yet moved to Washington, D.C., when word arrived of her husband's death one month after taking office.

Har·rod |'herəd|, Charles Henry (1800–85) English grocer and tea merchant. In 1853 he took over a shop in Knightsbridge, London, which, after expansion by his son **Charles Digby Harrod** (1841–1905), became the prestigious Harrod's department store.

Har·ry |'herē|, Deborah (1945–) U.S. punk rock vocalist. She was known as "Blondie" and performed with the group by the same name.

Hart |härt|, Johnny (1931–) U.S. cartoonist and author. Full name *John Lewis Hart*. He created the comic strips "B.C." and "The Wizard of Id."

Hart |härt|, Lorenz Milton (1895–1943) U.S. lyricist. His collaborations with composer Richard Rodgers include the scores for the Broadway shows *Babes in Arms* (1937) and *Pal Joey* (1940). Notable songs: "The Lady Is a Tramp," "My Funny Valentine," and "Blue Moon."

Hart |härt|, Moss (1904–61) U.S. playwright. His collaborations with George S. Kaufman include *You Can't Take It With You* (1936, Pulitzer Prize) and *The Man Who Came to Dinner* (1939).

Har·tack |'härtæk|, Bill (1932–) U.S. jockey. Full name *William John Hartack, Jr.*. He won the Kentucky Derby five times.

Harte |härt|, (Francis) Brett (1836–1902) U.S. short-story writer and poet. He is chiefly remembered for his stories about life in a Californian gold-mining settlement.

Hart·ley |'härtlē|, L. P. (Leslie Pôles) (1895–1972) English novelist and short-story writer.

Hart·nell |'härtnəl|, Sir Norman (1901–78) English couturier; dressmaker to Queen Elizabeth II (whose coronation gown he designed) and the Queen Mother.

Harun ar-Rashid |hä'rōōn är rä'sHed| (763–809) Also **Haroun-al-Raschid** (763–809), fifth Abbasid caliph of Baghdad (786–809). The most powerful of the Abbasid caliphs, he was made famous by his portrayal in the *Arabian Nights.*

Har·vard |'härvərd|, John (1607–38) American clergyman. He left his library and half of his estate to the newly founded college in Massachusetts which became Harvard University.

Har·vey |'härvē|, Alfred (1913–94) U.S. cartoonist. The founder of Harvey Comics, he created the cartoon character Casper the Friendly Ghost.

Har·vey |'härvē|, Paul (1918–) U.S. radio journalist and commentator. He is a syndicated columnist for the *Los Angeles Times* (1954–).

Har·vey |'härvē|, William (1578–1657) English physician, discoverer of the circulation of the blood. In *De Motu Cordis* (1628), Harvey described the motion of the heart and concluded that the blood leaves through the arteries and returns to the heart through the veins after it had passed through the flesh.

Has·dru·bal |hæz'drōōbəl| (died 221 BC) Carthaginian general. He accompanied his father-in-law, Hamilcar, to Spain in 237 and advanced the Carthaginian boundary to the Ebro.

Ha·šek |'häsHek|, Jaroslav (1883–1923) Czech novelist and short-story writer.

Hass |häs|, Robert (1947–) U.S. author. He was Poet Laureate of the U.S. (1995–97).

Has·sam |'hæsəm|, Childe (1859–1935) U.S. artist. Full name *Frederick Childe Hassam.*

Has·sel·blad |'häsel,bläd|, Victor (1906–78) Swedish inventor. He served as president of Hasselblad Photography, Inc. (1944–66).

Hass·ler |'häslər|, Ferdinand Rudolph (1770–1843) U.S. geodesist, born in Switzerland. He was superintendent of the U.S. Coast Survey (1816–18, 1832–43).

Has·tie |'hästē|, William H. (1904–76) U.S. jurist. He served as the first black federal judge (appointed 1937) and as governor of the U.S. Virgin Islands (1946–49).

Has·tings |'hästiNGz|, Thomas (1860–1929) U.S. architect. With John Merven Carrère (1858–1911), he designed the New York Public Library (1902 –11) and the Manhattan Bridge (1904–11).

Has·tings |'hästiNGz|, Warren (1732–1818) British colonial administrator. India's first governor general (1774–84), he introduced vital administrative reforms.

Hath·a·way |'hæTHə,wā|, Anne (*c.* 1556–1623) the wife of Shakespeare, whom she married in 1582.

Hat·shep·sut |hæt'sHep,sōōt| (died 1482 BC) Egyptian queen of the 18th dynasty, reigned *c.*1503–1482 BC. On the death of her husband Tuthmosis II, she became regent for her nephew Tuthmosis III. She then named herself Pharaoh and was often portrayed as male.

Haupt·mann |'howp(t),mæn|, Gerhart (1862–1946) German dramatist. An early pioneer of naturalism, he is known for *Before Sunrise* (1889) and *The Ascension of Joan* (1893). Nobel Prize for Literature (1912).

Ha·vel |'hävəl|, Václav (1936–) Czech dramatist and statesman, president of Czechoslovakia (1989–92) and of the Czech Republic since 1993. His plays, such as *The Garden Party* (1963), were critical of totalitarianism, and he was twice imprisoned as a dissident. He was elected president following the fall of the Communist leadership.

Hav·ell |'hævəl|, Robert, Jr. (1793–1878) U.S. engraver and painter. He made most of the plates for Audubon's *Birds of America.*

Hav·li·cek |'hæv,ləcHek|, John (1940–) U.S. basketball player.

Hawke |hawk|, Bob (1929–) Australian Labour statesman, prime minister (1983–91); full name *Robert James Lee Hawke.*

Haw·king |'hawkiNG|, Stephen (William) (1942–) English theoretical physicist. His main work has been on space–time, quantum mechanics, and black holes. His book *A Brief History of Time* (1988) proved a popular bestseller.

Haw·kins |'hawkinz|, Alma (1904–94) U.S. pioneer of modern dance.

Haw·kins |'hawkinz|, Coleman (Randolph) (1904–69) U.S. jazz saxophonist. During the 1920s and 1930s he was influential in making the tenor saxophone popular as a jazz instrument.

Haw·kins |'hawkinz|, Sir John (1532–95) English sailor. Also **Hawkyns**. Involved in the slave trade and privateering, he later helped build up the fleet that defeated the Spanish Armada in 1588.

Hawks |hawks|, Howard (Winchester) (1896–1977) U.S. movie director, producer, and screenwriter. He directed such movies as *The Big Sleep* (1946), *Gentlemen Prefer Blondes* (1953), and *Rio Bravo* (1959).

Hawks·moor |'hawks,mawr|, Nicholas (1661–1736) English architect. He worked with Vanbrugh at Castle Howard and Blenheim Palace and designed six London churches.

Hawn |hawn|, Goldie (1945–) U.S. actress. Notable movies: *Cactus Flower* (1969, Academy Award).

Ha·worth |'haw,wərTH|, Sir Walter Norman (1883–1950) English organic chemist. He was a pioneer in carbohydrate chemistry and was the first person to make a vitamin artificially when he synthesized vitamin C. Nobel Prize for Chemistry (1937).

Haw·thorne |'hawTHawrn| U.S. authors. **Nathaniel Hawthorne** (1804–64) was a novelist and short-story writer. Much of his fiction explores guilt, sin, and morality. Notable works: *Twice-Told Tales* (short stories, 1837) and *The House of Seven Gables* (novel, 1851). His son, **Julian Hawthorne** (1846–1934), wrote *Garth* (1877) and *Nathaniel Hawthorne and His Wife* (1884).

Hay |hā|, John Milton (1838–1905) U.S. diplomat and author. He was President Lincoln's private secretary (1861–65) and U.S. ambassador to Great Britain (1897–98). As U.S. secretary of state (1898–1905), he negotiated the Hay-Pauncefote Treaty (1901), making pos-

sible the construction of the Panama Canal.

Hay·den |'hād(ə)n|, Charles (1870–1937) U.S. banker and philanthropist. He donated the projector in the planetarium in New York City named in his honor.

Hay·den |'hād(ə)n|, Robert (1913–80) U.S. poet. Notable works: *Words in the Mourning Time* (1970) and *American Journal* (1978).

Hay·dn |'hīdn|, (Franz) Joseph (1732–1809) Austrian composer. A major exponent of the classical style, he taught both Mozart and Beethoven. His work includes 108 symphonies, 67 string quartets, 12 masses, and the oratorio *The Creation* (1796–98).

Hay·ek |'hīyek|, Friedrich August von (1899–1992) Austrian-born British economist. Strongly opposed to Keynesian economics, he was a leading advocate of the free market. Nobel Prize for Economics (1974).

Hayes |hāz|, Helen (1900–93) U.S. actress. Born *Helen Hayes Brown*; known as **the first lady of the American theater**. Her Broadway career spanned seven decades and included Tony-winning roles in *Happy Birthday* (1946) and *Time Remembered* (1957). Notable movies: *The Sin of Madelon Claudet* (1932, Academy Award) and *Airport* (1970, Academy Award).

Hayes |hāz|, Isaac (1942–) U.S. songwriter, pianist, and singer. His scoring for the film *Shaft* made him the first African-American composer to win an Academy Award (1971); his hits include "Walk On By" and "By the Time I Get to Phoenix."

Hayes |hāz|, Isaac Israel (1832–81) U.S. explorer and author. He made three expeditions to the Arctic and recounted his experiences in *An Arctic Boat Journey* (1860).

Hayes |hāz|, Roland (1887–1976) U.S. musician, a singer of classical music and spirituals. Spingarn Medal, 1925.

Hayes, Rutherford (Birchard) see box. **Lucy Ware Webb Hayes** (1831–89), wife of Rutherford Hayes and U.S. first lady (1877–81). She was known as **Lemonade Lucy** for her prohibition of alcoholic beverages in the White House.

Hayes, Rutherford Birchard
19th U.S. president

Life dates: 1822–1893
Place of birth: Delaware, Ohio
Mother: Sophia Birchard Hayes
Father: Rutherford Hayes, Jr.
Wife: Lucy Ware Webb Hayes
Children: Birchard, James, Rutherford, Joseph, George, Fanny, Scott, Manning
College/University: Kenyon College; Harvard Law School
Military service: officer in Ohio volunteers during Civil War; rose to the rank of brevet major general
Career: Farmer; lawyer
Political career: U.S. House of Representatives; governor of Ohio; president
Party: Republican
Home state: Ohio
Opponent in presidential race: Samuel J. Tilden
Term of office: March 4, 1877–March 3, 1881
Vice president: William Almon Wheeler
Notable events of presidency: railroad strikes of 1877; civil service reform, specie payments resumption; Bland-Allison Silver Purchase Act; Permanent Exhibition, Philadelphia; end of War with Idaho Indians
Other achievements: Admitted to the Ohio bar
Place of burial: Fremont, Ohio

Hayes |hāz|, Woody (1913–87) U.S. football coach. Full name *Wayne Woodrow Hayes*. He coached at Ohio State University (1951–78), where he won 13 Big Ten Championships and four Rose Bowl victories.

Hay•ward |'hāwərd|, Susan (1919–75) U.S. actress. Born *Edythe Marrener*. Notable movies: *I Want to Live* (1958, Academy Award).

Hay•worth |'hāwərTH|, Rita (1918–87) U.S. actress and dancer; born *Margarita Carmen Cansino*. She achieved stardom in movie musicals such as *Cover Girl* (1944) before going on to play roles in *film noir*, notably in *Gilda* (1946) and *The Lady from Shanghai* (1948).

Ha•zel•tine |'hāzəl,tin|, Louis Alan (1886–1964) U.S. electrical engineer. He invented the neutrodyne circuit, which suppressed the noise inherent in radio receivers and made commercial broadcasting possible.

Ha•zen |'hāzən|, Elizabeth Lee (1885–1975) U.S. microbiologist. With Rachel Brown, she developed Nystatin, the first nontoxic antifungal antibiotic.

Haz•litt |'hæzlət|, William (1778–1830) English essayist and critic. His diverse essays, collected in *Table Talk* (1821), were marked by a clarity and conviction that brought new vigor to English prose writing.

Haz•zard |'hæzərd|, Shirley (1931–) Australian author and diplomat. Notable works: *The Bay of Noon* (1970) and *Countenance of Truth* (1990).

H. D. see DOOLITTLE.

Head |hed|, Edith (1907–81) U.S. costume designer. She worked on a wide range of movies, winning Oscars for costume design in *All About Eve* (1950) and *The Sting* (1973).

Hea•ney |'hēnē|, Seamus (Justin) (1939–) Irish poet. Born in Northern Ireland, in 1972 he took Irish citizenship. Notable works: *North* (1975) and *The Haw Lantern* (1987). Nobel Prize for Literature (1995).

Hearst |hərst| U.S. family, including: **George Hearst** (1820–91), a mining magnate. He had holdings in Nevada, Utah, Montana, South Dakota, and Mexico. He served as a member of the U.S. Senate from California (1886–91). His son, **William Randolph Hearst** (1863–1951), was a newspaper publisher and tycoon. His introduction of features such as large headlines and sensational crime reporting revolutionized American journalism. He was the model for the central character of Orson Welles's movie *Citizen Kane* (1941). William Randolph Hearst's granddaughter, heiress **Patricia Campbell Hearst** (1954–), was kidnapped by the Symbionese Liberation Army (1974), found by FBI agents (1975), and convicted of bank robbery (1976). She was known as **Patty**.

Heath |hēTH|, Sir Edward (Richard George) (1919–) British Conservative statesman, prime minister (1970–74). He negotiated Britain's entry into the European Economic Community and faced problems caused by a marked increase in oil prices. Attempts to restrain wage rises led to widespread strikes, and he lost a general election after a second national coal strike.

Heat-Moon |'hētmo͞on|, William Least (1939–) U.S. author. Also known as **William Trogdon**. His books include *Blue Highways* (1982).

Heav·i·side |'hevē,sīd|, Oliver (1850–1925) English physicist and electrical engineer, important in the development of telephone communication and telegraphy. In 1902 he suggested (independently of A. E. Kennelly) the existence of a layer in the atmosphere responsible for reflecting radio waves back to earth.

Hecht |hekt|, Anthony Evan (1923–) U.S. poet. His books of verse include *The Hard Hours* (1967, Pulitzer Prize).

Hecht |hekt|, Ben (1894–1964) U.S. author and dramatist. With Charles MacArthur, he wrote *The Front Page* (1928).

Heck·er |'hekər|, Isaac Thomas (1819–88) U.S. clergyman. He founded the Congregation of the Missionary Priests of St. Paul the Apostle ("Paulists") and served as its first superior (1858–88).

Heck·e·wel·der |'hekə,weldər|, John Gottlieb Ernestus (1743–1823) U.S. missionary and author, born in England. A Moravian missionary to Indians of the Susquehanna Valley, he wrote *Account of the History, Manners, and Customs of the Indian Nationals Who Once Inhabited Pennsylvania* (1819).

Hedge |hej|, Frederic Henry (1805–90) U.S. clergyman and author. Notable works: *Prose Writers of Germany* (1848) and *Martin Luther and Other Essays* (1888).

He·din |he'dēn|, Sven Anders (1865–1952) Swedish explorer and geographer. Notable books: *Mount Everest* (1922) and *The Silk Road* (1938).

Hef·lin |'heflən|, Van (1910–71) U.S. actor. Notable movies: *Johnny Eager* (1942, Academy Award).

Hef·ner |'hefnər|, Hugh (1926–) U.S. publisher. He was the founder of *Playboy Magazine* (1953) and Playboy Clubs International, Inc. (1959).

He·gel |'hāgəl|, Georg Wilhelm Friedrich (1770–1831) German philosopher. In his *Science of Logic* (1812–16) Hegel described the three-stage process of dialectical reasoning, on which Marx based his theory of dialectical materialism. He believed that history, the evolution of ideas, and human consciousness all develop through idealist dialectical processes as part of the Absolute or God coming to know itself.

Hei·deg·ger |'hīdəgər|, Martin (1889–1976) German philosopher. In *Being and Time* (1927) he examined the ontology of being, in particular human existence as involvement with a world of objects (*Dasein*). His writings on *Angst* (dread) as a fundamental part of human consciousness due to radical freedom of choice and awareness of death had a strong influence on existentialist philosophers such as Sartre.

Hei·fetz |'hīfəts|, Jascha (1901–87) U.S. violinist, born in Lithuania. Recognized as a musical prodigy at age three, he made his U.S. debut at Carnegie Hall in 1917 and went on to become the most celebrated violinist of the century.

Hei·ne |'hīnə|, (Christian Johann) Heinrich (1797–1856) German poet; born *Harry Heine*. Much of his early lyric poetry was set to music by Schumann and Schubert. In 1830 Heine emigrated to Paris, where his works became more political.

Hein·lein |'hīn,līn|, Robert Anson (1907–88) U.S. author. Notable works of science fiction: *Stranger in a Strange Land* (1961) and *I Will Fear No Evil* (1970). His pseudonyms include Anson MacDonald, Lyle Monroe, John Riverside, Caleb Saunders, and Simon York.

Heinz |hīn(t)s|, Henry John (1844–1919) U.S. food manufacturer. In 1869 he established a family firm for the manufacture and sale of processed foods. Heinz devised the marketing slogan "57 Varieties" in 1896 and erected New York's first electric sign to promote his company's pickles in 1900.

Hei·sen·berg |'hīzən,bərg|, Werner Karl (1901–76) German mathematical physicist and philosopher. He developed a system of quantum mechanics based on matrix algebra in which he stated his famous uncertainty principle

(1927). For this and his discovery of the allotropic forms of hydrogen he was awarded the 1932 Nobel Prize for Physics.

Held |held|, John, Jr. (1889–1958) U.S. cartoonist, illustrator and artist. He visually defined Jazz Age with the images of flappers and flaming youths.

Hel·e·na |'helənə|, St. (c. 248–c. 328 AD) Roman empress and mother of Constantine the Great. In 326 she visited the Holy Land and founded basilicas on the Mount of Olives and at Bethlehem. She is credited with the finding of the cross on which Christ was crucified. Feast day (in Eastern Church) May 21; (in Western Church) August 18.

He·lio·gab·a·lus |ˌhēlēəˈgæbələs| (AD 204–22) Roman emperor (218–22). Also **Elagabalus**. Born *Varius Avitus Bassianus*. He took his name from the Syro-Phoenician sun god Elah-Gabal, of whom he was a hereditary priest. He became notorious for his dissipated lifestyle and neglect of state affairs; he and his mother were both murdered.

Hel·ler |'helər|, Joseph (1923–) U.S. novelist. His experiences in the U.S. Army Air Forces during World War II inspired his best-known novel *Catch-22* (1961), an absurdist black comedy satirizing war, the source of the expression "catch-22."

Hell·man |'helmən|, Lillian (Florence) (1905–84) U.S. dramatist. Her plays, such as *The Children's Hour* (1934) and *The Little Foxes* (1939), often reflected her socialist and feminist concerns. She lived with the detective-story writer Dashiell Hammett, and both were blacklisted during the McCarthy era.

Helm·holtz |'helm,hōlts|, Hermann Ludwig Ferdinand von (1821–94) German physiologist and physicist. He formulated the principle of the conservation of energy in 1847. Other achievements include his studies in sense perception, hydrodynamics, and non-Euclidean geometry.

Hel·mont |'helmänt|, Jan Baptista van (1579–1644) Belgian chemist and physician. He made early studies on the conservation of matter, was the first to distinguish gases, and coined the word *gas*.

Helms |helmz|, Jesse (1921–) U.S. senator from North Carolina (1973–).

Helms·ley |'helmzlē| U.S. business family, including **Harry B. Helmsley** (1909–97) and his wife **Leona Helmsley**. They built a real estate empire, Helmsley-Spear, Inc., but he was eventually convicted of tax evasion. She was president of Helmsley Hotels, Inc. (1980–) and also served time in prison for tax evasion.

Hé·lo·ïse |'elə,wēz| (c. 1098–1164) French abbess. She is known for her tragic love affair with the theologian Abelard, which began after she became his pupil. When the affair came to light, Abelard persuaded her to enter a convent; she later became abbess of the community of Paraclete. See also ABELARD.

Help·mann |'helpmən|, Sir Robert (Murray) (1909–86) Australian ballet dancer, choreographer, director, and actor. He joined the Vic-Wells Ballet shortly after coming to England in 1933, and in 1935 began a long partnership with Margot Fonteyn.

Hel·prin |'helprən|, Mark (1947–) U.S. author. Notable works: *Winter's Tale* (1983).

Hem·ings |'heminGz|, Sally (1773–1835) U.S. slave. A slave at Thomas Jefferson's estate, Monticello, she was reported to be his mistress in the *Richmond Recorder* (1802).

Hem·ing·way |'heminGgwā|, Ernest (Miller) (1899–1961) U.S. novelist, short-story writer, and journalist. He achieved success with *The Sun Also Rises* (1926), which reflected the disillusionment of the postwar "lost generation." Other notable works: *A Farewell to Arms* (1929), *For Whom the Bell Tolls* (1940), and *The Old Man and the Sea* (1952, Pulitzer Prize 1953). Nobel Prize for Literature (1954).

Hen·der·son |'hendərsən|, (James) Fletcher (1898–1952) U.S. jazz pianist, bandleader, and arranger. He was a big band leader during the swing era.

Hen·der·son |'hendərsən|, Richard (1735–85) U.S. colonizer. He sent Daniel Boone to explore beyond the Cumberland Gap (1769), and he helped to settle colonies in Kentucky and in Nashville, Tennessee.

Hen·der·son |ˈhendərsən|, Rickey (1958–) U.S. baseball player. He set a major league record by stealing 130 bases in one season (1982).

Hen·drick |ˈhendrik|, Burton Jesse (1870–1949) U.S. journalist and historian. Pulitzer Prize–winning works: *The Victory at Sea* (1920, written with Admiral William S. Sims), *The Life and Letters of Walter Hines Page* (1922), and *The Training of an American: The Earlier Life and Letters of Walter Hines Page* (1928).

Hen·dricks |ˈhendriks|, Thomas Andrews (1819–85) U.S. vice president (1885).

Hen·drix |ˈhendriks|, Jimi (1942–70) U.S. rock musician; full name *James Marshall Hendrix*. Remembered for the flamboyance and originality of his improvisations, he greatly widened the scope of the electric guitar. Notable songs: "Purple Haze" (1967), and "All Along the Watchtower" (1968).

Hen·gist and Horsa |ˈhenɡɡəst ænd ˈhawrsə| (died 488) semimythological Jutish leaders. According to Bede, the brothers were invited to Britain by the British king Vortigern in 449 to assist in defeating the Picts and later established an independent Anglo-Saxon kingdom in Kent.

Hen·ie |ˈhenē|, Sonja (1912–69) Norwegian figure skater. She won ten consecutive world championships (1927–36) and three Olympic gold medals (1928, 1932, 1936).

Hen·ley |ˈhenlē|, Beth (1952–) U.S. playwright. She won a Pulitzer Prize for *Crimes of the Heart* (1979).

Hen·ne·pin |ˈhenəpən|, Louis (1640–*c.* 1701) French missionary, explorer, and author. He accompanied La Salle through the Great Lakes.

Hen·ri |ˈhenrē|, Robert (1865–1929) U.S. painter. An advocate of realism, he believed that the artist must be a social force. The Ashcan School was formed largely as a result of his influence.

Hen·ri·et·ta |ˌhenrēˈetə|, Maria (1609–69) daughter of Henry IV of France, queen consort of Charles I of England (1625–49). Her Roman Catholicism heightened public anxieties about the court's religious sympathies and was a contributory cause of the English Civil War.

Hen·ry[1] |ˈhenrē| (1068–1135) the name of eight kings of England: **Henry I** (1068–1135; reigned 1100–35). King of England, youngest son of William I. His only son drowned in 1120, and although Henry extracted an oath of loyalty to his daughter Matilda from the barons in 1127, his death was followed almost immediately by the outbreak of civil war. **Henry II** (1133–89; reigned 1154–89); the son of Matilda. The first Plantagenet king, he restored order after the reigns of Stephen and Matilda. Opposition to his policies on reducing the power of the Church was led by Thomas à Becket, who was eventually murdered by four of Henry's knights. **Henry III** (1207–72; reigned 1216–72), the son of John. King of England. His ineffectual government caused widespread discontent, ending in Simon de Montfort's defeat and capture of Henry in 1264. Although he was restored a year later, real power resided with his son, who eventually succeeded him as Edward I. **Henry IV** (1366–1413; reigned 1399–1413), son of John of Gaunt. King of England; known as **Henry Bolingbroke**. He overthrew Richard II, establishing the Lancastrian dynasty. His reign was marked by rebellion in Wales and the north, where the Percy family raised several uprisings. **Henry V** (1387–1422; reigned 1413–22). King of England, son of Henry IV. He renewed the Hundred Years War soon after coming to the throne and defeated the French at Agincourt in 1415. **Henry VI** (1421–71; reigned 1422–61 and 1470–71), son of Henry V. King of England. He was unfit to rule effectively on his own due to a recurrent mental illness. Government by the monarchy became increasingly unpopular and after intermittent civil war with the House of York (the Wars of the Roses), Henry was deposed in 1461 by Edward IV. He briefly regained his throne following a Lancastrian uprising. **Henry VII** (1457–1509; reigned 1485–1509), the son of Edmund Tudor, Earl of Richmond. The first Tudor king; known as **Henry Tudor**. Although the grandson of

Owen Tudor, he inherited the Lancastrian claim to the throne through his mother, a great-granddaughter of John of Gaunt. He defeated Richard III at Bosworth Field and eventually established an unchallenged Tudor dynasty. **Henry VIII** (1491–1547; reigned 1509–47), son of Henry VII. King of England. Henry had six wives (Catherine of Aragon, Anne Boleyn, Jane Seymour, Anne of Cleves, Catherine Howard, Katherine Parr); he executed two and divorced two. His first divorce, from Catherine of Aragon, was opposed by the Pope, leading to England's break with the Roman Catholic Church.

Hen•ry[2] |'henrē| (1394–1460) Portuguese prince; known as **Henry the Navigator**. The third son of John I of Portugal, he organized many voyages of discovery, most notably south along the African coast, thus laying the foundation for Portuguese imperial expansion around Africa to the Far East.

Hen•ry[3] |'henrē| the name of seven kings of the Germans, six of whom were also Holy Roman emperors: **Henry I** (c. 876–936; reigned 919–936). King of the Germans; known as **Henry the Fowler**. He waged war successfully against the Slavs in Brandenburg, the Magyars, and the Danes. **Henry II** (973–1024; reigned 1002–24). King of the Germans. Holy Roman emperor (1014–24); also known as **Saint Henry. Henry III** (1017–56; reigned 1039–56). King of the Germans. Holy Roman emperor (1046–56). He brought stability and prosperity to the empire, defeating the Czechs and fixing the frontier between Austria and Hungary. **Henry IV** (1050–1106; reigned 1056–1105), son of Henry III. King of the Germans. Holy Roman emperor (1084–1105). Increasing conflict with Pope Gregory VII led Henry to call a council in 1076 to depose the Pope, who excommunicated Henry. Henry obtained absolution by doing penance before Gregory in 1077 but managed to depose him in 1084. **Henry V** (1081–1125; reigned 1099–1125). King of the Germans. Holy Roman emperor (1111–25). **Henry VI** (1165–97; reigned 1069–97). King of the Germans. Holy Roman emperor (1191–97). **Henry VII** (c.

1275–1313; reigned 1308–13). King of the Germans. Holy Roman emperor (1312–13).

Hen•ry IV |'henrē| (1553–1610) king of France 1589–1610; known as **Henry of Navarre**. Although leader of Huguenot forces in the latter stages of the French Wars of Religion, on succeeding the Catholic Henry III he became Catholic himself in order to guarantee peace. He established religious freedom with the Edict of Nantes (1598) and restored order after the prolonged civil war.

Hen•ry |'henrē|, Joseph (1797–1878) U.S. physicist and educator. His electrical inventions include the first electromagnetic motor (1829). He was the first secretary and director of the Smithsonian Institution (1846–77). The "henry" unit of inductance is named after him.

Hen•ry |'henrē|, Marguerite (1902–) U.S. author of children's books. Notable works: *Misty of Chincoteague* (1947, Newbery Award).

Hen•ry |'henrē|, O (1862–1910) U.S. short-story writer; pseudonym of *William Sydney Porter*. Jailed for embezzlement in 1898, he started writing short stories in prison. Collections include *Cabbages and Kings* (1904) and *The Voice of the City* (1908).

Hen•ry |'henrē|, Patrick (1736–99) American revolutionary. As a member of the Continental Congress (1774–76), he was a noted orator. He is best remembered for an impassioned speech in which he stated, "Give me liberty, or give me death."

Henry Bolingbroke |'bawliNG,br ͝ook| Henry IV of England (see HENRY[1]).

Henry the Fowler Henry I, king of the Germans (see HENRY[3]).

Henry Tudor Henry VII of England (see HENRY[1]).

Hen•son |'hensən|, Jim (1936–90) U.S. puppeteer. Full name *James Maury Henson*. He created the Muppets, the most commercially successful puppets in history. Since gaining fame as principal characters on television's "Sesame Street" (1969–), the Muppets have been featured in numerous television shows and movies.

Hen•son |'hensən|, Josiah (1789–1883) U.S. slave and clergyman. A Methodist preacher, he escaped from Maryland to Canada (1830). His autobiography, *The Life of Josiah Henson* (1849) includes an introduction by Harriet Beecher Stowe.

Hen·son |'hensən|, Matthew Alexander (1866–1955) U.S. explorer. He accompanied Peary on his 1908 expedition to the North Pole.

Hep·burn |'hepbərn|, Audrey (1929–93) British actress, born in Belgium. After pursuing a career as a stage and movie actress in England, she moved to Hollywood, where she starred in such movies as *Roman Holiday* (1953), for which she won an Oscar, and *My Fair Lady* (1964).

Hep·burn |'hepbərn|, Katharine (1907–) U.S. actress. She starred in a wide range of movies, often opposite Spencer Tracy; movies include *Woman of the Year* (1942), *The African Queen* (1951), and *On Golden Pond* (1981), for which she won her fourth Oscar.

Hep·ple·white |'hepəl,(h)wīt|, George (died 1786) English cabinetmaker and furniture designer. The posthumously published book of his designs, *The Cabinetmaker and Upholsterer's Guide* (1788), contains almost 300 designs, characterized by light and elegant lines, which sum up neoclassical taste.

Hep·worth |'hep,wərTH|, Dame (Jocelyn) Barbara (1903–75) English sculptor. A pioneer of abstraction in British sculpture, she worked in wood, stone, and bronze and is noted for her simple monumental works in landscape and architectural settings, including *The Family of Man* (nine-piece group, 1972).

Her·a·cli·tus |,herə'klītəs| (*c.* 540–480 BC) Greek philosopher. He believed that fire is the origin of all things and that permanence is an illusion, everything being in a (harmonious) process of constant change.

Her·bert |'hərbərt|, Sir A. P. (1890–1970) English writer and politician Full name *Alan Patrick Herbert*. He wrote novels, items for the magazine *Punch*, and libretti for comic operas.

Her·bert |'hərbərt|, George (1593–1633) English metaphysical poet. He was vicar of Bemerton, near Salisbury; his poems are pervaded by simple piety and reflect the spiritual conflicts he ex-

perienced before submitting his will to God.

Her·bert |'hərbərt|, Victor (1859–1924) U.S. cellist, conductor, and composer, born in Ireland. Notable operettas: *Babes in Toyland* (1903) and *Naughty Marietta* (1910).

Herbst |hərbst|, Josephine Frey (1892–1969) U.S. author and journalist. Her novel *Pity Is Not Enough* (1933) was the first in a popular trilogy based on her family's history from the Civil War to the Depression.

Her·e·ward the Wake |'herəwərd THə 'wāk| (11th cent) semilegendary Anglo-Saxon rebel leader. A leader of Anglo-Saxon resistance to William I's new Norman regime, he is thought to have been responsible for an uprising centered on the Isle of Ely in 1070.

Her·man |'hərmən|, Woody (1913–87) U.S. jazz clarinetist, saxophonist, and bandleader. Full name *Woodrow Charles Herman*; known as "the Boy Wonder of the Clarinet." The *Ebony Concerto*, written for him by Stravinsky, was performed at Carnegie Hall (1946).

He·ro |'hērō| (1st century) Greek mathematician and inventor; known as **Hero of Alexandria**. His surviving works are important as a source for ancient practical mathematics and mechanics. He described a number of hydraulic, pneumatic, and other mechanical devices, including elementary applications of the power of steam.

Her·od |'herəd| (*c.* 73–4 BC) ruler of ancient Palestine (37–34 BC). Known as **Herod the Great**. He built the palace of Masada and rebuilt the Temple in Jerusalem. According to the New Testament, the birth of Jesus during his reign led Herod to order the massacre of the innocents (Matt. 2:16).

Her·od Agrip·pa |'herəd ə'gripə| the name of two rulers of ancient Palestine: **Herod Agrippa I** (10 BC–AD 44; reigned AD 41–44), grandson of Herod the Great. King of Judaea. He imprisoned St. Peter and put St. James the Great to death. His son, **Herod Agrippa II** (*c.* AD 27–*c.* 93; reigned 50–*c.* 93). He was king of various territories in northern Palestine. He presided over the trial of St. Paul (Acts 25:13).

Her·od An·ti·pas |'herəd 'äntəpəs| (21 BC–39 AD) ruler of ancient Palestine, son of Herod the Great, tetrarch of Galilee and Peraea 4 BC–AD 40. He married Herodias and was responsible for the beheading of John the Baptist. According to the New Testament (Luke 23:7), Pilate sent Jesus to be questioned by him before the Crucifixion.

He·rod·o·tus |he'rädətəs| (5th century BC) Greek historian. His *History* tells of the Persian Wars of the early 5th century BC. He was the first historian to collect his materials systematically, test their accuracy to a certain extent, and arrange them in a well-constructed and vivid narrative.

He·roph·i·lus |hə'räfələs| (c. 335–c. 280 BC) Greek anatomist. He is regarded as the father of human anatomy for his fundamental discoveries concerning the anatomy of the brain, eye, and reproductive organs. Herophilus also studied the physiology of nerves, arteries, and veins.

Herr |her|, Herbert Thacker (1876–1933) U.S. engineer. He invented locomotive air-brake equipment and made improvements to turbine, oil, and gas engines.

Her·res·hoff |'herəs,hawf| U.S. family, including **James Brown Herreshoff** (1834–1930), an inventor. He invented a sliding seat for rowboats and improved marine steam boilers. His brother, **Nathanel Greene Herreshoff** (1848–1938), was a yacht manufacturer. He designed many America's Cup defenders, including *Vigilant* (1892) and *Defender* (1895); he also built the first seagoing torpedo boat for the U.S. Navy.

Her·rick |'herik|, Robert (1591–1674) English cavalier poet. He is best known for his collection *Hesperides* (1648), containing both secular and religious poems.

Her·rick |'herik|, Robert Welch (1868–1938) U.S. author and educator. Notable novels: *The Gospel of Freedom* (1898), *The Common Lot* (1904), and *Sometime* (1933).

Her·ri·man |'herəmən|, George Joseph (1880–1944) U.S. cartoonist and illustrator. He created the "Krazy Kat" comic strip and illustrated the "Archy and Mehitabel" books.

Her·ri·ot |'hereət|, James (1916–95) English short-story writer and veterinary surgeon; pseudonym of *James Alfred Wight*. His experiences as a veterinarian in North Yorkshire inspired a series of stories (the basis for a television series), including *All Creatures Great and Small* (1972).

Her·schel |'hərSHəl|, Sir (Frederick) William (1738–1822) German-born British astronomer. His cataloging of the skies resulted in the discovery of the planet Uranus. He was the first to appreciate the great remoteness of stars and developed the idea that the sun belongs to the star system of the Milky Way.

Her·schel |'hərSHəl|, Sir John (Frederick William) (1792–1871) English astronomer and physicist, son of William. He extended the sky survey to the southern hemisphere, carried out pioneering work in photography, and made contributions to meteorology and geophysics.

Her·sey |'hərsē|, John Richard (1914–93) U.S. author. Notable works: *A Bell for Adano* (1944, Pulitzer Prize) and *Hiroshima* (1946).

Her·shey |'hərSHē|, Alfred D. (1908–97) U.S. biologist. He conducted genetic research with Max Delbrück and Salvador Luria and discovered the recombination of viral DNA (1946). Nobel Prize for Physiology or Medicine, 1969.

Her·shey |'hərSHē|, Milton Snavely (1857–1945) U.S. industrialist. He established the Hershey chocolate company (1903).

Hertz |hərts|, Heinrich Rudolf (1857–94) German physicist and pioneer of radio communication. He continued the work of Maxwell on electromagnetic waves and was the first to broadcast and receive radio waves. Hertz also showed that light and radiant heat were electromagnetic in nature.

Herzl |'hərtsəl|, Theodor (1860–1904) Hungarian-born journalist, dramatist, and Zionist leader. The founder of the Zionist movement (1897), he worked for most of his life as a writer and journalist in Vienna.

Her·zog |'hərtsawg|, Werner (1942–) German movie director; born *Werner Stipetic*. Themes of remoteness in time and space are dominant elements throughout his movies, which include *Aguirre, Wrath of God* (1972) and *Fitz-carraldo* (1982).

He·si·od |ˈhesēəd| (*c.* 800 BC) Greek poet. One of the earliest known Greek poets, he wrote the *Theogony*, an epic poem on the genealogies of the gods, and *Works and Days*, which gave moral and practical advice and was the chief model for later ancient didactic poetry.

Hess |hes|, Harry Hammond (1906–69) U.S. geophysicist and educator. He made numerous discoveries regarding Pacific seamounts, island arcs, and seafloor spreading. He was chosen by NASA to be one of the first scientists to examine lunar rocks.

Hess |hes|, Dame Myra (1890–1965) English pianist. She was noted for her performances of the music of Schumann, Beethoven, Mozart, and Bach.

Hess |hes|, Rudolf (1894–1987) German Nazi politician, deputy leader of the Nazi Party (1934–41). Full name *Walther Richard Rudolf Hess*. In 1941, secretly and on his own initiative, he parachuted into Scotland to negotiate peace with Britain. He was imprisoned for the duration of the war and, at the Nuremberg war trials, sentenced to life imprisonment in Spandau prison, Berlin, where he died.

Hess |hes|, Victor Franz (1883–1964) Austrian-born U.S. physicist; born *Victor Franz Hess*. He showed that some ionizing radiation (later termed cosmic rays) was extraterrestrial in origin but did not come from the sun. Nobel Prize for Physics (1936), shared with C. D. Anderson.

Hes·se |ˈhesə|, Hermann (1877–1962) German-born Swiss novelist and poet. His work reflects his interest in spiritual values as expressed in Eastern religion and his involvement in Jungian analysis. Notable works: *Siddhartha* (1922), *Der Steppenwolf* (1927), and *The Glass Bead Game* (1943). Nobel Prize for Literature (1946).

Hes·ton |ˈhestən|, Charlton (1924–) U.S. actor. Notable movies: *Ben-Hur* (1959, Academy Award).

He·ve·sy |ˈhevəsHē|, George Charles de (1885–1966) Hungarian-born radio-chemist. He studied radioisotopes and invented the technique of labeling with isotopic tracers. Hevesy was also co-discoverer of the element hafnium (1923). Nobel Prize for Chemistry (1943).

Hew·itt |ˈhyo͞oət|, Abram Stevens (1822–1903) U.S. industrialist and politican. His iron manufacturing business featured the first open-hearth furnace (1862) in the U.S. and made the nation's first steel (1870). He served in the U.S. House of Representatives (1875–79, 1881–86) and as mayor of New York (1887–88).

Hew·itt |ˈhyo͞oət|, Don (1922–) U.S. television producer. He created and produced news programs and special events, including "60 minutes," the Kennedy-Nixon debates, and rocket launchings at Cape Canaveral.

Hew·lett |ˈhyo͞olət|, William R. (1913–) U.S. electrical engineer, inventor, and businessman. He invented an audio oscillator and cofounded the Hewlett-Packard Co. (1939).

Hey·er |ˈhīər|, Georgette (1902–74) English novelist. She is noted especially for her historical novels, which include numerous Regency romances such as *Regency Buck* (1935).

Hey·er·dahl |ˈhīərˌdäl|, Thor (1914–) Norwegian anthropologist. He is noted for his ocean voyages in primitive craft to demonstrate his theories of cultural diffusion, the best known of which was that of the balsa raft *Kon-Tiki* from Peru to the islands east of Tahiti in 1947.

Hey·ward |ˈhāwərd|, (Edwin) DuBose (1885–1940) U.S. author and poet. Full name *Edwin DuBose Heyward*. His first novel, *Porgy* (1925), dramatized with wife Dorothy, won a Pulitzer Prize and was made into the Gershwin opera *Porgy and Bess* (1935).

Hi·a·wa·tha |ˌhīəˈwäTHə| (*fl. c.* 1570) Mohawk Indian chief. Possibly a leader of mere legend, he is credited with establishing an Iroquois confederacy comprised of Onondaga, Mohawk, Oneida, Cayuga, and Seneca tribes. His name is said to mean "He Makes Rivers."

Hick·ok |ˈhikäk|, James Butler (1837–76) U.S. frontiersman and marshal; known as **Wild Bill Hickok**. The legend of his invincibility in his encounters with frontier desperadoes became something of a challenge to gunmen, and he was eventually murdered at Deadwood, South Dakota.

Hicks |'hiks|, Edward (1780–1849) U.S. artist. A primitive folk painter, he is noted for his *The Peaceable Kingdom* series of paintings.

Hicks |'hiks|, Sir John Richard (1904–89) English economist. He did pioneering work on general economic equilibrium (the theory that economic forces tend to balance one another rather than simply reflect cyclical trends), for which he shared a Nobel Prize with K. J. Arrow in 1972.

Hig·gin·both·am |'higən,bäTHəm|, A. Leon, Jr. (1928–) U.S. jurist. He became head of the U.S. Commission on Civil Rights in 1995. Awarded Spingarn Medal (1996).

Hig·gins |'higənz|, George Vincent (1939–) U.S. author. Notable novels *Friends of Eddie Coyle* (1971) and *Wonderful Years, Wonderful Years* (1988).

Hig·gin·son |'hēgənsən|, Thomas Wentworth Storrow (1823–1911) U.S. clergyman, journalist, and author. He was an activist for abolition and woman suffrage. He was also known for the correspondence he maintained with Emily Dickinson until her death (1886).

High·smith |'hīsmiTH|, Patricia (1921–95) U.S. writer of detective fiction; born *Patricia Plangman*. Her novels are noted for their black humor, particularly those featuring Tom Ripley, an amoral antihero resident in France. Her *Strangers on a Train* (1949) was filmed by Alfred Hitchcock in 1951.

Hi·jue·los |ē'hwelōs|, Oscar (1951–) U.S. author. His novels include *The Mambo Kings Play Songs of Love* (1989, Pulitzer Prize).

Hil·a·ry |'hilərē|, St. (*c.* 315–*c.* 367) French bishop. In *c.*350 he was appointed bishop of Poitiers, in which position he became a leading opponent of Arianism. Feast day, January 13.

Hil·da |'hildə|, St. (614–80) English abbess. Related to the Anglo-Saxon kings of Northumbria, she founded a monastery for both men and women at Whitby around 658, and was one of the leaders of the Celtic Church delegation at the Synod of Whitby. Feast day, November 17.

Hil·de·gard von Bing·en |'hildəgärd vawn 'biNGən|, St. (1098–1179) German abbess, scholar, composer, and mystic. A nun of the Benedictine order, she wrote scientific works, poetry, and music, and described her mystical experiences in *Scivias*.

Hil·dreth |'hildreTH|, Richard (1807–65) U.S. historian, author, and jurist. His works include the six-volume *A History of the United States* (1849–52).

Hil·fi·ger |'hil,figər|, Tommy (1952–) U.S. fashion designer

Hill |hil|, Anita (1956–) U.S. educator and author. Her book *Speaking Truth to Power* (1977), is based on her testimony of sexual harassment against Clarence Thomas during his Supreme Court nomination hearings (1991).

Hill |hil|, Benny (1925–92) English comedian; born *Alfred Hawthorne*. His risqué humor, as seen in the television series "The Benny Hill Show," had an international appeal.

Hill |hil|, George Roy (1922–) U.S. movie director. Notable movies: *The Sting* (1973, Academy Award).

Hill |hil|, (Norman) Graham (1929–75) English racecar driver. He became Formula One world champion in 1962 and 1975.

Hill |hil|, James Jerome (1838–1916) U.S. railroad executive, born in Canada.

Hill |hil|, Octavia (1838–1912) English housing reformer and cofounder of Britain's National Trust (1895).

Hill |hil|, Patty Smith (1868–1946) U.S. educator. She was an advocate in the nursery school movement.

Hill |hil|, Sir Rowland (1795–1879) English educationist, administrator, and inventor. He is chiefly remembered for his introduction of the penny postage-stamp system in 1840.

Hil·la·ry |'hilərē|, Sir Edmund (Percival) (1919–) New Zealand mountaineer and explorer. In 1953 Hillary and Tenzing Norgay were the first people to reach the summit of Mount Everest, as members of a British expedition.

Hil·lier |'hilyər|, James (1915–) U.S.

researcher and technology management executive. He co-invented and developed the first electron microscope in North America (1937).

Hill·man |ˈhilmən|, Sidney (1887–1946) U.S. labor leader, born in Lithuania. He helped to organize the Congress of Industrial Organizations (1935).

Hill·yer |ˈhilyər|, Robert Silliman (1895–1961) U.S. poet and educator. His *Collected Verse* (1933) won a Pulitzer Prize.

Hil·ton |ˈhiltən|, Conrad Nicholson (1887–1979) U.S. businessman. He formed the Hilton Hotels Corp. (1946).

Hil·ton |ˈhiltən|, James (1900–54) English author. Notable novels: *Lost Horizon* (1933), *Goodbye, Mr. Chips* (1934), and *Random Harvest* (1941).

Himes |hīmz|, Chester Bomar (1909–84) U.S. author. His books include a series of crime novels (1957–80) that feature the detective "Grave Digger" Johnson.

Himm·ler |ˈhimlər|, Heinrich (1900–45) German Nazi leader, chief of the SS (1929–45) and of the Gestapo (1936–45). He established and oversaw the systematic genocide of over 6 million Jews and other disfavored groups between 1941 and 1945. Captured by British forces in 1945, he committed suicide.

Hi·nault |ēˈnō|, Bernard (1954–) French racing cyclist. He won the Tour de France five times between 1978 and 1985 and won the Tour of Italy three times between 1980 and 1985.

Hin·de·mith |ˈhindəˌmiTH|, Paul (1895–1963) German composer. A leading figure in the neoclassical trend which began in the 1920s and an exponent of *Gebrauchsmusik* ("utility music"), he believed that music should have a social purpose. Notable works: *Mathis der Maler* (opera, 1938).

Hin·den·burg |ˈhindənˌbərg|, Paul Ludwig von Beneckendorff und von (1847–1934) German field marshal and statesman, president of the Weimar Republic (1925–34). Elected president in 1925 and reelected in 1932, he reluctantly appointed Hitler as chancellor in 1933.

Hine |hīn|, Lewis Wickes (1874–1940) U.S. photographer.

Hines |hīnz|, Earl (Kenneth) (1905–83) U.S. jazz pianist and band leader. Known as **Fatha Hines**. He originated the "trumpet style" of piano playing.

Hines |hīnz|, Gregory (1946–) U.S. dancer and choreographer.

Hin·gis |ˈhiNGgəs|, Martina (1981–) U.S. tennis player.

Hin·shel·wood |ˈhinsHəlˌwŏŏd|, Sir Cyril Norman (1897–1967) English physical chemist. He made fundamental contributions to reaction kinetics in gases and liquids. He later applied the laws of kinetics to bacterial growth, and suggested the role of nucleic acids in protein synthesis. Nobel Prize for Chemistry (1956).

Hin·ton |ˈhin(t)ən|, S. E. (Susan Eloise) (1948–) U.S. author. She is the author of young adult novels, including *That Was Then, This Is Now* (1971).

Hin·ton |ˈhin(t)ən|, William Augustus (1883–1959) U.S. physician. Noted for his development of tests for syphillis, he became the first black professor at Harvard Medical School (1949).

Hip·par·chus |hiˈpärkəs| (*c.* 146–127 BC) Greek astronomer and geographer. He is best known for his discovery of the precession of the equinoxes and is credited with the invention of trigonometry.

Hip·poc·ra·tes |hiˈpäkrətēz| (*c.* 460–377 BC) Greek physician, traditionally regarded as the father of medicine. His name is associated with the medical profession's Hippocratic oath from his attachment to a body of ancient Greek medical writings, probably none of which was written by him.

Hi·ro·hi·to |ˈhirōˈhitō| (1901–89) emperor of Japan (1926–89); full name *Michinomiya Hirohito*. Regarded as the 124th direct descendant of Jimmu, he refrained from involvement in politics, though he was instrumental in obtaining Japan's agreement to the unconditional surrender that ended World War II. In 1946 the new constitution imposed by the U.S. obliged him to renounce his divinity and become a constitutional monarch.

Hirsch·feld |ˈhərsHfeld|, Al (1903–) U.S. artist. He was a *New York Times* theater caricaturist (1925–); his murals and sculpture are represented in musuems nationally.

Hirsh·horn |'hərsHawrn|, Joseph Herman (1899–1981) U.S. financier and art collector, born in Latvia. He began as an office boy on Wall Street (1913) and built a fortune in mining and petroleum stocks; he built the Hirshhorn Museum in Washington, D.C. (1974) to house his art collection.

Hiss |his|, Alger (1904–96) U.S. public official. In 1948 he was accused of passing State Department documents to a Soviet agent. He pleaded innocent to these charges, but was later convicted of perjury in connection with the case, which became a political cause célèbre.

Hitch·cock |'hiCH,käk|, Sir Alfred (Joseph) (1899–1980) English movie director. Acclaimed in Britain for movies such as *The Thirty-Nine Steps* (1935), he moved to Hollywood in 1939. Among his later works, notable for their suspense and their technical ingenuity, are the thrillers *Strangers on a Train* (1951), *Psycho* (1960), and *The Birds* (1963).

Hitch·cock |'hiCH,käk|, Edward (1793–1864) U.S. geologist and educator. He performed a geological survey of Massachusetts (1830–33, 1837–41) and discovered dinosaur tracks in the Connecticut Valley; he also served as president of Amherst College (1845–54).

Hitch·ens |'hiCHənz|, Ivon (1893–1979) English painter. He is known chiefly for landscapes represented in an almost abstract style using areas of vibrant color.

Hit·ler |'hitlər|, Adolf (1889–1945) Austrian-born Nazi leader, chancellor of Germany (1933–45). He cofounded the National Socialist German Workers' (Nazi) Party in 1919, and came to prominence through his powers of oratory. While imprisoned for an unsuccessful putsch in Munich (1923–24) he wrote *Mein Kampf* (1925), an exposition of his political ideas. Becoming chancellor in 1933, he established the totalitarian Third Reich. His expansionist foreign policy precipitated World War II, while his fanatical anti-Semitism led to the Holocaust.

Hoag·land |'hōglənd|, Edward (1932–) U.S. author. His novels include *Seven Rivers West* (1986).

Ho·ban |'hōbən|, James (1762–1831) U.S. architect, born in Ireland. He designed the White House in Washington, D.C. (1793–1801) and its restoration and redesign after the War of 1812 (1815–29).

Ho·ban |'hōbən|, Russell Conwell (1925–) U.S. author and illustrator. His works include more than 50 children's books.

Ho·bart |'hōbərt; 'hōbärt|, Garret Augustus (1844–99) Vice president of the U.S. (1897–99).

Hob·be·ma |'häbəmə|, Meindert (*c.* 1638–1709) Dutch landscape painter. A pupil of Jacob van Ruisdael, he was one of the last 17th-century Dutch landscape painters.

Hobbes |häbz|, Thomas (1588–1679) English philosopher. Hobbes was a materialist, claiming that there was no more to the mind than the physical motions discovered by science, and he believed that human action was motivated entirely by selfish concerns, notably fear of death. In *Leviathan* (1651) he argued that absolute monarchy was the most rational, hence desirable, form of government.

Ho Chi Minh |'hō CHē ,min| (1890–1969) Vietnamese communist statesman, president of North Vietnam (1954–69); born *Nguyen That Thanh*. He led the Viet Minh against the Japanese during World War II, fought the French until they were defeated in 1954 and Vietnam was divided into North and South Vietnam, and deployed his forces in the guerrilla struggle that became the Vietnam War.

Hock·ing |'häkiNG|, William Ernest (1873–1966) U.S. educator and author. Notable books: *The Meaning of God in Human Experience* (1912) and *Science and the Idea of God* (1944).

Hock·ney |'häknē|, David (1937–) English painter and draftsman. He is best known for his association with pop art and for his Californian work of the mid-1960s, which depicts flat, almost shadowless architecture, lawns, and swimming pools.

Hodge |häj|, Frederick Webb (1864–1956) U.S. anthropologist and author. His books include the two-volume *Handbook of American Indians North of Mexico* (1907–10).

Hodg•es |'häjəz|, Johnny (1906–70) U.S. jazz alto saxophonist. Known as **Rabbit**. He was the mainstay of Duke Ellington's orchestra (1928–68), known for his earthy blues playing and ballad interpretation.

Hodg•kin |'häjkən|, Sir Alan Lloyd (1914–) English physiologist. With Andrew Huxley he demonstrated the role of sodium and potassium ions in the transmission of nerve impulses between cells. Nobel Prize for Physiology or Medicine (1963).

Hodg•kin |'häjkən|, Dorothy (Crowfoot) (1910–94) British chemist. She developed Sir Lawrence Bragg's X-ray diffraction technique for investigating the structure of crystals and applied it to complex organic compounds. Using this method she determined the structures of penicillin, vitamin B_{12}, and insulin. Nobel Prize for Chemistry (1964).

Hoe |hō|, Richard March (1812–86) U.S. inventor and industrialist. In 1846 he became the first printer to develop a successful rotary press, which greatly increased the speed of printing.

Hoff |hawf|, Marcian Edward, Jr. (1937–) U.S electronics engineer. His developments in computer technology include integrated circuits and the single-chip, general-purpose computer central processor.

Hof•fa |'hawfə|, Jimmy (1913–*c.* 75) U.S. labor union leader; full name *James Riddle Hoffa*. President of the Teamsters Union from 1957, he was imprisoned (1967–71) for attempted bribery of a federal court judge, fraud, and looting pension funds. His sentence was commuted by President Nixon and he was given parole in 1971 on condition that he resign as president of the union. He disappeared in 1975 and is thought to have been murdered.

Hoff•man |'hawfmən|, Dustin (Lee) (1937–) U.S. actor. A versatile method actor, he won Oscars for *Kramer vs Kramer* (1979) and *Rain Man* (1989).

Other notable movies: *The Graduate* (1967) and *Tootsie* (1983).

Hoff•man |'hawfmən|, Malvina (1887–1966) U.S. sculptor. He created bronzes of 110 racial types for the Field Museum in Chicago (1930–33).

Hoff•mann |'hawfmän|, E. T. A. (Ernst Theodor Amadeus) (1776–1822) German novelist, short-story writer, and music critic. His extravagantly fantastic stories provided the inspiration for Offenbach's opera *Tales of Hoffmann* (1881).

Hof•mann |'hawfmän|, Hans (1880–1966) U.S. artist, born in Germany. He was a leader in the style of abstract expressionism.

Hof•manns•thal |'hawfmän,stäl|, Hugo von (1874–1929) Austrian poet and dramatist. He wrote the libretti for many of the operas of Richard Strauss, including *Elektra* (1909). With Strauss and Max Reinhardt he helped found the Salzburg Festival.

Hof•stadt•er |'hōf,stætər|, Richard (1916–70) U.S. historian and author. Pulitzer Prize–winning works: *The Age of Reform: From Bryan to F.D.R.* (1955) and *Anti-Intellectualism in American Life* (1963).

Ho•gan |'hōgən|, Ben (1912–97) U.S. golfer.

Ho•garth |'hōgärTH|, Burne (1911–96) U.S. cartoonist. He created and illustrated the comic strip "Tarzan."

Ho•garth |'hōgärTH|, William (1697–1764) English painter and engraver. Notable works include his series of engravings on "modern moral subjects," such as *A Rake's Progress* (1735), which satirized the vices of both high and low life in 18th-century England.

Hogg |hawg|, James (1770–1835) Scottish poet.

Ho•kin•son |'hōkənsən|, Helen (1893–1949) U.S. cartoonist and author. She was best known for satirizing clubwomen; her cartoon characters, the "Hokinson Girls," frequently appeared in the *New Yorker* magazine.

Ho•ku•sai |'hōkŏŏ,sī|, Katsushika (1760–1849) Japanese painter and wood engraver. A leading artist of the *ukiyo-e* school, he represented aspects of Japanese everyday life in his woodcuts and strongly influenced European Impressionist artists.

Hol·a·bird |'häləbərd|, William (1854–1923) U.S. architect. With Martin Roche (1881), he began a firm that helped to develop the Chicago School of commercial architecture.

Hol·bein |'hōlbīn| German artists. **Hans Holbein** (c. 1465–1524); known as **Holbein the Elder**. His chiefly religious works include numerous cathedral altarpieces and such paintings as *Presentation of Christ* (1502) and *Fountain of Life* (1519). His son, **Hans Holbein** (c. 1497–1543), a painter and engraver, was known as **Holbein the Younger**. He became a well-known court portraitist in England and was commissioned by Henry VIII to supply portraits of the king's prospective brides. Notable works: *Dance of Death* (series of woodcuts, c. 1523–36); *Anne of Cleves* (miniature, 1539).

Hol·brook |'hōlbrook|, Hal (1925–) U.S. actor. A five-time Emmy winner, he is known for his stage portrayals of Mark Twain.

Hol·brook |'hōlbrook|, Josiah (1788–1854) U.S. educator.

Hol·den |'hōldən|, William (1918–81) U.S. actor. Born *William Beadle*. Notable movies: *Stalag 17* (1953, Academy Award).

Höl·der·lin |'hawldər,lēn; 'hœldər,lēn|, (Johann Christian) Friedrich (1770–1843) German poet. Most of his poems express a romantic yearning for harmony with nature and beauty. While working as a tutor he fell in love with his employer's wife, who is portrayed in his novel *Hyperion* (1797–99).

Hol·i·day |'hälədā|, Billie (1915–59) U.S. jazz singer; born *Eleanora Fagan*. She began her recording career with Benny Goodman's band in 1933, going on to perform with many small jazz groups. Her autobiography *Lady Sings the Blues* (1956) was made into a film in 1972.

Hol·in·shed |'hälənz,hed|, Raphael (died 1580) English chronicler. Although the named compiler of *The Chronicles of England, Scotland, and Ireland* (1577), Holinshed wrote only the *Historie of England* and had help with the remainder. The revised (1587) edition was used by Shakespeare.

Hol·land |'hälənd|, Clifford Milburn (1883–1924) U.S. civil engineer. He oversaw the construction of double subway tunnels under the East River in Manhattan and the Holland Tunnel under the Hudson River (1919–24).

Hol·land |'hälənd|, John Philip (1840–1914) U.S. inventor, born in Ireland. He designed the first submarine with an internal combustion engine for surface power and an electric motor for submerged cruising; his company became the Electric Boat Co.

Hol·lan·der |'hälləndər|, John (1929–) U.S. poet and educator. Since 1986, he has been the A. Bartlett Giamatti Professor of English at Yale University. Winner of the Bollingen Prize (1983), he has published more than 20 volumes of poetry as well as nonfiction, plays, anthologies, and children's books. Notable works: *The Night Mirror* (1971), *Reflections on Espionage* (1976), and *Powers of Thirteen* (1983).

Hol·lan·der |'hälləndər|, Nicole (1939–) U.S. cartoonist. She created the comic strip "Sylvia."

Hol·le·rith |'hälə,riTH|, Herman (1860–1929) U.S. engineer. He invented a tabulating machine using punched cards for computation, an important precursor of the electronic computer, and founded a company that later expanded to become the IBM Corp..

Hol·ley |'hälē|, Alexander Lyman (1832–82) U.S. engineer. He purchased the American rights to the Bessemer process (1863) and established the first steel plant in the U.S. (1865). He became known as "the father of modern American steel manufacture."

Hol·ly |'hälē|, Buddy (1936–59) U.S. rock-and-roll singer, guitarist, and songwriter; born *Charles Hardin Holley*. He recorded such hits as "That'll be the Day" with his band, The Crickets, before going solo in 1958. He was killed in an airplane crash.

Holm |hōm|, Celeste (1919–) U.S. actress. Notable movies: *Gentleman's Agreement* (1947, Academy Award).

Holmes |hōmz|, Arthur (1890–1965) English geologist, geophysicist and educator. He pioneered the isotopic dating of rocks and was one of the first supporters of the theory of continental drift. His *Principles of Physical Geology* (1944) became a standard text.

Holmes |hōmz|, Oliver Wendell (1809–94) U.S. physician, poet, and essayist. His best-known literary works are the humorous essays known as "table talks," which began with *The Autocrat of the Breakfast Table* (1857–58).

Holmes |hōmz|, Oliver Wendell (1841–1935) U.S. Supreme Court justice (1902–32). He became well known for his strong, articulate, and often dissenting opinions.

Holst |hōlst|, Gustav (Theodore) (1874–1934) English composer, of Swedish and Russian descent. He made his reputation with the orchestral suite *The Planets* (1914–16). Other notable works: *Choral Hymns from the Rig Veda* (1908–12).

Holt |hōlt| U.S. family, including: **Henry Holt** (1840–1926), a publisher and author. He organized Henry Holt and Co. (1873). His daughter **Winifred Holt** (1870–1945), a welfare worker, founded the New York Association for the Blind (1905).

Holt |hōlt|, John (1923–85) U.S. educational reformer and author. He was a leader in the home schooling movement in the 1970s. Notable works: *How Children Fail* (1964) and *How Children Learn.*

Ho·ly·field |'hōlē,fēld|, Evander (1962–) U.S. boxer. He was a three-time world heavyweight champion.

Ho·ly·oake |'hōlē,ōk|, Sir Keith (Jacka) (1904–83) New Zealand statesman, prime minister (1957 and 1960–72), governor general (1977–80).

Home of the Hirsel of Coldstream, Baron see DOUGLAS-HOME.

Ho·mer |'hōmər| (*c.* 7th–8th century BC) Greek epic poet. He is traditionally held to be the author of the *Iliad* and the *Odyssey*, though modern scholarship has revealed the place of the Homeric poems in a preliterate oral tradition. In later antiquity Homer was regarded as the greatest poet, and his poems were constantly used as a model and source by others.

Ho·mer |'hōmər|, Winslow (1836–1910) U.S. painter. He is best known for his seascapes, such as *Cannon Rock* (1895), painted in a vigorous naturalistic style considered to express the American pioneering spirit.

Hon·da |'händə|, Soichiro (1906–92) Japanese manufacturer. Opening his first factory in 1934, he began motorcycle manufacture in 1948 and expanded into car production during the 1960s.

Hon·eck·er |'hänəkər|, Erich (1912–94) East German communist statesman, head of state 1976–89. His repressive regime was marked by a close allegiance to the Soviet Union. He was ousted in 1989 as communism collapsed throughout eastern Europe.

Ho·neg·ger |'hänəgər|, Arthur (1892–1955) French composer, of Swiss descent. He lived and worked chiefly in Paris, where he became a member of the antiromantic group Les Six. His first major success was the orchestral work *Pacific 231* (1924).

Hooch |hōk|, Pieter de see DE HOOCH.

Hood |hŏŏd|, Raymond Mathewson (1881–1934) U.S. architect. Notable designs: the Tribune Tower (1922) in Chicago, and Rockefeller Center (1929–40) in New York City.

Hood |hŏŏd|, Thomas (1799–1845) English poet and humorist. He wrote much humorous verse but is chiefly remembered for serious poems such as "The Song of the Shirt".

Hooke |hŏŏk|, Robert (1635–1703) English scientist. He formulated the law of elasticity (Hooke's law), proposed an undulating theory of light, introduced the term *cell* to biology, postulated elliptical orbits for the earth and moon, and proposed the inverse square law of gravitational attraction. He also invented or improved many scientific instruments and mechanical devices, and designed a number of buildings in London after the Great Fire.

Hook·er |'hŏŏkər|, John Lee (1917–) U.S. blues singer and guitarist. He helped define the electric blues, which linked the blues with rock and roll.

Hook·er |'hŏŏkər|, Sir Joseph Dalton (1817–1911) English botanist and pioneer in plant geography. Hooker applied

Darwin's theories to plants and, with **George Bentham**, (1800–84), he produced a work on classification, *Genera Plantarum* (1862–83).

Hook·er |'hŏŏkər|, Thomas (c. 1586–1647) American clergyman, born in England. A founding settler of Hartford, Connecticut (1636), he wrote *Fundamental Orders* (1639), which was Connecticut's original constitution.

hooks |hŏŏks|, bell (c. 1955–   ) U.S. educator and author. Born *Gloria Watkins*. A champion of African-American and women's rights, she wrote *Teaching to Transgress: Education as Practice of Freedom* (1994).

Hooks |hŏŏks|, Benjamin Lawson (1925–   ) U.S. lawyer, clergyman, and civil rights leader. He was executive director of the NAACP (1977–93). Awarded Spingarn Medal (1986).

Hoo·ver |'hŏŏvər|, Herbert (Clark) see box. **Lou Henry Hoover** (1875–1944), wife of Herbert Clark Hoover and U.S. first lady (1929–33).

Hoo·ver |'hŏŏvər|, J. Edgar (1895–1972) U.S. government official, director of the FBI (1924–72); full name *John Edgar Hoover*. He reorganized the FBI into an efficient, scientific law-enforcement agency, but came under criticism for the organization's role during the McCarthy era and for its reactionary political stance in the 1960s.

Hoo·ver |'hŏŏvər|, William (Henry) (1849–1932) U.S. industrialist; manufacturer of Hoover vacuum cleaners.

Hope |hōp|, Bob (1903–   ) British-born U.S. comedian; born *Leslie Townes Hope*. He often adopted the character of a cowardly incompetent, cheerfully failing to become a romantic hero, as in the series of *Road* movies (1940–62).

Hope |hōp|, John (1868–1936) U.S. educator and civil rights leader. He was president of Morehouse College (1906–31) and of Atlanta University (1929–36).

Hope-Jones |hōp jōnz|, Robert (1859–1914) U.S. organ builder, born in England. He made numerous improvements in electrified organs. His Hope-Jones Organ Co. was sold to the Wurlitzer Co. (1910).

Hop·kins |'häpkənz|, Sir Anthony

Hoover, Herbert Clark
31st U.S. president

Life dates: 1874–1964
Place of birth: West Branch, Iowa (first president born west of the Mississippi River)
Mother: Hulda Randall Minthorn Hoover
Father: Jesse Clark Hoover
Wife: Lou Henry Hoover
Children: Herbert, Allan
College/University: Stanford University
Career: Mining engineer; entrepreneur
Political career: headed U.S. Food Administration in Europe during World War I; secretary of commerce; president; chairman of Commission on Organization of the Executive Branch of Government ("Hoover Commission")
Party: Republican
Home state: California
Opponents in presidential race: Alfred E. Smith
Term of office: March 4, 1929–March 3, 1933
Vice president: Charles Curtis
Notable events of presidency: Stock Market crash of October 1929; Great Depression; Reconstruction Finance Corporation created; London Naval Treaty; independence for the Philippines; "Star Spangled Banner" adopted as national anthem
Other achievements: Mining engineer/consultant in North America, Europe, Asia, Africa and Australia; after presidency, chairman of Famine Emergency Commission
Place of burial: West Branch, Iowa

(Philip) (1937–   ) Welsh actor. He won an Oscar for his performance in *The Silence of the Lambs* (1991). Other notable movies: *The Elephant Man* (1980) and *The Remains of the Day* (1993).

Hop·kins |'häpkənz|, Donald (1941–   ) U.S. public health physician. As a member of the U.S. delegation to the World Health Assembly in Geneva (1977–78, 1980–86) and deputy director of the Centers for Disease Control (1984–87), he worked to eradicate smallpox throughout the world.

Hop·kins |'häpkənz|, Sir Frederick Gowland (1861–1947) English biochemist. He carried out pioneering work on "accessory food factors" essential to the diet, later called vitamins. Nobel Prize for Physiology or Medicine (1929).

Hop·kins |'häpkənz|, Gerard Manley (1844–89) English poet. A shipwreck in 1876 inspired him to write "The Wreck of the Deutschland". Like his poems "Windhover" and "Pied Beauty" (both 1877), it makes use of Hopkins's "sprung rhythm" technique.

Hop·kins |'häpkənz|, Harry Lloyd (1890–1946) U.S. social worker and government official. He headed the Works Progress Administration (1935–38) and served as adviser to President Franklin D. Roosevelt.

Hop·kins |'häpkənz|, Mark (1802–87) U.S. philosopher and educator.

Hop·kins |'häpkənz|, Pauline (1859–1930) U.S. author. Her works include *Contending Forces: A Romance Illustrative of Negro Life North and South* (1900).

Hop·kins |'häpkənz|, Sam (1912–82) U.S. blues singer and guitarist. Known as **Lightnin'**.

Hop·kin·son |'häpkənsən|, Francis (1737–91) U.S. public official, musician, and author. He was a signer of the Declaration of Independence (1776) and helped design the first U.S. flag (1777). A gifted harpsichordist, he is considered the first native-born American composer of classical music.

Hop·per |'häpər|, Edward (1882–1967) U.S. realist painter. He is best known for his mature works, such as *Early Sunday Morning* (1930), often depicting isolated figures in bleak scenes from everyday urban life.

Hop·per |'häpər|, Grace Murray (1906–92) U.S. admiral, mathematician, and computer scientist.

Hop·per |'häpər|, Hedda (1890–1966) U.S. newspaper columnist. Born *Elda Furry*. She wrote a syndicated gossip column (1938–66).

Hor·ace |'hawrəs| (65–8 BC) Roman poet of the Augustan period; full name *Quintus Horatius Flaccus*. A notable satirist and literary critic, he is best known for his *Odes*, much imitated by later ages, especially by the poets of 17th-century England. His other works include *Satires* and *Ars Poetica*.

Hor·dern |'hawrdərn|, Sir Michael (Murray) (1911–95) English actor.

Hor·gan |'hawrgən|, Paul (1903–95) U.S. author. His books include *Great River* (1954, Pulitzer Prize).

Hork·heim·er |'hawrk,himər|, Max (1895–1973) German philosopher and sociologist. A leading figure of the Frankfurt School, he wrote *Dialectic of the Enlightenment* (1947), with his colleague Theodor Adorno, and *Critical Theory* (1968).

Hor·mel |hawr'mel|, George A. (1860–1946) U.S. businessman. The founder of Hormel Foods, he spoke out on economic issues and wrote a booklet called "The Golden Way to Unemployment Relief" (1935).

Horne |hawrn|, Lena Calhoun (1917–) U.S. singer and actress. In the early 1940s, she became the first African American to have a long-term contract with a Hollywood studio. Notable movies: *Stormy Weather* (1943) and *Till the Clouds Roll By* (1946). Awarded Spingarn Medal (1983).

Hor·ney |'hawrnī|, Karen (1885–1952) U.S. psychoanalyst, born in Germany. Born *Karen Danielsen*. Expelled from the New York Psychoanalytic Institute for her critique of Freudian practices (1941), she was the founder of the Association for Advancement of Psychoanalysis and the American Institute for Psychoanalysis.

Horns·by |'hawrnzbē|, Rogers (1896–1963) U.S. baseball player. Known as **Rajah**. Elected to Baseball Hall of Fame (1942).

Hor·nung |'hawrnəNG|, Paul (1935–) U.S. football player.

Ho·ro·witz |'hawrə,wits|, Vladimir (1903–89) Russian-born U.S. pianist. He first toured the U.S. in 1928, and settled there soon afterward. A leading international virtuoso, he was best known for his performances of Scarlatti, Liszt, Scriabin, and Prokofiev.

Hor·sa |'hawrsə| (died 455) see HENGIST AND HORSA.

Hor·ta |'hawrtə|, Victor (1861–1947) Belgian architect. He was a leading figure in art nouveau architecture and his work was notable for its innovative use of iron and glass.

Hotspur |'hätspər| The nickname of Sir Henry Percy (see PERCY).

Hou·di·ni |hoo͞'dēnē|, Harry (1874–1926) Hungarian-born U.S. magician and escape artist; born *Erik Weisz*. In the early 1900s he became famous for his ability to escape from all kinds of bonds and containers, from prison cells to aerially suspended straitjackets.

Hou·dry |'hoo͞drē; 'ōdrē|, Eugene Joules (1892–1962) French chemical engineer and inventor. In the 1920s, he discovered and developed a catalytic method for producing gasoline from crude oil. During World War II, he developed a method for producing synthetic rubber.

Hough·ton |'hōtn|, Henry Oscar (1823–95) U.S. publisher. His printing company, known as The Riverside Press, eventually became the Houghton Mifflin Co. (1864).

House·man |'howsmən|, John (1902–88) U.S. actor, born in Romania. Born *Jacques Haussmann*. Notable movies: *The Paper Chase* (1973, Academy Award).

Hous·man |'howsmən|, A. E. (Alfred Edward) (1859–1936) English poet and classical scholar. He is now chiefly remembered for the poems collected in *A Shropshire Lad* (1896), a series of nostalgic verses largely based on ballad forms.

Hous·ton |'hyoo͞stən|, Charles Hamilton (1895–1950) U.S. attorney and educator.

Hous·ton |'hyoo͞stən|, Samuel (1793–1863) U.S. soldier and politician. He was the first president of the Republic of Texas (1836–38; 1841–44) and the first U.S. senator from the state of Texas (1846–59). He was governor of Texas (1859–61) until ousted for refusing to swear allegiance to the Confederacy.

Hous·ton |'hyoo͞stən|, Whitney (1963–) U.S. singer. Her songs, a blend of gospel, ballad, pop, rock and rhythm and blues, include "I Will Always Love You" (1992).

How·ard |'howərd|, Catherine (*c.* 1520–42) fifth wife of Henry VIII. She married Henry soon after his divorce from Anne of Cleves in 1540. Accused of infidelity, she confessed and was beheaded.

How·ard |'howərd|, John (Winston) (1939–) Australian Liberal statesman, prime minister from 1996 with a Liberal–National Party coalition.

How·ard |'howərd|, Leslie (1893–1943) English actor; born *Leslie Howard Stainer*. He was best known for his roles as the archetypal English gentleman in movies such as *The Scarlet Pimpernel* (1935) and *Pygmalion* (1938). Other notable movies: *Gone with the Wind* (1939).

How·ard |'howərd|, Ron (1954–) U.S. actor and director. He was the child television star of "The Andy Griffith Show" (1960–68) and a star of "Happy Days" (1974–80). His film appearances include *The Music Man* (1962) and *American Graffiti* (1974). He directed *Backdraft* (1991) and *Apollo 13* (1995).

How·ard |'howərd|, Trevor (Wallace) (1916–88) English actor. He starred in *Brief Encounter* (1945) and *The Third Man* (1949) and later played character roles in movies such as *Gandhi* (1982).

Howe |how| . English officers. **Sir Richard Howe** (1726–99) was a naval officer. During the American Revolution, he was commander of the British fleet. His brother, **Sir William Howe** (1729–1814), was an army officer. He commanded the British troops at the Battle of Bunker Hill (1775) and succeeded Gage as commander in chief in North America (1775–78).

Howe |how| U.S. social reformers. **Samuel Gridley Howe** (1801–76). His success in educating a blind deaf-mute girl gained international attention. He was devoutly involved in such causes as public education, abolition, prison reform, and humane treatment of the mentally ill. His wife, **Julia Ward Howe** (1819–1910), was an author, poet, and social reformer. An activist in the causes of abolition, pacifism, and suffrage, she is best known as the author of "The Battle Hymn of the Republic" (1862). She was the first woman elected to the American Academy of Arts and Letters (1908).

Howe |how|, Elias (1819–67) U.S. mechanic and inventor. In 1846 he patented the first sewing machine. Its principles were adapted by Isaac Merrit Singer and others in violation of Howe's patent rights, and it took a seven-year litigation battle to secure the royalties.

Howe |how|, Gordie (1928–) U.S. hockey player.

Howe |how|, Irving (1920–93) U.S. educator, literary, and social critic. His books include *World of Our Fathers* (1976, National Book Award).

How·ells |'howəlz|, William Dean (1837–1920) U.S. novelist and critic. He was editor in chief of *Atlantic Monthly* (1971–81). His novels include *A Traveler from Altruria* (1894).

Howl·in' Wolf |'howlin ,woolf| (1910–76) U.S. blues singer, harmonica player, and guitarist. Born *Chester Arthur Burnett*. His hits include "Smokestack Lightnin'," "Little Red Rooster," and "I Ain't Superstitious."

Ho·xha |'hä,jə|, Enver (1908–85) Albanian statesman, founder of the Albanian Communist Party (1941), prime minister (1944–54), and first secretary of the Albanian Communist Party (1954–85). He rigorously isolated Albania from Western influences and implemented a Stalinist program of nationalization and collectivization.

Hoyle |hoil|, Sir Fred (1915–) English astrophysicist and writer. He was one of the proponents of the steady state theory of cosmology

Hua Guo Feng |,hwä ,gwō 'fəNG| (1920–) Chinese prime minister (1976-80) and chairman of the Communist Party (1976-81).

Hub·bard |'həbərd|, Cal (1900–77) U.S. sportsman. Full name *Robert Calvin Hubbard*. He was a football player and a baseball umpire, and was the only person to be a member of the halls of fame in both sports.

Hub·bard |'həbərd|, Elbert (1856–1915) U.S. author. His books include *A Message to Garcia* (1899).

Hub·bard |'həbərd|, Gardiner Greene (1822–97) U.S. lawyer. He was a financial backer of his son-in-law Alexander Graham Bell (from 1876) and the founder and first president of the National Geographic Society (1888–97).

Hub·bell |'həbəl|, Carl Owen (1903–88) U.S. baseball player. Known as **King Carl**. Elected to Baseball Hall of fame (1947).

Hub·ble |'həbəl|, Edwin Powell (1889–1953) U.S. astronomer. He studied galaxies and devised a classification scheme for them. In 1929 he proposed what is now known as Hubble's law with its constant of proportionality (Hubble's constant).

Hud·son |'hədsən|, Henry (*c.* 1575–1611) English explorer. He discovered the North American bay, river, and strait that bear his name. In 1610 he attempted to winter in Hudson Bay, but his crew mutinied and set Hudson and a few companions adrift, never to be seen again.

Hud·son |'hədsən|, Manley Ottmer (1886–1960) U.S. jurist. He was a judge at the Permanent Court of International Justice (1936–45) and author of *Progress in International Organization* (1932).

Hud·son |'hədsən|, William Henry (1841–1922) British naturalist and author, born in Argentina. An astute observer and lover of nature, he wrote *The Naturalist in La Plata* (1892) and *Nature in Downland* (1900).

Hug·gins |'həgənz|, Sir William (1824–1910) British astronomer. He pioneered spectroscopic analysis in astronomy, showing that nebulae are composed of luminous gas. He discovered the red shift in stellar spectra, attributing it to the Doppler effect and using it to measure recessional velocities.

Hughes |hyoōz|, Charles Evans (1862–1948) U.S. jurist and politcian. He was a U.S. Supreme Court justice (1910–16), a U.S. presidential candidate (1916), and Chief Justice of the U.S. (1930–41).

Hughes |hyoōz|, Howard (Robard) (1905–76) U.S. industrialist, movie producer, and aviator. He made his fortune through the Hughes Tool Co., made his debut as a movie director in 1926, and from 1935 to 1938 broke many world aviation records. Notable movies: *Hell's Angels* (1930) and *The Outlaw* (1941). For the last twenty-five years of his life he lived as a recluse.

Hughes |hyoōz|, (James Mercer) Langston (1902–67) U.S. writer. A leading voice of the Harlem Renaissance. He began a prolific literary career with *The Weary Blues* (1926), a series of poems on black themes using blues and jazz rhythms. Other poetry collections include *The Negro Mother* (1931).

Hughes |hyōōz|,Ted (1930–98) English poet; full name *Edward James Hughes*. His vision of the natural world as a place of violence, terror, and beauty pervades his work. He served as Britain's Poet Laureate (1984–98). Hughes was married to Sylvia Plath, a marriage he recounted in *Birthday Letters* (1998).

Hu•go |'hyōōgō|, Richard Franklin (1923–82) U.S. poet, author, and educator. Notable works: *A Run of Jacks* (1961) and *Selected Poems* (1979).

Hu•go |Y'gō; 'hyōōgō|,Victor (1802–85) French poet, novelist, and dramatist; full name *Victor-Marie Hugo*. A leading figure of French romanticism, he brought a new freedom to French poetry, and his belief that theater should express both the grotesque and the sublime of human existence overturned existing conventions. His political and social concern is shown in his novels. Notable works: *Hernani* (drama, 1830) and *Les Misérables* (novel, 1862).

Hui•zen•ga |hī'zeNGä|, (Harry) Wayne (1939–) U.S. businessman and corporate executive. The founder, chairman, and CEO of Blockbuster Entertainment Corp. (1987–94), he is an owner of the Florida Marlins, Miami Dolphins, and Florida Panthers.

Hull |həl|, Bobby (1939–) Canadian hockey player. Elected to the Hockey Hall of Fame, 1983.

Hull |həl|, Cordell (1871–1955) U.S. statesman. He served as a member of the U.S. House of Representatives (1907–21, 1923–31) and as U.S. secretary of state (1933–44). Received Nobel Peace Prize (1945).

Hull |həl|, Isaac (1773–1843) U.S. naval officer. As commander of the USS *Constitution* during the War of 1812, he won a stunning victory over the British *Guerrière*.

Hum•boldt |'həmbōlt|, Friedrich Heinrich Alexander Baron von (1769–1859) German explorer and scientist. He traveled in Central and South America (1799–1804) and wrote on natural history, meteorology, and physical geography.

Hume |'hyōōm|, David (1711–76) Scottish philosopher, economist, and historian. He rejected the possibility of certainty in knowledge and claimed that all the data of reason stem from experience. Notable works: *A Treatise of Human Nature* (1739–40) and *History of England* (1754–62).

Humes |hyōōmz|, H. L. (1926–) U.S. author. Full name *Harold Louis Humes*.

Hum•mel |'həmǝl|, Berta (1909–46) German artist. Also known as **Sister Maria Innocentia**. She created the sketches upon which M. I. Hummel figurines, made by the Franz Goebel Co., are based.

Hum•per•dinck |'həmpǝr,diNGk|, Engelbert (1854–1921) German composer. Influenced by Wagner, he is remembered as the composer of the opera *Hänsel und Gretel* (1893).

Hum•phrey |'həmfrē|, Doris (1895–1958) U.S. dancer and choreographer. She is known especially for her exploration of imbalance, fall, and recovery.

Hum•phrey |'həmfrē|, Hubert Horatio (1911–78) U.S. politican. He was vice president of the U.S. (1965–68) and a U.S. Democratic presidential candidate in 1968.

Hum•phreys |'həmfrēz|, David (1752–1818) U.S. author. During the American Revolution, he served as aide-de-camp to George Washington.

Hum•phreys |'həmfrēz|,Joshua (1751–1838) U.S. naval builder. Designed and supervised the construction of frigates (including the *Constitution* and *Constellation*) that formed the nucleus of the U.S. Navy in the War of 1812.

Hunt |hənt| U.S. family, including **William Morris Hunt** (1824&79), an artist. His paintings include *The Bathers* (1877). His brother, **Richard Morris Hunt** (1827–95), was an architect. Notable designs: Presbyterian Hospital (1872) in New York City, and Biltmore House (1895), a 225-room mansion in North Carolina.

Hunt |hənt|, Helen (1963–) U.S. actress. She won a 1997 Academy Award for *As Good as It Gets* and a 1997 Emmy Award for her role in the television series "Mad About You."

Hunt |hənt|, Henry Alexander (1866–1938) U.S. educator and social reformer. He was president of Fort Valley State College (1904–38). Spingarn Medal, 1930.

Hunt |hənt|, Ward (1810–86) U.S. Supreme Court justice (1873–82).

Hunt |hənt|, (William) Holman (1827–1910) English painter, one of the founders of the Pre-Raphaelite Brotherhood. He painted biblical scenes with extensive use of didactic and moral symbolism. Notable works: *The Light of the World* (1854) and *The Scapegoat* (1855).

Hun•ter |'hən(t)ər|, Holly (1958–   ) U.S. actress. Notable movies: *The Piano* (1993, Academy Award).

Hun•ter |'hən(t)ər|, Jim (1946–   ) U.S. baseball player. Full name *James Augustus Hunter*; known as **Catfish**. Elected to Baseball Hall of Fame (1987).

Hun•ter |'hən(t)ər|, John (1728–93) Scottish anatomist, regarded as a founder of scientific surgery. He also made valuable investigations in pathology, physiology, dentistry, and biology.

Hun•ting•ton |'hən(t)iNGtən|, Collis Potter (1821–1900) U.S. industrialist. He organized the Southern Pacific Railroad (1884).

Hunt•ley |'həntlē|, Chet (1911–74) U.S. television journalist. Born *Chester Robert Huntley*. With David Brinkley he coanchored *The Huntley-Brinkley Report* (1956–70).

Hurd |hərd|, Peter (1904–84) U.S. artist. He created sun-drenched landscapes of the American Southwest.

Hurs•ton |'hərstən|, Zora Neale (1903–60) U.S. novelist. Her novels reflect her interest in folklore, especially that of the Deep South. Notable works: *Jonah's Gourd Vine* (1934) and *Seraph on the Suwanee* (1948).

Hurt |hərt|, William (1950–   ) U.S. actor. Notable movies: *Kiss of the Spider Woman* (1985, Academy Award).

Husain variant spelling of HUSSEIN.

Hu•sák |'hoōsäk; 'hyoōsæk|, Gustáv (1913–91) Czechoslovak statesman, leader of the Communist Party of Czechoslovakia (1969–87) and president (1975–89). He succeeded Alexander Dubček following the Prague Spring of 1968 and purged the party of its reformist elements.

Huss |həs|, John (*c.* 1372–1415) Bohemian religious reformer; Czech name *Jan Hus*. A rector of Prague University, he supported the views of Wyclif, attacked ecclesiastical abuses, and was excommunicated in 1411. He was later tried and burnt at the stake. See also HUSSITE.

Hus•sein |hoō'sān|, ibn Talal (1935–99) Also **Husain**. King of Jordan (1953–99). Throughout his reign Hussein sought to maintain good relations both with the West and with other Arab nations, but his moderate policies created problems with the Palestinian refugees from Israel within Jordan. During the Gulf War he supported Iraq, but in 1994 he signed a treaty normalizing relations with Israel. He was succeeded by his son **Abdullah** (see ABDULLAH IBN HUSSEIN).

Hus•sein |hoō'sān|, Saddam (1937–   ) Also **Husain**. Iraqi president, prime minister, and head of the armed forces since 1979; full name *Saddam bin Hussein at-Takriti*. During his presidency Iraq fought a war with Iran (1980–88) and invaded Kuwait (1990), from which Iraqi forces were expelled in the Gulf War of 1991. He also ordered punitive attacks on Kurdish rebels in the north of Iraq and on the Marsh Arabs in the south.

Hus•serl |'hoōsərl|, Edmund (Gustav Albrecht) (1859–1938) German philosopher. His work forms the basis of the school of phenomenology; he rejected metaphysical assumptions about what actually exists, and explanations of why it exists, in favor of pure subjective consciousness as the condition for all experience, with the world as the object of this consciousness.

Hus•ton |'hyoōstən| U.S. acting family, including: Canadian-born **Walter Huston** (1884–1950). Born *Walter Houghston*. Notable movies: *Treasure of the Sierra Madre* (1948, Academy Award). His son, **John Huston** (1906–87), a director, was born in the U.S. but became an Irish citizen in 1964. He made his debut as a movie director in 1941 with *The Maltese Falcon*. Other notable movies: *The Treasure of the Sierra Madre* (1948; Academy Award), *The African Queen*

(1951), and *Prizzi's Honor* (1985). John's daughter, **Anjelica Huston** (1951–), is an actress. Notable movies: *Prizzi's Honor* (1985, Academy Award) and *The Addams Family* (1991).

Hutch·ins |'həCHənz|, Robert Maynard (1899–1977) U.S. educator and author.

Hutch·ins |'həCHənz|, Thomas (1730–89) U.S. cartographer. Appointed by Congress as "geographer to the U.S." (1781), he created maps that were the basis for all subsequent surveying in the West.

Hutch·in·son |'həCHənsən|, Anne Marbury (1591–1643) American religious leader, born in England. She was banished from Massachusetts Bay Colony in 1637 for her liberal views of grace and salvation. Having settled in New York in 1642, she and most of her family were killed by Indians.

Hut·son |'hətsən|, Don (1913–97) U.S. football player.

Hut·ton |'hətn|, James (1726–97) Scottish geologist. Although controversial at the time, his uniformitarian description of the processes that have shaped the surface of the earth is now accepted as showing that it is very much older than had previously been believed.

Hux·ley |'həkslē| English family, including: **Thomas Henry Huxley** (1825–95), a biologist. A surgeon and leading supporter of Darwinism, he coined the word *agnostic* to describe his own beliefs. Notable works: *Man's Place in Nature* (1863). His grandson, **Sir Julian Sorell Huxley** (1887–1975), was a biologist. He studied animal behavior and was a notable interpreter of science to the public. His brother, **Aldous (Leonard) Huxley** (1894–1963), was a novelist and essayist. After writing *Antic Hay* (1923) and *Brave New World* (1932), in 1937 he moved to California, where in 1953 he experimented with psychedelic drugs, writing of his experiences in *The Doors of Perception* (1954).

Huy·gens |'hoigənz|, Christiaan (1629–95) Dutch physicist, mathematician, and astronomer. His wave theory of light enabled him to explain reflection and refraction. He also patented a pendulum clock, improved the lenses of his telescope, discovered a satellite of Saturn, and recognized the nature of Saturn's rings, which had eluded Galileo.

Hy·att |'hīət|, Alpheus (1838–1902) U.S. zoologist and paleontologist. He helped to established the Marine Biological Labratory at Woods Hole, Massachusetts.

Hy·att |'hīət|, John Wesley (1837–1920) U.S. inventor. Creator of many inventions, including celluloid (1870).

Hyde, Edward see CLARENDON.

Hyde |hīd|, Henry Baldwin (1834–99) U.S. businessman. He founded the Equitable Life Assurance Society of the U.S. (1859).

Hy·pa·tia |,hī'pāSHə| (*c.* 370–415) Greek philosopher, astronomer, and mathematician. Head of the Neoplatonist school at Alexandria, she wrote several learned treatises as well as devising inventions such as an astrolabe.

Ii

Ia·coc·ca |ˌīə'kōkə|, Lee (1924–) U.S. industrialist. Full name *Lido Anthony Iacocca.* He is chairman of the board and chief executive officer of Chrysler Corp. (1979–).

Ibár·ruri Gó·mez |i'bäroorē 'gōmez|, Dolores (1895–1989) Spanish communist politician and leader of the Republicans during the Spanish Civil War; known as **La Pasionaria.**

Ibn Ba·tu·ta |ˌibən bæ'tootä| (*c.* 1304–68) Arab explorer. From 1325 to 1354 he journeyed through North and West Africa, India, and China, and wrote a vivid account of his travels in the *Rihlah.*

ibn Hus·sein, Abdullah see ABDULLAH IBN HUSSEIN.

Ibn Sa·ud |ˌibən sä'ood| (*c.* 1880–1953) king of Saudi Arabia (1932–53). Full name *Abd al-Aziz ibn Abd ar-Rahman ibn Faysal ibn Turki Abd Allah ibn Muhammad Al Saud.* A powerful Muslim leader, he founded Saudi Arabia (1932), having unified the various domains over which he had assumed sovereignty.

Ib·sen |'ibsən|, Henrik (1828–1906) Norwegian dramatist. He is credited with being the first major dramatist to write tragedy about ordinary people in prose. Ibsen's later works, such as *The Master Builder* (1892), deal increasingly with the forces of the unconscious and were admired by Sigmund Freud. Other notable works: *Peer Gynt* (1867), *A Doll's House* (1879), *Ghosts* (1881).

Ick·es |'ikəs|, Harold LeClair (1874–1952) U.S. lawyer and public official. He served as head of the federal Public Works Administration (1933–39) and as U.S. secretary of the interior (1933–46).

Ic·ti·nus |ik'tīnəs| (5th century BC) Greek architect. He is said to have designed the Parthenon in Athens with the architect Callicrates and the sculptor Phidias between 448 and 437 BC.

Igle·sias |ē'gläsyäs; i'gläzēəs|, Julio (1943–) Spanish singer. He has recorded more than sixty albums and is famous for love songs and ballads.

Ig·na·tius of Loy·o·la |ig'nāsHəs əv loi'ōlə|, St. (1491–1556) Spanish theologian and founder of the Society of Jesus (the Jesuit order). His *Spiritual Exercises* (1548), an ordered scheme of meditations, is still used in the training of Jesuits. Feast day, July 31.

Ig·na·tow, David (1914–97) U.S. poet. His works include *New and Collected Poems: 1970–1985* (1987).

Ikh·na·ton |ik'nät(ə)n| see AKHENATON.

Il·lich |'iliCH|, Ivan (1926–) Austrian-born U.S. educationist and writer. He advocated the deinstitutionalization of education, religion, and medicine. Notable works: *Deschooling Society* (1971) and *Limits to Medicine* (1978).

Iman |'ēmän| (1955–) U.S. model and entrepreneur, born in Somalia. The wife of David Bowie, she developed a line of cosmetics for women of color.

Im·ho·tep |im'hō,tep| (27th century BC) Egyptian architect and scholar, later deified. He probably designed the step pyramid built at Saqqara for the 3rd dynasty pharaoh Djoser.

Imus |'īməs|, Don (1940–) U.S. radio host and author. Host of the radio talk show "Imus in the Morning" (1988–) on WFAN, New York, as well as a television host for MS/NBC (1996–).

In·du·rain |'indyoo,rin|, Miguel (1964–) Spanish cyclist. He was the first person to win the Tour de France five consecutive times, (1991–95).

Ine |'inə| (688–726) king of Wessex (688–726). He extended the prestige and power of the throne, developing an extensive legal code.

Inge |'iNG|, William Motter (1913–73) U.S. playwright. Notable plays: *Come Back, Little Sheba* (1950), *Picnic* (1953), and *Bus Stop* (1955).

In·ger·soll |'iNGgər,sawl|, Robert Green (1833–99) U.S. lawyer and orator. During his lecture circuit (1870s), he promoted a secular religion that was labeled "agnosticism."

In·ger·soll |'iNGgər,sawl|, Robert Hawley (1859–1928) U.S. industrialist. He developed the mail-order business and chain-store system, and introduced the Ingersoll one-dollar watch (1892).

In·gra·ham |'iNGgrəhəm; 'iNGgrəm|, Prentiss (1843–1904) U.S. author. Using his own name as well as numerous pseudonyms, he wrote hundreds of dime novels, including *The Masked Spy* (1872).

In·gres |'æNGgrəs|, Jean Auguste Dominique (1780–1867) French painter. A pupil of Jacques-Louis David, he vigorously upheld neoclassicism in opposition to Delacroix's romanticism. Notable works: *Ambassadors of Agamemnon* (1801) and *The Bather* (1808).

In·man |'inmən|, Henry (1801–46) U.S. artist. A leading portraitist of his day, he helped found the National Academy of Design (1826).

In·ness |'inəs|, George (1825–94) U.S. artist. Notable paintings: *Peace and Plenty* (1865) and *The Home of the Heron* (1893).

In·sull |'insəl|, Samuel (1859–1938) U.S. financier, born in England. Private secretary to Thomas A. Edison, he built his financial empire based on holdings of electric companies. He fled the country when his businesses failed (1932).

Io·nes·co |yaw'neskō|, Eugène (1912–94) Romanian-born French dramatist, a leading exponent of the Theatre of the Absurd. Notable plays: *The Bald Soprano* (1950), *Rhinoceros* (1960).

Ipa·tieff |i'pät,yef|, Vladimir Nikolaievich (1867–1952) Russian-born U.S. chemist. He worked mainly on the catalysis of hydrocarbons, developing high octane fuels and techniques important to the petrochemical industry.

Iq·bal |,ik'bäl|, Sir Muhammad (1875–1938) Indian poet and philosopher, generally regarded as the father of Pakistan. As president of the Muslim League in 1930, he advocated the creation of a separate Muslim state in NW India; the demands of the League led ultimately to the establishment of Pakistan in 1947.

Ire·dell |'ī(ə)r,del|, James (1751–1799) U.S. Supreme Court justice (1790–99), born in England.

Ire·land |'īrlənd|, John (1838–1918) U.S. prelate, born in Ireland. He became Archbishop of St. Paul in 1884 and was a founder of Catholic University (1889) in Washington, D.C.

Ire·land |'īrlənd|, Patricia (1945–) U.S. lawyer and social reformer. She is president of the National Organization for Women (1991–).

Ire·nae·us |ī'rēnēəs|, St. (*c.* 130–*c.* 200 AD) Greek theologian, the author of *Against Heresies* (*c.*180), a detailed attack on Gnosticism. Feast day (in the Eastern Church) August 23; (in the Western Church) June 28.

Iron Chancellor see BISMARCK.

Iron Duke see WELLINGTON.

Iron Lady the nickname of Margaret Thatcher while she was British prime minister.

Irons |ī(ə)rnz|, Jeremy John (1948–) English stage, film, and television actor. Notable movies: *Reversal of Fortune* (1990, Academy Award).

Ir·ving |'ərviNG|, Sir Henry (1838–1905) English actor-manager; born *John Henry Brodribb*. He managed the Lyceum Theatre from 1878 to 1902, during which period he entered into a celebrated acting partnership with Ellen Terry.

Ir·ving |'ərviNG|, John (1942–) U.S. author. Notable works: *The Hotel New Hampshire* (1981) and *The World According to Garp* (1978).

Ir·ving |'ərviNG|, Washington (1738–1859) U.S. writer. He is best known for *The Sketch Book of Geoffrey Crayon, Gent* (1819–20), which contains such tales as "Rip Van Winkle" and "The Legend of Sleepy Hollow."

Is·a·bel·la I |,izə'belə| (1451–1504) queen of Castile (1474–1504) and of Aragon (1479–1504). Her marriage in 1469 to Ferdinand of Aragon helped to join together the Christian kingdoms of Castile and Aragon, marking the beginning of the unification of Spain. They instituted the Spanish Inquisition (1478) and supported Columbus's famous expedition of 1492.

Isa·bel·la of France |,izə'belə əv 'fræns| (1292–1358) daughter of Philip IV of France and wife of Edward II of England (1308–27). After returning to France in 1325, she organized an invasion of England in 1326 with her lover

Roger de Mortimer, murdering Edward and replacing him with her son, Edward III. Edward took control in 1330, executing Mortimer and sending Isabella into retirement.

Ish•er•wood |'isHər,wŏŏd|, Christopher (William Bradshaw) (1904–86) British-born U.S. novelist. Notable novels: *Mr. Norris Changes Trains* (1935), *Goodbye to Berlin* (1939; filmed as *Cabaret*, 1972).

Ishi•gu•ro |'isHi'gŏŏ,rō|, Kazuo (1954–) Japanese-born British novelist. Notable novels: *The Remains of the Day* (1989).

Is•i•dore of Se•ville |'izə,dawr əv sə 'vil|, St. (*c.* 560–636) Spanish archbishop and Doctor of the Church; also called **Isidorus Hispalensis**. He is noted for his *Etymologies*, an encyclopedic work used by many medieval authors. Feast day, April 4.

Isoc•ra•tes |ī'säkrə,tēz| (436–338 BC) Athenian orator whose written speeches are among the earliest political pamphlets.

Ito |'ē,tō|, Prince Hirobumi (1841–1909) Japanese statesman, premier four times between 1884 and 1901. He was prominent in drafting the Japanese constitution (1889) and helped to establish a bicameral national diet (1890). He was assassinated by a member of the Korean independence movement.

Ivan |'īvən; ē'vän| the name of six rulers of Russia: **Ivan I** (*c.* 1304–41). He was the grand duke of Muscovy (1328–40). He strengthened and enlarged the duchy, making Moscow the ecclesiastical capital in 1326. **Ivan II** (1326–59) was the grand duke of Muscovy (1353–59); known as **Ivan the Red**. **Ivan III** (1440–1505) was the grand duke of Muscovy (1462–1505); known as **Ivan the Great**. He consolidated and en-

larged his territory, defending it against a Tartar invasion in 1480 and adopting the title "Ruler of all Russia" in 1472. **Ivan IV** (1530–84), grand duke of Muscovy (1533–47) and first czar of Russia (1547–84); known as **Ivan the Terrible**. He captured Kazan, Astrakhan, and Siberia, but the Tartar siege of Moscow and the Polish victory in the Livonian War (1558–82) left Russia weak and divided. In 1581 Ivan killed his eldest son Ivan in a fit of rage, the succession passing to his mentally handicapped second son Fyodor. **Ivan V** (1666–96), nominal czar of Russia (1682–96). **Ivan VI** (1740–64), infant czar of Russia (1740–01).

Ivan the Great Ivan III of Russia (see IVAN).

Ivan the Terrible Ivan IV of Russia (see IVAN).

Ives |'īvz|, Burl (1909–95) U.S. actor and folk singer. Born *Icle Ivanhoe*. Notable movies: *The Big Country* (1958, Academy Award).

Ives |'īvz|, Charles (Edward) (1874–1954) U.S. composer, noted for his use of polyrhythms, polytonality, quartertones, and aleatoric techniques. Notable works: *The Unanswered Question* (chamber work, 1906) and *Three Places in New England* (for orchestra, 1903–14).

Ives |'īvz|, Frederic Eugene (1856–1937) U.S. inventor. He was responsible for many improvements in photographic printing, including the halftone photogravure process.

Ivo•ry |'īv(ə)rē|, James (1928–) U.S. movie director. He has made a number of movies in partnership with producer Ismail Merchant, including *Heat and Dust* (1983), *Howard's End* (1992), *A Room with a View* (1986), and *The Remains of the Day* (1993).

Jj

Jack·son |'jæksən|. U.S. pop singers: **Michael Jackson** (1958–) was the top-selling pop artist of the 1980s; his hit albums include *Dangerous* and *Thriller*. **Janet Damita Jackson** (1966–), his sister and the youngest of the Jackson family, sang hits including "That's the Way Love Goes" (1993).

Jack·son |'jæksən|, **Glenda** (1936–) British actress. Notable movies: *Women in Love* (1970, Academy Award).

Jack·son |'jæksən|, **Howell Edmunds** (1832–95) U.S. Supreme Court justice (1893–95).

Jack·son |'jæksən|, **Jesse (Louis)** (1941–) U.S. political and social activist; civil rights leader, U.S. civil rights activist, politician and clergyman. After working with Martin Luther King in the civil rights struggle, he competed for but failed to win the Democratic Party's 1984 and 1988 presidential nominations.

Jack·son |'jæksən|, **Mahalia** (1911–72) U.S. gospel singer and musician. Her 1947 recording of "Move Up a Little Higher" sold over a million copies.

Jack·son |'jæksən|, **Reggie** (1946–) U.S. baseball player. Full name *Reginald Martinez Jackson*; known as **Mr. October**. Elected to Baseball Hall of Fame (1993).

Jack·son |'jæksən|, **Robert Houghwout** (1892–1954) U.S. Supreme Court justice (1941–54). He was chief prosecutor for the U.S. at the Nuremberg war crimes tribunal (1945–46).

Jack·son |'jæksən|, **Scoop** (1912–83) U.S. politician. Full name *Henry Martin Jackson*. As a member of the U.S. Senate from Washington (1953–83), he led the Democratic neo-conservatives and twice campaigned unsuccessfully for the Democratic presidential nomination (1972 and 1976).

Jack·son |'jæksən|, **Shirley** (1919–65) U.S. author. She is best known for her tales of the macabre or supernatural. Notable novels: *The Bird's Nest* (1954) and *The Haunting of Hill House* (1959).

Jack·son |'jæksən|, **Stonewall** (1824–

Jackson, Andrew
7th U.S. president

Life dates: 1767–1845

Place of birth: in Carolinas, perhaps in Waxhaw, South Carolina

Mother: Elizabeth Hutchinson Jackson

Father: Andrew Jackson

Wife: Rachel Donelson Robards Jackson

Children: none (adopted his wife's nephew, renamed Andrew Jackson, Jr.)

Nickname: "Old Hickory"

College/University: none

Military service: served at the age of 13 in the S. Car. militia in the Revolutionary War; defeated Creek Indians, Battle of Horseshoe Bend, 1813; victorious over British at Battle of New Orleans, 1815; defeated Seminole Indians in Florida, 1817

Career: Lawyer; businessman

Political career: U.S. House of Representatives; U.S. Senate; justice, Tennessee Supreme Court; provisional governor of Florida; U.S. Senate; president

Home state: Tennessee

Party: Democratic

Opponents in presidential races: John Quincy Adams; Henry Clay

Term of office: March 4, 1829–March 3, 1837

Vice presidents: John Caldwell Calhoun; Martin Van Buren

Notable events of presidency: vetoed renewal of charter of the Bank of the United States; Indian Removal Act of 1830; proclamation opposing nullification issued; Specie Circular issued; Texas declaration of independence; Arkansas admitted as 25th state; Wisconsin Territory organized; Michigan admitted as 26th state; independence of Texas recognized

Other achievements: admitted to the North Carolina and Tennessee bars; successful real estate speculator; delegate to Tennessee State Constitutional Convention

Place of burial: The Hermitage, near Nashville, Tennessee

63) Confederate general. Full name *Thomas Jonathan Jackson*. The brilliant commander of the Shenandoah campaign (1861–62), he was mortally wounded by one of his own sharpshooters at Chancellorsville.

Jack·son |'jæksən|, William Henry (1843–1942) U.S. photographer. His photographs chronicled the expansion of the American West and particularly the construction of the Union Pacific Railroad.

Jack the Rip·per |jæk| (19th century) An unidentified English murderer. In 1888 at least six prostitutes were brutally killed in the East End of London, the bodies being mutilated in a way that indicated a knowledge of anatomy. The authorities received taunting notes from a person calling himself Jack the Ripper and claiming to be the murderer, but the cases remain unsolved.

Ja·co·bi |jə'kōbē; yä'kōbē|, Karl Gustav Jacob (1804–51) German mathematician. He worked on the theory of elliptic functions, in competition with Niels Abel.

Ja·cobs |'jākəbz|, Bernard B. (1916–) U.S. Broadway producer. With Gerald Schoenfeld (1924–), he took over the Shubert Organization.

Jacopo della Quercia see DELLA QUERCIA.

Jac·quard |zнä'kär(d)|, Joseph-Marie (1752–1834) French inventor. He invented the Jacquard loom (1801).

Ja·cuz·zi |jə'koōzē|, Candido (1903–) U.S. businessman. Developed the "jacuzzi," a portable aerating jet pump designed for home hydrotherapy.

Jag·ger |'jægər|, Mick (1943–) English rock singer and songwriter; full name *Michael Philip Jagger*. He formed the Rolling Stones *c.* 1962 with guitarist Keith Richards (1943–), a childhood friend.

Jakes |jāks|, John (1932–) U.S. author. Pseudonyms **Alan Payne** and **Jay Scotland**. He was a prolific author of such works as the *Kent Family Chronicles*.

Ja·kob·son |'yäkəbsən|, Roman (Osipovich) (1896–1982) Russian-born U.S. linguist. His most influential work described universals in phonology.

Jalal ad-Din ar-Rumi |jə'läl ооd'dēn ər 'roōmē| (1207–73) Persian poet and Sufi mystic, founder of the order of whirling dervishes; also called **Mawlana**.

James[1] the name of seven Stuart kings of Scotland: **James I** (1394–1437), son of Robert III, reigned 1406–37. A captive of the English until 1424, he returned to a country divided by baronial feuds, but managed to restore some measure of royal authority. **James II** (1430–60), son of James I, reigned 1437–60. He considerably strengthened the position of the Crown by crushing the powerful Douglas family (1452–55). **James III** (1451–88), son of James II, reigned 1460–88. His nobles raised an army against him in 1488, using his son, the future James IV, as a figurehead. The king was defeated and killed in battle. **James IV** (1473–1513), son of James III, reigned 1488–1513. He forged a dynastic link with England through his marriage to Margaret Tudor, the daughter of Henry VII, and revitalized the traditional pact with France. When England and France went to war in 1513 he invaded England, but died in defeat at Flodden. **James V** (1512–42), son of James IV, reigned 1513–42. During his reign Scotland was dominated by French interests. Relations with England deteriorated in the later years, culminating in an invasion by Henry VIII's army. **James VI** (1566–1625), James I of England (see JAMES[2]). **James VII** (1633–1701), James II of England (see JAMES[2]).

James[2] the name of two kings of England, Ireland, and Scotland: **James I** (1566–1625), son of Mary, Queen of Scots, king of Scotland (as James VI) 1567–1625, and of England and Ireland 1603–25. He inherited the throne of England from Elizabeth I, as great-grandson of Margaret Tudor, daughter of Henry VII. His declaration of the divine right of kings and his intended alliance with Spain made him unpopular with Parliament. **James II** (1633–1701), son of Charles I, king of England, Ireland, and (as James VII) Scotland 1685–88. His Catholic beliefs led to the rebellion of the Duke of Monmouth in

1685 and to James's later deposition in favor of William of Orange and Mary II. Attempts to regain the throne resulted in James's defeat at the Battle of the Boyne in 1690.

James³ |jāmz| U.S. family of intellectuals: **Henry James** (1811–82), father of Henry and William, a philosopher who wrote on theology and social philosophy and was a friend of many literary figures. His more prominent son, **Henry James** (1843–1916), an author and critic. His early novels, notably *The Portrait of a Lady* (1881), deal with the relationship between European civilization and American life, while later works, such as *What Maisie Knew* (1897), depict English life. **William James** (1842–1910), brother of Henry James the novelist. He was a psychologist, philosopher, and educator. A leading exponent of pragmatism, he sought a functional definition of truth, and in psychology he is credited with introducing the concept of the stream of consciousness.

James |jāmz|, Daniel, Jr. (1920–78) U.S. air force officer. Known as **Chappie**. He headed the North American Air Defense Command (1975–78), and became the first African American in U.S. military history to attain the rank of four-star general (1976).

James |jāmz|, Edmund Janes (1855–1925) U.S. political scientist and educator. He founded the American Economic Association (1885) and the American Academy of Political and Social Science (1889).

James |jāmz|, Etta (1938–) U.S. soul singer. Born *Jamesetta Hawkins*. Grammy Award, 1994.

James |jāmz|, Jesse Woodson (1847–82) U.S. outlaw. With brother Frank (1843–1915), he was a member of a notorious gang of train and bank robbers.

James |jāmz|, St. (died *c.* 44 AD) an Apostle, son of Zebedee and brother of John; known as **St. James the Great**. He was put to death by Herod Agrippa I; afterward, according to a Spanish tradition, his body was taken to Santiago de Compostela. Feast day, July 25.

James |jāmz|, St. (1st century) an Apostle; known as **St. James the Less**. Feast

day (in the Eastern Church) October 9; (in the Western Church) May 1.

James |jāmz|, St. (died *c.* 62 AD) leader of the early Christian Church at Jerusalem; known as **St. James the Just** or **the Lord's Brother**. He was put to death by the Sanhedrin. Feast Day, March 1.

James |jāmz|, Thomas (*c.* 1593–1635) English navigator. During his search for the Northwest Passage (1631, 1633), he explored the southern extension of Hudson Bay (James Bay).

Jame·son |'jāmsən|, John Franklin (1859–1937) U.S. historian and educator. He was a founder of the American Historical Association (1884) and headed the division of manuscripts at the Library of Congress (1928–37).

Ja·mi·son |'jāməsən|, Judith (1944–) U.S. dancer and choreographer. She performed with the Alvin Ailey American Dance Theater in New York City from 1965 and was star of the Broadway show *Sophisticated Ladies* (1980).

Ja·ná·ček |'yänə‚CHek|, Leoš (1854–1928) Czech composer. His works, much influenced by Moravian folk songs, include the opera *The Cunning Little Vixen* (1924) and the *Glagolitic Mass* (1927).

Jan·sen |'jænsən|, Cornelius Otto (1585–1638) Flemish Roman Catholic theologian and founder of Jansenism. A strong opponent of the Jesuits, he proposed a reform of Christianity through a return to St. Augustine.

Jansens (also **Janssen van Ceulen**) variant spelling of JOHNSON, CORNELIUS.

Jan·sky |'jænskē|, Karl Guthe (1905–50) U.S. electrical engineer. He founded the science of radio astronomy when he discovered radio waves that originated in distant space (1931).

Jan·son |'yänsawn|, Anton (1620–87) Dutch type designer. He designed the Janson typeface.

Jaques-Dal·croze |'zHäk däl'krōz|, Émile (1865–1950) Austrian-born Swiss music teacher and composer. He evolved the eurhythmics method of teaching music and dance, establishing a school for eurhythmics instruction in 1910.

Jar·man |'järmən|, Derek (1942–94) English movie director and painter.

Jar·rell |jə'rel|, Randall (1914–65) U.S. author, poet, and educator. His works include *The Woman at the Washington Zoo* (1960, National Book Award).

Jar·ry |'zнäri|, Alfred (1873–1907) French dramatist. His satirical farce *Ubu Roi* (1896) anticipated surrealism and the Theatre of the Absurd.

Ja·ru·zel·ski |ˌyärə'zelski|, Wojciech (1923–) Polish general and statesman, prime minister (1981–85), head of state (1985–89), and president (1989–90). He responded to the rise of Solidarity by imposing martial law and banning labor union activities, but following the victory of Solidarity in the 1989 elections he supervised Poland's transition to a democracy.

Jar·vik |'järvik|, Robert K. (1946–) U.S. biomedical research scientist. He patented an artificial heart driven by compressed air.

Ja·wor·ski |jə'wawrski|, Leon (1905–1982) U.S. lawyer and politician. He became the Watergate special prosecutor after Archibald Cox was fired (1973).

Jay |jā|, John (1745–1829) U.S. jurist and statesman. With James Madison and Alexander Hamilton, he was author of *The Federalist* (1787–88). He served as Chief Justice of the U.S. (1789–95).

Jean Paul |ˌzнän 'pawl| (1763–1825) German novelist; pseudonym of **Jo·hann Paul Friedrich Richter**. He is noted for his romantic novels, including *Hesperus* (1795), and for comic works such as *Titan* (1800–03).

Jeans |'jēnz|, Sir James Hopwood (1877–1946) English physicist and astronomer. Jeans proposed a theory for the formation of the solar system and was the first to propose that matter is continuously created throughout the universe, one of the tenets of the steady state theory.

Jef·fers |'jefərz|, Robinson (1887–1962) U.S. poet. Full name *John Robinson Jeffers*. Notable books of verse: *Tamar and Other Poems* (1924) and *The Women at Point Sur* (1927).

Jef·fer·son |'jefərsən|, Thomas see box.
Martha Wayles Skelton Jefferson (1748–82), wife of Thomas Jefferson.

Jefferson, Thomas
3rd U.S. president

Life dates: 1743–1826
Place of birth: Shadwell, Goochland (now Albemarle) County, Va.
Mother: Jane Randolph Jefferson
Father: Peter Jefferson
Wife: Martha Wayles Skelton
Children: Martha, Jane, Mary ("Marie," "Polly"), Lucy, Lucy Elizabeth
Nickname: Sage of Monticello
College/University: College of William and Mary
Career: Lawyer; writer
Political career: member of Virginia House of of Burgesses; delegate, Second Continental Congress; member, Virginia House of Delegates; governor of Virginia; U.S. House of Representatives; U.S. secretary of state; vice president (under John Adams); president
Party: Democratic-Republican
Home state: Virginia
Opponents in presidential races: John Adams, Thomas Pinckney; Aaron Burr, John Adams, Charles C. Pinckney; Charles C. Pinckney
Term of office: March 4, 1801–March 3, 1809
Vice presidents: Aaron Burr; George Clinton
Notable events of presidency: war with Barbary States; *Marbury vs. Madison* Supreme Court decision; Louisiana Territory purchased from France; Lewis and Clark expedition; Embargo Act; prohibition of the importation of slaves; Ohio admitted as 17th state; Michigan Territory established; Illinois Territory established; Non-Intercourse Act prohibiting trade with Grade Britain and France
Other achievements: Admitted to the Virginia bar; published influential pamphlet "A Summary View of the Rights of British America" (1774); chairman of the committee to prepare the Declaration of Independence; minister plenipotentiary to France; championed the founding of the University of Virginia
Place of burial: at Monticello, in Charlottesville, Va.

Jef·fer·son |'jefərsən|, Blind Lemon (1897–1930) U.S. blues singer and guitarist. His hit song "Booger Rooger

Blue" coined the term that became "boogie-woogie."

Jehu |'jē͵h(y)o͞o| (842–815 BC) king of Israel. He was famous for driving his chariot furiously (2 Kings 9).

Jel·li·coe |'jeləkō|, John Rushworth, 1st Earl (1859–1935) British admiral, commander of the Grand Fleet at the Battle of Jutland (1916).

Jen·kins |'jeNGkənz|, Roy (Harris), Baron Jenkins of Hillhead (1920–) English politician and scholar.

Jen·ney |'jenē|, William Le Baron (1832–1907) U.S. architect. His designs include the Home Insurance Co. Building (1884–85) in Chicago.

Jen·nings |'jeniNGz|, Peter Charles (1938–) U.S. television news anchorman, born in Canada. He anchors ABC's *World News Tonight* (1983–).

Jen·nings |'jeniNGz|, Waylon (1937–) U.S. country musician. Notable songs: "Momas Don't Let Your Babies Grow Up to be Cowboys" and "The Eagle."

Jen·son |'jensən|, Nicolas (c. 1420–80) French engraver and printer. An apprentice to Gutenberg, he established his own business in Venice and perfected roman type (1470).

Jer·e·miah |͵jerə'mīə| (c. 650–c. 585 BC) Hebrew prophet. He foresaw the fall of Assyria, the conquest of his country by Egypt and Babylon, and the destruction of Jerusalem. The biblical Lamentations are traditionally ascribed to him.

Je·rit·za |'yeritsə|, Maria (1887–1982) Czech operatic soprano. Born *Mizzi Jedička*. She sang with the Metropolitan Opera (1921–32).

Je·rome |jə'rōm|, St. (c. 342–420) Doctor of the Church. He is chiefly known for his compilation of the Vulgate Bible. Feast day, September 30.

Jer·vis |'jərvəs|, John, Earl St. Vincent (1735–1823) British admiral. In 1797, as commander of the British fleet, he defeated a Spanish fleet off Cape St. Vincent, for which he was created Earl St. Vincent.

Jes·per·sen |'yespərsən|, (Jens) Otto (Harry) (1860–1943) Danish philologist, grammarian, and educationist. He promoted the use of the "direct method" in language teaching with the publica-

tion of his theoretical work *How to Teach a Foreign Language* (1904). Other notable works: *Modern English Grammar* (1909–49).

Jes·sel |'jesəl|, George Albert (1898–1981) U.S. entertainer. He is best known as a master of ceremonies.

Je·sus |'jēzəs| (c. 6 BC–c. 30 AD) the central figure of the Christian religion. Also **Jesus Christ** or **Jesus of Nazareth**. Jesus conducted a mission of preaching and healing (with reported miracles) in Palestine in about AD 28–30, which is described in the Gospels. His followers considered him to be the Christ or Messiah and the Son of God, and belief in his resurrection from the dead is the central tenet of Christianity.

Jett |jet|, Joan (1960–) U.S. rock guitarist and singer. Notable albums: *Up Your Alley* (1988).

Jew·ett |'jo͞oət|, Charles Coffin (1816–68) U.S. librarian. He was the first librarian of the Smithsonian Institution (1848–54) and later became superintendent of the Boston Public Library (1855–68).

Jew·ett |'jo͞oət|, Sarah Orne (1849–1909) U.S. author and poet. Her works include *The Country of the Pointed Firs* (1896).

Jew·i·son |'jo͞oəsən|, Norman (1929–) Canadian movie director and producer. He is known particularly for the drama *The Cincinnati Kid* (1965) and *In the Heat of the Night* (1971), which won five Oscars, the musical *Fiddler on the Roof* (1971), and the romantic comedy *Moonstruck* (1987).

Je·ze·bel |'jezəbel| (9th century BC) a Phoenician princess, traditionally the great-aunt of Dido and in the Bible the wife of Ahab king of Israel. She was denounced by Elijah for introducing the worship of Baal into Israel (1 Kings 16:31, 21:5–15, 2 Kings 9:30–37). Her use of make-up shocked Puritan England.

Jiang Jie Shi variant form of CHIANG KAI-SHEK.

Ji·mé·nez de Cis·ne·ros |hi'menəs də sis'nerōs|, Francisco (1436–1517) Spanish cardinal and statesman, regent of Spain (1516–17). Also **Ximenes de Cisneros**. He was Grand Inquisitor for

Castile and Léon from 1507 to 1517, during which time he undertook a massive campaign against heresy, having some 2,500 alleged heretics put to death. **Jin•nah** |'jinə|, Muhammad Ali (1876–1948) statesman and founder of Pakistan. He headed the Muslim League in its struggle with the Hindu-oriented Indian National Congress over Indian independence, and in 1947 he became the first governor general and president of Pakistan.

Joan of Arc |jōn əv 'ärk|, St. (*c.* 1412–31) French national heroine; known as **the Maid of Orleans**. She led the French armies against the English in the Hundred Years War, relieving besieged Orleans (1429) and ensuring that Charles VII could be crowned in previously occupied Reims. Captured by the Burgundians in 1430, she was handed over to the English, convicted of heresy, and burnt at the stake. She was canonized in 1920. Feast day, May 30.

Jobs |jäbz|, Steven (Paul) (1955–) U.S. computer entrepreneur. He set up the Apple computer company in 1976 with *Steve Wozniak* (1950–), remaining chairman of the company until 1985.

Joel |jōl|, Billy (1949–) U.S. pop singer and songwriter. His many top 10 hits include "Just the Way You Are" (1977), "Tell Her About It" (1983), and "River of Dreams" (1993).

Jof•fre |'zHawfrə|, Joseph Jacques Césaire (1852–1931) French marshal, commander in chief of the French army on the Western Front during World War I.

Jof•frey |'jawfrē|, Robert (1930–88) U.S. ballet dancer and choreographer. Born *Abdullah Jaffa Anver Bey Khan*. He founded the Joffrey Ballet (1966).

John[1] |jän| (1165–1216) son of Henry II, king of England (1199–1216); known as **John Lackland**. He lost most of his French possessions, including Normandy, to Phillip II of France. In 1209 he was excommunicated for refusing to accept Stephen Langton as Archbishop of Canterbury. Forced to sign the Magna Carta by his barons (1215), he ignored its provisions and civil war broke out. **John**[2] |jän| the name of six kings of Por-

tugal: **John I** (1357–1433), reigned 1385–1433; known as **John the Great**. Reinforced by an English army, he defeated the Castilians at Aljubarrota (1385), winning independence for Portugal. **John II** (1455–95), reigned 1481–95. **John III** (1502–57), reigned 1521–57. **John IV** (1604–56), reigned 1640–56; known as **John the Fortunate**. The founder of the Braganza dynasty, he expelled a Spanish usurper and proclaimed himself king. **John V** (1689–1750), reigned 1706–50. **John VI** (1767–1826), reigned 1816–26.

John |jän|, Augustus (Edwin) (1878–1961) Welsh painter. Frequent subjects of his work are the gypsies of Wales; he was also noted for his portraits of the wealthy and famous, particularly prominent writers. He was the brother of Gwen John.

John |jän|, Sir Elton (Hercules) (1947–) English pop and rock singer, pianist, and songwriter; born *Reginald Kenneth Dwight*. Notable songs: "Goodbye, Yellow Brick Road" (1973) and "Can You Feel the Love Tonight?" (1994).

John |jän|, Gwen (1876–1939) Welsh painter. The sister of Augustus John, she settled in France. In 1913 she converted to Catholicism; her paintings, noted for their grey tonality, often depict nuns or girls in interior settings.

John |jän|, St. (1st century) an Apostle, son of Zebedee and brother of James; known as **St. John the Evangelist** or **St. John the Divine**. He has traditionally been credited with the authorship of the fourth Gospel, Revelation, and three epistles of the New Testament. Feast day, December 27.

John III |jän| (1624–96) king of Poland (1674–96); known as **John Sobieski**. In 1683 he relieved Vienna when it was besieged by the Turks, thereby becoming the hero of the Christian world.

John V |jän| (1689–1750) king of Portugal, reigned 1706–50.

John VI |jän| (1767–1826) king of Portugal, reigned 1816–26.

John of Da•mas•cus |,jän əv də 'mæskəs|, St. (*c.* 675–*c.* 749) Syrian theologian and Doctor of the Church. A champion of image worship against the iconoclasts, he wrote the influential encyclopedic work on Christian theology *The Fount of Wisdom*. Feast day, December 4.

John of Gaunt |ˌjän əv 'gawnt| (1340–99) son of England's Edward III. John of Gaunt was the effective ruler of England during the final years of his father's reign and the minority of Richard II. His son Henry Bolingbroke later became King Henry IV.

John of the Cross |ˌjän|, St. (1542–91) Spanish mystic and poet; born *Juan de Yepis y Alvarez*. A Carmelite monk and priest, he joined with St. Teresa of Ávila in founding the "discalced" Carmelite order in 1568. Feast day, December 14.

John the Baptist |ˌjän|, St. (1st century) Jewish preacher and prophet, a comtemporary of Jesus. In *c.*27 AD he preached and baptized on the banks of the Jordan River. Among those whom he baptized was Christ. He was beheaded by Herod Antipas after denouncing that latter's marriage to Herodias, the wife of Herod's brother Philip (Matt. 14:1–12). Feast day, June 24.

John the Evangelist, St (also **John the Divine**) see JOHN, ST.

John the Fortunate John IV of Portugal (see JOHN²).

John the Great John I of Portugal (see JOHN²).

John Paul II |ˌjän 'pawl| (1920–) Polish cleric, pope since 1978; born *Karol Jozef Wojtyla*. The first non-Italian pope since 1522, he traveled abroad extensively during his papacy and upheld the Roman Catholic Church's traditional opposition to artificial means of contraception and abortion, homosexuality, the ordination of women, and the relaxation of the rule of celibacy for priests.

Johns |ˈjänz|, Jasper (1930–) U.S. painter, sculptor, and printmaker. A key figure in the development of pop art, he depicted commonplace and universally recognized images. His notable series of works include *Flags*, *Targets*, and *Numbers* (all produced in the mid-1950s).

John·son |ˈjänsən| Andrew, see box.

Eliza McCardle Johnson (1810–76), wife of Andrew Johnson and U.S. first lady (1865–69).

Johnson, Andrew
17th U.S. president

Life dates: 1808–1875
Place of birth: Raleigh, N. Carolina
Mother: Mary McDonough Johnson
Father: Jacob Johnson
Stepfather: Turner Dougherty
Wife: Eliza McCardle Johnson
Children: Martha, Charles, Mary, Robert, Andrew
College/University: none
Military service: during Civil War, appointed by Lincoln as military governor of Tennessee
Career: Tailor
Political career: alderman and mayor; Greenville, Tenn.; Tennessee House of Representatives; U.S. House of Representatives; governor of Tennessee; U.S. Senate; vice president (under Lincoln); president; U.S. Senate
Party: Democratic; National Union Party
Home state: Tennessee
Opponents in presidential race: none (succeeded to the presidency after the assassination of Abraham Lincoln)
Term of office: Apr. 15, 1865–March 3, 1869
Vice president: none
Notable events of presidency: Reconstruction Act; Alaska Purchase; Thirteenth Amendment to the Constitution ratified, abolishing slavery; Nebraska admitted as 37th state; Tenure of Office Act; Fourteenth Amendment to the Constitution ratified; impeachment by U.S. House of Representatives and acquittal in U.S. Senate trial
Place of burial: Greenville, Tenn.

John·son |ˈjänsən|, Betsey (1942–) U.S. fashion designer.

John·son |ˈjänsən|, Byron Bancroft (1864–1931) U.S. baseball organizer. Known as **Ban**. He organized the American League (1900) and inaugurated the World Series.

John·son |ˈjänsən|, Cornelius (1593–*c*. 1661) English-born Dutch portrait painter. Also **Jansens** or **Janssen van Ceulen**. He painted for the court of Charles I; after the outbreak of the English Civil War, he emigrated to Holland (1643).

John·son |ˈjänsən|, Earvin (1959–) U.S. basketball player; known as **Magic Johnson**. He played for the Los

---

Johnson, Lyndon Baines
36th U.S. president

Life dates: 1908–1973
Place of birth: near Stonewall, Texas
Mother: Rebekah Baines Johnson
Father: Sam Ealy Johnson, Jr.
Wife: Lady Bird Johnson (born Claudia Alta Taylor)
Children: Lynda Bird, Luci
Nickname: LBJ
College/University: Southwest Texas State Teachers College
Military service: during World War II, served as a special duty officer, U.S. Naval Intelligence
Career: Teacher
Political career: U.S. House of Representatives; U.S. Senate (minority and majority leader); vice president (under Kennedy); president
Party: Democratic
Home state: Texas
Opponent in presidential race: Barry M. Goldwater
Term of office: Nov. 22, 1963–Jan. 20, 1969 (succeeded to the presidency after the assassination of John F. Kennedy)
Vice president: None (1st term); Hubert H. Humphrey (2nd term)
Notable events of presidency: Civil Rights Act; Voting Rights Act; Economic Opportunity Act; Nuclear Non-Proliferation Treaty; Vietnam War; Arab-Israeli War; Department of Transportation established
Other achievements: awarded Silver Star for gallantry, World War II
Place of burial: (near) Johnson City, Texas

Angeles Lakers from 1979 to 1991. After being diagnosed HIV-positive, he won an Olympic gold medal in 1992 and then briefly returned to the Lakers.

John•son |'jänsən|, Hiram Warren (1866–1945) U.S. politician. He served as governor of California (1911–17) and in the U.S. Senate (1917–45). A founder of the U.S. Progressive Party, he was the vice-presidential candidate on Theodore Roosevelt's "Bull Moose" ticket (1912).

John•son |'jänsən|, Howard Deering (c. 1896–1972) U.S. businessman. His Howard Johnson's restaurants were America's first franchise chain.

John•son |'jänsən|, Jack (1878–1946) U.S. boxer. He was the first black world heavyweight champion (1908–15).

John•son |'jänsən|, James P. (1894–1955) U.S. jazz pianist and composer. He wrote large-scale orchestral works such as *Harlem Symphony* (1932) and *Symphony in Brown* (1935), as well as songs.

John•son |'jänsən|, James Weldon (1871–1938) U.S. poet, novelist, and diplomat He was a leader in the civil rights movement and the Harlem Renaissance, and he edited *The Book of American Negro Poetry* (1922, enlarged 1931).

John•son |'jänsən|, John H. (1918–) U.S. publisher. He was chairman and chief executive officer of the Johnson Publishing Co., Inc. (1942–), the publisher of *Ebony* and *Jet* magazines. Spingarn Medal, 1966.

John•son |'jänsən| Lyndon Baines, see box. **Lady Bird Johnson**, born *Claudia Alta Taylor* (1912–), wife of Lyndon Johnson and U.S. first lady (1963–69).

John•son |'jänsən|, Martin Elmer (1884–1937) U.S. explorer and naturalist. He produced motion picures such as *Simba, the King of the Beasts* (1928); with his wife Osa Helen (1894-1953), who was also his pilot and a hunter, he coauthored several books.

John•son |'jänsən|, Mordecai W. (1890–1976) U.S. educator. Spingarn Medal, 1929.

John•son |'jänsən|, Philip Courtelyou (1906–) U.S. architect and author. He designed many buildings in New York City, including Lincoln Center, the AT&T headquarters building, and Bobst Library at New York University. He is the author of *Architecture Since 1922*.

John•son |'jänsən|, Reverdy (1796–1876) U.S. politician. He represented the defense in the Dred Scott Supreme Court case.

John•son |'jänsən|, Richard Mentor (1780–1850) vice president of the U.S. (1837–41).

John•son |'jänsən|, Robert (1911–38) U.S. blues singer and guitarist. Despite his mysterious early death, he was very influential on the 1960s blues movement. Notable songs: "I Was Standing at the Crossroads."

John•son |'jänsən|, Samuel (1709–84) English lexicographer, writer, critic, and conversationalist. Known as **Dr. Johnson.** A leading figure in the literary London of his day, he is noted particularly for his *Dictionary of the English Language* (1755), edition of Shakespeare (1765), and *The Lives of the English Poets* (1777). James Boswell's biography of Johnson records details of his life and conversation.

John•son |'jänsən|, Thomas (1732–1819) U.S. Supreme Court justice (1791–93).

John•son |'jänsən|, Walter Perry (1887–1946) U.S. baseball player. Known as **Big Train.** He pitched a record 113 career shutouts and led the American League in strikeouts for 12 seasons. Elected to Baseball Hall of Fame (1936).

John•son |'jänsən|, William (1771–1834) U.S. Supreme Court justice (1804–34).

John•ston |'jänstən|, Annie (1863–1931) U.S. author. She wrote a series of children's stories, beginning with "The Little Colonel" (1895).

John•ston |'jänstən|, Joseph Eggleston (1807–91) U.S. army officer and politician. He was defeated by Grant at Vicksburg and surrendered to Sherman. He was a member of the U.S. House of Representatives from Virginia (1879–81).

John•ston |'jänstən|, Lynn (1947–) Canadian cartoonist, author, and illustrator. She created the comic strip "For Better or For Worse."

Jo•liot |zHŌ'lyō|, Jean-Frédéric (1900–58) French nuclear physicist. Marie Curie's assistant at the Radium Institute; he worked with her daughter Irène (1897–1956) and they later married. Together they discovered artificial radioactivity. Nobel Prize for Chemistry (1935, shared with his wife).

Jo•liot-Cu•rie |zHŌ,lyōkyoō'rē|, Irène (1897–1956) French physicist. Nobel Prize for Chemistry, 1935.

Jol•liet |zHawl'ye; zHŌlē'(y)et|, Louis (1645–1700) French-Canadian explorer. With Jacques Marquette, he explored the upper Mississippi River.

Jol•son |'jōlsən|, Al (1886–1950) Russian-born U.S. singer, movie actor, and comedian; born *Asa Yoelson*. He made the Gershwin song "Swanee" his trademark, and appeared in blackface in the first full-length talking movie, *The Jazz Singer* (1927).

Jones |jōnz|, Bobby (1902–71) U.S. golfer; full name *Robert Tyre Jones*. In a short competitive career (1923–30), and as an amateur, he won thirteen major competitions, including four American and three British open championships.

Jones |jōnz|, Chuck (1912–) U.S. writer, producer, and director. Full name *Charles Martin Jones*. He was the creator of the cartoon characters Pepe le Pew, the Road Runner, Coyote, and others, and director of "How the Grinch Stole Christmas."

Jones |jōnz|, Daniel (1881–1967) British phonetician. He developed the International Phonetic Alphabet from 1907 and went on to invent the system of cardinal vowels. Notable works: *English Pronouncing Dictionary* (1917).

Jones |jōnz|, Edward D. (1856–1920) U.S. business journalist. With Charles Henry Dow, he founded Dow Jones & Co. (1882) and *The Wall Street Journal* (1889).

Jones |jōnz|, Howard Mumford (1892–1980) U.S. educator and author. Notable works: *O Strange New World* (1964, Pulitzer Prize).

Jones |jōnz|, Inigo (1573–1652) English architect and stage designer. He introduced the Palladian style to England; notable buildings include the Queen's House at Greenwich (1616) and the Banqueting Hall at Whitehall (1619).

Jones |jōnz|, James (1921–77) U.S. author. Notable works: *From Here to Eternity* (1951).

Jones |jōnz|, James Earl (1931–) U.S. actor. A star of stage, film, and television, he performed in the *Star Wars* movies and the play *Fences*.

Jones |jōnz|, Jennifer (1919–) U.S. actress. Born *Phyllis Isley*. Notable movies: *The Song of Bernadette* (1943, Academy Award).

Jones |jōnz|, Jo (1911–85) U.S. jazz drummer. Full name *Jonathan Jones*. He performed with Count Basie's

Orchestra (1934–48); his innovations revolutionized the timbre of the jazz rhythm section.

Jones |jōnz|, John Paul (1747–92) Scottish-born U.S. admiral; born *John Paul*. He became famous for his raids off the northern coasts of Britain during the American Revolution and in his ship *Bonhomme Richard* defeated the *Serapis* in 1779. He served in the Russian Navy in 1788–89.

Jones |jōnz|, Paula Corbin (1966–   ) U.S. plaintiff. Her 1994 suit charging President Bill Clinton with sexual harassment while he was governor of Arkansas in 1991 led to the exposure of Clinton's affair with Monica Lewinsky.

Jones |jōnz|, Quincy Delight, Jr. (1933–   ) U.S. composer, conductor, and jazz trumpeter. He founded his own recording label, Qwest Records, and wrote television and movie scores and the theme for "The Bill Cosby Show."

Jones |jōnz|, Shirley (1934–   ) U.S. stage, film, and television actress. Notable movies: *Elmer Gantry* (1960 Academy Award).

Jones |jōnz|, Tom (1940–   ) Welsh pop singer; born *Thomas Jones Woodward*. Hits include "It's Not Unusual" (1965), "The Green, Green Grass of Home" (1966), and "Delilah" (1968).

Jong |'jawNG|, Erica (Mann) (1942–   ) U.S. poet and novelist. She is best known for her picaresque novels *Fear of Flying* (1973), recounting the sexual exploits of its heroine Isadora Wing, and *Fanny* (1980), written in a pseudo-18th-century style.

Jon·son |'jänsən|, Ben (1572–1637) English dramatist and poet; full name *Benjamin Jonson*. With his play *Every Man in his Humour* (1598) he established his "comedy of humours," whereby each character is dominated by a particular obsession. He became the first Poet Laureate in the modern sense. Other notable works: *Volpone* (1606) and *Bartholomew Fair* (1614).

Jop·lin |'jäplin|, Janis (1943–70) U.S. singer. She died from a heroin overdose just before her most successful album, *Pearl*, and her number-one single "Me and Bobby McGee" were released.

Jop·lin |'jäplin|, Scott (1868–1917) U.S. pianist and composer. He was the first of the creators of ragtime to write down his compositions. Notable compositions: "Maple Leaf Rag" (1899), "The Entertainer" (1902), and "Gladiolus Rag" (1907).

Jor·daens |'yawrdäns|, Jacob (1593–1678) Flemish painter. Influenced by Rubens, he is noted for his boisterous peasant scenes painted in warm colors. Notable works: *The King Drinks* (1638).

Jor·dan |'jawrdən|, Barbara (1936–96) U.S. lawyer, educator, and politician. She was a member of the U.S. House of Representatives from Texas (1972–78) and a member of the Texas Senate (1966–72).

Jor·dan |'jawrdən|, Michael (Jeffrey) (1963–   ) U.S. basketball player. Playing for the Chicago Bulls (1984–93, 1995–98), he led them to six titles and was the NBA's (National Basketball Association) Most Valuable Player five times. He retired in 1993 to play professional baseball, but returned in 1995. He has endorsed products and appeared in movies.

Jo·seph |'jōzəf; 'jōsəf|, St. (1st cent. BC–1st cent. AD) husband of the Virgin Mary. A carpenter of Nazareth, he was betrothed to Mary at the time of the Annunciation. Feast day, March 19.

Jo·seph |'jōzəf; 'jōsəf|, Chief (1840–1904) American Indian chief. Indian name *Inmuttooyahlatlat*. As chief of the Nez Percé tribe, he defied the efforts of the U.S. government to move his people from Oregon until he was captured in 1877.

Jo·se·phine |'jōzəfēn; 'jōsəfēn| (1763–1814) Empress of France (1804–09); full name *Marie Joséphine Rose Tascher de la Pagerie*. She married to the Viscount de Beauharnais before marrying Napoleon in 1796. Their marriage proved childless, and she was divorced by Napoleon in 1809.

Jo·seph·son |'jōzəfsən; 'jōsəfsən|, Matthew (1899–1978) U.S. author. Notable works: *Zola and His Time* (1928) and *Infidel in the Temple* (1967).

Jo·se·phus |jō'sēfəs|, Flavius (*c.* 37–*c.* 100) Jewish historian, general, and Pharisee; born *Joseph ben Matthias*. His *Jewish War* gives an eyewitness account of the events leading up to the Jewish revolt against the Romans in 66, in which he was a leader.

Josh•ua |'jäSH(ə)wə| (c. 13th century BC) the Israelite leader who succeeded Moses and led his people into the Promised Land.

Josquin des Prez see DES PREZ.

Joule |jōōl|, James Prescott (1818–89) English physicist. Joule established that all forms of energy were interchangeable—the first law of thermodynamics. The Joule–Thomson effect, discovered with William Thomson, later Lord Kelvin, in 1852, led to the development of the refrigerator and to the science of cryogenics. Joule also measured and described the heating effects of an electric current passing through a resistance.

Joyce |jois|, James (Augustine Aloysius) (1882–1941) Irish author. One of the most important writers of the modernist movement, he made his name with *Dubliners* (short stories, 1914). His novel *Ulysses* (1922) revolutionized the structure of the modern novel and developed the stream-of-consciousness technique. Other notable novels: *A Portrait of the Artist as a Young Man* (1914–15) and *Finnegan's Wake* (1939).

Joy•ner |'joinər|, Florence Griffith (1959–98) U.S. track and field athlete. She established world records in the 100- and 200-meter races in 1988, winning three gold medals in the 1988 Olympic Games.

Joy•ner-Ker•see |'joinər 'kərsē|, Jackie (1962–) U.S. track and field athlete. She won gold medals in the heptathalon in the 1988 and 1992 Olympic Games.

Juan   Car•los |,(h)wän 'kärlōs| (1938–) grandson of Alfonso XIII, king of Spain since 1975; full name *Juan Carlos Victor María de Borbón y Borbón*. Franco's chosen successor, he became king after Franco's death. His reign has seen Spain's increasing liberalization and its entry into NATO and the European Community.

Juá•rez |'hwärez|, Benito Pablo (1806–72) Mexican statesman, president (1858–72). Between 1864 and 1867 he was replaced by Emperor Maximilian, who was supported by the French.

Judas |jōōdəs| see JUDE, ST.

Ju•das Is•car•iot |'jōōdəs is'kerēət| (1st century AD) an Apostle. He betrayed Jesus to the Jewish authorities in return for thirty pieces of silver; the Gospels leave his motives uncertain. Overcome with remorse, he later committed suicide.

Ju•das Mac•ca•bae•us |'jōōdəs ,mækə 'bēyəs| (died c. 161 BC) Jewish leader. Leading a Jewish revolt in Judaea against Antiochus IV Epiphanes from around 167, he recovered Jerusalem and dedicated the Temple anew. He is the hero of the two books of the Maccabees in the Apocrypha.

Jude |jōōd|, St. an Apostle, supposed brother of James; also known as **Judas**. Thaddaeus is traditionally identified with him. According to tradition, he was martyred in Persia with St. Simon. Feast day (with St. Simon), October 28.

Judge |jəj|, Mike (1962–) U.S. animator, producer, and movie director. He created the television comedies "Beavis and Butt-head" and "King of the Hill."

Jud•son |'jədsən|, Arthur Leon (1881–1975) U.S. musician and businessman. He organized a network of stations to air radio broadcasts of concerts (1927), which later became the Columbia Broadcasting System; he also formed Columbia Records.

Ju•gur•tha |jōō'gərTHə| (died 104 BC) joint king of Numidia (c.118–104). His attacks on his royal partners prompted intervention by Rome and led to the outbreak of the Jugurthine War (112–105). He was eventually captured by the Roman general Marius and executed in Rome.

Juil•li•ard |'jōōleärd|, Augustus D. (1840–1919) U.S. merchant and patron of music. He founded the Juilliard Musical Foundation (1920), which later became the Juilliard School of Music (1926).

Jul•ian |'jōōlyən| (c. 331–363 AD) Roman emperor (360–363), nephew of Constantine; full name *Flavius Claudius Julianus*; known as **the Apostate**. He restored paganism as the state cult in place of Christianity, but this move was reversed after his death during a campaign against the Persians.

Jul·ian |'jo͞olyən|, Percy Lavon (1899–1975) U.S. chemist. He synthesized cortisone and developed numerous soya protein derivatives. He was founder and president of Julian Laboratories (1953).

Jul·i·an of Nor·wich |'jo͞olyən əv 'nawriCH| (c. 1342–c. 1413) English mystic. She is said to have lived as a recluse outside St. Julian's Church, Norwich. She is chiefly associated with the *Revelations of Divine Love* (c.1393), a description of a series of visions she had in which she depicts the Holy Trinity as Father, Mother, and Lord.

Jul·i·us Cae·sar |'jo͞olyəs 'sēzər|, Gaius (100–44 BC) Roman general and statesman. He established the First Triumvirate (60) with Pompey and Crassus, and became consul in 59. Between 58 and 51 he fought the Gallic Wars, invaded Britain (55–54), and acquired immense power. After civil war with Pompey, which ended in Pompey's defeat at Pharsalus (48), Caesar became dictator at Rome and began to introduce reforms. He was murdered on the Ides (15th) of March in a conspiracy led by Brutus and Cassius.

Jung |yo͝oNG|, Carl (Gustav) (1875–1961) Swiss psychologist. He originated the concept of introvert and extrovert personality, and of the four psychological functions of sensation, intuition, thinking, and feeling. He collaborated with Sigmund Freud in developing the psychoanalytic theory of personality, but later disassociated himself from Freud's preoccupation with sexuality as the determinant of personality, preferring to emphasize a mystical or religious factor in the unconscious.

Jus·sieu |ZHo͞os'yOE|, Antoine Laurent de (1748–1836) French botanist. Jussieu grouped plants into families on the basis of common essential properties and, in *Genera Plantarum* (1789), developed the system on which modern plant classification is based.

Jus·tin |'jəstən|, St. (c. 100–165) Christian philosopher; known as **St. Justin the Martyr**. According to tradition he was martyred in Rome together with some of his followers. He is remembered for his *Apologia* (c.150). Feast day, June 1.

Jus·tin·i·an |jəs'tinēən| (483–565) Byzantine emperor (527–65); Latin name *Flavius Petrus Sabbatius Justinianus*. Through his general, Belisarius, he regained North Africa and Spain. He codified Roman law (529) and carried out a building program throughout the Empire, of which St. Sophia at Constantinople (532) was a part.

Ju·ve·nal |'jo͞ovənəl| (c. 60–c. 140) Roman satirist; Latin name *Decimus Junius Juvenalis*. His sixteen verse satires present a savage attack on the vice and folly of Roman society, chiefly in the reign of the emperor Domitian.

Kk

Ka·bi·la |kä'bēlə|, Laurent (1937–) African statesman, president of the Democratic Republic of Congo (formerly Zaire). Kabila's forces overthrew President Mobutu in 1997. On taking power Kabila changed the name of the country from Zaire to Democratic Republic of Congo.

Ká·dár |'kä,där|, János (1912–89) Hungarian statesman, First Secretary of the Hungarian Socialist Workers' Party (1956–88) and prime minister (1956–58 and 1961–65). After crushing the Hungarian uprising of 1956, Kádár consistently supported the Soviet Union. His policy of "consumer socialism" made Hungary the most affluent state in eastern Europe.

Kael |kāl|, Pauline (1919–) U.S. movie critic. She was a reviewer for *The New Yorker*; her collections of reviews include *Deeper into Movies* (1973, National Book Award).

Kaf·ka |'käfkə|, Franz (1883–1924) Czech novelist who wrote in German. His work is characterized by its portrayal of an enigmatic and nightmarish reality where the individual is perceived as lonely, perplexed, and threatened. Notable works: *The Metamorphosis* (1917) and *The Trial* (1925).

Ka·ha·na·mo·ku |kə,hänə'mōkōō|, Duke Paoa (1890–1968) U.S. swimmer and surfer. The developer of the flutter kick, he won the 100-yard freestyle gold medals in the 1912 and 1920 Olympic Games, as well as the 800-meter relay gold medal in the 1920 Olympics.

Kah·lo |'kälō|, Frieda (1907–54) Mexican artist. Her many self-portraits deal with her battle to survive after a crippling bus accident.

Kahn |kän|, Albert (1869–1942) U.S. architect. He designed the General Motors Building in Detroit, Michigan.

Kahn |kän|, Louis Isadore (1901–74) U.S. architect, born in Estonia. He designed the Salk Lab in La Jolla, California, and the Yale Art Gallery in New Haven, Connecticut.

Kahn |kän|, Otto Hermann (1867–1934) U.S. banker and philanthropist, born in Germany. He worked for the banking firm Kuhn, Loeb & Co. in New York from 1897. He is also noted as one of the greatest patrons of arts and served as president of the Metropolitan Opera Co. (1918–31).

Kai·ser |'kīzər|, Henry John (1882–1967) U.S. industrialist. He was an executive with companies involved in dam construction, shipbuilding, steel production, and automobile manufacture, and he founded the Kaiser Foundation for health services.

Kai·ser |'kīzər|, Georg (1878–1945) German dramatist. He is best known for his expressionist plays *The Burghers of Calais* (1914), and *Gas I* (1918) and *Gas II* (1920); the last two provide a gruesome vision of futuristic science, ending with the extinction of all life by poisonous gas.

Kai·ser Wil·helm Wilhelm II of Germany (see WILHELM II).

Kaler, James Otis (1848–1912) U.S. author. Pseudonym **James Otis**. He wrote stories for boys, including *Toby Tyler: or, Ten Weeks with a Circus* (1881).

Ka·li·da·sa |'kälē'däsə| (5th century AD) Indian poet and dramatist. He is best known for his drama *Sakuntala*, the love story of King Dushyanta and the maiden Sakuntala.

Ka·li·nin |kə'lēnin; kə'lyenyin|, Mikhail (Ivanovich) (1875–1946) Soviet statesman, head of state of the USSR 1919–46. He founded the newspaper *Pravda* (1912).

Ka·ma·li |kə'mälē|, Norma (1945–) U.S. fashion designer.

Ka·me·ha·me·ha |kä'mähä'mähä| five kings of Hawaii: **Kamehameha I** (*c.*1758–1819; reigned 1795–1819). Born *Paiea*; known as **Kamehameha the Great**. **Kamehameha II** (1797–1824; reigned 1819–24). Born *Liholiho*; son of Kamehameha I. **Kamehameha III** (1813–54; reigned 1825–54). Born *Kauikeaouli*; brother of Kamehameha II. **Kamehameha IV** (1834–63; reigned 1854–63). Also known as

Alexander Liholiho; nephew of Kamehameha III. **Kamehameha V** (1830–72; reigned 1863–72). Born *Lot*; brother of Kamehameha IV.

Ka·mer·lingh On·nes |'kämərliNG 'awnəs|, Heike (1853–1926) Dutch physicist. During his studies of cryogenic phenomena he achieved a temperature of less than one degree above absolute zero and succeeded in liquefying helium. Onnes discovered the phenomenon of superconductivity in 1911, and was awarded the Nobel Prize for Physics in 1913.

Kan·din·sky |kæn'dinskē|, Wassily (1866–1944) Russian painter. He pioneered abstract painting.

Kane |kān|, Bob (1916–) U.S. cartoonist. With neighbor Bill Finger, he was cocreator of the character Batman.

Kan·in |'kænən|, Garson (1912–) U.S. actor, director, and producer. Notable works: *Born Yesterday* (1946) and *Moviola* (1979).

Kant |känt|, Immanuel (1724–1804) German philosopher. In the *Critique of Pure Reason* (1781) he countered Hume's skeptical empiricism by arguing that any affirmation or denial regarding the ultimate nature of reality ("noumenon") makes no sense. He maintained that all we can know are the objects of experience ("phenomena"), interpreted by space and time and ordered according to twelve key concepts. Kant's *Critique of Practical Reason* (1788) affirms the existence of an absolute moral law—the categorical imperative.

Kap·lin |'kæplən|, Justin (1925–) U.S. author. Notable works: *Mr. Clemens and Mark Twain* (1966, Pulitzer Prize and National Book Award).

Ka·ra·džić |kä'räjiCH|, Vuk Stefanović (1787–1864) Serbian writer, grammarian, lexicographer, and folklorist. He modified the Cyrillic alphabet for Serbian written usage and compiled a Serbian dictionary in 1818. Widely claimed to be the father of modern Serbian literature, he collected and published national folk stories and poems.

Ka·ra·jan |'kärä‚yän|, Herbert von (1908–89) Austrian conductor, chiefly remembered as the principal conductor of the Berlin Philharmonic Orchestra (1955–89).

Ka·ra·man·lis |‚kerə'mænləs|, Constantine (1907–1998) Greek politician. He served as president of Greece (1980–85 and 1990–94), rebuilding democracy after a 1967–74 junta.

Ka·ran |'kerən; kə'ræn|, Donna (1948–) U.S. fashion designer.

Kar·loff |'kärlawf|, Boris (1887–1969) British-born U.S. actor; born *William Henry Pratt*. His name is chiefly linked with horror movies, such as *Frankenstein* (1931) and *The Body Snatcher* (1945).

Kar·pov |'kärpawf|, Anatoli (Yevgenevich) (1951–) Russian chess player. He was world champion from 1975 until defeated by Gary Kasparov in 1985.

Ka·sem |'käsəm|, Casey (1933–) U. S. radio disk jockey.

Kas·pa·rov |'kæspə‚rawf|, Gary (1963–) Russian chess player. He has been world chess champion since 1985.

Kas·se·baum |'kæsə‚bawm; 'kæsə‚bowm|, Nancy Landon (1932–) U.S. senator from Kansas (1979–96).

Kauff·mann |'kowfmən|, (Maria Anna Catherina) Angelica (1740–1807) Swiss painter. Also **Kauffman**. In London from 1766, she became well known for her neoclassical and allegorical paintings. She was a founding member of the Royal Academy of Arts (1768).

Kauf·man |'kawfmən|, George Simon (1889–1961) U.S. journalist, playwright, and director. He collaborated with George Gershwin to write *Of Thee I Sing* (1931, Pulitzer Prize), and with Moss Hart to write *You Can't Take It With You* (1936, Pulitzer Prize).

Kaunda, Kenneth (David) (1924–) Zambian statesman, president (1964–91). He led the United National Independence Party to electoral victory in 1964, becoming prime minister and the first president of independent Zambia.

Ka·wa·ba·ta |käwä'bätä|, Yasunari (1899–1972) Japanese novelist. Known as an experimental writer in the 1920s, he reverted to traditional Japanese novel forms in the mid 1930s. He was the first Japanese writer to win the Nobel Prize for Literature (1968).

Kaye |kā|, Danny (1913–87) U.S. actor

and comedian; born *David Daniel Kominski*. He was known for his mimicry, comic songs, and slapstick humor. Notable movies: *The Secret Life of Walter Mitty* (1947), *Hans Christian Andersen* (1952).

Ka·zan |kə'zæn|, Elia (1909–) Turkish-born U.S. movie and theater director; born *Elia Kazanjoglous*. In 1947 he co-founded the Actors' Studio, one of the leading centers of method acting. Kazan directed *A Streetcar Named Desire* on stage (1947) and then on screen (1953). Other notable movies: *On the Waterfront* (1954) and *East of Eden* (1955). He received an Academy Award for lifetime achievement 1999.

Kazin, Alfred (1915–98) U.S. literary critic. Notable works: *On Native Ground* (1942).

Kean |kēn|, Edmund (1787–1833) English actor, renowned for his interpretations of Shakespearean tragic roles, notably those of Macbeth and Iago.

Keane |kēn|, Bill (1922–) U.S. cartoonist. Full name *William Keane*. He created the comic strips "The Family Circus" and "Channel Chuckles."

Kea·ting |'kētiNG|, Paul (John) (1944–) Australian Labour statesman, prime minister (1991–96).

Kea·ton |'kētn|, Buster (1895–1966) U.S. actor and director; born *Joseph Francis Keaton*. His deadpan face and acrobatic skills made him one of the biggest comedy stars of the silent-movie era. He starred in and directed movies including *The Navigator* (1924) and *The General* (1926).

Kea·ton |'kētn|, Diane (1946–) U.S. actress. Born *Diane Hall*. Notable moves: *Annie Hall* (1977, Academy Award).

Keats |kēts|, Ezra Jack (1916–) U.S. children's author and illustrator.

Keats |kēts|, John (1795–1821) English poet. A principal figure of the romantic movement, he wrote all of his most famous poems, including "La Belle Dame sans Merci", "Ode to a Nightingale", and "Ode on a Grecian Urn", in 1818 (published in 1820).

Ke·ble |'kēbəl|, John (1792–1866) English churchman. His sermon on national apostasy (1833) is generally held to mark the beginning of the Oxford Movement, which he founded with John Henry Newman and Edward Pusey.

Keck·ley |'keklē|, Elizabeth (1827–1907) U.S. former slave. She earned her emancipation as a dressmaker and served Mrs. Abraham Lincoln. Notable works: *Behind the Scenes; or Thirty Years a Slave and Four Years in the White House* (1868), used by all Lincoln biographers.

Kee·ler |'kēlər|, Christine (1942–) English model and showgirl. She achieved notoriety in 1963 in a scandal arising from her affair with the Conservative cabinet minister John Profumo when she was also mistress of a Soviet attaché. Profumo resigned and Keeler was imprisoned on related charges.

Keene |kēn|, Charles Samuel (1823–91) English illustrator and caricaturist. He is remembered for his work in the weekly journal *Punch* from 1851.

Kee·shan |'kēsHən|, Robert James (1927–) U.S. actor and producer. He played Clarabell on the "Howdy Doody Show" (1947–52), and he produced and starred in "Captain Kangaroo" (1955–85).

Ke·fau·ver |'kē,fawvər|, (Carey) Estes (1903–63) U.S. politician. He was a member of the U.S. House of Representatives from Tennessee (1939–49), a member of the U.S. Senate (1949–63), and a Democratic vice presidential candidate (1956). As a senator, he conducted hearings to investigate organized crime in interstate commerce (1950–51).

Keil·lor |'kēlər|, Garrison (Edward) (1942–) U.S. writer and radio entertainer. He is creator of the radio program "A Prairie Home Companion" and the author of fiction such as *Wobegon Boy* (1996) and *The Sandy Bottom Orchestra* (1996, with J. Nilsson).

Keith |kēTH|, Damon Jerome (1922–) U.S. jurist. He served as a judge on the U.S. 6th Circuit Court of Appeals for Detroit (1977–). Spingarn Medal, 1974.

Ke·kulé |'kākoōlā|, Friedrich August (1829–96) German chemist; full name *Friedrich August Kekulé von Stradonitz*. One of the founders of structural organic chemistry, he is best known for discovering the ring structure of benzene.

Kel•ler |'kelər|, Helen (Adams) (1880–1968) U.S. writer, social reformer, and academic. Blind and deaf from the age of nineteen months, she learned how to read, type, and speak with the help of tutor Anne Sullivan. She went on to champion the cause of blind and deaf people throughout the world.

Kel•logg |'kelawg| U.S. nutritionists: **Will Keith Kellogg** (1860–1951), food manufacturer, collaborated with his brother, **John Harvey Kellogg** (1852–1943), a physician, to develop a breakfast cereal for sanatorium patients, of crisp flakes of rolled and toasted wheat and corn. He established the W. K. Kellogg company in 1906, whose successful breakfast cereals brought about a revolution in Western eating habits.

Kel•logg |'kelawg|, Frank Billings (1856–1937) U.S. statesman. As secretary of state (1925–29), he negotiated the Kellogg-Briand Pact of 1928 to outlaw war. Nobel Peace Prize, 1929.

Kel•logg |'kelawg|, Steven (1941–) U.S. children's author and illustrator.

Kel•ly |'kelē|, Emmett Lee (1898–1979) U.S. clown. He played the mournful tramp with the Ringling Brothers and Barnum and Bailey Circus (1942–57).

Kel•ly |'kelē|, Gene (1912–96) U.S. dancer and choreographer; full name *Eugene Curran Kelly*. He began his career on Broadway in 1938, making a successful transition to movies with *For Me and My Girl* (1942). He performed in and choreographed many movie musicals, including *An American in Paris* (1951) and *Singin' in the Rain* (1952).

Kel•ly |'kelē|, George (1887–1974) U.S. actor and playwright. Notable works: *Craig's Wife* (1925, Pulitzer Prize).

Kel•ly |'kelē|, Grace (Patricia) (1928–82) U.S. movie actress; also called (from 1956) **Princess Grace of Monaco**. She starred in *High Noon* (1952) and also made three Hitchcock movies, including *Rear Window* (1954), before retiring from movies in 1956 on her marriage to Prince Rainier III of Monaco. She died in an automobile accident.

Kel•ly |'kelē|, Ned (1855–80) Aus-

tralian outlaw; full name *Edward Kelly*. Leader of a band of horse and cattle thieves and bank robbers, he was eventually hanged.

Kel•ly |'kelē|, Walt (1913–73) U.S. cartoonist, book illustrator, and author. Full name *Walter Crawford Kelly*. He created the popular comic strip "Pogo."

Kel•vin |'kelvən|, William Thomson 1st Baron (1824–1907) British physicist and natural philosopher. Best known for introducing the absolute scale of temperature. He also reinstated the second law of thermodynamics and was involved in the laying of the first Atlantic cable, for which he invented several instruments.

Ke•mal Pa•sha |ke'mäl päshə| see ATATÜRK.

Kem•ble |'kembəl|, Fanny (1809–93) English actress; full name *Frances Anne Kemble*. The daughter of Charles Kemble and the niece of Sarah Siddons, she was a success in Shakespearean comedy and tragedy.

Kem•ble |'kembəl|, Gouverneur (1786–1875) U.S. manufacturer and politician. The producer of the finest cannon of his day, he was also a member of the U.S. House of Representatives from New York (1837–41).

Kem•ble |'kembəl|, John Philip (1757–1823) English actor-manager, brother of Sarah Siddons. Noted for his performances in Shakespearean tragedy, he was manager of Drury Lane (1788–1803) and Covent Garden (1803–17) theaters. His younger brother **Charles Kemble** (1775–1854) was also a successful actor-manager.

Kem•e•ny |'kemənē|, John George (1926–92) U.S. mathematician. At one time an assistant to Albert Einstein, he also contributed to the Manhattan Project and (with Thomas Kurtz) invented BASIC computer language (1964). He later became president of Dartmouth College (1970–91).

Kemp |kemp|, Jack F. (1935–) U.S. politician. He was a professional football player for 13 years and a member of the U.S. House of Representatives from New York (1971–); he was a Republican vice presidential candidate (1996).

Kempe |kemp|, Margery (c. 1373–c.

1440) English mystic. From about 1432 to 1436 she dictated one of the first autobiographies in English, *The Book of Margery Kempe*. It gives an account of her series of pilgrimages, as well as details of her mystic self-transcendent visions.

Kem•pis |'kempis|, Thomas à see THOMAS À KEMPIS.

Ken•dall |'kendl|, Edward Calvin (1886–1972) U.S. biochemist. He isolated crystalline thyroxine from the thyroid gland, and from the adrenal cortex he obtained a number of steroid hormones, one of which was later named cortisone. Nobel Prize for Physiology or Medicine (1950).

Ke•neal•ly |kə'nælē|, Thomas (Michael) (1935–) Australian novelist. He first gained recognition for *The Chart of Jimmy Blacksmith* (1972), but is probably best known for his prize-winning novel *Schindler's List* (1982), filmed by Steven Spielberg in 1993.

Ken•nan |'kenən|, George Frost (1904–) U.S. author and diplomat. He held ambassadorships to the Soviet Union and Yugoslavia. Notable works: *Russia Leave the Ward* (1956, Pulitzer Prize) and *Memoirs* (1967, Pulitzer Prize and National Book Award).

Ken•ne•dy |'kenədē| U.S. political family, including: **John Fitzgerald Kennedy** see box. His wife, **Jacqueline Kennedy** see ONASSIS. **Robert Francis Kennedy** (1925–68), U.S. attorney general (1961–64); known as **Bobby**. He closely assisted his brother John in domestic policy and was also a champion of the civil rights movement. He was assassinated during his campaign for the Democratic presidential nomination. **Edward Moore Kennedy** (1932–), brother of John and Robert, U.S. senator since 1962; known as **Ted** or **Teddy**. His political career has been overshadowed by his involvement in an automobile accident at Chappaquiddick Island (1969), in which his assistant Mary Jo Kopechne died. **John Fitzgerald Kennedy, Jr.**, (1960–), son of John Kennedy. U.S. lawyer and editor. He was cofounder and editor in chief of the magazine *George* (1995–98).

Ken•ne•dy |'kenədē|, Anthony McLeod

Kennedy, John Fitzgerald
35th U.S. president

Life dates: 1917–1963
Place of birth: Brookline, Mass.
Mother: Rose Elizabeth Fitzgerald Kennedy
Father: Joseph Patrick Kennedy
Wife: Jacqueline (Jackie) Lee Bouvier Kennedy
Children: Caroline; John, Jr.; Patrick (died 2 days after birth)
Nicknames: JFK; Jack
College/University: Harvard; Princeton; London School of Economics
Military service: U.S. Navy lieutenant and PT boat commander, World War II
Political career: U.S. House of Representatives; U.S. Senate; president
Party: Democratic
Home state: Massachusetts
Opponent in presidential race: Richard M. Nixon
Term of office: Jan. 20, 1961–Nov. 22, 1963 (assassinated)
Vice president: Lyndon Baines Johnson
Notable events of presidency: Peace Corps created; established Committee on Equal Employment Opportunity; Berlin Wall built; Cuban Missile Crisis; Nuclear Test-Ban Treaty; Alan Shepard first U.S. astronaut in space; President Diem and brother Ngo Dinh Nhu assassinated in Vietnam coup
Other achievements: Awarded Navy and Marine Corps Medal and Purple Heart; Pulitzer Prize for biography *Profiles in Courage*
Place of burial: Arlington National Cemetery, Va.

(1935–) U.S. Supreme Court justice (1988–).

Ken•ne•dy |'kenədē|, George (1925–) U.S. actor. Notable movies: *Cool Hand Luke* (1967, Academy Award).

Ken•ne•dy |'kenədē|, Joseph Patrick (1888–1969) U.S. businessman and diplomat. Father of John Fitzgerald, Robert Francis, and Edward T. Kennedy, he made his fortune in banking, the stock market, shipbuilding, and motion pictures.

Ken•ne•dy |'kenədē|, William (1928–) U.S. author. Notable works: *Ironweed* (1983, National Book Award and Pulitzer Prize).

Ken·nel·ly |'kenəlē|, Arthur Edwin (1861–1939) U.S. electrical engineer. His principal work was on the theory of alternating currents. Independently of O. Heaviside, he also discovered the layer in the atmosphere responsible for reflecting radio waves back to the earth.

Ken·neth I |'kenəTH| (died 858) king of Scotland (c.844–58); known as **Kenneth MacAlpin**. He is traditionally viewed as the founder of the kingdom of Scotland, which was established following his defeat of the Picts in about 844.

Kent |kent|, Rockwell (1882-1971.) U.S. author and artist. His books recount sea voyages and residences in the Arctic and South America.

Ken·ton |'ken(t)ən|, Stan (1912–79) U.S. bandleader, composer, and arranger; born *Stanley Newcomb*. He formed his own orchestra in 1940 and is particularly associated with the bigband jazz style of the 1950s.

Ken·yat·ta |ken'yätə|, Jomo (c. 1891–1978) Kenyan statesman, prime minister of Kenya (1963) and president (1964–78). Imprisoned for alleged complicity in the Mau Mau uprising (1952–61), on his release he was elected president of the Kenya African National Union and led Kenya to independence in 1963, subsequently serving as its first president.

Ken·zo |'kenzō| (1940–) Japanese fashion designer. Full name *Kenzo Takada*. His store, Jungle Jap, is known for trendsetting knitwear.

Kep·ler |'keplər|, Johannes (1571–1630) German astronomer. His analysis of Tycho Brahe's planetary observations led him to discover the three laws governing orbital motion.

Kern |kərn|, Jerome (David) (1885–1945) U.S. composer. A major influence in the development of the musical, he wrote several musical comedies, including *Showboat* (1927).

Kern |kərn|, John W. (1849–1917) U.S. politician. He was a member of the U.S. Senate from Indiana (1911–17) and a vice presidential Democratic candidate (1908).

Ker·ou·ac |'kerəwæk|, Jack (1922–69) U.S. novelist and poet, of French-Canadian descent; born *Jean-Louis Lebris de Kérouac*. A leading figure of the Beat Generation, he is best known for his semi-autobiographical novel *On the Road* (1957).

Kerr |kər; kär| U.S. authors: **Walter Francis Kerr** (1913–), a drama critic and playwright, wrote for the *New York Herald Tribune* (1951–66) and *The New York Times* (1966–83). Pulitzer Prize, 1978. **Jean Collins Kerr** (1923–) wrote *Please Don't Eat the Daisies* (1957) and collaborated with her husband Walter in writing plays.

Ker·ri·gan |'kerəgən|, Nancy (1969–) U.S. figure skater. The 1993 U.S. women's champion and an Olympic medalist (1992, bronze; 1994, silver), she was the victim of an assault planned by rival Tonya Harding.

Ker·tész |kər'tesH|, André (1894–1985) U.S. photographer, born in Hungary. He pioneered and refined the use of the handheld 35mm camera, and his photographs of Paris in the 1920s had a profound influence on modern photojournalism.

Ke·sey |'kēzē|, Ken (Elton) (1935–) U.S. novelist. His best-known novel, *One Flew over the Cuckoo's Nest* (1962), is based on his experiences as a ward attendant in a mental hospital.

Ketch·am |'keCHəm|, Hank (1920–) U.S. cartoonist and author. Full name *Henry King Ketcham*. He created the "Dennis the Menace" comic strip.

Ket·ter·ing |'ketəriNG|, Charles Franklin (1876–1958) U.S. automobile engineer. His first significant development was the electric starter (1912). As head of research at General Motors he discovered tetraethyl lead as an antiknock agent and defined the octane rating of fuels; he also did important work on diesel engines, synchromesh gearboxes, automatic transmissions, and power steering.

Ke·vor·kian |kə'vawrkēən|, Jack (1928–) U.S. physician. He was an advocate and practicioner of assisted suicide but was convicted of murder in the death of one of his patients.

Key |kē|, Francis Scott (1779–1843) U.S. lawyer and poet. A witness to the successful U.S. defense against the British bombardment of Fort McHenry in Baltimore (Sept. 13–14, 1814), he wrote the poem "Defence of Fort M'Henry." The poem was later set to music, renamed "The Star-Spangled Banner," and adopted as the U.S. national anthem (1931).

Key |kē|, Ted (1912–) U.S. cartoonist and writer. Full name *Theodore Key*. He is best known as the creator of "Hazel," which appeared in the *Saturday Evening Post*; he was also a cartoonist and writer for the *New Yorker* and other magazines.

Keynes |kānz|, John Maynard, 1st Baron (1883–1946) English economist. He laid the foundations of modern macroeconomics with *The General Theory of Employment, Interest and Money* (1936), in which he argued that full employment is determined by effective demand and requires government spending on public works to stimulate this. His theories influenced Roosevelt's decision to introduce the New Deal.

Kha·cha·tu·ri·an |ˌkäCHəˈtŏŏrēən|, Aram (Ilich) (1903–78) Soviet composer, born in Georgia. His music is richly romantic and reflects his lifelong interest in the folk music of Armenia, Georgia, and Russia. Notable works include *Gayane* (ballet, 1942), his Second Symphony (1943), and *Spartacus* (ballet, 1954).

Kha·ma |ˈkämə|, Sir Seretse (1921–80) Botswanan statesman, prime minister of Bechuanaland (1965) and first president of Botswana (1966–80).

Khan |kän|, Ayub see AYUB KHAN.

Kho·mei·ni |kōˈmānē|, Ruhollah (1900–89) Iranian Shiite Muslim leader; known as **Ayatollah Khomeini**. He returned from exile in 1979 to lead an Islamic revolution that overthrew the shah. He established Iran as a fundamentalist Islamic republic and relentlessly pursued the Iran–Iraq War (1980–89).

Khru·schev |krŏŏSHˈCHawf|, Nikita (Sergeevich) (1894–1971) Soviet statesman, premier of the USSR (1958–64). He was First Secretary of the Communist Party of the USSR (1953–64) after the death of Stalin, whom he denounced in 1956. He came close to war with the U.S. over the Cuban Missile Crisis in 1962 and also clashed with China, which led to his being ousted by Brezhnev and Kosygin.

Khu·fu |ˈkŏŏfŏŏ| see CHEOPS.

Kidd |kid|, William (1645–1701) Scottish pirate; known as **Captain Kidd**. Sent to the Indian Ocean in 1695 in command of an anti-pirate expedition, Kidd became a pirate himself. In 1699 he went to Boston in the hope of obtaining a pardon, but was arrested and later hanged in London.

Kid·der |kiddər|, (John) Tracy (1945–) U.S. author. Works include *The Soul of a New Machine* (1982, Pulitzer Prize, American Book Award).

Kid·man |ˈkidmən|, Nicole (1967–) U.S. actress. Notable movies: *To Die For* (1995), *Portrait of a Lady* (1996), and *Eyes Wide Shut* (1999). She is married to actor Tom Cruise.

Kier·ke·gaard |ˈkirkegärd|, Søren (Aabye) (1813–55) Danish philosopher. A founder of existentialism, he affirmed the importance of individual experience and choice and believed one could know God only through a "leap of faith," and not through doctrine. Notable works: *Either-Or* (1843) and *The Sickness unto Death* (1849).

Kie·slow·ski |kēˈslawfskē|, Krzysztof (1941–96) Polish movie director. Noted for their mannered style and their artistic, philosophical nature, his movies include *Dekalog* (1988), a series of visual interpretations of the Ten Commandments, and the trilogy *The Double Life of Véronique* (1991).

Kil·le·brew |ˈkiləˌbrŏŏ|, Harmon (1936–) U.S. baseball player. He led the American League in home runs six times.

Kil·ly |ˈkēyē|, Jean-Claude (1943–) French alpine skier. He won three gold medals at the 1968 Olympic Games and was a two-time World Cup champion.

Kil·mer |ˈkilmər|, Joyce (1888–1918) U.S. poet. Full name *Alfred Joyce Kilmer*. He was killed in action during World War I. Notable books: *Summer of Love* and *Trees and Other Poems* (1914).

Kim Il Sung |kim il sŏŏNG| (1912–94) Korean communist statesman, first premier of North Korea (1948–72) and president (1972–94); born *Kim Song Ju*.

He precipitated the Korean War (1950–53), and remained committed to the reunification of the country. He maintained a one-party state and created a personality cult around himself and his family; on his death he was quickly replaced in power by his son **Kim Jong Il**.
King |kɪNG| U.S. civil rights leaders. **Martin Luther King, Jr.** (1929–68), a Baptist minister, opposed discrimination against blacks by organizing nonviolent resistance and peaceful mass demonstrations, and was a notable orator. He was assassinated in Memphis. Nobel Peace Prize (1964). His birthday, January 15, is a legal holiday. **Coretta Scott King** (1927–   ), his wife, founded the Martin Luther King, Jr. Center for Nonviolent Social Change in Atlanta.
King |kɪNG|, Albert (1923–92) U.S. blues guitarist. Born *Albert Nelson*. Notable songs: "Laundromat Blues" (1966).
King |kɪNG|, B. B. (1925–   ) U.S. blues singer and guitarist; born *Riley B. King*. An established blues performer, he came to the notice of a wider audience in the late 1960s, when his style of guitar playing was imitated by rock musicians.
King |kɪNG|, Billie Jean (1943–   ) U.S. tennis player and promoter of professional women's tennis. She won a record twenty Wimbledon titles, including six singles titles (1966–68; 1972–73; 1975), ten doubles titles, and four mixed doubles titles.
King |kɪNG|, Carole (1942–   ) U.S. singer and songwriter. Born *Carole Klein*. With Gerry Goffin, she cowrote hits such as "Will You Still Love Me Tomorrow" (1961) and "Up on the Roof."
King |kɪNG|, Ernest J. (1878–1956) U.S. naval officer. He served as commander in chief of the U.S. Atlantic fleet (1940) and combined fleet (Dec. 1941), as chief of naval operations (1942–45), and as admiral of the fleet (1945).
King |kɪNG|, Larry (1933–   ) U.S. television and radio broadcaster. Born *Larry Zeiler*. He hosts the call-in television program "Larry King, Live."
King |kɪNG|, Rufus (1755–1827) U.S. politician. A member of the Continental Congress (1784–87), he ran unsuccessfully for U.S. vice president (1804 and 1808) and president (1816).
King |kɪNG|, Stephen Edwin (1947–   ) U.S. author. He is best known for his writings of horror and suspense. Notable novels: *Carrie* (1974), *The Shining* (1977), and *Bag of Bones* (1998).
King |kɪNG|, William Lyon Mackenzie (1874–1950) Canadian Liberal statesman, prime minister (1921–26, 1926–30, and 1935–48). The grandson of William Lyon Mackenzie, he played an important role in establishing the status of the self-governing nations of the Commonwealth.
King |kɪNG|, William Rufus de Vane (1786–1853) vice president of the U.S. (1853).
Kings•ley |ˈkɪNGzlē|, Charles (1819–75) English novelist and clergyman. He is remembered for his historical novel *Westward Ho!* (1855) and for his classic children's story *The Water-Babies* (1863).
King•sol•ver, Barbara (1955–   ) U.S. author. Notable works: *The Bean Trees* (1992) and *High Tide in Tucson: Essays Now or Never* (1995).
Kin•nell |kiˈnel|, Galway (1927–   ) U.S. author of fiction and poetry. Notable works: *Mortal Words, Mortal Acts* (1980).
Kin•sey |ˈkinzē|, Alfred Charles (1894–1956) American zoologist and sex researcher. He carried out pioneering studies into sexual behavior by interviewing large numbers of people. His best-known work, *Sexual Behavior in the Human Male* (1948, also known as the *Kinsey Report*), was controversial but highly influential.
Kip•ling |ˈkipliNG|, (Joseph) Rudyard (1865–1936) British novelist, short-story writer, and poet. Born in India, he is known for his poems, such as "If" and "Gunga Din," and his children's tales, notably *The Jungle Book* (1894) and the *Just So Stories* (1902). Nobel Prize for Literature (1907).
Kir•by |ˈkərbē|, Jack (1917–94) U.S. cartoonist. He made important contributions to the history of the comic book with the creation of the characters Captain America, Spider-Man, the Incredible Hulk, and the Fantastic Four.

Kir·by |'kərbē|, Rollin (1875–1952) U.S. cartoonist and author. He was a newspaper cartoonist and the writer of verse, short stories, and editorials for magazines. Pulitzer Prize for cartooning (1921, 1924, and 1928).

Kirch·hoff |'kerKHhawf|, Gustav Robert (1824–87) German physicist, a pioneer in spectroscopy. Working with Bunsen, he developed a spectroscope and discovered that solar absorption lines are specific to certain elements. He also developed the concept of black-body radiation and discovered the elements cesium and rubidium.

Kirch·ner |'kerKHnər|, Ernst Ludwig (1880–1938) German expressionist painter. In 1905 he was a founder of the first group of German expressionists. His paintings are characterized by the use of bright, contrasting colors and angular outlines and often depict claustrophobic street scenes.

Kirk·pat·rick |ˌkərk'pætrik|, Jeane Duane Jordan (1926–) U.S. political scientist and public official. U.S. representative to the U.N. (1981–85).

Kir·stein |'kərstīn|, Lincoln (1907–96) U.S. ballet promoter and author. With George Balanchine, he founded and then directed the School of American Ballet and the New York City Ballet.

Kis·sin·ger |'kisənjər|, Henry (Alfred) (1923–) German-born U.S. statesman and diplomat, Secretary of State 1973–77. In 1973 he helped negotiate the withdrawal of U.S. troops from South Vietnam, for which he shared the Nobel Peace Prize. He later restored U.S. diplomatic relations with Egypt in the wake of the Yom Kippur War and subsequently mediated between Israel and Syria. His numerous trips to foster Middle East negotiations led to the term "shuttle diplomacy."

Kitch·e·ner |'kiCH(ə)nər|, (Horatio) Herbert, 1st Earl Kitchener of Khartoum (1850–1916) British soldier and statesman. At the outbreak of World War I, he was made secretary of state for war. He had previously defeated the Mahdist forces at Omdurman in 1898, served as chief of staff in the Second Boer War, and been commander in chief (1902–09) in India.

Kit·tredge |'kitrij|, George Lyman (1860–1941) U.S. literary critic. Notable works: *Shakespeare* (1916).

Klap·roth |'kläp.rōt|, Martin Heinrich (1743–1817) German chemist, one of the founders of analytical chemistry. He discovered three new elements (zirconium, uranium, and titanium) in certain minerals, and contributed to the identification of others. A follower of Lavoisier, he helped to introduce the latter's new system of chemistry into Germany.

Klee |klā|, Paul (1879–1940) Swiss painter, resident in Germany from 1906. He joined Kandinsky's *Blaue Reiter* group in 1912 and later taught at the Bauhaus (1920–33). His work is characterized by his sense of color, and moves freely between abstraction and figuration. Although some of his paintings have a childlike quality, his later work became increasingly somber.

Klein |klīn|, Calvin (Richard) (1942–) U.S. fashion designer, known for his understated fashions for both men and women.

Klein |klīn|, Melanie (1882–1960) Austrian-born psychoanalyst. Klein was the first psychologist to specialize in the psychoanalysis of small children. Her discoveries led to an understanding of some of the more severe mental disorders found in children.

Klem·per·er |'klempərər|, Otto (1885–1973) German-born U.S. conductor and composer. While conductor at the Kroll Theatre in Berlin (1927–31), he was noted as a champion of new work. He became a U.S. citizen in 1937 and subsequently became known for his interpretations of Beethoven, Brahms, and Mahler.

Klerk |klerk|, F. W. de see DE KLERK.

Kliegl |'klēg(ə)l|, U.S. businessman, born in Germany. **Anton T. Kliegl** (1872–1927) and his brother **John H. Kliegl** (1869–1959) were pioneers in the development of electric stage lighting equipment.

Klimt |klimt|, Gustav (1862–1918) Austrian painter and designer. Co-founder of the Vienna Secession (1897), he is known for his decorative and allegorical paintings and his portraits of women. Notable works: *The Kiss* (1908).

Kline |klīn|, Kevin (1947–) U.S. actor. Notable movies: *A Fish Called Wanda* (1988, Academy Award).

Klugman |'kləgmən|, Jack (1922–) U.S. actor. Film credits include *Days of Wine and Roses* (1962). He starred in the television series "The Odd Couple" (1970–75) and "Quincy" (1976–83).

Knight |nīt|, Bob (1940–) U.S. basketball coach. He coached the 1984 gold medal Olympic team.

Knight |nīt|, Gladys (1944–) U.S. musician. She formed Gladys Knight and the Pips. Notable songs: "That's What Friends are For."

Knight |nīt|, John Shively (1894–1981) U.S. newspaper publisher. He merged his newspapers in Detroit, Chicago, New York, etc. with the Ridder Publications chain (1974) to form Knight-Ridder Newspapers, Inc., which includes 34 daily papers and 4 television stations.

Knight |nīt|, Philip H. (1938–) U.S. businessman. He was cofounder of the Blue Ribbon Sports athletic shoe company, which became Nike, Inc.

Knopf |(kə)'näpf|, Alfred A. (1892–1984) U.S. publisher. He was founder of Alfred A. Knopf (1915).

Knotts |näts|, Don (1924–) U.S. actor. Performer in movies and on television, and five-time Emmy Award winner for his supporting role as Barney Fife in the television series "The Andy Griffith Show."

Knowles |nōlz|, John (1926–) U.S. author. Notable works: *Selected Poems* (1982, Pulitzer Prize).

Knox |näks|, Frank (1874–1944) U.S. newspaper publisher and politician. Full name *William Franklin Knox*. He was a Republican vice presidential candidate (1936) and served as secretary of the U.S. Navy (1940–44).

Knox |näks|, Henry (1750–1806) American Revolutionary War general and first U.S. secretary of war (1785–94).

Knox |näks|, John (c. 1505–72) Scottish Protestant reformer. Knox played a central part in the establishment of the Church of Scotland within a Scottish Protestant state and led opposition to the Catholic Mary, Queen of Scots, when she returned to rule in her own right in 1561.

Koch |käCH|, Edward I. (1924–) U.S. politician. Mayor of New York City (1978–89).

Koch |käCH|, Kenneth (1925–) U.S. author and educator. Notable works: *Selected Poems* (1985). Bollingen Prize, 1995.

Köchel |'kОEKHəl; 'kərSHəl|, Ludwig Alois Ferdinand Ritter von (1800–77) Austrian music bibliographer. In his *Chronologisch-thematisches Verzeichnis* (1862), he numbered all of Mozart's works; hence the prefatory "K" or "KV" number on Mozart program listings.

Kodály |'kōdī; 'kōdäē|, Zoltán (1882–1967) Hungarian composer. His main source of inspiration was his native land; he was also involved in the collection and publication of Hungarian folk songs. Notable works: *Psalmus Hungaricus* (choral, 1923) and *Háry János* (operetta, 1925–27).

Koestler |'kest(l)ər|, Arthur (1905–83) Hungarian-born British novelist and essayist. His best-known novel *Darkness at Noon* (1940) exposed the Stalinist purges of the 1930s. He left money in his will to found a university chair in parapsychology.

Koffka |'kawfkə|, Kurt (1886–1941) German psychologist, educator, and author. Chief developer of Gestalt psychology and its application to child development.

Kofoid |'kō,foid|, Charles Atwood (1865–1947) U.S. zoologist. Played a major role in the establishment of the Scripps Institution of Oceanography and invented the Kofoid horizontal net and Kofoid self-closing bucket for the collection of plankton.

Kohl |kōl|, Helmut (1930–) German statesman, chancellor of the Federal Republic of Germany (1982–90), and of Germany (1990–98). As chancellor he showed strong commitment to NATO and to closer European unity within the European Union.

Kolff |kawlf|, Willem Johan (1911–) U.S. surgeon and educator, born in Holland. He developed an artificial kidney for clinical use (1943) and an oxygenator (1956).

Kooning |kōōniNG|, Willem de see DE KOONING.

Koontz |kōōnts|, Dean Ray (1945–) U.S. author. Pseudonyms **Richard Paige** and **Owen West**. He is the author of over 70 best-sellers including *Sole Survivor* (1996).

Koop |kōōp|, C. Everett (1916–) U.S. physician and government official. Full name *Charles Everett Koop*. U.S. surgeon general (1981–89).

Kop·lik |'käplik|, Henry (1858–1927) U.S. pediatrician. He described Koplik's spots to diagnose measles and established the first milk distribution center for infants of the poor.

Kor·but |'kawrbət|, Olga (1955–) Soviet gymnast, born in Belarus. She won two individual gold medals at the 1972 Olympic Games.

Kor·da |'kawrdə|, Sir Alexander (1893–1956) Hungarian-born British movie producer and director; born *Sándor Kellner*. He produced *The Thief of Baghdad* (1940) and *The Third Man* (1949) and produced and directed *The Private Life of Henry VIII* (1933).

Koren, Edward B. (1935–) U.S. cartoonist, author, and illustrator. He is best known for his creation of a cast of woolly characters appearing in the *New Yorker* magazine.

Kor·man |'kawrmən|, Harvey Herschel (1927–) U.S. actor. He starred in the television series "The Carol Burnett Show" (1967–70) and movies such as *Blazing Saddles* (1974) and *High Anxiety* (1978).

Kor·ni·lov |kawr'n(y)iləf|, Lavr Georgyevich (1870–1918) Russian general. He commanded the troops in Petrograd after the Bolshevik Revolution (1917) but was checked by the Bolsheviks in an attempt to make himself dictator.

Kos·cius·ko |,käsē'əs,kō|, Thaddeus (1746–1817) Polish soldier and patriot; full Polish name *Tadeusz Andrzej Bonawentura Kościuszko*. After fighting for the Americans during the Revolutionary War, he led a nationalist uprising against Russia in Poland in 1794.

Ko·sin·ski |kə'zinskē|, Jerzy (Nikodem) (1933–91) U.S. author, born in Poland. Notable works: *Being There* (1971).

Kos·suth |'kä,sōōTH|, Lajos (1802–94) Hungarian statesman and patriot. He led the 1848 insurrection against the Hapsburgs, but after a brief success the uprising was crushed and he began a lifelong period of exile.

Ko·sy·gin |kə'sēgən|, Aleksei (Nikolaevich) (1904–80) Soviet statesman, premier of the USSR (1964–80). He devoted most of his attention to internal economic affairs, being gradually eased out of the leadership by Brezhnev.

Kot·ze·bue |'kawtsə,bōō|, August von (1761–1819) German dramatist. His many plays were popular in both Germany and England. He was a political informant to Tsar Alexander I and was assassinated by the Germans.

Kou·fax |'kōfæks|, Sandy (1935–) U.S. baseball player. Elected to the Baseball Hall of Fame (1972).

Kous·se·vitz·ky |,kōōsə'vitskē|, Serge (1874–1951) U.S. conductor, born in Russia. He was director of the Boston Symphony Orchestra (1924–49) and organizer of the Berkshire Music Center at Tanglewood.

Ko·vacs |'kōvæks|, Ernie (1919–62) U.S. television comedian.

Krafft-Ebing |'kräf't ēbiNG|, Richard von (1840–1902) German physician and psychologist. He established the relationship between syphilis and general paralysis and pioneered the systematic study of aberrant sexual behaviour.

Kraft |kræft|, James Lewis (1874–1953) U.S. businessman, born in Canada. The founder of the Kraft Cheese Co., he patented a method of blending, pasteurizing, and packaging cheddar cheese (1916).

Krantz |kræn(t)s|, Judith (1928–) U.S. author. Notable works: *Princess Daisy* (1980).

Krebs |krebz|, Sir Hans Adolf (1900–81) German-born British biochemist. He discovered the cycle of reactions (Krebs cycle) by which urea is synthesized in the liver as a nitrogenous waste product. Nobel Prize for Physiology or Medicine (1953).

Krebs |krebz|, Johann Ludwig (1713–80) German organist and composer. He was a student of J. S. Bach.

Kreis·ler |'krīslər|, Fritz (1875–1962) Austrian-born U.S. violinist and composer. A noted virtuoso, in 1910 he gave the first performance of Elgar's violin concerto, which was dedicated to him.

Kress |kres|, Samuel Henry (1863–1955) U.S. merchant. He was the founder of S. H. Kress & Co., a chain of 5-, 10-, and 25-cent stores.

Krish·na·mur·ti |ˌkrisHnə'mərtē|, Jiddu (1895–1986) Indian spiritual leader. His spiritual philosophy is based on a rejection of organized religion and the attainment of self-realization by introspection.

Kris·tof·fer·son |kri'stawfərsən|, Kris (1936–) U.S. singer, songwriter, and actor.

Kroc |kräk|, Ray (1902–84) U.S. entrepreneur. Full name *Raymond Albert Kroc*. In 1955, he founded the franchise empire of McDonald's fast-food restaurants.

Kro·ne |'krōnə|, Julie (1963–) U.S. jockey. She was the first woman to capture a Triple Crown horse-racing title (1993).

Kro·pot·kin |krə'pätkən|, Prince Peter (1842–1921) Russian anarchist. Imprisoned in 1874, he escaped abroad in 1876 and did not return to Russia until after the Revolution. His works include *Modern Science and Anarchism* (1903).

Kru·ger |'krōōgər|, Stephanus Johannes Paulus (1825–1904) South African soldier and statesman, president of Transvaal (1883–99). He led the Afrikaners to victory in the First Boer War in 1881. His refusal to allow equal rights to non-Boer immigrants was one of the causes of the Second Boer War.

Kru·pa |'krōōpə|, Gene (1909–73) U.S. jazz drummer and bandleader. He was the first major popular drum soloist.

Krupp |krōōp; krəp|, Alfred (1812–87) German arms manufacturer. His company played a preeminent role in German arms production from the 1840s through the end of World War II.

Krutch |krōōCH|, Joseph Wood (1893–1970) U.S. educator and author. Notable work: *The Modern Temper* (1929).

Ku·be·lík |'kōōbəlik|, (Jeronym) Rafael (1914–) Czech conductor and composer. He served as director of the Chicago Symphony (1950–53), Covent Garden (1955–58), and the Bavarian Radio Orchestra (1961–80), and music

director of the Metropolitan Opera (1973-74).

Ku·blai Khan |ˌkōōblə 'kän| (1216–94) Mongol emperor of China, grandson of Genghis Khan. With his brother Mangu (then Mongol Khan) he conquered southern China (1252–59). After Mangu's death in 1259 he completed the conquest of China, founded the Yuan dynasty, and established his capital on the site of modern Beijing.

Ku·brick |'kōōbrik|, Stanley (1928–99) U.S. film director, producer, and writer. Notable films: *Dr. Strangelove* (1964), *2001: A Space Odyssey* (1968), and *A Clockwork Orange* (1971).

Kuhn |k(y)ōōn|, Maggie (1905–95) U.S. organization executive. Full name *Margaret Kuhn*. An advocate for women and the elderly, she was a founder of the Gray Panthers (1971) and author of *Maggie Kuhn on Aging* (1977).

Ku·min |'kōōmin|, Maxine (Winokur) (1925–) U.S. author. Notable works: *Up Country* and *Poems of New England* (1972, Pulitzer Prize).

Kun·de·ra |'kōōndərə|, Milan (1929–) Czech novelist. He emigrated to France in 1975 after his books were banned in Czechoslovakia following the Soviet military invasion of 1968. Notable works: *The Book of Laughter and Forgetting* (1979) and *The Unbearable Lightness of Being* (1984).

Ku·nitz |'kōōnits|, Stanley Jasspon (1905–) U.S. poet and editor. He is the author of *Selected Poems* (1958, Pulitzer Prize) and of reference works including *American Authors, 1600–1900* (1938, with Howard Haycraft).

Kunst·ler |'kəns(t)lər|, William (1919–95) U.S. attorney and civil rights activist. His clients included the Southern Christian Leadership Conference, the Black Panthers, and the Chicago Seven.

Ku·ralt |kə'rawlt|, Charles (1934–97) U.S. television and radio journalist. He chronicled life in America with his "On the Road" reports.

Ku·ro·sa·wa |ˌkōōrə'säwə|, Akira (1910–98) Japanese movie director. Notable movies: *Rashomon* (1950) and *Ran* (1985), a Japanese version of Shakespeare's *King Lear*.

Kurtz·man |'kərtsmən|, Harvey (1921–

93) U.S. illustrator and cartoonist. He helped to create *Mad* magazine.

Kurz·weil |'kərts‚wīl|, Raymond C. (1948–) U.S. computer scientist and entrepreneur. He is the chairman of Kurzweil Applied Intelligence, Inc. (1982–).

Ku·tu·zov |ko͞o'to͞ozəf; ko͞o'to͞o‚zawf|, Mikhail Illarionovich, Prince (1745–1813) Russian field marshal. He was an army commander in the wars against Napoleon (1805–12), the Turks (1811–12), and the French (1812).

Kwo·lek, Stephanie Louise (1923–) U.S. chemist. She invented processes that resulted in new polymers, the best known of which is Kevlar.

Kyd |kid|, Thomas (1558–64) English dramatist. His anonymously published *The Spanish Tragedy* (1592), an early example of revenge tragedy, was very popular on the Elizabethan stage.

Ll

La·ban |'läbən|, Rudolf von (1879–1958) Hungarian choreographer and dancer. A pioneer of the central European school of modern dance, in 1920 he published the first of several volumes outlining his system of dance notation.

la Bar·ca |lä 'bärkə|, Pedro Calderón de see CALDERÓN DE LA BARCA.

La·Belle |lə'bel|, Patti (1944–   ) U.S. singer and actress. Born *Patricia Louise Holt*. Grammy Award, 1991.

La Bru·yére |'lä broō'yer|, Jean de (1645–96) French writer and moralist. He is known for his *Caractères* (1688), consisting of a translation of the *Characters* based on Theophrastus and exposing the vanity and corruption of human behavior by satirizing Parisian society.

La·can |lä'käN|, Jacques (1901–81) French psychoanalyst and writer. A notable post-structuralist, he reinterpreted Freudian psychoanalysis, especially the theory of the unconscious, in the light of structural linguistics and anthropology.

La·chaise |lä'sHez|, Gaston (1882–1935) U.S. figurative sculptor, born in France. He is known for his massively proportioned female nudes, including *Standing Woman* (1912–27).

La·clos |lä'klō|, Pierre Choderlos de (1741–1803) French novelist; full name *Pierre-Ambroise-François Choderlos de Laclos*. He is chiefly remembered for his epistolary novel *Les Liaisons dangereuses* (1782).

Lad·is·laus I |'lädēs,läs| (*c.* 1040–95) king of Hungary (1077–95); canonized as **St. Ladislaus**. He extended Hungarian power and advanced the spread of Christianity. Feast day, June 27.

Lad·is·laus II |'lädēs,läs| (*c.* 1351–1434) king of Poland (1386–1434); Polish name *Władysław*. As grand duke of Lithuania, he acceded to the Polish throne on his marriage to the Polish monarch, **Queen Jadwiga**, thus uniting Lithuania and Poland.

La Farge |lə 'färzH; lə 'färj| U.S. family, including: **John La Farge** (1835–1910), an artist known for his panels in St. Thomas' Church (New York City) and for the stained glass at Second Presbyterian Church (Chicago). His son **Christopher Grant La Farge** (1862–1938), an architect. He designed the Roman Catholic chapel at West Point, New York. **Oliver (Hazard Perry) La Farge** (1901–63), son of Christopher Grant La Farge. He was an ethnologist and author who wrote *Laughing Boy* (1929, Pulitzer Prize).

La·fa·yette |,läfä'yet; ,läfē'yet; ,læfē 'yet|, Marie-Joseph-Paul-Yves-Roch-Gilbert du Motier, Marquis de (1757–1834) French soldier and statesman. He fought alongside the American colonists in the Revolutionary War and commanded the National Guard (1789–91) in the French Revolution.

La Fol·lette |lə'fälət|, Robert Marion (1855–1925) U.S. politician. He was a member of the U.S. House of Representatives from Wisconsin and a member of the U.S. Senate; he served as governor of Wisconsin and was a Progressive Party presidential candidate (1924).

La Fon·taine |'läfawn,tän|, Jean de (1621–95) French poet. He is chiefly remembered for his *Fables* (1668–94), drawn from oriental, classical, and contemporary sources.

La·ger·feld |'lägər,felt|, Karl (1938–   ) French fashion designer, born in Germany.

La·ger·löf |'lägər,lŏEv|, Selma (Ottiliana Lovisa) (1858–1940) Swedish novelist. She made her name with *Gösta Berlings Saga* (1891) and was the first woman to be the sole winner of a Nobel Prize (Literature, 1909).

La·grange |lä'gräNzH; lə'gränj|, Joseph-Louis Comte de (1736–1813) Italian-born French mathematician. He is remembered for his proof that every positive integer can be expressed as a sum of at most four squares, and for his work on mechanics and its application to the description of planetary and lunar motion.

La Guar·dia |lə'gwär͵dēə|, Fiorello Henry (1882–1947) U.S. politician. He was mayor of NewYork City (1933–45).

Lahr |lär|, Bert (1895–1967) U.S. comedian. Born *Irving Lahrheim*. He starred in *TheWizard of Oz* as the Cowardly Lion.

Laing |læNG|, R. D. (1927–89) Scottish psychiatrist; full name *Ronald David Laing*. He became famous for his controversial views on insanity and in particular on schizophrenia, linking what society calls insanity with politics and family structure.

Lake |lāk|, Simon (1866–1945) U.S. naval architect. He invented the even-keel submarine torpoedo boat.

La·lique |lä'lēk|, René (1860–1945) French jeweler, famous for his art nouveau brooches and combs and his decorative glassware.

La·mar |lə'mär|, Joseph Rucker (1857–1916) U.S. Supreme Court justice (1910–16).

La·mar |lə'mär|, Lucius Quintus Cincinnatus (1825–1893) U.S. Supreme Court justice (1888–93).

La·marck |lə'märk|, Jean-Baptiste de Monet de (1744–1829) French naturalist. French naturalist. He was an early proponent of organic evolution, although his theory is not widely accepted today. He suggested that species could have evolved from each other by small changes in their structure, and that the mechanism of such change (not now generally considered possible) was that characteristics acquired in order to survive could be passed on to offspring.

La·mar·tine |lämär'tēn|, Alphonse-Marie-Louis de Prat de (1790–1869) French poet, statesman, and historian. He was Minister of Foreign Affairs in the provisional government following the Revolution of 1848. Notable works: *Méditations poétiques* (1820).

Lamb |læm|, Charles (1775–1834) English essayist and critic.Together with his sister Mary he wrote *Tales from Shakespeare* (1807). Other notable works: *Essays of Elia* (1823).

Lamb |læm|, Wally (1950–) U.S. author. Notable works: *She's Come Undone* (1992) and *I Know This Much Is True* (1998).

Lamb |læm|, Willis Eugene, Jr. (1913–) U.S. physicist. He discovered the Lamb shift. Nobel Prize for Physics (1955).

Lam·bert |'læmbərt|, (Leonard) Constant (1905–51) English composer, conductor, and critic. He wrote the music for the ballet *Romeo and Juliet* (1926) and the jazz work *The Rio Grande* (1929), later becoming musical director of Sadler'sWells (1930–47).

L'Amour |lə'mawr; lə 'mo͞or|, Louis (Dearborn) (1908–88) U.S. author. Born *Louis LaMoore*. He wrote over 200 novels about the AmericanWest. Presidential Medal of Freedom, 1984.

Lam·pe·du·sa |͵læmpə'do͞osə|, Giuseppe Tomasi di (1896–1957) Italian novelist. His only novel *Il Gattopardo* (*The Leopard*) was originally rejected by publishers but won worldwide acclaim on its posthumous publication in 1958.

Lan·cas·ter |'læNG͵kæstər|, Burt (1913–94) U.S. movie actor; full name *Burton Stephen Lancaster*. He starred in movies such as *From Here to Eternity* (1953), *Elmer Gantry* (1960), for which he won an Oscar, and *Field of Dreams* (1989).

Land |lænd|, Edwin (1909–91) U.S. inventor. He invented a new polarizing filter with wide use in optical instruments; in 1937, he founded the Polaroid Corp. and introduced the first Polaroid Land Camera (1947).

Lan·dau |'læn͵dow|, Lev (Davidovich) (1908–68) Soviet theoretical physicist, born in Russia. Active in many fields, Landau was awarded the Nobel Prize for Physics in 1962 for his work on the superfluidity and thermal conductivity of liquid helium.

Lan·ders |'lændərz|, Ann (1918–) U.S. journalist. Born *Esther Pauline Friedman*. Author of the "Ann Landers" advice column, she competed with her twin sister, Abigail Van Buren ("Dear Abby").

Lan·don |'lændən|, Alfred Mossman (1887–1987) U.S. politician. He was a Republican presidential candidate (1936).

Lan·don |'lændən|, Michael (1936–91) U.S. actor. Born *Eugene Maurice*

Orowitz. He starred in the television series "Bonanza" (1959–73) and "Little House on the Prairie" (1974–82).

Lan·dor |ˈlændər|, Walter Savage (1775–1864) English poet and essayist. His works include the oriental epic poem *Gebir* (1798), and *Imaginary Conversations of Literary Men and Statesmen* (prose, 1824–8).

Lan·dry |ˈlændrē|, Tom (1924–) U.S. football coach and player. He was the Dallas Cowboys coach for 29 years.

Land·seer |ˈlæn(d)sir|, Sir Edwin Henry (1802–73) English painter and sculptor. He is best known for his animal subjects such as *The Monarch of the Glen* (1851). As a sculptor he is chiefly remembered for the bronze lions in London's Trafalgar Square (1867).

Land·stei·ner |ˈlän(d)ˌSHtīnər|, Karl (1868–1943) Austrian-born U.S. physician. In 1930 Landsteiner was awarded a Nobel Prize for devising the ABO system of classifying blood. He was also the first to describe the rhesus factor in blood.

Lane |lān|, John (19th c) U.S. blacksmith. He constructed the first steel plow (1833) and manufactured plows in Chicago (1824–97) with his son **John**.

Lang |ˈlæNG|, Fritz (1890–1976) Austrian-born movie director, resident in the U.S. from 1933. He directed the silent dystopian movie *Metropolis* (1927), making the transition to sound in 1931 with the thriller *M*. His later work included *The Big Heat* (1953).

Lange |ˈlæNG|, Dorothea (1895–1965) U.S. photographer. She is known for her documentary photographs of the Great Depression, including "White Angel Breadline"; her later photo-essays were published in *Life* magazine.

Lange |ˈlæNG|, Jessica (1949–) U.S. actress. Notable movies: *Tootsie* (1982, Academy Award).

Lang·er |ˈlæNGər|, Susanne K. (1895–1985) U.S. philosopher and educator. Notable works: *An Introduction to Symbolic Logic* (1937).

Lang·ford |ˈlæNGfərd|, Nathaniel Pitt (1832–1911) U.S. explorer and conservationist. He was instrumental in the creation of Yellowstone National Park (1872).

Lang·land |ˈlæNGlənd|, William (*c.* 1330–*c.*1400) English poet. He is best known for *Piers Plowman* (*c.*1367–70), a long allegorical poem which takes the form of a spiritual pilgrimage.

Lang·ley |ˈlæNGlē|, Samuel Pierpont (1834–1906) U.S. astronomer and aviation pioneer. He invented the bolometer (1879–81) and contributed to the design of early aircraft.

Lang·muir |ˈlæNGˌmyo͞or|, Irving (1881–1957) U.S. chemist and physicist. His principal work was in surface chemistry, especially applied to catalysis. He also worked on high-temperature electrical discharges in gases and studied atomic structure. Nobel Prize for Chemistry, 1932.

Lang·ton |ˈlæNGtən|, Stephen (*c.* 1150–1228) English prelate, Archbishop of Canterbury 1207–15; 1218–28. A champion of the English Church, he was involved in the negotiations leading to the signing of Magna Carta.

Lang·try |ˈlæNGtrē|, Lillie (1853–1929) British actress; born *Emilie Charlotte le Breton*. She made her stage debut in 1881 and later became the mistress of the Prince of Wales, later Edward VII.

Lans·bury |ˈlænzˌberē|, Angela Brigid (1925–) English actress. She starred in the television series "Murder, She Wrote" (1984–96) and the Broadway shows *Mame* (1966) and *Gypsy* (1974).

Lan·sing |ˈlænsiNG|, Robert (1864–1928) U.S. lawyer and public official. He was an authority on international law and served as U.S. secretary of state (1915-20).

Lan·ston |ˈlænstən|, Tolbert (1844–1913) U.S. inventor. He patented the typesetting machine (1887) and introduced Monotype (1897).

Lantz |ˈlæn(t)s|, Walter (1900–94) U.S. cartoonist, producer, painter, and animator. He was the creator of the cartoon character Woody Woodpecker. Academy Award, 1979.

Lan·vin, Jeanne (1867–1946) French couturier.

Lan·za |ˈlänzə|, Mario (1921–59) U.S. tenor. Born *Alfredo Arnold Cocozza*. He became an international star as the portrayer of Enrico Caruso in the movies

The Great Caruso (1951) and *The Seven Hills of Rome* (1958).

Lao-tzu |ˌlow'tsoo| (6th century BC) Chinese philosopher traditionally regarded as the founder of Taoism and author of the Tao-te-Ching, its most sacred scripture.

La•place |lä'pläs|, Pierre Simon de (1749–1827) French applied mathematician and theoretical physicist. His treatise *Méchanique céleste* (1799–1825) is an extensive mathematical analysis of geophysical matters and of planetary and lunar motion.

Lard•ner |'lärdnər|, Ring (1885–1933) U.S. author and journalist. Full name *Ringgold Wilmer Lardner*. Notable works: *How to Write Short Stories* (1924).

Lar•kin |'lärkən|, Philip (Arthur) (1922–85) English poet. His poetry is characterized by an air of melancholy and bitterness and by stoic wit. Notable works: *The Whitsun Weddings* (1964) and *High Windows* (1974).

La Roche•fou•cauld |lä ˌrōsHfoo'kō|, François de Marsillac, Duc de (1613–80) French writer and moralist. Notable works: *Réflexions, ou sentences et maximes morales* (1665).

La•rousse |lə'roos|, Pierre-Athanase (1817–75) French lexicographer and encyclopedist. He edited the fifteen-volume *Grand dictionnaire universel du XIXᵉ siècle* (1866–76), which aimed to treat every area of human knowledge. In 1852 he cofounded the publishing house of Larousse.

Lar•ro•quette |ˌlærə'ket|, John Bernard (1947–) U.S. actor. He starred in the television series "Night Court."

Lar•son |'lärsən|, Gary (1950–) U.S. cartoonist and author. His one-panel comic, "The Far Side," was syndicated in over 900 newspapers.

La Salle |lə'sæl|, René-Robert Cavelier de (1643–87) French explorer. He sailed from Canada down the Ohio and Mississippi Rivers to the Gulf of Mexico in 1682, naming the Mississippi basin Louisiana in honor of Louis XIV. In 1684 he led an expedition to establish a French colony on the Gulf of Mexico, but was murdered when his followers mutinied.

Lasch |læsH|, Christopher (1932–94) U.S. historian and social critic. Notable works: *The Culture of Narcissism* (1979).

Las•ker |'læskər|, Albert Davis (1880–1952) U.S. advertising executive and philanthropist, born in Germany. He owned the Chicago advertising firm Lord and Thomas (1912–42)

Las•ker |'læskər|, Emanuel (1868–1941) German chess player. He was the world champion from 1894 to 1921.

Las•ki |'læskē|, Harold Joseph (1893–1950) British political scientist, author, and educator. He was a prominent Labour party member who embraced Marxism in the 1930s. His *Authority in the Modern State* (1919) influenced socialist thinking.

Las•ky |'læsˌkē|, Jesse Louis (1880–1958) U.S. movie producer. He made over 1,000 movies, including *The Great Caruso* (1951).

Las•sus |'läsoos|, Orlandus de (1532–94) Flemish composer; Italian name *Orlando di Lasso*. A notable composer of polyphonic music, he wrote over 2,000 secular and sacred works.

Lath•rop |'läтнrəp|, George Parsons (1851–98) U.S. author and editor. He married Rose Hawthorne and edited her father Nathaniel Hawthorne's works. Notable works: *A Study of Hawthorne* (1876).

Lat•i•mer |'lætəmər|, Hugh (c. 1485–1555) English Protestant prelate and martyr. One of Henry VIII's chief advisers when the king broke with the papacy, under Mary I he was condemned for heresy and burnt at the stake at Oxford with Nicholas Ridley.

Lat•i•mer |'lætəmər|, Lewis H. (1848–1928) U.S. inventor. An associate of Thomas Edison, he supervised the installation of the first electric street lighting in New York City.

La Tour |lä 'toor|, Georges de (1593–1652) French painter. He is best known for his nocturnal religious scenes and his subtle portrayal of candlelight. Notable works: *St. Joseph the Carpenter* (1645) and *The Denial of St. Peter* (1650).

La•trobe |lə'trōb|, Benjamin H. (1764–1820) U.S. architect, born in England. He designed the south wing of the U.S. Capitol in Washington, D.C. and rebuilt the Capitol after its destruction by the British (1815–17).

Lat•ti•more |'lætə‚mawr|, Owen (1900–89) U.S. author and educator. Brother of Richmond Lattimore. He is noted for his writings on his travels, on geography and history, and on current events.

Lat•ti•more |'lætə‚mawr|, Richmond Alexander (1906–84) U.S. author. Brother of Owen Lattimore. His translations include Homer's *Illiad* (1951) and Aristophanes' *The Frogs* (1962).

Laud |lawd|, William (1573–1645) English prelate, Archbishop of Canterbury 1633–45. His attempts to restore some pre-Reformation practices in England and Scotland aroused great hostility and were a contributory cause of the English Civil War. He was executed for treason.

Lau•da |'lowdə|, Niki (1949–) Austrian racing-car driver; full name *Nikolaus Andreas Lauda.*

Lau•der |'lawdər|, Estee (1908–) U.S. businesswoman. She is chairman of the board of the Estee Lauder Co. (1946–).

Laugh•lin, James Laurence (1850–1933) U.S. educator and economist. He edited the *Journal of Political Economy* for 40 years.

Laugh•ton |'lawtn|, Charles (1899–1962) British-born U.S. actor. He is remembered for character roles such as Henry VIII (*The Private Life of Henry VIII*, 1933) and Captain Bligh (*Mutiny on the Bounty*, 1935); he also played Quasimodo in *The Hunchback of Notre Dame* (1939).

Lau•rel |'lawrəl|, Stan (1890–1965) British-born U.S. comedian. Full name *Arthur Stanley Jefferson Laurel.* He played the scatterbrained and tearful innocent alongside Oliver Hardy, his pompous, overbearing, and frequently exasperated friend. They brought their distinctive slapstick comedy to many movies from 1927 onwards.

Lau•ren |lə'ren|, Ralph (1939–) U.S. fashion and textile designer. Born *Ralph Lifshitz.* He began his Polo clothing line for men in 1968 and expanded to include a women's collection in 1971.

Lau•rence |'lawrəns|, (Jean) Margaret (1926–87) Canadian novelist. Her life in Somalia and Ghana (1950–57) influ-

enced her early work, including *This Side Jordan* (1960). Other notable works: *The Stone Angel* (1964).

Lau•rens |'lawrəns|, Henry (1724–92) U.S. merchant and colonial leader. He was president of the Second Continental Congress (1777–78).

Lau•rents |'lawrən(t)s|, Arthur (1918–) U.S. playwright and author. Notable works: *The Way We Were* (1972) and *The Turning Point* (1977).

Lau•ri•er |'lawrē‚ā|, Sir Wilfrid (1841–1919) Canadian Liberal statesman, prime minister (1896–1911). He was Canada's first French-Canadian and Roman Catholic prime minister. He worked to achieve national unity and oversaw the creation of the provinces of Alberta and Saskatchewan.

La•ver |'lāvər|, Rod (1938–) Australian tennis player; full name *Rodney George Laver.* In 1962 he became the second man (after Don Budge in 1938) to win the four major singles championships (British, American, French, and Australian) in one year, called the "Grand Slam"; in 1969 he was the first to repeat this.

La•voi•sier |lə‚vwä'zyā|, Antoine-Laurent (1743–94) French scientist, regarded as the father of modern chemistry. He caused a revolution in chemistry by his description of combustion as the combination of substances with air, or more specifically the gas oxygen.

Law |law|, (Andrew) Bonar (1858–1923) Canadian-born British Conservative statesman and prime minister (1922–23). He was leader of the Conservative Party (1911–21). He retired in 1921, but returned in 1922, following Lloyd George's resignation, to become prime minister for six months.

Law•less |'lawləs|, Theodore K. (1892–1971) U.S. physician. He was one of the first physicians to treat cancer with radium. Spingarn Medal, 1954.

Law•rence |'lawrəns|, St. (died 258) Roman martyr and deacon of Rome; Latin name *Laurentius.* According to tradition, Lawrence was ordered by the prefect of Rome to deliver up the treasure of the Church; when in response to this order he presented the poor people of Rome to the prefect, he was roasted to death on a gridiron. Feast day, August 10.

Law·rence |'lawrəns|, D. H. (1885–1930) English novelist, poet, and essayist; full name *David Herbert Lawrence.* His work is characterized by its condemnation of industrial society and by its frank exploration of sexual relationships, as in *The Rainbow* (1915) and *Lady Chatterley's Lover,* originally published in Italy in 1928, but not available in unexpurgated form until 1960. Other notable works: *Sons and Lovers* (1913).

Law·rence |'lawrəns|, Ernest Orlando (1901–58) U.S. physicist. 1939 Nobel Prize for Physics U.S. physicist. He developed the first circular particle accelerator, later called a cyclotron, and opened the way for high-energy physics. He also worked on providing fissionable material for the atom bomb. Nobel Prize for Physics (1939).

Law·rence |'lawrəns|, Jacob (1917–) U.S. artist and educator. His murals grace space at the Kingdome Stadium in Seattle and at Howard University; Spingarn Medal, 1970.

Law·rence |'lawrəns|, T. E. (1888–1935) British soldier and writer; full name *Thomas Edward Lawrence*; known as **Lawrence of Arabia.** From 1916 he helped to organize the Arab revolt against the Turks in the Middle East, contributing to General Allenby's eventual victory in Palestine in 1918. Lawrence described this period in *The Seven Pillars of Wisdom* (1926).

Law·rence |'lawrəns|, Sir Thomas (1769–1830) English painter. He achieved success with his full-length portrait (1789) of Queen Charlotte, the wife of King George III, and by 1810 he was recognized as the leading portrait painter of his time.

Law·son |'lawsən|, Thomas William (1857–1925) U.S. stockbroker. His sensational attacks on abusive money practices instigated an insurance investigation in 1905.

Lay·a·mon |'läə,män| (late 12th cent) English poet and priest. He wrote the verse chronicle known as the *Brut,* a history of England which introduces for the first time in English the story of King Arthur.

Laz·a·rus |'læzərəs|, Emma (1849–87) U.S. poet. She is known for her sonnet to the Statue of Liberty, which is carved on the pedestal of the statue.

Laz·a·rus |'læzərəs|, Mell (1929–) U.S. cartoonist. Full name *Melvin Lazarus.* He was creator of the comic strips "Miss Peach" and "Momma."

Leach·man |'lēCHmən|, Cloris (1930–) U.S. actress. She performed in the "Mary Tyler Moore Show" and starred in her own television program, "Phyllis" (1975–77). She won an Academy Award in 1971 for *The Last Picture Show.*

Lea·cock |'lē,käk|, Stephen (Butler) (1869–1944) Canadian humorist and economist. He is chiefly remembered for his many humorous short stories, parodies, and essays. Notable works: *Sunshine Sketches of a Little Town* (1912) and *Arcadian Adventures with Idle Rich* (1914).

Lea·key |'lēkē| British family of anthropologists and archaeologists, including: **Louis Seymour Bazett Leakey** (1903–72), a Kenyan-born anthropologist and author who discovered fossil hominids at the Olduvai Gorge in Tanzania. His wife **Mary (Douglas) Leakey** (1913–96), an archaeologist and anthropologist. She discovered fossilized footprints in Tanzania. Their son **Richard (Erskine Frere) Leakey** (1944–), a Kenyan-born archaeologist and anthropologist. He proved theories regarding the origins of *Homo sapiens.*

Lean |lēn|, Sir David (1908–91) English movie director. He made many notable movies, including *Lawrence of Arabia* (1962), *Doctor Zhivago* (1965), and *A Passage to India* (1984).

Lear |lir|, Edward (1812–88) English humorist and illustrator. He wrote *A Book of Nonsense* (1845) and *Laughable Lyrics* (1877).

Lear |lir|, Norman Milton (1922–) U.S. television writer, producer, and director. His award-winning shows include *All in the Family* and *Sanford and Son.*

Lear |lir|, William P. (1902–78) U.S.

inventor. He obtained over 150 patents for such inventions as the automobile radio, the eight-track stereo cartridge, and the Lear jet (1963).

Learn·ed |'lərnəd|, Michael (1939–) U.S. actress. She starred in the television series "The Waltons."

Leary |'lirē|, Timothy (Francis) (1920–96) U.S. psychologist. After experimenting with consciousness-altering drugs including LSD, he was dismissed from his teaching post at Harvard University in 1963 and became a symbol of the hippy drug culture.

Lea·vis |'lēvis|, F. R. (1895–1978) English literary critic; full name *Frank Raymond Leavis*. Founder and editor of the quarterly *Scrutiny* (1932–53), he emphasized the value of critical study of English literature to preserving cultural continuity. Notable works: *The Great Tradition* (1948).

Leav·itt |'levit|, Henrietta Swan (1868–1921) U.S. astronomer. She discovered four novae and some 2,400 variable stars.

Le Brun |lə'brəN|, Charles (1619–90) French painter, designer, and decorator. He was prominent in the development and institutionalization of French art and was a leading exponent of French classicism. In 1648 he helped to found the Royal Academy of Painting and Sculpture.

Le Car·ré |lə,kär'ā|, John (1931–) English novelist; pseudonym of *David John Moore Cornwell*. He is known for his unromanticized and thoughtful spy novels, which often feature the British agent George Smiley and include *The Spy Who Came in from the Cold* (1963) and *Tinker, Tailor, Soldier, Spy* (1974).

Le·conte de Lisle |lə'cōNt də ,lēl; lə 'cawnt də ,lēl|, Charles-Marie-René (1818–94) French poet and leader of the Parnassians. His poetry often draws inspiration from mythology, biblical history, and exotic Eastern landscape. Notable works: *Poèmes antiques* (1852).

Le Cor·bu·sier |ləkawrbʏzyā| (1887–1965) French architect and city planner, born in Switzerland; born *Charles Édouard Jeanneret*. A pioneer of the international style, he developed theories on functionalism, the use of new mate-

rials and industrial techniques, and the Modulor, a modular system of standard-sized units.

Led·bet·ter |'led,betər|, Huddie (1885–1949) U.S. blues singer. Known as **Leadbelly**. His many recordings include "Good Morning, Blues" (1940).

Le·der·berg |'lādər,bərg|, Joshua (1925–) U.S. geneticist. He won the 1958 Nobel Prize for Physiology or Medicine for his discovery of genetic recombination in bacteria.

Led·yard |'led,yərd|, John (1751–89) U.S. explorer. He joined Captain James Cook's last voyage to the Sandwich Islands.

Lee |lē| Family of early American statesmen. **Richard Henry Lee** (1732–94) was a delegate to the Continental Congress (1774–79) and authored a resolution that led to the writing of the Declaration of Independence; he was later elected to the U.S. Senate from Virginia (1789–92). His brother **Francis Lightfoot Lee** (1734–97) was a delegate to the Continental Congress (1775–79) and a signer of the Declaration of Independence. Their brother **Arthur Lee** (1740–92) was a member of the Continental Congress (1781–85) and the U.S. Treasury Board (1784–89).

Lee |lē| U.S. family, including: **Henry** (1756–1818), soldier and politician. Known as **Light-Horse Harry**. Noted as a brilliant Revolutionary War cavalry commander, he later became governor of Virginia (1792–95) and a member of the U.S. House of Representatives (1799–1801). His brother **Charles** (1758–1815) was attorney general of the U.S. (1795–1801). **Robert E. Lee** (1807–70), Confederate general and the son of Henry Lee. Full name *Robert Edward Lee*. He was the commander of the Confederate Army of Northern Virginia for most of the Civil War. A noted tactician and strategist, his invasion of the North was repulsed at the Battle of Gettysburg (1863), and he surrendered in 1865. **Fitzhugh Lee** (1835–1905), army officer and politician, nephew of Robert E. Lee and grandson of Henry Lee. He was the governor of Virginia (1886–90).

Lee |lē|, Ann (1736–84) U.S. religious

leader, born in England. Known as **Mother Ann**. A Shaker leader, she founded the first Shaker colony in the U.S. at Watervliet, NY (1776).

Lee |lē|, Bruce (1940–73) U.S. actor; born *Lee Yuen Kam*. An expert in kung fu, he starred in a number of martial arts movies, such as *Enter the Dragon* (1973). He also played Kato in the television series "The Green Hornet" (1966).

Lee |lē|, Gypsy Rose (1914–70) U.S. striptease artist; born *Rose Louise Hovick*. In the 1930s she became famous on Broadway for her sophisticated striptease act. He autobiography, *Gypsy* (1957) was filmed in 1962.

Lee |lē|, (Nelle) Harper (1926–) U.S. novelist. She won a Pulitzer Prize with her only novel, *To Kill a Mockingbird* (1960), about the sensational trial of a black man falsely charged with raping a white woman.

Lee |lē|, Henry D. (1849–1928) U.S. merchant and manufacturer. He invented Lee blue jeans.

Lee |lē|, Spike (1957–) U.S. movie director; born *Shelton Jackson Lee*. Lee's declared intention is to express the richness of black American culture; movies such as *Do the Right Thing* (1989) and *Malcolm X* (1992) sparked controversy with their treatment of racism.

Lee |lē|, Stan (1922–) U.S. publisher and author. He was the publisher of Marvel Comics and creator, former writer, and editor of "The Fantastic Four," "The Incredible Hulk," and "Spiderman."

Leeu·wen·hoek |'lāvən‚hook|, Antoni van (1632–1723) Dutch naturalist. He developed a lens for scientific purposes and was the first to observe bacteria, protozoa, and yeast. He accurately described red blood cells, capillaries, striated muscle fibers, spermatozoa, and the crystalline lens of the eye.

Lé·ger |lā'zHā|, Fernand (1881–1955) French painter. From about 1909 he was associated with the cubist movement, but then developed a style inspired by machinery and modern technology; works include the *Contrast of Forms* series (1913).

Le·Guin |lə'gwin|, Ursula (1929–) U.S. author. She has written science fic-

tion for children and adults, as well as novels and poetry, including *The Dispossessed* (1975).

Le·hár |'lā‚här|, Franz (Ferencz) (1870–1948) Hungarian composer. He is chiefly known for his operattas, of which the most famous is *The Merry Widow* (1905).

Leh·man |'lēmən; 'lämən|, Herbert Henry (1878–1963) U.S. banker and politician. He was a partner with Lehman Brothers bankers and served as governor of New York (1932–42) and as a member of the U.S. Senate from New York (1949–57).

Leh·mann |'lämən; 'lämän|, Lilli (1848–1929) German soprano. She was known especially as an interpreter of Wagner and Mozart and of lieder.

Leh·mann |'lämən; lämän|, Lotte (1888–1976) U.S. lyric soprano, born in Germany. She was known especially for her interpretations of Mozart, Beethoven, Wagner, Strauss, and Schumann.

Leh·rer |'lerər|, Jim (1934–) U.S. television journalist. Born *James Charles Lehrer*. With Robert MacNeil he co-anchored the *MacNeil/Lehrer News Hour* (1983–95) and now anchors the *NewsHour* (1995–).

Leib·niz |'līb‚nits|, Gottfried Wilhelm (1646–1716) German rationalist philosopher, mathematician, and logician. He argued that the world is composed of single units (monads), each of which is self-contained but acts in harmony with every other, as ordained by God, and so this world is the best of all possible worlds. Leibniz also made the important distinction between necessary and contingent truths and devised a method of calculus independently of Newton.

Lei·bo·vitz |'lēbə‚vits |, Annie (1949–) U.S. photographer. She was chief photographer of *Rolling Stone* magazine (1973–83) before moving to *Vanity Fair*.

Leicester, Earl of see DUDLEY.

Lei·dy |'līdē|, Joseph (1823–91) U.S. educator and anatomist. He was the first to identify extinct species of horse and tiger.

Leif Er·ics·son |'eriksən| see ERICSSON.

Leigh |lē|, Vivien (1913–67) British actress, born in India. Born *Vivian Hartley*. She won 1939 Academy Awards for her role as Scarlett O'Hara in *Gone With the Wind*.

Leigh•ton |'lātn|, Frederick, 1st Baron Leighton of Stretton (1830–96) English painter and sculptor. He was a leading exponent of Victorian neoclassicism and chiefly painted large-scale mythological and genre scenes.

Le•land |'lēlənd|, Henry Martyn (1843–1932) U.S. automobile manufacturer. He founded the Cadillac Motor Car Co. (1904) and the Lincoln Motor Co. (1917).

Le•land |'lēlənd|, Mickey (1944–89) U.S. politician. He was a member of the U.S. House of Representatives from Texas (1979–89) and a chairman of the Congressional Black Caucus.

Le•ly |'lēlē|, Sir Peter (1618–80) Dutch portrait painter, resident in England from 1641; Dutch name *Pieter van der Faes*. He became principal court painter to Charles II. Notable works include *Windsor Beauties*, a series painted during the 1660s.

Le•May |lə'mā|, Curtis Emerson (1906–90) U.S. air force officer. Known as **Old Iron Pants**. He was the commanding general of the U.S. Strategic Air Command (1948–57) and Air Force chief of staff (1961–65).

Lem•el•son |'leməlsən|, Jerome H. (1923–97) U.S. inventor. His more than 500 patents include the bar-code scanner, the fax machine, and the cassette drive mechanism.

Le•mieux |lə'myoō; lə'myOE|, Mario (1965–) U.S. hockey player, born in Canada.

Lem•mon |'lemən|, Jack (1925–) U.S. actor; born *John Uhler*. He made his name in comedy movies, such as *Some Like It Hot* (1959), later playing serious dramatic parts and winning an Oscar for *Save the Tiger* (1973).

Lem•nitz•er |'lem,nitsər|, Lyman Louis (1899–1988) U.S. army officer. He played a key role in the Allied invasions of Africa in World War II and in the negotiated surrender of Italy; later he served as commander of U.N. forces in Korea (1955–57) and as chairman of the U.S. joint chiefs of staff (1960–62).

Len•clos |länklō|, Ninon de (1620–1705) French courtesan; born *Anne de Lenclos*. She was a famous wit and beauty who advocated a form of Epicureanism in her book *La Coquette vengée* (1659) and later presided over one of the most distinguished literary salons of the age.

Len•dl |'lendl|, Ivan (1960–) Czechborn U.S. tennis player. He won many singles titles in the 1980s and early 1990s, including the U.S., Australian, and French Open championships.

L'En•fant |länfäN|, Pierre Charles (1754–1825) U.S. architect and soldier, born in France. He submitted plans for the design of Washington, D.C.

L'Eng•le |'leNGgəl|, Madeleine (1918–) U.S. author. She has written numerous works of adult and children's fiction and nonfiction, including *A Wrinkle in Time* (1962, Newbery Award).

Le•nin |'lenən| (1870–1924) the principal figure in the Russian Revolution and first premier of the Soviet Union (1918–24); born *Vladimir Ilich Ulyanov*. Lenin was the first political leader to attempt to put Marxist principles into practice. In 1917 he established Bolshevik control after the overthrow of the czar, and in 1918 became head of state (Chairman of the Council of People's Commissars). With Trotsky he defeated counter-revolutionary forces in the Russian Civil War but was forced to moderate his policies to allow the country to recover from the effects of war and revolution.

Len•non |'lenən|, John (1940–80) English pop and rock singer, guitarist, and songwriter. A founding member of the Beatles, he wrote most of their songs in collaboration with Paul McCartney. After the group broke up in 1970, he continued recording material, such as *Imagine* (1971), some with his second wife Yoko Ono. He was assassinated outside his home in New York.

Len•nox |'lenəks|, Annie (1954–) U.S. singer, born in Scotland. She was the lead singer of the Eurythmics before launching a solo career.

Le•no |'lenō|, Jay (1950–) U.S. actor

and comedian. Full name *James Douglas Muir Leno.* He replaced Johnny Carson as host of "The Tonight Show" (1992). Emmy Award, 1995.

Le Nô·tre |'lənōtrə|, André (1613–1700) French landscape gardener. He designed many formal gardens, including the parks of Vaux-le-Vicomte and Versailles, which incorporated his ideas on geometric formality and equilibrium.

Len·ox |'lenəks|, James (1800–80) U.S. philanthropist. His personal library became part of the New York Public Library.

Leo |'lē(y)ō| The name of thirteen popes, notably: **Leo I** (*c.* 400–461), pope from 440 and Doctor of the Church; known as **Leo the Great**; canonized as **St. Leo I**. He defined the doctrine of the Incarnation at the Council of Chalcedon (451) and extended the power of the Roman See to Africa, Spain, and Gaul. Feast day (in the Eastern Church), February 18; (in the Western Church), April 11. **Leo X** (1475–1521), pope from 1513; born *Giovanni de' Medici.* He excommunicated Martin Luther and bestowed on Henry VIII of England the title of Defender of the Faith. He was a noted patron of learning and the arts.

Leo III |'lē(y)ō| (*c.* 680–741) Byzantine emperor (717–41). He repulsed several Muslim invasions and carried out an extensive series of reforms. In 726 he banned icons and other religious images; the resulting iconoclastic controversy led to over a century of political and religious turmoil.

Leon·ard |'lenərd|, Elmore (John) (1925–) U.S. novelist and screenwriter Notable works: *Freaky Deaky* (1988), *Get Shorty* (1990), and *Be Cool* (1999).

Leon·ard |'lenərd|, Sugar Ray (1956–) U.S. boxer. Full name *Ray Charles Leonard.* He won world championship titles in three different weight divisions.

Le·o·nar·do da Vin·ci |ˌlē(y)ə'närdō də 'vinˌCHē| (1452–1519) Italian painter, scientist, and engineer. His paintings are notable for their use of the technique of *sfumato* and include *The Virgin of the Rocks* (1483–85), *The Last Supper*

(1498), and the enigmatic *Mona Lisa* (1504–05). He devoted himself to a wide range of other subjects, from anatomy and biology to mechanics and hydraulics: his nineteen notebooks include studies of the human circulatory system and plans for a type of aircraft and a submarine.

Le·on·ti·ef |lē'(y)awnˌtyef|, Wassily (1906–) U.S. economist, educator, and author, born in Russia. Notable works: The Structure of the American Economy, 1919–29 (2nd ed. 1976). Nobel Prize for Economics, 1973.

Le·o·pold I |'lē(y)əˌpōld| (1790–1865) first king of Belgium (1831–65). The fourth son of the Duke of Saxe-Coburg-Saalfield, Leopold was an uncle of Britain's Queen Victoria. In 1830 he refused the throne of Greece, but a year later he accepted that of the newly independent Belgium.

Leo the Great Pope Leo I (see LEO).

Le·pi·dus |'lepədəs|, Marcus Aemilius (died *c.* 13 BC) Roman statesman and triumvir. A supporter of Julius Caesar in the civil war against Pompey, he was elected consul in 46 and was appointed one of the Second Triumvirate with Octavian and Antony in 43.

Ler·ner |'lərnər|, Alan J. (1918–1986) U.S. lyricist and dramatist; full name *Alan Jay Lerner.* He wrote a series of musicals with composer Frederick Loewe (1904–88) that were also filmed, including *Paint Your Wagon* (1951; filmed 1969) and *My Fair Lady* (1956; filmed 1964). He won Oscars for the movies *An American in Paris* (1951) and *Gigi* (1958).

Le·sage |lə'säzH|, Alain-René (1668–1747) French novelist and dramatist. He is best known for the picaresque novel *Gil Blas* (1715–35).

Les·caze |ˌles'käz|, William (1896–1969) U.S. architect, born in Switzerland. He designed the Philadelphia Savings Fund Society building and the Church Peace Center building in New York City.

Les·seps |lā'seps; 'lesəps|, Ferdinand-Marie, Vicomte de (1805–94) French diplomat. From 1854 onwards, while in the consular service in Egypt, he devoted himself to the project of the Suez

Canal. In 1881 he embarked on the building of the Panama Canal, but the project was abandoned in 1889.

Les·sing |'lesiNG|, Doris (May) (1919–) British novelist and short-story writer, brought up in Rhodesia. An active communist in her youth, she frequently deals with social and political conflicts in her fiction, especially as they affect women. Notable novels: *The Grass is Singing* (1950), *Canopus in Argus* (1979–83), and *The Good Child* (1988).

Les·sing |'lesiNG|, Gotthold Ephraim (1729–81) German dramatist and critic. In his critical works, such as *Laokoon* (1766), he suggested that German writers look to English literature rather than the French classical school. He also wrote both tragedy and comedy.

Let·ter·man |'letərmən|, David (1947–) U.S. writer and comedian. He hosted "The David Letterman Show" and "Late Night with David Letterman"

Leu·tze |'loitsə|, Emanuel Gottlieb (1816–68) U.S. artist. He is noted for his historical paintings, especially *Washington Crossing the Deleware* (1851).

Le·ver·hulme |'levər,hyōōm|, 1st Viscount (1851–1925) English industrialist and philanthropist; born *William Hesketh Lever*. He and his brother manufactured soap; their company, Lever Bros., came to form the basis of the international corporation Unilever.

Lever·rier |ləvāryā|, Urbain-Jean-Joseph (1811–77) French mathematician. His analysis of the motions of the planets suggested that an unknown body was disrupting the orbit of Uranus. Le Verrier prompted the German astronomer **Johann Galle**, (1812–1910) to investigate, and the planet Neptune was discovered in 1846.

Lev·er·tov |'levər,tawf|, Denise (1923–97) U.S. poet, born in England. Notable works: *The Poet in the World* (1973).

Le·vi |'lāvē|, Primo (1919–87) Italian novelist and poet, of Jewish descent. His experiences as a survivor of Auschwitz are recounted in his first book *If This is a Man* (1947).

Lev·in |'levən|, Ira (1929–) U.S. author. Notable works: *Rosemary's Baby* (1967) and *Deathtrap* (1978).

Lev·in |'levən|, Meyer (1905–81) U.S. author. Notable works: *Compulsion* (1956).

Le·vine |lə'vēn|, David (1926–) U.S. caricaturist and painter. He was renowned for his political, social, and literary caricatures appearing in *Esquire* and the *New York Review of Books*.

Le·vine |lə'vēn|, Philip (1928–) U.S. poet and educator. Notable works: *Simple Truth* (1995, Pulitzer Prize).

Le·vin·son |'levən,sən|, Barry (1942–) U.S. director. Notable movies: *Rain Man* (1988, Academy Award).

Lé·vi-Strauss |,levē'strows|, Claude (1908–) French social anthropologist A pioneer in the use of a structuralist analysis to study cultural systems, he regarded language as an essential common denominator underlying cultural phenomena.

Le·win·sky |lə'winskē|, Monica (1973–) U.S. White House intern. She gained notoriety for her "inappropriate relationship" with President Bill Clinton.

Lew·is |'lōōəs|, Carl (1961–) U.S. track and field athlete; full name *Frederick Carleton Lewis*. He won Olympic gold medals in 1984, 1988, 1992, and 1996 (his ninth) for sprinting and the long jump and broke the world record for the 100 meters on several occasions.

Lew·is |'lōōəs|, Cecil Day see DAY LEWIS.

Lew·is |'lōōəs|, C. S. (1898–1963) British novelist, religious writer, and literary scholar; full name *Clive Staples Lewis*. He broadcast and wrote on religious and moral issues, and created the imaginary land of Narnia for a series of children's books. Notable works: *The Lion, the Witch, and the Wardrobe* (1950).

Lew·is |'lōōəs|, Henry (1932–1996) U.S. conductor. He was founder of the Los Angeles Chamber Orchestra (1958) and music director of the Los Angeles Opera (1965–68). He made his Metropolitan Opera conducting debut in 1972 in *La Bohème*.

Lew·is |'lōōəs|, Jerry Lee (1935–) U.S. rock-and-roll singer and pianist. In 1957 he had hits with "Whole Lotta Shakin' Going On" and "Great Balls of

Fire". His career was interrupted when his marriage to his fourteen-year-old cousin caused a public outcry.

Lew•is |'lōōəs|, John Llewellyn (1880–1969) U.S. labor leader. He headed the United Mine Workers (1920–60) and organized the Committee for Industrial Organization (1935), which became the Congress of Industrial Organizations.

Lew•is |'lōōəs|, Mel (1929–90) U.S. jazz drummer and orchestra leader. Born *Melvin Sokoloff*. He formed the Thad Jones-Mel Lewis Orchestra in 1965 and became the sole leader after 1979.

Lew•is |'lōōəs|, Meriwether (1774–1809) U.S. explorer. Together with William Clark he led an expedition to explore the newly acquired Louisiana Purchase (1804–06). They travelled from St. Louis to the Pacific Northwest and back. He then served as governor of Louisiana Territory (1807–09).

Lew•is |'lōōəs|, R.W. B. (1917–   ) U.S. literary critic and educator. Full name *Richard Warrington Baldwin Lewis*. Notable works: *The American Adam* (1955) and *Edith Warton* (1975, Pulitzer Prize).

Lew•is |'lōōəs|, Shari (1934–98) U.S. television puppeteer and ventriloquist. Born *Shari Hurwitz*. She was known for her children's television programs featuring the puppets Lamb Chop, Charlie Horse, and Hush Puppy.

Lew•is |'lōōəs|, (Harry) Sinclair (1885–1951) U.S. novelist, known for satirical works such as *Main Street* (1920), *Babbitt* (1922), and *Elmer Gantry* (1927). He was the first American writer to receive the Nobel Prize for Literature (1930).

Lew•is |'lōōəs|, (Percy) Wyndham (1884–1957) British novelist, critic, and painter, born in Canada. He was a leader of the vorticist movement, and with Ezra Pound edited the magazine *Blast* (1914–15). Notable novels: *The Apes of God* (1930).

Lib•by |'libē|, Willard Frank (1908–80) U.S. chemist. He was a member of the Atomic Energy Commission (1954–59) and won the Nobel Prize in Chemistry in 1960 for his discovery of radioactive carbon dating.

Lib•e•ra•ce |ˌlibəˈräCHē| (1919–87) U.S. pianist and entertainer; full name *Wladziu Valentino Liberace*. He was known for his romantic arrangements of popular piano classics and for his flamboyant costumes.

Lich•ten•stein |'liktən,stīn|, Roy (1923–97) U.S. painter and sculptor. A leading exponent of pop art, he became known for paintings inspired by comic strips. Notable works: *Whaam!* (1963).

Lid•dell |'lidəl|, Eric (Henry) (1902–45) British runner and missionary, born in China. In the 1924 Olympic Games he won the 400 meters in a world record time. His exploits were celebrated in the movie *Chariots of Fire* (1981).

Lid•dell Hart |ˌlidəl 'härt|, Sir Basil Henry (1895–1970) British military historian and theorist. He developed principles of mobile warfare, which were adopted by both sides in World War II.

Lie |lē|, Trygve Halvdan (1896–1968) Norwegian Labor politician, first secretary general of the United Nations (1946–53).

Lie•ber |'lēbər|, Francis (1800–1872) U.S. political philosopher, born in Germany. His work, *A Code for the Government of Armies* (1863), was reissued by the War Department as General Orders No. 100 and became a standard international work on military law and conduct of war.

Lie•big |'lēbig|, Justus von (Baron) (1803–73) German chemist and teacher. With Friedrich Wöhler he discovered the benzoyl radical, and demonstrated that such radicals were groups of atoms that remained unchanged in many chemical reactions.

Li•ge•ti |'ligətē|, György Sándor (1923–   ) Hungarian composer. His orchestral works *Apparitions* (1958–59) and *Atmosphères* (1961) dispense with the formal elements of melody, harmony, and rhythm.

Light•foot |'līt,fŏŏt|, Gordon (1938–   ) Canadian singer and songwriter. His hits include "If You Could Read My Mind" and "The Wreck of the Edmund Fitzgerald."

Li•li•u•o•ka•la•ni |liˌlēəwōkəˈlänē| (1838–1917) Hawaiian queen. Also known as **Lydia Paki Liliuokalani** and **Liliu Kamakaeha**. The last reigning queen of the Hawaiian Islands (1891–

93), she ascended the throne in 1891; she was deposed by U.S. marines in 1893 and formally renonced her royal claim in 1895.

Lim•baugh |limbaw|, Rush (1951–) U.S. talk show host and political commentator. His daily three-hour radio show, combining conservative political commentary with satire, has the largest audience of any radio talk show.

Li•món |lē'mōn|, José Arcadio (1908–72) U.S. modern dancer and choreographer, born in Mexico. He founded his own dance company (1947).

Lin |'lin|, Leslie Charles Bowyer (1907–93) U.S. author, born in Singapore. Pseudonym **Leslie Charteris**. He wrote popular thrillers featuring the character Simon Templar, the Saint. Notable works: *The Saint Steps In* (1943) and *Vendetta for Saint* (1964).

Lin |'lin|, Maya (1960–) U.S. architect. She designed the Vietnam Veterans' Memorial in Washington, D.C.

Lin•a•cre |linəkər|, Thomas (*c.* 1460–1524) English physician and classical scholar. In 1518 he founded the College of Physicians in London, and became its first president. He translated Galen's Greek works on medicine and philosophy into Latin, reviving studies in anatomy, botany, and clinical medicine in Britain.

Lin Biao |,lin 'byow| (*c.* 1907–71) Also **Lin Piao**. Chinese communist statesman and general. He was nominated to become Mao's successor in 1969. Having staged an unsuccessful coup in 1971, he was reported to have been killed in a plane crash while fleeing to the Soviet Union.

Lin•coln |'liNGkən|, Abraham see box. **Mary Todd Lincoln** (1818–82), wife of Abraham Lincoln and U.S. first lady (1861–65). Their son **Robert Todd Lincoln** (1843–1926), U.S. lawyer. The only one of four sons of Abraham Lincoln to live to adulthood, he served as secretary of war (1881–85) and as president of the Pullman Co. (1897–1911).

Lind |'lind|, Jenny (1820–87) Swedish soprano; born *Johanna Maria Lind Goldschmidt*. She was known as "the Swedish nightingale" for the purity and agility of her voice.

Lincoln, Abraham
16th U.S. president

Life dates: 1809–1865
Place of birth: Hodgenville, Hardin (now Larue) County, Ky.
Mother: Nancy Hanks Lincoln
Stepmother: Sarah Bush Johnston Lincoln
Father: Thomas Lincoln
Wife: Mary Todd Lincoln
Children: Robert, Edward, William, Thomas ("Tad")
Nickname: Honest Abe
College/University: None
Military service: captain, Company of Volunteers; private, U.S. Army, Black Hawk War
Career: Lawyer; surveyor; postmaster
Political career: Illinois General Assembly; U.S. House of Representatives; president
Party: Whig; Republican
Home state: Illinois
Opponents in presidential races: Stephen A. Douglas, John C. Breckinridge, John Bell; George B. McClellan
Term of office: Mar. 4, 1861–Apr. 15, 1865 (assassinated)
Vice presidents: Hannibal Hamlin; Andrew Johnson
Notable events of presidency: Civil War; Emancipation Proclamation; Homestead Act; Gettysburg Address; Morrill Land-Grant College Act; West Virginia and Nevada admitted as 35th and 36th states; Gen. Robert E. Lee surrendered to Gen. Ulysses S. Grant at Appomattox Courthouse, Va.
Other achievements: Admitted to the Illinois bar; Lincoln-Douglas debates in Illinois (senatorial campaign); first Republican president
Place of burial: Springfield, Ill.

Lind•bergh |'lin(d)bərg| U.S. family, including: **Charles (Augustus) Lindbergh** (1902–74), aviator. In 1927 he made the first solo transatlantic flight in a single-engined monoplane, *Spirit of St. Louis*, and was known thereafter as "Lucky Lindy." He recounted his adventures in the Pulitzer Prize-winning *The Spirit of St. Louis* (1953). His wife **Anne Morrow Lindbergh** (1906–), U.S. author and poet. Notable works: *North to the Orient* (1935) and *Listen! The Wind* (1938). With her husband Charles, she moved to Europe to escape the publicity surrounding the kidnap and murder of their two-year-old son in 1932.

Lind·gren |'lin(d)ˌgrən|, Astrid (1907–) Swedish author of children's books. Notable works: *Pippi Longstocking.*

Lind·say |'linzē| Family of Australian artists. **Sir Lionel Lindsay** (1874–1961) was an art critic, watercolor painter, and graphic artist. His brother **Norman Lindsay** (1879–1969) was a graphic artist, painter, critic, and novelist.

Lind·say |'linzē|, Howard (1889–1968) U.S. playwright, producer, and actor. With Russel Crouse (1893–1966) he co-authored Broadway shows, including *Anything Goes* (1934), *State of the Union* (1946, Pulitzer Prize) and *Sound of Music* (1959).

Lind·say |'linzē|, Vachel (1879–1931) U.S. poet. Full name *Nicholas Vachel Lindsay.* Notable books: *General William Booth Enters into Heaven and Other Poems* (1913), *The Congo and Other Poems* (1914), and *The Candle in the Cabin* (1926).

Link |liNGk|, Edwin Albert (1904–81) U.S. inventor and businessman. With brother George, he made a flight simulator for pilot classroom training (1929) and was the founder and president of Link Aviation, Inc. (1935–53).

Lin·nae·us |lə'nā(y)əs|, Carolus (1707–78) Swedish botanist, founder of modern systematic botany and zoology. Latinized name of *Carl von Linné.* He devised an authoritative classification system for flowering plants involving binomial Latin names (later superseded by that of Antoine Jussieu), and also a classification method for animals.

Lip·chitz |'lipˌSHits|, Jacques (1891–1973) Lithuanian-born French sculptor; born *Chaim Jacob Lipchitz.* After producing cubist works such as *Sailor with a Guitar* (1914), he explored the interpenetration of solids and voids in his series of "transparent" sculptures of the 1920s.

Li·pin·ski |lə'pinskē|, Tara (1982–) U.S. figure skater. She became the youngest woman to win the U.S. and

world figure skating championship (1997).

Li Po |'lē pō; 'lē 'bō| (AD 701–62) Also **Li Bo** or **Li T'ai Po**. Chinese poet. Typical themes in his poetry are wine, women, and the beauties of nature.

Lip·pi |'lipē|, Filippino (*c.* 1457–1504) Italian painter, son of Fra Filippo Lippi. Having trained with his father and Botticelli he completed a fresco cycle begun by Masaccio in the Brancacci Chapel, Florence; other works include the series of frescoes in the Carafa Chapel in Rome and the painting *The Vision of St. Bernard* (*c.*1486).

Lip·pin·cott |'lipən,kät|, Joshua Ballinger (1813–86) U.S. publisher. He founded J. B. Lippincott & Co. (1936).

Lipp·mann |'lipmən|, Gabriel-Jonas (1845–1921) French physicist. He is best known today for his production of the first fully orthochromatic color photograph in 1893.

Lipp·mann |'lipmən|, Walter (1889–1974) U.S. journalist. He was a founder and associate editor of *The New Republic* and a columnist for *The New York Herald Tribune* (1931–67). Pulitzer Prizes, 1958 and 1962.

Lip·ton |'liptən|, Sir Thomas Johnstone (1850–1931) Scottish merchant and yachtsman. He developed a chain of food stores in Scotland before investing in tea. He entered five yachts in the America's Cup races.

Li·sa |'lēsə|, Manuel (1772–1820) U.S. fur trader. He built Fort Manuel, the first trading post in Montana, and he formed the Missouri Fur Co. with members of the Chouteau family.

Lis·ter |'listər|, Joseph (1st Baron) (1827–1912) English surgeon, inventor of antiseptic techniques in surgery. He realized the significance of Louis Pasteur's germ theory in connection with sepsis, and in 1865 he used carbolic acid dressings on patients who had undergone surgery.

Lis·ton |'listən|, Sonny (1932?–70) U.S. heavyweight boxing champion; born *Charles Liston.*

Liszt |list|, Franz (1811–86) Hungarian composer and pianist. He was a key figure in the romantic movement; many of his piano compositions combine lyricism with great technical complexity, while his twelve symphonic poems (1848–58) created a new musical form.

Lith·gow |'liᴛʜgow|, John (1945–) U.S. actor. He won 1996–97 Emmy Awards for his role in the television show "Third Rock from the Sun."

Lit·tle |'litəl|, Arthur Dehon (1863–1935) U.S. chemical engineer. He organized a chemical consulting firm that was later reorganized as Arthur D. Little, Inc. (1909).

Lit·tle |'litəl|, Charles Coffin (1799–1869) U.S. publisher. With James Brown, he founded Little, Brown and Co. (1847), publishers of legal and general works.

Little Corporal a nickname for Napoleon.

Lit· Rich·ard |'litl 'riᴄʜərd| (1932–) U.S. rock and roll musician. Born *Richard Wayne Penniman*. His hits include "Tutti Frutti," "Long Tall Sally," and "Good Golly, Miss Molly."

Lit·tle Tur·tle |'litl 'tərtl| (1752?–1812) chief of the Miami Indians. He led raids on settlers in the Northwest Territory and was forced to sign the Treaty of Greenville (1795).

Lit·tle·wood |'litl,wŏŏd|, (Maudie) Joan (1914–) English theater director. She cofounded the Theatre Workshop (1945), and is particularly remembered for her production of the musical *Oh, What a Lovely War* (1963).

Lit·tré |lētrā|, Maximilien-Paul-Émile (1801–81) French lexicographer and philosopher. He was the author of the major *Dictionnaire de la langue française* (1863–77). A follower of Auguste Comte, he became the leading exponent of positivism after Comte's death.

Liv·er·pool |'livər,pŏŏl|, Robert Banks Jenkinson, 2nd Earl of (1770–1828) British Tory statesman, prime minister (1812–27).

Liv·ing·ston |'liviᴎGstən| Family of early American jurists and statesmen. **Robert R. Livingston** (1746–1813) was a member of the Continental Congress (1775–55, 1779–81) and one of the five drafters of the Declaration of Independence. His brother **Edward Livingston** (1764–1836) authored the penal code for Louisiana, which became the model for state penal codes throughout the U.S. and internationally. They were great-grandsons of Robert Livingston.

Liv·ing·ston |'liviᴎGstən|, Robert (1654–1728) U.S. fur trader, born in Scotland. He married Alida Van Rensselaer and established an estate of 160,000 acres in upstate New York; he became a prominent influence in New York state politics.

Liv·ing·ston |'liviᴎGstən|, Henry Brockholst (1757–1823) U.S. Supreme Court justice (1806–23).

Liv·ing·stone |'liviᴎGstən|, David (1813–73) Scottish missionary and African explorer. He went to Bechuanaland as a missionary in 1841. On extensive travels, he discovered Lake Ngami (1849), the Zambezi River (1851), and the Victoria Falls (1855). In 1866 he went in search of the source of the Nile, and was found in poor health by Sir Henry Morton Stanley in 1871.

Livy |'livē| (59 BC–AD 17) Roman historian; Latin name *Titus Livius*. His history of Rome from its foundation to his own time contained 142 books, of which thirty-five survive (including the earliest history of the war with Hannibal).

Llo·sa |'yōsə|, Mario Vargas see VARGAS LLOSA.

Lloyd |loid|, Harold (Clayton) (1894–1971) U.S. movie comedian. Performing his own hair-raising stunts, he used physical danger as a source of comedy in silent movies such as *High and Dizzy* (1920), *Safety Last* (1923), and *The Freshman* (1925).

Lloyd George |'loid 'jawrj|, David, 1st Earl Lloyd George of Dwyfor (1863–1945) British Liberal statesman, prime minister (1916–22). His coalition government was threatened by economic problems and trouble in Ireland, and he resigned when the Conservatives withdrew their support in 1922.

Lloyd Web·ber |'loid 'webər|, Sir Andrew, Baron Lloyd-Webber of Sydmonton (1948–) English composer. His many successful musicals, several of them written in collaboration with the lyricist Sir Tim Rice, include *Jesus Christ Superstar* (1970), *Cats* (1981), and *The Phantom of the Opera* (1986).

Lly·wel·yn |lo͞o'(w)elən| (died 1282) prince of Gwynedd in North Wales; also known as **Llywelyn ap Gruffydd**. Proclaiming himself prince of all Wales in 1258, he was recognized by Henry III in 1265. His refusal to pay homage to Edward I led the latter to invade and subjugate Wales (1277–84); Llewelyn died in an unsuccessful rebellion.

Lo·ba·chev·sky |ˌlōbə'CHefskē|, Nikolay Ivanovich (1792–1856) Russian mathematician. At about the same time as Gauss and **János Bolyai,** (1802–60), he independently discovered non-Euclidean geometry. His work was not widely recognized until the non-Euclidean nature of space–time was revealed by the general theory of relativity.

Lo·bo |'lōbō|, Rebecca (1973–) U.S. basketball player. She was the women's college basketball Player of the Year in 1995, when she led the University of Connecticut to an undefeated season and a national title. She was also on the 1996 U.S. Olympic women's basketball team and a premier player for the New York Liberty in the Women's National Basketball League.

Locke |läk|, Alain (LeRoy) (1886–1954) U.S. author and educator. His anthology *The New Negro: An Interpretation* (1925) started the Harlem Renaissance.

Locke |läk|, John (1632–1704) English philosopher, a founder of empiricism and political liberalism. His *Two Treatises of Government* (1690) argues that the authority of rulers has a human origin and is limited. In *An Essay concerning Human Understanding* (1690) he argued that all knowledge is derived from sense-experience.

Lock·yer |'läkyər|, Sir (Joseph) Norman (1836–1920) English astronomer. His spectroscopic analysis of the sun led to his discovery of a new element, which he named *helium*. He founded both the Science Museum in London and the scientific journal *Nature*, which he edited for fifty years.

Lodge |läj|, David (John) (1935–) English novelist and academic Honorary professor of Modern English Literature at the University of Birmingham since 1976, he often satirizes academia and literary criticism in his novels, which include *Changing Places* (1975) and *Small World* (1984).

Lodge[1] |läj|, Henry Cabot (1850–1924) U.S. politician and author. He was a member of the U.S. House of Representatives and the U.S. Senate from Massachusetts; the great-grandson of George Cabot and grandfather of Henry Cabot Lodge.

Lodge[2] |läj|, Henry Cabot (1902–85) U.S. politician and diplomat. He was a Republican vice presidential candidate (1960), ambassador to South Vietnam (1963–63, 1965–67), and chief negotiator at the Vietnam peace talks in Paris. He was grandson of Henry Cabot Lodge (1850–1924).

Lodge |läj|, Sir Oliver (Joseph) (1851–1940) English physicist. He made important contributions to the study of electromagnetic radiation, and was a pioneer of radio-telegraphy.

Loeb |lōb|, James Morris (1867–1933) U.S. banker and philanthropist. With the banking firm Kuhn, Loeb and Co. (1888–1901), he subsidized the publication of the *Loeb Classical Library* (1910).

Loes·ser |'lesər|, Frank Henry (1910–69) U.S. composer and lyricist. He composed movie scores and songs, including *Baby, It's Cold Outside* (1948, Academy Award) and *Guys and Dolls* (1950).

Loew |lō|, Marcus (1870–1927) U.S. theater owner and movie producer. He owned a chain of movie theaters and then formed Loew's Inc., which purchased Metro Pictures and Goldwyn Pictures to become Metro-Goldwyn-Mayer.

Loewe |lō|, Frederick (1901–88) U.S. composer. The collaboration he began with lyricist Alan Jay Lerner in 1942 became one of the most successful in the history of musical theater. Notable scores: *Brigadoon* (1947), *My Fair Lady* (1956), *Gigi* (1958), and *Camelot (1960)*.

Lof·ting |'lawfˌtiNG|, Hugh (1886–1947) British author and U.S. resident. He wrote numerous children's books, including *The Story of Dr. Doolittle* (1922) and its many sequels.

Lo·gan |'lōgən|, Joshua Lockwood

(1908–88) U.S. director and playwright. He directed Broadway shows, including *South Pacific* (1949), which he also cowrote, and *Annie Get Your Gun* (1946).

Lo·gan |'lōgən|, Rayford W. (1897–1982) U.S. historian and educator. Spingarn Medal, 1980

Lomb |läm|, Henry (1828–1908) U.S. optician. He was a cofounder of Bausch & Lomb Optical Co.

Lom·bar·di |läm'bärdē|, Vincent Thomas (1913–70) U.S. football coach. He coached the Green Bay Packers (1959–67) to five National Football League championships and two Super Bowl titles.

Lom·bar·do |ləm'bär,dō|, Guy Albert (1902–77) U.S. band leader, born in Canada. His dance band, the Royal Canadians (from 1927), played the "sweetest music this side of heaven," and his New Year's Eve broadcasts became a national tradition.

Lon·don |'ləndən|, Jack (1876–1916) U.S. novelist; pseudonym of *John Griffith Chaney*. The Klondike gold rush of 1897 provided the material for his famous works depicting struggle for survival. Notable works: *The Call of the Wild* (1903) and *White Fang* (1906).

Long |lawNG|, Huey Pierce (1893–1935) U.S. politician. Known as **the Kingfish**. He was governor of Louisiana (1928–31) and a U.S. senator (1932–35), known as a dictatorial demagogue with politically radical ideas, most notably his "Share the Wealth" program. Not long after he announced his plans to run for the U.S. presidency, he was assassinated.

Long |lawNG|, John Luther (1861–1927) U.S. author. He wrote the short story *Madame Butterfly* (1898), which was adapted for the stage and used as a source for Puccini's opera.

Long |lawNG|, Stephen Harriman (1784–1864) U.S. Army officer and explorer. His expeditions included the upper Mississippi and the Rocky Mountain region; he discovered Longs Peak in Colorado.

Long·a·cre |'lawNG,ākər|, James Barton (1794–1869) U.S. engraver. He created *The National Portrait Gallery of Distinguished Americans* (4 vols., 1834–39)

and was chief engraver of the U.S. Mint (1844–69).

Long·fel·low |'lawNG,felō|, Henry Wadsworth (1807–82) U.S. poet. He is known for "The Wreck of the Hesperus" and "The Village Blacksmith" (both 1841) and narrative poems such as *Evangeline* (1847), *The Song of Hiawatha* (1855), and *Paul Revere's Ride* (1861).

Lon·gi·nus |län'jīnəs| (1st century AD) Greek scholar. He is the supposed author of a Greek literary treatise *On the Sublime*, concerned with the moral function of literature, which influenced Augustan writers such as Dryden and Pope.

Long·street |'lawNG,strēt|, James (1821–1904) Confederate army officer. He surrendered with Robert E. Lee at Appomattox and recounted his experiences in *From Manassas to Appomattox* (1896).

Loos |'lo͞os|, Anita (1893–1981) U.S. author. She wrote books and movie scripts, including *Gentlemen Prefer Blondes* (1925).

Lor·ca |lawrkə|, Federico García (1898–1936) Spanish poet and dramatist. His works include *Gypsy Ballads* (verse, 1928) and intense, poetic tragedies evoking the passionate emotions of Spanish life, notably *Blood Wedding* (1933) and *The House of Bernada Alba* (1945).

Lorde |lawrd|, Audre (1934–92) U.S. poet. Notable works: *The Marvelous Arithmetics of Distance: Poems 1987–1992*.

Lo·ren |lə'ren|, Sophia (1934–) Italian actress; born *Sofia Scicolone*. She has starred in both Italian and American movies, including the slapstick comedy *The Millionairess* (1960) and the wartime drama *La Ciociara* (1961), for which she won an Oscar.

Lo·rentz |'lawrənts|, Hendrik Antoon (1853–1928) Dutch theoretical physicist. He worked on the forces affecting electrons and realized that electrons and cathode rays were the same thing. For their work on electromagnetic theory he and his pupil **Pieter Zeeman**, (1865–1943) shared the 1902 Nobel Prize for Physics.

Lo·renz |'lawrənz; 'lawrənts|, Konrad

(Zacharias) (1903–89) Austrian zoologist. He pioneered the science of ethology, emphasizing innate rather than learned behaviour or conditioned reflexes. Lorenz extrapolated his studies in ornithology to human behaviour patterns, and compared the ill effects of the domestication of animals to human civilizing processes. He shared a Nobel Prize in 1973 with Karl von Frisch and Nikolaas Tinbergen.

Lo·ren·zo de' Me·di·ci |lə'renzō dā 'medə,CHē; mə'dēCHē| (1449–92) Italian statesman and scholar. A patron of the arts and humanist learning, he supported Botticelli, Leonardo da Vinci, and Michelangelo, among others. He was also a noted poet and scholar in his own right.

Lor·i·mer |'lawrəmər|, George Horace (1867–1937) U.S. editor. He was editor in chief of the *Saturday Evening Post* (1889–1936).

Lor·rain, Claude |law'rān| see CLAUDE LORRAIN.

Lor·raine, Claude |law'rān| see CLAUDE LORRAINE.

Lor·re |'lawrē; 'lärē|, Peter (1904–64) Hungarian-born U.S. actor; born *Laszlo Lowenstein*. He was known for the sinister roles he played, as in the German movie *M* (1931), *The Maltese Falcon* (1941), and *The Raven* (1963).

Lo·throp |'lōTHrəp|, Harriet Mulford Stone (1844–1924) U.S. author. Pseudonym **Margaret Sidney**. Notable works: *Five Little Peppers and How They Grew* (1881).

Lo·ti |lō'tē|, Pierre (1850–1923) French novelist; pseudonym of *Louis Marie Julien Viaud*. His voyages as a naval officer provided the background for works such as *Pêcheur d'Islande* (1886) and *Matelot* (1893).

Lott |lät; 'lawt|, Trent (1941–) U.S. politician. Member of the U.S. House of Representatives from Michigan (1989–).

Lot·to |'lätō|, Lorenzo (c. 1480–1556) Italian painter. He chiefly painted religious subjects, though he also produced a number of notable portraits, such as *A Lady as Lucretia* (c.1533).

Lou·ga·nis |ˌloo'gänəs|, Greg (1960–) U.S. diver. He won two gold medals at the 1984 Olympic Games and two at the 1988 Olympics.

Lou·is II |'loo(w)ē| (846–79) king of France, reigned 877–79.

Lou·is |'loo(w)ē| The name of 18 kings of France: **Louis I** (778–840), son of Charlemagne. He was king of the West Franks and Holy Roman Emperor (814–40). **Louis II** (846–879; reigned 877–879). **Louis III** (863–882; reigned 879–882), son of Louis II. **Louis IV** (921–954; reigned 936–954). **Louis V** (967–987; reigned 979–987). **Louis VI** (1081–1137; reigned 1108–37). **Louis VII** (c.1120–80; reigned 1137–80). **Louis VIII** (1187–1226; reigned 1223–26). **Louis IX** (1214–70; reigned 1226–70), son of Louis VIII, canonized as **St. Louis**. He conducted two unsuccessful crusades, dying of plague in Tunis during the second. Feast day, August 25. **Louis X** (1289–1316; reigned 1314–16). **Louis XI** (1423–83; reigned 1461–83), son of Charles VII. He continued his father's work in laying the foundations of a united France ruled by an absolute monarchy. **Louis XII** (1462–1515; reigned 1498–1515). **Louis XIII** (1601–43; reigned 1610–43), son of Henry IV of France. During his minority the country was ruled by his mother Marie de Médicis. From 1624 he was heavily influenced in policy-making by his chief minister Cardinal Richelieu. **Louis XIV** (1638–1715; reigned 1643–1715), son of Louis XIII; known as **the Sun King**. His reign represented the high point of the Bourbon dynasty and of French power in Europe, and in this period French art and literature flourished. His almost constant wars of expansion united Europe against him, however, and gravely weakened France's financial position. **Louis XV** (1710–74; reigned 1715–74), great-grandson and successor of Louis XIV. He led France into the Seven Years' War (1756–63). **Louis XVI** (1754–93; reigned 1774–92), grandson and successor of Louis XV. His minor concessions and reforms in the face of the emerging French Revolution proved disastrous. As the Revolution became more extreme, he was executed with his wife, Marie Antoinette, and the monarchy was abolished. **Louis XVII** (1785–95), son of Louis XVI. He was the titular king who died in prison during the Revolution. **Louis XVIII** (1755–1824; reigned 1814–24), brother of Louis XVI. After his nephew Louis XVII's death he became titular king in exile until the fall of Napoleon in 1814, when he returned to Paris on the summons of Talleyrand and was officially restored to the throne.

Lou·is I |'lo͞o(w)ē| (1326–82) king of Hungary (1342–82) and of Poland (1370–82); known as **Louis the Great**. Under his rule Hungary became a powerful state; he fought two successful wars against Venice (1357–58; 1378–81), and the rulers of Serbia, Wallachia, Moldavia, and Bulgaria became his vassals.

Lou·is |'lo͞ois|, Joe (1914–81) U.S. heavyweight boxing champion; born *Joseph Louis Barrow*; known as the **Brown Bomber**. He was heavyweight champion of the world 1937–49, defending his title twenty-five times during that period. He retired undefeated and then lost a comback fight.

Lou·is |'lo͞owis|, Morris (1912–62) U.S. artist. Born *Morris Bernstein*. He was an abstract Expressionist painter influenced by Jackson Pollack.

Lou·is-Phi·lippe |'lo͞o(w)ē fə'lēp| (1773–1850) king of France (1830–48). After the restoration of the Bourbons he became the focus for liberal discontent and was made king, replacing Charles X. His regime was gradually undermined by radical discontent and eventually overthrown.

Louis the Great Louis I of Hungary (see LOUIS I).

Love·lace |'ləvləs|, Augusta Ada King, Countess of (1815–52) English mathematician. The daughter of Lord Byron, she became assistant to Charles Babbage and worked with him on his mechanical computer.

Love·lace |'ləvləs|, Maud Hart (1892–1980) U.S. author. She wrote children's fiction, including the "Betsy-Tacy" series.

Love·lace |'ləvləs|, Richard (1618–57) English poet. A supporter of Charles I, he was imprisoned during the English Civil War in 1642, when he probably

wrote his famous poem "To Althea, from Prison."

Lov·ell |'ləvəl|, Sir (Alfred Charles) Bernard (1913–) English astronomer and physicist, and pioneer of radio astronomy. He founded Manchester University's radio observatory at Jodrell Bank, where he directed the construction of the large radio telescope that is now named after him.

Lov·ell |'ləvəl|, James A., Jr. (1928–) U.S. astronaut. He was aboard the Apollo 8 first journey to the moon (1968) and the Apollo 13 aborted mission to the moon (1970).

Love·lock |'ləvläk|, James (Ephraim) (1919–) English scientist. He is best known for the *Gaia hypothesis*, first presented by him in 1972 and discussed in several popular books, including *Gaia* (1979).

Lov·ett |'ləvət|, Lyle (1957–) U.S. country singer and actor. Grammy Award, 1997. Notable movies: *The Player* and *Short Cuts*.

Low |lō|, Sir David (Alexander Cecil) (1891–1963) British cartoonist, born in New Zealand, famous for his political cartoons and for inventing the character Colonel Blimp.

Low |lō|, Juliette Gordon (1860–1927) U.S. youth leader. She founded the Girl Scouts of America (1912).

Lowe |lō|, Edwin S. (1910–86) U.S. manufacturer. He manufactured games such as bingo, Yahtzee, chess, and checkers.

Low·ell |'lōəl|, Amy (Lawrence) (1874–1925) U.S. poet. A leading imagist poet, she is known for her polyphonic prose and sensuous imagery. Notable works: *A Critical Fable* (1922) and *What's O'-Clock* (Pulitzer Prize, 1925).

Low·ell |'lōəl|, James Russell (1819–91) U.S. poet, essayist, and diplomat. He was the first editor of the *Atlantic Monthly* (1857–61).

Low·ell |'lōəl|, Percival (1855–1916) U.S. astronomer. Lowell inferred the existence of a ninth planet beyond Neptune, and when it was eventually discovered in 1930 it was given the name Pluto, with a symbol that also included his initials. He was the brother of Amy Lowell.

Low•ell |'lōəl|, Robert (Traill Spence) (1917–77) U.S. poet. His poetry, often describing his manic depression, is notable for its intense confessional nature and for its complex imagery.

Low•ry |'low(ə)rē|, Lois (1937–) U.S. author of novels for adolescents.

Low•ry |'low(ə)rē|, L. S. (1887–1976) English painter; full name *Laurence Stephen Lowry*. He painted small matchstick figures set against the iron and brick expanse of urban and industrial landscapes.

Low•ry |'low(ə)rē|, (Clarence) Malcolm (1909–57) English novelist. His experiences living in Mexico in the 1930s provided the background for his symbolic semi-autobiographical novel *Under the Volcano* (1947).

Loy |loi|, Myrna (1905–93) U.S. actress. Born *Myrna Williams*. She played Nora Charles in *The Thin Man* (1934).

Loyd |loid|, Samuel (1841–1911) U.S. puzzlemaker. He devised chess problems and invented the Parcheesi board game.

Lu•bitsch |'lōōbiCH|, Ernst (1892–1947) U.S. movie director, born in Germany. Notable works: *Heaven Can Wait* (1943).

Lu•can |'lōōkən| (AD 39–65) Roman poet, born in Spain; Latin name *Marcus Annaeus Lucanus*. His major work is *Pharsalia*, a hexametric epic in ten books dealing with the civil war between Julius Caesar and Pompey.

Lu•cas |'lōōkəs|, George (1944–) hollywood U.S. movie director, producer, and screenwriter. He wrote and directed the science-fiction movie *Star Wars* (1977), Steven Spielberg's *Raiders of the Lost Ark* (1981), and the two sequels of each movie.

Lu•cas van Ley•den |'lōōkəs væn 'līdən| (c. 1494–1533) Dutch painter and engraver. He produced his most significant work as an engraver, including *Ecce Homo* (1510). His paintings include portraits, genre scenes, and religious subjects.

Luce |lōōs| U.S. family, including: **Henry Robinson Luce** (1898–1967), editor and publisher. He was a co-founder of *Time, Fortune, Life,* and *Sports Illustrated* magazines. His wife **Clare Boothe Luce** (1903–87), playwright and public official. She served as a war correspondent for *Life* magazine during World War II and as ambassador to Italy (1953–57).

Luck•man |'ləkmən|, Sid (1916–) U.S. football player. Elected to the NFL Hall of Fame (1965).

Lu•cre•tius |lōō'krēSHəs| (c. 94–c. 55 BC) Roman poet and philosopher; full name *Titus Lucretius Carus*. His didactic hexametric poem *On the Nature of Things* is an exposition of the materialist atomist physics of Epicurus, which aims to give peace of mind by showing that fear of the gods and of death is without foundation.

Lu•den•dorff |'lōōdn,dawrf|, Erich (1865–1937) German general, Chief of Staff to General von Hindenburg during the First World War and later a Nazi Party support.

Lud•lum |'lədləm|, Robert (1927–) U.S. author. Pseudonyms **Jonathan Ryder, Michael Shepherd.** He has written suspense novels, including *The Bourne Identity* (1980).

Lud•wig |'lōōdwig; 'lədwig; 'lōōdvig| Name of three kings of Bavaria: **Ludwig I** (1786–1868; reigned 1825–48). He became unpopular due to his reactionary policies, lavish expenditure, and his domination by the dancer Lola Montez, and he was forced to abdicate in favor of his son **Maximilian II. Ludwig II** (1845–86; reigned 1864–86). A patron of the arts, he became a recluse and built a series of elaborate castles. He was declared insane and deposed in 1886. **Ludwig III** (1845–1921; reigned 1913–18).

Lu•gar |'lōōgər|, Richard Green (1932–) U.S. senator from Indiana (1977–).

Lu•go•si |lə'gōsē|, Bela (born Béla Ferenc Blasko) (1884–1956) Hungarian-born U.S. actor famous for his roles in horror movies such as *Dracula* (1931), *Mark of the Vampire* (1935), and *The Wolf Man* (1940).

Lu•han |,lōō'hän|, Mabel Dodge (Ganson) (1879–1962) U.S. author and patron of artists. Notable works: *Lorenzo in Taos* (1932) and *Intimate Memories* (4 vols., 1933–37).

Lu•kács |'lōō,käCH|, György (1885–

1971) Hungarian philosopher, literary critic, and politician. His best-known work is *History and Class Consciousness* (1923), in which he stresses the central role of alienation in Marxist thought.

Lu•kas |'lo͞okəs|, J. Anthony (1933–97) U.S. journalist and author. Notable works: *Common Ground* (1986, Pulitzer Prize).

Lu•kas |'lo͞okəs|, Paul (1895–1971) U.S. actor, born in Hungary. Notable movies: *Watch on the Rhine* (1943, Academy Award).

Luke |lo͞ok|, St. (1st century AD) an evangelist, closely associated with St. Paul and traditionally the author of the third Gospel and the Acts of the Apostles. Feast day, October 18.

Lul•ly |lY'lē; lo͞o'lē|, Jean-Baptiste (1632–87) French composer, born in Italy; Italian name *Giovanni Battista Lulli*. His operas, which include *Alceste* (1674) and *Armide* (1686), mark the beginning of the French operatic tradition.

Lu•miére |ˌlo͞omē'er|, Auguste-Marie-Louis-Nicolas (1862–1954) French inventors and movie pioneers. In 1895 the brothers patented their "Cinématographe," which combined a movie camera and projector. They also invented the improved "autochrome" process of color photography.

Lunce•ford |'lənsfərd|, Jimmie (1902–47) U.S. jazz band leader and saxophonist. Full name *James Melvin Lunceford*. Jimmie Lunceford's Orchestra (1929) had a national reputation as an outstanding black swing band.

Lun•den |'ləndən|, Joan (1950–) U.S. television journalist. She was co-host of ABC's "Good Morning, America" (1980–97).

Lu•pi•no |lə'pē,nō; lo͞o'pēnō|, Ida (1918–95) U.S. actress and director, born in England. She starred in *Anything Goes* (1936), *Artists and Models* (1937), and *the Sea Wolf* (1941).

Lu•ria |'lo͞orē(y)ə|, Salvador Edward (1912–91) U.S. microbiologist, born in Italy. He won a National Book Award for *Life: The Unfinished Experiment* (1974) and shared the 1969 Nobel Prize for Physiology or Medicine.

Lu•rie |'lo͞orē|, Alison (1926–) U.S. author and educator. She has written adult and children's fiction and nonfiction, including *The War Between the Tates* (1974).

Lur•ton |'lərt(ə)n|, Horace Harmon (1844–1914) U.S. Supreme Court justice (1910–14). He served in the Confederate army for three years.

Lu•ther |'lo͞oTHər|, Martin (1483–1546) German Protestant theologian, the principal figure of the German Reformation. He preached the doctrine of justification by faith rather than by works and attacked the sale of indulgences (1517) and papal authority. In 1521 he was excommunicated at the Diet of Worms. His translation of the Bible into High German (1522–34) contributed significantly to the development of German literature in the vernacular.

Lu•thu•li |lə'to͞olē|, Albert John Mvumbi (1898–1967) Also **Lutuli**. South African political leader. His presidency of the African National Congress (1952–60) was marked by a program of civil disobedience for which he was awarded the Nobel Peace Prize (1960).

Lu•to•slaw•ski |ˌlo͞otə'slawvskē|, Witold (1913–94) Polish composer noted for his orchestral music. From the early 1960s his works were characterized by a blend of notational composition and aleatroic sections.

Lut•yens |'lətyenz| English family, including: **Sir Edwin (Landseer) Lutyens** (1869–1944), architect. He established his reputation designing country houses, but is particularly known for his plans for New Delhi (1912), where he introduced an open garden-city layout, and for the Cenotaph in London (1919–21). His daughter **(Agnes) Elizabeth** (1906–83), composer. She was one of the first English composers to use the twelve-tone system, as in her *Chamber Concerto No. 1* (1939).

Lux•em•burg |'ləksəm,bərg|, Rosa (1870–1919) Polish-born German revolutionary leader. Together with the German socialist **Karl Liebknecht** (1871–1919) she founded the revolutionary group known as the Spartacus League in 1916 and the German Communist Party in 1918.

Ly·cur·gus |lī'kərgəs| (9th century BC) Spartan lawgiver. He is traditionally held to have been the founder of the constitution and military regime of ancient Sparta.

Lyd·gate |'lid,gāt|, John (c. 1370–c. 1450) English poet and monk. His copious output of verse, often in Chaucerian style, includes the poetical translations the *Troy Book* (1412–20) and *The Fall of Princes* (1431–38).

Ly·ell |'lī(ə)l|, Sir Charles (1797–1875) Scottish geologist. His textbook *Principles of Geology* (1830–33) influenced a generation of geologists and held that the earth's features were shaped over a long period of time by natural processes, thus clearing the way for Darwin's theory of evolution.

Ly·ly |'lilē|, John (c. 1554–1606) English prose writer and dramatist. His prose romance in two parts, *Euphues, The Anatomy of Wit* (1578) and *Euphues and his England* (1580) was written in an elaborate style that became known as *euphuism*.

Lynn |lin|, Loretta (1935–) U.S. country singer and songwriter. Born *Loretta Webb*. Notable songs: "Don't Come Home a Drinkin' (With Lovin' on Your Mind)" and "Coal Miner's Daughter."

Lynn |lin|, Dame Vera (1917–) English singer; born *Vera Margaret Lewis*. She is known chiefly for her rendering of such songs as "We'll Meet Again" and "White Cliffs of Dover", which she sang to the troops in World War II.

Ly·on |'līən|, Mary Mason (1797–1849) U.S. educator. She founded Mount Holyoke Seminary (later Mount Holyoke College) in South Hadley, Massachusetts (1837), and served as its first president (1837–49).

Lyo·tard |,lēə'tär|, Jean-François (1924–) French philosopher and literary critic. He outlined his "philosophy of desire," based on the politics of Nietzsche, in *L'Économie libidinale* (1974). In later books he adopted a postmodern quasi-Wittgensteinian linguistic philosophy.

Ly·san·der |lī'sændər| (died 395 BC) Spartan general. He defeated the Athenian navy in 405 and captured Athens in 404, so bringing the Peloponnesian War to an end.

Ly·sen·ko |li'seNGkō|, Trofim Denisovich (1898–1976) Soviet biologist and geneticist. He was an adherent of Lamarck's theory of evolution by the inheritance of acquired characteristics. Since his ideas harmonized with Marxist ideology he was favoured by Stalin and dominated Soviet genetics for many years.

Ly·sip·pus |'lī'sipəs| (4th century BC) Greek sculptor. He is said to have introduced a naturalistic scheme of proportions for the human body into Greek sculpture.

Lyt·ton |'litn|, 1st Baron (1803–73) British novelist, dramatist, and statesman; born *Edward George Earle Bulwer-Lytton*. He achieved literary success with *Pelham* (1828), a novel of fashionable society, and also wrote historical romances (such as *The Last Days of Pompeii*, 1834) and plays. As a diplomat, he served as Viceroy of India (1876–80).

Mm

Ma |mä|, Yo-Yo (1955–   ) U.S. cellist, born in Paris. Made his debut in New York's Carnegie Hall at age 9, and currently performs throughout the world with major orchestras.

Ma·bu·se |məˈbyzə|, Jan (c. 1478–c. 1532) Flemish painter; Flemish name *Jan Gossaert*. He was one of the first artists to disseminate the Italian style in the Netherlands.

MacAlpin |məkˈælpən|, Kenneth see KENNETH I.

Mac·Ar·thur |məˈkärᴛʜər|, Douglas (1880–1964) U.S. general. Commander of U.S. (later Allied) forces in the SW Pacific during World War II, he accepted Japan's surrender in 1945 and administered the ensuing Allied occupation. He was in charge of UN forces in Korea 1950–51, before being forced to relinquish command by President Truman.

Ma·cau·lay |məˈkawlē|, Dame (Emilie) Rose (1881–1958) English novelist and essayist. Notable novels: *Potterism* (1920), *The World My Wilderness* (1950), and *The Towers of Trebizond* (1956).

Ma·cau·lay |məˈkawlē|, Thomas Babington, 1st Baron (1800–59) English historian, essayist, and philanthropist. He was a civil servant in India, where he established a system of education and a new criminal code, before returning to Britain and devoting himself to literature and politics. Notable works: *The Lays of Ancient Rome* (1842) and *History of England* (1849–61).

Mac·beth |məkˈbeᴛʜ| (c. 1005–57) king of Scotland 1040–57. He came to the throne after killing his cousin Duncan I in battle, and was himself defeated and killed by Malcolm III. Shakespeare's tragedy *Macbeth* considerably embroiders the historical events.

Mac·ca·bae·us |ˌmækəˈbēyəs|, Judas see JUDAS MACCABAEUS.

Mac·Diar·mid |məkˈderməd|, Hugh (1892–1978) Scottish poet and nationalist; pseudonym of *Christopher Murray Grieve*. The language of his poems drew on the language of various regions of Scotland and historical periods. He was a founding member (1928) of the National Party of Scotland (later the Scottish National Party).

Mac·Don·ald |məkˈdänəld|, Dwight (1906–82) U.S. journalist and author. Notable works: *Against the American Grain* (1963).

Mac·Don·ald |məkˈdänəld|, Flora (1722–90) Scottish Jacobite heroine. She aided Charles Edward Stuart's escape from English pursuit after his defeat at Culloden in 1746, by smuggling him to the island of Skye, disguised as her maid.

Mac·don·ald |məkˈdänəld|, Sir John Alexander (1815–91) Scottish-born Canadian statesman, prime minister (1867–73 and 1878–91). He played a leading role in the confederation of the Canadian provinces and was appointed first prime minister of the Dominion of Canada.

Mac·Don·ald |məkˈdänəld|, (James) Ramsay (1866–1937) British Labour statesman, prime minister (1924, 1929–31, and 1931–35). He served as Britain's first Labour prime minister.

Mac·Dow·ell |məkˈdowəl|, Edward Alexander (1860–1908) U.S. composer. He is known for his symphonic poems, including *Hamlet and Ophelia* (1885). His widow established the MacDowell Colony for artists and musicians in 1910.

Ma·chia·vel·li |ˌmækēəˈvelē|, Niccolò di Bernardo dei (1469–1527) Italian statesman and political philosopher. His best-known work is *The Prince* (1532), which advises rulers that the acquisition and effective use of power may necessitate unethical methods.

Mack |mæk|, Connie (1862–1956) U.S. baseball player and manager. Born *Cornelius Alexander McGillicuddy*. A manager of the Philadelphia Athletics for 50 years, he led the team to 9 American League pennants and 5 World Series championships. He was elected to the Hall of Fame in 1937.

Mac·ken·zie |məˈkenzē|, Sir Alexander

(1764–1820) Scottish explorer of Canada. He discovered the Mackenzie River in 1789 and in 1793 became the first European to reach the Pacific Ocean by land along a northern route.

Mac·ken·zie |mə'kenzē|, Sir Compton (1883–1972) English novelist, essayist, and poet; full name *Edward Montague Compton Mackenzie*. He is best known for his novels, which include *Sinister Street* (1913–14) and *Whisky Galore* (1947).

Mac·ken·zie |mə'kenzē|, William Lyon (1795–1861) Scottish-born Canadian politician and journalist, involved with the movement for political reform in Canada. In 1837 he led an unsuccessful rebellion in Toronto and fled to New York.

Mack·in·tosh |'mækən‚täSH|, Charles Rennie (1868–1928) Scottish architect, designer, and painter. A leading exponent of art nouveau, he pioneered the new concept of functionalism in architecture and interior design. Notable among his designs is the Glasgow School of Art (1898–1909).

Mac·Lach·lan |mə'kläklən|, Patricia (1938–) U.S. children's author.

Mac·Laine |mə'klān|, Shirley (1934–) U.S. actress. Born *Shirley Beatty*. Notable movies: *Terms of Endearment* (1983, Academy Award).

Mac·lean |mə'klān|, Alistair (1922–87) Scottish novelist, writer of thrillers including *The Guns of Navarone* (1957) and *Where Eagles Dare* (1967).

Mac·lean |mə'klān|, Donald (Duart) (1913–83) British Foreign Office official and Soviet spy. After acting as a Soviet agent from the late 1930s he fled to the USSR with Guy Burgess in 1951.

Mac·Leish |mə'klēSH|, Archibald (1892–1982) U.S. poet. Pulitzer Prize-winning works: *Conquistador* (1932), *Collected Poems* (1952), and *J.B.* (1958).

Mac·leod |mə'klowd|, John James Rickard (1876–1935) Scottish physiologist. He directed the research on pancreatic extracts by F. G. Banting and C. H. Best that led to the discovery and isolation of insulin. Macleod shared a Nobel Prize for Physiology or Medicine with Banting in 1923.

Mac·Mil·lan |mək'milən|, Donald Baxter (1874–1970) U.S. explorer and author. He accompanied Robert Peary on his expeditions to the North Pole (1908–09) and to Greenland, Baffin Island, and Labrador (before 1950).

Mac·mil·lan |mək'milən|, (Maurice) Harold, 1st Earl of Stockton (1894–1986) British Conservative statesman, prime minister (1957–63). His term of office saw the signing of the Test Ban Treaty (1963) with the U.S. and the USSR. Macmillan resigned on grounds of ill health shortly after the scandal surrounding a member of his government, John Profumo.

Mac·Neice |mək'nēs|, (Frederick) Louis (1907–63) Northern Irish poet. His work, such as *Collected Poems* (1966), is characterized by the use of assonance, internal rhymes, and balladlike repetitions.

Mac·Neil |mək'nēl|, Robert Breckenridge Ware (1931–) U.S. broadcast journalist, born in Canada. With Jim Lehrer he co-anchored the *MacNeil/Lehrer News Hour* (1983–95).

Mac·Nel·ly |mək'nelē|, Jeff (1947–) U.S. political cartoonist. Full name *Jeffrey Kenneth MacNelly*. Pulitzer Prizes for Political Cartooning, 1972, 1978, and 1985.

Ma·con |'mākən|, Uncle Dave (1870–1952) U.S. country singer, banjo player, and comedian.

Mac·quar·ie |mə'kwärē|, Lachlan (1761–1824) Scottish-born Australian colonial administrator, governor of New South Wales (1809–21).

Ma·da·ri·a·ga y Ro·jo |‚mädərē'ägə ē 'rōhō|, Salvador de (1886–1978) Spanish writer and diplomat. He was a delegate to the League of Nations (1931–36). Notable works: *The Rise and Fall of the Spanish Empire* (1947).

Mad·dux |'mædəks|, Greg (1966–) U.S. baseball pitcher. He won an unprecedented four straight National League Cy Young Awards.

Mad·i·son |'mædəsən|, James see box.

Dolley Madison (1768–1849), born *Dorothea Payne Todd*, wife of James Madison and U.S. first lady (1809–17). She is remembered for saving the portrait of George Washington from the burning White House.

Madison, James
4th U.S. president

Life dates: 1751–1836
Place of birth: Port Conway, Va.
Mother: Eleanor ("Nelly") Rose Conway Madison
Father: James Madison
Wife: Dolley Payne Todd Madison
Children: none
Nickname: Father of the Constitution
College/University: College of New Jersey (now Princeton)
Military service: colonel, Orange County militia
Political career: Virginia State Council; Second Continental Congress; U.S. House of Representatives; U.S. secretary of state; president
Party: Democratic-Republican
Home state: Virginia
Opponents in presidential races: Charles Cotesworth Pinckney; DeWitt Clinton
Term of office: March 4, 1809–March 3, 1817
Vice president: George Clinton; Elbridge Gerry
Notable events of presidency: War of 1812; Washington D.C. burned by the British; "Star Spangled Banner" written by Francis Scott Key; Missouri Territory organized; Louisiana and Indiana admitted as the 18th and 19th states
Other achievements: Admitted to the Virginia bar; drafted Virginia guarantee of religious liberty and helped write state constitution; wrote essays on constitutional government for *The Federalist*; member, Virginia Ratification Convention; rector, University of Virginia; delegate to Virginia Constitutional Convention; chief author of the Bill of Rights
Place of burial: Montpelier, Va.

Ma•don•na |mə'dänə| (1958–) U.S. pop singer and actress; born *Madonna Louise Ciccone*. Albums such as *Like a Virgin* (1984) and her image as a sex symbol brought her international stardom from the mid-1980s. She starred in the movie *Desperately Seeking Susan* (1985).

Mae•ce•nas |ˌmīˈsēnəs|, Gaius (*c.* 70–8 BC) Roman statesman. He was a trusted adviser of Augustus and a notable patron of poets such as Virgil and Horace.

Mae•ter•linck |'metər,liNGk|, Count Maurice (1862–1949) Belgian poet, dramatist, and essayist. His prose dramas *La Princesse Maleine* (1889) and *Pelléas et Mélisande* (1892) established him as a leading figure in the symbolist movement. Nobel Prize for Literature (1911).

Ma•gel•lan |mə'jelən|, Ferdinand (*c.* 1480–1521) Portuguese explorer; Portuguese name *Fernão Magalhães*. In 1519 he sailed from Spain, rounding South America through the strait that now bears his name, and reached the Philippines in 1521. He was killed in a skirmish on Cebu; the survivors sailed back to Spain around Africa, completing the first circumnavigation of the globe (1522).

Ma•gritte |mə'grēt|, René (François Ghislain) (1898–1967) Belgian surrealist painter. His paintings display startling or amusing juxtapositions of the ordinary, the strange, and the erotic, depicted in a realist manner.

Mah•fouz |mä'fōōz|, Naguib (1911–) Egyptian novelist and short-story writer. He was the first writer in Arabic to be awarded the Nobel Prize for Literature (1988). Notable works: *Miramar* (1967).

Mah•ler |'mälər|, Gustav (1860–1911) Austrian composer, conductor, and pianist. Forming a link between romanticism and the experimentalism of Schoenberg, his works include nine complete symphonies (1888–1910) and the symphonic song cycle *Das Lied von der Erde* (1908).

Mai•ler |'mālər|, Norman (1923–) U.S. novelist and essayist. His novels, in which he frequently deals with the effect of war and violence on human relationships, include *The Naked and the Dead* (1948) and *Ancient Evenings* (1983). His nonfiction works combine a wide range of styles from autobiography to political commentary and include the prize-winning *The Armies of the Night* (1968) and *The Executioner's Song* (1979).

Mai•mo•ni•des |mī'mänədēz| (1135–1204) Jewish philosopher and Rabbinic scholar, born in Spain; born *Moses ben*

Maimon. His *Guide for the Perplexed* (1190) attempts to reconcile Talmudic scripture with the philosophy of Aristotle.

Main·te·non |ˌmæNt(ə)'nawN|, Françoise d'Aubigné, Marquise de (1635–1719) Mistress and later second wife of the French king Louis XIV.

Ma·jor |'mājər|, John (1943–) British Conservative statesman, prime minister (1990–97). His premiership saw the negotiations leading to the Maastricht Treaty and progress toward peace in Northern Ireland.

Ma·ka·ri·os III |mə'kärē,ōs| (1913–77) Greek Cypriot archbishop and statesman, first president of the republic of Cyprus (1960–77); born *Mikhail Christodolou Mouskos*. He was primate and archbishop of the Greek Orthodox Church in Cyprus from 1950.

Ma·la·mud |'mæləməd|, Bernard (1914–86) U.S. novelist and short-story writer. Notable works: *The Fixer* (1967), *Dubin's Lives* (1979), and *Stories of Bernard Malamud* (1983).

Mal·colm |'mælcəm| Name of four kings of Scotland: **Malcolm I** (died 954; reigned 943–54). **Malcolm II** (*c.* 953–1034; reigned 1005–34). **Malcolm III** (*c.* 1031–93; reigned 1058–93), son of Duncan I; known as **Malcolm Canmore** (from Gaelic *Ceann-mor*, "great head"). He came to the throne after killing Macbeth in battle (1057), and was responsible for helping to form Scotland into an organized kingdom. **Malcolm IV** (1141–65; reigned 1153–65), grandson of David I; known as **Malcolm the Maiden**. His reign witnessed a progressive loss of power to Henry II of England; he died young and without an heir.

Mal·colm X |'mælcəm 'eks| (1925–65) U.S. political activist; born *Malcolm Little*. He joined the Nation of Islam in 1946 and became a vigorous campaigner for black rights, initially advocating the use of violence. In 1964 he converted to orthodox Islam and moderated his views on black separatism; he was assassinated the following year.

Mal·den |'mawldən|, Karl (1914–) U.S. actor. Born Miaden Sekulovich. He starred in the television series "The Streets of San Francisco" (1972–77) and won an Academy Award for his role in *A Streetcar Named Desire* (1951).

Ma·len·kov |mə'len,kawf|, Georgi (Maksimilianovich) (1902–88) Soviet statesman, born in Russia. He became prime minister and first secretary of the Soviet Communist Party in 1953, but was forced to resign in 1955 following internal party struggles.

Ma·le·vich |mə'lāvicH|, Kazimir (Severinovich) (1878–1935) Russian painter and designer, founder of the suprematist movement. In his abstract works he used only basic geometrical shapes and a severely restricted range of color.

Malf·man, Theodore Harold (1927–) U.S. inventor of Ruby Laser Systems.

Mal·herbe |ˌmä'lərb|, François de (1555–1628) French poet. An architect of classicism in poetic form and grammar, he criticized excess of emotion and ornamentation and the use of Latin and dialectal forms.

Ma·li·now·ski |ˌmælə'nawfskē|, Bronisław Kaspar (1884–1942) Polish anthropologist. He initiated the technique of "participant observation" and developed the functionalist approach to anthropology.

Mal·lar·mé |ˌmälär'mä|, Stéphane (1842–98) French poet. A symbolist, he experimented with rhythm and syntax by transposing words and omitting grammatical elements. Notable poems: "Hérodiade" (*c.*1871) and "L'Aprèsmidi d'un faune" (1876).

Malle |mäl|, Louis (1932–95) French movie director. His movies *Ascenseur pour l'échafaud* (1958) and *Les Amants* (1959) are seminal examples of the French *nouvelle vague*. Other notable movies: *Pretty Baby* (1978) and *Au revoir les enfants* (1987).

Mal·lon |'mælən|, Mary (1870?–1938) U.S. cook. Known as **Typhoid Mary**. Immune to typhoid herself, she spread the disease while working in New York City; she was institutionalized for life from 1914 to protect others

Ma·lone |mə'lōn|, Dorothy (1925–) U.S. actress. Notable movies: *Written on the Wind* (1956, Academy Award).

Ma·lone |mə'lōn|, John C. (1941–)

U.S. telecommunications executive. He is the CEO of Tele-Communications, Inc. (1996–).

Ma·lone |mə'lōn|, Karl (1963–) U.S. basketball player.

Ma·lone |mə'lōn|, Moses (1955–) U.S. basketball player.

Mal·o·ry |'mælərē|, Sir Thomas (died 1471) English writer. His major work, *Le Morte d'Arthur* (printed 1483), is a prose translation of a collection of the legends of King Arthur, selected from French and other sources.

Mal·raux |ˌmäl'rō|, André (1901–76) French novelist, politician, and art critic. Involved in the Chinese communist uprising of 1927 and the Spanish Civil War, he was later appointed France's first minister of cultural affairs (1959–69). Notable novels: *La Condition humaine* (1933).

Mal·thus |'mawlTHəs|, Thomas Robert (1766–1834) English economist and clergyman. In *Essay on Population* (1798) he argued that without the practice of "moral restraint" the population tends to increase at a greater rate than its means of subsistence, resulting in the population checks of war, famine, and epidemic.

Mam·et |'mæmət|, David (1947–) U.S. dramatist, director, and screenwriter. Notable plays: *Glengarry Glen Ross* (Pulitzer Prize, 1984) and *Oleanna* (1992).

Man·ches·ter |'mæn,CHəstər|, William (1922–) U.S. historian and biographer. Notable works: *The Death of a President* (1967).

Man·ci·ni |ˌmæn'sēnē|, Henry (1924–94) U.S. composer and conductor. He wrote many movie themes, including "The Pink Panther."

Man·de·la |ˌmæn'delə| Family of South African political figures, including: **Nelson (Rolihlahla) Mandela** (1918–), president of South Africa since 1994. He was sentenced to life imprisonment in 1964 as an activist for the African National Congress (ANC). Released in 1990, as leader of the ANC he engaged in talks on the introduction of majority rule with President F. W. de Klerk, with whom he shared the Nobel Peace Prize in 1993. He became the country's first democratically elected president in 1994. His former wife **Winnie Mandela** (1934–). Despite her conviction on kidnapping and assault charges (1990), she continues to be a prominent figure in the African National Congress.

Man·del·brot |'mændl,brō|, Benoit (1924–) Polish-born French mathematician. Mandelbrot is known as the pioneer of fractal geometry.

Man·del·stam |'mändl,stäm|, Osip (Emilevich) (1891–1938) Also **Mandelshtam**. Russian poet, a member of the Acmeist group. Sent into internal exile in 1934, he died in a prison camp. Notable works: *Stone* (1913) and *Tristia* (1922).

Man·de·ville |'mændə,vil|, John (14th cent) English nobleman. He is remembered as the reputed author of a book of travels and travelers' tales that was actually compiled by an unknown hand from the works of several writers.

Ma·net |ˌmä'nā|, Édouard (1832–83) French painter. He adopted a realist approach that greatly influenced the Impressionists, using pure color to give a direct unsentimental effect. Notable works: *Déjeuner sur l'herbe* (1863), *Olympia* (1865), and *A Bar at the Folies-Bergère* (1882).

Man·e·tho |'mænə,THō| (3rd century BC) Egyptian priest. He wrote a history of Egypt from mythical times to 323, in which he arbitrarily divided the succession of rulers known to him into thirty dynasties, an arrangement that is still followed.

Man·kie·wicz |'mænkə,wits|, Joseph Leo (1909–93) U.S. director, producer, and screenwriter. Notable movies: *All About Eve* (1950, Academy Award).

Man·kil·ler |'mæn,kilər|, Wilma Pearl (1945–) U.S. Cherokee Nation tribal leader and historian. She is a women's rights leader and author of *Mankiller: A Chief and Her People* (1993).

Man·ley |'mænlē|, Michael (Norman) (1923–97) Jamaican statesman, prime minister (1972–80 and 1989–92). A socialist, he introduced policies to strengthen Jamaica's economy through the expansion of public works and the encouragement of local industry.

Mann |'mæn|, Horace (1796–1859)

U.S. educator and politician. Known as **the father of American public education.** While serving in the Massachusetts state legislature (1927–37), he helped establish the first state board of education, over which he presided (1937–48).

Mann |'män|, Thomas (1875–1955) German novelist and essayist. The role and character of the artist in relation to society is a constant theme in his works. Notable works: *Buddenbrooks* (1901), *Death in Venice* (1912), and *Dr. Faustus* (1947). Nobel Prize for Literature (1929).

Man·ner·heim |'mänər,hām|, Baron Carl Gustaf Emil von (1867–1951) Finnish soldier and politician. He planned and supervised the construction of the Mannerheim line of defense against Russia (1939–40), and he was president of Finland (1944–46).

Man·nes |'mænəs|, Leopold (1899–1964) U.S. scientist, musician, and inventor. He was a co-inventor of Kodachrome color film and a faculty member of the Mannes School of Music, which was founded by his father David (1866–1959).

Man Ray |'mæn 'rā| see RAY, MAN.

Man·sart |,män'sär(t)|, François (1598–1666) French architect. He rebuilt part of the château of Blois, which incorporated the type of roof now named after him.

Mans·field |'mæns,fēld|, Katherine (1888–1923) New Zealand short-story writer; pseudonym of *Kathleen Mansfield Beauchamp.* Her stories range from extended impressionistic evocations of family life to short sketches.

Man·son |'mænsən|, Charles (1934–) U.S. cult leader. He founded a commune based on free love and complete subordination to him. In 1969 its members carried out a series of murders, including that of the U.S. actress Sharon Tate, for which he and some followers received the death sentence (later commuted to life imprisonment).

Man·son |'mænsən|, Sir Patrick (1844–1922) Scottish physician, pioneer of tropical medicine. He discovered the organism responsible for elephantiasis and established that it was spread by the bite

of a mosquito; he then suggested a similar role for the mosquito in spreading malaria.

Man·stein |'män,stīn|, Fritz Erich von (1887–1973) German army officer. Born *Fritz Erich von Lewinski.* He planned an assault against France in World War II and was imprisoned for war crimes.

Man·te·gna |,män'tenyə|, Andrea (1431–1506) Italian painter and engraver, noted especially for his frescoes.

Man·tell |,mæn'tel|, Gideon Algernon (1790–1852) English geologist. Mantell is best known as the first person to recognize dinosaur remains as reptilian. In 1825 he published a description of the teeth of a "giant fossil lizard" which he named *Iguanodon.*

Man·tle |'mæn(t)əl|, Mickey Charles (1931–95) U.S. baseball player. Elected to the Baseball Hall of Fame, 1974.

Ma·nu·tius |mə'nōōSH(ē)əs|, Aldus see ALDUS MANUTIUS.

Man·zo·ni |,män'zōnē|, Alessandro (1785–1873) Italian novelist, dramatist, and poet. He is remembered chiefly as the author of the novel *I Promessi sposi* (1825–42), a historical reconstruction of 17th-century Lombardy.

Mao Ze·dong |'mow ,zə'dawNG| (1893–1976) Also **Mao Tse-tung** . Chinese statesman, chairman of the Communist Party of the Chinese People's Republic (1949–76) and head of state (1949–59). A cofounder of the Chinese Communist Party in 1921 and its effective leader from the time of the Long March (1934–35), he eventually defeated both the occupying Japanese and rival Kuomintang nationalist forces to create the People's Republic of China in 1949, becoming its first head of state. At first Mao followed the Soviet Communist model, but from 1956 he introduced his own measures, such as the economically disastrous Great Leap Forward (1958–60). Despite having resigned as head of state Mao instigated the Cultural Revolution (1966–68), during which he became the focus of a personality cult.

Ma·ra·do·na |,merə'dawnə|, Diego (Armando) (1960–) Argentinian soccer player. He captained the Argentina team that won the World Cup in 1986, arousing controversy when his apparent handball scored a goal in the quarterfinal match against England.

Ma·rat |mə'rä(t)|, Jean Paul (1743–93) French revolutionary and journalist. A virulent critic of the moderate Girondists, he was instrumental (with Danton and Robespierre) in their fall from power in 1793.

Mar·a·vich |'merə,viCH|, Pete (1948–88) U.S. basketball player. Known as **Pistol Pete**. Elected to the Basketball Hall of Fame (1986).

Mar·ceau |,mär'sō|, Marcel (1923–) French mime artist. He is known for appearing as the white-faced Bip, a character he developed from the French Pierrot character.

March |märCH|, Fredric (1897–1975) U.S. stage and movie actor. Born *Frederick Bickel*. Notable moveis: *Dr. Jekyll and Mr. Hyde* (Academy Award, 1932) and *The Best Years of Our Lives* (Academy Award, 1946).

Mar·ci·a·no |märsē'änō|, Rocky (1923–69) U.S. boxer; born *Rocco Francis Marchegiano*. He became world heavyweight champion in 1952 and successfully defended his title six times before he retired, undefeated, in 1956.

Mar·co·ni |mär'kōnē|, Guglielmo (1874–1937) Italian physicist, electrical engineer, and inventor. He produced the continuously oscillating wave (1912), which is essential for the transmission of sound. Known as the father of radio, he went on to develop short-wave transmissions over long distances and received the Nobel Prize for Physics (1909).

Mar·co Po·lo |'märkō 'pōlō| (*c.* 1254–1324) Italian explorer. With his father and uncle he traveled to China and the court of Kublai Khan via central Asia (1271–75). He eventually returned home (1291–95) via Sumatra, India, and Persia. His book recounting his travels spurred the European quest for Eastern riches.

Mar·cos |'mär,kōs|, Ferdinand Edralin (1917–89) President of the Philippines (1965–86). Amid charges of corruption and political intrigue, he was unable to secure his 1986 reelection and was forced into exile.

Mar·cus Au·re·lius |'märkəs aw'rēlēəs| see AURELIUS.

Mar·cu·se |mär'kōōzə|, Herbert (1898–1979) German-born U.S. philosopher. A member of the Frankfurt School, in *Soviet Marxism* (1958) he argued that revolutionary change can come only from alienated elites such as students.

Mare, Walter de la see DE LA MARE.

Mar·garet |'märgrət|, St. (*c.* 1046–93) Scottish queen, wife of Malcolm III. She exerted a strong influence over royal policy during her husband's reign, and was instrumental in the reform of the Scottish Church. Feast day, November 16.

Mar·garet, Prin·cess |'märgrət|, Margaret Rose (1930–) member of the British royal family, only sister of Elizabeth II.

Mar·gre·the II |mär'grātə| (1940–) queen of Denmark (1972–).

Ma·ria de' Med·i·ci |mə'rēə dä 'medəCHē; me'dēCHē| see MARIE DE MÉDICIS.

Ma·ria The·re·sa |mə'rēə tə'räsə| (1717–80) Archduchess of Austria, queen of Hungary and Bohemia (1740–80). The daughter of the Emperor Charles VI, she succeeded to the Habsburg dominions in 1740 by virtue of the Pragmatic Sanction. Her accession triggered the War of the Austrian Succession, which in turn led to the Seven Years War (1756–63).

Ma·rie An·toi·nette |mə'rē ,æntwə'net| (1755–93) French queen, wife of Louis XVI. A daughter of Maria Theresa, she married the future Louis XVI of France in 1770. Her extravagant lifestyle led to widespread unpopularity and, like her husband, she was executed during the French Revolution.

Ma·rie de Mé·di·cis |mə'rē də 'medə,sēs| (1573–1642) queen of France; Italian name *Maria de' Medici*. The second wife of Henry IV of France, she ruled as regent during the minority of her son Louis XIII (1610–17) and retained her influence after her son came to power.

Ma·rin |mə'rin|, John Cheri (1870–1953) U.S. artist. He is known especially for his expressionistic watercolor seascapes and views of Manhattan.

Ma·ri·net·ti |ˌmerə'nedē|, Filippo Tommaso (1876–1944) Italian poet and dramatist. He launched the futurist movement with a manifesto (1909) that exalted technology, glorified war, and demanded revolution in the arts.

Ma·ri·ni |mə'rēnē|, Marino (1901–80) Italian sculptor, painter, and graphic artist. He is known especially for his expressionistic horse-and-rider series (from 1935).

Ma·ri·no |mə'rēnō|, Dan (1961–) U.S. football player.

Mar·i·on |'merēən|, Francis (c. 1732–c. 1795) American Revolutionary commander. Known as **The Swamp Fox**. He commanded militia troops in South Carolina and evaded the British by hiding in swamps.

Mar·is |'merəs|, Roger Eugene (1934–85) U.S. baseball player. A New York Yankees right fielder, he broke Babe Ruth's record (60 home runs, 1927) for most home runs in a season by hitting 61 in 1961.

Mar·i·us |'merēəs|, Gaius (c. 157–86 BC) Roman general and politician. Elected consul in 107 BC, he defeated Jugurtha and invading Germanic tribes. After a power struggle with Sulla he was expelled from Italy, but returned to take Rome by force in 87 BC.

Mark |märk|, St. an Apostle, companion of St. Peter and St. Paul, traditional author of the second Gospel. Feast day, April 25.

Mar·ko·va |mär'kōvə|, Dame Alicia (1910–) English ballet dancer; born Lilian Alicia Marks. She founded the Markova–Dolin Ballet with Anton Dolin in 1935 and was prima ballerina with the London Festival Ballet 1950–52.

Marks |'märks|, Simon, 1st Baron Marks of Broughton (1888–1964) English businessman; established the retail chain Marks & Spencer.

Marl·bor·ough |'mär(l)ˌbərə|, John Churchill, 1st Duke of (1650–1722) British general. He was commander of British and Dutch troops in the War of the Spanish Succession and won a series of victories (notably at Blenheim in 1704) over the French armies of Louis XIV.

Mar·lette |mär'let|, Doug (1949–) U.S. editorial cartoonist. Full name Douglas Nigel Marlette. He was creator and author of the comic strip "Kudzu." Pulitzer Prize for Editorial Cartooning, 1988.

Mar·ley |'märlē|, Bob (1945–81) Jamaican reggae singer, guitarist, and songwriter; full name Robert Nesta Marley. Having formed the trio the Wailers in 1965, in the 1970s he was instrumental in popularizing reggae. His lyrics often reflected his commitment to Rastafarianism.

Mar·lowe |'märˌlō|, Christopher (1564–93) English dramatist and poet. As a dramatist he brought a new strength and vitality to blank verse; his work influenced Shakespeare's early historical plays. Notable plays: Doctor Faustus (c.1590) and The Jew of Malta (1592).

Mar·quand |ˌmär'kwänd|, J. P. (1893–1960) U.S. author. Full name John Phillips Marquand. He created the character Mr. Moto, a Japanese detective featured in several of his stories. Notable novels: The Late George Apley (1937, Pulitzer Prize), Point of No Return (1949), and Women and Thomas Harrow (1958).

Mar·quette |ˌmär'ket|, Jacques (1637–75) French Jesuit missionary and explorer. Arriving in Canada in 1666, he played a prominent part in the attempt to Christianize the American Indians, and explored the Wisconsin and Mississippi Rivers.

Már·quez |'märˌkes|, Gabriel García see GARCÍA MÁRQUEZ.

Mar·quis |'märkwəs|, Don (1878–1937) U.S. journalist and author. Full name Donald Robert Perry Marquis. Notable works: archy and mehitabel (1927) and sequels.

Mar·quis de Sade |säd| see SADE.

Mar·ri·ott |'meriˌät|, John Willard, Jr. (1932–) U.S. businessman. Founder of the Marriott hotel chain (1964), he is president and CEO (1972–) of Marriott Corp..

Mar·ry·at |'meriət|, Frederick (1792–1848) English novelist and naval officer; known as **Captain Marryat**. Notable works: Peter Simple (1833), Mr.

Midshipman Easy (1836), and *The Children of the New Forest* (1847).

Mar•sal•is |ˌmärˈsæləs|, Wynton (1961–) U.S. jazz trumpeter. He formed his own group in 1981 and was the first musician to win Grammy awards for both a jazz and a classical recording (1984). He is the brother of saxophonist Branford Marsalis.

Marsh |märSH|, James (1794–1842) U.S. clergyman and educator. He was influential in the American Transcendental movement and served as president of the University of Vermont (1826–33).

Marsh |märSH|, Dame Ngaio (Edith) (1889–1982) New Zealand writer of detective fiction. Her works include *Vintage Murder* (1937) and *Final Curtain* (1947).

Marsh |märSH|, Othniel Charles (1831–99) U.S. paleontologist. He was a nephew of George Peabody and the originator of "authentic skeletal restorations" of dinosaurs.

Marsh |märSH|, Reginald (1898–1954) U.S. artist. He is known especially for his paintings of New York City, including *The Bowery* (1930).

Mar•shall |ˈmärSHəl|, George C. (1880–1959) U.S. general and statesman; full name *George Catlett Marshall*. A career army officer, he served as U.S. Army chief of staff (1939–45) in World War II. As U.S. secretary of state (1947–49) he initiated the program of economic aid to European countries known as the Marshall Plan. Nobel Peace Prize (1953).

Mar•shall |ˈmärSHəl|, John (1755–1835) Chief Justice of the U.S. (1801–35). He is considered the father of the American system of constitutional law.

Mar•shall |ˈmärSHəl|, Thomas Riley (1854–1925) vice president of the U.S. (1913–21). He opposed woman's suffrage and prohibition, and he is noted for the remark "What this country needs is a really good five-cent cigar."

Mar•shall |ˈmärSHəl|, Thurgood (1908–93) U.S. Supreme Court justice (1967–93). The first black justice appointed to the U.S. Supreme Court, he had previously won 29 of the 32 cases he argued before the Court, including the land-

mark civil rights case *Brown v. Board of Education* (1954).

Mar•tel |märˈtel|, Charles see CHARLES MARTEL.

Mar•tial |ˈmärSHəl| (c. 40–c. 104 AD) Roman epigrammatist, born in Spain; Latin name *Marcus Valerius Martialis*. His fifteen books of epigrams, in a variety of meters, reflect all facets of Roman life.

Mar•tin |ˈmärtn|, Dean (1917–95) U.S. singer and actor; born *Dino Paul Crocetti*. He joined with Frank Sinatra and Sammy Davis, Jr. in a number of movies, including *Bells are Ringing* (1960), and had his own television show.

Mar•tin |ˈmärtn|, Glenn Luther (1886–1955) U.S. airplane manufacturer. He founded the Glenn L. Martin Co. (1917), which manufactured bombers, transoceanic flying boats, and clipper airplanes.

Mar•tin |ˈmärtn|, Mary (1913–90) U.S. actress. She starred in the Broadway musicals *South Pacific* (1949), *The Sound of Music* (1959), and *Peter Pan* (1954).

Mar•tin |ˈmärtn|, St. (c. 316–397) French bishop (Bishop of Tours from 371), a patron saint of France. When giving half his cloak to a beggar he received a vision of Christ, after which he was baptized. Feast day, November 11.

Mar•tin |ˈmärtn|, Steve (1945?–) U.S. actor and comedian. He made his name with farcical movie comedies such as *The Jerk* (1979) and went on to write, produce, and star in *Roxanne* (1987) and *LA Story* (1991).

Mar•ti•neau |ˈmärtə,nō|, Harriet (1802–76) English writer. She wrote mainly on social, economic, and historical subjects, and is known for her twenty-five-volume series *Illustrations of Political Economy* (1832–4) and her translation of Auguste Comte's *Philosophie positive* (1853).

Mar•ti•ni |ˌmärˈtēnē|, Simone (c. 1284–1344) Italian painter. His work is characterized by strong outlines and the use of rich color, as in *The Annunciation* (1333).

Mar•vell |ˈmärvəl|, Andrew (1621–78) English metaphysical poet. He was best known during his lifetime for his verse satires and pamphlets attacking the corruption of Charles II and his ministers; most of his poetry was published posthumously and was not recognized until the 20th century. Notable poems: "To his Coy Mistress" and "An Horatian Ode on Cromwell's Return from Ireland."

Mar·vin |'märvən|, Lee (1924–87) U.S. actor. Notable movies: *Cat Ballou* (1965, Academy Award).

Marx Brothers |märks| A family of U.S. comedians, consisting of the brothers **Chico** (Leonard, 1886–1961), **Harpo** (Adolph Arthur, 1893–1964), **Groucho** (Julius Henry, 1890–1977), and **Zeppo** (Herbert, 1901–79). Their movies, which are characterized by their anarchic humor, include *Duck Soup* (1933) and *A Night at the Opera* (1935).

Marx |märks|, Karl (Heinrich) (1818–83) German political philosopher and economist, resident in England from 1849. The founder of modern communism with Friedrich Engels, he collaborated with him in the writing of the *Communist Manifesto* (1848) and enlarged it into a series of books, most notably the three-volume *Das Kapital.*

Mary[1] |'merē| mother of Jesus; known as **the (Blessed) Virgin Mary,** or **St. Mary,** or **Our Lady.** According to the Gospels she was a virgin betrothed to Joseph and conceived Jesus by the power of the Holy Spirit. She has been venerated by Catholic and Orthodox Churches from the earliest Christian times. Feast days, January 1 (Roman Catholic Church), March 25 (Annunciation), August 15 (Assumption), September 8 (Immaculate Conception).

Mary[2] |'merē| Name of two queens of England: **Mary I** (1516–58, reigned 1553–58), daughter of Henry VIII; known as **Mary Tudor** or **Bloody Mary.** In an attempt to reverse the country's turn toward Protestantism she instigated the series of religious persecutions by which she earned her nickname. **Mary II** (1662–94; reigned 1689–94), daughter of James II. Having been invited to replace her Catholic father on the throne after his deposition in 1689, she insisted that her husband, William of Orange, be crowned along with her.

Mary, Queen of Scots |'merē| (1542–87) daughter of James V and queen of Scotland (1542–67); known as **Mary Stuart.** A devout Catholic, she was unable to control her Protestant lords and fled to England in 1567. She became the focus of several Catholic plots against Elizabeth I and was eventually beheaded.

Mary, St. see MARY[1].

Mary Mag·da·lene |'merē 'mægdələn; 'mægdə,lēn|, St. Also **Magdalen.** (in the New Testament) a woman of Magdala in Galilee. She was a follower of Jesus, who cured her of evil spirits (Luke 8:2); she is also traditionally identified with the "sinner" of Luke 7:37. Feast day, July 22.

Mary Stu·art |'merē 'stōōərt| see MARY, QUEEN OF SCOTS.

Ma·sac·cio |mə'zäCHō| (1401–28) Italian painter; born *Tommaso Giovanni di Simone Guidi.* The first artist to apply the laws of perspective to painting, he is remembered particularly for his frescoes in the Brancacci Chapel in Florence (1424–27).

Ma·sa·ryk |'mäsə,rik|, Tomáš (Garrigue) (1850–1937) Czechoslovak statesman, president (1918–35). He became Czechoslovakia's first president when the country achieved independence in 1918.

Mas·ca·gni |mä'skänyē|, Pietro (1863–1945) Italian composer and conductor. He is especially remembered for the opera *Cavalleria Rusticana* (1890).

Mase·field |'mās,fēld|, John (Edward) (1878–1967) English poet and novelist. He was appointed Poet Laureate in 1930. Notable works: *Salt-Water Ballads* (1902).

Mas·low |'mæzlō|, Abraham (1908–70) U.S. psychologist. He was a leader of the humanistic school of psychology, and he postulated a " hierarchy of needs" to explain human motivation.

Ma·son |'māsən|, Bobby Ann (1940–) U.S. author. Notable works: *Midnight Magic* (1998) and *In Country* (1985).

Ma·son |'māsən|, Charles (1728–86) English astronomer. With Jeremiah Dixon he surveyed the boundary line between Maryland and Pennsylvania (1763–68) that became known as the Mason-Dixon Line.

Ma·son |'māsən|, George (1725–92) U.S. political philosopher and politician. A Virginia statesman and Revolutionary leader, he refused to sign the Constitution because it lacked a Bill of Rights, which he wrote.

Ma·son |'māsən|, James (1909–84) English actor He acted in more than a hundred films, notably *A Star is Born* (1954), *Lolita* (1962), *Georgy Girl* (1966), and *The Verdict* (1982).

Ma·son |'māsən|, Lowell (1792–1872) U.S. musician. He founded the Boston Academy of Music (1833) and established the first public school music program in the U.S.

Mas·sa·soit |ˌmæsə'soit| (1580?–1661) chief of the Wampanoag Indians. He signed the treaty at Plymouth in 1621 and remained a friend to white settlers. His son was named King Philip.

Mas·sey |'mæsē|, Raymond (1896–1983) U.S. actor and producer, born in Canada.

Mas·sine |mə'sēn|, Léonide Fédorovitch (1896–1979) Russian-born choreographer and ballet dancer, a French citizen from 1944; born *Leonid Fyodorovich Myasin*. He was the originator of the symphonic ballet, and danced in and choreographed the movie *The Red Shoes* (1948).

Mas·sin·ger |'mæsənjər|, Philip (1583–1640) English dramatist. Notable works: *The Duke of Milan* (1621–22), *A New Way to Pay Old Debts* (1625–26), and *The City Madam* (1632).

Mas·son |mə'sän|, André (1896–1987) French painter and graphic artist. He joined the surrealists in the mid-1920s and pioneered "automatic" drawing, a form of fluid, spontaneous composition intended to express images emerging from the unconscious.

Mas·ters |'mæstərz|, Edgar Lee (1869–1950) U.S. writer. Notable books of verse: *Spoon River Anthology* (1915) and *Domesday Book* (1920). Notable biographies: *Lincoln—The Man* (1931) and *Mark Twain* (1938).

Mas·tro·ian·ni |ˌmästroi'änē|, Marcello (1924–96) Italian actor. He appeared in over 140 films, including *La Dolce Vita* (1960) and *Divorce, Italian Style* (1962).

Ma·ta Ha·ri |'mätə 'härē| (1876–1917) Dutch dancer and secret agent; born *Margaretha Geertruida Zelle*. She probably worked for both French and German intelligence services before being executed by the French in 1917.

Math·er |'mæTHər| Family of early New England clergymen, including: **Richard** (1596–1669), born in England. He helped define New England Congregationalism and broadened the power and membership of the Congregational Church. His son **Increase Mather** (1639–1723), clergyman and educator. He was a Congregational leader credited with ending executions for witchcraft. **Cotton Mather** (1663–1728), son of Increase Mather, Congregational clergyman and author. His ecclesiastical history of New England, *Magnalia Christi Americana* (1702), is considered a masterpiece of 17th-century scholarship.

Math·er |'mæTHər|, Stephen Tyng (1867–1930) U.S. conservationist. A descendant of Richard Mather, he organized and served as the first director of the National Parks Service (1917–29).

Math·ews |'mæTHyōōz|, Eddie (1931–) U.S. baseball player. Elected to the Baseball Hall of Fame (1978).

Math·ew·son |'mæTHyōōsən|, Christy (1880–1925) U.S. baseball player. He won 22 or more games for 12 straight years, for a total of 373 career wins. He pitched three shutouts in 1905 World Series. Elected to the Baseball Hall of Fame (1936).

Ma·thi·as |mə'THīəs|, Bob (1930–) U.S. track and field athlete and politician. He was the youngest winner of the decathlon with a gold medal in the 1948 Olympic Games and another in the 1952 Olympics; later he served as a member of the U.S. House of Representatives from California (1967–74).

Math·is |'mæTHəs|, Johnny (1935–) U.S. pop singer. His popular ballads include "Wonderful, Wonderful," "It's Not for Me to Say," and "Chances Are."

Ma·til·da |mə'tildə| (1102–67) English princess, daughter of Henry I and mother of Henry II; known as **the Empress Maud**. Henry's only legitimate child, she was named his heir, but her cousin

Stephen seized the throne on Henry's death in 1135. She waged an unsuccessful civil war against Stephen until 1148.

Ma·tisse |mə'tēs|, Henri (Emile Benoît) (1869–1954) French painter and sculptor. His use of nonnaturalistic color led him to be regarded as a leader of the Fauvists. His later painting and sculpture displays a trend toward formal simplification and abstraction and includes large figure compositions and abstracts made from cut-out colored paper.

Mat·lin |'mætlən|, Marlee (1965–) U.S. actress. Notable movies: *Children of a Lesser God* (1986, Academy Award).

Mat·thau |'mæTHow|, Walter (1920–) U.S. actor. Born *Walter Matuschanskayasky*. Notable stage performances: *The Odd Couple* (1964); notable movies: *The Fortune Cookie* (1966, Academy Award) and *The Odd Couple* (1966)

Mat·thew |'mæTHyoo|, St. an Apostle, a tax collector from Capernaum in Galilee, traditionally the author of the first Gospel. Feast day, September 21.

Mat·thew Pa·ris |'mæTHyoo 'perəs| (*c.* 1199–1259) English chronicler and Benedictine monk, noted for his *Chronica Majora*, a history of the world from the Creation to the mid-13th century.

Mat·thi·as |mə,THīəs|, St. an Apostle, chosen by lot after the Ascension to replace Judas. Feast day (in the Western Church) May 14; (in the Eastern Church) August 9.

Mat·thies·sen |'mæTH(y)əsən|, F. O. (1902–50) U.S. educator and author. Full name *Francis Otto Matthiessen*. Notable works: *American Renaissance* (1941).

Mat·thies·sen |'mæTH(y)əsən|, Peter (1927–) U.S. author. Notable works: *The Snow Leopard* (1978, National Book Award).

Mat·zel·i·ger |mət'seləgər|, Jan Ernst (1852–89) U.S. inventor, born in Suriname. His lasting machine, which revolutionized the shoe industry, was patented in 1883.

Mauch·ly |'mäklē|, John William (1907–80) U.S. physicist and engineer. With John P. Eckert he invented the first electronic computer, ENIAC (1946), and later models Binac and Univac I.

Maud·lin |'mawdlən|, William H. (1921–) U.S. cartoonist and author. He depicted the squalid life of the G.I. in World War II. Notable works: *Bill Maudlin's Army* (1951) and *The Brass Ring* (1971).

Maugham |'mawm|, (William) Somerset (1874–1965) British novelist, short-story writer and dramatist, born in France. Notable works: *Of Human Bondage* (1915), *The Moon and Sixpence* (1919), *East of Suez* (1922), and *Cakes and Ale* (1930).

Mau·pas·sant |,mōpə'sän|, (Henri René Albert) Guy de (1850–93) French novelist and short-story writer. He wrote about 300 short stories and six novels in a simple, direct narrative style. Notable novels: *Une Vie* (1883) and *Bel-Ami* (1885).

Mau·riac |,mawrē'äk|, François (1885–1970) French novelist, dramatist, and critic. His stories show the conflicts of convention, religion, and human passions suffered by prosperous bourgeoisie. Notable works: *Thérèse Desqueyroux* (1927). Nobel Prize for Literature (1952).

Mau·ry |'mawrē|, Matthew Fontaine (1806–73) U.S. oceanographer. He conducted the first systematic survey of oceanic winds and currents, and published charts of his findings.

Maw·la·na another name for JALAL AD-DIN AR-RUMI.

Max |mæks|, Peter (1937–) U.S. artist, born in Germany. His works include art for U.S. postage stamps, murals for border stations between the U.S. and Canada and the U.S. and Mexico, and an annual series of Statue of Liberty paintings.

Max·im U.S. family of inventors, including: **Sir Hiram Stevens Maxim** (1840–1916). He invented incandescent lamps and the Maxim machine gun. His brother **Hudson** (1853–1927), born *Isaac Maxim*. He was an inventor and explosives expert. **Hiram Percy Maxim** (1896–1936), son of Sir Hiram. He invented the Maxim firearms silencer and adapted the same idea to mufflers and air compressors.

Max·i·mil·ian |,mæksə'milyən| (1832–67) Austrian emperor of Mexico 1864–

7; full name *Ferdinand Maximilian Joseph*. Brother of Franz Josef, Maximilian was established as emperor of Mexico under French auspices in 1864. American pressure forced Napoleon III to withdraw his support in 1867. He was executed by a popular uprising led by President Benito Juárez.

Max·well |ˈmækswəl|, Elsa (1883–1963) U.S. columnist and socialite. She was a syndicated gossip columnist and legendary hostess for high society and royalty in Europe and U.S.

Max·well |ˈmækswəl|, James Clerk (1831–79) Scottish physicist. He extended the ideas of Faraday and Kelvin in his equations of electromagnetism and succeeded in unifying electricity and magnetism, identifying the electromagnetic nature of light, and postulating the existence of other electromagnetic radiation.

Max·well |ˈmækswəl|, (Ian) Robert (1923–91) Czech-born British publisher and media entrepreneur; born *Jan Ludvik Hoch*. He died in mysterious circumstances while yachting off Tenerife; it subsequently emerged that he had misappropriated company pension funds.

Max·well |ˈmækswəl|, William (1908–) U.S. author. Notable works: *So Long, See You Tomorrow* (1979).

Ma·ya·kov·sky |ˌmäyəˈkawfskē|, Vladimir (Vladimirovich) (1893–1930) Soviet poet and dramatist, born in Georgia. A fervent futurist, he wrote in a declamatory, aggressive avant-garde style, which he altered to have a comic mass appeal after the Bolshevik revolution.

May·all |ˈmäˌawl|, John Brumwell (1933–) English blues singer and musician. He formed the group John Mayall's Bluesbreakers in 1963.

May·beck |ˈmäˌbek|, Bernard Ralph (1862–1957) U.S. architect. He designed Hearst Hall and other buildings at the University of California, Berkeley.

May·er |ˈmäər|, Jean (1920–93) U.S. nutritionist and educator, born in France. His work on nutrition led to the expansion of the federal school lunch program and the food stamp program.

May·er |ˈmäər|, Louis B. (1885–1957) Russian-born U.S. movie executive; full name *Louis Burt Mayer*; born *Eliezer Mayer*. In 1924 he formed Metro-Goldwyn-Mayer (MGM) with Samuel Goldwyn; he headed the company until 1951.

May·er |ˈmīər|, Oscar F. (1859–1955) U.S. businessman, born in Germany. He founded the Oscar Mayer Co., best known for the Oscar Mayer weiner.

May·field |ˈmäˌfēld|, Curtis (1942–) U.S. musician. He performed with the Impressions (1958–70); his solo hits include the soundtrack to the film *Superfly* (1972).

Mayle |māl|, Peter (1939–) U.S. author. Notable works: *A Year in Provence* (1990) and *Under the Tuscan Sun* (1997).

Mayo |ˈmāō|, William Worrall (1819–1911) U.S. physician, born in England. With his sons **William James Mayo** (1861–1939) and **Charles Horace Mayo** (1865–1939), both surgeons, he helped the Sisters of St. Francis found St. Mary's Hospital in Rochester, Minnesota, with the Mayos as its sole staff (1889).

Mayo |ˈmāō|, George Elton (1880–1949) U.S. psychologist, born in Australia. He practiced social and industrial psychology.

Mayr |ˈmäər|, Ernst Walter (1904–) German-born U.S. zoologist. He argued for a neo-Darwinian approach to evolution in his classic *Animal Species and Evolution* (1963).

Mays |māz|, Benjamin E. (1895–1984) U.S. educator and civil rights leader.

Mays |māz|, Willie (1931–) U.S. baseball player. Known as **Say Hey Kid**. Elected to the Baseball Hall of Fame, 1979.

Ma·za·rin |ˈmäzərən|, Jules (1602–61) Italian-born French statesman; Italian name *Giulio Mazzarino*. Sent to Paris as the Italian papal legate (1634), he became a naturalized Frenchman, and was made a cardinal in 1641 and then chief minister of France (1642).

Maz·zi·ni |məˈzēnē|, Giuseppe (1805–72) Italian nationalist leader. He founded the patriotic movement Young Italy (1831) and was a leader of the Risorgimento. Following the country's unification as a monarchy in 1861, he continued to campaign for a republican Italy.

Mbo•ya |əm'boiyə|, Tom (1930–69) Kenyan statesman. Full name *Thomas Joseph Mboya*. As secretary of the Kenya Federation of Labour (1953–63), he successfully campaigned for Kenyan independence and more representation for blacks in the legislature. He served as minister of justice (1963) and minister of economic affairs (1964–69). Regarded as the likely successor to President Kenyatta, he was assassinated in Nairobi.

Mc•Al•lis•ter |mə'kæləstər|, (Samuel) Ward (1827–95) U.S. lawyer and social leader. He coined the term "The Four Hundred" to refer to the socialites left after he cut a guest list to 400 to accommodate Mrs. William Astor's Newport ballroom.

Mc•Car•thy |mə'kärTHē|, Cormac (1933–) U.S. author. Notable works: *The Orchard Keeper* (1965).

Mc•Car•thy |mə'kärTHē|, Joseph Raymond (1908–57) U.S. politician. A Wisconsin Republican, he was a U.S. senator (1947–57). Having charged the U.S. State Department with an infiltration of Communists, he headed a Senate subcommittee that investigated suspected government subversives. Marked by unsubstantiated accusations and highly questionable invasions of privacy, these investigations were finally halted and McCarthy was censured by the Senate (1954).

Mc•Car•thy |mə'kärTHē|, Mary (Therese) (1912–89) U.S. novelist and critic. Notable novels: *The Groves of Academe* (1952) and *The Group* (1963).

Mc•Cart•ney |mə'kärtnē|, Sir (James) Paul (1942–) English pop and rock singer, songwriter, and bass guitarist. A founding member of the Beatles, he wrote most of their songs in collaboration with John Lennon. After the group broke up in 1970 he formed the band Wings.

Mc•Cart•ney |mə'kärtnē|, Linda (1941–98) U.S. photographer and musician. Wife of former Beatle Paul McCartney.

Mc•Caw |mə'kaw|, Craig O. (1949–) U.S. communications executive. He founded McCaw Cellular Communications, Inc. (1968) and NextLink.

Mc•Cay |mə'kā|, Winsor Zenic (1869–1934) U.S. cartoonist. He is best known for the comic strip "Little Nemo in Slumberland."

Mc•Clel•lan |mə'klelən|, George Brinton (1826–85) U.S. army officer. Known as **Little Mac**. He became general in chief of the U.S. Army (1861) during the Civil War. Although the victor at Antietam (1862), he was removed from command due to a lack of military aggressiveness. The Democratic presidential candidate in 1864, he was defeated by incumbent Abraham Lincoln.

Mc•Clin•tock |mə'klin,(t)äk|, Barbara (1902–92) U.S. geneticist. The discovery of DNA vindicated her earlier findings of transposable genetic elements (1951), earning her the 1983 Nobel Prize for Physiology or Medicine.

Mc•Clos•ky |mə'klawskē|, Robert (1914–) U.S. children's author and illustrator. Notable works: *Make Way for Ducklings* (Caldecott Medal, 1958).

Mc•Cor•mack |mə'kawrmək|, John (1884–1945) U.S. tenor, born in Ireland. He sang with the Chicago, Boston, Metropolitan, and Monte Carlo opera companies.

Mc•Cor•mick |mə'kawrmək|, Cyrus Hall (1809–84) U.S. inventor and industrialist. His patented reaper (1834) was the cornerstone of his harvesting machinery company, and the innovative deferred-payment plans he offered customers became a model in American consumerism.

Mc•Cor•mick |mə'kawrmək|, Katharine Dexter (1875–1967) U.S. women's rights activist. She cofounded the League of Women Voters.

Mc•Court |mə'kawrt|, Frank (1930–) U.S. author. Notable works: *Angela's Ashes* (1996, Pulitzer Prize).

Mc•Cov•ey |mə'kəvē|, Willie (1938–) U.S. baseball player. Elected to the Baseball Hall of Fame (1986).

Mc•Cul•lers |mə'kələrz|, (Lula) Carson (1917–67) U.S. writer. Her work deals sensitively with loneliness and the plight of the eccentric. Notable works: *The Heart is a Lonely Hunter* (1940), *The Member of the Wedding* (1946), and *The Ballad of The Sad Cafe* (1951).

Mc•Cul•lough |mə'kələ(k)|, Colleen

(1937–) Australian author. Notable works: *The Thorn Birds* (1977) and *The Song of Troy* (1998).

Mc•Cutch•eon |mə'kəCHən|, John Tinney (1870–1949) U.S. cartoonist and author. He is best known for his cartoons depicting midwestern rural life.

Mc•Don•ald |mək'dänəld|, Maurice (1902–71) U.S. entrepeneur. With brother **Richard** he founded McDonald's hamburger restaurant, beginning the concept of fast-food drive-ins.

Mc•Dou•gall |mək'do͞ogl|, Alexander (1732–86) American Revolutionary patriot, born in Scotland. He was a member of the Contintental Congress (1781–82, 1784–85).

Mc•En•roe |'mækən,rō|, John (Patrick) (1959–) U.S. tennis player. A temperamental player, he dominated the game in the early 1980s. He won seven Wimbledon titles (three for singles: 1981, 1983, 1984) and four U.S. Open singles championships (1979–84).

Mc•En•tire |'mækən,tī(ə)r|, Reba (1954–) U.S. country singer. Her song credits include "You Lie," "The Greatest Man I Never Knew," and "Take It Back."

Mc•Gov•ern |mə(k)'gəvərn|, George S. (1922–) U.S. politician. He was a Democratic presidential candidate (1972).

Mc•Graw |mə(k)'graw|, John (1873–1934) U.S. baseball manager. He was manager of the New York Giants 1905–24. Elected to Baseball Hall of Fame (1936).

Mc•Guane, Thomas (1939–) U.S. author. Notable works: *Ninety-Two in the Shade* (1974).

Mc•Guf•fey |mə'gəfē|, William Holmes (1800–73) U.S. public education reformer. He is best known for his series of *Eclectic Readers*.

Mc•Gwire |mə(k)'gwī(ə)r|, Mark David (1963–) U.S. athlete. In 1998, he hit 70 home runs, breaking Roger Maris's record (61) for the most home runs in a season.

Mc•Iner•ney |'mækə,nərnē|, Jay (1955–) U.S. author. Notable works: *Bright Lights, Big City* (1984).

Mc•Kay |mə'kā|, Donald (1810–80) U.S. shipbuilder. He designed famous clipper ships, including *Flying Cloud,* as well as ships for the U.S. Navy.

Mc•Kay |mə'kā|, Jim (1921–) U.S. television sports commentator. He was commentator for the Winter and Summer Olympic Games (1960–84) and host of ABC's *Wide World of Sports* (1986–).

Mc•Ken•na |mə'kenə|, Joseph (1843–1926) U.S. Supreme Court justice (1898–1925).

Mc•Kim |mə'kim|, Charles F. (1847–1909) U.S. architect. He designed the Public Library in Boston, the Columbia University Library, and Penn Station in New York City.

Mc•Kim |mə'kim|, Charles M. (1920–) U.S. architect. He designed the KUHT-TV transmitter building in Houston, Texas.

Mc•Kin•ley |mə'kinlē|, John (1780–1852) U.S. Supreme Court justice (1837–52).

Mc•Kin•ley |mə'kinlē|, William see box. **Ida Saxton McKinley** (1847–1907), wife of William McKinley and U.S. first lady (1897–1901).

Mc•Ku•en |mə'kyo͞o(w)ən|, Rod (1933–) U.S. poet, composer, and singer.

Mc•Lach•lan |mə'kläklən|, Sarah (1968–) U.S. pop musician, born in Canada. Grammy Award, 1998.

Mc•Lean |mə'klēn|, John (1785–1861) U.S. Supreme Court justice (1829–61). He dissented in the Dred Scott case and was an unsuccessful candidate for the Republican nomination for the presidency (1856, 1860).

Mc•Lu•han |mə'klo͞oən|, (Herbert) Marshall (1911–80) Canadian writer and thinker. He became famous in the 1960s for his phrase "the medium is the message" and his argument that it is the characteristics of a particular medium rather than the information it disseminates that influence and control society.

Mc•Man•us |mək'mænəs|, George (1884–1954) U.S. cartoonist. He created the comic strip "Bringing Up Father."

Mc•Mas•ter |mək'mæstər|, John Bach (1852–1932) U.S. historian. Notable works: *History of the People of the U.S.* (8 vols.,1883–1912).

McKinley, William
25th U.S. president

Life dates: 1843–1901
Place of birth: Niles, Ohio
Mother: Nancy Campbell Allison McKinley
Father: William McKinley
Wife: Ida Saxton Mc Kinley
Children: Katherine, Ida
College/University: Allegheny College; Albany Law School
Military service: brevet major, Civil War
Career: Lawyer; teacher
Political career: U.S. House of Representatives; governor of Ohio; president
Party: Republican
Home state: Ohio
Opponent in presidential races: William Jennings Bryan
Term of office: Mar. 4, 1897–Sept. 14, 1901 (assassinated by Leon Czolgosz)
Vice presidents: Garret A. Hobart; Theodore Roosevelt
Notable events of presidency: Gold Rush in Klondike; Dingley Tariff Act; Hague Peace Conference; Treaty of Paris; Spanish-American War; Hawaii annexed to U.S.; Philippines, Puerto Rico, and Guam acquired from Cuba; American Samoa acquired by Treaty of 1900; Gold Standard Act
Other achievements: Admitted to the Ohio bar; prosecuting attorney, Stark County, Ohio
Place of burial: Canton, Ohio

Mc•Mil•lan |mək'milən|, Edwin Mattison (1907–91) U.S. physicist. He discovered neptunium. Nobel Prize for Chemistry, 1951.

Mc•Mur•try |mək'mərtrē|, Larry (1936–) U.S. author. Notable works: *Lonesome Dove* (1985).

Mc•Na•mara |'mæknə,merə|, Robert Strange (1916–) U.S. businessman and public official. He was secretary of the U.S. Department of Defense (1961–68) and president of the World Bank (1968–81).

Mc•Part•land |mək'pärtlənd|, Jimmy (1907–91) U.S. jazz trumpeter. Full name *James Dougald McPartland*. He defined the style that was later termed "Chicago jazz."

Mc•Phee |mək'fē|, John (Angus) (1931–) U.S. journalist and author.

Notable works: *Coming into the Country* (1977).

Mc•Rae |mə'krā|, Carmen (1922–94) U.S. jazz singer. She began as a club singer in New York City; she became an inventive scat singer directly influenced by the emergence of bop.

Mc•Rey•nolds |mək'renəl(d)z|, James C. (1862–1946) U.S. Supreme Court justice (1914–41).

Mc•Veigh |mək'vā|, Timothy (1968–) U.S. terrorist. He was convicted in 1997 of federal conspiracy, murder, and other charges for his role in the bombing of the Alfred P. Murrah Federal Building in Oklahoma City in 1995.

Mc•Wil•liams |mək'wilyəmz|, Carey (1905–80) U.S. journalist and author. He was editor of *The Nation* (1955–79). Notable works: *Factories in the Field* (1939).

Mead |mēd|, Margaret (1901–78) U.S. anthropologist and social psychologist. She worked in Samoa and the New Guinea area and wrote a number of studies of primitive cultures, including *Coming of Age in Samoa* (1928). Her writings made anthropology accessible to a wide readership and demonstrated its relevance to Western society.

Meade |mēd|, George Gordon (1815–72) U.S. army officer. He was the commander of the Army of the Potomac (1863–65) during the Civil War, and is most noted for his victory at Gettysburg (1863).

Mea•ny |'mēnē|, George (1894–1980) U.S. labor leader. He was president of the AFL-CIO (1955–79).

Meara |'mirə|, Anne (1929–) U.S. actress. She and her husband Jerry Stiller form the comedy duo Stiller & Meara.

Meat Loaf |'mēt ,lōf| (1947–) U.S. rock musician and actor. Born *Marvin Lee Aday*. Notable songs: "I'd Do Anything for Love (But I Won't Do That)"; notable movies: *The Rocky Horror Picture Show*.

Med•a•war |'medəwər|, Sir Peter (Brian) (1915–87) English immunologist. He studied the biology of tissue transplantation, and showed that the rejection of grafts was the result of an immune mechanism. Nobel Prize for Physiology or Medicine (1960).

Me•di•ci Also **de' Medici**. A powerful Italian family of bankers and merchants whose members effectively ruled Florence for much of the 15th century and from 1569 were grand dukes of Tuscany. **Cosimo** and **Lorenzo de' Medici** were notable rulers and patrons of the arts in Florence; the family also provided four popes (including **Leo X**) and two queens of France (**Catherine de' Medici** and **Marie de Médicis**).

Mé•di•cis |'medə,sēs|, Marie de see MARIE DE MÉDICIS.

Meh•ta |'mätä|, Zubin (1936–) U.S. symphony conductor, born in India. He has been music director of the Los Angeles Philharmonic (1962–78), the New York Philharmonic (1978–91), and the Israel Philharmonic (1991–).

Mei•er |'mīər|, Richard (1934–) U.S. architect. He designed the Getty Center Museum in Los Angeles and the High Museum of Art in Georgia.

Mei•ji Ten•no |,mäjē 'tenō| (1852–1912) emperor of Japan (1868–1912); born *Mutsuhito*. He took the name Meiji Tenno when he became emperor. He encouraged Japan's rapid modernization and political reform.

Mei•kle•john |'mīkl,jän|, Alexander (1872–1964) U.S. educator and social reformer, born in England. Notable works: *The Liberal College* (1920).

Me•ir |mä'ir|, Golda (1898–1978) Israeli stateswoman, prime minister (1969–74); born *Golda Mabovich*. Born in Ukraine, she emigrated to the U.S. in 1907 and then to Palestine in 1921. Following Israel's independence she served in cabinet posts from 1949 to 1966 before being elected prime minister. She resigned (1974) in the wake of criticism for Israel's losses in the Arab-Israeli War (1973).

Meit•ner |'mītnər|, Lise (1878–1968) Austrian-born Swedish physicist. She worked in the field of radiochemistry with Otto Hahn, discovering the element protactinium with him in 1917. She formulated the concept of nuclear fission with her nephew Otto Frisch.

Me•lanch•thon |mə'læNGkTHän|, Philipp (1497–1560) German Protestant reformer; born *Philipp Schwarzerd*. He succeeded Martin Luther as leader of the Reformation movement in Germany in 1521 and drew up the Augsburg Confession (1530).

Mel•ba |'melbə|, Dame Nellie (1861–1931) Australian operatic soprano; born *Helen Porter Mitchell*. She was born near Melbourne, from which city she took her professional name. Melba gained worldwide fame with her coloratura singing.

Mel•bourne |'melbərn|, William Lamb, 2nd Viscount (1779–1848) British Whig statesman, prime minister (1834 and 1835–41). He became chief political adviser to Queen Victoria after her accession in 1837.

Mel•chi•or |'melkē,awr|, Lauritz Lebrecht Hommel (1890–1973) U.S. tenor, born in Denmark. He was considered the outstanding heldentenor of his day.

Mel•e•a•ger |,mele'āgər| (1st century BC) Greek poet, best known as the compiler of *Stephanos*, one of the first large anthologies of epigrams.

Mel•len•camp |'melən,kæmp|, John (Cougar) (1951–) U.S. rock musician. Notable albums: *American Fool* (1982).

Mel•lon |'melən|, Andrew (William) (1855–1937) U.S. financier and philanthropist. He served as secretary of the treasury (1921–32). He donated his art collection and made gifts to establish the National Gallery of Art in Washington D.C. in 1941.

Mel•ville |'melvil|, Herman (1819–91) U.S. novelist and short-story writer. His experiences on a whaling ship formed the basis of several novels, notably *Moby Dick* (1851). Other notable works: *White-Jacket* (1850), *The Confidence Man* (1857), and *Billy Budd* (first published in 1924).

Me•nan•der |mə'nændər| (c. 342–292 BC) Greek dramatist. His comic plays deal with domestic situations and capture colloquial speech patterns. The sole complete extant play is *Dyskolos*.

Men•ci•us |'men,SHēəs| (c. 371–c. 289 BC) Chinese philosopher; Latinized name of *Meng-tzu* or *Mengzi* ("Meng the Master"). Noted for developing Confucianism, he believed that rulers should provide for the welfare of the people and that human nature is intrinsically good.

Menck·en |'meNGkən|, H. L. (1880–1956) U.S. journalist and literary and social critic; full name *Henry Louis Mencken.* From 1908 he attacked the political and literary establishment. In his book *The American Language* (1919) he opposed the dominance of European culture in America, arguing for and establishing the study of American English in its own right.

Men·del |'mendəl|, Gregor Johann (1822–84) Moravian monk, the father of genetics. From systematically breeding peas he demonstrated the transmission of characteristics in a predictable way by factors (genes) that remain intact and independent between generations and do not blend, though they may mask one another's effects.

Men·de·le·ev |ˌmendə'lāəf|, Dmitri (Ivanovich) (1834–1907) Russian chemist. He developed the periodic table and successfully predicted the discovery of several new elements.

Men·dels·sohn |'mendlsən|, Felix (1809–47) German composer and pianist; full name *Jakob Ludwig Felix Mendelssohn-Bartholdy.* His romantic music is elegant, light, and melodically inventive. Notable works include the oratorio *Elijah* (1846) and eight volumes of *Songs without Words* for piano.

Men·do·za |ˌmen'dōzə|, Antonio de (c. 1490–1552) Spanish colonial administrator, the first viceroy of New Spain (1535–50).

Me·nes |'mē,nēz| (c. 3100 BC) Egyptian pharaoh. He founded the first dynasty that ruled Egypt.

Meng-tzu |meNG 'tsōō| Also **Mengzi.** Chinese name for MENCIUS.

Men·nen |'menən|, Gerhard H. (1856–1902) U.S. manufacturer. He founded the Mennen Chemical Co. (1892), maker of talcum powder, creams, and beauty products.

Men·nin·ger |'menənjər|, Karl Augustus (1893–1990) U.S. psychiatrist. He founded the Menninger Clinic, where he began training psychiatrists in psychoanalysis.

Me·not·ti |mə'nätē|, Gian Carlo (1911–) U.S. composer, born in Italy.

Notable operas: *The Old Maid and the Thief* (1939; Pulitzer Prize) and *Amahl and the Night Visitors* (1951).

Men·u·hin |'menyōōin|, Sir Yehudi (1916–99) U.S.-born British violinist. He founded a school of music, named after him, in 1962.

Men·zies |'menzēz|, Sir Robert Gordon (1894–1978) Australian Liberal statesman, prime minister (1939–41 and 1949–66). He is Australia's longest-serving prime minister.

Mer·ca·tor |mər'kātər|, Gerardus (1512–94) Flemish geographer and cartographer, resident in Germany from 1552; Latinized name of *Gerhard Kremer.* He invented the system of map projection that is named after him.

Mer·cer |'mərsər|, Johnny (1909–76) U.S. songwriter. Full name *John Herndon Mercer.* He wrote lyrics for hundreds of popular songs, including "Moon River" (1961) and "Days of Wine and Roses" (1962).

Mer·chant |'mərCHənt|, Ismail (1936–) Indian movie producer. In 1961 he became a partner with James Ivory in Merchant Ivory Productions. Together they have made a number of movies, such as *Shakespeare Wallah* (1965), *The Bostonians* (1984), and *Howard's End* (1992).

Merckx |mərks|, Eddy (1945–) Belgian racing cyclist. During his professional career he won the Tour de France five times (1969–72 and 1974).

Mer·cou·ri |mərk(y)ōōrē|, Melina (1923–94) Greek actress and politician; born *Anna Amalia Mercouri.* Her movies include *Never on Sunday* (1960). Exiled for opposing the military junta in 1967, she was elected to Parliament in the socialist government of 1978, becoming minister of culture in 1985.

Mer·cu·ry |'mər,kyərē|, Freddie (1946–91) British pop star. He was the founder (1971) and lead singer of the heavy metal rock band Queen.

Mer·e·dith |'merə,diTH|, George (1828–1909) English novelist and poet. His semiautobiographical verse collection *Modern Love* (1862) describes the disillusionment of married love. Other notable works: *The Egoist* (1871).

Mer·e·dith |'merə,diTH|, James Howard

(1933–) U.S. business executive. He was the first African American to attend Jackson (Mississippi) State College (1960–62) after 3,000 troops quelled riots.

Mer•e•dith |'merə,diTH |, William (Morris) (1919–) U.S. poet. Notable works: *Partial Accounts* (1987, Pulitzer Prize).

Mer•gen•tha•ler |'mərgən,tälər|, Ottmar (1854–99) U.S. inventor, born in Germany. He developed the first Linotype typesetting machine (1884).

Mer•man |'mərmən|, Ethel (1908?–84) U.S. singer and actress. Born *Ethel Zimmerman*. The "queen of Broadway" for 3 decades, she performed in many Broadway plays and musicals, including *Gypsy* (1959) and *Hello, Dolly!* (1970).

Mer•ri•am |'merēəm| Brothers **George** (1803–80) and **Charles** (1806–87), U.S. publishers, formed the G. & C. Merriam Co., which published the first version of the Merriam-Webster dictionary.

Mer•rill |'merəl|, Frank Dow (1903–55) U.S. army officer. He organized the volunteer regiment known as "Merrill's Marauders," who trained for jungle warfare (1943).

Mer•rill |'merəl|, James (1926–95) U.S. poet. Notable works: *Nights and Days* (National Book Award, 1966) and *Divine Comedies* (1976, Pulitzer Prize). Bollingen Prize, 1973.

Mer•ton |'mərtən|, Thomas (1915–68) U.S. monk and author, born in France. He was ordained as Father M. Louis. Notable works: *The Seven Storey Mountain* (1948).

Mer•win |'mərwən|, W. S. (1927–) U.S. poet and author. Full name *William Stanley Merwin*. Notable works: *The Carrier of Ladders* (1970, Pulitzer Prize). Bollingen Prize, 1979.

Mes•mer |'mezmər|, Franz Anton (1734–1815) Austrian physician. Mesmer is chiefly remembered for introducing a therapeutic technique involving hypnotism; it was bound up with his ideas about "animal magnetism," however, and steeped in sensationalism.

Mes•sa•li•na |,mesə'lēnə|, Valeria (*c.* 22–48 AD) Also **Messallina**. Roman empress, third wife of Claudius. She be-

came notorious in Rome for the murders she instigated in court and for her extramarital affairs, and was executed on Claudius's orders.

Mes•ser•schmitt |'mesər,SHmit |, Willy (1898–1978) German aircraft designer and manufacturer of German warplanes.

Mes•sia•en |'mesā,ən |, Olivier (Eugène Prosper Charles) (1908–92) French composer. His music was influenced by Greek and Hindu rhythms, birdsong, Stravinsky and Debussy, and the composer's Roman Catholic faith. Notable works: *Quartet for the End of Time* (1941).

Mes•sick |'mesək|, Dalia (1906–) U.S. cartoonist. Pseudonym **Dale Messick**. She created the comic strip "Brenda Starr, Reporter."

Me•tes•ky |mə'teskē |, George (1903–) U.S. terrorist. Known as **The Mad Bomber.** He confessed to planting 32 bombs and causing 15 injuries between 1947 and 1957 in New York City.

Me•tho•di•us |mə'THōdēəs|, St. the brother of St. Cyril (see CYRIL, ST.).

Met•ter•nich |'metər,nik|, Klemens Wenzel Nepomuk Lothar, Prince of Metternich-Winneburg-Beilstein (1773–1859) Austrian statesman. As foreign minister (1809–48), he was one of the organizers of the Congress of Vienna (1814–15), which devised the settlement of Europe after the Napoleonic Wars.

Mey•er |'mīər|, Adolf (1866–1950) U.S. psychiatrist and educator, born in Switzerland. He was a leading exponent of psychobiology.

Mey•er•beer |'mīərbir|, Giacomo (1791–1864) German composer; born *Jakob Liebmann Beer*. He settled in Paris, establishing himself as a leading exponent of French grand opera with a series of works including *Les Huguenots* (1836).

Mey•er•hof |'mīərhawf|, Otto Fritz (1884–1951) German-born U.S. biochemist. He worked on the biochemical processes involved in muscle action and provided the basis for understanding the process by which glucose is broken down to provide energy. Nobel Prize for Physiology or Medicine (1922).

Mi•chel•an•ge•lo |,mikəl'ænjələ; ,mīkəl'ænjəlō| (1475–1564) Italian sculptor, painter, architect, and poet; full name *Michelangelo Buonarroti*. A leading figure of the High Renaissance, Michelangelo established his reputation with sculptures such as the *Pietà* (*c.*1497–1500) and *David* (1501–04). Under papal patronage he decorated the ceiling of the Sistine Chapel in Rome (1508–12) and painted the fresco *The Last Judgment* (1536–41), both important mannerist works. His architectural achievements include the completion of St. Peter's in Rome (1546–64).

Mi·che·lin |'misHələn|, André (1853–1931) French industrialist. He and his brother Édouard founded the Michelin Tire Co. in 1888 and pioneered the use of tires on automobiles.

Mi·che·loz·zo |,mēkə'lätsō| (1396–1472) Italian architect and sculptor; full name *Michelozzo di Bartolommeo*. In partnership with Ghiberti and Donatello he led a revival of interest in Roman architecture.

Mi·chel·son |'mīkəlsən|, Albert Abraham (1852–1931) U.S. physicist. He specialized in precision measurement in experimental physics, and in 1907 became the first American to be awarded a Nobel Prize.

Miche·ner |miCH(ə)nər|, James Albert (1907–97) U.S. author. Notable novels: *Tales of the South Pacific* (1947, Pulitzer Prize), *The Bridges at Toko-ri* (1953), and *Caribbean* (1989).

Mid·dle·ton |'midl-tən|, Thomas (*c.* 1570–1627) English dramatist. He is best known for the tragedies *The Changeling* (1622), written with the dramatist William Rowley, and *Women Beware Women* (1620–27).

Mid·ler |'midlər|, Bette (1945–) U.S. actress and musician. Known as **The Divine Miss M**. She is noted for her 1989 hit "Wind Beneath My Wings," taken from the movie in which she starred, *Beaches*.

Mies van der Rohe |,mēs ,væn dər 'rō|, Ludwig (1886–1969) German-born architect and designer. He designed the German pavilion at the 1929 International Exhibition at Barcelona and the Seagram Building in New York (1954–58), and was noted for his tubular steel furniture. He was director of the

Bauhaus 1930–33 before emigrating to the U.S. in 1937.

Miff·lin |'miflin|, George Harrison (1845–1921) U.S. publisher. He was president of Houghton Mifflin Co. (1908–21).

Mi·hai·lo·vić |mə'hīlə,viCH|, Draža (1893–1946) Yugoslav soldier; full name *Dragoljub Mihailović*. Leader of the Chetniks during World War II, in 1941 he became minister of war for the Yugoslav government in exile. After the war he was executed on the charge of collaboration with the Germans.

Mi·kan |'mīkən|, George (1924–) U.S. basketball player, born in Czechoslovakia. Elected to the Basketball Hall of Fame (1959).

Mi·ki·ta |mə'kētə|, Stanley (1940–) U.S. hockey player, born in Czechoslovakia. He led the NHL in scoring four times.

Mil·haud |mē'(y)ō|, Darius (1892–1974) French composer. A member of the group Les Six, he composed the music to Cocteau's ballet *Le Boeuf sur le toit* (1919). Much of his music was polytonal and influenced by jazz.

Mil·ken |'milkən|, Michael (1946–) U.S. junk bond trader. He was convicted of fraud and racketeering in 1989.

Mill |mil|, John Stuart (1806–73) English philosopher and economist. Mill is best known for his political and moral works, especially *On Liberty* (1859), which argued for the importance of individuality, and *Utilitarianism* (1861), which extensively developed Bentham's theory.

Mil·lais |mə'lā|, Sir John Everett (1829–96) English painter. A founding member of the Pre-Raphaelite Brotherhood, he went on to produce lavishly painted portraits and landscapes. Notable works: *Christ in the House of his Parents* (1850) and *Bubbles* (1886).

Mil·land |mə'lænd|, Ray (1905–86) U.S. actor. Notable movies: *The Lost Weekend* (1945, Academy Award).

Mil·lay |mə'lā|, Edna St. Vincent (1892–1950) U.S. poet and author. Notable works: *The Ballad of the Harp-Weaver* (1923, Pulitzer Prize).

Mille |mil|, Cecil B. de see DeMille.

Mil·ler |'milər|, Alfred Jacob (1810–

74) U.S. artist. His Rocky Mountain sketches of Indians and mountain men were first published to illustrate *DeVoto's Across the Wide Missouri* (1947).

Mil·ler |'milər|, Arthur (1915–) U.S. dramatist. He established his reputation with *Death of a Salesman* (1949; Pulitzer Prize). *The Crucible* (1953) used the Salem witch trials of 1692 as an allegory for McCarthyism in America in the 1950s. Miller was married to Marilyn Monroe (1955–61). Notable works: *All My Sons* (1947), *A View From the Bridge* (1955), and *After the Fall* (1964).

Mil·ler |'milər|, Glenn (1904–44) U.S. jazz trombonist and bandleader. Full name *Alton Glenn Miller*. He led a celebrated swing big band, with whom he recorded his signature tune "Moonlight Serenade." He died when his aircraft disappeared over the English Channel.

Mil·ler |'milər|, Henry (Valentine) (1891–1980) U.S. novelist. His autobiographical novels *Tropic of Cancer* (1934) and *Tropic of Capricorn* (1939) were banned in the U.S. until the 1960s due to their frank depiction of sex and use of obscenities.

Mil·ler |'milər|, J. D. (1923–96) U.S. country songwriter. Notable songs: "Honky-Tonk Angels."

Mil·ler |'milər|, Joaquin (1837–1913) U.S. author and poet. Born *Cincinnatus Hiner Miller*.

Mil·ler |'milər|, Roger Dean (1936–92) U.S. country singer and songwriter. Notable songs: "King of the Road" and "Dang Me," as well as music for the Broadway show, *Big River*.

Mil·ler |'milər|, Samuel Freeman (1816–90) U.S. Supreme Court justice (1862–90).

Mil·ler |'milər|, Shannon (1977–) U.S. gymnast. She won 5 medals in 1992 Olympics and 2 gold medals in the 1996 Olympics, and was the All-Around Women's World Champion in 1993 and 1994.

Mil·ler |'milər|, Steve (1943–) U.S. musician. He started his Steve Miller Blues Band in 1966.

Mil·let |mə'lā|, Jean (François) (1814–75) French painter. He was famous for the dignity he brought to the treatment of peasant subjects, which he concen-

trated on from 1850. Notable works: *The Gleaners* (1857).

Mil·lett |'milit|, Kate (1934–) U.S. feminist; full name *Katherine Millett*. She became involved in the civil rights movement of the 1960s, and advocated a radical feminism in *Sexual Politics* (1970).

Mil·li·kan |'miləkən|, Robert Andrews (1868–1953) U.S. physicist. He was the first to give an accurate figure for the electric charge on an electron. Nobel Prize for Physics, 1923.

Mills |milz|, Clark (1815–83) U.S. sculptor. He executed a bronze equestrian statue of Andrew Jackson in Washington, D.C.

Mills |milz|, John (1908–) U.S. actor. Notable movies: *Ryan's Daughter* (1970, Academy Award).

Mills |milz|, Sir John (Lewis Ernest Watts) (1908–) English actor. He is best known for his roles in war and adventure movies, such as *Scott of the Antarctic* (1948). He won an Oscar for his portrayal of a village idiot in *Ryan's Daughter* (1971). His daughters Juliet Mills (b.1941) and Hayley Mills (b.1946) have also had acting careers.

Mills |milz|, Robert (1781–1855) U.S. architect. He designed the Washington Monument in Washington, D.C.

Milne |'mil(n)|, A. A. (1882–1956) English writer of stories and poems for children; full name *Alan Alexander Milne*. He created the character Winnie the Pooh for his son Christopher Robin. Notable works: *Winnie-the-Pooh* (1926) and *When We Were Very Young* (verse collection, 1924).

Mi·losz |'mēlawSH|, Czeslaw (1911–) U.S. poet and author, born in Lithuania. Notable works: *Collected Poems* (1988). Nobel Prize, 1980.

Mil·sap |'mil,sæp|, Ronnie (1944–) U.S. country singer.

Mil·ton |'miltən|, John (1608–74) English poet. His three major works, completed after he had gone blind (1652), show his mastery of blank verse: they are the epic poems *Paradise Lost* (1667, revised 1674) and *Paradise Regained* (1671), and the verse drama *Samson Agonistes* (1671).

Min·ghel·la, Anthony (1954–) U.S.

director. Notable movies: *The English Patient* (Academy Award, 1996).

Min•gus |'miNGgəs|, Charles (1922–79) U.S. jazz bassist and composer. A leading figure of the 1940s jazz scene, he experimented with atonality and was influenced by gospel and blues. His compositions include "Goodbye Porkpie Hat."

Min•nel•li |mə'nelē| U.S. family, including: **Vincente Minnelli** (1910–86), movie director. He directed classic Hollywood musicals, including *Gigi* (1958, Academy Award). He was married to actress Judy Garland. His daughter **Liza Minnelli** (1946–), actress and entertainer. Notable movies: *Cabaret* (1972, Academy Award).

Min•ton |'min(t)ən|, Sherman (1890–1965) U.S. Supreme Court justice (1949–56).

Min•ton |'min(t)ən|, Thomas (1765–1836) English pottery manufacturer. He made majolica, bone china, and reproductions of works of della Robbia and Palissy.

Min•u•it |'minyəwət|, Peter (1580–1638) Dutch colonial administrator. He was the first director general of the North American Dutch colony of New Netherland (1626–31). He purchased Manhattan Island from the Algonquin Indians (1626) for 60 guilders ($24).

Mi•ra•beau |'mirə,bō|, Honoré Gabriel Riqueti, Comte de (1749–91) French revolutionary politician. Pressing for a form of constitutional monarchy, Mirabeau was prominent in the early days of the French Revolution.

Mi•ró |,mi'rō|, Joan (1893–1983) Spanish painter. One of the most prominent figures of surrealism, he painted a brightly colored fantasy world of variously spiky and amebic calligraphic forms against plain backgrounds.

Mi•shi•ma |'misHē,mä|, Yukio (1925–70) Japanese writer; pseudonym of *Hiraoka Kimitake*. His books include the four-volume *The Sea of Fertility* (1965–70), which looks at reincarnation and the sterility of modern life. An avowed imperialist, he committed hara-kiri after failing to incite soldiers against the postwar regime.

Mis•so•ni, Tai Otavio (1921–) Italian

fashion designer, born in Yugoslavia. With his wife Rosita, he founded the Missoni Co. in Milan (1953)

Mitch•ell |'miCHəl|, Billy (1879–1936) U.S. army officer, born in France. An outspoken advocate of air power, he was court-martialed for his criticism of the War and Navy Departments (1925).

Mitch•ell |'miCHəl|, John (1870–1919) U.S. labor leader. He was United Mine Workers president (1898–1908).

Mitch•ell |'miCHəl|, John (1913–88) U.S. statesman. He was U.S. attorney general under President Nixon (1969–72).

Mitch•ell |'miCHəl|, John Ames (1845–1918) U.S. artist, editor, and novelist. He founded and edited *Life* magazine (1883–1918).

Mitch•ell |'miCHəl|, Joni (1943–) Canadian singer and songwriter; born *Roberta Joan Anderson*. Starting to record in 1968, she moved from folk to a fusion of folk, jazz, and rock. Notable albums: *Blue* (1971) and *Hejira* (1976).

Mitch•ell |'miCHəl|, Margaret (1900–49) U.S. novelist, famous as the author of the Pulitzer Prize–winning novel *Gone with the Wind* (1936), set during the Civil War.

Mitch•ell |'miCHəl|, Maria (1818–89) U.S. astronomer. She established the orbit of a newly discovered comet (1847) and became the first woman elected to the American Academy of Arts and Sciences.

Mitch•ell |'miCHəl|, S. Weir (1829–1914) U.S. author. Full name *Silas Weir Mitchell*. Notable works: *Hugh Wynne, Free Quaker* (1897).

Mitch•um |'miCHəm|, Robert (1917–97) U.S. actor. He was a professional boxer before rising to stardom in movies such as *Out of the Past* (1947), and *Night of the Hunter* (1955).

Mit•ford |'mitfərd|, Nancy (Freeman) (1904–73) She and her sister **Jessica (Lucy)** (1917–96) were English writers. Nancy achieved fame with comic novels including *Love in a Cold Climate* (1949). Jessica became a U.S. citizen in 1944 and is best known for her works on American culture, notably *The American Way of Death* (1963). Among their four sisters were **Unity** (1914–48), who was an admirer of Hitler, and **Diana** (1910–), who married Sir Oswald Mosley in 1936.

Mith·ri·da·tes VI |ˌmiTHrəˈdāˌtēz| (*c.* 132–63 BC) Also **Mithradates VI.** king of Pontus (120–63 BC); known as **Mithridates the Great.** His expansionist policies led to three wars with Rome (88–85, 83–82, and 74–66 BC). He was finally defeated by Pompey.

Mit·ter·rand |ˈmitəˌrän(d) |, François (Maurice Marie) (1916–96) French statesman, president (1981–95). As president he initially moved to raise basic wages, increase social benefits, nationalize key industries, and decentralize government. The Socialist Party lost its majority vote in the 1986 general election and Mitterrand made the conservative Jacques Chirac prime minister, resulting in a reversal of some policies.

Mi·ya·ke, Issey (1938–) Japanese fashion designer. Worked with Guy Laroche, Hubert de Givenchy, and Geoffrey Beene before opening a design studio (1970).

Mö·bi·us |ˈmOEbēəs; ˈmōbēəs |, August Ferdinand (1790–1868) German mathematician and astronomer. He discovered the one-sided figure the Möbius strip (1958).

Mö·bi·us |ˈmOEbēəs; ˈmōbēəs |, Karl August (1825–1908) German zoologist. He introduced the concept of the ecosystem.

Mo·bu·tu Se·se Se·ko |məˈbo͞oto͞o ˈsāze ˈsākō| (1930–97) president of Zaire, now the Democratic Republic of Congo (1965–97); born *Joseph-Désiré Mobutu.* Seizing power in a military coup in 1965, he retained control despite opposition until 1997, when he was finally forced to resign.

Mo·di·glia·ni |ˌmōdēlˈyänē |, Amedeo (1884–1920) Italian painter and sculptor, resident in France from 1906. His portraits and nudes are noted for their elongated forms, linear qualities, and earthy colors.

Moholy-Nagy |ˈmawhəlē ˈnäj |, László (1895–1946) Hungarian-born U.S. painter, sculptor, and photographer. He pioneered the experimental use of plastic materials, light, photography, and movie.

Mois·san |ˌmwäˈsän |, Ferdinand Frédéric Henri (1852–1907) French chemist. In 1886 he succeeded in isolating the very reactive element fluorine. In 1892 he invented the electric-arc furnace that bears his name. Nobel Prize for Chemistry (1906).

Mo·lière |ˌmōlˈyer| (1622–73) French dramatist; pseudonym of *Jean-Baptiste Poquelin.* He wrote more than twenty comic plays about contemporary France, developing stock characters from Italian *commedia dell'arte.* Notable works: *Don Juan* (1665), *Le Misanthrope* (1666), and *Le Bourgeois gentilhomme* (1670).

Mol·nar |ˈmawlnär|, Ferenc (1878–1952) Hungarian playwright and novelist. Notable plays: *Liliom* (1909) and *The Good Fairy* (1930). Notable novels: *The Paul Street Boys* (1907) and *Andor* (1918).

Mo·lo·tov |ˈmäləˌtawf|, Vyacheslav (Mikhailovich) (1890–1986) Soviet statesman; born *Vyacheslav Mikhailovich Skryabin.* As commissar (later minister) for foreign affairs (1939–49; 1953–56), he negotiated the nonaggression pact with Nazi Germany (1939) and after 1945 represented the Soviet Union at meetings of the United Nations.

Molt·ke |ˈmawltkə|, Helmuth Karl Bernhard Graf von (1800–91) Prussian soldier. He devised strategic and tactical command methods for modern mass armies engaged on broad fronts.

Momm·sen |ˈmämsən|, Theodor (1817–1903) German historian. He is noted for his three-volume *History of Rome* (1854–56; 1885) and his treatises on Roman constitutional law (1871–88). Nobel Prize for Literature (1902).

Monck |məNGk|, George, 1st Duke of Albemarle (1608–70) English general. Initially a Royalist, he became a supporter of Oliver Cromwell and later suppressed the Royalists in Scotland (1651). Concerned at the growing unrest following Cromwell's death (1658), Monck negotiated the return of Charles II in 1660.

Mon·dale |ˈmänˌdāl |, Walter Frederick (1928–) U.S. vice president (1977–81). A Minnesota Democrat, he served in the U.S. Senate (1964–76). He ran for the U.S. presidency in 1984, losing to incumbent Ronald Reagan. He was U.S. ambassador to Japan (1993–96).

Mon·dri·an |'mawndrēən|, Piet (1872–1944) Dutch painter; born *Pieter Cornelis Mondriaan*. He was a cofounder of the De Stijl movement and the originator of neoplasticism, one of the earliest and strictest forms of geometrical abstract painting.

Mo·net |ˌmōˈnā|, Claude (1840–1926) French painter. A founding member of the Impressionists, his fascination with the play of light on objects led him to produce a series of paintings of single subjects painted at different times of day and under different weather conditions, such as the *Haystacks* series (1890–91), *Rouen Cathedral* (1892–95), and the *Water lilies* sequence (1899–1906; 1916 onward).

Mon·i·ca |'mänikə|, St. (332–c. 387) mother of St. Augustine of Hippo. She is often regarded as the model of Christian mothers for her patience with her son's spiritual crises, which ended with his conversion in 386. Feast day, August 27 (formerly May 4).

Mo·nier |'mawnˌyā|, Joseph (1823–1906) French gardener and inventor. He was the first to reinforce concrete with wire netting (1867).

Monk |məNGk|, Thelonious (Sphere) (1920–82) U.S. jazz pianist and composer, one of the founders of the bebop style in the early 1940s, he became popular in the late 1950s, as the new style of "cool" jazz reached a wider audience. Notable compositions: "Round Midnight," "Straight, No Chaser," and "Well, You Needn't."

Mon·mouth |'mänməTH|, James Scott, Duke of (1649–85) English claimant to the throne of England. The illegitimate son of Charles II, he became the focus for Whig supporters of a Protestant succession. In 1685 he led a rebellion against the Catholic James II, but was defeated at the Battle of Sedgemoor and executed.

Mo·nod |məˈnō(d)|, Jacques Lucien (1910–76) French biochemist; 1965 Nobel Prize for Physiology or Medicine French biochemist. Together with fellow French biochemist François Jacob (1920–), with whom he was awarded a Nobel Prize in 1965, he formulated a theory to explain how genes are activated and in 1961 proposed the existence of messenger RNA.

Mon·roe |mənˈrō|, James see box. **Elizabeth Kortright Monroe** (1768–1830), wife of James Monroe and U.S. first lady (1817–25).

Mon·roe |mənˈrō|, Bill (1911–96) U.S. country singer, songwriter, and man-

---

Monroe, James
5th U.S. president

Life dates: 1758–1831
Place of birth: Westmoreland County, Va.
Mother: Elizabeth Jones Monroe
Father: Spence Monroe
Wife: Elizabeth ("Eliza") Kortright Monroe
Children: Eliza, Maria
College/University: College of William and Mary
Military service: lieutenant colonel, Continental Army, Revolutionary War
Career: lawyer
Political career: Virginia Assembly; Congress of the Confederation; U.S. Senate; minister to Spain, France, and Great Britain; governor of Virginia; U.S. secretary of state; U.S. secretary of war; president
Party: Democratic-Republican
Home state: Virginia
Opponents in presidential races: Rufus King; John Quincy Adams
Term of office: March 4, 1817–March 3, 1825
Vice president: Daniel D. Tompkins
Notable events of presidency: construction of Erie Canal; Seminole Wars; Financial Panic of 1819; Missouri Compromise; Monroe Doctrine; legislation established flag of the United States; Rush-Bagot Agreement; Mississippi, Illinois, Alabama, Maine, and Missouri admitted as 20th–24th states
Other achievements: Delegate to Virginia state convention to ratify Federal Constitution; chairman, Virginia Constitutional Convention; headed diplomatic mission to Spain; commissioned to negotiate treaty with England
Place of burial: Richmond, Va.

dolin player. Known as **the father of bluegrass**. With his group the Blue Grass Boys, he joined the Grand Ole Opry (1939) and toured; his 1988 song "Southern Flavor" won the first Grammy for bluegrass music.

Mon•roe |mən'rō|, Marilyn (1926–62) U.S. actress; born *Norma Jean Mortenson*; later *Norma Jean Baker*. Her movie roles, largely in comedies, made her the definitive Hollywood sex symbol. Her husbands included playwright Arthur Miller and baseball player Joe DiMaggio. She is thought to have died of an overdose of sleeping pills. Notable movies: *Gentlemen Prefer Blondes* (1953), *Some Like it Hot* (1959), and *The Misfits* (1961).

Mon•ta•gna |mawn'tänyə|, Bartolommeo Cincani (*c.* 1450–1523) Italian painter. He is noted for his altarpiece *Sacra Conversazione* (1499).

Mon•taigne |män'tān|, Michel (Eyquem) de (1533–92) French essayist. Widely regarded as the originator of the modern essay, he wrote about prominent personalities and ideas of his age in his skeptical *Essays* (1580; 1588).

Mon•ta•le |ˌmōn'tälä|, Eugenio (1896–1981) Italian poet, critic, and translator. Nobel Prize for Literature, 1975

Mon•tana |män'tænə|, Bob (1920–75) U.S. cartoonist. He created the comic strip "Archie."

Mon•tana |män'tænə|, Joe (1956–) U.S. football player.

Mont•calm |ˌmän(t)'käm|, Louis Joseph de Montcalm-Gozon, Marquis de (1712–59) French general. He defended Quebec against British troops under General Wolfe, but was defeated and fatally wounded in the battle on the Plains of Abraham during the French and Indian War.

Mon•tes•pan |ˌmawntəs'pän|, Françoise-Athénaïs de Rochechouart, Marquise de (1641–1707) French noblewoman. She was mistress of Louis XIV from 1667 to 1679, and had seven children by him. She subsequently fell from favor when the king became attracted to the children's governess, Madame de Maintenon.

Mon•tes•quieu |ˌmän(t)əs'kyoō|, Charles Louis de Secondat, Baron de La Brède et de (1689–1755) French political philosopher. His reputation rests chiefly on *L'Esprit des lois* (1748), a comparative study of political systems in which he championed the separation of judicial, legislative, and executive powers as being most conducive to individual liberty.

Mon•tes•so•ri |ˌmän(t)ə'sawrē|, Maria (1870–1952) Italian educationist. In her book *The Montessori Method* (1909) she advocated a child-centered approach to education, developed from her success with mentally handicapped children.

Mon•teux |ˌmawn'tœ|, Pierre (1875–1964) U.S. conductor, born in France. He was a noted interpreter of 20th-century music.

Mon•te•ver•di |ˌmäntə'verdē|, Claudio (1567–1643) Italian composer. His madrigals are noted their use of harmonic dissonance; other important works include his opera *Ofeo* (1607) and his sacred *Vespers* (1610).

Mon•tez |män'tez|, Lola (1818–61) Irish dancer; born *Marie Dolores Eliza Rosanna Gilbert*. She became the mistress of Ludwig I of Bavaria in 1846 and exercised great influence over him until banished the following year.

Mon•te•zu•ma II |ˌmän(t)ə'zoōmə| (1466–1520) Aztec emperor (1502–20). The last ruler of the Aztec empire in Mexico, he was defeated and imprisoned by the Spanish under Cortés in 1519. He was killed while trying to pacify some of his former subjects during an uprising against his captors.

Mont•fort |'män(t)fərt| Family of soldiers, including: **Simon de Montfort** (*c.* 1165–1218), French soldier. From 1209 he led the Albigensian Crusade against the Cathars in southern France. His son **Simon de Montfort, Earl of Leicester** (*c.* 1208–65), English soldier, born in Normandy. He led the baronial opposition to Henry III, defeating the king at Lewes in 1264 and summoning a Parliament (1265). He was defeated and killed by reorganized royal forces under Henry's son (later Edward I).

Mont•gol•fier |ˌmän(t)'gawlfēər|, **Joseph Michel** (1740–1810) and **Jacques Étienne** (1745–99), French brothers; inventors and pioneers in hot-air ballooning. They built a large balloon from linen and paper and successfully lifted a number of animals; the first human ascents followed in 1783.

Mont•gom•ery |ˌmän(t)ˈgəm(ə)rē|, Bernard Law, 1st Viscount Montgomery of Alamein (1887–1976) British Field Marshal; known as **Monty**. His victory at El Alamein in 1942 proved the first significant Allied success in World War II. He commanded the Allied ground forces in the invasion of Normandy in 1944 and accepted the German surrender on May 7, 1945.

Mont•go•me•ry |ˌmän(t)ˈgəm(ə)rē|, L. M. (1874–1942) Canadian novelist; full name *Lucy Maud Montgomery*. She is noted for her best-selling first novel *Anne of Green Gables* (1908).

Mont•rose |ˈmäntrōz|, James Graham, 1st Marquis of (1612–50) Scottish general. Montrose supported Charles I in the English Civil War and inflicted a dramatic series of defeats on the stronger Covenanter forces in the north before being defeated. In 1650 he attempted to restore Charles II, but was betrayed to the Covenanters and hanged.

Moo•dy |ˈmoodē|, John (1868–1958) U.S. financial analyst. He published various investment magazines; in 1941 he merged with Henry V. Poor, and their firm became Standard and Poor.

Moo•dy |ˈmoodē|, William Henry (1853–1917) U.S. Supreme Court justice (1906–10).

Moon |moon|, Sun Myung (1920–) Korean industrialist and religious leader. In 1954 he founded the Holy Spirit Association for the Unification of World Christianity, which became known as the Unification Church. Disciples are popularly called "Moonies."

Moore |moor|, Alfred (1755–1810) U.S. Supreme Court justice (1799–1804).

Moore |moor|, Archie (1913?–) U.S. boxer.

Moore |moor|, Charles (1925–93) U.S. architect. He designed Sea Ranch near San Francisco and the Piazza d'Italia in Los Angeles.

Moore |moor|, Clement Clarke (1779–1863) U.S. author. His poetry includes "A Visit from St. Nicholas," published anonymously (1923).

Moore |moor|, Dudley (Stuart John) (1935–) English actor, comedian, and musician. He appeared with Peter Cook in the television shows "Beyond the Fringe" (1959–64) and "Not Only … But Also" (1964–70). His movies include *Arthur* (1981).

Moore |moor|, G. E. (1873–1958) English moral philosopher and member of the Bloomsbury Group; full name *George Edward Moore*. Notable works: *Principia Ethica* (1903).

Moore |moor|, George (Augustus) (1852–1933) Irish novelist. Notable works: *A Mummer's Wife* (1885) and *Esther Waters* (1894).

Moore |moor|, Gordon E. (1929–) U.S. businessman. He was cofounder of Intel Corp (1968) with Robert Norton Noyce.

Moore |moor|, Henry (Spencer) (1898–1986) English sculptor and draftsman. His work is characterized by semi-abstract reclining forms, large upright figures, and family groups, which Moore intended to be viewed in the open air.

Moore |moor|, Marianne Craig (1887–1972) U.S. poet. Notable works: *Collected Poems* (1951, Pulitzer Prize) and *Tell Me, Tell Me* (1966).

Moore |moor|, Mary Tyler (1936–) U.S. actress. She starred in the television series "The Dick Van Dyke Show" (1961–66) and "The Mary Tyler Moore Show" (1970–77).

Moore |moor|, Thomas (1779–1852) Irish poet and musician. He wrote patriotic and nostalgic songs set to Irish tunes, notably "The Harp that once through Tara's Halls" and "The Minstrel Boy," and is also known for the oriental romance *Lalla Rookh* (1817).

Moores |moors|, Dick (1909–86) U.S. cartoonist. Full name *Richard Moores*. He created the comic strip "Gasoline Alley."

Mo•ra•via |məˈrāvēə|, Alberto (1907–90) Italian author. Born *Alberto Pincherle*. His novels and short stories were censored by Fascists and condemned by the Vatican.

More |mawr|, Sir Thomas (1478–1535) English scholar and statesman, Lord Chancellor (1529–32); canonized as **St. Thomas More**. His *Utopia* (1516), describing an ideal city state, established him as a leading humanist of the Renaissance.

Mo·reau |mə'rō|, Jeanne (1928–) French actress. Notable movies: *Les Liaisons dangereuses* (1959), *Jules et Jim* (1961), and *Nikita* (1990).

Mo·renz, Howie (1902–37) Canadian hockey player. He was voted Outstanding Player of the Half-Century, 1950.

Mor·gan |'mawrgən|, Daniel (1736–1802) American Revolutionary soldier and politican. He served as a member of the U.S. House of Representatives (1797–99).

Mor·gan |'mawrgən|, J. P. (1837–1913) U.S. financier, philanthropist, and art collector; full name *John Pierpont Morgan*. He created General Electric (1891) and the U.S. Steel Corp. (1901). He bequeathed his large art collection to the Museum of Modern Art in New York.

Mor·gan |'mawrgən|, Thomas Hunt (1866–1945) U.S. geneticist. His studies on inheritance using the fruit fly *Drosophila* showed that the genetic information was carried by genes arranged along the length of the chromosomes. Nobel Prize for Physiology or Medicine (1933).

Mo·ri |,maw'rē|, Hanae (1926–) Japanese fashion designer.

Mor·i·son |'mawrəsən|, Samuel Eliot (1887–1976) U.S. historian. Notable works: *Oxford History of the United States* (1927), *Admiral of the Ocean Sea* (1942, Pulitzer Prize), and *John Paul Jones* (1959, Pulitzer Prize).

Mor·i·son |'mawrəsən|, Stanley (1889–1967) English typographer. He was on the staff of the London *Times* (1929–60); he designed Times New Roman typeface (1932).

Mo·ri·sot |,mawri'sō|, Berthe (Marie Pauline) (1841–95) French painter, the first woman to join the Impressionists. Her works typically depicted women and children and waterside scenes.

Mor·land |'mawrlənd|, George (1763–1804) English painter. Although indebted to Dutch and Flemish genre painters such as David Teniers the Younger, he drew his inspiration for his pictures of taverns, cottages, and farm-

yards from local scenes, as with *Inside a Stable* (1791).

Mor·ley |'mawrlē|, Edward Williams (1838–1923) U.S. chemist. In 1887 he collaborated with Albert Michelson in an experiment to determine the speed of light, the result of which disproved the existence of the ether.

Mo·ro |'maw,rō|, Aldo (1916–78) Italian statesman and Christian Democrat prime minister (1963–68, 1974–76). He was assassinated by the Red Brigades.

Mor·ris |'mawrəs|, Desmond John (1928–) British zoologist. He studied animal behavior and the implications for the human condition. Notable works: *The Naked Ape* (1967).

Mor·ris |'mawrəs|, Gouverneur (1752–1816) American politician. An active proponent of American independence, he represented New York as a member of the Continental Congress (1777–79), the Constitutional Convention (1787), and the U.S. Senate (1800–03). It was while serving as Robert Morris's assistant superintendent of finance (1781–85) that he proposed the adoption of a decimal monetary system based on dollars and cents.

Mor·ris |'mawrəs|, Robert (1734–1806) American politician and financier. He represented Pennsylvania as a member of the Continental Congress (1775–78) and was a reluctant signer of the Declaration of Independence. He provided extensive financial support for the colonial war effort and was later appointed superintendent of finance (1781–84) by the Continental Congress. After serving in the U.S. Senate (1789–95), he lost all his money in western land speculations and spent his final years in poverty.

Mor·ris[1] |'mawrəs|, William (1834–96) English designer, craftsman, poet, and writer. A leading figure in the Arts and Crafts Movement, in 1861 he established Morris & Co., an association of craftsmen whose members included Edward Burne-Jones and Dante Gabriel Rossetti, to produce hand-crafted goods for the home. His many writings include *News from Nowhere*, which portrays a socialist Utopia.

Mor·ris[2] |'mawrəs|, William (1873–

1932) U.S. theatrical agent. He organized the William Morris Agency.

Mor•ris |'mawrəs|, William Richard, 1st Viscount Nuffield (1877–1963) English automobile manufacturer and philanthropist.

Mor•ris |'mawrəs|, Wright (Marion) (1910–) U.S. author, educator and photographer. Notable works: *Earthly Delights, Unearthly Adornments* (1978).

Mor•ri•son |'mawrəsən|, Jim (1943–71) U.S. rock singer; full name *James Douglas Morrison*. Morrison was the lead singer of the Doors.

Mor•ri•son |'mawrəsən|, Toni (1931–) U.S. novelist; full name *Chloe Anthony Morrison*. Her novels depict the black American experience and heritage, often focusing on rural life in the South, as in *The Bluest Eye* (1970). *Beloved* (1987) won the Pulitzer Prize, and Morrison became the first black woman to receive the Nobel Prize for Literature in 1993. Notable works: *Sula* (1973), *Song of Solomon* (1977), *Tar Baby* (1981), and *Jazz* (1992).

Mor•ri•son |'mawrəsən|, Van (1945–) Northern Irish singer, instrumentalist, and songwriter; full name *George Ivan Morrison*. He developed a distinctive personal style from a background of blues, soul, folk music, and rock. Notable albums: *Astral Weeks* (1968) and *Moondance* (1970).

Mor•ris•sey |'mawrəsē|, Stephen Patrick (1959–) British rock musician.

Mor•ti•mer |'mawrtəmər|, Roger de, 8th Baron of Wigmore and 1st Earl of March (*c.* 1287–1330) English noble. In 1326 he invaded England with his lover Isabella of France, replacing her husband, England's Edward II, with her son, the future Edward III. When Edward III assumed royal power in 1330 he had Mortimer executed.

Mor•ton |'mawrtən|, Jelly Roll (1885–1941) U.S. jazz pianist, composer, and bandleader; born *Ferdinand Joseph La Menthe Morton*. He was one of the principal links between ragtime and New Orleans jazz.

Mor•ton[1] |'mawrtən|, John (*c.* 1420–1500) English prelate and statesman. He was appointed Archbishop of Canterbury in 1486 and Chancellor under Henry VII a year later. The Crown's stringent taxation policies made the regime in general and Morton in particular widely unpopular.

Mor•ton[2] |'mawrtən|, John (1724?–77) American Revolutionary patriot. He was a member of the Continental Congress (1774–77) and a signer of the Declaration of Independence.

Mor•ton |'mawrtən|, Julius Sterling (1832–1902) U.S. agriculturist. The U.S. secretary of agriculture (1893–97), he originated Arbor Day.

Mor•ton |'mawrtən|, Levi Parsons (1824–1920) vice president of the U.S. (1889–93) and governor of New York (1895–97).

Mor•ton |'mawrtən|, Oliver Hazard Perry Throck (1823–77) U.S. politican. A founder of the Indiana Republican Party, he served in the U.S. Senate (1867–77).

Mor•ton |'mawrtən|, Thomas (1590?–1647) U.S. colonist, born in England. He was arrested twice for anti-Puritan polemics and activites; his *New English Canaan* (1637) satirizes Myles Standish as "Captain Shrimp."

Mor•ton |'mawrtən|, William Thomas Green (1819–68) U.S. dentist and pioneer in surgical anesthesia.

Mo•san•der |mə'sændər|, Carl Gustaf (1797–1858) Swedish chemist. Mosander continued Berzelius's work on the rare earth elements and discovered the new elements lanthanum, erbium, and terbium, and the supposed element didymium.

Mose•ley |'mōzlē|, Henry Gwyn Jeffreys (1887–1915) English physicist. He determined the atomic numbers of elements from their X-ray spectra, demonstrated that an element's chemical properties are determined by this number, and showed that there are only 92 naturally occurring elements.

Mo•ses |'mōzəs| (*c.* 14th–13th century BC) Hebrew prophet and lawgiver, brother of Aaron. According to the biblical account, he was born in Egypt and led the Israelites away from servitude there, across the desert toward the Promised Land. During the journey he was inspired by God on Mount Sinai to write down the Ten Commandments on tablets of stone (Exod. 20).

Mo·ses |'mōzəs|, Edwin (1955–) U.S. track athlete; full name *Edwin Corley Moses*. He won Olympic gold medals for the 400-meters hurdles in 1976 and 1984, and set successive world records in the event throughout those years.

Mo·ses |'mōzəs|, Grandma (1860–1961) U.S. painter; full name *Anna Mary Robertson Moses*. She took up painting as a hobby when widowed in 1927, producing more than a thousand paintings in primitive style, mostly of American rural life.

Mo·ses |'mōzəs|, Robert (1889–1981) U.S. public official. As New York City parks commissioner (1934–60), he built 416 miles of parkways.

Moss |maws|, Jeffrey A. (1942–98) U.S. children's author and songwriter. He created the "Sesame Street" characters Cookie Monster and Oscar the Grouch and wrote *The Butterfly Jar.*

Moss |maws|, Stirling (1929–) English racecar driver.

Möss·bau·er |'maws,bowər|, Rudolf Ludwig (1929–) German physicist. He discovered the Mössmauer effect, for which he shared the 1961 Nobel Prize for Physics.

Mo·ten |'mōtn|, Bennie (1894–1935) U.S. jazz pianist. Full name *Benjamin Moten*. He was a principal developer of the "Southwestern" style of orchestral jazz.

Mother Te·re·sa |tə'rēsə; tə'rāsə| see TERESA, MOTHER.

Moth·er·well |'maṮHər,wel|, Robert (1915–91) U.S. artist. He was a founder and leading exponent of the New York school of abstract expressionism.

Mot·ley |'mätlē|, Willard (1912–65) U.S. author. Notable works: *Let No Man Write My Epitaph* (1958).

Mo·ton |'mōtn|, Robert Russa (1867–1940) U.S. educator. He was principal of the Tuskegee Normal and Industrial Institute (1915–35). Spingarn Medal, 1932.

Mott |mät|, Lucretia (Coffin) (1793–1880) U.S. social reformer. A progressive Quaker minister, she was a highly motivated activist in the causes of abolition, women's rights, and freedom of religion.

Mou·hot |,moo'ō|, Henri (1826–61) French naturalist and photographer. Full name *Alexandre-Henri Mouhot*. He discovered ancient Cambodian temples at Angkor (1860).

Mount·bat·ten |,mown(t)'bætn|, Louis (Francis Albert Victor Nicholas), 1st Earl Mountbatten of Burma (1900–79) British admiral and administrator. He was supreme Allied commander in Southeast Asia (1943–45) and the last viceroy (1947) and first governor general of India (1947–48). He was killed by an IRA bomb while on his yacht.

Moy·er |'moiər|, Andrew J. (1899–1959) U.S. inventor. He developed a method for the production of penicillin, which became a model for the development of all other antibiotic fermentations.

Moy·ers |'moiərz|, Bill (1934–) U.S. journalist. He worked for public and commercial television as a news analyst.

Moy·ni·han |'moinə,hæn|, Daniel Patrick (1927–) U.S. senator from New York (1977–).

Moy·roud, Louis Marius (1914–) French inventor. With Rene Higonnet, he built the first practical phototypesetting machine, the Lumitype, later known as the Photon (1946).

Mo·zart |'mō,tsärt|, (Johann Chrysostom) Wolfgang Amadeus (1756–91) Austrian composer. A child prodigy as a harpsichordist, pianist, and composer, he came to epitomize classical music in its purity of form and melody. A prolific composer, he wrote more than forty symphonies, nearly thirty piano concertos, over twenty string quartets, and sixteen operas, including *The Marriage of Figaro* (1786), *Don Giovanni* (1787), *Così fan tutte* (1790), and *The Magic Flute* (1791).

Mu·ba·rak |moo'bärək|, (Muhammad) Hosni (Said) (1928–) Egyptian statesman, president since 1981. He did much to establish closer links between Egypt and other Arab nations, while opposing militant Islamic fundamentalism in Egypt.

Mu·cha |'mookə|, Alphonse (1860–1939) Czech painter and designer; born

Alfons Maria. He was a leading figure in the art nouveau movement, noted for his flowing poster designs, typically featuring the actress Sarah Bernhardt.

Mudd |məd|, Roger Harrison (1928–) U.S. journalist. He was the CBS News chief Washington correspondent (1961–87).

Mu·ga·be |mŏŏ'gäbē|, Robert (Gabriel) (1924–) Zimbabwean statesman, prime minister (1980–87) and president since 1987. He became prime minister in Zimbabwe's first post-independence elections. In 1987 his party ZANU merged with ZAPU and Mugabe became executive president of a one-party state.

Mug·ler, Thierry (1948–) French fashion designer.

Mu·ham·mad |mə'häməd| (*c.* 570–632) Also **Mohammed**. Arab prophet and founder of Islam. In *c.*610 in Mecca he received the first of a series of revelations that, as the Koran, became the doctrinal and legislative basis of Islam. In the face of opposition to his preaching he and his small group of supporters were forced to flee to Medina in 622 (the Hegira). Muhammad led his followers into a series of battles against the Meccans. In 630 Mecca capitulated, and by his death Muhammad had united most of Arabia.

Mu·ham·mad |mə'häməd|, Elijah (1897–1975) U.S. activist. He directed the growth of the Black Muslim movement.

Mu·ham·mad |mə'häməd|, Mahathir (1925–) Malaysian statesman, prime minister since 1981.

Mu·ham·mad Ah·mad see MAHDI.

Mu·ham·mad A·li[1] |mə'häməd ¸älē| (1769–1849) Ottoman viceroy and pasha of Egypt (1805–49), possibly of Albanian descent. He modernized Egypt's infrastructure, making it the leading power in the eastern Mediterranean, and established a dynasty that survived until 1952.

Mu·ham·mad A·li[2] |mə'häməd ¸ä'lē| (1942–) U.S. boxer; born *Cassius Marcellus Clay.* He was an Olympic gold medalist as a light heavyweight in 1960. He won the world heavyweight title in 1964, 1974, and 1978, becoming the only boxer to be world heavyweight champion three times. After converting to Islam and changing his name, he was stripped of his title for refusing army service on conscientious objector grounds, a decision that was overthrown by the U.S. Supreme Court in 1971.

Mu·ji·bur Rah·man |mŏŏ'jēbŏŏr rə'män| (1920–75) Bangladeshi statesman, first prime minister of independent Bangladesh (1972–75) and president (1975); known as **Sheikh Mujib**. After failing to establish parliamentary democracy as prime minister, he assumed dictatorial powers in 1975. He and his family were assassinated in a military coup.

Mul·doon |məl'dōōn|, Sir Robert (David) (1921–92) New Zealand statesman, prime minister (1975–84). His premiership was marked by domestic measures to tackle low economic growth and high inflation.

Mul·ler |'mələr|, Hermann Joseph (1890–1967) U.S. geneticist. He discovered that X-rays induce mutations in the genetic material of the fruit fly *Drosophila* and thus recognized the danger of X-radiation to living things. Nobel Prize for Physiology or Medicine (1946).

Mül·ler |'mələr|, Johannes Peter (1801–58) German anatomist and zoologist. He was a pioneer of comparative and microscopical methods in biology.

Mül·ler |'mələr|, (Friedrich) Max (1823–1900) German-born British philologist. He is remembered for his edition of the Sanskrit *Rig-veda* (1849–75).

Mül·ler |'mələr|, Paul Hermann (1899–1965) Swiss chemist. He synthesized DDT in 1939 and soon patented it as an insecticide. Nobel Prize for Physiology or Medicine (1948).

Mul·li·gen |'mələgən|, Gerry (1927–96) U.S. jazz baritone saxophonist and songwriter. Full name *Gerald Joseph Mulligen.* He helped create the "Cool Jazz" idiom.

Mul·li·ken |'mələkən|, Robert Sanderson (1896–1986) U.S. chemist, physicist and educator. Nobel Prize for Chemistry, 1966.

Mul·lin |'mələn|, Willard (1902–78) U.S. cartoonist and artist. He created the characters of the baseball-playing "Bum" and "Kid."

Mul·ro·ney |məl'rōnē|, (Martin) Brian (1939–) Canadian Progressive Conservative statesman, prime minister (1984–93).

Mum·ford |'məmfərd|, Lewis (1895–1990) U.S. social philosopher. He was an expert on regional and city planning. Notable works: *The Myth of the Machine* (1967, 1971).

Munch |mYNSH|, Charles (1891–1968) French violinist and conductor. He was conductor of the Paris Philharmonic and the Boston Symphony and director of the Berkshire Music Center at Tanglewood.

Munch |mo͞oNGk|, Edvard (1863–1944) Norwegian painter and engraver. He infused his subjects with an intense emotionalism, exploring the use of vivid color and linear distortion to express feelings about life and death. Notable works: his *Frieze of Life* sequence, incorporating *The Scream* (1893).

Mun·ro |mən'rō|, Alice (1931–) Canadian author. Notable works: *The Moons of Jupiter* (1983) and *Selected Stories* (1996).

Mun·ro |mən'rō|, H. H. see SAKI.

Mu·ra·sa·ki Shi·ki·bu |,mo͞orə'säkē 'SHēkē,bo͞o| (*c.* 978–*c.* 1031) Japanese author. Notable works: the *Tale of Genji*.

Mu·rat |,myo͞o'rä|, Joachim (*c.* 1767–1815) French general, king of Naples 1808–15. Murat made his name as a cavalry commander in Napoleon's Italian campaign (1800) and was made king of Naples. He attempted to become king of all Italy in 1815, but was captured in Calabria and executed.

Mur·doch |'mərdäk|, Dame (Jean) Iris (1919–99) British novelist and philosopher, born in Ireland. She is primarily known for her novels, many of which explore complex sexual relationships and spiritual life. Notable novels: *The Sandcastle* (1957) and *The Sea, The Sea* (Booker Prize, 1978), and *The Philosopher's Pupil* (1983).

Mur·doch |'mərdäk|, (Keith) Rupert (1931–) Australian-born U.S. publisher and media entrepreneur. As the founder and head of the News International Communications empire he owns major newspapers in Australia, Britain, and the U.S., together with movie and television companies and the publishing firm HarperCollins.

Mu·ril·lo |m(y)o͞o'rēyō|, Bartolomé Esteban (*c.* 1618–82) Spanish painter. He is noted for his genre scenes of urchins and peasants and for his devotional pictures.

Mur·nau |'mo͞or,now|, F. W. (1888–1931) German movie director; born *Frederick Wilhelm Plumpe*. His revolutionary use of cinematic techniques to record and interpret human emotion paralleled the expressionist movement in art and drama. Notable movies: *Nosferatu* (1922), *Der letzte Mann* (1924), and *Sunrise* (1927), which won three Oscars.

Mur·phy |'mərfē|, Audie (1924–71) U.S. soldier and actor. The most decorated soldier of World War II, he appeared in war adventure movies such as *Beyond Glory* (1948) and *To Hell and Back* (1955).

Mur·phy |'mərfē|, Carl (1889–1967) U.S. journalist, publisher, and civil rights leader, and educator. He was editor of the *Baltimore Afro-American* (1922–61) and was on the board of directors of the NAACP. Spingarn Medal, 1955.

Mur·phy |'mərfē|, Eddie (1961–) U.S. actor. Notable movies: *Beverly Hills Cop* (1984) and *Coming to America* (1988).

Mur·phy |'mərfē|, Frank (1890–1949) U.S. Supreme Court justice (1940–49). Full name *William Francis Murphy*.

Mur·phy |'mərfē|, Turk (1915–87) U.S. jazz trombonist and band leader. Born *Melvin Edward Alton Murphy*. He formed his own band in 1947 and led it into the 1980s; he opened the Traditional Jazz Museum in San Francisco (1986).

Mur·ray |'mərē|, (George) Gilbert (Aimé) (1866–1957) Australian-born British classical scholar. His translations of Greek dramatists helped to revive interest in Greek drama. He was also a founder of the League of Nations and later a joint president of the United Nations.

Mur·ray |'mərē|, Sir James (Augustus

Henry) (1837–1915) Scottish lexicographer. He was chief editor of the *Oxford English Dictionary*, but did not live to see the work completed.

Mur·ray |'mərē|, Phillip (1886–1952) U.S. labor leader, born in Scotland. He served as president of the Congress of Industrial Organizations (1940–52) and as president of the United Steel Workers of America (1942–52).

Mur·row |'mərō|, Edward R. (1908–65) U.S. journalist. Born *Egbert Roscoe Murrow*. He produced and narrated the radio series "Hear It Now" and the television series "See It Now."

Mu·se·ve·ni, Yoweri (Kaguta) (1945–) Ugandan statesman, president since 1986. He came to power after ousting Milton Obote and brought some stability to a country that had suffered under the dictatorial Obote and Idi Amin.

Mu·si·al |'myōōzēəl|, Stan (1920–) U.S. baseball player. Known as **Stan the Man**. He led the National League in batting seven times. Elected to the Baseball Hall of Fame (1969).

Mus·kie |'məskē|, Edmund Sixtus (1914–96) U.S. lawyer and politician. He was a member of the U.S. Senate from Maine (1959–80) and a Democratic vice presidential candidate (1968); he also served as U.S. secretary of state (1980–81).

Mus·so·li·ni |ˌmōōsə'lēnē|, Benito (Amilcaro Andrea) (1883–1945) Italian Fascist statesman, prime minister (1922–43); known as **Il Duce** ("the leader"). He founded the Italian Fascist Party in 1919. He annexed Abyssinia in 1936 and entered World War II on Germany's side in 1940. Forced to resign after the Allied invasion of Sicily, he was rescued from imprisonment by German paratroopers, but was captured and executed by Italian communist partisans.

Mus·sorg·sky |mə'zawr(g)skē|, Modest (Petrovich) (1839–81) Also **Moussorgsky**. Russian composer. His best-known works include the opera *Boris Godunov* (1874), *Songs and Dances of Death* (1875–77) and the piano suite *Pictures at an Exhibition* (1874).

Mutsuhito see MEIJI TENNO.

My·ers |'mīərz|, Russell (1938–) U.S. cartoonist. He created the comic strip, "Broom Hilda."

Myr·dal |'m(i)ər,däl| Swedish family, including: **(Karl) Gunnar Myrdal** (1898–1987), economist. He was a leading analyst of Third World development policies. Nobel Prize for Economics, 1974. His wife **Alva Myrdal** (1902–86), sociologist, government official, and peace activist. With her husband she implemented a national program for children's welfare; she shared the 1982 Nobel Peace Prize with Alfonso Garcia Robles.

My·ron |'mīrən| (*c.* 480–440 BC) Greek sculptor. None of his original work is known to survive, but there are two certain copies, one being the *Discobolus* (*c.*450 BC), a figure of a man throwing the discus, which demonstrates a remarkable interest in symmetry and movement.

Nn

Na·bo·kov |'näbə,kawf|, Vladimir (Vladimorovich) (1899–1977) Russian-born U.S. novelist and poet. He is best known for *Lolita* (1958), his novel about a middle-aged man's obsession with a twelve-year-old girl.

Na·der |'nādər|, Ralph (1934–) U.S. consumer-rights advocate. His campaign on behalf of public safety gave impetus to the consumer-rights movement from the 1960s onward and prompted legislation concerning car design, radiation hazards, food packaging, and insecticides.

Na·ga·no |nä'gänō|, Osami (1880–1947) Japanese admiral. He planned and executed the attack on Pearl Harbor.

Na·gur·ski |nə'gərskē|, Bronko (1908–90) U.S. football player. He was a charter member of the college and professional football halls of fame.

Nagy |näj|, Imre (1896–1958) Hungarian communist statesman and prime minister (1953–55 and 1956). In 1956 he withdrew Hungary from the Warsaw Pact, seeking neutral status. He was executed after the Soviet Army crushed the uprising of 1956 later that year.

Nai·paul |'nī,pawl|, V. S. (1932–) Trinidadian writer of Indian descent, resident in Britain since 1950; full name *Sir Vidiadhar Surajprasad Naipaul*. He is best known for his satirical novels, such as *A House for Mr. Biswas* (1961); *In a Free State* (1971) won the Booker Prize.

Nai·smith |'nā,smiTH|, James A. (1861–1939) U.S. physical educator. He invented the game of basketball (1891).

Na·math |'nāməTH|, Joe (1943–) U.S. football player. Nicknamed "Broadway Joe," he was a professional quarterback (1965-78) who led the New York Jets to a 1969 Super Bowl title. Elected to the NFL Hall of Fame, 1985.

Na·nak |'nänək| (1469–1539) Indian religious leader and founder of Sikhism; known as **Guru Nanak**. Not seeking to create a new religion, he preached that spiritual liberation could be achieved through meditating on the name of God.

His teachings are contained in a number of hymns that form part of the Adi-granth.

Nan·sen |'nænsən|, Fridtjof (1861–1930) Norwegian Arctic explorer. In 1888 he led the first expedition to cross the Greenland ice fields, and five years later he sailed from Siberia for the North Pole, which he failed to reach, on board the *Fram*. He received the Nobel Peace Prize in 1922.

Na·po·le·on |nə'pōlyən; nə'pōlē(y)ən| three rulers of France: **Napoleon I** (1769–1821), emperor 1804–14 and 1815; full name *Napoleon Bonaparte*; known as **Napoleon**. In 1799 Napoleon joined a conspiracy which overthrew the Directory, becoming the supreme ruler of France. He declared himself emperor in 1804, establishing an empire stretching from Spain to Poland. After defeats at Trafalgar (1805) and in Russia (1812), he abdicated and was exiled to the island of Elba (1814). He returned to power in 1815, but was defeated at Waterloo and exiled to the island of St. Helena. **Napoleon II** (1811–1832), son of Napoleon I and Empress Marie-Louise; full name *Napoleon François Charles Joseph Bonaparte*. In 1814 Napoleon I abdicated on behalf of himself and Napoleon II, who had no active political role. **Napoleon III** (1808–73), emperor 1852–70; full name *Charles Louis Napoleon Bonaparte*; known as **Louis-Napoleon**. A nephew of Napoleon I, Napoleon III was elected President of the Second Republic in 1848 and staged a coup in 1851. He abdicated in 1870 after defeat in the Franco-Prussian War.

Na·ra·yan |nə'rīən|, R. K. (1906–) Indian novelist and short-story writer; full name *Rasipuram Krishnaswamy Narayan*. His best-known novels are set in an imaginary small Indian town, and portray its inhabitants in an affectionate yet ironic manner; they include *Swami and Friends* (1935) and *The Man-Eater of Malgudi* (1961)

Na·ra·ya·nan |nə'rīənən|, K. R.

(1920–   ) Indian statesman, president since 1997; full name *Kocheril Raman Narayanan.*

Nar·vá·ez |ˌnärväˈyez|, Pánfilo de (1470?–1528) Spanish conquistador. He landed near Tampa Bay (1528) and went as far as Tallahassee in search of gold.

Nash |næsH|, Graham (1942–   ) British rock musician. He was a guitarist, keyboardist, and singer with the group Crosby, Stills, Nash (and Young).

Nash |næsH|, John (1752–1835) English town planner and architect. He planned the layout of Regent's Park (1811–25), Trafalgar Square (1826–*c.*1835), and many other parts of London, and designed the Marble Arch.

Nash |næsH|, (Frederic) Ogden (1902–71) U.S. poet. His sophisticated light verse comprises puns, epigrams, and other verbal eccentricities.

Nash |næsH|, Paul (1889–1946) English painter and designer. He was a war artist in both world wars. Notable works: *Totes Meer* (1940–1).

Nash |næsH|, Richard (1674–1762) Welsh dandy; known as **Beau Nash**. He was an arbiter of fashion and etiquette in the early Georgian age.

Nashe |næsH|, Thomas (1567–1601) English pamphleteer, prose writer, and dramatist. Notable works: *The Unfortunate Traveller* (1594).

Nas·ser |ˈnæsər|, Gamal Abdel (1918–70) Egyptian colonel and statesman, prime minister (1954–56) and president (1956–70). He deposed King Farouk in 1952 and President Muhammad Neguib in 1954. His nationalization of the Suez Canal brought war with Britain, France, and Israel in 1956; he also waged two unsuccessful wars against Israel (1956 and 1967).

Nast |næst|, Thomas (1840–1902) U.S. cartoonist. He was staff artist of *Harper's Weekly* (1862–86) and creator of the Republican elephant and the Democratic donkey symbols as well as the U.S. image of Santa Claus.

Na·than |ˈnāTHən|, George Jean (1882–1958) U.S. journalist. He cofounded the magazine *American Mercury* (1924) and wrote the *Encyclopaedia of the Theatre* (1940).

Na·than |ˈnāTHən|, Robert (Gruntal) (1894–1985) U.S. author. Notable works: *Sleeping Beauty* (1950).

Na·tion |ˈnāsHən|, Carry Amelia (Moore) (1846–1911) U.S. temperance reformer. Her prohibitionist activism was characterized by scenes of hatchet-wielding saloon smashing, primarily in Kansas.

Na·var·ro |nəˈvärō; ˌnäˈvärō|, Fats (1923–50) U.S. jazz trumpeter. Full name *Theodore Navarro.* He was among the foremost players in the bop idiom.

Nav·ra·ti·lo·va |ˌnævrətəˈlōvə|, Martina (1956–   ) Czech-born U.S. tennis player. She dominated women's tennis throughout the 1980s and won nine Wimbledon singles titles (1978–79; 1982–87; 1990).

Nde·ti |n-ˈdetē; enˈdetē|, Cosmas (1971–   ) Kenyan runner. He won the Boston Marathon three times (1993, 1994, 1995) and set the course record of 2:07:15 (1994).

Neal |nēl|, John (1793–1876) U.S. author. Notable works: *The Down-Easters* (1833).

Neal |nēl|, Joseph Clay (1807–47) U.S. author. Notable works: *Charcoal Sketches; or, Scenes in a Metropolis* (1838).

Neal |nēl|, Patricia (1926–   ) U.S. stage and movie actress. Notable movies: *Hud* (1963, Academy Award).

Near·ing |ˈnēriNG|, Scott (1883–1983) U.S. environmentalist and economist. His book *Living the Good Life* (1954) became one of the foundations of the 1960s counterculture.

Neb·u·chad·nez·zar II |ˌnebəkəd ˈnezər| (*c.* 630–562 BC) king of Babylon (605–562 BC). He rebuilt the city with massive walls, a huge temple, and a ziggurat and extended his rule over neighboring countries. In 586 BC he captured and destroyed Jerusalem and deported many Israelites in what is known as the Babylonian Captivity.

Neck·er |ˈnekər|, Jacques (1732–1804) Swiss-born banker and director general of French finances (1777–81; 1788–89). In 1789 he recommended summoning the States General and was dismissed, this being one of the factors that triggered the French Revolution.

Need·ham |ˈnēdəm|, Joseph (1900–95)

English scientist and historian. Notable works: *History of Embryology* (1934) and *Science and Civilization in China* (1954).

Nee•son |'nēsən|, Liam (1952–) U.S. actor, born in Ireland. Notable movies: *Schindler's List* (1994).

Nef•er•ti•ti |ˌnefər'tētē| (14th century BC) Also **Nofretete**. Egyptian queen, wife of Akhenaten and half-sister of Tutankhamen. She is best known from the painted limestone bust of her, now in Berlin (*c.*1350).

Ne•he•mi•ah |ˌnēə'mīə| (5th century BC) Hebrew leader who supervised the rebuilding of the walls of Jerusalem (*c.*444) and introduced moral and religious reforms (*c.*432).

Neh•ru |'nāro͞o|, Jawaharlal (1889–1964) Indian statesman, prime minister (1947–64); known as **Pandit Nehru**. An early associate of Mahatma Gandhi, Nehru was elected leader of the Indian National Congress in 1929. He was imprisoned nine times by the British for his nationalist campaigns, but went on to become the first prime minister of independent India.

Neill |nēl|, A. S. (1883–1973) Scottish teacher and educationist; full name *Alexander Sutherland Neill*. He founded the progressive school Summerhill, which has attracted both admiration and hostility for its anti-authoritarian ethos.

Neill |nēl|, Sam (1948–) New Zealand actor; born *Nigel John Dermot*. He starred in the British television series "Reilly: The Ace of Spies" (1983) and achieved international recognition with *Jurassic Park* and *The Piano* (both 1993).

Nel•son |'nelsən| U.S. family of entertainers, including: **Ozzie Nelson** (1906–75), bandleader and actor. Full name *Oswald George Nelson*. He is best remembered as the father in "The Adventures of Ozzie and Harriet," a comedy series on radio (1944–54) and television (1952–66) starring Ozzie, his wife, Harriet Hilliard Nelson, and (from 1949) their sons, David and Ricky. His son **Ricky Nelson** (1940–85), musician and actor. Full name *Eric Hilliard Nelson*. He became a teen idol with many song hits including "Hello, Mary Lou."

Nel•son |'nelsən|, Byron (1912–)

U.S. golfer. He set the all-time PGA stroke average with 68.33 strokes per round over 120 rounds in 1945.

Nel•son |'nelsən|, Horatio, Viscount Nelson, Duke of Bronte (1758–1805) British admiral. Nelson became a national hero as a result of his victories at sea in the Napoleonic Wars, especially the Battle of Trafalgar, in which he was mortally wounded.

Nel•son |'nelsən|, Samuel (1792–1873) U.S. Supreme Court justice (1845–72).

Nel•son |'nelsən|, Willie (1933–) U.S. country singer and songwriter. He is noted for hits such as "A Good Hearted Woman" (1976) and the album *Red Haired Stranger* (1975).

Nem•e•rov |'neməˌrawv|, Howard (1920–91) U.S. poet and professor. U.S. poet laureate, 1988.

Nen•ni•us |'nenēəs| (*c.* 800) Welsh chronicler. He is traditionally credited with the compilation or revision of the *Historia Britonum*, which includes one of the earliest known accounts of King Arthur.

Nernst |nərnst|, Walther Hermann (1864–1941) German physical chemist. He is best known for his discovery of the third law of thermodynamics (also known as *Nernst's heat theorem*). Nobel Prize for Chemistry (1920).

Ne•ro |'nirō| (AD 37–68) Roman emperor 54–68; full name *Nero Claudius Caesar Augustus Germanicus*. Infamous for his cruelty, he wantonly executed leading Romans. His reign witnessed a fire that destroyed half of Rome in 64.

Ne•ru•da |nə'ro͞odə|, Pablo (1904–73) Chilean poet and diplomat; born *Ricardo Eliezer Neftali Reyes*. He took his pseudonym from the Czech poet Jan Neruda. His *Canto General* (completed 1950), is an epic covering the history of the Americas. Nobel Prize for Literature (1971).

Ner•va |'nərvə|, Marcus Cocceius (*c.* 30–98 AD) Roman emperor 96–8. He returned to a liberal and constitutional form of rule after the autocracy of his predecessor, Domitian.

Ner•vi |'nervē|, Pier Luigi (1891–1979) Italian engineer and architect. A pioneer of reinforced concrete, he codesigned the UNESCO building in Paris (1953) and designed the Pirelli skyscraper in Milan (1958) and San Francisco cathedral (1970).

Nes•bit |'nesbət|, E. (1858–1924) English novelist; full name *Edith Nesbit*. She is best known for her children's books, including *Five Children and It* (1902) and *The Railway Children* (1906).

Net•an•ya•hu |ˌnet(ə)n'yäho͞o|, Benjamin (1949–) Israeli Likud statesman, prime minister since 1996. Leader of the right-wing Likud coalition since 1993, he narrowly defeated Shimon Peres in the elections of 1996.

Neu•mann |'noimän|, John von (1903–57) Hungarian-born U.S. mathematician and computer pioneer. He pioneered game theory and the design and operation of electronic computers.

Neu•tra |'noitrə; 'n(y)o͞otrə|, Richard Josef (1892–1970) U.S. architect, born in Austria. Notable designs: Mathematics Park (New Jersey) and Orange County courthouse (California).

Neu•wirth |'n(y)o͞o'(w)ərTH|, Bebe (1958–) U.S. actress. Tony Award, 1997.

Nev•ers |'nevərz|, Ernest Alonzo (1903–76) U.S. athlete. A professional player of both baseball and football, he set an NFL single-game scoring record of 40 points (1929).

Nev•ille |'nevəl|, Richard see WARWICK, RICHARD NEVILLE.

Nev•ins |'nevənz|, Allan (1890–1971) U.S. historian and author. Notable works: *Grover Cleveland* (1932, Pulitzer Prize) and *Hamilton Fish* (1936, Pulitzer Prize).

Nev•sky |'nevskē|, Alexander see ALEXANDER NEVSKY.

New•cas•tle |'n(y)o͞oˌkæsəl|, Thomas Pelham-Holles, 1st Duke of (1693–1768) British Whig statesman, prime minister (1754–56 and 1757–62). During his second term in office he headed a coalition with William Pitt the Elder.

New•comb |'n(y)o͞okəm|, Simon (1835–1909) U.S. astronomer, born in Canada. His tables of the planetary system were used throughout the world.

New•combe |'n(y)o͞okəm|, John (1944–) Australian tennis player. He won Wimbledon three times and the U.S. and Australian championships twice each.

New•ell |'n(y)o͞oəl|, Robert Henry (1836–1901) U.S. journalist and humorist. Pseudonym **Orpheus C. Kerr** (a play on the words "office seeker&cqq). Notable works: *The Orpheus C. Kerr Papers* (1862–71).

New•hart |'n(y)o͞ohärt|, Bob (1929–) U.S. entertainer He starred in the television series "The Bob Newhart Show" (1971–78) and "Newhart" (1982–90).

New•house |'n(y)o͞ohows|, Samuel I., Jr. (1895–1979) U.S. publisher and philanthropist. He served as the chairman of Conde Nast Publications, Inc.

Ne Win |'ne 'win|, U (1911–) Burmese general and socialist statesman, prime minister (1958–60), head of state (1962–74), and president (1974–81). After the military coup in 1962 he established a military dictatorship and formed a one-party state.

New•lands |'n(y)o͞olən(d)z|, John Alexander Reina (1837–98) English industrial chemist. He proposed a form of periodic table shortly before Dmitri Mendeleev, based on a supposed *law of octaves* according to which similar chemical properties recurred in every eighth element.

New•man |'n(y)o͞omən|, Barnett (1905–70) U.S. painter A seminal figure in color-field painting, he juxtaposed large blocks of uniform color with narrow marginal strips of contrasting colors.

New•man |'n(y)o͞omən|, John Henry (1801–90) English prelate and theologian. A founder of the Oxford Movement, in 1845 he turned to Roman Catholicism, becoming a cardinal in 1879.

New•man |'n(y)o͞omən|, Paul (1925–) U.S. actor and movie director. Among his many movies are *Butch Cassidy and the Sundance Kid* (1969), *The Sting* (1973), *The Color of Money* (1987), for which he won an Oscar, and *The Glass Menagerie* (1987), which he also directed. He was also known for his philanthropic activities.

New•port |'n(y)o͞oˌpawrt|, Christopher (1565?–1617) English sailor. The founder of Jamestown, Virginia (1606–

7), he was shipwrecked on Bermuda (1609), procuring it as a colony for England.

New·ton |'n(y) o͞otn|, A. Edward (1863–1940) U.S. book collector and author. Full name *Alfred Edward Newton*.

New·ton |'n(y)o͞otn|, Sir Isaac (1642–1727) English mathematician and physicist, considered the greatest single influence on theoretical physics until Einstein. In his *Principia Mathematica* (1687), Newton gave a mathematical description of the laws of mechanics and gravitation, and applied these to planetary motion. *Opticks* (1704) records his optical experiments and theories, including the discovery that white light is made up of a mixture of colors. His work in mathematics included the binomial theorem and differential calculus.

Ney |nā|, Michel (1769–1815) French marshal. He was one of Napoleon's leading generals, and commanded the French cavalry at Waterloo (1815).

Nga·ta |'ᴺGätä; en'gätə|, Sir Apirana Turupa (1874–1950) New Zealand Maori leader and politician. As Minister for Native Affairs he devoted much time to Maori resettlement, seeking to preserve the characteristic elements of their life and culture.

Ngo Dinh Diem |(ə)'ᴺGō 'din di'(y)em| (1901–63) President of the Republic of South Vietnam (1956–63) He was assassinated in a military coup d'état.

Nich·o·las |'nik(ə)ləs|, St. (4th century) Christian prelate. Said to have been bishop of Myra in Lycia, he is the patron saint of children, sailors, Greece, and Russia. The persona of Santa Claus (a corruption of his name) originated from the Dutch custom of giving gifts to children on his feast day (December 6).

Nich·o·las I |'nikələs| two czars of Russia: **Nicholas I** (1796–1855; reigned 1825–55), brother of Alexander I. At home he pursued rigidly conservative policies, while his expansionism in the Near East led to the Crimean War. **Nicholas II** (1868–1918; reigned 1894–1917), son of Alexander III. Forced to abdicate after the Russian Revolution in 1917, he was shot along with his family a year later.

Nich·ols |'nikəlz|, Mike (1931–) U.S.

director. Born *Michael Igor Peschowsky*. Notable movies: *The Graduate* (1967, Academy Award).

Nich·ols |'nikəlz|, Red (1905–65) U.S. jazz cornetist and band leader. Full name *Ernest Loring Nichols*. He was the most prolifically recorded white jazz bandleader of the 1920s.

Nich·ols |'nikəlz|, Terry (1955–) U.S. terrorist. A coconspirator with Timothy McVeigh, he was sentenced to life imprisonment for his role in the bombing of Oklahoma City's Alfred P. Murrah Federal Building in 1995.

Nich·ols |'nikəlz|, Thomas Low (1815–1901) U.S. journalist and author. Notable works: *Forty Years of American Life: 1821–61* (1864).

Nich·ol·son |'nikəlsən|, Ben (1894–1981) English painter; full name *Benjamin Lauder Nicholson*. He was a pioneer of British abstract art, noted for his painted reliefs with circular and rectangular motifs.

Nich·ol·son |'nikəlsən|, Jack (1937–) U.S. actor. He won Oscars for *One Flew Over the Cuckoo's Nest* (1975), *Terms of Endearment* (1983), and *As Good As It Gets* (1997). Other movies include *Easy Rider* (1969), *Chinatown* (1974), *The Shining* (1980), *Prizzi's Honor* (1985), and *Batman* (1989).

Nick·laus |'nikləs|, Jack William (1940–) U.S. golfer. He has won more than eighty tournaments during his professional career, including six wins in the PGA championship, five in the Masters, four in the U.S. Open, and three in the British Open.

Nicks |niks|, Stevie (1948–) U.S. rock musician. Full name *Stephanie Nicks*. She performed with the group Fleetwood Mac.

Nic·o·lay |'nikə,lā|, John George (1832–1901) U.S. journalist, born in Germany. He was Abraham Lincoln's private secretary and biographer.

Ni·col·let |,nikə'let|, Joseph Nicolas (1786–1843) U.S. explorer, born in France. With John Fremont, he mapped the region between the upper Mississippi and Missouri rivers.

Nie·buhr |'nēbər|, Reinhold (1892–1971) U.S. theologian and political activist. Notable works: *Moral Man and*

Immoral Society (1932) and *The Irony of American History* (1952).

Niel·son |'nilsən|, Carl August (1865–1931) Danish composer. He is best known for his six symphonies (1890–1925).

Nie·mey·er |'nē‚mīər|, Oscar (1907–) Brazilian architect. An early exponent of modernist architecture in Latin America, he designed the main public buildings of Brasilia (1950–60).

Nie·möl·ler |'nē‚mOElər; 'nē‚mələr|, Martin (1892–1984) German Lutheran pastor. An outspoken opponent of Nazism, he was imprisoned in Sachsenhausen and Dachau concentration camps (1937–45).

Nietz·sche |'nēCHə; 'nēCHē|, Friedrich Wilhelm (1844–1900) German philosopher. He is known for repudiating Christianity's compassion for the weak, exalting the "will to power," and formulating the idea of the *Übermensch* (superman), who can rise above the restrictions of ordinary morality.

Nieuw·land |'n(y) o͞o‚lənd|, Julius Arthur (1878–1936) U.S. chemist and botanist, born in Belgium. He synthesized organic compounds, including rubber.

Night·in·gale |'nītn‚gāl|, Florence (1820–1910) English nurse and medical reformer. In 1854, during the Crimean War, she improved sanitation and medical procedures at the army hospital at Scutari, achieving a dramatic reduction in the mortality rate. She became known as the "Lady of the Lamp" for her nightly rounds.

Ni·jin·sky |ni'zHinskē; ni'jinskē|, Vaslav (Fomich) (1890–1950) Russian ballet dancer and choreographer. The leading dancer with Diaghilev's Ballets Russes from 1909, he went on to choreograph Debussy's *L'Après-midi d'un faune* (1912) and Stravinsky's *The Rite of Spring* (1913).

Nils·son |'nilsən|, (Märta) Birgit (1922–) Swedish operatic soprano. She gained international success in the 1950s, being particularly noted for her interpretation of Wagnerian roles.

Nim·itz |'nimits|, Chester William (1885–1966) U.S. naval officer. He was chief of the Bureau of Navigation

(1939–41) and became commander in chief of the Pacific Fleet after Pearl Harbor (1941). Aboard his flagship, the USS *Missouri*, he was the U.S. signatory on the occasion of Japanese surrender (1945). He then served as chief of naval operations (1945–47).

Nin |nēn|, Anaïs (1903–77) U.S. writer. She published her first novel, *House of Incest*, in 1936 and went on to produce collections of short stories, essays, diaries, and erotica.

Ni·ño |'nēn‚yō|, Pedro Alonzo (1468?–1505) Spanish navigator. He navigated the ship *Niña* on Columbus's first voyage to the New World.

Ni·ro |'nērō|, Robert De see DE NIRO.

Niv·en |'nivən|, David (1909–83) U.S. actor. Notable movies: *Separate Tables* (1958, Academy Award).

Nix·on |'niksən| Richard Milhous, see box. **Pat Nixon** (1912–93), wife of Richard Nixon and U.S. first lady (1969–74); born *Thelma Catherine Ryan*.

Nko·mo |(ə)NG'kawmō|, Joshua (Mqabuko Nyongolo) (1917–) Zimbabwean statesman, leader of the Zimbabwe African People's Union (ZAPU). He returned to the cabinet in 1988, when the Zimbabwe African National Union and ZAPU agreed to merge, and became vice president in 1990.

Nkru·mah |(ə)NG'kro͞omə|, Kwame (1909–72) Ghanaian statesman, prime minister (1957–60), president (1960–66). The first prime minister after independence, he became increasingly dictatorial and was finally overthrown in a military coup.

No·bel |nō'bel|, Alfred Bernhard (1833–96) Swedish chemist and engineer. He invented dynamite (1866), gelignite, and other high explosives, making a large fortune which enabled him to endow the prizes that bear his name.

No·gu·chi |nō'go͞oCHē|, Isamu (1904–88) U.S. sculptor and designer. Notable designs: two bridges for Peace Park (Hiroshima, 1952); the Billy Rose Sculpture Garden (the Israeli Museum, Jerusalem, 1960–65).

No·lan |'nōlən|, Sir Sidney Robert (1917–92) Australian painter, known

---

Nixon, Richard Milhous
37th U.S. president

Life dates: 1913–1994
Place of birth: Yorba Linda, California
Mother: Hannah Milhous Nixon
Father: Francis Anthony Nixon
Wife: Pat (Thelma Catharine Ryan) Nixon
Children: Patricia (Tricia), Julie
College/University: Whittier College; Duke University Law School
Military service: U.S. Navy lieutenant, World War II
Career: lawyer
Political career: U.S. House of Representatives; U.S. Senate; vice president (under Eisenhower); president
Party: Republican
Home state: California
Opponents in presidential races: defeated by John F. Kennedy in 1960; Hubert H. Humphrey, George C. Wallace (1968); George McGovern (1972)
Term of office: Jan. 20, 1969–Aug. 9, 1974 (resigned)
Vice presidents: Spiro T. Agnew (resigned); Gerald R. Ford
Notable events of presidency: U.S. troops sent to Cambodia and Laos; Kent State University incident; Environmental Protection Agency created; Daniel Ellsberg disclosed "Pentagon Papers"; Twenty-Sixth Amendment to the Constitution (lowering voting age to 18) ratified; U.S. combat ground troops departed from Vietnam; burglary of Democratic National Convention headquarters at Watergate Hotel; Watergate scandal; Wounded Knee incident; Arab-Israeli War; Federal Energy Administration created; impeachment hearings in the House Judiciary Committee
Other achievements: first president to visit Communist China; published *Six Crises*; *RN: The Memoirs of Richard Nixon*; and *The Real War*
Place of burial: Yorba Linda, California

---

for his paintings of famous characters and events from Australian history.

Noll |nôl|, Chuck (1932–   ) U.S. football coach. Full name *Charles Henry Noll*. He coached the Pittsburgh Steelers to four Super Bowl titles.

Nor·di·ca |ˈnawrdəkə|, Lillian (1857–

1914) U.S. soprano. Born Lillian Norton. She was the first American opera singer to gain international fame.

Nord·strom |ˈnawrdstrəm|, Ursula (1910–88) U.S. editor. She worked for Harper & Row from 1936 and became its first female vice president in 1960; she launched the careers of many authors, including Charlotte Zolotow and Maurice Sendak.

No·ri·e·ga |ˌnawrēˈägə|, Manuel (Antonio Morena) (1939–   ) Panamanian statesman and general, head of state 1983–9. Charged with drug trafficking by a U.S. grand jury in 1988, he eventually surrendered to U.S. troops sent into Panama and was brought to trial, convicted, and imprisoned in 1992.

Nor·man |ˈnawrmən|, Greg (1955–   ) Australian golfer; full name *Gregory John Norman*. He has won the world match-play championship three times (1980; 1983; 1986) and the British Open twice (1986; 1993).

Nor·man |ˈnawrmən|, Jessye (1945–   ) U.S. operatic soprano. She is noted for her interpretations of the works of Wagner, Schubert, and Mahler.

Nor·ris |ˈnawrəs|, Frank (1870–1902) U.S. author. Born *Benjamin Franklin Norris*. His unfinished trilogy *Epic of Wheat* documents the history of muckraking.

Nor·ris |ˈnawrəs|, George William (1861–1944) U.S. politician. As a member of the U.S. Senate from Nebraska (1913–43), he founded the Tennessee Valley Authority.

North |nawrTH|, Frederick, Lord (1732–92) British Tory statesman and prime minister 1770–82. He sought to avoid the Revolutionary War, but was regarded as responsible for the loss of the American colonies.

North |nawrTH|, Oliver (1943–   ) U.S. soldier. He provided testimony to Congress on the Iran-contra affair, saying he believed that all of his activities were authorized by his superiors (1986).

North·cliffe |ˈnawrTHklif|, Alfred Charles William Harmsworth, 1st Viscount (1865–1922) British newspaper publisher. He built up a large newspaper empire, including *The Times*, the *Daily Mail*, and the *Daily Mirror*.

Nor•ton |'nawrtən|, Charles Eliot (1827–1908) U.S. educator and author. He was the editor of *North American Review* (1864–68) and the first American professor of fine arts (Harvard, 1874–98).

Nor•ton |'nawrtən|, Eleanor Holms (1937–) U.S. lawyer and educator. She has been assistant director of the ACLU (1965–70) and professor of law at Georgetown University (1982–).

Nor•ton |'nawrtən|, Mary (1903–92) English author and actress. She wrote *The Borrowers* series of books for children.

Nos•tra•da•mus |ˌnawstrə'däməs| (1503–66) French astrologer and physician; Latinized name of *Michel de Nostredame*. His cryptic and apocalyptic predictions in rhyming quatrains appeared in two collections (1555 and 1558), and their interpretation continues to be the subject of controversy.

No•vel•lo |nō'velō|, Ivor (1893–1951) Welsh composer, songwriter, actor, and dramatist; born *David Ivor Davies*. In 1914 he wrote "Keep the Home Fires Burning," which became one of the most popular songs of World War I.

No•verre |naw'ver|, Jean-Georges (1727–1810) French choreographer and dance theorist, who stressed the importance of dramatic motivation in ballet as opposed to technical virtuosity.

No•vot•ný |'nawvawt,nē|, Antonín (1904–75) Czechoslovak communist statesman, president 1957–68. A founding member of the Czechoslovak Communist Party (1921), he played a major part in the communist seizure of power in 1948. He was ousted by the reform movement in 1968.

Noyce |nois|, Robert Norton (1927–90) U.S. engineer. He was a co-inventor of the integrated circuit, and with Gordon Moore he founded Intel Corp. (1968).

Noyes |noiz|, Alfred (1880–1958) English poet. Notable works: *The Flower of Old Japan* (1903) and *Drake* (1908).

Noyes |noiz|, John Humphrey (1811–86) U.S. social reformer. A propounder of the doctrine of Perfectionism, which held that human moral and spiritual perfection is attainable, he formed societies at Putney, Vermont (1839) and Oneida, New York (1848–79).

Nuf•field |'nəfēld|, William Richard Morris, 1st Viscount (1877–1963) British automotive manufacturer and philanthropist, who opened the first Morris automobile factory in Oxford in 1912. He endowed Nuffield College, Oxford (1937) and created the Nuffield Foundation (1943) for medical, social, and scientific research.

Nu•re•yev |nŏŏ'rāef; 'nŏŏrā,(y)ev|, Rudolf (1938–93) Russian-born ballet dancer and choreographer. He defected to the West in 1961, joining the Royal Ballet in London, where he began his noted partnership with Margot Fonteyn. He became a naturalized Austrian citizen in 1982.

Nur•mi |'nərmē|, Paavo Johannes (1897–1973) Finnish distance runner. He won seven Olympic gold medals (1920–28) and held a world record for the mile (1923–31).

Nye•re•re |nī'rerē|, Julius Kambarage (1922–) Tanzanian statesman, president of Tanganyika (1962–64) and of Tanzania (1964–85). He led Tanganyika to independence in 1961 and in 1964 successfully negotiated a union with Zanzibar, creating the new state of Tanzania.

Ny•ro |'nērō|, Laura (1947–97) U.S. songwriter and singer. Born *Laura Nigro*. Notable songs: "Wedding Bell Blues," "Blowin' Away," and "And When I Die."

Oo

Oak·ley |'ōklē|, Annie (1860–1926) U.S. markswomen; full name *Phoebe Anne Oakley Mozee*. In 1885 she joined Buffalo Bill's Wild West Show, of which she became a star attraction for the next 17 years.

Oates |'ōts|, Joyce Carol (1938–) U.S. author and educator. Notable works: *A Sentimental Education* (1981).

Oates |'ōts|, Titus (1649–1705) English clergyman and conspirator, remembered as the fabricator of the Popish Plot (1678). Convicted of perjury in 1685, Oates was imprisoned in the same year, but subsequently was released and granted a pension.

Oba·ta |,ō'bätə|, Gyo (1923–) U.S. architect. Notable designs: the National Air and Space Museum of the Smithsonian Institution (Washington, D.C.).

Obo·te |aw'baw,tā|, (Apollo) Milton (1924–) Ugandan statesman, prime minister (1962–66), president (1966–71 and 1980–85). Overthrown by Idi Amin in 1971, he was re-elected president in 1980. He was removed in a second military coup in 1985.

O'Bri·an |,ō'brīən|, Patrick (1932–) English author. He wrote the Aubrey-Maturin novels and works of British naval history.

O'Bri·en |ō'brīən|, Conan (1963–) U.S. television actor, producer, and writer. He wrote for "Saturday Night Live" and hosted the "Late Night" program.

O'Bri·en |ō'brīən|, Edna (1932–) Irish novelist and short-story writer, noted especially for her novel *The Country Girls* (1960).

O'Bri·en |ō'brīən|, Flann (1911–66) Irish novelist and journalist; pseudonym of *Brian O'Nolan*. Writing under the name of Myles na Gopaleen, he contributed a satirical column to the *Irish Times* for nearly twenty years. Notable novels: *At Swim-Two-Birds* (1939); *The Third Policeman* (1967).

O'Bri·en |ō'brīən|, Tim (1946–) U.S. author. Notable works: *Tomcat in Love* (1998), *In the Lake of the Woods* (1994), and *Going After Cacciato* (1978).

O'Ca·sey |ō'kāsē|, Sean (1880–1964) Irish dramatist. His plays, such as *The Shadow of a Gunman* (1923) and *Juno and the Paycock* (1924), deal with the Irish poor before and during the civil war that followed the establishment of the Irish Free State (1922). He also wrote an autobiography in several volumes.

Oc·cam, William of |'äkəm| see WILLIAM OF OCCAM.

Ochs |ōks|, Adolph Simon (1858–1935) U.S. publisher. He acquired *The New York Times* (1896) and made it one of the nation's preeminent newspapers.

Ochs |ōks|, Phil (1940–76) U.S. folksinger and songwriter. He was popular in 1960s protest circles for his songs "I Ain't a Marchin'" and "Draft Dodger Rag."

Ock·ham, William of see WILLIAM OF OCCAM.

O'Con·nell |ō'känəl|, Daniel (1775–1847) Irish nationalist leader and social reformer; known as **the Liberator**. His election to Parliament in 1828 forced the British government to grant Catholic Emancipation in order to enable him to take his seat in the House of Commons. In 1839 he established the Repeal Association to abolish the union with Britain.

O'Con·nor |ō'känər|, Carroll (1924–) U.S. actor, writer, and producer. He starred in the television series "All in the Family" (1971–79).

O'Con·nor |ō'känər|, Flannery (1925–64) U.S. novelist and short-story writer. Full name *Mary Flannery O'Connor*. Notable novels: *Wise Blood* (1952) and *The Violent Bear It Away* (1960).

O'Con·nor |ō'känər|, Sandra Day (1930–) U.S. Supreme Court justice (1981–). She was the first woman appointed to the U.S. Supreme Court.

O'Con·nor |ō'känər|, Sinéad (1966–) Irish pop singer.

Oc·ta·vi·an |äk'tāvēən| see AUGUSTUS.

Odets |ō'dets|, Clifford (1906–63) U.S.

dramatist. He was a founding member in 1931 of the avant garde Group Theater, which staged his best-known play, *Waiting for Lefty* (1935). His plays of the 1930s reflect the experiences of the Depression.

O'Don•nell |ō'dänəl|, Rosie (1962–) U.S. actress and talk show host. She has hosted television's "Rosie O'Donnell Show" since 1995; her acting credits include the movies *A League of Their Own* (1992) and *Harriet the Spy* (1996) and the stage musical *Grease* (1994).

Oer•ter |'awrtər|, Al (1936–) U.S. track and field athlete. He holds an Olympic record for consecutive medals, winning the discus 1956–68.

Of•fa |'awfə| (died 796) king of Mercia 757–96. He organized the construction of Offa's Dyke.

Of•fen•bach |'awfən,bäk|, Jacques (1819–80) German composer, resident in France fromx 1833; born *Jacob Offenbach*. He is associated with the rise of the operetta, whose style is typified by his *Orpheus in the Underworld* (1858). Other notable works: *The Tales of Hoffmann* (1881).

Og•den |'ägdən|, Peter Skene (1794–1854) Canadian explorer. He discovered the Humboldt River (1828); Ogden, Utah, is named for him.

Ogle•thorpe |'ōgəl,THawrp|, James Edward (1696–1785) British soldier, philanthropist, and member of Parliament (1722–54). He received the charter for the colony of Georgia (1732) and founded Savannah.

O'Ha•ra |ō'herə|, Frank (1926–66) U.S. poet and art critic. He won a National Book Award for *Selected Poems* (1973).

O'Ha•ra |ō'herə|, John (Henry) (1905–70) U.S. author. Notable works: *Butterfield 8* (1935); *A Rage to Live* (1949); and *From the Terrace* (1958).

O'Hig•gins |ō'higinz|, Bernardo (*c.* 1778–1842) Chilean revolutionary leader and statesman, head of state 1817–23. With the help of José de San Martín, he led the army that defeated Spanish forces in 1817 and paved the way for Chilean independence the following year.

Ohm |ōm|, Georg Simon (1789–1854) German physicist. The units ohm and

mho are named after him, as is Ohm's Law on electricity.

O'Keeffe |ō'kēf|, Georgia (1887–1986) U.S. painter. Her best-known paintings depict enlarged flowers and are often regarded as sexually symbolic (for example, *Black Iris*, 1926). She married photographer Alfred Stieglitz in 1924.

Olaf |'ō,läf; 'ōləf| five kings of Norway: **Olaf I Tryggvason** (969–1000; reigned 995–1000). **Olaf II Haraldsson** (*c.* 995–1030; reigned 1016–30). Canonized as **St. Olaf** for his attempts to spread Christianity in his kingdom, he is the patron saint of Norway. Feast day, July 29. **Olaf III Haraldsson** (died 1093; reigned 1066–93). **Olaf IV Haakonsson** (1370–87; reigned 1380–87). **Olaf V** (1903–91; reigned 1957–91). Full name *Olaf Alexander Edmund Christian Frederik.*

Ola•ju• |ə'läzHə,wän|, Hakeem (1963–) U.S. basketball player, born in Nigeria.

Ol•den•burg |'ōldən,bərg|, Claes Thure (1929–) U.S. pop artist and sculptor, born in Sweden.

Old Pretender see STUART, JAMES.

Olds |ōldz|, Ransom Eli (1864–1950) U.S. inventor and manufacturer. He created the Oldsmobile, the first commercially successful American car (1901).

Olds |ōldz|, Sharon (1942–) U.S. poet. Notable works: *The Father* (1993).

Oli•phant |'äləfənt|, Pat (1935–) U.S. political cartoonist and artist, born in Australia. He is syndicated internationally.

Ol•i•ver |'äləvər|, King (1885–1938) U.S. jazz cornetist and band leader. Full name *Joe Oliver*. In Chicago and New Orleans he played with newcomer Louis Armstrong in King Oliver's Creole Jazz Band.

Ol•i•ver |'äləvər|, Mary (1935–) U.S. poet. Notable works: *American Primitive* (1983, Pulitzer Prize) and *New and Selected Poems* (1992, National Book Award).

Ol•i•ver |'äləvər|, Sy (Melvin James) (1910–88) U.S. jazz trumpeter, composer, and conductor. He played with Tommy Dorsey's orchestra.

Oliv•ier |ə'livē,ā|, Laurence (Kerr), Baron Olivier of Brighton (1907–89)

English actor and director. Following his professional debut in 1924, he performed all the major Shakespearean roles; he was also director of the National Theatre (1963–73). His movies include *Rebecca* (1940), *HenryV* (1944), and *Hamlet* (1948).

Olm·sted |'ōm͵sted|, Frederick Law (1822–1903) U.S. architect. He designed Central Park in New York and Fairmount Park in Philadelphia.

Ol·sen |'ōlsən|, Kenneth H. (1926–) U.S. engineer and inventor. The inventor of magnetic core memory, he helped develop the modern computer.

Ol·sen |'ōlsən|, Tillie (1913–) U.S. author. Notable works: *Silences* (1978).

Omar I |'ō͵mär| (*c.* 581–644) Muslim caliph (634–44). He conquered Syria, Palestine, and Egypt.

Omar Khay·yám |'ō͵mär ͵kī'(y)äm; ͵kī(y)æm| (*c.*1048–1131) Persian poet, mathematician, and astronomer. His *rubáiyát* (quatrains), found in *The Rubáiyát of Omar Khayyám* (translation published 1859), are meditations on the mysteries of existence and celebrations of worldly pleasures.

Onas·sis |ō'næsəs|, Aristotle (Socrates) (1900?–75) Greek shipping magnate and international businessman. He owned a substantial shipping empire and founded the Greek national airline, Olympic Airways (1957).

Onas·sis |ō'næsəs|, Jacqueline Lee Bouvier Kennedy (1929–94) U.S. first lady; known as **Jackie O.** She married John F. Kennedy in 1953, serving as first lady during his presidency (1961–63). Widowed in 1963, she married Aristotle Onassis (1968). After his death (1975), she pursued a career in publishing.

On·daat·je |än'dätyə|, (Philip) Michael (1943–) Sri Lankan-born Canadian writer. Notable works: *Running in the Family* (autobiography, 1982); *The English Patient* (novel; Booker Prize, 1992).

O'Neal |ō'nēl|, Shaquille (1972–) U.S. basketball player.

O'Neill |ō'nēl|, Eugene (Gladstone) (1888–1953) U.S. dramatist. He was awarded the Pulitzer Prize for his first full-length play, *Beyond the Horizon* (1920). Other notable works: *The Em-*

peror Joves (1920), *Anna Christie* (1921), *Desire Under the Elms* (1924), *Mourning Becomes Electra* (1931), and *The Iceman Cometh* (1946). *Long Day's Journey into Night* appeared posthumously in 1956. Nobel Prize for Literature (1936).

Ono |'ōnō|, Yoko (1933–) U.S. musician and artist, born in Japan. She married John Lennon in 1969 and collaborated with him on various experimental recordings. Ono also recorded her own albums.

Oort |awrt|, Jan Hendrik (1900–92) Dutch astronomer. He proved that the Galaxy is rotating, and determined the position and orbital period of the sun within it.

Opel |'ōpel|, Wilhelm von (1871–1948) German automotive manufacturer. His company was the first in Germany to introduce assembly-line production, selling over one million cars.

Opie |'ōpē|, John (1761–1807) English painter. His work includes portraits and history paintings such as *The Murder of Rizzio* (1787).

Op·pen·hei·mer |'äp(ə)n͵hīmər|, Julius Robert (1904–67) U.S. theoretical physicist. He was director of the laboratory at Los Alamos during the development of the first atom bomb, but opposed the development of the hydrogen bomb after the Second World War.

Op·per |'äpər|, Frederick Burr (1857–1937) U.S. cartoonist. He is best known for the comic strips "Happy Hooligan," "And Her Name Was Maud!" and "Alphonse and Gaston."

Orange, William of William III of Great Britain and Ireland (see WILLIAM).

Or·bi·son |'awrbə͵sən|, Roy (1936–88) U.S. rock-and-roll singer and songwriter. Notable songs: "Only the Lonely" (1960) and "Oh, Pretty Woman" (1964).

Or·ca·gna |awr'känyä| (*c.* 1308–68) Italian painter, sculptor, and architect; born *Andrea di Cione*. His paintings include frescoes and an altarpiece in the church of Santa Maria Novella, Florence (1357).

Or·czy |'awrtsē|, Baroness Emmusca (1865–1947) Hungarian-born British novelist. Her best-known novel is *The Scarlet Pimpernel* (1905).

Orff |awrf|, Carl (1895–1982) German composer. He is best known for his secular cantata *Carmina Burana* (1937), based on a collection of characteristically bawdy medieval Latin poems.

Or·i·gen |'awri,jen| (*c.* 185–*c.* 254) Christian scholar and theologian, probably born in Alexandria, Egypt. His most famous work was the *Hexapla*, an edition of the Old Testament with six or more parallel versions. His Neoplatonist theology was ultimately rejected by Church orthodoxy.

Or·man·dy |'awrmǝndē|, Eugene (1899–1985) U.S. conductor, born in Hungary. Born *Jeno Blau*. He was conductor of the Philadelphia Orchestra from 1938 to 1980, the longest directorship in U.S. history.

Oroz·co |ō'rōskō; ō'rawskō|, José Clemente (1883–1949) Mexican artist. He was the most important 20th-century muralist to work in fresco.

Orr |awr|, Bobby (1948–) U.S. hockey player (1966–77), born in Canada. Full name **Robert Gordon Orr**. Led the National Hockey League in scoring twice and assists five times.

Or·te·ga |awr'tāgǝ|, Daniel (1945–) Nicaraguan statesman, president (1985–90); full name *Daniel Ortega Saavedra*. He became the leader of the Sandinista National Liberation Front (FSLN) in 1966 and became president after the Sandinista election victory in 1984.

Or·te·ga y Gas·set |,awr'tāgǝ ē 'gäsǝt|, José (1883–1955) Spanish philosopher. His works include *The Revolt of the Masses* (1930), in which he proposed leadership by an intellectual elite.

Or·ton |'awrtǝn|, Joe (1933–67) English dramatist; born *John Kingsley Orton*. He wrote a number of unconventional black comedies, examining corruption, sexuality, and violence; they include *Entertaining Mr. Sloane* (1964) and *Loot* (1965).

Or·well |'awr,wel|, George (1903–50) British novelist and essayist, born in India; pseudonym of *Eric Arthur Blair*. His work is characterized by his concern about social injustice. His most famous works are *Animal Farm* (1945), a satire on Communism as it developed under Stalin, and *Nineteen Eighty-four* (1949), a dystopian account of a future state in which every aspect of life is controlled by Big Brother.

Ory |'awrē|, Kid (1886–1973) U.S. jazz trombonist and bandleader. Full name *Edward Ory*. He composed "Muskrat Ramble" and was the leader of the Spikes' Seven Pods of Pepper, the first New Orleans style jazz band to record.

Os·borne |'äz,bawrn|, Thomas Mott (1859–1926) U.S. prison reformer. He resigned as warden of Sing Sing prison (1914–15) because of public hostility toward his system of self-government for inmates.

Os·bourne |'äz,bawrn; 'äzbǝrn|, John (James) (1929–94) English dramatist His first play, *Look Back in Anger* (1956), ushered in a new era of kitchen-sink drama; its hero Jimmy Porter personified contemporary disillusioned youth, the so-called "angry young man." Later plays include *The Entertainer* (1957) and *Luther* (1961).

Os·ce·o·la |,äsē'ōlǝ; ,ōsē'ōlǝ| (*c.* 1804–38) Native American leader of the Seminole Indians. A successful leader during the Seminole Wars (1835–42), he was captured while bearing a flag of truce.

Os·ler |'äslǝr|, Sir William (1849–1919) Canadian-born physician and classical scholar. His *Principles and Practice of Medicine* (1892) became the chosen clinical textbook for medical students.

Os·man I |'äs,män; 'äsmǝn| (1258–1326) Also **Othman**. Turkish conqueror, founder of the Ottoman (Osmanli) dynasty and empire. Osman reigned as sultan of the Seljuk Turks from 1288, conquering NW Asia Minor. He assumed the title of emir in 1299.

Os·ta·de |'äs,tädǝ|, Adriaen van (1610–85) Dutch painter and engraver. His work chiefly depicts lively genre scenes of peasants carousing or brawling in crowded taverns or barns.

O'Sul·li·van |ō'sǝlǝvǝn|, Maureen (1911–98) U.S. actress, born in Ireland. She starred as Jane in the *Tarzan* series and appeared in Woody Allen's *Hannah and Her Sisters*(1986).

O'Sul·li·van |ō'sǝlǝvǝn|, Timothy H. (1840–82) U.S. photographer. He took photographs of Civil War battles, the southwestern U.S., and Panama.

Os·wald |'äz,wawld|, Lee Harvey (1939–63) U.S. alleged assassin of President John F. Kennedy. He denied the charge of assassinating the president, but was murdered before he could be brought to trial. Oswald's role in the assassination remains the focus for a number of conspiracy theories.

Os·wald of York |'äs,wawld|, St. (*c.* 925–992) English prelate and Benedictine monk. As Archbishop of York, he founded several monasteries and, with St. Dunstan, revived the Church and learning in 10th-century England. Feast day, February 28.

Oth·man Variant form of OSMAN I.

Otho |'ōTHō|, Marcus Salvius (AD 32–69) Roman emperor (January–April 69). He was proclaimed emperor after he had procured the death of Galba in a conspiracy of the praetorian guard, but the German legions, led by their imperial candidate, Vitellius, defeated his troops, and Otho committed suicide.

Otis |'ōtəs|, Elisha Graves (1811–61) U.S. inventor and manufacturer. He produced the first efficient elevator with a safety device to prevent it from falling (1852).

Otis |'ōtəs|, James (1725–83) American revolutionary statesman. He led the majority in the Massachusetts legislature (1766–69) and opposed various revenue acts.

O'Toole |ō'tōōl|, Peter (Seamus) (1932–) Irish-born British actor. Notable movies include *Lawrence of Arabia* (1962) and *Goodbye Mr. Chips* (1969); he is especially noted for his portrayals of eccentric characters.

Ott |ät|, Mel (1909–58) U.S. baseball player. Full name *Melvin Thomas Ott*. He was the first to hit 500 home runs in the National League.

Ot·to |'ätō|, Nikolaus August (1832–91) German engineer whose name is given to the four-stroke cycle on which most internal-combustion engines work.

Ot·to I |'ätō| (912–73) king of the Germans 936–73, Holy Roman emperor 962–73; known as **Otto the Great**. As king of the Germans he carried out a policy of eastward expansion, and as

Holy Roman emperor he established a presence in Italy to rival that of the papacy.

Ot·way |'ätwā|, Thomas (1652–85) English dramatist. He is chiefly remembered for his two blank verse tragedies, *The Orphan* (1680) and *Venice Preserved* (1682).

Oui·da |'wēdə| (1839–1908) English novelist; pseudonym of *Marie Louise de la Ramée*. Her novels, such as *Under Two Flags* (1867), are romances that are typically set in a fashionable world far removed from reality.

Out·cault |'owt,kawlt|, Richard Felton (1863–1928) U.S. cartoonist. He created the characters Yellow Kid (1895) and Buster Brown (1902).

Ovid |'ävid| (43 BC–*c.* 17AD) Roman poet; full name *Publius Ovidius Naso*. He is particularly known for his elegiac love poems (such as the *Amores* and the *Ars Amatoria*) and for the *Metamorphoses*, a hexametric epic which retells Greek and Roman myths.

Ow·en |'ō(w)ən|, Sir Richard (1804–92) English anatomist and paleontologist. Owen made important contributions to evolution, taxonomy, and palaeontology and coined the word *dinosaur* in 1841. He was a strong opponent of Darwinism.

Ow·en |'ō(w)ən|, Robert Dale (1801–77) U.S. politician and social reformer, born in England. As a member of the U.S. House of Representatives from Indiana (1843–47), he drafted legislation to create the Smithsonian Institution; his letter to Abraham Lincoln, published as *Policy of Emancipation* (1863), influenced Lincoln's views.

Ow·ens |'ō(w)ənz|, Jesse (1913–80) U.S. track and field athlete; born *James Cleveland Owens*. In 1935 he equalled or broke six world records in 45 minutes, and in 1936 won four gold medals at the Olympic Games in Berlin. The success in Berlin of Owens, as a black man, outraged Hitler.

Oz |äz|, Frank Richard (1944–) U.S. puppeteer, born in England. He created many of the Muppet characters, including Miss Piggy, Grover, and Bert.

Oza·wa |ō'zäwə|, Seiji (1935–) Japanese conductor. He was conductor of the Toronto Symphony Orchestra from 1965 to 1970, and in 1973 he became music director and conductor of the Boston Symphony Orchestra. He conducts frequently with major symphony and opera companies.

Ozick |'ō,zik|, Cynthia (1928–　) U.S. author and critic. Notable works: *The Puttermesser Papers* (1997).

Ozu |'ōzōō|, Yasujirō (1903–63) Japanese movie director. He was the originator of films about lower middle class families, such as *Tokyo Monogatari* (1953).

Pp

Pabst |pæbst|, Captain Frederick (1836–1904) U.S. steamship captain and businessman. He entered his father-in-law's brewery business and turned it into the Pabst brewing company.

Pa•chel•bel |'päkнəl,bel|, Johann (1653–1706) German composer and organist. His compositions include seventy-eight chorale preludes, thirteen settings of the Magnificat, and the Canon and Gigue in D for three violins and continuo.

Pa•ci•no |pə'cнēnō|, Al (1940–   ) U.S. movie actor; full name *Alfredo James Pacino*. Nominated for an Oscar eight times, winning once for *Scent of a Woman* (1992), he first achieved recognition with *The Godfather* (1972). Other notable movies: *Scarface* (1983), *Dick Tracy* (1990), and *Carlito's Way* (1993).

Pack•wood |'pæk,wood|, Robert (1932–   ) U.S. politician. A member of the U.S. Senate from Oregon (1969–95), he resigned following charges of sexual harassment.

Pa•de•rew•ski |,pædə'refskē|, Ignacy Jan (1860–1941) Polish pianist, composer, and statesman, prime minister (1919). He was the first prime minister of independent Poland, but resigned after only ten months in office and resumed his musical career.

Pa•ga•ni•ni |,pägä'nēnē|, Niccolò (1782–1840) Italian violinist and composer. His virtuoso violin recitals, including widespread use of pizzicato and harmonics, established him as a major figure of the romantic movement.

Page |pāj|, Geraldine (Sue) (1924–87) U.S. actress. Her Broadway credits include *Sweet Bird of Youth* (1959), *Strange Interlude* (1963), and *Agnes of God* (1982). Notable movies: *The Trip to Bountiful* (1985, Academy Award).

Page |pāj|, Jimmy (1944–   ) British rock guitarist, composer, and producer.

Page |pāj|, Thomas Nelson (1853–1922) U.S. author. Notable works: *In Ole Virginia* (1887).

Page |pāj|, Walter Hines (1855–1918) U.S. diplomat, journalist, and philanthropist. A partner in Doubleday, Page & Co., he advocated mass education and welfare.

Pag•lia |'pæglēə|, Camille (Anna) (1947–   ) U.S. cultural critic. Her first book, *Sexual Personae* (1990), brought her to public attention. Other notable works: *Sex, Art, and American Culture* (1992) and *Vamps and Tramps* (1994).

Pa•gnol |pən'yōl|, Marcel (1895–1974) French dramatist, movie director, and writer. His novels include *La Gloire de mon père* (1957) and *Le Chateau de ma mère* (1958); the movies *Jean de Florette* and *Manon des Sources* (both 1986) were based on Pagnol's *L'Eau des collines* (1963).

Pah•la•vi |'päləvē| two shahs of Iran: **Reza Pahlavi** (1878–1944; ruled 1925–41). Born *Reza Khan*. An army officer, he took control of the Persian government after a coup in 1921. He was elected Shah in 1925 but abdicated following the occupation of Iran by British and Soviet forces. His son, **Muhammad Reza Pahlavi** (1919–80; ruled 1941–79). Also known as **Reza Shah**. Opposition to his regime culminated in the Islamic revolution of 1979 under Ayatollah Khomeini; he was forced into exile and died in Egypt.

Paige |pāj|, Satchel (1906–82) U.S. baseball player. Born *Leroy Robert Paige*. A pitcher for the Negro leagues (1924–47) and the major leagues, he pitched 55 career no-hitters. Elected to the Baseball Hall of Fame (1971).

Paine |pān|, Albert Bigelow (1861–1937) U.S. editor, dramatist, and biographer. He edited Mark Twain's letters and authored *The Great White Way* (1901).

Paine |pān|, John Knowles (1839–1906) U.S. organist and composer. He held the first chair of music in an American university (Harvard).

Paine |pān|, Thomas (1737–1809) English political writer. His pamphlet *Common Sense* (1776) called for American independence and *The Rights of Man* (1791) defended the French Revolution. His radical views prompted the British government to indict him for treason, and he fled to France. Other notable works: *The Age of Reason* (1794).

Pais•ley |'pāzlē|, Ian (Richard Kyle) (1929–) Northern Irish clergyman and politician. cofounder of the Ulster Democratic Unionist Party (1972), he has been a vociferous and outspoken defender of the Protestant Unionist position in Northern Ireland.

Pa•les•tri•na |ˌpælə'strēnə|, Giovanni Pierluigi da (*c.* 1525–94) Italian composer. Palestrina is chiefly known for his sacred music, including 105 masses, over 250 motets, and the *Missa Papae Marcelli* (1567).

Pa•ley |'pālē|, Grace (1922–) U.S. novelist and short story writer. Notable works: *Collected Stories* (1994).

Pa•ley |'pālē|, William Samuel (1901–90) U.S. television and radio executive. He built the CBS communications empire and served as its president (1928–46) and chairman of the board (1946–90).

Pal•grave |'pawlˌgrāv|, Francis Turner (1824–97) English critic and poet, known for his anthology *The Golden Treasury of Songs and Lyrical Poems in the English Language* (1861).

Pa•lis•sy |'pælisē|, Bernard (*c.* 1510–89) French potter, known for his richly colored earthenware decorated with reliefs of plants and animals.

Pal•la•dio |pə'lädēō|, Andrea (1508–80) Italian architect; born *Andrea di Pietro della Gondola*. He led a revival of classical architecture, in particular promoting the Roman ideals of harmonic proportions and symmetrical planning. A notable example of his many villas, palaces, and churches is the church of San Giorgio Maggiore in Venice.

Pal•me |'pälmə|, (Sven) Olof (Joachim) (1927–86) Swedish statesman, prime minister (1969–76 and 1982–86). He was killed by an unknown assassin.

Pal•mer |'pä(l)mər|, Arnold (Daniel) (1929–) U.S. golfer. His many championship victories include the Masters (1958; 1960; 1962; 1964), the U.S. Open (1960), and the British Open (1961–2). The huge galleries that were attracted by the ever-popular Palmer whenever he played came to be called "Arnie's Army."

Pal•mer |'pä(l)mər|, Erastus Dow (1817–1904) U.S. sculptor. Notable works: *The White Captive* (1859).

Pal•mer |'pä(l)mər|, Jim (1945–) U.S. baseball player. He won the Cy Young Award three times.

Pal•mer |'pä(l)mər|, Samuel (1805–81) English painter and etcher. His friendship with William Blake resulted in the mystical, visionary landscape paintings, such as *Repose of the Holy Family* (1824), for which he is best known. He was leader of a group of artists called The Ancients.

Pal•mer•ston |'pä(l)mərstən|, Henry John Temple, 3rd Viscount (1784–1865) British Whig statesman, prime minister (1855–58 and 1859–65). Palmerston declared the second Opium War against China in 1856 and oversaw the successful conclusion of the Crimean War in 1856 and the suppression of the Indian Mutiny in 1858. He also maintained British neutrality during the U.S. Civil War.

Pan•dit |'pændət|, Vijaya (Lakshmi) (1900–90) Indian politician and diplomat, sister of Jawaharlal Nehru. Imprisoned three times by the British for nationalist activities, after independence she became the first woman to serve as president of the United Nations General Assembly (1953–54).

Pa•net•ta |pə'netə|, Leon Edward (1938–) U.S. politician. He was White House chief of staff to President Clinton (1994–97).

Pa•ni•ni |'päninē| (*fl. c.* 400 BC) Indian grammarian. Sources vary as to when he lived, with dates ranging from the 4th to the 7th century BC. He is noted as the author of the *Eight Lectures*, a grammar of Sanskrit.

Pank•hurst |'pæNGkˌhərst|, Emmeline (1858–1928) English suffragette. In 1903 Emmeline and her daughters Christabel (1880–1958) and (Estelle) Sylvia (1882–1960) founded the Women's Social and Political Union, with the motto "Votes for Women." Following the imprisonment of Christabel in 1905, Emmeline initiated the militant suffragette campaign that continued until the outbreak of World War I.

Pao·loz·zi |pow'lätsē|, Eduardo (Luigi) (1924–) Scottish artist and sculptor, of Italian descent. He was a key figure in the development of pop art in Britain in the 1950s.

Pa·pa·dop·ou·los |ˌpäpə'däpələs|, Georgios (1919–) Greek military and political leader. He headed the military junta that ruled Greece from 1967 to 1973, after which he became prime minister (1967–73) and then president (1973).

Pa·pan·dre·ou |ˌpäpən'drāo͞o|, George (1888–1968) Greek political leader. He was exiled in 1936, headed the government-in-exile (1944–45), and was elected premier in 1963. He was arrested after a military coup in April 1967.

Pa·pi·neau |päpē'nō|, Louis Joseph (1786–1871) French-Canadian politician. The leader of the French-Canadian party in Lower Canada (later Quebec province), he campaigned against the union of Lower and Upper Canada (later Ontario) and pressed for greater French-Canadian autonomy. He was forced to flee the country after leading an abortive French rebellion against British rule in 1837.

Papp |pæp|, Joseph (1921–91) U.S. producer and director. Born *Joseph Papirofsky*. He was managing director of the Hollywood's Actors Laboratory (1948–50) and founded the Shakespearean Theatre Workshop (1954), which became the New York Shakespeare Festival.

Pap·pus |'pæpəs| (*fl. c.* 300–350) Greek mathematician; known as **Pappus of Alexandria**. Little is known of his life, but his *Collection* of six books (another two are missing) is the principal source of knowledge of the mathematics of his predecessors.

Pa·quin |'pækwin|, Anna (1982–) U.S. actress. Notable movies: *The Piano* (1993, Academy Award).

Pa·ra·cel·sus |ˌperə'selsəs| (*c.* 1493–1541) Swiss physician; born *Theophrastus Phillipus Aureolus Bombastus von Hohenheim*. He developed a new approach to medicine and philosophy based on observation and experience. He saw ill-

ness as having a specific external cause (rather than resulting from an imbalance of the bodily humors), and introduced chemical remedies to replace traditional ones.

Par·is |'peris|, Matthew see MATTHEW PARIS.

Park |pärk|, Mungo (1771–1806) Scottish explorer. He undertook a series of explorations in West Africa (1795–7), among them the navigation of the Niger. He drowned on a second expedition to the Niger (1805–6).

Park Chung Hee |ˌpärk CHƏNG 'hē| (1917–79) South Korean statesman, president (1963–79). After staging a coup in 1961 he was elected president, assuming dictatorial powers in 1971. Under Park's presidency South Korea emerged as a leading industrial nation.

Par·ker |'pärkər|, Alton Brooks (1852–1926) U.S. jurist and politician. He served as chief justice of the New York court of appeals (1898–1904) and was a Democratic presidential candidate in 1904.

Par·ker |'pärkər|, Bonnie (1911–34) U.S. bank robber. The romantic partner of Clyde Barrow, who was known for a criminal spree, she wrote a poem that inspired the movie *The Ballad of Bonnie and Clyde*.

Par·ker |'pärkər|, Charlie (1920–55) U.S. saxophonist; full name *Charles Christopher Parker*; known as **Bird** or **Yardbird**. From 1944 he played with Thelonious Monk and Dizzy Gillespie, and became one of the key figures of the bebop movement. He is noted especially for his recordings with Miles Davis in 1945.

Par·ker |'pärkər|, Dorothy (Rothschild) (1893–1967) U.S. humorist, literary critic, and writer. From 1927 Parker wrote book reviews and short stories for the *New Yorker* magazine, becoming one of its legendary wits.

Par·ker |'pärkər|, Francis Wayland (1837–1902) U.S. educator. A school principal and superintendent, he was a pioneer of progressive education in the U.S.

Par·ker |'pärkər|, Horatio William (1863–1919) U.S. composer. The dean of the Yale School of Music (1904–19), he wrote oratorios, operas, and choral works.

Par·ker |'pärkər|, Louis W. (1906–93) U.S. inventor, born in Hungary. He invented the first color television.

Par·ker |'pärkər|, Theodore (1810–60) U.S. clergyman and social reformer. A liberal and radical Unitarian and later Congregational minister, he was a leading Transcendentalist of his day.

Park·man |'pärkmən|, Francis (1823–93) U.S. historian. He traveled the Oregon Trail in 1846 to improve his health and later wrote an account of his journey, *The California and Oregon Trail* (1849).

Parks |pärks|, Gordon Roger Alexander Buchanan (1912–) U.S. movie director, composer, author, and photographer. He directed the movie *Shaft* (1972) and was the author of *Flash Photography* (1947); Spingarn Medal, 1972.

Parks |pärks|, Rosa L. (1913–) On December 1, 1955, she refused to give up her bus seat to a white man in Montgomery, Alabama; after the ensuing boycott and NAACP protest, bus segregation was ruled unconstitutional. Spingarn Medal, 1979.

Par·men·i·des |pär'menə,dēz| (5th century BC) Greek philosopher. Born in Elea in SW Italy, he founded the Eleatic school of philosophers. In his work *On Nature*, written in hexameter verse, he maintained that the apparent motion and changing forms of the universe are in fact manifestations of an unchanging and indivisible reality.

Par·mi·gia·ni·no |,pärməjə'nē,nō| (1503–40) Also **Parmigiano**. Italian painter; born *Girolano Francesco Maria Mazzola*. He made an important contribution to early mannerism with the graceful figure style of his frescoes and portraits. Notable works: *Madonna with the Long Neck* (1534).

Par·nell |pär'nel|, Charles Stewart (1846–91) Irish nationalist leader. Parnell became leader of the Irish Home Rule faction in 1880 and raised the profile of Irish affairs through obstructive parliamentary tactics. He was forced to retire from public life in 1890 after the exposure of his adultery with Mrs. Kitty O'Shea.

Parr |pär|, Katherine (1512–48) English queen, sixth and last wife of Henry VIII. Having married the king in 1543, she influenced his decision to restore the succession to his daughters Mary and Elizabeth (later Mary I and Elizabeth I, respectively).

Par·ry |'perē|, Sir (Charles) Hubert (Hastings) (1848–1918) English composer. Parry's best-known work is his setting of William Blake's poem "Jerusalem" (1916), which has acquired the status of a national song.

Par·sons |'pärsənz|, Sir Charles (Algernon) (1854–1931) British engineer, scientist, and manufacturer. He patented and built the first practical steam turbine in 1884, designed to drive electricity generators. He also developed steam turbines for marine propulsion, and his experimental vessel *Turbinia* caused a sensation in 1897.

Par·sons |'pärsənz|, Estelle (1927–) U.S. stage and movie actress. Notable movies: *Bonnie and Clyde* (1967, Academy Award).

Par·sons |'pärsənz|, John T. (1913–) U.S inventor. He built a machine that cut airplane wings automatically on a contour; the machine now has many applications in manufacturing.

Par·ton |'pärtn|, Dolly (Rebecca) (1946–) U.S. country music singer and songwriter. Her hits include "Jolene" (1974). She has also made a number of movies, including *Nine to Five* (1980) and *Steel Magnolias* (1989), and founded a theme park, Dollywood.

Pas·cal |pæ'skæl|, Blaise (1623–62) French mathematician, physicist, and religious philosopher. He founded the theory of probabilities and developed a forerunner of integral calculus, but is best known for deriving the principle that the pressure of a fluid at rest is transmitted equally in all directions. His *Lettres Provinciales* (1656–7) and *Pensées* (1670) argue for his Jansenist Christianity.

Pa·šić |'päsнісн|, Nikola (1845–1926) Serbian statesman, prime minister of Serbia five times between 1891 and 1918, and of the Kingdom of Serbs, Croats, and Slovenes (1921–24 and 1924–26). He was a party to the formation of the Kingdom of Serbs, Croats, and Slovenes (called Yugoslavia from 1929) in 1918.

Pa•so•li•ni |ˌpäsə'lēnē|, Pier Paolo (1922–75) Italian film director and novelist. A Marxist, he drew on his experiences in the slums of Rome for his work, but became recognized for his controversial, bawdy literary adaptation, such as *The Gospel According to St. Matthew* (1964) and *The Canterbury Tales* (1973).

Pass |pæs|, Joe (1929–94) U.S. jazz guitarist. Born *Joseph Anthony Jacobi Passalaqua*. He achieved recognition with his 1973 solo album, *Virtuoso*.

Pas•sos, John Dos see DOS PASSOS.

Pas•ter•nak |'pæstər,næk|, Boris (Leonidovich) (1890–1960) Russian poet, novelist, and translator. His best-known novel, *Doctor Zhivago* (1957), describes the experience of the Russian intelligentsia during the Revolution; it was banned in the Soviet Union. Pasternak was awarded the Nobel Prize for Literature in 1958, but turned it down under pressure from Soviet authorities.

Pas•teur |päs'tœr|, Louis (1822–95) French chemist and bacteriologist. He introduced pasteurization and made pioneering studies in vaccination techniques.

Pa•ter |'pātər|, Walter (Horatio) (1839–94) English essayist and critic. His *Studies in the History of the Renaissance* (1873) had a major impact on the development of the Aesthetic Movement.

Pa•ter•no |pə'tərnō|, Joe (1926–) U.S. college football coach.

Pat•er•son |'pætərsən|, William (1745–1806) U.S. Supreme Court justice (1793–1806), born in Ireland. He was a member of the Constitutional Convention (1787), a member of the U.S. Senate from New Jersey (1789–90), and governor of New Jersey (1790–93).

Pa•thé |pä'tā; pə'THā|, Charles (1863–1957) French movie pioneer. In 1896 he and his brothers founded a company that came to dominate the production and distribution of movies. It became internationally known for its newsreels, first introduced in France in 1909.

Pa•ton |'pātn|, Alan (Stewart) (1903–88) South African writer and politician. He is best known for his novel *Cry, the Beloved Country* (1948), a passionate indictment of the apartheid system.

Pa•tou |pə'tōō|, Jean (1887–1936) French couturier and perfume-maker.

Pat•rick |'pætrik|, St. (5th cent) Apostle and patron saint of Ireland. Of Romano-British parentage, he was taken as a slave to Ireland, where he experienced a religious conversion. He founded the archiepiscopal see of Armagh in about 454. Feast day, March 17.

Pat•ter•son |'pætərsən|, Floyd (1935–) U.S. boxer. An Olympic middleweight champion (1952), he was also world heavyweight champion (1956–59, 1960–62).

Pat•ter•son |'pætərsən| U.S. family of journalists, including: **Robert Wilson Patterson** (1850–1910), editor of the *Chicago Tribune* (1873–1910.). **Joseph Medill Patterson** (1879–1946), the son of Robert Patterson. With his cousin Robert McCormick he founded the *New York Daily News* (1925). **Eleanor Medill Patterson** (1884–1948), the daughter of Robert Patterson; known as **Cissy**. She was the editor and later the owner (1939) of the *Washington Herald*, which she merged with the *Washington Times*.

Pat•ti |'pætē|, Adelina (1843–1919) U.S. operatic soprano, born in Spain of Italian parentage. Born *Adela Juana Maria*. One of the greatest coloratura singers of the 19th century, she made her New York debut in 1859.

Pat•ton |'pætn|, George Smith (1885–1945) U.S. army general. During World War II, he commanded the ground forces in the Allied invasion of northwest Africa (1942–43) and the U.S. Third Army in the drive through France (1944). He wrote his autobiography, *War as I Knew It* (1947).

Paul III |pawl| (1468–49) Italian pope (1534–49); born *Alessandro Farnese*. He excommunicated Henry VIII of England in 1538, instituted the order of the Jesuits in 1540, and initiated the Council of Trent in 1545. Paul III was also a patron of Michelangelo.

Paul |pawl|, Les (1915–) U.S. jazz guitarist and guitar designer; born *Lester Polfus*. In 1946 he invented the solid-body electric guitar, which was promoted from 1952 as the Gibson Les Paul guitar. Paul was also among the first to use such recording techniques as over-dubbing. His style of play influenced many rock guitarists.

Paul |pawl|, St. (died *c.* 64) Christian missionary of Jewish descent; known as **Paul the Apostle**, or **Saul of Tarsus**, or **the Apostle of the Gentiles**. He first opposed the followers of Jesus, assisting at the martyrdom of St. Stephen. On a journey to Damascus he was converted to Christianity after a vision and became one of the first major Christian missionaries and theologians. His epistles form part of the New Testament. Feast day, June 29.

Paul•ding |'pawldiNG|, Hiram (1797–1878) U.S. naval officer. He was acting lieutenant on the *Ticonderoga* at the Battle of Lake Champlain (1814).

Paul•ding |'pawldiNG|, James Kirke (1778–1860) U.S. author. He authored *Westward Ho!* (1832) and served as secretary of the navy under Martin Van Buren (1838–41).

Paul•ey |'pawlē|, Jane (1950–) U.S. journalist. She cohosted NBC's *The Today Show* (1976–90) and is coanchor of *Dateline NBC* (1992–).

Paul•i |'powlē|, Wolfgang (1900–58) Austrian-born U.S. physicist. He made a major contribution to quantum theory with his exclusion principle, according to which only two electrons in an atom could occupy the same quantum level, provided they had opposite spins. In 1931 he postulated the existence of the neutrino, later discovered by Enrico Fermi. Nobel Prize for Physics (1945).

Paul•ing |'pawliNG|, Linus Carl (1901–94) U.S. chemist. He is renowned for his study of molecular structure and chemical bonding, for which he received the 1954 Nobel Prize for Chemistry. His suggestion of a helical structure for proteins formed the foundation for the elucidation of the structure of DNA.

Pau•sa•ni•as |paw'sānēəs| (2nd cent) Greek geographer and historian. His *Description of Greece* (also called the *Itinerary of Greece*) is a guide to the topography and remains of ancient Greece and is still considered an invaluable source of information.

Pa•va•rot•ti |ˌpävä'rawtē; ˌpævə'rätē|,

Luciano (1935–) Italian operatic tenor. He made his debut as Rodolfo in Puccini's *La Bohème* in 1961 and has since gained international acclaim and popularity for his bel canto singing.

Pa•ve•se |pə'vā,zā|, Cesare (1908–50) Italian novelist, poet, and translator. He is best known for his last novel *La Luna e i falò* (1950), in which he portrays isolation and the failure of communication as a general human predicament.

Pav•lov |'päv,lawv|, Ivan (Petrovich) (1849–1936) Russian physiologist. He was awarded a Nobel Prize in 1904 for his work on digestion, but is best known for his studies on the conditioned reflex. He showed by experiment with dogs how the secretion of saliva can be stimulated not only by food but also by the sound of a bell associated with the presentation of food.

Pav•lo•va |päv'lōvə|, Anna (Pavlovna) (1881–1931) Russian dancer, resident in Britain from 1912. Her highly acclaimed solo dance *The Dying Swan* was created for her by Michel Fokine in 1905. On settling in Britain she formed her own company.

Pay•ton |'pātn|, Walter (1954–) U.S. football player. He set an NFL career rushing record with 16,726 yards.

Paz |päz|, Octavio (1914–98) Mexican poet and essayist. His poems reflect a preoccupation with Aztec mythology. He also wrote essays in response to the brutal suppression of student demonstrations in 1968. Nobel Prize for Literature (1990).

Pea•body |'pē,bädē|, Elizabeth Palmer (1804–94) U.S. education pioneer. Her Boston bookshop became a focus for Transcendentalist activities, including the publication of the *Dial*. She also published elementary textbooks and founded the first American kindergarten (1860).

Pea•body |'pē,bädē|, George (1795–1869) U.S. banker and philanthropist. He founded the U.S. Peabody Education Fund and a number of scientific museums (Yale, Harvard, Baltimore).

Peake |pēk|, Mervyn (Laurence) (1911–68) British novelist, poet, and artist, born in China. He is principally remembered for the trilogy comprising

Titus Groan (1946), *Gormenghast* (1950), and *Titus Alone* (1959).

Peale |pēl| American family of artists, including: **Charles Willson Peale** (1741–1827). He painted more than 1,000 portraits of prominent Americans, including the first known portrait of George Washington (1772). **Rembrandt Peale** (1778–1860), his son. He painted historical scenes and portraits of George Washington, Thomas Jefferson, and Napoleon Bonaparte.

Peale |pēl|, Norman Vincent (1898–1993) U.S. clergyman. He preached "applied Christianity," encouraging people to think positively. Notable books: *The Art of Living* (1937) and *The Power of Positive Thinking* (1952).

Pearl |pərl|, Minnie (1912–96) U.S. comedian and country music singer. Born *Sarah Ophelia Colley Cannon*. She was a Grand Ole Opry star who made recordings and television appearances.

Pears |perz|, Sir Peter (1910–86) English operatic tenor. In his lifelong partnership with Benjamin Britten he performed the title roles in all of Britten's operas and with Britten cofounded the Aldeburgh Festival in 1948.

Pear·son |'pirsən|, Lester Bowles (1897–1972) Canadian diplomat and Liberal statesman, prime minister (1963–68). As secretary of state for External Affairs (1948–57) he acted as a mediator in the resolution of the Suez crisis (1956). Nobel Peace Prize (1957).

Pea·ry |'pirē|, Robert Edwin (1856–1920) U.S. explorer. He made eight Arctic voyages before becoming the first person to reach the North Pole, on April 6, 1909.

Peck |pek|, (Eldred) Gregory (1916–) U.S. actor. Peck won an Oscar for his role as the lawyer Atticus in the movie of the novel *To Kill a Mockingbird* (1962).

Peck·ham |'pekəm|, Rufus Wheeler (1838–1909) U.S. Supreme Court justice (1896–1909).

Peel |pēl|, Sir Robert (1788–1850) British Conservative statesman, prime minister (1834–35 and 1841–46). As home secretary (1828–30) he established (in the UK) the Metropolitan Police (hence the nicknames *bobby* and *peeler*). His repeal of the Corn Laws in 1846 split the Conservatives and forced his resignation.

Peerce |pirs|, Jan (1904–84) U.S. operatic tenor. Born *Jacob Pincus Perelmuth*. He was a regular soloist with Toscanini at Radio City Music Hall, and he sang with the Metropolitan Opera for 26 seasons beginning in 1941, as well as in films and on Broadway.

Peg·ler |'peglər|, (James) Westbrook (1894–1969) U.S. journalist. He wrote a syndicated column (Pulitzer Prize, 1941).

Pei |pā|, I. M. (1917–) U.S. architect, born in China. Full name *Iwoh Ming Pei*. He designed monumental public buildings, including the East Wing of the National Gallery of Art in Washington, D.C., and the Pyramid at the Louvre in Paris.

Pei·erls, Sir Rudolf Ernst (1907–95) British physicist, born in Germany. On staff at the Los Alamos National Laboratory, with Otto Frisch he was the first physicist to calculate that an atomic bomb could be made.

Peirce |pirs|, Charles Sanders (1839–1914) U.S. philosopher and logician. A founder of American pragmatism, he argued that the meaning of a belief is to be understood by the actions and uses to which it gives rise.

Pei·sis·tra·tus variant spelling of PISISTRATUS.

Pe·la·gius |pə'lāj(ē)əs| (*c.* 360–*c.* 420) British monk. He denied the doctrines of original sin and predestination, defending innate human goodness and free will. His beliefs were opposed by St. Augustine of Hippo and condemned as heretical by the Synod of Carthage in about 418.

Pe·lé |'pā,lā| (1940–) Brazilian soccer player; born *Edson Arantes do Nascimento*. Regarded as one of the greatest goalscorers of all time, he ended his career with the New York Cosmos (1975–77), and is credited with over 1,200 goals in first-class soccer.

Pel·ham |'peləm|, Henry (1696–1754) British Whig statesman, prime minister (1743–54).

Pelle·tier |ˌpel'tyā; ˌpelə'tir|, Pierre-Joseph (1788–1842) French chemist.

With his friend **Joseph-Bienaimé Caventou** (1795–1877), he isolated a number of alkaloids for the first time. Pelletier and Caventou also isolated the green pigment of leaves and gave it the name *chlorophyll*.

Pel·li |'pelē|, Cesar (1926–) U.S. architect. Notable designs: the World Financial Center and Carnegie Hall Tower (New York).

Pem·ber·ton |'pembərtən|, John Stith (1831–1888) U.S. inventor. He invented the soft drink Coca-Cola.

Pen·de·rec·ki |ˌpendə'retskē|, Krzysztof (1933–) Polish composer. His music frequently features sounds drawn from extramusical sources and note clusters, as in his *Threnody for the Victims of Hiroshima* (1960) for fifty-two strings. Notable religious works: *Stabat Mater* (1962) and *Polish Requiem* (1980–4).

Pen·der·gast |'pendərˌgæst|, Thomas Joseph (1872–1945) U.S. politician. A supporter of Harry Truman, he was the acknowledged Democratic boss of Kansas City and Missouri.

Pen·field |'penˌfēld|, Wilder Graves (1891–1976) Canadian neurologist. He devised a surgical method for treating epilepsy.

Penn |pen|, William (1644–1718) English Quaker, founder of Pennsylvania. Having been imprisoned in 1668 for his Quaker writings, he successfully petitioned King Charles II for a grant of land in North America to repay a debt. He founded the colony of Pennsylvania as a sanctuary for Quakers and other Nonconformists in 1682.

Pen·ney |'penē|, James Cash (1875–1971) U.S. businessman. He developed the J. C. Penney department store chain and served as the company's president (1913–17) and chairman (1917–46).

Pe·pin III |'pepin| (c. 714–768) King of the Franks (751–768). Called **Pepin the Short**. He founded the Carolingian dynasty (751) and was the father of Charlemagne.

Pep·per |'pepər|, Art, Jr. (1925–82) U.S. jazz alto saxophonist. Born *Arthur Edward Pepper, Jr.* He toured with Stan Kenton (1946–51) and was associated with "West Coast jazz."

Pep·per·rell |'pepərəl|, Sir William

(1696–1759) American jurist and naval hero. A Maine fish and lumber merchant, he was a hero in King George's War (1744).

Pepys |pēps|, Samuel (1633–1703) English diarist and naval administrator. He is particularly remembered for his *Diary* (1660–9), which describes events such as the Great Plague and the Fire of London.

Per·ce·val |'pərsəvəl|, Spencer (1762–1812) British Tory statesman, prime minister (1809–12). He was shot dead in the lobby of the House of Commons by a bankrupt merchant who blamed the government for his insolvency.

Per·cy |'pərsē|, Sir Henry (1364–1403) English soldier; known as **Hotspur** or **Harry Hotspur**. Son of the 1st Earl of Northumberland, he was killed at the battle of Shrewsbury during his father's revolt against Henry IV.

Per·cy |'pərsē|, Walker (1916–90) U.S. author. Notable works: *The Moviegoer* (1961, National Book Award).

Per·due |ˌpər'do͞o|, Frank (1920–) U.S. entrepreneur. He founded Perdue Farms, a company that raises and markets chickens.

Pe·rei·ra |pə'rerə|, William (1909–85) U.S. architect. Notable designs: Los Angeles International Airport and the Transamerica Building (San Francisco).

Pe·rel·man |'pər(ə)lmən|, S. J. (1904–79) U.S. humorist and writer; full name *Sidney Joseph Perelman*. In the early 1930s he worked in Hollywood as a scriptwriter, and from 1934 his name is linked with the *New Yorker* magazine, for which he wrote most of his short stories and sketches.

Pe·res |pə'rez|, Shimon (1923–) Polish-born Israeli statesman, prime minister (1984–86 and 1995–96); Polish name *Szymon Perski*. As foreign minister under Yitzhak Rabin he played a major role in negotiating the PLO–Israeli peace accord (1993). Nobel Peace Prize (1994), shared with Rabin and PLO leader Yasser Arafat.

Pé·rez de Cué·llar |'perez də 'kweyär|, Javier (1920–) Peruvian diplomat and secretary general of the United Nations 1982–91.

Per·i·cles |'perə,klēz| (c. 495–429 BC) Athenian statesman and general. A champion of Athenian democracy, he pursued an imperialist policy and masterminded Athenian strategy in the Peloponnesian War. He commissioned the building of the Parthenon in 447 and promoted the culture of Athens in a golden age that produced such figures as Aeschylus, Socrates, and Phidias.

Per·kin |'pərkən|, Sir William Henry (1838–1907) English chemist and pioneer of the synthetic organic chemical industry. He prepared and manufactured the first synthetic dyestuff, mauve, from aniline.

Per·kins |'pərkənz|, Carl (1932–98) U.S. singer and songwriter. A rockabilly artist, he wrote "Blue Suede Shoes."

Per·kins |'pərkənz|, Frances (1882–1965) U.S. public official. As U.S. secretary of labor (1933–45) and the first woman to hold a federal cabinet post, she promoted the adoption of the Social Security Act.

Per·kins |'pərkənz|, Max (1884–1947) U.S. editor. Full name *William Maxwell Evarts Perkins*. He was the intellectual champion and publisher of daring new writers, including F. Scott Fitzgerald and Ernest Hemingway.

Perl·man |'pərlmən|, Itzhak (1945–) Israeli violinist. He has appeared with most of the world's major orchestras and has won 6 Grammy awards.

Perl·man |'pərlmən|, Rhea (1948–) U.S. actress. She starred in the television series "Taxi" (1978–82) and "Cheers" (1982–93).

Perls |pərlz|, Fritz (1893–1970) U.S. psychiatrist, born in Germany. Born *Frederick Salomon Perls*. He was a founder and practitioner of Gestalt psychotherapy.

Pe·rón |pə'rōn| Argentinian political family, including: **Juan Domingo Perón** (1895–1974), soldier and statesman . He participated in the 1943 military coup and was later elected president (1946–55, 1973–74), winning popular support with his social reforms. The faltering economy and conflict with the Church led to his removal and exile. Perón returned to power in 1973, but died in office. **María Eva Duarte Ibar-**guren de Perón (1919–52), his second wife; known as **Evita**. A former actress, after her marriage in 1945 she became de facto minister of health and of labor until her death from cancer; her social reforms earned her great popularity with the poor.

Pe·rot |pə'rō|, H. Ross (1930–) U.S. businessman and politician. Full name *Henry Ross Perot*. He mounted a third-party candidacy for president of the U.S. in 1992.

Per·rault |pə'rō|, Charles (1628–1703) French writer. He is remembered for his *Mother Goose Tales* (1697), containing such fairy tales as "Sleeping Beauty," "Little Red Riding Hood," "Puss in Boots," and "Cinderella."

Per·rin |pə'ræN; 'perən|, Jean Baptiste (1870–1942) French physical chemist. He provided the definitive proof of the existence of atoms, proved that cathode rays are negatively charged, and investigated Brownian motion. Nobel Prize for Physics (1926).

Per·ry |'perē| Family of U.S naval officers, including: **Oliver Hazard Perry** (1785–1819) He built up and commanded the American fleet that fought the British on Lake Erie during the War of 1812. Upon defeating the British fleet (Sept. 10, 1813), he sent the dispatch to General William Henry Harrison, "We have met the enemy and they are ours." **Matthew Calbraith Perry** (1794–1858), his brother. He commanded (1837) the *Fulton*, the first steam vessel in the U.S. navy. He negotiated a treaty with Japan (signed 1854) that opened diplomatic relations and trade with the U.S.

Per·ry |'perē|, Bliss (1860–1954) U.S. educator, editor, and author. He edited *Atlantic Monthly* (1899–1909) and *The American Mind* (1912).

Per·ry |'perē|, Fred (1909–95) British-born U.S. tennis player; full name *Frederick John Perry*. His record of winning three consecutive singles titles at Wimbledon (1934–36) was unequaled until 1978.

Per·ry |'perē|, Harold R. (1916–91) U.S. religious leader. He became the first black American Roman Catholic bishop in the 20th century (1966).

Per·shing |'pərsHiNG; 'pərZHiNG |, John Joseph (1860–1948) U.S. army officer. Known as **Black Jack**. His early military years included active duty in Cuba (1898) and the Philippines (1899–1903). He led the force that pursued Pancho Villa into Mexico (1916–17) before becoming commander in chief of the American Expeditionary Forces (1917–19) in World War I. His Meuse-Argonne offensive (1918) led to the final collapse of the Germans. In 1919, he was named General of the Army and served as U.S. Army chief of staff (1921–24). His memoir, *My Experiences in the World War* (1931), won the Pulitzer Prize.

Perthes |pert |, Jacques Boucher de see BOUCHER DE PERTHES.

Pe·rutz |pə'rōōtz |, Max Ferdinand (1914–) British biochemist, born in Austria. He discovered the molecular structure of blood pigment; with John C. Kendrew, he won the 1962 Nobel Prize for Chemistry.

Pes·ci |'pesHē |, Joe (1943–) U.S. actor. Notable movies: *Good Fellas* (1990, Academy Award).

Pes·ta·loz·zi |ˌpestə'lawtsē |, Johann Heinrich (1746–1827) Swiss educational reformer. He pioneered education for poor children and had a major impact on the development of primary education.

Pé·tain |ˌpā'tæN |, (Henri) Philippe (1856–1951) French soldier and politician. He was the premier of the Fascist-dominated Vichy government in France (1940–44).

Pe·ter |'pētər |, St. (died *c.* 67) an Apostle. Born *Simon*. Peter ("stone") is the name given him by Jesus, signifying the rock on which he would establish his church. He is regarded by Roman Catholics as the first bishop of the church at Rome, where he is said to have been martyred in about AD 67. He is often represented as the keeper of the door of heaven. Feast day, June 29.

Pe·ter I |'pētər | (1672–1725) czar of Russia (1682–1725); known as **Peter the Great**. Peter modernized his armed forces before waging the Great Northern War (1700–21) and expanding his territory in the Baltic. His extensive administrative reforms were instrumental in transforming Russia into a significant European power. In 1703 he made the new city of St. Petersburg his capital.

Pe·ter the Hermit |ˌpētər | (*c.* 1050–1115) French monk. His preaching on the First Crusade was a rallying cry for thousands of peasants throughout Europe to journey to the Holy Land; most were massacred by the Turks in Asia Minor. Peter later became prior of an Augustinian monastery in Flanders.

Pe·ter·kin |'pētərkən |, Julia (Mood) (1880–1961) U.S. author. Notable works: *Scarlet Sister Mary* (1928, Pulitzer Prize).

Pe·ters |'pētərz |, Mike (1943–) U.S. editorial and political cartoonist. He created the comic "Mother Goose & Grimm."

Pe·ter·son |'pētərsən |, Charles Jacobs (1819–87) U.S. author and publisher. He founded *Ladies' National Magazine* (1842).

Pe·ter·son |'pētərsən |, Oscar (Emmanuel) (1925–) Canadian jazz pianist and composer. He became internationally famous in the 1960s, often appearing with Ella Fitzgerald.

Pe·ter·son |'pētərsən |, Roger Tory (1908–96) U.S. ornithologist and artist. Peterson produced his first book for identifying birds in the field in 1934, introducing the concept of illustrating similar birds in similar postures with their differences highlighted. The format of his field guides has become standard in field guides for all groups of animals and plants.

Pe·ti·pa |ˌpā'tēpə |, Marius (Ivanovich) (1818–1910) French ballet dancer and choreographer, resident in Russia from 1847. Petipa choreographed more than fifty ballets, working with Tchaikovsky on *Sleeping Beauty* (1890) and *The Nutcracker* (1892).

Pe·trarch |'peˌträrk | (1304–74) Italian poet; Italian name *Francesco Petrarca*. His reputation is chiefly based on the *Canzoniere* (*c.* 1351–53), a sonnet sequence in praise of a woman he calls Laura.

Pe·trie |'pētrē |, Sir (William Matthew) Flinders (1853–1942) English archaeologist and Egyptologist. He began excavating the Great Pyramid in 1880.

Petrie was the first to establish the system of sequence dating, now standard archaeological practice, by which sites are excavated layer by layer and historical chronology determined by the dating of artefacts found *in situ*.

Pe•tro•ni•us |pə'trōnēəs|, Gaius (died AD 66) Roman writer; known as **Petronius Arbiter**. Petronius is generally accepted as the author of the *Satyricon*, a work in prose and verse satirizing the excesses of Roman society.

Pe•try |'pētrē|, Ann (1908–   ) U.S. author. She was the first African-American woman author to receive broad critical acclaim. Notable works: *The Street* (1946).

Pet•ti•ford |'petəfərd|, Oscar (1922–60) U.S. jazz double bassist, cellist, and bandleader. He played with Dizzy Gillespie, Duke Ellington, and Woody Herman and is remembered for his lasting influence on bop style.

Pet•tit |'petət|, Bob (1932–   ) U.S. basketball player. Elected to the Basketball Hall of Fame (1970).

Pet•ty |'petē|, Richard (1937–   ) U.S. racecar driver. He was the first stock car driver to win $1 million in his career.

Pet•ty |'petē|, Tom (1952–   ) U.S. rock vocalist, composer, and guitarist. He formed his own band The Heartbreakers (1976); his solo releases include the album *Wildflowers* (1994).

Pevs•ner |'pevznər|, Antoine (1886–1962) Russian-born French sculptor and painter, brother of Naum Gabo. With his brother he was a founder of Russian constructivism; the theoretical basis of the movement was put forward in their *Realistic Manifesto* (1920).

Phei•dip•pi•des |fī'dipə,dēz| (5th century BC) Athenian messenger. He was sent to Sparta to ask for help after the Persian landing at Marathon in 490 and is said to have covered the 250 km (150 miles) in two days on foot.

Phid•i•as |'fidēəs| (5th century BC) Athenian sculptor. He is noted for the sculptures on the Parthenon (the Elgin marbles) and his vast statue of Zeus at Olympia (*c*.430), which was one of the Seven Wonders of the Ancient World.

Phil•by |'filbē|, Kim (1912–88) British Foreign Office official and spy; born

Harold Adrian Russell Philby. While working at the British Embassy in Washington, DC (1949–51), Philby was asked to resign on suspicion of being a Soviet agent. He defected to the USSR in 1963 and was officially revealed to have spied for the Soviets from 1933.

Phil•ip[1] |'filəp|, St. an Apostle. He is commemorated with St. James the Less on May 1.

Phil•ip[2] |'filəp|, St. deacon of the early Christian Church; known as **St. Philip the Evangelist**. He was one of seven deacons appointed to superintend the secular business of the Church at Jerusalem (Acts 6:5–6). Feast day, June 6.

Phil•ip[3] |'filəp| the name of five kings of ancient Macedonia, notably: **Philip II** (382–336 BC; reigned 359–336 BC), father of Alexander the Great; he reigned and was known as **Philip II of Macedon**. He unified and expanded ancient Macedonia as well as carrying out a number of army reforms. His victory over Athens and Thebes at the battle of Chaeronea in 338 established his hegemony over Greece. **Philip V** (238–179 BC; reigned 221–179 BC). His expansionist policies led to a series of confrontations with Rome, culminating in his defeat and resultant loss of control over Greece.

Phil•ip[4] |'filəp| the name of six kings of France: **Philip I** (1052–1108; reigned 1059–1108). **Philip II** (1165–1223; reigned 1180–1223), son of Louis VII; known as **Philip Augustus**. After mounting a series of campaigns against the English kings Henry II, Richard I, and John, Philip succeeded in regaining Normandy (1204), Anjou (1204), and most of Poitou (1204–05). **Philip III** (1245–1285; reigned 1270–85), known as **Philip the Bold**. **Philip IV** (1268–1314; reigned 1285–1314), son of Philip III; known as **Philip the Fair**. He continued to extend French dominions, waging wars with England (1294–1303) and Flanders (1302–05). **Philip V** (1294–1322; reigned 1316–1322), known as **Philip the Tall**. **Philip VI** (1293–1350; reigned 1328–50); known as **Philip of Valois**. The founder of the Valois dynasty, Philip came to the throne on the death of Charles IV, whose only child, a girl, was barred from ruling. His claim was challenged by Edward III of England; the dispute developed into the Hundred Years War.

Phil·ip[5] |'filəp| the name of five kings of Spain: **Philip I** (1478–1506; reigned 1504–06); known as **Philip the Handsome**. Son of the Holy Roman Emperor Maximilian I, in 1496 Philip married the infanta Joanna, daughter of Ferdinand of Aragon and Isabella of Castile. After Isabella's death he ruled Castile jointly with Joanna, establishing the Hapsburgs as the ruling dynasty in Spain. **Philip II** (1527–98; reigned 1556–98), son of Charles I (Holy Roman Emperor Charles V). Philip came to the throne following his father's abdication. His reign was dominated by an anti-Protestant crusade that exhausted the Spanish economy. **Philip III** (1578–1621; reigned 1598–1621). **Philip IV** (1605–1665; reigned 1621–1665). **Philip V** (1683–1746; reigned 1700–24 and 1724–46), grandson of Louis XIV. The selection of Philip as successor to Charles II, and Louis XIV's insistence that Philip remain an heir to the French throne, gave rise to War of the Spanish Succession (1701–14). In 1724 Philip abdicated in favor of his son Louis I, but returned to the throne following Louis's death.

Phil·ip[6] |'filəp|, Prince (1921–) Duke of Edinburgh and husband of Elizabeth II. The son of Prince Andrew of Greece and Denmark, he married Princess Elizabeth in 1947; on the eve of his marriage he was created Duke of Edinburgh.

Phil·ip Au·gus·tus |'filəp ə'gəstəs| Philip II of France (see PHILIP[4]).

Phil·ip the Bold Philip III of France (see PHILIP[4]).

Phil·ip the Fair Philip IV of France (see PHILIP[4]).

Phil·ip the Handsome Philip I of Spain (see PHILIP[5]).

Phil·ip the Tall Philip V of France (see PHILIP[4]).

Phil·ip of Valois |väl'wä| Philip VI of France (see PHILIP[4]).

Phil·lips |'filəps| U.S. entrepreneurs: Brothers **Frank Phillips** (1873–1950) and **Lee Eldas Phillips** (1876–1944) founded Phillips Petroleum Co.

Phil·lips |'filəps|, David Graham (1867–1911) U.S. journalist and novelist. His novels were written to expose corruption and other evils. Notable works: *Susan Lenox* (1917).

Phil·lips |'filəps|, Samuel (1752–1802) U.S. industrialist and political leader. He manufactured gunpowder for the Continental army and founded Phillips Academy at Andover (1778), the first endowed academy in America.

Phi·lo Ju·dae·us |'fīlō jŏŏ'dāəs| (c. 15 BC–c. 50 AD) Jewish philosopher of Alexandria. He is particularly known for his commentaries on the Pentateuch (written in Greek), which he interpreted allegorically in the light of Platonic and Aristotelian philosophy.

Phiz |fiz| (1815–82) English illustrator; pseudonym of *Hablot Knight Browne*. He illustrated many of Dickens's works, including *Martin Chuzzlewit, Pickwick Papers*, and *Bleak House*. He took his pseudonym to complement Dickens's "Boz."

Phoe·nix |'fēniks|, River (1970–93) U.S. actor.

Pho·ti·us |'fōtēəs| (c. 820–c. 891) Byzantine scholar and patriarch of Constantinople. His most important work is the *Bibliotheca*, a critical account of 280 earlier prose works and an invaluable source of information about many works now lost.

Phyfe |fīf|, Duncan (1768–1854) U.S. cabinetmaker, born in Scotland. He made chairs, sofas, and tables noted for their graceful proportions with simple ornaments precisely carved.

Piaf |'pēäf|, Edith (1915–63) French singer, cabaret artiste, and songwriter. Born *Edith Giovanna Gassion*; known as **The Kid**. She gained international fame with her songs of tragic love affairs.

Pia·get |ˌpēä'zнä|, Jean (1896–1980) Swiss psychologist. Piaget's work on the intellectual and logical abilities of children provided the single biggest impact on the study of the development of human thought processes. He described the mind as proceeding through a series of fixed stages of cognitive development, each being a prerequisite for the next.

Pi·cas·so |pə'käsō|, Pablo (1881–1973) Spanish painter, sculptor, and graphic artist, resident in France from 1904. His prolific inventiveness and technical versatility made him the dominant figure in avant-garde art in the first half of the 20th century. Following his Blue Period (1901–04) and Rose Period (1905–06), *Les Demoiselles d'Avignon* (1907) signaled his development of cubism (1908–14). In the 1920s and 1930s he adopted a neoclassical figurative style and produced semisurrealist paintings using increasingly violent imagery, notably *The Three Dancers* (1935) and *Guernica* (1937).

Pi•cas•so |pə'käsō|, Paloma (1949–) French jewelry designer. She is the daughter of Pablo Picasso.

Pick•er•ing |'pik(ə)riNG|, John (1777– 1846) U.S. linguist and lexicographer. The son of Timothy Pickering, he wrote the first dictionary of Americanisms.

Pick•er•ing |'pik(ə)riNG|, Timothy (1745–1829) U.S. government official. He was the U.S. secretary of war (1795) and secretary of state (1795–1800) as well as a member of the U.S. Senate (1803–11) and House of Representatives (1813–17).

Pick•er•ing |'pik(ə)riNG|, William Hayward (1910–) New Zealand-born U.S. engineer, director of the Jet Propulsion Laboratory (JPL) at the California Institute of Technology (1954–76). During his directorate the JPL launched America's first satellite, Explorer I (1958), and several unmanned probes to the moon and planets.

Pick•ett |'pikət|, George Edward (1825–75) U.S. army officer. Last in his class at West Point (1846), he became distinguished as a Confederate general during the Civil War. His military reputation was marred at Gettysburg (1863) when, under orders, he led a disastrous charge ("Pickett's Charge") across an open field.

Pick•ett |'pikət|, Wilson (1941–) U.S. soul-rock singer and songwriter. Notable songs: "In the Midnight Hour."

Pick•ford |'pikfərd|, Mary (1893–1979) Canadian-born U.S. actress; born *Gladys Mary Smith*. She was a star of silent movies, usually playing the innocent young heroine, as *Rebecca of Sunnybrook Farm* (1917), *Pollyanna* (1920).

She won an Academy Award for *Coquette* (1929). She also cofounded United Artists (1919).

Pierce |pirs|, Franklin (1804–69) see box. **Jane Means Appleton Pierce** (1806–63), wife of Franklin Pierce and U.S. first lady (1853–57).

Pier•cy |'pirsē|, Marge (1936–) U.S. author. Notable works: *City of Darkness, City of Light* (1996).

Pie•ro del•la Fran•ces•ca |'pyerō ˌdelə frän'CHeskə| (*c.* 1420–92) Italian painter. He used perspective, proportion, and geometrical relationships to create ordered and harmonious pictures in which the figures appear to inhabit real space. He is best known for his fres-

---

Pierce, Franklin
14th U.S. president

Life dates: 1804–1869
Place of birth: Hillsborough (now Hillsboro), New Hampshire
Mother: Anna Kendrick Pierce
Father: General Benjamin Pierce
Wife: Jane Means Appleton Pierce
Children: Franklin (died 3 days after birth), Frank, Benjamin
College/University: Bowdoin College
Military service: U.S. Army brigadier general, Mexican War
Career: lawyer
Political career: New Hampshire state legislature; U.S. House of Representatives; U.S. Senate; president
Party: Democratic
Home state: New Hampshire
Opponents in presidential race: Winfield Scott
Term of office: March 4, 1853–March 3, 1857
Vice president: William R. D. King
Notable events of presidency: Tariff Act of 1857; civil war in Kansas; first U.S. World's Fair; Ostend Manifesto; Gadsden Purchase; Treaty of Kanagawa; Republican Party formed; Japanese ports opened to American trade; Kansas-Nebraska Act
Other achievements: Admitted to the New Hampshire bar; declined appointment as U.S. attorney general under President Polk; member and president, New Hampshire Fifth State Constitutional Convention
Place of burial: Concord, N.H.

coes, notably a cycle in Arezzo depicting the story of the True Cross (begun 1452).

Pike |pīk|, Zebulon Montgomery (1779–1813) U.S. explorer. He led expeditions to the Louisiana Purchase region; Pike's Peak, Colorado, is named for him although he never climbed it.

Pi•late |'pīlət|, Pontius (died *c.* 36 AD) Roman procurator of Judaea *c.*26–*c.*36. He is remembered for presiding at the trial of Jesus Christ and authorizing his crucifixion.

Pills•bury |'pilz,berē|, Charles Alfred (1842–99) U.S. businessman. He began as a small flour miller in Minneapolis (1869) and became the largest flour producer in the world (1889).

Pin•cay |pin'kī|, Laffit, Jr. (1946–) U.S. jockey.

Pin•chot |'pinSHŌ|, Gifford (1865–1946) U.S. forester. He was the first professional American forester and a leader in the land conservation movement; he was also governor of Pennsylvania (1923–27, 1931–35).

Pinck•ney |'piNGknē| U.S. political family, including: **Charles Cotesworth Pinckney** (1746–1825). A Federalist, he ran unsuccessfully for U.S. vice president (1800) and president (1804, 1808). **Thomas Pinckney** (1750–1828, brother of Charles Cotesworth Pinckney. As Washington's minister to England (1792–96) he negotiated Pinckney's Treaty with Spain. **Charles Pinckney** (1757–1824), cousin of Thomas and Charles Cotesworth Pinckney. He was governor of South Carolina (1789–92, 1796–98, 1806–08) and a U.S. Senator (1819–21).

Pin•dar |'pin,där| (*c.* 518–*c.* 438 BC) Greek lyric poet. He is famous for his odes (the *Epinikia*), which celebrate victories in athletic contests at Olympia and elsewhere and relate them to religious and moral themes.

Pi•ne•ro |pi'nerō|, Sir Arthur Wing (1855–1934) English dramatist and actor. Notable works: *The Second Mrs. Tanqueray* (1893).

Pin•ker•ton |'piNGkərtən|, Allan (1819–84) Scottish-born U.S. detective. In 1850 he established the first American private detective agency, be-

coming famous after solving a series of train robberies. He served as *Dandy Dick* (1887). From 1889 he embarked on a number of serious plays dealing with social issues, especially the double standards of morality for men and women.

Pink•ham |'piNGkəm|, Lydia (1819–83) U.S. inventor and saleswoman. She concocted and marketed Mrs. Lydia E. Pinkham's Vegetable Compound, a patented herbal medicine for female complaints (1865).

Pi•no•chet |,pēnō'SHā|, Augusto (1915–) Chilean general and statesman, president (1974–90); full name *Augusto Pinochet Ugarte.* Having masterminded the military coup that overthrew President Allende in 1973, he imposed a military dictatorship until forced to call elections, giving way to a democratically elected president in 1990.

Pin•sky |'pinskē|, Robert (1940–) U.S. author, educator and poet. Notable works: *Sadness and Happiness* (1975) and *The Sounds of Poetry* (1997).

Pin•ter |'pintər|, Harold (1930–) English dramatist, actor, and director. His plays are associated with the Theatre of the Absurd and are typically marked by a sense of menace. Notable plays: *The Birthday Party* (1958), *The Caretaker* (1960), and *Party Time* (1991).

Pin•za |'pinzə|, Ezio (1892–1957) Italian operatic bass. He performed with the Metropolitan Opera for 22 years beginning in 1926 and was responsible for the return of Mozart's operas to the Met repertory by mid-century.

Pi•per |'pīpər|, John (1903–92) English painter and decorative designer. He is best known for his watercolors and aquatints of buildings and for his stained glass in Coventry and Llandaff cathedrals.

Pip•pen |'pipən|, Scottie (1965–) U.S. basketball player.

Pi•ran•del•lo |,pirən'delō|, Luigi (1867–1936) Italian dramatist and novelist. His plays, including *Six Characters in Search of an Author* (1921) and *Henry IV* (1922), challenged the conventions of naturalism. Notable novels: *The Outcast* (1901) and *The Late Mattia Pascal*

(1904). Nobel Prize for Literature (1934).

Pi•ra•ne•si |ˌpirə'nāzi|, Giovanni Battista (1720–78) Italian engraver. Notable works: *Prisons* (1745–61).

Pir•sig |'pərsig|, Robert Maynard (1928–) U.S. author. Notable works: *Zen and the Art of Motorcycle Maintenance* (1974).

Pi•san |'pēzän|, Christine de see DE PISAN.

Pi•sa•no[1] |pi'zänō| Italian sculptors: **Andrea** (*c*.1290–*c*.1348) and **Nino**, his son (died *c*.1368). Andrea created the earliest pair of bronze doors for the baptistery at Florence (completed 1336). Nino was one of the earliest to specialize in free-standing life-size figures.

Pi•sa•no[2] |pi'zänō| two Italian sculptors: **Nicola** (*c*.1220–*c*.1278) and his son **Giovanni** (*c*.1250–*c*.1314). Nicola's work departed from medieval conventions and signaled a revival of interest in classical sculpture. His most famous works are the pulpits in the baptistery at Pisa and in Siena cathedral. Giovanni's works include the richly decorated facade of Siena cathedral.

Pi•sis•tra•tus |pə'sistrətəs| (*c*. 600–*c*. 527 BC) Also **Peisistratus**. Tyrant of Athens. He seized power in 561 and after twice being expelled ruled continuously from 546 until his death. He reduced aristocratic power in rural Attica and promoted the financial prosperity and cultural pre-eminence of Athens.

Pis•sar•ro |pi'särō|, Camille (1830–1903) French painter and graphic artist. He was a leading figure of the Impressionist movement, typically painting landscapes and cityscapes. He also experimented with pointillism in the 1880s.

Pit•man |'pitmən|, Sir Isaac (1813–97) English inventor of a shorthand system, published as *Stenographic Sound Hand* (1837). Pitman shorthand is still widely used.

Pit•ney |'pitnē|, Mahlon (1858–1924) U.S. Supreme Court justice (1912–22).

Pitt |pit| the name of two British statesmen: **William**, 1st Earl of Chatham (1708–78); known as **Pitt the Elder**. As Secretary of State (effectively Prime Minister), he headed coalition govern-

ments 1756–61 and 1766–68. He brought the Seven Years War to an end in 1763 and also masterminded the conquest of French possessions overseas, particularly in Canada and India. **William** (1759–1806), Prime Minister 1783–1801 and 1804–06, the son of Pitt the Elder; known as **Pitt the Younger**. The youngest-ever Prime Minister, he introduced financial reforms to reduce the national debt.

Pitt |pit|, Brad (1963–) U.S. actor. He starred in the movie *Seven Years in Tibet* (1997).

Pitt-Rivers |ˌpit 'rivərz|, Augustus Henry Lane Fox (1827–1900) English archaeologist and anthropologist. He developed a new scientific approach to archaeology. His collection of weapons and artifacts from different cultures formed the basis of the ethnological museum in Oxford that bears his name.

Pi•us XII |'pīəs| (1876–1958) pope 1939–58; born *Eugenio Pacelli*. He upheld the neutrality of the Roman Catholic Church during World War II, and was criticized after the war for failing to condemn Nazi atrocities.

Pi•zan, Christine de see DE PISAN.

Pi•zar•ro |pi'zärō|, Francisco (*c*. 1475–1541) Spanish conquistador. He defeated the Inca empire of Peru and in 1533 set up a puppet monarchy at Cuzco, building his own capital at Lima (1535), where he was assassinated.

Planck |pläNGk|, Max (Karl Ernst Ludwig) (1858–1947) German theoretical physicist who founded quantum theory, announcing the radiation law named after him in 1900. Nobel Prize for Physics (1918).

Plank |plæNGk|, Charles J. (1915–89) U.S. inventor, born in India. With Edward Rosinski he developed the first commercially useful zeolite catalyst in the petroleum industry.

Plante |plænt|, Jacques (1929–86) Canadian hockey player. He was the first goalie to wear a mask during games. Elected to the Hockey Hall of Fame (1978).

Plath |plæTH|, Sylvia (1932–63) U.S. poet, wife of Ted Hughes. Her work is notable for its treatment of extreme and painful states of mind. In 1963 she committed suicide. Notable works: *Ariel* (poems, 1965) and *The Bell Jar* (novel, 1963).

Pla·to |'plātō| (*c.* 429–*c.* 347 BC) Greek philosopher. A disciple of Socrates and the teacher of Aristotle, he founded the Academy in Athens. An integral part of his thought is the theory of "ideas" or "forms," in which abstract entities or *universals* are contrasted with their objects or *particulars* in the material world. His philosophical writings are presented in the form of dialogues, with Socrates as the principal speaker; they include the *Symposium* and the *Timaeus*. Plato's political theories appear in the *Republic*, in which he explored the nature and structure of a just society.

Plau·tus |'plawtəs|, Titus Maccius (*c.* 250–184 BC) Roman comic dramatist. His plays, such as *Rudens*, are modeled on Greek New Comedy.

Play·er |'plāər|, Gary (1935–) South African golfer. He has won numerous championships including the British Open (1959; 1968; 1974), the Masters (1961; 1974; 1978), the PGA (1962; 1972), and the U.S. Open (1965).

Play·fair |'plā,fer|, John (1748–1819) Scottish mathematician and geologist. A friend of James Hutton, he summarized the latter's views for a wider readership in his *Illustrations of the Huttonian Theory of the Earth* (1802).

Plimp·ton |'plimptən|, George Ames (1927–) U.S. author, editor, and television host. He was editor in chief of *Paris Review* (1953–), a contributor to *Sports Illustrated* (1968–), and editor of *Writers at Work*.

Pliny[1] |'plinē| (23–79) Roman statesman and scholar; Latin name *Gaius Plinius Secundus*; known as **Pliny the Elder**. His *Natural History* (77) is a vast encyclopedia of the natural and human worlds. He died while observing the eruption of Vesuvius.

Pliny[2] |'plinē| (*c.* 61–*c.* 112) Roman senator and writer, nephew of Pliny the Elder; Latin name *Gaius Plinius Caecilius Secundus*; known as **Pliny the Younger**. He is noted for his books of letters, which deal with both public and private affairs and which include a de-

scription of the eruption of Vesuvius in 79.

Plo·ti·nus |plə'tīnəs| (*c.* 205–70) philosopher, probably of Roman descent. He was the founder and leading exponent of Neoplatonism; his writings were published after his death by his pupil Porphyry.

Plum·mer |'pləmər|, (Arthur) Christopher (Orme) (1929–) U.S. actor, born in Canada. His award-winning stage, television, and film credits include the movie *The Sound of Music* (1965, Academy Award).

Plu·tarch |'ploo͞,tärk| (*c.* 46–*c.* 120) Greek biographer and philosopher; Latin name *Lucius Mestrius Plutarchus*. He is chiefly known for *Parallel Lives*, a collection of biographies of prominent Greeks and Romans.

Po·ca·hon·tas |'pōkə'häntəs| (*c.* 1595–1617) American Indian, daughter of Powhatan, an Algonquian chief in Virginia. According to John Smith, Pocahontas rescued him from death at the hands of her father. In 1612 she was seized as a hostage by the English, and she later married colonist John Rolfe.

Pod·ho·retz |päd'hawrəts|, Norman (1930–) U.S. literary critic. The editor of *Commentary* (1960–), he authored *The Bloody Crossroads: Where Literature and Politics Meet* (1986).

Poe |pō|, Edgar Allan (1809–49) U.S. short-story writer, poet, and critic. His fiction and poetry are Gothic in style and characterized by their exploration of the macabre and the grotesque. Notable works: "The Fall of the House of Usher" (short story, 1840), "The Murders in the Rue Morgue" (detective story, 1841), and "The Raven" (poem, 1845).

Poin·ca·ré |,pwænkä'rā|, Jules-Henri (1854–1912) French mathematician and philosopher of science, who transformed celestial mechanics and was one of the pioneers of algebraic topology. He proposed a relativistic philosophy which implied the absolute velocity of light, which nothing could exceed.

Pois·son |,pwä'sōN|, Siméon-Denis (1781–1840) French mathematical physicist. His major contributions were in probability theory, in which he greatly improved Laplace's work and developed several concepts that are now named after him.

Poi·tier |'pwätē,ā|, Sidney (1924–) U.S. actor and movie director, the first black American actor to achieve superstar status. Notable movies: *Lilies of the Field* (1963) and *In the Heat of the Night* (1967).

Po·lan·ski |pə'lænskē|, Roman (1933–) French movie director, of Polish descent. His second wife, the actress **Sharon Tate** (1943–69), was one of the victims of a multiple murder by followers of the cult leader Charles Manson. Notable movies: *Rosemary's Baby* (1968) and *Chinatown* (1974).

Polk |pōk|, James Knox (1795–1849) see box. **Sarah Childress Polk** (1803–91), wife of James Knox Polk and U.S. first lady (1845–49).

Pol·lack |'pälək|, Sydney (1934–) U.S. television and movie director. Notable movies: *The Way We Were* (1973), *Three Days of the Condor* (1975), and *Out of Africa* (1985, Academy Award).

Pol·lai·uo·lo |ˌpōlī'wōlō| Italian sculptors, painters, and engravers: **Antonio** (c.1432–98) and **Piero** (1443–96). Both brothers worked on the monuments to Popes Sixtus IV and Innocent VIII in St. Peter's, and Antonio is particularly known for his realistic depiction of the human form.

Pol·lock |'pälək|, (Paul) Jackson (1912–56) U.S. painter. He was a leading figure in the abstract expressionist movement and from 1947 became the chief exponent of the style known as action painting. Fixing the canvas to the floor or wall, he poured, splashed, or dripped paint on it, covering the whole canvas and avoiding any point of emphasis in the picture.

Po·lo |'pōlō|, Marco see MARCO POLO.

Pol Pot |ˌpōl 'pät; ˌpäl 'pät| (1925–98) Cambodian communist leader of the Khmer Rouge, prime minister (1976–79); born *Saloth Sar*. During his regime the Khmer Rouge embarked on a brutal reconstruction program in which millions of Cambodians were killed. Overthrown in 1979, Pol Pot led the Khmer Rouge in a guerrilla war against the new Vietnamese-backed government. In 1997 he was denounced by the

---

Polk, James Knox
11th U.S. president

Life dates: 1795–1849
Place of birth: near Pineville, Mecklenburg County, North Carolina
Mother: Jane Knox Polk
Father: Samuel Polk
Wife: Sarah Childress Polk
Children: none
College/University: University of North Carolina
Career: lawyer
Political career: Tennessee state legislature; U.S. House of Representatives; Speaker of the House; governor of Tennessee; president
Party: Democratic
Home state: Tennessee
Opponent in presidential race: Henry Clay
Term of office: March 4, 1845–March 3, 1849
Vice president: George M. Dallas
Notable events of presidency: U.S. Naval Academy opened; Elias Howe patented sewing machine; Mexican War; California Gold Rush; Women's Rights Convention, Seneca Falls, New York; Oregon admitted as a territory; Department of Interior created; Texas, Iowa, and Wisconsin admitted as 28th, 29th, and 30th states
Other achievements: Admitted to the Tennessee bar
Place of burial: Polk Place, Nashville, Tennessee

Khmer Rouge and put under house arrest.

Po·lyb·i·us |pə'libēəs| (c. 200–c. 118 BC) Greek historian His forty books of *Histories* (only partially extant) chronicled the rise of the Roman Empire from 220 to 146 BC.

Pol·y·carp |'pälē,kärp|, St. (c. 69–c. 155) Greek bishop of Smyrna in Asia Minor. The leading Christian figure in Smyrna, he was arrested during a pagan festival, refused to recant his faith, and was burned to death. Feast day, February 23.

Pol·y·cli·tus |ˌpälē'klītəs| (5th century BC) Greek sculptor, known for his statues of idealized male athletes. Two Roman copies of his works survive, the *Doryphoros* (spear-bearer) and the *Diad-*

umenos (youth fastening a band around his head).

Pom·pa·dour |ˌpämpə'dawr|, Jeanne Antoinette Poisson, Marquise de (1721–64) French noblewoman; known as **Madame de Pompadour**. In 1744 she became the mistress of Louis XV, gaining considerable influence at court, but she later became unpopular as a result of her interference in political affairs.

Pom·pey |'pämpē| (106–48 BC) Roman general and statesman; Latin name *Gnaeus Pompeius Magnus*; known as **Pompey the Great**. He founded the First Triumvirate, but later quarreled with Julius Caesar, who defeated him at the battle of Pharsalus. He then fled to Egypt, where he was murdered.

Pom·pi·dou |'pämpə,dōō|, Georges (Jean Raymond) (1911–74) French statesman, prime minister (1962–68) and president (1969–74). He was instrumental in ending the conflict in Algeria between French forces and nationalist guerrillas.

Ponce de Le·ón |ˌpän(t)s də 'lēän; ˌpän(t)sə ˌdā lē'ōn|, Juan (*c.* 1460–1521) Spanish explorer. He accompanied Columbus on his second voyage to the New World in 1493, became governor of Puerto Rico (1510–12), and landed on the coast of Florida near what became St. Augustine in 1513, claiming the area for Spain.

Pons |pänz|, Lily (1898–1976) U.S. operatic soprano, born in France. Born *Alice-Joséphine Pons*. She made her debut at the Metropolitan Opera in 1931 as Lucia in *Lucia de Lammermoor* and was the reigning diva at the Met for 25 years.

Pon·selle |pän'sel|, Rosa (1897–1981) U.S. operatic soprano. Born *Rosa Ponzillo*. She sang with the Metropolitan Opera for 19 seasons, beginning in 1918 with her debut as Leonora in *Fidelio*.

Pon·te |'pōntā|, Lorenzo Da see DA PONTE.

Pon·ti·ac |'pän(t)ē,æk| (*c.* 1720–69) Ottawa Indian chief. He is credited with organizing and leading a rebellion against the British, during which he led a year-long siege of Fort Detroit (1763–64). He agreed to terms of peace in 1766.

Pon·tor·mo |pawn'tawr,mō|, Jacopo da (1494–1557) Italian painter, whose use of dynamic composition, anatomical exaggeration, and bright colors placed him at the forefront of early mannerism.

Pope |pōp|, Alexander (1688–1744) English poet. A major figure of the Augustan age, he is famous for his caustic wit and metrical skill, in particular his use of the heroic couplet. Notable works: *The Rape of the Lock* (1712; enlarged 1714) and *An Essay on Man* (1733–34).

Pope |pōp|, John Russell (1874–1937) U.S. architect. Notable designs: the National Gallery (Washington D.C.).

Pop·per |'päpər|, Sir Karl Raimund (1902–94) Austrian-born British philosopher. In *The Logic of Scientific Discovery* (1934) he argued that scientific hypotheses can never be finally confirmed as true, but are tested by attempts to falsify them. In *The Open Society and its Enemies* (1945) he criticized the historicist social theories of Plato, Hegel, and Marx.

Por·phy·ry |'pawrfərē| (*c.* 232–303) Neoplatonist philosopher; born *Malchus*. He was a pupil of Plotinus, whose works he edited after the latter's death.

Porsche |'pawrSH(ə)|, Ferdinand (1875–1952) Austrian car designer. In 1934 he designed the Volkswagen ("people's car"), while his name has since become famous for the high-performance sports and racing cars produced by his company, originally his designs.

Por·sen·na |pawr'senə|, Lars (6th century BC) Also **Porsena**. A legendary Etruscan chieftain, king of the town of Clusium. Summoned by Tarquinius Superbus after the latter's overthrow and exile from Rome, Porsenna subsequently laid siege to the city but did not succeed in capturing it.

Por·ter |'pawrtər|, Cole (1891–1964) U.S. songwriter. He made his name with a series of Broadway musicals and also wrote songs for films, including *High Society* (1956). Notable songs: "Let's Do It," "Night and Day," and "Begin the Beguine." Notable musicals *Anything Goes* (1934) and *Kiss Me, Kate* (1948).

Por·ter |'pawrtər|, David (1780–1843)

U.S. military leader. He served in the wars against France (1799) and Tripoli (1801–05) and in the War of 1812; David Glasgow Farragut was his adopted son.

Por·ter |'pawrtər|, Katherine Anne (1890–1980) U.S. short-story writer and novelist. Notable works: *Pale Horse, Pale Rider* (short stories, 1939), *Ship of Fools* (novel, 1962), and *Collected Short Stories* (1965), for which she won a Pulitzer Prize.

Por·ter |'pawrtər|, Peter (Neville Frederick) (1929–) Australian poet, resident chiefly in England since 1951.

Por·tis |'pawrtəs|, Charles (McColl) (1933–) U.S. author. Notable works: *True Grit* (1968).

Post |pōst|, Charles W. (1854–1914) U.S. inventor. He invented a coffee substitute called Postum, Grape Nuts cereal, and other food products.

Post |pōst|, Emily (Price) (1873–1960) U.S. author. Notable works: *Etiquette* (1922).

Post |pōst|, George Brown (1837–1913) U.S. architect. Notable designs: the New York Stock Exchange and the Wisconsin State Capitol (Madison).

Post |pōst|, Wiley (1899–1935) U.S. aviator. He was the first man to fly solo around the world (1933).

Po·tok, Chaim (1929–) U.S. author and artist. Notable works: *The Chosen* (1967) and *The Gift of Asher Lev* (1991).

Pot·ter |'pätər|, (Helen) Beatrix (1866–1943) English writer for children. She is known for her series of animal stories, illustrated with her own delicate watercolors, which began with *The Tale of Peter Rabbit* (first published privately in 1900).

Pou·lenc |'pōōläNGk|, Francis (Jean Marcel) (1899–1963) French composer. He was a member of Les Six. His work is characterized by lyricism as well as the use of idioms of popular music such as jazz. His work includes songs and the ballet *Les Biches* (1923).

Pound |pownd|, Ezra (Weston Loomis) (1885–1972) U.S. poet and critic, resident in Europe 1908–45. Initially associated with imagism, he later developed a highly eclectic poetic voice, drawing on a vast range of classical and other references and establishing a reputation as a modernist poet. In 1945 he was charged with treason following his pro-Fascist radio broadcasts from Italy during World War II; adjudged insane, he was committed to a mental institution until 1958. Notable works: *Hugh Selwyn Mauberley* (1920) and *Cantos* (series, 1917–70).

Pound |pownd|, Roscoe (1870–1964) U.S. educator. A scholar of modern jurisprudence, he wrote hundreds of books.

Pous·sin |pōō'seN|, Nicolas (1594–1665) French painter. He is regarded as the chief representative of French classicism and a master of the grand manner. His subject matter included biblical scenes (*The Adoration of the Golden Calf*, *c.*1635), classical mythology (*Et in Arcadia Ego*, *c.*1655), and historical landscapes.

Pow·der·ly |'powdərlē|, Terence Vincent (1849–1924) U.S. labor leader. He was largely responsible for the first Chinese Exclusion Act (1882) and the Contract Labor Act (1885).

Pow·ell |'powəl|, Adam Clayton, Jr. (1908–72) U.S. clergyman and politician. He was a long-time member of the U.S. House of Representatives from New York (1945–67; 1969–71) and authored over 50 pieces of social legislation.

Pow·ell |'powəl|, Anthony (Dymoke) (1905–) English novelist. He is best known for his sequence of twelve novels *A Dance to the Music of Time* (1951–75), a satirical portrayal of the English upper middle classes between the two world wars.

Pow·ell |'powəl|, Bud (1924–66) U.S. jazz pianist. Full name *Earl Powell*. He was the most important pianist in the early bop style.

Pow·ell |'powəl|, Colin Luther (1937–) U.S. army officer. Decorated for heroism in Vietnam, he later held a series of commands posts and became a White House assistant for national security affairs (1987–89). The first black American to become chairman of the Joint Chiefs of Staff (1989), he was commander in chief of the 1990–91 U.S. military operations (Desert Shield and Desert Storm) against Iraq.

Pow·ell |'powəl|, John Wesley (1834–1902) U.S. geologist and author. He directed the U.S. Geological Survey (1880–94).

Pow·ell |'powəl|, Lewis F., Jr. (1907–98) U.S. Supreme Court justice (1972–87).

Pow·ell |'powəl|, Mel (1923–98) U.S. composer. Born *Melvin Epstein*. He began as a jazz musician before studying with Paul Hindemith (1952).

Pow·ell |'powəl|, Michael (Latham) (1905–90) English movie director, producer, and scriptwriter. He founded The Archers Co. with the Hungarian scriptwriter **Emeric Pressburger** (1902–88); their movies included *The Red Shoes* (1948), *The Tales of Hoffman* (1951), and *A Matter of Life and Death* (1945).

Pow·ha·tan |pow'hætn| (c. 1550–1618) Algonquian Indian chief. Indian name *Wa-hun-sen-a-cawh* or *Wahunsonacock*. He was the leader of an alliance ("Powhatan's Confederacy") of some 30 tribes, primarily in eastern Virginia. He is thought to be the first Native American leader to have contact with English settlers in North America. Often noted for his ruthlessness, he made peace with the colonists after his daughter Pocahontas married Englishman John Rolfe (1614).

Prandtl |'präntl|, Ludwig (1875–1953) German physicist. He established the existence of the boundary layer and made important studies on streamlining.

Prax·it·e·les |,præk'sitl,ēz| (mid 4th century BC) Athenian sculptor. Only one of his works, *Hermes Carrying the Infant Dionysus*, survives. He is also noted for a statue of Aphrodite, of which there are only Roman copies.

Prem·in·ger |'preminjər|, Otto (Ludwig) (1906–86) Austrian-born U.S. movie director. Notable productions: *The Moon is Blue* (1953), *The Man with the Golden Arm* (1955), and *Bonjour Tristesse* (1959).

Pren·der·gast |'prendər,gæst|, Maurice Brazil (1859–1924) U.S. artist, born in Canada. A post-Impressionist watercolorist, he painted *Central Park* (1901) and *Promenade* (1914–15).

Pres·cott |'preskät|, William Hickling (1796–1859) U.S. historian. An expert in Spanish history, he authored *The History of the Reign of Ferdinand and Isabella the Catholic* (1838).

Pres·ley |'preslē; 'prezlē|, Elvis (Aron) (1935–77) U.S. singer and actor known as **King of Rock and Roll**. He was the dominant personality of early rock and roll with songs such as "Heartbreak Hotel," "Don't Be Cruel," and "Hound Dog" and was noted for the frank sexuality of his performances. He also made numerous movies, including *King Creole* (1958). He became a cult figure after his death.

Prev·in |'prevən|, André (George) (1929–) German-born U.S. conductor, pianist, and composer. He is most famous as a conductor, notably with the London Symphony Orchestra (1968–79), the Pittsburgh Symphony Orchestra (1976–86), and the Royal Philharmonic Orchestra (1987–91).

Pré·vost d'Ex·iles |,prä'vō deg'zēl|, Antoine-François (1697–1763) French novelist; known as **Abbé Prévost**. A Benedictine monk and priest, he is remembered for his novel *Manon Lescaut* (1731), which inspired operas by Jules Massenet and Puccini.

Prez |prā|, Josquin des see DES PREZ.

Price |prīs|, Edison Avery (1918–97) U.S. inventor of track lighting.

Price |prīs|, George (1901–95) U.S. cartoonist. He was a regular contributor to the *New Yorker* magazine.

Price |prīs|, Leontyne (1927–) Full name *Mary Violet Leontyne Price*. U.S. singer. Her 1952 Broadway successes in *Four Saints in Three Acts* and *Porgy and Bess* led to an international career as an operatic and concert soprano. She made her Metropolitan Opera debut in 1961.

Price |prīs|, Vincent (1911–93) U.S. actor, best known for his performances in a series of movies based on stories by Edgar Allan Poe.

Priest·ley |'prēs(t)lē|, J. B. (1894–1984) English novelist, dramatist, and critic; full name *John Boynton Priestley*. Notable works: *The Good Companions* (1929), a picaresque novel, and the mystery drama *An Inspector Calls* (1947).

Priest·ley |'prēs(t)lē|, Joseph (1733–

1804) English scientist and theologian. Priestley was the author of about 150 books, mostly theological or educational. His chief work was on the chemistry of gases, in which his most significant discovery was of "dephlogisticated air" (oxygen) in 1774; he demonstrated that it was important to animal life, and that plants give off this gas in sunlight.

Pri·mo de Ri·ve·ra |'prēmō ˌdā rē-'verä|, Miguel (1870–1930) Spanish general and statesman, head of state 1923–30. He assumed dictatorial powers after leading a military coup. His son, **José Antonio Primo de Rivera** (1903–36), founded the Falange in 1933 and was executed by Republicans in the Spanish Civil War.

Prince |prins| (1958–) U.S. rock, pop, and funk singer, songwriter, and musician; full name *Prince Rogers Nelson*. An eccentric, prolific performer with an enormously varied output, Prince is perhaps best known for the album and movie *Purple Rain* (1984).

Prince |prins|, Harold S. (1928–) U.S. theatrical producer. He produced *Fiorello* (Pulitzer Prize), *Cabaret*, *Evita*, and *Phantom of the Opera*.

Prince Albert, Prince Charles, etc. see ALBERT, PRINCE; CHARLES, PRINCE, etc.

Princes in the Tower, see EDWARD V.

Princess Anne, Princess Margaret, etc. see ANNE, PRINCESS; MARGARET, PRINCESS, etc.

Pri·scian |'prisH(ē)ən| (6th century AD) Byzantine grammarian; full name *Priscianus Caesariensis*. His *Grammatical Institutions* became one of the standard Latin grammatical works in the Middle Ages.

Pritch·ett |'pricHət|, Sir V. S. (1900–97) English writer and critic; full name *Victor Sawdon Pritchett*. He is chiefly remembered for his short stories.

Pro·co·pi·us |prō'kōpēəs| (*c.* 500–*c.* 532) Byzantine historian, born in Caesarea in Palestine. He accompanied Justinian's general Belisarius on his campaigns between 527 and 540. His principal works are the *History of the Wars of Justinian* and *On Justinian's Buildings*.

Proc·tor |'präktər|, William C. (1862–

1934) U.S. businessman. Beginning in 1890, he headed the company that invented and marketed Ivory soap. He instituted labor reforms such as profit-sharing and pensions.

Pro·fu·mo |prə'f(y)ōōmō|, John (Dennis) (1915–) British Conservative politician. In 1960 he was appointed secretary of state for war under Harold Macmillan. Three years later news broke of his relationship with Christine Keeler, the mistress of a Soviet diplomat, precipitating a government crisis and his resignation.

Pro·ko·fi·ev |prō'kawfē ˌef|, Sergei (Sergeevich) (1891–1953) Russian composer. Notable works include seven symphonies, the opera *The Love for Three Oranges* (1919), the *Lieutenant Kijé* suite (1934), the ballet music for *Romeo and Juliet* (1935–36), and *Peter and the Wolf* (1936), a young person's guide to the orchestra.

Pro·per·tius |prō'pərsH(ē)əs|, Sextus (*c.* 50–*c.* 16 BC) Roman poet. His four books of elegies are largely concerned with his love affair with a woman whom he called Cynthia.

Prost |prawst|, Alain (1955–) French racecar driver, four-time winner of the Formula One championship (1985–86, 1989, 1993).

Prou·dhon |prō'dōN|, Pierre-Joseph (1809–65) French social philosopher and journalist. His pamphlet *What Is Property?* (1840) argues that property, in the sense of the exploitation of one person's labor by another, is theft.

Proulx |prōō|, E. Annie (1935–) U.S. author. Notable works: *The Shipping News* (1994, Pulitzer Prize).

Proust |prōōst|, Joseph-Louis (1754–1826) French analytical chemist. He proposed the law of constant proportions, demonstrating that any pure sample of a chemical compound (such as an oxide of a metal) always contains same elements in fixed proportions.

Proust |prōōst|, Marcel (1871–1922) French novelist, essayist, and critic. He devoted much of his life to writing his novel *À la recherche du temps perdu* (published in seven sections between 1913 and 1927). Its central theme is the recovery of the lost past and the releasing of its creative energies through the stimulation of unconscious memory.

Prout |prowt|, William (1785–1850) English chemist and biochemist. He developed the hypothesis that hydrogen is the primary substance from which all other elements are formed, which, although incorrect, stimulated research in atomic theory.

Prou•ty |'prowtē|, Olive Higgins (1882–1974) U.S. author. Notable works: *Stella Dallas* (1922).

Prud•homme |ˌproo'dəm|, Paul (1940–) U.S. chef. Established as an expert in traditional cajun and creole cooking, he became renowned for his innovative blackened fish and meats. Notable cookbooks: *Paul Prudhomme's Louisiana Kitchen* (1984).

Ptol•e•my |'täləmē| (2nd century) Greek astronomer and geographer. His teachings had enormous influence on medieval thought, the geocentric view of the cosmos being adopted as Christian doctrine until the late Renaissance. Ptolemy's *Geography*, giving lists of places with their longitudes and latitudes, was also a standard work for centuries, despite its inaccuracies.

Puc•ci |'pooCHē|, Emilio (1914–) Italian skiwear designer.

Puc•ci•ni |poo'CHēnē|, Giacomo (1858–1924) Italian composer. Puccini's sense of the dramatic, gift for melody, and skillful use of the orchestra have contributed to his enduring popularity. Notable operas: *La Bohème* (1896), *Tosca* (1900), and *Madama Butterfly* (1904).

Puck•ett |'pəkət|, Kirby (1961–) U.S. baseball player. He led the Minnesota Twins to World Series titles in 1987 and 1991.

Pu•las•ki |pə'læskē|, Casimir (1747–79) Polish count and commissioned American cavalry officer. Having fled from his involvement in a Polish rebellion (1768–72), he arrived in America (1777) on the recommendation of Benjamin Franklin. He joined the cause of American independence and soon became a general (1778). He was invaluable in the defense of Charleston (1779) and was mortally wounded at the siege of Savannah.

Pul•it•zer |'poolətsər; 'pyoolətsər|, Joseph (1847–1911) Hungarian-born U.S. newspaper proprietor and editor. A pioneer of popular journalism, he owned a number of newspapers, including the *New York World*, and competed for readers with William Randolph Hearst. He made provisions in his will for the establishment of the annual Pulitzer Prizes.

Pul•len |'poolən|, Don (Gabriel) (1941–95) U.S. jazz pianist. His style mixed bop, soul, and free jazz.

Pull•man |'poolmən|, George Mortimer (1831–97) U.S. industrialist. The founder of the Pullman Palace Car Co. (1867), he converted railroad coaches into sleeping cars.

Pur•cell |'pərsəl; pər'sel|, Henry (1659–95) English composer. Organist for Westminster Abbey (1679–95), he composed choral odes and songs for royal occasions. His main interest was music for the theater; he composed the first English opera *Dido and Aeneas* (1689) and the incidental music for many plays.

Pu•sey |'pyoozē|, Edward Bouverie (1800–82) English theologian. In 1833, while professor of Hebrew at Oxford, he founded the Oxford Movement and became its leader after the withdrawal of John Henry Newman (1841). His many writings include a series of *Tracts for the Times*.

Push•kin |'pooSH,kin|, Aleksandr (Sergeevich) (1799–1837) Russian poet, novelist, and dramatist. He wrote prolifically in many genres; his first success was the romantic narrative poem *Ruslan and Ludmilla* (1820). Other notable works include the verse novel *Eugene Onegin* (1833) and the blank-verse historical drama *Boris Godunov* (1831).

Putt•nam |'pətnəm|, Sir David (Terence) (1941–) English movie director. He directed *Chariots of Fire* (1981), which won four Oscars, *The Killing Fields* (1984), and *The Mission* (1986).

Pu•zo |'poozō|, Mario (1920–) U.S. author. Notable works: *The Godfather* (1969) and *The Last Don* (1996).

Pyle |pil|, Ernest Taylor (1900–45) U.S. journalist. A syndicated war correspondent, he won a Pulitzer Prize (1944).

Pym |pim|, Barbara (Mary Crampton)

(1913–80) English novelist. She wrote a number of novels dealing satirically with English middle-class village life, including *Excellent Women* (1952), *Less than Angels* (1955), and *Quartet in Autumn* (1977).

Pyn•chon |'pinCHən|, Thomas (Ruggles) (1937–) U.S. novelist. He is an elusive author who shuns public attention, while his works abandon the normal conventions of the novel. Notable works: *V* (1963), *The Crying of Lot 49* (1966), *Gravity's Rainbow* (1973, National Book Award), *Vineland* (1990), and *Mason and Dixon* (1997).

Pyr•rho |'pirō| (*c.* 365–*c.* 270 BC) Greek philosopher, regarded as the founder of skepticism. He is credited with arguing that happiness comes from suspending judgment because certainty of knowledge is impossible.

Pyr•rhus |'pirəs| (*c.* 318–272 BC) king of Epirus *c.*307–272. After invading Italy in 280, he defeated the Romans at Asculum in 279, but sustained heavy losses; the term *pyrrhic victory* is named in allusion to this.

Py•thag•o•ras |pə'THægərəs| (*c.* 580–500 BC) Greek philosopher; known as **Pythagoras of Samos**. Pythagoras sought to interpret the entire physical world in terms of numbers, and founded their systematic and mystical study; he is best known for the theorem of the right-angled triangle. His analysis of the courses of the sun, moon, and stars into circular motions was not set aside until the 17th century.

Qq

Quant |kwänt|, Mary (1934–) English fashion designer. She was a principal creator of the "1960s look," launching the miniskirt in 1966 and promoting bold colors and geometric designs. She was also one of the first to design for the ready-to-wear market.

Qua·si·mo·do |ˌkwäzēˈmōˌdō|, Salvatore (1901–68) Italian poet, whose early work was influenced by French symbolism. His later work is more concerned with political and social issues. Nobel Prize for Literature (1959).

Quayle |kwāl|, James Danforth (1947–) vice president of the U.S. (1989–93). He served as a member of the U.S. Senate from Indiana (1981–89).

Queen |kwēn|, Ellery. U.S. writer of detective novels; pseudonym of *Frederic Dannay* (1905–82) and *Manfred Bennington Lee* (1905–71), who wrote as a team. Their novels feature a detective also called Ellery Queen.

Quer·cia |ˈkwerCHä|, Jacopo della see DELLA QUERCIA.

Que·zon y Mo·li·na |ˈkäzän ē mōˈlēnə|, Manuel Luis (1878–1944) Filipino politician. He was the first president of the Commonwealth of the Philippines (1935–44).

Quin·cey |ˈkwinsē|, Thomas De see DE QUINCEY.

Quind·len |ˈkwindlən|, Anna (1953–) U.S. author and journalist. She wrote *One True Thing* and won a Pulitzer Prize for commentary in *The New York Times* (1992).

Quine |kwīn|, Willard Van Orman (1908–) U.S. philosopher and logician. A radical critic of modern empiricism, Quine took issue with the philosophy of language proposed by Rudolf Carnap, arguing that "no statement is immune from revision" and that even the principles of logic themselves can be questioned and replaced. In *Word and Object* (1961) he held that there is no such thing as satisfactory translation.

Quinn |kwin|, Anthony Rudolph Oaxaca (1915–) U.S. actor. Notable movies: *Viva Zapata!* (1952, Academy Award).

Quinn |kwin|, Jane Bryant (1939–) U.S. journalist. She writes a syndicated financial column (1974–) and authored *Everyone's Money Book* (1979).

Quin·te·ro |kwin'terō; kēn'terō|, Jose Benjamin (1924–) U.S. theatrical director, born in Panama. He directed *A Moon for the Misbegotten, Long Days Journey into Night,* and *Strange Interlude.*

Quin·til·ian |kwin'tilyən| (c. 35–c. 96 AD) Roman rhetorician; Latin name *Marcus Fabius Quintilianus.* He is best known for his *Education of an Orator,* a comprehensive treatment of the art of rhetoric and the training of an orator.

Rr

Ra |rä|, Sun (*c.* 1915–93) U.S. jazz bandleader, pianist, and composer.

Ra·banne, Paco (1934–   ) Spanish fashion designer.

Rab·bitt |'ræbət|, Eddie (1944–98) U.S. singer and songwriter. Born *Edward Thomas Rabbitt*. He wrote pop and country music, including "Kentucky Rain" and "Suspicious."

Rabe, David (1940–   ) U.S. author and playwright. Notable works: *Streamers* (1977).

Rab·e·lais |'ræbə‚lā|, François (*c.* 1483–1553) French satirist. His writings are noted for their earthy humor, their parody of medieval learning and literature, and their affirmation of humanist values. Notable works: *Pantagruel* (*c.*1532) and *Gargantua* (1534).

Ra·bi |'räbē|, Isidor Isaac (1898–1988) U.S. physicist, born in Austria. He invented the resonance method to measure the magnetic properties of atomic nuclei and won the Nobel Prize in Physics (1944).

Ra·bin |rä'bēn|, Yitzhak (1922–95) Israeli statesman and military leader, prime minister (1974–77 and 1992–95). In 1993 he negotiated a PLO–Israeli peace accord with Yasser Arafat, for which he shared the 1994 Nobel Peace Prize with Arafat and Shimon Peres. He was assassinated by a Jewish extremist.

Rach·ma·ni·nov |räk'mänənawf|, Sergei (Vasilevich) (1873–1943) Russian composer and pianist, resident in the U.S. from 1917. Part of the Russian romantic tradition, he is primarily known for his compositions for piano, including concertos and the Prelude in C sharp minor (1892).

Ra·cine |rə'sēn|, Jean (1639–99) French dramatist, the principal tragedian of the French classical period. Central to most of his tragedies is a perception of the blind folly of human passion, continually enslaved and unsatisfied. Notable works: *Andromaque* (1667) and *Phèdre* (1677).

Rack·ham |'rækəm|, Arthur (1867–1939) English illustrator, noted for his

illustrations of books such as the Grimm brothers' *Fairy Tales* (1900) and Washington Irving's *Rip Van Winkle* (1905).

Ra·dis·son |‚rädə'sōN|, Pierre Espirit (1636–1710) French explorer. A fur trader in the Lake Superior region, he inspired the organization of the Hudson's Bay Co. (1670).

Rad·ner |'rædnər|, Gilda (1946–82) U.S. comedian and actress. She was an original cast member of "Saturday Night Live."

Rae·burn |'rā‚bərn|, Sir Henry (1756–1823) Scottish artist. The leading Scottish portraitist of his day, he depicted the local intelligentsia and Highland chieftains in a bold and distinctive style.

Raf·fi |'ræfē| (1948–   ) Canadian songwriter and children's entertainer. Full name *Raffi Cavoukian*.

Raf·fles |'ræfəlz|, Sir (Thomas) Stamford (1781–1826) British colonial administrator. As lieutenant general of Sumatra (1818–23), he persuaded the East India Company to purchase the undeveloped island of Singapore (1819), undertaking much of the preliminary work for transforming it into an international port and center of commerce.

Ra·fi·nesque |‚räfē'nesk|, Constantine Samuel (1783–1840) U.S. educator and naturalist, born in Turkey.

Raf·san·ja·ni |‚räfsən'jänē|, Ali Akbar Hashemi (1934–   ) Iranian statesman and religious leader, president (1989–97). In 1978 he helped organize the mass demonstrations that led to the shah's overthrow. As leader of Iran he sought to improve the country's relations with the West.

Ra·ha·krish·nam |‚rähä'krēsHnäm|, Sir Sarvepalli (1888–1975) Indian philosopher and statesman, president (1962–67). He introduced classiscal Indian philosophy to the West through works such as *Indian Philosophy* (1923–27).

Rah·man |'rämän| see ABDUL RAHMAN, MUJIBUR RAHMAN.

Rahv |räv|, Philip (1908–73) U.S. editor and educator, born in Ukraine. He cofounded and edited the *Partisan Review* (1933).

Rain•ey |'rānē|, Joseph Hayne (1832–87) U.S. politician. He was the first African American elected to the U.S. House of Representatives, from South Carolina (1870–79).

Rain•ey |'rānē|, Ma (1886–1939) U.S. blues singer. Full name *Gertrude Rainey*. She made over 100 recordings with Louis Armstrong and her Georgia Jazz Band.

Rain-in-the-Face (d. 1905) Teton Sioux commander. With Sitting Bull and others, he annihilated the forces under Custer at Little Bighorn (1876).

Raitt |rāt|, Bonnie (1949–) U.S. singer, songwriter, and guitarist. Her style incorporates blues, pop, folk, and rhythm and blues; her album *Nick of Time* won a 1990 Grammy Award.

Raj•neesh |,räj'nēSH|, Bhagwan Shree (1931–90) Indian guru; born *Chandra Mohan Jain*; known as **the Bhagwan** (Sanskrit, "lord"). He founded an ashram in Poona, India, and a commune in Oregon, becoming notorious for his doctrine of communal therapy and salvation through free love. He was deported from the U.S. in 1985 for immigration violations.

Rá•ko•si |'räkəsHē|, Mátyás (1892–1971) Hungarian Communist statesman, first secretary of the Hungarian Socialist Workers' Party 1945–56 and prime minister (1952–53 and 1955–56). After the Communist seizure of power in 1945 he did much to establish a firmly Stalinist regime. He was ousted as premier by the more liberal Imre Nagy in 1953.

Ra•leigh |'rälē|, Sir Walter (*c.* 1552–1618) Also **Ralegh**. English explorer, courtier, and writer. A favorite of Elizabeth I, he organized several voyages of exploration and colonization to the Americas and introduced potato and tobacco plants to England. Imprisoned in 1603 by James I on a charge of conspiracy, he was released in 1616 to lead an expedition in search of El Dorado, but was executed on the original charge when he returned empty-handed.

Ra•ma•krish•na |,rämə'krisHnə| (1836–86) Indian yogi and mystic; born

Gadadhar Chatterjee. He condemned lust, money, and the caste system, preaching that all religions leading to the attainment of mystical experience are equally good and true.

Ra•man |'rämən|, Sir Chandrasekhara Venkata (1888–1970) Indian physicist. He discovered the Raman effect, one of the most important proofs of the quantum theory of light. Nobel Prize for Physics (1930).

Ra•ma•nu•jan |rə'mänəjən|, Srinivasa Aaiyangar (1887–1920) Indian mathematician. He made a number of original discoveries in number theory, especially, in collaboration with **G. H. Hardy**, 1877–1947, a theorem concerning the partition of numbers into a sum of smaller integers.

Ram•bert |,räm'ber|, Dame Marie (1888–1982) British ballet dancer, teacher, and director, born in Poland; born *Cyvia Rambam*. After moving to London in 1917 she formed and directed the Ballet Club, which became known as the Ballet Rambert in 1935.

Ra•meau |,rä'mō|, Jean-Philippe (1683–1764) French composer, musical theorist, and organist. He is best known for his four volumes of harpsichord pieces (1706–41), which are noted for their bold harmonies and textural diversity.

Ra•món y Ca•jal |rə'mōn ē kə'häl|, Santiago (1852–1934) Spanish physician and histologist. He was a founder of the science of neurology, identifying the neuron as the fundamental unit of the nervous system. Nobel Prize for Physiology or Medicine (1906), shared with Camillo Golgi.

Ram•say |'ræmzē|, Allan (1713–84) Scottish portrait painter. His style is noted for its French rococo grace and sensitivity, particularly in his portraits of women.

Ram•say |'ræmzē|, Sir William (1852–1916) Scottish chemist, discoverer of the noble gases. He first discovered argon, helium, and (with the help of **M. W. Travers**, 1872–1961) neon, krypton, and xenon, determing their atomic weights and places in the periodic table. In 1910, with Frederick Soddy and **Sir Robert Whytlaw-Gray**, 1877–1958, he identified the last noble gas, radon. Nobel Prize for Chemistry (1904).

Ram·ses |'ræmzēz; 'ræmsēz| also **Rameses**. the name of eleven Egyptian pharaohs, notably: **Ramses II** (died *c.*1225 BC), reigned *c.*1292–*c.*1225 BC; known as **Ramses the Great**. The third pharaoh of the 19th dynasty, he built vast monuments and statues, including the two rock temples at Abu Simbel. **Ramses III** (died *c.*1167 BC), reigned *c.*1198–*c.*1167 BC. The second pharaoh of the 20th dynasty, he fought decisive battles against the Libyans and the Sea Peoples. After his death the power of Egypt declined.

Rand |rænd|, Ayn (1905–82) Russian-born U.S. writer and philosopher; born *Alissa Rozenbaum*. She developed a philosophy of "objectivism," arguing for "rational self-interest," individualism, and laissez-faire capitalism, which she presented in both non-fiction works and novels. Notable novels: *The Fountainhead* (1943) and *Atlas Shrugged* (1957).

Ran·dall |'rændəl|, Tony (1920–) U.S. actor. Born *Leonard Rosenberg*. He starred in the television series "The Odd Couple" (1970–74).

Ran·dolph |'ræn,dawlf| American colonial political family, including: **Peyton Randolph** (*c.* 1721–75), the president of the First Continental Congress. **Edmund Jennings Randolph** (1753–1813). The nephew of Peyton Randolph, he was a member of the Continental Congress (1779–82), governor of Virginia (1786–88), U.S. attorney general (1789–94), and U.S. secretary of state (1794–95).

Ran·dolph |'ræn,dawlf|, Asa Philip (1889–1979) U.S. labor and civil rights leader.

Ran·dolph |'ræn,dawlf|, Jennings (1902–98) U.S. politician. He was a Democratic member of the U.S. Senate from West Virginia (1958–85).

Ran·dolph |'ræn,dawlf|, John (1773–1833) U.S. politician. Known as **John Randolph of Roanoke**. A member of the U.S. House of Representatives from Virginia (1799–1813, 1815–17, 1819–25, 1827–29), he was a vigorous proponent of states' rights.

Ran·jit Singh |'rənjət 'siNG| (1780–1839) Indian maharaja, founder of the Sikh state of Punjab; known as the **Lion of the Punjab**. He proclaimed himself maharaja of Punjab in 1801 and went on to make it the most powerful state in India. Most of his territory was annexed by Britain after the Sikh Wars that followed his death.

Rank |ræNGk|, J. Arthur, 1st Baron (1888–1972) English industrialist and film executive; full name *Joseph Arthur Rank*. In 1941 he founded the Rank Organization, a movie production and distribution company that acquired control of the leading British studios and movie theaters in the 1940s and 1950s.

Ran·som |'rænsəm|, John Crowe (1888–1974) U.S. poet and critic. With *The New Criticism* (1941) he started a school of criticism that rejected the Victorian emphasis on literature as a moral force and advocated a close analysis of textual structure in isolation from the social background of the text.

Rao |row|, P. V. Narasimha (1921–) Indian statesman and prime minister (1991–96); full name *Pamulaparti Venkata Narasimha Rao*.

Raph·a·el |'ræfēəl; ˌräfi'el| (1483–1520) Italian painter and architect; Italian name *Raffaello Sanzio*. Regarded as one of the greatest artists of the Renaissance, he is particularly noted for his madonnas, including his altarpiece the *Sistine Madonna* (*c.*1513).

Ras·mus·sen |'ræsˌmo͞osən|, Knud Johan Victor (1879–1933) Danish explorer and ethnologist of Greenland.

Ra·spu·tin |ræs'pyo͞otn|, Grigori (Efimovich) (1872–1916) Russian monk. He came to exert great influence over Tsar Nicholas II and his family during World War I; this influence, combined with his reputation for debauchery, steadily discredited the imperial family, and he was assassinated by a group loyal to the tsar.

Ra·ta·na |rə'tänə|, Tahupotiki Wiremu (1870–1939) Maori political and religious leader in New Zealand. He founded the Ratana Church (1920), a religious revival movement that aimed to unite all Maori people.

Rath·er |'ræTHər|, Dan (1931–) U.S. journalist. He is managing editor and anchorman for *CBS Evening News* (1981–).

Rat·ti·gan |'rætəgən|, Sir Terence (Mervyn) (1911–77) English dramatist. Notable plays: *The Winslow Boy* (1946), *The Browning Version* (1948), and *Ross* (1960), based on the life of T. E. Lawrence.

Rat·tle |'rætəl|, Sir Simon (Denis) (1955–) English conductor. He was principal conductor with the City of Birmingham Symphony Orchestra 1980–91 and is noted particularly for his interpretation of works by early 20th-century composers such as Mahler.

Rau·schen·berg |'rowSHən,bərg|, Robert (1925–) U.S. artist. His series of "combine" paintings, such as *Charlene* (1954) and *Rebus* (1955), incorporate three-dimensional objects such as nails, rags, and bottles.

Ra·vel |rə'vel|, Maurice (Joseph) (1875–1937) French composer. Noted for their colorful orchestration, his works have a distinctive tone and make use of unresolved dissonances. Notable works: *Daphnis and Chloë* (ballet) (1912); *Boléro* (orchestral work) (1928).

Raw·lings |'rawliNGz|, Marjorie Kinnan (1896–1953) U.S. journalist and author. Notable works: *The Yearling* (1938, Pulitzer Prize).

Rawls |rawlz|, John (1921–) U.S. philosopher. His books *A Theory of Justice* (1971) and *Political Liberalism* (1993) consider the basic institutions of a just society as those chosen by rational people under conditions that ensure impartiality.

Ray |rā|, Man (1890–1976) U.S. photographer, painter, and filmmaker; born *Emmanuel Rudnitsky*. A leading figure in the New York and European Dada movements, he is perhaps best known for his photograph the *Violin d'Ingres* (1924), which achieved the effect of making the back of a female nude resemble a violin.

Ray |rā|, Satyajit (1921–92) Indian movie director, the first to bring Indian movies to the attention of Western audiences. Notable movies: *Pather Panchali* (1955).

Ray·burn |'rā,bərn|, Samuel Taliaferro (1882–1961) U.S. politician. He was a member of the House of Representatives from Texas (1913–61) and speaker of the House (1940–46; 1949–61).

Ray·leigh |'rālē|, John William Strutt (3rd Baron) (1842–1919) English physicist. He established the electrical units of resistance, current, and electromotive force. With William Ramsay he discovered argon and other inert gases. Nobel Prize for Physics (1904).

Ray·mond |'rāmənd|, Alex (1909–56) U.S. cartoonist. Full name *Alexander Gillespie Raymond*. He created the comic strips "Secret Agent X-9," "Flash Gordon," "Jungle Jim," and "Rip Kirby."

Ray·mond |'rāmənd|, Henry Jarvis (1820–69) U.S. journalist. He founded *The New York Times* (1851), which helped launch the Republican Party (1854).

Reade |rēd|, Charles (1814–84) English novelist and dramatist, remembered for his historical romance *The Cloister and the Hearth* (1861).

Rea·gan |'rāgən|, Ronald (Wilson) (1911–) see box. **Nancy Reagan** (1923–), wife of Ronald Reagan and U.S. first lady (1981–89). Born *Anne Frances Robbins Davis*. She campaigned for young people to "Just Say No" to drugs.

Ré·au·mur |'rāə,myŏŏr|, René Antoine Ferchault de (1683–1757) French naturalist. He is chiefly remembered for his thermometer scale, now obsolete, which set the melting point of ice at 0° and the boiling point of water at 80°. Réaumur also carried out pioneering work on insects and other invertebrates.

Red Cloud |'red 'klowd| (1822–1909) Native American leader of the Oglala Indians. Indian name *Mahpiua Luta*. He opposed the U.S. government's attempts to build forts along the Bozeman Trail in Wyoming and Montana.

Red·ding |'rediNG|, Otis (1941–67) U.S. soul singer. One of the most influential soul singers of the late 1960s, it was not until the Monterey pop festival in 1967 that he gained widespread recognition. "Dock of the Bay," released after Redding's death in an airplane crash, became a number-one hit in 1968.

Red·en·bach·er |'redn,bäkər|, Orville (1907–95) U.S. agricultural scientist.

Reagan, Ronald Wilson
40th U.S. president

Life dates: 1911–
Place of birth: Tampico, Illinois
Mother: Nelle Clyde Wilson Reagan
Father: John Edward Reagan
Wives: Jane Wyman (born Sarah Jane Fulks); divorced 1948; married Nancy Davis (born Anne Frances Robbins) in 1952
Children: (with first wife) Maureen, Michael (adopted); (with second wife) Patricia, Ronald (Skip)
Nickname: Dutch
College/University: Eureka College
Military service: U.S. Army Air Forces during World War II
Career: Radio announcer; motion picture and television actor
Political career: Governor of California
Party: Republican (Democrat until 1962)
Home state: California
Opponents in presidential races: Jimmy Carter, John Anderson; Walter F. Mondale
Term of office: Jan. 20, 1981–Jan. 20, 1989
Vice president: George Bush
Notable events of presidency: Economic Recovery Tax Act of 1981; assassination attempt by John Hinckley Jr.; dismissal of 13,000 striking air traffic controllers; Sandra Day O'Connor appointed first woman Supreme Court justice; 241 die in bombing of U.S. Marine Corps building in Lebanon; U.S. invasion of Caribbean island of Grenada; space shuttle *Challenger* disaster; Chernobyl nuclear power plant disaster; Intermediate-Range Nuclear Forces Treaty; Iran-contra affair
Other achievements: president, Screen Actors Guild (six terms, five consecutively); television series host

---

He founded the Orville Redenbacher popcorn company.

Red·field |'redfĕld|, William C. (1789–1857) U.S. scientist. He discovered that hurricanes are revolving storms (1840) and served as the first president of the American Asssociation for the Advancement of Science.

Red·ford |'redfərd|, (Charles) Robert (1937–) U.S. movie actor and director. He made his name playing opposite Paul Newman in *Butch Cassidy and the Sundance Kid* (1969), costarring again with him in *The Sting* (1973). Other notable movies include *The Way We Were* (1973), *The Great Gatsby* (1974), *All the President's Men* (1976), and *Ordinary People* (1980), for which he won an Oscar as director. He sponsors the annual Sundance Film Festival for independent filmakers

Red·grave |'red‚grāv| the name of a family of English actors, notably: **Sir Michael (Scudamore)** (1908–85). A well-known stage actor, he played numerous Shakespearean roles and also starred in films such as *The Browning Version* (1951) and *The Importance of Being Earnest* (1952). **Vanessa** (1937–), Sir Michael's eldest daughter. Her successful career in the theater and movies includes the films *Mary Queen of Scots* (1972), *Julia* (1976), for which she won an Oscar, and *Howard's End* (1992) Her sister **Lynn** (1943–) has appeared in many films, including *Georgy Girl* (1966, Academy Award) and *Gods and Monsters* (1998)..

Red Jack·et |'red 'jækət| (c. 1758–1830) Native American leader of the Seneca Indians. He received a symbolic medal from President Washington (1792).

Red·man |'redmən|, Don (1900–64) U.S. composer, bandleader, and saxophonist. Full name *Donald Matthew Redman*. He formed his own band (1931) and is noted for such songs as "Flight of the Jitterbugs" (1939) and "Deep Purple."

Red·mond |'redmənd|, John (Edward) (1856–1918) Irish politician, leader of the Irish Nationalist Party in the House of Commons 1891–1918. The Home Rule Bill of 1912 was introduced with his support, although it was never implemented because of World War I.

Re·don |rə'dawn; rə'dõN|, Odilon (1840–1916) French painter and graphic artist. He was a leading exponent of symbolism and forerunner of surrealism, especially in his early charcoal drawings of fantastic or nightmarish subjects.

Red·stone |'red‚stōn|, Sumner Murray (1923–) U.S. businessman and lawyer. He is president and CEO of National Amusements, Inc. (1967–) and chairman of the board of Viacom, Inc. (1987–).

Reed |rēd|, Donna (1921–86) U.S. actress. Born *Donna Belle Mullenger*. Notable movies: *From Here to Eternity* (1953, Academy Award).

Reed |rēd|, Ishmael (1938–) U.S. author. Full name *Ishmael Scott Emmett Coleman Reed*. Notable works: *Japanese by Spring* (1993).

Reed |rēd|, John (1887–1920) U.S. journalist and poet. He organized the first communist party in the U.S. (1919) and edited its journal *The Voice of Labor*.

Reed |rēd|, Lou (1942–) U.S. rock singer, guitarist, and songwriter; full name *Lewis Allan Reed*. Reed led the Velvet Underground, his literate songs dealing with hitherto taboo subjects such as heroin addiction and sadomasochism. His best-known solo recordings are the song "Walk on the Wild Side" and album *Transformer* (both 1972).

Reed |rēd|, Stanley Forman (1884–1980) U.S. Supreme Court justice (1938–57).

Reed |rēd|, Willis (1942–) U.S. basketball player.

Reeve |rēv|, Christopher (1952–) U.S. actor and director. Notable movies: *Superman* (1978).

Reeve |rēv|, Tapping (1744–1823) U.S. lawyer and educator. He founded the Litchfield Law School (1784), the first law school in the U.S.

Reeves |rēvz|, Jim (1924–64) U.S. country singer and songwriter. Notable songs: "Four Walls."

Reeves |rēvz|, Martha (1941–) U.S. pop and soul singer. She was the lead singer of Martha and the Vandellas. Notable songs: "Dancing in the Streets," "Heat Wave," and Jimmy Mack."

Rehn·quist |'ren,kwist|, William Hubbs (1924–) Chief Justice of the U.S. (1986–). As President Nixon's assistant attorney general (1969–71), he held to a conservative stance that opposed civil rights legislation. He was appointed U.S. Supreme Court justice in 1972 and chief justice in 1986.

Re·ho·bo·am |,rē(h)ə'bōəm| (*c.* 930–*c.*

915) son of Soloman, king of anicent Israel (*c.*930–*c.*915 BC). His reign witnessed the secession of the northern tribes and their establishment of a new kingdom under Jeroboam, leaving Rehoboam as the first king of Judah (1 Kings 11–14).

Reich |rīk|, Steve (1936–) U.S. composer; full name *Stephen Michael Reich*. A leading minimalist, he uses the repetition of short phrases within a simple harmonic field. Influences include Balinese and West African music.

Reid |rēd|, Whitelaw (1837–1912) U.S. journalist and diplomat. He was the managing editor of *The New York Tribune* (1872–1905) and the U.S. minister to France and ambassador to England.

Rei·ner |'rīnər| U.S. family of actors. **Carl Reiner** (1922–) produced and wrote for the television series "The Dick Van Dyke Show." **Rob Reiner** (1947–), his son, acted in the television series "All in the Family" and directed the movies *Stand By Me* (1986) and *The Princess Bride* (1987).

Rein·hardt |'rīn,härt|, Django (1910–53) Belgian jazz guitarist; born *Jean Baptiste Reinhardt*. He became famous in Paris in the 1930s for his improvisational style, blending swing with influences from his gypsy background.

Rein·hardt |'rīn,härt|, Max (1873–1943) Austrian director and impresario; born *Max Goldmann*. He produced large-scale versions of such works as Sophocles' *Oedipus Rex* (1910), and helped establish the Salzburg Festival, with Richard Strauss and Hugo von Hofmannsthal.

Rein·king |'rinkiNG|, Ann (1950–) U.S. actress and dancer. Her stage, film, and television appearances include *A Chorus Line*, *All That Jazz*, and *Chicago* (1997, Tony Award).

Reith |rēTH|, John (Charles Walsham), 1st Baron (1889–1971) Scottish administrator and politician, first general manager (1922–27) and first director general (1927–38) of the BBC.

Re·marque |rə'märk|, Erich Maria (1898–1970) German-born U.S. novelist. His first novel, *All Quiet on the Western Front* (1929, movie 1930), was a huge international success. All of his ten novels deal with the horror of war and its aftermath.

Rem·brandt |'rem,brænt| (1606–69) Dutch painter; full name *Rembrandt Harmensz van Rijn*. He made his name as a portrait painter with the *Anatomy Lesson of Dr Tulp* (1632). With his most celebrated painting, the *Night Watch* (1642), he used chiaroscuro to give his subjects a more spiritual and introspective quality, a departure that was to transform the Dutch portrait tradition. Rembrandt is especially identified with the series of more than sixty self-portraits painted from 1629 to 1669.

Re·ming·ton |'remiNGtən|, Frederic (1861–1909) U.S. painter and sculptor. He painted scenes of the American West. Notable sculptures: *Bronco Buster.*

Re·nan |rə'nän|, (Joseph) Ernest (1823–92) French historian, theologian, and philosopher. He provoked a controversy with the publication of his *Life of Jesus* (1863), which rejected the supernatural element in Jesus' life.

Re·nault |rə'nō|, Louis (1877–1944) French engineer and automotive manufacturer. He and his brothers established the Renault company in 1898, manufacturing racing cars, and later industrial and agricultural machinery and military technology.

Re·nault |rə'nō|, Mary (1905–83) British novelist, resident in South Africa from 1948; pseudonym of *Mary Challans*. She wrote historical novels set in the ancient world, notably a trilogy dealing with Alexander the Great (1970–81).

Ren·dell |'rendəl|, Ruth (Barbara) (1930–) English writer of detective fiction and thrillers. She is noted for her psychological crime novels and her character Chief Inspector Wexford; she also writes under the pseudonym of Barbara Vine.

Re·no |'renō|, Janet (1938–) U.S. attorney general (1993–). She was the first woman to be appointed to this office.

Re·noir |,ren'wär| French family, including: **(Pierre) Auguste Renoir** (1841–1919), French painter. An early Impressionist, he developed a style characterized by light, fresh colors and indistinct, subtle outlines. Notable works:

Les Grandes baigneuses (1884–87). **Jean Renoir** (1894–1979), French movie director, his son. He is famous for movies including *La Grande illusion* (1937) and *La Règle du jeu* (1939).

Ren·wick |'renwik|, James, Jr. (1818–95) U.S. architect. Notable designs: St. Patrick's Cathedral (New York, 1853); the Smithsonian Institution (1848); and Vassar College (1865).

Res·nais |rə'nā|, Alain (1922–) French movie director. One of the foremost directors of the *nouvelle vague*, he used experimental techniques to explore memory and time. Notable movies: *Hiroshima mon amour* (1959) and *L'Année dernière à Marienbad* (1961).

Re·spig·hi |rə'spēgē|, Ottorino (1879–1936) Italian composer. He is best known for his suites the *Fountains of Rome* (1917) and the *Pines of Rome* (1924), based on the poems of Gabriele d'Annunzio.

Reu·ter |'roitər|, Paul Julius, Baron von (1816–99) German pioneer of telegraphy and news reporting; born *Israel Beer Josaphat*. After establishing a service for sending commercial telegrams in Aachen (1849), he moved his headquarters to London, where he founded the news agency Reuters.

Reu·ther |'rooTHər|, Walter (1907–70) U.S. labor leader. He was president of the United Automobile Workers (1946–70) and of the Congress of Industrial Organizations (1952–55).

Rev·els |'revəlz|, Hiram Rhoades (1822–1901) U.S. politician, educator, and clergyman. He was the first African American elected to the U.S. Senate, from Mississippi (1870–71).

Re·vere |rə'vir|, Paul (1735–1818) American patriot and silversmith. In 1775 he rode from Boston to Lexington to warn fellow American revolutionaries of the approach of British troops, immortalized in Longfellow's poem "Paul Revere's Ride" (1863).

Rex·roth |'reks,rawTH|, Kenneth (1905–82) U.S. poet and critic. Notable works: *New Poems* (1974); *Classics Revisited* (1969).

Rey·nolds |'renəldz|, Albert (1933–) Irish Fianna Fáil statesman, prime minister (1992–94). He was involved with British prime minister John Major in drafting the Downing Street Declaration (1993), intended as the basis of a peace initiative in Northern Ireland.

Rey•nolds |'renəldz|, Sir Joshua (1723–92) English painter. The first president of the Royal Academy (1768), he sought to raise portraiture to the status of historical painting by adapting poses and settings from classical statues and Renaissance paintings.

Re•za Shah |'räzə 'SHä| see PAHLAVI.

Rhead, Louis John (1857–1926) U.S. artist. His work was often featured on the covers of magazines such as *Harper's*.

Rhee |rē|, Syngman (1875–1965) president of the Republic of Korea (1948–60). Having been the principal leader in the movement for Korean independence, he became president of the exiled Korean provisional government (1919–41). Following World War II, he returned from exile and became the first elected president of the Republic of Korea (South Korea). Amid social and political unrest, he resigned one month into his fourth term (1960) and went into exile in Hawaii.

Rhine |rīn|, Joseph Banks (1895–1980) U.S. parapsychologist. He was founder and director of the Institute of Parapsychology in North Carolina (1964–68), which investigated extra-sensory perception.

Rhodes |rōdz|, Cecil (John) (1853–1902) British-born South African statesman, prime minister of Cape Colony (1890–96). He expanded British territory in southern Africa, annexing Bechuanaland (now Botswana) in 1884 and developing Rhodesia from 1889. By 1890 he had acquired 90 percent of the world's production of diamonds.

Rhodes |rōdz|, Richard Lee (1937–) U.S. author. Notable works include *The Making of the Atomic Bomb* (1988, Pulitzer Prize).

Rhys |rēs|, Jean (1894–1979) British novelist and short-story writer, born in Dominica; pseudonym of *Ella Gwendolen Rees Williams*. Her novels include *Good Morning, Midnight* (1939) and *Wide Sargasso Sea* (1966).

Rib•ben•trop |'rib(ə)n,träp|, Joachim von (1893–1946) German Nazi politician. As foreign minister (1938–45) he signed the nonaggression pact with the Soviet Union (1939). He was convicted as a war criminal in the Nuremberg trials and hanged.

Ri•be•ra |rə'berə|, José (or Jusepe) de (c. 1591–1652) Spanish painter and etcher, resident in Italy from 1616; known as **Lo Spagnoletto** ("the little Spaniard"). He is best known for his religious and genre paintings, for example the *Martyrdom of St. Bartholomew* (c. 1630).

Rice |rīs|, Anne (1941–) U.S. author. Notable works: *Pandora: New Tales of the Vampire* (1998).

Rice |rīs|, Jerry (1962–) U.S. football player. He set NFL records in pass receptions and passing touchdowns.

Rice |rīs|, Thomas Dartmouth (1808–60) U.S. minstrel singer and playwright. He introduced the song and dance "Jim Crow" (1828).

Rice |rīs|, Sir Tim (1944–) English lyricist and entertainer; full name *Timothy Miles Bindon Rice*. Together with Andrew Lloyd Webber he cowrote a number of hit musicals, including *Joseph and the Amazing Technicolor Dreamcoat* (1968), *Jesus Christ Superstar* (1971), and *Evita* (1978). He has also won two Oscars for best original movie song (1992 and 1994).

Rich |riCH|, Adrienne (Cecile) (1929–) U.S. author and poet. Notable works: *Dark Fields of the Republic: Poems, 1991–1995* (1995).

Rich |riCH|, Buddy (1917–87) U.S. jazz drummer and bandleader; born *Bernard Rich*. He played for bandleaders such as Artie Shaw and Tommy Dorsey and formed his own band in 1946.

Rich |riCH|, Charlie (1932–95) U.S. country singer and songwriter. Known as **Silver Fox**. Notable songs: "Behind Closed Doors" and "The Most Beautiful Girl."

Rich |riCH|, Frank (1949–) U.S. journalist. He wrote for *The New York Times* as a drama critic (1980–93) and an op-ed columnist (1994–).

Rich•ard I |'riCHərd| (1157–99) king of England son of Henry II, reigned

1189–99; known as **Richard Coeur de Lion** or **Richard the Lionheart**. He led the Third Crusade, defeating Saladin at Arsuf (1191), but failing to capture Jerusalem. Returning home, he was held hostage by the Holy Roman Emperor Henry VI until being released in 1194 on payment of a huge ransom.

Rich•ard II |'riCHərd| (1367–1400) king of England son of the Black Prince, reigned 1377–99. Following his minority, he executed or banished most of his former opponents. His confiscation of John of Gaunt's estate on the latter's death provoked Henry Bolingbroke's return from exile to overthrow him.

Rich•ard III |'riCHərd| (1452–85) king of England brother of Edward IV, reigned 1483–85. He served as Protector to his nephew Edward V, who, after two months, was declared illegitimate and subsequently disappeared. Richard's brief rule ended at Bosworth's Field, where he was defeated by Henry Tudor and killed.

Rich•ard |'riCHərd|, Cliff (1940–) British pop singer, born in India; born *Harry Roger Webb.*

Rich•ard |'riCHərd|, Maurice (1921–) Canadian hockey player. He was the first player to score 50 goals in one season.

Richard Coeur de Lion Richard I of England (see RICHARD).

Rich•ards |'riCHərdz|, I. A. (1893–1979) English literary critic and poet; full name *Ivor Armstrong Richards.* He emphasized the importance of close textual study, and praised irony, ambiguity, and allusiveness. Notable works: *Practical Criticism* (1929).

Rich•ards |'riCHərdz|, Keith (1943–) British rock guitarist and vocalist. He performed with the Rolling Stones; his solo albums include *Main Offender* (1992).

Rich•ards |'riCHərdz|, Laura Elizabeth (1850–1943) U.S. author. She wrote over 80 children's books and, with her sister Maud Howe Elliott, a biography of their mother, *Julia Ward Howe* (1915, Pulitzer Prize).

Rich•ards |'riCHərdz|, Michael (1949–) U.S. actor. He is noted for his role in the television show "Seinfeld" (1990–98).

Rich•ard•son |'riCHərdsən|, Elliot Lee (1920–) U.S. lawyer. The U.S. attorney general under President Nixon, he resigned in protest when Nixon fired Watergate special prosecutor Archibald Cox (1973).

Rich•ard•son |'riCHərdsən|, Henry Hobson (1838–86) U.S. architect. A pioneer in designing an indigenous American style of architecture, he created Trinity Church (Boston, 1872–77) and the Marshall Field Building (Chicago, 1885–87).

Rich•ard•son |'riCHərdsən|, Natasha (1963–) U.S. actress. Notable movies: *The Parent Trap* (1998).

Rich•ard•son |'riCHərdsən|, Sir Ralph (David) (1902–83) English actor. He played many Shakespearean roles as well as leading parts in plays including Harold Pinter's *No Man's Land* (1975) and movies including *Oh! What a Lovely War* (1969).

Rich•ard•son |'riCHərdsən|, Samuel (1689–1761) English novelist. His first novel *Pamela* (1740–41), entirely in the form of letters and journals, popularized the epistolary novel. He experimented further with the genre in *Clarissa Harlowe* (1747–48).

Richard the Lionheart Richard I of England (see RICHARD).

Rich•e•lieu |'rishəl,(y)o͞o|, Armand Jean du Plessis, duc de (1585–1642) French cardinal and statesman. As chief minister of Louis XIII (1624–42) he dominated French government. In 1635 he established the Académie Française.

Rich•ie |'riCHē|, Lionel B., Jr. (1949–) U.S. singer, songwriter, and producer. His hits include "We Are the World" (1985), "Truly" (1982), and "Say You, Say Me" (1987).

Rich•ler |'riCHlər|, Mordecai (1931–) Canadian writer. His best-known novel is probably *The Apprenticeship of Duddy Kravitz* (1959). Notable works: *St. Urbain's Horseman* (1971), and *Simon Gursky Was Here* (1989).

Rich•ter |'riktər|, Conrad (Michael) (1890–1968) U.S. author. Notable works: *The Town* (1950, Pulitzer Prize).

Richt•ho•fen |'rikt,hawfən|, Manfred,

Freiherr von (1882–1918) German fighter pilot; known as **the Red Baron**. He joined a fighter squadron in 1915, flying a distinctive bright red aircraft. He was eventually shot down after destroying eighty enemy planes.

Rick•ey |'rikē|, Branch (1881–1965) U.S. baseball manager. He revolutionized the game with the creation of the modern farm system, and he integrated the major leagues when he brought Jackie Robinson to the Brooklyn Dodgers (1947).

Rick•o•ver |'rik,ōvər|, Hyman George (1900–86) U.S. naval officer, born in Poland (then part of Russia). A rear admiral in 1953 and a vice admiral in 1959, he was the individual most responsible for creating the U.S. nuclear-powered navy. The world's first nuclear-powered submarine, the USS *Nautilus*, was launched under his direction (1954). He received the Presidential Medal of Freedom (1980).

Ride |'rīd|, Sally (1951–) U.S. astronaut. She was the first U.S. woman to travel in space, on the shuttle *Challenger* (1983).

Rid•ley |'ridlē|, Nicholas (c. 1500–55) English Protestant bishop and martyr. He was appointed bishop of Rochester (1547) and then of London (1550). He opposed the Catholic policies of Mary I, for which he was burnt at the stake.

Rie |rē|, Lucie (1902–95) Austrian-born British potter. Her pottery and stoneware were admired for their precise simple shapes and varied subtle glazes.

Rie•fen•stahl |'rēfən,stawl|, Leni (1902–) German filmmaker and photographer; full name *Bertha Helene Amalie Riefenstahl*. She is chiefly known for *Triumph of the Will* (1934), a depiction of the 1934 Nuremberg Nazi Party rallies. Though she was not working for the Nazi Party, outside Germany her work was regarded as Nazi propaganda.

Riel |rē'el|, Louis (1844–85) Canadian political leader. He led the rebellion of the Metis at Red River Settlement in 1869, later forming a provisional government and negotiating terms for the union of Manitoba with Canada. He was

executed for treason after leading a further rebellion.

Rie•mann |'rēmän|, (Georg Friedrich) Bernhard (1826–66) German mathematician. He founded Riemannian geometry, which is of fundamental importance to both mathematics and physics. The *Riemann hypothesis*, about the complex numbers which are roots of a certain transcendental equation, remains an unsolved problem.

Riis |rēs|, Jacob August (1849–1914) U.S. journalist and reformer, born in Denmark. He was police reporter for *The New York Tribune* (1877–88) and *The New York Evening Sun* (1888–99) and a crusader for parks, playgrounds, and improved schools and housing in urban areas.

Riles |rīlz|, Wilson Camanza (1917–) U.S. educational consultant. Spingarn Medal, 1973.

Ri•ley |'rīlē|, Bridget (Louise) (1931–) English painter. A leading exponent of op art, she worked with flat patterns to create optical illusions of light and movement. Notable paintings: *Fall* (1963).

Ri•ley |'rīlē|, James Whitcomb (1849–1916) U.S. poet. Notable works: *The Old Swimmin'-Hole and 'Leven More Poems* (1883).

Ri•ley |'rīlē|, Pat (1945–) U.S. professional basketball player and coach. He coached the Los Angeles Lakers to four of their five NBA titles.

Ril•ke |'rilkə|, Rainer Maria (1875–1926) Austrian poet, born in Bohemia; pseudonym of *René Karl Wilhelm Josef Maria Rilke*. His conception of art as a quasi-religious vocation culminated in his best-known works, the *Duino Elegies* and *Sonnets to Orpheus* (both 1923).

Ril•lieux, Norbert (1806–94) U.S. inventor. He revolutionized the sugar-refining industry (1846) .

Rim•baud |ræm'bō|, (Jean Nicholas) Arthur (1854–91) French poet. Known for poems such as "Le Bateau ivre" (1871) and the collection of symbolist prose poems *Une Saison en enfer* (1873), and for his stormy relationship with Paul Verlaine, he stopped writing at about the age of 20 and spent the rest of his life traveling.

Rimes |rīmz|, LeAnn (1982–) U.S. country singer and songwriter. Grammy Award, 1997.

Rimsky-Korsakov |ˌrimskē 'kawrsə kawf|, Nikolai (Andreevich) (1844–1908) Russian composer. He achieved fame with his orchestral suite *Scheherazade* (1888) and his many operas drawing on Russian and Slavic folk tales.

Rines |rīnz|, Robert Harvey (1922–) U.S. inventor and lawyer. He invented high-resonance image-scanning radar and sonar.

Rip·ken |'ripkin|, Cal, Jr. (1960–) U.S. baseball player. He holds the major league record of 2,632 consecutive games.

Rip·ley |'riplē|, George (1802–80) U.S. critic and reformer. A Unitarian minister who withdrew from the profession, he became associated with the New England Transcendentalists and founded the Brook Farm commune (1841–47). He created the first daily book review in U.S., at the *New York Tribune* (1849–80).

Rit·ten·house |'rit(ə)n‚hows|, David (1732–96) U.S. astronomer, surveyor, and clockmaker. He settled the dispute over the boundaries of the Mason-Dixon line.

Rit·ter |'ritər|, Tex (1907–74) U.S. country singer, songwriter. Notable songs: "Jingle, Jangle, Jingle."

Ri·ve·ra |rə'verə|, Diego (1886–1957) Mexican painter. He inspired a revival of fresco painting in Latin America and the U.S. His largest mural is a history of Mexico for the National Palace in Mexico City (unfinished, 1929–57).

Riv·ers |'rivərz|, Joan (1937–) U.S. entertainer. She has appeared on many television shows with her trademark line, "Can we talk?"

Ro·bards |'rō‚bärds|, Jason Nelson, Jr. (1922–) U.S. actor. Notable movies: *Long Day's Journey into Night* (1962) and *All The President's Men* (1976, Academy Award).

Robbe-Grillet |ˌräbgrē'ye|, Alain (1922–) French novelist. His first novel, *The Erasers* (1953), was an early example of the *nouveau roman*. He also wrote essays and screenplays.

Rob·bia |'rawbyä| see DELLA ROBBIA.

Rob·bins |'räbənz|, Harold (1916–97) U.S. novelist He wrote best-sellers such as *The Carpetbaggers* (1961) and *The Betsy* (1971).

Rob·bins |'räbənz|, Jerome (1918–98) U.S. ballet dancer and choreographer. He choreographed a number of successful musicals, including *The King and I* (1951), *West Side Story* (1957), and *Fiddler on the Roof* (1964).

Rob·bins |'räbənz|, Marty (1925–82) U.S. country singer and songwriter. Notable songs: "A White Sport Coat and a Pink Carnation."

Rob·bins |'räbənz|, Tom (1936–) U.S. author. Notable works: *Even Cowgirls Get the Blues* (1976) and *Half Asleep in Frog Pajamas* (1994).

Rob·ert |'räbərt| the name of three kings of Scotland: **Robert I** (1274–1329), reigned 1306–29; known as **Robert the Bruce**. He campaigned against Edward I and defeated Edward II at Bannockburn (1314). He re-established Scotland as a separate kingdom, negotiating the Treaty of Northampton (1328). **Robert II** (1316–90), grandson of Robert the Bruce, reigned 1371–90. He was steward of Scotland from 1326 to 1371 and the first of the Stuart line. **Robert III** (*c.*1337–1406), son of Robert II, reigned 1390–1406; born *John*. An accident made him physically disabled, resulting in a power struggle among members of his family.

Rob·erts |'räbərts|, Cokie (1943–) U.S. journalist. Full name *Corinne Boggs Roberts*. She is a correspondent for National Public Radio. (1977–), a co-anchor on the television program "This Week" (1996–), and the author of *We Are Our Mother's Daughters* (1998).

Rob·erts |'räbərts|, Frederick Sleigh, 1st Earl Roberts of Kandahar (1832–1914) British field marshal.

Rob·erts |'räbərts|, Owen Josephus (1875–1955) U.S. Supreme Court justice (1930–45). He also served as dean of the University of Pennsylvania Law School (1948–51).

Rob·ert·son |'räbərtsən|, Cliff (1925–) U.S. actor. Notable movies: *Charly* (1968, Academy Award).

Rob·ert·son |'räbərtsən|, Oscar (1938–) U.S. basketball player. He led the 1960 U.S. Olympic team to a gold medal.

Rob·ert the Bruce see ROBERT.

Robe·son |'rōb(ə)sən|, Paul (Bustill) (1898–1976) U.S. singer and actor. His singing of "Ol' Man River" in the musical *Showboat* (1927) established his international reputation. As an actor Robeson was particularly identified with the title role of *Othello*. His black activism and Communist sympathies led to ostracism in the 1950s.

Robes·pierre |ˌrōbz'pyer|, Maximilien François Marie Isidore de (1758–94) French revolutionary. As leader of the radical Jacobins in the National Assembly he backed the execution of Louis XVI, implemented a purge of the Girondists, and initiated the Terror, but the following year he fell from favor and was guillotined.

Rob·in·son |'räbənsən|, Brooks (1937–   ) U.S. baseball player. He led the American League in fielding 12 times (1960–72).

Rob·in·son |'räbənsən|, Edward G. (1893–1972) Romanian-born U.S. actor; born *Emanuel Goldenberg*. He appeared in a number of gangster movies in the 1930s, starting with *Little Caesar* (1930).

Rob·in·son |'räbənsən|, Edwin Arlington (1869–1935) U.S. poet. His verse was largely unnoticed until 1905, when President T. Roosevelt praised his dramatic, often ironic work, setting into motion much recognition. Pulitzer Prize–winning works: *Collected Poems* (1921), *The Man Who Died Twice* (1924), and *Tristram* (1927).

Rob·in·son |'räbənsən|, Frank (1935–   ) U.S. baseball player and manager. He won MVP honors in both the National League and the American League, and became the first African-American manager in the major leagues (1975).

Rob·in·son |'räbənsən|, Jackie (1919–72) U.S. baseball player (1947–56). Born *Jack Roosevelt Robinson*. Joining the Brooklyn Dodgers in 1947, he became the first black player in the major leagues. In 1949, he led the National League with a .342 batting average and was named the league's Most Valuable

Player. Elected to the Baseball Hall of Fame (1962).

Rob·in·son |'räbənsən|, Joseph Taylor (1872–1937) U.S. politician. He was a member of the U.S. House of Representatives (1903–13) and of the U.S. Senate from Arkansas (1913–37) and a Democratic vice presidential candidate (1928).

Rob·in·son |'räbənsən|, Mary (Terese Winifred) (1944–   ) Irish Labour stateswoman, president (1990–97). She became Ireland's first woman president, noted for her platform of religious toleration and her liberal attitude. She became United Nations High Commissioner for Human Rights in 1997.

Rob·in·son |'räbənsən|, Max (1939–88) U.S. television journalist. He became the first African American to anchor a network news show (1978).

Rob·in·son |'räbənsən|, Smokey (1940–   ) U.S. soul singer and songwriter; born *William Robinson*. He is known for a series of successes with his group the Miracles, such as "Tracks of my Tears" (1965).

Rob·in·son |'räbənsən|, Sugar Ray (1920–89) U.S. boxer; born *Walker Smith*. He was world welterweight champion and seven times middleweight champion.

Rob Roy |'räb 'roi| (1671–1734) Scottish outlaw; born *Robert Macgregor*. His reputation as a Scottish Robin Hood was exaggerated in Sir Walter Scott's novel of the same name (1817).

Rob·son |'räbsən|, Dame Flora (1902–84) English actress. She was noted for her performance as the Empress Elizabeth in *Catherine the Great* (1934), and later for her many character roles.

Ro·cham·beau |ˌrawSHəm'bō|, Jean Baptiste Donatien de Vimeur, Comte de (1725–1807) French soldier. He commanded a French force that came to George Washington's aid at White Plains, New York, during the Revolutionary War (1781).

Roche |rōSH|, (Eamonn) Kevin (1922–   ) U.S. architect, born in Ireland. Notable designs: the Oakland Museum (Oakland, California, 1961–68) and the UN Plaza (New York, 1969–75).

Roch·es·ter |'räCHəstər|, John Wilmot,

2nd Earl of (1647–80) English poet and courtier. Infamous for his dissolute life at the court of Charles II, he wrote sexually explicit love poems and verse satires.

Rock |räk|, John (1890–1984) U.S. obstetrician-gynecologist. With Gregory Pincus and M.C. Chang he pioneered oral contraceptive pills (1960).

Rock·e·fel·ler |'räkə,felər| U.S. business and political family, including: **John D. Rockefeller**, (1839–1937), U.S. industrialist and philanthropist; full name *John Davison Rockefeller*. He founded the Standard Oil company in 1870, and by 1880 he exercised a virtual monopoly over oil refining in the U.S. Both he and his son, **John D. Rockefeller, Jr.** (1874–1960), established many philanthropic institutions. **Nelson Rockefeller** (1908–1979), son of John D. Rockefeller, Jr., and U.S. vice president (1974–77), known as **Rocky**. He held several government posts under Presidents F. D. Roosevelt, Truman, and Eisenhower before becoming governor of New York (1958–73). Nominated by Gerald Ford, he was named vice president when Ford acceded to the presidency following President Nixon's resignation (1974).

Rock·ne |'räknē|, Knute (1888–1931) U.S. college football coach. He coached Notre Dame to three consecutive national titles.

Rock·well |'räk,wel|, Norman (Percevel) (1894–1978) U.S. illustrator. Known for his typically sentimental portraits of small-town American life, he was an illustrator for *The Saturday Evening Post*, for which he created 317 covers (1916–63).

Rod·den·ber·ry |'rädn,berē|, Gene (1921–91) U.S. television producer and scriptwriter; full name *Eugene Wesley Roddenberry*. He created and wrote many scripts for the television science-fiction drama series "Star Trek," first broadcast 1966–69.

Rod·dick |'rädək|, Anita (Lucia) (1943–) English businesswoman. In 1976 she opened a shop selling cosmetics with an emphasis on environmentally conscious products. This developed into the Body Shop chain.

Rod·gers |'räjərz|, Jimmie (1897–1933) U.S. country singer and songwriter. Full name *James Charles Rodgers*; known as **The Singing Brakeman**. After retiring from his work on the railroad, he recorded over 100 songs, including "Waiting for a Train" and "T for Texas."

Rod·gers |'räjərz|, Richard (Charles) (1902–79) U.S. composer. He worked with lyricist **Lorenz Hart** (1895–1942) before collaborating with Oscar Hammerstein II on a succession of popular musicals, including *Oklahoma!* (1943), *South Pacific* (1949), *The King and I* (1951), and *The Sound of Music* (1959).

Ro·din |,rō'dæN|, Auguste (1840–1917) French sculptor. He was chiefly concerned with the human form. Notable works: *The Thinker* (1880) and *The Kiss* (1886).

Rod·man |'rädmən|, Dennis (1961–) U.S. basketball player. He led the National Basketball Association in rebounding six years in a row (1991–97).

Rod·ney |'rädnē|, Red (1927–94) U.S. jazz trumpeter. Born *Robert Chudnick*. Originally a swing player, he modernized his style after hearing Dizzy Gillespie and Charlie Parker; he played bop style in Charlie Parker's quintet (1949–51).

Ro·dri·go |raw'drēgō|, Joaquín (1901–) Spanish composer. He is best known for his guitar concerto (1939) and for his *Concerto Pastorale* (1978) for flute and orchestra, commissioned by James Galway.

Roe |rō|, Sir (Edwin) Alliott Verdon (1877–1958) English engineer and aircraft designer. With his brother H.V. Roe he founded the Avro Co. and built a number of planes, including the Avro 504 biplane of World War I; in 1928 he formed the Saunders-Roe Co. to design and manufacture flying boats.

Roeb·ling |'rōbliNG|, John Augustus (1806–69) U.S. engineer and bridge builder, born in Germany. He designed the railroad span at Niagara Falls (1851–55) and made plans for the Brooklyn Bridge, which his son Washington Augustus Roebling (1837–1926) completed as chief engineer of construction.

Roeg |rōg|, Nicholas (Jack) (1928–)

English movie director. His work is often impressionistic, and uses cutting techniques to create disjointed narratives. Notable works: *Performance* (1970) and *The Man Who Fell to Earth* (1975).

Roeth·ke |'retkē; 'reTHkē|, Theodore (1908–63) U.S. educator and poet. Notable works: *The Waking* (1953, Pulitzer Prize) and *Words for the Wind* (1958, Bollingen Prize).

Rog·ers |'räjərz|, Edith (1881–1960) U.S. politician. Born *Edith Nourse*. As a member of the U.S. House of Representatives from Massachusetts (1925–60), she introduced legislation that created the Women's Army Corps and the GI Bill of Rights.

Rog·ers |'räjərz|, Fred McFeely (1928–   ) U.S. television producer, actor, and author. He created and stars in the television program "Mister Rogers' Neighborhood" (1965–   ).

Rog·ers |'räjərz|, Ginger (1911–95) U.S. actress and dancer; born *Virginia Katherine McMath*. She is known for her dancing partnership with Fred Astaire, during which she appeared in movie musicals, including *Top Hat* (1935). Her solo acting career included the movie *Kitty Foyle* (1940), for which she won an Oscar.

Rog·ers |'räjərz|, Henry Huttleston (1840–1909) U.S. financier. While an executive with Standard Oil, he patented machinery for separating naphtha from crude oil and originated the idea of pipeline transportation.

Rog·ers |'räjərz|, James Gamble (1897–1947) U.S. architect. Notable designs: the Columbia-Presbyterian Medical Center (New York) and much of Yale University.

Rog·ers |'räjərz|, Kenny (1938–   ) U.S. country singer. Full name *Kenneth Ray Rogers*. His hits include "Lucille," "The Gambler," and "We've Got Tonight."

Rog·ers |'räjərz|, Sir Richard (George) (1933–   ) British architect, born in Italy. A leading exponent of high-tech architecture, his major works include the Pompidou Centre in Paris (1971–77), designed with the Italian architect Renzo Piano, and the Lloyd's Building in London (1986).

Rog·ers |'räjərz|, Roy (1912–98) U.S. actor and singer. Born *Leonard Slye*. He was one of the "Original Sons of the Pioneers" country singers.

Rog·ers |'räjərz|, Will (1879–1935) U.S. humorist and actor. Full name *William Penn Adair Rogers*. A vaudeville headliner with his rope twirling and homespun humor (from 1902), he wrote a syndicated column for *The New York Times* (1922–35). He died in a plane crash with aviator Wiley Post.

Ro·get |rō'ZHā|, Peter Mark (1779–1869) English scholar. He worked as a physician but is remembered as the compiler of *Roget's Thesaurus of English Words and Phrases*, first published in 1852.

Roh·mer |'rōmər|, Sax (1883–1959) British author. Born *Arthur Sarsfield Ward*. Under the pseudonym Sax Rohmer he wrote novels featuring the fictional Chinese criminal Fu Manchu.

Rohr·er |'rawrər|, Heinrich (1933–   ) U.S. physicist, born in Switzerland. He invented the scanning tunneling microscope (Nobel Prize, 1986).

Rolfe |rawlf|, John (1585–1622) Virginia colonist, born in England. He perfected the process of curing tobacco, and he was married to the American Indian Pocahontas.

Rol·land |raw'läN|, Romain (1866–1944) French novelist, dramatist, and essayist. His interest in genius led to a number of biographies, and ultimately to *Jean-Christophe* (1904–12), a cycle of ten novels about a German composer. Nobel Prize for Literature (1915).

Rolls |rōlz|, Charles Stewart (1877–1910) English automotive and aviation pioneer. He and Henry Royce formed the company Rolls-Royce Ltd in 1906. Rolls, the first Englishman to fly across the English Channel, was killed in an airplane crash. The Rolls-Royce company established its reputation with luxury cars such as the Silver Ghost and the Silver Shadow, and produced aircraft engines used in both world wars, and later for commercial airliners.

Röl·vaag |'rōl,väg|, Öle Edvart (1876–1931) U.S. author and educator, born in Norway. Notable novels: *Giants in the Earth* (1927) and *Their Fathers' God* (1931).

Rom·berg |'räm,bǝrg|, Sigmund (1887–1951) Hungarian-born U.S. composer. He wrote a succession of popular operettas, including *The Student Prince* (1924), *The Desert Song* (1926), and *New Moon* (1928).

Rom·mel |'rämǝl|, Erwin (1891–1944) German field marshal; known as **the Desert Fox**. As commander of the Afrika Korps he deployed a series of surprise maneuvers and succeeded in capturing Tobruk (1942), but was defeated by Montgomery at El Alamein later that year. He was forced to commit suicide after being implicated in the officers' conspiracy against Hitler in 1944.

Rom·ney[1] |'rämnē|, George (1734–1802) English portrait painter. From the early 1780s he produced over fifty portraits of Lady Hamilton in historical costumes and poses.

Rom·ney[2] |'rämnē|, George (1907–95) U.S. businessman and politician, born in Mexico. He was president of American Motors, governor of Michigan (1963–69), and U.S. secretary of Housing and Urban Development (1969–72).

Ron·stadt |'rän,stæt|, Linda (1946–) U.S. pop and folk musician. Notable songs: "You're No Good" and "I Can't Help It If I'm Still in Love with You" (Grammy Award, 1975).

Rönt·gen |'rentgǝn; 'rOEntgǝn|, Wilhelm Conrad (1845–1923) German physicist, the discoverer of X-rays. He was a skillful experimenter and worked in a variety of areas as well as radiation. He was awarded the first Nobel Prize for Physics (1901).

Roo·ney |'roōnē|, Andy (1919–) U.S. journalist and author. Full name *Andrew Aitkin Rooney*. He is a writer and producer for CBS News (1959–), a syndicated columnist (1979–), and a commentator on television's "60 Minutes" (1978–).

Roo·ney |'roōnē|, Mickey (1920–) U.S. actor; born *Joseph Yule, Jr.* He played Andy Hardy in sixteen comedy-drama films about the Hardy family. He received Oscar nominations for his roles in *Babes in Arms* (1939) and *The Human Comedy* (1943).

Roo·se·velt |'rōzǝ,velt| **Theodore Roosevelt** see box. **Alice Hathaway**

Lee Roosevelt (1861–84), first wife of Theodore Roosevelt, whom she married in 1880. **Edith Kermit Carow Roosevelt** (1861–1948), wife of Theodore Roosevelt and U.S. first lady (1901–09).

Roo·se·velt |'rōzǝ,velt| **Franklin D. Roosevelt** see box. **(Anna) Eleanor Roosevelt** (1884–1962), wife of Franklin D. Roosevelt and U.S. first lady (1933–45). She was the niece of

---

Roosevelt, Theodore
26th U.S. president

Life dates: 1858–1919
Place of birth: New York, New York
Mother: Martha Bulloch Roosevelt
Father: Theodore Roosevelt
Wife: Alice Hathaway Lee (died 1884); Edith Kermit Carow (married 1886)
Children: (by first wife) Alice Lee; (by second wife) Theodore, Jr., Kermit, Ethel, Archibald, Quentin
Nicknames: Teddy; TR
College/University: Harvard
Military service: during Spanish-American War, organized and commanded a volunteer cavalry known as the "Rough Riders"
Career: Rancher; soldier; writer
Political career: New York State Assembly; U.S. Civil Service Commissioner; governor of New York; vice president (under McKinley); president; organized Progressive (Bull Moose) Party
Party: Republican
Home state: New York
Opponents in presidential races: Alton B. Parker (1904); William Howard Taft, Woodrow Wilson (1912)
Term of office: Sept. 14, 1901 (succeeded to the presidency after the assassination of William McKinley)–March 3, 1909
Vice president: none (first term); Charles W. Fairbanks (second term)
Notable events of presidency: breaking up of trusts; Sherman Anti-Trust Act; Department of Commerce and Labor created; U.S. Forest Service established; Panama Canal Zone acquired by U.S.; Federal Food and Drugs Act; Oklahoma admitted as 46th state
Other achievements: Awarded Nobel Prize in 1906 for mediation leading to the Russo-Japanese Peace Treaty
Place of burial: Oyster Bay, New York

Theodore Roosevelt and married Franklin Roosevelt in 1905. She was involved in a wide range of liberal causes; as chair of the U.N. Commission on Human Rights she helped draft the Declaration of Human Rights (1948).

Root |ro͞ot|, Elihu (1845–1937) U.S. lawyer and diplomat. He served as secretary of war (1898–1904) and as secretary of state (1905–09). He won the Nobel Peace Prize for the Root-Takahira Agreement with the Japanese (1912).

Root |ro͞ot|, John Wellborn (1887–1963) U.S. architect. He designed the Palmo-

---

Roosevelt, Franklin Delano
32nd U.S. president

Life dates: 1882–1945
Place of birth: Hyde Park, New York
Mother: Sara Roosevelt
Father: James Roosevelt
Wife: (Anna) Eleanor Roosevelt
Children: Anna Eleanor, James, Franklin Delano, Jr. (died in infancy, 1909), Elliott, Franklin Delano Jr. (born 1914), John
Nickname: FDR
College/University: Harvard; Columbia University Law School
Career: lawyer; bank officer
Political career: New York Senate; assistant secretary of the Navy; governor of New York; president
Party: Democratic
Home state: New York
Opponents in presidential races: Herbert C. Hoover (1932); Alfred M. Landon (1936); Wendell Lewis Willkie (1940); Thomas E. Dewey (1944)
Term of office: March 4, 1933–Apr. 12, 1945 (died during fourth term)
Vice presidents: John Nance Garner; Henry A. Wallace (third term); Harry S. Truman (fourth term)
Notable events of presidency: banking crisis ended with bank holiday declaration; New Deal programs enacted; Federal Housing Administration authorized; Federal Communications Commission created; Social Security Act; Fair Labor Standards Act; World War II; "Four Freedoms" enunciated; Lend-Lease Act; Yalta Conference
Other achievements: vice president, Fidelity and Deposit Company
Place of burial: Hyde Park, New York

---

live Building (Chicago) and the Hotel Statler (Washington, D.C.).

Ro•sa |'rōzə|, Salvator (1615–73) Italian painter and etcher. The picturesque and "sublime" qualities of his landscapes, often peopled with bandits and containing scenes of violence in wild natural settings, were an important influence on the romantic art of the 18th and 19th centuries.

Ros•ci•us |'räsH(ē)əs| (died 62 BC) Roman actor; full name *Quintus Roscius Gallus*. Many notable English actors from the 16th century onward were nicknamed in reference to his great skill.

Rose |rōz|, Axl (1962–) U.S. hard rock vocalist. Born *William Bailey*. He formed the Guns 'n' Roses band with Izzy Stradlin (1985).

Rose |rōz|, Fred (1898–1954) U.S. country singer, songwriter and musician. Notable songs: "Honest and Truly" and "Deed I Do."

Rose |rōz|, Pete (1941–) U.S. baseball player and manager. He holds the major league record for hits with 4,256.

Rose•anne |rō'zæn| (1952–) U.S. actress. Born *Roseanne Barr*. She was the award-winning star of the television program "Roseanne" (1988–97).

Rose•bery |'rōz,berē|, Archibald Philip Primrose, 5th Earl of (1847–1929) British Liberal statesman, prime minister (1894–95).

Ro•sen•berg |'rōzən,bərg| U.S. spies. **Ethel Greenglass Rosenberg** (1915–53) and her husband **Julius Rosenberg** (1918–53) were Communist Party members executed for espionage.

Ro•sen•berg |'rōzən,bərg|, Howard (1942–) U.S. journalist. A writer for the *Los Angeles Times*, he won a Pulitzer Prize for criticism (1985).

Ro•so•li•no |,räsə'lēnō|, Frank (1926–78) U.S. jazz trombonist. He performed with Howard Rumsey's Lighthouse All Stars (1954–60) and with Donn Trenner's band on television's "Steve Allen Show" (1962–64).

Ross |raws| British explorers. **Sir John Ross** (1777–1856) led an expedition to Baffin Bay in 1818 and another in search of the Northwest Passage between 1829 and 1833. His nephew, **Sir James Clark Ross** (1800–62), discovered the north magnetic pole in 1831 and headed an expedition to the Antarctic from 1839 to 1843, in the course of which he discovered Ross Island, Ross Dependency, and the Ross Sea.

Ross |raws|, Betsy (1752–1836) American patriot and seamstress. Full name *Elizabeth Griscom Ross*. She is credited with having made the first flag of the U.S. (June 1776).

Ross |raws|, Diana (1944–   ) U.S. pop and soul singer. Originally the lead singer of the Supremes, she went on to become a successful solo artist. She received an Oscar for her role as Billie Holiday in the movie *Lady Sings the Blues* (1973).

Ross |raws|, Harold Wallace (1892–1951) U.S. editor. He was founder and editor of *The New Yorker* magazine (1925–51).

Ross |raws|, Sir Ronald (1857–1932) British physician. Ross confirmed that the *Anopheles* mosquito transmitted malaria, and went on to elucidate the stages in the malarial parasite's life cycle. Nobel Prize for Physiology or Medicine (1902).

Ros·sel·li·ni |ˌrawsəˈlēnē|, Roberto (1906–77) Italian movie director. He is known for his neorealist movies, particularly his quasidocumentary trilogy about World War II, *Open City* (1945).

Ros·set·ti |rəˈzetē| English family, including: **Dante Gabriel Rossetti** (1828–82), poet and painter; full name *Gabriel Charles Dante Rossetti*. A founding member of the Pre-Raphaelite brotherhood (1848), he is best known for his idealized images of women, including *Beata Beatrix* (c.1863) and *The Blessed Damozel* (1871–79). **Christina (Georgina) Rossetti** (1830–94), his sister and a poet. She wrote much religious poetry (reflecting her High Anglican faith), love poetry, and children's verse. Notable works: *Goblin Market and Other Poems* (1862).

Ros·si·ni |rəˈsēnē|, Gioacchino Antonio (1792–1868) Italian composer, one of the creators of Italian bel canto. He wrote over thirty operas, including *The Barber of Seville* (1816) and *William Tell* (1829).

Ros·tand |ˈrästənd|, Edmond (1868–

1918) French dramatist and poet. He romanticized the life of the 17th-century soldier, duelist, and writer Cyrano de Bergerac in his poetic drama of that name (1897).

Ros·ten |ˈrawstən|, Leo (Calvin) (1908–97) U.S. political scientist and humorist, born in Poland. Pseudonym **Leonard Q. Ross**. Notable works: *The Joys of Yinglish* (1989).

Ros·tro·po·vich |ˌrawstrəˈpōvicH|, Mstislav Leopoldovich (1927–   ) Russian cellist, pianist, and conductor. He was music director and conductor of the National Symphony Orchestra in Washington, D.C. (1977–94).

Roth |rawTH|, Ann (1931–   ) U.S. costume designer. She was a leading costumer for Broadway plays from the late 1950s and for Hollywood films from the mid 1960s.

Roth |rawTH|, Henry (c. 1906–   ) U.S. author, born in Austria. Notable works: *Call It Sleep* (1934).

Roth |rawTH|, Philip (Milton) (1933–   ) U.S. novelist and short-story writer. He often writes with irony and humor about the complexity and diversity of contemporary American Jewish life. Notable works: *Portnoy's Complaint* (1969), which records the intimate confessions of an adolescent boy to his psychiatrist; *Zuckerman Bound* (1985); and *American Pastoral* (1997).

Roth·ko |ˈrawTHkō|, Mark (1903–70) U.S. painter, born in Latvia; born *Marcus Rothkovich*. A leading figure in color-field painting, he painted hazy and apparently floating rectangles of color.

Roth·schild |ˈrawTH,CHīld|, Meyer Amschel (1743–1812) German financier. He founded the Rothschild banking house in Frankfurt at the end of the 19th century and was financial adviser to the landgrave of Hesse. His five sons all entered banking.

Rou·ault |rooˈō|, Georges (Henri) (1871–1958) French painter and engraver. Associated with expressionism, he used vivid colors and simplified forms enclosed in thick black outlines.

Rous |rows|, (Francis) Peyton (1879–1970) U.S. pathologist. He was a pioneering cancer researcher; in 1966 he won the Nobel Prize for Physiology or Medicine with C. B. Huggins for the discovery of tumor-inducing viruses (1910).

Rous·seau |rŏŏ'sō|, Henri (Julien) (1844–1910) French painter; known as **le Douanier** ("customs officer"). After retiring as a customs official in 1893, he created bold and colorful paintings of fantastic dreams and exotic jungle landscapes, such as *Sleeping Gypsy* (1897) and *Tropical Storm with Tiger* (1891).

Rous·seau |rŏŏ'sō|, Jean-Jacques (1712–78) French philosopher and writer, born in Switzerland. He believed that civilization warps the fundamental goodness of human nature, but that the ill effects can be moderated by active participation in democratic consensual politics. Notable works: *Émile* (1762) and *The Social Contract* (1762).

Rous·seau |rŏŏ'sō|, (Pierre Étienne) Théodore (1812–67) French painter. A leading landscapist of the Barbizon School, his works typically depict the scenery and changing light effects of the forest of Fontainebleau, for example *Under the Birches, Evening* (1842–44).

Ro·vere, Richard (Halworth) (1915–79) U.S. journalist. A writer for *The New Yorker* (1944–79), he also wrote *Arrivals and Departures* (1976).

Row·an |'rōən|, Carl Thomas (1925–) U.S. journalist. He has written a nationally syndicated column since 1965; he was U.S. ambassador to Finland (1963–64) and director of the U.S. Information Agency (1964–65).

Rowe |rō|, Nicholas (1647–1718) English dramatist. Notable works: *Tamerlane* (1701) and *The Fair Penitent* (1703).

Row·land·son |'rōlən(d)sən|, Mary White (*c.* 1635–*c.* 1678) American writer. She and her three children were abducted (1676) by hostile Indians during King Philip's War; she published her narrative in 1682.

Row·land·son |'rōlən(d)sən|, Thomas (1756–1827) English painter, draftsman, and caricaturist. Some of his watercolors and drawings are featured in the series *Tours of Dr. Syntax* (1812–21).

Rowles, Jimmy (1918–96) U.S. jazz composer and pianist. Born *James George Hunter*. He was an accompanist to singers such as Billie Holiday and Peggy Lee.

Royce |rois|, Sir (Frederick) Henry (1863–1933) English engine designer. He founded the company of Rolls-Royce Ltd. with Charles Stewart Rolls in 1906, becoming famous as the designer of the Rolls-Royce Silver Ghost automobile and later also becoming known for his aircraft engines.

Roy·ko |'roikō|, Mike (1932–) U.S. journalist. A reporter and columnist for the *Chicago Daily News* (1959–78) and *Chicago Tribune* (1984–97), he won a Pulitzer Prize for commentary (1972).

Roy·ster |'roistər|, Vermont Connecticut (1914–96) U.S. journalist. On the staff of *The Wall Street Journal* for 60 years (1936–96), he won a Pulitzer Prize for commentary (1984).

Rub·bra |'rəbrə|, (Charles) Edmund (1901–86) English composer and pianist. He wrote many songs and eleven symphonies.

Ru·bens |'rŏŏbenz|, Sir Peter Paul (1577–1640) Flemish painter. The foremost exponent of northern Baroque, he is best known for his portraits and mythological paintings featuring voluptuous female nudes, as in *Venus and Adonis* (*c.* 1635).

Ru·bik |'rŏŏbik|, Ernö (1944–) Hungarian professor and inventor. He devised the Rubik's Cube puzzle (1974).

Ru·bin |'rŏŏbən|, Benjamin A. (1917–) U.S. inventor. He invented the bifurcated vaccination needle, which can be used in primitive conditions.

Ru·bin |'rŏŏbən|, Jerry (1938–94) U.S. radical. A 1960s standard-bearer of counterculture, he led student opposition to Vietnam War.

Ru·bin·stein |'rŏŏbən,stīn|, Anton (Grigorevich) (1829–94) Russian composer and pianist. In 1862 he founded the St. Petersburg Conservatory and was its director 1862–67 and 1887–91. He composed symphonies, operas, songs, and piano music.

Ru·bin·stein |'rŏŏbən,stīn|, Artur (1888–1982) Polish-born U.S. pianist. He toured extensively in Europe and the U.S. and among his many recordings are the complete works of Chopin.

Ru·bin·stein |'rŏŏbən,stīn|, Helena

(1882–1965) U.S. beautician and businesswoman. Her organization became an international cosmetics manufacturer and distributor.

Ru·by |'roobē|, Jack (1911–67) U.S. assassin. He shot and killed Lee Harvey Osward, the man accused of murdering President Kennedy.

Ruck·ey·ser, Muriel (1913–80) U.S. poet and author. Her poetry reflects her liberal political activism.

Rud·kin |'rədkin|, Margaret Fogarty (1897–1967) U.S. entrepreneur. She began the Pepperidge Farms company by baking bread at home.

Ru·dolph |'roodawlf|, Paul (1918–) U.S. architect. Notable designs: the Jewitt Art Center (Wellesley College) and the Art and Architecture building at Yale University.

Ru·dolph |'roodawlf|, Wilma (1940–94) U.S. runner. She was the first woman to win three gold medals in track and field in one Olympics (1960).

Ruis·dael |'roisdäl|, Jacob van (c. 1628–82) Dutch landscape painter. Also **Ruysdael**. Born in Haarlem, he painted the surrounding landscape from the mid-1640s until his move to Amsterdam in 1657.

Ru·iz de Alar·cón y Men·do·za |roo 'ēs dä ˌälär'kawn ē ˌmen'dōsə|, Juan (1580–1639) Spanish dramatist, born in Mexico City. His most famous play, the moral comedy *La Verdad sospechosa*, was the basis of Corneille's *Le Menteur* (1642).

Ru·key·ser |'roo,kīzər|, Louis (1933–) U.S. economic commentator. He hosts the television program "Wall Street Week."

Rund·stedt |'roond,stet|, Karl Rudolf Gerd von (1875–1953) German field marshal. He was the German commander in chief on the Western Front during World War II (1942–45).

Run·yon |'rənyən|, (Alfred) Damon (1884–1946) U.S. author and journalist. His short stories about New York's Broadway underworld characters are written in a highly individual style with much use of colorful slang. His collection *Guys and Dolls* (1932) formed the basis for the musical of the same name (1950).

Ru·pert, Prince |'roopərt| (1619–82) English Royalist general, son of Frederick V (elector of the Palatinate) and nephew of Charles I. The Royalist leader of cavalry, he initially won a series of victories, but was defeated by Parliamentarian forces at Marston Moor (1644) and Naseby (1645).

Rupp |rəp|, Adolph (1901–77) U.S. college basketball coach. He coached the University of Kentucky to four NCAA championships.

Rush |rəsн|, Benjamin (1745–1813) American physician, educator, and patriot. He was a member of the Continental Congress (1776–77) and a signer of the Declaration of Independence. As surgeon general of the Continental Army, he established the first free dispensary in the U.S. (1786).

Rush·die |'rəsнdē|, (Ahmed) Salman (1947–) Indian-born British novelist. His work, chiefly associated with magic realism, includes the prize-winning *Midnight's Children* and *The Satanic Verses* (1988). The latter, regarded by Muslims as blasphemous, caused Iran's Ayatollah Khomeini to issue a fatwa (death penalty) in 1989 condemning Rushdie to death. Other works: *Haroun and the Sea of Stories* (1990, for children) and *The Moor's Last Sigh* (1995).

Rush·ing |'rəsнing|, Jimmy (1903–72) U.S. blues singer. Full name *James Andrew Rushing*; known as **Mr. Five by Five**. He performed with Count Basie's Band (1935–50).

Rusk |rəsk|, (David) Dean (1909–94) U.S. educator and statesman. He was secretary of state under Presidents Kennedy and Johnson (1961–69).

Rus·kin |'rəskən|, John (1819–1900) English art and social critic. His prolific writings include attacks on Renaissance art in *The Stone of Venice* (1851–53), capitalism in "The Political Economy of Art" (1857), and utilitarianism in *Unto This Last* (1860).

Rus·sell |'rəsəl|, Bertrand (Arthur William), 3rd Earl Russell (1872–1970) British philosopher, mathematician, and social reformer. In *Principia Mathematica* (1910–13) he and A. N. Whitehead attempted to express all of mathematics in formal logic terms. He expounded logical atomism in *Our Knowledge of the External World* (1914) and neutral monism in *The Analysis of Mind* (1921). A conscientious objector during World War I, he also campaigned for women's suffrage and against nuclear arms. Nobel Prize for Literature (1950).

Rus·sell |'rəsəl|, Bill (1934–) U.S. basketball player and coach. He became the first African-American head coach in the NBA (1966).

Rus·sell |'rəsəl|, Charles Marion (1865–1926) U.S. artist. He was noted for his paintings of cowboy and Indian life and Western landscapes.

Rus·sell |'rəsəl|, George William (1867–1935) Irish poet and journalist. After the performance of his poetic drama *Deirdre* (1902) Russell became a leading figure in the Irish literary revival.

Rus·sell |'rəsəl|, Henry Norris (1877–1959) U.S. astronomer. He worked mainly in astrophysics and spectroscopy, and is best known for his independent discovery of the relationship between stellar magnitude and spectral type, which he represented diagrammatically.

Rus·sell |'rəsəl|, John, 1st Earl Russell (1792–1878) British Whig statesman, prime minister (1846–52 and 1865–66). He was responsible for introducing the Reform Bill of 1832 into Parliament and resigned his second premiership when his attempt to extend the franchise further was unsuccessful.

Rus·sell |'rəsəl|, Ken (1927–) English movie director. Full name *Henry Kenneth Alfred Russell*. Characterized by extravagant and extreme imagery, his movies, for example *Women in Love* (1969), have often attracted controversy for their depiction of sex and violence.

Rus·sell |'rəsəl|, Pee Wee (1906–69) U.S. jazz clarinetist. Full name *Charles Ellsworth Russell*. He played dixieland music mainly in New York and intermittently with Eddie Condon for 30 years.

Russ·wurm |'rəs,wərm|, John Brown (1799–1851) U.S. publisher. With Samuel E. Cornish he founded the nation's first black newspaper, *Freedom's Journal* (1827, New York).

Rus·tin |'rəstən|, Bayard (1910–87) U.S. civil rights leader. He helped organized the March on Washington (1963).

Ruth |rōōTH|, Babe (1895–1948) U.S. baseball player; born *George Herman Ruth*; also known as the **Bambino**. He played for the Boston Red Sox (1914–19), New York Yankees (1919–34), and Boston Braves (1935). Originally a pitcher, he later became noted for his hitting, setting a record of 714 career home runs that remained unbroken until 1974 and a single-season record in 1927 of 60 home runs that was not broken until 1961. In 1936 he became one of the original inductees into the Baseball Hall of Fame.

Ruth·er·ford |'rəTHərfərd|, Johnny (1938–) U.S. racecar driver. He won the Indy 500 championship three times.

Ruth·er·ford |'rəTHərfərd|, Dame Margaret (1892–1972) English actress. Chiefly remembered for her roles as a formidable but jovial eccentric, she won an Oscar for *The VIPs* (1963).

Rut·ledge |'rətləj|, John (1739–1800) U.S. Supreme Court justice (1789–91). He was appointed Chief Justice of the U.S. in 1795 and served one term but was not confirmed by the U.S. Senate.

Rut·ledge |'rətləj|, Wiley Blount, Jr. (1894–1949) U.S. Supreme Court justice (1943–49).

Ruys·dael variant spelling of RUISDAEL.

Ry·an |'rīən|, Nolan (1947–) U.S. baseball player. He holds the pitching records for no-hitters (7) and strikeouts (5,714).

Ry·an |'rīən|, Thomas Fortune (1851–1926) U.S. financier. Among many investments, he was a founder of the American Tobacco Co. in the early 1890s.

Ry·der |'rīdər|, Albert Pinkham (1847–1917) U.S. artist. He is known for seascapes and pastoral landscapes.

Ry·der |'rīdər|, Winona (1971–) U.S. actress. Born *Winona Laura Horowitz*. Notable movies: *Age of Innocence* (1993) and *Little Women* (1994).

Ry·kiel, Sonia (1930–) French fashion designer.

Ryle |rīl|, Gilbert (1900–76) English philosopher. In *The Concept of Mind* (1949) he attacks the mind–body dualism of Descartes. He was a cousin of the astronomer Sir Martin Ryle.

Ryle |rīl|, Sir Martin (1918–84) English astronomer. His demonstration that remote objects appeared to be different from closer ones helped to establish the big bang theory of the universe. Nobel Prize for Physics (1974). He was a cousin of the philosopher Gilbert Ryle.

Ry·sa·nek |'rēzä,nek|, Leonie (1926–98) Austrian operatic soprano. She made her debut at Innsbruck in 1949 as Agathe in *Der Freischütz*, and with the New York Metropolitan Opera in 1959 as Lady Macbeth; for the next 37 years she sang 299 performances of 24 roles.

Ss

Saa·di variant spelling of SADI.

Saa·ri·nen |'särənən|, Eero (1910–61) U.S. architect, born in Finland. Notable designs: Memorial Arch in St. Louis (1948) and the U.S. Embassy in London (1955–60).

Sa·bin |'sābən|, Albert Bruce (1906–93) U.S. physician, born in Russia. He developed an oral vaccine against poliomyelitis (adopted by World Health Organization 1957).

Sa·ble |'sābəl|, Jean Baptiste Point (*c.* 1750–1818) U.S. fur trader and pioneer, born in Haiti. Also known as *Point du Sable.* He founded a trading settlement at the present site of Chicago (1779).

Sac·a·ja·wea |ˌsækəjə'wēə; ˌsækəjə 'wāə| (*c.* 1786–1812) Shoshone guide and interpreter. Also **Sacagawea** ("Bird Woman"). She joined the Lewis and Clark expedition in what is now North Dakota and guided their expedition through the wilderness and across the Rockies (1804–05).

Sac·co |'sækō|, Nicola (1891–1927) U.S. political radical. Along with Bartolomeo Vanzetti, she was accused of murder in a sensational trial.

Sachs |zäks; sæks|, Hans (1494–1576) German poet and dramatist. Some of his poetry celebrated Luther and furthered the Protestant cause, while other pieces were comic verse dramas.

Sack·ler |'sæklər|, Howard (1929–82) U.S. playwright and director. Notable works: *The Great White Hope* (1967; Pulitzer Prize).

Sackville-West |'sækˌvil 'west|, Vita (1892–1962) English novelist and poet. Full name *Victoria Mary Sackville-West.*

Sa·dat |sə'dät|, (Muhammad) Anwar al- (1918–81) Egyptian statesman, president 1970–81.

Saddam Hussein See HUSSEIN, Saddam.

Sade |säd|, Donatien-Alphonse-François, Comte de (1740–1814) French writer and soldier; known as **the Marquis de Sade**. His career as a cavalry officer was interrupted by periods of imprisonment for cruelty and debauchery. While in prison he wrote a number of sexually explicit works, including *Les 120 Journées de Sodome* (1784) and *Justine* (1791).

Sa·di |sä'dē| (*c.* 1213–*c.* 1291) Persian poet; born *Sheikh Muslih Addin.* His principal works were the collections known as the *Bustan* (1257) and the *Gulistan* (1258).

Sa·fer |'säfər|, Morley (1931–) U.S. journalist, born in Canada. He cohosts the television program "60 Minutes" (1971–).

Saf·ire |'sæfˌīr|, William (1929–) U.S. journalist and author. He is a conservative political commentator and writer of the "On Language" column for *The New York Times.*

Sa·gan |'sāgən|, Carl (Edward) (1934–96) U.S. astronomer. Sagan showed that amino acids can be synthesized in an artificial primordial soup irradiated by ultraviolet light—a possible origin of life on the earth. He wrote several popular science books, and was coproducer of the television series *Cosmos* (1980).

Sa·gan |'sāgən|, Françoise (1935–) French novelist, dramatist, and short-story writer; pseudonym of *Françoise Quoirez.* She rose to fame with her first novel, *Bonjour Tristesse* (1954); in this and subsequent novels she examined the transitory nature of love as experienced in brief liaisons. Notable works: *Un Certain sourire* (1956) and *Aimez-vous Brahms?* (1959).

Sa·gen·dorf |'sægənˌdawrf|, Bud (1915–94) U.S. cartoonist. Full name *Forrest Cowles Sagendorf.* He was assistant to the creator of Popeye and continued Popeye after the death of the creator (Elzie Segar).

Sa·ha |'sähä|, Meghnad (1894–1956) Indian theoretical physicist. Saha worked on thermal ionization in stars and laid the foundations for modern astrophysics. He devised an equation expressing the relationship between ionization and temperature.

Sa·id |sä'ēd|, Edward W. (1935–) U.S. critic, born in Palestine; full name

Edward Wadi Said. He came to public notice with *Orientalism* (1978), a study of Western attitudes towards Eastern culture. Other notable works: *Culture and Imperialism* (1993).

Saint |sānt|, Eva Marie (1924–) U.S. actress. Her television, stage, and film credits include *On the Waterfront* (1954, Academy Award).

Sainte-Beuve |seNt'bOEv|, Charles Augustin (1804–69) French critic and writer. In his criticism he concentrated on the influence of social and other factors in the development of character.

Saint-Exupéry |ˌseNtāgzYpā'rē|, Antoine-Marie-Roger de (1900–44) French writer and aviator, best known for the fable *The Little Prince* (1943). Other works: *Night Flight* (1931).

Saint-Gaudens |sānt'gawdnz|, Augustus (1848–1907) U.S. sculptor, born in Ireland. Notable works: *Farragut* (in Madison Square, New York City) and *Shaw Memorial* on Boston Common.

Saint Lau·rent |ˌseNlaw'räN|, Yves (Mathieu) (1936–) French couturier. After working with Christian Dior, he opened his own fashion house in 1962, later launching Rive Gauche boutiques to sell ready-to-wear garments and expanding the business to include perfumes.

Saint-Saëns |seN'säN|, (Charles) Camille (1835–1921) French composer, pianist, and organist. He is best known for his Third Symphony (1886), the symphonic poem *Danse macabre* (1874), and the *Carnaval des animaux* (1886).

Saint-Simon |ˌseNsē'mawN|, Claude-Henri de Rouvroy, Comte de (1760–1825) French social reformer and philosopher. Later claimed as the founder of French socialism, he argued that society should be organized by leaders of industry and given spiritual direction by scientists.

Saint-Simon |ˌseNsē'mawN|, Louis de Rouvroy, Duc de (1675–1755) French writer. He is best known for his *Mémoires*, a detailed record of court life between 1694 and 1723, in the reigns of Louis XIV and XV.

Sa·jak |'sā,jæk|, Pat (1947–) U.S. game show host. He is host of the television game show "Wheel of Fortune" (1981–).

Sa·kha·rov |'säKHə,rawf; 'säkə,rawv|, Andrei (Dmitrievich) (1921–89) Russian nuclear physicist and civil rights campaigner. Having helped to develop the Soviet hydrogen bomb, he campaigned against nuclear proliferation. He fought for reform and human rights in the USSR, for which he was awarded the Nobel Peace Prize in 1975 but was also sentenced to internal exile 1980–86.

Sa·ki |'säkē| (1870–1916) British short-story writer, born in Burma; pseudonym of *Hector Hugh Munro*. His stories encompass the satiric, comic, macabre, and supernatural and frequently depict animals as agents seeking revenge on humankind.

Sal·a·din |'sæləd(ə)n| (1137–93) sultan of Egypt and Syria 1174–93; Arabic name *Salah-ad-Din Yusuf ibn-Ayyub*. Saladin reconquered Jerusalem from the Christians in 1187, but he was defeated by Richard the Lionheart at Arsuf (1191). He earned a reputation not only for military skill but also for honesty and chivalry.

Sa·lam |sä'läm|, Abdus (1926–96) Pakistani theoretical physicist. He independently developed a unified theory to explain electromagnetic interactions and the weak nuclear force. In 1979 he shared the Nobel Prize for Physics.

Sa·la·zar |'sælə,zär|, Antonio de Oliveira (1889–1970) Portuguese statesman and prime minister (1932–68). During his long premiership he ruled the country as a virtual dictator, enacting a new authoritarian constitution along Fascist lines. Salazar maintained Portugal's neutrality throughout the Spanish Civil War and World War II.

Sa·lie·ri |säl'yerē|, Antonio (1750–1825) Italian composer. Salieri was hostile to Mozart and a rumor arose that he poisoned him, though the story is now thought to be without foundation.

Sal·in·ger |'sælənjər|, J. D. (1919–) U.S. novelist and short-story writer; full name *Jerome David Salinger*. He is best known for his influential colloquial novel of adolescence *The Catcher in the Rye* (1951). He lived reclusively and did not publish after 1965. Other notable works: *Franny and Zooey* (1961), *Raise High the Roof Beam, Carpenter* (1963), and *Seymour: An Introduction* (1963), all short-story collections.

Salis·bury |'sawlz₁berē; 'sawlzb(ə)rē|, Robert Arthur Talbot Gascoyne-Cecil, 3rd Marquess of (1830–1903) British Conservative statesman and prime minister (1885–86, 1886–92, and 1895–1902). He supported the policies that resulted in the Second Boer War (1899–1902).

Salk |'saw(l)k|, Jonas Edward (1914–95) American microbiologist. He developed the standard *Salk vaccine* against polio, using virus inactivated by formalin, in the early 1950s, and later became the director of the institute in San Diego that now bears his name.

Sal·lust |'sæləst| (*c.* 86–35 BC) Roman historian and politician; Latin name *Gaius Sallustius Crispus.* As a historian he was concerned with the political and moral decline of Rome after the fall of Carthage in 146 BC. His chief surviving works deal with the Catiline conspiracy and the Jugurthine War.

Sam·pras |'sæmprəs|, Peter (1971–) U.S. tennis player. He was the youngest man ever to win the U.S. Open, in 1990, and repeated as champion in 1993 and 1995–96. He won the Wimbledon title in 1993–95 and 1997–98, as well as the Australian Open in 1994 and 1997.

Sam·so·nov |₁səm'sawnəf|, Aleksandr Vasiliyevich (1859–1914) Russian military leader. He commanded the army that invaded East Prussia (August 1914).

Sam·u·el·son |'sæmyə(wə)lsən|, Paul Anthony (1915–) U.S. economist. He has held many international advisory positions, including a seat on the Federal Reserve Board (1965–). Nobel Prize, 1970.

Sand |säN(d); sænd|, George (1804–76) French novelist; pseudonym of *Amandine-Aurore Lucile Dupin, Baronne Dudevant.* Her earlier novels, including *Lélia* (1833), portray women's struggles against conventional morals; she later wrote a number of pastoral novels, such as *La Mare au diable* (1846). Sand had a ten-year affair with Chopin.

Sand·burg |'sæn(d)₁bərg|, Carl (1878–1967) U.S. poet and biographer. Notable books of verse: *Chicago Poems* (1915), *Smoke and Steel* (1920), and *Complete Poems* (1950, Pulitzer Prize). Notable biographies: *Abraham Lincoln—The Prairie Years* (1926) and *Abraham Lincoln—The War Years* (1939, Pulitzer Prize).

San·de·man |'sændəmən|, Robert (1718–71) U.S. clergyman, born in Scotland. He was the leader of the religious sect known as the Sandemanians.

San·ders |'sændərz|, Barry (1968–) U.S. football player. He was twice named NFL Player of the Year.

San·ders |'sændərz|, Colonel Harland David (1890–1980) U.S. entrepreneur. He founded Kentucky Fried Chicken.

San·ders |'sændərz|, Lawrence (1920–) U.S. author. Notable works: *Guilty Pleasures* (1998) and *McNally's Puzzle* (1996).

San·ford |'sænfərd|, Edward Terry (1865–1930) U.S. Supreme Court justice (1923–30).

Sang·er |'sæNGər|, Margaret Louise (Higgins) (*c.* 1879–1966) U.S. birth-control campaigner. Her experiences as a nurse prompted her to distribute the pamphlet *Family Limitation* in 1914 and to found the first American birth-control clinic in 1916. She was the first president of the International Planned Parenthood Federation (1953).

San Mar·tín |₁sän mär'tēn|, José Francisco de (1778–1850) Argentinian soldier and statesman. Having assisted in the liberation of his country from Spanish rule (1812–13), he went on to aid Bernardo O'Higgins in the liberation of Chile (1817–18) and Peru (1820–4). He was also involved in gaining Peruvian independence and was Protector of Peru (1821–22).

San·som |'sænsəm|, Art (1920–91) U.S. cartoonist and author. Full name *Arthur Baldwin Sansom.* He originated the character Brutus Applethorp for the syndicated comic strip "The Born Loser."

San·so·vi·no |₁sänsə'vēnō|, Jacopo Tatti (1486–1570) Italian sculptor and architect. He was city architect of Venice, where his buildings, including the Palazzo Corner (1533) and St. Mark's Library (begun 1536), show the development of classical architectural style for contemporary use.

San·ta An·na |ˌsæntə 'ænə; ˌsäntə 'änə|, Antonio López de (1794–1876) Mexican general and political leader. A militant revolutionary, he controlled Mexico as its president (1833–36), its dictator (1844–45), and again its president (1853–55). In most of the interim years, he was essentially still in control and engaged in several military actions against the U.S., including his defeat at San Jacinto (1836) and Buena Vista (1847).

San·ta·na |ˌsæn'tænə|, Carlos (1947–) U.S. rock musician, born in Mexico. He formed the Afro-Latin rock group Santana (1968); his eighth solo album hit, "Blues for Salvador," won a 1987 Grammy Award.

San·ta·ya·na |ˌsäntə'yänə|, George (1863–1952) Spanish philosopher and writer; born *Jorge Augustin Nicolás Ruiz de Santayana*. His works include *The Realms of Being* (1924), poetry, and the novel *The Last Puritan* (1935).

Sa·pir |sə'pir|, Edward (1884–1939) German-born U.S. linguistics scholar and anthropologist. One of the founders of American structural linguistics, he carried out important research on American Indian languages and linguistic theory.

Sap·pho |'sæfō| (c. 610 BC–c. 580 BC) Greek lyric poet who lived on Lesbos. Many of her poems express her affection and love for women and have given rise to her association with female homosexuality.

Sa·ran·don |sə'rændən|, Susan (1946–) U.S. actress. Born *Susan Tomalin*. Notable movies: *Thelma and Louise* (1991), *The Client* (1994), and *Dead Man Walking* (1995).

Sar·a·zen |'særəzən|, Gene (1902–99) U.S. golfer. He was one of only four players to win all four Grand Slam titles.

Sa·rett |sə'ret|, Lewis Hastings (1917–) U.S. inventor. He prepared the first synthetic cortisone.

Sar·gent |'särjənt|, Sir (Harold) Malcolm (Watts) (1895–1967) English conductor and composer. In 1921 he made an acclaimed debut conducting his own *Impressions of a Windy Day*.

Sar·gent |'särjənt|, John Singer (1856–1925) U.S. painter. He is best known for his portraiture in a style noted for its bold brushwork. He was much in demand in Parisian circles, but following a scandal over the supposed eroticism of *Madame Gautreau* (1884) he moved to London.

Sar·gon |'sär,gän| (2334–2279 BC) the semi-legendary founder of the ancient kingdom of Akkad.

Sar·gon II |'sär,gän| (died 705 BC) king of Assyria 721–705. He was probably a son of Tiglath-pileser III and is famous for his conquest of cities in Syria and Palestine.

Sar·noff |'sär,nawf|, David (1891–1971) U.S. broadcaster and businessman. He pioneered the development of radio and televison broadcasting in the U.S.; later he became chairman of RCA and founder of NBC.

Sa·roy·an |sə'roiən|, William (1908–81) U.S. author. Notable books of short stories: *The Daring Young Man on the Flying Trapeze* (1934) and *My Name Is Aram* (1940). Notable plays: *The Time of Your Life* (1939) and *Razzle Dazzle* (1942). Notable novels: *The Human Comedy* (1943) and *The Laughing Matter* (1953).

Sar·raute |sä'rōt|, Nathalie (1902–) French author, born in Russia.

Sar·to |'särtō|, Andrea del (1486–1531) Italian painter; born *Andrea d'Agnolo*. He worked chiefly in Florence, where his works include fresco cycles in the church of Santa Annunziata and the series of grisailles in the cloister of the Scalzi (1511–26).

Sar·ton |'särtn|, (Eleanor) May (1912–95) U.S. author and poet, born in Belgium.

Sar·tre |särt; 'särtrə|, Jean-Paul (1905–80) French philosopher, novelist, dramatist, and critic. A leading existentialist, he dealt in his work with the nature of human life and the structures of consciousness. In 1945 he founded the review *Les Temps modernes* with his lifelong associate, Simone de Beauvoir. He refused the Nobel Prize for Literature in 1964. Notable works: *Nausée* (novel, 1938), *Being and Nothingness* (treatise,

1943), and *Huis clos* (play, 1944).

Sas·soon |sə'sōōn|, Vidal (1928–) English hairstylist. Opening a London salon in 1953, he introduced the cut and blow-dry styles that became popular for both men and women.

Sas·soon |sæ'sōōn|, Siegfried (Lorraine) (1886–1967) English poet and novelist. He is known for his starkly realistic poems written while serving in World War I, expressing his contempt for war leaders as well as compassion for his comrades.

Sa·tie |sä'tē|, Erik (Alfred Leslie) (1866–1925) French avant-garde composer. He formed an irreverent avant-garde artistic set associated with Les Six, Dadaism, and surrealism. Notable works: *Gymnopédies* (1888).

Sa·to |'sätō|, Eisaku (1901–75) Japanese prime minister (1964-72). He shaped post-war economic growth and improved relations with Asian neighbors; in 1974 he shared the Nobel Peace Prize for his opposition to nuclear weapons.

Saul |sawl| (11th century BC) (in the Bible) the first king of Israel (11th century BC).

Saul of Tarsus see PAUL, ST.

Saus·sure |sō'syr|, Ferdinand de (1857–1913) Swiss linguistics scholar. He was one of the founders of modern linguistics, and his work is fundamental to the development of structuralism. Saussure made a distinction between *langue* (the total system of language) and *parole* (individual speech acts), and stressed that linguistic study should focus on the former.

Sav·age |'sævij|, Michael Joseph (1872–1940) New Zealand Labor statesman and prime minister (1935–40).

Sa·vo·na·ro·la |ˌsævənə'rōlə|, Girolamo (1452–98) Italian preacher and religious reformer. A Dominican monk and strict ascetic, he became popular for his passionate preaching against immorality and corruption. Savonarola became virtual ruler of Florence (1494–95) but in 1497 he was excommunicated and later executed as a heretic.

Saw·yer |'soiər; 'sawyər|, (L.) Diane (1945–) U.S. journalist. She is co-anchor of the television program "60 Minutes" (1981–).

Say·ers |'sāərz|, Dorothy Leigh (1893–1957) English novelist and dramatist; full name *Dorothy Leigh Sayers*. She is chiefly known for her detective fiction featuring the amateur detective Lord Peter Wimsey; titles include *The Nine Tailors* (1934).

Say·ers |'sāərz|, Gale (Eugene) (1943–) U.S. football player. He set an NFL record of 22 touchdowns in his rookie year (1965).

Sca·lia |skə'lē(y)ə|, Antonin (1936–) U.S. Supreme Court justice (1986–)

Scal·i·ger |'skæləjər|, Joseph Justus French family, including: **Julius Caesar Scaliger** (1484–1558), Italian-born French classical scholar and physician. **Joseph Justus Scaliger** (1540–1609), French scholar, his son. His *De Emendatione Temporum* (1583) gave a more scientific foundation to the understanding of ancient chronology by comparing and revising the computations of time made by different civilizations, including those of the Babylonians and Egyptians.

Scar·lat·ti |skär'lätē| two Italian composers. **(Pietro) Alessandro (Gaspare)** (1660–1725) was an important and prolific composer of operas which carried Italian opera through the baroque period and into the classical. His son **(Giuseppe) Domenico** (1685–1757) wrote over 550 sonatas for the harpsichord, and his work made an important contribution to the development of the sonata form.

Scar·ry |'skærē; 'skerē|, Richard (McClure) (1919–94) U.S. author and illustrator. As a writer of books for children, he has penned and illustrated more than 250 titles.

Schaw·low |'sHawlō|, Arthur Leonard (1921–) U.S. inventor. With Charles H. Townes he invented the laser. Nobel Prize (1981).

Schee·le |'sHālə|, Carl Wilhelm (1742–86) Swedish chemist. He discovered a number of substances including glycerol, chlorine, and oxygen.

Schell |sHel|, Maximilian (1930–) U.S. actor. Notable movies: *Judgment at Nuremberg* (1961, Academy Award).

Schenck |sHeNGk|, Joseph M. (1878–1961) U.S. corporate executive, born in Russia. He founded Twentieth Century Pictures.

Schia·pa·rel·li |ˌsk(y)äpəˈrelē; ˌsHäpəˈrelē|, Elsa (1896–1973) Italian-born French fashion designer.

Schia·pa·rel·li |ˌsk(y)äpəˈrelē; ˌsHäpəˈrelē|, Giovanni Virginio (1835–1910) Italian astronomer. He studied the nature of cometary tails, and observed Mars in detail.

Schick |sHik|, Lieutenant Colonel Jacob (1877–1937) U.S. inventor. He invented the dry shaver.

Schie·le |ˈsHēlə|, Egon (1890–1918) Austrian painter and draughtsman. His style is characterized by an aggressive linear energy and a neurotic intensity. Notable works: *The Cardinal and the Nun* (1912) and *Embrace* (1917).

Schil·ler |ˈsHilər|, (Johann Christoph) Friedrich von (1759–1805) German dramatist, poet, historian, and critic. Initially influenced by the *Sturm und Drang* movement, he was later an important figure of the Enlightenment. His historical plays include the trilogy *Wallenstein* (1800), *Mary Stuart* (1800), and *William Tell* (1804). Among his best-known poems is "Ode to Joy," which Beethoven set to music in his Ninth Symphony.

Schin·dler |ˈsHindlər|, Oskar (1908–74) German industrialist. He saved more than 1,200 Jews from concentration camps by employing them first in his enamelware factory in Cracow and then in an armaments factory that he set up in Czechoslovakia in 1944. This was celebrated in the film *Schindler's List* (1993).

Schle·gel |ˈsHlägəl|, August Wilhelm von (1767–1845) German romantic poet and critic, who was among the founders of art history and comparative philology.

Schles·in·ger |ˈsHläziNGər|, Arthur Meier (1888–1965) U.S. historian. Notable works: *The Colonial Merchants and the American Revolution, 1763–1776* (1918) and *The American Reformer* (1950).

Schles·in·ger |ˈslesənjər; ˈslesiNGər|, John Richard (1926–) British movie, telvision, and theater director. Notable movies: *Midnight Cowboy* (1969, Academy Award).

Schles·sin·ger |ˈslesənjər; ˈslesiNGər|, Laura U.S. radio psychologist and author. Known as **Dr. Laura**. She offers advice to callers on her syndicated radio show.

Schlick |sHlik|, Friedrich Albert Moritz (1882–1936) German philosopher and physicist, founder of the Vienna Circle. Notable works: *General Theory of Knowledge* (1918).

Schlie·mann |ˈsHlē,män|, Heinrich (1822–90) German archaeologist. In 1871 he began excavating the mound of Hissarlik on the NE Aegean coast of Turkey, where he discovered the remains of nine superimposed cities, identifying the second oldest as Homer's Troy, although it was later found to be pre-Homeric. He subsequently undertook excavations at Mycenae (1876).

Schmidt |sHmit|, Helmut (Heinrich Waldemar) (1918–) German politician. He was chancellor of the Federal Republic of Germany (1974–82).

Schmidt |sHmit|, Mike (1949–) U.S. baseball player. Full name *Michael Jack Schmidt*.

Schna·bel |ˈsHnäbəl|, Artur (1882–1951) U.S. pianist, born in Austria. He is known for his performances of Beethoven, Brahms, and Schubert; he also composed works for piano, orchestra, and voice, and he edited and recorded Beethoven's piano sonatas.

Schnei·der |ˈsnīdər|, Ralph Edward (1909–64) U.S. businessman and inventor. He launched the Diners Club, which offered the world's first credit card.

Schoen·berg |ˈsHOEn,berg; ˈsHärn,bərg|, Arnold (Franz Walter) (1874–1951) Austrian-born U.S. composer and music theorist. His major contribution to modernism was the development of atonality and serialism. He introduced atonality into his second string quartet (1907–08), while *Serenade* (1923) is the first example of the technique of serialism.

Scholl |sHōl|, William (1882–1968) U.S. doctor, inventor, and manufacturer. Known as **Dr. Scholl**. He developed and patented arch-support and other foot products and wrote *The Human Foot: Anatomy, Deformities & Treatment* (1915).

Schon•berg |'sHŏn,bərg|, Harold C. (1915–) U.S. journalist and author. A writer on music and culture for *The New York Times* (1950–85), he won a Pulitzer Prize for criticism (1971).

School•craft |'skŏol,kræft|, Henry Rowe (1793–1864) U.S. ethnologist and explorer. He discovered the source of the Mississippi River at Lake Itasca, Minnesota (1832), and he married an Ojibwa woman and wrote pioneering works on American Indian ethnology.

Scho•pen•hau•er |'sHŏpən,(h)owər|, Arthur (1788–1860) German philosopher. According to his philosophy, as expressed in *The World as Will and Idea*, the will is identified with ultimate reality and happiness is only achieved by abnegating the will (as desire).

Schrei•ner |'sHrīnər|, Olive (Emilie Albertina) (1855–1920) South African novelist and feminist. Notable works: *The Story of an African Farm* (novel, 1883) and *Woman and Labour* (1911).

Schrö•ding•er |'sHrōdiNGər|, Erwin (1887–1961) Austrian physicist. He founded the study of wave mechanics, deriving the equation whose roots define the energy levels of atoms. Nobel Prize for Physics (1933).

Schroe•der |'sHrOEdər; 'sHrōdər|, Gerhard (Fritz Kurt) (1944–) German politician. The chancellor of Germany (1998–), he is a Social Democrat allied with the Green Party.

Schroe•der |'sHrōdər|, Patricia (Scott) (1940–) U.S. politician. She was a member of the U.S. House of Representatives from Colorado (1973–).

Schu•bert |'sHŏobərt|, Franz (Peter) (1797–1828) Austrian composer. His music is associated with the romantic movement for its lyricism and emotional intensity, but belongs in formal terms to the classical age. His works include more than 600 songs, the "Trout" piano quintet (1819), and nine symphonies.

Schul•berg |'skŏol,bərg|, Budd (Wilson) (1914–) U.S. author and screenwriter. He won an Academy Award for his screenplay *On the Waterfront* (1954).

Schul•yer |'sHŏolyer|, James (Marcus) (1923–91) U.S. author. Notable works: *The Morning of the Poet* (1980, Pulitzer Prize).

Schulz |sHŏolts|, Charles (Monroe) (1922–) U.S. cartoonist. He is the creator of the widely syndicated "Peanuts" comic strip., featuring a range of characters including the boy Charlie Brown and the dog Snoopy.

Schu•ma•cher |'sHŏo,mäkər|, E. F. (1911–77) German economist and conservationist; full name *Ernst Friedrich Schumacher*. His most famous work is *Small is Beautiful: Economics as if People Mattered* (1973), which argues that mass production needs to be replaced by smaller, more energy-efficient enterprises.

Schu•mann |'sHŏo,män|, Robert (Alexander) (1810–56) German composer. He was a leading romantic composer, particularly noted for his songs (including settings of poems by Heinrich Heine and Robert Burns) and piano music. His other works include four symphonies and much chamber music. His wife **Clara** (1819–96) was a noted pianist and composer.

Schurz |sHŏorts; 'sHərts|, Carl (1829–1906) U.S. political reformer, journalist, and army officer, born in Germany. He served as a Union army general at Bull Run and Gettysburg and as a member of the U.S. Senate from Missouri (1869–75); later he was an editorial writer for *Harper's* (1892–98) and president of the National Civil Service Reform League (1892–1901).

Schu•ster |'sHŏostər|, Max Lincoln (1897–1970) U.S. publisher. He was co-founder and partner of Simon and Schuster book publishers (1924).

Schütz |sHŏots|, Heinrich (1585–1672) German composer and organist. He is regarded as the first German baroque composer, and composed what is thought to have been the first German opera (*Dafne*, 1627; now lost).

Schwab |sHwäb|, Charles Michael (1862–1939) U.S. steel industrialist. He was the first President of the U.S. Steel Corp. (1901–03) and the founder of the Bethlehem Steel Co. (1903).

Schwann |sHwän; sHwän|, Theodor

Ambrose Hubert (1810–82) German physiologist. He showed that animals (as well as plants) are made up of individual cells and that the egg begins life as a single cell. He is best known for discovering the cells forming the myelin sheaths of nerve fibres (Schwann cells).

Schwann |SHwän|, William Joseph (1913–98) U.S. organist, musicologist, and publisher. He founded the Schwann catalog of recordings.

Schwartz |SHwawrts|, Delmore (1913–66) U.S. author. He was editor of *The Partisan Review* (1943–55) and author of *Summer Knowledge* (1959, Bollingen Prize).

Schwar•ze•neg•ger |'SHwawrtzə-ˌnegər|, Arnold (Alois) (1947–) Austrian-born U.S. actor. He won the bodybuilding title Mr. Olympia seven times (1970–75; 1980) before retiring to concentrate on acting. Noted for his action roles, for instance in *The Terminator* (1984), he diversified in films such as the comedy *Kindergarten Cop* (1990) and the spy thriller *True Lies* (1994).

Schwarz•kopf |'SHwawrts,kaw(p)f; SHwarts,kä(p)f|, Dame (Olga Maria) Elisabeth (Friederike) (1915–) German operatic soprano. She is especially famous for her roles in works by Richard Strauss, such as *Der Rosenkavalier*.

Schwarz•kopf |'SHwawrts,kaw(p)f; SHwarts,kä(p)f|, H. Norman (1934–) U.S. army officer. He was deputy commander of U.S. forces during the invasion of Grenada (1983). Promoted to full general in 1988 and appointed commander in chief of the U.S. Central Command (1988–91), he led the Allied forces against Iraq in the Persian Gulf War (1991). He retired in 1991.

Schweit•zer |'SHwītsər|, Albert (1875–1965) German theologian, musician, and medical missionary born in Alsace. *The quest for the Historical Jesus* (1906) emphasized the importance of understanding Jesus within the context of the Jewish apocalyptic thought of his day. In 1913 he qualified as a doctor and went as a missionary to Gabon, where he established a hospital. Nobel Peace Prize (1952).

Scip•io Ae•mil•i•an•us |'sipē,ō ə,milē

'änəs| (*c.* 185–129 BC) Roman general and politician; full name *Publius Cornelius Scipio Aemilianus Africanus Numantinus Minor*, adoptive grandson of Scipio Africanus. He achieved distinction in the siege of Carthage (146 BC) during the third Punic War and in his campaign in Spain (133BC).

Scip•io Af•ri•can•us |'sipē,ō ˌæfri-'känəs| (236–*c.* 184 BC) Roman general and politician; full name *Publius Cornelius Scipio Africanus Major*. He was successful in concluding the second Punic War, firstly by the defeat of the Carthaginians in Spain in 206 BC and then by the defeat of Hannibal in Africa At Zama in 202 BC.

Scor•se•se |ˌskawr'säzē|, Martin (1942–) U.S. movie director. Notable works: *Mean Streets* (1973), *Taxi Driver* (1976), and *The Last Temptation of Christ* (1988).

Scott |skät|, Dred (*c.* 1795–1858) U.S. slave. He brought suit for his freedom based on his five-year residence in free territories, but the U.S. Supreme Court ruled against him (1857) in a case that became the focus of much heated political controversy. Scott was emancipated later that year and became a hotel porter in St. Louis.

Scott |skät|, George C. (1927–) U.S. actor. Full name: *George Campbell Scott*. Notable movies: *Patton* (1970 Academy Award).

Scott |skät|, Paul Mark (1920–78) British novelist. Notable works: *Raj Quartet.*

Scott |skät|, Sir Peter (Markham) (1909–89) English naturalist and artist, son of Sir Robert Scott. In 1946 he founded the Wildfowl Trust at Slimbridge in Gloucestershire.

Scott |skät|, Ridley (1939–) English movie director. Notable works: *Alien* (1979), *Blade Runner* (1982), and *Thelma and Louise* (1991).

Scott |skät|, Sir Robert (Falcon) (1868–1912) English explorer and naval officer. In 1910–12 Scott and four companions made a journey to the South Pole by sled, arriving there in January 1912 to discover that Roald Amundsen had beaten them by a month. Scott and his companions died on the journey back to base; their bodies and diaries were discovered eight months later.

Scott |skät|, Sir Walter (1771–1832) Scottish novelist and poet. He established the form of the historical novel in Britain and was influential in his treatment of rural themes and use of regional speech. Notable novels: *Waverley* (1814), *Ivanhoe* (1819), *Kenilworth* (1821), and *Quentin Durward* (1823).

Scott |skät|,Winfield (1786–1866) U.S. army officer. Known as **Old Fuss and Feathers.** A hero of the War of 1812, he became supreme commander of the U.S. Army (1841–61). During the Mexican War, he waged a victorious campaign from Veracruz to Mexico City (1847). He ran for the office of U.S. president as the Whig candidate (1852) but was defeated by Democrat Franklin Pierce.

Scria•bin |skrē'äbən|,Aleksandr (Nikolayevich) (1872–1915) Russian composer and pianist. Also **Skryabin.** Notable works: *The Divine Poem* (symphony, 1903) and *Prometheus: The Poem of Fire* (symphonic poem, 1909–10).

Scrib•ner |'skribnər|, Charles (1821–71) U.S. publisher. With Isaac D. Baker he founded the publishing company Baker & Scribner (1846), later Scribner's Sons.

Scripps |'skrips| U.S. newspaper publishers. **Edward Wyllis Scripps** (1854–1926) founded the Scripps-McRae League newspaper chain (1894) with his brother George Scripps and Milton A. McRae, and in 1907 he organized the United Press Association. His son, **Robert Paine Scripps** (1895–1938), founded the Scripps-Howard newspapers (1922) with Roy W. Howard.

Sea•borg |'sē,bawrg|, Glenn (Theodore) (1912–) American nuclear chemist. During 1940–58 Seaborg and his colleagues produced nine of the transuranic elements (plutonium to nobelium) in a cyclotron. Seaborg and his early collaborator **Edwin McMillan** (1907–91) shared the Nobel Prize for Chemistry in 1951.

Seale |sēl|, John Clement (1942–) U.S. cinematographer, born in Australia. Notable movies: *Rainman* (1988).

Sea•man |'sēmən|, Elizabeth Cochrane (1867–1922) U.S. journalist. Pseudonym **Nelly Bly.** Her employer Joseph Pulitzer dispatched her to make reality out of Jules Verne's fictional *Around the World in 80 Days.* She returned in 72 days, 6 hours, and 11 minutes (1889–90).

Searle |sərl|, Ronald (William Fordham) (1920–) English artist and cartoonist.

Sears |sirz|, Richard Warren (1863–1914) U.S. businessman. He founded his first mail-order business in Minneapolis (1886), moved to Chicago and sold it, then began a partnership with A. C. Roebuck in a new business, which became Sears, Roebuck & Co. (1893).

Se•at•tle |sē'ætl|, Chief (1786–1866) Native American leader of the Suquamish and Dewamish tribes. He signed the Treaty of Port Elliott (1855), guaranteeing a reservation for his people in what became the state of Washington.

Sea•ver |'sēvər|, Tom (1944–) U.S. baseball player. Full name *George Thomas Seaver.* He won three Cy Young Awards.

Se•bas•tian |sə'bæscHən|, St. (late 3rd cent) Roman martyr. According to legend he was a soldier who was shot by archers on the order of Diocletian, but who recovered, confronted the emperor, and was then clubbed to death. Feast day, January 20.

Se•da•ka |sə'dækə|, Neil (1939–) U.S. singer and songwriter. Notable songs: "Love Will Keep Us Together" and "Laughter in the Rain"

See•ger |'sēgər|, Pete (1919–) U.S. folk musician and songwriter. Seeger was a prominent figure in the American folk revival. He was also concerned with environmental issues, especially on the Hudson River. Notable songs: "If I Had a Hammer" (*c.*1949) and "Where Have All the Flowers Gone?" (1956).

Se•gar |'sē,gär|, Elzie Crisler (1894–1938) U.S. cartoonist. He was the creator of "Popeye."

Se•go•via |sə'gōvēə|, Andrés (1893–1987) Spanish guitarist and composer. He was largely responsible for the revival of the classical guitar, elevating it to use as a concert instrument and making a large number of transcriptions of classical music to increase the repertoire of the instrument.

Sein•feld |'sīn‚feld|, Jerry (1955–) U.S. comedian and actor. He was star of the television sitcom "Seinfeld."

Sel•craig see SELKIRK.

Sel•den |'seldən|, George Baldwin (1846–1922) U.S. lawyer and inventor. He received the first American patent for a gasoline-driven car (1895), and he sold rights to the patent on a royalty basis.

Sel•es |'seləs|, Monica (1973–) U.S. tennis player, born in Yugoslavia. She became the youngest woman to win a grand slam singles title with her victory in the French Open in 1990. She was stabbed on court by a fan of Steffi Graf in 1993, but she returned to play in 1995 and won the Australian Open in 1996.

Se•leu•cus I |sə'lookəs| (died 281 BC) King of the Seleucid Empire (306–281 BC). Also known as **Seleucus Nicator**. A Macedonian general under Alexander the Great, he founded the Seleucid Empire.

Sel•kirk |'sel‚kərk|, Alexander (1676–1721) Scottish sailor; also called *Alexander Selcraig*. While on a privateering expedition in 1704, Selkirk quarreled with his captain and was put ashore, at his own request, on one of the uninhabited Juan Fernandez Islands, where he remained until 1709. His experiences formed the basis of Daniel Defoe's novel *Robinson Crusoe* (1719).

Sel•lers |'selərz|, Peter (1925–80) English comic actor. Full name *Peter Richard Henry Sellers*. He is best known for the "Pink Panther" series of movies of the 1960s and 1970s, in which he played the French detective Inspector Clouseau. Other notable films: *The Lady Killers* (1955) and *Dr. Strangelove* (1964).

Se•lous |sə'loos|, Frederick Courteney (1851–1917) English explorer, naturalist, and soldier. From 1890 he was involved in the British South Africa Company, negotiating mineral and land rights. The Selous Game Reserve in Tanzania is named after him.

Sel•ye |'selyā|, Hans Hugo Bruno (1907–82) Austrian-born Canadian physician. He showed that environmental stress and anxiety could result in the release of hormones that, over a long period, could produce biochemical and physiological disorders.

Selz•nick |'selznik|, David O. (1902–65) U.S. movie producer; full name *David Oliver Selznick*. He produced such movies as *King Kong* (1933) for RKO and *Anna Karenina* (1935) for MGM before establishing his own production company in 1936 and producing such screen classics as *Gone with the Wind* (1939) and *Rebecca* (1940).

Sem•mel•weis |'zeməl‚vīs|, Ignaz Philipp (1818–65) Hungarian obstetrician; Hungarian name *Ignác Fülöp Semmelweis*. He discovered the infectious character of puerperal fever and advocated rigorous cleanliness and the use of antiseptics by doctors examining patients.

Se•na•na•yake |‚sänänä'yäkä|, Don Stephen (1884–1952) Sinhalese statesman, prime minister of Ceylon (now Sri Lanka) (1947–52). As prime minister he presided over Ceylon's achievement of full dominion status within the Commonwealth.

Sen•dak |'sen‚dæk|, Maurice Bernard (1928–) U.S. author and illustrator of children's books. He received a Caldecott Award for *Where the Wild Things Are* (1963).

Sen•e•ca |'senikə|, Roman writers. **Marcus (or Lucius) Annaeus Seneca** (*c.* 55 BC–*c.* 39 AD), was a Roman rhetorician born in Spain and known as **Seneca the Elder**. He is best known for his works on rhetoric, only parts of which survive. **Lucius Annaeus Seneca** (*c.* 4 BC–AD 65), his son, was a Roman statesman, philosopher, and dramatist known as **Seneca the Younger**. He became tutor to Nero in 49 and was appointed consul in 57. His *Epistulae Morales* is a notable Stoic work.

Sen•ghor |säN'gawr|, Léopold Sédar (1906–) president of Senegal (1960–80). His *Poèmes* were published in 1984.

Sen•nach•er•ib |sə'nækə‚rib| (died 681 BC) king of Assyria (705–681), son of Sargon II. In 701 he put down a Jewish rebellion, laying siege to Jerusalem but sparing it from destruction (according to 2 Kings 19:35). He also rebuilt the city of Nineveh and made it his capital.

Sen•nett |'senət|, Mack (1880–1960) U.S. movie director, producer, and actor, born in Canada. Born *Michael Sinnott*. He produced over 1,000 slapstick comedy shorts and created the Keystone Kops; his films include *The Shriek of Araby* (1923).

Se•quoya |sə'kwoiə| (*c.* 1770–1843) Cherokee scholar. Also **Sequoia**; also known (in later years) as **George Guess**. He invented a writing system for the Cherokee language (1809–21) and with it taught thousands of Cherokee Indians to read and write. The giant sequoia trees of California are named for him.

Se•raph•ic Doc•tor the nickname of St. Bonaventura.

Ser•gi•us |'sərjēəs|, St. (1314–92) Russian monastic reformer and mystic; Russian name *Svyatoi Sergi Radonezhsky*. He founded forty monasteries, reestablishing the monasticism that had been lost through the Tartar invasion, and inspired the resistance that saved Russia from the Tartars in 1380. Feast day, September 25.

Ser•ling |'sərliNG|, Rod (1924–75) U.S. writer and television producer. He hosted the television series "The Twilight Zone" (1959–65).

Ses•sions |'seSHənz|, Roger Huntington (1896–1985) U.S. composer. He composed eight symphonies, as well as operas and the cantata *When Lilacs Last in the Dooryard Bloom'd* (1970). Pulitzer Prizes, 1974 and 1981.

Se•ton |'sētn|, St. Elizabeth Ann (Bayley) (1774–1821) U.S. religious leader, educator, and social reformer. She became the first native-born American to be canonized as a saint (1975).

Seu•rat |sə'rä|, Georges-Pierre (1859–91) French painter. The founder of neo-Impressionism, he is chiefly associated with pointillism, which he developed during the 1880s. Among his major paintings using this technique is *Sunday Afternoon on the Island of La Grande Jatte* (1884–6).

Seuss |sōōs|, Dr. see GEISEL, THEODOR SEUSS.

Sev•a•reid |'sevə,rīd|, Eric (Arnold) (1912–92) U.S. broadcast journalist and author.

Se•ve•rus |sə'virəs|, Septimius (146–211) Roman emperor 193–211; full name *Lucius Septimius Severus*. He reformed the imperial administration and the army. In 208 he led an army to Britain to suppress a rebellion in the north of the country and later died at York.

Sew•all |'sōōəl|, Samuel (1652–1730) American colonial merchant and jurist. He presided over the Salem witchcraft trials (1692); his *Diary* (published 1878–82) covers the years 1674–77 and 1685–1729.

Sew•ard |'sōō(w)ərd|, William Henry (1801–72) U.S. statesman and politician. An outspoken antislavery politician, he was governor of New York (1839–43), U.S. senator (1849–61), and U.S. secretary of state (1861–69). He negotiated the purchase of Alaska from Russia (1867), which was widely mocked as "Seward's Icebox" and "Seward's Folly."

Sex•ton |'sekstən|, Anne (1928–74) U.S. poet. Notable works: *Live or Die* (1966, Pulitzer Prize).

Sey•mour |'sē,mawr|, Jane (*c.* 1509–37) third wife of Henry VIII and mother of Edward VI. She married Henry in 1536 and finally provided the king with the male heir he wanted, although she died twelve days later.

Sey•mour |'sē,mawr|, Lynn (1939–   ) Canadian ballet dancer; born *Lynn Springbett*. From 1957 she danced for the Royal Ballet. Her most acclaimed roles came in Frederick Ashton's *Five Brahms Waltzes in the Manner of Isadora Duncan* and *A Month in the Country* (both 1976).

Sha•ba•ka |'SHæbəkə| (died 695 BC) Egyptian pharaoh, founder of the 25th dynasty, reigned 712–698 BC; known as **Sabacon**. He promoted the cult of Amun and revived the custom of pyramid burial in his own death arrangements.

Shack•le•ton |'SHækəltən|, Sir Ernest Henry (1874–1922) British explorer. During one of his Antarctic expeditions (1914–16), Shackleton's ship *Endurance* was crushed in the ice. Shackleton and his crew eventually reached an island, from where he and five others made a 800-mile (1,300-km) open-boat voyage to South Georgia Island to get help.

Shaftes·bury |'SHæf(t)s,berē|, Anthony Ashley Cooper, 7th Earl of (1801–85) English philanthropist and social reformer. A dominant figure of the 19th-century social reform movement, he inspired much of the legislation designed to improve conditions for the large working class created as a result of the Industrial Revolution. His reforms included the introduction of the ten-hour work day (1847).

Shah |SHä|, Karim Al-Hussain see AGA KHAN.

Shah |SHä|, Reza see PAHLAVI.

Shahn |SHän|, Ben (1898–1969) U.S. artist, born in Lithuania. His paintings are devoted to political and social themes.

Sha·ka |'SHäkə| (c. 1787–1828) Also **Chaka**. Zulu chief (1816–28). He reorganized his forces and waged war against the Nguni clans, subjugating them and forming a Zulu empire in SE Africa.

Shake·speare |'SHāk,spir|, William (1564–1616) English dramatist. His plays are written mostly in blank verse and include comedies, such as *A Midsummer Night's Dream* and *As You Like It*; historical plays, including *Richard III* and *Henry V*; the Greek and Roman plays, which include *Julius Caesar* and *Antony and Cleopatra*; enigmatic comedies such as *All's Well that Ends Well* and *Measure for Measure*; the great tragedies, *Hamlet, Othello, King Lear*, and *Macbeth*; and the group of tragicomedies with which he ended his career, such as *The Winter's Tale* and *The Tempest*. He also wrote more than 150 sonnets, published in 1609.

Sha·li·kash·vi·li |,SHälē,käSH'vēlē|, John Malchase (1936–) U.S. army officer, born in Poland. He was chairman of the Joint Chiefs of Staff (1993–97).

Shal·ma·ne·ser III |,SHælmə'nēzər| (died 824 BC) king of Assyria (859–824 BC). Most of his reign was devoted to the expansion of his kingdom and the conquest of neighboring lands. According to Assyrian records he defeated an alliance of Syrian kings and the king of Israel in a battle at Qarqar on the Orontes in 853 BC.

Sha·mir |SHə'mir|, Yitzhak (1915–) Polish-born Israeli statesman, prime minister (1983–84 and 1986–92); Polish name *Yitzhak Jazernicki*. Under his leadership Israel did not retaliate when attacked by Iraqi missiles during the Gulf War, thereby possibly averting an escalation of the conflict.

Shan·kar |'SHäNG,kär|, Ravi (1920–) Indian sitar player and composer. From the mid-1950s he toured Europe and the U.S. giving sitar recitals, doing much to stimulate contemporary Western interest in Indian music.

Shan·kar |'SHäNG,kär|, Uday (1900–77) Indian dancer, brother of Ravi Shankar. He introduced Anna Pavlova to Indian dance and performed with her in his ballet *Krishna and Radha* (1923). He later toured the world with his own company, introducing Indian dance to European audiences.

Shank·er |'SHæNGkər|, Albert (1928–97) U.S. labor organizer. As head of the American Federation of Teachers, he was responsible for doubling its size.

Shan·non |'SHænən|, Claude Elwood (1916–) American engineer. He was the pioneer of mathematical communication theory, which has become vital to the design of both communication and electronic equipment. He also investigated digital circuits, and was the first to use the term *bit* to denote a unit of information.

Sha·pi·ro |SHə'pirō|, Karl (Jay) (1913–) U.S. author and educator. Notable works: *V-Letter and Other Poems* (1944, Pulitzer Prize).

Shap·ley |'SHæplē|, Harlow (1885–1972) American astronomer. He carried out an extensive survey of galaxies and used his studies on the distribution of globular star clusters to locate the likely centre of the Galaxy and to infer its structure and dimensions. He found that the solar system is located on the Galaxy's edge and not at its center.

Shar·ma |'SHärmə|, Shankar Dayal (1918–) Indian statesman, president (1992–97). A member of the Congress

Party, Sharma served as vice president (1987–92).

Sharp |ˈsHärp|, Cecil (James) (1859–1924) English collector of folk songs and folk dances.

Sharp |ˈsHärp|, William (1856–1905) Scottish author. Also called **Fiona Macleod**.

Sharp•ton |ˈsHärptən|, Al (1954–) U.S. civil rights activist and Baptist minister. Full name *Alfred Charles Sharpton, Jr.*

Shat•ner |ˈsHætnər|, William (1931–) U.S. actor, director, and producer, born in Canada. He starred in the "StarTrek" movies and television series.

Shaw |sHaw|, Artie (1910–) U.S. jazz clarinetist and bandleader. Born *Arthur Jacob Arshawsky*. He was a leading musician of the swing period and formed several small groups, including the Gramercy Five.

Shaw |sHaw|, George Bernard (1856–1950) Irish dramatist and writer. His best-known plays combine comedy with a questioning of conventional morality and thought; they include *Man and Superman* (1903), *Pygmalion* (1913), and *St. Joan* (1923). A socialist, he became an active member of the Fabian Society. Nobel Prize for Literature (1925). Other noted works: *Candida* (1897) and *Major Barbara* (1905).

Shaw |sHaw|, Henry Wheeler (1818–85) U.S. author. Pseudonym **Josh Billings**. Notable works: *Josh Billings, His Sayings* (1865).

Shaw |sHaw|, Irwin (1913–84) U.S. author. Notable works: *Bury the Dead* (1936) and *Rich Man, Poor Man* (1970).

Shear•er |ˈsHirər|, Moira (1926–) Scottish ballet dancer and actress; full name *Moira Shearer King*. A ballerina with Sadler's Wells from 1942, she is perhaps best known for her portrayal of a dedicated ballerina in the film *The Red Shoes* (1948).

Shear•er |ˈsHirər|, Norma (1902–83) U.S. actress, born in Canada. Born *Edith Norma Shearer*. She made a successful transition from silent to talking movies. Notable movies: *The Divorcee* (1929–30 Academy Award).

Sheed |sHēd|, Wilfrid (John Joseph) (1930–) U.S. author, born in Eng-

land. Notable works: *A Middle Class Education* (1961).

Shee•han |ˈsHēən|, John Clark (1915–92) U.S. research chemist. He invented semisynthetic penicillin.

Shee•ler |ˈsHēlər|, Charles (1883–1965) U.S. artist. He photographed and painted industrial-commercial subjects.

Shel•don |ˈsHeldən|, Charles Monroe (1857–1946) U.S. clergyman and author. A Congregational minister, he edited the *Christian Herald* and wrote *In His Steps* (1896).

Shel•don |ˈsHeldən|, Edward (Brewster) (1886–1946) U.S. author. Notable works: *The Nigger* (1909).

Shel•don |ˈsHeldən|, Sidney (1917–) U.S. novelist. Notable works: *Tell Me Your Dreams* (1998).

Shel•ley |ˈsHelē| English writers. **Percy Bysshe Shelley** (1792–1822) was a leading poet of the romantic movement with radical politcal views. Notable works include *Queen Mab* (political poems, 1813), *Prometheus Unbound* (lyrical drama, 1820), *The Defence of Poetry* (essay, 1821), and *Adonais* (1821), an elegy on the death of Keats. His wife, **Mary (Wollstonecraft) Shelley** (1797–1851), daughter of William Godwin and Mary Wollstonecraft, eloped with him in 1814 and married him in 1816. She is chiefly remembered as the author of the Gothic novel *Frankenstein, or the Modern Prometheus* (1818).

Shep•ard |ˈsHepərd|, Sam (1943–) U.S. playwright and actor. Born *Samuel Shepard Rogers*. He wrote the plays *Buried Child* (1979, Pulitzer Prize) and *Fool for Love* (1984); he acted in the movies *Fool for Love* (1985) and *Baby Boom* (1987).

Shep•hard |ˈsHepərd|, Thomas (1605–49) U.S. clergyman, born in England. He helped found Harvard and wrote *The Sincere Convert* (1641).

Shep•herd |ˈsHepərd|, Cybill (1950–) U.S. actress. She appeared in the movie *The Last Picture Show* (1971) and had a starring role in the television series "Moonlighting."

Sher•er |ˈsHirər|, Moshe (1921–98) U.S. rabbi. He contributed to the rise of Jewish Orthodoxy in the U.S.

Sher•i•dan |ˈsHerəd(ə)n|, Philip Henry

(1831–88) U.S. army officer. A severe and effective Union cavalry commander in the Civil War, he was noted for his decisive victories and plundering raids.In April 1865, he cut off the Confederate retreat at Appomattox, forcing the surrender of General Lee.

Sher·i·dan |'sHerəd(ə)n|, Richard Brinsley (1751–1816) Irish dramatist and Whig politician. His plays are comedies of manners; they include *The Rivals* (1775) and *The School for Scandal* (1777). In 1780 he entered Parliament, becoming a celebrated orator and holding senior government posts.

Sher·man |'sHərmən|, James Schoolcraft (1855–1912) vice president of the U.S. (1909–12).

Sher·man |'sHərmən|, Roger (1721–93) American politician. A Connecticut legislator and jurist, he was an avid proponent of American independence. He was the only person to sign all of the following: the Articles of Association (1774), the Declaration of Independence (1776), the Articles of Confederation (1777), and the Constitution (1787).

Sher·man |'sHərmən|, William Tecumseh (1820–91) U.S. general. In 1864 in the Civil War he was appointed commander of Union forces in the West. He set out with 60,000 men on a "March to the Sea" through Georgia from Atlanta to Savannah, then north through the Carolinas, during which he crushed Confederate forces and broke civilian morale by his policy of deliberate destruction of the territory he passed through. He served as commander of the army (1869–84).

Sher·ring·ton |'sHeriNGtən|, Sir Charles Scott (1857–1952) English physiologist. He contributed greatly to the understanding of the nervous system and introduced the concept of reflex actions and the reflex arc. Nobel Prize for Physiology or Medicine (1932).

Shev·ard·na·dze |,sHevərd'nädzə|, Eduard (Amvrosiyevich) (1928–) Soviet statesman. He was Minister of Foreign Affairs 1985–90 under President Gorbachev before becoming head of state of his native Georgia in 1992.

Shields |sHēldz|, (Christa) Brooke

(Camille) (1965–) U.S. actress. She began her career as a model, before acting in movies and in the starring role of the television program "Suddenly Susan."

Shields |sHēldz|, Carol Ann (1935–) U.S. author. Notable works: *Larry's Party* (1997).

Shil·la·ber |'sHil,äbər|, Benjamin Penhallow (1814–90) U.S. editor and humorist. He edited a weekly humor magazine called *The Carpet-Bag* (1851–53) and wrote *The Life and Sayings of Mrs. Partington* (1854).

Shi·ma |'sHēmə|, Hideo (1901–98) Japanese engineer. He designed the Shinkansen bullet train.

Ship·ley |'sHiplē|, Jenny (1952–) New Zealand stateswoman. Full name *Jennifer Mary Shipley*. She is the prime minister of New Zealand (1997–).

Shi·ras |'sHīrəs|, George, Jr. (1832–1924) U.S. Supreme Court justice (1892–1903).

Shi·va·ji |'sHiväjē| (1627–80) Indian raja of the Marathas (1674–80). Also **Sivaji**. He raised a successful Hindu revolt against Muslim rule in 1659 and expanded Maratha territory. After being crowned raja, he blocked Mogul expansionism by forming an alliance with the sultans in the south.

Shock·ley |'sHäklē|, William (Bradford) (1910–89) U.S. physicist. Shockley and his researchers at Bell Laboratories developed the transistor in 1948, and in 1958 he shared with them the Nobel Prize for Physics. He later became a controversial figure because of his views on a supposed connection between race and intelligence.

Shoe·maker |'sHŌŌ,mākər|, Willie (1931–) U.S. jockey. Full name *William Lee Shoemaker*. He holds the record for all-time career wins (8,833).

Sholes |sHōlz|, Christopher Latham (1819–90) U.S. journalist and inventor. With his two collaborators, Samuel W. Soulé and Carols Glidden, he received a patent for the first practical typewriter.

Sho·lo·khov |'sHawlə,KHawf|, Mikhail Aleksandrovich (1905–84) Soviet novelist. Notable works: *Quiet Flows the Don*. Nobel Prize for Literature, 1965.

Sho·lom Alei·chem |'sHōləm ə'lākəm|

(1859–1916) U.S. author, born in Ukraine. Born *Solomon Rabinowitz*. *Fiddler on the Roof* is based on his writings.

Shore |SHawr|, Dinah (Frances Rose) (1921–93) U.S. singer. She was a radio, television, and film star, as well as host of the television programs "Dinah's Place" (1970–74) "Dinah!" (1974–79), and "Dinah! And Friends." She won 10 Academy Awards.

Sho·sta·ko·vich |ˌSHästə'kōviCH|, Dmitri (Dmitriyevich) (1906–75) Russian composer. He developed a highly personal style, and, although he experimented with atonality and twelve-note techniques, his music always returned to a basic tonality. He is best known for his fifteen symphonies.

Shri·ver |'SHrīvər|, (Robert) Sargent, Jr. (1915–) U.S. lawyer and politician. He was a Democratic vice presidential candidate (1972)

Shu·la |'SHo͞olə|, Don (Francis) (1930–) U.S. football coach. He retired with the NFL record of 347 career wins. Elected to the NFL Hall of Fame (1997).

Shu·ster |'SHo͞ostər|, Joe (1914–92) U.S. cartoonist. He was the co-creator of Superman with childhood friend Jerry Siegel.

Shute |SHo͞ot|, Nevil (1899–1960) English novelist; pseudonym of *Nevil Shute Norway*. After World War II he settled in Australia, which provides the setting for his later novels. Notable works: *A Town Like Alice* (1950) and *On the Beach* (1957), which depicts a community facing gradual destruction in the aftermath of a nuclear war.

Si·be·li·us |sə'bālēəs|, Jean (1865–1957) Finnish composer; born *Johan Julius Christian Sibelius*. His affinity for his country's landscape and legends, especially the epic *Kalevala*, is expressed in a series of symphonic poems including *The Swan of Tuonela* (1893), *Finlandia* (1899), and *Tapiola* (1925).

Sick·ert |'sikərt|, Walter Richard (1860–1942) British painter, of Danish and Anglo-Irish descent. His subjects are mainly urban scenes and figure compositions, particularly pictures of the theater and music hall, and drab domestic interiors.

Sid·dons |'sidnz|, Sarah (1755–1831) English actress, sister of John Kemble; born *Sarah Kemble*. She was an acclaimed tragic actress, noted particularly for her role as Lady Macbeth.

Sid·ney |'sidnē|, Sir Philip (1554–86) English poet, courtier, and soldier. His best-known work is *Arcadia* (published posthumously in 1590), a pastoral prose romance including poems in a wide variety of verse forms.

Sie·gel |'sēgəl|, Jerry (1914–96) U.S. cartoonist. Full name *Jerome Siegel*. He was the co-creator of Superman with childhood friend Joe Shuster

Sie·mens |'zēmənz| German family of scientific entrepreneurs and engineers. **Ernst Werner von Siemens** (1816–92) was an electrical engineer who developed the process of electroplating, devised an electric generator which used an electromagnet, and pioneered electrical traction. His brother **Karl Wilhelm** (1823–83) (also known as *Sir Charles William Siemens*) moved to England, where he developed the open-hearth steel furnace and designed the cable-laying steamship *Faraday*. Their brother **Friedrich** (1826–1904) applied the principles of the open-hearth furnace to glass-making.

Si·gnac |sēn'yäk|, Paul (1863–1935) French neo-Impressionist painter. A pointillist painter, he had a technique that was freer than Seurat's and was characterized by the use of small dashes and patches of pure color rather than dots.

Si·ha·nouk |'sēə,no͞ok|, Norodom (1922–) Cambodian king (1941–55 and since 1993), prime minister (1955–60), and head of state (1960–70 and 1975–76). After Cambodian independence in 1953, Sihanouk abdicated in favor of his father in order to become prime minister. On his father's death Sihanouk proclaimed himself head of state. He was ousted in a U.S.-backed coup and was briefly reinstated by the Khmer Rouge. Sihanouk was crowned for the second time in 1993.

Si·kor·ski |SHē'kawrskē|, Wladyslaw Eugeniusz (1881–1943) Polish general and statesman. He was prime minister of Poland (Dec. 1922–May 1923), as well as minister of war (1924–25) and prime minister in exile (1939–43).

Si·kor·sky |sə'kawrskē|, Igor (Ivanovich) (1889–1972) Russian-born American aircraft designer. He built the first large four-engined aircraft, the Grand (1913), in his native country and went on to establish the Sikorsky company in the US. In 1939 he developed the first mass-produced helicopter.

Sil·li·toe |'silə,tō|, Alan (1928–   ) English writer, noted for his novels about working-class provincial life. Notable works: *The Loneliness of the Long-Distance Runner* (1959) and *Saturday Night and Sunday Morning* (1958).

Sills |silz|, Beverly (1929–   ) U.S. singer. Born *Belle Miriam Silverman*; known as **Bubbles**. Her association with the New York City Opera included a brilliant career as a soprano (1955–80) and the positions of general director (1979–88) and president (1989–90). She became the first woman chairperson of the Lincoln Center for the Performing Arts (1993–   ).

Sil·ver·stein |'silvər,stīn; 'silvər,stēn|, Shel (1932–99) U.S. author. Full name *Shelby Silverstein*. Notable works: *A Light in the Attic* (1981), *The Giving Tree* (1964), and *Where the Sidewalk Ends* (1974).

Si·me·non |ˌsēme'nawN|, Georges-Joseph-Christian (1903–89) Belgian-born French novelist. He is best known for his series of detective novels featuring Commissaire Maigret.

Sim·n Sty·li·tes |'simēən stī'lītēz|, St. (*c.* 390–459) Syrian monk. After living in a monastic community he became the first to practise an extreme form of asceticism which involved living on top of a pillar.

Sim·ic |'simik|, Charles (1938–   ) U.S. author, born in Yugoslavia. Notable works: *The World Doesn't End* (1989, Pulitzer Prize).

Sim·jian |'simyən|, Luther (1905–97) U.S. inventor, born in Turkey. He holds more than 200 patents for mechanisms including a 1960 bank-deposit machine that was the basis for the modern automatic teller machine, the teleprompter,

and the automatic postal meter machine.

Sim·mons |'simənz|, Al (1902–56) U.S. baseball player. Full name *Aloysius Harry Simmons*; born *Aloys Szymanski*. He twice led the American League in batting.

Sim·mons |'simənz|, Gene (1949–   ) U.S. rock musician, born in Israel. He was founder and member of the group Kiss (1973).

Simms |simz|, William Gilmore (1806–70) U.S. author. He wrote frontier romances and historical novels about the history of South Carolina.

Si·mon |'sīmən|, Carly (1945–   ) U.S. singer and songwriter. Notable songs: "You're So Vain," "Let the River Run," and "Anticipation."

Si·mon |'sīmən|, (Marvin) Neil (1927–   ) U.S. dramatist. Most of his plays are wry comedies portraying aspects of middle-class life; they include *Barefoot in the Park* (1963) and *The Odd Couple* (1965). Many of his plays were made into movies.

Si·mon |'sīmən|, Paul (1942–   ) U.S. singer and songwriter. He achieved fame with **Art Garfunkel** (1941–   ) for the albums *Sounds of Silence* (1966) and *Bridge Over Troubled Water* (1970). The duo split up in 1970 and Simon went on to pursue a successful solo career, recording albums such as *Graceland* (1986).

Si·mon |'sīmən|, Richard Leo (1899–1960) U.S. publisher. He was cofounder of Simon and Schuster book publishers (1924).

Si·mon |'sīmən|, St. an Apostle; known as **Simon the Zealot**. According to one tradition he preached and was martyred in Persia along with St. Jude. Feast day (with St. Jude), October 28.

Si·mon·i·des |sī'mänə,dēz| (*c.* 556–*c.* 468 BC) Greek lyric poet. Much of his poetry, which includes elegies, odes, and epigrams, celebrates the heroes of the Persian Wars.

Simp·son |'sim(p)sən|, Sir James Young (1811–70) Scottish surgeon and obstetrician. He discovered the usefulness of chloroform as an anesthetic shortly after the first use of ether.

Simp·son |'sim(p)sən|, George Gaylord (1902–84) U.S. paleontologist. He excavated and researched North American vertebrae fossils.

Simp·son |'sim(p)sən|, O. J. (1947–   ) U.S. football player, actor, and celebrity; full name *Orenthal James Simpson.* Following a successful career as a running back, Simpson became a sports commentator on television. He was arrested in 1994, accused of murdering his ex-wife and her male companion, but was acquitted after a lengthy, high-profile trial.

Simp·son |'sim(p)sən|, Wallis (1896–1986) U.S.-born wife of Edward, Duke of Windsor (Edward VIII); born *Wallis Warfield.* Her relationship with the king caused a scandal in view of her impending second divorce and forced the king's abdication in 1936. The couple were married shortly afterward, and she became the Duchess of Windsor.

Sims |simz|, Zoot (1925–85) U.S. jazz tenor saxophonist and bandleader. Full name *John Haley Sims.* He performed with Woody Herman's big band (1947–49) as one of the Four Brothers.

Si·na·tra |sə'nätrə|, Frank (1915–98) U.S. singer and actor; full name *Francis Albert Sinatra.* He became a star in the 1940s with a large teenage following; his many hits include "Night and Day" and "My Way". Notable movies: *From Here to Eternity* (1953), for which he won an Oscar.

Sin·clair |'sin,kler; sin'kler|, Sir Clive (Marles) (1940–   ) English electronics engineer and entrepreneur.

Sin·clair |sin'kler|, Upton (Beall) (1878–1968) U.S. novelist and social reformer. He agitated for social justice in seventy-nine books, including *The Jungle* (1906) and the eleven-volume "Lanny Budd" series (1940–53).

Sing·er |'siNGər|, Isaac Bashevis (1904–91) Polish-born U.S. novelist and short-story writer. His work blends realistic detail and elements of fantasy, mysticism, and magic to portray the lives of Polish Jews from many periods. Notable works: *The Magician of Lublin* (novel, 1955), *The Slave* (novel, 1962), *The Spinoza of Market Street* (short stories, 1961), and *Collected Stories* (1982). Nobel Prize for Literature (1978).

Sing·er |'siNGər|, Isaac Merritt (1811–75) U.S. inventor. In 1851 he designed and built the first commercially successful sewing machine, which included features already developed by Elias Howe. Singer's company became the world's largest sewing machine manufacturer.

Sin·gle·ton |'siNGgəltən|, Zutty (1898–1975) U.S. jazz drummer. Full name *Arthur James Singleton.* He was among the first drummers to use sock cymbals and wire brushes.

Sis·kel |'siskəl|, Gene (1946–99) U.S. movie critic. Full name *Eugene Kal Siskel.* He wrote for the *Chicago Tribune* (1969–98) and was co-host of the syndicated television program "Siskel & Ebert & the Movies" (1986–98).

Sis·ler |'sislər|, George Harold (1893–1973) U.S. baseball player. He set a record of 257 hits (1920).

Sis·ley |sislē; sē'slä|, Alfred (1839–99) French Impressionist painter, of English descent. He is chiefly remembered for his paintings of the countryside around Paris in the 1870s, with their concentration on reflecting surfaces and fluid brushwork.

Sit·ting Bull |,sitiNG 'bʊl| (c. 1831–90) Sioux chief; Sioux name *Tatanka Iyotake.* As the main chief of the Sioux peoples from about 1867, Sitting Bull led the Sioux in the fight to retain their lands; this resulted in the massacre of Lt. Col. George Custer and his men at Little Bighorn. He was killed by reservation police during the Ghost Dance turmoil.

Sit·well |'sit,wel; 'sitwəl|, Dame Edith (Louisa) (1887–1964) English poet and critic. Her early verse, with that of her brothers **Osbert** (1892–1969) and **Sacheverell** (1897–1988) marked a revolt against the prevailing Georgian style of the day.

Si·va·ji variant spelling of SHIVAJI.

Skel·ton |'skeltn|, John (c. 1460–1529) English poet. Court poet to Henry VIII, he wrote verse consisting of short irregular rhyming lines with rhythms based on colloquial speech.

Skel·ton |'skeltn|, Red (1913–97) U.S. comedian. Born *Richard Skelton.* A stage, circus, and movie performer, he starred in the television series "The Red Skelton Show" (1951–71).

Skid•more |'skid,mawr|, Louis (1897–1962) U.S. architect. Notable designs: U.S. Air Force Academy.

Skin•ner |'skinər|, B. F. (1904–90) U.S. behavioral psychologist. Full name *Burrhus Frederic Skinner*. He promoted the view that the proper aim of psychology should be to predict behavior, and hence be able to control it.

Skrya•bin variant spelling of SCRIABIN.

Sla•ter |'slātər|, Samuel (1768–1835) U.S. industrialist, born in England. He established textile mills at Pawtucket, Rhode Island, (1793) and elsewhere in New England.

Slick |slik|, Grace (1943–   ) U.S. rock vocalist. Born *Grace Barnett Wing*. She was a member of the Haight-Ashbury rock group Jefferson Airplane, which later became Jefferson Starship. Notable songs: "Somebody to Love" and "White Rabbit."

Sloan |slōn|, Alfred Pritchard, Jr. (1875–1966) U.S. industrialist. He was an executive with General Motors (1923–66).

Sloan |slōn|, John French (1871–1951) U.S. artist. He depicted scenes of New York City and gained fame as part of the "Ashcan School."

Sloane |slōn|, Sir Hans (1660–1753) Irish physician and naturalist. He endowed the Chelsea Physic Garden, and his books and specimens formed the basis of the British Museum Library and the Natural History Museum in London.

Slo•cum |'slōkəm|, Joshua (1844–*c.* 1910) U.S. mariner and author, born in Canada. He was the first man to sail alone around the world (1900).

Smalls |smawlz|, Robert (1839–1915) U.S. naval officer and politician. Born a slave, after he was impressed into the Confederate navy he commandeered a frigate, delivered it into Union hands, and became a pilot in the Union navy (1862). He later became a member of the U.S. House of Representatives from South Carolina (1875–79, 1881–87).

Smea•ton |'smētn|, John (1724–92) English engineer. He produced the first diving bell fed by compressed air, and founded the Society of Engineers (1771).

Sme•ta•na |'smetn-ə|, Bedřich (1824–84) Czech composer. Regarded as the founder of Czech music, he was dedicated to the cause of Czech nationalism, as is apparent in his operas, such as *The Bartered Bride* (1866) and in the cycle of symphonic poems *Ma Vlast ("My Country"* 1874–9).

Smi•ley |'smīlē|, Jane Graves (1949–   ) U.S. author. Notable works: *A Thousand Acres* (1991) and *Moo* (1995).

Smith |smiTH|, Adam (1723–90) Scottish economist and philosopher. Often regarded as the founder of modern economics, he advocated minimal state interference in economic matters and discredited mercantilism. Notable works: *Inquiry into the Nature and Causes of the Wealth of Nations* (1776).

Smith |smiTH|, Alfred Emanuel (1873–1944) U.S. politician. He served as governor of New York (1919–20 and 1923–28) and was a Democratic presidential candidate (1928).

Smith |smiTH|, Andrew (*c.* 1836–94) U.S. manufacturer. His cough drops were among the first "factory-filled" boxes of any confection.

Smith |smiTH|, Ashbel (1805–86) U.S. politician and physician. He negotiated a treaty by which Mexico acknowledged the independence of Texas (1845).

Smith |smiTH|, Bessie (1894–1937) Full name *Elizabeth Smith*. U.S. blues singer. She made over 150 recordings, including some with Benny Goodman and Louis Armstrong.

Smith |smiTH|, Betty (Wehner) (1904–72) U.S. author. Notable works: *A Tree Grows in Brooklyn* (1943).

Smith |smiTH|, Clarence (1904–29) U.S. jazz pianist and singer. Known as **Pinetop**. His recording "Pinetop's Boogie Woogie" (1928–29) was a pioneer of boogie-woogie.

Smith |smiTH|, David (Roland) (1906–65) U.S. sculptor. His early work is marked by recurring motifs of human violence and greed. These later give way to a calmer, more monumental style, as in the *Cubi* series.

Smith |smiTH|, Dean (Edwards) (1931–   ) U.S. college basketball coach. He coached the U.S. Olympic team to a gold medal in 1976 and remains number one on the all-time Division I victory list.

Smith |smiTH|, Emmitt J., III (1969–) U.S. football player. He was a three-time NFL rushing leader.

Smith |smiTH|, Horace (1808–93) U.S. inventor and manufacturer. With Daniel Baird Wesson he patented and manufactured revolvers (1854, 1857).

Smith |smiTH|, Ian (Douglas) (1919–) Rhodesian statesman and prime minister (1964–79). In 1965 he issued a unilateral declaration of independence from Britain because he would not agree to black majority rule. He eventually resigned in 1979 but remained active in politics in the independent state of Zimbabwe.

Smith |smiTH|, Jedediah Strong (1799–1831) U.S. explorer. He made expeditions in the Rocky Mountains (1822–26), California, and the Oregon coast (1826–69).

Smith |smiTH|, John (c. 1580–1631) American colonist, born in England. One of the leading promoters of English colonization in America, he helped found the colony of Jamestown (1607) and served as its president (1608–09).

Smith |smiTH|, Joseph (1805–44) U.S. religious leader and founder of the Church of Jesus Christ of Latter-Day Saints (the Mormons). In 1827, according to his own account, he was led by divine revelation to find the sacred texts written by the prophet Mormon, which he published as *The Book of Mormon* in 1830. He founded the Mormon Church in the same year and later established a large community in Illinois, where he was arrested and murdered by a mob.

Smith |smiTH|, Kate (1909–86) U.S. singer. Full name *Kathryn Elizabeth Smith*. She began a radio show in 1931 and started singing her trademark song "God Bless America" in 1938.

Smith |smiTH|, Lee (Arthur) (1957–) U.S. baseball pitcher. He retired in 1997 as the all-time saves leader with 478.

Smith |smiTH|, Lillian (Eugenia) (1897–1966) U.S. author and civil rights activist. Her *Strange Fruit* (1944),

an interracial love story, became a best-seller.

Smith |smiTH|, (Lloyd) Logan Pearsall (1865–1946) U.S. author. Notable works: *Reperusals and Re-collections* (1936).

Smith |smiTH|, Maggie (1934–) U.S. actress. Notable movies: *The Prime of Miss Jean Brodie* (1969, Academy Award).

Smith |smiTH|, Margaret Chase (1897–1995) U.S. senator from Maine (1940–73).

Smith |smiTH|, Richard (1735–1803) colonial American lawyer. A signer of the Declaration of Independence, he wrote a detailed diary of the Continental Congress.

Smith |smiTH|, Robert Weston (1938–95) U.S. radio, television, and movie entertainer. Known as **Wolfman Jack**. He was a rock and roll radio disk jockey based in San Diego (1987–95); his movies include *American Graffiti* (1973).

Smith |smiTH|, Samuel (1752–1839) U.S. politician. He was a Revolutionary War leader, a member of the U.S. House of Representatives from Maryland (1793–1803, 1816–22), and a U.S. senator (1803–15, 1835–38).

Smith |smiTH|, Samuel Francis (1808–95) U.S. clergyman. He wrote the hymn "America" (1831).

Smith |smiTH|, Seba (1792–1868) U.S. journalist. Pseudonym **Major Jack Downing**. He founded Maine's *Portland Courier* (1829); his letters were an inspiration to homespun political philosophers.

Smith |smiTH|, (Robert) Sidney (1877–1935) U.S. cartoonist. He drew the cartoon "The Gumps" from 1917–1935.

Smith |smiTH|, Stevie (1902–71) English poet and novelist; pseudonym of *Florence Margaret Smith*. She is mainly remembered for her witty, caustic, and enigmatic verse; collections include *A Good Time Was Had by All* (1937) and *Not Waving But Drowning* (1957).

Smith |smiTH|, Sydney (1771–1845) English Anglican churchman, essayist, and wit. He is notable for his *Letters of Peter Plymley* (1807), which defended Catholic Emancipation.

Smith |smiTH|, Theobald (1859–1934) U.S. microbiologist. Known for his work on the causes and nature of infectious and parasitic diseases, he developed the theory of immunization (1884–86).

Smith |smiTH|, William (1769–1839) English geologist. An English land surveyor and geologist, he pioneered the study of stratigraphical geology.

Smith |smiTH|, Willie (1897–1973) U.S. jazz pianist. Born *William Henry Joseph Bonaparte Bertholoff*; known as **The Lion**. His is known for his stride style solo recordings in 1939.

Smith•son |'smiTHsən|, James (1765–1829) English chemist. Known as **James Louis Macie** until 1801. He bequeathed money for the establishment of the Smithsonian Institution.

Smol•lett |'smälət|, Tobias (George) (1721–71) Scottish novelist. His humorous and fast-moving picaresque novels include *The Adventures of Roderick Random* (1748) and *The Adventures of Peregrine Pickle* (1751).

Smuck•er |'sməkər|, Jerome (1858–1948) U.S. businessman. He founded the J. M. Smucker Co., a manufacturer of apple butter; his sons expanded the company to include jellies and preserves.

Smuts |smⱮts; smⱭts|, Jan (Christiaan) (1870–1950) South African statesman, soldier, and prime minister (1919–24 and 1939–48). He led Boer forces during the Second Boer War, but afterwards supported the policy of Anglo-Boer cooperation. He commanded Allied troops against German East Africa (1916) and later helped to found the League of Nations.

Snead |snēd|, Sam (1912–) U.S. golfer. Full name *Samuel Jackson Snead*. He holds the PGA Tour career victory record (81).

Snod•grass |'snäd,græs|, W. D. (1926–) U.S. poet and educator. Full name *William DeWitt Snodgrass*. Notable works: *Heart's Needle* (1959, Pulitzer Prize).

Snor•ri Stur•lu•son |'snawrē 'stərləsən| (1178–1241) Icelandic historian and poet. A leading figure of medieval Icelandic literature, he wrote the *Younger Edda* or *Prose Edda* and the

Heimskringla, a history of the kings of Norway from mythical times to the year 1177.

Snow |snō|, C. P., 1st Baron Snow of Leicester (1905–80) English novelist and scientist; full name *Charles Percy Snow*. He is best known for his sequence of eleven novels *Strangers and Brothers*, which deals with moral dilemmas in the academic world, and for his lecture "The Two Cultures" (1959).

Sny•der |'snīdər|, John P. (1926–97) U.S. chemical engineer and cartographer. He determined the method for converting a spherical globe to a flat map.

Soane |sōn|, Sir John (1753–1837) English architect. His later work avoided unnecessary ornament and adopted structural necessity as the basis of design. His designs included the Bank of England (1788–1833, since rebuilt) and his house in London, now a museum.

So•bies•ki |sō'byeskē|, John see JOHN III.

So•bre•ro |sō'brerō|, Ascanio (1812–88) Italian chemist. He discovered nitroglycerin (1847).

Soc•ra•tes |'säkrə,tēz| (*c.* 470–399 BC) ancient Athenian philosopher. As represented in the writings of his disciple Plato, he engaged in dialogue with others in an attempt to reach understanding and ethical concepts by exposing and dispelling error (the *Socratic method*). Charged with introducing strange gods and corrupting the young, he committed suicide as required.

Sol•o•mon |'säləmən| (*c.* 970–*c.* 930 BC) son of David, king of ancient Israel (*c.*970–*c.*930 BC). In the Bible, Solomon is traditionally considered the writer of the Song of Solomon, Ecclesiastes, and Proverbs, and he is proverbial for his wisdom. Discontent with his rule, however, led to the secession of the northern tribes in the reign of his son Rehoboam.

So•lon |'sōlən; 'sō,län| (*c.* 630–*c.* 560 BC) Athenian statesman and lawgiver. One of the Seven Sages, he revised the code of laws established by Draco, making it less severe. His division of the citizens into four classes based on wealth rather than birth laid the foundations of Athenian democracy.

Sol·ti |'SHŌltē|, Sir Georg (1912–97) Hungarian-born British conductor. He revivified Covent Garden as musical director (1961–71) and was conductor of the Chicago Symphony Orchestra (1969–91) and the London Philharmonic Orchestra (1979–83).

Sol·zhe·ni·tsyn |,sōlzHə'nētsən|, Alexander (1918–) Russian novelist; Russian name *Aleksandr Isayevich Solzhenitsyn*. He spent eight years in a labor camp for criticizing Stalin and began writing on his release. From 1963 his books were banned in the Soviet Union, and he was exiled in 1974, eventually returning to Russia in 1994. Notable works: *One Day in the Life of Ivan Denisovich* (1962), *The First Circle* (1968), *August 1914* (1971), and *The Gulag Archipelago* (1974). Nobel Prize for Literature (1970).

So·mo·za |sə'mōsə| the name of a family of Nicaraguan statesmen: **Anastasio** (1896–1956), president 1937–47 and 1951–56; full name *Anastasio Somoza García*. He took presidential office following a military coup in 1936. Somoza ruled Nicaragua as a virtual dictator and was assassinated. **Luis** (1922–67), president 1957–63, son of Anastasio; full name *Luis Somoza Debayle*. **Anastasio** (1925–80), President 1967–79, younger brother of Luis; full name *Anastasio Somoza Debayle*. His dictatorial regime was overthrown by the Sandinistas, and he was assassinated while in exile in Paraguay.

Sond·heim |'sänd,hīm|, Stephen (Joshua) (1930–) U.S. composer and lyricist. He became famous with his lyrics for Leonard Bernstein's *West Side Story* (1957). He has since written a number of musicals, including *A Little Night Music* (1973), *Sweeney Todd* (1979), and *Sunday in the Park with George* (1984).

Son·tag |'sän,tæg|, Susan (1933–) U.S. writer and critic. She established her reputation as a radical intellectual with *Against Interpretation* (essays, 1966). Other notable works: *On Photography* (1976) and *Illness as Metaphor* (1979).

Sont·hei·mer |'sänt,hīmər|, Carl G. (c. 1915–98) U.S. electronics engineer and entrepreneur. He brought the Cuisinart food processor to the U.S.

Soph·o·cles |'säfə,klēz| (c. 496–406 BC) Greek dramatist. His seven surviving plays are notable for their complexity of plot and depth of characterization, and for their examination of the relationship between mortals and the divine order. Notable plays: *Antigone, Electra,* and *Oedipus Rex* (also called *Oedipus Tyrannus*).

Sop·with |'säpwiTH|, Sir Thomas (Octave Murdoch) (1888–1989) English aircraft designer. During the First World War he designed the fighter biplane the Sopwith Camel, while in World War II, as chairman of the Hawker Siddeley company, he was responsible for the production of aircraft such as the Hurricane fighter.

Sor·en |'sawrən|, Tabitha L. (1967–) U.S. television newscaster and writer.

Sou·sa |'sōōzə|, John Philip (1854–1932) U.S. composer and band conductor, known as the "March King." He wrote more than a hundred marches, including *The Stars and Stripes Forever, Semper Fidelis,* and *The Washington Post March.* The sousaphone, invented in 1898, was named in his honor.

Sou·ter |'sōōtər|, David Hackett (1939–) U.S. Supreme Court justice (1990–).

Sou·they |'sowTHē; 'səTHē|, Robert (1774–1843) English poet. Associated with the Lake Poets, he is best known for his shorter poems, such as the "Battle of Blenheim" (1798). He was made Poet Laureate in 1813.

Sou·tine |sōō'tēn|, Chaim (1893–1943) French painter, born in Lithuania. A major exponent of expressionism, he produced pictures of grotesque figures during the 1920s, while from 1925 he increasingly painted still lifes.

So·yin·ka |swoi'iNGkə|, Wole (1934–) Nigerian dramatist, novelist, and critic. Born *Akinwande Oluwole Soyinka*. In 1986 he became the first African to receive the Nobel Prize for Literature. Notable works: *The Lion and the Jewel* (play, 1959) and *The Interpreters* (novel, 1965).

Spaak |späk|, Paul-Henri Charles (1899–1972) Belgian statesman. As prime minister of Belgium (1938–39, 1946, 1947–50), he helped draft the charters of the UN, NATO, and the Common Market.

Spaatz |späts|, Carl (1891–1974) U.S. air force officer. Born *Carl Spatz*; known as **Tooey**. He led the U.S. bombing force in Germany (1944) and Japan (1945) and was the first chief of staff of the independent U.S. air force (1947).

Spahn |spän|, Warren (Edward) (1921–) U.S. baseball player. He holds the pitching record for most career wins by a left-hander (363).

Spal·lan·za·ni |ˌspälänt'sänē|, Lazzaro (1729–99) Italian physiologist and biologist. He is known today for his experiments in subjects such as the circulation of the blood and the digestive system of animals. He also disproved the theory of spontaneous generation.

Span·ier |'spænyər|, Muggsy (1906–67) U.S. jazz cornetist and bandleader. Full name *Francis Joseph Spanier*. He organized his Ragtime Band (1939) and made 16 recordings that helped revive interest in New Orleans jazz in 1940s.

Spark |spärk|, Dame Muriel (1918–) Scottish novelist. Notable works: *The Prime of Miss Jean Brodie* (1961) and *The Mandelbaum Gate* (1965).

Spark·man |'spärkmən|, John Jackson (1899–1985) U.S. politician. He served as an Alabama member of the U.S. House of Representatives (1937–46) and of the U.S. Senate (1946–79); he also was a Democratic vice presidential candidate (1952).

Spar·ta·cus |'spärtəkəs| (died *c.* 71 BC) Thracian slave and gladiator. He led a revolt against Rome in 73, but was eventually defeated by Crassus in 71 and crucified.

Spas·sky |'spæskē|, Boris (Vasilyevich) (1937–) Russian chess player, world champion (1969–72).

Spea·ker |'spēkər|, Tris (1888–1958) U.S. baseball player. Full name *Tristram E. Speaker*. He is the all-time leader in outfield assists (449) and doubles (793).

Speare |spir|, Elizabeth George (1908–94) U.S. author. She wrote historical fiction for children, including *The Witch of Blackbird Pond* (Newbery Award, 1958), *The Bronze Bow* (Newbery Award,

1961), and *Life in Colonial America* (1963).

Spec·tor |'spektər|, Phil (1940–) U.S. record producer and songwriter. Full name *Phillip Harvey Spector*. He pioneered a "wall of sound" style, using echo and tape loops, and had a succession of hit recordings in the 1960s with groups such as the Ronettes and the Crystals.

Speer |spir; SHpär|, Albert (1905–81) German architect and Nazi government official, designer of the Nuremberg stadium for the 1934 Nazi Party congress. He was also minister for armaments and munitions. Following the Nuremberg trials, he served twenty years in Spandau prison.

Speke |spēk|, John Hanning (1827–64) English explorer. With Sir Richard Burton, he became the first European to discover Lake Tanganyika (1858). He also discovered Lake Victoria, naming it in honor of the queen.

Spel·ling |'speliNG|, Aaron (*c.* 1928–) U.S. television producer and writer. He produced numerous television programs, including "Dynasty."

Spence |spens|, Sir Basil (Urwin) (1907–76) British architect, born in India.

Spen·cer |'spensər|, Herbert (1820–1903) English philosopher and sociologist. He sought to apply the theory of natural selection to human societies, developing social Darwinism and coining the phrase the "survival of the fittest" (1864).

Spen·cer |'spensər|, Sir Stanley (1891–1959) English painter. He is best known for his religious and visionary works in the modern setting of his native village of Cookham in Berkshire, such as *Resurrection: Cookham* (1926).

Spen·der |'spendər|, Sir Stephen Harold (1909–) British poet and critic. Notable works: *Poems of Dedication* (1946) and *World within World* (1951).

Speng·ler |SHpeNGglər; 'speNGglər|, Oswald (1880–1936) German philosopher. In his book *The Decline of the West* (1918–22) he argues that civilizations undergo a seasonal cycle of a thousand years and are subject to growth and decay analogous to biological species.

Spen·ser |'spensər|, Edmund (*c.* 1552–99) English poet. He is best known for his allegorical romance the *Faerie Queene* (1590; 1596), celebrating Queen Elizabeth I and written in the Spenserian stanza.

Sper·ry |'sperē|, Elmer Ambrose (1860–1930) U.S. electrical engineer, industrialist, and inventor. He founded eight manufacturing companies and held over 400 patents, including the Sperry Gyroscopic Compass (1910).

Spie·gel·man |'spēgəlmən|, Art (1948–) U.S. artist and author, born in Sweden. Notable works: *Maus* (1986, Pulitzer Prize), *Raw* (1989), and *Open Me—I'm a Dog* (1997).

Spiel·berg |'spēl,bərg|, Steven (1947–) U.S. filmmaker. Notable films: *Jaws* (1975), *Close Encounters of the Third Kind* (1977), *E. T. the Extra-Terrestrial* (1982), *Jurassic Park* (1993), *Schindler's List* (1993), and *Saving Private Ryan* (1998).

Spil·lane |spə'lān|, Mickey (1918–) U.S. writer; pseudonym of *Frank Morrison Spillane*. His popular detective novels include *I, the Jury* (1947), *My Gun Is Quick* (1950), and *The Big Kill* (1951).

Spin·garn |'spin,gärn|, Joel Elias (1875–1939) U.S. author. The founder of the National Association for the Advancement of Colored People (1909), he was also a founder of Harcourt, Brace & Co. (1919–32).

Spi·no·za |spi'nōzə|, Baruch (or Benedict) de (1632–77) Dutch philosopher, of Portuguese-Jewish descent. He espoused a pantheistic system, seeing "God or nature" as a single infinite substance, with mind and matter being two incommensurable ways of conceiving the one reality.

Spitz |spits|, Mark (Andrew) (1950–) U.S. swimmer. He won seven gold medals in the 1972 Olympic Games at Munich and set twenty-seven world records for freestyle and butterfly (1967–72).

Spock |späk|, Benjamin McLane (1903–98) U.S. pediatrician and writer; known as **Dr. Spock**. His influential manual *The Common Sense Book of Baby and Child Care* (1946) challenged traditional ideas in child-rearing in favor of a psychological approach.

Spotts·wood |'späts,wŏŏd|, Stephen Gill (1897–1974) He was chairman of the NAACP (1961–74).

Spring·field |'spriNG,fēld|, Dusty (1939–99) British pop-rock vocalist. Born *Mary O'Brien*. Her hits include "You Don't Have to Say You Love Me" (1966) and "What Have I Done to Deserve This" (1987).

Spring·steen |'spriNG,stēn|, Bruce (Frederick Joseph) (1949–) U.S. rock singer, songwriter, and guitarist, noted for his songs about working-class life in the U.S. Notable albums: *Born to Run* (1975) and *Born in the USA* (1984).

Spru·ance |'sprōōəns|, Raymond Ames (1886–1969) U.S. admiral. He was commander in chief of the U.S. Pacific fleet (1945–46).

Spy·ri |'sHpērē|, Johanna (1827–1901) Swiss author. Her children's story *Heidi's Years of Wandering and Learning* (1880) was published in the U.S. as *Heidi* (1884).

Squan·to |'skwäntō| (died 1622) Pawtuxet Indian. He befriended the Pilgrims in Plymouth Colony (1621), acting as an interpreter and giving them advice on planting and fishing, assistance that proved vital to their survival.

Squibb |skwib|, Edward Robinson (1819–1900) U.S. navy physician and businessman. He founded a pharmaceutical company to provide a source of reliable drugs and vitamins to the armed forces (1859).

Staël |stäl|, Mme de see DE STAËL.

Stagg |stæg|, Amos Alonzo (1862–1965) U.S. athlete, football coach, and inventor. A coach at the University of Chicago and College of the Pacific, he invented the tackling dummy; he was elected to both the college football and basketball halls of fame.

St. Agnes, St. Barnabas, etc. see AGNES, ST., BARNABAS, ST.

Stahl |stäl|, Lesley Rene (1941–) U.S. journalist. She is a correspondent for CBS News, appearing on the television program "60 Minutes."

Stai·ner |'stānər|, Sir John (1840–1901) English composer. He is remembered for his church music, including hymns, cantatas, and the oratorio *Crucifixion* (1887).

Sta·lin |'stälən|, Joseph (1879–1953) Soviet statesman, general secretary of the Communist Party of the USSR 1922–53; born *Iosif Vissarionovich Dzhugashvili*. His adoptive name Stalin means "man of steel." Having isolated his political rival Trotsky, by 1927 Stalin was the uncontested leader of the Communist Party. In 1928 he launched a succession of five-year plans for rapid industrialization and the enforced collectivization of agriculture; as a result of this process some 10 million peasants are thought to have died. His large-scale purges of the intelligentsia in the 1930s were equally ruthless. After the World War II victory over Hitler in 1945 he maintained a firm grip on neighboring Communist states.

Stal·lone |stə'lōn|, Sylvester Enzio (1946–) U.S. actor, director, and producer. He is best known for his *Rocky* and *Rambo* movies.

Stan·dish |'stændisH|, Myles (*c.* 1584–1656) American colonist, from England. First name also **Miles**. He accompanied the Pilgrims to America (1620) and became the military leader of Plymouth Colony. He was a cofounder of Duxbury, Massachusetts (1631). He is romanticized as the lovelorn suitor in Longfellow's fictional poem "The Courtship of Miles Standish."

Stan·ford |'stænfərd|, A. Leland (1824–93) U.S. railroad official and philanthropist. Full name *Amasa Leland Stanford*. He was governor of California (1861–63); a member of the U.S. Senate (1885–93); promoter, financier, and director of two railroads, the Central Pacific and the Southern Pacific; and founder of Stanford University (1885).

Stan·ford |'stænfərd|, Sir Charles (Villiers) (1852–1924) British composer, born in Ireland. He is noted especially for his Anglican church music and numerous choral works.

Stan·ier |'stænir|, Sir William (Arthur) (1876–1965) English railroad engineer. He is chiefly remembered for his standard locomotive designs for the London Midland and Scottish Railway.

Stan·i·slaus |'stænə‚slaws|, St. (1030–79) patron saint of Poland; Polish name *Stanislaw*; known as **St. Stanislaus of Cracow**. As bishop of Cracow (1072–79) he excommunicated King Boleslaus II. According to tradition Stanislaus was murdered by Boleslaus while taking Mass. Feast day, April 11 (formerly May 7).

Stan·i·slav·sky |‚stænə'släfskē|, Konstantin (Sergeyevich) (1863–1938) Russian theater director and actor; born *Konstantin Sergeyevich Alekseyev*. Stanislavsky trained his actors to take a psychological approach and use latent powers of self-expression when taking on roles; his theory and technique were later developed into method acting.

Stan·ley |'stænlē| U.S. inventors. **Francis Edgar Stanley** (1849–1918) and his twin brother **Freelan Oscar Stanley** (1849–1940) designed and built steam cars (1902–17).

Stan·ley |'stænlē|, Sir Henry Morton (1841–1904) Welsh explorer; born *John Rowlands*. As a newspaper correspondent he was sent in 1869 to central Africa to find David Livingstone; two years later he found him at Lake Tanganyika. After Livingstone's death in 1873, Stanley continued his explorations in Africa, charting Lake Victoria, tracing the course of the Congo, and mapping Lake Albert.

Stan·ley |'stænlē|, William, Jr. (1858–1916) U.S. electrical engineer and inventor. He installed the first alternating current distribution system (1886, Great Barrington, Massachusetts).

Stan·ton |'stæntən|, Edwin McMasters (1814–69) U.S. lawyer and public official. He was secretary of war under Abraham Lincoln and played a pivotal role in the impeachment proceedings against President Andrew Johnson; in 1869 he was appointed to the U.S. Supreme Court but died before taking office.

Stan·ton |'stæntən|, Elizabeth (Cady) (1815–1902) U.S. social reformer. With Lucretia Mott, she organized the first U.S. women's rights convention, in Seneca Falls, New York (1848). From 1852, she led the women's rights movement with Susan B. Anthony. She was president of the National Woman Suffrage Association (1869–90) and editor of the radical feminist magazine *Revolution* (1868–70).

Sta·ple·ton |'stāpəltən|, Maureen (1925–) U.S. actress. Notable movies: *Reds* (1981, Academy Award).

Star·ling |'stärliNG|, Ernest Henry (1866–1927) English physiologist and founder of the science of endocrinology. He demonstrated the existence of peristalsis, and coined the term *hormone* for the substance secreted by the pancreas which stimulates the secretion of digestive juices.

Starr |stär|, Bart (1934–) U.S. football player. Full name *Bryan B. Starr*. Elected to the Football Hall of Fame (1977).

Starr |stär|, Kenneth Winston (1946–) U.S. attorney. He was appointed independent counsel (1994) to investigate the Clinton Whitewater real estate venture and other scandals, including the president's affair with Monica Lewinsky.

Starr |stär|, Ringo (1940–) English rock and pop drummer; born *Richard Starkey*. He became the drummer for the Beatles in 1962. After the band split up (1970), he pursued a solo career.

Sta·ti·us |'stāsHəs|, Publius Papinius (*c.* 45–96 AD) Roman poet. He is best known for the *Silvae*, a miscellany of poems addressed to friends, and the *Thebais*, an epic concerning the bloody quarrel between the sons of Oedipus.

Stau·bach |'staw,bäk; 'stawbæk|, Roger (Thomas) (1942–) U.S. football player. He was a five-time passing leader in the National Football Conference.

Stau·ding·er |'sHtowdiNGər|, Hermann (1881–1965) German chemist. His studies of polymers won him the Nobel Prize for Chemistry in 1953.

Ste·ber, Eleanor (1916–90) U.S. operatic soprano. She sang with the Metropolitan Opera for 22 seasons, beginning with her debut in 1940 as Sophie.

Steel |stēl|, Danielle (Fernande) (1947–) U.S. author. Notable works: *Full Circle* (1984), *Five Days in Paris* (1995), and *Long Road Home* (1998).

Steele |stēl|, Sir Richard (1672–1729) Irish essayist and dramatist. He founded and wrote for the periodicals the

Tatler (1709–11) and the *Spectator* (1711–12), the latter in collaboration with Joseph Addison.

Stef·fens |'stefənz|, (Joseph) Lincoln (1866–1936) U.S. journalist. The leader of the muckraking movement, he was editor of *McClure's* (1902–06).

Steg·ner |'stegnər|, Wallace (Earle) (1909–93) U.S. author and professor. Notable works: *Angle of Repose* (1971, Pulitzer Prize) and *The Spectator Bird* (1976, National Book Award).

Stei·chen |'stīkən|, Edward Jean (1879–1973) U.S. photographer, born in Luxembourg. First name originally *Edouard*. He is credited with transforming photography to an art form.

Steig |stīg|, William (1907–) U.S. cartoonist and artist. He created the "Small Fry" drawings appearing in *The New Yorker* magazine.

Stei·ger |'stīgər|, Rod (1925–) U.S. actor. Notable movies: *In the Heat of the Night* (1967, Academy Award).

Stein |stīn|, Gertrude (1874–1946) U.S. writer. Stein developed an esoteric stream-of-consciousness style, notably in *The Autobiography of Alice B. Toklas* (1933). Her home in Paris became a focus for the avant-garde during the 1920s and 1930s.

Stein·beck |'stīn,bek|, John (Ernst) (1902–68) U.S. novelist. His work, for example *Of Mice and Men* (1937) and *The Grapes of Wrath* (1939), is noted for its sympathetic and realistic portrayal of the migrant agricultural workers of California. His later novels include *Cannery Row* (1945) and *East of Eden* (1952). Nobel Prize for Literature (1962).

Stein·bren·ner |'stīn,brenər|, George Michael III (1930–) U.S. businessman. The principal owner of the New York Yankees (1973–), he is also chairman of the board of the American Ship Building Co. (1978–).

Stei·nem |'stīnəm|, Gloria (1934–) U.S. social reformer and journalist. A women's rights activist, she cofounded and edited *Ms.* magazine (1971–87).

Stei·ner |'stīnər|, Rudolf (1861–1925) Austrian philosopher, founder of anthroposophy. He founded the Anthroposophical Society in 1912, aiming to integrate the practical and psychological in education. The society has contributed to child-centered education, especially with its Steiner schools.

Stein·metz |'stīn‚mets|, Charles Proteus (1865–1923) German inventor. Born *Karl August Rudolf Steinmetz*. His theories for alternating current enabled the expansion of the electric power industry in U.S.

Stein·way |'stīn‚wā|, Henry (Engelhard) (1797–1871) German pianobuilder, resident in the U.S. from 1849; born *Heinrich Engelhard Steinweg*. He founded his famous piano-making firm in New York in 1853.

Stel·la |'stelə|, Frank (Philip) (1936–) U.S. painter, an important figure in minimalism known for his series of all-black paintings.

Stel·ler |'sHtelər; 'stelər|, Georg Wilhelm (1709–46) Last name originally *Stoeller*. German naturalist and geographer. Steller was a research member of Vitus Bering's second expedition to Kamchatka and Alaska and described many new birds and mammals, several of which now bear his name.

Sten·dhal |steN'däl; sten'däl| (1783–1842) French novelist; pseudonym of *Marie Henri Beyle*. His two best-known novels are *Le Rouge et le noir* (1830), relating the rise and fall of a young man from the provinces, and *La Chartreuse de Parme* (1839).

Sten·gel |'steNGgəl|, Casey (c. 1890–1975) U.S. baseball player and manager. Full name *Charles Dillon Stengel*. He guided the New York Yankees to ten American League pennants and seven World Series (1949–60).

Sten·nis |'stenəs|, John Cornelius (1901–95) U.S. politician. He was a U.S. senator from Mississippi for more than 41 years (1947–89).

Ste·pha·no·pou·los |‚stefə'näpələs|, George (1961–) U.S. political official. He was a senior adviser during the Clinton administration.

Ste·phen |'stēvən| (c. 1097–1154) grandson of William the Conqueror, king of England 1135–54. Stephen seized the throne from Matilda a few months after the death of Henry I. Civil war followed until Matilda was defeated and forced to leave England in 1148.

Ste·phen |'stēvən|, St. (died c. 35 AD) Christian martyr. One of the original seven deacons in Jerusalem appointed by the Apostles, he was charged with blasphemy and stoned, thus becoming the first Christian martyr. Feast day (in the Western Church) December 26; (in the Eastern Church) December 27.

Ste·phen |'stēvən|, St. (c. 977–1038) king and patron saint of Hungary (reigned 1000–38). The first king of Hungary, he took steps to Christianize the country. Feast day, September 2 or (in Hungary) August 20.

Stern |stərn|, Howard (Allan) (1954–) U.S. disk jockey and talkshow host. He has been labeled a "shock jock" for his trademark broadcasting of crass and explicit material.

Stern |stərn|, Isaac (1920–) U.S. violinist, born in Russia. He made his New York debut in 1937 in Carnegie Hall; he was the first American to perform in Russia after World War II (1956), and he was invited to China in 1979.

Stern |stərn|, Otto (1888–1969) U.S. physicist, born in Germany. He used molecular beams to establish the existence of atomic magnetic moments. Nobel Prize for Physics, 1943.

Stern |stərn|, Richard (Gustave) (1928–) U.S. author. Notable works: *Other Men's Daughters* (1973) and *A Father's Words: A Novel* (1986).

Sterne |stərn|, Laurence (1713–68) Irish novelist. He is best known for his nine-volume work *The Life and Opinions of Tristram Shandy* (1759–67), which parodied the developing conventions of the novel form. Other notable works: *A Sentimental Journey through France and Italy* (1768).

Stet·son |'stetsən|, John Batterson (1830–1906) U.S. entrepreneur. He created the Stetson hat and gave financial support to Stetson University in Florida.

Steu·ben |'sHtoibən; 'stoobən|, Friedrich von (1730–94) American army officer, born in Prussia. Full name *Friedrich Wilhelm Ludolf Gerhard Augustin von Steuben*. Arriving in America in December 1777, he joined Washington at Valley Forge, where he introduced European methods of training and discipline. Appointed inspector general of the Continental Army (1778), he turned raw troops into a legitimate military force.

Ste•vens |'stēvənz|, George (*c.* 1904–75) U.S. director. Notable movies: *A Place in the Sun* (1951 Academy Award).

Ste•vens |'stēvənz|, John Paul (1920–) U.S. Supreme Court justice (1975–)

Ste•vens |'stēvənz|, Wallace (1879–1955) U.S. poet. He wrote poetry privately and mostly in isolation from the literary community, developing an original and colorful style. His *Collected Poems* (1954) won a Pulitzer Prize.

Ste•ven•son |'stēvənsən|, Adlai Ewing (1900–65) U.S. statesman and politician. A popular supporter of social reform and internationalism, he was governor of Illinois (1949–53) and was twice the unsuccessful Democratic candidate for the presidency (1952, 1956).

Ste•ven•son |'stēvənsən|, James (*c.* 1929–) U.S. cartoonist, author, and illustrator. His books for children include *Are We Almost There?* (1985) and *The Supreme Souvenir Factory* (1988).

Ste•ven•son |'stēvənsən|, Robert Louis (Balfour) (1850–94) Scottish novelist, poet, and travel writer. Stevenson made his name with the adventure story *Treasure Island* (1883). He is also known for *A Child's Garden of Verses*, a collection of poetry. Other notable works: *The Strange Case of Dr. Jekyll and Mr. Hyde* and *Kidnapped* (both 1886).

Stew•art |'stoŏərt|, Jackie (1939–) Scottish racecar driver and television commentator; born *John Young Stewart*. He was three times world champion (1969; 1971; 1973).

Stew•art |'stoŏərt|, James (Maitland) (1908–97) U.S. actor, famous for roles in which he was seen as embodying the all-American hero. His movies include *The Philadelphia Story* (1940), which earned him an Oscar, Frank Capra's *It's a Wonderful Life* (1946), Alfred Hitchcock's *Vertigo* (1958), and westerns such as *The Man from Laramie* (1955).

Stew•art |'stoŏərt|, Martha (1941–) U.S. businesswoman. She turned her home decorating and cooking ideas into an industry, including an "Ask Martha" radio talk show, a television program, a magazine, and a signature line of housewares.

Stew•art |'stoŏərt|, Mary (1916–) English author. Notable works: *The Hollow Hills* (1973).

Stew•art |'stoŏərt|, Potter (1915–85) U.S. Supreme Court justice (1958–81). He upheld the First Amendment claim in the Pentagon Papers case, and he was noted for his 1964 opinion on pornography, "I know it when I see it."

Stew•art |'stoŏərt|, Rod (1945–) English pop singer and songwriter; full name *Roderick David Stewart*.

Stibitz |'stibəts|, George Robert (1904–95) U.S. inventor. Considered the father of the modern digital computer, he helped design the Model I complex number calculator.

Stick•ley |'stiklē|, Gustave (1858–1942) U.S. furniture designer and manufacturer. His style came to be known as Craftsman.

Stieg•litz |'stēglitz|, Alfred (1864–1946) U.S. photographer, husband of Georgia O'Keefe. He was important for his pioneering work to establish photography as a fine art in the U.S.

Stif•fel |'stifəl|, Theodopholous A. (1899–1971) U.S. businessman. The designer of Stiffel Lamps, he began marketing moderately priced creations and then changed to more elegant productions.

Stiles |stīlz|, Ezra (1727–95) U.S. scholar, teacher, lawyer, and minister. A Congregational minister, he was a president of Yale College (1778–95) and a founder of Brown University.

Stil•ler |'stilər|, Jerry (1926–) U.S. actor. He and his wife Anne Meara form the comedy duo Stiller and Meara.

Stills |stilz|, Stephen (1945–) U.S. rock musician. He was a rock guitarist and keyboardist, as well as a singer with the group Crosby, Stills, Nash (and Young).

Stil•well |'stil,wel|, Joseph Warren (1883–1946) U.S. army officer. Known as **Uncle Joe** or **Vinegar Joe**. He commanded U.S. troops in the China-Burma-India theater (1942–44), U.S. army ground forces under Douglas

MacArthur (1945), and the U.S. 10th Army in the Pacific (1945–46).

Stim·son |'stimsən|, Henry Lewis (1867–1950) U.S. lawyer and statesman. He was the first American to serve in the cabinets of four presidents; among these posts, he served as secretary of state (1929–33) and twice as secretary of war (1911–13 and 1940–45). He authored the Stimson Doctrine against Japan.

Stine |stīn|, R. L. (1943–) U.S. author. He wrote the "Goosebumps" series for children.

Sting |stiNG| (1951–) British pop musician. Born *Gordon Matthew Sumner.* Formerly the lead singer with The Police, as a solo artist he has recorded "If Ever I Lose My Faith in You" (1993, Grammy Award) and "Fields of Gold" (1993).

Stir·ling |'stərliNG|, Sir James Frazer (1926–92) Scottish architect. Working at first in a brutalist style, he became known for his use of geometric shapes and colored decoration in public buildings such as the Neuestaatsgalerie in Stuttgart (1977).

Stitt |stit|, Sonny (1924–82) U.S. jazz saxophonist. Full name *Edward Stitt.* He was a disciple of Charlie Parker.

Stock·hau·sen |'sHtäk,howzən|, Karlheinz (1928–) German composer. An important avant-garde composer and exponent of serialism, he cofounded an electronic music studio for West German radio and in 1980 embarked on his *Licht* cycle of musical ceremonies.

Sto·ker |'stōkər|, Bram (1847–1912) Irish novelist and theater manager; full name *Abraham Stoker.* He is chiefly remembered as the author of the vampire story *Dracula* (1897).

Stokes |stōks|, Carl (1927–1996) U.S. politician. He was the first African-American mayor of a major U.S. city (Cleveland, 1967–72).

Sto·kow·ski |stə'kowskē|, Leopold (1882–1977) British-born U.S. conductor, of Polish descent. Full name *Leopold Antoni Stanislaw Boleslawowicz Stokowski.* He is best known for arranging and conducting the music for Walt Disney's movie *Fantasia* (1940), which

sought to bring classical music to cinema audiences by means of cartoons.

Stone |stōn|, Edward Durell (1902–78) U.S. architect. Notable designs include the U.S. Embassy in India and the Museum of Modern Art (New York, 1938–39).

Stone |stōn|, Harlan Fiske (1872–1946) Chief Justice of the U.S. (1941–46) and U.S. Supreme Court justice (1925–41).

Stone |stōn|, Lucy (1818–93) U.S. feminist and abolitionist. The first woman in Massachusetts to earn a college degree, she traveled widely during the 1850s lecturing on women's rights, and she founded the American Woman Suffrage Association (1869)

Stone |stōn|, Oliver (1946–) U.S. movie director, screenwriter, and producer. He won Oscars for his adaptation of the novel *Midnight Express* (1978) and his direction of *Platoon* (1986) and *Born on the Fourth of July* (1989), both of which indict U.S. involvement in the Vietnam War. Other notable films: *JFK* (1991) and *Natural Born Killers* (1994).

Stone |stōn|, Robert (1937–) U.S. author. Notable works: *Images of War* (1986) and *Outerbridge Reach* (1992).

Stone |stōn|, Sharon (1958–) U.S. actress.

Sto·ner |'stōnər|, Eugene (1922–97) U.S. gun designer. He built the prototype for the M-16, a standard-issue weapon of the American soldier.

Stookey |'stŏŏkē|, (Noel) Paul (1937–) U.S. guitarist and singer. He was part of the singing trio Peter, Paul and Mary (see TRAVERS).

Stop·pard |'stäpərd|, Sir Tom (1937–) British dramatist, born in Czechoslovakia; born *Thomas Straussler.* His best-known plays are comedies, often dealing with metaphysical and ethical questions, for example *Rosencrantz and Guildenstern are Dead* (1966), which is based on the characters in *Hamlet.* Other notable works: *Jumpers* (1972), *The Real Thing* (1982), and *Arcadia* (1993).

Sto·ry |'stawrē|, Joseph (1779–1845) U.S. Supreme Court justice (1811–45). He was a pioneer in organizing and directing teaching at Havard Law School.

Stouf•fer |'stōfər|, Vernon (1901–74) U.S. businessman. He founded the restaurant chain and frozen food business that bear his name.

Stout |stowt|, Rex (Todhunter) (1886–1975) U.S. author. He created the *Nero Wolfe* detective novels.

Stowe |stō|, Harriet (Elizabeth) Beecher (1811–96) U.S. novelist. She won fame with her antislavery novel *Uncle Tom's Cabin* (1852), which strengthened the contemporary abolitionist cause with its descriptions of the sufferings caused by slavery.

Stra•bo |'strābō| (*c.* 63 BC–*c.* 23 AD) historian and geographer of Greek descent. His only extant work, *Geographica*, in seventeen volumes, provides a detailed physical and historical geography of the ancient world during the reign of Augustus.

Stra•chey |'strāCHē|, (Giles) Lytton (1880–1932) British biographer. Notable works: *Eminent Victorians* (1969).

Stra•di•va•ri |ˌsträdə'värē; ˌstrædə 'verē|, Antonio (*c.* 1644–1737) Italian violin-maker. He devised the proportions of the modern violin, giving a more powerful and rounded sound than earlier instruments possessed. About 650 of his celebrated violins, violas, and violoncellos are still in existence.

Strand |strænd|, Mark (1934–) U.S. poet and author, born in Canada. He was Poet Laureate of the U.S. (1990–91). Notable works: *Selected Poems* (1980) and *Mr. And Mrs. Baby and Other Stories* (1985).

Strand |strænd|, Paul (1890–1976) U.S. photographer and documentary cameraman. He is known for his landscapes.

Stras•berg |'stræsˌbərg|, Lee (1901–82) U.S. actor, director, and drama teacher; born in Austria; born *Israel Strassberg*. As artistic director of the Actors' Studio in New York City (1948–82), he was the leading figure in the development of method acting in the U.S.

Strat•e•mey•er |'strætəˌmīər|, Edward (1863–1930) U.S. author. Pseudonyms **Arthur M. Winfield** and **Laura Lee Hope**. He authored the *Bobbsey Twins* and *Nancy Drew* series. Father of Harriet Stratemeyer Adams.

Strauss |SHtrows| the name of two Austrian composers: **Johann** (1804–49), a leading composer of waltzes; known as **Strauss the Elder**. His best-known work is the *Radetzky March* (1838). **Johann** (1825–99), son of Strauss the Elder; known as **Strauss the Younger**. He became known as "the waltz king," composing many famous waltzes, such as *The Blue Danube* (1867). He is also noted for the operetta *Die Fledermaus* (1874).

Strauss |strows|, Levi (*c.* 1829–1902) U.S. manufacturer, born in Germany. He established Levi Strauss & Co. (1850) to sell pants made of tent canvas to gold miners.

Strauss |SHtrows|, Richard (Georg) (1864–1949) German composer. With the librettist Hugo von Hofmannsthal he produced operas such as *Der Rosenkavalier* (1911). Often regarded as the last of the 19th-century romantic composers, Strauss is also well known for the symphonic poem *Also Sprach Zarathustra* (1896).

Stra•vin•sky |strə'vinskē|, Igor (Fyodorovich) (1882–1971) Russian-born composer, resident in the U.S. from 1939. He made his name with the ballets *The Firebird* (1910) and *The Rite of Spring* (1913); both shocked Paris audiences with their irregular rhythms and frequent dissonances. Stravinsky later developed a neoclassical style typified by *The Rake's Progress* (opera, 1948–51) and experimented with serialism in *Threni*.

Stray•horn |'strāˌhawrn|, Billy (1915–67) U.S. jazz composer and pianist. Full name *William Thomas Strayhorn*; known as **Swee' Pea**. He was in close collaboration with Duke Ellington for 30 years; his ballads include "Lush Life," "Chelsea Bridge," and "Lotus Blossom."

Streep |strēp|, Meryl (1949–) U.S. actress; born *Mary Louise Streep*. She won Oscars for her parts in *Kramer vs. Kramer* (1980) and *Sophie's Choice* (1982). Other notable movies: *The French Lieutenant's Woman* (1981), *Out of Africa* (1986), and *One True Thing* (1998).

Stree•ter |'strētər|, Edward (1891–

1976) U.S. author. Notable works: *Father of the Bride* (1949).

Strei·sand |'strī,sænd; 'strī,zænd|, Barbra (Joan) (1942–   ) U.S. singer, actress, and movie director. She won an Oscar for her performance in *Funny Girl* (1968). She later played the lead in *A Star is Born* (1976); the movie's song "Evergreen", composed by Streisand, won an Oscar. Streisand also starred in, produced, and directed *Yentl* (1983).

Strind·berg |'strin(d),bərg|, (Johan) August (1849–1912) Swedish dramatist and novelist. His satire *The Red Room* (1879) is regarded as Sweden's first modern novel. His later plays are typically tense, psychic dramas, such as *A Dream Play* (1902).

Stro·heim |'strō,hīm; 'SHtrō,hīm|, Eric (1885–1957) U.S. movie actor and director, born in Austria. Born *Erich Oswald Stroheim*. He acted in *La Grande Illusion* (1937) and was director of *The Merry Widow* (1925).

Strong |strawNG|, William (1808–95) U.S. Supreme Court justice (1870–80). He wrote the majority opinion in the Supreme Court's reversal of its decision declaring the Legal Tender Act of 1862 unconstitutional (1871).

Stu·art |'stōōərt|, Charles Edward (1720–88) son of James Stuart, pretender to the British throne; known as **the Young Pretender** or **Bonnie Prince Charlie**. He led the Jacobite uprising of 1745–46. However, he was driven back to Scotland and defeated at the Battle of Culloden (1746).

Stu·art |'stōōərt|, Gilbert Charles (1755–1828) U.S. artist. He is best known for his portraits of the early presidents, especially his five life-size portrayals of George Washington.

Stu·art |'stōōərt|, James (Francis Edward) (1688–1766) son of James II (James VII of Scotland), pretender to the British throne; known as **the Old Pretender**. He arrived in Scotland too late to alter the outcome of the 1715 Jacobite uprising and left the leadership of the 1745–46 uprising to his son Charles Edward Stuart.

Stu·art |'stōōərt|, Jeb (1833–64) Confederate cavalry officer. Full name *James Ewell Brown Stuart*. He was known for

his brazen missions of reconnaissance during the Civil War. His stunning raid that surrounded McClellan's army (1862) is praised as a superb military action. He was mortally wounded at Yellow Tavern.

Stu·art |'stōōərt|, Mary see MARY, QUEEN OF SCOTS.

Stubbs |stəbz|, George (1724–1806) English painter and engraver. He is particularly noted for his sporting scenes and paintings of horses and lions, such as the *Mares and Foals in a Landscape* series (*c.*1760–70).

Stubbs |stəbz|, William (1825–1901) English historian and ecclesiastic. He wrote the influential *Constitutional History of England* (three volumes 1874–78).

Stu·de·ba·ker |'stōōdə,bākər|, Clement (1831–1901) U.S. wagon and carriage manufacturer. With his brother Henry (1826–95), he founded H & C Studebaker (1852), which became Studebaker Brothers (1868); the company experimented with automobiles and manufactured Studebaker automobiles after 1901.

Stur·geon |'stərjən|, Theodore (Hamilton) (1918–85) U.S. author. His works of fantasy and science fiction include *More Than Human* (1953).

Sturt |stərt|, Charles (1795–1869) English explorer. He led three expeditions into the Australian interior, becoming the first European to discover the Darling River (1828) and the source of the Murray (1830).

Stuy·ve·sant |'stīvəsənt|, Peter (*c.* 1610–72) Dutch administrator in North America. First name originally *Petrus.* Appointed colonial governor of New Netherland in 1647, he served until the colony was captured by English forces (1664).

Sty·ron |'stīrən|, William (1925–   ) U.S. author. Notable works: *Sophie's Choice* (1979) and *A Tidewater Morning: Three Tales from Youth* (1993).

Suck·ling |'səkliNG|, Sir John (1609–42) English poet, dramatist, and Royalist leader, one of the Cavalier poets in the court of Charles I.

Suckow, Ruth (1892–1960) U.S. author. Her birthplace, rural Iowa, is the setting for most of her fiction.

Su•cre |'sōͦˌkrä|, Antonio José de (1795–1830) Venezuelan revolutionary and statesman, president of Bolivia (1826–28). He served as Simón Bolívar's chief of staff, liberating Ecuador, Peru, and Bolivia from the Spanish, and was the first president of Bolivia.

Sue•to•ni•us |swē'tōnēəs| (c. 69–c. 140 AD) Roman biographer and historian; full name *Gaius Suetonius Tranquillus*. His surviving works include *Lives of the Caesars*.

Su•har•to |sōͦ'härtō|, Raden (1921–) Indonesian president (1967–98).

Sui, Anna (1955–) U.S. fashion designer. She founded Anna Sui Inc. (1992).

Su•kar•no |sōͦ'kärnō|, Achmed (1901–70) Indonesian statesman, president (1945–67). He led the struggle for independence, which was formally granted in 1949, but lost power in the 1960s after having been implicated in the abortive communist coup of 1965.

Su•lei•man I |ˌsōͦlä'män| (c. 1494–1566) sultan of the Ottoman Empire (1520–66). Also **Soliman** or **Solyman**; also known as **Suleiman the Magnificent** or **Suleiman the Lawgiver**. The Ottoman Empire reached its fullest extent under his rule.

Sul•la |'sōͦlə| (138–78 BC) Roman general and politician; full name *Lucius Cornelius Sulla Felix*. After a victorious campaign against Mithridates VI, Sulla invaded Italy in 83. He was elected dictator in 82 and implemented constitutional reforms in favor of the Senate.

Sul•li•van |'mäsē|, Anne (1866–1936) U.S. teacher. Married name *Anne Sullivan Macy*. She was the constant companion of Helen Keller.

Sul•li•van |'sələvən|, Sir Arthur (Seymour) (1842–1900) English composer. His fame rests on the fourteen light operas which he wrote in collaboration with the librettist W. S. Gilbert.

Sul•li•van |'sələvən|, Ed (1902–74) U.S. actor. Full name *Edward Vincent Sullivan*. He was host of television's "Ed Sullivan Show" (1948–71) where he gave national exposure to many performers, including Elvis Presley and the Beatles.

Sul•li•van |'sələvən|, Harry Stack (1892–1949) U.S. psychiatrist. He developed techniques for the treatment of schizophrenia.

Sul•li•van |'sələvən|, John Lawrence (1858–1918) U.S. boxer. The world heavyweight champion (1882–92), he was the last of the bare-knuckle champions.

Sul•li•van |'sələvən|, Louis Henry (1856–1924) U.S. architect. He developed modern functionalism in architecture by designing skyscrapers. Notable works: the Auditorium Building (Chicago, 1886–90).

Sul•ly |'səlē|, Thomas (1783–1872) U.S. painter. He painted portraits of the Marquis de Lafayette, Thomas Jefferson, James Madison, and Andrew Jackson.

Sulz•ber•ger |'səlts¸bərgər|, Arthur Ochs (1926–) U.S. publisher. He worked for *The New York Times* from 1951, serving as its president fron 1963 to 1979.

Sum•ner |'səmnər|, Charles (1811–74) U.S. politician. He served as a member of the U.S. Senate from Massachusetts (1851–74), where he was a leader in the anti-slavery movement. One of his orations attacked Andrew Butler, and in response, Butler's nephew, Preston S. Brooks, brutally caned Sumner in the Senate chamber.

Sun King the nickname of Louis XIV of France (see LOUIS).

Sun Yat-sen |'sōͦn 'yät 'sen| (1866–1925) Chinese statesman. Also **Sun Yixian**. He was provisional president of the Republic of China (1911–12) and president of the Southern Chinese Republic (1923–25). He organized the Kuomintang force and played a vital part in the revolution of 1911 that overthrew the Manchu dynasty. Following opposition, however, he resigned as president to establish a secessionist government at Guangzhou.

Sur•tees |'sər¸tēz|, Robert Smith (1803–64) English journalist and novelist. He is best remembered for his comic sketches of Mr. Jorrocks, the sporting Cockney grocer, collected in *Jorrocks's Jaunts and Jollities* (1838).

Su•sann |sōͦ'zæn|, Jacqueline (c.

1926–74) U.S. author. Notable works include *Valley of the Dolls* (1968).

Suth·er·land |'sǝTHǝrlǝnd|, George (1862–1942) U.S. Supreme Court justice (1922–38). He wrote many opinions opposing Franklin Roosevelt's programs.

Suth·er·land |'sǝTHǝrlǝnd|, Graham (Vivian) (1903–80) English painter. During World War II he was an official war artist. His postwar work included the tapestry *Christ in Majesty* (1962) in Coventry cathedral.

Suth·er·land |'sǝTHǝrlǝnd|, Dame Joan (1926–) Australian operatic soprano, noted for her dramatic coloratura roles, particularly the title role in Donizetti's *Lucia di Lammermoor.*

Sut·ton |'sǝtn|, Walter Stanborough (1877–1916) U.S. geneticist. He made the first clear formulation of the theory that chromosomes carry physical units determining inheritance.

Su·zu·ki |sǝ'zo͞okē|, Shinichi (1898–1998) Japanese musician. He developed the Suzuki method of teaching young children to play the violin.

Swan |swän|, Sir Joseph Wilson (1828–1914) English physicist and chemist. He devised an electric light bulb in 1860 and in 1883 he formed a partnership with Thomas Edison to manufacture it.

Swan·son |'swänsǝn|, Gloria (1899–1983) U.S. actress; born *Gloria May Josephine Svensson.* She was a major star of silent movies such as *Sadie Thompson* (1928) but is chiefly known for her performance as the fading movie star in *Sunset Boulevard* (1950).

Swayne |swān|, Noah Haynes (1804–84) U.S. Supreme Court justice (1862–81).

Swe·den·borg |'swēdn,bawrg|, Emanuel (1688–1772) Swedish scientist, philosopher, and mystic. The spiritual beliefs that he expounded after a series of mystical experiences blended Christianity with pantheism and theosophy.

Swen·son |'swensǝn|, May (1919–89) U.S. poet. Notable works: *The Complete Poems to Solve* (1993).

Sweyn I |svän| (died 1014) king of Denmark (*c.*985–1014). Also **Sven**; known as **Sweyn Forkbeard**. From 1003 he launched a series of attacks on England, finally driving Ethelred the Unready to flee to Normandy at the end of 1013. Sweyn then became king of England but died five weeks later. He was the father of Canute.

Swift |swift|, Gustavus Franklin (1839–1903) U.S. meat packer. He commissioned the development of the refrigerated railroad car (1877) and incorporated his business as Swift and Co. (1885).

Swift |swift|, Jonathan (1667–1745) Irish satirist, poet, and Anglican cleric; known as **Dean Swift**. He is best known for *Gulliver's Travels* (1726), a satire on human society in the form of a fantastic tale of travels in imaginary lands. He also wrote *A Modest Proposal* (1729), ironically urging that the children of the poor should be fattened to feed the rich.

Swin·burne |'swin,bǝrn|, Algernon Charles (1837–1909) English poet and critic. Associated as a poet with the Pre-Raphaelites, he also contributed to the revival of interest in Elizabethan and Jacobean drama and produced influential studies of William Blake and the Brontës.

Swin·ner·ton |'swinǝrt(ǝ)n|, James Guilford (1875–1974) U.S. cartoonist. He is best known for the comic strip "Little Jimmy."

Swith·in |'swiTHǝn|, St. (died 862) English ecclesiastic. Also **Swithun**. He was bishop of Winchester from 852. The tradition that if it rains on St. Swithin's Day it will do so for the next forty days may have its origin in the heavy rain said to have occurred when his relics were to be transferred to a shrine in Winchester cathedral. Feast day, July 15.

Swit·zer |'switsǝr|, Robert (1904–97) U.S. inventor. With his brother Joseph, he invented fluorescent paint and founded the Day-Glo Co..

Synge |siNG|, J. M. (1871–1909) Irish dramatist; full name *Edmund John Millington Synge.* His play *The Playboy of the Western World* (1907) caused riots at the Abbey Theatre, Dublin, because of its explicit language and its implication that Irish peasants would condone a brutal murder.

Szell |sel|, George (1897–1970) U.S. pianist and conductor, born in Hungary.

First name originally *Georg*. He was conductor of the Cleveland Orchestra (1946–70).

Szent-Györgyi |ˌsänt 'jawrj|, Albert von Nagyrapolt (1893–1986) American biochemist, born in Hungary. He discovered ascorbic acid, later identified with vitamin C.

Szi•lard |'zil,ärd; zə'lärd|, Leo (1898–1964) U.S. physicist, born in Hungary. He fled from Nazi Germany to the U.S., where he became a central figure in the Manhattan Project to develop the atom bomb.

Tt

Tac·i·tus |'tæsətəs| (c. 56–c. 120 AD) Roman historian; full name *Publius*, or *Gaius*, *Cornelius Tacitus*. His *Annals* (covering the years 14–68) and *Histories* (69–96) are major works on the history of the Roman Empire.

Taft |tæft|, U.S. political family, including: **William Howard Taft** (1857–1930) see box. **Helen Herron Taft** (1861–1943), wife of William Howard Taft and U.S. first lady (1909–13). **Robert Alphonso Taft** (1889–1953), their son, known as **Mr. Republican**. A prominent Ohio conservative, he was a U.S. senator (1938–53) who opposed President Franklin D. Roosevelt's New Deal and Fair Deal programs. He coauthored the Taft-Hartley Act (1947), which imposed new restrictions on labor. In the 1950s, he defended the antisubversive activities of Senator Joseph McCarthy.

Tag·li·a·bue |'tæglēə,b(y)oo|, Paul (1940–) U.S. journalist. He is the commissioner of the National Football League (1989–).

Ta·gore |tə'gawr|, Rabindranath (1861–1941) Indian writer and philosopher. His poetry pioneered the use of colloquial Bengali, and his own translations established his reputation in the West. Nobel Prize for Literature (1913).

Tail·le·ferre |,tīə'fer|, Germaine (1892–1983) French composer and pianist. A member of Les Six, she composed concertos for unusual combinations of instruments.

Tal·bert |'tælbərt|, Mary Burnett (1866–1923) U.S. educator and civil rights advocate. She served as president of the National Association of Colored Women (1916–21) and was a crusader for the Dyer anti-lynching bill (1921). She was the first African-American woman to win the Spingarn Medal (1922).

Tal·bot |'tawlbət|, (William Henry) Fox (1800–77) English pioneer of photography. He produced the first photograph on paper in 1835. Five years later he discovered a process for producing a neg-

---

Taft, William Howard
27th U.S. president

Life dates: 1857–1930
Place of birth: Cincinnati, Ohio
Mother: Louise Maria Torrey Taft
Father: Alphonso Taft
Wife: Helen Herron Taft
Children: Robert, Helen, Charles
College/University: Yale; Cincinnati Law School
Career: Lawyer; judge; law professor
Political career: U.S. Solicitor General; U.S. Federal Circuit Court judge; civil governor-general of the Philippine Islands; U.S. secretary of war; president; U.S. Supreme Court chief justice
Party: Republican
Home state: Ohio
Opponents in presidential races: William Jennings Bryan; Woodrow Wilson; Theodore Roosevelt
Term of office: March 4, 1909–March 3, 1913
Vice president: James Schoolcraft Sherman
Notable events of presidency: Tariff Board established; parcel post service authorized; New Mexico admitted as 47th state; Arizona admitted as 48th state; Alaska granted full territorial government
Other achievements: admitted to the Ohio bar; Superior Court judge, Cincinnati; dean, University of Cincinnati Law School; professor of law, Yale
Place of burial: Arlington National Cemetery, Arlington, Va.

---

ative from which multiple positive prints could be made, though the independently developed daguerreotype proved to be superior.

Tal·ley·rand |'tælē,rænd|, Charles Maurice de (1754–1838) French statesman; full surname *Talleyrand-Périgord*. Involved in the coup that brought Napoleon to power, he became head of the new government after the fall of Napoleon (1814) and was later instrumental in the overthrow of Charles X and the accession of Louis Philippe (1830).

Tal·lis |'tæləs|, Thomas (c. 1505–85) English composer. Organist of the Chapel Royal jointly with William Byrd, he served under Henry VIII, Edward VI, Mary, and Elizabeth I. His works include the 40-part motet *Spem in Alium*.

Tam·bo |'tämbō|, Oliver (1917–93) South African politician. He joined the African National Congress in 1944, became its acting president in 1967, and was president from 1977 until 1991, when he resigned in favor of Nelson Mandela, recently released from prison.

Tam·er·lane |'tæmər,lān| (1336–1405) Mongol ruler of Samarkand (1369–1405). Also **Tamburlaine**; Tartar name *Timur Lenk* ("lame Timur"). Leading a force of Mongols and Turks, he conquered Persia, northern India, and Syria and established his capital at Samarkand. He was the ancestor of the Mogul dynasty in India.

Tames |tämz|, George (1919–94) U.S. photographer. He chronicled presidents and political leaders.

Tan |tæn|, Amy (1952–) U.S. author. Notable works: *The Joy Luck Club* (1989) and *The Kitchen God's Wife* (1991).

Ta·na·ka |tə'näkə|, Tomoyuki (1909–97) Japanese movie producer.

Tan·dy |'tændē|, Jessica (1909–94) U.S. actress, born in England. She made many stage appearances, some with her husband Hume Cronyn, including *The Gin Game*; her films include *Driving Miss Daisy* (1989, Academy Award)

Ta·ney |'tawnē|, Roger Brooke (1777–1864) Chief Justice of the U.S. (1836–64). He upheld the principle of federal supremacy over states' rights.

Tange |'täNGgä|, Kenzo (1913–) Japanese architect. His work, which includes the Peace Center at Hiroshima (1955), is characterized by the use of modern materials while retaining a feeling for traditional Japanese architecture.

Ta·ni·za·ki |,tänē'zäkē|, Jun'ichiro (1886–1965) Japanese novelist and playwright. Notable works: *Some Prefer Nettles* (1955) and *Diary of an Old Man* (1965).

Tann·häu·ser |'tän,hoizər| (c. 1200–c. 1270) German poet. In reality a Minnesinger whose works included lyrics

and love poetry, he became a legendary figure as a knight who visited Venus's grotto and spent seven years in debauchery, then repented and sought absolution from the Pope.

Tan·sen |'tæn,sen| (c. 1500–89) Indian musician and singer. A leading exponent of northern Indian classical music, he became an honored member of the court of Akbar the Great.

Ta·ran·ti·no |,tærən'tēnō|, Quentin (Jerome) (1963–) U.S. movie director, screenwriter, and actor. He came to sudden prominence with *Reservoir Dogs* (1992), followed in 1994 by *Pulp Fiction*. Both aroused controversy for their amorality and violence but also won admiration for their wit and style.

Tar·bell |'tärbəl|, Ida M. (1857–1944) U.S. author. She was a leader of the muckraking movement and a writer for *McClure's* magazine. Notable works: *The History of the Standard Oil Co.* (1904).

Tar·ken·ton |'tärkəntən|, Fran (1940–) U.S. football player. He passed for 47,003 yards and 342 touchdowns, both NFL records.

Tar·king·ton |'tärkiNGtən|, Booth (1869–1946) U.S. author. Full name *Newton Booth Tarkington*. Notable novels: *The Magnificent Ambersons* (1918) and *Alice Adams* (1921).

Tar·kov·sky |tär'kawfskē|, Andrei (Arsenevich) (1932–86) Russian movie director. Featuring a poetic and impressionistic style, his movies include *Ivan's Childhood* (1962), *Solaris* (1972), and *The Sacrifice* (1986), which won the special grand prize at the Cannes Film Festival.

Tar·quin·i·us |tär'kwinēəs| the name of two semi-legendary Etruscan kings of ancient Rome; anglicized name *Tarquin*: **Tarquinius Priscus**, died 578 BC; reigned c.616–c.578 BC; full name *Lucius Tarquinius Priscus*. According to tradition he was murdered by the sons of the previous king. **Tarquinius Superbus**, reigned c.534–c.510 BC; full name *Lucius Tarquinius Superbus*; known as **Tarquin the Proud**. According to tradition he was the son or grandson of Tarquinius Priscus. Noted for his cruelty, he was expelled from the city and the Republic was founded. He repeatedly but unsuccessfully attacked Rome, assisted by Lars Porsenna.

Tar·ti·koff |'tärti,kawf|, Brandon (1949–97) U.S. television network executive. He began as a director of comedy programs and later became president of NBC (1980–).

Tas·man |'täsmän|, Abel (Janszoon) (1603–c. 1659) Dutch navigator. Sent in 1642 by the Governor General of the Dutch East Indies, Anthony van Diemen (1593–1645), to explore Australian waters, he reached Tasmania (which he named Van Diemen's Land) and New Zealand, and in 1643 arrived at Tonga and Fiji.

Tas·so |'tæsō|, Torquato (1544–95) Italian poet, known for his epic poem *Gerusalemme liberata* (1581).

Tate |tāt|, James (Vincent) (1943–) U.S. poet and educator. Notable works: *Selected Poems* (1992, Pulitzer Prize) and *Worshipful Company of Fletchers* (1994, National Book Award).

Tate |tāt|, (John Orley) Allen (1899–1979) U.S. author and educator. He was a leader of the "New Criticism" and the author of poetry, biography, literary criticism, and anthologies.

Tate |tāt|, Nahum (1652–1715) Irish dramatist and poet, resident in London from the 1670s. He was appointed Poet Laureate in 1692.

Ta·ti |tä'tē|, Jacques (1908–82) French movie director and actor; born *Jacques Tatischeff*. He introduced the comically inept character Monsieur Hulot in *Monsieur Hulot's Holiday* (1953), seen again in movies including the Oscar-winning *Mon oncle* (1958).

Ta·tum |'tātəm|, Art (1910–56) U.S. jazz pianist; full name *Arthur Tatum*. Born with cataracts in both eyes, he was almost completely blind. He became famous in the 1930s for his solo and trio work.

Ta·tum |'tātəm|, Edward Lawrie (1909–75) U.S. biochemist. He shared the 1958 Nobel Prize for Physiology or Medicine with George Wells Beadle (1903–89) for his work showing that one gene codes for one enzyme.

Tave·ner |'tævənər|, John (Kenneth) (1944–) English composer. His music is primarily religious and has been influenced by his conversion to the Russian Orthodox Church.

Tav·er·ner |'tævə(r)nər|, John (c. 1490–1545) English composer, an influential writer of early polyphonic church music.

Tay·lor |'tālər|, Art (1929–95) U.S. jazz drummer. Full name *Arthur S. Taylor, Jr.* He performed and recorded with many different groups and was host of a radio interview program.

Tay·lor |'tālər|, Edward Thompson (1793–1871) U.S. Methodist minister. Known as **Father Taylor**. Herman Melville based Father Mapple's sermon in *Moby Dick* on Taylor's style.

Tay·lor |'tālər|, Elizabeth (1932–) U.S. actress, born in England. Notable movies include *National Velvet* (made when she was still a child in 1944), *Cleopatra* (1963), and *Who's Afraid of Virginia Woolf?* (1966), for which she won an Oscar. She has been married numerous times, including twice to the actor Richard Burton.

Tay·lor |'tālər|, Frederick Winslow

Taylor, Zachary
12th U.S. president

Life dates: 1784–1850
Place of birth: near Barboursville, Va.
Mother: Sarah Dabney Strother Taylor
Father: Richard Taylor
Wife: Margaret Mackall Smith Taylor
Children: Anne, Sarah, Octavia, Margaret, Mary Elizabeth, Richard
Nickname: "Old Rough and Ready"
College/University: none (privately tutored)
Military service: served during the War of 1812; defeated the Seminoles in Florida in 1837; won several battles during the Mexican War
Career: Farmer; soldier
Political career: none prior to the presidency
Party: Whig
Home state: Kentucky
Opponents in presidential race: Lewis Cass
Term of office: March 4, 1849–Jul. 9, 1850 (died in office)
Vice president: Millard Fillmore
Notable events of presidency: Clayton-Bulwer Treaty with Great Britain
Place of burial: Louisville, KY

(1856–1915) U.S. industrial engineer. His time and motion studies became known as the "Taylorization" of mass labor production.

Tay·lor |'tālər|, Henry (Splawn) (1942–) U.S. author and educator. Notable works: *The Flying Change* (1985, Pulitzer Prize).

Tay·lor |'tālər|, James (1948–) U.S. pop musician. His hit songs include "You've Got a Friend" and "Fire and Rain."

Tay·lor |'tālər|, Jeremy (1613–67) English Anglican churchman and writer. Chaplain to Charles I during the English Civil War, he is now remembered chiefly for his devotional writings.

Tay·lor |'tālər|, John (1753–1824) U.S. politician and agriculturist. Known as **John Taylor of Caroline**. He was a member of the U.S. Senate from Virginia (1792–94, 1803, and 1822–24) and a strong advocate of states' rights.

Tay·lor |'tālər|, Lawrence (1959–) U.S. football player. He played in a record ten professional bowl games.

Tay·lor |'tālər|, Paul (1930–) U.S. choreographer. He performed with Martha Graham and the New York City Ballet, before forming his own Paul Taylor Dance Co. (1955).

Tay·lor |'tālər| Zachary, see box. **Margaret Mackall Smith Taylor** (1788–1852), wife of Zachary Taylor and U.S. first lady (1849–50).

Tchai·kov·sky |CHī'kawfskē|, Pyotr (Ilich) (1840–93) Russian composer. Notable works include the ballets *Swan Lake* (1877) and *The Nutcracker* (1892), the First Piano Concerto (1875), the opera *Eugene Onegin* (1879), the *1812 Overture* (1880), and his sixth symphony, the "Pathétique" (1893).

Te Ka·na·wa |tā 'känəwə|, Dame Kiri (Janette) (1944–) New Zealand operatic soprano, resident in Britain since 1966. She made her debut in London in 1970 and since then has sung in the world's leading opera houses.

Tea·gar·den |'tē,gärdn|, Jack (1905–64) U.S. jazz trombonist and singer.

Teale |tēl|, Edwin Way (1899–1980) U.S. author. Notable works: *Wandering Through Winter* (1965, Pulitzer Prize).

Teas·dale |'tēz,dāl|, Sara (1884–1933) U.S. poet. Notable works: *Love Songs* (1917, special Pulitzer award).

Te·cum·seh |tə'kəmsə| (1768–1813) Shawnee chief. Also **Tecumtha**. His plans to organize a military confederacy of tribes to resist U.S. encroachment was thwarted by the defeat of his brother, Tenskatawa ("the Prophet"), at Tippecanoe (1811). An ally of the British in the War of 1812, he fought and died in the Battle of the Thames.

Teil·hard de Char·din |tā'yär də SHär-'deN|, Pierre (1881–1955) French Jesuit philosopher and palaeontologist. He is best known for his theory, blending science and Christianity, that man is evolving mentally and socially towards a perfect spiritual state. The Roman Catholic Church declared his views unorthodox, and his major works (e.g. *The Phenomenon of Man*, 1955) were published posthumously.

Tel·e·mann |'telə,män|, Georg Philipp (1681–1767) German composer and organist. His prolific output includes 600 cantatas, 44 Passions, and 40 operas.

Tel·ford |'telfərd|, Thomas (1757–1834) Scottish civil engineer.

Tel·ler |'telər|, Edward (1908–) Hungarian-born U.S. physicist. After moving to the U.S. he worked on the first atomic reactor and the first atom bombs. Work under his guidance led to the detonation of the first hydrogen bomb in 1952.

Tem·pest |'tempəst|, Dame Marie (1864–1942) English actress; born *Mary Susan Etherington*. She was noted for her playing of elegant middle-aged women; the role of Judith Bliss in *Hay Fever* (1925) was created for her by Noel Coward.

Tem·ple |'tempəl|, Shirley (1928–) U.S. child star and political figure; married name *Shirley Temple Black*. In the 1930s she appeared in a succession of movies, such as *Rebecca of Sunnybrook Farm* (1938). She later became active in Republican politics and represented the U.S. at the United Nations and as an ambassador.

Te·niers |tə'nirs; 'tenyərz|, David (1610–90) Flemish painter; known as **David Teniers the Younger**. From

1651 he was court painter to successive regents of the Netherlands.

Ten·niel |'tenēəl|, Sir John (1820–1914) English illustrator and cartoonist. He illustrated Lewis Carroll's *Alice's Adventures in Wonderland* (1865) and *Through the Looking Glass* (1871).

Ten·ny·son |'tenəsən|, Alfred, 1st Baron Tennyson of Aldworth and Freshwater (1809–92) known as *Alfred, Lord Tennyson*. English poet, Poet Laureate from 1850. His reputation was established by *In Memoriam* (1850), a long poem concerned with immortality, change, and evolution. Other notable works: "The Charge of the Light Brigade" (1854).

Ten·zing Nor·gay |'tenziNG 'nawr,gā| (1914–86) Sherpa mountaineer. In 1953, as members of the British expedition, he and Sir Edmund Hillary were the first to reach the summit of Mount Everest.

Ter·ence |'terəns| (*c.* 190–159 BC) Roman comic dramatist; Latin name *Publius Terentius Afer*. His six surviving comedies are based on the Greek New Comedy; they are marked by more realism and a greater consistency of plot than the works of Plautus.

Te·re·sa |tə'rēsə; tə'rāsə|, Mother (1910–97) Roman Catholic nun and missionary. Also **Theresa**; born *Agnes Gonxha Bojaxhiu* in what is now Macedonia, of Albanian parentage. She became an Indian citizen in 1948. She founded the Order of Missionaries of Charity, which became noted for its work among the poor in Calcutta and now operates in many parts of the world. Nobel Peace Prize (1979).

Te·re·sa of Á·vi·la |'ävēlə|, St. (1515–82) Spanish Carmelite nun and mystic. She instituted the "discalced" reform movement with St. John of the Cross. Her writings include *The Way of Perfection* (1583) and *The Interior Castle* (1588). Feast day, October 15.

Te·re·sa of Li·sieux |lēz'yOE|, St. (1873–97) French Carmelite nun. Also **Thérèse**; born *Marie-Françoise Thérèse Martin*. In her autobiography, *L'Histoire d'une âme* (1898), she taught that sanctity can be attained through continual renunciation in small matters, and not only through extreme self-mortification. Feast day, October 3.

Te·resh·ko·va |,terəsH'kawvə|, Valentina (Vladimirovna) (1937–   ) Russian cosmonaut. In June 1963 she became the first woman in space.

Ter·hune |tər'hyOōn|, Albert Payson (1872–1942) U.S. author. His fiction about collies includes *Lad: A Dog* (1919).

Ter·kel |'tərkəl|, Studs Louis (1912–   ) U.S. author and radio and television journalist. Notable works: *The Good War* (1984, Pulitzer Prize).

Ter·man |'tərmən|, Lewis Madison (1877–1956) U.S. psychologist and educator. He revised the Binet-Simon Intelligence Tests and introduced the term "intelligence quotient."

Ter·ry |'terē|, Dame (Alice) Ellen (1847–1928) English actress. She played in many of Henry Irving's Shakespearean productions, and George Bernard Shaw created a number of roles for her.

Ter·ry |'terē|, Eli (1772–1852) U.S. manufacturer and inventor. He invented the mantel clock and was the first to mass-produce clocks.

Ter·ry |'terē|, Paul (1887–1971) U.S. cartoonist. He was the animator of Mighty Mouse.

Ter·tul·lian |tər'təlyən| (*c.* 160–*c.* 220) early Christian theologian; Latin name *Quintus Septimius Florens Tertullianus*. His writings include Christian apologetics and attacks on pagan idolatry and Gnosticism.

Tes·la |'teslə|, Nikola (1856–1943) American electrical engineer and inventor, born in what is now Croatia of Serbian descent. He developed the first alternating-current induction motor, as well as several forms of oscillators, the tesla coil, and a wireless guidance system for ships.

Te·traz·zi·ni |,tāträ'tsēnē|, Luisa (1871–1940) Italian operatic soprano. She made her debut in Florence in 1890 as Inès and toured extensively worldwide.

Thack·er·ay |'THækərē; 'THækə,rā|, William Makepeace (1811–63) British novelist. He established his reputation with *Vanity Fair* (1847-8), a satire of the upper middle class of early 19th-century society.

Thad·dae·us |'THædēəs| (1st century AD) an Apostle named in St. Matthew's Gospel, traditionally identified with St. Jude.

Tha·les |'THā,lēz| (c. 624–c. 545 BC) Greek philosopher, mathematician, and astronomer, living at Miletus. Judged by Aristotle to be the founder of physical science, he is also credited with founding geometry. He proposed that water was the primary substance from which all things were derived.

Thant |THänt; THænt|, U (1909–74) Burmese statesman. He served as secretary general of the UN (1961–71).

Tharp |THärp|, Twyla (1941–) U.S. dancer and choreographer. She performed with the Paul Taylor Dance Co., the Joffrey Ballet, and the American Ballet Theater and later formed her own modern dance troupe (1965).

Thatch·er |'THæCHər|, Margaret (Hilda), Baroness Thatcher of Kesteven (1925–) British Conservative stateswoman, prime minister (1979–90). She was Britain's first woman prime minister, and became the longest-serving British prime minister of the 20th century. Her period in office was marked by an emphasis on monetarist policies, privatization of nationalized industries, and labor union legislation. She became known for her determination and her emphasis on individual responsibility and enterprise.

Thaves, Bob (1924–) U.S. cartoonist. He created the "Frank and Ernest" comic strip.

Thax·ter |'THækstər|, Celia Laighton (1835–94) U.S. author. Notable works: *An Island Garden* (1894).

Thay·er |'THāər|, Abbott Handerson (1849–1921) U.S. artist. His study of protective coloration led to the development of camouflage.

The·mis·to·cles |THə'mistə,klēz| (c. 528–460 BC) Athenian statesman. He helped build up the Athenian fleet, and defeated the Persian fleet at Salamis in 480.

The·oc·ri·tus |THē'äkrətəs| (c. 310–c. 250 BC) Greek poet, born in Sicily. He is chiefly known for his *Idylls*, hexameter poems presenting the lives of imaginary shepherds which were the model for Virgil's *Eclogues*.

The·o·do·ra |THēə'dawrə| (c. 500–48) Byzantine empress, wife of Justinian. As Justinian's closest adviser, she exercised a considerable influence on political affairs and the theological questions of the time.

The·o·do·ra·kis |,THēədə'räkis|, Mikis (1925–) Greek composer and politician. He was imprisoned by the military government for his left-wing political activities (1967–70). His compositions include the ballet *Antigone* (1958), and the score for the movie *Zorba the Greek* (1965).

The·od·o·ric |,THē'ädərik| (c. 454–526) king of the Ostrogoths 471–526; known as **Theodoric the Great**. At its greatest extent his empire included Italy, Sicily, Dalmatia, and parts of Germany.

The·o·do·sius I |,THēə'dōsHəs| (c. 346–95) Roman emperor 379–95; full name *Flavius Theodosius*; known as **Theodosius the Great**. Proclaimed co-emperor by the Emperor Gratian in 379, he took control of the Eastern Empire and ended the war with the Visigoths. A pious Christian, he banned all forms of pagan worship in 391.

The·o·phras·tus |,THēə'fræstəs| (c. 370–c. 287.) Greek philosopher and scientist, the pupil and successor of Aristotle. The most influential of his works was *Characters*, a collection of sketches of psychological types.

The·re·sa, Mother |tə'rēsə; tə'rāsə| see TERESA, MOTHER.

The·roux |THə'rōō|, Paul (1941–) U.S. author. He has written fiction and nonfiction, including *The Mosquito Coast* (1982) and *Kowloon Tong* (1997).

Thes·i·ger |'THesəjər|, Wilfred (Patrick) (1910–) English explorer. He explored many countries, notably Saudi Arabia and Oman. Notable works: *Arabian Sands* (1959) and *The Marsh Arabs* (1964).

Thes·pis |'THespəs| (6th century BC) Greek dramatic poet, regarded as the founder of Greek tragedy.

Thom |täm|, Alexander (1894–1985) Scottish expert on prehistoric stone circles. An engineer, he began a detailed survey of the stone circles of Britain and Brittany in the 1930s.

Tho•mas |'täməs|, Clarence (1948–) U.S. Supreme Court justice (1991–). His appointment to the Court was approved only after a lengthy and controversial Senate hearing in which he had to respond to charges of sexual harassment.

Tho•mas |'täməs|, Danny (1914–91) U.S. television producer and actor. Born *Amos Jacobs*; father of actress Marlo Thomas. He starred in the television series "Make Room for Daddy" (1953–64).

Tho•mas |'täməs|, Dylan (Marlais) (1914–53) Welsh poet. In 1953 he narrated on radio *Under Milk Wood*, a portrait of a small Welsh town, interspersing poetic alliterative prose with songs and ballads. Other notable works: *Portrait of the Artist as a Young Dog* (prose, 1940).

Tho•mas |'täməs|, (Philip) Edward (1878–1917) English poet. His work offers a sympathetic but unidealized depiction of rural English life, adapting colloquial speech rhythms to poetic meter.

Tho•mas |'täməs|, George Henry (1816–70) U.S. army officer. A Virginia loyalist, he commanded volunteers and won several key battles in the Civil War.

Tho•mas |'täməs|, Isaiah (1749–1831) U.S. printer and publisher. He founded the American Antiquarian Society (1812) and authored *The History of Printing in America* (1810).

Tho•mas |'täməs|, Norman (1884–1968) U.S. social reformer and politician. He helped found the American Civil Liberties Union (1920) and was a Socialist Party presidential candidate six times (1928–48).

Tho•mas |'täməs|, St. (1st century AD) Apostle; known as **Doubting Thomas**. He earned his nickname by saying that he would not believe that Christ had risen again until he had seen and touched his wounds (John 20:24–9). Feast day, December 21.

Tho•mas à Kem•pis |'täməs ə 'kempəs| (*c.* 1380–1471) German theologian; born *Thomas Hemerken*. He is the probable author of *On the Imitation*

of Christ (*c.*1415–24), a manual of spiritual devotion.

Tho•mas Aqui•nas |'täməs ə'kwīnəs|, St. see AQUINAS, ST. THOMAS.

Tho•mas More |'täməs mawr|, St. see MORE.

Thomp•son |'täm(p)sən|, Benjamin, Count Rumford. (1753–1814) U.S. scientist and inventor. He established the kinetic theory of heat and invented the drip coffeepot and the Rumford stove. He was a loyalist during the American Revolution.

Thomp•son |'täm(p)sən|, Daley (1958–) English decathlon athlete.

Thomp•son |'täm(p)sən|, Emma (1959–) English actress and screenwriter. Her movies include *Howard's End* (1992), for which she won an Oscar for best actress; *Sense and Sensibility* (1996), for which she also wrote the Oscar-winning screenplay; and *Primary Colors* (1998).

Thomp•son |'täm(p)sən|, Flora (Jane) (1876–1947) English writer. She is remembered for her semi-autobiographical trilogy *Lark Rise to Candleford* (1945).

Thomp•son |'täm(p)sən|, Francis (1859–1907) English poet. His best-known work, such as *The Hound of Heaven* (1893), uses powerful imagery to convey intense religious experience.

Thomp•son |'täm(p)sən|, J. Walter (1847–1928) U.S. businessman. Full name *James Walter Thompson*. He established an advertising firm in New York City (1878) and developed it into one of the most successful in U.S.

Thomp•son |'täm(p)sən|, Smith (1768–1843) U.S. Supreme Court justice (1823–43).

Thom•son |'tämsən|, Elihu (1853–1937) U.S. electrical engineer and inventor, born in England. He was the inventor of electric welding and of the standard three-phase, alternating-current generator (1890); his company merged with Thomas Edison's to form the General Electric Co. (1892).

Thom•son |'tämsən|, British family of scientists, including: **Sir Joseph John** (1856–1940), English atomic physicist. He discovered the electron, deducing its existence as a particle smaller than the atom from his experiments. Thomson received the 1906 Nobel Prize for Physics for his research into the electrical conductivity of gases. His son, **Sir George Paget Thomson** (1892–1975), shared the 1937 Nobel Prize for Physics for his discovery of electron diffraction by crystals.

Thom·son |'tämsən|, Roy Herbert, 1st Baron (1894–1976) British newspaper publisher and businessman, born in Canada. He owned television stations and a chain of newspapers in Canada, England, and Scotland.

Thom·son |'tämsən|, Tom (1877–1917) Canadian painter; full name *Thomas John Thomson*. Notable works: *Northern Lake* (1913), *The West Wind* (1917), and *The Jack Pine* (1917).

Thom·son |'tämsən|, Virgil Garnett (1896–1989) U.S. composer, music critic, and conductor. He was music critic of the *New York Herald Tribune* (1940–54). His movie score for *Louisiana Story* won the 1949 Pulitzer Prize.

Tho·reau |THə'rō|, Henry David (1817–62) U.S. essayist and poet. A key figure of Transcendentalism, he is best known for his book *Walden, or Life in the Woods* (1854), an account of a two-year experiment in self-sufficiency at Walden Pond in Concord, Massachusetts. His essay "On the Duty of Civil Disobedience" (1849) influenced Mahatma Gandhi's policy of passive resistance.

Thorn·dike |'THawrn,dīk|, Dame (Agnes) Sybil (1882–1976) English actress. She played the title part in the first London production of George Bernard Shaw's *St. Joan* (1924).

Thorn·ton |'THawrnt(ə)n|, William (1759–1828) U.S. architect, born in the British West Indies. He designed the Capitol building in Washington, D.C. (1792).

Thorpe |'THawrp|, Jim (1888–1953) U.S. athlete. After winning Olympic gold medals in the pentathlon and decathlon (1912), he played both baseball and football professionally.

Thor·vald·sen |'tōor,välsən|, Bertel (c. 1770–1844) Danish sculptor. Also **Thorwaldsen**. Major works include a statue of Jason in Rome (1803) and the tomb of Pius VII (1824–31).

Thrale |THrāl|, Hester Lynch (1741–1821) English writer; second married name *Hester Lynch Piozzi* She was a close friend of Dr. Samuel Johnson, who lived with her and her husband for several years.

Thu·cyd·i·des |THōo'sidə,dēz| (c. 455–c. 400 BC) Greek historian. He is remembered for his *History of the Peloponnesian War*, which analyzes the origins and course of the war; he fought in the conflict on the Athenian side.

Thumb |THəm|, General Tom (1838–83) U.S. circus entertainer. Born *Charles S. Stratton*. A 40-inch-tall dwarf, he worked as a sideshow attraction in the shows of P. T. Barnum.

Thur·ber |'THərbər|, James (Grover) (1894–1961) U.S. humorist and cartoonist. He published many of his essays, stories, and sketches in *The New Yorker* magazine. His collections of essays, stories, and sketches include *My World—And Welcome to It* (1942), which contains the story "The Secret Life of Walter Mitty."

Thur·mond |'THərmənd|, (James) Strom (1902–) U.S. politician. He was governor of South Carolina (1947–51) and a member of the U.S. Senate from South Carolina (1955–); he was a States' Rights Party presidential candidate (1948).

Tib·bett |'tibət|, Lawrence (1896–1960) U.S. operatic baritone. He sang for 27 seasons with the Metropolitan Opera, beginning with his debut in 1923 as Lovitsky.

Ti·be·ri·us |tī'birēəs| (42 BC–AD 37) Roman emperor (AD 14–37); full name *Tiberius Julius Caesar Augustus*. The adopted successor of his stepfather and father-in-law Augustus, he became increasingly tyrannical, and his reign was marked by a growing number of treason trials and executions.

Ti·bul·lus |tə'bələs|, Albius (c. 50–19 BC) Roman poet. He is known for his elegiac love poetry and for his celebration of peaceful rural life.

Tick·nor |'tiknər|, William Davis (1810–64) U.S. publisher. He founded a publishing company (1832), which became Ticknor and Fields (1854), publishers of the *Atlantic Monthly*

(1859), as well as works by Emerson, Thoreau, Hawthorne, and Longfellow.

Tie·po·lo |tēˈepə,lō|, Giovanni Battista (1696–1770) Italian painter. He painted numerous rococo frescoes and altarpieces including the *Antony and Cleopatra* frescoes in the Palazzo Labia, Venice (*c.*1750), and the decoration of the residence of the Prince-Bishop at Würzburg (1751–3).

Tif·fa·ny |ˈtifənē|, Louis Comfort (1848–1933) U.S. glass-maker and interior decorator. A leading exponent of American art nouveau, he established a decorating firm in New York that produced stained glass, vases, lamps, and mosaic.

Tiglath-pileser |ˈtig,læTHˈpīˈlēzər| the name of three kings of Assyria, notably: **Tiglath-pileser I**, reigned *c.*1115–*c.*1077 BC. He extended Assyrian territory, taking Cappadocia, reaching Syria, and defeating the king of Babylonia. **Tiglath-pileser III**, reigned *c.*745–727 BC. He brought the Assyrian empire to the height of its power, subduing large parts of Syria and Palestine, and conquered Babylonia.

Til·den |ˈtildən|, Bill (1893–1953) U.S. tennis player. He led the U.S. to seven straight Davis Cup victories (1920–26).

Til·den |ˈtildən|, Samuel Jones (1814–86) U.S. politician. He was a Democratic candidate in the 1876 presidential election, which he won by popular vote but lost by settlement of electoral commission. He contributed to the endowment of the New York Public Library.

Til·lich |ˈtilik|, Paul (Johannes) (1886–1965) German-born U.S. theologian and philosopher. He proposed a form of Christian existentialism. Notable works: *Systematic Theology* (1951–63).

Ti·mo·shen·ko |,timəˈsHeNGkō|, Semyon Konstantinovich (1895–1970) Soviet army commander. He directed the defense of Stalingrad (1941–42).

Tim·o·thy |ˈtiməTHē|, St. (1st century AD) convert and disciple of St. Paul. Traditionally he was the first bishop of Ephesus and was martyred in the reign of the Roman emperor Nerva. Feast day, January 22 or 26.

Tin·ber·gen |ˈtin,berg(ə)n| Dutch family including: **Niko Tinbergen** (1907–88); full name *Nikolaas Tinbergen*, a zoologist. He studied social patterns among animals and applied many findings on animal aggression to humans. He shared the 1973 Nobel Prize for Physiology or Medicine with Konrad Lorenz and Karl von Frisch. His brother **Jan Tinbergen** (1903–94), an economist, shared the first Nobel Prize for Economics (1969) with Ragnar Frisch for his pioneering work on econometrics.

Tin·to·ret·to |,tintəˈretō| (1518–94) Italian painter; born *Jacopo Robusti*. His work was typified by a mannerist style, including unusual perspectives and chiaroscuro effects.

Tip·pett |ˈtipət|, Sir Michael (Kemp) (1905–98) English composer. He established his reputation with the oratorio *A Child of Our Time* (1941), which drew on jazz, madrigals, and spirituals in addition to classical sources. Other works include five operas, four symphonies, and several song cycles.

Tir·pitz |ˈtirpəts|, Alfred von (1849–1930) German naval commander. As secretary of state in the Imperial Navy department (1897–1916), he created the German high seas fleet.

Ti·tian |ˈtisHən| (*c.* 1488–1576) Italian painter; Italian name *Tiziano Vecellio*. The most important painter of the Venetian school, he experimented with vivid colors and often broke conventions of composition. He painted many sensual mythological works, including *Bacchus and Ariadne* (*c.*1518–23).

Ti·to |ˈtētō| (1892–1980) Yugoslav Marshal and statesman, prime minister (1945–53) and president (1953–80); born *Josip Broz*. He organized a communist resistance movement against the German invasion of Yugoslavia (1941). He became head of the new government at the end of the war, establishing Yugoslavia as a non-aligned Communist state with a federal constitution.

Tit·tle |ˈtitl|, Y. A. (1926–) U.S. football player. Full name *Yelberton Abraham Tittle*. Elected to the Football Hall of Fame (1971).

Ti·tus |ˈtītəs| (AD 39–81) Roman emperor 79–81, son of Vespasian; born

Titus Flavius Vespasianus. In 70 he ended a revolt in Judaea with the conquest of Jerusalem.

Ti•tus |'tītəs|, St. (1st century AD) Greek churchman. A convert and helper of St. Paul, he was traditionally the first bishop of Crete. Feast day (in the Eastern Church) August 23; (in the Western Church) February 6.

To•bi•as |tə'bīəs|, Channing Heggie (1882–1961) U.S. religious and civic leader. He was secretary of the National Council of the YMCA (1911–23) and chairman of the board of the NAACP (1953–59). Spingarn Medal, 1948.

To•bit |'tōbət| a pious Israelite living during the Babylonian Captivity (597–538 BC), described in the Apocrypha.

Tocque•ville |'tōk,vil|, Alexis de (1805–59) French politician and historian. Full name *Alexis Charles Henri Maurice Clèrel de Tocqueville.* He is best known for his classic work of political analysis, *Democracy in America* (1835).

Todd |täd|, Baron Alexander Robertus (1907–   ) British biochemist. He won a 1957 Nobel Prize for Chemistry for his work in determining the chemical structure of nucleotides.

Todd |täd|, Mabel Loomis (1856–1932) U.S. author. She edited Emily Dickinson's *Poems* (1890–91, 1896) and *Letters of Emily Dickinson* (1894).

Todd |täd|, Thomas (1765–1826) U.S. Supreme Court justice (1807–26).

Tof•fler |'tawflər|, Alvin (1928–   ) U.S. author. Known for his futurist nonfiction, he first gained popularity with the publication of *Future Shock* (1971).

To•jo |'tō,jō|, Hideki (1884–1948) Japanese military leader and statesman, prime minister (1941–44). He initiated the Japanese attack on Pearl Harbor, and by 1944 he had assumed virtual control of all political and military decision-making. After Japan's surrender, he was tried and hanged as a war criminal.

To•klas |'tōkləs|, Alice Babette (1877–1967) U.S. author. She was a companion and secretary of Gertrude Stein.

Tol•kien |'tōl,kēn; 'täl,kēn|, J. R. R. (1892–1973) British novelist and literary scholar, born in South Africa; full name *John Ronald Reuel Tolkien.* He is famous for the fantasy adventures *The Hobbit* (1937) and *The Lord of the Rings* (1954–5), set in Middle Earth.

Tol•son |'tawlsən|, Melvin Beaunorus (1898–1966) U.S. author. Notable works: *Black Boy* (1963).

Tol•stoy |'tawl,stoi; 'tōl,stoi|, Count Leo (1828–1910) Russian writer; Russian name *Lev Nikolaevich Tolstoi.* He is best known for the novels *War and Peace* (1863–9), an epic tale of the Napoleonic invasion, and *Anna Karenina* (1873–77).

Tom•baugh |'täm,baw|, Clyde William (1906–97) American astronomer. His chief discovery was that of the planet Pluto on March 13, 1930, which he made from the Lowell Observatory in Arizona. Tombaugh subsequently discovered numerous asteroids.

To•mei |tō'mā|, Marisa (1964–   ) U.S. actress. Notable movies: *My Cousin Vinny* (1992, Academy Award).

Tom•lin |'tämlən|, Lily (1939–   ) U.S. comedian and actress. Born *Mary Jean Tomlon.* She has starred in the television series "Rowan & Martin's Laugh-In" (1969–73) and a one-woman Broadway show *The Search for Signs of Intelligent Life in the Universe* (Tony Award, 1985). Notable movies: *Nine to Five* (1980).

Tomp•kins |'täm(p)kənz|, Daniel D. (1774–1825) vice president of the U.S. (1817–25).

Tone |tōn|, (Theobald) Wolfe (1763–98) Irish nationalist. In 1794 he promoted a French invasion of Ireland that failed to overthrow English rule. Tone was captured by the British during the Irish insurrection in 1798 and committed suicide in prison.

Toole |tōol|, John Kennedy (1937–69) U.S. author. Notable works: *A Confederacy of Dunces* (1980, Pulitzer Prize), published posthumously.

Too•mer |'tōomər|, Jean (1894–1967) U.S. author. Notable works: *Cane* (1923).

Tor•que•ma•da |,tawrkə'mädə|, Tomás de (*c.* 1420–98) Spanish cleric and Grand Inquisitor. A Dominican monk, he became confessor to Ferdinand and Isabella, whom he persuaded to institute the Inquisition in 1478. He was also the prime mover behind the expulsion of the Jews from Spain in and after 1492.

Tor·rence |'tawrəns|, (Frederic) Ridgely (1875–1950) U.S. author. Notable works: *Poems* (1941, 1952).

Tor·rey |'tawrē|, John (1796–1873) U.S. chemist, botanist, and author. With Asa Gray, he published *A Flora of North America* (two vols., 1838–43).

Tor·ri·cel·li |ˌtawrə'CHelē|, Evangelista (1608–47) Italian mathematician and physicist. He invented the mercury barometer, with which he demonstrated that the atmosphere exerts a pressure sufficient to support a column of mercury in an inverted closed tube.

Tor·te·lier |ˌtawrtl'yä|, Paul (1914–90) French cellist. He was noted for his interpretations of Bach and Elgar and was appointed professor at the Paris Conservatoire in 1957.

Tos·ca·ni·ni |ˌtäskə'nēnē|, Arturo (1867–1957) Italian conductor. He was musical director at La Scala in Milan (1898–1903; 1906–8) before becoming conductor of the Metropolitan Opera, New York (1908–21) and the New York Philharmonic Orchestra (1928–36). He founded the NBC Symphony Orchestra (1937).

Tough |təf|, Dave (1908–48) U.S. jazz drummer. Full name *David Jaffray Tough*. He played with Tommy Dorsey's Band and with the Benny Goodman Orchestra.

Toulouse-Lautrec |tə,lo͞oz- lō'trek|, Henri (Marie Raymond) de (1864–1901) French painter and lithographer. His reputation is based on his color lithographs from the 1890s, depicting actors, music-hall singers, prostitutes, and waitresses in Paris; particularly well known is the *Moulin Rouge* series (1894).

Tous·saint L'Ou·ver·ture |to͞o'seN ˌlo͞over'tYr|, Pierre Dominique (*c.* 1743–1803) Haitian revolutionary leader. One of the leaders of a rebellion (1791) that emancipated the island's slaves, he was appointed governor general by the revolutionary government of France in 1797. In 1802 Napoleon (wishing to restore slavery) took over the island, and Toussaint died in prison in France.

Townes |townz|, Charles Hard (1915–) U.S. physicist. His development of microwave oscillators and am-

plifiers led to his invention of the maser in 1954. Townes later showed that an optical maser (a laser) was possible, though the first working laser was constructed by others. Nobel Prize for Physics (1964).

Town·send |'townzənd|, Willard (1895–1957) U.S. labor organizer. He organized the United Transport Service Employees, or "redcaps" (1935).

Town·shend |'townzənd|, Peter Dennis Blandford (1945–) British rock musician. He performed with The Who and composed the rock opera *Tommy* (Tony Award, 1993).

Toyn·bee |'toinbē|, Arnold (1852–83) English economist and social reformer. He taught both undergraduates and adult education classes in Oxford and worked with the poor in London's East End. He is best known for his pioneering work *The Industrial Revolution* (1884).

Toyn·bee |'toinbē|, Arnold (Joseph) (1889–1975) English historian. He is best known for his twelve-volume *Study of History* (1934–61), in which he traced the pattern of growth, maturity, and decay of different civilizations.

Tra·cy |'trāsē|, Spencer (1900–67) U.S. actor, particularly known for his screen partnership with Katharine Hepburn, with whom he costarred in movies such as *Guess Who's Coming to Dinner?* (1967). Other notable movies: *Captains Courageous* (1937, for which he won an Oscar); *Boys Town* (1938, for which he won an Oscar); *Adam's Rib* (1949); *Inherit the Wind* (1960); and *Judgment at Nuremberg* (1961).

Tra·herne |trə'hərn|, Thomas (1637–74) English religious writer and metaphysical poet. His major prose work *Centuries* (1699) was rediscovered in 1896 and republished as *Centuries of Meditation* (1908).

Tra·jan |'trājən| (*c.* 53–117 AD) Roman emperor 98–117; Latin name *Marcus Ulpius Traianus*. His reign is noted for the many public works undertaken and for the Dacian wars (101–6), which ended in the annexation of Dacia as a province.

Trav·ers |'trævərz|, Mary (1937–) U.S. folk singer. She was part of trio Peter, Paul, and Mary from the early

1960s through 1990s; their songs, reflecting the social concerns of the 1960s, include "Blowin' in the Wind" and "If I Had a Hammer."

Trav·is |'trævəs|, Merle (1917–83) U.S. country singer, guitarist, and songwriter.

Tre·vi·no |trə'vēnō|, Lee (Buck) (1939–) U.S. golfer. In 1971 he became the first man to win all three Open championships (Canadian, U.S., and British) in the same year.

Trev·or |'trevər|, William (1928–) Irish novelist and short-story writer; pseudonym of *William Trevor Cox*. His works deal insightfully with the elderly, the lonely, and the unsuccessful. They include the novels *The Old Boys* (1964) and *Fools of Fortune* (1983).

Tril·lin |'trilən|, Calvin (1935–) U.S. journalist and author. Notable works: *Remembering Denny* (1993).

Tril·ling |'triliNG| U.S. family of writers, including: **Lionel Trilling** (1905–75), a literary critic. Notable works: *The Liberal Imagination* (1950). **Diana Trilling** (1905–), his wife and an author. Notable works: *Mrs. Harris* (1981).

Trim·ble |'trimbəl|, Robert (1777–1828) U.S. Supreme Court justice (1826–28).

Tris·ta·no |tris'tänō|, Lennie (1919–78) U.S. jazz pianist and teacher. Full name *Leonard Joseph Tristano*. He founded a school of jazz in New York, where he excelled as a teacher.

Trol·lope |'träləp| English family of writers, including: **Anthony Trollope** (1815–82), a novelist. He is best known for the six Barsetshire novels, including *The Warden* (1855) and *Barchester Towers* (1857), and for the six political Palliser novels. **Frances Trollope** (1780–1863), his mother, and the author of *Domestic Manners of the Americans* (1832).

Trot·sky |'trätskē|, Leon (1879–1940) Russian revolutionary; born *Lev Davidovich Bronstein*. He helped to organize the October Revolution with Lenin and built up the Red Army. He was expelled from the party by Stalin in 1927 and exiled in 1929. He settled in Mexico in 1937, where he was later murdered by a Stalinist assassin.

Troyes |trwä|, Chrétien de see CHRÉTIEN DE TROYES.

Tru·deau |troo'dō|, Garry B. (1948–) U.S. cartoonist. He was the creator of "Doonesbury." Pulitzer Prize, 1975.

Tru·deau |troo'dō|, Pierre (Elliott) (1919–) Canadian Liberal statesman, prime minister of Canada (1968–79 and 1980–84). Noted for his commitment to federalism, Trudeau held a provincial referendum in Quebec in 1980, which rejected independence, and saw the transfer of residual constitutional powers from Britain to Canada in 1982.

Truf·faut |troo'fō|, François (1932–84) French movie director. His first feature movie, *The 400 Blows* (1959), established him as a leading director of the *nouvelle vague*. Other movies include *Jules et Jim* (1961) and *The Last Metro* (1980).

Tru·ji·llo |troo'hēyō|, Rafael (1891–1961) Dominican statesman, president of the Dominican Republic (1930–38 and 1942–52); born *Rafael Leónidas Trujillo Molina*; known as **Generalissimo**. Although he was formally president for only two periods, he wielded dictatorial powers from 1930 until his death.

Tru·man |'troomən| U.S. family, including: **Harry S Truman** see box. **Bess Truman** (1885–1982), wife of Harry S Truman and U.S. first lady (1945–53); born *Elizabeth Virginia Wallace*. **Margaret Truman** (1924–), their daughter, a novelist; married name *Margaret Truman Daniel*. Notable novels: *Murder in the White House* (1980) and *Murder in the Pentagon* (1991).

Trum·bo |'trəmbō|, Dalton (1905–76) U.S. author and screenwriter. Notable works: *Johnny Got His Gun* (1939), *Exodus*, and *Spartacus* (1960).

Trum·bull |'trəmbəl|, John (1756–1843) U.S. artist. He created paintings for the rotunda of the Capitol building in Washington, D.C., and painted several portraits of George Washington.

Trump |trəmp|, Donald John (1946–) U.S. real estate developer.

Truth |trooTH|, Sojourner (*c.* 1797–1883) U.S. evangelist and reformer; previously *Isabella Van Wagener*. Born into slavery, she was sold to Isaac Van Wagener, who released her in 1827. She

Truman, Harry S
33rd U.S. president

Life dates: 1884–1972
Place of birth: Lamar, Missouri
Mother: Martha Ellen Young Truman
Father: John Anderson Truman
Wife: Bess (Elizabeth Virginia) Wallace Truman
Children: (Mary) Margaret
College/University: none
Military service: Missouri National Guard; during World War I served in combat in France
Career: Farmer; owner, men's clothing store
Political career: U.S. Senate; vice president (under Franklin D. Roosevelt); president
Party: Democratic
Home state: Missouri
Opponents in presidential race: Thomas E. Dewey, Henry A. Wallace, James Strom Thurmond
Term of office: Apr. 12, 1945–Jan. 20, 1953 (succeeded to the presidency on the death of Franklin D. Roosevelt)
Vice president: Alben W. Barkley
Notable events of presidency: Germany surrenders to Allied forces; Potsdam Conference; atomic bombing of Hiroshima and Nagasaki, Japan; Japan surrenders, ending World War II; Truman Doctrine; Labor-Management Relations Act (Taft-Hartley Act); Economic Cooperation Administration created (European Recovery Program or Marshall Plan); North Atlantic Treaty Organization (NATO) established; Korean War begins
Other achievements: chairman, Special Senate Committee to Investigate the National Defense Program (Truman Committee)
Place of burial: Independence, Missouri

became a zealous evangelist, preaching in favor of black rights and women's suffrage.

Tshom•be |'CHawmbā|, Moise (1919–69) Prime minister of Belgian Congo (1964–65).

Tsiol•kov•sky |ˌCHēəl'kawfskē|, Konstantin (Eduardovich) (1857–1935) Russian aeronautical engineer. Tsiolkovsky carried out pioneering theoretical work on multistage rockets, jet engines, and space flight, and his pro-posal for the use of liquid fuel pre-dated the work of R. H. Goddard by nearly forty years.

Tsu•bo•u•chi |ˌtso͞obə'o͞oCHē|, Shōyō (1859–1935) Japanese writer, scholar, translator. He began the *shingeki* (New Theater) movement, translated Shakespeare into Japanese, and wrote the first major work of modern Japanese literary criticism.

Tubb |təb|, Ernest (1914–84) U.S. country singer, songwriter, guitarist. Notable songs: "The Yellow Rose of Texas."

Tub•man |'təbmən|, Harriet (c. 1820–1913) U.S. aboloitionist. Known as **the Moses of Her People**. She was born a slave in Maryland, but escaped via the Underground Railroad (1849). Following what she called direct messages from God, she returned to Maryland numerous times, leading some 300 slaves to safety. During the Civil War, she went on many spying missions for the Union.

Tub•man |'təbmən|, William Vacanarat Shadrach (1895–1971) president of Liberia (1944–71).

Tuch•man |'təkmən|, Barbara (1912–89) U.S. historian and author. Notable works: *The Guns of August* (1962, Pulitzer Prize) and *Stilwell and the American Experience in China, 1911–45* (1971, Pulitzer Prize).

Tuck•er |təkər|, Richard (1913–75) U.S. operatic tenor. Born *Rubin Ticker*. He sang with the Metropolitan Opera for 30 seasons, beginning with his debut in 1945.

Tuck•er |təkər|, Sophie (1884–1966) U.S. burlesque and vaudeville entertainer, born in Russia. Born *Sophie Abuza*. She joined the Ziegfeld Follies (1909) and later starred in the Schubert Gaieties and the Earl Carroll Vanities; she was known as the "last of the red hot mamas."

Tuck•er |təkər|, Tanya (1958–) U.S. country and pop musician. Notable album: *Can't Run From Yourself* (1992).

Tu•dor |'to͞odər|, Henry. Henry VII of England (see HENRY).

Tu•dor |'to͞odər|, Mary. Mary I of England (see MARY).

Tu Fu |'do͞o 'fo͞o| (AD 712–70) Chinese poet. Also **Du Fu**. He is noted for his bitter satiric poems attacking social injustice and corruption at court.

Tull |təl|, Jethro (1674–1741) English agriculturalist. In 1701 he invented the seed drill, a machine that could sow seeds in accurately spaced rows at a controlled rate, reducing the need for farm laborers.

Tul·ley |'təlē|, John (c. 1639–1701) U.S. author, born in England. He wrote the first continuous series of humorous almanacs in the U.S., beginning in 1687.

Tul·ly |'təlē|, Alice (1902–93) U.S. singer, philanthropist, and arts patron.

Tul·si·das |'toolsē,däs| (c. 1543–1623) Indian poet. A leading Hindu devotional poet, he is chiefly remembered for the *Ramcaritmanas* (c. 1574–7), a work consisting of seven cantos based on the Sanskrit epic, the *Ramayana*.

Tune |toon|, Tommy (1939–) U.S. dancer and choreographer. Notable musicals: *The Best Little Whorehouse in Texas* (1978).

Tu·nick |'toonək|, Jonathan (1938–) U.S. musician. He orchestrated Broadway shows, including *Promises, Promises* (1968), *A Little Night Music* (1973), and *A Chorus Line* (1975).

Tun·ney |'tənē|, Gene (James Joseph) (1898–1978) U.S. heavyweight boxer. He was a world heavyweight champion with a career record of 76 wins and one loss.

Tu·po·lev |'toopəlyif|, Andrei Nikolaievich (1888–1972) Soviet aeronautical engineer. He designed over 100 military and passenger aircraft and created the first supersonic airliner (1969).

Tup·per |'təpər|, Earl (1907–83) U.S. inventor. He invented the plastic food storage containers known as Tupperware (1946).

Tur·ge·nev |toor'gänyəf|, Ivan (Sergeevich) (1818–83) Russian novelist, dramatist, and short-story writer. His novels, such as *Fathers and Sons* (1862), examine individual lives to illuminate the social, political, and philosophical issues of the day.

Tu·ring |'tooriNG|, Alan Mathison (1912–54) British mathematician. He developed the concept of a theoretical computing machine, a key step in the development of the first computer, and carried out important code-breaking work in World War II. He also investigated artificial intelligence.

Tur·ner |'tərnər|, Frederick Jackson (1861–1932) U.S. historian, educator and author. He revolutionized the study of the American frontier with his book *The Significance of Sections in American History* (1932, Pulitzer Prize).

Tur·ner |'tərnər|, J. M. W. (1775–1851) English painter; full name *Joseph Mallord William Turner*. He made his name with landscapes and stormy seascapes, becoming increasingly concerned with depicting the power of light by the use of primary colors, often arranged in a swirling vortex. Notable works: *Rain, Steam, Speed* (1844); *The Fighting Téméraire* (1838).

Tur·ner |'tərnər|, Joe (1911–85) U.S. rock and blues singer. He was a blues shouter of hits such as "Shake, Rattle, and Roll" and "Chains of Love."

Tur·ner |'tərnər|, Nat (1800–31) U.S. slave leader. Hanged on charges of murder and insurrection, he had organized a slave uprising in Southampton, Virginia, in which at least 50 whites were killed (August 1831).

Tur·ner |'tərnər|, Ted (1938–) U.S. broadcasting executive. Full name *Robert Edward Turner III*. His Turner Broadcasting System includes the television networks TBS ("the SuperStation"), Cable News Network (CNN), Turner Classic Movies (TCM), and the Cartoon Network. He owns the Atlanta Braves baseball team and the Atlanta Hawks basketball team. An accomplished yachtsman, he won the America's Cup (1977).

Tur·ner |'tərnər|, Tina (1939–) U.S. rock musician. Born *Anna Mae Bullock*. With her husband she was part of the duo Ike and Tina Turner; her hits include "What's Love Got to Do with It" and "We Don't Need Another Hero."

Tu·row |'toorō|, Scott F. (1949–) U.S. author. Notable works: *Laws of Our Fathers* (1996) and *Presumed Innocent* (1996).

Tur·pin |'tərpən|, Dick (1706–39) English highwayman. He was a cattle and deer thief in Essex before entering into partnership with Tom King, a notorious highwayman. Turpin was hanged at York for horse-stealing.

Tus·saud |'tōōsō; tə'sawd|, Madame (1761–1850) French founder of Madame Tussaud's waxworks museum, resident in Britain from 1802; née *Marie Grosholtz*. She took death masks in wax of prominent victims of the French Revolution and later toured Britain with her wax models. In 1835 she founded a permanent waxworks exhibition in London.

Tut·ankh·a·men |ˌtōō,täNG'kämən| (died *c.* 1352 BC) Egyptian pharaoh of the 18th dynasty, reigned *c.*1361–*c.*1352 BC. Also **Tutankhamun**. His tomb, with its rich and varied contents, was discovered virtually intact by the English archaeologist Howard Carter in 1922.

Tuth·mo·sis III |tōōt'mōsəs| (died *c.* 1450 BC) son of Tuthmosis II, Egyptian pharaoh of the 18th dynasty *c.*1504–*c.*1450 BC. His reign was marked by extensive building; the monuments he erected included Cleopatra's Needles (*c.*1475 BC).

Tu·tu |'tōō,tōō|, Desmond (Mpilo) (1931–) South African clergyman. As General Secretary of the South African Council of Churches (1979–84), he became a leading voice in the struggle against apartheid. He was archbishop of Cape Town 1986–96. Nobel Peace Prize (1984).

Twain |twān|, Mark (1835–1910) U.S. novelist and humorist; pseudonym of *Samuel Langhorne Clemens*. After gaining a reputation as a humorist with early work, he wrote his best-known novels, *The Adventures of Tom Sawyer* (1876) and *The Adventures of Huckleberry Finn* (1885), which give a vivid evocation of Mississippi frontier life.

Tweed |twēd|, William Marcy (1823–78) U.S. politician. Known as **Boss Tweed**. A New York Democrat, he served in the U.S. House of Representatives (1853–55) and as New York City commissioner of schools (1856–57). By the time he was elected to the state senate (1867–71), he had become the leader of a ring of political corruption, which, until exposed in 1870, swindled the state treasury out of as much as $200

million. He was convicted (1873) but fled to Cuba and Spain (1875–76). He was extradited (1876) and returned to a New York jail, where he died.

Twich·ell |'twiCHəl|, Joseph Hopkins (1838–1918) U.S. Congregational clergyman. He was a member of the Nook Farm community in Hartford, Connecticut, where Mark Twain lived.

Twit·ty |'twitē|, Conway (1933–93) U.S. country singer, songwriter, and guitarist. Born *Harold Lloyd Jenkins*. Notable songs: "Hello, Darlin'" and "After the Fire is Gone."

Ty·cho Bra·he |'tīkō 'brähē| see BRAHE.

Ty·ler |'tīlər|, Anne (1941–) U.S. author. Notable works: *A Patchwork Planet* (1998) and *The Accidental Tourist* (1986).

Ty·ler |'tīlər| John, see box. **Letitia**

***

Tyler, John
10th U.S. president

Life dates: 1790–1862
Place of birth: Charles City County, Va.
Mother: Mary Marot Armistead Tyler
Father: John Tyler
Wife: Letitia Christian Tyler (died 1842); Julia Gardiner (married 1844)
Children: (by first wife) Mary, Robert, John, Letitia, Elizabeth, Anne, Alice, Tazewell; David, John, Julia, Lachlan, Lyon, Robert, Pearl
College/University: College of William and Mary
Career: Farmer; lawyer
Political career: Virginia House of Delegates; U.S. House of Representatives; governor of Virginia; U.S. Senate; vice president (under Harrison); president; elected to Confederate House of Representatives
Party: Democratic; Whig
Home state: Virginia
Opponents in presidential race: none
Term of office: Apr. 6, 1841–March 3, 1845 (succeeded to the presidency on the death of William Henry Harrison)
Vice president: none
Notable events of presidency: Pre-Emption Act; treaty with China; annexation of Texas; Florida admitted as the 27th state
Other achievements: admitted to the Virginia bar
Place of burial: Richmond, Va.

Christian Tyler (1790–1842), wife of John Tyler and U.S. first lady (1841–42).

Julia Gardener Tyler (1820–89), wife of John Tyler and U.S. first lady (1844–45).

Ty·ler |ˈtīlər|, Moses Coit (1835–1900) U.S. historian and educator. He helped organize the American Historical Association (1884). Notable works: *A History of American Literature, 1607–1765* (1878) and *The Literary History of the American Revolution, 1763–83* (1897).

Ty·ler |ˈtīlər|, Wat (died 1381) English leader of the Peasants' Revolt of 1381. He captured Canterbury and went on to take London and secure Richard II's concession to the rebels' demands, which included the lifting of the newly imposed poll tax. He was killed by royal supporters.

Tyn·dale |ˈtindəl|, William (*c.* 1494–1536) English translator and Protestant martyr. Faced with ecclesiastical opposition to his project for translating the Bible into English, Tyndale left England in 1524. His translations of the Bible later formed the basis of the authorized version. He was burnt at the stake as a heretic in Antwerp.

Ty·son |ˈtīsən|, Mike (1966–) U.S. heavyweight boxing champion; full name *Michael Gerald Tyson*.

Ty·us |ˈtīəs|, Wyomia (1945–) U.S. track and field athlete. She was the first woman to win consecutive Olympic gold medals (1964, 1968) in the 100-meter dash.

Tza·ra |ˈtsärə|, Tristan (1896–1963) Romanian-born French poet; born *Samuel Rosenstock*. He was one of the founders of the Dada movement and wrote its manifestos. His poetry, with its continuous flow of unconnected images, helped form the basis for surrealism.

Uu

Uc·cel·lo |ōō'CHelō|, Paolo (c. 1397–1475) Italian painter; born *Paolo di Dono*. His paintings are associated with the early use of perspective and include *The Rout of San Romano* (c.1454–57) and *A Hunt in a Forest* (after 1460), one of the earliest known paintings on canvas.

Udall |'yōō,dawl|, Morris King (1922–98) U.S. politician. He was a member of the U.S. House of Representatives from Arizona (1961–91).

Uhry |'yōōrē|, Alfred (1937–) U.S. playwright. Notable works: *Driving Miss Daisy* (1987, Pulitzer Prize).

Ula·no·va |yōō'länəvə|, Galina (Sergeyevna) (1910–98) Russian ballet dancer. She gave notable interpretations of *Swan Lake* and *Giselle*, and also danced the leading roles, composed especially for her, in all three of Prokofiev's ballets.

Ul·fi·las |'əlfə,læs| (c. 311–c. 381) Christian bishop and translator. Also **Wulfila**. Believed to be of Cappadocian descent, he became bishop of the Visigoths in 341. His translation of the Bible from Greek into Gothic (of which fragments survive) is the earliest known translation of the Bible into a Germanic language. Ulfilas is traditionally held to have invented the Gothic alphabet, based on Latin and Greek characters.

Ull·man |'əlmən|, Tracey (1959–) English actress.

Ul·pi·an |'əlpēən| (died c. 228) Roman jurist, born in Phoenicia; Latin name *Domitius Ulpianus*. His numerous legal writings provided one of the chief sources for Justinian's *Digest* of 533.

Ul·ya·nov |'ōōlyə,nawf|, Vladimir Ilich see LENIN.

Un·cas |'əNGkəs| (c. 1600–1683) chief of the Mohegan Indians. He sided with the British in the Pequot War (1637).

Un·der·wood |'əndər,wōōd|, William (1787–1864) U.S. businessman. He founded a cannery (1821), whose "red devil" is thought to be the oldest registered food trademark.

Un·ga·ro, Emanuel Matteotti (1933–) French fashion designer.

Uni·tas |yōō'nītəs|, Johnny (1933–) U.S. football player. Full name *John Constantine Unitas*. He led the Baltimore Colts to 2 NFL titles and a Super Bowl win.

Un·ser |'ənsər|, Al (1939–) U.S. racecar driver. He retired in 1994, ranked third on the all-time Indy car list with 39 wins.

Un·ter·mey·er |'əntər,mīər|, Louis (1885–1977) U.S. author. He published critical anthologies, including *Modern American Poetry* (1919, with many revisions), as well as his own poetry.

Up·dike |'əp,dīk|, John (Hoyer) (1932–) U.S. novelist, poet, and short-story writer. He is noted for his quartet of novels *Rabbit, Run* (1960), *Rabbit Redux* (1971), *Rabbit is Rich* (1981, Pulitzer Prize), and *Rabbit at Rest* (1990, Pulitzer Prize). Other novels include *The Witches of Eastwick* (1984), and *S* (1998).

Up·john |'əp,jän|, Richard (1802–78) U.S. architect. Notable designs: Trinity Church (New York).

Urann, Marcus Libby (1873–1963) U.S. lawyer and businessman. He founded Ocean Spray Preserving Co. in order to mass-market cranberry sauce.

Ur·bahn |'ōōr,bän|, Max O. (1912–95) U.S. architect. Notable works: Vehicle Assembly Building (Cape Canaveral, Florida).

Urey |'yōōrē|, Harold Clayton (1893–1981) U.S. chemist He discovered deuterium in 1932, pioneered the use of isotope labeling, and became director of the Manhattan Project at Columbia University. Nobel Prize for Chemistry (1934).

Uris |'yōōrəs|, Leon Marcus (1924–) U.S. author. Notable works: *QB VII* (1970) and *Trinity* (1976).

Usti·nov |'yōōstə,nawf|, Sir Peter (Alexander) (1921–) British actor, director, and dramatist, of Russian descent. He has written and acted in a number of plays, including *Romanoff* *and Juliet* (1956). Notable movies: *Spartacus* (1960) and *Death on the Nile* (1978).

Uta·ma·ro |ˌo͞otə'märō|, Kitagawa (1753–1806) Japanese painter and printmaker; born *Kitagawa Nebsuyoshi*. A leading exponent of the ukiyo-e school, he was noted for his sensual depictions of women.

Utril·lo |o͞o'trēō|, Maurice (1883–1955) French painter, chiefly known for his depictions of Paris street scenes, especially the Montmartre district.

Vv

Va·ga·no·va |vəˈgänəvə|, Agrippina Yakovlevna (1879–1951) Russian ballet teacher. He codified a Soviet ballet technique that developed acrobatic virtuousity.

Vail |vāl|, Theodore Newton (1845–1920) U.S. businessman. He began as a telegraph operator for Western Union in New York City (1864–66) and general manager of Bell Telephone (1878–87). In 1885 he incorporated the American Telephone & Telegraph company (AT&T) to unify the industry and provide long-distance service; he served as the company's president (1885–89, 1907–19).

Va·len·ti |vəˈlentē|, Jack Joseph (1921–) U.S. movie executive. He is the CEO of the Motion Picture Association of America, Inc. (1966–) and chairman of the Alliance of Motion Picture and television Producers, Inc. (1966–).

Val·en·ti·no |ˌvælənˈtēnō|, Mario (1933–) Italian fashion designer.

Val·en·ti·no |ˌvælənˈtēnō|, Rudolph (1895–1926) Italian-born U.S. actor; born *Rodolfo Alfonzo Raffaelo Pierre Filibert Guglielmi di Valentina d'Antonguolla*. He played the romantic hero in silent movies such as *The Sheikh* (1921).

Va·le·ra |vəˈlerə|, Eamon de see DE VALERA.

Va·le·rian |vəˈlirēən| (died 260) Roman emperor 253–60; Latin name *Publius Licinius Valerianus*. He renewed the persecution of the Christians initiated by Decius.

Va·lé·ry |ˌväləˈrē|, Paul (1871–1945) Full name *Ambroise Paul Toussaint Jules Valéry*. French poet, essayist, and critic. His poetry includes *La Jeune parque* (1917) and "Le Cimetière marin" (1922).

Val·ois |välˈwä|, Dame Ninette de see DE VALOIS.

Van Al·len |væn ˈælən|, James Alfred (1914–) U.S. physicist who discovered Van Allen belts. He used balloons and rockets to study cosmic radiation in the upper atmosphere, showing that specific zones of high radiation were the result of charged particles from the solar wind being trapped in two belts around the earth.

Van Brock·lin |væn ˈbräklən|, Norm (1926–83) U.S. football player. Full name *Norman Mack Van Brocklin*. He led the NFL in passing three times and punting twice.

Van·brugh |ˈvænbrə|, Sir John (1664–1726) English architect and dramatist. His comedies include *The Relapse* (1696) and *The Provok'd Wife* (1697); among his architectural works are Castle Howard (1702) and Blenheim Palace (1705), both produced in collaboration with Nicholas Hawksmoor.

Van Bu·ren |væn ˈbyŏŏrən|, Martin (1782–1862) see box. Hannah Hoes Van Buren (1783–1819), wife of Martin Van Buren.

Van·cou·ver |vænˈkŏŏvər|, George (1757–98) English navigator. He led an

---

Van Buren, Martin
8th U.S. president

Life dates: 1782–1862
Place of birth: Kinderhook, New York
Mother: Maria Hoes Van Buren
Father: Abraham Van Buren
Wife: Hannah Hoes Van Buren
Children: Abraham, John, Martin, Smith
College/University: none
Career: Lawyer
Political career: New York Senate; U.S. Senate; governor of New York; U.S. secretary of state; vice president; president
Party: Democratic-Republican; Democratic
Home state: New York
Opponents in presidential races: William Henry Harrison
Term of office: March 4, 1837–March 3, 1841
Vice president: Richard M. Johnson
Notable events of presidency: Financial panic of 1837; Iowa territorial government authorized; Aroostook War; independent federal treasury system created
Place of burial: Kinderhook, New York

exploration of the coasts of Australia, New Zealand, and Hawaii (1791–92), and later charted much of the west coast of North America between southern Alaska and California. Vancouver Island and the city of Vancouver, Canada, are named after him.

Van de Graaf |'væn də ˌgræf|, Robert Jemison (1901–67) U.S. physicist. He invented the high-voltage *Van de Graaf generator* in about 1929, which was later adapted for use as a particle accelerator and as a high-energy X-ray generator for medical treatment and industrial use.

Van·den·berg |'vændənbərg|, Arthur Hendrick (1884–1951) U.S. journalist and politician. He was editor of the *Grand Rapids Herald* (1906–28); as a member of the U.S. Senate from Michigan (1928–51), he led the Republican opposition to President Franklin Roosevelt's foreign policy but later became a chief Republican architect of bipartisan foreign policy.

Van·der·bilt |'vændərˌbilt|, Cornelius (1794–1877) U.S. businessman and philanthropist. He amassed a fortune from shipping and railroads and made an endowment to found Vanderbilt University in Nashville, Tennessee (1873).

Van·der·lyn |'vændərlən|, John (1775–1852) U.S. artist. A neoclassicist, he painted *The Landing of Columbus* (1842–44) for the U.S. Capitol rotunda.

Van der Post |'væn dər ˌpōst|, Sir Laurens (Jan) (1906–96) South African explorer and writer. His books, including *Venture to the Interior* (1952) and *The Lost World of the Kalahari* (1958), combine travel writing and descriptions of fauna with philosophical speculation.

Van De·van·ter |'væn də'væntər|, Willis (1859–1941) U.S. Supreme Court justice (1910–37).

van de Vel·de |ˌvæn də 'veldə|, family of Dutch painters, including: **Willem** (1611–93); known as **Willem van de Velde the Elder**. He painted marine subjects and was official artist to the Dutch fleet. He also worked for Charles II. **Willem** (1633–1707), son of Willem the Elder; known as **Willem van de Velde the Younger**. He was also a notable marine artist who painted for Charles II. **Adriaen** (1636–72); son of

Willem the Elder. He painted landscapes, portraits, and biblical and genre scenes.

van de Vel·de |ˌvæn də 'veldə|, Henri (Clemens) (1863–1957) Belgian architect, designer, and teacher, who pioneered the development of art nouveau design and architecture in Europe. His buildings include the Werkbund Theatre in Cologne (1914).

Van Do·ren |væn 'dawrən| U.S. writers. **Carl (Clinton) Van Doren** (1885–1950), a historian and literary critic, is noted as the author of *Benjamin Franklin* (1938, Pulitzer Prize). His brother, **Mark (Albert) Van Doren** (1894–1972), was a poet and educator. Notable works: *Collected Poems* (1939, Pulitzer Prize).

Van Dru·ten |væn 'drōotn|, John (William) (1901–57) U.S. playwright and author, born in England. Notable works: *I Remember Mama* (1944).

van Duyn |væn 'dīn|, Mona (1921–   ) U.S. poet. Poet Laureate of the U.S., 1992–93.

Van Dyck |væn 'dīk|, Sir Anthony (1599–1641) Flemish painter. Also **Vandyke**. He is famous for his portraits of members of the English court, which determined the course of portraiture in England for more than 200 years.

Van Dyke |væn 'dīk|, Dick (1925–   ) U.S. actor. He starred in the television series "The Dick Van Dyke Show" (1961–66) and the movie *Mary Poppins* (1965).

Van Eyck |vän 'āk; væn 'īk|, Jan (*c.* 1370–1441) Flemish painter. He made innovative use of oils, bringing greater flexibility, richer and denser color, and a wider range from light to dark. Notable works: *The Adoration of the Lamb* (known as the Ghent Altarpiece, 1432) in the church of St. Bavon in Ghent and *The Arnolfini Marriage* (1434).

Van Gogh |væn 'gō|, Vincent (Willem) (1853–90) Dutch painter. He is best known for his post-Impressionist work, influenced by contact with Impressionist painting and Japanese woodcuts after he moved to Paris in 1886. His most famous pictures include several studies of sunflowers and *A Starry Night* (1889). Suffering from severe depression, he cut off part of his own ear and eventually committed suicide.

Van Ha·len |væn ˈhälən|, Eddie (1957–ᅟ) U. S. rock musician, born in the Netherlands. Grammy Award, 1991.

van Ley·den |v&aen. ˈlīdən |, Lucas see LUCAS VAN LEYDEN.

Van Rens·se·laer |ˌvæn ˌrensəˈlir; ˌvæn ˈrensələr|, Stephen (1764–1839) U.S. army officer and politician. He was a member of the U.S. House of Representatives from New York (1822–29) and founded the technical school (1824) that became Rensselaer Polytechnic Institute.

Van Vech·ten |væn ˈvektən|, Carl (1880–1964) U.S. art and music critic. Notable works: *Nigger Heaven* (1926).

Van·zet·ti |vænˈzetē |, Bartolomeo (1888–1927) U.S. political radical, born in Italy. Along with Nicola Sacco, he was accused of murder in a sensational trial.

Va·rèse |vəˈrez |, Edgard (1883–1965) U.S. composer and conductor, born in France. Born *Edgar Victor Achille Charles Varèse*. He was a pioneer in electronic music. Notable works: *Nocturnal* (1961).

Var·gas |ˈvärgəs |, Getúlio Dornelles (1883–1954) Brazilian statesman, president (1930–45 and 1951–54). After seizing power he ruled as a virtual dictator until overthrown by a coup. Returned to power after elections in 1951, he later committed suicide after widespread calls for his resignation.

Var·gas Llo·sa |ˈvärgəs ˈyōsə|, Mario (1936–ᅟ) Full name *Jorge Mario Pedro Vargas Llosa*. Peruvian novelist, dramatist, and essayist. Novels include *Aunt Julia and the Scriptwriter* (1977), *The War of the End of the World* (1982), and *A Fish in the Water* (1994).

Var·ro |ˈværō |, Marcus Terentius (116–27 BC) Roman scholar and satirist. His works covered many subjects, including philosophy, agriculture, the Latin language, and education.

Va·sa·rely |ˌväsəˈrelē |, Viktor (1908–97) Hungarian-born French painter. A pioneer of op art, he was best known for a style of geometric abstraction that used repeated geometric forms and interacting colors to create visual disorientation.

Va·sa·ri |väˈzärē |, Giorgio (1511–74)

Italian painter, architect, and biographer. His *Lives of the Most Excellent Painters, Sculptors, and Architects* (1550, enlarged 1568) laid the basis for later study of art history in the West.

Vas·co da Ga·ma see DA GAMA.

Vaughan |vawn |, Henry (*c.*1621–95) Welsh religious writer and metaphysical poet.

Vaughan |vawn |, Sarah Lois (1924–90) U.S. jazz singer. Known as **The Divine One**. She made her first recording with Billy Eckstine's Orchestra (1944).

Vaughan |vawn |, Stevie Ray (1955–90) U.S. blues-rock guitarist. Notable songs: "Pride and Joy."

Vaughn Wil·liams |ˌvawn ˈwilyəmz |, Ralph (1872–1958) English composer. His strongly melodic music frequently reflects his interest in Tudor composers and English folk songs. Notable works: *Fantasia on a Theme by Thomas Tallis* (1910), *A London Symphony* (1914), and the Mass in G minor (1922).

Vaux |vōz; vawks; vōks |, Calvert (1824–95) U.S. architect and landscape gardener. He is known for his work in New York City, including, with Frederick Law Olmsted, the design of Central Park.

Veb·len |ˈveblən |, Thorstein (Bunde) (1857–1929) U.S. economist and social scientist. His works include the critique of capitalism *The Theory of the Leisure Class* (1899) and *The Theory of Business Enterprise* (1904).

Ve·ga |ˈvāgə |, Lope de (1562–1635) Spanish dramatist and poet; full name *Lope Felix de Vega Carpio*. He is regarded as the founder of Spanish drama.

Ve·láz·quez |vəˈläs,kās |, Diego Rodríguez de Silva y (1599–1660) Spanish painter, court painter to Philip IV. His portraits humanized the formal Spanish tradition of idealized figures. Notable works: *Pope Innocent X* (1650), *The Toilet of Venus* (known as The Rokeby Venus, *c.*1651), and *Las Meninas* (*c.*1656).

Ve·láz·quez de Cuél·lar |vəˈläs,kās dä ˈkwä,är |, Diego (*c.* 1465–1524) Spanish conquistador. After sailing with Columbus to the New World in 1493, he began the conquest of Cuba in 1511; he later initiated expeditions to conquer Mexico.

Vel·de, van de |'veldə|,Willem and sons see VAN DE VELDE.

Vel·de, van de |'veldə|, Henri see VAN DE VELDE.

Vel·le·ius Pa·ter·cu·lus |vəˈlēəs pəˈtərkyələs| (*c.* 19 BC–*c.* 30 AD) Roman historian and soldier. His *Roman History*, covering the period from the early history of Rome to AD 30, is notable for its eulogistic depiction of Tiberius.

Ven·ing Mei·nesz |'veniNG 'mānəs|, Felix Andries (1887–1966) Dutch geophysicist. He devised a technique for making accurate gravity measurements with the aid of a pendulum and pioneered the use of submarines for marine gravity surveys. He located negative gravity anomalies in the deep trenches near island arcs in the Pacific, correctly interpreting them as being due to the downward buckling of the oceanic crust.

Ven·tu·ra |ven'to͝orə; ven'CHo͝orə|, Jesse (1951–) U.S. politician. Born *James George Janos*. A former professional wrestler (known as **The Body**), he is the governor of Minnesota (1998–).

Ven·tu·ri |ven'tyo͝orē; ven'CHo͝orē|, Robert (Charles) (1925–) U.S. architect, pioneer of postmodernist architecture. Among his buildings are the Humanities Classroom Building of the State University of NewYork (1973) and the Sainsbury Wing of the National Gallery in London (1991).

Ve·nu·ti |ve'no͞otē|, Joe (1903–78) U.S. jazz violinist. Born *Guiseppe Venuti*. The first great jazz violinist, he led a big band (1935–43) before returning to small groups.

Ve·ra Cruz |,verə 'kro͞oz|, Phillip (1905–94) U.S. social reformer, born in the Philipines. He helped found the United Farm Workers Union.

Ver·di |'verdē|, Giuseppe (Fortunino Francesco) (1813–1901) Italian composer. His many operas, such as *La Traviata* (1853), *Aida* (1871), and *Otello* (1887), emphasize the dramatic element, treating personal stories on a heroic scale and often against backgrounds that reflect his political interests. He is also famous for his *Requiem* (1874).

Ver·gil variant spelling of VIRGIL.

Ver·laine |ver'len|, Paul Marie (1844–96) French symbolist poet. Notable collections of poetry include *Poèmes saturniens* (1867), *Fêtes galantes* (1869), and *Romances sans paroles* (1874).

Ver·meer |vər'mir|, Jan (1632–75) Dutch painter. He generally painted domestic genre scenes, for example *The Kitchen Maid* (*c.*1658). His work is distinguished by its clear design and simple form.

Verne |vərn|, Jules (1828–1905) French novelist. One of the first writers of science fiction, he often anticipated later scientific and technological developments, as in *Twenty Thousand Leagues under the Sea* (1870). Other novels include *Journey to the Center of the Earth* (1864) and *Around the World in Eighty Days* (1873).

Ve·ro·ne·se |,verə'nāzē|, Paolo (*c.* 1528–88) Italian painter; born *Paolo Caliari*. He gained many commissions in Venice, including the painting of frescoes in the Doges' Palace. He is particularly known for his richly colored feast scenes (for example *The Marriage at Cana*, 1562).

Ver·ra·za·no |,verät'sänō|, Giovanni da (*c.* 1480–1528) Italian navigator in the service of France. He was the first European to enter New York Bay (1524).

Ver·sa·ce |vər'säCHē|, Gianni (1946–97) Italian fashion designer.

Ver·woerd |fər'vo͝ort|, Hendrik (Frensch) (1901–66) South African statesman, prime minister (1958–66). As minister of Bantu Affairs (1950–58) he developed the segregation policy of apartheid. As premier he banned the African National Congress and the Pan-Africanist Congress in 1960, following the Sharpeville massacre. He withdrew South Africa from the Commonwealth and declared it a republic in 1961.

Ve·ry |'verē|, Jones (1813–80) U.S. poet and religious thinker. He was incarcerated in an asylum for the insane; his mystical poetry and essays were published under the patronage of Ralph Waldo Emerson (1839).

Ve·sa·li·us |vəˈsālēəs|, Andreas (1514–64) Flemish anatomist, the founder of modern anatomy. His major work, *De Humani Corporis Fabrica* (1543), contained accurate descriptions of human anatomy, but owed much of its great historical impact to the woodcuts of his dissections.

Ves·pa·sian |vəs'pāzHən| (AD 9–79) Roman emperor (69–79) and founder of the Flavian dynasty; Latin name *Titus Flavius Sabinus Vespasianus*. He was acclaimed emperor by the legions in Egypt during the civil wars following the death of Nero and gained control of Italy after the defeat of Vitellius. His reign saw the restoration of financial and military order and the initiation of a public building program.

Ves·puc·ci |vəs'pōōCHē|, Amerigo (1451–1512) Italian merchant and explorer. He traveled to the New World, reaching the coast of Venezuela on his first voyage (1499–1500) and exploring the Brazilian coastline in 1501–02. The Latin form of his first name is believed to have given rise to the name of America.

Viar·dot |vyär'dō|, Pauline (1821–1910) French operatic mezzo-soprano. She made her debut in London in 1839 as Desdemona in *Otello* and sang at Covent Garden (1849–55) and with the Paris Opera until 1860.

Vi·cen·te |vē'säntā|, Gil (*c.* 1465–*c.* 1536) Portuguese dramatist and poet. He is regarded as Portugal's most important dramatist; many of his works were written to commemorate national or court events and include religious dramas, farces, pastoral plays, and satirical comedies.

Vi·co |'vēkō|, Giambattista (1668–1744) Italian philosopher. In *Scienza Nuova* (1725) he asserted that civilizations are subject to recurring cycles of barbarism, heroism, and reason, accompanied by corresponding cultural, linguistic, and political modes. His historicist approach influenced later philosophers such as Marx.

Vic·tor Em·man·u·el II |'viktər i 'mænyəwəl| (1820–78) ruler of the kingdom of Sardinia 1849–61 and first king of united Italy 1861–78. He hastened the drive toward Italian unification by appointing Cavour as premier of Piedmont in 1852. After being crowned king of Italy he added Venetia to the kingdom in 1866 and Rome in 1870.

Vic·tor Em·man·u·el III |'viktər i 'mænyəwəl| (1869–1947) last king of Italy 1900–46. He invited Mussolini to form a government in 1922 and lost all political power. After the loss of Sicily to the Allies (1943), he acted to dismiss Mussolini and conclude an armistice. He abdicated in 1946.

Vic·to·ria |vik'tawrēə|, Tomás Luis de (1548–1611) Spanish composer. His music, all of it religious, resembles that of Palestrina in its contrapuntal nature; it includes motets, masses, and hymns.

Vic·to·ria |vik'tawrēə| (1819–1901) queen of Great Britain and Ireland 1837–1901 and empress of India 1876–1901. Full name *Alexandrina Victoria*. She took an active interest in the policies of her ministers, but largely retired from public life after the death of her husband, Prince Albert, in 1861. Her reign was the longest in British history.

Vi·dal |vi'däl|, Gore (1925–) U.S. novelist, dramatist, and essayist; born *Eugene Luther Vidal*. His novels, many of them satirical comedies, include *Williwaw* (1946) and *Myra Breckenridge* (1968) and *Creation* (1981), as well as historical fiction such as *Lincoln* (1984).

Vigée-Lebrun |vē'ZHā lə'broEN|, (Marie Louise) Élisabeth (1755–1842) French painter. She is known for her portraits of women and children, especially Marie Antoinette and Lady Hamilton.

Vi·gno·la |vēn'yōlə|, Giacomo Barozzi da (1507–73) Italian architect. His designs were mannerist in style and include the Palazzo Farnese near Viterbo (1559–73) and the church of Il Gesù in Rome (begun 1568).

Vi·gny |vēn'yē|, Alfred Victor, Comte de (1797–1863) French poet, novelist, and dramatist. His poetry reveals his faith in "man's unconquerable mind." Other works include the play *Chatterton* (1835).

Vi·go |'vēgō|, Jean (1905–34) French movie director. His experimental movies, which combine lyrical, surrealist, and realist elements, include *Zéro de conduite* (1933) and *L'Atalante* (1934).

Vil·la |'vē(y)ə|, Pancho (1878–1923) Mexican revolutionary. Full name *Francisco Villa*; born *Doroteo Arango*. After playing a prominent role in the revolution of 1910–11 he overthrew the dictatorial regime of General Victoriano Huerta in 1914 together with Venustiano Carranza, but then rebelled against Carranza's regime with Emiliano Zapata.

Villa-Lobos |ˌvēlə-'lōbōs|, Heitor (1887–1959) Brazilian composer. He used folk music in many of his instrumental compositions, notably the nine *Bachianas brasileiras* (1930–45).

Vil·lard |vē'lär(d)|, Henry U.S. journalists and businessmen, born in Germany. **Henry Villard** (1835–1900), born *Ferdinand Heinrich Gustav Hilgard,* served as president (1881–84) and later chairman (1889–93) of the Northern Pacific Railroad. He also was president of the Edison General Electric Co. (1890–92) and purchased the *New York Evening Post* (1881). **Oswald Garrison Villard** (1872–1949), his son, was president of the *New York Evening Post* (1900–18) and editor (1918–32) and owner (1918–35) of *The Nation.*

Vil·lon |vē'yawN|, François (1431–63) French poet; born *François de Montcorbier* or *François des Loges.* He is best known for *Le Lais* or *Le Petit testament* (1456) and the longer, more serious *Le Grand testament* (1461).

Vin·cent de Paul |'vinsənt də 'pawl|, St. (1581–1660) French priest. He devoted his life to work among the poor and the sick and established institutions to continue his work, including the Daughters of Charity (Sister of Charity of St. Vincent de Paul) (1633). Feast day, July 19.

Vin·ci |'vinCHē|, Leonardo da see LEONARDO DA VINCI.

Vine |vīn|, Frederick John (1939–) English geologist. Vine and his colleague **Drummond H. Matthews** (1931–97) contributed to the theory of plate tectonics, showing that magnetic data from the earth's crust under the Atlantic Ocean provided evidence for sea-floor spreading.

Vin·son |'vinsən|, Frederick Moore (1890–1953) U.S. Supreme Court justice (1946–53).

Vir·chow |'firkō|, Rudolf Karl (1821–1902) German physician and patholo-gist, founder of cellular pathology. He argued that the cell was the basis of life and that diseases were reflected in specific cellular abnormalities. Virchow also stressed the importance of environmental factors in disease.

Vir·gil |'vərjəl| (70–19 BC) Roman poet. Also **Vergil**; Latin name *Publius Vergilius Maro.* He wrote three major works: the *Eclogues,* ten pastoral poems, blending traditional themes of Greek bucolic poetry with contemporary political and literary themes; the *Georgics,* a didactic poem on farming; and the *Aeneid* (see AENEID), an epic poem about the Trojan Aeneas.

Virgin Mary mother of Jesus (see MARY).

Vis·con·ti |vis'käntē|, Luchino (1906–76) Italian movie and theater director; full name *Don Luchino Visconti, Conte di Modrone.* His movies include *The Leopard* (1963) and *Death in Venice* (1971). His first movie, *Obsession* (1942), was regarded as the forerunner of neorealism.

Vi·tel·li·us |və'telēəs|, Aulus (15–69) Roman emperor. He was acclaimed emperor in January 69 by the legions in Germany during the civil wars that followed the death of Nero. He defeated Otho but was killed by the supporters of Vespasian.

Vi·tru·vi·us |və'trōōvēəs| (1st century BC) Roman architect and military engineer; full name *Marcus Vitruvius Pollio.* He wrote a comprehensive ten-volume treatise on architecture that includes matters such as acoustics and water supply as well as the more obvious aspects of architectural design, decoration, and building.

Vi·tus |'vītəs|, St. (died *c.* 300) Christian martyr. He was the patron of those who suffered from epilepsy and certain nervous disorders, including St. Vitus's dance (Sydenham's chorea). Feast day, June 15.

Vi·val·di |vi'väldē|, Antonio (Lucio) (1678–1741) Italian composer and violinist, one of the most important baroque composers. His feeling for texture and melody is evident in his numerous compositions such as *The Four Seasons* (concerto, 1725).

Vi·ve·ka·nan·da |ˌvivəkə'nändə|,

Swami (1863–1902) Indian spiritual leader and reformer; born *Narendranath Datta.* He spread the teachings of the Indian mystic Ramakrishna and introduced Vedantic philosophy to the U.S. and Europe.

Viz•e•tel•ly |ˌvizə'telē|, Frank Horace (1864–1938) U.S. lexicographer and editor, born in England. He edited Funk and Wagnall's *New Standard Dictionary.*

Vla•di•mir I |'vlædə,mir| (956–1015) grand prince of Kiev (980–1015); known as **Vladimir the Great**; canonized as **St. Vladimir.** His marriage to a sister of the Byzantine emperor Basil II resulted in his conversion to Christianity and in Christianity in Russia developing close association with the Orthodox Church. Feast day, July 15.

Vla•minck |vlə'meNk|, Maurice de (1876–1958) French painter and writer. With Derain and Matisse he became a leading exponent of Fauvism, though later his color became more subdued.

Vol•ta |'vōltə|, Alessandro Giuseppe Antonio Anastasio (1745–1827) Italian physicist. He discovered methane gas (1778) and developed the first electric battery (1800). The volt, a unit of electrical potential, is named after him.

Vol•taire |vōl'ter| (1694–1778) French writer, dramatist, and poet; pseudonym of *François-Marie Arouet.* He was a leading figure of the Enlightenment, and frequently came into conflict with the establishment as a result of his radical views and satirical writings. Notable works: *Lettres philosophiques* (1734) and the satire *Candide* (1759).

Vol•wi•ler |'vawl,wīlər|, Ernest H. (1893–1992) U.S. inventor. With Donalee Tabern he invented Pentothal while looking for an anesthetic for direct injection into the bloodstream.

von Braun |vän 'brown|, Wernher Magnus Maximilian see BRAUN.

Von Für•sten•berg |vän 'fərstən,bərg|, Diane Halfin (1946–   ) U.S. fashion designer, born in Belgium.

von Kar•man |vän 'kärmən|, Theodore

(1881–1963) U.S. physicist and aeronautical engineer, born in Hungary. He was instrumental in the development of rocket technology and was a cofounder of the Jet Propulsion Laboratory (1944).

von Laue |vän 'lowə|, Max Theodor Felix (1879–1960) German physicist. He won a 1914 Nobel Prize for Physics for his discovery of diffraction of X-rays by atoms or ions in crystals.

Von•ne•gut |'vänəgət|, Kurt, Jr. (1922–   ) U.S. novelist and short-story writer. His works blend elements of realism, science fiction, fantasy, and satire, and include *Cat's Cradle* (1963), *Slaughterhouse Five* (1969), and *Hocus Pocus* (1991).

von Neu•mann |vän 'noōmən|, John (1903–57) U.S. mathematician, born in Hungary. He contributed to the development of high-speed computers and of the hydrogen bomb; he coined the term "cybernetics."

von Stern•berg |vän 'stərn,bərg|, Josef (1894–1969) Austrian-born U.S. movie director. His best-known movie *Der Blaue Engel* (1930; *The Blue Angel*) made Marlene Dietrich an international star.

Vo•ro•shi•lov |vərə'sHēləf|, Kliment Yefremovich (1881–1969) Soviet statesman and marshal. He was president after Stalin's death (1953-60).

Vree•land |'vrēlənd|, Diane (*c.* 1903–89) U.S. editor, born in France. She edited *Harper's Bazaar* (1939–62) and *Vogue* (1962–71) and was a fashion consultant to the Metropolitan Museum of Art in New York.

Vuil•lard |ˌvwē'yär(d)|, (Jean) Édouard (1868–1940) French painter and graphic artist. Full name *Jean-Édouard Vuillard.* A member of the Nabi Group, he produced decorative panels, murals, paintings, and lithographs, particularly of domestic interiors and portraits.

Vy•shin•sky |və'sHinskē|, Andrei Yanuaryevich (1883–1954) Soviet lawyer and statesman. He was foreign minister (1949–53) and served as chief prosecuter in Stalin's "purge trials."

Ww

Wade |wād|, (Sarah) Virginia (1945–)
English tennis player.

Wag·ner |'wægnər|, Honus (1874–
1955) U.S. baseball player and coach.
Full name *John Peter Wagner*; known as
the Flying Dutchman. Elected to Baseball Hall of Fame (1936).

Wag·ner |'vägnər|, (Wilhelm) Richard
(1813–83) German composer. He developed an operatic genre which he
called music drama, synthesizing music,
drama, verse, legend, and spectacle. Notable works: *The Flying Dutchman*
(opera, 1841), *Der Ring des Nibelungen*
(a cycle of four operas, 1847–74), *Tristan and Isolde* (music drama, 1859), and
the *Siegfried Idyll* (1870).

Wain |wān|, John (Barrington) (1925–
94) English writer and critic. One of the
"Angry Young Men" of the early 1950s,
he was later professor of poetry at Oxford (1973–8).

Wain·wright |'wān,rīt|, Jonathan May-
hew (1883–1953) U.S. army officer. He
was forced to surrender at Corregidor
(1942) and was held as a prisoner of war
until 1945.

Waite |wāt|, Morrison Remick (1816–
88) Chief Justice of the U.S. (1874–88).
He wrote over 100 opinions, including
the Granger cases (1877), which upheld
the power of state governments to reg-
ulate business.

Waits |wāts|, Tom (1949–) U.S.
singer and songwriter. His *Bone Machine*
album won a 1992 Grammy Award.

Wajda |'wīdə|, Andrzej (1926–) Pol-
ish movie director. Notable movies:
Ashes and Diamonds (1958), *Man of Iron*
(1981), and *Danton* (1983).

Waks·man |'wæksmən|, Selman Abra-
ham (1888–1973) U.S. biochemist,
born in Russia. Russian-born American
microbiologist. He discovered the an-
tibiotic streptomycin, used especially
against tuberculosis. Nobel Prize for
Physiology or Medicine, 1952.

Wal·cott |'wawlkət|, Charles Doolittle
(1850–1927) U.S. geologist and pale-
ontologist. He was director of the U.S.
Geological Survey (1894–1907) and

Secretary of the Smithsonian Institution
(1907–).

Wald |wawld|, Lillian D. (1867–1940)
U.S. nurse and social worker. She organized the Visiting Nurse Service known
as the Henry Street Settlement in New
York City (1893).

Wald·heim |'väld,hīm|, Kurt
(1918–) Austrian diplomat and
statesman, president (1986–92). He was
Secretary General of the United Nations (1972–81). His later career was
blemished by revelations about his service as a German officer in World War
II.

Walesa |və'lensə; və'wensə|, Lech
(1943–) Polish labor leader and
statesman, president (1990–95). As
shipyard worker in Gdańsk, he founded
the labor union called Solidarity (1980),
and was imprisoned 1981–82 after the
movement was banned. After Solidarity's landslide victory in the 1989 elec-
tions he became president. Nobel Peace
Prize (1983).

Wales, Prince of |wālz| see PRINCE OF
WALES; CHARLES, PRINCE.

Wal·green |'wawl,grēn|, Charles
Rudolph (1873–1939) U.S. businessman. He founded the drugstore chain
that bears his name (1902).

Walk·er |'wawkər|, Alice (Malsenior)
(1944–) U.S. writer and critic. No-
table novels: *The Color Purple* (Pulitzer
Prize, 1982), *In Search of Our Mothers'
Gardens: Womanist Prose* (1983), and
Possessing the Secret of Joy (1992).

Walk·er |'wawkər|, Jimmy (1881–1946)
U.S. politician. Full name *James John
Walker*. He was mayor of New York City
(1926–32) but resigned when his involvement in fraud was exposed.

Walk·er |'wawkər|, John (1952–)
New Zealand track athlete. He was the
first athlete to run a mile in less than 3
minutes 50 seconds (1975).

Walk·er |'wawkər|, Margaret Abigail
(1915–) U.S. poet. Notable works:
For My People (1942) and *Jubilee* (1965).

Walk·er |'wawkər|, Mort (1923–)
U.S. cartoonist. Full name *Addison*

Morton Walker. He was the creator of the comic strip "Beetle Baily" and the co-creator of the strip "Hi and Lois."

Walk·er |'wawkər|, Ralph Thomas (1889–1973) U.S. architect. Notable designs: the New York Telephone building and the IBM Research Lab (New York).

Walk·er |'wawkər|, Robert (1801–69) U.S. politician. He was a member of the U.S. Senate from Mississippi (1835–45); he also served as U.S. secretary of the treasury (1845–49) and was largely responsible for creation of the Department of the Interior (1849).

Walk·er |'wawkər|, Sarah Breedlove (1867–1919) U.S. businesswoman. Known as **Madame C. J.** She invented and marketed a preparation to straighten kinky hair (1905) and built her business into the largest African-American–owned firm in the U.S, the Madame C. J. Walker Manufacturing Co. She bequeathed her fortune to educational institutions and charities.

Walk·er |'wawkər|, T-Bone (1910–75) U.S. guitarist. Full name *Aaron Thibeaux Walker*; known as **Daddy of the Blues**. He pioneered the electric blues guitar sound. Notable songs: "Viola Lee Blues" and "Stormy Monday Blues."

Wal·lace |'wawləs; 'wäləs|, Alfred Russel (1823–1913) English naturalist and a founder of zoogeography. He independently formulated a theory of the origin of species that was very similar to that of Charles Darwin.

Wal·lace |'wawləs; 'wäləs|, (Richard Horatio) Edgar (1875–1932) English novelist, screenwriter, and dramatist, noted for his crime novels.

Wal·lace |'wawləs; 'wäləs|, Henry Agard (1888–1965) U.S. politician and editor. He was editor of *Wallaces' Farmer* and its successor (1910–33). He served as vice president of the U.S. (1941–45) and was a Progressive party candidate for president (1948).

Wal·lace |'wawləs; 'wäləs|, George Corley (1919–98) U.S. politician. A four-term governor of Alabama (1963–67, 1971–79, 1983–87), he gained national attention in the early 1960s when he defied the civil rights legislation that outlawed segregation in public schools. After losing the 1968 presidential race as a third-party candidate, he sought the presidential nomination as a Democrat (1972). While campaigning, he was shot and paralyzed by would-be assassin Arthur Bremner.

Wal·lace |'wawləs; 'wäləs|, Lewis (1827–1905) U.S. soldier and author. He served as major general in the Mexican War and the Civil War. Notable works: Ben Hur (1880).

Wal·lace |'wawləs; 'wäləs|, Mike (1918–) U.S. journalist. Born *Myron Leon Wallace.* A radio and television news commentator, he appears on the television program "60 Minutes."

Wal·lace |'wawləs; 'wäləs|, Sir William (c. 1270–1305) Scottish national hero. He was a leader of Scottish resistance to Edward I, defeating the English army at Stirling in 1297. After Edward's second invasion of Scotland in 1298, Wallace was defeated and subsequently executed.

Wal·lace |'wawləs; 'wäləs|, William Roy DeWitt (1889–1981) U.S. editor and publisher. With his wife Lila, he founded and edited the *Reader's Digest* magazine; they donated much of their fortune to charity.

Wal·len·berg |'wawlən,bərg; 'wälən-,bərg|, Raoul Gustav (1912–47) Swedish diplomat. In 1944 in Budapest he helped many thousands of Jews to escape death by issuing them Swedish passports. In 1945 he was arrested by Soviet forces and imprisoned in Moscow. Although the Soviet authorities stated that Wallenberg had died in prison in 1947, his fate remains uncertain.

Wal·ler |'wawlər; 'wälər|, Fats (1904–43) U.S. jazz pianist, composer, bandleader, and singer. Full name *Thomas Waller.* He was a stride style pianist and a composer of hits such as "Ain't Misbehavin'" (1928) and "Honeysuckle Rose" (1929).

Wal·ler |'wawlər; 'wälər|, Robert James (1939–) U.S. author. Notable works: *The Bridges of Madison County* (1992).

Wal·lis |'wawləs; 'wäləs|, Sir Barnes Neville (1887–1979) English inventor. His designs include the bouncing bomb used against the Ruhr dams in Germany in the Second World War.

Wal·pole |'wawl͵pōl|, Horace, 4th Earl of Orford (1717–97) English writer and Whig politician, son of Sir Robert Walpole. He wrote *The Castle of Otranto* (1764), one of the first Gothic novels.

Wal·pole |'wawl͵pōl|, Sir Hugh (Seymour) (1884–1941) British novelist, born in New Zealand. He is best known for *The Herries Chronicle* (1930–33), a historical sequence set in England's Lake District.

Wal·pole |'wawl͵pōl|, Sir Robert, 1st Earl of Orford (1676–1745) British Whig statesman, First Lord of the Treasury and chancellor of the Exchequer (1715–17 and 1721–42), father of Horace Walpole. Walpole is generally regarded as the first British prime minister, having presided over the cabinet for George I and George II.

Wal·sing·ham |'wawlziNGəm|, Sir Francis (*c.* 1530–90) English politician. As secretary of state to Queen Elizabeth I he developed a spy network that gathered information about Catholic plots against the queen.

Wal·ter |'wawltər|, Bruno (1876–1962) U.S. conductor, born in Germany. Born *Bruno Walter Schlesinger.* He is noted as the standard interpreter of Mozart and as a supreme conductor of Brahms, Mahler, and Bruckner.

Wal·ters |'wawltərz|, Barbara (1931–) U.S. television journalist. She appears on the television program "20/20" (1979–).

Wal·ton |'wawltn|, Ernest Thomas Sinton (1903–95) Irish physicist. In 1932 he succeeded, with Sir John Cockcroft, in splitting the atom. Nobel Prize for Physics (1951, shared with Cockcroft).

Wal·ton |'wawltn|, Izaak (1593–1683) English writer. He is chiefly known for *The Compleat Angler* (1653; largely rewritten, 1655), which combines practical information on fishing with folklore, interspersed with pastoral songs and ballads.

Wal·ton |'wawltn|, Sam (1918–92) U.S. businessman. He was the founder of Wal-Mart discount stores.

Wal·ton |'wawltn|, Sir William (Turner) (1902–83) English composer. Notable works: *Façade* (1921–3, a setting of poems by Edith Sitwell for recitation), the oratorio *Belshazzar's Feast* (1930–1), and movie scores for three Shakespeare plays and the movie *The Battle of Britain* (1969).

Wam·baugh |'wäm͵bow|, Joseph Aloysius, Jr. (1937–) U.S. author. Notable works: *Floaters* (1996).

Wan·a·ma·ker |'wänə͵mākər|, John (1838–1922) U.S. businessman. He was a pioneering department store merchant; in 1861 he founded a men's clothing store in Philadelphia, which he expanded into a department store (1877). He served as U.S. postmaster general (1889–93).

Wang |wäNG|, An (1920–90) U.S. computer engineer, born in China. The founder of Wang Laboratories (1951), he held 40 patents.

Wan·kel |'wæNGkəl; 'väNGkəl|, Felix Heinrich (1902–88) German engineer. He was the inventor and developer of the practical rotary combustion engine.

War·beck |'wawr͵bek|, Perkin (1474–99) Flemish claimant to the English throne. In an attempt to overthrow Henry VII, he claimed to be one of the Princes in the Tower. After attempting to begin a revolt, he was captured and imprisoned in the Tower of London in 1497 and later executed.

War·burg |'wawr͵bərg|, Aby (Moritz) (1866–1929) German art historian. From 1905 he built up a library in Hamburg, dedicated to preserving the classical heritage of Western culture. In 1933 it was transferred to England and housed in the Warburg Institute (part of the University of London).

War·burg |'wawr͵bərg|, Otto Heinrich (1883–1970) German biochemist. He pioneered the use of the techniques of chemistry for biochemical investigations, especially for his work on intracellular respiration. Nobel Prize for Physiology or Medicine (1931); he was prevented by the Nazi regime from accepting a second one in 1944 because of his Jewish ancestry.

Ward |wawrd|, Aaron Montgomery (1843–1913) U.S. businessman. In 1872 he founded founded a dry-goods business, which became the first mail-order firm in the U.S., Montgomery Ward & Co..

Ward |wawrd|, Artemas (1727–1800) American politician and soldier. He served as a Revolutionary War commander, second in command to George Washington; later he was a member of the Continental Congress (1780–82) and of the U.S. House of Representatives (1791–95).

Ward |wawrd|, Mrs. Humphry (1851–1920) English writer and anti-suffrage campaigner, niece of Matthew Arnold; née *Mary Augusta Arnold.* She is best known for several novels dealing with social and religious themes, especially *Robert Elsmere* (1888). An active opponent of the women's suffrage movement, she became the first president of the Anti-Suffrage League in 1908.

Ware |wer|, Henry (1764–1845) U.S. clergyman and educator. He was responsible for the separation of the Unitarians from the Congregationalists, and he developed a curriculum for Harvard Divinity School (1816).

War·hol |'wawr,hawl|, Andy (c. 1928–87) U.S. painter, graphic artist, and movie-maker; born *Andrew Warhola.* A major exponent of pop art, he achieved fame for a series of silk-screen prints and acrylic paintings of familiar objects (such as Campbell's soup cans) and famous people (such as Marilyn Monroe), treated with objectivity and precision.

War·ner |'wawrnər|, Charles Dudley (1829–1900) U.S. author. Notable works: *The Gilded Age* (1873), with Samuel Clemens.

War·ner |'wawrnər|, Harry (1881–1958) U.S. movie executive, born in Poland. Born *Harry Morris Eichelbaum.* With brothers Albert (1884–1967), Samuel Louis (1887–1927), and Jack Leonard (1892–1978, born in Canada), he founded Warner Brothers Pictures (1923). The company produced *The Jazz Singer* (1927), the first talking movie.

War·ner |'wawrnər|, Pop (1871–1954) U.S. football coach. Full name *Glenn Scobey Warner.* He coached Olympic gold medalist and football player Jim Thorpe, as well as the football teams at

Pittsburgh (1915–23) and at Stanford University (1924–32).

War·ren |'wawrən; 'wärən| U.S. family of physicians. **Joseph Warren** (1741–75), a Revolutionary War patriot, was killed at the Battle of Bunker Hill. His brother, **John Warren** (1753–1815), was a leading medical practitioner in New England, a surgeon in the Revolutionary War, and the founder of Harvard Medical School (1783). **John Collins Warren** (1778–1856), son of John Warren, founded Massachusetts General Hospital (1811).

War·ren |'wawrən; 'wärən|, Charles (1868–1954) U.S. attorney and constitutional law scholar. Notable works: *A History of the American Bar...to 1860* (1911), *The Supreme Court in U.S. History* (two vols., revised 1937) and *Congress, the Constitution, and the Supreme Court* (1935).

War·ren |'wawrən; 'wärən|, Earl (1891–1974) Chief Justice of the U.S. (1953–69). He did much to extend civil liberties, including prohibiting segregation in schools. He is also remembered for heading the Warren Commission (1964) into the assassination of President Kennedy.

War·ren |'wawrən; 'wärən|, Leonard (1911–60) U.S. operatic baritone. Born *Leonard Warrenoff.* He sang for 22 seasons with the Metropolitan Opera, beginning with his debut in 1939. He collapsed and died onstage during a battle scene in *La Forza del Destino.*

War·ren |'wawrən; 'wärən|, Mercy Otis (1728–1814) U.S. author and political satirist. Notable works: *The Adulateur* (1773).

War·ren |'wawrən; 'wärən|, Robert Penn (1905–89) U.S. poet, novelist, and critic. An advocate of New Criticism, he was the first person to win Pulitzer Prizes in both fiction and poetry, and in 1986 he was made the first American Poet Laureate.

War·wick |'wawrwik|, Dionne (1941–) U.S. singer. Notable songs: "Do You Know the Way to San Jose" and "I'll Never Fall in Love Again."

War·wick |'wawr(w)ik|, Richard Neville, Earl of (1428–71) English statesman; known as **Warwick the**

Kingmaker. During the Wars of the Roses he fought first on the Yorkist side, helping Edward IV to gain the throne (1461), and then on the Lancastrian side, briefly restoring Henry VI to the throne (1470). Warwick was killed at the Battle of Barnet.

Wash·a·kie |'wäsHəkē| (c. 1804–1900) chief of the Shoshone Indians. He was an ally of the U.S. against the Blackfoot, Cheyenne and Sioux tribes and was given a military funeral.

Wash·ing·ton |'wawSHiNGtən; 'wäSHiNGtən| George, see box. **Martha Dandridge Custis Washington** (1731–

Washington, George
1st U.S. president

Life dates: 1732–1799
Place of birth: Westmoreland County, Va.
Mother: Mary Ball Washington
Father: Augustine Washington
Wife: Martha Dandridge Custis Washington
Children: none
Nickname: "Father of His Country"
College/University: none
Military service: aide-de-camp, French and Indian War; general and commander-in-chief, Army of the United Colonies during the Revolutionary War
Career: Farmer; surveyor; soldier
Political career: Virginia House of Burgesses; First Continental Congress; Second Continental Congress; president
Party: Federalist
Home state: Virginia
Term of office: Apr. 30, 1789–March 3, 1797
Vice president: John Adams
Notable events of presidency: Post Office Department created; first U.S. census; Bank of the United States chartered; District of Columbia established; Vermont admitted as the 14th state; Bill of Rights; Kentucky admitted as 15th state; Tennessee admitted as the 16th state; cornerstone of White House and Capitol laid
Other achievements: commander-in-chief, Virginia armed forces; appointed Lieutenant-General and Commander-in-Chief of all the armies of the United States by President John Adams
Place of burial: Mount Vernon, Va.

1802), wife of George Washington and U.S. first lady (1789–97).

Wash·ing·ton |'wawSHiNGtən; 'wäSHiNGtən|, Booker T. (1856–1915) U.S. educationist; full name *Booker Taliaferro Washington*. A leading commentator for black Americans, Washington established the Tuskegee Institute in Alabama (1881) and published his influential autobiography *Up from Slavery* in 1901. His support for segregation and his emphasis on black people's vocational skills attracted criticism from other black leaders.

Wash·ing·ton |'wawSHiNGtən; 'wäSHiNGtən|, Bushrod (1762–1829) U.S. Supreme Court justice (1798–1829).

Wash·ing·ton |'wawSHiNGtən; 'wäSHiNGtən|, Denzel (1954–) U.S. actor. Notable movies: *Glory* (1989, Academy Award).

Wash·ing·ton |'wawSHiNGtən; 'wäSHiNGtən|, Dinah (1924–63) U.S. jazz singer. Born *Ruth Lee Jones*; known as **the Queen of the Blues**. Notable songs: "What a Difference a Day Makes" (1959).

Wash·ing·ton |'wawSHiNGtən; 'wäSHiNGtən|, Harold (1922–87) U.S. politician. He was the first African-American mayor of Chicago (1983–87).

Was·ser·man |'wäsərmən|, Lew R. (1913–) U.S. corporate executive. Full name *Lewis Robert Wasserman*. He is an executive with Music Corp. of America, Inc.

Was·ser·stein |'wäsər,stīn; 'wäsər,stēn|, Wendy (1950–) U.S. playwright. Notable works: *The Heidi Chronicles* (1989).

Wa·ter·house |'wawtər,hows; 'wätər,hows|, Alfred (1830–1905) English architect.

Wa·ter·house |'wawtər,hows; 'wätər,hows|, Benjamin (1754–1846) U.S. physician. He established a safe vaccination method as a general practice in America.

Wa·ters |'wawtərz; 'wätərz|, Ethel (1896–1977) U.S. jazz and blues singer. He began as "cake-walking baby" and moved to mainstream popular music.

Wa·ters |'wawtərz; 'wätərz|, Muddy (1915–83) U.S. blues singer and guitarist; born *McKinley Morganfield*. He became famous with his song "Rollin' Stone" (1950). Waters impressed new rhythm-and-blues bands such as the Rolling Stones, who took their name from his 1950 song.

Wat·son |'wätsən|, James Dewey (1928–) American biologist. Together with Francis Crick he proposed a model for the structure of the DNA molecule. He shared the Nobel Prize for Physiology or Medicine with Crick and Maurice Wilkins in 1962.

Wat·son |'wätsən|, John Broadus (1878–1958) U.S. psychologist. Founder of the school of behaviorism. He held that the role of the psychologist was to discern, through observation and experimentation, the innate and acquired behavior in an individual.

Wat·son |'wätsən|, Johnny (1935–96) U.S. rhythm and blues guitarist.

Wat·son |'wätsən|, Thomas John (1874–1956) U.S. businessman. He worked for Computing-Tabulating-Recording Co., which became known in 1924 as International Business Machines; he served as the company's president (1914–49) and chairman (1949–56).

Wat·son |'wätsən|, Tom (1949–) U.S. golfer. He is a six-time PGA Player of the Year.

Watson-Watt |ˌwätsən'wät|, Sir Robert Alexander (1892–1973) Scottish physicist. He led a team that developed radar into a practical system for locating aircraft; this played a vital role in the Second World War.

Wat·teau |wä'tō|, Jean Antoine (1684–1721) French painter, of Flemish descent. An initiator of the rococo style, he is also known for his invention of the *fête galante*, the depiction of elegantly dressed people at play in a rural setting.

Wat·ter·son |'wawtərsən; 'wätərsən|, Bill (1958–) U.S. cartoonist and author. He created the comic strip "Calvin and Hobbes."

Wat·ter·son |'wawtərsən; 'wätərsən|, Henry (1840–1921) U.S. journalist. He was editor of the Louisville (Kentucky) *Courier-Journal*, which he controlled for 51 years.

Watts |wäts|, George Frederick (1817–1904) English painter and sculptor. He is best known for his portraits of public figures, including Gladstone, Tennyson, and J. S. Mill. He was married to the actress Ellen Terry from 1864 to 1877.

Watts |wäts|, Isaac (1674–1748) English hymn writer and poet, remembered for hymns such as "O God, Our Help in Ages Past" (1719).

Waugh |waw|, Evelyn (Arthur St. John) (1903–66) English novelist. His work was profoundly influenced by his conversion to Roman Catholicism in 1930. Notable works: *Decline and Fall* (1928); and *Brideshead Revisited* (1945).

Wa·vell |'wävəl|, Archibald Percival, 1st Earl (1883–1950) British army officer. The commander in chief of British forces in the Middle East (1938–41), he was defeated by Rommel; he later became viceroy of India (1943–47).

Wayne |wān|, Anthony (1745–96) American revolutionary officer. Known as **Mad Anthony**. Noted for his courage and military brilliance, he participated in several critical Revolutionary War battles and is credited with saving West Point from British occupation following Benedict Arnold's betrayal. He retired in 1783, but returned to active duty in the 1790s, defeating the Indians at the Battle at Fallen Timbers (1794).

Wayne |wān|, James Moore (1790–1867) U.S. Supreme Court justice (1835–67).

Wayne |wān|, John (1907–79) U.S. actor; born *Marion Michael Morrison*. Associated with the movie director John Ford from 1930, Wayne became a Hollywood star with *Stagecoach* (1939) and appeared in classic westerns such as *Red River* (1948), *The Searchers* (1956) and *True Grit* (1969), for which he won an Oscar.

Webb |web| English socialists, economists, and historians. (Martha) Beatrice Potter Webb (1858–1943) and her husband Sidney (James) Webb, Baron Passfield (1859–1947), were prominent members of the Fabian Society and helped to establish the London School of Economics (1895). They wrote *The History of Trade Unionism* (1894) and *Industrial Democracy* (1897), as well as founding the *New Statesman* (1913).

Webb |web|, Chick (1902–39) U.S. jazz

band leader and drummer. Full name *William Henry Webb*. His band at the Savoy Ballroom in New York, became an outstanding band of the swing period.

Webb |web|, Jack (1920–82) U.S. actor and producer. He starred in the television series "Dragnet" (1952–59, 1967–70).

Webb |web|, Mary (Gladys Meredith) (1881–1927) English novelist. Her novels, such as *Gone to Earth* (1917) and *Precious Bane* (1924), are representative of regional English fiction popular at the beginning of the century.

We·ber |'vābər|, Carl Maria (Friedrich Ernst) von (1786–1826) German composer. He is regarded as the founder of the German romantic school of opera. Notable operas: *Der Freishütz* (1817–21), *Euryanthe* (1822–3).

We·ber |'vābər|, Max (1864–1920) German economist and sociologist, regarded as one of the founders of modern sociology. Notable works: *The Protestant Ethic and the Spirit of Capitalism* (1904) and *Economy and Society* (1922).

We·ber |'vābər|, Wilhelm Eduard (1804–91) German physicist. He proposed a unified system for electrical units and determined the ratio between the units of electrostatic and electromagnetic charge.

We·bern |'vābərn|, Anton (Friedrich Ernst) von (1883–1945) Austrian composer, a leading exponent of atonality and 12-tone composition. His music is marked by its brevity: *Five Pieces for Orchestra* (1911–13) lasts under a minute.

Web·ster |'webstər|, Ben (1909–73) U.S. jazz tenor saxophonist. Full name *Benjamin Francis Webster*. He played with Duke Ellington's band (1940–43).

Web·ster |'webstər|, Daniel (1782–1852) U.S. statesman and lawyer. A famed orator, he represented New Hampshire in the U.S. House of Representatives (1813–17) and Massachusetts in the U.S. House (1823–27) and Senate (1827–41, 1845–50). As secretary of state (1841–43) under President W. H. Harrison, he negotiated the Webster-Ashburton Treaty, which settled boundary disputes with Canada. He was again secretary of state (1850–52) under President Fillmore.

Web·ster |'webstər|, John (*c.* 1580–*c.* 1625) English dramatist. Notable works: *The White Devil* (1612) and *The Duchess of Malfi* (1623), both revenge tragedies.

Web·ster |'webstər|, Noah (1758–1843) U.S. lexicographer. His *American Dictionary of the English Language* (1828) in two volumes and containing 70,000 words was the first dictionary to give comprehensive coverage of American usage.

We·de·kind |'vādə,kint|, Frank (1864–1918) German dramatist. A key figure of expressionist drama, he scandalized contemporary German society with the explicit and sardonic portrayal of sexual awakening in *The Awakening of Spring* (1891).

Wedg·wood |'wej,wŏod|, Josiah (1730–95) English inventor and potter. He founded Wedgwood China and created many patterns for monarchs and aristocrats.

We·ge·ner |'vāgənər|, Alfred Lothar (1880–1930) German meteorologist and geologist. He was the first serious proponent of the theory of continental drift.

Weid·man |'wīdmən|, Jerome (1913–) U.S. author. Notable works: *I Can Get It For You Wholesale* (1937) and, with George Abbott, *Fiorello!* (1960, Pulitzer Prize).

Weil |vīl|, Simone (1909–43) French essayist, philosopher, and mystic. During World War II she joined the resistance movement in England and died of tuberculosis while weakened by voluntary starvation with her French compatriots.

Weill |vīl|, Kurt (Julian) (1900–50) German composer, resident in the U.S. from 1935. He is best known for the operas he wrote with Bertolt Brecht, political satires including *The Threepenny Opera* (1928).

Wein·berg |'wīn,bərg|, Steven (1933–) American theoretical physicist. He devised a theory to unify electromagnetic interactions and the weak forces within the nucleus of an atom, for which he shared the Nobel Prize for Physics in 1979.

Weis·mann |'vīs,män|, August Friedrich Leopold (1834–1914) German biologist and one of the founders of modern genetics. He expounded the theory of germ plasm, which ruled out the transmission of acquired characteristics and suggested that variability in individuals came from the recombination of chromosomes during reproduction.

Weiss·mul·ler |'wīs,mələr|, Johnny (1904–84) U.S. swimmer and actor; full name *Peter John Weissmuller*. He won three Olympic gold medals in 1924 and two in 1928. In the 1930s and 1940s he was the star of the Tarzan movies and later starred on television.

Weiz·mann |'vītsmən|, Chaim (Azriel) (1874–1952) Russian-born Israeli statesman, president (1949–52). He played an important role in persuading the U.S. government to recognize the new state of Israel (1948) and became its first president.

Welch |welCH; welSH|, John Francis, Jr. (1935–) U.S. businessman. He is the CEO of General Electric (1981–).

Welch |welCH; welSH|, Thomas B. (1825–1903) U.S. inventor and businessman. A dentist who invented nonalcoholic grape juice to replace wine used in his church's communion services, he founded Welch's Grape Juice (1869).

Welch |welCH; welSH|, William Henry (1850–1934) U.S. physician. He helped organize the Johns Hopkins Medical School (1893) and Hospital (1889) and made notable contributions to bacteriology and immunology.

Welles |welz|, (George) Orson (1915–85) U.S. movie director and actor. His realistic radio dramatization in 1938 of H. G. Wells's *The War of the Worlds* persuaded many listeners that a Martian invasion was really happening. Notable movies: *Citizen Kane* (1941), *The Lady from Shanghai* (1948), and *The Third Man* (1949).

Wel·ling·ton |'weliNGtən|, Arthur Wellesley, 1st Duke of (1769–1852) British soldier and Tory statesman, prime minister (1828–30 and 1834); known as **the Iron Duke**. He served as commander of the British forces in the Peninsular War (1808–14) and in 1815 defeated Napoleon at the Battle of Waterloo, so ending the Napoleonic Wars.

Wells |welz|, Henry (1805–78) U.S. pioneer in express shipping. He founded the American Express Co. (1850) and (with William G. Fargo) Wells, Fargo & Co. (1852).

Wells |welz|, H. G. (1866–1946) English novelist; full name *Herbert George Wells*. He wrote some of the earliest science-fiction novels, such as *The War of the Worlds* (1898), which combined political satire with warnings about the powers of science.

Wells |welz|, Horace (1815–48) U.S. physician. He discovered anesthesia in the U.S., but his demonstration in 1845 before a Harvard medical class failed.

Wells |welz|, Ida Bell (1862–1931) U.S. journalist. Last name also **Wells-Barnett**. The editor of *Memphis Free Speech* (1891–92), she founded the Negro Fellowship League (1910).

Wells |welz|, Mary (1943–92) U.S. pop singer. She was associated with the Motown sound. Notable songs: "My Guy" (1964).

Wel·ty |'weltē|, Eudora (1909–) U.S. novelist, short-story writer, and critic. Welty's novels chiefly focus on life in the South and contain Gothic elements; they include *The Optimist's Daughter* (1972), which won the Pulitzer Prize. Other works: *Collected Stories of Eudora Welty* (1980).

Wen·ce·slas |'wensəs,läs| (1361–1419) king of Bohemia (as Wenceslas IV, 1378–1419). Also **Wenceslaus**. He became king of Germany, Holy Roman emperor, and king of Bohemia in the same year, but was deposed by the German Electors in 1400.

Wen·ce·slas |'wensəs,läs|, St. (c. 907–929) Duke of Bohemia and patron saint of the Czech Republic. Also **Wenceslaus**; also known as **Good King Wenceslas**. He worked to Christianize the people of Bohemia but was murdered by his brother; he later became venerated as a martyr. Feast day, September 28.

Wer·ner |'vernər|, Abraham Gottlob (1749–1817) German geologist. He was the chief exponent of the theory of Neptunism, eventually shown to be incorrect, and attempted to establish a universal stratigraphic sequence.

Wes·ley |'weslē; 'wezlē|, John (1703–91) English preacher and cofounder of Methodism. Wesley was a committed Christian evangelist who won many working-class converts, often through open-air preaching. The opposition they encountered from the Church establishment led to the Methodists forming a separate denomination in 1791. His brother **Charles** (1707–88) was also a founding Methodist, and both wrote many hymns.

Wes·son |'wesən|, Daniel Baird (1825–1906) U.S. inventor and manufacturer. With Horace Smith he patented and manufactured revolvers (1854, 1857).

West |west|, Benjamin (1738–1820) U.S. painter, resident in Britain from 1763. He became historical painter to George III in 1769 and the second president of the Royal Academy in 1792. Notable works: *The Death of General Wolfe* (1771).

West |west|, Dorothy (1907–98) U.S. author. A writer of the Harlem Renaissance, she became a best-selling novelist at age 88 with *The Wedding* (1995).

West |west|, Dottie (1932–91) U.S. country singer and songwriter. Her Grand Ole Opry songs include "Here Comes My Baby."

West |west|, Jerry (1938–) U.S. basketball player and team executive. His silhouette serves as the NBA's logo. Elected to the Basketball Hall of Fame (1979).

West |west|, Mae (c. 1892–1980) U.S. actress and author. She made her name on Broadway in her own comedies *Sex* (1926) and *Diamond Lil* (1928), memorable for their spirited approach to sexual matters, before embarking on her successful Hollywood career in the 1930s.

West |west|, Nathanael (1903–40) U.S. novelist. Pseudonym of *Nathan Wallenstein Weinstein*. He wrote mainly during the Great Depression of the 1930s. Notable works: *Miss Lonelyhearts* (1933) and *The Day of the Locust* (1959).

West |west|, Dame Rebecca (1892–1983) Irish-born British writer and feminist; born *Cicily Isabel Fairfield*. She is best remembered for her study of the Nuremberg trials, *The Meaning of Treason* (1949). Other notable works: *The Fountain Overflows* (novel, 1957).

West·hei·mer |'west,hīmər|, (Karola) Ruth Siegel (1929–) U.S. psychologist, born in Germany. Known as **Dr. Ruth**. In her radio and television talk shows she dispenses advice on sexual matters.

West·ing·house |'westiNG,hows|, George (1846–1914) U.S. inventor and manufacturer. His achievements covered several fields, but he is best known for developing vacuum-operated safety brakes and electrically controlled signals for railways. He built up a huge company, Westinghouse Electric, to manufacture his products.

Wes·ton |'westən|, Edward (1886–1958) U.S. photographer. A pioneer of modern photography with an emphasis on sharp realism, he is known for his landscapes of the American West.

West·o·ver |'wes,tōvər|, Russ (1887–1966) U.S. cartoonist. Full name *Russell Channing Westover*. He created the popular flapper comic strip "Tillie the Toiler."

Wex·ler |'wekslər|, Jerry (1917–) U.S. record producer. He is credited with coining the term "rhythm and blues," a label he used to describe black popular music in his *Billboard* column (1948–51). As co-owner of Atlantic Records (1953–78), he produced the works of such recording artists as Ray Charles, Otis Redding, Aretha Franklin, and Wilson Pickett.

Wey·den |'vīdn|, Rogier van der (c. 1400–64) Flemish painter; French name *Rogier de la Pasture*. He was particularly influential in the development of Dutch portrait painting. Notable works: *The Last Judgment* and *The Deposition in the Tomb* (both c.1450).

Whar·ton |'(h)wawrtn|, Edith (Newbold) (1862–1937) U.S. novelist and short-story writer, resident in France from 1907. Her novels are concerned with the conflict between social and individual fulfillment. They include *The Age of Innocence* (1920), which won a Pulitzer Prize.

Wheat·ley |'(h)wētlē|, Phillis (c. 1752–

84) U.S. poet. She was born in Africa and sold as a slave at age eight to the John Wheatley family of Boston. She was educated by them and then sent to London, where she published her first volume of poems, *Poems on Various Subjects, Religious and Moral* (1773). Her *Memoirs and Poems* were published in 1834.

Whea·ton |'(h)wētn|, Henry (1785–1848) U.S. jurist and diplomat. Notable works: *Elements of International Law* (1836) and *History of the Law of Nations* (1845).

Wheat·stone |'(h)wēt,stōn|, Sir Charles (1802–75) English physicist and inventor. He is best known for his electrical inventions, which included an electric clock, the Wheatstone bridge, the rheostat, and, with Sir W. F. Cooke, the electric telegraph.

Whee·ler |'(h)wēlər|, John Archibald (1911–) U.S. theoretical physicist. He worked with Niels Bohr on nuclear fission, and collaborated with Richard Feynman on problems concerning the retarded effects of action at a distance. He coined the term "black hole" in 1968.

Whee·ler |'(h)wēlər|, William Almon (1819–87) vice president of the U.S. (1877–81).

Whee·lock |'(h)wē,läk|, Eleazar (1711–79) U.S. clergyman and educator. He founded Dartmouth College (1769) and served as its first president (1770–79).

Whip·ple |'(h)wipəl|, Fred Lawrence (1906–) U.S. astronomer. He discovered six new comets.

Whis·tler |'(h)wislər|, James (Abbott) McNeill (1834–1903) U.S. painter and etcher. Notable works: *Arrangement in Gray and Black: The Artist's Mother* (portrait, 1872).

White |(h)wīt| U.S. family, including: **Richard Grant White** (1821–85), author and literary critic. His edition of Shakespeare was republished as the Riverside text. **Stanford White** (1853–1906), his son, an architect. Notable designs: the Washington Arch in Washington Square Park (New York) and Madison Square Garden (New York).

White |(h)wīt|, Andrew Dickson (1832–1918) U.S. educator and diplomat. With Ezra Cornell, he cofounded Cornell University and served as its first president (1867–85); he was also first president of the American Historical Association and chairman of the U.S. delegation to the Hague Peace Conference (1899).

White |(h)wīt|, Byron R. (1917–) U.S. Supreme Court justice (1962–93).

White |(h)wīt|, E. B. (1899–85) U.S. author. Full name *Elwyn Brooks White*. He was a chief contributor to *The New Yorker* and the author of the children's classics *Stuart Little* (1945) and *Charlotte's Web* (1952). Special Pulitzer Prize, 1978.

White |(h)wīt|, Edward Douglas (1845–1921) Chief Justice of the U.S. (1910–21) and U.S. Supreme Court justice (1894–1910).

White |(h)wīt|, Edward Higgins, II (1930–67) U.S. astronaut. The first U.S. astronaut to maneuver in space outside a spacecraft (1965), he was killed in a flash fire in the Apollo 1 capsule.

White |(h)wīt|, John (c. 1577–c. 1593) English artist. He was a Virginia colonist on Roanoke Island (1585); his watercolors were the first authentic pictorial records of life in the New World.

White |(h)wīt|, Patrick (Victor Martindale) (1912–90) Australian novelist, born in Britain. White's reputation is chiefly based on his two novels *The Tree of Man* (1955) and *Voss* (1957). Nobel Prize for Literature (1973).

White |(h)wīt|, Paul Dudley (1886–) U.S. physician. A heart specialist and the author of *Heart Disease* (1931), he was Eisenhower's specialist at the time of the president's heart attack (1955).

White |(h)wīt|, Pearl Fay (1889–1938) U.S. actress. Her movie credits include *The Perils of Pauline* (1914).

White |(h)wīt|, T. H. (1906–64) British novelist, born in India; full name *Terence Hanbury White*. He is best known for the tetralogy *The Once and Future King*, his reworking of the Arthurian legend that began with *The Sword in the Stone* (1937).

White |(h)wīt|, Walter Francis (1893–1955) U.S. civil rights leader and author. He served as executive secretary of the NAACP (1931–55).

White |(h)wīt|, William Allen (1868–

1944) U.S. journalist. Known as the **Sage of Emporia**. He edited Kansas's *Emporia Gazette* from 1895; he won a Pulitzer Prize for his editorials (1923) and another for his autobiography (1946).

White·head |'(h)wīt,hed|, Alfred North (1861–1947) English philosopher and mathematician. He is remembered chiefly for *Principia Mathematica* (1910–13), on which he collaborated with his pupil Bertrand Russell.

White·man |'(h)wītmən|, Paul (1891–1967) U.S. symphony conductor. Known as **Pops**. He conducted the premiere of George Gershwin's *Rhapsody in Blue* (1924), which introduced symphonic jazz.

Whit·lam |'(h)witləm|, (Edward) Gough (1916–) Australian Labour statesman and prime minister (1972–75). Whitlam ended compulsory military service and relaxed the immigration laws. In 1975 he refused to call a general election and became the first elected prime minister to be dismissed by the British Crown.

Whit·man |'(h)witmən|, Marcus (1802–47) U.S. missionary physician and pioneer. He was murdered in Oregon by Cayuse Indians.

Whit·man |'(h)witmən|, Charles Otis (1842–1910) U.S. zoologist. He was the founder and first director of the Marine Biological Laboratory at Woods Hole, Massachusetts (1893–1908).

Whit·man |'(h)witmən|, Christine Todd (1946–) U.S. politician and governor of New Jersey (1994–).

Whit·man |'(h)witmən|, Walt (1819–92) U.S. poet; full name *Walter Whitman*. In 1855 he published the free verse collection *Leaves of Grass*, incorporating "I Sing the Body Electric" and "Song of Myself"; eight further editions followed in Whitman's lifetime. Other notable works: *Drum-Taps* (1865) and *Sequel to Drum-Taps* (1865).

Whit·ney |'(h)witnē| U.S. family, including: **Josiah Dwight Whitney** (1819–96). He was the state geologist of California (1860–74) and the person for whom Mount Whitney was named. **William Dwight Whitney** (1827–94), his brother, a philologist and educator.

He edited the *Century Dictionary* (1889–91).

Whit·ney |'(h)witnē|, Eli (1765–1825) U.S. inventor. He is best known for his invention of the cotton gin (patented 1794), a machine for automating the removal of seeds from raw cotton. He also is known to have developed the idea of mass-producing interchangeable parts. This he applied in his fulfillment of a contract (1797) to supply muskets for the U.S. government.

Whit·ney |'(h)witnē|, Gertrude Vanderbilt (1876–1942) U.S. sculptor and philanthropist. She sculpted the *Titanic Memorial* in Washington, D.C., and founded the Whitney Museum of American Art, the first museum in the U.S. devoted exclusively to native art (1931). Daughter of Cornelius Vanderbilt.

Whit·ney |'(h)witnē|, William Collins (1841–1904) U.S. financier and politician. As U.S. secretary of the navy (1885–89), he laid the basis for the modern "steel navy."

Whit·ta·ker |'(h)witikər|, Charles Evans (1901–73) U.S. Supreme Court justice (1957–62).

Whit·ti·er |'(h)witēər|, John Greenleaf (1807–92) U.S. poet and abolitionist. He is best known for his poems on rural themes, especially "Snow-Bound" (1866).

Whit·ting·ton |'(h)witiNGtən|, Dick (*c.* 1358–1423) English merchant and Lord Mayor of London; full name *Sir Richard Whittington*. He was a dry goods merchant who became Lord Mayor three times (1397–98; 1406–07; 1419–20). The legend of his early life as a poor orphan was first recorded in 1605.

Whit·tle |'(h)witl|, Sir Frank (1907–96) English aeronautical engineer, test pilot, and inventor of the jet aircraft engine. He took out the first patent for a turbojet engine in 1930, and in 1941 the first flight using Whittle's jet engine was made.

Whit·worth |'(h)wit,wərTH|, Kathy (1939–) U.S. golfer. She is a seven-time LPGA Player of the Year.

Whorf |wawrf|, Benjamin Lee (1897–1941) U.S. linguist and insurance executive, known for his contribution to the Sapir-Whorf hypothesis, which states that the structure of a language influences the culture in which it is spoken.

Whym·per |'(h)wimpər|, Edward (1840–1911) English mountaineer. After seven attempts he finally succeeded in climbing the Matterhorn in 1865, but on the way down, four of his fellow climbers fell to their deaths.

Wide·man |'wīdmən|, John Edgar (1941–) U.S. author. Notable works: *Fatheralong: A Meditation on Father and Sons, Race and Society* (1994).

Wie·ner |'wēnər|, Norbert (1894–1964) American mathematician. He is best known for establishing the science of cybernetics in the late 1940s. Wiener made major contributions to the study of stochastic processes, integral equations, harmonic analysis, and related fields.

Wie·sel |vē'zel|, Elie (1928–) Romanian-born U.S. human rights campaigner, novelist, and academic; full name *Eliezer Wiesel*. A survivor of Auschwitz and Buchenwald concentration camps, Wiesel became an authority on the Holocaust, documenting and publicizing Nazi war crimes. Nobel Peace Prize (1986).

Wie·sen·thal |'vēzən,täl; 'wēzən,THäl|, Simon (1908–) Austrian Jewish investigator of Nazi war crimes. After spending three years in concentration camps, he began a campaign to bring Nazi war criminals to justice, tracing some 1,000 unprosecuted criminals, including Adolf Eichmann.

Wig·gin |'wigən|, Kate Douglas (1856–1923) U.S. author. Notable works: *Rebecca of Sunnybrook Farm* (1903).

Wig·gles·worth |'wigəlz,wərTH|, Michael (1631–1705) U.S. clergyman and poet, born in England. Notable works include the theological poem *The Day of Doom* (1662).

Wig·more |'wig,mawr|, John Henry (1863–1943) U.S. legal scholar. The dean of the law faculty at Northwestern University (1901–29), he wrote the *Treatise on the Anglo-American System of Evidence* (1904–5).

Wig·ner |'wignər|, Eugene Paul (1902–) U.S. mathematical physicist, born in Hungary. He formulated the laws governing the mechanics of nuclear

particles and shared a Nobel Prize with Maria Mayer and J. H. D. Jensen (1963).

Wil·ber·force |'wilbər,fawrs|, William (1759–1833) English politician and social reformer. He was a prominent campaigner for the abolition of the slave trade, his efforts resulting in its outlawing in the British West Indies (1807) and in the 1833 Slavery Abolition Act.

Wil·bur |'wilbər|, Richard (Purdy) (1921–) U.S. poet and professor. Poet Laureate of the U.S., 1987–88. Notable works: *Things of This World* (1956, Pulitzer Prize), *New and Collected Poems* (1988), and *Runaway Opposites* (1995).

Wil·cox |'wil,käks|, Ella Wheeler (1850–1919) U.S. poet, novelist, and short-story writer. She wrote many volumes of romantic verse, the most successful one being *Poems of Passion* (1883).

Wilde |wīld|, Oscar (Fingal O'Flahertie Wills) (1854–1900) Irish dramatist, novelist, poet, and wit. His advocacy of "art for art's sake" is evident in his only novel, *The Picture of Dorian Gray* (1890). As a dramatist he achieved success with the comedies *Lady Windermere's Fan* (1892) and *The Importance of Being Earnest* (1895). Wilde was imprisoned (1895–97) for homosexual offenses and died in exile.

Wil·der |'wīldər|, Billy (1906–) Austrian-born U.S. movie director and screenwriter; born *Samuel Wilder*. He earned recognition as a writer-director with the *film noir* classic *Double Indemnity* (1944). Other movies include *Sunset Boulevard* (1950), *Some Like It Hot* (1959), and *The Apartment* (1960), which won three Oscars.

Wil·der |'wīldər|, Gene (1935–) U.S. actor. Born *Jerome Silberman*. He cowrote and starred in *Young Frankenstein* (1974) and *Blazing Saddles* (1973).

Wil·der |'wīldər|, Laura Ingalls (1867–1957) U.S. author. Notable works: *Little House on the Prairie* (1935).

Wil·der |'wīldər|, Thornton (Niven) (1897–1975) U.S. novelist and dramatist. He won several Pulitzer Prizes. Notable works: *The Bridge of San Luis Rey* (novel, 1927), *Our Town* (play, 1938), and *Skin of Our Teeth* (play, 1942).

Wil·helm I |'vil,helm| (1797–1888) king of Prussia (1861–88) and emperor of

Germany (1871–88). His reign saw the unification of Germany. He became the first emperor of Germany after Prussia's victory against France in 1871. The latter part of his reign was marked by the rise of German socialism, to which he responded with harsh, repressive measures.

Wil·helm II |'vil,helm| (1859–1941) emperor of Germany 1888–1918, grandson of Wilhelm I and also of Queen Victoria; known as **Kaiser Wilhelm**. After forcing Bismarck to resign in 1890, he proved unable to exercise a strong or consistent influence over German policies. He was vilified by Allied propaganda as the instigator of the First World War. In 1918 he abdicated and went into exile.

Wil·hel·mi·na |ˌvilhel'mēnə| (1880–1962) queen of the Netherlands 1890–1948. During World War II she maintained a government in exile in London and through frequent radio broadcasts became a symbol of resistance among the Dutch people. She returned to the Netherlands in 1945.

Wil·kens |'wilkənz|, Lenny (1937–) U.S. basketball player and coach. He was inducted into the Basketball Hall of Fame in 1988.

Wilkes |wilks|, Charles (1798–1877) U.S. naval officer. He was the surveyor who determined that Antarctica is a continent (1838–42); Wilkes Land was named in his honor.

Wil·kie |'wilkē|, Sir David (1785–1841) Scottish painter. He made his name with the painting *Village Politicians* (1806). His style contributed to the growing prestige of genre painting.

Wil·kins |'wilkənz|, Maurice Hugh Frederick (1916–) New Zealand-born British biochemist and molecular biologist. From X-ray diffraction analysis of DNA, he and his colleague Rosalind Franklin confirmed the double helix structure proposed by Francis Crick and James Watson in 1953. Nobel Prize for Physiology or Medicine (1962, shared with Crick and Watson).

Wil·kins |'wilkənz|, Roy (1901–81) U.S. civil rights leader. He served as executive secretary of the NAACP (1955–77). Presidential Medal of Freedom, 1969.

Will |wil|, George F. (1941–) U.S. journalist. A columnist and television commentator, he won a Pulitzer Prize for commentary (1977).

Wil·lard |'wilərd|, Archibald MacNeal (1836–1918) U.S. painter. His *Yankee Doodle, or the Spirit of '76* was exhibited at the Centennial exposition in Philadelphia (1876).

Wil·lard |'wilərd|, Emma (1787–1870) U.S. educational reformer. She founded a boarding school in Vermont (1814) to teach subjects not then available to women, such as mathematics and philosophy. The school moved to New York (1821) as the Troy Female Seminary; it served as a model for subsequent women's colleges in the U.S. and Europe.

Wil·lard |'wilərd|, Frances Elizabeth Caroline (1839–98) U.S. women's rights and temperance activist. She was president of the Women's Christian Temperance Union (1879) and an organizer of the Prohibition party.

Wil·lard |'wilərd|, Frank (1893–1958) U.S. cartoonist. He created the comic strip "Moon Mullins" in the early 1920s.

Wil·liam |'wilyəm| (c. 1027–87) the name of two kings of England and two of Great Britain and Ireland: **William I** (c. 1027–87), reigned 1066–87, the first Norman king of England; known as **William the Conqueror**. He invaded England and defeated Harold II at the Battle of Hastings (1066). He introduced Norman institutions and customs (including feudalism) and instigated the Domesday Book. **William II** (c. 1060–1100), son of William I, reigned 1087–1100; known as **William Rufus**. William crushed rebellions in 1088 and 1095 and also campaigned against his brother Robert, Duke of Normandy (1089–96), ultimately acquiring the duchy. He was killed by an arrow while out hunting. **William III** (1650–1702), grandson of Charles I, husband of Mary II, reigned 1689–1702; known as **William of Orange**. In 1688 he deposed James II at the invitation of disaffected politicians and, having accepted the Declaration of Rights, was crowned along with his wife Mary.

William IV (1765–1837), son of George III, reigned 1830–37; known as **the Sailor King**. Having served in the Royal Navy, he came to the throne after the death of his brother George IV. In 1834 he intervened in political affairs by imposing the Conservative Robert Peel as Prime Minister, despite a Whig majority in Parliament.

Wil·liam I[1] |'wilyəm| (1143–1214) grandson of David I, king of Scotland (1165–1214); known as **William the Lion**. He attempted to reassert Scottish independence but was forced to pay homage to Henry II of England after being captured by him in 1174.

Wil·liam I[2] |'wilyəm| (1533–84) prince of the House of Orange, chief magistrate of the United Provinces of the Netherlands (1572–84); known as **William the Silent**. He led a revolt against Spain from 1568 and was assassinated by a Spanish agent.

Wil·liam of Oc·cam |'wilyəm əv 'äkəm| (c. 1285–1349) English philosopher and Franciscan friar. Also **Ockham**. He is known for the maxim called "Occam's razor," which states that in explaining a thing, no more assumptions should be made than are necessary.

Wil·liam of Orange |'wilyəm| William III of Great Britain and Ireland (see WILLIAM).

Wil·liam Rufus |'wilyəm 'roofəs| William II of of England (see WILLIAM).

Wil·liams |'wilyəmz| U.S. country singers and songwriters: **Hank Williams** (1923–53); born *Hiram King Williams*. He had the first of many country hits, "Lovesick Blues," in 1949; "Your Cheatin' Heart" (recorded 1952) was released after his sudden death. **Hank Williams, Jr.**, his son. Notable songs: "Texas Women" (1981).

Wil·liams |'wilyəmz|, Cootie (1911–85) U.S. jazz trumpeter and band leader. Full name *Charles Melvin Williams*. He performed with Duke Ellington (1929–40), who was inpired by his playing to write "Concerto for Cootie" (1940) and "New Concerto for Cootie" (1963).

Wil·liams |'wilyəmz|, Daniel Hale (1858–1931) U.S. physician. He performed one of the first two open-heart operations (1893) and was the first African American elected as a fellow of the American College of Surgeons.

Wil·liams |'wilyəmz|, Ephraim (1714–55) U.S. army officer. He served as captain of the Massachusetts militia patrolling the northern Massachusetts border. He bequeathed funds for the school that became Williams College.

Wil·liams |'wilyəmz|, Jody (1950–) U.S. political activst. She won a Nobel Peace Prize in 1997 for her work to ban landmines.

Wil·liams |'wilyəmz|, John (1664–1729) U.S. clergyman and author. He was taken captive by Indians and ransomed (1706); after his release he wrote *The Redeemed Captive Returning to Zion* (1707).

Wil·liams |'wilyəmz|, John Towner (1932–) U.S. composer and conductor. He conducted the Boston Pops Orchestra (1980–98) and wrote the movie scores to *Jaws*, the *Star Wars* trilogy, *Raiders of the Lost Ark*, and *Close Encounters of the Third Kind*.

Wil·liams |'wilyəmz|, J. R. (1888–1957) U.S. cartoonist, born in Canada. Full name *James Robert Williams*. He created the panel "Out Our Way" in 1922.

Wil·liams |'wilyəmz|, Mary Lou (1914–81) U.S. jazz pianist and composer. She composed "Trumpet No End" (1946) for Duke Ellington; her sacred works include *Christ of the Andes* (1963) and three masses.

Wil·liams |'wilyəmz|, Robert R., Jr. (1886–1965) Indian inventor. He synthesized Vitamin B[1].

Wil·liams |'wilyəmz|, Robin (1952–) U.S. actor. His stage, television, and film credits include *Dead Poets Society* (1989) and *Mrs. Doubtfire* (1993).

Wil·liams |'wilyəmz|, Roger (c. 1603–83) American clergyman and founder of Rhode Island (1644).

Wil·liams |'wilyəmz|, Ted (1918–) U.S. baseball player. Full name *Theodore Samuel Williams*. He was the last player to bat over .400 for a season (1941). Elected to the Baseball Hall of Fame (1966).

Wil·liams |'wilyəmz|, Tennessee (1911–83) U.S. dramatist; born *Thomas Lanier Williams*. He achieved success with *The

Glass Menagerie (1944) and *A Streetcar Named Desire* (1947), which deal with the tragedy of vulnerable heroines living in fragile fantasy worlds shattered by brutal reality. Other notable works: *Cat on a Hot Tin Roof* (1955) and *The Night of the Iguana* (1962).

Wil·liams |'wilyəmz|, William Carlos (1883–1963) U.S. physician and writer. His poetry is characterized by avoidance of emotional content and the use of American vernacular. Collections include *Spring and All* (1923).

Wil·liam·son |'wilyəmsən|, Henry (1895–1977) English novelist. His works include *Tarka the Otter* (1927) and the fifteen-volume semi-autobiographical sequence *A Chronicle of Ancient Sunlight* (1951–69).

Wi·liam the Conqueror |'wilyəm| William I of England (see WILLIAM).

Will·kie |'wilkē|, Wendell Lewis (1882–1944) U.S. politician and lawyer. He was a Republican presidential candidate (1940).

Wills |wilz|, Bob (1905–75) U.S. country singer, bandleader, and songwriter. Full name *Robert James Wills*. His group, the Texas Playboys, popularized western swing.

Wil·son |'wilsən|, Sir Angus (Frank Johnstone) (1913–91) English novelist and short-story writer. His works display his satiric wit, acute social observation, and a love of the macabre and the farcical. Notable novels: *The Old Men at the Zoo* (1961).

Wil·son |'wilsən|, August (1945–) U.S. author and playwright. Notable works: *Fences* (1986, Pulitzer Prize), *The Piano Lesson* (1990, Pulitzer Prize), and *Seven Guitars* (1996).

Wil·son |'wilsən|, Brian (1942–) U.S. rock musician. He popularized the California surfing sound of the Beach Boys, which he formed in 1961 with his brothers Dennis Wilson (1944–83) and Carl Wilson (1946–).

Wil·son |'wilsən|, Charles Thomson Rees (1869–1959) Scottish physicist. He is chiefly remembered for inventing the cloud chamber, which became a major tool of particle physicists. Nobel Prize for Physics (1927).

Wil·son |'wilsən|, Edmund (1895–

1972) U.S. critic, essayist, and short-story writer. He is remembered chiefly for works of literary and social criticism, including *Axel's Castle* (1931), *To the Finland Station* (1940), and *Patriotic Gore: Studies in the Literature of the American Civil War* (1962).

Wil·son |'wilsən|, Edward Osborne (1929–) American social biologist. He has worked principally on social insects, extrapolating his findings to the social behavior of other animals including humans. Notable works: *Sociobiology: the New Synthesis* (1975).

Wil·son |'wilsən|, Gahan (1930–) U.S. cartoonist and author. His macabre cartoons were mainly published in *Playboy* magazine.

Wil·son |'wilsən|, (James) Harold, Baron Wilson of Rievaulx (1916–95) British Labour statesman, prime minister (1964–70 and 1974–76). In both terms of office he faced severe economic problems. His government introduced a number of social reforms and renegotiated Britain's terms of entry into the European Economic Community, which was confirmed after a referendum in 1975.

Wil·son |'wilsən|, Harriet (1808–*c.* 1870) U.S. author. She wrote *Our Nig: Sketches from the Life of a Free Black, in a Two-Story White House, North, Showing That Slavery's Shadows Fall Even There* (1859), the first novel by an African American published in the U.S.

Wil·son |'wilsən|, Harry Leon (1867–1939) U.S. author. Notable works: *Merton of the Movies* (1922).

Wil·son |'wilsən|, Henry (1812–75) U.S. politician. Born *Jeremiah Jones Colbath*. He was a founder of the Republican party, a member of the U.S. Senate from Massachusetts (1855–73), and vice president of the U.S. (1873–75).

Wil·son |'wilsən|, James (1742–98) U.S. Supreme Court justice (1789–98).

Wil·son |'wilsən|, John Tuzo (1908–93) Canadian geophysicist. Wilson was a pioneer in the study of plate tectonics, introducing the term *plate* in this context and identifying transform faults.

Wil·son |'wilsən|, Lanford (1937–) U.S. playwright. Notable works: *Talley's Folly* (1979, Pulitzer Prize).

> **Wilson, Woodrow**
> *28th U.S. president*
>
> **Life dates:** 1856–1924
> **Place of birth:** Staunton, Virginia
> **Mother:** Janet (Jessie) Woodrow Wilson
> **Father:** Joseph Ruggles Wilson
> **Wives:** Ellen Louise Axson Wilson (died 1914); Edith Bolling Galt Wilson (married 1915)
> **Children:** Margaret, Jessie Woodrow, Eleanor
> **College/University:** Princeton University; University of Virginia Law School; Johns Hopkins University
> **Career:** Lawyer; professor
> **Political career:** governor of New Jersey
> **Party:** Democratic
> **Home state:** New Jersey
> **Opponents in presidential races:** William Howard Taft, Theodore Roosevelt; Charles Evans Hughes
> **Term of office:** March 4, 1913–March 3, 1921
> **Vice president:** Thomas R. Marshall
> **Notable events of presidency:** Federal Reserve Act; Federal Trade Commission established; Clayton Anti-Trust Act; World War I; sinking of the *Lusitania*; Fourteen Points speech to Congress; 18th Amendment to the Constitution ratified (Prohibition)
> **Other achievements:** Ph.D. in political science from Johns Hopkins University; president, Princeton University; awarded 1919 Nobel Peace Prize
> **Place of burial:** Washington, D.C.

Wil·son |'wilsən|, Nancy Sue (1937–) U.S. jazz and pop singer.

Wil·son |'wilsən|, Teddy (1912–86) U.S. jazz pianist. Full name *Theodore Shaw Wilson*. He performed with Benny Goodman (1935–39).

Wil·son |'wilsən|, Tom (1931–) U.S. cartoonist. He created the cartoon character Ziggy.

Wil·son |'wilsən| (Thomas) Woodrow, see box. **Ellen Louise Axson Wilson** (1860–1914), wife of Woodrow Wilson and U.S. first lady (1913–14). **Edith Bolling Galt Wilson** (1872–1961), wife of Woodrow Wilson and U.S. first lady (1915–21).

Winck·el·mann |'viNGkəl‚män|, Johann (Joachim) (1717–68) German archaeologist and art historian, born in Prussia. He took part in the excavations at Pompeii and Herculaneum and his best-known work, *History of the Art of Antiquity* (1764), was particularly influential in popularizing the art and culture of ancient Greece.

Wind·ing, Kai (1922–83) U.S. jazz trombonist, born in Denmark.

Wind·sor, Duke of |'winzər|, the title conferred on Edward VIII on his abdication in 1936.

Wines |wīnz|, Enoch Cobb (1806–79) U.S. reformer. He tried to make prisons into places of reform and correction instead of punishment.

Win·frey |'winfrē|, Oprah (1954–) U.S. actress and television talk show host. She began her confessional-style "Oprah Winfrey Show" in 1986.

Win·ston |'winstən|, Harry (1896–1978) U.S. businessman. He founded a famous jewelry store in New York City.

Win·ter·hal·ter |'vintər‚hältər|, Franz Xaver (1806–73) German painter. He painted many portraits of European royalty and aristocracy.

Win·ter·son |'wintərsən|, Jeanette (1959–) English writer. She has received several honors for her fiction, including a Whitbread Award (1985).

Win·throp |'winTHrəp|, American colonists and politicians, born in England: **John Winthrop** (1588–1649) was the first governor of the Massachusetts Bay Colony (from 1629). **John Winthrop, Jr.**, his eldest son (1606–76), was an early astronomer and the governor of Connecticut (1657, 1659–76).

Win·throp |'winTHrəp|, John (1714–79) U.S. astronomer and physicist. He was the first American to practice rigorous experimental science, predicting the return of Halley's Comet in 1759 and giving laboratory demonstrations of electricity (1746). He was descended from Governor John Winthrop.

Win·tour |'wintər|, Anna (1949–) U.S. journalist, born in England. She was creative director of *Vogue* (1983–86) and editor of *House and Garden* (1987–88).

Win·wood |'win‚wŏŏd|, Steve (1948–) British pop musician. Notable songs: "Higher Love" (1986, Grammy Award).

Wise |wīz|, Isaac Mayer (1819–1900) U.S. rabbi and scholar, born in Germany. Born *Isaac Mayer Weis*. He founded Reformed Judaism in the U.S. and established Hebrew Union College (1875).

Wise |wīz|, John (1652–1725) American clergyman. He was a Congregational pastor in Ipswich, Massachusetts, who opposed the Mathers' attempts to regulate churches. Notable works: *A Vindication of the Government of New England Churches* (1717).

Wis·sler |'wislər|, Clark (1870–1947) U.S. anthropologist and author. He was the curator of the American Museum of Natural History (1906–41).

Wis·tar |'wistər|, Caspar (1761–1818) U.S. educator and author. He was a professor of anatomy at the University of Pennsylvania and a leader in the intellectual life of Philadelphia; the genus *Wisteria* was named for him.

With·er·spoon |'wiTHər,spoon|, John (1723–94) colonial American clergyman and educator, born in Scotland. As president of the College of New Jersey (now Princeton University) (1768–94), he was a signer of the Declaration of Independence and a member of the Continental Congress (1776–79, 1780–81).

Witt |vit|, Katarina (1965–) German figure skater. A four-time world champion, she won Olympic gold medals for East Germany in 1984 and 1988.

Witt·gen·stein |'vitgən,SHtīn|, Ludwig (Josef Johann) (1889–1951) British philosopher, born in Austria. His two major works, *Tractatus Logico-Philosophicus* (1921) and *Philosophical Investigations* (1953), examine language and its relationship to the world.

Władysław II see LADISLAUS II.

Wode·house |'wood,hows|, Sir P. G. (1881–1975) English writer; full name *Pelham Grenville Wodehouse*. His best-known works are humorous stories of the upper-class world of Bertie Wooster and his valet, Jeeves.

Wolf |woolf|, Hugo (Philipp Jakob) (1860–1903) Austrian composer. He is chiefly known as a composer of lieder, some of which are settings of Goethe and Heinrich Heine.

Wolfe |woolf|, James (1727–59) British

general. One of the leaders of the expedition sent to seize French Canada, he commanded the attack on the French capital, Quebec (1759). He was fatally wounded while leading his troops to victory on the Plains of Abraham, the scene of the battle that led to British control of Canada.

Wolfe |woolf|, Thomas (Clayton) (1900–38) U.S. novelist. His intense, romantic works, including his first, autobiographical novel, *Look Homeward Angel* (1929), dwell idealistically on America. Other notable works: *Of Time and the River* (1935), *The Web and the Rock* (1938), and *You Can't Go Home Again* (1940).

Wolfe |woolf|, Tom (1931–) U.S. writer; born *Thomas Kennerley Wolfe, Jr.* Having been a news reporter for the *Washington Post* and the *Herald Tribune*, he examined contemporary American culture in *The Electric Kool-Aid Acid Test* (1968), the novel *The Bonfire of the Vanities* (1988), and *A Man in Full* (1998).

Wolff |woolf|, Tobias (1945–) U.S. author. Notable works: *This Boy's Life: A Memoir* (1989).

Wolf·man Jack see SMITH, ROBERT WESTON.

Wol·las·ton |'woolastan|, William Hyde (1766–1828) English chemist and physicist. He discovered palladium and rhodium, and pioneered techniques in powder metallurgy. Wollaston also demonstrated that static and current electricity were the same, invented a kind of slide rule for use in chemistry, and was the first to observe the dark lines in the solar spectrum.

Woll·stone·craft |'woolstan,kræft|, Mary (1759–97) English writer and feminist, of Irish descent. Her best-known work, *A Vindication of the Rights of Woman* (1792), defied assumptions about male supremacy and championed educational equality for women. In 1797 she married William Godwin and died shortly after giving birth to their daughter, Mary Shelley.

Wol·per |'wōlpər|, David Lloyd (1928–) U.S. movie and television executive. He is the president of Wolper Pictures, Ltd. (1958–) and an executive producer at Warner Bros., Inc. (1976–).

Wol•sey |'wo͝olzē|, Thomas (*c.* 1474–1530) English prelate and statesman; known as **Cardinal Wolsey**. Wolsey dominated foreign and domestic policy in the early part of Henry VIII's reign, but incurred royal displeasure through his failure to secure the papal dispensation necessary for Henry's divorce from Catherine of Aragon. He was arrested on a charge of treason and died on his way to trial.

Won•der |'wəndər|, Stevie (1950–) U.S. singer, songwriter, and musician; born *Steveland Judkins Morris*. His repertoire has included soul, rock, funk, and romantic ballads, as heard on albums such as *Innervisions* (1973). He has been blind since birth.

Wood |wo͝od|, Mrs. Henry (1814–87) English novelist; born *Ellen Price*. Her ingenious and sensational plots about murders, thefts, and forgeries make her one of the forerunners of the modern detective novelist. Notable works: *East Lynne* (1861).

Wood |wo͝od|, Sir Henry (Joseph) (1869–1944) English conductor. In 1895 he instituted the first of the Promenade Concerts, which he conducted every year until he died. He arranged the *Fantasia on British Sea Songs* (including "Rule, Britannia").

Wood |wo͝od|, Grant De Volsen (1892–1942) U.S. artist. Notable paintings: *American Gothic* (1930) and *Daughters of Revolution* (1932).

Wood |wo͝od|, Natalie (1938–81) U.S. actress. She played the vulnerable adolescent heroine of *Rebel Without A Cause* (1955) and similar roles in *Cry in the Night* (1956), *West Side Story* (1961), and *Inside Daisy Clover* (1966).

Wood•bu•ry |'wo͝od,berē; 'wo͝odbərē|, Levi (1789–1851) U.S. Supreme Court justice (1845–51).

Wood•en |'wo͝odn|, John (1910–) U.S. college basketball player and coach. He coached UCLA to ten national titles.

Woods |wo͝odz|, Granville T. (1856–1910) U.S. inventor. He invented the air brake and the third-rail system now used in subways.

Woods |wo͝odz|, Rose Mary (1917–) U.S. government employee. She was Richard Nixon's personal secretary (1951–75) and is best known for her role in the Watergate coverup.

Woods |wo͝odz|, Tiger (1975–) U.S. golfer; born *Eldrick Woods*.

Woods |wo͝odz|, William Burnham (1824–87) U.S. Supreme Court justice (1880–87).

Wood•son |'wo͝odsən|, Carter Godwin (1875–1950) U.S. historian. He founded the Association for the Study of Negro Life and History (1916).

Wood•ward |'wo͝odwərd|, C. Vann (1908–) U.S. historian of the American South. Full name *Comer Vann Woodward*. Notable works: *Oxford History of the U.S.* (11 vols., 1982–) and *Mary Chesnut's Civil War* (1981, Pulitzer Prize).

Wood•ward |'wo͝odwərd|, Joanne (1930–) U.S. actress. Notable movies: *The Three Faces of Eve* (1957, Academy Award)

Wood•ward |'wo͝odwərd|, Robert Burns (1917–79) American organic chemist. He was the first to synthesize quinine, cholesterol, chlorophyll, and vitamin B$_{12}$, and with the Polish-born American chemist **Roald Hoffmann**, (1937–) discovered symmetry-based rules governing the course of rearrangement reactions involving cyclic intermediates. Nobel Prize for Chemistry (1965).

Wood•ward |'wo͝odwərd|, Robert Upshur (1943–) U.S. journalist. He was assistant managing editor of *The Washington Post* (1981–) and co-author with Carl Bernstein of *All the President's Men* (1974).

Woolf |wo͝olf|, Virginia (1882–1941) English novelist, essayist, and critic; born *Adeline Virginia Stephen*. A member of the Bloomsbury Group, she gained recognition with *Jacob's Room* (1922). Subsequent novels, such as *Mrs. Dalloway* (1925) and *To the Lighthouse* (1927), characterized by their poetic Impressionism, established her as an exponent of modernism.

Wooll•cott |'wo͝olkət|, Alexander (Humphreys) (1887–1943) U.S. critic and actor. *The Man Who Came to Din-*

ner, a play by Moss Hart and George S. Kaufman, is based on the character of Woollcott, who appeared in the leading role (1939).

Wool·ley |'wŏolē|, Sir (Charles) Leonard (1880–1960) British archaeologist. He directed a British-American excavation of the Sumerian city of Ur (1922–34), which uncovered rich royal tombs and thousands of clay tablets.

Wool·worth |'wŏol,wərTH|, Frank Winfield (1852–1919) U.S. businessman. He pioneered the concept of low-priced retailing in 1878 and from this built a large international chain of stores.

Worces·ter |'wŏostər|, Joseph Emerson (1784–1865) U.S. lexicographer. He published gazetteers and school texts (mainly dictionaries); his dictionary rivaled that of Noah Webster.

Words·worth |'wərdz,wəTH|, William (1770–1850) English poet. Much of his work was inspired by the geography of England's Lake District. His *Lyrical Ballads* (1798), which was composed with Samuel Taylor Coleridge and included "Tintern Abbey," was a landmark in Romanticism. Other notable poems: "I Wandered Lonely as a Cloud" (sonnet, 1815), and *The Prelude* (1850). He was appointed Poet Laureate in 1843.

Worth |wərTH|, Charles Frederick (1825–95) English couturier, resident in France from 1845. Regarded as the founder of Parisian *haute couture,* he is noted for designing gowns with crinolines and for introducing the bustle.

Wouk |wōk; wŏok|, Herman (1915–) U.S. author. Notable novels: *The Caine Mutiny: A Novel of World War II* (1951), *Marjorie Morningstar* (1955), and *The Winds of War* (1971).

Woz·ni·ak |'wäznē,æk|, Steve (1950–) U.S. inventor. With Steve Jobs he created the first successful personal computer.

Wren |ren|, Sir Christopher (1632–1723) English architect. Following the Fire of London (1666), Wren was responsible for the design of the new St. Paul's Cathedral (1675–1711) and many of the city's churches. Other works include the Greenwich Observatory (1675) and a partial rebuilding of Hampton Court (1689–94).

Wren |ren|, P. C. (1885–1941) English novelist; full name *Percival Christopher Wren.* He is best known for his romantic adventure stories dealing with life in the French Foreign Legion, the first of which was *Beau Geste* (1924).

Wright |rīt|, Elizur (1804–85) U.S. reformer and actuary. As the Massachusetts commissioner of insurance (1858–66), he lobbied the state legislature for reform of life insurance practices.

Wright |rīt|, Fanny (1795–1852) U.S. reformer, born in Scotland. Born *Frances Wright.* With Robert Dale Owen she published the *Free Enquirer* from 1829, and she was active in the U.S. women's rights movement.

Wright |rīt|, Frank Lloyd (1869–1959) U.S. architect. His "prairie-style" houses revolutionized American domestic architecture. He advocated an "organic" architecture, characterized by a close relationship among building, landscape, and the materials used. Notable buildings include the Kaufmann House, which incorporated a waterfall, in Pennsylvania (1935–39) and the Guggenheim Museum of Art in New York (1956–59).

Wright |rīt|, Mickey (1935–) U.S. golfer.

Wright |rīt|, Orville (1871–1948) U.S. aviation pioneer. In 1903 he and his brother **Wilbur Wright** (1867–1912) were the first to make brief, powered, sustained and controlled flights in an airplane, which they had designed and built themselves. They were also the first to make and fly a fully practical powered airplane (1905) and a passenger-carrying airplane (1908).

Wright |rīt|, Richard Nathaniel (1908–60) U.S. author. Notable novels: *Native Son* (1940) and *The Long Dream* (1958). Notable nonfiction: *Black Power* (1954) and *White Man, Listen!* (1957).

Wright |rīt|, Sewall (1889–1988) U.S. geneticist and mathematician. He developed the concept of genetic drift known as the Sewall Wright effect.

Wright |rīt|, Willard Huntington (1888–1939) U.S. author. Pseudonym **S. S. Van Dine**. He created the master sleuth

Philo Vance, who appeared in various novels, including *The Benson Murder Case* (1926).

Wrig•ley |'riglē|, William, Jr. (1861–1932) U.S. businessman. He began as a manufacturer's sales representative for his father's soap company, giving free gum as an incentive; in 1891 he went into business for himself manufacturing chewing gum.

Wurde•mann |'wərdmən|, Audrey (1911–60) U.S. poet and novelist. Notable works: *Splendor in the Grass* (1936) and *Bright Ambush* (1934, Pulitzer Prize). She was wife of Joseph Auslander.

Wur•lit•zer |'wərlitsər|, Rudolph (1831–1914) U.S. businessman, born in Germany. He introduced the jukebox in 1934 and founded Wurlitzer Instruments.

Wurst•er |'wərstər|, William (1895–1973) U.S. architect. Notable designs: Ghirardelli Square (San Francisco).

Wy•att |'wīət|, James (1746–1813) English architect. He was both a neoclassicist and a leading figure in the Gothic revival, the latter seen most notably in his design for Fonthill Abbey in Wiltshire (1796–1807).

Wy•att |'wīət|, Sir Thomas (1503–42) English poet. He went to Italy (1527) as a diplomat in the service of Henry VIII; this visit probably stimulated his translation of Petrarch. His work also includes sonnets, rondeaux, songs for the lute, and satires.

Wych•er•ley |'wiCHərlē|, William (c. 1640–1716) English dramatist. His Restoration comedies are characterized by their acute examination of sexual morality and marriage conventions. Notable works: *The Country Wife* (1675).

Wyc•liffe |'wiklif; 'wīklif|, John (c. 1330–84) English religious reformer. Also **Wycliffe**. He criticized the wealth and power of the Church and upheld the Bible as the sole guide for doctrine; his teachings were disseminated by itinerant preachers and are regarded as precursors of the Reformation. Wyclif instituted the first English translation of the complete Bible. His followers were known as Lollards.

Wy•eth |'wīəTH|, U.S. family of artists: **N. C. Wyeth** (1882–1945); full name *Newell Convers Wyeth*. He created thousands of oil-paint illustrations, which appeared in countless publications, including such classic novels as Daniel Defoe's *Robinson Crusoe*, Robert Louis Stevenson's *Treasure Island*, and James Fenimore Cooper's *The Deerslayer*. **Andrew Newell Wyeth** (1917–), his son. Notable paintings: *Christina's World* (1948) and The Helga Pictures (a series, 1971–85). **Jamie Wyeth** (1946–), son of Andrew Newell Wyeth; full name *James Browning Wyeth*. Notable paintings: *Portrait of J.F.K.* (1965) and *Wolfbane* (1984).

Wy•ler |'wīlər|, William (1902–81) U.S. director. Notable movies: *Mrs. Miniver* (1942, Academy Award).

Wy•lie |'wīlē|, Eleanor (Hoyt) (1885–1928) U.S. poet and novelist. Notable works: *Nets To Catch the Wind* (1921).

Wynd•ham |'windəm|, John (1903–69) English writer of science fiction; pseudonym of *John Wyndham Parkes Lucas Beynon Harris*. His fiction often examines the psychological impact of catastrophe. Notable novels: *The Day of the Triffids* (1951), *The Chrysalids* (1955), and *The Midwich Cuckoos* (1957).

Wy•nette |wī'net|, Tammy (1942–98) U.S. country singer; born *Tammy Wynette Pugh*. Her unique lamenting voice brought her success with songs such as "Apartment No. 9" (1966) and "Stand by Your Man" (1968).

Wythe |wiTH|, George (1726–1806) colonial American jurist and statesman. He was a signer of the Declaration of Independence and a judge in the Virginia high court of chancery (1778–1806).

Xx

Xan·thip·pe |zænˈtipē| (5th century BC) wife of the philosopher Socrates. Also **Xantippe**. Her allegedly bad-tempered behavior toward her husband has made her proverbial as a shrew.

Xa·vi·er |ˈzāvēər|, St. Francis (1506–52) Spanish Catholic missionary; known as **the Apostle of the Indies**. One of the original seven Jesuits, from 1540 he traveled to southern India, Sri Lanka, Malacca, the Moluccas, and Japan, makng thousands of converts. Feast day, December 3.

Xe·na·kis |zəˈnäkis|, Iannis (1922–) French composer and architect, of Greek descent. He is noted for his use of electronic and aleatory techniques in music.

Xe·noph·a·nes |zəˈnäfə,nēz| (c. 570–c. 480 BC) Greek philosopher. A member of the Eleatic school, he argued for a form of pantheism, criticizing belief in anthropomorphic gods.

Xen·o·phon |ˈzenəfən| (c. 435–c. 354 BC) Greek historian, writer, and military leader. From 401 he fought with Cyrus the Younger against Artaxerxes II, and led an army of 10,000 Greek mercenaries in their retreat of about 900 miles (1,500 km) after Cyrus was killed; the campaign and retreat are recorded in the *Anabasis*. Other notable writings include the *Hellenica*, a history of Greece.

Xer·xes I |ˈzərk,sēz| (c. 519–465 BC) son of Darius I, king of Persia 486–465. His invasion of Greece achieved victories in 480 at Artemisium and Thermopylae, but defeats at Salamis (480) and Plataea (479) forced him to withdraw.

Yy

Yale |yāl|, Elihu (1649–1721) English colonial administrator. Because of his gift of books and goods to the Collegiate School in Saybrook, Connecticut, the school changed its name to Yale College (1718).

Yale |yāl|, Linus (1821–68) U.S. inventor and manufacturer. He invented the pin tumbler cylinder lock and the combination lock, and he founded the Yale Lock Manufacturing Co. (1868).

Ya·ma·gu·chi |ˌyämə'gōōCHē|, Kristi (1971–) U.S. figure skater. In 1992 she won national, world, and Olympic titles.

Ya·ma·mo·to |ˌyämə'mōtō|, Isoroku (1884–1943) Japanese admiral. As commander in chief of the Combined Fleet (air and naval forces) from 1939, he was responsible for planning the Japanese attack on Pearl Harbor (1941).

Ya·ma·sa·ki |ˌyämə'säkē|, Minoru (1912–86) U.S. architect. He designed the influential barrel-vaulted St. Louis Municipal Airport Terminal (1956) and the World Trade Center in New York (1972).

Yan·cey |'yænsē|, Jimmy (1894–1951) U.S. jazz pianist. Full name *James Edward Yancey*. He appeared with his wife, Mama Yancey, at Carnegie Hall in 1948.

Yang |yäNG|, Chen Ning (1922–) U.S. physicist, born in China. He shared the 1957 Nobel Prize for Physics with Tsun-Dao Lee for his discovery that parity is not conserved in the weak interaction.

Yard |yärd|, Molly (*c.* 1910–) U.S. journalist. She was president of the National Organization for Women (1986–91).

Yard·ley |'yärdlē|, Jonathan (1939–) U.S. journalist and author. A book critic for the *Washington Post* (1981–), he won a Pulitzer Prize for criticism (1981).

Yar·row |'yærō|, Peter (1938–) U.S. guitarist and singer. He was part of the trio Peter, Paul, and Mary.

Yas·trzem·ski |yə'stremskē|, Carl Michael (1939–) U.S. baseball player. Known as **Yaz**. He led the American League in batting three times. Elected to the Baseball Hall of Fame (1989).

Yea·ger |'yāgər|, Chuck (1923–) U.S. pilot; full name *Charles Elwood Yeager*. He became the first person to break the sound barrier when he piloted the Bell X-1 rocket research aircraft at high altitude to a level-flight speed of 670 mph in 1947.

Yeats |yāts|, W. B. (1865–1939) Irish poet and dramatist; full name *William Butler Yeats*. His play *The Countess Cathleen* (1892) and his collection of stories *The Celtic Twilight* (1893) stimulated Ireland's theatrical, cultural, and literary revival. Notable poetry: *The Tower* (1928), containing "Sailing to Byzantium" and "Leda and the Swan", and *The Winding Stair* (1929). Nobel Prize for Literature (1923).

Yelt·sin |'yeltsən|, Boris (Nikolayevich) (1931–) Russian statesman, president of the Russian Federation since 1991. Impatient with the slow pace of Gorbachev's reforms, Yeltsin resigned from the Communist Party after becoming president of the Russian Soviet Federative Socialist Republic in 1990. As president of the independent Russian Federation he faced opposition to his reforms and in 1993 survived an attempted coup, but he was re-elected in 1996.

Yer·by |'yərbē|, Frank (Garvin) (1916–91) U.S. author. After the success of *The Foxes of Harrow* (1946), he turned from stories about racial injustice to historical adventure novels.

Yer·kes |'yərkēz|, Charles Tyson (1837–1905) U.S. financier. He established his own banking house (1862) but was jailed for embezzlement (1871); made a second fortune in street railroad operations in Philadelphia and Chicago.

Yer·kes |'yərkēz|, Robert Mearns (1876–1956) U.S. psychologist and educator. A pioneer in the study of animal behavior, he was a leading authority on comparative psychology and psychobiology. Notable works: *The Mental Life of Monkeys and Apes* (1916).

Yev·tu·shen·ko |ˌyevtə'SHeNGkō|, Yevgeni (Aleksandrovich) (1933–) Russian poet. *Third Snow* (1955) and *Zima Junction* (1956) were regarded as encapsulating the feelings and aspirations of the post-Stalin generation, and he incurred official hostility because of the outspoken nature of some of his poetry, notably *Babi Yar* (1961).

Ye·zier·ska |yəz'yirskə|, Anzia (1885–1970) U.S. author, born in Russia. She wrote novels and short story collections including *Bread Givers* (1925), as well as an autobiography, *Red Ribbon on a White Horse* (1950), with an introduction by W. H. Auden.

Yo·len |'yōlən|, Jane H. (1939–) U.S. children's author and editor. Notable works: *The Girl Who Cried Flowers and Other Tales* (1974).

Yo·shi·mo·to |ˌyōSHē'mōtō|, Banana (1964–) Japanese author.

Young |yəNG|, Andrew Jackson, Jr. (1932–) U.S. clergyman, politician, and civil rights leader. He served as U.S. ambassador to the United Nations (1977–79) and as mayor of Atlanta, Georgia (1982–). Spingarn Medal, 1978.

Young |yəNG|, Art (1866–1943) U.S. cartoonist. Full name *Arthur Henry Young*. He was a political radical and satirist who published in *The Masses* (1911–17).

Young |yəNG|, Brigham (1801–77) U.S. Mormon leader. He succeeded Joseph Smith as the leader of the Mormons in 1844, led them westward, and established their headquarters at Salt Lake City, Utah. He served as governor of the territory of Utah from 1850 until 1857.

Young |yəNG|, Chic (1901–73) U.S. cartoonist. Full name *Murat Bernard Young*. He created the comic strip "Blondie."

Young |yəNG|, Coleman Alexander (1918–) U.S. politician. He was the longest-serving mayor of Detroit (1974–94).

Young |yəNG|, Denton True (1867–1955) U.S. baseball player. Known as **Cy Young**. He was the all-time pitching leader in wins (511), complete games (750), and innings pitched (7,355).

Young |yəNG|, Loretta (Gretchen) (1913–) U.S. actress. Notable movies: *The Farmer's Daughter* (1947, Academy Award).

Young |yəNG|, Mahonri (Mackintosh) (1877–1957) U.S. sculptor. He is known for his bronzes *Stevedore* and *Man with Pick*; he is a grandson of Brigham Young.

Young |yəNG|, Neil (Percival) (1945–) Canadian singer, songwriter, and guitarist. He performs both solo and with his group Crazy Horse, combining plaintive acoustic material with distinctively distorted electric-guitar playing. Notable albums: *Harvest* (1972).

Young |yəNG|, Owen D. (1874–1962) U.S. lawyer and corporate executive. He formulated the Young Plan for German reparations at the end of World War I and was president of General Electric (1922–39).

Young |yəNG|, Pres (1909–59) U.S. jazz tenor saxophonist and composer. Full name *Lester Willis Young*. He often accompanied Billie Holiday on records. Notable songs: "Lady Be Good" and "Lester Leaps In."

Young |yəNG|, Steve (1961–) U.S. football player. He was the only quarterback to lead the NFL in passer rating for four straight years.

Young Pretender see STUART.

Your·ce·nar |ˌyo͞orsə'när|, Marguerite (1903–87) French writer. Born *Marguerite de Crayencour*. Many of her novels are meticulous historical reconstructions, including *Mémoires d'Hadrian* (1951). Her interest in male homosexuality is reflected in the novel *Alexis ou le Traité du vain combat* (1929).

Yu·ka·wa |yo͞o'käwə|, Hideki (1907–81) Japanese physicist. He won the 1949 Nobel Prize for Physics for his prediction of the existence of the particle pi-meson (pion) in 1935.

Zz

Za·har·i·as |zə'hærēəs|, Babe (1914–56) U.S. track and field athlete and golfer. Full name *Mildred Ella Didrikson Zaharias*. After winning two gold medals in the 1932 Olympics, she became a professional golfer and won 12 major titles; she helped found the LPGA (1949).

Zam·bo·ni |zæm'bōnē|, Frank J. (1901–) U.S. inventor. He invented the Zamboni ice-resurfacing machine.

Za·mo·ra |zə'mawrə|, Pedro (1972–94) U.S. AIDS activist, born in Cuba.

Zan·uck |'zænək|, Darryl Francis (1902–79) U.S. movie producer; full name *Darryl Francis Zanuck*. He was the controlling executive of Twentieth Century Fox, and its president from 1965 until his retirement in 1971.

Za·pa·ta |zə'pätə|, Emiliano (1879–1919) Mexican revolutionary. He attempted to implement his program of agrarian reform by means of guerrilla warfare. From 1914 he and Pancho Villa fought against the regimes of General Huerta and Venustiano Carranza.

Zap·pa |'zæpə|, Frank (1940–93) U.S. rock singer, musician, and songwriter. Full name *Francis Vincent Zappa, Jr.*. In 1965 he formed the Mothers of Invention, who combined psychedelic rock with elements of jazz and satire. In Zappa's later career he often mixed flowing guitar improvisations with scatological humor.

Za·to·pek |'zätō,pek|, Emil (1922–) Czech long-distance runner. In the 1952 Olympic Games he won gold medals in the 5,000 meters, 10,000 meters, and marathon.

Zee·man |'zā,män|, Pieter (1865–1943) Dutch physicist. His work on the interaction of light and magnets yielded what is now known as the Zeeman effect. Nobel Prize for Physics, 1902.

Zef·fi·rel·li |,zefə'relē|, Franco (1923–) Italian movie and theater director; born *Gianfranco Corsi*. His operatic productions are noted for the opulence of their sets and costumes. Notable movies: *Romeo and Juliet* (1968), *Brother Sun, Sister Moon* (1973),

and the television movie *Jesus of Nazareth* (1977).

Ze·no[1] |'zēnō| (*c.*495–*c.*430 BC) Greek philosopher; known as **Zeno of Elea**. A member of the Eleatic school, he defended Parmenides' theories by formulating paradoxes that appeared to demonstrate the impossibility of motion, one of which shows that once Achilles has given a tortoise a start he can never overtake it, since each time he arrives where it was, it has already moved on.

Ze·no[2] |'zēnō| (*c.*355–263 BC) Greek philosopher; known as **Zeno of Citium**. He founded the school of Stoic philosophy (*c.* 300), but all that remains of his treatises are fragments of quotations.

Ze·no·bia |zə'nōbēə| (3rd century AD) queen of Palmyra *c.*267–272. Full name *Septimia Zenobia*. She conquered Egypt and much of Asia Minor. When she proclaimed her son emperor, the Roman emperor Aurelian attacked, defeated, and captured her.

Zep·pe·lin |'zep(ə)lin|, Ferdinand (Adolf August Heinrich), Count von (1838–1917) German aviation pioneer. An army officer until his retirement in 1890, he devoted the rest of his life to the development of the dirigible named after him.

Zeux·is |'zōōksəs| (*fl.* late 5th century BC) Greek painter, born at Heraclea in southern Italy. His works are known only through the reports of ancient writers, who make reference to monochrome techniques and his use of shading to create an illusion of depth, while his verisimilitude is the subject of many anecdotes.

Zhou En·lai |'jō 'en'lī| (1898–1976) Chinese Communist statesman and prime minister of China (1949–76). Also **Chou En-lai**. A founder of the Chinese Communist Party, he organized a Communist workers' revolt in 1927 in Shanghai in support of the Kuomintang forces surrounding the city. As premier, he was a moderating influence during the Cultural Revolution and presided over the moves towards détente with the U.S. in 1972–73.

Zhu De |'j͞oo 'dä| (1886–1976) Chinese military and political leader. He was founder and commander in chief of the Chinese People's Liberation Army and was closely associated with Mao Zedong.

Zhu·kov |'zH͞oo,kawf|, Georgi (Konstantinovich) (1896–1974) Soviet military leader, born in Russia. In the course of World War II he defeated the Germans at Stalingrad (1943), lifted the siege of Leningrad (1944), and led the final assault on Germany and the capture of Berlin (1945). After the war he commanded the Soviet zone in occupied Germany.

Zia-ul-Haq |'zēə əl 'häk|, Muhammad (1924–88) Pakistani general, statesman, and president (1978–88). As chief of staff he led the coup that deposed President Zulfikar Bhutto in 1977. He banned all political parties and began to introduce strict Islamic laws.

Zi·aur |zē'owr|, Rahman (1935–81) Bengali nationalist and president of Bangladesh (1977–81).

Zieg·feld |'zēg,feld|, Florenz (1869–1932) U.S. theater manager. In 1907 he produced the first of a series of revues in New York, based on those of the Folies-Bergère, entitled the *Ziegfeld Follies*. Among the many famous performers he promoted were W. C. Fields and Fred Astaire.

Zin·del |'zindəl|, Paul (1936–) U.S. playwright. Notable works: *The Effect of Gamma Rays on Man-in-the-Moon Marigolds* (1964, Pulitzer Prize).

Zinne·mann |zinmən|, Fred (1907–97) Austrian-born U.S. movie director. He joined MGM in 1937 and won Oscars for the short *That Mothers Might Live* (1938) and the feature movies *From Here to Eternity* (1953) and *A Man For All Seasons* (1966).

Zof·fany |'zäfənē|, Johann (c. 1733–1810) German-born painter, resident in England from 1758. Many of his earlier paintings depict scenes from the contemporary theater and feature the actor David Garrick (e.g. *The Farmer's Return*, 1762).

Zog I |zōg| (1895–1961) Albanian prime minister (1922–24), president (1925–28), and king (1928–39); full name *Ahmed Bey Zogu*. He initially headed a republican government, proclaiming himself king in 1928. His autocratic rule resulted in relative political stability, but when the country was invaded by Italy in 1939 he went into exile. He abdicated in 1946 after Albania became a Communist state.

Zo·la |zō'lä|, Émile (Édouard Charles Antoine) (1840–1902) French novelist and critic. His series of twenty novels collectively entitled *Les Rougon-Macquart* (1871–93), including *Nana* (1880), *Germinal* (1885), and *La Terre* (1887), attempts to show how human behavior is determined by environment and heredity. In 1898 he published *J'accuse*, a noted pamphlet in support of Alfred Dreyfus.

Zo·rach |'zawr,äk|, William (1887–1966) U.S. sculptor. Notable works include *Mother and Child* (1930) and *Spirit of Dance* (1932).

Zo·ro·as·ter |'zawrō,æstər| (c. 628–c. 551 BC) Persian prophet and founder of Zoroastrianism; Avestan name *Zarathustra*. Little is known of his life, but traditionally he was born in Persia and began to preach the tenets of what was later called Zoroastrianism after receiving a vision from Ahura Mazda.

Zsig·mon·dy |'zHig,mawndē|, Richard Adolf (1865–1929) Austrian-born German chemist. He investigated the properties of various colloidal solutions and invented the ultramicroscope for counting colloidal particles. Nobel Prize for Chemistry (1925).

Zu·kor |'z͞ookər|, Adolph (1873–1976) U.S. movie producer and corporate executive. He founded Famous Players Film Co. (1912), which merged with another company to become Paramount Pictures, Inc.

Zur·ba·rán |,z͞oorbə'rän|, Francisco de (1598–1664) Spanish painter. He carried out commissions for many churches and for Philip IV, for whom he painted *The Defence of Cadiz* (1634) and the series *The Labors of Hercules* (1634). Much of his subject matter is religious.

Zwing·li |'zwiNGlē; 'tsfiNGglē|, Ulrich (or *Huldreich*) (1484–1531) Swiss

Protestant reformer, the principal figure of the Swiss Reformation. He rejected papal authority and many orthodox doctrines, and although he had strong local support in Zurich, his ideas met with fierce resistance in some regions. Zwingli was killed in the civil war that resulted from his reforms.

Zwor·y·kin |ˈzwawrəkin|, Vladimir Kosma (1889–1982) Russian-born U.S. physicist and television pioneer. He invented a precursor of the television camera, the first to scan the image electronically.

Appendixes

PRESIDENTS OF THE UNITED STATES OF AMERICA

Name and life dates	Party (term in office)
1. George Washington 1732-99	Federalist (1789-97)
2. John Adams 1735-1826	Federalist (1797-1801)
3. Thomas Jefferson 1743-1826	Democratic-Republican (1801-09)
4. James Madison 1751-1836	Democratic-Republican (1809-17)
5. James Monroe 1758-1831	Democratic-Republican (1817-25)
6. John Quincy Adams 1767-1848	Independent (1825-29)
7 Andrew Jackson 1767-1845	Democrat (1829-37)
8. Martin Van Buren 1782-1862	Democrat (1837-41)
9. William H. Harrison 1773-1841	Whig (1841)
10. John Tyler 1790-1862	Whig, then Democrat (1841-45)
11. James K. Polk 1795-1849	Democrat (1845-49)
12. Zachary Taylor 1784-1850	Whig (1849-50)
13. Millard Fillmore 1800-74	Whig (1850-53)
14. Franklin Pierce 1804-69	Democrat (1853-57)
15. James Buchanan 1791-1868	Democrat (1857-61)
16. Abraham Lincoln 1809-65	Republican (1861-65)
17. Andrew Johnson 1808-75	Democrat (1865-69)
18. Ulysses S. Grant 1822-85	Republican (1869-77)
19. Rutherford B. Hayes 1822-93	Republican (1877-81)
20. James A. Garfield 1831-81	Republican (1881)
21. Chester A. Arthur 1830-86	Republican (1881-85)
22. Grover Cleveland 1837-1908	Democrat (1885-89)
23. Benjamin Harrison 1833-1901	Republican (1889-93)
24. Grover Cleveland (see above)	Democrat (1893-97)
25. William McKinley 1843-1901	Republican (1897-1901)
26. Theodore Roosevelt 1858-1919	Republican (1901-09)
27. William H. Taft 1857-1930	Republican (1909-13)
28. Woodrow Wilson 1856-1924	Democrat (1913-21)
29. Warren G. Harding 1865-1923	Republican (1921-23)
30. Calvin Coolidge 1872-1933	Republican (1923-29)
31. Herbert Hoover 1874-1964	Republican (1929-33)
32. Franklin D. Roosevelt 1882-1945	Democrat (1933-45)
33. Harry S Truman 1884-1972	Democrat (1945-53)
34. Dwight D. Eisenhower 1890-1969	Republican (1953-61)
35. John F. Kennedy 1917-63	Democrat (1961-63)
36. Lyndon B. Johnson 1908-73	Democrat (1963-69)
37. Richard M. Nixon 1913-94	Republican (1969-74)
38. Gerald R. Ford 1913-	Republican (1974-77)
39. James Earl Carter 1924-	Democrat (1977-81)
40. Ronald W. Reagan 1911-	Republican (1981-89)
41. George H.W. Bush 1924-	Republican (1989-93)
42. William J. Clinton 1946-	Democrat (1993-)

MONARCHS OF ENGLAND AND BRITAIN

House	Monarch	Reign
Wessex (West Saxon)	Egbert	802-839
	Ethelwulf	839-856
	Ethelbald	856-860
	Ethelbert	860-866
	Ethelred I	866-871
	Alfred the Great	871-899
	Edward the Elder	899-924
	Athelstan	925-939
	Edmund I	939-946
	Edred	946-955
	Edwy	955-957
	Edgar	959-975
	Edward the Martyr	975-978
	Ethelred II (the Unready)	978-1016
	Edmund II (Ironside)	1016
Danish		
	Canute (Cnut)	1016-1035
	Harold I	1035-1040
	Hardecanute	1040-1042
West Saxon (restored)	Edward II (the Confessor)	1042-1066
	Harold II	1066
Normandy	William I (the Conqueror)	1066-1087
	William II	1087-1100
	Henry I	1100-1135
	Stephen	1135-1154
Plantagenet (Anjou)	Henry II	1154-1189
	Richard I (the Lion-heart)	1189-1199
	John	1199-1216
	Henry III	1216-1272
	Edward I	1272-1307
	Edward II	1307-1327
	Edward III	1327-1377
	Richard II	1377-1399
Lancaster	Henry IV	1399-1413
	Henry V	1413-1422
	Henry VI	1422-1461
York	Edward IV	1461-1483
	Edward V	1483
	Richard III	1483-1485
Tudor	Henry VII	1485-1509
	Henry VIII	1509-1547
	Edward VI	1547-1553
	Jane (Lady Jane Grey)	1553

House	Monarch	Reign
	Mary I (Bloody Mary)	1553-1558
	Elizabeth I	1558-1603
(monarchs of Britain)		
Stuart	James I	1603-1625
	Charles I	1625-1649
Commonwealth	Long Parliament	1649-1660
Protectorate	Oliver Cromwell	1653-1658
	Richard Cromwell	1658-1660
Stuart	Charles II	1660-1685
	James II	1685-1688
interregnum		1688-1689
	William III and Mary II	1689-1694
	Anne	1702-1714
Hanover	George I	1714-1727
	George II	1727-1760
	George III	1760-1820
	George IV	1820-1830
	William IV	1830-1837
Saxe-Coburg-Gotha	Victoria	1837-1901
	Edward VII	1901-1910
Windsor	George V	1910-1936
	Edward VIII	1936
	George VI	1936-1952
	Elizabeth II	1952-

PRIME MINISTERS OF GREAT BRITAIN AND THE UNITED KINGDOM

Name	Party	Dates in Power
Sir Robert Walpole	Whig	1721-1742
Earl of Wilmington	Whig	1742-1743
Henry Pelham	Whig	1743-1754
Duke of Newcastle	Whig	1754-1756
Earl of Bute	Tory	1762-1763
George Grenville	Whig	1763-1765
Marquis of Rockingham	Whig	1765-1766
Earl of Chatham	Whig	1766-1768
Duke of Grafton	Whig	1768-1770
Lord North	Tory	1770-1782
Marquis of Rockingham	Whig	1782
Earl of Shelburne	Whig	1782-1783
Duke of Portland	coalition	1783
William Pitt	Tory	1783-1801
Henry Addington	Tory	1801-1804
William Pitt	Tory	1804-1806
Lord William Grenville	Whig	1806-1807
Duke of Portland	Tory	1807-1808
Spencer Perceval	Tory	1809-1812
Earl of Liverpool	Tory	1812-1827
George Canning	Tory	1827
Viscount Goderich	Tory	1827-1828
Duke of Wellington	Tory	1828-1830
Earl Grey	Whig	1830-1834
Viscount Melbourne	Whig	1834
Duke of Wellington	Tory	1834
Sir Robert Peel	Conservative	1834-1835
Viscount Melbourne	Whig	1835-1841
Sir Robert Peel	Conservative	1841-1846
Lord John Russell	Whig	1846-1852
Earl of Derby	Conservative	1852
Earl of Aberdeen	coalition	1852-1855
Viscount Palmerston	Liberal	1855-1858
Earl of Derby	Conservative	1858-1859
Viscount Palmerston	Liberal	1859-1865
Earl Russell	Liberal	1865-1866
Earl of Derby	Conservative	1866-1868
Benjamin Disraeli	Conservative	1868
William Ewart Gladstone	Liberal	1868-1874
Benjamin Disraeli	Conservative	1874-1880
William Ewart Gladstone	Liberal	1880-1885
Marquis of Salisbury	Conservative	1885-1886
William Ewart Gladstone	Liberal	1892-1894
Earl of Rosebery	Liberal	1894-1895
Marquis of Salisbury	Conservative	1895-1902
Arthur James Balfour	Conservative	1902-1905
Sir Henry Campbell-Bannerman	Liberal	1905-1908
Herbert Henry Asquith	Liberal	1908-1916
David Lloyd George	coalition	1916-1922

Name	Party	Dates in Power
Andrew Bonar Law	Conservative	1922-1923
Stanley Baldwin	Conservative	1923-1924
James Ramsay MacDonald	Labour	1924
Stanley Baldwin	Conservative	1924-1929
James Ramsay MacDonald	coalition	1929-1935
Stanley Baldwin	coalition	1935-1937
Neville Chamberlain	coalition	1937-1940
Sir Winston Spencer Churchill	coalition	1940-1945
Clement Attlee	Labour	1945-1951
Sir Winston Spencer Churchill	Conservative	1951-1955
Sir Anthony Eden	Conservative	1955-1957
Harold Macmillan	Conservative	1957-1963
Sir Alec Douglas-Home	Conservative	1963-1964
Harold Wilson	Labour	1964-1970
Edward Heath	Conservative	1970-1974
Harold Wilson	Labour	1974-1976
James Callaghan	Labour	1976-1979
Margaret Thatcher	Conservative	1979-1990
John Major	Conservative	1990-1997
Anthony Blair	Labour	1997-

ACADEMY AWARD WINNERS

Note: The movie for which the award was given follows the individual's name, in parentheses.

1928
Best actor: Charles Chaplin (*The Circus*)
Best actress: Janet Gaynor (*Seventh Heaven*)
Best director (drama): Frank Borzage (*Seventh Heaven*)
Best director (comedy): Lewis Milestone (*Two Arabian Knights*)

1929
Best actor: Warner Baxter (*In Old Arizona*)
Best actress: Mary Pickford (*Coquette*)
Best director: Frank Lloyd (*The Divine Lady*)

1930
Best actor: George Arliss (*Disraeli*)
Best actress: Norma Shearer (*The Divorceé*)
Best director: Lewis Milestone (*All Quiet on the Western Front*)

1931
Best actor: Lionel Barrymore (*A Free Soul*)
Best actress: Marie Dressler (*Min and Bill*)
Best director: Norman Taurog (*Skippy*)

1932
Best actors: Wallace Berry (*The Champ*), Frederic March (*Dr. Jekyll and Mr. Hyde*)
Best actress: Helen Hayes (*The Sin of Madelon Claudet*)
Best director: Frank Borzage (*Bad Girl*)

1933
Best actor: Charles Laughton (*The Private Life of Henry VIII*)
Best actress: Katharine Hepburn (*Morning Glory*)
Best director: Frank Lloyd (*Cavalcade*

1934
Best actor: Clark Gable (*It Happened One Night*)
Best actress: Claudette Colbert (*It Happened One Night*)
Best director: Frank Capra (*It Happened One Night*)

1935
Best actor: Victor McLaglen (*The Informer*)
Best actress: Bette Davis (*Dangerous*)
Best director: John Ford (*The Informer*)

1936
Best actor: Paul Muni (*The Story of Louis Pasteur*)
Best actress: Luise Rainer (*The Great Ziegfeld*)
Best director: Frank Capra (*Mr. Deeds Goes to Town*)

1937
Best actor: Spencer Tracy (*Captains Courageous*)
Best actress: Luise Rainer (*The Good Earth*)
Best director: Leo McCarey (*The Awful Truth*)

1938
Best actor: Spencer Tracy (*Boys Town*)
Best actress: Bette Davis (*Jezebel*)
Best director: Frank Capra (*You Can't Take It With You*)

1939
Best actor: Robert Donat (*Goodbye Mr. Chips*)
Best actress: Vivien Leigh (*Gone with the Wind*)
Best director: Victor Fleming (*Gone with the Wind*)

1940
Best actor: James Stewart (*The Philadelphia Story*)
Best actress: Ginger Rogers (*Kitty Foyle*)
Best director: John Ford (*The Grapes of Wrath*)

1941
Best actor: Gary Cooper (*Sergeant York*)
Best actress: Joan Fontaine (*Suspicion*)
Best director: John Ford (*How Green Was My Valley*)

1942
Best actor: James Cagney (*Yankee Doodle Dandy*)
Best actress: Greer Garson (*Mrs. Miniver*)
Best director: William Wyler (*Mrs. Miniver*)

1943
Best actor: Paul Lukas (*Watch on the Rhine*)
Best actress: Jennifer Jones (*The Song of Bernadette*)
Best director: Michael Curtiz (*Casablanca*)

1944
Best actor: Bing Crosby (*Going My Way*)
Best actress: Ingrid Bergman (*Gaslight*)
Best director: Leo McCarey (*Going My Way*)

1945
Best actor: Ray Milland (*The Lost Weekend*)
Best actress: Joan Crawford (*Love Letters*)
Best director: Billy Wilder (*The Lost Weekend*)

1946
Best actor: Frederic March (*The Best Years of Our Lives*)
Best actress: Olivia De Havilland (*To Each His Own*)
Best director: William Wyler (*The Best Years of Our Lives*)

1947
Best actor: Ronald Colman (*A Double Life*)
Best actress: Loretta Young (*The Farmer's Daughter*)
Best director: Elia Kazan (*Gentleman's Agreement*)

1948
Best actor: Laurence Olivier (*Hamlet*)
Best actress: Jane Wyman (*Johnny Belinda*)
Best director: John Huston (*The Treasure of the Sierra Madre*)

1949
Best actor: Broderick Crawford (*All the King's Men*)
Best actress: Olivia De Havilland (*The Heiress*)
Best director: Joseph L. Mankiewicz (*A Letter to Three Wives*)

1950
Best actor: Jose Ferrer (*Cyrano De Bergerac*)
Best actress: Judy Holliday (*Born Yesterday*)
Best director: Joseph L. Mankiewicz (*All About Eve*)

1951
Best actor: Humphrey Bogart (*The African Queen*)
Best actress: Vivien Leigh (*A Streetcar Named Desire*)
Best director: George Stevens (*A Place in the Sun*)

1952
Best actor: Gary Cooper (*High Noon*)
Best actress: Shirley Booth (*Come Back, Little Sheba*)
Best director: John Ford (*The Quiet Man*)

1953
Best actor: William Holden (*Stalag 17*)
Best actress: Audrey Hepburn (*Roman Holiday*)
Best director: Fred Zinnemann (*From Here to Eternity*)

1954
Best actor: Marlon Brando (*On the Waterfront*)
Best actress: Grace Kelly (*The Country Girl*)
Best director: Elia Kazan (*On the Waterfront*)

1955
Best actor: Ernest Borgnine (*Marty*)
Best actress: Anna Magnani (*The Rose Tattoo*)
Best director: Delbert Mann (*Marty*)

1956
Best actor: Yul Brynner (*The King and I*)
Best actress: Ingrid Bergman (*Anastasia*)
Best director: George Stevens (*Giant*)

1957
Best actor: Alec Guinness (*The Bridge on the River Kwai*)
Best actress: Joanne Woodward (*The Three Faces of Eve*)
Best director: David Lean (*The Bride on the River Kwai*)

1958
Best actor: David Niven (*Separate Tables*)
Best actress: Susan Hayward (*I Want to Live!*)
Best director: Vincente Minnelli (*The Defiant Ones*)

1959
Best actor: Charlton Heston (*Ben-Hur*)
Best actress: Simone Signoret (*Room at the Top*)
Best director: William Wyler (*Ben-Hur*)

1960
Best actor: Burt Lancaster (*Elmer Gantry*)
Best actress: Elizabeth Taylor (*Butterfield 8*)
Best director: Billy Wilder (*The Apartment*)

1961
Best actor: Maximilian Schell (*Judgment at Nuremberg*)
Best actress: Sophia Loren (*Two Women*)
Best director: Jerome Robbins, Robert Wise (*West Side Story*)

1962
Best actor: Gregory Peck (*To Kill a Mockingbird*)
Best actress: Anne Bancroft (*The Miracle Worker*)
Best director: David Lean (*Lawrence of Arabia*)

1963
Best actor: Sydney Poitier (*Lilies of the Field*)
Best actress: Patricia Neal (*Hud*)
Best director: Tony Richardson (*Tom Jones*)

1964
Best actor: Rex Harrison (*My Fair Lady*)
Best actress: Julie Andrews (*Mary Poppins*)
Best director: George Cukor (*Mary Poppins*)

1965
Best actor: Lee Marvin (*Cat Ballou*)
Best actress: Julie Christie (*Darling*)
Best director: Robert Wise (*The Sound of Music*)

1966
Best actor: Paul Scofield (*A Man for All Seasons*)
Best actress: Elizabeth Taylor (*Who's Afraid of Virginia Wolf?*)
Best director: Fred Zinnemann (*A Man for All Seasons*)

1967
Best actor: Rod Steiger (*In the Heat of the Night*)
Best actress: Katharine Hepburn (*Guess Who's Coming to Dinner*)
Best director: Mike Nichols (*The Graduate*)

1968
Best actor: Cliff Robertson (*Charly*)
Best actress: Barbra Streisand (*Funny Girl*)
Best director: Carol Reed (*Oliver!*)

1969
Best actor: John Wayne (*True Grit*)
Best actress: Maggie Smith (*The Prime of Miss Jean Brodie*)
Best director: John Schlesinger (*Midnight Cowboy*)

1970
Best actor: George C. Scott (*Patton*)
Best actress: Glenda Jackson (*Women in Love*)
Best director: Franklin J. Schaffner (*Patton*)

1971
Best actor: Gene Hackman (*The French Connection*)
Best actress: Jane Fonda (*Klute*)
Best director: William Friedkin (*The French Connection*)

1972
Best actor: Marlon Brando (*The Godfather*)
Best actress: Liza Minnelli (*Cabaret*)
Best director: Bob Fosse (*Cabaret*)

1973
Best actor: Jack Lemmon (*Save the Tiger*)
Best actress: Glenda Jackson (*A Touch of Class*)
Best director: George Roy Hill (*The Sting*)

1974
Best actor: Art Carney (*Harry and Tonto*)
Best actress: Ellen Burstyn (*Alice Doesn't Live Here Anymore*)
Best director: Francis Ford Coppola (*The Godfather, Part II*)

1975
Best actor: Jack Nicholson (*One Flew Over the Cuckoo's Nest*)
Best actress: Louise Fletcher (*One Flew Over the Cuckoo's Nest*)
Best director: Milos Forman (*One Flew Over the Cuckoo's Nest*)

1976
Best actor: Peter Finch (*Network*)
Best actress: Faye Dunaway (*Network*)
Best director: John G. Avildsen (*Rocky*)

1977
Best actor: Richard Dreyfuss (*The Goodbye Girl*)
Best actress: Diane Keaton (*Annie Hall*)
Best director: Woody Allen (*Annie Hall*)

1978
Best actor: Jon Voight (*Coming Home*)
Best actress: Jane Fonda (*Coming Home*)
Best director: Michael Cimino (*The Deer Hunter*)

1979
Best actor: Dustin Hoffman (*Kramer vs. Kramer*)
Best actress: Sally Field (*Norma Rae*)
Best director: Robert Benton (*Kramer vs. Kramer*)

1980
Best actor: Robert De Niro (*Raging Bull*)
Best actress: Sissy Spacek (*Coal Miner's Daughter*)
Best director: Robert Redford (*Ordinary People*)

1981
Best actor: Henry Fonda (*On Golden Pond*)
Best actress: Katharine Hepburn (*On Golden Pond*)
Best director: Warren Beatty (*Reds*)

1982
Best actor: Ben Kingsley (*Gandhi*)
Best actress: Meryl Streep (*Sophie's Choice*)
Best director: Richard Attenborough (*Gandhi*)

1983
Best actor: Robert Duvall (*Tender Mercies*)
Best actress: Shirley MacLaine (*Terms of Endearment*)
Best director: James L. Brooks (*Terms of Endearment*)

1984
Best actor: F. Murray Abraham (*Amadeus*)
Best actress: Sally Field (*Places in the Heart*)
Best director: Milos Forman (*Amadeus*)

1985
Best actor: William Hurt (*Kiss of the Spider Woman*)
Best actress: Geraldine Page (*The Trip to Bountiful*)
Best director: Sydney Pollack (*Out of Africa*)

1986
Best actor: Paul Newman (*The Color of Money*)
Best actress: Marlee Matlin (*Children of a Lesser God*)
Best director: Oliver Stone (*Platoon*)

1987
Best actor: Michael Douglas (*Wall Street*)
Best actress: Cher (*Moonstruck*)
Best director: Bernardo Bertolucci (*The Last Emperor*)

1988
Best actor: Dustin Hoffman (*Rain Man*)
Best actress: Jodie Foster (*The Accused*)
Best director: Barry Levinson (*Rain Man*)

1989
Best actor: Daniel Day-Lewis (*My Left Foot*)
Best actress: Jessica Tandy (*Driving Miss Daisy*)
Best director: Oliver Stone (*Born on the Fourth of July*)

1990
Best actor: Jeremy Irons (*Reversal of Fortune*)
Best actress: Kathy Bates (*Misery*)
Best director: Kevin Costner (*Dances with Wolves*)

1991
Best actor: Anthony Hopkins (*The Silence of the Lambs*)
Best actress: Jodie Foster (*The Silence of the Lambs*)
Best director: Jonathan Demme (*The Silence of the Lambs*)

1992
Best actor: Al Pacino (*Scent of a Woman*)
Best actress: Emma Thompson (*Howards End*)
Best director: Clint Eastwood (*Unforgiven*)

1993
Best actor: Tom Hanks (*Philadelphia*)
Best actress: Holly Hunter (*The Piano*)
Best director: Steven Spielberg (*Schindler's List*)

1994
Best actor: Tom Hanks (*Forrest Gump*)
Best actress: Jessica Lange (*Blue Sky*)
Best director: Robert Zemeckis (*Forrest Gump*)

1995
Best actor: Nicolas Cage (*Leaving Las Vegas*)
Best actress: Susan Sarandon (*Dead Man Walking*)
Best director: Mel Gibson (*Braveheart*)

1996
Best actor: Geoffrey Rush (*Shine*)
Best actress: Frances McDormand (*Fargo*)
Best director: Anthony Minghella (*The English Patient*)

1997
Best actor: Jack Nicholson (*As Good As It Gets*)
Best actress: Helen Hunt (*As Good As It Gets*)
Best director: James Cameron (*Titanic*)

1998
Best actor: Robert Benigni (*Life is Beautiful* [*La Vita è Bella*])
Best actress: Gwyneth Paltrow (*Shakespeare in Love*)
Best director: Steven Spielberg (*Saving Private Ryan*)

BASEBALL HALL OF FAME INDUCTEES

(elected by the Baseball Writers Association of America)

Year of Induction	Player
1999	George Brett
	Nolan Ryan
	Robin Yount
1998	Don Sutton
1997	Phil Niekro
1995	Mike Schmidt
1994	Steve Carlton
1993	Reggie Jackson
1992	Rollie Fingers
	Tom Seaver
1991	Rod Carew
	Ferguson Jenkins
	Gaylord Perry
1990	Jim Palmer
	Joe Morgan
1989	Johnny Bench
	Carl Yastrzemski
1988	Willie Stargell
1987	Billy Williams
	Catfish Hunter
1986	Willie McCovey
1985	Lou Brock
	Hoyt Wilhelm
1983	Juan Marichal
	Brooks Robinson
1982	Hank Aaron
	Frank Robinson
1981	Bob Gibson
1980	Al Kaline
	Duke Snider
1979	Willie Mays
1978	Eddie Mathews
1977	Ernie Banks
1976	Bob Lemon
	Robin Roberts
1975	Ralph Kiner
1974	Whitey Ford
	Mickey Mantle
1973	Warren Spahn
	Roberto Clemente
1972	Yogi Berra
	Sandy Koufax
	Early Wynn
1970	Lou Boudreau
1969	Roy Campanella
	Stan Musial
1968	Joe Medwick
1967	Red Ruffing
	Ted Williams
1964	Luke Appling
1962	Bob Feller
	Jackie Robinson
1956	Joe Cronin
	Hank Greenberg
1955	Joe DiMaggio
	Gabby Hartnett
	Ted Lyons
	Dazzy Vance
1954	Bill Dickey
	Rabbit Maranville
	Bill Terry
1953	Dizzy Dean
	Al Simmons
1952	Harry Heilmann
	Paul Waner
1951	Jimmie Foxx
	Mel Ott
1949	Charlie Gehringer
1948	Herb Pennock
	Pie Traynor
1947	Michey Cochrane
	Frank Frisch
	Lefty Grove
	Carl Hubbell
1942	Rogers Hornsby
1939	Eddie Collins
	Lou Gehrig
	Willie Keeler
	George Sisler
1938	Grover Alexander
1937	Nap Lajoie
	Tris Speaker
	Cy Young
1936	Ty Cobb
	Walter Johnson
	Christy Mathewson
	Babe Ruth
	Honus Wagner

(elected by the Veterans Committee)

Year of Induction	Player
1998	George Davis
	Larry Doby
	Lee MacPhail
	Wilbur Rogan

Year of Induction	Player
1997	Tommy Lasorda
	Nellie Fox
	Willie J. Wells, Sr.
1996	Jim Bunning
	Earl Weaver
	Ned Hanlon
	Bill Foster
1995	Richie Ashburn
	Leon Day
	William Hulbert
	Vic Willis
1994	Leo Durocher
	Phil Rizzuto
1992	Hal Newhouser
	Bill McGowen
1991	Bill Veeck
	Tony Lazzeri
1989	Al Barlick
	Red Schoendienst
1987	Ray Dandridge
1986	Bobby Doerr
	Ernie Lombardi
1985	Enos Slaughter
	Arky Vaughan
1984	Rick Ferrell
	Pee Wee Reese
1983	Walter Alston
	George Kell
1982	Happy Chandler
	Travis Jackson
1981	Johnny Mize
	Rube Foster
1980	Chuck Klein
	Tom Yawkey
1979	Hack Wilson
	Warren Giles
1978	Larry MacPhail
	Addie Joss
1977	Al Lopez
	Amos Rusie
	Joe Sewell
1976	Roger Connor
	Cal Hubbard
	Fred Lindstrom
1975	Earl Averill
	Bucky Harris
	Billy Herman
1974	Jim Bottomley
	Jocko Conlan
	Sam Thompson
1973	Billy Evans
	George Kelly
	Mickey Welch
1972	Lefty Gomez
	William Harridge
	Ross Youngs
1971	Dave Bancroft
	Jake Beckley
	Chick Hafey
	Harry Hopper
	Joe Kelley
	Rube Marquard
	George Weiss
1970	Earle Combs
	Ford Frick
	Jesse Haines
1969	Stan Coveleski
	Waite Hoyt
1968	Kiki Cuyler
	Goose Goslin
1967	Branch Rickey
	Lloyd Waner
1966	Casey Stengel
1965	Pud Galvin
1964	Red Faber
	Burleigh Grimes
	Miller Huggins
	Tim Keefe
	Heine Manush
	John Ward
1963	John Clarkson
	Elmer Flick
	Sam Rice
	Eppa Rixey
1962	Bill McKechnie
	Edd Roush
1961	Max Carey
	Billy Hamilton
1959	Zack Wheat
1957	Sam Crawford
	Joe McCarthy
1955	Frank Baker
	Ray Schalk
1953	Ed Barrow
	Chief Bender
	Thomas Connolly
	Bill Klem
	Bobby Wallace
	Harry Wright
1949	Mordecai Brown
	Kid Nichols
1946	Jesse Burkett
	Frank Chance
	Jack Chesbro
	Johnny Evers
	Clark Griffith
	Tommy McCarthy
	Joe McGinnity

	Eddie Plank	1938	Alexander Cartwright, Jr.
	Joe Tinker		Henry Chadwick
	Rube Waddell	1936	Morgan Bulkeley
	Ed Walsh		Ban Johnson
1945	Roger Bresnahan		John McGraw
	Dan Brouthers		Connie Mack
	Fred Clarke		George Wright
	Jimmy Collins		
	Ed Delahanty		
	Hugh Duffy		
	Hugh Jennings		
	Michael Kelly		
	Jim O'Rourke		
	Wilbert Robinson		
1944	Kenesaw Mountain		
	Landis		
1939	Cap Anson		
	Charles Comiskey		
	Candy Cummings		
	Buck Ewing		
	Hoss Radbourn		
	Al Spalding		

(elected by the Negro League Committee)

Year of Induction	Player
1977	Pop Lloyd
	Martin Dihigo
1976	Oscar Charleston
1975	Judy Johnson
1974	Cool Papa Bell
1973	Monte Irvin
1972	Josh Gibson
	Buck Leonard
1971	Satchel Paige

PRO FOOTBALL HALL OF FAME INDUCTEES

1999
Eric Dickerson
Tom Mack
Ozzie Newsome
Billy Shaw
Lawrence Taylor

1998
Paul Krause
Tommy McDonald
Anthony Munoz
Mike Singletary
Dwight Stephenson

1997
Mike Haynes
Wellington Mara
Don Shula
Mike Webster

1996
Lou Creekmur
Dan Dierdorf
Joe Gibbs
Charlie Joiner
Mel Renfro

1995
Jim Finks
Henry Jordan
Steve Largent
Lee Roy Selmon
Kellen Winslow

1994
Tony Dorsett
Harry (Bud) Grant
Jimmy Johnson
Leroy Kelly
Jackie Smith
Randy White

1993
Dan Fouts
Larry Little
Chuck Noll
Walter Payton
Bill Walsh

1992
Lem Barney

Al Davis
John Mackey
John Riggins

1991
Earl Campbell
John Hannah
Stan Jones
Tex Schramm
Jan Stenerud

1990
Junious (Buck) Buchanan
Bob Griese
Franco Harris
Ted Hendricks
Jack Lambert
Tom Landry
Bob St. Clair

1989
Mel Blount
Terry Bradshaw
Art Shell
Willie Wood

1988
Fred Bilentnikoff
Mike Ditka
Jack Ham
Alan Page

1987
Larry Csonka
Len Dawson
Joe Greene
John Henry Johnson
Jim Langer
Don Maynard
Gene Upshaw

1986
Paul Hornung
Ken Houston
Willie Lanier
Frank Tarkenton
Doak Walter

1985
Frank Gatski
Joe Namath

Pete Rozelle
O.J. Simpson
Roger Stauback

1984
Willie Brown
Mike McCormack
Charley Taylor
Arnie Weinmeister

1983
Bobby Bell
Sid Gillman
Sonny Jurgensen
Bobby Mitchell
Paul Warfield

1982
Doug Atkins
Sam Huff
George Musso
Merlin Olsen

1981
Morris (Red) Badgro
George Blanda
Willie Davis
Jim Ringo

1980
Herb Adderley
David (Deacon) Jones
Bob Lilly
Jim Otto

1979
Dick Butkus
Yale Lary
Ron Mix
Johnny Unitas

1978
Lance Alworth
Weeb Ewbank
Alphonse (Tuffy)
  Leemans
Ray Nitschke
Larry Wilson

1977
Frank Gifford
Forrest Gregg
Gale Sayers
Bart Starr
Bill Willis

1976
Ray Flaherty
Len Ford
Jim Taylor

1975
Roosevelt Brown
George Connor
Dante Lavelli
Lenny Moore

1974
Tony Canadeo
Bill George
Lou Groza
Dick (Night Train) Lane

1973
Raymond Berry
Jim Parker
Joe Schmidt

1972
Lamar Hunt
Gino Marchetti
Ollie Matson
Clarence (Ace) Parker

1971
Jim Brown
Bill Hewitt
Frank (Bruiser) Kinard
Vince Lombardi
Andy Robustelli
Y.A. Tittle
Norm Van Brocklin

1970
Jack Christiansen
Tom Fears
Hugh McElhenny
Pete Pihos

1969
Glen (Turk) Edwards
Earle (Greasy) Neale
Leo Nomellini

Joe Perry
Ernie Stautner

1968
Cliff Battles
Art Donovan
Elroy (Crazylegs) Hirsch
Wayne Millner
Marion Motley
Charley Trippi
Alex Wojciechowicz

1967
Chuck Bednarik
Charles Bidwill
Paul Brown
Bobby Layne
Dan Reeves
Ken Strong
Joe Stydahar
Emlen Tunnell

1966
Bill Dudley
Joy Guyon
Arnie Herber
Walt Kiesling
George McAfee
Steve Owen
Hugh (Shorty) Ray
Clyde (Bulldog) Turner

1965
Guy Chamberlin
John (Paddy) Driscoll
Dan Fortmann
Otto Graham
Sid Luckman
Steve Van Buren
Bob Waterfield

1964
Jimmy Conzelman
Ed Healey
Clark Hinkle
Roy (Link) Lyman
August (Mike)
Michaelske
Art Rooney
George Trafton

1963
Sammy Baugh
Bert Bell
Joe Carr

Earl (Dutch) Clark
Red Grange
George Halas
Mel Hein
Wilbur (Pete) Henry
Cal Hubbard
Don Hutson
Earl (Curly) Lambeau
Tim Mara
George Preston Marshall
Johnny Blood (McNally)
Bronko Nagurski
Ernie Nevers
Jim Thorpe

BASKETBALL HALL OF FAME INDUCTEES

Year inducted	Players
1998	Larry Bird
	Arnie Risen
1996	Alex English
	Bailey Howell
1995	George Gervin
	Gail Goodrich
	David Thompson
	George Yardley
1994	Kareem Abdul-Jabbar
	Vern Mikkelsen
1993	Harold E. "Buddy" Jeanette
1992	Walt Bellamy
	Julius "Dr. J" Erving
	Dan Issel
	Dick McGuire
	Calvin Murphy
	Bill Walton
1991	Connie Hawkins
	Bob Lanier
1990	Nate "Tiny" Archibald
	Dave Cowens
	Harry "The Horse" Gallatin
1989	Dave Bing
	Elvin "The Big E" Hayes
	Neil Johnston
	Earl "The Pearl" Monroe
1988	William "Pop" Gates
	K.C. Jones
	Lenny Wilkens
1987	Clyde Lovellette
	Wes Unseld
1986	Rick Barry
	Walt "Clyde" Frazier
	Robert Houbregs
	Pete Maravich
	Bobby Wanzer
1985	Billy Cunningham
	Tom Heinsohn
1984	Al Cervi
	Nate Thurmond
1983	John Havlicek
	Sam Jones
1982	Bill Bradley
	Dave DeBusschere
	Jack Twyman
1981	Hal Greer
	Slater Martin
	Frank Ramsey
	Willis Reed
1979	Jerry Lucas
	Oscar Robertson
	Jerry West
1978	Wilt Chamberlain
1977	Paul Arizin
	Joe Fulks
	Cliff Hagan
	Jim Pollard
1976	Elgin Baylor
1975	Tom Gola
	Bill Sharman
1974	Bill Russell
1972	Dolph Schayes
1970	Bob Cousy
	Bob Pettit
1969	Bob Davies
1966	Joe Lapchick
1964	John "Honey" Russell
1961	Andy Phillip
1960	Edward "Easy Ed" Macauley
1959	George Mikan

Year inducted	Coaches
1998	Alex Hannum
	Lenny Wilkens
1996	Pete Carril
1993	Charles J. "Chuck" Daly
1991	Al McGuire
	Jack Ramsay
1985	William "Red" Holzman
1976	Frank McGuire
1975	Harry Litwack
1968	Arnold "Red" Auerbach
1967	Alvin "Doggie" Julian
1964	Ken Loeffler

Year inducted	Contributors
1990	Larry Fleisher
	Larry O'Brien

1980	J. Walter Kennedy
1979	Lester Harrison
1978	Pete Newell
1973	Maurice Podoloff
1971	Eddie Gottlieb
1965	Walter Brown
	Bill Mokray
1964	Edward "Ned" Irish
1959	Harold Olsen

Year inducted	Referees
1994	Earl Strom
1979	J. Dallas Shirley
1978	Jim Enright
1977	John Nucatola
1959	Matthew "Pat" Kennedy

ROCK AND ROLL HALL OF FAME INDUCTEES

1999
Billy Joel
Curtis Mayfield
Paul McCartney
Del Shannon
Dusty Springfield
Bruce Springsteen
Staple Singers

Non-Performer
George Martin

Early Influences
Charles Brown
Bob Wills and His Texas Playboys

1998
Eagles
Fleetwood Mac
Mamas and Papas
Lloyd Price
Santana
Gene Vincent

Non-Performer
Allen Toussaint

Early Influence
Jelly Roll Morton

1997
Bee Gees
Buffalo Springfield
Crosby, Stills and Nash
Jackson Five
Joni Mitchell
Parliament-Funkadelic
(Young) Rascals

Non-Performer
Syd Nathan

Early Influences
Mahalia Jackson
Bill Monroe

1996
David Bowie
Jefferson Airplane
Little Willie John
Gladys Knight and the Pips
Pink Floyd
Shirelles
Velvet Underground

Non-Performer
Tom Donahue

Early Influence
Pete Seeger

1995
The Allman Brothers Band
Al Green
Janis Joplin
Led Zeppelin
Martha and the Vandellas
Neil Young
Frank Zappa

Non-Performer
Paul Ackerman
1995 (cont.)
Early Influence
Orioles

1994
Animals
The Band
Duane Eddy
Grateful Dead
Elton John
John Lennon
Bob Marley
Rod Stewart

Non-Performer
Johnny Otis

Early Influence
Willie Dixon

1993
Ruth Brown
Cream
Creedence Clearwater Revival
Doors
Etta James
Frankie Lymon and the Teenagers
Van Morrison
Sly and the Family Stone

Non-Performers
Dick Clark
Milt Gabler

Early Influence
Dinah Washington

1992
Bobby "Blue" Bland
Booker T. and the M.G.'s
Johnny Cash
Jimi Hendrix
Isley Brothers
Sam and Dave
Yardbirds

Non-Performers
Leo Fender
Bill Graham
Doc Pomus

Early Influences
Elmore James
Professor Longhair

1991
La Vern Baker
Byrds
John Lee Hooker
Impressions
Wilson Pickett
Jimmy Reed
Ike and Tina Turner

Non-Performers
Dave Bartholomew
Ralph Bass

Early Influence
Howlin' Wolf

Lifetime Achievement
Nesuhi Ertegun

1990
Hank Ballard
Bobby Darin
Four Seasons
Four Tops
Kinks
Platters
Simon and Garfunkel
The Who

Non-Performers
Gerry Goffin and Carole King
Holland, Dozier, and Holland

Early Influences
Louis Armstrong
Charlie Christian
Ma Rainey

1989
Dion
Otis Redding
Rolling Stones
Temptations
Stevie Wonder

Non-Performer
Phil Spector
1989 (cont.)
Early Influences
The Ink Spots
Bessie Smith
Soul Stirrers

1988
Beach Boys
Beatles
Drifters
Bob Dylan
Supremes

Non-Performer
Berry Gordy, Jr.

Early Influences
Woody Guthrie
Lead Belly
Les Paul

1987
Coasters
Eddie Cochran

1987 (cont.)
Bo Diddley
Aretha Franklin
Marvin Gaye
Bill Haley
B. B. King
Clyde McPhatter
Ricky Nelson
Roy Orbison
Carl Perkins
Smokey Robinson
Big Joe Turner
Muddy Waters
Jackie Wilson
Non-Performers
Leonard Chess
Ahmet Ertegun
Jerry Leiber and Mike Stoller
Jerry Wexler

Early Influences
Louis Jordan
T-Bone Walker
Hank Williams

1986
Chuck Berry
James Brown
Ray Charles
Sam Cooke
Fats Domino
Everly Brothers
Buddy Holly
Jerry Lee Lewis
Elvis Presley
Little Richard

Non-Performers
Alan Freed
Sam Phillips

Early-Influences
Robert Johnson
Jimmie Rodgers
Jimmy Yancey

Lifetime Achievement
John Hammond

Dictionary of Places

Aa

Aa·ben·raa |'awbən,raw| (also **Åbenrå**) port and resort town in SE Jutland, Denmark. Pop. 21,000.

Aa·chen |'äкHən| (French name **Aix-La-Chapelle**) industrial city and spa in western Germany, in North Rhine–Westphalia; Charlemagne's capital and favorite residence. Pop. 244,440.

Aal·borg |'awl,bawrg| (also **Ålborg**) industrial city and port in N Jutland, Denmark. Pop. 155,000.

Aa·len |'älən| industrial city in S Germany, on the Kocher River, E of Stuttgart. Pop. 65,000. The city is noted for its old half-timbered houses. It gives its name to the Aalen period in geological history.

Aale·sund |'awlə,sōōn| commercial seaport and fishing town in W Norway, on three islands. Pop. 36,000. It is linked by tunnel to several offshore islands.

Aals·meer |'äls,mer| town in W central Netherlands, SW of Amsterdam. Pop. 22,000. It is famous for its huge flower market.

Aalst |'älst| industrial city in W central Belgium. Pop. 77,000.

Aa·re River |'ärə| river (184 mi./295 km. long) in Switzerland. Rising in the Bernese Alps, it flows NW to the Rhine opposite the German town of Waldshut and is the longest river entirely in Switzerland.

Aar·gau |'är,gow| canton in N Switzerland, in a fertile agricultural region. Area: 543 sq. mi./1,405 sq. km. Pop. 490,000. Capital: Aarau.

Aar·hus |'awr,hōōs| (also **Århus**) city on the coast of E Jutland, Denmark. Pop. 261,440.

A·ba |ə'bä| industrial city in S Nigeria, NE of Port Harcourt. Pop. 264,000.

Aba·co Islands |'æbə,kō| forested island group in the N Bahamas.

Aba·dan |,äbə'dän| major port and oil-refining center on an island of the same name on the Shatt al-Arab waterway in W Iran. Pop. 308,000.

Aba·kan |,äbə'kän; ,əbə'kän| (until 1931 **Ustabakanskoe**) industrial city in S central Russia, capital of the republic of Khakassia. Pop. 154,000.

Abbe·ville[1] |äbə'vēl| industrial and commercial town in N France. Pop. 25,000. It gives its name to early Paleolithic pickaxe industries (*c.* 500,000 B.C.), remains of which were found here. □ **Abbevillian** *adj. & n.*

Ab·be·ville[2] |'æbē,vil| historic city in NW South Carolina. Pop. 5,778.

Ab·bey Road |'æbē| road in NW London, England, W of Regents Park, site of recording studios associated with the Beatles and other pop music figures.

Ab·bey Theatre |'æbē| theater in Abbey Street, Dublin, Ireland, opened in 1904 and associated with Yeats and other writers and with Irish culture in general.

Ab·bots·ford |'æbətsfərd| district municipality in SW British Columbia, near the Washington border. Pop. 18,864.

Ab·bot·ta·bad |'æbətə,bäd| resort city in N Pakistan, in the foothills of the Himalayas. Pop. 66,000.

ABC Islands |'ā'bē'sē| acronym for the Dutch Caribbean islands of Aruba, Bonaire, and Curaçao.

Ab·de·ra |æb'dirə| city in ancient Greece, on the Aegean Sea, E of the mouth of the Mesta River. It was home to several prominent Greek philosophers, among them Protagoras and Democritus.

Abé·ché |,äbā'sHä| (also **Abeshr**) historic commercial city in E Chad. Pop. 188,000. Once capital of the Ouaddaï Empire, it is a trade center for the Sahel.

Abe·o·ku·ta |ä'bäōkōō,tä| city in SW Nigeria, capital of the state of Ogun. Pop. 308,800.

Aber·deen[1] |'æbər,dēn| town in NE Maryland, on Chesapeake Bay. Pop. 13,087. A major military test range is nearby.

Aber·deen[2] |'æbər,dēn| city and seaport in NE Scotland, the administrative capital of Grampian region. It is a center of the offshore North Sea oil industry. Pop. 201,100.

Aber·deen[3] |,æbər'dēn| city in NE South Dakota, a dairy center. Pop. 24,927.

Aber·deen·shire |,æbər'dēnsHər; ,æbər'dēn,sHir| former county of NE Scotland. It became a part of Grampian region in 1975.

Aber·fan |,æbər'væn| village in S Wales where, in 1966, a slag heap collapsed, overwhelming houses and a school and killing 28 adults and 116 children.

Aber·foyle |,æbər'foil| resort village in SW Scotland, in the Trossachs, N of Glasgow. It is associated with the writings of Sir Walter Scott.

Abe·ryst·wyth |,æbə'rist,wiTH| resort and

cultural town on Cardigan Bay, W Wales. Pop. 10,000.

Ab•ha |'äb,hä| (also **Ebha; Ibha**) city in SW Saudi Arabia, in the highland area of Asir province. Pop. 112,000.

Abi•djan |,æbə'jän| chief port of Côte d'Ivoire, the capital 1935–83. Pop. 1,850,000.

Abi•lene[1] |'æbə,lēn| commercial city in E central Kansas, famed as the first terminus of the Chisholm Trail. Pop. 6,242.

Abi•lene[2] |'æbə,lēn| city in N central Texas, an agricultural and oil industry center. Pop. 106,654.

Abi•quiu |,æbə'kēōō| ranching community in N New Mexico, noted as the longtime home of artist Georgia O'Keeffe.

Ab•kha•zia |äb'кнäzēə| autonomous territory in the NW republic of Georgia, S of the Caucasus Mts. on the Black Sea. Pop. 537,500. Capital: Sokhumi. In 1992 Abkhazia unilaterally declared itself independent, sparking armed conflict with Georgia, and the following year drove Georgian forces from its territory. □ **Abkhazian** adj. & n. **Abkhazi** adj. & n.

Abo•mey |,æbə'mā; ə'bōmē| town in S Benin, capital of the former kingdom of Dahomey. Pop. 54,400.

Abra•ham, Plains of |'abrə,hæm| see PLAINS OF ABRAHAM.

Abruz•zi |ə'brōōtsē| mountainous region of E central Italy. Capital: Aquila.

Ab•sa•ro•ka Range |æb'sawrkē| range of the Rocky Mts. in Montana and Wyoming.

A•bu Dha•bi |,äbōō 'däbē| **1** the largest of the seven member states of the United Arab Emirates, lying between Oman and the Persian Gulf coast. Pop. 670,125. The former sheikhdom joined the federation of the United Arab Emirates in 1971. **2** the capital of this state. Pop. 242,975. It is also the federal capital of the United Arab Emirates.

Abu•ja |ə'bōōjə| newly built city in central Nigeria, designated in 1982 to replace Lagos as the national capital. Pop. 378,670.

Abu•kir |,äbōō'kir| see ABU QIR,.

Abu Mu•sa |,äbōō 'mōōsə| small island in the Persian Gulf. Formerly held by the emirate of Sharjah, it has been occupied by Iran since 1971.

Abu Qir |ä'bōō 'kir| (also **Abukir** or **Aboukir**) village in N Egypt, NE of Alexandria, on Abu Qir Bay. The British won the Battle of the Nile (1798) in the bay. Ancient Canopus was in this locality.

Abu Sim•bel |,äbōō 'simbəl| (also **Ipsambul**) former village in S Egypt. Rock tem-

ples here were removed to high ground in the 1960s, after building of the Aswan Dam on the Nile River.

Aby•dos[1] |ə'bīdes| town of ancient Egypt, on the Nile River N of Thebes, the site of burial of many early pharaohs.

Aby•dos[2] |ə'bīdes| town of ancient Asia Minor, in present-day NW Turkey, on the S side of the Dardanelles. It is across from Sestos and NE of modern Canakkale, and is associated with the legend of Hero and Leander.

Abys•si•nia |,æbə'sinēə| former name for ETHIOPIA. □ **Abyssinian** adj. & n.

Aca•dia |ə'kādēə| former French colony established in 1604 in the territory that later formed Nova Scotia. It was contested by France and Britain until it was ceded to Britain in 1763. Acadians were deported to other parts of North America; some migrated to Louisiana (where they became known as Cajuns). □ **Acadian** adj. & n.

Aca•jut•la |,äkə'hōōtlə| seaport town in W El Salvador, the leading Pacific port in the country. Pop. 17,000.

Aca•pul•co |,äkə'pōōlkō| port and resort in S Mexico, on the Pacific coast. Pop. 592,290. Full name **Acapulco de Juárez.**

Ac•cra |ə'krä| capital of Ghana, a port on the Gulf of Guinea. Pop. 867,000.

Aceh |'ä,cнä| (also **Atjeh; Achin**) province and special region of Indonesia, on N Sumatra. Area: 21,395 sq. mi./55,392 sq. km. Pop. 2,611,000. Capital: Banda Aceh.

Achaea |ə'kēə| region of ancient Greece on the North coast of the Peloponnese. □ **Achaean** adj. & n.

Ache•lous River |,ækə'lōōəs| second-longest river in Greece (137 mi./219 km). It rises in the Pindus Mts. and flows into the Ionian Sea near the Gulf of Patras.

Ache•ron River |'ækə,rän| in Greek mythology, a river that flowed through Hades. The name is also given to several rivers in Greece that pass through underground caverns and caves.

Achill Island |'ækəl| island in County Mayo, NW Ireland, a noted fishing center.

Áco•ma |'äkə,maw; 'ækə,maw| Indian community atop a mesa in NW New Mexico, one of the oldest known human settlements in North America.

Acon•ca•gua |,ækən'kägwə| extinct volcano in the Andes, on the border between Chile and Argentina, rising to 22,834 ft./6,960 m. It is the highest mountain in the W hemisphere.

Aço•res |ə'sawris| Portuguese spelling for AZORES Islands.

Acre[1] |'äkrə| state of western Brazil, on the border with Peru. Capital: Rio Branco.

Acre[2] |'äkər; 'äkər| industrial seaport of NW Israel. Pop. 39,100. Also called **Akko**.

Ac·ro·po·lis, the |ə'kräpələs| hill (260 ft./80 m. high) in Athens, Greece, atop which is the Parthenon, a temple to Athena, and other ancient sites, some built as early as the 5th century B.C. The Acropolis was destroyed by the Persians in 480 B.C.

Ac·te |'äktē| peninsula in NE Greece, one of three fingers at the end of Chalcidice, extending into the Aegean Sea between the Strymonic Gulf and Singitic Gulf. Mount Athos is at its tip.

Adak |'ä,dæk| island in the Aleutian Islands of SW Alaska, site of a U.S. naval base.

Ada·ma·wa |,ädə'mä-wə| plateau region of W Africa, in N central Cameroon and E Nigeria. It is also the name of a Nigerian state and a province of Cameroon.

Adam's Bridge |'ædəmz| line of shoals lying between NW Sri Lanka and the SE coast of Tamil Nadu in India, separating the Palk Strait from the Gulf of Mannar.

Adam's Peak |'ædəmz| mountain in S central Sri Lanka, rising to 2,243 m./7,360 ft. It is regarded as sacred by Buddhists, Hindus, and Muslims.

Ada·na |,ädə'nä| a town in S Turkey, capital of a province of the same name. Pop. 916,150.

Ada·pa·za·ri |,ädə,päzə'rə| commercial and industrial city in NW Turkey, in Sakarya province. Pop. 171,000.

Ad Dam·mam |,äd dä'mäm| port town in Saudi Arabia, on the Persian Gulf coast. Pop. 1,224,000.

Ad·dis Aba·ba |,ædəs 'æbəbə| capital and largest city of Ethiopia, in the central plateau. Pop. 2,113,000. It is the commercial and cultural center of Ethiopia, and has light industries.

Ad·di·son |'ædəsən| village in NE Illinois, a suburb NW of Chicago. Pop. 32,058.

Ade·laide |'ædl,äd| industrial port city, the capital of South Australia state, Australia. Pop. 1,050,000.

Adé·lie Land |ə'dālē| (also **Adélie Coast**) section of the Antarctic continent S of the 60th parallel, between Wilkes Land and King George V Land.

Aden, Gulf of |'ädn; 'ædn| part of the E Arabian Sea lying between the S coast of Yemen and the Horn of Africa.

Aden |'ädən| port in Yemen at the mouth of the Red Sea. Pop. 417,370. Aden was formerly under British rule, first as part of British India (from 1839), then from 1935

as a Crown Colony. It was capital of the former South Yemen from 1967 until 1990.

Adi·ge River |'ädə,jā| river (255 mi./408 km.) in NE Italy, rising in the Rhaetian Alps and flowing into the Adriatic Sea between Venice and the mouth of the Po River.

Adi·ron·dack Mountains |,ædə'rän,dæk| (also **the Adirondacks**) range of mountains in New York, source of the Hudson and Mohawk rivers. It is part of the Canadian Shield.

Adi·ron·dack Park |,ædə'rän,dæk| state preserve in N central New York, the largest park in the contiguous U.S.

Adis A·be·ba |,ædəs 'æbəbə| variant spelling of ADDIS ABABA.

Adi·ya·man |,ädēə'män| city in SE Turkey, capital of Adiyaman province. Pop. 100,000.

Ad·mi·ral·ty Islands |'ædm(ə)rəltē| group of about forty islands in the W Pacific, part of Papua New Guinea.

Ado-Ekiti |,ädō,ä'kētē| city in SW Nigeria, in the Yoruba Hills. Pop. 317,000.

Adrar des Ifo·ras |ä'drär dō,zēfaw'rä| massif region in the central Sahara, on the border between Mali and Algeria.

Adri·an |'ädrēən| city in SE Michigan. Pop. 22,097

Adri·at·ic Sea |,ädrē'ætik| arm of the Mediterranean Sea between the Balkans and the Italian peninsula.

Ad·wa |'ädwə| (also **Adua**) historic commercial town in N Ethiopia, in Tigré province, site of an 1896 defeat of the Italians by Menelik II. Pop. 25,000.

Ady·gea |,ädə'gäə| autonomous republic in the NW Caucasus in SW Russia, with a largely Muslim population. Pop. 432,000. Capital: Maikop. Full name **Adygei Autonomous Republic.**

Ad·zha·ria |ə'järēə| (also **Adjaria** or **Adzharistan**) autonomous republic in the Republic of Georgia, on the Black Sea. Its capital is Batumi. Pop. 382,000.

Ae·ge·an Islands |i'jēən| group of islands in the Aegean Sea, forming a region of Greece. The principal islands of the group are Chios, Samos, Lesbos, the Cyclades, and the Dodecanese.

Ae·ge·an Sea |i'jēən| part of the Mediterranean Sea lying between Greece and Turkey, bounded to the S by Crete and Rhodes and linked to the Black Sea by the Dardanelles, the Sea of Marmara, and the Bosporus.

Ae·gi·na |i'jīnə| resort and seaport in E Greece, on the Saronic Gulf, SW of Athens. Pop. 11,000.

Ae•go•spo•ta•mi |ˌēgəˈspätəˌmī| small river of ancient Thrace flowing into the Hellespont (now the Dardanelles). Near its mouth the Athenian fleet was defeated by Lysander in 405 B.C., ending the Peloponnesian War.

Ae•o•lian Islands |ēˈōlyən| ancient name for LIPARI ISLANDS.

Ae•o•lis |ˈēələs| ancient Greek colony in NW Asia Minor (present-day Turkey).

Ae•to•lia |iˈtōlyə| region of ancient Greece, now part of the modern department of Aetolia and Acarnania, in central Greece. Pop. 231,000. The capital is Mesolóngion.

Afar |əˈfär| desert region of NE Ethiopia, on the borders of Eritrea and Djibouti.

Af•ghan•i•stan |æfˈgænəˌstæn| mountainous landlocked republic in central Asia. Area: 250,173 sq. mi./647,697 sq. km. Pop. 16,600,000. Languages, Pashto and Dari (Persian). Capital and largest city: Kabul. Long dominated by British and Russian interests, Afghanistan has been in turmoil since Soviet withdrawal in 1989. Most of the country is in the Hindu Kush; agriculture, textiles, and natural gas are important to the economy. □ **Afghan** *adj. & n.*

Afghanistan

Af•ri•ca |ˈæfrikə| the second largest (11.62 million sq. mi./30.1 million sq. km.) continent, a S projection of the Old World land mass divided roughly in two by the equator and surrounded by sea except where the Isthmus of Suez joins it to Asia. Largest country: Sudan. Largest city: Cairo, Egypt. In the N Africa is dominated by the Sahara Desert, S of which is the transitional Sahel, with a central plateau and surrounding tropical lowlands farther S. In the far S, much of South Africa is temperate. □ **African** *adj. & n.*

Af•ton |ˈæftən| (also **Afton Water** stream in SW Scotland, in the Strathclyde region, immortalized by the poet Robert Burns.

Af•yon |äfˈyōn| (also **Afyonkarahisar**) city in W Turkey, capital of Afyon province.

Pop. 96,000. The area is noted for its opium production.

Aga•dir |ˌägəˈdir| seaport and resort on the Atlantic coast of Morocco. Pop. 110,500.

Aga•na |əˈgänyə| the capital of Guam, on the Philippine Sea. Pop. 1,139.

Agar•ta•la |ˌəgərtlˈä| city in the far NE of India, capital of the state of Tripura, near the border with Bangladesh. Pop. 157,640.

Agas•siz, Lake prehistoric glacial lake of the Pleistocene epoch, covering parts of present-day Minnesota, North Dakota, Manitoba, and Ontario.

Age•nais |äzHəˈnä| ancient region of SW France. The major town is Agen. The region corresponds roughly to the present department of Lot-et-Garonne.

Aghi•os Ni•ko•la•os |ˈäyē‚aws niˈkōlä‚aws| fishing port and resort on the N coast of Crete, E of Heraklion. Pop. 8,100. Greek name **Áyios Nikólaos**.

Agin•court |ˈæjən‚kawrt; ˈäzHən‚ko͞or| village in the Pas-de-Calais, N France. In 1415, during the Hundred Years War, King Henry V of England defeated a much larger French force here. Modern French name, **Azincourt**.

Agou•ra Hills |əˈgawrə| city in SW California, a suburb NW of Los Angeles. Pop. 20,390.

Ag•ra |ˈägrə| city on the Jumna River in Uttar Pradesh state, N India. Pop. 899,000. Founded in 1566, Agra was the capital of the Mogul empire until 1658. It is the site of the TAJ MAHAL.

Ag•ri |ˈärē; äˈrə| capital of Agri province in extreme E Turkey, near the Armenian and Iranian borders. Pop. 58,000.

Ag•ri•gen•to |ˌägriˈjen‚tō| market and tourist center in Sicily, in S Italy, capital of Agrigento province. Pop. 57,000. On a hill overlooking the Mediterranean Sea, the town has many ancient monuments.

Agua Pri•e•ta |ˈägwəprēˈätə| city in Sonora, NW Mexico, near the Arizona border. Pop. 38,000.

Aguas•ca•lien•tes |ˌägwəskälˈyen‚täs| **1** state of central Mexico. Area: 2,217 sq. mi./5,471 sq. km. Pop. 720,000. **2** its capital, a health resort noted for its hot springs. Pop. 506,000.

Agul•has, Cape |əˈgələs| the most southerly (34° 52' S) point of the continent of Africa, in the province of Western Cape, South Africa.

Agul•has Current |əˈgələs| ocean current flowing S along the E coast of Africa.

Ah•len |ˈälən| industrial city in NW Germany, S of Münster. Pop. 53,000.

Ah·ma·da·bad |'ämədə,bäd| (also **Ahmedabad**) industrial city in the state of Gujarat in W India. Pop. 2,873,000.

Ah·mad·na·gar |,äməd'nəgər| (also **Ahmednagar**) commercial and industrial city in W central India, in Maharashtra state. Pop. 222,000.

Ahua·cha·pán |,äwəchə'pän| commercial city in SW El Salvador, capital of Ahuachapán department. Pop. 25,000. It is in an area noted for its coffee and its geothermal power production.

Ah·vaz |ä'wäz| (also **Ahwaz**) historic commercial and industrial city in W Iran, in an oil-producing area. Pop. 725,000.

Ah·ve·nan·maa |'ävänən,mä| Finnish name for **Åland Islands**.

Ai·ken |'äken| resort city in W central South Carolina. Pop. 19,872.

Ain·tab |ïn'tæb| former name (until 1921) for GAZIANTEP, Turkey.

Ain·tree |'äntrē| suburb of Liverpool, England, site of a racecourse over which the Grand National steeplechase is run.

Aire River |ær; er| river in W Yorkshire, England. Leeds lies on it, and its upper valley, **Airedale**, gave its name to the dog breed.

Aisne River |en; än| river (150 mi./240 km.) that rises in the Argonne area in NE France and flows NW to meet the Oise River at Compiègne.

Aix-en-Pro·vence |eks äN prō'väNs| historic spa and cultural city in Provence in S France. Pop. 126,850.

Aix-la-Cha·pelle |,eks lä sHä'pel| French name for AACHEN.

Ai·zawl |ï'zowl| city in the far NE of India, capital of the state of Mizoram. Pop. 154,000.

Ajac·cio |ä'yäCHō; äzHäks'yō| port on the W coast of Corsica. Pop. 59,320. It is the capital of the department of Corse-du-Sud.

Ajan·ta Caves |ə'jəntə| series of caves in the state of Maharashtra, S central India, containing Buddhist frescos and sculptures dating from the 1st century B.C. to the 7th century A.D.

Ajax |'ā,jæks| industrial town in S Ontario. Pop. 57,350.

Aj·man |æj'män; äj'mæn| **1** smallest of the seven emirates of the United Arab Emirates. Pop. 64,320. **2** its capital city.

Aj·mer |əj'mir; əj'mer| commercial city in NW India, in Rajasthan. Pop. 402,000.

Ajo·dhya |ə'yōdyə| see AYODHYA, India.

Akar·naí |ä,kärnä'ē| (also **Akharnai**, **Acharnae**) town in S Greece, N of Athens. Aristophanes set his play *The Acharnians* here. Pop. 40,000.

Aka·shi |'äkə,sHē; ə'käsHē| industrial port city in W central Japan, on SW Honshu. Pop. 271,000. Standard time for Japan is set here.

Ak·he·ta·ten |,äkə'tätn| ancient Egyptian capital built by Akhenaten in *c.* 1375 B.C. when he established the new worship of the sun disc Aten, but abandoned after his death. See also AMARNA, TELL EL-.

Aki·ta |ä'kētə| industrial port city in NE Japan, on N Honshu. Pop. 302,000.

Ak·kad |'æk,æd; 'äk,äd| ancient city on the Euphrates River in central Mesopotamia, its exact location unknown. It gave its name to the Akkadian Empire and language. □ **Akkadian** *adj. & n.*

Ak-Mechet |,äk mə'CHet| former name for SIMFEROPOL, Ukraine.

Ak·mo·la |äk'mawlə| alternate spelling for AQMOLA, Kazakhstan.

Ako·la |ə'kōlə| commercial and industrial city in W central India, in Maharashtra state. Pop. 328,000.

Ak·ron |'ækrən| city in NE Ohio. Pop. 223,000. Through much of the 20th century it was the center of the tire and rubber industry in the U.S.

Ak·sai Chin |'äk,sī 'CHin| region of the Himalayas between Tibet and Xinjiang, occupied by China since 1950. It is claimed by India as part of Kashmir.

Ak·su |'äk'soō| city in Xinjiang, W China, on the Aksu River in the foothills of the Tian Shan range. Pop. 341,000. It was the Mongol capital in the 14th century.

Ak·sum |'äk,soōm| (also **Axum**) a town in the province of Tigray in N Ethiopia. It was a religious center and the capital of a powerful kingdom between the 1st and 6th centuries A.D. □ **Aksumite** *adj. & n.*

Ak·tyu·binsk |ək'tyoōbinsk| **1** subdivision of W central Kazakhstan. Pop. 753,000.

Aku·mal |,äkoō'mäl| village in SE Mexico, in Quintana Roo state, on the Gulf of Mexico, noted as a diving and beach resort.

Ala·bama |,ælə'bæmə| see box, p. 6. □ **Alabaman** *adj. & n.*

Ala·bama River |,ælə'bæmə| river in S Alabama, flowing 315 mi./507 km. into the Mobile River.

Ala·goas |,älə'gōəs| state in E Brazil, on the Atlantic coast. Pop. 2,513,000. Capital: Maceió.

Alai Range |'ä,lī| mountain range in SW Kyrgyzstan. The highest peak reaches 19,554 ft./5,960 m.

Ala·me·da[1] |,ælə'mēdə| port city in N central California, just SW of Oakland on San Francisco Bay. Pop. 76,459.

Alabama

Capital: Montgomery
Largest city: Birmingham
Other cities: Athens, Decatur, Dothan, Gadsden, Huntsville, Mobile, Tuscaloosa
Population: 4,040,587 (1990); 4,351,999 (1998); 4,631,000 (2005 proj.)
Population rank (1990): 22
Rank in land area: 30
Abbreviation: AL; Ala.
Nicknames: The Heart of Dixie; Yellowhammer State
Motto: *Audemus jura nostra defendere* (Latin: 'We Dare Defend Our Rights')
Bird: flicker; yellowhammer
Fish: tarpon
Flower: camellia
Tree: Southern longleaf pine
Song: "Alabama"
Noted physical features: Appalachian Mountains
Tourist attractions: Azalea Trail Festival; Civil Rights Memorial/Museum, Alabama Shakespeare Festival; Carver Museum; W.C. Handy Home & Museum; Alabama Space and Rocket Center; Moundville State Monument; Pike Pioneer Museum; USS *Alabama* Memorial Park; Russell Cave National Monument; Vulcan Statue.
Admission date: December 14, 1819
Order of admission: 22
Name origin: For the Alabama River, which was possibly named for Choctaw Indians who lived along it.

Ala·me·da² |ˌäləˈmädə| public park in the center of Mexico City, Mexico, named for its cottonwood trees.
Ala·mo, the |ˈæləˌmō| historic site in San Antonio, Texas. In 1836 Mexican forces overwhelmed American defenders here.
Ala·mo·gor·do |ˌæləməˈgawrdō| city in S New Mexico. Pop. 27,596. White Sands and other military and aerospace facilities are nearby.
Åland Islands |ˈawˌlän| (Finnish name **Ahvenanmaa**) group of islands in the Gulf of Bothnia, forming an autonomous region of Finland. Capital: Mariehamn (known in Finnish as Maarianhamina).
Ala·nia |əˈlänyä| (formerly **Caucasian Republic of North Ossetia**), republic in S Russia, on the N slopes of the central Caucasus Mts. Pop. 695,000. The capital is Vladikavkaz.
Alap·pu·zha |ˌələˈpōōzə| see ALLEPEY, India.

Alas·ka |əˈlæskə| see box. □ **Alaskan** *adj.* & *n.*
Alas·ka, Gulf of |əˈlæskə| part of the NE Pacific, bounded by the Alaska Peninsula and the Alexander Archipelago.
Alas·ka Highway |əˈlæskə| see ALCAN HIGHWAY.
Alas·ka Peninsula |əˈlæskə| peninsula on the S coast of Alaska. It extends SW into the NE Pacific between the Bering Sea and the Gulf of Alaska, and is continued in the Aleutian Islands.
Alas·ka Range |əˈlæskə| mountain chain lying across S Alaska. Mt. McKinley (20,320 ft./6,194 m.) is its high point.
Ála·va |ˈäləvə| largest of the three Basque provinces in N Spain. Pop. 272,000. Capital: Vitoria.

Alaska

Capital: Juneau
Largest city: Anchorage
Other cities: Barrow, Fairbanks, Ketchikan, Kodiak, Nome, Sitka
Population: 550,043 (1990); 614,010 (1998); 700,000 (2005 proj.)
Population rank (1990): 49
Rank in land area: 1
Abbreviation: AK; Alas.
Nicknames: Great Land; Sourdough State; Last Frontier; Land of the Midnight Sun
Motto: 'North to the Future'
Bird: willow ptarmigan
Fish: chinook (king salmon)
Flower: forget-me-not
Tree: Sitka spruce
Song: "Alaska's Flag"
Noted physical features: Glacier Bay, Prudhoe Bay; Prince William Sound; Gulf of Alaska; Gastineau Channel; Malaspina Glacier; Mount McKinley (Alaska Range); Chilkoot Pass; Kenai, Alaska, Seward peninsulas; Alexander Archipelago; Whitehorse Rapids; Beaufort Sea; Bering Strait
Tourist attractions: Mount McKinley; Portage Glacier, Mendenhall Glacier; Ketchikan Totems; Glacier Bay National Park and Preserve; Denali National Park; Mt. Roberts Tramway; Pribilof Islands; St. Michael's Russian Orthodox Cathedral; Katmai National Park & Preserve.
Admission date: January 3, 1959
Order of admission: 49
Name origin: From the Aleutian word *alakshak*, meaning 'peninsula,' 'great land,' or 'mainland.'

Al·ba·ce·te |ˌälbə'sāˌtā| commercial city, in an agricultural province of the same name in SE Spain. Pop. 134,600.

Al·ba Iu·lia |ˌälbə 'yo͞olyə| city in W central Romania, to the N of the Transylvanian Alps. Pop. 72,330. Founded by the Romans in the 2nd century A.D., it was the capital of Transylvania.

Al·ba Lon·ga |ˌælbə 'lawnGgə| ancient city in the Alban Hills in central Italy, according to legend the birthplace of Romulus and Remus, founders of Rome.

Al·ba·nia |æl'bānēə; awl'bānēschwa.| republic in SE Europe, in the Balkan Peninsula, on the Adriatic Sea. Area: 11,104 sq. mi./28,748 sq. km. Pop. 3,300,000. Language, Albanian. Capital and largest city: Tirana. Part of the Byzantine, later the Ottoman, empires, Albania became independent in 1912. After World War II until 1992 it was an isolationist communist state. Agriculture has given way to industry in many areas, but the economy remains underdeveloped. □ **Albanian** *adj. & n.*

Albania

Al·ba·ny[1] |ˌawl'benē; æ'bānē| commercial city in SW Georgia. Pop. 78,122.

Al·ba·ny[2] |'awlbənē| state capital of New York, an industrial port and commercial and educational center on the Hudson River. Pop. 101,080.

Al·ba·ny[3] |'awlbənē| city in NW Oregon. Pop. 29,462.

Al·be·marle Sound |'ælbəˌmärl| inlet of the Atlantic in NE North Carolina, inside the Outer Banks.

Al·bert, Lake |'ælbərt| lake in the Rift Valley of E central Africa, on the border between the Democratic Republic of the Congo (formerly Zaire) and Uganda. It is linked to Lake Edwards by the Semliki River and to the White Nile by the Albert Nile. Also called **Lake Mobutu Sese Seko**.

Al·ber·ta |æl'bərtə| prairie province in W Canada, bounded on the S by the U.S. and on the W by the Rocky Mts. Area: 255,287 sq. mi./661,190 sq. km. Pop. 2,545,553. Capital: Edmonton. Largest city: Calgary. Oil and gas, wheat and other crops, and tourism are important to the economy of Alberta, which also has various industries in its urban centers. □ **Albertan** *adj. & n.*

Al·bert Canal |'ælbərt| canal in NE Belgium, 80 mi./128 km. long, that links the Meuse and Scheldt rivers, connecting the cities of Liège and Antwerp.

Al·bert Nile |äber'vēl| upper part of the White Nile, flowing through NW Uganda between Lake Albert and the Ugandan–Sudanese border.

Al·bert·ville |ælbərtˌvil| winter resort in SE France, in the Rhône-Alps region, near the Italian border. Pop. 18,000. The 1992 Winter Olympics were held here.

Al·bi |ˌäl'bē| town in S France. Pop. 48,700. The Albigensian heretical movement of the 12th and 13th centuries took its name from **Albiga**, the ancient name of the town, a center of the movement.

Al·bi·on |'ælbēən| ancient and literary name for the island of Great Britain.

Al·bu·quer·que |'ælbəˌkərkē| city in N central New Mexico, on the Rio Grande. Pop. 384,736. A commercial and research center, it is the largest city in New Mexico.

Al·bu·ry |'awlbərē| commercial town in SE Australia, on the N side of the Murray River in New South Wales. Pop. 40,000.

Al·ca·lá de He·na·res |ˌälkä'lä dä ə'näˌräs| city in central Spain, on the Henares River NE of Madrid. Pop. 162,780.

Al·can Highway |'ælˌkæn| (also **Alaska Highway**) military road, built during World War II to link Dawson Creek, in the Yukon Territory, with Fairbanks, Alaska, as part of a supply route to the Soviet Union and the Pacific.

Al·ca·traz |'ælkəˌtræz| rocky island in San Francisco Bay, California. It was, between 1934 and 1963, the site of a maximum security Federal prison, nicknamed "The Rock."

Al·cá·zar, the |ˌælkə'zär; æl'kæzər| 12th-century Moorish palace in Seville, SW Spain, later used by Spanish kings. The term is also applied to palaces in Toledo and other Spanish cities.

Al·cor·cón |ˌälkawr'kōn| SW suburb of Madrid, in central Spain. Pop. 140,000.

Al·da·bra |æl'dæbrə| coral island group in the Indian Ocean, NW of Madagascar. Formerly part of the British Indian Ocean Territory, it became an outlying dependency of the Seychelles in 1976.

Al·dan River |əl'dän| river (1,400 mi./

2,240 km.) in E Siberia, Russia. It rises in the Stanovoy Khrebet Mts. and flows into the Lena River E of Yakutsk.

Al·de·burgh |'äldəbərə| town on the coast of Suffolk, E England. Pop. 3,000. It is the site of an annual music festival established (1948) by Benjamin Britten.

Al·der·ney |'awldərnē| island in the English Channel, to the NE of Guernsey. Pop. 2,130. It is the third largest of the Channel Islands. French name **Aurigny**.

Al·der·shot |'awldər,sнät| town in S England, in Hampshire, site of a major military training center. Pop. 54,358.

Alek·san·drovsk |,ælik'ændrəfsk| former name (until 1921) for ZAPORIZHZHYA, Ukraine.

Alen·çon |äläN'sawN| capital of the department of Orne, NW France. Pop. 35,000. The town is known for its fine lace.

Alen·te·jo |ə,leN'tezн͞o͞o| region and former province of E central Portugal.

Alep·po |ə'lepō| city in N Syria. Pop. 1,355,000. This ancient city was formerly an important commercial center on the trade route between the Mediterranean and the countries of the East. Arabic name **Halab**.

Ales·san·dria |,älə'sändrēə| agricultural market and industrial center in NW Italy, capital of Alessandria province. Pop. 93,000.

Aletsch·horn |'älicн,hawrn| mountain in Switzerland, in the Bernese Alps, rising to 13,763 ft./4,195 m. Its glaciers are among the largest in Europe.

Aleu·tian Islands |ə'l͞o͞osнən| (also **the Aleutians**) chain of volcanic islands in Alaska, extending W and S from the Alaska Peninsula.

Aleu·tian Range |ə'l͞o͞osнən| extension of the Coast Ranges in SW Alaska. It contains many volcanoes.

Alex·an·der Archipelago |,ælg'zændər| group of about 1,100 islands off the coast of SE Alaska, the remnants of a submerged mountain system.

Alex·an·dret·ta |,ælig,zæn'dretə| former name for ISKENDERUN, Turkey.

Alex·an·dria[1] |,ælig'zændrēə| the chief port of Egypt. Pop. 2,893,000. Alexandria was a major center of Hellenistic culture, renowned in ancient times for its library and for the Pharos lighthouse. □ **Alexandrian** adj. & n.

Alex·an·dria[2] |,ælig'zændrēə| industrial city in central Louisiana, on the Red River. Pop. 49,188.

Alex·an·dria[3] |,ælig'zændrēə| city in N Virginia, on the Potomac River opposite Washington, D.C. Pop. 111,183.

Al·föld |'awl,foeld| great central plain of Hungary, extending into Serbia and W Romania. On the main invasion route to W Europe, it has often been a battleground. It is now an agricultural and cattle-raising area. The Little Alföld, W Hungary, extends into Austria and S Slovakia.

Al·gar·ve, the |äl'gärvə| the southernmost province of Portugal, on the Atlantic coast, noted as a resort area. Capital: Faro.

Al·ge·ci·ras |,æljə'sirəs| ferry port and resort in S Spain. Pop. 101,365.

Al·ge·ria |æl'jirēə| republic on the Mediterranean coast of N Africa. Area: 919,595 sq. mi./2.32 million sq. km. Pop. 25,800,000. Language, Arabic. Capital and largest city: Algiers. The second-largest African nation, Algeria is dominated in the S by the Sahara Desert. France held it as a colony from the 19th century until 1962. Oil and gas are now central to the economy, and there is some agriculture in the N. □ **Algerian** adj. & n.

Algeria

Al·giers |æl'jirz| the capital and largest city of Algeria, one of the leading Mediterranean ports of N Africa. Pop. 1,722,000.

Al·goa Bay |æl'gōə| inlet of the Indian Ocean in SE South Africa, in the Cape province. Port Elizabeth is here.

Al·gon·quin Pro·vin·cial Park |æl'gäNGkwin| park in S central Ontario, noted for its lakes and scenery.

Al·ham·bra, the |æl'hæmbrə; æl'hämbrə| Moorish palace and citadel in Granada, Spain. Built 1248–1354, it is an important example of Moorish architecture.

Al·ham·bra |æl'hæmbrə; æl'hämbrə| city in SW California, a suburb NE of Los Angeles. Pop. 82,106.

Al Hil·lah |æl 'hilə| commercial port city in central Iraq, on an irrigation canal branching off from the Euphrates River. Pop. 220,000.

Ali·can·te |ˌälə'käntä; ˌælə'käntē| seaport on the Mediterranean coast of SE Spain, the capital of a province of the same name. Pop. 270,950.

Alice |'æləs| city in S Texas. Pop. 19,788.

Alice Springs |'æləs| town, a railway terminus and supply center serving the outback of Northern Territory, Australia. Pop. 20,450.

Ali·garh |ˌälē'gär; ˌälē'gər| city in N India, in Uttar Pradesh. Pop. 480,000. The city comprises the ancient fort of Aligarh and the former city of Koil.

Al Ji·zah |æl 'jēzə| variant form of GIZA, Egypt.

Al·ju·bar·ro·ta |ˌälzHōōbə'rōtə| village in W central Portugal. The most important battle in Portuguese history took place here in 1385 when John I defeated invaders from Castile.

Al Ka·rak |äl'kärək; ˌælkə'räek| (also **Karak**; ancient name **Kir Moab**) historic commercial city in W Jordan, near the S end of the Dead Sea. Pop. 50,000. It was a Moabite city in biblical times.

Alk·maar |'älk,mär| city in the NW Netherlands. Pop. 91,000. It has a famous Edam cheese market.

Al·la·gash River |'ælə,gæsH| river in N Maine, noted as a canoeing route.

Al·la·ha·bad |ˌäləhə'bäd| city in the state of Uttar Pradesh, N central India. Pop. 806,000. Situated at the confluence of the sacred Juma and Ganges rivers, it is a place of Hindu pilgrimage.

All-American Canal |ˌawl ə'merəkən| water conduit from the Colorado River across S California, supplying the Imperial Valley and nearby farm areas.

Al·le·ghe·ny Mountains |ˌælə'gänē| (also **the Alleghenies**) a relatively low (2,000-4,000 ft./610-1,460 m.) mountain range of the Appalachian system in the U.S. extending through Pennsylvania, Maryland, Virginia, West Virginia. Its E slopes are called the Allegheny Front.

Al·le·ghe·ny River |ˌælə'gänē| river that flows 325 mi./523 km. through New York and Pennsylvania, joining the Monongahela River at Pittsburgh, Pennsylvania to form the Ohio River.

Al·len, Bog of |'ælən| series of peat bogs in central Ireland, between Dublin and the Shannon River. It covers 375 sq. mi./970 sq. km.

Al·len·town |'ælən,town| commercial and industrial city in E Pennsylvania, on the Lehigh River. Pop. 105,090.

Al·lep·pey |ə'lepē| (also called **Alappuzha**) commercial port city in S India, on the Malabar Coast of Kerala state. Pop. 265,000. .

All·gau Alps |'awl,goi| (in German, **Allgäuer Alpen**) a range of the Alps that separates Bavaria from the Austrian Tyrol. Madelegabel is the highest peak: 8,678 ft./2,645 m.

Al·li·ance |ə'līəns| city in NE Ohio. Pop. 23,393.

Al·lier |äl'yā| river of central France that rises in the Cévennes and flows 258 mi./410 km. NW to meet the Loire.

Al·lo·way |'ælə,wā| village in Strathclyde, SW Scotland, the birthplace (1759) of the poet Robert Burns.

Al·ma |'ælmə| city in S central Quebec, on the Saguenay River. Pop. 25,910.

Alma-Ata |ˌælmə'ətä| older name for ALMATY, Kazakhstan.

Al·ma·dén |ˌälmə'dän| town in S central Spain, in the Sierra Morena Mts. Pop. 15,000. Mercury mines are located nearby.

Al·ma·di·es, Cape |ˌælmə'dēəs| westernmost point of Africa, a promontory NW of Dakar, Senegal, at 17° 33′ W.

Al Ma·di·nah |ˌæl mə'dēnə| Arabic name for MEDINA.

Al·ma·ty |əl'mätē| (also **Alma-Ata**) largest city and former capital (until 1998) of Kazakhstan, an industrial, research, and educational center. Pop. 1,515,300. Former name (until 1921) **Verny**.

Al·me·ría |ˌälmə'rēə| industrial port city, capital of Almería province, Andalusia, S Spain. Pop. 157,760.

Al·mi·ran·te Brown |ˌälmə'rän,tä 'brown| city in E Argentina, forming part of the Buenos Aires metropolitan area. Pop. 449,100.

Alo·ha |ə'lō,hä| community in NW Oregon, a suburb W of Portland. Pop. 34,284.

Alo·ha State |əlō,hä| informal name for HAWAII.

Alor Se·tar |'äl,awr sē'tär| the capital of the state of Kedah in Malaysia, near the W coast of the central Malay Peninsula. Pop. 71,682.

Al·phe·us River |æl'fēəs| river in S Greece, rising in Arcadia and flowing NW into the Ionian Sea near Pyrgos. In Greek mythology it ran underground to the fountain of Arethusa, in Syracuse, Sicily. Also **Alphios**.

Alps |ælps| mountain system in Europe consisting of several ranges extending in a curve from the coast of SE France through

NW Italy, Switzerland, Liechtenstein, and S Germany into Austria. The highest peak of the Alps, Mont Blanc, rises to 15,771 ft./4,807 m. □ **Alpine** *adj.*

Al Qa·hi·ra |æl 'kähē,raw| Arabic name for CAIRO, Egypt.

Al·sace |æl'säs; æl'sæs| region of NE France, on the borders with Germany and Switzerland. Alsace was annexed by Prussia, along with part of Lorraine (forming *Alsace-Lorraine*), after the Franco-Prussian War of 1870–1, and restored to France after World War I. Alsace is noted for its industry, agriculture, and historic sites. □ **Alsatian** *adj. & n.*

Al·ta·de·na |,æltə'dēnə| residential suburb in SW California, just N of Pasadena. Pop. 42,658.

Al·tai |'æl,tī| (also **Altay**) a krai (administrative territory) of Russia in SW Siberia, on the border with Kazakhstan. Capital: Barnaul.

Al·tai Mountains |'æl,tī| mountain system of central Asia extending about 1,000 mi./1,600 km. E from Kazakhstan into W Mongolia and N China.

Al·ta·mi·ra[1] |,ältə'mirə| city in N central Brazil, on the Xingu River in Pará state, a commercial center in the Amazon basin. Pop. 79,000.

Al·ta·mi·ra[2] |,ältə'mirə| cave in NE Spain, site of noted prehistoric rock paintings. Discovered in 1879, the art depicts bison, deer, and other animals.

Al·ta·mont |'æltə,mänt| site in N central California, NE of Livermore, scene of a famous 1969 rock concert.

Alt·dorf |'ält,dawrf| town in central Switzerland, near Lucerne, the capital of Uri canton. Pop. 8,000. Altdorf was the home of the legendary William Tell.

Al·ten·burg |'ältən,bərg| industrial city in eastern Germany, on the Pleisse River. Pop. 53,000.

Al·ti·pla·no |,awltə'plänō| high plains region in the Andes Mts. in W Bolivia and S Peru. Lake Titicaca and the city of La Paz are in this region, where agriculture and mining are important and where most Bolivians live.

Al·to A·di·ge |,ältō 'ädə,jā| autonomous German-speaking region in NE Italy. Pop. 891,000. It includes the N part of the former Trentino–Alto Adige region.

Al·ton |'awltn| industrial city in SW Illinois, on the Mississippi River N of St. Louis, Missouri. Pop. 32,905.

Al·to·na |äl'tōnə; æl'tōnə| former city, incorporated into Hamburg, N Germany,

in 1937. The city is a port on the Elbe River.

Al·too·na |æl'tōōnə| city in S central Pennsylvania, in the Allegheny Mts. Pop. 51,881. A famed railroad center, it is near Horseshoe Curve, where rails first crossed the Alleghenies.

Al·tus |'æltəs| city in SW Oklahoma. Pop. 21,910.

Al Uq·sur |äl'ōōksōōr| Arabic name for LUXOR, Egypt.

Al·vin |'ælvən| city in SE Texas. Pop. 19,220.

Al·war |'əlwər| industrial and commercial city in N central India, in Rajasthan state. Pop. 211,000.

Ama·ga·sa·ki |ə,mägə'säkē| industrial port city in W central Japan, on S Honshu. Pop. 499,000.

Amal·fi |ə'mälfē| port and resort on the W coast of Italy, on the Gulf of Salerno. Pop. 5,900.

Ama·na Colonies |ə'mænə| group of seven villages in E central Iowa. Settled by a German religious group, they are famous for manufacturing appliances.

Ama·pá |,ämə'pä| state of N Brazil, on the Atlantic coast, lying between the Amazon delta and the border with French Guiana. Capital: Macapá. It is a region of dense rainforest. Pop. 289,000.

Ama·ril·lo |,æmə'rilō| industrial and commercial city in NW Texas, in the Panhandle. Pop. 157,615.

Amar·na, Tell el- |'tel ,el ə'märnə| the site of the ruins of the ancient Egyptian capital Akhetaten, on the E bank of the Nile.

Amas·ya |,äməs'yä| (ancient name **Amasia**) historic commercial city in N Turkey, the capital of Amasya province. Pop. 163,000. It was a Cappadocian capital.

Ama·zon River |'æmə,zän| river in South America, flowing over 4,150 mi./6,683 km. through Peru, Colombia, and Brazil into the Atlantic. It drains two-fifths of the continent, and in terms of water flow it is the largest river in the world. □ **Amazonian** *adj. & n.*

Ama·zo·nas |,æmə'zōnəs| largest (604,266 sq. mi./1,564,445 sq. km.) state of NW Brazil. Capital: Manaus. It is traversed by the Amazon and its numerous tributaries. Pop. 2,103,000.

Ama·zo·nia |,æmə'zōnēə| **1** region surrounding the Amazon River, principally in Brazil but also extending into Peru, Colombia, and Bolivia. It contains about one third of the world's remaining tropical rainforest. **2** national park protecting 3,850 sq.

mi./10,000 sq. km. of rainforest in the state of Pará, N Brazil.

Am·ba·to |äm'bätō| market town in the Andes of central Ecuador. Pop. 229,190.

Am·ber Coast |'æmbər| name for the N coast of the Dominican Republic, on the Atlantic around Puerto Plata. Nearby mountains are the leading world source of amber.

Am·berg |'ämberk| city in S central Germany, on the Vils River, E of Nuremberg. Pop. 43,000.

Am·boise |ˌäɴ'bwäz| town in N central France, in the Loire valley. It is known chiefly for its Gothic and Renaissance chateau, of which only parts remain. Leonardo da Vinci died at Amboise and is buried in its chapel.

Am·bon |äm'bawn; 'æm,bän| (also **Amboina**) 1 mountainous island in E Indonesia, one of the Moluccas Islands. 2 port on this island, the capital of the Moluccas. Pop. 80,000.

Am·brym |'ämbrim| (also **Ambrim**) island in NE Vanuatu, noted for its folk arts and black volcanic ash.

Am·chit·ka |æm'cHitkə| island in the Aleutian Islands of SW Alaska. It has been used as a military base and for nuclear testing.

Amer·i·ca |ə'merəkə| 1 (also **the Americas**) land mass of the W hemisphere consisting of the continents of North and South America joined by the Isthmus of Panama. The continent was originally inhabited by American Indians and Inuit peoples. The NE coastline of North America was visited by Norse seamen in the 8th or 9th century, but European colonization followed the explorations of Columbus, who reached the West Indies in 1492 and the South American mainland in 1498. 2 widely used informal name for the United States. The name **America** dates from the early 16th century and is believed to derive from the Latin form (*Americus*) of the given name of Amerigo Vespucci, who explored the E coast of South America in at least two voyages between 1499 and 1502. Vespucci's explorations convinced Europeans that these lands were not part of Asia (as Columbus thought) but rather a "New World." The name first appeared on maps by German cartographer Martin Weldseemüller in 1507. □ **American** adj. & n.

Amer·i·can River |ə'merəkən| river in N central California, joining the Sacramento River at Sacramento. Gold was discovered here in 1848, setting off the California gold rush.

Amer·i·can Sa·moa |ə'merəkən sə'mōə| unincorporated overseas territory of the U.S. comprising a group of islands in the S Pacific, to the E of the state of SAMOA and S of the Kiribati group. Pop. 46,770. Capital: Fagatogo. In 1899 the U.S. took control of the islands by agreement with Germany and Britain.

American Samoa

Amer·i·cus |ə'merəkəs| city in SW Georgia. Pop. 16,512.

Amers·foort |'ämərs,fawrt| transportation and manufacturing center in the central Netherlands. Pop. 102,000.

Ames |āmz| city in central Iowa, home to Iowa State University. Pop. 47,198.

Am·ha·ra |äm'härə| region and former kingdom of NW Ethiopia, which gave its name to the Amharic language. Gondar is the principal city in the area.

Am·herst[1] |'æm(h)ərst| town in W central Massachusetts, home to several colleges. Pop. 35,228.

Am·herst[2] |'æm(h)ərst| town in W New York, a suburb NE of Buffalo. Pop. 111,711.

Ami·ens |äm'yeɴ| commercial and industrial city in N France. Pop. 136,230. An historic textile center, it attracts tourism.

Amin·di·vi Islands |ˌəmən'dēvē| the northernmost group of islands in the Indian territory of Lakshadweep in the Indian Ocean.

Ami·ran·te Islands |'æmə,rænt| group of coral islands in the Indian Ocean, forming part of the Seychelles.

Amish Country |'ämisH| name for areas, chiefly in SE Pennsylvania and NE Ohio, inhabited by the Amish, an agricultural religious sect.

Am·man |ə'män| the capital, largest city, and industrial and commercial center of Jordan. Pop. 1,160,000.

Amol |'aw,mōl| (also **Amul**) commercial city in N Iran, in the foothills of the Elburz Mts. Pop. 140,000.

Amoy |ä'moi| another name for XIAMEN, China.

Am·ra·va·ti |əm'rävətē; äm'rävətē| industrial and commercial city in W central India, in Maharashtra state. Pop. 434,000. It has the largest cotton market in India.

Am·rit·sar |əm'ritsər; äm'ritsər| city in the state of Punjab in NW India. Pop. 709,000. The center of the Sikh faith and the site of its holiest temple, the Golden Temple.

Am·ro·ha |əm'rōhə| town in N India, in Uttar Pradesh state. Pop. 137,000. It is a Muslim center of pilgrimage.

Am·stel·veen |'ämstəl,vān| industrial suburb of Amsterdam, the Netherlands. Pop. 70,000. Schiphol International Airport is located here.

Am·ster·dam[1] |'æmpstər,dæm| the capital and largest city of the Netherlands. Pop. 702,440. Although Amsterdam is the capital, the country's seat of government and administrative center is at The Hague. Amsterdam, a European commercial and cultural center, is crossed by canals, which have made it known as the Venice of the N.

Am·ster·dam[2] |'ämstər,däm; 'æmstər,dæm| city in E central New York, on the Mohawk River and the Erie Canal. Pop. 20,714.

Amu Dar·ya |,ämōō 'däryə| river of central Asia, rising in the Pamirs and flowing 1,500 mi./2,400 km. into the Aral Sea. In classical times it was known as the Oxus.

Amund·sen Gulf |'ämənsən| arm of the Beaufort Sea N of the mainland Northwest Territories and Nunavut and S of Banks Island, in the Canadian arctic.

Amund·sen Sea |'ämənsən| arm of the South Pacific Ocean on the coast of Antarctica, off Marie Byrd Land.

Amur River |ə'mōōr| (Chinese name **Heilong Jiang**) river of NE Asia, flowing 1,786 mi./2,874 km. along the Russia-China border then NE through Russia to the Tatar Strait.

Ana·con·da |,ænə'kändə| mining city in SW Montana. Pop. 10,278.

Ana·cos·tia |,ænə'kawstēə; ,ænə'kästēə| residential section of SE Washington, D.C., across the Anacostia River from the rest of the District of Columbia.

Ana·dyr River |,änə'dir| river (694 mi./1,117 km.) in NE Siberian Russia. It rises in the mountains S of Chukotshoye Nagor'ye and flows into the Gulf of Anadyr.

Ana·heim |'ænə,hīm| city in California, on the SE side of metropolitan Los Angeles. Pop. 266,400. It is the site of the amusement park Disneyland.

Aná·huac |ə'nä,wäk| name for the central plateau of Mexico, including the Mexico City area (the Valley of Mexico).

Aná·po·lis |ä'näpōō,lēs| commercial city in central Brazil, in Goiás state. Pop. 265,000. It is a rail center shipping coffee and other agricultural and mine products.

Ana·to·lia |,ænə'tōlēə| the W peninsula of Asia, bounded by the Black Sea, the Aegean, and the Mediterranean, that forms the greater part of Turkey. □ **Anatolian** adj. & n.

An·chor·age |'æNGk(ə)rij| the largest city in Alaska, a seaport on Cook Inlet, off the Pacific. Pop. 226,340.

An·co·na |äNG'kōnə; æNG'kōnə| port on the Adriatic coast of central Italy, capital of Marche region. Pop. 103,270.

An·cy·ra |æn'sīrə| ancient Roman name for ANKARA, Turkey.

An·da |'ändä| city in Heilongjiang province, NE China, between Daqing and Harbin. Pop. 423,000.

An·da·lu·sia |ändə'lōōsēə| the southernmost region of Spain, bordering on the Atlantic and the Mediterranean. Capital: Seville. The region was under Moorish rule from 711 to 1492. Spanish name **Andalucía**. □ **Andalusian** adj. & n.

An·da·man and Ni·co·bar Islands |'ændəmən ən 'nikə,bär| two groups of islands in the Bay of Bengal, constituting a Union Territory of India. Pop. 279,110. Capital: Port Blair.

An·der·lecht |'ändər,leKHt| industrial suburb of Brussels, Belgium. Pop. 88,000. It was the home of the scholar Erasmus in the 16th century.

An·der·son[1] |'ændərsən| industrial city in E central Indiana. Pop. 59,459.

An·der·son[2] |'ændərsən| city in NW South Carolina. Pop. 26,184.

An·der·son·ville |'ændərsən,vil| village in SW Georgia, near Americus, site of a major Confederate prison camp during the Civil War.

An·des |'ændēz| major mountain system running the length of the Pacific coast of South America. It extends over some 5,000 mi./8,000 km., with a continuous height of more than 10,000 ft./3,000 m. Its highest peak is Aconcagua, which rises to a height of 22,834 ft./6,960 m. □ **Andean** adj.

Andh·ra Pra·desh |'ändrə prə'deSH| state in SE India, on the Bay of Bengal. Pop. 66,305,000. Capital: Hyderabad.

An·di·zhan |,ändi'zän| (also **Andijon**) **1** administrative subdivision in E Uzbekistan. Area: 1,660 sq. mi./4,299 sq. km. Pop.

1,795,000. **2** its capital, an industrial city. Pop. 298,000.

An·dor·ra |æn'dawrə| small (181 sq. mi./468 sq. km.) autonomous principality in the S Pyrenees, between France and Spain. Pop. 55,000. Languages: Catalan, Spanish, and French. Capital: Andorra la Vella. Its independence dates from the late 8th century, when Charlemagne is said to have granted the Andorrans self-government for their help in defeating the Moors. It has a pastoral and resort economy, with international offices. □ **Andorran** *adj. & n.*

Andorra

An·do·ver |'æn,dōvər; 'ændəvər| town in NE Massachusetts, home to Phillips Academy, a famous prep school. Pop. 29,151.

An·dre·an·of Islands |,ændrē'æn,awf; ,ændrē'ænəf| island group in SW Alaska, part of the Aleutian Islands.

An·dros[1] |'ændrəs| largest (2,300 sq. mi./5,955 sq. km.) island of the Bahamas, in the W part.

An·dros[2] |'ændrəs; 'æn,draws| island in Greece, northernmost island of the Cyclades, in the Aegean Sea. Pop. 9,000. Its capital is Andros.

An·dro·scog·gin River |,ændrə'skägən| river that flows 175 mi./280 km. from N New Hampshire through SW Maine to the Atlantic.

Ané·ho |ä'nähō| commercial port town in S Togo, E of Lomé. Pop. 14,000. It was formerly a colonial capital and slave-trade center.

Ane·to, Pi·co de |'pēkō ,dä ə'netō| mountain peak in the Maladeta range in NE Spain, just S of the French border. It is the tallest peak in the Pyrénées (11,168 ft./3,404 m.).

An·ga·ra River |,ängə'rä| river (1.039 mi./1,779 km.) in SE Siberia, Russia. It flows from Lake Baikal NW and W, meeting the Yenisei River S of Yeniseysk.

An·garsk |ən'gärsk| industrial city in E

Siberia, Russia, NW of Irkutsk. Pop. 267,000.

An·gel Falls |'änjəl| waterfall in the Guiana Highlands of SE Venezuela. It is the highest waterfall in the world, with an uninterrupted descent of 3,210 ft./978 m. The falls were discovered in 1935 by the American aviator and prospector James Angel.

An·gel Island |'änjəl| island in San Francisco Bay, N central California, that was the chief immigration station on the U.S. W coast. It is now a state park.

An·geln |'äNGgəln| region in NW Schleswig-Holstein, Germany, noted as a cattle-raising area and as the traditional home of the Angles, who invaded Britain in the 5th century.

An·gers |äN'zHä| industrial and commercial city in W France, capital of the former province of Anjou. Pop. 146,160.

Ang·kor |'æNGkawr; 'äNG,kawr| the capital of the ancient kingdom of the Khmer in NW Cambodia; long abandoned, the site was rediscovered in 1860, and is noted for its temples, especially the Angkor Wat (mid 12th century).

An·gle·sey |'æNGgəl,sē| island of NW Wales, separated from the mainland by the Menai Strait. The ferry port at Holyhead is on Holy Island, just NW.

An·glia |'æNGglēə| Latin name for England, the land of the Angles (Latin *Angli*), a Germanic people who settled here in the 5th century. *England* has the same meaning.

An·go·la |æNG'gōlə; æn'gōlə| republic on the W coast of southern Africa. Area: 481,186 sq. mi./1.25 million sq. km. Pop. 10,301,000. Capital and largest city: Luanda. Languages, Portuguese (official), Bantu languages. Held by the Portuguese for almost 400 years before 1975, Angola has a central plateau with headwaters of the Congo and Zambezi rivers. Timber, coffee, tobacco, and diamonds are important to the economy. Oil is central especially to the

Angola

coastal exclave of Cabinda. □ **Angolan** *adj. & n.*

An•go•ra |æNG'gawrə; æn'gawrə| old name for ANKARA, Turkey, source of the name of a type of wool.

An•go•stu•ra |ˌæNGə'st(y)o͞orə| old name for CIUDAD BOLÍVAR, Venezuela.

An•gou•lême |ˌäNGgo͞o'lem| industrial and transportation center in W France, on the Charente River. Pop. 46,000.

An•guil•la |æNG'gwilə; æn'gwilə| the most northerly of the Leeward Islands in the West Indies. Pop. 7,020. Languages, English (official), English Creole. Capital: The Valley. Formerly a British colony, and briefly united with St. Kitts and Nevis (1967), the island is now a self-governing dependency of the UK. □ **Anguillan** *adj. & n.*

An•gus |'æNGgəs| former county of NE Scotland, known from the 16th century until 1928 as Forfarshire. It became an administrative district of Tayside region in 1975.

An•hui |'än'hwā| (also **Anhwei**) province in E China. Pop. 59,380,000. Capital: Hefei.

An•jou[1] |'æn,jo͞o; äN'ZHo͞o| former province of W France, on the Loire. It was an English possession from 1154 to 1204. Angers was the chief town. □ **Angevin** *adj. & n.*

An•jou[2] |äNZHo͞o| residential city in S Quebec, immediately NE of Montreal. Pop. 37,210.

An•ka•ra |'æNGkərə; 'äNGkərə| the capital of Turkey since 1923. Pop. 2,559,470. Prominent in Roman times as Ancyra, it later declined in importance until chosen by Kemal Atatürk in 1923 as his seat of government. Former name (until 1930) **An•gora**.

Ann, Cape |æn| peninsula in NE Massachusetts, noted for its resorts and scenery.

An•na•ba |ˌæn'äbə| port of NE Algeria. Pop. 348,000. The modern town is adjacent to the site of Hippo Regius, a prominent city in Roman Africa and the home and bishopric of St. Augustine of Hippo from 396 to 430. Former name **Bône**.

An Na•jaf |ˌän nə'yäf| (also called **Mashad Ali**) city in S central Iraq, on a lake W of the Euphrates River. Pop. 243,000. The tomb of Ali, son-in-law of the Prophet Muhammad, is here.

An•nam |ə'næm; ə'näm| former independent kingdom (c.10th to 19th centuries) in SE Asia, in territory that is now a region in central Vietnam. □ **Annamese** *adj. & n.*

An•nan•dale |'ænən,dāl| residential sub-

urb in N Virginia, SW of Washington, D.C. Pop. 50,975.

An•na•po•lis |ə'næp(ə)liəs| city, the capital of Maryland, on Chesapeake Bay. Pop. 33,190. It is the home of the U.S. Naval Academy.

An•na•po•lis Roy•al |ə'næp(ə)ləs 'roiəl| historic town in SW Nova Scotia, on the Annapolis River. Pop. 633.

An•na•pur•na |ˌænə'po͝ornə| ridge of the Himalayas, in N central Nepal. Its highest peak rises to 26,503 ft./8,078 m.

Ann Ar•bor |æn 'ärbər| city in SE Michigan, home to the University of Michigan. Pop. 109,592.

Anne•cy |än'sē| capital of the department of Haute-Savoie, in SE France. Pop. 51,000. It is an industrial center and resort.

An Nhon |'än'nōn| (formerly **Binh Dinh**) city in SE Vietnam, SSE of Da Nang, near Quy Nhon. It was once the capital of Annam.

An•nis•ton |'ænə,stən| industrial and military city in NE Alabama. Pop. 26,623.

An•no•bón |ˌänō'bawn| island of Equatorial Guinea, in the Gulf of Guinea. Also called **Pagalu**.

An•qing |'än'CHiNG| city in Anhui province, E China, at the mouth of the Yangtze River. Pop. 441,000.

An•shan |'än'sHän| city in Liaoning, China. Pop. 1,370,000. Anshan is situated close to major iron-ore deposits and China's largest iron-and-steel complex is nearby.

An•shun |'än'sHo͞on| city in Guizhou province, S China, noted for green tea and sugar production. Pop. 174,000.

An•tak•ya |ˌäntä'kyä| Turkish name for ANTIOCH.

An•tal•ya |ˌäntl'yä| port in S Turkey. Pop. 378,200.

An•ta•na•na•ri•vo |ˌäntə,nänə'rēvō| capital, largest city, and commercial center of Madagascar, situated in the central plateau. Pop. 802,390. Former name (until 1975) **Tananarive**.

Ant•arc•ti•ca |ænt'är(k)tikə| continent surrounding the South Pole, situated mainly within the Antarctic Circle and almost entirely covered by ice sheets. Area: 5.4 million sq. mi./13.9 million sq. km.

Ant•arc•tic Circle |ænt'är(k)tik| the parallel of latitude 66° 33' S of the equator. It marks the southernmost point at which the sun is visible on the S winter solstice and the northernmost point at which the midnight sun can be seen on the S summer solstice.

Antarctica

Antigua & Barbuda

Ant•arc•tic Convergence |ˌæn'(t)är(k)tik kən'vərjəns; ænt'är(k)tik| the zone of the Antarctic Ocean where cold, nutrient-laden Antarctic surface water sinks beneath the warmer waters to the N.

Ant•arc•tic Ocean |ænt'är(k)tik| the sea surrounding Antarctica, consisting of parts of the S Atlantic, the S Pacific, and the S Indian Ocean. Also called **Southern Ocean**.

Ant•arc•tic Peninsula |ænt'är(k)tik| mountainous peninsula of Antarctica between the Bellingshausen sea and the Weddell Sea, extending N toward Cape Horn and the Falkland Islands.

An•thra•cite Belt |'ænTHrə,sīt| area of NE Pennsylvania, around Scranton and Wilkes-Barre, where hard coal has been central to economic development.

An•tibes |äN'tēb| fishing port and resort in SE France, on the Riviera. Pop. 70,690. Just S is the well-known Cap d'Antibes.

An•ti•cos•ti Island |ˌæntə'kawstē| largely uninhabited island in E Quebec, in the mouth of the Saint Lawrence River.

An•tie•tam |æn'tētəm| historic site on Antietam Creek, in NW Maryland, SE of Sharpsburg, scene of a major Civil War battle in September 1862.

An•ti•go•nish |ˌæntəgi'nisH| town in N central Nova Scotia. Pop. 4,924.

An•ti•gua |æn'tēgwə| (also **Antigua Guatemala**) historic town in the central highlands of Guatemala. Pop. 26,630.

An•ti•gua and Bar•bu•da |æn'tigwə ənd ˌbär'bōōdə; än'tēgwə ənd ˌbär'bōōdə; æn-'tēg(w)ənd bär'bōōdə| republic consisting of two islands in the Leeward Islands in the West Indies. Area: 171 sq. mi./442 sq. km. Pop 80,000. Languages: English (official), Creole. Capital: St. John's (on Antigua). Discovered in 1493 by Columbus and settled by the English in 1632, Antigua became a British colony with Barbuda as its dependency; the islands gained independence within the Commonwealth in 1981. Tourism and sugar have been mainstays of the economy. □ **Antiguan** *adj. & n.*

Anti-Lebanon Mountains |ˌænti'lebə-nən| range of mountains running N to S along the border between Lebanon and Syria, E of the Lebanon range.

An•til•les |æn'tilēz| group of islands, forming the greater part of the West Indies. The *Greater Antilles*, extending roughly E to W, comprise Cuba, Jamaica, Hispaniola (Haiti and the Dominican Republic), and Puerto Rico; the *Lesser Antilles*, to the SE, include the Virgin Islands, Leeward Islands, Windward Islands, and various small islands to the N of Venezuela. See also NETHERLANDS ANTILLES.

An•ti•och[1] |'æntē,äk| city in N central California. Pop. 62,195.

An•ti•och[2] |'æntē,äk| city in S Turkey, near the Syrian border. Pop. 123,871. Antioch was the ancient capital of Syria under the Seleucid kings, who founded it. Turkish name **Antakya**.

An•tip•o•des, the |æn'tipəd,ēz| from the term for any two points opposite each other on the earth's surface, an old (chiefly British) popular name for Australia and New Zealand.

An•to•fa•gas•ta |ˌäntōfə'gästə| industrial port city in N Chile, the capital of Antofagasta region. Pop. 227,000. Mining and tourism are central to its economy.

An•trim |'æntrəm| **1** one of the Six Counties of Northern Ireland. **2** town in this county, on the NE shore of Lough Neagh. Pop. 21,000.

An•si•ra•be |ˌäntsir'äbā| spa town in central Madagascar, in the Ankaratra Mts. Pop. 120,000.

An•tung |'än'dōōNG| former name for DANDONG, China.

Ant•werp |'æn,twərp| port in N Belgium, on the Scheldt. Pop. 467,520. By the 16th century it became a leading European commercial and financial center. French name **Anvers**, Flemish name **Antwerpen**.

An·ra·dha·pu·ra |ˌənəˌrädəˈpo͝orə| city in N central Sri Lanka, capital of a district of the same name. Pop. 36,000. The ancient capital of Sri Lanka, it is a center of Buddhist pilgrimage.

An·vers |änˈver(s)| French name of ANTWERP, Belgium.

An·yang |ˈänˈyäNG| industrial city in Henan province, central China. Pop. 480,000. It was the last capital (1330–1066 B.C.) of the Shang dynasty.

An·za Bor·re·go |ˈænzə bəˈrägō| desert region, much of it a state park, in S California.

An·zio |ˈäntsēˌō; ˈænzēō| seaport, W Italy, S of Rome. Pop. 36,000. It was a popular resort for citizens of ancient Rome. Allied troops landed here in January 1944; amid fierce fighting, to begin their drive on Rome.

Ao·mo·ri |ˌäōˈmawrē| industrial port city in N Japan, on N Honshu. Pop. 288,000.

Ao·ran·gi |owˈräNGē| Maori name for MOUNT COOK, New Zealand.

Aos·ta |äˈawstə| city in NW Italy, capital of Valle d'Aosta region. Pop. 36,095.

Ao·te·a·roa |ˌowˌtāəˈrōə| Maori name for NEW ZEALAND.

Aou·zou Strip |owˈzo͞o| narrow corridor of disputed desert land in N Chad, stretching the full length of the border between Chad and Libya.

Apa·che Junction |əˈpæCHē| city in S central Arizona, a suburb SE of Phoenix. Pop. 18,100.

Apa·la·chi·co·la River |ˌæpəˌlæCHiˈkōlə| see CHATTAHOOCHEE RIVER.

Apel·doorn |äpəlˌdawrn| town in the E central Netherlands. Pop. 148,200. The site of the summer residence of the Dutch royal family.

Apen·nines |ˈæpəˌnīnz| mountain range running 880 mi./1,400 km. down the length of Italy, from the NW to the S tip of the peninsula. □ **Apennine** adj.

Aphro·di·si·as |ˌæfrəˈdizēəs| ancient city of W Asia Minor, site of a temple dedicated to Aphrodite. Now in ruins, it is situated 50 mi./80 km. W of Aydin, Turkey.

Apia |äˈpēə| port city, the capital and economic and cultural center of the state of Samoa (Western Samoa). Pop. 32,200.

Apos·tle Islands |əˈpäsəl| island group in N Wisconsin, in Lake Superior.

Ap·pa·la·chia |ˌæpəˈläSHə; ˌæpəˈlæCHə| term for areas in the Appalachian Mts. of the E U.S. that exhibit longterm poverty and distinctive folkways. □ **Appalachian** adj.

Ap·pa·la·chian Mountains |ˌæpəˈläSHən; ˌæpəˈlæCHən| (also **the Appalachians**) a mountain system of E North America, stretching from Quebec and Maine in the N to Georgia and Alabama in the S. Its highest peak is Mount Mitchell in North Carolina, which rises to 6,684 ft./2,037 m. Other ranges in the Appalachian system include the White Mts. of New Hampshire, the Green Mts. of Vermont, the Catskills of New York, and the Allegheny, Blue Ridge, and Cumberland mountains. □ **Appalachian** adj.

Ap·pa·la·chian Trail |ˌæpəˈläSHən; ˌæpəˈlæCHən| 2,000-mi./3,200-km. footpath through the Appalachian Mts., from Mount Katahdin in Maine to Springer Mt. in Georgia.

Ap·pian Way |ˈæpēən| the principal road S from Rome in classical times, named after Appius Claudius Caecus, who in 312 B.C. built the section to Capua; it was later extended to Brindisi. Latin name **Via Appia**.

Ap·ple Isle |ˈæpəl| (also **Apple Island**) an informal Australian name for Tasmania.

Ap·ple·ton |ˈæpəltən| industrial and academic city in E central Wisconsin. Pop. 65,695.

Ap·ple Valley[1] |ˈæpəl| town in SW California, a suburb NE of Los Angeles. Pop. 46,079.

Ap·ple Valley[2] |ˈæpəl| city in SE Minnesota, a suburb S of Minneapolis. Pop. 34,598.

Ap·po·mat·tox |ˌæpəˈmætəks| historic site in central Virginia, at the head of the Appomattox River, where Robert E. Lee surrendered his Confederate forces in April 1865, ending the Civil War.

Ap·ra Harbor |ˈäprə| military and commercial port on Guam. Pop. 7,956.

Apu·lia |əˈp(y)o͞olyə| region of SE Italy, extending into the "heel" of the peninsula. Capital: Bari. Italian name **Puglia**.

Apu·re River |äˈpo͝orə| river that flows 500 mi./800 km. from the Andes in Colombia across W central Venezuela, into the Orinoco River.

Apu·ri·mac River |ˌäpəˈrēˌmäk| river that flows 430 mi./690 km. through central Peru, to join the Urubamba River in forming the Ucayali River, an important headwater of the Amazon.

Aqa·ba |äkəkəbə; ˈækəbə| Jordan's only port, at the head of the Gulf of Aqaba. Pop. 40,000.

Aqa·ba, Gulf of |äkˈmawlətow.; ˈækəbə|

part of the Red Sea extending N between the Sinai and Arabian peninsulas.

Aq·mo·la |äk'mawlə| (also **Akmola**) former name of ASTANA.

Aq·taū |'äk‚tow| (formerly **Shevchenko**) town in SW Kazakhstan, on the E coast of the Caspian Sea. Pop. 169,000.

Aq·tö·be |äk'tœbe| (formerly known as **Aktyubinsk**) industrial city in Kazakhstan, in the S foothills of the Ural Mts. Pop. 261,000.

Aquid·neck former name of the largest island in Narragansett Bay, now called Rhode Island; part of the state of Rhode Island.

Aqui·la |'äkwilə| city in E central Italy, capital of Abruzzi region. Pop. 67,820. Italian name **L'Aquila.**

Aqui·taine |'ækwə‚tān| region and former province of SW France, on the Bay of Biscay, centered on Bordeaux. It was an English possession 1259–1453. Latin name **Aquitania.**

Ara·bia |ə'rābēə| (also **Arabian Peninsula**) a peninsula of SW Asia, largely desert, lying between the Red Sea and the Persian Gulf and bounded on the N by Jordan and Iraq. The original homeland of the Arabs and the historic center of Islam, it comprises the states of Saudi Arabia, Yemen, Oman, Bahrain, Kuwait, Qatar, and the United Arab Emirates. □ **Arabian** adj. & n.

Ara·bian Desert |ə'rābēən| desert in E Egypt, between the Nile and the Red Sea. Also called the **Eastern Desert.**

Ara·bian Gulf another name for the PERSIAN GULF.

Ara·bian Peninsula |ə'rābēən| another name for ARABIA.

Ara·bian Sea |ə'rābēən| the NW part of the Indian Ocean, between Arabia and India.

Ara·by |'ærəbē| archaic term for ARABIA.

Ara·ca·jú |‚ärəkə'ZHŌŌ| port in E Brazil, on the Atlantic coast, capital of the state of Sergipe. Pop. 404,828.

Arad |ä'räd| commercial and industrial city in W Romania, capital of Arad county, on the Mures River. Pop. 191,000.

Ara·fu·ra Sea |‚ærə'fŏŏrə| sea lying between N Australia, the islands of E Indonesia, and New Guinea.

Ara·gon |'ærə‚gän| (Spanish name **Aragón**) autonomous region of NE Spain, bounded on the N by the Pyrenees and on the E by Catalonia and Valencia. Capital: Saragossa. Formerly an independent kingdom, it was united with Catalonia in 1137 and with Castile in 1479. □ **Aragonese** adj. & n.

Ara·guaía River |‚ærə'gwīyə| river that flows 1,300 mi./2,100 km. from Mato Grosso state, S central Brazil, N to the Tocantins River. Bananal Island, which lies in its course, is over 200 mi./320 km. long.

Arak |ə'räk| commercial city in W central Iran, in the Zagros Mts. SW of Tehran. Pop. 331,000. It is famous for its carpets.

Araks River |ə'räks| (ancient name **Araxes**; Turkish name **Aras**) river that flows 566 mi./900 km. E from Armenia to the Caspian Sea, at times forming the Turkey-Iran and Armenia-Azerbaijan borders. Its valley has been claimed to be the legendary Garden of Eden.

Aral Sea |'ærəl| inland sea in central Asia, on the border between Kazakhstan and Uzbekistan. Its area was reduced to two-thirds of its original size between 1960 and 1990, after water was diverted for irrigation, with serious consequences for the environment.

Aram |'ærəm| ancient country of SW Asia, roughly the equivalent of present-day Syria. Its language, Aramaic, was a lingua franca in the region, and came to be spoken by many Jews.

Aran Islands |'ærən| group of three islands, Inishmore, Inishmaan, and Inisheer, off the W coast of the Republic of Ireland.

Aran·juez |‚ärän'hwäTH| agricultural market town and former royal summer residence in central Spain, near Madrid. Pop. 36,000.

Ara·rat, Mount |'ærə‚ræt| pair of volcanic peaks in E Turkey, near the borders with Armenia and Iran. The higher peak, which rises to 16,946 ft./5,165 m., is the traditional site of the resting place of Noah's ark after the Flood (Gen. 8:4).

Arau·ca·nia |‚är‚owkä'nēə| region of S Chile, S of the Bío-Bío River. Temuco is its capital. The Araucanian Indians lived in the area before Europeans arrived, and resisted settlement until the 1880s. □ **Araucanian** adj.

Ara·val·li Range |ə'rävəlē| mountain range in NW India, running from N Gujarat state to central Rajasthan state.

Ar·bil |'är‚bēl| (also **Erbil; Irbil**) historic city in N Iraq, capital of the Kurdish province of Arbil. Pop. 334,000.

Ar·broath |är'brōTH| port town in Tayside, E Scotland. Pop. 24,000. The independence of Scotland from England was proclaimed here in 1320.

Ar·buck·le Mountains |'är‚bəkəl| low

range in S central Oklahoma, a recreational resource.

Ar·ca·dia[1] |är'kādēə| city in SW California, a suburb NE of Los Angeles. Pop. 48,290. The Santa Anita racetrack is here.

Ar·ca·dia[2] |är'kādēə| (also **Arcady**; Greek name **Arkhadia**) mountainous district in the Peloponnese of S Greece. In poetic fantasy it represents a pastoral paradise and in Greek mythology it is the home of Pan. □ **Arcadian** adj.

Ar·ca·ta |är'kātə| city in NW California, on Humboldt Bay off the Pacific. Pop. 15,197.

Arch·an·gel |'är‚kānjəl| industrial port of NW Russia, on the White Sea. Pop. 419,000. It is named after the monastery of the Archangel Michael situated here. Russian name **Arkhangelsk**.

Ar·chi·pié·la·go de Co·lón |‚ärcH'pyälä‚gō ‚dä kə'lōn| official Ecuadorian name for GALAPAGOS ISLANDS.

Arc·tic, the |'är(k)tik| regions on or N of the Arctic Circle.

Arc·tic Archipelago |'är(k)tik| name for all the islands lying N of mainland Canada and the Arctic Circle. Sparsely populated, they have varied mineral resources and wildlife. Baffin Island is the largest in the group.

Arc·tic Circle |'är(k)tik| the parallel of latitude 66° 33′ N of the equator. It marks the northernmost point at which the sun is visible on the N winter solstice and the southernmost point at which the midnight sun can be seen on the N summer solstice.

Arc·tic National Wildlife Refuge |'är(k)tik| preserve on the North Slope of NE Alaska, scene of controversies over oil exploration and drilling.

Arc·tic Ocean |'är(k)tik| ocean that surrounds the North Pole, lying within the Arctic Circle. Much of it is covered with pack ice throughout the year.

Ar·da·bil |‚ärdə'bēl| (also **Ardebil**) historic city in NW Iran. Pop. 311,000. It is famous for its carpets and rugs.

Ar·dèche |är'desH| department in E France, in the Rhône-Alpes region. Area: 2,136 sq. mi./5,529 sq. km. Pop. 278,000. The capital is Privas.

Ar·den, Forest of |'ärdən| forest in Warwickshire, central England, remnant of a much greater wilderness and associated with *As You Like It* by Shakespeare. The name has come to connote idyllic pastoral life.

Ar·dennes |är'den| forested upland region extending over parts of SE Belgium, NE

France, and Luxembourg. It was the scene of fierce fighting in both world wars.

Ard·more |'ärd‚mawr| city in S Oklahoma, in an oil-producing and agricultural area. Pop. 23,079.

Ard·na·mur·chan |‚ärdnə'mərKHən| peninsula on the coast of Highland Region in W Scotland.

Are·ci·bo |‚ärə'sēbō| community in NW Puerto Rico, W of San Juan. Pop. 49,545. It is an academic center noted for its huge radio telescope facility.

Are·op·a·gus |‚ærē'äpəgəs| rocky hill in Athens, Greece, W of the Acropolis. Once the meeting place of the prime council (the Areopagus) of Greece, it was the site of Saint Paul's address to the Athenians.

Are·qui·pa |‚ärə'kēpə| commercial city in the Andes of S Peru. Pop. 634,500.

Are·thu·sa |‚ærə'THōōzə; ‚ærə'THōōsə| see ALPHEUS river, Greece.

Arez·zo |ə'retsō| agricultural trade center in central Italy, capital of Arezzo province. Pop. 92,000.

Ar·gen·teuil |ärzHən'twœi| industrial NW suburb of Paris, on the Seine River. Pop. 94,000. Many painters have worked in Argenteuil, including Monet.

Ar·gen·tia |är'jenCHə| locality in SE Newfoundland, on Placentia Bay, former site of naval facilities important in World War II.

Ar·gen·ti·na |‚ärjən'tēnə| republic occupying much of the S part of South America. It is the second largest country in the continent. Area: 1,073,809 sq. mi./2,780,092 sq. km. Pop. 32,646,000; official language, Spanish. Capital and largest city: Buenos Aires. Also called **the Argentine Republic.** With the Andes in the W, the pampa in the center, and the Atlantic coast in the E, Argentina is a major producer of grains and cattle. Oil, gas, and minerals are also important, and there is much industry. □ **Argentine** n. **Argentinian** adj. & n.

Argentina

Ar·geş River |'är‚jɛsʜ| river in S Romania that rises in the Transylvanian Alps and flows S to the Danube River SE of Bucharest; it is linked to the city by canals.

Ar·go·lis |'ärgələs| ancient region of the Peloponnese, SE Greece, dominated by Argos and home to the Argives. A modern prefecture retains the name.

Ar·gonne |är'gawn; är'gän| wooded plateau in NE France, near the Belgian border. The region is thinly populated. A major Allied offensive was staged here during World War I; during World War II the region was occupied by Germany in 1940–44.

Ar·gos |'är‚gəs| city in the NE Peloponnese of Greece. Pop. 20,702. One of the oldest cities of ancient Greece, it dominated the Peloponnese and the W Aegean in the 7th century B.C. □ **Argive** *adj. & n.*

Ar·gyll·shire |är'gīl‚sʜir; är'gīlsʜər| former county on the W coast of Scotland. It was divided between Strathclyde and Highland regions in 1975.

Ar·i·a·na |‚ærē'änə; ‚ärē'änə| name for E provinces of the ancient Persian Empire lying to the S of the Oxus (present-day Amu Darya) River.

Ar·i·ca |ä'rēkə| port city in extreme N Chile, near the Peruvian border. Pop. 195,000. It provides foreign trade facilities for landlocked Bolivia, to the E.

Ar·i·ma·thea |‚ærəmə'ʜēə| (also **Arimathaea**) unidentified biblical town, the home of Joseph who placed Jesus in his tomb and who is identified with the AVALON legend.

Ar·i·zo·na |‚ærə'zōnə| see box. □ **Arizonan** *adj. & n.*

Ar·kan·sas |'ärkən‚saw| see box. □ **Arkansan** *adj. & n.*

Ar·kan·sas River |'ärkən‚saw; är'kænzəs| river in the SW U.S., flowing 1,450 mi./2,320 km. from the Rockies in Colorado to join the Mississippi River in Arkansas. It has been made navigable by oceangoing vessels as far W as Tulsa, Oklahoma.

Ar·khan·gelsk |‚ər'ᴋʜängilsk; är'kæn‚gelsk| Russian name for ARCHANGEL.

Arl·berg |'ärl‚berk; 'ärlbərg| mountain valley and pass in the Tyrolean Alps, W Austria. A tunnel (6.3 mi./10.1 km.) through the pass, completed in 1884, links Bludenz, Landeck, and Innsbruck.

Arles |ärl| historic city in SE France. Pop. 52,590. It was the capital of the medieval kingdom of Arles, formed in the 10th century by the union of the kingdoms of Provence and Burgundy.

Ar·ling·ton[1] |'ärliNGtən| town in E Massa-

Arizona

Capital/largest city: Phoenix
Other cities: Flagstaff, Glendale, Mesa, Phoenix, Scottsdale, Tempe, Tucson
Population: 3,665,228 (1990); 4,668,631 (1998); 5,230,000 (2005 proj.)
Population rank (1990): 24
Rank in land area: 6
Abbreviation: AZ; Ariz.
Nickname: Grand Canyon State
Motto: *Ditat Deus* (Latin: 'God Enriches')
Bird: cactus wren
Flower: blossom of the saguaro cactus
Tree: paloverde
Songs: "Arizona March Song"; "Arizona"
Noted physical features: Grand Canyon; Sonora Desert, Painted Desert; Petrified Forest; Canyon de Chelly; Meteor Crater; London Bridge; Biosphere 2; Navajo National Monument.
Tourist attractions: Grand Canyon; Painted Desert; Petrified Forest; Hoover Dam
Admission date: February 14, 1912
Order of admission: 48
Name origin: From the Pima or Papago Indian word *arizonac*, which may mean 'place of small springs.'

Arkansas

Capital/largest city: Little Rock
Other cities: Fayetteville, Fort Smith, Hot Springs, North Little Rock, Pine Bluff
Population: 2,350,725 (1990); 2,538,303 (1998); 2,750,000 (2005 proj.)
Population rank (1990): 33
Rank in land area: 29
Abbreviation: AR; Ark.
Nickname: Land of Opportunity
Motto: *Regnat populus* (Latin: 'The People Rule')
Bird: mockingbird
Flower: apple blossom
Tree: pine
Songs: "Arkansas"; "The Arkansas Traveler"
Noted physical features: Magazine Mountain
Tourist attractions: Hot Springs National Park; Eureka Springs; Ozark Folk Center; Crater of Diamonds; Toltec Mounds Archaeological State Park.
Admission date: June 15, 1836
Order of admission: 25
Name origin: From the French name for the Quapaw tribe of the Sioux, whose name is translated 'downstream people.'

chusetts, a suburb NW of Boston. Pop. 44,630.

Ar·ling·ton² |'ärliNGtən| industrial city in N Texas, between Dallas and Fort Worth. Pop. 261,720.

Ar·ling·ton³ |'ärliNGtən| county in N Virginia, forming a suburb of Washington, D.C. Pop. 170,936. It is the site of the Pentagon and the Arlington National Cemetery.

Ar·ling·ton Heights |'ärliNGtən 'hīts| village in NE Illinois, a suburb NW of Chicago. Pop. 75,460.

Ar·lon |är'lawN| town in SE Belgium, capital of the province of Luxembourg. Pop. 23,420.

Ar·ma·ged·don |,ärmə'gedn| biblical hill of **Megiddo**, an archaeological site on the plain of Esdraelon, S of present-day Haifa, Israel. In the book of Revelation, Armageddon is the site of the last battle between good and evil.

Ar·magh |är'mä; 'är,mä| **1** one of the Six Counties of Northern Ireland, formerly an administrative area. **2** the chief town of this county. Pop. 12,700. It has been the religious capital of Ireland since the 5th century.

Ar·ma·gnac |,ärmən,yäk; ,ärmən'yæk| region in SW France, in Aquitaine, constituting most of the department of Gers. It is best known for its medieval fortified villages (*bastides*) and its brandy.

Ar·ma·vir |ər,mə'vir| industrial city and transportation center in S central Russia, in the foothills of the Caucasus Mts. Pop. 162,000.

Ar·me·nia¹ |är'mänyə| city in W central Colombia, in a coffee growing district. Pop. 212,000.

Ar·me·nia² |är'mēnēə| landlocked republic in the Caucasus of SE Europe. Area: 11,510 sq. mi./29,800 sq. km. Pop. 3,360,000. Languages, Armenian and Russian. Capital and largest city: Yerevan. The remnant of a much larger historical

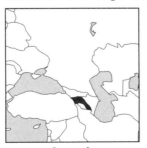

Armenia

country, Armenia has been dominated by Turkey and by Russia, and became independent in 1992 after the Soviet Union dissolved. Cotton, rice, fruit, tobacco, and small manufactures are important. Christian Armenia has had uneasy relations with its Muslim neighbors. □ **Armenian** adj. & n.

Ar·men·tières |,ärmäN'tyer| industrial town in extreme N France. Pop. 26,000. It became known through the World War I song "Mademoiselle from Armentières."

Ar·mor·i·ca |är'mawrikə| ancient region of NW France between the Seine and the Loire. It is usually identified with all or the N part of Brittany. □ **Armorican** adj. & n.

Arn·hem |'ärn,hem; 'ärnəm| town in the E Netherlands, on the Rhine River, capital of the province of Gelderland. Pop. 131,700. During World War II, in September 1944, British airborne troops made a landing nearby but were overwhelmed by German forces.

Arn·hem Land |'ärnəm ,lænd| peninsula in Northern Territory, Australia whose chief town is Nhulunbuy. In 1976 Arnhem Land was declared an Aboriginal reservation.

Ar·no River |'ärnō| river that rises in the Apennines of N Italy and flows W 150 mi. (240 km.) through Florence and Pisa to the Ligurian Sea.

Arns·berg |'ärns,berk| industrial city in western Germany, on the Ruhr River. Pop. 76,000.

Aroos·took County |ə'rōōstək; ə'rōōstək| northernmost and largest county in Maine, noted for its potato production.

Ar·rah |'ərə| (also **Ara**) industrial city in NE India, in Bihar state. Pop. 157,000.

Ar Ra·ma·di |,är rə'mädē| (also **Ramadie; Rumadiya**) town in central Iraq, on the Euphrates River. Pop. 137,000.

Ar·ran |'ærən| island in the Firth of Clyde, in the W of Scotland.

Ar·ras |ä'räs| town in NE France, in the Pas-de-Calais. Pop. 42,700. In medieval times, it was the capital of Artois, and a center for the manufacture of tapestries.

Ar·row·head Region |'ærə,hed| highland region of NE Minnesota, largely on the Canadian Shield, noted for its mines and wilderness recreation.

Ar·thur's Seat |'ärTHərz 'sēt| volcanic hill in and overlooking Edinburgh, Scotland, from which King Arthur is supposed to have watched his army defeat the forces of the Picts.

Ar·tois |är'twä| region and former province

of NW France. Known in Roman times as Artesium, the area gave its name to a type of well, which was first sunk in the 12th century.

Aru·ba |ə'rōōbə| island in the Caribbean Sea, close to the Venezuelan coast. Pop. 60,000. Capital: Oranjestad. Formerly part of the Netherlands Antilles, it separated from that group in 1986 to become a self-governing territory of the Netherlands. It is a popular resort destination.

Aruba

Aru·na·chal Pra·desh |ˌärə'näCHəl prə-'deSH| mountainous state in the far NE of India, lying on the borders of Tibet to the N and Burma (Myanmar) to the E. Capital: Itanagar.

Aru·sha |ə'rōōSHə| industrial city in N Tanzania, the capital of the Arusha region. Pop. 140,000. It is a safari base in a coffee-growing area. Mount Kilimanjaro is nearby.

Ar·va·da |är'vædə; är'vädə| city in N central Colorado, a suburb NW of Denver. Pop. 89,235.

Ar·za·mas |ˌär,zə'mäs| town and rail junction in W Russia, S of Nizhni Novgorod. Pop. 111,000.

Asa·hi·ka·wa |ˌä,sähē'käwə; ˌäsä'hēkäwə| commercial and industrial city in N Japan, on central Hokkaido. Pop. 359,000.

Asan·sol |ˌəsən'sōl| industrial city in NE India, in West Bengal, NW of Calcutta. Pop. 262,000.

As·bes·tos |ˌäbes'tōs; æz'bestəs| city in S Quebec, E of Montreal, a center of asbestos mining. Pop. 6,487.

As·bury Park |'æz,berē 'pärk; 'æzb(ə)rē 'pärk| city in E central New Jersey, on the Atlantic shore, long a noted resort. Pop. 16,799.

As·ca·lon |'äskə,lawn; 'æskə,län| ancient Greek name for ASHQELON, Israel.

Ascen·sion Island |ə'senCHən| small island in the South Atlantic, incorporated with St. Helena, with which it is a dependency and strategic asset of the U.K. Pop. 1,007.

Aschaf·fen·burg |ä'sHäfən,bŏŏrk| river port in S Germany, on the Main River, ESE of Frankfurt am Main. Pop. 64,000.

As·co·li |'äskəlē| (also **Ascoli Piceno**) tourist resort and market town in the Marche region of E central Italy and capital of Ascoli Piceno province. Pop. 53,000.

As·cot |'æs,kät| town in Berkshire, England, SW of Windsor. Its racetrack on Ascot Heath is the site of the annual Royal Ascot races.

ASEAN |'äsē,än| acronym for the Association of South East Asian Nations, founded in 1967 by Indonesia, Malaysia, the Philippines, Singapore, and Thailand. Brunei joined in 1984. ASEAN has economic, security, and diplomatic purposes.

Ashan·ti |ə'sHäntē| (also **Asante**) region of central and S Ghana. From the 17th century it was the center of the Ashanti Empire, with its capital at Kumasi, whose king occupied the Golden Stool. With a complex, matrilinal, village-centered social organization, the Ashanti people dominated the region, which is noted for its agriculture, especially cacao production, gold mining and goldwork, and colorful Kente cloth. Conflict with British colonial incursions marked much of the 19th century and finally the Ashanti region was annexed by Britain in 1902, becoming part of the former British colony of the Gold Coast.

Ash·dod |'äsH,däd; äsH,dōd| seaport on the Mediterranean coast of Israel, situated to the S of Tel Aviv. Pop. 62,000.

Ashe·ville |'æsHvəl; 'æsH,vil| city in W North Carolina, a resort in the Blue Ridge Mts. Pop. 61,607. The famed Biltmore estate is here.

Ash·ford |'æsHfərd| industrial town in Kent, SE England. Pop. 91,000. One terminus of the Channel Tunnel from France is here.

Ash·ga·bat |'äsHgə,bät| (also **Ashkhabad**) the capital of the central Asian republic of Turkmenistan. Pop. 407,200. Former name (1919–27) **Poltoratsk**.

Ashi·ka·ga |ˌäsHə'kägə| commercial city in N central Japan, on central Honshu. Pop. 168,000. It gave its name to a Japanese dynasty.

Ash·kha·bad |'äsHkə,bäd| variant spelling of ASHGABAT, Turkmenistan.

Ash·land[1] |'æsHlənd| city, a coal industry center, in NE Kentucky, on the Ohio River. Pop. 23,622.

Ash·land[2] |'æsHlənd| city in N central Ohio. Pop. 20,079.

Ash·more and Car·tier Islands |'æsHmôr ən 'kärtyā| external territory of Australia in the Indian Ocean, comprising the uninhabited Ashmore Reef and Cartier Islands.

Ash·qe·lon |'äsHkə,lōn; 'æsHkə,län| (also **Ashkelon**) ancient Mediterranean city, situated to the S of modern Tel Aviv, in Israel. Greek name **Ascalon**.

Ash Sha·ri·qah |äsH'shärēkə| variant form of SHARJAH, United Arab Emirates.

Ash·ta·bu·la |,æsHtə'byōōlə| port city in NE Ohio, on Lake Erie. Pop. 21,633.

Ash·ta·roth |'æsHtə,räTH; 'æsHtə,rōTH| ancient city in SW Syria, E of the Sea of Galilee, a center of worship of the Phoenician goddess Astarte.

Asia |'āzHə| largest (17 million sq. mi./44 million sq. km.) of the world's continents, constituting nearly one-third of the land mass, lying N of the equator except for some SE Asian islands. It is connected to Africa by the Isthmus of Suez, and borders Europe (part of the same land mass) along the Ural Mts., the Caspian Sea, the Caucasus Mts., and the Black Sea. Largest country: Russia. Largest cities: Seoul, South Korea; Calcutta and Bombay, India; Tokyo, Japan. □ **Asian** adj. & n. **Asiatic** adj.

Asia Minor |'āzHə 'mīnər| the W peninsula of Asia, which now constitutes the bulk of Turkey (Anatolia). For over 2,500 years before the 6th century A.D., it was a center of Asian and European cultures.

Asir Mountains |ä'sir| range of mountains in SW Saudi Arabia, running parallel to the Red Sea.

As·ma·ra |æs'märə| industrial and commercial center, the capital and largest city of Eritrea. Pop. 358,000.

Asnières-sur-Seine |än'yer sōōr 'sen| industrial NW suburb of Paris, France, on the Seine River. Pop. 72,000.

Aso Mountain |'äsō| (Japanese name **Asosan**) volcano with five peaks in S Japan, on Kyushu. Its crater is one of the world's largest: 75 mi./121 km. in circumference.

As·pen |'æspən| resort city in S central Colorado. Pop. 6,850. Formerly a silver-mining town, it is now a thriving recreational center, noted particularly for its skiing facilities.

As·sam |ä'sæm| state in NE India. Capital: Dispur. Most of the state lies in the valley of the Brahmaputra River; it is noted for the production of tea. □ **Assamese** adj. & n.

As·sa·teague Island |'æsə,tēg| barrier island in SE Maryland and NE Virginia, on the Atlantic, noted for its wild ponies.

As·si·ni·boine River |ə'sinə,boin| river that flows 590 mi./950 km. from E Saskatchewan into Manitoba, joining the Red River at Winnipeg.

As·si·si |ə'sēsē; ə'sēzē| town in the province of Umbria in central Italy. Pop. 24,790. It is famous as the birthplace of St. Francis, whose tomb is here.

As Su·lay·ma·ni·yah |äs ,sōōli,mä'nēyə| variant form of SULAYMANIYAH, Iraq.

As·sur |ä'sōōr; 'äsôr| (also **Asur** or **Ashur**) an ancient city-state of Mesopotamia, situated on the present-day Tigris River to the south of modern Mosul, Iraq. The Assyrian empires were centered on the city.

As·syr·ia |ə'sirēə| ancient country in what is now N Iraq. From the early part of the 2nd millennium B.C. Assyria was the center of a succession of empires; it was at its peak in the 8th and late 7th centuries B.C., when its rule stretched from the Persian Gulf to Egypt. It fell in 612 B.C. to a coalition of Medes and Chaldeans. □ **Assyrian** adj. & n.

Asta·na |äs'tänə| capital of Kazakhstan (since 1998). Pop. 287,000. Formerly called **Aqmola** and, earlier, **Tselinograd**.

As·ti |'ästē| city in NW Italy and capital of Asti province. Pop.77,000. It is at the center of a wine-producing region.

As·to·ria[1] |ə'stawrēə| section of NW Queens, New York City, noted for its large Greek-American population.

As·to·ria[2] |ə'stawrēə| city in NW Oregon, near the mouth of the Columbia River on the Pacific coast. Pop. 10,069. In the 19th century it was a famous fur-trading center.

As·tra·khan |'æstrə,kæn| city in S Russia, on the delta of the Volga River. Pop. 509,000. Astrakhan fleeces were given their name because traders from the city brought them into Russia from central Asia.

As·tu·ri·as |ä'stŏŏryäs| autonomous region and former principality of NW Spain. Capital: Oviedo. □ **Asturian** adj. & n.

Asun·ci·ón |ä,sōōnsē'ōn| the capital, largest city, industrial center, and chief port of Paraguay, on the Paraguay River. Pop. 729,300.

As·wan |äs'wän| city on the Nile in S Egypt, 10 mi./16 km. N of Lake Nasser. Pop. 195,700. Two dams across the Nile have been built nearby. The controlled release of water from Lake Nasser behind the High

Dam produces the greater part of Egypt's electricity.

As•yut |ˌäs'yo͞ot| industrial and commercial city in E central Egypt, on the Nile River. Pop. 313,000. It was the ancient Lycopolis.

Ata•ca•ma Desert |ˌätə'kämə| arid region of W Chile, extending roughly 600 mi./965 km. S from the Peruvian border.

Atas•ca•de•ro |ə,tæskə'derō| city in SW California. Pop. 23,138.

Atchaf•a•laya River |(ə),CHæfə'līə| river in S central Louisiana that flows 170 mi./275 km. S to the Gulf of Mexico. It is used to control flooding on the Red and Mississippi rivers.

Atch•i•son |'æCHisən| city in NE Kansas, the birthplace of the Santa Fe (Atchison, Topeka & Santa Fe) Railroad. Pop. 10,656.

Ath•a•bas•ca River |ˌæTHə'bæskə| river that flows 765 mi./1,230 km. NE from the Rocky Mts. across Alberta to Lake Athabasca, the fourth-largest lake within Canada. The river valley has large oil tar deposits.

Ath•ens[1] |'æTHənz| city in NE Georgia, seat of the University of Georgia. Pop. 45,734.

Ath•ens[2] |'æTHənz| the capital of Greece. Pop. 3,096,775. A flourishing city-state of ancient Greece, Athens was an important cultural center from the 5th century B.C. It came under Roman rule in 146 B.C. and fell to the Goths in A.D. 267. After its capture by the Turks in 1456 Athens declined in status until chosen as the capital of a newly independent Greece in 1834. Greek name transliterated **Athínai.** □ **Athenian** *adj. & n.*

Ath•ens[3] |'æTHənz| city in SE Ohio, seat of Ohio University. Pop. 21,265.

Ath•er•ton Tableland |'æTHərtən| plateau in the Great Dividing Range in NE Queensland, Australia.

Athí•nai |ə'THē,nä| transliteration for the Greek name ATHENS.

Ath•os, Mount |'æ,THäs; 'ä,THäs| narrow, mountainous peninsula in NE Greece, projecting into the Aegean Sea. It is inhabited by monks of the Orthodox Church, who forbid women and even female animals to set foot on the peninsula. □ **Athonite** *adj. & n.*

Atit•lán |ˌätēt'län| dormant volcano in central Guatemala, SW of Guatemala City; 11,633 ft./3,546 m. **Lake Atitlán,** in a crater on the N, is famed for its scenery.

At•lan•ta |ət'læntə| the state capital of Georgia and its largest city. Pop. 394,000. Founded at the end of a railway line in

1837, the city was originally called Terminus; in 1843 it was incorporated as Marthasville, and in 1845 its name was finally changed to Atlanta. During the Civil War it was an important Confederate supply depot, but much of the city was burned after its capture in 1864 by Sherman. In recent decades the Atlanta metropolitan area has grown tremendously, and is a major center of industry and commerce. □ **Atlantan** *adj. & n.*

At•lan•tic City |ət'læntik| resort city in SE New Jersey, on the Atlantic. Pop. 37,986. It is famed for its gambling casinos.

Atlantic Intracoastal Waterway |ət'læntik 'intər,kōstəl| route that allows sheltered boat passage for 1,900 mi./3,100km. along the Atlantic coast between Boston, Massachusetts and Key West, Florida.

At•lan•tic Ocean |ət'læntik| the ocean lying between Europe and Africa to the E and N and South America to the W. It is divided by the equator into the N Atlantic and the S Atlantic oceans.

At•lan•tic Provinces |ət'læntik| name for the MARITIME PROVINCES of Canada together with NEWFOUNDLAND AND LABRADOR.

At•lan•tis |ət'læntəs| legendary island that sank in a volcanic explosion in ancient times, destroying a great civilization. Some place it in the Atlantic, W of Gibraltar. Others identify it with the Greek island of THERA.

At•las Mountains |'ætləs| range of mountains in N Africa extending from Morocco to Tunisia in a series of chains.

At•ti•ca[1] |'ætikə| triangular promontory of E mainland Greece. With the islands in the Saronic Gulf it forms a department of Greece, of which Athens is the capital. □ **Attic** *adj. & n.*

At•ti•ca[2] |'ætikə| town in W New York, scene of a bloody 1971 prison uprising. Pop. 7,383.

At•tle•boro |'ætlbərə| industrial city in SE Massachusetts, NE of Providence, Rhode Island. Pop. 38,383.

At•tu |'æ,to͞o| westernmost of the Aleutian Islands in SW Alaska. During World War II it was occupied by Japanese forces.

At•wa•ter |'æt,wawtər; 'æt,wätər| city in central California. Pop. 22,282.

Aube |ōb| department in NE France. Area: 2,319 sq. mi./6,004 sq. km. Pop. 289,000. The capital is Troyes. The area is part of the region that produces champagne.

Au•ber•vil•liers |ˌōber,vēl'yä| industrial town NE of Paris, in N central France. Pop.

68,000. It was a medieval pilgrimage destination.

Au·burn[1] |'awbərn| academic city in E Alabama, home to Auburn University. Pop. 33,830.

Au·burn[2] |'awbərn| industrial city in SW Maine, on the Androscoggin River opposite Lewiston. Pop. 24,309.

Au·burn[3] |'awbərn| industrial and commercial city in W central New York, on Owasco Lake. Pop. 31,258.

Au·burn[4] |'awbərn| industrial city in W central Washington. Pop. 33,102.

Au·burn Hills |'awbərn| city in SE Michigan, a residential and commercial suburb E of Pontiac and NE of Detroit. Pop. 17,076.

Au·bus·son |ˌōbY'sawN| town in central France, on the Creuse River. It is famous for its tapestry and carpet works, which date to the 15th century. There is also some light industry.

Auck·land |'awklənd| the largest city and chief seaport of New Zealand, on North Island. Pop. 309,400. It was the site of the first Parliament of New Zealand in 1854, remaining the capital until 1865.

Aude |ōd| department in SW France. Area: 2,371 sq. mi./6,139 sq. km. Pop. 299,000. The capital is Carcassonne.

Augh·rim |'awgrəm| village in E Galway, W Ireland, scene of a conclusive victory by the Protestant William of Orange over Catholic forces on July, 12, 1691 (Orangemen's Day in Northern Ireland).

Au·gra·bies Falls |aw'gräbēz| series of waterfalls on the Orange River in the province of Northern Cape, South Africa.

Augs·burg |'owks,bŏŏrk; 'awgz,bərg| historic commercial and industrial city in S Germany, in Bavaria. Pop. 259,880.

Au·gus·ta[1] |ə'gəstə| commercial and resort city in E Georgia. Pop. 44,640. The Augusta National golf course is here.

Au·gus·ta[2] |ə'gəstə| state capital of Maine, on the Kennebec River. Pop. 21,320.

Au·lis |'awləs; 'owləs| small port in ancient Greece, from which, in Homeric legend, the Greeks sailed against Troy at the start of the Trojan War.

Au·rang·a·bad |ow'rəNG(g)ə,bäd| commercial and industrial city in W India, in Maharashtra state. Pop. 572,000. The magnificent mausoleum of the wife of the Mogul emperor Aurangzeb is here.

Au·ri·gnac |awrēn'yäk| village, S France, in the foothills of the Pyrenees, SW of Toulouse. Significant remains from the Paleolithic era were found in a cave here in 1860; the Aurignacian period takes its name from the village.

Au·ro·ra[1] |ə'rawrə| city in N central Colorado, a largely residential suburb E of Denver. Pop. 222,103.

Au·ro·ra[2] |ə'rawrə| industrial city in NE Illinois. Pop. 99,581.

Au·ro·ra[3] |ə'rawrə| town in S Ontario, a suburb N of Toronto. Pop. 29,454.

Ausch·witz |'owSH,vits; 'owSH,wits| (Polish name **Oświęcim**) town in S Poland, near Cracow. Site of one of the largest and most infamous of the Nazi concentration camps during World War II.

Aus·ter·litz |'owstər,lits; 'awstə,lits| agricultural town in the SE Czech Republic. On December 2, 1805, in the "battle of the three emperors" here, Napoleon defeated Austrian troops under Emperor Francis II and Russian troops led by Czar Alexander I.

Aus·tin[1] |'awstən| city in SE Minnesota, noted for its meatpacking industry. Pop. 21,907.

Aus·tin[2] |'awstən| capital of Texas, on the Colorado River in the S central part. Pop. 465,622. A research and industrial center, it is also known as the seat of the University of Texas.

Aus·tral·asia |ˌawstrə'lāzHə| the region consisting of Australia, New Zealand, New Guinea, and the neighboring islands of the Pacific. □ **Australasian** adj. & n.

Aus·tra·lia |aw'strālyə| island country and continent of the S hemisphere, in the SW Pacific. Area: 2.97 million sq. mi./7.68 million sq. km. Pop. 17,500,000. Language, English. Capital: Canberra. Largest city: Sydney. Noted for its unique fauna, Australia was inhabited by Aboriginal peoples of mixed stock before British colonization began in the late 18th century. Largely flat plains, the country has strong agricultural and livestock-raising sectors, along with extensive mining and varied industry. □ **Australian** adj. & n.

Australia

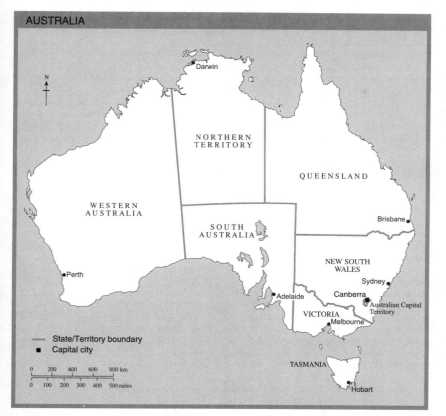

AUSTRALIA

Aus·tra·lian Alps |aw'strālyən 'ælps| the SE section of the E highlands of Australia, in the states of Victoria and New South Wales.

Aus·tra·lian Ant·arc·tic Territory |aw'strālyən ænt'är(k)tik| area of Antarctica administered by Australia, lying between longitudes 142° E and 136° E.

Aus·tra·lian Cap·i·tal Territory |ˌaw'strālyən| federal territory in New South Wales, Australia, consisting of one enclave ceded by New South Wales in 1911 to contain Canberra. Formerly included Jervis Bay 1915–88.

Aus·tra·sia |aw'strāzHə| kingdom of the Merovingian Franks in the 6th–8th centuries, incorporating N European lands from E France to Bohemia.

Aus·tria |'awstrēə| mountainous landlocked republic in central Europe. Area: 32,389 sq. mi./83,854 sq. km. Pop. 7,700,000. Language, German. Capital and largest city: Vienna. German name **Österreich**. Long the center of the Habsburg and Austro-Hungarian empires, the republic was dominated by Nazi Germany in 1938–45. Its economy is based on agriculture and forest industries, mining, tourism, and manufacturing. Vienna is a great cultural center. □ **Austrian** *adj. & n.*

Austria-Hungary |'awstrēə'həNGgərē| (also **Austro-Hungarian Empire** or **Dual Monarchy**) kingdom that existed from 1867 until the outbreak of World War I. Austria and Hungary were sovereign states, and parts of present-day Croatia, Slovakia, Romania, Slovenia, Italy, Poland, Bosnia, and the Czech Republic were subject to the crown.

Aus·tro·ne·sia |ˌawstrə'nēzHə| name sometimes used to designate the islands of the Pacific, where Austronesian, or Malayo-Polynesian, languages are spoken. These languages, however, extend as far W as Madagascar. □ **Austronesian** *adj. & n.*

Au·teuil |ō'tœ| district in Paris, France. Formerly a town, between the Seine River and the SE entrance to the Bois de Boulogne, it was absorbed into Paris 1860.

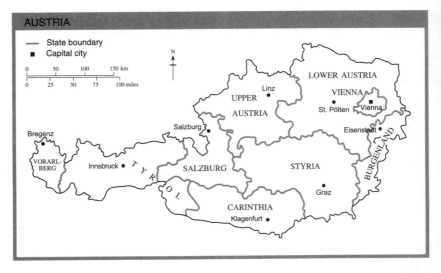

AUSTRIA

— State boundary
■ Capital city

0   50   100   150 km
0   25   50   75   100 miles

N

UPPER
AUSTRIA

Linz

LOWER AUSTRIA

VIENNA
St. Pölten   Vienna

Bregenz

Salzburg

Eisenstadt

VORARL-
BERG

Innsbruck

T
Y
R
O
L

SALZBURG

STYRIA

BURGENLAND

Graz

CARINTHIA

Klagenfurt

Au·vergne |ō'vern(yə)| region of S central France and a province of the Roman Empire. The region is mountainous and contains the extinct volcanic cones known as the Puys.

Au·xerre |ō'ser| commercial town and capital of Yonne district in N central France. Pop. 40,000. It is the center of the Chablis wine trade.

Au·yu·it·tuq National Park |ˌow'yo͞oətək| preserve on Baffin Island in Nunavut, the first Canadian park within the Arctic Circle.

Ava·lon |'ævə,län| in Arthurian legend, the land of the dead, long identified with Glastonbury, in Somerset, SW England, where an ancient abbey was said to have been founded by Joseph of Arimathea.

Ava·lon Peninsula |'ævə,län| historic region in SE Newfoundland, home to most residents of the province since early European settlement.

Ave·bury |'ävb(ə)rē| village in Wiltshire, SW England, site of one of Britain's major henge monuments of the late Neolithic period. The monument consists of a bank and ditch containing the largest known stone circle, with two smaller circles within it.

Avei·ro |ə'väro͞o; ə'vero͞o| seaport town on the Aveiro lagoon in SW Portugal, capital of Aveiro district. Pop. 35,000.

Avel·la·ne·da |ˌäväzнä'nä'uädä| city in E Argentina, a major industrial suburb of Buenos Aires. Pop. 347,000.

Avel·li·no |ˌävel'lēnō| market and manufacturing center in S Italy, E of Naples. Pop. 56,000. The town has suffered significant

earthquake damage, but many medieval buildings survive.

Aver·nus |ə'vərnəs| lake near Naples in Italy, which fills the crater of an extinct volcano. It was described by Virgil and other Latin writers as the entrance to the underworld.

Avey·ron |ˌävā'rōN| department in S France, at the S edge of the Massif Central. Area: 3,374 sq. mi./8,735 sq. km. Pop. 270,000. The capital is Rodez.

Avi·gnon |ˌvēn'yawN| city on the Rhône in SE France. Pop. 89,440. From 1309 until 1377 it was the residence of the popes during their exile from Rome, and was papal property until the French Revolution.

Avi·la |ə'vēlə| (also **Avila de los Caballeros**) ancient city in N central Spain, the capital of Avila province. Pop. 50,000. Its medieval buildings attract tourists.

Avi·lées |ˌävē'läs| port and industrial center in N Spain, on the Bay of Biscay. Pop. 84,000.

Avo·ca |ə'vōkə| short river and its valley (the **Vale of Avoca**) in Wicklow, E Ireland, S of Dublin, famed for its beauty.

Avon[1] |'ävən| river of central England that rises near the Leicestershire-Northamptonshire border and flows 96 mi./154 km. SW through Stratford to the Severn River.

Avon[2] |'ävən| river of SW England that rises near the Gloucestershire-Wiltshire border and flows 75 miles (121 km) through Bath and Bristol to the River Severn.

Avon[3] |'ävən| county of SW England, formed in 1974 from parts of N Somerset and Gloucestershire; county seat, Bristol.

Axis, the |'æksəs| term for Germany, Italy, and Japan, along with countries allied to them, during World War II.

Ax·min·ster |'æk,sminstər| town in Devon, SW England. Pop. 5,000. It was formerly famous for its carpets.

Ax·um |'äk,so͞om| variant spelling of AKSUM, Ethiopia.

Aya·cu·cho |,ī·ə'ko͞oCHō| historic commercial city in the Andes of S central Peru. Pop. 101,600.

Ay·din |ī'din| (ancient name **Tralles**) historic commercial city in SW Turkey, on the Menderes River. Pop. 107,000. It is the capital of Aydin province, a mining region.

Ayers Rock |ærz| red rock mass in Northern Territory, Australia, SW of Alice Springs. One of the largest monoliths in the world, it is 1,143 ft./348 m. high and about 6 mi./9 km. in circumference. It is named after Sir Henry Ayers, premier of South Australia 1872–73. Aboriginal name **Uluru**.

Ayles·bury |'älzb(ə)rē| town in S central England, the county seat of Buckinghamshire. Pop. 50,000.

Ayl·mer |'älmər| city in SW Quebec, a suburb just W of Hull and NW of Ottawa, Ontario. Pop. 32,244.

Ayodh·ya |ə'yōdyə| (also **Ajodhya**) village in N central India, part of the city of Faizabad, in Uttar Pradesh state. It is one of Hinduism's seven sacred sites.

Ayr·shire |'ær,SHir; 'ær,SHər| former county of SW Scotland, on the Firth of Clyde. It became a part of Strathclyde region in 1975.

Ayut·la |ä'yo͞otlə| (official name **Ayutla de los Libres**) historic town in Guerrero state, S Mexico, noted for the 1854 Plan of Ayutla, a protest and statement of principles for a new government.

Ayut·tha·ya |,äyo͞o'tīyə| historic city in S central Thailand, N of Bangkok. Pop. 61,000.

Azad Kash·mir |ä'zäd käSH'mēr| autonomous state in NE Pakistan, formerly part of Kashmir; administrative center, Muzaffarabad. It was established in 1949 after Kashmir was split as a result of the partition of India.

Aza·nia |ə'zänēə| alternative name for South Africa, proposed in the time of apartheid by some supporters of majority rule for the country.

Azer·bai·jan |,æzər,bī'ZHän| republic in the Caucasus of SE Europe, on the W shore of the Caspian Sea. Area: 33,450 sq. mi./86,600 sq. km. Pop. 7,219,000. Languages, Azerbaijani, Russian. Capital and largest city: Baku. Dominated for centuries by Persia and then Russia, Azerbaijan became independent in 1991, on the breakup of the Soviet Union. The mountainous country has an economy based on agriculture and oil. □ **Azerbaijani** *adj. & n.*

Azerbaijan

Azores |'ā,zawrz| group of volcanic islands in the Atlantic, W of Portugal, in Portuguese possession but partially autonomous. Pop. 241,590. Capital: Ponta Delgada. Portuguese name **Açores**.

Azov, Sea of |ə'zawf; 'æ,zawf| inland sea of S Russia and Ukraine, separated from the Black Sea by the Crimea and linked to it by a narrow strait.

Azu·sa |ə'zo͞osə| city in SW California, an industrial and residential suburb NE of Los Angeles. Pop. 41,333.

Az Zar·qa |ä'zärkə| variant form of ZARQA, Jordan.

Bb

Baal·bek |'bäl,bek| town in E Lebanon, site of the ancient city of Heliopolis.

Ba·ba·ho·yo |,bäbə'hōyō| commercial town in W Ecuador, in tropical lowlands along the Babahoyo River. Pop. 50,000.

Ba·bar Islands |'bä,bär| island group in E Indonesia, in the Banda Sea between Timor and the Taninbar Islands.

Ba·bel |'bābəl; 'bæbəl| biblical site of a tower built in the plain of Shinar, Mesopotamia, in an attempt to reach heaven.

Bab el Man·deb |'bæb el 'män,deb| strait, 17 mi./27 km. wide, between E Africa and the Arabian Peninsula, linking the Red Sea with the Gulf of Aden, part of the Indian Ocean.

Ba·bine Lake |bæ'bēn| lake in central British Columbia, noted for its fishing and salmon spawning grounds. The Babine Mts. run along its W side.

Ba·bi Yar |,bäbē 'yär| ravine near Kiev, Ukraine, where in two days in 1943 Nazis slaughtered 33,000 Jews. In all, the Nazis are believed to have killed 100,000 persons, primarily Jews, Gypsies, and Russian prisoners of war, over a period of months here.

Ba·bol |bä'bōl; bäbōōl| (also **Babul**) commercial city in N Iran, just S of the Caspian Sea. Pop. 137,000.

Ba·bo·qui·vi·ri Mountains |,bäbōkə-'värē| range in S Arizona, rising to 7,734 ft./2,357 m. at Baboquiviri Peak.

Bab·ru·isk |bə'brōoisk| (also **Babruysk, Bobruisk,** or **Bobruysk**) a river port in central Belarus, on the Berezina River SE of Minsk. Pop. 222,900.

Ba·bu·yan Islands |,bäbōō'yän| group of twenty-four volcanic islands lying to the N of the island of Luzon in the N Philippines.

Bab·y·lon[1] |'bæbələn; 'bæbə,län| ancient city in Mesopotamia, the capital of Babylonia in the 2nd millennium B.C. The city (of which only ruins now remain) lay on the Euphrates River and was noted for its luxury, its fortifications, and particularly for the Hanging Gardens of Babylon. □ **Babylonian** adj. & n.

Bab·y·lon[2] |'bæbələn; 'bæbə,län| town on the South Shore of Long Island, New York, including Babylon, Amityville, and other villages. Pop. 202,889.

Bab·y·lo·nia |,bæbə'lōnēə| ancient region of Mesopotamia, formed when the kingdoms of Akkad in the N and Sumer in the S combined the first half of the 2nd millennium B.C. Babylonia was dominated by Assyria, formerly its dependency, from the 14th to the 7th century B.C. The throne was held by the Chaldeans from 625 to 539 B.C., and Babylonia was conquered by Cyrus the Great of Persia in 539 B.C. □ **Babylonian** adj. & n.

Ba·ca·bal |,bəkə'bäl| commercial city in NE Brazil, on the Rio Mearim. Pop. 99,000.

Ba·cău |bə'kow| industrial town in NE Romania, in the foothills of the Carpathian Mts., on the Bistriţa. River. Pop.193,000.

Bac·ca·rat |,bäkə'rä| town in NE France, on the W edge of the Vosges Mts. The town is famous for its crystal works, established in 1764.

Back Bay |bæk| historic residential and commercial district of W Boston, Massachusetts, on land along the Charles River that was reclaimed in the 19th century.

Ba·co·lod |bə'kō,lōd| city on the NW coast of the island of Negros in the central Philippines. Pop. 364,180. It is the chief city of the island and a major port.

Bac·tria |'bæktrēə| ancient country in central Asia, corresponding to the N part of modern Afghanistan. Traditionally the home of Zoroaster, it was the seat of a powerful Indo-Greek kingdom in the 3rd and 2nd centuries B.C. □ **Bactrian** adj. & n.

Ba·da·csóny |'bädə,CHōnē| district in Hungary, NW of Lake Balaton, noted for its white wines.

Ba·da·joz |,bädə'hōs| market center and industrial city in W Spain, capital of Badajoz province. Pop. 130,000.

Ba·da·lo·na |,bädə'lōnə| seaport in NE Spain, NE of Barcelona, on the Mediterranean Sea. Pop. 206,000.

Ba·den |'bädn| spa town in Austria, S of Vienna. Pop. 24,000. It was a royal summer retreat and fashionable resort in the 19th century.

Baden-Baden |'bädn'bädn| spa town in the Black Forest, SW Germany. Pop. 48,700. It was a fashionable resort in the 19th century.

Baden-Württemberg |,bädn'vyrtəm-,berg| state of western Germany. Capital: Stuttgart.

Bad·ger State |'bæjər| nickname for WISCONSIN.

Bad Hom·burg |,bät 'awm,bŏŏrg| (also called **Homburg** or **Bad Homburg vor der**

Höhe) spa and resort in the Taunus Mts., in central Germany. Homburg hats originated here.

Bad Kreuz·nach |ˌbät 'kroit,snäk| historic spa and industrial city in western Germany, in Rhineland-Palatinate. Pop. 43,000.

Bad·lands, the |'bæd,lændz| highland region chiefly in SW South Dakota, S of the Black Hills, noted for its harsh terrain.

Bad·min·ton |'bædmintn| name of two villages in SW England. Badminton House, a local estate, gave its name to the game first played here.

Baf·fin Bay |'bæfən| extension of the N Atlantic between Baffin Island and Greenland, linked to the Arctic Ocean by three passages. It is largely icebound in winter.

Baf·fin Island |'bæfən| large island in the Canadian Arctic, situated at the mouth of Hudson Bay. It is separated from Greenland by Baffin Bay.

Ba·fous·sam |bä'fōōsəm| commercial city in W Cameroon, in a coffee-producing region. Pop. 113,000.

Bagh·dad |'bæg,dæd; bæg'dæd| capital of Iraq, on the Tigris River. Pop. 4,648,600. A thriving city under the Abbasid caliphs in the 8th and 9th centuries, it was taken by the Ottoman sultan Suleiman in 1534 and remained under Ottoman rule until World War I. In 1920 it became the capital of the newly created state of Iraq. Today it is the administrative, commercial, and cultural center of the country.

Ba·guio |'bägēō| summer capital of the Philippines, a mountain resort on NW Luzon. Pop. 183,000. Noted for its woodcarvings, it is also the center of a major gold-producing area.

Ba·ha·mas |bə'häməz| (official name **Commonwealth of the Bahamas**) republic consisting of an archipelago off the SE coast of Florida. Area: 5,380 sq. mi./13,939 sq. km. Pop. 225,050. Languages, English, Creole. Capital and largest city: Nassau. It was on one of these West

Indian islands that Columbus made his first landfall in the New World. The islands were a British colony from the 18th century until they gained independence in 1973. Tourism, finance, fishing, and some industry are important to the economy. □ **Bahamian** adj. & n.

Ba·ha·ram·pur |'bähərəm,pŏŏr| town in NE India, in West Bengal state, near the border with Bangladesh. Pop. 126,000.

Ba·ha·wal·pur |bə'häwəl,pŏŏr| city of central Pakistan, in Punjab province. Pop. 250,000. It was formerly the capital of a princely state established by the nawabs of Bahawalpur.

Ba·hia |bä'ēə| **1** State of E Brazil, on the Atlantic coast. Pop. 11,855,000. Capital: Salvador. **2** an earlier name for SALVADOR.

Ba·hía Blanca |bä'ēə 'blänɢkə| port in Argentina serving the S part of the country. Pop. 271,500.

Bah·raich |bə'rīk| commercial town in N India, in Uttar Pradesh state, NE of Lucknow. Pop. 135,000. It is a place of pilgrimage for Hindus and Muslims.

Bah·rain |bä'rān| sheikhdom consisting of a group of islands in the Persian Gulf. Area: 255 sq. mi./691 sq. km. Pop. 518,000. Language, Arabic. Capital and largest city: Manama. Formerly under Portuguese, Persian, and British domination, Bahrain became independent in 1971. Pearls were once central to the economy; today oil refining and exporting are. □ **Bahraini** adj. & n.

Bahrain

Bahr al-Ghazal |ˌbär æl gə'zäl| river in S Sudan, a tributary to the White Nile. The name was also formerly that of a province of S Sudan.

Ba·ia Ma·re |'bīə 'märə| industrial city in NW Romania, capital of Maramureş county. Pop. 150,000.

Bai·cheng |'bī'CHəNG| city in Jilin province, NE China. Pop. 218,000.

Bahamas

Bai·kal, Lake |bīˈkawl; bīˈkæl| (also **Baykal**) large lake in S Siberia, the largest freshwater lake in Eurasia and, with a depth of 5,714 ft./1,743 m., the deepest lake in the world.

Baie-Comeau |bā ˈkōmō; ˌbākōˈmō| industrial port city in SE Quebec, at the mouth of the Manicouagan River on the St. Lawrence River, NE of Quebec City. Pop. 26,012.

Bai·ko·nur |ˌbīkəˈnoͅor| (also **Baykonur**) mining town in central Kazakhstan. The world's first satellite (1957) and the first manned space flight (1961) were launched from the former Soviet space center nearby.

Bain·bridge Island |ˈbānbrij| island in W Washington, in Puget Sound, a largely-residential suburb W of Seattle.

Bai·ri·ki |ˈbīˌrēkē| capital of Kiribati, on South Tarawa Island. Pop. 2,200.

Bai·yin |ˈbīˈyin| industrial city in Gansu province, central China, NE of Lanzhou. Pop. 548,000.

Ba·ja Cal·i·for·nia |ˈbähä ˌkælᵻˈfawrnyə| mountainous peninsula in NW Mexico, which extends S from the border with California and separates the Gulf of California from the Pacific Ocean. It consists of two states of Mexico: *Baja California* (capital, Mexicali) and *Baja California Sur* (capital, La Paz). Also called **Lower California**.

Ba·ker Island |ˈbākər| uninhabited island in the central Pacific, near the equator, claimed by the U.S. in 1857. Once a guano source, it is now a wildlife refuge.

Ba·ker Lake |ˈbākər| settlement in Nunavut, on the Thelon River W of Hudson Bay, home to the only inland Inuit community in Canada. Pop. 1,186.

Ba·kers·field |ˈbākərzˌfēld| industrial city in S central California, an oil industry center in the San Joaquin Valley. Pop. 174,820.

Ba·ker Street |ˈbākər| commercial street in W central London, England, S of Regent's Park, associated with the fictional detective Sherlock Holmes.

Bakh·chi·sa·rai |ˌbäКНСHisəˈrī| town in S Ukraine, on the Crimean Peninsula. The palace of the khans there was restored by Potemkin while he was governor of Crimea.

Bakh·ta·ran |ˌbäКНtəˈrän| (also called **Kermanshah**) commercial and industrial city in W Iran, in the Zagros Mts. Pop. 624,000.

Ba·ku |bäˈkoͅo| the capital of Azerbaijan, on the Caspian Sea. Pop. 1,780,000. It is an industrial port and a center of the oil industry.

Ba·la·kla·va |ˌbələˈklävə| (also **Balaclava**) village in S Ukraine, on the SW coast of the Crimean Peninsula. During the Crimean War, the famous Charge of the Light Brigade took place here. The so-called Balaklava helmet was first worn during that war.

Ba·la·ko·vo |ˌbələˈkawvə| city in W Russia, WNW of Saratov, E of the Volga River. Pop. 200,000.

Ba·la·shi·kha |ˌbələˈsHēkə| city in W Russia, NE of Moscow. Pop. 137,000.

Bal·a·ton, Lake |ˈbawləˌtōn| large shallow lake in W central Hungary, situated in a resort and wine-producing region to the S of the Bakony Mts.

Bal·boa |bælˈbōə| town in S Panama, on the Gulf of Panama of the Pacific Ocean. Pop. 3,000. It was the administrative center for the U.S.-controlled Panama Canal Zone, and is at the W entrance of the canal.

Bal·brig·gan |bælˈbrigən| port and resort town in E Ireland, N of Dublin. Pop. 8,000. Its textiles are famous.

Bal·cones Escarpment |bælˈkōnəs| geologic fault separating the plains of E Texas from highlands to the W. San Antonio, Austin, and Waco lie near or on it.

Bald·win Park |ˈbawldwən| city in SW California, a suburb E of Los Angeles. Pop. 69,330.

Bâle |bäl| French name for BASLE, Switzerland.

Bal·e·ar·ic Islands |ˌbælēˈærik| (also **the Balearics**) group of Mediterranean islands off the E coast of Spain, forming an autonomous region of that country, with four large islands (Majorca, Minorca, Ibiza, Formentera) and seven smaller ones. Capital: Palma (on Majorca).

Ba·li |ˈbälē; ˈbalē| mountainous island of Indonesia, to the E of Java; chief city, Denpasar. Pop. 2,856,000. It is noted for its beauty and the richness of its culture. □ **Balinese** *adj. & n.*

Ba·li·ke·sir |ˌbälikəˈsir| city in NW Turkey, a textile center and capital of Balikesir province. Pop. 171,000.

Ba·lik·pa·pan |ˌbälikˈpäˌpän| port and oil center in Indonesia, on E Borneo. Pop. 344,000.

Bal·kan Mountains |ˈbawlkən| (also called **Balkans**) range of mountains stretching across Bulgaria to the Black Sea. The highest peak is Botev Peak (7,793 ft./2,375 m.). □ **Balkan** *adj.*

Bal·kans |ˈbawlkənz| the countries occupying the part of SE Europe lying S of the Danube and Sava rivers, forming the

Balkan Peninsula, bounded by the Adriatic and Ionian seas in the W, the Aegean and Black seas in the E, and the Mediterranean in the south. At the crossroads of Europe and Asia, of Christianity and Islam, and of Byzantine and Western Roman Christianity, this mountainous region is noted for fierce ethnic and religious conflicts among its varied peoples—Greeks, Slavs, Turks, Albanians, and Gypsies. The peninsula was taken from the Byzantine Empire by the Ottoman Turks in the 14th and 15th centuries, and parts remained under Turkish control until 1912–13. After World War I the peninsula was divided among Greece, Albania, Bulgaria, and Yugoslavia (which broke up in 1991–3), with Turkey retaining only a small area including Constantinople (Istanbul). Balkan countries formed from the breakup of Yugoslavia include Slovenia, Croatia, Bosnia and Herzegovina, and Macedonia. □ **Balkan** *adj.*

Balkh |bawlk| historic town in N central Afghanistan, W of Mazar-e-Sharif. Pop. 7,000.

Bal·la·rat |'bælə,ræt| mining and sheep-farming center in Victoria, Australia. Pop. 64,980. It is the site of the discovery in 1851 of the largest gold reserves in Australia.

Balls Bluff |bawlz| historic locality on the Potomac River in NE Virginia, near Leesburg, site of an October 1861 Confederate victory.

Bal·ly |'bälē| (also **Bali**) industrial town in E India, N of Calcutta in West Bengal state. Pop. 182,000.

Bal·ly·me·na |,bælē'mēnə| town in Northern Ireland, to the N of Lough Neagh, in County Antrim. Pop. 28,000.

Bal·mor·al Castle |bæl'mawrəl| holiday residence of the British royal family, in NE Scotland, on the Dee River near Braemar.

Bal·qash, Lake |,bäl'käsн| (also **Balkhash, Balkash**) shallow salt lake in Kazakhstan, 350 mi./560 km. long.

Bal·sas, Rio |,rēō 'bawlsəs| river that flows 450 mi./725 km. through central Mexico, through Puebla, Guerrero, and Michoacán states, into the Pacific.

Bal·tic Sea |'bawltik| sea in N Europe. Nearly landlocked by Scandinavia, the Baltic states, and Germany, it is linked with the North Sea by the Kattegat strait and the Øresund channel.

Bal·tic States |'bawltik| **1** the republics of Estonia, Latvia, and Lithuania. **2** the ten members of the Council of Baltic States es-

tablished in 1992: Denmark, Estonia, Finland, Germany, Latvia, Lithuania, Norway, Poland, Russia, and Sweden.

Bal·ti·more |'bawltə,mawr| historic industrial seaport, the largest city in Maryland, on Chesapeake Bay. Pop. 736,000.

Bal·ti·more County |'bawltə,mawr| county in N central Maryland, surrounding but not including the city of Baltimore. Towson is its seat. Pop. 692,134.

Bal·ti·stan |,bawltə'stæn| region of N Pakistan, in the Karakoram range of the Himalayas, to the S of K2. Also called **Little Tibet**.

Ba·lu·chi·stan |bə,lōōCHə'stæn| **1** a mountainous region of W Asia, which includes part of SE Iran, SW Afghanistan, and western Pakistan. **2** a province of western Pakistan. Capital: Quetta.

Ba·ma·ko |'bämə,kō| the capital of Mali, in the south of the country, an industrial port and historic cultural center on the Niger River. Pop. 646,000.

Bam·berg |'bæm,bərg| industrial port and commercial center on the Regnitz River in S Germany. It was once a renowned ecclesiastical center. Pop. 71,000.

Ba·men·da |bə'mendə| commercial and resort city in NW Cameroon. Pop. 138,000.

Ba·mi·an |,bämē'än| city in central Afghanistan. Pop. 8,000. Nearby are the remains of two colossal statues of Buddha and the ruins of the city of Ghulghuleh, which was destroyed by Genghis Khan *c.*1221.

Ba·na·ba |bə'näbə; 'bänəbə| island in the W Pacific, just S of the equator, to the W of the Gilbert Islands. Formerly within the Gilbert and Ellice Islands, the island has been part of Kiribati since 1979. Also called **Ocean Island**.

Ba·nat |'bän,ät| former province, now divided between Hungary and Romania, E of the Tisza River.

Ban·bury |'bænb(ə)rē; 'bæmb(ə)rē| commercial town in Oxfordshire, central England, noted for its market cross and for its cakes. Pop. 37,000.

Ban·dar Ab·bas |,bändər ə'bäs| (also **Benderabbas**) port city in S Iran, on the Strait of Hormuz at the mouth of the Persian Gulf. Pop. 250,000. It has long been one of the main ports of Iran.

Ban·dar Lam·pung |,bändər läm'pōōNG| city at the S tip of Sumatra, in Indonesia. Pop. 284,275. It was created in the 1980s as a result of the amalgamation of the city of Tanjungkarang and the nearby port of Telukbetung.

Ban·dar Se·ri Be·ga·wan |ˌbändər ˌserē bəˈgäˌwän| the capital of Brunei. Pop. 46,000.

Ban·da Sea |ˈbändə| sea in E Indonesia, between the central and S Moluccas Islands.

Ban·dung |ˈbänˌdo͞oNG| industrial and cultural city in Indonesia. Pop. 2,056,900. Founded by the Dutch in 1810, it was the capital of the former Dutch East Indies.

Banff |bæmf| resort town in SW Alberta, in the Rocky Mts. W of Calgary. Pop. 5,688.

Banff·shire |ˈbæmfsHər; ˈbæmfˌsHir| former county of NE Scotland that became a part of Grampian region in 1975.

Ban·ga·lore |ˈbäNGgəˌlawr| city in S central India, capital of the state of Karnataka. Pop. 2,651,000. It is a center of high-tech and other industries.

Bang·ka |ˈbæNGkä; ˈbäNGkä| (also **Banka**) island in Indonesia, SE of Sumatra, one of the world's foremost tin-producing centers. Chief town: Pangkalpinang.

Bang·kok |ˈbæNGˌkäk; bæNGˈkäk| industrial and commercial city, the capital and chief port of Thailand, on the Chao Phraya waterway, 25 mi./40 km. upstream from its outlet into the Gulf of Thailand. Pop. 5,876,000.

Ban·gla·desh |ˌbäNGgləˈdesH| republic of the Indian subcontinent, in the Ganges delta. Area: 55,813 sq. mi./143,998 sq. km. Pop. 107,992,140. Official language, Bengali. Capital and largest city: Dhaka. Long part of British India, then (1947–71) the E part of Pakistan, Bangladesh became independent in 1971. A densely populated, fertile agricultural low country, it is prone to repeated monsoonal flooding, and is one of the poorest countries in the world. □ **Bangladeshi** *adj. & n.*

Bangladesh

Ban·gor¹ |ˈbæNGgər| industrial city in E central Maine, on the Penobscot River, formerly a lumbering center. Pop. 33,181.

Ban·gor² |ˈbæNGˌgawr; ˈbænˌgawr; ˈbæNG-

gər| resort town in Northern Ireland, E of Belfast on Belfast Lough. Pop. 71,000.

Ban·gor³ |ˈbæNGgər; ˈbæNGˌgawr| academic and industrial town in Gwynedd, N Wales, at the N end of the Menai Strait. Pop. 12,000.

Ban·gui |bäNGˈgē; ˈbäNGˌgē| the capital of the Central African Republic, a port on the Ubangi River. Pop. 596,800.

Ban·ja Lu·ka |ˌbänyə ˈlo͞okə| spa town in N Bosnia and Herzegovina. Pop. 143,000. It served as a base for Bosnian Serbs in their ethnic war against Bosnian Muslims in the 1990s.

Ban·jar·ma·sin |ˌbänjərˈmäsən| (also **Bandjarmasin**) a deepwater port and capital of the province of Kalimantan in Indonesia, on the island of Borneo. Pop. 480,700.

Ban·jul |ˈbænˌjo͞ol| the capital of the Gambia. Pop. 44,540. Until 1973 it was known as Bathurst.

Banks Island |bæNGks| westernmost island in the Arctic Archipelago of N Canada. Sparsely populated, it is home to abundant wildlife.

Banks·town |ˈbæNGksˌtown| city in Australia, a residential suburb WSW of Sydney, in New South Wales. Pop. 154,000.

Ban·nock·burn |ˈbænəkˌbərn; ˌbænəkˈbərn| village in central Scotland, S of Stirling, site of a Scottish victory over the English in 1314.

Bann River |bæn| longest (80 mi./130 km.) river of Northern Ireland, which flows through Lough Neagh and NW to the Atlantic. It is noted for salmon and eel fishing.

Ban·ská Bys·tri·ca |ˈbänkə ˈbistritˌsä| town in central Slovakia, at the confluence of the Hron and Bystrica rivers. Pop. 178,000.

Ban·tam |ˈbänˌtäm; ˈbæntəm| (also **Banten**; **Bantan**) ruined port town in Indonesia, on NW Java. The small domestic fowl known as "bantams" are named after it.

Ban·try Bay |ˈbæntrē| inlet of the N Atlantic in County Cork, SW Ireland, long used by fishing and naval fleets. It now has an oil terminal.

Ban·tu·stan |ˈbæto͞oˌstæn| name, *often offensive*, for any of the partially self-governing homelands reserved for black South Africans before 1994. Bophuthatswana was an example.

Bao·ding |ˈbowˈdiNG| city in Hebei province, E China, an agricultural distribution center on the Fu River. Pop. 483,000.

Bao·ji |'bow'jē| industrial city in Shaanxi province, central China, on the Wei River in the foothills of the Qin Ling Mts. Pop. 338,000.

Bao·shan |'bow'sHän| industrial city in Yunnan province, S China, between the Lancang and Nu rivers. Pop. 697,000. It is a major iron and steel center.

Bao·tou |'bow'tō| industrial city in Inner Mongolia, N China, on the Yellow River. Pop. 1,180,000.

Ba·ra·cal·do |ˌbärə'käldō| industrial city in N Spain, on the Nervion River. Pop. 105,000.

Ba·ra·coa |ˌbärə'kōə| port city in extreme E Cuba, on the N coast. Pop. 50,000. It is the oldest (1512) European settlement in Cuba.

Ba·ra·ho·na |ˌbärə'ōnə| port city in the SW Dominican Republic, on the Caribbean Sea. Pop. 158,000.

Ba·ra·no·vi·chi |bə'ränə,vēcHē| (also **Baranavichy**) industrial city in W Belarus. Pop. 163,000.

Ba·ra·ta·ria Bay |ˌbärə'tærēə| inlet of the Gulf of Mexico in SE Louisiana, S of New Orleans, associated with Jean Lafitte and other early 19th-century outlaws.

Bar·ba·dos |bär'bādəs| the most easterly of the Caribbean islands, a republic in the Windward Islands group. Area: 166 sq. mi./431 sq. km. Pop. 260,480. Official language, English. Capital: Bridgetown. Barbados became a British colony in the 1630s and remained British until 1966, when it gained independence. Tourism, sugar, and fishing are important to its economy. □ **Barbadian** *adj. & n.*

Barbados

Bar·ba·ry |'bärb(ə)rē| (also **Barbary States**) a former name for the Saracen countries of N and NW Africa, together with Moorish Spain. The area was noted between the 16th and 18th centuries as a haunt of pirates. Compare with MAGHRIB.

Bar·ba·ry Coast[1] |'bärb(ə)rē| former name for the Mediterranean coast of N Africa from Morocco to Egypt.

Bar·ba·ry Coast[2] |'bärb(ə)rē| historic district of central San Francisco, California, famed in the 19th century for its lawlessness.

Bar·ber·ton |'bärbərtən| city in NE Ohio, a suburb SW of Akron. Pop. 27,623.

Bar·bi·can |'bärbikən| section of E central London, England, NE of St. Paul's Cathedral, redeveloped after World War II bombing.

Bar·bi·zon |bärbə'zawN| village in the forest of Fontainebleau, N central France. It gave its name to a group of 19th-century landscape painters who worked here; they include Corot, Daubigny, and Millet.

Bar·bu·da |bär'bōōdə| see ANTIGUA AND BARBUDA. □ **Barbudan** *adj. & n.*

Bar·ce·lo·na[1] |ˌbärsə'lōnə| city on the coast of NE Spain, capital of Catalonia. Pop. 1,653,175. It is a large seaport and industrial city and a leading cultural center. It was the seat of the Republican government during the Spanish Civil War.

Bar·ce·lo·na[2] |ˌbärsə'lōnə| port and industrial city in NE Venezuela, on the Neveri River, near the Caribbean Sea. Pop. 222,000.

Bar·ce·los |bär'selōs| town in N Portugal, on the Cávado River. Pop. 5,000. The Barcelos cockerel is the national emblem.

Bard·dha·man |'bərdəmən; 'bärdəmən| city in NE India, in West Bengal state on the Damodar River. Pop. 245,000.

Bar·de·jov |'bärdəyawf| town in E Slovakia, on the Topla River, near the Polish border. Pop. 79,000. It is known for its hot springs.

Bar·do·li·no |ˌbärdə'lēnō| resort town in NE Italy, on the E shore of Lake Garda. Pop. 6,000. It is famous for its red wine.

Ba·reil·ly |bə'rälē| industrial city in N India, in Uttar Pradesh. Pop. 583,000.

Ba·rents Sea |'bærənts| part of the Arctic Ocean to the N of Norway and Russia, bounded to the W by Svalbard, to the N by Franz Josef Land, and to the E by Novaya Zemlya.

Bar Harbor |bär| resort town in S central Maine, on Mount Desert Island. Pop. 4,443.

Ba·ri |'bärē| industrial seaport on the Adriatic coast of SE Italy, capital of Apulia region. Pop. 353,030.

Ba·ri·nas |bə'rēnəs| commercial city in W Venezuela, the capital of Barinas state, a cattle- and oil-producing area. Pop. 154,000.

Ba·ri·sal |'bærə,säl| river port in S Bangladesh, on the Ganges delta. Pop. 180,010.

Bar·king and Dag·en·ham |'bärkiNG ən 'dægənəm| industrial borough of Greater London, England, N of the city center. Pop. 140,000.

Bark·ly Tableland |'bärklē| plateau region lying to the NE of Tennant Creek in Northern Territory, Australia.

Bar·let·ta |bär'letə| seaport and commercial center in SE Italy. Pop. 89,000. A famous duel between French and Italian knights took place near here in 1503.

Bar·na·ul |,bärnə'ool| the capital of Altai territory of S Russia, an industrial port on the Ob River. Pop. 603,000.

Bar·ne·gat Bay |'bärni,gæt; 'bärnigət| tidal body in SE New Jersey, shielded from the Atlantic by barrier islands, and the site of numerous resorts.

Bar·net |'bärnət| largely residential borough of N Greater London, England. Pop. 283,000.

Barns·ley |'bärnzlē| town in N England, a mining center in South Yorkshire. Pop. 217,300.

Barn·sta·ble |'bärnstəbəl| town in SE Massachusetts, on the SW part of Cape Cod. It is the commercial center for a resort area. Pop. 40,949.

Ba·ro·da |bə'rōdə| **1** former princely state of W India, now part of Gujarat. **2** former name (until 1976) for VADODARA.

Ba·ros·sa Valley |bə'raqsə| wine-producing region in Australia, N of Adelaide in South Australia.

Ba·rot·se·land |bə'rätsə,lænd| historic name for what is now the Western Province of Zambia. The Barotse people live in the area, along the Zambezi River.

Bar·qui·si·me·to |,bärkēsē'mätō| commercial city in NW Venezuela. Pop. 602,620.

Bar·ra |'bærə| small island toward the S end of the Outer Hebrides, Scotland, to the S of South Uist, from which it is separated by the Sound of Barra.

Bar·rack·pore |'bərək,pōr| (also **Barrackpur**) historic military town in NE India, in West Bengal state, N of Calcutta. Pop. 133,000.

Bar·ra Man·sa |,bärə 'mäNsə| industrial city in SE Brazil, NW of Rio de Janeiro. Pop. 165,000.

Bar·ran·quil·la |,bärən'kēeə| the chief port of Colombia. Pop. 1,018,700. Founded in 1629, the city lies at the mouth of the Magdalena River, near the Caribbean Sea.

Bar·ren Lands |'bærən| name for tundra areas of northern Canada.

Bar·rie |'bærē| city in S Ontario, on Lake Simcoe, NW of Toronto. Pop. 62,728.

Bar·row |'bærō| city in N central Alaska, a commercial center on the Arctic Ocean. It is the northernmost U.S. city. Pop. 3,469. Nearby Point Barrow is the northernmost point in the U.S., at 71° 23′ N.

Barrow-in-Furness |'bærō ən 'fərnəs| industrial port city in Cumbria, NW England, on the Furness Peninsula. Pop. 74,000.

Bar·stow |'bär,stō| city in S central California, in the Mojave Desert NE of Los Angeles. Pop. 21,472.

Bar·tles·ville |'bärtlz,vil| city in NE Oklahoma, an oil industry center. Pop. 34,256.

Bart·lett |'bärtlət| town in SW Tennessee, a suburb NE of Memphis. Pop. 26,989.

Ba·ry·saw |bə'rēsəf| industrial city in central Belarus. Pop. 147,000. Formerly **Borisov**.

Bash·kiria |bäsH'kirēə| autonomous republic in central Russia, W of the Urals. Pop. 3,964,000. Capital: Ufa. Also called **Bashkir Autonomous Republic, Bashkortostan**.

Ba·sil·don |'bæzldən| town in SE England. Pop. 157,500. It was developed as a new town (planned urban center) from 1949.

Ba·si·li·ca·ta |bə,zēlē'kätə| region of S Italy, lying between the 'heel' of Apulia and the 'toe' of Calabria. Capital: Potenza.

Basin and Range Province |'bäsən ən 'rānj| largely arid intermountain region of the SW U.S., chiefly in Nevada, Utah, and California. The Great Basin and Death Valley are parts of the region.

Basle |bäl| commercial and industrial city on the Rhine in NW Switzerland. Pop. 171,000. French name **Bâle**, German name **Basel**.

Basque Country |bæsk| region of the W Pyrenees in both France and Spain, the homeland of the Basque people. French name **Pays Basque**.

Basque Provinces |bæsk| autonomous region of N Spain, on the Bay of Biscay. Capital: Vitoria.

Bas·ra |'bäsrə; 'äzrə| oil port of Iraq, on the Shatt al-Arab waterway. Pop. 616,700. It is a Shiite center with a long cultural history.

Bas-Rhin |bä 'ræN| department in NE France, between the Rhine River and the Vosges Mts. Area: 1,849 sq. mi./4,787 sq. km. Pop. 953,000. The capital and commerical center is Strasbourg.

Bas·sein |bə'sān| port on the Irrawaddy delta in SW Burma. Pop. 144,100.

Basse-Normandie |ˌbäs ˌnawrmäNdē| region of NW France, on the coast of the English Channel, including the Cherbourg Peninsula and the city of Caen.

Basse·terre |bäs'ter| the capital of St. Kitts and Nevis in the Leeward Islands, on the island of St. Kitts. Pop. 12,600.

Basse-Terre |bäs 'ter| the main island of the French overseas department of Guadeloupe, in the West Indies.

Bass Strait |bæs| channel separating Tasmania from the mainland of Australia.

Ba·stia |bäst'yä; 'bästēə| the chief port of Corsica. Pop. 38,730.

Bas·tille, the |bäs'tēl| (*hist.*) fortress and state prison in E Paris, France, near the present Place de la Bastille, built in the 14th century. The storming of the prison by revolutionaries on July 14, 1789, is considered to mark the beginning of the French Revolution. Demolition of the prison began the next day.

Bas·togne |bä'stōn(yə)| town, SE Belgium. Pop. 11,000. It was the scene of heavy fighting during the Battle of the Bulge in World War II.

Ba·su·to·land |bə'sootō,lænd| former name (until 1966) for LESOTHO.

Ba·ta |'bätə| seaport in Equatorial Guinea. Pop. 17,000.

Ba·taan |bə'tæn; bə'tän| peninsula and province in the Philippines, on W Luzon, bounded by Manila Bay (E) and the South China Sea (W); scene of World War II battles and the infamous "Death March." Pop. 426,000.

Ba·tal·ha |bə'tälyə| town in central Portugal. Pop. 3,000. Its Dominican abbey was built in 1388 in honor of Portugal's independence from Spain; Portuguese forces had defeated the Spanish in a battle nearby, in 1385.

Ba·tan·gas City |bə'täNGgəs| industrial and commercial port city in the Philippines, on SW Luzon. Pop. 144,000.

Ba·tan Islands |bə'tän| the most northerly islands of the Philippines.

Ba·ta·via |bə'tävēə; bə'tävēə| former name (until 1949) for DJAKARTA, Indonesia. It derives from an earlier name for the Netherlands.

Bath |bæTH; bäTH| spa town in SW England, in Avon. Pop. 79,900. The town was founded by the Romans, who called it Aquae Sulis, and was a fashionable spa in the 18th century.

Bath·urst Island |'bæTHərst| island in the Queen Elizabeth group in Nunavut, Canada, near which the North Magnetic Pole lies in the Arctic Ocean.

Bat·man |bät'män| city in SE Turkey, in Batman province on the Batman River, near its junction with the Tigris River. Pop. 147,000.

Bat·na |bət'nä| industrial city in NE Algeria, SW of Constantine. Pop. 184,000.

Bat·on Rouge |ˌbætn 'roozH| the state capital of Louisiana, on the Mississippi River N of New Orleans. Pop. 219,530.

Bat·tam·bang |'bätəm,bäNG| (also **Batdambang**) the capital of a province of the same name in W Cambodia, a commercial center in a rice-growing area. Pop. 551,860.

Bat·ten·berg |'bätn,berg| village in Hesse, western Germany. The name was used for a branch of the German royal family; members married into the British royal family and their descendants later assumed the name Mountbatten.

Bat·ter·sea |'bætərsē| district of SW London, England, part of the borough of Wandsworth, on the S side of the Thames River, across from Chelsea.

Bat·tery, the |'bætərē| historic area at the S end of Manhattan Island, New York City.

Bat·ti·ca·loa |ˌbətikə'lōə| city on the E coast of Sri Lanka. Pop. 42,900.

Bat·tle |'bætl| town in SE England, in East Sussex, actual site of the Battle of Hastings (1066). Pop. 6,000.

Bat·tle Creek |'bætl| city in S Michigan, noted as a cereal industry center. Pop. 53,540.

Ba·tu·mi |bə'toomē| port city, capital of Adzharia, in the Republic of Georgia, on the Black Sea. Pop. 383,000.

Ba·tu Pa·hat |'bätoo 'pä,hät| (also called **Bandar Penggaram**) port town in Malaysia, on the Strait of Malacca in W Johor.

Bat Yam |'bät 'yäm| city in central Israel, a suburb S of Tel Aviv, on the Mediterranean Sea. Pop. 142,000.

Bau·chi |'bowCHē| town in NE Nigeria, a tin mining center. Pop. 186,000. It is the capital of Bauchi state, part of a former kingdom of the same name.

Bau·rú |bow'roo| commercial city in S Brazil, NW of São Paulo, in an agricultural region. Pop. 265,000.

Ba·var·ia |bə'værēə| state of S Germany, formerly an independent kingdom. Capital: Munich. German name **Bayern**.
□ **Bavarian** *adj. & n.*

Bax·ter State Park |'bækstər| preserve in N Maine that incorporates Mount

Katahdin and the N end of the Appalachian Trail.

Ba·ya·mo |bə'yämō| industrial and commercial city in SE Cuba, the capital of Granma province. Pop. 125,000. Bayamo was prominent in the 1890s revolt against Spanish rule.

Ba·ya·món |ˌbīä'mōn| community in NE Puerto Rico, an industrial and residential suburb SW of San Juan. Pop. 202,103

Bay Area |bā| region around San Francisco Bay, in N central California. Oakland is the hub of the East Bay, San Jose of the South Bay.

Bay City |bā| industrial city in E Michigan, on the Saginaw River near Lake Huron. Pop. 38,936.

Bay·ern |'bīərn| German name for BAVARIA.

Ba·yeux |bī'yœ| market town in NW France, near the English Channel. Pop. 15,000. It was the first city liberated by the Allies after D-day, during World War II. It is famous for the medieval Bayeux tapestry, actually an embroidery, which recounts the story of the Norman Conquest of England in 1066.

Bay·ko·nur |ˌbīkə'noͻr| locality in central Kazakhstan, NE of Aral Sea. The Soviet Union maintained a missile- and rocket-testing site here.

Bay of for names beginning thus, see the other element, e.g., FUNDY, BENGAL, etc.

Ba·yonne[1] |ˌbā'ōn| port and industrial town in SW France, in the Basque region in the Pyrénées-Atlantiques. Pop. 42,000. In the 16th and 17th centuries, Bayonne produced cutlery; the word "bayonet" is derived from its name.

Bay·onne[2] |bā'yawn| industrial port city in NE New Jersey, on New York Bay. Pop. 61,444.

Bay·ou Teche |'bī,oo 'tesh| water route in S central Louisiana, at the heart of Cajun Country. Also called **the Teche.**

Bay·ping name formerly used in English for BEIJING (approximation of **Peiping**).

Bay·reuth |bī'roit; 'bī,roit| industrial and cultural city in Bavaria, S Germany. Pop. 73,000. The composer Richard Wagner is buried here, and festivals of his operas are held regularly.

Bay State |bā| nickname for MASSACHUSETTS.

Bays·wa·ter |'bāz,wawtər; 'bāz,wätər| residential district of W central London, England, N of Hyde Park.

Bay·town |'bā,town| city in SE Texas, an oil industry center E of Houston. Pop. 63,850.

Beachy Head |bēchē 'hed| high chalk headland on the coast of East Sussex, SE England, on the English Channel, near which the French won a naval victory in 1690.

Bea·con Hill |'bēkən 'hil| historic neighborhood in downtown Boston, Massachusetts, on high ground N of the Boston Common.

Bea·cons·field |'bēkənz,fēld| town in S central England, in Buckinghamshire, NW of London, associated with the 19th-century politician and writer Benjamin Disraeli and with other literary figures. Pop. 11,000.

Bea·gle Channel |'bēgəl| channel through the islands of Tierra del Fuego at the S tip of South America, named for the ship in which Charles Darwin passed through in the 1830s.

Beale Street |bēl| historic commercial street in downtown Memphis, Tennessee, associated with black music and commerce.

Beard·more Glacier |bird,mawr| glacier in Antarctica, flowing from the Queen Maud Mts. to the Ross Ice Shelf, at the S edge of the Ross Sea.

Bé·arn |bā'ärn| former province in SE France, now part of the department of Pyrénées-Atlantique.

Be·as |'bē,äs| river of N India that rises in the Himalayas and flows through Himachal Pradesh to join the Sutlej River in Punjab. In ancient times called the Hyphasis, it marked the E limit of Alexander the Great's conquests.

Beau·bourg |bō'boͻr| see POMPIDOU CENTER, Paris, France.

Beauce |bōs| agricultural plain in N central France, SW of Paris. Its chief town is Chartres. A variety of crops are grown in its fertile soil, including wheat, corn, potatoes, barley, and oats.

Beau·fort Sea |'bōfərt| part of the Arctic Ocean lying to the N of Alaska and Canada.

Beau·jo·lais |ˌbōzhə'lā| wine-growing region in E central France, between Mâcon and Lyons W of the Saône River. The chief town is Villefrance-sur-Saône.

Beau·mont |'bō,mänt| industrial port in SE Texas, an oil industry center on the Neches River. Pop. 114,323.

Beau·port |bō'pawr| city in SE Quebec, a suburb on the Saint Lawrence River NE of Quebec City. Pop. 69,158.

Beau·vais |bō'vä| manufacturing town in N central France, N of Paris. Pop. 56,000. Beauvais had a renowned tapestry works, which were moved to Gobelins in 1940 after suffering damage in World War II. Its Gothic cathedral has the highest choir vault in the world.

Bea·ver·ton |'bēvərtən| city in NW Oregon, a suburb W of Portland, noted for its electronics industry. Pop. 53,310.

Bech·u·a·na·land |bĕCH'wänə,lænd| former British colony in southern Africa, now largely the nation of BOTSWANA. A section became part of present-day South Africa. *Bechuana* is an old name for the Tswana people.

Bed·ford[1] |'bedfərd| town in S central England, on the Ouse River, the county seat of Bedfordshire. Pop. 89,200.

Bed·ford[2] |'bedfərd| city in NE Texas, a suburb NE of Fort Worth. Pop. 43,762.

Bed·ford·shire |'bedfərd,SHir; 'bedfərd-SHər| county of S central England; county seat, Bedford.

Bedford-Stuyvesant |'bedfərd 'stīvəsənt| residential and commercial section of N Brooklyn, New York, home to one of the largest U.S. black communities.

Bed·lam |'bedləm| popular name for St. Mary of Bethlehem hospital, founded in London, England in 1247, and by the 14th century a well-known mental hospital.

Bed·ling·ton |'bedliNGtn| town in NE England, in Northumberland. Pop. 13,000. It gave its name to a breed of terrier.

Bee·hive State |'bē,hīv| nickname for UTAH.

Beer·she·ba |bir'SHēbə| historic commercial city in S Israel, on the N edge of the Negev desert. Pop. 138,100.

Bei·an |'bā'än| city in Heilongjiang province, NE China, in the foothills of the Xiao Hinggan Ling Mts. Pop. 205,000.

Bei·hai |'bā'hī| port city in Guangxi, S China, on the Gulf of Tonkin. Pop. 113,000. It is an industrial and fishing center.

Bei·jing |bā'jiNG; 'bā'zhiNG| the capital and second-largest city of China, in the NE of the country. Pop. 6,920,000. Beijing became the capital in 1421, at the start of the Ming period. The political and cultural center of China, it is also an industrial hub. Also called **Peking**; formerly called **Peiping**.

Bei·ra |'bārə| port on the coast of Mozambique, capital of Sofala province. Pop. 299,300.

Bei·rut |bā'rōōt| the capital and chief port of Lebanon. Pop. 1,500,000. The city was badly damaged during the Lebanese civil war of 1975–89. It has a long history as a commercial center and resort.

Be·jaïa |bə'jīə| (French name **Bougie**) port city in NE Algeria, on the Gulf of Bejaïa, an inlet of the Mediterranean Sea. Pop. 124,000. It has long been a political and academic center.

Be·kaa |bə'kä| (also **El Beqa'a**) a fertile valley in central Lebanon between the Lebanon and Anti-Lebanon Mts.

Bel Air |bel 'er; bel 'ær| affluent residential section of Los Angeles, California.

Be·la·rus |,byälə'rōōs; ,belə'rōōs| republic in eastern Europe. Area: 80,185 sq. mi./207,600 sq. km. Pop. 10,328,000. Official language, Belorussian. Capital and largest city: Minsk. Also called **Belorussia**, **White Russia**. Largely flat plains, with extensive marshes along the Dnieper River, Belarus is both agricultural and industrial. It was part of the Soviet Union 1921–91. □ **Belarussian** *adj. & n.* **Belorussian** *adj. & n.*

Belarus

Be·la·ya River |'byeləyə| river in the Bashkir Republic, E European Russia, flowing 700 mi./1,210 km. NW from the Ural Mts. to the Kama River.

Be·la·ya Tser·kov |'byeləyət'serkəf| (Ukrainian name **Bila Tserkva**) industrial city in Ukraine, S of Kiev. Pop. 200,500.

Bel·cher Islands |'belCHər| island group in SE Hudson Bay, in Nunavut, Canada.

Be·lém |bə'lem| city and port of N Brazil, at the mouth of the Amazon, capital of the state of Pará Pop. 1,244,640.

Bel·fast |'bel,fæst; bel'fæst| capital, largest city, and chief port of Northern Ireland. Pop. 280,970. Famed for its shipyards, the city suffered damage and population decline from the early 1970s as a result of sectarian violence.

Bel·fort |,bel'fawr| industrial city in E France, in the historically important

Belfort Gap between the Vosges and Jura mountains. Pop. 51,900.

Bel·gaum |bel'gowm| industrial city in W India, in the state of Karnataka. Pop. 326,000.

Bel·gian Con·go |'beljən 'käNGgō| former (1908–60) name for the Congo (formerly Zaire).

Bel·gium |'beljəm| low-lying republic in W Europe, on the S of the North Sea and English Channel. Area: 11,796 sq. mi./30,540 sq. km. Pop. 9,978,700 (1991); languages, Flemish and French (Walloon). Capital and largest city: Brussels. French name **Belgique**, Flemish name **België**. Belgium separated from the Netherlands in 1830. It suffered heavily in both world wars, but is one of the most industrial countries in Europe, as well as home to many European Union offices. □ **Belgian** *adj. & n.*

Belgium

Bel·go·rod |'byelgərət| industrial city in S Russia, on the Donets River close to the border with Ukraine. Pop. 306,000.

Bel·grade |'bel,gräd; bel'gräd| capital of Serbia and Yugoslavia, the industrial and commercial center and largest city of Serbia, on the Danube River. Pop. 1,168,450. Serbian name **Beograd**.

Bel·gra·via |bel'grävēə| fashionable district of London, England, S of Knightsbridge, noted for its diplomatic and literary associations.

Be·li·tung |bə'lē,tōoNG| (also **Billiton**) Indonesian island in the Java Sea, between Borneo and Sumatra.

Be·lize |bə'lēz| country on the Caribbean coast of Central America. Area: 8,867 sq. mi./22,965 sq. km. Pop. 190,800. Languages, English (official), Creole, Spanish. Capital: Belmopan. Largest city: Belize City. Former name (until 1973) **British Honduras**. Belize, which became independent in 1981, relies on tourism and subsistence agriculture. Its people are largely of African extraction □ **Belizian** *adj. & n.*

Belize

Be·lize City |bə'lēz| the principal seaport and former capital (until 1970) of Belize. Pop. 46,000.

Bell |bel| city in SW California, a suburb SE of Los Angeles. Pop. 34,365.

Bel·lary |bə'lärē| industrial city in Karnataka state, S India. Pop. 245,800.

Bel·leau Wood |bel'ō| (French name **Bois de Belleau**) forest E of Paris, France, and just E of Château-Thierry, scene of a June 1918 victory by American forces over the Germans.

Belle Glade |bel| city in SE Florida, a sugarcane-producing hub. Pop. 16,177.

Belle Isle, Strait of |bel 'īl| ocean passage between Newfoundland and Labrador, at the mouth of the Gulf of St. Lawrence in E Canada.

Belle·ville[1] |'bel,vil| section of E Paris, France. It is a working-class district famous for Père Lachaise cemetery, which contains the tombs of many famous people.

Belle·ville[2] |'bel,vil| industrial city in SW Illinois. Pop. 42,785.

Belle·ville[3] |'bel,vil| industrial township in NE New Jersey. Pop. 34,213.

Belle·ville[4] |'bel,vil| city in SE Ontario, near Lake Ontario. Pop. 37,243.

Belle·vue[1] |'bel,vyōō| city in E Nebraska. Pop. 30,982.

Belle·vue[2] |'bel,vyōō| historic municipal hospital in lower Manhattan, New York City.

Bell·flow·er |'bel,flow-ər| city in SW California, a suburb SE of Los Angeles. Pop. 61,815.

Bell Gardens |bel| unincorporated suburb E of Los Angeles, California. Pop. 42,355.

Bel·ling·ham |'beliNG,hæm| industrial port city in NW Washington, on Bellingham Bay off Puget Sound. Pop. 52,179.

Bel·lings·hau·sen Sea |'beliNGz,howzən| part of the SE Pacific off the coast of Antarctica, bounded to the E and S by the Antarctic Peninsula and Ellsworth Land.

Bel·lin·zo·na |ˌbelən'zōnə; ˌbelənt'sōnə| historic resort town in S Switzerland, near the Italian border. Pop. 17,000.

Bel·lo |'bāyō| town in NW Colombia, just N of Medellín, of which it is a suburb.

Bell·wood |'bel,wŏŏd| village in NE Illinois, a suburb W of Chicago. Pop. 20,421.

Bel·mont[1] |'bel,mänt| city in N central California, a suburb SE of San Francisco. Pop. 24,127.

Bel·mont[2] |'bel,mänt| town in E Massachusetts, a suburb NW of Boston. Pop. 24,720.

Bel·mo·pan |ˌbelmō'pæn| the capital of Belize. Founded in 1970 to succeed Belize City, it is one of the smallest capitals in the world. Pop. 3,850.

Be·lo Ho·ri·zon·te |ˌbälō ˌawre'zawNntē| city in E Brazil, capital of the state of Minas Gerais. Pop. 2,020,160. It is a center for regional mining and agricultural industries.

Be·loit |bə'loit| industrial and academic city in SE Wisconsin. Pop. 35,573.

Be·los·tok |ˌbyelə'stawk| Russian name for BIALYSTOK, Poland.

Bel·sen |'belzən| village near Bergen, in Lower Saxony, NW Germany, site of a World War II Nazi concentration camp (also called **Bergen-Belsen**).

Belts·ville |'belts,vil; 'beltsvəl| unincorporated village in central Maryland, just NE of Washington, D.C. Pop. 14,476. The U.S. Department of Agriculture has its chief experimental station here.

Bel·tsy |'byeltsē| (Romanian name **Bălți**) city in N central Moldova. Pop. 164,800.

Belt·way, the |'belt,wā| circular highway around Washington, D.C., in Maryland and Virginia. The U.S. government is said to exist "inside the Beltway."

Bel·ve·dere, the |'belvə,dir| former court of the Vatican, in Rome, Italy, now a famous art museum.

Be·mid·ji |bə'mijē| city in NW Minnesota, near the head of the Mississippi River. Pop. 11,245.

Be·mis Heights |'bēməs| historic village in E New York, SE of Saratoga Springs, site of two 1777 Revolutionary War battles.

Be·na·res |bə'närəs| former name for VARANASI, India.

Ben·be·cu·la |ben'bekyŏŏlə| small island in the Outer Hebrides, Scotland, between North and South Uist and linked to them by causeways.

Ben Bul·ben |ben 'bəilbən| small mountain in County Sligo, NW Ireland, at the

SW foot of which, in Drumcliff, the poet W.B. Yeats is buried.

Bend |bend| city in central Oregon. Pop. 20,469.

Ben·dery |bən'derē| former Russian name for TIGHINA, Moldova.

Ben·di·go |'bendi,gō| commercial, and former gold-mining town in the state of Victoria, Australia. Pop. 57,430.

Be·ne Be·raq |bə,nä bə'räk| city in central Israel, a suburb N of Tel Aviv, noted for its Talmudic schools. Pop. 127,000.

Be·ne·lux |'benl,əks| collective name for Belgium, the Netherlands, and Luxembourg (an acronym of *Bel*gium, *Neth*erlands, and *Lux*embourg), especially with reference to their economic union.

Ben·gal, Bay of |ben'gawl; beNG'gawl| part of the Indian Ocean lying between India to the W and Burma and Thailand to the E.

Ben·gal |ben'gawl; beNG'gawl| region in the NE of the Indian subcontinent, containing the Ganges and Brahmaputra river deltas. In 1947 the province was divided into West Bengal, which has remained a state of India, and East Bengal, now Bangladesh. □ **Bengali** *adj. & n.*

Beng·bu |'bəNG'bŏŏ| city in Anhui province, E China, an agricultural trade center. Pop. 623,000.

Ben·gha·zi |ben'gäzē| Mediterranean port in NE Libya. Pop. 485,400. It was the joint capital (with Tripoli) from 1951 to 1972.

Beng·ku·lu |beNG'kŏŏlŏŏ| port city in SW Sumatra, Indonesia. Pop. 173,000.

Ben·gue·la |ben'gwelə| port and railway terminal in Angola, on the Atlantic coast. Pop. 155,000.

Ben·gue·la Current |ben'gwelə| cold ocean current that flows from Antarctica N along the W coast of S Africa as far as Angola.

Be·ni River |'bänē| river that flows 1,000 mi./1,600 km. from central to N Bolivia, along the E of the Andes, into the Madeira River.

Be·ni·cia |bə'nēsHə| city in N central California, N of San Francisco Bay. Pop. 24,437.

Be·nin, Bight of |bə'nēn| wide bay on the coast of Africa N of the Gulf of Guinea, bordered by Togo, Benin, and SW Nigeria. Lagos is its chief port.

Be·nin |bə'nēn| republic of W Africa, immediately W of Nigeria. Area: 43,483 sq. mi./112,622 sq. km. Pop. 4,883,000. Languages, French (official), West African languages. Capital: Porto Novo. Largest city:

Benin

Cotonou. The country, whose name recalls an earlier African kingdom, was conquered by the French in 1893 and became part of French West Africa. In 1960 it became fully independent. Cotton, cacao, oil, and subsistence farming are important. Former name (until 1975) DAHOMEY. □ **Beninese** *adj. & n.*

Ben Nev·is |ben 'nevəs| mountain in western Scotland. Rising to 4,406 ft./1,343 m., it is the highest mountain in the British Isles.

Ben·ning·ton |'beniNGtən| historic town in SW Vermont. Pop. 16,451.

Be·no·ni |bə'nōnē| city in South Africa, in the province of Gauteng, E of Johannesburg. Pop. 206,800. It is a gold-mining center.

Ben·son·hurst |'bensən,hərst| residential section of SW Brooklyn, New York.

Ben·ton Harbor |'bentn| industrial city in SW Michigan. Pop. 12,818.

Bent's Fort |bents| historic site in E central Colorado, NE of La Junta, on the Arkansas River and the former Santa Fe Trail.

Be·nue River |'bānwā| river that flows 870 mi./1,400 km. from N Cameroon into Nigeria, where it joins the Niger River.

Ben·xi |'ben'sHē| city in NE China, in the province of Liaoning. Pop. 920,000. It is a center for metal and other heavy industries.

Be·o·grad |'bāə,gräd| Serbian name for BELGRADE.

Bep·pu |'bepo͞o| resort city in SW Japan, on NW Kyushu, famed for its hot springs. Pop. 130,000.

Ber·bera |'bərbərə| port on the N coast of Somalia. Pop. 65,000.

Berch·tes·ga·den |berKHtəs,gädn| town in S Germany, in the Bavarian Alps close to the border with Austria. Pop. 8,186. Adolf Hitler's fortified retreat, the "Eagle's Nest," was here.

Ber·dyansk |bir'dyänsk| port city in SE Ukraine, on the Sea of Azov. Pop. 134,000.

Be·rea |bə'rēə| city in central Kentucky, home to Berea College. Pop. 9,126.

Be·re·zi·na River |bər'yāzHinə| river that flows 370 mi./600 km. SE across Belarus to the Dnieper River. It was the scene of an 1812 retreat by Napoleon's armies, and of 1941 battles between German and Soviet forces.

Be·rez·ni·ki |bər'yawznəkē| port city on the Kama River in the W Urals, Russia, center of a chemical-processing complex. Pop. 201,000.

Ber·ga·ma |bər'gämə| commercial town in W Turkey, N of Izmir. Pop. 101,000. Ancient Pergamum, a cultural and political center under the Mysians and Romans, was here.

Ber·ga·mo |'bergə,mō| city in Lombardy, N Italy, in the foothills of the Alps. Pop. 118,000. It has historic upper and industrial lower sections.

Ber·gen[1] |'bergən| Flemish name for MONS, Belgium.

Ber·gen[2] |'bergən| seaport in SW Norway. Pop. 213,344. It is a center of the fishing and North Sea oil industries.

Ber·gen·field |,bərgən,fēld| suburban borough in NE New Jersey. Pop. 24,458.

Ber·gen op Zoom |'berKHən awp 'zōm| commercial town in the SW Netherlands, on the Zoom River and the Scheldt estuary. Pop. 47,000.

Ber·ge·rac |bərzHə'räk| wine-producing region in the Dordogne valley in SW France.

Ber·ing Sea |'beriNG| arm of the N Pacific lying between NE Siberia and Alaska, bounded to the S by the Aleutian Islands. It is linked to the Arctic Ocean by the Bering Strait.

Ber·ing Strait |'beriNG| narrow sea passage that separates the E tip of Siberia from Alaska and links the Arctic Ocean with the Bering Sea, about 53 mi./85 km. wide at its narrowest point. During the Ice Age, as a result of a drop in sea levels, the *Bering land bridge* formed between the two continents, allowing the migration of animals and dispersal of plants in both directions, including the earliest human arrivals in the Americas.

Berke·ley |'bərklē| city in W California, on San Francisco Bay, site of the University of California at Berkeley. Pop. 102,724.

Berke·ley Springs |'bərklē| (official name **Bath**) town in E West Virginia. Pop. 735. It is a famous spa.

Berk·shire |'bärkSHər; 'bärk,SHir| county of S England, W of London; county seat, Reading.

Berk·shire Hills |'bərkSHər| upland in W Massachusetts, noted as a resort area.

Ber·lin |bər'lin| the capital of Germany, an industrial, commercial, and cultural city on the Spree River, in the NE. The capital of the German Empire from 1871, it was divided into East Berlin and West Berlin after World War II. The former was the capital of East Germany, while Bonn became capital of West Germany. In 1990 Berlin was reunified. Pop. 3,102,500.

Ber·lin Wall |bər'lin| fortified and heavily guarded wall built in 1961 by the communist authorities on the boundary between East and West Berlin, chiefly to curb the flow of East Germans to the West. Regarded as a symbol of the division of Europe into the communist countries of the East and the democracies of the West, it was opened in November 1989 after the collapse of the communist regime in East Germany, and subsequently dismantled.

Ber·me·jo River |ber'māhō| river that flows 650 mi./1,045 km. SE from N Argentina to the Paraguay River, at the Paraguayan border.

Ber·mu·da |bər'myōōdə| (also **the Bermudas**) British crown colony, made up of about 150 small islands (20.5 sq. mi./53 sq. km.), about 650 mi./1,046 km. E of the coast of North Carolina. Pop. 58,000. Language, English. Capital: Hamilton. Inhabited since 1609, Bermuda now has internal self-government. Most of its people are of African extraction. Tourism, finance, fishing, and light industry are important. □ **Bermudan** adj. & n. **Bermudian** adj. & n.

Bermuda

Ber·mu·da Hundred |bər'myōōdə| locality SE of Richmond, Virginia, site of an 1864 Civil War battle.

Ber·mu·da Tri·an·gle |bər,myōōdə 'trī-,æNGgəl| area of the Atlantic between Florida, Bermuda, and Puerto Rico, the scene of many mysterious ship and aircraft disappearances.

Bern |bern; 'bərn| (also **Berne**) the capital of Switzerland since 1848, an industrial and administrative city in the W central part of the country. Pop. 134,620. □ **Bernese** adj. & n.

Ber·nese Alps |,bər'nēz; bər'nēs| (also **Bernese Oberland**) range of the Alps in central and W Switzerland. Finsteraarhorn (14,022 ft./4,274 m.), the Jungfrau, and the Eiger are here.

Ber·ni·na Alps |bər'nēnə| section of the Rhaetian Alps in S Switzerland and N Italy, reaching 13,284 ft./4,049 m. at Piz Bernina.

Ber·ry |be'rē| former province of central France; chief town, Bourges.

Ber·wick·shire |'berwik,SHir; 'beriksHər| former county of SE Scotland, on the border with England. It became a part of Borders region (now Scottish Borders) in 1975.

Berwick-upon-Tweed |'berik əpən 'twēd| town at the mouth of the Tweed River in NE England, close to the Scottish border. Pop. 13,000. It was ceded by Scotland to England in 1482.

Ber·wyn |'bərwən; 'bər,win| city in NE Illinois, a suburb W of Chicago. Pop. 45,426.

Be·san·çon |bəzäN'sawN| the capital of Franche-Comté in NE France, a precision-industry center. Pop. 119,200.

Bes·kids |bes'kēdz| forested mountain range along the borders of Slovakia with Poland and the Czech Republic, reaching 5,659 ft./1,725 m. at Babia Góra, and noted for iron mining and resorts.

Bes·sa·ra·bia |,besə'räbēə| region in E Europe between the Dniester and Prut rivers, from 1918 to 1940 part of Romania. The major part of the region now is in Moldova, the remainder in Ukraine. □ **Bessarabian** adj. & n.

Bes·se·mer |'besəmər| city in N central Alabama, a steel and industrial center SW of Birmingham. Pop. 33,497.

Beth·a·ny |'beTHənē| city in central Oklahoma, a suburb W of Oklahoma City. Pop. 20,075.

Beth·el[1] |'beTHəl| city in SW Alaska, a fishing center. Pop. 4,674.

Beth·el[2] |'beTHəl| town in the Catskill Mts., SE New York. Pop. 3,693. It is the actual site of the 1969 Woodstock music festival.

Beth·el[3] |'beTHəl| ancient city of Palestine, N of Jerusalem in the West Bank, where in the biblical account Abraham built his first altar.

Beth·el Park |'beTHəl| borough in SW Pennsylvania, a suburb S of Pittsburgh. Pop. 33,823.

Be·thes·da[1] |bə'THezdə| in the Bible, a pool in Jerusalem with miraculous healing properties.

Be·thes·da[2] |bə'THezdə| affluent unincorporated suburb in central Maryland, N of Washington, D.C. It is home to the National Institutes of Health. Pop. 62,936.

Beth·le·hem[1] |'beTHli,hem; 'beTHlēəm| small town 5 mi./8 km. S of Jerusalem, in the Israeli-occipied West Bank. Pop. 14,000. It was the native city of King David and is the reputed birthplace of Jesus.

Beth·le·hem[2] |'beTHli,hem; 'beTHlēəm| industrial city in E Pennsylvania, on the Lehigh River. Pop. 71,428. It is a famed steelmaking center.

Beth·sa·i·da |beTH'sāədə| ancient city of Palestine, believed to have been near the Sea of Galilee, the birthplace of several followers of Jesus.

Bet·ten·dorf |'betn,dawrf| industrial city in SE Iowa, on the Mississippi River. It is one of the Quad Cities.

Betws-y-Coed |,betōōsə'koid| resort community in NW Wales, on the Conway River, noted for its scenery and as an outdoor center. Pop. 800.

Bev·er·ly |'bevərlē| industrial and resort city in NE Massachusetts. Pop. 38,195.

Bev·er·ly Hills |'bevərlē| largely residential city in California, on the NW side of the Los Angeles conurbation. Pop. 31,970. It is famous as the home of movie stars.

Bex·ley |'bekslē| borough of Greater London, England, comprising industrial and residential suburbs SE of the city. Pop. 211,000.

Bé·ziers |bā'zy| industrial town in S France, on the Orb River. Pop. 72,000. It is a communication center and a trade center for the wine industry.

Bha·gal·pur |'bägəl,pŏŏr| industrial and commercial city in Bihar, NE India, on the Ganges River. Pop. 262,000.

Bha·rat |'bərət| Hindi name for INDIA.

Bhat·pa·ra |bät'pärə| industrial city in West Bengal, E India, on the Hooghly River. Formerly an academic center, it now makes textiles and paper. Pop. 304,000.

Bhav·na·gar |bow'nəgər| industrial port in NW India, in Gujarat, on the Gulf of Cambay. Pop. 401,000. It was the capital of a former Rajput princely state of the same name.

Bhi·lai·na·gar |bi'lī,nəgər| (also **Bhilai**) industrial city in Madhya Pradesh, central India, a steel center. Pop. 399,000.

Bho·pal |bō'päl| city in central India, the capital of the state of Madhya Pradesh. Pop. 1,604,000. In December 1984 leakage of poisonous gas from an American-owned pesticide factory in the city caused the death of about 2,500 people.

Bhu·ba·nes·war |bŏŏbə'nəsHwər| administrative and industrial city in E India, capital of the state of Orissa. Pop. 412,000.

Bhu·tan |bŏŏ'tän; bŏŏtæn| kingdom on the SE slopes of the Himalayas, a protectorate of India. Area: 18,000 sq. mi./46,620 sq. km. Pop. 600,000. Languages, Dzongkha (official), Nepali. Capital: Thimphu. It is a country of subsistence farmers living in valleys and on the slopes of some of the highest mountains in the world. □ **Bhutanese** *adj. & n.*

Bhutan

Bi·a·fra |bē'æfrə; bē'äfrə| state proclaimed in 1967, when part of E Nigeria, inhabited chiefly by the Ibo people, sought independence from the rest of the country. In the ensuing civil war the new state's troops were overwhelmed by numerically superior forces, and by 1970 it had ceased to exist. □ **Biafran** *adj. & n.*

Bi·ak |'bē'äk| island off N Irian Jaya, Indonesia, scene of World War II battles. Air and naval facilities and fishing are important to its economy.

Białys·tok |'byowə,sHtawk| industrial city in NE Poland, close to the border with Belarus. Pop. 270,568. Russian name **Belostok**.

Biar·ritz |,bēə'rits| seaside resort in SW France, on the Bay of Biscay. Pop. 28,890.

Bible Belt |'bībəl ,belt| term for parts of the U.S. where fundamentalist Christianity is a major social force, especially in the upper S.

Bid·de·ford |'bidəfərd| industrial city in SW Maine. Pop. 20,710.

Bie·le·feld |'bēlə,felt| industrial city in North Rhine–Westphalia in western Germany. Pop. 322,130.

Bielsko-Biala |'byelskaw'byäwə| (German name **Bielitz**) industrial city in S Poland, on the Biala River. Pop. 181,000.

Bien Hoa |'byen 'hwä| industrial city in S Vietnam, N of Ho Chi Minh City. Pop. 314,000. A major U.S. airbase was here during the Vietnam War.

Big Apple |big 'æpəl| nickname for New York City.

Big Bear Lake |'big 'ber| reservoir and recreational center in S California, in the San Bernardino Mts. ENE of Los Angeles.

Big Ben |big 'ben| popular name for the bell, and also for the clock tower it hangs in, of the Houses of Parliament, in Westminster, London, England. Hung in 1859, Big Ben has become emblematic of Britain.

Big Bend National Park |big 'bend| U.S. national park in a bend of the Rio Grande, in the desert lands of S Texas on the border with Mexico, in which were discovered, in 1975, fossil remains of the pterosaur.

Big Black River |big 'blæk| river in Mississippi, flowing 330 mi./530 km. into the Mississippi River near Vicksburg.

Big·horn Mountains |'big,hawrn| range of the Rocky Mts. in Montana and Wyoming. The Bighorn River flows along its W side.

Big Island |big| popular name for the island of HAWAII.

Big Mud·dy |big 'mədē| popular name for the Missouri River, whose waters are much less clear than those of the Mississippi.

Big Sioux River |big 'sōō| river in South Dakota and Iowa, flowing 420 mi./680 km. into the Missouri River.

Big Spring |big 'spriNG| city in W Texas, an oil industry center NE of Midland. Pop. 23,093.

Big Sur |big 'sər| scenic locality in W central California, S of Monterey on the Pacific coast.

Big Thick·et |big 'THikit| forested area of E Texas, N of Beaumont, noted for its biological diversity.

Bi·hac |'bēihäCH| town in NW Bosnia and Herzegovina, near the Croatian border. Ruled by Turkey before 1878, it is largely Muslim. In 1993 it was the site of fierce fighting between the Muslim population and Bosnian government forces. Pop. 46,000.

Bi·har |bi'här| state in NE India. Pop. 86,339,000. Capital: Patna. □ **Bihari** *adj. & n.*

Bi·ja·pur |bi'jäpōor| largely Muslim city in Karnataka, SW India. Pop. 193,000.

Bi·ka·ner |,bikə'ner| historic city in Rajasthan, NW India, near the Thar Desert. Pop. 415,000.

Bi·ki·ni |bi'kēnē| atoll in the Marshall Islands, in the W Pacific, used by the U.S. between 1946 and 1958 as a site for testing nuclear weapons.

Bi·las·pur |bi'läs,pōor| commercial city in Madhya Pradesh, central India. Pop. 234,000.

Bil·bao |bil'bow| seaport and industrial city in N Spain, in the Basque Country. Pop. 372,200.

Bille·rica |bil'rikə| town in NE Massachusetts, S of Lowell. Pop. 37,609.

Bil·lings |'biliNGz| commercial city in S central Montana. Pop. 81,151. It is Montana's largest city.

Bil·lings·gate |'biliNGz,gāt| London fish market dating from the 16th century. In 1982 the market moved to London's East End.

Bi·loxi |bə'ləksē| city in SE Mississippi, on the Gulf of Mexico. Pop. 46,319. It is a noted fishing and tourist center.

Bim·i·ni |'bimənē| (also **Biminis**) resort islands in the NW Bahamas. The legendary Fountain of Youth sought by Ponce de León was thought to be here.

Bing·en |'biNGen| (official name **Bingen am Rhein**) port city on the Rhine River in Rhineland-Palatinate, western Germany. Pop. 25,000.

Bing·ham·ton |'biNGəmtən| industrial city in S central New York, on the Susquehanna River near the Pennsylvania border. Pop. 53,008.

Binh Dinh[1] |'bin 'din| agricultural province of central Vietnam, on the South China Sea. Pop. 1.37 million. It was heavily bombed during the Vietnam War.

Binh Dinh[2] |'bin 'din| see AN NHON, Vietnam.

Bio·ko |bē'ōkō| island of Equatorial Guinea, in the E part of the Gulf of Guinea. Its chief town is Malabo, the capital of Equatorial Guinea. It was known as Fernando Póo until 1973, and from 1973 to 1979 as Macias Nguema.

Bir Ha·cheim |'bir hä'KHām| (Arabic name **Bir al Hakkayim**) oasis town in N Libya, SW of Tobruk, scene of World War II battles in 1942.

Bir·ke·nau |'birkə,now| village in S Poland, site of a Nazi concentration camp associated with nearby Auschwitz.

Bir·ken·head |'bərkən,hed| town in NW

England on the Mersey River opposite Liverpool. Pop. 116,000.

Bir·ming·ham[1] |'bərmiNG,hæm| industrial city in N central Alabama. Pop. 265,968.

Bir·ming·ham[2] |'bərmiNG,hæm| city in W central England, in West Midlands. Pop. 934,900. The second-largest British city, it is a center of heavy industry, high technology, and education. It is locally called Brum (a shortening of Brummagem).

Bir·ming·ham[3] |'bərmiNG,hæm; 'bərmiNGəm| city in SE Michigan, a suburb N of Detroit. Pop. 19,997.

Bis·bee |'bizbē| resort city in SE Arizona, near the Mexican border. Pop. 6,288. It was formerly a noted mining center.

Bis·cay, Bay of |bis'kā| part of the N Atlantic between the N coast of Spain and the W coast of France, noted for its strong currents and storms.

Bis·cayne Bay |bis'kān| inlet of the Atlantic in SE Florida, S of Miami, noted for its islands and resorts.

Bish·kek |bisH'kek| the capital of Kyrgyzstan, an industrial and administrative city. Pop. 625,000. From 1926 to 1991 the city was named Frunze. Former name (until 1926) **Pishpek**.

Bi·sho |'bēsHō| town in southern South Africa, the capital of the province of Eastern Cape, situated near the coast to the NE of Port Elizabeth. Pop. (with East London) 270,130.

Bis·kra |'biskrə| city in N Algeria, between the Sahara Desert and the Aurès Mts. Pop. 129,000. An oasis, then a resort, it is now a growing commercial and industrial center.

Bis·marck |'bizmärk| the state capital of North Dakota. Pop. 49,256. A terminus of the Northern Pacific Railroad, it took the name of the German chancellor in recognition of German financial support to the railroad.

Bis·marck Archipelago |'bizmärk| island group in the W Pacific, part of Papua New Guinea. Held by Germany from 1884 to World War I, it includes New Britain, New Ireland, and several hundred other islands.

Bis·marck Sea |'bizmärk| arm of the Pacific NE of New Guinea and N of New Britain.

Bis·sa·gos Islands |bə'sägəs| group of islands off the coast of Guinea-Bissau, W Africa.

Bis·sau |bi'sow| port city, the capital and largest city of Guinea-Bissau. Pop. 125,000.

Bis·triţ·a |'bēstrit,sä| commercial city in N Romania. Pop. 87,000.

Bi·thyn·ia |bə'THinēə| region of NW Asia Minor (present-day Turkey) W of ancient Paphlagonia, bordering the Black Sea and the Sea of Marmara.

Bi·to·la |bə'tawlə| (also **Bitolj**, formerly **Monastir**) historic commercial city in S Macedonia. Pop. 76,000.

Bit·ter·root Range |'bitə,rōōt| part of the Rocky Mts. in W Montana and E Idaho.

Bi·wa, Lake |'bē,wä| largest lake in Japan, just N of Kyoto, in central Honshu. It is noted for its resorts, fishing, and pearl industry.

Biysk |bēsk| (also **Biisk**) industrial port city on the Biya River in Siberia, E Russia. Pop. 234,000.

Bi·zer·ta |bə'zərtə| (also **Bizerte**) a seaport on the N coast of Tunisia. Pop. 94,500.

Black Belt |'blæk 'belt| agricultural district in central Alabama and Mississippi, named for its rich soils.

Black·burn |'blækbərn| industrial town in NW England, in Lancashire. Pop. 132,800.

Black Country |blæk| district of the English Midlands with heavy industry.

Black Earth |blæk 'ərTH| see CHERNOZEM region.

Black Forest |blæk| hilly wooded region of SW Germany, lying to the E of the Rhine valley. German name **Schwarzwald**.

Black·heath |'blæk,hēTH| historic common and suburban district of S London, England, chiefly in Lewisham. Wat Tyler's rebels camped here in 1381.

Black Hills |blæk| range of mountains in E Wyoming and W South Dakota. The highest point is Harney Peak (7,242 ft./2,207 m.); the range also includes the sculptured granite face of Mount Rushmore.

Black Mesa |blæk| upland in NE Arizona, home to many of the Navajo. The Hopi live on extensions to the S.

Black Mountain |blæk| resort town in W North Carolina, noted as the former site of avant-garde Black Mountain College. Pop. 5,418.

Black Mountains |blæk| range of the Appalachian Mts. in W North Carolina. Mount Mitchell (6684 ft./2039 m.) is the high point.

Black·pool |'blæk,pōōl| seaside resort in Lancashire, NW England. Pop. 144,500.

Black River |blæk| river that flows 300 mi./480 km. SE through Missouri and Arkansas, along the E edge of the Ozark Plateau.

Blacks·burg |'blæks,bərg| town in SW Virginia, in the Appalachian Mts., home to Virginia Polytechnic Institute. Pop. 34,590.

Black Sea |blæk| tideless, highly saline, and almost landlocked sea bounded by Ukraine, Russia, Georgia, Turkey, Bulgaria, and Romania, and connected to the Mediterranean through the strait of Bosporus and the Sea of Marmara.

Black·stone River |'blæk,stōn| river that flows 50 mi./80 km. S through Worcester, Massachusetts to Pawtucket, Rhode Island, below which it is called the Seekonk River. The Blackstone Valley was a site of early U.S. industrial development.

Black War·ri·or River |blæk 'wawryər| river that flows 178 mi./287 km. across N Alabama to join the Tombigbee River. Tuscaloosa and the Birmingham area lie along its course.

Bla·go·ev·grad |,blä'gōəvgräd| spa town in SW Bulgaria, in the Pirin Mts. Pop. 86,000. Blagoevgrad is built on the ruins of an ancient Thracian town.

Bla·go·vesh·chensk |,bləgəv'yäsH-CHinsk| transportation center and city in E Siberia, SE Russia, near the Chinese border. Pop. 208,000.

Blaine |blān| city in SE Minnesota, a suburb N of Minneapolis. Pop. 38,975.

Blan·tyre |blæn'tīr| the chief commercial and industrial city of Malawi. Pop. 331,600 (with Limbe, a town 5 mi./8 km. SE of Blantyre).

Blar·ney |'blärnē| village in County Cork, S Ireland, just NW of Cork. Those who kiss the Blarney Stone, at its castle, are said to then possess the power to cajole.

Blas·ket Islands |'blæskit| island group off the Dingle Peninsula in SW Ireland, in County Kerry, uninhabited since 1953.

Blen·heim |'blenəm| village in S Germany, site of a victory by British and Austrian troops, led by the Duke of Marlborough, over the French in 1704. The Duke took the village's name for his country seat in Woodstock, England.

Bli·da |'blēdə| (Arabic name **El Boulaïda**) city in N Algeria, SW of Algiers, at the feet of the Atlas Mts. Pop. 191,000. It is a famed agricultural and horticultural center.

Block Island |bläk| resort island in S Rhode Island, in the Atlantic at the E end of Long Island Sound.

Bloem·fon·tein |'blōōm,fän,tān| the capital of Free State and judicial capital of South Africa. Pop. 300,150. An industrial center, it is also called **Mangaung**.

Blois |blə'wä| historic and commercial town in central France, in the Loire valley.

Pop. 52,000. Blois is the capital of the Loire-et-Cher department.

Bloom·field |'blōōm,fēld| township in NE New Jersey, an industrial suburb N of Newark. Pop. 45,061.

Bloom·ing·ton[1] |'blōōmiNGtən| commercial city in central Illinois. Pop. 51,972.

Bloom·ing·ton[2] |'blōōmiNGtən| city in S central Indiana, home to Indiana University and to a noted limestone industry. Pop. 60,633.

Bloom·ing·ton[3] |'blōōmiNGtən| city in SE Minnesota, a suburb S of Minneapolis. It is home to the huge Mall of America. Pop. 86,335.

Blooms·bury |'blōōmz,berē| area of central London noted for its large squares and gardens and for its associations with the literary and artistic circle called the Bloomsbury Group. The British Museum is located here.

Blue·fields |'blōō,fēldz| port on the Mosquito Coast of Nicaragua, situated on an inlet of the Caribbean Sea. Pop. 18,000.

Blue·grass State |'blōō,græs| nickname for KENTUCKY, referring to the Bluegrass Region, a rich central plateau famed for its horse farms.

Blue Grotto, the |blōō 'grätō| cavern on the N shore of the Isle of Capri, in the Bay of Naples, Italy. Half filled with water, the grotto is famous for the unusual blue light inside.

Blue Mosque |blōō 'mäsk| (also **Sultan Ahmet Mosque**) mosque in Istanbul, Turkey, with six minarets, built 1609–16, regarded as one of the finest in the world, and a widely known symbol of the region and the Islamic world.

Blue Mountains[1] |blōō| section of the Great Dividing Range in New South Wales, Australia.

Blue Mountains[2] |blōō| range of mountains in E Jamaica.

Blue Mountains[3] |blōō| range of mountains running from central Oregon to SE Washington State in the U.S.

Blue Nile |blōō 'nīl| one of the two principal headwaters of the Nile. Rising from Lake Tana in NW Ethiopia, it flows some 1,000 mi./1,600 km. SW then NW into Sudan, where it meets the White Nile at Khartoum.

Blue Ridge Mountains |'blōō ,rij| range of the Appalachian Mts. in the E U.S., stretching from S Pennsylvania to N Georgia. Mount Mitchell is the highest peak, rising to a height of 6,684 ft./2,037 m.

Blue Springs |blōō| city in W central

Missouri, a residential suburb E of Kansas City. Pop. 40,153.

Blu·me·nau |blōōmə'now| commercial city in S Brazil, in an agricultural area in Santa Caterina state. Pop. 231,000. The culture of its 19th-century German settlers still dominates.

Blythe·ville |'blīvəl| city in NE Arkansas. Pop. 22,906.

Boa Vis·ta |'bōə 'vēSHtə| town in N Brazil, capital of the state of Roraima. Pop. 130,426.

Bobo-Dioulasso |'bōbō,dyōōlä'sō| commercial and industrial city in SW Burkina Faso. Pop. 269,000. It is an agricultural market and rail center.

Bob·ruysk |bäb'rōoisk| (also **Babruysk, Bobruisk**) city in Belarus. Pop. 223,000. It is a port on the Berezina River and an industrial center.

Bo·ca Ra·ton |,bōkə rə'tōn| city in SE Florida, on the Atlantic N of Fort Lauderdale. A noted resort, it also has varied industries. Pop. 61,492.

Bo·chum |'bōKHōōm| industrial city in the Ruhr valley, North Rhine–Westphalia, western Germany. Pop. 398,580.

Bo·den·see |'bōdn,zā| German name for Lake Constance (see CONSTANCE, LAKE).

Bodh·ga·ya |,bōd'gīə| (also **Buddh Gaya**) a village in the state of Bihar, NE India, where the Buddha attained enlightenment.

Bod·nath |bōd'nät| site of a massive Buddhist stupa in Nepal, E of Kathmandu, the biggest in Nepal and one of the biggest in the world.

Bo·drum |bō'drōōm| resort town on the Aegean coast of W Turkey, site of the ancient city of Halicarnassus.

Boe·o·tia |bē'ōSHə| department of central Greece, to the N of the Gulf of Corinth, and a region of ancient Greece of which the chief city was Thebes. □ **Boeotian** adj. & n.

Bo·fors |'bōfawrs| town in S central Sweden. The eponymous antiaircraft gun was made here in a factory owned by Alfred Nobel, founder of the Nobel prizes. Bofors is a major armaments center.

Bo·ga·lu·sa |,bōgə'lōōsə| city in SE Louisiana, on the Pearl River, a forest industry and agricultural center. Pop. 14,280.

Bo·gaz·köy |,bō,(g)äz'koi| village in central Turkey, E of Ankara, on the site of ancient Hattusas, the Hittite capital of the 15th–13th centuries B.C.

Bo·gor |'bō,gawr| resort town in Indonesia, on NW Java, S of Djakarta, famous for its botanical gardens. Pop. 271,000.

Bo·go·tá |,bōgə'taw; ,bōgəgə'tä| the capital of Colombia, situated in the E Andes at about 8,560 ft./2,610 m. Pop. 4,921,200. It was founded by the Spanish in 1538 on the site of a pre-Columbian center of the Chibcha culture. Official name **Santa Fé de Bogotá**.

Bo Hai |'bō 'hī| (also **Po Hai**) a large inlet of the Yellow Sea, on the coast of E China. Also called **Gulf of Chihli**.

Bo·he·mia |bō'hēmēə| region forming the W part of the Czech Republic. Formerly a Slavic kingdom, it became a province of the newly formed Czechoslovakia by the Treaty of Versailles in 1919. The term *Bohemian*, referring to a subculture that chooses not to live by the standards of the dominant culture, derives from the popular 19th-century association of Bohemia with the Gypsies. □ **Bohemian** adj. & n.

Bo·he·mi·an Forest |bō'hēmēən| wooded mountain range along the boundary between Germany and the Czech Republic. Its highest peak is Arber, in Bavaria: 4,780 ft./1,457 m.

Bo·hol |bō'hawl| island lying to the N of Mindanao in the central Philippines; chief town, Tagbilaran.

Bois de Bou·logne |,bwä də bōō'lōn| park in W Paris, France. Covering 2,137 acres/865 hectares, it was formerly a royal hunting ground. It now comprises wooded areas, restaurants, lakes, two racetracks, and gardens.

Boi·se |'boisē; 'boizē| the state capital of Idaho, an administrative and commercial city. Pop. 125,738.

Bo·ka·ro Steel City |bō'kärō 'stēl| steel-producing city in E India, in the coalfields of Bihar state. Pop. 416,000. It has one of Asia's largest steel plants.

Bo·kha·ra |bō'KHärə| see BUKHORO, Uzbekistan.

Boks·burg |'bäks,bərg| city in NE South Africa, a gold-mining center E of Johannesburg. Pop. 196,000.

Bole |bōl| (also called **Bortala**) Kazakh town in Xinjiang, NW China, N of the Tian Shan range. Pop. 141,000.

Bo·ling·brook |'bōliNGbrōōk| village in NE Illinois, a suburb SW of Chicago. Pop. 40,843.

Bo·li·var, Pi·co |'pēkō ,bō'lē,vär| peak in W Venezuela, in the Cordillera de Mérida, near the Colombian border, the highest in the country: 16,411 ft./5,002 m. It is part of a mountain called La Columna.

Bo·liv·ia |bə'livēə| landlocked republic in South America. Area: 424,162 sq.

Bolivia

mi./1,098,580 sq. km. Pop. 6,420,800; languages, Spanish (official), Aymara, Quechua. Capital and largest city: La Paz; legal capital and seat of the judiciary, Sucre. An Inca country, then until 1825 a Spanish colony, Bolivia depends on agriculture in the Altiplano, oil and gas, and mining. Political instability has held back development. □ **Bolivian** *adj. & n.*

Bo•lo•gna |bə'lōn(y)ə| commercial and industrial city in N Italy, capital of Emilia-Romagna region. Pop. 411,800. Its university, which dates from the 11th century, is the oldest in Europe.

Bol•ton |'bōltn| historic industrial city in NW England, in Greater Manchester. Pop. 253,300.

Bol•za•no |bawlt'sänō| commercial and resort city in NE Italy, capital of the Trentino–Alto Adige region. Pop. 100,380. German name **Bozen**

Bo•ma |'bōmə| port city in W Congo (formerly Zaire), on the Congo River estuary. Pop. 246,000. It was the capital of the Belgian Congo before 1926.

Bom•bay |bäm'bā| port city on the W coast of India, capital of the state of Maharashtra. Pop. 9,990,000. Official name (from 1995) **Mumbai**. It is a center of textile and other industries.

Bo•mu River |'bōmōō| (also **M'Bomou**) river that flows 500 mi./800 km. from NE Congo (formerly Zaire), to join the Uele River in forming the Ubangi River. It forms part of the border between Congo and the Central African Republic.

Bon, Cape |bän| peninsula of NE Tunisia, extending into the Mediterranean Sea.

Bon•aire |bə'ner| one of the two principal islands of the Netherlands Antilles (the other is Curaçao); chief town, Kralendijk. Pop. 10,190.

Bo•nam•pak |bə'näm,päk| ruined city of the Maya, found in the 1940s in the jungles of E Chiapas state, SE Mexico.

Its frescoes give much detail on Maya life.

Bo•nan•za Creek |bə'nænzə| stream in the W central Yukon Territory, near Dawson, site of the 1896 discovery that set off the Klondike gold rush.

Bon•di |'bändē| coastal resort in New South Wales, Australia, a suburb of Sydney. It is noted for its beach and surfing.

Bon•doc |bawn'dawk| peninsula in the Philippines, on S Luzon, bounded by Mompog Pass (W) and Ragay Gulf (E).

Bône |bōn| former name for ANNABA, Algeria.

Bon•gor |bäNG'gawr| commercial town in SW Chad, across the Logone River from Cameroon. Pop. 195,000.

Bo•nin Islands |'bōnən| (Japanese name **Ogasawara-gunto**) volcanic island group of Japan in the NW Pacific, S of Tokyo.

Bonn |bän; bawn| industrial and university city in the state of North Rhine–Westphalia in Germany. Pop. 296,240. From 1949 until the reunification of Germany in 1990 Bonn was the capital of the Federal Republic of Germany.

Bon•ne•ville Dam |'bänə,vil| hydroelectric dam built in the 1930s on the Columbia River, E of Portland, Oregon.

Bon•ne•ville Salt Flats |'bänə,vil| desert in NW Utah, W of the Great Salt Lake, noted as the site of automotive speed trials.

Boot•heel portion of the state of Missouri in the southeast corner, jutting down between Arkansas and Tennessee, having the appearance on a map of a bootheel.

Boo•thia, Gulf of |'bōoTHēə| gulf in the Canadian Arctic, between the Boothia Peninsula and Baffin Island, in Nunavut.

Boo•thia Peninsula |'bōoTHēə| peninsula of N Canada, in Nunavut, situated between Victoria and Baffin islands.

Boot Hill |bōot| name for a cemetery in several cowboy towns, such as Dodge City, Kansas, or Deadwood, South Dakota.

Boo•tle |'bōotl| industrial port town in NW England, a suburb of Liverpool on the Mersey River. Pop. 71,000.

Bo•phu•tha•tswa•na |,bōpōōtät'swänə| former homeland established in South Africa for the Tswana people, now part of North-West and Mpumalanga provinces.

Bora-Bora |'bawrə 'bawrə| island of the Society Islands group in French Polynesia.

Bo•rås |bōo'raws| industrial city in SW Sweden, a textile center. Pop. 101,770.

Bor•deaux |bawr'dō| port of SW France on the Garonne River, capital of Aquitaine. Pop. 213,270. It is a center of the wine trade.

Bor·ders |'bawrdərz| general term for the lands on either side of the England-Scotland border, and, since 1975, name of a local government region on the Scottish side.

Bor·der States those US states that were slave states but did not secede from the Union during the Civil War, including Delaware, Maryland, Kentucky, and Missouri.

Bo·rin·quén |ˌbawrin'kän| local (Arawakan) name for Puerto Rico. Also, **Boriquén**.

Bor·neo |'bawrnēō| large island of the Malay Archipelago, comprising Kalimantan (a region of Indonesia), Sabah and Sarawak (states of Malaysia), and Brunei. □ **Bornean** adj.

Born·holm |'bawrnˌhō(l)m| Danish island in the Baltic Sea, SE of Sweden.

Bor·no |'bawrnō| (also **Bornu**) state in NE Nigeria, bordering Chad, Niger, and Cameroon. Much of the historic kingdom of Bornu occupied its agricultural plains.

Bo·ro·bu·dur |ˌbōrəbōō'dŏŏr| (also **Boroboedoer**) vast Buddhist temple complex in Indonesia, on central Java. Built in the 8th or 9th century, it is the biggest religious monument in SE Asia.

Bo·ro·di·no |ˌbōrədē'naw| village in W Russia, W of Moscow. It was the site of a major battle between Russian and French troops during the Napoleonic Wars, before Napoleon occupied Moscow.

Bo·ro·vets |'bawrə,(y)vets| ski resort in the Rila Mts. of W Bulgaria.

Bor·ro·me·an Islands |ˌbawrə'mēən| four small islands in Lake Maggiore, in N Italy. Isola Bella, the largest, is site of the 17th-century Borromeo Palace, with spectacular terraced gardens.

Borscht Belt |bawrsHt| popular name for region of the Catskill Mts., in SE New York, famed for its Jewish resorts.

Bor·stal |'bawrstəl| village in SE England, near Rochester, Kent, that gave its name to a system of reformatories for young offenders.

Bo·ru·jerd |ˌbōrōō'yerd| (also **Burujird**) city in W Iran, in the Zagros Mountains. Pop. 201,000.

Bose |bōs| city in Guangxi, S China, on the You River. Pop. 275,000.

Bos·kop |'baws,kawp| town in South Africa, in the North-West province, where a skull fossil was found in 1913. The fossil is undated and morphologically shows no primitive features. At the time this find was regarded as representative of a distinct "Boskop race" but is now thought to be related to the San-Nama (Bushman-Hottentot) types.

Bos·nia |'bäznēə| **1** short for BOSNIA AND HERZEGOVINA. **2** a region in the Balkans forming the larger, N part of Bosnia and Herzegovina. □ **Bosnian** adj. & n.

Bosnia

Bos·nia and Her·ze·go·vi·na |'bäznēə ən ˌhərtsəgō'vēnə| (also **Bosnia–Herzegovina**) country in the Balkans, formerly a constituent republic of Yugoslavia. Area: 19,748 sq. mi./51,128 sq. km. Pop. 4,365,000. Capital and largest city: Sarajevo. Almost landlocked, Bosnia and Herzegovina was long dominated by the Ottoman Empire, then by Austria-Hungary. It was part of Yugoslavia 1918–92. Ethnic warfare since independence has severly damaged its economy.

Bos·po·rus |'bäsp(ə)rəs| (also **Bosphorus**) strait connecting the Black Sea with the Sea of Marmara, and separating Europe from the Anatolian peninsula of W Asia. Istanbul is located at its S end.

Bos·ra |'bäsrə| (also called **Busra esh-Sham**) village in SW Syria, near the border with Jordan, site of the ruined city of Bostra, which was important in Roman times.

Bos·sier City |'bōzHər| city in NW Louisiana, on the Red River, just NE of Shreveport. Pop. 52,721. It is an oil and gas industry center.

Bos·ton[1] |'bawstən| commercial port town in E England, in Lincolnshire. Pop. 26,000. Puritans left here in 1633 for Massachusetts Bay.

Bos·ton[2] |'bawstən| the state capital and largest city in Massachusetts. Pop. 574,280. □ **Bostonian** adj. & n.

Bos·worth Field |'bäzwərTH| site in central England, near Market Bosworth, Leicestershire, scene of the last battle (1485) of the Wars of the Roses, in which the Yorkist king Richard III was defeated.

Bot·a·ny Bay |'bätn-ē| inlet of the Tasman Sea in New South Wales, Australia, just S of Sydney. It was the site of Captain James Cook's landing in 1770 and of an early British penal settlement.

Bo·tev Peak |'baw,tef| mountain in Bulgaria, highest peak in the Balkan Mts.: 7,793 ft./2,376 m.

Both·nia, Gulf of |'bäTHnēə| N arm of the Baltic Sea, between Sweden and Finland.

Bo·to·sa·ni |bätəsHän(yə)| market town in NE Romania, on the Moldavian Plain, near the Ukrainian border, capital of Botosani county. Pop. 120,000.

Bot·swa·na |bät'swänə| landlocked republic in southern Africa. Area: 231,800 sq. mi./600,360 sq. km. Pop. 1,300,000. Languages, Setswana and English. Capital and largest city: Gaborone. Arid tableland, much of it part of the Kalahari Desert, dominates Botswana, which was the British colony of Bechuanaland from 1885 until 1966. Herding, agriculture, and mining are important. □ **Botswanan** adj. & n.

Botswana

Bot·trop |'baw,trawp| industrial city in western Germany, N of Essen. Pop. 119,000. It was formerly a center of coal production.

Boua·ké |bwä'kä| (also **Bwake**) commercial city in central Côte d'Ivoire, a rail- and textile-industry center. Pop. 390,000.

Bou·cher·ville |'bōōsHər,vil| city in S Quebec, a suburb NE of Montreal. Pop. 33,796.

Bouches-du-Rhône |,bōōsH dY 'rōn| department in SE France, on the Rhône delta. Area: 1,974 sq. mi./5,112 sq. km. Pop. 1,750,000. The capital city is Marseilles.

Bou·gain·ville |'bōōgən,vil; 'bōgən,vil| volcanic island in the S Pacific, the largest of the Solomon Islands.

Boul·der |'bōldər| city in N central Colorado, NW of Denver, home to the University of Colorado. Pop. 83,312.

Bou·logne |bōō'lawn(yə)| ferry port and fishing town in N France. Pop. 44,240. Full name **Boulogne-sur-Mer.**

Bound·a·ry Waters |'bownd(ə)rē| region of NE Minnesota, along the Ontario border, famed as a canoeing center.

Boun·ti·ful |'bowntəfəl| city in N Utah, a suburb N of Salt Lake City. Pop. 36,659.

Bour·bon County |'bərbən| county in N central Kentucky, in the Bluegrass region, birthplace of the American whiskey type.

Bour·bon Island |'bōōrbən; bōōr'bawN| former name for the French Indian Ocean island of RÉUNION. It gave its name to the bourbon rose.

Bour·bon·nais |,bōōrbə'nā| former duchy and province of central France; chief town, Moulins.

Bourges |bōōrZH| city and capital of the department of Cher, in central France. Pop. 80,000. An industrial and transportation center, it has a section with numerous Renaissance buildings.

Bour·gogne |bōōr'gawn(yə)| French name for BURGUNDY.

Bourne·mouth |'bawrnməTH; 'bōōrnməTH| resort on the S coast of England, a unitary council traditionally in Dorset. Pop. 154,400.

Bourse |bōōrs| (full name **Palais de la Bourse**) the stock exchange in Paris, France, on the Rue Vivienne.

Bou·vet Island |'bōōvā| uninhabited island in the S Atlantic, a former whaling station and dependency of Norway.

Bow |bō| (full name **St. Mary-le-Bow**) parish in E central London, England, in Cheapside, within the sound of whose bells the true Cockney is said to be born.

Bow·ery |'bow(ə)rē| street and district in lower Manhattan, New York City, historically associated with vagrant men and cheap hotels.

Bow·ie |'bōē| town in W central Maryland, a suburb NE of Washington, D.C. Pop. 37,589.

Bowl·ing Green[1] |bōliNG 'grēn| city in W central Kentucky. Pop. 40,641.

Bowl·ing Green[2] |bōliNG 'grēn| historic park in S Manhattan, New York City, just N of the Battery.

Bow River |bō| river that flows 315 mi./507 km. from the Rocky Mts. SE across Alberta to the South Saskatchewan River. Calgary lies on it.

Boyne River |boin| river in E Ireland that flows NE from the Bog of Allen to the Irish Sea near Drogheda, near which, in 1690, the Protestant army of William of Orange defeated Catholic supporters of James II.

Boyn·ton Beach |'bointən| resort city in SE Florida. Pop. 46,194.

Boys Town |boiz| village in E central Nebraska, just W of Omaha, famed as a home for troubled youth. Pop. 794.

Boz·caa·da |ˌbōzjə'dä| island off NW Turkey, in the Aegean Sea just S of the Dardanelles. As ancient **Tenedos**, it was a base for the Persian attack on Greece under Xerxes, and according to legend was the Greek base against nearby Troy.

Boze·man |'bōzmən| city in SW Montana. Pop. 22,660.

Bra·bant |brə'bænt| former duchy in W Europe, lying between the Meuse and Scheldt rivers. Its capital was Brussels. It is now divided into two provinces in two countries: North Brabant in the Netherlands, of which the capital is 's-Hertogenbosch; and Brabant in Belgium, of which the capital remains Brussels.

Bra·den·ton |'brādntən| city in SW Florida, noted as a resort and for citrus processing. Pop. 43,779.

Brad·ford |'brædfərd| industrial city, a longtime textile center, in N England, traditionally in Yorkshire. Pop. 449,100.

Brae·mar |brā'mär| historic village in NE Scotland, in the Grampian region, where the first Jacobite Rising began in 1715. It is famous for its summer Highland Games.

Bra·ga |'brägə| city in N Portugal, capital of a mountainous district of the same name. Pop. 90,535.

Bra·gan·za |brə'gäNs| city in NE Portugal, capital of a mountainous district of the same name. Pop. 16,550. It was the original seat of the Braganza dynasty. Portuguese name **Bragança**.

Brah·ma·pu·tra Ri·ver |ˌbrämə'pōōtrə| river in S Asia, rising in the Himalayas and flowing 1,800 mi./2,900 km. through Tibet, NE India, and Bangladesh, to join the Ganges at its delta on the Bay of Bengal.

Brǎ·i·la |brə'ēlə| industrial city and port on the Danube, in E Romania. Pop. 236,300.

Brain·tree |'brān,trē| town in E Massachusetts, a suburb S of Boston. Pop. 32,836.

Bramp·ton |'bræmtən| city in S Ontario, an industrial and residential suburb W of Toronto. Pop. 234,445.

Bran·den·burg |'brændən,bərg| state of NE Germany. Capital: Potsdam. The modern state corresponds to the W part of the former Prussian electorate, of which the E part was ceded to Poland after World War II.

Bran·den·burg Gate |'brændən,bərg| only surviving city gate of Berlin (built 1788–91). It was designed as a triumphal arch commemorating the military successes of Prussia, especially of Frederick the Great (1712–86). After the construction of the Berlin Wall in 1961 it stood just behind the Wall in East Berlin. German name **Brandenburgertor**.

Bran·don |'brændən| city in SW Manitoba. Pop. 38,567.

Bran·dy·wine Creek |'brændē,wīn| historic stream in SE Pennsylvania and N Delaware, birthplace of the U.S. gunpowder industry.

Bran·ford |'brænfərd| town in S central Connecticut, a suburb E of New Haven. Pop. 27,603.

Bran·son |'brænsən| city in SW Missouri, on the Ozark Plateau, noted as a resort based on country music. Pop. 3,706.

Brant·ford |'bræntfərd| industrial city in S Ontario. Pop. 81,997.

Bra·sí·lia |brə'zilyə| the capital, since 1960, of Brazil. Pop. 1,601,100. Designed by Lúcio Costa in 1956, the city was located in the center of the country with the intention of drawing people away from the crowded coastal areas.

Bra·şov |brə'sHawv| second-largest city of Romania, an industrial and transportation center in the Carpathians. Pop. 352,640. It belonged to Hungary until after World War I, and was ceded to Romania in 1920. Hungarian name **Brassó**.

Bras·só |'bræsō| Hungarian name for BRAȘOV, Romania.

Bra·ti·sla·va |ˌbrätə'slävə| the capital of Slovakia, an industrial port on the Danube River. Pop. 441,450. From 1526 to 1784 it was the capital of Hungary. German name **Pressburg**; Hungarian name **Pozsony**.

Bratsk |brätsk| city in central Siberia, E Russia, on the Angara River. Pop. 258,000.

Brat·tle·bo·ro |'brædl,bərə| town in SE Vermont, on the Connecticut River. Pop. 12,241.

Braun·schweig |'brown,sHfīk| German name for BRUNSWICK.

Bray[1] |brā| village in S England, in Berkshire, on the Thames River, setting for the ballad "The Vicar of Bray," about 16th-century religious upheavals.

Bray[2] |brā| resort and port town in E Ireland, in County Wicklow, S of Dublin, on the Irish Sea. Pop. 25,000.

Bra·zil |brə'zil| the largest country in South America. Area: 3.29 million sq. mi./8.51 million sq. km. Pop. 146,825,475 (1991); language, Portuguese. Capital: Brasilia. Largest city: São Paulo. Portuguese name

BRAZIL

State/Territory boundary
■ Capital city

N

0   500   1000 km
0   250   500   750 miles

Boa Vista ●
RORAIMA

AMAPA
Macapá ●

Belém ●
São Luis ●

Manaus ●

AMAZONAS

PARÁ

MARANHÃO
Teresina ●
Fortaleza ●
CEARÁ
RÍO GRANDE DO NORTE
● Natal
João Pessoa ●
PARAIBA
PERNAMBUCO ● Recife

ACRE
Río Branco ●
Porto Velho ●
RONDÔNIA

MATO GROSSO

TOCANTINS
PIAUI

Palmas ●

BAHIA

Maceió
ALAGOAS
Aracajú
SERGIPE

Cuiabá ●

GOIÁS
FD
Brasilia ■
Goiânia ●

Salvador ●

MINAS GERAIS

MATO GROSSO DO SUL
Campo Grande ●

SÃO-PAULO
São Paulo ●

Belo Horizonte ●

ESPÍRITO SANTO
Vitória ●

RIO DE JANEIRO
Rio de Janeiro ●

PARANÁ
Curitiba ●

SANTA CATARINA
Florianópolis ●

RIO GRANDE DO SUL
Pôrto Alegre ●

FD FEDERAL DISTRICT

Brasil. The fifth-largest country in the world, Brazil was inhabited by Tupi and Guarani peoples, then colonized by the Portuguese, gaining independence in 1822. The N half lies in the Amazon basin, and the interior is largely undeveloped. Tropical and plains agriculture, mining, and industry are all important. The population is diverse. □ **Brazilian** *adj. & n.*

Braz·os River |'bræzəs| river that flows 840 mi./1350 km. SE across Texas, from the Panhandle to the Gulf of Mexico. The cities at its mouth are called collectively Brazosport.

Braz·za·ville |'bräzə,vil| the capital of the Republic of the Congo, an industrial port on the Congo River. Pop. 2,936,000. It was founded in 1880 by the French explorer Savorgnan de Brazza (1852–1905) and was

capital of French Equatorial Africa from 1910 to 1958.

Brea |brēə| city in S California, an oil and industrial center E of Los Angeles. Pop. 32,873.

Bread Bas·ket of Amer·ica the Midwestern US states that are major producers of grain products.

Brecon·shire |'brekən,sнir; 'brekənsнər| (also **Brecknockshire**) a former county of S central Wales. It was divided between Powys and Gwent in 1974.

Bre·da |brā'dä; 'brādə| historic manufacturing town in the SW Netherlands. Pop. 124,800.

Bre·genz |'brägents| city in W Austria, on the E shores of Lake Constance. Pop. 27,240. It is the capital of the state of Vorarlberg.

Breizh |brezH| Breton name for BRITTANY.

Bre·men |'brämən; 'bremən| **1** state of NE Germany. Divided into two parts, which center on the city of Bremen and the port of Bremerhaven, it is surrounded by the state of Lower Saxony. **2** its capital, an industrial city linked by the Weser River to the port of Bremerhaven and the North Sea. Pop. 537,600.

Brem·er·ha·ven |'bremər,hävən| (formerly **Wesermünde**) seaport in NW Germany, on the North Sea coast N of Bremen. Pop. 131,000. Bremerhaven is one of the largest seaports and fishing centers in Europe. The first regular shipping service between the U.S. and Europe began here.

Brem·er·ton |'bremərtən| city in W central Washington, on Puget Sound, home to large naval shipyards. Pop. 38,142.

Bren·ner Pass |'brenər| Alpine pass at the border between Austria and Italy, on the route between Innsbruck and Bolzano, at an altitude of 4,450 ft./1,371 m.

Brent |brent| largely residential borough of NW Greater London, England. Pop. 226,000. Wembley stadium is here.

Brent·ford |'brentfərd| suburban community in S England, within the Greater London borough of Hounslow, N of the Thames River.

Brent·wood[1] |'brent,wŏŏd| town in SE England, a suburb in Essex, E of London. Pop. 51,000.

Brent·wood[2] |'brent,wŏŏd| affluent residential section of W Los Angeles, California.

Brent·wood[3] |'brent,wŏŏd| village in central Long Island, New York. Pop. 45,218.

Bre·scia |'bräSHə| industrial city in Lombardy, in N Italy. Pop. 196,770.

Bres·lau |'bres,low| German name for WROCŁAW, Poland.

Brest[1] |brest| river port and industrial city in Belarus, situated close to the border with Poland. Pop. 268,800. A peace treaty between Germany and Russia was signed here in March 1918. Former name (until 1921) **Brest-Litovsk**. Polish name **Brześć nad Bugiem.**

Brest[2] |brest| port and naval base on the Atlantic coast of Brittany, in NW France. Pop. 153,100.

Bre·tagne |brə'tänyə| French name for BRITTANY.

Bret·ton Woods |'bretn| resort in the White Mts. of N central New Hampshire, noted as the site of United Nations conferences at the end of World War II.

Bre·vard County |brə'värd| county in E central Florida, on the Atlantic, the site of Cape Canaveral and large citrus and resort industries. Pop. 398,978.

Bridge of Sighs |'sīz| bridge across a canal in Venice, Italy, so called because prisoners were led across it between the Ducal Palace and the nearby prison. Italian name **Ponte dei Sospiri.**

Bridge·port |'brij,pawrt| industrial city in SW Connecticut, on Long Island Sound. Pop. 141,686.

Bridge·town |'brij,town| the capital of Barbados, a port on the S coast. Pop. 6,720.

Brie |brē| region in N France, E of Paris, between the Seine and the Marne rivers. The area is famous for its soft cheese.

Brigh·ton |'brītn| resort town on the S coast of England, in East Sussex. Pop. 133,400. It was patronized by the Prince of Wales (later George IV), and is noted for its Regency architecture, as well as for its pleasure pier.

Brigh·ton Beach |'brītn| section of S Brooklyn, New York, E of Coney Island, famed for its Jewish community, and now home to a large Russian immigrant population.

Brin·di·si |'brindizē| capital of Brindisi province, a port in SE Italy, on the Adriatic Sea. Pop. 93,000. It was the S terminus of the Appian Way, and a historic link between Italy and the E Mediterranean.

Bris·bane |'brizbən; 'briz,bān| the capital of Queensland, Australia, an industrial port on the E coast. Pop. 1,273,500.

Bris·tol[1] |'bristəl| industrial city and township in W central Connecticut. Pop. 60,640.

Bris·tol[2] |'bristəl| city in SW England. Pop. 370,300. Situated on the Avon River about 6 mi./10 km. from the Bristol Channel, it has been a leading port since the 12th century, and was key in the exploration and settling of North America.

Bris·tol[3] |'bristəl| industrial city in E Tennessee, adjoining Bristol, Virginia. Pop. 23,421.

Bris·tol Channel |'bristəl| wide inlet of the Atlantic between S Wales and the SW peninsula of England, narrowing into the estuary of the Severn River.

Brit·ain |'britn| the island containing England, Wales, and Scotland, and including the small adjacent islands. The name is broadly synonymous with Great Britain, but the longer form is more usual for the political unit. See also GREAT BRITAIN.
□ **British** adj. & n. **Britisher** n.

Bri·tan·nia Latin name of the Roman province, later applied as a literary term for the entire island of Britain or for the British Empire. Also used of the personification of Great Britain, depicted as a seated woman holding a trident and wearing a helmet.

Brit·ish Ant·arc·tic Territory |ˌbritisH æntär(k)tik| that part of Antarctica claimed by Britain. Designated in 1962 from territory that was formerly part of the Falkland Islands Dependencies, it includes some 150,058 sq. mi./388,500 sq. km. of the continent of Antarctica as well as the South Orkney and South Shetland islands in the South Atlantic.

Brit·ish Co·lum·bia |ˌbritisH kə'ləmbēə| province on the W coast of Canada. Area: 365,947 sq. mi./947,800 sq. km. Pop. 3,282,061. Capital: Victoria. Largest city: Vancouver. Formed in 1866 by the union of Vancouver Island (a former British colony) and the mainland area, then called New Caledonia, the province includes the Queen Charlotte Islands. Forest industries, tourism and recreation, fishing, mining, hydroelectric power, and manufacturing are all important.

Brit·ish Gui·ana |ˌbritisH ˌgī'änə| name until 1966 for GUYANA.

Brit·ish Hon·du·ras |ˌbritisH hän'd͞ōrəs| name until 1973 for BELIZE.

Brit·ish In·dia |ˌbritisH 'indēə| that part of the Indian subcontinent administered by the British from 1765, when the East India Company acquired control over Bengal, until 1947, when India became independent and Pakistan was created. By 1850 British India was coterminous with India's boundaries in the W and N and by 1885 it included Burma in the E. The period of British rule was known as the Raj. See also INDIA.

Brit·ish In·di·an Ocean Territory |'britisH 'indēən 'ōsHən| British dependency in the Indian Ocean, comprising the islands of the Chagos Archipelago and (until 1976) some other groups now belonging to the Seychelles. Ceded to Britain by France in 1814, the islands became a separate dependency in 1965. There are no permanent inhabitants, but British and U.S. naval personnel occupy the island of Diego Garcia.

Brit·ish Isles |ˌbritisH 'īlz| group of islands lying off the coast of NW Europe, from which they are separated by the North Sea or the English Channel. They include Britain, Ireland, the Isle of Man, the He-brides, the Orkney Islands, the Shetland Islands, the Scilly Isles, and the Channel Islands.

Brit·ish North Amer·i·ca |'britisH ˌnawrTH ə'merəkə| term for British possessions in North America after the U.S. gained independence. In 1867 most became parts of Canada.

Brit·ish So·ma·li·land |ˌbritisH sə'mälēˌlænd| former British protectorate established on the Somali coast of E Africa in 1884. In 1960 it united with former Italian territory to form the independent republic of Somalia.

Brit·ish Vir·gin Islands |'britisH ˌvərjən| see VIRGIN ISLANDS.

Brit·tany |'britn-ē| region and former duchy of NW France, forming a peninsula between the Bay of Biscay and the English Channel. It was occupied in the 5th and 6th centuries by Celtic Britons fleeing the Saxons, and was not incorporated into France until 1532. The Breton language is still spoken widely here. French name **Bretagne**. Breton name **Breizh**. □ **Breton** adj. & n.

Brive-la-Gaillard |ˌbrēv lä gī'yär(d)| market town in SW France, E of Périgueux. Pop. 53,000.

Brix·ton |'brikstən| district of S London, England, in Lambeth borough, home to the major black community in the city.

Br·no |'bərnō| industrial city in the Czech Republic. Pop. 388,000. It is the capital of Moravia. German name **Brünn**.

Broads |brawdz| often **the Norfolk Broads** a network of shallow freshwater lakes, traversed by slow-moving rivers, in an area of Norfolk and Suffolk. They were formed by the gradual natural flooding of medieval peat diggings.

Broad·stairs |'brawdˌsterz| coastal resort town in SE England, in the Isle of Thanet, Kent, associated with Charles Dickens, who lived here. Pop. 23,000.

Broad·way |'brawdˌwā| street traversing the length of Manhattan, New York. It is famous for its theater district, and its name has become synonymous with the New York professional theater business. It is also known as the Great White Way, in reference to its brilliant illuminated theater marquees and other signs.

Brock·en |'bräkən| peak in the Harz Mts. of N central Germany, rising to 3,747 ft./1,143 m. It is noted for the phenomenon of the Brocken specter, a cloud effect, and for witches' revels that reputedly took place here on Walpurgis night.

Brock·ton |'bräktən| industrial city in SE Massachusetts, S of Boston, noted especially for shoe manufacture. Pop. 92,788.

Bro·ken Ar·row |'brōkən 'ærō| city in NE Oklahoma, a suburb SE of Tulsa. Pop. 58,043.

Brok·en Hill[1] |'brōkən| town in New South Wales, Australia. Pop. 23,260. It is a center of lead, silver and zinc mining.

Brok·en Hill[2] |brōkən| former name (1904–65) for KABWE, Zambia.

Brom·berg |'bräm,bərg| German name for BYDGOSZCZ, Poland.

Brom·ley |'brämlē| residential borough of SE Great London, England. Pop. 282,000. On the Kent border, it includes the site of the former Crystal Palace.

Bronx, the |bräNGks| largely residential and industrial borough in NE New York City. It is the only part of the city on the mainland, and is coextensive with Bronx County. Pop. 1,203,789. □ **Bronxite** n.

Brook Farm |'brŏŏk 'färm| historic commune that existed in the 1840s in West Roxbury, now a SW section of Boston, Massachusetts, associated with Margaret Fuller and other writers.

Brook·field |'brŏŏk,fēld| city in SE Wisconsin, a suburb W of Milwaukee. Pop. 35,184.

Brook·ha·ven |'brŏŏk,hāvən| town in E Long Island, New York, including Brookhaven, Stony Brook, and other villages. It is home to a noted nuclear laboratory. Pop. 407,779.

Brook·lands |'brŏŏklən(d)z| motor-racing circuit near Weybridge in Surrey, England, opened in 1907. During World War II the course was converted for aircraft manufacture.

Brook·line |'brŏŏk,līn| town in E Massachusetts, a suburb on the W side of Boston and almost surrounded by the city. Pop. 54,718.

Brook·lyn |'brŏŏklən| largely residential and the most populous borough of New York City, coextensive with Kings County, at the SW corner of Long Island. It is famed for its neighborhoods. Pop. 2,300,664. □ **Brooklynite** n.

Brook·lyn Bridge |'brŏŏklən| suspension bridge between S Manhattan and N Brooklyn, New York City. Completed in 1883, it was one of the period's engineering marvels, and is celebrated in art and literature.

Brook·lyn Park |'brŏŏklən| city in SE Minnesota, a suburb N of Minneapolis. Pop. 56,381.

Brooks Range |brŏŏks| mountain chain that lies across N Alaska. It is the NW extreme of the Rocky Mts., and the North Slope lies on its N.

Bros·sard |braw'sär| city in S Quebec, a suburb E of Montreal, across the Saint Lawrence River. Pop. 64,793.

Brow·ard County |'browərd| county in SE Florida, on the Atlantic, N of Miami. Fort Lauderdale is its seat. Pop. 1,255,488.

Browns Ferry |brownz| locality on the Tennessee River in N Alabama, site of a major nuclear power plant.

Browns·ville[1] |'brownz,vil| section of E Brooklyn, New York, noted in the early 20th century for its Jewish community, today a struggling inner-city neighborhood. Local name the 'Ville.

Browns·ville[2] |'brownz,vil| city in S Texas, on the Rio Grande and the Mexican border. Pop. 98,962.

Bruce Peninsula |brŏŏs| peninsula in S Ontario that extends NW across Lake Huron, separating Georgian Bay, to the N, from the main body.

Bruges |brŏŏZH| city in NW Belgium, capital of the province of West Flanders. Pop. 117,000. A center of the Flemish textile trade until the 15th century, it is a well-preserved medieval city surrounded by canals. Flemish name **Brugge**.

Brug·ge |'brYkə; 'brŏŏgə| Flemish name for BRUGES, Belgium.

Brum |brəm| Brit. an informal name for the city of Birmingham, England, an abbreviation of the dialectal form of the city's name, **Brummagemo**.

Bru·nei |brŏŏ'nī| oil-rich sultanate on the NW coast of Borneo. Area: 2,226 sq. mi./5,765 sq. km. Pop. 264,000. Languages, Malay, English, Chinese. Capital: Bandar Seri Begawan. Official name **Brunei Darussalam**. □ **Bruneian** adj. & n.

Brunei

Bruns·wick[1] |'brənzwik| **1** former duchy and state of Germany, mostly incorporated into Lower Saxony. German name **Braunschweig. 2** the capital of this former duchy, an industrial city in Lower Saxony, Germany. Pop. 259,130.

Bruns·wick[2] |'brənzwik| town in SW Maine, home to Bowdoin College. Pop. 20,906.

Brus·sels |'brəsəlz| the capital of Belgium and of the province of Brabant. Pop. 954,000. It is a major European commercial, financial, and administrative center. The headquarters of the European Commission is here. French name **Bruxelles**; Flemish name **Brussel**.

Brux·elles |brʏ(k)'sel| French name for BRUSSELS, Belgium.

Bry·an |'brīən| city in E central Texas. Pop. 55,002.

Bry·ansk |brē'änsk| industrial city in European Russia, SW of Moscow, on the Desna River. Pop. 456,000.

Bryce Canyon |brīs| region in S central Utah, site of a national park noted for spectacular rock formations.

Brześć nad Bu·giem |bə'ZHesCH näd 'bŏŏg,yem| Polish name for BREST, Belarus.

Bu·bas·tis |byŏŏ'bæstəs| city of ancient N Egypt, in the Nile Delta, near present-day Zagazig. It has been much excavated.

Bu·ca·ra·man·ga |,bŏŏkərə'mäNGgə| commercial city in N central Colombia. Pop. 353,000. It is in a noted coffee- and tobacco-producing region.

Bu·cha·rest |'b(y)ŏŏkə,rest| the capital of Romania and former capital of Wallachia. Pop. 2,343,800. A cultural and industrial center, it was founded in the 14th century on the trade route between Europe and Constantinople. Romanian name **Bucureşti**.

Bu·chen·wald |'bŏŏKHən,wält| village in central Germany, near Weimar. It was the site of a Nazi concentration camp during World War II.

Buck·eye State |'bək,ī| nickname for OHIO.

Buck·ing·ham Palace |'bəkiNGəm; 'bəkiNG,hæm| official residence of the British monarch, in central London, in Westminster, on the W of St. James's Park and just W of the Houses of Parliament.

Buck·ing·ham·shire |'bəkiNGəm,SHir; 'bəkiNGəmsHər| county of central England; county seat, Aylesbury. Abbreviation: **Bucks**.

Bucks County |bəks| county in SE Penn-

sylvania, on the Delaware River, noted for its affluent Philadelphia suburbs and its artists' colonies. Its seat is Doylestown. Pop. 541,174.

Bu·cu·reşti |,bŏŏkŏŏ'resHtē| Romanian name for BUCHAREST.

Bu·da·pest |'b(y)ŏŏdə,pest; 'bŏŏdə,pesHt| the capital, largest city, and commercial, industrial, and cultural center of Hungary. Pop. 2,000,000. The city was formed in 1873 by the union of the hilly city of Buda on the W bank of the Danube River with the low-lying city of Pest on the E.

Bud·weis |'bŏŏt,vīs| German name for ČESKÉ BUDĚJOVICE, Czech Republic. It gave this name to a type of beer.

Bue·na Park |,byŏŏnə 'pärk| city in S California, SE of Los Angeles. Its tourist attractions include Knott's Berry Farm, a famous theme park. Pop. 68,784.

Bue·na·ven·tu·ra |,bwänəven't(y)ŏŏrə| the chief Pacific port of Colombia. Pop. 122,500.

Bue·na Vis·ta |,bwänə 'vēstə| village in N Mexico, in Coahuila state, near Saltillo, where U.S. forces under Zachary Taylor won a major battle against Mexican forces under Santa Anna in February 1847.

Bue·nos Ai·res |'bwänəs ,ærēz| the capital, largest city, commercial and industrial center, and chief port of Argentina, on the Plata River. Pop. 2,961,000.

Buf·fa·lo |'bəfə,lō| industrial city in W New York. Pop. 328,120. Situated at the E end of Lake Erie, it is a major port on the Great Lakes–St. Lawrence Seaway.

Buf·fa·lo River |'bəfə,lō| river that flows 132 mi./213 km. through the Ozark Plateau in NW Arkansas and is a designated national preserve.

Bug River |bŏŏg| (also **Western Bug River**) river (481 mi./774 km.) in E central Poland that rises in SW central Ukraine and flows into the Vistula River near Warsaw.

Bu·gan·da |b(y)ŏŏ'gændə| former kingdom in E Africa, now part of UGANDA. It was centered around Kampala, N of Lake Victoria.

Bu·jum·bu·ra |,bŏŏjəm'bŏŏrə| the capital of Burundi, at the NE end of Lake Tanganyika. Pop. 235,440. It was known as Usumbura until 1962.

Bu·ka·vu |bŏŏ'kävŏŏ| town in E Congo (formerly Zaire), S of Lake Kivu. Pop. 210,000. A commercial and tourist center, it was formerly called Costermansville.

Bu·kho·ro |bə'KHärə| (also **Bukhara, Bokhara**) city in the central Asian republic of Uzbekistan. Pop. 246,200. In an extensive cotton-growing district, it is one of the oldest trade centers in central Asia, and is also noted for the production of karakul fleeces.

Bu•ko•vi•na |ˌbo͞okəˈvēnə| region of SE Europe in the Carpathians, divided between Romania and Ukraine. Formerly a province of Moldavia, it was ceded to Austria by the Turks in 1775. After World War I it was made part of Romania, the N part being incorporated into the Ukrainian SSR in World War II.

Bu•la•wa•yo |ˌbo͞oləˈwīˌō| industrial and commercial city in W Zimbabwe, the second-largest in the country. Pop. 620,940.

Bul•gar•ia |ˌbəlˈgerēə| republic in SE Europe, on the W shore of the Black Sea. Area: 42,840 sq. mi./110,912 sq. km. Pop. 8,798,000. Capital and largest city: Sofia. Language: Bulgarian. The Balkan Mts. traverse Bulgaria, which was Turkish-dominated from the 14th through the late 19th century. Independence was achieved in 1908. Agriculture has been joined since World War II by industry as economic mainstays. □ **Bulgarian** *adj. & n.* **Bulgar** *n.*

Bulgaria

Bull•head City |ˈbo͞olˌhed| city in NW Arizona, on the Colorado River, a resort and casino center. Pop. 21,951.

Bull Run |bo͞ol| small river in E Virginia, scene of two Confederate victories (also called the battles of Manassas), in 1861 and 1862, during the Civil War.

Bun•bury |ˈbənbərē| seaport and resort to the S of Perth in Western Australia. Pop. 24,000.

Bun•combe County |ˈbəngəm| county in the Blue Ridge Mts. of W North Carolina. Its seat is Asheville. Pop. 174,821. The term *bunkum* or *bunk* arose from a long, inconsequential speech made by the area's congressman in the 1820s.

Bun•ker Hill |ˌbəNGkər| hill in the Charlestown section of N Boston, Massa-

chusetts. The 1775 battle of Bunker Hill was actually fought on nearby Breed's Hill.

Bur•bank |ˈbərˌbæNGk| city in S California, on the N side of Los Angeles. Pop. 93,640. It is a center of the film, television, and aerospace industries.

Bur•gas |bo͞orˈgäs| industrial port and resort in SE Bulgaria, on the Black Sea. Pop. 226,120.

Bur•gen•land |ˈbo͞orgənˌlänt| state of E Austria. Capital: Eisenstadt.

Bur•gos |ˈbo͞orˌgōs| town in N Spain. Pop. 169,280. It was the capital of Castile during the 11th century, and the official seat of Franco's Nationalist government (1936-39).

Bur•gun•dy |ˈbərgəndē| region and former duchy of E central France, centered on Dijon. French name **Bourgogne**. □ **Burgundian** *adj. & n.*

Bur•han•pur |bərˈhänˌpo͞or| historic city in W central India, in Madhya Pradesh state. Pop. 173,000.

Bur•ki•na Fa•so |bo͞orˈkēnə ˈfäsō| (or **Burkina**) landlocked republic in W Africa, in the Sahel. Area: 105,870 sq. mi./274,200 sq. km. Pop. 9,271,000. Official language, French. Capital and largest city: Ouagadougou. A French protectorate from 1898, it became an autonomous republic within the French Community in 1958 and a fully independent republic in 1960. Its economy is based largely on subsistence farming. Former name (until 1984) UPPER VOLTA. □ **Burkinan** *adj. & n.* **Burkinabè** *adj. & n.*

Burkina

Bur•lin•game |ˈbərlənˌgām| city in N central California, on San Francisco Bay, a suburb S of San Francisco. Pop. 26,801.

Bur•ling•ton[1] |ˈbərliNGtən| city in N central North Carolina, noted as a textile center. Pop. 39,498.

Bur•ling•ton[2] |ˈbərliNGtən| city in S Ontario, on Lake Ontario SW of Toronto. Pop. 129,600.

Bur·ling·ton³ |'bərliNGtən| largest city in Vermont, in the NW part, on Lake Champlain. Pop. 39,127.

Bur·ma |'bərmə| country in SE Asia, on the Bay of Bengal. Area: 261,220 sq. mi./ 676,560 sq. km. Pop. 42,528,000. Language, Burmese. Capital and largest city: Rangoon (Yangon). Official name (since 1989) **Union of Myanmar**; also called **Myanmar**. In NW Indochina, Burma is dominated by the Irrawaddy River. It has a monsoonal climate, and grows rice, teak, and other forest and tropical crops. Mining and oil are also important. The army has controlled Burman politics since 1962. □ **Burmese** *adj. & n.* **Burman** *adj.*

Burma

Bur·ma Road |'bərmə| route linking Lashio in Burma to Kunming in China, covering 717 mi./1,154 km. Completed in 1939, it was built by the Chinese in response to the Japanese occupation of the Chinese coast, to serve as a supply route to the interior.

Bur·na·by |'bərnəbē| municipality in SW British Columbia, an industrial and residential center just E of Vancouver. Pop. 158,858.

Burn·ley |'bərnlē| industrial town in NW England, in Lancashire, N of Manchester. Pop. 89,000.

Burns·ville |'bərnz,vil| city in SE Minnesota, a suburb S of Minneapolis. Pop. 51,288.

Bur·sa |'bərsə| city in NW Turkey, capital of a province of the same name. Pop. 834,580. It was the capital of the Ottoman Empire 1326–1402.

Burton-upon-Trent |'bərtn ə,pän 'trent| town in W central England, in Staffordshire, on the Trent River NE of Birmingham. Pop. 59,600. It is noted for its breweries.

Bu·run·di |bə'rōondē| central African republic, on the E side of Lake Tanganyika, to the S of Rwanda. Area: 10,747 sq. mi./27,834 sq. km. Pop. 5,800,000. Languages, French and Kirundi. Capital and largest city: Bujumbura. Independent since 1962, Burundi has been torn by strife between its agricultural Hutu majority and the more urban Tutsi minority. □ **Burundian** *adj. & n.*

Burundi

Bury |'berē| industrial town in NW England, in Greater Manchester, noted for its textile and paper industries. Pop. 61,000.

Bur·yat·ia |bōor'yätyə| (also **Buryat Republic**) an autonomous republic in SE Russia, between Lake Baikal and the Mongolian border. Pop. 1,049,000. Capital: Ulan-Ude.

Bury Saint Ed·munds |,berē sənt 'edmən(d)z| historic commercial town in SE England, in Suffolk. Pop. 31,000. The body of King (later Saint) Edmund was interred here in the 10th century, but *Bury* is the equivalent of *burg* or *borough*.

Bu·shehr |bōōsHer| (also **Bushire**) commercial port city in S Iran, on the Persian Gulf. Pop. 133,000.

Butte |byōot| city in SW Montana, famed as a mining center. Pop. 33,336.

Bu·tu·an |bōō'tōō,än| commercial port city in the Philippines, on NE Mindanao. Pop. 172,000.

Bu·zau |bōō'zow| industrial city in SE Romania, on the Buzau River, capital of Buzau county. Pop. 145,000.

Buz·zards Bay |'bəzərdz| inlet of the Atlantic in SE Massachusetts, just W of Cape Cod.

Byb·los |'biblə| ancient Mediterranean seaport, situated on the site of present-day Jebeil, to the N of Beirut in Lebanon. It became a thriving Phoenician city in the 2nd millennium B.C.

Byd·goszcz |'bidgawsH(CH)| industrial river port in N central Poland. Pop. 381,530. Twenty thousand of its citizens were massacred by Nazis in September 1939. German name **Bromberg**.

By·tom |'bi,tawm| city in S Poland, NW of Katowice. Pop. 231,200. It was in Prussia until 1945. German name **Beuthen**.

By·zan·ti·um |bə'zæntēəm| ancient Greek city, founded in the 7th century B.C., at the S end of the Bosporus, site of present-day Istanbul, Turkey. It was rebuilt by Constantine the Great in A.D. 324–30 as Constantinople, after which it became the center of the Eastern Roman or Byzantine Empire. □ **Byzantine** *adj. & n.*

Cc

Ca·ba·na·tuan |ˌkäbänä'twän| city in the Philippines, on central Luzon, N of Manila. Pop. 173,000.

Ca·be·za Pri·e·ta |kə'bāzə prē'ātə| national wildlife refuge in SW Arizona, in the Sonoran Desert. The Cabeza Prieta Mts. give their name to the preserve, which is home to bighorn sheep and other species.

Ca·bi·mas |kä'bēməs| industrial town in NW Venezuela, on the North shore of Lake Maracaibo. Pop. 166,000. It is an oil industry center.

Ca·bin·da |kə'bində| 1 exclave of Angola at the mouth of the Congo River, separated from the rest of Angola by part of the Democratic Republic of Congo (formerly Zaire). 2 the capital of this area, an oil industry center. Pop. 163,000.

Ca·bo·ra Bas·sa |kə,bawrə 'bäsə| lake on the Zambezi River in W Mozambique. Its waters are enclosed by a dam and form part of a massive hydroelectric complex.

Cab·ot Strait |'kæbət| ocean passage between Newfoundland and Nova Scotia, linking the Gulf of Saint Lawrence with the Atlantic.

Cá·ce·res |'käsərās| walled city in W Spain, on the Cáceres River, capital of Cáceres province. Pop. 81,000.

Cad·il·lac Mountain |'kædl,æk| peak on Mount Desert Island in SE Maine, within Acadia National Park. At 1,532 ft./467 m. it is the highest point on the U.S. E coast.

Ca·diz |kə'diz| city and port on the coast of SW Spain. Pop. 156,560. Founded by the Phoenicians, it was later a major center for journeys to the Americas.

Caen |käɴ| industrial city and river port in Normandy in N France, on the Orne River, capital of the region of Basse-Normandie. Pop. 115,620.

Caer·nar·fon |kär'närvən| (also **Caernarvon**) a town in NW Wales on the Menai Strait, the administrative center of Gwynedd. Pop. 9,400.

Caer·nar·fon·shire |kär'närvənsʜər; ,kär-'närvənsʜir| (also **Caernarvonshire**) a former county of NW Wales, part of Gwynedd from 1974.

Caer·phil·ly |kïr'filē| commercial town in S Wales, in Mid Glamorgan. Pop. 42,000. It gave its name to a kind of white cheese, and has a famous castle.

Cae·sa·rea |ˌsē zə'rēə| ancient port on the Mediterranean coast of present-day Israel, one of the principal cities of Roman Palestine.

Cae·sa·rea Ma·za·ca |ˌsēzə'rēə 'mæzəkə; ,sezə'rēə| former name for KAYSERI, Turkey.

Cae·sa·rea Phil·ip·pi |ˌsēzə'rēə 'filə,pï; ,sezə'rēə| city in ancient Palestine, on the site of the present-day village of Baniyas in the Golan Heights.

Ca·ga·yan de Oro |ˌkägə'yän dä 'ōrō| industrial port city in the Philippines, on NW Mindanao. Pop. 340,000.

Ca·ga·yan Islands |ˌkägə'yän| group of seven small islands in the Sulu Sea in the W Philippines.

Ca·glia·ri |'käl,yärē| the capital of Sardinia, a port on the S coast. Pop. 211,720.

Cagnes-sur-Mer |ˌkän(yə) sʏr 'mer| fishing port and resort in SE France, on the Riviera just W of Nice. Pop. 41,000.

Ca·guas |'kägwäs| commercial and industrial community in E central Puerto Rico, S of San Juan. Pop. 92,429.

Ca·ho·kia |kə'hōkēə| village in SW Illinois, across the Mississippi River from St. Louis, Missouri. Pop. 17,550. The Cahokia Mounds, major pre-Columbian earthworks, are to the NE.

Ca·hors |kä'awr| industrial town, capital of the department of Lot in S central France. Pop. 21,000. It retains many medieval buildings.

Cairn·gorm Mountains |'kern,gawrm| (also **the Cairngorms**) a mountain range in N Scotland.

Cairns |'kernz| resort town in NE Australia, in NE Queensland. Pop. 64,000. It is one of the main sugar ports in Australia.

Cai·ro[1] |'kïrō| the capital of Egypt and the largest city in Africa, a port on the Nile near the head of its delta. Founded in the 10th century, it is an industrial, commercial, transportation, and cultural center. Pop. 13,300,000. Arabic name **Al Qahira**. □ **Cairene** adj.

Cai·ro[2] |'kārō| city in S central Illinois, at the junction of the Ohio and Mississippi rivers. Pop. 4,846.

Caith·ness |'kāтʜnes| former county in the extreme NE of Scotland. It became part of Highland region in 1975.

Ca·ja·mar·ca |ˌkähə'märkə| commercial city in NW Peru, in the Andes. Pop. 93,000. It is in the middle of a mining district, and produces textiles and leather goods.

Ca·jun Country |'kājən| region of S Louisiana inhabited largely by Cajuns, descendants of 18th-century exiles from Acadia, now Nova Scotia.

Ca·la·bar |ˌkælə'bär| seaport in SE Nigeria. Pop. 126,000.

Ca·la·bria |kä'läbrēə| region of SW Italy, forming the "toe" of the Italian peninsula. Capital: Reggio di Calabria. □ **Calabrian** *adj. & n.*

Ca·lais |kæ'lā| ferry port in N France. Pop. 75,840. Captured by Edward III in 1347 after a long siege, it remained an English possession until it was retaken by the French in 1558.

Ca·lais, Pas de French name for the Strait of Dover, connecting the English Channel and the North Sea.

Ca·la·ma |kə'lämə| city in N Chile, between the Andes Mts. and the Atacama Desert. Pop. 121,000. Nearby are the huge Chuquicamata copper mines.

Ca·la·ma·ta |ˌkælə'mätə; ˌkälə'mätə| capital and principal trading port of Messinia prefecture, S Greece. Pop. 41,000. Greek name **Kalámai** or **Kalamáta**.

Ca·lam·ba |kä'lämbə| commercial and industrial town in the Philippines, on S Luzon, SE of Manila. Pop. 173,000.

Că·lă·ra·și |ˌkələ'räsн(ē)| city in SE Romania, capital of Călărași county. Pop. 76,000.

Ca·la·ver·as County |ˌkælə'verəs| largely rural county in E central California, in the Sierra Nevada, associated with the 1840s gold rush and the writing of Mark Twain.

Cal·cut·ta |kæl'kətə| port and industrial center in E India, capital of the state of West Bengal and the largest city in India. Pop. 10,916,000. It is situated on the Hooghly River near the Bay of Bengal. □ **Calcuttan** *adj. & n.*

Cal·e·do·nia |ˌkælə'dōnyə| Roman name for the N part of Britain, present-day SCOTLAND. □ **Caledonian** *adj. & n.*

Cal·e·do·nian Canal |ˌkælə'dōnyən| system of lochs and canals crossing Scotland from Inverness on the E coast to Fort William on the W. With canals built by Thomas Telford, it was opened in 1822. It traverses the Great Glen, part of its length being formed by Loch Ness.

Ca·lex·i·co |kə'leksikō| city in S California, across the border from Mexicali, Mexico. Pop. 18,633.

Cal·ga·ry |'kælgərē| commercial and industrial city in S Alberta, the largest in the province. Pop. 710,680.

Ca·li |'kälē| industrial city in W Colombia,

in the Cauca River valley. Pop. 1,624,400. An agricultural trade center, it was the reputed hub of cocaine traffic.

Cal·i·cut |'kæli,kət| seaport in the state of Kerala in SW India, on the Malabar Coast. Pop. 420,000. In the 17th and 18th centuries Calicut became a center of the textile trade with Europe. The cotton fabric known as calico originated here. Also called **Kozhikode.**

Cal·i·for·nia |ˌkælə'fawrnyə| see box. □ **Californian** *adj. & n.*

Cal·i·for·nia, Gulf of |ˌkælə'fawrnyə| arm

California
Capital: Sacramento
Largest city: Los Angeles
Other cities: Anaheim, Burbank, Long Beach, Oakland, Pasadena, San Diego, San Francisco, San Jose
Population: 29,760,021 (1990); 32,666,550 (1998); 34,441,000 (2005 proj.)
Population rank (1990): 1
Rank in land area: 3
Abbreviation: CA; Cal.; Calif.
Nickname: The Golden State
Motto: *Eureka* (Greek: 'I Have Found It')
Bird: California Valley quail
Fish: California golden trout
Flower: golden poppy
Tree: California redwood
Song: "I Love You, California"
Noted physical features: Monterey Bay, San Diego Bay, San Francisco Bay; Lake Tahoe; Golden Gate Bridge; Big Sur; Cape Mendocino; Mohave Desert, Colorado Desert; San Andreas Fault; Palisade Glacier; Death Valley; Lassen Volcano
Tourist attractions: RMS *Queen Mary*, Long Beach; Palomar Observatory; Disneyland, Anaheim; J. Paul Getty Museum, Malibu; Universal Studios, Hollywood; Los Angeles County Art Museum; San Diego Zoo; Knotts Berry Farm; Napa Valley; Monterey Peninsula; Fisherman's Wharf; Shasta Dam; Sutters Mill; Channel Islands, Kings Canyon, Lassen Volcanic, Redwood, Sequoia and Yosemite national parks; Alcatraz, Folsom Prison, San Quentin Prison
Admission date: September 9, 1850
Order of admission: 31
Name origin: Named Alta ('upper') California by Spanish explorers moving north from Baja ('lower') California, the Mexican peninsula to the south.

of the Pacific separating the Baja California peninsula from mainland Mexico.

Cal·i·for·nia Current |ˌkælə'fawrnyə| cold ocean current of the E Pacific that flows S along the W coast of North America.

Cal·lao |kə'yow| the principal seaport of Peru. Pop. 369,770.

Ca·lo·o·can |ˌkälə'ō,kän| (also **Kalookan**) city in the Philippines, on S Luzon, a suburb NW of Manila. Pop. 763,000.

Cal·u·met City |'kælyə,met| city in NE Illinois, a suburb S of Chicago, on the Indiana border. Pop. 37,840. The surrounding industrial region, in both states, is called the Calumet.

Cal·va·dos |'kælvə,dōs| department in NW France, along the English Channel, in Basse-Normandie. Area: 2,143 sq.mi./5,548 sq. km. Pop. 618,000. The capital is Caen. An apple-growing area, it gave its name to a type of brandy.

Cal·va·ry |'kælv(ə)rē| Latin name for the hill outside Jerusalem on which Jesus was crucified. The Greek name is **Golgotha**.

Cal·y·don |'kælə,dän| ancient city in central Greece, near the coast of the Gulf of Patras. The legendary Calydonian boar hunt was the search for a savage boar sent by the goddess Artemis to destroy Calydon.

Cam, River |kæm| (ancient name **Granta**) river that flows 40 mi./65 km. NE from Essex, SE England, through Cambridge to join the Ouse River near Ely.

Ca·ma·güey |ˌkämə'gwā; ˌkæmə'gwā| commercial city in E Cuba, the capital of Camagüey province. Pop. 295,000. The surrounding region produces livestock and various crops.

Ca·margue |kə'märg| (also **the Camargue**) a region of the Rhône delta in SE France, characterized by numerous shallow salt lagoons. It is known for its white horses and as a nature reserve.

Cam·a·ril·lo |ˌkæmə'rilō| city in SW California, W of Los Angeles. Pop. 52,303.

Ca·mau Peninsula |kə'mow| (also called **Mui Bai Bung**) cape at the S end of Vietnam; marks the SE corner of the Gulf of Thailand.

Cam·bay, Gulf of |kæm'bā| (also **Gulf of Khambat**) an inlet of the Arabian Sea on the Gujarat coast of W India, N of Bombay.

Cam·bo·dia |kæm'bōdēə| country in SE Asia, in Indochina between Thailand and southern Vietnam. Area: 69,884 sq. mi./181,040 sq. km. Pop. 8,660,000. Language, Khmer. Capital and largest city: Phnom Penh. Also officially called the **Khmer Republic** (1970–75) and **Kam-**

Cambodia

puchea (1976–89). Remnant of a great Khmer empire, Cambodia was controlled by the French (1863–1953). During the Vietnam War it suffered U.S. bombing and incursions, followed by a civil war that led to massive atrocities under the Khmer Rouge (1975–79). The Mekong River and Tonlé Sap (lake) dominate this country, whose economy relies on agriculture and fishing. □ **Cambodian** adj. & n.

Cam·brai |käN'bre| industrial city in NW France, on the Escaut River in the Nord-Pas-de-Calais. Pop. 34,000. The Flemish version of the town's name, Kambryk, became the name of a linen or cotton fabric, in English cambric.

Cam·bria |'kämbrēə; 'kæmbrēə| ancient name for WALES, which is mostly occupied by the **Cambrian Mountains,** a rugged upland that gave its name to geologic terminology. □ **Cambrian** adj.

Cam·bridge[1] |'kämbrij| city in E England, the county seat of Cambridgeshire. Pop. 101,000. Cambridge University is located here, and there are light industries. □ **Cantabrigian** adj. & n.

Cam·bridge[2] |'kābrij| city in E Massachusetts, across the Charles River from Boston. Pop. 95,800. Harvard University and the Massachusetts Institute of Technology are here.

Cam·bridge[3] |'kābrij| city in S Ontario, W of Toronto, a research and industrial center. Pop. 92,722.

Cam·bridge·shire |'kämbrij,SHir; 'kämbrijSHər| county of E England; county seat, Cambridge. Pop. 641,000.

Cam·bu·luc |ˌkämbōō'lōōk| see BEIJING, China.

Cam·den[1] |'kæmdən| borough of N central London, England, immediately N of Westminster. Pop. 170,000. Bloomsbury, Hampstead, and Highgate are among its constituent parts.

Cam·den[2] |'kæmdən| industrial city in SW

New Jersey, across the Delaware River from Philadelphia, Pennsylvania. Pop. 87,492.

Cam·e·lot |'kæmə,lät| in Arthurian legend, the place where King Arthur, the Celtic hero of 5th-century England, had his court. Winchester is among sites suggested as having been Camelot.

Cam·em·bert |'kæməm,ber| village in the Orne department of Normandy, in NW France. It gave its name to the soft cheese.

Cam·er·on Highlands |'kæm(ə)rən| hill resort region in Pahang, Malaysia.

Cam·er·oon |,kæmə'rōōn| republic on the W coast of Africa, between Nigeria and Gabon. Area: 183,569 sq. mi./475,442 sq. km. Pop. 12,081,000. Languages, French, English, W African languages. Capital: Yaoundé Largest city: Douala. French name **Cameroun**. Controlled by the Germans, French, and English, Cameroon gained independence in 1960. It relies on tropical agriculture and forest products, along with oil. □ **Cameroonian** *adj. & n.*

Cameroon

Cam·er·oon, Mount |,kæmə'rōōn| active volcano in SW Cameroon, near the Atlantic Ocean. At 13,354 ft./4,070 m. it is the highest point in W Africa S of the Sahara.

Ca·mi·no Re·al |kə'mē,nō rā'æl| name ("royal road") for various routes established by the Spanish during early settlement of the U.S. SW. Notable examples led from Mexico to San Francisco Bay and to Santa Fe, New Mexico.

Cam·pa·gna di Ro·ma |käm'pänyə dē 'rōmə| plain surrounding the city of Rome, in central Italy. It was a popular ancient residential area but was later abandoned because of unhealthy (malarial) conditions. It has been reclaimed and now is farmland.

Cam·pa·nia |käm'pänēə| region of W central Italy. Capital: Naples. □ **Campanian** *adj. & n.*

Camp·bell |'kæmbəl| city in W central Cal-

ifornia, SW of San Jose, part of the Silicon Valley research and industrial complex. Pop. 36,048.

Camp·bell·town |'kæmbəl,town| city in Australia, in New South Wales, a suburb S of Sydney. Pop. 138,000.

Camp Da·vid |kæmp 'dāvid| retreat in the Catoctin Mts. of Maryland, NW of Washington, D.C., used by U.S. presidents since the 1940s.

Cam·pe·che |Käm'päCHä; kæm'pēCHē| 1 state of SE Mexico, on the Yucatán Peninsula. Area: 19,626 sq. mi./50,812 sq. km. Pop.: 529,000. 2 its capital, a seaport on the Gulf of Mexico. Pop. 172,200.

Cam·per·down |'kämpər,down| (Dutch name **Camperduin**) village in the W Netherlands, on the North Sea. In a 1797 naval battle near here the British defeated Dutch forces.

Cam·pi·na Gran·de |käm'pēnə 'grändē| commercial city in E Brazil, NW of Recife in Paraíba state. Pop. 326,000.

Cam·pi·nas |käm'pēnəs| commercial city in SE Brazil, NW of São Paulo, a center for the coffee and high-tech industries. Pop. 835,000.

Cam·po·bas·so |,kämpō'bäsō| city in central Italy, capital of Molise region. Pop. 51,300.

Cam·po·bel·lo Island |,kæmpə'belō| resort island in SW New Brunswick, off Eastport, Maine, noted as the vacation home of Franklin D. Roosevelt.

Cam·po Gran·de |'kämpōō 'grändē| city in SW Brazil, capital of the state of Mato Grosso do Sul. Pop. 489,000.

Cam·pos |'kämpōōs| (full name **Campos dos Goytacazes**) city in SE Brazil, on the Paraíba River, NE of Rio de Janeiro. Pop. 391,000. It is a sugar-producing and oil industry-servicing center.

Cam Ranh Bay |'kæm 'rän| inlet of the South China Sea, southern central Vietnam. It has been a major base for France, Japan, the former Soviet Union, and the U.S., which had a major installation here during the Vietnam War.

Camu·lo·du·num |,kæmələ'dōōnəm| Roman name for COLCHESTER, England.

Ca·na |'kānə| biblical village in Galilee, N Israel, N of Nazareth, where Jesus performed his first miracle at a wedding. It was perhaps within present-day Kafr Kana, an Arab town (pop. 12,000).

Ca·naan |'kānən| the biblical name for the area of ancient Palestine W of the Jordan River, the Promised Land of the Israelites, who conquered and occupied it during the

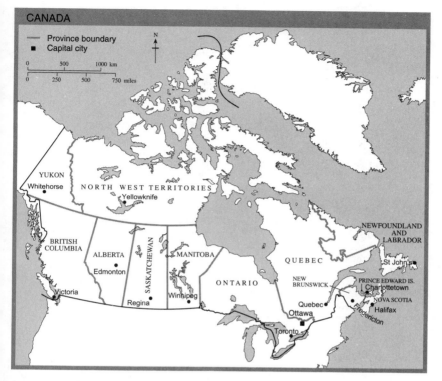

CANADA
- Province boundary
- ■ Capital city

0   500   1000 km
0   250   500   750 miles

YUKON — Whitehorse
NORTH WEST TERRITORIES — Yellowknife
BRITISH COLUMBIA
ALBERTA — Edmonton
SASKATCHEWAN
MANITOBA
Victoria
Regina — Winnipeg
ONTARIO
QUEBEC
NEWFOUNDLAND AND LABRADOR
St John's
NEW BRUNSWICK
PRINCE EDWARD IS. — Charlottetown
NOVA SCOTIA
Quebec — Halifax
Ottawa — Fredericton
Toronto

latter part of the 2nd millennium B.C. □ **Canaanite** *adj. & n.*

Can·a·da |ˈkænədə| the second-largest country in the world, covering N North America except for Alaska. Area: 3.85 million sq. mi./9.98 million sq. km. Pop. 27,296,859; Languages, English and French. Capital: Ottawa. Largest cities: Montreal, Calgary, Toronto. The object of a long power struggle between France and Britain, Canada became a dominion, essentially independent, in 1867. Its early economy was based on the fur trade. Today, mining, plains agriculture, fishing, hydropower, and heavy and light industry are all important. □ **Canadian** *adj. & n.*

Ca·na·di·an River |kəˈnādēən| river that flows 900 mi./1,450 km. from E New Mexico across the Texas Panhandle and Oklahoma. Oklahoma City lies on it. It is also called the South Canadian River.

Ca·na·di·an Shield |kəˈnādēən| massive plateau that occupies over two-fifths of the land area of Canada and is drained by rivers generally flowing into Hudson Bay. Extending N from the Great Lakes and including the Adirondacks of New York and the Arrowhead Region of Minnesota, it is the oldest portion of the North American continent, being permanently elevated above sea level since the Precambrian Era. Also called **Laurentian Plateau.**

Canal Zone |kəˈnæl| see PANAMA CANAL.

Ca·nar·ies Current |kəˈnerēz| cold ocean current in the North Atlantic that flows SW from Spain to meet equatorial waters near the Canary Islands.

Ca·nar·sie |kəˈnärsē| residential section of SE Brooklyn, New York, along Jamaica Bay, named for a local tribe.

Ca·nary Islands (also **the Canaries**; Spanish name **Islas Canarias**) group of islands in the Atlantic, off the NW coast of Africa, forming an autonomous region of Spain. Capital: Las Palmas. Pop. 1,557,530. The group includes the islands of Tenerife, Gomera, La Palma, Hierro, Gran Canaria, Fuerteventura, and Lanzarote.

Ca·nav·er·al, Cape |kəˈnæv(ə)rəl| cape on the E coast of Florida, known as Cape Kennedy from 1963 until 1973. It is the site of the John F. Kennedy Space Center, from which U.S. space missions are launched.

Can·ber·ra |ˈkænb(ə)rə| the capital of Australia and seat of the federal government, in Australian Capital Territory, an enclave of New South Wales. Pop. 310,000.

Can·cún |kæn'kōōn| beach resort in SE Mexico, on the NE coast of the Yucatán Peninsula. Pop. 27,500.

Can·dia |'kændēə| Venetian name for the Greek island of Crete, the city of Heraklion, and the part of the Aegean Sea that lies between the Cyclades and Crete. The ruins of the city of Knossos are near the modern city of Candia.

Ca·nea |kə'nēə| (also **Khaniá**) ancient city on Crete, in Greece. The modern city is a port and capital of Khaniá prefecture.

Cang·zhou |'zæNG'jō| city in Hebei province, E China, on the Grand Canal S of Tianjin. Pop. 303,000.

Can·nae |'kænē| battlefield in SE Italy, near Barletta. During the Second Punic War, in 216 B.C., Rome suffered one of its worst defeats here at the hands of Hannibal.

Cannes |kän; kæn| resort on the Mediterranean coast of France, in Alpes-Maritimes. Pop. 69,360. An international film festival is held here annually.

Ca·no·as |'kä'nōəs| city in S Brazil, a suburb N of Pôrto Alegre in Rio Grande do Sul state. Pop. 278,000.

Ca·no·pus |kə'nōpəs| resort city of ancient N Egypt, in the Nile Delta, E of Alexandria, near present-day Abu Qir (Abukir). It gave its name to canopic (burial) jars.

Can·so, Strait of |'kænsō| ocean passage between Cape Breton Island and the mainland of Nova Scotia, bridged since the 1950s. Also, **the Canso Gut.**

Can·ta·bria |kən'täbrēə| autonomous region of N Spain, between Asturias and the Basque provinces. Pop. 527,000. Capital: Santander. □ **Cantabrian** adj. & n.

Can·ter·bury[1] |'kæntər,berē| city in Kent, SE England, the seat of the Archbishop of Canterbury, head of the Church of England. Pop. 39,700. St. Augustine established a church and monastery here in 597. After the 1170 murder of Thomas à Becket, Canterbury became a place of medieval pilgrimage.

Can·ter·bury[2] |'kæntər,berē| region on the central east coast of South Island, New Zealand, including the Canterbury Plains.

Can·ton and En·der·bury |'kæntn ən 'endər,berē| two islands in Kiribati, in the Phoenix Islands group, that were held by the U.S. and the United Kingdom before 1980. Canton is also spelled **Kanton.**

Can·ton[1] |'kæn,tän| see GUANGZHOU, China.

Can·ton[2] |'kæntn| industrial city in NE

Ohio. Pop. 84,161. The Professional Football Hall of Fame is in the city.

Can·tons de l'Est |kæn'tän də 'lest| French name for the EASTERN TOWNSHIPS, Quebec.

Canyon de Chel·ly |də 'sHä(lē)| national monument in NE Arizona, on the Navajo Indian Reservation, noted for cliff dwellings and other ruins.

Can·yon·lands |'kænyən,læn(d)z| region of SE Utah, many of whose noted rock formations are preserved in the Canyonlands National Park.

Cap-de-la-Madeleine |,käp də ,lä mäd 'len| industrial city in S Quebec, across the St. Maurice River from Trois-Rivières. Pop. 33,716.

Cape Bret·on Island |käp 'bretn| island forming the NE part of the province of Nova Scotia. It takes its name from the cape at its NE tip.

Cape Che·lyus·kin |CHel'yōōskən| cape on the Taimyr Peninsula, in Siberia, Russia. At 77° 45′N, it is the northernmost point on the Asian mainland.

Cape Cod |käd| sandy peninsula in SE Massachusetts. Forming an arm-shaped curve enclosing Cape Cod Bay, it includes many popular summer resorts. The Pilgrims landed on the N tip in November 1620, before proceeding to Plymouth.

Cape Colony |'kälənē| early name (1814–1910) for the former CAPE PROVINCE of South Africa.

Cape Cor·al |'kawrəl; 'kärəl| resort city in SW Florida, S of Fort Myers. Pop. 74,991.

Cape Dor·set |'dōrsit| Inuit community on an island off SW Baffin Island, in Nunavut. Remains found here gave their name to the Cape Dorset Culture of up to 2,500 years ago. Inuit name **Kinngait.**

Cape Fear River |'käp 'fir| river that flows 200 mi./320 km. across E North Carolina to enter the Atlantic near Wilmington, at Cape Fear.

Cape Gi·rar·deau |jə'rärdō| city in SE Missouri, on the Mississippi River. Pop. 34,438.

Cape John·son Depth |'jänsən 'depTH| the deepest point of the Philippine or Mindanao Trench, off the E coast of the Philippines, dropping to 34,440 ft./10,497 m. below sea level. It is named after the USS *Cape Johnson.*

Cape May |mā| resort city in extreme S New Jersey, on the Atlantic. Pop. 4,668.

Cape Pi·ai |pē'ī| cape in Malaysia at the tip of the Malay Peninsula, at 01° 16′ N the most southerly point of the Asian mainland.

Cape Prov•ince |'kāp 'prävəns| former province of South Africa, containing the Cape of Good Hope. The area became a British colony in 1814; it was known as Cape Colony from then until 1910, when it joined the Union of South Africa. In 1994 it was divided into the provinces of Northern Cape, Western Cape, and Eastern Cape.

Ca•per•na•um |kə'pərnēəm| biblical village on the N shore of the Lake of Galilee, on the site of present-day Kefar Nahum, Israel, a center of the work of Jesus and home to several of his disciples.

Cape Ro•ca |'rōkə| peninsula in Portugal, W of Lisbon, the westernmost point on the European mainland. Portuguese name **Cabo da Roca**.

Cape Ta•ri•fa |tə'rēfə| peninsula on the coast of S Spain. At 36° 00′ N, it is the southernmost point on mainland Europe.

Cape Town |'kāp ,town| the legislative capital of South Africa and administrative capital of the province of W Cape. Pop. 776,600. It is an historic port and an industrial center.

Cape Ver•de |,kāp 'vərd| republic consisting of a group of ten islands in the Atlantic off the coast of Senegal, named after the most westerly cape of Africa. Area: 1,557 sq. mi./4,033 sq. km. Pop. 383,000. Languages, Portuguese, Creole. Capital: Praia. Largest city: Mindela. Previously uninhabited, the islands were settled by the Portuguese in the 15th century. In 1975, an independent republic was established. Farming, fishing, and salt extraction are important. □ **Cape Verdean** adj. & n.

Cape Verde Islands

Cape Wrath |ræTH; 'räTH| headland at the NW tip of the mainland of Scotland.

Cape York |'yawrk| the northernmost point of the continent of Australia, on the Torres Strait at the tip of the sparsely populated Cape York Peninsula in Queensland.

Cap-Haïtien |kāp 'hāSHən| historic port city in N Haiti. Pop. 133,000. A former Haitian capital and the second-largest city in the country, it is associated with the early political leader Henri Christophe.

Cap•i•tol Hill |'kæpətl 'hil| the region around the U.S. Capitol building in Washington, D.C. (often an allusive reference to the U.S. Congress itself).

Cap•i•to•line |'kæpətl,īn| (also **Capitoline Hill**) highest of the seven hills of Rome and historic center of the city, overlooking the Forum. Atop the hill is a complex of buildings on a site designed by Michelangelo. In the center is a famous equestrian statue of Marcus Aurelius.

Cap•i•tol Reef National Park |'kæpətl 'rēf| preserve in S central Utah, noted for its fossils and rock formations.

Cap•pa•do•cia |,kæpə'dōSHə| ancient region of central Asia Minor (present-day Turkey), between Lake Tuz and the Euphrates, N of Cilicia. It was an important center of early Christianity. □ **Cappadocian** adj. & n.

Ca•pre•ra |kə'prärə| island off the NE coast of Sardinia, Italy. It was the home of the Italian nationalist leader Giuseppe Garibaldi, who is buried here.

Ca•pri |'käprē; kə'prē| island off the W coast of Italy, S of Naples; it has been a noted resort since ancient Roman times.

Ca•pri•vi Strip |kə'prēvē| narrow strip of Namibia that extends toward Zambia from the NE corner of Namibia and reaches the Zambezi River.

Cap•rock, the |'kæp,räk| escarpment in N Texas, separating the Llano Estacado from the central Texas prairies. The Llano Estacado itself is sometimes called the Caprock.

Ca•rac•as |kə'rækəs; kə'räkəs| the capital and largest city of Venezuela, in the N near the Caribbean. Pop. 1,824,890. It is the commercial, industrial, and cultural center of Venezuela.

Ca•ra•vag•gio |,kærə'väjō| agricultural and industrial town in N Italy, on the Lombardy Plain. Pop. 14,000. The Mannerist painter Caravaggio was born here.

Car•bon•dale |'kärbən,dāl| city in S central Illinois, a coal center and home to Southern Illinois University. Pop. 27,033.

Car•cas•sonne |,kärkə'sawn| walled commercial city in SW France, the capital of Aude department, in Languedoc-Roussillon near the Spanish border. Pop. 45,000.

Car•che•mish |'kär,kemiSH| ancient city on the upper Euphrates, NE of present-day Aleppo, Syria.

Car·da·mom Mountains |'kärdəməm; 'kärdə,mäm| range of forested mountains in W Cambodia, along the Thai border, rising to 5,886 ft./1,813 m. at its highest point.

Cár·de·nas |kär'dānəs; 'kärdn-əs| industrial port in N central Cuba, E of Havana. Pop. 63,000.

Car·diff |'kärdəf| the capital of Wales, a seaport on the Bristol Channel. Pop. 272,600. Welsh name **Caerdydd**.

Car·di·gan·shire |'kärdəgənSHər; 'kärdəgən,SHir| former county of SW Wales. It became part of Dyfed in 1974; the area became a county once more in 1996, as Ceredigion.

Car·ia |'kerēə| ancient region of SW Asia Minor, S of the Maeander River and NW of Lycia. □ **Carian** adj. & n.

Ca·ri·a·ci·ca |,kärēə'sēkə| city in E Brazil, a suburb of Vitória, in Espírito Santo state. Pop. 252,000.

Ca·rib·be·an National Forest |,kærə-'bēən; kə'ribēən| preserve in NE Puerto Rico, noted for its rainforest vegetation and wildlife. Also called **El Yunque**.

Ca·rib·be·an Sea |,kærə'bēən; kə'ribēən| the part of the Atlantic lying between the Antilles and the mainland of Central and South America.

Car·i·boo Mountains |'kærə,boo| range in E central British Columbia, part of the Rocky Mts., scene of an 1860s gold rush.

Ca·rin·thia |kə'rinTHēə| Alpine state of S Austria. Capital: Klagenfurt. German name **Kärnten**. □ **Carinthian** adj. & n.

Car·lisle¹ |kär'līl; 'kär,līl| industrial and commercial town in NW England, the county seat of Cumbria. Pop. 99,800.

Car·lisle² |kär'līl; 'kär,līl| historic borough in S Pennsylvania, SW of Harrisburg. Pop. 18,419. It is home to the Army War College.

Car·low |'kärlō| **1** county of the Republic of Ireland, in the province of Leinster. Pop. 41,000. **2** its capital, on the Barrow River. Pop. 11,000.

Carls·bad¹ |'kärlz,bæd| city in SW California, on the Pacific coast N of San Diego. Pop. 63,126.

Carls·bad² |'kärls,bät| see KARLOVY VARY, Czech Republic.

Carls·bad³ |'kärlz,bæd| city in SE New Mexico, on the Pecos River. Pop. 24,952. To the SW is Carlsbad Caverns, a vast cave complex.

Car·ma·gno·la |,kärmən'yōlə| commune, in NW Italy, on the Po. Pop. 24,000. The carmagnole, a style of clothing worn by Piedmontese workmen and adopted by in-

surrectionists during the French Revolution in 1792, is thought to have taken its name from the village.

Car·mar·then |kər'märTHən| town in SW Wales, the administrative center of Carmarthenshire. Pop. 54,800. Welsh name **Caerfyrddin**.

Car·mar·then·shire |kər'märTHnsHər; ,kär'märTHnsHir| county of S Wales; administrative center, Carmarthen. It was part of Dyfed between 1974 and 1996.

Car·mel, Mount |'kärməl| group of mountains near the Mediterranean coast in NW Israel, sheltering the port of Haifa. In the Bible it is the scene of the defeat of the priests of Baal by the prophet Elijah.

Car·mel |kär'mel| city in W central California, a resort on the Pacific S of Monterey. Pop. 4,239.

Car·mi·chael |'kär,mīkəl| community in N central California, a suburb NE of Sacramento. Pop. 48,702.

Car·na·by Street |'kärnəbē| street in W central London, England, W of Soho, made famous in the 1960s as the center of the teenage fashion industry.

Car·nac |'kär,næk| village in NW France, in Brittany, on the Atlantic coast. It is best known for its prehistoric stone monuments, huge standing stones aligned in long avenues or in semicircular or rectangular enclosures.

Car·nat·ic |,kär'nætik| (also **Karnatic**) term sometimes applied to all of S India, but more usually used of the plains of the SE, to the E of the Eastern Ghats mountain range, where France and Britain struggled for control of India in the 18th century.

Car·ne·gie Hall |'kärnəgē 'hawl; kär'negē| famed concert hall in central Manhattan, New York City, traditionally the goal of any serious musician.

Car·nic Alps |'kärnik| (German name **Karnische Alpen**) range of the Alps on the border of S Austria and NE Italy, reaching 9,124 ft./2,781 m. at Monte Coglians (Hohe Warte).

Car·nio·la |,kärn'yōlə; 'kärnē'ōlə| historic region of Slovenia on the border with Italy. After being occupied by Rome and then settled by Slovenes, it belonged to Austria and then was divided between Italy and Yugoslavia in 1919. Since 1947 it has been part of Yugoslavia and then Slovenia.

Car·ol City |'kærəl| suburban community in SE Florida, N of Miami. Pop. 53,331.

Car·o·li·na¹ |,kærə'līnə| commercial and residential suburb E of San Juan, Puerto Rico. Pop. 162,404.

Ca·ro·li·na² |,kærə'līnə| 17th-century English colony in SE North America, which eventually became North Carolina and South Carolina (the Carolinas).

Car·o·line Islands (also **the Carolines**) group of islands in the W Pacific Ocean, N of the equator, forming the Federated States of MICRONESIA.

Car·ol Stream |'kærəl| village in NE Illinois, a suburb W of Chicago. Pop. 31,716.

Ca·ro·ni River |,kärə'nē| river in E Venezuela that flows 550 mi./880 km. N from the Pacaraima Range to the Orinoco River. The Guri Reservoir is along it.

Car·pa·thi·an Mountains |kär'päTHēən| (also **the Carpathians**) a mountain system extending SE from S Poland and the Czech Republic into Romania. See KARPATHOS.

Car·pen·tar·ia, Gulf of |'kärpən'terēə; 'kärpən'tærēə| large bay on the N coast of Australia, between Arnhem Land and the Cape York Peninsula.

Car·ran·tuo·hill |,kærən'tōōəl| highest peak in Ireland, in Macgillicuddy's Reeks, County Kerry, in the SW: 3,415 ft./1,041 m.

Car·ra·ra |kə'rärə| town in Tuscany in NW Italy, famous for the white marble quarried here since Roman times. Pop. 68,480. □ **Carrarese** adj. & n.

Car·ri·a·cou |,kærə'kōō| largest (13 sq. mi./21 sq. km.) island in the Grenadines, in the Windward Islands group in the West Indies. Pop. 5,000. Hillsborough is the chief town. Administered by Grenada, Carriacou has some agriculture and a tourist trade.

Car·rick·fer·gus |,kærək'fərgəs| historic port town in E Northern Ireland, NE of Belfast on Belfast Lough, in County Antrim. Pop. 31,000.

Carrick-on-Shannon |'kærik än 'sHænən| the county seat of Leitrim in the Republic of Ireland, on the Shannon River. Pop. 6,168.

Car·ri·zo Plain |kə'rēzō| lowland in W central California, along the San Andreas Fault, noted for its earthquakes and wildlife.

Car·roll·ton |'kærəltən| city in NE Texas, a suburb N of Dallas. Pop. 82,169.

Car·son |'kärsən| city in SW California, an industrial suburb S of Los Angeles. Pop. 83,995.

Car·son City |'kärsən| the state capital of Nevada, in the W, near the California line. Pop. 40,440. It was a famed 19th-century silver town, site of the Comstock Lode and later of a branch of the U.S. Mint.

Car·ta·ge·na¹ |,kärtə'hänə| port city, resort, and oil-refining center in NW Colombia, on the Caribbean Sea. Pop. 688,300.

Car·ta·ge·na² |,kärtə'hänə| port in SE Spain. Pop. 172,150. Originally named Mastia, it was refounded as Carthago Nova (New Carthage) by Hasdrubal in c.225 B.C., as a base for the Carthaginian conquest of Spain.

Car·thage |'kärTHij| ancient city on the coast of N Africa near present-day Tunis. Founded by the Phoenicians c.814 B.C., Carthage became a major force in the Mediterranean, and came into conflict with Rome in the Punic Wars. It was finally destroyed by the Romans in 146 B.C. □ **Carthaginian** adj. & n.

Car·tier Islands |,kärtē'ä| see ASHMORE AND CARTIER ISLANDS, Australia.

Ca·ru·a·ru |,kärōōə'rōō| city in NE Brazil, in Pernambuco state. Pop. 214,000. It is the commercial center of a farming and livestock-producing area.

Cary |'kærē| town in E central North Carolina, a commercial and research center. Pop. 43,858.

Cas·a·blan·ca |,käsə'bläNGkə; 'kæsə 'blæNGkə| the largest city and commercial center of Morocco, a seaport on the Atlantic coast. Pop. 2,943,000.

Ca·sa Gran·de |'käsə 'grändē; 'grädä| city in S central Arizona, S of Phoenix. Pop. 19,082. It is named for nearby pre-Columbian ruins.

Cas·cade Range |kæs'kād| range of volcanic mountains in W North America, extending from S British Columbia through Washington and Oregon to N California. Its highest peak, Mount Rainier, rises to 14,410 ft./4,395 m. The range also includes the active volcano Mount St. Helens.

Cas·co Bay |'kæskō| inlet of the Atlantic in S Maine, known for its hundreds of islands and protected anchorages. Portland lies on it.

Ca·ser·ta |kə'zertə| commercial center in S central Italy, the capital of Caserta province. Pop. 70,000. Nearby is Caserta Vecchia, a medieval town.

Cash·el |'kæsHəl| town in S Ireland, in County Tipperary, dominated by the 200-ft./60-m. **Rock of Cashel**, seat of the kings of Munster in the 4th–12th centuries. A chapel now surmounts the Rock.

Cash·mere |'kæzH,mēr; 'kæsH,mir| see KASHMIR.

Cas·per |'kæspər| city in E central

Wyoming, on the North Platte River. Pop. 46,742. Oil is central to its economy.

Cas·pi·an Sea |'kæspēən| large landlocked salt lake, bounded by Russia, Kazakhstan, Turkmenistan, Azerbaijan, and Iran. It is the world's largest (143,524 sq. mi./370,992 sq. km.) body of inland water. Its surface lies 92 ft./28 m. below sea level.

Cas·tal·ia |kə'stālyə| spring on Mount Parnassus, in central Greece, that was sacred to Apollo and to the Muses; it was said to inspire those who bathed in it. □ **Castalian** *adj.*

Ca·stel·lam·ma·re di Sta·bia |käs,telə-'märä dē 'stäbyə| fortified seaport in S Italy, on the Bay of Naples. Pop. 69,000.

Cas·tel Gan·dol·fo |,käs,tel gän'dawlfō| the summer residence of the pope, situated on the edge of Lake Albano near Rome.

Cas·tel·li Ro·ma·ni |käs,telē rō'mänē| region in the Alban Hills E of Rome, central Italy. The region is known for its vineyards and for the numerous castles belonging to popes and wealthy Italian families, including Castel Gandolfo.

Cas·tel·lón de la Pla·na |kästə(l)'yōn də lä 'plänə| seaport and industrial city in E Spain, on the Mediterranean Sea, and capital of Castellón province. Pop. 137,000.

Cas·ter·bridge |'kæstər,brij| name given by Thomas Hardy in his novels to DORCH-ESTER[1], the county seat of Dorset, SW England.

Cas·tile |kæ'stēl| region of central Spain, on the central plateau of the Iberian Peninsula, formerly an independent Spanish kingdom. The marriage of Isabella of Castile to Ferdinand of Aragon in 1469 linked these two powerful kingdoms and led eventually to the unification of Spain. □ **Castilian** *adj. & n.*

Castilla–La Mancha |kä'stē(l)yə lä 'mänCHə| autonomous region of central Spain. Capital: Toledo.

Castilla-León |kä'stē(l)yə lā'ōn| autonomous region of N Spain. Capital: Valladolid.

Cas·tle·bar |,kæsəl'bär| the county seat of Mayo, in the Republic of Ireland. Pop. 6,070.

Cas·tries |kä'strē; 'kæs,trēs| capitol of the Caribbean island nation of St. Lucia, a seaport on the NW coast. Pop. 14,055.

Cas·tro, the |'kæstrō| popular name for a neighborhood of central San Francisco, California, noted as a center of gay politics and culture.

Castrop-Rauxel |'käs,trawp 'rowksəl| industrial city in the Ruhr district of western Germany. Pop. 79,000.

Cat·a·li·na Island |,kætl'ēnə| see SANTA BARBARA ISLANDS, California.

Cat·a·lo·nia |,kætl'ōnyə| autonomous region of NE Spain. Pop. 6,059,000. Capital: Barcelona. The region has a strong separatist tradition; the normal language for everyday purposes is Catalan, which has also won acceptance in recent years for various official purposes. Catalan name **Catalunya**; Spanish name **Cataluña**.

Cat·a·mar·ca |,kätə'märkə| mining and commercial town in NW Argentina, the capital of Catamarca province. Pop. 110,000.

Ca·ta·nia |kə'tänyə| seaport situated at the foot of Mount Etna, on the E coast of Sicily. Pop. 364,180.

Ca·tan·za·ro |,kätän(d)'zärō| chief town of the Calabria region of S Italy. Pop. 104,000. A commercial center, it is the capital of Catanzaro province.

Ca·taw·ba River |kə'tawbə; kə'täbə| river that flows 300 mi./480 km. from the Blue Ridge Mts. in North Carolina across much of South Carolina.

Ca·thay |kə'THā; kæ'THā| the name by which China was known to medieval Europe. Also called **Khitai**.

Ca·the·dral City |kə'THēdrəl| city in S California, a resort SE of Palm Springs. Pop. 30,085. It takes its name from a local canyon.

Cath·er·ine, Mount |'kæTH(ə)rin| (Arabic name **Jebel Katherina**) mountain at the S end of the Sinai Peninsula, NE Egypt, the highest point in the country: 8,652 ft./2,637 m. A monastery on its slopes is said to be on the site of the burning bush of *Genesis*.

Ca·tons·ville |'kätnz,vil| community in central Maryland, a suburb SW of Baltimore. Pop. 35,233.

Cats·kill Mountains |'kæt,skil| (also **the Catskills**) range of mountains in SE New York, W of the Hudson River, part of the Appalachian system. Among its many resorts are those of the Borscht Belt.

Cau·ca River |'kowkə| river in W Colombia that flows N for 800 mi./1,300 km. from the Andes to the Magdalena River.

Cau·ca·sus |'kawkəsəs| (also **Caucasia**) mountainous region of SE Europe, lying between the Black and the Caspian seas, in Georgia, Armenia, Azerbaijan, and SE Russia. Mount Elbrus, at 18,481 ft./5,642 m., is the highest point. The region has given its name to both language and racial categories. □ **Caucasian** *adj. & n.*

Cau·very River |'kawvərē| (also **Kaveri**) river in S India that flows 475 mi./764 km. from the Western Ghats to the Bay of Bengal. After the Ganges, it is India's most sacred river.

Cav·an |'kævən| **1** county of the NW Republic of Ireland, part of the old province of Ulster. Pop. 53,000. **2** its county seat. Pop. 3,330.

Ca·vi·te |kə'vētē| historic port city in the Philippines, on SW Luzon, SW of Manila. Pop. 92,000.

Caw·dor |'kawdər| village in N Scotland, in the Highlands near Nairn. Cawdor Castle figures in *Macbeth* by Shakespeare.

Cawn·pore |'kawn,pawr| another spelling for KANPUR, India.

Ca·xi·as |kä'sHēəs| commercial city in NE Brazil, on the Itapecuru River in Maranhão state. Pop. 134,000.

Ca·xi·as do Sul |'käsHēəs dōō 'sōol| industrial city in S Brazil, in Rio Grande do Sul state. Pop. 263,000.

Cay·enne |kī'en| the capital and chief port of French Guiana. Pop. 41,600. It gave its name to a type of hot pepper.

Cay·man Islands |'kāmən| (also **the Caymans**) group of three islands in the Caribbean Sea, S of Cuba. Pop. 31,930. Official language, English. Capital: George Town. A resort and financial center, the Caymans are a British dependency.

Cayman Islands

Cay·u·ga, Lake |kə'yōōgə; kā'(y)ōōgə| one of the Finger Lakes, in W central New York. Ithaca lies at its S end.

Ce·a·nan·nus Mor |,sēə'nænəs ,mawr| (also **Kells**) town in E Ireland, in County Meath, the source, in its monastery, of the *Book of Kells*, the famous illuminated gospel manuscript now in Dublin, and given the town's alternate name.

Ce·a·rá |,sāə'rä| state in NE Brazil, on the Atlantic coast. Pop. 6,363,000. Capital: Fortaleza.

Ce·bu |sābōō| **1** island of the S central

Philippines. **2** its chief city and port. Pop. 610,000.

Ce·dar Falls |'sēdər| city in NE Iowa, on the Cedar River. Pop. 34,298.

Ce·dar Ra·pids |'sēdər| industrial and commercial city in E central Iowa, on the Cedar River. Pop. 108,751.

Ce·la·ya |sā'līə| commercial city in W central Mexico, in Guanajuato state, in an agricultural area. Pop. 215,000.

Cel·e·bes |'selə,bēz| former name for SULAWESI, Indonesia.

Cel·e·bes Sea |'selə,bēz| part of the W Pacific between the Philippines and Sulawesi, bounded to the W by Borneo. It is linked to the Java Sea by the Makassar Strait.

Ce·les·tial Empire |sə'lescHəl| old term for CHINA.

Ce·lje |'tselye| spa and industrial town in central Slovenia, on the Savinja River. Pop. 41,000.

Cel·le |'tselə; 'kælə| manufacturing city in N Germany, on the Aller River. Pop. 70,000.

Cel·tic Sea |'keltik; 'seltik| the part of the Atlantic between S Ireland and SW England.

Cen·ten·ni·al State |,sen'tenēəl| nickname for COLORADO.

Cen·tral Af·ri·can Republic |'sentrəl ,æfrikən| republic in the Sahel of central Africa. Area: 241,313 sq. mi./625,000 sq. km. Pop. 3,113,000. Languages: French (official), Sango. Capital and largest city: Bangui. Formerly a French colony, it became a republic in 1958 and fully independent in 1960. Ranging from tropical forest to semidesert, it is essentially agricultural. Former name (until 1958) UBANGHI SHARI. In 1966–79 called the CENTRAL AFRICAN EMPIRE.

Central African Republic

Cen·tral A·me·ri·ca |,sentrəl ə'merəkə| the southernmost part of North America, linking the continent to South America and consisting of the countries of Guatemala, Belize, Honduras, El Salvador, Nicaragua, Costa Rica, and Panama. □ **Central American** *adj. & n.*

Cen·tral Asia |'sentrəl 'āzHə| parts of the Asian land mass generally taken to include regions E of European Russia and W of China; much of the area is vast grasslands (steppes).

Cen·tral Asian States |'sentrəl 'āzHən| association, formed in 1994, of the former Soviet Central Asian republics that are now independent Kazakhstan, Kyrgyzstan, and Uzbekistan.

Cen·tral Eu·rope |'sentrəl 'yŏŏrəp| loosely defined term for parts of Europe W of Eastern Europe, N of Southern Europe, and E of Western Europe, usually taken to include most of Germany, Switzerland, Austria, and sometimes the Czech Republic and parts of Poland.

Cen·tral Park |'sentrəl| large public park in the center of Manhattan, New York City. Created in the 1850s–70s, it was the model for U.S. urban parks.

Cen·tral Valley |'sentrəl| lowland of central California. In the N it is drained by the Sacramento River, and also called the Sacramento Valley. In the S, it is called the San Joaquin Valley after the major river here. It is a significant producer of agricultural products.

Centre |säNtr| region of central France, including departments on the Loire River. Its capital is Orleans.

Ceph·a·lo·nia |ˌsefə'lōnēə| Greek island in the Ionian Sea. Pop. 29,400. Greek name **Kefallinía.**

Ce·ram |'sā,räm| (also **Seram; Serang**) island in E Indonesia, in the central Moluccas. Chief town: Masohi.

Ce·ram Sea |'sā,räm| (also **Seram Sea**) the part of the W Pacific Ocean at the center of the Moluccas Islands.

Ce·ra·sus |'serəsəs| see GIRESUN, Turkey.

Cer·ri·tos |sə'rētəs| city in SW California, a suburb SE of Los Angeles. Pop. 53,240.

Cer·ro de Pas·co |'serō dā 'päskō| mining city in central Peru, in the Andes Mts. at 14,216 ft./4,333 m. Pop. 30,000. Once a key silver source, it today provides vanadium and other metals.

Cer·ro Gor·do |ˌserō 'gawrdō| mountain pass in E Mexico, between Veracruz and Jalapa, scene of an 1847 victory by U.S. forces in the Mexican War.

Cer·ro Ma·ra·vil·la |'serō ˌmärə'vēə| peak in the Cordillera Central of S Puerto Rico, near Ponce, site of a much-debated 1978

incident in which two independence activists were killed.

Cer·tal·do |CHer'täldō| village in central Italy, SW of Florence. Pop. 16,000. It was the childhood home of the poet Boccaccio.

Ce·se·na |CHā'zānə| agricultural and industrial town in N Italy. Pop. 90,000. Its Malatesta Library is one of the oldest monastic libraries extant.

Če·ské Bu·dě·jo·vice |'CHeskā 'bŏŏdyə ˌyawvət,sā| city in the S of the Czech Republic, on the Vltava River. Pop. 173,400. A tourist center, it is also noted for the production of beer. German name **Budweis.**

Ce·ti·nje |'tse,tēnyə| historic town in Montenegro. Pop. 20,000. It was formerly the capital of Montenegro, and is a monastic center.

Ceu·ta |'THā,ŏŏtə; 'sā,ŏŏtə| Spanish exclave, a port and military post on the coast of N Africa, in Morocco. Pop. 67,615.

Cé·vennes |sā,ven| mountain range on the SE edge of the Massif Central in France.

Cey·han |jā'hän| (ancient name **Pyramus**) river that flows 300 mi./480 km. S through central Turkey to the Gulf of Iskenderun in the Mediterranean Sea. The city of **Cey·han** (pop. 85,000) lies on its course.

Cey·lon |si'län; sā'län| former name (until 1972) for SRI LANKA.

Cha·blais |sHā'blā| former region in E France, S of Lake Geneva. It is now part of Haut-Savoie department.

Cha·blis |sHā'blē| village in central France, in Burgundy (Bourgogne), famous for its white wines.

Cha·co |'CHäkō| see GRAN CHACO, South America.

Chad |CHæd| landlocked republic in N central Africa. Area: 495,752 sq. mi./1,284,000 sq. km. Pop. 5,828,000. Official languages: French and Arabic. Capital and largest city: N'Djamena. Independent from France in 1960, Chad is dominated by the Sahara Desert in the N and the Lake Chad watershed, in the Sahel, in the S. Mining, agri-

Chad

culture, and herding are important. □ **Cha-dian** *adj. & n.*

Chad, Lake |CHæd| shallow lake on the borders of Chad, Niger, and Nigeria in N central Africa. Its size varies seasonally from *c.*4,000 sq. mi./10,360 sq. km. to *c.*10,000 sq. mi./25,900 sq. km.

Cha·gos Archipelago |'CHägəs| island group in the Indian Ocean forming the British Indian Ocean Territory.

Chal·ce·don |'kælsə,dän| former city on the Bosporus in Asia Minor, now part of Istanbul, Turkey. The site was quarried for building materials, including chalcedony, during the construction of Constantinople by the Romans. Turkish name **Kadiköy**. □ **Chalcedonian** *adj. & n.*

Chal·cid·i·ce |kæl'sidesē| peninsula in N Greece, with three long headlands extending into the Aegean Sea SE of Thessaloníki.

Chal·cis |'kælsəs; 'kælkəs| the chief town of the island of Euboea, on the coast opposite mainland Greece. Pop. 44,800. Greek name **Khalkís**.

Chal·dea |kæl'dēə| ancient country of the Chaldeans, in what is now S Iraq. □ **Chaldean** *adj. & n.*

Chal·leng·er Deep |'CHælənjər 'dēp| See MARIANA TRENCH, Pacific Ocean.

Châlons-sur-Marne |SHä'lawNSYr,märn| industrial and wine-making city and capital of the Marne department in NE France. Pop. 52,000.

Chalon-sur-Saône manufacturing city in E central France, at the junction of the Saône and Loire rivers. Pop. 56,000.

Cham·bers·burg |'CHämbərz,bərg| historic borough in S Pennsylvania, SW of Harrisburg. Pop. 16,647.

Cham·bé·ry |SHäNbä'rē| commercial and administrative city in Savoie department, in E France. Pop. 55,600.

Cham·bord |SHäN'bawr| village in N central France, in the Loire valley. King Francis I built an immense Renaissance chateau here, sited in an enormous park.

Cha·mi·zal, the |'SHæmə,zæl; ,chämē'säl| district divided between El Paso, Texas, and Ciudad Juarez, Mexico, on the Rio Grande, whose shifts have caused border disputes. Both countries maintain parks here.

Cha·mo·nix |SHämaw'nē| ski resort at the foot of Mont Blanc, in the Alps of E France. Pop. 9,255. Full name **Chamonix-Mont-Blanc**.

Cham·pa |'CHämpə; 'CHæmpə| former independent kingdom (2nd to *c.*14th centuries) in territory now in central and southern Vietnam; home of the Chams, related to Cambodians.

Cham·pagne |SHäN'pän(yə); sham'pän| region and former province of NE France, which now corresponds to the Champagne-Ardenne administrative region. The region is noted for the white sparkling wine first produced there in about 1700.

Champagne-Ardenne |SHäN,pän yär-'den| region in NE France, comprising part of the Ardennes forest and the vine-growing area of Champagne.

Cham·pagne Castle |SHäN'pän| peak in the Drakensberg Range of NE South Africa, the highest in the country: 11,073 ft./3,375 m.

Cham·paign |SHæm'pän| city in E central Illinois, home to the University of Illinois. Pop. 63,502.

Champigny-sur-Marne |SHäNpēn'yē sYr ,märn| residential suburb SE of Paris, on the Marne River. Pop. 80,000. It was a battleground during the Franco-Prussian War.

Cham·plain, Lake |SHæm'plän| glacial lake in North America, to the E of the Adirondack Mts. It forms part of the border between New York and Vermont, and its N tip extends into Quebec. The Champlain Valley is noted for its scenery and history.

Champs Ély·sées |'SHäNz älē'zā| avenue in Paris, leading from the Place de la Concorde to the Arc de Triomphe. It is noted for its fashionable shops and restaurants.

Chan·cel·lors·ville |'CHæns(ə)lərz,vil| historic locality in E central Virginia, W of Fredericksburg, site of a Civil War battle in May 1863.

Chan Chan |'CHän 'CHän| the capital of the pre-Inca civilization of the Chimu. Its extensive adobe ruins are situated on the coast of N Peru.

Chan-chiang |'CHän jē'äNG| see ZHANG-JIANG, China.

Chan·der·na·gore |,CHəndərnə'gôr| (also **Chandanaggar**) town in E India, in West Bengal state, a suburb N of Calcutta. Pop. 122,000.

Chan·di·garh |'CHəndēgər| **1** Union Territory of NW India, created in 1966. **2** city in this territory. Pop. 503,000. The present city was designed in 1950 by Le Corbusier as a new capital for the Punjab and is now the capital of the states of Punjab and Haryana.

Chan·dler |'CHændlər| city in S central Arizona, a suburb and resort SE of Phoenix. Pop. 90,533.

Chan·dra·pur |,CHəndrə'poor| historic

city in central India, in Maharashtra state on the Irar River. Pop. 226,000.

Chang |CHäNG| (also **Ko Chang**) resort island, second-largest in Thailand, in the Gulf of Thailand.

Chang'an |'CHäNG'än| name of XI'AN, China, when it was the capital of the Han (206 B.C.–A.D. 220) and Sui (581–618) dynasties.

Chang·chia·kow |'jäNG'jē'ä'kō| see ZHANGJIAKOU, China.

Chang·chun |'CHäNG'CHŏŏn| industrial city in NE China, capital of Jilin province. Pop. 2,070,000. It is a center of vehicle and machinery production and of technical education.

Chang·de |'CHäNG'də| city and river port in Hunan province, SE central China, on the Yuan River. Pop. 301,000. It is an administrative and light industrial center.

Chang Jiang |'CHäNG jē'äNG| another name for the YANGTZE.

Chang·kia·kow |'jäNGjē'ä 'kō| see ZHANGJIAKOU.

Chang·sha |'CHäNG'SHä| the capital of Hunan province in E central China. Pop. 1,300,000.

Chang·shu |'CHäNG'SHŏŏ| town in Jiangsu province, E China, an industrial port near the mouth of the Yangtze River. Pop. 214,000.

Ch'ang·won |'CHäNG'wän| industrial city in S South Korea, on a bay off the Korea Strait. Pop. 482,000.

Chang·zhi |'CHäNG'jē| city in Shanxi province, E central China, W of Anyang. Pop. 317,000.

Chang·zhou |'CHäNG'jō| city in Jiangsu province, E China, on the Grand Canal N of Shanghai. Pop. 670,000.

Chan·ia |kän'yä| port on the N coast of Crete, capital of the island from 1841 to 1971. Pop. 47,340. Greek name **Khaniá**.

Chan·nel Islands¹ |'CHænl| another name for the SANTA BARBARA ISLANDS, California.

Chan·nel Islands² |'CHænl| group of islands in the English Channel off the NW coast of France, of which the largest are Jersey, Guernsey, and Alderney. Smaller islands include Sark, Herm, and Jethou. Pop. 146,000. Formerly part of the dukedom of Normandy, they have owed allegiance to England since 1066. French name **Îles Anglo-Normandes**.

Chan·nel Tunnel |'CHænl| rail tunnel under the English Channel, extending 31 mi./49 km. and linking England and France. The tunnel (popularly called the

Channel Islands

Chunnel) opened in 1994 after eight years of construction to link Holywell, near Folkestone, England, and Sangatte, near Calais, France.

Chan·til·ly |ˌshäntē'yē| town N of Paris, in N central France. Pop. 10,000. The town is noted for its chateau, which houses the Musée Condéc, a collection of medieval art; its racecourse; its fine lace; and its flavored whipped cream.

Chao·hu |'CHow'hŏŏ| city in Anhui province, E China, on the E shore of Chao Lake (Chao Hu). Pop. 741,000.

Chao Phra·ya |CHow 'prīə| major waterway of central Thailand, formed by the junction of the Ping and Nan rivers.

Chao·yang |'CHow'yäNG| city in Liaoning province, NE China, on the Daling River NE of Beijing. Pop. 328,000.

Cha·pa·la, Lake |CHə'pälə| largest (50 mi./80 km. long) lake in Mexico, in the W central states of Jalisco and Michoacán. It is a resort and fishing center.

Chap·el Hill |'CHæpəl| town in N central North Carolina, home to the University of North Carolina and to many research facilities. Pop. 38,719.

Chap·pa·quid·dick Island |ˌCHæpə-'kwidik| small resort island off the coast of Massachusetts, E of Martha's Vineyard, the scene of a car accident in 1969 involving Senator Edward Kennedy in which his assistant Mary Jo Kopechne drowned.

Cha·pul·te·pec |CHə'pŏŏltə,pek| hill ("Grasshopper Hill") in the major park of Mexico City, Mexico. It is the ancient seat of Aztec emperors, and is surmounted by a castle that was captured by U.S. forces in September 1847.

Cha·rente |shä'räNt| river of W France, which rises in the Massif Central and flows 225 mi./360 km. W to enter the Bay of Biscay at Rochefort.

Cha·ri River |shä'rē| (also **Shari**) river that flows 660 mi./1,060 km. through the Central African Republic, Chad, and Cameroon. Emptying into Lake Chad, it is the longest river in the African continent that drains internally.

Cha·ri·kar |CHÄrē'kär| city in NE Afghanistan, in the Hindu Kush Mts., N of Kabul. Pop. 100,000.

Char·ing Cross |,CHæriNG 'kraws| district in central London, England, in the borough of Westminster, just SE of Trafalgar Square. Distances from London are measured from Charing Cross.

Char·jew |CHär'jōō| (also **Chardzhou** or **Charjui**) commercial city in E Turkmenistan, on the Amu Darya River. Pop. 166,000. It is a cotton-trade center.

Char·le·roi |,sHärlə'(r)wä| industrial city in SW Belgium. Pop. 206,200.

Charles·bourg |sHärl'bōōr| city in S Quebec, a suburb just NE of Quebec City. Pop. 70,788.

Charles River |CHärlz| river that flows 60 mi./100 km. through E Massachusetts, between Cambridge and Boston, to Boston Harbor.

Charles·ton[1] |'CHärlstən| historic port city in South Carolina, on the Ashley and Cooper rivers. Pop. 80,410. The bombardment in 1861 of Fort Sumter, in the harbor, by Confederate troops marked the beginning of the Civil War. Charleston is a commercial city and a center of tourism.

Charles·ton[2] |'CHärlstən| the state capital of West Virginia, an industrial city on the Kanawha River. Pop. 57,290.

Charles·town[1] |'CHärlz,town| neighborhood of N Boston, Massachusetts, N of the Charles River. Bunker Hill is here.

Charles·town[2] |'CHärlz,town| chief town of Nevis, in the federation of St. Kitts and Nevis, in the West Indies. Pop. 1,700. It is a port linked with Basseterre, on St. Kitts.

Char·lotte |'sHärlət| commercial city in S North Carolina, a major banking and financial center. Pop. 395,930.

Char·lotte Ama·lie |'sHärlət ə'mälyə| the capital of the U.S. Virgin Islands, a resort hub and port on the island of St. Thomas. Pop. 52,660.

Char·lottes·ville |'sHärləts,vil; 'sHärlətsvəl| city in central Virginia, in the Blue Ridge Mts., home to the University of Virginia. Pop. 40,341. Monticello, the home of Thomas Jefferson, is nearby.

Char·lotte·town |'sHärlət,town| the capital and chief port of Prince Edward Island. Pop. 33,150.

Char·tres |'sHärt(rə)| city in N France.

Pop. 41,850. It is noted for its huge Gothic cathedral.

Char·treuse |sHär'trœz| (also **La Grande Chartreuse**) mountainous region in SE France. Its famous green and yellow liqueurs were first made in the monastery of La Grande Chartreuse, near Grenoble.

Cha·ryb·dis |kə'ribdes| in Greek mythology, a female monster thrown into the sea by Zeus. She landed across from Scylla and spewed out water, creating a whirlpool later identified with Galofalo, in the Strait of Messina, Sicily.

Cha·teau·guay |'sHætəgē; 'sHætə,gā| city in S Quebec, a suburb SW of Montreal. Pop. 39,833.

Cha·teau·roux |sHätō'rōō| industrial city and capital of the department of Indre in N France, on the Indre River. Pop. 53,000.

Chateau-Thierry |sHæ,tō tye'rē| town in the Picardy region of N France, on the Marne River. Pop. 15,000. It was a major battlefield during World War I; there is a monument to the U.S. soldiers who took the town from German occupiers in 1918, and a military cemetery.

Chat·ham[1] |'CHætəm| port town in SE England, on the Medway River E of London, in Kent. Pop. 65,000. It was long a major naval base.

Chat·ham[2] |'CHætəm| city in S Ontario, E of Detroit, Michigan. Pop. 43,557.

Chat·ham Islands |'CHætəm| group of two islands, Pitt and Chatham islands, in the SW Pacific to the E of New Zealand, to which they belong.

Chats·worth |'CHæts,wərTH| estate, the seat of the Dukes of Devonshire, in N Derbyshire, N central England. It is one of the most famous and frequently visited British great houses.

Chat·ta·hoo·chee River |,CHætə'hōō-CHē| river that flows 435 mi./700 km. through Georgia, to the Florida border, where it continues as the Apalachicola River, into the Gulf of Mexico.

Chat·ta·noo·ga |,CHætn'ōōgə| city in SE Tennessee, on the Tennessee River near the Georgia border, a rail and industrial center. Pop. 152,466.

Chau·bu·na·gun·ga·maug, Lake |CHaw-,bənə'gəNGgə,mawg| small lake in S Massachusetts, S of Worcester, in the town of Webster. The full form of its name, Chargoggagoggmanchaugagoggchaubunagungamaugg, is said to be the longest American place name.

Chau·diere River |sHōd'yer| river that flows 120 mi./190 km. from the Maine border N through Quebec, emptying into the Saint Lawrence River opposite Quebec City.

Chau·mont |sHō'mawN| manufacturing town and capital of the department of Haute-Marne in NE France. Pop. 29,000. Chaumont served as the headquarters of the U.S. Expeditionary Force in World War I.

Chau·tau·qua |sHə'tawkwə| resort town in SW New York, on Chautauqua Lake, famed as the birthplace of a 19th-century popular education movement. Pop. 4,554.

Cha·vin de Huán·tar |CHə'vēn dä 'wän- ˌtär| agricultural town in W central Peru near which are major pre-Columbian ruins, left by the pre-Inca Chavin culture of 3,000 years ago.

Chea·dle |'CHēdl| (official name **Cheadle and Gatley**) industrial town in NW England, in Greater Manchester. Pop. 60,000.

Cheap·side |'CHēp,sīd| historic commercial district in the city of London, England, near St. Paul's Cathedral.

Che·bo·ksa·ry |ˌCHebäk'särē| city in W central Russia, on the Volga River, W of Kazan, capital of the autonomous republic of Chuvashia. Pop. 429,000.

Chech·nya |'CHECHnēə| (also **Chechenia**) autonomous republic in the Caucasus in SW Russia, on the border with Georgia. Pop. 1,290,000. Capital: Grozny. The republic declared itself independent of Russia in 1991; Russian troops invaded in 1994, but withdrew after the signing of a peace treaty in 1996. Also called **Chechen Republic**. □ **Chechen** *adj. & n.*

Ched·dar |'CHedər| village in Somerset, SW England, that gave its name to the type of cheese. It is a center for tourists, especially those visiting nearby Cheddar Gorge in the Mendip Hills.

Cheek·to·wa·ga |ˌCHēktə'wägə| town in W New York, an industrial suburb E of Buffalo. Pop. 99,314.

Che·foo |'jə'fōō| see YANTAI, China.

Che·ju |'CHä'jōō| **1** island province of South Korea, S of the mainland in the North China Sea. Pop. 505,000. **2** its capital, a fishing port. Pop. 259,000.

Che·kiang |'jəjē'äNG| see ZHEJIANG, China.

Che·lan, Lake |sHə'læn| recreational lake in N central Washington, in the Cascade Mts.

Chelles |sHel| town in N France on the Marne River. The dating of prehistoric remains found here led to the designation

"Chellean period" for that epoch in prehistory.

Chelm |KHelm; helm| industrial city in E Poland, the capital of Chelm county. Pop. 66,000.

Chelm·no |KHelmnō; helmnō| **1** industrial city in N central Poland, in the Vistula River valley. Pop. 22,000. **2** site of a Nazi concentration camp near Łodz, Poland.

Chelms·ford |'CHelmsfərd| cathedral city in SE England, the county seat of Essex. Pop. 152,418.

Chel·sea[1] |'CHelsē| fashionable residential district of London, England, on the N bank of the Thames River. The Kings Road here was a center of "Swinging London" of the 1960s.

Chel·sea[2] |'CHelsē| industrial and commercial city in NE Massachusetts, just N of Boston. Pop. 28,710.

Chel·sea[3] |'CHelsē| fashionable residential section of S Manhattan, New York City, on the West Side.

Chel·ten·ham |'CHeltn,əm| town in W England, in Gloucestershire. Pop. 85,900. It became a fashionable spa in the 19th century.

Chel·ya·binsk |&chel'yäbinsk| industrial city in S Russia, in a mining district on the E slopes of the Ural Mts. Pop. 1,148,000.

Chem·nitz |'kemnits| industrial city in eastern Germany, on the Chemnitz River. Pop. 310,000. Former name (1953–90) **Karl-Marx-Stadt**.

Che·nab |CHə'näb| river of N India and Pakistan, which rises in the Himalayas and flows through Himachal Pradesh and Jammu and Kashmir, to join the Sutlej River in Punjab. It is one of the five rivers that gave Punjab its name.

Chen-chiang |'jənjē'äNG| see ZHENJIANG, China.

Cheng·chow |'jəNG'jō| see ZHENGZHOU, China.

Cheng·de |'CHəNG'də| city in Hebei province, N China, on the Luan River. Pop. 247,000. It was the summer capital of the Manchu emperors.

Cheng·du |'CHəNG'dōō| the capital of Sichuan province in W central China. Pop. 2,780,000.

Che·non·ceaux |sHənawN'sō| village in W central France, on the Cher River. It is famous for its romantic Renaissance chateau, whose arches span the Cher. During World War II the line separating occupied France from Vichy France ran through the Cher and thus through the chateau itself.

Cheq·uers |'CHekərz| estate in Buckinghamshire, central England, NW of London, since 1917 a country retreat for the British prime minister.

Cher |'SHer| river in central France, which rises in the Massif Central, flowing 220 mi./350 km. N to meet the Loire near Tours.

Cher·bourg |SHer'boŏr; 'SHer,boŏrg| seaport and naval base in Normandy, N France, formerly a key transatlantic harbor. Pop. 28,770.

Che·re·po·vets |,CHirəpə'vyets| industrial city in NW Russia, on the Rybinsk reservoir. Pop. 313,000.

Cher·ka·sy |CHir'käsē| port in central Ukraine, on the Dnieper River. Pop. 297,000. Russian name **Cherkassy**.

Cher·kessk |CHir'kesk| city in the Caucasus in S Russia, capital of the republic of Karachai-Cherkessia. Pop. 113,000.

Cher·ni·hiv |CHir'nēiv| port in N Ukraine, on the Desna River. Pop. 301,000. Russian name **Chernigov**.

Cher·niv·tsi |CHirnift'sē| city in W Ukraine, in the foothills of the Carpathians, close to the border with Romania; the economic hub of Bukovina. Pop. 257,000. It was part of Romania between 1918 and 1940. Russian name **Chernovtsy**; Romanian name **Cernăuţi**; German name **Czernowitz**.

Cher·no·byl |CHər'nōbəl| town near Kiev in Ukraine where, in April 1986, an accident at a nuclear power plant resulted in a serious escape of radioactive material and the subsequent contamination of parts of what are now Ukraine and Belarus, as well as other parts of Europe.

Cher·no·zem |,CHirnə'zHawm| semiarid regions in S Russia and N Kazakhstan that take their name from their fertile black soil, rich in humus. Also **Black Earth regions**.

Cher·ra·pun·ji |CHərə'poŏnjē| (also **Cherrapunjee**) commercial town in NE India, in Meghalaya state, on the S slope of the Khasi Hills. It is reputedly the wettest inhabited place in the world, with an average annual rainfall of 450 in./1,100 cm.

Cher·ry Hill |'CHerē| township in SW New Jersey, a suburb SE of Philadelphia, Pennsylvania. Pop. 69,359.

Cher·so·nese |'kərsə,nēz| ancient name for the Gallipoli Peninsula in Turkey. The name is also applied to other peninsulas, including the Crimea and the Malay Peninsula (the **Golden Chersonese**).

Ches·a·peake |'CHesə,pēk| port city in central Virginia, in the Hampton Roads area. Pop. 151,976.

Ches·a·peake Bay |'CHesə,pēk| large inlet of the North Atlantic on the E U.S. coast, extending 200 mi./320 km. inland through the states of Virginia and Maryland, and famed for the richness of its marine life.

Chesh·ire |'CHesHər; 'CHes,ir| county of W central England; county seat, Chester.

Che·sil Beach |'CHezəl| (also **Chesil Bank**) a shingle beach in S England, off the Dorset coast.

Ches·ter[1] |'CHestər| historic city in W England, the county seat of Cheshire. Pop. 115,000.

Ches·ter[2] |'CHestər| city in SE Pennsylvania, on the Delaware River SW of Philadelphia. Pop. 41,856.

Ches·ter·field[1] |'CHestər,fēld| industrial town in Derbyshire, central England. Pop. 99,700.

Ches·ter·field[2] |'CHestər,fēld| city in E central Missouri, a suburb W of St. Louis. Pop. 37,991.

Chest·nut Hill[1] |'CHes,nət| affluent suburban area W of Boston, Massachusetts, partly in Brookline, partly in Newton.

Chest·nut Hill[2] |'CHes,nət| affluent residential section of N Philadelphia, Pennsylvania.

Che·tu·mal |,CHätoŏ'mäl| port in SE Mexico, on the Yucatán Peninsula at the border with Belize, capital of the state of Quintana Roo. Pop. 40,000.

Chev·i·ot Hills |'CHevēət; 'CHēvēət| (also **the Cheviots**) a range of hills on the border between England and Scotland.

Chevy Chase[1] |'CHevē 'CHās| see OTTERBURN, England.

Chevy Chase[2] |'CHevē 'CHās| fashionable suburb N of Washington, D.C., in Montgomery County, Maryland. Pop. 8,559.

Chey·enne |SHī'æn; SHī'en| commercial city, the capital of Wyoming, in the SE. Pop. 50,008. Government, cattle, and tourism are central to its economy.

Chey·enne River |SHī'æn; SHī'en| river that flows 530 mi./850 km. from NE Wyoming into W South Dakota, joining the Missouri River at Lake Oahe.

Chiai |CHēä'ē| (also **Chia-i**) city, W Taiwan, a distribution center for agricultural products from the surrounding region. Pop. 259,000.

Chiang·mai |CHē'äNG'mī| city in NW Thailand. Pop. 164,900.

Chi·an·ti |kē'äntē| region in Tuscany, in central Italy, NW of Siena, noted for its dry red wine.

Chi·a·pas |CHē'äpəs| state of S Mexico, bordering Guatemala. Area: 28,664 sq.

mi./74,211 sq. km. Pop. 3,204,000. Capital: Tuxtla Gutiérrez. Heavily Indian in population, Chiapas has long struggled with poverty and chafed at Mexican government control.

Chi•ba |ˈCHēbə| industrial city in Japan, on the island of Honshu, E of Tokyo. Pop. 829,470.

Chi•ca•go |SHəˈkägō; SHeˈkawgō| city in Illinois, on Lake Michigan. Pop. 2,783,730. Selected as a terminal for the Illinois and Michigan canal (1848), and for railroads to the E (1852), Chicago developed during the 19th century as a major grain market and food-processing center. It is the third-largest city in the U.S., and a major center of commerce, industry, culture, and education. □ **Chicagoan** *adj.* & *n.*

Chi•chén It•zá |CHiˈCHen ētˈsä| site in central Yucatán, SE Mexico, a center of the Mayan empire until around the year 1200. Its pyramids, wells, temples, and other structures have been partly restored.

Chich•es•ter |ˈCHiCHəstər| city in S England, the county seat of West Sussex. Pop. 27,200.

Chick•a•mau•ga Creek |ˌCHikəˈmawgə| stream that flows from NW Georgia into the Tennessee River, near Chattanooga, Tennessee. A brutal Civil War battle was fought along it in September 1863.

Chi•cla•yo |CHēˈklīyō| commercial city in NW Peru, between the Andes and the Pacific, in an irrigated desert area. Pop. 426,000.

Chi•co |ˈCHēkō| city in N California, at the N end of the Sacramento Valley. Pop. 40,079.

Chic•o•pee |ˈCHikə,pē| city in S central Massachusetts, an industrial center on the N side of Springfield. Pop. 56,632.

Chi•cou•ti•mi |SHiˈkōōtəmē| industrial city in SE Quebec, on the Saguenay River N of Quebec City. Pop. 62,670.

Chiem, Lake |kēm| in S Germany, SE of Munich, in a resort area. It is the largest lake in Bavaria (31 sq. mi./81 sq. km.).

Chie•ti |kēˈetē| commercial town in central Italy on the Pescara River and capital of Chieti province. Pop. 57,000.

Chi•feng |ˈCHərˈfəNG| (Mongolian name **Ulanhad**) city, Inner Mongolia, NE China. Pop. 392,000. It is a distribution center for agricultural products from the surrounding region.

Chi•ga•sa•ki |ˌCHēgäˈsäkē| resort and industrial city in E central Japan, on central Honshu. Pop. 202,000.

Chih•li, Gulf of |ˈjirˈli; ˈCHēˈlē| see BO HAI, China.

Chi•hua•hua |CHəˈwäwə| **1** largest state of Mexico, in the N, bordering Texas and New Mexico. Area: 94,607 sq. mi./244,938 sq. km. Pop. 2,440,000. **2** its capital, the principal city of N central Mexico. Pop. 530,490.

Chile |ˈCHēlə; ˈCHilē| republic occupying a long Pacific coastal strip in SW South America. Area: 292,132 sq. mi./756,622 sq. km. Pop. 13,232,000. Capital and largest city: Santiago. Language, Spanish. Part of the Inca empire, the country achieved independence from Spanish Peru in 1818. Much of the N is the mineral-rich Atacama Desert. In the S, grazing lands and forest predominate. Mining, agriculture, and fishing are important. □ **Chilean** *adj.* & *n.*

Chile

Chil•lán |CHēˈyän| commercial city in S central Chile, in a rich agricultural valley NE of Concepción. Pop. 146,000.

Chil•li•cothe |ˌCHiləˈkäTHē; ˌCHiləˈkawTHē| historic city in S central Ohio, an early capital of the state. Pop. 21,921.

Chil•lon |SHēˈyawN| castle in Vaud, W Switzerland, at the E end of Lake Geneva. The Swiss patriot François Bonivard, hero of Byron's poem *The Prisoner of Chillon*, was kept here.

Chil•pan•cin•go |ˌCHēlpänˈsingō| city in SW Mexico, capital of the state of Guerrero. Pop. 120,000.

Chil•tern Hills |ˈCHiltərn| (also **the Chilterns**) range of chalk hills in S England, N of the Thames River and W of London.

Chi•lung |ˈjēˈlōōNG| (also **Chi-lung**; also called **Keelung**) chief port and naval base of Taiwan, at the N tip of the island. Pop. 357,000. Shipbuilding, fishing, and chemicals are important industries.

Chim•bo•ra•zo |ˌCHimbəˈräzō| the highest Andean peak in Ecuador, rising to 20,487 ft./6,310 m.

Chim·bo·te |CHĕm'bō,tā| industrial port city in W central Peru, on the Pacific N of Lima. Pop. 297,000. It is a major fishing center.

Chim·kent |SHim'kent| see SHYMKENT, Kazakhstan.

Chi·na |'CHīnə| country in E Asia, the third-largest and most populous in the world. Area: 3.7 million sq. mi./9.6 million sq. km. Pop. 1,151,200,000. Language, Chinese (Mandarin is official). Capital: Beijing. Largest city: Shanghai. Official name **People's Republic of China**. One of the oldest known cultures, China has been a republic since 1912, and a communist state since 1949. Almost all its people live in the E third of the country, the W being mostly arid and mountainous. Agriculture, mining, and manufacturing are all important. □ **Chinese** *adj. & n.*

Chi·na, Republic of |'CHīnə| official name for TAIWAN.

Chi·na Sea |'CHīnə| the part of the Pacific Ocean off the coast of China, divided at the island of Taiwan into the *East China Sea* at the N and the *South China Sea* at the S.

Chi·na·town |'CHīnə,town| generic term for a Chinese-dominated commercial district in any of various U.S. or Canadian cities. Noted examples are in San Francisco, New York, and Vancouver.

Chin·co·teague Island |'SHiNGkə,tēg; 'CHiNGkə,tēg| island in E Virginia, W of Assateague Island and noted for its wild horses and much visited.

Chin·dwin |'CHin'dwin| river that rises in northern Burma and flows southwards for 500 mi./885 km. to meet the Irrawaddy.

Chin Hills |CHin| range of hills in W Burma, close to the borders with India and Bangladesh.

Chin·ju |'jin'jōō| commercial and industrial city in S South Korea. Pop. 330,000.

Chin·kiang |'jin'jäNG| see ZHENJIANG, China.

Chi·no |'CHēnō| city in SW California, an outer suburb E of Los Angeles. Pop. 59,682.

Chi·non |SHē'nawN| medieval town in W central France, in the Loire valley. Pop. 9,000. It is dominated by the ruins of its chateau, where Joan of Arc first presented herself to the Dauphin of France. The town produces fine wines.

Chi·nook Belt |SHə'nŏŏk; CHə'nŏŏk| term

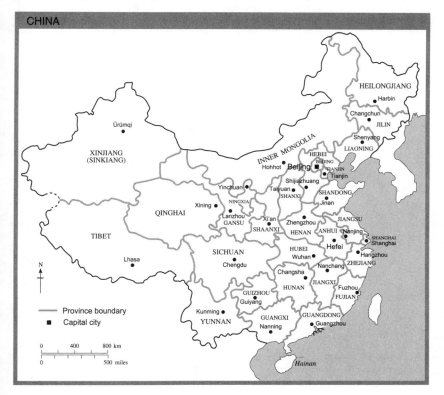

CHINA

for region of the U.S. and Canada just E of the Rocky Mts., where warm *chinook* winds mitigate winter cold.

Chi•os |ˈkē͵äs| Greek island in the Aegean Sea. Pop. 52,690. Greek name **Khios**. □ **Chian** *adj. & n.*

Chi•pa•ta |CHēˈpätə| (formerly **Fort Jameson**) commercial town in E Zambia, near the Malawi border. Pop. 146,000.

Chir•chik |CHirˈCHēk| (also **Chirciq**) industrial city in NE Uzbekistan, NE of Tashkent. Pop. 157,000.

Chi•ri•ca•hua Mountains |͵CHiriˈkäwə| range in SE Arizona, on the Mexican border, noted in the 19th century as controlled by Cochise and other Apache leaders.

Chis•holm Trail |ˈCHisəm| historic route over which 19th-century cowboys drove cattle 1,500 mi./2,400 km. N from Texas to Abilene and other Kansas cities reached by developing railroads.

Chi•și•năŭ |͵kēsHəˈnow| the capital and largest city of Moldova. Pop. 665,000. Russian name **Kishinyov** or **Kishinev**.

Chis•wick |ˈCHizik| largely residential district of W London, England, N of the Thames River in the borough of Hounslow. It is associated with Alexander Pope, William Morris, and other cultural figures.

Chi•ta |CHiˈtä| city in SE Siberia, Russia, on the Trans-Siberian Railway. Pop. 349,000.

Chit•ta•gong |ˈCHitə͵gawNG| seaport in SE Bangladesh, on the Bay of Bengal. Pop. 1,566,070.

Chi•tun•gwi•za |͵CHētoͦoNGˈgwēzə| city in NE Zimbabwe, a suburb SE of Harare. Pop. 274,000.

Chka•lov |CHəˈkäləf| former name (1938–57) for ORENBURG, Russia.

Cho•be |ˈCHōbə| district of N Botswana, site of a national park noted for its wildlife.

Cho•fu |ˈCHō͵foͦo| city in E central Japan, on E central Honshu, a residential and industrial suburb of Tokyo. Pop. 198,000.

Choi•seul |sHwäˈzœl| volcanic island in the Solomon Islands, E of Bougainville, a scene of fighting in World War II.

Choi•sy |sHwäˈzē| (full name **Choisy-le-Roi**) commune, an industrial SE suburb of Paris, France. Pop. 38,000.

Cho•lon |ˈCHōˈlawn| industrial and commercial district of Ho Chi Minh City, Vietnam. It was an important port before Saigon developed, and has long been heavily Chinese.

Cho•lu•la |CHōˈloͦolə| (official name **Cholula de Rivadabia**) city in Puebla state, E central Mexico. Pop. 54,000. It is

famed for its Aztec pyramids, churches, and other historic sites.

Chong•jin |ˈCHəNGˈjin| industrial port city on the NE coast of North Korea. Pop. 754,100.

Chong•ju |ˈCHəNGˈjoͦo| commercial and industrial city in W central South Korea, capital of N Chungchong province. Pop. 531,000.

Chong•qing |ˈCHoͦoNGˈCHiNG; ˈCHoͦoNGˈkiNG| (formerly **Chungking**) industrial city in Sichuan province, central China, on the Yangtze River. It produces steel, chemicals, textiles, and motorcycles. It was the capital of China from 1938 to 1945.

Chon•ju |ˈCHənˈjoͦo| commercial and industrial city in SW South Korea, capital of N Cholla province, in the heart of a rice-producing region. Pop. 563,000.

Cho Oyu |ˈCHō ōˈyoͦo| peak in the Himalayas, on the Nepal-Tibet border, first climbed in 1954. 26,750 ft./8,150 m.

Chor•ril•los |CHōˈrē-ōs| town in W central Peru, a resort and suburb S of Lima. Pop. 213,000.

Cho•rzów |ˈkō͵zHoͦof| transportation and industrial center in S Poland. Pop. 133,000. It is in a mining region.

Chotts |sHäts| term, from the Arabic, for saline lakes, especially in Algeria and Tunisia. Their vicinity is used for herding.

Christ•church |ˈkrīs͵CHərCH| commercial city, the largest on South Island, New Zealand. Pop. 303,400.

Chris•ti•a•nia |͵krisCHēˈænēə; ͵kristēˈænēə| (also **Kristiania**) former name (1624–1924) for OSLO, Norway.

Chris•tian•sted |ˈkrisCHən͵sted| resort town on Saint Croix Island in the U.S. Virgin Islands, once the capital of the Danish West Indies. Pop. 2,555.

Christ•mas Island[1] |ˈkrisməs| island in the Indian Ocean 200 mi./350 km. S of Java, administered as an external territory of Australia since 1958. Pop. 1,275.

Christ•mas Island[2] |ˈkrisməs| former name (until 1981) for KIRITIMATI, Kiribati.

Chu•bu |ˈCHoͦoˈboͦo| mountainous region of Japan, on the island of Honshu. Capital: Nagoya.

Chu•gach Mountains |ˈCHoͦo͵gæCH; ˈCHoͦo͵gæsH| range of mountains, part of the Coast Ranges, in S Alaska. Anchorage lies at its feet, and it is noted for glaciers that flow S into the Gulf of Alaska.

Chu•go•ku |CHoͦoˈgōkoͦo| region of Japan, on the island of Honshu. Capital: Hiroshima.

Chuk•chi Sea |ˈCHoͦokCHē; ˈCHəkCHē| part

of the Arctic Ocean lying between North America and Asia and to the N of the Bering Strait.

Chu·la Vis·ta |ˌCHo͞olə 'vistə| city in SW California, S of San Diego and near the Mexican border. Pop. 135,163.

Chun·chon |'CHo͞on'CHən| industrial city in NE South Korea, the capital of Kangwon province. Pop. 179,000.

Chung·king |CHəNG'kiNG| see CHONGQING, China.

Chung-shan |'jo͞oNG'SHän| see ZHONGSHAN, China.

Chu·qui·sa·ca |ˌCHo͞oke͞e'säkə| former name (1539–1840) for SUCRE, Bolivia.

Church·ill |'CHərCHəl; 'CHər,CHil| settlement in NE Manitoba, a warm-weather port on Hudson Bay. Pop. 1,143.

Church·ill Downs |'CHər,CHil; 'CHərCHəl| horse-racing facility in Louisville, Kentucky, site of the annual Kentucky Derby.

Church·ill River[1] |'CHərCHəl; 'CHər,CHil| river that flows 600 mi./1,000 km. from the Canadian Shield across E Labrador to the Labrador Sea. Its high falls generate hydroelectric power. It was formerly called the Hamilton River.

Church·ill River[2] |'CHərCHəl; 'CHər,CHil| river that flows 1,000 mi./1,600 km. from N Saskatchewan across Manitoba to Hudson Bay at Churchill. It was important in the early fur trade.

Chu·va·shia |CHo͞o'väSHēə| autonomous republic in European Russia, E of Nizhni Novgorod. Pop. 1,340,000. Capital: Cheboksary. □ **Chuvash** *adj. & n.*

Chu·xiong |'CHo͞oSHe'awNG| city in Yunnan province, S China, W of Kunming on a tributary of the Jinsha River. Pop 383,000.

Chu·zhou |'CHo͞o'jō| city in Anhui province, E China, NW of Nanjing. Pop. 370,000.

Ci·bo·la |'sibələ| legendary land of wealth, sometimes seven cities of gold, that enticed early Spanish explorers in the SW U.S. The name survives in various localities.

Cic·ero |'sisə,rō| town in NE Illinois, an industrial and residential suburb just W of Chicago. Pop. 67,436.

Cien·fue·gos |ˌsē-en'fwägōs| port city in S central Cuba, on Cienfuegos Bay in the Caribbean Sea, the capital of Cienfuegos province. Pop. 124,000.

Ci·li·cia |sə'liSHə| ancient region on the coast of SE Asia Minor, corresponding to the present-day province of Adana, Turkey. □ **Cilician** *adj. & n.*

Ci·li·cian Gates |se'liSHən| mountain pass in the Taurus Mts. of S Turkey, historically

forming part of a route linking Anatolia with the Mediterranean coast.

Cim·ar·ron River |'simə,rän; 'simə,rōn| river that flows 600 mi./1,000 km. from New Mexico across Oklahoma to the Arkansas River near Tulsa. The W Panhandle of Oklahoma was once known as the Territory of Cimarron.

Cim·me·ri·an Bos·po·rus |sə'mirēən 'bäspərəs| historical name for the Kerch Strait, which links the Sea of Azov and the Black Sea at the E of the Crimean Peninsula of the Ukraine. The Cimmerians, peoples from this region, overran Asia Minor (present-day Turkey) in the 7th century B.C.

Cim·pu·lung |ˌkimpə'lo͞oNG| commercial and resort town in central Romania, on the S slopes of the Transylvanian Alps. Pop. 40,000.

Cin·cin·nati |ˌsinsə'nætē| industrial city in SW Ohio, a port on the Ohio River. Pop. 364,000.

Cinque Ports |'siNGk 'pawrts| group of medieval ports in Kent and East Sussex, SE England, which were formerly allowed trading privileges in exchange for providing the bulk of England's navy. The five original Cinque Ports were Hastings, Sandwich, Dover, Romney, and Hythe; later Rye and Winchelsea were added.

Ci·pan·go |si'pæNGgō| (also **Zipango**) medieval name given to an island described by Marco Polo and thought to be Japan.

Cir·cas·sia |sər'kæSHə| historic region covering the area between the Black Sea, the Kuban River, and the Caucasus Mts., and roughly equivalent to the Krasnodar Territory in present-day SE Russia. □ **Circassian** *adj. & n.*

Cir·cum·po·lar regions |ˌsərkəm'pōlər| term for regions near or around a pole, used especially in describing areas and related peoples, such as the Inuit, of N Asia and N North America.

Ci·re·bon |'CHēre'bawn| industrial port city in Indonesia, on the N coast of W Java. Pop. 254,000.

Ci·ren·ces·ter |'sīren,sestər; 'sisitər| town in Gloucestershire, SW England. Pop. 14,000. It was a major town in Roman Britain, when it was known as Corinium Dobunorum.

Cis·al·pine Gaul |sis'æl,pīn 'gawl| see GAUL.

Cis·at·lan·tic |ˌsisət'læn(t)ik| on one's own side of the Atlantic; a term used chiefly by Europeans.

Cis·kei |'sis,kī| former homeland established in South Africa for the Xhosa people, now part of the province of Eastern Cape.

Ci•teaux |sē'tō| (Latin name **Cistercium**) village in E France, about 16 mi./26 km. SE of Dijon. The Cistercian order of Roman Catholic monks was founded here in 1098.

Ci•thae•ron |sə'THērən| (also **Kithairon**) mountain in Greece (4,623 ft./1,409 m.). It is the site of many events in Greek mythology.

Cities of the Plain see SODOM.

Ci•ti•um |'sēsH(ē)əm| (also called **Cition;** biblical name **Kittim** or **Chittim**) ancient city of SE Cyprus, on the site of present-day Larnaca. It was a Phoenician and Assyrian center.

Ci•tlal•té•petl |sēt,läl'tä,petl| the highest peak in Mexico, in the E of the country, N of the city of Orizaba. It rises to a height of 18,503 ft./5,699 m. and is an extinct volcano. Spanish name **Pico de Orizaba**. The name is from the Aztec and literally means 'star mountain.'

Cit•rus Heights |'sitrəs| community in N central California, a suburb NE of Sacramento. Pop. 107,439.

City of Lon•don |'ləndən| the part of London, England, within the ancient city boundaries and governed by the Lord Mayor and Corporation. It is noted as Britain's chief financial district. Also referred to as **the City**.

Ciu•dad Bo•lí•var |syōō'däd bō'lē,vär| city in E Venezuela, a port on the Orinoco River. Pop. 225,850. Formerly called Angostura, it was renamed in 1846 to honor the country's liberator, Simón Bolívar.

Ciu•dad del Es•te |syōō'däd del 'estä| port city in SE Paraguay, on the Paraná River, near the Itaipu Dam. Pop. 134,000. Before 1989 it was called **Puerto Presidente Stroessner.**

Ciu•dad Gua•ya•na |syōō'däd gī'änə| (also **Santo Tomé de Guayana**) industrial city in E Venezuela, at the junction of the Caroní and Orinoco rivers. Pop. 543,000. It is a steel- and aluminum-producing center.

Ciu•dad Juá•rez |syōō'däd 'hwäres| (also **Juárez**) commercial and industrial city in Chihuahua state, N Mexico, across the Rio Grande from El Paso, Texas. Pop. 790,000.

Ciu•dad Ma•de•ro |syōō'däd mə'därō| city in E Mexico, a suburb and oil industry center just N of Tampico, in the state of Tamaulipas. Pop. 160,000.

Ciu•dad Obre•gón |syōō'däd ,ōbrā'gōn| commercial city in Sonora state, NW Mexico, in an irrigated farming district. Pop. 160,000.

Ciu•dad Re•al |syōō'däd rā'äl| agricultural market town in central Spain, between the Guadiana and Jablón rivers, and capital of Ciudad Real province. Pop. 475,000.

Ciu•dad Tru•jil•lo |syōō'däd trōō'hēyō| former name (1936–61) for SANTO DOMINGO, Dominican Republic.

Ciu•dad Vic•to•ria |syōō'däd vēk'tōryə| city in NE Mexico, capital of the state of Tamaulipas. Pop. 207,830.

Ci•vi•ta•vec•chia |,CHēvētə'vekēə| port on the W central coast of Italy, on the Tyrrhenian Sea. Pop. 51,000. Originally built as the chief port for Rome, it still serves in that role.

Clack•man•nan |klæk'mænən| (also **Clackmannanshire**) administrative region and former county of central Scotland; administrative center, Alloa.

Clacton-on-Sea |'klæktənän,sē| seaside resort in Essex, SE England, E of London. Pop. 40,000.

Clair•vaux |kler'vō| hamlet in NE France, near Ville-sous-la-Ferté, in the Aube department. The former Cistercian abbey here was founded 1115 by St. Bernard of Clairvaux.

Clap•ham |'klæpəm| residential district in SW London, England, in the borough of Wandsworth, noted for its major rail junction.

Clare |klær| county of the Republic of Ireland, on the W coast, in the province of Munster; county seat, Ennis. Pop. 91,000.

Clare•mont |'klær,mänt| city in SW California, a suburb and academic center E of Los Angeles. Pop. 32,503.

Clark Fork River |'klärk 'fôrk| river that flows 360 mi./580 km. from W Montana into E Idaho, into the Columbia River.

Clarks•dale |'klärks,dāl| city in NW Mississippi, a Delta cotton center also associated with the development of blues music. Pop. 19,717.

Clarks•ville |'klärks,vil; 'klärksvəl| industrial and commercial city in N central Tennessee, on the Cumberland River. Pop. 75,494.

Clear•field |'klir,fēld| city in N Utah, SW of Ogden and Hill Air Force Base, which is central to its economy. Pop. 21,435.

Clear Lake |'klir 'lāk| section of SE Houston, Texas, home to major U.S. space flight facilities and many of their workers.

Clear•wa•ter |'klir,wädər| city in W central

Florida, on the Gulf of Mexico, W of Tampa. It is a noted resort center. Pop. 98,784.

Clear·wa·ter Mountains |'klir,wawtər; 'klir,wätər| range in N Idaho, part of the Rocky Mts., noted for their forests and mining.

Clee·thorpes |'klē,THawrps| resort town in NE England, on the Humber estuary next to Grimsby, in Humberside. Pop. 67,000.

Clem·son |'klemsən| city in NW South Carolina, home to Clemson University. Pop. 11,096.

Cle·o·pa·tra's Needle |klēə'pætrəz 'nēdl| popular name for either of two ancient Egyptian obelisks, one on the Victoria Embankment in London, England, the other in Central Park, New York City.

Clermont-Ferrand |,kler,mawN fə'räN| industrial city in central France, capital of the Auvergne region, at the center of the Massif Central. Pop. 140,170.

Cleve·land[1] |'klēvlənd| former county on the North Sea coast of NE England, formed in 1974 from parts of Durham and North Yorkshire and replaced in 1996 by the unitary councils of Middlesbrough, Hartlepool, Stockton-on-Tees, and Redcar and Cleveland.

Cleve·land[2] |'klēvlənd| major port and industrial city in NE Ohio, on Lake Erie and the Cuyahoga River. Pop 505,600. It is a historic center of heavy industry, including oil, machinery, and metals.

Cleve·land[3] |'klēvlənd| city in SE Tennessee, NE of Chattanooga. Pop. 30,354.

Cleve·land Heights |'klēvlənd| city in NE Ohio, a residential suburb on the NE side of Cleveland. Pop. 54,052.

Cleves |klēvz| town in western Germany, between the Rhine River and the border with the Netherlands. Pop. 45,000. Its economy is based on tourism and manufacturing. German name **Kleve**.

Clif·den |'klifdən| coastal resort town in County Galway, W Ireland, near which Alcock and Brown landed after the first transatlantic airplane flight in 1919.

Clif·ton[1] |'kliftən| suburb of Bristol, SW England, site of a noted suspension bridge built by Isambard Brunel across the Avon Gorge.

Clif·ton[2] |'kliftən| industrial city in NE New Jersey, immediately W of Passaic. Pop. 71,742.

Clinch River |klinCH| river that flows 300 mi./480 km. from SW Virginia into Tennessee, where it passes the Norris Dam and

Oak Ridge before joining the Tennessee River.

Clin·ton |'klintən| city in E central Iowa, on the Mississippi River. Pop. 29,201.

Clip·per·ton Island |'klipərtən| uninhabited French island in the E Pacific, SW of Mexico. A phosphate source, it is named for an 18th-century English pirate.

Clon·mac·noise |,klänmək'noiz| village in W central Ireland, on the Shannon River, site of the ruins of a 6th-century monastery that was a major academic center.

Clon·mel |klän'mel| the county seat of Tipperary, in the Republic of Ireland. Pop. 14,500.

Clo·vis[1] |'klōvəs| city in central California, in the San Joaquin Valley, a suburb NE of Fresno. Pop. 50,323.

Clo·vis[2] |'klōvəs| agricultural city in E New Mexico. Pop. 30,954. The Clovis Culture of 10,000 years ago is named for artifacts found nearby.

Cluj–Napoca |'klooZH 'näpōkə| city in W central Romania. Pop. 321,850. It was founded in the 12th-century by German-speaking colonists; by the 19th century it belonged to Hungary and was the cultural center of Transylvania. The name was changed from Cluj in the mid-1970s to incorporate the name of a nearby ancient settlement. Also called **Cluj**; Hungarian name **Kolozsvár**; German name **Klausenburg**.

Clu·ny |kloo'nē| town in the Burgundy region of E France. Pop. 5,000. Cluny was once a leading religious center; its 12th-century abbey (now destroyed) was the largest in the world.

Clu·tha River |'klooTHə| gold-bearing river at the S end of South Island, New Zealand. It flows 213 mi./338 km. to the Pacific Ocean.

Clwyd |'klooəd| former county of NE Wales, replaced in 1996 by Denbighshire and Flintshire.

Clyde |klīd| river in W central Scotland that flows 106 mi./170 km. from the Southern Uplands to the Firth of Clyde, formerly famous for the shipbuilding industries along its banks, in the CLYDEBANK area.

Clyde, Firth of |,fərTH əv 'klīd| the estuary of the Clyde River in W Scotland.

Clydes·dale |'klīdz,dāl| valley of the upper Clyde River, in central Scotland, an agricultural district that gave its name to breeds of draft horses and dogs.

Cni·dus |'nīdəs| ancient Greek city of Asia Minor, in present-day SW Turkey, on Cape Krio in the Aegean Sea, N of Rhodes. It was noted for its artists and schools.

Co·a·hui·la |ˌkōə'wēlə| state of N Mexico, on the border with Texas. Area: 57, 930 sq. mi./149,982 sq. km. Pop. 1,971,000. Capital: Saltillo.

Coast Mountains |kōst| range that curves 1,000 mi./1,600 km. from British Columbia NW to Alaska, extending the line of the Cascade Mts. Mount Waddington (13,104 ft./3,994 m.) is the high point.

Coast Rang·es |kōst| name for various ranges that extend from S California along the Pacific coast to Alaska. Parallel to, and W of, the Coast Mts., they reach 19,524 ft./5,951 m. at Mount Logan, in the Yukon Territory.

Coats Land |'kōts ˌlænd| region of Antarctica, to the E of the Antarctic Peninsula.

Co·at·za·co·al·cos |kəˌwätsəkə'wälkōs| industrial port city in SE Mexico, on the Bay of Campeche in the Gulf of Mexico, in Veracruz state. Pop. 199,000. An oil industry center, it is at the mouth of the Coatzacoalcos River, which flows N across the Isthmus of Tehuantepec.

Co·bán |kō'bän| commercial city in central Guatemala, a coffee industry center in the highlands. Pop. 34,000.

Cobb County |käb| county in NW Georgia, containing many NW suburbs of Atlanta. Its seat is Marietta. Pop. 447,745.

Cobh |kōv| (formerly **Queenstown**) seaport and resort in County Cork, S Ireland, immediately S of Cork. Pop. 6,000.

Co·burg |'kō,bərg| city in S Germany, on the Itz River. Pop. 45,000. Between 1826 and 1918 it alternated with Gotha as the capital of Saxe-Coburg-Gotha.

Co·cha·bam·ba |ˌkōCHə'bämbə| industrial and commercial city in W central Bolivia, at the center of a rich agricultural region. Pop. 404,100.

Co·chin |kō'CHin| seaport and naval base on the Malabar Coast of SW India, in the state of Kerala. Pop. 504,000.

Cochin-China |'kōCHin'CHīnə| the former name for the S region of what is now Vietnam. Part of French Indo-China from 1862, in 1946 it became a French overseas territory, then merged officially with Vietnam in 1949.

Cock·aigne, land of |kä'kān| (also **Cockayne**) in medieval English folklore, a land of luxurious idleness. The name has nothing to do with *cocaine*.

Cock·er·mouth |'käkərməTH; 'käkərˌmowTH| commercial town in Cumbria, NW England, birthplace of William Wordsworth. Pop. 8,000.

Co·co·nut Creek |'kōkəˌnət| city in SE Florida, a residential suburb NW of Fort Lauderdale. Pop. 27,485.

Co·co·nut Grove |'kōkəˌnət| district of SW Miami, Florida, with a history as an arts colony and a thriving tourist trade.

Co·co River |'kō,kō| (formerly **Segovia**) river that flows 450 mi./720 km. from SW Honduras, forming much of the Honduras-Nicaragua border, into the Caribbean Sea.

Co·cos Islands |ˌkōkəs| group of twenty-seven small coral islands in the Indian Ocean, administered as an external territory of Australia since 1955. Pop. 603. The islands were discovered in 1609 by Captain William Keeling of the East India Company. Also called **Keeling Islands**.

Cod·ring·ton |'kädriNGtən| only settlement on the island of Barbuda, in Antigua and Barbuda, West Indies. Pop. 1,000.

Co·dy |'kōdē| city in NW Wyoming, associated with Buffalo Bill Cody, who lived here. Tourism is important to its economy. Pop. 7,897.

Coeur d'Alene |ˌkawr dl'ān| commercial and resort city in NW Idaho, on Coeur d'Alene Lake, which is fed by the Coeur d'Alene River. Pop. 24,563.

Co·gnac |kawn'yäk; 'kōn,yæk| city in W France, on the Charentes River. Pop. 23,000. It is known for premium brandy, produced since the 17th century.

Coi·hai·que |koi'īkā| military and administrative city in the Aisén region of S Chile. Pop. 43,000. It is the chief town of S Chile.

Coim·ba·tore |'koimbə,tŏŏr| commercial and industrial city in the state of Tamil Nadu, in S India. Pop. 853,000.

Co·im·bra |kŏŏ'imbrə| university city in central Portugal. Pop. 96,140.

Col·ca Canyon |'kōlkə| gorge in the Andes Mts. in S Peru, N of Arequipa. With sides rising to 14,300 ft./4,360 m., it is thought to be the deepest canyon in the world.

Col·ches·ter |'kōlCHəstər| commercial town in Essex, SE England. Pop. 82,000. It was prominent in Roman Britain, when it was known as Camulodunum.

Col·chis |'kälkəs| ancient region S of the Caucasus Mts. at the E end of the Black Sea. In classical mythology it was the goal of Jason's expedition for the Golden Fleece. Greek name **Kolkhis**.

Col·ditz |'kōldits| town in eastern Germany, SE of Leipzig. Its castle was used as a top-security prison for Allied prisoners during World War II.

Cold Spring Harbor |'kōld ˌspriNG| village on the North Shore of Long Island, New York, in Huntington town, famed as a whaling port and today for biological research. Pop. 4,789.

Cold·stream |'kōld,strēm| town in SE Scotland, in the Borders region, where the Coldstream Guards were formed for a 1660 foray into England to restore Charles II to the throne.

Cole·raine |kōl'rān; 'kōl,rān| industrial port and university town in the N of Northern Ireland, on the Bann River in County Londonderry. Pop. 16,000.

Co·li·ma |kə'lēmə| **1** a state of SW Mexico, on the Pacific coast. Area: 2,005 sq. mi./5,191 sq. km. Pop. 425,000. **2** its capital city. Pop. 58,000.

Col·lege Park |'kälij| city in central Maryland, just NE of Washington, D.C., home to the University of Maryland. Pop. 21,927.

Col·lege Station |'kälij| city in E central Texas, home to Texas A&M University. Pop. 52,456.

Col·mar |'kōl,mär| industrial port city on the Ill River, capital of the department of Haut-Rhin, NE France. Pop. 67,000. Also **Kolmar.**

Co·logne |kə'lōn| industrial and university city in western Germany, in North Rhine–Westphalia. Pop. 956,690. Founded by the Romans and situated on the Rhine River, Cologne is notable for its medieval cathedral. German name **Köln.**

Co·lo·ma |kə'lōmə| historic locality in NE California, on the American River NE of Sacramento, where gold was discovered in 1848 on John (Johann) Sutter's mill site, leading to the California gold rush.

Co·lombes |kō'lawNb; kə'lōm| industrial NW suburb of Paris, France, on the Seine River. Pop. 76,000.

Co·lom·bia |kə'ləmbēə| republic in the extreme NW of South America, having coastlines on both the Atlantic and the Pacific. Area: 440,365 sq. mi./1,140,105 sq. km. Pop. 34,479,000. Language, Spanish. Capital and largest city: Bogotá. Colombia was conquered by the Spanish in the early 16th century and achieved independence in 1819. Gran Colombia, as it was then known, has been reduced to the present-day boundaries. Largely in the Andes, with cities in the valleys, Colombia has an economy largely dependent on mining and agriculture. □ **Colombian** *adj. & n.*

Co·lom·bo |kə'ləmbō| the capital, largest city, and chief port of Sri Lanka. Pop. 615,000.

Co·lón |kə'lōn| the chief port of Panama, at the Caribbean end of the Panama Canal. Pop. 140,900. It was founded in 1850 by the American William Aspinwall, after whom it was originally named.

Co·lo·nia |kə'lōnyə| (official name **Colonia del Sacramento**) port and resort city in S Uruguay, across the Plate River from Buenos Aires, Argentina. Pop. 22,000.

Col·o·ra·do |,kälə'rædō; ,kälə'rädō| see box.

Colorado

Capital/largest city: Denver
Other cities: Arvada, Aurora, Boulder, Colorado Springs, Golden, Pueblo, Telluride
Population: 3,294,394 (1990); 3,970,971 (1998); 4,468,000 (2005 proj.)
Population rank (1990): 26
Rank in land area: 8
Abbreviation: CO; Colo.
Nickname: The Centennial State
Motto: *Nil sine Numine* ('Nothing without Providence')
Bird: lark bunting
Flower: columbine
Tree: blue spruce
Song: "Where the Columbines Grow"
Noted physical features: Black Canyon; Royal Gorge; Mount Elbert
Tourist attractions: Four Corners; Garden of the Gods; Continental Divide; Dinosaur, Great Sand Dunes, Black Canyon of Gunnison, and Colorado national monuments; Grand Mesa National Forest; Georgetown Loop Historic Mining Railroad Park, Cumbres & Toltec Scenic Railroad; Estes, Mesa Verde and Rocky Mountain national parks; Aspen Ski Resort
Admission date: August 1, 1876
Order of admission: 38
Name origin: Bestowed by the Spanish conquistadors (possibly by Cortez). It was the name of an imaginary island, an earthly paradise, in *Las Serges de Esplandian,* a Spanish romance written by Montalvo in 1510.

Colombia

Col·o·ra·do Desert |ˌkälə'rædō; ˌkälə-'rädō| region of S California and N Baja California, Mexico. The Salton Sea, Palm Springs, and the Imperial Valley are here.

Col·o·ra·do Plateau |ˌkälə'rædō; ˌkälə-'rädō| region of arid uplands in the SW U.S., along the Colorado River, in Colorado, Utah, New Mexico, and Arizona, noted for its scenery.

Col·o·ra·do River[1] |ˌkälə'rædō; ˌkälə'rädō| river that rises in the Rocky Mts. of N Colorado and flows generally SW for 1,468 mi./2,333 km. to the Gulf of California, passing through the Grand Canyon.

Col·o·ra·do River[2] |ˌkälə'rædō; ˌkälə'rädō| river that flows 900 mi./1,450 km. E across Texas, from the Llano Estacado to the Gulf of Mexico. Austin lies on it.

Col·o·ra·do Springs |ˌkälə'rædō; ˌkälə-'rädō| city in central Colorado, S of Denver, at the foot of the Front Range of the Rocky Mts. A resort with many military installations, it is home to the U.S. Air Force Academy. Pop. 281,140.

Co·los·sae |kə'läsē| ancient city of Phrygia, Asia Minor, in present-day SW Turkey, near Denizli. Early Christians here (Colossians) were addressed in an epistle by Paul.

Col·os·se·um |ˌkälə'sēəm| amphitheater in Rome, begun by the Emperor Vespasian c. A.D. 75. It held 50,000 spectators, its sections connected by an elaborate network of stairs, and was the scene of various kinds of combat.

Co·los·sus |kə'läsəs| huge bronze statue of Helios, the sun-god, at Rhodes, in ancient Greece; one of the Seven Wonders of the World. Said to be more than 100 ft./30 m. tall, it was destroyed in an earthquake in 224 B.C.

Col·ton |'kōltn| city in SW California, immediately SW of San Bernardino. Pop. 40,213.

Co·lum·bia, District of |kə'ləmbēə| see DISTRICT OF COLUMBIA.

Co·lum·bia[1] |kə'ləmbēə| residential community in central Maryland, between Baltimore and Washington, D.C., planned and established in the 1960s. Pop. 75,883.

Co·lum·bia[2] |kə'ləmbēə| city in central Missouri, home to the University of Missouri. Pop. 69,101.

Co·lum·bia[3] |kə'ləmbēə| industrial city, the capital of South Carolina, in the central part. Pop. 98,052.

Co·lum·bia River |kə'ləmbēə| river in NW North America that rises in the Rocky Mts. of SE British Columbia, and flows 1,230

mi./1,953 km. generally SW into the U.S., where it winds across the COLUMBIA PLATEAU of central Washington, then turns W to form the Washington-Oregon border and enters the Pacific near Astoria, Oregon.

Co·lum·bus[1] |kə'ləmbəs| industrial city in W Georgia, on the Chattahoochee River, noted as a textile center. Pop. 179,278.

Co·lum·bus[2] |kə'ləmbəs| industrial city in S central Indiana. Pop. 31,802.

Co·lum·bus[3] |kə'ləmbəs| commercial, industrial, and university city, the capital of Ohio, in the central part. Pop. 632,910.

Co·ma·ya·gua |ˌkōmə'yägwə| historic city in W central Honduras, a former capital of the country. Pop. 36,000.

Co·mil·la |kə'milə| (also **Komilla**) city in E Bangladesh, SE of Dhaka. Pop. 165,000.

Co·mi·no |kə'mēnō| the smallest of the three main islands of Malta.

Co·mi·tán |ˌkōmē'tän| (official name **Comitán de Domínguez**) commercial city in Chiapas, S Mexico, near the Guatemalan border. Pop. 48,000.

Com·mon·wealth, the |'kämən,welTH| (official name **the Commonwealth of Nations**) association of nations and dependencies that were formerly part of the British Empire.

com·mon·wealth official designation of four U.S. states: Kentucky, Massachusetts, Pennsylvania, and Virginia.

Com·mon·wealth of In·de·pen·dent States (abbrev. **C.I.S.**) confederation of the former constituent republics of the Soviet Union, established in 1991. The member states are Armenia, Belarus, Kazakhstan, Kyrgyzstan, Moldova, Russia, Tajikistan, Turkmenistan, Ukraine, and Uzbekistan.

Com·mun·ism Peak |'kämyə,nizəm| highest peak in the Pamir Mts. of Tajikistan, rising to 24,590 ft./7,495 m. It was the highest mountain in the former Soviet Union. Former names **Mount Garmo** (until 1933) and **Stalin Peak** (until 1962).

Co·mo, Lake |'kōmō| lake in the foothills of the Alps in N Italy. The resort city of COMO (pop. 87,000) is at the SW end.

Co·mo·do·ro Ri·va·da·via |ˌkōmō'dawrō ˌrēvə'dävēə| port in S Argentina on the Atlantic coast of Patagonia. Pop. 124,000.

Co·moé River |ˌkōmō'ā| river that flows 475 mi./765 km. from Burkina Faso through Côte d'Ivoire, to the Gulf of Guinea. In NE Côte d'Ivoire, a national park along the river is noted for its wildlife.

Com·o·rin, Cape |'kämərin| cape at the S tip of India, in the state of Tamil Nadu.

Com·o·ros |ˈkämə‚rōz; kəˈmawrōz| republic consisting of a group of islands in the Indian Ocean, N of Madagascar. Area: 690 sq. mi./1,787 sq. km. Pop. 492,000. Languages, French (official), Arabic (official), Comoran Swahili. Capital: Moroni. Arab influence was dominant in the islands until, in the mid-19th century, they came under French control. In 1974 all but one (Mayotte) of the four major islands voted for independence. Plantation agriculture, producing foods, fibers, and essences, predominates. □ **Comoran** *adj. & n.*

Comoros

Com·piègne |kawNˈpyen(yə)| city in N France on the Oise River. Pop. 45,000. The armistice that ended World War I was signed in the forest nearby on November 11, 1918; the armistice between France and Germany was signed on the same spot in 1940.

Comp·ton |ˈkämptən| industrial city in SW California, immediately S of Los Angeles. Pop. 90,454.

Com·stock Lode |ˈkäm‚stäk| historic gold and silver source in the Virginia Mts. of W Nevada, S of Reno, basis of a boom that lasted from the 1850s through the late-19th century.

Con·a·kry |ˈkänəkrē| the capital, largest city, and chief port of Guinea, on Tombo Island in the Atlantic. Pop. 950,000.

Con·car·neau |‚kōNkärˈnō| port city in Finistère department, Brittany, NW France. Pop. 19,000. It is a fishing center and artists' retreat.

Con·cep·ci·ón |‚kawnsepsˈyōn| industrial city in S central Chile, in a mining and agricultural district. Pop. 294,000.

Con·cord[1] |ˈkäNGkərd; ˈkäNG‚kawrd| city in N central California, NE of Oakland. Naval facilities are key to its economy. Pop. 111,348.

Con·cord[2] |ˈkäNGkərd; ˈkäNG‚kawrd| historic suburban town in E Massachusetts, on the Concord River. Pop. 17,080. Battles here and at Lexington in April 1775 marked the start of the Revolutionary War.

Con·cord[3] |ˈkäNGkərd; ˈkäNG‚kawrd| the state capital of New Hampshire, on the Merrimack River in the S central part. Pop. 36,006.

Con·cord[4] |ˈkäNGkərd; ˈkäNG‚kawrd| industrial city in S central North Carolina, a textile center. Pop. 27,347.

Con·corde, Place de la |ˈpläs də lä ‚kawNˈkōrd| square adjoining the Tuileries, in Paris, France. Built in the late 18th century and originally called the Place Louis XV, it became the place of execution during the French Revolution; Louis XVI and Marie Antoinette were beheaded here.

Con·cor·dia |kənˈkōrdēə| port city in NE Argentina, in a farming region of Entre Ríos province, on the Uruguay River and the border with Uruguay. Pop. 139,000.

Condé-sur-L'Escaut |kawNəˈdäsyrlesˈkō| village in N France near the Belgian border. The name was attached to a branch of the royal house of Bourbon, and princes of Condé have played a major role in French history. The family owned the chateau at Chantilly.

Con·es·to·ga |‚känəˈstōgə| township in SE Pennsylvania, near Lancaster, birthplace of the Conestoga wagon that helped settle the western U.S. Pop. 3,470.

Co·ney Island |ˈkōnē| beach resort, amusement park, and residential district on the Atlantic coast in Brooklyn, New York.

Confederate States of America |kənˈfed(ə)rət ˈstäts əv əˈmerikə| (also **the Confederacy**) the eleven Southern states (Alabama, Arkansas, Florida, Georgia, Louisiana, Mississippi, North Carolina, South Carolina, Tennessee, Texas, and Virginia) that seceded from the United States in 1860–61, leading to the Civil War.

Con·go[1] |ˈkäNGgō| (official name **Democratic Republic of Congo**; formerly **Zaïre**; also **Congo-Kinshasa**) equatorial country in central Africa with a short coastline on

Congo[1]

the Atlantic. Area: 905,350 sq. mi./2.34 million sq. km. Pop. 38,473,000. Languages, French (official), Kongo, Lingala, Swahili, others. Capital and largest city: Kinshasa. A Belgian colony from 1885, it was the Belgian Congo 1908–60. Independence led to civil war. The dictator Mobutu Sese Seko, in power 1965–97, changed the name to Zaïre in 1971. Most of the country is in the Congo River basin, and is heavily forested. Copper and various minerals abound.

Con•go[2] |'käNGgō| (official name, **People's Republic of the Congo**; often **the Congo** or **Congo-Brazzaville**) equatorial country in Africa, with a short Atlantic coastline. Area: 132,046 sq. mi./342,000 sq. km. Pop. 2,351,000. Languages, French (official), Kikongo, and other Bantu languages. Capital and largest city: Brazzaville. Part of the former French Congo, the country, independent since 1960, is separated from the former Zaire by the Congo and Ubangi rivers. It produces oil, timber, coffee, and tobacco. □ **Congolese** adj. & n.

Con•go River |'käNGgō| major river of central Africa, which rises as the Lualaba to the S of Kisangani in N Congo (formerly Zaire) and flows 2,800 mi./4,630 km. in a great curve W, turning SW to form the border between the Congo and the Democratic Republic of Congo before emptying into the Atlantic. Also called **Zaire River**.

Con•nacht |'känawt| (also **Connaught**) province in the W of the Republic of Ireland, including Counties Sligo, Roscommon, Mayo, Leitrim, and Galway.

Con•nect•i•cut |kə'netikət| see box.

Con•nect•i•cut River |kə'netikət| longest river in New England, flowing 407 mi./655 km. from N New Hampshire, on the Quebec border, between New Hampshire and Vermont, then through W Massachusetts and central Connecticut, to Long Island Sound, on the Atlantic.

Con•ne•ma•ra |ˌkänə'märə| mountainous coastal region of Galway, in the W of the Republic of Ireland.

Con•roe |'känrō| city in E Texas, a longtime lumber and oil center now a suburb N of Houston. Pop. 27,610.

Con Son |'kōn 'sōn| island in the South China Sea, off the S coast of Vietnam.

Con•stance, Lake |'känstən(t)s| lake in SE Germany on the N side of the Swiss Alps, at the meeting point of Germany, Switzerland, and Austria, forming part of the course of the Rhine River. German name **Bodensee**.

Connecticut

Capital: Hartford
Largest city: Bridgeport
Other cities: New Haven, New London, Stamford, Waterbury
Population: 3,287,116 (1990); 3,274,069 (1998); 3,317,000 (2005 proj.)
Population rank (1990): 27
Rank in land area: 48
Abbreviation: CT; Conn.
Nicknames: The Constitution State; Nutmeg State; Land of Steady Habits; Blue Law State
Motto: *Qui Transtulit Sustinet* (Latin: 'He Who Transplanted Still Sustains')
Bird: American robin
Flower: mountain laurel
Tree: white oak
Song: "Yankee Doodle"
Noted physical features: Long Island Sound; Connecticut and Housatonic rivers
Tourist attractions: Mystic Seaport & Aquarium; Mark Twain House; Peabody Museum; Gillette Castle; U.S.S. *Nautilus* Memorial; Foxwoods Casino & Resort, Mohegan Sun Casino; Essex Steam Train.
Admission date: January 9, 1788
Order of admission: 5
Name origin: For the Connecticut River, from an Algonquian word translated 'long river place.'

Con•stan•ţa |kən'stäntsə| (also **Constanza**) the chief port of Romania, on the Black Sea. Pop. 349,000. Founded in the 7th century B.C. by the Greeks, it was under Roman rule from 72 B.C. Formerly called Tomis, it was renamed after the Roman emperor Constantine the Great in the 4th century.

Con•stan•tine |'känstən,tēn| commercial city in NE Algeria. Pop. 449,000. The capital of the Roman province of Numidia, it was destroyed in 311 but rebuilt by the Roman emperor Constantine the Great and given his name.

Con•stan•ti•no•ple |ˌkän,stæntə'nōpəl| the former name for Istanbul, Turkey, from A.D. 330 (when it was given its name by the Roman emperor Constantine the Great) to the capture of the city by the Turks in 1453.

Con•sti•tu•tion State |ˌkänstə't(y)ōō-shən| informal name for CONNECTICUT.

Con•ta•do•ra |ˌkäntə'dawrə| resort island in Panama, in the Pearl Island, in the Gulf of Panama, that gave its name to a group of nations (Colombia, Panama, Venezuela, and Mexico) that sought, in 1983, to resolve Central American conflicts.

Con·ta·gem |ˌkōntə'zнäm| city in Minas Gerais state, SE Brazil, an industrial suburb W of Belo Horizonte. Pop. 491,000.

Con·ti·nen·tal Divide |ˌkäntn'entl di'vīd| the main series of mountain ridges in W North America, chiefly the crests of the Rocky Mts., which form a watershed separating the rivers flowing E into the Atlantic or the Gulf of Mexico from those flowing W into the Pacific. Also called the **Great Divide**.

Con·tra Cos·ta County |ˌkäntrə 'kästə; 'kawstə| county in N central California, including many industrial and port cities along upper San Francisco Bay. Its seat is Martinez. Pop. 803,732.

Con·way[1] |'kän,wā| city in central Arkansas. Pop. 26,481.

Con·way[2] |'kän,wā| town in N central New Hampshire, a gateway to White Mt. resorts, noted especially for the village of North Conway. Pop. 7,940.

Con·wy |'känwē| (also **Conway**) commercial and resort town in NW Wales, in Gwynedd. Pop. 13,000.

Cooch Be·har |ˌko͞oсн bə'här| (also **Koch Bihar**) commercial town in E India, in W. Bengal state. Pop. 71,000.

Cook, Mount |ko͝ok| the highest peak in New Zealand, in the Southern Alps on South Island, rising to a height of 12,349 ft./3,764 m. Maori name **Aorangi**.

Cook County |ko͝ok| county in NE Illinois, embracing Chicago and most of its closer suburbs. Pop. 5,105,067.

Cook Inlet |ko͝ok| inlet of the Gulf of Alaska, W of the Kenai Peninsula in S Alaska. Anchorage lies at its N end.

Cook Islands |ko͝ok| group of fifteen islands in the SW Pacific Ocean between Tonga and French Polynesia, which have the status of a self-governing territory in free association with New Zealand. Pop. 18,000. Languages, English (official), Rarotongan (a Polynesian language). Capital: Avarua, on Rarotonga.

Cook Strait |ko͝ok| the strait separating the North and South islands of New Zealand.

Coon Rapids |ko͞on| city in SE Minnesota, on the Mississippi River N of Minneapolis. Pop. 52,978.

Co·op·er·a·tive Republic of Guy·ana |gī'änə| official name for GUYANA.

Coo·pers·town |'ko͞opərz,town| resort village in central New York, on Otsego Lake,

site of the Baseball Hall of Fame. Pop. 2,180.

Coos Bay |ko͞os| city in SW Oregon, on the Pacific coast. Pop. 15,076.

Co·pa·ca·bana Beach |ˌkōpəkə'bænə| resort on the Atlantic coast of Brazil, part of Rio de Janeiro.

Co·pán |kō'pän| ancient Mayan city, in W Honduras near the Guatemalan border, the southernmost point of the Mayan empire.

Co·pen·ha·gen |'kōpən,hägən| the capital and chief port of Denmark, a city occupying the E part of Zealand and N part of the island of Amager. Pop. 466,700. Danish name **København**.

Co·pia·pó |ˌkōpēə'pō| industrial city in N Chile, on the S of the Atacama Desert. Pop. 79,000. It is a mining-industry center.

Cop·ley Square |'käplē| neighborhood in Back Bay, Boston, Massachusetts.

Cop·per·belt |'käpər,belt| a mining region of central Zambia with rich deposits of copper, cobalt, and uranium; chief town, Ndola.

Cop·per Canyon |'käpər| (Spanish name **Barranca del Cobre**) canyon in Chihuahua state, N Mexico, in the Sierra Madre Occidental. Named for the color of its walls, it is crossed by railroad and is a tourist attraction.

Cop·per·mine |'käpər,mīn| community in Nunavut, at the mouth of the Coppermine River on the Arctic Ocean. Pop. 1,116. Inuit name **Kugluktuk**.

Co·quim·bo |kō'kēmbō| port city in N Chile, in the Coquimbo region. Pop. 117,000. It is the port for La Serena, in a copper- and manganese-producing region.

Cor·al Ga·bles |ˌkawrəl 'gäbləz; ˌkärəl| resort and commercial city in SE Florida, just SW of Miami on Biscayne Bay. Pop. 40,091.

Cor·al Sea |ˌkawrəl; ˌkärəl| part of the W Pacific lying between Australia, New Guinea, and Vanuatu, the scene of a naval battle between U.S. and Japanese aircraft carriers in 1942.

Cor·al Springs |ˌkawrəl; ˌkärəl| residential city in SE Florida. Pop. 79,443.

Cor·bières |kawr'byer| wine-producing district in the S of the Languedoc region of France, between Narbonne and the Spanish border.

Cor·co·va·do |ˌkawrkə'vädo͞o| peak rising to 2,310 ft./711 m. on the S side of Rio de Janeiro, Brazil. A gigantic statue of Christ, 131 ft./40 m. high, stands on its summit.

Cor·cy·ra |kawr'sīrə| ancient Greek name for CORFU.

Cor·dil·le·ra Cen·tral |'kawrdē'yerə sen-

'träl| name in several Spanish-speaking countries for the chief mountain range. There are such *cordilleras* in Peru, Colombia, the Dominican Republic, Puerto Rico, and the Philippines.

Cór·do·ba[1] |'kawrdəbə| city in central Argentina, capital of Córdoba province. Pop. 1,198,000. It is a commercial center and the second-largest city in the country.

Cór·do·ba[2] |'kawrdəbə| commercial city in E central Mexico, in Veracruz state, in a coffee-, sugar-, and fruit-producing region. Pop. 131,000. An 1821 treaty signed here established Mexican independence.

Cór·do·ba[3] |'kawrdəbə| (also **Cordova**) city in Andalusia, S Spain. Pop. 309,200. Founded by the Carthaginians, it was under Moorish rule from 711 to 1236, and was renowned for its learning and for its architecture, particularly the Great Mosque. Spanish name **Córdoba.**

Cor·fu |kawr'foo| Greek resort island, one of the largest of the Ionian Islands, off the W coast. It was known in ancient times as Corcyra. Pop. 105,350. Greek name **Kérkira.**

Cor·inth |'kawrinTH; 'kärinTH| city on the N coast of the Peloponnese, Greece. Pop. 27,400. The modern city, built in 1858, is a little to the NE of the site of the prominent ancient city. Greek name **Kórinthos.** □ **Corinthian** *adj. & n.*

Cor·inth, Gulf of |'kawrinTH; 'kärinTH| inlet of the Ionian Sea extending between the Peloponnese and central Greece. Also called **Gulf of Lepanto.**

Cor·inth, Isthmus of |'kawrinTH; 'kärinTH| narrow neck of land linking the Peloponnese with central Greece and separating the Gulf of Corinth from the Saronic Gulf.

Cor·inth Canal |'kawrinTH; 'kärinTH| shipping channel across the narrowest part of the Isthmus of Corinth (a distance of 4 mi./ 6.4 km.). Opened in 1893, it links the Gulf of Corinth and the Saronic Gulf.

Co·rin·to |kə'rēntō| town in NW Nicaragua, the leading Pacific port in the country, exporting coffee, sugar, wood, and other products. Pop. 17,000.

Cork |kawrk| **1** largest (2,880 sq. mi./7,459 sq. km.) and second-most populous (410,000) county of the Republic of Ireland, in the SW in the province of Munster. **2** its county seat, a port on the Lee River and the second-largest city in the Republic. Pop. 127,000.

Corn Belt |kawrn| name for parts of the U.S. Midwest, especially Illinois and Iowa, where corn is a major crop.

Cor·ner Brook |kawrnər| industrial port city in W Newfoundland, a paper industry center. Pop. 22,410.

Cor·ning |'kawrniNG| industrial city in S central New York, noted for glass production. Pop. 11,938.

Corn Islands |kawrn| (Spanish name **Islas de Maíz**) two small islands in the Caribbean Sea off E Nicaragua, used as a U.S. Marine base (1916–71).

Corn·wall[1] |'kawrn,wawl; 'kawrnwəl| county occupying the extreme SW peninsula of England. Pop. 469,000. County town: Truro. It was a Celtic region with its own language, which survived until about 250 years ago, and customs. □ **Cornish** *adj. & n.*

Corn·wall[2] |'kawrn,wawl; 'kawrnwəl| city in E Ontario, a port on the Saint Lawrence River across from Massena, New York. Pop. 47,137.

Co·ro |'kōrō| (also **Santa Ana de Coro**) city in NW Venezuela, an oil center near the Paraguaná Peninsula. Pop. 125,000.

Co·ro·man·del Coast |,kawrə'mændl| the S part of the E coast of India, from Point Calimere to the mouth of the Krishna River.

Co·ro·na[1] |kə'rōnə| city in SW California, an industrial and residential suburb SW of Riverside. Pop. 76,095.

Co·ro·na[2] |kə'rōnə| residential and commercial section of N Queens, New York City.

Co·ro·nel |,kawrə'nel| port city in S central Chile, S of Concepción. Pop. 83,000. It is a resort, and coal is mined in the area.

Cor·pus Chris·ti |,kawrpəs 'kristē| city, an industrial and fishing port in S Texas. Pop. 257,400. It is situated on Corpus Christi Bay, an inlet of the Gulf of Mexico.

Cor·reg·i·dor |kə'regə,dawr| island in the Philippines just S of the Bataan Peninsula on Luzon Island; scene of World War II battles and now a national shrine.

Cor·rien·tes |,kawrē'entās| port city in NE Argentina, on the Paraná River across from Resistencia and near the Paraguayan border. Pop. 269,000.

Corse |kawrs| French name for CORSICA.

Cor·si·ca |'kawrsikə| mountainous island off the W coast of Italy, forming an administrative region of France. Pop. 249,740. Chief towns, Bastia (N department) and Ajaccio (S department). It was the birthplace of Napoleon I. French name **Corse.** □ **Corsican** *adj. & n.*

Cor·si·ca·na |ˌkawrsiˈkænə| city in E central Texas, an oil center. Pop. 22,911.

Cor·ti·na d'Am·pez·zo |kawrˈtēnə dämˈpetsō| popular winter resort town in NE Italy, in the Dolomites. Pop. 7,000. The 1956 Winter Olympics were held here.

Ço·rum |CHawˈrōōm| commercial city in N central Turkey, the capital of Çorum province. Pop. 117,000.

Cor·val·lis |kawrˈvæləs| city in W Oregon, on the Willamette River. Pop. 44,757. Oregon State University is here.

Cor·vo |ˈkawrvō| northernmost and smallest of the Azores Islands, part of Portugal. Area: 6.8 sq. mi./17.5 sq. km.

Co·sen·za |kōˈzentsə| market town in Calabria, S Italy, capital of Cosenza province. Pop. 105,000.

Cos·ta Blan·ca |ˌkōstə ˈbläNGkə| resort region on the Mediterranean coast of SE Spain.

Cos·ta Bra·va |ˌkōstə ˈbrävə| resort region to the N of Barcelona, on the Mediterranean coast of NE Spain.

Cos·ta del Sol |ˌkōstə del ˈsōl| resort region on the Mediterranean coast of S Spain.

Cos·ta Do·ra·da |ˌkōstə dōˈrädə| resort region, in Spain, on the E coast S of Barcelona, on the Mediterranean Sea.

Cos·ta Mesa |ˌkōstə ˈmāsə; ˌkästə| city in SW California, on the Pacific S of Los Angeles. Pop. 96,357.

Cos·ta Ri·ca |ˌkästə ˈrēkə; ˌkawstə| republic in Central America, on the Isthmus of Panama. Area: 19,707 sq. mi./51,022 sq. km. Pop. 3,301,210. Language, Spanish. Capital and largest city: San José. A former Spanish colony, Costa Rica achieved full independence in 1838. With temperate highlands and tropical lowlands, it produces timber, coffee, cacao, and sugar. Tourism is also important. □ **Costa Rican** adj. & n.

Costa Rica

Co·ta·ba·to |ˌkōtəˈbätō| port city in the Philippines, on W Mindanao, near the mouth of the Mindanao River. Pop. 127,000.

Côte d'Azur |ˌkōtdäˈzYr; ˌkōt dəˈZHōōr| coastal area of SW France, along the Mediterranean Sea. The area covered is roughly coterminous with the French Riviera and includes the towns of Cannes, Saint Tropez, Juan-les-Pins, and Antibes and the city of Nice. It also includes the principality of Monaco.

Côte d'Ivoire |ˌkōt dēˈvwär| (English name **Ivory Coast**) republic in W Africa, on the Gulf of Guinea. Area: 124,550 sq. mi./322,462 sq. km. Pop.: 12,000,000. Languages, French, W African languages. Capital: Yamoussoukro. Largest city: Abidjan. Controlled by the French from 1842, the country became independent in 1960. Largely savanna and tropical forest, it produces timber, coffee, cacao, bananas, rubber, and palm oil. It is one of the more developed and stable African states.

Côte d'Or |ˌkōt ˈdawr| department in central France, in Burgundy (Bourgogne), famous for its wines. Area: 3,385 sq. mi./8,763 sq. km. Pop. 494,000. The capital is Dijon.

Co·ten·tin Peninsula |ˌkōtäNˈtæN| region of NW France, in Normandy, that juts out into the English Channel. At its tip is the port city of Cherbourg.

Co·to·nou |ˌkōtōˈnōō; ˌkōtnˈōō| largest city, chief port, and chief commercial and political center of Benin, on the coast of W Africa. Pop. 536,830.

Co·to·paxi |ˌkōtəˈpäksē| the highest active volcano in the world, rising to 19,142 ft./5,896 m. in the Andes of central Ecuador.

Cots·wold Hills |ˈkät,swōld; ˈkätswəld| (also **the Cotswolds**) range of limestone hills in SW England, largely in the county of Gloucestershire.

Cott·bus |ˈkät,bōōs| industrial city in SE Germany, in Brandenburg, on the Spree River. Pop. 123,320.

Cot·tian Alps |ˈkätēən| section of the W Alps on the border between SE France and NW Italy. The highest point is Mount Viso (12,634 ft./3,851 m.).

Cot·ton Belt |ˈkätn| region of the U.S. South where cotton is the historic main crop, especially parts of Georgia, Alabama, and Mississippi.

Coun·cil Bluffs |ˈkowntsəl| industrial and commercial city in SW Iowa, on the Missouri River opposite Omaha, Nebraska. Pop. 54,315.

Cour·an·tyne River |ˈkawrən,tīn| (Dutch

name **Corantijn**) river that flows 450 mi./725 km. N between Guyana and Suriname, into the Atlantic.

Cour·be·voie |ˌko͞orbəˈvwä| industrial city and residential suburb, NW of Paris, France. Pop. 60,000.

Cour·land |ˈko͞or,länt; ˈko͞orlənd| (also **Kurland**) historical name for region of W Latvia on the shores of the Baltic Sea.

Cour·trai |ko͞orˈträ| French name for KORTRIJK, Belgium.

Cov·ent Garden |ˌkəvənt ˈgärdən| district in central London, England, originally the garden of the Abbey of Westminster. It was the site for 300 years of London's chief fruit and vegetable market, which in 1974 was moved to Battersea. Covent Garden is also famed as a home to theater and opera.

Cov·en·try |ˈkəvəntrē| industrial city in the W Midlands of England, the heart of the British auto industry. Pop. 292,600. The city center was destroyed in a November 1940 German air raid, and subsequently rebuilt.

Co·vi·na |kōˈvēnə| city in SW California, a suburb E of Los Angeles. Pop. 43,207.

Cowes |kowz| town on the Isle of Wight, S England. Pop. 16,300. It is famous as a yachting center.

Cox's Ba·zar |ˌkäks(iz) bəˈzär| port and resort town on the Bay of Bengal, near Chittagong, S Bangladesh. Pop. 29,600.

Co·yo·a·cán |ˌkoi-ōəˈkän| municipality within the Federal District of Mexico, a suburb of Mexico City. Pop. 640,000. It has historic associations with Hernán Cortés, Trotsky, and Frida Kahlo.

Co·zu·mel |ˌkōso͞oˈmel; ˈkōzə,mel| resort island in the Caribbean, off the NE coast of the Yucatán Peninsula of Mexico.

Cra·cow |ˈkrä,ko͞of; ˈkräk,ow| industrial and university city in S Poland, on the Vistula River. Pop. 750,540. It was the capital of Poland from 1320 until replaced by Warsaw in 1609. Polish name **Kraków**.

Cra·io·va |krīˈōvə| industrial city in SW Romania, in Oltenia. Pop. 300,030.

Cran·ston |ˈkrænstən| industrial city in central Rhode Island, a suburb S of Providence. Pop. 76,060.

Cra·ter Lake |ˈkrātər| lake filling a volcanic crater in the Cascade Range of SW Oregon. With a depth of more than 1,968 ft./600 m., it is the deepest lake in the U.S.

Craw·ley |ˈkrawlē| town in SE England, in West Sussex, an industrial and residential suburb near Gatwick Airport. Pop. 87,000.

Crays Mal·ville |kremälˈvēl| site of the first

commercial-style nuclear reactor, "Super-Phénis," near Lyons, in E France.

Cré·cy |krāˈsē| (also **Crécy-en-Ponthieu**) village in N France, in Picardy. The English won their first great victory in the Hundred Years War here in 1346, with the defeat of King Philip VI by King Edward III and Edward, the Black Prince.

Cre·mo·na |krəˈmōnə| commercial city in Lombardy, N Italy. Pop. 75,160. In the 16th–18th centuries the city was home to three renowned families of violinmakers: the Amati, the Guarneri, and the Stradivari.

Crest·ed Butte |ˈkrestid ˈbo͞ot| resort town in W central Colorado, a center for skiing and mountain biking. Pop. 878.

Crete |krēt| Greek island in the E Mediterranean. Pop. 536,980. Capital: Heraklion. It is noted for the remains of the Minoan civilization that flourished here in the 2nd millennium B.C. It fell to Rome in 67 B.C. and was subsequently ruled by Byzantines, Venetians, and Turks. Crete played an important role in the Greek struggle for independence from the Turks in the late 19th and early 20th centuries. Greek name **Kríti**. □ **Cretan** *adj. & n.*

Cré·teil |krāˈtā| city, a SE suburb of Paris, France, on the Marne River. Pop. 82,000. It has some light industry.

Crewe |kro͞o| industrial town and railway junction in Cheshire, W central England. Pop. 47,800.

Cri·mea |krīˈmēə| (usu. **the Crimea**) a peninsula of Ukraine lying between the Sea of Azov and the Black Sea. It was the scene of the Crimean War in the 1850s. The majority of the population is Russian. □ **Crimean** *adj.*

Crip·ple Creek |ˈkripəl| city in central Colorado, W of Colorado Springs, scene of a gold-mining boom in the 1890s. Pop. 584.

Croagh Pat·rick |ˌkrō ˈpætrik| mountain in W Ireland, near Westport, County Mayo, said to be where St. Patrick began his missionary work.

Cro·a·tia |krōˈāSHə| country in SE Europe, on the Adriatic Sea, formerly a constituent republic of Yugoslavia. Area: 21,838 sq. mi./56,538 sq. km. Pop. 4,760,000. Language, Croatian. Capital and largest city: Zagreb. Croatian name **Hrvatska**. After almost 1,000 years of Hungarian control, interrupted at times by Turkish power, Croatia in 1918 became part of what was later named Yugoslavia. Poor relations with neighboring Serbia were exacerbated by the Croatian alliance with Nazi Germany in 1941–45, and when Yugoslavia dissolved, strife ensued. Croatia produces coal, oil, grain, livestock, and timber. Coastal resorts are important. □ **Croatian** *adj. & n.* **Croat** *n.*

Croatia

Cro-Magnon |krōmän'yōN| cave in SW France, near Périgueux, where remains were found of an Upper Paleolithic prototype of Homo sapiens, or modern man. This population of early humans is now known as Cro-Magnon man.

Cro·mar·ty Firth |'krämərtē| inlet of the Moray Firth on the coast of Highland region, N Scotland.

Cro·to·ne |krə'tōnā| industrial town in Calabria, S Italy. Pop. 56,000. It was the site of an ancient Greek republic and the home of the mathematician Pythagoras.

Cro·ton River |'krōtn| short river in E New York, flowing into the Hudson River. It is the source of much New York City water.

Crown Heights |krown| neighborhood of N Brooklyn, New York, noted for its West Indian and Orthodox Jewish communities.

Crown Point |krown| resort town in NE New York, on Lake Champlain, scene of much 18th-century military action.

Croy·don |'kroiden| borough of S Greater London, England. Pop. 300,000. A light industrial and commercial center, it was the site of London's first (1915) airport.

Cro·zet Islands |krō'zā| group of five small islands in the S Indian Ocean, under French administration.

Crys·tal Palace |'kristl| iron and glass exhibition structure erected in Hyde Park, London, England, in 1851, then moved to Sydenham, near Croydon. It burned in 1936. The area around its Sydenham site is also called Crystal Palace.

Ctes·i·phon |'tesə,fän| ancient city on the Tigris near Baghdad, capital of the Parthian kingdom from *c.*224 and then of Persia under the Sassanian dynasty. It was taken by the Arabs in 636 and destroyed in the 8th century.

Cuauh·té·moc |kwow'tāmək| district of Mexico City, Mexico, named for the last Aztec emperor and incorporating most of the downtown area, including the Alameda and Zócalo.

Cuau·tla |'kwowtlə| commercial and resort city in Morelos state, S central Mexico. Pop. 120,000.

Cu·ba |'kyōobə| republic in the Caribbean, the largest and westernmost of the islands of the West Indies, at the mouth of the Gulf of Mexico. Area: 42,820 sq. mi./110,860 sq. km. Pop. 10,977,000. Language, Spanish. Capital and largest city: Havana. A Spanish colony, Cuba was controlled by the U.S. from 1898, and became autonomous in 1934. After a 1959 revolution it became gradually a Soviet client state, and the U.S. enforced a trade embargo. Cuba produces sugar, tobacco, seafood, and some mine and industrial products. Tourism is regaining importance. □ **Cuban** *adj. & n.*

Cuba

Cu·ban·go |kōō'bäNGgō| Angolan name for the OKAVANGO River.

Cu·ca·mon·ga |,kōōkə'mäNGgə| see RANCHO CUCAMONGA, California.

Cú·cu·ta |'kōōkōō,tə| industrial and commercial city in N Colombia, near the Venezuelan border, in the Andes. Pop. 450,000.

Cud·da·lore |'kədl,awr| port in S India, on the Coromandel Coast of Tamil Nadu state, S of Pondicherry. Pop. 144,000.

Cud·da·pah |'kədəpə| commercial and industrial city in S central India, in Andhra Pradesh state. Pop. 121,000.

Cuen·ca |'kweNGkə| city in the Andes in S Ecuador. Pop. 239,900. Founded in 1557, it is known as the 'marble city' because of its many fine buildings.

Cuer·na·va·ca |,kwernə'väkə| highland resort town in central Mexico, capital of the state of Morelos. Pop. 400,000.

Cu·ia·bá |ˌko͞oyə'bä| river port in W central Brazil, on the Cuiabá River, capital of the state of Mato Grosso. Pop. 389,070.

Cu·ia·bá River |ˌko͞oyə'bä| river of W Brazil, which rises in the Mato Grosso plateau and flows for 300 mi./483 km. to join the São Lourenço River near the border with Bolivia.

Cu·le·bra |ko͞o'läbrə| island community off the E coast of Puerto Rico, formerly a naval reserve, now a resort and wildlife preserve. Pop. 1,542.

Cu·lia·cán Ro·sa·les |ˌko͞olyə'kän ˌrō-'säləs| commercial city in NW Mexico, capital of the state of Sinaloa. Pop. 662,110.

Cul·lo·den |kə'lädn| village in NE Scotland, near Inverness. At nearby Culloden Moor, in April 1746, English forces won the last pitched battle on British soil, ending the Jacobite uprising.

Cul·ver City |ˌkəlvər| city in SW California, W of Los Angeles, an industrial and filmmaking center. Pop. 38,793.

Cu·mae |'kyōōmē| ancient city in SW Italy, near Naples. It is believed to be the site of the earliest Greek colony in Italy or Sicily, founded around 750 B.C. The priestess called the Cumaean Sybil lived in a nearby cave. □ **Cumaean** adj.

Cu·ma·ná |ˌko͞omä'nä| historic port city in NE Venezuela, capital of Sucre state, on the Manzanares River. Pop. 212,000. It is said to be the oldest European settlement in South America.

Cum·ber·land |'kəmbərlənd| former county of NW England. In 1974 it was united with Westmorland and part of Lancashire to form the county of Cumbria.

Cum·ber·land Gap |'kəmbərlənd| historic pass through the Appalachian Mts., from SW Virginia into SE Kentucky. In the 18th century it was the main route of the western settlement.

Cum·ber·land River |'kəmbərlənd| river that flows 690 mi./1,110 km. from the Cumberland Plateau in SE Kentucky across N Tennessee and back into Kentucky, where it joins the Ohio River near Paducah. Nashville lies along it.

Cum·ber·nauld |ˌkəmbər'nawld| town in central Scotland, in North Lanarkshire, near Glasgow, for which it was built to house an expanding population. Pop. 48,760.

Cum·bria |'kəmbrēə| county of NW England. County town: Carlisle. Cumbria was an ancient British kingdom, and the name continued to be used for the hilly NW region of England containing the Lake Dis-

trict and much of the N Pennines. The county of Cumbria was formed in 1974, largely from the former counties of Westmorland and Cumberland. □ **Cumbrian** adj. & n.

Cu·naxa |kyo͞o'næksə| town of ancient Babylonia, NW of Babylon, near the Euphrates River, scene of a battle in 401 B.C. from which the events in the Anabasis of Xenophon followed.

Cu·ne·ne |ko͞o'nänə| river of Angola, which rises near the city of Huambo and flows 156 mi./250 km. S as far as the border with Namibia, which then follows it W to the Atlantic.

Cu·neo |'ko͞onēō| industrial and market town in N Italy, capital of Cuneo province. Pop. 56,000.

Cu·per·ti·no |ˌko͞opər'tēnō| city in N central California, W of San Jose. It is part of the Silicon Valley complex. Pop. 40,263.

Cu·ra·çao |ˌk(y)o͞orə'sow; ˌk(y)o͞orə'sō| the largest island of the Netherlands Antilles, in the Caribbean Sea 37 mi./60 km. N of the Venezuelan coast. Pop. 144,100. Chief town: Willemstad.

Cu·re·pipe |ko͞or'pēp| resort town in W central Mauritius, in the highlands. Pop. 67,000.

Cu·ria |'kyo͞orēə| the papal court and government departments in the Vatican City, Rome, Italy.

Cu·ri·có |ˌko͞orē'kō| city in central Chile, in the agricultural Maule region. Pop. 104,000. It is the center of a wine-making district.

Cu·ri·ti·ba |ˌko͞orə'tēbə| industrial and commercial city in S Brazil, capital of the state of Paraná. Pop. 1,315,035.

Cur·ragh, the |'kərə| plain in County Kildare, E Ireland, noted as a military training site and center for horse racing.

Cur·zon Line |'kərzən| line defining the Russian-Polish border, named for British foreign secretary Lord Curzon, who proposed it in 1919, and modified in later years.

Cush |ko͞oSH| (also **Kush**) ancient kingdom of the upper Nile valley, in Nubia (present-day Egypt and Sudan). It gave its name to the Cushitic peoples and languages.

Cut·tack |'kətək| industrial and commercial port city in E India, in Orissa state. Pop. 402,000. It is a historical and religious center.

Cux·ha·ven |ko͞oks'häfən| seaport in NW Germany, on the Elbe River. Pop. 60,000.

Cuy·a·ho·ga River |ˌkīə'hōgə; kə'hōgə| river that flows 80 mi./130 km. through N

Ohio, emptying into Lake Erie at Cleveland. The industrial suburb of **Cuyahoga Falls** (pop. 48,950) lies along it near Akron.

Cuz•co |'kōōskō| city in the Andes in S Peru. Pop. 275,000. It was the capital of the Inca empire until the Spanish conquest in 1533.

Cwm•bran |kōōm'brän| town in SE Wales, administrative center of Monmouthshire. Pop. 44,800.

Cyc•la•des |'siklə,dēz| large group of islands in the S Aegean Sea, regarded in antiquity as circling around the sacred island of Delos. The Cyclades form a department of modern Greece. Greek name **Kikládhes**.

Cym•ru |'kəmrē| Welsh name for WALES.

Cy•press |'sīprəs| city in S central California, a suburb SE of Los Angeles. Pop. 42,655.

Cy•press Hills |'sīprəs| forested upland in SW Saskatchewan and SE Alberta.

Cy•prus |'sīprəs| the third-largest Mediterranean island, a republic lying 50 mi./80 km. S of the Turkish coast. Area: 3,573 sq. mi./9,251 sq. km. Pop. 708,000. Languages, Greek and Turkish. Capital and largest city: Nicosia. An ancient Greek colony, Cyprus was controlled by Turkey 1571–1878, then by Britain until independence in 1960, which was preceded by Greek-Turkish fighting. In 1974 Turkish forces took over part of the island, but the Turkish Republic of Northern Cyprus has not been recognized. Fruit, wine, and clothing are among the products of Cyprus. □ **Cypriot** *adj. & n.*

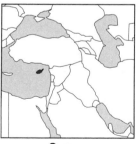

Cyprus

Cy•re•na•ica |,sirə'nāekə| region of NE Libya, bordering on the Mediterranean Sea, settled by the Greeks *c.* 640 B.C. □ **Cyrenaic** *adj.*

Cy•re•ne |sī'rēnē| ancient Greek city in N

Africa, near the coast in Cyrenaica. From the 4th century B.C. it was a great intellectual center.

Cy•the•ra |sə'THirə| (Greek name **Kithira**) a rocky island in S Greece, in the Aegean Sea off the coast of the Peloponnese.

Czech•o•slo•va•kia |,CHekəsləväkēə| former country in central Europe, now divided between the Czech Republic and Slovakia. Capital: Prague. □ **Czechoslovak** *n.* **Czechoslovakian** *adj. & n.*

Czechoslovakia

Czech Republic |CHek| country in central Europe, the W part of the former Czechoslovakia. Area: 30,461 sq. mi./ 78,864 sq. km. Pop. 10,298,700. Language, Czech. Capital and largest city: Prague. Comprising the former Bohemia, Moravia, and Silesia, the Czech Republic came into being in 1993. It has important heavy industry and mining sectors. Tourism is also important.

Czech Republic

Czer•no•witz |'CHernə,vits| German name for CHERNIVTSI, Ukraine.

Czę•sto•cho•wa |,CHENstə'kōvə| industrial city in S central Poland. Pop. 258,000. It is famous for the religious icon of the "Black Madonna" in its monastery, an object of pilgrimage.

Dd

Da·bro·wa Gór·ni·cza |dawN'brawvə gŏor 'nēcHə| mining and manufacturing city in S Poland. Pop. 137,000.

Dac·ca |'däkə| another spelling for DHAKA, Bangladesh.

Da·chau |'dä,KHow| city in Bavaria, SW Germany, on the Amper River near Munich. Pop. 33,000. The Nazis operated a concentration camp here 1933–45.

Dach·stein |'däKH,SHtīn| **1** mountain range in central Austria, in the Salzkammergut resort area, with many mountain lakes and glaciers. **2** the highest peak in the range: 9,829 ft./2,996 m.

Da·cia |'dāsHə| ancient country of SE Europe in what is now NW Romania. It was annexed by Trajan in A.D. 106 as a province of the Roman Empire. □ **Dacian** *adj. & n.*

Dade County |dād| county in SE Florida, on the Atlantic coast, embracing Miami and many suburbs as well as much of the Everglades. Pop. 1,937,044. Formally **Miami-Dade County.**

Da·dra and Na·gar Ha·ve·li |də'drä ænd 'nəgər ə'velē| Union Territory in W India, on the Arabian Sea. Pop. 138,500. Capital: Silvassa.

Dag·en·ham |'dægənəm| see BARKING AND DAGENHAM, London, England.

Dag·e·stan |,dägə'stän| autonomous republic in SW Russia, on the western shore of the Caspian Sea. Pop. 1,823,000. Capital: Makhachkala.

Da·ho·mey |də'hōmē| former name (until 1975) for BENIN. It is an alternate name for the Fon, the chief ethnic group in Benin.

Dai·qui·ri |,dīkē'rē| village in E Cuba, near Santiago de Cuba. U.S. troops landed here and at nearby Siboney in 1898, in the Spanish-American War. The rum drink is said to be named for the village.

Dai·ren |'dī'rən| former name for DALIAN.

Da·kar |dä'kär| the capital of Senegal, a port on the Atlantic coast. Pop. 1,641,350. It is one of W Africa's major commercial and industrial centers.

Dakh·la |'däklə| (also **ad Dakhla**) port town in Western Sahara, on the Atlantic coast. Pop. 30,000. A Moroccan provincial capital, it was the chief town of the Spanish colony of Rio Oro, and was called **Villa Cisneros**.

Da·ko·ta |də'kōtə| former territory of the U.S., organized in 1889 into the states of North Dakota and South Dakota. □ **Dakotan** *adj.*

Da·lar·na |'dälər,nä| (formerly **Dalecarlia**) forested region in W central Sweden. Its people are known for their distinctive dialect and customs.

Da Lat |'dä 'lät| city in southern Vietnam. Pop. 87,000. It is a resort, a market town, and one of Vietnam's foremost educational centers.

Da·le·car·lia |,dälə'kärlēə| another name for DALARNA, Sweden.

Dales, the |dālz| (also **Yorkshire Dales**) series of valleys of small rivers in N England that drain through Yorkshire to the North Sea. Among them are Teesdale, Wensleydale, Wharfedale, and Airedale.

Da·li |'dä'lē| city in Yunnan, S China, on the W shore of Er Hai. It is a noted marble-producing center. Pop. 399,000.

Da·lian |'däl'yän| port and shipbuilding center on the Liaodong Peninsula in NE China, now part of the urban complex of Luda. Pop. 2,524,000. Former name **Dairen.**

Dal·las |'dæləs| commercial, industrial, and cultural city in NE Texas, noted as a center of the oil and banking industries. Pop. 1,006,877. Dallas–Fort Worth Airport is one of the largest in the world.

Dalles, The |dælz| (official name **The City of the Dalles**) inland port city in N central Oregon, on the Columbia River. Pop. 11,060.

Dal·ma·tia |dæl'māsHə| ancient region in what is now SW Croatia, comprising mountains and a narrow coastal plain along the Adriatic, together with offshore islands. It once formed part of the Roman province of Illyricum. □ **Dalmatian** *adj. & n.*

Dal·ri·a·da |dæl'rīədə| ancient Gaelic kingdom in northern Ireland whose people (the Scots) established a colony in SW Scotland from about the late 5th century. By the 9th century Irish Dalriada had declined, but the people of Scottish Dalriada gradually acquired dominion over the whole of Scotland.

Dal·ton |'dawltn| city in NW Georgia, a textile center. Pop. 21,761.

Da·ly City |'dālē| city in N central California, a suburb on the SW side of San Francisco. Pop. 92,311.

Da·man and Diu |də'män ən 'dēyŏŏ|

Union Territory in India, on the W coast N of Bombay. Pop. 101,400. Capital: Daman. It consists of the district of Daman and the island of Diu, and until 1987 was administered with Goa.

Da•man•hur |ˌdämən'hōor| (ancient name **Heliopolis Parva**) commercial and industrial city in N Egypt, in the Nile delta. Pop. 216,000.

Da•ma•ra•land |dəˈmärə,lænd; ˈdämərə-ˌlænd| plateau region of central Namibia inhabited chiefly by the Damara and Herero peoples.

Da•mas•cus |dəˈmæskəs| the capital of Syria since the country's independence in 1946. Pop. 1,497,000. It has existed for over 4,000 years, and is the largest Syrian city, as well as the commercial and financial center.

Da•ma•vand, Mount |ˌdäməˈvänd| peak in N Iran, in the Elburz range. It is the highest peak in Iran: 18, 376 ft./5,601 m.

Da•mi•et•ta |ˌdæmēˈetə| **1** the E branch of the Nile Delta, in N Egypt. **2** port at the mouth of the delta. Pop. 113,000. Arabic name **Dumyat**.

Dan |dæn| biblical city, the northernmost of the Holy Land, thought to have been just W of present-day Baniyas, Syria.

Dan•a•kil Depression |ˈdænə,kil| long low-lying desert region of NE Ethiopia and N Djibouti, between the Red Sea and the Great Rift Valley.

Da Nang |däˈnäNG; dəˈnæNG| port city in central Vietnam, on the South China Sea. Pop. 382,670. During the Vietnam War it was used as a U.S. military base. Former name **Tourane**.

Da•na Point |ˈdänə| city in SW California, on the Pacific coast. Pop. 31,896.

Dan•bury |ˈdæn,berē; ˈdænb(ə)rē| city in W central Connecticut, formerly noted for its hat industry. Pop. 65,585.

Dan•dong |ˈdänˈdōoNG| port in Liaoning province, NE China, near the mouth of the Yalu River, on the border with North Korea. Pop. 660,500. Former name **Antung**.

Dane•law |ˈdän,law| the part of N and E England occupied or administered by Danes from the late 9th century until after the Norman Conquest.

Dan•ish West In•dies |ˈdänisH ,west ˈindēz| former name for the U.S. Virgin Islands, held by Denmark 1754–1917.

Dan•jiang•kou |ˈdänjeˈäNGˈkō| city in Hubei province, E central China, at the S end of the Danjiangkou Reservoir. Pop. 431,000.

Dan•mark |ˈdän,märk| Danish name for DENMARK.

Dan River |dæn| river that flows 180 mi./290 km. from SW Virginia into North Carolina, to the Roanoke River.

Dan•ube River |ˈdæn,yōob| river that rises in the Black Forest in SW Germany and flows about 1,700 mi./2,736 km. into the Black Sea. It is the second-longest river in Europe after the Volga; the cities of Vienna, Bratislava, Budapest, and Belgrade are situated on it. German name **Donau**. □ **Danubian** adj. & n.

Da•nu•bi•an Principalities |dəˈnyōo-bēən| the former European principalities of Moldavia and Wallachia. In 1861 they united to form the state of Romania.

Dan•vers |ˈdænvərz| town in NE Massachusetts, NE of Boston. Pop. 24,174.

Dan•ville¹ |ˈdæn,vil; ˈdænvəl| city in N central California, NE of Oakland. Pop. 31,306.

Dan•ville² |ˈdæn,vil; ˈdænvəl| city in E central Illinois. Pop. 33,828.

Dan•ville³ |ˈdæn,vil; ˈdænvəl| city in S Virginia, on the Dan River, noted for its tobacco and textile industries. Pop. 53,056.

Dan•zig |ˈdäntsig| German name for GDAŃSK, Poland.

Dão |ˈdãō; dow| river and wine-growing region in N central Portugal. The river (50 mi./80 km.) rises in the Serra de Lapa and flows SW into the Mondego River near Coimbra.

Dap•sang |däpˈsäNG| another name for K2.

Da•qing |ˈdäˈCHiNG| (also **Taching**) major industrial city in NE China, in Heilongjiang province. Pop. 996,800.

Dar•bhan•ga |dərˈbəNGgə| commercial city in NE India, in Bihar state. Pop. 218,000.

Dar•da•nelles |ˌdärdnˈelz| narrow strait between European and Asiatic Turkey (called the Hellespont in classical times), linking the Sea of Marmara with the Aegean Sea. It is 38 mi./60 km. long. In 1915, it was the scene of an unsuccessful attack on Turkey by Allied troops (see GALLIPOLI).

Dar es Sa•laam |ˌdär ,es səˈläm| (also **Da-ressalam**) the chief port and long the capital of Tanzania. Pop. 1,360,850. It was founded in 1866 by the sultan of Zanzibar. Although it retains some key functions, the capital is officially Dodoma, and the transition has been in progress through the 1990s.

Dar•fur |ˈdär,fōor| region in the W of Sudan. Until 1874 it was an independent kingdom.

Dar·i·en, Gulf of |ˌdærēˈen| part of the Caribbean Sea between Panama and Colombia.

Da·rién |ˌdærēˈen| sparsely populated province of E Panama. The name was formerly applied to the whole of the Isthmus of Panama.

Dar·jee·ling |därˈjēliNG| (also **Darjiling**) hill station at an altitude of 7,054 ft./2,150 m. in W Bengal, NE India, near the Sikkim border. Pop. 73,090. The area is famous for its tea.

Dark Continent nickname for AFRICA, used esp. in the nineteenth century.

Dar·khan |ˈdärˌKHän| (also **Darhan**) industrial and mining city in N Mongolia, the second largest in the country, established in 1961. Pop. 80,100.

Dar·ling River |ˈdärliNG| river of SE Australia, flowing 1,712 mi./2,757 km. in a generally SW course to join the Murray River.

Dar·ling·ton |ˈdärliNGtən| industrial town in Durham, NE England. Pop. 96,700.

Darm·stadt |ˈdärmˌSHtät| city in Hesse, western Germany, a heavy industrial and European space agency center. Pop. 140,040.

Dart·ford |ˈdärtfərd| town in Kent, SE England, an industrial and residential suburb E of London on the Thames River. Pop. 62,000.

Dart·moor |ˈdärtˌmawr| moorland district in Devon, SW England, that was a royal forest in Saxon times, now a national park. A famed prison is here.

Dart·mouth[1] |ˈdärtməTH| port in Devon, SW England. Pop. 6,210. It is the site of the Royal Naval College.

Dart·mouth[2] |ˈdärtməTH| city in S central Nova Scotia, across Halifax Harbour from Halifax. Pop. 67,798.

Dar·win |ˈdärwən| the capital of Northern Territory, Australia, a remote military and tourist city on the Timor Sea. Pop. 73,300.

Dash·howuz |ˌdəSHəˈwōōs| (formerly **Tashauz**) oasis city in N Turkmenistan, in the Amu Darya valley near the Uzbekistan border. Pop. 114,000.

Da·tong |ˈdäˈtōōNG| industrial and mining city in N China, in Shanxi province. Pop. 1,090,000. The nearby Yungang caves are famed for their ancient stone carvings.

Dau·gav·pils |ˈdowgəvˌpils| transportation center and commercial city in SE Latvia, on the Western Dvina River. Pop. 127,000. Former Russian name **Dvinsk**.

Dau·lat·a·bad |ˌdawlətəˈbäd| (formerly **Deogiri**) historic town in W India, in Maharashtra state, NW of Aurangabad.

Dau·phi·né |ˌdawfēˈnä| region and former province of SE France, in the Dauphiné Alps. Its capital was Grenoble.

Da·van·ge·re |ˈdəvəngərē| commercial and industrial city in S India, in Karnataka state. Pop. 287,000.

Da·vao |ˈdäˌvow| seaport in the S Philippines, on the island of Mindanao. Pop. 850,000. Founded in 1849, it is the largest city on the island and the third-largest in the Philippines.

Dav·en·port |ˈdævənˌpawrt| industrial city in SE Iowa, on the Mississippi River, one of the Quad Cities. Pop. 95,333.

Da·vis |ˈdāvəs| academic and agricultural city in N central California, W of Sacramento. Pop. 46,209.

Da·vis Mountains |ˈdāvəs| range in SW Texas, site of the Mount Locke observatory and several resorts.

Da·vis Strait |ˈdāvəs| sea passage 400 mi./645 km. long separating Greenland from Baffin Island and connecting Baffin Bay with the Atlantic.

Da·vos |däˈvōs| resort and winter-sports center in E Switzerland. Pop. 10,500.

Daw·son |ˈdawsən| town in the W central Yukon Territory, on the Klondike and Yukon rivers, center of a gold rush after 1896.

Da·xian |ˈdäSHēˈän| (also **Dachuan**) city in Sichuan province, central China, on the Zhou River N of Chongqing. Pop. 218,000.

Day·ton[1] |ˈdātn| industrial city in W Ohio. Pop. 182,000. It was the home of the aviation pioneers the Wright brothers and is still a center of aerospace research.

Day·ton[2] |ˈdātn| city in SE Tennessee, famed as the site of the 1925 trial of John Scopes for teaching evolution. Pop. 5,671.

Day·to·na Beach |däˈtōnə| resort city in NE Florida, on the Atlantic coast. Pop. 61,921.

Da·zu |ˈdädˈzōō| important Buddhist archeological site, Sichuan province, central China, in the hills 100 mi./160 km. NW of Chongqing, with over 50,000 9th–13th century stone carvings.

DDR abbreviation for DEUTSCHE DEMOKRATISCHE REPUBLIK.

Dead Sea |ded| salt lake or inland sea in the Jordan valley, on the Israel–Jordan border. Its surface is 1,300 ft./400 m. below sea level.

Dead·wood |ˈdedˌwŏŏd| city in W South Dakota, in the Black Hills, famed for its 1870s gold rush and Boot Hill cemetery. Pop. 1,830.

Deal |dēl| port and resort town in SE England, one of the Cinque Ports in Kent. Pop. 26,000. Julius Caesar is said to have landed here in his invasion of Britain in A.D.55.

Dear·born |'dir,bawrn; 'dirbərn| city in SE Michigan, on the SW side of Detroit, home to the Ford auto company and to Greenfield Village, a large historical restoration complex. Pop. 89,286.

Death Valley |deTH| desert basin, extending to 282 ft./86 m. below sea level, in SE California and SW Nevada, the lowest, hottest, and driest part of North America.

Deau·ville |'dō'vēl| resort town in Normandy, N France, on the English Channel. Long a fashionable resort, it has a famous casino and racetrack.

De·bre·cen |'debrət,sen| industrial and commercial city in E Hungary, in the Great Alfold. Pop. 217,290. It is the second-largest city in Hungary.

De·cap·o·lis |də'kæpələs| federation of ancient Greek cities in Palestine, mostly N and NE of the Sea of Galilee, formed under Roman protection in the 1st century B.C. Damascus was the most important.

De·ca·tur[1] |də'kātər| industrial city in N Alabama, on the Tennessee River. Pop. 48,761.

De·ca·tur[2] |də'kātər| industrial and commercial city in central Illinois. Pop. 83,885.

Dec·can |'dekən| triangular plateau in S India, bounded by the Malabar Coast in the W, the Coromandel Coast in the E, and by the Vindhaya Mts. and the Narmada River in the N.

Ded·ham |'dedəm| town in E Massachusetts, a suburb SW of Boston. Pop. 23,782.

Dee[1] |dē| river in NE Scotland, which rises in the Grampian Mts. and flows E past Balmoral Castle to the North Sea at Aberdeen.

Dee[2] |dē| river that rises in North Wales and flows past Chester and into the Irish Sea.

Deep South |'dēp 'sowTH| parts of the SE U.S. regarded as most embodying Southern traditions. Mississippi, Alabama, and South Carolina are regarded as at its heart. See also SOUTH, THE.

Deer·field |'dir,fēld| historic town in NW Massachusetts, on the Connecticut River. Pop. 5,018. It suffered major Indian attacks in 1675 and 1704.

Deer·field Beach |'dir,fēld| resort city in SE Florida, N of Fort Lauderdale. Pop. 46,325.

De·fense, la |,lä dā'fäNs| business complex just W of Paris, France. Ultramodern, sleek buildings and sculptures characterize the area.

De·hi·wa·la |,dähē'wələ| resort town on the W coast of Sri Lanka. Pop. 174,000. It has one of the best-regarded zoos in Asia.

Deh·ra Dun |'dərə 'doon| city in N India, in a valley at the foot of the Himalayas in Uttar Pradesh state. Pop. 270,000. The Indian military academy and a noted forestry research institute are here.

De Kalb |di'kælb| industrial city in N central Illinois. Pop. 34,925.

De·la·no |də'länō| agricultural city in S central California. Pop. 22,762.

Del·a·ware |'delə,wær| see box.

Del·a·ware River |'delə,wær| river of the NE U.S. Rising in the Catskill Mts. in New York State, it flows some 280 mi./450 km. S to N Delaware, where it meets the Atlantic at Delaware Bay. For much of its length it forms the E border of Pennsylvania.

Delft |delft| town in the Netherlands, in the province of South Holland. Pop. 89,400. The home of the painters Pieter de Hooch and Jan Vermeer, it is noted for its pottery.

Del·hi |'delē| Union Territory in N central

Delaware

Capital: Dover
Largest city: Wilmington
Other cities: Brookside, Claymont, Edgemoor, Newark, Smyrna
Population: 666,168,000 (1990); 743,603 (1998); 800,000 (2005 proj.);
Population rank (1990): 46
Rank in land area: 49
Abbreviation: DE; Del.
Nicknames: First State; Diamond State; Blue Hen State
Motto: 'Liberty and Independence'
Bird: blue hen chicken
Fish: weakfish
Flower: peach blossom
Tree: American holly
Song: "Our Delaware"
Noted physical features: Delaware Bay, Rehoboth Bay
Tourist attractions: E.I. du Pont de Nemours; Ft. Christina Monument, Holy Trinity (Old Swedes) Church; Hagley Museum, Winterthur Museum and Gardens; Rehoboth Beach; Dover Downs International Speedway
Admission date: December 7, 1787
Order of admission: 1
Name origin: Name first given to the river by Capt. Samuel Argall, who explored it in 1610, for Lord De La Warr, early governor of Virginia; then used of the Lenni-Lenape Indians, and finally of the state.

India, containing the cities of Old and New Delhi. Pop. 7,175,000. *Old Delhi*, a walled city on the Jumna River, was made the capital of the Mogul Empire in 1638 by Shah Jahan (1592–1666). *New Delhi*, the capital of India, was built 1912–29 to replace Calcutta as the capital of British India.

Del·mar·va Peninsula |del'märvə| region comprising part of *Dela*ware, the Eastern Shore of *Mary*land, and part of *Virgin*ia. Chesapeake Bay lies to the W.

Del·men·horst |'delmən,hawrst| industrial city in NW Germany, near Bremen. Pop. 76,000.

De·los |'dē,läs| small Greek island in the Aegean Sea, regarded as the center of the Cyclades. Now virtually uninhabited, in classical times it was considered to be sacred to Apollo, and according to legend was the birthplace of Apollo and Artemis. Greek name **Dhílos**. □ **Delian** *adj. & n.*

Del·phi |'del,fī| one of the most important religious sanctuaries of ancient Greece, dedicated to Apollo and situated on the lower S slopes of Mount Parnassus above the Gulf of Corinth. Thought of as the "navel" of the earth, it was the seat of the Delphic Oracle, whose riddling responses to a wide range of questions were delivered by Apollo's priestess, the Pythia. Greek name **Dhelfoí**. □ **Delphic** *adj.*

Del·ray Beach |'del,rā| resort city in SE Florida, N of Fort Lauderdale. Pop. 47,181.

Del Rio |del 'rēō| city in SW Texas, on the Rio Grande. Pop. 30,705.

Del·ta, the |'deltə| region in N Mississippi, lying between the Yazoo and Mississippi rivers, famed for its cotton and for blues music. Also called the **Yazoo Delta** or **Mississippi Delta.**

Del·ta |'deltə| municipality in SW British Columbia, SE of Vancouver. Pop. 88,978.

De·me·rara[1] |,demə'rærə| former Dutch colony in South America, now part of Guyana.

De·me·rara[2] |,demə'rærə| river of N Guyana. Rising in the Guiana Highlands, it flows about 200 mi./320 km. N to the Atlantic.

Demp·ster Highway |'dempstər| road opened in 1979 to connect the Yukon Territory with the Mackenzie delta, in the Northwest Territories. It is the only highway in Canada to cross the Arctic Circle.

De·na·li |də'nälē| another name for MOUNT MCKINLEY, Alaska, and the name of the national park that surrounds it.

Den·bigh·shire |'denbēsHər; 'denbēsHir| county of N Wales; administrative center, Ruthin. It was divided between Clwyd and Gwynedd between 1974 and 1996.

Den Haag |dən 'häg| Dutch name for the HAGUE.

Den Hel·der |dən 'heldər| chief North Sea naval base of the Netherlands, opposite the island of TEXEL. Pop. 62,000.

Den·i·son |'denəsən| city in N Texas, on the Red River. Pop. 21,505.

De·niz·li |,deniz'lē| commercial city in SW Turkey, capital of Denizli province. Pop. 203,000. Ruins of ancient Laodicea ad Lycum, nearby, draw tourists.

Den·mark |'den,märk| (official name **Kingdom of Denmark**; Danish name **Danmark**) country in N Europe, in Scandinavia, on the Jutland peninsula and neighboring islands, between the North and Baltic seas. Area: 16,631 sq. mi./43,075 sq. km. Pop. 5,100,000. Language, Danish. Capital and largest city: Copenhagen. Denmark emerged as a separate country during the Viking period (10th–11th centuries). It is both industrial and agricultural; dairying is important, as is tourism. Greenland and the Faeroe Islands are overseas territories. □ **Danish** *adj.* **Dane** *n.*

Denmark

Den·mark Strait |'den,märk| arm of the N Atlantic Ocean between Iceland and Greenland.

Den·pa·sar |dən'päs,är| the chief city of the island of Bali, Indonesia, a seaport on the S coast. Pop. 261,200.

Den·ton |'dentn| commercial and educational city in NE Texas. Pop. 66,270.

D'En·tre·cas·teaux Islands |,däNtrəkäs-'tō| island group in SE Papua New Guinea, off the SE coast of New Guinea, of which the largest are Goodenough, Fergusson, and Normanby islands.

Dents du Mi·di |,däN dY mē'dē| mountain group in SE France, in the W Alps, between the Rhône River at Martigny and Mont

Blanc. The highest point is Dent du Midi (10,695 ft./3,260 m.).

Den·ver |'denvər| the state capital and largest city of Colorado. Pop. 467,600. Situated at an altitude of 5,280 ft./1,608 m. on the E side of the Rocky Mts., Denver developed in the 1870s as a silver-mining town. The "Mile-High City" is now an administrative, industrial, and commercial center, the metropolis of the mountain region.

De·o·la·li |ˌdāō'lälē| commercial and resort town in W India, in Maharashtra state. Pop. 51,000.

Der·bent |dyir'byent| city in S Russia, in Dagestan on the W shore of the Caspian Sea. Pop. 80,000.

Der·by |'därbē; 'dərbē| industrial city in the Midlands of England, on the Derwent River. Pop. 214,000.

Der·by·shire |'därbē,sHir; 'därbēsHər| county of N central England; county seat, Matlock.

Der·ry |'derē| see LONDONDERRY, Northern Ireland.

Der·went |'dərwənt| name of four short rivers in N and N central England, in Cumbria, Derbyshire, Durham and Northumberland, and Yorkshire. **Derwent Water** is a lake on the first of these, in the Lake District in Cumbria.

Des·er·et |ˌdezə'ret| name proposed in the 1840s by Mormon settlers for what became Utah.

Des Moines |də 'moin| the state capital and largest city of Iowa. Pop. 193,200.

Des·na River |dyiz'nä| river (550 mi./885 km.) in W Russia and Ukraine, rising E of Smolensk and flowing into the Dnieper River near Kiev.

De So·to |də 'sōtō| city in NE Texas, a suburb S of Dallas. Pop. 30,544.

Des Plaines |des 'plänz| city in NE Illinois, a suburb NW of Chicago. Pop. 53,223. O'Hare International Airport is on its S side.

Des·sau |'des,ow| industrial city in Germany, on the Mulde River, in Anhalt about 70 mi./112 km. SW of Berlin. Pop. 95,100. The famed Bauhaus design institute was here 1925–32.

Det·mold |'det,mawlt| city and capital of North Rhine–Westphalia, in NW Germany. Pop. 67,000. A resort on the N edge of the Teutoburg Forest, it is also a manufacturing center.

De·troit |di'troit; 'dē,troit| industrial city and Great Lakes port in SE Michigan. Pop. 1,028,000. Its metropolitan area is the center of the U.S. automobile industry. It is popularly known as either **Motor City** or **Motown.**

Deut·sche De·mo·kra·tische Re·pub·lik |'doicHə ˌdemōkrätisHə ˌräpōō'blēk| German name for the former state of East Germany.

Deutsch·land |'doicH,länt| German name for GERMANY.

De·va |'dävə| market town in W central Romania, on the Mures River. Pop. 77,000.

De·ven·ter |'dävəntər| industrial city in E Netherlands, on the IJssel River. Pop. 68,000.

Dev·il's Island |'devəlz| rocky island off the coast of French Guiana, used 1852–1953 as a penal settlement, especially for political prisoners.

Dev·il's Tower |'devəlz| rock column in NE Wyoming, a national monument on the Belle Fourche River. It is 865 ft./264 m. high.

Dev·on |'devən| (also **Devonshire**) a county of SW England; county seat, Exeter.

Dev·on Island |'devən| southernmost of the Queen Elizabeth Is., in the Arctic Archipelago of Nunavut. It has some plant and animal life.

Dews·bu·ry |'d(y)ōōz,berē| textile-manufacturing town in N England, near Leeds. Pop. 50,000.

De·yang |də'yæNG| industrial city in Sichuan province, central China, N of Chengdu. Pop. 768,000.

Dez·ful |dez'fōōl| (also **Desful; Disful**) commercial town in W Iran, on the Dez River. Pop. 181,000.

Dezh·nev, Cape |'dyezHnəf| (also **East Cape**) cape at E end of Chukchi Peninsula, E Russia, projecting into the Bering Strait.

De·zhou |'də'jō| city in Shandong province, E China, on the Grand Canal NW of Jinan. Pop. 283,000.

Dhah·ran |dä'rän; ˌdähə'rän| oil town in E Saudi Arabia. Pop. 74,000. It was an Allied forces port and military base during the Persian Gulf War.

Dha·ka |'däkə| (also **Dacca**) the capital and largest city of Bangladesh, a commercial center in the Ganges delta. Pop. 3,637,890.

Dhan·bad |'dänbäd| city in Bihar, NE India, center of a coal-mining district. Pop. 818,000.

Dha·ram·sa·la |därm'sälə| (also **Dharmshala**) hill resort in N India, in Himachal Pradesh state. Pop. 17,000. The Dalai Lama's Tibetan government-in-exile is here.

Dhar·war |där'wär| textile-manufacturing city in S India, in Karnataka state, twinned with Hubli. Pop. 648,000.

Dhau·la·gi·ri |,dowlə'girē| mountain massif in the Himalayas, in Nepal, with six peaks, rising to 26,810 ft./8,172 m. at its highest point.

Dhel·foí |THel'fē| Greek name for DELPHI.

Dhí·los |'THē,laws| Greek name for DELOS.

Dhu·lia |'doōlēə| (also **Dhule**) ndustrial city in W India, in Maharashtra state, NE of Bombay. Pop. 278,000.

Di·ab·lo Canyon |dē'æblō| nuclear power plant site in SW California, near San Luis Obispo, controversial because it was built over a geologic fault.

Di·a·man·ti·na River |,dīəmən'tēnə| intermittent river in E central Australia, flowing 560 mi./890 km. from central Queensland to South Australia.

Dia·mond Head |'dī(ə)mənd| an extinct volcano (761 ft./232 m.) overlooking the port of Honolulu on the Hawaiian island of Oahu.

Di·as·po·ra, the |dī'æsp(ə)rə| from a Greek term for 'scattering,' the world outside historical Palestine, into which the Jews were dispersed from the 6th century B.C.

Die·go Gar·cia |dē,āgō gär'sēə| the largest island of the Chagos Archipelago in the middle of the Indian Ocean, site of a strategic Anglo-American naval base established in 1973.

Dien Bien Phu |,dyen ,byen 'foō| village in NW Vietnam, in 1954 the site of a French military post that was captured by the Vietminh after a 55-day siege, effectively ending French power in the region.

Di·eppe |dē'ep| channel port in N France, from which ferries run to Newhaven and other English ports. Pop. 36,600. In August 1942, it was the scene of an unsuccessful British-Canadian commando raid.

Dig·by |'digbē| port town in W Nova Scotia, off the Bay of Fundy. Pop. 2,311.

Di·jon |dē'zHawN| industrial city in E central France, the former capital of Burgundy. Pop. 151,640.

Di·li |'dilē| seaport on the Indonesian island of Timor, which was (until 1975) the capital of the former Portuguese colony of East Timor. Pop. 60,150.

Di·mi·tov·grad |di'mētrəf,grät| industrial town in W Russia, NW of Samara. Pop. 133,000.

Di·naj·pur |di'näj,poōr| commercial city in NW Bangladesh, capital of Dinajpur district. Pop. 128,000.

Di·na·ric Alps |də'nærik| mountain range in the Balkan peninsula, running parallel to the Adriatic coast from Slovenia in the NW, through Croatia, Bosnia, and Montenegro, to Albania in the SE. The Karst region is here.

Din·digul |'dindi,gəl| commercial town in S India, in Tamil Nadu state. Pop. 182,000. It is noted for its cheroots.

Din·gle |'diNGgəl| port town in SW Ireland, at the W end of the **Dingle Peninsula,** on the N side of **Dingle Bay,** in County Kerry. Pop. 1,300. It is the westernmost town in Europe.

Di·o·mede Islands |'dīə,mēd| two islands in the Bering Strait. Big Diomede belongs to Russia, and Little Diomede belongs to the United States. They are separated by the International Date Line.

Di·re·da·wa |'dērā'dowə| industrial and commercial city in E Ethiopia, on the rail line from Addis Ababa to Djibouti. Pop. 165,000.

Dis·ko |'diskō| island with extensive coal deposits on the W coast of Greenland. Its chief settlement is Godhavn.

Dis·mal Swamp |'dizməl| wetland in SE Virginia and NE North Carolina, famed in legend and history. Also, **Great Dismal Swamp.**

Dis·ney·land |'diznē,lænd| amusement park in Anaheim, California, opened in 1955.

Dis·ney World |'diznē ,wərld| amusement park in Lake Buena Vista, SW of Orlando, Florida, opened in 1971. Formally **Walt Disney World.**

Dis·pu·ra |dis'poōrə| (also **Dispur**) city in NE India, capital of Assam state.

Dis·trict of Co·lum·bia |kə'ləmbēə| (abbrev.: **D.C.**) federal district of the U.S., coextensive with the city of WASHINGTON, on the Potomac River between Virginia and Maryland. Created in 1790, it had its Virginia components (now Arlington County and Alexandria) returned to that state in 1846.

Dis·tri·to Fe·de·ral |dēs'trētō ,fādā'räl| (abbrev. **D.F.;** English name **Federal District**) governmental district of Mexico, surrounding and including Mexico City. Pop. 8.2 million.

Diu |'dēoō| a constituent part of Daman and Diu Union Territory, W India, comprising mainly an island and port town of the same name.

Di·vi·nó·po·lis |jēvē'nawpōlēs| commercial city in SE Brazil, in Minas Gerais state. Pop. 172,000.

Dix·ie |'diksē| popular name for the U.S. South, especially the pre-Civil War South. Also **Dixieland.**

Di·yar·ba·kir |di,yärbä'kir| commercial city in SE Turkey, capital of a province of the same name. Pop. 381,100. It has a large Kurdish community.

Dja·ja·pu·ra |,jäyä'pŏŏrə| see JAYAPURA, Indonesia.

Dja·kar·ta |jə'kärtə| (also **Jakarta**) the capital and largest city of Indonesia, situated in NW Java. Pop. 8,222,500. Former name (until 1949) **Batavia**. It is the commercial, cultural, and administrative center of Indonesia.

Djam·bi |'jämbē| (also **Jambi**) port city in Indonesia, on SE Sumatra. Pop. 340,000.

Djer·ba |'jərbə; 'jerbə| (also **Jerba**) resort island in the Gulf of Gabès off the coast of Tunisia.

Dji·bou·ti |jə'bŏŏtē| (also **Jibuti**) **1** republic on the NE coast of Africa, on the Gulf of Aden. Area: 9,003 sq. mi./23,310 sq. km. Pop. 441,000. Languages, Arabic (official), French (official), Somali and other Cushitic languages. It is largely desert. **2** its capital, a port that handles much Ethiopian trade. Pop. 290,000. □ **Djiboutian** *adj. & n.*

Djibouti

DMZ abbreviation for Demilitarized Zone, a strip of land separating North and South Korea, intended to keep the hostile forces apart. A similar zone was also in use during the Vietnam War, separating North and South Vietnam.

Dnie·per River |(də)'nēpər| river of E Europe, rising in Russia W of Moscow and flowing S some 1,370 mi./2,200 km. through Ukraine to the Black Sea. Ukrainian name **Dnipro.**

Dnies·ter River |(də)'nēstər| river of E Europe, rising in the Carpathian Mts. in W Ukraine and flowing 876 mi./1,410 km. to the Black Sea near Odessa. Russian name **Dnestr**, Ukrainian name **Dnister.**

Dni·pro·dzer·zhinsk |(də),nyeprədzir-'zhinsk| industrial city and river port in Ukraine, on the Dnieper River. Pop. 283,600. Former name (until 1936) **Kamenskoye.**

Dni·pro·pe·trovsk |(də),neyprōpə'trawfsk| industrial city and river port in Ukraine, on the Dnieper River. Pop. 1,187,000. It was known as Yekaterinoslav (Ekaterinoslav) until 1926.

Do·brich |'dawbrēch| city in NE Bulgaria, the center for an agricultural region. Pop. 115,800. It was formerly called Tolbukhin (1949–91).

Dob·ru·ja |'dawbrŏŏ,jä| district in E Romania and NE Bulgaria on the Black Sea coast, bounded on the N and W by the Danube River.

Do·dec·a·nese |dō'dekə,nēz| group of twelve major and many smaller Greek islands in the SE Aegean, of which the largest is Rhodes.

Dodge City |däj| city in SW Kansas. Pop. 21,129. Established in 1872 as a railhead on the Santa Fe Trail, it rapidly gained a reputation as a rowdy frontier town.

Do·do·ma |'dōdəmə| the official capital of Tanzania, in the center of the country. Pop. 203,830. See also DAR ES SALAAM

Do·do·na |də'dōnə| ancient town in NW Greece. It was the site of an early oracle of Zeus, believed to originate when a dove landed in an oak tree here; believers interpreted the rustling of the leaves and other sounds to divine Zeus's message.

Dog·ger Bank |'dawgər 'bæNGk| submerged sandbank in the North Sea, about 70 mi./115 km. off the NE coast of England. It is an important fishing zone.

Dog·patch |'dawg,pæch| home of Li'l Abner and others in the comic strip of Al Capp, a fictional setting somewhere on the Ozark Plateau.

Do·ha |'dōhə| the capital of Qatar; pop. 300,000.

Dol·drums |'dōldrəmz| area of the earth, just N of the equator and near the trade winds, where seas give birth to hurricanes but may also be characterized by extended periods of calm.

Dollard-des-Ormeaux |dō'lärdəzor'mō| city in S Quebec, a residential suburb SW of Montreal. Pop. 46,922.

Dol·o·mite Mountains |'dōlə,mīt; 'dälə-,mīt| (also **the Dolomites**) range of the Alps in N Italy, so named because of the characteristic rock of the region is dolomitic limestone. Marmolada, at 10,965 ft./3,342 m., is the high point.

Do·lo·res Hi·dal·go |də'lōrəs ē'dälgō| historic commercial city in central Mexico, in Guanajuato state. Pop. 40,000. Here Father Miguel Hidalgo issued the 1810 declaration (the *Grito de Hidalgo*) initiating the Mexican war of independence.

Dom, the |dōm| mountain in the Mischabelhörner group of the Pennine Alps, in S Switzerland. It is the highest mountain entirely in Switzerland: 14,911 ft./4,545 m.

Dome of the Rock Islamic shrine in E Jerusalem, surrounding the rock on which Abraham is said to have prepared to sacrifice his son Isaac, and from which Muhammad ascended into heaven. It is built on Mt. Moriah, sacred to Jews as the site of the Temple of Solomon.

Dom·i·ni·ca |,dämə'nēkə; də'minikə| mountainous island commonwealth in the West Indies, the loftiest of the Lesser Antilles and the northernmost and largest (290 sq. mi./751 sq. km.) of the Windward Islands. Pop. 71,790. Languages, English (official), Creole. Capital and largest community: Roseau. Tropical crops are important. The island came into British possession at the end of the 18th century, becoming independent in 1978. □ **Do·minican** *adj. & n.*

Dominica

Do·mi·ni·can Republic |də'minikən| country in the Caribbean occupying the E part of the island of Hispaniola. Area: 18,704 sq. mi./48,442 sq. km. Pop. 7,770,000. Language, Spanish. Capital and largest city: Santo Domingo. The Dominican Republic is the former Spanish colony of Santo Domingo. It was proclaimed a republic in 1844. The mountainous country relies on agriculture, mining, light industry, and tourism. □ **Dominican** *adj. & n.*

Dom·re·my |'dawNrä'mē| (also called **Domremy-la-Pucelle**) village in NE France, SW of Nancy, on the Meuse River. It is the birthplace of Joan of Arc.

Dominican Republic

Don, River[1] |dän| river in N England that rises in the Pennines and flows 70 mi./112 km. E to join the Ouse shortly before it, in turn, joins the Humber.

Don, River[2] |dän| river in Scotland that rises in the Grampians and flows 82 mi./131 km. E to the North Sea at Aberdeen.

Do·nau |'dō,now| German name for the DANUBE River.

Don·bas |'dän,bæs| Ukrainian name for DONETS BASIN.

Don·bass |dən'bäs; 'dän,bæs| Russian name for DONETS BASIN.

Don·cas·ter |'däNGkəstər| industrial town and rail center in N England, formerly part of Yorkshire. Pop. 284,300.

Don·e·gal |,däni'gawl; ,dəni'gawl| county in the extreme NW of the Republic of Ireland, part of the old province of Ulster. Pop. 128,000. Capital: Lifford.

Do·nets |də'n(y)ets| river in E Europe, rising near Belgorod in S Russia and flowing SE for some 630 mi./1,000 km. through Ukraine before re-entering Russia and joining the Don near Rostov.

Do·nets Basin |də'n(y)ets| coal-mining and industrial region of SE Ukraine, stretching between the valleys of the Donets and lower Dnieper rivers. Ukrainian name **Donbas**.

Do·netsk |də'n(y)etsk| the leading city of the Donets Basin in Ukraine. Pop. 1,117,000. The city was called **Yuzovka** from 1872 until 1924, and **Stalin** or **Stalino** from 1924 until 1961.

Dong-nai River |'dawNG 'ni| (also **Donnai**) river in Vietnam that flows 300 mi./483 km. from S central Vietnam to join the Saigon River below Ho Chi Minh City.

Dong·ting, Lake |'dooNG 'tiNG| (Chinese name **Dongting Hu**) shallow lake in Hunan province, E central China, the second-largest freshwater lake in China; area 1,089 sq. mi./2,820 sq. km.

Dong·ying |'dooNG 'yiNG| city in Hebei

province, E China, near the mouth of the Yellow River, in an area rich in oil. Pop. 540,000.

Don Mills |'dän 'milz| planned industrial, commercial, and residential community in North York, Ontario, just NE of Toronto.

Don•ner Pass |'dänər| site in the Sierra Nevada of NE California where some members of an 1844 emigrant party survived a blizzard partly by eating the dead.

Don•ny•brook |'dänē,brook| suburb to the SE of Dublin, Ireland, scene (1204–1855) of an annual fair famous for its fighting and riotous behavior.

Don River |dän| river in Russia that rises near Tula, SE of Moscow, and flows for a distance of 1,224 mi./1,958 km. to the Sea of Azov.

Doon River |doon| short river in SW Scotland, in the Strathclyde region, celebrated in the poetry of Robert Burns. It flows through **Loch Doon**, a widening, and into the Firth of Clyde.

Doone Valley |doon| valley in N Devon, SW England, N of Exmoor, Somerset, setting for the events in R.D. Blackmore's popular novel *Lorna Doone*.

Door•nik |'dawrnik| Flemish name for TOURNAI, Belgium.

Door Peninsula |dawr| resort region of NE Wisconsin, lying between Green Bay and Lake Michigan.

Dor•ches•ter[1] |'dawrCHəstər; 'dawr,CHestər| town in S England, the county seat of Dorset. Pop. 14,000.

Dor•ches•ter[2] |'dawrCHəstər; 'dawr,CHestər| residential section of Boston, Massachusetts, S of downtown.

Dor•dogne[1] |dawr'dōn(ye)| department of SW France. It contains caves that have yielded abundant remains of early humans and their artifacts and art, such as that at Lascaux.

Dor•dogne[2] |dawr'dōn(ye)| river of W France that rises in the Auvergne and flows 297 mi./472 km. W to meet the Garonne and form the Gironde estuary.

Dor•drecht |'dawr,dreKHt| industrial city and river port in the Netherlands, near the mouth of the Rhine (there called the Waal), 12 mi./20 km. SE of Rotterdam. Pop. 110,500. Also called **Dort**.

Do•ris |'dawrəs| ancient name for a mountainous district in central Greece. It was home to the Dorians, one of the four main groups of ancient Greeks.

Dor•set |'dawrsət| county of SW England; county seat, Dorchester. Pop. 645,000. It is central to the writings of Thomas Hardy.

Dort•mund |'dawrt,moont| industrial city and canal port in NW Germany, in North Rhine-Westphalia, a center for steel and brewing. Pop. 601,000.

Dor•val |dawr'väl| city in S Quebec, a suburb W of Montreal and home to its older airport. Pop. 17,249.

Dos Her•ma•nas |,dōs er'mänəs| industrial commune in SW Spain, SE of Seville. Pop. 77,000.

Do•than |'dōTHən| city in SE Alabama, near the Florida line. Pop. 53,589.

Dou•ai |dwe; doo'ä| industrial and commercial town in NW France, on the Scarpe River near Lille. Pop. 44,000. Douai was the center of the textile trade in the Middle Ages.

Dou•a•la |doo'älə| the chief port and largest city of Cameroon. Pop. 1,200,000.

Doubs River |doo| river (270 mi./435 km.) that rises in the Jura Mts., E France, flows NE, becoming part of the French-Swiss border, flows into Switzerland , and then turns W to return to France, finally joining the Saône River.

Doug•las |'dəgləs| resort town, the capital of the Isle of Man, in the Irish Sea. Pop. 22,210.

Doun•reay |doon'rā| village in extreme N Scotland, in Caithness, site of two now inactive nuclear breeder reactors and of an experimental wave-power station in the Pentland Firth.

Dou•ro |'dō,roo| river of the Iberian Peninsula, rising in central Spain and flowing W for 556 mi./900 km/ through Portugal to the Atlantic near Oporto. Spanish name **Duero**.

Do•ver[1] |'dōvər| the state capital of Delaware. Pop. 23,500.

Do•ver[2] |'dōvər| ferry port in Kent, SE England, on the English Channel. Pop. 34,300. It is mainland Britain's nearest point to the Continent, being only 22 miles (35 km) from Calais, France.

Do•ver[3] |'dōvər| industrial city in SE New Hampshire. Pop. 25,042.

Do•ver, Strait of |'dōvər| sea passage between England and France, connecting the English Channel with the North Sea. At its narrowest it is 22 mi./35 km. wide.

Down |down| one of the Six Counties of Northern Ireland, formerly an administrative area; chief town, Downpatrick. Pop. 339,000.

Down East |down 'ēst| name for NE New England and/or the Maritime Provinces, deriving from an old term for sailing downwind, to the E.

Dow·ners Grove |'downərz| village in NE Illinois, a suburb W of Chicago. Pop. 46,858.

Dow·ney |'downē| city in SW California, an industrial suburb SE of Los Angeles. Pop. 91,444.

Down·ing Street |'downiNG| street in central London, England, in Westminster, next to Whitehall. The official residence of the British prime minister is at 10 Downing St., and other key residences and offices are here as well.

Down·pat·rick |ˌdown'pætrik| town in SE Northern Ireland, the seat of County Down. Pop. 8,000. It is associated with St. Patrick, who was long thought to have been buried here along with Saints Columba and Brigid.

Downs |downz| region of chalk hills in S England, forming parallel ranges. The **North Downs** are in Surrey and Kent, the **South Downs** in Sussex.

Down Under nickname for Australia and New Zealand.

Doyles·town |'doilzˌtown| township in SE Pennsylvania, noted for its museums. Pop. 14,510.

Dra·chen·fels Mountain |'dräKHənˌfels| hill in the Siebengebirge, near Bonn, S Germany, rising 1,053 ft./321 m. The legendary character Siegfried is supposed to have slain a dragon here.

Dra·kens·berg Mountains |'dräkənzˌbərg| range of mountains in southern Africa, stretching in a NE–SW direction for 700 mi./1,126 km. through Lesotho and parts of South Africa. The highest peak is Thabana Ntlenyana (11,425 ft./3,482 m.).

Drake Passage |drāk| area of ocean, noted for its violent storms, connecting the South Atlantic with the South Pacific and separating the S tip of South America (Cape Horn) from the Antarctic Peninsula.

Drakes Bay |drāks| inlet of the Pacific Ocean, NW of San Francisco, California, visited by Francis Drake in 1579.

Dra·ma |'drämə| department in N Greece. Area: 1,339 sq. mi./3,468 sq. km. Pop. 97,000. Its capital is Drama.

Dram·men |'drämən| seaport in SE Norway, on an inlet of Oslofjord. Pop. 51,900.

Dran·cy |dräNsē| industrial town, a NE suburb of Paris, France. Pop. 61,000. During World War II there was a Nazi internment camp here.

Dra·va River |'drävə| (also **Drave**), river that rises in N Italy and flows 456 mi./725 km. through S Austria, Slovenia, and Croa-tia to join the Danube near Osijek. It forms part of the border between Hungary and Croatia.

Dres·den |'drezdən| city in eastern Germany, the capital of Saxony, on the Elbe River. Pop. 485,130. Famous for its baroque architecture and china industry, it was almost totally destroyed by Allied bombing in 1945.

Dri·na River |'drēnə| river, 285 mi./459 km. long, that flows into the Sava River W of Belgrade, Serbia. It constitutes part of the border between Bosnia and Herzegovina and Serbia.

Drobeta-Turnu Se·ve·rin |drō'bātə 'tōōrnōō ˌsävə'rēn| industrial port city in SW Romania, on the Danube River. Pop. 116,000.

Dro·ghe·da |'draw-ədə; 'droiədə| port city in the NE Republic of Ireland, in Louth. Pop. 23,000. In 1649 the inhabitants were massacred after refusing to surrender to Oliver Cromwell's forces. The Battle of the Boyne was fought nearby in 1690.

Drôme |drōm| department in SE France. Area: 2,520 sq. mi./6,525 sq. km. Pop. 414,000. The capital is Valence.

Drott·ning·holm |'drōōtniNGˌhō(l)m| the winter palace of the Swedish royal family, on an island to the W of Stockholm.

Drouzh·ba |'drōōzHbə| (also **Druzba**) resort town on the Black Sea coast of Bulgaria, N of Varna. Also called **Sveti Konstantin**.

Drum·cliff |ˌdrəm'klif| see BEN BULBEN, Ireland.

Drum·mond·ville |'drəməndˌvil| industrial city in S Quebec, E of Montreal. Pop. 35,462.

Dru·ry Lane |'drōōrē| street in central London, England, NE of Covent Garden, site since 1663 of the most famous British theaters, and thus a term for the theater itself.

Druze, Je·bel |'jebəl 'drōōz| (also **Jebel ed Druz**) **1** region in S Syria, home of the Druze, E of the Sea of Galilee, on the border with N Jordan. **2** mountain in this area: 5,900 ft./1,800 m.

Dry Tor·tu·gas |ˌdrī tawr'tōōgəz| island group in SW Florida, W of Key West, noted for its wildlife and for Fort Jefferson, built during the Civil War. Also **the Tortugas** or **Tortugas Keys**.

Duar·te, Pi·co |'pēkō 'dwärtə| (formerly **Monte Trujillo**) peak in the Cordillera Central of the central Dominican Republic, at 10,417 ft./3,175 m. said to be the highest in the Caribbean.

Du·bai |dōō'bī| **1** member state of the United Arab Emirates. Area: 1,506 sq. mi./3,900 sq. km. Pop. 674,100. **2** its capital city, a port on the Persian Gulf. Pop. 265,700.

Dub·lin |'dəblin| **1** the capital and largest city of the Republic of Ireland, an industrial port on the Irish Sea at the mouth of the Liffey River. Pop. 477,700. It is a cultural center associated with writers including Jonathan Swift, Oscar Wilde, and James Joyce. Irish name **Baile Átha Cliath**. **2** the most populous county in Ireland, including the city and many suburbs. Pop. 1,024,000. □ **Dubliner** *n*.

Du·brov·nik |dōō'brawvnik| port and resort on the Adriatic coast of Croatia. Pop. 66,100. A major medieval port, famed for its architecture, it was damaged during a Serbian siege in 1991. Italian name (until 1918) **Ragusa**.

Du·buque |də'byōōk| industrial and commercial city in NE Iowa, on the Mississippi River. Pop. 57,546.

Dud·ley |'dədlē| industrial and commercial city in the West Midlands of England, near Birmingham. Pop. 187,000.

Duf·fel |'dəfəl| town in S Belgium. Pop. 7,000. The coarse woolen cloth known as *duffel* originated here.

Du·four·spit·ze |də'fōōr'sнpitsə| second-highest peak in the Alps and the highest in Switzerland: 15,203 ft./4,634 m. It is in the Monta Rosa group of the Pennine Alps, on the Swiss-Italian border.

Dug·way |'dəg,wā| community in NW Utah, in the Great Salt Lake Desert, site of an Army range where chemical and biological weapons have been tested. Pop. 1,761.

Duis·burg |'dys,berk; 'd(y)ōōz,bərg| industrial city in NW Germany, in North Rhine-Westphalia. Pop. 537,440. It is the largest inland port in Europe, at the Rhine-Ruhr junction.

Du·luth |də'lōōтн| port in NE Minnesota, at the western end of Lake Superior. Pop. 92,800. With its neighbor Superior, Wisconsin, it is a leading grain- and ore-exporting port.

Dum·bar·ton |,dəm'bärtn| town in Scotland on the Clyde W of Glasgow, in West Dunbartonshire. Pop. 21,960.

Dum·bar·ton Oaks |'dəm,bärtn 'ōks| historic site in Washington, D.C., an estate at which plans for the United Nations were formulated in a 1944 meeting.

Dum Dum |'dəm ,dəm| city in NE India, in West Bengal state, near Calcutta. Pop. 41,000. The "dum-dum" bullet was first made here while the city was headquarters for British artillery.

Dum·fries |,dəm'frēs| market town in SW Scotland, administrative center of Dumfries and Galloway region. Pop. 32,130.

Dum·fries and Gal·lo·way |'dəm'frēs ən 'gælə,wā| administrative region in SW Scotland, formed in 1975; administrative center, Dumfries.

Dum·fries·shire |,dəm'frēsнər; ,dəm'frē ,sнir| former county of SW Scotland, which became part of Dumfries and Galloway region in 1975.

Dum·yat |dōōm'yät| Arabic name for DAMIETTA, Egypt.

Du·na·új·vá·ros |'dōōnow,värōsн| industrial town in central Hungary, on the Danube River. Pop. 60,000.

Dun·bar·ton·shire |dəm'bärtnsнər; dəm-'bärtn,sнir| (also **Dumbartonshire**) administrative region and former county of W central Scotland, on the Clyde, divided into *East Dunbartonshire* and *West Dunbartonshire*.

Dun·dalk[1] |,dən'daw(l)k| the county seat of Louth, in the Republic of Ireland, a port on the E coast. Pop. 25,800.

Dun·dalk[2] |'dən,dawk| community in N central Maryland, a port and suburb just SE of Baltimore. Pop. 65,800.

Dun·dee |dən'dē| industrial port and university city in E Scotland, on the N side of the Firth of Tay. Pop. 165,500.

Dun·e·din[1] |dən'ēdən| resort city in W Florida, on the Gulf of Mexico W of Tampa. Pop. 34,012.

Dun·e·din[2] |dən'ēdən| industrial port city on South Island, New Zealand. Pop. 113,900.

Dun·ferm·line |dən'fərmlən| industrial city in Fife, central Scotland, near the Firth of Forth. Pop. 55,000.

Dun·gar·van |dən'gärvən| town on the S coast of the Republic of Ireland, the administrative center of Waterford. Pop. 6,920.

Dunge·ness |,dənjə'nes; 'dənjə,nes| locality in NW Washington, on the Olympic Peninsula, that gave its name to a kind of crab.

Dun·hua |'dōōn'hwä| industrial city in Jilin province, NE China, on the Mudan River NW of Yanji. Pop. 450,000.

Dun·huang |'dōōn'hwäнg| town in Gansu province, NW China, on the old Silk Road near the site of the earliest known Buddhist cave shrines in China (4th century A.D.).

Dun·kirk |dən'kərk; 'dən,kərk| (French name **Dunkerque**) port in N France, on the English Channel. Pop 71,070. It was the scene of the evacuation to Britain in 1940 of 335,000 Allied troops who were rescued by warships, requisitioned civilian ships, and a host of small boats, under constant attack by German aircraft.

Dun Laoghaire |ˌdən 'lirē| ferry port and resort town in the Republic of Ireland, on Dublin Bay just SE of Dublin. Pop. 54,715. Earlier names **Dunleary** and (1820–1921) **Kingstown.**

Dun•net Head |'dənət 'hed| headland on the N coast of Scotland, between Thurso and John o'Groats. It is the most northerly point on the British mainland.

Dun•si•nane |dən'sinən; 'dənsə,nān| hill in central Scotland, in Tayside, in the Sidlaw Hills, the scene of the final defeat of Macbeth in the play of Shakespeare, based on events of the year 1054.

Dun•sta•ble |'dənstəbəl| historic industrial town in S England, N of the Chiltern Hills in Bedfordshire, at the junction of the ancient Watling Street and Icknield Way. Pop. 31,000.

Du•que de Ca•xi•as |'dōōkē dē kä'sHēəs| city in SE Brazil, a suburb of Rio de Janeiro. Pop. 1,352,160.

Dura-Europos |'dōōrə yōō'rōpəs| ancient city of Syria, on the Euphrates River, E of Palmyra. Founded in the 3rd century B.C., it was abandoned about 550 years later.

Du•ran•go |d(y)ōō'ræNGgō| **1** state of N central Mexico. Area: 47,579 sq. mi./123,181 sq. km. Pop. 1,352,000. **2** its capital city. Pop. 414,000. Full name **Victoria de Durango.**

Dur•ban |'dərbən| seaport and resort in South Africa, on the coast of KwaZulu/Natal. Pop. 1,137,380. Former name (until 1835) **Port Natal.**

Dü•ren |'dYrən| industrial city and transportation center in W Germany, on the Ruhr River. Pop. 83,000.

Durg |dōōrg| commercial town in central India, in Madhya Pradesh state. Pop. 151,000. It is twinned with Bhilainagar.

Dur•ga•pur |'dōōrgə,pōōr| industrial city in NE India, in the state of West Bengal. Pop. 415,990.

Dur•ham[1] |'dərəm; 'dōōrəm| **1** city on the Wear River, in NE England. Pop. 85,800. It is famous for its 11th-century cathedral, which contains the tomb of the Venerable Bede, and its university. **2** (also **County Durham**) a county of NE England. Pop. 590,000. County town, Durham.

Dur•ham[2] |'dərəm; 'dōōrəm| industrial and academic city in N central North Carolina, noted for its tobacco business and as the home of Duke University. Pop. 136,611.

Dur•rës |'dōōrəs| port and resort in Albania, on the Adriatic coast. Pop. 72,000. Italian name **Durazzo.**

Du•shan•be |d(y)ōō'sHäm,bä| industrial city, the capital of Tajikistan. Pop. 602,000. Former name (1929–61) **Stalinabad.**

Düs•sel•dorf |'dYsəl,dawrf| industrial, commercial, and cultural city of NW Germany, on the Rhine, capital of North Rhine-Westphalia. Pop. 577,560.

Dust Bowl |'dəs(t),bōl| popular name for parts of the U.S. Great Plains where 1930s windstorms blew topsoil across a wide area. Kansas, Oklahoma, and N Texas were at its center.

Dutch East In•dies |'dəcH ēst 'indēz| former name (until 1949) for INDONESIA.

Dutch•ess County |'dəcHəs| county in SE New York, E of the Hudson River, traditionally agricultural but increasingly suburban. Its seat its Poughkeepsie. Pop. 259,462.

Dutch Gui•a•na |'dəcH gē'änə| former name (until 1948) for SURINAME.

Dutch New Gui•nea |ˌdəcH n(y)ōō 'ginē| former name (until 1963) for IRIAN JAYA, Indonesia.

Du•yun |'dōō'yōōn| agricultural and industrial city in Guizhou province, S China, on the Longtou River SE of Guiyang. Pop. 392,000.

Dvi•na River |d(ə)vē'nä| river (634 mi./1,020 km.) that rises in Russia's Valai Hills and flows SW across Belarus and Latvia into the Gulf of Riga.

Dy•fed |'dəvēd| former county of SW Wales 1974–96, comprising the former counties of Cardiganshire, Carmarthenshire, and Pembrokeshire.

Dzaud•zhi•kau |(d)zow'jēkō| former name (1944–54) for VLADIKAVKAZ, Russia.

Dzer•zhinsk |jer'zHinsk| city in W central Russia, W of Nizhni Novgorod. Pop. 286,000. Former names **Chernorechye** (until 1919) and **Rastyapino** (1919–29).

Dzier•zo•niów |jer'zHawnyōōf| (German name **Reichenbach**) manufacturing town, in SW Poland. Pop. 38,000. It is known for its textiles.

Dzun•ga•ria |zōōNG'gærēə| (also **Junggar** or **Junggar Basin**) sparsely populated semidesert region of Xinjiang, NW China, between the Tien Shan and Altai Shan ranges.

Ee

Ea·gan |'ēgən| city in SE Minnesota, a suburb just S of Saint Paul. Pop. 47,409.

Ea·gle Pass |'ēgəl| city in SW Texas, on the Rio Grande. Pop. 20,651.

Ea·ling |'ēliNG| residential borough of W Greater London, England. Pop. 264,000. It is noted as the longtime center of the British film industry.

East, the |'ēst| countries to the E of Europe. See NEAR EAST, MIDDLE EAST, and FAR EAST. In the 20th century, communist countries from the Soviet satellites of E Europe through China have also been referred to as the East.

East Af·ri·ca |ēst 'æfrikə| the E part of the African continent, especially the countries of Kenya, Uganda, and Tanzania.

East An·glia |,ēst 'æNGglēə| region of E England consisting of the counties of Norfolk, Suffolk, and parts of Essex and Cambridgeshire.

East Ben·gal |,ēst ben'gäl| the part of the former Indian province of Bengal that was ceded to Pakistan in 1947, forming the greater part of the province of East Pakistan. It gained independence as Bangladesh in 1971.

East Ber·lin |,ēst bər'lin| the E half of the city of Berlin (divided in 1945) and, until German reunification in 1990, part of the German Democratic Republic. It was separated from West Berlin in 1961 by the Berlin Wall.

East·bourne |'ēst,bawrn| resort town on the S coast of England, in East Sussex. Pop. 78,000.

East Chi·ca·go |,ēst SHə'kägō; shə'kawgō| industrial port city in NW Indiana, on Lake Michigan SE of Chicago, Illinois. Pop. 33,892.

East Chi·na Sea see CHINA SEA.

East Co·ker |,ēst 'kōkər| village in SW England, in Somerset, S of Yeovil, the ancestral home and burial place of the poet T.S. Eliot.

East End |ēst 'end| the part of London, England, east of the City as far as the Lea River, including the Docklands. □ **East Ender** *n.*

Eas·ter Island |'ēstər| (Polynesian name **Rapa Nui**) island in the SE Pacific, W of Chile. Pop. 2,000. It has been administered by Chile since 1888. The island, first settled by Polynesians in about A.D. 400, is famous for its monolithic statues of human heads, believed to date from the period 1000–1600.

East·ern bloc the nations of eastern and central Europe that were under Soviet domination from the end of World War II until the collapse of the Soviet communist system in 1989-91, usually considered to include Poland, East Germany, Czechoslovakia, Hungary, Romania, Bulgaria, and Yugoslavia.

East·ern Cape |'ēstərn| province of SE South Africa, formerly part of the Cape province. Pop. 6,504,000. Capital: Bisho.

East·ern Desert |'ēstərn| another name for the ARABIAN DESERT, Egypt.

East·ern Eur·ope |'ēstərn 'yo͞orəp| portion of the European landmass lying east of Germany and the Alps and west of the Ural Mountains. It includes the former Eastern bloc countries of Poland, the Czech Republic and Slovakia (formerly as Czechoslovakia), Hungary, Romania, and Bulgaria, as well as the Baltic republics of Estonia, Latvia, and Lithuania, and the former Soviet republics of Belarus and Ukraine, along with Russia west of the Urals.

East·ern Hemisphere |'ēstərn| the half of the earth containing Europe, Asia, and Africa.

East·ern Shore |'ēstərn| region of E Maryland on the Delmarva Peninsula, on the E side of Chesapeake Bay.

East·ern Townships |'ēstərn| region of SE Quebec, E of Montreal, settled in the 19th century by English speakers, but today mostly French-speaking. French name **Cantons de l'Est,** also **Estrie.**

East·ern Trans·vaal |'ēstərn trænz'väl| former province of NE South Africa, formerly part of Transvaal, and now MPUMALANGA. Capital: Nelspruit.

East Flan·ders |ēst 'flændərz| province of N Belgium. Pop. 1,336,000. Capital: Ghent. See also FLANDERS.

East Fri·sian Islands |ēst 'frizHən| see FRISIAN ISLANDS, Germany.

East Ger·many |ēs(t) 'jərmənē| (official name **German Democratic Republic**) former independent nation created in 1949 from the area of Germany occupied by the Soviet Union after World War II. It was reunited with West Germany after the fall of its communist government in 1990. German name **Deutsche Demokratische Republik.**

East Hamp·ton |ēst 'hæmptən| resort town in E Long Island, New York, noted for its artists' colony. Pop. 16,132.

East Har·lem |ēst 'härləm| neighborhood of Harlem, in N Manhattan, New York City. Parts of it have been called Italian Harlem and Spanish Harlem, reflecting local ethnic history.

East Hart·ford |ēst 'härtfərd| industrial town in central Connecticut, across the Connecticut River from Hartford. Pop. 50,452.

East In·dies |ēst 'indēz| **1** the islands of SE Asia, especially the Malay Archipelago. **2** (archaic) the whole of SE Asia to the east of and including India. □ **East Indian** adj. & n.

East Kil·bride |ˌēst kil'brīd| town in W central Scotland, in South Lanarkshire. Pop. 81,400.

East Lan·sing |ēst 'lænsiNG| city in S central Michigan, home to Michigan State University. Pop. 50,677.

East Liv·er·pool |ēst 'livərpōōl| city in E Ohio, on the Ohio River, famed for its ceramics industry. Pop. 13,654.

East Lon·don |ēst 'ləndən| industrial port and resort in South Africa, on the Eastern Cape coast. Pop. 270,130.

East Los An·ge·les |ˌēst laws 'ænjələs| community in SW California, a largely Hispanic suburb on the E side of Los Angeles. Pop. 126,379.

East Lo·thi·an |ˌēs(t) 'lōTHēən| administrative region and former county of E central Scotland.

East·main River |'ēst,mān| river in W central Quebec that flows 470 mi./760 km. into Hudson Bay. The Eastmain region was an early fur trade center, and is today the site of major hydroelectric developments.

East New York |ˌēst n(y)ōō 'yawrk| largely residential section of E Brooklyn, New York City.

Eas·ton |'ēstən| industrial city in E Pennsylvania, on the Lehigh and Delaware rivers. Pop. 26,276.

East Orange |ēst 'är(i)nj; 'awr(i)nj| city in NE New Jersey, a suburb NW of Newark. Pop. 73,552.

East Pak·i·stan |'ēs(t) ˌpækə'stæn| former part of Pakistan, bounded by India to the N, W, and E and by Burma to the SE; the largely Muslim Indian state of East Bengal before 1947, it became Bangladesh in 1971.

East Point |'ēst 'point| city in NW Georgia, a residential and industrial suburb S of Atlanta. Pop. 34,402.

East·port |'ēst,pawrt| maritime city in E Maine, on an island in Passamaquoddy Bay Pop. 1,965. It is the easternmost U.S. city.

East Prov·i·dence |ēst 'prävədəns| city in E Rhode Island, an industrial and commercial suburb across the Seekonk River from Providence. Pop. 50,380.

East Prus·sia |ēst 'prəSHə| the NE part of the former kingdom of Prussia, on the Baltic coast, later part of Germany and divided after World War II between the Soviet Union (now Russia) and Poland.

East Ri·ding of York·shire |ēst 'rīdiNG əv 'yawrksHər; 'yawrk,sHir| administrative region in NE England, formerly one of the traditional ridings or divisions of the county of Yorkshire.

East River |'ēst| strait running from Long Island Sound to Upper New York Bay, in New York City, separating Manhattan and the Bronx from Brooklyn and Queens.

East Saint Louis |ˌēst sānt 'lōōwəs| city in SW Illinois, an industrial and commercial center across the Mississippi River from Saint Louis. Pop. 40,944.

East Si·be·ri·an Sea |ˌēst sī'birēən| part of the Arctic Ocean lying between the New Siberian Islands and Wrangel Island, to the N of E Siberia.

East Side |'ēst 'sīd| part of Manhattan, New York City, lying between the East River and Fifth Avenue. The **Upper East Side**, S of East Harlem, is generally affluent. The **Lower East Side**, below 14th Street, is famed as home to immigrants.

East Sus·sex |ēst 'səsiks| county of SE England. Pop. 671,000. County town, Lewes.

East Ti·mor |ēst 'tē,mawr; tē'mawr| the E part of the island of Timor in the S Malay Archipelago; chief town, Dili. Formerly a Portuguese colony, the region declared itself independent in 1975. In 1976 it was invaded by Indonesia, which annexed and claimed it as the 27th state of Indonesia, a claim that has never been recognized by the

East Timor

United Nations. Since then the region has been the scene of bitter fighting and of alleged mass killings by the Indonesian government and military forces.

East•wood |'ēst,wŏŏd| mining village in central England, in Nottinghamshire, the birthplace of the writer D.H. Lawrence.

East York |ēst 'yawrk| residential borough in S Ontario, immediately N of Toronto. Pop. 102,696.

Eau Claire |ō 'kler| industrial city in W central Wisconsin. Pop. 58,856.

Eb•bw Vale |'ebŏŏ| industrial town in S Wales, in Gwent, N of Cardiff. Pop. 9,000. Once a noted coal- and steel-producing center, it now has light industries.

Eb•la |'eblə| city in ancient Syria, to the SW of Aleppo. It became very powerful in the mid-3rd millennium B.C., when it dominated a region corresponding to present-day Lebanon, N Syria, and SE Turkey.

Ebo•ra•cum |i'bawrəkəm| Roman name for YORK, England.

Ebro River |ābrō| the principal river of NE Spain, rising in the mountains of Cantabria and flowing 570 mi./910 km. SE into the Mediterranean Sea.

Eca•te•pec de Mo•re•los |ā,kätə'pec 'dā mə'rālōs| industrial city in central Mexico, a suburb NE of Mexico City in the state of Mexico. Pop. 1,218,000.

Ec•bat•a•na |ek'bætn-ə| see HAMADAN, Iran.

Ech Chlef |,esH shə'lef| (also **Ech Chéliff** or **Chlef**) industrial and commercial town in N Algeria, on the Chéliff River SW of Algiers. Pop. 130,000.

Ec•ua•dor |'ekwə,dawr| equatorial republic in South America, on the Pacific coast. Area: 109,484 sq. mi./270,670 sq. km. Pop. 11,460,100. Languages, Spanish (official), Quechua. Capital and largest city: Quito. Stretching from coastal plains to the Andes and Amazonian jungles, Ecuador is largely agricultural, and produces oil. The Gala-

Ecuador

pagos Islands are an external territory. □ **Ecuadorean** *adj. & n.*

Edam |'ēdəm| market town in the Netherlands, to the NE of Amsterdam, noted for its cheese. Pop. 24,840.

Ed•dy•stone Rocks |'edēstōn| rocky reef off the coast of Cornwall, England, 14 mi./22 km. SW of Plymouth. It was the site of the earliest lighthouse (1699) built on rocks fully exposed to the sea.

Ede[1] |'ādə| industrial city in E Netherlands. Pop. 96,000.

Ede[2] |'ā,dā| industrial town in SW Nigeria, NE of Ibadan, in a predominantly Yoruba region. Pop. 271,000.

Eden |'ēdn| biblical paradise, the original garden abode of Adam and Eve. It is usually located in the EUPHRATES River valley, but has sometimes been placed as far E as the Araks River, on the Turkey-Armenia border.

Eden Prai•rie |'ēdn| city in SE Minnesota, a suburb SW of Minneapolis. Pop. 39,311.

Edes•sa |i'desə| (also **Edhessa** or **Vodena**) commercial city in NE Greece. Pop. 18,000. It was the ancient seat of kings of Macedonia.

Edge•hill |'ej,hil| (also **Edge Hill**) locality in central England, on the Warwickshire-Oxfordshire border, NW of Banbury, where the first major battle of the English Civil War was fought in 1642.

Edge•wood |'ej,wŏŏd| community in NE Maryland, noted for its U.S. arsenal. Pop. 23,903.

Edi•na |ē'dīnə| city in SE Minnesota, a suburb SW of Minneapolis. Pop. 46,070.

Ed•in•burg |'edn,bərg| city in S Texas, in the Rio Grande Valley. Pop. 29,885.

Ed•in•burgh |'edn,bərə| the capital of Scotland, lying on the S shore of the Firth of Forth. Pop. 421,200. The city grew up around an 11th-century castle built by Malcolm III, which dominates the landscape. It is an administrative, commercial, and cultural center.

Edir•ne |ā'dirnā| (ancient name **Adrianopolis**) historic commercial city in European Turkey, NW of Istanbul. Pop. 102,000. It is the capital of Edirne province.

Ed•mond |'edmənd| city in central Oklahoma, a residential suburb and oil industry center N of Oklahoma City. Pop. 52,315.

Ed•monds |'edmən(d)z| city in W central Washington, on Puget Sound, a suburb N of Seattle. Pop. 30,744.

Ed•mon•ton |'edməntən| the capital of Alberta, on the North Saskatchewan River E of the Rockies. Pop. 703,070. It is an oil and petrochemical center.

Edo |'edō| (also **Yedo**) former name (until 1868) of Japan's capital, Tokyo.

Edom |'ēdəm| (also **Seir**) ancient land S of the Dead Sea. According to the Bible, its people were descendants of Esau. Its capital was Petra (in present-day Jordan). Edom was later the Roman Idumaea. □ **Edomite** *adj. & n.*

Ed·ward, Lake |'edwərd| lake on the border between Uganda and the Democratic Republic of Congo (former Zaire), linked to Lake Albert by the Semliki River.

Ed·wards Air Force Base |'edwərdz| facility in S central California, NE of Los Angeles and on the W of the Mojave Desert, noted as a center for air and space experimentation.

Ed·wards Plateau |'edwərdz| highland region of SW Texas, between the Llano Estacado and the Balcones Escarpment, noted for its ranchlands.

Ee·lam |'ē,läm| the proposed homeland of the Tamil people of Sri Lanka, for which the Tamil Tigers separatist group have been fighting since the early 1980s.

Efa·te |ā'fätā| (also **Vaté**; formerly **Sandwich Island**) island in central Vanuatu, site of the capital, Vila.

Ega·di Islands |'ā,gädē| group of small islands in the Mediterranean Sea off the W coast of Sicily, in Italy. The principal islands are Marettimo, Favignana, Levanzo, and Stagnone.

Eger |'egər| spa town in the N of Hungary, noted for the 'Bull's Blood' red wine produced in the surrounding region. Pop. 63,365.

Eg·mont, Mount |'eg,mänt| volcanic peak in North Island, New Zealand, rising to a height of 8,260 ft./2,518 m. Maori name **Taranaki.**

Egypt |'ējəpt| republic in northeasternmost Africa, bordering on the Mediter-

ranean Sea. Area: 386,900 sq. mi./1.0 million sq. km. Pop. 53,087,000. Official language, Arabic. Capital and largest city: Cairo. Mostly desert in the W, Egypt is dominated in the E by the Nile River and its delta. Known to history for over 5,000 years, it was conquered by the Arabs in A.D. 642. Agriculture, petroleum, and textiles are important industries today. □ **Egyptian** *adj. & n.*

Eh·ren·breit·stein |,ārən'brīt,SHtīn| former town, now part of Koblenz, in western Germany. Its powerful fortress was built c. A.D. 1000.

Ei·fel |'īfəl| plateau in western Germany, N of the Moselle River and E of the Ardennes, forming the NW part of the Rhenish Slate Mts. It is composed of limestone and is a generally barren region, with a history of mining.

Eif·fel Tower |'īfəl| iron tower, 984 ft./300 m. tall, in Paris, France, constructed for the 1889 World's Fair and since then the unofficial symbol of Paris. A popular tourist attraction, it also has a meteorological station and broadcasting antennae.

Ei·ger |'īgər| mountain peak in the Bernese Alps in central Switzerland, which rises to 13,101 ft./3,970 m.

Ei·lat |ā'lät| (also **Elat**) the southernmost city in Israel, a port and resort at the head of the Gulf of Aqaba. Pop. 36,000. Founded in 1949 near the ruins of biblical Elath, it is Israel's only outlet to the Red Sea.

Eind·ho·ven |'īnt,hōvən| industrial city in the S of the Netherlands. Pop. 193,000. It is a major producer of electrical and electronic goods.

Eire |'erə| the Gaelic name for Ireland, the official name of the Republic of Ireland from 1937 to 1949.

Ei·se·nach |'īzə,näKH| resort and industrial town in central Germany. Pop. 51,000.

Ei·sen·hüt·ten·stadt |'īzən,hYtn,SHtät| industrial and trade city in eastern Germany, on the Oder River near the Polish border. Pop. 49,000.

Ei·sen·stadt |'īzən,SHtät| city in E Austria, capital of the state of Burgenland and historic seat of the Esterházy family. Pop. 10,500.

Eis·rie·sen·welt |'īs,rēzən,velt| cave system in the Tennen massif, S of Salzburg, Austria. It is believed to be the largest system of ice caves in the world: 25 mi./40 km. long.

Eka·te·rin·burg |yi'kætərən,bərg| (also **Yekaterinburg**) industrial city in central Russia, in the E foothills of the Urals. Pop.

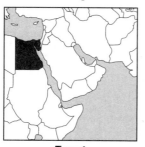

Egypt

1,372,000. In 1924–91 it was known as **Sverdlovsk**.

Eki·bas·tuz |ˌekēˈbäsˌto͞os| coal-mining town in E Kazakhstan, SW of Pavlodar. Pop. 93,000.

El Aaiún |ˌel īˈo͞on| Arabic name for LAʼYOUN, Western Sahara.

El Ala·mein |ˌelˈælə,mān| (also **Alamein**) historic town in N Egypt, on the road along the Mediterranean coast W of Alexandria, where British forces stopped a German advance in 1942.

Elam |ˈēləm| ancient state in SW Iran, E of the Tigris, established in the 4th millennium B.C. Susa was one of its chief cities. □ **Elamite** adj. & n.

Ela·zig |ˌeläˈzi| commercial city in E central Turkey, E of the upper Euphrates River. Pop. 205,000. It is the capital of Elazig province.

El·ba |ˈelbə| small island off the W coast of Italy, famous as the place of Napoleon's first exile (1814–15).

El·ba·san |ˌelbäˈsän| industrial and commercial town in central Albania. Pop. 83,000.

El·be River |ˈelbə; elb| river of central Europe, flowing 720 mi./1,159 km. from the Czech Republic through Germany, past Dresden, Magdeburg, and Hamburg, to the North Sea.

El·bert, Mount |ˈelbərt| mountain in Colorado, to the E of the resort town of Aspen. Rising 14,431 ft./4,399 m., it is the highest peak in the Rocky Mts.

El·blag |ˈelblawNGk| seaport city in N Poland, on the Elblag River near the Baltic Sea, SE of Gdańsk. Pop. 125,000.

El·brus, Mount |elˈbro͞os; ˈel,bro͞os| peak in the Caucasus Mts., on the border between Russia and Georgia. Rising to 18,481 ft./5,642 m., it is the highest mountain in Europe.

El·burz Mountains |elˈbo͞orz| mountain range in NW Iran, close to the S shore of the Caspian Sea. Damavand is the highest peak, rising to 18,386 ft./5,604 m.

El Ca·jon |ˌel kəˈhōn| city in SW California, a suburb E of San Diego. Pop. 88,693.

El Cap·i·tan |ˌel ˌkæpiˈtæn| peak in Yosemite National Park, California, famed for its sheer walls rising over 3,000 ft./1,000 m. above its base.

El Cen·tro |ˌel ˈsentrō| city in S California, commercial center of the Imperial Valley. Pop. 31,384.

El·che |ˈelCHä| town in the province of Alicante in SE Spain. Pop. 181,200.

El Djem |ˌel ˈjem| town in E Tunisia, noted for its well-preserved Roman amphitheater.

El Do·ra·do |ˌel dəˈrädō; dəˈrädō| land of wealth in legends of early American exploration, named for a ruler, perhaps somewhere in modern Colombia, who was said to be inaugurated with gold dust.

Elea |ˈēlēə| (also known as **Velia**) ancient town in S Italy, founded by Greeks in 536 B.C. It was the home of the Eleatic school of philosophers, led by Parmenides. □ **Eleatic** adj. & n.

Elek·tro·stal |el,yektrəˈstäl| industrial city in W Russia, E of Moscow. Pop. 153,000.

El·e·phan·ta Island |ˌeləˈfæntə| (Hindu name **Gharapuri**) small island in W India, in Bombay Harbor, Maharashtra state. It is known for its centuries-old caves with carvings and sculptures.

El·e·phant Pass |ˈeləfənt| narrow strip of land at the N end of Sri Lanka, linking the Jaffna peninsula with the rest of the island.

Eleu·sis |əˈlyo͞osis| ancient city in E Greece, NW of Athens, on the site of present-day Elévsis. It was the home of the Eleusinian Mysteries, which celebrated the goddess Demeter, and the birthplace of the playwright Aeschylus.

Eleu·thera |əˈlo͞oTHərə| island in the central Bahamas, over 100 mi./160 km. long. Settled by the British in the 1640s, it has a pop. of 9,000.

El Faiyum |ˌel fāˈ(y)o͞om| (also **Fayum** or **Al Fayyum**) historic oasis town in N Egypt, SW of Cairo. Pop. 244,000. It now has many light industries.

El Fer·rol |ˌel ferˈrawl| seaport in NW Spain, on the Atlantic. Pop. 87,000. Spain's most important naval base is here.

El·gin[1] |ˈeljin| industrial city in NE Illinois, W of Chicago, formerly noted for its watch manufacturing. Pop. 77,010.

El·gin[2] |ˈelgin| historic town in NE Scotland, a commercial and religious center in the Moray district of the Grampian region. Pop. 19,000.

El·gon, Mount |ˈel,gän| extinct volcano on the border between Kenya and Uganda, rising to 14,178 ft./4,321 m.

Elis |ˈēlis| ancient city in SW Greece, on the Kyllini Peninsula. It was famous for its temple of Zeus at Olympia and for a time controlled the Olympian games.

Elis·a·beth·ville |əˈlizəbəTH,vil| former name (until 1966) for LUBUMBASHI, Congo (formerly Zaire).

Elis·ta |əˈlistə| city in SW Russia, capital of the autonomous republic of Kalmykia. Pop. 85,000.

Eliz·a·beth |ə'lizəbəTH| industrial port city in NE New Jersey, on Newark Bay. Pop. 110,002.

El Ja·di·da |el 'jädēdə| (formerly **Mazagan**) port and resort town in N Morocco, on the Atlantic coast SW of Casablanca. Pop. 119,000.

Elk·hart |'el‚kärt| industrial city in N Indiana, a rail center long noted for manufacture of musical instruments. Pop. 43,627.

Elk Hills |elk| range in S central California, near Bakersfield, site of an oil reserve involved in the 1920s Teapot Dome scandal.

Elles·mere Island |'elz‚mir| the northernmost and third-largest island of the Canadian Arctic.

Elles·mere Port |'elz‚mir| industrial port in NW England, in Cheshire, on the estuary of the Mersey River. Pop. 65,800.

El·lice Islands |'eləs| former name for TUVALU.

El·li·cott City |'elikət| historic community in N central Maryland, W of Baltimore, primarily a residential suburb. Pop. 41,396.

El·lis Island |'eləs| island in New York Bay that from 1892 until 1943 served as an entry point for immigrants to the U.S., and later (until 1954) as a detention center for deportees. It is now a museum site and the focus of a territorial dispute between New York and New Jersey,

El·lo·ra |ə'lawrə| (also **Elura**) a village in W India, in Maharashtra state, NW of Aurangabad. It is known for its rock temples.

Ells·worth Land |'elzwərTH| plateau region of Antarctica between the Walgreen Coast and Palmer Land. It rises at the Vinson Massif, the highest point in Antarctica, to 16,863 ft./5,140 m.

El Ma·hal·la el Ku·bra |‚el mə'hælə 'el 'kōōbrə| industrial city in N Egypt, in the Nile Delta W of the Damietta branch. Pop. 400,000.

El Man·su·ra |‚el män'sōōrə| (also **Al Mansurah**) industrial city in NE Egypt, in the Nile Delta, on the Damietta branch. Pop. 362,000. It is a cotton trade center.

Elm·hurst¹ |'elm‚hərst| city in NE Illinois, W of Chicago. Pop. 42,029.

Elm·hurst² |'elm‚hərst| largely residential section of N Queens, New York City, noted for the diversity of its population.

El Min·ya |el 'minyə| (also **Al Minya**) industrial city in N central Egypt, on the Nile River. Pop. 203,000.

Elm·mi·ra |el'mīrə| industrial city in S central New York, near the Pennsylvania line. Pop. 33,724.

El Mi·sti |el 'mēstē| dormant volcano in S Peru, rising to 19,031 ft./5,822 m. NE of Arequipa. It has been important in Inca and Peruvian religion and legend.

El Mon·te |el 'mäntē| city in SW California, a suburb E of Los Angeles. Pop. 106,209.

El Mor·ro |el 'mawrō| historic fortress in San Juan, Puerto Rico, begun in 1539. Also **Morro Castle.**

El Ni·ño |el 'nēnyō| popular name for a complex of climate fluctuations in the equatorial regions of the Pacific, especially cyclical warming of ocean currents off the NW shores of South America. The name is from the Spanish for the infant Jesus, as effects intensify around Christmas.

El Nor·te |el 'nawrtä| common term used in Mexico and elsewhere in Latin America to refer to the US; Spanish "the North."

El Obeid |‚el ə'bād| (also **Al Ubayyid**) desert city in central Sudan, in the Kordofan region, where local foces under the Mahdi defeated the British in 1883.

El Paso |el 'pæsō| industrial city in W Texas, on the Rio Grande, across from Ciudad Juárez, Mexico. Pop. 515,342.

El Qa·hi·ra |'kähērə| variant spelling of Al Qahira, the Arabic name for CAIRO, Egypt.

El Sal·va·dor |el 'sælvä‚dawr| republic in Central America, on the Pacific coast. Area: 8,260 sq. mi./21,393 sq. km. Pop. 5,048,000. Language, Spanish. Capital and largest city: San Salvador. Independent from Spain in 1821, El Salvador is dominated by volcanic ranges and subtropical valleys. Coffee, cotton, and sugar are the chief products. □ **Salvadorean** *adj. & n.*

El Salvador

El·si·nore |'elsē‚nawr| port on the NE coast of the island of Zealand, Denmark. Pop. 56,750. It is the site of the 16th-century Kronborg Castle, which is the setting for Shakespeare's *Hamlet.* Danish name **Helsingør.**

Els·tree |'el‚strē| village in SE England, in

Hertfordshire, NW of London. Pop. 5,000. It is a center of the British film industry.

El Ta·jín |ˌel təˈhēn| archaeological site in E central Mexico, in Veracruz state, noted for its Totonac Pyramid of the Niches.

El To·ro |el ˈtawrō| suburban community in SW California, SE of Los Angeles, formerly site of a Marine air base. Pop. 62,685.

El Uq·sur |el ˈooksoor| (also **Al Uqsur**) Arabic name for LUXOR, Egypt.

Ely, Isle of |ˈēlē| former county of England extending over the N part of present-day Cambridgeshire. Before widespread drainage it formed a fertile 'island' in the surrounding fenland.

Ely[1] |ˈēlē| cathedral city in the fenland of Cambridgeshire, SE England, on the Ouse River. Pop. 9,100.

Ely[2] |ˈēlē| city in E central Nevada, a famed mining center. Pop. 4,756.

Elyr·ia |əˈlirēə| industrial city in N Ohio, W of Cleveland. Pop. 56,746.

Ely·sée Palace |ˌālāˈzā| official residence (since 1873) of the president of France, in Paris. Built in 1718, it was once the property of the Marquise de Pompadour, mistress of King Louis XV.

Ely·si·um |əˈlizhəm| (also **Elysian Fields**) in ancient Greek myth, a land far to the W, or in the underworld, where heroes lived happily after death. □ **Elysian** adj.

El Yunque popular name for the CARIBBEAN NATIONAL FOREST.

Em·den |ˈemdən| port in NW Germany, on the North Sea in the estuary of the Ems River. Pop. 51,000. The city's development was encouraged by the industrial growth of the Ruhr Valley and by the construction of the Dortmund-Ems Canal.

Emei Shan |ˈəmˈā ˈshän| (formerly **O-mei Shan**) mountain in Sichuan province, S central China, SW of Chengdu. A sacred Buddhist site, it has many temples and images.

Em·er·ald Coast |ˈem(ə)rəld| name given to part of the coast of Brittany, NW France. It includes the towns of Dinard, Paramé, Saint-Briac, and Saint-Lunaire.

Em·er·ald Isle poetic name for Ireland.

Eme·sa |ˈeməsə| city in ancient Syria, on the Orontes River on the site of present-day Homs. It was famous for its temple to the sun god Elah-Gabal.

Emi Kous·si |ä'mē ˈkoosē| volcanic mountain in the Sahara, in N Chad, rising to 11,202 ft./3,415 m., the highest peak in the Tibesti Mts.

Emilia-Romagna |äˈmēlyə rōˈmänyə| region of N Italy. Capital: Bologna.

Em·ma·us[1] |əˈmāəs| ancient town, NW of Jerusalem, probably now Imwas, in Israeli-occupied Jordan. Judas Maccabeus won a notable victory here in 166 B.C.

Em·ma·us[2] |əˈmāəs| borough in E Pennsylvania, S of Allentown, noted as the home of Rodale Press, exponent of organic farming. Pop. 11,157.

Em·men |ˈemən| industrial city in the NE Netherlands. Pop. 93,000.

Em·men·tal |ˈemən,täl| valley of the Emme River, in W central Switzerland. The region gives its name to the characteristic Swiss cheese.

Emo·na |iˈmōnə| Roman name for LJU-BLJANA, Slovenia.

Em·pire State nickname for NEW YORK.

Em·pire State Building |ˈem,pīr ˈstāt| office building in Manhattan, New York City. At 1,454 ft./443 m., it was the tallest building in the world from 1931 until 1971.

Em·po·ria |emˈpawrēə| commercial city in E central Kansas, associated with William Allen White and his Emporia *Gazette*, which he published 1895–1944. Pop. 25,512.

Empty Quarter another name for the RUB' AL KHALI, Saudi Arabia.

Ems River |ems; emz| river (208 mi./335 km.), rising in the Teutoburger Wald of NW Germany and flowing into the North Sea near Emden. The Dortmund-Ems Canal runs parallel to the river.

En·ci·ni·tas |ˌensiˈnētəs| city in SW California, a suburb NW of San Diego. Pop. 55,386.

En·der·bury Island |ˈendər,berē| see CANTON AND ENDERBURY, Kiribati.

En·der·by Land |ˈendərbē| part of Antarctica claimed by Australia.

En·field |ˈen,fēld| residential and industrial borough of N Greater London, England. Pop. 249,000. It gave its name to the Enfield rifle.

En·ga·dine |ˌeNGgəˈdēn| valley of the Inn River in E Switzerland, in the Rhaetian Alps. Noted for its beauty and climate, the region has many resorts, including Saint Moritz and Pontresina.

Eng·land |ˈiNG(g)lənd| country forming the largest and southernmost part of Great Britain and of the United Kingdom, and containing the capital, London. Area: 50,397 sq. mi./130,478 sq. km. Pop. 46,170,000. □ **English** adj. & n.

Eng·lish Channel |ˈiNG(g)lish| (French name **la Manche**) the sea channel separating S England from N France. It is 22 mi./35 km. wide at its narrowest point. A

ENGLAND

County boundary
■ Capital city

0 50 100 km
0 25 50 75 miles

NORTHUMBERLAND

TYNE AND WEAR

DURHAM CLEVELAND

CUMBRIA

N

NORTH YORKSHIRE

ISLE OF MAN

LANCASHIRE WEST YORKSHIRE HUMBERSIDE

MERSEYSIDE GREATER MANCHESTER SOUTH YORKSHIRE

CHESHIRE DERBYSHIRE LINCOLNSHIRE

NOTTINGHAMSHIRE

STAFFORDSHIRE

NORFOLK

SHROPSHIRE LEICESTERSHIRE

W. MIDLANDS

CAMBRIDGE-SHIRE

HEREFORD AND WORCESTER WARWICKSHIRE NORTHAMPTONSHIRE SUFFOLK

BEDFORDSHIRE

GLOUCESTER-SHIRE OXFORD-SHIRE BUCKINGHAMSHIRE HERTFORD-SHIRE ESSEX

GREATER LONDON ■London

AVON BERKSHIRE

WILTSHIRE SURREY KENT

SOMERSET HAMPSHIRE

WEST SUSSEX EAST SUSSEX

DEVON DORSET

ISLE OF WIGHT

CORNWALL

ISLES OF SCILLY CHANNEL IS.

railway tunnel beneath it linking England and France was opened in 1994 (the Channel Tunnel).

Enid |ˈēnid| city in N central Oklahoma, home to Vance Air Force Base. Pop. 45,309.

Eni·we·tok |ˌenəˈwēˌtäk| (also **Enewetak**) uninhabited island in the North Pacific, one of the Marshall Islands. Cleared of its native population, it was used by the U.S. as a testing ground for nuclear weapons from 1948 to 1954.

En·nis |ˈenəs| county seat of Clare, in the Republic of Ireland. Pop. 14,000.

En·nis·kil·len |ˌenəˈskilən| county seat of

Fermanagh, Northern Ireland. Pop. 10,000. Former spelling *Inniskilling.*

En·sche·de |ˈenskəˌdā| industrial and university city in the E Netherlands. Pop. 147,000.

En·se·na·da |ˌensəˈnädə| city in NW Mexico, in Baja California state, on the Pacific. Pop. 260,000. It is a cruise ship port and industrial center.

En·teb·be |enˈtebā; enˈtebē| town in S Uganda, on the N shore of Lake Victoria. Pop. 42,000. It was the capital of Uganda during the period of British rule, from 1894 to 1962.

Entre-deux-Mers |'äNtrədœ'mer| region in SW France, between the Dordogne and the Garonne rivers. The area is noted for its wines.

Enu·gu |ā'nōōgōō| industrial city in SE Nigeria, capital of the state of Enugu. Pop. 293,000. In a coal producing-region, it was the capital of BIAFRA.

Éper·nay |ˌāpər'ne| town in NE France, on the Marne River. Pop. 28,000. Many well-known makers of champagne are headquartered here, and tourists come to visit the wine caves.

Eph·e·sus |'efəsəs| ancient Greek city on the W coast of Asia Minor, in present-day Turkey, noted in ancient times as site of the temple of Diana, one of the Seven Wonders of the World. It was an important center of early Christianity; St. Paul preached here and St. John is said to have lived here.

Eph·ra·ta |'efrətə| historic borough in SE Pennsylvania, SW of Reading, settled by German pietists and now a tourist and crafts center. Pop. 12,133.

Ep·i·dau·rus |'epəˌdawrəs| ancient Greek city and port on the NE coast of the Peloponnese. Greek name **Epídhavros**.

Epi·nal |ˌāpē'näl| manufacturing town, capital of the department of Vosges in E France, on the Moselle River. Pop. 40,000.

Epi·rus |i'pīrəs| **1** coastal region of NW Greece. Capital: Ioánnina. Greek name **Ipiros**. **2** an ancient country of which the modern region corresponds to the SW part, extending N to Illyria and E to Macedonia and Thessaly.

Ep·ping |'epiNG| town in SE England, a residential suburb NE of London, in Essex. Pop. 11,000. **Epping Forest,** now a park, is what remains of the former Waltham Forest, a royal preserve that included all of Essex.

Ep·som |'epsəm| town in Surrey, SE England. Pop. 68,500. Its natural mineral waters were used in the production of the purgative known as Epsom salts. The annual Derby and Oaks horse races are held at Epsom Downs.

equa·tor, the |ə'kwātər| imaginary line around the earth, equidistant from the poles and having a latitude of 0°. It divides the earth into N and S hemispheres. The equator is generally thought of as a zone (the *equatorial* regions) of great heat.

Equa·to·ri·al Gui·nea |ˌekwə'tawrēəl 'ginē| republic in W Africa on the Gulf of Guinea, comprising several offshore islands and a coastal settlement between Camer-

Equatorial Guinea

oon and Gabon. Area: 10,830 sq. mi./ 28,051 sq. km. Pop. 426,000. Languages, Spanish (official), local Niger–Congo languages, pidgin. Capital: Malabo (on the island of Bioko). Formerly a Spanish colony, the country became fully independent in 1968. It is the only independent Spanish-speaking state in Africa. Cacao, coffee, and timber are its chief exports. □ **Equatorial Guinean** *adj. & n.*

Er·e·bus, Mount |'erəbəs| volcanic peak on Ross Island, Antarctica. Rising to 12,452 ft./3,794 m., it is the world's most southerly active volcano.

Erech |'ē,rek| biblical name for URUK, Iraq.

Er·furt |'er,fŏort| industrial city in central Germany, capital of Thuringia. Pop. 205,000.

Erie, Lake |'irē| one of the five Great Lakes of North America, between Canada and the U.S. It is linked to Lake Huron by the Detroit River and to Lake Ontario by the Welland Canal and by the Niagara River, which is its only natural outlet. Cleveland and Buffalo lie on its shores.

Erie |'irē| industrial port city in extreme NW Pennsylvania, on Lake Erie. Pop. 108,718.

Erie Canal |'irē| historic canal that connected the Hudson River at Albany, in E New York, with the Niagara River and the Great Lakes. Opened in 1825, it spurred the growth of New York City. Today it is chiefly recreational.

Erin |'erən| archaic poetic or literary name for Ireland.

Er·i·trea |ˌerə'trēə; ˌerə'trāə| independent state in NE Africa, on the Red Sea. Area: 36,183 sq. mi./93,769 sq. km. Pop. 3,500,000. Language, Tigray and Cushitic languages. Capital and largest city: Asmara. Half Muslim, half Christian, Eritrea separated fully from Ethiopia in 1993. Agriculture and mining are important. □ **Eritrean** *adj. & n.*

Eritrea

Er·lan·gen |'er,läNGən| industrial city in S Germany, on the Regnitz River. Pop. 102,000.

Er·na·ku·lum |ər'näkələm| city in S India, in Kerala state, near Kochi. Its Jewish community is thought to date back to the 2nd or 3rd century.

Erne |'ərn| river that flows 72 mi./115 km. from N Republic of Ireland into Northern Ireland, to the Atlantic at Donegal Bay. Along its route are two widenings, Upper and Lower Lough Erne, between which the town of Enniskillen lies.

Erode |i'rōd| cotton-processing city in S India, in Tamil Nadu state. Pop. 357,000.

Er·ro·man·go |,erō'mäNGgō| (also **Erromanga**) volcanic island in S Vanuatu, noted for its coral formations and bays.

Ery·man·thus |,ere'mænTHəs| mountain group in S Greece, in NW Peloponnesus. According to Greek mythology, the mountains were the home of the Erymanthian boar captured by Hercules.

Erz·ge·bir·ge |'ertsgə,birgə| range of mountains on the border between Germany and the Czech Republic. Also called the **Ore Mountains**.

Er·zin·can |,erzin'jän| (also **Erzinjan**) historic town in E central Turkey, in agricultural Erzincan province. Pop. 91,000.

Er·zu·rum |,erzə'ro͞om| commercial city in NE Turkey, capital of mountainous Erzurum province. Pop. 242,000.

Es·bjerg |'esbyer| port in Denmark, on the W coast of Jutland. Pop. 82,000. It has ferry links with Britain and the Faroe Islands.

Es·ca·na·ba |,eskə'näbə| port city in the Upper Peninsula of NW Michigan, on Lake Michigan. Pop. 13,659.

Es·caut |es'kō| French name for the SCHELDT River.

Es·con·di·do |,eskən'dēdō| commercial city in SW California, N of San Diego. Pop. 108,635.

Es·co·ri·al, el |,el ,eskawr'yäl| 16th-century building complex in central Spain, NW of Madrid, comprising a palace, a monastery, a church, and the mausoleums of several Spanish sovereigns.

Es·dra·e·lon |,ezdrə'ēlən| (also called **Plain of Jezreel**) plain in N Israel that separates Galilee (N) from Samaria (S).

Eskil·stu·na |'eskil,stynə| industrial city in SE Sweden, between Lakes Hjälmaren and Mälaren, W of Stockholm. Pop. 90,000.

Es·ki·se·hir |,eskisHə'hir| industrial and spa city in W central Turkey, the capital of Eskisehir province. Pop. 413,000.

Es·me·ral·das |,esmə'räldəs| port city in NW Ecuador, the capital of Esmeraldas province. Pop. 99,000.

Es·pa·ña |es'pänyə| Spanish name for SPAIN.

Es·pí·ri·to San·to |esH'pērəto͞o 'säNto͞o| state of E Brazil, on the Atlantic coast. Capital: Vitória.

Es·pi·ri·tu San·to |es'pērəto͞o 'säntō| volcanic island in NW Vanuatu, the largest in the country. Largely agricultural, it was the site of U.S. bases during World War II.

Es·poo |'espō| (Swedish name **Esbo**) city in S Finland; a W suburb of Helsinki. Pop. 173,000. It is the second-largest city in Finland.

Es·qui·pu·las |,eskē'po͞oləs| town in SE Guatemala, near the border with Honduras. Pop. 19,000. Noted for the image of the "Black Christ of Esquipulas" in its church, the town is a center of pilgrimage.

Es·sa·oui·ra |,esə'wirə| (formerly **Mogador**) port city in SW Morocco, on the Atlantic coast. Pop. 54,000.

Es·sen |'esən| industrial city in the Ruhr valley, in NW Germany. Pop. 627,000. It is home to the Krupp steelworks.

Es·se·qui·bo |,esə'kwēbō| river in Guyana, rising in the Guiana Highlands and flowing about 600 mi./965 km. N to the Atlantic.

Es·sex |'esiks| county of E England, NE of London. Pop. 1,496,000. County town, Chelmsford.

Ess·ling·en |'esliNGən| industrial city in SW Germany, on the Neckar River near Stuttgart. Pop. 91,000.

Es·sone |e'sawn| department S of Paris in the Île-de-France, in N central France. Pop. 1,084,000. The capital is Evry.

Es·te |'estä| agricultural town in NE Italy. Pop. 17,000. Many Roman ruins are in the area.

Es·te·rel |,ester'el| mountainous region in S France, along the coasts of the departments of Var and Alpes-Maritimes. Its highest point is Mont Vinaigre (2,020 ft./616 m.).

Es·tes Park |'estēz| resort town in N central Colorado, a gateway to Rocky Mountain National Park. Pop. 3,184.

Es·to·nia |e'stōnēə| Baltic republic on the S coast of the Gulf of Finland. Area: 17,420 sq. mi./45,100 sq. km. Pop. 1,591,000. Languages, Estonian (official), Russian. Capital and largest city: Tallinn. Dominated by Russia for over two centuries, Estonia regained independence in 1991. Flat and characterized by forests and wetlands, it has a maritime and forest-industry economy. □ **Estonian** adj. & n.

Estonia

Es·to·ril |ˌeSHtə'ril| resort on the Atlantic coast of Portugal, W of Lisbon. Pop. 25,000.

Es·tre·ma·du·ra |ˌiSHtrəmə'dŏŏrə| coastal region and former province of W central Portugal.

Es·trie |'estrē| see EASTERN TOWNSHIPS, Quebec.

Esz·ter·gom |'estər,gōm| historic town and river port on the Danube in Hungary, NW of Budapest. Pop. 30,000.

Eta·wah |ə'täwə| commercial town in N India, in Uttar Pradesh state, SE of Agra. Pop. 124,000.

Ethi·o·pia |ˌēTHē'ōpēə| landlocked republic in NE Africa. Area: 472,432 sq. mi./1.22 million sq. km. Pop. 45,892,000. Lan-

Ethiopia

guages, Amharic (official), several other Afro-Asiatic languages. Capital and largest city: Addis Ababa. Former name **Abyssinia**. The oldest independent African country, Ethiopia was dominated by Italy in 1935–41. Most of its people are subsistence farmers, who struggle against repeated droughts. Separatist struggles in Eritrea and Tigray have characterized recent decades. □ **Ethiopian** adj. & n.

Et·na, Mount |'etnə| volcano in E Sicily, rising to 10,902 ft./3,323 m. It is the highest and most active volcano in Europe.

Eto·bi·coke |i'tōbə,kōk| city in S Ontario, an industrial and residential center W of Toronto. Pop. 309,993.

Etoile, Place de l' |ˌpläs də ˌlā'twäl| circular intersection in Paris, in N central France. Twelve avenues meet at L'Etoile, at one end of the Champs Elysées. In the center is the Arc de Triomphe, constructed in 1806 by Napoleon I to commemorate his military victories. The Tomb of the Unknown Soldier rests at the base of the Arc.

Eton |'ētn| town in SE England, in Buckinghamshire, N across the Thames River from Windsor, and W of London, noted as the home of Eton College, the famous school for boys. Pop. 4,000.

Eto·sha Pan |ē'tōSHə 'pæn| depression in the plateau of N Namibia, filled with salt water and having no outlets, extending over an area of 1,854 sq. mi./4,800 sq. km.

Etre·tat |ˌātrə'tä| town in NW France, in Normandy, on the English Channel N of Le Havre. It is noted for its beaches and for its dramatic white cliffs.

Etru·ria |i'trŏŏrēə| ancient state of W Italy, situated between the Arno and Tiber rivers and corresponding approximately to present–day Tuscany and parts of Umbria. It was the center of the Etruscan civilization, which flourished in the middle centuries of the 1st millennium B.C. □ **Etruscan** adj. & n.

Eu·boea |yŏŏ'bēə| island of Greece in the W Aegean Sea, separated from the mainland by only a narrow channel at its capital, Chalcis. Greek name **Évvoia**.

Eu·clid |'yŏŏklid| city in NE Ohio, an industrial and residential suburb NE of Cleveland. Pop. 54,875.

Eu·gene |yŏŏ'jēn| city in W central Oregon, on the Willamette River. An industrial and commercial center, it is also home to the University of Oregon. Pop. 112,659.

Eu·phra·tes |yŏŏ'frätēz| river of SW Asia

that rises in the mountains of E Turkey and flows 1,700 mi./2,736 km. through Syria and Iraq to join the Tigris, forming the Shatt al-Arab waterway. The two rivers define MESOPOTAMIA.

Eur·a·sia |yŏŏ'rāzнə| term used to describe the total continental land mass of Europe and Asia combined. □ **Eurasian** adj.

Eure |œr| 1 department in NW France, in Haute-Normandie. Pop. 514,000. The capital is Evreux. 2 river in NW France, rising in the Perche Hills and flowing NW for 142 mi./225 km. to the Seine River near Rouen.

Eu·re·ka |yŏŏ'rēkə| port city in NW California, on Humboldt Bay off the Pacific, a noted lumbering center. Pop. 27,025.

Eu·ro Dis·ney |'yŏŏrō 'diznē| (also called **Disneyland Paris**) theme park, in Marne-la-Valée, 19 mi./30 km. E of Paris, in N central France, opened in 1992. The park is modeled on Disney's U.S. parks.

Eu·ro·land |'yŏŏrō,lænd| popular term for the eleven European nations that in 1998 initiated use of the *euro*, a common currency.

Eu·rope |'yŏŏrəp| continent of the N hemisphere, separated from Africa to the S by the Mediterranean Sea and from Asia to the E roughly by the Dardanelles, Sea of Marmara, and the Bosporus, the Black Sea, the Caucasus Mts., the Caspian Sea, and the Ural Mts. Area: 3.8 million sq. mi./9.9 million sq. km. Europe contains approximately 10 percent of the world's population. Europe consists of the W part of the land mass of which Asia forms the E (and far greater) part, and includes the British Isles, Iceland, and most of the Mediterranean islands. Its recent history has been dominated by the decline of European states from their former colonial and economic pre-eminence, the emergence of the European Union among the wealthy democracies of W Europe, and the collapse of the Soviet Union with consequent changes of power in central and E Europe. □ **European** adj. & n.

Eu·ro·pe·an Com·mu·ni·ty |,yŏŏrə'pēən| (abbreviated **EC**) organization of W European countries, formed in 1967 by merging the earlier European Economic Community (EEC) and other bodies for purposes of economic and political integration. It was superseded in 1993 by the EUROPEAN UNION.

Eu·ro·poort |'yŏŏrə,pawrt| major European port in the Netherlands, near Rotterdam, created in 1958.

Eus·ca·di |,ʏskä'dē| (also known as **Basque Country** and, in French, **Pays Basque**) the territory on both sides of the Pyrénées, in France and Spain, occupied by the Basque people, including the Basque Provinces of N Spain and most of Pyrénées-Atlantique department in SW France.

Eux·ine Sea |'yŏŏksin; 'yŏŏk,sīn| ancient name (in Latin **Pontus Euxinus**) for the BLACK SEA.

Ev·ans·ton |'evənstən| city in NE Illinois, a suburb just N of Chicago, home to Northwestern University and to various industries. Pop. 73,233.

Ev·ans·ville |'evənz,vil| industrial port city in SW Indiana, on the Ohio River. Pop. 126,272.

Ev·er·est, Mount |'ev(ə)rəst| mountain in the Himalayas, on the border between Nepal and Tibet. Rising to 29,028 ft./8,848 m., it is the highest mountain in the world; its summit was first reached in 1953 by New Zealander Edmund Hillary and Nepalese Tenzing Norgay.

Ev·er·ett[1] |'ev(ə)rət| industrial city in NE Massachusetts, just N of Boston. Pop. 35,701.

Ev·er·ett[2] |'ev(ə)rət| industrial port city in NW Washington, N of Seattle, noted for its huge Boeing aircraft-assembly plant. Pop. 69,961.

Ev·er·glades |'evər,glādz| vast area of marshland and coastal mangrove in S Florida, part of which is protected as a national park.

Evian-les-Bains |ā'vyäɴ lā 'bæɴ| resort and spa in E France, on Lake Geneva. Pop. 6,000. Its bottled mineral water is popular around the world.

Évo·ra |'evərə| commercial center and city in S Portugal, capital of Évora district. Pop. 35,000.

Evreux |ā'vrœ| industrial town, capital of Eure department, in Haute-Normandie, in NW France. Pop. 51,000.

Ex·e·ter[1] |'eksətər; 'egzətər| the county seat of Devon, SW England, on the Exe River. Pop. 101,000. Exeter was founded by the Romans, who called it Isca.

Ex·e·ter[2] |'eksətər; 'egzətər| historic town in SE New Hampshire, home to the Phillips (Exeter) Academy. Pop. 12,481.

Ex·moor |'ek,smŏŏr; 'ek,smawr| area of moorland in N Devon and W Somerset, SW England, rising to 1,706 ft./520 m. at

Dunkery Beacon. The area is designated a national park.

Ex·tre·ma·du·ra |ˌestrəmə'do͞orə| autonomous region of W Spain, on the border with Portugal. Capital: Mérida. Spanish name **Estremadura.**

Ex·u·ma Cays |igˈzo͞omə ˈkēz; ikˈso͞omə| group of some 350 small islands in the Bahamas.

Eyre, Lake |ær; er| Australia's largest salt lake, in South Australia.

Ff

Fa·en·za |fä'enzə| town in Emilia-Romagna, N Italy. Pop. 54,000. It gave its name to the type of pottery known as faience.

Fair·banks |'fær,bæNGks| second-largest city in Alaska, in the central part, near the junction of the Chena and Tanana rivers. With a mining history, it is now chiefly commercial. Pop. 30,843.

Fair·born |'fær,bawrn| city in SW Ohio, NE of Dayton. In a farm area, it is also adjacent to Wright-Patterson Air Force Base. Pop. 31,300.

Fair·fax County |'færfæks| county in NE Virginia that incorporates many suburbs of Washington, D.C. Pop. 818,584.

Fair·field[1] |'fær,fēld| city in N central California, an agricultural processing center. Pop. 77,211.

Fair·field[2] |'fær,fēld| residential town in SW Connecticut, with many suburban villages. Pop. 53,418.

Fair·field[3] |'fær,fēld| city in SW Ohio, N of Cincinnati. Pop. 39,729.

Fair Isle |'fær 'īl| one of the Shetland Islands of Scotland, lying about halfway between Orkney and the main Shetland group. It gave its name to a knitting style.

Fair·mount Park |'færmänt| park in Philadelphia, Pennsylvania, noted as the site of the 1876 U.S. Centennial Exposition.

Fai·sa·la·bad |,fī'sälə'bäd| industrial city in Punjab, Pakistan. Pop. 1,092,000. Until 1979 it was known as Lyallpur.

Faiz·a·bad |'fīzə,bäd| commercial and industrial city in N India, in Uttar Pradesh state. Pop. 178,000.

Fa·laise |fä'lāz| market town in Normandy, NW France. Pop. 8,000. Heavy fighting occurred here after the Allied D-Day invasion in June 1944.

Fal·kirk |'fawl,kərk| town in central Scotland, administrative center of Falkirk region. Pop. 37,000. Edward I defeated the Scots here in 1298.

Falk·land Islands |'fawklənd| (also **the Falklands**) group of islands in the South Atlantic, forming a British Crown Colony. Pop. 2,121. Capital: Stanley (on East Falkland). In 1982 Argentina, which calls the islands **Las Malvinas,** and Britain fought a brief war for control.

Falk·land Islands Dependencies |'fawklənd| overseas territory of the U.K. in the South Atlantic, consisting of the South Sandwich Islands and South Georgia, which is administered from the Falkland Islands.

Falkland Islands

Fall·ing·wa·ter |'fawliNG,wawtər; 'fawliNG,wätər| house designed by Frank Lloyd Wright that stands over Bear Run, a stream in SW Pennsylvania, near the Maryland line.

Fall Line |fawl| in the U.S., imaginary line between the points at which rivers drop from the PIEDMONT into the Atlantic coastal plain. Many eastern industrial cities lie on the Fall Line.

Fall River |fawl| industrial city in SE Massachusetts, a longtime textile center associated with the Lizzie Borden legend. Pop. 92,703.

Falls Road |fawlz| road in the Catholic neighborhoods of Belfast, Northern Ireland, parallel to the Shankill Road, which passes through Protestant neighborhoods to the S.

Fal·mouth[1] |'fælməTH| historic port town in SW England, in Cornwall. Pop. 18,000. The westernmost port on the N of the English Channel, it is a yachting and shipbuilding center.

Fal·mouth[2] |'fælməTH| commercial town in SE Massachusetts, on the SW of Cape Cod. The Woods Hole ocean science complex is here. Pop. 27,960.

Fal·ster |'fälstər| Danish island in the Baltic Sea, S of Zealand.

Fa·ma·gus·ta |,fämə'gōōstə| historic city in Turkish-occupied E Cyprus. Pop. 8,000. Important during the Crusades, it is a ferry port and resort.

Far·al·lon Islands |'færə,län| small, uninhabited island group in the Pacific Ocean just W of San Francisco, California. Also, the **Farallones.**

Far East |'fär 'ēst| informal term for China, Japan, and other countries of E Asia. □ **Far Eastern** *adj.*

Fare·well, Cape[1] |fær'wel| the southernmost point of Greenland. Danish name **Kap Farvel.**

Fare·well, Cape[2] |fær'wel| the northernmost point of South Island, New Zealand. The cape was named by Captain James Cook as the last land sighted before he left for Australia in March 1770.

Far·go |'färgō| largest city in North Dakota, in the SE part, across the Red River of the North from Moorhead, Minnesota. Pop. 74,111.

Fa·ri·da·bad |fə'rēdə‚bäd| industrial city in N India, S of Delhi, in the state of Haryana. Pop. 614,000.

Farm Belt the states of the Midwest that are noted particularly for their agricultural production: Iowa, Kansas, Minnesota, Nebraska, North Dakota, and South Dakota.

Farm·ing·ton |'färmiNGtən| city in NW New Mexico, an energy industry center. Pop. 33,997.

Farn·bor·ough |'färnb(ə)rə| town in S England, in Hampshire. Pop. 48,000. Noted as a center of aviation, it is the site of an annual air show.

Farne Islands |färn| group of seventeen small islands off the coast of Northumberland, NE England, noted for their wildlife.

Fa·ro |'färoō| seaport on the S coast of Portugal, capital of the Algarve. Pop. 32,000.

Far·oe Islands |'færō; 'ferō| (also **Faeroe Islands** or **the Faroes**)a group of islands in the N Atlantic between Iceland and the Shetland Islands, belonging to Denmark but partly autonomous. Pop. 44,000; languages, Faroese (official), Danish. Capital: Tórshavn. □ **Faroese** *adj. & n.*

Far·ra·ka Barrage dam on the Ganges River, on the border between India and Bangladesh, completed in 1975.

Far·rukh·a·bad |fə'roōkə‚bäd| commercial city in N India, in Uttar Pradesh state. Pop. 208,000 (with neighboring Fategarh).

Fars |färs| an area in SW Iran roughly equivalent to the ancient province of Pars, the nucleus of the Persian Empire.

Far West |'fär 'west| the regions of North America in the Rocky Mts. and along the Pacific coast.

Fa·sho·da |fə'sHōdə| village in SE Sudan, on the White Nile River, that gave its name to an 1898 confrontation between France

and Great Britain over African territory. After the "Fashoda Incident" was resolved, the village's name was changed to Kodok.

Fast·net |'fæs(t)nət| rocky islet off the SW coast of Ireland.

Fá·ti·ma |fə'tēmə| village in W central Portugal, NE of Lisbon. Pop. 5,000. It became a center of Roman Catholic pilgrimage after the reported sighting here in 1917 of the Virgin Mary.

Faw |faw| (also called **Al Faw; Fao**) port city in SE Iraq, near the Persian Gulf.

Fay·ette·ville[1] |'fāət‚vil; 'fāətvəl| commercial city in NW Arkansas, home to the University of Arkansas. Pop. 42,099.

Fay·ette·ville[2] |'fāət‚vil; 'fāətvəl| commercial city in S central North Carolina. Fort Bragg and other military installations are central to its economy. Pop. 75,695.

Fed·er·al Way |'fed(ə)rəl| city in W central Washington, a suburb lying between Seattle and Tacoma. Pop. 67,554.

Fei·ra de San·ta·na |'färə dä sän'tänə| commercial and industrial city in NE Brazil, in Bahia state, NW of Salvador. Pop. 393,000. It is a beef industry center.

Feld·berg Mountain |'feltberg| mountain peak in Baden-Wurttemberg, SW Germany. It is the highest peak in the Black Forest (4,898 ft./1,493 m.).

Fe·lix·stowe |'fēlik‚stō| port on the E coast of England, in Suffolk. Pop. 23,000.

Fen·no·scan·dia |‚fenə'skændēə| land mass in NW Europe comprising Scandinavia, Finland, and the adjacent area of NE Russia.

Fens, the |fenz| (also **Fen Country** or **Fenland**) low-lying wetlands in E England, principally in Lincolnshire, reclaimed since the 17th century for agricultural use. The Wash lies N and E.

Fen·way, the |'fen‚wä| park system incorporating wetlands in Boston, Massachusetts. Nearby is Fenway Park, the famous baseball stadium.

Fer·ga·na |‚färgə'nä| **1** administrative subdivision in E Uzbekistan. Pop. 2,226,000. **2** (formerly **Novy Margelan** and **Skobelev**) its capital, a city in the Fergana Valley. Pop. 183,000.

Fer·ma·nagh |fər'mænə| one of the Six Counties of Northern Ireland, formerly an administrative area. Pop. 51,000; chief town, Enniskillen.

Fer·nan·do de No·ro·nha |fər'nändoō dē naw'rōnyə| territory of NE Brazil, a group of volcanic islands in the S Atlantic, NE of Natal. Long used as a penal colony, it is now in part a national park.

Fer·nan·do Póo |fər'nændō 'pō| former name (to 1973) for the island of BIOKO, Equatorial Guinea.

Fer·ney |fer'nā| (also called **Ferney-Voltaire**) village in E France, near the Swiss border. The French philosopher Voltaire lived here.

Fern Hill |'fərn 'hil| farm at Llangain, near Carmarthen, SW Wales, in Dyfed, setting of a well-known poem ("Fern Hill") by Dylan Thomas.

Fer·ra·ra |fə'rärə| city in N Italy, capital of a province of the same name. Pop. 141,000. Ferrara grew to prominence in the 13th century under the rule of the Este family.

Fer·tile Cres·cent |,fərtl 'kresənt| crescent-shaped area of fertile land in the Middle East extending from the E Mediterranean coast through the valley of the Tigris and Euphrates rivers to the Persian Gulf. It was the center of the Neolithic development of agriculture (from 7000 B.C.), and the cradle of the Assyrian, Sumerian, and Babylonian civilizations.

Fer·tő Tó |'fertœ'tō| Hungarian name for the NEUSIEDLER SEE.

Fez |fez| (also **Fès**) historic city in N Morocco, founded in 808. Pop. 564,000. A textile center, it gave its name to the hat style.

Fez·zan |fe'zæn| (Arabic name **Fazzan**) historic desert and oasis region of SW Libya, known to Europeans since pre-Roman times.

Fi·an·a·ran·tsoa |,fëänäräN'tsōə| town in E central Madagascar, a noted academic center in an agricultural area. Pop. 124,000.

Fie·so·le |'fyāzə,lā| tourist center and village outside Florence, in central Italy, on a hill overlooking the city. Pop. 4,000.

Fife |fīf| administrative region and former county of E central Scotland; administrative center, Glenrothes.

Fi·ji |'fējē| republic in the S Pacific consisting of a group of some 840 islands, of which about a hundred are inhabited. Area: 7,078 sq. mi./18,333 sq. km. Pop. 800,000. Languages, English (official), Fijian, Hindi. Capital and largest community: Suva, on Viti Levu. Independent since 1970, Fiji is peopled chiefly by Polynesians and Indians. Subsistence agriculture and the export of sugar, copra, and spices dominate the economy. □ **Fijian** *adj. & n.*

Fíl·ip·poi |'fēlepē| Greek name for PHILIPPI.

Fill·more, the |'fil,mawr| popular name for a neighborhood of San Francisco, California, W of downtown, that was central to 1960s youth culture.

Find·horn |'find,hawrn| village in N Scotland, in the Grampian region W of Elgin, site of a noted New Age agricultural community.

Find·lay |'fin(d)lē| industrial city in NW Ohio. Pop. 35,675.

Fin·gal's Cave |'fiNGgəlz| cave on the island of Staffa in the Inner Hebrides, Scotland, noted for the basaltic pillars that form its cliffs. It is said to have been the inspiration for Mendelssohn's overture *The Hebrides*.

Fin·ger Lakes |'fiNGgər| region of central New York named for its series of narrow glacial lakes that lie parallel in a N–S orientation. Canandaigua, Keuka, Seneca, and Cayuga are among the better known. Farms and resorts surround the lakes.

Fin·is·tère |,fēnē'ster| department of Brittany, in NW France. Pop. 839,000. The capital is Quimper. It is the westernmost department in France.

Fin·is·terre, Cape |,fēnē'ster| promontory of NW Spain, forming the westernmost point of the mainland. The shipping forecast area *Finisterre* covers part of the Atlantic off NW Spain, W of the Bay of Biscay.

Fin·land |'finlənd| republic on the Baltic Sea, between Sweden and Russia. Area: 130,608 sq. mi./338,145 sq. km. Pop. 4,999,000. Languages, Finnish and Swedish. Capital and largest city: Helsinki.

Fiji

Finland

Finnish name **Suomi**. Heavily forested and with thousands of islands, Finland has been dominated by Russia during much of its history. Wood, paper, and manufacturing industries are important. □ **Finnish** *adj.* **Finn** *n.*

Fin·land, Gulf of |ˈfinlənd| arm of the Baltic Sea between Finland and Estonia, extending E to St. Petersburg in Russia.

Fin·ster·aar·horn Mountain |ˌfinsterˈär-ˌhawrn| highest peak in the Bernese Alps, in Switzerland: 14,022 ft./4,274 m.

Fire Island |fīr| barrier island on the S shore of Long Island, New York, site of numerous small resort communities.

Fi·ren·ze |feˈrentsä| Italian name for FLORENCE.

Fi·ro·za·bad |firˈōzə,bäd| commercial and industrial town in N central India, in Uttar Pradesh state. Pop. 271,000.

First World |ˈfərst ˈwərld| see THIRD WORLD.

Fish River |fiSH| river that flows 300 mi./480 km. from central Namibia into the Orange River at the border with South Africa.

Fitch·burg |ˈfiCH,bərg| city in N central Massachusetts, NW of Boston, noted especially for its plastics industry. Pop. 41,194.

Fitz·roy, Cer·ro |ˈsärō ˈfēts,roi| (English name **Fitzroy Mountains**) range in Patagonia, on the border of S Argentina and S Chile, rising to 11,073 ft./3,375 m.

Fiu·me |ˈfyōōmä| Italian name for RIJEKA, Croatia.

Flag·staff |ˈflæg,stæf| city in N central Arizona, near the San Francisco Peaks, home to Lowell Observatory and the University of Northern Arizona. Pop. 45,857.

Flam·bor·ough Head |ˈflæm,b(ə)rə| rocky promontory on the E coast of England, in the East Riding of Yorkshire.

Fla·min·i·an Way |fləminēən ˈwā| (in Latin **Via Flaminia**) ancient road in Italy that led N from Rome to Rimini, extending more than 200 mi./322 km.

Flan·ders |ˈflændərz| region in the SW part of the Low Countries, now divided between Belgium (where it forms the provinces of East and West Flanders), France, and the Netherlands. It was a powerful medieval principality and the scene of prolonged fighting during the World War I. □ **Flemish** *adj.* **Fleming** *n.*

Flat·bush |ˈflæt,bŏŏSH| residential and commercial section of central Brooklyn, New York.

Flat·head Range |ˈflæt,hed| range of the Rocky Mts. in NW Montana. The **Flat-head River**, which flows through the area, is a tributary of the Clark Fork River, and an important recreational resource.

Fleet Street |ˈflēt ,strēt| street in central London, England, along which the offices of British national newspapers were located until the mid-1980s. The term is used to refer to the British press.

Flens·burg |ˈflents,bŏŏrg; ˈflenz,berg| industrial seaport in NW Germany, on the Flensburg fjord of the Baltic Sea. Pop. 87,000. Before 1867 it belonged to Denmark. It is Germany's northernmost city.

Flevo·land |ˈflävō,länt| province of the Netherlands, created in 1986 from land reclaimed from the Zuider Zee during the 1950s and 1960s.

Flin·ders Island |ˈflindərz| the largest island in the Furneaux group, in the Bass Strait between Tasmania and mainland Australia.

Flin·ders Ranges |ˈflindərz| mountain range in South Australia state, Australia.

Flint |flint| industrial city in SE Michigan, an auto industry center since the Buick Company was established here in 1903. Pop. 140,761.

Flint·shire |ˈflintsHir| county of NE Wales; administrative center, Mold. It was part of Clwyd from 1974 to 1996.

Flod·den |ˈflädn| (also **Flodden Field**) battle site in N England, near Branxton, Northumberland and the Scottish border, where English forces in 1513 defeated the Scots, inflicting devastating losses.

Flor·ence[1] |ˈflawrəns| industrial and commercial city in NW Alabama, on the Tennessee River E of Muscle Shoals. Pop. 36,426.

Flor·ence[2] |ˈflawrəns| city in W central Italy, the capital of Tuscany, on the Arno River. Pop. 408,000. Florence was a leading center of the Italian Renaissance from the 14th to the 16th centuries, especially under the rule of the Medici family during the 15th century. Italian name **Firenze**. □ **Florentine** *adj. & n.*

Flor·ence[3] |ˈflawrəns| commercial city in NE South Carolina. Pop. 29,813.

Flo·ren·cia |flawˈrensēä| commercial town in S Colombia, the capital of Caquetá department, in an agricultural area. Pop. 108,000.

Flo·res |ˈflawrəs| the largest of the Lesser Sunda Islands in Indonesia.

Flo·ri·a·nó·po·lis |ˌflawrēəˈnawōpŏŏlis| city in S Brazil, on the Atlantic coast, capital of the state of Santa Catarina. Pop. 293,000.

Flor·i·da |'flawrədə; 'flärədə| see box.
□ **Floridian** *adj. & n.*

Flor·i·da Keys |'flawredə; 'flärədə| chain of small islands off the tip of the Florida peninsula. Linked to each other and to the mainland by a series of causeways and bridges forming the Overseas Highway, the islands extend SW over 100 mi./160 km. Key Largo, the longest, is closest to the mainland, and the highway extends as far as Key West.

Flor·is·sant |'flawrəsənt| historic city in E central Missouri, NW of St. Louis. Pop. 51,206.

Flush·ing[1] |'fləSHiNG| port in the SW Netherlands. Pop. 44,000. Dutch name **Vlissingen**.

Florida

Capital: Tallahassee
Largest city: Jacksonville
Other cities: Clearwater, Daytona Beach, Ft. Lauderdale, Hialeah, Miami, Orlando, St. Petersburg, Tampa
Population: 12,937,926 (1990); 14,915,980 (1998); 16,279,000 (2005 proj.)
Population rank (1990): 4
Rank in land area: 22
Abbreviation: FL; Fla.
Nickname: Sunshine State
Motto: 'In God We Trust'
Bird: mockingbird
Fish: largemouth bass (freshwater); Atlantic sailfish (saltwater)
Flower: orange blossom
Trees: sabal palmetto palm (cabbage palm)
Song: "Old Folks at Home" (also known as "Swanee River")
Noted physical features: Apalachee, Biscayne, Waccasassa bays; Cape Canaveral, Cape Sable; Gulf of Mexico; Atlantic Ocean; Rainbow Springs, Silver Springs; Everglades and Okefenokee swamps
Tourist attractions: Walt Disney World, Epcot Center, Disney-MGM Studios; Universal Studios; Marine Land; Miami Beach; Ringling Bros. Museum of Circus; Everglades National Park; Cypress Gardens; Busch Gardens
Admission date: March 3, 1845
Order of admission: 27
Name origin: Named *Pascua Florida* ('Flowery Easter') by Juan Ponce de Leon.

Flush·ing[2] |'fləSHiNG| commercial and residential section of N Queens, New York City, noted for its diverse population.

Fly River |flī| longest river in Papua New Guinea, flowing 750 mi./1,200 km. from the border with Irian Jaya, Indonesia into the Gulf of Papua. It is noted for its wide estuary and its crocodiles.

Fly·over jocular term for the central US between the east and west coast metropolitan regions, esp. between New York City and Los Angeles. This disparaging reference to the majority of the country and its population is said to have been promulgated by frequent-flying executives of the broadcast industry.

Foc·sani |fōk'SHän(yə)| industrial city in E central Romania, in the foothills of the Transylvanian Alps. Pop. 99,000.

Fog·gia |'fawjə| industrial town in SE Italy, in Apulia. Pop. 160,000.

Fog·gy Bot·tom |'fawgē 'bätəm| low-lying part of the District of Columbia, along the Potomac River, home to the U.S. State Department, which is sometimes also called Foggy Bottom.

Fo·go |'fōgō| island in S Cape Verde. São Filipe is its chief town.

Folke·stone |'fōkstən| seaport and resort in Kent, on the SE coast of England. Pop. 44,000. The English terminal of the Channel Tunnel is at Cheriton, nearby.

Fol·som[1] |'fōlsəm| city in N central California, NE of Sacramento. Pop. 29,802.

Fol·som[2] |'fōlsəm| village in NE New Mexico that gave its name to an ancient culture whose artifacts, especially spear points, were found here.

Fond du Lac |'fändl,æk; 'fänjə,læk| industrial and commercial city in SE Wisconsin, on Lake Winnebago. Pop. 37,757.

Fon·se·ca, Gulf of |fän'säkə| inlet of the Pacific Ocean in W Central America. El Salvador lies on its N, Honduras on its E, and Nicaragua on its S.

Fon·taine·bleau |,fawNten'blō; 'fäntn,blō| town, SE of Paris, in N central France. Pop. 20,000. In the Renaissance chateau in its vast forest, King Louis XIV revoked the Edict of Nantes and Napoleon I signed his first abdication.

Fon·tana |fän'tænə| city in SW California, a steel center E of Los Angeles. Pop. 87,535.

Fon·te·noy |fawNt'nwä| village in SW Belgium. The French won a celebrated victory over English, Irish, Dutch, and Hanoverian troops here in 1745.

Foo·chow |'foo'CHow| see FUZHOU, China.

For·bid·den City[1] |fər'bidn| area of Beijing, China containing the former imperial palaces, to which entry was forbidden to all except the members of the imperial family and their servants.

For·bid·den City[2] |fər'bidn| name given to Lhasa, Tibet.

Ford·ham |'fawrdəm| section of the central Bronx, New York City, that takes its name from Fordham University.

For·est Hills |'fawrəst; 'färəst| affluent residential section of central Queens, New York City, associated with the U.S. Open (tennis), played here until 1978.

For·far |'fawrfər| town in E Scotland, administrative center of Angus region. Pop. 13,000. It is noted for its castle, the meeting place in 1057 of an early Scottish Parliament and the home of several Scottish kings.

For·far·shire |'fawrfər,SHir; 'fawfərSHər| former name (from the 16th century until 1928) for ANGUS, Scotland.

For·lì |fawr'lē| industrial town in NE Italy. Pop.110,000. It is the capital of Forlì province.

For·men·te·ra |,fawrmen'tärə| small island in the Mediterranean, S of Ibiza. It is the southernmost of the Balearic Islands of Spain.

For·mo·sa |fawr'mōsə| former (Portuguese) name for TAIWAN. □ **Formosan** adj.

For·ta·le·za |,fawrtläzə| port and resort city in NE Brazil, on the Atlantic coast, capital of the state of Ceará. Pop. 1,769,000.

Fort Ben·ning |'beniNG| military installation in W Georgia, outside Columbus, a center of infantry training.

Fort Bragg |bræg| military installation in central North Carolina, outside of Fayetteville, a center for airborne training.

Fort Col·lins |'kälinz| commercial and industrial city in N central Colorado, home to Colorado State University. Pop. 87,758.

Fort-de-France |,fawrdə'fräNs| the capital of Martinique. Pop. 102,000. □ **Foyalais** adj. & n.

Fort Dix |diks| military installation in S central New Jersey, major U.S. training center during World War II.

Fort Dodge |däj| commercial and mining city in NW Iowa. Pop. 25,894.

Forth |fawrTH| river of central Scotland, rising on Ben Lomond and flowing E through Stirling into the North Sea.

Forth, Firth of |'ferTH əv; 'fōrTH| the estuary of the Forth River, spanned by a cantilever railway bridge (opened 1890) and a road suspension bridge (1964).

Fort Hood |hood| military installation in central Texas, near Killeen, an armored training center.

Fort Knox |näks| U.S. military reservation in Kentucky, famous as the site of the depository (built in 1936) that holds the bulk of U.S. gold bullion in its vaults.

Fort La·my |,fawr lə'mē| former name (until 1973) for N'DJAMENA, Chad.

Fort Lau·der·dale |'lawdər,dāl| resort, commercial, and industrial city in SE Florida, N of Miami. Pop. 149,377.

Fort Lee |lē| commercial and residential borough in NE New Jersey, across the Hudson River from New York City. Pop. 31,997.

Fort Mc·Hen·ry |mik'henrē| historic site in the harbor of Baltimore, Maryland, scene of an 1812 British siege that inspired Francis Scott Key to write "The Star Spangled Banner."

Fort My·ers |'mīərz| resort and commercial city in SW Florida. Pop. 45,206.

Fort Peck Dam |,fawrt 'pek| dam on the Missouri River in NE Montana, built in 1940, that created Fort Peck Lake, the largest reservoir in the state.

Fort Pierce |piərs| resort and port city in E central Florida. Pop. 36,830.

Fort Sill |sil| military installation in SW Oklahoma, N of Lawton. A cavalry base in the 19th century, it now is an artillery training center.

Fort Smith |smiTH| industrial city in W Arkansas, on the Arkansas River. Pop. 72,798.

Fort Sum·ter |'səmtər| historic site in the harbor of Charleston, South Carolina. Confederate forces fired on U.S. troops here in April 1861, beginning the Civil War.

Fort Wayne |wān| industrial and commercial city in NE Indiana. Pop. 173,072.

Fort Wil·liam |'wilyəm| town in W Scotland, on Loch Linnhe near Ben Nevis. Pop. 11,000.

Fort Worth |fawrt 'wərTH| industrial and commercial city in N Texas, W of Dallas. Pop. 447,619.

forty-ninth parallel |'fawrtē,nīnTH 'pærə,lel| the parallel of latitude 49° N of the equator, especially as forming the boundary between Canada and the U.S.W of the Lake of the Woods, Minnesota.

Fo·shan |'fōsHän| (formerly **Fatshan**; **Namhoi**) industrial city in Guangdong province, S China, SW of Guangzhou, known for its silk and porcelain. Pop. 303,000.

Fosse Way |'fäs wā| ancient road in Britain. It ran from Axminster to Lincoln, via Bath and Leicester (about 200 mi./320 km.), and marked the limit of the first stage of the Roman occupation (mid-1st century A.D.)

Foth·er·in·gay |'fäTHəriNG,gā; 'fäTHərNG-,hä| village in Northamptonshire, S England, on the Nene River, scene of the birth of Richard III and the execution of Mary, Queen of Scots.

Foun·tain of Youth |'fowntn əv 'yōoTH| see under BIMINI, Bahamas.

Foun·tain Valley |'fowntn| city in SW California, a suburb SE of Los Angeles. Pop. 53,691.

Four Cor·ners |fawr 'kawrnərz| point where Arizona, New Mexico, Colorado, and Utah meet. The only such site in the U.S., it is surrounded by Navajo and Ute reservations.

Fourth World |'fawrTH 'wərld| term used to designate the poorest countries in the THIRD WORLD, especially Asian, Latin American, and African states.

Fou·ta Djal·lon mountainous district in W Guinea, in a Fulani homeland. The headstreams of the Niger and Senegal rivers are here.

Fox·bor·ough |'fäks,bərō| suburban town in E Massachusetts, SW of Boston, site of Foxborough (Shaeffer) Stadium. Pop. 14,637.

Foxe Basin |fäks| shallow inlet of the Atlantic in Nunavut, Canada, between Baffin Island and the mouth of Hudson Bay.

Fox·woods |'fäks,wŏodz| gambling resort on the Mashantucket Pequot reservation in the town of Ledyard, in SE Connecticut, N of New London.

Fra·ming·ham |'frāmiNG,hæm| industrial and commercial town in E Massachusetts. Pop. 64,994.

Fran·ca |'fräNGkə| industrial and commercial city in S Brazil, in São Paulo state, in a coffee-, diamond-, and livestock-producing area. Pop. 267,000.

France |fræns| republic in W Europe. Area: 211,208 sq. mi./547,026 sq. km. Pop. 56,556,000. Language, French. Capital and largest city: Paris. French name **République française,** abbrev. **RF.** The Gaul of the Roman period, France emerged in the Middle Ages, and has been a major European power since the 16th century. It is industrial and agricultural, but is perhaps best known for its cultural strengths. □ **French** adj. & n.

Franche-Comté |,fräNshkawN'tā| region of E France, in the N foothills of the Jura Mts.

Fran·cis·town |'frænsəs,town| industrial and commercial town in NE Botswana, in a mining area. Pop. 65,000.

Fran·co·nia |fræNG'kōnēə| medieval duchy of S Germany, inhabited by the Franks.

Fran·co·nia Notch |fræ&ng'kōnēə 'näCH| valley in the White Mts. of N New Hampshire, noted for its scenery, including the Old Man of the Mountains, the famous rock formation.

Fran·ken·thal |'fräNGkən,täl| industrial city in western Germany, NW of Mannheim. Pop. 47,000.

Frank·fort |'fræNGkfərt| the state capital of Kentucky. Pop. 25,968.

Frank·furt |'fräNGkfŏort; 'fræNGkfərt| commercial city in western Germany, in Hesse. Pop. 654,000. The headquarters of the Bundesbank is here. Full name **Frankfurt am Main.**

Frank·lin Mountains |'fræNGklən| range in the W Northwest Territories, E of the Mackenzie River.

Franz Jo·sef Land |,fräns 'jōsəf| group of islands in the Arctic Ocean, discovered in 1873 by an Austrian expedition and annexed by the USSR in 1928.

Fra·scati |fräs'kätē| town in central Italy. Pop. 20,000. A popular summer resort since the Roman era, it is known for its white wine.

Fra·ser |'frāzər; 'frāzHər| river of British Columbia. It rises in the Rocky Mts. and flows in a wide curve 850 mi./1,360 km. into the Strait of Georgia, just S of Vancouver.

Fray Ben·tos |fri 'bäntaws| port and meatpacking center in W Uruguay. Pop. 20,000.

Fred·er·ick |'fred(ə)rik| city in N Maryland. Fort Detrick is nearby. Pop. 40,148.

Fred·er·icks·burg[1] |'fred(ə)riks,bərg| resort city in central Texas, in the Hill Country. Pop. 6,934.

Fred·er·icks·burg[2] |'fred(ə)riks,bərg| historic commercial city in NE Virginia, on the Rappahannock River. Pop. 19,027.

Fred·er·ic·ton |'fred(ə)riktən| the capital of New Brunswick, in the SW, on the St. John River. Pop. 46,466. The city was founded in 1785 by United Empire Loyalists, colonists who left the U.S. after the Revolutionary War.

Fred·er·iks·berg |'freTHrigz,ber| W suburb of Copenhagen, Denmark. Pop. 86,000.

Free·port[1] |'frē,pawrt| port city in the N Bahamas, on Grand Bahama Island. Pop.

FRANCE

0 50 100 150 200 km
0 25 50 75 100 miles

Regional boundary
Department boundary
■ Capital City
• Regional capital

Departments of the Paris Region

VAL-D'-OISE
HAUTS-DE-SEINE
SEINE-SAINT-DENIS
YVELINES
Paris
VAL-DE-MARNE
SEINE-ET-MARNE
ESSONNE

Regions

1. Alsace
2. Aquitaine
3. Auvergne
4. Bourgogne
5. Bretagne
6. Centre
7. Champagne-Ardenne
8. Franche-Comté
9. Languedoc-Roussillon
10. Limousin
11. Lorraine
12. Midi-Pyrénées
13. Nord-Pas-de-Calais
14. Basse Normandie
15. Haute Normandie
16. Pays de La Loire
17. Picardie
18. Poitou-Charentes
19. Provence-Alpes-Côte d'Azur
20. Rhône-Alpes
21. Ile-de-France

27,000. It is a resort and commercial center.

Free·port[2] |'frē͵pawrt| commercial and industrial city in NW Illinois. Pop. 25,840.

Free·port[3] |'frē͵pawrt| commercial village in Hempstead town, Long Island, New York. Pop. 39,894.

Free States |'frē 'stāts| in U.S. history, those states in which slavery was not legal before the Civil War.

Free·town |'frē͵town| the capital and chief port of Sierra Leone. Pop. 505,000.

Frei·berg |'frī͵berg| industrial center and rail junction in eastern Germany, in the foothills of the Ore Mts. Pop. 51,000. It is in a mining region.

Frei·burg |'frī,boͦork; 'frī,bərg| industrial city in SW Germany, in Baden-Württemberg, on the edge of the Black Forest. Pop. 194,000. Full name **Freiburg im Breisgau.**

Fre·man·tle |'frē,mæntl| the principal port of Western Australia, part of the Perth metropolitan area. Pop. 24,000.

Fre·mont |'frē,mänt| industrial and commercial city in N central California, S of Oakland off San Francisco Bay. Pop. 173,339.

French Com·mu·ni·ty |'frenCH kə-'myoͦonətē| (French name **Communauté française**) organization established in 1958 linking France with overseas territories and departments, as well as with seven former African colonies. It ceased to have practical importance by the early 1960s.

French Con·go |ˌfrenCH 'kängō| early name for FRENCH EQUATORIAL AFRICA, now the People's Republic of Congo.

French Equa·to·rial Af·ri·ca |frenCH ˌekwə'tawrēəl 'æfrikə| former federation of French territories in W central Africa (1910–58). Previously called French Congo, its constituent territories were Chad, Ubangi Shari (now the Central African Republic), Gabon, and Middle Congo (now the Republic of the Congo).

French Gui·a·na |frenCH gē'änə| overseas department of France, in N South America. Area: 35,126 sq. mi./90,976 sq. km. Pop. 96,000. Capital: Cayenne. A low, tropical land, it produces timber, rum, and fish.

French Guiana

French Indo·china |'frenCH,indō'CHīnə| former French colonial territory of SE Asia, comprising the present countries of Vietnam, Cambodia, and Laos.

French Pol·y·ne·sia |frenCH ˌpälə'nēzHə|

overseas territory of France in the South Pacific. Pop. 200,000. Capital: Papeete (on Tahiti). French Polynesia comprises the Society Islands, the Gambier Islands, the Tuamotu Archipelago, the Tubuai Islands, and the Marquesas. It became an overseas territory of France in 1946, and was granted partial autonomy in 1977.

French So·ma·li·land |frenCH sə'mälēˌlænd| former name (until 1967) for DJIBOUTI.

French South·ern and Ant·arc·tic Territories |'frenCH 'saTHərn ənd ænt'är(k)tik| overseas territory of France, comprising Adélie Land in Antarctica, and the Kerguelen and Crozet archipelagos and the islands of Amsterdam and St. Paul in the S Indian Ocean.

French Sudan former name for MALI.

French West Af·ri·ca |frenCH west æfrikə| former federation of French territories in NW Africa (1895–1959). Its constituent territories were Senegal, Mauritania, French Sudan (now Mali), Upper Volta (now Burkina Faso), Niger, French Guinea (now Guinea), the Côte d'Ivoire, and Dahomey (now Benin).

Fres·nil·lo |frez'nēyō| city in N central Mexico, in Zacatecas state, in a silver-mining region. Pop. 75,000. It has a noted mining school.

Fres·no |'freznō| city in central California, in the San Joaquin Valley, in an agricultural and oil-producing area. Pop. 354,202.

Fri·bourg |frē'boͦor| (in German **Freiburg**) canton in W Switzerland, on a plateau in the foothills of the Alps. Area: 644 sq. mi./1,672 sq. km. Pop. 204,000. The area is agricultural.

Frie·drichs·ha·fen |'frēdriKHs'häfən| industrial and port city in S Germany, on the Lake of Constance. Pop. 52,000.

Friend·ly Islands |'fren(d)lē| another name for TONGA.

Fries·land[1] |'frēs,länt| the W part of the ancient region of Frisia.

Fries·land[2] |'frēs,länt| N province of the Netherlands, bounded to the W and N by the IJsselmeer and the North Sea. Capital: Leeuwarden.

Fri·sia |'frizHə; 'frēzHə| ancient region of NW Europe. It consisted of the Frisian Islands and parts of the mainland corresponding to the present-day provinces of Friesland and Groningen in the Netherlands and the regions of Ostfriesland and Nordfriesland in NW Germany. □ **Frisian** *adj. & n.*

Fri•sian Islands |'frizHən; 'frēzHən| chain of islands lying off the coast of NW Europe, extending from the IJsselmeer in the Netherlands to Jutland. The islands consist of three groups: the *West Frisian Islands* form part of the Netherlands, the *East Frisian Islands* form part of Germany, and the *North Frisian Islands* are divided between Germany and Denmark.

Fri•u•li |'frē-ōō͞,lē; frē'ōōlē| historic region of SE Europe now divided between Slovenia and the Italian region of Friuli-Venezia Giulia. A Rhaeto-Romance dialect is spoken locally. □ **Friulian** *adj. & n.*

Friuli–Venezia Giu•lia |'frē-ōō͞,lē və-'netsēə 'jōōlya; frē'ōōlē| region in NE Italy, on the border with Slovenia and Austria. Capital: Trieste.

Fro•bi•sher Bay |'frōbisHər| inlet of the Atlantic at the S end of Baffin Island, in Nunavut. Iqaluit, the town at its head, was formerly also called Frobisher Bay.

Front Range |frənt| easternmost range of the Rocky Mts., chiefly in Colorado, reaching 14,270 ft./4,349 m. at Grays Peak. Pikes Peak is also here.

Frun•ze |'frōōnzə| former name (1926–91) for BISHKEK, Kyrgyzstan.

Fu•chu |'fōōCHōō| industrial and residential city in E central Japan, on Honshu, a suburb of Tokyo. Pop. 209,000.

Fuer•te•ven•tu•ra |,fwertävän'tōōrə| second-largest of the Canary Islands, belonging to Spain, in the Atlantic. Area:655 sq. mi./1,722 sq. km. Its chief town is Puerto del Rosario.

Fu•jai•rah |fōō'jīrə| (also **Al Fujayrah**) **1** one of the seven member states of the United Arab Emirates. Pop. 76,000. **2** its capital.

Fu•ji, Mount |'fōōjē| dormant volcano in the Chubu region of Japan. Rising to 12,385 ft./3,776 m., it is Japan's highest mountain, with a symmetrical, conical, snow-capped peak. Its last eruption was in 1707. Regarded by the Japanese as sacred, it has been celebrated in art and literature for centuries. Also called **Fujiyama**.

Fu•jian |'fōōjēan| (formerly **Fukien**) mountainous province, SE China, across the Taiwan Strait from Taiwan. Pop. 27.49 million. Capital: Fuzhou.

Fu•ji•sa•wa |,fōōjē'säwä| city and resort town in central Japan on E Honshu, a suburb SW of Tokyo. Pop. 350,000.

Fu•kui |fōō'kōōē| industrial city in W central Japan, on central Honshu. Pop. 253,000.

Fu•ku•o•ka |,fōōkōō'ōka| industrial city and port in S Japan, capital of Kyushu island. Pop. 1,237,000.

Fu•ku•shi•ma |,fōōkōō'sHēmə; fōō'kōō-sHēmə| main commercial city of NE Japan, on N Honshu. Pop. 278,000.

Fu•ku•ya•ma |,fōōkōō'yämä| industrial and commercial port in W Japan, on SW Honshu. Pop. 366,000.

Ful•da |'fōōldə| headwater of the Weser River, in western Germany. It flows 137 mi./218 km. to join the Werra River, forming the Weser.

Ful•ham |'fōōləm| district of W London, England, part of the borough of **Hammersmith and Fulham**.

Fu•ling |'fōō'liNG| city in Sichuan province, central China, on the Yangtze River at its junction with the Wu River. Pop. 986,000.

Ful•ler•ton |'fōōlərtən| city in SW California, SE of Los Angeles. Pop. 114,144.

Fu•na•ba•shi |,fōōnä'bäsHē| city in central Japan, on E Honshu, a residential and industrial suburb of Tokyo. Pop. 533,000.

Fu•na•fu•ti |,f(y)ōōnə'f(y)ōōtē| the capital of Tuvalu, situated on an island of the same name. Pop. 2,500.

Fu•nan |'fōō'nän| former kingdom of SE Asia (1st to 6th centuries) in territory occupied by much of present-day Cambodia and southern Vietnam.

Fun•chal |fōōn'sHäl| the capital and chief port of Madeira, on the S coast of the island. Pop. 110,000.

Fun•dy, Bay of |'fəndē| arm of the Atlantic extending between the Canadian provinces of New Brunswick and Nova Scotia. It is subject to fast-running tides, the highest in the world, which reach 50–80 ft./12–15 m. and are used to generate electricity.

Fur•neaux Islands |'fərnō| group of Australian islands off the coast of NE Tasmania, in the Bass Strait. The largest is Flinders Island.

Fur•ness |'fərnəs| peninsular region of NW England, NW of Morecambe Bay in Cumbria. The chief town is BARROW-IN-FURNESS.

Fur Seal Islands another name for the PRIBILOF ISLANDS.

Fürth |fyrt| industrial city in S Germany, suburb of Nuremberg, on the Rednitz and Pegnitz rivers. Pop. 105,000,

Fu•shun |'fōō'sHōōn| coal-mining city in NE China, in the province of Liaoning. Pop. 1,330,000.

Fu•tu•na Islands |foo͞'too͞nə| see WALLIS AND FUTUNA ISLANDS, French Polynesia.

Fu•xin |'foo͞sHin| (also **Fou-hsin**) industrial city in NE China, in Liaoning province. Pop. 743,000.

Fu•zhou |'foo͞'jō| (also **Foochow**) port in SE China, capital of Fujian province. Pop. 1,270,000.

Fyn island |fyn| island, part of Denmark, situated between Jutland and Zealand. Area: Pop. 459,000. The chief town is Odense.

Gg

Ga·bès |'gäb,es; gäb'es| (also **Qabis**) industrial seaport in E Tunisia. Pop. 99,000.

Ga·bon |gä'bawN| equatorial republic in W Africa, on the Atlantic coast. Area: 103,386 sq. mi./267,667 sq. km. Pop. 1,200,000. Languages, French (official), Fang, other W African languages. Capital and largest city: Libreville. A French territory from 1888 to 1958, Gabon became independent in 1960. Oil, timber, and minerals are important to its economy. □ **Gabonese** *adj. & n.*

Gabon

Ga·bo·rone |,gäbə'rōnā| the capital of Botswana, in the S of the country near the border with South Africa. Pop. 133,000.

Ga·bro·vo |'gäbrō,vō| industrial city in central Bulgaria, on the Yantra River. Pop. 88,000. Bulgaria's chief textile center, it is situated on an approach to the Shipka Pass through the Balkan Mts.

Ga·dag |'gədəg| commercial town in SW India, in Karnataka state. Pop. 134,000 (with neighboring Betgeri).

Gads·den |'gædzdən| industrial city in NE Alabama. Pop. 42,523.

Gads·den Purchase |'gædzdən| area in New Mexico and Arizona, near the Rio Grande. Extending over 30,000 sq. mi./77,700 sq. km., it was purchased from Mexico in 1853 by the American diplomat James Gadsden (1788-1858), with the intention of ensuring a southern railroad route to the Pacific.

Gael·tacht |'gāl,täxt| (**the Gaeltacht**) region of Ireland in which the vernacular language is Irish, particularly in Connacht.

Gaf·sa |'gæfsə| (Arabic name **Qafsah**; Roman name **Capsa**) oasis and industrial town in W central Tunisia. Pop. 71,000. It gave its name to the Paleolithic Capsian culture.

Gaines·ville |'gānz,vil; 'gānzvəl| city in N central Florida, home to the University of Florida. Pop. 84,770.

Gai·thers·burg |'gāTHərz,bərg| city in central Maryland, a residential and corporate center NW of Washington, D.C. Pop. 39,542.

Ga·la·pa·gos Islands |gə'läpəgəs; gə-'læpəgəs| Pacific archipelago on the equator, about 650 mi./1,045 km. W of Ecuador, to which it belongs. Pop. 9,750. Spanish name **Archipiélago de Colón**. The islands are noted for their abundant wildlife, including giant tortoises and many other endemic species. They were the site of Charles Darwin's observations of 1835, which helped him to form his theory of natural selection.

Ga·laţi |gə'läts| industrial city in E Romania, a river port on the lower Danube. Pop. 324,000.

Ga·la·tia |gə'lāsHə| ancient region in central Asia Minor (present-day Anatolian Turkey), settled by invading Gauls (the Galatians) in the 3rd century B.C. It later became a province of the Roman Empire. □ **Galatian** *adj. & n.*

Gales·burg |'gālz,bərg| commercial and industrial city in W central Illinois. Pop. 33,530.

Ga·li·cia¹ |gə'lisHə| region of E central Europe, north of the Carpathian Mountains. A former province of Austria, it now forms part of SE Poland and W Ukraine. Hasidic Judaism developed here. □ **Galician** *adj. & n.*

Ga·li·cia² |gə'lisHə| autonomous region and former kingdom of NW Spain. Capital: Santiago de Compostela. □ **Galician** *adj. & n.*

Gal·i·lee, Sea of |'gælə,lē| lake in N Israel. The River Jordan flows through it from N to S. Also called **Lake Tiberias, Lake Kinneret**.

Gal·i·lee |'gælə,lē| N region of ancient Palestine, W of the Jordan River, associated with the ministry of Jesus. It is now part of Israel. □ **Galilean** *adj. & n.*

Gal·le |gäl; gæl| seaport on the SW coast of Sri Lanka. Pop. 77,000.

Gal·li·po·li |gə'lipəlē| (Turkish name **Galibolu**) peninsula in European Turkey, between the Dardanelles and the Aegean Sea, scene of a bloody and unsuccessful Allied attack on Turkish positions in 1915–16, during World War I.

Gal·lo·way |ˈgælə‚wā| area of SW Scotland consisting of the two former counties of Kirkcudbrightshire and Wigtownshire, and now part of Dumfries and Galloway region.

Gal·ves·ton |ˈgælvəstən| port in Texas, SE of Houston. Pop. 59,070. It is situated on Galveston Bay, an inlet of the Gulf of Mexico.

Gal·way |ˈgawl‚wā| **1** county of the Republic of Ireland, on the W coast in the province of Connacht. Pop. 180,000. **2** its county seat, a seaport at the head of Galway Bay. Pop. 51,000.

Gal·way Bay |ˈgawl‚wā| inlet of the Atlantic on the W coast of Ireland.

Gam·bia |ˈgæmbēə; ˈgämbēə| (also **the Gambia**) a country on the coast of W Africa. Area: 4,363 sq. mi./11,295 sq. km. Pop. 900,000. Languages, English (official), Malinke and other indigenous languages. Capital: Banjul. A narrow strip on the Gambia River, within the territory of Senegal (with which it has been politically joined at times), Gambia relies on tourism, fishing, and agriculture to sustain its economy. See also SENEGAMBIA. □ **Gambian** adj. & n.

Gambia

Gam·bia River |ˈgæmbēə; ˈgämbēə| river of W Africa that rises near Labé in Guinea and flows 500 mi./800 km. through Senegal and Gambia to the Atlantic at Banjul.

Gam·bier Islands |ˈgæm‚bir| group of coral islands in the S Pacific, forming part of French Polynesia.

Gän·cä |gänˈjä| industrial city in Azerbaijan. Pop. 281,000. The city was formerly called Elizavetpol (1804–1918) and Kirovabad (1935–89). Russian name **Gyandzhe**.

Gan·der |ˈgændər| town on the island of Newfoundland, on Lake Gander. Pop. 10,339. Its airport served the first regular transatlantic flights, during World War II.

Gan·dhi·na·gar |‚gərdiˈnəgər| city in W India, capital of the state of Gujarat. Pop. 122,000.

Gan·ga |ˈgəNGge| Hindi name for the GANGES River.

Gan·ga·na·gar |ˈəNGgə‚nəgər| commercial town in NW India, in Rajasthan state, near the border with Pakistan. Pop. 161,000.

Gan·ges |ˈgæn‚jēz| river of N India and Bangladesh, which rises in the Himalayas and flows some 1,678 mi./2,700 km. SE to the Bay of Bengal, where it forms the world's largest delta. The river is regarded by Hindus as sacred. Hindi name **Ganga**. □ **Gangetic** adj.

Gang·tok |ˈgəng‚tawk| city in N India, in the foothills of the Kanchenjunga mountain range, capital of the state of Sikkim. Pop. 25,000.

Gan·su |ˈgän‚so͞o| (also **Kansu**) a province of NW central China, between Mongolia and Tibet. Pop. 22.37 million. Capital: Lanzhou. This narrow, mountainous province forms a corridor through which the Silk Road passed.

Gao |gow| port town in NE Mali, on the Niger River. Pop. 40,000.

Gap |gäp| tourist center, manufacturing town, and capital of the Hautes-Alpes department in SE France, in the foothills of the Dauphiné Alps. Pop. 36,000.

Gard |gär| department in S France, in the lower Rhône Valley. Area: 2,260 sq. mi./5,853 sq. km. Pop. 585,000. The capital is Nîmes.

Gar·da, Lake |ˈgärdə| largest lake in Italy, in the NE, between Lombardy and Venetia.

Gar·de·na |gärˈdēnə| city in SW California, an industrial suburb S of Los Angeles. Pop. 49,847.

Gar·den City |ˈgärdn| commercial village in Hempstead town, Long Island, New York. Pop. 21,686. The historic air facility Roosevelt Field was here.

Gar·den Grove |ˈgärdn| city in SW California, an industrial and residential suburb SE of Los Angeles. Pop. 143,050.

Gar·den State |ˈgärdn| informal name for NEW JERSEY.

Gar·land |ˈgärlənd| city in NE Texas, an industrial and residential suburb on the NE side of Dallas. Pop. 180,650.

Garmisch-Partenkirchen |ˈgärmisH ‚pärtn‚kirKHən| resort town in S Germany, in the Bavarian Alps near Oberammergau. Pop. 27,000. It hosted the 1936 Winter Olympic Games.

Gar·mo, Mount |ˈgärmō| former name

(until 1933) for COMMUNISM PEAK, Kyrgyzstan.

Ga•ronne |gä'rawn| river of SW France, which rises in the Pyrenees and flows 400 mi./645 km. NW through Toulouse and Bordeaux to join the Dordogne at the Gironde estuary.

Ga•roua |gə'rōōə| river port in N Cameroon, on the Bénoué River. Pop. 78,000.

Gary |'gærē| industrial port city in NW Indiana, a steel center on Lake Michigan SE of Chicago. Pop. 116,646.

Gas•co•ny |'gæskənē| region and former province of SW France, in the N foothills of the Pyrenees. It was held by England between 1154 and 1453. French name **Gascogne**. □ **Gascon** adj. & n.

Gaspé Peninsula |gæs'pā| region of SE Quebec between the Saint Lawrence River and New Brunswick. Fishing, agriculture, and tourism are important to its economy.

Ga•stein•er Valley |gä'sHtīnər| (also called **Gasteintal**) river valley in the Hohe Tauern range, W Austria. It is known for its scenery and for the spas of Bad Hofgastein and Badgastein.

Gas•to•nia |gæ'stōnēə| industrial city in SW North Carolina, a noted textile center. Pop. 54,732.

Gat•chi•na |'gächinə| city in NW Russia. Pop. 84,000. It is the site of a former imperial palace, built in the late 18th century and a favorite residence of the czars.

Gates•head |'gāts,hed| industrial town in NE England, on the S bank of the Tyne River opposite Newcastle. Pop. 196,000.

Gath |gæTH| biblical city in Philistia, E of present-day Ashdod, Israel, the home of the giant Goliath.

Gat•i•neau |,gætn'ō| city in SW Quebec, a largely French-speaking suburb across the Ottawa River from Ottawa, Ontario. Pop. 92,284.

Ga•tun Lake |gə'tōōn| (Spanish name **Lago Gatún**) lake in Panama, created by the damming of the Chagres River during construction of the Panama Canal. The Gatun Locks control passage on the Canal.

Gat•wick |'gætwik| international airport in SE England, to the S of London in West Sussex.

Gau•ha•ti |gow'hätē| industrial city in NE India, in Assam, a river port on the Brahmaputra. Pop. 578,000.

Gaul |gawl| (Latin name **Gallia**) ancient region of Europe, corresponding to modern France, Belgium, the S Netherlands, SW Germany, and N Italy. The area S of the Alps was conquered in 222 B.C. by the Romans, who called it *Cisalpine Gaul*. The area N of the Alps, known as *Transalpine Gaul*, was taken by Julius Caesar between 58 and 51 B.C. □ **Gallic** adj.

Gaunt |gawnt| former name for GHENT, Belgium.

Gau•teng |'gow,teNG| province of NE South Africa, formerly part of Transvaal. Capital: Johannesburg. Former name (until 1995) **Pretoria-Witwatersrand-Vereeniging**.

Ga•var•nie |,gävär'nē| village in SW France, in the central Pyrenees. Nearby are a waterfall (1,385 ft./422 m.) and a huge natural amphitheater, the Cirque de Gavarnie.

Gäv•le |'yevlə| seaport in E central Sweden, on the Gulf of Bothnia, N of Stockholm. Pop. 89,000. It is the capital of Gävleborg county.

Ga•ya |gə'yä| city in NE India, in the state of Bihar S of Patna. Pop. 291,000. It is a place of Hindu pilgrimage.

Ga•zan•ku•lu |,gäzən'kōōlōō| former homeland established in South Africa for the Tsonga people, now part of the provinces of Northern province and Mpumalanga.

Ga•za Strip |'gäzə; 'gæzə| strip of territory in Palestine, on the SE Mediterranean coast, including the town of Gaza. Pop. 748,000. Administered by Egypt from 1949, and occupied by Israel from 1967, it became a self-governing Palestinian enclave under an agreement with Israel in 1994 and elected its own legislative council in 1996.

Ga•zi•an•tep |,gäzēän'tep| commercial and industrial city in S Turkey, near the border with Syria. Pop. 603,000. Former name (until 1921): **Aintab**.

Gdańsk |gə'dänsk; gə'dænsk| (German name **Danzig**) industrial port and shipbuilding center in N Poland, on an inlet of the Baltic Sea. Pop. 465,000. Disputed between Prussia and Poland during the 19th century, it was a free city under a League of Nations mandate from 1919 until 1939, when it was annexed by Nazi Germany, precipitating hostilities with Poland and the outbreak of World War II. In the 1980s the Gdańsk shipyards were the site of the activities of the Solidarity movement, which eventually led to the collapse of the communist regime in Poland in 1989.

GDR abbreviation for GERMAN DEMOCRATIC REPUBLIC.

Gdy•nia |gə'dinēə| port and naval base in

N Poland, on the Baltic Sea NE of Gdańsk. Pop. 251,000.

Gee·long |jēˈlawNG| port and oil-refining center on the S coast of Australia, in the state of Victoria. Pop. 126,000.

Ge·hen·na |gəˈhenə| biblical name for Hinnom, a valley near Jerusalem where children were burned in sacrifice to Moloch and other gods. Gehenna came to signify torment and misery.

Ge·jiu |ˈgəjēˈo͞o| (also **Geju**)a tin-mining city in S China, near the border with Vietnam. Pop. 384,000.

Ge·la |ˈjälə| port and industrial center in S Sicily, S Italy. Pop. 72,000.

Gel·der·land |ˈgeldər,lænd| province of the Netherlands, on the border with Germany. Capital: Arnhem. Formerly a duchy, the province was variously occupied by the Spanish, the French, and the Prussians until 1815.

Gel·sen·kir·chen |,gelzənˈkirKHən| industrial city in western Germany, in North Rhine-Westphalia NE of Essen. Pop. 294,000.

Gems·bok National Park |ˈgemz,bäk| preserve in SW Botswana and an adjoining part of South Africa, in the Kalahari Desert. It is noted for its dunes and wildlife.

Ge·ne·ral San Mar·tín |,KHänäˈräl ,sän märˈtēn| (also **San Martín**) city in E Argentina, a NW suburb of Buenos Aires. Pop. 408,000.

Ge·ne·ral San·tos |,KHänäˈräl ˈsäntōs| (also called **Dadiangas**) port city in the Philippines, on S Mindanao, on Saragani Bay. Pop. 250,000.

Ge·ne·ral Sar·mien·to |,KHänäˈräl ,särˈmyentō| (also **Sarmiento** or **San Miguel**) city in E Argentina, a suburb W of Buenos Aires, in a cattle-producing district. Pop. 647,000.

Gen·e·see River |,jenəˈsē; ˈjenə,sē| river that flows 144 mi./232 km. from NW Pennsylvania through W New York, into Lake Ontario at Rochester.

Ge·ne·va |jəˈnēvə| city in SW Switzerland, on Lake Geneva. Pop. 167,000. It is the headquarters of international bodies such as the Red Cross, various organizations of the United Nations, and the World Health Organization. French name **Genève**. It was the site of the Geneva Conventions (1846–1949), which established rules for the conduct of war, and was the headquarters of the League of Nations (1920–46).

Ge·ne·va, Lake |jəˈnēvə| lake in SW central Europe, between the Jura Mts. and the Alps. Its S shore forms part of the border between France and Switzerland. French name **Lac Léman**.

Genk |KHeNGk| (also **Genck**) town in NE Belgium. Pop. 61,000.

Gen·oa |ˈjenəwə| seaport on the NW coast of Italy, capital of Liguria region. Pop. 701,000. It was the birthplace of Christopher Columbus. Italian name **Genova**. □ **Genoese** *adj. & n.*

Gent |KHent| Flemish name for GHENT, Belgium.

George, Lake |jawrj| resort lake in NE New York, NE of Albany, near the Vermont line, scene of many 18th-century military actions.

Georges Bank |ˈjawrjəz| underwater rise in the Atlantic, between Massachusetts and Nova Scotia, site of important U.S. and Canadian fishing zones.

George·town[1] |ˈjawrj,town| the capital of Guyana, a port at the mouth of the Demerara River. Pop. 188,000.

George·town[2] |ˈjawrj,town| affluent section of NW Washington, D.C., home to government officials, shopping districts, and Georgetown University.

George Town[1] |ˈjawrj ,town| the capital of the Cayman Islands, on the island of Grand Cayman. Pop. 12,000.

George Town[2] |ˈjawrj ,town| the chief port of Malaysia and capital of the state of Penang, on Penang island. Pop. 219,000. It was founded in 1786 by the British East India Company. Also called **Penang**.

Geor·gia, Strait of |ˈjawrjə| ocean passage between Vancouver Island and the mainland of British Columbia and Washington.

Geor·gia[1] |ˈjawrjə| a republic of SE Europe, on the E shore of the Black Sea. Area: 26,905 sq. mi./69,700 sq. km. Pop. 5,500,000 (1994). Languages, Georgian (official), Russian, and Armenian. Capital and largest city: Tbilisi. A medieval kingdom, Georgia was dominated by Russia in the 19th–20th centuries, regaining inde-

Georgia

pendence in 1991. It is both agricultural and industrial. □ **Georgian** *adj. & n.*

Geor•gia[2] |'jawrjə| see box. □ **Georgian** *adj. & n.*

Geor•gian Bay |'jawrjən| inlet of Lake Huron, in central Ontario, separated from the rest of the lake by the Bruce Peninsula.

Ge•ra |'gärä| industrial city in eastern central Germany, in Thuringia. Pop. 127,000.

Ger•ald•ton |'jerəl(d)tən| seaport and resort on the W coast of Australia, to the N of Perth. Pop. 24,000.

Ger•man Dem•o•cratic Republic official name for the former state of East Germany.

Ger•man East Af•ri•ca |'jərmən ēst 'æfrikə| former German protectorate in East Africa (1891–1918), corresponding to present-day Tanzania, Rwanda, and Burundi.

Ger•man South West Af•ri•ca |'jərmən ˌSOWTH west 'æfrikə| former German protectorate in SW Africa (1884–1918), corresponding to present-day Namibia.

Ger•man•town |'jərmən,town| historic residential section of NW Philadelphia, Pennsylvania, scene of a 1777 battle.

Georgia

Capital/largest city: Atlanta
Other cities: Albany, Athens, Augusta, Columbus, Macon, Marietta, Savannah, Augusta, Sparta
Population: 6,478,216 (1990); 7,642,207 (1998); 8,413,000 (2005 proj.)
Population rank (1990): 11
Rank in land area: 24
Abbreviation: GA; Ga.
Nicknames: Empire State of the South; Peach State; Goober State; Peachtree State
Motto: 'Wisdom, Justice, Moderation'
Bird: brown thrasher
Fish: largemouth bass
Flower: Cherokee rose
Tree: live oak
Song: "Georgia"
Noted physical features: Warm Springs; Okefenokee Swamp; Brasstown Bald Peak
Tourist attractions: Andersonville National Cemetery; Fort Frederica, Fort Pulaski and Ocmulgee national monuments
Admission date: January 2, 1788
Order of admission: 4
Name origin: Named by early settler James Oglethorpe for King George II of England, who in 1732 granted Oglethorpe a royal charter to the land.

Ger•many |'jərmənē| republic in central Europe. Area: 137,838 sq. mi./357,000 sq. km. Pop. 78,700,000. Language, German. Capital and largest city: Berlin; seat of government, Bonn. German name **Deutschland**. Ranging from N coastal plains to the Alps, Germany unified in the mid-19th century, and became a world power in the 20th. Divided, after World War II, into WEST GERMANY and EAST GERMANY, it was reunified in 1990. It is an industrial and economic power, which also has a strong agricultural sector and an important cultural position. □ **German** *adj. & n.*

Ger•mis•ton |'jərməstən| city in South Africa, in the province of Gauteng, SE of Johannesburg. Pop. 134,000. It is the site of a large gold refinery, which serves the Witwatersrand gold-mining region.

Ge•ro•na |hā'rōnə| industrial city in NE Spain, on the Oñar River, NE of Barcelona. Pop. 67,000. It is the capital of Gerona province.

Ge•ta•fe |he'täfä| industrial and market center in central Spain, near Madrid. Pop. 135,000.

Geth•sem•a•ne |ˌgeTH'semənē| biblical garden, between Jerusalem and the Mount of Olives, the scene of the agony of Jesus and his betrayal.

Get•tys•burg |'getēz,bərg| historic agricultural and commercial borough in S central Pennsylvania, scene of a critical Civil War battle in July 1863. Pop. 7,025.

Gey•sir |'gāsir| (also **Great Geysir**) hot spring in SW Iceland, active in the 1890s, that gave its name to the term *geyser*.

Ge•zi•ra, El |ˌel jə'zērə| (also **Al Jazirah**) region of central Sudan, S of Khartoum, between the White Nile and Blue Nile, a center of irrigated agriculture.

Gha•da•mis |gə'dämis| (also **Ghadames** or **Ghudamis**) oasis town in W Libya, on the Algerian border and near the Tunisian border. Pop. 52,000.

Gha•ga•ra Ri•ver |gə'gärə; 'gägərə| (also **Gogra**; Nepalese **Karnali**) river in S central Asia that flows 570 mi./900 km. from SW Tibet through Nepal into India, where it joins the Ganges River.

Gha•na |'gänə| republic of W Africa, with its S coastline on the Atlantic. Area: 92,100 sq. mi./238,537 sq. km. Pop. 16,500,000. Languages, English (official), W African languages. Capital and largest city: Accra. Known as the Gold Coast 1874–1957, Ghana was the first British African colony to gain independence. It produces cacao,

coffee, coconuts, timber, and other crops.
□ **Ghanaian** *adj. & n.*

Gha·ry·an |gär'yän| city in NW Libya, S of
Tripoli. Pop. 118,000.

Ghats |gawts| two mountain ranges in cen-
tral and S India. Known as *the Eastern Ghats*
and *the Western Ghats*, they run parallel to
the coast on either side of the Deccan
plateau.

Gha·zi·a·bad |'gäzēə,bäd| city in N India,
in Uttar Pradesh E of Delhi. Pop. 461,000.

Ghaz·ni |'gäznē| commercial city in E cen-

Ghana

tral Afghanistan, SW of Kabul. Pop. 33,000. It is famous for sheepskin coats.

Ghent |gent| city in Belgium, capital of the province of East Flanders. Pop. 230,200. Founded in the 10th century, it became the capital of the medieval principality of Flanders. It was formerly known in English as Gaunt (surviving in names, e.g., John of Gaunt). Flemish name **Gent.**

Ghet•to |'getō| term for a section of a city where residents of a particular race or ethnic identity are forced to live. The term was first used for a site in 16th-century Venice, Italy (*ghetto is the Italian word for 'foundry'*).

Giant's Cause•way |'jīənts 'kawz,wā| formation of basalt columns, dating from the Tertiary period, on the N coast of Northern Ireland. It was once believed to be the end of a road made by a legendary giant to STAFFA in the Inner Hebrides, where there is a similar formation.

Gib•e•on |'gibēən| biblical town, NW of Jerusalem in the present-day West Bank, whose inhabitants, the Gibeonites, allied themselves with the Israelites under Joshua.

Gi•bral•tar |jə'brawltər| British dependency near the S tip of the Iberian Peninsula, at the E end of the Strait of Gibraltar. Area: 2.26 sq. mi./5.86 sq. km. Pop. 28,000. Languages, English (official), Spanish. Occupying a site of great strategic importance, Gibraltar consists of fortified town and military base at the foot of a rocky headland, the **Rock of Gibraltar**. Britain captured it during the War of the Spanish Succession in 1704 and is responsible for its defense, external affairs, and internal security. □ **Gibraltarian** *adj. & n.*

Gibraltar

Gi•bral•tar, Strait of |jə'brawltər| channel between the S tip of the Iberian Peninsula and N Africa, forming the only outlet of the Mediterranean Sea to the Atlantic. It is some 38 mi./60 km. long and varies in width from 15 mi./24 km. to 25 mi./40 km. at its W extremity.

Gib•son Desert |'gibsən| desert region in Western Australia, to the SE of the Great Sandy Desert.

Gies•sen |'gēsən| industrial city and rail junction in central Germany, on the Lahn River. Pop. 72,000.

Gi•fu |'gē,foo; gē'foo| industrial city in central Japan, on the island of Honshu, noted for paper production. Pop. 410,000.

Gi•jón |hē'hōn| port and industrial city in N Spain, on the Bay of Biscay. Pop. 260,000.

Gi•la River |'hēlə| river that flows 645 mi./1,045 km. from New Mexico across S Arizona to the Colorado River. Phoenix is in its valley.

Gil•bert and El•lice Island |'gilbərt ən(d) 'elis| former British colony (1915–75) in the central Pacific, consisting of two groups of islands: the Gilbert Islands, now a part of Kiribati, and the Ellice Islands, now Tuvalu.

Gil•boa, Mount |gil'bōə| mountain in NE Israel, in the Samarian highlands above the plain of Esdraelon, where in the biblical account Saul was defeated by the Philistines and killed himself.

Gil•git |'gilget| commercial town in the NW Himalayas, controlled by Pakistan, capital of the Gilgit region. Pop. 44,000.

Gil•ling•ham |'jiliNGəm| residential town on the Medway estuary SE of London, England. Pop. 94,000.

Gil•roy |'gil,roi| agricultural city in W central California, noted for its garlic production. Pop. 31,487.

Gin•za, the |'gēnzə| shopping and entertainment district of Tokyo, Japan.

Gi•re•sun |,gērə'soon| port city in NE Turkey, on the Black Sea. Pop. 68,000. The capital of Giresun province, it was the ancient Cerasus, whose name, from a famous local product, is the source of the word *cherry*.

Gi•ronde |zHē'rawNd| **1** estuary in SW France, formed at the junction of the Garonne and Dordogne rivers, N of Bordeaux, and flowing NW for 45 mi./72 km. into the Bay of Biscay. **2** a department in Aquitaine, SW France. Pop. 1,213,000. Capital, Bordeaux.

Gis•borne |'gizbərn| port and resort on the E coast of North Island, New Zealand. Pop. 31,000.

Gi•te•ga |gē'tāgə| commercial town in central Burundi, E of Bujumbura. Pop. 102,000.

Giur•giu |'joorjoo| port city in S Romania, on the Danube River. Pop. 72,000. Giurgiu is linked by bridge with Ruse, Bulgaria.

Gi·za |'gēzə| suburban city SW of Cairo in N Egypt, on the W bank of the Nile, site of the Pyramids and the Sphinx. Pop. 2,156,000. Also called **El Giza**; Arabic name **Al Jizah**.

Gji·ro·ka·stër |ˌgyērō'kästər| historic city in S Albania, on the Drino River. Pop. 25,000.

Gla·cier Bay National Park |'glāsHər| preserve in SE Alaska, on the Pacific coast. Extending over an area of 4,975 sq. mi./12,880 sq. km, it contains the terminus of the Grand Pacific Glacier.

Glad·beck |'glät,bek| industrial city in W Germany, in the Ruhr district. Pop. 80,000.

Gla·mor·gan |glə'mawrgən| former county of S Wales.

Glar·ner Alps |'glärnər| (also **Glarner Alps**) range in the Alps, in NE Switzerland between Lake Lucerne and the Rhine River. Glärnissch (9,560 ft./2,914 m.) has one of the steepest faces in the Alps. The commune of Glarus, at the foot of Glärnisch, is the capital of Glarus canton.

Glas·gow |'glæz,gō; 'glæsgō| largest city in Scotland on the Clyde River. Pop. 655,000. Formerly a major shipbuilding center and still an important commercial and cultural center. □ **Glaswegian** *adj. & n.*

Glas·ton·bury |'glæstənb(ə)rē; 'glæstən,berē| town in Somerset, SW England. Pop. 7,000. It is the legendary burial place of King Arthur and Queen Guinevere and the site of a ruined abbey held by legend to have been founded by Joseph of Arimathea.

Glen Canyon see POWELL, LAKE.

Glen·coe |glen'kō| valley in W Scotland, in the Highlands SE of Fort William, scene of a 1692 massacre of Jacobite Macdonald clansmen by soldiers of the Protestant William III.

Glen·dale[1] |'glen,dāl| city in S central Arizona, a residential and commercial suburb NW of Phoenix. Pop. 148,134.

Glen·dale[2] |'glen,dāl| city in SW California, a commercial and residential suburb N of Los Angeles. Pop. 180,038.

Glen·da·lough |'glendə,läKH| (also **Vale of Glendalough**) valley in Wicklow, SE Ireland, noted for its beauty and for its cluster of medieval religious ruins.

Glen·do·ra |glen'dawrə| city in SW California, a suburb NE of Los Angeles. Pop. 47,828.

Glen·ea·gles |glen'ēgəlz| valley in E Scotland, SW of Perth, site of a noted hotel and golfing center.

Glen Gar·ry |glen'gærē| valley in W Scot

land, in the Highlands N of Fort William, that gave its name to the *glengarry,* a characteristic Scottish cap.

Glen More |glen 'mawr| another name for the GREAT GLEN of Scotland.

Glen·roth·es |glen'räTHəs| town in E Scotland, administrative center of Fife region. Pop. 39,000.

Glit·ter·tind |'glitər,tin| mountain in Norway, in the Jotunheim range. Rising to 8,104 ft./2,470 m., it is the highest peak in the country.

Gli·wi·ce |gli'vētsə| mining and industrial city in S Poland, near the border with the Czech Republic. Pop. 214,000.

Glom·ma river |'glawmə| longest river in Norway (365 mi./590 km.), rising in the SE and flowing S to the Skagerrak at Frederikstad.

Glouces·ter[1] |'glästər; 'glawstər| city in SW England, the county seat of Gloucestershire. Pop. 92,000. It was founded by the Romans, who called it Glevum, in A.D. 96.

Glouces·ter[2] |'glästər; 'glawstər| city in NE Massachusetts, on Cape Ann, a famed fishing and resort center. Pop. 28,716.

Glouces·ter·shire |'glästərshər; 'glawstərshər| county of SW England. Pop. 521,000; county seat, Gloucester.

Glynde·bourne |'glīn(d),bawrn| estate in SE England, near Lewes, East Sussex, scene of a famed summer opera festival.

Gniez·no |gə'nyeznaw| historic town in W central Poland. Pop. 70,000. It was the first capital of Poland and the site of royal coronations until 1320.

Goa |'gōə| state on the W coast of India. Capital: Panaji. Formerly a Portuguese territory, it was seized by India in 1961. It formed a Union Territory with Daman and Diu until 1987, when it was made a state. □ **Goan** *adj. & n.* **Goanese** *adj. & n.*

Go·bi Desert |'gōbē| barren plateau of S Mongolia and N China. Covering over 500,000 sq. mi./1.2 million sq. km., it is noted for its fossils.

Go·da·va·ri |gō'dävərē| river in central India that rises in the state of Maharashtra and flows about 900 mi./1,440 km. SE across the Deccan plateau to the Bay of Bengal.

God·havn |'gōTH,hown| (Inuit name **Qeqertarsuaq**) town in W Greenland, on the S coast of the island of Disko.

Go·doy Cruz |gōdoi krōōs| city in W Argentina, S of Mendoza. Pop. 180,000. It is a wine-making center.

Godt·håb |'gawt,hawp| former name (until 1979) for NUUK, Greenland.

Godwin-Austen, Mount |'gädwin 'awstən| former name for K2.

Go·ge·bic Range |gō'gēbik| range of iron-bearing hills in the W Upper Peninsula of Michigan and adjacent parts of Wisconsin.

Goi·â·nia |goi'änyə| city in S central Brazil, capital of the state of Goiás. Pop. 998,000. Founded as a new city in 1933, it replaced Goiás as state capital in 1942.

Goi·ás |goi'äs| state in S central Brazil. Capital: Goiânia.

Go·lan Heights |'gō,län 'hīts| range of hills on the border between Syria and Israel, NE of the Sea of Galilee. Formerly under Syrian control, the area was occupied by Israel in 1967 and annexed in 1981. Negotiations for the withdrawal of Israeli troops from the region began in 1992.

Gol·con·da |gäl'kändə| historic ruined city in S central India, in Andhra Pradesh state. It was famous for its diamonds.

Gold Beach |gōld| name given to the W section of the beach at Normandy where British troops landed on D-day in June 1944. It lies E of Arromanches.

Gold Coast[1] |'gōld 'cōst| term for any of various affluent residential or resort districts in the U.S., either in a city like New York or Chicago or along an actual coast, such as that S of Miami, Florida.

Gold Coast[2] |'gōld 'cōst| resort region on the E coast of Australia, to the S of Brisbane.

Gold Coast[3] |'gōld 'cōst| former name (until 1957) for GHANA.

Gol·den |'gōldən| city in N central Colorado, NW of Denver, a mining, brewing, and academic center. Pop. 13,116.

Gol·den Gate |'gōldən 'gæt| deep channel connecting San Francisco Bay, California, with the Pacific Ocean, spanned by the Golden Gate suspension bridge (completed 1937).

Gol·den Horde |'gōldən 'hawrd| (also **Kipchak Empire**) Mongol empire of the 14th century, centered along the Volga River, with its capital at Sarai, at first near present-day Astrakhan, later near present-day Volgograd. It controlled much of what is now Russia.

Gol·den Horn |'gōldən 'hawrn| curved inlet of the Bosporus forming the harbor of Istanbul. Turkish name **Haliç**.

Gol·den Sands |'gōldən 'sændz| (Bulgarian name **Zlatni Pyasuti**) resort town in E Bulgaria, on the Black Sea N of Varna.

Gol·den State |'gōldən 'stāt| nickname for CALIFORNIA.

Gol·den Tri·an·gle |'gōldən 'trī,æŋgəl| region in SE Asia covering parts of Burma, Laos, and Thailand, a major source of opium and heroin.

Golds·boro |'gōldz,bərō| city in E North Carolina, a noted tobacco center. Pop. 40,709.

Gol·go·tha |'gälgəTHə; gäl'gäTHə| Greek name, from the Hebrew for skull, for CALVARY.

Go·ma·ti River |'gawmətē| river in N India, in Uttar Pradesh state, that flows 500 mi./800 km. from the foothills of the Himalayas to join the Ganges River near Varanasi.

Go·mel |gaw'm(y)el| Russian name for HOMEL, Belarus.

Gó·mez Pa·la·cio |'gōmes pä'läsēō| commercial and industrial city in N Mexico, in Durango state, in an agricultural region. Pop. 233,000.

Go·mor·rah |gə'mawrə| see SODOM, biblical city.

Go·na·ïves |,gōnä'ēv| port town in W Haiti, on the Gulf of Gonâve. Pop. 63,000. The independence of Haiti from France was proclaimed here in 1804.

Gon·dar |'gawndər| (also **Gonder**) commercial city in NW Ethiopia, in Amhara province. Pop. 112,000. An historic center for both Christians and Jews (Falashas), it was the capital of Ethiopia before 1855.

Gond·wa·na·land |gän'dwänə,lænd| (also **Gondwana**) supercontinent thought to have existed in the S hemisphere before breaking apart into Africa, South America, Antarctica, Australia, the Arabian Peninsula, and the Indian subcontinent.

Good Hope, Cape of |good 'hōp| mountainous promontory S of Cape Town, South Africa, near the S extremity of Africa. Sighted toward the end of the 15th century by Bartolomeu Dias, it was rounded for the first time by Vasco da Gama in 1497.

Good·win Sands |'goodwin 'sændz| area of sandbanks in the Strait of Dover, SE England. Often exposed at low tide, the sandbanks are a hazard to shipping.

Go·rakh·pur |'gawrək,poor| industrial city in NE India, in Uttar Pradesh near the border with Nepal. Pop. 490,000.

Go·raz·de |gə'räzhdə| predominantly Muslim town in E Bosnia and Herzegovina that was attacked repeatedly by Bosnian Serbs in 1993–94 in the ethnic fighting that followed the breakup of Yugoslavia in 1991. Pop. 17,000.

Gor·bals |'gawrbəlz| district of Glasgow, Scotland, on the south bank of the Clyde

River, formerly noted for its slums and tenement buildings.

Gor·di·um |'gawrdēəm| ancient city of Asia Minor (now NW Turkey), the capital of Phrygia in the 8th and 9th centuries B.C. Alexander the Great here cut the Gordian knot.

Go·rée Island |gaw'rā| (French name **Île de Gorée**) island near Dakar, Senegal, held by various European powers for centuries, and noted as an embarkation point for slaves.

Gö·reme |'gawrəmə| valley in Cappadocia in central Turkey, noted for its cave dwellings hollowed out of the soft tufa rock. In the Byzantine era these contained hermits' cells, monasteries, and more than 400 churches.

Gor·gan |'gawr'gawn| (formerly **Asterabad; Astarabad**) town in NE Iran, in the NE foothills of the Elburz Mts. Pop. 162,000.

Gor·gon·zo·la |ˌgawrgən'zōlə| village in N Italy, NE of Milan, known for its rich, veined cheese. Pop. 16,000.

Gori |'gōrē| industrial city in central Republic of Georgia, on the Kura River. Pop. 62,000.

Go·ri·zia |gə'rētsyə| town in NE Italy, NW of Trieste. Pop. 39,000. It is the capital of Gorizia province.

Gor·ky |'gawrkē| former name (1932–91) for NIZHNI NOVGOROD, Russia.

Gor·litz |'gœr,litz| industrial town in E Germany, on the Neisse River, E of Dresden at the Polish border. Pop. 70,000.

Gor·lov·ka |'gawrləfkə| industrial city in SE Ukraine, in the Donets Basin. Pop. 338,000.

Gorno-Altai |'gawrnəäl'tī| autonomous republic in S central Russia, on the border with Mongolia. Pop. 192,000. Capital: Gorno-Altaisk.

Gor·zow Wiel·ko·pol·ski |'gōZHŏŏf ˌvyelkə'pawlskē| transportation and trade center in W Poland, on the Warthe River. Pop. 121,000.

Go·saint·han |ˌgō,sīn'tän| (also called **Xixabangma Feng**) peak in the Himalayas in S Tibet near Nepal. It is the highest peak entirely within China: 26,287 ft./ 8,012 m.

Go·shen |'gōSHən| fertile area of NE ancient Egypt, E of the Nile delta, where the biblical Jacob and his descendants lived on land granted by the pharaoh before the Exodus.

Gos·port |'gäs,pawrt| port town in S England, on Portsmouth Harbour in Hampshire. Pop. 70,000. It is a former naval port, now a yachting center.

Gö·ta·land Canal |'yœtə,länd| 240-mi./386-km. system of lakes, rivers, and canals in S Sweden, connecting Göteborg and Stockholm. The canals, incorporating 58 locks, make up half the system's length. Built in 1832, they reach a height of 300 ft./91 m.

Gö·te·borg |'yœtə,bawr(yə)| Swedish name for GOTHENBURG.

Go·tha |'gōtə| city in central Germany, in Thuringia. Pop. 58,000. From 1640 until 1918 it was the residence of the dukes of Saxe-Gotha and Saxe-Coburg-Gotha.

Go·tham[1] |'gōtəm| village in Nottinghamshire, England. It is associated with the folk tale *The Wise Men of Gotham*, in which the inhabitants of the village demonstrated cunning by feigning stupidity.

Go·tham[2] |'gäTHəm| nickname for New York City, used originally in satires by Washington Irving. □ **Gothamite** n.

Goth·en·burg |'gäTHən,bərg| seaport in SW Sweden, on the Kattegat strait. Pop. 433,000. It is the second-largest city in Sweden. Swedish name **Göteborg**.

Got·land |'gawt,länt; 'gät,lænd| island and province (including neighboring smaller islands) of Sweden, in the Baltic Sea. Pop. 57,000. Capital: Visby.

Go·to Is·lands |'gōtō| (also called **Gotoretto**) island group in SW Japan, in the East China Sea off W Kyushu.

Göt·ting·en |'gœtiNGən| town in N central Germany, on the Leine River. Pop. 124,000. It is noted for its university.

Gou·da |'gŏŏdə| market town in the Netherlands, just NE of Rotterdam. Pop. 66,000. It is noted for its cheese.

Gough Island |gawf; gäf| island in the S Atlantic, S of Tristan da Cunha. In 1938 it became a dependency of the British Crown Colony of St. Helena.

Go·ver·na·dor Va·la·da·res |ˌgŏŏvərnə-'dawr ˌvälə'däris| industrial and commercial city in SE Brazil, in Minas Gerais state. Pop. 231,000.

Go·zo |'gawdzō| Maltese island, to the NW of the main island of Malta.

Grace·land |'gräslənd; 'gräs,lænd| home and burial place of Elvis Presley, a major tourist attraction in Memphis, Tennessee.

Gra·cias a Di·os, Cape |'gräsēəs ä'dē-aws| cape forming the easternmost extremity of the Mosquito Coast in Central America, on the border between Nicaragua and Honduras. Its name in Spanish means thanks (be) to God. It was so named by

Columbus, who, becalmed off the coast in 1502, was able to continue his voyage with the arrival of a following wind near this point.

Gra·ham Land |'grāəm| the N part of the Antarctic Peninsula, the only part of Antarctica lying outside the Antarctic Circle. Discovered in 1831–2 by the English navigator John Biscoe (1794–1843), it now forms part of British Antarctic Territory, but is claimed also by Chile and Argentina.

Gra·ian Alps |'grāən; 'grīən| W range of the Alps, along the French-Italian border S of Mont Blanc. It reaches 13,323 ft./4,061 m. at Gran Paradiso, in Italy.

Gram·pi·an |'græmpēən| former local government region in NE Scotland, dissolved in 1996.

Gram·pi·an Mountains[1] |'græmpēən| mountain range in SE Australia, in Victoria. It forms a spur of the Great Dividing Range at its W extremity.

Gram·pi·an Mountains[2] |'græmpēən| mountain range in N central Scotland. Its S edge forms a natural boundary between the Highlands and the Lowlands.

Gra·na·da[1] |grə'nädə| city in Nicaragua, on the NW shore of Lake Nicaragua. Pop. 89,000. Founded by the Spanish in 1523, it is the oldest city in the country.

Gra·na·da[2] |grə'nädə| city in Andalusia in S Spain. Pop. 287,000. Founded in the 8th century, it became the capital of the Moorish kingdom of Granada in 1238. It is the site of the Alhambra.

Gran·by |'grænbē| city in S Quebec, E of Montreal. Pop. 42,804.

Gran Ca·na·ria |,gränGkə'näryə| volcanic island off the NW coast of Africa, one of the Canary Islands of Spain. Its chief town, Las Palmas, is the capital of the Canaries.

Gran Cha·co |grän 'CHäcō| (also **Chaco**) a lowland plain in central South America, extending from S Bolivia through Paraguay to N Argentina.

Gran Co·lom·bia |,grän kə'lōmbēə| country formed in NW South America in 1819, from lands liberated from Spanish rule. It comprised present-day Colombia, Venezuela, Panama, and Ecuador, and dissolved in 1830.

Grand Ba·ha·ma |bə'hämə; bə'hāmə| fourth-largest island in the Bahamas, in the NW. Freeport is its chief town. Grand Bahama is a tourist center.

Grand Banks |grænd 'bænks| submarine plateau of the continental shelf off the SE coast of Newfoundland, Canada. It is a

meeting place of the warm Gulf Stream and the cold Labrador Current; this promotes the growth of plankton, making the waters an important feeding area for fish.

Grand Canal[1] |,grand kə'næl| series of waterways in E China, extending from Beijing S to Hangzhou, a distance of 1,060 mi./1,700 km. Its original purpose was to transport rice from the river valleys to the cities. Its construction proceeded in stages between 486 B.C. and A.D. 1327.

Grand Canal[2] |grand kə'næl| the main waterway of Venice, Italy. It is lined on each side by fine palaces and spanned by the Rialto Bridge.

Grand Can·yon |grand 'kænyən| deep gorge in Arizona, formed by the Colorado River. It is about 277 mi./440 km. long, 5 to 15 mi./8 to 24 km. wide, and, in places, 6,000 ft./1,800 m. deep. The area was designated a national park in 1919.

Grand Canyon of the Snake another name for HELL'S CANYON.

Grand Cou·lee Dam |grænd 'ko͞olē| dam on the Columbia River in E central Washington, completed in 1942.

Grande Com·o·ro |,gräNd kaw'mawr| the largest-island of the Comoros, off the NW coast of Madagascar. Pop. 233,500. Chief town (and capital of the Comoros), Moroni.

Grande-Terre |gräNd'ter| second largest of the islands that make up the French department of Guadeloupe, in the E West Indies. The department's largest town, Point-à-Pitre, is here.

Grand Forks |'grænd 'fawrks| city in NE North Dakota, on the Red River of the North and the Minnesota line. Pop. 49,425.

Grand Island |grænd ,īlənd| commercial and industrial city in S central Nebraska. Pop. 39,386.

Grand Junction |græn(d) 'jəNGkSHən| city in W Colorado, at the junction of the Colorado (formerly the Grand) and Gunnison rivers. Pop. 29,034.

Grand Port·age |grænd 'pawrtij| historic locality in NE Minnesota, on Lake Superior, where early traders began a portage around the falls of the Pigeon River.

Grand Prairie |grænd 'prārē| industrial city in NE Texas, between Dallas and Fort Worth. Pop. 99,616.

Grand Pré |'græn 'prā| historic locality in W central Nova Scotia, on the Minas Basin, scene of the 1755 expulsion of Acadians recounted in *Evangeline.*

Grand Rapids |grænd 'ræpədz| industrial

city in SW Michigan, on the Grand River, noted for its furniture production. Pop. 189,126.

Grand Strand |grænd 'strænd| name for the NE coast of South Carolina, site of many resorts including Myrtle Beach.

Grand Te·ton National Park |grænd 'tē-,tän| preserve in NW Wyoming, just S of Yellowstone National Park, named for the highest of its peaks. Jackson Hole is here.

Gran·ite State |'grænit| nickname for NEW HAMPSHIRE.

Gran Sas·so d'Ita·lia |grän 'säsō dē'tälyə| limestone massif in E central Italy, in the Apennine range. Its highest peak is the Corno Grande (9,554 ft./2,914 m.). It has the only glacier in the Apennines.

Gran·ta |'græntə| alternate name for the Cam River, England.

Gras·mere |'græs,mir| village in Cumbria, NW England, beside a small lake of the same name. Pop. 1,000. William and Dorothy Wordsworth lived here.

Grasse |gräs| town near Cannes in SE France, center of the French perfume industry. Pop. 42,000.

Graves |gräv| district in the department of Gironde, SW France, extending from the banks of the Garonne River to S of Bordeaux. It is known for its wines.

Graves·end |gräv'zend| (official name **Gravesham**) industrial town in SE England, in the Thames estuary E of London, in Kent. Pop. 90,000. It is the burial place of Pocahontas.

Grave·yard of the At·lan·tic nickname for CAPE HATTERAS, noted for the many shipwrecks that have occurred near it.

Grays Harbor |gräz 'härbər| inlet of the Pacific Ocean in W Washington, just S of the Olympic Peninsula, a noted fishing and lumbering area.

Graz |gräts| industrial city in S Austria, on the Mur River, capital of the state of Styria. Pop. 232,000. It is the second-largest city in Austria.

Great Aus·tra·lian Bight |aw'strālyən 'bīt| wide bay on the S coast of Australia, part of the S Indian Ocean.

Great Bar·rier Reef |'bærēər| coral reef in the W Pacific, off the coast of Queensland, Australia. It extends for about 1,250 mi./2,000 km., roughly parallel to the coast, and is the largest coral reef in the world.

Great Basin |'bāsən| arid region of the western U.S. between the Sierra Nevada and Rocky Mts., including most of Nevada and parts of the adjacent states. Death

Valley and the Great Salt Lake are within the Basin.

Great Bear Lake fourth-largest North American lake, in the Northwest Territories, Canada. It drains into the Mackenzie River via the Great Bear River.

Great Brit·ain |grāt 'britn| England, Wales, and Scotland considered as a unit. The name is also often used loosely to refer to the United Kingdom. Wales was politically incorporated with England in the 16th century, and in 1604 James I, the first king of both England and Scotland, was proclaimed 'King of the Great Britain'; this name was adopted at the Union of the English and Scottish Parliaments in 1707. In 1801 Great Britain was united with Ireland (from 1921, only Northern Ireland) as the United Kingdom.

Great Dis·mal Swamp |'dizməl| (also **Dismal Swamp**) an area of swampland in SE Virginia and NE North Carolina.

Great Divide popular name for the CONTINENTAL DIVIDE in the western U.S.

Great Di·vid·ing Range mountain system in E Australia. Curving roughly parallel to the coast, it extends from E Victoria to N Queensland. Also called **Great Divide**.

Great·er An·til·les |än'tilēz| see ANTILLES.

Great·er Lon·don |'ləndən| metropolitan area comprising central London and the surrounding regions. It is divided administratively into the City of London, thirteen inner London boroughs, and nineteen outer London boroughs. Pop. 6,379,000.

Great·er Man·ches·ter |'mæn,CHestər; 'mænCHəstər| metropolitan county of NW England including the city of Manchester and adjacent areas. Pop. 2,445,000.

Great·er Sun·da Islands |'sŏondə| see SUNDA ISLANDS.

Great Falls |fawlz| industrial city in N central Montana, on the Missouri River. Pop. 55,097.

Great Glen |glen| large fault valley in Scotland, extending from the Moray Firth SW for 60 mi./37 km. to Loch Linnhe, and containing Loch Ness. Also called **Glen More**.

Great In·di·an Desert |'indēən| another name for the THAR DESERT.

Great Lakes |grāt lāks| group of five large interconnected lakes in central North America, consisting of Lakes Superior, Michigan, Huron, Erie, and Ontario, and constituting the largest area of fresh water in the world. Lake Michigan is wholly within the U.S., and the others lie on the Canada–U.S. border. Connected to the Atlantic by the St. Lawrence Seaway, the Great Lakes form an important commercial waterway.

Great Lakes–St. Law•rence Seaway |'lawrəns| waterway in North America that flows 2,342 mi./3,768 km. from near Duluth, Minnesota through the Great Lakes and along the course of the St. Lawrence River to the Atlantic. A number of artificial sections bypass rapids in the river. It is open along its entire length to oceangoing vessels; it was inaugurated in 1959.

Great Plain see ALFOLD.

Great Plains vast area of plains to the E of the Rocky Mts. in North America, extending from the valley of the Mackenzie River in Canada to S Texas. The North Slope of Alaska is considered an extension of the Plains. Areas closer to the Rockies and of higher elevation are called the High Plains.

Great Rift Valley large system of rift valleys in E Africa and the Middle East, forming the most extensive such system in the world and running for some 3,000 mi./4,285 km. from the Jordan valley in Syria, along the Red Sea into Ethiopia, and through Kenya, Tanzania, and Malawi into Mozambique. It is marked by a chain of lakes and a series of volcanoes, including Mount Kilimanjaro.

Great St. Ber•nard Pass |'sānt bər'närd| see ST. BERNARD PASS.

Great Salt Lake salt lake in N Utah, W of Salt Lake City, in the Great Basin. With an area of some 1,000 sq. mi./2,590 sq. km., it is the largest salt lake in North America.

Great Sand Sea area of desert in NE Africa, on the border between Libya and Egypt.

Great Sandy Desert[1] large tract of desert in N central Western Australia.

Great Sandy Desert[2] another name for the RUB' AL KHALI, chiefly in Saudi Arabia.

Great Slave Lake fifth-largest (11,030 sq. mi./28,568 sq. km.) North American lake, in the Northwest Territories. The deepest lake in North America, it reaches 2,015 ft./615 m. The Mackenzie River flows out of it.

Great Smoky Mountains |'smōkē| (also **Smoky Mountains** or **Smokies**) range of the Appalachian Mts. in SW North Carolina and E Tennessee. A noted tourist attraction, they are named for a frequent haze.

Great Vic•to•ria Desert |vik'tawrēə| desert region of Australia, which straddles the boundary between Western Australia and South Australia.

Great Wall of Chi•na former defensive wall in N China, extending 4,187 mi./6,700 km. from Gansu province to Yellow Sea NE of Beijing. The first wall was constructed by unifying existing smaller walls during the Qin dynasty c.210 B.C., and the present wall dates largely from the Ming dynasty (1368–1644). The intent was to keep nomadic invaders, chiefly Mongols, from attacking.

Great Whale River |(h)wāl| (French name **Grande Rivière de la Baleine**) river that flows 365 mi./590 km. W across NW Quebec to Hudson Bay, subject of recent controversy over power development.

Great White Way nickname for the theater district of BROADWAY, New York City.

Great Zim•ba•bwe |zim'bäbwā| complex of stone ruins in a fertile valley in Zimbabwe, about 175 mi./270 km. S of Harare, discovered by Europeans in 1868. They are the remains of a city that was the center of a flourishing civilization in the 14th and 15th centuries. The circumstances of its decline and abandonment are unknown.

Greece |grēs| republic in SE Europe, on the Aegean, Mediterranean, and Ionian seas. Area: 50,488 sq. mi./130,714 sq. km. Pop. 10,269,000. Language, Greek. Capital and largest city: Athens. Official name: **The Hellenic Republic**. Greek name: **Ellás**. A great power and center of culture in the 5th century B.C., Greece passed through two thousand years of eclipse and domination by Macedonians, Romans, Turks, and others before gaining independence in 1830. It is now both agricultural and industrial, and its cultural history draws visitors. □ **Greek** *adj. & n.*

Greece

Gree•ley |'grēlē| agricultural and commercial city in N central Colorado. Pop. 60,536.

Green Bay |'grēn 'bā| industrial port city in NE Wisconsin, on Green Bay, an inlet of Lake Michigan. Pop. 96,466.

Green Gab·les |'grēn 'gābəlz| home of the fictional Anne of Green Gables, on Prince Edward Island. Sites identified with her story are now tourist attractions.

Green·land |'grēnlənd| largest island (840,325 sq. mi./2.2 million sq. km.) in the world, lying to the NE of North America and mostly within the Arctic Circle. Pop. 55,000. Capital: Nuuk (Godthåb). Danish name **Grønland**; called in Inuit **Kalaallit Nunaat**. □ **Greenlander** *n.*

Greenland

Green·land Sea |'grēnlənd| sea that lies between the E coast of Greenland and the Svalbard archipelago, forming part of the Arctic Ocean.

Green Mountains |grēn| range of the Appalachians that extends N to S through Vermont, reaching 4,393 ft./1,340 m. at Mount Mansfield.

Green Mountain State |grēn| nickname for VERMONT.

Green·ock |'grēnək| port in W central Scotland, on the Firth of Clyde. Pop. 55,000.

Green River |grēn| river that flows 730 mi./1,130 km. from Wyoming through Colorado and Utah, into the Colorado River.

Greens·boro |'grēnz,bərə| city in N central North Carolina. Pop. 183,521. Textiles are its best-known manufacture.

Green·ville[1] |'grēn,vil; 'grēnvəl| city in NW Mississippi, in the Delta. Pop. 45,226.

Green·ville[2] |'grēn,vil; 'grēnvəl| industrial city in NW South Carolina. Pop. 58,282.

Green·wich[1] |'grenicH; 'grenij| town in SW Connecticut, on Long Island Sound. Pop. 58,441. It is chiefly an affluent New York suburb.

Green·wich[2] |'grenicH; 'grēn,wicH| London borough on the S bank of the Thames, the original site of the Royal Greenwich Observatory. Pop. 201,000. The prime meridian (0° longitude) is here, and Green-

wich Time is the standard from which times around the world are determined.

Green·wich Village |'grenicH 'vilij; 'grenij| district of New York City on the Lower West Side of Manhattan, traditionally associated with writers, artists, and musicians.

Greifs·wald |'grifs,fält| port and manufacturing city in NE Germany, near the Baltic Sea. Pop. 66,000.

Gre·na·da |grə'nādə| republic in the West Indies, consisting of the island of Grenada (the southernmost of the Windward Islands) and the S Grenadine Islands. Area: 133 sq. mi./345 sq. km. Pop. 94,800. Languages, English (official), English Creole. Capital: St. George's. Colonized by the French and British, Grenada became independent in 1974. Agriculture and tourism are important to its economy. □ **Grenadian** *adj. & n.*

Grenada

Gren·a·dine Islands |,grenə'dēn| (also **the Grenadines**) a chain of small islands in the Caribbean, part of the Windward Islands. They are divided administratively between ST. VINCENT AND THE GRENADINES and GRENADA.

Gre·no·ble |grə'nawbl(ə)| industrial, resort, and academic city in SE France, in the Dauphiné Alps. Pop. 154,000.

Gresh·am |'gresHəm| city in NW Oregon, a suburb E of Portland. Pop. 68,235.

Gret·na Green |'gretnə 'grēn| village in Scotland just N of the English border, near Carlisle, formerly a popular place for runaway couples from England to be married without the parental consent required in England for people under a certain age.

Gri·mal·di Caves |gri'mäldē| resort village near Ventimiglia, NW Italy, at the French border. Prehistoric remains, including human skeletons, have been found in caves here.

Grims·by |'grimzbē| fishing port in NE England, on the S of the Humber estuary.

Pop. 89,000. Official name **Great Grims-by**.

Grin·del·wald |'grindəl,vält| Alpine resort in S central Switzerland, in the Jungfrau region of the Bernese Alps. Pop. 4,000.

Gri·qua·land |'grēkwə,lænd| former territory of S South Africa, created in 1862 by the mixed-race Griquas and annexed to the Cape Province in 1879–80. Kokstad and Kimberly are the chief towns in the area.

Gris-Nez, Cape |grē 'nā| headland, N France, extending into the Strait of Dover 15 mi./24 km. SW of Calais. It is the point in France closest to Great Britain.

Gri·sons |gre'zawN| mountainous canton in SW Switzerland. Pop. 170,000. Its capital is Chur. The canton includes several popular ski resorts, including Saint Moritz and Davos.

Grod·no |'grawdnə| Russian name for HRODNA, Belarus.

Gro·ning·en |'grōniNGən| commercial and industrial city in the N Netherlands, capital of a province of the same name. Pop. 169,000.

Gros·se·to |grō'sätō| market center and capital of Grosseto province, W central Italy, in the Maremma coastal region. Pop. 71,000.

Gross·glock·ner |'grōs,glawknər| the highest mountain in Austria, in the E Tyrolean Alps, rising to 12,457 ft./3,797 m.

Grot·on |'grätn| town in SE Connecticut, on the Thames River and Long Island Sound. Pop. 45,144. It is noted for the manufacture of submarines.

Group of Sev·en name given to seven leading industrial nations, as when they meet to discuss international policy. Members are the U.S., Japan, Germany, France, the United Kingdom, Italy, and Canada. They are also called the **G-7** or **G7**.

Groz·ny |'grawznē; 'gräznē| city in SW Russia, near the border with Georgia, capital of Chechnya. Pop. 401,000.

Gru·dziadz |'grōō,jawnts| port and industrial city in N central Poland, on the Vistula River. Pop. 100,000.

Gru·yère |grY'yer; grē'yer| village in W Switzerland, SW of Fribourg. The well-known hard cheese was first made here.

Gryt·vi·ken |'grit,vēkən| the chief settlement on the island of South Georgia, in the South Atlantic, a former whaling station.

Gstaad |gə'sHtät| winter-sports resort in W Switzerland.

Gua·da·la·ja·ra¹ |,gwädl-ə'härə| second-largest city in Mexico, an industrial, commercial, and arts center and the capital of the state of Jalisco, in the W central part. Pop. 2,847,000.

Gua·da·la·ja·ra² |,gwädl-ə'härə| commercial city in central Spain, to the NE of Madrid, the capital of Guadalajara province. Pop. 67,000.

Gua·dal·ca·nal |,gwädlkə'næl| island in the W Pacific, the largest of the Solomon Islands. Pop. 71,000. During the World War II it was the scene of the first major U.S. offensive against the Japanese (August 1942).

Gua·dal·quiv·ir |,gwädlki'vir| river of Andalusia in S Spain. It flows for 410 mi./657 km. through Cordoba and Seville to reach the Atlantic NW of Cadiz.

Gua·da·lu·pe Hi·dal·go |'gwädl-ōōp(ä)hi-'dälgō| name for part of present-day GUSTAVO MADERO, central Mexico. The Basilica de Guadalupe, a shrine to Our Lady of Guadalupe, and the object of pilgrimage since the 1550s, is here.

Gua·da·lu·pe Mountains |'gwädl,ōōp; ,gwädl'ōōpē| range in W Texas and S New Mexico. Guadalupe Peak (8,749 ft./2,668 m.) is the highest point in Texas. The Carlsbad Caverns are in the New Mexico section.

Gua·de·loupe |,gwädl'ōōp| group of islands in the Lesser Antilles, forming an overseas department of France. Pop. 387,000 (1991). Languages, French (official), French Creole. Capital: Basse-Terre. □ **Guadeloupian** *adj. & n.*

Guadeloupe

Gua·dia·na |gwä'dyänə| river of Spain and Portugal. Rising in a plateau region SE of Madrid, it flows SW for some 360 mi./580 km., entering the Atlantic at the Gulf of Cadiz. For the last part of its course it forms the border between Spain and Portugal.

Gual·la·ti·ri |,gwäyə'tirē| volcano in N Chile, in the Andes along the Bolivian border. At 19,892 ft./6,063 m., it is the highest active volcano in South America.

Guam |gwäm| the largest and southernmost of the Mariana Islands, administered as an unincorporated territory of the U.S. Pop. 133,152. Languages, English (official), Austronesian languages. Capital: Agaña. Guam was ceded to the U.S. by Spain in 1898. □ **Guamanian** *adj. & n.*

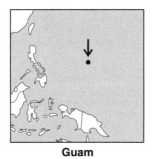

Guam

Gua·na·ba·ra Bay |ˌgwänə'bärə| (also **Rio de Janeiro Bay**) inlet of the S Atlantic in SE Brazil. Rio de Janeiro lies on its SW.

Gua·na·cas·te |ˌgwänə'kästā| region of NW Costa Rica, E of the Cordillera de Guanacaste, that draws tourists to Pacific resorts and wildlife preserves.

Gua·na·jua·to |ˌgwänə'hwätō| **1** state of central Mexico. Area: 11,777 sq. mi./30,491 sq. km. Pop. 3,890,000. **2** its capital city. Pop. 45,000. The city developed as a silver-mining and silver-working center after 1558.

Guang·dong |'gwäNG'dŏoNG| (also **Kwangtung**) a province of S China, on the South China Sea. Pop. 63.64 million. Capital: Guangzhou (Canton).

Guang·xi Zhuang (formerly **Kwangsi**) autonomous region, S China, on the border with Vietnam. Pop. 39.46 million. Capital: Nanning.

Guang·zhou |'gwäNG'jō| (also **Kwangchow**) a city in S China, the capital of Guangdong province. Pop. 3,918,000. It is one of the leading industrial and commercial centers of S China. Also called **Canton**.

Guan·tá·na·mo Bay |gwän'tänə‚mō| bay on the SE coast of Cuba. It is the site of a U.S. naval base established in 1903, the source of U.S. and Cuban disputes in recent decades. The city of **Guantanamo**, pop. 200,000, is to the W.

Gua·po·ré |ˌgwäpə'rä| river that flows NW for 1,090 mi./1,745 km. from SW Brazil, forming much of the Brazil-Bolivia border, to the Mamoré River.

Gua·ru·lhos |gwä'rŏolyŏos| industrial and commercial city in SE Brazil, a suburb NE of São Paulo. Pop. 973,000.

Gua·te·ma·la |ˌgwäte'mälə| republic in Central America, bordering on the Pacific and with a short coastline on the Caribbean Sea. Area: 42,056 sq. mi./108,889 sq. km. Pop. 10,621,200. Language, Spanish. Capital and largest city: Guatemala City. A Mayan land, Guatemala was a Spanish colony 1523–1828. It has a largely agricultural economy. □ **Guatemalan** *adj. & n.*

Guatemala

Gua·te·ma·la City |ˌgwätə'mälə| the capital of Guatemala. Pop. 1,167,000. Situated at an altitude of 4,920 ft./1,500 m. in the central highlands, the city was founded in 1776 to replace the former capital, Antigua Guatemala, which was destroyed by an earthquake in 1773. The largest Central American city, it is an industrial and commercial center.

Gua·via·re River |gwäv'yärä| river that flows 650 mi./1,040 km. E from the Andes in Colombia to join the Orinoco River at the Venezuelan border.

Gua·ya·quil |ˌgwĭə'kēl| industrial city in Ecuador, the country's principal port and second-largest city. Pop. 1,877,000.

Guay·mas |'gwĭmäs| port city in NW Mexico, in Sonora state, on the Gulf of California. Pop. 87,000. It is a resort and the port for Hermosillo, to the N.

Guay·na·bo |gwĭ'näbō| community in NE Puerto Rico, a suburb S of San Juan. Pop. 73,385.

Guelph |gwelf| industrial and academic city in S Ontario. Pop. 87,976.

Guer·ni·ca |ger'nēkə| town in Vizcaya, one of the Basque Provinces of N Spain, to the E of Bilbao. Pop. 18,000. Formerly the seat of a Basque parliament, it was bombed in 1937, during the Spanish Civil War, by German planes in support of Franco, an event depicted in a famous painting by Picasso. Full name **Guernica y Luno**.

Guern·sey |'gərnzē| island in the English

Channel, to the NW of Jersey. Pop. 59,000. Capital: St. Peter Port. It is the second-largest of the Channel Islands.

Guer·re·ro |gə'rerō| state of SW central Mexico, on the Pacific coast. Area: 24,828 sq. mi./64,281 sq. km. Pop. 2,622,000. Capital: Chilpancingo.

Gui·a·na |gē'änə| region in N South America, bounded by the Orinoco, Negro, and Amazon rivers and the Atlantic. It now comprises Guyana, Suriname, French Guiana, and the Guiana Highlands.

Gui·a·na Highlands |gē'änə 'hīləndz| mountainous plateau region of N South America, lying between the Orinoco and Amazon River basins, largely in SE Venezuela and northern Brazil. Its highest peak is Roraima (9,094 ft./2,774 m.).

Guild·ford |'gildfərd| largely residential cty in S England, in Surrey. Pop. 63,000.

Gui·lin |'gwē'lin| (also **Kweilin**) a city in S China, on the Li River, in the autonomous region of Guangxi Zhuang. Pop. 552,000.

Gui·ma·rães |ˌgēmə'rīNSH| city in NW Portugal. Pop. 48,000. It was the first capital of Portugal.

Guin·ea |'ginē| republic on the W coast of Africa. Area: 94,962 sq. mi./245,857 sq. km. Pop. 6,909,300. Languages, French (official), Fulani, Malinke, and other languages. Capital and largest city: Conakry. Part of the medieval Fulani empire, Guinea was a French colony before independence in 1958. Mining and agriculture are central to its economy. See also GUINEA-BISSAU and EQUATORIAL GUINEA. □ **Guinean** *adj. & n.*

Guinea

Guin·ea, Gulf of |'ginē| large inlet of the Atlantic along the S coast of West Africa.

Guinea-Bissau |ˌginēbi'sow| republic on the W coast of Africa, between Senegal and Guinea. Area: 13,953 sq. mi./36,125 sq. km. Pop. 1,000,000. Languages, Portuguese (official), W African languages, Creoles. Capital and largest city: Bissau. A

Portuguese colony and slave trade center, Guinea-Bissau gained independence in 1974. Fishing and tropical agriculture are key to its economy.

Guinea-Bissau

Gui·púz·coa |gē'pōōTHkəwə| smallest of the three Basque provinces in N Spain. Pop. 676,000. The capital is San Sebastian.

Guise |gēz| town in N France. Pop. 7,000. It gave its name to the dukes of Guise, the ruins of whose 16th-century castle still exist.

Gui·yang |'gwē'yäng| (also **Kweiyang**) an industrial city in S China, capital of Guizhou province. Pop. 1,490,000.

Gui·zhou |'gwē'jō| (also **Kweichow**) mountainous province of S China. Pop. 32.4 million. Capital: Guiyang.

Gu·ja·rat |ˌgōōjə'rät| state in W India, with an extensive coastline on the Arabian Sea. Capital: Gandhinagar. Formed in 1960 from the N and W parts of the former state of Bombay, it is one of the most industrialized parts of the country. □ **Gujarati** *adj. & n.*

Guj·ran·wa·la |ˌgōōjrən'wälə| city in Pakistan, in Punjab province, NW of Lahore. Pop. 597,000. It was the birthplace of the Sikh ruler Ranjit Singh, and was an important center of Sikh influence in the early 19th century.

Guj·rat |gōōj'rät| city in Pakistan, in Punjab province, N of Lahore. Pop. 154,000.

Gu·lag Archipelago |'gōō,läg| name given to the chain of forced-labor camps (gulags) that operated in Russia 1918–1956. Alexander Solzhenitsyn, the Russian Nobelist, wrote a book under this title, documenting the existence of the gulag and the horrific conditions there.

Gul·bar·ga |ˌgōōlbər,gä| city in S central India, in the state of Karnataka. Pop. 303,000. Formerly the seat of the Bahmani kings of the Deccan (1347–*c*.1424), it is now a center of the cotton trade.

Gulf of Aden, Gulf of Boo·thia |'ädn,

|'bŏŏTHēə| for entries beginning thus, see under the other name element, e.g., ADEN, GULF OF; BOOTHIA, GULF OF.

Gulf In·tra·coast·al Water·way route that allows sheltered boat passage along the coast of the Gulf of Mexico between Key West, Florida, and Brownsville, Texas.

Gulf·port |'gəlf,pawrt| city in S Mississippi, on the Gulf of Mexico W of Biloxi. Pop. 40,775.

Gulf States[1] |'gəlf| the states bordering on the Persian Gulf (Iran, Iraq, Kuwait, Saudi Arabia, Bahrain, Qatar, the United Arab Emirates, and Oman).

Gulf States[2] |'gəlf| the states of the U.S. bordering on the Gulf of Mexico (Florida, Alabama, Mississippi, Louisiana, and Texas).

Gulf Stream |'gəlf| warm ocean current that flows from the Gulf of Mexico N along the American coast toward Newfoundland, continuing across the Atlantic Ocean toward NW Europe as the North Atlantic Drift.

Gul·ja |'gŏŏljə| see YINING, China.

Gun·ni·son River |'gənəsən| river that flows 180 mi./290 km. through W Colorado to the Colorado River. It is noted for its "Black Canyon."

Gun·tur |gŏŏn'tŏŏr| historic commerical city in E India, in Andhra Pradesh. Pop. 471,000.

Gup·ta Em·pire |'gŏŏptə| empire of the Hindu Gupta dynasty (4th to 6th centuries) in territory roughly equivalent to present-day N India.

Gur·kha |'gŏŏrkə; 'gərkə| (also **Gorkha**) area in E central Nepal known for its fighting men, many of whom served with distinction in the British and Indian armies.

Gur·yev |'gŏŏryəf| (also known as **Atyraū**) **1** administrative subdivision in Kazakhstan. Pop. 447,000. **2** its capital, a seaport town. Pop. 157,000.

Gus·ta·via |gŏŏst'ävyə| capital of the French island of Saint-Barthélémy, in the Leeward Islands, West Indies.

Gu·ters·loh |'gytərz,lō| industrial city in NW Germany. Pop. 84,000.

Guy·ana |gi'änə| country on the NE coast of South America. Area: 83,082 sq. mi./214,969 sq. km. Pop. 737,950. Languages, English (official), English Creole, Hindi. Capital and largest city: Georgetown. Official name **Cooperative Republic of Guyana**. Occupied by the British

Guyana

1796–1966, and known as British Guiana, Guyana produces sugar, rice, bauxite, timber, and fish. Its interior is largely tropical forest. □ **Guyanese** *adj. & n.*

Guy·enne |gē'en| (also **Guienne**) region and former province of S France, stretching from the Bay of Biscay to the SW edge of the Massif Central.

Gwa·li·or |'gwälē,awr| industrial city in Gwalior district in Madhya Pradesh, central India. Pop. 693,000. Noted for its 6th-century fortress.

Gwent |gwent| former county of SE Wales, formed in 1974 from most of Monmouthshire, part of Breconshire, and Newport, and dissolved in 1996.

Gwe·ru |'gwärŏŏ| (formerly **Gwelo**) city in central Zimbabwe. Pop. 128,000. It is a commercial and rail center in a mining district.

Gwyn·edd |'gwinəTH| **1** county of NW Wales, formed in 1974 from Anglesey, Caernarfonshire, part of Denbighshire, and most of Merionethshire and re-formed in 1996 with a smaller area; administrative center, Caernarfon. **2** a former principality of North Wales. Powerful in the mid-13th century under Llewelyn, it was subjugated by the English forces of Edward I in 1282.

Gyan·dzhe |gyän'jä| Russian name for GÄNCÄ, Azerbaijan.

Györ |dyŏŏr| (German **Raab**) city in NW Hungary near the border with Slovakia. Pop. 131,000. It is a transportation hub and an industrial center.

Gyum·ri |'gyŏŏmrē| industrial city in NW Armenia, close to the border with Turkey. Pop. 123,000. Founded as a fortress in 1837, the city was destroyed by an earthquake in 1926 and again in 1988. It was formerly called Aleksandropol (1840–1924) and Leninakan (1924–91). Russian name **Kumayri**.

Hh

Haar·lem |'härləm| city in the Netherlands, near Amsterdam. Pop. 148,000. It is the capital of the province of North Holland and the center of the Dutch bulb industry.

Haar·lem·mer·meer |'härləmər,mēr| (also known as **Hoofddorp**) city in W Netherlands, built on land reclaimed from the Harlem Meer, a branch of the Zuider Zee. Pop. 98,000.

Ha·bi·ki·no |hä'bēkē,nō| city in W central Japan, on S Honshu, SSE of Osaka. Pop. 115,000.

Habs·burg |'häps,bŏŏrk; 'hæps,bərg| castle in N Switzerland, near the Aare River. Built c. 1030, it was the family seat of the counts of Habsburg, whose descendants ruled various countries, including Germany and Austria, for nearly 700 years.

Ha·chi·no·he |,häCHē'nōhä| industrial and commercial port city in N Japan, on N Honshu. Pop. 241,000.

Ha·chi·o·ji |,häCHē'ōjē| industrial city in E central Japan, on E central Honshu, W of Tokyo. Pop. 466,000. It is noted for its silk-weaving

Hack·en·sack |'hæk ən,sæk| city in NE New Jersey, E of Paterson. Pop. 37,049.

Hack·ney |'hæk,nē| industrial and residential borough of NE London, England, just N of Tower Hamlets. Pop. 164,000. It probably gave its name to the *hackney* or *hack*, a horse-drawn cab.

Ha·da·no |hä'dänō| commercial city in E central Japan, on central Honshu, SW of Tokyo. Pop. 156,000.

Ha·dhra·maut |,hädrä'mawt| narrow region on the S coast of Yemen, separating the Gulf of Aden from the desert land of the S Arabian peninsula.

Ha·dri·an's Wall |'hādrēənz| defensive wall across N England, from the Solway Firth in the W to the mouth of the Tyne River in the E, built by the Romans in the 2nd century to protect against attacking N tribes.

Hae·ju |'hī'jōō| industrial port city in SW North Korea, on the Yellow Sea. Pop. 195,000.

Ha·fun, Cape |hä'fōōn| (Arabic name **Ras Hafun**) peninsula in NE Somalia, on the Indian Ocean. At 51° 23′ E, it is the easternmost point in Africa.

Ha·gen |'hägən| industrial city in NW Germany, in North Rhine-Westphalia. Pop. 214,000.

Ha·gers·town |'hāgərz,town| city in NW Maryland. Pop. 35,445.

Ha·gia So·phi·a |'hājēə sō'fēə| (also **Saint Sophia**) domed monument of Byzantine architecture in Istanbul, Turkey, built as a Christian church in the 6th century, converted to a mosque in 1453, and a museum since 1935.

Hague |hāg| (**The Hague**) the seat of government and administrative center of the Netherlands, on the North Sea coast, capital of the province of South Holland. Pop. 444,000. The International Court of Justice is based here. Dutch name **Den Haag**; also called **'s-Gravenhage**.

Hai·fa |'hīfə| the chief port of Israel, in the NW on the Mediterranean coast. Pop. 248,000.

Haight-Ash·bury |'hāt'asH,berē| residential and commercial section of central San Francisco, California, associated with youth culture of the 1960s.

Hai·kou |'hī'kō| industrial seaport, S China, capital and largest city of the island province of Hainan. Pop. 280,000.

Ha·il |hīl| (also **Hail; Hayel**) city in NW Saudi Arabia, on the pilgrimage route from Iraq to Mecca. Pop. 177,000.

Hai·lar |'hī'lär| market town, Inner Mongolia, NE China, on the Hailar River W of the Da Hinggang Mts. Pop. 185,000.

Hai·nan |'hī'nän| island province, S China, between the South China Sea and Gulf of Tonkin. Pop. 6.42 million. Capital: Haikou.

Hai·naut |ä'nō| province of S Belgium, N of the Ardennes. Pop. 77,000. Capital: Mons.

Hai·phong |'hī'fawNG| industrial port in northern Vietnam, on the delta of the Red River in the Gulf of Tonkin. Pop. 783,000. It was damaged during the Vietnam War.

Hai River |hī| (Chinese name **Hai He**) river in E China that flows 677 mi./1,090 km. from the Taihang Shan range to the Bo Hai E of Tianjin.

Hai·ti |'hātē| republic in the Caribbean, occupying the W third of the island of Hispaniola. Area: 10,718 sq. mi./27,750 sq. km. Pop. 7,041,000. Official languages, Haitian Creole, French. Capital and largest city: Port-au-Prince. A French colony 1697–1804, Haiti gained independence through a slave rebellion. A series of dictatorships and U.S. domination have charac-

Haiti

terized its history. Tropical fruits and bauxite are leading products, but the country is poor. Its culture is strongly African. □ **Haitian** *adj. & n.*

Hajj |häj| (also **Hadj**) the pilgrimage to Mecca, Saudi Arabia, that each Muslim is required to make once in a lifetime. JEDDAH is a major port on the pilgrimage, which also flows through the airports of Arabia.

Ha·ko·da·te |,häkō'dätä| port in N Japan, on the S tip of the island of Hokkaido. Pop. 307,000.

Ha·ko·ne |hä'kōnä| mountain resort in E central Japan, on E central Honshu. Pop. 19,000. It is in the center of Fuji-Hakone-Izu National Park, in an area famous for its hot springs and scenic beauty.

Ha·lab·ja |hä'ləbzHə| (also **Alabja**) Kurdish town in NE Iraq, close to the Iranian border, where thousands died during a gas attack by Iraqi planes in 1988.

Ha·le·a·ka·la |,hälä,äkə'lä| dormant volcano on E Maui, Hawaii that draws many visitors.

Hales·o·wen |,häl'zōən| engineering town in the West Midlands of England, W of Birmingham. Pop. 58,000.

Ha·liç |hä'lēCH| Turkish name for GOLDEN HORN.

Hal·i·car·nas·sus |,hæləkär'næsəs| ancient Greek city on the SW coast of Asia Minor, at what is now the Turkish city of Bodrum. It was the birthplace of the historian Herodotus and the site of the Mausoleum of Halicarnassus, one of the Seven Wonders of the World.

Hal·i·fax[1] |'hælə,fæks| industrial town in N England, on the Calder River, formerly in Yorkshire. Pop. 77,000.

Hal·i·fax[2] |'hælə,fæks| historic port city, the capital of Nova Scotia. Pop.114,455. It is Canada's principal ice-free port on the Atlantic coast.

Hal·lan·dale |'hælən,däl| resort city in SE Florida, N of Miami. Pop. 30,996.

Hal·le |'hälə| city in east central Germany, on the Saale River, in Saxony-Anhalt. Pop. 303,000. HALLE-NEUSTADT (pop. 91,000) is just NE.

Hall·stadt |'häl,SHtät| (also **Hallstatt**) village in W central Austria. Graves from as early as c. 1000 B.C. have been discovered here. The site gave its name to the Hallstadt culture of the Iron Age.

Hal·ma·he·ra |,hælmə'herə| the largest of the Molucca Islands of Indonesia.

Halm·stad |'hälm,städ| seaport in SW Sweden, on the Kattegat, capital of Halmstad county. Pop. 81,000.

Häl·sing·borg |'helsiNG,bawr(yə)| Swedish name for HELSINGBORG.

Ha·ma |'hämä| (also **Hamah**) an industrial city in W Syria, on the Orontes River. Pop. 229,000. It was the center of an Aramaean kingdom in the 11th century B.C. Much of the modern city was destroyed during an unsuccessful uprising against the government in 1982.

Ha·ma·dan |,hämä'dän| commercial city in W Iran, in the Zagros Mts. between Tehran and Bakhtaran. Pop. 350,000. It is on the site of the ancient city of Ecbatana, which became the capital of the kingdom of Media in the 6th century B.C.

Ha·ma·matsu |,hämä'matsōō| industrial city on the S coast of the island of Honshu, Japan. Pop. 535,000.

Ham·burg[1] |'häm,bōōrg| industrial port city in N Germany, on the Elbe River. Pop. 1,669,000. Founded by Charlemagne in the 9th century, and largely destroyed by bombing during World War II, it is now the largest port in Germany, with extensive shipyards.

Ham·burg[2] |'hæm,bərg| town in W New York, containing suburbs S of Buffalo. Pop. 53,735.

Ham·burg·er Hill |'hæm,bərgər| name given to mountain in central Vietnam, near the border with Laos, where hundreds of American soldiers were killed in a 1969 assault during the Vietnam War.

Ham·den |'hæmdən| town in S central Connecticut, a residential and industrial suburb on the N side of New Haven. Pop. 52,434.

Hä·meen·lin·na |,hämän'linä| (Swedish name **Tavastehus**) industrial city in SW Finland, on Lake Vanajavesi. Pop. 43,000.

Ha·meln |'häməln| (also **Hamelin**) a town in NW Germany, in Lower Saxony, on the Weser River. Pop. 57,000. A medieval market town, it is the setting of the legend of the Pied Piper of Hamelin.

Ham·hung |'häm'hŏONG| industrial city in E North Korea. Pop. 775,000. It was the center of government of NE Korea during the Yi dynasty of 1392–1910.

Ha·mi |'hä'mē| (also called **Kumul**) city and oasis in Xinjiang, NW China, on the trade route SE from Ürümqi. Pop. 275,000.

Ham·il·ton[1] |'hæməl,tən| the capital of Bermuda. Pop. 1,100.

Ham·il·ton[2] |'hæməl,tən| township in W central New Jersey, containing suburbs on the SE side of Trenton. Pop. 86,553.

Ham·il·ton[3] |'hæməl,tən| city on North Island, New Zealand. Pop. 149,000.

Ham·il·ton[4] |'hæməl,tən| industrial city in SW Ohio, N of Cincinnati. Pop. 61,368.

Ham·il·ton[5] |'hæməl,tən| port and industrial city in S Ontario, Canada, at the W end of Lake Ontario. Pop. 318,499.

Ham·il·ton[6] |'hæməl,tən| town in South Lanarkshire, S Scotland, near Glasgow. Pop. 50,000.

Hamm |häm| industrial city in NW Germany, in North Rhine-Westphalia, on the Lippe River. Pop. 180,000.

Ham·mer·fest |'hæmər,fest| ice-free port in N Norway, on North Kvaløy island. Pop. 7,000. It is the northernmost town in Europe.

Ham·mer·smith |'hæmər,smiTH| industrial and residential district of W London, England, now part of the borough of **Hammersmith and Fulham** (pop. 136,000), on the N side of the Thames. BBC television is based here.

Ham·mond |'hæmənd| industrial port city in NW Indiana, on Lake Michigan, SE of Chicago, Illinois. Pop. 84,236.

Hamp·shire |'hæmpsHər; 'hæmp,sHir| county on the coast of S England. Pop. 1,512,000; county seat, Winchester.

Hamp·stead |'hæm(p),sted| residential suburb of NW London, England, part of the borough of Camden. **Hampstead Heath** is one of the best-known parks in London.

Hamp·ton[1] |'hæm(p)tən| district of the borough of Richmond upon Thames, in W Greater London, England, N of the Thames River. **Hampton Court** is a 16th-century palace used by monarchs from Henry VIII through George II.

Hamp·ton[2] |'hæm(p)tən| historic city in SE Virginia, in the Hampton Roads complex, on Chesapeake Bay. Pop. 133,793.

Hamp·ton Roads |'hæm(p)tən| deep-water estuary 4 mi./6 km. long, formed by the James River where it joins Chesapeake Bay, on the Atlantic coast in SE Virginia.

The ports of Newport News and Hampton are situated on it.

Hamp·tons, the |'hæm(p)tənz| cluster of resort villages in E Long Island, New York, including Southampton, East Hampton, and Amagansett.

Ha·nau |'hä,now| (full name **Hanau am Main**) river port and industrial city in central Germany, E of Frankfurt on the Main River. Pop. 84,000.

Han·dan |'hän'dän| industrial city in S Hebei province, E China, a communications and transportation hub on the Fuyang River N of Anyang. Pop. 1,110,000.

Han·ford |'hænfərd| government reservation in Richland, SE Washington, former U.S. plutonium-production site.

Hang·zhou |'häNG'jō| (also **Hangchow**) the capital of Zhejiang province in E China, situated on Hangzhou Bay, an inlet of the Yellow Sea, at the S end of the Grand Canal. Pop. 2,589,500.

Han·ni·bal |'hænəbəl| port city in NE Missouri, on the Mississippi River. Pop. 18,004. It is noted as the boyhood home of Mark Twain.

Ha·noi |hæ'noi| the capital of Vietnam, an industrial city on the Red River in the N of the country. Pop. 1,090,000. It was the capital of French Indochina from 1887 to 1946, and of North Vietnam before the reunification of North and South Vietnam.

Han·o·ver[1] |hä'nōvər| **1** industrial city in NW Germany, on the Mittelland Canal. Pop. 517,000. It is the capital of Lower Saxony. German name **Hannover**. **2** a former state and province in northern Germany. In 1714 the Elector of Hanover succeeded to the British throne as George I, and from then until the accession of Victoria (1837) the same monarch ruled both Britain and Hanover. □ **Hanoverian** adj. & n.

Han·o·ver[2] |'hæn,ōvər| town in W central New Hampshire, on the Connecticut River. Pop. 9,212. It is home to Dartmouth College.

Han River |hän| **1** (Chinese name **Han Shui**) river of E China that flows 952 mi./1,532 km. SE from SW Shaanxi province to the Yangtze River in Hubei province. **2** (Chinese name **Han Jiang**) river in S China, rising in SE Fujian province and flowing 210 mi./338 km. S to the South China Sea at Shantou in Guangdong province.

Han·se·at·ic League |,hænsē'ætik| association of N German port cities on the Baltic Sea, founded in the 13th century to enhance trade. Lübeck was its center, and

Hamburg and Bremen major partners. Non-German cities as far away as London and Novgorod were associates. It declined by the 17th century. Member cities were known as **Hanse towns.**

Han·zhong |'hän'jōōNG| city in Shaanxi province, central China, SW of Xi'an on the N bank of the Han River. Pop. 420,000.

Ha·ran |hä'rän| (also **Harran:** ancient name **Charan** or **Carrhae**) historic city in SE Turkey, in Urfa province, near the Syrian border. On Mesopotamian trade routes, it was the scene of several important battles in antiquity.

Ha·rap·pa |hə'ræpə| ancient city of the Indus valley civilization (*c.*2600–1700 B.C.), in N Pakistan. The site of the ruins was discovered in 1920.

Ha·ra·re |hə'rärä| the capital, largest city, and commercial center of Zimbabwe. Pop. 1,184,000. Former name (until 1982) **Salisbury.**

Har·bin |'härbin; här'bin| the capital of Heilongjiang province in NE China, an industrial city and rail center on the Songhua River. Pop. 3,597,000.

Har·dang·er Fjord |här'däNGər| fjord on the SW coast of Norway, extending inland for 75 mi./120 km. It is Norway's second-largest fjord.

Har·dwar |'här,dwär| city in Uttar Pradesh, N India, on the Ganges River. Pop. 189,000. It is a place of Hindu pilgrimage.

Har·fleur |är'flŒr| town in N France, at the mouth of the Seine River on the English Channel. Pop. 10,000. Formerly a flourishing port, it lost its importance as its harbor silted up.

Har·gei·sa |här'gäsə| (also **Hargeysa**) commercial city in NW Somalia, former capital of British Somaliland. Pop. 400,000.

Har·in·gey |'hæriNG,gä| industrial and residential borough of NE London, England, just N of Hackney. Pop. 187,000. Highgate and Tottenham are among its districts.

Har·lan County |'härlən| county in the Cumberland Mts. of SE Kentucky, famed scene of strife between coal miners and mine owners. Pop. 36,574.

Har·lech |'härleKH| village on the W coast of Wales, in Gwynedd. It is noted for the ruins of its 13th-century castle.

Har·lem |'härləm| district of New York City, situated to the N of 96th Street in NE Manhattan. It has long had a large black population, and from the 1920s was noted for its musical and night life. The literary and artistic movement known as the Harlem

Renaissance flourished here after World War I. □ **Harlemite** *n.*

Har·ley Street |'härlē| street in central London, England, where many eminent physicians and surgeons have consulting rooms.

Har·lin·gen |'härlinjən| city in S Texas, NW of Brownsville. Pop. 48,735. It is the hub of a vegetable-producing region.

Har·low |'härlō| town in W Essex, SE England, N of London. Pop. 80,000.

Har·ney Peak |'härnē| peak in the Black Hills of SW South Dakota. At 7,242 ft./2,209 m., it is the highest in the U.S. E of the Rocky Mts.

Har·pers Ferry |'härpərz| town in Jefferson County, West Virginia, at the confluence of the Potomac and Shenandoah rivers. Pop. 308. In October 1859 John Brown and a group of abolitionists briefly captured a Federal arsenal here, hoping to spur a slave rebellion.

Har·ris |'hærəs| the S part of the island of Lewis and Harris in the Outer Hebrides of Scotland, famous for its tweeds.

Har·ris·burg |'hærəs,bərg| the state capital of Pennsylvania, on the Susquehanna River in the central part. Pop. 52,376. The nearby nuclear power station at Three Mile Island suffered a serious accident in 1979.

Har·ri·son·burg |'hærisən,bərg| commercial and academic city in N Virginia, in the Shenandoah Valley. Pop. 30,707.

Har·rods·burg |'hærədz,bərg| historic city in central Kentucky. Pop. 7,335. Established in 1774, it was the first English settlement W of the Allegheny Mts.

Har·ro·gate |'hærə,gät| town in N England, in N Yorkshire, N of Leeds. Pop. 69,000. It is a noted spa.

Har·row |'hærō| largely residential borough of NW Greater London, England. Pop. 194,000. The Harrow School was founded here in 1572. □ **Harrovian** *adj. & n.*

Hart·ford |'härtfərd| the state capital of Connecticut, on the Connecticut River in the central part. Pop. 139,739. An industrial city, it is also an insurance center.

Har·tle·pool |'härtlē,pōōl| port on the North Sea coast of NE England, in Cleveland. Pop. 92,000.

Har·wich |'hærij; 'hæriCH| ferry port in Essex, on the North Sea coast of SE England. Pop. 17,000.

Ha·ry·a·na |,härē'änə| state of N India. Pop. 16.32 million. Capital: Chandigarh. It was formed in 1966, largely from Hindi-speaking parts of the former state of Punjab.

Harz Mountains |härtz| range of mountains in central Germany, the highest of which is the Brocken. The mountains figure in much folklore.

Has•selt |'häsǝlt| city in NE Belgium, on the Demer River, capital of the province of Limburg. Pop. 67,000.

Has•tings¹ |'hāstiNGz| resort and residential town in SE England, in East Sussex, one of the Cinque Ports, on the English Channel. Pop. 75,000. The Battle of Hastings (1066) was fought nearby at BATTLE.

Has•tings² |'hāstiNGz| industrial city in New Zealand, on North Island, near Napier. Pop. 58,000.

Ha•to Rey |'ätō'rā| district of central San Juan, Puerto Rico, site of much of the Commonwealth's business activity.

Hat•ter•as, Cape |'hætǝrǝs| peninsula in E North Carolina. The treacherous waters around it have been called "the Graveyard of the Atlantic."

Hat•ties•burg |'hætēz,bǝrg| industrial, commercial, and academic city in SE Mississippi. Pop. 41,882.

Hat•tu•sa the capital of the ancient Hittite Empire, situated in present-day central Turkey about 22 mi./35 km. E of Ankara.

Hau•sa•land |'howsǝ,lænd| historical name for the highland regions of N Nigeria that were home to the Hausa people and language before the 19th century. Kano was the chief town.

Haute-Garonne |,ōtgä'rōn| department in S France, in the Midi-Pyrénées region. Pop. 926,000. The capital city is Toulouse.

Haute-Normandie |,ōt,nawrmäN'dē| region of N France, on the coast of the English Channel, including the city of Rouen.

Haute-Saône |,ōt'sōn| department in E France, in the Franche-Comté region. Pop. 230,000. The area is largely agricultural. The capital is Vesoul.

Haute-Vienne |,ōt'vyen| department in central France, in the Limousin region. Pop. 354,000. The capital city is Limoges.

Haut-Rhin |ō'reN| department in E France, in the Alsace region. Pop. 671,000. The capital city is Colmar.

Hauts-de-Seine |,ōdǝ'sen| department in central France, in the Île-de-France region. Pop. 1,392,000. The capital city is Nanterre.

Ha•va•na |,hǝ'vænǝ| the capital and chief port of Cuba, on the N coast. Pop. 2,160,000. It was founded in 1519, and is an industrial center with a tourist industry

beginning to recover from isolation since the 1959 Cuban revolution. Spanish name **La Habana**.

Hav•ant |'hævǝnt| engineering town in SE Hampshire, England. Pop. 50,000.

Ha•va•su, Lake |'hævǝ,sōō| reservoir and recreational site on the Colorado River between Arizona and SE California. **Lake Havasu City** (pop. 24,363), in Arizona, is home to the reconstructed 19th-century London Bridge.

Ha•ver•hill |'hāv(ǝ)rǝl| industrial city in NE Massachusetts, on the Merrimack River. Pop. 51,418.

Ha•ver•ing |'hāvǝriNG| easternmost borough of Greater London, England, N of the Thames River. Pop. 224,000. It is mostly residential.

Ha•waii |hǝ'wä(y)ē| see box. □ **Hawaiian** *adj. & n.*

Ha•worth |'haw-wǝrTH| town in N Eng-

Hawaii

Capital/largest city: Honolulu
Other cities: Aiea, Kailua, Kaneohe, Pearl City
Population: 1,108,229 (1990);1,193,001 (1998); 1,342,000 (2005 proj.)
Population rank (1990): 41
Rank in land area: 43
Abbreviation: HI; Haw.
Nicknames: Aloha State; Paradise of the Pacific
Motto: *Ua mau ke ea o ka aina i ka pono* (Hawaiian: 'The Life of the Land is Perpetuated in Righteousness')
Bird: nene or Hawaiian goose
Fish: humuhumunukunukuapuaa
Flower: pua aloalo (hibiscus)
Tree: kukui or candlenut
Song: "Hawaii Ponoi"
Noted physical features: Halawa, Kamohio, Kaneohe, Kawaihae, Kiholo, Mamala, Maunalua, Pohue, Waiagua bays; Waikiki Beach; Waimea Canyon; Aua, Kaiwi, Kalohi, Pailolo channels; Kilauea and Punchbowl craters; Kau Desert; Pearl Harbor; Diamond Head; Iao and Manoa valleys; Haleakala, Kilauea, Mauna Kea, Mauna Loa volcanos
Tourist attractions: Lahaina; Haleakala National Park; Hawaiian volcanos; Pearl Harbor; *U.S.S. Arizona* Memorial
Admission date: August 21, 1959
Order of admission: 50
Name origin: Possibly derived from the native Polynesian word meaning 'homeland.'

land, in W Yorkshire, N of Halifax, noted as the home of the Brontë sisters, the writers.

Haw·thorne |'haw,THawrn| city in SW California, an industrial suburb S of Los Angeles. Pop. 71,349.

Hay·mar·ket Square |'hā,märkət| historic site in Chicago, Illinois, site of an 1886 bombing during a labor demonstration.

Hay·ward |'hāwərd| city in N central California, S of Oakland on San Francisco Bay. Pop. 111,498.

Heard and Mc·Don·ald Island |hərd ænd mik'dänld| group of uninhabited islands in the S Indian Ocean, administered by Australia since 1947 as an external territory.

Heart |härt| commercial and industrial city in W Afghanistan. Pop. 177,000.

Heath·row |'hēTHrō| international airport situated 15 mi./25 km. W of the center of London, England, in the borough of Hillingdon.

He·bei |'hə'bā| (also **Hopeh**) a province of NE central China. Pop. 61.08 million. Capital: Shijiazhuang.

Heb·ri·des |'hebrə,dēz| group of about 500 islands off the NW coast of Scotland. Also called **Western Isles**. The **Inner Hebrides** include the islands of Skye, Mull, Jura, Islay, Iona, Coll, Eigg, Rhum, Staffa, and Tiree. The Little Minch separates this group from the **Outer Hebrides**, which include the islands of Lewis and Harris, North and South Uist, Benbecula, Barra, and the isolated St. Kilda group. Norse occupation has influenced the language, customs, and place names, although most of the present-day population have Celtic affinities and Gaelic is still spoken on several of the islands. □ **Hebridean** *adj. & n.*

He·bron |'hēbrən| Palestinian city on the West Bank of the Jordan. Pop. 75,000. As the home of Abraham it is a holy city of both Judaism and Islam. Israeli forces withdrew from all but a small part of the city in 1997.

Heer·len |'herlən| industrial city and transportation center in the SE Netherlands, near Maastricht. Pop. 95,000.

He·fei |'hə'fā| (also **Hofei**; formerly **Lu-chow**) an industrial city in E China, capital of Anhui province. Pop. 1,541,000.

He·gang |'hə'gäNG| city in Heilongjiang province, NE China, NE of Harbin. Pop. 650,000.

Hei·del·berg |'hīdl,bərg| city in SW Germany, on the Neckar River, in Baden-Württemberg. Pop. 139,000. Its famed university received its charter in 1386 and is the oldest in Germany.

Heil·bronn |'hīl,brän| industrial city in SW Germany, a port on the Neckar River, in Baden-Württemberg. Pop. 117,000.

Hei·long Jiang |'hī'lōōNG jē'äNG| see AMUR RIVER, China.

Hei·long·jiang |'hī'lōōNG jē'äNG| (formerly **Heilungkiang**) province of NE China, on the Russian border, the most northerly Chinese province. Pop. 35.22 million. Capital: Harbin.

He·jaz |he'jæz| (also **Hijaz**) coastal region of W Saudi Arabia, extending along the Red Sea. Mecca and Medina are here.

Hek·la |'heklə| intermittently active volcano in SW Iceland, rising to 4,840 ft./1,491 m.

Hel·e·na |'helənə| the state capital of Montana, a former mining center, in the W central part. Pop. 24,569.

Hel·go·land |'helgə,lænd| German name for HELIGOLAND.

Hel·i·con , Mount |'helə,kän| mountain in Boeotia, central Greece, to the N of the Gulf of Corinth, rising to 5,741 ft./1,750 m. It was believed by the ancient Greeks to be the home of the Muses.

Hel·i·go·land |'heləgō,lænd| small island in the North Sea off the coast of Germany, one of the North Frisian Islands. The island was Danish from 1714 until seized by the British navy in 1807 and later ceded officially to Britain. In 1890 it was returned to Germany. German name **Helgoland**.

He·li·op·o·lis[1] |,hēlē'äpələs| ancient Egyptian city situated near the apex of the Nile delta at what is now Cairo. It was the original site of the obelisks known as Cleopatra's Needles.

He·li·op·o·lis[2] |,hēlē'äpələs| ancient Greek name for BAALBEK, Lebanon.

Hel·las |'heləs| Greek name for GREECE.

Hel·les·pont |'helə,spänt| the ancient name for the Dardanelles, after the legendary Helle, who fell into the strait and was drowned while escaping with her brother Phrixus from their stepmother, Ino, on a golden-fleeced ram.

Hell's Canyon |helz| chasm in Idaho, cut by the Snake River and forming the deepest gorge in the U.S. Flanked by the Seven Devils Mts., the canyon drops to a depth of 7,900 ft./2,433 m.

Hell's Kit·chen |helz| former neighborhood in W Manhattan, New York City, noted for its violence. Times Square is nearby. The area is now called Clinton.

Hel·mand |'helmənd| the longest river in Afghanistan. Rising in the Hindu Kush, it flows 700 mi./1,125 km., generally SW, before emptying into marshland near the Iran–Afghanistan border.

Hel·sing·borg |'helsiNG,bawr(yə)| port in S Sweden, on the Øresund opposite Elsinore in Denmark. Pop. 109,000. Swedish name **Hälsingborg.**

Hel·sing·fors |'helsiNG,fawrz| Swedish name for HELSINKI, Finland.

Hel·sing·ør |,helsiNG'œr| Danish name for ELSINORE.

Hel·sin·ki |,hel'siNGkē| the capital, largest city, and cultural center of Finland, an industrial port in the S on the Gulf of Finland. Pop. 492,000. Swedish name **Helsingfors.**

Hel·ve·tia |hel'vēSHə| Latin name for SWITZERLAND.

Hel·wan |hel'wän| (also **Hilwan**) industrial city in N Egypt, a suburb S of Cairo and E of the Nile River. Pop. 328,000.

Hem·el Hemp·stead |,hemǝl'hem(p)sted| town in SE England, in Hertfordshire. Pop. 80,000.

Hem·et |'hemet| city in S California, SE of Riverside, in an agricultural area. Pop. 36,094.

Hemp·stead |'hem(p),sted| town in W Long Island, NewYork, on the E boundary of Queens, New York City. Pop. 725,639. Hempstead, Rockville Centre, Levittown, and many other suburban villages are here.

He·nan |'hǝ'nän| (also **Honan**) a province of N central China. Pop. 85.51 million. Capital: Zhengzhou.

Hen·der·son |'hendǝrsǝn| city in SE Nevada, SE of LasVegas, home to a large chemical industry. Pop. 64,942.

Heng·e·lo |'heNGǝ,lō| industrial town in the Netherlands, near the German border. Pop. 76,000.

Heng·yang |'hǝNG'yäNG| city in Hunan province, SE China, on the Xiang River S of Changsha. Pop. 616,000. It is a transportation and industrial center.

Hen·ley |'henlē| (also **Henley-on-Thames**) town in SE England, in Oxfordshire, on theThames River. Pop. 10,000. It is famous as the home of an annual rowing regatta begun in 1839.

He·rak·li·on |hǝ'ræklēən| the capital of Crete, a port on the N coast of the island. Pop. 117,000. Greek name **Iráklion.**

Hé·rault |ā'rō| department in S France, in the Languedoc region. Pop. 795,000. The capital is Montpellier.

Her·cu·la·ne·um |,hǝrkyǝ'lānēǝm| ancient Roman town, near Naples, on the lower slopes of Vesuvius. The volcano's eruption in A.D. 79 buried it deeply under

volcanic ash, along with Pompeii, and thus largely preserved it until its accidental rediscovery by a well digger in 1709.

Her·e·ford |'herǝfǝrd| city in W central England, administrative center of Herefordshire, on the Wye River. Pop. 50,000.

Here·ford and Worce·ster |'herǝfǝrd ǝn 'wo͝ostǝr| former county ofW central England, formed in 1974 from the counties of Herefordshire and Worcestershire, which were reinstated in 1998.

Here·ford·shire |'herǝfǝrd,SHir; 'herǝfǝrd-SHǝr| county of W central England, between 1974 and 1998 part of the county of Hereford and Worcester.

Her·ford |'her,fawrt| manufacturing city in NW Germany, on the Werre River. Pop. 62,000.

Her·mit·age, the[1] |'hǝrmǝtij| famed art museum in Saint Petersburg, Russia. It is housed in an adjunct to the Winter Palace constructed in 1764 by Catherine the Great, who started its collection.

Her·mit·age, the[2] |'hǝrmǝtij| estate, the home of Andrew Jackson, in central Tennessee, NE of Nashville.

Her·mon, Mount |'hǝrmǝn| the S part of the Anti-Lebanon range on the Syria-Lebanon border.

Her·mo·sil·lo |,ermō'sēyō| city in NW Mexico, an agricultural trade center and capital of the state of Sonora. Pop. 449,000.

Herne |hern| port and industrial city in NW Germany, NE of Essen, on the Rhine-Herne Canal. Pop. 179,000.

Her·ning |'herniNG| manufacturing city in Jutland, central Denmark. Pop. 57,000. It is an important textile center.

Her·shey |'hǝrSHē| village in SE Pennsylvania, created by Hershey, the chocolate manufacturer. Pop. 11,860. It is a popular tourist destination.

Her·stal |'her,stäl| industrial city in E Belgium. Pop. 38,000.The birthplace of Pepin II, it is now a center of the armament industry.

Her·ten |'hertn| manufacturing city in NW Germany, N of Essen. Pop. 70,000.

Hert·ford |'härtfǝrd| the county seat of Hertfordshire, England. Pop. 21,000.

Hert·ford·shire |'härtfǝrd,SHir; 'härtfǝrd-SHǝr| county of SE England, one of the Home Counties, NW of London. Pop. 952,000; county seat, Hertford.

Her·ze·go·vi·na |,hertsǝ'gōvǝnǝ| (also **Hercegovina**) a region in the Balkans forming the S part of BOSNIA AND HERZEGOVINA and separated from the Adriatic by

part of Croatia. Its chief town is Mostar.
□ **Herzegovinian** *adj. & n.*

Her·zliy·ya |ˌhɛrtsəˈleyə| (also **Hertseliya;
Herzliya; Herzlia**) resort city in central Israel. Pop. 84,000. It was named after the founder of Zionism, Theodor Herzl.

Hes·pe·ria |heˈspirēə| city in S California, a suburb N of San Bernardino. Pop. 50,418.

Hes·per·i·des, Garden of the |heˈsperə ˌdēz| in Greek myth, land where the daughters of Atlas guarded a tree with golden apples, at the westernmost extreme of the world; the garden is conflated with the mythical Islands of the Blessed, or Western Islands, a vision of paradise.

Hesse |ˈhes(ə)| state of western Germany. Pop. 5,600,000. Capital: Wiesbaden. German name **Hessen**. □ **Hessian** *adj. & n.*

He·ze |ˈhəˈzə| (also called **Caozhou**) city and transportation center in W Shandong province, E China, S of the Yellow River. Pop. 1,017,000.

Hi·a·le·ah |ˌhīəˈleə| city in SE Florida, a largely Hispanic suburb NW of Miami. Pop. 188,004.

Hib·bing |ˈhibiNG| city in NE Minnesota, a mining center in the Mesabi Range. Pop. 18,046.

Hi·ber·nia |hīˈbərniə| Latin and literary name for Ireland. □ **Hibernian** *adj. & n.*

Hick·o·ry |ˈhik(ə)rē| city in W central North Carolina, noted for its furniture industry. Pop. 28,301.

Hicks·ville |ˈhiksˌvil| village in central Long Island, New York, the commercial hub of a suburban area. Pop. 40,174.

Hi·dal·go |ēˈdälgō| state of S Mexico. Pop. 1,881,000. Capital: Pachuca de Soto. Mountainous Hidalgo was long a mining center.

Hi·ga·shi·hi·ro·shi·ma |hēˈgäsHēhēˈrōsH ēmä| city in W Japan, on SW Honshu, E of Hiroshima. Pop. 94,000.

Hi·ga·shi·ku·ru·me |hēˈgäsHēkoōˈroōmä| city in E central Japan, on E central Honshu, a residential suburb of Tokyo. Pop. 114,000.

Hi·ga·shi·mat·su·ya·ma |hēˈgäsHēmät soō̄ˈyämä| city in E central Japan, on E central Honshu, a suburb of Tokyo. Pop. 84,000.

Hi·ga·shi·mu·ra·ya·ma |hēˈgäsHēmoō̄rä ˈyämä| city in E central Japan, on E central Honshu, NW of Tokyo. Pop. 134,000.

Hi·ga·shi·o·sa·ka |hēˈgäsHēˈōsäkä| city in W central Japan, on S Honshu, a residential and industrial suburb E of Osaka. Pop. 518,000.

Hi·ga·shi·ya·ma·to |hēˈgäsHēyäˈmätō|

city in E central Japan, on E central Honshu, N of Shinjuku. Pop. 75,000.

High·gate |ˈhīˌgāt| largely residential district of NE London, England, part of the borough of Haringey, NE of Hampstead Heath, noted especially for its cemetery.

High·lands |ˈhīlən(d)z| region of N Scotland, traditionally the mountainous areas N of a line from Dumbarton in the SW to Stonehaven, near Aberdeen, in the NE. It included the Hebrides and other islands to the W. The present-day **Highland** administrative region covers approximately the N half of Scotland.

High Plains see GREAT PLAINS.

High Point |ˈhīˌpoint| industrial city in N central North Carolina. Pop. 69,496. Furniture and tobacco are central to its economy.

High Wy·combe |hīˈwikəm| industrial town in S England, in Buckinghamshire. Pop. 70,000. It is noted especially for its furniture.

Hi·güey town, in the E Dominican Republic, the capital of La Altagracia province. Pop. 84,000.

Hi·ko·ne |hiˈkōnä| city in central Japan, on S Honshu, on the E shore of Lake Biwa. Pop. 100,000.

Hil·den |ˈhildən| manufacturing city in NW Germany, SE of Düsseldorf. Pop. 55,000.

Hil·des·heim |ˈhildəsˌhīm| industrial city in Lower Saxony, NW Germany. Pop. 106,000.

Hill Country region of S central Texas, NW of San Antonio and the Balcones Escarpment, with many recreational resources.

Hil·le·rød |ˈhiləˌrœTH| industrial and tourist town in Denmark. Pop. 33,000. It is the site of the notable 17th-century Frederiksborg Castle.

Hil·ling·don |ˈhiliNGdən| residential and industrial borough of W Greater London, England. Pop. 226,000. Heathrow Airport is here.

Hills·bo·ro |ˈhilzˌbərō| commercial and industrial city in NW Oregon. Pop. 37,520.

Hi·lo |ˈhēlō| port community in Hawaii, on the N coast of the island of Hawaii. Pop. 37,808.

Hil·ton Head Island |ˈhiltnˈhed| resort island in S South Carolina, one of the Sea Islands.

Hil·ver·sum |ˈhilvərsəm| town in the Netherlands, in North Holland province, near Amsterdam. Pop. 85,000. It is the center of the Dutch radio and television network.

Hi·ma·chal Pra·desh |hə'mäCHəl prə 'deSH| mountainous state in N India. Pop. 44.82 million. Capital: Simla.

Hi·ma·la·yas |ˌhiməˈläəz; hiˈmäl(ə)yəz| a vast mountain system in S Asia, extending 1,500 mi./2,400 km. from Kashmir eastward to Assam. It covers most of Nepal, Sikkim, and Bhutan and forms part of the N boundary of the Indian subcontinent. The Himalayas consist of a series of parallel ranges rising up from the Ganges basin to the Tibetan plateau, at over 9,840 ft./3,000 m. above sea level, and include the Karakoram, Zaskar, and Ladakh ranges. The backbone is the Great Himalayan Range, the highest mountain range in the world, with several peaks rising to over 25,000 ft./7,700 m., the highest being Mount Everest. □ **Himalayan** *adj.*

Hi·ma·may·lan |ˌhēmäˈmīˌlän| town in the Philippines, on W Negros, on Panay Gulf. Pop. 81,000.

Hi·me·ji |hēˈmäjē| industrial city in W central Japan, on S Honshu, WNW of Kobe. Pop. 454,000.

Hin·den·burg |ˈhindənˌbərg| former German name (1915–45) for ZABRZE, Poland.

Hin·den·burg Line |ˈhindənˌbərg| defensive line established by Germany along its borders with France and Belgium during World War I. Fortifications stretched from Lille SE to Metz.

Hin·du Kush |ˈhindo͞oˈko͞oSH| range of high mountains in N Pakistan and Afghanistan, forming a W continuation of the Himalayas. Several peaks exceed 20,000 ft./6,150 m., the highest being Tirich Mir.

Hin·du·stan |ˌhindo͞oˈstæn| *hist.* the Indian subcontinent in general, more specifically that part of India N of the Deccan, especially the plains of the Ganges and Jumna rivers.

Hin·nom |ˈhinˌäm; ˈhinəm| see GEHENNA, biblical site.

Hi·no |hēnō| city in E central Japan, on E central Honshu, a residential suburb W of Tokyo. Pop. 166,000.

Hip·po·crene |ˈhipəˌkrēn; ˌhipəˈkrēnē| spring on Mount HELICON that was, according to Greek mythology, created by Pegasus and considered sacred to the Muses and a source of inspiration.

Hip·po Re·gi·us |ˈhipō ˈrējēəs| see ANNABA, Algeria.

Hi·ra·ka·ta |ˌhēräˈkätä| city in W central Japan, on S Honshu, near Osaka. Pop. 391,000.

Hi·ra·tsu·ka |hēˈräts(ə)kä| commercial city

in E central Japan, on E central Honshu, SW of Yokohama. Pop. 246,000.

Hi·ro·sa·ki |ˌhērōˈsäkē| city in N Japan, on N Honshu, S of Aomori. Pop. 175,000.

Hi·ro·shi·ma |ˌhirəˈSHēmə; həˈrōSHəmə| city on the S coast of the island of Honshu, W Japan, capital of Chugoku region. Pop. 1,086,000. It was the target of the first atomic bomb, which was dropped by the United States on August 6, 1945 and resulted in the deaths of about one third of the city's population of 300,000.

His·pan·io·la |ˌhispənˈyōlə| island of the Greater Antilles in the Caribbean. After its European discovery by Columbus in 1492, Hispaniola was colonized by the Spanish, who ceded the W part (now Haiti) to France in 1697. The eastern part became the Dominican Republic.

His·sar·lik |ˌhisərˈlik| see TROY, ancient city.

Hi·ta·chi |hēˈtäCHē| industrial city in E central Japan, on the E coast of Honshu, NE of Mito. Pop. 202,000.

Hi·va Oa |ˌhēvä ˈöä| volcanic island in the Marquesas Islands, French Polynesia. The commercial center of the Marquesas, it is also the site of the grave of artist Paul Gauguin.

Hka·ka·bo Ra·zi |käˈkäbō ˈräzē| peak in N Burma on an outlier of the Himalayas, on the frontier with China. It is the highest peak in Burma: 19,295 ft./5,881 m.

Ho·bart |ˈhōˌbärt| the capital and chief port of Tasmania, Australia. Pop. 127,000.

Ho·bo·ken |ˈhōˌbōkən| industrial city in NE New Jersey, on the Hudson River opposite New York City. Pop. 33,397.

Ho Chi Minh City |ˌhōCHēˈmin| (former name, before 1975: **Saigon**) city and port on the S coast of Vietnam; pop. 3,016,000. It was the capital of the French colony of Cochin China, established in Vietnam in the 19th century, becoming capital of South Vietnam in the partition of 1954. After the communist victory in the Vietnam War, it was renamed. The largest Vietnamese city, it is an industrial center on the Saigon River.

Ho Chi Minh Trail |ˌhōCHēˈmin| a covert system of trails along Vietnam's W frontier, a major supply route for North Vietnamese forces during the Vietnam War.

Ho·dei·da |hōˈdādə| the chief port of Yemen, on the Red Sea. Pop. 246,000. Arabic name **Al-Hudayda**.

Hoek van Hol·land |ˌho͞ok vän ˈhawlänt| Dutch name for HOOK OF HOLLAND.

Hof |hôf; hawf| town in S Germany, on the Saale River, near the Czech border. Pop.

53,000. Before Germany's reunification in 1990, Hof was a major checkpoint for travelers between East and West Germany.

Hof·burg |'hōfbŏŏrk; 'hawf‚bŏŏrg| complex of buildings in Vienna, Austria, including the former imperial palace. It was the seat of government for the emperors of Germany until 1806 and for the rulers of Austria until 1918.

Ho·fei |'hə'fā| see HEFEI, China.

Ho·fu |'hōfŏŏ| city in W Japan, on SW Honshu, SW of Hiroshima. Pop. 118,000.

Hog·gar Mountains |'hägər; hə'gär| mountain range in the Saharan desert of S Algeria, rising to a height of 9,573 ft./2,918 m. at Tahat. Also called **Ahaggar Mountains**.

Ho·hen·lin·den |‚hōən'lindən| village in S Germany, E of Munich. A French victory here in 1800 over the Austrians helped pave the way to the Peace of Lunéville in 1801.

Ho·hen·zol·lern |'hōənt‚sälərn| former province of Germany, now part of the state of Baden-Württemberg. The Hohenzollern family ruled the region as emperors of Germany 1871–1918. After 1945 it became part of the state of Württemberg-Hohenzollern, and in 1952 it took its present name.

Ho·he Tau·ern Mountains |‚hōə'towərn| range in the E Alps, S Austria. The highest peak is Grossglockner: 12,457 ft./3,797 m.

Hoh·hot |'hə'hawt| (also **Huhehot**) the capital of Inner Mongolia autonomous region, NE China. Pop. 1,206,000. Former name (until 1954) **Kweisui**.

Hok·kai·do |hä'kīdō| the most northerly of the four main islands of Japan, constituting an administrative region. Pop. 5,644,000. Capital: Sapporo.

Hol·guín |awl'gēn| commercial city in NE Cuba, the capital of Holguín province. Pop. 246,000. Gibara, its port, is to the N.

Hol·land[1] |'hälənd| **1** another name for the NETHERLANDS. **2** former province of the Netherlands, comprising the coastal parts of the country. It is now divided into **North Holland** and **South Holland**

Hol·land[2] |'hälənd| city in SW Michigan, noted for its Dutch heritage. Pop. 30,745.

Hol·lan·dia |hä'lændēə| former name for JAYAPURA, Indonesia.

Hol·ly Springs |'hälē| historic city in N Mississippi. Pop. 7,261.

Hol·ly·wood[1] |'hälē‚wŏŏd| resort and retirement city in SE Florida, N of Miami, on the Atlantic. Pop. 121,697.

Hol·ly·wood[2] |'hälē‚wŏŏd| district of Los Angeles, the principal center of the American film and television industry.

Ho·lon |'hō‚län; KHaw'lawn| manufacturing town in W central Israel, part of the Tel Aviv-Jaffa metropolitan area. Pop. 164,000.

Hol·royd |'hawl‚roid| city in SE Australia, in New South Wales, a residential suburb of Sydney. Pop. 79,000.

Hol·stein |'hōl‚SHtīn| former duchy of the German kingdom of Saxony, situated in the S part of the Jutland peninsula. A duchy of Denmark from 1474, it was taken by Prussia in 1866 and incorporated with the neighboring duchy of Schleswig as the province of Schleswig-Holstein.

Hol·y·head |'hälē‚hed| port on Holy Island in Wales, off Anglesey. Pop. 13,000. It is the chief port for ferries between Great Britain and Ireland.

Ho·ly Island |'hōlē| another name for LINDISFARNE, England.

Ho·ly Land |'hōlē'lænd| region on the E shore of the Mediterranean, in what is now Israel and Palestine, revered by Christians as the place in which Christ lived and taught, by Jews as the land given to the people of Israel, and by Muslims.

Hol·yoke |'hōlē‚ōk; 'hō(l)‚yōk| industrial city in W central Massachusetts, NW of Springfield. Pop. 43,704.

Ho·ly Ro·man Em·pire |‚hōlē ‚rōmən 'empīr| empire that was proclaimed in A.D. 800 and formally dissolved in 1806. Established by the papacy to ensure secular rule in Europe, it gradually became a rival centered in Germany, and later in Austria. Its boundaries were in constant flux.

Hol·y·rood |'hälē‚rŏŏd| 16th-century palace, the official residence of the British monarch in Edinburgh, Scotland.

Ho·ly See |'hōlē 'sē| the papal court, or governing center of the Roman Catholic Church, thus often taken as synonymous with the VATICAN CITY.

Home Counties |'hōm| the English counties surrounding London, into which London has extended. They comprise chiefly Essex, Kent, Surrey, and Hertfordshire.

Ho·mel |haw'm(y)el| industrial city in SE Belarus. Pop. 506,000. Russian name **Gomel**.

Home·stead |'hōm‚sted| agricultural and suburban city in SE Florida, SW of Miami. Pop. 28,866.

Homs |hawmz| (also **Hims**) industrial city in western Syria, on the Orontes River. Pop. 537,000. It was named in 636 by the Muslims and occupies the site of ancient Emesa.

Ho·nan |'hō'nän| see HENAN, China.

Hon·du·ras |hän'd(y)ŏŏrəs| republic of Central America, bordering on the Caribbean Sea and with a short coastline on the Pacific. Area: 43,294 sq. mi./112,088 sq. km. Pop. 5,294,000. Language, Spanish. Capital and largest city: Tegucigalpa. See also BRITISH HONDURAS. A Spanish colony for over 300 years, Honduras gained independence in 1821. It is primarily agricultural, much of its land undeveloped. Bananas and other tropical crops grow in the lowlands, coffee in the highlands. □ **Honduran** adj. & n.

Hon·fleur |awN'flœr| port and resort on the Normandy coast, NW France, on the Seine estuary. Pop. 8,000.

Hong Kong |'häNG'käNG; 'hawNG,kawNG| (Chinese name **Xianggang**) special administrative region governed by China, on its SE coast, formerly (until 1997) a British dependency. Area: 414 sq. mi./1,071 sq. km. Pop. 5,900,000. Official languages, English and Cantonese. Capital: Victoria. The area comprises Hong Kong Island, which was ceded by China in 1841, the Kowloon peninsula, ceded in 1860; and the New Territories, additional areas of the mainland that were leased for 99 years in 1898. Hong Kong has become one of the world's major financial and manufacturing centers, with the third-largest container port in the world.

Hong Kong

Hong·shui |'həNG,SHwē| (Chinese name **Hongshui He**; formerly **Hungshui River**) river, S China, flowing 900 mi./1,448 km. S and E from E Yunnan to join the You River near Guiping to form the Xi.

Ho·ni·a·ra |,hōnē'ärə| port and the capital of the Solomon Islands, on the NW coast of the island of Guadalcanal. Pop. 35,000.

Hon·o·lu·lu |,hän-l-'lŏŏ,lŏŏ; ,hōn-l'ŏŏ,lŏŏ| the state capital and principal port of Hawaii, on the SE coast of the island of Oahu. Pop. 365,272.

Hon·shu |'hänSHŏŏ| the largest (89,184 sq. mi./230,897 sq. km.) of the four main islands of Japan. Pop. 99,254,000. Tokyo is the chief city.

Hood, Mount |'hŏŏd| peak in the Cascade Range in NW Oregon, E of Portland. At 11,239 ft./3,426 m. it is the highest point in the state.

Hoogh·ly |'hŏŏg,lē| (also **Hugli**) the most westerly of the rivers of the Ganges delta, in West Bengal, India. It flows for 120 mi./192 km. into the Bay of Bengal and is navigable to Calcutta.

Hook of Holland |'häländ| cape and port of the Netherlands, near The Hague, linked by ferry to the British isles. Dutch name **Hoek van Holland**.

Hoorn |hawrn| city in the Netherlands, on an inlet of the IJsselmeer. Pop. 58,000. It is a popular yachting center and agricultural market.

Hoo·sier State |'hŏŏZHər| nickname for INDIANA. The meaning of *Hoosier* is unclear.

Ho·peh |'hə'bä; 'hō'pä| see HEBEI, China.

Ho·reb, Mount |'hawr,eb| biblical mountain in Sinai, probably identical with Mount SINAI.

Hor·liv·ka |'hawrlivkə| industrial city in SE Ukraine, in the Donets Basin. Pop. 338,000. Russian name **Gorlovka**.

Hor·muz, Strait of |'hawrməz;hawr'mŏŏz| strait linking the Persian Gulf with the Gulf of Oman, which leads to the Arabian Sea, and separating Iran from the Arabian Peninsula. It is of strategic and economic importance as a waterway through which sea traffic to and from the oil-rich states of the Gulf must pass.

Hor·muz |'hawrməz; hawr'mŏŏz| (also **Ormuz**) an Iranian island at the mouth of the Persian Gulf, in the Strait of Hormuz. It is the site of an ancient city, which was an important center of commerce in the Middle Ages.

Horn, Cape |'hawrn| the southernmost point of South America, on a Chilean island S of Tierra del Fuego. The region is notorious for its storms, and until the opening of the Panama Canal in 1914 constituted the only sea route between the Atlantic and Pacific. Also called **the Horn**.

Horn of Af·ri·ca |'æfrikə| peninsula of NE Africa, comprising Somalia and parts of Ethiopia. It lies between the Gulf of Aden and the Indian Ocean. Also called **Somali Peninsula**.

horse latitudes |hawrs| belt of light winds about 30° from the equator in both the N and the S hemispheres, between the westerlies (closer to the equator) and trade winds. Sailing vessels often were becalmed here.

Hor·sens |'hawrsəns| port on the E coast of Denmark, situated at the head of Horsens Fjord. Pop. 55,000.

Hos·pet |'hōsH,pet| commercial town in S India, in Karnataka state, E of Hubli. Pop. 135,000.

Hos·pi·ta·let |ˌōspētä'let| (also **Hospitalet de Llobregat**) city and S suburb of Barcelona, in NE Spain. Pop. 269,000.

Ho·tan |'haw'tän| (formerly **Khotan**) town in Xinjiang, NW China, an oasis in the foothills of the Kunlun Shan range, on the caravan route on the S edge of the Taklimakan Desert. Pop. 121,000.

Hot Springs spa city in central Arkansas. Pop. 32,462.

Hou·ma |'hōmə| city in SE Louisiana, in the Cajun Country, SW of New Orleans. Pop. 30,495.

Houns·low |'hownz,lō| largely residential borough of W Greater London, England, N of the Thames River. Pop. 193,000.

Hou·sa·ton·ic River |ˌhōōsə'tänik| river that flows 130 mi./210 km. from the Berkshire Hills in W Massachusetts through Connecticut, to Long Island Sound.

Hous·ton |'(h)yōōstən| industrial port and the largest city in Texas, linked to the Gulf of Mexico by the Houston Ship Canal, a major oil industry and transshipment center. Pop. 1,630,553. Since 1961 it has been the headquarters for U.S. space research and manned space flight; it is the site of NASA's Johnson Space Center.

Hove |'hōv| resort town on the S coast of England, adjacent to Brighton. Pop. 67,000.

How·land Island |'howlənd| uninhabited island in the central Pacific, near the equator, held by the U.S. It is a wildlife refuge.

How·rah |'howrə| (also **Haora**) heavy industrial city and rail center in E India, on the Hooghly River opposite Calcutta. Pop. 947,000.

Howth |hōTH| suburban district of E Dublin, Ireland, a port and resort whose hill dominates the N side of Dublin Bay.

Hoya |'hoiə| city in E central Japan, on E central Honshu, a residential suburb of Tokyo. Pop. 95,000.

Hra·dec Krá·lo·vé |'hrädets 'krälō,ve| town in the N Czech Republic, capital of East Bohemia region on the Elbe River. Pop. 162,000. German name **Königgrätz**.

Hrod·na city in W Belarus, on the Neman River near the borders with Poland and

Lithuania. Pop. 277,000. Russian name **Grodno**.

Hsin·chu |'sHin'CHōō| (also **Hsin-chu**) port on the NW coast of Taiwan. Pop. 293,000. The city is an important computer and electronics center.

Hsü-chou |'sHY'jō| see XUZHOU, China.

Hua·cho |'wächō| port city in W central Peru, NW of Lima. Pop. 51,000.

Huai·bei |'hwī'bā| industrial city in N Anhui province, E China, SW of Xuzhou. Pop. 1,308,000.

Huai·hua |'hwī'hōōä| city in Hunan province, S central China, on a bend of the Wu River. Pop. 436,000.

Huai·nan |'hwī'nän| city in the province of Anhui, in E central China, in a mining district. Pop. 1,228,000.

Huai·yin |'hwī'yin| city in Jiangsu province, E China, on the Grand Canal N of Yangzhou, and E of Hongze Lake. Pop. 391,000.

Hua·lla·ga |wä'yägä| river in central Peru, one of the headwaters of the Amazon. Rising in the central Andes, it flows, generally NE for 700 mi./1,100 km. and emerges into the Amazon Basin at Lagunas.

Huam·bo |'wämbō| city in the mountains in W Angola. Pop. 400,000. Founded in 1912, it was known by its Portuguese name of Nova Lisboa until 1978.

Huan·ca·yo |wäNG'kīō| commercial city in S central Peru, on the Mantaro River, in a mining district of the Andes. Pop. 97,000.

Huang Hai |'hwäNG'hī| Chinese name for the YELLOW SEA.

Huang He |'hwäNG'hə| (also **Huang Ho**) see YELLOW RIVER, China.

Huang·pu |'hwäNG'pōō| (formerly **Whampoa**) port and industrial city in S Guangdong province, S China, on an island in the Pearl River. Economically tied to Guangzhou (Canton) to its W, it is the site of a military academy founded by the Kuomintang party.

Huang Shan |'hwäNG'sHän| (English name **Yellow Mountains**) mountain range in S Anhui province, E China, to the S of the Yangtze River. Its cloud-swept landscape has been popular with Chinese poets and painters.

Huang·shan |'hwäNG'sHän| town in S Anhui province, E China, situated N of the Huang Shan range. Pop. 151,000.

Huang·shi |'hwäNG'sHē| (formerly **Hwangshih**) industrial city in Hubei province, E central China, on the Yangtze River S of Wuhan. Pop. 458,000. It has iron and steel and other heavy industries.

Hua·nu·co |'wäno͞o,kō| commercial city in central Peru, on the Huallaga River in the Andes. Pop. 73,000. It is the capital of Huánuco province, and the ancient Temple of Kotosh is nearby.

Hua·ráz |wä'räs| commercial and resort city in W Peru, the capital of Ancash department. Pop. 44,000. HUASCARÁN national park is just W.

Huas·ca·rán |wäskä'rän| extinct volcano in the Peruvian Andes, W central Peru, rising to 22,205 ft./6,768 m. It is the highest peak in Peru.

Hub, the |həb| popular nickname for Boston, Massachusetts, the "Hub of the Universe."

Hu·bei |'ho͞o'bā| (formerly **Hupeh**) province of E central China, mountainous in the N and traversed by the Yangtze River in the S. Pop. 53.97 million. Capital: Wuhan.

Hub·li |'ho͞obli| (also **Hubli-Dharwad**) industrial city and rail junction in SW India. Pop. 648,000. It was united with the adjacent city of Dharwad in 1961.

Hud·ders·field |'hədərs,fēld| town in N England, formerly in Yorkshire. Pop. 149,000. It is an historic textile center.

Hud·din·ge |'hədiNGə| city in E Sweden, a suburb S of Stockholm. Pop. 76,000.

Hud·son Bay |'hədsən| body of water in NE Canada. It is the largest inland sea in the world (over 475,000 sq. mi,/1.23 million sq. km.) and is connected to the N Atlantic via the Hudson Strait.

Hud·son River |'həd,sən| major river of E North America, which rises in the Adirondack Mts. and flows S for 350 mi./560 km. past Albany, where it is connected with the Erie Canal, and into the Atlantic at New York City.

Hué |ho͞o'ā; (h)wā| industrial port city in central Vietnam, the former (1802–1945) capital. Pop. 219,000.

Hue·co Mountains |'wākō| range in S New Mexico and W Texas, near El Paso, rising to 6,717 ft./2,049 m.

Huel·va |'welvə| industrial city and port in S Spain, near the Portuguese border; capital of Huelva province. Pop. 144,000.

Hues·ca |'weskə| marketing and industrial town in NE Spain, at the base of the Pyrenees, the capital of Huesca province. Pop. 50,000.

Hui·zhou |'hwē'jō| port city in Guangdong province, S China, on the Dong River to the east of Guangzhou (Canton). Pop. 161,000.

Hull[1] |həl| (official name **Kingston-upon-Hull**) city and port in NE England, at the junction of the Hull and Humber rivers. Pop. 252,000.

Hull[2] |həl| industrial and administrative city in SW Quebec, across the Ottawa River from Ottawa, Ontario. Pop. 60,707.

Hum·ber |'həmbər| estuary in NE England, flowing 38 mi./60 km. E from the junction of the Rivers Ouse and Trent to the North Sea. It has the major port of Hull on its N bank and is spanned by the world's largest suspension bridge, opened in 1981 and having a span of 4,626 ft./1,410 m.

Hum·ber·side |'həmbər,sīd| former county of NE England, formed in 1974 from parts of the East and West Ridings of Yorkshire and the N part of Lincolnshire. It was dissolved in 1996.

Hum·boldt Current |'həm,bōlt| another name for the PERUVIAN CURRENT.

Hum·boldt River |'həm,bōlt| river that flows 300 mi./480 km. across N Nevada, disappearing in the NW into a basin called the Humboldt Sink.

Hu·nan |'ho͞o'nän| province of E central China. Pop. 60.66 million. Capital: Changsha. □ **Hunanese** *adj. & n.*

Hu·ne·doa·ra |'ho͞onä,dwärä| industrial city in W central Romania. Pop. 86,000.

Hun·ga·ry |'həNGgə,rē| republic in central Europe. Area: 35,934 sq. mi./93,033 sq. km. Pop. 10,600,000. Language, Hungarian (Magyar). Capital and largest city: Budapest. Hungarian name **Magyarország**. Settled by the Magyars in the 9th century, Hungary came under the Habsburgs in the 17th century, and gained independence in 1918. It was a communist state from the end of World War II until 1989. Once chiefly agricultural, it is increasingly industrial. □ **Hungarian** *adj. & n.*

Hungary

Hun·jiang |'ho͞oNGjē'äNG| industrial city in Jilin province, NE China, near the border with North Korea. Pop. 694,000.

Hun·ting·don·shire |'həntiNGdən,SHir; 'hətiNGdənSHər| former county of SE England. It became part of Cambridgeshire in 1974.

Hun·ting·ton[1] |'həntiNGtən| town in N Long Island, New York, containing Huntington, Cold Spring Harbor, and other largely residential villages. Pop. 191,474.

Hun·ting·ton[2] |'həntiNGtən| industrial city in West Virginia, on the Ohio River. Pop. 54,840.

Hun·ting·ton Beach |'həntiNGtən| city in S California, on the Pacific coast, to the S of Long Beach. Pop. 181,519.

Hunts·ville[1] |'hənts,vil| city in N Alabama. Pop. 159,789. It is a center for space exploration and solar energy research.

Hunts·ville[2] |'hənts,vil| city in E Texas, N of Houston. Pop. 27,925.

Hu·ron, Lake |'(h)yo͞orən; '(h)yo͞or,än| the second-largest (24,361 sq. mi./63,096 sq. km.) of the five Great Lakes of North America, between Ontario and Michigan. Georgian Bay is its NE extension, separated by the Bruce Peninsula of Ontario.

Hur·ri·cane Alley |'hərə,kän| popular term for areas of the U.S. and Caribbean, such as Florida and the Gulf Coast, especially prone to hurricanes.

Hutch·in·son |'həCHən,sən| city in S central Kansas. Pop. 39,308.

Hu·zhou |'ho͞o'jō| (formerly **Wuxing**) city in N Zhejiang province, E China, W of Shanghai and S of Tai Lake. Pop. 218,000.

Hvar |hvär| island, part of Bosnia and Herzegovina, in the Adriatic Sea off the Dalmatian coast. It was a popular tourist destination before the Balkan wars of the 1990s.

Hwan·ge |'(h)wäNGgā| town in W Zimbabwe. Pop. 39,000. Nearby is the Hwange National Park, established as a game reserve in 1928. Fomer name (until 1982) **Wankie**.

Hy·an·nis |hī'ænis| commercial village, in SE Massachusetts, on Cape Cod, in a resort area. Pop. 14,120.

Hyde Park[1] |hīd| the largest British royal park, in W central London. Its Serpentine and Speakers' Corner are well-known to visitors.

Hyde Park[2] |hīd| town in SE New York, on the Hudson River N of Poughkeepsie, associated with the family of Franklin D. Roosevelt. Pop. 21,320.

Hy·der·a·bad[1] |'hīd(ə)rə,bäd| **1** commercial and university city in central India, capital of the state of Andhra Pradesh. Pop. 3,005,000. **2** former large princely state of S central India, divided in 1956 among Maharashtra, Mysore, present-day Karnataka, and Andhra Pradesh.

Hy·der·a·bad[2] |'hīd(ə)rə,bäd| commercial and industrial city in SE Pakistan, in the province of Sind, on the Indus River. Pop. 1,000,000.

Hy·dra |'hīdrə| island in Greece, in the S Aegean Sea, off the E coast of Peloponnese. It is mostly rocky and barren.

Hy·met·tus |hī'metəs| mountain ridge SE of Athens, Greece, reaching 3,366 ft./1,026 m, and noted for its marble.

Hy·pha·sis |'hifəsis| ancient Greek name for the BEAS River, India.

Ii

Ia·şi |'yäSHē| commercial and industrial city in E Romania. Pop. 338,000. From 1565 to 1859 it was the capital of the principality of Moldavia. German name **Jassy**.

Iba·dan |ē'bädän; ē'bädn| the second largest city of Nigeria, a commercial center 100 mi./160 km. NE of Lagos. Pop. 1,295,000.

Iba·gué |ˌēbə'gā| city in W central Colombia, capital of Tolima department. Pop. 334,000. An Andes market center, it is also noted for its music conservatory and festivals.

Iba·ra·ki |ē'bärəkē; ˌēbä'räkē| city in W central Japan, on S Honshu, near Osaka. Pop. 254,000.

Ibar·ra |ē'bärə| historic city in N Ecuador, the capital of Imbabura province, N of Quito. Pop. 81,000. It is a center for commerce and folk arts.

Ibe·ri·an Peninsula |ī'birēən| the extreme SW peninsula of Europe (ancient **Iberia**, land of the Iberes), containing present-day Spain and Portugal. It was colonized by Carthage before the Third Punic War (149–146 B.C.), after which it came increasingly under Roman influence. It was invaded by the Visigoths in the 4th–5th centuries A.D. and by the Moors in the 8th century.

Ibi·za |i'bēzä| **1** the westernmost of the Balearic Islands of Spain. **2** its capital city and port. Pop. 25,000. □ **Ibizan** adj. & n.

Ica |'ēkä| commercial city in SW Peru, on the Ica River, the capital of Ica department. Pop. 109,000. Its name is also that of a pre-Incan culture that flourished nearby.

Ice·land |'īslənd| an island republic in the N Atlantic. Area: 39,714 sq. mi./102,820 sq. km. Pop. 300,000. Language, Icelandic. Capital and largest city: Reykjavik. Icelandic name **Island** (meaning 'iceland').

Settled by Vikings in the 9th century, Iceland was ruled by Norway, then Denmark, until 1944. Volcanically active, it relies on geothermal energy, fishing, and mining. □ **Icelandic** adj. **Icelander** n.

Ichi·ha·ra |ē'CHē,härə| industrial city in E central Japan, on central Honshu, SE of Tokyo. Pop. 258,000.

Ichi·ka·wa |ē'CHē,käwə| industrial city in W central Japan, on E Honshu, NE of Tokyo. Pop. 437,000.

Ichi·no·mi·ya |ˌēCHē'nōmēə| industrial city in central Japan, on S central Honshu, NW of Nagoya. Pop. 262,000.

Ichun |'ē'CHo͞on| see YICHUN, China.

Ick·nield Way |'ik,nēld| ancient pre-Roman track that crosses S England in a wide curve from Wiltshire on the S coast to Norfolk, on the E coast.

Ida |'īdə| mountain in central Crete, associated in classical times with the god Zeus. Rising to 8,058 ft./2,456 m., it is the highest peak on the island.

Ida·ho |'īdə,hō| see box.

Idaho

Capital/largest city: Boise
Other cities: Idaho Falls, Lewiston, Moscow, Pocatello, Twin Falls
Population: 1,006,749 (1990); 1,228,684 (1998); 1,480,000 (2005 proj.)
Population rank (1990): 42
Rank in land area: 14
Abbreviation: ID; Ida.
Nicknames: Gem State; Light on the Mountain
Motto: Esto perpetua (Latin: 'May it endure forever')
Bird: mountain bluebird
Fish: cutthroat trout
Flower: syringa
Tree: Western white pine
Song: "Here We Have Idaho"
Noted physical features: Moyie, Shosone and Upper Mesa falls; Hooper, Lavahot and Soda springs; Borah Peak
Tourist attractions: Sun Valley; Continental Divide; Brownlee Dam, Oxbow Dam; Craters of the Moon National Park; Hells Canyon; Shoshone Falls; River of No Return Wilderness Area; Redfish Lake
Admission date: July 3, 1890
Order of admission: 43
Name origin: Said to be a coined name with the invented meaning 'gem of the mountains.' Another theory suggests Idaho may be a Kiowa Apache term for the Comanche.

Iceland

Ida·ho Falls |ˈīdə‚hō| city in SE Idaho, on the Snake River. Pop. 43,929.

Idi·ta·rod River |īˈditə‚räd| river in W Alaska, scene of a 1908 gold rush. It is on the route of the Iditarod dog sled race, which goes from Anchorage to Nome.

Id·lib |ˈid‚lib| commercial town in NW Syria, SW of Aleppo. Pop. 100,000. Ancient Ebla lay to the S.

Id·u·mae·a |‚id(y)o͞oˈmēə| another name for ancient EDOM.

Ie·per |ēpər| Flemish name for YPRES, Belgium.

If |ēf| small island off the S coast of France, 2 mi./3 km. from Marseilles. On it is the Château d'If, a famous fortress prison.

Ife |ˈēfä| industrial city in SW Nigeria. Pop. 241,000. It was a center of the Yoruba kingdom from the 14th to the 17th centuries.

If·ni |ˈifnē| former overseas province of Spain, on the SW coast of Morocco, ceded to Morocco in 1969.

Igua·çu |‚ēgwəˈso͞o| river of S Brazil. It rises in the Serra do Mar in SE Brazil and flows W for 800 mi./1,300 km. to the Paraná River, which it joins shortly below the noted Iguaçu Falls. Spanish name **Iguazú**

Igua·la |ēˈgwälä| (official name **Iguala de la Independencia**) historic city in S Mexico, in Guerrero state. Pop. 83,000. In a mining region, it was the scene of a noted 1821 announcement of independence.

IJs·sel |ˈīsəl| river in the E Netherlands, flowing 72 mi./115 km. N to the IJsselmeer.

IJs·sel·meer |ˈīsəl‚mer| shallow lake in the NW Netherlands, created in 1932 by the building of a dam across the entrance to the old Zuider Zee. Large areas have since been reclaimed as polders.

Ika·ría |‚ēkəˈrēə| (also **Icaria**) island of Greece, part of the Southern Sporades group, in the Aegean Sea, named for the mythical figure Icarus, who flew too close to the sun and fell into the sea.

Ike·da |ēˈkädə| city in W central Japan, on S Honshu, an industrial and residential suburb N of Osaka. Pop. 104,000.

Ike·ja |ēˈkäjə| industrial town in SW Nigeria, just NW of Lagos. Murtala Muhammad International Airport is here. Pop. 60,000.

Ik·san |ˈēk‚sän| commercial city in SW South Korea, in an agricultural region. Pop. 323,000.

Ila |ˈēlə| commercial town in SW Nigeria, in an agricultural area. Pop. 233,000.

Île-de-France |‚ēl də fräⁿs| region of N central France, incorporating the city of Paris and surrounding departments.

Ile de la Ci·té |‚ēl də lä sēˈtä| island in the Seine River, in Paris, France. The site of the first settlement in Paris and later the center of the Roman colony, it is now the site of the cathedral of Notre-Dâme and other historic buildings and government offices.

Ile·sha |ēˈläsHə| city in SW Nigeria, an agricultural trade center. Pop. 342,000.

Il·hé·us |ēlˈyäo͞os| port city in E Brazil, in S Bahia state. Pop. 224,000. It is historically the leading cacao exporting center in Brazil.

Ili·gan |ēˈlēˈgän| industrial port city in the Philippines, on W central Mindanao, on Iligan Bay. Pop. 227,000.

Ili River |ˈēlē| river in central Asia, formed in NW Xinjiang, China, by the conjunction of the Tekes and Künes rivers, whose headwaters rise in the Tian Shan range. It flows 590 mi./950 km. W and NW to the S end of Lake Balkash in Kazakhstan.

Il·i·um |ˈilēəm| the alternative name for ancient TROY, especially the 7th-century B.C. Greek city.

Il·li·nois |‚iləˈnoi; ‚iləˈnoiz| see box.

Illinois

Capital: Springfield
Largest city: Chicago
Other cities: Aurora, Bloomington, Decatur, Elgin, Peoria, Rockford
Population: 11,430,602 (1990); 12,045,326 (1998); 12,266,000 (2005 proj.)
Population rank (1990): 6
Rank in land area: 25
Abbreviation: IL; Ill.
Nicknames: Prairie State; Land of Lincoln
Motto: 'State Sovereignty, National Union'
Bird: cardinal
Fish: bluegill
Flower: violet
Tree: white oak
Song: "Illinois"
Noted physical features: Shawnee Hills; Charles Mound
Tourist attractions: Chicago; Abraham Lincoln home and tomb; Lincoln Trail; Starved Rock State Park; Shawnee National Forest; Illinois State Museum
Admission date: December 3, 1818
Order of admission: 21
Name origin: From the French collective noun for the Illini or Inini Indians, whose name is from an Algonquin word meaning 'men' or 'warriors.'

Il·li·nois River |ˌiləˈnoi; ˌiləˈnoiz| river that flows 273 mi./440 km. SW through Illinois to the Mississippi River.

Il·lyr·ia |iˈlirēə| ancient region along the E coast of the Adriatic Sea, including Dalmatia and what is now Montenegro and N Albania. □ **Illyrian** *adj. & n.*

Ilo·cos |ēˈlōkōs| region in the Philippines, on NW Luzon. Pop. 4.22 million. Ilocos Norte and Ilocos Sur are two of the four provinces in the region.

Ilo·i·lo |ˌēlōˈēlō| port on the S coast of the island of Panay in the Philippines. Pop. 310,000.

Ilo·rin |ēˈlawren| industrial city in W Nigeria. Pop. 390,000. In the 18th century it was the capital of a Yoruba kingdom that was eventually absorbed into a Fulani state in the early 19th century.

Ima·ba·ri |ˌēmäˈbärē| industrial port city in W Japan, on the NW coast of Shikoku. Pop. 123,000.

Im·bros |ˈēmˌbraws| Turkish island in the NE Aegean Sea, near the entrance to the Dardanelles. Turkish name **Imroz**.

Im·pe·ra·triz |ēmˌperəˈtrēs| commercial city in NE Brazil, on the Tocantins River in Maranhão state. Pop. 228,000. It ships regional farm and forest products.

Im·pe·ri·al Valley |imˈpirēəl| irrigated section of the Colorado Desert, in SE California, site of a major agricultural industry.

Im·phal |ˈimpˌhəl| the capital of the state of Manipur in the far NE of India, lying close to the border with Burma. Pop. 157,000. It was the scene of an important victory in 1944 by Anglo-Indian forces over the Japanese.

Im·roz |imˈrawz| Turkish name for IMBROS.

Inch·cape Rock |ˈinCHˌkāp| (also **Bell Rock**) sandstone reef in the North Sea, off the mouth of the Tay River in Scotland, subject of a ballad by Robert Southey.

In·chon |ˈinˌCHän| industrial port on the W coast of South Korea, on the Yellow Sea near Seoul. Pop. 1,818,000. It is the site of a U.S. amphibious landing in the Korean War (1950).

In·de·pend·ence |ˌindəˈpendəns| historic suburban city in NW Missouri, E of Kansas City. Pop. 112,301.

In·dia |ˈindēə| republic of S Asia, occupying most of the Indian subcontinent, on the Indian Ocean. Area: 1.23 million sq. mi./3.18 million sq. km. Pop. 859,200,000. Languages, Hindi, English, fourteen others including Bengali, Gujarati, Marathi, Tamil, Telugu, Urdu. Capital: New Delhi. Largest cities: Bombay (Mumbai), Calcut-

ta. Hindi Name **Bharat**. Settled since at least the 3rd millennium B.C., India has been dominated by Aryans, Muslims, and Europeans, especially the British. It achieved independence from the U.K. in 1947, then split into Hindu (India) and Muslim (Pakistan) states. Although 83% Hindi, India still has the third-largest Muslim community in the world. Many Indians are subsistence farmers, but mining and industry are also important. □ **Indian** *adj. & n.*

In·di·ana |ˌindēˈænə| see box.

In·di·an·ap·o·lis |ˌindēəˈnæp(ə)ləs| the capital and largest city of Indiana. Pop. 741,952. A commercial and industrial center, it is also noted as host to the annual Indianapolis 500 motor race (held in Speedway, a city enclosed by Indianapolis).

In·di·an Ocean |ˈindēən| the ocean to the S of India and neighboring Asia, extending from the E coast of Africa to the East Indies and Australia.

In·di·an subcontinent |ˈindēən| the part of Asia S of the Himalayas that forms a peninsula extending into the Indian Ocean,

---

Indiana

Capital/largest city: Indianapolis
Other cities: Bloomington, Evansville, Ft. Wayne, Gary, Hammond, Lafayette, South Bend, Terre Haute
Population: 5,544,159 (1990); 5,899,195 (1998); 6,215,000 (2005 proj.)
Population rank (1990): 14
Rank in land area: 38
Abbreviation: IN; Ind.
Nickname: Hoosier State
Motto: 'The Crossroads of America'
Bird: cardinal
Flower: peony
Tree: tulip tree (yellow poplar)
Song: "On the Banks of the Wabash, Far Away"
Noted physical features: Wyandotte Cave; Greensfort Top Mountain; Indiana Dunes
Tourist attractions: Lincoln Boyhood National Monument; New Harmony; Indian mounds
Admission date: December 11, 1816
Order of admission: 19
Name origin: A Latinized or Spanish form of *Indian* meaning 'land of the Indians'; used in 1768 by the Philadelphus Trading Company for territory ceded to them by the Iroquois.

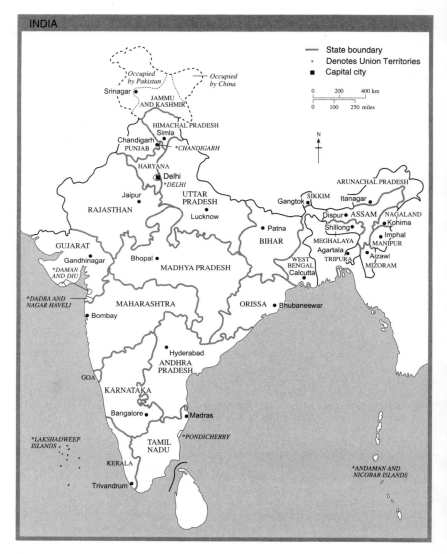

INDIA

State boundary
• Denotes Union Territories
■ Capital city

---

between the Arabian Sea and the Bay of Bengal. Historically forming the whole territory of greater India, the region is now divided among India, Pakistan, and Bangladesh. Geologically, the Indian subcontinent is a distinct unit, formerly part of the ancient supercontinent of Gondwanaland. As a result of continental drift it became joined to the rest of Asia, perhaps as recently as 40 million years ago, in a collision that created the Himalayas.

In·dies |ˈindēz| archaic term for the EAST INDIES.

In·di·gir·ka |ˌindəˈgirkə| river of far E Siberia, which flows N for 1,112 mi./1,779 km. to the Arctic Ocean, where it forms a wide delta.

In·dio |ˈindēˌō| desert city in S California, SE of Palm Springs. Pop. 36,793.

In·di·ra Gan·dhi Canal |inˈdirə ˈgändē| canal in NW India, bringing water to the Thar Desert of Rajasthan from the Harike Barrage on the Sutlej River. The canal, which is 406 mi./650 km. long, was completed in 1986. Former name **Rajasthan Canal**.

In·do·chi·na |ˌindōˈCHīnə| (also **Indo-China**) the peninsula of SE Asia containing Burma, Thailand, Malaysia, Laos, Cambodia, and Vietnam; especially, the part of this area consisting of Laos, Cambodia, and Vietnam, which was a French dependency (FRENCH INDOCHINA) from 1862 to 1954. □ **Indochinese** *adj. & n.*

In·do·ne·sia |ˌindəˈnēzHə; ˌindəˈnēsHə| SE Asian republic consisting of many islands in the Malay Archipelago. Area: 735,638 sq. mi./1.90 million sq. km. Pop. 184,300,000. Languages, Indonesian (Bahasa Indonesia: official), Malay, Balinese, Chinese, Javanese, others. Capital and largest city: Djakarta (on Java). Former name **Dutch East Indies**. Controlled by the Dutch for two centuries before 1949, Indonesia is predominantly agricultural. Rice, rubber, palm oil, timber, tin, other metals, and oil and gas are all important products. □ **Indonesian** *adj. & n.*

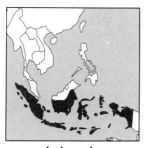

Indonesia

In·dore |inˈdawr| manufacturing city of Madhya Pradesh in central India. Pop. 1,087,000.

In·dus |ˈindəs| river of S Asia, about 1,800 mi./2,900 km. in length, flowing from Tibet through Kashmir and Pakistan to the Arabian Sea. Along its valley an early civilization flourished from *c.*2600 to 1760 B.C., whose economic wealth was derived from sea and land trade with the rest of the Indian subcontinent.

In·gle·wood |ˈiNGgəlˌwo͝od| city in SW California, an industrial and residential suburb S of Los Angeles. Pop. 109,602.

In·gol·stadt |ˈiNGgəlˌsHtät| industrial and commercial city in SW Germany, on the Danube River. Pop. 107,000.

In·gu·she·tia |ˌiNGgo͝oˈsHēsHə| (also **Ingush Republic**) autonomous republic of Russia, N of Georgia. Until the breakup of the Soviet Union in 1991, it was united with Chechnya. Its capital is Nazran.

In·ker·man |ˈiNGkərmən| village in Ukraine, near the mouth of the Chernaya

River E of Sevastopol. The Russians were defeated by English and French forces here in a battle (1854) during the Crimean War.

In·land Empire |ˈinlənd| popular name for highland agricultural regions of central Washington, E of the Cascade Range.

In·land Sea |ˈinlənd| arm of the Pacific, enclosed by the Japanese islands of Honshu, Shikoku, and Kyushu. Its chief port is Hiroshima.

In·land Wa·ter·way another name for ATLANTIC INTRACOASTAL WATERWAY or GULF INTRACOASTAL WATERWAY.

In·ner Mon·go·lia |mäNGˈgōlyə| (Chinese name **Nei Monggol**) autonomous region of N China, on the border with Mongolia. Pop. 21.46 million. Capital: Hohhot.

In·nis·free |ˌinisHˈfrē| island in County Sligo, NW Ireland, in Lough Gill, that is the setting for a well-known poem by W.B. Yeats.

Inn River |in| river in W Europe that rises in the Rhaetian Alps of Switzerland and flows 320 mi./508 km. through the Austrian Tyrol past Innsbruck into S Germany, where it flows into the Danube River at Passau.

Inns·bruck |ˈinsˌbro͝ok| resort and industrial city in W Austria, capital of Tyrol. Pop. 115,000.

In·side Passage |ˈinˌsīd| water route from Seattle, Washington, to Alaska, passing through islands in Washington, British Columbia, and SE Alaska.

Inter-American Highway |ˌintərəˈmerəkən| name for the section of the PAN-AMERICAN HIGHWAY between the U.S.-Mexico border (at Nuevo Laredo, Mexico) and Panama City, Panama.

In·ter·la·ken |ˈintərˌläkən| the chief town of the Bernese Alps in central Switzerland, on the Aare River between Lakes Brienz and Thun. Pop. 5,000.

In·ter·mon·tane Region |ˌintərmänˈtān| (also **Intermountain Region**) term for the mountain and basin regions lying between the Rocky Mts. and the mountains of the U.S. W coast.

In·ter·na·tion·al Date Line |ˌin(t)ərˈnæsHənl| imaginary line at 180° longitude, halfway around the earth from Greenwich, England. Points immediately W are 12 hours ahead of Greenwich Mean Time, points immediately E 12 hours behind. In the Pacific, the line bends in various places to avoid dividing populations.

In·tra·coast·al Wa·ter·way see ATLANTIC

INTRACOASTAL WATERWAY; GULF INTRA-
COASTAL WATERWAY.

In·va·lides, Hôtel des |ō'tel dez ˌäNvä'lēd| building complex in Paris, France. Originally built as a home for aged soldiers by King Louis XIV, it is now a military museum. The sarcophagus of Napoleon I rests beneath the classical dome.

In·ver·car·gill |ˌinvər'kärgil| city in New Zealand, capital of Southland region, South Island. Pop. 52,000.

In·ver·ness |ˌinvər'nes| city in N Scotland, administrative center of Highland region, at the mouth of the Ness River. Pop. 41,000.

In·yo Mountains |'inyō| range in E central California that includes Mount Whitney, at 14,495 ft./4,418 m. the highest point in the U.S. outside Alaska.

Io·án·ni·na |yō'änēnə| department in NW Greece. Pop. 157,000. The capital is Ioánnina.

Iona |ī'ōnə| small island in the Inner Hebrides, Scotland, off the W coast of Mull. It is the site of a monastery founded by St. Columba in about 563.

Io·nia |ī'ōnēə| in classical times, the central part of the W coast of Asia Minor, which had long been inhabited by Hellenic people (the Ionians) and was again colonized by Greeks from the mainland from about the 8th century B.C. □ **Ionian** adj. & n.

Io·ni·an Islands |ī'ōnēən| chain of about forty Greek islands off the W coast of mainland Greece, in the Ionian Sea, including Corfu, Cephalonia, Ithaca, and Zakinthos.

Io·ni·an Sea |ī'ōnēən| the part of the Mediterranean Sea between W Greece and S Italy, at the mouth of the Adriatic.

Io·wa |'īəwə| see box. □ **Iowan** adj. & n.

Io·wa City |'īəwə| city in E Iowa. Pop. 59,738. Founded in 1838, it was the state capital until replaced by Des Moines in 1858. The University of Iowa is here.

Ip·a·ne·ma |ˌipə'nēmə| beachfront section of S Rio de Janeiro, Brazil, just SW of Copacabana.

Ipi·ran·ga |ˌēpē'räNGgə| stream and district SE of central São Paulo, Brazil, site where Brazilian independence from Portugal was declared in 1822.

Ipoh |'ēpō| the capital of the state of Perak in W Malaysia. Pop. 383,000. It replaced Taiping as state capital in 1937.

Ips·wich |'ip,swiCH| the county seat of Suffolk, E England, a port and industrial center on the estuary of the Orwell River. Pop. 116,000.

Iowa

Capital/largest city: Des Moines
Other cities: Cedar Rapids, Davenport, Dubuque, Perry, Sioux City, Waterloo
Population: 2,776,755 (1990); 2,862,447 (1998); 2,941,000 (2005 proj.)
Population rank (1990): 30
Rank in land area: 26
Abbreviation: IA; Ia.
Nicknames: The Hawkeye State; Corn State
Motto: 'Our Liberties We Prize and Our Rights We Will Maintain'
Bird: eastern goldfinch
Flower: wild rose
Tree: oak
Song: "The Song of Iowa"
Tourist attractions: Amana Colonies; first apple orchard; Little Brown Church; Herbert Hoover National Historic Site; Effigy Mounds National Monument
Admission date: December 28, 1846
Order of admission: 29
Name origin: For the Iowa River, which was named for the Iowa Indians of Siouan linguistic stock; the name is a French version of the Dakota name for the tribe, said to mean 'the sleepy ones.'

Iqa·lu·it |ē'kälōoit| (formerly **Frobisher Bay**) capital of Nunavut Territory, Canada, in S Baffin Island. Pop. 3,552.

Iqui·que |ē'kēkä| port city in N Chile, in the Tarapacá region. Pop. 149,000. It exports nitrates from the Atacama Desert as well as fish.

Iqui·tos |ē'kētōs| city in NE Peru, a port on the Amazon River. Pop. 252,000. It is a commercial, oil industry, and cultural center in the tropical rainforest.

Irá·kli·on |ē'räklē,awn| Greek name for HERAKLION, Crete.

Iran |i'rän; i'ran; ī'ran| republic in the Middle East, between the Caspian Sea and the Persian Gulf. Area: 636,539 sq. mi./1.65

Iran

million sq. km. Pop. 54,600,000. Languages, Farsi (Persian) (official), Azerbaijani, Kurdish, Arabic, others. Capital and largest city: Tehran. Successor to Persia, Iran took its current name in 1935. Its monarchy was overthrown in 1979, and a theocratic Islamic republic established. Oil, textiles, and foods are major products in this largely desert country. □ **Iranian** *adj. & n.*

Ira·pua·to |ˌērə'pwätō| commercial city in central Mexico, in Guanjuato state. Pop. 265,000. Its region is famous for flower, fruit, and vegetable production.

Iraq |i'räk; i'ræk; ĭ'ræk| republic in the Middle East, on the Persian Gulf. Area: 169,300 sq. mi./438,317 sq. km. Pop. 17,583,450. Language, Arabic (minorities speak Kurdish and Turkoman). Capital and largest city: Baghdad. The site of ancient Mesopotamia, Iraq was conquered by Arabs in the 7th century. After centuries of domination by the Turks and then the British, it gained independence in 1932. Its economy relies heavily on oil. Wars with its neighbors Iran and Kuwait and strife with Kurdish and Marsh Arab minorities have characterized recent decades. □ **Iraqi** *adj. & n.*

Iraq

Ir·bid |ir'bid; 'irbid| commercial city in N Jordan, N of Amman on the Jordan River. Pop. 170,000. It is an administrative and cultural center in a grain-producing region.

Ir·bil |'ər,bēl; 'ir,bēl| see ARBIL, Iraq.

Ire·land, Republic of |'īrlənd| country comprising approximately four-fifths of Ireland. Area: 27,146 sq. mi./70,282 sq. km. Pop. 3,523,400. Languages, Irish (official), English. Capital and largest city: Dublin. Also called **Irish Republic**. Comprising 26 of the 32 counties of Ireland, the Republic separated itself from British rule gradually in 1921–37. Its traditional pastoral and agricultural economy is shifting toward light industry. Tourism is important. □ **Irish** *adj. & n.*

Ire·land |'īrlənd| island of the British Isles, lying W of Great Britain. Approximately four-fifths of the area (32,327 sq. mi./83,694 sq. km.) of Ireland forms the Republic of Ireland, with the remainder forming NORTHERN IRELAND.

Iri·an Ja·ya |'ir,ēän 'jīə| province of E Indonesia comprising the W half of the island of New Guinea together with the adjacent small islands. Pop. 1.83 million. Capital: Jayapura. Until its incorporation into Indonesia in 1963 it was known as Dutch New Guinea. Also called **West Irian**.

Irish Republic |'īrisH| see IRELAND, RE-PUBLIC OF.

Irish Sea |'īrisH| the sea separating Ireland from England and Wales.

Ir·kutsk |ir'kŏotsk| industrial and cultural city of Siberia, near the W shore of Lake Baikal in E Russia. Pop. 635,000.

Iron·bot·tom Sound |'ī(ə)rn,bätəm| name given by U.S. forces in 1942 to the waters N of Guadalcanal, in the Solomon Islands. Especially around Savo Island, the ocean floor here was considered to be covered with sunken ships.

Iron Cur·tain |ˌī(ə)rn| cold war dividing line between the Soviet Union and its satellites and the West, defined by Winston Churchill in 1946 as extending from eastern Germany in the N to Trieste, on the Italy-Yugoslavia border, in the S.

Iron Gate |ī(ə)rn| gorge through which a section of the Danube River flows, forming part of the boundary between Romania and Serbia. Navigation was improved by means of a ship canal constructed through it in 1896. Romanian name **Porţile de Fier**, Serbo-Croat name **Gvozdena Vrata**.

Ir·ra·wad·dy |ˌirə'wädē| the principal river of Burma, 1,300 mi./2,090 km. long. It flows in a large delta into the E part of the Bay of Bengal.

Ir·tysh |ir'tisH| river of central Asia, which rises in the Altai Mts. in N China and flows W into NE Kazakhstan, where it turns NW into Russia, joining the Ob River near its mouth. Its length is 2,655 mi./4,248 km.

Iru·ma |ē'rŏomə| city in E central Japan, on E central Honshu, a residential and industrial suburb NW of Tokyo. Pop. 138,000. It is noted for cultivation of green tea.

Irún |ē'rŏon| river port and industrial town in N Spain, on the Bidassoa River. Pop. 54,000.

Ir·ving |'ərviNG| industrial city in NE Texas, between Dallas and Fort Worth. Pop. 155,037.

Ir·ving·ton |'erviNGtən| industrial and res-

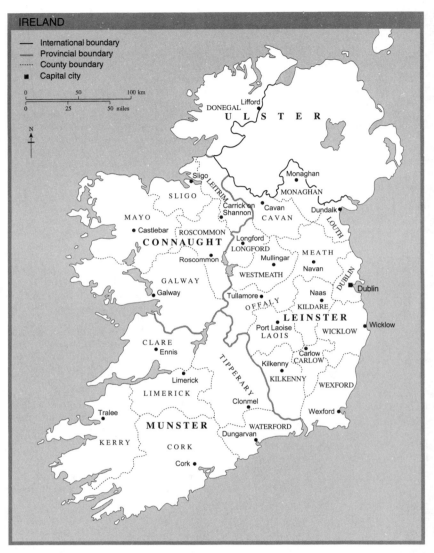

IRELAND

— International boundary
— Provincial boundary
······ County boundary
■ Capital city

0   50   100 km
0   25   50 miles

N

idential township in NE New Jersey, on the W side of Newark. Pop. 61,010.

Is·chi·a |'iskēə| resort island in the Tyrrhenian Sea off the W coast of Italy, about 16 mi./26 km. W of Naples. The 'Emerald Isle' is noted for its hot springs.

Ise |'ēsā| city in central Honshu, Japan, on Ise Bay. Pop. 104,000. Former name (until 1956) **Ujiyamada**.

Isère River |ē'zer| river in E France that rises in the Alps near Val d'Isère and flows 180 mi./290 km., meeting the Rhône River near Valence.

Iser·lohn |ˌēzər'lōn| commercial and industrial city in western Germany. Pop. 93,000. In the 19th century it was the most populous city in Westphalia.

Ise·sa·ki |ˌēsā'säkē| city in N central Japan, on central Honshu, NW of Tokyo. Pop. 116,000.

Ise·yin |ē'sāin| commercial and industrial town in SW Nigeria, N of Ibadan, Pop. 192,000. In a tobacco-growing region, it also has noted textile industries.

Is·fa·han |ˌisfə'hän| (also **Esfahan, Ispa·han**) historic industrial city in central Iran, the country's third-largest city. Pop.

1,127,000. It was the capital of Persia from 1598 until 1722.

Ish•i•ka•ri River |ˌēSHē'kärē| river in N Japan, on W Hokkaido, that flows 225 mi./362 km. from the interior of Hokkaido to Ishikari Bay on the Sea of Japan; second-longest river in Japan.

Ishim River |i'shim| river (1,330 mi./2,140 km.) in N central Kazakhstan and W Asian Russia. It rises in the central steppes of Kazakhstan and flows N to the Irtysh at Ust-Ishim.

Ishi•no•ma•ki |ˌēSHēnō'mäkē| commercial and fishing port in NE Japan, on the NE coast of Honshu. Pop. 122,000.

Isis |'īsis| local and poetic name for the Thames River, in S England, especially in and around Oxford.

Is•ken•de•run |ˌiskendə'rōōn| port and naval base in S Turkey, on the Mediterranean coast. Pop. 159,000. Formerly named Alexandretta, it lies on or near the site of Alexandria ad Issum, founded by Alexander the Great in 333 B.C.

Is•lam•a•bad |is'lämə,bäd| the capital of Pakistan, a modern planned city in the N of the country, which replaced Rawalpindi as capital in 1967. Pop. 201,000.

Is•la Mu•je•res |'ēslä mōō'hārəs| island in SE Mexico, in the Gulf of Mexico off Quintana Roo state. It is a popular resort.

Is•lay |'īlə; 'ī,lä| island that is the southernmost of the Inner Hebrides, Scotland, S of Jura.

Isle of Wight |'wīt| see WIGHT, ISLE OF.

Isle Roy•ale |īl 'roiəl| island in Michigan, in W Lake Superior, near Grand Portage, Minnesota, part of a national park and noted for its wildlife.

Is•ling•ton |'izliNGtən| residential and industrial borough of N London, England. Pop. 155,000. Sadler's Wells Theatre is here.

Is•mai•lia |ˌizmāə'lēə| (Arabic name **Al Is-mailiyah**) port city in NE Egypt, on the Suez Canal, halfway between Port Said and Suez. Pop. 247,000.

Is•ra•el |'izrēəl; 'izräəl| country in the Middle East, on the Mediterranean Sea. Area: 8,022 sq. mi./20,770 sq. km. Pop. 4,600,000. Languages, Hebrew (official), English, Arabic. Capital (not recognized as such by the U.N.), Jerusalem; most embassies in Tel Aviv. Established in 1948 as a Jewish homeland in part of British-controlled Palestine, Israel has been in continual conflict with its Arab neighbors, and today occupies territories taken in war, in-

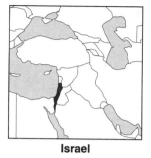

Israel

cluding the WEST BANK and Syrian GOLAN HEIGHTS. Irrigated agriculture, industry, tourism, and the support of Jews in the DIASPORA are key to the well-being of Israel. See also PALESTINE. □ **Israeli** *adj. & n.*

Issyk-Kul, Lake |ˌisik'kōōl| (also **Issiq Köl**) lake in NE Kyrgyzstan, in a mountain range at 5,279 ft./1,609 m., site of several ancient cultures.

Is•tan•bul |ˌistän'bōōl| historic port, the largest city in Turkey, on the Bosporus, lying partly in Europe, partly in Asia. Pop. 7,309,000. Formerly the Roman city of Constantinople (330–1453), it was built on the site of the ancient Greek city of Byzantium. It was captured by the Ottoman Turks in 1453 and was the capital of Turkey from that time until 1923. Istanbul has long been a commercial and religious center.

Is•tria |'ēstrēə| (also **Istrian Peninsula**) mountainous peninsula jutting into the N Adriatic Sea and belonging to Croatia and Slovenia. The peninsula is primarily agricultural. The NW section, including Trieste, belongs to Italy.

Ita•bu•na |ˌētə'bōōnə| city in E Brazil, in Bahia state. Pop. 185,000. It is a center for cacao and cattle industries.

Ita•i•pú Dam |ē'tīpōō| dam on the Paraná River between SW Brazil and E Paraguay, operational since 1984. One of the largest hydroelectric projects in the world, it impounds the huge **Itaipú Reservoir**.

Ital•ian East Af•ri•ca former African possessions of Italy, including Eritrea, Ethiopia, and Italian Somaliland (now part of Somalia).

It•aly |'itl-ē| republic in S Europe. Area: 116,348 sq. mi./301,225 sq. km. Pop. 57,746,160. Language, Italian. Capital and largest city: Rome. Italian name **Italia**. Successor to Rome, Italy achieved unification in the 19th century. In addition to its rich cultural heritage, it has a strong industrial

ITALY

Region boundary
■ Capital city

0   50   100   150   200 km
0   25   50   75   100 miles

TRENTINO-ALTO ADIGE
Trento
FRIULI-VENEZIA GIULIA
Trieste
•Aosta
VALLE D'AOSTA
LOMBARDY
VENETIA
Venice
Turin
Milan
PIEDMONT
LIGURIA
Genoa
EMILIA-ROMAGNA
Bologna
Florence
Ancona
TUSCANY
THE MARCHES
Perugia
UMBRIA
L'Aquila
Rome
ABRUZZI
LATIUM
MOLISE
Campobasso
Naples
Bari
CAMPANIA
APULIA
Potenza
BASILICATA
SARDINIA
Cagliari
CALABRIA
Palermo
Reggio
SICILY

N

base. The agricultural S is less prosperous. Sicily and Sardinia are the largest Italian islands in the Mediterranean. □ **Italian** *adj. & n.*

Ita•mi |ē'tämē| city in W central Japan, on S Honshu, a residential suburb N of Osaka. Pop. 186,000.

Ita•na•gar city in the far NE of India, N of the Brahmaputra River, capital of the state of Arunachal Pradesh. Pop. 17,000.

Ith•a•ca[1] |'iTHəkə| island off the W coast of Greece in the Ionian Sea, the legendary home of Odysseus.

Ith•a•ca[2] |'iTHəkə| academic city in central New York, at the S end of Cayuga Lake, home to Cornell University. Pop. 29,541.

Itsu·ku·shi·ma |ˌēts(o͞o)'ko͞o'sHēmä| (also called **Miyajima**) island in W Japan, in the Inland Sea, off SW Honshu. It is noted for its beauty and its historic and sacred buildings.

Ivano-Frankovsk |ē,vänōfräNG'kawfsk| (formerly known as **Stanislav**) industrial city in W Ukraine. Pop. 220,000.

Iva·no·vo |i'vänəvə| textile city in W Russia, NE of Moscow, capital of Ivanovo Oblast. Pop. 482,000.

Ivo·ry Coast |'īv(ə)rē| English name for CÔTE D'IVOIRE.

Ivry-sur-Seine |ē,vrēsYr'sen| industrial SE suburb of Paris, France. Pop. 56,000.

Iwa·ki |ē'wäkē| industrial city in NE Japan, on the E coast of Honshu, between Sendai and Mito. Pop. 356,000.

Iwa·ku·ni |ˌēwä'ko͞onē| industrial city in W Japan, on the SW coast of Honshu. Pop. 110,000.

Iwo |'ēwō| commercial city in SW Nigeria, NE of Ibadan, in a cacao producing area. Pop. 262,000.

Iwo Ji·ma |ˌiwə 'jēmə| largest of the Volcano Islands in the W Pacific, 760 mi./1,222 km. S of Tokyo. During World War II it was the heavily fortified site of a Japanese airbase, and its attack and capture in 1944–45 was one of the bloodiest campaigns in the Pacific. It was returned to Japan in 1968.

Izal·co |ē'sälkō| volcano in W El Salvador, N of Sonsonate, that rises to 7,828 ft./2,386 m. Long called the Lighthouse of the Pacific, it last erupted in 1966 but is active.

Izhevsk |'ē,zHevsk| industrial city in central Russia, capital of the republic of Udmurtia. Pop. 642,000. Former name (1984–87) **Ustinov.**

Iz·ma·il |ˌēzmä'yēl| (also known as **Ismayil**) city in Ukraine, on the N side of the Danube Delta near the Black Sea. Pop. 95,000.

Iz·mir |iz'mir| seaport and naval base in W Turkey, on an inlet of the Aegean Sea. Pop. 1,757,000. It is the third-largest city in Turkey. Former name **Smyrna.**

Iz·mit |iz'mit| port city in NW Turkey, on the Gulf of Izmit, an inlet of the Sea of Marmara. Pop. 257,000.

Iz·ta·cal·co |ˌēstə'kälkō| (also **Ixtacalco**) industrial city, a constituent of the Distrito Federal, just S of Mexico City, Mexico. Pop. 448,000.

Iz·tac·ci·huatl |ˌēstäk'sē,wätl| (also **Ixtaccihuatl**) dormant volcano in central Mexico, reaching 17,342 ft./5,286 m. Neighbor to POPOCATÉPETL, it is SE of Mexico City, from which it can be seen in clear weather.

Iz·ta·pa·la·pa |ˌēstəpə'läpə| (also **Ixtapalapa**) community in central Mexico, a constituent of the DISTRITO FEDERAL, SE of downtown Mexico City. Pop. 1,490,000.

Izu·mi |ē'zo͞omē| city in W central Japan, on S Honshu, a residential and industrial suburb S of Osaka. Pop. 138,000.

Jj

Ja•bal•pur |'jəbəl,pŏŏr| industrial city and military post in Madhya Pradesh, central India. Pop. 760,000.

Ja•blon•ec nad Ni•sou |'yäblō,nets ,näd 'nē,sŏŏ| city in the N central Czech Republic. Pop. 88,000. It is a center of the Bohemian glassmaking industry.

Ja•blo•ni•ca Pass (also known as **Tatar Pass** or **Delatyn Pass**) pass through the E Carpathian Mts., Ukraine, SW of Kolomyya.

Ja•bo•a•tão |,zHäb,wätowN| commercial city in NE Brazil, in Pernambuco state, a suburb W of Recife. Pop. 487,000.

Ja•ca•rei |,zHäkərāyē| industrial and commercial city in SE Brazil, E of São Paulo. Pop. 168,000.

Jack•son[1] |'jæksən| industrial city in S central Michigan. Pop. 37,446.

Jack•son[2] |'jæksən| industrial and commercial city, the capital of Mississippi, in the central part, on the Pearl River. Pop. 196,637.

Jack•son[3] |'jæksən| commercial city in W Tennessee. Pop. 48,949.

Jack•son Heights |,jæksən 'hīts| commercial and residential section of N Queens, New York City.

Jack•son Hole |,jæksən 'hōl| valley on the Snake River in NW Wyoming, partly in Grand Teton National Park. It is a fashionable resort.

Jack•son•ville[1] |'jæksən,vil| industrial city and port in NE Florida. Pop. 635,230.

Jack•son•ville[2] |'jæksən,vil| city in SE North Carolina, a service town for nearby Camp Lejeune and other military facilities. Pop. 30,013.

Ja•én |hä'ān| market and manufacturing city in S Spain. Pop. 106,000.

Jaf•fa |'jäfə; 'yäfə| city and port on the Mediterranean coast of Israel, forming a S suburb of Tel Aviv and since 1949 united with Tel Aviv. Pop. (with Tel Aviv) 355,000. Inhabited since prehistoric times, Jaffa was a Byzantine bishopric until captured by the Arabs in 636; later, it was a stronghold of the Crusaders. Hebrew name **Yafo**; biblical name **Joppa**.

Jaff•na |'jäfnə| city and port on the Jaffna Peninsula at the N tip of Sri Lanka. Pop. 129,000.

Jag•ga•nath (also **Juggernaut**) see PURI, India.

Jai•pur |'jī,pŏŏr| cultural and industrial city in W India, the capital of Rajasthan. Pop. 1,455,000.

Ja•kar•ta |jə'kärtə| another spelling for DJAKARTA, Indonesia.

Ja•lal•a•bad |jə'lälə,bäd| city in E Afghanistan, E of Kabul, near the border with Pakistan. Pop. 61,000.

Ja•lan•dhar |'jələndər| (formerly **Jullundur**) industrial and commercial city in N India, in Punjab state. Pop. 520,000.

Ja•la•pa |hä'läpä| (also **Xalapa**) commercial city in E central Mexico, capital of the state of Veracruz, in an agricultural area. Pop. 288,000. Full name **Jalapa Enríquez**.

Jal•gaon |jäl,gown| commercial city in W central India, in Maharashtra state. Pop. 242,000.

Ja•lis•co |hä'lēskō| state of W central Mexico, on the Pacific coast. Area: 31,223 sq. mi./80,836 sq. km. Pop. 5,279,000. Capital: Guadalajara.

Jal•na |'jälnə| town in W central India, in Maharashtra state, SW of Aurangabad. Pop. 175,000.

Ja•mai•ca[1] |jə'mākə| island republic in the Caribbean, SE of Cuba. Area: 4,230 sq. mi./10,956 sq. km. Pop. 2,314,480. Language, English. Capital and largest city: Kingston. Colonized by the Spanish from the 15th century, and seized by the British in 1655, Jamaica gained independence in 1962. Its economy relies on bauxite extraction, agriculture, and tourism. □ **Jamaican** adj. & n.

Jamaica

Ja•mai•ca[2] |jə'mākə| commercial and residential section of E central Queens, New York City.

Jam•bi |'jämbē| (also **Djambi**) commercial city in Indonesia, on S Sumatra, on the Hari River. Pop. 340,000.

James Bay |'jāmz| shallow S arm of Hudson Bay, Canada, once a fur trading center, now the focus of disputes over hydroelectric projects.

James River¹ |,jāmz| (also **Dakota River**) river that flows 700 mi./1,100 km. from North Dakota through South Dakota, into the Missouri River.

James River² |,jāmz| river that flows 340 mi./550 km across E Virginia, past Richmond and into the Tidewater region, into Hampton Roads. Colonial Jamestown was on its estuary.

James•town¹ |'jāmz,town| city in SW New York, on Lake Chautauqua. It is both industrial and a resort service center. Pop. 34,681.

James•town² |'jāmz,town| the capital and chief port of the Atlantic island of St. Helena. Pop. 1,500.

James•town³ |'jāmz,town| British settlement established on the James River in Virginia in 1607, abandoned when the colonial capital was moved to Williamsburg at the end of the 17th century.

Jam•mu |'jəmoō| town in NW India. Pop. 206,000. It is the winter capital of the state of Jammu and Kashmir.

Jam•mu and Kash•mir |'jəmoō; 'kæsH-,mir| mountainous state of NW India at the W end of the Himalayas, formerly part of Kashmir. Pop. 7.72 million. Capitals: Srinagar (in summer) and Jammu (in winter).

Jam•na•gar |jäm'nəgər| port and walled city in the state of Gujarat, W India. Pop. 325,000.

Jam•shed•pur |'jämsHed,poōr| industrial city in the state of Bihar, NE India. Pop. 461,000.

Janes•ville |'jānz,vil| industrial city in S Wisconsin, on the Rock River. Pop. 52,133.

Jan May•en |'yän 'mīən| barren and virtually uninhabited island in the Arctic Ocean between Greenland and Norway, annexed by Norway in 1929.

Ja•pan, Sea of |jə'pæn| the sea between Japan and the mainland of Asia.

Ja•pan |jə'pæn| country in E Asia, occupying a chain of islands in the Pacific roughly parallel with the E coast of the Asian mainland. Area: 145,931 sq. mi./377,815 sq. km. Pop. 122,626,000. Language, Japanese. Capital and largest city: Tokyo. Japanese name **Nippon** (Land of the Rising Sun). In existence from around the 6th century B.C., Japan became a modern state in the late 19th century. It has few natural resources, but has made itself an industrial and commercial power. Expansionist

Japan

drives of the early 20th century came to an end with the Japanese loss in World War II. □ **Japanese** adj. & n.

Ja•pan Current |jə'pæn| (also **Japanese Current**) another name for KUROSHIO.

Ja•pu•rá River |,zHäpoō'rä| (Colombian name **Caquetá**) river that flows 1,750 mi./2,815 km. from SW Colombia into Brazil, to join the Amazon River.

Jar•row |'jərō| town in NE England, on the Tyne estuary. Pop. 31,000. From the 7th century until the Viking invasions its monastery was a center of Northumbrian Christian culture. Its name is also associated with hunger marches to London by the unemployed during the Depression of the 1930s.

Jär•ven•pää |'yärven,pä| town in S Finland, notes as home to the composer Sibelius. Pop. 32,000.

Jas•sy |yäsH| German name for IAŞI, Romania.

Jaun•pur |'jown,poōr| commercial city in NE India, in Uttar Pradesh state. Pop. 136,000.

Ja•va |'jävə| volcanic island in the Malay Archipelago, forming part of Indonesia. Pop. 112.16 million. Heavily forested and agricultural, with most of the population of Indonesia, Java is noted for its cultural history. □ **Javan** adj. & n. **Javanese** adj. & n.

Ja•va•ri River |,zHävä'rē| (Peruvian name **Yavari**) river that flows NE for 500 mi./810 km. from E Peru along the Peru-Brazil border, to the Amazon River.

Ja•va Sea |'jävə| sea in the Malay Archipelago of SE Asia, surrounded by the islands of Borneo, Java, and Sumatra.

Ja•ya•pu•ra |,jäyä'poōrä| (also **Djajapura**) port city in Indonesia, capital of Irian Jaya province on W New Guinea. Pop. 46,000.

Ja•zi•rah, al |,æljä'zērä| region in Iraq, NW of Baghdad, in the Tigris-Euphrates valley; an important trading center in both ancient and medieval times.

Jeb·el Mu·sa |'jebəl'm͞oͦsə| mountain in N Morocco, just W of Ceuta; 2,790 ft./850 m. With the Rock of Gibraltar, it is one of the Pillars of Hercules, flanking the Strait of Gibraltar.

Jef·fer·son City |'jefərsən| commercial and industrial city, the capital of Missouri. Pop. 35,481.

Je·hol former province of NE China, now divided among Inner Mongolia, Hebei, and Liaoning.

Je·le·nia Gó·ra |yə'lenyä 'gawrä| industrial and commercial city in SW Poland. Pop. 93,000.

Jel·ga·va |'yelgəvä| (also **Yelgava**) historic commercial city in S Latvia, on the Lielupe River. Pop. 75,000.

Je·mez Mountains |'hāmes| range in N New Mexico, NW of Santa Fe, site of Valle Grande, an enormous caldera. Chicoma Peak (11,950 ft./3,642 m.) is the high point.

Je·na |'yānə| university town in central Germany, in Thuringia. Pop. 101,000. It was the scene of a battle (1806) in which Napoleon defeated the Prussians. It is noted as a manufacturing center for optical and precision instruments.

Je·rez |hä'res; hä're_TH_| town in Andalusia, Spain. Pop. 184,000. It is the center of the sherry (from *jerez*) making industry. Full name **Jerez de la Frontera**.

Jer·i·cho |'jerə,kō| town in Palestine, in the West Bank N of the Dead Sea. It has been occupied from at least 9000 B.C. According to the Bible, Jericho was a Canaanite city destroyed by the Israelites after they crossed the Jordan into the Promised Land; its walls were flattened by the shout of the army of Joshua and the blast of the trumpets. Occupied by the Israelis since the Six Day War of 1967, in 1994 Jericho was the first area given partial autonomy under the PLO-Israeli peace accord.

Jer·sey |'jərzē| the largest (45 sq. mi./116 sq. km.) of the Channel Islands of Britain. Pop. 83,000. Capital: St. Helier.

Jer·sey City |'jərzē| industrial city in NE New Jersey, on the Hudson River opposite New York City. Pop. 228,537.

Je·ru·sa·lem |jə'r͞oͦs(ə)ləm; jə'r͞oͦz(ə)-ləm| the holy city of the Jews, sacred also to Christians and Muslims, lying in the Judaean hills about 20 mi./30 km. from the Jordan River. Pop. 562,000. The city was captured from the Canaanites by King David of the Israelites, who made it his capital. As the site of the Temple, built by Solomon (957 B.C.), it also became the center of the Jewish religion. Since then it has shared the troubled history of the area—destroyed by the Babylonians in 586 B.C. and by the Romans in A.D. 70, and fought over by Saracens and Crusaders in the Middle Ages. From 1947 the city was divided between the states of Israel and Jordan until the Israelis occupied the whole city in June 1967 and proclaimed it the capital of Israel. It is revered by Christians as the place of Christ's death and resurrection, and by Muslims as the site of the Dome of the Rock.

Jer·vis Bay Territory |'järvis| territory on Jervis Bay on the SE coast of Australia. Incorporated in 1915 as a sea outlet for the Australian Capital Territory, it separated from the Capital Territory in 1988.

Jes·sore |je,'sawr| commercial city in SW Bangladesh, on the Bhairab River. Pop. 176,000.

Jew·ish Republic |'j͞oͦ i SH| autonomous oblast in extreme E Russia, in the basins of the Biro and Bidzhan rivers. Pop. 212,000. Although it was intended as a home for Jews, only a small percentage of its population is Jewish.

Jez·re·el see ESDRAELON.

Jhang Sa·dar (also called **Jhang-Maghiana**) commercial town in central Pakistan, W of Lahore. Pop. 196,000.

Jhan·si |'jänsē| city in the state of Uttar Pradesh, N India. Pop. 301,000.

Jhe·lum |'jäləm| river that rises in the Himalayas and flows through the Vale of Kashmir into Punjab, where it meets the Chenab River. In ancient times it was called by the Greek name Hydaspes.

Jia·ling River |jē'ä'liNG| (Chinese name **Jialing Jiang**) river, central China, rising in the area around the S Gansu-Shaanxi border and flowing 600 mi./965 km. S through Sichuan to the Yangtze River at Chongqing.

Jia·mu·si |jē'ä'm͞oͦ'sē| city in Heilongjiang province, NE China, on the Sungari River NE of Harbin. Pop. 493,000.

Jiang·men |jē'äNG'men| city in Guangdong province, S China, on a branch of the Pearl River SW of Guangzhou (Canton). Pop. 231,000.

Jiang·su |jē'äNG's͞oͦ| (also **Kiangsu**) a province of E China. Pop. 67,006,000. Capital: Nanjing. It includes much of the Yangtze delta.

Jiang·xi |jē'äNG'sē| (also **Kiangsi**) a province of SE China. Pop. 37,710,000. Capital: Nanchang.

Jiao·zu·o |jē'owd'zwō| city in Henan

province, E central China, NW of Zhengzhou. Pop. 409,000.

Jia·xing |jē'ä'sHiNG| (formerly **Kashing**) city in Zhejiang province, E China, on the Grand Canal SW of Shanghai. Pop. 697,000.

Ji·ca·ril·la Mountains |ˌhēkə'rēə| range in S central New Mexico, reaching 8,200 ft./2,500 m. at Jicarilla Mt.

Jid·dah |'jidə| (also **Jeddah**) seaport on the Red Sea coast of Saudi Arabia, near Mecca. It is the Saudi administrative capital. Pop. 1,400,000.

Ji·lin |'jē'lin| (also **Kirin**) **1** a province of NE China. Pop. 24,660,000. Capital: Changchun. **2** an industrial city in Jilin province. Pop. 2,252,000.

Ji·nan |'ji'nän| (also **Tsinan**) city in E China, the capital of Shandong province. Pop. 2,290,000.

Jing·de·zhen |'jiNG'də'jen| (formerly **Fowliang**) city in Jiangxi province, SE China, E of Poyang Lake. Pop. 281,000. It has been a porcelain center since the Han dynasty, reaching its height during Sung times.

Jin·zhou |'jin'jō| city in Liaoning province, NE China, near the Gulf of Liaodong at the N end of the Bo Hai. Pop. 569,000.

Ji·pi·ja·pa |ˌhēpē'häpə| commercial town in W Ecuador, a noted center for Panama-hat production. Pop. 32,000.

Jiu·jiang |jē'ōōjē'äNG| city in N Jiangxi province, E central China, on the Yangtze River, N of Poyang Lake and SE of Wuhan. Pop. 291,000. Bricks, tiles, and textiles are produced.

Ji·xi |'jē'sHē| city in Heilongjiang province, NE China, on the Muling River E of Harbin. Pop. 684,000.

João Pes·soa |'zHownpe'sōwə| resort and industrial city in NE Brazil, on the Atlantic coast, capital of the state of Paraíba. Pop. 484,000.

Jo·burg |'jō,bərg| informal name for Jo-HANNESBURG, South Africa.

Jodh·pur |'jädpər; 'jäd,pŏŏr| **1** city in W India, in Rajasthan. Pop. 649,000. **2** a former princely state of India, now part of Rajasthan.

Jod·rell Bank |'jädrəl| scientific site in Cheshire, NW England, home to the Nuffield Radio Astronomy Laboratory, with one of the world's largest radio telescopes.

Jog·ja·kar·ta |ˌjawkjə'kärtə| variant spelling of YOGYAKARTA, Indonesia.

Jo·han·nes·burg |jō'hänəs,bərg; jō'hæn-əs,bərg| city in South Africa, the capital of the province of Gauteng. Pop. 1,916,000. It is the largest city in South Africa and the center of its gold-mining industry.

Jo·han·nis·berg |yō'hänis,berg| village in central Germany, near the Rhine River. Best known for its wine, it is also a health resort.

John Day River |'jän 'dā| river that flows 280 mi./450 km. across N Oregon to join the Columbia River E of The Dalles.

John o'Groats |ˌjän ə'grōts| village at the extreme NE point of the Scottish mainland.

John·son City |'jänsən| industrial city in NE Tennessee, part of a complex with Bristol and Kingsport. Pop. 49,381.

John·ston Atoll |'jänstən| atoll in the central Pacific, SW of Hawaii, controlled by the U.S. and used for military operations.

Johns·town |'jänz,town| industrial city in SW Pennsylvania, SE of Pittsburgh, noted as the site of a devastating 1889 flood. Pop. 28,134.

Jo·hor |jə'hawr| (also **Johore**) state of Malaysia, at the southernmost point of mainland Asia, joined to Singapore by a causeway. Pop. 2.1 million. Capital: Johor Baharu.

Jo·hor Ba·ha·ru |jə'hawr 'bähə,rōō| the capital of the state of Johor in Malaysia. Pop. 329,000.

Jo·li·et |ˌjōlē'et| industrial and commercial city in NE Illinois. Pop. 76,836.

Jo·lo |'hō,lō| (also called **Sulu**) **1** island in the Philippines, chief island in the Sulu Archipelago, between the Sulu Sea and the Celebes Sea. **2** its chief town. Pop. 53,000.

Jones·bo·ro |'jōnz,bərō| city in NE Arkansas. Pop. 46,535.

Jones·town |'jōnz,town| former religious settlement in the jungle of Guyana, established by Reverend Jim Jones with some 1,000 followers, almost all of whom died in a mass suicide in late 1978.

Jön·kö·ping |'yœn,sHœpiNG| industrial city in S Sweden, at the S end of Lake Vättern. Pop. 111,000.

Jon·quière |ˌzHawn'kyär| industrial city in S Quebec, on the Saguenay River just W of Chicoutimi. Pop. 57,993.

Jop·lin |'jäplən| industrial and commercial city in SW Missouri. Pop. 40,961.

Jop·pa biblical name for JAFFA.

Jor·dan |'jawrdn| country in the Middle East, east of the Jordan River. Area: 35,475 sq. mi./89,206 sq. km. Pop. 4,000,000. Language, Arabic. Capital and largest city: Amman. Official name **Hashemite King-**

dom of Jordan. In an area dominated by successive empires for centuries, Jordan gained independence from Britain in 1946. In 1948–49 it took over the WEST BANK, but lost it to Israel in 1967. The country is now home to many Palestinian refugees. Mining and tourism are important to its economy. □ **Jordanian** *adj. & n.*

Jordan

Jor•dan River |'jawrdn| river flowing S for 200 mi./320 km. from the Anti-Lebanon Mts. through the Sea of Galilee into the Dead Sea. John the Baptist baptized Christ in the Jordan. It is regarded as sacred not only by Christians but also by Jews and Muslims.

Jor•na•da del Muer•to |hawr'nädə del 'mwer₁tō| desert region in S New Mexico, near White Sands, famed as the "journey of death" for the difficulties it presented early travelers.

Josh•ua Tree National Park |'jäsHəwə| preserve in S California, noted for its desert plant and animal life.

Jo•tun•heim |'yōtn₁häm| **1** mountain range in S central Norway. Its highest peak is Glittertind 8,110 ft./2,472 m. **2** in Norse mythology, a part of the universe inhabited by giants.

Juan de Fu•ca Strait |'(h)wän dä 'fyōōkə| ocean passage between Vancouver Island, British Columbia, and the Olympic Peninsula of Washington.

Juan Fer•nan•dez Islands |'hwän fer-'nän₁däs| group of three almost uninhabited islands in the Pacific Ocean 400 mi./640 km. W of Chile.

Juan-les-Pins |₁ZHwäeNlä'peN| resort on the S coast of France, part of Antibes, on the Riviera, between Nice and Cannes, known for its fine beaches.

Juá•rez |'hwär₁es| another name for CIUDAD JUÁREZ, Mexico.

Juà•zei•ro do Nor•te |₁ZHwä'särōō dōō 'nawrtä| city in NE Brazil, in Ceará state,

an agricultural processing center. Pop. 186,000.

Ju•ba |'jōōbə| capital of the S region of Sudan, on the White Nile. Pop. 100,000.

Jub•ba |'jōōbə| (also **Juba**) a river in E Africa, rising in the highlands of central Ethiopia and flowing S for about 1,000 mi./1,600 km. through Somalia to the Indian Ocean. The surrounding territory was formerly known as **Jubaland**.

Ju•daea |jōō'dēə| the S part of ancient Palestine, corresponding to the former kingdom of Judah. The Jews returned to the region after the Babylonian Captivity, and in 165 B.C. the Maccabees again established it as an independent kingdom. It became a province of the Roman Empire in 63 B.C., and was subsequently amalgamated with Palestine. Also spelled **Judea**. □ **Judaean** *adj. & n.*

Juiz de Fo•ra |₁ZHwēz dē 'fawrə| industrial city in E Brazil, in Minas Gerais state, a textile-producing and rail center. Pop. 386,000.

Ju•juy |hōō'hwē| (official name **San Salvador de Jujuy**) historic city in extreme NW Argentina, capital of Jujuy province. Pop. 183,000. It processes sugar and other crops and has many manufacturers.

Ju•lian Alps |'jōōlyən| Alpine range in W Slovenia and NE Italy, rising to a height of 9,395 ft./2,863 m. at Triglav.

Jul•lun•dur |'jələndər| see JALANDHAR, India.

Jum•na |'jəmnə| river of N India, which rises in the Himalayas and flows in a large arc S and SE, through Delhi, joining the Ganges below Allahabad. Its source (Yamunotri) and its confluence with the Ganges are both Hindu holy places. Hindi name **Yamuna**.

Ju•na•ghad |jōō'nägəd| (also **Junagarh**) commercial town in W India, in Gujarat state. Pop. 167,000.

Jun•diai |₁ZHōōndyä'ē| industrial city in S Brazil, in São Paulo state. Pop. 286,000.

Ju•neau |'jōōnō| the capital of Alaska, a seaport on an inlet of the Pacific in the S panhandle. Pop. 26,751.

Jung•frau |'yōōNG₁frow| mountain in the Swiss Alps, 13,642 ft./4,158 m. high.

Ju•no Beach |'jōōnō| name given to one of three sections of the beach on the Normandy coast, NW France, that was the landing site for British troops on D-day in June 1944. It is centered around the village of Courseulles sur Mer.

Ju•ra¹ |'jōōrə| system of mountain ranges on the border of France and Switzerland.

It has given its name to the Jurassic period, when most of its rocks were laid down.

Ju•ra² |'jo͞orə| island of the Inner Hebrides, Scotland, N of Islay and S of Mull, separated from the W coast of Scotland by the Sound of Jura.

Ju•rong |'jo͞o'rawNG| industrial town, developed since the 1970s, in SW Singapore. Much of the Singapore workforce is employed here.

Ju•ruá River |zho͞or'wä| river that flows 1,500 mi./2,400 km. from E Peru through NW Brazil, into the Amazon River.

Jut•land |'jət,lənd| peninsula of NW Europe, forming the mainland of Denmark to-gether with the N German state of Schleswig-Holstein. Danish name **Jylland**.

Ju•ven•tud, Isla de la |'ēslä ,dā ,lä ,ho͞ovän 'to͞od| (English name **Isle of Youth**; formerly **Isle of Pines**) island off SW Cuba, in the Caribbean Sea. Pop. 71,000. Long a source of jurisdictional disputes between Cuba and the U.S., it has been a resort and prison colony. It was renamed in 1978 and has many facilities dedicated to youth.

Jyl•land |'yʏ,län| Danish name for JUT-LAND.

Jy•väs•ky•lä |'yʏväs,kʏlä| industrial port city in central Finland. Pop. 67,000.

Kk

K2 |'kä'toͦo| the highest mountain in the Karakoram range, on the border between Pakistan and China. It is the second highest peak in the world, rising to 28,250 ft./8,611 m. It was discovered in 1856 and named K2 because it was the second peak to be surveyed in the Karakoram range. It was also formerly known as Mount Godwin-Austen after Col. H. H. Godwin-Austen, who first surveyed it. Also called **Dapsang.**

Kaa·ba |'käbə| (also **Caaba**) a shrine within the Great Mosque at Mecca, Saudi Arabia, the focal point of the Muslim haj, or pilgrimage.

Ka·ba·le·ga Falls |,käbə'lägə| waterfall on the lower Victoria Nile near Lake Albert, in NW Uganda. Former name **Murchison Falls.**

Kabardino-Balkaria |,kəbər'dyēnəbawl'kärēə| autonomous republic of SW Russia, on the border with Georgia. Pop. 768,000. Capital: Nalchik. Also called **Kabarda-Balkar Republic.**

Ka·bul |'käbəl; 'kä,boͦol| the capital of Afghanistan. Pop. 700,000. It is situated in the NE of the country, with a strategic position commanding the mountain passes through the Hindu Kush, especially the Khyber Pass. It was capital of the Mogul Empire 1504–1738 and in 1773 replaced Kandahar as capital of an independent Afghanistan.

Ka·bwe |'käb,wä| mining town in central Zambia, to the N of Lusaka. Pop. 167,000. It is the site of a cave that has yielded human fossils associated with the Upper Pleistocene period. Former name (1904–65) **Broken Hill.**

Ka·by·lia |kä'bēlyə| name for regions of the Atlas Mts. in Algeria that are occupied by the Kabyle, a Berber people.

Ka·chin |.kä'CHin| state in N Burma, on the frontier with China and India. Pop. 804,000. Capital: Myitkyina.

Ka·di·köy |kä'dəkœi| Turkish name for CHALCEDON.

Ka·do·ma |.kä'dōmä| city in W central Japan, on S Honshu, an industrial and residential suburb N of Osaka. Pop. 142,000.

Kae·song |'gä'sawNG| commercial and industrial city in S North Korea, on the 38th Parallel (the South Korean border). Pop. 346,000. An ancient city, it was the scene of armistice talks at the end of the Korean War.

Ka·fue River |kä'foͦoä| river that flows 600 mi./965 km. from N Zambia across the country to the Zambezi River. Kafue National Park lies in its floodplains.

Ka·ge·ra River |kä'gärä| river that flows 250 mi./400 km. from NW Tanzania, along the Rwanda and Uganda borders, into Lake Victoria. It is the farthest headwater of the Nile River.

Ka·go·shi·ma |kägō'SHēmə| city and port in Japan. Pop. 537,000. Situated on the S coast of Kyushu, on the Satsuma Peninsula, it is noted for its porcelain (Satsuma ware).

Ka·ho·o·la·we |kä,hō-ō'läwä| island in Hawaii, SW of Maui, formerly used as a military range.

Kah·ra·man·ma·raş historic commercial city in central Turkey, capital of Kahramanmaraş province. Pop. 228,000. It was a Hittite center in the 9th century B.C.

Kai·bab Plateau |'kī,bæb| highland region of NW Arizona, N of the Grand Canyon, and adjoining S Utah.

Kai·feng |'kī'fəNG| city in Henan province, E China, on the Yellow River. Pop. 693,000. One of the oldest cities in China, as Bianliang it was the Chinese capital from A.D. 907 to A.D. 1127.

Kai Islands |'kī| island group in Indonesia, in the SE Moluccas, in the Banda Sea between Ceram Island (NW) and the Aru Islands (E).

Kai·las |kī'läs| (also called **Kangrinboqê Feng**) peak, SW Tibet; the highest peak in the Kailas, or Gangdisê, Mts.: 22,027 ft./6,714 m. It is near the headwaters of the Indus and Brahmaputra rivers and is sacred to Hindus.

Kai·lua |kī'loͦoə| community in SE Oahu, Hawaii, on the Pacific NE of Honolulu. Pop. 36,818.

Kai·pa·ro·wits Plateau |kī'pärəwits| highland region in S central Utah, N of Lake Powell.

Kair·ouan |ker'wän| city in NE Tunisia. Pop. 72,000. It is a Muslim holy city and a place of pilgrimage.

Kai·sers·lau·tern |,kīzərz'lowtərn| industrial city in western Germany, in Rhineland-Palatinate. Pop. 101,000.

Ka·ki·na·da |,käki'nädə| (formerly **Cocanada**) commercial port city in SE India, on the Bay of Bengal in Andhra Pradesh state. Pop. 327,000.

Ka•ko•ga•wa |ˌkäkōʹgäwä| industrial city in W central Japan, on S Honshu, W of Kobe. Pop. 240,000.

Ka•laal•lit Nu•naat |käˈlä(t)lēt nooʹnät| Inuit name for GREENLAND.

Ka•la•ha•ri Desert |ˌkäləʹhärē| high, vast, arid plateau in southern Africa N of the Orange River. It comprises most of Botswana with parts in Namibia and South Africa.

Kal•a•ma•ta |ˌkäləʹmätə| see CALAMATA, Greece.

Kal•a•ma•zoo |ˌkæləməʹzoo| industrial and commercial city in SW Michigan. Pop. 80,277.

Kal•gan |ˈkælʹgæn| Mongolian name for ZHANGJIAKOU, China.

Kal•goor•lie |kælʹgoorlē| gold-mining town in Western Australia, focus of a gold rush in the 1890s. Pop. 11,000.

Ka•li•man•tan |ˌkälēʹmän,tän| region of Indonesia, comprising the S part of the island of Borneo.

Kalinin |kəˈlēnen| former name (1931–91) for TVER, Russia.

Ka•li•nin•grad |kəˈlēnen,grəd| **1** port on the Baltic Sea, capital of the Russian region of Kaliningrad. Pop. 406,000. It was known by its German name of Königsberg until 1946, when it was ceded to the Soviet Union and renamed in honor of Soviet President Mikhail Kalinin. Its port is ice-free all year round and is a major naval base. **2** region of Russia, an exclave on the Baltic coast of E Europe. Capital: Kaliningrad. It is separated from Russia by the territory of Lithuania, Latvia, and Belarus.

Ka•lisz |ˈkälēsH| industrial city in central Poland. Pop. 106,000.

Kal•mar |ˈkäl,mär| port in SE Sweden, on the Kalmar Sound opposite Öland. Pop. 56,000.

Kal•mar Sound |ˈkäl,mär| narrow strait between the mainland of SE Sweden and the island of Öland, in the Baltic Sea.

Kal•my•kia |kælʹmikēə| autonomous republic in SW Russia, on the Caspian Sea. Pop. 325,000. Capital: Elista. Official name **Republic of Kalmykia-Khalmg Tangch**.

Ka•lu•ga |kəˈloogə| industrial city and river port in European Russia, on the Oka River SW of Moscow. Pop. 314,000.

Kal•yan |kəlˈyän| commercial and industrial city on the W coast of India, in the state of Maharashtra, NE of Bombay. Pop. 1,014,000.

Ka•ma River |ˈkämə| river (1,128 mi./1,805 km.) in Russia that rises in the central Ural Mts. and flows to the Volga River near Kazan.

Ka•ma•ku•ra |ˌkämäʹkoo,rä| historic town in E central Japan, on E central Honshu. Pop. 174,000. It is noted chiefly as a religious center.

Ka•mar•ha•ti |ˌkämərʹhätē| industrial city in NE India, in West Bengal state, a suburb of Calcutta. Pop. 266,000.

Kam•chat•ka |kəmʹcHätkə| vast mountainous peninsula of the NE coast of Siberian Russia, separating the Sea of Okhotsk from the Bering Sea; chief port, Petropavlovsk.

Ka•men•skoye |ˈkäminskəyə| former name (until 1936) for DNIPRODZERZHINSK, Ukraine.

Kamensk-Uralsky |ˈkäminsk ooˈrälskyē| industrial city in central Russia, in the E foothills of the Urals. Pop. 208,000.

Ka•menz |ˈkä,ments| industrial city in E Germany, on the Schwarze Elster River. Pop. 19,000.

Ka•mien•na Gó•ra |käˈmyenä ʹgoorə| (German name **Landshut**) industrial and commercial center in W Poland. Pop. 93,000.

Kam•loops |ˈkæm,loops| city in S central British Columbia, an administrative, commercial, and transportation center. Pop. 67,057.

Kam•pa•la |kämʹpälə| the capital of Uganda. Pop. 773,000. It is situated on the N shores of Lake Victoria and replaced Entebbe as capital when the country became independent in 1963.

Kam•pu•chea |ˌkämpəʹcHēə; ˌkæmpə ʹcHēə| former name (1976–89) for CAMBODIA. □ **Kampuchean** adj. & n.

Ka•nan•ga |kəˈnänGgə| (formerly **Luluabourg**) commercial city in S central Congo (formerly Zaire), on the Lulua River. Pop. 372,000. It is in an agricultural and diamond-mining area.

Ka•na•ta |kəˈnætə| city in SE Ontario, an industrial and residential suburb W of Ottawa. Pop. 37,344.

Ka•na•wha River |kəˈnaw-wə; kəˈnoi| river in W central West Virginia that connects the New River with the Ohio River. Charleston and other industrial centers lie along it.

Ka•na•za•wa |ˌkänäʹzäwä| port city in central Japan, on central Honshu. Pop. 443,000. An agricultural, industrial and tourist center, it was once the seat of powerful feudal lords.

Kan•chen•jun•ga |ˌkəncHənʹjooNGgə| (also **Kangchenjunga** or **Kinchinjunga**) a mountain in the Himalayas, on the border between Nepal and Sikkim. Rising to a height of 28,209 ft./8,598 m., it is the world's third-highest mountain.

Kan·chi·pu·ram |kənˈCHēpərəm| (formerly **Conjeeveram**) city in S India, in Tamil Nadu state, W of Madras. Pop. 171,000. An ancient city with many temples, it is one of the most sacred Hindu towns in India.

Kan·da·har |ˌkəndəˈhär| city in S Afghanistan. Pop. 225,000. It was Afghanistan's first capital after independence (1748), until being replaced by Kabul in 1773.

Kan·dy |ˈkændē| city in Sri Lanka. Pop. 104,000. It was the capital (1480–1815) of the former independent kingdom of Kandy and contains one of the most sacred Buddhist shrines, the Dalada Maligava (Temple of the Tooth). □ **Kandyan** adj. & n.

Ka·ne·o·he |ˌkänäˈōhä| community in E Oahu, Hawaii, a largely residential suburb NE of Honolulu. Pop. 35,448.

Kan·gar |ˈkäNGˌgär| the capital of the state of Perlis in N Malaysia, near the W coast of the Malay Peninsula. Pop. 13,000.

Ka·Ngwa·ne |käNGˈ(g)wänä| former homeland established in South Africa for the Swazi people, now part of the province of Mpumalanga.

Kan·ka·kee |ˌkæNGkəˈkē| city in NE Illinois, on the Kankakee River. Pop. 27,575.

Kan·kan |käNˈkäN| commercial town in E central Guinea, a rail center and port on the Milo River. Pop. 100,000.

Ka·no |ˈkänō| commercial, industrial, and cultural city in N Nigeria. Pop. 553,000.

Kan·pur |ˈkän,pŏŏr| (also **Cawnpore**) industrial city in Uttar Pradesh, N India, on the Ganges River. Pop. 2,100,000.

Kan·sas |ˈkænzəs| see box. □ **Kansan** adj. & n.

Kan·sas City |ˌkænzəs| each of two adjacent cities in the U.S., at the junction of the Missouri and Kansas rivers, one in NE Kansas (pop. 149,767) and the other in NW Missouri (pop. 435,146). Together they are an industrial, commercial, and rail complex.

Kan·su |ˈkänˈsŏŏ| see GANSU, China.

Kan·to |ˈkäntō| region of Japan, on the island of Honshu. Capital: Tokyo.

Kao·hsiung |ˈgowSHēˈŏŏNG| the chief port of Taiwan, on the SW coast. Pop. 1,390,000.

Ka·pa·chi·ra Falls waterfall on the Shire River in S Malawi. Former name **Murchison Rapids**.

Kansas

Capital: Topeka
Largest city: Wichita
Other cities: Kansas City, Lawrence, Leavenworth, Overland Park, Salina
Population: 2,477,574 (1990); 2,629,067 (1998); 2,668,000 (2005 proj.)
Population rank (1990): 32
Rank in land area: 15
Abbreviation: KS; Kans.
Nicknames: Sunflower State; Wheat State; Breadbasket of America; Jayhawk State
Motto: Ad Astra per Aspera (Latin: 'To the Stars Through Difficulties')
Bird: western meadowlark
Flower: sunflower
Tree: cottonwood
Song: "Home on the Range"
Noted physical features: Great Plains, Osage Plains; Mount Sunflower
Tourist attractions: Eisenhower Center; Fort Riley, Fort Scott; Haskell Institute Indian Training School; Leavenworth Penitentiary; Tuttle Creek Reservoir
Admission date: January 29, 1861
Order of admission: 34
Name origin: For the Kansas River, the name of which first applied to Indians living along it; the name is a Siouan word, Kansa, translated 'people of the south wind.'

Kap Far·vel |ˌkæp ˈfär,vel| Danish name for Cape FAREWELL, Greenland.

Ka·pi·la·vas·tu |ˌkəpiləˈvəstŏŏ| town and principality of ancient India, birthplace of the Buddha (c.563 B.C.); in present-day Nepal.

Ka·pos·var |ˈkawpōSH,vär| commercial city in SW Hungary. Pop. 74,000. It is the capital of Somogy county.

Kara-Bogaz Gol |kä'rä bə'gäz'gawl| (also **Garabogazkol**) shallow salt lake in NW Turkmenistan, an inlet of the Caspian Sea separated by dike in the 1970s. Chemical industries are important in the area.

Karachai-Cherkessia autonomous republic in the N Caucasus, SW Russia. Pop. 436,000. Capital: Cherkessk. Official name **Karachai-Cherkess Republic**.

Ka·ra·chi |kəˈräCHē| major city and port in Pakistan, capital of Sind province. Pop. 6,700,000. Situated on the Arabian Sea, it was the capital of Pakistan 1947–59 before being replaced by Rawalpindi.

Ka·ra·fu·to |ˌkärä'fo͞otō| the Japanese name for the S part of the island of Sakhalin.

Ka·ra·gan·da |ˌkärə'gändə| Russian name for QARAGHANDY, Kazakhstan.

Ka·raj |kä'räj| city in N Iran, to the west of Tehran. Pop. 442,000.

Kar·a·ko·ram |ˌkärə'kawrəm| great mountain system of central Asia, extending over 300 mi./480 km. SE from NE Afghanistan to Kashmir and forming part of the borders of India and Pakistan with China. One of the highest mountain systems in the world, it consists of a group of parallel ranges, forming a W continuation of the Himalayas, with many peaks over 26,000 ft./7,900 m., the highest being K2. Virtually inaccessible, it also contains the highest passes in the world, at elevations over 16,000 ft./4,900 m., including Karakoram Pass and Khardungla Pass.

Kar·a·ko·rum |ˌkärə'kawrəm| ancient city in central Mongolia, now ruined, which was the capital of the Mongol Empire, established by Genghis Khan in 1220. The capital was moved to Khanbaliq (modern Beijing) in 1267, and Karakorum was destroyed by Chinese forces in 1388.

Ka·ra Kul, Lake |ˌkärä 'ko͞ol| (also **Qara Kul**) lake in E Tajikistan, in the Pamirs plateau.

Ka·ra Kum |ˌkärə 'ko͞om| desert in central Asia, to the E of the Caspian Sea, covering much of Turkmenistan. Russian name **Karakumy**.

Ka·ra Sea |'kärə| arm of the Arctic Ocean off the N coast of Russia, bounded to the E by the islands of Severnaya Zemlya and to the W by Novaya Zemlya.

Ka·ra·wan·ken Alps |ˌkärə'väNGkən| (Italian name **Caravanche**) range of the E Alps along the Austria-Slovenia border, rising to 7,341 ft./2,238 m. at Hochstule.

Kar·ba·la |'kärbələ| city in S Iraq. Pop. 185,000. A holy city for Shiite Muslims, it is the site of the tomb of Husayn, grandson of Muhammad, who was killed here in A.D. 680.

Ka·re·lia |kə'rēlyə| region of NE Europe on the border between Russia and Finland. Following Finland's declaration of independence in 1917, part of Karelia became a region of Finland and part an autonomous republic of the Soviet Union. After the Russo-Finnish war of 1939–40 the greater part of Finnish Karelia was ceded to the Soviet Union. The remaining part of Karelia constitutes a province of eastern Finland. □ **Karelian** adj. & n.

Ka·ren State |kə'ren| state in SE Burma, on the border with Thailand. Capital: Pa-an. Inaugurated in 1954 as an autonomous state of Burma, it was given the traditional Karen name of Kawthoolay in 1964, but reverted to Karen after the 1974 constitution limited its autonomy. Starting in 1995 a rebel army, the Karen National Union, engaged in armed conflict with the Burmese government in an attempt to gain independence. Also called **Kawthoolay**, **Kawthulei**.

Ka·ri·ba, Lake |kə'rēbə| artificial lake on the Zambia–Zimbabwe border in central Africa. It was created by the damming of the Zambezi River by the Kariba Dam, and is the chief source of hydroelectric power for Zimbabwe and Zambia.

Ka·ri·ba Dam |kə'rēbə| concrete arch dam on the Zambezi River, 240 mi./385 km. downstream from the Victoria Falls. It was built in 1955–59.

Ka·ri·ya |kä'rēyä| industrial city in central Japan, on central Honshu, SE of Nagoya. Pop. 120,000.

Karl-Marx-Stadt |'kärl 'märks ˌSHtät| former name (1953–90) for CHEMNITZ, Germany.

Kar·lo·vac |'kärlə,väts| industrial town in NW Croatia, on the Kupa River. Pop. 60,000.

Kar·lo·vy Va·ry |'kärlōvē 'värē| spa town in the W Czech Republic. Pop. 56,000. It is famous for its alkaline thermal springs. German name **Karlsbad**.

Karls·kro·na |ˌkärl'skro͞onə| seaport and fishing center in SE Sweden, on the Baltic Sea, capital of Belkinge province. Pop. 59,000.

Karls·ru·he |'kärls,ro͞oə| industrial town and port on the Rhine in western Germany. Pop. 279,000.

Karl·stad |'kärl,städ| industrial town in central Sweden, on the N shore of Lake Vänern. Pop. 76,000.

Kar·nak |'kär,næk| village in Egypt on the Nile, now largely amalgamated with Luxor. It is the site of the N complex of monuments of ancient Thebes, including the great temple of Amun.

Kar·nal |kər'näl| historic city in NW India, in Haryana state. Pop. 176,000.

Kar·na·ta·ka |ˌkär'nätəkə| state in SW India. Pop. 44.82 million. Capital: Bangalore. Former name (until 1973) **Mysore**.

Kärn·ten |'kernten| German name for CARINTHIA, Austria.

Ka·roo, the |kə'ro͞o| (also **Karroo**) elevated semidesert plateau in South Africa, used for grazing.

Kár·pa·thos |ˈkärpə,THaws| island in Greece, in the Aegean Sea between Crete and Rhodes. Pop.5,000. Its largest town is Karpathos.

Kars |kärs| city in NE Turkey, in Kars province. Pop. 78,000. A historic Armenian city, Kars is noted for its crafts.

Kar·shi |ˈkärsHē| (also **Qarshi**; formerly **Bek-Budi**) transportation center in SE Uzbekistan. Pop. 168,000.

Karst |kärst| (in Slovenian **Kras**) limestone region near Trieste in Slovenia, noted for its geologic formations. Its name is used by geologists to describe similar limestone regions elsewhere.

Ka·sai River |käˈsī| (also **Cassai**) river that flows 1,100 mi./1,800 km. from central Angola through S and central Congo (formerly Zaire), into the Congo River. In its lower 500 mi./800 km. it is an important trade route.

Ka·shan |käˈsHän| oasis town in central Iran, N of Isfahan. Pop. 155,000. It has long been noted for its carpets.

Ka·shi |ˈkäˈsHē| (also called **Kashgar**) chief commercial city of W Xinjiang, NW China, on the Kashgar River. Pop. 175,000. It is a fertile oasis on the former Silk Road.

Ka·shi·wa |käˈsHēwä| city in E central Japan, on E central Honshu, NE of Tokyo. Pop. 305,000.

Kash·mir, Vale of |ˈkæsH,mir; kæsHˈmir| Himalayan valley in Jammu and Kashmir, N India, on the Jhelum River and lakes, noted for its beauty.

Kash·mir |ˈkæsH,mir; kæsHˈmir| region on the N border of India and NE Pakistan. Formerly a state of India, it has been disputed between India and Pakistan since partition in 1947, with sporadic outbreaks of fighting. The NW part is controlled by Pakistan, most of it forming the state of Azad Kashmir, while the remainder is incorporated into the Indian state of Jammu and Kashmir. Formerly spelled **Cashmere**. □ **Kashmiri** adj. & n.

Kas·sa·la |ˈkäsə,lə| (also **Kasala**) historic commercial town in E Sudan, near the Eritrean border. Pop. 146,000.

Kas·sel |ˈkäsəl| industrial city in central Germany, in Hesse. Pop. 197,000. It was the capital of the kingdom of Westphalia (1807–13) and of the Prussian province of Hesse-Nassau (1866–1944).

Kas·ser·ine Pass |ˈkäsə,rēn| historic site near the village of Al-Qasrayn, N central Tunisia. A gap in an extension of the Atlas Mts., it was fought over by German and American forces in February 1943.

Ka·su·gai |käˈsōōgī| industrial city in central Japan, on S central Honshu, a suburb N of Nagoya. Pop. 267,000.

Ka·su·ka·be |,käs(ōō)ˈkäbä| city in E central Japan, on E central Honshu, N of Tokyo. Pop. 189,000.

Ka·sur |käˈsōōr| city in Punjab province, NE Pakistan. Pop. 155,000.

Ka·tah·din, Mount |kəˈtädn| (also **Ktaadn**) peak in N central Maine, in Baxter State Park. At 5,267 ft./1,606 m., it is the highest point in the state. The N end of the Appalachian Trail is here.

Ka·tan·ga |kəˈtaNGgə| former name (until 1972) for SHABA, Congo (formerly Zaire).

Ka·thi·a·war |,kätēəˈwär| peninsula on the W coast of India, in the state of Gujarat, separating the Gulf of Kutch from the Gulf of Cambay.

Kath·man·du |,kätmænˈdōō| (also **Katmandu**) historic city, the capital of Nepal. Pop. 419,000. It is situated in the Himalayas at an altitude of 4,450 ft./1,370 m.

Kat·mai National Park |ˈkæt,mī| preserve in SW Alaska, on the Alaska Peninsula, noted for its volcanic activity and wildlife.

Ka·to·wi·ce |,kätəˈvētsə| city in SW Poland. Pop. 349,000. It is the industrial center of the Silesian coal-mining region.

Ka·tsi·na |ˈkätsēnə| commercial and industrial city in N Nigeria, near the Niger border and NW of Kano. Pop. 182,000. It was the capital of the Kingdom of Katsina, part of HAUSALAND.

Kat·te·gat |ˈkætə,gæt; ˈkät.ə,gät| strait, 140 mi./225 km. in length, between Sweden and Denmark. It is linked to the North Sea by the Skagerrak and to the Baltic Sea by the Øresund.

Kau·ai |ˈkow,ī| island in the state of Hawaii, separated from Oahu by the Kauai Channel; chief town, Lihue.

Kau·nas |ˈkownəs| industrial city and river port in southern Lithuania, at the confluence of the Viliya and Neman rivers. Pop. 430,000. It was the capital of Lithuania 1918–40.

Ka·vál·la |käˈvälä| port on the Aegean coast of NE Greece. Pop. 57,000. Originally a Byzantine city and fortress, it was Turkish until 1912, when it was ceded to Greece.

Ka·ve·ri |ˈkävərē| see CAUVERY River, India.

Ka·wa·goe |käˈwägō,ā| city in E central Japan, on E central Honshu, NW of Tokyo. Pop. 305,000.

Ka·wa·gu·chi |,käwäˈgōōCHē| industrial city in E central Japan, on E central Honshu, a suburb N of Tokyo. Pop. 439,000.

Ka·wa·sa·ki |ˌkäwəˈsäkē| industrial city on the SE coast of the island of Honshu, Japan. Pop. 1,174,000.

Kaw·thoo·lay |ˌkawTHo͞oˈlä| (also **Kaw-thulei**) former name (1964–74) for KAREN STATE, Burma.

Kay·se·ri |ˈkīsərē| city in central Turkey, capital of a province of the same name. Pop. 421,000. Known as Kayseri since the 11th century, it was formerly called Caesarea Mazaca and was the capital of Cappadocia.

Ka·zakh·stan |kəzäkˈstän| (also spelled **Kazakstan**) republic in central Asia, on the S border of Russia, extending from the Caspian Sea E to the Altai Mts. and China. Area: 1.05 million sq. mi./2.72 million sq. km. Pop.: 16,899,000. Languages, Kazakh (official), Russian. Capital: Aqmola (Akmola). Largest city: Almaty. A Turkic homeland later dominated by Mongols, Kazakhstan eventually was absorbed into the Russian Empire. In 1991 it gained independence as the Soviet Union dissolved. Rich in reources, the country is characterized by nomadic pastoralism, crops including cotton and grains, and growing industry. □ **Kazakh** adj. & n

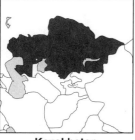

Kazakhstan

Ka·zan |kəˈzän(yə)| port on the Volga River to the E of Nizhni Novgorod in Russia, capital of the autonomous republic of Tatarstan. Pop. 1,103,000.

Ka·zan·luk |ˌkäzänˈlək| (also **Kazanlik**) industrial city in central Bulgaria, near the Valley of the Roses. Pop. 62,000.

Kaz·bek |kəzˈbyek| extinct volcano in Georgia, in the central Caucasus Mts., rising over the Daryal Pass. Height: 16,558 ft./5,056 m.

Kear·ny |ˈkärnē| industrial town in NE New Jersey, on Newark Bay, just W of Jersey City. Pop. 34,874.

Keb·ne·kai·se |ˌkebneˈkīsə| the highest peak in Sweden, in the N of the country, rising to a height of 6,962 ft./2,117 m.

Ke·dah |ˈkedə| state of NW Malaysia, on

the W coast of the Malay Peninsula. Pop. 1,413,000. Capital: Alor Setar.

Ke·di·ri |kāˈdirē| city in Indonesia, on E Java. Pop. 250,000. It is famous for handicrafts such as batik.

Kee·ling Islands |ˈkēliNG| another name for COCOS ISLANDS.

Kee·lung |ˈkēˈlo͝oNG| see CHILUNG, Taiwan.

Keene |kēn| city in SW New Hampshire. Pop. 22,430.

Ke·fal·lin·ía |ˌkefälēˈnēä| Greek name for CEPHALONIA.

Kef·la·vik |ˈkyeblə,vēk; ˈkeflə,vik| fishing port in SW Iceland. Pop. 8,000. Iceland's international airport is located nearby.

Ke·lang |kəˈläNG| (also called **Port Kelang**; also **Klang**) port city in Malaysia, on the Strait of Malacca in Selangor state. Pop. 368,000. It is Malaysia's busiest international port.

Ke·lan·tan |kəˈlän,tän| state of N Malaysia, on the E coast of the Malay Peninsula. Pop. 1,220,000. Capital: Kota Baharu.

Kells |kelz| see CEANNANUS MOR, Ireland.

Kelmscott |ˈkelmskət; ˈkelm,skät| (also **Kelmscot**) village in Oxfordshire, S England, longtime home of the writer and designer William Morris, and associated with the Arts and Crafts movement of the late 19th century.

Ke·low·na |kiˈlōnə| city in S British Columbia, on Okanagan Lake, in an agricultural and resort area. Pop. 75,950.

Ke·me·ro·vo |ˈkyemə,rōvə; ˈkyemərə,vō| industrial city in S central Russia, to the E of Novosibirsk. Pop. 521,000.

Ke·nai Peninsula |ˈkē,nī| region in S Alaska, in the Gulf of Alaska just S of Anchorage.

Ken·dal |ˈkendəl| resort town in Cumbria, NW England, in the Lake District. Pop. 24,200.

Ken·il·worth |ˈkenl,wərTH| commercial town in central England, in Warwickshire, SW of Coventry. Pop. 17,000. It is associated with the novels of Walter Scott.

Ke·ni·tra |kəˈnētrə| (formerly **Port Lyautey**) river port city in N Morocco, NE of Rabat and near the Atlantic coast, on the Sebou River. Pop. 293,000.

Ken·ne·bec River |ˈkenə,bek| river that flows 150 mi./240 km. through W central Maine to the Atlantic. Waterville, Augusta, and Bath lie on it.

Ken·ner |ˈkenər| city in SE Louisiana, a suburb W of New Orleans. Pop. 72,033.

Ken·ne·wick |ˈkenə,wik| city in SE Washington, on the Columbia River. The nuclear industry at nearby Hanford has been central to its economy. Pop. 42,155.

Ke·no·sha |kəˈnōSHə| industrial port city in SE Wisconsin, on Lake Michigan. Pop. 80,352.

Ken·sing·ton |ˈkensiNGtən; ˈkenziNGtən| fashionable residential district in central London, England, part of the borough of Kensington and Chelsea. Pop. 128,000.

Kent[1] |kent| county on the SE coast of England. Pop.: 1,486,000; county seat, Maidstone. □ **Kentish** *adj. & n.*

Kent[2] |kent| city in NE Ohio, home to Kent State University. Pop. 28,835.

Ken·tucky |kənˈtəkē| see box. □ **Kentuckian** *adj. & n.*

Ken·ya, Mount |ˈkenyə; ˈkēnyə| mountain in central Kenya, just S of the equator, rising to a height of 17,058 ft./5,200 m. The second-highest mountain in Africa, it gave its name to the country Kenya.

Ken·ya |ˈkenyə; ˈkēnyə| equatorial republic in E Africa, on the Indian Ocean. Area: 225,047 sq. mi./582,646 sq. km. Pop. 25,016,000. Languages, Swahili (official), English (official), Kikuyu. Capital and largest city: Nairobi. Peopled largely by Bantu speakers, Kenya came under British domination in the early 20th century, and gained independence in 1963. Tea and coffee are important products, and tourism is also important. Most of the N is sparsely populated semidesert. □ **Kenyan** *adj. & n.*

Kenya

Ke·o·kuk |ˈkēəˌkək| city in SE Iowa, on the Mississippi River. Pop. 12,451.

Ke·ra·la |ˈkerələ| state on the coast of SW India. Pop. 29,010,000. Capital: Trivandrum. It was created in 1956 from the former state of Travancore-Cochin and part of Madras. □ **Keralite** *adj. & n.*

Kerch |ˈkerCH| city in S Ukraine, the chief port and industrial center of the Crimea, at the E end of the Kerch Peninsula. Pop. 176,000.

Kentucky

Official name: Commonwealth of Kentucky
Capital: Frankfort
Largest city: Louisville
Other cities: Bowling Green, Covington, Lexington, Paducah
Population: 3,685,296 (1990); 3,936,499 (1998); 4,098,000 (2005 proj.)
Population rank (1990): 23
Rank in land area: 37
Abbreviation: KY; Ky.
Nicknames: Bluegrass State; Dark and Bloody Ground
Motto: 'United We Stand, Divided We Fall'
Bird: cardinal
Fish: bass
Flower: goldenrod
Tree: Kentucky coffee tree
Song: "My Old Kentucky Home"
Noted physical features: Bluegrass Basin; Mammoth Cave; Land Between the Lakes; Cumberland Gap; Cumberland Plateau; Black Mountain
Tourist attractions: Birthplace of Abraham Lincoln; Fort Knox; Mammoth Cave National Park; Kentucky Derby; Churchill Downs; Wilderness Trail
Admission date: June 1, 1792
Order of admission: 15
Name origin: Named when the territory was established as a county of Virginia in 1776, from a Wyandot word *ken-tah-teh*, meaning 'land of tomorrow.'

Ker·gue·len Islands |ˈkərgəˌlən; ˌkergāˈlen| group of islands in the S Indian Ocean, comprising the island of Kerguelen and some 300 small islets, forming part of French Southern and Antarctic Territories.

Kér·ki·ra |ˈkerkirə| modern Greek name for CORFU.

Kerk·ra·de |ˈkərkˌrädə| mining town in the S Netherlands, on the German border. Pop. 53,000. An international music competition is held here every four years.

Ker·mad·ec Islands |kərˈmədek| group of uninhabited islands in the W South Pacific, N of New Zealand, administered by New Zealand since 1887.

Ker·man |kərˈmän| (formerly called **Carmana**) historic desert city in SE Iran. Pop. 312,000.

Ker·man·shah |kərˌmänˈSHä| another name for BAKHTARAN, Iran.

Ker·ry |ˈkerē| county of the Republic of Ireland, on the SW coast in the province of

Munster. Pop. 122,000; county seat, Tralee.

Ker·u·len River |'kerə,len| (also called **Herlen**) river of NE Mongolia and NE China. Rising in the Hentiyn Nuruu range NE of Ulan Bator, Mongolia, it flows 785 mi./1,263 km. S and E to Hulun Lake in Heilongjiang province, China.

Kes·te·ven |kes'tēvən| one of three administrative divisions of Lincolnshire, England before the local government reorganization of 1974, now administered as the districts of North and South Kesteven.

Kes·wick |'kezik| market and resort town on the shores of Derwent Water in Cumbria, NW England. Pop. 6,000.

Ket River |'ket| river (842 mi./1,355 km) in SE Russia. It rises N of Krasnoyarsk and flows W into the Ob River at Kolpashevo.

Ketch·i·kan |'keCHi,kæn| city in SE Alaska, on Revillagigedo Island in the Alexander Archipelago. Pop. 8,263.

Ket·ter·ing |'ketəriNG| city in SW Ohio, an industrial and residential suburb SE of Dayton. Pop. 60,569.

Kew Gardens |'kyoo| the Royal Botanic Gardens at Kew, in Richmond, SW London, England.

Key Largo |'kē 'lär,gō| resort island off the S coast of Florida, the S and the longest of the Florida Keys.

Key·stone State |'kē,stōn| nickname for PENNSYLVANIA.

Key West |'kē 'west| resort city in southern Florida, at the S tip of the Florida Keys. Pop. 24,832. It is the southernmost city in the U.S. outside Hawaii.

Kha·ba·rovsk |kə'bärərəfsk| industrial city in Siberian Russia, on the Amur River and the Chinese border. Pop. 608,000.

Kha·kas·sia |kə'käsyə| autonomous republic in S central Russia. Pop. 569,000. Capital: Abakan.

Kha·li·stan |,kälə'stän| the name given by Sikh nationalists to a proposed independent Sikh state, created chiefly from Indian territory.

Khal·kís |KHäl'kēs| Greek name for CHALCIS.

Khan·ba·lik |,känbä'lēk| see BEIJING, China.

Kha·niá |KHän'yä| Greek name for CHANIA, Crete.

Khan·ka, Lake |'käNGkə| lake that lies on the boundary between China and Primorsky Krai, SE Russia, N of Vladivostok. Most of the lake lies in Russia.

Kha·rag·pur |'kərəg,poor| industrial town in NE India, in West Bengal state, W of Calcutta. Pop. 280,000.

Kharg Island |'kärg| small island at the head of the Persian Gulf, site of Iran's principal deep-water oil terminal.

Khar·kiv |'KHärkəf| (formerly **Kharkov**) industrial and commercial city in NE Ukraine, in the Donets basin. Pop. 1,618,000. It was the capital of Soviet Ukraine 1919–34, before Kiev.

Khar·toum |kär'toom| the capital of Sudan, situated at the junction of the Blue Nile and the White Nile. Pop. 925,000. Originally a 19th-century military garrison, it now has administrative and industrial zones.

Khas·ko·vo |'käskə,vō| capital city of Khaskovo province, central Bulgaria. Pop. 95,000. It processes tobacco.

Khay·lit·sa |'kī,lētsə| township 25 mi./40 km. SE of Cape Town, South Africa. Pop. 190,000. It was built in 1983 for African workers from several nearby squatter camps.

Kha·zar·ia |kə'zärēə| ancient region of SE Russia, important for its strategic location along trade routes between the Black and Caspian seas.

Kher·son |KHer'sawn| industrial and oil port in S Ukraine, on the Dnieper estuary near the Black Sea. Pop. 361,000.

Khe Sanh |'kä'sän| site, in N central Vietnam, of one of the costliest battles of the Vietnam War.

Khi·os |'KHē,aws| Greek name for CHIOS.

Khi·va |'KHēvä| (ancient name **Chorasmia**) former khanate on the left bank of the Amu Darya River, in what is now NW Uzbekistan. The region is largely desert. Its capital is the oasis town of Khiva.

Khmel·nit·sky |KHmel'nitskē| (also **Khmelnytskyy**) industrial city in W Ukraine, SW of Kiev. Pop. 241,000.

Khmer Republic |kə'mer| former official name (1970–75) for CAMBODIA.

Khon Kaen |'kawn 'kän| town in E central Thailand, on the Korat Plateau, NE of Bangkok. Pop. 131,000.

Kho·per River |KHə'pyawr| river (625 mi./1,010 km.) in SW Russia. It rises SW of Penza and flows into the Don River.

Khor·ram·shahr |,kawrəm'sHHər| oil port on the Shatt al-Arab waterway in W Iran. It was almost totally destroyed during the Iran-Iraq War of 1980–88. Former name (until 1924) **Mohammerah**.

Khudzhand |KHoo'jät| (also **Khodzhent**; formerly **Leninabad**; earlier, **Khojend**) town in NW Tajikistan, on the Syr Darya

River. Pop. 165,000. It is a textile center and one of the oldest towns in central Asia.

Khul·na |'kōōlnä| industrial city in S Bangladesh, on the Ganges delta. Pop. 601,000.

Khun·je·rab Pass |'kənjə,rəb| high-altitude pass through the Himalayas, on the Karakoram highway at a height of 16,088 ft./4,900 m., linking China and Pakistan.

Khu·ze·stan |ˌKHŌŌZHi'stän| province in SW Iraq. Pop. 3,176,000. Capital: Ahvaz. It is rich in oil fields.

Khy·ber Pass |'kībər| mountain pass in the Hindu Kush, on the border between Pakistan and Afghanistan at a height of 3,520 ft./1,067 m. The pass was once of great commercial and strategic importance, the route by which successive invaders entered India, and was garrisoned by the British intermittently between 1839 and 1947.

Kiang·si |jēäNG'ē| see JIANGXI, China.

Kiang·su |jē'äNG'sōō| see JIANGSU, China.

Kid·der·min·ster |'kidər,minstər| town in W central England, in Worcestershire, on the Stour River. Pop. 51,000. It is known for its carpets.

Kid·ron |'kidrən; ki'drōn| valley in the Israeli-occupied West Bank, and an intermittent stream flowing through it from East Jerusalem to the Dead Sea, both mentioned in the Bible.

Kiel |kēl| naval port in N Germany, capital of Schleswig-Holstein, on the Baltic Sea coast at the E end of the Kiel Canal. Pop. 247,000.

Kiel Canal |kēl| waterway, 61 mi./98 km. in length, in NW Germany, running W from Kiel to Brunsbüttel at the mouth of the Elbe. It connects the North Sea with the Baltic and was constructed in 1895 to provide the German navy with a shorter route between these two seas. German name **Nord-Ostsee Kanal**.

Kiel·ce |'kyeltsə| heavy industrial city in S Poland. Pop. 214,000.

Ki·ev |'kē,ef; 'kē,ev| capital of Ukraine, an industrial city and port on the Dnieper River. Pop. 2,616,000. Founded in the 8th century, and the medieval capital of Kievan Rus, it became capital of the Ukrainian Soviet Socialist Republic in 1934. In 1991 it became capital of independent Ukraine.

Ki·ga·li |ki'gälē| the capital of Rwanda, a commercial city E of Lake Kivu. Pop. 234,000.

Ki·go·ma |kē'gōmä| port town in W Tanzania, on Lake Tanganyika. It has rail connections to Dar es Salaam, and has been a trade center for centuries, transshipping goods from central Africa.

Ki·klá·dhes |ki'kläTHis| Greek name for the CYCLADES.

Ki·lau·ea |ˌkēlow'äə| volcano with a crater roughly 5 mi./8 km. long by 3 mi./5 km. broad on the island of Hawaii, on the eastern flanks of Mauna Loa at an elevation of 4,090 ft./1,247 m.

Kil·dare |kil'dær; kil'der| county of the Republic of Ireland, in the E, in the province of Leinster. Pop. 123,000; county seat, Naas.

Kil·i·man·ja·ro, Mount |ˌkiləmən'järō| extinct volcano in N Tanzania. It has twin peaks, the higher of which, Kibo 19,340 ft./5,895 m., is the highest mountain in Africa.

Kil·ken·ny |kil'kenē| **1** county of the Republic of Ireland, in the SE, in the province of Leinster. Pop. 74,000. **2** its county seat. Pop. 9,000.

Kil·lar·ney |ki'lärnē| town in the SW of the Republic of Ireland, in County Kerry, famous for the beauty of the nearby lakes and mountains. Pop. 7,000.

Kil·leen |ki'lēn| city in E central Texas. Pop. 63,535. Nearby Fort Hood is key to its economy.

Kil·ling Fields, the name given to all or parts of Cambodia under the Khmer Rouge regime (1975–79), which was responsible for the deaths of a million or more Cambodians.

Kil·mar·nock |kil'märnək| town in W central Scotland, administrative center of East Ayrshire. Pop. 44,000.

Kim·ber·ley[1] |'kimbərlē| (also **the Kimberleys**) plateau region in the far N of Western Australia. A mining and cattle-rearing region, it was the scene of a gold rush in 1885.

Kim·ber·ley[2] |'kimbərlē| city in South Africa, in the province of Northern Cape. Pop. 167,000. It has been a diamond-mining center since the early 1870s.

Kim·chaek |'kēm'CHæk| (formerly **Somgjin**) industrial port city in E North Korea, on the Sea of Japan. Pop. 281,000.

Kin·a·ba·lu, Mount |ˌkēn'äbälōō| mountain in the state of Sabah in E Malaysia, on the N coast of Borneo. Rising to 13,431 ft./4,094 m., it is the highest peak of Borneo and of SE Asia.

Kin·car·dine·shire |kin'kärdnsHər; kin'kärdn,sHir| former county of E Scotland. In 1975 it became part of Grampian region and in 1996 part of Aberdeenshire.

Kings Canyon National Park |'kiNGZ

|'kænyən| national park in the Sierra Nevada, California, to the N of Sequoia National Park. Established in 1940, it preserves groves of ancient sequoia trees, including some of the largest in the world.

Kings County county in New York state coextensive with the borough of Brooklyn.

King's Lynn |'kiNGz 'lin| (also **Lynn Regis** or **Lynn**) port and market town in E England, near the Wash and the mouth of the Ouse. Pop. 37,000.

Kings·port |'kiNGz,pawrt| industrial city in NE Tennessee, part of a complex with Johnson City and Bristol. Pop. 36,365.

Kings·ton¹ |'kiNGstən| the capital, largest city, and chief port of Jamaica. Pop. 538,000. Founded in 1693, it became capital in 1870.

Kings·ton² |'kiNGstən| historic city in SE New York, on the Hudson River. Pop. 23,095.

Kings·ton³ |'kiNGstən| industrial port in SE Ontario, on Lake Ontario, at the head of the St. Lawrence River. Pop. 56,597.

Kingston-upon-Hull |'kiNGstənə,pän 'həl| official name for HULL, England.

Kings·ton upon Thames |'kiNGztən ə ,pawn 'temz| industrial and commercial borough of SW Greater London, England. Pop. 130,000.

Kings·town |'kiNG,stown| the capital and chief port of St. Vincent and the Grenadines, in the West Indies. Pop. 26,000.

King Wil·liam Island |kiNG 'wilyəm| island in the Arctic Archipelago of Nunavut, Canada. Gjoa Haven, important in the history of the Northwest Passage, is on the S shore.

Kin·ki |'kinkē| region of Japan, on the island of Honshu. Capital: Osaka. Kyoto, Kobe, and Nara are here.

Kinross-shire |kin'rawssHər; kin'raws ,sHir| former county of E central Scotland.

Kin·sale |kin'sāl| historic port and resort town in SW Ireland, in S County Cork. Off **Old Head of Kinsale**, a cape to the S, the *Lusitania* was sunk in 1915.

Kin·sha·sa |kin'sHäsə| the capital, largest city, and industrial center of the Democratic Republic of Congo (formerly Zaire), a port on the Congo River, in the SW. Pop. 3,804,000. Founded in 1881 by the explorer Sir Henry M. Stanley, it became the capital of Zaire in 1960. Former name (until 1966) **Léopoldville.**

Kin·ston |'kinz,tən| industrial and commercial city in E North Carolina. Pop. 25,295. Tobacco is central to its economy.

Kin·tyre |kin'tīr| peninsula on the W coast of Scotland, to the W of Arran, extending S for 40 mi./64 km. into the North Channel and separating the Firth of Clyde from the Atlantic. Its S tip is the Mull of Kintyre.

Kir·ghi·zia |kir'gēzHə| another name for KYRGYZSTAN.

Ki·ri·ba·ti |,kirə'bätē; 'kirə,bæs| republic in the SW Pacific including the Gilbert Islands, the Line islands, the Phoenix Islands, and Banaba (Ocean Island). Area: 277 sq. mi./717 sq. km. Pop. 71,000. Official languages, English and I-Kiribati (local Austronesian language). Capital: Bairiki (on Tarawa). The Micronesian islands were dominated by Britain 1892–1975. Phosphate mining was formerly the main economic base; today tuna fishing and copra are important. □ **Kiribatian** *adj. & n.*

Kiribati

Ki·rin |'kē'rin| see JILIN province, China.

Ki·ri·ti·ma·ti |kə'risməs| island in the Pacific Ocean, one of the Line Islands of Kiribati. Pop. 3,000. The largest atoll in the world, it was discovered by Captain James Cook on Christmas Eve, 1777 and was British until it became part of an independent Kiribati in 1979. Former name (until 1981) **Christmas Island.**

Kirk·cal·dy |kə(r)'kawdē| industrial town and port in Fife, SE Scotland, on the N shore of the Firth of Forth. Pop. 47,000.

Kirk·cud·bright |kə(r)'kōōbrē| town in Dumfries and Galloway, SW Scotland, on the Dee River. Pop. 3,000.

Kirk·cud·bright·shire |kə(r)'kōōbrēsHər; kə(r)'kōōbrē,sHir| former county of SW Scotland. It became part of the region of Dumfries and Galloway in 1975.

Kirk·land |'kərklənd| city in W central Washington, a suburb NE of Seattle. Pop. 40,052.

Kir·kuk |kir'kōōk| industrial city in N Iraq, center of the oil industry in that region. Pop. 208,000.

Kirk·wall |'kərkwəl; 'kər,kwawl| port in the

Orkney Islands, Scotland. Pop. 6,000. Situated on the island of Mainland, it is the chief town of the islands.

Ki·rov |'kē,rawf| former name (1934–92) for VYATKA, Russia.

Ki·ro·va·bad |,kērəvə'bät| former name (1935–89) for GĂNCĂ, Azerbaijan.

Ki·ro·vo·hrad |,kērəvə'hräd| industrial city in central Ukraine, on the Ingul River, capital of Kirovohrad oblast. Pop. 274,000. Former name **Kirovograd**.

Ki·ru·na |'kērōō,nä| the northernmost town of Sweden, in the Lapland iron-mining region. Pop. 26,000.

Kir·yu |'kiryōō; kir'yōō| city in N central Japan, on central Honshu, NNW of Tokyo. Pop. 126,000. It has been a major center of silk production since the 8th century.

Ki·san·ga·ni |,kēsän'gänē| city in the northernmost part of the Democratic Republic of Congo (formerly Zaire), on the Congo River. Pop. 373,000. Former name (until 1966) **Stanleyville**.

Kish |'kisH| major city of ancient Mesopotamia, on a former channel of the Euphrates River. Its ruins lie E of those of Babylon, and E of present-day Hillah, Iraq.

Ki·shi·nev |'kisHi,nef| Russian name for CHIŞINĂU, Moldova.

Ki·shi·wa·da |,kēsHē'wädä| city in W central Japan, on S Honshu, an industrial and residential suburb S of Osaka. Pop. 189,000.

Kis·ka Island |'kiskə| island in the Aleutian Islands, in SW Alaska. Site of naval facilities, it was occupied by the Japanese during World War II.

Kis·sim·mee |ki'simē| resort and agricultural city in central Florida. Pop. 30,050.

Ki·ta·kyu·shu |kē'täkyōō,sHōō| industrial port in S Japan, a steelmaking center on the N coast of Kyushu. Pop. 1,026,000.

Kitch·e·ner |'kicHənər| city in SE Ontario. Pop. 168,282. Settled by German Mennonites in 1806, it is an industrial and university center.

Kitt Peak |'kit| peak in the Quinlan Mts., in S Arizona, site of a large observatory complex.

Kit·ty Hawk |'kitē,hawk| resort town on the Outer Banks, on the Atlantic coast of North Carolina. Pop. 1,973. It was near here, in Kill Devil Hills, in 1903, that the Wright Brothers made the first powered airplane flight.

Kit·we |'kē,twä| city in the Copperbelt mining region of N Zambia. Pop. 338,000.

Kitz·bühel |'kits,byōō(ə)l| town in the

Tyrol, W Austria. Pop. 8,000. It is a popular winter resort center.

Ki·vu, Lake |'kēvōō| lake in central Africa, on the border between the Democratic Republic of Congo (formerly Zaire) and Rwanda.

Ki·zil Ir·mak |,ki'zil ir'mäk| (ancient name **Halys**) longest river of Turkey, flowing 715 mi./1,150 km. in a great curve through central Anatolia to the Black Sea.

Klad·no |'klädnaw| industrial city in the NW Czech Republic. Pop. 72,000.

Kla·gen·furt |'klägən,fŏŏrt| city in S Austria, capital of Carinthia. Pop. 89,000.

Klai·pe·da |'klīpədə| industrial city, the chief port of Lithuania, on the Baltic Sea. Pop. 206,000. Former name (1918–23 and 1941–44, when under German control) **Memel**.

Klam·ath Mountains |'klæməTH| ranges in SW Oregon and N California, through which the **Klamath River** flows to the Pacific.

Klau·sen·burg |'klowzen,bŏŏrk| German name for CLUJ–NAPOCA, Romania.

Klerks·dorp |'klerks,dawrp| commercial city in South Africa, in North-West Province, SW of Johannesburg. Pop. 239,000.

Klon·dike |'klän,dīk| tributary of the Yukon River, in Yukon Territory, NW Canada, which rises in the Ogilvie Mts. and flows 100 mi./160 km. W to join the Yukon at Dawson. It gave its name to the surrounding region, which became famous when gold was found in nearby Bonanza Creek in 1896, touching off the Klondike Gold Rush of 1897–98.

Klos·ters |'klawstərz| Alpine winter-sports resort in E Switzerland, near Davos and the Austrian border.

Knights·bridge |'nīts,brij| district in the West End of London, England, to the S of Hyde Park, noted for its fashionable and expensive shops, including Harrods Department Store.

Knos·sos |'näsəs| the principal city of Minoan Crete, the remains of which are on the N coast. The site was occupied from Neolithic times until c. 1200 B.C. Excavations from 1899 onwards revealed the remains of what became known as the Palace of Minos.

Knox·ville |'näks,vil; 'näksvəl| industrial city on the Tennessee River, in E Tennessee. Pop. 165,121. The early 19th-century state capital, it is home to the University of Tennessee.

Ko·be |'kōbā| industrial port in central

Japan, on the island of Honshu. Pop. 1,477,000. The city was severely damaged by an earthquake in 1995.

Kø·ben·havn |ˌkœbən'hown| Danish name for COPENHAGEN.

Ko·blenz |'kō,blents| (also **Coblenz**) manufacturing city in western Germany, at the confluence of the Moselle and Rhine rivers. Pop. 110,000.

Ko·chi |'kōCHē| commercial port in W Japan, on the S coast of Shikoku. Pop. 317,000.

Kocs |'kōCH| village in NW Hungary. The English word "coach" for a horse-drawn carriage is derived from its name.

Ko·dai·ra |kō'dī| city in E central Japan, on E central Honshu, a suburb E of Tokyo. Pop. 164,000.

Ko·di·ak Island |'kōdē,æk| island in the Gulf of Alaska, in SW Alaska, noted for its wildlife and sites of early European settlement.

Ko·dor |kōdawr| see FASHODA.

Ko·fu |'kōfōō| industrial city in central Japan, on Honshu, W of Tokyo. Pop. 201,000. It was the seat of powerful feudal lords.

Ko·hi·ma |'kōhēmə| city in the far NE of India, capital of the state of Nagaland. Pop. 53,000.

Koil |koil| see ALIGARH, India.

Ko·kand |kō'känt| (Uzbek name **Qŭqon**) city in E Uzbekistan, a rail and trade center. Pop. 175,000.

Ko·ko·mo |'kōkə,mō| industrial city in N central Indiana. Pop. 44,962.

Ko·la Peninsula |'kōlə| peninsula on the NW coast of Russia, separating the White Sea from the Barents Sea. The port of Murmansk lies on its N coast.

Kol·ha·pur |'kōlə,pŏŏr| industrial city in the state of Maharashtra, W India. Pop. 405,000.

Kol·khis Greek name for COLCHIS.

Köln |'kœln| German name for COLOGNE.

Ko·lozs·vár |'kōlōZH,vär| Hungarian name for CLUJ–NAPOCA, Romania.

Kol·we·zi |kōl'wäzē| industrial city in SE Congo (formerly Zaire), in the Shaba region. Pop. 545,000. It is a mining center.

Ko·ly·ma |ˌkälē'mä| river of far E Siberia, which flows approximately 1,500 mi./2,415 m. N to the Arctic Ocean.

Ko·man·dor·ski Islands |ˌkəmən 'dawrskyē| island group in extreme E Russia, off the E Kamchatka Peninsula. The Danish explorer Vitus Bering died (1741) at Bering Island here, and U.S. naval forces defeated the Japanese nearby in 1943.

Ko·ma·ti River |ˌkō'mätē| (also **Rio Incomati**) river that flows 500 mi./800 km. from the Drakensberg Range in South Africa, through Swaziland, South Africa, and Mozambique, to the Indian Ocean N of Maputo.

Ko·mi |'kōmē| autonomous republic of NW Russia. Pop. 1,265,000. Capital: Syktyvkar.

Ko·mo·do |kə'mōdō| island in Indonesia, in the Lesser Sunda Islands, between Sumbawa and Flores, home to the komodo dragon, the largest species of lizard.

Kom·pong Som |'kawm,pawNG sawm| (also **Kampong Som**; formerly **Sihanoukville**) port city in S Cambodia, on the Gulf of Thailand. Pop. 75,000. It is the principal deepwater port and commercial center of Cambodia, and has resort trade.

Kom·so·molsk |ˌkämsə'mawlsk| industrial city in the far E of Russia, on the Amur River. Pop. 318,000. It was built in 1932 by members of the Komsomol, the Soviet communist youth organization. Also called **Komsomolsk-on-Amur**.

Ko·na Coast |'kōnə| name for part of the SW coast of the island of Hawaii, noted for its resorts and coffee production.

Kong |'kawNG| 18th-century kingdom of W Africa whose name survives in a region and town in E central Côte d'Ivoire.

Kon·go |'käNGgō| former kingdom in W central Africa, in the area of the Congo River. It was established in the 14th century and declined under Portuguese influence until absorbed into what is now Angola and Congo (formerly Zaire).

Kö·nig·grätz |'kōnik,grets| German name for HRADEC KRÁLOVÉ, Czech Republic.

Kö·nigs·berg |'kœniks,berk| German name for KALININGRAD, Russia.

Kon·ya |kawn'yä| commercial city in SW central Turkey. Pop. 513,000. An ancient Phrygian settlement, it became the capital of the Seljuk sultans toward the end of the 11th century.

Koo·te·nai River |'kōōtn-,ā| (also **Kootneya**) river that flows 450 mi./720 km. from SE British Columbia into Montana and Idaho, then back into British Columbia, where it joins the Columbia River.

Kor·do·fan |ˌkawrdə'fæn| region of central Sudan. El Obeid is the chief town.

Ko·rea |kə'rēə| region of E Asia forming a peninsula between the Sea of Japan and the Yellow Sea, now divided into the countries of North Korea and South Korea.

Ko·rea Bay |kə'rēə| arm of the Yellow Sea

along the coast of NW North Korea. The Yalu River enters the sea here.

Ko•rea Strait |kə'rēə| channel between the Sea of Japan, to the N, and the East China Sea, to the S. South Korea lies to the NW, Japan to the SE. In the middle is the Japanese island of Tsushima; waters to the SE of the island are called Tsushima Strait.

Kó•rin•thos |'kōrin,THaws| Greek name for CORINTH.

Ko•ri•ya•ma |,kawrē'yämä| industrial city in NE Japan, on N central Honshu, S of Fukushima. Pop. 315,000.

Ko•ror |'kawr,awr| (also **Oreor**) capital of the Republic of Palau, in the W Pacific, on Koror Island (pop. 10,000).

Kort•rijk |'kawr,trīk| city in W Belgium, a textile center in West Flanders. Pop. 76,000. French name **Courtrai**.

Ko•rup National Park |'kawrəp| national park in W Cameroon, on the border with Nigeria. It was established in 1961 to protect a large area of tropical rainforest.

Kos |kaws; käs| (also **Cos**) a Greek island in the SE Aegean, one of the Dodecanese group.

Kos•ci•us•ko, Mount |,käzē'əskō| peak in SE Australia, in the Great Dividing Range in SE New South Wales. Rising to 7,234 ft./2,228 m., it is the highest mountain in Australia.

Ko•shi•ga•ya |kō'sHēgäyä| city in E central Japan, on E central Honshu, a suburb N of Tokyo. Pop. 285,000.

Ko•ši•ce |'kōsHētse| industrial city in S Slovakia. Pop. 235,000.

Ko•so•vo |'kawsə,vō| autonomous province of Serbia. Capital: Priština. It borders on Albania and the great majority of the people are of Albanian descent. Unrest, spurred by opposition to Serbian rule, gripped the region in the late 1990s. □ **Kosovar** *adj. & n.*

Kos•rae |'kaws,rī| island in the Caroline Islands, constituting a state in the Federated States of Micronesia. Pop. 7,000.

Kos•tro•ma |kə,strä'mä| industrial city in European Russia, on the Volga River to the NW of Nizhni Novgorod. Pop. 280,000.

Ko•ta |'kōtə| industrial city in Rajasthan state, in NW India, on the Chambal River. Pop. 536,000.

Ko•ta Ba•ha•ru |'kōtə 'bähə,boo| city in Malaysia, on the east coast of the Malay Peninsula, the capital of the state of Kelantan. Pop. 219,000.

Ko•ta Ki•na•ba•lu |'kōtə ,kinəbə'loo| port in Malaysia, on the N coast of Borneo, capital of the state of Sabah. Pop. 56,000.

Kot•ka |'kätkə| port on the S coast of Finland. Pop. 57,000.

Ko•tor |'kō,tawr| (also **Cattaro**) seaport and commercial center in Montenegro, on the Gulf of Kotor. Pop. 22,000.

Kot•ze•bue |'kätsə,boo| city in NW Alaska, on Kotzebue Sound. Pop. 2,751.

Kou•rou |koo'roo| town on the N coast of French Guiana. Pop. 11,000. Nearby is a satellite-launching station of the European Space Agency.

Kov•rov |kəv'rawf| industrial town in W Russia E of Moscow. Pop. 162,000. It is a railroad junction.

Kow•loon |'kow'loon| densely populated peninsula on the SE coast of China, forming part of Hong Kong. It is separated from Hong Kong Island by Victoria Harbour.

Kra, Isthmus of |'krä| the narrowest part of the Malay Peninsula, forming part of S Thailand.

Kra•gu•je•vac |'krägooyə,väts| city in central Serbia. Pop. 147,000. It was the capital of Serbia 1818–39.

Kraj•i•na |krä'yēnə| predominantly Serbian region of E Croatia that attempted to secede following Croatia's separation from Yugoslavia in 1991.

Kra•ka•toa |,krækə'tōə| (also **Krakatau**) small volcanic island in Indonesia, lying between Java and Sumatra, scene of an eruption in 1883 that destroyed most of the island and is the most powerful explosion in recorded history.

Kra•ków |'krä,koof; 'kräk,ow| Polish name for CRACOW.

Kra•lje•vo |'krälye,vō| industrial and market town in central Serbia, near the confluence of the Ibar and Morava rivers. Pop.122,000.

Kra•ma•torsk |,krämə'tawrsk| industrial city and transportation hub in E Ukraine, in the Donets Basin. Pop. 201,000.

Kras•no•dar |,kräsnə'där| industrial port on the lower Kuban River in SW Russia, in a wheat growing area near the Black Sea. Pop. 627,000. It was known before 1922 as Yekaterinodar (Ekaterinodar).

Kras•no•yarsk |,kräsnə'yärsk| port and rail center on the Yenisei River in central Siberian Russia. Pop. 922,000. Some 40 mi./64 km. N of the city was a secret Soviet reactor used to produce military materials.

Kre•feld |'krä,felt| industrial port city, a textile center, on the Rhine in western Germany, in North Rhine-Westphalia. Pop. 246,000.

Kre•men•chuk |,kremen'CHook| industrial city in E central Ukraine, on the Dnieper River. Pop. 238,000. Russian name **Kremenchug**.

Krem·lin, the |'kremlən| citadel in Moscow, Russia, on RED SQUARE. A walled complex built over several hundred years and containing churches and palaces, it is the seat of the Russian government and was earlier the seat of the government of the Soviet Union.

Krish·na River |'krisHnə| (also **Kistna**)river that rises in theWestern Ghats of S India and flows 805 mi./1,288 km. to the Bay of Bengal.

Kris·tian·sand |'krisCHən,sæn(d)| ferry port on the S coast of Norway, in the Skagerrak. Pop. 66,000.

Kris·tian·stad |'krisCHən,städ| industrial and commercial town in SE Sweden, on the Helge River, capital of Kristianstad county. Pop. 72,000.

Krí·ti |'krētē| Greek name for CRETE.

Kri·voy Rog |kryi'voi 'rawk| Russian name for KRYVY RIH, Ukraine.

Krk |kərk| largest island of Croatia, in the Adriatic Sea. Pop. 13,000. It is a resort area with several small towns.

Kron·stadt[1] |'krōn,SHtät| German name for BRAṢOV, Romania.

Kron·stadt[2] |'krōn,SHtät| (also **Kronshtadt**) port city on Kotlin Island, W Russia, W of Saint Petersburg. Pop. 45,000. The fortress here was built by Peter the Great and was important in Russia's strategic defense system, especially during the siege of Leningrad inWorldWar II.

Kru Coast |'krōō| section of the coast of Liberia to the NW of Cape Palmas, inhabited by the Kru people.

Kru·ger National Park |'krōōgər| preserve in South Africa, in Mpumalanga, on the Mozambique border. It was originally a game reserve established in 1898 by South African President Paul Kruger.

Kru·gers·dorp |'krōōgərz,dawrp| industrial town in Gauteng province, NE South Africa, W of Johannesburg, in a region where gold, asbestos, and uranium are mined. Pop. 196,000.

Kru·se·vac |'krōōSHe,väts| industrial town in S central Serbia, near the confluence of the Rasina and Morava rivers. Pop. 133,000.

Kry·vy Rih |kri'vē 'riKH| industrial city in S Ukraine, at the center of an iron-ore-mining region. Pop. 717,000. Russian name **Krivoy Rog**.

Kua·la Lum·pur |,kwälə 'lōōm,pōōr| the capital of Malaysia, in the SW of the Malay

Peninsula. Pop. 1,145,000. It is a major commercial center in the middle of a rubber-growing and tin-mining region.

Kua·la Treng·ga·nu |'kwälə təreNG 'gänōō| (also **Kuala Terengganu**) the capital of the state of Trengganu in Malaysia, on the E coast of the Malay Peninsula at the mouth of the Trengganu River. Pop. 229,000.

Kuan·tan |'kwän,tän| the capital of the state of Pahang in Malaysia, on the E coast of the Malay Peninsula. Pop. 199,000.

Ku·ban River |kōō'bän| river (584 mi./934 km.) in S Russia. It rises in the Greater Caucasus Mts. and flows into the Sea of Azov.

Ku·ching |'kōōCHiNG| port in Malaysia, on the Sarawak River near the NW coast of Borneo, capital of the state of Sarawak. Pop. 148,000.

Kui·by·shev |'kōōēbəsHəf| former name (1935–91) for SAMARA, Russia.

Ku·li·ko·vo |,kōōli'kawvə| plain in SW Russia, near the source of the Don River. A major battle here in 1380 was important in freeing Russia from Mongol domination.

Ku·ma·ga·ya |,kōōmä'gäyä| industrial city in E central Japan, on E central Honshu, NW of Tokyo. Pop. 152,000.

Ku·ma·mo·to |,kōōmə'mōtō| industrial and commercial city in S Japan, on the W coast of Kyushu island. Pop. 579,000.

Ku·ma·no·vo |kōō'mänawvō| city in N Macedonia, NE of Skopje, in a tobacco-growing region. Pop. 136,000. It is the scene of a Serbian victory over the Turks in 1912.

Ku·ma·si |kōō'mäsi| commercial city in S Ghana. Pop. 376,000. It is the capital of the Ashanti region.

Ku·may·ri |'kōō,mīrē| Russian name for GYUMRI, Armenia.

Kum·ba·ko·nam |,kōōmbə'kōnəm| (also **Combaconum**) commercial city in S India, in Tamil Nadu state. Pop. 151,000. Noted for its many Hindu temples, it is a center of Brahmanism and a pilgrimage site.

Kun·lun Shan |'kōōn'lōōn 'sHän| range of mountains in W China, on the N edge of the Tibetan plateau, extending E for over 1,000 mi./1,600 km. from the Pamir Mts. Its highest peak is Muztag, which rises to 25,338 ft./7,723 m.

Kun·ming |'kōōn'miNG| industrial city in SW China, capital ofYunnan province, on Lake Dianchi. Pop. 1,612,000.

Kuo·pio |'kwawpē,aw| resort and industrial city in S Finland, capital of Kuopio province. Pop. 81,000.

Ku·ra River |kə'rä; 'kᴏᴏrə| river that flows 940 mi./1,510 km. from NE Turkey through Georgia and Azerbaijan, into the Caspian Sea. It is important for irrigation, hydroelectric power, and navigation.

Kur·di·stan |ˌkᴏᴏdə'stæn; 'kərdə,stæn| extensive region in the Middle East S of the Caucasus, the traditional home of the Kurdish people. The area includes large parts of E Turkey, N Iraq, W Iran, E Syria, Armenia, and Azerbaijan. The creation of the separate state of Kurdistan, proposed by the Allies after World War I, has long been opposed by Iraq, Iran, Syria, and Turkey. Following persecution of the Kurds by Iraq in the aftermath of the Gulf War of 1991, certain areas designated safe havens were established for the Kurds in N Iraq, although these havens are not officially recognized as a state.

Ku·re |'kᴏᴏrā| city in S Japan, a shipbuilding center on the S coast of Honshu, near Hiroshima. Pop. 217,000.

Kur·gan |kᴏᴏr'gän| city in central Russia, commercial center for an agricultural region. Pop. 360,000.

Ku·rile Islands |'k(y)ᴏᴏr,ēl; kyᴏᴏ'rēl| (also **Kuril Islands** or **the Kurils**) chain of 56 islands between the Sea of Okhotsk and the N Pacific, stretching from the S tip of the Kamchatka Peninsula of Russia to the NE corner of the Japanese island of Hokkaido. The islands were given to Japan in exchange for the N part of Sakhalin island in 1875, but were returned to the Soviet Union in 1945. They are the subject of dispute between Russia and Japan.

Kur·nool |kər'nᴏᴏl| (also **Karnul**) commercial town in S India, in Andhra Pradesh state. Pop. 275,000.

Ku·ro·shio |kᴏᴏr'ōsʜēō| warm current flowing in the Pacific NE past Japan and toward Alaska. Also called **Japanese Current, Japan Current**.

Kursk |kᴏᴏrsk| industrial city in SW Russia. Pop. 430,000. It was the scene of an important Soviet victory over the Germans in World War II.

Ku·ruk·shet·ra |ˌkᴏᴏrᴏᴏk'sʜätrə| city in N India, in Haryana state. Pop. 81,000. It is a Hindu pilgrimage site.

Kur·ze·me |'kᴏᴏrzə,mä| (also **Kurland**) former province in W Latvia, along the Baltic Sea and the SW shore of the Gulf of Riga. It is an agricultural, wooded region.

Kuş·a·da·si |ˌkᴏᴏsʜädä'si| resort town on the Aegean coast of western Turkey. Pop. 32,000.

Ku·shi·ro |kᴏᴏ'sʜērō| fishing port and industrial city in N Japan, on the SE coast of Hokkaido. Pop. 206,000.

Küss·nacht |'kʏs,näкʜt| village in N central Switzerland, E of Lucerne. Pop. 8,000. According to legend, William Tell shot the Austrian bailiff Gessler nearby.

Ku·ta·i·si |ˌkᴏᴏtä'ēsē| industrial city in central Georgia. Pop. 236,000. One of the oldest cities in Transcaucasia, it has been the capital of various kingdoms, including Colchis and Abkhazia.

Kutch, Gulf of |'kəcʜ| inlet of the Arabian Sea on the W coast of India.

Kutch, Rann of |'kəcʜ| vast salt marsh in the NW of the Indian subcontinent, on the shores of the Arabian Sea, extending over the boundary between SE Pakistan and the state of Gujarat in NW India.

Ku·wait |kə'wāt| country on the Arabian Peninsula, on the NW coast of the Persian Gulf. Area: 6,880 sq. mi./17,818 sq. km. Language, Arabic. Capital: Kuwait City. With a history as a fishing and trading sheikhdom, Kuwait since the 1930s has become one of the world's leading oil producers. Iraqi claims on the area led to the 1990–91 occupation and resulting Gulf War. □ **Kuwaiti** adj. & n.

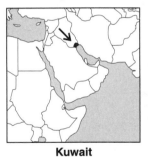

Kuwait

Ku·wait City |kə'wāt| port on the Persian Gulf, the capital city of Kuwait. Pop. 150,000.

Kuz·bass |kᴏᴏz'bäs| another name for Kuznets Basin of Russia.

Kuz·nets Basin |kᴏᴏz'nyetsk| (also **Kuznetsk**) industrial region of S Russia, in the valley of the Tom River, between Tomsk and Novokuznetsk. The region is rich in iron and coal deposits. Also called **Kuzbass**.

Kwa·ja·lein |'kwäjələn; 'kwäjə,lān| largest atoll in the Marshall Islands, in the W central Pacific. During World War II it was fought over by U.S. and Japanese forces.

Kwa Nde·be·le |ˌkwändə'bälä| former

homeland established in South Africa for the Ndebele people, now part of the province of Mpumalanga.

Kwan•do River |'kwändō| (also **Cuando** or **Linyanti**) river that flows 500 mi./800 km. from central Angola, along the Angola-Zambia border, into the Caprivi Strip of Namibia, and along the N border of Botswana, where the Chobe River extends its course to the Zambezi River.

Kwang•chow |'gwäNG'jō| see GUANG-ZHOU, China.

Kwang•cho•wan |'gwäNG'jō'wän| (Chinese name **Zhanjiang**) former French territory in Guangdong province, S China. Leased for 99 years in 1898, it was returned in 1945.

Kwang•ju |'gawNG'jōō| industrial city in SW South Korea. Pop. 1,145,000.

Kwang•si |'gwäNG'SHē| see GUANGXI, China.

Kwang•tung |'gwäNG'ōōNG| see GUANG-DONG, China.

Kwan•tung |'gwän'dōōNG| (Japanese name **Kanto**) former territory, S Liaoning province, NE China, on the Liaodong Peninsula. Leased by China to Russia in 1898, the area was under Japanese control from 1905 to 1945. Dairen (now Dalian) and Port Arthur (now Lüshun) were part of Kwantung.

KwaZulu/Natal |kwaä'zōōlōōnä'täl| province of E South Africa, on the Indian Ocean. Capital: Pietermaritzburg. Formerly called Natal, it became one of the new provinces of South Africa following the democratic elections of 1994. See also NATAL².

Kwa•Zu•lu |kwä'zōōlōō| former homeland established in South Africa for the Zulu people, now part of the province of KwaZulu/Natal. The general area was formerly known as Zululand.

Kwei•chow |'gwä'jō| see GUIZHOU, China.

Kwei•lin |'kgä'lin| see GUILIN, China.

Kwei•yang |'gwä'yäNG| see GUIYANG, China.

Kyo•ga, Lake |'kyōgə| (also **Kioga**) shallow lake in S central Uganda, on the Victoria Nile River, N of Lake Victoria, to which it was once joined.

Kyong•ju |'kyawNG'jōō| historic city in SE South Korea. Pop. 274,000. It was the cap-

ital of the Silla dynasty for a millennium, to A.D. 935, and is a tourist center today.

Kyo•to |kē'ōtō| industrial city in central Japan, on the island of Honshu. Pop. 1,461,000. Founded in the 8th century, it was the imperial capital from 794 until 1868, and has many noted buildings and sites.

Ky•re•nia |kə'rēnēə| historic port in N central Cyprus, N of Nicosia. Turkish forces landed here in 1974 in their invasion of the island.

Kyr•gyz Republic |kir'gēz| another name for KYRGYZSTAN.

Kyr•gyz•stan |,kirgə'stän| mountainous republic in central Asia, on the NW border of China. Area: 76,640 sq. mi./198,500 sq. km. Pop. 4,448,000. Official language, Kyrgyz. Capital and largest city: Bishkek. Also called **Kirghizia**; **Kyrgyz Republic**. Under Russian control 1864–1991, Kyrgyzstan has an economy based on agriculture, mining, and hydropower production. □ **Kyrgyz** *adj. & n.* **Kirgis** *adj. & n.*

Kyrgyzstan

Kyu•shu |kē'yōōSHōō| the most southerly of the four main islands of Japan, constituting an administrative region. Pop. 13,296,000. Capital: Fukuoka.

Kyu•sten•dil |,kyōōsten'dil| market city in SW Bulgaria, near the Serbian border. Pop. 55,000. Famed for its mineral springs, it is also a spa.

Ky•zyl |ki'zil| city in S central Russia, on the Yenisei River, capital of the republic of Tuva. Pop. 80,000.

Ky•zyl Kum |ki'zil kōōm| arid desert region in central Asia, extending E from the Aral Sea to the Pamir Mts. and covering part of Uzbekistan and S Kazakhstan.

Ll

La·bé |läˈbä| commercial town in W central Guinea, in the Fouta Djallon region. It is predominantly Fulani and an Islamic center. Pop. 110,000.

La Belle Province |ləˈbel| nickname for QUEBEC (French, literally 'the Beautiful Province').

Lab·ra·dor |ˈlæbrəˌdawr| coastal region of E Canada, which forms the mainland part of the province of Newfoundland and Labrador. Largely on the barren Canadian Shield, it has mining and fishing centers.

Lab·ra·dor Current |ˈlæbrəˌdawr ˈkərənt| cold ocean current that flows S from the Arctic Ocean along the NE coast of North America. It meets the warm Gulf Stream in an area off the coast of Newfoundland that is noted for its dense fogs.

Lab·ra·dor Peninsula |ˈlæbrəˌdawr| broad peninsula of E Canada, between Hudson Bay, the Atlantic, and the Gulf of St. Lawrence. Consisting of the Ungava Peninsula and Labrador, it contains most of Quebec and the mainland part of the province of Newfoundland and Labrador. Also called **Labrador-Ungava**.

Lab·ra·dor Sea |ˈlæbrəˌdawr| section of the Atlantic between Labrador and S Greenland, noted for its icebergs.

La·bu·an |ləˈbo͞oən| Malaysian island off the N coast of Borneo. Pop. 26,000. Capital: Victoria.

Lac·ca·dive Islands |ˈlækədīv| one of the groups of islands forming the Indian territory of Lakshadweep in the Indian Ocean.

La·ce·dae·mon |ˌlæsəˈdēmən| see SPARTA, Greece. □ **Lacedaemonian** adj. & n.

La Ce·i·ba |lä ˈsābä| seaport on the Caribbean coast of Honduras. Pop. 68,000.

La Chaux-de-Fonds |ləsHōd(ə)ˈfawN| commune in W Switzerland, in the Jura Mts., NW of Bern. Pop. 36,000. It is a major watch-manufacturing center.

La·chine |ləˈsHēn| industrial city in S Quebec, just SW of Montreal, site of a canal that in the 1820s opened the upper Saint Lawrence River to commerce.

Lach·lan |ˈläklən| river of New South Wales, Australia, which rises in the Great Dividing Range and flows some 920 mi./1,472 km. to join the Murrumbidgee River near the border with Victoria.

Lack·a·wan·na |ˌlækəˈwänə| industrial city in W New York, on Lake Erie and the W side of Buffalo. Pop. 20,585.

Lac Lé·man |ˌläklä'mäN| French name for Lake Geneva (see GENEVA, LAKE), Switzerland.

La·co·ni·a |ləˈkōnēə| (also **Lakonia**) modern department and ancient region of Greece, in the SE Peloponnese. Throughout the classical period the region was dominated by its capital, Sparta. □ **Laconian** adj. & n.

La Co·ru·ña |ˌläkawˈro͞onyä| (also **Corunna**) port in NW Spain. Pop. 251,000. It was the point of departure for the Spanish Armada in 1588 and the site of a battle in 1809 in the Peninsular War, at which British forces under Sir John Moore defeated the French.

La Crosse |ləˈkraws| industrial and commercial city in W Wisconsin, on the Mississippi River. Pop. 51,003.

La·dakh |ləˈdäk| high-altitude region of NW India, Pakistan, and China, containing the Ladakh and Karakoram mountain ranges and the upper Indus valley; chief town, Leh (in India).

Lad·o·ga, Lake |ˈlædəgə| lake in NW Russia, NE of St. Petersburg, near the border with Finland. It is the largest lake in Europe, with an area of 6,837 sq. mi./17,700 sq. km.

La·dy·smith |ˈlādēˌsmiTH| town in E South Africa, in KwaZulu/Natal, scene of famous siege by Boer forces in 1899–1900.

Lae |lä| industrial seaport on the E coast of Papua New Guinea, the country's second-largest city. Pop. 81,000.

La·fay·ette[1] |ˌläfēˈet| industrial and commercial city in NW Indiana. Pop. 43,764.

La·fay·ette[2] |ˌläfēˈet; ləˈfäət| city in S Louisiana, an oil industry center in the Cajun Country. Pop. 94,440.

La·gash |ˌläˈgæsH| (also **Shirpurla**) ancient Sumerian city in present-day S Iraq, between the Tigris and Euphrates rivers.

La·gos |ˈläˌgäs; ˈläˌgōs| the chief city of Nigeria, a port on the Gulf of Guinea. Pop. 1,347,000. Originally a center of the slave trade, it became capital of the newly independent Nigeria in 1960. It was replaced as capital by Abuja in 1991.

La Grande River |ləˈgränd; lə ˈgrænd| river that flows 500 mi./800 km. across central Quebec to Hudson Bay. It is the site of huge, and controversial, power projects.

La Guai·ra |läˈgwīrə| port city in N Venezuela, on the Caribbean Sea. Pop.

24,000. It is the port for Caracas, just S, and the leading port of the country, with an international airport and cruise ship facilities.

La Ha·bra |lə 'häbrə| city in SW California, SE of Los Angeles. Pop. 51,266.

La·hai·na |lə'hīnə| resort and agricultural community in W Maui, Hawaii. Pop. 9,073.

La·hore |lə'hawr| commercial city, the capital of Punjab province and second largest city of Pakistan, situated near the border with India. Pop. 3,200,000.

Lah·ti |'lätē| industrial city and lake port in S Finland, at the S end of Lake Päijänne. Pop. 93,000.

Lai·bach |'lībäкн| German name for LJUBLJANA, Slovenia.

La Jol·la |lə'hoiə| resort and institutional section of N San Diego, California, on the Pacific Ocean.

Lake Al·bert, Lake Bai·kal &, etc. for lakes, see the other element in the place name, e.g., ALBERT, BAIKAL, SUPERIOR, etc.

Lake Charles |'CHär(ə)lz| industrial port city in SW Louisiana, on the Calcasieu River. Pop. 70,580.

Lake District |lāk| region of lakes and mountains in Cumbria, NW England, noted for its resorts and associated with artists and writers, including English poets Wordsworth, Coleridge, and Southey (the Lake Poets).

Lake·hurst |'lākhərst| borough in E central New Jersey, site of a naval facility associated with the 1937 crash of the dirigible *Hindenburg.*

Lake·land¹ |'läklənd| another term for the LAKE DISTRICT, England.

Lake·land² |'læklənd| city in central Florida, noted for its resorts and its citrus industry. Pop. 70,576.

Lake Lou·ise |lə'wēz| resort in SW Alberta, in the Rocky Mts., noted for the beauty of the lake that gives it its name.

Lake of the Ozarks |'ō,zärks| lake in central Missouri, a noted recreational resource created by a dam built in 1931.

Lake of the Woods |wōōdz| lake on the border between Canada and the U.S., to the W of the Great Lakes. It is bounded to the W by Manitoba, to the N and E by Ontario, and to the S by Minnesota. See also NORTHWEST ANGLE.

Lake Plac·id |'plæsid| resort village in the Adirondack Mts., in NE New York, site of Olympic competition in 1932 and 1980. Pop. 2,485.

Lake·wood¹ |'lāk,wŏŏd| city in SW Cali-

fornia, a suburb SE of Los Angeles. Pop. 73,557.

Lake·wood² |'lāk,wŏŏd| city in N central Colorado, a suburb on the W side of Denver. Pop. 126,481.

Lake·wood³ |'lāk,wŏŏd| city in NE Ohio, a suburb W of Cleveland, on L. Erie. Pop. 59,718.

Lak·shad·weep Islands |lək'sнäd,wēp| group of islands off the Malabar Coast of SW India, constituting a Union Territory in India. Pop. 52,000. Capital: Kavaratti. The group consists of the Laccadive, Minicoy, and Amindivi islands.

La La·gu·na |lä lə'gōōnə| university town and tourist center on Tenerife, in the Spanish Canary Islands. Pop. 117,000.

La Lou·vière |lə lōō'vyer| industrial city in SW Belgium, in the province of Hainaut W of Charleroi. Pop. 76,000.

La Man·cha |lə 'mänCHə| flat, arid plateau in S central Spain, once part of New Castile and now mostly in the region of Castilla-La Mancha. Cervantes wrote *Don Quixote* while imprisoned in La Mancha.

Lam·ba·ré·né |,lämbə'rānä| town in W central Gabon, on the Ogooué River, SE of Libreville, longtime base of the missionary doctor Albert Schweitzer. Pop. 15,000.

Lam·beth |'læmbəTH| borough of inner London, England, on the S bank of the Thames. Pop. 220,000. **Lambeth Palace** is the London residence of the Archbishop of Canterbury, ecclesisastical head of the Church of England.

La·mía |lä'mēə| (formerly known as **Zitu·ni**) historic market city in E central Greece. Pop. 44,000.

Lam·mer·muir Hills |'læmər,myŏŏr| (also **Lammermoor**) low range of hills in SE Scotland, in East Lothian and the Borders.

Lam·pe·du·sa |,lämpə'dōōsə| island in the Mediteranean Sea between Malta and N Africa, administered by Italy. It is the largest of the Pelagian group. Pop. 4,000.

La·nai |lə'nī| island in Hawaii, W of Maui. It is primarily agricultural, with some resorts.

Lan·ark·shire |'lænərk,sн(i)ər; 'lænərksнər| former county of SW central Scotland, now divided into the administrative regions of **North Lanarkshire** and **South Lanarkshire**.

Lan·ca·shire |'læNGkə,sнir; 'læNGkəsнər| county of NW England, on the Irish Sea. Pop. 1,365,000; administrative center, Preston.

Lan·cas·ter¹ |'læNG,kæstər; 'læNGkəstər| city in SW California, NE of Los Angeles, on the edge of the Mojave Desert. Pop. 97,291. Edwards Air Force Base is nearby.

Lan·cas·ter[2] |'læNGkəstər; 'læNG,kæstər| city in Lancashire, NW England, on the estuary of the Lune River. Pop. 44,000. It was the county seat of Lancashire until 1974. □ **Lancastrian** *adj. & n.*

Lan·cas·ter[3] |'læNG,kæstər; 'læNGkəstər| city in SE Pennsylvania, primarily a commercial center for the Pennsylvania Dutch Country. Pop. 55,551.

Lan·chow |'län'CHOW| see LANZHOU, China.

Landes |'lændz| department in SW France, along the Atlantic coast in Aquitaine. Pop. 331,000. The main economic activities are forestry, agriculture, and tourism. The capital is Mont-de-Marsan.

Land of the Ris·ing Sun popular name for Japan, a rough translation of *Nippon*, derived from a Chinese name for the island nation.

Land's End |'læn(d)z 'end| rocky promontory in SW Cornwall, which forms the westernmost point of England and Britain. The approximate distance by road from Land's End to Britain's northeastermost point at John o'Groats in Scotland is 876 mi./1,400 km.

Lands·hut |'länts,ho͞ot| industrial city in S Germany, on the Isar River NE of Munich. Pop. 60,000.

Lang·fang |'läNG'fäNG| city in Hebei province, E China, between Beijing and Tianjin. Pop. 533,000.

Lang·ley |'læNGlē| community in NE Virginia, just NW of Washington, D.C., home to the Central Intelligence Agency.

Lan·gue·doc |läNG'dawk; ,læNGgə'däk| former province of S France, which extended from the Rhône valley to the N foothills of the E Pyrenees. Its name derives from *langue d'oc*, the term for the form of medieval French spoken in the South, the predecessor of modern Provencal.

Languedoc-Roussillon |läNNG'dawk ,ro͞osē'yawN| region of S France, on the Mediterranean coast, extending from the Rhône delta to the border with Spain.

L'Anse aux Mead·ows |,læns ō 'medōz| historic site in NW Newfoundland, where remains of Viking settlement dating from about A.D. 1000, possibly the legendary VINLAND, have been found.

Lan·sing |'lænsiNG| industrial city, the capital of Michigan. Pop. 127,321.

Lan·tau |'län'dow| island of Hong Kong, to the W of Hong Kong Island and form-

ing part of the New Territories. Chinese name **Tai Yue Shan**.

La·nús |lä'no͞os| city in E Argentina, an industrial suburb S of Buenos Aires. Pop. 467,000.

Lan·za·ro·te |,länsə'rōtä| one of the Canary Islands of Spain, the most easterly of the group; chief town, Arrecife. A series of volcanic eruptions in about 1730 dramatically altered the island's landscape, creating an area of volcanic cones in the SW known as the 'Mountains of Fire.'

Lan·zhou |'læn'zHo͞o| (also **Lanchow**) industrial city in N China, on the upper Yellow River, capital of Gansu province. Pop. 1,480,000.

Laois |lēsH; läsH| (also **Laoighis, Leix**) county of the Republic of Ireland, in the province of Leinster. Pop. 53,000; county seat, Portlaoise. Former name **Queen's County**.

Laon |läN| historic commercial town, capital of Aisne department, N France. Pop. 29,000. It formerly served as the capital of France (8th–10th centuries).

Laos |lows; 'lä,ōs; 'lä,äs| landlocked country in SE Asia, in Indochina. Area: 91,464 sq. mi./236,800 sq. km. Pop. 4,279,000. Language, Laotian. Capital and largest city: Vientiane. A kingdom from the 14th century, dominated by the French 1898–1949, Laos underwent a 25-year civil war, and is now a communist republic. Most of its people are subsistence farmers, and many of its resources are undeveloped. □ **Laotian** *adj. & n.* **Lao** *adj. & n.*

Laos

La Pal·ma |lə 'pälmə| one of the Canary Islands of Spain, the most northwesterly in the group. It is the site of an astronomical observatory.

La Paz[1] |lə 'päs; lə 'päz| the capital of Bolivia, an industrial city in the NW near the border with Peru. Pop. 711,000. (The judicial capital is Sucre.) Situated in the Andes at an altitude of 12,000 ft. (3,660 m), La Paz is the highest capital city in the world.

La Paz[2] |lə 'päs| city in Mexico, near the S tip of the Baja California peninsula, capital of the state of Baja California Sur. Pop. 100,000.

La Pé•rouse Strait |ˌlä pə'roos| (also **Soya Strait**) strait separating Hokkaido, N Japan, from Sakhalin Island, Russia. The Sea of Okhotsk lies to the E, the Sea of Japan to the W.

Lap•land |'læpˌlænd; 'læplənd| region of N Europe that extends from the Norwegian Sea to the White Sea and lies mainly within the Arctic Circle. It consists of the N parts of Norway, Sweden, and Finland, and the Kola Peninsula of Russia. It is inhabited by a nomadic people, the Lapps or Laplanders.

La Pla•ta |lə 'plætə; lə 'plätə| port in Argentina, on the Plate River (Río de la Plata) SE of Buenos Aires. Pop. 640,000.

Lap•tev Sea |'læpˌtef; 'læpˌtev| part of the Arctic Ocean that lies to the N of Russia between the Taymyr Peninsula and the New Siberian Islands.

Lapu-Lapu |ˌläpoo 'läpoo| (formerly **Opon**) city in the Philippines, on the NW coast of Mactan. Pop. 146,000.

L'Aqui•la |'läkwēlə| city in the Abruzzi region of E central Italy. Pop. 68,000. It is a summer resort.

Lar•a•mie |'lerəˌmē| industrial and resort city in SE Wyoming. Pop. 26,687. It was settled in 1868, during construction of the Union Pacific Railroad.

La•re•do |lə'rādō| industrial port city in S Texas, across the Rio Grande from Nuevo Laredo, Mexico. Pop. 122,899.

Lar•go |'lärˌgō| resort city in W central Florida, on the SW side of Clearwater. Pop. 65,674.

La Rio•ja[1] |ˌlä rē'ōhä| commercial city in NW Argentina, the capital of La Rioja province, in the Andes. Pop. 105,000.

La Rio•ja[2] |ˌlä rē'ōhä| autonomous region of N Spain, in the wine-producing valley of the Ebro River. Capital: Logroño.

La•ris•sa |lə'risə| city in Greece, the chief town of Thessaly. Pop. 113,000. Greek name **Lárisa**.

Lar•ka•na |lär'känə| commercial city in S central Pakistan, N of Karachi. Pop. 275,000.

Lar•na•ca |'lärnəkə| historic port city in SE Cyprus, in the Greek-controlled zone. Pop. 44,000. On the site of ancient Citium, it is an industrial and resort center.

La Ro•chelle |ˌlä raw.'sHel| port on the At-

lantic coast of W France. Pop. 74,000. It was a 17th-century Huguenot stronghold.

La Roche-sur-Yon |ˌlä 'rawsHsYr'yawN| capital of the department of the Vendée in W France. Pop. 49,000. It is an agricultural and transportation center.

La Ro•ma•na |lə rō'mänə| port city in the SE Dominican Republic. Pop. 133,000. It has an airport and cruise ship facilities, and is a resort center.

La Salle |lə 'sæl| city in S Quebec, a residential and industrial suburb SW of Montreal. Pop. 73,804.

La Sca•la |lä 'skälə| opera house, built 1776–78, in Milan, Italy, long famed the largest and most prestigious in the world.

Las•caux |lä'skō; læs'kō| village in SW France, in the Périgord region, site of a cave with famed Paleolithic paintings and drawings. The cave was closed to the public in 1963 in order to preserve the art.

Las Cru•ces |läs'kroosəs| city in S New Mexico, on the Rio Grande. Pop. 62,126.

La Se•re•na |lä sā'ränä| historic city in N central Chile, a coastal resort and the capital of Coquimbo province. Pop. 120,000. Chilean independence was declared here in 1818.

Las Pal•mas |läs 'pälməs| port and resort on the N coast of the island of Gran Canaria, capital of the Canary Islands. Pop. 372,000. Full name **Las Palmas de Gran Canaria**.

La Spe•zia |lä'spetsēə| industrial port in NW Italy. Pop. 103,000. Since 1861 it has been Italy's chief naval station.

Las•sen Peak |'læsən| (also **Mount Lassen**) dormant volcano in the Cascade Range, in N California. It rises to 10,457 ft./3,187 m.

Las Ve•gas |läs 'vāgəs| city in S Nevada. Pop. 258,295. It is noted for its casinos and nightclubs, and is the center of one of the fastest-growing metropolitan areas in the U.S.

Lat•a•kia |ˌlätə'kēə| seaport on the coast of W Syria, opposite the NE tip of Cyprus. Pop. 293,000.

La Tène |lä'ten| site near Lake Neuchâtel in Switzerland where ancient Celtic artifacts were found, giving a name to the second phase of the European Iron Age, from the 5th century B.C. to the Roman conquest.

Lat•er•an |'lætərən| complex in SE Rome, Italy, including the cathedral church of Rome. Formerly the residence of the popes, it is associated with several ecclesiastical councils and treaties.

Lat·in A·mer·i·ca |ˌlætn əˈmerikə| the parts of the American continent where Spanish or Portuguese is the main national language (i.e., Mexico and, in effect, the whole of Central and South America including many of the Caribbean islands). □ **Latin American** *adj. & n.*

Lat·in Quarter |ˈlætn ˈkwawrtər| section of Paris, France, on the Left Bank (S side) of the Seine River) and centered around the Sorbonne. It has attracted students, writers, and intellectuals for centuries.

La·ti·um |ˈlāsн(ē)əm| ancient region of W central Italy, W of the Apennines and S of the Tiber River. Settled during the early part of the 1st millennium B.C. by a branch of the Indo-European people known as the Latini, it had become dominated by Rome by the end of the 4th century B.C.; it is now part of the modern region of Lazio.

La·tur |läˈto͞or| town in S central India, in Maharashtra state, NW of Hyderabad. Pop. 197,000.

Lat·via |ˈlætviə| republic on the E shore of the Baltic Sea, between Estonia and Lithuania. Area: 24,947 sq. mi./64,589 sq. km. Pop. 2,693,000. Language, Latvian (Lettish). Capital and largest city: Riga. Long dominated by Poland, Sweden, or Russia. Latvia was independent 1918–40, then became a constituent of the Soviet Union. Independence was regained in 1991. Farming and commerce are essential to its economy. □ **Latvian** *adj. & n.*

Latvia

Laugh·lin |ˈläklən; ˈläflən| community in S Arizona, across the Colorado River from Bullhead City, Arizona. Pop. 4,791. It is a gambling resort.

Laun·ces·ton |ˈlawnsəstən| city in N Tasmania, Australia, on the Tamar estuary, the second-largest city of the island. Pop. 67,000.

Laur·a·sia |lawˈrāzнə| supercontinent thought to have existed in the N hemisphere before breaking up into North

America, Greenland, Europe, and most of Asia (excluding the Indian subcontinent and the Arabian Peninsula).

Lau·rel |ˈlawrəl| city in central Maryland, a largely residential center between Washington, D.C. and Baltimore. Pop. 19,438.

Lau·ren·tian Plateau |lawˈrenCHən| another name for the CANADIAN SHIELD. The Laurentian Mountains are a resort area in S Quebec, NW of Montreal.

Lau·sanne |lōˈzän| resort town in SW Switzerland, on the N shore of Lake Geneva. Pop. 123,000. It is headquarters for the International Olympic Committee.

La·val[1] |läˈväl| industrial center and capital city of the department of Mayenne, in NW France. Pop. 53,000. It is noted for its linen products.

La·val[2] |läˈväl| city in S Quebec, a suburb on the Île Jésus, just N of Montreal. Pop. 314,398.

La Ve·ga |lä ˈvāgə| commercial city in the central Dominican Republic, the capital of La Vega province. Pop. 73,000.

La Ven·ta |lä ˈväntə| village in SE Mexico, in mangrove swamps in W Tabasco state, site of major Olmec archaeological finds. The La Venta culture of 2,500 years ago takes its name from the vicinity.

Law·rence |ˈlawrəns; ˈlärəns| city in NE Kansas, home to the University of Kansas. Pop. 65,608. It was the scene of bloody fighting before and during the Civil War.

Law·ton |ˈlawtn| city in SW Oklahoma. Pop. 80,561. Fort Sill is just N.

La'youn |līˈo͞on| (also **Laayoune**) the capital of Western Sahara, on the Atlantic coast. Pop. 97,000. Arabic name **El Aaiún**.

Lay·ton |ˈlātn| city in N Utah, S of Ogden. Pop. 41,784.

La·zio |ˈlätsēō| administrative region of W central Italy, on the Tyrrhenian Sea, including the ancient region of Latium. Capital: Rome.

Lead·ville |ˈled,vil| historic mining city in central Colorado. Pop. 2,629. At 10,190 ft./3,108 m., it is the highest U.S. city.

Leam·ing·ton Spa |ˌlemiNGtən ˈspä| town in central England, in Warwickshire, SE of Birmingham. Pop. 57,000. Noted for its saline springs, it was granted the status of royal spa after a visit by Queen Victoria in 1838. Official name **Royal Leamington Spa**.

Leav·en·worth |ˈlevən,wərTH| city in NE Kansas, on the Missouri River. Several noted prisons are in or near the city, which also has military facilities. Pop. 38,495.

Leb·a·non[1] |ˈlebənən; ˈlebəˌnän| republic

in the Middle East, NE of Israel, with a coastline on the Mediterranean Sea. Area: 4,037 sq. mi./10,452 sq. km. Pop. 2,700,000. Language, Arabic. Capital and largest city: Beirut. Successor to ancient Phoenicia, long dominated by the Turks, later the French, Lebanon gained independence in 1943. Its commercial and tourist economy suffered severe damage during civil war in the 1980s. □ **Lebanese** *adj. & n.*

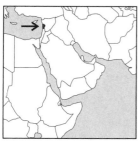

Lebanon

Leb·a·non[2] |'lebənən; 'lebə,nän| industrial city in SE Pennsylvania, in the Pennsylvania Dutch Country. Pop. 24,800.

Leb·a·non Mountains |'lebənən; 'lebə,nän| range of mountains in Lebanon. Running parallel to the Mediterranean coast, it rises to 10,022 ft./3,087 m. at Qornet es Saouda. It is separated from the Anti-Lebanon Mts., on the border with Syria, by the Bekaa Valley.

Le Bour·get |lə bŏŏr'zHā| town in N central France, 25 mi./40 km. N of Paris. It was the site of Le Bourget airport, now closed, where Charles Lindbergh landed after his solo transatlantic flight in May 1927.

Le·bo·wa |lə'bōə| former homeland established in South Africa for the North Sotho people, now part of Northern Province.

Lec·ce |'lacHā| ancient market town in SE Italy, capital of Lecce province. Pop. 102,000. It is noted for its Baroque architecture.

Lec·co |'lakō| town on Lake Lecco, a SE branch of Lake Como, in N Italy. Pop. 46,000.

Leeds |lēdz| industrial city in N England, formerly in Yorkshire. Pop. 674,000. It developed as a wool town in the Middle Ages, becoming a center of the clothing trade in the Industrial Revolution.

Lee's Summit |,lēz| industrial city in NW Missouri, SE of Kansas City. Pop. 46,418.

Leeu·war·den |'lā,värdn| market town in N Netherlands, capital of Friesland province. Pop. 85,000.

Lee·ward Islands |'lēwərd; 'lōōərd| group of islands in the West Indies, constituting the N part of the Lesser Antilles. The group includes Guadeloupe, Antigua, St. Kitts, and Montserrat. *Leeward* refers to the islands' situation farther downwind (in terms of the prevailing southeasterly winds) than the Windward Islands.

Lef·ko·sia |,lefkə'sēyə| Greek name for NICOSIA, Cyprus, and the name of the district surrounding the city.

Left Bank |'left 'bæNGk| district of the city of Paris, France, on the S bank of the Seine River. The site of educational and arts institutions including the Sorbonne and the Académie des Beaux-Arts, as well as the surrounding Latin Quarter, it is an area noted for its intellectual and artistic life. French name **Rive Gauche.**

Le·gaz·pi |lä'gäspē| (also **Legaspi**) port city in the Philippines, on SE Luzon, on Albay Gulf. Pop. 121,000. It is at the base of the active Mayon Volcano.

Leg·horn |'leg,hawrn| another name for LIVORNO, Italy.

Leg·ni·ca |leg'nētsə| textile center and manufacturing town, capital of Legnica county, in SW Poland. Pop. 105,000. German name **Liegnitz.**

Leh |lā| town in Jammu and Kashmir, N India, to the E of Srinagar near the Indus River. Pop. 9,000. It is the chief town of the Himalayan region of Ladakh, and the administrative center of Ladakh district.

Le Ha·vre |lə 'häv(rə)| industrial port in N France, on the English Channel at the mouth of the Seine. Pop. 197,000.

Le·high River |'lē,hī| river that flows 103 mi./166 km. through E Pennsylvania, to the Delaware River. The Lehigh Valley is heavily industrial, with Bethlehem and Allentown among its centers.

Leices·ter |'lestər| industrial city in central England, on the Soar River, the county seat of Leicestershire. Pop. 271,000. It was founded as a Roman settlement on the Fosse Way (AD 50–100).

Leices·ter·shire |'lestərsHir; 'lestərsHər| county of central England. Pop. 860,000; county seat, Leicester.

Lei·den |'līdn| (also **Leyden**) city in the W Netherlands, 9 mi./15 km. NE of The Hague. Pop. 112,000. It is the site of the country's oldest university, founded in 1575.

Lein·ster |'lenstər| province of the Republic of Ireland, in the SE, comprising twelve counties centered on Dublin.

Leip·zig |'līpsig| industrial city in E central Germany. Pop. 503,000. A publishing and music center, it is associated with J. S. Bach, who is buried here.

Lei·ria |lā'rēə| town in central Portugal. Capital of Leiria district, on the Liz River. Pop. 28,000.

Leith |lēTH| former port city in SE Scotland, now part of Edinburgh.

Lei·trim |'lētrəm| county of the Republic of Ireland, in the province of Connacht. Pop. 25,000; county seat, Carrick-on-Shannon.

Lei·zhou Peninsula |'lā'jō| (formerly **Luichow Peninsula**) peninsula in S Guangdong province, S China, across the Hainan Strait from Hainan Island. The former French territory of Kwangchowan was on the E coast.

Le Mans |lə 'mäN; lə 'män(z)| industrial town in NW France. Pop. 148,000. It is the site of a famed motor-racing circuit, on which a 24-hour endurance race is held each summer.

Lem·berg |'lem,bərg| German name for LVIV, Ukraine.

Lem·nos |'lem,näs; 'lemnəs| Greek island in the N Aegean Sea, off NW Turkey; chief town, Kástron. Greek name **Límnos**.

Le·na |'lānə| river in Siberia, which rises in the mountains on the W shore of Lake Baikal and flows for 2,750 mi./4,400 km. into the Laptev Sea. It is famous for the goldfields in its basin.

Le·nin·a·kan |lə,nēnə'kän| former name (1924–91) for GYUMRI, Armenia.

Len·in·grad |'lenən,græd| former name (1924–91) for ST. PETERSBURG, Russia. The German siege of Leningrad (1941–44) was one of the most destructive in history.

Len·in Peak |'lenin| (formerly **Kaufman Peak**) mountain in the Trans Alai Range, between Kyrgyzstan and Tajikistan. It was the second-highest peak in the former Soviet Union (23,405 ft./7,134 m.) and is the highest in the Trans Alai.

Len·ox |'lenəks| resort town in W Massachusetts, in the Berkshire Hills. Pop. 5,069. Tanglewood, the noted summer music complex, is here.

Lens |läNs| industrial city in N France. Pop. 38,000.

Leom·in·ster |'lemənstər| industrial city in N central Massachusetts. Pop. 38,145.

Le·ón[1] |lā'ōn| industrial city in Guanajuato state, central Mexico. Pop. 872,000.

Le·ón[2] |lā'ōn| industrial and university city

in W Nicaragua, the second-largest city in the country. Pop. 159,000.

Le·ón[3] |lā'ōn| city in N Spain. Pop. 146,000. It is the capital of the province and former kingdom of León, now part of Castilla-León region.

Le·o·nine City |'lēə,nīn| the part of Rome, Italy in which the Vatican stands, walled and fortified by Pope Leo IV.

Lé·o·pold·ville |'lēə,pōlkd,vil; 'lāə,pold,vil| former name (until 1966) for KINSHASA, Congo (formerly Zaire).

Le·pan·to, Gulf of |lə'päntō; lə'pæntō| another name for the Gulf of Corinth (see CORINTH, GULF OF), Greece.

Le·pon·tine Alps |li'pän,tīn; 'lepən'tīn| range of the central Alps on the Italian-Swiss border, just N of the Italian lake district, reaching 11,683 ft./3,563 m. at Monte Leone. The range extends into central Switzerland.

Lep·tis Mag·na |'leptəs 'mægnə| ancient seaport and trading center on the Mediterranean coast of N Africa, near present-day Al Khums in Libya. Founded by the Phoenicians, it became one of the three chief cities of Tripolitania and was later a Roman colony under Trajan.

Lé·ri·da |lārēdä| industrial city in NE Spain, on the Segre River, capital of Lérida province. Pop. 119,000. The surrounding area is agricultural.

Ler·wick |'lərwik| the capital of the Shetland Islands, Scotland, on the island of Mainland. Pop. 7,000. The most northerly town in the British Isles, it is a fishing center and a service port for the oil industry.

Les Abymes |lā zä'bēm| town on Grand-Terre, in Guadeloupe, in the West Indies. Pop. 63,000. The department's international airport is here.

Les Baux-de-Provence |lā'bō də prō-'väNs| village in Bouches-du-Rhône department, SE France. A tourist attraction atop a hill, it gave its name to the mineral bauxite.

Les·bos |'lez,bäs| Greek island in the E Aegean, off the coast of NW Turkey. Pop. 104,000; chief town, Mytilene. Its artistic golden age of the late 7th and early 6th centuries B.C. produced the poets Alcaeus and Sappho. Greek name **Lésvos**.

Les Cayes |lā 'kā| (also **Cayes** or **Aux Cayes**) port city in SW Haiti, on the Caribbean Sea. Pop. 38,000.

Le·so·tho |lə'so͞otō; lə'sōtō| landlocked mountainous kingdom forming an enclave within South Africa. Area: 11,717 sq. mi./30,335 sq. km. Pop. 1,816,000. Official

Lesotho

languages, Sesotho and English. Capital and largest city: Maseru. Formerly Basutoland, and independent since 1966, Lesotho sends many of its workers to South Africa. Agriculture and handicrafts are also important.

Les·ser An·til·les |ˈlesər ænˈtiléz| see ANTILLES.

Les·ser Sun·da Islands |ˈlesər ˈsəndə; ˈso͞ondə| see SUNDA ISLANDS.

Lés·vos |ˈlez,vaws| Greek name for LESBOS.

Leth·bridge |ˈleTHbrij| city in S Alberta, on the Oldman River. It is an industrial, academic, and research center. Pop. 60,974.

Lethe |ˈlēTHē| in Greek mythology, river of the underworld. When the dead drank its waters, they forgot their life on earth.

Le·ti·cia |ləˈtēsyə| town and river port at the S tip of Colombia, on the upper reaches of the Amazon on the border with Brazil and Peru. Pop. 24,000.

Leu·ven |ˈlœvən| historic university town in Belgium, E of Brussels. Pop. 85,000. It was the capital of Brabant (11th–15th century). French name **Louvain**.

Levallois-Perret |lə,væwäpəˈrā| industrial and residential suburb NW of Paris, France. Pop. 54,000.

Le·vant |ləˈvænt| historical term for the E part of the Mediterranean with its islands and coastal regions, from the French *levant*, 'rising' (in reference to the sun).

Le·ver·ku·sen |ˈlāvər,ko͞ozən| industrial city in western Germany, in North Rhine-Westphalia, on the Rhine River N of Cologne. Pop. 161,000.

Levis-Lauzon |lā,vēlōˈzawN| industrial city in S Quebec, across the Saint Lawrence River from Quebec City. Pop. 39,452.

Lev·it·town |ˈlevət,town| village in central Long Island, New York, developed after World War II. Pop. 53,286. It was noted for its "cookie-cutter" houses. There were also Levittowns in New Jersey, Pennsylvania, and Puerto Rico.

Lew·es |ˈlo͞oəs| town in S England, NE of Brighton, the county seat of East Sussex. Pop. 15,000.

Lew·is |ˈlo͞oəs| the northern part of the island of Lewis and Harris in the Outer Hebrides, Scotland.

Lew·is and Clark Trail |ˈlo͞oəs ən ˈklärk| (official name **Lewis and Clark National Historic Trail**) route of the Lewis and Clark expedition, which in 1804–06 explored the Louisiana Purchase from St. Louis, Missouri to the Pacific Coast.

Lew·is and Har·ris |ˈlo͞oəs ənd ˈhærəs| (also **Lewis with Harris**) the largest and northernmost island of the Outer Hebrides in Scotland; chief town, Stornoway. The island, which is separated from the mainland by the Minch, consists of a N part, Lewis, and a smaller and more mountainous S part, Harris.

Lew·i·sham |ˈlo͞oəSHəm| largely residential borough of SE Greater London, England, S of the Thames River. Pop. 215,000.

Lew·is·ton[1] |ˈlo͞oəstən| industrial city in NW Idaho, on the Snake River. Pop. 28,082.

Lew·is·ton[2] |ˈlo͞oəstən| industrial city in SW Maine, on the Androscoggin River opposite Auburn. Pop. 39,757.

Lex·ing·ton[1] |ˈleksiNGtən| historic commercial city in central Kentucky. Pop. 225,366. It is a noted horse-breeding center.

Lex·ing·ton[2] |ˈleksiNGtən| residential town NW of Boston, Massachusetts. Pop. 28,974. It was the scene in 1775 of the first battle in the Revolutionary War.

Ley·te |ˈlātē; ˈlātä| island in the central Philippines. Pop. 1,362,000; chief town, Tacloban.

Ley·te Gulf |ˈlātē; ˈlātä| inlet of the Philippine Sea, E Philippines, between Leyte and Samar. A Japanese fleet was destroyed here during World War II, in 1944.

Le·zhë |ˈläzHə| (also **Lesh**; ancient name **Lissus**; Italian name **Alessio**) historic town in NW Albania, the burial place of the national hero Skanderbeg.

Lha·sa |ˈläsə| the capital of Tibet. Pop. 140,000. It is situated in the N Himalayas at an altitude of 11,800 ft./3,600 m., on a tributary of the Brahmaputra. The historic center of Tibetan Buddhism, it was the seat of the Dalai Lama until a Chinese takeover in 1959.

Lian·yun·gang |lēˈänˈyʏnˈgäNG| deepwater port in Jiangsu province, E China, on the Yellow Sea. Pop, 354,000. It is a special economic zone in a mining and agricultural region.

Liao River |lē'ow| river in NE China, rising in Inner Mongolia and flowing 864 mi./1,390 km. through Liaoning province to the Gulf of Liaodong at the N end of the Bo Hai.

Liao•dong Peninsula |lē'ow'dŏoNG| peninsula in NE China, which extends S into the Yellow Sea between Bo Hai and Korea Bay.

Liao•ning |lē'ow'niNG| province in NE China, separated on the E from North Korea by the Yalu River. Pop. 39,460,000. Capital: Shenyang. An important industrial region, it is a leading producer of iron, steel, coke, and chemicals.

Liao•yang |lē'ow'yäNG| city in Liaoning province, NE China, SE of Shenyang. Pop. 493,000. An agricultural distribution center with light industries, it was the site of a Japanese victory (1904) during the Russo-Japanese War.

Liao•yuan |lē'owyY'en| city in Jilin province, NE China, in the Jilin Hada Ling mountains to the S of Changchun. Pop. 378,000.

Li•ard River |'lē,ärd; lē'ärd| river that flows 570 mi./920 km. from the Yukon Territory through British Columbia and the Northwest Territories to the Mackenzie River.

Li•be•rec |'lēbə,rets| industrial city in the N central Czech Republic. Pop. 48,000. The city is a center of textile manufacturing, especially woolens.

Li•be•ria |lī'birēə| republic on the Atlantic coast of W Africa. Area: 37,757 sq. mi./97,754 sq. km. Pop. 2,639,000. Languages, English (official), English-based pidgin. Capital and largest city: Monrovia. Founded in 1822 for freed U.S. slaves, Liberia gained independence in 1847. Civil war in 1980–96 severely damaged its econ-

Liberia

omy, which is based on mining and other extractive industries. □ **Liberian** *adj. & n.*

Lib•er•ty Island |'libərtē| island in New York Bay, off Jersey City, New Jersey, site, since 1885, of the Statue of Liberty.

Li•bre•ville |'lēbrə,vil| the capital of Gabon, a port on the Atlantic coast at the mouth of the Gabon River. Pop. 352,000.

Lib•ya |'libēə| country in North Africa, on the Mediterranean, with most of its S in the Sahara Desert. Area: 685,786 sq. mi./1.78 million sq. km. Pop. 4,714,000. Capital and largest city: Tripoli. Part of Roman and Turkish empires, later controlled by Italy, Libya gained independence in 1951. Oil, discovered in 1959, is key to its economy. □ **Libyan** *adj. & n.*

Libya

Lib•yan Desert |'libēən| name for the NE Sahara Desert, W of the Nile in Egypt, Libya, and NW Sudan. In Egypt it is also called the Western Desert.

Lich•field |'liCH,fēld| town in central England, in Staffordshire N of Birmingham. Pop. 26,000. It was the birthplace of lexicographer Samuel Johnson.

Li•di•ce |'lēd(y)ət,sä| village, 5 mi./8 km. W of Kladno, in the Czech Republic. In June 1942 Nazis killed all the male inhabitants, sent the women to concentration camps and the children to German institutions, then destroyed the entire village in retaliation for the assassination of a high Nazi official.

Li•dingö |'lē,dēNGœ| island suburb of Stockholm in Sweden, in the NE of the city. Pop. 38,000.

Li•do |'lēdō| **1** an island reef off the coast of NE Italy, in the N Adriatic. It separates the Lagoon of Venice from the Gulf of Venice. Full name **Lido di Malamocco. 2** (also **the Lido**) a town and beach resort in NE Italy, on the Lido reef opposite Venice. Pop. 21,000.

Liech•ten•stein |'liKHtən,SHtīn| small (62 sq. mi./160 sq. km.) independent principality in the Alps, between Switzerland and Austria. Pop. 28,880; official language, German. Capital and largest town: Vaduz. Created in 1719 and independent since 1866, Liechtenstein is economically integrated with Switzerland. Finance and tourism are important. □ **Liechtensteiner** *n.*

Liechtenstein

Li•ège |lē'ezH| **1** province of E Belgium. Formerly ruled by independent prince-bishops, it became a part of the Netherlands in 1815 and of Belgium in 1830. Flemish name **Luik. 2** its capital city, an industrial port on the Meuse River. Pop. 195,000.

Lie•pä•ja |'lyepäyə| seaport in Latvia, on the Baltic Sea. Pop. 115,000. It has a naval base as well as a commercial harbor.

Lif•fey |'life| river of E Ireland, which flows for 50 mi./80 km. from the Wicklow Mts. to Dublin Bay. The city of Dublin is situated at its mouth.

Lif•ford |'lifərd| the county seat of Donegal, in the NW Republic of Ireland. Pop. 1,500.

Li•gu•ria |lə'gyŏŏrēə| coastal region of NW Italy, which extends along the Mediterranean coast from Tuscany to the border with France. Capital: Genoa. In ancient times Liguria extended as far as the Atlantic seaboard. □ **Ligurian** *adj. & n.*

Li•gur•i•an Alps |li'gyŏŏrēən| spur of the Alps extending from the Maritime Alps along the French border into NE Italy, to the Apennines. The **Ligurian Sea** is the section of the Mediterranean just to the S.

Li•ka•si |li'käsē| (formerly **Jadotville**) mining city in SE Congo (formerly Zaire), in the Shaba region. Pop. 280,000. The region produces copper and cobalt.

Lille |'lēl| industrial city in N France, a textile and technology center near the border with Belgium. Pop. 178,000.

Lil•le•ham•mer |'lilə,hämər| resort town and capital of Oppland county, S Norway.

Pop. 23,000. The 1994 Winter Olympics were held here.

Li•long•we |lə'lawNGwä| commercial city, founded as the capital of Malawi in 1975. Pop. 234,000.

Li•ma[1] |'līmə| industrial city in NW Ohio, N of Dayton. Pop. 45,549.

Li•ma[2] |'lēmə| the capital of Peru. Pop. 5,706,000. Founded in 1535 by Francisco Pizarro, it was the capital of the Spanish colonies in South America until the 19th century. Today it is an industrial center with a Pacific port at Callao.

Li•mas•sol |,lēmə'sawl| port on the Greek-controlled S coast of Cyprus, on Akrotiri Bay. Pop. 143,000.

Lim•be |'limbä| (formerly **Victoria**) port and resort town in SW Cameroon, on the Atlantic coast W of Douala. Pop. 45,000. It is a former colonial capital.

Lim•burg |'lim,bərg| former duchy of Lorraine, divided in 1839 between Belgium and the Netherlands. It now forms a province of NE Belgium (capital, Hasselt) and a province of SE Netherlands (capital, Maastricht). French name **Limbourg**.

Li•mei•ra |lē'märə| city in S Brazil, in São Paulo state. Pop. 230,000. It is a commercial and processing center in an area known for orange production.

Lim•er•ick |'lim(ə)rik| **1** county of the Republic of Ireland, in the W in the province of Munster. Pop. 162,000. **2** its county seat, on the Shannon River. Pop. 52,000.

Lím•nos |'lēmnaws| Greek name for LEMNOS.

Li•moges |lə'mōzH| city in W central France, the principal city of Limousin. Pop. 136,000. Famous in the late Middle Ages for enamel work, it has been noted since the 18th century for the production of porcelain.

Li•món |lē'mōn| port on the Caribbean coast of Costa Rica. Pop. 75,000. Also called **Puerto Limón**.

Li•mou•sin |lēmŏŏ'zeN| region and former province of central France, centered on Limoges.

Lim•po•po |lim'pōpō| river of SE Africa. Rising as the Crocodile River near Johannesburg, it flows 1,100 mi./1,770 km. in a sweeping curve to the N and E to meet the Indian Ocean in Mozambique, N of Maputo. For much of its course it forms South Africa's boundary with Botswana and Zimbabwe.

Li•na•res[1] |lē'närās| commercial city in S central Chile, in the Maule region, in an agricultural district. Pop. 76,000.

Li·na·res[2] |lē'närās| industrial town in S Spain, in a silver- and lead-mining area. Pop. 57,000.

Lin·coln[1] |'liNGkən| city in E England, the county seat of Lincolnshire. Pop. 82,000. It was founded by the Romans as Lindum Colonia.

Lin·coln[2] |'liNGkən| the state capital of Nebraska. Pop. 191,972. The second-largest Nebraska city, it is a university and commercial center.

Lin·coln·shire |'liNGkən,SHir; 'liNGkən-SHər| county on the E coast of England. Pop. 574,000; county seat, Lincoln. The former N part of the county, included in Humberside 1974–96, is now divided into *North Lincolnshire* and *North East Lincolnshire*.

Lin·den |'lindən| industrial city in NE New Jersey, S of Elizabeth, noted for its oil refineries. Pop. 36,701.

Lin·dis·farne |'lindəs,färn| small island off the coast of Northumberland, N of the Farne Islands. Linked to the mainland by a causeway exposed only at low tide, it is the site of a church and monastery founded by St. Aidan in 635. Also called **Holy Island**.

Lind·sey |'linzē| one of three administrative divisions of Lincolnshire before the local government reorganization of 1974 (the others were Holland and Kesteven), comprising the N part of the country.

Line Islands |līn| group of eleven islands in the central Pacific, straddling the equator S of Hawaii. Eight of the islands, including Kiritimati (Christmas Island), form part of Kiribati; the remaining three (Jarvis, Palmyra, and Kingman Reef) are uninhabited dependencies of the U.S.

Lin·fen |'lin'fən| city in Shanxi province, E central China, on the Fen River S of Taiyuan. Pop. 187,000.

Lin·ga·yen |,liNGgä'yen| 1 inlet of the South China Sea, in central Luzon, the Philippines. 2 port town in the Philippines, central Luzon, on the Lingayen Gulf. Pop. 79,000.

Lin·hai |'lin'hī| city in Zhejiang province, E China, NW of Jiaojiang on the Ling River. Pop. 1,012,000.

Lin·he |'lin'hə| city in Inner Mongolia, N China, W of Baotou near the bend of the Yellow River. Pop. 347,000.

Lin·kö·ping |'lin'CHœ'piNG| industrial town in SE Sweden. Pop. 122,000. It was a noted cultural and ecclesiastical center in the Middle Ages.

Lin·lith·gow |lin'liTHgō| historic town in central Scotland, in West Lothian. Pop. 10,000. Its palace, home to Scottish kings and birthplace of Mary, Queen of Scots, is now a ruin.

Lin·qing |'lin'CHiNG| city in Shandong province, E China, on the Grand Canal, W of Jinan. Pop. 124,000.

Lin·yi |'lin'yē| city in Shandong province, E China, on the Yi River, SE of Jinan. Pop. 325,000.

Linz |lin(t)s| industrial city in N Austria, on the Danube River, capital of the state of Upper Austria. Pop. 203,000.

Lip·a·ri Islands |'lipərē| group of seven volcanic resort islands in the Tyrrhenian Sea, off the NE coast of Sicily, and in Italian possession. Believed by the ancient Greeks to be the home of Aeolus, the islands were formerly known as the Aeolian Islands.

Li·petsk |'lēpitsk| industrial city in SW Russia, on the Voronezh River. Pop. 455,000.

Li·piz·za |'lēpētsə| (Slovenian name **Lipica**) village in Slovenia, a horse breeding center since Roman times. It gave its name to the white Lipizzaner horses.

Lip·pe |'lipə| former state in N central Germany, since 1947 part of the state of North Rhine-Westphalia. Its capital was Detmold.

Lis·bon |'lizbən| the capital and chief port of Portugal, an industrial and cultural center on the Atlantic coast at the mouth of the Tagus River. Pop. 678,000. Much of the city was rebuilt after a 1755 earthquake. Portuguese name **Lisboa**.

Lis·burn |'lizbərn| town in County Antrim, Northern Ireland, to the SW of Belfast, on the border with County Down. Pop. 40,000.

Lis·doon·var·na |lis'dōon,värnə| spa town in the Republic of Ireland, in County Clare. Pop. 600.

Li·shui |'lē'SHwē| city in Zhejiang province, SE China, NW of Wenzhou on a tributary of the Ou River. Pop. 303,000.

Li·sieux |lēz'yœ| town in Calvados, N France. Pop. 25,000. It is the site of a shrine of Saint Theresa of Lisieux, who was canonized in 1925.

Litch·field |'liCH,fēld| historic town in NW Connecticut. Pop. 8,365.

Lith·u·a·nia |,liTHə'wānēə| republic on the SE shore of the Baltic Sea. Area: 25,183 sq. mi./65,200 sq. km. Pop. 3,765,000. Languages, Lithuanian (official), Russian. Capital and largest city: Vilnius. Long tied to Poland, Lithuania was dominated by Russia in the 18th–20th centuries, regaining independence in 1991. Traditionally agricultural, it has since 1940 become increasingly industrial. □ **Lithuanian** *adj. & n.*

Lithuania

Lit·tle A·mer·i·ca |ə'merikə| name given five former U.S. exploration bases in Antarctica between 1929 and 1958. All were on or near the Bay of Whales in the Ross Sea.

Lit·tle Ar·a·rat |'ærə,ræt| see ARARAT, MOUNT.

Lit·tle Belt channel between the Kattegat and the Baltic Sea that separates the mainland of Denmark from Fyn Island.

Lit·tle Big·horn River |,litl 'big,hawrn| river in N Wyoming and SE Montana, scene of the 1876 defeat of George Custer's cavalry by Cheyenne and Sioux warriors.

Lit·tle Mis·sou·ri River |mə'zoorē| river that flows 560 mi./900 km. from Wyoming through Montana and the Dakotas, to the Missouri River.

Lit·tle Rock |'litl ,räk| the capital of Arkansas, an industrial city on the Arkansas River. Pop. 175,795.

Lit·tle Rus·sia |'rəsHə| term formerly applied chiefly to the Ukraine, but also to neighboring regions in historic RUTHENIA.

Lit·tle St. Ber·nard Pass |,sänt bə(r)-'närd| see ST. BERNARD PASS.

Lit·tle Ti·bet |tə'bet| another name for BALTISTAN.

Lit·tle·ton |'lidltən| industrial city in N central Colorado, S of Denver. Pop. 33,685.

Liu·zhou |lē'oo'jō| (also **Liuchow**) an industrial city in S China, in Guangxi Zhuang province NE of Nanning. Pop. 740,000.

Liv·er·more |'livər,mawr| city in N central California, E of Oakland, noted as home to the Lawrence Livermore nuclear laboratory. Pop. 56,741.

Liv·er·pool |'livər,pool| industrial port city in NW England, on the E side of the mouth of the Mersey River. Pop. 448,000. Liverpool developed as a port in the 17th cen-

tury with the import of cotton from America and the export of textiles produced in Lancashire and Yorkshire, and in the 18th century became an important center of shipbuilding and engineering.

Liv·ing·stone |'liviNGstən| former name for MARAMBA, Zambia.

Li·vo·nia¹ |lə'vōnēə| region on the E coast of the Baltic Sea, N of Lithuania, comprising most of present-day Latvia and Estonia. German name **Livland**. □ **Livonian** *adj. & n.*

Li·vo·nia² |lə'vōnēə| industrial city in SE Michigan, W of Detroit. Pop. 100,850.

Li·vor·no |lə'vawr,nō| port in NW Italy, in Tuscany, on the Ligurian Sea. Pop. 171,000. It is the site of the Italian Naval Academy. Also called **Leghorn**.

Liz·ard, the |'lizərd| promontory in SW England, in Cornwall. Its S tip, Lizard Point, is the southernmost point of the British mainland.

Lju·blja·na |lē,ooblē'änə| the capital of Slovenia. Pop. 267,000. The city was founded (as Emona) by the Romans in 34 B.C. Long the capital of Illyria, it is a modern industrial city. German name **Laibach**.

Llan·dud·no |hlän'didnō| resort town in Conwy, N Wales, on the Irish Sea. Pop. 14,000.

Lla·nel·li |hlä'nehlē| industrial port in S Wales, in Dyfed, on Carmarthen Bay, a former center of steel and tin manufacturing. Pop. 73,000.

Llan·gol·len |hlä'gawhlən| resort town in NE Wales, in Clwyd. Pop. 3,000. A tourist center, it is home to the annual international *eisteddfod* (arts festival).

Llano Es·ta·ca·do |'yänō ,estə'kädō| (also **Staked Plain**) high section of the Great Plains in the Texas Panhandle and SE New Mexico.

Lla·nos |'yänōs| vast grassy plains or savannas in tropical South America, especially in the Orinoco River basin. They are known as the home of cattle-tending *llaneros*, South American cowboys.

Lo·bam·ba |lō'bämbə| village in W central Swaziland, SE of Mbabane, that is the royal and legislative capital of the kingdom.

Lo·bi·to |lō'bētō| seaport and natural harbor on the Atlantic coast of Angola. Pop. 150,000.

Lo·car·no |lō'kärnō| resort in S Switzerland, at the N end of Lake Maggiore. Pop. 14,000.

Lock·er·bie |'läkərbē| town in SW Scotland, in Dumfries and Galloway. Pop. 4,000. In 1988 the wreckage of a Pan Am jetliner, bound for NewYork, but destroyed by a terrorist bomb, crashed on the town, killing all those on board and eleven people on the ground.

Lock·port |'läk,pawrt| city in W NewYork, NE of Buffalo, on the Erie Canal route. Pop. 24,426.

Lo·cris |'lōkrəs| region in the central part of ancient Greece, eventually divided into parts. It was a very early state, probably predating the arrival of the Phocians.

Lod |lōd| (also **Lydda**) historic city in central Israel, SE of Tel Aviv. Pop. 51,000.

Lo·di[1] |'lawdē| city in N central California, N of Stockton, in the San Joaquin Valley. Pop. 51,874.

Lo·di[2] |'lō'dī| town in N Italy, SE of Milan. Pop. 42,000. French troops led by Napoleon defeated Austrian troops here in 1796.

Łódź city in central Poland. Pop. 842,000.

Lo·fo·ten Islands |'lōfōtn| island group off the NW coast of Norway. They are situated within the Arctic Circle, SW of the Vesterålen group.

Lo·gan, Mount |'lōgən| mountain in the SW Yukon Territory, in Kluane National Park, near the border with Alaska. Rising to 19,850 ft./6,054 m., it is the highest peak in Canada and the second-highest peak in North America.

Lo·gan |'lōgən| city in N Utah, in an agricultural area. Pop. 32,762.

Lo·gro·ño |lō'grōnyō| market town in N Spain, on the Ebro River, capital of La Rioja region. Pop. 127.000.

Loire |lə'wär| longest river of France. It rises in the Massif Central and flows 630 mi./1,015 km. N and W to the Atlantic at St. Nazaire. Its valley is noted for its historic chateaus.

Lo·ja |'lōhä| commercial and university city in S Ecuador, the capital of Loja province. Pop. 94,000.

Lol·land |'law,län| Danish island in the Baltic Sea, to the S of Zealand and W of Falster.

Lo·mas de Za·mo·ra |'lōmäs dä sə-'mawrə| city in E Argentina, an industrial suburb S of Buenos Aires. Pop. 573,000.

Lom·bard Street |'läm,bärd| street in the financial district of London, England, containing many leading banks.

Lom·bar·dy |'läm,bärdē; 'lämbərdē| region of N central Italy, between the Alps and the Po River. Capital: Milan. Italian name **Lombardia**. □ **Lombard** adj. & n.

Lom·bok |'läm,bäk| volcanic island of the Lesser Sunda group in Indonesia, between

Bali and Sumbawa. Pop. 2,500,000; chief town, Mataram.

Lo·mé |'lōmä| the capital and chief port of Togo, on the Gulf of Guinea. Pop. 450,000.

Lo·mond, Loch |läk 'lōmənd; läkH| lake in W central Scotland, to the NW of Glasgow. The largest freshwater lake in Scotland, it is the subject of songs and folklore.

Lom·poc |'läm,päk| city in SW California, NW of Santa Barbara. Pop. 37,649. Its economy relies on agriculture and government installations.

Lon·don[1] |'ləndən| industrial and commercial city in S Ontario, on the Thames River to the N of Lake Erie. Pop. 303,165.

Lon·don[2] |'ləndən| the capital of the United Kingdom, situated in SE England on the River Thames. Pop. 6,379,000. London was settled as a river port and trading center, called Londinium, shortly after the Roman invasion in A.D. 43, and since the Middle Ages has been a leading world city. Devastated by the Great Plague (1665–66) and the Fire of London (1666), the city was rebuilt in the late 17th century. Damage duringWorld War II again led to substantial reconstruction. It is divided administratively into the City of London, known as the Square Mile, which is the British financial center, and thirty-two boroughs of Greater London. It is the seat, atWestminster, of the British government. □ **Londoner** n.

Lon·don Bridge |'ləndən| name of several successive bridges over the RiverThames in London, England, beginning with a wood structure of the 10th century. The stone bridge of the 1830s was moved in 1968 to Lake Havasu City, Arizona, where it is a tourist attraction.

Lon·don·der·ry |'ləndən,derē| **1** one of the Six Counties of Northern Ireland, formerly an administrative area. Pop. 187,000. **2** its chief town, a port city on the Foyle River near the N coast. Pop. 63,000. It was formerly called Derry, a name still used by many. In 1613 it was granted to the City of London for colonization and became known as Londonderry.

Lon·dri·na |lōn'drēnə| commercial city in S Brazil, in Paraná state, in an agricultural area. Pop. 413,000.

Lone Star State |'lōn ,stär| nickname for TEXAS, whose flag contains one star.

Long Beach |'lawNG ,bēcH| port and resort city in S California, just S of Los Angeles. Pop. 429,433.

Long Branch |'lawNG ,bræncH| city in E central New Jersey, on the Atlantic, long a noted summer resort. Pop. 28,658.

Long·champs |lōN'SHäN| famed racetrack in Paris, France, in the Bois de Boulogne, long a resort for the fashionable.

Long·ford |'lawNGfərd| **1** county in the central Republic of Ireland, in the province of Leinster. Pop. 30,000. **2** its county seat. Pop. 6,000.

Long Island |lawNG 'īlənd| island of New York State, extending E of Manhattan for 118 mi./210 km. roughly parallel to the coast of Connecticut, from which it is separated by Long Island Sound. Its W tip, comprising the New York boroughs of Brooklyn and Queens, is separated from Manhattan and the Bronx by the East River. To the E are suburban NASSAU COUNTY and SUFFOLK COUNTY.

Long Island City |lawNG 'īlənd| section of Queens, New York City, across the East River from Manhattan, and both industrial and residential.

Long·mont |'lawNG,mänt| city in N Colorado, an agricultural and industrial center. Pop. 51,555.

Lon·gueuil |lawNG'gāl| city in S Quebec, an industrial suburb across the St. Lawrence River from Montreal. Pop. 129,874.

Long·view[1] |'lawNG,vyo͞o| city in E Texas, in an oil-producing area. Pop. 70,311.

Long·view[2] |'lawNG,vyo͞o| port city in SW Washington, on the Cowlitz and Columbia rivers. Pop. 31,499.

Long·yan |'lo͞oNG'yän| industrial and agricultural city in Fujian province, SE China, NW of Xiamen. Pop. 386,000.

Look·out Mountain |'lo͞ok,owt| Appalachian ridge on the Cumberland Plateau in Alabama, Georgia, and Tennessee, where near Chattanooga it was the scene of a November 1863 Civil War battle.

Loop, the |lo͞op| commercial district at the center of Chicago, Illinois, named for the railway tracks that circle around part of it.

Lop Nor |'lōp 'nawr| (also **Lop Nur**) dried-up salt lake in the arid basin of the Tarim River in NW China, used since 1964 for nuclear testing.

Lo·rain |law'rān| port city in N central Ohio, on Lake Erie W of Cleveland. Pop. 71,245.

Lor·ca |'lawrkə| market town in Murcia, SE Spain, on the Guadalentin River. Pop. 67,000.

Lord Howe Island |lawrd 'how| volcanic island in the SW Pacific off the E coast of Australia, administered as part of New South Wales. Pop. 320.

Lord's |lawrdz| cricket ground in St. John's Wood, N London, England, headquarters since 1814 of the Marylebone Cricket Club (MCC), the sport's unofficial governing body.

Lo·re·lei |'lawrə,lī| rock cliff on the Rhine River S of Coblenz, western Germany, in legend the home of a siren whose song lures boatmen to destruction. The cliff is noted for its echo.

Lo·re·to |lə'rātō| town in E Italy, near the Adriatic coast to the S of Ancona. Pop. 11,000. It is the site of the 'Holy House', said to be the home of the Virgin Mary and to have been brought from Nazareth by angels in 1295.

Lo·rient |lawr'yäN| shipbuilding port in NW France, on the S coast of Brittany. Pop. 62,000.

Lor·raine |law'ren; lə'rān| region of NE France, between Champagne and the Vosges mountains. The modern region corresponds to the southern part of the medieval kingdom of Lorraine (from the ancient name **Lotharingia**), which extended from the North Sea to Italy.

Los Al·a·mos |laws 'æləmōs| community in N New Mexico, on the Pajarito Plateau. Pop. 11,455. It has been a center for nuclear research since the 1940s, when it was built to be the site of the development (in the Manhattan Project) of the first nuclear bombs.

Los An·ge·les[1] |laws 'ænjələs| city on the Pacific coast of S California, the second-largest city in the U.S. Pop. 3,485,398. Founded by the Spanish in 1781, it developed after the arrival of the Southern Pacific Railroad and the discovery of oil in 1894. It has become a major center of industry, filmmaking, and television in the 20th century, its metropolitan area having expanded to include towns such as Beverly Hills, Hollywood, Santa Monica, and Pasadena. **Los Angeles County** is the largest in the U.S.: pop. 8,863,164.

Los An·ge·les[2] |laws'ænjələs| city in S central Chile, a processing center in the agricultural Bío-Bío River valley. Pop. 142,000.

Los Gat·os |laws 'gætəs| city in N central California, SW of San Jose. Pop. 27,357.

Los Mo·chis |laws 'mōcHēs| commercial city in W Mexico, in Sinaloa state. Pop. 163,000.

Lost Colony see ROANOKE ISLAND.

Los Te·ques |laws 'tākes| commercial and resort city in N Venezuela, the capital of Miranda state. Pop. 141,000.

Lot |lawt| river of S France, which rises in

the Auvergne and flows 300 mi./480 km.W to meet the Garonne SE of Bordeaux.

Lo·thi·an |'lōTHēən| former local government region in central Scotland, now divided into *East Lothian, Midlothian,* and *West Lothian.*

Louang·phra·bang |'lwäNGprä'bäNG| variant spelling of LUANG PRABANG, Laos.

Lough·bor·ough |'ləfb(ə)rə| town in Leicestershire, England, on the River Soar N of Leicester. Pop. 46,000.

Lou·is·bourg |'lōōəs,bərg| historic town in E Cape Breton Island, Nova Scotia, captured by British and New England forces during 18th-century fighting. Pop. 1,261.

Lou·i·si·ade Archipelago |lōō,ēzē| island group in extreme SE Papua New Guinea. Tagula is the largest island.

Lou·i·si·ana |lə,wēzē'ænə; ,lōō(ə)zē'ænə| see box. □ **Louisianan** *adj. & n.*

Lou·i·si·ana Purchase |lə,wēzē'ænə; ,lōō(ə)zē'ænə| region W of the Mississippi River, bought from France by the U.S. in 1803. Including most of the present-day U.S. N of Texas and E of the Continental Divide, it was explored by the Lewis and Clark expedition.

Lou·is·ville |'lōōi,vil| industrial city and river port in N Kentucky, on the Ohio River across from Indiana. Pop. 269,063. It is the site, at Churchill Downs, of the annual Kentucky Derby horse race.

Lourdes |lōōrdz| town in SW France, at the foot of the Pyrenees. Pop. 17,000. It has been a major place of Roman Catholic pilgrimage since 1858, when a young peasant girl, Marie Bernarde Soubirous (St. Bernadette), claimed to have had a series of visions of the Virgin Mary in a grotto here.

Lou·ren·ço Mar·ques |lō'ränsōō mär'käSH| former name (until 1976) for MAPUTO, Mozambique.

Louth |lowTH; lowT͟H| county of the Republic of Ireland, on the E coast in the province of Leinster. Pop. 91,000; county seat, Dundalk.

Lou·vain |lōō'veN| French name for LEUVEN, Belgium.

Louvre, the |'lōōv(rə)| art museum in Paris, France. Housed in a Renaissance palace, the museum is one of the largest in the world, with such famous works as the *Mona Lisa* and the *Venus de Milo.*

Love Canal |'ləv| section of Niagara Falls, New York that was evacuated after 1970s exposure that chemical wastes underlay its residential neighborhood. It has been partially reoccupied.

Love·land |'ləvlænd; 'ləvlənd| city in N central Colorado, between Denver and Fort Collins. Pop. 37,352.

Low Countries general term for the Netherlands, Belgium, and Luxembourg. French name **Pays-bas.**

Low·ell |'lōəl| city in NE Massachusetts, on the Concord and Merrimack rivers, developed after 1822 as a planned industrial community, based on textile manufacturing. Pop. 103,439.

Low·er Aus·tria |'awstrēə| state of NE Austria. Pop. 1,481,000. Capital: St. Pölten. German name **Niederösterreich.**

Low·er Cal·i·for·nia |,kælə'fawrnyə| another name for BAJA CALIFORNIA, Mexico.

Low·er Can·a·da |'kænədə| the mainly French-speaking region of Canada around the lower St. Lawrence River, in what is now S Quebec. It was a British colony under this name in 1791–1841. See also UPPER CANADA.

Low·er East Side |'lōər ,ēst 'sīd| district of SE Manhattan, New York City, famed as home to immigrants, especially Jews, from the 1880s through the early 20th century.

Low·er Egypt |'ējipt| see UPPER EGYPT.

Low·er Forty-eight States term for the

Louisiana

Capital: Baton Rouge
Largest city: New Orleans
Other cities: Alexandria, Lafayette, Lake Charles, Shreveport
Population: 4,219,973 (1990); 4,368,967 (1998); 4,535,000 (2005 proj.)
Population rank (1990): 21
Rank in land area: 31
Abbreviation: LA; La.
Nicknames: Pelican State; Bayou State
Motto: 'Union, Justice, and Confidence'
Bird: Eastern brown pelican
Flower: magnolia
Tree: bald cypress
Songs: "Give Me Louisiana"; "You Are My Sunshine"
Noted physical features: Head of the Passes; coastal marshlands; Mississippi Delta; Gulf of Mexico; Five Islands Salt Domes; Driskill Mountain
Tourist attractions: New Orleans (French Quarter, Bourbon Street, Mardi Gras festival); Bayou Country
Admission date: April 30, 1812
Order of admission: 18
Name origin: Named in 1682 to honor France's King Louis XIV by French explorer Robert Cavelier, Sieur de La Salle.

48 contiguous United States, excluding Alaska and Hawaii.

Low·er Hutt |'hət| city in New Zealand, NE of Wellington. Pop. 64,000. It is the site of the Prime Minister's official residence, Vogel House.

Low·er Sax·o·ny |'sæksənē| state of NW Germany. Pop. 7,238,000. Capital: Hanover. It corresponds to the NW part of the former kingdom of Saxony. German name **Niedersachsen**.

Lowes·toft |'lō(ə),stawft| fishing port and resort town on the North Sea coast of E England, in NE Suffolk. Pop. 60,000. It is the most easterly English town.

Loy·al·ty Islands |'loi(ə)ltē| group of islands in the SW Pacific, forming part of the French overseas territory of New Caledonia. Pop. 18,000.

Lu·a·la·ba |,lōōə'läbə| river of central Africa, which rises near the S border of the Democratic Republic of Congo (formerly Zaire) and flows N for about 400 mi./640 km., joining the Lomami to form the Congo River.

Lu·an·da |lə'wändə| the capital of Angola, a port on the Atlantic coast. Pop. 2,250,000.

Luang Pra·bang |lōō'äNG prə'bäNG| (also **Louangphrabang**) city in NW Laos, on the Mekong River. Pop. 44,000. It was the royal residence and Buddhist religious center of Laos until the end of the monarchy in 1975.

Lu·ang·wa River |lōō'äNGwə| river that flows 500 mi./800 km. from NE Zambia, to form part of the Zambia-Mozambique border, before emptying into the Zambezi River.

Lu·an·shya |lōō'änsHä| industrial city in central Zambia, near the border with Congo (formerly Zaire). It is in a region producing copper, uranium, peanuts, and other crops. Pop. 146,000.

Lub·bock |'ləbək| commercial and industrial city in NW Texas, an agricultural processing hub. Pop. 186,206.

Lü·beck |'lYbek| historic port city in N Germany, on the Baltic coast of Schleswig-Holstein. Pop. 211,000. It was a leading city in the Hanseatic League (14th–19th centuries).

Lub·lin |'lōōblən; 'lōō,blēn| manufacturing city in E Poland. Pop. 351,000.

Lu·bum·bashi |,lōōbōōm'bäsHē| city in the SE of the Democratic Republic of Congo (formerly Zaire), near the border with Zambia, capital of the mining region of Shaba. Pop. 739,000. Former name (until 1966) **Elisabethville**.

Luc·ca |'lōōkə| city in N Italy, a noted silk- and olive-producing center in Tuscany, W of Florence. Pop. 86,000.

Lu·ce·na |lōō'sänä| commercial city in the Philippines, on S Luzon. Pop. 151,000.

Lu·cerne, Lake |lōō'sərn| (also **Lake of Lucerne**) lake in central Switzerland, surrounded by the four cantons of Lucerne, Nidwalden, Uri, and Schwyz. Also called **Lake of the Four Cantons**; German name **Vierwaldstättersee**.

Lu·cerne |lōō'sərn| resort city on the W shore of Lake Lucerne, in central Switzerland. Pop. 59,000. German name **Luzern**.

Lu·chow |'lōō'jō| **1** see HEFEI, China. **2** see LUZHOU, China.

Luck·now |'lək,now| city in N India, capital of the state of Uttar Pradesh. Pop. 1,592,000. The former capital of Oudh, it is noted for its crafts industries.

Lü·da |'lY'dä| industrial center and port on the SE tip of the Liaodong Peninsula in Liaoning province, NE China, consisting of the cities of Dalian and Lüshun. Pop. 1,630,000.

Lü·den·scheid |'lYdensHīt| industrial city in western Germany. Pop. 76,000.

Ludh·i·a·na |,lōōdē'änə| industrial and commercial city in NW India, in Punjab, SE of Amritsar. Pop. 1,012,000.

Lud·low |'lədlō| commercial and tourist town in W England, in Shropshire. Pop. 9,000.

Lud·wigs·burg |'lōōdviks,bōōrk| transportation center and industrial city in SW Germany. Pop. 79,000.

Lud·wigs·ha·fen | ,lōōdviks'häfen| industrial river port in W central Germany, SW of Mannheim, on the Rhine in the state of Rhineland-Palatinate. Pop. 165,000.

Lu·ga·no |lōō'gänō| resort and financial town in S Switzerland, on the N shore of Lake Lugano. Pop. 26,000.

Lu·go |'lōōgō| walled city and trade center in NW Spain, on the Minho River. Pop. 87,000. It is the capital of Lugo province, in an agricultural region.

Lu·hansk |lōō'hänsk| industrial city in E Ukraine, in the Donets Basin. Pop. 501,000. Former name **Voroshilovgrad**. Russian name **Lugansk**.

Lui·chow Peninsula |lə'wēcHow| see LEIZHOU PENINSULA, China.

Luik |loik| Flemish name for LIÈGE, Belgium.

Lu·leå |'lōōlə,aw| seaport in N Sweden, on the Gulf of Bothnia, capital of Norrbotten county. Pop. 68,000.

Lund |lŏŏnd| city in SW Sweden, just NE of Malmö. Pop. 88,000. Its university was founded in 1666.

Lun•dy |'ləndē| granite island in the Bristol Channel, off the coast of N Devon, SW England.

Lü•ne•burg Heath |'lYne,bŏŏrg| sandy heath between the Elbe and Aller rivers in N Germany. Part of it is a military training site, and part is a nature preserve. German name **Lüneberger Heide**.

Lu•nen |'lŏŏnən| manufacturing city in N central Germany on the Lippe River. Pop. 86,000.

Luo•yang |lə'waw'yäNG| industrial city in Henan province, E central China, on the Luo River. Pop. 1,160,000. It was founded in the 12th century B.C. in the Zhou (Chou) dynasty and was the capital of several subsequent dynasties.

Lu•que |'lŏŏkā| historic city in S Paraguay. Pop. 84,000. A capital of the country in the 19th century, it is now a suburb of Asunción.

Lu•sa•ka |lŏŏ'säkə| the capital of Zambia, an industrial city and transportation center in an agricultural area. Pop. 982,000.

Lu•sa•tia |'lŏŏsāsHə| region of E Germany and SW Poland. Upper, or South, Lusatia is largely agricultural; Lower Lusatia, in the N, is forested. The inhabitants of the region have periodically sought independence. □ **Lusatian** adj. & n.

Lü•shun |'lY'sHŏŏn| (formerly **Port Arthur**) port on the Liaodong Peninsula, NE China, now part of the urban complex of Lüda. It was leased by Russia as a Pacific naval port in 1898 and seized by the Japanese in 1904.

Lu•si•ta•nia |,lŏŏsə'tānēə| ancient Roman province in the Iberian Peninsula, corresponding to modern Portugal. □ **Lusitanian** adj. & n.

Lu•te•tia |lŏŏ'tēsH(ē)ə| Roman name for the settlement that became PARIS, France.

Lu•ton |'lŏŏtn| industrial town to the NW of London, England, formerly in Bedfordshire. Pop. 167,000.

Lutsk |lŏŏtsk| (Polish name **Luck**) river port and industrial city in NW Ukraine, on the Styr River. Pop. 210,000.

Lüt•zen |'lYtsən| town in S central Germany. It was the site of a Napoleonic victory, in 1813, over Russian and Prussian forces.

Lux•em•bourg[1] |'ləksəm,bərg| **1** country in W Europe, between Belgium, Germany, and France. Area: 999 sq. mi./2,586 sq. km. Pop. 378,000. Languages, Luxem-

bourgish, French, and German. An independent grand duchy since 1815, Luxembourg has had close ties with Belgium and the Netherlands. Iron and steel are key to its economy. **2** its capital, a commercial, cultural, and industrial center. Pop. 76,000. It is the seat of the European Court of Justice. **3** a province of SE Belgium, until 1839 a province of the Grand Duchy of Luxembourg. Capital: Arlon. □ **Luxembourger** n.

Luxembourg

Lux•em•bourg[2] |'ləksəm,bərg| **1** the **Luxembourg Gardens**, a park in Paris, France, on the Left Bank, near the Sorbonne. **2** the **Palace of Luxembourg**, a palace in the Luxembourg Gardens, built in 1615–20. It now houses the French Senate.

Lux•or |'lək,sawr; 'lŏŏk,sawr| city in E Egypt, on the E bank of the Nile. Pop. 142,000. It is the site of the S part of ancient Thebes and contains the ruins of the temple built by Amenhotep III and of monuments erected by Ramses II. Arabic name **El Uqsur**.

Lu•zhou |'lŏŏ'jō| (formerly **Luchow**) city in Sichuan province, central China, on the Yangtze River SW of Chongqing. Pop. 263,000.

Lu•zon |lŏŏ'zän; lŏŏ'zawn| the most northerly and the largest (40,420 sq. mi./104,688 sq. km.) island in the Philippines. Its chief towns are Quezon City and Manila, the national capital.

Lviv |lə'vēō; lə'vēf| industrial and commercial city in W Ukraine, near the border with Poland. Pop. 798,000. Russian name **Lvov**.

Ly•all•pur |'līəl,pŏŏr| former name (until 1979) for FAISALABAD, Pakistan.

Ly•ce•um, the |lī'sēəm| gymnasium and garden near ancient Athens, Greece, where Aristotle taught his philosophy.

Ly•cia |'lisHə| ancient region on the coast of SW Asia Minor (present-day SW

Turkey), between Caria and Pamphylia. □ **Lycian** *adj. & n.*

Lyd•ia |'lidēə| ancient region of W Asia Minor (present-day W Turkey), S of Mysia and N of Caria. It became a powerful kingdom in the 7th century B.C., but in 546 was absorbed into the Persian Empire. □ **Lydian** *adj. & n.*

Lyme |līm| town in SE Connecticut, on the Connecticut River, which gave its name to Lyme disease. Pop. 1,949.

Lynch•burg |'linCH,bərg| city in W central Virginia, near the Blue Ridge Mts. Pop. 66,049.

Lynn |lin| city in NE Massachusetts, on Massachusetts Bay NE of Boston, noted for its shoe and other industries. Pop. 81,245.

Ly•ons |lyawN| industrial and commercial city and river port in SE France, at the confluence of the Rhône and Saône rivers. Pop. 422,000. The Roman Lugdunum, it was an important city of Gaul. Its cuisine is famous. French name **Lyon**.

Mm

Maas |'mäs| Dutch name for the MEUSE River.

Maas·tricht |mä'striᴋʜt| industrial city in the Netherlands, capital of the province of Limburg, on the Maas (Meuse) River near the Belgian and German borders. Pop. 117,000. The Treaty of the European Union was signed here in 1992.

Ma·cao |mə'kow| (Portuguese name **Macau**) Portuguese dependency, SE China, on the Pearl River estuary opposite Hong Kong. Area: 6.5 sq. mi./17 sq. km. Pop. 467,000. Capital: Macao City. Comprising Macao peninsula and two neighboring islands, the colony was established as a trading settlement in 1557. Tourism, gambling, and fishing are its economic mainstays. It is due to return to Chinese control in 1999. □ **Macanese** *adj. & n.*

Macao

Ma·ca·pá |ˌmäkä'pä| town in N Brazil, on the Amazon delta, capital of the state of Amapá. Pop. 167,000.

Ma·cau |mə'kow| see MACAO.

Mac·cles·field |'mækəlz,fēld| industrial town in W England, in Cheshire. Pop. 48,000. Once a silk industry center, it now has various manufactures.

Mac·Don·nell Ranges |mək'dänl| series of mountain ranges extending W from Alice Springs in Northern Territory, Australia. The highest peak is Mount Liebig: 4,948 ft./1,524 m.

Mac·e·do·nia[1] |ˌmæsə'dōnēə| ancient country in SE Europe, at the N end of the Greek peninsula. In the 4th century B.C. it was a kingdom that under Philip II and Alexander the Great became a great empire. The region is now divided among Greece, Bulgaria, and the republic of Macedonia.

Mac·e·do·nia[2] |ˌmæsə'dōnēə| landlocked republic in the Balkan peninsula. Area: 9,932 sq. mi./25,713 sq. km. Pop. 2,038,000. Language, Macedonian. Capital: Skopje. Formerly a constituent republic of Yugoslavia, Macedonia became independent after a referendum in 1991. It is both agricultural and industrial. □ **Macedonian** *adj. & n.*

Macedonia

Mac·e·do·nia[3] |ˌmæsə'dōnēə| region in the northeast of modern Greece. Pop. 2,263,000. Capital: Thessaloníki.

Mac·eió |ˌmäsä'ō| port in E Brazil, on the Atlantic coast. Pop. 700,000. It is the capital of the state of Alagoas.

Ma·ce·ra·ta |ˌmäcʜä'rätä| agricultural and industrial town in E central Italy, capital of the province of Macerata. Pop. 44,000.

Mac·gil·li·cud·dy's Reeks |mə'giləkədēz 'rēks| range of hills in County Kerry, SW Ireland. It rises to 3,415 ft./1,041 m. at Carrantuohill, highest point in Ireland.

Ma·cha·la |mä'cʜälä| commercial town in S Ecuador, capital of El Oro province, in an agricultural area. Pop. 144,000.

Ma·chi·da |mä'cʜēdä| city in E central Japan, on E central Honshu, an industrial and residential suburb SW of Tokyo. Pop. 349,000.

Ma·chi·li·pat·nam |mɔcʜ'lēpətnəm| port city in E India, in Andhra Pradesh state, on the Bay of Bengal. Pop. 159,000.

Ma·chu Pic·chu |'mäcʜoō 'pikcʜoō| fortified Inca town in the Andes in Peru. It is famous for its dramatic position, high on a steep-sided ridge. It contains a palace, a temple to the sun, and extensive cultivation terraces. Rediscovered in 1911, it was named after the mountain that rises above it.

Ma·ci·as Ngue·ma |mä'sēäs əNG'wämä|

former name (1973–79) for BIOKO, Equatorial Guinea.

Mac•kay |mə'kā| port in NE Australia, on the coast of Queensland. Pop. 40,000.

Mac•ken•zie Mountains | mə'kenzē| range of the N Rocky Mts., chiefly along the border between the Yukon Territory and the Northwest Territories.

Mac•ken•zie River | mə'kenzē| the longest river in Canada, flowing 1,060 mi./1,700 km. NW from the Great Slave Lake in the Northwest Territories to its delta and mouth on the Beaufort Sea.

Mack•i•nac, Straits of | 'makə,naw| passage between Lakes Huron and Michigan, crossed since 1957 by the Mackinac Bridge. The Upper Peninsula of Michigan lies to the N, and historic Mackinac Island lies just to the E.

Ma•con |'mākən| industrial and commercial city in central Georgia, on the Ocmulgee River. Pop. 106,612.

Mâ•con |'mākən| town, the capital of Saône-et-Loire department, E central France, on the Saône River. Pop. 39,000. At the center of a wine-producing region, it is also a transportation hub and an industrial center.

Mac•quar•ie River | mə'kwerē| river in New South Wales, Australia, rising on the W slopes of the Great Dividing Range and flowing 600 mi./960 km. NW to join the Darling River, of which it is a headwater.

Mac•tan |mäk'tän| island in the Philippines, off the E coast of Cebu. The Portuguese navigator Ferdinand Magellan was killed here in 1521.

Mad•a•gas•car |,mædə'gæskər| island country in the Indian Ocean, off the E coast of Africa. Pop. 12,016,000. Official languages, Malagasy and French. Capital: Antananarivo. The fourth-largest island in the world, Madagascar resisted colonization until the French took control in 1896. Independent as the Malagasy Republic in 1960, it changed its name back in 1975. Its predominantly agricultural people are a mix of African, Polynesian, and Arab. □ **Madagascan** *adj. & n.*

Ma•dei•ra[1] |mə'derə| river in NW Brazil, which rises on the Bolivian border and flows about 900 mi./1,450 km. to meet the Amazon E of Manaus. It is navigable to large ocean-going vessels as far as Pôrto Velho. □ **Madeiran** *adj.*

Ma•dei•ra[2] |mə'derə| island in the Atlantic off NW Africa, the largest of the Madeiras, a group that constitutes an autonomous region of Portugal. Pop. 270,000. Capital: Funchal. Encountered by the Portuguese in 1419, the islands are known for the fortified wine produced here, and have agricultural and crafts industries.

Ma•de•leine, Isles de la |'ēl dä lä mawd-'len| (English name **Magdalen Islands**) island group in SE Quebec, in the Gulf of St. Lawrence N of Prince Edward Island.

La Ma•de•leine |lə mæ'dlen| church in Paris, France. Begun in 1806 by Napoleon, it has the form and shape of a Greek temple, with 52 Corinthian columns running around the exterior. The church is unusual in having no windows.

Ma•dhya Pra•desh |'mädēə prə'desH| state in central India, the largest (171,261 sq. mi./443,446 sq. km.) Indian state, formed in 1956. Pop. 66.14 million. Capital: Bhopal.

Mad•i•son |'mædəsən| the state capital of Wisconsin, an industrial and university city in the central part, largely on Lakes Mendota and Monona. Pop. 191,262.

Mad•i•son Avenue |'mædəsən| street in Manhattan, New York City, associated with the advertising industry, which has many offices here.

Mad•i•son Square |'mædəsən| park in Manhattan, New York City, at the S end of Madison Ave. The original **Madison Square Garden**, the famous sports arena, was here. Today the arena is on 34th Street.

Ma•di•un |mädē'yo͞on| (also **Madioen**) industrial and commercial municipality in Indonesia, on E Java, W of Surabaya. Pop. 170,000.

Ma•dras |'mædrəs| **1** industrial seaport on the SE coast of India, capital of Tamil Nadu. Pop. 3,795,000. Official name (since 1995) **Chennai**. **2** former name (until 1968) for the state of Tamil Nadu.

Ma•drid |mə'drid| the capital and largest city of Spain. Pop. 2,985,000. Situated on a high plateau in the center of the country, it replaced Valladolid as capital in 1561. It is an industrial and cultural center.

Madagascar

Ma·du·ra |'mæjərə| agricultural island of Indonesia, off the NE coast of Java. Its chief town is Pamekasan.

Ma·du·rai |mədə'rī| historic city in Tamil Nadu in S India. Pop. 952,000.

Mae·an·der |mē'(y)ændir| ancient name for the MENDERES River, Turkey.

Mae·ba·shi |mä'ēbäsHē| (also **Maye-bashi**) city in N central Japan, on central Honshu. Pop. 286,000. It is noted for silk-worm growing and silk production.

Mael·strom, the |'māl,sträm| powerful current and whirlpool that passes through a channel in the Norwegian Sea off the NW coast of Norway, in the Lofoten Islands.

Maf·e·king |'mæfə,kiNG| (also **Mafikeng**) a town in South Africa, in North-West Province, scene of an 1899–1900 siege during which a British force outlasted Boer attackers.

Ma·fe·teng |mäfə'teNG| town in W Lesotho, in an agricultural district SW of Maseru. Pop. 206,000.

Ma·ga·dan |məgä'dän| port and naval base in E Siberia, Russia, on the Sea of Okhotsk. Pop. 154,000.

Ma·ga·dha |'məgädä| ancient kingdom of NE India (7th century B.C.–A.D. 325) on territory within present-day Bihar state.

Ma·ga·di, Lake |mäg'ädē| salt lake in the Great Rift Valley, in S Kenya, with extensive deposits of sodium carbonate and other minerals.

Mag·da·le·na |,mægdə'lēnə| the principal river of Colombia, rising in the Andes and flowing N for about 1,000 mi./1,600 km. to enter the Caribbean at Barranquilla.

Mag·de·burg |'mægdə,bərg| industrial city in Germany, the capital of Saxony-Anhalt, a port on the Elbe River and linked to the Rhine and Ruhr by the Mittelland Canal. Pop. 290,000.

Ma·gel·lan, Strait of |mə'jelən| passage separating Tierra del Fuego and other islands of Chile and Argentina from mainland South America, connecting the Atlantic and Pacific.

Ma·gen·ta |mə'jen(t)ə| commune in N Italy, W of Milan. Pop. 23,000. French and Sardinian armies defeated Austrian forces here in 1859. In honor of the victory, the town's name was given to a reddish-purple dye.

Mag·giore, Lake |mə'jawrē| the second-largest of the lakes of N Italy, extending into S Switzerland. It is surrounded by mountains and has many resorts along its shores.

Ma·ghrib |'mæ,grib| (also **Maghreb**) Arabic name for the region of N and NW Africa

between the Atlantic and Egypt, comprising the coastal plain and Atlas Mtns. of Morocco, together with Algeria, Tunisia, and sometimes also Libya, forming a well-defined zone bounded by sea or desert. Moorish Spain was also considered part of this region during the Arab rule here. Compare with BARBARY.

Ma·gi·not Line |,mä(d)zHē'nō ,līn| line of defensive fortifications, completed in 1936, along France's NW frontier, extending from Switzerland to Luxembourg. In World War II, although the defenses held, the Germans went around its end through Belgium, and conquered France.

Mag·na Grae·cia |'mægnə 'grāsH(ē)ə| term for ancient Greek port colonies in present-day S Italy, excluding Sicily. Chief cities included Tarentum (now Tarento), Crotona (Crotone), Cumae, and Sybaris.

Mag·ne·sia |mæg'nēzHə| the name of two ancient cities in Lydia, in Asia Minor, now part of Turkey: Magnesia on the Maeander, the site of a temple to Artemis Leukophryne, and Magnesia at Sipulus, near modern MANISA.

mag·net·ic pole | mæg,netik 'pōl| either of two places on earth where a compass needle will dip vertically. The South Magnetic Pole is in Antarctica, the North Magnetic Pole near Bathurst Island in the Arctic Archipelago of Canada. The location of each fluctuates.

Mag·ni·to·gorsk |məg'n(y)itä'gōrsk| industrial city, a metallurgical center in S Russia, on the Ural River close to the border with Kazakhstan. Pop. 443,000.

Mag·no·lia State nickname for MISSISSIPPI.

Mag·ya·ror·szág |'mädyär,awr,säg; 'mäj-,är,awr'säg| Hungarian name for HUNGARY.

Ma·ha·bad |mää'bäd| city in NW Iran, near the Iraqi border, with a chiefly Kurdish population. Pop. 63,000. In 1941–46 it was the center of a Soviet-supported Kurdish republic.

Ma·ha·jan·ga |mä'zäNGgä| port city in NW Madagascar, on the Mozambique Channel of the Indian Ocean. Pop. 122,000.

Ma·ha·na·di River |mä'hänədē| river in central India, flowing 550 mi./885 km. from the Eastern Ghats to the Bay of Bengal.

Ma·ha·rash·tra |,mä(h)ə'räsHtrə| state in W India bordering on the Arabian Sea, formed in 1960 from the SE part of the former Bombay State. Pop. 78,750,000. Capital: Bombay. □ **Maharashtrian** *adj. & n.*

Ma•ha•we•li |ˌmä(h)əˈwelē| the largest river in Sri Lanka. Rising in the central highlands, it flows 206 mi./330 km. to the Bay of Bengal near Trincomalee.

Mahe |ˌməˈhä| largest island of the Seychelles. Pop. 63,000. Victoria, the capital, is here. The economy relies on fishing, tourism, and agriculture.

Ma•hi•lyow |məgiˈlyawf| industrial city and railway center in E Belarus, on the Dnieper River. Pop. 363,000. Russian name **Mogilev**.

Mahon |məˈhon; məˈhōn| (also **Port Mahón**) the capital of the island of Minorca in the Balearic Islands of Spain, a port on the SE coast. Pop. 22,000.

Ma•ho•ning River |məˈhōniNG| river in E Ohio and NW Pennsylvania whose valley was the 19th-century hub of the U.S. steel industry.

Ma•hore |məˈhōr; məˈhawr| another name for the French Indian Ocean island group of MAYOTTE.

Maid•en•head |ˈmādnˌhed| industrial town in Berkshire, S England, W of London on the Thames River. Pop. 60,000.

Maid•stone |ˈmādˌstōn| town in SE England, on the River Medway, the county seat of Kent. Pop. 133,000.

Mai•du•gu•ri |mīˈdo͞ogərē| commercial and industrial town in NE Nigeria, near Lake Chad. Pop. 282,000.

Mai•kop |mīˈkawp| city in SW Russia, capital of the republic of Adygea. Pop. 120,000.

Main |mān| river of Germany that rises in N Bavaria and flows 310 mi./500 km. W, through Frankfurt, to meet the Rhine at Mainz.

Maine[1] |mān| historic region and former province in NW France, S of Normandy and E of Brittany. It comprises the present departments of Mayenne and Sarthe and parts of the departments of Loire-et-Cher, Eure-et-Loir, and Orne. The commercial center is Le Mans. The Maine River, 8 mi./13 km. long, formed by the confluence of the Sarthe and Mayenne rivers near Angers, flows into the Loire River.

Maine[2] |mān| see box.

Main•land |ˈmān,lænd| in Scotland: **1** (also called **Pomona**) the largest (178 sq. mi./460 sq. km.) of the Orkney Islands. Chief town: Kirkwall. Scapa Flow and Skara Brae are here. **2** the largest (225 sq. mi./580 sq. km.) of the Shetland Islands. Chief town: Lerwick.

Main Line |ˈmān,līn| popular name for a series of affluent suburbs W of Philadel-

---

Maine

Capital: Augusta
Largest city: Portland
Other cities: Auburn, Bangor, Brunswick, Lewiston
Population: 1,227,928 (1990); 1,244,250 (1998); 1,285,000 (2005 proj.)
Population rank (1990): 38
Rank in land area: 39
Abbreviation: ME
Nickname: Pine Tree State
Motto: *Dirigo* (Latin: 'I direct')
Bird: chickadee
Fish: landlocked salmon
Flower: white pine cone and tassel
Tree: Eastern white pine
Song: "State of Maine Song"
Noted physical features: Casco; Penobscot, Passamaquoddy bays; Desert of Maine Sand Dunes; Mount Katahdin
Tourist attractions: Acadia National Park; Allagash Wilderness Waterway; Old Orchard Beach; West Quoddy Head lighthouse
Admission date: March 15, 1820
Order of admission: 23
Name origin: For the former province of Maine in western France; also reflects an older reference to the mainland as distinct from the offshore islands.

---

phia, Pennsylvania, along the old Pennsylvania Railroad main line.

Mainz |mīn(t)s| commercial city in W Germany, capital of Rhineland-Palatinate, situated at the confluence of the Rhine and Main rivers. Pop. 183,000. Johannes Gutenberg built the first printing press here c.1448.

Mai•po River |ˈmīpō| river that flows 155 mi./250 km. W from the Chilean Andes, near Santiago, to the Pacific. Its valley is a noted wine-producing center.

Maj•da•nek |mīˈdänek| (also **Maidanek**) village near Lublin, SE Poland, site of a major Nazi death camp during World War II.

Ma•jor•ca |məˈjawrkə| the largest of the Balearic Islands. Pop. 614,000. Capital: Palma. Spanish name **Mallorca**. □ **Majorcan** *adj*.

Ma•kas•sar Strait |məˈkäsər| stretch of water separating the islands of Borneo and Sulawesi and linking the Celebes Sea in the N with the Java Sea in the S. Makassar is also the former name of Ujung Padang, Indonesia.

Ma•ka•ti |mäˈkätē| town just SE of Manila,

the Philippines, a residential and high-tech industrial suburb of the capital. Pop. 453,000.

Ma·kga·di·kga·di Pans |mə͵gædē͵gædē| extensive area of salt pans in N central Botswana, a game preserve.

Ma·khach·ka·la |məkhəcHkäˈlä| port in SW Russia, on the Caspian Sea, capital of the autonomous republic of Dagestan. Pop. 327,000. Former name (until 1922) **Port Petrovsk**.

Ma·ke·yev·ka |məˈkāyef(v)kæ(ə)| (also **Makeevka**) industrial city and coal-mining center in E Ukraine, NE of Donetsk. Pop. 424,000.

Mak·kah |ˈmekä| Arabic name for MECCA, Saudi Arabia.

Mal·a·bar Coast |ˈmælə͵bär| the S part of the W coast of India, including the coastal region of Karnataka and most of the state of Kerala.

Ma·la·bo |ˈmælə͵bō| seaport, the capital of Equatorial Guinea, on the island of Bioko. Pop. 10,000. Former name **Santa Isabel**.

Ma·la·bon |mälä'bōn| (also called **Ta-nong**) industrial and commercial port town in the Philippines, on S Luzon, just N of Manila. Pop. 278,000.

Ma·la·ca·nang Palace official residence of the president of the Philippines, in Manila, SW Luzon, on the Pasig River.

Ma·lac·ca, Strait of |məˈläkə| the channel between the Malay Peninsula and the Indonesian island of Sumatra, an important sea passage linking the Indian Ocean to the South China Sea. The ports of Melaka and Singapore lie on this strait.

Ma·la·ga |ˈmäləgə| seaport and resort on the Andalusian coast of S Spain. Pop. 525,000. Spanish name **Málaga**.

Mal·a·gasy Republic |ˈmælə'gæsē| former name (1960–75) for MADAGASCAR.

Ma·lang |mäˈläNG| commercial and industrial city in Indonesia, on E Java, S of Surabaya. Pop. 695,000.

Mä·la·ren |ˈmelären| lake in SE Sweden, extending inland from the Baltic Sea. The city of Stockholm is situated at its outlet.

Ma·la·tya |mäˈlätyä| (ancient name **Me-litene**) historic city in E central Turkey, capital of Malatya province. Pop. 282,000. It is in an important agricultural region.

Ma·la·wi, Lake |məˈläwē| another name for Lake Nyasa (see NYASA, LAKE).

Ma·la·wi |məˈläwē| landlocked republic of S central Africa, in the Great Rift Valley. Area: 45,764 sq. mi./118,484 sq. km. Pop. 8,796,000. Official languages, English and Nyanja. Capital: Lilongwe. Largest city:

Blantyre. From 1891 to 1964 it was Nyasaland, under British control. Largely agricultural, it depends on Mozambique for access to overseas trade. □ **Malawian** adj. & n.

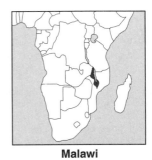

Malawi

Ma·laya |məˈlāə| former country in SE Asia, consisting of the S part of the Malay Peninsula and some adjacent islands (originally including Singapore), now forming the W part of the federation of Malaysia and known as West Malaysia. The area was colonized by the Dutch, Portuguese, and the British, who eventually became dominant; the several Malay states federated under British control in 1896. Malaya was occupied by the Japanese 1941–45. The country became independent in 1957, the federation expanding to become Malaysia in 1963.

Ma·lay Archipelago |ˈmā͵lā| an extended group of islands, including Sumatra, Java, Borneo, the Philippines, and New Guinea, lying between SE Asia and Australia. They

constitute the bulk of the area formerly known as the East Indies.

Ma·lay Peninsula |'mā,lā| peninsula in SE Asia separating the Indian Ocean from the South China Sea. It extends approximately 700 mi./1,100 km. S from the Isthmus of Kra and comprises the S part of Thailand and the whole of Malaya (West Malaysia).

Ma·lay·sia |mə'lāZHə| country in SE Asia, on the Malay Peninsula (West Malaysia) and N Borneo (East Malaysia). Area: 127,369 sq. mi./329,758 sq. km. Pop. 18,294,000. Language, Malay. Capital and largest city: Kuala Lumpur. A historic Malay kingdom was later dominated by Hindus, Muslims, the Dutch, the Portuguese, and the British. Independent since 1963, it is largely agricultural, exporting forest products, rubber, tin, palm oil, and oil. □ **Malaysian** *adj. & n.*

Mal·den |'mawldən| city in E Massachusetts, a suburb just N of Boston. Pop. 53,884.

Mal·dives |'mawldīvz; 'mawldēvz| (also **Maldive Islands**) republic consisting of a chain of coral islands in the Indian Ocean SW of Sri Lanka. Area: 115 sq. mi./298 sq. km. Pop. 221,000. Language, Maldivian (Sinhalese). Capital and largest settlement: Malé. Long under Arab influence, and a British colony 1887–1965, the Maldives depend on fishing, tourism, and tropical fruits for income. □ **Maldivian** *adj. & n.*

Mal·don |'mawldən| commercial town in SE England, on the Blackwater River estuary in E Essex. Pop. 15,000. A battle against

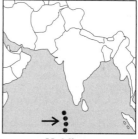

Maldives

the Danes here in A.D.991 gave rise to a famous Anglo-Saxon poem.

Ma·lé |māl| the capital and largest atoll of the Maldives. Pop. 55,000.

Ma·le·gaon |mä'lägown| city in W India, in Maharashtra NE of Bombay. Pop. 342,000.

Ma·li |'mälē| landlocked republic in W Africa, S of Algeria. Area: 479,024 sq. mi./1.24 million sq. km. Pop. 8,706,000. Languages, French (official), others main-

Mali

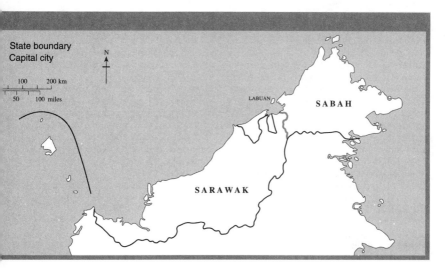

State boundary
Capital city

N

100   200 km

50   100 miles

LABUAN

SABAH

SARAWAK

ly of the Mande group. Capital and largest city: Bamako. Former name (until 1960) **French Sudan**. Largely in the Sahara and Sahel, Mali takes its name from a medieval trade empire. It became independent from France in 1959. Agriculture, fishing, and extractive industries are key to its economy. □ **Malian** *adj. & n.*

Mal·i·bu |'mælə,bōō| resort community, part of Los Angeles, on the Pacific coast of S California. It is noted for its beaches, for its elaborate oceanview residences, and as the home of the J. Paul Getty Museum.

Ma·lin·che |mä'lēnCHä| dormant volcano in central Mexico, on the border of Tlaxcala and Puebla: 14,636 ft./4,461 m.

Ma·lin·di |mä'lēndē| port city in SE Kenya, on the Indian Ocean. Pop. 51,000. It is a former Portuguese colonial capital, and earlier was an Arab trade center.

Ma·lines |mə'lēn| French name for MECHELEN, Belgium.

Mal·lor·ca |mə'yawrkə| Spanish name for MAJORCA, Balearic Islands.

Mal·mai·son |,mälmā'zawn| chateau, now a museum in Rueil-Malmaison, a W suburb of Paris, France. Built in 1669, it was the favorite home of the Empress Josephine, the first wife of Napoleon I. She died here in 1814.

Mal·mé·dy |'mälmādē| tourist and industrial town in E Belgium, in the Ardennes, scene of heavy fighting and a massacre of captured Americans in 1944. Pop. 10,000.

Malmö |'mäl,mō| port and industrial city in SW Sweden, on the Øresund opposite Copenhagen. Pop. 234,000.

Ma·lo·los |mä'lōlōs| commercial town in the Philippines, on SW Luzon, N of Manila. Pop. 125,000. It was the capital of the Philippine Republic proclaimed by revolutionaries in 1898.

Mal·pla·quet |'mælplæ,ket| village in N France, on the border with Belgium. In 1709 British and Austrian troops won a victory there over the French in a major battle of the War of the Spanish Succession.

Mal·ta |'mawltə| island republic in the central Mediterranean, about 60 mi./100 km. S of Sicily. Area: 122 sq. mi./316 sq. km. Pop. 356,000. Official languages, Maltese and English. Capital and chief settlement: Valletta. Important to maritime peoples since the Phoenicians, Malta was held by the British 1814–1964. As its naval importance has declined, tourism has grown. □ **Maltese** *adj. & n.*

Mal·vern Hills |'mawlvərn| (also **the Malverns**) range of limestone hills in W

Malta

England, in Herefordshire and Worcestershire. The highest point is Worcestershire Beacon (1,394 ft./425 m.).

Mal·vi·nas, Islas | mäl'vēnəs| Argentinian name for the FALKLAND ISLANDS.

Mam·moth Cave National Park |'mæməTH| preserve in W central Kentucky, site of the largest known cave system. It consists of over 300 mi./480 km. of charted passageways and contains spectacular rock formations.

Ma·mo·ré River |məmōō'rā| river that flows 600 mi./970 km. from central Bolivia to the border with W Brazil. It joins the Beni River to form the Madeira River.

Ma·mou·tzu the capital (since 1977) of the French Indian Ocean territory of Mayotte (Mahore). Pop. 12,000.

Man, Isle of |'il əv 'mæn| island in the Irish Sea that is a British Crown possession having home rule, with its own legislature (the Tynwald) and judicial system. Pop. 70,000. Capital: Douglas. The island was part of the Norse kingdom of the Hebrides in the Middle Ages, passing into Scottish hands in 1266; the English gained control in the early 15th century. Its ancient Gaelic language, Manx, is still occasionally used for ceremonial purposes. □ **Manx** *adj. & n.*

Ma·na·do |mä'nädō| commercial port in Indonesia, on NE Sulawesi. Pop. 217,000.

Ma·na·gua |mə'nägwə| the capital, commercial and industrial center, and largest city of Nicaragua. Pop. 682,000. The city was devastated by an earthquake in 1972, and damaged further during the civil strife of the late 1970s.

Ma·na·ma |mə'nämə| seaport capital of Bahrain, a center for oil refining and finance. Pop. 140,000.

Ma·na Pools National Park |'mänä 'pōōlz| national park and wildlife habitat in N Zimbabwe, in the Zambezi valley NE of Lake Kariba, established in 1963.

Ma·nas·sas |məˈnæsəs| see BULL RUN, Virginia.

Ma·naus |mäˈnows| city in NW Brazil, capital of the state of Amazonas. Pop. 1,012,000. It is the principal commercial center of the upper Amazon region.

Manche, la |mawnSHˌlä| French name for the ENGLISH CHANNEL.

Manche |mawnSH| department in NW France, coextensive with the Cotentin Peninsula, Normandy. Pop. 480,000. The region is largely agricultural. The main towns are Cherbourg and the capital, Saint Lô.

Man·ches·ter[1] |ˈmænCHəstər| industrial city in NW England. Pop. 397,000. Founded in Roman times, it developed in the 18th and 19th centuries as a center of the English textile industry, and is an important industrial and trade center, with access to the sea via the Manchester Ship Canal. □ **Mancunian** *adj. & n.*

Man·ches·ter[2] |ˈmænCHəstər| largest city in New Hampshire, on the Connecticut River in the S part. It is an industrial center long noted for textile production. Pop. 99,567.

Man·chou·li |ˈmänˈCHo͞oˈlē| see MANZHOULI, China.

Man·chu·kuo |mänˈCHo͞okwaw| (also **Manzhouguo**) country created 1932 by the invading Japanese in NE China. Claimed to be a Manchu state, it was in fact a puppet, and was abolished in 1945.

Man·chu·ria |mænˈCHo͞orēə| mountainous region forming the NE portion of China, now comprising the provinces of Jilin, Liaoning, and Heilongjiang. In 1932 it was declared an independent state by Japan and renamed Manchukuo; it was restored to China in 1945. □ **Manchurian** *adj. & n.*

Man·da·lay |ˈmændəlā| port on the Irrawaddy River in central Burma. Pop. 533,000. Founded in 1857, it was the capital until 1885 of the Burmese kingdom. It is an important Buddhist religious center.

Man·da·lu·yong |ˌmändälo͞oˈyawNG| industrial town in the Philippines, on S Luzon, a suburb of Manila. Pop. 245,000.

Man·fre·do·nia |mänfreˈdōnyä| seaport in SE Italy, on the Gulf of Manfredonia. Pop. 59,000.

Man·hat·tan[1] |mænˈhætn| commercial city in NE Kansas. Pop. 37,712. Fort Riley is just to the W.

Man·hat·tan[2] |mænˈhætn| island near the mouth of the Hudson River, forming the best-known borough of the City of New York. The site of the original Dutch settlement of New Amsterdam (1625), it was taken by the British in 1664. Manhattan, coextensive with New York County, is the commercial and cultural center of New York City. Pop. 1,487,526. □ **Manhattanite** *n.*

Ma·ni·ca·land |məˈnēkəˌlænd| goldmining province of E Zimbabwe. Capital: Mutare.

Man·i·coua·gan River |mænēˈkwägən| river that flows 280 mi./450 km. from central Quebec to the Saint Lawrence River. It is the site of huge hydroelectric projects, and a reservoir that fills a circular meteorite impact zone 60 mi./100 km. in diameter.

Ma·nila |məˈnilə| the capital, chief port, and financial and industrial center of the Philippines, on the island of Luzon. Pop. 1,599,000. Founded in 1571, it was an important trade center of the Spanish until taken by the U.S. in 1898.

Ma·ni·pur |ˈmænəˌpo͞o(ə)r| state in the far E of India, E of Assam, on the border with Burma. Pop. 1.83 million. Capital: Imphal.

Ma·ni·sa |ˌmäneˈsä| (ancient name **Magnesia**) historic commercial city in W Turkey, capital of Manisa province. Pop. 158,000. Its area produces minerals, cotton, and other crops.

Man·i·to·ba |ˌmænəˈtōbə| prairie province of central Canada, noted for its many lakes and rivers, with a coastline on Hudson Bay. Area: 250,947 sq. mi./649,950 sq. km. Pop. 1,091,942. Capital and largest city: Winnipeg. The area was part of Rupert's Land from 1670 until it was transferred to Canada by the Hudson's Bay Company and became a province in 1870. Farming, mining, and manufacturing are all important. □ **Manitoban** *adj. & n.*

Man·i·tou·lin Island |ˌmänəˈto͞olēn| island in Ontario, in N Lake Huron. At 1,068 sq. mi./2,766 sq. km., it is the largest lake island in the world. It has numerous fishing and resort villages.

Man·i·za·les |ˌmäneˈzäläs| commercial city in W central Colombia, in the Andes, the capital of Caldas department. Pop. 327,000. It is a center for the coffee industry.

Man·ka·to |mänˈkätō| city in S central Minnesota, in an agricultural and quarrying district. Pop. 31,477.

Man·nar, Gulf of |mənˈnär| inlet of the Indian Ocean lying between NW Sri Lanka and the S tip of India. It lies to the S of Adam's Bridge, which separates it from the Palk Strait.

Man·nar |mənˈnär| **1** island off the NW

coast of Sri Lanka, linked to India by the chain of coral islands and shoals known as Adam's Bridge. **2** a town on this island. Pop. 14,000.

Man·ner·heim Line |'mänərhām; 'mænərhīm| fortifications erected by Finland across the Karelian isthmus during the Finnish-Russian War. Begun in 1939 and never completed, the fortifications extended 80 mi./129 km. from the Gulf of Finland to Lake Ladoga.

Mann·heim |'mæn,hīm| industrial port at the confluence of the Rhine and the Neckar in Baden-Württemberg, SW Germany. Pop. 315,000.

Ma·no |'mæ,nō| river of W Africa. It rises in NW Liberia and flows 200 mi./320 km. to the Atlantic, forming for part of its length the boundary between Liberia and Sierra Leone.

Man·re·sa |män'rāsä| industrial city in NE Spain, on the Cardoner River. Pop. 66,000.

Mans, Le |lə 'mawn| see LE MANS, France.

Mans·field, Mount |'mæns,fēld| peak in N Vermont, at 4,393 ft./1,340 m. the highest in the state and in the Green Mts.

Mans·field[1] |'mæns,fēld| industrial town in central England, N of Nottingham. Pop. 72,000. Sherwood Forest is to the E.

Mans·field[2] |'mæns,fēld| industrial city in N central Ohio. Pop. 50,627.

Man·ta |'mæntə| port city in W Ecuador, NW of Guayaquil. Pop. 126,000. Its name is also that of an ancient culture of the area.

Man·te·ca |män'tēkæ| city in central California, in the San Joaquin Valley, in an agricultural area. Pop. 40,773.

Man·ti·nea |mändē'nä(y)ä| city of ancient Greece, in E Arcadia. It was the scene of three major battles, including one in the Peloponnesian War.

Man·tua |'mænCHəwə| (Italian name **Mantova**) town in N Italy. Pop. 54,000. It is an agricultural, industrial, and tourist center. It was an important cultural center during the Renaissance. □ **Mantuan** adj. & n.

Ma·nus |'mänōōs| largest island in the Admiralty Islands, N Papua, New Guinea, in the Manus administrative district. Volcanic and hilly, it has coconut plantations but is largely uninhabited.

Man·za·ni·llo[1] |,mänzä'nēyō| port city in SE Cuba, on the Caribbean Sea. Pop. 98,000. It exports sugar, tobacco, and other regional crops.

Man·za·ni·llo[2] |,mänzä'nēyō| commercial city in SW Mexico, in Colima state. Pop. 68,000. It is a leading Pacific port and a resort.

Man·zhou·li |män'zHōlē| (formerly **Manchouli**) city in Inner Mongolia, NE China, on the Russian and near the Mongolian border. Pop. 120,000.

Man·zi·ni |män'zēnē| (formerly **Bremersdorp**) industrial city in central Swaziland. Pop. 19,000. It was a colonial capital before 1902.

Ma·pu·to |mə'pōōtō| the capital and chief port of Mozambique, on the Indian Ocean in the S of the country. Pop. 1,098,000. Founded as a Portuguese fortress in the late 18th century, it became the capital of Mozambique in 1907. Former name (until 1976) **Lourenço Marques**.

Mar·a·cai·bo |,merə'kībō| city and port in NW Venezuela, situated on the channel linking the Gulf of Venezuela with Lake Maracaibo. Pop. 1,401,000. Founded in 1571, the city expanded rapidly after the discovery of oil in the region in 1917.

Mar·a·cai·bo, Lake |,märä'kībō| lake in NW Venezuela, the largest (5,120 sq. mi./13,261 sq. km.) in South America, linked by a narrow channel to the Gulf of Venezuela and the Caribbean Sea.

Ma·ra·cay |märə'kī| industrial and commercial city in N Venezuela, capital of Aragua state. Pop. 354,000. It is a cattle industry center.

Ma·ra·di |'mərädē| industrial and commercial town in S Niger, near the Nigerian border. Pop. 113,000.

Ma·rais, le |lə mä'rā| section of Paris, France, on the Right Bank of the Seine. An old section of narrow streets and ancient buildings, the once run-down Marais, home to Paris's Jewish community, has been largely restored and has become fashionable. At its center is the Place des Vosges.

Ma·ra·jó |,märä'zHō| island in NE Brazil, at the mouth of the Amazon, with the Pará River on its SE side. Flat and over 150 mi./240 km. long, it is used for cattle raising and has prehistoric sites.

Ma·ram·ba |mə'rämbə| city in S Zambia, about 3 mi./5 km. from the Zambezi River and the Victoria Falls. Pop. 95,000. Formerly called Livingstone, it was the capital of Northern Rhodesia from 1911 until Lusaka succeeded it in 1935.

Ma·ra·nhão |,märän'yown| state of NE Brazil, on the Atlantic coast. Pop. 4,930,000. Capital: São Luís.

Ma·ra·ñón |,märän'yōn| river of N Peru, which rises in the Andes and flows 1,000 mi./1,600 km., forming one of the principal headwaters of the Amazon.

Mar·a·thon |'merə‚THän| village and plain in SE Greece, NE of Athens. In 490 B.C. the Athenians and Plataeans defeated a Persian army here, and the messenger Pheidippides ran 20 mi./32 km. to Athens to bring the news.

Mar·be·lla |mär'bāə| resort town on the Costa del Sol of S Spain, in Andalusia. Pop. 81,000.

Mar·ble·head |'märbəlhed| coastal town in NE Massachusetts, a noted yachting and fishing port. Pop. 19,971.

Mar·burg |'märbərg| (officially **Marburg an der Lahn**) **1** city in the state of Hesse, in west central Germany. Important in the history of Protestantism, it draws tourists and has light industries. Pop. 71,000. **2** German name for **Maribor**, Slovenia.

Marche¹ |'märCH| agricultural region of central France, on the NW edge of the Massif Central, comprising the department of Creuse and parts of the departments of Haut-Vienne, Indre, and Charente. Guèret is the chief town.

Marche² |'märCH| (also **the Marches**) region in E central Italy, between the Apennine Range and the Adriatic Sea. Pop. 1,436,000. The area is hilly or mountainous, and farming is the chief industry.

Mar·co Po·lo Bridge |'märkō 'pōlō| marble bridge spanning the Yongding River at Lugouqiao, 9 mi./14 km. SW of Beijing, China. In July 1937 a clash between Japanese and Chinese troops here marked the beginning of the Second Sino-Japanese War (1937–45).

Mar del Pla·ta |‚mär dəl 'plätə| fishing port and resort in Argentina, on the Atlantic coast S of Buenos Aires. Pop. 520,000.

Ma·ren·go |mə'reNGgō| village near Turin, NW Italy. In 1800 Napoleon I defeated an Austrian army here.

Mar·ga·ri·ta |‚märgə'rētə| island in the Caribbean Sea, off the coast of Venezuela. Visited by Columbus in 1498, it was used as a base by Simón Bolívar in 1816 in the struggle for independence from Spanish rule.

Mar·gate |'mär‚gāt| port and resort town in SE England, E of London in the Isle of Thanet, Kent. Pop. 53,000.

Mar·gi·lan |‚märgə'län| (also **Margelan**) town in E Uzbekistan, adjacent to the city of Kokand. Pop. 125,000. It is an important silk center.

Ma·ri |'märē| ancient city on the W bank of the Euphrates, in Syria, near the Iraqi border. Its period of greatest importance was from the late 19th to the mid 18th centuries B.C.; the vast palace of the last king, Zimri-Lin, has yielded an archive of 25,000 cuneiform tablets, which are the principal source for the history of N Syria and Mesopotamia at that time.

Ma·ri·ana Islands |‚merē'ænə; ‚märē'änə| (also **the Marianas**) a group of islands in the W Pacific, comprising Guam and the Northern Marianas. Visited by Magellan in 1521, the islands were colonized by Spain in 1668. Guam was ceded to the U.S. in 1898 and the remaining islands were sold to Germany in the following year. Administered by Japan after World War I, they became part of the Pacific Islands Trust Territory, administered by the U.S., in 1947. In 1975 the Northern Marianas voted to establish a commonwealth in union with the U.S., and became self-governing three years later. See also GUAM; NORTHERN MARIANAS

Ma·ri·a·nao |‚märēə'now| city in NW Cuba, a residential suburb W of Havana. Pop. 134,000. It has resort beaches and some industry.

Ma·ri·ana Trench |‚merē'ænə; ‚märē'änə| ocean trench to the SE of the Mariana Islands in the W Pacific, with the greatest known ocean depth (36,201 ft./11,034 m. at the Challenger Deep).

Ma·rián·ské Lázně |‚märē'änske 'läznye| (also **Marienbad**) spa town in W Bohemia, Czech Republic. Pop. 15,000. World-famous for its healing springs, it was popular with writers.

Ma·ri Auton·o·mous Republic |'märē| another name for MARI EL, Russia.

Ma·rib |'märib| ancient city, now in ruins, in E Yemen, E of Sana'a. It was one of the chief cities of the kingdom of Sheba (c. 1000 B.C.)

Ma·ri·bor |'märēbōr| industrial city in NE Slovenia, on the Drava River near the border with Austria. Pop. 104,000. German name **Marburg**.

Mar·i·co·pa County |‚meri'cōpə| county in S central Arizona. Its seat is Phoenix, which, with nearby suburbs, is home to more than half of all Arizonans. Pop. 2,122,101.

Ma·rie Byrd Land |mä'rē 'bərd| region of Antarctica bordering the Pacific, between Ellsworth Land and the Ross Sea.

Ma·ri El |mə'rē 'el| autonomous republic in European Russia, E of Moscow and N of the Volga. Pop. 754,000. Capital: Yoshkar-Ola. Also called **Mari Autonomous Republic**.

Marien·bad German name for MARIÁNSKÉ LÁZNĚ.

Ma·ri·ki·na |ˌmäreˈkēnä| (also **Mariquina**) commercial town in the Philippines, on S Luzon, E of Manila. Pop. 310,000.

Ma·rí·lia |ˈmärēlyə| commercial and agricultural city in SE Brazil, in W São Paulo state. Pop. 178,000.

Ma·rin County |ˈmärˈən| county in NW California, across the Golden Gate from San Francisco. Many affluent suburbs are here. Pop. 230,096.

Ma·rin·gá |ˈmärēnˌgä| commercial city in SE Brazil, in Paraná state. Pop. 269,000. Coffee is among its agricultural products.

Mar·i·on[1] |ˈmærēən| industrial city in E central Indiana. Pop. 32,618.

Mar·i·on[2] |ˈmærēən| industrial city in N central Ohio. Pop. 34,075.

Mar·i·time Alps |ˈmærəˌtīm| section of the Alps, in NW Italy and SW France. The highest peak is Punta Argentera (10,817 ft./3,297 m.)

Mar·i·time Provinces |ˈmærəˌtīm| (also **the Maritimes**) the Canadian provinces of New Brunswick, Nova Scotia, and Prince Edward Island, with coastlines on the Gulf of St. Lawrence and the Atlantic. These provinces, with Newfoundland and Labrador, are also known as the Atlantic Provinces.

Ma·ri·tsa |məˈritsə| river of S Europe, which rises in the Rila Mts. of SW Bulgaria and flows 300 mi./480 km. S to the Aegean Sea. It forms part of the border between Bulgaria and Greece and that between Greece and European Turkey. Its ancient name is the Hebros or Hebrus. Turkish name **Meriç**; Greek name **Évros**.

Ma·ri·u·pol |märēˈ o͞opōl| industrial port on the S coast of Ukraine, on the Sea of Azov. Pop. 517,000. Former name (1948–89) **Zhdanov.**

Marl |märl| industrial and mining center in western Germany, in the Ruhr district. Pop. 90,000.

Marl·bor·ough |ˈmärlbərō| industrial city in E central Massachusetts. Pop. 31,813.

Mar·ma·ra, Sea of |ˈmärmərə| small sea in NW Turkey. Connected by the Bosporus to the Black Sea and by the Dardanelles to the Aegean, it separates European Turkey from Anatolia. In ancient times it was known as the Propontis.

Marne |märn| river of E central France, which rises in the Langres plateau N of Dijon and flows 328 mi./525 km. N and W to join the Seine near Paris. Its valley was the scene of two important battles in World War I. The first (September 1914) halted and repelled the German advance on Paris; the second (July 1918) ended the final German offensive.

Ma·roua |ˈmärо͞oä| town in N Cameroon, S of L. Chad. Pop. 143,000. It is the trade center for a large region.

Mar·que·sas Islands |märˈkāsäz| group of volcanic islands in the S Pacific, forming part of French Polynesia. Pop. 8,000. The islands were annexed by France in 1842. The largest is Hiva Oa, on which the French painter Gauguin spent the last years of his life.

Mar·quette |märˈket| port city in the Upper Peninsula of Michigan, on Lake Superior. Pop. 21,977.

Mar·ra·kesh |ˌmerəˈkeSH| (also **Marrakech**) industrial and tourist city in W Morocco, in the foothills of the High Atlas Mts. Pop. 602,000. It was founded in 1062 as the capital of the Muslim Almoravid dynasty. It was the capital of Morocco until 1147, and again 1550–1660.

Mar·sa·la |märˈsälə| seaport in Sicily, S Italy, on the Mediterranean Sea. Pop. 81,000. It gave its name to a sweet red wine.

Mar·seilles |märˈsä| industrial city and port on the Mediterranean coast of France. Pop. 808,000. French name **Marseille**. The second-largest city in France, settled in the 6th century B.C. as the Greek Massilia, it was the chief port for the French colonization of Algeria.

Mar·shall Islands |ˈmärSHəl| republic consisting of two chains of islands in the NW Pacific. Area: 70 sq. mi./181 sq. km. Pop. 43,420. Languages, English (official), local Austronesian languages. Capital: Majuro. Formerly controlled by the Germans and Japanese, the Marshalls were administered by the U.S. in 1947–86, then entered into free association with the U.S. Tourism is important. Kwajalein, Bikini, and Eniwetok have all been used for nuclear or

Marshall Islands

other military tests. □ **Marshallese** *adj. & n.*

Mars•ton Moor |ˈmärstən ˌmawr| moor in N England, just W of York, site of the largest battle (1644) of the English Civil War, a victory for Parliamentarians under Thomas Fairfax and Oliver Cromwell.

Mar•ta•ban, Gulf of |ˈmärtəˌbän| inlet of the Andaman Sea, a part of the Indian Ocean, on the coast of SE Burma E of Rangoon.

Mar•tha's Vineyard |ˈmärTHəz ˈvinyərd| resort island in the Atlantic off the coast of Massachusetts, to the S of Cape Cod; its chief town is Edgartown.

Mar•ti•nez |märˈtēnez| industrial port in N central California, on Suisun Bay, N of Oakland. Pop. 31,808.

Mar•ti•nique |ˌmärtnˈēk| French island in the West Indies, in the Lesser Antilles. Pop. 360,000. Capital: Fort-de-France. □ **Martiniquan** *adj. & n.* **Martinican** *adj. & n.*

Martinique

Ma•ry |məˈrē| commercial city in SE Turkmenistan, in a natural gas- and cotton-producing area. Pop. 95,000. It was formerly called **Merv,** and is near the site of the ancient Merv, a town of great historical and religious importance.

Mar•y•land |ˈmerələnd| see box. □ **Marylander** *n.*

Ma•sa•da |məˈsädə| site in Israel of the ruins of a palace and fortification built by Herod the Great on the SW shore of the Dead Sea in the 1st century B.C. It was a Jewish stronghold in the Zealots' revolt against the Romans (A.D. 66–73) and was the scene in A.D. 73 of mass suicide by the Jewish defenders when the Romans breached the citadel after a siege of nearly two years.

Ma•san |ˈmäˌsän| port city in SE South Korea, on an inlet of the Western Channel (the Korea Strait). Pop. 497,000. It is the center of a free-trade zone, with textile and other industries.

Maryland

Capital: Annapolis
Largest city: Baltimore
Other cities: Bethesda, Columbia, Frederick, Hagerstown
Population: 4,781,468 (1990); 5,134,808 (1998); 5,467,000 (2005 proj.)
Population rank (1990): 19
Rank in land area: 42
Abbreviation: MD; Md.
Nicknames: Old Line State; Free State
Motto: *Fatti maschii, parole femine* (Italian: 'Manly deeds, womanly words')
Bird: Baltimore oriole
Fish: rockfish or striped bass
Flower: black-eyed Susan
Tree: white oak
Song: "Maryland, My Maryland"
Noted physical features: Chesapeake Bay; Pocoson Swamp; Great Valley, Hagerstown Valley; Backbone Mountain
Tourist attractions: Fort McHenry; Antietam National Battlesite; U.S. Naval Academy; Camp David Presidential Retreat
Admission date: April 28, 1788
Order of admission: 7
Name origin: For Queen Henrietta Maria (1609-99), wife of Charles I of England.

Ma•sa•ya |mäˈsäyä| commercial and industrial city in W Nicaragua, the capital of Masaya province, SE of Managua. Pop. 80,000.

Mas•ba•te |mäsˈbätä| island, noted as a mining district, in the central Philippines. Pop. 599,000. The chief town is Masbate.

Mas•ca•rene Islands |ˌmæskəˈrēn| (also **the Mascarenes**) group of three islands in the W Indian Ocean, E of Madagascar, comprising Réunion, Mauritius, and Rodrigues.

Ma•se•ru |ˈmæzəˌrōō| the capital of Lesotho, situated on the Caledon River near the border with the province of Free State in South Africa. Pop. 367,000.

Mash•had |məˈsHäd| (also **Meshed**) city in NE Iran, close to the border with Turkmenistan. Pop. 1,463,000. The burial place in A.D. 809 of the Abbasid caliph Harun ar-Rashid and in 818 of the Shiite leader Ali ar-Rida, it is a holy city of the Shiite Muslims. It is the second-largest city in Iran, and is noted for its textiles.

Ma•sho•na•land |məˈsHōnəlænd| area of N Zimbabwe, occupied by the Shona people. A former province of S Rhodesia, it is now divided into the three provinces of Mashonaland East, West, and Central.

Ma•son City |ˈmāsn| industrial city in N central Iowa. Pop. 29,040.

Mason-Dixon Line |ˈmāsnˈdiksən| boundary between Maryland and Pennsylvania, named for its two 1760s surveyors. By extension, it is popularly considered the boundary between the U.S. North and South.

Mas•sa•chu•setts |ˌmæsəˈCHo͞osəts| see box.

Mas•sa•chu•setts Bay |ˌmæsəˈCHo͞osəts| inlet of the Atlantic between Cape Cod and Cape Ann, in E Massachusetts. Boston Harbor is an inlet of Massachusetts Bay.

Mas•sa•wa |məˈsäwə| (also **Mitsiwa**) the chief port of Eritrea, on the Red Sea. Pop. 27,000. It serves as an outlet for Ethiopian trade.

Mas•sif Central |məˈsef ˌsänˈträl| mountainous plateau in S central France. Covering almost one-sixth of the country, it rises to a height of 6,188 ft./1,887 m. at Puy de Sancy in the Auvergne.

Mas•sil•lon |ˈmæsələn| city in NE Ohio, S of Akron. Pop. 31,007.

Ma•su•ria |məˈzo͞oreä| low-lying forested lakeland region of NE Poland. Formerly part of East Prussia, it was assigned to Poland after World War I. Also called **Masurian Lakes**. □ **Masurian** adj.

Ma•ta•be•le•land |ˌmätəˈbālə,lænd| former province of Southern Rhodesia, lying between the Limpopo and Zambezi rivers and occupied by the Matabele people. It is now divided into the two Zimbabwean provinces of Matabeleland North and South.

Ma•ta•di |mäˈtädē| commercial city in W Congo (formerly Zaire), on the Congo River 80 mi./130 km. from the Atlantic. Pop. 173,000. It is the chief port of Congo.

Mat•a•gor•da Bay |ˌmætəˈgôrdə| inlet of the Gulf of Mexico in SE Texas, at the mouth of the Colorado River.

Mat•a•mo•ros |mätäˈmōrōs| (also **Heroica Matamoros**) commercial city in NE Mexico, in Tamaulipas state, across the Rio Grande from Brownsville, Texas. Pop. 303,000.

Mat•a•nus•ka Valley |ˌmætəˈno͞oskə| agricultural region in S central Alaska, NE of Anchorage.

Ma•tan•zas |mətˈänzəs| port city in N Cuba, capital of Matanzas province, E of Havana. Pop. 114,000. Once a pirate center, it now exports sugar and other crops.

Ma•ta•ram |ˈmätäräm| former Muslim sul-

Massachusetts

Official name: Commonwealth of Massachusetts

Capital/largest city: Boston

Other cities: Agawam, Brockton, Cambridge, Holyoke, New Bedford, Pittsfield, Springfield, Worcester

Population: 6,016,425 (1990); 6,147,132 (1998); 6,310,000 (2005 proj.)

Population rank (1990): 13

Rank in land area: 44

Abbreviation: MA; Mass.

Nicknames: (Old) Bay State; Old Colony State; Puritan State; Baked Bean State

Motto: *Ense petit placidam sub libertate quietem* (Latin: 'By the sword we seek peace, but peace only under liberty')

Bird: chickadee

Fish: cod

Flower: mayflower (also called ground laurel or trailing arbutus)

Tree: American elm

Song: "All Hail to Massachusetts"

Noted physical features: Buzzard's Bay; Cape Ann, Cape Cod; Mount Greylock

Tourist attractions: Boston (many historic and cultural sites); Walden Pond; Plymouth Rock; Cape Cod National Seashore; Old Sturbridge Village

Admission date: February 6, 1788

Order of admission: 6

Name origin: From Algonquian (Natick) Indian words *massa* meaning 'great' and *wachuset* meaning 'hill,' probably referring to the Blue Hills near Boston, then used of the Indians living near them, and later of the bay.

---

tanate in the Malay Archipelago. At its most powerful (17th century), it controlled most of Java.

Ma•te•ra |mäˈtärä| town in S Italy, capital of Matera province. Pop. 55,000. It is an agricultural and industrial center.

Ma•thu•ra |ˈmətərə| (formerly **Muttra**) city in N India, in Uttar Pradesh state. Pop. 233,000. It is the reputed birthplace of the Hindu god Krishna.

Mat•ma•ta |mätmäˈtä| village in SE Tunisia, in the Matmata hills S of Gabés, noted for its cave dwellings.

Ma•to Gros•so |ˌmäto͞o ˈgrōso͞o| high plateau region of SW Brazil, forming a watershed between the Amazon and Plate river systems. The region is divided into two states, *Mato Grosso* (Pop. 2,020,000; Capital: Cuiabá) and MATO GROSSO DO SUL.

Ma•to Gros•so do Sul |ˈmäto͞o ˈgrōso͞o|

Ma·tsu |'mätso͞o| island, SE China, off the coast of Fujian province, E of Fuzhou. Under the control of the Nationalist government on Taiwan after the fall of the mainland, it was subjected (with Quemoy) to periodic shelling during the 1950s.

Ma·tsu·ba·ra |mä'tso͞obärä| city in W central Japan, on S Honshu, an industrial and residential suburb S of Osaka. Pop. 136,000.

Ma·tsu·do |mä'tso͞odō| city in E central Japan, on E central Honshu, a suburb of Tokyo. Pop. 456,000.

Ma·tsue |mät'so͞oä| (also **Matsuye**) port city in W Japan, on SW Honshu. Pop. 143,000.

Ma·tsu·mo·to |mä'tso͞omōtō| commercial city in central Japan, on central Honshu, NE of Nagoya. Pop. 201,000.

Ma·tsu·shi·ma islands |mä'tso͞osHēmä| group of islands in Japan, in Matsushima Bay, N Honshu. The soft volcanic rock of these hundreds of small islands has been worn into fantastic shapes by the sea.

Ma·tsu·ya·ma |ˌmätso͞o'yämə| city in Japan, the capital and largest city of the island of Shikoku. Pop. 443,000.

Mat·ter·horn |'mædər,haw(ə)rn| mountain in the Pennine Alps, on the border between Switzerland and Italy. Rising to 14,688 ft./4,477 m., it was first climbed in 1865 by the English mountaineer Edward Whymper. French name **Mont Cervin**; Italian name **Monte Cervino**.

Ma·tu·rín |mäto͞o'rēn| commercial city in NE Venezuela, capital of Monagas state. Pop. 207,000.

Mauá |mæo͞o'ä| city in SE Brazil, a suburb SE of São Paulo. Pop. 345,000.

Maui |'mowē| the second-largest of the Hawaiian islands, lying to the NW of the island of Hawaii.

Mau·na Kea |ˌmownə 'käə| extinct volcano on the island of Hawaii, in the central Pacific. Rising to 13,796 ft./4,205 m., it is the highest peak in the Hawaiian islands. The summit is the site of several large astronomical telescopes.

Mau·na Loa |ˌmownə 'lōə| active volcano on the island of Hawaii, to the S of Mauna Kea, rising to 13,678 ft./4,169 m. The volcano Kilauea is situated on its flanks.

Mau·re·ta·nia |ˌmawrə'tānēə| ancient region of N Africa, corresponding to the N part of Morocco and W and central Algeria. Originally occupied by the Moors

(Latin *Mauri*) and conquered by the Arabs in the 7th century. □ **Mauretanian** *adj. & n.*

Mau·ri·ta·nia |ˌmawrə'tānēə| republic in W Africa with a coastline on the Atlantic. Area: 398,107 sq. mi./1.03 million sq. km. Pop. 2,023,000. Languages, Arabic (official), French. Capital and largest city: Nouakchott. Mauritania was a center of Berber power in the 11th and 12th centuries, at which time Islam became established in the region. Later, nomadic Arab tribes became dominant, while on the coast European nations, especially France, established trading posts. Controlled by the French from 1902, Mauritania achieved independence in 1961. Its people are largely nomadic pastoralists; fishing and mining are also important. □ **Mauritanian** *adj. & n.*

Mauritania

Mau·ri·tius |maw'risHəs| island republic in the Indian Ocean, about 550 mi./850 km. E of Madagascar. Area: 788 sq. mi./2,040 sq. km. Pop. 1,105,740. Languages, English (official), French Creole, Indian languages. Capital and largest city: Port Louis. Held by the Portuguese, Dutch, French, and British, Mauritius gained independence in 1968. Its economy is centered on sugar. □ **Mauritian** *adj. & n.*

Ma·ya·güez |mīyä'gwäz| industrial port in W Puerto Rico, on the Mona Passage. Pop. 83,010.

Mauritius

Ma·yenne |mä'yen| **1** department of NW France. Pop. 278,000. **2** river in W France, a headwater of the Maine.

May·er·ling |'mīerliNG| village in E Austria, in the Vienna Woods. Crown Prince Rudolf and Baroness Maria Vetsera died in unexplained circumstances in a hunting lodge here in January 1889.

May·fair |'mā,fæ(ə)r| fashionable and opulent district in the West End of London, England.

May·kop |mī'kawp| (also **Maikop**) industrial town in S Russia, in the N foothills of the Caucasus Mts. Pop. 120,000.

May·nooth |mā'nooTH| village in Country Kildare, in the Republic of Ireland. Pop. 1,300. It is the site of St. Patrick's College, founded in 1795, the academic center of Irish Catholicism.

Mayo |'māō| county in the NW Republic of Ireland, in the province of Connacht. Pop. 111,000; county seat, Castlebar.

Ma·yon Volcano |mä'yōn| active volcano in the Philippines, on SE Luzon. It is considered to be one of the most perfect cones on Earth.

Ma·yotte |mä'yawt| island to the E of the Comoros in the Indian Ocean. Pop. 94,000. Languages, French (official), local Swahili dialect. Capital: Mamoutzu. When the Comoros became independent in 1974, Mayotte remained an overseas territory of France. Also called **Mahore**.

Mayotte

Mazar-e-Sharif |mə'zäresHə'rēf| industrial city in N Afghanistan. Pop. 131,000. The city, whose name means 'tomb of the saint', is the reputed burial place of Ali, son-in-law of Muhammad.

Ma·za·tlán |mäsät'län| seaport and resort city in Mexico, on the Pacific coast in the state of Sinaloa. Pop. 314,000. Founded in 1531, it developed as a center of Spanish trade with the Philippines.

Ma·zo·via |mə'zōvēə| ancient principality in Poland, E of the Vistula River. At one time semi-independent, it was incorporated into Poland by the early 16th century.

Mba·bane |əmbä'bänä| the administrative capital of Swaziland, a resort in the high veld. Pop. 38,000.

Mban·da·ka |əmbän'däkä| (formerly **Coquilhatville**) commercial and industrial city in N Congo (formerly Zaire), a port on the Congo River. Pop. 166,000.

Mbe·ya |əm'bāä| commercial town in S Tanzania, NW of Lake Malawi. Pop. 93,000. It is a former gold-mining center.

Mbuji-Mayi |əm'boojē mäyē; 'mīē| (formerly **Bakwanga**) commercial city in S central Congo (formerly Zaire). Pop. 603,000. It is a famed diamond-mining center.

Mc·Al·len |mə'kælən| city in S Texas, in the agricultural Rio Grande valley. Pop. 84,021.

Mc·Kees·port |mə'kēzpōrt| city in SW Pennsylvania, an industrial suburb SE of Pittsburgh. Pop. 26,016.

Mc·Kin·ley, Mount |mə'kinlē| mountain in S central Alaska. Rising to 20,110 ft./6,194 m., it is the highest peak in North America. Also called **Denali**, it is in Denali National Park.

Mead, Lake |mēd| largest U.S. reservoir, in SE Nevada, created after 1933 by the Hoover Dam on the Colorado River.

Mead·ow·lands, the |'medō,lændz| entertainment and sports complex in NE New Jersey, in the meadows of the Hackensack River, NW of New York City.

Meath |mēTH| county in the E part of the Republic of Ireland, in the province of Leinster. Pop. 106,000; county seat, Navan.

Meaux |mō| industrial city in N France, on the Marne River. Pop. 45,000.

Mec·ca |,mekə| city in W Saudi Arabia, an oasis town in the Red Sea region of Hejaz, E of Jiddah, considered by Muslims to be the holiest city of Islam. Pop. 618,000. The birthplace in A.D. 570 of the prophet Muhammad, it was the scene of his early teachings before his emigration (the Hegira) to Medina in 622. On his return to Mecca in 630 it became the center of the new Muslim faith. It is the site of the Great Mosque and the Kaaba, and is a center of Islamic ritual, including the hajj pilgrimage. The city is closed to non-Muslims. Arabic name **Makkah**.

Me·che·len |'mäKHələn| city in N Belgium, N of Brussels. Pop. 75,000. It is noted for its cathedral and for Mechlin lace. French name **Malines**.

Meck·len·burg |'meklən,bərg| former

state of NE Germany, on the Baltic coast, now part of Mecklenburg–West Pomerania.

Mecklenburg-West Pomerania |'mek-lən,bȯrg| state of NE Germany, on the coast of the Baltic Sea. Pop. 2,100,000. Capital: Schwerin. It consists of the former state of Mecklenburg and the W part of Pomerania.

Me•dan |mä,dän| city in Indonesia, in NE Sumatra near the Strait of Malacca. Pop. 1,730,000. It was established as a trading post by the Dutch in 1682 and became a leading commercial center.

Me•de•llín |mädä'yēn| city in E Colombia, the second-largest city in the country. Pop. 1,581,000. A major center of coffee production, it has in recent years gained a reputation as the hub of the Colombian drug trade.

Med•ford[1] |'medfərd| city in NE Massachusetts, a suburb just NW of Boston. Pop. 57,407.

Med•ford[2] |'medfərd| commercial city in SW Oregon, in an agricultural area near the California line. Pop. 46,951.

Me•dia |'mēdēə| ancient region of Asia to the SW of the Caspian Sea, corresponding approximately to present-day Azerbaijan, NW Iran, and NE Iraq. The region is roughly the same as that inhabited today by the Kurds. Originally inhabited by the Medes, the region was conquered in 550 B.C. by Cyrus the Great of Persia. □ **Median** adj.

Med•i•cine Bow Mountains |'medəsin bō| range of the Rocky Mts., extending the Front Range of Colorado into S Wyoming.

Med•i•cine Hat |'medəsən ,hæt| commercial and industrial city in SE Alberta, on the South Saskatchewan River. Pop. 43,625.

Me•di•na |mə'dēnə| city in W Saudi Arabia, around an oasis some 200 mi./320 km. N of Mecca. Pop. 500,000. Medina was the refuge of Muhammad's infant Muslim community from its removal from Mecca in A.D. 622 until its return there in 630. It was renamed Medina, meaning 'city', by Muhammad and made the capital of the new Islamic state until it was superseded by Damascus in 661. It is Muhammad's burial place and the site of the first Islamic mosque, constructed around his tomb. It is considered by Muslims to be the second-most holy city after Mecca, and a visit to the prophet's tomb at Medina often forms a sequel to the formal pilgrimage to Mecca. Arabic name **Al Madinah**.

Med•i•ter•ra•nean Sea |,medətə'rānēən| almost landlocked sea between S Europe, the N coast of Africa, and SW Asia. It is connected with the Atlantic by the Strait of Gibraltar, with the Red Sea by the Suez Canal, and with the Black Sea by the Dardanelles, the Sea of Marmara, and the Bosporus.

Me•doc |'mä,däk| district in Aquitaine, in SW France, NW of Bordeaux between the Bay of Biscay and the Gironde River estuary. It contains some of France's most famous vineyards. The main towns are Pauillac and Lesparre.

Mee•rut |'märət| industrial and commercial city in N India, in Uttar Pradesh NE of Delhi. Pop. 850,000. It was the scene in 1857 of the first uprising against the British in the Indian Mutiny.

Meg•a•lóp•o•lis |,megə'läpələs| city in ancient SE Greece, founded by citizens from many other cities for defense against Sparta. The name means 'large city.'

Mé•ga•ra |'megərə| city of E central Greece, on the Gulf of Saronica. The philosopher Euclid founded the Megarian school of philosophy (5th century B.C.). □ **Megarian** adj.

Me•gha•la•ya |,māgə'läə| state in the extreme NE of India, on the N border of Bangladesh. Pop. 1,761,000. Capital: Shillong. It was created in 1970 from part of Assam.

Me•gid•do |mi'gi'dō| ancient city of NW Palestine, situated to the SE of Haifa in present-day Israel. Founded in the 4th millennium B.C., it controlled an important route linking Syria and Mesopotamia with the Jordan valley, Jerusalem, and Egypt. Its commanding location made the city the scene of many battles throughout history. It is believed to be the site referred to by the biblical name *Armageddon* (possibly meaning 'hill of Megiddo') in Revelation 16.

Meis•sen |'mīsən| city in E Germany, in Saxony, on the Elbe River NW of Dresden. Pop. 39,000. It is famous for its porcelain.

Mei•xian city in Guangdong province, S China, on the Mei River, NW of Shantou. Pop. 749,000.

Me•ke•le |'mākələ| city in N Ethiopia, the capital of Tigray province. Pop. 62,000.

Mek•nès |mek'nès| historic commercial city in N Morocco, in the Middle Atlas Mts. W of Fez. Pop. 120,000. In the 17th century it was the residence of the Moroccan sultan.

Me•kong |'mä'kawNG| river of SE Asia, which rises in Tibet and flows SE and S for 2,600 mi./4,180 km. through S China,

Laos, Cambodia, and Vietnam to its extensive delta on the South China Sea. It forms much of the boundary between Laos and its W neighbors Burma and Thailand.

Me·la·ka |mä'läkä| (also **Malacca**) **1** state of Malaysia, on the SW coast of the Malay Peninsula, on the Strait of Malacca. **2** its capital and chief port. Pop. 88,000. It was conquered by the Portuguese in 1511 and played an important role in the development of trade between Europe and the East, especially China.

Mel·a·ne·sia |ˌmelə'nēzнə| region of the W Pacific to the S of Micronesia and W of Polynesia. It contains the Bismarck Archipelago, the Solomon Islands, Vanuatu, New Caledonia, Fiji, and the intervening islands, and is the area of earliest human settlement in the Pacific. □ **Melanesian** *adj. & n.*

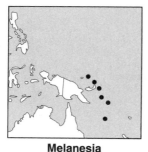

Melanesia

Mel·bourne[1] |'melbərn| the capital of Victoria, SE Australia, on the Bass Strait opposite Tasmania. Pop. 2,762,000. It became state capital in 1851 and was capital of Australia 1901–27. It is a major port and commercial center and the second-largest city in Australia.

Mel·bourne[2] |'melbərn| resort city in E central Florida, just S of Cape Canaveral. Pop. 59,646.

Me·li·lla |mə'lēyə| Spanish exclave on the Mediterranean coast of Morocco. Pop. (with Ceuta) 57,000. It was occupied by Spain in 1497.

Me·li·to·pol |ˌmelə'tawpəl| industrial city in S Ukraine, on the Sea of Azov. Pop. 176,000.

Me·los |'mēläs| Greek island in the Aegean Sea, in the SW of the Cyclades group. It was the center of a flourishing civilization in the Bronze Age and is the site of the discovery in 1820 of a Hellenistic marble statue of Aphrodite, the *Venus de Milo*. □ **Melian** *adj. & n.*

Mel·rose |'mel,rōz| town in S Scotland, in the Borders region, on the Tweed River, site of Melrose Abbey, a ruin known for its beauty and associations with Walter Scott.

Me·lun |mə'lən| industrial town in N central France, SE of Paris; capital of the Seine-et-Marne department. Pop. 36,000.

Me·mel |'mäməl| **1** former district of East Prussia. Centered on the city of Memel (Klaipeda). It became an autonomous region of Lithuania in 1924. In 1938 it was taken by Germany, but it was restored to Lithuania by the Soviet Union in 1945. See also KLAJPEDA. **2** the Neman River in its lower course (see NEMAN).

Mem·phis[1] |'mem(p)fəs| ancient city of Egypt, whose ruins are situated on the Nile just S of Cairo. It is thought to have been founded as the capital of the Old Kingdom of Egypt by Menes, the ruler of the first Egyptian dynasty, who united the kingdoms of Upper and Lower Egypt. Associated with the god Ptah, it remained one of Egypt's principal cities even after Thebes was made the capital of the New Kingdom, and is the site of the pyramids of Saqqara and Giza and the Sphinx.

Mem·phis[2] |'mem(p)fəs| river port on the Mississippi in the extreme SW of Tennessee. Pop. 610,337. Founded in 1819, it was a major cotton trading center just N of the Mississippi Delta, and today is a commercial and medical hub. It is the scene of the 1968 assassination of Martin Luther King, and the home and burial place of Elvis Presley.

Men·ai Strait |'me,nī| channel separating Anglesey from the mainland of NW Wales, noted for two bridges built 1819–26 and 1846–50.

Men·de·res |mende'res| river of SW Turkey. Rising in the Anatolian plateau, it flows for some 240 mi./384 km., entering the Aegean Sea S of the Greek island of Samos. Known in ancient times as the Maeander, and noted for its winding course, it gave its name to the verb *meander*.

Men·dip Hills |'mendip| (also **the Mendips**) a range of limestone hills in SW England.

Men·do·ci·no |ˌmendə'sēnō| resort community in NW California, on the Pacific coast. **Cape Mendocino,** the westernmost point in the state, is farther to the N.

Men·do·za |men'dōzə| city in W Argentina, in the foothills of the Andes at the center of a wine-producing region. Pop. 122,000.

Men·lo Park[1] |'menlō| city in N central California, an industrial and commercial suburb S of San Francisco. Pop. 28,040.

Men•lo Park[2] |'menlō| historic community in central New Jersey, in Edison Township, NE of New Brunswick. It was the scene of the laboratory, and many inventions, of Thomas Edison.

Me•nor•ca |mə'nawrkə| Spanish name for MINORCA, in the Balearic Islands.

Men•ton |mawn'tōn| resort town in SE France, near the Italian border on the French Riviera. Pop. 29,000.

Me•ra•no |mä'ränō| tourist and health resort in NE Italy, NW of Bolzano, on the S slope of the Alps. Pop. 33,000.

Mer•ced |mər'sed| city in central California, an agricultural processing hub in the San Joaquin Valley. Pop. 56,216.

Mer•cia |'mersH(ē)ə| former kingdom of central England. It was established by invading Angles in the 6th century A.D. in the border areas between the new Anglo-Saxon settlements in the east and the Celtic regions in the west. □ **Mercian** *adj. & n.*

Mer•iç |me'rēCH| Turkish name for the MARITSA River.

Mé•ri•da[1] |'mērēdə| city in SE Mexico, capital of the state of Yucatán. Pop. 557,000. It is a major agricultural trade center.

Mé•ri•da[2] |'mērēdə| historic city in W Spain, on the Guadiana River, capital of Extremadura region and formerly of Roman Lusitania. Pop. 50,000.

Mé•ri•da[3] |mä'rēdə| city in W Venezuela, in the N Andes, S of Lake Maracaibo, the capital of Mérida province. Pop. 168,000. It is a religious and tourist center.

Mer•i•den |'merədən| industrial city in S central Connecticut. Pop. 59,479.

Me•rid•i•an |mə'ridēən| city in E Mississippi, a commercial, transportation, and military center. Pop. 41,036.

Mer•i•on•eth•shire |,merē'änəTHSHir| former county of NW Wales. It became a part of Gwynedd in 1974.

Mer•lo |'merlō| town in E Argentina, a suburb W of Buenos Aires. Pop. 390,000.

Mer•oe |'merōwē| ancient city on the Nile, in present-day Sudan NE of Khartoum. Founded in *c.*750 B.C., it was the capital of the ancient kingdom of Cush from *c.*590 B.C. until it fell to the invading Aksumites in the early 4th century A.D. □ **Meroitic** *adj. & n.*

Mer•ri•mack River |'merə,mæk| river that flows 110 mi./180 km. from New Hampshire through E Massachusetts to the Atlantic. Its valley, site of Manchester, Con-

cord, and Nashua, New Hampshire, and Lowell, Lawrence, and Haverhill, Massachusetts, is often considered the birthplace of American industry.

Mer•sa Ma•truh |',mərsə mə'trōō| naval and resort town on the Mediterranean coast of Egypt, W of Alexandria. Pop. 113,000.

Mer•sey |'mərzē| river in NW England, which rises in the Peak District of Derbyshire and flows 70 mi./112 km. to the Irish Sea near Liverpool.

Mer•sey•side |'mərzē,sīd| metropolitan county of NW England; its chief city is Liverpool. Pop. 1,377,000.

Mer•sin |mer'sēn| industrial port in S Turkey, on the Mediterranean SW of Adana. Pop. 422,000.

Mer•thyr Tyd•fil |',mərTHər 'tidvil| industrial town in S Wales, in a historic mining area. Pop. 59,000.

Mer•ton |'mərtən| largely residential borough of SW Greater London, England. Pop. 162,000. The tennis center at Wimbledon is here.

Merv |'merv| earlier name for MARY, and name of the ancient city nearby.

Me•sa |'māsə| city in S central Arizona, an industrial and residential suburb E of Phoenix. Pop. 288,091.

Me•sa•bi Range |mə'säbē| low hills in NE Minnesota, site of one of the largest iron sources in the world. Hibbing is a regional mining center.

Me•sa Ver•de |'māsə 'verdē| high plateau in S Colorado, in a national park with the remains of many prehistoric cliff dwellings.

Mes•o•a•mer•i•ca |'mezōə'merəkə| (also **Meso-America**) the central region of America, from central Mexico to Nicaragua, especially as a region of ancient civilizations and native cultures before the arrival of Europeans. □ **Mesoamerican** *adj. & n.*

Me•so•lón•gi•on |,mesō'lōNGyin| Greek name for MISSOLONGHI.

Mes•o•po•ta•mia |,mesəpə'tämēə| ancient region of SW Asia in present-day Iraq, lying between the Tigris and Euphrates rivers ; its name derives from Greek *mesos* ('middle') + *potamos* ('river'). Its alluvial plains were the site of the early civilizations of Akkad, Sumer, Babylonia, and Assyria. □ **Mesopotamian** *adj. & n.*

Mes•quite |me'skēt| city in NE Texas, an industrial and commercial suburb on the E side of Dallas. Pop. 101,484.

Mes•se•nia |mäs'sēnēə| division of ancient

Greece in the SW Peloponnese, a center of Mycenaean culture.

Mes·si·na |mə'sēnə| industrial port city in NE Sicily. Pop. 275,000. Founded in 730 B.C. by the Greeks, it is situated on the Strait of Messina.

Mes·si·na, Strait of |mə'sēnə| channel separating the island of Sicily from the 'toe' of Italy. It forms a link between the Tyrrhenian and Ionian seas. The strait, which is 20 mi./32 km. in length and 2.5 to 12 mi./4 to 19 km. wide, is noted for the strength of its currents. It is traditionally identified as the location of the legendary sea monster Scylla and the whirlpool Charybdis.

Me·ta River |'mātə| river that flows 650 mi./1,050 km. from central Colombia to the NE, forming part of the Colombia-Venezuela boundary, into the Orinoco River.

Met·air·ie |'metərē| community in SE Louisiana, the largest residential suburb of New Orleans, on its NW side. Pop. 149,428.

Me·te·o·ra |mə'tāōrä| group of monasteries in N central Greece, in Thessaly. The monasteries, built between the 12th and the 16th centuries, are perched on the summits of curiously shaped rock formations.

Me·trop·o·lis |mə'träpələs| see THERA.

Metz |mets| historic industrial city in Lorraine, NE France, on the Moselle River. Pop. 124,000. Once the capital of Frankish Austrasia, it has more recently been an iron and steel center.

Meu·don |mə'dōn| town, a suburb of Paris, in N central France. Pop. 49,000.

Meuse |'myōoz| river of W Europe, which rises in NE France and flows 594 mi./950 km. through Belgium and the Netherlands to the North Sea S of Dordrecht. Flemish and Dutch name **Maas**.

Mex·i·cali |ˌmeksə'kälē| the capital of the state of Baja California, in NW Mexico, adjacent to Calexico, California. Pop. 602,000.

Mex·i·co, Gulf of |'meksəkō| extension of the W Atlantic. Bounded in a sweeping curve by the U.S. to the N, by Mexico to the W and S, and by Cuba to the SE, it is linked to the Atlantic by the Straits of Florida and to the Caribbean Sea by the Yucatán Channel.

Mex·i·co, State of |'meksəkō| (Spanish name **México**) state in central Mexico, surrounding the Distrito Federal. Area: 8,245 sq. mi./21,355 sq. km. Pop. 9,816,000. Capital: Toluca.

Mex·i·co, Valley of |'meksəkō| basin in central Mexico, the site of Mexico City and the Distrito Federal. Its many shallow lakes have been largely drained, and the valley is now densely populated.

Mex·i·co |'meksəkō| republic in North America, with extensive coastlines on the Gulf of Mexico and the Pacific Ocean, bordered by the U.S. to the N. Area: 756,200 sq. mi./1.96 million sq. km. Pop. 81,140,920. Language, Spanish. Capital and largest city: Mexico City. The center of the Mayan and Aztec civilizations, it was conquered by Spain in the 1520s, gaining independence in 1821. In the early 19th century it lost much territory to the U.S. Today it has 31 states and a federal district, and is both agricultural and industrial, with an important oil industry and much cross-border trade with the U.S. Tourism is important. □ **Mexican** *adj. & n.*

Mex·i·co City |'meksəkō| the capital of Mexico. Pop. 13,636,000. Founded in about 1300 as the Aztec capital Tenochtitlán, it was destroyed in 1521 by the Spanish conquistador Cortés, who rebuilt it as the capital of New Spain. A financial, cultural, and commercial center, it is one of the most populous cities in the world.

Mez·zo·gior·no |ˌmetsō'j(ē)awrnō| term for the S part of Italy from Abruzzi and Campania S, and including Sicily and Sardinia. The name in Italian means 'midday,' and refers to the strength of the sun in the region. See also MIDI.

Mi·ami |mī'æmē| port city on the coast of SE Florida. Pop. 358,548. Its subtropical climate and miles of beaches make this and the resort island of Miami Beach, separated from the mainland by Biscayne Bay, a year-round holiday resort. Miami is also a major Hispanic commercial and cultural center.

Mi·ami Beach |mī'æmē| city in SE Florida, on the Atlantic, across Biscayne Bay from Miami. It is a famous resort, known recently especially for its South Beach (Art Deco) district. Pop. 92,639.

Mich·i·gan, Lake |'misHigən| one of the five Great Lakes of North America. Bordered by Michigan, Wisconsin, Illinois, and Indiana, it is the only one of the Great Lakes to lie wholly within the U.S. Chicago is at its SW corner.

Mich·i·gan |'misHigən| see box, p. 233. □ **Michigander** *n.*

Mi·cho·a·cán |ˌmēcHōä'kän| mountainous state of W Mexico, on the Pacific coast. Pop. 3,534,000. Capital: Morelia.

Mi·chu·rinsk |mə'cHŌŌrənsk| transporta-

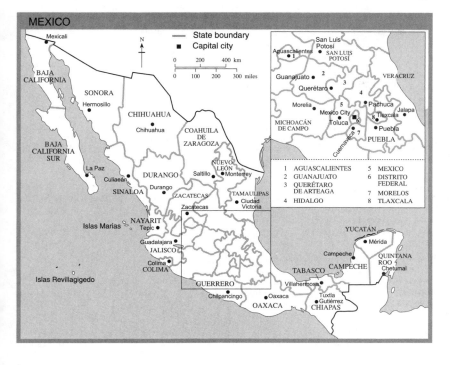

MEXICO

State boundary
■ Capital city

Mexicali
Baja California
Sonora
Hermosillo
Chihuahua
Chihuahua
Coahuila de Zaragoza
Baja California Sur
La Paz
Culiacán
Durango
Durango
Saltillo
Nuevo León
Monterrey
Sinaloa
Zacatecas
Zacatecas
Tamaulipas
Ciudad Victoria
Islas Marias
Nayarit
Tepic
Guadalajara
Jalisco
Colima
Colima
Islas Revillagigedo
Guerrero
Chilpancingo
Oaxaca
Oaxaca
Tuxtla Gutiérrez
Chiapas

San Luis Potosí
Aguascalientes 1 San Luis Potosí
Guanajuato 2 Veracruz
Querétaro 3
Morelia 5 4 Pachuca
Michoacán de Campo Mexico City Jalapa
Toluca 6 Tlaxcala
7 Puebla
Cuernavaca Puebla

1 AGUASCALIENTES   5 MEXICO
2 GUANAJUATO   6 DISTRITO
3 QUERÉTARO   FEDERAL
   DE ARTEAGA   7 MORELOS
4 HIDALGO   8 TLAXCALA

Yucatán
Mérida
Campeche
Quintana Roo
Chetumal
Campeche
Tabasco
Villahermosa

Michigan

Capital: Lansing
Largest city: Detroit
Other cities: Ann Arbor, Bay City, Flint, Grand Rapids, Marquette, Muskegon, Saginaw
Population: 9,295,297 (1990); 9,817,242 (1998); 9,763,000 (2005 proj.)
Population rank (1990): 8
Rank in land area: 11
Abbreviation: MI; Mich.
Nicknames: Wolverine State; Water Wonderland; Upper Peninsula often referred to as the Land of Hiawatha
Motto: *Si quaeris peninsulam amoenam, circumspice* (Latin: 'If you seek a pleasant peninsula, look about you')
Bird: robin
Fish: brook trout
Flower: apple blossom
Tree: white pine
Song: "Michigan, My Michigan"
Noted physical features: Saginaw Bay, Lake St. Clair; Mackinac Straits
Tourist attractions: Mackinac Bridge; Soo Canal, Sault Ste. Marie Canal; Holland Tulip Festival; Isle Royale National Park; Greenfield Village
Admission date: January 26, 1837
Order of admission: 26
Name origin: Named in 1805 apparently for Lake Michigan, itself named from an Indian word, possibly Chippewa *Michigama*, meaning 'great lake.'

tion center and industrial city in W Russia, SE of Moscow. Pop. 109,000.
Mi·cro·ne·sia, Federated States of
|ˌmīkrəˈnēzHə| group of associated island states comprising the 600 islands of the Caroline Islands, in the W Pacific to the N of the equator. Area: 271 sq. mi./701 sq. km. Pop. 108,000. Languages, English (official), Austronesian languages. Capital: Palikir (on Pohnpei). The group, which includes the islands of Yap, Kosrae, Truk, and Pohnpei, was administered by the U.S. as part of the Pacific Islands Trust Territory from 1947 and entered into free association with the U.S. as an independent state in 1986. Subsistence agriculture and fishing are important. □ **Micronesian** *adj. & n.*
Mi·cro·ne·sia |ˌmīkrəˈnēzHə| region of the W Pacific to the N of Melanesia and N and W of Polynesia. It includes the Mariana, Caroline, and Marshall island groups, and Kiribati.
Mid-Atlantic Ridge |ˌmidətˈlæn(t)ik ˈrij| submarine ridge that lies under the Atlantic, from Iceland in the N to near Antarctica in the S. It roughly parallels the outlines of the continents to either side, and is considered to mark where continental plates are separating, allowing new crustal

Micronesia

material to rise.The islands of Iceland, the Azores, Ascension, St. Helena, and Tristan da Cunha are situated on it.

Mid-Atlantic States term for the US states between New England and the South that are on or near the Atlantic coast, usually including NewYork, New Jersey, and Pennsylvania, and sometimes also Delaware and Maryland.

Mid·dle A·mer·i·ca |'midəl ə'merəkə| general name for the region that includes Mexico and the countries of Central America, and usually also the West Indies.

Mid·dle At·lan·tic |'midəl ; ət'læn(t)ik| region of the U.S., generally including New Jersey, Pennsylvania, and Delaware, and often also New York and Maryland.

Mid·dle East |'midəl 'ēst| extensive area of SW Asia and N Africa, stretching from the shores of the W Mediterranean to Pakistan and including the Arabian Peninsula. □ **Middle Eastern** adj.

Mid·dle Passage |'midəl 'pæsij| historical term for the route taken by slave ships from W Africa to the Americas.

Mid·dles·brough |'midəlzbrə| port in NE England, the county seat of Celeveland, on the estuary of theTees River. Pop. 141,000.

Mid·dle·sex |'midəl‚seks| former county of SE England, to the NW of London. In 1965 it was divided among Hertfordshire, Surrey, and Greater London.

Mid·dle·town[1] |'midəltown| commercial and industrial city in central Connecticut, on the Connecticut River S of Hartford, home to Wesleyan University. Pop. 42,762.

Mid·dle·town[2] |'midəltown| industrial city in SW Ohio, between Cincinnati and Dayton. Pop. 46,029.

Mid Gla·mor·gan |'mid glə'mawrgən| former county of South Wales formed in 1974 from parts of Breconshire, Glamorgan, and Monmouthshire and dissolved in 1996.

Mi·di |mē'dē| term for the S of France.The name in French means 'midday' and refers

to the strength of the sun in the region. See also MEZZOGIORNO.

Mid·i·an |'midēən| biblical name for a region of the NW Arabian Peninsula, home of the Midianites, enemies of the Israelites. Situated E of the Gulf of Aqaba, it may have been the equivalent of present-day Madian, Saudi Arabia.

Midi-Pyrénées |‚midēpērə'nā| region of S France, between the Pyrenees and the Massif Central, centered on Toulouse.

Mid·land[1] |'midlənd| city in central Michigan, best known as home to the Dow Chemical Company. Pop. 38,053.

Mid·land[2] |'midlənd| city in W Texas, an oil industry center in the Permian Basin. Pop. 89,443. Its sister city is Odessa.

Mid·lands, the | 'midləndz| general name for inland counties of central England, from just NW of London (Buckinghamshire) N to Nottinghamshire and W to West Midlands.

Mid·lo·thi·an |mid'lōTHēən| administrative region and former county of central Scotland; administrative center, Dalkeith.

Midnight Sun, Land of the |'midnīt 'sən| popular term for Arctic regions where the sun remains above the horizon through the night in midsummer, especially for N Norway.

Mid·way Islands |'midwā| two small islands with a surrounding coral atoll, in the central Pacific in the W part of the Hawaiian chain.The islands were annexed by the U.S. in 1867 and remain a U.S. territory and naval base.They were the scene in 1942 of the Battle of Midway, in which the U.S. Navy repelled a Japanese invasion fleet, sinking four aircraft carriers.

Mid·west |'mid'west| the region of N states of the U.S. from Ohio W through the Dakotas. □ **Midwestern** adj. **Midwesterner** n.

Mid·west City |'mid'west| city in central Oklahoma, a suburb just E of Oklahoma City. Tinker Air Force Base is nearby. Pop. 52,267.

Mí·ko·nos |'mēkōnōs| Greek name for MYKONOS.

Mi·lan |mə'län| industrial city in NW Italy, capital of Lombardy region. Pop. 1,432,000. A politically powerful city in the past, particularly from the 13th to the 15th centuries. Milan today is a leading fashion, finacial, cultural, and commercial center. Italian name **Milano**. □ **Milanese** adj. & n.

Mi·le·tus |mī'lētəs| ancient city of the Ionian Greeks in SW Asia Minor. In the 7th and 6th centuries B.C. it was a powerful port, from which more than sixty colonies were founded on the shores of the Black Sea and in Italy and Egypt. It was the home of the pre-Socratic philosophers Thales, Anaximander, and Anaximenes.

Mil·ford |ˌmilfərd| city in SW Connecticut, a suburb W of New Haven. Pop. 49,938.

Mil·ford Ha·ven |ˈmilfərd ˈhāvən| (Welsh name **Aberdaugleddau**) historic industrial port in SW Wales, in Dyfed. Pop. 14,000. It is today a major oil port and refinery center.

Milk River |ˈmilk| river that flows 625 mi./1,000 km. through NW Montana and S Alberta, into the Missouri River. It is the northwesternmost part of the Missouri-Mississippi system.

Mill·ville |ˈmilˌvil| city in S New Jersey, across the Maurice River from Vineland. It is a longtime glass industry center. Pop. 25,992.

Mí·los |ˈmēlōs| Greek name for MELOS.

Mil·ton Keynes |ˈmiltən| residential and academic town in Buckinghamshire, S central England. Pop. 172,000.

Milvian Bridge see SAXA RUBRA.

Mil·wau·kee |milˈwawkē| industrial port city in SE Wisconsin, on the W shore of Lake Michigan. Pop. 628,088. It is noted for its brewing industry and German culture.

Mi·na·ma·ta |mēˈnämätä| industrial city in SW Japan, on SW Kyushu, S of Kumamoto, scene of a 1960s mercury poisoning episode. Pop. 35,000.

Mi·nas Bas·in |ˈmīnəs| inlet of the Bay of Fundy in W central Nova Scotia, scene of some of the most extreme tides in the world.

Mi·nas Ge·rais |ˈmēnə ZHēˈrīs| state of SE Brazil. Pop. 15.73 million. Capital: Belo Horizonte. It has major deposits of iron ore, coal, gold, and diamonds.

Mi·na·ti·tlán |ˌmēnätēˈtlän| industrial port in E Mexico, in Veracruz state, on the Coatzacoalcos River. Pop. 200,000. It is an oil industry center.

Minch |minCH| (also **the Minch**) a channel of the Atlantic, between the mainland of Scotland and the Outer Hebrides. The N stretch is called the *North Minch*, the S stretch, NW of Skye, is called the *Little Minch*. Also called **the Minches**.

Min·da·nao |ˌmindəˈnäō| the second largest (39,400 sq. mi./102,000 sq. km.) island in the Philippines, in the SE of the group. Pop. 14.30 million. Its chief town is Davao.

Min·den |ˈmindən| industrial city and transportation center in NW Germany, on the Weser River and the Midland Canal. Pop. 75,000.

Min·do·ro |minˈdōrō| island in the Philippines, situated to the SW of Luzon.

Min·gre·lia |minˈgrēlēyə| lowland region in the Republic of Georgia, bordering on the Black Sea. Its major products are tea and grapes. Poti is the main port. The area corresponds to the former country of Colchis.

Mi·nho |ˈmēnyōō| Portuguese name for the MIÑO River.

Min·i·coy Islands |ˈminəkoi| one of the groups of islands forming the Indian territory of Lakshadweep in the Indian Ocean.

Min·ne·ap·o·lis |ˌminēˈæpələs| industrial city and port on the Mississippi River in SE Minnesota. Pop. 368,383, the largest city in the state. It is adjacent to the state capital, St. Paul; the two are referred to as the *Twin Cities.* Minneapolis is the major agricultural processing center of the upper Midwest and is a commercial and technological center.

Min·ne·so·ta |ˌminəˈsōtə| see box. □ **Minnesotan** *adj. & n.*

Min·ne·so·ta River |ˌminəˈsōtə| river that

Minnesota

Capital: St. Paul
Largest city: Minneapolis
Other cities: Bloomington, Duluth, Rochester, St. Cloud
Population: 4,375,099 (1990); 4,725,419 (1998); 5,005,000 (2005 proj.)
Population rank (1990): 20
Rank in land area: 12
Abbreviation: MN; Minn.
Nicknames: North Star State; Gopher State; Bread and Butter State
Motto: *L'Etoile du Nord* (French: 'The North Star')
Bird: common loon
Fish: walleye
Flower: moccasin flower; pink and white lady's slipper
Tree: Norway (red) pine
Song: "Hail! Minnesota"
Noted physical features: Big Bog; Northwest Angle; Minnehaha Falls; Eagle Mountain
Tourist attractions: Paul Bunyan Monument; Pipestone and Grand Portage national monuments; Voyageurs' National Park; Kensington Rune Stone
Admission date: May 11, 1858
Order of admission: 32
Name origin: For the Minnesota River; from the Siouan word *Menesota,* meaning "cloudy water," or possibly "water reflecting cloudy skies."

flows 320 mi./530 km. through Minnesota, to join the Mississippi River just S of the Twin Cities.

Mi•ño |mē'nyō| river that rises in NW Spain and flows S to the Portuguese border, which it follows before entering the Atlantic N of Viana do Castelo. Portuguese name **Minho**.

Mi•nor•ca |mə'nawrkə| most easterly of the Balearic Islands of Spain, in the W Mediterranean Sea. Pop. 59,000. The second-largest of the Balearic chain at 271 sq. mi./702 sq. km., it is largely agricultural, and is a popular tourist destination.

Mi•not |'mīnät| commercial and industrial city in N central North Dakota. Pop. 34,544.

Minsk |'minsk| the capital of Belarus, an industrial city in the central region of the country. Pop. 1,613,000.

Miq•ue•lon |'mēk,län| see St. Pierre and Miquelon.

Mi•ra•bel |,mērə'bel| city in S Quebec, a suburb NW of Montreal, and site of its international airport. Pop. 17,971.

Mir•a•flor•es |,mērä'flawrez| residential suburb of Lima, W central Peru, a beach resort just S of the city. Pop. 87,000.

Mir•za•pur |'mərzäpoor| city in N India, in Uttar Pradesh state. Pop. 169,000. It includes the Hindu pilgrimage center, Vindhyachal.

Mi•sha•wa•ka |mi'sHäwawkə| industrial city in NE Indiana, on the E side of South Bend. Pop. 42,608.

Mi•shi•ma |mē'sHēmä| resort city in E central Japan, on central Honshu, NE of Shizuoka. Pop. 105,000.

Mis•kolc |'misHkōlts| industrial and university city in NE Hungary. Pop. 191,000.

Mis•ra•tah |mēs'rätə| (also **Misurata**) oasis and port city in NW Libya, on the Mediterranean Sea E of Tripoli. Pop. 178,000.

Mis•sion•ary Ridge |'misHə,nerē| historic site SE of Chattanooga, Tennessee, on the Georgia line, scene of a November 1863 Civil War battle following that at nearby Lookout Mt.

Mis•sis•sau•ga |,misi'sawgə| city in S Ontario, on the W shore of Lake Ontario. Pop. 463,388. It is an industrial and residential SW suburb of Toronto.

Mis•sis•sip•pi |,misə'sipē| see box. □ **Mississippian** *adj. & n.*

Mis•sis•sip•pi River |,misə'sipē| major river of the U.S., which rises in N Minnesota near Bemidji and Lake Itasca and flows S to a delta in Louisiana on the Gulf of Mexico. With its chief tributary, the Mis-

---

Mississippi

Capital/largest city: Jackson
Other cities: Biloxi, Gulfport, Greenville, Hattiesburg, Meridian, Tupelo
Population: 2,573,216 (1990); 2,752,092 (1998); 2,908,000 (2005 proj.)
Population rank (1990): 31
Rank in land area: 32
Abbreviation: MS; Miss.
Nickname: The Magnolia State
Motto: *Virtute et armis* (Latin: 'By valor and arms')
Bird: mockingbird
Fish: largemouth bass or black bass
Flower: magnolia blossom
Tree: magnolia
Song: "Go, Mississippi"
Noted physical features: Yazoo Basin Delta; Tennessee Hills and Loess Bluffs; Black Prairie, Jackson Prairie; Mississippi River; Woodall Mountain
Tourist attractions: Natchez Trace; Vicksburg National Military Park; Gulf Islands National Seashore
Admission date: December 10, 1817
Order of admission: 20
Name origin: For the Mississippi River; from Algonquian *meeche* or *mescha*, meaning 'great,' and *cebe*, meaning 'river, water,' thus 'great river.'

---

souri, it is 3,710 mi./5,970 km. long, and drains over one-third of the U.S. The Ohio River flows into it at Cairo, Illinois. It has been a major route for transportation since the 17th century, and remains important for commercial shipping, forming a major portion of the border of 10 states. Important cities along the Mississippi include Minneapolis and St. Paul, Minnesota; Dubuque and Davenport, Iowa; St. Louis, Missouri; Memphis, Tennessee; and Baton Rouge and New Orleans, Louisiana.

Mis•so•lon•ghi |,misə'lawNGē| city in W Greece, on the N shore of the Gulf of Patras. Pop. 11,000. It is noted as the place where the poet Byron, who had joined the fight for Greek independence from the Turks, died of malaria in 1824. Greek name **Mesolóngion**.

Mis•sou•la |mə'soolə| commercial city in W Montana, on the Clark Fork River. Pop. 42,918.

Mis•sou•ri |mə'zoorē| see box, p. 237. □ **Missourian** *adj. & n.*

Mis•sou•ri River |mə'zoorē| a major river of the U.S., one of the main tributaries of the Mississippi. It rises in the Rocky Mts.

Missouri

Capital: Jefferson City
Largest city: St. Louis
Other cities: Columbia, Kansas City, Springfield, St. Joseph
Population: 5,117,073 (1990); 5,438,559 (1998); 5,718,000 (2005 proj.)
Population rank (1990): 15
Rank in land area: 21
Abbreviation: MO; Mo.
Nicknames: The Show Me State; Mother of the West
Motto: *Salus populi suprema lex esto* (Latin: 'The welfare of the people shall be the supreme law')
Bird: bluebird
Flower: hawthorn blossom
Tree: flowering dogwood
Song: "Missouri Waltz"
Noted physical features: Big Spring; Till Plains, Osage Plains; Ozark Plateau; Taum Sauk Mountain
Tourist attractions: Branson; Osage Dam
Admission date: August 10, 1821
Order of admission: 24
Name origin: For the Missouri River; the name was that of an Indian tribe that lived near the mouth of the river.

in Montana and flows 2,315 mi./3,736 km. through the Dakotas, Nebraska, Iowa, Kansas, and Missouri to meet the Mississippi just N of St. Louis. A major transportation route, dammed for Great Plains agriculture, it is popularly called the Big Muddy.

Mi•ta•ka |mē'täkä| city in E central Japan, on E central Honshu, a suburb W of Tokyo. Pop. 166,000.

Mi•ti•lí•ni |,mitə'lēnē| Greek name for MYTILENE.

Mit•la |'mētlə| ancient city in S Mexico, to the E of the city of Oaxaca, now a noted archaeological site. Believed to have been established as a burial site by the Zapotecs, it was eventually overrun by the Mixtecs in about A.D. 1000.

Mi•to |'mētō| city in E central Japan, a prefectural capital in central Honshu. Pop. 235,000. It contains one of the greatest landscape gardens in Japan.

Mit•tel•land Canal |'mitəlländ| canal in NW Germany, which was constructed between 1905 and 1930. It is part of an inland waterway network linking the Rhine and Elbe rivers.

Mix•co |'mēsHkō| city in S central Guatemala, a suburb just W of Guatemala City. Pop. 413,000.

Mi•ya•ji•ma |mēyä'jēmə| earlier name for ITSUKUSHIMA.

Mi•ya•za•ki |mē'yäzäkē| port and resort city in SW Japan, on SE Kyushu. Pop. 288,000. A great Shinto shrine dedicated to the first emperor of Japan is here.

Mi•zo•ram |mə'zawrəm| state in the far NE of India, lying between Bangladesh and Burma. Pop. 686,000. Capital: Aizawl. Separated from Assam in 1972, it was administered as a Union Territory in India until 1986, when it became a state.

Mla•da Bo•les•lav |əm'lädä 'bawləzläf| (German name **Jungbunzlau**) industrial city in the N central Czech Republic. Pop. 48,000.

Mma•ba•tho |mäbätō| the capital of North-West Province in South Africa, near the border with Botswana. Pop. 28,000. It was the capital of the former homeland of Bophuthatswana.

Mo•ab |'mōæb| the ancient kingdom of the Moabites, situated to the E of the Dead Sea, in present-day Jordan. □ **Moabite** *adj. & n.*

Mo•bile |'mō,bēl| industrial port city on the coast of S Alabama. Pop. 196,278. It is situated at the head of Mobile Bay, an inlet of the Gulf of Mexico.

Mo•cha |'mōkə| (also **Mokha**) port in SW Yemen, on the Red Sea coast. Pop. 6,000. It gave its name to a type of coffee once exported from here.

Mo•de•na |'mōdānə| industrial city in N Italy, NW of Bologna. Pop. 117,000.

Mo•des•to |mə'destō| city in N central California, in the San Joaquin Valley, an agricultural processing and wine-making center. Pop. 164,730.

Mo•doc Plateau |'mōdäk| volcanic highland in N California and S Oregon, former home of the Modoc people.

Moers |mœrz| industrial city in western Germany, in North Rhine–Westphalia. Pop. 105,000.

Moe•sia |'mēsHə| ancient country and Roman province in SE Europe, corresponding to parts of modern Bulgaria and Serbia.

Mog•a•di•shu |,mōgə'dēsHо̄о̄| the capital of Somalia, a port on the Indian Ocean. Pop. 377,000. Also called **Muqdisho**; Italian name **Mogadiscio**.

Mo•gi das Cru•zes |'mōzHē däz 'kro͞ozes| industrial city in SE Brazil, an iron and steel industry center E of São Paulo. Pop. 262,000.

Mo·gi·lyov |mägi'lyawf| (also **Mogilev**) Russian name for MAHILYOW.

Mo·gol·lon Plateau |məgē'ōn; mōgə'yōn| highland region of E central Arizona. Its S boundary is the **Mogollon Rim,** an escarpment also called the Mogollon Mts., but not to be confused with a range of that name in New Mexico.

Mo·gul Empire |'mōgəl| (also **Moghul** or **Mughal**) Muslim empire in N and central India, established in the 16th century, and expanded until the 18th. It declined until the British abolished it in 1857.

Mo·hács |'mōhäCH| river port and industrial town on the Danube in S Hungary, close to the borders with Croatia and Serbia. Pop. 21,000. It was the site of a battle in 1526 in which the Hungarians were defeated by a Turkish force, as a result of which Hungary became part of the Ottoman Empire.

Mo·ham·me·rah |mə,hämä'rä| former name (until 1924) for KHORRAMSHAHR, Iran.

Mo·hawk River |'mō,hawk| river that flows 140 mi./230 km. across central New York, joining the Hudson River above Albany. The Mohawk Valley is the site of much of the Erie Canal, and has long been a transportation corridor.

Mohenjo-Daro |mō'henyō'därō| ancient city of the civilization of the Indus valley (c.2600–1700 B.C.), now a major archaeological site in Pakistan, SW of Sukkur.

Mo·ja·ve Desert |mō'hävē| (also **Mohave**) desert in S California, to the SE of the Sierra Nevada and N and E of Los Angeles.

Mo·jo·ker·to |mōjō'kertō| (also **Modjokerto**) industrial town in Indonesia, on E Java, SW of Surabaya. Pop. 100,000.

Mok·po |'mäk,pō| port city in extreme SW South Korea. Pop. 253,000.

Mol·dau |'mawl,dow| German name for the VLTAVA River.

Mol·da·via |mäl'dāvēə| **1** a former principality of SE Europe. Formerly a part of the Roman province of Dacia, it came under Turkish rule in the 16th century. In 1861 Moldavia united with Wallachia to form Romania. **2** another name for MOLDOVA.

Mol·do·va |mäl'dōvə| landlocked republic in SE Europe, between Romania and Ukraine. Area: 13,017 sq. mi./33,700 sq. km. Pop. 4,384,000. Languages, Moldavian (official), Russian. Capital and largest city: Chişinău. Also called **Moldavia**. Part of Romania, then (1940–91) a republic of the Soviet Union, Moldova is a fertile agri-

Moldava

cultural country. □ **Moldovan** adj. & n. **Moldavian** adj. & n.

Mol·do·vea·nu |,mōdōl'vyänōō| mountain peak in Romania, in the Transylvanian Alps SE of Sibiu. It is the highest peak in Romania (8,346 ft./2,544 m.).

Mo·line |'mō'lēn| city on the Rock and Mississippi rivers in NW Illinois, one of the Quad Cities and home to a noted farm machinery industry. Pop. 43,202.

Mo·li·se |mō'lēzā| region of E Italy, on the Adriatic coast. Pop. 336,000. Capital: Campobasso.

Mo·lo·kai |,mōlō'kī| island of Hawaii, E of Oahu, site of numerous resorts.

Mo·lo·tov |'mälə,tawf| former name (1940–57) for PERM, Russia.

Mo·luc·cas Islands |mō'ləkəz| island group in Indonesia, between Sulawesi and New Guinea; chief city, Amboina. Settled by the Portuguese in the early 16th century, the islands were taken a century later by the Dutch. They were formerly known as the Spice Islands. Indonesian name **Maluku**. □ **Moluccan** adj. & n.

Mom·ba·sa |mōm'bäsä| seaport and industrial city in SE Kenya, on the Indian Ocean. Pop. 465,000. It is the leading port and second-largest city of Kenya.

Mo·na |'mōnə| ancient and literary name for either the island of ANGLESEY, Wales, or the Isle of MAN.

Mon·a·co |'mänəkō| principality forming an enclave (0.75 sq. mi./1.95 sq. km.) within French territory, on the Mediterranean coast near the Italian border. Pop. 30,000; official language, French. Capital: Monaco-Ville. Ruled by the Grimaldi family since 1297, and the smallest sovereign state, except for the Vatican, Monaco relies on tourism and its casinos for income. □ **Monacan** adj. & n. **Monégasqu** adj. & n.

Mo·nad·nock, Mount |mə'näd,näk| isolated peak in SW New Hampshire whose name stands for any mountain of its type.

Monaco

Mon•a•ghan |'mänə,hæn| **1** county of the Republic of Ireland, part of the old province of Ulster. Pop. 51,000. **2** its county seat. Pop. 6,000.

Mo•na Passage |'mōnə| ocean passage between Puerto Rico and the Dominican Republic, leading from the Atlantic into the Caribbean Sea, and noted for its difficult waters.

Mo•nash•ee Mountains |mə'näsHē| range of the N Rocky Mts. in SE British Columbia, reaching 10,560 ft./3,219 m. at Hallam Peak.

Mön•chen•glad•bach |,mənKHen'glädbäk| industrial city in NW Germany. Pop. 263,000. It is the site of the NATO headquarters for N Europe.

Mon•clo•va |mäNG'klōvα| industrial city in NE Mexico, in Coahuila state. Pop. 178,000. It is an iron and steel center.

Monc•ton |'məNGktən| commercial and academic city in SE New Brunswick, on the Petitcodiac River. Pop. 57,010.

Mo•nem•va•sía |,mōnemvä'sēä| (also known as **Monembasia**) village in S Greece, on a small island off the coast of Laconia, in the Peloponnese. It is known for its wine, called malmsey or malvasia.

Mon•go•lia |mäNG'gōlēə| republic of E Asia, between Siberian Russia and China. Area: 604,480 sq. mi./1.56 million sq. km. Pop. 2,184,000. Language, Mongolian.

Mongolia

Capital and largest city: Ulan Bator. Center of the former Mongol Empire, it was later a Chinese province (Outer Mongolia, to distinguish it from Inner Mongolia). It has great mineral resources, but most of its people remain nomadic pastoralists. □ **Mongolian** *adj. & n.*

Mon•mouth•shire |'mänmǝTHSHi(ǝ)r| county of SE Wales, on the border with England; administrative center, Cwmbran. The major part of it was part of Gwent 1974–96.

Mo•no Lake |'mōnō| saline lake in E central California, near the Nevada line, noted for its rock formations, many exposed when local waters were diverted to the Los Angeles area.

Mo•non•ga•he•la River |mä,nängä'hēlä| river that flows 128 mi./206 km. from West Virginia into W Pennsylvania, to Pittsburgh, where it joins the Allegheny River to form the Ohio River. Its valley is highly industrial.

Mon•roe |mən'rō| industrial and commercial city in N central Louisiana, in a natural gas producing area. Pop. 54,909.

Mon•ro•via[1] |mən'rōvēə| industrial city in SW California, NE of Los Angeles. Pop. 35,761.

Mon•ro•via[2] |mən'rōvēə| the capital and chief port of Liberia. Pop. 500,000. Founded in 1822 for resettled American slaves, it was later named for President James Monroe.

Mons |mawnz| industrial town in S Belgium, capital of the province of Hainaut. Pop. 92,000. It was the scene in August 1914 of the first major battle of World War I between British and German forces. Flemish name **Bergen**.

Mon•tana |män'tænə| see box, p. 240. □ **Montanan** *adj. & n.*

Mont•au•ban |mäntə'bän| market center in S France, capital of the Tarn-et-Garonne department in the Midi-Pyrénées. Pop. 53,000.

Mont Blanc |,mawn 'bläNGk| peak in the Alps on the border between France and Italy, rising to 15,771 ft./4,807 m. The highest peak in the Alps and in W Europe, it was first climbed in 1786.

Mont Ce•nis |mōn sǝ'nē| (Italian name **Monte Cenisio**) Alpine pass linking Modane, France, and Susa, Italy. The nearby Mont Cenis Tunnel, opened 1871, was the first major tunnel through the Alps. It links Modane and Bardonnecchia, Italy.

Mont Cer•vin |mawn ser'ven| French name for the MATTERHORN.

Mont•clair |mänt'klär| township in NE

Montana

Capital: Helena
Largest city: Billings
Other cities: Bozeman, Butte, Great Falls, Missoula
Population: 799,065 (1990); 880,453 (1998); 1,006,000 (2005 proj.)
Population rank (1990): 44
Rank in land area: 4
Abbreviation: MT; Mont.
Nickname: Treasure State; Big Sky Country
Motto: *Oro y Plata* (Spanish: 'Gold and Silver')
Bird: Western meadowlark
Fish: black-spotted (cutthroat) trout
Flower: bitterroot
Tree: Ponderosa pine
Song: "Montana"
Noted physical features: Great Falls; Granite Peak
Tourist attractions: Continental Divide; Custer Cemetery; Glacier and Yellowstone national parks
Admission date: November 8, 1889
Order of admission: 41
Name origin: From Latin *montana*, meaning 'mountainous region.'

New Jersey, an affluent suburb NW of Newark. Pop. 37,729.

Mon·te Al·bán |ˈmōnte älˈbän| ancient city, now in ruins, in Oaxaca, S Mexico. Occupied from the 8th century B.C., it was a center of the Zapotec culture from about the 1st century B.C. to the 8th century A.D.

Mon·te Car·lo |ˌmän(t)ē ˈkärˌlō| resort in Monaco, forming one of the four communes of the principality. Pop. 12,000. It is famous as a gambling center.

Mon·te Cas·si·no |ˌmän(t)ā kəˈsēˌnō| hill in central Italy near the town of Cassino, the site of the principal monastery of the Benedictines, founded by St. Benedict *c.*529.

Mon·te Cer·vi·no |ˌmän(t)ā serˈvēnō| Italian name for the MATTERHORN.

Mon·te Cris·to |ˌmän(t)ā ˈkristō| uninhabited Italian island in the Tyrrhenian Sea, S of Elba, associated with the novel *The Count of Monte Cristo* by Alexandre Dumas.

Mon·te·go Bay |mənˈtē go| free port and beach resort on the N coast of Jamaica. Pop. 82,000.

Mon·té·li·mar |ˌmäntä lēˈmär| manufacturing town in Dauphiné, SE France, noted for nougat production. Pop. 31,000.

Mon·te·ne·gro |ˌmäntəˈne gro| mountainous, landlocked republic in the Balkan peninsula. Area: 5,335 sq. mi./13,812 sq. km. Pop. 632,000. Official language, Serbo-Croat. Capital: Podgorica. Long tied to Serbia, Montenegro remains a nominal constituent of the much reduced Yugoslavia. Its economy is based on livestock raising, agriculture, mining, and iron and steel. □ **Montenegrin** *adj. & n.*

Mon·te·rey |ˌmäntəˈrā| city and fishing port on the coast of central California, founded by the Spanish in the 18th century. Pop. 31,954. The harbor is the site of the Monterey Bay Aquarium, and of Cannery Row, featured in the writing of John Steinbeck.

Mon·te·ría |ˌmäntəˈrēä| commercial city in N Colombia, a port on the Sinú River and capital of Córdoba department. Pop. 266,000.

Mon·ter·rey |ˌmäntəˈrā| city in NE Mexico, capital of the state of Nuevo León and the third largest city in Mexico. Pop. 2,522,000. It is an iron and steel and heavy industrial center.

Mon·te Sant'An·gel·o |ˈmäntəsænˈtænjälō| commune in SE Italy. Pop. 15,000. The archangel Michael is said to have appeared at a grotto here; a 5th-century sanctuary at the site has long been a pilgrimage destination.

Mon·tes Cla·ros |ˌmōnCHēz ˈklärōs| industrial and agricultural city in E Brazil, in Minas Gerais state. Pop. 271,000.

Mon·te·vid·eo |ˌmäntəvəˈdāo| the capital and chief port of Uruguay, on the Plate River. Pop. 1,360,000. It is the commercial and financial center of Uruguay.

Mon·te·zu·ma, Halls of |ˌmäntəˈzōōmə| in the U.S. Marine anthem, Mexico City, especially CHAPULTEPEC, as a scene of Marine activity.

Mont·gom·ery |mənˈ(t)ˈgəm(ə)rē| the state capital of Alabama, an industrial and commercial city on the Alabama River. Pop. 187,106.

Mont·gom·ery County |mənˈ(t)ˈgəm(ə)rē| county in central Maryland, containing many suburbs on the N side of Washington, D.C. Rockville is its seat. Pop. 757,027.

Mont·gom·ery·shire | mənˈ(t)ˈgəmrēsHir; mənˈ(t)ˈgəmrēsHīər| former county of central Wales. It became a part of Powys in 1974.

Mon·ti·cel·lo |ˌmäntəˈCHelō| historic estate just SE of Charlottesville, in central Virginia, the home of Thomas Jefferson.

Mont·mar·tre |ˌmän'märtrə| district in N Paris, on a hill above the Seine, much frequented by artists in the late 19th and early 20th centuries when it was a separate village. Topped by the basilica of Sacré Coeur, it is the site of the Moulin Rouge and the Place Pigalle.

Mont·par·nasse |ˌmänpär'näs| district of Paris, on the left bank of the River Seine. Frequented in the late 19th century by writers and artists, it is traditionally associated with Parisian cultural life.

Mont·pe·lier |ˌmän(t)'pēlyər| the state capital of Vermont, in the N central part on the Winooski River. Pop. 8,247.

Mont·pel·lier |ˌmänpəl'yā| city in S France, near the Mediterranean coast, capital of Languedoc-Roussillon. Pop. 211,000. A medical school and university, world famous in medieval times, was founded here in 1221.

Mont·re·al |ˌmäntrē'awl| port city on the St. Lawrence River in S Quebec. Pop. 1,017,666. Founded in 1642, it was under French rule until 1763; almost two-thirds of its current population are French-speaking. Montreal, one of the largest French cities in the world, is an industrial, commercial, and cultural center. French name **Montréal**.

Mon·treuil |mōn'troi| town, an E suburb of Paris, France. Pop. 95,000. It has a variety of light industries.

Mon·treux |mən'trō| resort town in SW Switzerland, at the E end of Lake Geneva. Pop. 20,000. Since the 1960s it has hosted annual festivals of jazz and television.

Mont St. Mi·chel |ˌmawn ˌsän mē'sHel| rocky prominence off the coast of Normandy, NW France. An island only at high tide, it is surrounded by sandbanks and linked to the mainland by a causeway. It is crowned by a medieval Benedictine abbey-fortress.

Mont·ser·rat |ˌmäntsə'rät| island in the Caribbean, one of the Leeward Islands.

Montserrat

Pop. 12,000. Capital: Plymouth. It was colonized by Irish settlers in 1632 and is now a British dependency. Since 1995, it has been severely affected by the ongoing eruption of the Soufrière Hills volcano, causing the evacuation of the S part of the island, including Plymouth. □ **Montserratian** *adj. & n.*

Mon·u·ment Valley |'mänyəmənt| region of NE Arizona and S Utah, W of the Four Corners, whose scenery has been the backdrop for many movies.

Mon·za |'mäntsä| industrial city in N Italy, NE of Milan, a textile and motor-racing center. Pop. 123,000.

Moon, Mountains of the |mo͞on| see Ruwenzori, Uganda.

Mo·o·rea |mōē'rāyä| (formerly **Eimeo**) volcanic island in Windward (E) group of the Society Islands, French Polynesia. Tourism is important on this mountainous island.

Moor·head |'mo͝o(ə)r,hed| commercial city in W Minnesota, a transportation hub across the Red River of the North from Fargo, North Dakota. Pop. 32,295.

Moose·head Lake |'mo͞oshed| largest lake in Maine, in the W central section. Small resorts lie along its forested shores.

Moose Jaw |'mo͞os ,jaw| city in S central Saskatchewan, a transportation and processing center W of Regina. Pop. 33,593.

Mo·rad·a·bad |mə'rədäbäd| city and railway junction in N India, in Uttar Pradesh. Pop. 417,000.

Mor·ar, Loch |'mawrər| loch in W Scotland. At 1,017 ft./310 m., it is Scotland's deepest.

Mo·ra·va |'mawrävä| river (240 mi./385 km.) that flows SW through the Czech Republic, forming part of its border with Slovakia, into the Danube River.

Mo·ra·via |mə'rāvēə| region of the Czech Republic, situated S of the Sudeten Mts., between Bohemia in the W and the Carpathians in the E; chief town, Brno. A province of Bohemia from the 11th century, it was made an Austrian province in 1848, becoming a part of Czechoslovakia in 1918. □ **Moravian** *adj. & n.*

Mo·ra·vi·an Gate |mə'rāvēyən| historic pass in the N Czech Republic, between the E end of the Sudeten Mts. and the W end of the Carpathian Mts.

Mor·ay |'mərē| (also **Morayshire**) administrative region and former county of N Scotland, bordered on the N by the Moray Firth; administrative center, Elgin.

Mor·ay Firth |'mərē| deep inlet of the

North Sea on the NE coast of Scotland. Inverness is near its head.

Mor·bi·han |mawrbē'yän| department in Brittany, NW France, on the Atlantic. Pop. 620,000. The capital is Vannes.

Mord·vin·ia |mawrd'vēnēə| (also **Mordovia**) autonomous republic in European Russia, SE of Nizhni Novgorod. Pop. 964,000. Capital: Saransk.

More·cambe Bay |'mōrkəm| inlet of the Irish Sea, on the NW coast of England between Cumbria and Lancashire.

Mo·re·lia |mō'rälyä| city in central Mexico, capital of the state of Michoacán. Pop. 490,000. Founded in 1541, it was known as Valladolid until 1828.

Mo·re·los |mō'rälōs| state of central Mexico, in the W of Mexico City. Pop. 1,195,000. Capital: Cuernavaca.

Mo·re·no Valley |mə'ränō| city in SW California, a suburb just E of Riverside. Pop. 118,779.

Mor·gan·town |'mōrgən,town| commercial city in N West Virginia, home to West Virginia University. Pop. 25,879.

Mo·ri·ah, Mount |mə'rīyä| biblical name for the hill in present-day E Jerusalem on which the Temple of Solomon was built. It may also be the place where Abraham was to sacrifice his son Isaac.

Mo·rio·ka |mōrē'ōkə| industrial and commercial city in NE Japan, on N Honshu. Pop. 235,000.

Mo·roc·co |mə'räkō| kingdom in NW Africa, with coastlines on the Mediterranean Sea and Atlantic. Area: 177,184 sq. mi./458,730 sq. km. Pop. 25,731,000. Languages, Arabic (official), Berber, Spanish, French. Capital: Rabat. Largest city: Casablanca. Conquered by the Arabs in the 7th century, later controlled by the Portuguese, Spanish, and French, Morocco regained independence in 1956. Mining, agriculture, tourism, and fishing are important. □ **Moroccan** *adj. & n.*

Morocco

Mo·ro Gulf |'mō,rō| inlet of the N Celebes Sea, SW of Mindanao in the Philippines.

Mo·rón |'mō,rawn| city in E Argentina, a suburb SW of Buenos Aires. Pop. 642,000.

Mo·ro·ni |mə'rōnē| the capital of Comoros, on the island of Grande Comoré Pop. 22,000.

Mor·ris Jes·up, Cape |'mawrəs 'jesəp| northernmost (83° 38′ N) point of land in the world, at the N tip of Greenland, 439 mi./706 km. from the North Pole.

Mor·ro Castle |'mawrō| name for two forts in Cuba, in the harbors of Havana and Santiago de Cuba. The fort in Santiago was attacked and taken by U.S. troops in 1898, during the Spanish-American War.

Mos·cow[1] |'mäs,kow| city in NW Idaho, home to the University of Idaho. Pop. 18,519.

Mos·cow[2] |'mäs,kow| the capital of Russia, an industrial and cultural hub at the center of the vast plain of European Russia, on the Moskva River. Pop. 9,000,000. First mentioned in medieval chronicles in 1147, it soon became the chief city of the increasingly powerful Muscovite princes. Moscow became the capital when Ivan the Terrible proclaimed himself the first czar of Russia in the 16th century. Peter the Great moved his capital to St. Petersburg in 1712, but after the Bolshevik Revolution of 1917 Moscow was made the capital of the USSR and seat of the new Soviet government, with its center in the Kremlin, the fortress that was the citadel of the medieval city. Russian name **Moskva**. □ **Muscovite** *adj. & n.*

Mo·selle |mō'zel| (also **Moselle**) river of W Europe, which rises in the Vosges Mts. of NE France and flows 346 mi./550 km. NE through Luxembourg and Germany to meet the Rhine at Koblenz.

Mo·shi |'mōsHē| commercial city in N Tanzania, just S of Mount Kilimanjaro, in a coffee-growing region. Pop. 95,000.

Mos·kva |'mäskvə| Russian name for Moscow.

Mos·qui·to Coast |mə'skētō| sparsely populated coastal strip of swamp, lagoon, and tropical forest comprising the Caribbean coast of Nicaragua and NE Honduras, occupied by the Miskito people after whom it is named.

Mos·so·ró |mōsō'raw| city in NE Brazil, in Rio Grande do Norte state, a salt and mining center. Pop. 192,000.

Most |mawst| industrial city and rail junction in the NW Czech Republic, near the German border. Pop. 71,000.

Mos·ta·ga·nem |mawstägä'nem| commercial port city in NW Algeria, on the Mediterranean Sea, E of Oran. Pop. 115,000.

Mo·star |'mōstär| predominantly Muslim city in central Bosnia and Herzegovina. Pop. 110,000. It was nearly destroyed in 1992–93 by Serb and Croat forces trying to eliminate the Muslim presence in the city.

Mo·sto·les |'mōstōles| city in central Spain, SW of Madrid. Pop. 176,000.

Mo·sul |mō'sŏol| city in N Iraq, on the Tigris River, opposite the ruins of Nineveh. Pop. 571,000. It gives its name to muslin, a cotton fabric first produced here.

Moth·er Lode |'məTHər| popular name for the area, on the W of the Sierra Nevada in N central California, where much of the gold sought after 1848 in local rivers is thought to have come.

Motor City (also **Motown**) nickname for Detroit, the center of the US automobile industry.

Mo·town |'mō,town| see DETROIT, Michigan.

Moul·mein |'mŏol,mān| port in SE Burma, capital of the state of Mon . Pop. 220,000.

Moun·dou |'mŏondŏo| commercial city in S Chad. Pop. 281,000.

Mountain State |'mowntn| nickname for WEST VIRGINIA.

Mountain States |'mowntn| region of the U.S. comprising states that contain part of the Rocky Mts. New Mexico, Colorado, Wyoming, Utah, Idaho, and Montana are generally considered Mountain States.

Moun·tain View |'mowntn| city in N central California, near the S end of San Francisco Bay, part of the Silicon Valley complex. Pop. 67,460.

Mount Ararat, Mount Carmel, etc. see ARARAT, MOUNT; CARMEL, MOUNT, etc.

Mount Des·ert Island |'mownt'dəsərt| island in the Atlantic in SE Maine, site of Bar Harbor and other resorts. Most of the island is in Acadia National Park.

Mount Isa |'mownt'īzə| lead- and silver-mining town in NE Australia, in W Queensland. Pop. 24,000.

Mount Ver·non[1] |'mownt 'vərnən| city in SE New York, a suburb on the N side of the Bronx, New York City. Pop. 67,153.

Mount Ver·non[2] |'mownt 'vərnən| property in NE Virginia, about 15 mi./24 km. from Washington D.C., on a site overlooking the Potomac River. Built in 1743, it was the home of George Washington from 1747 until his death in 1799. It remains a popular tourist attraction, and is the site of Washington's grave.

Mourne Mountains |mōrn| range of hills in SE Northern Ireland, in County Down. Slieve Donard (2,796 ft./853 m.) is the high point in the province.

Mo·zam·bique |,mōzæm'bēk| republic on the E coast of southern Africa. Area: 308,760 sq. mi./799,380 sq. km. Pop. 16,142,000. Languages, Portuguese (official), Bantu languages. Capital and largest city, Maputo. Controlled by Portugal for over 400 years before independence in 1975, Mozambique relies chiefly on subsistence agriculture, with some mining. □ **Mozambican** adj. & n.

Mozambique

Mo·zam·bique Channel |,mōzæm'bēk| arm of the Indian Ocean separating the E coast of mainland Africa from the island of Madagascar.

Mpu·ma·lan·ga |,əmpŏomə'läNGä| province of NE South Africa, formerly East Transvaal. Capital: Nelspruit.

Mu·dan·jiang |'mŏo'dän'yäNG| city in Heilongjiang province, NE China, on the Mudan River, SE of Harbin. Pop. 572,000.

Mu·fu·li·ra |,mŏofŏolē'rä| industrial and commercial city in N central Zambia, on the border of Congo (formerly Zaire), in a copper-mining area. Pop. 153,000.

Mühl·haus·en |'myŏolhowzən| German name for MULHOUSE, France.

Mühl·haus·en in Thü·ring·en |'myŏolhowzən in 'tyŏoriNGən| manufacturing city in Thuringia, in central Germany, on the Unstrut River. Pop. 44,000.

Mu·ka·che·ve |,mŏokə'cHŏvə| (also **Mukachevo;** Hungarian name **Munkács**) historic industrial town in the W Ukraine. Pop. 88,000. It has changed hands repeatedly since the 9th century.

Mu·kal·la |mŏo'kælə| port on the S coast of Yemen, in the Gulf of Aden. Pop. 154,000.

Muk·den |'mo͝okdən| former name for SHENYANG, China.

Mul·ha·cén |mo͞olä'THän| mountain in S Spain, SE of Granada, in the Sierra Nevada range. Rising to 11,424 ft./3,482 m., it is the highest mountain in the country.

Mül·heim |'myo͞olhīm| industrial city in western Germany, in North Rhine-Westphalia, SE of Essen. Pop. 117,000. Full name **Mülheim an der Ruhr**.

Mul·house |mə'lo͞oz| industrial city in NE France, in Alsace. Pop. 110,000. It was a free imperial city until it joined the French Republic in 1798. In 1871, after the Franco-Prussian War, the city became part of the German Empire until it was reunited with France in 1918. German name **Mühlhausen**.

Mull |məl| large island of the Inner Hebrides; chief town, Tobermory. It is separated from the coast of Scotland near Oban by the Sound of Mull.

Mul·lin·gar |ˌmələn'gär| the county seat of Westmeath, in the Republic of Ireland. Pop. 14,000.

Mul·tan |məl'tän| commercial city in Punjab province, E central Pakistan. Pop. 980,000.

Mün·chen |mo͞onkHən| German name for MUNICH.

Mun·cie |'mənsē| industrial city in E central Indiana, noted as home to Ball Company, maker of glass containers, and as the 'Middletown' of sociological literature. Pop. 71,035.

Mun·ger |'mənger| (also **Monghyr**) city in E India, in Bihar state. Pop. 150,000. It has one of the largest cigarette factories in India.

Mu·nich |'myo͞onək| city in SE Germany, capital of Bavaria. Pop. 1,229,000. Munich is noted for the architecture of the medieval city center and as an artistic and cultural center. German name **München**.

Mun·kács |'myo͞oNGkäcH| Hungarian name for MUKACHEVE.

Mun·ster[1] |'mənstər| village in NE France, SW of Strasbourg, in the Haut-Rhin. The village gave its name to the well-known cheese.

Mun·ster[2] |'mənstər| province of the Republic of Ireland, in the SW of the country, comprising Counties Cork, Clare, Kerry, Tipperary, Limerick, and Waterford.

Mün·ster |'myo͞onstər| industrial port city in NW Germany. Pop. 250,000. It was formerly the capital of Westphalia; the Treaty of Westphalia, ending the Thirty Years War, was signed here in 1648.

Muq·di·sho alternate form of MOGADISHU, Somalia.

Mur River |myo͝or| river that rises in the E part of the Hohe Tauern and flows 279 mi./170 km. through Austria and Slovenia, draining into the Drava River.

Mu·ra·no |mo͝or'änō| N suburb of Venice, Italy, on five small islands in the Lagoon of Venice. It is famous for its colorful glass.

Mur·chi·son Falls |mərcHəsən| former name for KABALEGA FALLS, Uganda.

Mur·chi·son Rapids |'mərcHəsən| former name for KAPACHIRA FALLS, Malawi.

Mur·cia |'mərSHə| **1** autonomous region in SE Spain. In the Middle Ages, along with Albacete, it formed an ancient Moorish kingdom. **2** its capital, an industrial city on the Segura River. Pop. 329,000.

Mu·res River |'mo͝oresH| (in Hungarian **Maros**) river (470 mi./755 km.) that rises in the Carpathians in Romania and flows W into Hungary, meeting the Tisza at Szeged.

Mur·frees·boro |mərfrēz'bərō| commercial city in central Tennessee, SE of Nashville. A Civil War battle fought near here (January 1863) is also called the battle of Stones River.

Mur·gab river |mo͝or'gäb| (also **Morghab**; **Murghab**) river in NW Afghanistan and SE Turkmenistan, flowing 600 mi./965 km. from the W Hindu Kush to the Kara-Kum desert, where it disappears into the sand.

Mur·mansk |mo͝or'mænsk| port in NW Russia, on the N coast of the Kola Peninsula, in the Barents Sea. Pop. 472,000. It is the largest city N of the Arctic Circle and its port is ice-free throughout the year.

Mu·rom |'mo͝orəm| port and transportation center in W Russia. Pop. 127,000. First mentioned in in 862, it is one of the oldest Russian cities.

Mu·ro·ran |mo͝oo'rōrän| industrial port city in N Japan, on SW Hokkaido. Pop. 118,000.

Mur·ray River |mərē| the principal river of Australia, which rises in the Great Dividing Range in New South Wales and flows 1,610 mi./2,590 km. generally NW, forming part of the border between the states of Victoria and New South Wales, before turning S in South Australia to empty into the Indian Ocean SE of Adelaide.

Mur·rum·bidg·ee |ˌmərəm'bijē| river of SE Australia, in New South Wales. Rising in the Great Dividing Range, it flows 1,099 mi./1,759 km. W to join the Murray, of which it is a major tributary.

Mu·ru·roa |ˌmo͞oro͝o'rōə| remote South Pacific atoll in the Tuamotu archipelago, in French Polynesia, used as a nuclear testing site from 1966.

Mu·sa·la, Mount |myōōsä'lə| (also **Mousalla**) the highest peak in Bulgaria, in the Rila Mountains, rising to 9,596 ft./ 2,925 m.

Mu·sa·shi·no |mōō'sä,shēnō| city in E central Japan, on E central Honshu, a suburb of Tokyo. Pop. 139,000.

Mus·cat |'məskät| (also **Masqat**) the capital of Oman, a port on the SE coast of the Arabian Peninsula. Pop. 41,000.

Mus·cat and Oman |'məsket| former name (until 1970) for OMAN.

Mus·cle Shoals |'məsəl| industrial city in NW Alabama, on the Tennessee River, near the Wilson Dam and the former site of the Mussel (or Muscle) Shoals shallows. Pop. 9,611.

Mus·co·vy |məs'kōvē| **1** medieval principality in W central Russia, centered on Moscow, which formed the nucleus of present-day Russia. Founded in the late 13th century by Daniel, son of Alexander Nevsky, Muscovy gradually expanded despite Tartar depredations, finally overcoming the Tartars in 1380. Princes of Muscovy became the rulers of Russia; in 1472 Ivan III completed the unification, overcoming rivalry from the principalities of Novgorod, Tver, and Vladimir and adopted the title "Ruler of all Russia." In 1547 Ivan IV (Ivan the Terrible) became the first czar of the new empire, and made Moscow its capital. **2** archaic name for Russia. □ **Muscovite** adj. & n.

Mu·shin |'mōō'sHin| industrial city in SW Nigeria, a suburb NW of Lagos. Pop. 294,000.

Mus·ke·gon |məs'kēgən| industrial port in W Michigan, on Lake Michigan. Pop. 40,283.

Mus·ko·gee |mə'skōgē| commercial city in E central Oklahoma, on the Arkansas River. Pop. 37,708.

Mus·tique |mə'stēk| small resort island in the N Grenadines, in the Caribbean to the S of St. Vincent.

Mu·ta·re |mōō'tärä| industrial town in the E highlands of Zimbabwe. Pop. 70,000. Former name (until 1982) **Umtali**.

Mu·zaf·far·a·bad |mōō'zəfərə'bäd| town in NE Pakistan, the administrative center of Azad Kashmir.

Mu·zaf·far·na·gar |mōō'zəfərnəgər| commercial town in N India, in Uttar Pradesh state, N of Delhi. Pop. 248,000.

Mu·zaf·far·pur |mōō'zəfərpōōr| town in

NE India, in Bihar state, N of Patna. Pop. 240,000.

Muz·tag |muz'tag; mōōz'tag| **1** (also **Ulugh Muztagh**) peak in W China on the Tibet-Xinjiang border near the Karamiran Pass; the highest peak in the Kunlun Shan Mts.: 25,338 ft./7,723 m. **2** (also **Muztagh**) peak in W China, S Xinjiang region near the Kashmir border: 23,885 ft./7,282 m. high.

Muz·ta·ga·ta |mōōz,tägä'tä| (also **Muztagh Ata**) peak in the Muztagata range, in Xinjiang, W China, near the Tajikistan border: 24,757 ft./7,546 m. high.

Mwan·za |'mwänzä| commercial city in N Tanzania, a port on Lake Victoria, in an agricultural area. Pop. 260,000.

Mwe·ru, Lake |'mwärōō| (also **Moero**) lake on the border of Zambia and Congo (formerly Zaire), W of Lake Tanganyika. The Luapula River flows through this fishing resource.

Myan·mar, Union of official name of BURMA.

My·ce·nae |mī'sēnē| ancient city in Greece, situated near the coast in the NE Peloponnese, the center of the late Bronze Age Mycenaean civilization. The capital of King Agamemnon, it was at its most prosperous c. 1400–1200 B.C.; systematic excavation of the site began in 1840. □ **Mycenaean** adj. & n.

Myit·kyi·na |myitCHē'nä| town in N Burma, capital of Kachin state, near the Chinese border. Pop. 56,000.

My·ko·la·yiv |,mikō'läyēv| industrial city in S Ukraine, on the Southern Bug river near the N tip of the Black Sea. Pop. 508,000. Russian name **Nikolaev**.

Myk·o·nos |'mikə,näs| Greek island in the Aegean, one of the Cyclades. Greek name **Míkonos**.

My Lai |'mē'lī| village in Son My district, central Vietnam, S of Quang Ngai, site of a 1968 massacre of Vietnamese civilians by U.S. troops during the Vietnam War.

My·men·singh |'mīmən'siNG| port on the Brahmaputra River in central Bangladesh. Pop. 186,000.

Myr·tle Beach |'mərtəl| resort city in NE South Carolina, the hub of the part of the Atlantic coast called the Grand Strand. Pop. 24,848.

My·sia |'mishēə| ancient region of NW Asia Minor (present-day NW Turkey), on the Mediterranean coast S of the Sea of Marmara. □ **Mysian** adj. & n.

My·sore |mī'sōr| **1** city in the Indian state of Karnataka. Pop. 480,000. It was the capital of the princely state of Mysore and is noted for the production of silk, incense, and sandalwood oil. **2** former name (until 1973) for KARNATAKA.

Myt·i·le·ne |mitəl'ēnē| the chief town of the Greek island of Lesbos. Pop. 24,000. Greek name **Mitilíni**.

My·tish·chi |mə'tiSHCHē| manufacturing city in W Russia, NE of Moscow. Pop. 154,000.

Nn

Naas |näs| county seat of Kildare in the central Republic of Ireland, in Leinster. Pop. 11,000.

Na·be·rezh·nye Chel·ny |nəbir'ezнniyə cHil'nē| (formerly **Brezhnev**; earlier, **Chelny**) city in W Russia, on the Kama River. Pop. 514,000.

Na·beul |nə'bool| (also **Nabul**) resort town in NE Tunisia, on the Cape Bon peninsula. Pop. 39,000.

Nab·lus |'näbləs| commercial city, largely Palestinian, in the Israeli-occupied West Bank, N of Jerusalem. Pop. 120,000. It is near the site of ancient Shechem.

Na·ca·la |nä'kälə| deepwater port on the E coast of Mozambique. Pop. 104,000. It is linked by rail with landlocked Malawi.

Nac·og·do·ches |näkə'dōcHes| historic city in E Texas, on the Angelina River. Pop. 30,872.

Na·di·ad |nədē'äd| commercial and industrial town in W India, in Gujarat state. Pop. 170,000.

Na·fud |næ'food| (also **Nefud**; **An Nafud**) desert region in N Saudi Arabia, in a large oval depression surrounded by curiously-shaped sandstone outcrops.

Na·ga |'nägä| (formerly **Nueva Caceres**) commercial city in the Philippines, on SE Luzon. Pop. 115,000. It was one of the earliest Spanish settlements.

Na·ga·land |'nägə,lænd| state in the far NE of India, on the border with Burma. Pop. 1,216,000. Capital: Kohima. It was created in 1962 from parts of Assam. The Naga Hills straddle the India-Burma border.

Na·ga·no |nä'gänō| commercial and industrial city in central Japan, on central Honshu. Pop. 347,000. It is the site of a major Buddhist shrine.

Na·ga·o·ka |nägä'ōkä| industrial city in N central Japan, on central Honshu. Pop. 186,000.

Na·ga·sa·ki |,nägə'säkē| city and port in SW Japan, on the W coast of Kyushu island. Pop. 445,000. A center of shipbuilding, it is the Japanese port nearest to China, and in 1639–1854 was the only Japanese port open (on the island of Dejima) to foreign trade. It was the target of the second atomic bomb dropped by the United States, on August 9, 1945.

Na·ger·coil |'nägərkoil| industrial city in S India, in Tamil Nadu state. Pop. 189,000. The southernmost city in India, it is an important Christian center in a mainly Hindu area.

Nagorno-Karabakh |nə',gawrnə,kerə-'bäk| region of Azerbaijan in the S foothills of the Caucasus. Pop. 192,000. Capital: Xankändi. Formerly a Persian khanate, it was absorbed into the Russian Empire in the 19th century, later becoming an autonomous region of the Soviet Union, within Azerbaijan. Fighting between Azerbaijan and Armenia began in 1985, with the majority Armenian population desiring to be separated from Muslim Azerbaijan and united with Armenia; the region declared unilateral independence in 1991, and most Azeris have now left the area.

Na·go·ya |nə'goiə| city in central Japan, a center of heavy industry on the S coast of the island of Honshu, capital of Chubu region. Pop. 2,155,000.

Nag·pur |,näg'poor| city in central India, in the state of Maharashtra. Pop. 1,622,000. The former center of the Gond dynasty, it is now an administrative and commercial center.

Nags Head |'nægs hed| resort town in E North Carolina, in the Outer Banks. Pop. 1,838.

Na·ha |'nähä| industrial port in S Japan, capital of Okinawa island. Pop. 305,000.

Na·ha·vand |nähə'vænd| (also **Neha-vand**) commercial town in W Iran, S of Hamadan. Pop. 59,000. The Arabs defeated the Persians here *c.*641, marking the de facto end of the Persian Empire.

Na·huel Hua·pí |nä'welwä'pē| lake in W central Argentina, in the Andes near the Chilean border. The ski resort of San Carlos de Bariloche lies on its S, and the lake and surrounding national park are also popular.

Nairn·shire |'nærnsHēr; 'nærnsHir| former county of NE Scotland, on the Moray Firth. It was part of the Highland region in 1975–96

Nai·ro·bi |nī'rōbē| the capital of Kenya. Pop. 1,346,000. It is situated on the central Kenyan plateau at an altitude of 5,500 ft./1,680 m., and is an administrative, commercial, light industrial, and tourist center.

Na·jaf |'näjäf| (also **An Najaf**) city in S Iraq, on the Euphrates. Pop. 243,000. It contains the shrine of Ali, the prophet Muhammad's son-in-law, and is a holy city for the Shiite Muslims.

Na·khi·che·van |ˌnäkəCHə'vän| see NAX-ÇIVAN, Azerbaijan.

Na·khod·ka |nə'kawtkə| port and naval base in extreme E Russia, on the Sea of Japan E of Vladivostok. Pop. 163,000. It is the E terminus of the Trans-Siberian Railroad.

Na·khon Pa·thom |nəkawn pä'təm| city in SW Thailand, NW of Bangkok. Pop. 45,000. The most sacred Buddhist shrine in Thailand is here.

Na·khon Rat·cha·si·ma |räkawn räCHə-sēmä| (also **Khorat**; **Korat**) commercial city in NE Thailand, on the Takhong River. Pop. 204,000.

Na·ku·ru |nə'kō͞orō͞o| industrial city in W Kenya. Pop. 163,000. Nearby is Lake Nakuru, famous for its spectacular flocks of flamingos.

Nal·chik |'nälCHik| city in the Caucasus, SW Russia, capital of the republic of Kabardino-Balkaria. Pop. 237,000.

Na·man·gan |ˌnämən'gän| city in E Uzbekistan, an agricultural processing center near the border with Kyrgyzstan. Pop. 312,000.

Na·ma·qua·land |nə'mäkwəˌlænd| region in SW Africa, the homeland of the Nama people. **Little Namaqualand** lies immediately to the S of the Orange River and is in the South African province of Northern Cape, while **Great Namaqualand** lies to the N of the river, in Namibia.

Na·men |'nämən| Flemish name for NAMUR, Belgium.

Na·mib Desert |'nämib| desert of SW Africa. It extends for 1,200 mi./1,900 km. along the Atlantic coast, from the Curoca River in SW Angola through Namibia to the border between Namibia and South Africa.

Na·mib·ia |nə'mibēə| republic in SW Africa, on the Atlantic. Area: 318,382 sq. mi./824,292 sq. km. Pop. 1,834,000. Languages, English, Bantu and Khoisan languages, Afrikaans. Capital and largest city:

Namibia

Windhoek. Formerly controlled by Germany, then South Africa, and known as South West Africa, Namibia gained independence in 1990. Largely desert, it has an economy based on livestock raising, fishing, and mining. □ **Namibian** adj. & n.

Nam·po |'näm'pō| (also **Chinnampo**) industrial city in W North Korea, SW of Pyongyang, for which it is the port. Pop. 691,000.

Nam·pu·la |näm'pō͞olə| commercial city in NE Mozambique, capital of Nampula province. Pop. 203,000.

Na·mur |nə'mō͞or| **1** province in central Belgium. It was the scene of the last German offensive in the Ardennes in 1945. Flemish name **Namen**. **2** the capital of this province, at the junction of the Meuse and Sambre rivers. Pop. 103,000.

Na·nai·mo |nə'nī,mō| lumbering port on the E coast of Vancouver Island in British Columbia. Pop. 60,129.

Nan·chang |nän'CHäNG| industrial city in SE China, capital of Jiangxi province. Pop. 1,330,000.

Nan·cy |'nænsē| industrial and cultural city in NE France, chief town of Lorraine. Pop. 102,000.

Nan·ded |'nändəd| (also **Nander**) commercial city in central India, in Maharashtra state. Pop. 309,000. It is an important Sikh pilgrimage site.

Nan·ga Par·bat |'näNGgə 'pərbət| mountain in N Pakistan, highest peak in the W Himalayas. It rises to 26,660 ft./8,126 m.

Nan·jing |næn'jiNG| (formerly **Nanking**) industrial city and capital of Jiangsu province, E China, on the Yangtze River. Pop. 3,682,000. It was the capital of China from 1368 to 1421 and from 1912 to 1937. The bloody Japanese capture of the city (1937) during the Second Sino-Japanese War is known as the "rape of Nanking."

Nan·ning |'nän'dziNG| industrial city, the capital of Guangxi Zhuang autonomous region in S China. Pop. 1,070,000.

Nan·terre |nän'ter| industrial city, capital of the Hauts-de-Seine department, and a W suburb of Paris, in N central France. Pop. 96,000.

Nantes |nänt| historic port city in W France, on the Loire, chief town of Pays de la Loire region. Pop. 252,000.

Nan·tong |'nän'tō͞oNG| (formerly **Nantung**) port city in Jiangsu province, E central China, near the mouth of the Yangtze River. Pop. 343,000. It is a special economic zone and textile center.

Nan·tuck·et |næn'təkət| island off the

coast of Massachusetts, S of Cape Cod and E of Martha's Vineyard. It was an important whaling center in the 18th and 19th centuries. It is now a summer resort.

Nan•yang |'nän'yäNG| city in Henan province, E central China, on the Bai River, SW of Zhengzhou. Pop. 304,000.

Na•pa |'næpə| commercial city in N central California, hub of the wine-making Napa Valley. Pop. 61,842.

Na•per•ville |'näpər,vil| city in NE Illinois, an outer suburb W of Chicago, with many high-technology businesses. Pop. 85,351.

Na•pier |'näpēər| seaport on Hawke Bay, North Island, New Zealand. Pop. 52,000.

Na•ples[1] |'näpəlz| resort city in SW Florida, on the Gulf of Mexico. Pop. 19,505.

Na•ples[2] |'näpəlz| port city on the W coast of Italy, capital of Campania region. Pop. 1,206,000. It was formerly the capital of the kingdom of Naples and Sicily (1816–60). Italian name **Napoli**. □ **Neapolitan** adj. & n.

Na•po•li |'näpōlē| Italian name for NAPLES[2].

Na•ra |'närä| city in central Japan, on the island of Honshu. Pop. 349,000. It was the first capital of Japan (710–784) and an important center of Japanese Buddhism.

Na•ra•shi•no |närä'sHēnō| city in E central Japan, on E central Honshu, an industrial suburb E of Tokyo. Pop. 151,000.

Na•ra•yan•ganj |nə'räyən,gənj| river port in Bangladesh, on the Ganges delta SE of Dhaka. Pop. 406,000.

Nar•bonne |när'bawn| city in S France, in Languedoc-Roussillon, just inland from the Mediterranean. Pop. 47,000. It was founded by the Romans in 118 B.C. as the capital of Gallia Narbonensis, and was a prosperous medieval port until its harbor silted up in the 14th century.

Na•ri•ta |nä'rētə| city in E central Japan, on E central Honshu. Pop. 87,000. The Tokyo International Airport is here.

Nar•ma•da |nər'mədə| river that rises in Madhya Pradesh, central India, and flows generally W for 778 mi./1,245 km. to the Gulf of Cambay. It is regarded by Hindus as sacred.

Nar•ra•gan•sett Bay |,nerə'gænsit| inlet of the Atlantic in S and central Rhode Island. Providence, Newport, and many resorts lie on it.

Nar•va |'närvə| industrial city in NE Estonia, on the Narva River. Pop. 82,000. It is a major textile-manufacturing center.

Nar•vik |'när,vik| ice-free port on the NW coast of Norway, N of the Arctic Circle.

Pop. 19,000. It is an iron-ore exporting center.

Nase•by |'näzbē| village in central England, in Northamptonshire, scene of the last major battle (1645) of the English Civil War, in which Parliamentary armies won a conclusive victory.

Nash•ua |'næsHəwə| industrial city on the Merrimack River in S New Hampshire. Pop. 79,662.

Nash•ville |'næsH,vil| the state capital of Tennessee. Pop. 488,374. It is a financial and commercial center, also known for its music industry, and is the site of Opryland U.S.A. (an entertainment complex) and the Country Music Hall of Fame.

Na•sik |'näsik| (also **Nashik**) city in W India, in Maharashtra, on the Godavari River NE of Bombay. Pop. 647,000.

Nas•sau[1] |'nä,saw| port on the island of New Providence, capital of the Bahamas and a resort and financial center. Pop. 172,000.

Nas•sau[2] |'nä,saw| former duchy of western Germany, centered on the small town of Nassau, from which a branch of the House of Orange arose. It corresponds to parts of the present-day states of Hesse and Rhineland-Palatinate.

Nas•sau County |'nä,saw| county in central Long Island, New York, immediately E of Queens and home to many New York suburbs. Pop. 1,287,348.

Nas•ser, Lake |'näsər| lake in SE Egypt created in the 1960s by the building of two dams on the Nile at Aswan.

Na•tal[1] |nə'täl| port on the Atlantic coast of NE Brazil, capital of the state of Rio Grande do Norte. Pop. 606,000.

Na•tal[2] |nə'täl| former province of South Africa, on the E coast. Having been a Boer republic and then a British colony, it acquired internal self-government in 1893 and became a province of the Union of South Africa in 1910. The province was renamed KwaZulu/Natal in 1994.

Natch•ez |'næCHiz| historic port city on the Mississippi River in SW Mississippi. Pop. 19,460. The **Natchez Trace**, leading from here to Nashville, Tennessee, was a 19th-century route for riverboatmen returning N from trips to New Orleans.

Na•tion•al City |'næsHənəl| city in SW California, S of San Diego, site of numerous naval facilities. Pop. 54,249.

Na•tion•al•ist Chi•na term once used for the Chinese government established on Taiwan after 1949, for many years the only Chinese government recognized by the US.

Na·tion·al Road |'næsHənəl| historic highway that in the early 19th century led from Maryland through the Appalachian Mts., to St. Louis, Missouri. It was once the major route for W expansion.

NATO |'nātō| acronym for the NORTH ATLANTIC TREATY ORGANIZATION.

Nat·ron, Lake |'nātrən| lake in N Tanzania, on the border with Kenya, containing large deposits of salt and soda.

Na·u·cal·pan de Jua·rez |now'kälpän dä 'hwäres| industrial city in central Mexico, a suburb on the NW side of Mexico City. Pop. 773,000.

Nau·cra·tis |'nawkrətis| ancient Greek commercial city in N Egypt, SE of present-day Damanhur.

Nau·ga·tuck |'nawgə,tək| industrial borough in SW Connecticut, on the Naugatuck River next to Waterbury. Pop. 30,625.

Nau·plia |'nawplēə| (also called **Na**) port on the Gulf of Argolis in S Greece. Pop. 11,000. It was the first capital of independent Greece. The ruins of the ancient city of Tiryns are nearby.

Na·u·ru |nä'ōōrōō| island republic in the SW Pacific, near the equator. Area: 8 sq. mi./21 sq. km. Pop. 10,000. Languages, Nauruan (an Austronesian language) and English; no official capital. Independent since 1968, it has the world's richest deposits of phosphates. □ **Nauruan** *adj. & n.*

Nauru

Na·vad·wip |nəvəd'vēp; nəvəd'wēp| (also **Nabadwip**; formerly **Nadia**) commercial and industrial city in E India, in West Bengal state. Pop. 155,000. It is a noted Hindu educational center.

Nav·an |'nævən| the county seat of Meath, in the Republic of Ireland. Pop. 3,000.

Na·va·ri·no |,nævə'rēnō| (Greek name **Pylos**) seaport in SW Peloponnese, Greece. Nearby are the ruins of an ancient Mycenaean city. In 1827 Greeks and their allies defeated Turkish and Egyptian naval forces here.

Na·varre |nə'vär| autonomous region of N Spain, on the border with France. Capital: Pamplona. It represents the S part of the former kingdom of Navarre, which was conquered by Ferdinand in 1512 and attached to Spain, while the N part passed to France in 1589 through inheritance by Henry IV. Spanish name **Navarra**.

Na·vas·sa Island |nä'väsə| island in the Caribbean Sea W of Haiti, held by the U.S. and used as a Coast Guard base.

Na·vo·joa |nä'vōhōä| commercial city in NW Mexico, in Sonora state, an agricultural processing center. Pop. 83,000.

Na·vo·tas |nä'vōtä| (also **Nabotas**) port town in the Philippines, on S Luzon. Pop. 187,000. It is the largest fishing port in the Philippines.

Nav·pak·tos |'näfpäktōs| (in Italian **Lepanto**) port in central Greece, on the Gulf of Corinth. In the Battle of Lepanto, in 1571, Christian naval forces under Don John of Austria defeated those of the Ottoman Empire.

Na·wab·ganj |nə'wäbgənj| commercial city in W Bangladesh, NW of Rajshahi. Pop. 121,000.

Nax·çi·van |nəkēCHi'vän| **1** predominantly Muslim Azerbaijani autonomous republic, situated on the borders of Turkey and N Iran and separated from the rest of Azerbaijan by a narrow strip of Armenia. Pop. 300,000. Russian name **Nakhichevan**. **2** the capital city of this republic. Pop. 51,000.

Nax·os |'näksōs| Greek island in the S Aegean, the largest (165 sq. mi./428 sq. km.) of the Cyclades. Pop. 14,000. It is associated with the legend of Theseus and Ariadne.

Na·ya·rit |,nīyä'rēt| state of W Mexico, the Pacific coast. Area: 10,420 sq. mi./26,979 sq. km. Pop. 816,000. Capital: Tepic.

Naz·a·reth |'næzərəTH| historic town in lower Galilee, in present-day N Israel. Pop. 39,000. Mentioned in the Gospels as the home of Mary and Joseph, it is closely associated with the childhood of Jesus and is a center of Christian pilgrimage.

Naz·ca |'näskä| (also **Nasca**) city and province in SW Peru, noted for the artifacts of a pre-Incan civilization, especially the huge "Nazca lines" on the desert floor. Pop. 23,000.

N'Dja·me·na |ənjä'mänə| the capital of Chad. Pop. 531,000. Former name (1900–1973) Fort Lamy. It is a communications, agricultural processing, and university center.

Ndo•la |ən'dōlə| commercial city in the Copperbelt region of central Zambia. Pop. 376,000.

Neagh, Lough |'läk 'nā| shallow lake in Northern Ireland, the largest (147 sq. mi./382 sq. km.) freshwater lake in the British Isles.

Ne•an•der•thal |nē'ændər,tawl| valley E of Düsseldorf, in western Germany, where remains of the first fossil to be identified as belonging to *Homo sapiens*, or modern man, were found in 1856; the skeleton was called Neanderthal man.

Near East |,nēr 'ēst| (**the Near East**) a term originally applied to the Balkan states of SE Europe, but now generally applied to the countries of SW Asia between the Mediterranean and India (including the Middle East), especially in historical contexts. □ **Near Eastern** *adj.*

Near Islands |nēr| island group at the W end of the Aleutian Islands, in SW Alaska. Attu is one of the Near Islands.

Neath |nēTH| industrial town in S Wales on the Neath River. Pop. 49,000. Welsh name **Castell-Nedd**.

Neb•li•na, Pico da see PICO DA NEBLINA, Brazil.

Ne•bo, Mount |'nēbō| biblical mountain, identified with a peak in N central Jordan, NE of the Dead Sea, from which Moses viewed the Promised Land. Pisgah is an alternate name, or the name of one part of Mount Nebo.

Ne•bras•ka |nə'bræskə| see box. □ **Nebraskan** *adj. & n.*

Neck•ar |'nekär| river of western Germany, which rises in the Black Forest and flows 228 mi./367 km. N and W through Stuttgart to meet the Rhine at Mannheim.

Ne•der•land |'nādər,lænd| Dutch name for the NETHERLANDS.

Nee•nah |'nēnə| city in E Wisconsin, on the Fox River, a flour and paper-milling center. Pop. 23,219.

Ne•gri Sem•bi•lan |'nāgərē səm'bēlən| state of Malaysia, on the SW coast of the Malay Peninsula. Pop. 724,000. Capital: Seremban.

Neg•ev |'ne,gev| (also **the Negev**) an arid region forming most of S Israel, between Beersheba and the Gulf of Aqaba, on the Egyptian border. Large areas are irrigated for agriculture.

Ne•gom•bo |nā'gawm,bō| port and resort on the W coast of Sri Lanka, N of Colombo. Pop. 61,000.

Nebraska
Capital: Lincoln
Largest city: Omaha
Other cities: Fremont, Grand Island, Hastings, North Platte, Scottsbluff
Population: 1,578,385 (1990); 1,662,719 (1998); 1,761,000 (2005 proj.)
Population rank (1990): 36
Rank in land area: 16
Abbreviation: NE; Neb. or Nebr.
Nickname: Cornhusker State; Tree Planters' State
Motto: 'Equality Before the Law'
Bird: Western meadowlark
Flower: goldenrod
Tree: cottonwood
Song: "Beautiful Nebraska"
Noted physical features: Badlands; Sand Hills, Drift Hills, Loess Hills; Chimney Rock; Ogalla Aquifer
Tourist attractions: Boys' Town; Scott's Bluff and Agate Fossil Beds national monuments
Admission date: March 1, 1867
Order of admission: 37
Name origin: From the Oto Indian word *nebrathka*, meaning 'flat water,' applied to both the Platte and Nebraska rivers.

Neg•ril |'negril| resort township near the W end of Jamaica, noted for its beaches.

Ne•gro, Rio |'rēō 'nāgrō| see RIO NEGRO.

Ne•gros |'nāgrōs| island in the Visayan group, the fourth-largest of the Philippines. Pop. 3,182,000; chief city, Bacolod.

Nei•jiang |'nā'jyæNG| river port and rail center in Sichuan province, central China, on the Tuo River, W of Chongqing. Pop. 310,000.

Neis•se[1] |'nīsə| river in central Europe, which rises in the N of the Czech Republic and flows over 140 mi./225 km. generally N, forming the S part of the border between Germany and Poland (the Oder–Neisse Line) and joining the Oder River NE of Cottbus. German name **Lausitzer Neisse**; Polish name **Nysa Luzycka**.

Neis•se[2] |'nīsə| river of S Poland, which rises near the border with the Czech Republic and flows 120 mi./195 km. generally NE, through the town of Nysa, joining the Oder River SE of Wrocław. German name **Glatzer Neisse**. Polish name **Nysa Kłodzka**.

Nei•va |'nāvä| commercial city in S central

Colombia, on the Magdalena River, the capital of Huila department. Pop. 233,000.

Nejd |nejd| arid plateau region in central Saudi Arabia, N of the Rub' al Khali desert, at an altitude of about 5,000 ft./1,500 m. It is home to many Bedouins, who gather in its oases.

Nel·lore |ne'lawr| port city in SE India, in Andhra Pradesh, on the Penner River. Pop. 316,000. Situated close to the mouth of the river, it is one of the chief ports of the Coromandel Coast.

Nel·son |'nelsən| port in New Zealand, on the N coast of South Island. Pop. 47,000.

Nel·son River |'nelsən| river that flows 400 mi./640 km. across E Manitoba, to Hudson Bay. Once a fur trade route, it is now an important source of hydroelectric power.

Nels·pru·it |nels'proit| town in E South Africa, the capital of the province of Mpumalanga, situated on the Crocodile River to the W of Kruger National Park. Pop. 62,000.

Ne·man |'nemən| river of E Europe, which rises S of Minsk in Belarus and flows 597 mi./955 km. W and N to the Baltic Sea. Its lower course, which forms the boundary between Lithuania and the Russian enclave of Kaliningrad, is called the Memel. Lithuanian name **Nemunas**, Belorussian name **Nyoman**.

Ne·mea |'nēmēə| city of ancient Greece, in N Argolis. A great Temple of Zeus was located here. It was home to the Nemean Games, which drew participants from all over Greece and which took place in the second and fourth years of each Olympiad. □ **Nemean** adj.

Ne·mi, Lake |'nāmē| lake in the Alban Hills, central Italy, SE of Rome. In ancient times there were a temple and a grove to Diana nearby.

Ne·mours |nə'moŏr| town, SE suburb of Paris, in N central France. Pop. 12,000.

Nen River |'nən| (Chinese name **Nen Jiang**; formerly **Nonni River**) river, NE China, the chief tributary of the Sungari. It flows 740 mi./1,190 km. S from the Da Hinggan Ling mountains to the Sungari W of Harbin.

Ne·nets |ne'nets| autonomous region in N Russia, comprising the tundra coast N of the Komi Republic. Pop. 55,000. Its people, the Nenets, are also known as Samoyeds.

Ne·o·sho River |nē'ōsHŌ| (also, **Grand River**) river that flows 460 mi./740 km. from central Kansas through NE Oklahoma, into the Arkansas River.

Ne·pal |ˌnä'päl| mountainous landlocked kingdom in S Asia, in the Himalayas (and including Mount Everest). Area: 56,849 sq. mi./147,181 sq. km. Pop. 19,406,000. Language, Nepali. Capital and largest city: Kathmandu. Conquered by the Gurkhas in the 18th century, Nepal has since remained independent. It exports clothing, carpets, leather, and grain. □ **Nepalese** adj. & n.

Nepal

Ne·pe·an |ni'pēən| city in SE Ontario, a research and industrial center on the SW side of Ottawa. Pop. 107,627.

Ne·se·bur |ne'sebər| historic town in E Bulgaria, on the Black Sea. Pop. 9,000. The ancient Mesembria, it now draws tourists.

Loch Ness |'lawk 'nes| deep lake in NW Scotland, in the Great Glen. Forming part of the Caledonian Canal, it is 24 miles (38 km.) long, with a maximum depth of 755 ft. (230 m.). It is well known as home to an aquatic monster whose existence has been disputed for centuries.

Neth·er·lands |'neTHərlən(d)z| **1** kingdom in W Europe, on the North Sea. Area: 14,412 sq. mi./37,313 sq. km. Pop. 15,010,000. Language, Dutch. Capital: Amsterdam; seat of government, The Hague. Dutch name **Nederland**. Also called **Holland**. Independent since 1648, the Netherlands has been a leading colonial power. Low and densely populated, it has a maritime and industrial economy. **2**

Netherlands

hist. the Low Countries. □ **Netherlander** *n.* **Netherlandish** *adj.*

Neth·er·lands An·til·les |'neTHərlən(d)z æn'tilēz| two widely separated groups of islands in the Caribbean, in the Lesser Antilles. Capital: Willemstad, on Curaçao. Pop. 189,000. The southernmost group, just off the N coast of Venezuela, comprises Bonaire and Curaçao, and until 1986 also included Aruba. The N group comprises St. Eustatius, St. Martin, and Saba. The islands were visited in the 16th century by the Spanish and were settled by the Dutch in the mid-17th century. In 1954 they were granted self-government and became an autonomous region of the Netherlands.

Netherlands Antilles

Ne·tza·hual·có·yotl |nät,säwäl'kō,yōtl| (also **Ciudad Netzahualcóyotl**) city in central Mexico, in México state, a suburban part of the Mexico City area. Pop. 1,255,000.

Neu·bran·den·burg |noi'brändənbərg| industrial city in NE Germany. Pop. 88,000.

Neu·châ·tel, Lake |nooSHä'tel| the largest lake lying wholly within Switzerland, situated at the foot of the Jura Mts. in W Switzerland.

Neu·châ·tel |,nooSHə'tel| canton in the Jura Mts. of W Switzerland. Pop. 161,000. Its capital is Neuchâtel.

Neuilly-sur-Seine |noi'yēsərsän| city, a suburb of Paris, in N central France. Pop. 64,000. Primarily a wealthy residential community, Neuilly also has some industry. The American Hospital of Paris is here.

Neu·mün·ster |noi'moonster| industrial city and transportation center in NW Germany, N of Hamburg. Pop. 81,000.

Neun·kir·chen |noin'kirkhən| industrial city in NW Germany. Pop. 52,000.

Neu·quén |neoo'kän| city in W Argentina, the capital of Neuquén province. Pop. (with nearby Plottier) 183,000. On the Neuquén

River, it is a port and agricultural processing center.

Neu·sie·dler See |'noi,zēdlər,zā| shallow lake in the steppe region between E Austria and NW Hungary. Hungarian name **Fertö Tó.**

Neuss |nois| industrial city and canal port in western Germany, on the Rhine River, W of Düsseldorf. Pop. 148,000.

Neu·stadt an der Wein·stras·se |'noisHtät än der 'vīnsHträsə| industrial city and wine center in western Germany, W of the Rhine River and SW of Mannheim. Pop. 53,000.

Neus·tria |'noostreə| in France, during the Merovingian dynasty (6th–8th centuries), the western portion of the kingdom of the Franks. It consisted of the area around the Seine and the Loire rivers and lands to the north.

Neu·tral Zone |'nootrəl 'zōn| area between N Saudi Arabia and SE Iraq, W of Kuwait, that formerly had no recognized sovereignty but is now divided, roughly equally, between Saudi Arabia and Iraq.

Ne·va |'nyēvə| river in NW Russia that flows 46 mi./74 km. W from Lake Ladoga to the Gulf of Finland, passing through St. Petersburg. Alexander Nevsky took his name from this river after defeating the Swedes here in 1240.

Ne·va·da |nə'vædə| see box. □ **Nevadan** *adj. & n.*

Nevada	
Capital: Carson City	
Largest city: Las Vegas	
Other cities: Reno	
Population: 1,201,833 (1990); 1,746,898 (1998); 2,070,000 (2005 proj.)	
Population rank (1990): 39	
Rank in land area: 7	
Abbreviation: NV; Nev.	
Nickname: Silver State; Sagebrush State	
Motto: 'All for Our Country'	
Bird: mountain bluebird	
Fish: Lahontan cutthroat trout	
Flower: sagebrush	
Tree: single-leaf pinon; bristlecone pine	
Song: "Home Means Nevada"	
Noted physical features: Great Basin; Gypsum Cave; Sonoran Desert; Lake Mead; Columbia Plateau; Boundary Peak	
Tourist attractions: Las Vegas; Comstock Lode; Davis and Hoover dams; Tule, Punch Bowl, and Steam Boat hot springs	
Admission date: October 31, 1864	
Order of admission: 36	
Name origin: From the Spanish word *nevada*, meaning 'snow-covered,' shortened from Sierra Nevada, the mountain range in western Nevada along the California border.	

Never-Never |'nevər'nevər| **1** the unpopulated desert country of the interior of Australia; the remote outback. **2** (**Never-Never Land** or **Country**) a region of Northern Territory, Australia, SE of Darwin; chief town, Katherine.

Ne·vers |nə'ver| city in central France, on the Loire. Pop. 44,000. It was capital of the former province of Nivernais.

Ne·ves |'nevis| city in SE Brazil, an industrial suburb NE of Rio de Janeiro and just N of Niterói, on Guanabara Bay. Pop. 151,000.

Ne·vis |'nēvis| one of the Leeward Islands in the Caribbean, part of St. Kitts and Nevis. Pop. 9,000. Capital: Charlestown. □ **Nevisian** *adj. & n.*

Nev·sky Pros·pekt |'nevskē 'prawspekt| main thoroughfare in Saint Petersburg, Russia, along which are ranged the Winter Palace, the Hermitage, and other buildings of historic and architectural interest.

New Al·ba·ny |n(y)o͞o 'awlbənē| industrial city in S Indiana, across the Ohio River from Louisville, Kentucky Pop. 36,322.

New Am·ster·dam |n(y)o͞o 'æm(p)stər ,dæm| former name for NEW YORK CITY.

New·ark[1] |'n(y)o͞o,ärk| city in NW Delaware, home to the University of Delaware. Pop. 25,098.

New·ark[2] |'n(y)o͞owərk| industrial port city in N New Jersey, the largest city in the state. Pop. 275,221.

New·ark[3] |'n(y)o͞owərk| industrial and commercial city in central Ohio. Pop. 44,389.

New Bed·ford |n(y)o͞o 'bedfərd| industrial port city in SE Massachusetts, on Buzzards Bay, a famed 19th-century whaling center. Pop. 99,922.

New Bern |'n(y)o͞o 'bərn| historic commercial city in E North Carolina. Pop. 17,363.

New Braun·fels |n(y)o͞o 'brownfəlz| city in S central Texas. Pop. 27,334.

New Brit·ain[1] |'n(y)o͞o 'britən| industrial city in central Connecticut, noted for its hardware manufacturing. Pop. 75,491.

New Brit·ain[2] |'n(y)o͞o 'britən| mountainous island in the South Pacific, largest of the Bismarcks and part of Papua New Guinea, lying off the NE coast of New Guinea. Pop. 312,000. Capital: Rabaul.

New Bruns·wick[1] |,n(y)o͞o 'brənz,wik| city in central New Jersey, on the Raritan River, home to Rutgers, the state university. Pop. 41,711.

New Bruns·wick[2] |,n(y)o͞o 'brənz,wik| maritime province on the SE coast of Canada. Area: 28,355 sq. mi./73,440 sq. km. Pop. 723,900. Capital: Fredericton. Largest city: St. John. Settled in the early 17th century by the French, the area was ceded to Britain in 1713. New Brunswick, created in 1784 from Nova Scotia, became one of the original four provinces in the Dominion of Canada in 1867. Tourism, fishing, mining, and forest industries are important.

New·burgh |'n(y)o͞o,bərg| historic industrial city in SE New York, on the Hudson River. Pop. 26,454.

New·bury·port |'n(y)o͞obərēpawrt| historic port city, now chiefly residential, in NE Massachusetts, at the mouth of the Merrimack River. Pop. 16,317.

New Cal·e·do·nia |,n(y)o͞o ,kælə'dōnēə| island in the South Pacific, E of Australia. Pop. 178,000. Capital: Nouméa. Since 1946 it has formed, with its dependencies, a French overseas territory. It was inhabited by Melanesians for at least 3,000 years before the French annexed the island in 1853, and after the discovery of nickel in 1863 it assumed some economic importance for France. There has been a movement for independence in recent years. □ **New Caledonian** *adj. & n.*

New Caledonia

New·cas·tle |'n(y)o͞o,kæsəl| industrial port on the SE coast of Australia, in New South Wales. Pop. 262,000.

Newcastle-under-Lyme |'n(y)o͞o,kæsəl ,əndər līm| industrial town in Staffordshire, W central England, just SW of Stoke-on-Trent. Pop. 117,000.

Newcastle-upon-Tyne |'n(y)o͞o,kæsəl ə,pän 'tīn| industrial city in NE England, a port on the River Tyne. Pop. 263,000. It was long famed for its coal.

New·chwang |'no͞o CHwäNG; 'nyo͞o- 'CHwäNG| see YINGKOU, China.

New Del·hi |,n(y)o͞o 'delē| see DELHI, India.

New Eng·land |,n(y)o͞o 'iNG(g)lənd| area in the NE U.S., comprising the states of

Maine, New Hampshire, Vermont, Massachusetts, Rhode Island, and Connecticut. The name was originally applied to the region by the English explorer John Smith in 1614. □ **New Englander** *n.*

New Forest |ˌn(y)o͞o 'fawrəst| area of heath and woodland in S Hampshire, S England. It has been reserved as Crown property since 1079, originally as a royal hunting area, and is noted for its ponies.

New·found·land |'n(y)o͞ofən(d)lən(d)| island off the E coast of Canada, at the mouth of the St. Lawrence River. Area: 43,359 sq. mi./112,300 sq. km. A British colony from the 16th century, in 1949 it was united with Labrador (as Newfoundland and Labrador) to form a province of Canada. Fishing, forest industries, mining, and oil are important to the economy. □ **Newfoundlander** *n.*

New·found·land and Lab·ra·dor |'n(y)o͞ofən(d)lən(d) ænd 'læbrəˌdaw(ə)r| province of Canada, comprising the island of Newfoundland and the Labrador coast of the Ungava Peninsula. Area: 156,649 sq. mi./404,517 sq. km. Pop. 568,474. Capital: St. John's. Newfoundland was united with Labrador and joined the Dominion of Canada in 1949. The provincial economy relies on fishing, mining, and forest industries.

New France term for French colonial area in the New World.

New·gate |'n(y)o͞oˌgāt| former prison in London, England, at the W gate to the City, on a site today occupied by the Central Criminal Court. It was notorious for its unsanitary conditions. It burned during a 1780 riot.

New Geor·gia |ˌn(y)o͞o 'jawrjə| volcanic island group in the W central Solomon Islands. **New Georgia Sound,** along the N side, was called "the Slot" by Americans during World War II, when the area saw heavy fighting with Japanese forces.

New Gra·na·da |ˌn(y)o͞o grə'nädə| (Span. name **Nuevo Granada**) former S[p]... colony, a viceroyalty, roughly c[o]... present-day Colombia, Panam[a]... and Venezuela. Colombia an[d]...,000 called New Granada 18[ ]... Green-

New Guin·ea |ˌn(y)o͞o [ ]al divisions; S Pacific, off the [N]aya, a province second-largest [f]orms part of Papua sq. km.) isl[and]... **Guinean** *adj. & n.* land). It [ ]... the W [ ]... of J[ ]... N[ ]...

New·ham |'n(y)o͞oəm| industrial and residential borough of E London, England. Pop. 200,000. In the docklands area of London, it incorporates East Ham and West Ham.

New Hamp·shire |ˌn(y)o͞o 'hæm(p)sHər| see box.

New Ha·ven |'n(y)o͞ohāvən| industrial city in S central Connecticut, on Long Island Sound, home to Yale University. Pop. 130,474.

New·ha·ven |ˌn(y)o͞o'hāvən| port town in S England, in East Sussex, a terminus for ferries across the English Channel. Pop. 10,000.

New Heb·ri·des |ˌn(y)o͞o 'hebrədēz| former name (until 1980) for VANUATU.

New Hope |'no͞o 'hōp| borough in SE Pennsylvania, on the Delaware River, a well-known tourist destination and artists' colony. Pop. 1,400.

New Ibe·ria |n(y)o͞o ī'birēə| city in S Louisiana, on the Bayou Teche in Cajun Country, in a salt- and oil-producing area. Pop. 31,828.

New Ire·land |ˌn(y)o͞o 'īrlənd| island in the South Pacific, part of Papua New Guinea, lying to the N of New Britain. Pop. 87,000. Capital: Kavieng.

New Hampshire

Capital: Concord
Largest city: Manchester
Other cities: Dover, Nashu[a]
Population: 1,109,252 (1[ ])
  (1998); 1,281,000 (2[ ])
Population rank (1[ ])
Rank in land ar[ea]
Abbreviation[ ]shire"
Nickname[ ]eatures: Lake Win-
Motto: [ ]
Bird[ ]ite Mountains
F[r]actions: Great Stone Face;
[W]ashington; Kinsman's Notch,
[ ]ham Notch, Crawford Notch, and
[Fr]anconia Notch

Admission date: June 21, 1788
Order of admission: 9
Name origin: Named by Capt. John
Mason (1586-1636) to honor the county
of Hampshire, England; he received a
grant to a portion of the territory later occupied by the colony and state.

New Jersey

Capital: Trenton
Largest city: Newark
Other cities: Atlantic City, Camden, Jersey City, Paterson
Population: 7,730,188 (1990); 8,115,011 (1998); 8,392,000 (2005 proj.)
Population rank (1990): 9
Rank in land area: 47
Abbreviation: NJ; N.J.
Nickname: Garden State
Motto: 'Liberty and Prosperity'
Bird: Eastern goldfinch
Flower: purple violet
Tree: red oak
Noted physical features: Palisades, Sandy Hook; Delaware Bay; Cape May
Tourist attractions: Atlantic City; Jersey shore; Delaware Water Gap
Admission date: December 18, 1787
Order of admission: 3
Name origin: For the island of Jersey in the English Channel; probably named by James, Duke of York, for his friend, Sir George Carteret, who was born on Jersey and was its principal royal defender during the English Commonwealth.

New Mexico

Capital: Santa Fe
Largest city: Albuquerque
Other cities: Las Cruces, Los Alamos, Roswell
Population: 1,515,069 (1990); 1,736,931 (1998); 2,016,000 (2005 proj.)
Population rank (1990): 37
Rank in land area: 5
Abbreviation: NM; N.M. or N. Mex.
Nickname: Land of Enchantment
Motto: Crescit Eundo (Latin: 'It Grows as it Goes')
Bird: roadrunner
Fish: cutthroat trout
Flower: yucca
Tree: pinon
Song: "O, Fair New Mexico"
Noted physical features: Tularosa Basin; Jornada de Muerto Desert; Wheeler Peak
Tourist attractions: Carlsbad Caverns; Four Corners; Butte and Elephant dams; Los Alamos National Laboratory
Admission date: January 6, 1912
Order of admission: 47
Name origin: Named by the Spanish explorer Francisco de Ilbarra in 1562 for the country of Mexico, of which it was a territory until the end of the Mexican War (1846-48).

New Jer•sey |,n(y)o͞o 'jərzē| see box.
□ **New Jerseyan** n.
New Lon•don |,n(y)o͞o 'ləndən| industrial port city in SE Connecticut, across the Thames River from Groton and on Long Island Sound. Pop. 28,540.

w **Mad•rid** |,n(y)o͞o mə'drid| commercial n SE Missouri, on the Mississippi the center of an area devastated earthquake along the **New** New

'lēnz| rǒǒmärkət| town in Suf- city in the sed horse racing cen- shipping and in destination. Pop. 49 ə̄kō| see box. by the French in 1718; o͞o or- 1763, it was ceded back to F ̣gest then sold to the U.S. in the Lou chase. It is noted for its annual Mard celebrations and for its association with development of jazz.

New Plym•outh |,n(y)o͞o 'plimərH| port in New Zealand, on the W coast of North Island. Pop. 49,000.

New•port [1] |'n(y)o͞o,pawrt| historic port city in S Rhode Island, on Rhode Island, famed as a resort and home to naval facilities. Pop. 28,277.
New•port [2] |'n(y)o͞o,pawrt| industrial town and port in S Wales, on the Bristol Channel. Pop. 130,000. Welsh name **Casnewydd**.
New•port Beach |'n(y)o͞o,pawrt| resort, residential, and industrial city in SW California, SE of Los Angeles. Pop. 66,643.
New•port News |'n(y)o͞o,pawrt| city in SE Virginia, at the mouth of the James River on the Hampton Roads estuary. Pop. 170,045. Settled around 1620, it is a major seaport and shipbuilding center.
New Prov•i•dence |n(y)o͞o 'prawvidəns| land in the central Bahamas, site of the al, Nassau. Pop. 172,000. It is home of the people of the Bahamas.
o͞o **New** ̣ec |n(y)o͞o kwi'bek| (French 320 mi. ̣-Québec) vast, lightly pop- N Quebec, between Bay, that was part ries before 1912. ver that flows Carolina

through Virginia and into West Virginia, where it enters the Kanawha River.

New Ro•chelle |ˌn(y)o͞o rə'sHel; rō'sHel| city in SE New York, a suburb NE of New York City, on Long Island Sound. Pop. 67,265.

New•ry |'n(y)o͞orē| industrial port town in the SE of Northern Ireland, in County Down. Pop. 19,000.

New Si•be•ri•an Islands |ˌn(y)o͞o sī'bērē-ən| group of uninhabited islands in E Siberia, Russia, in the Arctic Ocean. They are divided into two parts by the Sannikov Strait.

New South Wales |ˌn(y)o͞o ˌsowTH 'wālz| state of SE Australia. Pop. 5,827,000. Capital: Sydney. First colonized from Britain in 1788, it was federated with the other states of Australia in 1901. Agriculture and mining are important.

New Spain |ˌn(y)o͞o 'spān| former Spanish viceroyalty established in Central and North America in 1535, centered on present-day Mexico City. It comprised all the land under Spanish control N of the Isthmus of Panama, including parts of the S U.S. It also came to include the Spanish possessions in the Caribbean and the Philippines. The viceroyalty was abolished in 1821, when Mexico achieved independence.

New Territories |ˌn(y)o͞o 'terəˌtawrēz| part of Hong Kong along the S coast of mainland China, lying to the N of the Kowloon peninsula, also including the islands of Lantau, Tsing Yi, and Lamma. It comprises 92 percent of the land area of Hong Kong.

New•ton |'n(y)o͞otn| city in E Massachusetts, a residential and industrial suburb on the Charles River, W of Boston. Pop. 82,585.

New•town•ab•bey |'n(y)o͞otn'æbē| suburban town in E Northern Ireland, on Belfast Lough, just NE of Belfast, in County Antrim. Pop. 73,000.

New West•min•ster |n(y)o͞o ˌwes(t)'mɪstər| port city in SW British Colum(later King James II). Because of the is-suburb E of Vancouver. Pop. 43,5

New World |ˌn(y)o͞o 'wərld| South America regarded c lation to Europe, Asia, cially after the early explorers.

New York |'n(y)... mouth of the Hud-**Yorker** *n.* 2,564. The city is situ-

New York

city, ir
the
s

New York

Capital: Albany
Largest city: New York
Other cities: Binghamton, Buffalo, Islip, Rochester, Syracuse
Population: 17,990,455 (1990); 18,175,301 (1998); 18,250,000 (2005 proj.)
Population rank (1990): 3
Rank in land area: 27
Abbreviation: NY; N.Y.
Nickname: The Empire State; Excelsior State
Motto: *Excelsior* (Latin: 'Ever upward')
Bird: bluebird
Fish: brook or speckled trout
Flower: rose
Tree: sugar maple
Song: "I Love New York"
Noted physical features: Adirondack Mountains; Finger Lakes; Hudson Valley; Niagara Falls; Mohawk Valley
Tourist attractions: New York City (many sites); Baseball Hall of Fame; Fire Island
Admission date: July 26, 1788
Order of admission: 11
Name origin: For James, Duke of York and Albany (1633-1701), later King James II of England; name applied from 1664 as Yorkshire, to the territory east of the Hudson, later as New York, as distinct New Jersey.

---

ated mainly on islands and The boroughs: Manhattan, P-(on the mainland), and were land. Manhattan ers in 1609, tural heart of ists are said to art galleri attan Island from headqu erchandise traditionally and t establishing a settlement H ey called New Amsterdam. In was captured by the British, who amed it in honor of the Duke of York (later King James II). Because of the island's small area and population density Manhattan has been built upward, with many tall buildings that give it its characteristic skyline. □ **New Yorker** *n.*

New Zea•land |ˌn(y)o͞o 'zēlənd| island country in the S Pacific about 1,200 mi./1,900 km. E of Australia. Area: 103,455 sq. mi./267,844 sq. km. Pop. 3,434,950. Languages, English (official), Maori. Capital: Wellington. Maori name **Aotearoa**. Maoris lived in the islands before the Dutch arrived in 1642. The British took control in 1840, and independence came in 1931. Agriculture, especially livestock raising and mining, form the backbone of the economy. □ **New Zealander** *n.*

New Zealand

Ne•ya•ga•wa |nāyä'gäwä| city in W central Japan, on S Honshu, a suburb N of Osaka. Pop. 257,000.

Ney•sha•bur |nāsHä'boŏr| (also **Nishapur**) historic commercial and cultural city in NE Iran, W of Mashhad. Pop. 136,000. In an agricultural region, it was a center of Persian life. The poet Omar Khayyam was born and is buried here.

Nga•li•e•ma, Mount |əNG,gälē'ämä| Congolese name for Mount Stanley (see STANLEY, MOUNT).

ʼga•mi•land |əNG'gämē,laend| region in ˮ Botswana, N of the Kalahari Desert. ˮes the Okavango marshes and Lake

is ˮ |,əNGawrōNG'gōrō| extinct educaˮ the Great Rift Valley in Niˮ mi./326 sq. km. in falls on the Niˮ principal parts seˮmercial port the Horseshoe Falls aˮ316,000. It dian) bank, which fall 1ˮs, and the American Falls adjoining ˮ which fall 167 ft./50 m. They are a pˮ tourist attraction, long a noted destinaˮ for honeymooners. In 1859 Charles Blondin was the first to walk across the gorge on a tightrope and in 1901 Annie Edson Taylor was the first person to go over

the falls in a barrel. **2** city in upper New York State situated on the E bank of the Niagara River beside the Falls. Pop. 61,840. **3** city in S Ontario, on the W bank of the Niagara River beside the Falls. Pop. 75,399.

Ni•ag•a•ra River |nī'æg(ə)rə| river of North America, flowing northward for 35 miles (56 km) from Lake Erie to Lake Ontario, and forming part of the border between Canada and the U.S. The Niagara Falls are halfway along its course. It is a major source of hydroelectric power.

Nia•mey |'nyä,mā| the capital of Niger, a commercial city and port on the Niger River. Pop. 410,000.

Ni•caea |nī'sēə| ancient city in Asia Minor, on the site of present-day Iznik, Turkey, which was important in Roman and Byzantine times. It was the site of two ecumenical councils of the early Christian Church (in 325 and 787).

Nic•a•ra•gua, Lake |nikə'rägwə| lake near the W coast of Nicaragua, the largest (3,100 sq. mi./8,029 sq. km.) lake in Central America. Granada is on its NW shore.

Nic•a•ra•gua |nikə'rägwə| the largest country in Central America, a republic with a coastline on both the Atlantic and the Pacific. Area: 46,448 sq. mi./120,254 sq. km. Pop. 3,975,000. Language, Spanish. Capital and largest city: Managua. A Spanish colony, Nicaragua gained full independence in 1838. Coffee, cotton, bananas, sugar, and meat are leading products. □ **Nicaraguan** *adj. & n.*

Nicaragua

ˮ**re** |nēīs| resort city on the French Riviera near the border with Italy. Pop. ˮAnnexed from Italy in 1860, it is Turkeˮ fAlpes-Maritimes department. Empire bˮˮ**nds** |'nikəbär| see ANˮAR ISLANDS, India.

ˮēdēə| ancient city of ˮ of Izmit, NW ˮthe Byzantine

Nic·o·sia |ˌnikəˈsēə| the capital of Cyprus. Pop. 186,000. Since 1974 it has been divided into Greek and Turkish sectors.

Nie·der·ö·ster·reich |ˈnēdəˈrōstərˌräik| German name for LOWER AUSTRIA.

Nie·der·sach·sen |ˈnēdərˌzäksən| German name for LOWER SAXONY.

Ni·ger |ˈnijər| landlocked republic in West Africa, on the S edge of the Sahara. Area: 489,378 sq. mi./1.27 million sq. km. Pop. 7,909,000. Languages, French (official), Hausa, and other W African languages. Capital and largest city: Niamey. Part of French West Africa from 1922, it became fully independent in 1960. Its people are overwhelmingly pastoral, although mining is also important.

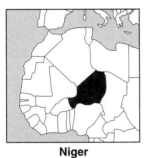

Niger

Ni·ge·ria |nīˈjirēə| republic on the coast of W Africa, bordered by the Niger River to the N. Area: 356,805 sq. mi./923,768 sq. km. Pop. 88,514,500. Languages, English (official), Hausa, Ibo, Yoruba, and others. Capital: Abuja. Largest city: Lagos. The most populous country in Africa, Nigeria was controlled by the British from the 19th century until independence in 1960. Traditionally focused on agriculture, fishing, and forest industries, Nigeria has since the 1960s become a major oil producer. □ **Nigerian** *adj. & n.*

Ni·ger River |ˈnijər| river in NW Africa, which rises on the NE border of Sierra Leone and flows 2,550 mi./4,100 km. NE to Mali, then SE through W Niger and Nigeria, before turning S into the Gulf of Guinea.

Ni·i·ga·ta |nēˈgätä| industrial port in central Japan, on the NW coast of the island of Honshu. Pop. 486,000.

Nii·ha·ma |ˈnēhämä| fishing port in W Japan, on N Shikoku. Pop. 129,000.

Ni·i·hau |ˈnēhow| island in Hawaii, SW of Kauai, whose residents are all native Hawaiians.

Ni·i·za |ˈnēzä| city in central Japan, on Honshu, a suburb of Tokyo. Pop. 139,000.

Nij·me·gen |ˈnäˌmāgən| industrial town in the E Netherlands, S of Arnhem. Pop. 146,000.

Nik·ko |ˈnēkkō| historic city and mountain resort in N central Japan, on central Honshu, in Nikko National Park. Pop. 20,000.

Ni·ko·la·ev |ˌnikəˈläyəf| Russian name for MYKOLAYIV, Ukraine.

Ni·ko·pol |nēˈkawpōl| industrial city in S Ukraine, on the Dnieper River. Pop. 158,000.

Nile |nīl| river in E Africa, the longest river in the world, which rises in E central Africa near Lake Victoria and flows 4,160 mi./6,695 km. generally N through Uganda, Sudan, and Egypt to empty through a large delta into the Mediterranean. See also BLUE NILE, ALBERT NILE, VICTORIA NILE, WHITE NILE.

Nil·gi·ri Hills |ˈnilgərē| range in S India, in W Tamil Nadu, rising to 8,648 ft./2,636 m. at Doda Betta. They form a branch of the Western Ghats.

Ni·ló·po·lis |niˈlawpəlis| city in SE Brazil, a suburb NW of Rio de Janeiro. Pop. 155,000.

Nîmes |nēm| city in S France, capital of the Gard department. Pop. 134,000. It is noted for its many well-preserved Roman ruins and for its textile industry; the fabric *denim* takes its name from Nimes.

Nim·rud |nimˈrood| modern name of an ancient Mesopotamian city on the E bank of the Tigris S of Nineveh, near present-day Mosul, Iraq. It was the capital of Assyria 879–722 B.C. The city was known in biblical times as Calah; the modern name arose through association in Islamic mythology with the biblical figure of Nimrod.

Nin·e·veh |ˈninəvə| ancient city on the E bank of the Tigris, opposite present-day Mosul, Iraq. It was the oldest city of the Assyrian empire, and its capital, until it was destroyed by a coalition of Babylonians and Medes in 612 B.C.

Nigeria

Ning·bo |'niNG'bō| (formerly **Ningpo**) port city in Zhejiang province, E China, at the junction of the Fenghua, Tong, and Yuyao rivers. Pop. 1,090,000. A special economic zone, it is a oil-refining, shipbuilding, and fishing center.

Ning·xia (formerly **Ningsia**) autonomous region, N central China. Area: 25,492 sq. mi./66,000 sq. km. Pop. 4,660,000. Capital: Yinchuan. It is an agricultural province on the Loess Plateau.

Niort |nyawr| commercial and industrial town in W France, capital of Deux-Sèvres department. Pop. 59,000.

Nip·i·gon, Lake |'nipigän| lake in NW Ontario, NE of Thunder Bay, used largely for recreational purposes.

Nip·is·sing, Lake |'nipəsiNG| lake in E central Ontario. The city of North Bay is on its shore.

Nip·pon |ni'pän| old name for Japan (from the Chinese, 'land of the Rising Sun'). □ **Nipponese** *adj. & n.*

Nip·pur |ni'pŏŏr| ancient city of Babylonia and Sumeria, in SE present-day Iraq, on a former course of the Euphrates River. It was occupied more than 4,000 years ago.

Niš |nēSH| (also **Nish**) historically dominant industrial city in SE Serbia, on the Nišava River near its confluence with the Morava. Pop. 175,000.

Ni·shi·no·mi·ya |'nēSHē'nōmēyə| industrial port city in W central Japan, on S Honshu. Pop. 427,000.

Ni·te·rói |ˌnētā'roi| industrial port on the coast of SE Brazil, on Guanabara Bay opposite the city of Rio de Janeiro. Pop. 455,000.

Ni·tra |nyēt'rä| agricultural market town in W Slovakia, on the Nitra River. Pop. 90,000. It is the site of the oldest church and castle in the country, dating from c. 830.

Niue |nē'ŏŏä| island territory of New Zealand in the S Pacific, to the E of Tonga. Pop. 2,200. Languages, English (official),

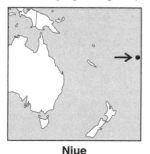

Niue

local Austronesian. Capital: Alofi. Annexed in 1901, the island achieved self-government in free association with New Zealand in 1974. Niue is the world's largest coral island.

Ni·ver·nais |nēver'nā| former duchy and province of central France. Its capital was the city of Nevers.

Ni·zam·a·bad |nē'zäməbäd| commercial city in central India, in Andhra Pradesh state. Pop. 241,000.

Nizh·ne·var·tovsk |niZHnē'värtəfsk| city in W Siberia, Russia. Pop. 246,000. It is near one of the world's largest oil fields.

Nizh·ni Nov·go·rod |'niZHnē 'nawvˌgərəd| industrial river port in European Russia, on the Volga. Pop. 1,443,000. Between 1932 and 1991 it was named Gorky after the writer Maxim Gorky, who was born here.

Nizh·ni Ta·gil |'niZHnē tə'gil| industrial and metal-mining city in central Russia, in the Urals N of Ekaterinburg. Pop. 440,000.

Nkong·sam·ba |əNGkawNG'sämbə| (also **N'Kongsamba**) commercial city in SW Cameroon, NW of Yaounde. It is a tourist center near Mount Nlonako. Pop. 85,000.

No·be·o·ka |nō'bēōkə| industrial and commercial port city in SW Japan, on SE Kyushu. Pop. 131,000.

Nob Hill |näb| commercial district of N San Francisco, California, long noted for the homes of the wealthy ("nobs").

No·da |'nōdä| commercial and industrial city in E central Japan, on E central Honshu. Pop. 114,000.

No·gal·es |nə'gælās| commercial city in NW Mexico, in Sonora state, on the U.S. border across from Nogales, Arizona. Pop. 106,000.

No·ginsk |nō'ginsk| manufacturing city in W Russia, E of Moscow. Pop. 123,000.

Nome |nōm| city in W Alaska, on the S coast of the Seward Peninsula. Pop. 3,500. Founded in 1896, it was a center of the Alaskan gold rush.

non·aligned na·tions term for those independent nations that were not formally allied with either of the two Cold War superpowers, the United States and the Soviet Union; examples: India and Egypt.

Non·tha·bu·ri |'nōn'tə'bŏŏrē| (also **Nondaburi**) town in S Thailand, a suburb N of Bangkok. Pop. 248,000.

Noot·ka Island |'nŏŏtkə| island in SW British Columbia, off SW Vancouver Island, noted for its native culture.

Nord·kapp |'nawrkäp| Norwegian name for NORTH CAPE.

Nord·kyn |'nawrdkin| promontory on the N coast of Norway, to the E of North Cape. At 71° 8′ N, it is the northernmost point of the European mainland, North Cape being on an island.

Nord-Pas-de-Calais |nawr'pädəkä'le| region of M France, on the border with Belgium.

Nordrhein-Westfalen |'nawrtrīn,vest-'fälən| German name for NORTH RHINE–WESTPHALIA.

Nor·folk[1] |'nawrfək| county on the E coast of England, E of the Wash. Pop. 737,000; county seat, Norwich.

Nor·folk[2] |'nawrfək| industrial and naval port city in SE Virginia, on Hampton Roads. Pop. 261,229.

Nor·folk Island |'nawrfək| island in the Pacific, off the E coast of Australia, administered since 1913 as an external territory of Australia. Pop. 1,912. Discovered by Captain James Cook in 1774, it was used from 1788 to 1814 as a penal colony.

Norfolk Islands

Nor·ge |'nawrgə| Norwegian name for NORWAY.

Nor·ic Alps |'nōrik ælps| range of the E Alps in S Austria, along the borders of Styria and Carinthia, reaching 8,006 ft./2,440 m. at Eisenhut.

Nor·i·cum |'nawrikəm| ancient Roman province, a Celtic homeland S of the Danube River in present-day Austria and Bavaria.

No·rilsk |nə'rēlsk| city in N Siberia, Russia, within the Arctic Circle and the northernmost city in Russia. Pop. 173,000. It was founded as a prison camp and is thought to be the coldest city in the world.

Nor·mal |'nawrməl| town in central Illinois, home to Illinois State University (originally a *normal*, or teachers', school). Pop. 40,023.

Nor·man |'nawrmən| city in central Oklahoma, S of Oklahoma City, home to the University of Oklahoma. Pop. 80,071.

Nor·man·dy |'nawrməndē| former province of NW France with its coastline on the English Channel, now divided into the two regions of Lower Normandy (Basse-Normandie) and Upper Normandy (Haute-Normandie); chief town, Rouen. Farming and orcharding are key to the economy of Normandy, which was the historic home to the Normans who invaded England in 1066, and which was the scene of the D-Day landings in June, 1944. □ **Norman** *adj. & n.*

Norr·kö·ping |'nawr,SHŌpiNG| industrial city and seaport on an inlet of the Baltic Sea in SE Sweden. Pop. 121,000.

North Af·ri·ca |,nawrTH 'æfrəkə| the N part of the African continent, especially the countries bordering the Mediterranean and the Red seas. □ **North African** *adj. & n.*

North·al·ler·ton |nawr'THælərtən| town in the N of England, the administrative center of North Yorkshire. Pop. 14,000.

North Amer·i·ca |,nawrTH ə'merəkə| continent comprising the N half of the American land mass. Connected to South America by the Isthmus of Panama. It contains Canada, the United States, Mexico, and the countries of Central America. □ **North American** *adj. & n.*

North·amp·ton[1] |nawr'THæm(p)tən| town in S central England, on the Nene River, the county seat of Northamptonshire. Pop. 178,000.

North·amp·ton[2] |nawr'THæm(p)tən| industrial and commercial city in W central Massachusetts, on the Connecticut River. It is home to Smith College. Pop. 29,289.

North·amp·ton·shire |nawr'THæm(p)-tən,SHi(ə)r| county of central England. Pop. 569,000; county seat, Northampton.

North At·lan·tic Drift |,nawrTH ət'læn-(t)ik| continuation of the Gulf Stream across the Atlantic and along the coast of NW Europe, where it has a significant warming effect on the climate.

North At·lan·tic Ocean |,nawrTH ət-'læn(t)ik| see ATLANTIC OCEAN.

North At·lan·tic Treaty Organization |,nawrTH ət'læn(t)ik 'trētē ,awrgənə'zā-SHən| (also **NATO**) military association of European and North American nations, formed in 1949 to guard against perceived Soviet expansionism. Its headquarters are in Brussels, Belgium. In the 1990s some former Soviet bloc nations were invited to join NATO.

North Bay |,nawrTH 'bā| city in E central

Ontario, a commercial and transportation hub on Lake Nipissing. Pop. 55,405.

North Ca·na·di·an River |ˌnawrTH kə-ˈnādēən| (also **Beaver River**) river that flows 800 mi./1,300 km. from NE New Mexico through Texas and Oklahoma, to the Canadian River. Oklahoma City lies on it.

North Cape |ˌnawrTH ˈkāp| promontory on Magerøya, an island off the N coast of Norway. North Cape is the northernmost point of the world accessible by road. Norwegian name **Nordkapp**.

North Car·o·li·na |ˈnawrTH ˌkerəˈlīnə| see box. □ **North Carolinian** *adj. & n.*

North Channel |ˌnawrTH ˈCHænəl| the stretch of sea separating SW Scotland from Northern Ireland and connecting the N Irish Sea to the Atlantic.

North Charles·ton |ˌnawrTH ˈCHärəlstən| city in SE South Carolina, a residential suburb with naval facilities. Pop. 70,218.

North Chi·ca·go |ˌnawrTH SHiˈkawgō| industrial city in NE Illinois, on Lake Michigan just S of Waukegan. Pop. 34,978.

North Country[1] |ˈnawrTH ˈkəntrē| in England, traditional term for areas N of the River Humber.

North Country[2] |ˈnawrTH ˈkəntrē| in New York state, areas N of the Mohawk and Hudson rivers, extending to the St. Lawrence valley and Lake Ontario.

North Da·ko·ta |ˈnawrTH dəˈkōdə| see box. □ **North Dakotan** *adj. & n.*

North·east region of the US, usually thought to include the six New England states, New Jersey, and the eastern portions of New York State and Pennsylvania.

North·east King·dom nickname for the region including the three most northerly counties of Vermont.

North Carolina

Capital: Raleigh
Largest city: Charlotte
Other cities: Durham, Fayetteville, Greensboro, Greenville, High Point, Winston-Salem
Population: 6,628,637 (1990); 7,546,493 (1998); 8,227,000 (2005 proj.)
Population rank (1990): 10
Rank in land area: 28
Abbreviation: NC; N.C, N. Car.
Nickname: Tarheel State
Motto: *Esse quam videri* (Latin: 'To be rather than to seem')
Bird: cardinal
Fish: channel bass
Flower: dogwood blossom
Tree: pine
Song: "The Old North State"
Noted physical features: Outer Banks; Cape Fear, Cape Hatteras, Cape Lookout; Pamlico Sound; Dismal Swamp; Mount Mitchell
Tourist attractions: Great Smoky Mountain National Park (with Tennessee); Cape Lookout; Cape Hatteras; Wright Brothers National Memorial
Admission date: November 21, 1789
Order of admission: 12
Name origin: For Charles I of England, who called the territory *Carolana*, "land of Charles," in a 1629 land grant to Sir Robert Heath; the area had already been named *Carolina* in 1562 by French explorer Jean Ribaut to honor Charles IX, king of France; *Carolina* was used from 1663. The northern portion of the orig-inial Carolina came to be called 'North Carolina' after the colony was divided in 1729.

North Dakota

Capital: Bismarck
Largest city: Fargo
Other cities: Grand Forks, Minot
Population: 638,800 (1990); 638,244 (1998); 677,000 (2005 proj.)
Population rank (1990): 47
Rank in land area: 19
Abbreviation: ND; N.D, N. Dak.
Nickname: Flickertail State; Sioux State; Land of the Dakotas; Peace Garden State
Motto: 'Liberty and Union, Now and For-ever, One and Inseparable'
Bird: western meadowlark
Fish: northern pike
Flower: wild prairie rose
Tree: American elm
Song: "North Dakota Hymn"
Noted physical features: Williston Basin; The Slope; Red River Valley; Little Missouri National Grasslands; White Butte
Tourist attractions: Garrison Dam; Theodore Roosevelt National Park
Admission date: November 2, 1889
Order of admission: 39
Name origin: For the Dakota (Sioux) Indian confederation, in whose language the word means 'allies,' referring to the friendly compact that joined seven small-er tribes. The original Dakota Territory was divided into north and south regions in 1889.

North·east Passage |ˌnawrTH'ēst 'pæsij| passage for ships along the N coast of Europe and Asia, from the Atlantic to the Pacific via the Arctic Ocean, sought for many years as a possible trade route to the East. It was first navigated in 1878–79 by the Swedish explorer Baron Nordenskjöld.

North Equa·to·ri·al Current |ˌnawrTH ˌekwə'tawrēəl 'kerənt| ocean current that flows W across the Pacific just N of the equator.

North·ern Neck region in E Virginia between the Potomac and Rappahannock rivers, a tidewater peninsula.

North·ern Cape |'nawrTHərn 'kāp| largest (139,700 sq. mi./362,000 sq. km.) province of South Africa, in the SW, formerly part of Cape Province. Pop. 749,000. Capital: Kimberley. Northern Cape is largely Karoo scrubland.

North·ern Cir·cars |'nawrTHərn ser'kärz| former name for the coastal region of E India between the Krishna River and Orissa, now in Andhra Pradesh.

north·ern hem·i·sphere the half of the earth that is N of the equator.

North·ern Ire·land |ˌnawrTHərn 'ī(ə)rlənd| province of the United Kingdom occupying the NE part of Ireland. Area: 1,944 sq. mi./5,032 sq. km. Pop. 1,570,000. Capital and largest city: Belfast. Northern Ireland, which comprises six of the nine historic counties of Ulster, was established as a self-governing province in 1920, having refused to be part of the Irish Free State. It has long been dominated by Unionist parties, which represent the Protestant majority. Many members of the Roman Catholic minority favor union with the Republic of Ireland. Discrimination against Catholics led to violent conflicts and (from 1969) the presence of British army units in an attempt to keep the peace. Terrorism and sectarian violence by paramilitary groups representing both sides of the conflict continued into the late 1990s. Industry in Belfast and agriculture are key to the local economy.

North·ern Ma·ri·an·as, Commonwealth of the |'nawrTHərn märē'änəs| self-governing territory in the W Pacific, comprising the Mariana Islands with the exception of the southernmost, Guam. Area: 184 sq. mi./477 sq. km. Pop. 43,345. Languages, English (official), Austronesian languages. Capital: Chalan Kanoa (on Saipan). The Northern Marianas are constituted as a self-governing commonwealth

Northern Mariana Islands

in union with the United States. Military bases are important to their economy.

North·ern Province |'nawrTHərn| province of N South Africa, formerly part of Transvaal. Capital: Pietersburg. Mining and farming are important.

North·ern Rho·de·sia |ˌnawrTHərn rō-'dēzHə| former name (until 1964) for ZAMBIA.

North·ern Territory |ˌnawrTHərn 'terəˌtawrē| state of N central Australia. Pop. 158,000. Capital: Darwin. The territory was annexed by the state of South Australia in 1863, and administered by the Commonwealth of Australia from 1911. It became a self-governing territory in 1978 and a full state in 1995. Mining is important.

North Fri·sian Islands |nawrTH 'frizHən| see FRISIAN ISLANDS.

North Island |nawrTH 'īlənd| the northern of the two main islands of New Zealand, separated from South Island by Cook Strait. Area: 44,180 sq. mi./114,383 sq. km. Pop. 2,553,000.

North Ko·rea |nawrTH kə'rēə| republic in E Asia, occupying the N part of the peninsula of Korea. Area: 46,558 sq. mi./120,538 sq. km. Pop. 22,227,000. Language, Korean. Capital and largest city: Pyongyang. Official name **Democratic People's Republic of Korea**. Formed when Korea was partitioned in 1948, North Korea is an in-

North Korea

creasingly isolated communist state. Industry and mining are important, as is agriculture, although famine is a recurrent problem. □ **North Korean** *adj. & n.*

North Lit·tle Rock |nawrTH 'litəl räk| city in central Arkansas, an industrial center across the Arkansas River from Little Rock. Pop. 61,741.

North Os·se·tia |nawrTH aw'sēSHə| autonomous republic of Russia, in the Caucasus on the border with Georgia. Pop. 638,000. Capital: Vladikavkaz. Since 1994 it has been called Alania. See also OSSETIA.

North Platte River |nawrTH 'plat| river that flows 620 mi./960 km. from N Colorado across Wyoming and Nebraska, to the Platte River. Its valley was part of the Oregon Trail.

North Rhine-Westphalia |,nawrTH 'rīn-,west'fälyə| the most populous state of Germany, in the W. Area: 13,159 sq. mi./ 34,070 sq. km. Pop. 17,104,000. Capital: Düsseldorf. German name **Nordrhein-Westfalen.**

North Sea |'nawrTH 'sē| shallow arm of the Atlantic lying between the mainland of Europe and the coast of Britain, important for its oil and gas deposits and for its fishing grounds.

North Slope |nawrTH 'slōp| name for regions of Alaska N of the Brooks Range, extending to the Arctic Ocean. Sparsely populated, it is the scene of much oil exploration and extraction.

North Syd·ney |nawrTH 'sidnē| town in SE Australia, in New South Wales, a commercial and industrial suburb N of Sydney. Pop. 50,000.

North Ton·a·wan·da |nawrTH ,tänə'wändə| industrial city in W New York, on the Niagara River N of Buffalo, at the W end of the historic Erie Canal. Pop. 34,989.

North·um·ber·land |nawr'THəmbərlən(d)| county in NE England, on the Scottish border. Pop. 301,000; county seat, Morpeth.

North·um·ber·land Strait |nawr'THəmbərlənd| ocean passage in the Gulf of St. Lawrence, separating Prince Edward Island from New Brunswick and Nova Scotia.

North·um·bria |nawr'THəmbrēə| **1** area of NE England comprising the counties of Northumberland, Durham, and Tyne and Wear. **2** an ancient Anglo-Saxon kingdom in NE England extending from the Humber to the Forth. □ **Northumbrian** *adj. & n.*

North Vi·et·nam |nawrTH vē,et'näm| former communist republic in SE Asia, in the N part of Vietnam, created in 1954 when Vietnam was partitioned; after defeating noncommunist South Vietnam in the Vietnam War, it declared a reunited, socialist republic (1976).

North·west An·gle |,nawrTH'west 'æNGəl| forested region of N Minnesota, separated from the rest of the state and the U.S. by Lake of the Woods. It is the northernmost part of the contiguous U.S.

North-West Fron·tier Province |,nawrTH'west frən'tēr| province of western Pakistan, on the border with Afghanistan. Pop. 12,290,000. Capital: Peshawar.

Northwest Passage |,nawrTH'west 'pæsəj| sea passage along the N coast of the American continent, through the Canadian Arctic from the Atlantic to the Pacific. It was sought for many years as a possible trade route; it was first navigated in 1903-06 by Roald Amundsen, but has no commercial value.

North-West Province |,nawrTH'west| province of N South Africa, formed in 1994 from the NE part of Cape Province and SW Transvaal. Pop. 3,349,000. Capital: Mmabatho.

North·west Territories |,nawrTHwest 'terə,tawrēz| territory of NW Canada, between Yukon Territory and Nunavut. Capital: Yellowknife. Much of it consists of sparsely inhabited forests and tundra. The Northwest Territories, then including the land that is now Nunavut, was ceded by Britain to Canada in 1870. Nunavut became a separate territory in 1999.

North·west Territory |,nawrTHwest 'terə,tawrē| region and former territory of the U.S. lying E of the Mississippi and N of the Ohio rivers. It was acquired in 1783 after the Revolutionary War and now forms the states of Indiana, Ohio, Michigan, Illinois, Wisconsin, and part of Minnesota. Also called the **Old Northwest.**

North York |,nawrTH 'yawrk| city in S Ontario, a largely residential suburb N of Toronto. Pop. 562,564.

North York·shire |,nawrTH 'yawrk,SHir| county in NE England. Pop. 699,000; administrative center, Northallerton. It was formed in 1974 from parts of the former North, East, and West ridings of Yorkshire. The city of York is here.

Nor·walk[1] |'nawrwawk| city in SW California, a suburb SE of Los Angeles. Pop. 94,279.

Nor·walk[2] |'nawrwawk| industrial city in SW Connecticut, on Long Island Sound. Pop. 78,331.

Nor·way |'nawrwā| mountainous European kingdom, on the N and W coastline of Scandinavia. Area: 125,098 sq. mi./323,878 sq. km. Pop. 4,249,830. Language, Norwegian. Capital and largest city: Oslo. Norwegian name **Norge**. Norway gained independence, after longtime domination by either Denmark or Sweden, in 1905. Maritime and forest industries have been supplemented, since the 1960s, by North Sea oil. □ **Norwegian** *adj. & n.*

Norway

Nor·we·gian Sea |nawr'wējən| sea that lies between Iceland and Norway and links the Arctic Ocean with the NE Atlantic.

Nor·wich[1] |'nawr(w)icH| industrial city in SE Connecticut, on the Thames River. Pop. 37,391.

Nor·wich[2] |'nawr(w)icH| commercial and university city in E England, the county seat of Norfolk. Pop. 121,000.

Nos·sob River |'nōsäb| (also **Nosop**) river that flows 500 mi./800 km. from Namibia across the Kalahari Desert into Botswana, where it forms part of the border with South Africa and empties into the Auob River.

Notre-Dame |'nōtrə 'däm| cathedral church of Paris, France, on the Ile de la Cité In 1163 Pope Alexander III laid the cornerstone for the church, built in early Gothic style, and most of the construction was completed within 30 years. During the French Revolution the church became a "Temple of Reason," and many of the sculptures on the façade were destroyed. Restoration was undertaken in 1845 by Viollet-le-Duc.

No·tre Dame Mountains |'nōdər 'däm; 'nōtrə 'däm| Appalachian range in S Quebec, extending S of the St. Lawrence River into the Gaspé Peninsula, where they include the Shickshock Mts.

Not·ting·ham |'nätiNG,hæm| industrial city in E central England, the county seat of Nottinghamshire. Pop. 261,000.

Not·ting·ham·shire |'nätiNGəm,sHi(ə)r|

county in central England. Pop. 981,000; county seat, Nottingham.

Not·ting Hill |'nätiNG 'hil| residential area of N central London, England, N of Holland Park, a center of the city's West Indian population.

Nouad·hi·bou |,nwädē'boo| the principal port of Mauritania, on the Atlantic coast at the border with Western Sahara. Pop. 22,000. Former name **Port-Étienne**.

Nouak·chott |nw'äksHät| the capital of Mauritania, on the Atlantic coast. Pop. 850,000 .

Nou·méa |noo'māə| the capital of the island and French overseas territory of New Caledonia. Pop. 65,000. Former name **Port de France**.

Nouvelle-Calédonie |voo'velkə'lädōnē| French name for NEW CALEDONIA.

No·va Igua·çu |'nawvä ,ēgwä'soo| city in SE Brazil, an industrial suburb NW of Rio de Janeiro. Pop. 801,000.

No·va Lis·boa |,nōvə liz'bōə| former name (until 1978) for HUAMBO, Angola.

No·va·ra |nō'värə| agricultural and industrial town in N Italy, capital of Novara province. Pop. 103,000.

No·va Sco·tia |,nōvə 'skōsHə| **1** a peninsula on the SE coast of Canada, projecting into the Atlantic and separating the Bay of Fundy from the Gulf of St. Lawrence. **2** a province of E Canada, comprising the peninsula of Nova Scotia and the adjoining Cape Breton Island. Area: 21,425 sq. mi./55,490 sq. km. Pop. 899,942. Capital and largest city: Halifax. Settled by the French as ACADIA, it changed hands several times befor being controlled by the British in 1713. One of the original four provinces in Canada in 1867, it has maritime, iron and steel, and lumber industries, and tourism is important. □ **Nova Scotian** *adj. & n.*

No·va·to |nə'vätō| city in NW California, N of San Francisco. Pop. 47,585.

No·va·ya Zem·lya |,nōvəyə ,zem'l(y)ä| two large uninhabited islands in the Arctic Ocean off the N coast of Siberian Russia. The name means 'new land.'

Nov·go·rod |'nawv,gərəd| commercial city in NW Russia, on the Volkhov River at the N tip of Lake Ilmen. Pop. 232,000. Russia's oldest city, it was settled by the Varangian chief Rurik in 862 and ruled by Alexander Nevsky between 1238 and 1263, when it was an important center of medieval E Europe.

No·vi Pa·zar |'nōvē pə'zär| historic commercial city in Serbia, on a tributary of the Ibar River. Pop. 86,000.

No·vi Sad |'nōvē 'säd| industrial city in Serbia, on the Danube River, capital of the autonomous province of Vojvodina. Pop. 179,000.

No·vo·cher·kassk |ˌnōvəCHər'käsk| industrial city in W Russia, NE of Rostov. Pop. 188,000.

No·vo Ham·bur·go |'nōvōō æm'bōōrgōō| industrial and commercial city in S Brazil, in Rio Grande do Sul state. Pop. 207,000. It was settled by Germans in the 19th century.

No·vo·kuz·netsk |ˌnōvəkōōz'n(y)etsk| industrial city in the Kuznets Basin in S central Siberian Russia. Pop. 601,000.

No·vo·mos·kovsk |ˌnōvəmä'kawfsk| industrial city in W Russia, S of Moscow. Pop. 146,000.

No·vo·ros·siysk |nōvərə'sēsk| naval base and seaport in SW Russia, on the Black Sea coast. Pop. 190,000.

No·vo·si·birsk |ˌnōvəsi'bərsk| industrial city and rail center in central Siberian Russia, to the W of the Kuznets Basin, on the Ob River. Pop. 1,443,000.

Noy·on |nwæ'yæn| industrial and commercial town in N France. Pop. 15,000. In 768 Charlemagne was crowned King of the Franks here.

Nu·bia |'nōōbēə| ancient region of S Egypt and northern Sudan, including the Nile valley between Aswan and Khartoum and the surrounding area. Much of Nubia is now covered by the waters of Lake Nasser, formed by the building of the two dams at Aswan. Nubia fell under ancient Egyptian rule from the time of the Middle Kingdom, soon after 2000 B.C., and from about the 15th century B.C. was ruled by an Egyptian viceroy. The country was Egyptianized, and trade (especially in gold) flourished. By the 8th century B.C., however, as Egypt's centralized administration disintegrated, an independent Nubian kingdom emerged, and for a brief period extended its power over Egypt. Nubians constitute an ethnic minority group in present-day Egypt. The **Nubian Desert** lies between the Nile and the Red Sea. □ **Nubian** *adj. & n.*

Nu·e·ces River |nōō'äsəs| river that flows 315 mi./515 km. from central Texas into the Gulf of Mexico at Nueces Bay. The city of Corpus Christi is at its mouth.

Nue·va San Sal·va·dor |'nwävə sæn 'sælvədawr| (also **Santa Tecla**) city in SW El Salvador, a suburb W of San Salvador in coffee-growing country. Pop. 96,000. It was established after an 1850s earthquake destroyed San Salvador.

Nue·vo La·re·do |'nwävō lə'rädō; nōō'ävō| commercial city in E Mexico, in Tamaulipas state, across the Rio Grande from Laredo, Texas. Pop. 218,000. It is a rail and road terminus and international trade center.

Nue·vo Le·ón |'nwävō lā'ōn; nōō'ävō| state of NE Mexico, on the border with the U.S. Area: 25,077 sq. mi./64,924 sq. km. Pop. 3,086,000. Capital: Monterrey.

Nu·ku'a·lo·fa |ˌnōōkōōə'lōfə| the capital of Tonga, situated on the island of Tongatapu. Pop. 30,000.

Nu·ku Hi·va |'nōōkōō 'hēvə| largest (127 sq. mi./329 sq. km.) of the Marquesas Islands, in French Polynesia. It is mountainous and has several good harbors.

Nu·kus |nōō'kōōs| industrial city in S Uzbekistan, on the right bank of the Amu Darya River. Pop. 180,000.

Null·ar·bor Plain |'nələrbər| vast arid plain in SW Australia, stretching inland from the Great Australian Bight. It contains no surface water, has sparse vegetation, and is almost uninhabited.

Nu·ma·zu |nōō'mäzōō| industrial port city in central Japan, on central Honshu. Pop. 212,000.

Nu·mid·ia |nōō'midēə| ancient kingdom, later a Roman province, situated in N Africa in an area N of the Sahara corresponding roughly to present-day Algeria. □ **Numidian** *adj. & n.*

Nu·na·vut territory in N Canada, comprising the eastern part of the original Northwest Territories and including most of the islands of the Arctic Archipelago. It is the homeland of the Inuit people.

Nun·a·wa·ding |'nənəwəˌdiNG| city in Australia, in Victoria, a suburb E of Melbourne. Pop. 91,000.

Nun·ea·ton |nə'nētən| industrial city in central England, in Warwickshire, a textile center. Pop. 82,000.

Nu·ni·vak Island |'nōōnəvæk| island in the Bering Sea, in SW Alaska, home to Inuit hunters and fishermen and to much wildlife.

Nür·bur·gring |'nyōōrbərgriNG| auto racetrack in Nürburg, Rhineland-Palatinate, W central Germany.

Nu·rem·berg |'nōōr(ə)m,bərg| commercial, industrial, and cultiral city in S Germany, in Bavaria. Pop. 497,000. In the 1930s Nazi Party congresses and annual rallies were held in the city, and in 1945–46 it was the scene of the Nuremberg trials, in which Nazi war criminals faced an international tribunal. German name **Nürnberg**.

Nu•ri•stan |no͝orə'stæn| mountainous region of NE Afghanistan, scene of heavy fighting during the Soviet occupation of the 1980s.

Nürn•berg |nyern,berg| German name for NUREMBERG.

Nut•meg State |'nətmeg| nickname for CONNECTICUT.

Nuuk |'no͞ok| capital of Greenland, a port on the Davis Strait. Pop. 12,000. It was known by the Danish name Godthåb until 1979.

Nyan•za |nē'ænzə| agricultural province of NW Kenya; pop. 3.89 million. Its capital is Kisumu. The Bantu term *nyanza* is also an element in the names of several major African lakes.

Nya•sa, Lake |'nyäsä| lake in E central Africa, the third largest lake in Africa. About 360 mi./580 km. long, it forms most of the E border of Malawi with Mozambique and Tanzania. Also called **Lake Malawi**.

Nya•sa•land |'nyäsəlænd| former name (until 1966) for MALAWI.

Nyi•regy•há•za |'nyērej 'häzaw| commercial and industrial city in E Hungary. Pop. 115,000.

Ny•kø•ping |'no͝oCHo͞opēNG| port in SE Sweden, on the Baltic Sea, capital of Södermanland county. Pop. 66,000.

Nym•phen•burg |'nimpfenbərg| complex of palaces in Munich, S Germany (Bavaria). The Nymphenburg chateau was built in the late 17th century. A porcelain factory was later established here.

Ny•sa |'nisə| Polish name for the NEISSE River.

Ny•stad |'no͞ostäd| Swedish name for UUSIKAUPUNKI.

Oo

Oahe, Lake |ōˈwähē| reservoir NW of Pierre, South Dakota, in the Missouri River, created since 1963 by the huge, earthen Oahe Dam.

Oa·hu |ōˈwähoo| the third-largest of the Hawaiian islands. Its principal community, Honolulu, is the state capital of Hawaii. The U.S. naval base at Pearl Harbor is here.

Oak·land |ˈōklənd| industrial port city on the E side of San Francisco Bay in N California. Pop. 372,242.

Oak Park |ōk ˈpärk| village in NE Illinois, a largely residential suburb W of Chicago. Pop. 53,648.

Oak Ridge |ˈōk ˌrij| city in E Tennessee, on the Clinch River, established in 1942 as part of U.S. nuclear development, and still a research and industrial center. Pop. 27,310.

Oak·ville |ˈōkˌvil| port city in S Ontario, on L. Ontario SW of Toronto, an industrial and residential suburb. Pop. 114,670.

Oa·xa·ca |wäˈhäkə| **1** state of S Mexico. Area: 36,289 sq. mi./93,952 sq. km. Pop. 3,022,000. **2** its capital city, an historic cultural and commercial center. Pop. 213,000. Full name **Oaxaca de Juárez.**

Ob |äb| the principal river of the W Siberian lowlands and one of the largest rivers in Russia. Rising in the Altai Mts., it flows generally N and W for 3,481 mi./5,410 km. before entering the Gulf of Ob (or Ob Bay), an inlet of the Kara Sea, a part of the Arctic Ocean.

Oban |ˈōbən| port and tourist resort on the W coast of Scotland, in Argyll and Bute, opposite the island of Mull. Pop. 8,000.

Ober·am·mer·gau |ˌōbərˈämərgow| village in the Bavarian Alps of SW Germany. Pop. 5,000. It is the site of the most famous of the few surviving passion plays, which has been performed by the villagers every tenth year (with few exceptions) since 1634 as a result of a vow made during an epidemic. The villagers divide the parts among themselves and are responsible also for the production, music, costumes, and scenery.

Ober·hau·sen |ˈōbərˌhowzən| industrial city in western Germany, in the Ruhr valley in North Rhine–Westphalia. Pop. 225,000.

Ober·land |ˈōbərˌlænd| in German, generic term for mountainous or upland region. It appears in such German or Swiss names as Bernese Oberland.

Ober·lin |ˈōbərlən| city in N central Ohio, home to Oberlin College. Pop. 8,191.

Ober·ö·ster·reich |ˌōbəˌrōstər ˌraik| German name for UPPER AUSTRIA.

Obi·hi·ro |ōbēˈhērō| city in N Japan, on N central Hokkaido, E of Sapporo. Pop. 167,000.

Obi Islands |ˈōbē| (also called **Ombi Islands**) island group in Indonesia, in the N central Moluccas, in the Ceram Sea between Halmahera (N) and Ceram (S).

Ocala |ōˈkälə| industrial and resort city in N central Florida. Pop. 42,045.

Oc·ci·dent, the |ˈawksidənt| literary term for Europe, America, or both, as distinct from the ORIENT. It derives from the Latin word for 'setting' (used of the sun). □ **Occidental** adj. & n.

Oce·an·ia |ˌōshēˈænēə| (also **Oceanica**) the islands of the Pacific and adjacent seas, variously defined. Also, **Oceanica.** □ **Oceanian** adj. & n.

Ocean Island |ˈōshən| another name for BANABA, Kiribati.

Ocean·side |ˈōshənsīd| residential and commercial city in SW California, N of San Diego. Nearby Camp Pendleton, a Marine base, is central in its life. Pop. 128,398.

Ocean State |ˈōshən| nickname for RHODE ISLAND.

Ocho Ri·os |ˈōchō ˈrēōs| resort town in N Jamaica, a port on the Caribbean Sea, famed for its waterfalls. Pop. 8,000.

Ocra·coke Island |ˈōkrəkōk| barrier island in E North Carolina, part of the Outer Banks. Fishing and resort trade are central to its economy.

Oda·wa·ra |ōdäˈwärə| city in E central Japan, on E central Honshu, SW of Tokyo. Pop. 193,000.

Oden·se |ˈōdənsə| industrial port in E Denmark, on the island of Fyn. Pop. 178,000.

Oder |ˈōdər| river of central Europe that rises in the mountains in the W of the Czech Republic and flows N through W Poland to meet the Neisse River, then continues N forming the N part of the border between Poland and Germany before flowing into the Baltic Sea. This border between Poland and Germany, known as the Oder–Neisse Line, was adopted at the Potsdam Conference in 1945. Czech and Polish name **Odra.**

Odes·sa¹ |ōˈdesə| city in SW Texas, with its neighbor Midland an oil industry center in the Permian Basin. Pop. 89,699.

Odes•sa[2] |ō'desə| city and naval, industrial, and resort port on the S coast of Ukraine, on the Black Sea. Pop. 1,106,000. Ukrainian name **Odesa**.

Odra |'ōdər| Polish name for the ODER River.

Of•fa•ly |'awfəlē| county in the central part of the Republic of Ireland, in the province of Leinster. Pop. 58,000; county seat, Tullamore.

Of•fa's Dyke |'awfəz 'dīk| series of earthworks along the England-Wales border, attributed to Offa, 8th-century king of Mercia, whose aim was to mark the boundary established in wars with the Welsh.

Of•fen•bach |'awfən,bäk| (also **Offenbach am Main**) industrial city in W Germany, on the Main River. Pop. 116,000.

Oga•den |ō'gäden| (**the Ogaden**) desert region in SE Ethiopia, largely inhabited by Somali nomads. It has been claimed by successive governments of neighboring Somalia.

Oga•ki |ō'gäkē| city in central Japan, on central Honshu, W of Gifu. Pop. 148,000.

Ogal•lala Aq•ui•fer vast groundwater resource under eight U.S. states, used esp. for crop irrigation. It stretches from southern South Dakota to W Texas and E New Mexico.

Og•bo•mo•sho |,ōgbō'mōsHō| city and agricultural market in SW Nigeria, N of Ibadan. Pop. 661,000. Its people are largely Yoruba.

Og•den |'ägdən| industrial and military city in N Utah, N of Salt Lake City. Pop. 63,909.

Og•dens•burg |'ägdənz,bərg| industrial city in N New York, on the St. Lawrence River. Pop. 13,521.

Ogo•oué River |ōgō'wä| (also **Ogowe**) river that flows 560 mi./900 km. from the SW Congo across Gabon to the Gulf of Guinea in the Atlantic. It is key to Gabon's economy.

O'Hare In•ter•na•tion•al Airport |ō'her ,intər'næsHənl| facility in NE Illinois, NW of Chicago, on the S side of Des Plaines. It is one of the busiest airports in the world.

Ohio |ō'hīō| see box. □ **Ohioan** *adj. & n.*

Ohio River |ō'hīō| river that flows 980 mi./1,580 km. from Pittsburgh, Pennsylvania, where it is formed by the Allegheny and Monongahela rivers, through the E Midwest to join the Mississippi River at Cairo, Illinois. Now heavily industrial and a route of commerce, it was a key corridor of 19th-century W expansion.

Ohio

Capital: Columbus
Largest city: Cleveland
Other cities: Akron, Canton, Cincinnati, Dayton, Toledo, Youngstown
Population: 10,847,115 (1990); 11,209,493 (1998); 11,428,000 (2005 proj.)
Population rank (1990): 7
Rank in land area: 34
Abbreviation: OH; O.
Nickname: Buckeye State
Motto: 'With God, All Things Are Possible'
Bird: cardinal
Flower: scarlet carnation
Tree: buckeye
Song: "Beautiful Ohio"
Noted physical features: Ohio River; Lake Erie
Tourist attractions: Pro Football Hall of Fame; Rock and Roll Hall of Fame
Admission date: March 1, 1803
Order of admission: 17
Name origin: Named for the river, which itself was named by French explorers after similar words in several Indian languages; the name is from the Iroquoian *oheo*, 'beautiful,' *ohion-hiio*, 'beautiful river,' or possibly Wyandot *ohezuh*, 'great; fair to look upon.'

Ohrid, Lake |'ōkrēd| lake in SE Europe, on the border between Macedonia and Albania.

Oil Rivers |oil| general term for the delta of the Niger River, in S Nigeria.

Oise River |wäz| river in S Belgium and N France, rising in the Ardennes Mts. and flowing 189 mi./302 km. SW, meeting the Seine River near Pointoise.

Oi•ta |'awē,tä| commercial and industrial port city in SW Japan, on NE Kyushu. Pop. 409,000.

Ojai |'ōhī| city in SW California, NW of Los Angeles, a resort and artists' colony. Pop. 7,613.

Oka River |ō'kä| **1** river (530 mi./853 km. long) in S central Russia. It flows N from the Sayan Mts. into the Angara River. **2** river (919 mi./1,479 km. long) in W Russia, rising in Kursk oblast and flowing into the Volga River at Nizhny Novgorod; it is the main tributary of the Volga.

Oka•na•gan, Lake |ōkə'nägən| lake in S British Columbia, noted for its resorts and for Ogopogo, a rumored marine inhabitant.

Oka•ra |ō'kärə| commercial city in NE Pakistan, in Punjab province. Pop. 154,000.

Oka•van•go river of SW Africa that rises in central Angola and flows 1,000 mi./1,600 km. SE to Namibia, where it turns E to form part of the border between Angola and Namibia before entering Botswana, where it drains into the extensive Okavango marshes of Ngamiland. Also called **Cubango.**

Oka•ya•ma |'ōkä'yämä| industrial city and major railroad junction in SW Japan, on the SW coast of Honshu. Pop. 594,000.

Oka•za•ki |'ōkä'zäkē| city in central Japan, on S central Honshu, S of Nagoya. Pop. 307,000.

O.K. Cor•ral |'ō'kä kə'ræl| see TOMBSTONE, Arizona.

Okee•cho•bee, Lake |,ōkə'CHōbē| lake in S Florida. Fed by the Kissimmee River from the N, it drains into the Everglades in the S, this drainage being controlled by embankments and canals. It forms part of the Okeechobee Waterway, which crosses the Florida peninsula from W to E, linking the Gulf of Mexico with the Atlantic.

Oke•fe•no•kee Swamp |,ōkəfə'nōkē| extensive area of swampland in SE Georgia and NE Florida, associated with the cartoon character Pogo.

Okhotsk, Sea of |ə'kätsk| inlet of the N Pacific on the E coast of Russia (Siberia), between the Kamchatka Peninsula and the Kurile Islands. Magadan is the chief port here.

Oki•na•wa |ōki'näwä| an island group of Japan, in the S Ryukyu Islands. Pop. 1,222,000. Capital: Naha. Controlled after World War II by the U.S., the islands were returned to Japan in 1972, but many U.S. military facilities remain. □ **Okinawan** adj. & n.

Ok•la•ho•ma |,ōklə'hōmə| see box. □ **Oklahoman** adj. & n.

Ok•la•ho•ma City |,ōklə'hōmə| the capital of Oklahoma and largest city in the state, an industrial and commercial center. Pop. 444,719. It expanded rapidly after the discovery in 1928 of underlying oil fields.

Öland |'ō,länd| narrow island in the Baltic Sea off the SE coast of Sweden, the largest in the country, separated from the mainland by Kalmar Sound. Pop. 26,000.

Ola•the |ō'lāTHə| industrial city in NE Kansas, SW of Kansas City. Pop. 63,352.

Old Bai•ley |,ōld 'bālē| name for the Central Criminal Court of London, England, originally in a courtyard (bailey) of the city walls, since 1906 on the site of NEWGATE prison.

Old Cas•tile |ōld kæ'stēl| former province

Oklahoma

Capital/largest city: Oklahoma City
Other cities: Lawton, Norman, Tulsa
Population: 3,145,585 (1990); 3,346,713 (1998); 3,491,000 (2005 proj.)
Population rank (1990): 28
Rank in land area: 20
Abbreviation: OK; Okla.
Nickname: Sooner State; Boomer State
Motto: Labor omnia vincit (Latin: 'Labor conquers all things')
Bird: scissor-tailed flycatcher
Fish: white (sand) bass
Flower: mistletoe
Tree: redbud
Song: "Oklahoma!"
Noted physical features: Panhandle; Black Mesa
Tourist attractions: American Indian Hall of Fame; National Cowboy Hall of Fame
Admission date: November 16, 1907
Order of admission: 46
Name origin: From Choctaw okla, 'people,' and humma or homma, 'red,' thus, 'land of the red people.'

---

in N Spain, now part of N Castile. It comprises the modern provinces of Avila, Burgos, Cantabria, La Rioja, Palencia, Segovia, Soria, and Valladolid.

Old Del•hi |ōld 'delē| see DELHI, India.

Ol•den•burg |'ōldən,bɔrg| market town and industrial center of NW Germany, on the Hunte River, W of Bremen. Pop. 146,000.

Old•ham |'ōld,hæm| industrial town in NW England, NE of Manchester. Pop. 100,000.

Old Sar•um |,ōld 'serəm| ancient hill city in S England, in Wiltshire, just N of Salisbury (New Sarum). Fortified since the Iron Age, it had a cathedral, then declined until, in the early 19th century, it was a classic "rotten borough," represented in Parliament although it had almost no inhabitants.

Ol•du•vai Gorge |'awldə,vī 'gawrj| gorge in N Tanzania, 30 mi./48 km. long and up to 300 ft./90 m. deep. Its exposed strata contain numerous fossils (especially hominids) spanning the full range of the Pleistocene period.

Old World |ōld wər(ə)ld| Europe, Asia, and Africa, regarded collectively as the part of the world known before the discovery of the Americas. Compare with NEW WORLD.

Ole•nek River |əli'nyōk| river (1,350

m./2,175 km.) in Russia that rises in the central Siberian plateau and flows NE to the Laptev Sea.

Olé·ron, Ile d' |ˌēldawlä'rawn| resort island in the Bay of Biscay, off the W coast of France. It is the largest island in the Bay of Biscay: 66 sq. mi./171 sq. km. The main towns are Saint-Pierre and Le Château.

Olin·da |ō'lində| historic city in E Brazil, in Pernambuco state, just N of Recife. Pop. 341,000. A Portuguese colonial capital and longtime cultural center, it also has many nearby beaches.

Ol·ives, Mount of |'awləvz| the highest point in the range of hills to the E of Jerusalem, in the West Bank. It is a holy place for both Judaism and Christianity and is frequently mentioned in the Bible. The Garden of Gethsemane is nearby.

Olo·mouc |'awlawmōts| historic industrial city on the Morava River in N Moravia, in the Czech Republic. Pop. 106,000.

Olon·ga·po |ō,lawNGgə'pō| port city in the Philippines, on central Luzon. Pop. 193,000.

Olsz·tyn |'awlsHtən| city in N Poland, in the lakeland area of Masuria. Pop. 164,000. Founded in 1348 by the Teutonic Knights, it was a part of Prussia between 1772 and 1945. German name **Allenstein**.

Olt River |awlt| river (348 mi./557 km.) in S Romania that rises in the Carpathian Mts. and flows S, meeting the Danube River at Turnu Măgurele.

Ol·te·nia |awl'tēnēə| region of S Romania, the W part of Wallachia.

Olym·pia[1] |ə'limpēə| plain in Greece, in the western Peloponnese. In ancient times it was the site of the chief sanctuary of the god Zeus, the place where the original Olympic Games were held.

Olym·pia[2] |ə'limpēə| the capital of the state of Washington, a port on Puget Sound. Pop. 33,840.

Olym·pic Peninsula |ə'limpik| region of NW Washington, on the Pacific and Juan de Fuca Strait. The Olympic Mts. and Olympic National Park are here.

Olym·pus, Mount[1] |ə'limpəs| mountain in Cyprus, in the Troodos range. Rising to 6,400 ft./1,951 m., it is the highest peak on the island.

Olym·pus, Mount[2] |ə'limpəs| mountain in N Greece, at the E end of the range dividing Thessaly from Macedonia; height 9,570 ft./2,917 m. It was the abode of the gods in Greek mythology.

Olyn·thus |ō'linTHəs| ancient city in NE Greece, on the peninsula of Chalcidice. It

was the head of the Chalcidian League, formed to oppose the hegemony of Athens and Sparta.

Omagh |ō'mä| town in Northern Ireland, principal town of County Tyrone. Pop. 15,000.

Oma·ha |'ōmə,hä| largest city in Nebraska, an industrial and market center in the E, on the Missouri River. Pop. 335,795.

Oma·ha Beach |'ōmə,hä| name used during the D-Day landing in June 1944 for one part of the Norman coast where U.S. troops landed. It is at the mouth of the Vire River, at the village of Saint-Laurent-sur-Mer, NW of Bayeux.

Oman, Gulf of |ō'män| inlet of the Arabian Sea, N of Oman, connected by the Strait of Hormuz to the Persian Gulf.

Oman |ō'män| country at the E corner of the Arabian Peninsula. Area: 82,030 sq. mi./212,458 sq. km. Pop. 1,600,000. Language, Arabic. Capital and largest city: Muscat. The sultanate, a regional power in the 19th century, when it was known as Muscat and Oman, is now an oil producer. □ **Omani** adj. & n.

Oman

Om·dur·man |ˌawmdər'män| city in central Sudan, on the Nile opposite Khartoum. Pop. 229,000. In 1898 it was the site of a battle that marked the final British defeat of local Mahdist forces.

Ome |'ōmā| city in central Japan, on Honshu, W of Tokyo. Pop. 126,000.

O-mei Shan |'ōmā 'sHän| see EMEI SHAN, China.

Omi·ya |ōw'mēyä| city in E central Japan, on E central Honshu, a suburb N of Tokyo. Pop. 404,000.

Omo·lon River |əmə'lawn| river (715 mi./1,150 km.) in E Russia. Rising in the Kolyma Mts., it flows into the Kolyma River.

Omsk |awmsk| industrial city in S central Russia, a port on the Irtysh and Om rivers. Pop. 1,159,000.

Omu·ta |'ōmootä| industrial city in SW Japan, on W Kyushu. Pop. 150,000.

On·do |'awndō| commercial city in SW Nigeria, NE of Lagos, capital of Ondo state. Pop. 150,000.

One·ga, Lake |ə'negə| lake in NW Russia, near the border with Finland, the second-largest (3,710 sq. mi./9,609 sq. km.) European lake, after Lake LADOGA..

Onei·da |ō'nīdə| city in central New York, near Oneida Lake, noted for its silverware industry, a legacy of a 19th-century religious community. Pop. 10,850.

Onit·sha |ō'nēCHə| industrial and commercial city in S Nigeria, a port on the Niger River. Pop. 328,000.

Ono·mi·chi |ōnōmēCHē| city in W Japan, on SW Honshu, W of Okayama. Pop. 97,000. It has noted Buddhist temples.

On·tar·io, Lake |awn'terēō| the smallest and most easterly of the Great Lakes, lying on the U.S.–Canadian border between Ontario and New York State.

On·tar·io[1] |awn'terēō| commercial city in SW California, E of Los Angeles, in an agricultural area. Pop. 133,179.

On·tar·io[2] |awn'terēō| province of E Canada, between Hudson Bay and the Great Lakes. Area: 412,581 sq. mi./1.069 million sq. km. Pop. 9,914,200. Capital and largest city: Toronto. Settled by the French and English in the 17th century, ceded to Britain in 1763, Ontario (formerly Upper Canada) became one of the original four provinces in the Dominion of Canada in 1867. It is agricultural and industrial, and Ottawa and Toronto conduct much of the administration and business of Canada. □ **Ontarian** adj. & n.

Oost·en·de |ō'stendə| Flemish name for OSTEND, Belgium.

OPEC |'ōpek| acronym for the **Organization of Petroleum Exporting Countries**, founded in 1960 and based in Vienna, Austria. Members are Algeria, Gabon, Indonesia, Iran, Iraq, Kuwait, Libya, Nigeria, Qatar, Saudi Arabia, the United Arab Emirates, and Venezuela.

Ophir |'ōfər| country of riches, especially gold and precious stones, mentioned in the Bible. It may have been in the SE Arabian Peninsula, or in E Africa.

Opo·le |aw'pawle| (in German **Oppeln**) industrial port city in S Poland, on the Oder River. Pop. 127,000.

Opor·to |ō'pawrtoo| the principal city and port of N Portugal, near the mouth of the Douro River, famous for port wine. Pop. 311,000. Portuguese name **Porto**.

Ora·dea |aw'rädyä| industrial city in W Romania, near the border with Hungary. Pop. 222,000.

Oradour-sur-Glane |awrə'doorsoorglän| village in W central France, near Limoges, site of a World War II massacre. In June 1944, just after D-day, Nazis murdered the entire populace of approximately 700 persons, with the exception of a few who escaped, and then burned the entire village. The burned remains have been left as a reminder; a new village has developed nearby.

Oral |'awrəl| (former Russian name **Uralsk**) market city in NW Kazakhstan, on the Ural River. Pop. 207,000.

Oran |aw'rän| port on the Mediterranean coast of Algeria, an industrial center and the second-largest Algerian city. Pop. 664,000.

Or·ange[1] |'awrənj| city in SW California, SE of Los Angeles in an agricultural area. Pop. 110,658.

Or·ange[2] |'awrənj| town in S France, on the Rhône, home of the ancestors of the Dutch royal house.

Or·ange County |'awrənj| county in SW California, between Los Angeles and San Diego. Santa Ana, its seat, is one of many cities here. Pop. 2,410,556.

Or·ange Free State |'awrənj 'frē ,stāt| area and former province in central South Africa, to the north of the Orange River. First settled by Boers after the Great Trek, the area became a province of the Union of South Africa in 1910 and in 1994 became one of the new provinces of South Africa. The province was renamed **Free State** in 1995.

Or·ange River |'awrənj| the longest river in South Africa, which rises in the Drakensberg Mts. in NE Lesotho and flows generally W for 1,155 mi./1,859 km. to the Atlantic, forming the border between Namibia and South Africa in its lower course.

Ora·ni·en·burg |aw'ränēənbərg| city in NE Germany, on the Havel River. It was the site of one of the earliest Nazi concentration camps. Pop. 29,000.

Oran·je·stad |aw'ränyəstät| the capital of the Dutch island of Aruba in the Caribbean. Pop. 25,000.

Ora·şul Stalin former name for BRAŞOV, Romania.

Or·du |'awrdoo| (ancient name **Cotyora**) port city in N Turkey, the capital of Ordu province, on the Black Sea. Pop. 102,000.

Or·dzho·ni·kid·ze |,awrjäni'kijə| former

name (1954–93) for VLADIKAVKAZ, Russia.

Öre·bro |awrə'brōō| industrial city in S central Sweden. Pop. 121,000.

Or·e·gon |'awrə,gän; 'awrə,gən| see box. □ **Oregonian** *adj. & n.*

Or·e·gon Trail |'awrə,gän; 'awrə,gən| pioneer route across the W U.S., from Independence, Missouri, to Fort Vancouver in the Willamette Valley of W Oregon Territory, some 2,000 mi./3,000 km. in length. It was used chiefly from 1842–1860 by settlers moving W.

Orekhovo-Zuyevo |,ər'yəкнəvə'zōōyəvə| industrial city in W Russia, E of Moscow, on the Klyazma River. Pop. 137,000.

Orel |aw'rel| historic industrial city in SW Russia, S of Moscow on the Oka and Orlik rivers. Pop. 342,000.

Orem |'ōrəm| city in N central Utah, a suburb of Provo. Pop. 67,561.

Ore Mountains |'aw(ə)r| English name for the ERZGEBIRGE, in Germany and the Czech Republic.

Oren·burg |'ōrən,bərg| industrial and commercial city in S Russia, on the Ural River. Pop. 552,000. It was known as Chkalov from 1938 to 1957.

Oren·se |aw'rensä| city in NW Spain, on the Miño River, in an agricultural region, capital of Orense province. Pop. 106,000.

Oregon

Capital: Salem
Largest city: Portland
Other cities: Eugene, Medford, Portland
Population: 2,842,321 (1990); 3,281,974 (1998); 3,613,000 (2005 proj.)
Population rank (1990): 29
Rank in land area: 9
Abbreviation: OR; Ore., Oreg.
Nickname: Beaver State
Motto: 'The Union'
Bird: Western meadowlark
Fish: chinook salmon
Flower: Oregon grape
Tree: Douglas fir
Song: "Oregon, My Oregon"
Noted physical features: Coos Bay; Marble Hills Caves; Cascade Range and Mount Hood
Tourist attractions: Columbia River Gorge; Crater Lake National Park; Sea Lion Caves
Admission date: February 14, 1859
Order of admission: 33
Name origin: Possibly from a former name of the Columbia River; the exact origin of the name is in dispute.

Øre·sund |'əresən| narrow channel between Sweden and the Danish island of Zealand. It connects the Kattegat (N) with the Baltic Sea. Also called **the Sound**.

Organization of African Unity |,awrgən-ə'zāsHən əv 'æfrəkən 'yōōnədē| (abbreviated **OAU**) organization founded in 1963 for cooperation among independent African states. It now has over 50 members and is headquartered in Addis Ababa, Ethiopia.

Organization of American States |,awr-gənə'zāsHən əv ə'merəkən stāts| (abbreviated **OAS**) organization founded in 1948 to promote political and economic cooperation among states of North America, South America, and the Caribbean. Cuba was denied participation in 1962. Headquarters are in Washington, D.C.

Ori·ent, the |'awrēənt| literary name for countries of E Asia, or of all of Asia. Originally it referred to the Near East. It derives from the Latin term for 'rising' (used of the sun). □ **Oriental** *adj. & n.*

Oril·lia |ō'rilyə| city in S Ontario, on Lake Simcoe N of Toronto. Pop. 25,925.

Ori·no·co |,awrə'nōkō| river in N South America, which rises in SE Venezuela and flows 1,280 mi./2,060 km., entering the Atlantic through a vast delta. For part of its length it forms the border between Colombia and Venezuela.

Oris·sa |aw'risə| state in E India, on the Bay of Bengal. Pop. 31,510,000. Capital: Bhubaneswar.

Ori·za·ba |,ōrē'säbə| commercial and resort city in E central Mexico, in Veracruz state. Pop. 114,000. Nearby is the **Pico de Orizaba**, or CITLALTÉPETL, the highest peak in the country.

Ork·ney Islands |'awrknē| (also **Orkney** or **the Orkneys**) a group of more than 70 islands off the NE tip of Scotland, constituting an administrative region of Scotland. Pop. 19,000; chief town, Kirkwall. Colonized by the Vikings in the 9th century, they came into Scottish possession (together with Shetland) in 1472, having previously been ruled (together with Shetland) by Norway and Denmark.

Or·kon River |'awrkän| (also **Orkhon**) river in N Mongolia, flowing 698 mi./1,123 km. from the N edge of the Gobi Desert until it joins the Selenga River near the Russian border.

Or·lan·do |awr'lændō| city in central Florida. Pop. 164,693. It is a popular tourist destination, situated near the John F. Kennedy Space Center and Disney World.

Or·lé·a·nais |awrlāə'ne| region and former

province of N central France, centered around Orléans.

Orl•é•ans, Île d' |ˌēldawrlä'än| historic residential and resort island in the St. Lawrence River in S Quebec, just NE of Quebec City.

Orl•e•ans |'awrlē(ə)nz| commercial city in central France, on the Loire, capital of Loiret department. Pop. 108,000. In 1429 it was the scene of Joan of Arc's first victory over the English during the Hundred Years War. French name **Orléans**.

Or•ly |'awr'lē| SW suburb of Paris, in N central France, site of an international airport.

Or•moc |awr'mäk| (also called **MacArthur**) commercial port city in the Philippines, on W Leyte. Pop. 129,000. It was a Japanese military base during World War II, until captured by U.S. troops in 1944.

Or•mond Beach |'awrmənd| resort city in NE Florida, N of Daytona Beach. Pop. 29,721.

Orne River |awrn| river (95 mi./152 km.) in NW France, rising in the Orne department and flowing through Calvados, past Caen into the English Channel.

Oro•no |'ōrə,nō| town in E central Maine, on the Penobscot River N of Bangor, home to the University of Maine. Pop. 10,573.

Oron•tes |aw'rawntēz| river in SW Asia that rises near Baalbek in N Lebanon and flows 355 mi./571 km. through W and N Syria before turning W through S Turkey to enter the Mediterranean. It is an important source of water for irrigation, especially in Syria.

Or•re•fors |awrre'fawrs| town in SE Sweden, NW of Kalmar, noted for its crystal and glassware.

Or•sha |'awrsHə| city in NE Belarus. Pop. 112,000. It is a rail and industrial center.

Orsk |awrsk| industrial city in S Russia, in the Urals on the Ural River near the border with Kazakhstan. Pop. 271,000.

Oru•mi•yeh |ōō,rōō'mēyə| (also **Urumiyeh**) 1 shallow salt lake in NW Iran, W of Tabriz. 2 city in NW Iran. Pop. 357,000. According to tradition, the religious leader Zoroaster was born here.

Oru•ro |aw'rōōrō| city in W Bolivia. Pop. 183,000. It is the center of an important mining region.

Or•vie•to |awr'vyätō| town in Umbria, central Italy. Pop. 22,000. It lies at the center of a wine-producing area.

Osage River |ō'säj| river that flows 360 mi./580 km. through Missouri to the Missouri River. The Lake of the Ozarks is along it.

Osa•ka |ō'säkə| port and commercial and industrial city in central Japan, on the island of Honshu, capital of Kinki region. Pop. 2,642,000. It is the third-largest Japanese city.

Osa•sco |ōō'säskōō| city in S Brazil, a suburb W of São Paulo. Pop. 622,000.

Osh |awsH| city in W Kyrgyzstan, near the border with Uzbekistan. Pop. 236,000. It was an important post on an ancient trade route to China and India.

Osh•a•wa |'äsHəwə| city in Ontario, on the shore of Lake Ontario E of Toronto. Pop. 174,010. It is the center of the Canadian automobile industry.

Osh•kosh |'äsHkäsH| industrial city in E central Wisconsin, on L. Winnebago. Pop. 55,006.

Osho•gbo |ō'sHōgbō| commercial and industrial city in SW Nigeria, NE of Ibadan. Pop. 421,000.

Osi•jek |'ōsēyek| industrial city in E Croatia, on the Drava River. Pop. 105,000.

Öskemen |'awskemən| (formerly **Ust-Kamenogosk**) industrial city in NE Kazakhstan, on the Irtysh River. Pop. 330,000.

Os•lo |'äz,lō| the capital, largest city, and chief port of Norway, on the S coast at the head of Oslofjord. Pop. 458,000. Founded in the 11th century, it was known as Christiania (or Kristiania) from 1624 until 1924.

Os•na•brück |äsnəbrōōk| industrial city in NW Germany, in Lower Saxony. Pop. 165,000.

Osor•no |ōs'awrnō| commercial city in S Chile, in the lake resort district. Pop. 117,000. It is home to many descendants of German immigrants.

Os•sa, Mount[1] |'äsə| mountain in Thessaly, NE Greece, south of Mount Olympus, rising to a height of 6,489 ft./1,978 m. In Greek mythology the giants piled Mount Ossa onto Mount Pelion in an attempt to reach Olympus and destroy the gods.

Os•sa, Mount[2] |'äsə| the highest mountain on the island of Tasmania, rising to a height of 5,305 ft./1,617 m.

Os•se•tia |aä'sēsHə| region of the central Caucasus. It is divided by the boundary between Russia and Georgia into two parts, North Ossetia (now Alania) and South Ossetia, and between 1989 and 1992 was the scene of ethnic conflict.

Os•si•ning |'awsəniNG| town in SE New York, on the Hudson River, noted as the home of Sing Sing prison. Pop. 34,124.

Os•tend |ä'stend| port on the North Sea coast of NW Belgium, in West Flanders. Pop. 68,000. It is a major ferry port. Flemish name **Oostende**; French name **Ostende**.

Os•tia |'ästēə| ancient city and harbor that was situated on the W coast of Italy at the mouth of the Tiber River; siltation eventually left it several miles inland. It was the first colony founded by ancient Rome and was a major port and commercial center.

Ostra•va |'awstrəvə| industrial city in the Moravian lowlands of the NE Czech Republic. Pop. 328,000. It is in the coal-mining region of Silesia.

Os•we•go |äs'wēgō| industrial port city in N central New York, on Lake Ontario and the Oswego River. Pop. 19,195.

Ota |'ōtə| industrial city in N central Japan, on central Honshu, NE of Tokyo. Pop. 140,000.

Ota•go |ō'tägō| region of New Zealand, on the SE coast of South Island. Dunedin is the chief setlement.

Ota•ru |ō'tä,rōō| industrial and commercial port city in N Japan, on W Hokkaido. Pop. 163,000.

Otran•to, Strait of |aw'träntō| channel linking the Adriatic Sea with the Ionian Sea and separating the 'heel' of Italy from Albania.

Otsu |'ōtsōō| industrial port city in central Japan, on S Honshu, E of Kyoto. Pop. 260,000.

Ot•ta•wa |'ätə,wä| the federal capital of Canada, in SE Ontario on the Ottawa River. Pop. 313,987. Founded in 1827, it was named Bytown until 1854.

Ot•ta•wa River |'ätə,wä| river that flows 700 mi./1,100 km. through E Canada, forming much of the border between Ontario and Quebec, into the St. Lawrence River.

Ot•ter•burn |'ätər,bərn| village in N England, in Northumberland, scene of a 1388 Scottish victory over the English, celebrated in the ballads "Chevy Chase" and "Otterburn."

Ot•to•man Empire |'ätəmən 'em,pī(ə)r| Muslim empire of the Turks, established in 1299 and finally dissolved in 1922. In the 16th century it dominated the E Mediterranean and much of SE Europe.

Ouach•i•ta Mountains |'wäSHitaw| low range in W Arkansas and E Oklahoma, S of the Ozark Plateau. Magazine Mt., at 2,753 ft./840 m., is the high point in Arkansas.

Ouach•i•ta River |'wäSHitaw| river that flows 600 mi./970 km. across W Arkansas and into N Louisiana, where it is known in part as the Black River and empties into the Red River.

Oua•ga•dou•gou |,wägə'dōōgōō| the capital of Burkina Faso, a commercial and administrative city, formerly capital of the Mossi empire. Pop. 634,000.

Ou•de•naar•de |,awdən'ärdə| town in East Flanders, Belgium, site of a British and Austrian victory over French troops in 1708. Pop. 27,000.

Oudh |awd| (also **Audh** or **Awadh**) region of N India. In 1877 it joined with Agra and in 1902 it formed the United Provinces of Agra and Oudh. This was renamed Uttar Pradesh in 1950.

Oues•sant |we'sän| (also **Ushant**) island 10 mi./16 km. off the coast of Brittany, in NW France. Its lighthouse marks the S entrance to the English Channel.

Oui•dah |'wēdə| (also **Whydah** or **Wida**) port town in S Benin, W of Cotonou on the Gulf of Guinea. Pop. 32,000. In the 17th–19th centuries it was a major slave-exporting center.

Ouj•da |ōō'jdä| (also **Oudjda**) commercial city in NE Morocco, near the Algerian border, in a mining district. Pop. 357,000.

Ou•lu |'aw,lōō| city in central Finland, on the W coast, capital of a province of the same name. Pop. 101,000. Swedish name **Uleåborg**.

Ouro Prê•to |'ōrōō 'prätōō| historic city in E Brazil, in Minas Gerais state. Pop. 62,000. A cultural and former gold rush town, it draws tourists.

Ouse |ōōz| name of several English rivers (especially the **Great Ouse**), which rises in Northamptonshire and flows 160 mi./257 km. E then northward through East Anglia to the Wash near King's Lynn.

Out•back, the |'owt ,bæk| popular name for isolated, sparsely populated, rural areas of Australia.

Out•er Banks |'owtər 'bænks| series of barrier islands on the Atlantic coast in E North Carolina. It is noted for its resorts, and for the older culture of inhabitants called "Bankers."

Out•er Mon•go•lia |'owdər mäNG'gōlēyə| see MONGOLIA.

Ou•tre•mont |'ōōtrə,mänt| residential city in S Quebec, under Mount Royal from downtown Montreal. Pop. 22,935.

Ov•am•bo•land |ō'væmbō,lænd| semiarid region of N Namibia, the homeland of the Ovambo people.

Over•ijs•sel |,ōvər'äsəl| province of the E central Netherlands, N of the IJssel River, on the border with Germany. Pop. 1,026,000. Capital: Zwolle.

Over•land Park |'ōvər,lænd| city in NE

Kansas, a commercial and residential suburb SW of Kansas City. Pop. 111,790.

Ovie•do |aw'vyedō| industrial city in NW Spain, capital of the Asturias region and Oviedo province. Pop. 203,000.

Owa•ton•na |ˌōwə'tänə| commercial city in SE Minnesota, in a dairy farming region. Pop. 19,386.

Owen•do |ō'wendō| village in NW Gabon, on the Gabon River just SE of Libreville, for which it is the deepwater port, and just upstream from the Atlantic.

Ow•ens•boro |'ōwənz,bərō| industrial port city in NW Kentucky, on the Ohio River. Pop. 53,549.

Owen Stan•ley Range |'ōwən 'stænlē| mountains extending SE to NW across New Guinea Island, Papua New Guinea, reaching 13,363 ft./4,073 m. at Mount Victoria.

Owens Valley |'ōwənz| valley of the Owens River, in E central California, between the Sierra Nevada and the Inyo Mts., the source since 1913 of much of the water supply for Los Angeles.

Ox•ford[1] |'äksfərd| industrial and cultural city in central England, on the Thames River, the county seat of Oxfordshire. Pop. 109,000. Oxford University is here.

Ox•ford[2] |'äksfərd| town in N central Mississippi, home to the University of Mississippi and associated with novelist William Faulkner. Pop. 9,984. See also YOKNAPATAWPHA COUNTY.

Ox•ford•shire |'äksfərd,SHi(ə)r| county of S central England. Pop. 554,000; county seat, Oxford.

Ox•nard |'äks,närd| city in SW California, in an agricultural area NW of Los Angeles, on the Pacific coast. Pop. 142,216.

Ox•us |'äksəs| ancient name for the AMU DARYA River.

Ox•y•rhyn•chus |ˌäksə'riNGkəs| archaeological site in NE Egypt, on the Nile River S of El Faiyum, where many important papyri have been recovered. The present-day village of Al-Bahnasa (or Behnesa) is here.

Oya•ma |ō'yä,mä| industrial city in N central Japan, on central Honshu, N of Tokyo. Pop. 148,000.

Oyo |'ōyō| commercial and agricultural city in SW Nigeria, N of Ibadan. Pop. 226,000.

Oys•ter Bay |'oistər| town in central Long Island, New York, containing Hicksville, Farmingdale, Oyster Bay, and other suburban villages. Pop. 292,657.

Oz nickname for AUSTRALIA.

Ozark Mountains |'ō,zärk| (also **the Ozarks**) heavily forested highland plateau dissected by rivers, valleys, and streams, lying between the Missouri and Arkansas rivers and within the states of Missouri, Arkansas, Oklahoma, Kansas, and Illinois. The Ozarks are noted for their rural culture.

Pp

Paarl |pärl| town in SW South Africa, in the province of Western Cape, NE of Cape Town. Pop. 71,000. It is at the center of a noted wine-producing region.

Pa·chu·ca de So·to |pəˈCHo͞okə di ˈsōtō| (officially **Pachuca de Soto**) city in Mexico, capital of the state of Hidalgo. Pop. 179,000.

Pa·cif·i·ca |pəˈsifikə| city in N central California, a suburb just S of San Francisco, on the Pacific. Pop. 37,670.

Pa·cif·ic Crest Trail |pəˈsifik| recreational trail that extends from the Mexican to the Canadian border, through California, Oregon, and Washington, following mountain ridges for 2,600 mi./4,200 km.

Pa·cif·ic Islands, Trust Territory of the |pəˈsifik| United Nations trusteeship established in 1947 under U.S. administration, and dissolved in 1994. It included the Caroline, Marshall, and Mariana islands, today all components of the Marshall Islands, the Northern Mariana Islands, the Federated States of Micronesia, or Palau.

Pa·cif·ic Ocean |pəˈsifik| the largest of the world's oceans, lying between North and South America to the E and Asia and Australasia to the W, and occupying roughly one-third of the surface of the earth. The explorer Magellan named it for its relatively calm weather. See also SOUTH SEA.

Pa·cif·ic Rim |pəˈsifik| the countries and regions bordering the Pacific Ocean, especially the nations of E Asia that experienced rapid economic growth in the 1980s and 1990s.

Pa·dang |ˈpädˌäNG| seaport of Indonesia, the largest city on the W coast of Sumatra. Pop. 481,000.

Pad·ding·ton |ˈpädiNGtən| largely residential district of W central London, England, known for its railroad station, which serves W England and Wales.

Pa·der·born |ˈpädərbawrn| agricultural market and industrial city in Germany, E of Münster. Pop. 126,000. The Holy Roman Empire was born here in a meeting between Charlemagne and Pope Leo III in 799.

Pad·ma |ˈpädmə| river of S Bangladesh, formed by the confluence of the Ganges and the Brahmaputra in the Ganges delta near Rajbari.

Pa·do·va |ˈpädōvə| Italian name for PADUA.

Pad·re Island |ˈpädrä| barrier island in S Texas, on the Gulf of Mexico, noted for its resorts and its wildlife. It is 113 mi./183 km. long.

Pad·ua |ˈpäjo͞oə| historic industrial and commercial city in NE Italy. Pop. 218,000. Italian name **Padova**.

Pa·du·cah |pəˈd(y)o͞okə| historic commercial city in W Kentucky, on the Ohio River near the mouth of the Tennessee River. Pop. 27,256.

Paes·tum |ˈpestəm| ancient city in S Italy, on the Gulf of Salerno. It was founded in the 6th century B.C. by Greek colonists.

Pa·ga·lu |pəˈgälo͞o| former name (1973–79) for ANNOBÓN, Equatorial Guinea.

Pa·gan |ˈpägən| town in Burma, situated on the Irrawaddy SE of Mandalay. It is the site of an ancient city that was the capital of a powerful Buddhist dynasty the 11th–13th centuries.

Pa·go Pa·go |ˌpägō ˈpägō| chief port of American Samoa, on Tutuila Island. Pop. 4,000. Fagatogo, the territorial capital, is just to the E.

Pa·hang |pəˈhæNG| mountainous forested state of Malaysia, on the E coast of the Malay Peninsula. Capital: Kuantan.

Paign·ton |ˈpān(t)ən| resort town in SW England, on the S coast of Devon. Pop. 41,000.

Paint·ed Desert |ˈpäntəd| region of NE Arizona noted for its colorful eroded landscapes.

Pais·ley |ˈpāzlē| town in central Scotland, to the W of Glasgow, administrative center of Renfrewshire. Pop. 75,000. A center of handweaving by the 18th century, it became famous for its distinctive shawls.

Pak·i·stan |ˈpækəˌstæn| republic in the NW of the Indian subcontinent. Area: 310,522 sq. mi./803,943 sq. km. Pop. 115,588,000. Languages, Urdu (official), Punjabi, Sindhi, Pashto. Capital: Islamabad. Largest city: Karachi. Created in 1947 from Indian territory as an Islamic nation, Pakistan lost East Pakistan (as the new Bangladesh) in 1972. Predominantly agricultural, it has growing industry. □ **Pak·istani** adj. & n.

Pak·se |päkˈsä| (also **Pakxe**) largest town in S Laos, on the Mekong River. Pop. 25,000. The 7th-century ruins of the

Pakistan

ancient Khmer capital of Wat Phou lie to the S.

Pa·lat·i·nate |pə'lætnət| name given to two regions of Germany during the Holy Roman Empire: the Rhenish or Lower Palatinate, now part of Rhineland-Palatinate, and the Upper Palatinate, now in NE Bavaria.

Pal·a·tine |'pælə,tīn| village in NE Illinois, a suburb NW of Chicago. Pop. 39,253.

Pa·lau |pə'law| (also called **Belau**) island republic in the W Pacific, in the Caroline Islands. Area: 188 sq. mi./488 sq. km. Pop. 16,400. Capital: Koror (to be replaced by Babelthuap). Held by Spain, Germany, and the U.S. before 1994, the islands have an economy based on fishing and tourism.

Pa·la·wan |pə'lawən| long, narrow, mountainous island in the W Philippines, separating the Sulu Sea from the South China Sea; chief town, Puerto Princesa.

Pale, the |pāl| **1 English Pale** or **Irish Pale** the part of Ireland controlled by the British from the 11th century until the 16th century, when complete control was achieved. **2 Jewish Pale** parts of Poland in which Jews were traditionally allowed to live.

Pa·lem·bang |pälem'bäNG| historic commercial city in Indonesia, in the SE part of the island of Sumatra, a port on the Musi River. Pop. 1,141,000.

Pa·len·cia |pə'lensēə| industrial city in NW Spain, site of the first Spanish university (1208), and capital of Palencia province. Pop. 77,000.

Pa·len·que |pə'leNGkä| site of a former Mayan city in N Chiapas, SE Mexico, SE of present-day Villahermosa. The well-preserved ruins of the city, which existed from about A.D. 300 to 900, include notable examples of Mayan architecture and extensive hieroglyphic texts.

Pa·ler·mo |pə'lər,mō| the capital of the Italian island of Sicily, an industrial port on

the N coast. Pop. 734,000. It was founded by the Phoenicians in the 8th century B.C.

Pal·es·tine |'pælə,stīn| territory in the Middle East on the E coast of the Mediterranean Sea. It has had many changes of frontier and status in the course of history, and contains several places that are sacred to Christians, Jews, and Muslims. In biblical times Palestine comprised Israel and Judah. The land was controlled at various times by the Egyptian, Assyrian, Persian, and Roman empires before being conquered by the Arabs in A.D. 634. It remained in Muslim hands, except for the period during the Crusades (1098–1197), until World War I, being part of the Ottoman Empire from 1516 to 1918. The name Palestine was used as the official political title for the land W of the Jordan mandated to Britain in 1920. In 1948 the state of Israel was established in what was traditionally Palestine, but the name continued to be used in the context of the struggle for territory and political rights of displaced Palestinian Arabs. Agreements from 1993 and subsequently between Israel and the Palestine Liberation Organization gave limited autonomy to the Gaza Strip and the West Bank and set up the Palestine National Authority and a police force. □ **Palestinian** adj. & n.

Pa·les·tri·na |,pælə'strēnə| agricultural market town in central Italy. Pop. 14,000. It is built on the site of a town, Praeneste, that was a summer resort for wealthy residents of ancient Rome.

Pal·ghat |'pälgät| (also **Pulicat; Palakkad**) commercial town in SE India, in Kerala state. Pop. 180,000. It commands a major pass through the Western Ghats.

Pa·li·kir |,pälē'kir| capital of the Federated States of Micronesia, on Pohnpei. It succeeds nearby Kolonia.

Pal·i·sades, the |,pælə'sādz| (also **Palisades of the Hudson**) cliffs that line the W side of the Hudson River, in New Jersey and New York, across from New York City and N to Newburgh, New York.

Palk Strait |pälk| inlet of the Bay of Bengal separating N Sri Lanka from the coast of Tamil Nadu in India. It lies to the N of Adam's Bridge, which separates it from the Gulf of Mannar.

Pall Mall |,päl 'mäl| street in central London, England, in Westminster, N of St. James's Park, noted for its clubs and as a resort of high society. It gave its name to the term *mall*.

Pal·ma |'pälmə| the capital of the Balearic

Islands of Spain, an industrial port and resort on the island of Majorca. Pop. 309,000. Full name **Palma de Mallorca**.

Pal•mas |'pälməs| town in central Brazil, on the Tocantins River, capital of the state of Tocantins. Pop. 6,000.

Palm Bay |pälm| residential city in E central Florida, just SW of Melbourne. Pop. 62,632.

Palm Beach |pälm| fashionable resort town in SE Florida, on a barrier island between the Atlantic and Lake Worth (a lagoon). Pop. 9,814.

Palm•dale |'pälmdāl| city in SW California, a suburb N of Los Angeles, near Edwards Air Force Base. Pop. 68,842.

Pal•mer•ston North |',pä(l)mərstən 'nawrᴛH| commercial city in the SW part of North Island, New Zealand. Pop. 69,000.

Pal•met•to State |päl'metō| nickname for SOUTH CAROLINA.

Pal•mi•ra |'pälmīrə| city in W Colombia, in Valle del Cauca department, an agricultural commerce and research center. Pop. 175,000.

Palm Springs |,pä(l)m 'spriNGz| resort city in the Colorado Desert of S California, E of Los Angeles, noted for its hot mineral springs and affluent lifestyle. Pop. 40,181.

Pal•my•ra[1] |päl'mīrə| town in W New York, SE of Rochester, noted as the early home of Joseph Smith, Mormon church founder. Pop. 7,690.

Pal•my•ra[2] |päl'mīrə| ancient city of Syria, an oasis in the Syrian desert NE of Damascus on the site of present-day Tadmur.

Pal•my•ra Atoll |'pälmīrə| atoll in the central Pacific, part of the Line Islands and formerly part of Hawaii, but excluded at statehood in 1959.

Pa•lo Al•to |'pælō 'æltō| city in W California, S of San Francisco. Pop. 55,900. It is a noted center for electronics and computer technology, and the residential center for nearby Stanford University.

Pal•o•mar, Mount |'pælə,mär| mountain in S California, NE of San Diego, rising to a height of 6,126 ft./1,867 m. It is the site of a noted astronomical observatory.

Pa•los |'pälōs| former seaport in SW Spain. Pop. 7,000. Christopher Columbus sailed from here on his first voyage to the New World, in 1492.

Pa•lu |'pälōō| city in Indonesia, on W Sulawesi. Pop. 299,000.

Pa•mir Mountains |pə'mir| (also **the Pamirs**) mountain system of central Asia, centered in Tajikistan and extending into Kyrgyzstan, Afghanistan, Pakistan, and W China. The highest peak in the Pamirs, Communism Peak in Tajikistan, rises to 24,590 ft./7,495 m.

Pam•li•co Sound |'pæmli,kō| inlet of the Atlantic in E North Carolina, inside the Outer Banks islands. Albemarle Sound is to its N.

Pam•pas |'pämpəz| (also **Pampa**) wide treeless plains of South America, in central Argentina and S Uruguay. Humid and grass-covered, they are used for cattle and grain production.

Pam•phyl•ia |pæm'filyə| ancient coastal region of S Asia Minor, between Lycia and Cilicia, to the E of the modern port of Antalya, Turkey. □ **Pamphylian** adj. & n.

Pam•plo•na |pæm'plōnə| industrial city in N Spain, capital of the former kingdom and modern region of Navarre. Pop. 191,000. It is noted for the fiesta of San Fermin, held in July, which is celebrated with the running of bulls through the streets of the city.

Pa•na•ji |pä'näjē| (also **Panjim**) city in W India, a port on the Arabian Sea. Pop. 85,000. It is the capital of the state of Goa.

Pan•a•ma |'pænə,mä| republic in Central America, in the Isthmus of Panama. Area: 29,773 sq. mi./77,082 sq. km. Pop. 2,329,330. Language, Spanish. Capital and largest city: Panama City. A Spanish colony, Panama became part of Colombia in 1821, and gained independence in 1903. The U.S. controlled the Canal Zone, splitting the country, until 1979. Panama is primarily agricultural, with Canal-based business also important. □ **Panamanian** adj. & n.

Panama

Pan•a•ma, Isthmus of |'pænə,mä| (formerly the **Isthmus of Darien**) in the narrowest sense, the site of the Panama Canal. More broadly, all the territory of Panama, or the entire region connecting North and South America.

Pan•a•ma Canal |'pænə,mä kə'næl| canal

about 50 mi./80 km. long, across the Isthmus of Panama, connecting the Atlantic and Pacific. Its construction, begun by Ferdinand de Lesseps in 1881 but abandoned in 1889, was completed by the U.S. between 1904 and 1914. Control of the canal by the U.S. is due to be ceded to Panama in 1999. The surrounding territory, the (Panama) Canal Zone, was administered by the U.S. until 1979, when it was returned to Panama.

Pan·a·ma City[1] |'pænə,mä| port city in NW Florida, a resort center in the Panhandle. Pop. 34,378.

Pan·a·ma City[2] |'pænə,mä| the capital of Panama, situated on the Pacific coast (the Gulf of Panama) close to the Panama Canal. Pop. 585,000.

Pan-American Highway |,pæn'əmerəkən| road system initiated in the 1920s to link nations of the W hemisphere from Alaska to Chile. Gaps remain in Panama and Colombia. The **Inter-American Highway** is the section from the Texas-Mexico border S to Panama City.

Pan·a·mint Range |'pænəmint| mountain range in E central California, W of Death Valley, noted for its high walls and deep canyons.

Pa·nay |pə'nī| island in the Visayas group, in the central Philippines; chief town, Iloilo.

Pan·chiao |'pæn'CHiow| (also **Pan-ch'iao**; formerly **Pankiao**) city in N Taiwan, a suburb SW of Taipei. Pop. 544,000.

Pan·dhar·pur |'pəndər,poŏr| town in W central India, in Maharashtra state. Pop. 64,000. It is a Hindu pilgrimage site.

Pa·ne·ve·žys |pänyə,və'ZHēz| industrial city in Lithuania, NE of Kaunas. Pop. 132,000.

Pan·gaea |pæn'jēə| name for earth's hypothetical single land mass prior to its separation into distinct continents between 300 and 200 million years ago.

Pan·han·dle |'pæn,hæ(d)əl| popular name for part of any of various U.S. states that projects from its main body. Examples are those of SE Alaska, NW Florida, N Texas, and W Oklahoma.

Pa·ni·ha·ti |pänē'hätē| industrial and commercial city in NE India, in West Bengal state, a suburb N of Calcutta. Pop. 275,000.

Pa·ni·pat |'pänēpət| historic town in NW India, in Haryana state, N of Delhi. Pop. 191,000.

Pan·mun·jom |'pan'moŏn'jawm| village in the demilitarized zone between North and South Korea. It was here that the armistice

ending the Korean War was signed on July 27, 1953. International talks have been held here since.

Pan·no·nia |pə'nōnēə| ancient country of S Europe lying S and W of the Danube, in present-day Austria, Hungary, Slovenia, and Croatia.

Pan·ta·nal |päntä'näl| vast region of tropical swampland in the upper reaches of the Paraguay River in SW Brazil.

Pan·tel·le·ria |,pæn(t)ələ'rēə| volcanic Italian island in the Mediterranean, situated between Sicily and the coast of Tunisia. It was used as a place of exile by the ancient Romans, who called it Cossyra. Pop. 7,000.

Pan·the·on, the |'pænTHē,än| secular temple in Paris, France. Constructed 1759–89 in the classical style, it contains the tombs of many illustrious French writers, including Voltaire and Victor Hugo.

Pa·pal States |'pāpəl ,stāts| the temporal dominions formerly (756–1870) belonging to the Pope, in central Italy. See also VATICAN CITY.

Pa·pe·e·te |,päpä'ātä| the capital of French Polynesia, situated on the NW coast of Tahiti. Pop. 24,000.

Paph·la·go·nia |,pæflə'gōnēə| ancient region of N Asia Minor (present-day Turkey), on the Black Sea coast between Bithynia and Pontus, to the N of Galatia. □ **Paphlagonian** adj. & n.

Pa·phos |'pā,fôs| historic port and resort town in SW Cyprus. Pop. 29,000. According to Greek legend, the goddess Aphrodite was born on the waves near here.

Pap·ua |'päpoŏə| the SE part of the island of New Guinea, now part of the independent state of Papua New Guinea.

Pap·ua New Guinea country in the W Pacific comprising the E half of the island of New Guinea together with some neighboring islands. Area: 178,772 sq. mi./462,840 sq. km. Pop. 3,530,000. Languages, English (official), Tok Pisin, and several hundred Austronesian and Papuan languages.

Papua New Guinea

Capital and largest city: Port Moresby. Formed administratively in 1949, under Australian control, Papua New Guinea gained independence in 1975. It is largely agricultural, with mining also important. □ **Papua New Guinean** *adj. & n.*

Pa•rá |pe'rä| **1** name for the E mouth of the Amazon River, also at the mouth of the To-cantins River, in N Brazil. **2** state in N Brazil, on the Atlantic coast at the delta of the Amazon. Pop. 5,182,000. Capital: Belém. It is a region of dense rainforest.

Pa•ra•cel Islands |,pärə'sel| (also **the Paracels**) group of about 130 small barren coral islands and reefs in the South China Sea to the SE of the Chinese island of Hainan. The islands are claimed by both China and Vietnam.

Paracel Islands

Par•a•dise |'perə,dīs| suburban community in SE Nevada, just S of Las Vegas. Pop. 124,682.

Par•a•guay |'perə,gwī| landlocked republic in central South America. Area: 157,108 sq. mi./406,752 sq. km. Pop. 4,120,000. Languages, Spanish (official), Guarani. Capital and largest city: Asunción. Independent of Spanish rule in 1811, Paraguay has warred with its neighbors in 1865–70 and 1932–35. Ranching, agriculture, and textiles are leading industries. □ **Paraguayan** *adj. & n.*

Par•a•guay River |'perə,gwī| river that

Paraguay

flows 1,584 mi./2,549 km. from the Mato Grosso of W Brazil into Paraguay, and into the Paraná River. It is navigable by larger vessels as far as Concepción.

Pa•ra•í•ba |pärä'ēbä| state of E Brazil, on the Atlantic coast. Pop. 3,201,000. Capital: João Pessoa.

Pa•ra•mar•i•bo |,perə'merə,bō| the capital of Suriname, a port on the Atlantic coast. Pop. 201,000.

Pa•ra•mount |'perə,mownt| city in SW California, a suburb SE of Los Angeles. Pop. 47,669.

Pa•ram•us |pə'ræməs| borough in NE New Jersey, a commercial and residential suburb NE of Paterson. Pop. 25,101.

Pa•ra•ná[1] |'pärä'nä| river port in E Argentina, on the Paraná River. Pop. 276,000.

Pa•ra•ná[2] |,pärä'nä| state of S Brazil, on the Atlantic coast. Pop. 8,443,000. Capital: Curitiba.

Pa•ra•ná[3] |,pärä'nä| river of South America, which rises in SE Brazil and flows some 2,060 mi./3,300 km. S to the Plate River estuary in Argentina. For part of its length it forms the SE border of Paraguay.

Pa•ra•na•guá |'päränäg'wä| port city in SE Brazil, in Paraná state. Pop. 108,000. It is a coffee-exporting center.

Pa•ra•ña•que |,pärə'nyäkä| commercial and residential town in the Philippines, on S Luzon, S of Manila. Pop. 308,000.

Par•bha•ni |'pərbənē| commercial town in central India, in Maharashtra state. Pop. 190,000.

Par•du•bi•ce |'pärdoo,bitsē| industrial city in the N central Czech Republic, on the Elbe River. Pop. 96,000.

Pa•ra•í•ba River |pär'äbə| river that flows 650 mi./1,050 km. across S Brazil, from São Paulo state through Rio de Janeiro state, to the Atlantic at Campos. Its valley is a key agricultural region.

Pa•ri•cu•tin |pä'rēkootēn| volcano in W central Mexico, in Michoacán state, that appeared in 1943 and grew until 1952, burying a village and being studied closely by scientists.

Par•is[1] |'pærəs| the capital of France, on the Seine River. Pop. 2,175,000. Paris was held by the Romans, who called it Lutetia, and from the 5th century by the Franks, and was established as the capital in 987. It was organized into three parts, the Île de la Cité (an island in the Seine), the Right Bank, and the Left Bank, during the reign of Philippe-Auguste (1180–1223). The city's neoclassical architecture dates from modernization in the Napoleonic era; this continued under Napoleon III, when the bridges and boulevards of the modern city were built. Famous landmarks are the Eiffel Tower, the Louvre, and Notre-Dame cathedral. Paris is a world cultural and administrative center. □ **Parisian** adj. & n.

Par·is[2] |'pærəs| commercial city in NE Texas. Pop. 24,699.

Park Avenue |'pärk| commercial and residential street in Manhattan, New York City, regarded as emblematic of worldly success.

Par·kers·burg |'pärkərzbərg| industrial city in NW West Virginia, on the Ohio River. Pop. 33,862.

Park Range |'pärk| range of the Rocky Mts. in S Wyoming and N Colorado, W of the Front Range. It is noted for its resorts.

Par·lia·ment Hill |'pärlə,mənt| locality in Ottawa, Ontario, site of the chief buildings and offices of the government of Canada.

Par·ma[1] |'pärmə| **1** province of N Italy, S of the Po River in Emilia-Romagna. **2** its capital. Pop. 194,000. Founded by the Romans, it became a bishopric in the 9th century A.D. and capital of the duchy of Parma and Piacenza in about 1547.

Par·ma[2] |'pärmə| city in NE Ohio, a residential and industrial suburb S of Cleveland. Pop. 87,876.

Par·na·í·ba |pärnä'ēbä| commercial city in NE Brazil, in N Piauí state, on the Parnaíba River near the Atlantic. Pop. 128,000.

Par·nas·sus, Mount |pär'næsəs| mountain in central Greece, just N of Delphi, rising to a height of 8,064 ft./2,457 m. Held to be sacred by the ancient Greeks, as was the spring of Castalia on its S slopes, it was associated with Apollo and the Muses and regarded as a symbol of poetry. Greek name **Parnassós**. □ **Parnassian** adj. & n.

Pa·ros |'pær,äs| Greek island in the S Aegean, in the Cyclades. It is noted for the translucent white Parian marble that has been quarried here since the 6th century B.C. □ **Parian** adj. & n.

Par·ral |päh'räl| (official name **Hidalgo del Parral**) city in N Mexico, in Chihuahua state, a mining center. Pop. 91,000.

Par·ra·mat·ta |,perə'mätə| city in SE Australia, in New South Wales, an industrial suburb W of Sydney. Pop. 132,000. It is one of the oldest settlements in Australia.

Parsippany–Troy Hills |pär'sēpənētrōi| commercial and residential township in N New Jersey. Pop. 48,478.

Par·the·non |'pärTHə,nän| see the ACROPOLIS, Athens, Greece.

Par·thia |'pärTHēə| ancient Asian kingdom SE of the Caspian Sea. At its height, it ruled an empire that stretched from the Euphrates to the Indus. □ **Parthian** adj. & n.

Pas, The |'pä| commercial town in W Manitoba, on the Saskatchewan River. Pop. 6,166.

Pas·a·de·na[1] |,pæsə'dēnə| industrial city in S California, in the San Gabriel Mts/ NE of Los Angeles. Pop. 131,591. It is the site of the Rose Bowl football stadium.

Pas·a·de·na[2] |,pæsə'dēnə| industrial port city in SE Texas, on the E side of Houston. Pop. 119,363.

Pa·sar·ga·dae |pə'särgə,dē| ruined city of ancient Persia, capital of Cyrus the Great; it was NE of present-day Shiraz, Iran.

Pa·say |'päsī| commercial city in the Philippines, on S Luzon, just S of Manila. Pop. 374,000.

Pas·ca·gou·la |,pæskə'gōōlə| industrial port city in SE Mississippi, a shipbuilding center on the Gulf of Mexico. Pop. 25,899.

Pas de Ca·lais |pädkä'le| **1** department in NW France, on the English Channel. Pop. 1,433,000. The capital is Arras. **2** French name for the **Strait of Dover** (21 mi./34 km. wide), which connects the English Channel and the North Sea.

Pa·sig |'päsig| commercial town in the Philippines, on S Luzon, E of Manila. Pop. 395,000.

Pa·so Ro·bles |,pæsō 'rōbəlz| (official name **El Paso de Robles**) resort and agricultural city in W central California. Pop. 18,583.

Pas·sa·ic |pə'sāik| industrial city in NE New Jersey, on the Passaic River. Pop. 58,041.

Pas·sa·ma·quod·dy Bay |,pæsəmə 'kwädē| (also **Quoddy Bay**) inlet of the Bay of Fundy at the border of Maine and New Brunswick, noted for its powerful tides.

Pas·sau |'päs,ow| town in S Germany at the confluence of the Danube, the Inn, and the Ilz rivers. Pop. 51,000. It has an annual trade fair.

Pass·chen·dae·le |'päsHən,dälə| village in W Belgium. During World War I the British Ypres advance of 1917 was halted here after bloody fighting.

Pas·so Fun·do |'päsōō'fōōndōō| city in S Brazil, in Rio Grande do Sul state. Pop. 147,000. It is the commercial center of an agricultural region.

Pas·to |'pästō| historic commercial city in SW Colombia, the capital of Nariño department, in an agricultural district. Pop. 303,000.

Pat·a·go·nia |,pætə'gōnēə| region of South America, in S Argentina and Chile. Consisting largely of a dry barren plateau, it extends from the Colorado River in central Argentina to the Strait of Magellan and from the Andes to the Atlantic coast. □ **Patagonian** *adj. & n.*

Pa·ta·li·pu·tra |ˌpätäli'pōͅotrə| ancient name for PATNA, India.

Pa·tan |'pätən| town in W India, in Gujarat state, NW of Ahmadabad. Pop. 120,000. It is noted for its Jain temples.

Pat·er·son |'pætərsən| historic industrial city in NE New Jersey, on the Passaic River. It is famed for its silk and other manufactures. Pop. 140,891.

Pa·than·kot |pə'tänkōt| commercial city in W India, in Punjab state Pop. 147,000.

Pa·ti·a·la |ˌpətē'älə| (also **Puttiala**) commercial and industrial city in NW India, in Punjab state. Pop. 269,000.

Pat·mos |'pæt,maws| Greek island in the Aegean Sea, one of the Dodecanese group. It is believed that St. John was living here in exile when he had the visions described in the book of Revelation.

Pat·na |'pətnə| city in NE India, on the Ganges, capital of the state of Bihar. Pop. 917,000. Important in ancient times, it had become deserted by the 7th century but was refounded in 1541 by the Moguls and became a viceregal capital. Former name **Pataliputra**.

Pa·tras |'pätrəs| industrial port in the NW Peloponnese, W Greece, on the Gulf of Patras. Pop. 155,000. Taken by the Turks in the 18th century, it was the site in 1821 of the outbreak of the Greek war of independence. It was finally freed in 1828. Greek name **Pátrai**.

Pat·ta·ya |pə'tīyə| beach resort on the coast of S Thailand, SE of Bangkok.

Pátz·cua·ro |'pätskwärō| city in W central Mexico, in Michoacán state, a commercial and resort center on Lake Pátzcuaro. Pop. 42,000.

Pau |pō| resort and industrial town in the Aquitaine region of SW France, capital of the department of Pyrénées-Atlantique. Pop. 84,000.

Pauil·lac |pō'yäk| commune in the Médoc region of Aquitaine, in SW France, near Bordeaux. Pauillac is noted for its wines and produces some of the greatest red wines in France.

Pa·via |pə'vēə| university city in N Italy, capital of Pavia province. Pop. 80,000.

Pav·lo·dar |pävlä'där| **1** administrative district in NE Kazakhstan. Pop. 957,000. **2** its capital, a city on the Irtysh River. Pop. 337,000.

Paw·tuck·et |pə'təkət| industrial city in NE Rhode Island, on the Blackstone River, NE of Providence, site of pioneering metal and textile plants. Pop. 72,644.

Pays-Bas French name for the LOW COUNTRIES.

Pays Basque |'päz 'bæsk| French name for BASQUE COUNTRY.

Pays de la Loire |päd lä'l wär| region of W France centered on the Loire valley. Nantes is the chief city.

Pa·zar·dzhik |'päzärjēk| spa town and industrial center in central Bulgaria, on the Maritsa River. Pop. 138,000.

Pea·body |'pē,bədē| industrial city in NE Massachusetts. Pop. 47,039.

Peace River |pēs| river that flows 1,194 mi./1,923 km. from N British Columbia into Alberta, to the Slave River. Its valley is noted for grain production.

Peach State |pēCH| nickname for the U.S. state of GEORGIA.

Peak District |'pēk ',distrik(t)| limestone plateau in Derbyshire, N central England, at the S end of the Pennines, rising to 2,088 ft./636 m. at Kinder Scout.

Pearl Harbor |'pərl 'härbər| harbor on the island of Oahu, in Hawaii, the site of American Pacific Fleet headquarters, where a surprise attack on December 7, 1941 by Japanese carrier aircraft inflicted heavy damage and brought the U.S. into World War II.

Pearl River[1] |pərl| river of S China, flowing from Guangzhou (Canton) S to the South China Sea and forming part of the delta of the Xi River. Its lower reaches widen to form the Pearl River estuary, the inlet between Hong Kong and Macao.

Pearl River[2] |pərl| river that flows 485 mi./780 km. across central Mississippi to form part of the border with Louisiana. It empties into the Gulf of Mexico.

Pea·ry Land |'pirē| mountainous region on the Arctic coast of N Greenland.

Peb·ble Beach |'peb(ə)l| resort on the Monterey Peninsula, in W central California, site of a famous golf course.

Peć |peCH| (also **Pech**) market town in SW Serbia, near the Albanian border. Pop. 111,000.

Pe·chen·ga |pə'CHengə| region of NW Russia, lying W of Murmansk on the border with Finland. Formerly part of Finland, it was ceded to the Soviet Union in 1940. It was known by its Finnish name, Petsamo, from 1920 until 1944.

Pe·cho·ra |pə'CHawrə| river of N Russia,

which rises in Urals and flows some 1,125 mi./1,800 km. N and E to the Barents Sea.

Pe·con·ic Bay |pə'känik| inlet of the Atlantic Ocean in the East End of Long Island, New York, separating the North Fork and South Fork of the island.

Pe·cos River |'pā͵kōs| river that flows 925 mi./1,490 km. from N New Mexico through W Texas, to the Rio Grande.

Pécs |pāCH| industrial city in SW Hungary. Pop. 172,000, formerly the capital of the S part of the Roman province of Pannonia.

Pee Dee River |'pē͵dē| river that flows 230 mi./370 km. through North Carolina and South Carolina, to an inlet on the Atlantic S of the Grand Strand.

Peeks·kill |'pēkskil| commercial city in SE New York, on the Hudson River. Pop. 19,536.

Pee·ne·mun·de |͵pēnə'mo͞ondə| village in NE Germany, on a small island just off the Baltic coast. During World War II it was the chief site of German rocket research and testing.

Pe·gu |pe'go͞o| city and river port of S Burma, on the Pegu River NE of Rangoon. Pop. 150,000. Founded in 825 as the capital of the Mon kingdom, it is a center of Buddhist culture.

Pei-ching variant spelling of BEIJING, China.

Pei·ping former name for BEIJING, China.

Pei·pus, Lake |'pīpəs| (also called **Lake Chudo**) lake in E Estonia, on the Russian border. It drains into the Narva River.

Pe·ka·long·an |pəkä'lawngən| (also **Pecalongan**) industrial and commercial city in Indonesia, on N Java. Pop. 243,000.

Pe·kan·ba·ru |pe'känbäro͞o| (also **Pakanbaru**) port and oil town in Indonesia, on central Sumatra. Pop. 399,000.

Pe·king (also **Pekin**) former spelling of BEIJING, China.

Pe·la·gi Islands |pe'läjē| (also **Pelagian;** Italian name **Isole Pelagie**) three islands in the Mediterranean Sea, S of Sicily and held by Italy: Lampedusa, Linosa, and Lampione.

Pe·lée, Mount |pə'lā| volcano on the island of Martinique, in the Caribbean. Its eruption in 1902 destroyed the island's then capital St. Pierre, killing its population of some 30,000.

Pe·le·lieu |͵pālə'lēo͞o| island in S Palau, in the W Pacific, noted for the fierce battle fought here between Japanese and American forces in 1944.

Pe·li·on |'pēlēən| wooded mountain in Greece, near the coast of SE Thessaly, rising to 5,079 ft./1,548 m. It was held in Greek mythology to be the home of the centaurs, and the giants were said to have piled Pelion onto Mount Ossa in their attempt to reach heaven and destroy the gods.

Pel·la |'pelə| ancient capital of Greek Macedonia, the birthplace of Alexander the Great in 356 B.C.

Pel·ly Mountains |'pelē| range in the S central Yukon Territory. The **Pelly River** flows N of the range to the Yukon River.

Pel·o·pon·nese |͵peləpə'nēsəs| (**the Peloponnese;** also **Peloponnesus**) the mountainous S peninsula of Greece, connected to central Greece by the Isthmus of Corinth. Greek name **Pelopónnisos**.

Pe·lo·tas |pe'lōtæs| city in S Brazil, in Rio Grande do Sul state, a canal port and beef industry center. Pop. 277,000.

Pem·ba¹ |'pembə| seaport in N Mozambique, on the Indian Ocean. Pop. 41,000. Formerly **Porto Amelia**.

Pem·ba² |'pembə| island off the coast of Tanzania, in the W Indian Ocean N of Zanzibar, noted for clove production.

Pem·broke |'pem͵brōk| port in SW Wales, in Pembrokeshire. Pop. 16,000. It was a Norman stronghold from the 11th century, and was long a naval dockyard center. Welsh name **Penfro**.

Pem·broke Pines |'pembrōk| city in SE Florida, a residential suburb NW of Miami. Pop. 65,452.

Pem·broke·shire |'pəmbro͞oksHər| county of SW Wales; administrative center, Haverfordwest. It was part of Dyfed from 1974 to 1996.

Pe·nang |pə'næNG| (also **Pinang**) **1** island of Malaysia, situated off the W coast of the Malay Peninsula. In 1786 it was ceded to the East India Company as a British colony. Known as Prince of Wales Island until 1867, it united with Malacca and Singapore in a union of 1826, which in 1867 became the British colony called the Straits Settlements. It joined the federation of Malaya in 1948. **2** a state of Malaysia, consisting of this island and a coastal strip on the mainland. Capital: George Town (also called Penang, on Penang island). The mainland strip was united with the island in 1798 as part of the British colony.

Pen·de·li·kón Mountain |͵pendelē'kōn| mountain in E central Greece, NE of Athens. Height: 3,639 ft./1,109 m.

Pend Oreille, Lake |pändə'rā| lake in N Idaho, noted for its trout fishing. The **Pend Oreille River** flows from its N end into

Washington and British Columbia, to the Columbia River.

Pen·in·su·la, the |pə'nins(ə)lə| the Iberian Peninsula in SW Europe, comprising Spain and Portugal. A phase of the Napoleonic Wars was fought here, in which the combined forces of Spain, Portugal, and Britain successfully repulsed the French.

Pen·nine Hills |'pen,īn| (also **Pennine Chain** or **the Pennines**) range of hills in N England, extending from the Scottish border S to the Peak District in Derbyshire. Its highest peak is Cross Fell in Cumbria, which rises to 2,930 ft./893 m.

Penn·syl·vania |,pensəl'vānyə| see box. □ **Pennsylvanian** *adj. & n.*

Penn·syl·vania Avenue |,pensəl'vānyə| street in Washington, D.C. along whose route are the White House (at number 1600) and Capitol Hill.

Penn·syl·vania Dutch Country |,pensəl-

Pennsylvania

Official name: Commonwealth of Pennsylvania
Capital: Harrisburg
Largest city: Philadelphia
Other cities: Allentown, Bethlehem, Erie, Hershey, Pittsburgh, Scranton
Population: 11,881,643 (1990); 12,001,451 (1998); 12,281,000 (2005 proj.)
Population rank (1990): 5
Rank in land area: 33
Abbreviation: PA; Pa., Penn., Penna.
Nickname: Keystone State; Quaker State
Motto: 'Virtue, Liberty, and Independence'
Bird: ruffed grouse
Fish: brook trout
Flower: mountain laurel
Tree: eastern hemlock
Noted physical features: Appalachian Mountains; Allegheny Front and Allegheny Mountains; Great Valley; Piedmont Plateau; Pocono Mountains
Tourist attractions: Gettysburg Battle Site; Philadelphia: Liberty Bell, Independence Hall; Valley Forge
Admission date: December 2, 1787
Order of admission: 2
Name origin: Named in 1681 in charter for the land granted by Charles II of England, to honor Admiral Sir William Penn (1621-70), father of William Penn (1644-1718), who received the royal charter and was the founder of Pennsylvania.

'vānyə| popular name, from a corruption of *Deutsch*, for areas in E Pennsylvania settled and dominated by Germans. Lancaster is often considered the chief city.

Pe·nob·scot River |pə'näbskät| river that flows 350 mi./560 km. through central Maine, into Penobscot Bay on the Atlantic. Bangor lies on it, and its upper reaches are lumbering and recreational areas.

Pen·rith |'penriTH| city in SE Australia, in New South Wales, a suburb W of Sydney. Pop. 150,000.

Pen·sa·cola |,pensə'kōlə| industrial and port city in NW Florida, in the Panhandle near the Alabama line. It is a naval center. Pop. 58,165.

Pen·ta·gon, the |'pen(t)ə,gän| building in Arlington County, N Virginia, across the Potomac River from Washington, D.C. It is home to the U.S. Defense Department.

Pent·land Firth |'pentlənd firTH| channel separating the Orkney Islands from the N tip of mainland Scotland. It links the North Sea with the Atlantic.

Pen·za |'penzə| city in S central Russia. Pop. 548,000. Situated on the Sura River, a tributary of the Volga, it is an industrial and transportation center.

Pen·zance |pen'zæns| resort and port town in SW England, on the S coast of Cornwall near Land's End. Pop. 20,000.

People's Republic of China |'pēpəlz rē 'pəblik| official name (since 1949) of CHINA.

Pe·o·ria |pē'ōrēə| river port and industrial city in central Illinois, on the Illinois River. Pop. 113,504. The city developed around a fort built by the French in 1680.

Pe·rak |'perək| state of Malaysia, on the W side of the Malay Peninsula. Capital: Ipoh. It is a major tin-mining center.

Perche |persH| former province in N France. Its territory is now divided among the Orne, Eure-et-Loir, and Eure departments. Its capitals were Nogent-le-Rotrou and Mortagne. The breed of draft horses known as Percherons came from Perche.

Pe·rei·ra |pə'rārə| commercial city in W central Colombia, capital of Risaralda department, in the agricultural Cauca River valley. Pop. 336,000.

Père Lachaise |perlä'sHeyz| cemetery in BELLEVILLE¹, in Paris, France, resting place for many French and other notables.

Per·ga·mum |'pərgəməm| city in ancient Mysia, in W Asia Minor (present-day W Turkey), to the N of Izmir on a rocky hill close to the Aegean coast. The capital in the 3rd and 2nd centuries B.C. of the Attalid dynasty, it was one of the greatest of the Hellenistic cities and was famed for its cultural institutions, especially its library, which was second only to that at Alexandria. □ **Pergamene** *adj. & n.*

Pé·ri·gord |pārē'gawr| area of SW France, in the SW Massif Central. It became a part of Navarre in 1470, and of France in 1670.

Pe·ri·gueux |pārē'gœ| commercial city, capital of the Dordogne department in SW France. Pop. 33,000. It is particularly famous for its foods, especially its pâtes.

Per·lis |'pərləs| the smallest state of Malaysia and the most northerly of those on the Malay Peninsula. Pop. 188,000. Capital: Kangar.

Perm |pərm| industrial city in Russia, in the W foothills of the Ural Mts. Pop. 1,094,000. Former name (1940–57) **Molotov.**

Per·mi·an Basin |'pərmēən| region of W Texas, a major oil and gas source in which the cities of Midland and Odessa are production centers.

Per·nam·bu·co |,pernəm'bōō,kōō| state of E Brazil, on the Atlantic coast. Pop. 7,123,000. Capital: Recife (also formerly called Pernambuco).

Per·nik |'pernik| industrial city in W Bulgaria, in a coal-mining region. Pop. 121,000.

Per·pi·gnan |pārpēn'yän| city in S France, in the NE foothills of the Pyrenees, close to the border with Spain. Pop. 108,000. A former fortress town, it was the capital of the old province of Roussillon.

Per·rier |,perē'yā| spring at Vergèze, S France, SW of Nîmes. Its name is given to the effervescent water that is bottled and sold commercially.

Per·sep·o·lis |pər'sepələs| city in ancient Persia, to the NE of present-day Shiraz. It was founded in the late 6th century B.C. by Darius I as the ceremonial capital of Persia under the Achaemenid dynasty. The city is noted for ruins including functional and ceremonial buildings and cuneiform inscriptions in Old Persian, Elamite, and Akkadian.

Per·sia |'pərzhə| former country of SW Asia, now called Iran. The ancient kingdom of Persia, corresponding to the modern district of Fars in SW Iran, became in the 6th century B.C. the domain of the Achaemenid dynasty. Under Cyrus the Great in the 6th century B.C. Persia became the center of a powerful empire that included all of W Asia, Egypt, and parts of E Europe; the empire, defied by the Greeks in the Persian Wars of the 5th century B.C., was eventually overthrown by Alexander the Great in 330 B.C. The country was subsequently ruled by a succession of dynasties until it was conquered by the Muslim Arabs between A.D. 633 and 651. Taken by the Mongols in the 13th century, Persia was ruled by the Kajar dynasty from 1794 until 1925, when Reza Khan Pahlavi became shah. It was renamed Iran in 1935. □ **Persian** *adj. & n.*

Per·sian Gulf |,pərzhən 'gəlf| arm of the Arabian Sea, to which it is connected by the Strait of Hormuz and the Gulf of Oman. It extends NW between the Arabian Peninsula and the coast of SW Iran. Also called **Arabian Gulf**; informally **the Gulf.**

Per·sian Gulf States |,pərzhən 'gəlf| see GULF STATES.

Perth¹ |pərth| the capital of the state of Western Australia, on the Indian Ocean. Pop. 1,019,000 (including the port of Fremantle). Founded by the British in 1829, it developed rapidly after the discovery in 1890 of nearby gold.

Perth² |pərth| town in E Scotland, at the head of the Tay estuary. Pop. 41,000. The administrative center of Perth and Kinross region, it was the capital of Scotland from 1210 until 1452.

Perth Am·boy |'pərth 'æm,boi| historic industrial city in NE New Jersey, on the Raritan River and across the Arthur Kill from Staten Island, New York. Pop. 41,967.

Perth·shire |'pərthshīr; 'pərthshər| former county of central Scotland. It became a part of Tayside region in 1975 and of Perth and Kinross in 1996.

Pe·ru¹ |pə'rōō| commercial city in N central Indiana, on the Wabash River. Pop. 12,843.

Pe·ru² |pə'rōō| republic in South America, on the Pacific coast, traversed throughout its length by the Andes. Area: 496,414 sq. mi./1.28 million sq. km. Pop. 22,048,000. Official languages, Spanish and Quechua. Capital and largest city: Lima. The center

Peru

of the Inca empire, Peru was controlled by Spain 1532–1824. Its economy relies chiefly on agriculture, mining, and fishing. □ **Peruvian** *adj. & n.*

Pe·ru·gia |pə'roōjə| historic university city in central Italy, the capital of Umbria. Pop. 151,000. It flourished in the 15th century as a center of the Umbrian school of painting. A papal possession from 1540, it became a part of united Italy in 1860.

Pe·ru·vi·an Current |pə'roōvēən| cold ocean current that moves N from the S Pacific along the coast of Chile and Peru before turning W into the South Equatorial Current.

Per·vo·uralsk |pirvə'rälsk| city in central Russia, near Yekaterinburg. Pop. 129,000.

Pe·sa·ro |'pāzärō| port and resort town on the Foglia River in E central Italy, in the Marche district and capital of Pesaro province. Pop. 90,000.

Pes·ca·do·res |,peskə'dōrēz| (Chinese name **P'eng-hu Ch'ün-tao**) group of 64 small Taiwanese islands in the Taiwan Strait, between Taiwan and China. Pop. 120,000. The largest and most populous island is Penghu.

Pe·sca·ra |pes'kärä| tourist resort and seaport in E central Italy, on the Pescara River, capital of Pescara province. Pop. 129,000.

Pe·sha·war |pə'sHäwər| the capital of North-West Frontier Province, in Pakistan. Pop. 555,000. Mentioned in early Sanskrit literature, it is one of Pakistan's oldest cities. Under Sikh rule from 1834, it was occupied by the British between 1849 and 1947. Situated near the Khyber Pass on the border with Afghanistan, it is of strategic and military importance.

Pest |pest| **1** county in central Hungary. Pop. 954,000. Its capital is Budapest. **2** town on the W bank of the Danube River, since 1873 a component, with the town of Buda, of Budapest.

Pe·tach Tik·va |'petək 'tikvə| (also **Petah Tikva; Petah Tiqwa**) industrial city in W central Israel, E of Tel Aviv. Pop. 152,000. It was founded in the late 19th century as one of the first modern agricultural Jewish settlements in Palestine.

Pe·ta·ling Ja·ya |pə'täliNG 'jīə| industrial city in SW Malaysia, SW of Kuala Lumpur. Pop. 208,000.

Pet·a·lu·ma |,petəl'oōmə| city in NW California, a suburb and poultry-producing center N of San Francisco. Pop. 43,184.

Pe·ta·re |pe'tärä| city in N Venezuela, a suburb E of Caracas. Pop. 338,000.

Pe·ter·bor·ough[1] |'pētər,bərə| industrial

city in E central England, formerly in Cambridgeshire. Pop. 149,000. An old city with a 12th-century cathedral, it has been developed as a planned urban center since the late 1960s.

Pe·ter·bor·ough[2] |'pētər,bərō| city in E Ontario, on the Trent Canal E of Toronto. Pop. 68,371.

Pe·ters·burg |'pēdərz,bərg| industrial and commercial city in SE Virginia, S of Richmond, scene of heavy fighting in the Civil War. Pop. 38,386.

Pe·tra |'petrə| ancient city of SW Asia, in present-day Jordan. The city, which lies in a hollow surrounded by cliffs, is accessible only through narrow gorges. Its extensive ruins include temples and tombs hewn from "rose-red" sandstone cliffs.

Pet·ri·fied Forest |'petrəfīd| highland area of E central Arizona, noted for its agates and plant fossils. It is now a national park.

Pet·ro·dvo·rets |pitrədvä'ryets| (formerly **Leninsk**; earlier, **Peterhof**) port and resort city in W Russia, on the S bank of Neva River. Pop. 81,000. The Peterhof, the Tsarist summer palace, is here.

Pet·ro·grad |'petrə,gräd| former name (1914–24) for St. Petersburg, Russia.

Pe·tro·li·na |petrō'lēnä| city in E central Brazil, in Pernambuco state, a port on the São Francisco River, across from Juàzeiro, Bahia. Pop. 175,000.

Pet·ro·pav·lovsk[1] |,petrə'pæv,lawfsk| (also **Petropavl**) industrial and commercial city in N Kazakhstan, on the Trans-Siberian Railroad. Pop. 248,000.

Pet·ro·pav·lovsk[2] |,petrə'pævlawfsk| Russian fishing port and naval base on the E coast of the Kamchatka Peninsula in E Siberia. Pop. 245,000. Full name **Petropavlovsk-Kamchatsky**.

Pe·tró·po·lis |pə'träpələs| historic resort city in SE Brazil, in hills N of Rio de Janeiro. Pop. 294,000. It was the longtime summer capital of the emperor of Brazil.

Pet·ro·za·vodsk |,petrəsə'vätsk| city in NW Russia, on Lake Onega, capital of the republic of Karelia. Pop. 252,000.

Pet·sa·mo |'petsə,mō| former Finnish name (1920–44) for Pechenga, Russia.

Pforz·heim |'fawrts,(h)īm| city in SW Germany, on the edge of the Black Forest. Pop. 116,000. It was an important medieval trade center and is now the center of Germany's jewelry and watch-making industries.

Phan Thiet |'pän 'tyet| port city in southern Vietnam, E of Ho Chi Minh City. Pop. 151,000.

Pha·ros |'fe,raws| peninsula, formerly an island, in Alexandria, Egypt, site of a lighthouse built in the 3rd century B.C. that was one of the Seven Wonders of the Ancient World. An earthquake destroyed it in the 14th century.

Pharr |fär| city in S Texas, in the agricultural Rio Grande valley. Pop. 32,921.

Phar·sa·lus |fär'sāləs| town in E central Greece; nearby, on the Pharsalian Plain, Julius Caesar decisively defeated Pompey the Great in 48 B.C.

Phil·a·del·phia |ˌfilə'delfēə| the chief city of Pennsylvania, an industrial port on the Delaware River. Pop. 1,585,577. Established as a Quaker colony by William Penn and others in 1681, it was the site in 1776 of the signing of the Declaration of Independence and in 1787 of the adoption of the Constitution of the United States, and was now the second largest city on the E coast, and a major commercial and cultural center. □ **Philadelphian** adj. & n.

Phil·ip·pi |fə'lipē| city in ancient Macedonia, the scene in 42 B.C. of two battles in which Mark Antony and Octavian defeated Brutus and Cassius, the assassins of Julius Caesar. Its ruins lie close to the Aegean coast in NE Greece, near the port of Kaválla (ancient Neapolis). Greek name **Fílippoi.**

Phil·ip·pines |ˌfilə'pēnz| republic in SE Asia consisting of an archipelago of over 7,000 islands separated from the Asian mainland by the South China Sea. Area: 115,875 sq. mi./300,000 sq. km. Pop. 60,685,000. Official languages, Pilipino (Tagalog) and English. Capital and largest city: Manila. Controlled by Spain 1565–1898, the islands were then held by the U.S. until 1946. Their economy is based on agriculture, mining, timbering, and various manufactures. □ **Philippine** adj. **Filipino** adj. & n.

Phil·ip·pine Sea | ˌfilə'pēn| section of the

Philippines

W Pacific on the E of the Philippine Islands, and extending N to Japan. During World War II several major battles, including that at LEYTE GULF, were fought here.

Phil·ip·pop·o·lis |fili'päpōlis| ancient Greek name for PLOVDIV, Bulgaria.

Phi·lis·tia |fə'listēə| ancient land of the Philistines, a seafaring people who in biblical times occupied the coast of Palestine. Their chief cities were Gaza, Ashkelon, Ashdod, Gath, and Ekron. After defeat by the Israelites around 1000 B.C., Philistia declined.

Phnom Penh |pə'nawm 'pen| the capital of Cambodia, a port at the junction of the Mekong and Tonlé Sap rivers. Pop. 920,000. It became the capital of a Khmer kingdom in the mid-15th century. Between 1975 and 1979 the Khmer Rouge forced a great many of its population (then 2.5 million) to leave the city and resettle in the country.

Pho·caea |fō'sēə| ancient city of Asia Minor, in present-day NW Turkey, on the Aegean Sea on the site of Foça. It was a maritime power from about 3,000 to about 2,500 years ago.

Pho·cis |'fōsəs| ancient district in central Greece, N of the Gulf of Corinth, that included the site of the Delphic oracle, as well as Mount Parnassus.

Phoe·ni·cia |fə'niSHə| ancient country on the shores of the E Mediterranean, corresponding to modern Lebanon and the coastal plains of Syria. It consisted of a number of city-states, including Tyre and Sidon, and was a flourishing center of Mediterranean trade and colonization during the early part of the 1st millennium B.C. □ **Phoenician** adj. & n.

Phoe·nix |'fēniks| industrial and commercial city, the state capital of Arizona. Pop. 983,403. Its dry climate makes it a popular winter resort and retirement location.

Phoe·nix Islands |'fēniks| group of eight islands lying just S of the equator in the W Pacific. They form a part of Kiribati.

Phoe·nix Park |'fēniks| public park in Dublin, Ireland, W of the city center, along the Liffey River, associated with literary figures as well as with sensational 1882 political murders.

Phryg·ia |'frijēə| ancient region of W central Asia Minor (present-day Turkey) to the S of Bithynia. Centered on the city of Gordium, it dominated Asia Minor after the decline of the Hittites in the 12th century B.C., reaching the peak of its power in the 8th century under King Midas. It was eventually absorbed into the kingdom of Lydia in the 6th century B.C. □ **Phrygian** *adj. & n.*

Phu·ket |ˌpo͞o'ket| **1** an island of Thailand, situated at the head of the Strait of Malacca off the W coast of the Malay Peninsula. **2** a port at the S end of Phuket island, a major resort center and outlet for the Indian Ocean. Pop. 24,000.

Pia·cen·za |pyä'CHen(t)sə| commune in N Italy, on the Po River, SE of Milan, capital of Piacenza province. Pop. 103,000. It is an agricultural and industrial center.

Piatra-Neamţ |ˈpyäträ'nyäms| industrial city in NE Romania. Pop. 116,000.

Piauí |ˈpyawē| state of NE Brazil, on the Atlantic coast. Pop. 2,581,000. Capital: Teresina.

Pic·ar·dy |ˈpikərdē| region and former province of N France, centered on the city of Amiens. It was the scene of heavy fighting in World War I. French name **Picardie**.

Pic·cadilly |ˌ'pikə,dilē| street in central London, England, extending from Hyde Park E to Piccadilly Circus, noted for its fashionable shops, hotels, and restaurants.

Pic du Mi·di |pēk do͞o 'mēdē| (also **Pic du Midi de Bigorre**) mountain peak (9,409 ft./2,868 m.) in the W central Pyrenees, in SW France.

Pick·er·ing |ˈpik(ə)riNG| town in S Ontario, NE of Toronto on Lake Ontario, site of a major nuclear power development. Pop. 68,631.

Pi·co da Ne·bli·na |ˈpēko dä 'nəblēnä| mountain in NW Brazil, close to the border with Venezuela. Rising to 9,888 ft./3,014 m., it is the highest peak in Brazil.

Pi·co de Ane·to |ˈpēko dä ä'netō| highest peak in the Pyrenees, in N Spain. Height: 11,168 ft./3,404 m.

Pi·co de Ori·za·ba |ˈpēko dä ōrē'zäbä| another name for CITLALTÉPETL, Mexico.

Pi·co Ri·ve·ra |ˌpēko ri'verə| city in SW California, an industrial suburb E of Los Angeles. Pop. 59,177.

Pied·mont[1] |ˈpēd,mänt| region of NW Italy, in the foothills of the Alps. Capital: Turin. Dominated by Savoy from 1400, it became a part of the kingdom of Sardinia in 1720. It was the center of the movement for a united Italy in the 19th century. Italian name **Piemonte**. □ **Piedmontese** *n. & adj.*

Pied·mont[2] |ˈpēd,mänt| in the U.S., highland areas between the Appalachian Mts. and the Atlantic coast. The Piedmont ends at the Fall Line, where rivers drop to the coastal plain.

Pi·e·ria |pī'irēä| in ancient Greece, the name for a plain in Macedonia where the Muses were born. □ **Pierian** *adj.*

Pierre |pē'e(ə)r| the capital of South Dakota, a commercial city on the Missouri River. Pop. 12,906.

Pie·tar·saa·ri |ˈpyetär,säri| industrial and port city in W Finland, on the Gulf of Bothnia. Pop. 20,000.

Pie·ter·mar·itz·burg |ˌpētər'merəts,bərg| industrial city in E South Africa, the capital of KwaZulu/Natal. Pop. 229,000.

Pie·ters·burg |ˈpētərz,bərg| town in N South Africa, the capital of Northern Province. Pop. 55,000. In 1994 it took the official name Polokwane.

Pi·galle |pi'gäl| area of Paris, France, on the Right Bank, near Montmartre. The Place Pigalle is noted for its disreputable bars and nightspots.

Pig Island |pig| nickname for New Zealand, said to be so named because of the pigs left here by Captain Cook.

Pigs, Bay of |ˈpigz| bay on the SW coast of Cuba, scene of an unsuccessful attempt in 1961 by U.S.-backed Cuban exiles to invade the country and overthrow the regime of Fidel Castro.

Pikes Peak |ˈpīks| mountain in the Front Range of the S Rocky Mts., near Colorado Springs, Colorado. At 14,110 ft./4,300 m., it has long been a guide for travelers on the plains.

Pik Po·be·dy |ˈpēk pä'byedē| mountain in E Kyrgyzstan, close to the border with China. Rising to a height of 24,406 ft./7,439 m., it is the highest peak in the Tien Shan range.

Pil·co·ma·yo River |ˌpilkə'mäyō| river that flows 1,000 mi./1,600 km. from the Andes of W Bolivia, along the Argentina-Paraguay border, and joins the Paraguay River at Asunción, Paraguay.

Pillars of Her·cu·les |ˈhərkyəlēz| two promontories at the E end of the Strait of Gibraltar. Calpe is today known as the Rock of Gibraltar. Abyla is either Mount Acho or the Jebel Musa, in Morocco. Said to have been pushed into place by Hercules, the Pillars were long thought of as the end of the known world.

Pil·sen |ˈpilzən| industrial city in the W part of the Czech Republic. Pop. 173,000. It is noted for the production of lager (pilsener) beer. Czech name **Plzeň**.

Pilt·down |ˈpilt,down| hamlet in SE England, in East Sussex, scene of the 1912 "discovery" of Piltdown Man, shown in the 1950s to be a hoax.

Pim·li·co¹ |'pimli,kō| residential district in central London, England, N of the River Thames in Westminster, adjacent to Belgravia.

Pim·li·co² |'pimli,kō| neighborhood in NW Baltimore, Maryland, site of a famous horseracing track, home to the Preakness.

Pi·nar del Rio |pē'när del 'rēō| city in W Cuba, capital of Pinar del Rio province. Pop. 101,000. It is a tobacco industry center.

Pi·na·tu·bo, Mount |,pinə'tōōbō| volcano on the island of Luzon, in the Philippines. It erupted in 1991, killing more than 300 people and destroying the homes of more than 200,000.

Pin·dus Mountains |'pindəs| range of mountains in W central Greece, stretching from the border with Albania S to the Gulf of Corinth. The highest peak is Mount Smolikas, which rises to 8,136 ft./2,637 m. Greek name **Píndhos**.

Pine Barrens |'pīn| region of S New Jersey, lightly populated and characterized by sandy soils, stunted conifer forests, and numerous small rivers.

Pine Bluff |'pīn| industrial city in SE Arkansas, on the Arkansas River, site of a large arsenal. Pop. 57,140.

Pine Ridge |'pīn| village in SW South Dakota, headquarters for the Pine Ridge Indian Reservation. Pop. 2,596.

Pines, Isle of¹ |'pīnz| see JUVENTUD, ISLA DE LA, Cuba.

Pines, Isle of² |'pīnz| (French name **Île des Pins**) island in the S Pacific, off SE New Caledonia, long a French penal colony, now a resort.

Ping·ding·shan |'ping'ding'sHæn| city in Henan province, E central China, S of Zhengzhou. Pop. 843,000.

Ping·tung |'ping'dəng| (also **P'ing-tung**) city, SW Taiwan, E of Kaohsiung. Pop. 213,000. It is an industrial and food-processing center in an agricultural region.

Ping·xiang |'ping'siǎng| city in Jiangxi province, SE China, in the foothills of the Luoxiao Shan range, SE of Changsha. Pop. 1,305,000.

Pink·ham Notch |'piNGkəm| valley in the White Mts. of N New Hampshire, just E of the Presidential Range. It is a recreational center.

Pinsk |'pinsk| city, a shipping and manufacturing center, in SW Belarus. Pop. 122,000.

Pi·ra·ci·ca·ba |pērăsē'käbä| city in SE Brazil, in São Paulo state. Pop. 303,000. In an agricultural region. It is a processing and academic center.

Pi·rae·us |pī'rāəs| the chief port of Athens, Greece, situated on the Saronic Gulf 5 mi./8 km. SW of the city. Pop. 183,000. Greek name **Piraiévs** or **Piraiéus**.

Pi·sa |'pēzə| industrial city in N Italy, in Tuscany, on the Arno River. Pop. 101,000. It is noted for the 'Leaning Tower of Pisa', a circular bell tower that leans about 17 ft./5 m. from the perpendicular over its height of 181 ft./55 m.

Pis·cat·a·way |'pi'skætə,wā| suburban township in central New Jersey, across the Raritan River from New Brunswick. Pop. 47,089.

Pis·gah |'pizgə| see Mount NEBO.

Pish·pek |pisH'pek| former name (until 1926) for BISHKEK, Kyrgyzstan.

Pi·sid·ia |pə'sidēə| ancient region of Asia Minor (present-day Turkey), between Pamphylia and Phrygia. It was incorporated into the Roman province of Galatia in 25 B.C. □ **Pisidian** *adj. & n.*

Pis·mo Beach |'pizmō| city in SW California, S of San Luis Obispo, a resort center in an oil producing area. Pop. 7,669.

Pi·sto·ia |pēs'tōyä| city at the foot of the Apennine Range in N central Italy, NW of Florence. Pop. 90,000. It is the capital of Pistoia province.

Pit·cairn Islands |'pit,kärn| British dependency comprising a group of volcanic islands in the S Pacific, E of French Polynesia. The only settlement is Adamstown, on Pitcairn Island, the chief island of the group. Pop. 54. Pitcairn Island was discovered in 1767, and remained uninhabited until settled in 1790 by mutineers from HMS *Bounty*. The island is named after the midshipman who first sighted the islands.

Pitcairn Island

Pi·teş·ti |pe'tesHt| industrial town and rail junction in an oil-producing area of S Romania, on the Argeş River, NW of Bucharest. Pop. 163,000.

Pitt Island |pit| see CHATHAM ISLANDS, New Zealand.

Pitts·burg |'pitsbərg| industrial port city in N central California, on Suisun Bay NE of Oakland. Pop. 47,564.

Pitts·burgh |'pits,bərg| industrial city in SW Pennsylvania, at the junction of the Allegheny and Monongahela rivers (forming the Ohio River). Pop. 369,879. The city, originally named Fort Pitt, was founded in 1758 on the site of a French settlement. An important center of steel production for many years, its economic base has shifted to transportation services and high technology.

Pitts·field |'pitsfēld| industrial city in W Massachusetts, on the Housatonic River. It is the commercial center of the Berkshire Hills. Pop. 48,622.

Piu·ra |'pyŏŏrä| commercial city in NW Peru, the capital of Piura department. Pop. 324,000. In a coastal desert, it is a processing center for an irrigated agricultural district.

Pla·cen·tia Bay |plə'sencHə| inlet of the Atlantic in SE Newfoundland, site of early European settlement and 20th-century naval activity.

Plain·field |'plānfēld| industrial city in NE New Jersey. Pop. 46,567.

Plain of Jars |'plän| plain in central Laos where over 300 jars, about 1,500 to 2,000 years old and 3 ft./1m.-10 ft./3 m. tall, are scattered; their origin and function are unknown. The plain was the scene of heavy fighting during the Vietnam War.

Plain of Reeds |'plän| swampy region of southern Vietnam, N of the Mekong Delta.

Plains of A·bra·ham |plänz əv 'ābrəhæm| plateau beside the city of Quebec, overlooking the St. Lawrence River. It was the scene in 1759 of a battle in which the British army under General Wolfe, having scaled the heights above the city under cover of darkness, surprised and defeated the French. The battle led to British control over Canada.

Plains States the US states dominated by the GREAT PLAINS, generally including North and South Dakota, Nebraska, and Kansas, and sometimes Iowa and Missouri.

Pla·no |'plānō| city in NE Texas, an industrial and commercial suburb NE of Dallas. Pop. 128,713.

Plan·ta·tion |plæn'tāsHən| city in SE Florida, a residential suburb W of Fort Lauderdale. Pop. 66,692.

Plas·sey |'plæsē| village in NE India, in West Bengal, NW of Calcutta. It was the scene in 1757 of a battle in which a small British army under Robert Clive defeated the forces of the nawab of Bengal, establishing British supremacy in Bengal.

Pla·taea |plə'tēə| ancient city of Greece. The Greeks defeated the Persians here in 479 B.C. Repeatedly captured and sacked, it was rebuilt by Alexander the Great.

Plate, River |'plāt| wide estuary on the Atlantic coast of South America between Argentina and Uruguay, formed by the confluence of the Paraná and Uruguay rivers. The cities of Buenos Aires and Montevideo lie on its shores. Spanish name **Río de la Plata**.

Platte River |'plæt| river that is formed by the North Platte and South Platte rivers in SW Nebraska, and flows 310 mi./500 km. to the Missouri River near Omaha.

Platts·burgh |'plætsbərg| city in NE New York, on Lake Champlain, a papermaking center and the site of battles in the 18th and 19th centuries. Pop. 21,255.

Pleas·an·ton |'plesəntən| city in N central California, a suburb SE of Oakland. Pop. 50,553.

Plei·ku |'plā'kŏŏ| (also **Play Cu**) commercial city in the central highlands of Vietnam. Pop. 126,000.

Plen·ty, Bay of |'plentē| region of North Island, New Zealand, extending around the bay of the same name. The port of Tauranga is situated on it.

Ple·ven |'plevən| industrial city in N Bulgaria, NE of Sofia. Pop. 168,000. An important fortress town and trading center of the Ottoman Empire, it was taken from the Turks by the Russians in the Russo-Turkish War of 1877, after a siege of 143 days.

Plock |plōtsk| port in central Poland, capital of Plock county, on the Vistula River. Pop. 123,000.

Plo·ieş·ti |plō'yesHt| oil-refining city in central Romania, N of Bucharest. Pop. 254,000.

Plov·div |'plōvdif| industrial and commercial city in S Bulgaria. Pop. 379,000. Known to the ancient Greeks as Philippopolis and to the Romans as Trimontium, it assumed its present name after World War I, and is the second-largest Bulgarian city.

Ply·mouth[1] |'pliməTH| port and naval base in SW England, on the Devon coast. Pop. 239,000. In 1620 it was the scene of the Pilgrims' departure to North America in the *Mayflower*.

Ply·mouth[2] |'pliməTH| resort town in SE Massachusetts, on the Atlantic coast S of Boston. Pop. 45,608. The site in 1620 of the landing of the Pilgrims, it was the earliest permanent European settlement in New England.

Ply•mouth³ |'plimǝTH| city in SE Minnesota, a suburb NW of Minneapolis. Pop. 50,889.

Ply•mouth⁴ |'plimǝTH| the capital of the island of Montserrat in the Caribbean. Pop. 3,500. It was abandoned following the eruption of the Soufrière Hills volcano from 1995.

Ply•mouth Rock |ˌplimǝTH 'räk| granite boulder at Plymouth, Massachusetts, onto which the Pilgrims are said to have stepped from the *Mayflower.*

Pl•zen |'pǝl,zen| Czech name for PILSEN.

Po |pō| longest river of Italy. It rises in the Alps near the border with France and flows 415 mi./668 km. eastward to the Adriatic.Turin is on the Po, Milan in its valley.

Po•ca•tel•lo |ˌpōkǝ'telō| industrial and commercial city in SE Idaho. Pop. 46,080.

Po•co•no Mountains |'pōkǝ,nō| range in NE Pennsylvania, noted for its resorts.

Pod•go•ri•ca |'pädgǝ,rētsǝ| industrial city, the capital of Montenegro. Pop. 118,000. It was under Turkish rule from 1474 until 1878. Between 1946 and 1993 it was named Titograd in honor of Yugoslav leader Marshal Tito.

Po•do•lia |pǝ'dōlēǝ| former region, now in W Ukraine, between the Southern Bug and Dniester rivers. It has belonged to Lithuania, Poland, Turkey, Austria, and Russia.

Po•dolsk |pō'dǝlsk| industrial and technological city in Russia, S of Moscow. Pop. 209,000.

Po•dunk |'pō,dǝNGk| in the U.S., an insignificant rural place, perhaps originally from a Connecticut Indian locality name.

Po Hai |'bō 'hī| see BO HAI, China.

P'o•hang |'pō'häNG| industrial port city in SE South Korea, on the Sea of Japan. Pop. 509,000. It is a steel industry center.

Pohn•pei |'pänpā| (formerly **Ponape**) volcanic island, forming with surrounding atolls one of the four Federated States of MICRONESIA. Pop. 33,000. Kolonia, the capital, is here.

Pointe-à-Pitre |ˌpwäntǝpē'trǝ| the chief port and commercial capital of the French island of Guadeloupe in the West Indies. Pop. 26,000.

Pointe-Noire |ˌpwänt'nwär| the chief seaport of the Republic of Congo, an industrial city and oil terminal on the Atlantic coast. Pop. 576,000.

Point Pe•lée National Park |'pēlē| preserve in SW Ontario, on the W end of Lake Erie, at the southernmost point on the mainland of Canada.

Pois•sy |ˌpwæ'sē| commune in N France, on the Seine River NW of Paris. Pop. 37,000. The Villa Savoye (1929–30), by Le Corbusier, is an important example of the International Style of architecture.

Poi•tiers |ˌpwätyä| city in W central France, the chief town of Poitou-Charentes region and capital of the former province of Poitou. Pop. 82,000.

Poi•tou |pwä'tōō| former province of W central France, now united with Charente to form the region of Poitou-Charentes. Formerly part of Aquitaine, it was held by the French and English in succession until it was finally united with France at the end of the Hundred Years War.

Poitou-Charentes |pwä'tōōsHä'rät| region of W France, on the Bay of Biscay, centered on Poitiers.

Po•kha•ra |'pōkǝrǝ| city in central Nepal, NW of Kathmandu. Pop. 95,000.

Po•land |'pōlǝnd| republic in central Europe with a coastline on the Baltic Sea. Area: 117,599 sq. mi./304,463 sq. km. Pop. 38,183,000. Language, Polish. Capital and largest city: Warsaw. Polish name **Polska**. A nation since the 11th century, Poland was a regional power in the 16th century, but has since suffered domination by Russia, Germany, and other neighbors. It has an industrial economy; agriculture and mining are also important. □ **Polish** *adj.* **Pole** *n.*

Poland

Po•land Spring |'pōlǝnd| former spa in the town of Poland, in SW Maine, known today for its bottled water.

Po•lish Corridor |'pōlisH| former name for a region of Poland that extended N to the Baltic coast and separated East Prussia from the rest of Germany, granted to Poland after World War I to ensure Polish access to the coast. Its annexation by Germany in 1939, and the German invasion of the rest of Poland, was the beginning of WorldWar II. After the war the area was restored to Poland.

Polokwane see PIETERSBURG.

Po•lon•na•ru•wa |pōlō'nərōōwä| town in NE Sri Lanka. Pop. 12,000. Succeeding Anuradhapura in the 8th century as the capital of Ceylon, it became an important Buddhist center in the 12th century. It was subsequently deserted until a modern town was built here in the 20th century.

Pol•ska |'pōlskä| Polish name for POLAND.

Pol•ta•va |pəl'tävə| industrial and agricultural city in E central Ukraine. Pop. 317,000.

Pol•y•ne•sia |ˌpälə'nēZHə| region of the central Pacific, lying to the E of Micronesia and Melanesia and containing the easternmost of the three great groups of Pacific islands, including Hawaii, the Marquesas Islands, Samoa, the Cook Islands, and French Polynesia. □ **Polynesian** *adj. & n.*

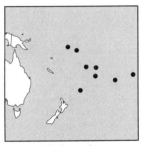

Polynesia

Pom•er•a•nia |ˌpämə'rānēə| region of N Europe, extending along the S shore of the Baltic Sea between Stralsund in NE Germany and the Vistula River in Poland. The region was controlled variously by Germany, Poland, the Holy Roman Empire, Prussia, and Sweden, until the larger part was restored to Poland in 1945, the western portion becoming a part of the German state of Mecklenburg–West Pomerania.

Po•mo•na |pə'mōnə| industrial and commercial city in SW California, in an agricultural area E of Los Angeles. Pop. 131,723.

Pom•pa•no Beach |ˌpämpə,nō| resort city in SE Florida, N of Fort Lauderdale, on the Atlantic. Pop. 72,411.

Pom•peii |päm'pā| ancient city in W Italy, SE of Naples. It was buried by an eruption of MountVesuvius in 79 AD; excavations of the site began in 1748, revealing well-

preserved remains of buildings, mosaics, furniture, and the personal possessions of inhabitants.

Pom•pi•dou Center | pawNpē'dōō| (also **Centre Pompidou**; informally known as **Beaubourg**), cultural center in Paris, France, on the Right Bank (N of the Seine River). Most of the building, which opened in 1977, is occupied by the National Museum of Modern Art.

Pon•ca City |'päNGkə| industrial city in N central Oklahoma, an oil-industry center. Pop. 26,359.

Ponce |päns| industrial port in S Puerto Rico, on the Caribbean Sea. Pop. 159,151.

Pon•di•cher•ry |ˌpändə'cHerē| **1** Union Territory of SE India, on the Coromandel Coast, formed from several widely separated former French territories and incorporated into India in 1954. Pop. 789,000. **2** its capital city. Pop. 203,000.

Pon•ta Del•ga•da |ˌpäntə del'gädə| resort and port on the island of São Miguel in the Portuguese Azores. Pop. 21,000.

Pon•ta Gros•sa |'pōntä 'grōsä| commercial city in S Brazil, in Paraná state. Pop. 253,000. It processes farm and forest products of the region.

Pont-Aven |pawntə'ven| village in Brittany, NW France, associated with Paul Gauguin and other late-19th-century French artists.

Pont•char•train, Lake |'päncHər,trän| shallow lake in SE Louisiana, N of New Orleans and Metairie, noted for its long causeway and as a seafood producer.

Pont du Gard |pawn dōō 'gär| Roman aqueduct built C.A.D.14 across the Gard River in S France to supply water to Nîmes. It consists of three tiers of arches and is 900 ft./270 m. long and 160 ft./50 m. high.

Pon•te Vec•chio |'pōnte 'vecHō| bridge in Florence, Italy, over the Arno River. Built in the 14th century, the shop-lined structure is the only Florentine bridge to survive World War II.

Pon•te•ve•dra |ˌpōntä,vädrä| port in NW Spain, capital of Pontevedra province. Pop. 75,000.

Pon•ti•ac |'päntēæk| industrial city in SE Michigan, NW of Detroit, an auto-industry center. Pop. 71,166.

Pon•ti•a•nak |ˌpäntē'änək| seaport in Indonesia, on the W coast of Borneo at the delta of the Kapuas River. Pop. 305,000.

Pon•tine Marshes |'pän,tēn ,märsHəz| area of marshland in W Italy, on the Tyrrhenian coast S of Rome. It became infested with malaria in ancient times, and it was not until 1928 that an extensive scheme to drain the marshes was begun. Several new towns have since been built in the region, which is now a productive agricultural area. Italian name **Agro Pontino**.

Pon·tus |'päntəs| ancient region of N Asia Minor, on the Black Sea coast N of Cappadocia. It reached its height between 120 and 63 B.C. under Mithridates VI, when it dominated the whole of Asia Minor; by the end of the 1st century B.C. it had been defeated by Rome and absorbed into the Roman Empire.

Pon·tus Eux·i·nus ancient Greek name for the BLACK SEA.

Poole |pool| port and resort town on the S coast of England, in Dorset, just W of Bournemouth. Pop. 131,000.

Poo·na |'poonə| (also **Pune**) industrial city in Maharashtra, W India, in the hills SE of Bombay. Pop. 1,560,000. A Maratha capital, it became a military and administrative center under British rule.

Po·pa·yán |ˌpōpə'yän| historic cultural city in SW Colombia, the capital of Cauca department. Pop. 204,000.

Po·po·ca·té·petl |ˌpōpə'kætəpetəl| active volcano in Puebla state, Mexico, SE of Mexico City, which rises to 17,887 ft./5,452 m. It is one of twin peaks (the other is Ixtaccihuatl) visible from the city in clear weather.

Por·ban·dar |pōr'bəndər| port town in W India, in Gujarat state. Pop. 160,000. Mohandas Gandhi, father of Indian independence, was born here.

Por·cu·pine River |'pawrkyəpīn| river that flows 450 mi./720 km. from the Yukon Territory into NE Alaska, to the Yukon River.

Po·ri |'pawrē| industrial port in SW Finland, on the Gulf of Bothnia. Pop. 76,000.

Por·tage[1] |'pawrtij| port city in NW Indiana, on L. Erie E of Gary. Pop. 29,060.

Por·tage[2] |'pawrtij| city in SW Michigan, a suburb S of Kalamazoo. Pop. 41,042.

Port Ar·thur[1] |'ärTHər| former name (1898–1905) for LÜSHUN, China.

Port Ar·thur[2] |'ärTHər| city in SE Texas, an oil industry center on the Neches and Sabine rivers near the Gulf Coast. Pop. 58,724.

Port-au-Prince |ˌpawrtə'prins| the capital of Haiti, a port on the W coast of Hispaniola. Pop. 1,255,000. Founded by the French in 1749, it became capital of the new republic in 1806.

Port Blair |'blār| port city on the S tip of South Andaman Island, India, in the Bay

of Bengal. Pop. 75,000. It is the capital of the Andaman and Nicobar Islands.

Port Co·quit·lam |kō'kwitləm| industrial and commercial city in SW British Columbia, on the Fraser River E of Vancouver. Pop. 36,773.

Port de France |fræns| former name for NOUMÉA, in French New Caledonia.

Port Dick·son |'diksən| port and resort town in Malaysia, on the Strait of Malacca, SW of Seremban. Pop. 48,000.

Port Eliz·a·beth |ə'lizä,beTH| port city in South Africa, on the coast of the province of Eastern Cape. Pop. 853,000. Settled by the British in 1820, it is now an auto manufacturing city and beach resort.

Port-Étienne[2] |ˌpōrtä'tyen| former name for NOUADHIBOU, Mauritania.

Port-Gentil |'pōr ˌZHän'tä| the principal port city of Gabon, on the Atlantic coast S of Libreville. Pop. 76,000.

Port Har·court |'här,kawrt| principal port of SE Nigeria, an industrial city on the Gulf of Guinea at the E edge of the Niger delta. Pop. 371,000.

Port Hed·land |'hedlənd| seaport on the NW coast of Western Australia. Pop. 14,000.

Port Hue·ne·me |wī'nēmē| industrial and military port city in SW California, NW of Los Angeles. Pop. 20,319.

Port Hu·ron |'hyooŏrən; 'hyooŏrän| industrial port city in SE Michigan, on Lake Huron and the St. Clair River. Pop. 33,694.

Por·ţi·le de Fier |pōr'tselede'fyer| Romanian name for the IRON GATE.

Port·land, Isle of |'pawrtlənd| rocky limestone peninsula on the S coast of England, in Dorset. Its southernmost tip is known as the Bill of Portland or Portland Bill. The peninsula is quarried for its building stone.

Port·land[1] |'pawrtlənd| largest city in Maine, on Casco Bay off the Atlantic, in the SW part. It is an industrial, commercial, and tourist center. Pop. 64,358.

Port·land[2] |'pawrtlənd| industrial port city in NW Oregon, on the Willamette River near its confluence with the Columbia River. Pop. 437,319. Founded in 1845, it developed as a supply center in gold rushes of the 1860s and 1870s, and as a lumber port. It is the largest city in Oregon.

Port·laoi·se |pawrt'lēsHə| (also **Port-laoighise**) the county seat of Laois, in the S central Republic of Ireland. Pop. 9,000.

Port Lou·is |pawr'lwē| the capital of Mauritius, a port on the NW coast. Pop. 144,000.

Port Moo·dy |'moŏdi| city in SW British

Columbia, an industrial port on Burrard Inlet, just E of Vancouver. Pop. 17,712.

Port Mores·by |'mōrzbē| the capital of Papua New Guinea, situated on the S coast of the island of New Guinea, on the Coral Sea. Pop. 193,000.

Port Na·tal former name (until 1835) for DURBAN, South Africa.

Por·to |'pōr,tōō| Portuguese name for OPORTO.

Pôr·to Ale·gre |'pawrtōō ä'ləgre| major port and commercial city in SE Brazil, capital of the state of Rio Grande do Sul. Pop. 1,263,000. It is situated on the Lagoa dos Patos, a lagoon separated from the Atlantic by a sandy peninsula.

Por·to·bel·lo Road |pawrtō'bälō| street in W central London, England, N of Notting Hill, noted for its open-air market.

Por·to·fi·no |pawrtō'fēnō| village, a resort in NW Italy, SE of Genoa. Pop. 600. Its picturesque port attracts visitors.

Port-of-Spain |'pawrdəv'spān| the capital of Trinidad and Tobago, a port on the NW coast of the island of Trinidad. Pop. 46,000.

Por·to No·vo |'pawrtō 'nō,vō| the capital of Benin, a port on the Gulf of Guinea close to the border with Nigeria. Pop. 179,000. It was a center of the Portuguese slave trade in the 17th century.

Pôr·to Vel·ho |'pawrtōō 'velyōō| city in W Brazil, capital of the state of Rondônia, in a mining and lumbering district. Pop. 286,000.

Por·to·vie·jo |pawrtōvē'āhō| commercial city in W Ecuador, on the Portoviejo River NW of Guayaquil, in an agricultural district. Pop. 201,000.

Port Pe·trovsk former name (until 1922) for MAKHACHKALA, Russia.

Port Pirie |'pirē| port city on the coast of South Australia, on the Spencer Gulf N of Adelaide, in a mining district. Pop. 15,000.

Port Roy·al |'rōyäl| port town in SE Jamaica, on the peninsula enclosing Kingston harbor. A notorious buccaneering center, it was destroyed by a 1692 earthquake. In 1907 another quake occurred. It continues to be used for shipyards.

Port-Royal |',pawrt 'roiäl| abbey for women, later also a boys' school, founded in 1204, W of Paris, in N central France. It was moved to Paris in 1626. A center of Jansenism, the abbey was closed by papal bull in 1704.

Port Said |sī'ēd| port city in Egypt, on the Mediterranean coast at the N end of the Suez Canal. Pop. 461,000. It was founded in 1859 at the start of the construction of

the Suez Canal, and is today both an industrial center and a resort.

Port Saint Lu·cie |'lōōsē| resort and retirement city in E central Florida. Pop. 55,866.

Ports·mouth[1] |'pawrtsməTH| port city and naval base on the S coast of England, formerly in Hampshire. Pop. 175,000. A naval dockyard was established here in 1496.

Ports·mouth[2] |'pawrtsməTH| historic port city in SE New Hampshire, on the Piscataqua River off the Atlantic. Pop. 25,925.

Ports·mouth[3] |'pawrtsməTH| commercial and naval city in SE Virginia, on Hampton Roads W of Norfolk. Pop. 103,907.

Port Su·dan |sōō'dæn| the chief port city of Sudan, on the Red Sea. Pop. 207,000.

Port Town·send |'townzənd| historic port city in NW Washington, on the Olympic Peninsula. Pop. 7,001.

Por·tu·gal |'pōrCHəgəl| republic occupying the W part of the Iberian peninsula in SW Europe. Area: 35,563 sq. mi./92,072 sq. km. Pop. 10,393,000. Language, Portuguese. Capital and largest city: Lisbon. Portugal broke from Spain in the 12th century, and was a colonial power in the 15th–16th centuries. Today, agriculture, tourism, mining, and some industry are important. □ **Portuguese** *adj. & n.*

Portugal

Por·tu·guese India |,pōrCHəgēz| former Portuguese colonial possessions in India, comprising Goa, Daman and Diu, and Dadra and Nagar-Haveli. By 1961 all had been repossessed by India.

Port Vi·la |vē'lä| see VILA, Vanuatu.

Po·sa·das |pō'sädäs| industrial and commercial city in NE Argentina, on the Paraná River opposite Encarnación, Paraguay. Pop. 220,000.

Po·sen |'pōzən| German name for POZNAŃ, Poland.

Po·ten·za |pō'tentsä| market town in S Italy, capital of Basilicata region. Pop. 68,000.

Po·to·mac |pə'tōmək| river of the E U.S., which rises in the Appalachian Mts. in West Virginia and flows about 285 mi./459 km., into Chesapeake Bay on the Atlantic coast. Washington, D.C. is on the Potomac.

Po·to·sí |pə'tōsē| mining city in S Bolivia. Pop. 112,000. Situated at an altitude of about 13,780 ft./4,205 m., it is one of the highest cities in the world.

Pots·dam |'päts,dæm| city in eastern Germany, the capital of Brandenburg, just SW of Berlin on the Havel River. Pop. 95,000. It is the site of the rococo Sans Souci palace built for Frederick the Great of Prussia in 1745–47.

Pot·ter·ies, the |'pätərēz| industrial district in central England, in N Staffordshire, in the Trent River valley. The ceramic industry in Stoke-on-Trent and other "Five Towns" peaked here at the end of the 18th century.

Potts·town |'pätstown| industrial borough in SE Pennsylvania, on the Schuylkill River NW of Philadelphia. Pop. 21,381.

Potts·ville |'pätsvil| industrial and commercial city in SE Pennsylvania, on the Schuylkill River NW of Philadelphia. Pop. 16,603.

Pough·keep·sie |pə'kipsē| industrial city in SE New York, on the Hudson River, noted as the home of Vassar College. Pop. 28,844.

Pow·der River |'powdər| river that flows 485 mi./780 km. from NE Wyoming into S Montana, to the Yellowstone River.

Pow·ell, Lake |'powel| reservoir on the Colorado River in S Utah, formed since the 1960s by the Glen Canyon Dam. The lake inundated famed Glen Canyon.

Pow·ys |'päəs| county of E central Wales, on the border with England, formed in 1974 from the former counties of Montgomeryshire, Radnorshire, and most of Breconshire. Pop. 116,000; administrative center, Llandrindod Wells. Its name is that of a former Welsh kingdom.

Po·yang Lake |'pōyəNG| (Chinese name **Poyang Hu**) lake in Jiangxi province, SE central China; the largest freshwater lake in China: 1,383 sq. mi./3,583 sq. km. It is linked to the Yangtze River, for which it serves as an overflow reservoir.

Po·za Ri·ca |'pōzä 'rēkä| (official name **Poza Rica de Hidalgo**) city in E central Mexico, an oil industry center in Veracruz state. Pop. 152,000.

Poz·nań |'pōz,næn| city in NW Poland. Pop. 590,000. An area of German colonization since the 13th century, it was

under German control almost continuously until World War I, and was overrun by the Germans again in 1939. It was severely damaged during World War II. German name **Posen**.

Po·zsony |'pōzHōnē| Hungarian name for BRATISLAVA, Slovakia.

Poz·zuo·li |pōt'tswawlē| seaport on the Bay of Naples, W Italy. Pop. 65,000. It has extensive Roman ruins and is a tourist center.

Prades |präd| village in S France, SW of Perpignan, site of a music festival founded by Pablo Casals, who settled here in 1939 in protest against the Franco government in Spain.

Pra·do, the |'prädō| national art gallery in Madrid, Spain, established in 1815 and housing a famed collection of Spanish art, as well as art from other countries.

Prague |präg| the capital of the Czech Republic, in the NE on the Vltava River. Pop. 1,212,000. Czech name **Praha**. Prague was the capital of Czechoslovakia from 1918 until the partition of 1993. The capital of Bohemia from the 14th century, it was the scene of much religious conflict. In 1618 Protestant citizens threw Catholic officials from the windows of Hradčany Castle, an event, known as the **Defenestration of Prague**, which contributed to the outbreak of the Thirty Years War. Modern Prague is an industrial and cultural center, noted for its beauty.

Praia |'prīə| the capital of Cape Verde, a port on the island of São Tiago. Pop. 62,000.

Prai·rie du Chien |'prərē də 'sHen| historic commercial city in SW Wisconsin, near the mouth of the Wisconsin River on the Mississippi River. Pop. 5,659.

Pra·to |'prätō| city in Tuscany, N Italy, NW of Florence. Pop. 167,000.

Pres·cott |'pres,kät| historic city in W central Arizona, a mining and tourist center. Pop. 26,455.

Pres·i·den·tial Range |,prezədenCHl| range in the White Mts., in N New Hampshire, including Mount Washington, at 6,288 ft./1,918 m. the highest peak in the NE U.S.

Pre·šov |'presHaw| market town in E Slovakia, on the Torysa River. Pop. 88,000.

Press·burg |'pres,bərg| German name for BRATISLAVA, Slovakia.

Pres·ton |'prestən| industrial city in NW England, the administrative center of Lancashire, on the Ribble River. Pop. 126,000. It was the site in the 18th century of the first English cotton mills.

Prest•wick |'prest,wik| resort town to the S of Glasgow in South Ayrshire, SW Scotland, the site of an international airport. Pop. 14,000.

Pre•to•ria |prə'tawrēə| the administrative capital of South Africa, in Gauteng province. Pop. 1,080,000. Founded in 1855, it is an industrial and university city.

Prib•i•lof Islands |'pribə,lawf| (also **Fur Seal Islands**) group of four islands in the Bering Sea, off the coast of SW Alaska. First visited in 1786 by the Russian explorer Gavriil Loginovich Pribylov, they came into U.S. possession after the purchase of Alaska in 1867.

Pri•lep |'prēlep| commercial and industrial city in S Macedonia. Pop. 100,000.

Prime Me•rid•i•an, the |prīm mə'ridēən| 0° longitude, which runs through Greenwich, England. Other longitudes are based on it. See also INTERNATIONAL DATE LINE.

Pri•mor•sky Krai |prē'mōrski krī| krai (administrative territory) in the far SE of Siberian Russia, between the Sea of Japan and the Chinese border. Pop. 2,281,000. Capital: Vladivostok.

Prince Al•bert |'prints 'älbərt| industrial and commercial city in central Saskatchewan. Pop. 34,181.

Prince Ed•ward Island |,prins 'edwərd| island in the Gulf of St. Lawrence, in E Canada, the country's smallest (2,185 sq. mi./5,660 sq. km.) province. Capital and largest city: Charlottetown. Explored and colonized by the French, it was ceded to the British in 1763. It became a province of Canada in 1873. Fishing and tourism are important industries. A bridge to mainland New Brunswick was opened in 1997.

Prince George |'prints 'jōrj| city in central British Columbia, a transportation and commercial hub on the Fraser River. Pop. 69,653.

Prince George's County |'prints 'jōrjəz| county in S central Maryland, site of many SE suburbs of Washington, D.C. Pop. 729,268.

Prince of Wales Island[1] |'prints əv 'wälz| largest island in the Alexander Archipelago, in SE Alaska. It is the home of the Haida people.

Prince of Wales Island[2] |'prints əv 'wälz| an island in the Canadian Arctic, in Nunavut, NW of the Boothia Peninsula.

Prince of Wales Island[3] |'prints əv 'wälz| former name for PENANG, Malaysia.

Prince Ru•pert |prints 'rōōpərt| industrial port city in W central British Columbia,

on Chatham Sound and the Inside Passage. Pop. 16,620.

Prince•ton |'prinstən| historic academic borough in W central New Jersey, home to Princeton University. Pop. 12,016.

Prince Wil•liam Sound |'prints 'wilyəm| inlet of the Pacific in S central Alaska, scene of a huge 1989 oil tanker spill. Cordova and Valdez are the main ports.

Prin•ci•pe Island |'prin(t)səpə| volcanic island in the Gulf of Guinea, W Africa, that constitutes part of the nation of São Tomé and Príncipe. Pop. 5,000.

Pri•pyat |'prēpyət.| (also **Pripet**) river of NW Ukraine and S Belarus, which rises in Ukraine near the border with Poland and flows some 440 mi./710 km. E through the Pripyat Marshes to join the Dnieper River N of Kiev.

Priš•ti•na |'prēsHtēnä| city in S Serbia, the capital of the autonomous province of Kosovo. Pop. 108,000. The capital of medieval Serbia, it was under Turkish control from 1389 until 1912.

Priz•ren |'prizren| market town in Kosovo, S Serbia, near the Albanian border. Pop. 135,000.

Pro•bo•ling•go |,prōbō'liNGō| (also **Prabalingga; Perobolinggo**) port city in Indonesia, on NE Java, SE of Surabaya. Pop. 177,000.

Pro•ko•pyevsk |prə'kawpyəfsk| coal-mining city in S Russia, in the Kuznets Basin industrial region to the S of Kemerovo. Pop. 274,000.

Prom•ised Land |'prämisd| in the Bible, land promised the Jews by God, and viewed by their leader, Moses, from Mt. Pisgah, at the end of his life.

Prom•on•to•ry Mountains |'präməntōrē| short range that forms a peninsula in the N Great Salt Lake, in N Utah. The first transcontinental railroad passed through Promontory, N of the range. Today trains pass Promontory Point, at the S end, via a causeway across the lake.

Pro•pon•tis |prə'päntəs| ancient name for the Sea of Marmara (see MARMARA, SEA OF).

Pro•vence |prō'väns| former province of SE France, on the Mediterranean coast E of the Rhône. Settled by the Greeks in the 6th century B.C., the area around Marseilles became, in the 1st century B.C., part of the Roman colony of Gaul. It was united with France in 1481 and is now part of the region of Provence–Alpes–Côte d'Azur. The language and culture of Provence are distinctive. □ **Provencal** adj. & n.

Provence-Alpes-Côte d'Azur |prə'vänsälpkōtdä'zyōr| mountainous region of SE France, on the border with Italy and including the French Riviera. Pop. 4,258,000. Marseilles is the chief city.

Prov·i·dence |'prävə,dens| the state capital of Rhode Island, a port on the Atlantic coast. Pop. 160,728. It was founded in 1636 as a haven for religious dissenters by Roger Williams (1604–83), who had been banished from the colony at Plymouth, Massachusetts. It developed in the 18th century as a major port for trade with the West Indies, and is today an industrial and financial center.

Prov·i·dence Plan·ta·tions |'prävə,dens| the mainland portion of the state of Rhode Island.

Prov·ince·town |'prävən,stown| port town in SE Massachusetts, a famed resort and artists' community at the N tip of Cape Cod. Pop. 3,561.

Pro·vo |'prōvō| industrial and commercial city in N central Utah, S of Salt Lake City. It is home to Brigham Young University. Pop. 86,835.

Prud·hoe Bay |',prōͦodō| inlet of the Arctic Ocean on the N coast of Alaska. Since 1968 it has been a major center of Alaskan oil production.

Prus·sia |'prəsHə| former kingdom of Germany. Originally a small country on the SE shores of the Baltic, under Frederick the Great it became a major European power controlling much of modern NE Germany and Poland. After the Franco-Prussian War of 1870–71 it became the center of Bismarck's new German Empire, but following Germany's defeat in World War I the Prussian monarchy was abolished. Its nucleus was an area E of the Vistula, taken in the 13th century by the Teutonic Knights and passing in 1618 to the electors of Brandenburg. The kingdom of Prussia was proclaimed in 1701, with its capital at Berlin. □ **Prussian** adj. & n.

Prut |'prōͦot| (also **Pruth**) river of SE Europe, which rises in the Carpathian Mts. in S Ukraine and flows SE for 530 mi./ 850 km., joining the Danube near Galați in Romania. For much of its course it forms the border between Romania and Moldova.

Pskov |pskōf| ancient city in W Russia, in an agricultural area SW of Saint Petersburg. Pop. 206,000.

Pu·call·pa |pōͦo'kīpä| commercial town in E Peru, capital of Ucayali department, a port on the Ucayali River. Pop. 153,000.

Pu·ch'on |pōͦo'CHawn| (also **Puchon**) industrial and agricultural city in NW South Korea, W of Seoul. Pop. 779,000.

Pue·bla |'pweblə| **1** state of S central Mexico. Pop. 4,118,000. **2** its capital city. Pop. 1,055,000. The fourth-largest Mexican city, an industrial center, it lies at the edge of the central plateau. Full name **Puebla de Zaragoza.**

Pueb·lo |'pweblō| industrial city in S central Colorado, on the Arkansas River at the foot of the Front Range of the Rocky Mts. Pop. 98,640.

Puer·to Bar·rios |'pwertō 'bärēōs| port city in E Guatemala, on the Bay of Amatique in the Caribbean Sea. Pop. 29,000. The capital of Izabal department, it was long a key banana-export center.

Puer·to Ca·bel·lo |kä'vāyō| historic industrial port city in N Venezuela, W of Caracas. Pop. 129,000. It exports fruit and ores and has oil and chemical facilities.

Puer·to Cor·tés |kawr'tās| port in NW Honduras, on the Caribbean coast at the mouth of the Ulua River. Pop. 40,000.

Puer·to Es·con·di·do |eskän'didō| resort town in S Mexico, on the Pacific coast in Oaxaca state. Pop. 8,000.

Puer·to Montt |mawnt| port city in S central Chile, on the Gulf of Ancud off the Pacific. Pop. 131,000. It has resort and fishing trade, and is the S terminus of Chilean railroads.

Puer·to Pla·ta |'plætə| resort town and cruise port in the Dominican Republic, on the N coast (the Amber Coast). Pop. 96,000.

Puer·to Prin·ce·sa |pren'sesə| commercial town in the Philippines, on E central Palawan. Pop. 92,000.

Puer·to Ri·co |'pwertō 'rikō; 'pawrto| island of the Greater Antilles, in the Caribbean. Area: 3,460 sq. mi./8,959 sq. km. Pop. 3,522,040. Official languages, Spanish and English. Capital and largest city: San Juan. One of the earliest Spanish settlements in the New World, it was ceded

Puerto Rico

to the U.S. in 1898 after the Spanish-American War, and in 1952 it became a commonwealth in voluntary association with the U.S., with full powers of local government. Its economy, based on manufacturing, agriculture, and tourism, is highly dependent on the U.S. □ **Puerto Rican** *adj. & n.*

Puer·to Ri·co Trench |ˌpwertō 'rikō| ocean trench extending in an E–W direction to the N of Puerto Rico and the Leeward Islands. It reaches a depth of 28,397 ft./9,220 m.

Puer·to Val·lar·ta |väyärtə| resort and port city in W Mexico, on the Pacific in Jalisco state. Pop. 94,000. It is noted for its fishing, yachting, and hotel facilities.

Pu·get Sound |ˌpyo͞ojət| island-filled inlet of the Pacific on the coast of Washington State in the U.S. It is linked to the ocean by the Strait of Juan de Fuca and is overlooked by the city of Seattle, which is situated on its E shore.

Pu·glia |'po͞olyä| Italian name for APULIA.

Pu·la |'po͞olə| port, industrial center, and resort town in W Croatia, on the Adriatic Sea, on the S tip of the Istrian Peninsula. Pop. 62,000.

Pull·man |'po͞olmən| commercial city in SE Washington, on the Palouse River, home to Washington State University. Pop. 23,478.

Pun·jab |'pən,jäb| (also **the Punjab**) region of NW India and Pakistan, a wide, fertile plain traversed by the Indus and the five tributaries that gave the region its name. □ **Punjabi** *adj. & n.*

Pu·no |'po͞onō| commercial city in SE Peru, the capital of Puno department, on Lake Titicaca. Pop. 100,000. It is a tourist and cultural center.

Punt |po͞ont| land visited by Egyptian traders as early as the 15th century B.C., probably the coast of present-day Eritrea and Djibouti

Pun·ta Are·nas |',po͞ontə ə'ränəs| port in S Chile, on the Strait of Magellan. Pop. 114,000.

Pun·ta del Es·te |del 'ästä| resort city in S Uruguay, in Maldonado department, E of the mouth of the Rio de la Plata. Pop. 8,000. It has been the scene of international conferences.

Punx·su·taw·ney |ˌpəNGksə'tawni| borough in W central Pennsylvania, noted as the home of Punxsutawney Phil, a groundhog whose movements are closely observed by the media each February 2.

Pu·qi town in Hubei province, E central China, SW of Wuhan. Pop. 413,000.

Pur·cell Mountains |'pərsəl| range of the N Rocky Mts. in SE British Columbia, E of the Selkirk Mts.

Pu·ri |'po͞orē| (also called **Jagannath; Juggernaut**) port city in E India, in Orissa state. Pop. 125,000. It is the center of worship of the Hindu god Jagannath.

Pur·nia |'po͞ornëä| (also **Purnea**) commercial town in E India, in Bihar state. Pop. 137,000.

Pu·rus River |pə'ro͞os| river that flows NE for 2,100 mi./3,400 km. from the Andes in E Peru into NW Brazil, where it joins the Amazon.

Pu·san |ˌpo͞o'sän| port city on the SE coast of South Korea. Pop. 3,798,000. A center of heavy industry, it is the second-largest South Korean city.

Push·kar Lake |'po͞oSHker| lake in NW India, in E central Rajasthan state. It is a religious site with the only temple in India dedicated to the Hindu god Brahma.

Push·kin |'po͞oSH,kin| (formerly **Detskoye Selo** and, earlier, **Tsarskoye Selo**) residential and resort suburb of Saint Petersburg, Russia. The site was given by Peter the Great to his wife as a summer residence. After the 1917 Revolution, it became known as Detskoye Selo ('children's village') and was a health resort. In 1937 it was renamed Pushkin, for the poet.

Put·u·ma·yo River |ˌpo͞otə'mīō| river that flows 1,000 mi./1,610 km. from the Andes in SW Colombia, along the borders with Ecuador and Peru, into NW Brazil, where it joins the Amazon.

PWV *abbrev. for* Pretoria–Witwatersrand–Vereeniging, former South African province, now GAUTENG.

Pya·ti·gorsk |ˌpitē'görsk| (also **Piatigorsk**) spa in W Russia, on the Kuma River, NW of Grozny, Chechnya. Pop. 129,000. The city also has some industry.

Pyong·yang |'pyawNG'yæNG| the capital of North Korea, on the Taedong River. Pop. 2,000,000. The oldest city on the Korean peninsula, it was first mentioned in records of 108 B.C. It developed as an industrial city during the Japanese occupation of 1910–45.

Pyr·e·nees |'pirə,nēz| range of mountains extending along the border between France and Spain from the Atlantic coast to the Mediterranean. Its highest peak is the Pico de Aneto in northern Spain, which rises to a height of 11,168 ft./3,404 m. □ **Pyrenean** *adj. & n.*

Qq

Qa·ra·ghan·dy |kärə'gändə| industrial city in E Kazakhstan, at the center of a major coal-mining region. Pop. 613,000. Russian name **Karaganda**.

Qa·tar |'kä,tär| sheikhdom occupying a peninsula on the W coast of the Persian Gulf. Area: 4,416 sq. mi./11,437 sq. km. Pop. 402,000. Language, Arabic. Capital and largest city: Doha. The country was a British protectorate from 1916 until 1971, when it became independent. Oil is the chief source of revenue. □ **Qatari** *adj. & n.*

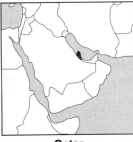

Qatar

Qat·ta·ra Depression |kə'tärə| extensive, low-lying, and largely impassable area of desert in NE Africa, to the W of Cairo, that falls to 436 ft./133 m. below sea level.

Qaz·vin |käz'vēn| (also **Kazvin; Kasbin**) industrial and commercial city in NW Iran, NW of Tehran. Pop. 279,000.

Qena |'kēnə| (also **Kena**; ancient name **Caene**) town in S central Egypt, on the Nile River, in an agricultural area. Pop. 137,000.

Qi·lian Shan |'CHi'lyän 'SHän| mountain range in N China, on the border between Gansu and Qinghai provinces, rising to a height of 19,114 ft./5,826 m.

Qing·dao |'CHĒNG'dow| port in E China, in Shandong province on the Yellow Sea coast. Pop. 2,040,000.

Qing·hai |'CHĬNG'hī| (also **Tsinghai**) mountainous province in N central China. Pop. 4,457,000. Capital: Xining.

Qing·hai Lake |'CHĒNG'hī| (Chinese name **Qinghai Hu**) salt lake in Qinghai province, N central China; the largest lake in the country. Area: 1,770 sq. mi./4,583 sq. km.

Qin·huang·dao |'CHin'hwäNG'dow| industrial port in Hebei province, NE China, on the Bo Hai near the Liaoning border. Pop. 448,000. A special economic zone, it is linked by pipeline to the oil fields at Daqing.

Qin·zhou |'CHēn'jō| city in Guangxi, S China, on an inlet of the Gulf of Tonkin, S of Nanning. Pop. 944,000.

Qi·qi·har |'CHē'CHē'här| port on the Nen River, in Heilongjiang province, NE China. Pop. 1,370,000.

Qi·shon |'kīSHən| (also **Kison; Kishon**) river in N Israel that flows 45 mi./72 km., from near Mount Gilboa to the Mediterranean Sea at Haifa.

Qi·tai·he |'CHē'tī'hə| industrial city in Heilongjiang province, NE China, E of Harbin near the Russian border. Pop. 327,000.

Qom |'kōm| (also **Qum** or **Kum**) industrial city in central Iran. Pop. 780,000. It is a holy city and center of learning and pilgrimage for Shiite Muslims.

Qos·ta·nay |kəstə'nī| (also known as **Kustanay**) **1** administrative subdivision in N Kazakhstan. Pop. 1,074,000. **2** its capital city, a mining and agricultural center. Pop. 234,000.

Quad Cities |kwäd| industrial complex on the Mississippi River, composed of Davenport and Bettendorf, SE Iowa, and Moline and Rock Island, NW Illinois. A second Quad Cities, in N Alabama on the Tennessee River, consists of Florence, Sheffield, Tuscumbia, and Muscle Shoals.

Quai d'Orsay |'kā dawr'sä| riverside street on the Left (S) Bank of the Seine in Paris. The French ministry of foreign affairs has its headquarters in this street.

Quang Tri |'kwæNG 'trē| province in central Vietnam, NW of Hue. The center of the Demilitarized Zone (DMZ) during the Vietnam War, it suffered heavy deforestation by U.S. forces.

Quan·ti·co |'kwäntə,kō| town in NE Virginia, on the Potomac River, SW of Washington, D.C. Pop. 670. Nearby are major Marine and FBI training centers.

Quan·zhou |'CHwæn'jō| city in Fujian province, SE China, NE of Xiamen. Pop. 444,000. It was one of the great Chinese ports during the Middle Ages.

Qua·tre Bras |'kätrə 'brä| village in central Belgium, SE of Brussels, site of an 1815 battle in which the English under Wellington defeated French troops.

Que·bec¹ |k(w)ə'bek| province in E Canada. Area: 594,860 sq. mi./1.67 million sq. km. Pop. 6,845,700. Settled by the French in 1608, it was ceded to the British in 1763, and became one of the original four provinces in the Dominion of Canada in 1867. The majority of its residents are French-speaking and its culture remains predominantly French. It has some political independence from the rest of Canada, and is the focal point of the French-Canadian nationalist movement. Varied manufacturing, mining, forest industries, fishing, hydropower, and tourism are all important. French name **Québec**. □ **Québecois** *adj. & n.* **Quebecer** *n.*

Que·bec² |k(w)ə'bek| (also **Quebec City**) the capital city of Quebec province, a port on the St. Lawrence River. Pop. 167,517. Founded on the site of a Huron village (Stadacona) in 1608, it is Canada's oldest city. It was a center of the struggle between the French and British for control of North America and it was captured by a British force in 1759 after the battle of the Plains of Abraham. It became capital of Lower Canada (later Quebec) in 1791.

Qued·lin·burg |'kfedlinbərg| historic industrial and market city in central Germany. Pop. 29,000.

Queen Char·lotte Islands |'sнärlət| group of more than 150 islands off the W coast of Canada, in British Columbia, noted for fishing and lumbering.

Queen City nickname for CINCINNATI, Ohio.

Queen Eliz·a·beth Islands |ə'lizə,beTH| name for all islands in the Arctic Archipelago of Canada N of the Parry Channel (approximately 74° N). Mostly unpopulated, and often ice-covered, they were formerly called the Parry Islands.

Queen Maud Land |mowd| part of Antarctica bordering the Atlantic, claimed since 1939 by Norway.

Queens |kwēnz| largest and second most populous borough of New York City, co-extensive with Queens County, at the W end of Long Island. Pop. 1,951,598. It is noted for its diverse populace and residential and light industrial neighborhoods.

Queen's County |kwēnz| former name for County LAOIS, Ireland.

Queens·land |'kwēnzlənd| state comprising the NE part of Australia. Pop. 2,922,000. Capital: Brisbane. Established in 1824 as a penal settlement, Queensland was constituted a separate colony in 1859, having previously formed part of New South Wales, and was federated with the other states of Australia in 1901. Agricul-

ture and mining are key to the economy. □ **Queenslander** *n.*

Queens·ton |'kwēnztən| historic locality, now in Niagara-on-the-Lake, E Ontario, just N of Niagara Falls, site of fighting in the War of 1812.

Quel·i·ma·ne |kelē'mänə| (also **Quilimane** or **Kilimane**) port town in E central Mozambique, near the Indian Ocean on the Quelimane River. Pop. 146,000.

Que·luz |ke'lōōSH| town in central Portugal, N of Lisbon. Pop. 44,000. Its 18th-century palace was a royal residence.

Que·moy |ki'moi| island group, SE China, off the coast of Fujian province, E of Xiamen. Under the control of the Nationalist government on Taiwan after the communist takeover of the mainland, it was subjected to periodic shelling during the 1950s.

Que·ré·ta·ro |kə'retə,rō| **1** state of central Mexico. Area: 4,422 sq. mi./11,449 sq. km. Pop. 1,044,000. **2** its capital city, an industrial and tourist center. Pop. 454,000. In 1847 it was the scene of the signing of the treaty ending the U.S.–Mexican war.

Quet·ta |'kwetə| city in western Pakistan, the capital of Baluchistan province. Pop. 350,000.

Quet·zal·te·nan·go |ketsälte'näNGō| city in SW Guatemala, capital of Quetzaltenango department. Pop. 246,000. It is an industrial center and the second-largest Guatemalan city.

Que·zon City |'kāsōn| city on the island of Luzon in the N Philippines, on the outskirts of Manila. Pop. 1,667,000. It was established in 1940 and from 1948 to 1976 was the capital of the Philippines.

Qu·fu |'CHōō'fōō| small town in Shandong province in E China, where Confucius was born in 551 BC and lived for much of his life.

Quib·dó |kēb'dō| town in W Colombia, the capital of Chocó department. Pop. 119,000. It is a mining and tropical agriculture center.

Qui·be·ron |kēb'rōn| **1** peninsula in Brittany, NW France. **2** fishing port and resort at its tip. Pop. 5,000.

Quil·mes |'kēlmes| industrial city in E Argentina, a suburb SE of Buenos Aires. Pop. 509,000.

Qui·lon |kwē'lōn| (also **Kollam**) commercial port in SW India, on the Malabar Coast in Kerala state. Pop. 362,000.

Quil·pué |kēl'pwā| commercial and resort city in central Chile, E of Valparaiso. Pop. 107,000.

Quin•cy¹ |'kwinsē| industrial and commercial city in W central Illinois, on the Mississippi River. Pop. 39,681.

Quin•cy² |'kwinsē| historic industrial city in E Massachusetts, on Boston Harbor, just SE of Boston, a noted shipbuilding center. Pop. 84,985.

Qui Nhon |kwē 'nyawn| (also **Quy Nhon**) industrial and commercial city in SE Vietnam, on the South China Sea. Pop. 202,000. A naval station and military base during the Vietnam War, it was the center of heavy fighting.

Quin•ta•na Roo |kēn'tänä 'rōō| state of SE Mexico, on the Yucatán Peninsula. Area: 19,394 sq. mi./50,212 sq. km. Pop. 494,000. Capital: Chetumal.

Quir•i•nal |'kwirənəl| one of the seven original hills on which Rome was built. The Quirinal Palace, built for the Pope, has been home to kings, and now is home to the president of Italy.

Qui•to |'kētō| the capital and educational and cultural center of Ecuador. Pop. 1,401,000. It is situated in the Andes just S of the equator, at an altitude of 9,350 ft./2,850 m.

Qui•vi•ra |kī'vērä| legendary land of wealth, somewhere in what is now the U.S. SW, sought by Spanish adventurers. The 1540 Coronado expedition followed rumors as far as Great Bend, Kansas.

Qum•ran |koōm'ræn| region on the W shore of the Dead Sea, in the West Bank. The Dead Sea scrolls were found (1947–56) in caves at nearby Khirbet Qumran, the site of an ancient Jewish (probably Essene) settlement.

Qwa•qwa |'kwäkwə| (also **QwaQwa**) former homeland established in South Africa for the South Sotho people, in the Drakensberg Mts. in what is now Free State province.

Qy•zyl•or•da |kə͵silər'dä| (also **Kzyl-Orda**) **1** administrative subdivision in S Kazakhstan, E of the Aral Sea. Pop. 665,000. **2** its capital. Pop. 158,000.

Rr

Ra·bat |rə'bät| the capital of Morocco, an industrial port on the Atlantic coast. Pop. 1,220,000. It was founded as a fort in the 12th century by the Almohads, and is today an administrative and textile center.

Ra·baul |rä'bowl| the chief town and port of the island of New Britain, in Papua New Guinea. Pop. 17,000.

Ra·ci·bóorz |rä'CHĕboŏsH| (German name **Ratibor**) industrial port town in S Poland, on the Oder River. Pop. 62,000.

Ra·cine |rə'sēn; rä'sēn| industrial city in SE Wisconsin, on Lake Michigan. Pop. 84,298.

Rǎ·dǎ·u·ţi |,rədə'ŏŏtsē| industrial town in N Romania, in Bukovina. Pop. 31,000.

Rad·nor·shire |'rædnərsHiər; sHər; rædnərsHir| former county of E Wales. It became part of Powys in 1974.

Ra·dom |'rä,dawm| industrial city in central Poland. Pop. 228,000.

Rae Ba·re·li |rī bə'rä,lē| city in N central India, in Uttar Pradesh state, SSE of Lucknow. Pop. 130,000.

Rae·tia |'rē,sHēə| (also **Rhaetia**) ancient Roman province, S of the Danube River in what is now E Switzerland and part of the Tyrol.

Ra·gu·sa[1] |rə'gŏŏsə| Italian name (until 1918) for DUBROVNIK, Croatia. It is the probable source of the word *argosy*, referring to large and richly-freighted merchant ships of the 16th century.

Ra·gu·sa[2] |rə'gŏŏsə| industrial town in SE Sicily, S Italy, capital of Ragusa province. Pop. 69,000.

Rah·way |'raw,wā| industrial city in NE New Jersey, SW of Elizabeth. Pop. 25,325.

Ra·ia·tea |,rīə'tāə| volcanic island, the largest in the Leeward group of the Society Islands, French Polynesia. It has been thought the homeland from which Polynesian migrations spread across the Pacific.

Rai·chur |'rīCHər| commercial town in S central India, in Karnataka state. Pop. 171,000.

Rain·bow Bridge |'rānbō| bridge of natural rock, the world's largest, in S Utah, just N of the border with Arizona. Its span is 278 ft./86 m.

Rai·nier, Mount |,rā'nēr| volcanic peak in the SW of Washington State in the U.S. Rising to a height of 14,410 ft./4,395 m., it is the highest peak in the Cascade Range.

Rainy River |'rā,nē| short river that flows W along the Minnesota-Ontario border, past International Falls and into the Lake of the Woods. One of its sources is Rainy Lake, also on the border.

Rai·pur |'rī,pawr| city in central India, in Madhya Pradesh, an agricultural processing center. Pop. 438,000.

Ra·jah·mun·dry |,räjə'mŏŏndrē| commercial and industrial city in E central India, in Andhra Pradesh state. Pop. 404,000,

Ra·ja·sthan |'räjə,stän| state in W India, on the Pakistani border. Pop. 43.88 million. Capital: Jaipur. The W part of the state consists largely of the Thar Desert and is sparsely populated. □ **Rajasthani** *adj. & n.*

Ra·ja·sthan Canal |'räjə,stän| former name for the INDIRA GANDHI CANAL, India.

Raj·kot |'räj,kōt| administrative city in Gujarat, W India, in an agricultural area. Pop. 556,000.

Raj·pu·ta·na |,räjpə'tänə| ancient region of India consisting of a collection of princely states ruled by dynasties. Following independence from Britain in 1947, they united to form the state of Rajasthan, parts also being incorporated into Gujarat and Madhya Pradesh.

Raj·sha·hi |,räj'sHä,hē| industrial port on the Ganges River in W Bangladesh. Pop. 325,000.

Ra·leigh |'rawlē; 'rälē| the state capital of North Carolina, a research and industrial center in a tobacco growing region. Pop. 207,951.

Ra·mat Gan |rə'mät 'gän| industrial city in W central Israel, adjacent to Tel Aviv. Pop. 122,000.

Ram·bouil·let |,ränbŏŏ'yä| town in N France, in the Forest of Rambouillet. Pop. 25,000. The chateau here, formerly a royal residence, is now the summer home of the French president, and a conference center.

Ra·mil·lies |'rämē'yē| village in central Belgium, site of a 1706 battle in which English troops defeated French forces.

Ram·pur |'ræm,pŏŏr| town in N India, in Uttar Pradesh state. Pop. 243,000. It is noted for a collection of rare manuscripts and Mogul miniature paintings.

Ran·ca·gua |,rän'kägwə| historic city in central Chile, capital of the Libertador General Bernardo O'Higgins region. Pop. 190,000. Copper mining, manufacturing, and agriculture are important here.

Ran·chi |'rænCHē| industrial and educational city in Bihar, NE India. Pop. 598,000.

Ran·cho Cor·do·va |'ræn,CHŌ 'kawr-,dəvə| industrial suburb in N central California, NE of Sacramento. Pop. 48,731.

Ran·cho Cu·ca·mon·ga |'ræn,CHŌ ,kōō-kə'mäNGə| (also **Cucamonga**) city in SW California, a residential and industrial suburb E of Los Angeles. Pop. 101,409.

Rand |rænd| also **the Rand** another name for WITWATERSRAND, South Africa.

Ran·ders |'rænərz| port of Denmark, on the Randers Fjord on the E coast of the Jutland peninsula. Pop. 61,000.

Rand·olph |'ræn,dawlf| town in E Massachusetts, a suburb S of Boston. Pop. 30,093.

Rand·stad |'ränd,städ| urban region in the NW of the Netherlands that stretches in a horseshoe shape from Dordrecht and Rotterdam to Utrecht and Amersfoort via The Hague, Leiden, Haarlem, and Amsterdam. The majority of the people of the Netherlands live in this area.

Range·ley Lakes |'ränj,lē| resort region in W Maine, near the New Hampshire line, noted for Rangeley, Mooselookmeguntic, and other lakes and the Mahoosuc Range, which stands just S.

Ran·goon |ræNG'gōōn| the capital of Burma, a port in the Irrawaddy delta. Pop. 2,459,000. For centuries a Buddhist religious center, it is the site of the Shwe Dagon Pagoda, built over 2,500 years ago. The modern city was established by the British in the mid-19th century and became capital in 1886. Burmese name **Yangon**.

Rang·pur |'rəNG,pawr| city in NW Bangladesh. Pop. 221,000. It is noted for its cotton carpets.

Rann of Kutch see KUTCH, RANN OF, India.

Ra·pal·lo |rə'pä,lō| seaport and resort in NW Italy, on the Riviera, on the Gulf of Genoa. Pop. 27,000.

Ra·pa Nui |,rä,pä 'nōō,ē| Polynesian name for EASTER ISLAND.

Rap·id City |'ræ,pid| city in SW South Dakota, commercial center for Black Hills and Mount Rushmore tourism. Pop. 54,523.

Rap·pa·han·nock River |,ræpə'hænək| river that flows 210 mi./340 km. across E Virginia, into the Tidewater region. Fredericksburg lies on it, the Northern Neck to the N.

Rar·i·tan River |'rærə,tən| short river in central New Jersey that flows past New Brunswick and Perth Amboy, into Raritan Bay, an arm of New York Bay and the Atlantic.

Rar·o·ton·ga |,rärə'tawNGə| mountainous island in the S Pacific, the chief island of the Cook Islands. Its chief town, Avarua, is the capital of the Cook Islands. □ **Rarotongan** adj. & n.

Ras al Khai·mah |'räs ,el'kämə| **1** one of the seven member states of the United Arab Emirates. Pop. 144,000. It joined the UAE in 1972, after the British withdrawal from the Persian Gulf. **2** its capital, a port on the Gulf. Pop. 42,000.

Ra·shid |rə'sHēd| (formerly **Rosetta**) port city in N Egypt, E of Alexandria at the Rashid (Rosetta) branch of the delta of the Nile River. Pop. 52,000. The Rosetta stone, key to deciphering Egyptian hieroglyphics, was found here in 1799.

Rasht |ræsHt| (also **Resht**) commercial and industrial city in N Iran, near the Caspian Sea. Pop. 341,000.

Rath·lin Island |'ræTH,lin| island in the North Channel, off County Antrim, Northern Ireland, associated with ancient connections between Ireland and Scotland.

Ra·ting·en |'rätiNG,ən| industrial city in NW Germany, N of Dusseldorf. Pop. 91,000.

Rat Islands |'ræt| island group in the Aleutian Islands, in SW Alaska. Lying between the Near and Andreanof islands, they include Amchitka and Kiska.

Rat·lam |,rət'läm| (also **Rutlam**) commercial city in W central India, in Madhya Pradesh state. Pop. 196,000.

Ra·ton |rə'tōn| commercial city in NE New Mexico, at the Colorado border. It grew below Raton Pass, which was key in the development of the Santa Fe Trail and Santa Fe Railroad.

Ra·ven·na |rə'venə| city near the Adriatic coast in N central Italy. Pop. 137,000. It became the capital of the Western Roman Empire in 402 and then of the Ostrogothic kingdom of Italy, afterward serving as capital of Byzantine Italy. It is noted for its ancient mosaics dating from the early Christian period. The oil industry and tourism are important today.

Ra·vens·brück |,rävenz'brōōk| village in Brandenburg, NE Germany, N of Berlin. The Nazis maintained a concentration camp here during World War II.

Ra·vi |'rä,vē| river in the N of the Indian subcontinent, one of the headwaters of the Indus, which rises in the Himalayas in Himachel Pradesh, NW India, and flows 450 mi./725 km. generally SW into Pakistan, where it empties into the Chenab River just N of Multan.

Ra·wal·pin·di |,räwəl'pindē| industrial city

in Punjab province, N Pakistan, in the foothills of the Himalayas. Pop. 955,000. A former military station, it was the interim capital of Pakistan, 1959–67, during the construction of Islamabad.

Raw•son |'rawsən| port town in S Argentina, in Patagonia, on the Atlantic coast, capital of Chubut province. Pop. 19,000.

Read•ing[1] |'rediNG| the county seat of Berkshire, in S England, on the Kennet River near its junction with the Thames. Pop. 123,000.

Read•ing[2] |'rediNG| industrial and commercial city in SE Pennsylvania, on the Schuylkill River. Pop. 78,380.

Re•ci•fe |re'sēfē| port and resort city on the Atlantic coast of NE Brazil, capital of the state of Pernambuco. Pop. 1,298,000. Former name **Pernambuco**.

Reck•ling•hau•sen |,rəkliNG'howzən| industrial city in NW Germany, S of Münster. Pop. 126,000.

Red Bank |'rəd| resort and commercial borough in E New Jersey. Pop. 10,636.

Red•bridge |'red,brij| largely residential borough of NE Greater London, England. Pop. 221,000. On the Essex border, it includes much of Epping Forest.

Red China term used of mainland China, in reference to to its communist government.

Red Deer |'red,dir| industrial city in central Alberta, an oil industry center between Edmonton and Calgary. Pop. 58,134.

Red•ding |'rədiNG| commercial and resort city in N California, at the N end of the Sacramento Valley. Pop. 66,462.

Red•ditch |'redicH| industrial town in W central England, a Birmingham suburb in Worcestershire. Pop. 77,000.

Red Hook |'red| industrial port section of Brooklyn, New York, on New York Bay across from Governor's Island.

Red•lands |'redlənz| commercial and resort city in S California, near the San Bernardino Mts. Pop. 60,394.

Red•mond |'redmənd| city in W central Washington, a suburb NE of Seattle, noted as the home of the Microsoft corporation. Pop. 35,800.

Re•don•do Beach |,rā'dändō| city in SW California, a largely residential suburb on Santa Monica Bay, S of Los Angeles. Pop. 60,167.

Red River[1] |red| river in SE Asia, which rises in S China and flows 730 mi./1,175 km. generally SE through N Vietnam to the Gulf of Tonkin. Chinese name **Yuan Jiang**. Vietnamese name **Song Hong**.

Red River[2] |red| **1** river in the S U.S., a tributary of the Mississippi, which rises in N Texas and flows 1,222 mi./1,966 km. generally SE, forming part of the border between Texas and Oklahoma, and enters the Mississippi in Louisiana. Also called **Red River of the South**. **2** river in the N U.S. and Canada, which rises in North Dakota and flows 545 mi./877 km. N, forming for most of its length the border between North Dakota and Minnesota, before entering Manitoba, passing Winnipeg, and emptying into Lake Winnipeg. Also called **Red River of the North**.

Red Sea |red| long, narrow nearly landlocked sea separating Africa from the Arabian Peninsula. It is linked to the Indian Ocean in the S by the Bab el Mandab and Gulf of Aden and to the Mediterranean in the N by the Suez Canal.

Red Square |red| large public square in Moscow, Russia, bounded on one side by the Kremlin and on another by Saint Basil's cathedral.

Red•wood City |'red,wŏod| port city in N central California, on SW San Francisco Bay, now part of the Silicon Valley complex. Pop. 66,072.

Reel•foot Lake |'rēl,fŏot| lake in the NW corner of Tennessee, near the Mississippi River, formed during the 1811 earthquake centered on nearby New Madrid, Missouri.

Re•gens•burg |'rāgəmz,bərg| port city, a tourist and industrial center in SE Germany, at the confluence of the Danube and Regen rivers. Pop. 123,000.

Reg•gio di Ca•la•bria |'red,jō ,dē ,kä'läbrēə| port at the S tip of the 'toe' of Italy, on the Strait of Messina, capital of Calabria region. Pop. 183,000. The original settlement was founded about 720 B.C. by Greek colonists as Rhegion (Latin, Rhegium).

Reg•gio Emi•lia |,ä'mēlyə| industrial city in N Italy. Pop. 130,000. It is capital of a province of the same name (also called **Reggio Emilia**) in Emilia-Romagna.

Re•gi•na |rə'jīnə| the capital of Saskatchewan, situated in the center of the wheat-growing plains of S central Canada. Pop. 179,178. It was the administrative headquarters of the Northwest Territories until 1905, and is today a wheat, oil, and steel center.

Re•ho•vot |ri'hō,vōt| (also **Rehovoth; Rehoboth**) industrial town in central Israel, SW of Ramala. Pop. 85,000.

Reich |rīk| German word for 'state or nation', used for particular German governments. The First Reich was the Holy

Roman Empire; the Second Reich was the German Empire (1871–1919); the Third Reich was the Nazi regime (1933–1945).

Rei·chen·bach |'rīkʜən‚bäk| waterfall in SW Switzerland, with five cascades dropping more than 200 ft./61 m.

Reich·stag, the |'rīkʜ‚stæg| historic name for the lower house of the German parliament. Hitler charged that communists had set a major fire that destroyed most of the Reichstag in 1933; the Nazis won the next election, starting their rise to power. The Reichstag was abolished in 1949, but its restored building stands in the Tiergarten park in Berlin.

Reims |rēmz| (also **Rheims**) city of N France, chief town of Champagne-Ardenne region. Pop. 185,000. It was the traditional coronation place of most French kings and is noted for its 13th-century Gothic cathedral and as the center of the champagne industry.

Re·ma·gen |'rämä‚gən| town in western Germany, on the Rhine River, where the Allies first crossed the Rhine, taking the Ludendorff Bridge, in 1945.

Rem·scheid |'rem‚sʜīt| industrial city in NW Germany, E of Düsseldorf. Pop. 124,000.

Ren·do·va |‚ren'dōvə| island in the W central Solomon Islands, off the coast of New Georgia, the scene of 1943 fighting between U.S. and Japanese forces.

Ren·frew·shire |'renfrōō‚sʜir; sʜər| administrative region and former county of W central Scotland, on the Firth of Clyde, divided into *Renfrewshire* and *East Renfrewshire.*

Rennes |ren| industrial and educational city in NW France. Pop. 204,000. It was established as the capital of a Celtic tribe, the Redones, later becoming the capital of the ancient kingdom of Brittany.

Re·no |'rēnō| city in W Nevada, on the Truckee River. Pop. 133,850. It is noted as a gambling resort and was long the scene of many quick marriages and divorces.

Ren·ton |'rentən| city in W central Washington, a residential and industrial suburb SE of Seattle, on Lake Washington. Pop. 41,688.

Re·pub·li·can River |‚ri'pəblikən| river that flows 445 mi./715 km. from NE Colorado through S Nebraska and into Kansas, where it joins the Smoky Hill River to form the Kansas River.

Re·search Tri·an·gle Park |'rē‚sərcʜ 'trīæNG‚gəl| research complex in central

North Carolina, between Durham, Raleigh, and Chapel Hill, created in the 1950s by Duke and North Carolina State universities and the University of North Carolina.

Re·sis·ten·cia |‚räsis'tensēə| city in NE Argentina, capital of Chaco province, across the Paraná River from Corrientes. Pop. 291,000. It exports agricultural produce and has some industries.

Re·şi·ta |'re‚sʜētsä| industrial city in the foothills of the Transylvanian Alps, W Romania, capital of Caraş-Severin county. Pop. 110,000.

Res·ton |'restən| planned residential and commercial community in N Virginia, NW of Washington, D.C., established in the 1960s. Pop. 48,556.

Re·thondes |‚rə'tawn| village in N France, near Compiègne. The armistice that ended World War I was signed here on November 11, 1918, and Hitler demanded that the French surrender in 1940 be signed in the same railway car.

Re·thym·non |'re.ʜēm‚nawn| port on the N coast of Crete. Pop. 18,000. Greek name **Réthimnon**.

Ré·u·nion |rē'yōōnyən| volcanically active, subtropical island in the Indian Ocean E of Madagascar, one of the Mascarene Islands. Pop. 597,000. Capital: Saint-Denis. A French possession since 1638, the island became an administrative region of France in 1974.

Réunion

Re·us |'re‚ōōs| commercial and industrial town in NE Spain. Pop. 88,000. It has an international airport.

Reut·ling·en |'roitliNG‚ən| industrial city in western Germany, S of Stuttgart. Pop. 106,000.

Re·vere |rə'vir| suburban city in E central Massachusetts, on Massachusetts Bay NE of Boston, famed for its beach. Pop. 42,786.

Re·vil·la·gi·ge·do Islands |rə‚viləgə 'gēdō| (also **Revilla Gigedo**) island group in the Pacific off the W coast of Mexico, part of Colima state. Socorro is the largest.

Reyes, Point |'rāz| promontory in NW California, N of Drakes Bay, in Marin County, noted for its winds, fog, and wildlife.

Reyk·ja·vik |'rākyə,vik| the capital and oldest and largest city of Iceland, a port on the W coast. Pop. 98,000. It is the northernmost capital in the world.

Rey·no·sa |,rā'nōsə| commercial city in NE Mexico, in Tamaulipas state, across the Rio Grande from Hidalgo, Texas. Pop. 266,000. Agriculture and oil are important in the area.

Rhein |rīn| German name for the RHINE River.

Rhein·gau |'rīn,gow| wine-growing region in central Germany, on the Rhine River. It produces what are considered Germany's best white wines.

Rhein·land |'rīn,lænd| German name for the RHINELAND.

Rheinland-Pfalz |'rīn,lænd,fälts| German name for the state of RHINELAND-PALATI-NATE.

Rhine |rīn| river in W Europe that rises in the Swiss Alps and flows for 820 mi./1,320 km. to the North Sea, forming part of the German–Swiss border, before flowing through Germany, along the French border, and the Netherlands. On its course it flows through major cities including Basle (the head of navigation), Mannheim, Mainz, Cologne, and Düsseldorf. The Rhine is central to German culture and tourism, but has serious pollution problems today. German name **Rhein**; French name **Rhin**.

Rhine·land |'rīn,lænd| the region of western Germany through which the Rhine flows, especially the part to the W of the river. German name **Rheinland**.

Rhineland-Palatinate |'rīnləndpə'lætənāt| state of western Germany. Pop. 3,702,000. Capital: Mainz. German name **Rheinland-Pfalz**.

Rhode Island see box. □ **Rhode Islander** *n.*

Rhodes |rōdz| **1** Greek island in the SE Aegean, off the Turkish coast, the largest of the Dodecanese and the most easterly island in the Aegean. Pop. 98,000. Greek name **Ródhos**. **2** its capital, a port on the northernmost tip. Pop. 42,000. It was founded *c.*408 B.C. and was the site of the Colossus of Rhodes, one of the Seven Wonders of the Ancient World.

Rho·de·sia |rō'dēZHə| the former name of

Rhode Island

Capital/largest city: Providence
Other cities: Cranston, Kingston, East Providence, Newport, Pawtucket, Warwick, Woonsocket
Population: 1,003,464 (1990); 988,480 (1998); 1,012,000 (2005 proj.)
Population rank (1990): 43
Rank in land area: 50
Abbreviation: RI; R.I.
Official name: State of Rhode Island and Providence Plantations
Nickname: Ocean State; Little Rhody
Motto: 'Hope'
Bird: Rhode Island Red chicken
Flower: violet
Tree: red maple
Song: "Rhode Island"
Noted physical features: Narragansett Bay; Block Island Sound; Jerimoth Hill; Point Judith
Tourist attractions: Newport; Block Island
Admission date: May 29, 1790
Order of admission: 13
Name origin: For Rhode Island in Narragansett Bay, which Italian explorer Giovanni da Verrazano is said to have named for its likeness to the Mediterranean isle of Rhodes, off the coast of Turkey.

---

a large territory in south central Africa that was divided into Northern Rhodesia (now Zambia) and Southern Rhodesia (now Zimbabwe). The region was developed by Cecil Rhodes through the British South African Company, which administered it until Southern Rhodesia became a self-governing British colony in 1923 and Northern Rhodesia a British protectorate in 1924. From 1953 to 1963 Northern and Southern Rhodesia were united with Nyasaland (now Malawi) to form the Federation of Rhodesia and Nyasaland. The name Rhodesia was adopted by Southern Rhodesia when Northern Rhodesia left the Federation in 1963 to become the independent republic of Zambia; Rhodesia became independent Zimbabwe in 1979. □ **Rhodesian** *adj. & n.*

Rhod·o·pe Mountains |'rä,dəpē| mountain system in the Balkans, SE Europe, on the border between Bulgaria and Greece, rising to a height of over 6,600 ft./2,000 m. and including the Rila Mts. in the NW.

Rhond·da |'rändə| urbanized district of S Wales, which extends along the valleys of the Rhondda Fawr and Rhondda Fach rivers. It was formerly noted as a coal-mining area.

Rhône |rōn| river in SW Europe that rises in the Swiss Alps and flows 505 mi./812 km., through Lake Geneva into France, then to Lyons, Avignon, and the Mediterranean W of Marseilles, where it forms a wide delta that includes the Camargue.

Rhône-Alpes |'rōnälp| region of SE France, extending from the Rhône valley to the borders with Switzerland and Italy and including much of the former duchy of Savoy.

Rhum |rōōm| (also **Rum**) island in the Inner Hebrides of Scotland, to the S of Skye, a nature reserve.

Ri•al•to[1] |rē'æl,tō| city in SW California, a suburb W of San Bernardino. Pop. 72,388.

Ri•al•to[2] |rē'æl,tō| island in Venice, containing the old mercantile quarter of medieval Venice. The Rialto Bridge, completed in 1591 and lined with shops, crosses the Grand Canal between Rialto and San Marco islands. It gives its name to lively commercial zones including the theater district of central Manhattan, New York City.

Ri•au Archipelago |'rē,aw| island group in Indonesia, off the SE end of the Malay Peninsula, at the entrance to the Strait of Malacca.

Ri•bei•rão Prê•to |'rēbā,rown 'prā,tōō| city in SE Brazil, in São Paulo state. Pop. 453,000. It is an agricultural center in a coffee-producing region.

Rich•ard•son |'riCHərdsən| city in NE Texas, a suburb on the NE side of Dallas. Pop. 74,840.

Rich•field |'riCH,fēld| city in SE Minnesota, a suburb S of Minneapolis. Pop. 35,710.

Rich•land |'riCHlənd| city in SE Washington, on the Columbia and Yakima rivers near Kennewick and Pasco, with which it has become a service center for the Hanford nuclear reservation. Pop. 32,315.

Rich•mond[1] |'riCHmənd| city in SW British Columbia, a suburb just S of Vancouver. Pop. 126,624.

Rich•mond[2] |'riCHmənd| industrial port city in N central California, on E San Francisco Bay, just N of Berkeley. Pop. 87,425.

Rich•mond[3] |'riCHmənd| industrial city in E central Indiana. Pop. 38,705.

Rich•mond[4] |'riCHmənd| residential borough of Greater London, England, on the Thames. Pop. 155,000. It contains Hampton Court Palace and the Royal Botanic Gardens at Kew. Full name **Richmond-upon-Thames**.

Rich•mond[5] |'riCHmənd| the state capital of Virginia, a port on the James River. Pop. 203,056. During the American Civil War it was the Confederate capital after July 1861. It is a tobacco, heavy industry, and educational center.

Rich•mond County |'riCHmənd| see STATEN ISLAND.

Ri•deau Canal |,ri'dō| waterway in E Ontario, created in the 1820s, linking Ottawa and the Ottawa River with Kingston and Lake Ontario.

Rie•sen•ge•bir•ge Mountains |'rēzənGə ,bərgə| mountain range on the border between SW Poland and the N Czech Republic, part of the Sudetês Mts.

Rif Mountains |'rif| (also **Er Rif**) mountain range of N Morocco, running parallel to the Mediterranean for about 180 mi./290 km. E from Tangier. Rising to over 7,000 ft./2,250 m., it forms a W extension of the Atlas Mts. The mountains are a noted retreat of Berber tribes.

Ri•ga |'rēgə| industrial port on the Baltic Sea, capital and largest city of Latvia. Pop. 915,000. It was a 13th-century hub of the Hanseatic League.

Right Bank |'rīt 'bæŋk| district of the city of Paris, France, to the N of the Seine River. The historic home to commerce and the middle class of Paris, the area contains the Champs Élysées and the Louvre. French name **Rive Droite**.

Ri•je•ka |ri'yekə| industrial port on the Adriatic coast of Croatia. Pop. 168,000. Before 1918 it was the chief Austro-Hungarian naval base. Italian name **Fiume**.

Ri•la Mountains |'rē,lä| range in W Bulgaria, forming the westernmost extent of the Rhodope Mts. It is the highest range in Bulgaria, rising to 9,596 ft./2,925 m. at Mount Musala.

Ri•mi•ni |'rēminē| port and resort on the Adriatic coast of NE Italy. Pop. 131,000. It is a cultural center associated with the medieval Malatesta family.

Ri•mou•ski |,ri'mōōskē| industrial port city in SE Quebec, on the Saint Lawrence River NE of Quebec City. Pop. 30,873.

Ring of Fire |'riNG ,əv 'fīr| term for the volcanically and seismically active regions around the Pacific, including the Andes Mts., the Aleutian Islands, the Japanese and Philippine islands, and many other island and continental zones.

Ri•o•bam•ba |'rē,ō'bämbə| historic city in central Ecuador, capital of Chimborazo province. Pop. 96,000. It is an industrial and commercial center. The first Ecuadorian constitution was drawn up here in 1830.

Rio Bran•co |'bräNG,ko͞o| city in W Brazil, a rubber industry center and capital of the state of Acre. Pop. 197,000.

Rio Cla•ro |'klä,ro͞o| industrial and commercial city in SE Brazil, in São Paulo state. Pop. 153,000.

Río Cuar•to |'kwär,tō| commercial city in central Argentina, on the Cuarto River in Córdoba province. Pop. 139,000.

Rio de Ja•nei•ro |,dä zHə'nerō| 1 state of E Brazil, on the Atlantic coast. Pop. 12.78 million. 2 (also **Rio**) its capital. Pop. 5,481,000. The chief port of Brazil, it was the capital from 1763 until 1960, when it was replaced by Brasilia. Its skyline is dominated by two rocky peaks: Sugar Loaf Mts. to the E and Corcovado, with its statue of Christ, to the S. A leading financial, cultural, and tourist center, Rio is noted for its Copacabana and Ipanema beach resorts, and its annual Carnival.

Río de Oro |dä 'aw,rō| arid region on the Atlantic coast of NW Africa, forming the S part of Western Sahara. It was united with Saguia el Hamra in 1958 to form the province of Spanish Sahara (now Western Sahara).

Rio Gran•de |'rēō 'grænd; 'grändä| river of North America that rises in the Rocky Mts. of SW Colorado and flows 1,880 mi./3,030 km. generally SE to the Gulf of Mexico, forming the U.S.–Mexico border from El Paso, Texas to the sea. Mexican name **Rio Bravo (del Norte).**

Rio Gran•de do Nor•te |'grän,dä do͞o 'nawr,tä| semiarid state of NE Brazil, on the Atlantic coast. Pop. 2,414,000. Capital: Natal.

Rio Gran•de do Sul |'grän,dä ,do͞o 'so͞ol| state of Brazil, on the Atlantic coast at the southern tip of the country, on the border with Uruguay. Pop. 9,135,000. Capital: Pôrto Alegre.

Rí•o•ha•cha |,rēyō'äCHə| historic port town in N Colombia, on the Caribbean Sea. Pop. 126,000. Coal, gold, and pearls have all been important local products.

Rio Mu•ni |'m(y)o͞onē| the part of Equatorial Guinea that lies on the mainland of W Africa, consisting largely of lowlands along the Mbini River. Its chief town is Bata.

Rio Ne•gro |'näg,rō| river of South America, which rises as the Guainia in E Colombia and flows for about 1,400 mi./2,255 km. through NW Brazil before joining the Amazon near Manaus.

Río Pie•dras |'pyädräs| academic and commercial section of San Juan, Puerto Rico, home to the University of Puerto Rico.

Rio Ran•cho |'rænCHō| city in N central New Mexico, a residential and industrial suburb NW of Albuquerque. Pop. 32,505.

Rip•on |'ripän| historic city in E Wisconsin, home to Ripon College and regarded as the birthplace of the Republican party. Pop. 7,241.

Ri•shon le-Ziyyon |,rē'sHawn,lətsē'yawn| (also **Rishon Le-Zion; Rishon Lezion; Rishon le Tsiyon**) mainly residential city in W Israel, S of Tel Aviv. Pop. 160,000.

Rish•ra |'risHrə| town in E India, in West Bengal state, N of Calcutta. Pop. 103,000.

Ri•sing Sun, Land of the |'rīziNG'sən| name for Japan, a translation of Chinese NIPPON.

Riv•er•side |'rivər,sīd| industrial and residential city in S California, in an orange-growing region E of Los Angeles. Pop. 226,505.

Ri•vi•era |,rivē'erə| Mediterranean coastal region from Marseilles, France, E to La Spezia, Italy, famed for its beauty and climate, and scene of many famed resorts. See also CÔTE D'AZUR.

Ri•vi•era Beach |,ri'virə| resort and industrial city in SE Florida, N of West Palm Beach. Pop. 27,639.

Riv•ne |'rivnə| industrial city in W Ukraine, NE of Lviv. Pop. 233,000. Russian name **Rovno.**

Ri•yadh |rē'yäd| the capital and comercial center of Saudi Arabia. Pop. 2,000,000. Situated on a high plateau in the center of the country, it has extensive new suburbs.

Road Town |'rōd| the capital of the British Virgin Islands, on the island of Tortola. Pop. 6,000.

Ro•a•noke |'rōə,nōk| industrial city in W central Virginia, a rail center in the Shenandoah Valley. Pop. 96,397.

Ro•a•noke Island |'rōə,nōk| island in E North Carolina, E of Croatan Sound, inside the Outer Banks, scene of the first English settlement in America, the "Lost Colony," established in 1585, which disappeared mysteriously by 1591.

Ro•a•noke River |'rōə,nōk| river that flows 410 mi./660 km. from SW Virginia, across North Carolina, to Albemarle Sound. Roanoke, Virginia and Roanoke Rapids, North Carolina along its course.

roar•ing for•ties |'rōriNG 'fawr,tēz| (**the roaring forties**) stormy ocean tracts between latitudes 40° and 50° S.

Rob•ben Island |,räbən| island in Table

Bay, off CapeTown, South Africa. Formerly a military reservation, then a prison colony that held Nelson Mandela among others, it is now a resort.

Rob·in·son Cru·soe Island |'räbin,sən 'kro͞o,sō| (also **Mas á Tierra**) island in the JUAN FERNANDEZ group off W Chile, associated with Alexander Selkirk, the model for the protagonist of the Defoe novel, who was marooned here in 1704.

Ro·ca·ma·dour |rō'kämä,dawr| medieval pilgrimage village, built into a cliff in SW France, in Quercy. Pilgrims climbed the 223 stone steps to the tomb of Saint Amadour as part of their trek to Santiago de Compostela. The site is now a popular tourist attraction.

Roch·dale |'räCH,dāl| industrial town in NW England, N of Manchester. Pop. 97,000. A textile center, it was the birthplace in 1844 of the British cooperative movement.

Roche·fort |'rōSH,fawr| (also called **Rochefort-sur-Mer**) industrial port in W France, on the Charente River S of La Rochelle, formerly an important naval base. Pop. 27,000.

Roch·es·ter[1] |'räCHəstər| town on the Medway estuary SE of London, England. Pop. 24,000.

Roch·es·ter[2] |'räCHəstər| industrial city in SE Minnesota, home to the famed Mayo Clinic, established in 1889. Pop. 70,475.

Roch·es·ter[3] |'räCHəstər| city in NW New York State, on Lake Ontario, a manufacturing center noted for its photographic and optical industries. Pop. 231,636.

Roch·es·ter Hills |'rä,CHestər| residential and industrial city in SE Michigan, just NE of Pontiac. Pop. 61,766.

Rock·all |'räk,awl| rocky islet in the N Atlantic, about 250 mi./400 km. NW of Ireland. It was formally annexed by Britain in 1955 but has since become the subject of territorial dispute among Britain, Denmark, Iceland, and Ireland.

Rock·e·fel·ler Center |'räkə,felər| business building complex in midtown Manhattan, New York City. Radio City Music Hall is here.

Rock·ford |'räkfərd| industrial city in N central Illinois, on the Rock River. Pop. 139,426.

Rock·hamp·ton |räk'hæmptən| port on the Fitzroy River, in Queensland, NE Australia. Pop. 56,000. It is the center of Australia's largest beef-producing area.

Rock Hill |'räk| industrial city in N South Carolina. Pop. 41,643.

Rock Island |'räk| industrial city in NW Illinois, on the Mississippi River, one of the Quad Cities. It is noted for its arsenal. Pop. 40,552.

Rock·land County |'räk,lən(d)| largely suburban county in SE New York, on the W side of the Hudson River and the New Jersey line. Pop. 265,475.

Rock of Gi·bral·tar |,ji'brältər| see GIBRALTAR.

Rock·port |'räk,pärt| town in NE Massachusetts, a resort and fishing community on Cape Ann. Pop. 7,482.

Rock, the nickname for ALCATRAZ.

Rock·ville |'räk,vil| city in central Maryland, a residential suburb with many government offices, NW of Washington, D.C. Pop. 44,835.

Rocky Mount |'rä,kē| industrial city in E central North Carolina, a tobacco industry center. Pop. 48,997.

Rocky Mountains |,räkē| (also **the Rockies**) the chief mountain system of North America, which extends from the U.S.–Mexico border to the Yukon Territory of N Canada. It separates the Great Plains from the W intermountain and coastal states and forms the Continental Divide. Several peaks rise to over 14,000 ft./4,300 m., the highest being Colorado's Mount Elbert at 14,431 ft./4,399 m.

Ró·dhos |'rōdōs| Greek name for RHODES.

Rod·ri·guez |,räd'rēgəs| (also **Rodrigues**) mountainous island in the W Indian Ocean, NE of Mauritius, of which it is a dependency. Pop. 35,000. Fishing and tourism are important here.

Roe·se·la·re |,ro͞osə'lärə| textile manufacturing town in NW Belgium, in West Flanders. Pop. 58,000. French name **Roulers**.

Rogue River |'ro͞oZH| river that flows 200 mi./320 km. W across S Oregon, to the Pacific. In an agricultural area, it is noted for its fishing.

Rohn·ert Park |'rōnərt| city in NW California, a suburb N of San Francisco. Pop. 36,326.

Roh·tak |'rōtək| commercial town in NW India, in Haryana state. Pop. 216,000.

Ro·ma |'rōmə| Italian name for ROME.

Ro·ma·gna |rō'mänyə| historic region, formerly under papal control, in N central Italy, on the Adriatic Sea. Its territory is now part of several Italian regions: Emilia-Romagna, Marche, and Tuscany.

Ro·man Empire |'rōmən| areas controlled by Rome during the time of its emperors, from the 1st century B.C. until its collapse in A.D. 476. Its greatest extent was from Armenia and Mesopotamia in the E to Iberia in the W, and from Britain in the N to N Africa in the S. In A.D. 395 it was divided into the EASTERN EMPIRE and WESTERN EMPIRE.

Ro•ma•nia |rō'mānēə| (also **Rumania**) republic in SE Europe with a coastline on the Black Sea. Area: 88,461 sq. mi./229,027 sq. km. Pop. 23,276,000. Language, Romanian. Capital and largest city: Bucharest. The Dacia of Roman times, the country was later Wallachia and Moldavia, independent from the Ottoman Empire in 1878. From 1945 to 1989 it was a communist state. With sizable Hungarian, Gypsy, and German communities, it has an economy based on industry, mining, oil and gas, and some agriculture. □ **Romanian** adj. & n.

Romania

Rome[1] |rōm| industrial city in NW Georgia, on the Coosa River. Pop. 30,326.

Rome[2] |rōm| (Italian name **Roma**) the capital of Italy and of the Lazio region, situated on the Tiber River about 16 mi./25 km. inland from the Tyrrhenian Sea. Pop. 2,791,000. Italian name **Roma**. According to tradition the city was founded by Romulus (after whom it was named) in 753 B.C. on the Palatine Hill; as it grew it spread to the other six hills of Rome (Aventine, Caelian, Capitoline, Esquiline, and Quirinal). Rome was ruled by kings until the expulsion of Tarquinius Superbus in 510 B.C. led to the establishment of the Roman Republic. By the mid-2nd century B.C. Rome had subdued all of Italy and had come to dominate the W Mediterranean and the Hellenistic world in the E, acquiring the first of the overseas possessions that became the ROMAN EMPIRE. By the time of the empire's fall in the 5th century A.D. the city was overshadowed politically by Constantinople, but emerged as the seat of the papacy and as the spiritual capital of Western Christianity. In the 14th and 15th centuries Rome became a center of the Re-

naissance. It remained part of the Papal States until 1871, when it was made the capital of a unified Italy. Today it is a center of culture, finance, fashion, and international organizations. □ **Roman** adj. & n.

Rome[3] |rōm| industrial city in central New York, on the Mohawk River. Pop. 44,350.

Ron•ces•valles |ˌrawnsəs'välyāz| (in French **Roncevaux**) mountain pass in the Pyrenees, between Pamplona, Spain and Saint-Jean-Pied-de-Port, France. Part of Charlemagne's army was defeated here in 788; the feats and death of one of his nobles, Roland, are celebrated in the *Chanson de Roland.*

Ron•champ |ˌrawn'sHän| commune in E central France, near the Swiss and German borders. A massive, free-standing chapel designed by French architect Le Corbusier was erected here in 1950–55.

Ron•dô•nia |rawn'dō,nyə| state of NW Brazil, in the Amazon basin on the border with Bolivia. Pop. 1,131,000. Capital: Pôrto Velho.

Rong•e•lap |'rawNGə,læp| atoll in the W Pacific, in the N Marshall Islands at the NW end of the Ratak group, E of Bikini. It was evacuated in the 1980s because of contamination from 1950s nuclear tests at ENIWETOK.

Roo•se•velt Island |'rōzə,velt| (formerly **Blackwell's Island** and **Welfare Island**) residential island in the East River, New York City, between Manhattan and Queens.

Roo•se•velt Roads |'rōzə,velt| (official name **Atlantic Fleet Weapons Training Facility**) naval reserve on the E coast of Puerto Rico.

Roquefort-sur-Soulzhon |rōk'fawrso͞or ˌso͞ol'zawn| village in S France, in the S foothills of the Massif Central. It is famous for its blue-veined cheese, which is aged in limestone caves.

Ro•rai•ma |raw'rīmə| **1** mountain in the Guiana Highlands of South America, at the junction of the borders of Venezuela, Brazil, and Guyana. Rising to 9,094 ft./2,774 m., it is the highest peak in the range. **2** state of N Brazil, on the borders with Venezuela and Guyana. Pop. 216,000. Capital: Boa Vista.

Ro•sa•rio |rō'särēō| inland port on the Paraná River in E central Argentina. Pop. 1,096,000. An outlet for Pampas agriculture, it is also industrial.

Ros•com•mon |räs'kämən| **1** county in the N central part of the Republic of Ireland, in the province of Connacht. Pop. 52,000. **2** its county seat. Pop. 18,000.

Ro•seau |ˌrōˈzō| the capital of the island commonwealth of Dominica, in the Caribbean. Pop. 16,000.

Rose•mead |ˈrōz·mēd| city in SW California, a residential suburb E of Los Angeles. Pop. 51,638.

Rose•ville[1] |ˈrōzˌvil| city in NE California, a suburb NE of Sacramento. Pop. 44,685.

Rose•ville[2] |ˈrōzˌvil| city in SE Michigan, a suburb NE of Detroit. Pop. 51,412.

Rose•ville[3] |ˈrōzˌvil| city in SE Minnesota, a suburb N of St. Paul. Pop. 33,485.

Ros•kil•de |ˈrawsˌkilə| port in Denmark, on the island of Zealand, W of Copenhagen. Pop. 49,000. It was the seat of Danish kings from *c.*1020 and the capital of Denmark until 1443.

Ross and Crom•ar•ty |ˈräs ˈkrawmərˌtē| former county of N Scotland, stretching from the Moray Firth to the North Minch. In 1975 it became part of the Highland region. Dingwall is the chief town.

Ross•lare |ˌräsˈler| ferry port on the SE coast of the Republic of Ireland, in County Wexford.

Ross Sea |ˈraws| large arm of the Pacific forming a deep indentation in the coast of Antarctica. At its head is the Ross Ice Shelf, the world's largest body of floating ice, which is approximately the size of France. On the E shores of the Ross Sea lies Ross Island, which is the site of Mount Erebus and of Scott Base, an Antarctic station established by New Zealand in 1957.

Ros•tock |ˈrästäk| industrial port on the Baltic coast of NE Germany. Pop. 244,000.

Ros•tov |rəsˈtawf| port and industrial city in SW Russia, on the Don River near its entry into the Sea of Azov. Pop. 1,025,000. The city is built around a fortress erected by the Turks in the 18th century. Full name **Rostov-on-Don**.

Ros•well[1] |ˈräzˌwel| city in NW Georgia, a suburb N of Atlanta. Pop. 47,923.

Ros•well[2] |ˈräzˌwel| agricultural and military city in SE New Mexico, the scene of a mysterious crash in July 1947. Controversy has surrounded claims by some investigators that the crashed object was a UFO. Pop. 44,654.

Ro•ta |ˈrōtə| island in the W Pacific, in the S Northern Mariana Islands, NE of Guam. Pop. 2,000. The scene of heavy World War II fighting and of an important U.S. air base, it now draws tourists.

Roth•er•ham |ˈräTHərəm| industrial town in N England, a steel center formerly in South Yorkshire. Pop. 247,000.

Ro•to•rua |ˌrōtōˈrōōə| city and health resort on North Island, New Zealand, on the SW shore of Lake Rotorua. Pop. 54,000. It lies at the center of a region of thermal springs and geysers.

Rot•ter•dam |ˈrätərˌdæm| city in the Netherlands, at the mouth of the Meuse River, 15 mi./25 km. inland from the North Sea. Pop. 582,000. It is one of the world's largest ports, with extensive shipbuilding, oil refining, and petrochemical industries. See also EUROPOORT.

Rott•weil |ˈrawtˌwīl; ˈrawtˌvīl| town in SW Germany, on the Neckar River, SW of Stuttgart. It gave its name to Rottweiler dogs, formerly used here by drovers.

Rou•baix |ˌrōōˈbā| industrial town in N France, near Lille on the Belgian border. Pop. 98,000. It is part of one of the most important textile-manufacturing regions in France.

Rou•en |ˈrwän| port on the Seine River in NW France, chief town of Haute-Normandie. Pop. 105,000. Rouen was in English possession from the time of the Norman Conquest until captured by the French in 1204, and again 1419–49; in 1431 Joan of Arc was tried and burned at the stake there. The modern city is an industrial and tourist center.

Rouge, River |ˈrōōZH| short river with several branches in and around Detroit, Michigan.

Rou•lers |rōōˈlers| French name for ROESELARE, Belgium.

Round Rock |ˈrownd| city in central Texas, a suburb N of Austin. Pop. 30,923.

Rous•sil•lon |ˌrōōsēˈyawn| former province of S France, on the border with Spain in the E Pyrenees, now part of Languedoc-Roussillon. Part of Spain until 1659, Roussillon retains many of its Spanish characteristics; Catalan is widely spoken.

Route 128 |rōōt wən ˈtwen(t)ēˌyāt; rowt| highway that circles Boston, Massachusetts in the N, W, and S, noted for its complex of high-technology industries.

Route 66 |rōōt ˈsikstē siks; rowt| former interstate highway from Chicago, Illinois to Santa Monica, California, designated in 1926 and today supplanted by such newer routes as Interstates 40 and 44.

Rouyn-Noranda |ˈrōōˌwinˌnawˈrændə| industrial city in SW Quebec, center of a major mining district. Pop. 26,448.

Ro•va•nie•mi |ˈrōväˌnyəmē| the principal town of Finnish Lapland, just S of the Arctic Circle. Pop. 33,000.

Rov•no |'rawvnə| Russian name for RIVNE, Ukraine.

Rox•burgh•shire |'rawksbərə,SHər; SHir| former county in S Scotland, now part of the Scottish Borders region. Hawick is the chief town.

Rox•bury |'rawksbə,rē| district of Boston, Massachusetts, today the center of the city's black community.

Roy•al, Mount |'roiyəl| hill in Montreal, Quebec, rising to 763 ft./233 m. Topped by recreational parks, it dominates the city and gives it its name.

Roy•al Gorge |'roiyəl| (also the **Grand Canyon of the Arkansas**) steep defile on the Arkansas River in S central Colorado, near Cañon City, a noted tourist attraction.

Roy•al Oak |'roiyəl| city in SE Michigan, a residential and industrial suburb NW of Detroit. Pop. 65,410.

Ruanda-Urundi |,rōō'wändə,ōō'rōōndē| former Belgian and United Nations trust territory, now the nations of RWANDA and BURUNDI.

Rub' al Kha•li |'rəb ,äl'kälē| vast desert in the Arabian peninsula, extending from central Saudi Arabia S to Yemen and E to the United Arab Emirates and Oman. It is also known as the Great Sandy Desert or Empty Quarter.

Ru•bi•con River |'rōōbi,kawn| small river that flows into the Adriatic Sea in NE Italy near San Marino that marked the ancient boundary between Cisalpine Gaul and Italy. In 49 B.C. Julius Caesar led his army across it into Italy, breaking the law forbidding a general to lead an army out of his province, and so committing himself to war against the Senate and Pompey. The ensuing civil war resulted in victory for Caesar after three years.

Rub•tsovsk |,rōōp'tsawfsk| city in W Siberia, S Russia. Pop. 172,000.

Ru•by Mountains |'rōō,bē| range in NE Nevada, noted for its alpine scenery.

Rud•ny |'rōōdnē| (also **Rudnyy**) city in NW Kazakhstan, on the Tobol River. Pop. 128,000. It is in an iron-mining region.

Ru•fisque |rōō'fēsk| port city in W Senegal, a suburb E of Dakar. Pop. 112,000.

Rug•by |'rəgbē| commercial and engineering town in central England, on the Avon River in Warwickshire. Pop. 60,000. Rugby School, where the game of rugby was developed in the early 19th century, was founded here in 1567.

Rü•gen |'rōō,gən| island in the Baltic Sea off the NE coast of Germany, to which it is linked by a causeway. It forms part of the state of Mecklenburg–West Pomerania.

Ruhr |'rōōr| region of coal mining and heavy industry in North Rhine–Westphalia, western Germany. It is named after the Ruhr River, which flows through it, meeting the Rhine near Duisburg.

Ru•iz, Ne•va•do del |,ne'vädō ,del ,rōō-'wēs| active volcano in Tolima department, W central Colombia, in the Cordillera Central of the Andes: 17,720 ft./5,400 m.

Ru•me•lia |rōō'mēlyə| (also **Roumelia**) the territories in Europe that formerly belonged to the Ottoman Empire, including Macedonia, Thrace, and Albania.

Run•corn |'rəNGkərn| industrial town in NW England, on the Mersey River and canals in Cheshire. Pop. 65,000.

Run•ny•mede |'rənē,mēd| meadow on the S bank of the River Thames near Windsor, in Surrey, England. It is associated with the Magna Carta, signed by King John in 1215 here or nearby.

Ru•pert's Land |'rōōpərts| (also **Prince Rupert's Land**) historic region of N and W Canada, roughly corresponding to what are now Manitoba, Saskatchewan, Yukon, Alberta, and S parts of the Northwest Territories and Nunavut. It was granted in 1670 by Charles II to the Hudson's Bay Company and named after Prince Rupert, the first governor of the Company; it was purchased by Canada in 1870.

Ruse |'rōōsā| (also **Rousse**) industrial city and the principal river port of Bulgaria, on the Danube. Pop. 210,000. Turkish during the Middle Ages, it was captured by Russia in 1877 and ceded to Bulgaria. Former name **Ruschuk**.

Rush•more, Mount |'rəSH,mawr| mountain in the Black Hills of South Dakota, near Rapid City, noted for its giant relief carvings of four U.S. presidents— Washington, Jefferson, Lincoln, and Theodore Roosevelt—carved (1927–41) under the direction of the sculptor Gutzon Borglum.

Rus•sia |'rəSHə| republic in E Europe and N Asia, the largest country in the world. Area: 6.6 million sq. mi./17.1 million sq. km. Pop. 148,930,000. Official language, Russian. Capital and largest city: Moscow. Official name **Russian Federation**. Russia developed from medieval Muscovy into a great empire by the 18th century. After the revolution of 1917, it became the largest constituent of the Soviet Union, which broke up in 1991. A land of vast distances and numerous national groups, Russia is a leading industrial and agricultural state engaged in adjusting to life after communism. □ **Russian** *adj. & n.*

Russia

Rus·sian Federation |'rəsHən| official name for RUSSIA.

Rus·ta·vi |ˌrōō'stävē| industrial city in the Republic of Georgia, on the Kura River. Pop. 160,000.

Rust Belt |'rəst 'belt| popular name for regions of the U.S. NE and Midwest where heavy industry has declined. Steel-producing cities in Pennsylvania and Ohio are at its center.

Rus·ton |'rəstən| commercial city in N Louisiana. Pop. 20,027.

Ru·the·nia |rōō'THēnyə| region of central Europe on the S slopes of the Carpathian Mts., now forming the Transcarpathian region of W Ukraine. Formerly part of the Austro-Hungarian Empire, it was divided among Poland, Czechoslovakia, and Romania. Gaining independence for a single day in 1938, it was occupied by Hungary and in 1945 ceded to the Soviet Union, becoming part of Ukraine. □ **Ruthenian** *adj. & n.*

Rut·land[1] |'rətlənd| county in the E Midlands, the smallest (153 sq. mi./396 sq. km.) county in England; county seat, Oakham. Between 1974 and 1997 it was part of Leicestershire.

Rut·land[2] |'rətlənd| industrial and commercial city in S central Vermont. Pop. 18,230.

Ru·wen·zo·ri |ˌrōōwən'zawrē| mountain range in central Africa, on the Uganda–Congo (formerly Zaire) border between Lake Edward and Lake Albert, rising to 16,765 ft./5,110 m. at Margherita Peak on Mount Stanley. The range is generally thought to be the 'Mountains of the Moon' mentioned by Ptolemy, and as such the supposed source of the Nile.

Rwan·da |rə'wändə| landlocked republic in central Africa, to the N of Burundi and the S of Uganda. Area: 10,173 sq. mi./26,338 sq. km. Pop. 7,403,000. Official languages, Rwanda (a Bantu language) and French. Capital and largest city: Kigali. Official name **Rwandese Republic**. Dominated by Germany, then Belgium, from the late 19th century, Rwanda became independent in 1962. Densely populated and mainly agricultural, it has seen repeated bloodshed between its Hutu majority and Tutsi minority. □ **Rwandan** *adj. & n.* **Rwandese** *adj. & n.*

Rwanda

Rya·zan |ˌrēə'zän(yə)| industrial city in European Russia, a port on the Oka River SE of Moscow. Pop. 522,000.

Ry·binsk |'ribyinsk| city in NW Russia, a port on the Volga River. Pop. 252,000. It was formerly known as Shcherbakov (1946–57) and, in honor of former President Yuri Andropov of the Soviet Union, as Andropov (1984–89).

Ryb·nik |'ribnik| transportation center and industrial town in S Poland. Pop. 140,000.

Ry·dal |'rīdl| village in NW England, in the Lake District in Cumbria, on Rydal Water. It is the site of Rydal Mount, longtime home of the poet Wordsworth.

Ryde |rīd| resort town in S England, in the Isle of Wight, on Spithead Channel, SW of Portsmouth. Pop. 25,000.

Rye[1] |rī| resort town in SE England, in East Sussex. Pop. 4,000. Once one of the later CINQUE PORTS, it has more recently been associated with writers and artists.

Rye[2] |rī| city in SE New York, a suburb on Long Island Sound, N of New York City. Pop. 14,936.

Ry·sy |'risē| peak in the Tatra Mts., the highest in Poland: 8,197 ft./2,499 m.

Ryu·kyu Islands |rē'ōōˌkyōō| chain of islands in the W Pacific, stretching for about

600 mi./960 km. from the S tip of the island of Kyushu, Japan, to Taiwan. The largest island is Okinawa. Part of China in the 14th century, the archipelago was incorporated into Japan by 1879 and was held under U.S. military control between 1945 and 1972.

Rze•szow |'zHe,sHo͞of| industrial town in SW Poland, capital of Rzeszow county, on the Wislik River. Pop. 153,000.

Ss

Saa•le |'zälə; 'sälə| river of E central Germany. Rising in N Bavaria near the border with the Czech Republic, it flows 265 mi./425 km. N to join the Elbe near Magdeburg.

Saa•nich |'sänicH| municipality in SW British Columbia, on Vancouver Island, a suburb on the NW side of Victoria. Pop. 95,577.

Saar |sär; zär| **1** river of W Europe. Rising in the Vosges Mts. in E France, it flows 150 mi./240 km. N to join the Mosel River in Germany, just E of the border with Luxembourg. French name **Sarre**. **2** the Saarland.

Saar•brück•en |zär'brʏkən; sär'brŏŏkən| industrial city in W Germany, the capital of Saarland, on the Saar River close to the border with France. Pop. 362,000.

Saar•land |'zär‚länt; 'sär‚lænd| state of W Germany, on the border with France. Pop. 1,077,000. Capital: Saarbrücken. Rich in coal and iron-ore and long dominated by France, the area became a German state in 1957.

Sa•ba¹ |'säbə| ancient kingdom in SW Arabia, famous for its trade in gold and spices; the biblical Sheba.

Sa•ba² |'säbə; 'säbə| island in the Netherlands Antilles, in the Caribbean. Pop. 1,130. The smallest island in the group, it is to the NW of St. Kitts.

Sa•ba•dell |säbä'del| manufacturing city in NE Spain, near Barcelona, on the Ripoll River. Pop. 184,000. It is a leading textile center.

Sa•bah |'säbä| state of Malaysia, comprising the N part of Borneo and some offshore islands. Capital: Kota Kinabalu. A British protectorate from 1888, it joined Malaysia in 1963.

Sab•ha |'säb‚hä| oasis town in W central Libya, in the Sahara Desert. Pop. 113,000.

Sa•bine River |sə'bēn| river that flows 360 mi./580 km. from E Texas to form the border with Louisiana, reaching the Gulf of Mexico at Sabine Pass.

Sa•ble Island |'säbəl| island in SE Nova Scotia, in the Atlantic 175 mi./285 km. SE of Halifax. It has been called the Graveyard of the Atlantic for the many shipwrecks that have occurred nearby.

Sab•ra•tha |'sabrəTHə| (also **Sabrata**) one of the three ancient Phoenician cities of Tripolitania; near present-day Tripoli, Libya.

Sab•ze•var |‚sæbzə'vär| commercial city in NE Iran. Pop. 148,000.

Sach•sen |'zäksən| German name for SAXONY.

Sachsen-Anhalt |'zäksən'än‚hält| German name for SAXONY-ANHALT.

Sac•ra•men•to |‚sækrə'mentō| the capital of California, on the Sacramento River to the NE of San Francisco. Pop. 369,365.

Sac•ra•men•to Mountains |‚sækrə'mentō| range in S New Mexico and W Texas. The Jicarilla, Sierra Blanca, and Guadalupe mountains are all considered part of the Sacramentos.

Sac•ra•men•to River |‚sækrə'mentō| river of N California, which rises near the border with Oregon and flows 380 mi./611 km. S to San Francisco Bay, through the Central Valley.

Sa•do Island |'sädō| island in N central Japan, in the Sea of Japan off the W coast of Honshu.

Sa•fed Koh Mountains |sä'fed 'kō| (also **Safid Koh, Sefid Koh**) mountain range in E Afghanistan, on border with Pakistan; the Khyber Pass crosses a spur of the range.

Sa•fi |'säfē| (also **Saffi**) industrial port city in W central Morocco, on the Atlantic coast. Pop. 262,000.

Sa•ga |'sägä| industrial city in SW Japan, on W Kyushu. Pop. 170,000.

Sa•ga•mi•ha•ra |sä‚gämē'härə| industrial city in E central Japan, on E central Honshu. Pop. 532,000.

Sa•ga•mi Sea |sä'gämē| inlet of the N Pacific, off the SE coast of Honshu, S central Japan.

Sagar |'sägər| (also **Saugor**) commercial town in central India, in Madhya Pradesh state. Pop. 257,000.

Sag Harbor |sæg| resort village in E Long Island, New York, famous as a 19th-century whaling port. Pop. 2,134.

Sag•i•naw |'sægə‚naw| industrial and commercial city in E central Michigan, on the Saginaw River. Pop. 69,512.

Sag•ue•nay River |‚sægə'nä| river that flows 110 mi./180 km. through S Quebec, from the Lac Saint-Jean to the St. Lawrence River. Chicoutimi and Jonquière are among industrial cities along it.

Sa•guia el Ham•ra |'sägēə el '(h)ämrə| intermittent river in the N of the Western

Sahara. It flows into the Atlantic W of La'youn. The name is also used for the region through which it flows. A territory of Spain from 1934, it united with Río de Oro in 1958 to become a part of Spanish Sahara.

Sa•gun•to |sä'gōōntō| seaport city in E Spain, on the Mediterranean Sea. Pop. 19,000. The capture by Hannibal in 219 B.C. of this Roman outpost began the Second Punic War.

Sa•hara Desert |sə'herærə; sə'härə| (also **the Sahara**) vast desert in N Africa, extending from the Atlantic in the W to the Red Sea in the E, and from the Mediterranean and the Atlas Mts. in the N to the Sahel in the S. The largest desert in the world, it covers an area of about 3,500,000 sq. mi./9,065,000 sq. km, almost one-third of Africa. In recent years it has been extending S into the Sahel. □ **Saharan** adj.

Sa•ha•ran•pur |sə'härən,pŏŏr| commercial and industrial city in N India, in Uttar Pradesh state. Pop. 374,000.

Sa•hel |sə'hel| vast semiarid region of N Africa, to the S of the Sahara, which forms a transitional zone at the S of the desert and comprises the northern part of the region known as the Sudan. The Sahel covers about one-fifth of Africa. □ **Sahelian** adj. & n.

Sa•hi•wal |'sähēwäl| commercial city in E central Pakistan, SW of Lahore. Pop. 151,000.

Sai•da |sī'dä| Arabic name for SIDON, Lebanon.

Sai•gon |sī'gän| name before 1975 for HO CHI MINH CITY, Vietnam.

Saint Al•bans |sənt 'awlbənz| city in Hertfordshire, SE England. Pop. 56,000. It developed around an abbey, which was founded in Saxon times on the site of the martyrdom in the 3rd century of St. Alban, a Christian Roman from the nearby Roman city of Verulamium.

Saint Al•bert |sānt 'ælbərt| city in central Alberta, a suburb on the NW side of Edmonton. Pop. 42,146.

Saint An•drews |sānt 'ændrōōz| town in E Scotland, in Fife, on the North Sea. Pop. 14,000. It is noted for its university, founded in 1410, and its championship golf courses.

Saint Au•gus•tine |sānt 'awgə,stēn| historic port city in NE Florida, SE of Jacksonville, on the Atlantic coast. Founded by the Spanish in 1565, it is often called "the oldest city in America." Pop. 11,692.

Saint-Bar•thé•le•my |seN ,bärtāl'mē| (familiarly **St. Bart's**) resort island in the West Indies, in the Leeward Islands. Pop. 5,000. Gustavia is its capital. St. Bart's is a dependency of Guadeloupe, which is to the SE.

Saint Ber•nard Pass |,sānt bər'närd| either of two passes across the Alps in S Europe. The *Great St. Bernard Pass*, on the border between SW Switzerland and Italy, rises to 8,100 ft./2,469 m. The *Little St. Bernard Pass*, on the French–Italian border SE of Mont Blanc, rises to 7,178 ft./2,188 m. They are named after the hospices founded on their summits in the 11th century by the French monk St. Bernard.

Saint Cath•e•rines |sānt 'kæTH(ə)rənz| industrial and commercial city in S Ontario, on Lake Ontario NW of Niagara Falls. Pop. 129,300.

Saint Charles |sānt CHärlz| historic commercial city in E central Missouri, on the Missouri River. Pop. 54,555.

St. Chris•to•pher and Nevis, Federation of |sānt 'kristəfər ən 'nevəs| see ST. KITTS AND NEVIS.

Saint Clair River |sənt 'klær| short river that flows from Lake Huron, forming the boundary between Michigan and Ontario, into Lake Saint Clair, which in turn is drained into Lake Erie by the Detroit River.

Saint Cloud |sānt 'klowd| industrial and commercial city in E central Minnesota, on the Mississippi River NW of Minneapolis. Pop. 48,812.

Saint-Cloud |seN'klōō| residential and resort W suburb of Paris, in N central France. It has a famous racetrack.

Saint Croix | sānt 'kroi| island in the Caribbean, the largest of the U.S. Virgin Islands. Pop. 50,000; chief town, Christiansted. Purchased by Denmark in 1753, it was sold to the U.S. in 1917.

Saint Croix River[1] |sānt 'kroi| river that flows 75 mi./120 km. from E Maine to form the boundary with New Brunswick, before entering Passamaquoddy Bay. The first French settlement in North America was established in 1604 on Dochet Island, near its mouth.

Saint Croix River[2] |sānt 'kroi| river that flows 164 mi./265 km. from NW Wisconsin to form part of the boundary with Minnesota, before emptying into the Mississippi River.

Saint-Cyr-l'Ecole |,sæN'sirlä'kōl| commune in N France, 3 mi./5 km. W of Versailles, site of a famed military school (founded 1808).

Saint David's |sənt 'dāvidz| city near the coast of SW Wales, in Pembrokeshire. Pop.

1,800. Its 12th-century cathedral houses the shrine of St. David, the patron saint of Wales. Welsh name **Tyddewi**.

Saint-Denis[1] |ˌsæN dəˈnē| municipality in France, now an industrial N suburb of Paris. Pop. 91,000.

Saint-Denis[2] |ˌsæN dəˈnē| the capital of the French island of Réunion, a port on the N coast. Pop. 122,000.

Sainte-Anne-de-Beaupré |seNt,ändəbō-ˈprä| city in S Quebec, on the St. Lawrence River NE of Quebec City, site of a shrine that is the object of many pilgrimages. Pop. 3,146.

Sainte-Foy |seNt ˈfwä| city in S Quebec, a suburb just SW of Quebec City. Pop. 71,133.

Saint Eli•as Mountains |ˌsänt əlˈīəs| section of the Coast Ranges in SE Alaska and the neighboring Yukon Territory. Mount Logan, the highest point in Canada, is here, along with other high peaks and numerous glaciers.

Saint Émi•lion |seNt āmēlˈyōN| town in the Gironde department of SW France, on the Dordogne River, that gave its name to a group of Bordeaux wines.

Saint-Étienne |seNt äˈtyen| city in S central France, the capital of Loire department, SW of Lyons. Pop. 202,000. It is one of the leading French heavy industry centers.

Saint Eu•sta•ti•us |ˌsänt yo͞oˈstäsHəs| small volcanic island in the Caribbean, in the Netherlands Antilles. Pop. 2,000. Dutch name **Sint Eustatius;** locally, **Statia**.

Saint Fran•cis River |sänt ˈfränsis| river that flows 425 mi./685 km. from SE Missouri into E Arkansas, emptying into the Mississippi River near Helena.

Saint Gall |sänt ˈgawl| (in German **Sankt Gallen**) town in NE Switzerland, capital of Saint Gall canton. Pop. 73,000. It has a famous abbey, founded by Saint Gall in the 7th century, with a renowned collection of medieval manuscripts; the abbey was a major center of learning during the Middle Ages.

Saint George |sänt ˈjawrj| historic resort city in SW Utah, near the Arizona line. Pop. 28,502.

Saint George's |sänt jōrjiz| the capital of Grenada in the West Indies, a port in the SW of the island. Pop. 36,000.

St. George's Channel |sänt jōrjiz| channel between S Wales and SE Ireland, linking the Irish Sea with the Celtic Sea (the Atlantic Ocean).

Saint-Germain |ˌseNzHərˈmeN| **1** section of Paris, France, on the Left Bank (S of the Seine). A colorful quarter of narrow streets and cafes, it was the favorite haunt of postwar intellectuals and writers. In recent years it has become increasingly fashionable. **2** church of Saint-Germain-des-Prés, in the district. There has been a church on this spot since the 6th century, but the oldest parts of the present church date from the 11th century.

Saint-Germain-en-Laye |ˌseNzHərˈmen-äNˈlā| residential and resort suburb W of Paris, in N central France. Pop. 42,000. The town has a notable promenade. A treaty of 1919 signed here dissolved the Austro-Hungarian Empire.

St. Gott•hard Pass |sänt ˈgätərd; seN gə-ˈtär| mountain pass in the Alps in S Switzerland, situated at an altitude of 6,916 ft./2,108 m. It is named after a former chapel and hospice (14th century), dedicated to an 11th-century bishop of Hildesheim in Germany.

St. He•le•na |ˌsänt həˈlēnə| solitary island in the South Atlantic, a British dependency. Pop. 6,000. Capital: Jamestown. It was administered by the East India Company from 1659 until 1834 when it became a British colony. Ascension, Tristan da Cunha, and Gough Island are dependencies of St. Helena. It is famous as the place of Napoleon's exile (1815–21) and death. □ **St. Helenian** *adj. & n.*

St Helena

St. Hel•ens, Mount |sänt ˈhelənz| active volcano in SW Washington, in the Cascade Range, rising to 8,312 ft./2,560 m. A dramatic eruption in May 1980 reduced its height by several hundred meters and spread volcanic ash and debris over a large area.

St. Hel•ens |sənt ˈhelənz| industrial town in NW England, in Merseyside NE of Liverpool. Pop. 175,000.

St. Hel•ier |sənt ˈhelyər| the capital of Jersey, in the Channel Islands of Britain, situated on the S coast. Pop. 28,000.

Saint-Hubert |ˌseNt Yˈberǀ city in S Quebec, a suburb across the St. Lawrence River from Montreal. Pop. 74,027.

Saint Ives ǀsənt ˈīvzǀ in England: **1** fishing port and resort town in the SW, in Cornwall. Pop. 11,000. Its arts colony is well known. **2** commercial town in the SE, in Cambridgeshire. Pop. 15,000. The nursery rhyme riddle pertains to the latter.

Saint James's Palace ǀsənt ˈjāmzəzǀ former residence of the British royal family, in Westminster, London, from 1697 until BUCKINGHAM PALACE replaced it in the 19th century. The **Court of St. James** is the official term for the British court, to which ambassadors are accredited.

Saint-Jean, Lac ǀˌlä seNˈzHäNǀ lake in S central Quebec, NW of Quebec City. Drained by the Saguenay River, it is the site of many resorts.

Saint-Jean-de-Luz ǀseNˈzHäNdəˈlYzǀ town, SW France, on the Bay of Biscay near the Spanish border. Pop. 13,000. Formerly a fishing village, it is now primarily a resort.

Saint-Jean-sur-Richelieu ǀseN,zHäNsYrˌrēsHəlˈyœ ǀ commercial city in S Quebec, SE of Montreal. Pop. 37,607.

St. John[1] ǀsänt ˈjänǀ island in the Caribbean, smallest of the three principal islands of the U.S. Virgin Islands. Pop. 3,504.

St. John[2] ǀsänt ˈjänǀ (usu. **Saint John**) largest city in New Brunswick, an industrial port on the Bay of Fundy at the mouth of the St. John River. Pop. 74,969.

St. John's[1] ǀsänt ˈjänzǀ the capital of Antigua and Barbuda, on the NW coast of Antigua. Pop. 36,000.

St. John's[2] ǀsänt ˈjänzǀ the capital of Newfoundland, a port on the SE coast of the island. Pop. 95,770. One of the oldest European settlements in North America, it was inhabited seasonally by the British from 1583.

Saint Joseph ǀsänt ˈjōzefǀ port city in NW Missouri, an industrial and commercial hub on the Missouri River. Pop. 71,852.

St. Kil•da ǀsənt ˈkildəǀ small island group of the Outer Hebrides of Scotland, in the Atlantic 40 mi./64 km. W of Lewis and Harris. The islands are now uninhabited and are a nature reserve.

St. Kitts and Nevis ǀsänt ˈkits ən(d) ˈnevəsǀ country in the Caribbean consisting of two adjoining islands of the Leeward Islands. Area: 101 sq. mi./261 sq. km. Pop.

St Kitts

44,000. Languages, English (official), Creole. Capital and largest town: Basseterre (on St. Kitts). Official name **Federation of St. Christopher and Nevis.** Colonized by Britain from 1623, the islands became fully independent in 1983. Tourism, sugar, and some light industry sustain the economy. □ **Kittitian** *adj. & n.* **Nevisian** *adj. & n.*

Saint Law•rence Island ǀsänt ˈlawrənsǀ island in W Alaska, in the Bering Sea. Most of its few inhabitants are Inuit.

St. Law•rence River ǀsänt ˈlawrənsǀ river of North America, which flows for some 750 mi./1,200 km. from Lake Ontario along the border between Canada and the U.S. to the Gulf of St. Lawrence on the Atlantic coast. The Thousand Islands, Montreal, and Quebec City lie along it. See also GREAT LAKES–ST. LAWRENCE SEAWAY.

St. Law•rence Seaway ǀsänt ˈlawrənsǀ see GREAT LAKES–SAINT LAWRENCE SEAWAY.

Saint-Lô ǀseNˈlōǀ town, capital of the Manche department, in Normandy, NW France. Pop. 23,000. It was almost completely destroyed during the Allied invasion during World War II and has since been rebuilt.

Saint-Louis ǀˌseNləˈwēǀ port city in NW Senegal, on St.-Louis Island in the Senegal River delta, near the Mauritanian border. Pop. 126,000. It is a former colonial capital of both Senegal and Mauritania.

St. Lou•is ǀsänt ˈlo͞oəsǀ historic port city in E Missouri, on the Mississippi just S of its confluence with the Missouri. Pop. 396,685. Founded by the French as a fur-trading post in the 1760s, it passed to the Spanish, the French again, and finally in 1803 to the U.S. as part of the Louisiana Purchase. It was long the gateway to settlement of the Louisiana Purchase and other western regions.

Saint Lou•is Park ǀsänt ˈlo͞oəsǀ city in SE Minnesota, a suburb SW of Minneapolis. Pop. 43,787.

St. Lu•cia |sānt 'lōōSHə| country in the West Indies, one of the Windward Islands. Area: 238 sq. mi./616 sq. km. Pop. 133,310. Languages, English (official), French Creole. Capital and largest town: Castries. France and Britain disputed control of St. Lucia for over 200 years until France yielded in 1814. Independence came in 1979. Tourism, agriculture, and light industries sustain the economy. □ **St. Lucian** *adj. & n.*

St Lucia

St. Ma•lo |ˌseNmä'lō| walled town and port on the N coast of Brittany, in NW France. Pop. 49,000.

Saint Marks |sānt 'märks| see SAN MARCO.

St. Mar•tin |sānt 'märtn| small island in the Caribbean, one of the Leeward Islands. Pop. 32,000. The S section is administered by the Dutch, forming part of the Netherlands Antilles; the larger N section is part of the French overseas department of Guadeloupe. Dutch name **Sint Maarten**.

Saint Mar•tin•ville |sānt 'märtin,vil| city in S Louisiana, a Cajun Country center on the Bayou Teche. Pop. 7,137.

Saint-Maur-des-Fosses |seN,mawrdə- faw'sä; ,sän'mawrdäfä'sə| industrial city, a suburb of Paris, in N central France, on the Marne River. Pop. 81,000.

Saint Mau•rice, Rivière |ˌseN maw'rēs; sānt 'mawrəs| river that flows 325 mi./525 km. through S Quebec, emptying into the St. Lawrence River at Trois-Rivières. Industrial cities along it include Shawinigan and Grand-Mère. Its valley is called **La Mauricie.**

Saint-Mihiel |ˌseNmē'yel| commune in NE France. Pop. 5,000. Fighting independently for the first time in World War I, U.S. troops took the village from the Germans in September 1918.

St. Mo•ritz |sānt 'mawrits| resort and winter sports center in SE Switzerland.

St.-Nazaire |ˌseNnä'zär| naval and industrial port city in NW France, on the Atlantic

at the mouth of the Loire River. Pop. 66,000.

St. Ni•co•las |seN ˌnēkaw'lä| French name for SINT-NIKLAAS, Belgium.

St. Paul |sānt 'pawl| the state capital of Minnesota, a commercial and university city on the Mississippi adjacent to Minneapolis, with which it forms the Twin Cities. Pop. 272,235.

Saint Paul's Cathedral |sənt pawlz| cathedral on Ludgate Hill, in central London, England, built by Christopher Wren 1675–1711. It often serves as a symbol of London, or of England.

Saint Pe•ter Port |sānt 'pētər| town, the commercial and administrative center of Guernsey, in the British Channel Islands. Pop. 16,000.

Saint Pe•ter's |sānt 'pētərz| principal and largest Christian church in the world, the seat of the Catholic faith, in the Vatican City, in Rome, Italy. The current building dates from the 16th century; the famous dome follows a design by Michelangelo.

St. Pe•ters•burg[1] |sānt 'pētərz,bərg| resort and industrial city in W Florida, on the Gulf of Mexico. Pop. 238,630.

St. Pe•ters•burg[2] |sānt 'pētərz,bərg| city and seaport in NW Russia, in the delta of the Neva River, on the E shores of the Gulf of Finland. Pop. 5,035,000. Former names **Petrograd** (1914–24) and **Leningrad** (1924–91). Founded in 1703 by Peter the Great, it was the capital of Russia from 1712 until the Russian Revolution. During World War II, as Leningrad, it was subjected to a siege that lasted from 1941 to 1944. A city of waterways and bridges, it is an industrial and cultural center.

St. Pierre and Miq•ue•lon |sānt 'pir ən(d) 'mikə,län| group of eight small islands in the North Atlantic, off the S coast of Newfoundland. Pop. 6,390. An overseas territory of France, the islands form the last remaining French possession in North America. Fishing is key to the economy.

St Pierre & Miquelon

Saint Pöl·ten |sänt 'pōltən| see SANKT
PÖLTEN.

Saint-Quentin |ˌseNkäN'teN| industrial
commune in N France, on the Somme
River. Pop. 62,000.

Saint-Remy-de-Provence |ˌseNrä'mēdə-
praw'väNs; ˌsænrä'mēdə'prō'väns| town in
SE France, about 15 mi./24 km. NE of
Arles. A popular tourist destination, it is
known for its Roman ruins and its association with the artist Van Gogh.

Saint So·phia |sänt sə'fēə| see HAGIA
SOPHIA, Istanbul, Turkey.

Saint Thom·as |sänt 'täməs| industrial city
in S Ontario, just N of Lake Erie. Pop.
29,990.

St. Thom·as |sänt 'täməs| resort island in
the Caribbean, the second-largest of the
U.S. Virgin Islands, to the E of Puerto Rico.
Pop. 48,170; chief town, Charlotte Amalie.
Settled by the Dutch in 1657, it passed nine
years later to the Danes, who sold it to the
U.S. in 1917.

St.-Tropez |ˌseNtraw'pe; sän,trō'pe| fishing
port and resort on the Mediterranean coast
of S France, SW of Cannes. Pop. 6,000.

St. Vin·cent, Cape |sänt 'vinsənt| head-
land in SW Portugal, at the SW tip of the
country. It was the site of a sea battle in
1797 in which the British fleet defeated the
Spanish. Portuguese name **São Vincente**.

St. Vin·cent and the Gren·a·dines |sänt
'vinsənt; ˌgrenə'dēnz| island state in the
Windward Islands in the Caribbean, consisting of the mountainous island of St. Vincent and some of the Grenadines. Area: 150
sq. mi./389 sq. km. Pop. 108,000. Languages, English (official), English Creole.
Capital and largest town: Kingstown. Controlled by Britain 1783–1979, the islands
have an economy based on agriculture and
tourism. □ **Vincentian** *adj. & n.*

St Vincent & Grenadines

Sai·pan |sī'pæn| the largest of the islands
comprising the Northern Marianas in the
W Pacific.

Sa·ïs |'sä-is| ancient city of N Egypt, on the
old Canopic branch of the Nile River delta.
It was the capital of Lower Egypt.

Sa·kai |'säk,ī| industrial city in Japan, on
Osaka Bay just S of the city of Osaka. Pop.
808,000.

Sa·kha, Republic of |'säkə| official name
for YAKUTIA, Russia.

Sa·kha·lin |ˌsäkə'lēn; 'sækə,lēn| Russian is-
land in the Sea of Okhotsk, off the coast of
E Russia and separated from it by the Tartar Strait. Pop. 709,000. Capital: Yuzhno-
Sakhalinsk. From 1905 to 1946 it was divided into a N part held by Russia, and a S
part (Karafuto), occupied by Japan.

Sa·kur·a |sə'ko͝orə| city in E central Japan,
on E central Honshu, N of Chiba. Pop.
145,000.

Sa·la·do, Río |ˌrēō sə'läTHō| (also **Río Sal-
ado del Norte**) river that flows 1,250
mi./2,010 km. across N Argentina, from the
Andes, to join the Paraná River at Santa Fe.
Its lower course has been channeled for irrigation. Argentina has several smaller
rivers also called Río Salado.

Sa·la·man·ca |ˌsælə'mäNGkə| industrial
and agricultural city in W Spain, in Castil-
la-León. Pop. 186,000.

Sal·a·mis |'sæləməs| island in the Saronic
Gulf in Greece, to the W of Athens. The
strait between the island and the mainland
was the scene in 480 B.C. of a crushing defeat of the Persian fleet under Xerxes I by
the Greeks under Themistocles.

Sa·lang Pass |sä'läNG| high-altitude route
across the Hindu Kush in Afghanistan. A
road and tunnel were built by the Soviet
Union during the 1960s to improve military and commercial access to Kabul.

Sa·la·vat |sə'lävät| city in Bashkortostan,
W Russia, S of Ufa. Pop. 152,000.

Sa·lé |sä'lä| industrial port city in N Mo-
rocco, on the Atlantic, NE of Rabat. Pop.
580,000. It was once home to the Sallee
Rovers, a group of Barbary pirates.

Sa·lem[1] |'säləm| industrial city in Tamil
Nadu in S India. Pop. 364,000.

Sa·lem[2] |'säləm| port city in NE Massa-
chusetts, on the Atlantic coast N of Boston.
Pop. 38,091. It was the scene in 1692 of a
notorious series of witchcraft trials.
Tourism is important today.

Sa·lem[3] |'säləm| the capital of Oregon, an
industrial city on the Willamette River SW
of Portland. Pop. 107,786.

Sa·ler·no |sə'lernō| port on the W coast of
Italy, on the Gulf of Salerno SE of Naples.
Pop. 151,000.

Sal·ford |'sawlfərd| industrial city in NW

England, in Greater Manchester. Pop. 218,000.

Sa·li·na |sə'lī:nə| industrial and commercial city in central Kansas. Pop. 42,303.

Sa·li·nas |sə'lēnəs| city in W central California, a commercial center in the agriculturally important Salinas Valley. Pop. 108,777.

Salis·bury[1] |'sawlz,berē; 'sawlzbərē| market city in S England, in the Salisbury Plain in Wiltshire. Pop. 35,000. It is noted for its 13th-century cathedral, whose spire, at 404 ft./123 m. is the highest in England. Its diocese is known as Sarum, an old name for the city.

Salis·bury[2] |'sawlz,berē; 'sawlzbərē| industrial city in W central North Carolina. Pop. 23,087.

Salis·bury[3] |'sawlz,berē; 'sawlzbərē| former name (until 1982) for HARARE, Zimbabwe.

Salm·on River |'sæmən| river that flows 425 mi./685 km. through central Idaho. With its branches, it is noted as a salmon breeding and river sports resource.

Sa·lon·i·ca |sə'länikə; ,sælə'nēkə| another name for THESSALONÍKI, Greece.

Sal·op |'sæləp| another name for SHROPSHIRE, England. It was the official name of the county 1974–80. □ **Salopian** adj. & n.

Sal·ta |'sältə| commercial city in NW Argentina, capital of Salta province. Pop. 370,000. It ships agricultural products.

Sal·ti·llo |säl'tē(y)ō| industrial and university city in N Mexico, capital of the state of Coahuila, in the Sierra Madre SW of Monterrey. Pop. 441,000.

Salt Lake City | sawlt| the capital and largest city of Utah, situated near the SE shore of the Great Salt Lake. Pop. 159,936. Founded in 1847 by Brigham Young, the city is the world headquarters of the Church of Latter-Day Saints (Mormons). It is a center of high-tech industry.

Sal·to |'sältō| city in NW Uruguay, capital of Salto department, on the Uruguay River across from Concordia, Argentina. Pop. 93,000. It is a commercial and transportation center.

Sal·ton Sea |'sawltn| salt lake in SE California, created in the dry **Salton Sink** by a 1905 diversion of the Colorado River. It is a recreational resource and wildlife refuge.

Sal·va·dor |,sælvə'dawr; 'sælvə,dawr| port on the Atlantic coast of E Brazil, capital of the state of Bahia. Pop. 2,075,000. Founded in 1549, it was the capital of the Portuguese colony until 1763, when the seat of government was transferred to Rio de Janeiro. Former name **Bahia**.

Sal·ween |'sæl,wēn| river of SE Asia, which rises in Tibet and flows for 1,500 mi./2,400 km. SE and S through Burma to the Gulf of Martaban, an inlet of the Andaman Sea.

Salz·burg |'zälts,bŏŏrk| city in W Austria, near the border with Germany, the capital of a state of the same name; pop. 144,000. It is noted for its annual music festivals, one dedicated to the composer Mozart, who was born here in 1756.

Salz·git·ter |'zälts,gitər| industrial city in Germany, in Lower Saxony SE of Hanover. Pop. 115,000.

Salz·kam·mer·gut |'zält,skämər,gŏŏt| resort area of lakes and mountains in the states of Salzburg, Upper Austria, and Styria, in W Austria.

Sa·mar |'sä,mär| island in the Philippines, situated to the SE of Luzon. It is the third-largest island of the group. The island-enclosed **Samar Sea** lies to the W.

Sa·ma·ra |sə'märə| industrial city and river port in SW Russia, situated on the Volga at its confluence with the Samara River. Pop. 1,258,000.

Sa·mar·ia |sə'mærēə| **1** an ancient city of central Palestine, founded in the 9th century B.C. as the capital of the northern Hebrew kingdom of Israel. The ancient site is in the modern West Bank, NW of Nablus. **2** the region of ancient Palestine around this city, between Galilee in the N and Judaea in the S. □ **Samaritan** adj. & n.

Sam·a·rin·da |,sæmə'rində| commercial city in Indonesia, capital of East Kalimantan, in E Borneo. Pop. 265,000.

Sa·mar·kand |'sæmər,kænd| (also **Samarqand**) city in E Uzbekistan. Pop. 370,000. One of the oldest cities of Asia, it was founded in the 3rd or 4th millennium B.C. It grew to prominence as a center of the silk trade, situated on the Silk Road, and in the 14th century became the capital of Tamerlane's Mongol Empire.

Sa·mar·ra |sə'märə| city in Iraq, a Shiite center on the Tigris River N of Baghdad. Pop. 62,000.

Sam·bal·pur |'səmbəl,pŏŏr| city in E central India, NW of Cuttack in Orissa state. Pop. 193,000.

Sam·bhal |'səmbəl| commercial city in N India, in Uttar Pradesh state. Pop. 150,000.

Sam·ni·um |'sæmnēəm| ancient country in what is now central Italy, comprising Abruzzi and part of Campania. It was conquered by Rome in 290 B.C. □ **Samnite** adj. & n.

Sa•moa |sə'mōə| **1** group of islands in Polynesia, divided between American Samoa and the state of Samoa. **2** (also **Western Samoa**) independent state comprising a group of nine islands in the SW Pacific. Area: 1,098 sq. mi./2,842 sq. km. Pop. 160,000. Languages, Samoan and English. Capital, Apia. Controlled by Germany, then New Zealand, Samoa became independent in 1962. It exports coconut products and other foods and spices. See also AMERICAN SAMOA. □ **Samoan** *adj. & n.*

Sa•mos |'sämaws| Greek island in the Aegean, close to the coast of W Turkey.

Sam•o•thrace |'sæmə,THrās; ,sæmə 'THrāsē| island in NE Greece, in the Aegean Sea. The island's peak, at 5,577 ft.,/1,700 m., is the tallest of any Aegean island. The statue *Victory of Samothrace*, popularly known as *Winged Victory*, found here, is now in the Louvre in Paris.

Sam•sun |säm'soon| historic port city in N Turkey, the capital of Samsun province. Pop. 304,000. The leading Turkish port on the Black Sea, it is also a tobacco-industry center.

Sana'a |sæn'ä| (also **Sanaa**) the capital of Yemen. Pop. 500,000. A handicrafts center claimed to be the oldest city in the world, it is noted for its huge medina (walled city).

Sa•nan•daj |,sänən'däj| a mostly Kurdish city in NW Iran, in the Zagros Mts. Pop. 244,000.

San An•dre•as Fault |,sæn æn'drāəs| fault line extending for some 600 mi./965 km. through coastal California. Seismic activity is common along its course, caused by two crustal plates sliding past each other. The city of San Francisco lies close to the fault, and such movement caused the devastating earthquake of 1906 and a further convulsion in 1989.

San An•drés |,sæn æn'drāəs| resort island in the Caribbean Sea, E of Nicaragua but part of an archipelago held by Colombia. Pop. 40,000. Tourism and duty-free commerce are important.

San An•ge•lo |sæn 'ænjəlō| commercial and industrial city in W central Texas. Pop. 84,474.

San An•to•nio |sæn ān'tōnē,ō| industrial, commercial, and military city in S central Texas. Pop. 935,933. It is the site of the Alamo.

San Ber•nar•di•no |,sæn ,bərnə(r)'dēnō| industrial and commercial city in S California, E of Los Angeles. Pop. 164,164. It is the seat of **San Bernardino County**, the largest (20,064 sq. mi./51,966 sq. km.) in the U.S. The **San Bernardino Mountains** lie mostly N of the city.

San Ber•nar•do |,sän ber'närdō| industrial and commercial city in central Chile, in Maipo province, S of Santiago. Pop. 188,000.

San Bru•no |sæn 'broonō| city in N central California, a suburb on San Francisco Bay, S of San Francisco. Pop. 38,961.

San Car•los |sæn 'kärlōs| **1** city in the Philippines, on central Luzon. Pop. 125,000. **2** port city in the Philippines, on E Negros. Pop. 106,000.

San Car•los de Ba•ri•lo•che |sæn 'kawrlōs də ,bärē'lōCHä| ski resort in the Andes of Argentina, on the shores of Lake Nahuel Huapi. Pop. 48,000.

San•chi |'sänCHē| village in central India, in Madhya Pradesh state, site of the best-preserved Buddhist monuments in India.

San•chung |'sæn'jooNG| (also **San-ch'ung**) city in N Taiwan, W of Taipei and N of Panchiao. Pop. 382,000.

San Cle•men•te |,sæn klə'mentē| city in SW California, on the Pacific SE of Los Angeles, noted as the home of Richard Nixon. Pop. 41,100.

San Cris•to•bal |,sänkrē'stōbäl| (also **Makira** or **San Cristoval**) volcanic island in the S Solomon Islands, SE of Guadalcanal.

San Cris•tó•bal[1] |sän krē'stōbäl| historic commercial city in the S Dominican Republic, in an agricultural area. Pop. 88,000.

San Cristóbal[2] |,sänkrē'stōbäl| industrial and commercial city in W Venezuela, the capital of Táchira state. Pop. 221,000.

Sanc•ti Spí•ri•tus |'säNGktē 'spērē,toos| historic commercial city in W central Cuba, the capital of Sancti Spíritus province. Pop. 86,000.

San•da•kan |,sändä'kän| commercial port city in Malaysia, on NE Borneo. Pop. 157,000.

San•dal•wood Island |'sændəl,wood| another name for SUMBA, Indonesia.

Sand Hills |sænd| large plains area of W central Nebraska, noted as a ranching district.

Sand•hills |'sænd,hilz| (also **Sand Hills**) line of low, sandy hills lying across the Carolinas and Georgia, at the boundary of the coastal plain and the Piedmont.

Sand•hurst |'sænd,hərst| town in S central England, in Berkshire, original home to the British Royal Military College, now at Camberley, in Surrey.

San•dia Mountains |sæn'dēə| range in

central New Mexico, rising to 10,678 ft./3,255 m. at Sandia Peak, near Albuquerque.

San Di•e•go |sæn dē'āgō| industrial, institutional, and retirement city and naval port on the Pacific coast of S California, just N of the border of Mexico. Pop. 1,110,549. It was founded as a mission in 1769.

San•dring•ham |'sændriNGəm| village in SE England, in Norfolk, NE of King's Lynn, site of one of the holiday retreats of the British royal family.

San•dus•ky |sən'dəskē; sæn'dəskē| industrial port city in N Ohio, on Lake Erie at Sandusky Bay. Pop. 29,764.

Sand•wich¹ |'sæn(d)wiCH| resort town in SE England, in Kent, one of the CINQUE PORTS. Pop. 4,000.

Sand•wich² |'sæn(d)wiCH| town in SE Massachusetts, on Cape Cod, a resort with a history of glassmaking. Pop. 15,489.

Sand•wich Islands |'sæn(d)wiCH| former name for HAWAII.

Sandy |'sændē| city in N central Utah, a residential and commercial suburb S of Salt Lake City. Pop. 75,058.

Sandy Hook |'sændē 'hŏŏk| peninsula in NE New Jersey, S of New York City, separating Raritan Bay from the Atlantic. It is noted for its lighthouse, beaches, and forts.

Sandy•mount |ˌsændē,mownt| residential SE section of Dublin, Ireland, the birthplace of the poet W.B.Yeats. Nearby **Sandycove,** to the E of Dun Laoghaire, is associated with the writer James Joyce.

San Fer•nan•do¹ |ˌsæn fər'nændō| port city in E Argentina, just N of Buenos Aires. Pop. 145,000.

San Fer•nan•do² |ˌsæn fər'nændō| **1** commercial port town in the Philippines on N central Luzon, NW of Baguio. Pop. 85,000. **2** industrial town in the Philippines, on central Luzon, NW of Manila. Pop. 158,000.

San Fer•nan•do³ |ˌsæn fər'nændō| (formerly **Isla de León**) port city in S Spain. Pop. 82,000. It has a naval academy and an arsenal.

San Fer•nan•do Valley |ˌsæn fər'nændō| (popularly **the Valley**) irrigated district NW of downtown Los Angeles, California, comprising city neighborhoods and nearby suburbs.

San•ford |'sænfərd| resort and commercial city in N central Florida. Pop. 32,387.

San Fran•cis•co |ˌsæn frən'siskō; fræn 'siskō| historic city and seaport on the coast of California, situated on a peninsula between the Pacific and San Francisco Bay. Pop. 723,959. It is a major center of commerce, finance, industry, and culture. Founded as a mission by Mexican Jesuits in 1776, it was taken by the U.S. in 1846. The fine natural harbor of San Francisco Bay is entered by the channel known as the Golden Gate. The city suffered severe damage from an earthquake in 1906, and has been frequently shaken by less severe earthquakes. □ **San Franciscan** adj. & n.

San Fran•cis•co Peaks |ˌsæn frən'siskō; fræn'siskō| mountain group in N Arizona, N of Flagstaff, including Humphreys Peak, at 12,633 ft./3,851 m. the highest point in the state.

San Ga•bri•el Mountains |sæn 'gābrēəl| range in S California, on the N of (and partly in) the city of Los Angeles. Mount San Antonio, at 10,080 ft./3,105 m., is the high point. The Mount Wilson observatory is here. The city of **San Gabriel** (pop. 37,120) is a suburb E of Los Angeles.

San Gi•mi•gna•no |ˌsän jēmē'nyänō| medieval town in central Italy. Pop. 7,000. Set atop a hill, the walled town, with its 14 towers, is a major tourist attraction.

San•gli |'säNGgli| commercial town in W India, in Maharashtra state. Pop. 364,000.

San•gre de Cris•to Mountains |ˌsæNGgrē də 'kristō| range in S Colorado and N New Mexico, an extension of the Front Range of the Rocky Mts. The Pecos and Canadian rivers rise here.

San•i•bel Island |'sænəbəl| resort island in SW Florida, SW of Fort Myers, famed among seashell collectors.

San Isi•dro |ˌsän ē'sēTHrō| city in E Argentina, a suburban part of the Buenos Aires area. Pop. 299,000.

San Ja•cin•to River |ˌsæn jə'sin,tō| river in SE Texas that flows into Galveston Bay, E of Houston. The 1836 battle that won Texas independence from Mexico was fought on its bank.

San Joa•quin River |ˌsæn wä'kēn| river that flows 350 mi./560 km. from S central California, to join the Sacramento River and enter San Francisco Bay. The agricultural and oil producing lands surrounding it are known as the San Joaquin Valley, part of the Central Valley.

San Jo•se |ˌsæn (h)ō'zā; ə'zā| city in W California, to the S of San Francisco Bay. Pop. 782,248. It is the largest city in Silicon Valley, a center of high-tech industries.

San Jo•sé |ˌsän haw'sā; ˌsæn hō'zā| the capital and chief port of Costa Rica. Pop. 319,000.

San Juan¹ |ˌsæn 'wän| city in W Argentina,

the capital of San Juan province, in the E Andes. Pop. 353,000. It produces foods and wines.

San Juan[2] |ˌsæn 'wän| the capital and chief port of Puerto Rico, a commercial and tourist center on the N coast. Pop. 437,745.

San Juan Cap·is·tra·no |sæn 'wän ˌkæpəs 'tränō| city in SW California, between Los Angeles and San Diego, site of a 1776 mission to which migrating swallows famously return each March 19. Pop. 26,183.

San Juan Hill[1] |sän 'hwän| hill near Santiago de Cuba, E Cuba, scene of a July 1898 battle in the Spanish-American War.

San Juan Hill[2] |sæn '(h)wän| former neighborhood in Manhattan, New York City, where the cultural complex of Lincoln Center now stands.

San Juan Islands |sæn '(h)wän| island group in NW Washington, N of Puget Sound and S of the Strait of Georgia. San Juan and Orcas are the largest islands in the group.

San Juan Mountains |sæn '(h)wän| range of the Rocky Mts. in SW Colorado and N New Mexico, source of the Rio Grande, which here flows through the agricultural San Juan Valley.

Sankt Pöl·ten |zäNGkt 'pœltn| industrial city and transportation center in N central Austria, capital of Lower Austria. Pop. 49,000.

San·ku·ru River |säNG'kōōrōō| river that flows 750 mi./1,200 km. from the S central Congo (formerly Zaire) into the Kasai River. In its upper third it is called the Lubilash River.

San Le·an·dro |ˌsæn lē'ændrō| city in N central California, a suburb on the SE side of Oakland, in an agricultural area. Pop. 68,223.

San Lo·ren·zo |ˌsän lō'renzō| industrial and commercial city in central Paraguay, just E of Asunción. Pop. 133,000.

San Lu·cas, Ca·bo |ˌkävō sän 'lōōkäs| (English name **Cape San Lucas**) cape at the S end of Baja California, Mexico, on the W end of the mouth of the Gulf of California, noted for its scenery and as a resort.

San Lu·is Obis·po |ˌsæn ˌlōōəs ə'bispō| city in W central California, in an agricultural area NW of Los Angeles. Pop. 41,958.

San Lu·is Pot·o·sí |ˌsän lōōˌēs ˌpōtə'sē| **1** state of N central Mexico. Area: 24,360 sq. mi./63,068 sq. km. Pop. 2,002,000. **2** its capital, an industrial and silver-mining city. Pop. 526,000.

San Mar·co |sän 'märkō| one of the two large islands that make up Venice, in NE

Italy. It is also the name of that city's famous square, the Piazza San Marco, dominated by the Byzantine Cathedral of San Marco.

San Mar·cos[1] |sæn 'märkəs| city in SW California, a suburb N of San Diego. Pop. 38,974.

San Mar·cos[2] |sæn 'märkəs| city in S central Texas, S of Austin. Pop. 28,743.

San Ma·ri·no[1] |ˌsæn mä'rēnō| city in SW California, a suburb NE of Los Angeles. Pop. 12,959.

San Ma·ri·no[2] |ˌsæn mä'rēnō| republic forming a small (23.5 sq. mi./61 sq. km.) enclave in Italy, near Rimini. Pop. 23,000. Language, Italian. Capital: the town of San Marino. Perhaps Europe's oldest state, claiming to have been independent almost continuously since its foundation in the 4th century, it is said to be named after Marino, a Dalmatian stonecutter who fled here to escape the persecution of Christians under Diocletian. Agriculture and crafts are the backbone of the economy.

San Marino

San Ma·teo |ˌsæn mə'tāō| commercial and industrial city in N central California, on San Francisco Bay S of San Francisco. Pop. 85,486.

San Mi·guel |ˌsän mē'gel| industrial and commercial city in E El Salvador, on the Pan-American Highway. Pop. 183,000.

San Mi·guel de Allen·de |ˌsän mē'gel dä ä'yendə| city in central Mexico, in Guanajuato state. Pop. 49,000. It is a commercial and tourist center, and has a noted arts colony.

San Mi·guel de Tu·cu·mán |ˌsän 'mēgel də ˌtōōkōō'män| (also **Tucumán**) historic city in N Argentina, the capital of Tucumán province. Pop. 622,000. It is a sugar industry center. Argentine independence was proclaimed here in 1816.

San Ni·co·lás |ˌsän ˌnēkō'läs| (official name **San Nicolás de los Arroyos**) industrial and commercial city in central

Argentina, on the Paraná River, SE of Rosario. Pop. 115,000.

San Ni•co•lás de los Gar•za |ˌsän ˌnēkō 'läs dä lōs 'gärsä| city in N Mexico, in Nuevo León state, a suburb N of Monterrey. Pop. 437,000.

San Pab•lo[1] |sæn 'päblō| city in N central California, on San Pablo Bay N of Oakland. Pop. 25,158.

San Pab•lo[2] |sän 'päblō| commercial city in the Philippines, on S Luzon. Pop. 162,000.

San Pe•dro |sæn 'pēdrō; 'pädrō| section of S Los Angeles, California, on San Pedro Bay, site of the city's harbor facilities.

San Pe•dro de Ma•co•rís |sän 'pädrō dä ˌmäkō'rēs| industrial port city in the SE Dominican Republic, capital of San Pedro de Macorís province. Pop. 124,000. It is a famous producer of baseball players.

San Pe•dro Su•la |sän 'pädrō 'sōōlə| second-largest city in Honduras, an industrial and commercial center near the Caribbean coast. Pop. 326,000.

San Quen•tin |sæn 'kwentn| site in Marin County, NW California, across the Golden Gate from San Francisco, where a famous state prison is located.

San Ra•fael |ˌsæn rə'fel| city in NW California, on San Rafael Bay, N of San Francisco. Pop. 48,404.

San Re•mo |sän 'rämō| resort on the Riviera, in NW Italy, on the Ligurian Sea. Pop. 64,000. It is also a major flower market.

San Sal•va•dor[1] |sän ˌsälvä'dawr; sæn 'sælvəˌdawr| (also **Watlings**) island in the SE Bahamas, believed to be the site where Columbus first landed in the New World in 1492. Pop. 2,000.

San Sal•va•dor[2] |sän ˌsälvä'dawr; sæn 'sælvəˌdawr| the capital of El Salvador, a trade and light industrial center. Pop. 423,000.

San Sal•va•dor[3] |sän ˌsälvä'dawr; sæn 'sælvəˌdawr| see JUJUY.

San Sebastián |ˌsän säbäst'yän| port and resort in N Spain, in the Basque Country, on the Bay of Biscay close to the border with France. Pop. 174,000.

San Sim•e•on |sæn 'simēən| community in W central California, on the Pacific coast, site of the Hearst Estate, a noted tourist attraction.

Sans Sou•ci |ˌsäN sōō'sē| see POTSDAM.

San•ta Ana[1] |ˌsæntə 'ænə| industrial and commercial city in S California, SE of Los Angeles. Pop. 293,742. To the E are the

Santa Ana Mountains, source of the hot, dry Santa Ana winds.

San•ta Ana[2] |ˌsäntə 'änə| city in El Salvador, in an agricultural region close to the border with Guatemala. Pop. 202,000.

San•ta Ana[3] |ˌsäntə '| highest volcano in El Salvador, SW of the city of Santa Ana. It rises to 7,730 ft./2,381 m.

San•ta Bar•ba•ra |ˌsæntə 'bärb(ə)rə| resort city in California, on the Pacific coast NW of Los Angeles. Pop. 85,571.

San•ta Bar•ba•ra Islands |ˌsæntə 'bärb(ə)rə| (also **Channel Islands**) island group in SW California, off the Pacific coast. Santa Catalina (also called Catalina) is a tourist destination.

San•ta Ca•ta•ri•na |ˌsäntä ˌkätä'rēnə| state of S Brazil, on the Atlantic coast. Pop. 4,538,000. Capital: Florianópolis.

San•ta Clara[1] |ˌsæntə 'klærə| city in N central California, a longtime fruit-producing center now at the heart of Silicon Valley. Pop. 93,613.

San•ta Clara[2] |ˌsäntä 'klärä| commercial and industrial city in central Cuba, the capital of Villa Clara province. Pop. 217,000.

San•ta Clar•i•ta |ˌsæntə klə'rētə| city in SW California, a suburb NW of Los Angeles. Pop. 110,642.

San•ta Co•lo•ma de Gra•ma•net |ˌsäntä kō'lōmä dä ˌgrämä'net| commune in NE Spain, a suburb of Barcelona. Pop. 132,000.

San•ta Cruz[1] |ˌsäntä 'krōōs| industrial and commercial city in the central region of Bolivia. Pop. 695,000.

San•ta Cruz[2] |ˌsæntə 'krōōz| resort and academic city in W central California, on Monterey Bay. Pop. 49,040.

San•ta Cruz[3] |ˌsäntä 'krōōs| port and the chief city of the island of Tenerife, in the Canary Islands. Pop. 192,000. Full name **Santa Cruz de Tenerife.**

San•ta Cruz Islands |ˌsæntə 'krōōz| island group in the SE Solomon Islands, in the SW Pacific, scene of an October 1942 naval battle between U.S. and Japanese forces.

San•ta Fe[1] |'säntä 'fä| city in N Argentina, a port on the Salado River near its confluence with the Paraná. Pop. 395,000.

San•ta Fe[2] |ˌsæntə 'fä| the capital of New Mexico. Pop. 55,859. It was founded as a mission by the Spanish in 1610. From 1821 until the arrival of the railroad in 1880 it was the terminus of the Santa Fe Trail. Taken by U.S. forces in 1846 during the Mexican War, it became the capital of New Mexico in 1912. It is today an administrative and tourist center.

San•ta Fe Trail |ˌsæntə ˈfā| historic route, established in the 1820s, from St. Louis, Missouri, to Santa Fe, New Mexico. Merchants and settlers used it until the Santa Fe Railroad was built in the 1870s.

San•ta Is•a•bel Island |ˌsæntə ˈizäˌbel| mountainous island in the central Solomon Islands, in the SW Pacific. Pop. 14,000.

San•ta Lu•cia Range |ˌsæntə lo͞oˈsēə| range in W central California, part of the Coast Ranges, noted for its resorts and wineries.

San•ta Ma•ria[1] |ˌsäntə mäˈrēə| commercial, industrial, and military city in S Brazil, in Rio Grande do Sul state. Pop. 218,000.

San•ta Ma•ria[2] |ˌsæntə məˈrēə| commercial city in SW California, in an agricultural area. Pop. 61,284.

San•ta Mar•ta |ˌsäntə ˈmärtə| historic port city in N Colombia, the capital of Magdalena department. Pop. 286,000.

San•ta Mon•i•ca |ˌsæntə ˈmänikə| resort city on the coast of SW California, just W of Los Angeles. Pop. 86,905.

San•tan•der |ˌsänˌtänˈder| industrial port in N Spain, on the Bay of Biscay, capital of Cantabria. Pop. 194,000.

San•ta•rém[1] |ˌsäntəˈrem| commercial city in N Brazil, in Pará state, a port on the Amazon River. 243,000.

San•ta•rém[2] |ˌsäntəˈrem| town in central Portugal, capital of Santaém province, on the Tagus River, NE of Lisbon. Pop. 15,000.

San•ta Ro•sa |ˌsæntə ˈrōzə| commercial city in NW California, in an agricultural area N of San Francisco. Pop. 113,313.

San•tee River |sænˈtē| river that flows 140 mi./230 km. through E South Carolina, to the Atlantic.

San•ti•a•go |ˌsäntēˈägō| the capital and largest city of Chile, situated to the W of the Andes in the central part of the country. Pop. 5,181,000. It is the industrial and cultural center of Chile.

San•ti•a•go de Com•pos•te•la |ˌsäntēˈägō də ˌkawmpōˈstälä| city in NW Spain, capital of Galicia. Pop. 106,000. The remains of St. James the Great (Spanish *Sant Iago*) are said to have been brought there after his death; it is an important place of pilgrimage.

San•ti•a•go de Cu•ba |ˌsäntēˈägō də ˈko͞obä| industrial port on the coast of SE Cuba, the second-largest city on the island. Pop. 433,000.

San•ti•a•go del Es•te•ro |ˌsäntēˈägō del äˈstärō| city in N central Argentina, the capital of Santiago del Estero province. Pop. 264,000. One of the oldest cities in Ar-

gentina, it is a spa and agricultural trade center.

San•ti•a•go de los Ca•ba•lle•ros |ˌsäntēˈägō dä lōs ˌkäbäˈyärōs| commercial city in the N central Dominican Republic, an agricultural trade center. Pop. 365,000.

San•to An•dré |ˌsäntōo änˈdre| city in S Brazil, an industrial and commercial suburb of São Paulo. Pop. 625,000.

San•to Do•min•go |ˌsäntō dōˈmiNGgō| the capital and largest city of the Dominican Republic, a port on the S coast. Pop. 2,055,000. Founded in 1496 by the brother of Christopher Columbus, it is the oldest European settlement in the Americas. From 1936 to 1961 it was called Ciudad Trujillo.

San•to Do•min•go de los Co•lo•ra•dos |ˌsäntō dōˈmiNGgō dälōs ˌkōlawˈrädōs| commercial city in NW Ecuador, in Pichincha province on the W of the Andes. Pop. 114,000. Its name derives from the local Colorados Indians.

San•to•ri•ni |ˌsæntəˈrēnē| another name for THERA, Greece.

San•tos |ˈsæntōos| industrial port on the coast of Brazil, SE of São Paulo. Pop. 429,000.

San•tur•ce |sänˈto͞orsä| commercial and residential district of San Juan, Puerto Rico, with noted beaches.

São Ber•nar•do do Cam•po |sowN berˈnärdōo dōo ˈkämpōo| city in SE Brazil, an industrial suburb SE of São Paulo. Pop. 659,000.

São Ca•e•ta•no do Sul |sowN kīˈtänōo dōo so͞ol| city in SE Brazil, a commercial suburb SE of São Paulo. Pop. 141,000.

São Car•los |sowN ˈkärlōs| commercial and industrial city in SE Brazil, in NW São Paulo state. Pop. 175,000.

São Fran•cis•co |sowN fränˈsēskō| river of E Brazil. It rises in Minas Gerais and flows for 1,990 mi./3,200 km. N then E, meeting the Atlantic to the N of Aracajú.

São Gon•ça•lo |sowN ˈgōNˈsälōo| city in SE Brazil, an industrial and commercial suburb E of Rio de Janeiro, on Guanabara Bay. Pop. 721,000.

São João de Me•ri•ti |sowN ˈ zHwowN də ˈmireˈtē| city in SE Brazil, a largely residential suburb NW of Rio de Janeiro. Pop. 425,000.

São Jo•sé do Rio Prê•to |ˌsowN zHōˈzä dōo ˈrēōo ˈpretō| commercial and industrial city in SE Brazil, in São Paulo state. Pop. 323,000.

São Jo•sé dos Cam•pos |ˌsowN zHōˈzä dōosH ˈkämpōos| industrial and commercial city in SE Brazil, in São Paulo state. Pop. 486,000.

São Le·o·pol·do |ˌsowN ˌlāōˈpōldōō| industrial city in S Brazil, in Rio Grande do Sul state. Pop. 168,000.

São Lu·ís |sowN ləˈwēs| port in NE Brazil, on the Atlantic coast, capital of the state of Maranhão. Pop. 695,000.

Saône |sōn| river of E France, which rises in the Vosges Mts. and flows 298 mi./480 km. SW to join the Rhône at Lyons.

São Pau·lo |sowN ˈpowlōō| **1** state of S Brazil, on the Atlantic coast. Pop. 31.55 million. **2** its capital. Pop. 9,700,000. It is the largest city in Brazil and second-largest in South America, and is the financial, industrial, and institutional center of Brazil.

São Tia·go |sowN ˈtyägōō| (also **Santiago**) largest (383 sq. mi./992 sq. km.) island of Cape Verde. Pop. 176,000. Praia, the capital, is here. Agriculture is central to the economy.

São To·mé and Prín·ci·pe |ˌsowN təˈmä ən(d) ˈprinsəpə| country consisting of two main islands and several smaller ones in the Gulf of Guinea. Pop. 120,000. Languages, Portuguese (official), Portuguese Creole. Capital São Tomé. The islands were settled by Portugal from 1493 and became independent in 1975.

Sao Tome and Principe

São Vi·cen·te, Cabo de |ˈkabōō dä sowN vēˈsäNtē| Portuguese name for Cape St. Vincent (see ST. VINCENT, CAPE).

São Vi·cen·te |sowN vēˈsäNtē| historic resort city in SE Brazil, a suburb of Santos, on an Atlantic island in São Paulo state. Pop. 280,000.

São Vi·cen·te Island |sowN vēˈsäNtē| island in NW Cape Verde, in the Windward group. Pop. 51,000. Fishing and mining are important here.

Sa·pe·le |səˈpälä| port city in S Nigeria, in the Niger River delta. Pop. 123,000. It is a timber industry center.

Sap·po·ro |säˈpawrō| city in N Japan, capital of the island of Hokkaido, a manufacturing and winter sports center. Pop. 1,672,000.

Saq·qa·ra |səˈkärə| (also **Sakkara**) archaeological site in N Egypt, just S of Cairo, near the Nile River, noted for its ancient ruins and burial structures.

Sar·a·gos·sa |ˌsærəˈgawsə| industrial city in N Spain, capital of Aragon, situated on the Ebro River. Pop. 614,000. The ancient settlement here was taken in the 1st century B.C. by the Romans, who called it Caesaraugusta (from which the modern name is derived). Spanish name **Zaragoza**.

Sa·rai |säˈrī| former city in SW Russia, E of the lower Volga River, near Leninsk. In the 13th–15th centuries it was the capital of the Mongol state, the Empire of the Golden Horde.

Sa·ra·je·vo |ˌsärəˈyävō| industrial city, the capital of Bosnia and Herzegovina. Pop. 200,000. Taken by the Austro-Hungarians in 1878, it became a center of Slav opposition to Austrian rule. It was the scene in June 1914 of the assassination by a Bosnian Serb of Archduke Franz Ferdinand, the heir to the Austrian throne, an event that triggered the outbreak of World War I. The city suffered severely from the ethnic conflicts that followed the breakup of Yugoslavia in 1991, and was beseiged by Bosnian Serb forces in the surrounding mountains from 1992 to 1994.

Sar·a·nac Lakes |ˈsærəˌnæk| group of resort lakes in NE New York, in the Adirondack Park, site of a pioneering tuberculosis sanatorium.

Sa·ransk |səˈränsk| city in European Russia, capital of the autonomous republic of Mordvinia, to the S of Nizhni Novgorod. Pop. 316,000.

Sar·a·so·ta |ˌsærəˈsōtə| resort city in SW Florida, on Sarasota Bay off the Gulf of Mexico, long noted as a winter base for circuses. Pop. 50,961.

Sa·ras·va·ti River |ˈsärəsˌvətē| (also **Saraswati**) river in W India, flowing 120 mi. /195 km., from E of Palanpur in S Rajasthan state to Little Rann of Kutch, in Gujarat state.

Sar·a·to·ga |ˌsærəˈtōgə| agricultural city in W central California, SW of San Jose. Pop. 28,061.

Sar·a·to·ga Springs |ˈsærəˈtōgə| city in E New York, N of Albany, a spa noted for horse racing and for two battles fought nearby during the American Revolution. Pop. 25,001.

Sa·ra·tov |sə'rätəf| industrial city in SW Russia, on the Volga River N of Volgograd. Pop. 909,000.

Sa·ra·wak |sə'räwä(k)| state of Malaysia, comprising the NW part of Borneo. Pop. 1,669,000. Capital: Kuching.

Sar·din·ia |sär'dinēə| large (9,305 sq. mi./24,090 sq. km.) Italian island in the Mediterranean Sea to the W of Italy. Pop. 1,664,000. Capital: Cagliari. In 1720 it was joined with Savoy and Piedmont to form the kingdom of Sardinia; the kingdom formed the nucleus of the Risorgimento, becoming part of a unified Italy under Victor Emmanuel II of Sardinia in 1861. Italian name **Sardegna**.

Sar·dis |'särdəs| ancient city of Asia Minor, the capital of Lydia, whose ruins lie near the W coast of modern Turkey, to the NE of Izmir.

Sar·gas·so Sea |sär'gæsō| region of the W Atlantic between the Azores and the Caribbean, so called because of the prevalence in it of floating sargasso seaweed. It is the breeding place of eels from the rivers of Europe and E North America, and is known for its usually calm conditions.

Sar·go·dha |sər'gōdə| market city and rail junction in N central Pakistan. Pop. 294,000.

Sarh |sär| (formerly **Fort-Archambault**) city in S Chad, on the Chari River. Pop. 130,000. It is a cotton industry center.

Sa·ri |'särē| commercial and industrial port city in N Iran, near the Caspian Sea. Pop. 168,000.

Sark |särk| one of the British Channel Islands, lying to the E of Guernsey. A tourist destination, it has its own parliament.

Sar·ma·tia |sär'mäsʜə| ancient region to the N of the Black Sea, extending originally from the Urals to the Don and inhabited by Slavic peoples. The term has also been used to refer to Poland. □ **Sarmatian** adj. & n.

Sar·nath |sär'nät| Buddhist shrine in N India, in Uttar Pradesh state, E of Varanasi. According to legend, Buddha gave his first sermon here, c.528 B.C.

Sar·nia |'särnēə| (offiical name **Sarnia-Clearwater**) industrial port in S Ontario, on Lake Huron and the St. Clair River. It is a major oil-industry center. Pop. 74,376.

Sa·ron·ic Gulf |sə'ränik| inlet of the Aegean Sea on the coast of SE Greece. Athens and the port of Piraeus lie on its N shores.

Sarre |sär| French name for the SAAR.

Sarthe |särt| **1** department in W France.

Pop. 514,000. **2** river in NW France that flows 178 mi./285 km. S from the department of Orne past Le Mans to Angers, where it meets the Loir and the Mayenne rivers.

Sar·um |'særəm| old name for Salisbury, England, still used as the name of its diocese. See also OLD SARUM.

Sa·se·bo |'säsä͵bō| commercial and industrial port city in SW Japan, on W Kyushu. Pop. 245,000.

Sas·katch·e·wan |sə'skæcʜəwən| prairie province of central Canada. Area: 251,866 sq. mi./652,330 sq. km. Pop. 994,000. Capital: Regina. Largest city: Saskatoon. Administered by the Hudson's Bay Company before 1870, it became part of the Northwest Territories, then, in 1905, a province. It is a major producer of grains.

Sas·katch·e·wan River |sə'skæcʜəwən| river of Canada. Rising in two headstreams, the North and South Saskatchewan, in the Rocky Mts., it joins and flows E for 370 mi./596 km. to Lake Winnipeg. Its waters continue via the Nelson River to Hudson Bay.

Sas·ka·toon |͵sæskə'tōōn| industrial city in S central Saskatchewan, in the Great Plains on the South Saskatchewan River. Pop. 186,060. It is the largest city in the province.

Sas·sa·ri |'säsəre| administrative and trade center in NW Sardinia, Italy, capital of Sassari province. Pop. 120,000.

Sa·tsu·ma |sæt'sōōmə; 'sätsə͵mä| former province of SW Japan. It comprised the major part of the SW peninsula of Kyushu, also known as the Satsuma Peninsula.

Sa·tu Ma·re |'sätōō 'märā| transportation junction and city in NW Romania, capital of Satu Mare county, on the Someş River near the Hungarian border. It is the original home of the Satmar sect of Orthodox Jews. Pop. 138,000.

Sau·di Ara·bia |'sowdē ə'räbēə; 'sawdē| kingdom in SW Asia occupying most of the

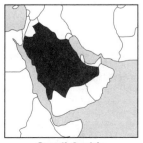

Saudi Arabia

Arabian Peninsula. Area: 829,996 sq. mi./2.15 million sq. km. Pop. 15,431,000. Language, Arabic. Capital and largest city: Riyadh. Administrative capital: Jeddah. Largely desert, it is the birthplace of Islam in the 7th century. An independent kingdom since 1932, it was revolutionized in 1938 by the discovery of oil. Mecca, the Islamic holy city, draws millions of visitors annually. □ **Saudi Arabian** adj. & n. **Saudi** adj. & n.

Sau·gus |'sawgəs| town in E Massachusetts, a suburb N of Boston that was the site of the first U.S. ironworks (1646). Pop. 25,549.

Sault Sainte Ma·rie |ˌsoo ˌsānt mə'rē| each of two North American river ports that face each other across the falls of the St. Mary's River, between Lakes Superior and Huron. The N port (pop. 72,822) lies in Ontario, while the S port (pop. 14,700) is in Michigan. The region is popularly known as **the Soo**.

Sau·mur |so'mYr| town in W central France, on the Loire River, in a wine-producing region. Pop. 32,000.

Sau·sa·li·to |ˌsawsə'lētō| city in NW California, across the Golden Gate from San Francisco. It is residential and has an artists' colony. Pop. 7,152.

Sau·ternes |so'tern; so'tərn| region in SW France, S of Bordeaux, known for its sweet white wines.

Sa·va River |'sävä| river (580 mi./930 km.) that rises in the Julian Alps of W Slovenia and flows SE through Croatia and Serbia to the Danube at Belgrade.

Sa·vai'i |sə'vī-ē| (also **Savaii**) mountainous volcanic island in the SW Pacific, the largest (700 sq. mi./1,813 sq. km.) of the Samoan islands.

Sa·van·nah |sə'vænə| industrial port in Georgia, just S of the border with South Carolina, on the Savannah River close to its outlet on the Atlantic. Pop. 137,560. It is noted for its 18th-century town design and architecture.

Sa·vann·ah River |sə'vænə| river that flows 315 mi./506 km., mostly along the border of Georgia and South Carolina, to reach the Atlantic near Savannah. Augusta, Georgia, lies on its course.

Sa·van·na·khet |sə,vänə'ket| (also **Savannaket**) town in S Laos, on the Mekong River at the border with Thailand. Pop. 51,000. It is a center for Thai-Lao trade.

Sa·vo Island |'sävō| volcanic island in the central Solomon Islands, in the SW Pacific, across Ironbottom Sound N of Guadal-

canal. Its waters were the scene of a defeat of U.S. naval forces by the Japanese in 1942.

Sa·vo·na |sə'vōnə| seaport in NW Italy, on the Gulf of Genoa, capital of Genoa province. Pop. 67,000.

Sa·von·lin·na |'sävawn,lēnnə| resort town in SE Finland, noted for its opera festival. Pop. 29,000.

Sa·voy |sə'voi| area of SE France bordering on NW Italy, a former duchy ruled by the counts of Savoy from the 11th century. In 1720 it was joined with Sardinia and Piedmont to form the kingdom of Sardinia, but in 1861, when Sardinia became part of a unified Italy, Savoy was ceded to France. French name **Savoie**. □ **Savoyard** adj. & n.

Sa·voy Theatre |sə'voi| theater in London, England, famed especially for its presentations of operettas by Gilbert and Sullivan, whose devotees came to be called Savoyards. The name was repeated in such other sites as the Savoy Ballroom in Harlem, New York City.

Sa·vu Sea |'sävoo| part of the Indian Ocean that is encircled by the Indonesian islands of Sumba, Flores, Savu, and Timor, N of Australia.

Sa·watch Range |sə'wäcH| range of the Rocky Mts. in central Colorado that includes Mount Elbert, at 14,433 ft./4,399 m., the highest peak in the state and in the entire Rocky Mt. system.

Saw·tooth Range |'sawtootH| range of the N Rockies in S central Idaho, noted for its jagged peaks. It is a noted recreational area.

Sa·xa Ru·bra |ˌsæksə 'roobrə| town in ancient Etruria, N of Rome, Italy. In A.D. 312 the Emperor Constantine here defeated a rival, Maxentius, who drowned while crossing the Milvian Bridge. Legend holds that a sign then appeared in the sky that led Constantine to accept Christianity and to become emperor of the Western as well as of the Eastern Roman Empire.

Sax·o·ny |'sæksənē| **1** state in eastern central Germany. Its capital is Dresden. Pop. 5,000,000. **2** region and former kingdom of Germany, including the present-day states of Saxony in the SE, Saxony-Anhalt in the center, and Lower Saxony in the NW. German name **Sachsen**.

Saxony-Anhalt |'säksənē'änhält| state of Germany, on the plains of the Elbe and the Saale rivers. Pop. 2,823,000. Capital: Magdeburg. It corresponds to the former duchy of Anhalt and the central part of the former kingdom of Saxony. German name **Sachsen-Anhalt**.

Sa•ya•ma |sä'yämä| resort town and industrial center in E central Japan, on E central Honshu. Pop. 157,000.

Sayre•ville |'sāər‚vil; 'servil| industrial and residential borough in E New Jersey. Pop. 34,986.

Sa•zan |'sä‚zän| (Italian name **Saseno**) island in SW Albania, in Vlorë Bay off the Gulf of Otranto (the Adriatic Sea). It was held by the Italians as a naval base 1914–47, and later used by Soviet and Chinese submarines.

Sca•fell Pike |'skaw‚fel| mountain in the Lake District of NW England, in Cumbria. Rising to a height of 3,210 ft./978 m., it is the highest peak in England.

Scan•di•na•via |‚skændə'nāvēə| **1** large peninsula in NW Europe, occupied by Norway and Sweden. It is bounded by the Arctic Ocean in the N, the Atlantic in the W, and the Baltic Sea in the S and E. **2** a cultural region consisting of the countries of Norway, Sweden, and Denmark and sometimes also of Iceland, Finland, and the Faroe Islands. □ **Scandinavian** adj. & n.

Scapa Flow |‚skæpə 'flō| strait in the Orkney Islands, N Scotland. It was an important British naval base, especially in World War I. The German High Seas Fleet was interned here after its surrender, and was scuttled in 1919 as an act of defiance against the terms of the Versailles peace settlement.

Scar•bor•ough¹ |'skärb(ə)rə| fishing port and resort on the coast of North Yorkshire, England. Pop. 38,000.

Scar•bor•ough² |'skärb(ə)rə| industrial and residential city in S Ontario, part of metropolitan Toronto. Pop. 524,598.

Scars•dale |'skärz‚dāl| residential town in SE New York, an affluent suburb of New York City. Pop. 16,987.

Schaff•hau•sen |sHäf'howzən| canton in N Switzerland, N of the Rhine River. Pop. 72,000. Its capital is Schaffhausen.

Schaum•burg |'sHawm‚bərg| residential and industrial village in NE Illinois, a suburb NW of Chicago. Pop. 68,586.

Scheldt |skelt| river of N Europe. Rising in N France, it flows 270 mi./432 km. through Belgium and the Netherlands to the North Sea. Also called **Schelde**; French name **Escaut**.

Sche•nec•ta•dy |skə'nektədē| industrial city in E New York, NW of Albany. Pop. 65,566. It is a center of electrical and related industries.

Schip•hol |'sHip‚ōl| see AMSTELVEEN, Netherlands.

Schles•wig |'sHles‚viKH| former Danish duchy, in the S part of the Jutland peninsula. Taken by Prussia in 1866, it was incorporated with the neighboring duchy of Holstein as the province of Schleswig-Holstein. The N part of Schleswig was returned to Denmark in 1920 after a plebiscite held in accordance with the Treaty of Versailles.

Schleswig-Holstein |'sHles‚viKH 'hōl‚sHtīn| state of NW Germany, occupying the S part of the Jutland peninsula. Pop. 2,649,000. Capital: Kiel.

Schmal•kal•den |'sHmäl‚käldən| town in central Germany. Pop. 18,000. It has been a center of metalworking since the Middle Ages. In 1531 Protestant princes met here to form the Schmalkaldic League to fight against the Holy Roman Empire.

Schön•brunn, Palace of |'sHœn‚broŏn| palace in Vienna, Austria, built in the late 17th–early 18th centuries as the summer residence of the Austrian emperor. In the Austrian Baroque style, it is graced by extensive gardens.

Schuyl•kill River |'skoŏl‚kil; 'skoŏkəl| river that flows 130 mi./210 km. through E Pennsylvania, joining the Delaware River at Philadelphia.

Schwa•ben |'sHfäbən| German name for SWABIA.

Schwä•bisch Gmünd |'sHfebisH 'gmYnt| (also **Gmünd**) industrial city in SW Germany, to the E of Stuttgart. Pop. 56,000.

Schwarz•wald |'sHfärts‚vält| German name for the BLACK FOREST.

Schwein•furt |'sHfīn‚foŏrt| industrial city in S Germany, in Bavaria. Pop. 55,000.

Schweiz |'sHfīts| German name for SWITZERLAND.

Schwe•rin |sHfä'rēn| industrial and commercial city in NE Germany, capital of Mecklenburg–West Pomerania, on the SW shore of Lake Schwerin. Pop. 126,000.

Schwyz |'sHfēts| city in central Switzerland, to the E of Lake Lucerne, capital of a canton of the same name. Pop. 13,000. The canton was one of the three original (13th-century) members of the Swiss Confederation, to which it gave its name.

Scil•ly Isles |'sili| (also **Isles of Scilly** or **the Scillies**) group of about 140 small islands (of which five are inhabited) off the SW tip of England. Pop. 3,000. Capital: Hugh Town (on St. Mary's). □ **Scillonian** adj. & n.

Scone |skoŏn| ancient Scottish settlement N of Perth, where the kings of medieval

Scotland were crowned on the Stone of Destiny. It is believed to be on the site of a Pictish capital.

Sco•pus, Mount |'skōpəs| peak in Israel, N of Jerusalem. It has long been of strategic importance in the defense of the city.

Scores•by Sound |'skawrzbē| inlet of the Greenland Sea in E central Greenland, noted for its fjords.

Sco•tia |'skōsHə| literary name for Scotland, from medieval Latin.

Scot•land |'skätlənd| country forming the northernmost part of Great Britain and of the United Kingdom. Area: 29,805 sq. mi./77,167 sq. km. Pop. 4,957,300. Capital: Edinburgh. Largest city: Glasgow. Peopled by Celts who resisted Roman and later English domination, Scotland finally became part of the United Kingdom in 1707. It produces textiles, timber, whisky, and foods. North Sea oil and tourism are also important. □ **Scottish** adj. **Scot** n.

Scot•land Yard |'skätlənd| headquarters of the London Metropolitan Police, in England, originally in Great Scotland Yard, off Whitehall in Westminster, later in two different locations called New Scotland Yard.

Scot•tish Borders |'skätisH| administrative region of S Scotland; administrative center, Melrose.

Scotts•bluff |'skäts,bləf| commercial city in W Nebraska. Pop. 13,711. It is named for a nearby promontory that was a pioneer landmark.

Scotts•dale |'skäts,dāl| city in S central Arizona, a suburb E of Phoenix. Pop. 130,069. Taliesin West, the architectural school of Frank Lloyd Wright, is here.

Scran•ton |'skræntn| industrial city in NE Pennsylvania, a steel center in the anthracite-mining region. Pop. 81,805.

Scroo•by |'skroōbē| village in central England, in N Nottinghamshire, the original home of several of the Pilgrims.

Scun•thorpe |'skən,THawrp| industrial town in NE England, in North Lincolnshire. Pop. 60,000.

Scu•ta•ri[1] |'skoōtərē| Italian name for SHKODËR, Albania.

Scu•ta•ri[2] |'skoōtərē| former name for Üsküdar, near Istanbul, Turkey, site of a British army hospital in which Florence Nightingale worked during the Crimean War.

Scyth•ia |'siTHēə| ancient region of SE Europe and Asia. The Scythian Empire, which existed between the 8th and 2nd centuries B.C., was centered on the N

shores of the Black Sea and extended from S Russia to the border of Persia. □ **Scythian** adj. & n.

Sea Islands |'sē| chain of islands off the Atlantic coast of N Florida, Georgia, and South Carolina. They include many resorts and nature preserves, and are noted for their African-derived Gullah culture.

Seal Beach |'sēl| city in SW California, just SE of Long Beach. Pop. 25,098.

Sea•ly•ham |'sēlēəm| location in S Wales, in Dyfed, S of Fishguard, that gave its name to a breed of terrier.

Sea of Azov, Sea of Galilee, etc. see AZOV, SEA OF; GALILEE, SEA OF; etc.

Sears Tower |sirz| office building in Chicago, Illinois, formerly the tallest occupied structure in the world, at 1,454 ft./443 m.

SEATO |'sētō| see SOUTHEAST ASIA TREATY ORGANIZATION.

Se•at•tle |sē'ætəl| port and industrial city in the state of Washington, on the E shore of Puget Sound. Pop. 516,259. First settled in 1852, it is now the largest city in the NW U.S. Aircraft manufacturing, commerce, and tourism are important.

Se•bas•to•pol |sə'bæstə,pōl| fortress and naval base in Ukraine, near the S tip of the Crimea. Pop. 361,000. The focal point of military operations during the Crimean War, it fell to Anglo-French forces in September 1855 after a year-long siege. Russia and Ukraine have recently disputed control and use of its harbor. Ukrainian and Russian name **Sevastopol**.

Se•bring |'sēbriNG| city in S central Florida. Pop. 8,900. In an agricultural area, it is a famed home to sports car racing.

Se•cau•cus |si'kawkəs| industrial town in NE New Jersey. Pop. 14,061. It is noted for its warehouses and outlet stores.

Sec•ond City nickname for CHICAGO.

Se•cun•der•a•bad |si'kəndərə,bäd; si 'kəndərə,bäd| (also **Sikandarabad**) city in S central India, in Andhra Pradesh state. Pop. 136,000. Once one of the largest British military stations in India, it is now a major Indian army base.

Se•da•lia |si'dälyə| industrial and commercial city in W central Missouri. Pop. 19,800.

Se•dan |sə'dän| town in NE France, on the Meuse River. Pop. 22,000. The decisive battle of the Franco-Prussian War took place here in 1870; the French defeat led to the end of the Second Empire. The town has been a textile center since the 16th century.

Se·do·na |si'dōnə| resort city in N central Arizona, a popular New Age center. Pop. 7,720.

Se·go·via |sə'gōvēə| city in N central Spain, N of Madrid. Pop. 58,000. Taken by the Moors in the 8th century, it was reclaimed by Castile in 1079, and was long a royal residence.

Sei·kan Tunnel |'sā,kän| rail tunnel in Japan, joining the islands of Honshu and Hokkaido. Completed in 1988, it is the longest undersea tunnel in the world: 32.3 mi./51.7 km.

Seine |sān; sen| river of N France. Rising N of Dijon, it flows NW for 473 mi./761 km., through the cities of Troyes and Paris to the English Channel near Le Havre.

Sekondi-Takoradi |'sekən'dē ,täkə'rädē| joint city and industrial seaport in SW Ghana, on the Gulf of Guinea. It is capital of the W region of Ghana, and one of the most important W African ports. Pop. 615,000.

Se·lang·or |sə'läNGŌor| state of Malaysia, on the W coast of the Malay Peninsula. Capital: Shah Alam.

Sel·borne |'sel,bawrn| village in S England, in Hampshire, the home of 18th-century naturalist Gilbert White.

Selebi-Phikwe |sə'läbē'pē,kä| mining town in E Botswana, S of Francistown. Pop. 40,000.

Se·len·ga River |,siliNG'gä| river in Mongolia and Russia, flowing 980 mi./1,568 km. from NW Mongolia to Lake Baikal in Russia.

Se·leu·cia |sə'lōōSHə| ancient city on the Tigris River, just S of present-day Baghdad, Iraq, a capital of the Seleucid Empire from the 4th century B.C. to the 2nd century A.D.

Sel·kirk Mountains |'sel,kərk| range of the Rocky Mts. in British Columbia, between the Monashees (W) and the Purcells (E).

Sel·kirk·shire |'sel,kərkSHər; 'säl,kərk- ,SHīr| former county of SE Scotland. It was made a part of Borders region (now Scottish Borders) in 1975.

Sel·la·field |'selə,fēld| the site of a nuclear power station and reprocessing plant on the coast of Cumbria in NW England. It was the scene in 1957 of a fire that caused a serious escape of radioactive material. Former name (1947–81) **Windscale**.

Sel·ma |'selmə| industrial city in S central Alabama, on the Alabama River. Pop. 23,755.

Se·ma·rang |sə'mär,äNG| port and commercial and industrial city in Indonesia, on the N coast of Java. Pop. 1,249,000.

Se·mei |'semā| (also **Semey**) industrial city and river port in E Kazakhstan, on the Irtysh River close to the border with Russia. Pop. 339,000. Founded in the 18th century, it was known as Semipalatinsk until 1991.

Se·me·ru |sə'merōō| (also called **Mahemeru; Mahameroe**) volcanic peak in Indonesia, at the E end of the island of Java and the island's highest point: 12,060 ft./3,676 m.

Se·mi·pa·la·tinsk |,semēpə'lätinsk| former name (until 1991) for SEMEI, Kazakhstan.

Sem·me·ring Pass |'semməriNG| mountain pass in the E Alps of Austria that connects the states of Styria and Lower Austria. The Semmeringbahn, built 1848–54, was the first major mountain railroad in Europe.

Sen·dai |sen'dī| industrial and university city in Japan, near the NE coast of Honshu. Pop. 918,000. It is the capital of the region of Tohoku.

Sen·e·ca Falls |'senikə| town in W central New York, W of Cayuga Lake. Pop. 9,384. It was the scene in 1848 of the first women's rights convention in the U.S.

Sen·e·ca Lake |'senikə| largest of the Finger Lakes in W central New York. Geneva is on its N, Watkins Glen on its S.

Sen·e·gal |,seni'gawl| republic on the coast of W Africa. Area: 75,984 sq. mi./196,722 sq. km. Pop. 7,632,000. Languages, French (official), Wolof, and other W African languages. Capital and largest city: Dakar. Part of the medieval Mali Empire, Senegal was controlled by the French before independence in 1959. Largely rural and semidesert, it almost encloses the Gambia. □ **Senegalese** adj. & n.

Sen·e·gal River |,seni'gawl| (also **Sénégal**) river of W Africa whose headstreams

Senegal

are in the Fouta Djallon of N Guinea. It flows 680 mi./1,088 km., through Mali and then along the Senegal-Mauritania border, to the Atlantic at St.-Louis, Senegal.

Sen•e•gam•bia |ˌseni'gämbēə| **1** region of W Africa consisting of the Senegal and Gambia rivers and lands between them, mostly in Senegal and W Mali. **2** short-lived (1982–89) confederation of Senegal and the Gambia. □ **Senegambian** adj. & n.

Seoul |sōl| the capital of South Korea, in the NW of the country on the Han River. Pop. 10,628,000. It was the capital of the Yi dynasty from the late 4th century until 1910, when Korea was annexed by the Japanese. Extensively developed under Japanese rule, it became the capital of South Korea after the partition of 1945. It is a world industrial, financial, and commercial center.

Se•quoia National Park |si'kwoiə| preserve in the Sierra Nevada of California, E of Fresno. It was established in 1890 to protect groves of giant sequoia trees, of which the largest, the General Sherman Tree, is though to be between 3,000 and 4,000 years old.

Se•raing |səNreN| industrial town in Belgium, on the Meuse River just SW of Liège. Pop. 61,000.

Ser•am•pore |'serəmˌpawr| (also **Serampur; Shrirampur**) industrial town in E India, West Bengal state. Pop. 137,000. It originated as a Danish settlement in the 18th century.

Ser•bia |'sərbēə| republic in the Balkan Peninsula, part of Yugoslavia. Area: 34,129 sq. mi./88,361 sq. km. Pop. 9,660,000. Language, Serbo-Croat. Capital and largest city: Belgrade. Serbian name **Srbi•ja**. Independent by the 6th century, Serbia was dominated by the Turks from the 14th century until 1878. From World War I until 1991, it was the dominant partner in Yugoslavia; today only Montenegro remains in the Yugoslav confederation with Serbia. Recent decades have seen strife with neighboring Croatia and Bosnia, and within Serbia with the nominally autonomous regions of Kosovo (largely Albanian) and Vojvodina (largely Hungarian). □ **Serbian** adj. & n. **Serb** n.

Se•rem•ban |sə'rembən| the capital of the state of Negri Sembilan in Malaysia, in the SW of the Malay Peninsula. Pop. 136,000.

Ser•en•dib |'serənˌdib| see SRI LANKA.

Se•ren•ge•ti |ˌserən'getē| vast plain in Tanzania, to the W of the Great Rift Valley. In 1951 the Serengeti National Park was cre-

ated to protect the area's large numbers of wildebeest, zebra, and Thomson's gazelle.

Ser•gi•pe |serZHēpē| state in E Brazil, on the Atlantic coast. Pop. 1,492,000. Capital: Aracajú.

Ser•gi•yev Po•sad |sir'gyāyif pä'säd| (formerly **Zagorsk**) industrial town in W Russia, NE of Moscow. Pop. 115,000.

Ser•pu•khov |ser'pōōkəf| industrial city in W Russia, S of Moscow, on the Oka River. Pop. 145,000.

Ses•tos |'sestōs| ancient town in present-day European Turkey, on the N side of the Dardanelles narrows opposite ABYDOS. The Persian king Xerxes attempted to bridge the strait here to attack Greece in the 5th century B.C.

Sète |set| (formerly **Cette**) town in S France, in Languedoc, on the Mediterranean Sea. Pop. 42,000. It is a major commercial and fishing port and a shipping center, with canals running through the town.

Sé•tif |sā'tēf| commercial and industrial city in NE Algeria. Pop. 170,000. It was a center of a 1945 uprising against French colonial rule.

Se•tú•bal |sə'tōōbəl| port and industrial town on the coast of Portugal, S of Lisbon. Pop. 84,000.

Se•vas•to•pol |se'västəˌpōl| Russian name for SEBASTOPOL, Ukraine.

Sev•en Hills |'sevən| original site of the city of Rome, Italy. The hills are the Aventine, Caelian, Capitoline, Esquiline, Palatine, Quirinal, and Viminal. According to legend, the city was founded by Romulus on the Palatine hill in 753 B.C. The name Seven Hills has since been applied to prominences in such cities as San Francisco, California, and to regions like the Siebengebirge of Germany.

Sev•en Wonders of the World (also **Seven Wonders of the Ancient World**) traditional list of the most spectacular man-made structures in the world, dating from the 2nd century and usually comprising the Pyramids of Egypt; the Hanging Gardens of Babylon; the Mausoleum of Halicarnassus; the Temple of Diana at Ephesus; the Colossus of Rhodes; the statue of Zeus at Olympia; and the Pharos at Alexandria.

Sev•ern |'sevərn| river of SW Britain. Rising in central Wales, it flows NE, then S, in a broad curve for some 180 mi./290 km. to its mouth on the Bristol Channel. The estuary is spanned by a suspension bridge N of Bristol, opened in 1966, and a second bridge a few miles to the S, opened in 1996.

Se•ver•na•ya Zem•lya |'syevirnəyə zemlē

'ä| group of uninhabited islands in the Arctic Ocean off the N coast of Russia, to the N of the Taimyr Peninsula.

Se·ve·ro·do·netsk |ˌsyevirədəˈnetsk| city in SE Ukraine, NW of Lugansk. Pop. 132,000.

Se·ve·rod·vinsk |ˌsyevirədˈvinsk| industrial port in NW Russia, on the White Sea coast W of Archangel. Pop. 250,000.

Se·vier River |səˈvir| river that flows 325 mi./525 km. through central Utah, irrigating the E edge of the Great Basin.

Se·ville |səˈvil| industrial port city in S Spain, the capital of Andalusia, on the Guadalquivir River. Pop. 683,000. A leading cultural center of Moorish Spain, it was reclaimed by the Spanish in 1248, and rapidly became prominent as a center of trade with the colonies of the New World. Spanish name **Sevilla**.

Sè·vres |ˈsevrə| town and SW suburb of Paris, in N central France. Pop. 22,000. Sèvres produced fine porcelains especially during the 18th and 19th centuries.

Sew·ard Peninsula |ˈso͞oərd| region of NW Alaska on the Bering Strait and the Chukchi Sea. Nome lies on its S coast.

Sey·chelles |sāˈsHel(z)| (also **the Seychelles**) republic consisting of a group of about ninety islands in the SW Indian Ocean, about 600 mi./1,000 km. NE of Madagascar. Land area: 175 sq. mi./453 sq. km. Pop. 69,000. Languages, French Creole (official), English, French. Capital: Victoria (on Malé island). Uninhabited but known to Arab traders, the islands were annexed by France in the 18th century. The British took control during the Napoleonic Wars. Independence came in 1976. Tourism, fishing, and copra and spice production are important. □ **Seychellois** adj. & n.

Seychelles

Sey·han |sāˈhän| river that flows 350 mi./560 km. through central Turkey to the Mediterranean Sea. Adana is on its course.

Sfax |sfæks| (also **Safaqis**) port on the E coast of Tunisia. Pop. 231,000. It is a center for the region's phosphate industry.

's Graven·hage Dutch name for THE HAGUE.

Shaan·xi |ˈsHänˈsHē| (also **Shensi**) mountainous province of central China. Pop. 32,880,000. Capital: Xi'an. It is the site of the earliest settlements of the ancient Chinese civilizations.

Sha·ba |ˈsHäbə| copper-mining region of SE Congo (formerly Zaire). Capital: Lubumbashi. Former name (until 1972) **Katanga**. The most populous Congolese region, and a major cobalt producer, it has been subject to repeated secessionist pressures.

Shah Alam |ˈsHä ˈäläm| the capital of the state of Selangor in Malaysia, near the W coast of the Malay Peninsula. Pop. 24,000.

Shah·ja·han·pur |ˌsHäjəˈhän͵po͝or| commercial city in N central India, in Uttar Pradesh state. Pop. 260,000. It was founded by and named for the Mogul emperor Shah Jahan (1647).

Shak·er Heights |ˈsHākər| city in NE Ohio, an affluent suburb E of Cleveland. Pop. 30,831.

Shakh·ty |ˈsHäkti| coal-mining city in SW Russia, in the Donets Basin NE of Rostov. Pop. 227,000.

Shan |sHän| state in E central Burma. Pop. 3,719,000. Its people are mostly Shans, whose Shan States flourished in much of this area between the 12th and 16th centuries.

Shan·dong |ˈsHänˈdo͝oNG| (formerly **Shantung**) province in E China, on the Yellow Sea. Pop. 84,890,000. Capital: Jinan. It is a leading industrial and agricultural province.

Shan·dong Peninsula |ˈsHänˈdo͝oNG| peninsula in E Shandong province, NE China, separating the Bo Hai from the Yellow Sea. It is the largest peninsula in China.

Shang·hai |ˈsHæNGˌhī; sHæNGˈhī| city on the E coast of China, a port on the estuary of the Yangtze. Pop. 7,780,000. Opened for trade with the W in 1842, Shanghai contained until World War II areas of British, French, and American settlement. It was the site in 1921 of the founding of the Chinese Communist Party. It is now China's most populous city.

Shang·qiu |ˈsHänCHēˈo͞o| city in NE Henan province, E China, SE of Zhengzhou. Pop. 165,000. It was the site of a Northern Song (Sung) dynasty imperial residence.

Shangri-La |ˌSHæNGgrə'lä| Tibetan utopia in the 1933 novel *Lost Horizon* by James Hilton. The name has been applied to various retreats from worldly care, notably CAMP DAVID, the presidential resort in Maryland.

Shan·kill Road |'SHæNGkil| road in the Protestant neighborhoods of Belfast, Northern Ireland, parallel to Falls Road, which passes through Roman Catholic neighborhoods to the N.

Shan·non |'SHænən| the longest river of Ireland. It rises in County Leitrim near Lough Allen and flows 240 mi./390 km. S and W to its estuary on the Atlantic. Near its mouth, W of Limerick, is the international airport also called Shannon.

Shan·si |'SHän'SHē| see SHANXI, China.

Shan·tou |'SHän'tō| port in the province of Guangdong in SE China, on the South China Sea at the mouth of the Han River. Pop. 860,000. It was designated a treaty port in 1869. Former name **Swatow**.

Shan·tung |'SHän'dəNG| see SHANDONG, China.

Shan·tung Peninsula |'SHän'dəNG| see SHANDONG PENINSULA, China.

Shan·xi |'SHän'SHē| (also **Shansi**) a province of N central China, to the S of Inner Mongolia. Pop. 28,760,000. Capital: Taiyuan.

Shao·guan |'SHow'gwän| city in Guangdong province, S China, on the Bei River N of Guangzhou (Canton). Pop. 350,000.

Shao·xing |'SHow'SHiNG| commercial city in Zhejiang province, E China, in a rice-growing region on the Grand Canal SE of Hangzhou. Pop. 180,000.

Shao·yang |'SHow'yäNG| city in Hunan province, SE central China, SW of Changsha. Pop. 247,000. It is a coal- and iron-mining center.

Shar·jah |'SHärjə| **1** one of the seven member states of the United Arab Emirates. Pop. 400,000. Arabic name **Ash Shariqah**. **2** its capital city, on the Persian Gulf. Pop. 125,000.

Sharm al-Sheikh |'SHärm æl'SHāk| (also **Ras Nasrani**) cape at the S of the Sinai Peninsula, NE Egypt. Its commanding position on the Gulf of Aqaba led to fighting between Egyptian and Israeli forces in 1956 and 1967. Israel occupied it 1967–82.

Shar·on |'SHærən| fertile coastal plain in Israel, lying between the Mediterranean Sea and the hills of Samaria.

Sha·shi |'SHä'SHē| inland port and commercial center in Hubei province, E central China, on the Yangtze River W of Wuhan. Pop. 281,000.

Shas·ta, Mount |'SHæstə| peak in N California, the highest point (14,162 ft./4,317 m.) in the Cascade Range within the state. Recreational Shasta Lake lies on its S.

Shatt al-Arab |'SHæt æl 'ærəb| river of SW Asia, formed by the confluence of the Tigris and Euphrates and flowing 120 mi./195 km. through SE Iraq to the Persian Gulf. Its lower course forms the border between Iraq and Iran.

Sha·win·i·gin |SHə'winəgən| industrial city in S Quebec, on the St.-Maurice River N of Trois-Rivières. Pop. 19,931.

Shaw·mut Peninsula |'SHawmət| promontory on which the city of Boston, Massachusetts was founded in the 1630s. Beacon Hill is the only survivor of the three that gave the settlement its early name, Trimountaine.

Shaw·nee[1] |SHaw'nē; SHänē| city in NE Kansas, a suburb SW of Kansas City. Pop. 37,993.

Shaw·nee[2] |SHaw'nē; SHänē| industrial city in central Oklahoma, in an oil- and gas-producing region. Pop. 26,017.

She·ba |'SHēbə| the biblical name of Saba, in SW Arabia. The queen of Sheba visited King Solomon in Jerusalem (1 Kings 10).

She·boy·gan |SHi'boigən| industrial city in E Wisconsin, a port on Lake Michigan. Pop. 49,676.

Shef·field |'SHef,ēld| industrial city in N England, formerly in Yorkshire. Pop. 500,000. Sheffield is famous for the manufacture of cutlery and silverware and for the production of steel.

Shel·ton |'SHeltn| industrial city in SW Connecticut. Pop. 35,418.

Shen·an·do·ah National Park |ˌSHenən-'dōə| national park in the Blue Ridge Mts. of N Virginia, to the SE of the Shenandoah River.

Shen·an·do·ah River |ˌSHenən'dōə| river of Virginia, rising in two headstreams, one on each side of the Blue Ridge Mts., and flowing some 150 mi./240 km. N to join the Potomac at Harpers Ferry, West Virginia. Its valley is famed for its beauty and Civil War history.

Shen·si |'SHen'SHē| see SHAANXI, China.

Shen·yang |'SHen'yäNG| city in NE China. Pop. 4,500,000. An important Manchurian city between the 17th and early 20th centuries, it is now the capital of the province of Liaoning. Former name **Mukden**.

Shen·zhen |'SHen'jen| industrial city in S China, just N of Hong Kong. Pop. 875,000.

Shep·herd's Bush |ˈsHepərdz| largely residential district of W London, England, W of Kensington, noted as the site of BBC television studios.

Sher·brooke |ˈsHər,bro͝ok| commercial and industrial city in S Quebec, in the Eastern Townships E of Montreal. Pop. 76,429.

Sher·i·dan |ˈsHerədn| city in N central Wyoming. Pop. 13,900.

Sher·man |ˈsHərmən| commercial and industrial city in NE Texas. Pop. 31,601.

's Her·to·gen·bosch |ser,tōKHən,baws| commercial city in the S Netherlands, the capital of North Brabant. Pop. 92,000.

Sher·wood Forest |ˈsHər,wo͝od| former forest that covered much of Nottinghamshire, central England, associated with legends of Robin Hood. A few remnants are preserved.

Shet·land Islands |ˈsHetlənd| (also **Shetland** or **the Shetlands**) group of about 100 islands off the N coast of Scotland, NE of the Orkneys, constituting the administrative region of Shetland. Pop. 22,000; chief town, Lerwick. Together with the Orkney Islands the Shetland Islands became a part of Scotland in 1472, having previously been ruled by Norway and Denmark. Noted for the production of knitwear, they have provided in the late 20th century a base for the North Sea oil and gas industries. □ **Shetlander** *n.*

Shi·bam |sHiˈbäm| commercial town in SE Yemen. A fortress town, it is noted for the height of its houses, which have from six to nine stories.

Shick·shock Mountains |ˈsHik,sHäk| (French name **Monts Chic-Chocs**) range of the Appalachian Mts. that extends NE through the Gaspé Peninsula of Quebec.

Shi·ga·tse |sHiˈgätse| see XIGAZÊ, China.

Shi·he·zi |ˈsHiˈhəd'zə| city in Xinjiang, NE China, in the N foothills of the Tian Shan mountains, W of Ürümqi. Pop. 300,000.

Shi·jia·zhuang |ˈsHējēˈäjo͞oˈäNG| industrial city in NE China, capital of Hebei province. Pop. 1,320,000.

Shi·ko·ku |sHiˈkōko͞o| the smallest (7,260 sq. mi./18,795 sq. km.) of the four main islands of Japan, constituting an administrative region. Pop. 4,195,000. Capital: Matsuyama. It is divided from Kyushu to the W and S Honshu to the N by the Inland Sea.

Shi·li·gu·ri |sHiˈlē,go͞orē| town in E India, in West Bengal state, SSE of Darjeeling. Pop. 227,000.

Shil·le·lagh |sHəˈlālē| village in SE Ireland,

in County Wicklow, that gave its name to a cudgel made from a kind of oak or blackthorn that grows locally.

Shil·long |sHəˈlawNG| city in the far NE of India, capital of the state of Meghalaya. Pop. 131,000.

Shi·loh[1] |ˈsHīlō| biblical place where the Ark of the Covenant was kept after Canaan was conquered. Present-day Khirbat Saylun, in the Israeli-occupied West Bank NE of Jerusalem, is on the site.

Shi·loh[2] |ˈsHīlō| historic site in SW Tennessee, near Pittsburg Landing on the Tennessee River, scene of a major Civil War battle in April 1862.

Shi·ma·ba·ra |sHiˈmä,bärä| (also **Simabara**) city in SW Japan, on the Shimabara Peninsula on NW Kyushu. Pop. 45,000.

Shi·mi·zu |sHiˈmēzo͞o| port city in E central Japan, on the S coast of central Honshu. Pop. 242,000.

Shi·mo·da |sHiˈmōdä| port city in E central Japan, in central Honshu. Pop. 30,000. The first U.S. consulate to Japan was opened here in 1856.

Shi·mo·no·se·ki |ˈsHimōnō,sekē| industrial port city in W Japan, at the extreme SW of Honshu. Pop. 263,000.

Ship·ka Pass |ˈsHipkä| pass through the Balkan Mts., central Bulgaria, near which Russian and Bulgarian forces won a major victory over the Turks in 1878.

Ship·rock |ˈsHiprák| eroded volcanic feature that stands above the desert in NW New Mexico near the Four Corners. It was sacred to the Navajo and a landmark for travelers.

Shi·raz |sHiˈräz| city in S central Iran. Pop. 965,000. It is noted for the school of miniature painting based here between the 14th and 16th centuries, and for the manufacture of carpets and wine.

Shire River |ˈsHir,ā| (also **Shiré**) river that flows 250 mi./400 km. from Lake Malawi in Malawi into Mozambique, where it joins the Zambezi River. The **Shire Highlands** on the E side in Malawi, are a fertile agricultural area.

Shi·shou |ˈsHiˈsHō| city in Hubei province, E central China, on the Yangtze River S of Shashi. Pop. 558,000.

Shit·tim |ˈsHitəm| biblical land, E of Jericho, where the Israelites stopped before reaching the Promised Land.

Shi·yan |ˈsHiˈyän| city in N Hubei province, E central China, on the Wudang Shan range W of the Danjiangkou Reservoir. Pop. 274,000.

Shi·zu·o·ka |,sHizo͞oˈōkä| port on the S

coast of the island of Honshu in Japan. Pop. 472,000.

Shko•dër |'sнkōdər| city in NW Albania, near the border with Montenegro. Pop. 82,000. Italian name **Scutari.**

Shkum•bin River |sнkoōm'bin| river that flows across central Albania, from near Lake Ohrid, past Elbasan, to the Adriatic Sea. It divides the country between Gheg speakers to the N and Tosk speakers to the S.

Sho•la•pur |'sнōlə,poor| city in W India, a textile center on the Deccan plateau in the state of Maharashtra. Pop. 604,000.

Show Me State |'sнō mē| nickname for MISSOURI.

Shreve•port |'sнrēv,pawrt| industrial city in NW Louisiana, on the Red River near the border with Texas. Pop. 198,525. Founded in 1839, it grew rapidly after the discovery of oil and gas in the region in 1906.

Shrews•bury |'sнrōōz,bərē| town in W England, the county seat of Shropshire, on the Severn River near the border with Wales. Pop. 59,000.

Shrop•shire |'sнräp,sнər| county of W England, on the border with Wales. Pop. 402,000; county seat, Shrewsbury. Also called **Salop.**

Shuang•ya•shan |'sнoōäNG'yä'sнän| city in Heilongjiang province, NE China, NE of Harbin and S of the Sungari (Songhua) River. Pop. 386,000.

Shu•bra el Khei•ma |'sнōbrä el 'kämä| (also **Shubra al-Khayma**) city in NE Egypt, an industrial suburb N of Cairo. Pop. 812,000.

Shu•men |'sнoō,men| industrial and cultural city in NE Bulgaria. Pop. 126,000.

Shym•kent |cнim'kent| (also **Chimkent**) **1** former administrative district of Kazakhstan, now called South Kazakhstan. Pop. 1,879,000. **2** its capital, an industrial city N of Tashkent. Pop. 438,000.

Sia•chen Glacier |'syäcнin| glacier in the Karakoram Mts. in NW India, at an altitude of some 17,800 ft./5,500 m. Extending over 44 mi./70 km., it is one of the world's longest glaciers.

Si•al•kot |sē'äkōt| industrial city in the province of Punjab, in Pakistan. Pop. 296,000.

Si•am, Gulf of |sī'æm| former name for the Gulf of Thailand (see THAILAND, GULF OF).

Si•am |sī'æm| former name (until 1939) for THAILAND. □ **Siamese** adj. & n.

Siau•liai |'sнow'lä| manufacturing city in N Lithuania, NW of Kaunas. Pop. 149,000.

Ši•be•nik |'sнēbenēk| industrial city and port in Croatia, on the Adriatic coast. Pop. 41,000.

Si•be•ria |sī'birēə| vast region of Russia, including some three-quarters of the republic and extending from the Urals to Kamchatka in the Pacific and from the Arctic coast to the N borders of Kazakhstan, Mongolia, and China. It was occupied by the Russians in successive stages from 1581 when a Cossack expedition ousted the Tartar khanate of Sibir, which gave the region its name. After the opening in 1905 of the Trans-Siberian Railway, Siberia became more accessible and attracted settlers from European Russia. Noted for the severity of its winters, it was traditionally used as a place of exile; it is now a major source of minerals and hydroelectric power. □ **Siberian** adj. & n.

Si•biu |'sēbyoō| industrial city in central Romania. Pop. 188,000.

Si•bo•ney |,sēbō'nä| town in E Cuba, in Santiago de Cuba province, with nearby Daiquiri the landing place of U.S. troops in 1898, during the Spanish-American War.

Si•bu•yan |,sēboō'yän| island in the central Philippines, in the Sibuyan Sea S of Luzon.

Si•chuan |'si'cнwän| (also **Szechuan** or **Szechwan**) province of W central China. Pop. 107,220,000. Capital: Chengdu. Surrounded by mountains, it is largely agricultural. □ **Sichuanese** adj. & n.

Si•ci•lia |sē'cнēlyä; si'silyə| Italian name for SICILY.

Sic•i•lies, Kingdom of the Two |'sisilēz| unification under one crown of Sicily and S Italy (the kingdom of Naples, or lands S of the Papal States), first effected in 1442, and last official in 1816–60.

Sic•i•ly |'sisilē| island, the largest (9,929 sq. mi./25,706 sq. km.) in the Mediterranean, off the SW tip of Italy. Pop. 5,197,000. Capital and largest city: Palermo. It is separated from the Italian mainland by the Strait of Messina and its highest point is the volcano Mount Etna. Settled successively by Phoenicians, Greeks, and Carthaginians, it became a Roman province in 241 B.C. after the first Punic War. It was conquered toward the end of the 11th century by the Normans, who united the island with S Italy as the kingdom of the Two Sicilies. Conquered by Charles of Anjou in 1266, the island subsequently passed to the House of Aragon. It was reunited with S Italy in 1442. The kingdom was claimed in 1816 by the Spanish Bourbon King Ferdinand, but was liberated in 1860 by Garibaldi and incorporated into the new state of Italy. Italian name **Sicilia**. □ **Sicilian** *adj. & n.*

Si·di bel Ab·bès |'sēdē bel ä'bes| commercial and industrial town in N Algeria, to the S of Oran. Pop. 186,000. It is the former home of the French Foreign Legion.

Si·don |'sīdn| port city in Lebanon, on the Mediterranean coast S of Beirut. Pop. 38,000. Founded in the 3rd millennium B.C., it was a Phoenician seaport and city-state. Arabic name **Saida**.

Sid·ra, Gulf of |'sidrə| (also **Gulf of Sirte**) broad inlet of the Mediterranean on the coast of Libya, between Benghazi and Misratah.

Sie·ben·ge·bir·ge Mountains |'sēbengebērge| mountain range in western Germany, on the Rhine River, SE of Bonn. The highest peak is the Grosser Olberg (1,509 ft./460 m.). The scenic region attracts many tourists.

Sie·gen |'sēgen| industrial town in western Germany, on the Sieg River, in an iron-producing region. Pop. 111,000.

Sieg·fried Line |'sēg,frēd| line of defensive fortification built in western Germany before World War II, facing the French Maginot Line and extending from the Swiss border on the S to Cleve on the N, generally parallel to the Rhine River. Allied forces first broke through the line in late 1944.

Si·em Re·ap |,sēəm 'reəp| town in NW Cambodia, on the Siem Reap River The ruins of the ancient city of Angkor are just to the N.

Si·e·na |sē'enə| commercial and cultural city in W central Italy, in Tuscany. Pop. 58,000. In the 13th and 14th centuries it was the center of a flourishing school of art. Its central square is the venue for the noted Palio horse race. □ **Sienese** *adj. & n.*

Si·er·ra Le·one |sē'erə lē'onē| republic on the coast of W Africa. Area: 27,709 sq. mi./71,740 sq. km. Pop. 4,239,000. Languages, English (official), English Creole,

Sierra Leone

Temne, and other W African languages. Capital and largest city: Freetown. Coastal areas were controlled by the British from the late 18th century, inland areas in 1896. Independence came in 1961. Agriculture and mining are both important. □ **Sierra Leonean** *adj. & n.*

Si·er·ra Mad·re |sē'erə 'mädrä| mountain system in Mexico, extending from the border with the U.S. in the N to the S border with Guatemala. Regarded as an extension of the Rocky Mts., it reaches 18,697 ft./5,699 m. at CITLALTÉPETL, SE of Mexico City.

Si·er·ra Ma·es·tra |sē'erä mä'esträ| mountain range in SE Cuba, reaching 6,470 ft./1,972 m. at Pico Turquino. Forested and rich in minerals, the mountains are famous as the base of 1950s rebels under Fidel Castro.

Si·er·ra Ne·va·da[1] |sē'erə nə'vädə| mountain range in E California. Rising sharply from the Great Basin in the E, it descends more gently to California's Central Valley in the W. Its highest peak is Mount Whitney, which rises to 14,495 ft./4,418 m.

Si·er·ra Ne·va·da[2] |sē'erə nə'vädə| mountain range in S Spain, in Andalusia, SE of Granada. Its highest peak is Mulhacén, which rises 11,424 ft./3,482 m.

Si·er·ra Ne·va·da de Mé·ri·da |sē'erə nə-'vädə de 'meridä| (also **Cordillera de Mérida**) range of the Andes Mts. in NW Venezuela, reaching 16,420 ft./5,000 m. at Pico Bolívar, the highest peak in the country.

Si·er·ra Ne·va·da de San·ta Mar·ta |sē-'erə nə'vädə de 'sæntə 'märtə| mountain range in N Colombia, near the Caribbean Sea and the Venezuela border, reaching 19,020 ft./5,797 m. at Pico Cristóbal Colón, the highest peak in the country.

Si·ghi·şoa·ra |,sēgə'sHwärə| industrial and resort city in central Romania, in Transylvania. Pop. 38,000.

Sig·ma·ring·en |'sigmä,riNGən| city in SW Germany, on the Danube River. Pop. 16,000. Its castle became the home of the Hohenzollerns, rulers of Germany, in 1535.

Si·ha·nouk·ville |sē'hänōōk,vil| see KOMPONG SOM, Cambodia.

Si·kang |'sHē'käNG| former province (1928–55) in S China, now divided between Tibet and Sichuan.

Si·king |'sHē'kiNG| former name for XI'AN, China.

Sik·kim |'sikim| state of NE India, in the E Himalayas between Bhutan and Nepal, on the border with Tibet. Pop. 405,000. Capital: Gangtok. After British rule it became an Indian protectorate, becoming a state of India in 1975. □ **Sikkimese** *adj. & n.*

Sil·ches·ter |'sil,CHestər| village in Hampshire, S England, SW of Reading. It is the site of an important town of pre-Roman and Roman Britain, known to the Romans as Calleva Atrebatum.

Si·le·sia |sī'lēZHə| region of central Europe, centered on the upper Oder valley, now largely in SW Poland. It was partitioned at various times among the states of Prussia, Austria–Hungary, Poland, and Czechoslovakia. It is known for its coal deposits and forests. □ **Silesian** *adj. & n.*

Sil·i·con Valley |'silikən; 'silikän| name given to an area between San Jose and Palo Alto in Santa Clara County, California, noted for its computer and electronics industries.

Silk Road |'silk| (also **Silk Route**) ancient caravan route linking Xi'an in central China with the E Mediterranean. Skirting the N edge of the Taklimakan Desert and passing through Turkestan, it covered a distance of some 4,000 mi./6,400 m. It was established during the period of Roman rule in Europe, and took its name from the silk that was brought W from China. It was also the route by which Christianity spread E. A railway (completed in 1963) follows the Chinese part of the route, from Xi'an to Urumqi.

Si·lo·am |si'lōəm| biblical spring and pool just SE of Jerusalem, from which water was drawn through a tunnel to the city.

Sil·ver Spring |'silvər| residential and commercial suburb in central Maryland, just N of Washington, D.C. Pop. 76,046.

Sil·ver State |'silvər| nickname for NEVADA.

Sim·birsk |sim'birsk| city in European Russia, a port on the Volga River SE of Nizhni Novgorod. Pop. 638,000. Between 1924 and 1992 it was called Ulyanovsk, in honor of Lenin (Vladimir Ilich Ulyanov), who was born here in 1870.

Sim·coe, Lake |'simkō| recreational lake in S Ontario, N of Toronto, in an agricultural area.

Sim·fer·o·pol |,simfə'rawpəl| city in the Crimea, Ukraine. Pop. 349,000. It was settled by the Tartars in the 16th century, when it was known as Ak-Mechet, and was seized in 1736 by the Russians.

Si·mi Valley |sē'mē| city in SW California, a residential suburb NW of Los Angeles. Pop. 100,217.

Sim·la |'simlə| resort city in NE India, cap-

ital of the state of Himachal Pradesh. Pop. 110,000.

Sim·plon |'sim,plawn| pass in the Alps in S Switzerland, consisting of a road built by Napoleon 1801–5 at an altitude of 6,591 ft./2,028 m. and a railway tunnel (built in 1922) that links Switzerland and Italy.

Simp·son Desert |'sim(p)sən| desert in central Australia, situated between Alice Springs and the Channel Country to the E.

Si·nai |'sī,nī| (**the Sinai**) arid mountainous peninsula in NE Egypt, extending into the Red Sea between the Gulf of Suez and the Gulf of Aqaba. It was occupied by Israel between 1967 and 1982, when it was fully restored to Egypt following the Camp David agreement. In the S is Mount Sinai, where, according to the Bible, Moses received the Ten Commandments. □ **Sinaitic** *adj.*

Si·na·loa |,sēnə'lōə| state on the Pacific coast of Mexico. Area: 22,529 sq. mi./58,328 sq. km. Pop. 2,211,000. Capital: Culiacán Rosales.

Sin·ce·le·jo |,sēnsā'lāhō| commercial city in N Colombia, the capital of Sucre department. Pop. 168,000.

Sind |sind| province of SE Pakistan, traversed by the lower reaches of the Indus. Pop. 21.68 million. Capital: Karachi.

Si·nes |'sēnisн| industrial port in SW Portugal, the birthplace of the explorer Vasco da Gama. Pop. 10,000.

Sin·ga·pore |'siNG(g)ə,pawr| republic in SE Asia consisting of the island of Singapore (linked by a causeway to the S tip of the Malay Peninsula) and some fifty-four smaller islands. Area: 239 sq. mi./618 sq. km. Pop. 3,045,000. Official languages, Malay, Chinese, Tamil, and English. Capital and largest city: Singapore City. An East India Company trading post from 1819, ruled by the British from 1867, Singapore gained independence in 1965, after two years as part of Malaysia. Long a commercial and naval hub, it remains a financial

Singapore

and trade center. □ **Singaporean** *adj. & n.*
see OSSINING.

Si•ning |'sē'niNG| see XINING, China.

Sin•kiang |'siNG'kyæNG| see XINJIANG, China.

Si•nop |se'nōp| (ancient name **Sinope**) historic port town in N Turkey, the capital of Sinop province. Pop. 26,000. Founded by Ionian Greeks in the 8th century B.C., it was the birthplace of Diogenes, the Cynic philosopher.

Sint Maar•ten |sint 'märtin| Dutch name for ST. MARTIN, in the Antilles.

Sint-Niklaas |sint 'nēkläs| industrial town in N Belgium, SW of Antwerp. Pop. 68,000. French name **St. Nicolas**.

Sin•tra |'sintrə| (also **Cintra**) historic town in W Portugal, in a mountainous area NW of Lisbon. Pop. 20,000.

Sin•ui•ju |'SHi'nwē'jōō| industrial port city in North Korea, on the Yalu River near its mouth on the Yellow Sea. Pop. 500,000.

Sioux City |sōō| commercial and industrial city in NW Iowa, on the Missouri and Big Sioux rivers. Pop. 80,505.

Sioux Falls |sōō| largest city in South Dakota, a commercial and industrial center in the SE, on the Big Sioux River. Pop. 100,814.

Si•ping |'sə'piNG| city in Jilin province, NE China, SW of Changchun near Liaoning province. Pop. 317,000.

Si•ra•cu•sa |,sirə'kōōzə| Italian name for SYRACUSE.

Sir•dar•yo |sirdär'yō| river of central Asia. Rising in two headstreams in the Tien Shan mountains in E Uzbekistan, it flows for some 1,380 miles (2,220 km) W and NW through southern Kazakhstan to the Aral Sea. Russian name **Syr-Darya**.

Si•ret River |sē'ret| river (280 mi./448 km.) in Ukraine and Romania, rising in the Carpathian Mts. and flowing S to meet the Danube River near Galaţi.

Sir•mio•ne |sēr'myōnā| (formerly **Sermione**) resort and historic port on Sirmione Peninsula, N Italy, on the S shore of Lake Garda.

Sis•ki•you Mountains |'siski,yōō| forested range of the Klamath Mts. in NW California and SW Oregon.

Sis•op•hon |'sē'sō'pən| commercial town in W Cambodia, in a forested area near the border with Thailand.

Sis•sing•hurst |'sisiNG,hərst| estate in SE England, in Kent, noted in the 20th century as a literary retreat owned by Harold Nicolson and Victoria Sackville-West.

Sis•tine Chapel |'si,stēn| chapel in the Vat-

ican City, built by Pope Sixtus V, and best know for its ceiling, painted by Michelangelo.

Sit•ka |'sitkə| city in the Panhandle of SW Alaska, on Baranof Island. A historic trade center, it draws tourists. Pop. 8,588.

Sit•tang |'si,täNG| river of S Burma. Rising in the Pegu Mts., it flows some 350 mi./560 km. S into the Bay of Bengal at the Gulf of Martaban.

Sit•twe |'sitwē| port and rice-milling center in W Burma. Pop. 108,000.

Si•vas |si'väs| (ancient name **Sebaste** or **Sebastea**) historic city in central Turkey, the capital of Sivas province, on the Kizil Irmak River. Pop. 222,000. Important under the Romans and Byzantines, it is industrial and commercial.

Si•vash Sea |si'væSH| (also known as **Putrid Sea**) area of marshes and salt lagoons in S Ukraine, in the N and NE Crimea.

Si•wa•lik Hills |si'wälik| range of foothills in the S Himalayas, extending from NE India across Nepal to Sikkim.

Six Counties |'siks| the counties of Northern Ireland: Antrim, Down, Armagh, Londonderry, Tyrone, and Fermanagh. Along with Cavan, Donegal, and Monaghan, now in the Irish Republic, they formed historic Ulster.

Sjæl•land |'SHe,län| Danish name for ZEALAND.

Skag•er•rak |'skægə,ræk| (also **the Skagerrak**) strait separating S Norway from the NW coast of Denmark. It links the Baltic Sea (SE) to the North Sea via the Kattegat.

Skag•way |'skæg,wā| city in SW Alaska, in the Panhandle. Pop. 692. A cruise ship port, it was a gateway to the 1897–98 Klondike gold rush.

Skå•ne |'skōne| (also known as **Scania**) historic province of S Sweden, now divided between Malmöhus and Kristianstad counties. It was formerly held by Denmark.

Ska•ra Brae |,skerə 'brā| Stone Age settlement on Mainland, in the Orkney Islands of Scotland, one of the leading prehistoric sites of N Europe.

Skee•na River |'skēnə| river that flows 360 mi./580 km. through central British Columbia to the Pacific.

Skel•e•ton Coast |'skelətn| arid coastal area in Namibia. Comprising the N part of the Namib Desert, it extends from Walvis Bay in the S to the border with Angola.

Skel•ligs, the |'skeligz| three rocky islands

off County Kerry, SW Ireland, formerly a noted pilgrimage site.

Ski·a·thos |'skīə,THäs| Greek island in the Aegean Sea, the most westerly of the Northern Sporades group. Greek name **Skíathos**.

Skid Row |'skid 'rō| term for a marginal city district where alcoholics and drifters congregate. The original was Skid Road, where loggers gathered, in Seattle, Washington.

Sko·kie |'skōkē| residential and industrial village in NE Illinois, a suburb NW of Chicago. Pop. 59,432.

Skop·je |'skawpye; 'skawpyä| the capital of the republic of Macedonia, in the N on the Vardar River. Pop. 440,000. Founded by the Romans, it was controlled by the Turks for over 500 years before World War I.

Skye |'skī| mountainous island of the Inner Hebrides, recently linked to the W coast of Scotland by a bridge; chief town, Portree. It is the largest and most northerly island of the group.

Sky·ros |'skē,raw| island, largest of the Northern Sporades, in Greece, in the Aegean Sea.

Slave Coast |slāv| name given by Europeans to the coastal region of W Africa roughly from present-day Togo to the Niger River delta. This was the primary source of slaves in the 16th–19th centuries.

Sla·vo·nia |slä'vōnēə| historic region in Croatia. It was originally part of the Roman province of Pannonia, became a Slavic state, and was later dominated by Turkey.

Slav·yansk |'slävyänsk| (also **Slovyansk**) industrial city in E Ukraine, N of Donetsk. Pop. 137,000.

Sleepy Hollow |'slēpē| town in SE New York, E of the Hudson River and N of Tarrytown. It is associated with the writings of Washington Irving.

Sli·dell |slī'del| city in SE Louisiana, NE of New Orleans, noted as a center for science related to space exploration. Pop. 24,124.

Sli·go |'slīgō| **1** county of the Republic of Ireland, in the W in the province of Connacht. Pop. 55,000. **2** its county seat, a seaport on Sligo Bay, an inlet of the Atlantic. Pop. 17,000.

Sli·ven |'slēven| commercial city in E central Bulgaria, in the foothills of the Balkan Mts. Pop. 150,000.

Slot, the |'slät| name given in World War II by U.S. forces to New Georgia Sound, in the central Solomon Islands. Japanese

forces trying to defend Guadalcanal were seen as coming consistently down this passage from the NW.

Slough |sləf| industrial town in S central England, in Berkshire, W of London. Pop. 97,000.

Slo·va·kia |slō'väkēə| republic in central Europe. Area: 18,940 sq. mi./49,035 sq. km. Pop. 5,268,935. Language, Slovak. Capital and largest city: Bratislava. Slovak name **Slovensko**. Independent of Hungary in 1918, Slovakia joined Bohemia and Moravia to form Czechoslovakia, then became independent in 1993. Agricultural until World War II, it is increasingly industrial. □ **Slovak** *adj. & n.* **Slovakian** *adj. & n.*

Slovakia

Slo·ve·nia |slō'vēnēə| nearly landlocked republic in SE Europe, formerly a constituent republic of Yugoslavia. Area: 7,822 sq. mi./20,251 sq. km. Pop. 1,962,000. Language, Slovene. Capital and largest city: Ljubljana. Slavic since the 6th century, Slovenia was part of the Austrian Empire before 1919, when it was made part of what became Yugoslavia. In 1991 it became independent. Mineral-based industries and tourism are important. □ **Slovene** *adj. & n.*

Słupsk |'slо̄opsk| industrial city in N Poland, on the Slupia River. It is the capital of Słupsk county. Pop. 101,000.

Slovinia

Smith·field[1] |'smiTH,fēld| part of London, England, just NW of the City, noted as a site of meat and horse markets, scene of the annual Bartholomew Fair, and execution place.

Smith·field[2] |'smiTH,fēld| town in S Virginia, in the Tidewater, famed for its ham production. Pop. 4,686.

Smith·so·ni·an Institution foundation for scientific research, established in 1838 and based in Washington, D.C. It operates over a dozen museums and institutes in Washington and other cities.

Smith·town |'smiTH,town| residential town on the North Shore of Long Island, New York. Pop. 113,406.

Smoky Hill River |'smōkē 'hil| river that flows 540 mi./870 km. from Colorado across Kansas. Its valley was long a route for W migration.

Smo·lensk |smō'lensk| industrial city in E European Russia, on the Dnieper River close to the border with Belarus. Pop. 346,000.

Smyr·na |'smirnə; 'smɑrnə| ancient city on the W coast of Asia Minor, on the site of present-day Izmir, Turkey.

Snake River |'snāk| river of the NW U.S. Rising in Yellowstone National Park in Wyoming, it flows for 1,038 mi./1,670 km. through Idaho into the state of Washington, where it joins the Columbia River. Irrigation systems made its valley an important agricultural area.

Sneek |snāk| town in the Netherlands, a water-sports center with a large yachting harbor. Pop. 29,000.

Snow·don |'snōdən| mountain in NW Wales. Rising to 3,560 ft./1,085 m., it is the highest mountain in Wales. Welsh name **Yr Wyddfa**.

Snow·do·nia |snō'dōnēə| massif region in NW Wales, forming the heart of the Snowdonia National Park. Its highest peak is Snowdon.

So·chi |'sōCHē| Black Sea port and resort in SW Russia, in the W foothills of the Caucasus, close to the border with Georgia. Pop. 339,000.

So·ci·ety Islands |sə'sī,itē| group of islands in the S Pacific, forming part of French Polynesia. Pop. 163,000.

So·co·tra |sə'kōtrə| island in the Arabian Sea near the mouth of the Gulf of Aden. Capital: Tamridah. It is administered by Yemen.

Sö·der·täl·je |sədər'telye| industrial W suburb of Stockholm, Sweden, on the Södertälje Canal. Pop. 82,000.

Sod·om |'sädəm| city of biblical Palestine, one of the Cities of the Plain, probably S of the Dead Sea, destroyed along with neighboring Gomorrah because of the wickedness of its inhabitants.

So·fia |sō'fēə| the capital, largest city, and industrial and cultural center of Bulgaria. Pop. 1,221,000. An ancient Thracian settlement, it became a province of Rome in the first century A.D. It was held by the Turks between the late 14th and late 19th centuries and became the capital of Bulgaria in 1879.

Sogne Fjord |'sawnə| fjord on the W coast of Norway. The longest and deepest fiord in the country, it extends inland for some 125 mi./200 km., with a maximum depth of 4,291 ft./1,308 m. Norwegian name **Sognafjorden**.

So·ho[1] |'sō,hō| commercial and entertainment district in the West End of London, England, around Soho Square, noted for its night life and long an immigrant quarter.

So·Ho[2] |'sō,hō| district of S Manhattan, New York City, famed for its artist-occupied industrial lofts and galleries. Its name derives from *So*uth of *Ho*uston Street.

Sois·sons |swäsawN| agricultural and industrial city in N France, on the Aisne River. Pop. 30,000. Settled by the Romans and an early religious center, it has been the site of many battles.

So·ka |'sōkä| city in E central Japan, on E central Honshu, a suburb NE of Tokyo. Pop. 206,000.

So·ko·to |sō'kōtō| industrial and commercial city in NW Nigeria, capital of Sokoto state, in a region once part of the Muslim Fulani Empire. Pop. 181,000.

So·le·dad |'sōlə,dæd| city in the Salinas Valley of W central California, home to a noted state prison. Pop. 7,146.

So·lent |'sōlənt| (also **the Solent**) channel between the NW coast of the Isle of Wight and the mainland of S England.

So·leure |sawlœr| French name for SOLOTHURN, Switzerland.

So·li·hull |,sōlə'həl| industrial and residential town in the West Midlands of England, forming part of the Birmingham metropolitan area . Pop. 95,000.

So·li·kamsk |səli'kämsk| town in central Russia, in the W foothills of the Ural Mts. Pop. 110,000.

So·ling·en |'zōliNGən; 'sōliNGən| industrial city in western Germany, in the Ruhr Valley, E of Düsseldorf. Pop. 166,000.

Sol·o·mon Islands |'säləmən| (also **the Solomons**) country consisting of a group

Solomon Islands

of islands in the SW Pacific, to the E of New Guinea. Area: 10,643 sq. mi./27,556 sq. km. Pop. 326,000. Languages, English (official), Pidgin, local Austronesian languages. Capital: Honiara (on Guadalcanal). Divided between Britain and Germany in the 19th century, with Australia replacing Germany in 1920, the islands became independent in 1978. They are sparsely populated and chiefly agricultural. The N part of the chain is part of Papua New Guinea. □ **Solomon Islander** *n.*

So·lo·thurn |'zōlə͵to͝orn| **1** canton in NW Switzerland, in the Jura Mts. Pop. 227,000. French name **Soleure. 2** its capital, a town on the Aare River. Pop. 15,000.

So·lu·tré |sōlətrā| (also called **Solutré-Pouilly**), village in E central France, in Burgundy. The area is known for its white wines. A site containing a rock shelter and a prehistoric burial, discovered here in 1867, gave a name to the Solutrean phase of the Paleolithic era.

Sol·way Firth |'sawlwā| inlet of the Irish Sea, separating Cumbria (in England) from Dumfries and Galloway (in Scotland).

So·ma·lia |sə'mälyə| republic in the Horn of Africa, NE Africa. Area: 246,294 sq. mi./637,657 sq. km. Pop. 8,041,000. Official languages, Somali and Arabic. Capital and largest city: Mogadishu. Controlled in parts by Britain and Italy, Somalia became

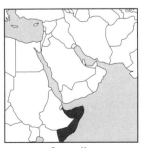

Somalia

independent in 1960. Civil war has beset the largely agricultural country since 1988. □ **Somali** *adj. & n.*

So·ma·li Peninsula |sə'mälē| another name for the HORN OF AFRICA.

Som·er·set |'səmər͵set| county of SW England, on the Bristol Channel. Pop. 459,000; county seat, Taunton.

Som·er·ville |'səmər͵vil| industrial and residential city in E Massachusetts, a suburb immediately NW of Boston. Pop. 76,210.

Somme |'sawm| river of N France. Rising E of Saint-Quentin, it flows 153 mi./245 km. through Amiens to the English Channel NE of Dieppe. The area around it was the scene of heavy fighting in World War I.

Som·nath |'sōmnät| (also called **Patan Somnath; Patan; Prabhas Patan**) port town in W central India, in Gujarat state. It is famous in Hindu mythology as the spot where Krishna was accidentally killed by a hunter's arrow.

Song·hai Empire |säNG'gī| (also **Songhay**) Berber, later Muslim, empire that flourished in the 8th–16th centuries along the Niger River. It was centered in present-day Mali, around Gao.

Song·hua River |'səNG'hwä| (Chinese name **Songhua Jiang**) see SUNGARI River, China.

Song·nam |'səNG'näm| city in NW South Korea, a suburb SE of Seoul. Pop. 869,000.

So·no·ma County |sə'nōmə| county in NW California, famed for its wineries and agriculture. Pop. 388,222.

So·no·ra |sə'nawrə| state of NW Mexico, on the Gulf of California. Area: 70,317 sq. mi./182,052 sq. km. Pop. 1,822,000. Capital: Hermosillo.

So·no·ra Desert |sə'nawrə| arid region of North America, comprising much SE California and SW Arizona in the U.S. and, in Mexico, much of Baja California and the W part of Sonora. The Mojave and Colorado deserts in California are extensions.

Soo, the |'so͞o| popular name for the region around and including the twin cities of Sault Ste. Marie, in Michigan and Ontario, from a pronunciation of *sault*, French for 'rapid.'

Soo·chow |'so͞o'CHOW| see SUZHOU, China.

Soon·er State |'so͞onər| nickname for OKLAHOMA, which was settled in part in the 1890s by those who arrived *sooner* than the official opening day for land claims.

So·rac·te |saw'räktē| isolated mountain in central Italy, NE of Rome. Height:

2,267ft./691 m. In ancient times there was a temple of Apollo at the top, and the mountain was mentioned in the poetry of Horace and Ovid.

Sor•bonne, the |sawr'bən; sawr'bawn| seat of the faculty of arts and letters of the University of Paris, in Paris, in N central France. The Sorbonne opened in 1253 on the Left Bank (S side of the Seine River) as a school of theology. It became part of the University of Paris in 1808.

So•ro•ca•ba |ˌsawrō'käbä| industrial and commercial city in S Brazil, in São Paulo state. Pop. 431,000.

Sor•ren•to |sə'rentō| resort town on the W coast of central Italy, on a peninsula separating the Bay of Naples, which it faces, from the Gulf of Salerno. Pop. 17,000.

Sos•no•wiec |saw'snōv,yets| industrial and mining town in SW Poland, W of Cracow. Pop. 259,000.

Sou•fri•ère[1] |ˌsoōfrē'yər| dormant volcano on the French island of Guadeloupe in the Caribbean. Rising to 4,813 ft./1,468 m., it is the highest peak in the Lesser Antilles.

Sou•fri•ère[2] |ˌsoōfrē'yər| active volcanic peak on the island of St. Vincent in the Caribbean. It rises to a height of 4,006 ft. (1,234 m).

Sousse |soōs| (also **Susah, Susa**) port and resort on the E coast of Tunisia. Pop. 125,000.

South, the in the U.S., term with several definitions, most commonly the eleven states of the 1861–65 Confederacy: Alabama, Arkansas, Florida, Georgia, Louisiana, Mississippi, North Carolina, South Carolina, Tennessee, Texas, and Virginia. □ **Southern** *adj.* **Southerner** *n.*

South Af•ri•ca |ˌsowTH 'æfrəkə| republic occupying the southernmost part of the continent of Africa. Area: 471,625 sq. mi./1.22 million sq. km. Pop. 36,762,000. Languages, English, Afrikaans, Zulu, Xhosa, and others. Administrative capital: Pretoria; seat of legislature: Cape Town; judicial capital: Bloemfontein; largest city: Johannesburg. Settled and then fought over at the end of the 19th century by the Dutch and English, South Africa achieved self-government (by the white minority) in 1910. From 1948 its policy of

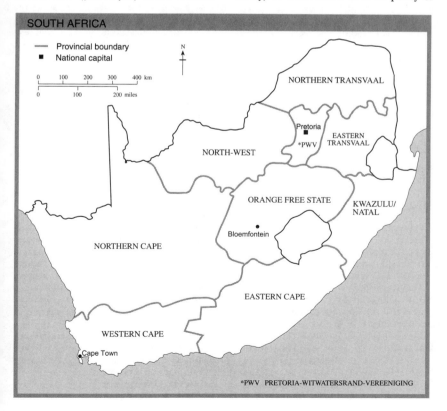

SOUTH AFRICA

— Provincial boundary
■ National capital

0   100   200   300   400 km
0   100   200 miles

N

NORTHERN TRANSVAAL

Pretoria ■
*PWV   EASTERN TRANSVAAL

NORTH-WEST

ORANGE FREE STATE

KWAZULU/ NATAL

Bloemfontein •

NORTHERN CAPE

EASTERN CAPE

WESTERN CAPE

● Cape Town

*PWV PRETORIA-WITWATERSRAND-VEREENIGING

racial separation (apartheid) brought increasing international isolation, which receded as apartheid collapsed after 1990. Majority (African) rule was achieved in 1994. Its mining, agriculture, and industry make South Africa one of the most prosperous African nations. □ **South African** *adj. & n.*

South Amer•i•ca |ˌsowTH əˈmerikə| continent comprising the S half of the American land mass, connected to North America by the Isthmus of Panama. It includes the Falkland Islands, the Galapagos Islands, and Tierra del Fuego. (See also AMERICA.) □ **South American** *adj. & n.*

South•amp•ton[1] |ˌsowTHˈ(h)æm(p)tən| industrial city and seaport on the S coast of England, formerly in Hampshire. Pop. 194,000. It lies at the end of Southampton Water, an inlet of the English Channel opposite the Isle of Wight.

South•amp•ton[2] |ˌsowTHˈ(h)æm(p)tən| resort and residential town in SE New York, at the E end of Long Island. Pop. 44,976.

South At•lan•tic Ocean |sowTH ætˈlæntik| see ATLANTIC OCEAN.

South Aus•tra•lia |ˌsowTH awsˈtrālyə| state comprising the S central part of Australia. Area: 380,069 sq. mi./984,000 sq. km. Pop. 1,454,000. Capital: Adelaide. Constituted as a semi-independent colony in 1836, it became a Crown Colony in 1841 and was federated with the other states of Australia in 1901. Irrigated agriculture is important.

South Bank |ˈsowTH| district of London, England, across the Thames River from Parliament, developed since the 1950s as an arts center.

South Beach |ˈsowTH| fashionable resort district of Miami Beach, Florida, noted for its Art Deco buildings.

South Bend |ˈsowTH| industrial city in N Indiana. Pop. 105,511. The university community of Notre Dame is just N of the city.

South Bos•ton |ˈsowTH| residential district of E Boston, Massachusetts, noted for its Irish working-class community. Familiarly, **Southie.**

South Car•o•li•na |ˌsowTH ˌkerəˈlīnə| see box. □ **South Carolinean** *adj. & n.*

South Chi•na Sea |ˈsowTH ˈCHīnə| see CHINA SEA.

South Da•ko•ta |ˌsowTH dəˈkōtə| see box, p. 347. □ **South Dakotan** *adj. & n.*

South Dum Dum |ˈsowTH ˈdəm dəm| city in NE India, in West Bengal, near Calcutta. Pop. 231,000.

South Carolina
Capital/largest city: Columbia
Other cities: Charleston, Greenville, North Charleston, Spartanburg
Population: 3,486,703 (1990); 3,835,962 (1998); 4,033,000 (2005 proj.)
Population rank (1990): 25
Rank in land area: 40
Abbreviation: SC; S. Car.
Nickname: Palmetto State
Motto: *Animis opibusque parati* ("Prepared in mind and resources")
Bird: Carolina wren
Fish: striped bass
Flower: Carolina jessamine (yellow jasmine)
Tree: palmetto
Song: "Carolina"
Noted physical features: Piedmont Plateau; Sassafras Mountain
Tourist attractions: Hilton Head Island; Myrtle Beach; Saluda Dam; Fort Sumter; Cypress Gardens
Admission date: May 23, 1788
Order of admission: 8
Name origin: For *Carolina*, see at *North Carolina*. The southern portion of the original Carolina colony came to be called 'South Carolina' after the colony was divided in 1729.

Southeast Asia Treaty Organization (abbrev. **SEATO**) a defense alliance that existed between 1954 and 1977 for countries of SE Asia and part of the SW Pacific, to further a US policy of containing communism. Its members were Australia, Britain, France, New Zealand, Pakistan, the Philippines, Thailand, and the US.

Southend-on-Sea |ˈsowTHˌendˌänˈsē| resort town in Essex, England, on the Thames estuary E of London. Pop. 154,000.

South Equa•to•ri•al Current |ˌsowTH ˌēkwäˈtawrēəl| ocean current that flows W across the Pacific just S of the equator.

South•ern Alps |ˈsəTHərn ˈælps| mountain range in South Island, New Zealand. Running roughly parallel to the W coast, it extends almost the entire length of the island. At Mount Cook, its highest peak, it rises to 12,349 ft./3,764 m.

south•ern hem•i•sphere the half of the earth that is S of the equator.

South•ern Ocean |ˈsəTHərn| the expanse of ocean surrounding Antarctica. Also **Antarctic Ocean.**

South•ern Pines |ˈsəTHərn ˈpīnz| resort

South Dakota

Capital: Pierre
Largest city: Sioux Falls
Other cities: Aberdeen, Rapid City, Sioux Falls, Watertown
Population: 696,004 (1990); 738,171 (1998); 810,000 (2005 proj.)
Population rank (1990): 45
Rank in land area: 17
Abbreviation: SD; S.D., S. Dak.
Nickname: Coyote State
Motto: 'Under God the People Rule'
Bird: ring-necked pheasant
Fish: walleye
Flower: American pasque
Tree: Black Hills spruce (white spruce)
Song: "Hail, South Dakota"
Noted physical features: Black Hills; Missouri River; Lake Oahe
Tourist attractions: Mt. Rushmore National Memorial; Wounded Knee; Oahe Dam; Homestake Mine; Badlands and Wind Cave national parks
Admission date: November 2, 1889
Order of admission: 40
Name origin: For *Dakota* see at *North Dakota*. The original Dakota Territory was divided into north and south regions in 1889.

---

town in S central North Carolina, noted for its golf courses. Pop. 9,129.

South•ern Rho•de•sia |'sǝTHǝrn rō 'dēzHyä| see ZIMBABWE.

South•field |'sowTH'fēld| residential and industrial city in SE Michigan, a suburb NW of Detroit. Pop. 75,728.

South Gate |'sowTH ˌgāt| industrial city in SW California, SE of Los Angeles. Pop. 86,284.

South Geor•gia |'sowTH 'jawrjǝ| barren island in the South Atlantic, situated 700 mi./1,120 km. E of the British Falkland Islands, of which it is a dependency. It was first explored in 1775 by Captain James Cook, who named the island after George III.

South Gla•mor•gan |'sowTH glæ'mawrgǝn| former county of S Wales, on the Bristol Channel, dissolved in 1996.

South Had•ley |'sowTH 'hædlē| town in W Massachusetts, on the Connecticut River N of Springfield, noted as home to Mount Holyoke College. Pop. 16,685.

South Island |'sowTH| the more southerly and larger (58,406 sq. mi./151,215 sq. km.) of the two main islands of New Zealand, separated from North Island by Cook Strait. Pop. 882,000.

South Ko•rea |'sowTH kaw'rēyǝ| republic in E Asia, occupying the S part of the peninsula of Korea. Area: 38,340 sq. mi./99,263 sq. km. Pop. 42,793,000. Language, Korean. Capital and largest city: Seoul. Official name **Republic of Korea**. Formed in 1948, when Korea was partitioned along the 38th parallel, South Korea has a strong agricultural sector but is primarily an emerging industrial power. □ **South Korean** *adj. & n.*

South Korea

South Ork•ney Islands |'sowTH 'awrknē| group of uninhabited islands in the South Atlantic, lying to the NE of the Antarctic Peninsula. Discovered in 1821, they are administered as part of the British Antarctic Territory.

South Os•se•tia |'sowTH ō'sēsHǝ| autonomous region of Georgia, situated in the Caucasus on the border with Russia. Capital: Tskhinvali. (See also OSSETIA.)

South Pass |'sowTH| valley in the Wind River Mts. of SW Wyoming that was a major route for settlers moving W through the Rockies in the 19th century.

South Platte River |'sowTH 'plæt| river that flows 425 mi./685 km. from the Rocky Mts. in Colorado, through Denver, and across Colorado to Nebraska, where it joins the North Platte to form the Platte.

South Pole |'sowTH 'pōl| 90° S, the southernmost point on earth. It is on a plateau in central Antarctica, and was first reached in 1911 by Roald Amundsen. See also MAGNETIC POLE.

South•port |'sowTH,pawrt| resort and suburban town in NW England, on the Irish Sea coast n of Liverpool. Pop. 91,000.

South Sand•wich Islands |'sowTH 'sæn ˌ(d)wicH| group of uninhabited volcanic islands in the South Atlantic, lying 300 mi./480 km. SE of South Georgia. They are administered from the British Falkland Islands.

South Sea |'sowTH| (also **South Seas**) historical name for the S Pacific, whose various islands have been called the **South Sea Islands**.

South Shet·land Islands |'sowTH 'SHetlənd| group of uninhabited islands in the South Atlantic, lying N of the Antarctic Peninsula. Discovered in 1819, they are administered as part of the British Antarctic Territory.

South Shields |'sowTH 'SHēldz| industrial port on the coast of NE England, at the mouth of the Tyne opposite North Shields. Pop. 87,000.

South Side |sowTH sīd| area S of central Chicago, Illinois, in the 20th century home to the largest U.S. black community.

South Vi·et·nam |'sowTH vē'etnäm| former republic in SE Asia, established in the southern part of Vietnam in 1954. After its defeat in the Vietnam War, it was reunited with North Vietnam to form Vietnam.

South·wark |'səTHərk| borough of SE London, England, on the Thames River. Pop. 196,000. Residential and industrial, it is noted as the former site of the Globe Theatre.

South West Af·ri·ca former name for NAMIBIA.

South York·shire |,sowTH 'yawrkSHər| metropolitan county of N England. Pop. 1,249,000. Sheffield is the major city.

So·vi·et Union |'sōvē,et| former federation of communist republics occupying the N half of Asia and part of E Europe. Capital: Moscow. Full name **Union of Soviet Socialist Republics**. Created from the Russian Empire in the aftermath of the 1917 Russian Revolution, the Soviet Union was the largest country in the world. It comprised fifteen republics: Russia, Belarus, Ukraine, Georgia, Armenia, Moldova, Azerbaijan, Kazakhstan, Kyrgyzstan, Turkmenistan, Tajikistan, Uzbekistan, and the three Baltic states (annexed in 1940). After World War II, in which it was invaded by Germany and sustained some 20 million casualties, the Soviet Union emerged as a superpower in rivalry with the U.S., leading to the Cold War. Decades of repression and economic failure eventually led to attempts at liberalization and economic reform under President Mikhail Gorbachev during the 1980s. This resulted, however, in a resurgence of nationalist feeling in the republics. The USSR was formally dissolved in 1991, some of its constituents joining a looser confederation, the Commonwealth of Independent States. □ **Soviet** *adj.*

So·we·to |sə'wetō| largely residential city, formerly several townships, in South Africa SW of Johannesburg. Pop. 597,000. In 1976 demonstrations against the compulsory use of Afrikaans in schools resulted in violent police activity and the deaths of hundreds here. The name is from *So(uth) We(stern) To(wnships)*. □ **Sowetan** *adj. & n.*

Spa |spä| town in E Belgium, SE of Liège. Pop. 10,000. It has been celebrated since medieval times for the curative properties of its mineral springs, and its name became generic.

Spain |spān| kingdom in SW Europe, occupying the greater part of the Iberian Peninsula. Area: 194,959 sq. mi./504,750 sq. km. Pop. 39,045,000. Languages, Spanish (official), Catalan. Capital and largest city: Madrid. Spanish name **España**. Dominated in various periods by Carthaginians, Romans, Visigoths, and Moors, Spain became a great power under the Habsburgs by the 16th century, and controlled one of the largest colonial empires. In the 19th century the empire largely dissolved. Modern Spain retains its agricultural base, but is also heavily industrial in some regions. □ **Spanish** *adj. & n.*

Span·dau |'spæn,dow| industrial district of Berlin, Germany; its 16th-century fortress was more recently a prison, and several condemned Nazi war criminals, including Rudoph Hess, were held here after the Nuremberg trials.

Span·ish Amer·i·ca |'spænisH| the parts of America once colonized by the Spanish and in which Spanish is still generally spoken, including most of Central and South America (except Brazil) and part of the Caribbean.

Span·ish Main the former name for the NW coast of South America between the Orinoco River and Panama, and adjoining parts of the Caribbean Sea.

Span·ish Sa·hara former name (1958–75) for WESTERN SAHARA.

Span·ish Steps famous stairs in Rome, Italy, built 1721–25 to connect the Piazza di Spagna with the church of the Trinità Dei Monti.

Span·ish Town second-largest town in Jamaica, W of Kingston; it is a former capital of Jamaica. Pop. 110,000.

Sparks |spärks| commercial city in W Nevada, NE of Reno. Pop. 53,367.

SPAIN

Region boundary
Province boundary
■ Capital city

Spar·ta |'spärtə| city (modern Greek name **Spartí**) in the S Peloponnese in Greece, capital of the department of Laconia. Pop. 13,000. It was a powerful city-state in the 5th century B.C., defeating its rival Athens in the Peloponnesian War to become the leading city of Greece. The ancient Spartans (also called Lacedaemonians) were renowned for the military organization of their state and for their rigorous discipline, courage, and austerity. □ **Spartan** *adj. & n.*

Spar·tan·burg |'spärtən,bərg| industrial and commercial city in NW South Carolina. Pop. 43,467.

Spey |spā| river of E central Scotland. Rising in the Grampian Mts. E of the Great Glen, it flows 108 mi./171 km. NE to the North Sea.

Spey·er |'SHpīər| river port and industrial center in SW Germany, on the Rhine River. Pop. 44,000.

Sphinx, the colossal desert structure near Giza, N Egypt, with a lion's body and the head of a man. A funerary monument, it dates from the 3rd millennium B.C.

Spice Islands |'spīs| former name for the MOLUCCA ISLANDS.

Spit·head |,spit'hed| channel between the NE coast of the Isle of Wight and the main-land of S England. It offers sheltered access to Southampton Water (the inlet of the Solent) and deep anchorage. It has long been a naval anchorage.

Spits·ber·gen |'spits,bərgən| Norwegian island in the Svalbard archipelago, in the Arctic Ocean N of Norway; principal settlement, Longyearbyen.

Split |split| port city in S Croatia, on the Adriatic coast. Pop. 189,000. An industrial and resort center, it contains the ruins of the palace of the Roman emperor Diocletian (3rd century A.D). Ancient name **Spalatum**.

Spo·kane |spō'kæn| industrial and commercial city in E Washington, in the Inland Empire, at the falls of the Spokane River, near the border with Idaho. Pop. 177,196.

Spo·le·to |spə'lātō| town in Umbria, in central Italy. Pop. 38,000. It was one of Italy's principal cities from the 6th to the 8th century A.D. It is a cultural center, the site of an annual arts festival.

Spoon River |'spoon| river that flows 160 mi./260 km. through central Illinois, associated with the verse of Edgar Lee Masters.

Spor·a·des |'spawrə,dēz| two groups of Greek islands in the Aegean Sea. The *Northern Sporades*, which lie close to the E coast of mainland Greece, include the islands of Euboea, Skiros, Skiathos, and Skopelos. The *Southern Sporades*, situated off the W coast of Turkey, include Rhodes and the other islands of the Dodecanese.

Spot·syl·va·nia County |ˌspätsilˈvānēə| rural county in NE Virginia, scene of Civil War battles including Fredericksburg and Spotsylvania Court House.

Sprat·ly Islands |ˈsprætlē| group of small islands and coral reefs in the South China Sea, between Vietnam and Borneo. Dispersed over a distance of some 600 mi./965 km., the islands are variously claimed by China, Taiwan, Vietnam, the Philippines, and Malaysia. There are nearby undersea oil deposits.

Spratley Islands

Spree River |ˈsHprä| river (247 mi./400 km.) in E Germany, rising in mountains near the Czech border and flowing N to join the Havel River at Spandau.

Spring·dale |ˈspriNGˌdāl| commercial and agricultural city in NW Arkansas. Pop. 29,941.

Spring·field[1] |ˈspriNGˌfēld| industrial and commercial city, the capital of Illinois, in the central part. Pop. 105,227.

Spring·field[2] |ˈspriNGˌfēld| industrial city in SW Massachusetts, on the Connecticut River. Pop. 156,983.

Spring·field[3] |ˈspriNGˌfēld| industrial and commercial city in SW Missouri, on the N edge of the Ozark Mts. Pop. 140,494.

Spring Green |ˈspriNG ˈgrēn| town in S Wisconsin, NW of Madison, noted as the site of Taliesin, the home and studio of Frank Lloyd Wright. Pop. 1,343.

Spring·hill |ˈspriNGˌhil| town in N central Nova Scotia, formerly a noted coal-mining center. Pop. 4,373.

Springs |spriNGz| industrial city in NE South Africa, in Gauteng province, in a coal-, gold-, and uranium-producing region. Pop. 158,000.

Square Mile informal name for the financial district of London, England.

Squaw Valley |ˈskwaw| resort in NE California, on Lake Tahoe, site of the 1960 Winter Olympics.

Sreb·re·ni·ca |ˌsrebrəˈnētsə| town in E Bosnia and Herzegovina, in a mining area. It was a target of "ethnic cleansing" by Serbian forces in the fighting between Muslims and Serbs that followed the breakup of Yugoslavia in 1991.

Sri Lanka |ˌsrē ˈläNGkə; ˌsHrēˌläNGkə| island republic off the SE coast of India. Area: 24,895 sq. mi./64,453 sq. km. Pop. 17,194,000. Languages, Sinhalese (official), Tamil, English. Capital and largest city: Colombo. Former name (until 1972) **Ceylon**. Arabic name **Serendib**. With a history of over 2,000 years, Ceylon was dominated by colonial powers from the 16th century, and annexed by Britain in 1815. Since independence in 1972 there has been friction, often open warfare, between the government and Tamil separatists. Sri Lanka is largely agricultural. □ **Sri Lankan** *adj. & n.*

Sri Lanka

Sri·na·gar |srēˈnägər; ˌsHrēˈnägər| city in NW India, the summer capital of the state of Jammu and Kashmir, on the Jhelum River in the foothills of the Himalayas. Pop. 595,000.

Staf·fa |ˈstæfə| small uninhabited island of the Inner Hebrides of Scotland, W of Mull. It is the site of Fingal's Cave and is noted for its basalt columns.

Staf·ford |ˈstæfərd| industrial and commercial town in central England, the county seat of Staffordshire, to the S of Stoke-on-Trent. Pop. 62,000.

Staf·ford·shire |ˈstæfərdˌsHər| county of central England. Pop. 1,020,000; county seat, Stafford.

Sta·gi·ra |stäˈjīrə| town in NE Greece, on the E Chalcidice Peninsula. The philosopher Aristotle was born here in 384 B.C.

Staked Plain |stāktplān| another name for LLANO ESTACADO.

Sta·kha·nov |stə'känōv| mining city in SE Ukraine, S of the Donets River. Pop. 112,000.

Sta·lin·grad |'stälən,græd| former name (1925–61) for VOLGOGRAD, Russia. In the 1942–43 battle of Stalingrad, Soviet forces wore down and defeated Nazi armies.

Sta·lin Peak |'stälən| former name (1933–62) for COMMUNISM PEAK.

Stam·boul |stæm'bōōl| archaic name for ISTANBUL, Turkey.

Stam·ford |'stæmfərd| commercial city in SW Connecticut, on Long Island Sound. Pop. 108,056. It is noted for its corporate headquarters.

Stand·ing Rock |'stændıNG| Sioux Indian reservation that straddles the North Dakota–South Dakota border, W of the Missouri River.

Stan·ley, Mount |'stænlē| mountain in the Ruwenzori range in central Africa, on the border between the Democratic Republic of Congo (formerly Zaire) and Uganda. Its highest point, Margherita Peak, which rises to 16,765 ft./5,110 m., is the third-highest in Africa. African name **Mount Ngaliema**.

Stan·ley |'stænlē| (also **Port Stanley**) the chief port and town of the British Falkland Islands, on the island of East Falkland. Pop. 1,557.

Stan·ley·ville |'stænlē,vil| former name (1882–1966) for KISANGANI.

Sta·ra Za·gora |'stärä zä'gawrä| industrial city in E central Bulgaria. Pop. 188,000. A former Thracian settlement, it was held by the Turks from 1370 until 1877, then destroyed by them during the Russo-Turkish War. It has since been rebuilt as a modern planned city.

Starn·ber·ger See |'sHtärnbergər 'zā| (formerly **Würmsee**) lake in Bavaria, Germany, surrounded by summer palaces of the region's aristocracy and public parks and beaches. It is a popular vacation area.

Sta·ry Os·kal |'stäri ä'skōl| (also **Staryy Oskal**) industrial and mining city in W Russia, W of Voronezh. Pop. 184,000.

State College borough in central Pennsylvania, in the Nittany Valley, home to Pennsylvania State University. Pop. 38,923.

Stat·en Island |stætn| island borough of New York City, in the SW across New York Bay from Manhattan. Pop. 378,977. It is coextensive with Richmond County.

Staun·ton |'stæn(t)ən| city in N central Virginia, in the Shenandoah Valley. Pop. 24,461.

Sta·vang·er |stə'væNGər| seaport in SW Norway. Pop. 98,000. It is an important center servicing offshore oil fields in the North Sea.

Stav·ro·pol[1] |stäv'rawpəl; stäv'rōpəl| former name (until 1964) for TOGLIATTI, Russia.

Stav·ro·pol[2] **1** krai (administrative territory) in S Russia, in the N Caucasus. **2** its capital city. Pop. 324,000.

Steam·boat Springs |'stēm,bōt| resort city in NW Colorado, a famed skiing center. Pop. 6,695.

Stei·er·mark |'sHtīər,märk| German name for STYRIA.

Stel·len·bosch |'stelən,baws; 'stelən,bōōsH| university town in Cape province, SW South Africa, just E of Cape Town. Pop. 74,000.

Sten·dal |sten'däl; stæn'däl| city and rail junction in central Germany, in Saxony-Anhalt. Pop. 76,000. Its name was adopted by the French writer Marie Henry Beyle (Stendhal).

Ste·pa·na·kert |stepänä'kert| Russian name for XANKÄNDI.

Steppes, the |steps| region of extensive flat grasslands in W central Asia, particularly in central Kazakhstan. The term is also used of such areas as the ALFOLD, in Hungary.

Ster·ling Heights |'stərlıNG 'hīts| city in SE Michigan, a residential and industrial suburb N of Detroit. Pop. 117,810.

Ster·li·ta·mak |,stirlitä'mäk| industrial city in S Russia, on the Belaya River to the N of Orenburg. Pop. 250,000.

Stet·tin |sHte'tēn| German name for SZCZECIN.

Steu·ben·ville |'stōōbən,vil| industrial city in E Ohio, on the Ohio River. Pop. 22,125.

Ste·ven·age |'stēvənij| industrial town in Hertfordshire, SE England. Pop. 75,000.

Ste·vens Point |'stēvənz| industrial and commercial city in central Wisconsin, on the Wisconsin River. Pop. 23,006.

Stew·art Island |'stōōərt| island of New Zealand, off the S coast of South Island, from which it is separated by the Foveaux Strait; chief settlement, Oban.

Steyr |'sHtīər| industrial city in N Austria. Pop. 39,000.

Sti·kine River |sti'kēn| river that flows 335 mi./540 km. across British Columbia to the Pacific.

Still·wa·ter |'stil,wätər| city in N central Oklahoma, home to Oklahoma State University. Pop. 36,676.

Still•well Road |'stilwel| WorldWar II military highway that connected NE India with China by way of Burma. It was 1,044 mi./1,680 km. long.

Stil•ton |'stiltən| village in SE England, in Cambridgeshire, which gave its name to a cheese made in Leicestershire and first sold here at the Bell Inn.

Stir•ling |'stərliNG| university town in central Scotland, on the Forth River, administrative center of Stirling region. Pop. 28,000.

Stock•bridge |'stäk,brij| resort town in W Massachusetts, in the Berkshire Hills. Pop. 2,408. Tanglewood estate, site of a famed summer music festival, is here.

Stock•holm |'stäk,hō(l)m| the capital of Sweden, a port on the E coast, situated on the mainland and on numerous adjacent islands. Pop. 674,000. It is the largest city and the economic and cultural center of the country.

Stock•port |'stäk,pawrt| industrial town in NW England, in Greater Manchester. Pop. 130,000.

Stock•ton |'stäktən| industrial city in N central California, a port on the San Joaquin River. Pop. 210,943.

Stockton-on-Tees |'stäktən än 'tēz| industrial town in NE England, a port on the Tees River near its mouth on the North Sea. Pop. 170,000. The town developed after the opening in 1825 of the Stockton and Darlington Railway, the first passenger rail service in the world.

Stoke-on-Trent |'stōk än 'trent| city on the Trent River in W central England, formerly part of Staffordshire. Pop. 245,000. It has long been the center of the Staffordshire pottery industries.

Stoke Po•ges |'stōk 'pōjis| village in S central England, in Buckinghamshire N of Slough, whose churchyard is the burial place of Thomas Grey and the presumed setting for his "Elegy Written in a Country Church Yard."

Stone•henge |'stōn,henj| megalithic monument in SW England, on Salisbury Plain in Wiltshire. Its standing stones, whose origin and purpose are debated, are often taken as a symbol of England.

Stone Mountain |'stōn| granite mass E of Atlanta, Georgia, site of the Confederate National Monument, created (1917–67) to a design by Gutzon Borglum.

Stones River see MURFREESBORO.

Ston•ey Creek |'stōnē| suburban city in S Ontario, on Lake Ontario next to Hamilton. Pop. 49,968.

Stony Brook |'stōnē| resort and academic village in E Long Island, NewYork. Pop. 13,726.

Stor•mont |'stawr,mänt| suburb to the E of Belfast, Northern Ireland, seat of the Northern Irish parliament (suspended since 1972), and thus a term for British rule in the province.

Stor•no•way |'stawrnə,wā| port on the E coast of Lewis, in the Outer Hebrides of Scotland. Pop. 6,000. The administrative center of the Western Isles, it is noted for the manufacture of Harris tweed.

Story•ville |'stawrē,vil| former entertainment district of New Orleans, Louisiana, closed in 1917 but associated with the early development of jazz music.

Stour |stōr| 1 river of central England that rises W of Wolverhampton and flows SW through Stourbridge and Kidderminster to meet the Severn at Stourport-on-Severn. 2 river of S England that rises in W Wiltshire and flows SE to meet the English Channel E of Bournemouth.

Stowe |stō| town in N central Vermont, a noted skiing and resort center. Pop. 3,433.

Straits Settlements |strāts| former British Crown Colony in SE Asia. Established in 1867, it comprised Singapore, Penang, and Malacca, and later included Labuan, Christmas Island, and the Cocos Islands. It was disbanded in 1946.

Stral•sund |'strälsənd| resort town and fishing port in N Germany, on the Baltic coast opposite the island of Rügen. Pop. 72,000.

Stran•raer |stræn'rär| port and market town in SW Scotland, in Dumfries and Galloway. Pop. 10,000. It is the terminus of a ferry service from Larne, in Northern Ireland.

Stras•bourg |'sträs,bŏŏrg| industrial and commercial city in NE France, in Alsace, close to the border with Germany. Pop. 256,000. Annexed by Germany in 1870, it was returned to France after World War I. It is the headquarters of the Council of Europe and of the European Parliament.

Strat•ford[1] |'strætfərd| industrial town in SW Connecticut, E of Bridgeport, former home to the American Shakespeare Festival. Pop. 49,389.

Strat•ford[2] |'strætfərd| city in S Ontario, on the Avon River, noted for its summer Shakespeare Festival. Pop. 27,666.

Stratford-upon-Avon |,strætfərd,əpän 'āvän| town in Warwickshire, central England, on the Avon River. Pop. 20,000. Famous as the birth and burial place of

William Shakespeare, it is the site of the Royal Shakespeare Theatre.

Strath•clyde |stræTH'klīd| former local government region in W central Scotland, dissolved in 1996. It took its name from a Celtic kingdom of the 5th–11th centuries, centered on Dumbarton.

Strom•bo•li |'strämbōlē| volcanic island in the Mediterranean, the most north-easterly of the Lipari Islands, NE of Sicily. Its volcano has been in a state of continual mild eruption throughout history.

Stru•ma River |'strōmä| river that rises in the Vitosha Mts. of Bulgaria and flows 216 mi./346 km. through Greece, draining into the Aegean Sea near Thessaloniki.

Stur•bridge |'stərbrij| town in S central Massachusetts, noted for its historical recreation Old Sturbridge Village. Pop. 7,775.

Stutt•gart |'stŏŏt,gärt| industrial and commercial city in western Germany, the capital of Baden-Württemberg, on the Neckar River. Pop. 592,000. It is an auto manufacturing center.

Stym•pha•lis, Lake |stim'fälis| lake in NE Peloponnese, Greece. In Greek mythology, Hercules slew the man-eating birds, the Stymphalians, here.

Styr•ia |'stirēə| mountainous state of SE Austria. Pop. 1,185,000. Capital: Graz. German name **Steiermark**.

Styx |stiks| in Greek mythology, river of the underworld, over which Charon ferried the souls of the dead. □ **Stygian** *adj.*

Su•bic Bay |'sōŏbik| inlet of the South China Sea in the Philippines, off central Luzon. A large U.S. naval facility here, closed in 1992, has become an industrial zone.

Sub•lime Porte |sə'blīm 'pawrt| name for the court of the sultan in Constantinople, the capital of the Ottoman Empire (present-day Istanbul, Turkey). It refers to the "imperial gate" leading to the sultan's audience chamber.

Su•bo•ti•ca |,sōŏbə'tētsə| industrial city and transportation center in Serbia, near the Hungarian border. Pop. 102,000.

sub-Sa•har•an Af•ri•ca the part of Africa to the south of the Sahara Desert, beginning with the southern regions of Mali, Niger, Chad, and Sudan and extending south to South Africa.

Su•cea•va |sōŏ'CHyävə| industrial town in NE Romania, in the E foothills of the Carpathian Mts., capital of Suceava county. Pop. 106,000.

Sü•chow |'sōŏ'CHow| see XUZHOU.

Su•cre |'sōŏ,krä| historic city, the judicial capital and seat of the legislature of Bolivia. Pop. 131,000. It is situated in the Andes, at an altitude of 8,860 ft./2,700 m. Named Chuquisaca by the Spanish in 1539, the city was renamed in 1825 in honor of Antonio José de Sucre, the first president of Bolivia.

Su•dan |sōŏ'dæn| (also **the Sudan**) **1** republic in NE Africa, S of Egypt, with a coastline on the Red Sea. Area: 967,940 sq. mi./2.51 million sq. km. Pop. 25,855,000. Languages, Arabic (official), Dinka, Hausa, and others. Capital and largest city: Khartoum. Ruled by the Arabas from the 13th century, by Egypt from 1822, Sudan revolted in the 1880s and finally achieved independence in 1956, after a period of British dominance. Largely agricultural, it has suffered from struggles between the Islamic central government and separatist S provinces. **2** vast region of N Africa, extending across the width of the continent from the S edge of the Sahara to the tropical equatorial zone in the S. □ **Sudanese** *adj. & n.*

Sudan

Sud•bury |'səd,bərē| city in central Ontario. Pop. 92,884. It lies at the center of Canada's largest mining region, the Sudbury Basin.

Su•de•ten•land |sōŏ'dātn,lænd| area in the NW part of the Czech Republic, on the border with Germany. Allocated to Czechoslovakia after World War I, it became an object of Nazi expansionist policies and was ceded to Germany as a result of the Munich Agreement of September 1938. In 1945 the area was returned to Czechoslovakia. Czech name **Sudety**.

Su•de•tes |sōŏ'dētēz| (also **Sudeten** or **Sudety**) mountain range on the border between Poland and the Czech Republic.

Su•ez, Isthmus of |sōŏ'əz| isthmus between the Mediterranean and the Red seas, connecting Egypt and Africa to the Sinai Peninsula and Asia. The port of Suez lies in the S, at the head of the Gulf of Suez, an arm of the Red Sea. The isthmus is traversed by the Suez Canal.

Su·ez Canal |soo'əz| shipping canal connecting the Mediterranean at Port Said, Egypt with the Red Sea. It was constructed between 1859 and 1869 by Ferdinand de Lesseps. In 1875 it came under British control; it was nationalized by Egypt in 1956. It is 106 mi./171 km. long, providing the shortest route for sea traffic between Europe and Asia.

Suf·folk[1] |'səfək| county of E England, on the coast of East Anglia. Pop. 630,000; county seat, Ipswich.

Suf·folk[2] |'səfək| commercial and agricultural city in S Virginia, in the Hampton Roads area. Pop. 52,141.

Suf·folk County |'səf,ək| suburban, agricultural, and resort county in SE NewYork, on the E end of Long Island. Pop. 1,321,864.

Sug·ar Loaf Mountain |'SHoogər 'lōf| rocky peak to the NE of Copacabana Beach, in Rio de Janeiro, Brazil. It rises to a height of 1,296 ft./390 m.

Suhl |sool| industrial town in eastern Germany. Pop. 59,000. Until the reunification of Germany, the name was also used for the district surrounding the town.

Su·i·ta |soo'ētä| city in W central Japan, on S Honshu, N of Osaka. Pop. 345,000.

Su·ka·bu·mi |sookä'boomē| resort and commercial town in Indonesia, on W Java, S of Jakarta. Pop. 120,000.

Su·kho·tai |',sookə'tī| town in NW Thailand. Pop. 23,000. It was formerly the capital of an independent state of the same name, which flourished from the mid-13th to the mid-14th centuries.

Su·khu·mi |soo'koomē| port city and capital of the autonomous republic of Abkhazia, in the Republic of Georgia, on the E coast of the Black Sea. It is also a resort known since Roman times for its sulfur baths. Pop. 122,000.

Suk·kur |sə'koor| commercial and industrial city in SE Pakistan, on the Indus River. Pop. 350,000. Nearby is the Sukkur Barrage, a dam across the Indus that directs water through irrigation channels to a large area of the Indus valley.

Su·la Islands |soolä| (also **Soela Islands**) group of islands in Indonesia, part of the Moluccas group, between Sulawesi (W) and the Ceram Sea (E).

Su·la·we·si |,soolə'wāsē| mountainous island in the Greater Sunda group in Indonesia, to the E of Borneo; chief town,

Ujung Pandang. It is noted as the habitat of numerous endemic species. Former name **Celebes**.

Su·lay·ma·ni·yah |soolīmä'nēye| town in NE Iraq, in mountainous S Kurdistan. Pop. 279,000. It is the capital of a Kurdish governorate of the same name. Full name **As Sulaymaniyah**; also spelled **Sulaimaniya**.

Sul·mo·na |sool'mōnä| commercial and industrial city in central Italy, on the Gizio River. Pop. 25,000.

Su·lu Sea |'sooloo| sea in the Malay Archipelago. The NE coast of Borneo lies SW, and islands of the Philippines, including the Sulu Archipelago, surround the sea on its other sides.

Su·ma·tra |sə'mätrə| large (164,000 sq. mi./424,700 sq. km.) island of Indonesia, to the SW of the Malay Peninsula, from which it is separated by the Strait of Malacca; chief city, Medan. □ **Sumatran** adj. & n.

Sum·ba |'soombä| island of the Lesser Sunda group in Indonesia, lying to the S of the islands of Flores and Sumbawa; chief town, Waingapu. Also called **Sandalwood Island**.

Sum·ba·wa |soom'bäwä| island in the Lesser Sunda group in Indonesia, between Lombok and Flores.

Su·mer |'soomər| ancient region of SW Asia, in present-day Iraq, comprising the S part of Mesopotamia. From the 4th millennium B.C. it was the site of an early civilization, and its city states became part of ancient Babylonia. □ **Sumerian** adj. & n.

Sum·ga·it |soomgä'yēt| Russian name for SUMQAYIT.

Sum·mer·side |'səmər,sīd| port town, the second-largest community on Prince Edward Island. Pop. 7,474.

Sum·mit |'səmət| city in NE New Jersey, an affluent suburb W of Newark. Pop. 19,757.

Sum·qay·it |soomkä'yēt| industrial city in E Azerbaijan, on the Caspian Sea. Pop. 235,000. Russian name **Sumgait**.

Sum·ter |'səmtər| commercial and industrial city in E central South Carolina. Pop. 41,943.

Su·my |'soomē| industrial city in NE Ukraine, near the border with Russia. Pop. 296,000.

Sun·belt, the |'sən,belt| (also **Sun Belt**) region of the U.S. originally known for its resorts, now more for the move of much business and commerce here from the N and E. It includes Florida, Texas, Arizona, and California.

Sun•chon |'so͞on'CHən| **1** industrial city in W North Korea, NE of Pyongyang, in a mining district. Pop. 356,000. **2** commercial city in SW South Korea, in an agricultural district. Pop. 249,000.

Sun City[1] |'sən| retirement community in S central Arizona, a suburb NW of Phoenix. Pop. 38,126.

Sun City[2] |'sən| resort in the North West province of South Africa, built in the 1980s in the former BOPHUTHATSWANA to attract tourists, especially from other parts of South Africa, with gambling and other entertainments.

Sun•da Islands |'so͞ondä| chain of islands in the SW part of the Malay Archipelago, consisting of two groups: the *Greater Sunda Islands*, which include Sumatra, Java, Borneo, and Sulawesi, and the *Lesser Sunda Islands*, which lie to the E of Java and include Bali, Sumbawa, Flores, Sumba, and Timor. The Sunda Strait passes between Sumatra and Java, connecting the Java Sea with the Indian Ocean.

Sun•dar•bans |'səndər,bənz| region of swampland in the Ganges delta, extending from the mouth of the Hooghly River in West Bengal, E India to that of the Tetulia in Bangladesh.

Sun•der•land |'səndərlənd| industrial city in Tyne and Wear, NE England, a North Sea port at the mouth of the Wear River. Pop. 287,000.

Sund•svall |'sənds,väl| port and manufacturing center in E Sweden, on the Gulf of Bothnia. Pop. 94,000.

Sun•flow•er State |'sən,flowər| nickname for KANSAS.

Sun•ga•ri River |'so͞ongərē| (also called **Songhua**) river of NE China, flowing 1,150 mi./1,850 km. N from the Changbai Shan range through Jilin and Heilongjiang provinces to the Amur River at the Russian border.

Sun•ny•vale |'sənē,väl| city in N central California, one of the technological centers of Silicon Valley. Pop. 117,229.

Sun•rise |'sən,rīz| city in SE Florida, a retirement and commercial suburb W of Fort Lauderdale. Pop. 64,407.

Sun•set Boulevard |'sən,set| road that links the center of Los Angeles, California, with the Pacific Ocean 30 mi./48 km. to the W. The E section, between Fairfax Avenue and Beverly Hills, is known as the Sunset Strip.

Sun•shine Coast |'sən,SHīn| name given

to the Pacific coast of Australia between Noosa Heads and Bribie Island, in Queensland, noted for its fine beaches.

Sun•shine State nickname for FLORIDA.

Sun Valley |'sən| city in S central Idaho, a famed winter sports resort. Pop. 938.

Suo•mi |'swawmē| Finnish name for FINLAND.

Su•pe•ri•or, Lake |sə'pirēər| the largest of the five Great Lakes of North America, lying between Michigan, Wisconsin, and Minnesota in the U.S. and Ontario, Canada. With an area of 31,800 sq. mi./82,350 sq. km., it is the largest freshwater lake in the world.

Su•pe•ri•or |sə'pirēər| port city in NW Wisconsin, on Lake Superior adjacent to Duluth, Minnesota. Pop. 27,134.

Sur, Point |'so͝or| see BIG SUR, California.

Su•ra•ba•ya |,so͞orə'bīə| industrial port in Indonesia, on the N coast of Java. Pop. 2,473,000. It is Indonesia's principal naval base and its second-largest city.

Su•ra•kar•ta |,so͞orə'kärtə| (also called **Solo; Sala**) city in Indonesia, on central Java, SE of Semarang. Pop. 504,000. It is an industrial, commercial, and cultural center.

Su•rat |so͞o'ræt; 'so͝orət| city in the state of Gujarat in W India, a port on the Tapti River near its mouth on the Gulf of Cambay. Pop. 1,497,000. It was the site of the first trading post of the East India Company, established in 1612.

Su•ren•dra•na•gar |sə'rendrənəgər| commercial and industrial town in W central India, in Gujarat state. Pop. 106,000.

Su•resnes |so͞o'rän| residential and industrial W suburb of Paris, France. Pop. 37,000. There is a U.S. military cemetery here.

Sur•gut |so͝or'go͝ot| oil- and gas-producing town and port in W Siberia, in Russia. Pop. 256,000.

Su•ri•ba•chi, Mount |,so͞ori'bäCHi| small dormant volcano on IWO JIMA, in the W Pacific, scene of a February 1945 flagraising by U.S. Marines that was the subject of a famous World War II photograph and a monument in the Arlington National Cemetery, Virginia.

Su•ri•gao |,so͞orē'gow| port and commercial city in the Philippines, on SE Mindanao. Pop. 100,000. It is one of the oldest Spanish settlements in the Philippines.

Su•ri•name |'so͞orə,näm| (also **Surinam**) republic on the NE coast of South America. Area: 63,061 sq. mi./163,265 sq. km. Pop. 457,000. Languages, Dutch (official),

Surinam

Creole, Hindi. Capital and largest city: Paramaribo. Former name (until 1948) **Dutch Guiana** or **Netherlands Guiana**. Colonized by the Dutch and the British, Suriname became independent in 1975. The largely African and Asian population relies on sugar, timber, and bauxite exports. □ **Surinamese** *adj. & n.* **Surinamer** *n.*

Sur•rey¹ |'sərē| municipality in SW British Columbia, an industrial and commercial suburb SE of Vancouver. Pop. 245,173.

Sur•rey² |'sərē| county of SE England. Pop. 997,000; county seat, Guildford. Surrey contains many London suburbs.

Surt•sey³ |'sərtsē| small island to the S of Iceland, formed by a volcanic eruption in 1963.

Su•sa¹ |'so͞ozə| ancient city of SW Asia, one of the chief cities of the kingdom of Elam and later capital of the Persian Achaemenid dynasty.

Su•sa² |'so͞ozə| another name for SOUSSE.

Sus•que•han•na River |ˌsəskwə'hænə| river of the NE U.S. It has two headstreams, one rising in New York State and one in Pennsylvania, which meet in central Pennsylvania. The river then flows 150 mi./240 km. S to Chesapeake Bay.

Sus•sex |'səsəks| former county of S England. It was divided in 1974 into the counties of East Sussex and West Sussex. Sussex was originally the kingdom of the South Saxons.

Suth•er•land |'səTHərlənd| former county of Scotland, since 1975 a district of Highland region.

Sut•lej |'sətlij| river of N India and Pakistan that rises in the Himalayas in SW Tibet, and flows for 900 mi./1,450 km. W through India into Punjab province in Pakistan, where it joins the Chenab to form the Panjnad and eventually join the Indus.

Sut•ton |'sətn| largely residential borough of S Greater London, England, W of Croydon. Pop. 164,000.

Sut•ton Cold•field |'sətn| largely residential town in the West Midlands of England, just N of Birmingham. Pop. 86,000.

Su•va |'so͞ovə| the capital of Fiji, a port on the SE coast of the island of Viti Levu. Pop. 72,000.

Su•wan•nee |'s(ə)wänē| (also **Swanee**) river of the SE U.S. Rising in SE Georgia, it flows for some 250 mi./400 km. SW through N Florida to the Gulf of Mexico.

Su•won |'so͞o'wən| historic industrial city in NW South Korea, S of Seoul. Pop. 2,449,000. The capital of Kyonggi province, it is an agricultural research and administrative center.

Suz•dal |'so͞ozdəl| city in central Russia, now part of NE Moscow. With its ancient buildings, its major industry is tourism.

Su•zhou |'so͞o'CHow| (also **Suchou** or **Soochow**) city in E China, in the province of Jiangsu, W of Shanghai on the Grand Canal. Pop. 840,000. Founded in the 6th century B.C., it was the capital of the ancient Wu kingdom.

Su•zu•ka |so͞o'zo͞okä| industrial city in central Japan, on S Honshu. Pop. 174,000.

Sval•bard |'sväl,bärd| group of islands in the Arctic Ocean about 400 mi./640 km. N of Norway. Pop. 3,700. They came under Norwegian sovereignty in 1925. The chief settlement (on Spitsbergen) is Longyearbyen.

Svalbard

Sverd•lovsk |ˌsvərd'lawfsk| former name (1924–91) for EKATERINBURG.

Sver•drup Islands |'sferdrəp| icebound island group in the Canadian Arctic, W of Ellesmere Island. Explored by the Norwegian Otto Sverdrup in 1898, they did not become Canadian until 1931.

Sve•ri•ge |sve'rēyə| Swedish name for SWEDEN.

Svir River |'svir| river (140 mi./320 km. long) in NW Russia. It flows from Lake Onega to Lake Ladoga. During World War

II it was the battle line between Russian and Finnish troops.

Sviz·ze·ra |'zvĕttserä| Italian name for SWITZERLAND.

Swa·bia |'swābēə| former duchy of medieval Germany. The region is now divided among SW Germany, Switzerland, and France. German name **Schwaben**. □ **Swabian** *adj. & n.*

Swains Island |swānz| (also **Quiros**) privately owned island in the S central Pacific, N of and under the jurisdiction of American Samoa. It was formerly part of Tokelau, New Zealand.

Swa·kop·mund |'sfäkawpmənt| resort town in W Namibia, on the Atlantic coast. Pop. 18,000. It was formerly the chief port of German Southwest Africa.

Swan River |'swän| river of Western Australia. Rising as the Avon to the SE of Perth, it flows N and W through Perth to the Indian Ocean at Fremantle. It was the site of the first free (nonpenal) European settlement in Western Australia.

Swan·sea |'swänzē| industrial port city in S Wales, on the Bristol Channel. Pop. 182,000. Welsh name **Abertawe**.

Swat |swät| river in N Pakistan, flowing 400 mi./645 km., from a SE spur of the Hindu Kush into the Kabul River NE of Peshawar.

Swa·tow |'swä'tow| former name for SHANTOU.

Swa·zi·land |'swäzē,lænd| landlocked kingdom in southern Africa, bounded by South Africa and Mozambique. Area: 6,706 sq. mi./17,363 sq. km. Pop. 825,000. Official languages, Swazi and English. Capital and largest city: Mbabane. Legislative capital: Lobamba. Controlled by South Africa and Britain, Swaziland became independent in 1968. It is largely agricultural.

Swaziland

Swe·den |'swēdən| kingdom occupying the E part of the Scandinavian Peninsula. Area: 173,798 sq. mi./449,964 sq. km. Pop.

Sweden

8,591,000. Language, Swedish. Capital and largest city: Stockholm. Swedish name **Sverige**. A nation from the 12th century, Sweden was an independent kingdom by 1523; in 1814–1905 it was united with Norway. Mining, forest industries, and manufacturing are key to the economy. □ **Swedish** *adj. & n.* **Swede** *n.*

Swift Current |'swift| industrial and commercial city in SW Saskatchewan. Pop. 14,815.

Swin·don |'swindən| industrial town in central England. Pop. 100,000. An old market town, it developed rapidly after railroad engineering works were established in 1841 and again in the 1950s as an overspill town for London.

Swiss Confederation |'swis| the confederation of cantons forming Switzerland, and the official name of the country.

Swit·zer·land |'switsərlənd| mountainous, landlocked republic in W central Europe. Area: 15,949 sq. mi./41,293 sq. km. Pop. 6,673,850. Official languages, French, German, Italian, and Romansch. Capital: Bern. Largest city: Zurich. French name **Suisse**, German name **Schweiz**, Italian name **Svizzera**; also called by its Latin name **Helvetia**. Independent from the 14th–15th centuries, when it threw off Hapsburg and other rulers, Switzerland has a history of neutrality and as a home to international organizations. Tourism, high technology, dairying, and finance are among key industries. □ **Swiss** *adj. & n.*

Sword Beach |sawrd| easternmost of the Normandy beaches used during the D-day landing in June 1944, at the village of Lion-sur-Mer. British forces landed here.

Syb·a·ris |'sibərəs| ancient city of MAGNA GRAECIA, on the Gulf of Tarentum (Taranto) in S Italy. Its luxury gave rise to the term *sybarite*.

Syd·ney[1] |'sidnē| industrial city in E Nova Scotia, on Cape Breton Island. Pop.

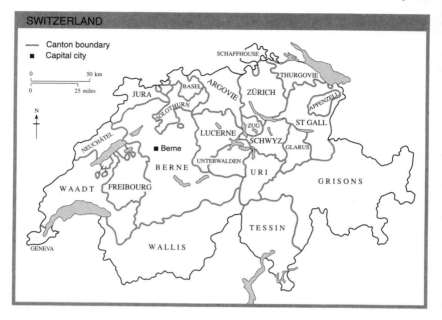

SWITZERLAND

— Canton boundary
■ Capital city

SCHAFFHOUSE
THURGOVIE
ZÜRICH
APPENZELL
JURA
BASEL
ARGOVIE
SOLOTHURN
ST GALL
ZUG
LUCERNE
SCHWYZ
GLARUS
NEUCHÂTEL
■ Berne
UNTERWALDEN
URI
BERNE
WAADT   FREIBOURG
GRISONS
GENEVA   WALLIS
TESSIN

26,063. It is a coal-mining and steelmaking center.

Syd·ney[2] |'sidnē| the capital of New South Wales in SE Australia. Pop. 3,098,000. It was the first British settlement in Australia and is the country's largest city and chief port. It has a fine natural harbor, crossed by the Sydney Harbour Bridge (opened 1932), and a striking opera house (opened 1973).

Syk·tyv·kar |siktif'kär| city in NW Russia, capital of the autonomous republic of Komi. Pop. 235,000.

Sylt |'sŏŏlt| island in the North Sea, largest of the Frisian Islands of Germany. Area: 36 sq. mi./96 sq. km. Its largest towns are Westerland, a resort, and Kampen.

Syr·a·cuse[1] |'sirə,kyŏŏs| industrial city in central New York, to the SE of Lake Ontario. Pop. 163,860. It was a center of salt production during the 19th century, and is now a manufacturing center.

Syr·a·cuse[2] |'sirə,kyŏŏs| port on the E coast of Sicily. Pop. 125,000. It was a flourishing center of Greek culture, especially in the 5th and 4th centuries B.C. under the rule of Dionysius I and II. It was taken by the Romans at the end of the 3rd century B.C. Italian name **Siracusa.**

Syr Dar·ya River |sir'däryə| river (1,370 mi./2,204 km.) in Kyrgyzstan, Uzbekistan, and Kazakhstan, flowing through the Fergana Valley to the Aral Sea.

Syr·ia |'sirēə| republic in the Middle East with a coastline on the E Mediterranean Sea. Area: 71,089 sq. mi./184,050 sq. km. Pop. 12,824,000. Language, Arabic. Capital and largest city: Damascus. An ancient country, Syria became an Islamic center in the 7th century, and was dominated by the Turks from the 16th century until World War I. It gained independence in 1941. In 1958–61 it was a member, with Egypt, of the United Arab Republic. Traditionally agricultural, it is now also industrial and an oil producer. □ **Syrian** adj. & n.

Syria

Syr·i·an Desert |'sirēən| region of SW Asia, a N extension of the Arabian Desert, in SE Syria, E Jordan, SW Iraq, and N Saudi Arabia. Mesopotamia lies to the E.

Syz·ran |siz'rən| river port and industrial

city in W Russia, on the Volga River. Pop. 175,000.

Szcze•cin |'shchet,shēn| industrial city in NW Poland, a port on the Oder River near the border with Germany. Pop. 413,000. German name **Stettin.**

Sze•chwan |'se(t)sh',wän| see SICHUAN.

Sze•ged |'seged| city in S Hungary, a port on the Tisza River near the border with Serbia. Pop. 178,000. It is noted for food production.

Szé•kes•fe•hér•vár |'sekesh,fehärvär| industrial and transportation center in W Hungary, the capital of Féjer county. Pop. 110,000. The kings of Hungary were crowned and buried here from the 11th to the 16th centuries.

Szi•get•vár |'sēget,vär| historic city in SW Hungary. Pop. 12,000. Its medieval fortress was defended by Nicholas Zrinyi against Sulayman I, the Ottoman sultan, in 1566.

Szol•nok |'sōl,nōk| agricultural and transportation center in E Hungary, capital of Solnok county. Pop. 80,000. It was founded as a fortress town in 1076.

Szom•bat•hely |'sōmbawt,hä| transportation center and capital of Vas county in W Hungary, near the Austrian border. Pop. 86,000.

Tt

Ta·bas·co |tə'bæskō| state of SE Mexico, on the Gulf of Mexico. Area: 9,759 sq. mi./25,267 sq. km. Pop. 1,501,000. Capital: Villahermosa. Agriculture and oil are key to its economy.

Ta·ble Mountain |,tābəl| flat-topped mountain near the SW tip of South Africa, overlooking Cape Town and Table Bay, rising to a height of 3,563 ft./1,087 m.

Ta·bor, Mount |'tābər| (Hebrew name **Har Tavor**) mountain in N Israel, rising to 1,938 ft./588 m. above the Plain of Jezreel.

Tà·bor |'täb,awr| historic city in the S central Czech Republic. Pop. 36,000. The economy is based on agriculture and mining.

Ta·bo·ra |tə'bawrə| commercial city in W central Tanzania, the capital of the Tabora region. Pop. 120,000.

Ta·briz |tə'brēz| city in NW Iran. Pop. 1,089,000. The capital of East Azerbaijan and a former Armenian and Persian capital, it has been subject to frequent destructive earthquakes. Textile, carpet, and other industries are important.

Ta·chi·ka·wa |,tä'CHe'käwä| commercial city in E central Japan, on E central Honshu, a suburb W of Tokyo. Pop. 153,000.

Ta·ching |'tä'CHiNG| see DAQING.

Ta·clo·ban |tä'klōbän| commercial port city in the Philippines, on NE Leyte. Pop. 137,000.

Tac·na |'täknə| city in extreme S Peru, the capital of Tacna department, an irrigated agricultural region. Pop. 116,000. The Tacna region was long fought over by Peru, Bolivia, and Chile.

Ta·co·ma |tə'kōmə| industrial port city in W central Washington, on Puget Sound S of Seattle. Pop. 176,664.

Ta·con·ic Mountains |tə'känik| (also **the Taconics**) range of the Appalachian system along the E border of New York with Connecticut, Massachusetts, and Vermont.

Tae·gu |'tæg'ōō; 'tī'gōō| industrial city in SE South Korea. Pop. 2,229,000. The third-largest South Korean city, a communications center, it has historic Buddhist sites.

Tae·jon |'tæj'awn; 'tī'jawn| industrial and technological city in central South Korea. Pop. 1,062,000.

Ta·gan·rog |'tægən,rawg| industrial port in SW Russia, on the Gulf of Taganrog, an inlet of the Sea of Azov. Pop. 293,000. It was founded in 1698 by Peter the Great as a fortress and naval base.

Ta·gus |'tägəs| river in SW Europe, the longest of the Iberian Peninsula, which rises in the mountains of E Spain and flows over 625 mi./1,000 km. generally W into Portugal, where it turns SW, emptying into the Atlantic near Lisbon. Spanish name **Tajo**, Portuguese name **Tejo**.

Ta·hi·ti |tə'hētē| island in the central S Pacific, one of the Society Islands, forming part of French Polynesia. Pop. 116,000. Capital: Papeete. One of the largest islands in the S Pacific, it was claimed for France in 1768. Tourism and fruit production are key to its economy.

Tah·le·quah |'tælə,kwaw.| commercial city in E Oklahoma, former capital of the Cherokee nation. Pop. 10,398.

Ta·hoe, Lake |'tä,hō| mountain lake on the border of N central California with Nevada, noted for its resorts.

Tai'an |'tī'än| industrial and agricultural city in NE China, in Shandong province. Pop. 1,370,000.

Tai·chung |'tī'CHŏŏNG| commercial and cultural city in W central Taiwan. Pop. 774,000.

Ta'if |'täif| city in W Saudi Arabia, to the SE of Mecca in the Asir Mts. Pop. 205,000. It is the unofficial seat of government of Saudi Arabia during the summer.

Tai·myr Peninsula |tī'mir| (also **Taymyr**) vast, almost uninhabited peninsula on the N coast of central Russia, extending into the Arctic Ocean and separating the Kara Sea from the Laptev Sea. Its N tip, Cape Chelyuskin, is the northernmost point of Asia.

Tai·nan |'tī'nän| industrial city on the SW coast of Taiwan. Pop. 690,000. Settled from mainland China in 1590, it is one of the oldest cities on the island and was its capital from 1684 until 1885, when it was replaced by Taipei. Its original name was Taiwan, the name later given to the whole island.

Tai·pei |'tī'pā; 'tī,bā| the capital of Taiwan. Pop. 2,718,000, an important center of commerce, finance, and industry. It developed as an industrial city in the 19th century, and became the capital in 1885.

Tai·ping |'tī'piNG| city in central peninsular Malaysia, in the foothills of the Bintang

Mts. Pop. 146,000. The only city in Malaysia with a Chinese name, it was developed by immigrant Chinese in the 1840s.

Tai·wan |'tī'wän| island republic off the SE coast of China. Area: 14,000 sq. mi./35,980 sq. km. Pop. 20,400,000. Official language, Mandarin Chinese. Capital: Taipei. Official name **Republic of China**. Former (Portuguese) name **Formosa**. Held at times by the Portuguese and Japanese, the island became in 1949 the refuge of nationalist Chinese fleeing the communist takeover of the mainland. It has since developed a strong industrial economy, despite friction between the exiles and natives and despite loss of UN recognition in 1971 in favor of the mainland, which regards Taiwan as one of its provinces. □ **Taiwanese** *adj. & n.*

Taiwan

Tai·yuan |'tīyōō'än| industrial city in N China, capital of Shanxi province. Pop. 1,900,000.

Ta'iz |tä'ēz| city in SW Yemen. Pop. 290,000. It was the administrative capital of Yemen from 1948 to 1962.

Ta·jik·i·stan |tä,jiki'stän| (also **Tadzhikistan**) mountainous republic in central Asia, N of Afghanistan. Area: 55,272 sq. mi./143,100 sq. km. Pop. 5,412,000. Languages, Tajik (official), Russian. Capital and largest city: Dushanbe. A Mongol ter-

Tajikistan

ritory absorbed into the Russian Empire in the 19th century, Tajikistan is inhabited by an Iranian, Sunni Muslim people. Independent from the Soviet Union since 1991, it has an economy based on agriculture and mineral extraction. □ **Tajik** *adj. & n.*

Taj Ma·hal |,täzH mə'häl| mausoleum in N central India, near the Jumna River in Agra, completed c. 1648 by Mogul emperor Shah Jahan for his favorite wife.

Ta·jo |'tähō| Spanish name for TAGUS.

Ta·ka·ma·tsu |,täkä'mätsōō| ferry port and industrial center in W Japan, on NE Shikoku. Pop. 330,000.

Ta·ka·o·ka |tä'kowkä| industrial city in central Japan, on central Honshu. Pop. 175,000. It is a center for the Japanese aluminum industry.

Ta·ka·ra·zu·ka |tä,kärä'zōōkä| city in W central Japan, on S Honshu, NW of Osaka. Pop. 202,000. It is a suburb and a resort serving the Osaka and Kobe areas.

Ta·ka·sa·ki |,täkä'säkē| industrial city in N central Japan, on central Honshu. Pop. 236,000.

Ta·kat·su·ki |tä'kätskē| city in W central Japan, on S Honshu, NNE of Osaka. Pop. 360,000.

Ta·kli·ma·kan Desert |,täkləmə'kän| (also **Takla Makan**) desert in the Xinjiang autonomous region of NW China, lying between the Kunlun Shan and Tien Shan mountains and forming the greater part of the Tarim Basin.

Ta·ko·ra·di |,täkō'rädē| seaport in W Ghana, on the Gulf of Guinea. Pop. 615,000. It is part of the joint urban area of Sekondi-Takoradi and is one of the major seaports of W Africa.

Ta·la·ra |tä'lärä| port town in extreme NW Peru, an oil industry center. Pop. 90,000.

Ta·la·ve·ra de la Rei·na |,tälä'värä,dä lä 'ränä| town in central Spain, on the Tagus River. Pop. 69,000. It is known for its fine ceramics.

Tal·ca |'tälkä| city in central Chile, capital of the Maule region. Pop. 164,000. It is a wine industry center.

Tal·ca·hua·no |,tälkä'wänō| city in S central Chile, a commercial and naval port in the Bío-Bío region. Pop. 247,000.

Tal·ie·sin |täl'yesən; tælē'əsən| see SPRING GREEN, Wisconsin and SCOTTSDALE, Arizona.

Tal·la·de·ga |,tælə'dāgə; ,tælə'dēgə| industrial city in E central Alabama, a mining center also noted for its Talladega Superspeedway. Pop. 18,175.

Tal·la·has·see |,tælə'hæsē| university and

Tal•la•poo•sa River |ˌtælə'pōōsə| river that flows 268 mi./430 km. from NW Georgia into Alabama, where it joins the Coosa to form the Alabama River.

Tal•linn |'tælən| the capital of Estonia, an industrial port on the Gulf of Finland. Pop. 505,000. Before 1917 it was called Revel.

Ta•ma |'tämä| city in E central Japan, on E central Honshu, W of Shinjuku. Pop. 144,000.

Ta•ma•le |tä'mälä| commercial and academic city in N Ghana, capital of the Northern region. Pop. 136,000.

Ta•mal•pa•is, Mount |ˌtæməl'pīəs| mountain in Marin County, NW California, N of San Francisco across the Golden Gate, and center of a recreational area.

Tam•an•ras•set |ˌtæmən'ræsət| commercial town in S Algeria, at the edge of the Hoggar Mts. and the Sahara. Pop. 38,000. It is a center for the Tuareg people.

Ta•mar |'tämər| river in SW England that rises in NW Devon and flows 60 mi./98 km. generally southward, forming the boundary between Devon and Cornwall and emptying into the English Channel through Plymouth Sound.

Tam•a•rac |'tæmə,ræk| city in SE Florida, a retirement center NW of Fort Lauderdale. Pop. 44,822.

Ta•mau•li•pas |tämow'lēpäs| state of NE Mexico with a coastline on the Gulf of Mexico. Area: 30,662 sq. mi./79,384 sq. km. Pop. 2,244,000. Capital: Ciudad Victoria.

Tam•bo•ra, Gu•nung |'gōō,nōōNG 'tämbrə| active volcano in Indonesia, on N Sumbawa. Its 1815 eruption was one of the most destructive in the history of the world.

Tam•bov |täm'bawf| industrial city in SW Russia. Pop. 307,000.

Ta•mil Na•du |ˌtæməl 'nädōō| state in the extreme SE of the Indian peninsula, on the Coromandel Coast, with a largely Tamil-speaking, Hindu population. Pop. 55,640,000. Capital: Madras. Tamil Nadu was also an ancient kingdom comprising a much larger area, stretching N to Orissa and including the Lakshadweep Islands and part of the Malabar Coast. Former name (until 1968) **Madras**.

Tam•ma•ny Hall |ˌtæmənē| name for the traditional Democratic Party in New York City, regarded as occupying a social hall in lower Manhattan. Actual headquarters moved many times.

Tam•mer•fors |ˌtämər'farsH| Swedish name for TAMPERE.

Tam•pa |'tæmpə| industrial port and resort on the W coast of Florida. Pop. 280,015.

Tam•pa Bay |'tæmpə| inlet of the Gulf of Mexico in SW Florida, on which lie Tampa, St. Petersburg, and other cities and resorts.

Tam•pe•re |'tämpərə| industrial and commercial city in SW Finland. Pop. 173,000. Swedish name **Tammerfors**.

Tam•pi•co |tæm'pē,kō| one of Mexico's principal ports, an oil, fishing, and resort center in Tamaulipas state, on the Gulf of Mexico. Pop. 272,000.

Tam•worth |'tæm,wərTH| industrial town in central England, in Staffordshire. Pop. 65,000.

Ta•na, Lake |'tänə| lake in N Ethiopia, the largest in the country and the source of the Blue Nile.

Ta•na |'tänə| longest river in Kenya. It flows 500 mi./800 km. from near Mount Kenya to the Indian Ocean N of Malindi.

Tan•a•gra |'tænəgrə| town in ancient Greece, in Boeotia E of Thebes, where the Spartans defeated the Athenians in 457 B.C. during the Peloponnesian War.

Ta•na•na•rive |tə'nœnə,rēv| former name (until 1975) for ANTANANARIVO.

Tan•a•na River |'tænə,naw| river that flows 600 mi./1,000 km. from the Yukon Territory across Alaska, meeting the Yukon River W of Fairbanks.

Tan•dil |tän'dēl| city in E Argentina, S of Buenos Aires. Pop. 90,000. It is a resort and agricultural and university center.

Tan•ga |'täNGgä| one of the principal ports of Tanzania, in the NE, on the Indian Ocean, opposite Pemba island. Pop. 188,000.

Tan•gan•yi•ka, Lake |ˌtæNGgən'yēkə| lake in E Africa, in the Great Rift Valley. The deepest lake in Africa and the longest (420 mi./680 km.) freshwater lake in the world, it forms most of the border of the Democratic Republic of Congo (formerly Zaire) with Tanzania and Burundi.

Tan•gan•yi•ka |ˌtæNGgən'ēkə| former republic in E Africa, since 1964 part of TANZANIA. Before independence in 1962, it was colonized by the Germans and the British.

Tan•gier |tæn'jir| (also **Tangiers, Tanger**) seaport on the N coast of Morocco, on the Strait of Gibraltar commanding the W entrance to the Mediterranean. Pop. 307,000. Portuguese from the end of the 15th century, Tangier was ruled by the sultan of Morocco from 1684 until 1904, when it came under international control; it passed to the newly independent monarchy of Morocco in 1956.

Tan·gle·wood see STOCKBRIDGE.

Tang·shan |'täNG'sHän| industrial city in Hebei province, NE China. Pop. 1,500,000. The city was rebuilt after a devastating earthquake in 1976.

Ta·nim·bar Islands |tə'nim,bär| group of islands in Indonesia, between the Aru Islands and Timor in the Banda Sea.

Tan·jung·ka·rang |ˌtänjo͞oNG'käräNG| see BANDAR LAMPUNG.

Tan·nen·berg |'tänən,berg| (Polish name **Stebark**) village in NE Poland (formerly in East Prussia), scene of two historic battles In 1410 Poles and allies defeated the invading Teutonic Knights nearby. In 1914 the Germans won a major victory over Russian troops here.

Tannu-Tuva |ˌtäno͞o'to͞ovə| former name for TUVA.

Tan·ta |'täntə| industrial and commercial city in NE Egypt, N of Cairo in the Nile delta. Pop. 372,000. It is a center of Sufism. The ruins of SAÏS are nearby.

Tan·za·nia |ˌtænzə'nēə| republic in E Africa with a coastline on the Indian Ocean. Area: 362,940 sq. mi./939,652 sq. km. Pop. 27,270,000. Official languages, Swahili and English. Capital: Dodoma. Largest city: Dar es Salaam. A 1964 unification of Tanganyika and Zanzibar, Tanzania stretches from high plateaus including the Serengeti E to the ocean. It is largely agricultural, producing coffee, cotton, sisal, and other export crops. Mount Kilimanjaro and other sites draw tourists. □ **Tanzanian** *adj. & n.*

Tanzania

Ta·or·mi·na |ˌtowr'mēnə| resort town on the E coast of Sicily. Pop. 11,000. It was founded by Greek colonists in the 4th century B.C. and was an an important city until the 15th century.

Taos |tows; 'tä,ōs| town in N New Mexico, in the Sangre de Cristo Mts., a noted resort and arts center. Pop. 4,065.

Ta·pa·chu·la |ˌtäpä'CHo͞olä| city in extreme SE Mexico, in Chiapas state, near the Guatemalan border. Pop. 223,000. It is a commercial and transportation center in a coffee-producing region.

Ta·pa·jós |ˌtäpə'ZHawsH| (also **Tapajoz**) river that with its headstreams flows 1,256 mi./2,010 km. N from the Mato Grosso in central Brazil, to join the Amazon W of Santarém.

Tap·pan Zee |'tæpən 'zē; 'tæ,pæn| broadening of the Hudson River in SE New York, near Tarrytown. Bridged in 1955, it is a well-known fishing and recreational site.

Tara |'tærə| hill in County Meath, E central Ireland, site in early times of the residence of the high kings of Ireland and still marked by ancient earthworks.

Ta·ra·bu·lus Al-Gharb |tə'räbələs äl 'gärb| Arabic name for TRIPOLI (in sense 1).

Ta·ra·bu·lus Ash-Sham |tə'räbələs esH 'sHæm| Arabic name for TRIPOLI (in sense 2).

Ta·ra·na·ki |ˌtärä'näkē| Maori name for Mount Egmont (see EGMONT, MOUNT).

Ta·ran·to |'tärän,tō| seaport and naval base in Apulia, SE Italy. Pop. 244,000. Founded by the Greeks in the 8th century B.C., it came under Roman rule in 272 B.C.

Ta·ras·con |ˌtärä'skawN| commercial town in SE France, on the Rhone River N of Arles, associated with the writing of Alphonse Daudet. Pop. 12,000.

Ta·ra·wa |tə'räwə; 'tärə,wä| atoll in the S Pacific, one of the Gilbert Islands. Pop. 29,000. It is the location of Bairiki, the capital of Kiribati. Tarawa was the scene of intense fighting in World War II.

Tarbes |tärb| industrial and market town in SW France, the capital of the Hautes-Pyrénées department. Pop. 50,000.

Tar Heel State |'tär,hēl| informal name for NORTH CAROLINA.

Ta·ri·ja |tä'rēhä| city in SE Bolivia, capital of Tarija department, on the Guadalquivir River. Pop. 90,000. It is a highland agricultural center.

Ta·rim |'tä'rēm; 'dä'rēm| river of NW China, in Xinjiang autonomous region. It rises at the Yarkand in the Kunlun Shan mountains and flows for over 1,250 mi./2,000 km. generally E through the dry Tarim Basin, petering out in the Lop Nor depression. For much of its course the river follows no clearly defined bed and is subject to much evaporation.

Ta·rim Basin |'tä'rēm; 'dä'rēm| vast, dry low-lying region in Xinjiang, NW China, lying between the Kunlun Shan and Tian Shan mountains. It includes the Talkimakan Desert and Turfan Depression.

Tar·lac |'tär,läk| commercial town in the Philippines, on central Luzon, N of Manila. Pop. 209,000.

Tarn |tärn| river of S France, which rises in the Cévennes and flows 235 mi./380 km/ generally SW through deep gorges before meeting the Garonne NW of Toulouse.

Tar·nów |'tär,nŏŏf| industrial city in S Poland. Pop. 74,000.

Tar·pe·ian Rock |tär'pēən| cliff in ancient Rome, at the SW corner of the Capitoline Hill, from which murderers and traitors were thrown.

Tar·pon Springs |'tärpən| city in SW Florida, on the Gulf of Mexico, home to a famed sponge-diving industry. Pop. 17,906.

Tar·qui·nia |tär'kwēnyə| industrial town in central Italy, NW of Rome. Pop. 14,000. Once capital of the Etruscan League, it came under Roman domination in the 4th century B.C.

Tar·ra·go·na |,tärə'gōnə| port and commercial center in E Spain, on the Mediterranean Sea, capital of Tarragona province. Pop. 113,000.

Tar·ra·sa |tə'räsə| (also **Terrassa**) industrial city in Catalonia, NE Spain, N of Barcelona. Pop. 154,000.

Tar·ry·town |'tærē,town| residential and industrial village in SE New York, on the Tappan Zee of the Hudson River. Pop. 10,739.

Tar·sus |'tärsəs| ancient city of Asia Minor (present-day S Turkey), the capital of Cilicia and the birthplace of St. Paul. It is now a market town.

Tar·ta·ry |'tärtərē| historical region of Asia and E Europe, especially the high plateau of central Asia and its NW slopes, which formed part of the Tartar Empire of Genghis Khan, with its capital at Samarkand, in the Middle Ages.

Tar·tu |'tär,tŏŏ| industrial and port city in E Estonia, on the Ema River. Pop. 115,000.

Tash·kent |tæsH'kent| the capital of Uzbekistan, in the far NE of the country in the western foothills of the Tian Shan mountains: pop. 2,094,000. One of the oldest cities in central Asia, Tashkent was an important center on the trade route between Europe and the Orient. It became part of the Mongol Empire in the 13th century, was captured by the Russians in 1865,

and replaced Samarkand as capital of Uzbekistan in 1930.

Ta·sik·ma·la·ya |,täsikmə'līə| (also **Tasikmalaja**) commercial city in Indonesia, on W Java. Pop. 166,000.

Tas·man, Mount |'tæzmən| peak in the Southern Alps range, on South Island, New Zealand; the second-highest in New Zealand: 11,473 ft./3,497 m.

Tas·ma·nia |tæz'mānēyə; tæz'mānyə| state of Australia consisting of the mountainous island of Tasmania itself and several smaller islands. Pop. 458,000. Capital and largest city: Hobart. It was known as Van Diemen's Land until 1855. Agriculture and mining are important. □ **Tasmanian** adj. & n.

Tas·man Sea |'tæzmən| arm of the South Pacific lying between Australia and New Zealand.

Ta·ta·bán·ya |'tätä,bänyä| town in N Hungary, in a coalfield W of Budapest. Pop. 77,000.

Ta·tar City |'tä'tär| (also called **Inner City**) walled section of Beijing, China, lying N of the Chinese, or Outer, City. It includes the Forbidden City and most government offices and embassies.

Ta·tar·stan |,tätər'stæn| autonomous republic in European Russia, in the valley of the Volga River. Pop. 3,658,000. Capital: Kazan.

Tate Gallery |tāt| noted art gallery in central London, England, on the N bank of the Thames in the Millbank section, opened in 1897.

Tat·ra Mountains |'tätrə| (also **the Tatras**) range in E Europe on the Polish–Slovak border, the highest range in the Carpathians, rising to 8,710 ft./2,655 m. at Mount Gerlachovsky.

Tau·ba·té |,towbə'tä| commercial city in SE Brazil, in São Paulo state. Pop. 220,000. It is a processing center in the agricultural Paraíba River valley.

Taung·gyi |'town'jē| (also **Tawnggyi**) hill resort town in central Burma, SE of Mandalay. Pop. 108,000.

Taun·ton[1] |'tawntn| the county seat of Somerset, in SW England. Pop. 49,000. It is a center of textile and cider production.

Taun·ton[2] |'tawntn| industrial city in SE Massachusetts. Pop. 49,832.

Tau·po, Lake |'towpō| the largest lake of New Zealand, in the center of North Island. The town of Taupo is on its northern shore. Maori name **Taupomoana**.

Tau·ran·ga |tow'räNGə| industrial port on the Bay of Plenty, North Island, New Zealand. Pop. 64,000.

Tau·rus Mountains |'tawrəs| (Turkish name **Toros Daglari**) range in S Turkey, parallel to the Mediterranean coast. Rising to 12,250 ft./3,734 m. at Mount Aladaë, it forms the S edge of the Anatolian plateau.

Ta·voy |tə'voi| commercial town in Tenasserim division, S Burma, near the mouth of the Tavoy River. Pop. 102,000.

Tax·co |'täskō| (official name **Taxco de Alarcón**) historic city in S Mexico, in Guerrero state, famed as a silver-mining and silversmithing center, and for its colonial architecture. Pop. 42,000.

Tay, Firth of |'fərTH əv 'tā| the estuary of the Tay River, on the North Sea coast of Scotland. It is spanned by the longest railroad bridge in Britain, a structure opened in 1888 that has 85 spans and a total length of 11,653 ft./3,553 m.

Tay |tā| the longest river in Scotland, flowing 120 mi./192 km. E through Loch Tay, and entering the North Sea through the Firth of Tay.

Tay·lor |'tālər| city in SE Michigan, a suburb SW of Detroit. Pop. 70,811.

Tay Ninh |'tī 'nin| commercial city in southern Vietnam, NW of Ho Chi Minh City. Pop. 37,000. It is the capital of Tay Ninh province, scene of some of the fiercest fighting during the Vietnam War.

Ta·za |'täzə| commercial and industrial city in NE Morocco, E of Fez. Pop. 121,000.

Tbi·li·si |təbī'lēsē| the capital of the republic of Georgia, on the Kura River in the Caucasus. Pop. 1,267,000. From 1845 until 1936 its name was Tiflis. An ancient city, it is now a commercial and industrial center.

Tchad French name for CHAD.

Tea·neck |'tē,nek| township in NE New Jersey, a largely residential suburb. Pop. 37,825.

Tea·pot Dome |'tē,pät 'dōm| oil field in SE Wyoming, which as a naval reserve was the focus of a 1920s corruption scandal.

Té·bes·sa |te'besə| (ancient name **Theveste**) historic commercial and industrial city in NE Algeria, near the Tunisian border. Pop. 112,000.

Tees |tēz| river of NE England that rises in Cumbria and flows 80 mi./128 km. generally SE to the North Sea at Middlesbrough.

Tees·side |'tē(z),sīd| industrial region in NE England around the lower Tees valley, in Celeveland, including Middlesbrough.

Te·gal |tā'gäl| industrial port town in Indonesia, on central Java. Pop. 230,000.

Te·gern·see |'tāgərn,zā| lake in Bavaria, in SW Germany, SE of Munich, in the foothills of the Alps, a popular resort area.

Te·gu·ci·gal·pa |tə,gōōsə'gælpə| capital and largest city of Honduras. Pop. 670,000. Once a mining center, it now has various industries.

Te·hach·a·pi Mountains |ti'hæCHə,pē| range that lies across California, just N of the Transverse Ranges. It is sometimes considered the divider between N and S California.

Teh·ran |,tāə'ræn; ,tāə'rän| (also **Teheran**) the capital and largest city of Iran, an industrial center in the foothills of the Elburz Mts. Pop. 6,750,000. It replaced Isfahan as capital of Persia in 1788.

Te·hua·cán |,tāwä'kän| city in S central Mexico, in Puebla state. Pop. 139,000. It is a commercial center and a famed spa.

Te·huan·te·pec, Isthmus of |tə'wäntə-,pek| lowland region in S Mexico, between the Gulf of Campeche (the Gulf of Mexico) on the N and the Gulf of Tehuantepec (the Pacific Ocean) on the S. Highland Chiapas lies to the E, Oaxaca to the W.

Tei·de, Pi·co de |'pēkō dā 'tā,dā| volcano on Tenerife, in the Spanish Canary Islands, in the Atlantic. At 3,718 m./12,198 ft., it is the highest peak in Spain.

Te·jo |'tā,ZHōō| Portuguese name for TAGUS.

Te·kir·dağ |te'kir,däg| port city in European Turkey, W of Istanbul on the Sea of Marmara, the capital of Tekirdağ province. Pop. 80,000.

Tel Aviv |,tel ə'vēv| (also **Tel Aviv–Jaffa**) industrial and administrative city on the Mediterranean coast of Israel. Pop. 355,000. It was founded as a suburb of Jaffa by Russian Jewish immigrants in 1909 and named Tel Aviv a year later. The capital of Israel 1948–50, it is still regarded as such by many governments.

Tel·e·graph Hill |'telə,græf| hill neighborhood in San Francisco, California, named for the signal stations that surmounted it in the 19th century.

Tel·e·mark |'telə,märk| mountain and lake region in S Norway. The highest peak is Gausta (6,178 ft./1,883 m.).

Tel·ford |'telfərd| industrial town in Shropshire, W central England. Pop. 115,000.

Tell el-Amarna |'tel ,el ə'märnə| see AMARNA, TELL EL-.

Tel·li·cher·ry |,teli'CHerē| (also called **Thalassery**) port town in S India, on the Malabar Coast of Kerala state. Pop. 104,000.

Tel·lu·ride |'telyə,rīd| resort town in SW Colorado, a former mining center. Pop. 1,309.

Te·ma |'tämä| industrial port city in SE

Ghana, just E of Accra. Pop. 100,000. Developed from the 1950s, it has the largest artificial harbor in Africa.

Te·mes·vár |'temesH,vär| Hungarian name for TIMIŞOARA.

Te·mir·tau |'tämirtow| coal-mining town in Kazakhstan, NW of Qaraghandy. Pop. 213,000.

Tem·pe, Vale of |'tempē| valley in E central Greece, between Mount Olympus and Mount Ossa. Its beauty was celebrated by the ancient Greek poets.

Tem·pe |,tem'pē; 'tempē| city in S central Arizona, a suburb E of Phoenix and home to Arizona State University. Pop. 141,865.

Tem·ple |'tempəl| industrial and commercial city in central Texas. Pop. 46,109.

Tem·ple, Mount |'tempəl| name for Mount MORIAH, in Jerusalem, as the site of the Temple of Solomon.

Te·mu·co |tä'mōōkō| industrial and commercial city in S central Chile, capital of Araucania region. Pop. 212,000.

Te·na·li |tä'nälē| commercial city in S India, in Andhra Pradesh state, SE of Hyderabad. Pop. 144,000.

Ten·der·loin, the |'tendər,loin| generic term for an urban district notorious for vice. It was first used of part of W Manhattan, New York City, in the 19th century.

Ten·e·dos |'tenə,däs| see BOZCAADA.

Ten·er·ife |,tenə'rēfē; ,tenə'rif| volcanic island in the Atlantic, the largest of the Spanish Canary Islands. Pop. 771,000. Capital: Santa Cruz.

Ten·nes·see |,tenə'sē| see box. □ **Tennessean** adj. & n.

Ten·nes·see River |,tenə'sē| river in the SE U.S., flowing some 875 mi./1,400 km. in a great loop, generally W through Tennessee and Alabama, then N to re-enter Tennessee, joining the Ohio River in W Kentucky. Its flooding was controlled and its flow harnessed for hydroelectric power by the projects of the Tennessee Valley Authority, beginning in 1933.

Te·noch·ti·tlán |tä,nawCHtēt'län| the capital of the Aztec empire in ancient Mexico.

Te·ó·fi·lo Oto·ni |tä'awfē,lōō ō'tōnē| (also **Theophilo Ottoni**) city in E central Brazil, in Minas Gerais state. Pop. 127,000. It is a center for the mining and cutting of semiprecious stones.

Te·o·ti·hua·cán |,täaw,tēwä'kän| the largest city of pre-Columbian America, situated about 25 mi./40 km. NE of present-day Mexico City. Built c. 300 B.C., it reached its zenith c. 300–600 A.D., when it was the center of an influential culture that spread

---

Tennessee

Capital: Nashville
Largest city: Memphis
Other cities: Chattanooga, Clarksville, Fayetteville, Jackson, Knoxville, Lexington
Population: 4,877,185 (1990); 5,430,621 (1998); 5,966,000 (2005 proj.)
Population rank (1990): 17
Rank in land area: 36
Abbreviation: TN; Tenn.
Nickname: Volunteer State; Big Bend State
Motto: 'Agriculture and Commerce'
Bird: mockingbird
Flower: iris (cultivated flower) or maypop (wildflower)
Tree: tulip poplar
Songs: "When It's Iris Time in Tennessee"; "The Tennessee Waltz"; "My Tennessee"; "My Homeland, Tennessee"; "Rocky Top"
Noted physical features: Nashville Basin; Appalachian Mountains; Cumberland Plateau; Clingman's Dome; Tennessee River
Tourist attractions: Graceland (Memphis); Grand Ole Opry House (Nashville); The Hermitage; Cumberland Gap, Great Smoky Mountains (with North Carolina) and Shiloh national parks
Admission date: June 1, 1796
Order of admission: 16
Name origin: For an important Cherokee village, *Tanasi*, on the Little Tennessee River in the eastern part of the state; the meaning of the name is unknown.

---

throughout Mesoamerica. By 650 it was declining, and it was sacked by invading Toltecs c. 900. Among its monuments are palatial buildings, plazas, and temples, including the Pyramids of the Sun and the Moon and the temple of Quetzalcóatl.

Te·pic |tä'pēk| city in W Mexico, capital of the agricultural state of Nayarit. Pop. 238,000.

Te·pli·ce |'teplētse| (also **Teplitz**) industrial and transportation center in the NW Czech Republic. Pop. 55,000. In a mining region, it is also a spa.

Ter·cei·ra |tər'serə| central and third-largest island in the Portuguese Azores, in the N Atlantic.

Te·re·si·na |,tärə'zēnə| river port in NE Brazil, on the Parnaíba river, capital of the state of Piauí. Pop. 591,000.

Te·re·só·po·lis |ˌtārā'zawpo͞o,lēs| resort city in SE Brazil, in highlands in Rio de Janeiro state. Pop. 123,000.

Ter·mez |ter'mez| town in S Uzbekistan, on the N bank of the Amu Darya River, on the Afghan border. Pop. 90,000.

Ter·na·te |tər'nätē| volcanic island in Indonesia, in the Moluccas, W of Halmahera. Chief town: Ternate.

Ter·ni |'ternē| industrial town in central Italy, on the Nera River, capital of Terni province. Pop. 110,000.

Ter·no·pol |ter'nōpəl| (also **Tarnopol**) 1 administrative district in W Ukraine, N of the Dniester River. Pop. 1,175,000. 2 its capital, an industrial city. Pop. 218,000.

Ter·re·bonne |'terə,bän| city in S Quebec, a suburb N of Montreal. Pop. 39,768.

Ter·re Haute |ˌterə 'hōt; 'hət| commercial and industrial city in W Indiana, on the Wabash River. Pop. 57,483.

Te·ruel |tāroͦo'wel| market town in E central Spain, on the Turia River, capital of Teruel province. Pop. 31,000.

Tes·sin |te'seN| French and German name for TICINO.

Te·te |'tätə| commercial town in W central Mozambique, on the Zambezi River. Pop. 112,000. It is the capital of Tete province.

Te·thys Sea |'tēTHis| former sea on the E of PANGAEA, thought to have lain along the line between Gondwanaland and Laurasia, roughly from present-day Iberia E to SE Asia.

Té·touan |tāt'wän| (also **Tetuán**) industrial and tourist city in N Morocco. Pop. 272,000.

Te·to·vo |'tetōvō| city in NW Macedonia, a ski resort and commercial center W of Skopje. Pop. 181,000. It is an Albanian ethnic center.

Teu·to·bur·ger·wald |'toitə,boͦorgər,vält| (also called **Teutoburg Forest**) forested range in NW Germany, between Paderborn and Osnabrück. Its highest peak reaches 1,465 ft./447 m.

Te·ve·re |'tävärä| Italian name for the TIBER River.

Tewks·bury |'toͦoksb(ə)rē| town in NE Massachusetts, SE of Lowell. Pop. 27,266. It is an industrial and residential suburb.

Tex·ar·kana |ˌteksär'kænə| twin cities on the Texas-Arkansas border. The Texas city (pop. 31,656) is home to an army ordnance center. The Arkansas city (pop. 22,631) is also industrial and commercial.

Tex·as |'teksəs| see box. ☐ **Texan** *adj. & n.*

Tex·as City |'teksəs| port city in SE Texas, on Galveston Bay SE of Houston. Pop.

Texas

Capital: Austin
Largest city: Houston
Other cities: Abilene, Corpus Christi, Dallas, El Paso, Fort Worth, Galveston, Laredo, Lubbock, San Antonio, Waco
Population: 16,986,510 (1990); 19,759,614 (1998); 21,487,000 (2005 proj.)
Population rank (1990): 3
Rank in land area: 2
Abbreviation: TX; Tex.
Nickname: Lone Star State
Motto: 'Friendship'
Bird: mockingbird
Flower: bluebonnet
Tree: pecan
Songs: "Texas, Our Texas"; "The Eyes of Texas"
Noted physical features: Corpus Christi Bay; Port Corpus Christi, Port Galveston, Port Houston; Guadalupe Peak
Tourist attractions: The Alamo; Big Bend National Park; Guadalupe Mountains; Lyndon B. Johnson Space Center; Padre Island National Seashore
Admission date: December 29, 1845
Order of admission: 28
Name origin: From the Caddo Indian word *teyshas*, 'allies,' used by various native groups to refer to their mutual alliances; in the 1540s, Spanish explorers took this to be a tribal name, recording it as *Teyas* or *Tejas*, and applying it to the land north of the Rio Grande.

40,822. This oil and chemical industry center was the scene of a devastating explosion in April 1947.

Tex·co·co, Lake |tās'kōkō| (also **Tezcuco**) dry lake in central Mexico, E of present-day Mexico City. It was the site, on islands, of the Aztec capital Tenochtitlán.

Tex·el |'tesəl| island, largest of the West Frisian Islands of the Netherlands, in the North Sea.

Tha·ba·na Ntlen·ya·na |tä'bänä ntlen-'yänä| mountain in the Drakensberg Range, in Lesotho. At 11,424 ft./3,482 m., it is the highest peak in Africa S of Mount Kilimanjaro.

Thai·land, Gulf of |'tī,lænd; 'tīlənd| inlet of the South China Sea between the Malay Peninsula to the W and Thailand and Cambodia to the E. It was formerly known as the Gulf of Siam.

Thai·land |'tī,lænd; 'tīlənd| kingdom in SE Asia, on the Gulf of Thailand. Area:

Thailand

198,190 sq. mi./513,115 sq. km. Pop. 56,303,000. Language, Thai. Capital and largest city: Bangkok. Former name (until 1939) **Siam**. A regional power from the 14th to the 19th century, Siam lost territory to British and French colonialism in the 19th century. It was occupied by Japan in World War II and supported the U.S. in the Vietnam War, later experiencing a large influx of refugees from Cambodia, Laos, and Vietnam. The absolute monarchy was abolished in 1931, although the king remained head of state. Thailand produces rice and other crops, tin and other metals, and textiles and consumer goods. □ **Thai** *adj. & n.*

Thames |'temz| river of S England, flowing 210 mi./338 km. E from the Cotswolds in Gloucestershire through London to the North Sea. In Oxfordshire it is also called the **Isis**.

Thames River¹ |'ᴛʜᴀmz; 'tāmz; 'temz| estuarial river in SE Connecticut that flows from Norwich past New London and Groton to Long Island Sound.

Thames River² |'temz| river that flows 160 mi./260 km. across S Ontario, past London. It was the scene of an 1813 battle in which Tecumseh died.

Thane |'tänə| (also **Thana**) industrial and commercial town in W India, in Maharashtra state. Pop. 797,000.

Than·et, Isle of |'ᴛʜænət| E peninsula of Kent, in SE England, once separated by channels from the mainland. The resorts of Margate and Ramsgate are here. The Jutes are thought to have landed here in A.D. 449.

Than·ja·vur |ˌtənjə'vōor| (also **Tanjore**) city in S India, in Tamil Nadu state. Pop. 200,000. It is noted for its temples and is a leading center of dance and music in S India.

Thap·sus |'ᴛʜæpsəs| ancient seaport of NE Tunisia, S of present-day Sousse, the scene of a victory by Julius Caesar over

Pompey in 46 B.C., during the Roman civil war.

Thar Desert |'tär; 'tər| desert region to the E of the Indus River, in Rajasthan and Gujarat states of NW India and the Punjab and Sind regions of SE Pakistan. Also called **Great Indian Desert**.

Thá·sos |'ᴛʜᴀˌsaws| island in Greece, in the N Aegean Sea. Its capital is Límen.

Thebes¹ |'ᴛʜēbz| Greek name for an ancient city of Upper Egypt, whose ruins lie on the Nile about 420 mi./675 km. S of Cairo. It was the capital of Egypt under the 18th dynasty (*c.* 1550–1290 B.C.) and is the site of the temples of Luxor and Karnak.

Thebes² |'ᴛʜēbz| city in Greece, in Boeotia, NW of Athens. It became a major power following the defeat of the Spartans at the battle of Leuctra in 371 B.C. It was destroyed by Alexander the Great in 336 B.C. Modern Greek name **Thívai**. □ **Theban** *adj. & n.*

The·lon River |'ᴛʜēˌlawn| river that rises in the Northwest Territories and flows 550 mi./900 km. across Nunavut to Hudson Bay.

The·o·dore Roo·se·velt National Park |'ᴛʜēəˌdawr 'rōzəˌvelt| preserve in W North Dakota, incorporating the ranch home of the president as well as extensive badlands areas.

The·ra |'ᴛʜirə| Greek island in the S Cyclades. The island suffered a violent volcanic eruption in about 1500 B.C.; remains of an ancient Minoan civilization have been preserved beneath the pumice and volcanic debris. Also called **Santorini**. Greek name **Thíra**. In legend Metropolis, the capital of Atlantis, was here.

Ther·mop·y·lae |ᴛʜər'mäpəlē| pass between the mountains and the sea in Greece, about 120 mi./200 km. NW of Athens, originally narrow but now much widened by the recession of the sea. In 480 B.C. it was the scene of a heroic defense against the Persian army of Xerxes I by 6,000 Greeks; among them were 300 Spartans, all of whom, including their king Leonidas, were killed.

Thes·pi·ae |'ᴛʜespēˌē| ancient city of Greece, at the foot of Mount Helicon (present Elikón), where, according to Greek mythology, the Muses performed.

Thes·sa·lo·ní·ki |ˌᴛʜesələ'nēkē| industrial port in NE Greece, the second-largest city in Greece and capital of the Greek region of Macedonia. Pop. 378,000. Also called **Salonica**; Latin name **Thessalonica**.

Thes·sa·ly |ˈTHesəlē| ancient and modern region of NE Greece. Greek name **Thessalía**. □ **Thessalian** adj. & n.

Thet·ford Mines |ˈTHetfərd| industrial city in S Quebec, in the Notre Dame Mts. Pop. 17,273. It has been a major asbestos producer.

Thiès |ˈtyes| commercial and industrial city in W Senegal, E of Dakar. Pop. 201,000.

Thim·phu |THim'po͞o| (also **Thimbu**) the capital since 1952 of Bhutan, in the Himalayas. Pop. 30,000.

Thing·vel·lir |ˈTHiNG(g),vet,lēr| lava plain in W Iceland, NE of Reykjavik, seat from A.D. 930 of the Althing, the oldest parliament in the world. It is now a national park.

Thí·ra |ˈTHirə| Greek name for THERA.

Third River |ˈTHərd| huge drainage canal in Iraq, between the Euphrates and Tigris rivers, completed 1992 as part of a land reclamation project, which is controversial as threatening the way of life of the Marsh Arabs of S Iraq.

Third World |ˈTHərd 'wərld| term used during the Cold War to designate countries not aligned with either the capitalist West (the First World) or the communist East (the Second World). It came to connote underdevelopment. See FOURTH WORLD.

Thí·vai |ˈTHē,vi| Greek name for THEBES².

Thorn·ton |ˈTHawrntn| city in N central Colorado, a residential and commercial suburb S of Denver. Pop. 55,031.

Thou·sand Islands¹ |ˈTHowzənd| group of about 100 small islands off the N coast of Java, forming part of Indonesia. Indonesian name **Pulau Seribu**.

Thou·sand Islands² |ˈTHowzənd| noted resort area, a group of about 1,500 islands in a widening of the St. Lawrence River, just below Kingston, Ontario. Some of the islands are in Ontario, some in New York.

Thou·sand Oaks |ˈTHowzənd| industrial city in SW California, NW of Los Angeles. Pop. 104,352.

Thrace |ˈTHrās| ancient country lying W of the Black Sea and N of the Aegean. It is now divided among Turkey, Bulgaria, and Greece. □ **Thracian** adj. & n.

Thread·nee·dle Street |ˈTHred,nēdl| street in central London, containing the premises of the Bank of England ("the Old Lady of Threadneedle Street").

Three Gor·ges Dam |THrē 'gawrjəz| dam under construction on the Yangtze River N of Yichang, in Hubei province, E central China. Potentially the largest hydroelectric

project in the world, the dam will flood the scenic Yangtze gorges.

Three Mile Island |ˈTHrē ,mīl 'īlənd| island in the Susquehanna River near Harrisburg, Pennsylvania, site of a nuclear power station. In 1979 an accident damaged the reactor core, provoking strong reactions against the nuclear industry in the U.S.

Three Sis·ters |THrē 'sistərz| glacier-covered volcanic peaks in W central Oregon, in the Cascade Range, a noted wilderness area.

Throgs Neck |ˈTHrägz ,nek| peninsula in the SE Bronx, New York City, that gives its name to a major bridge to Queens (Long Island).

Thu·le¹ |ˈto͞olē; 'THo͞olē| settlement on the NW coast of Greenland, founded in 1910 by the Danish explorer Knud Rasmussen. Inuit name **Qaanaaq**.

Thu·le² |ˈto͞olē; 'THo͞olē| country described by the ancient Greek explorer Pytheas as being six days' sail N of Britain, most plausibly identified with Norway. It was regarded by the ancients as the northernmost part of the world (in Latin **Ultima Thule**).

Thun |to͞on| 1 town in the N foothills of the Bernese Alps, central Switzerland, on the Aare River. Pop. 37,000. 2 a lake in central Switzerland, formed by a widening of the Aare.

Thun·der Bay |ˈTHəndər| city on an inlet W of Lake Superior in SW Ontario. Pop. 113,946. One of Canada's major ports, an outlet for grain from the prairies, it was formed by the amalgamation in 1970 of Fort William and Port Arthur.

Thu·rin·gia |THo͝o'rinj(ē)ə| densely forested state of E central Germany, N of the Ore Mountains. Pop. 2,572,000. Capital: Erfurt. German name **Thüringen**.

Thur·so |ˈTHərsō| fishing port on the N coast of Scotland, in Highland region, the northernmost town on the mainland of Britain. Pop. 9,000.

Tia·hua·na·co |,tēäwä'näkō| archaeological site in W Bolivia, at in the Andes highlands at the SE shore of Lake Titicaca. Its pre-Incan monuments include the Gateway of the Sun.

Tian·an·men Square |tē'enə(n),men| large public square in Beijing, China. On the S edge of the Tatar, or Inner, City, it is the site of the Great Hall of People, museums, monuments, and Mao Zedong's tomb. During April–June 1989, massive antigovernment demonstrations were held here until brutally suppressed.

Tian·jin |tē'än'jin| (also **Tientsin**) industrial port in NE China, in Hubei province, the third-largest city in the country. Pop. 5,700,000.

Tian Shan |tē'än'sHän| (formerly **Tien Shan**) mountain range to the N of the Tarim Basin in Xinjiang, China, extending to the W into Kyrgyzstan.

Tian•shui |tē'än'sH(w)ē| city in Gansu province, central China, in the N foothills of the Qin Ling mountains W of Baoji, Shaanxi. Pop. 1,967,000.

Ti•ber |'tībər| river of central Italy, upon which Rome stands. It rises in the Tuscan Apennines and flows 252 mi./405 km. generally SW, entering the Tyrrhenian Sea at Ostia. Italian name **Tevere**.

Ti•be•ri•as, Lake |tī'birēəs| another name for Sea of Galilee (see GALILEE, SEA OF).

Ti•be•ri•as |tī'birēəs| resort town in NE Israel, on the Sea of Galilee. Pop. 36,000. It was a center of Jewish learning from the 2nd century, and the scholar Maimonides is buried here.

Ti•bes•ti Mountains |tə'bestē| mountain range in N central Africa, in the Sahara in N Chad and S Libya. It rises to 11,201 ft./3,415 m. at Emi Koussi, the highest point in the Sahara.

Ti•bet |tə'bet| mountainous country in Asia on the N side of the Himalayas, since 1965 forming an autonomous region in the W of China. Area: 474,314 sq. mi./1.23 million sq. km. Pop. 2,196,000. Official languages, Tibetan and Chinese. Capital and largest city: Lhasa. Chinese name **Xizang**. On the "roof of the world," Tibet has an average elevation of over 12,500 ft./4,000 m. Ruled by Buddhist lamas since the 7th century, it has been dominated by Mongols, Manchus, and China since the 13th century. After China crushed a revolt in 1959, the Dalai Lama fled into exile, and sporadic unrest continued in this largely pastoral region. □ **Tibetan** adj. & n.

Ti•ci•no |tī'CHēnō| predominantly Italian-speaking canton in S Switzerland, on the Italian border. Capital: Bellinzona. It joined the Swiss Confederation in 1803. French and German name **Tessin**.

Ti•con•der•o•ga |ˌtī,kändə'rōgə| industrial village in NE New York, in lowlands between Lakes George and Champlain. Pop. 2,770. Nearby Fort Ticonderoga was fought over repeatedly in the 1750s–80s.

Tide•wa•ter, the |'tī,wawtər; 'tīd,wätər| coastal regions of E Virginia, in which tidal water flows up the Potomac, Rappahannock, York, James, and smaller rivers. Early

17th-century British settlement focused here.

Ti•do•re |tē'dōrä| island in Indonesia, in the Moluccas, W of Halmahera.

Tien Shan |tē'en'sHän| see TIAN SHAN.

Tien•tsin |tē'ent'sin| see TIANJIN.

Tier•ra del Fue•go |tē'erə del 'fwägō| island at the S extremity of South America, separated from the mainland by the Strait of Magellan. Discovered by Ferdinand Magellan in 1520, it is now divided between Argentina and Chile.

Tie•tê River |tyä'tä| river that flows 500 mi./800 km. across S Brazil, from near the Atlantic coast, past São Paulo, to the Paraná River.

Tif•fin |'tifən| industrial city in NW Ohio, on the Sandusky River. Pop. 18,604.

Tif•lis |'tifləs| former official Russian name (1845–1936) for TBILISI.

Ti•ghi•na |ti'gēnə| (also known as **Bendery**) manufacturing town in Moldova, near the Dniester River. Pop. 142,000.

Ti•gray |ti'grā| (also **Tigré**) province of Ethiopia, in the N of the country, bordering Eritrea. Capital: Mekele. An ancient kingdom, Tigray was annexed as a province of Ethiopia in 1855. It engaged in a bitter guerrilla war against the government of Ethiopia 1975–91, during which time the region suffered badly from drought and famine. □ **Tigrayan** adj. & n.

Ti•gre |'tēgrä| city in E Argentina, a port and resort N of Buenos Aires. Pop. 256,000.

Ti•gris |'tīgrəs| river in SW Asia, the more easterly of the two rivers of ancient Mesopotamia. It rises in the mountains of E Turkey and flows 1,150 mi./1,850 km. SE through Iraq, passing through Baghdad, to join the Euphrates, forming the Shatt al-Arab, which flows into the Persian Gulf.

Ti•hwa |'dē'hwä| former name (until 1954) for URUMQI.

Ti•jua•na |ˌtēə'wänə| town in NW Mexico, in Baja California just S of the U.S. border. Pop. 743,000. A tourist center, it has a reputation for rowdiness.

Ti•kal |tē'käl| ancient Mayan city in the tropical Petén region of N Guatemala, with great plazas, pyramids, and palaces. It flourished A.D. 300–800.

Ti•krit |ti'krēt| (also **Tekrit**) town in N central Iraq, NW of Baghdad. The Muslim sultan Saladin (c.1138) and Iraqi president Saddam Hussein (1937) were born here.

Til•burg |'til,bərg| industrial city, a textile center, in the S Netherlands, in the province of North Brabant. Pop. 159,000.

Til•bury |'tilb(ə)rē| the principal port of

London and SE England for container ships, on the N bank of the Thames River in Essex.

Til·la·mook |'tiləmək; 'tilə,mo͞ok| city in NW Oregon. Pop. 3,001. It is the seat of Tillamook County, a dairying center, and is on Tillamook Bay, a fishing and resort hub.

Tim·a·ru |'timə,ro͞o| port and resort on the E coast of South Island, New Zealand. Pop. 28,000.

Tim·buk·tu |ˌtimbək'to͞o| (also **Timbuctoo**) town in N Mali. Pop. 20,000. It was formerly a trading center for gold and salt on trans-Saharan trade routes, reaching the height of its prosperity in the 16th century but falling into decline after its capture by the Moroccans in 1591. French name **Tombouctou**.

Times Beach |'tīmz| abandoned city in E central Missouri, SW of St. Louis, site of a 1980s evacuation due to chemical contamination.

Times Square |'tīmz| a focal point of Manhattan, New York City, around the intersection of Broadway and 42nd St. Its long-held reputation for seediness is giving way to redevelopment.

Tim·gad |'tim,gæd| (ancient name **Thamugadi**) historic city in NE Algeria, near Batna, founded by the Romans in the 1st century A.D. and abandoned by the 7th century.

Ti·miş·oa·ra |ˌtēmē'sHwärə| industrial and university city in W Romania. Pop. 325,000. Formerly part of Hungary, and the chief city of the Banat region, it has substantial Hungarian and German-speaking populations. Demonstrations here in 1989 led to the collapse of the communist government. Hungarian name **Temesvár**.

Tim·mins |'timinz| industrial city in E central Ontario, in a major mining district. Pop. 47,461.

Ti·mor |'tē,mawr; tē'mawr| the largest of the Lesser Sunda Islands, in the S Malay Archipelago. Pop.: East Timor 714,000, West Timor 3,383,000. The island was formerly divided into Dutch West Timor and Portuguese East Timor. In 1950 West Timor was absorbed into the newly formed Republic of Indonesia. In 1975 East Timor declared itself independent but was invaded and occupied by Indonesia (see EAST TIMOR). □ **Timorese** *adj. & n.*

Ti·mor Sea |'tē,mawr; tē'mawr| arm of the Indian Ocean between Timor and NW Australia.

Tin·douf |tēn'do͞of| oasis town in extreme W Algeria, in the Sahara Desert. Pop. 14,000. It has been involved in tensions between Morocco and Algeria over the WESTERN SAHARA.

Ti·ni·an |'tinēən| island in the W Pacific, in the Northern Mariana Islands. Pop. 2,000. Used by U.S. forces during World War II, it is noted as the site from which the planes that dropped atomic bombs on Hiroshima and Nagasaki took off.

Tin·ker Creek |'tiNGkər| stream in SW Virginia, near Roanoke, a focus of the nature writing of Annie Dillard.

Tin Pan Alley |ˌtin pæn 'ælē| name for the U.S. popular music business, taken from no particular street, but long associated with lower Manhattan, New York City.

Tin·ta·gel |tin'tæjəl| village on the coast of N Cornwall, England. Nearby are the ruins of Tintagel Castle, the legendary birthplace of King Arthur.

Tin·tern Abbey |'tintərn| 12th-century ruin in SE Wales, in Gwent, on the Wye River, immortalized in a poem by Wordsworth.

Tip·pe·ca·noe River |ˌtipəkə'no͞o| river that flows 170 mi./275 km. through Indiana. Battle Ground, near its meeting with the Wabash, is the site of the 1811 battle of Tippecanoe.

Tip·pe·rary |ˌtipə'rerē| county in the center of the Republic of Ireland, in the province of Munster. Pop. 134,000; county seats, Nenagh, Clonmel.

Ti·ra·na |ti'ränə| (also **Tiranë**) the capital and largest city of Albania, on the Ishm River in the central part. Pop. 210,000. Founded by the Turks in the 17th century, it became capital of Albania in 1920, and is the country's industrial and cultural center.

Ti·ras·pol |ti'ræspəl| manufacturing city in E Moldova, on the Dniester River NW of Odessa. Pop. 186,000.

Tir·go·vi·şte |tər'gōvēsHte| town in S central Romania, in an oil-producing region. Pop. 101,000.

Tir·gu Jiu |'tərgo͞o 'ZHēo͞o| capital of Gorj county in SW Romania. Pop. 93,000.

Tîr·gu Mu·reş |'tərgo͞o 'mo͞o,resH| industrial and commercial city in central Romania, on the Mureş River. Pop. 165,000.

Ti·rich Mir |'tiricH'mir| the highest peak in the Hindu Kush, in NW Pakistan, rising to 25,230 ft./7,690 m.

Tir-nan-Og |ˌtirnə'nawg| in Irish folklore, a land of eternal youth, the equivalent of ELYSIUM.

Ti·rol |tə'rōl| German name for TYROL.

Tir·u·chi·ra·pal·li |ˌtirəCHə'räpəlē| (also **Tiruchchirappalli**) industrial city and rail junction in Tamil Nadu, S India. Pop. 387,000. Also called **Trichinopoly**.

Ti·ru·nel·ve·li |ˌtiro͞o'nelvəlē| commercial and industrial city in S India, in Tamil Nadu state. Pop. 366,000. The Christian saint Francis Xavier began his Indian ministry here in the 1540s.

Ti·ru·pa·ti |'tiro͞o,pätē| city in S India, in Andhra Pradesh state, NW of Madras. Pop. 189,000. It is a major Hindu religious site.

Ti·rup·pur |'tirə,po͞or| commercial town in S India, in Tamil Nadu state. Pop. 306,000. A temple here to the Hindu god Shiva is a pilgrimage site.

Ti·ryns |'tirənz; 'tīrənz| ancient city of Argolis Greece, in the NE Peloponnese. It figures prominently in Greek legend.

Ti·sa |'tēsä| Serbian name for TISZA.

Ti·sza |'tisaw| river in SE Europe, the longest tributary of the Danube, which rises in the Carpathian Mountains of W Ukraine and flows 600 mi./960 km. W into Hungary, then S, joining the Danube in Serbia NW of Belgrade. Serbian name **Tisa**.

Ti·ta·no, Monte |tē'tänō| mountain in the Republic of San Marino, notable for its three peaks. Height: 2,437 ft./743 m.

Ti·ti·ca·ca, Lake |ˌtiti'käkə; ˌtētē'käkə| lake in the Andes, on the border between Peru and Bolivia. At 12,497 ft./3,809 m., it is the highest large (3,200 sq. mi./8,288 sq. km.) lake in the world.

Ti·to·grad |'tētō,gräd| former name (1946–93) for PODGORICA.

Ti·to·vo Uži·ce |'tētaw,vaw 'o͞oZHētse| commercial and industrial city in W Serbia. Pop. 83,000.

Ti·tov Ve·les |'tētawv 'veles| commercial city in central Macedonia, on the Vardar River SE of Skopje. Pop. 65,000.

Ti·tus·ville¹ |'tītəs,vil| commercial and resort city in E central Florida, near Cape Canaveral. Pop. 39,394.

Ti·tus·ville² |'tītəs,vil| historic city in NW Pennsylvania, on Oil Creek. Pop. 6,434. The first operative oil well was drilled here in 1859.

Ti·vo·li |'tivəlē| commune NE of Rome. Pop. 51,000. A major tourist center, it is known for its waterfalls on the Aniene River and for its many opulent villas, chief among them the Villa d'Este and the remains of the villa of the Emperor Hadrian.

Ti·vo·li Gardens |'tivəlē| amusement park in central Copenhagen, Denmark, with theaters, rides, games, a lake, and a concert hall.

Ti·zi Ou·zou |tē'zi'o͞o'zo͞o| commercial and industrial town in N Algeria, E of Algiers. Pop. 101,000. It is the chief town of **Kabylia**.

Tlal·ne·pan·tla |ˌtlälnä'päntlə| (official name **Tlalnepantla de Baz**) city in central Mexico, just N of Mexico City, of which it is an industrial suburb. Pop. 702,000.

Tlal·pan |tläl'pän| (also **Tlalpam**) city in central Mexico, in the Distrito Federal, just S of Mexico City, of which it is a suburb. Pop. 485,000.

Tla·que·pa·que |ˌtläkä'päkä| town in SW Mexico, in Jalisco state, just SE of Guadalajara, of which it is a suburb. Pop. 328,000. Its folk arts are well known.

Tlax·ca·la |tlä'skälə| **1** state of E central Mexico, the smallest in the country. Area: 1,551 sq. mi./4,016 sq. km. Pop. 764,000. **2** its capital city. Pop. 25,000.

Tlem·cen |tlem'sen| industrial city in NW Algeria. Pop. 146,000. In the 13th–15th centuries it was the capital of a Berber dynasty.

To·a·ma·si·na |ˌto͞oəməsēnə| (formerly **Tamatave**) port city in E Madagascar, on the Indian Ocean. Pop. 127,000. On a rail line from Antananarivo, it is the chief port in Madagascar.

To·bac·co Road |tə'bækō| term for economically marginal parts of the U.S. upper South, drawn from a road along which early tobacco growers transported their product to river ports.

To·ba·go |tə'bāgō| island in the Lesser Antilles, West Indies, a constituent of TRINIDAD AND TOBAGO. Lying NE of Trinidad, it is 116 sq. mi./300 sq. mi. in area and has a pop. of 50,000. Scarborough is its capital.

To·bol River |tə'bawl| river (1,042 mi./1,677 km.) in Kazakhstan and W Russia in Asia, rising in the SE foothills of the Ural Mts. and flowing into the Irtysh River at Tobolsk.

To·bolsk |tə'bawlsk| industrial town in W Russia, in Siberia, on the Irtysh River. Pop. 94,000. Its industries center around oil and gas production.

To·bruk |'tō,bro͞ok; tō'bro͞ok| port on the Mediterranean coast of NE Libya. Pop. 94,000. It was the scene of fierce fighting during World War II. Arabic name **Tubruq**.

To·can·tins |ˌtōkən'tēNz| **1** river of South America, which rises in central Brazil and flows 1,640 mi./2,640 km. N, joining the Pará to enter the Atlantic through a large estuary at Belém. **2** state of central Brazil, formerly the N part of Goias. Pop. 920,000. Capital: Palmas.

Todd River |'täd| river in central Australia that flows only in wet years, 200 mi./320 km. from the MacDonnell Ranges to the Simpson Desert.

Tog·gen·burg |'tawgən,bo͞org| district in NE Switzerland, on the Thur River. Farming and tourism are the major industries.

To·gliat·ti |tawl'yätē| industrial city and river port in SW Russia, on the Volga River. Pop. 642,000. It was founded in 1738 but relocated in the mid-1950s to make way for the Kuibyshev reservoir. Former name (until 1964) **Stavropol**. Russian name **Tolyatti**.

To·go |'tōgō| republic in W Africa with a short coastline on the Gulf of Guinea. Area: 21,933 sq. mi./56,785 sq. km. Pop. 3,761,000. Languages, French (official), W African languages. Capital: Lomé. Official name **Togolese Republic**. The former Togoland, lying between Ashanti and Dahomey (Benin), was controlled by Germany and then Britain before independence in 1960. It is agricultural and has mineral resources. □ **Togolese** *adj. & n.*

Togo

To·ho·ku |tō'hōko͞o| region of Japan, in NE Honshu. Capital: Sendai.

To·kaj |'taw,kī| (also **Tokay**) town in NE Hungary, on the Tisza River. The well-known sweet wine is produced here.

To·ke·lau |'tōkə,low| group of three atolls in the W Pacific, between Kiribati and Samoa, forming an overseas territory of New Zealand. Pop. 1,200. Formerly **Union Islands**.

To·ko·ro·za·wa |,tōkō'rōzäwä| city in E central Japan, on E central Honshu, a suburb NE of Tokyo. Pop. 303,000.

To·ku·shi·ma |,tōko͞o'sHēmä| port city in W Japan, on SE Shikoku. Pop. 263,000.

To·ku·ya·ma |,tōko͞o'yämä| port city in W Japan, on SW Honshu, at W end of Inland Sea. Pop. 111,000.

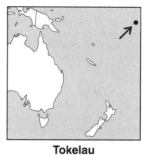

Tokelau

To·kyo |'tōkē,ō| the capital and largest city of Japan, capital of Kanto region, on Tokyo Bay, E central Honshu. Pop. 8,163,000. Formerly called Edo (or Yedo), it was the center of the military government under the shoguns (1603–1867). It was renamed Tokyo ("eastern capital") in 1868, when it replaced Kyoto ("western capital") as the imperial capital. An industrial, commercial, financial, and cultural center, it is also, with nearby Yokohama, a major port. The Tokyo metropolitan area, with a pop. of 28 million, is by some calculations the largest in the world.

Tol·bu·khin |tawl'bo͞oKHin| former name (1949–91) for DOBRICH.

To·le·do[1] |tə'lēdō| industrial city and port on Lake Erie, in NW Ohio. Pop. 332,943.

To·le·do[2] |tō'lädō| port city in the Philippines, on central Cebu. Pop. 120,000.

To·le·do[3] |tō'lädō| historic city in central Spain, on the Tagus River, capital of Castilla-La Mancha region. Pop. 64,000. It was a preeminent city and cultural center of Castile. Toledan steel and sword blades have been famous since the first century B.C.

Tol·lund |'tälənd| wetland in central Jutland, Denmark, where the remains of a much-studied Iron Age (c.500 B.C.–A.D. 400) man were found in 1950.

Tol·pud·dle |'täl,pədəl| village in SW England, in Dorset, made famous by the "Tolpuddle Martyrs," farmworkers whose 1830s attempts to form a union led to transportation as criminals to Australia.

To·lu·ca |tō,lo͞okä| commercial and industrial city in central Mexico, capital of the state of Mexico. Pop. 488,000. It lies at the foot of the extinct volcano Nevado de Toluca, at an altitude of 8,793 ft./2,680 m. Full name **Toluca de Lerdo**.

Tol·yat·ti |tawl'yätē| Russian name for TOGLIATTI.

Tom River |,tawm| river (450 mi./725 km.

long) in central Russia. It rises in the Altai Mts. and flows NNW into the Ob River near Tomsk.

To·ma·ko·mai |tō'mäkō,mī| industrial port city in N Japan, on S Hokkaido, SE of Sapporo. Pop. 160,000.

Tom·big·bee River |täm'bigbē| river that flows 400 mi./640 km. from NE Mississippi through W Alabama, to the Alabama River. In the 1980s the **Tennessee-Tombigbee Waterway** connected it with the Tennessee River.

Tom·bouc·tou |,tōNbōōk'tōō| French name for TIMBUKTU.

Tomb·stone |'tōōm,stōn| historic frontier city in SE Arizona. Pop. 1,220. It is the scene of the 1881 gunfight at the O.K. Corral.

To·mis |'tōməs| ancient name for CONSTANŢA.

Tomsk |tämsk| industrial city in S Siberian Russia, a port on the Tom River. Pop. 506,000.

Ton·a·wan·da |,tänə'wändə| industrial city in W New York, on the Niagara River N of Buffalo. Pop. 17,284.

Ton·ga |'täNG(g)ə| kingdom in the S Pacific consisting of an island group SE of Fiji. Area: 258 sq. mi./668 sq. km. Pop. 98,000. Official languages, Tongan and English. Capital: Nuku'alofa. Also called the **Friendly Islands**. Comprising some 170 islands and atolls, Tonga was controlled by Britain 1900–70. Fishing and tropical agriculture are important. □ **Tongan** adj. & n.

Tonga

Tong·a·ri·ro, Mount |,täNG(g)ə'rirō| mountain in North Island, New Zealand. It rises to a height of 6,457 ft./1,968 m. and is held sacred by the Maoris.

Ton·gass National Forest preserve in SE Alaska, the largest U.S. national forest, in the Panhandle and on islands in the Alexander Archipelago, focus of 1990s disputes over logging.

Tong·a·ta·pu |,täNG(g)ä'täpōō| largest

(100 sq. mi./260 sq. km.) island of Tonga. Nuku'alofa, the capital, is here.

Tong·chuan |'təNG'CHōō(w)än| industrial city in Shaanxi province, central China, N of Xi'an. Pop. 404,000.

Tong·hua |'təNG'hwä| city in Jilin province, NE China, E of Shenyang. Pop. 373,000

Ton·gi |'tawNGgē| (also **Tungi**) industrial city in central Bangladesh, N of Dhaka. Pop. 165,000.

Tong·ling |'tōōNG'liNG| city in Anhui province, E China, in the Yangtze River valley SW of Nanjing. Pop. 228,000.

Ton·kin, Gulf of |'tän'kin; 'täNG,kin| arm of the South China Sea, bounded by the coasts of S China and northern Vietnam and the island of Hainan. Its chief port is Haiphong. A disputed naval incident here in 1964 was followed by greatly increased U.S. military involvement in Vietnam.

Ton·kin |'tän'kin; 'käNG'kin| (also **Tongking; Tonking**) former French protectorate in SE Asia, on territory, centered on the Red River delta, constituting most of present-day northern Vietnam.

Ton·lé Sap |,tänlä'säp| lake in central Cambodia, linked to the Mekong River by the Tonlé Sap river. It triples in size during the wet season (June–Nov.), and has fisheries. Angkor stands on the NW shore.

Too·ele |tōō'welə| city in NW Utah. Pop. 13,887. Once a mining center, it has also been engaged in the building and dismantling of weapons.

Too·woom·ba |tə'wōōmbə| town in Queensland, Australia, to the W of Brisbane. Pop. 76,000. It was formerly known as The Swamps.

To·pe·ka |tə'pēkə| industrial city, the capital of Kansas, in the E central part. Pop. 119,883.

Top·ka·pi Palace former residence of the Ottoman sultans in Istanbul (then Constantinople), Turkey. It is now a museum famed for its jewels and for belongings of the prophet Muhammad.

Tor·bay |,tawr'bā| borough in Devon, SW England, on Tor Bay. Pop. 121,000. It was formed in 1968 from the amalgamation of the seaside resorts Torquay, Paignton, and Brixham.

Tor·de·sil·las |tawrdä'sē(l)yäs| village in N Spain, on the Duero River. A treaty signed here in 1494 between Spain and Portugal established the boundary between their respective colonial properties worldwide.

Tor·gau |'tawr,gow| port city in eastern central Germany, on the Elbe River. Pop.

22,000. The first meeting between U.S. and Soviet troops as they advanced into Germany in 1945 took place here.

To·ri·no |tō'rēnō| Italian name for TURIN.

Torn·gat Mountains |'tawrngæt| section of the E edge of the Canadian Shield, in E Labrador, rising to 5,420 ft./1,652 m. at Mt. Caubvick, on the Quebec border.

Tor·nio |'tawrnē,ō| river that rises in NE Sweden and flows 356 mi./566 km. generally S, forming the border between Sweden and Finland before emptying into the Gulf of Bothnia. Swedish name **Torne Älv**.

To·ron·to |tə'räntō| the capital of Ontario and center of the largest metropolitan area in Canada, on the north shore of Lake Ontario. Pop. 635,395; metropolitan area pop. 3,893,000. Founded in 1793, it was originally named York but in 1834 was renamed Toronto, from a Huron word mean 'meeting place.' It is the financial, commercial, and industrial hub of Canada.

Tor·quay |tawr'kē| resort town in SW England, in Devon, administratively part of Torbay since 1968. Pop. 57,000.

Tor·rance |'tawrəns| commercial and industrial city in SW California, S of Los Angeles. Pop. 133,107.

Tor·re An·nun·zia·ta |'tawrä ä,nŏŏnsē-'yätä| port city and seaside resort in S Italy, on the Bay of Naples at the foot of Mount Vesuvius. Pop. 56,000.

Tor·re del Gre·co |'tawrä del 'grekō| port and seaside resort in S Italy, on the Bay of Naples, near Mount Vesuvius. Pop. 104,000. It has suffered repeatedly from eruptions from Mount Vesuvius.

Tor·re·ón |,tawrä'ōn| industrial and commercial city in N Mexico, in Coahuila state. Pop. 460,000.

Tor·res Strait |'tawriz| channel separating the N tip of Queensland, Australia, from the island of New Guinea and linking the Arafura and the Coral seas.

Tor·res Ve·dras |'tawrəs 'vädrəsH| commune in W Portugal, N of Lisbon. Pop. 11,000. The town is known for its line of fortifications, erected in 1809 to defend against the French.

Tor·ring·ton |'tawriNGtən| historic industrial and commercial city in NW Connecticut, on the Naugatuck River. Pop. 33,687.

Tórs·havn |'tawrs,houn| (also **Thorshavn**) the capital of the Faroe Islands, a port on the island of Strømø. Pop. 14,000. It has been a governmental center since the 9th century.

Tor·to·la |tawr'tōlə| the principal island of the British Virgin Islands. Its chief town, Road Town, is the capital of the islands.

Tor·tu·ga Island |tawr'tōōgə| (French name **Île de la Tortue**) island off the N coast of Haiti, in the Atlantic, a notorious haunt of pirates in the 17th century.

To·ry Island |'tō,rē| small island off the coast of NW Ireland, in County Donegal, a noted pirate haven in legend.

To·sca·na |tō'skänə| Italian name for TUSCANY.

Tot·ten·ham |'tätnəm| district of N Greater London, England, part of the borough of Haringey.

Tot·to·ri |tō'tōrē| port city in W Japan, on S Honshu. Pop. 142,000.

Toub·kal, Mount |tōōb'käl| (Arabic name **Djebel Toubkal**) peak in S central Morocco, S of Marrakech. At 13,665 ft./4,165 m., it is the highest point in the Atlas Mts. and in N Africa.

Toul |tōōl| fortress town in NE France, on the Moselle River. Pop. 17,000. Primarily agricultural, it also has some light industry.

Tou·lon |tōō'lawN| port and naval base on the Mediterranean coast of S France. Pop. 170,000.

Tou·louse |tōō'lōōz| city in SW France, on the Garonne River, principal city of the Midi-Pyrénées region. Pop. 366,000. It is a high-tech industrial and educational center.

Tou·raine |tōō'rēn| region and former province in W central France, comprising the area around Tours. It is known for its wines and for the medieval and Renaissance chateaus that dot the Loire valley.

Tou·rane |tōō'rän| former name for DA NANG.

Tour·coing |tōōr'kweN| textile-manufacturing town in NW France, near the Belgian border. Pop. 94,000.

Tour·nai |tōōr'nā| town in Belgium, a textile center on the Scheldt River near the French border. Pop. 68,000. It was controlled by the counts of Flanders from the 9th century until taken by France in 1188; it returned to the Netherlands in 1814. Flemish name **Doornik**.

Tours |'tōōr| industrial and ecclesiastical city in W central France, on the Loire River. Pop. 133,000.

Tow·er Ham·lets |'tow,ər 'hæmləts| industrial and residential borough of E London, England, along the N of the Thames River. Pop. 154,000. Bethnal Green, Bow, Limehouse, Millwall, and Wapping are here.

Tow·er of Lon·don |'towər əv 'ləndən|

fortress in London, England, just E of the old City walls, on the N side of the River Thames. Begun in the 11th century, it now draws tourists to such attractions as the crown jewels.

Town 'n' Coun·try |'town ən 'kəntrē| residential community in W Florida, NW of Tampa. Pop. 60,946.

Tow·son |'towsən| suburban community in N Maryland, N of Baltimore. Pop. 49,445.

Towns·ville |'townz,vil| industrial port and resort on the coast of Queensland, NE Australia. Pop. 101,000.

To·ya·ma |tō'yämä| industrial port city in central Japan, on central Honshu. Pop. 321,000.

To·yo·ha·shi |,tōyō'häsHē| city in central Japan, on S central Honshu, S of Nagoya. Pop. 338,000.

To·yo·na·ka |,tōyō'näkä| city in W central Japan, on S Honshu, a suburb N of Osaka. Pop. 410,000.

To·yo·ta |toi'ōtə| (also **Toyoda**) industrial city in central Japan, on S central Honshu. Pop. 332,000. It is dominated by the Toyota Motor Company.

Trab·zon |træb'zän| port on the Black Sea in N Turkey. Pop. 144,000. In 1204, after the sack of Constantinople by the Crusaders, an offshoot of the Byzantine Empire was founded with Trabzon as its capital, which was annexed to the Ottoman Empire in 1461. Also called **Trebizond**.

Tra·cy |'trāsē| commercial and industrial city in N central California, in the San Joaquin Valley. Pop. 33,558.

Trades, the |'trādz| ocean regions in which the trade winds blow steadily from the NE (in the N hemisphere) or SE (in the S hemisphere). They lie within about 25° from the equator in each hemisphere, inside the **horse latitudes** and outside the equatorial **doldrums**.

Tra·fal·gar, Cape |trə'fælgər| cape on the coast of S Spain. The British navy won a decisive battle here against the French and Spanish navies in 1805, during the Napoleonic Wars.

Tra·fal·gar Square |trə'fælgər| public square in central London, England, in Westminster. Charing Cross is on the S side, the National Gallery on the N side, of this focal point.

Trail |trāl| industrial city in SE British Columbia, a mining and metal industry center. Pop. 7,919.

Trail of Tears |'trāl əv 'tērz| historic route or routes over which the Cherokee and other tribes moved W toward Oklahoma after being expelled from Georgia and neighboring states in the 1830s and 1840s.

Tra·lee |trə'lē| the county seat of Kerry, a port on the SW coast of the Republic of Ireland. Pop. 17,000.

Trans Alai Mountains |'trænz ə'lī| range in Kyrgyzstan, Tajikistan, and China. Lenin Peak, at 23,382 ft./7,127 m., is the highest in the range.

Trans-Alaska Pipeline |'trænzə'læskə| oil conduit that extends 800 mi./1,300 km. from Prudhoe Bay, on the North Slope of Alaska, to Valdez, on Prince William Sound.

Trans·ant·arc·tic Mountains |,trænz-,ænt'ärk,tik| mountain chain extending across Antarctica, separating Greater Antarctica from Lesser Antarctica and the Ross Ice Shelf. It reaches 14,275 ft./4,351 m. at Mount Markham.

Trans-Canada Highway |,trænz'kænədə| route between Victoria, British Columbia, and Saint John's, Newfoundland. At 4,860 mi./7,820 km., it is claimed to be the longest national highway in the world.

Trans·cau·ca·sia |,trænzkaw'kāzHə| region lying to the S of the Caucasus Mts., between the Black Sea and the Caspian, and comprising the present-day republics of Georgia, Armenia, and Azerbaijan. It was created the Transcaucasian Soviet Federated Socialist Republic in 1922, but was broken up into its constituent republics in 1936. □ **Transcaucasian** adj.

Trans·jor·dan |trænz'jawrdn| former name (until 1949) of the region E of the Jordan River now forming the main part of the kingdom of Jordan. □ **Transjordanian** adj.

Trans·kei |træn(t)'skī| former homeland established in South Africa for the Xhosa people, now part of the province of Eastern Cape.

Trans-Siberian Railway |trænsī'birēən| rail line that links European Russia with the Pacific coast. Built 1891–1904, it extends from Moscow through Vladivostok to the Sea of Japan, a distance of 5,786 mi./9,311 km. An extension stretches 1,952 mi./3,102 km. from Ust-Kut to the Pacific.

Trans·vaal |træns'väl| (also **the Transvaal**) former province in NE South Africa, lying N of the Vaal River. In 1994 it was divided into Northern Transvaal (now Northern), Eastern Transvaal (now Mpumalanga), Pretoria-Witwatersrand-Vereeniging (now Gauteng), and the E part of North-West Province.

Trans·verse Ranges |trænz'vərs| term

for various mountain ranges that cross S California, and are often considered the divider between N and S. See also TEHACHAPI Mts.

Tran·syl·va·nia[1] |ˌtrænsəlˈvānēə| large tableland region of NW Romania, separated from the rest of the country by the Carpathian Mts. and the Transylvanian Alps. Part of Hungary until it became a principality of the Ottoman Empire in the 16th century, it was returned to Hungary at the end of the 17th century and was incorporated into Romania in 1918. From Latin *trans* 'across, beyond' + *silva* 'forest'. □ **Transylvanian** *adj.*

Tran·syl·va·nia[2] |ˌtrænsəlˈvānēə| in U.S. history, unrecognized fourteenth colony that was proposed in the 1770s in what is now central Kentucky and neighboring Tennessee.

Tra·pa·ni |ˈträpänē| port and trade center on the NW coast of Sicily, in S Italy, capital of Trapani province. Pop. 73,000.

Tra·si·me·no, Lake |ˌträziˈmänō| lake in central Italy, W of Perugia. Hannibal defeated the Romans here in 217 B.C. in the Second Punic War, and there was heavy fighting between German and British troops during World War II.

Trás-os-Montes |ˈtræˌzōōzH ˈmōnˌtēsH| mountainous region of NE Portugal, N of the Douro River.

Trav·an·core |ˈtrævənˌkawr| (also **Tiruvankur**) region and former state in SW India, between the Malabar Coast and the Western Ghats in present-day Kerala state.

Trav·erse City |ˈtrævərs| resort and industrial port in Michigan, in the NW of the Lower Peninsula, on Lake Michigan. Pop. 15,155.

Trav·nik |ˈträvnēk| town in W central Bosnia and Herzegovina. Pop. 64,000. It was the capital of Bosnia 1686–1850.

Treb·bia River |ˈtrebyä| river (71 mi./114 km. long) in NW Italy that rises E of Genoa and flows into the Po River NW of Piacenza.

Treb·i·zond |ˈtrebəˌzänd| another name for TRABZON.

Tre·blin·ka |trəˈbliNGkə| site of a World War II Nazi concentration camp outside Warsaw, Poland.

Trem·blant, Mont |ˌmō ˈtremˌblänt; ˌmō ˌträˈblä| peak of the Laurentians in S Quebec, NW of Montreal, a noted ski resort.

Treng·ga·nu |treNGˈgänōō| (also **Terengganu**) state of Malaysia, on the E coast of the Malay Peninsula. Capital: Kuala Trengganu.

Trent |trent| the chief river of central England, which rises in Staffordshire and flows 170 mi./275 km. generally northeastward, uniting with the River Ouse 15 mi./25 km. W of Hull to form the Humber estuary.

Trent Canal |trent| (also **Trent-Severn Waterway**) waterway in S Ontario that connects Lake Huron (at Port Severn on Georgian Bay) with Lake Ontario (at Trenton). It was begun in the 1830s.

Trentino–Alto Adi·ge |trenˈtēnō ˌältō ˈädēˌjä| region of NE Italy. Capital: Bolzano. On the border with Austria, it includes the Dolomites.

Tren·to |ˈtrentō| historic industrial and commercial city on the Adige River in N Italy. Pop. 102,000.

Tren·ton[1] |ˈtrentən| industrial city, the capital of New Jersey, in the W central part on the Delaware River. Pop. 88,675.

Tren·ton[2] |ˈtrentən| industrial port city in SE Ontario, on the Bay of Quinte off Lake Ontario. Pop. 16,908. It is the E terminus of the Trent Canal.

Trèves |trev| the French name for TRIER.

Tre·vi·so |träˈvēzō| agricultural market and industrial city in NE Italy, capital of the province of Treviso, on the Sile and Botteniga rivers. Pop. 84,000.

Tri·Be·Ca |trīˈbēkə| residential and commercial section of S Manhattan, New York City, noted for its lofts. Its name derives from *Tri*angle *Be*low *Ca*nal Street.

Tri·bor·ough Bridge |ˈtrībəˌrō| bridge complex linking the Bronx, Queens, and Manhattan, in New York City, opened in 1936.

Trich·i·nop·o·ly |ˌtriCHəˈnäpəlē| another name for TIRUCHIRAPALLI.

Tri·chur |triˈCHōōr| (also **Thrissur**) commercial town in S India, in Kerala state. Pop. 275,000. It is an important Hindu religious center.

Tri·den·tine Alps |trīˈdenˌdīn| another name for the DOLOMITE Mts.

Trier |ˈtrir| city on the Mosel River in Rhineland-Palatinate, western Germany. Pop. 99,000. French name **Trèves**. Established by a Germanic tribe, the Treveri, *c.*400 B.C., Trier is one of the oldest cities in Europe. It was a powerful archbishopric from 815 until the 18th century, but fell into decline after the French occupation in 1797. Today it is noted as a wine and industrial center.

Tri·este |trēˈest| city in NE Italy, the largest port on the Adriatic and capital of Friuli–Venezia Giulia region. Pop. 231,000. Formerly held by Austria (1382–

1918), Trieste was annexed by Italy after World War I. The Free Territory of Trieste was created after World War II but returned to Italy in 1954.

Tri•glav |'trē͵gläv| mountain in the Julian Alps, NW Slovenia, near the Italian border. Rising to 9,392 ft. (2,863 m), it is the highest peak in the mountains E of the Adriatic.

Tri•ka•la |'trəkälä| (also **Trikala**) commercial city in Trikkala department, N central Greece. Pop. 41,000. It is said to be the birthplace of Aesculapius, the father of medicine, and was noted in ancient times for its medical school.

Tri•mon•ti•um |trē'mawntēyəm| Roman name for PLOVDIV.

Trin•co•ma•lee |͵triNGkōmə'lē| the principal port of Sri Lanka, on the E coast. Pop. 44,000. It was the chief British naval base in SE Asia during World War II after the fall of Singapore.

Trin•i•dad and To•ba•go |'trinədæd ən tə-'bāgō| republic in the West Indies consisting of two islands of the NE coast of Venezuela. Area: 1,981 sq. mi./5,128 sq. km. Pop. 1,249,000. Languages, English (official), Creole. Capital and largest city: Port-of-Spain (on Trinidad). Trinidad, much larger and inhabited by Arawaks, was a Spanish colony. Tobago, a Carib island, was colonized by France and Britain. Britain controlled both by the early 19th century. Independence came in 1962. Oil refining and trade are central to the economy. □ **Trinidadian** *adj. & n.* **Tobagan** *adj. & n.*

Trinidad & Tobago

Trin•i•ty Mountains |'triniətē| forested range of the Klamath Mts. in NW California. The Trinity River flows from it.

Trin•i•ty River |'trinitē| river that flows 550 mi./900 km. across Texas to the Gulf of Mexico. It rises in four main headstreams, the West, Clear, Elm, and East forks.

Trip•o•li¹ |'tripəlē| port in NW Lebanon.

Pop. 160,000. It was founded *c.*700 B.C. and was the capital of the Phoenician triple federation formed by the city-states Sidon, Tyre, and Arvad. Today it is a major port and commercial center of Lebanon. Arabic name **Tarabulus Ash-Sham** ('eastern Tripoli'); also **Trâblous**.

Trip•o•li² |'tripəlē| the capital and chief port of Libya, on the Mediterranean coast in the NW of the country. Pop. 991,000. Founded by Phoenicians in the 7th century BC, its ancient name was Oea. Arabic name **Tarabulus Al-Gharb** ('western Tripoli').

Trip•o•lis |'tripələs| summer resort and commercial center in S Greece, in the Peloponnesus. Pop. 22,000. It is the capital of Arcadia department.

Trip•o•li•ta•nia |͵tripələ'tānēə| coastal region surrounding Tripoli in North Africa, in what is now NE Libya. □ **Tripolitanian** *adj. & n.*

Tri•pu•ra |'tripərə| state in the far NE of India, on the E border of Bangladesh. Pop. 2,745,000. Capital: Agartala. An ancient Hindu kingdom, Tripura acceded to India after independence in 1947, and achieved full status as a state in 1972.

Tris•tan da Cu•nha |͵tristən də 'kōͦn(y)ə| the largest of a small group of volcanic islands in the S Atlantic 1,320 mi./2,112 km. SW of the British colony of St. Helena, of which it is a dependency. Pop. 292. It was discovered in 1506 by the Portuguese admiral Tristão da Cunha and annexed to Britain in 1816.

Tri•van•drum |tri'vændrəm| the capital of the state of Kerala, a port on the SW (Malabar) coast of India. Pop. 524,000.

Tr•na•va |'tərnəvə| market and ecclesiastical town in W Slovakia, NE of Bratislava. Pop. 72,000.

Tro•ad |'trō͵æd| (also **Troas**) ancient region of NW Asia Minor, of which ancient Troy was the chief city.

Tro•bri•and Islands |'trōbrē͵ænd| small group of islands in the SW Pacific, in Papua New Guinea, off the SE tip of the island of New Guinea.

Tro•ca•de•ro |͵träkə'derō| plaza in Paris, France, on the Right Bank of the Seine, opposite the Eiffel Tower. The plaza, built for a 1937 World's Fair, is the site of a major art museum.

Trois-Rivières |͵trwärēv'yer| (English name **Three Rivers**) historic industrial city in S Quebec, on the St. Lawrence River at the mouth of the St.-Maurice River. Pop. 49,426.

Trom•sø |'trōͦm͵sōͦ| the principal city of

Arctic Norway, situated on an island in Troms County. Pop. 51,000.

Trond·heim |'trōōn,hīm| historic port city in W central Norway, the second-largest city in the country. Pop. 138,000. It was the capital of Norway during the Viking period.

Troon |trōōn| town on the W coast of Scotland, In South Ayrshire, noted for its golf course. Pop. 14,000.

Trop·ics, the |'träpiks| region that lies between 23° 27′ N (the **Tropic of Cancer**) and 23° 27′ S (the **Tropic of Capricorn**). These are the outer limits of the zone in which the sun is ever directly overhead (June 21 in the N, Dec. 22 in the S). □ **tropical** adj.

Tros·sachs |'träsəks| (also **the Trossachs**) picturesque wooded valley in central Scotland, between Loch Achray and the lower end of Loch Katrine.

Trou·ville |trōōvēl| (also called **Trouville-sur-Mer**) resort and seaport on the English Channel, in NW France. Pop. 7,000.

Trow·bridge |'trō,brij| town in SW England, the county seat of Wiltshire. Pop. 23,000.

Troy[1] |troi| (also **Ilium, Ilion,** or **Troia**) ancient city of NW Asia Minor, S of the Dardanelles in present-day Turkey, according to legend besieged and destroyed by Greek forces 3,200 years ago. Its remains have been found at Hissarlik, on the Menderes River. □ **Trojan** adj. & n.

Troy[2] |troi| residential and commercial city in SE Michigan. Pop. 72,884.

Troy[3] |troi| industrial city in E New York, on the Hudson and Mohawk rivers just NE of Albany. Pop. 54,269.

Troyes |trwä| town in N France, on the Seine River. Pop. 61,000. It was capital of the former province of Champagne. It gave its name to a system of weights and measures first used at the medieval fairs held here.

Tru·cial States |'trōōsHəl| former name (until 1971) for UNITED ARAB EMIRATES, deriving from the 1836 maritime truce they signed with Britain.

Tru·jil·lo |trōō'hēyō| industrial city on the coast of NW Peru, capital of La Libertad department. Pop. 509,000.

Truk Islands |trōōk; trək| (also **Chuuk**) group of fourteen volcanic islands and numerous atolls in the W Pacific, in the Caroline Islands, forming part of the Federated States of Micronesia. Pop. 54,000. There was a Japanese naval base here during World War II.

Trum·bull |'trəmbəl| town in SW Connecticut, an affluent suburb NE of Bridgeport. Pop. 32,016.

Tru·ro[1] |'trōōrō| the county seat of Cornwall, in SW England. Pop. 19,000.

Tru·ro[2] |'trōōrō| resort town in E Massachusetts, near the end of Cape Cod. Pop. 1,573. It is a well-known arts colony.

Tru·ro[3] |'trōōrō| commercial and industrial town in central Nova Scotia, on Minas Basin. Pop. 11,683.

Truth or Con·se·quen·ces |,trōōTH 'känsə,kwensəz| commercial city in SW New Mexico, on the Rio Grande. Pop. 6,221. Formerly Hot Springs, it took its current name in 1950 to obtain a live radio broadcast from the city.

Tsa·ri·tsyn |tsə'rētsən| former name (until 1925) for VOLGOGRAD.

Tsar·sko·ye Se·lo |'tsärskəyə sə'law| earlier name for PUSHKIN.

Tse·li·no·grad |tsi'lēnə,gräd| former name for ASTANA, Kazakhstan.

Tsi·nan |'jē'nän| see JINAN.

Tsing·hai |'CHiNG'hī| see QINGHAI.

Tsing·tao |'CHiNG'dow| see QINGDAO.

Tsi·tsi·har |'CHi'CH'här| see QIQIHAR.

Tskhin·va·li |'tskinvəlē| the capital of South Ossetia, in the republic of Georgia. Pop. 43,000.

Tsu |(t)sōō| commercial and industrial port city in central Japan, on S Honshu, NW of Nagoya. Pop. 157,000.

Tsu·chi·u·ra |(t)sōō'CHēōōrä| commercial city and cultural center in E central Japan, on central Honshu, a suburb in the Tokyo-Yokohama area. Pop. 127,000.

Tsu·ga·ru Strait |(t)sōō'gärōō| strait in N Japan, between Honshu and Hokkaido islands, connecting the Sea of Japan with the Pacific; approximately 100 mi./161 km. long.

Tsu·ku·ba |(t)sōō'kōōbä| city in E central Japan, on central Honshu. Pop. 143,000. The government-planned Tsukuba City research and technology center here is home to 46 national research facilities.

Tsu·shi·ma |(t)sōō'sHēmä| Japanese island in the Korea Strait, between South Korea and Japan. In 1905 it was the scene of a defeat for the Russian navy during the Russo-Japanese War.

Tu·a·mo·tu Archipelago |,tōōə'mōtōō| group of about eighty coral islands forming part of French Polynesia, in the S Pacific. Pop. 12,000. It is the largest group of coral atolls in the world. The islands of Mururoa and Fangataufa have been used by the French since 1966 for nuclear testing.

Tü·bing·en |'tybiNGən| city in SW Germany, on the Neckar River. An educational and publishing center, it retains its medieval core. Pop. 75,000.

Tu·bruq |tŏŏ'brŏŏk| Arabic name for TOBRUK.

Tu·bu·ai Islands |tŏŏ'bwäē| group of volcanic islands in the S Pacific, forming part of French Polynesia; chief town, Mataura (on the island of Tubuai). Pop. 6,500. Also called the **Austral Islands**.

Tuc·son |'tŏŏ,sän| city in SE Arizona, a center of manufacturing and tourist destination with a desert climate. Pop. 405,390.

Tu·ge·la River |tŏŏ'gälə| river that flows 300 mi./483 km. from KwaZulu-Natal province, South Africa, to the Indian Ocean. **Tugela Falls,** with a total drop of 3,110 ft./948 m., is the highest in Africa.

Tui·ler·ies |,twēlə're| public gardens adjacent to the Louvre, in Paris, France, on the Right Bank. The grounds were originally bought by Catherine de Medici in 1563 for a garden next to the Tuileries Palace (demolished 1871).

Tu·la¹ |'tŏŏlə| the ancient capital city of the Toltecs, generally identified with a site near the town of Tula in Hidalgo State, central Mexico.

Tu·la² |'tŏŏlə| industrial city in European Russia, to the S of Moscow. Pop. 543,000.

Tu·la·gi |tŏŏ'lägē| (also **Tulaghi**) small island in the central Solomon Islands, just S of Florida Island and N of Guadalcanal, the scene of an Allied attack on Japanese troops in August 1942.

Tu·lare |tŏŏ'lærē; tŏŏ'lær| commercial city in S central California, an agricultural center in the San Joaquin Valley. Pop. 33,249.

Tul·cea |'tŏŏlcHä| industrial town in SE Romania, in the Danube delta, capital of Tulcea county. Pop. 95,000.

Tu·le Lake |'tŏŏlē| lake in N California, on the Modoc Plateau, a noted wildfowl refuge and scene of fighting in the 1870s Modoc War.

Tul·la·more |,tələ'mōr| the county seat of Offaly, in the Republic of Ireland. Pop. 9,000.

Tulle |tŏŏl| industrial city, capital of Corrège department in S central France. Pop. 21,000. The cloth known as tulle was first made here.

Tul·sa |'tələsə| commercial and industrial city, on the Arkansas River in NE Oklahoma. Pop. 367,302.

Tu·lum |,tŏŏ'lŏŏm| archaeological site in SE Mexico, a 6th-century Mayan city on the Caribbean coast of Quintana Roo state.

Tum·kur |tŏŏm'kŏŏ| commercial city and health resort in S central India, in the Devarayadurga Hills in Karnataka state. Pop. 180,000.

Tunb Islands |'tŏŏnəb| two small islands (Greater and Lesser Tunb) in the Persian Gulf, administered by the emirate of Ras al Khaimah until occupied by Iran in 1971.

Tun·bridge Wells |'tənbrij 'welz| spa town in Kent, SE England. Pop. 58,000. Founded in the 1630s after the discovery of iron-rich springs, the town was patronized by royalty throughout the 17th and 18th centuries. Official name **Royal Tunbridge Wells.**

Tung·shan |'tŏŏNG'sHän| see XUZHOU.

Tun·gu·ra·hua |,tŏŏNGgŏŏ'räwä| active volcano in the Andes in central Ecuador: 16,457 ft./5,016 m. It gives its name to surrounding Tungurahua province.

Tun·gu·ska |tŏŏNG'gŏŏskə| two rivers in Siberian Russia, the *Lower Tunguska* and *Stony Tunguska*, flowing W into the Yenisei River through the forested, sparsely populated Tunguska Basin. The area was the scene in 1908 of a devastating explosion believed to have been due to the disintegration in the atmosphere of a meteorite or small comet.

Tu·nis |'t(y)ŏŏnəs| the capital of Tunisia, an industrial port on the Mediterranean coast of N Africa, near the site of ancient Carthage. Pop. 597,000.

Tu·ni·sia |t(y)ŏŏ'nēzHə| republic in N Africa, on the Mediterranean. Area: 63,403 sq. mi./164,150 sq. km. Pop. 8,223,000. Language, Arabic. Capital and largest city: Tunis. The sucessor to classical Carthage, Tunisia was long controlled by the Turks and (1886–1956) by France. Agriculture, oil and mineral extraction, and tourism are all important to its economy. □ **Tunisian** *adj. & n.*

Tun·ja |'tŏŏNG,hä| historic commercial city

Tunisia

in central Colombia, the capital of Boyacá department. Pop. 112,000.

Tuol Sleng prison in Phnom Penh, Cambodia, a notorious execution site of the 1970s Khmer Rouge regime, now a museum of the history of the period.

Tu·ol·um·ne River |tōō'äləmē| river that flows from Yosemite National Park, California. It is impounded in the Hetch Hetchy Reservoir, which supplies San Francisco with water.

Tu·pe·lo |'t(y)ōōpə,lō| industrial city in NE Mississippi. Pop. 30,685. Site of Civil War battles, it is also the birthplace of Elvis Presley.

Tu·ran |tōō'rän| region of steppes and deserts in central Asia, S and E of the Aral Sea, extending from Kazakhstan through Uzbekistan and Turkmenistan; home of the Turanian people.

Tur·fan Depression |tōor'fän| see TURPAN DEPRESSION.

Tu·rin |'t(y)ōōrən| industrial and commercial city in NW Italy, on the Po River, capital of Piedmont region. Pop. 992,000. Turin was the capital of the kingdom of Sardinia from 1720 and became the first capital of a unified Italy (1861–64). It is a center of publishing, auto, and other industries. Italian name **Torino**.

Tur·ka·na, Lake |tōōr'känə| salt lake in NW Kenya and extending into S Ethiopia; it has no outlet, and is increasing in salinity. Also called **the Jade Sea.**

Tur·ke·stan |,tərkə'stæn| (also **Turkistan**) region of central Asia between the Caspian Sea and the Gobi Desert, inhabited mainly by Turkic peoples. It is divided by the Pamir and Tien Shan mountains into E Turkestan, now the Xinjiang autonomous region of China, and W Turkestan, which comprises present-day Turkmenistan, Kazakhstan, Uzbekistan, Tajikistan, and Kyrgyzstan.

Tur·key |'tərkē| republic comprising the whole of the Anatolian peninsula in W Asia,

as well as a peninsula in SE Europe. Area: 301,063 sq. mi./779,452 sq. km. Pop. 56,473,000. Language, Turkish. Capital: Ankara. Largest city: Istanbul. The center of the Ottoman Empire before World War I, Turkey became a secular republic in the 1920s. It has a sizable Kurdish minority in the E. Agriculture, coal mining, industry, and tourism are all important. □ **Turkish** adj. **Turk** n

Turk·me·ni·stan |tərk'menə,stæn| republic in central Asia, lying between the Caspian Sea and Afghanistan. Area: 188,528 sq. mi./488,100 sq. km. Pop. 3,861,000. Languages, Turkoman (official), Russian. Capital and largest city: Ashgabat. Also called **Turkmenia**. The Karakum Desert comprises 90% of Turkmenistan, which had been Turkestan and then (1924–91) a constituent republic of the Soviet Union. Traditionally pastoral, the country has substantial mineral resources. □ **Turkmen** adj. & n.

Turkmenistan

Turks and Cai·cos Islands |'tərks ən 'kākəs ,| British dependency in the Caribbean, comprising two island groups between Haiti and the Bahamas. Pop. 12,000. Capital: Cockburn Town (on the island of Grand Turk).

Tur·ku |'tōōrkōō| industrial port in SW Finland. Pop. 159,000. It was the capital of Finland until 1812. Swedish name **Åbo**.

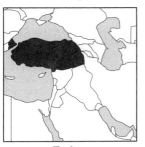
Turkey

Turks & Caicos

Tur·lock |'tər,läk| commercial city in N central California, in the San Joaquin Valley. Pop. 42,198. It is an agricultural hub.

Tur·nu Ro·şu |'tōōrnōō 'raw,SHōō| historic mountain pass in the Transylvanian Alps of central Romania. It is traversed by the Olt River.

Tur·nu Se·ve·rin |'tōōrnōō ,sāve'rēn| see DROBETA–TURNU SEVERIN, Romania.

Tur·pan Depression |'tōōr'pän| (also called **Turfan Depression**) deep depression in Xinjiang, W China, in the Tarim Basin, the lowest point in the country: 505 ft./154 m. below sea level. Area: 20,000 sq. mi./50,000 sq. km.

Tur·qui·no, Pi·co |'pēkō tōōr'kēnō| see SIERRA MAESTRA, Cuba.

Tus·ca·loo·sa |,təskə'lōōsə| industrial city in W central Alabama, on the Black Warrior River. Pop. 77,759. The University of Alabama is here.

Tus·can Archipelago |'təskən| group of small islands, belonging to Italy, in the Mediterranean Sea between France, Corsica, and Italy. Among the islands are Elba and Pianosa.

Tus·ca·ny |'təskənē| region of W central Italy, on the Ligurian Sea. Pop. 3,563,000. Capital: Florence. Italian name **Toscana**.

Tus·ca·ro·ra Mountains |,təskə'rōrə| range in NE Nevada that has been the scene of gold and silver booms.

Tus·cu·lum |'təsk(y)ələm| ancient town in Italy, SE of Rome. According to legend, it was a rival to Rome until defeated; later it became a resort for wealthy citizens of the city.

Tus·cum·bia |təsk'əmbēə| industrial city in NW Alabama, in the Muscle Shoals area on the Tennessee River. Pop. 8,413. The writer Helen Keller was born here.

Tus·ke·gee |təsk'ēgē| city in E central Alabama, home to Tuskegee Uinversity. Pop. 12,257.

Tus·tin |'təstən| city in SW California, a suburb SE of Los Angeles. Pop. 50,689.

Tu·ti·co·rin |,tōōtikə'rin| industrial port city in S India, in Tamil Nadu state. Pop. 284,000.

Tu·va |'tōōvə| autonomous republic in S central Russia, on the border with Mongolia. Pop. 314,000. Capital: Kyzyl. Former name **Tannu-Tuva**.

Tu·va·lu |tōō'välōō| country in the SW Pacific consisting of a group of nine main islands, formerly called the Ellice Islands. Area: 10 sq. mi./26 sq. km. Pop. 8,500. Official languages, English and Tuvaluan (an Austronesian language). Capital: Funafu-

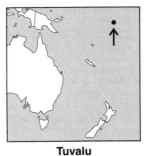

Tuvalu

ti. The islands formed part of the British colony of the Gilbert and Ellice Islands but separated from the Gilberts after a referendum in 1975. Tuvalu became independent in 1978. The chief product is coconuts. □ **Tuvaluan** adj. & n.

Tux·e·do Park |tək'sēdō| village in SE New York. Pop. 706. Developed in the 1880s as a refuge for the rich, it gave its name to the evening jacket.

Tux·tla Gu·ti·ér·rez |'tōōstlä gōōtē'yärās| commercial city in SE Mexico, capital of the state of Chiapas. Pop. 296,000.

Tuz·la |'tōōzlä| town in NE Bosnia. Pop. 132,000. A Muslim enclave, it suffered damage and heavy casualties when besieged by Bosnian Serb forces in 1992–94.

Tver |tver| industrial port in European Russia, on the Volga River NW of Moscow. Pop. 454,000. It was known as Kalinin from 1931 until 1991. Tver is also the name of a historic principality in the area.

Tweed |twēd| river that rises in the Southern Uplands of Scotland and flows 97 mi./155 km. generally E, crossing into NE England and entering the North Sea at Berwick-upon-Tweed. For part of its lower course it forms the border between Scotland and England.

Twen·ty·nine Palms |'twentē,nīn ,pälmz| desert city in S California, E of Los Angeles, just S of the Twentynine Palms Marine Corps air center. Pop. 11,821.

Twick·en·ham |'twikənəm| residential district of the borough of Richmond-upon-Thames, W London, England, headquarters to the Rugby Football Union and former home to poet Alexander Pope.

Twin Cities |twin| popular name for the adjacent cities of Minneapolis and Saint Paul, Minnesota.

Twin Falls |twin| commercial and industrial city in S central Idaho, on the Snake River. Pop. 27,591.

Ty·burn |'tībərn| place in London, England, near Marble Arch, where public hangings were held *c.*1300–1783.

Ty·chy |'təhə| industrial town in S Poland, S of Katowice. Pop. 192,000.

Ty·ler |'tīlər| industrial city in E Texas. Pop. 75,450. It is a center of horticultural industries, famed for its roses.

Tyne |tīn| river in NE England, formed by the confluence of two headstreams, the North Tyne, which rises in the Cheviot Hills, and the South Tyne, which rises in the N Pennines. It flows 31 mi./50 km. generally E, entering the North Sea at Tynemouth.

Tyne and Wear |'tīn ən 'wir| metropolitan county of NE England. Pop. 1,087,000. County town: Newcastle upon Tyne.

Tyne·side |'tīn,sīd| industrial urban region on the banks of the Tyne River, in NE England, stretching from Newcastle-upon-Tyne to the coast. □ **Tynesider** *n.*

Tyre |tīr| historic port on the Mediterranean in S Lebanon. Pop. 14,000. Founded in the 2nd millennium B.C. as a colony of Sidon, it was for centuries a Phoenician port and trading center, before its decline in the 14th century. □ **Tyrian** *adj. & n.*

Ty·rol |tə'rōl| Alpine state of W Austria. Capital: Innsbruck. The S part was ceded to Italy after World War I. German name **Tirol.** □ **Tyrolean** *adj. & n.* **Tyrolese** *adj. & n.*

Ty·rone |ti'rōn| one of the Six Counties of Northern Ireland, W of Lough Neagh. Pop. 144,000; chief town, Omagh.

Tyr·rhe·ni·an Sea |tə'rēnēən| part of the Mediterranean Sea between mainland Italy and the islands of Sicily and Sardinia.

Tyu·men |tyoo'men| city in W Siberian Russia, in the E foothills of the Ural Mts. Pop. 487,000. Founded in 1586 on a Tartar site, it is regarded as the oldest city in Siberia.

Tzu-po |'dzə'bō| see ZIBO.

Uu

Uban·gi River |(y)o͞o'bæNGgē| (French spelling **Oubangui**) river that flows 660 mi./1,060 km. from the border of the Central African Republic and Congo (formerly Zaire), along the border of the latter with the Republic of Congo, to join the Congo River, of which it is the chief N tributary.

Ubangi-Shari |(y)o͞o'bæNGgē 'sHärē| former name (until 1958) for CENTRAL AFRICAN REPUBLIC.

Ube |'o͞obē| industrial port city in W Japan, on SW Honshu. Pop. 175,000.

Ube·ra·ba |ˌo͞obe'räbə| commercial city in E Brazil, in Minas Gerais state, in an agricultural and cattle-raising region. Pop. 232,000.

Uber·lân·dia |'o͞obər'ländēə| commercial city in E Brazil, in Minas Gerais state, in an agricultural and cattle-raising area. Pop. 437,000.

Ubon Rat·cha·tha·ni |o͞o'bən, räCHə'tänē| (also **Ubol Rajadhani**) commercial town in E Thailand, on the Mun River just below its junction with the Chi. Pop. 99,000.

Uca·ya·li River |ˌo͞okə'yälē| river that flows 1,000 mi./1,600 km. through central and N Peru. It joins the Marañón River to form the Amazon.

Uc·cle |'əklə| (also **Ukkel**) commune in central Belgium. Pop. 76,000. It is a suburb of Brussels.

Udai·pur |o͞o'dīˌpo͝or| historic city in NW India, on Lake Pichola in Rajasthan state. Pop. 308,000.

Udha·ga·man·da·lam |ˌo͞odəgəmən'däləm| (also **Udagamandalam**) historic hill resort town in S India, in Tamil Nadu state. Pop. 82,000.

Udi·ne |'o͞odē,nä| manufacturing city in NE Italy, capital of Udine province. Pop. 99,000.

Ud·mur·tia |o͞od'mo͝orsHə| autonomous republic in central Russia. Pop. 1,619,000. Capital: Izhevsk. Also called **Udmurt Republic**.

Ue·da |o͞o'ädä| (also **Uyeda**) industrial and resort city in central Japan, on central Honshu, S of Nagano. Pop. 119,000.

Ue·le River |'welē| (also **Welle**) river that flows 700 mi./1,125 km. across N Congo (formerly Zaire), joining the Bomu River to form the Ubangi River.

Ufa |o͞o'fä| industrial city, the capital of Bashkiria, S central Russia, in the Ural Mts. Pop. 1,094,000.

Ufa River |o͞o'fä| river (580 mi./933 km) in W Russia. It rises in W Chelyabinsk oblast and flows through the Southern Ural Mts. into the Belaya River at Ufa.

Uf·fi·zi Gallery |o͞o'fitsē; o͞o'fētsē| art museum in Florence, Italy, housed in a Renaissance palace, that is home to some of the best-known Renaissance masterworks.

Ugan·da |(y)o͞o'gændə| landlocked republic in E Africa. Area: 93,140 sq. mi./241,139 sq. km. Pop. 16,876,000. Languages, English (official), Swahili, and others. Capital and largest city: Kampala. Ethnically diverse Uganda was controlled by Britain before independence in 1962. It exports coffee, tea, tobacco, cotton, and other products. □ **Ugandan** adj. & n.

Uganda

Uga·rit |o͞ogə'rēt| ancient port and Bronze Age trading city in N Syria, founded in Neolithic times and destroyed by the Sea Peoples in about the 12th century B.C. Late Bronze age remains include a palace, temples, and private residences containing legal, religious, and administrative cuneiform texts in Sumerian, Akkadian, Hurrian, Hittite, and Ugaritic languages. Its people spoke Ugaritic, a Semitic language written in a distinctive cuneiform alphabet, whose study has contributed to better understanding of biblical Hebrew. □ **Ugaritic** adj. & n.

Ui·jong·bu |'wē,jəNG'bo͞o| industrial city in NW South Korea, a satellite of Seoul. Pop. 276,000.

Uin·ta Mountains |yo͞o'intə| range of the Rocky Mts. in NE Utah. Kings Peak, at 13,528 ft./4,123 m. is its high point, and the high point in Utah.

Uist |'(y)o͞oist| two islands in the Outer Hebrides, Scotland, *North Uist* and *South Uist*, lying to the S of Lewis and Harris and separated from each other by the island of Benbecula.

Uji |'ōōjē| Resort city in W central Japan, on S Honshu, S of Kyoto. Pop. 177,000.

Uji•ji |ōō'jējē| commercial town in W Tanzania, on Lake Tanganyika just S of Kigoma, noted as the place where journalist Henry M. Stanley "found" explorer David Livingstone in 1871.

Uji•ya•ma•da |ˌōōjēyä'mädä| former name (until 1956) for ISE.

Uj•jain |'ōōˌjīn| historic city in W central India, in Madhya Pradesh, a Hindu holy site. Pop. 376,000.

Ujung Pan•dang |'ōōˌjōōNG'pän,däNG| the chief seaport of the island of Sulawesi in Indonesia. Pop. 944,300. Former name (until 1973) **Makassar**.

Uki•ah |yōō'kīə| city in NW California, on the Russian River. Pop. 14,599.

Ukraine |yōō'krān| (also formerly called **the Ukraine**) republic in E Europe, to the N of the Black Sea. Area: 233,179 sq. mi./603,700 sq. km. Pop. 51,999,000. Languages, Ukrainian and Russian. Capital and largest city: Kiev. The home of the Scythians and Sarmatians, Ukraine was united with Russia by the 9th century. It was an original republic of the Soviet Union, becoming independent in 1991. Its vast steppes produce grain, and heavy industry dominates the Donets Basin. Mining is also a key to the economy. □ **Ukrainian** *adj. & n.*

Ukraine

Ula•la |ōō'lälə| former name (until 1932) for GORNO-ALTAISK.

Ulan Ba•tor |ˌōōˌlän 'bä,tawr| (also **Ulaanbaatar**) the capital of Mongolia. Pop. 575,000. It was founded in the 17th century as a Buddhist center. Former name (until 1924) **Urga**.

Ulan-Ude |ˌōōˌlänōō'dä| industrial city in S Siberian Russia, capital of the republic of Buryatia. Pop. 359,000. Former name (until 1934) **Verkhneudinsk**.

Ule•å•borg |'ōōleō'bawrē| Swedish name for OULU.

Ul•has•na•gar |ˌōōlhəs'nägər| city in W India, in the state of Maharashtra. Pop. 369,000.

Uli•thi |ōō'lēTHē| atoll in the W Caroline Is., in the Federated States of Micronesia. U.S. forces took its harbor from the Japanese in 1944.

Ulm |'ōōlm| industrial city on the Danube River in Baden-Württemberg, S Germany. Pop. 112,000. It is noted for its Gothic cathedral, with a spire 528 ft./161 m. tall.

Ul•san |'ōōl'sän| industrial port on the S coast of South Korea. Pop. 683,000.

Ul•ster |'əlstər| former province of Ireland, in the N of the island. The nine counties of Ulster are now divided between Northern Ireland (Antrim, Down, Armagh, Londonderry, Tyrone, and Fermanagh) and the Republic of Ireland (Cavan, Donegal, and Monaghan). □ **Ulsterman** *n.* **Ulsterwoman** *n.*

Ul•ster County |'əlstər| county in SE New York, W of the Hudson River. Pop. 165,304. Many Catskills resorts are here.

Ul•ti•ma Thule |ˌəltimə'tōōlē| see THULE.

Ulugh Muz•tagh |'ōōˌlōōg mōōztäg| see MUZTAG.

Ulun•di |ōō'lōōndē| town in KwaZulu/Natal, South Africa, formerly the seat of Zulu kings, later capital of Zululand and KwaZulu. Pop. 11,000.

Ulu•ru |ōō'lōōrōō| Aboriginal name for AYERS ROCK.

Ul•ya•novsk |ōōl'yänəfsk| former name (1924–92) for SIMBIRSK.

Uman |ōō'män| historic industrial city in central Ukraine, S of Kiev. Pop. 93,000.

Um•bria |'əmbrēə| predominantly agricultural region of central Italy, in the valley of the Tiber. Pop. 823,000. Capital: Perugia.

Umeå |'ōōmä,ō| port city in NE Sweden, on an inlet of the Gulf of Bothnia. Pop. 91,000.

Umm al Qai•wain |'ōōm äl kī'wīn| **1** one of the seven member states of the United Arab Emirates. Pop. 35,000. **2** its capital city.

Um•ta•li |ōōm'tälē| former name (until 1982) for MUTARE.

Umåtaåta |ōōm'tätä| commercial town in S South Africa, in Eastern Cape province. Pop. 55,000. It was formerly the capital of TRANSKEI.

Una River |'ōōnä| river, 159 mi./256 km. long, that forms part of the border between Bosnia and Herzegovina and Croatia, emptying into the Sava River.

Un·a·las·ka |ˌənəˈlæskə| island in the E Aleutian Islands of Alaska. The naval base of Dutch Harbor and the city of Unalaska are the chief settlements.

Un·ga·va |ənˈgävə| (also **Labrador-Ungava**) peninsular region of E Canada, in N Quebec and Labrador. Thinly populated, it has vast hydroelectric and mineral resources.

Un·ion |ˈyo͞onyən| industrial and residential township in NE New Jersey. Pop. 50,024.

Un·ion City¹ |ˈyo͞onyən| city in N central California, a reidential and industrial suburb S of Oakland. Pop. 53,762.

Un·ion City² |ˈyo͞onyən| industrial city in NE New Jersey, across the Hudson River from New York City. Pop. 58,102.

Un·ion·dale |ˈyo͞onyən,dāl| residential and commercial village in SE New York, on Long Island, site of the Nassau Memorial Coliseum. Pop. 20,328.

Un·ion Square |ˈyo͞onyən| park in S Manhattan, New York City, noted as a former theater and, later, labor union hub.

Un·ion Territory |ˈyo͞onyən| any of several territories of India that are administered by the central government.

Un·ion·town |ˈyo͞onyən,town| historic city in SW Pennsylvania, in the Allegheny foothills and on the former National Road. Pop. 12,034.

United Arab Emirates |yo͞oˈnītəd ˈerəb ˈemərits| abbrev. **UAE**) independent state on the S coast of the Persian Gulf, W of the Gulf of Oman. Area: 30,010 sq. km./77,700 sq. km. Pop. 2,377,000. Language, Arabic. Capital: Abu Dhabi. The United Arab Emirates was formed in 1971 by the federation of the independent sheikhdoms formerly called the Trucial States: Abu Dhabi, Ajman, Dubai, Fujairah, Ras al Khaimah (joined early 1972), Sharjah, and Umm al Qaiwain. Oil and gas, fishing, and manufacturing are important to the economy.

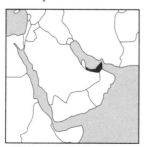

United Arab Emirates

United Arab Republic |yo͞oˈnītəd ˈerəb rəˈpəblik| abbrev. **UAR**) former political union established by Egypt and Syria in 1958. It was seen as the first step toward the creation of a pan-Arab union in the Middle East, but only Yemen entered into loose association with it (1958–66) and Syria withdrew in 1961. Egypt retained the name United Arab Republic until 1971.

United Kingdom |yo͞o,nītəd ˈkiNGdəm| abbrev. **U.K.**) country of W Europe consisting of England, Wales, Scotland, and Northern Ireland. Area: 94,295 sq. mi./244,129 sq. km. Pop. 55,700,000. Language, English. Capital and largest city: London. Full name **United Kingdom of Great Britain and Northern Ireland**. England (with Wales) and Scotland have had the same monarch since 1603, and were formally joined in 1707. Ireland was joined to Great Britain in 1801, but all except present-day Northern Ireland broke away in 1921. The U.K. has been a great maritime, colonial, industrial, and financial power; this historic prominence contributes to the reluctance of many Britons to enter fully into the European Union.

United Kingdom

United Nations |yo͞o,nītəd ˈnāsHənz| international organization headquartered on the East Side of Manhattan, New York City, but with offices (and subsidiary headquarters) in cities around the world.

United Provinces¹ |yo͞o,nītəd ˈprävinsəz| Indian administrative division formed by the union of Agra and Oudh and called Uttar Pradesh since 1950.

United Provinces² |yo͞o,nītəd ˈprävinsəz| *hist.* the seven provinces, united in 1579, that formed the basis of the republic of the Netherlands.

United Provinces of Cen·tral Amer·i·ca |yo͞o,nītəd ˈprävinsəz əv ˈsentrəl əˈmerikə| former federal republic in Central America, formed in 1823 to unite the states of Guatemala, El Salvador, Honduras,

Nicaragua, and Costa Rica, all newly independent from Spain. The federation collapsed in 1838.

United States of Amer·i·ca |yōō'nītəd 'stāts əv ə'merikə| (abbrev. **U.S.** or **USA;** see map, next page) federal republic occupying most of the S half of North America and including also Alaska and the Hawaiian Islands. Area: 3.62 million sq. mi./9.37 million sq. km. Pop. 248,710,000. Capital: Washington, D.C. Largest city: New York City. Established under the constitution of 1787, the U.S. now comprises 50 states and the District of Columbia. Since emerging from World War II as the leading power in the non-communist world, it has held a dominant military, industrial, financial, and cultural position.

Uni·ver·sal City |'yōōnə,vərsəl| district of NW Los Angeles, California, in the San Fernando Valley, home to Universal Studios and other entertainment facilities.

Uni·ver·sity City |,yōōnə'vərsətē| city in E Missouri, on the W boundary of St. Louis, home to Washington University. Pop. 40,087.

Uni·ver·sity Park |,yōōnə'vərsətē| city in NE Texas, enclosed by N Dallas, home to Southern Methodist University. Pop. 22,259.

Un·na |'ŏŏnə| industrial city in NW Germany, E of Dortmund. Pop. 64,000.

Un·ter den Lin·den |,ŏŏntər den 'lindən| tree-lined ("under the lindens") avenue in Berlin, Germany, stretching from the Brandenburg Gate to the Spree River .

Up·land |'əplənd| city in SW California, a suburb E of Los Angeles and N of Ontario. Pop. 63,374.

Upo·lu |ŏŏ'pōlŏŏ| volcanic island in the SW Pacific, the most populous of the republic of Samoa. Pop. 163,000. Apia, the capital, is here. Vailima, the last home of Robert Louis Stevenson, is now a government residence.

Up·per Aus·tria |'awstrēə; 'ästrēə| state of NW Austria. Capital: Linz. German name **Oberösterreich.**

Up·per Can·a·da |'cænədə| the mainly English-speaking region of Canada N of the Great Lakes and W of the Ottawa River, in what is now S Ontario. A British colony in 1791–1841, it was then united with Lower Canada.

Up·per Dar·by |'därbē| suburban township in S Pennsylvania, just SW of Philadelphia. Pop. 81,177.

Up·per Egypt |'ējipt| term for regions of Egypt S of Cairo and the delta of the Nile

River. They are "up" the Nile from the region around its delta, which is called **Lower Egypt.**

Up·per Peninsula |pə'ninsələ| the N section of Michigan, with shores on Lake Superior (N) and Lake Michigan (S) and Lake Huron (SE). Sparsely populated, it has fishing, mining, and resort industries.

Up·per Vol·ta |'vätə| former name (until 1984) for Burkina Faso.

Upp·sa·la |'əpsələ| industrial and cultural city in E Sweden. Pop. 167,000. Its university, founded in 1477, is the oldest in N Europe.

Upstate |,əp'stāt| in New York, parts of the state N of New York City, thought of as distinct culturally and politically.

Ur |ər; ŏŏr| ancient Sumerian city on the Euphrates, in S present-day Iraq. It was one of the oldest cities of Mesopotamia, dating from the 4th millennium B.C., and reached its zenith in the late 3rd millennium B.C. According to the Bible it was Abraham's place of origin. Much of the city was sacked and destroyed by the Alamites, but it recovered and underwent a revival under Nebuchadnezzar. Ur was conquered by Cyrus the Great in the 6th century B.C., after which it fell into decline and was finally abandoned in the 4th century B.C. The site was excavated 1922–34, revealing spectacular royal tombs and vast ziggurats.

Ura·ga |ŏŏ'rägä| port in central Japan, on Uraga Strait on SE Honshu. It was here that U.S. emissaries were repulsed when they first tried to establish relations with Japan in 1846.

Ural Mountains |'yŏŏrəl| (also **the Urals**) mountain range in N Russia, extending 1,000 mi./1,600 km.) S from the Arctic Ocean to the Aral Sea, in Kazakhstan, and rising to 6,214 ft./1,894 m. at Mount Narodnaya. It forms part of the conventional boundary between Europe and Asia.

Ural River |'yŏŏrəl| river (1,575 mi./2,534 km.) rising at the S end of the Ural Mts. in W Russia and flowing through W Kazakhstan to the Caspian Sea at Atyraū.

Ura·wa |ŏŏ'räwä| commercial city and cultural center in E central Japan, on E central Honshu, a suburb of the Tokyo-Yokohama metropolitan area. Pop. 418,000.

Ur·bana |ər'bænə| industrial and commercial city in E central Illinois, with neighboring Champaign home to the University of Illinois. Pop. 36,344.

Ur·bi·no |ŏŏr'bēnō| historic town in the Marches region of central Italy. Pop.

15,000. The palace here is a noted example of Renaissance architecture and contains a collection of Renaissance masterpieces.

Ur·fa |'ŏŏrfä| (also **Sanliurfa**; ancient name **Edessa**) commercial city in SE Turkey, the capital of Urfa province. Pop. 279,000. It is at the center of an agricultural district.

Ur·ga |'ŏŏrgə| former name (until 1924) for ULAN BATOR.

Ur·ganch |ŏŏr'gyenCH| (also **Urgench**) commercial city in W Uzbekistan, on Amu Darya River. Pop. 130,000.

Urua·pán |ŏŏ'rwä,pän| commercial city in W Mexico, in Michoacán state. Pop. 217,000. A Tarascan Indian center, it is noted for its folk arts. The surrounding district is agricultural.

Uru·guay |'(y)ŏŏrə,gwī| republic on the Atlantic coast of South America, S of Brazil. Area: 68,063 sq. mi./176,215 sq. km. Pop. 3,110,000. Language, Spanish. Capital and largest city: Montevideo. Liberated from Spanish colonial rule in 1825, Uruguay is a land of grassy plains devoted to livestock-raising, with fishing and light industries also important. □ **Uruguayan** *adj. & n.*

Uruguay

Uruk |'ŏŏrŏŏk| ancient city in S Mesopotamia, to the NW of Ur. One of the greatest cities of Sumer, it was built in the 5th millennium B.C. and is associated with the legendary hero Gilgamesh. Excavations begun in 1928 revealed great ziggurats and temples. Arabic name **Warka**; biblical name **Erech**.

Ürüm·qi |ŏŏ'rŏŏmCHē| (formerly **Urumchi; Tihwa**) industrial city and capital of Xinjiang, NW China. Pop. 1,100,000. At the junction of ancient caravan routes, Ürümqi has long been an important trading center.

Uşak |'ŏŏSHäk| commercial city in W Turkey, the capital of Uşak province, an agricultural area. Pop. 105,000.

Us·hua·ia |ŏŏ'swäyä| port in Argentina, in Tierra del Fuego. Pop. 11,000. It is the southernmost town in the world.

Üs·kü·dar |,ŏŏskŏŏ'där| suburb of Istanbul, Turkey, on the E side of the Bosporus where it joins the Sea of Marmara. Pop. 396,000. Former name **Scutari**.

Us·pal·la·ta Pass |,ŏŏspä'yätä; ,ŏŏspä-'ZHätä| pass over the Andes near Santiago,

— State boundary
■ Capital city

VT	VERMONT	MD	MARYLAND
NH	NEW HAMPSHIRE	DEL	DELAWARE
MASS	MASSACHUSETTS	WV	WEST VIRGINIA
NY	NEW YORK	VA	VIRGINIA
RI	RHODE ISLAND	KEN	KENTUCKY
CONN	CONNECTICUT	TEN	TENNESSEE
PA	PENNSYLVANIA	MIS	MISSISSIPPI
NJ	NEW JERSEY	ALB	ALABAMA

in S South America, linking Argentina with Chile. The statue 'Christ of the Andes' is here.

Us·su·riysk |ˌo͞oso͞o'rēsk| coal-mining center and transportation junction in E Russia, N of Vladivostok. Pop. 161,000.

Ust-Abakanskoe |o͞ost ˌäbə'känsko͞o| former name (until 1931) for ABAKAN.

Us·ti nad La·bem |'o͞ostyě 'näd lä,bem| industrial city in the NW Czech Republic. Pop. 107,000. It is a river port and transportation hub.

Us·ti·nov |'o͞ostə,nawf| former name (1984–87) for IZHEVSK.

Usu·ma·cin·ta River |ˌo͞oso͞omä'sēntä| river that flows 600 mi./1,000 km. from W Guatemala, where its headstreams include the Chixoy, along the border with Chiapas,

Mexico, then N through Mexico to the Gulf of Campeche.

Usum·bu·ra |ˌo͞osəmˈbo͞orə| former name (until 1962) for BUJUMBURA.

Utah |ˈyo͞oˌtaw; ˈyo͞oˌtä| see box. □ **Utahan** adj. & n.

Utah Beach |ˈyo͞oˌtaw; ˈyo͞oˌtä| name given to the westernmost of the beaches, N of Carentan in Normandy, where U.S. troops landed on D-day in June 1944.

Uti·ca[1] |ˈyo͞otikə| industrial city in central New York, on the Mohawk River. Pop. 68,637.

Uti·ca[2] |ˈyo͞otikə| ancient Phoenician city in N Africa, in present-day N Tunisia, NW of Tunis. It was for a time a Roman provin-

---

Utah

Capital/largest city: Salt Lake City
Other cities: Ogden, Provo
Population: 1,722,850 (1990); 2,099,758 (1998); 2,411,000 (2005 proj.)
Population rank (1990): 35
Rank in land area: 13
Abbreviation: UT; Ut.
Nickname: Beehive State
Motto: 'Industry'
Bird: California gull
Fish: rainbow trout
Flower: sego lily
Tree: blue spruce
Song: "Utah, We Love Thee"
Noted physical features: Great Basin; Great Salt Lake; Sevier Desert; Colorado Plateau, Tavaputs Plateau, Uinta Mountains, Wasatch Plateau and Range
Tourist attractions: Bonneville Salt Flats; Rainbow Bridge; Glen Canyon Dam, Flaming Gorge; Golden Spike National Historic Site; Dinosaur and Natural Bridges national monuments; Arches, Bryce Canyon, Canyonlands, Capital Reef and Zion national parks
Admission date: January 4, 1896
Order of admission: 45
Name origin: For the Ute Indians, who lived in the area; Ute or Eutaw is vaiously translated as 'in the tops of the mountains,' 'high up,' 'the hill dwellers,' 'the land of the sun,' or 'the land of plenty.'

---

cial capital, and declined by the 3rd century A.D.

Utrecht |ˈo͞oˌtreKHt; ˈyo͞oˌtrekt| commercial and cultural city in the central Netherlands, capital of a province of the same name. Pop. 231,000.

Utsu·no·mi·ya |ˌo͞otso͞oˈnōmēyä| industrial city in N central Japan, on central Honshu. Pop. 427,000.

Ut·tar Pra·desh |ˌo͞otə prəˈdāsh; prəˈdesh| state in N India, bordering on Tibet and Nepal. Pop. 139.03 million. Capital: Lucknow. It was formed in 1950 from the United Provinces of Agra and Oudh.

Uu·si·kau·pun·ki |ˈo͞osēˈkä,po͞oNGkē| (Swedish name **Nystad**) industrial port in SW Finland, on the Gulf of Bothnia. Pop. 14,000.

Ux·mal |o͞osHˈmäl| archaeological site in SE Mexico, in Yucatán state S of Mérida, the remains of a Mayan city built from about 600 A.D.

Uz·bek·i·stan |o͞ozˈbekə,stæn; o͞ozˈbekə-ˌstän| republic in central Asia, lying S and SE of the Aral Sea. Area: 172,808 sq. mi./447,400 sq. km. Pop. 20,955,000. Language, Uzbek. Capital and largest city: Tashkent. Home to a Turkic people, Uzbekistan was part of the Soviet Union 1924–91. It has vast irrigated agricultural and pasture land, mineral wealth, and some heavy industry. □ **Uzbek** adj. & n.

Uzbekistan

Uzh·go·rod |ˈo͞ozHgərət| (also **Uzhhorod**) industrial city and transportation hub in W Ukraine, in the foothills of the Carpathian Mountains. Pop. 120,000.

Vv

Vaal |väl| river of South Africa, the chief tributary of the Orange River, rising in the Drakensberg Mts. and flowing 750 mi./1,200 km) SW to the Orange River near Douglas, in Northern Cape.

Vaa·sa |'väsä| port in W Finland, on the Gulf of Bothnia. Pop. 53,000. Swedish name **Vasa**.

Vac·a·ville |'væka,vil| city in W central California, SW of Sacramento. Pop. 71,479. It is an agricultural trade center.

Va·do·dara |və'dōdərə| city in the state of Gujarat, W India. Pop. 1,021,000. The capital of the former state of Baroda, the city was known as Baroda until 1976.

Va·duz |fä'do͞ots| the capital of Liechtenstein. Pop. 5,000.

Vail |väl| town in N Colorado, a noted ski resort. Pop. 3,659.

Val·dai Hills |väl'dī| glacial highland in NW Russia, in the upper Volga region. The highest point is 1,053 ft./321 m.

Val-de-Marne |,väldə'märn| department in N France, in the Île-de-France, SE of Paris. Pop. 1,216,000. The capital is Créteil.

Val·dez |væl'dēz| port city in SE Alaska, on Prince William Sound, the S terminus of the Trans-Alaska Pipeline. Pop. 4,068.

Val·di·via |väl'dēvēə| industrial city in S central Chile, in the Los Lagos region. Pop. 114,000.

Val-d'Oise |väl'dwäz| department in N France, in the Île-de-France, N of Paris. Pop. 1,050,000. The capital is Pontoise.

Val-d'Or |väl'dawr| city in SW Quebec, a gold-mining center. Pop. 23,842.

Val·dos·ta |væl'dästə| industrial city in S Georgia. Pop. 39,806.

Va·lence |va'läNs| manufacturing city, capital of Drôme department , in SE France, on the Rhône River. Pop. 66,000.

Va·len·cia[1] |və'lensēə| **1** autonomous region of E Spain, on the Mediterranean coast. It was formerly a Moorish kingdom (1021–1238). **2** its capital, a port on the Mediterranean coast. Pop. 777,000.

Va·len·cia[2] |və'lensēə| industrial city in N Venezuela, on Lake Valencia. Pop. 903,000.

Va·len·ci·ennes |,väläN'syen| town in N France. Pop. 39,000. Its name is given to a decorative type of lace produced from the 15th century.

Va·le·ra |və'lärə| commercial city in W Venezuela, in Trujillo state. Pop. 111,000.

Val·hal·la |væl'hælə| in Scandinavian myth, the hall assigned to heroes who have died in battle. Here they feast with the god Odin.

Val·la·do·lid[1] |,väyädō'lēd| former name (until 1828) for MORELIA.

Val·la·do·lid[2] |,väyädō'lēd| city in N Spain, capital of Castilla-León region. Pop. 345,000. It was the principal residence of the kings of Castile in the 15th century.

Val·le d'Aos·ta |,välädä'awstə| largely French-speaking Alpine region in the NW corner of Italy. Capital: Aosta.

Val·le·du·par |,väyädo͞o'pär| commercial city in N Colombia, the capital of César department. Pop. 252,000.

Val·le·jo |və'laō; və'lä,hō| industrial port city in N central California, on San Pablo Bay NE of San Francisco. Pop. 109,199.

Val·let·ta |və'letə| the capital and chief port of Malta. Pop. 9,000; urban harbor area pop. 102,000.

Val·ley, the |'vælē| capital of Anguilla, in the West Indies. Pop. 2,000. It is a tourist center.

Val·ley Forge |'vælē 'fawrj| site on the Schuylkill River in Pennsylvania, about 20 mi./32 km. NW of Philadelphia, where George Washington's Continental Army spent the winter of 1777–78 in conditions of extreme hardship during the Revolutionary War.

Val·ley of the Kings valley near ancient Thebes in Egypt where the pharaohs of the New Kingdom (c. 1550–1070 B.C.) were buried. Most of the tombs were looted in antiquity; the exception was that of Tutankhamen, almost untouched until discovered in 1922.

Val·ley of the Sun nickname for the valley in central Arizona in which Phoenix and most of its suburbs lie.

Val·ley Stream |,vælē 'strēm| industrial and commercial village in W central Long Island, SE New York. Pop. 33,946.

Val·my |väl'mē| village in NE France, in the Argonne region. Pop. 290. The first engagement of the French Revolutionary Wars, between the French and the Prussians, was fought here on September 20, 1792.

Va·lois |väl'wä| medieval duchy of N France, home of the Valois royal dynasty (1328–1589).

Va·lo·na |və'lōnə| Italian name for VLORË.

Val·pa·raí·so |,välpärä'ēzō| the principal

port of Chile, in the center of the country, near Santiago. Pop. 277,000.

Val•pa•rai•so |ˌvælpəˈräzō| commercial and industrial city in NW Indiana. Pop. 24,414.

Van |væn| commercial town in E Turkey, capital of Van province. Pop. 153,000. A Kurdish center, it is on the SE shore of saline **Lake Van**, the largest (1,450 sq. mi./3,755 sq. km.) in the country.

Va•nad•zor |ˈvänädˌzawr| (formerly **Kirovakan**) industrial city in N Armenia. Pop. 169,000. It is a rail and manufacturing center.

Van•cou•ver[1] |vænˈkoovər| port city in SW British Columbia, on the mainland opposite Vancouver Island. Pop. 471,844. It is the largest city in W Canada, and its chief Pacific port.

Van•cou•ver[2] |vænˈkoovər| industrial port city in SW Washington, on the Columbia River N of Portland, Oregon. Pop. 46,380.

Van•cou•ver Island |vænˈkoovər| large island off the Pacific coast of Canada, in SW British Columbia. Its capital, Victoria, is the capital of British Columbia. It became a British Crown Colony in 1849, later uniting with British Columbia.

Van•da |ˈvändə| Swedish name for VANTAA.

Van•den•berg Air Force Base |ˈvændənˌbərg| facility on the Pacific coast of SW California, N of Santa Barbara, an important space program site.

Van•der•bijl•park |ˌvändərˌbilˌpärk| steel-manufacturing city in South Africa, in the province of Gauteng, S of Johannesburg. Pop. 540,000 (with Vereeniging).

Van Die•men's Land |vænˈdēmənz| former name (until 1855) for TASMANIA.

Vä•nern |ˈvenərn| (also **Vaner**) lake in SW Sweden, the largest (1,450 sq. mi./3,755 sq. km.) lake in Sweden and the third-largest in Europe.

Va•ni•ko•lo |ˌvänēˈkōlō| (also **Vanikoro**) island in the S central Solomon Islands, in the Santa Cruz group, scene of the 1788 loss of the French explorer La Pérouse.

Vannes |vän| agricultural and tourist center, capital of the department of Morbihan, in Brittany, NW France. Pop. 48,000.

Van Nuys |vænˈīz| industrial and residential section of NW Los Angeles, California, a center of aerospace manufacturing.

Van•taa |ˈväntä| city in S Finland, a N suburb of Helsinki. Pop. 155,000.

Va•nua Le•vu |vəˌnooə ˈlāvoo| (formerly **Sandalwood Island**) island in N Fiji, in the SW Pacific. At 2,146 sq. mi./5,556 sq.

km. it is the second-largest island in the country.

Va•nu•atu |ˌvänəˈwäˌtoo| republic consisting of a group of islands in the SW Pacific. Area: 5,716 sq. mi./14,800 sq. km. Pop. 156,000. Official languages, Bislama, English, and French. Capital: Vila (on Efate). The Melanesian islands were administered jointly by Britain and France 1906–80 as the condominium of the New Hebrides. Vanuatu became independent in 1980. Copra and fish are among its local products. □ **Vanuatuan** *adj. & n.*

Vanuatu

Var |vär| department in extreme SW France. Pop. 815,000. The capital is Toulon.

Va•ra•na•si |vəˈränəsē| historic city on the Ganges, in Uttar Pradesh, N India. Pop. 926,000. It is a holy city and a place of pilgrimage for Hindus, who undergo ritual purification in the Ganges. Former name **Benares**.

Var•dar River |ˈvärˌdär| (Greek name **Axios**) river that flows 240 mi./390 km. from W Macedonia into NE Greece, into the Gulf of Salonika in the Aegean Sea.

Va•re•se |vəˈräsä| town in Lombardy, N Italy, in a resort region. Pop. 88,000.

Varna |ˈvärnə| industrial port and resort in E Bulgaria, on the W shore of the Black Sea. Pop. 321,000.

Va•sa |ˈväsä| Swedish name for VAASA.

Vas•lui |väsˈlooē| commercial city in E Romania, capital of Vaslui county. Pop. 74,000.

Väs•ter•ås |ˌvestəˈraws| port on Lake Mälaren in E Sweden, the capital of Västmannland county. Pop. 120,000.

Vat•i•can City |ˈvætikən| independent papal state in the city of Rome, the seat of government of the Roman Catholic Church. Pop. 1,000. It covers an area of 109 acres/44 hectares around St. Peter's Basilica and the palace of the Vatican. Having been suspended after the incorporation of the former Papal States into Italy in 1870, the temporal power of the pope was restored by the Lateran Treaty of 1929. Castel Gandolfo and several churches in Rome constitute extraterritorial possessions.

Vät·tern |'vetərn| large lake in S Sweden, connected to the North and Baltic seas by canal. Jönköping lies on its S.

Vau·cluse |vō'klyz| department in SE France, in Provence. Pop. 467,000. The capital city is Avignon. The scenery of the Vaucluse attracts tourists.

Vaud |vō| canton on the shores of Lake Geneva in W Switzerland. Pop. 584,000. Capital: Lausanne. German name **Waadt.**

Vaude·ville |,vawd(ə)'vēl| corruption of the name of the valley **Vau-de-Vire** in NW France, home of Olivier Basselin, a 15th-century musician who supposedly composed the light love and drinking songs that first became known as vaudeville.

Vaux |vō| 1 village in NE France, NE of Verdun. The village experienced fierce fighting during World War I and was captured by German forces in June 1916. 2 Vaux-le-Vicomte, 17th-century chateau built for Nicolas Fouquet, finance minister to Louis XIV. Its magnificence so enraged the king that he had Fouquet jailed; it also inspired him to build the chateau at Versailles.

Väx·jö |'vek,shœ| industrial town in S Sweden, a glassmaking center and capital of Kronoborg county. Pop. 47,000.

Ve·ii |'vēī| ancient city in Etruria, N of Rome. It was an important member of the Etruscan League and fought against Rome for centuries before being captured after a 10-year siege.

Vel·bert |'fel,bert| manufacturing city in NW Germany, NE of Düsseldorf. Pop. 90,000.

veld |velt| (also **veldt**) high, treeless interior grasslands and savanna of South Africa and of Zimbabwe. The Boers settled much of the area in their Great Trek of the 1830s, and used it for grazing.

Ve·li·ki·ye Lu·ki |və'lēkēə 'lōōkē| transportation center and town in W Russia, W of Tver. Pop. 116,000.

Ve·li·ko Tur·no·vo |'veli,kaw 'tərnəvō| historic town in central Bulgaria, a former (1187–1396) capital, in the N foothills of the Balkan Mts. Pop. 100,000.

Vel·la La·vel·la |,velə lə'velə| island in the central Solomon Islands, in the SW Pacific, in the New Georgia group, NW of Guadalcanal, site of a 1943 victory by U.S. naval forces over the Japanese.

Vel·lore |və'lawr| historic commercial town in S India, in the foothills of the Eastern Ghats in Tamil Nadu state. Pop. 305,000.

Vel·sen |'velsən| seaport in N Netherlands, near the mouth of the North Sea Canal. Pop. 61,000.

Vence |väns| resort town in SE France, W of Nice. Pop. 15,000. It is a noted arts center.

Ven·da |'vendə| former homeland established in South Africa for the Venda people, now part of Northern Province.

Ven·dée |vän'dā| largely agricultural department in W France, on the Bay of Biscay. Pop. 509,000. The capital is La-Roche-sur-Yon. It was the center of 1790s rebellion against the Revolutionary government in Paris.

Ven·dôme |vän'dawm| 1 manufacturing town in N central France. Pop. 17,000. The title of duke of Vendôme was created by Henri IV and given to an out-of-wedlock son in 1598. 2 **Place Vendôme** square in Paris, France, on the Right Bank built 1687–1720, in classical style. In the center is a column cast from cannons captured by Napoleon I at the Battle of Austerlitz, topped by a statue of the emperor.

Ve·ne·to |'vänə,tō| (also **Venetia**) largely agricultural autonomous region in NE Italy The capital is Venice. Pop. 4,385,000.

Ve·ne·zia |və'netsēə| Italian name for Venice.

Ve·ne·zia Giu·lia |və'netsēə 'jōōlyä| former region in NE Italy, on the Adriatic Sea. Much of it was ceded to Yugoslavia after World War II; the rest merged with the province of Udine to form Friuli–Venezia Giulia.

Ven·e·zu·e·la |,venəz(ə)'wālə| republic on the N coast of South America, with a coastline on the Caribbean Sea. Area: 352,279 sq. mi./912,050 sq. km. Pop. 20,191,000. Language, Spanish. Capital and largest city: Caracas. Venezuela won independence from Spain in 1821, and seceded from Colombia in 1830. A major oil exporter, it

Venezuela

also mines metals and grows coffee and other crops. □ **Venezuelan** *adj. & n.*

Ven·ice[1] |'venəs| city in NE Italy, capital of the Veneto region. Pop. 318,000. Italian name **Venezia**. Situated on a lagoon of the Adriatic, it is built on numerous islands that are separated by canals and linked by bridges. It was a powerful republic in the Middle Ages and from the 13th to the 16th centuries a leading sea power, controlling trade to and ruling parts of the E Mediterranean. Its commercial importance declined after the Cape route to India was discovered at the end of the 16th century, but it remained an important center of art and music. After the Napoleonic Wars Venice was placed under Austrian rule and was incorporated into a unified Italy in 1866. □ **Venetian** *adj. & n.*

Ven·ice[2] |'venəs| beachfront section of Los Angeles, California, W of downtown.

Vè·nis·sieux |ˌvänē'syœ| town in E France, a SE suburb of Lyons. Pop. 61,000.

Ven·lo |'venlō| industrial and commercial city in Limbourg province, SE Netherlands, near the German border. Pop. 65,000.

Ven·ti·mi·glia |ˌventē'mēlyä| beach resort and seaport in NW Italy, on the Ligurian Sea, on the Italian Riviera near the French border. Pop. 26,000. It has a major flower market.

Ven·tu·ra |ven'CHŌōrə| (official name **San Buenaventura**) city in S California, on the Pacific, in an oil-producing and agricultural area. Pop. 92,575.

Ve·ra·cruz |ˌverə'krōōz| **1** state of E central Mexico, with a long coastline on the Gulf of Mexico. Capital: Jalapa Enriquez. **2** city and port in Veracruz state, on the Gulf of Mexico. Pop. 328,000.

Ver·cel·li |vər'CHelē| market town and industrial center in NW Italy, capital of Vercelli province. Pop. 50,000. It is in a rice-growing area.

Ver·dun[1] |ver'dəN| fortified town on the Meuse River in NE France. Pop. 23,000. The site of one of the longest and bloodiest battles in World War I, Verdun has large military cemeteries and several war memorials.

Ver·dun[2] |vər'dən| city in S Quebec, a suburb just S of Montreal on the St. Lawrence River. Pop. 61,307.

Ve·ree·ni·ging |və'rēnikiNG| industrial city in South Africa, in the province of Gauteng. Pop. 774,000 (with Vanderbijlpark).

Verkh·ne·u·dinsk |ˌvyerknə'ōōdinsk| former name (until 1934) for ULAN-UDE.

Ver·kho·yansk |ˌverkə'yänsk| river port and fur-trading town in Siberia, W Russia, NE of Yakutsk. Near the Arctic Circle and one of the coldest places on Earth, it was formerly used to house political exiles.

Ver·mont |vər'mänt| see box. □ **Vermonter** *n.*

Verny |'vərnyē| former name (until 1921) for ALMATY.

Ve·ro Beach |'virō| resort and commercial city in E central Florida. Pop. 17,350.

Ve·ro·na |və'rōnə| commercial and industrial city on the Adige River, in NE Italy. Pop. 259,000.

Verrazano-Narrows Bridge |ˌverə,zänō 'næröz| suspension bridge linking Staten Island, and Brooklyn, New York, completed in 1964. It crosses the Narrows of New York Bay.

Ver·sailles |ver'sī; vər'sī| town, SW of Paris, in N central France, capital of the department of Yvelines. Pop. 91,000. The opulent palace of Versailles, built by King Louis XIV, with its expansive gardens, was the royal residence until 1789. International treaties, including that ending World War I, have been signed here.

Ver·viers |ver'vyä| manufacturing town in E Belgium; pop 53,000.

Vermont

Capital: Montpelier
Largest city: Burlington
Other cities: Brattleboro, Rutland, Stowe
Population: 562,758 (1990); 590,883 (1998); 638,000 (2005 proj.)
Population rank (1990): 48
Rank in land area: 45
Abbreviation: VT; Vt.
Nickname: Green Mountain State
Motto: 'Freedom and Unity'
Bird: hermit thrush
Fish: brook trout (cold water); walleye pike (warm water)
Flower: red clover
Tree: sugar maple
Song: "Hail, Vermont!"
Noted physical features: Green Mountains
Tourist attractions: ski resorts
Admission date: March 4, 1791
Order of admission: 14
Name origin: From French *vert*, 'green,' and *mont*, 'mountain,' originally applied to the Green Mountains east of Lake Champlain by French explorer Samuel de Champlain on his map of 1612.

Ves•ter•å•len |'vestə,raw| group of islands of Norway, N of the Arctic Circle.

Vest•man•na•ey•jar |'vest,män'ā,yär| Icelandic name for WESTMANN ISLANDS.

Ve•su•vi•us |və'sōōvēəs| active volcano near Naples, in S Italy, 4,190 ft./1,277 m. high. A violent eruption in A.D. 79 buried the nearby towns of Pompeii and Herculaneum.

Vesz•prém |'ves,präm| town in W Hungary. Pop. 65,000. A commercial center, it is popular with tourists.

Vet•lu•ga River |vit'lōōgä| river (528 mi./850 km. long) in W Russia, flowing into the Volga River in the SW of Mari El Republic.

Ve•vey |və'vā| commune and tourist resort in W Switzerland, on the NE shore of Lake Geneva, SE of Lausanne. Pop. 16,000.

Via Ap•pia |,vēə 'æpēə; 'vīə| Latin name for APPIAN WAY.

Via•reg•gio |,vēä'rejō| beach resort and seaport on the Tyrrhenian Sea in W Italy. Pop. 57,000. The body of the English poet Shelley washed up on shore near here.

Vi•borg |'vē,bawr| historic rail junction and commercial town in N Denmark. Pop. 29,000.

Vi•cen•te Ló•pez |vē,sentä 'lōpes| city in E central Argentina, a suburb just NW of Buenos Aires. Pop. 289,000.

Vi•cen•za |vē'cHensä| industrial city in NE Italy, capital of Vicenza province. Pop. 109,000. It is noted for its Renaissance architecture.

Vi•chy |'vēsHē| town in S central France. Pop. 28,000. A noted spa, it is a source effervescent mineral water. During World War II it was the headquarters of the regime (1940–44) set up under Marshal Pétain after the German occupation of N France, to administer unoccupied France and the colonies, which functioned as a puppet for the Nazis.

Vicks•burg |'viks,bərg| city on the Mississippi River, in W Mississippi. Pop. 20,908. In 1863 it was successfully besieged by Union forces under U.S. Grant. It was the last Confederate outpost on the river, and its loss effectively split the Confederacy in half.

Vic•to•ria[1] |vik'tawrēə| state of SE Australia. Pop. 4,394,000. Capital: Melbourne. Originally a district of New South Wales, it became a separate colony in 1851 and was federated with the other states of Australia in 1901.

Vic•to•ria[2] |vik'tawrēə| port at the S tip of Vancouver Island, capital of British Columbia. Pop. 71,228.

Vic•to•ria[3] |vik'tawrēə| business center, port, and capital of Hong Kong, S China. Pop. 591,000. Victoria Harbor is one of the greatest natural harbors in the world and has excellent dockyard facilities.

Vic•to•ria[4] |vik'tawrēə| the capital of the Seychelles, a port on the island of Mahé. Pop. 24,000.

Vic•to•ria[5] |vik'tawrēə| city in S Texas, a center of the oil and cattle industries. Pop. 55,076.

Vic•to•ria, Lake |vik'tawrēə| the largest (26,820 sq. mi./69,464 sq. km.) lake in Africa, with shores in Uganda, Tanzania, and Kenya, and drained by the Nile. Also called **Victoria Nyanza**.

Vic•to•ria de Du•ran•go |vik'tawrēä dä dōō,räNggō| full name for the city of DURANGO, Mexico.

Vic•to•ria Falls |vik'tawrēä| waterfall 355 ft./109 m. high on the Zambezi River, on the Zimbabwe–Zambia border.

Vic•to•ria Island |vik'tawrēä| third-largest island in the Canadian Arctic, divided between the Northwest Territories and Nunavut. The administrative center of Cambridge Bay is on its SE coast.

Vic•to•ria Nile |vik'tawrēə 'nīl| the upper part of the White Nile, between Lake Victoria and Lake Albert.

Vic•to•ria Ny•an•za |vik'tawrēə nē'ænzə; nī'ænzə| another name for Lake Victoria (see VICTORIA, LAKE).

Vic•tor•ville |'viktər,vil| industrial and residential city in S California, NE of Los Angeles. Pop. 40,674.

Vi•da•lia |və'dālyə| city in SE Georgia, in an area noted for onion production. Pop. 11,708.

Vi•din |'vēdin| port city in extreme N Bulgaria, on the Danube River. Pop. 91,000. It is known for wine and ceramics.

Vi•en•na |vē'enə| the capital of Austria, an historic administrative, financial, and cultural center in the NE on the Danube River. Pop. 1,533,000. From 1278 to 1918 it was the seat of the Habsburg dynasty. It has long been a center of the arts, especially music, associated with famed composers. German name **Wien**. □ **Viennese** adj. & n.

Vi•en•na Woods |vē'enə| English name for WIENERWALD.

Vienne |vyen| **1** department in W central France, in the Poitou-Charentes region. Pop. 380,000. The capital is Poitiers. **2** river in central France that rises near Limoges and flows N and W for 220 mi./350 km., into the Loire River SE of Saumur. **3** the French form of VIENNA.

Vien·tiane |vyen'tyän| the capital and chief port of Laos, on the Mekong River. Pop. 377,000.

Vie·ques |vē'äkās| (English name **Crab Island**) island municipality in E Puerto Rico, a resort and naval firing range. Pop. 8,602.

Vier·sen |'firzən| industrial city in western Germany, W of Düsseldorf. Pop. 78,000.

Vier·wald·stät·ter·see |fir'vält,stetər,zā| German name for Lake Lucerne (see LUCERNE, LAKE).

Vi·et·nam |vē'et'näm; ,vēet'næm| republic in SE Asia, with a coastline on the South China Sea. Area: 127,295 sq. mi./329,566 sq. km. Pop. 67,843,000. Language, Vietnamese. Capital: Hanoi. Largest city: Ho Chi Minh City. Long dominated by China, Vietnam was part of French Indochina 1862–1954.With French withdrawal, it was partitioned into North and South Vietnam, and was reunified in 1975, following the Vietnam War. Its economy is traditionally based on agriculture. □ **Vietnamese** *adj. & n.*

Vietnam

Vi·go |'vēgō| port city in Galicia, NW Spain, on the Atlantic. Pop. 277,000.

Vi·ja·ya·na·gar |,vijəyə'nəgər| ruined city in S India, near present-day Hampi in Karnataka state; capital of the Hindu Vijayanagar empire of the 14th to 16th centuries.

Vi·ja·ya·wa·da |,vijəyə'wädä| commercial and religious city on the Krishna River in Andhra Pradesh, SE India. Pop. 701,000.

Vi·jo·së River |vē'ōsə| river (148 mi./238 km. long) in NW Greece that flows through Albania to the Adriatic Sea N of Vlorë

Vi·la |'vēlə| (also **Port Vila**) the capital of Vanuatu, on the SW coast of the island of Efate. Pop. 20,000.

Vi·la No·va de Ga·ia |,vēlə 'nawvə dä 'gīə| city in NW Portugal, an industrial suburb of Oporto. Pop. 68,000.

Vi·la Re·al |,vēlə rē'äl| town on the Corgo River in N Portugal, capital of Vila Real district. Pop. 15,000.

Vi·la Ve·lha |,vēlə 'velyə| port city in E Brazil, in Espírito Santo state, just S of Vitória. Pop. 269,000.

Vil·lach |'fil,äкн| industrial town and transportation center in S Austria. Pop. 55,000.

Vil·la d'Este |,vilä'destä| villa near Tivoli, E of Rome, Italy. Built for a cardinal of the Catholic Church in 1550, it is famous for its gardens.

Vil·lage, the |'vilij| see GREENWICH VILLAGE, New York City.

Vil·la·her·mo·sa |,vēyäer'mōsä| city in SE Mexico, capital of the state of Tabasco. Pop. 390,000. Full name **Villahermosa de San Juan Bautista**.

Vil·la·no·va |,vilə'nōvə| academic community in SE Pennsylvania, NW of Philadelphia, home to Villanova University.

Vil·la·vi·cen·cio |,vēyävē'sensē,ō| commercial city in central Colombia, the capital of Meta department. Pop. 233,000. It is the trading center for agricultural E Colombia.

Villefranche-sur-Mer |vēl'fräNSHSYr 'mer| seaport and resort, SE France, on the Riviera, E of Nice. Pop. 8,000.

Ville·juif |vēlZHə'wēf| commune, a S suburb of Paris, in N central France. Pop. 49,000.

Vil·leur·banne |,vēlYœr'bän| industrial E suburb of Lyons, E France. Pop. 120,000.

Villingen-Schwenningen |'viliNGən 'SHfeniNGən| twin manufacturing city in SW Germany, E of Freiburg. Combined pop. 80,000.

Vil·ni·us |'vilnēəs| historic industrial and academic city, the capital of Lithuania, on the Neris River. Pop. 593,000.

Vi·lyui River |vil'yōōē| (also **Vilyuy**) river (1,520 mi./2,450 km. long) in Asian Russia, flowing into the Lena River, NW of Yakutsk.

Vim·i·nal |'vimənl| one of the seven hills upon which Rome, Italy, was built.

Vi·my Ridge |vē'mē| ridge near commune of Vimy, in N France, N of Arras. It was captured by Canadian forces in 1917, after bloody fighting.

Vi·ña del Mar |,vēnyə del 'mär| city in central Chile, a seaside resort and suburb just N of Valparaiso. Pop. 281,000.

Vin·cennes[1] |veN'sen| industrial and residential E suburb of Paris, France. Pop.

45,000. A former royal residence here is now a museum.

Vin·cennes² |vin'senz| historic commercial and industrial city in SW Indiana, on the Wabash River. Pop. 19,859.

Vin·dhya Range |'vindyə| range in central India extending from Gujarat to the Ganges Valley; historically, the dividing line between N and S India.

Vine·land |'vīnlənd| commercial and industrial city in S New Jersey, in an agricultural area. Pop. 54,780.

Vinh Long |'vin 'lawNG| (also **Vinhlong**) port city in southern Vietnam, SW of Ho Chi Minh City. Pop. 82,000.

Vin·land |'vinlənd| region of the NE coast of North America that was visited in the 11th century by Norsemen led by Leif Ericsson. It was so named from the report that grapevines were found growing there. The exact location is uncertain: sites from the northernmost tip of Newfoundland (see L'ANSE AUX MEADOWS) to Cape Cod and even Virginia have been proposed.

Vin·ny·tsya |'vēnitsyə| industrial city in central Ukraine. Pop. 379,000. Russian name **Vinnitsa**.

Vin·son Mas·sif |'vinsən 'mæsif| the highest mountain range in Antarctica, in Ellsworth Land, rising to 16,863 ft./ 5,140 m.

Vire |vēr| **1** commercial town in NW France, on the Vire River **2** river in NW France, flowing N past Vire and Saint Lô into the Bay of the Seine. Its estuary was the dividing point between Omaha and Utah beaches in the D-day landings, June 1944.

Vir·gi·lio |vir'jēlēō| commune in N Italy, S of Mantova. Pop. 7,600. Ancient Andes, on this site, was the birthplace of the poet Virgil.

Vir·gin·ia |vər'jinyə| see box. □ **Virginian** *adj. & n.*

Vir·gin·ia Beach |vər'jinyə| city and resort on the Atlantic coast of SE Virginia. Pop. 393,069.

Vir·gin·ia City |vər'jinyə| historic settlement in W Nevada, S of Reno, site of the 1850s–60s Comstock Lode gold and silver boom.

Vir·gin Islands |'vərjən| group of Caribbean islands at the E extremity of the Greater Antilles, divided between British and U.S. administration. The islands were encountered by Columbus in 1493 and settled, mainly in the 17th century, by British and Danish sugar planters, who introduced African slaves. The British Virgin Islands

US Virgin Islands

consists of about forty islands in the NE of the group. Pop. 17,000. Capital: Road Town (on Tortola). They have constituted a British Crown Colony since 1956, having

Virginia
Official name: Commonwealth of Virginia
Capital: Richmond
Largest city: Norfolk
Other cities: Arlington, Hampton, Lexington, Newport News, Charlottesville, Roanoke, Virginia Beach, Williamsburg
Population: 6,187,358 (1990); 6,791,345 (1998); 7,324,000 (2005 proj.)
Population rank (1990): 12
Rank in land area: 35
Abbreviation: VA; Va.
Nickname: Old Dominion; Mother of Presidents; Mother of States
Motto: *Sic semper tyrannis* (Latin: 'Thus ever to tyrants')
Bird: cardinal
Flower: American dogwood flower
Tree: American dogwood
Song: "Carry Me Back to Old Virginia"
Noted physical features: Chesapeake Bay; Natural Bridge; Luray Caverns; Newport News, Norfolk, Portsmouth, Richmond (ports)
Tourist attractions: Bull Run, Chancellorsville, Fair Oaks, Fredericksburg, Manassas, Petersburg, Richmond, Seven Pines, Spotsylvania, Wilderness and Yorktown battle sites; Monticello, Mount Vernon, Stratford Hall and Williamsburg historical sites; George Washington Birthplace National Monument; Virginia Beach; Shenandoah National Park
Admission date: June 25, 1788
Order of admission: 10
Name origin: For Elizabeth I of England, "the Virgin Queen"; the name originally applied to all the territory claimed by the British in North America.

previously been part of the Leeward Islands. The remaining islands (about fifty) make up the U.S. unincorporated territory of the Virgin Islands. Pop. 101,809. Capital: Charlotte Amalie (on St. Thomas). They were purchased from Denmark in 1917 because of their strategic position.

Vi·run·ga |vē'rꝊNGgə| (also **Mfumbira**) mountain range in E central Africa, in the Rift Valley and N of Lake Kivu on the border of Congo (formerly Zaire) with Rwanda and Uganda. It reaches 14,787 ft./4,507 m. at Karisimbi, and has several active volcanoes.

Vis |vēs| island in the Adriatic Sea, part of Croatia. Pop. 4,000. A resort, its main towns are Vis and Komiža.

Vi·sa·kha·pat·nam |,vēsäkə'pətnəm| port on the coast of Andhra Pradesh, in SE India. Pop. 750,000.

Vi·sa·lia |vi'sālyə| city in S central California, an agricultural hub in the San Joaquin Valley. Pop. 75,636.

Vi·sa·yan |vē'sīən| (also **Visayas; Bisayas**) island group in the central Philippines, between Luzon and Mindanao.

Vis·by |'vizbē| port on the W coast of the Swedish island of Gotland, of which it is the capital. Pop. 57,000.

Vis·ta |'vistə| city in SW California, a suburb N of San Diego. Pop. 71,872.

Vis·tu·la |'visCHələ| river in Poland that rises in the Carpathian Mts. and flows 592 mi./940 km. generally N, through Cracow and Warsaw, to the Baltic near Gdańsk. Polish name **Wisła**.

Vi·tebsk |vē'tepsk| Russian name for VIT-SEBSK.

Vi·ter·bo |vē'terbō| agricultural center in central Italy, capital of Viterbo province. Pop. 60,000.

Vi·ti Le·vu |'vētē 'lävꝊ| the largest (4,028 mi./10,429 sq. km.) of the Fiji islands. Its chief settlement is Suva.

Vi·tim River |və'tēm| river (1,133 mi./1,823 km. long) in S Russia. It rises in central Buryatia and flows NE into the Lena River on the SW border of Sakha.

Vi·to·ria |vē'tawrēə| industrial city in NE Spain, capital of the Basque Provinces. Pop. 209,000.

Vi·tó·ria |vē'tawrēə| port in E Brazil, capital of the state of Espírito Santo. Pop. 276,000.

Vi·tó·ria da Con·qui·sta |vē'tawrēyə dä kawn'kēstä| city in E Brazil, in Bahia state. Pop. 264,000. It is a cattle industry center in the Batalha Mts.

Vitry-sur-Seine |vē,trē sYr 'sen| industri-

al suburb of Paris, in N central France. Pop. 85,000.

Vit·sebsk |'vētsyipsk| industrial city in NE Belarus, on the Western Dvina River. Pop. 356,000. Russian name **Vitebsk**.

Vit·to·ria |vi'tawrēə| city in SE Sicily, a center of wine and olive-oil production. Pop. 54,000.

Vit·to·rio Ve·ne·to |vi'tawrēō 'venä,tō| commune in NE Italy. Pop. 29,000. After winning a decisive battle here against Austrian forces, Italians achieved an armistice with Austro-Hungarian forces in World War I.

Viz·ca·ya |vis'kī(y)ə| province in N Spain, in the Basque Country, bordering on France. Pop. 1,155,000. The capital is Bilbao.

Viz·i·a·na·ga·ram |,vizēə'nəgərəm| commercial and industrial city in S India, in Andhra Pradesh state. Pop. 177,000.

Vlaar·ding·en |'vlärdiNGgən| industrial city in SW Netherlands, on the Nieuwe Maas River. Pop. 74,000.

Vla·di·kav·kaz |,vlədi,kəf'käz| city in SW Russia, capital of the autonomous republic of North Ossetia. Pop. 306,000. Former names **Ordzhonikidze** (1931–44 and 1954–93) and **Dzaudzhikau** (1944–54).

Vlad·i·mir |vlə'dē,mir; 'vlædə,mi(ə)r| historic industrial city in European Russia, E of Moscow. Pop. 353,000. It is the former (12th–13th century) capital of the principality of Vladimir.

Vla·di·vos·tok |,vlædəvə'stäk; ,vlædə-'västäk| city in the extreme SE of Russia, on the Sea of Japan, capital of Primorsky Krai. Pop. 643,000. It is the chief port of Russia's Pacific coast and terminus of the Trans-Siberian Railway.

Vlis·sing·en |'vlisiNGə| Dutch name for FLUSHING.

Vlo·rë |'vlawr| naval and commercial port in SW Albania, on the Adriatic coast. Pop. 56,000. Also called **Vlona**, Italian name **Valona**.

Vl·ta·va |'vəltəvə| river of the Czech Republic, which rises in the Bohemian Forest on the German border and flows 270 mi./435 km. generally N, passing through Prague before joining the Elbe N of the city. German name **Moldau**.

Voj·vo·di·na |'voivə,dēnə| mainly Hungarian-speaking province of N Serbia, on the Hungarian border. Pop. 2,035,000. Capital: Novi Sad.

Vol·ca·no Islands |väl'kānō; vawl'kānō| island group of Japan, in the W Pacific, S of Bonin Island; the largest is Iwo Jima.

Vol·ga |ˈvōlgə| the longest river in Europe, which rises in NW Russia and flows 2,292 mi./3,688 km. generally E to Kazan, where it turns SE to the Caspian Sea. It has been dammed at several points to provide hydroelectric power, and is navigable for most of its length.

Vol·go·donsk |ˌvəlgəˈdawnsk| city in W Russia, on the Don River NE of Rostov. Pop. 178,000.

Vol·go·grad |ˌvəlgəˈgrät| industrial city in SW Russia, at the junction of the Don and Volga rivers. Pop. 1,005,000. Former names **Tsaritsyn** (until 1925) and **Stalingrad** (1925–61).

Vol·hyn·ia |välˈhinēə| (also **Volynia**) historic region in NW Ukraine, originally a Russian principality. It is now largely an agricultural and coal-mining area.

Vo·log·da |ˈvawləgdə| industrial city in N Russia, on the Vologda River. Pop. 286,000.

Vo·los |ˈvaw‚laws; ˈvō‚läs| port on an inlet of the Aegean Sea, in Thessaly, E Greece. Pop. 77,000. Greek name **Vólos**.

Vol·scian Mountains |ˈvawlsHən| (also called **Lepini Mountains**) range in central Italy. Its highest peak rises to 5,039 ft./1,536 m.

Vol·ta |ˈvältə; ˈvōltə| river of W Africa, which is formed in central Ghana by the junction of its headwaters, the Black Volta, the White Volta, and the Red Volta, which rise in Burkina Faso. At Akosombo in SE Ghana it has been dammed, creating Lake Volta, one of the world's largest manmade lakes.

Vol·ta Re·don·da |ˌvawltə reˈdändə| industrial city in SE Brazil, in Rio de Janeiro state, on the Paraíba River. Pop. 229,000. It is a steel industry center.

Vol·ter·ra |vawlˈterə| town in central Italy. Pop. 13,000. An Etruscan stronghold later controlled Florence, it contains Etruscan and Roman structures.

Vol·tur·no River |vawlˈtoornō| river (109 mi./175 km.) in S central Italy that rises in the Apennine range and flows into the Gulf of Gaeta SE of Gaeta. Its valley was the scene of heavy fighting in World War II.

Vo·lu·bi·lis |vəˈloobiləs| Roman town in ancient Mauretania Tingitana, now an area of ruins near Meknès, NW Morocco.

Vol·un·teer State |ˌvälənˈtir| nickname for TENNESSEE.

Volzh·sky |ˈvawlsHkē| industrial city in SW Russia, on the Volga near Volgograd. Pop. 275,000.

Vor·arl·berg |ˈfawr‚ärl‚bərg| Alpine state of W Austria. Pop. 331,000. Capital: Bregenz.

Vor·ku·ta |vawrˈkootə| city in Russia, in the N Ural Mts., above the Arctic Circle. Pop. 117,000. It was founded as a prison labor camp during the Stalin era.

Vo·ro·nezh |vəˈrawnizH| industrial city in Russia, S of Moscow on the Voronezh River. Pop. 895,000.

Vo·ro·shi·lov·grad |ˌvərəsHə‚lowˈgrät| former (1935–91) name for LUHANSK.

Vosges |vōzH| mountain system of E France, in Alsace near the border with Germany, rising to 4,669 ft./1,423 m.

Vos·tok |väˈstawk| Russian scientific station in central Antarctica, near the S magnetic pole, cited as the coldest known place on earth.

Vot·kinsk |ˈvawt‚kinsk| industrial city in W Russia, on the Kama River. Pop. 104,000.

Voy·a·geurs National Park |ˌvoiäˈzHər| preserve in N Minnesota, along the Ontario border, whose name recalls the French fur traders of the 18th century.

Vra·tsa |ˈvrätsə| industrial city in NW Bulgaria, in the foothills of the Balkan Mountains. Pop. 102,000.

Vrin·da·van |ˈvrindəvən| (also **Brindaban; Bindraban; Vrindaban**) historic town in N India, in Uttar Pradesh state, S of Delhi. Pop. 48,000. It is a Hindu holy city.

Vu·ko·var |ˈvookə‚vär| town in extreme E Croatia, on the Danube River (the border with Serbia). Pop. 45,000.

Vung Tau |ˈvoong ˈtow| port in southern Vietnam, SE of Ho Chi Minh City, on the South China Sea. Pop. 134,000.

Vyat·ka |ˈvyätkə| industrial town in N central European Russia, on the Vyatka River. Pop. 487,000. Former name (1934–92) **Kirov**.

Vy·borg |ˈvē‚bawrg| (Swedish name **Viborg**: Finnish name **Vipuri**) seaport in NW Russia, on the Gulf of Finland, NE of Saint Petersburg and near the Finnish border. Pop. 80,000.

Vy·cheg·da River |ˈvicHegdə| river (700 mi./1,120 km. long) in W Russia, rising in the N Ural Mts. and flowing W to join the Northern Dvina River at Kotlas.

Ww

Waadt |vät| German name for VAUD.

Waal |väl| river of the S central Netherlands. The more southerly of two major tributaries of the Rhine, it flows for 52 mi./84 km. from the point where the Rhine forks, just W of the border with Germany, to the estuary of the Meuse (Maas) on the North Sea.

Wa·bash River |'waw,bæSH| river that flows 475 mi./765 km. from W Ohio across Indiana and then along the Indiana-Illinois border, to the Ohio River.

Wa·co |'wākō| commercial and industrial city in E central Texas. Pop. 103,590.

Wa·di Hal·fa |'wädē 'hälfə| town in N Sudan, on the border with Egypt. Situated on the Nile at the S end of Lake Nasser, it is the terminus of the railroad from Khartoum.

Wad Me·da·ni |wäd 'medn-ē| (also **Wad Madani**) city in E Sudan, capital of Gezira state, SE of Khartoum on the Blue Nile. Pop. 141,000. It is the center of a cotton-producing region.

Wag·ga Wag·ga |'wägə ,wägə| agricultural town on the Murrumbidgee River, in New South Wales, SE Australia. Pop. 41,000.

Wa·gram |'vä,gräm| village in E Austria, site of a battle (July 5–6, 1809) won by Napoleon against troops led by Archduke Charles Louis of Austria.

Wah |wä; vä| town in central Pakistan, S of Hasan Abdal. Pop. 122,000. A famous Mogul garden is here.

Wai·ka·to |wī'kätō| the longest river of New Zealand, which flows 270 mi./434 km. generally NW from Lake Taupo, at the center of North Island, to the Tasman Sea.

Wai·ki·ki |,wīki'kē| Hawaiian beach resort, a suburb of Honolulu, on the island of Oahu.

Wai·mea Canyon |wī'māə| (also **the Grand Canyon of the Pacific**) deep canyon in W Kauai Island, Hawaii, a tourist attraction.

Wai·tan·gi |'wī,täNGgē| historic village in New Zealand, on North Island, site of the signing of the Treaty of Waitangi, which formed the basis for British annexation of New Zealand (1840).

Wa·ka·ya·ma |,wäkə'yämə| commercial and industrial city in W central Japan, on S Honshu. Pop. 397,000.

Wake·field |'wāk,fēld| industrial town in E Massachusetts, N of Boston. Pop. 24,825.

Wake Forest |wāk| town in N central North Carolina, the original home of Wake Forest University, now in Winston-Salem. Pop. 5,769.

Wake Island |wāk| coral atoll in the Pacific, N of the Marshall Islands. Controlled by the U.S. since 1898, it was the scene of World War II fighting after the Japanese occupied it in December 1941.

Wak·han Salient |wä'KHän 'sālēənt| narrow corridor of land, 188 mi./300. km in length, in the NE corner of Afghanistan, which was formerly a demarcating line between Russian and British spheres of influence.

Wal·brzych |'välbzHik| coal-mining and industrial city in SW Poland. Pop. 141,000.

Wal·deck |'väl,dek| administrative district, a former principality, in Hesse, central Germany.

Wal·den Pond |'wawldən| pond in Concord, Massachusetts, associated with the writer Henry David Thoreau. It is now within a state park.

Wales |wālz| principality of Great Britain and a constituent of the United Kingdom, to the W of central England. Area: 8,020 sq. mi./20,766 sq. km. Pop. 2,798,000. Capital and largest city: Cardiff. Welsh name **Cymru**. Wales is mainly mountainous and forms a large peninsula extending into the Irish Sea. The earliest inhabitants appear to have been overrun by Celtic peoples in the Broze and Iron ages. The Romans established outposts linked by a system of roads. After the Roman withdrawal in the 5th century the Celtic Welsh successfully maintained independence against the Anglo-Saxons who settled in England, and in the 8th century Offa, king of Mercia, built an earthwork, Offa's Dyke, marking the border. In the Dark Ages Christianity was spead through Wales by missionaries, but the country remained somewhat isolated. Colonization from Norman England began in the 12th century, and was assured by Edward I's conquest (1277–84). Wales was formally brought into the English legal and parliamentary system in 1536, but has retained a distinct cultural identity; the Welsh language is still widely used. In the 1990s moves toward greater autonomy grew. □ **Welsh** adj. & n.

Wall·a·bout Bay |'wawlə,bowt| former inlet of the East River in Brooklyn, New York, scene of the imprisonment during the Revolutionary War of thousands of American prisoners, many of whom died here.

Wal·la·chia |wə'läkēə| (also **Walachia**) former principality of SE Europe, between the Danube and the Transylvanian Alps. In 1861 it was united with Moldavia to form Romania. □ **Wallachian** adj. & n.

Wal·la·sey |'wäləsē| residential town in Merseyside, NW England, on the Wirral Peninsula. Pop. 63,000.

Wal·la Wal·la |,wälə 'wälə| historic commercial and industrial city in SE Washington. Pop. 26,478.

Wal·ling·ford |'wawliNGfərd| industrial town in S central Connecticut. Pop. 40,822.

Wal·lis and Fu·tu·na Islands |'wälis ənd fə'to͞onə| overseas territory of France comprising two groups of islands to the W of Samoa in the central Pacific. Pop. 15,000. Capital: Mata-Uta (on Uvea).

Wallis & Fatuna

Wal·loo·nia |wä'lo͞onēə| (also **Wallonia**) French-speaking region in S Belgium, comprising the provinces of Hainaut, Liège, Luxembourg, Namur, and part of Brabant.

Wal·lops Island |'wäləps| island in E Virginia, on the Delmarva Peninsula, site of a U.S. rocket and high-altitude balloon facility.

Wal·lowa Mountains |wä'lawə| range in NE Oregon, noted for its alpine topography and plants. The Wallowa River valley, on its E, is home to the Nez Perce Indians.

Wall·send |'wawl,zend| industrial town in NE England, in Tyne and Wear, on the Tyne River. Pop. 45,000.

Wall Street |wawl| street at the S end of Manhattan, New York City, where the New York Stock Exchange and other leading financial institutions are located. □ **Wall Streeter** n.

Wal·nut Creek |'wäl,nət| residential and industrial city in N central California, a suburb NE of Oakland. Pop. 60,569.

Wal·sall |'wawl,sawl| industrial town in the West Midlands of England. Pop. 256,000.

Wal·sing·ham |'wawlziNGəm| village in E central England, in Norfolk, formerly site of Walsingham Abbey, a major place of pilgrimage.

Wal·tham |'wawl,THæm| historic industrial and academic city in E Massachusetts, on the Charles River W of Boston. Pop. 57,878.

Wal·tham Forest |'wawltəm; 'wawlTHəm| residential borough of NE Greater London, England. Pop. 203,400. **Waltham Abbey**, burial place of King Harold, last pre-Norman English king, is just N, in Essex.

Wal·vis Bay |'wawlvəs| port in Namibia. Pop. 25,000. It was an exclave of the former Cape Province, South Africa until it was transferred to Namibia in 1994.

Wands·worth |'wän(d)z,wərTH| largely residential borough of S London, England, S of the Thames River. Pop. 238,000. Battersea and Putney are here.

Wan·ga·nui |,wäNGgə'no͞oē| port in New Zealand, on the W coast of North Island. Pop. 41,000.

Wan·kie |'wäNGkē| former name (until 1982) for HWANGE.

Wann·see |'vän,zä| lakeside resort site, near Berlin, Germany, of a 1942 conference at which the Nazis set forth their doctrine of the "final solution," calling for the extermination of the Jews.

Wan·xian |'wänsHē'än| city in Sichuan province, central China, an inland port on the Yangtze River above the Yangtze Gorges. Pop. 157,000.

Wap·si·pin·i·con River |,wäpsə'pinikən| river that flows 225 mi./360 km. across E Iowa, to the Mississippi. Its valley is associated with the regional painting of Grant Wood and others.

Wa·ran·gal |'wawrəNGgəl| commercial and industrial city in S central India, in Andhra Pradesh state. Pop. 467,000.

War·dha |'wawrdə| **1** city in central India, in Maharashtra state, SW of Nagpur. Pop. 103,000. It was the headquarters of Mohandas Gandhi, father of Indian independence. **2** river in central India that flows 290 mi./465 km., from NW of Maharashtra state to its S border, where it meets the Wainganga to form the Pranhita.

War·ka |'värkə| Arabic name for URUK.

Warley |'wawrlē| industrial town in W central England, in the West Midlands, just W of Birmingham. Pop. 152,000.

Warm Springs |wärm| resort city in NW Georgia, associated with Franklin D. Roosevelt and his "Little White House," where he died. Pop. 407.

War·ner Rob·ins |ˌwärnər 'räbinz| industrial and military city in central Georgia. Pop. 43,726.

War·ren¹ |'wawrən; 'wärən| industrial city, an auto center, in SE Michigan, just N of Detroit. Pop. 144,864.

War·ren² |'wawrən; 'wärən| industrial city in NE Ohio, on the Mahoning River. Pop. 50,793.

War·ring·ton |'wawriNGtən| industrial town on the Mersey River in Cheshire, NW England. Pop. 83,000.

Warr·nam·bool |'wärnəm,bo͞ol| coastal resort and former whaling port in SE Australia, in Victoria. Pop. 24,000.

War·saw |'wawr,saw| historic city, the capital of Poland, on the Vistula River. Pop. 1,656,000. The city suffered severe damage and the loss of 700,000 lives during World War II and since has been almost completely rebuilt. It is a cultural and industrial center. Polish name **Warszawa.**

War·saw Pact |'wawr,saw| military alliance, formed by a 1955 treaty and surviving until 1991, of countries allied with the Soviet Union. A response to NATO, it included also Bulgaria, Czechoslovakia, Hungary, Poland, Romania, and (until 1968) Albania.

War·ta River |'värtə| river (502 mi./808 km. long) in Poland, rising NW of Craków and flowing W into the Oder River.

War·wick¹ |'wär,wik; 'wawr(w)ik| city in E central Rhode Island, an industrial and residential suburb S of Providence. Pop. 85,427.

War·wick² |'wärik; 'wawr(w)ik| the county seat of Warwickshire, in central England, on the Avon River. Pop. 22,000.

War·wick·shire |'wärik,sHir; 'wäriksHər| county of central England. Pop. 477,000; county seat, Warwick.

Wa·satch Range |'wawsæCH| range of the Rocky Mts., extending S from Idaho into central Utah, where Salt Lake City and its suburbs lie on its W, along the **Wasatch Front.**

Wash, the inlet of the North Sea in E England, between Lincolnshire and Norfolk. Boston and King's Lynn lie near it.

Wash·ing·ton¹ |'wawsHiNGtən; 'wäsHingtən| industrial town in NE England. Pop. 49,000. The original village of Wash-

ington was the ancestral home of George Washington, first President of the United States.

Wash·ing·ton² |'wawsHiNGtən; 'wäsHingtən| historic city in W Pennsylvania, SW of Pittsburgh. Pop. 15,864.

Wash·ing·ton³ |'wawsHiNGtən; 'wäsHingtən| see box. □ **Washingtonian** adj. & n.

Wash·ing·ton⁴ |'wawsHiNGtən; 'wäsHingtən| the capital of the U.S. Pop. 606,900. It is coextensive with the District of Columbia, a federal district on the Potomac River between Virginia and Maryland. Founded in 1790, it was planned and built as a capital. In addition to government, it is a business, cultural, and tourist center. Generally known as **Washington, D.C..** □ **Washingtonian** adj. & n.

Wash·ing·ton, Mount |'wäsHiNGtən; 'wäsHingtən| peak in N central New Hampshire, highest in the Presidential Range of the White Mts. and in the NE U.S.: 6,288 ft./1,918 m.

Wash·ing·ton Crossing |'wawsHiNGtən; 'wäsHingtən| historic site on the Delaware River N of Trenton, New Jersey, where George Washington and American forces crossed from Pennsylvania for an attack on

---

Washington

Capital: Olympia
Largest city: Seattle
Other cities: Everett, Spokane, Tacoma
Population: 4,866,692 (1990); 5,689,263 (1998); 6,258,000 (2005 est.)
Population rank (1990): 18
Rank in land area: 18
Abbreviation: WA; Wash.
Nickname: The Evergreen State
Motto: Alki (Chinook: 'By and By')
Bird: willow goldfinch
Fish: steelhead trout
Flower: coast rhododendron
Tree: Western hemlock
Song: "Washington, My Home"
Noted physical features: Puget Sound, Rosario Sound
Tourist attractions: Bonneville Dam, Grand Coulee Dam; Mount Rainier, Olympic, and North Cascades national parks
Admission date: November 11, 1889
Order of admission: 42
Name origin: For George Washington (1732-99), the first president of the United States.

Hessian troops on Christmas, 1776. There are parks on both sides of the river.

Wash·ing·ton Square |'wawSHiNGtən; 'wäSHiNGtən| park in lower Manhattan, NewYork City, a focal point of Greenwich Village.

Wash·i·ta River |'wäSHə,taw; 'wawSHə,taw| river that flows 500 mi./800 km. from theTexas Panhandle across S Oklahoma to the Red River at LakeTexoma.

Wa States |'wä| mountainous region of Burma, in Shan state E of the Salween River, inhabited by theWa; it constitutes a large part of the GOLDEN TRIANGLE.

Wa·ter·bury |'wawtər,berē; 'wätər,berē| industrial city in W Connecticut, on the Naugatuck River. Pop. 108,961. It is an historic brass-manufacturing center.

Wa·ter·ford[1] |'wawtərfərd; 'wätərfərd| town in SE Connecticut, a largely residential suburb of New London. Pop. 17,930.

Wa·ter·ford[2] |'wawtərfərd; 'wätərfərd| **1** county in the SE of the Republic of Ireland, in the province of Munster. Pop. 92,000; main administrative center, Dungarvan. **2** its county seat, a port on an inlet of St. George's Channel. Pop. 40,000. It is noted for its colorless flint glass, known asWaterford crystal.

Wa·ter·ford[3] |'wawtərfərd; 'wätərfərd| residential suburb NW of Pontiac, in SE Michigan. Pop. 66,692.

Wa·ter·gate, the |'wätər,gāt; 'wätər,gāt| apartment and office complex inWashington, D.C., site of a 1972 break-in at Democratic headquarters that led eventually to the resignation of President Richard Nixon.

Wa·ter·loo[1] |,wawtər'lōō; wätər'lōō| village in central Belgium. Pop. 28,000. The Battle ofWaterloo (1815) ended in Napoleon's decisive defeat by the British troops of the Duke of Wellington and Prussian troops.

Wa·ter·loo[2] |,wawtər'lōō; wätər'lōō| industrial and commercial city in NE Iowa. Pop. 66,467.

Wa·ter·loo[3] |,wawtər'lōō; wätər'lōō| commercial and industrial city in S Ontario, next to Kitchener. Pop. 71,181.

Wa·ter·town[1] |'wawtər,town; 'wätər,town| industrial town in E Massachusetts, on the Charles River just W of Boston. Pop. 33,284.

Wa·ter·town[2] |'wawtər,town; 'wätər,town | industrial and commercial city in N central NewYork, near Lake Ontario and theThousand Islands. Pop. 29,429.

Wa·ter·town[3] |'wawtər,town; 'wätər,town |

industrial city in S centralWisconsin. Pop. 19,142.

Wa·ter·ville |'wawtərvil; 'wätər,vil| commercial city in S central Maine, on the Kennebec River. Pop. 17,173.

Wa·ter·vliet |'wawtər,vlēt; wätər,vlēt| historic industrial city in E New York, just NE of Albany on the Hudson River. Pop. 11,061. The site of the first U.S. Shaker settlement and a large arsenal are here.

Wat·ford |'wätfərd| industrial town in Hertfordshire, SE England. Pop. 74,000.

Wat·kins Glen |'wätkinz| resort village in W central NewYork, at the S end of Seneca Lake. Pop. 2,207.

Wat·ling Street |'wätliNG| Roman road (now largely underlying modern roads) running NW across England, from Richborough in Kent through London and St. Albans toWroxeter in Shropshire.

Wat·son·ville |'wätsən,vil| city in W central California, in an agricultural area S of San Jose. Pop. 31,099.

Watts |wäts| district of S Los Angeles, California, home to much of the black population of the city.

Watts Bar |'wäts 'bär| locality on theTennessee River, NE of Chattanooga, Tennessee, site of major hydroelectric and nuclear facilities.

Wau·ke·gan |waw'kēgən| industrial port city in NE Illinois, on Lake Michigan. Pop. 69,392.

Wau·ke·sha |'wawki,SHaw| industrial city in SE Wisconsin, W of Milwaukee. Pop. 56,958.

Wau·sau |'waw,saw| industrial and commercial city in central Wisconsin. Pop. 37,060.

Wau·wa·to·sa |,waw-wə'tōsə| city in SE Wisconsin, a suburbW of Milwaukee. Pop. 51,308.

Wa·ver·ley |'wāvərlē| **1** town in Australia, a residential suburb E of Sydney, in New South Wales. Pop. 59,000. **2** town in SE Australia, a suburb SE of Melbourne, in Victoria. Pop. 118,000.

Wax·a·hach·ie |,wawksə'hæCHē| industrial and commercial city in NE Texas, S of Dallas. Pop. 18,168.

Wax·haw |'wæk,shä| town in S North Carolina, near the South Carolina border. Pop 1,294. Andrew Jackson was born in a settlement in the area in 1767, in which state is unclear.

Wayne[1] |wān| industrial city in SE Michigan, a suburb SW of Detroit. Pop. 19,899.

Wayne[2] |wān| residential and commercial

township in NE New Jersey, just NW of Paterson. Pop. 47,025.

Wayne County |wān| county in SE Michigan, site of Detroit and many suburbs. Pop. 2,111.687.

Wa•zir•i•stan |wə͵ziri'stän| arid mountainous region of NW Pakistan, on the border with Afghanistan.

Weald |wēld| formerly wooded district of SE England including parts of Kent, Surrey, and East Sussex.

Web•ster Groves |͵webstər 'grōvz| city in E Missouri, a residential and academic suburb SW of St. Louis. Pop. 22,987.

Wed•dell Sea |'wedl| arm of the Atlantic Ocean, off the coast of Antarctica.

Wee•nen |'vēnen| town in KwaZulu-Natal province, E South Africa, SE of Ladysmith, scene of an 1838 massacre of Boer settlers (Voortrekkers) by Zulu forces.

Wei•fang |'wā'fäNG| industrial city in Shandong province, E China. Pop. 565,000. Former name **Weihsien.**

Wei•hai |'wā'hī| city in Shandong province, E China, a port on the Yellow Sea. It was leased from 1898 to 1930 by the British, who called it Port Edward. Pop. 129,000.

Wei•mar |'vī͵mär| city in Thuringia, central Germany. Pop. 59,000. It was famous in the late 18th and early 19th century for its intellectual and cultural life. The German National Assembly ratified the Treaty of Versailles here in 1919, and established a government called the **Weimar Republic,** which lasted until 1933.

Wei•nan |'wā'nän| city in Shaanxi province, central China, NE of Xi'an, on the Wei River. Pop. 709,000.

Wei River |wā| (Chinese name **Wei Shui**) river of N central China, flowing 537 mi./864 km. from SE Gansu province to the Yellow River at Huatin. XIAN lies on the Wei.

Weir•ton |'wirtn| industrial city in N West Virginia, on the Ohio River. Pop. 22,124.

Wel•kom |'velkəm| mining town in central South Africa, in Free State. Pop. 185,000.

Wel•land |'welənd| industrial and commercial city in S Ontario, on the Welland Canal. Pop. 47,914.

Wel•land Canal |'welənd| (also **Welland Ship Canal**) canal in S Ontario, 26 mi./42 km. long, linking Lake Erie with Lake Ontario, bypassing Niagara Falls and forming part of the Great Lakes–St. Lawrence Seaway.

Welles•ley |'welzlē| town in E Massachusetts, a suburb W of Boston. Pop. 26,615. It is home to Wellesley College.

Well•fleet |'wel͵flēt| resort town in SE Massachusetts, near the tip of Cape Cod, noted for its arts colony. Pop. 2,493.

Wel•ling•ton |'weliNGtən| the capital of New Zealand, situated at the S tip of North Island. Pop. 150,000. It became the capital in 1865, succeeding Auckland.

Wells |welz| city in SW England, in Somerset, site of one of the best-known medieval cathedrals in Britain. Pop. 9,000.

Wels |vels| industrial and market town in N Austria, SW of Linz. Pop. 53,000. It was important during the Roman period.

Welsh Marches |welsH| name for the countryside on either side of the border between Wales and England. *March* is an old word for 'boundary.'

Wel•wel |'wel͵wel| pastoral village in SE Ethiopia, in the Ogaden, scene of a 1934 clash that preceded the Italo-Ethiopian War of 1935–36.

Wel•wyn Garden City |'welən| industrial city in SE England, in Hertfordshire. Pop. 41,000. Established in 1920 to ease crowding in London, to the S, it is also a commuter suburb.

Wem•bley |'wemblē| residential district of W Greater London, England, in the borough of Brent. It is famous for its sports stadium.

We•natch•ee |wə'næcHē| city in central Washington, an agricultural-procesing center on the Columbia River near the Wenatchee Mts. Pop. 21,756.

Wens•ley•dale |'wenzlē͵dāl| upper valley of the Ure River in North Yorkshire, N England, which gave its name to types of cheese and sheep.

Wen•zhou |'wen'jō| (also **Wen-Chou**) industrial city in Zhejiang province, E China. Pop. 1,650,000.

Wer•ri•bee |'werəbē| town in SE Australia, in Victoria, SW of Melbourne. Pop. 72,000.

We•sel |'vāzəl| industrial and port city in western Germany, on the Rhine River. The city was nearly destroyed in March 1945, when the Allies crossed the Rhine, and has has been rebuilt.

We•ser |'wāzər| river of NW Germany, which is formed at the junction of the Werra and Fulda rivers in Lower Saxony and flows 182 mi./292 km. N to the North Sea near Bremerhaven.

Wes•sex |'wesiks| the kingdom of the West Saxons, established in Hampshire in the early 6th century and gradually extended to include much of S England. Under Alfred the Great and his successors it formed the nucleus of the Anglo-Saxon kingdom of England. Athelstan, Alfred's grandson, became king of England. The name was revived in the 19th century by Thomas Hardy to designate the SW counties of England (especially Dorset) in which his novels are set.

West, the |west| in 20th-century politics, the largely capitalist nations of W Europe and the Americas.

West Af•ri•ca |'æfrikə| the W part of the African continent, especially the countries bounded by and including Mauritania, Mali, and Niger in the N and Gabon in the S. □ **West African** adj. & n.

West Al•lis |'æləs| industrial city in SE Wisconsin, a suburb of Milwaukee. Pop. 63,221.

West Bank |'west 'bæNGk| region west of the Jordan River and NW of the Dead Sea. Covering some 2,270 sq. mi./5,879 sq. km., it contains Jericho, Hebron, Nablus, Bethlehem, and other settlements. It became part of Jordan in 1948 and was occupied by Israel following the Six Day War of 1967. In 1993 an agreement was signed that granted limited autonomy to the Palestinians, who comprise 97 percent of its inhabitants; withdrawal of Israeli troops began in 1994.

West Bend |'west 'bend| industrial city in SE Wisconsin, on the Milwaukee River. Pop. 23,916.

West Ben•gal |ben'gäl| state in E India. Pop. 67.98 million. Capital: Calcutta. It was formed in 1947 from the predominantly Hindu area of former Bengal.

West Ber•lin |bər'lin| the W half of the city of Berlin (divided in 1945) and, until German reunification in 1990, a state of the Federal Republic of Germany. Surrounded on all sides by East Germany, it was occupied by U.S., French, and British troops and separated from East Berlin in 1961 by the Berlin Wall.

West Branch |'west ,brænCH| agricultural city in E central Iowa, the birthplace of Herbert Hoover. Pop. 1,908.

West Brom•wich |'brämwiCH| industrial town in the West Midlands, England, NW of Birmingham. Pop. 155,000.

West•ches•ter County |'wes,CHestər| suburban county in SE New York, just NE of New York City. Pop. 874,866. White Plains is its seat.

West Country |west| the SW counties of England, specifically Cornwall, Devon, Somerset, Avon, Wiltshire, and W Dorset.

West Co•vi•na |kō'vēnə| city in SW California, a suburb E of Los Angeles. Pop. 96,086.

West End |'west'end| the W part of central London, England, long noted for its theaters, clubs, and shopping.

Wes•ter•ly |'westərlē| industrial and resort town in SW Rhode Island, on the Connecticut border. Pop. 21,605.

West•ern Aus•tra•lia |aws'trālyə| state comprising the W part of Australia. Area: 975,473 sq. mi./2.53 million sq. km. Pop. 1,643,000. Capital: Perth. It was colonized by the British in 1826, and was federated with the other states of Australia in 1901.

West•ern Cape |'western 'kāp| province of SW South Africa, formerly part of Cape Province. Pop. 3,635,000. Capital: Cape Town.

West•ern Channel |'western 'CHænl| channel between South Korea and the Japanese island of Tsushima; it connects the Sea of Japan with the Yellow and the East China seas.

West•ern Desert |'western 'dezərt| Egyptian name for the LIBYAN DESERT.

West•ern Em•pire |'western 'em,pīr| the W part of the ROMAN EMPIRE from the 3rd to the 5th centuries A.D. It included Italy, Gaul, Spain, Britain, Illyricum (the E coast of the Adriatic Sea), and N Africa.

West•ern hem•i•sphere |'western 'hemə-,sfēr| the half of the earth containing the Americas.

West•ern Isles |'western 'īlz| **1** another name for the HEBRIDES. **2** an administrative region of Scotland, consisting of the Outer Hebrides. Pop. 29,000; administrative center, Stornoway.

West•ern Re•serve |'western ri'zərv| historic region of the U.S., comprising lands formerly owned by Connecticut, in present-day NE Ohio. Cleveland is the largest city.

West•ern Sa•hara |'western sə'hærə| region of NW Africa, on the Atlantic coast between Morocco and Mauritania. Area: 97,383 sq. mi./252,126 sq. km. Pop. 187,000. Capital: La'youn. Formerly the

Western Sahara

Spanish Sahara, the region has been controlled since 1976 by Morocco (Mauritania briefly controlled a part). The Polisario Front has continued to struggle for independence as the Saharabi Arab Democratic Republic. The area has vast rock phosphate deposits.

West·ern Sa·moa |'western sə'mōə| see republic of SAMOA.

Western Samoa

West·ern Wall |'western 'wawl| (also called **Wailing Wall**) wall in Jerusalem, Israel, originally part of the temple structure built by Herod the Great and destroyed by the Romans in A.D. 70. A place of Jewish prayer, it also forms the W wall of the sanctuary enclosing the Muslim holy place, the Dome of the Rock.

Wes·ter·ville |'wester,vil| city in central Ohio, a suburb NE of Columbus. Pop. 30,193.

Wes·ter·wald |'vester,vält| mountainous region in western Germany, stretching E from Koblenz and the Rhine River for 70 mi./115 km. Its highest peak, Fuchskauten, reaches 2,156 ft./657 m.

West·fa·len |'vest,fälen| German name for WESTPHALIA.

West·field[1] |'west,fēld| industrial city in W Massachusetts. Pop. 38,372.

West·field[2] |'west,fēld| historic town in NE New Jersey, a suburb W of Elizabeth. Pop. 28,870.

West Flan·ders |'flændərz| province of NW Belgium. Pop. 1,107,000. Capital: Bruges.

West Fri·sian Islands |'frēzHən| see FRISIAN ISLANDS.

West Ger·ma·ny |'jərmənē| (officially **Federal Republic of Germany**) former republic in Europe, formed in 1949 from the German zones occupied after World War II by the U.S., France, and Great Britain. Bonn was its acting capital. It was reunited with East Germany in 1990. German name **Bundesrepublik Deutschland**.

West Gla·mor·gan |glə'mawrgən| former county of S Wales, formed in 1974 and dissolved in 1996.

West Ham |west 'hæm| see NEWHAM, London, England.

West Hart·ford |west 'härtfərd| town in central Connecticut, a residential and industrial suburb W of Hartford. Pop. 60,110.

West Ha·ven |west 'hāvən; 'west ,hāvən| city in SW Connecticut, a suburb W of New Haven. Pop. 54,021.

West Hills |west 'hilz| section of the town of Huntington, New York, on Long Island, the birthplace of Walt Whitman.

West Hol·ly·wood |'hälē,wŏŏd| city in SW California, a largely residential suburb NE of Beverly Hills. Pop. 36,118.

West In·dies |west 'indēz| chain of islands extending from the Florida peninsula to the coast of Venezuela, lying between the Caribbean and the Atlantic. They consist of three main island groups, the Greater and Lesser Antilles and the Bahamas, with Bermuda lying farther to the N. Originally inhabited by Arawak and Carib Indians, the islands were visited by Columbus in 1492 and named by him in the belief that he had reached the coast of India. The Spanish settlements of the 16th and 17th centuries were fiercely contested by other European powers, principally the British, the French, and the Dutch; the region became notorious for buccaneering and piracy in the 17th century. Many of the islands became British colonies in the 17th and 18th centuries, and were centers for the cultivation of sugar and large plantations worked by slaves imported from W Africa. The islands now include a number of independent states and British, French, Dutch, and U.S. dependencies. □ **West Indian** adj. & n.

West Ir·i·an |'irē,än| see IRIAN JAYA.

West Jor·dan |west 'jawrdn| city in N central Utah, a largely residential suburb S of Salt Lake City. Pop. 42,892.

West La·fay·ette |läfä'yet| city in W central Indiana, a suburb of Lafayette and home to Purdue University. Pop. 25,907.

West·mann Islands |'westmən| group of fifteen volcanic islands off the S coast of Iceland. Icelandic name **Vestmannaeyjar**.

West·meath |west'mēTH| county of the central Republic of Ireland, in the province of Leinster. Pop. 62,000; county seat, Mullingar.

West Mem·phis |'memfəs| industrial and commercial city in NE Arkansas, across the

Mississippi River from Memphis, Tennessee. Pop. 28,259.

West Mid·lands |'midləndz| metropolitan county of central England. Pop. 2,500,000. County town: Brimingham.

West Mif·flin |'miflən| industrial borough in SW Pennsylvania, SE of Pittsburgh. Pop. 23,644.

West·min·ster¹ |'wes(t),minstər| industrial and commercial city in SW California, SE of Los Angeles. Pop. 78,118.

West·min·ster² |'wes(t),minstər| city in N central Colorado, a suburb NW of Denver. Pop. 74,625.

West·min·ster³ |'wes(t),minstər| inner borough of London, England, which contains the Houses of Parliament and many government offices. Pop. 181,000. Full name **City of Westminster**. The name is also used in reference to the British Parliament.

West·min·ster Ab·bey |'wes(t),minstər| church of St. Peter in Westminster, London, England, facing the Houses of Parliament. It is the site of royal coronations and burials, and is famous for its Poet's Corner, with the graves of many literary notables.

West·mor·land |'westmərlənd; west 'mawrlənd| former county of NW England. In 1974 it was united with Cumberland and N parts of Lancashire to form the county of Cumbria.

West·mount |'westmownt| affluent residential city in S Quebec, just SW of Montreal. Pop. 20,329.

West New York |n(y) o͞o 'yawrk| industrial and residential town in NE New Jersey, on the Hudson River across from New York City. Pop. 38,125.

Weston-super-Mare |'westən,so͞opər 'mer| resort in Avon, SW England, on the Bristol Channel. Pop. 62,000.

West Orange |'awr(y)nj; 'ärənj| suburban township in NE New Jersey, NW of Newark. Pop. 39,013.

West Pak·i·stan |'pæki'stæn; ,päki'stän| see PAKISTAN.

West Palm Beach |,west ,pä(l)m 'beCH| commercial and industrial city in SE Florida. Pop. 67,643.

West·pha·lia |,west'fälyə| former province of NW Germany. Previously a duchy of the archbishop of Cologne, it became a province of Prussia in 1815. In 1946 the major part was incorporated in the state of North Rhine–Westphalia, the northern portion becoming part of Lower Saxony. German name **Westfalen**. □ **Westphalian** *adj. & n.*

West Point |west 'point| community in SE New York, on the Hudson River, home to the U.S. Military Academy. Pop. 8,024.

West·port¹ |'west,pawrt| town in SW Connecticut, an affluent suburb W of Bridgeport. Pop. 24,410.

West·port² |'west,pawrt| former town, now part of Kansas City, Missouri, that was a 19th-century gateway to the westbound Santa Fe Trail.

West Prus·sia |'prəsHə| former province in Prussia, NE Germany, on the Baltic Sea. After World War I it was divided between Poland and Germany; at the end of World War II the entire region was given to Poland. Its capital was Danzig.

West Quod·dy Head |'kwädē| easternmost (66° 57′ W) point of the U.S., in Lubec, Maine, S of Passamaquoddy Bay.

West River |,west| see XI RIVER.

West Rox·bury |'räks,berē| SW district of Boston, Massachusetts. Largely residential, it was a separate town until 1874, and was the site of the experimental Brook Farm.

West Sen·e·ca |'senikə| town in W New York, a suburb SE of Buffalo. Pop. 47,830.

West Side |'west 'sīd| in Manhattan, New York City, the residential and commercial districts W of Fifth Avenue, regarded in general as less affluent, more diverse, and more intellectual than the East Side.

West Sus·sex |'səsiks| county of SE England. Pop. 693,000; county seat, Chichester. It was formed in 1974 from part of the former county of Sussex.

West Val·ley City |west 'vælē| city in N central Utah, a residential suburb S of Salt Lake City. Pop. 86,976.

West Vir·gin·ia |vər'jinyə| see box, p. 408. □ **West Virginian** *adj. & n.*

West·wood |'west,wo͝od| section of W Los Angeles, California, home to the University of California at Los Angeles (UCLA).

West York·shire |'yawrksHər| metropolitan county of N England. Pop. 1,985,000. County town: Wakefield.

Weth·ers·field |'weTHərz,fēld| historic town in central Connecticut, just S of Hartford on the Connecticut River. Pop. 25,651.

Wet·ter·stein Mountains |'vetər,sHtīn| range in S Germany. It includes the ZUGSPITZE, the highest peak in Germany.

Wetz·lar |'vet,slär| manufacturing city in central Germany, N of Frankfurt. Pop. 51,000.

We·wak |'wā,wäk; 'wē,wæk| town in N New Guinea Island, Papua New Guinea, the capital of Sepik district. Pop. 23,000. It

West Virginia

Capital: Charleston
Largest city: Huntington
Other cities: Morgantown, Parkersburg, Vienna, Weirton, Wheeling
Population: 1,793,477 (1990); 1,811,156 (1998); 1,849,000 (2005 proj.)
Population rank (1990): 34
Rank in land area: 41
Abbreviation: WV; W. Va.
Nickname: Mountain State; Panhandle State
Motto: *Montani Semper Liberi* (Latin: 'Mountaineers Are Always Free')
Bird: cardinal
Fish: brook trout
Flower: big laurel
Tree: sugar maple
Songs: "The West Virginia Hills"; "West Virginia, My Home Sweet Home"; "This Is My West Virginia"
Noted physical features: Seneca Cavern; Allegheny Plateau; Seneca Rock; Berkeley Springs, White Sulphur Springs; Spruce Knob
Tourist attractions: Harper's Ferry; Cumberland National Road
Admission of admission: June 20, 1863
Order of admission: 35
Name origin: The area was part of Virginia until the time of the Civil War. When Virginia voted to secede, the western counties that comprise West Virginia objected strongly and chose instead to remain loyal to the Union, forming a new state.

was the scene of fighting between U.S. and Japanese forces in World War II.

Wex·ford |'weksfərd| **1** county of the Republic of Ireland, in the SE, in the province of Leinster. Pop. 102,000. **2** its county seat, a port on the Irish Sea. Pop. 10,000.

Wey·mouth[1] |'wāməTH| resort and port on the coast of Dorset, S England. Pop. 38,000.

Wey·mouth[2] |'wāməTH| town in E Massachusetts, an industrial and residential suburb SE of Boston. Pop. 54,063.

Wham·poa |'hwäm'pwä| see HUANGPU.

Whang·a·rei |ˌ(h)wäNGə'rā| port on the NE coast of North Island, New Zealand. Pop. 44,000.

Whea·ton |'wētn| suburban city in NE Illinois, W of Chicago, noted for its many religious institutions. Pop. 51,464.

Whee·ler Peak |ˌ(h)wēlər| highest peak in New Mexico, in the Sangre de Cristo Mts. NE of Taos; 13,161 ft./4,011 m.

Whee·ling |'(h)wēliNG| historic industrial city in N West Virginia, on the Ohio River. Pop. 34,822.

Whid·bey Island |'(h)widbē| island in NW Washington, just N of Puget Sound. It is agricultural, residential, and a tourist attraction.

Whis·tler |'(h)wis(ə)lər| municipality in SW British Columbia, N of Vancouver, noted as a ski resort. Pop. 4,459.

Whit·by[1] |'(h)witbē| port town on the coast of North Yorkshire, NE England, a former ecclesisastical center. Pop. 13,000.

Whit·by[2] |'(h)witbē| town in SE Ontario, a largely residential suburb E of Toronto on Lake Ontario. Pop. 61,281.

White Bear Lake |'wīt 'ber| city in SE Minnesota, a suburb NE of St. Paul. Pop. 24,704.

White·chap·el |'(h)wīt,CHæpəl| district in the East End of London, England, E of the Tower of London, notorious as the scene of murders by Jack the Ripper in 1888. It is today more affluent.

White·hall |'(h)wīt,hawl| street in Westminster, London, England, in which many government offices are located; the name is used in reference to the British government.

White Hill |'(h)wīt| (also **White Mountain**) hill near Prague, the Czech Republic, where, in November 1620, Czech Protestants were decisively defeated by Catholic forces, ending the independence of Bohemia and marking the start of the Thirty Years War.

White Horse, Vale of the |'(h)wīt 'hawrs| district in S central England, around Wantage in Oxfordshire, named for the huge figure of a horse carved out of a hill at Uffington. Its date is uncertain.

White·horse |'(h)wīt,hawrs| the capital of Yukon Territory. Pop. 17,925. Situated on the Alaska Highway, it is the center of a copper-mining and fur-trapping region.

White House, the |'(h)wīt ,hows| official home of the U.S. president, on the N side of the Mall, at 1600 Pennsylvania Avenue, in Washington, D.C. Built 1792–1800, it was rebuilt after being burned by the British in 1814. Its Oval Office, East Room, and Rose Garden are especially familiar.

White Mountains[1] |'(h)wīt| range in E Arizona, rising to 11,420 ft./3,481 m. at Baldy Peak (also, White Mt.), and home to the White Mountain Apache.

White Mountains[2] |'(h)wīt| range of the Appalachian system in N New Hampshire, rising to 6,288 ft./1,918 m. at Mount Washington, in the Presidential Range. Known for their resorts, the Whites continue NE into Maine as the Longfellow Mts.

White Nile |'(h)wīt 'nīl| the name for the main, W branch of the Nile between the Uganda–Sudan border and its confluence with the Blue Nile at Khartoum.

White Pass |'(h)wīt| pass from Skagway, Alaska into British Columbia that provided a route for gold seekers in the 1890s Klondike rush. A railroad here, opened in 1900, draws tourists.

White Plains |'(h)wīt 'plānz| commercial city in SE NewYork, the seat ofWestchester County. Pop. 48,718.

White River[1] |'(h)wīt| river that flows 720 mi./1,160 m. from NW Arkansas across the Ozark Plateau, to the Mississippi River.

White River[2] |'(h)wīt| river that flows in two main branches through Indiana, past Indianapolis, to the Wabash River.

White River[3] |'(h)wīt| river that flows 500 mi./800 km. from NW Nebraska into South Dakota, to the Missouri River.

White Rus·sia |'(h)wīt 'rəsHə| another name for BELARUS. □ **White Russian** adj. & n.

White Sands |'wīt 'sændz| area of gypsum flats in central New Mexico, designated a national monument in 1933. It is surrounded by a large missile-testing range, which in 1945 was the site of the detonation of the first nuclear weapon.

White Sea |'(h)wīt| inlet of the Barents Sea on the coast of NW Russia.

White·stone |'(h)wīt,stōn| largely residential section of N Queens, NewYork, on the East River across from the Bronx, to which it is joined by the Bronx-Whitestone Bridge.

White Sul·phur Springs |,(h)wīt ,səlfər 'spriNGz| historic resort city in SE West Virginia, in the Allegheny Mts. Pop. 2,779.

Whit·ney, Mount |'(h)witnē| mountain in the Sierra Nevada in California. Rising to 14,495 ft./4,418 m., it is the highest peak in the continental U.S. outside Alaska.

Whit·ti·er |'(h)witēər| industrial city in SW California, a suburb SE of Los Angeles. Pop. 77,671.

Why·al·la |(h)wī'ælə| steel-manufacturing town on the coast of South Australia, on the Spencer Gulf. Pop. 26,000.

Wich·i·ta |'wiCHə,taw| largest city in Kansas, in the S on theArkansas River. Pop. 304,011. It has aircraft and other industries and is an agricultural and commercial center.

Wich·i·ta Falls |'wiCHə,taw| industrial and commercial city in N central Texas. Pop. 96,259.

Wick·low |'wiklō| 1 county of the Republic of Ireland, in the E, in the province of Leinster, S of Dublin. Pop. 97,000. 2 its county seat, on the Irish Sea. Pop. 6,000.

Wick·low Mountains |'wiklō| low range in SE Ireland, S of Dublin, covering much of CountyWicklow. Its famed beauty spots include AVOCA and GLENDALOUGH.

Wie·licz·ka |vye'lēCHkə| commune in S Poland, SE of Cracow, a salt-mining center. Pop. 17,000.

Wien |'vēn| German name for VIENNA.

Wie·ner Neu·stadt |,vēnər 'noi,sHtät| industrial town in NE Austria. Pop. 35,000. It is a manufacturing center and a rail junction.

Wie·ner·wald |'vēnər,vält| (also called **Vienna Woods**) a forested range in NE Austria, justW ofVienna. A picturesque region of hills and streams, it is a popular vacation area.

Wies·ba·den |'wēsbädn| city in western Germany, the capital of the state of Hesse, on the Rhine opposite Mainz. Pop. 264,000. It has been a spa town since Roman times.

Wig·an |'wigən| industrial town in NW England, in Greater Manchester. Pop. 89,000.

Wight, Isle of |wīt| island off the S coast of England, a county since 1974. Pop. 127,000. Administrative center: Newport. It lies at the entrance to Southampton Water and is separated from the mainland by the Solent and Spithead channels.

Wil·ber·force |'wilbər,fawrs| village in SW Ohio, NE of Xenia, home to Wilberforce University. Pop. 2,702.

Wil·der·ness, the |'wildərnəs| wooded region of Spotsylvania County, NE Virginia, site of an inconclusive Civil War battle in 1864.

Wil·der·ness Road |'wildərnəs| historic route opened by Daniel Boone in the 1770s and used until the 1840s, allowing W migration through the Allegheny Mts. by way of the Cumberland Gap betweenTennessee and Kentucky.

Wild·spit·ze |'vilt,sHpitsə| highest peak in the Otztaler Alps, in the Tyrol, W Austria, and second-highest in Austria: 12,382 ft./3,774 m.

Wild·wood |'wīl'd,wŏŏd| resort city in S New Jersey, on the Atlantic. Pop. 4,484.

Wil·helm, Mount |'vil,helm| peak in central New Guinea Island, Papua New

Guinea, the highest in the country: 14,739 ft./4,509 m.

Wil•helms•ha•ven |'wil,helmz,häfən| port and resort in NW Germany, on the North Sea. Pop. 91,000. It was a major naval base until 1945.

Wilkes-Barre |'wilks,bærə; 'wilks,bærē| industrial city in NE Pennsylvania, on the Susquehanna River in the Wyoming Valley. Pop. 47,523.

Wilkes Land |'wilks| region of Antarctica with a coast on the Indian Ocean. It is claimed by Australia.

Wil•lam•ette River |wə'læmət| river that flows 300 mi./480 km. through W Oregon, through Portland, to the Columbia River. Its fertile valley was the goal of 19th-century settlers.

Wil•lem•stad |'viləm,stät| the capital of the Netherlands Antilles, on the SW coast of the island of Curaçao. Pop. 50,000.

Wil•liams•burg¹ |'wilyəmz,bərg| residential and industrial section of N Brooklyn, New York, noted for its Hasidic Jewish community and arts colony.

Wil•liams•burg² |'wilyəmz,bərg| city in SE Virginia, between the James and York rivers. Pop. 11,530. First settled as Middle Plantation in 1633, it was the capital of Virginia from 1699, when it was renamed in honor of William III, until 1799, when Richmond became the state capital. Much of the town has been reconstructed to appear as it was during the colonial era.

Wil•liams•port |'wilyəmz,pawrt| industrial city in N central Pennsylvania, on the Susquehanna River. Pop. 31,933. It is noted as the birthplace of Little League baseball.

Will•ing•bo•ro |'wiliNG,bərə| residential township in W central New Jersey, near the Delaware River. Pop. 36,291. It was founded as Levittown in 1959.

Wil•lis•ton Lake |'wilistən| largest North American reservoir, on the Peace River in NE British Columbia, created by the W.A.C. Bennett Dam (completed 1968).

Wil•lough•by |'wiləbē| city in SE Australia, a residential suburb N of Sydney, in New South Wales. Pop. 52,000.

Wil•ming•ton¹ |'wilmiNGtən| largest city in Delaware, an industrial and commercial hub on the Delaware River, in the NE. Pop. 71,529.

Wil•ming•ton² |'wilmiNGtən| industrial port city in SE North Carolina, on the Cape Fear River and the Atlantic. Pop. 55,530.

Wil•son, Mount |'wilsən| peak in the San Gabriel Mts. of SW California, near Pasadena, site of a major astronomical observatory.

Wil•son |'wilsən| industrial city in E central North Carolina. Pop. 36,930.

Wil•ton |'wiltn| historic town in SW England, in Wiltshire. Pop. 4,000. Once the seat of the kings of Wessex, it is known for its carpet industry.

Wilt•shire |'wilt,sHir; 'wiltsHər| county of SW England. Pop. 553,000 ; county seat, Trowbridge.

Wim•ble•don |'wimbəldən| residential district of SW London, England, in the borough of Merton, famed as home to the All England Lawn Tennis and Croquet Club and its annual tennis tournament.

Wim•mera |'wimərə| **1** river in SE Australia, in Victoria, that flows 155 mi. /249 km. from the Great Dividing Range to Lake Hindmarsh. **2** wheat-growing area through which the river flows.

Win•ches•ter¹ |'win,CHestər; 'winCHəstər| historic city in S England, the county seat of Hampshire. Pop. 36,000. Known to the Romans, it became capital of the kingdom of Wessex in 519.

Win•ches•ter² |'win,CHestər; 'winCHəstər| historic city in NW Virginia, an agricultural center in the Shenandoah Valley. Pop. 21,947.

Wind Cave National Park |wind| preserve in the Black Hills of South Dakota, noted for its caves and wildlife.

Win•der•mere |'wində(r),mir| lake in Cumbria, in the Lake District. At about 10 mi./17 km. in length, it is the largest lake in England. The town of Windermere lies on its E shore.

Wind•hoek |'vint,hook| the capital of Namibia, in the center of the country. Pop. 59,000. It was the capital of the former German protectorate of South West Africa from 1892 until 1919, emerging as capital of independent Namibia in 1990.

Win•dow Rock |'windō| community in NE Arizona, capital of the Navajo Indian reservation. Pop. 3,306. It is named for a limestone formation.

Wind River Range |wind| range of the Rocky Mts. in W Wyoming, rising to 13,804 ft./4,207 m. at Gannett Peak, the highest in the state. The Wind River flows from the range.

Wind•scale |'win(d),skāl| former name (1947–81) for SELLAFIELD.

Wind•sor¹ |'winzər| commercial and residential town in N central Connecticut, N of Hartford. Pop. 27,817. **Windsor Locks,**

just N, is the site of Bradley International Airport.

Wind·sor[2] |'winzər| town in S England, on the Thames River opposite Eton. Pop. 32,000. It is the site of Windsor Castle, the primary residence of the British royal family.

Wind·sor[3] |'winzər| industrial city and port in S Ontario, on Lake Ontario opposite Detroit, Michigan. Pop. 191,435.

Wind·ward Islands[1] |'windwərd| group of islands in the E Caribbean. Constituting the S part of the Lesser Antilles, they include Martinique, Dominica, St. Lucia, Barbados, St. Vincent and the Grenadines, and Grenada. Their name refers to their position farther upwind (in terms of the prevailing SE winds) than the Leeward Islands.

Wind·ward Islands[2] |'windwərd| (French name **Iles du Vent**) island group in the E Society Islands, French Polynesia, including Moorea and Tahiti.

Wind·ward Passage |'windwərd| ocean channel between Cuba, on the W, and Haiti, on the E, connecting the Caribbean Sea with the Atlantic.

Windy City |'windē 'sitē| nickname for Chicago, Illinois, given not for its winds but for the volubility of its 19th-century promoters.

Win·ne·ba·go, Lake |,winə'bāgō| largest lake in Wisconsin, in the E central part. The city of Oshkosh and many resorts lie on it.

Win·ne·muc·ca |,winə'məkə| commercial and industrial city in N central Nevada, on the Humboldt River. Pop. 6,134.

Win·net·ka |wi'netkə| affluent residential village in NE Illinois, a suburb N of Chicago. Pop. 12,174.

Win·ni·peg, Lake |'winə,peg| large lake in the province of Manitoba in Canada, to the N of the city of Winnipeg. Fed by the Saskatchewan, Winnipeg, and Red rivers from the E and S, the lake is drained by the Nelson River, which flows NE to Hudson Bay.

Win·ni·peg |'winə,peg| the capital of Manitoba, an agricultural processing and administrative city in the S of the province at the confluence of the Assiniboine and Red rivers, to the S of Lake Winnipeg. Pop. 616,790. First settled as a French trading post in 1738, it became a post of the Hudson's Bay Company in 1821.

Win·ni·peg·o·sis, Lake |,winəpə'gōsis| lake in S central Manitoba whose waters drain E into Lake Manitoba, and thence into Lake Winnipeg.

Win·ni·pe·sau·kee, Lake |,winəpə'säkē| largest lake in New Hampshire, a resort center in the E central part.

Wi·no·na |wə'nōnə| industrial city in SE Minnesota, on the Mississippi River. Pop. 25,399.

Winston-Salem |,winstən'sāləm| industrial and commercial city in N central North Carolina, a tobacco-processing center. Pop. 143,485.

Win·ter Ha·ven |'wintər ,hāvən| resort and industrial city in central Florida. Pop. 24,725.

Win·ter Palace |,wintər 'pæləs| former Russian imperial palace in Saint Petersburg, one of the largest in the world and now an art museum. It was stormed in 1917 by Revolutionary forces.

Win·ter Park |,wintər| resort and citrus-growing city in E central Florida, NE of Orlando. Pop. 22,242.

Win·ter·thur[1] |'wintər,THoor| former estate of the du Pont family in N Delaware, in Centerville, now noted for its art and craft museums.

Win·ter·thur[2] |'vintər,toor| industrial town in N Switzerland, in Zurich canton. Pop. 86,000.

Win·throp |'winTHrəp| resort and residential town in NE Massachusetts, on the N of Boston Harbor. Pop. 18,127.

Wir·ral, the |'wirəl| peninsula in NW England, between the Dee River and the Mersey estuary, SW of Liverpool, to which it is connected by tunnels. It contains industrial and residential suburbs, including Birkenhead.

Wis·con·sin |wis'känsən| see box, p. 412. □ **Wisconsinite** n.

Wis·con·sin River |wis'känsən| river that flows 430 mi./690 km. through central Wisconsin to the Mississippi River at Prairie du Chien. The **Dells of the Wisconsin** are a popular scenic area.

Wis·ła |'vēswä| Polish name for VISTULA.

Wis·mar |'vis,mär| port in NE Germany, on the Baltic Sea, between Rostock and Lübeck. Pop. 54,000.

Wit·bank |'wit,bæNGk| industrial town in NE South Africa, a mining center in Mpumalanga province. Pop. 173,000.

Wit·ten |'vitn| industrial city on the Ruhr River E of Essen, in western Germany. Pop. 106,000.

Wit·ten·berg |'vitn,berk| town in eastern Germany, on the Elbe River NE of Leipzig. Pop. 87,000. It was the scene in 1517 of Martin Luther's campaign against the Roman Catholic Church, a major factor in the rise of the Reformation.

Wisconsin

Capital: Madison
Largest city: Milwaukee
Other cities: Eau Claire, Green Bay, Kenosha, Oshkosh, Racine, Sheboygan, Wausau, West Allis
Population: 4,891,769 (1990); 5,223,500 (1998); 5,479,000 (2005 proj.)
Population rank (1990): 16
Rank in land area: 23
Abbreviation: WI; Wis.
Nickname: Badger State; America's Dairyland
Motto: 'Forward'
Bird: robin
Fish: muskellunge
Flower: wood violet
Tree: sugar maple
Song: "On, Wisconsin!"
Noted physical features: Kettle Moraine Glacial Hills; The Dells Rock Formations; Timms Hill
Tourist attractions: Apostle Islands National Lakeshore
Admission date: May 29, 1848
Order of admission: 30
Name origin: For the Wisconsin River, which flows through the central part of the state; itself named probably from Ojibwa *Wees-kon-san*, meaning 'the gathering of the waters.'

Wit·wa·ters·rand |'wit,wawtərz,ränd| (also **the Witwatersrand**) region of South Africa, around the city of Johannesburg. Consisting of a series of parallel rocky ridges, it forms a watershed between the Vaal and Olifant rivers. The region contains rich gold deposits, first discovered in 1886. Also called **the Rand**.

Wło·cła·wek |'vlätslävek| agricultural market center and industrial city in central Poland, on the Vistula River. Pop. 122,000.

Wo·burn[1] |'w˜,bərn| village in S central England, in Berkshire, noted as the site of Woburn Abbey, 18th-century seat of the dukes of Bedford, now a major tourist attraction.

Wo·burn[2] |'wσσ,bərn; 'wōbərn| industrial city in NE Massachusetts, NW of Boston. Pop. 35,943.

Wo·dis·ław Sląs·ki |vō'jēswäf 'slawNskē| industrial city in S Poland, in a coal-mining region. Pop. 112,000.

Wo·king |'wōkiNG| residential town in Surrey, SE England. Pop. 82,000.

Wolds, the |wōldz| upland district in NE England, in Lincolnshire, Yorkshire, and

Humberside, composed of a range of chalk hills.

Wol·fen·büt·tel |'vawlfen,bytl| agricultural market and manufacturing city in N central Germany, on the Oker River. Pop. 52,000.

Wolf River |wσσlf| river that flows 210 mi./340 km. through central Wisconsin. With a lumbering history, it is also noted for its fishing.

Wolfs·berg |'vawlfs,berk| industrial town and summer resort in S Austria. Pop. 28,000.

Wolfs·burg |'vawlfs,bσσrk| industrial city on the Mittelland Canal in Lower Saxony, NW Germany, noted as the home of the Volkswagen company. Pop. 129,000.

Wol·lon·gong |'wσσlən,gawNG| industrial port city on the coast of New South Wales, SE Australia. Pop. 211,000.

Wol·ver·hamp·ton |'wσσlvər,hæm(p)tən| industrial city in the West Midlands, England, NW of Birmingham. Pop. 240,000.

Wol·ver·ine State |,wσσlvə'rēn| informal name for MICHIGAN.

Won·ju |'wawn'jσσ| industrial and military city in N South Korea, SE of Seoul. Pop. 237,000.

Won·san |'wawn'sän| industrial port city in E North Korea, on the Sea of Japan. Pop. 350,000.

Wood·bridge |'wσσd,brij| industrial, commercial, and residential township in NE New Jersey. Pop. 93,086.

Wood Buf·fa·lo National Park |'wσσd ,bəfəlō| preserve in N Alberta and the S Northwest Territories, the largest Canadian national park.

Wood·land |'wσσdlənd| city in N central California, in an agricultural area NW of Sacramento. Pop. 39,802.

Wood·land Hills |'wσσdlənd| affluent residential section of NW Los Angeles, California, in the San Fernando Valley.

Wood·lawn |'wσσd,lawn| residential section of the N Bronx, New York City, site of the noted Woodlawn Cemetery.

Woods Hole |'wσσdz 'hōl| village in Falmouth, SE Massachusetts, at the SW corner of Cape Cod, a resort and noted ocean research center.

Wood·stock[1] |'wσσd,stäk| town in central England, in Oxfordshire, NW of Oxford. Pop. 3,000. Nearby is Blenheim Palace, the 18th-century house built for the Duke of Marlborough, and birthplace of statesman Winston Churchill.

Wood·stock[2] |'wσσd,stäk| resort town in SE New York, near the Catskills. Pop.

6,290. It gave its name in the summer of 1969 to a huge rock festival actually held in Bethel, 60 mi./96 km. to the SW.

Wood·stock[3] |'wŏŏd,stäk| industrial city in S Ontario, on the Thames River. Pop. 30,075.

Wool·lah·ra |wŏŏ'lärə| city in SE Australia, a suburb SE of Sydney, in New South Wales. Pop. 51,000.

Woo·me·ra |'wŏŏmərə| town in central South Australia, the site of a vast military testing ground used in the 1950s for nuclear tests and since the 1960s for tracking space satellites.

Woon·sock·et |wŏŏn'säkət; 'wŏŏn'säkət| industrial city in N Rhode Island, on the Blackstone River. Pop. 43,877.

Woos·ter |'wŏŏstər| industrial and academic city in N central Ohio. Pop. 22,191.

Worces·ter[1] |'wŏŏstər| cathedral city in W England, on the River Severn, the administrative center of Worcestershire. Pop. 81,000. It was the scene in 1651, during the English Civil War, of a battle in which Oliver Cromwell defeated a Scottish army under Charles II. It has been a center of porcelain manufacture since 1751.

Worces·ter[2] |'wŏŏstər| industrial and university city in central Massachusetts, on the Blackstone River.

Worces·ter·shire |'wŏŏstər,sHir; 'wŏŏstərsHər| county of W central England, part of Hereford and Worcester between 1974 and 1998.

World's View |'wərldz 'vyŏŏ| height in S Zimbabwe, in the Matopo Hills SE of Bulawayo, where the British colonialist Cecil Rhodes is buried.

World Trade Center twin-towered office complex in S Manhattan, at 1,368 ft./417 m. the tallest building in New York City. It opened in 1973.

Worms |vawrms; 'wərmz| industrial town in western Germany, on the Rhine NW of Mannheim. Pop. 77,000. It was the scene in 1521 of the condemnation of Martin Luther's teaching, at the Diet of Worms.

Wor·thing |'wərTHiNG| resort town on the S coast of England, in West Sussex. Pop. 92,000.

Wound·ed Knee |,wŏŏndəd 'nē| village in SW South Dakota, on the Pine Ridge Indian reservation, scene of an 1890 massacre and 1973 demonstrations.

Wran·gel Island |'ræNGgəl| island in the East Siberian Sea, off the coast of NE Russia.

Wran·gell Mountains |'ræNGgəl| range in SE Alaska, within the Wrangell–St. Elias

National Park, along the Pacific coast and the border of the Yukon Territory.

Wre·kin, the |'rēkən| volcanic hill in W England, in Shropshire, that figures in the poetry of A. E. Housman.

Wrex·ham |'reksəm| mining and industrial town in NE Wales, in Clwyd. Pop. 41,000.

Wro·cław |'vrawt,swäf| industrial port city on the Oder River in W Poland. Pop. 643,000. Held by the Habsburgs from the 16th century, it was taken by Prussia in 1741. It passed to Poland in 1945. German name **Breslau**.

Wu·hai |'wŏŏ'hī| industrial city in Inner Mongolia, N China, on the Yellow River N of Yinchuan. Pop. 264,000.

Wu·han |'wŏŏ'hän| port in E China, the capital of Hubei province. Pop. 3,710,000. Situated at the confluence of the Han and the Yangtze rivers, it consists of three adjacent towns (Hankow, Hanyang, and Wuchang), administered jointly since 1950.

Wu·hsi |'wŏŏ'sHē| see WUXI.

Wu·hsien |'ŏŏsHē'en| see SUZHOU.

Wu·hu |'wŏŏ'hŏŏ| deepwater port on the Yangtze River in Anhui province, E China, SW of Nanjing. Pop. 426,000. It is an important agricultural processing and distribution center.

Wup·per·tal |'vŏŏpər,täl| industrial city in western Germany, in North Rhine–Westphalia NE of Düsseldorf. Pop. 385,000.

Wu River |wŏŏ| (Chinese name **Wu Jiang**) river of central China, flowing 700 mi./1,130 km. from central Guizhou province to the Yangtze River at Fuling, Sichuan, below Chongqing.

Würt·tem·berg |'vŏŏrtəm,berk| former state in SW Germany, now part of Baden-Württemberg.

Würz·burg |'vŏŏrts,bŏŏrk| industrial city on the Main River in Bavaria, S Germany. Pop. 128,000.

Wu·tai Shan |'wŏŏ'tä'sHän| mountain in Shanxi province, NE China, N of Taiyuan: 10,000 ft./3,060 m. high. It is sacred to Buddhism and a pilgrimage site.

Wu·xi |'wŏŏ'sHē| (also **Wu-hsi**) city, a textile center, on the Grand Canal in Jiangsu province, E China. Pop. 900,000.

Wu·xing |'wŏŏ'siNG| see HUZHOU.

Wu·zhou |'wŏŏ'jō| city in Guangxi, S China, on the Xun River, W of Guangzhou (Canton). Pop. 210,000.

Wy·an·dotte |'wīən,dät| industrial city in SE Michigan, S of Detroit. Pop. 30,938.

Wye |wī| river that rises in the mountains of W Wales and flows 132 mi./208 km. gen-

---

Wyoming

Capital: Cheyenne
Largest city: Casper
Other cities: Green River, Laramie, Rock Springs, Sheridan
Population: 453,588 (1990); 480,907 (1998); 568,000 (2005 proj.)
Population rank (1990): 50
Rank in land area: 10
Abbreviation: WY; Wyo.
Nickname: Equality State; Cowboy State
Motto: 'Equal Rights'
Bird: meadowlark
Flower: Indian paintbrush
Tree: plains cottonwood
Song: "Wyoming"
Noted physical features: Jackson Hole; Wyoming Basin; Shoshone Cave; Thermopolis Hot Springs; Gannett Peak
Tourist attractions: Buffalo Bill Center; Shoshone Dam; Fort Laramie; Fort Bridger Historical Preserve; Thunder Basin National Grassland; Devil's Tower and Fossil Butte National Monuments; Grand Teton and Yellowstone National Parks; Flamingo Gorge Reservoir
Admission date: July 10, 1890
Order of admission: 44
Name origin: From the Delaware Indian words *maugh-wau-wa-ma,* 'large plains' or 'upon the great plain'; originally applied to a valley in northeastern Pennsylvania.

---

erally SE, entering the Severn estuary at Chepstow. In its lower reaches it forms part of the border between Wales and England.

Wy·o·ming |wī'ōmiNG| see box.

Wy·o·ming Valley |wī'ōmiNG| valley in NE Pennsylvania, along the Susquehanna River, in an anthracite-producing industrial region. Wilkes-Barre is the chief city.

Wy·ong |'wī,äNG; 'wīawNG| town in SE Australia, in New South Wales, N of Sydney. Pop. 100,000.

Xx

Xai•xai |'SHĪ'SHĪ| (also **Xai-Xai;** formerly **Vila de João Belo**) town in S Mozambique, a seaport at the mouth of the Limpopo River on the Indian Ocean. Pop. 94,000.

Xan•a•du |'zænə‚do͞o| old name for Shangdu, Inner Mongolia, China. The imperial summer residence here, built during the Yuan dynasty, in the late 13th century, was the inspiration for Samuel Taylor Coleridge's famous poem "Kubla Khan: A Vision in a Dream."

Xan•kän•di |zän'kændē| the capital of Nagorno-Karabakh, in S Azerbaijan. Pop. 58,000. Russian name **Stepanakert.**

Xán•thi |'ksänTHē| **1** department in NE Greece. Pop. 90,000. **2** its capital. Pop. 32,000.

Xan•thus |'zænTHəs| (also **Xanthos**) ancient city of Lycia, in S Asia Minor (present-day SW Turkey), on the Xanthus (now Koca) River in Muğla province.

Xe•nia |'zēnyə| commercial and industrial city in SW Ohio. Pop. 24,664.

Xia•men |SHē'ä'mən| (also **Hsia-men**) port in Fujian province, SE China. Pop. 639,000. Also called **Amoy.**

Xi'an |SHē'än| (formerly **Sian; Siking; Chang'an**) industrial city and capital of Shaanxi province, N China. Pop. 2,710,000. Inhabited since the 11th century B.C., the city was the capital of the Qin (Ch'in), Han, and Sui dynasties and was the W capital of the Tang (T'ang) dynasty. The tomb of Qin emperor Shi Huangdi (c. 259–210 B.C.), guarded by 10,000 terracotta soldiers, was discovered nearby in 1974.

Xiang•fan |SHē'äNG'fän| city in Hubei province, E central China, NW of Wuhan, on the Han River. Pop. 410,000.

Xiang•gang Pinyin name for HONG KONG.

Xiang River |SHē'äNG| (Chinese **Xiang Jiang;** formerly **Siang River**) river, S central China, rising in NE Guangxi province and flowing 715 mi./1,150 km. N through Hunan to Lake Dongting.

Xiang•tan |SHē'äNG'tän| industrial city in Hunan province, S central China, on the Xiang River SW of Changsha. Pop. 442,000.

Xian•yang |SHē'ä'yäNG| city in Shaanxi province, central China, to the N of the Wei River, NW of Xi'an. Pop. 352,000.

Xi•chang |'SHē'CHäNG| city in S Sichuan province, central China. Pop. 436,000.

Xi•ga•zê |'SHē'gäd'zə| (formerly **Shigatse**) city in S Tibet, to the S of the Yarlung Zangbo (Brahmaputra) River, SW of Lhasa; the second-largest city in Tibet. Pop. 84,000. The Tashi Lumpo monastery to the W is the traditional seat of the Panchen Lama.

Xing•tai |'SHiNG'tī| industrial city in NE China, to the S of Shijiazhuang in the province of Hebei. Pop. 1,167,000.

Xin•gú |SHiNG'go͞o| river that rises in the Mato Grosso of W Brazil and flows 1,230 mi./1,979 km. generally N to join the Amazon delta.

Xi•ning |'SHē'niNG| (formerly **Sining**) industrial city and capital of Qinghai province, W central China. Pop. 698,000. An old trading town on the Tibetan caravan route, it is now an agricultural processing and distribution center.

Xin•jiang |'SHinjē'äNG| (formerly **Sinkiang**) autonomous region in NW China. Area: 636,100 sq. mi./1,646,800 sq. km. Pop. 15.17 million. Capital: Ürümqi. Occupying one sixth of China, Xinjiang includes the Tian Shan mountains and the vast Taklimakan Desert. The region has important mineral resources.

Xin•xiang |'SHinSHē'äNG| city in Henan province, E central China, NE of Zhengzhou, on the Wei River. Pop. 474,000.

Xin•yang |'SHin'yäNG| city in S Henan province, E central China, in the foothills of the Tongbai Shan range. Pop. 193,000.

Xin•yu |'SHin'yo͞o| industrial city in Jiangxi province, SE central China, an iron and steel center SW of Nanchang, on the Yuan River. Pop. 226,000.

Xi River |SHē| (English name **West River;** Chinese name **Xi Jiang;** formerly **Si River**) river, SE China. Rising in Yunnan province, where it is known as the Hongshui, the Xi flows 1,250 mi./2,010 km. E through Guangxi and Guangdong provinces to a large delta on the South China Sea, where Guangzhou (Canton), Hong Kong, and Macao are situated.

Xi•xa•bang•ma Feng |‚SHēSHə'bäNG‚mä 'feNG| see GOSAINTHAN.

Xi•zang |'SHi'zäNG| see TIBET.

Xo•chi•cal•co |‚sōCHē'kälkō| archaeological site in central Mexico, SW of Cuernavaca in Morelos state. Religious and military, the ruins reflect the influence of several different ancient cultures.

Xo•chi•mil•co |ˌsōCHē'mēlkō| town in central Mexico, in the Distrito Federal, S of Mexico City. Pop. 271,000. It is famous for its Floating Gardens, remnants of a 2,000-year-old system of lake shore agriculture.

Xu•chang |'SHY'CHäNG| city in Henan province, E central China, S of Zhengzhou. Pop. 254,000.

Xu•zhou |'SHo͞o'jō| (also **Hsu-chou, Su-chow**) city in Jiangsu province, E China. Pop. 910,000. Former name (1912–45) **Tongshan**.

Yy

Ya'an |'yä'än| (formerly **Yachow**) city in Sichuan province, central China, SW of Chengdu. Pop. 282,000. It is an important tea processing center.

Ya·blo·no·vy Range |'yä,blənəvē| mountain range in SE Siberia, S Russia, extending NE from the Mongolian border to E of Lake Baikal. The highest peak is Sokhondo (7,192 ft./2,192 m.).

Ya·chi·yo |'yäCHē,ō; yä'CHēō| city in E central Japan, on E central Honshu, N of Chiba. Pop. 149,000.

Ya·cui·ba |yä'kwēbə| commercial town in S Bolivia, in Tarija department, on the Argentine border, in the Gran Chaco region. Pop. 31,000.

Yad·kin River |'yädkən| river that flows 200 mi./320 km. through W North Carolina, joining the Uwharrie to form the Pee Dee River.

Ya·fo |'yäfō| Hebrew name for JAFFA.

Yai·zu |īzōō| port city in E central Japan, on central Honshu. Pop. 112,000.

Ya·ke·shi |'yä'kə'sHē| city in Inner Mongolia, NE China, on the Hailar River E of Hailar. Pop. 393,000.

Yak·i·ma |'yækə,maw| commercial and industrial city in S central Washington. Pop. 54,827.

Ya·ku·tia |yä'kōōsHə| autonomous republic in E Russia. Pop. 1,081,000. Capital: Yakutsk. It is the coldest inhabited region of the world, with 40 percent of its territory lying to the N of the Arctic Circle. Official name **Republic of Sakha**.

Ya·kutsk |yə'kōōtsk| city in E Russia, on the Lena River, capital of the republic of Yakutia. Pop. 187,000.

Ya·la |'yälə| town in SW Thailand, S of Pattani. Pop. 69,000.

Ya·long River |'yä'lōōNG| (Chinese name **Yalong Jiang**) river, S China, flowing 800 mi./1,290 km. S from S Qinghai province through W Sichuan to the Yangtze River at the Sichuan-Yunnan border; one of the longest tributaries of the Yangtze.

Yal·ta |'yawltə| port and spa in S Ukraine, on the Black Sea. It was the site of an Allied conference in 1945 that was attended by Roosevelt, Churchill, and Stalin, who laid the initial plans for post–World War II Europe.

Ya·lu River |'yä'lōō| river of E Asia, which rises in the mountains of Jilin province in NE China and flows 500 mi./800 km. generally SW to the Yellow Sea, forming most of the border between China and North Korea. In November 1950 the advance of UN troops toward the Yalu precipitated the Chinese advance into Korea.

Ya·ma·ga·ta |'yä,mägä,tä| industrial city in NE Japan, on N Honshu, W of Mount Zao. Pop. 250,000.

Ya·ma·gu·chi |,yämä'gōōCHē| commercial city in W Japan, on SW Honshu. Pop. 129,000. It has many Buddhist temples.

Ya·ma·to |yä'mätō| city in E central Japan, on E central Honshu, SW of Tokyo. Pop. 195,000.

Yamato-koriyama |yä'mätō,kawrē'yämä| city in W central Japan, on S Honshu, S of Nara. Pop. 93,000.

Yam·bol |'yäm,bōl| (also **Jambol**) port city in SE Bulgaria, on the Tundzha River. Pop. 99,000.

Ya·mous·sou·kro |,yämə'sōōkrō| the capital of Côte d'Ivoire. Pop. 120,000. It was designated as capital in 1983, replacing Abidjan.

Yam·pa River |'yæmpä| river that flows 250 mi./400 km. across NW Colorado to join the Green River. It is a recreational attraction.

Ya·mu·na |'yəmənə| Hindi name for JUMNA.

Yan'an |'yän'än| (formerly **Yenan**) market and tourist city in Shaanxi province, central China. Pop. 113,000. The destination of the communists' Long March during the Chinese civil war, it was the site of the communist headquarters for most of 1936–49.

Yan·cheng |'yän'&chəNG| (also **Yen-cheng**) industrial city in Jiangsu province, E China. Pop. 380,000.

Yang·chow |'yäNG'jō| see YANGZHOU.

Yan·gon |yäNG'gōn| Burmese name for RANGOON.

Yang·quan |'yäNGCHōō'än| city in Shanxi province, E China, E of Taiyuan, in a coal-and iron-mining region. Pop. 362,000.

Yang·tze River |'yäNG(t)'sē| (Chinese name **Chang Jiang**) principal and longest river of China: 3,964 mi./6,380 km. It rises as the Jinsha in the Tibetan highlands and flows S, then E through central China, entering the East China Sea at Shanghai.

Yang·zhou |'yäNG'jō| (formerly **Yang-chow**) city in Jiangsu province, E China, on the Grand Canal. Pop. 313,000. It was a capital of the Sui dynasty and important cultural and religious center under the Tang (T'ang) dynasty.

Yan·ji |'yän'jē| city in Jilin province, NE China, W of Tumen. Pop. 231,000.

Yank·ton |'yæNGktən| commercial and industrial city in SE South Dakota. Pop. 12,703.

Yan·tai |'yän'tī| (also **Yen-tai**) port on the Yellow Sea in Shandong province, E China. Pop. 3,204,600. Former name (3rd century B.C.–15th century) **Chefoo**.

Yan·tra River |'yäntrə| 178 mi./287 km. long, that rises in Bulgaria in the Balkan Mts. and flows N into the Danube River E of Nikopol.

Yao |yow; 'yäō| city in W central Japan, on S Honshu, a residential suburb S of Osaka. Pop. 278,000.

Ya·oun·dé |yown'dā| the capital of Cameroon, an agricultural trade center. Pop. 800,000.

Yap |yäp; yæp| (also **Uap**) island group in the SW Pacific, one of the four Federated States of Micronesia. Pop. 14,000. Previously held by Germany, then Japan, it was captured by U.S. forces in 1945.

Ya·qui River |yä'kē| river in NW Mexico that with headstreams flows 420 mi./680 km. from N Sonora state into the Gulf of California near Guaymas.

Ya·ren |'yä,ren| unofficial capital of the Pacific nation of Nauru.

Yar·kand River |yär'känd| (also called **Yarkant**; Chinese name **Yarkant He**) river in Xinjiang, W China. Rising near K2 in the Karakorum Mts. it flows 500 mi./800 km. NE to join the Kashgar and form the Tarim River.

Yar·mouth[1] |'yärməTH| resort town in SE Massachusetts, on S Cape Cod. Pop. 21,174.

Yar·mouth[2] |'yärməTH| port town in SW Nova Scotia. Pop. 7,781.

Yar·muk River |yär'mōōk| river that flows 50 mi./80 km. W from NW Jordan, to the Jordan River just S of the Sea of Galilee. It forms part of the Jordan-Syria border.

Ya·ro·slavl |,yärä'slävəl| port in European Russia, on the Volga River NE of Nizhni Novgorod. Pop. 636,000.

Yar·row Water |'yærō| river that flows from the Borders region in SE Scotland into Ettrick Water and the Tweed River near Selkirk. It is celebrated by English and Scottish poets.

Yas·na·ya Po·lya·na |'yäsnəyə pəl'yänə| village in W Russia, S of Tula. It was the birthplace of Leo Tolstoy, and he is buried at his estate here.

Ya·tsu·shi·ro |yät'sōō,sHērō| commercial city in SW Japan, on W Kyushu, on Yatsushiro Bay. Pop. 108,000.

Ya·vat·mal |'yävət,mäl| (also **Yeotmal**) commercial town in E central India, in Maharashtra state. Pop. 122,000.

Ya·wa·ta |yä'wätə| city in W central Japan, on S Honshu, S of Kyoto. Pop. 76,000.

Yax·chi·lan |,yäsHCHē'län| archaeological site in SE Mexico, in Chiapas state near the Guatemalan border, on the Usumacinta River. Mayan ruins here remain largely cloaked in jungle foliage.

Yazd |'yäzd| (also **Yezd**) historic city in central Iran, in a desert region. Pop. 275,000. It is known for its silk weaving.

Yaz·oo River |yæ'zōō| river that flows 190 mi./305 km. from N Mississippi to join the Mississippi River at Vicksburg. The fertile land between the rivers is the Mississippi **Delta**, or **Yazoo Delta**.

Ybor City |'ēbawr| industrial and commercial section of Tampa, Florida, noted for its Cuban culture and cigar industry.

Ye·do |'yedō| earlier name for TOKYO, Japan. Also, **Edo**.

Ye·lets |yil'yets| (also **Elets**) industrial city in W Russia, S of Moscow. Pop. 121,000.

Yel·low·head Pass |'yelō,hed| rail and highway pass through the Rocky Mts. W of Edmonton, Alberta.

Yel·low·knife |'yelō,nīf| the capital since 1967 of the Northwest Territories, on the N shore of Great Slave Lake. Pop. 15,179.

Yel·low River |'yelō| the second largest river in China, which rises in the mountains of W central China and flows over 3,000 mi./4,830 km. in a huge semicircle before entering the gulf of Bo Hai. Chinese name **Huang Ho**.

Yel·low Sea |'yelō| arm of the East China Sea, separating the Korean peninsula from the E coast of China. Chinese name **Huang Hai**.

Yel·low Springs |'yelō| academic village in SW Ohio, home to Antioch College. Pop. 3,972.

Yel·low·stone National Park |'yelə,stōn| preserve in NW Wyoming and Montana. Its features include Old Faithful, a geyser that erupts every 45 to 80 minutes to a height of about 100 ft./305 m.

Yem·en |'yemən| republic in the S and SW of the Arabian Peninsula. Area: 208,960 sq. mi./540,000 sq. km. Pop. 12,533,000. Language: Arabic. Capital and largest city: Sana'a. Economic and commercial capital: Aden. Islamic since the 7th century, Yemen was part of the Ottoman Empire from the

Yemen

16th century, then dominated by the British from the 19th century until 1967, when the country split into South Yemen (the People's Democratic Republic) and North Yemen (the Arab Republic). Reunification occurred in 1990. Oil, coffee, cotton, and trade are key to the economy. □ **Yemeni** *adj. & n.*

Ye·na·ki·ye·ve |ye'näkēyivə| (formerly **Ordzhonikidze** city in E Ukraine. Pop. 120,000. It is a suburb of Donetsk.

Yen·an |'yä'nän| see YAN'AN.

Ye·nan·gyaung |'yenän'jowNG| town in W central Burma, on the Irrawaddy River N of Magwe; the main oil-producing center in Burma.

Ye·ni·sei |ˌyenə'sä| river in Siberia, which rises in the mountains on the Mongolian border and flows 2,566 mi./4,106 km. generally N to the Arctic coast, emptying into the Kara Sea.

Yeo·vil |'yō,vil| commercial and industrial town in SW England, in Somerset. Pop. 37,000.

Yer·ba Bue·na |ˌyərbä 'bwenä| name of an island in San Francisco Bay, California, and also the 1820s mainland settlement that became the city of San Francisco.

Ye·re·van |ˌyerə'vän| (also **Erevan**) industrial city, the capital of Armenia, in the S Caucasus. Pop. 1,202,000.

Yes·sen·tu·ki |ˌyəsənto͞o'kē| resort town in W Russia, a spa on the N slopes of the Caucasus Mts., W of Pyatigorsk.

Yev·pa·to·ri·ya |ˌyefpä'tawrēəä| (also **Eupatoria**) seaport in Ukraine, on the W coast of the Crimean Peninsula. Pop. 111,000.

Ye·zo |'yezō| see HOKKAIDO.

Yi·bin |'ē'bin| commercial and industrial city in Sichuan province, central China, on the Min River S of Chengdu. Pop. 806,000.

Yi·chang |'ē'CHäNG| city in Hubei province, E central China, at the head of navigation on the Yangtze River, W of Wuhan. Pop. 372,000.

Yi·chun |'ē'CHo͞on| (also **I-chun**) city in Heilongjiang province, NE China. Pop. 882,000.

Yin·chuan |'yin'CHwän| industrial city, the capital of Ningxia province, NE China. It produces textiles, rubber goods, chemicals, and machine tools. Pop. 658,000.

Ying·kou |'yiNG'kō| (formerly **Newchwang**) city in Liaoning province, NE China, a port on the Liao River near where it flows into Liaodong Bay. Pop. 422,000.

Yi·ning |'yē'niNG| (also called **Gulja**) city in Xinjiang, NW China, a former caravan trading center in the W Tian Shan mountains. Pop.177,000.

Yi·yang |'yē'yäNG| city in Hunan province, E central China, an industrial port on the Zi River, NW of Changsha. Pop. 372,000.

Yog·ya·kar·ta |ˌyägy'kərtə| (also **Jogjakarta**) city in S central Java, Indonesia. Pop. 412,000. It was formerly the capital of Indonesia (1945–49).

Yo·ho National Park |'yōhō| preserve in the Rocky Mts. in SE British Columbia. Kicking Horse Pass, opened for the Canadian Pacific Railway, is here, as is the Burgess Shale, a famed fossil resource.

Yok·kai·chi |yō'kīCHē| industrial port city in central Japan, on S Honshu. Pop. 274,000.

Yok·na·pa·taw·pha County |ˌyawknəpə-'tawfə| fictional county in N Mississippi, the setting for most of the work of William Faulkner.

Yo·ko·ha·ma |ˌyōkə'hämə| seaport on the island of Honshu, Japan, S of Tokyo. Pop. 3,220,000. It is the second-largest city in Japan.

Yo·ko·su·ka |yō'kōsəkä| port city and naval base in E central Japan, on E central Honshu. Pop. 433,000.

Yol·la Bol·ly Mountains |'yälə ˌbälē| range of the Klamath Mts. in NW California, noted for its wilderness and wildlife.

Yo·na·go |yō'nägō| port city in W Japan, on S Honshu. Pop. 131,000.

Yo·ne·za·wa |yō'näzä,wä; ˌyōnə'zäwə| city in NE Japan, on N Honshu, S of Yamagata. Pop. 95,000. It has long been noted for silk weaving.

Yon·kers |'yäNGkərz| industrial city in SE New York, on the Hudson River just N of the Bronx, New York City. Pop. 188,082.

Yonne |yawn| **1** department in NE France. Pop. 323,000. The capital is Auxerre. **2** river, 184 mi./293 km. long, in central France that flows NW into the Seine River near Montereau.

Yor·ba Lin·da |ˌyawrbə 'lində| city in SW

California, a suburb SE of Los Angeles and the birthplace of Richard Nixon. Pop. 52,422.

York[1] |yawrk| historic commercial city in N England, on the Ouse River. Pop. 101,000. The Romans occupied the site, known as Eboracum, from A.D. 71 until about A.D. 400; in A.D. 867 it was taken by the Vikings. It is the seat of the Archbishop of York and is noted for its cathedral, York Minster.

York[2] |yawrk| suburban city in S Ontario, just N of Toronto. Pop. 140,525. York is also the early name for Toronto itself.

York[3] |yawrk| commercial and industrial city in SE Pennsylvania. Pop. 42,192.

York, Cape[1] |yawrk| the northernmost point in Australia, on the Torres Strait in N Queensland, at the tip of the Cape York Peninsula.

York, Cape[2] |yawrk| SW tip of Hayes Peninsula, on Baffin Bay, Greenland. It served as a base for U.S. explorer Robert E. Peary's polar expedition. A 100-ton meteorite found here was brought to the U.S. by Peary.

York•shire |'yawrksHər; 'yawrk,sHir| former county of N England, traditionally divided into East, West, and North Ridings. Since 1996 the N part of the area has formed the county of North Yorkshire, while the rest of the Yorkshire area consists of separately administered regions. □ **York-shireman** n. **Yorkshirewoman** n.

York•town |'yawrk,town| historic site in SE Virginia, on the York River N of Newport News, scene of both the last (October 1781) battle of the American Revolution and a Civil War battle (1862).

York•ville[1] |'yawrk,vil| district of the Upper East Side of Manhattan, New York City, long German in character.

York•ville[2] |'yawrk,vil| fashionable shopping and arts district of Toronto, Ontario.

Yo•ru•ba•land |'yawrəbə,lænd| (also **Yoruba**) region of coastal W Africa, home to the Yoruba people, and centered in SW Nigeria, in and around Lagos, Ibadan, and Oshogbo.

Yo•sem•i•te National Park |yō'semətē| preserve in the Sierra Nevada in central California. It includes Yosemite Valley, with sheer granite cliffs and the mile-high rock face of El Capitan and several famed waterfalls, including Yosemite Falls, the highest in the U.S., with a drop of 2,425 ft./ 739 m.

Yoshkar-Ola |yəsH'kärə'lä| industrial city, the capital of the republic of Mari El, in E central Russia. Pop. 246,000.

Yo•su |'yə'sōō| port city in S South Korea, on the Korea Strait. Pop. 184,000. It is a fishing, tourist, and oil refining center.

Youghal |yawl| historic port town in County Cork, S Ireland, on Youghal Bay, at the mouth of the Blackwater River. Pop. 6,000.

Yough•io•ghe•ny River |,yäkə'gānē| river that flows 135 mi./220 km. from West Virginia into Pennsylvania, joining the Monongahela River at McKeesport.

Youngs•town |'yəNGZ,town| industrial city in NE Ohio, in the Mahoning River valley. Pop. 95,372. It is an historic steel center.

Yous•sou•fia |yōō'sōōfēə| (formerly **Louis Gentil**) town in W central Morocco, NE of Safi, in a phosphate-mining area. Pop. 60,000.

Yoz•gat |yawz'gät| city in central Turkey, E of Ankara, capital of Yozgat province. Pop. 50,000.

Ypres |'ēpr(ə)| town in NW Belgium, near the border with France, in the province of West Flanders. Pop. 35,000. Ypres was the scene of some of the bitterest fighting of World War I. Flemish name **Ieper**.

Yp•si•lan•ti |,ipsə'læntē| industrial city in SE Michigan, near Ann Arbor. Pop. 24,846.

Yre•ka |wī'rēkə| commercial and resort city in N California, near the Oregon border. Pop. 6,948.

Yser River |ē'zer| river that flows through France and Belgium for 48 mi./77 km., emptying into the North Sea near Nieuwpoort, Belgium.

Yu•ba City |'yōōbə| commercial city in N central California, in an agricultural area NW of Sacramento. Pop. 27,437.

Yu•cai•pa |yōō'kīpə| suburban city in S California, SE of San Bernardino. Pop. 32,824.

Yu•ca•tán |,yōōkä'tän| state of SE Mexico, at the N tip of the Yucatán Peninsula. Area: 14,833 sq. mi./38,402 sq. km. Pop. 1,364,000. Capital: Mérida.

Yu•ca•tán Peninsula |,yōōkä'tän| peninsula in S Mexico, lying between the Gulf of Mexico and the Caribbean Sea. The region was the seat of the Mayan civilization.

Yuc•ca Mountain |'yəkə| mountain in SW Nevada, NW of Las Vegas, that is the proposed storage site for the most hazardous U.S. radioactive wastes.

Yu•ci |'yōō'zē| industrial city in Shanxi province, E China, SE of Taiyuan. Pop. 425,000.

Yue•yang |yōō'ä'yæNG| city in Hubei province, E central China, SW of Wuhan, on the NE shore of Lake Dongting. Pop. 303,000.

Yu·go·sla·via |ˌyo͞ogəˈslävēə| federation of states in SE Europe, in the Balkans. Created as the Kingdom of the Serbs, Croats, and Slovenes after World War I, it took the name Yugoslavia in 1929, its capital at Belgrade. In the 1990s, four of its republics (Croatia, Slovenia, Bosnia and Herzegovina, and Macedonia) seceded, amid regional conflicts. Serbia and Montenegro in 1992 declared a new Yugoslavia, but this has not received widespread recognition. □ **Yugoslavian** *adj. & n.*

Yugoslavia

Yu·kon River |ˈyo͞oˌkän| river that rises in the Yukon Territory and flows 1,870 mi./3,020 km. W through central Alaska to the Bering Sea.

Yu·kon Territory |ˈyo͞oˌkän| territory of NW Canada, on the border with Alaska. Area: 186,661 sq. mi./482,515 sq. km. Pop. 27,797. Capital and largest city: White-

horse. Mountainous, isolated, and undeveloped, the Yukon has little economic activity except for mining. The population increased briefly during the Klondike gold rush (1897–99).

Yu·lin |ˈyo͞oˈlin| industrial and commercial city in Guangxi, S China, E of Nanning, on the Nanliu River. Pop. 1,255,000.

Yu·ma |ˈyo͞omə| historic commercial city in SW Arizona, on the Colorado and Gila rivers near the California and Mexico borders. Pop. 54,923.

Yu·men |ˈyʏˈmən| (also called **Laojunmiao**) city in NW Gansu province, N China. Near the Jade Gate of the Great Wall, it is an important petroleum center. Pop. 109,000.

Yun·dum |ˈyo͞onˌdo͞om| village in W Gambia, SW of Banjul and site of its international airport.

Yun·nan |ˈyʏˈnæn| province of SW China, on the border with Vietnam, Laos, and Burma. Pop. 36.97 million. Capital: Kunming.

Yu·yao |ˈyʏˈyow| city in Zhejiang province, E China, NW of Ningbo. Pop. 778,000.

Yuzhno-Sakhalinsk |ˈyo͞ozHnə səkHəˈlinsk| chief town on Sakhalin Island, in far E Russia. Pop. 165,000.

Yu·zov·ka |ˈyo͞ozefkə| former name (1872–1924) for DONETSK.

Yve·lines |ēvˈlēn| department W of Paris in N central France. Pop. 1,307,000. The capital is Versailles.

Yver·don |ēverˈdôN| (also **Yverdon-les-Bains**) spa town in W Switzerland, N of Lausanne. Pop. 22,000.

Zz

Zaan•dam |zän'däm| manufacturing municipality in W Netherlands, near Amsterdam. Pop. 130,000. Peter the Great of Russia lived here (1697) in order to study shipbuilding.

Zaan•stad |'zän,stät| industrial town in W Netherlands. Pop. 131,000.

Zab•rze |'zäbzнe| industrial and mining city in Upper Silesia, S Poland. Pop. 205,000. From 1915 to 1945 it was a German city bearing the name Hindenburg.

Za•ca•te•cas |,säkə'täkəs| **1** state of N central Mexico. Area: 28,293 sq. mi./73,252 sq. km. Pop. 1,278,000. **2** its capital, a silver-mining city situated at an altitude of 8,200 ft. (2,500 m). Pop. 165,000.

Za•dar |'zä,där| port town and resort in W Croatia, on the Adriatic Sea. Pop. 76,000.

Za•ga•zig |zə'gäzig| (also **Zaqaziq**) commercial ity in the Nile delta, N Egypt. Pop. 279,000. Ancient Bubastis is nearby.

Za•greb |'zä,greb| the capital of Croatia, an industrial and communications center on the Sava River. Pop. 707,000.

Zag•ros Mountains |zäg'rəs| range in W Iran, rising to 14,921 ft./4,548 m. at Zard Kuh. Most of Iran's oil fields lie along the W foothills.

Za•he•dan |,zähi'dän| city in SE Iran, near the borders with Afghanistan and Pakistan. Pop. 362,000.

Zah•le |zä'lä| commercial and resort town in central Lebanon, E of Beirut in the Bekaa Valley. Pop. 200,000.

Za•ire |zä'ir| (also **Zaïre**) former name for the Democratic Republic of the CONGO.

Za•ire River |zä'ir| another name for the CONGO River.

Za•kin•thos |'zäkēn,тнaws| (also **Zakynthos**) island off the SW coast of mainland Greece, in the Ionian Sea, most southerly of the Ionian Islands. Pop. 33,000. Also called **Zante**.

Za•ko•pa•ne |,zäkə'pänə| a winter-sports resort in the Tatra Mts. of S Poland. Pop. 29,000.

Za•la•e•ger•szeg |'zawlaw,eger,seg| market town in W Hungary, on the Zala River. Pop. 63,000. It is the capital of Zala county.

Za•ma¹ |'zämə; 'zämə.| ancient town in N Africa, probably SW of Carthage (near Tunis, Tunisia), where the Roman Scipio Africanus defeated Carthaginian forces under Hannibal in 202 B.C.

Za•ma² |'zämä| city in E central Japan, on E central Honshu, W of Yokohama. Pop. 112,000.

Zam•be•zi River |zæm'bēzē| river of East Africa, which rises in NW Zambia and flows for 1,600 mi./2,560 km. S through Angola and Congo (formerly Zaire) to the Victoria Falls, turning E along the border between Zambia and Zimbabwe, before crossing Mozambique and entering the Indian Ocean.

Zam•bia |'zæmbēə| landlocked republic in central Africa, divided from Zimbabwe by the Zambezi River. Area: 290,696 sq. mi./752,613 sq. km. Pop. 8,373,000. Languages, English (official), various Bantu languages. Capital and largest city: Lusaka. A British colony from 1889, called Northern Rhodesia 1911–64, Zambia exports copper, cobalt, and other minerals. □ **Zambian** adj. & n.

Zambia

Zam•bo•an•ga |,zämbō'äNGgə| port on the W coast of Mindanao, in the S Philippines. Pop. 442,000.

Za•mo•ra |sä'mawrə| communications and marketing center in NW Spain, on the Duero River. Pop. 62,000.

Za•mość |'zä,mawsнcн| industrial town in SE Poland, SE of Lublin. Pop. 59,000.

Zand•voort |'zänt,vawrt| resort town in the Netherlands, on the North Sea coast. Pop. 16,000.

Zanes•ville |'zānz,vil| industrial city in N central Ohio, E of Columbus. Pop. 26,778. On the old National Road, it is a noted ceramics center.

Zan•jan |zæn'jän| commercial city in NW Iran, at the W end of the Elburz Mts. Pop. 254,000.

Zan•te |'dzäntä| another name for ZAKINTHOS.

Zan·zi·bar |'zænzə‚bär| island off the coast of E Africa, part of Tanzania. Pop. 641,000. Under Arab rule from the 17th century, Zanzibar was a prosperous trading port. It became a British protectorate in 1890 and an independent Commonwealth state in 1963, but in the following year the sultan was overthrown and the country became a republic, uniting with Tanganyika to form Tanzania. □ **Zanzibari** *adj. & n.*

Zao·zhuang |'zow'ZHwäNG| (also **Tsaochuang**) city in Shandong province, E China, a center for coal mining, heavy industry, and agricultural trade. Pop. 3,192,000.

Za·po·pan |‚säpō'pän| commercial town in SW Mexico, in Jalisco state, a satellite just W of Guadalajara. Pop. 668,000.

Za·po·rizh·zhya |‚zäpə'rawzHə| industrial city of Ukraine, on the Dnieper River. Pop. 891,000. It developed as a major industrial center after the construction of a hydroelectric dam in 1932. Russian name **Zaporozhye**; former name (until 1921) **Aleksandrovsk**.

Za·qa·ziq |‚zäkə'zēk| variant spelling of ZAGAZIG.

Za·ra·go·za |'zärə'gōsə| Spanish name for SARAGOSSA.

Zá·ra·te |'zärä‚tä| (formerly **General Uriburu**) commercial town in E Argentina, a port in the delta of the Paraná River, NW of Buenos Aires.

Za·ria |'zärēə| city in N Nigeria, an agricultural and light industrial center. Pop. 345,000.

Zar·qa |'zärkə| (also **Az Zarqa**) industrial city in NW Jordan, NE of Amman. Pop. 359,000.

Za·wier·cie |zä'vyerCHe| industrial city in S Poland, NW of Katowice, on the Warta River. Pop. 60,000.

Zea·land |'zēlənd| the principal island of Denmark, situated between the Jutland peninsula and the S tip of Sweden. Its chief city is Copenhagen. Danish name **Sjælland**.

Zee·brug·ge |'zā‚brYkə| industrial and ferry port on the coast of Belgium, linked by canal to Bruges.

Zee·land |'zā‚länt; 'zēlənd| agricultural province of the SW Netherlands, at the estuary of the Maas and Scheldt rivers. Pop. 357,000. Capital: Middelburg.

Ze·fat |'tse‚fät| (also **Safed; Safad; Tsefat**) historic city in N Israel, NNW of the Sea of Galilee. Pop. 22,000. It is one of Israel's four holy cities.

Zeist |zīst| residential community in central Netherlands, near Utrecht. Pop. 62,000.

Zeitz |tsīts; sīts| industrial city in eastern central Germany, on the Weisse Elster River, SSW of Leipzig. Pop. 44,000.

Ze·la·zo·wa Wo·la |zell‚äzawvä'vawlə| village in E central Poland, W of Warsaw, birthplace of the composer Chopin.

Ze·ni·ca |'zenētsə| (also **Zenitsa**) industrial town in central Bosnia and Herzegovina. Pop. 133,000.

Zen·tsu·ji |zent'sōōjē| city in W Japan, on N Shikoku, SW of Takamatsu. Pop. 38,000. The founder of the Shingon sect of Buddhism was born here.

Zer·matt |tsər'mät| Alpine ski resort and mountaineering center near the Matterhorn, in S Switzerland.

Ze·ya River |'zāyə| river (800 mi./1,290 km. long) in E Russia, rising in the Stanovoy Range and flowing S into the Amur River at Blagoveshchensk.

Zgierz |zgēsh| town in central Poland, a textile center. Pop. 59,000.

Zham·byl |jäm'bil| (formerly **Dzhambul**) industrial city, capital of Zhambyl region, S Kazakhstan. Pop. 312,000.

Zhang·jia·kou |'jäNGjē'ä'kō| (also **Changchiakow**) city along the Great Wall in Hebei province, NE China, in an ironmining area. Pop. 720,000. Mongolian name **Kalgan**.

Zhang·ye |'jäNG'yə| commercial and industrial city in Gansu province, N China, in the N foothills of the Qilian Shan mountains. Pop. 400,000.

Zhang·zhou |'jäNG'jō| city in Fujian province, SE China, W of Xiamen. Pop. 318,000.

Zhan·jiang |'jänjē'äNG| (also **Chan-chiang**) port in Guangdong province, S China. Pop. 1,049,000.

Zhao·dong |'jow'dōōNG| agricultural and industrial city in Heilongjiang province, NE China, NW of Harbin. Pop. 754,000.

Zhao·tong |'jow'tōōNG| city in NE Yunnan province, S China, E of the Jinsha (Yangtze) River. Pop. 560,000.

Zhda·nov |'ZHdänəf| former name (1948–89) for MARIUPOL.

Zhe·jiang |'jəjē'äNG| (formerly **Chekiang**) mountainous province in E China to the S of Yangtze River. Pop. 41.45 million. Capital: Hangzhou. It is the smallest mainland province in land area (39,230 sq. mi./101,800 sq. km.).

Zhe·lez·no·do·ro·zhnyy |ZHə‚liznədə-'rawzHnē| (also **Zheleznodorozhny**) industrial city in W Russia, E of Moscow. Pop. 99,000.

Zhe·lez·no·gorsk |ZHə,liznə'gawrsk| city in W Russia, NW of Kursk. Pop. 88,000.

Zheng·zhou |jəNG'jō| (also **Chengchow**) the capital of Henan province, in NE central China. Pop. 1,660,000.

Zhen·jiang |'jənjē'äNG| (also **Chen-chiang, Chinkiang**) port in Jiangsu province, on the Yangtze River, E China. Pop. 1,280,000.

Zhez·qaz·qhan |ZHəzkäz'KHän| (also **Zhezkazgan**; formerly **Dzezjazgab**) copper-mining city in central Kazakhstan. Pop. 110,000.

Zhi·to·mir |ZHi'taw,mir| Russian name for ZHYTOMYR.

Zhlo·bin |ZHlōbyin| industrial city in SE Belarus, on the Dnieper River. Pop. 57,000.

Zhob river |zhōb| seasonal river in central Pakistan, flowing 230 mi./370 km., from the Toba-Kakar Range to the Gomal River.

Zhong·shan |'jo͞oNG'sHän| (also **Chung-shan**) agricultural and industrial city in Guangdong province, SE China, the birthplace of political leader Sun Yat-sen. Pop. 1,073,000.

Zhu·kov·skiy |ZHo͞o'kawfskē| (also **Zhukovsky**) industrial city in W Russia, SE of Moscow. Pop. 101,000.

Zhu River |jo͞o| see PEARL RIVER.

Zhu·zhou |'jo͞o'jō| city in Hunan province, S central China, on the Xiang River S of Changsha. Pop. 410,000.

Zhy·to·myr |ZHi'taw,mir| industrial city in central Ukraine. Pop. 296,000. Russian name **Zhitomir**.

Zi·bo |'dzə'bō| (also **Tzu-po**) industrial city in Shandong province, E China. Pop. 2,484,000.

Zie·lo·na Go·ra |ZHə'lawnə'go͝oə| industrial town in W Poland, capital of Zielona Gora county. Pop. 114,000.

Zi·gong |'dzə'go͞oNG| industrial and agricultural city in Sichuan province, central China, SE of Chengdu, a center of salt production. Pop. 1,673,000.

Zi·guin·chor |,zēgeN'sHawr| commercial city in SW Senegal, an inland port on the Casamance River. Pop. 149,000.

Zi·hua·ta·ne·jo |,sēwätä'nähō| resort and fishing and cruise ship port in S Mexico, on the Pacific coast in Guerrero state.

Zi·le |zi'lä| commercial town in N central Turkey, in Tokat province. Pop. 46,000. As ancient **Zela**, it was the place from which Julius Caesar, after a victory, sent the mes-

sage "Veni, vidi, vici (I came, I saw, I conquered)."

Ži·li·na |'ZHēli,nä| industrial town in NW Slovakia, on the Váh River. Pop. 84,000.

Zil·ler·ta·ler Alps |tsili,tälər| range of the E Alps on the border between Austria and Italy. The Brenner Pass divides it from the Otztal Alps to the W.

Zim·ba·bwe |zim'bäb,wä| landlocked republic in SE Africa, divided from Zambia by the Zambezi River. Area: 151,058 sq. mi./391,090 sq. km. Pop. 10,080,000. Languages, English (official), Shona, Ndebele, and others. Capital and largest city: Harare. An ancient civilization that gave the country its name was overrun by Bantu peoples 500 years ago. The British dominated what was called Rhodesia from the late 19th century. In 1965–79 a white minority government declared independence. Majority (African) rule came in 1979. Mining and agriculture are the basis of the economy. □ **Zimbabwean** adj. & n.

Zimbabwe

Zin·der |zin'der| commercial town in S Niger. Pop. 121,000. A walled town on ancient caravan routes, it was a French colonial capital before 1926.

Zi·on |'zīən| (also **Mount Zion** or **Sion**) part of the city of Jerusalem, originally the hill (see MORIAH, MOUNT) on which the Temple of Solomon was built. The name came to mean Jerusalem itself, and the Promised Land in general.

Zi·on National Park |'zīən| preserve in SW Utah, noted for its colorful sandstone formations and deep canyons.

Zi·tá·cua·ro |,sētä'kwärō| historic city in S Mexico, in Michoacán state. Pop. 108,000. It was important during the Mexican War of Independence.

Zla·to·ust |zlätä'o͞ost| industrial city in central Russia, in the S Ural Mts. Pop. 208,000.

Zlin |zlēn| industrial town in the E central Czech Republic. Pop. 85,000. It is a center of the Czech shoe-manufacturing industry.

Zó•ca•lo |sōʹkälō| central public square in a Mexican city, especially the Plaza de la Constitución in Mexico City, one of the largest city squares in the world, the site of the National Palace and other important buildings.

Zoe•ter•meer |ˌzōōtərʹmer| industrial and administrative town in W Netherlands, N of Rotterdam. Pop. 103,000.

Zom•ba |ʹzōmbə| commercial city in S Malawi, in the agricultural Shire Highlands. Pop. 63,000. It was the first capital of Malawi.

Zo•na Ro•sa |ˌsōnə ʹrōsä| entertainment district of Mexico City, Mexico, just E of Chapultepec Park along the Paseo de la Reforma.

Zon•gul•dak |ˌzawNGgōōlʹdäk| port city in N Turkey, on the Black Sea, capital of Zonguldak province, a coal mining district. Pop. 120,000.

Zoue•rate |zwēʹrät| (also **Zouîrâte**) mining town in N central Mauritania, near the Western Sahara border. Pop. 26,000.

Zoug |tsōōk| French name for ZUG.

Zren•ja•nin |ʹzrenyəinin| (formerly called **Petrovgrad** and, earlier, **Velike Beçkerek**) port town in Vojvodina, N Serbia, on the Begej River. Pop. 81,000.

Zug |tsōōk| 1 mainly German-speaking canton in central Switzerland. Pop. 85,000. The smallest (265 sq. mi./685 sq. km.) canton, it joined the confederation in 1352. 2 its capital. Pop. 21,000. French name **Zoug**.

Zug•spit•ze |ʹtsōōk,SHpitsə| peak in the Wetterstein Mts. of the Bavarian Alps, S Germany, near the Tyrol. It is the highest peak in Germany (9,720 ft./2,963 m.).

Zui•der Zee |ˌzīdər ʹzā| former large shallow inlet of the North Sea, in the Netherlands. In 1932 a dam across the entrance was completed, and large parts have been drained and reclaimed as polders. The remainder forms the IJsselmeer.

Zu•lu•land |ʹzōōlōō,lænd| see KWAZULU.

Zun•yi |ʹdzōōnʹē| city in Guizhou province, S China, N of Guiyang. Pop. 354,000.

Zu•rich |ʹtsYriKH; ʹzōōrik| city in N central Switzerland, on Lake Zurich. Pop. 343,000. The largest city in Switzerland, it is an international financial center and a tourist destination.

Zut•phen |ʹzYtfə| historic industrial and commercial town in E central Netherlands, on the IJssel River. Pop. 31,000.

Zvi•sha•va•ne |ˌzvēSHəʹvänī| (formerly **Shabani**) mining town in S central Zimbabwe, E of Bulawayo. Pop. 27,000. It is an asbestos producing center.

Zwei•brück•en |ʹsfībrYkən| historic industrial city in western Germany, in Rhineland-Palatinate near the Saarland border. Pop. 35,000.

Zwick•au |ʹtsfikow| mining and industrial city in SE Germany, in Saxony. Pop. 113,000.

Zwol•le |ʹzwawlə| town in the E Netherlands, capital of Overijssel province. Pop. 96,000.

Appendixes

OCEANS AND SEAS OF THE WORLD

	Area		Maximum depth	
	Sq. miles	Sq. km.	Feet	Meters
Oceans				
Pacific Ocean	63,800	165,250	36,200	11,034
Atlantic Ocean	31,830	82,440	30,246	9,219
Indian Ocean	28,360	73,440	24,442	7,450
Arctic Ocean	5,400	14,090	17,881	5,450
Seas				
South China Sea	1,331	3,447	18,241	5,560
Caribbean Sea	1,063	2,754	25,197	7,680
Mediterranean Sea	967	2,505	16,470	5,020
Sea of Okhotsk	610	1,580	11,063	3,372
Gulf of Mexico	596	1,544	14,370	4,380
Hudson Bay	475	1,230	850	259
Sea of Japan	389	1,007	12,280	3,733
East China Sea	290	752	9,126	2,782
North Sea	222	575	2,170	659
Black Sea	178	461	7,360	2,237
Red Sea	169	438	7,370	2,240
Baltic Sea	163	422	1,440	437
Yellow Sea	161	417	300	91

WORLD LAND AREA BY CONTINENT

	Area		Percent of the
	Sq. miles	Sq. km.	world's land
Asia	17,100,000	44,350,000	29.6
Africa	11,700,000	30,300,000	20.2
North America	9,350,000	24,250,000	16.2
South America	6,900,000	17,800,000	11.8
Antarctica	5,500,000	14,250,000	9.5
Europe	4,050,000	10,500,000	7.0
Oceania (incl. Australia and New Zealand	3,300,000	8,500,000	5.7
TOTAL	57,900,000	149,950,000	100.0

WORLD POPULATION BY CONTINENT

	Pop. (1990)	Pop. density (people/sq. mile)
Asia	3,112,700,000	293
Africa	642,111,000	54
Europe	498,371,000	249
North America	427,226,000	34
South America	296,716,000	44
Oceania	26,481,000	8
TOTAL	5,292,200,000	101

MAJOR MOUNTAINS OF THE WORLD

Mountain	Location	Feet	Meters
Everest	Nepal-China	29,028	8,848
K2	Kashmir	28,250	8,611
Kanchenjunga	Nepal-India	28,209	8,598
Annapurna	Nepal	26,503	8,078
Communism Peak	Tajikstan	24,590	7,495
Aconcagua	Argentina-Chile	22,834	6,960
Ojos del Salado	Argentina-Chile	22,664	6,908
Bonete	Argentina	22,546	6,872
McKinley	Alaska, USA	20,110	6,194
Logan	Yukon, Canada	19,850	6,054
Kilimanjaro	Tanzania	19,340	5,895
Elbrus	Caucasus, Russia	18,481	5,642
Citlaltépetl	Mexico	18,503	5,699
Kenya	Kenya	17,058	5,200
Ararat	Turkey	16,946	5,165
Vinson Massif	Antarctica	16,863	5,140
Margherita Peak	Uganda-Zaire	16,763	5,109
Mont Blanc	France-Italy	15,771	4,807
Wilhelm	Papua New Guinea	14,739	4,509
Whitney	California, USA	14,495	4,418
Matterhorn	Italy-Switzerland	14,688	4,477
Elbert	Colorado, USA	14,431	4,399
Pikes Peak	Colorado, USA	14,110	4,300
Jungfrau	Switzerland	13,642	4,158
Cook	New Zealand	12,349	3,764
Hood	Oregon, USA	11,239	3,426
Olympus	Greece	9,570	2,917
Kosciusko	Australia	7,234	2,228

MAJOR VOLCANOES OF THE WORLD

Volcano	Location	Height (feet)	Last eruption (other notable eruptions)
Cameroon	Cameroon	13,354	1982
El Chichon	Mexico	7,300	1982
Erebus	Ross Is., Antarctica	12,450	1998
Etna	Italy	10,990	1998
Fuji	Honshu, Japan	12,368	1708
Kelud	Java, Indonesia	5,679	1990
Kilauea	Hawaii, USA	4,090	1998
Krakatau (Krakatoa)	Indonesia	2,667	1995 (1883)
Mauna Loa	Hawaii, USA	13,678	1984
Nevado del Ruiz	Colombia	17,457	1991 (1985)
Pelée	Martinique	4,583	1932 (1902)
Pinatubo	Luzon, Philippines	5,249	1995
Rainier	Washington, USA	14,410	1894
St. Helens	Washington, USA	8,312	1991 (1980)
Santa Maria	Guatemala	12,375	1998 (1902)
Santorini	Greece	1,850	1950 (c. 1500 B.C.)
Shasta	California, USA	14,162	1786
Stromboli	Italy	3,038	1998
Taal	Luzon, Philippines	984	1977 (1911)
Unzen	Japan	4,462	1996 (1792)
Vesuvius	Italy	4,190	1944 (A.D. 79)
Wrangell	Alaska, USA	14,269	1907

MAJOR NATURAL LAKES OF THE WORLD

	Area	
	Sq. miles	Sq. km.
Caspian Sea	143,240	370,992
Lake Superior	32,526	84,243
Lake Victoria	26,820	69,464
Aral Sea	24,904	64,501
Lake Huron	24,361	63,096
Lake Michigan	22,300	57,757
Lake Tanganyika	12,650	32,764
Lake Baikal	12,160	31,494
Great Bear Lake	12,095	31,328
Lake Nyasa	11,150	28,879
Great Slave Lake	11,030	28,568
Lake Erie	9,966	25,812
Lake Winnipeg	9,416	24,387
Lake Ontario	7,336	19,001
Lake Balkhash	7,115	18,428
Lake Ladoga	6,835	17,703
Lake Chad*	6,300	16,317
Lake Maracaibo	5,120	13,261
Patos	3,920	10,153
Lake Onega	3,710	9,609
Lake Eyre*	3,600	9,320
Lake Titicaca	3,200	8,288
Lake Nicaragua	3,100	8,029
Lake Mai-Ndombe*	3,100	8,029
Lake Athabasca	3,064	7,935

*indicates large seasonal variations

MAJOR RIVERS OF THE WORLD

River	Length Miles	Km.
Nile	4,160	6,695
Amazon	4,150	6,683
Yangtze (Chiang Jiang)	3,964	6,380
Mississippi-Missouri-Red Rock	3,741	6,019
Ob-Irtysh	3,481	5,410
Yenesei-Angara	3,100	4,989
Yellow (Huang He)	3,000	4,830
Congo	2,800	4,630
Lena	2,750	4,400
Amur-Shilka	2,744	4,390
Mackenzie-Peace-Finlay	2,635	4,241
Mekong	2,600	4,180
Missouri-Red Rock	2,564	4,125
Niger	2,550	4,100
Mississippi	2,470	3,975
Plate-Paranà	2,450	3,943
Murray-Darling	2,331	3,751
Missouri	2,315	3,736
Volga	2,292	3,688
Purus	2,100	3,400
São Francisco	1,990	3,200
Rio Grande	1,880	3,030
Yukon	1,870	3,020
Tunguska, Lower	1,861	2,995
Brahmaputra	1,800	2,900
Indus	1,800	2,900
Japurà	1,750	2,815
Danube	1,700	2,736
Euphrates	1,700	2,736
Ganges	1,678	2,700
Para-Tocantins	1,640	2,640
Nelson-S. Saskatchewan-Bow	1,600	2,560
Zambezi	1,600	2,560
Paraguay	1,584	2,549
Ural	1,575	2,534
Amu Darya	1,500	2,400
Kolyma	1,500	2,400
Salween	1,500	2,400
Colorado	1,468	2,333
Arkansas	1,450	2,320
Dnieper	1,370	2,200
Syr Darya	1,370	2,200
Orange	1,155	1,859
St. Lawrence	750	1,200

LARGEST METROPOLITAN AREAS OF THE WORLD

Metropolitan Area	Country	Pop. (1990) in millions
Mexico City	Mexico	20.2
Tokyo	Japan	18.1
São Paulo	Brazil	17.4
New York City	USA	16.2
Shanghai	China	13.4
Bombay (Mumbai)	India	12.6
Los Angeles	USA	11.9
Calcutta	India	11.8
Buenos Aires	Argentina	11.5
Seoul	Korea	11.0
Beijing	China	10.8
Rio de Janeiro	Brazil	10.7
Tianjin	China	9.4
Jakarta	Indonesia	9.3
Cairo	Egypt	9.0
Delhi	India	8.8
Moscow	Russia	8.8
Manila	Philippines	8.5
Osaka	Japan	8.5
Paris	France	8.5